सीताराम

तुलसीदास

कृत

रामचरितमानस

Tulsi Ramayana

the

Hindu Bible

Ramcharitmanas

with English Translation & Transliteration

तुलसीदास

tulsīdās

Published by: only **RAMA** only

(an Imprint of e1i1 Corporation)

Title: Tulsi Ramayana—The Hindu Bible
Sub-Title: Ramcharitmanas with English Translation & Transliteration

Author: Goswami Tulsidas

Translators: Baldev Prasad Saxena, Vidya Wati
Cover Design: Sushma

Identifiers

Library of Congress Control Number: **2016960422**
ISBN: **978-1-945739-01-9** (Paperback)
ISBN: **978-1-945739-03-3** (Hardcover)

—o—

About the Book: Ramcharitmanas—the Glorious-Lake of the enactments of Lord God Rama—is the Awadhi rendering of the Ramayana narrative. This Holy-Book, which is studied religiously by millions of people of Sanatana Dharma across the world every day, was composed—as the legend has it—by Lord Shiva, and then it passed on down through several different narrators, until finally reaching the present era it was penned down by the medieval saint Tulsidas.
This bilingual edition of Tulsidas' Text contains a word-to-word Transliteration alongside the Original Devanagari Text. An English Translation in natural communicative style follows group of verses.

About the Author: Goswami Tulsidas (1497-1623), a poet-saint, reformer and philosopher of India is renowned for his devotion to Lord Rama. A composer of several popular works, he is best known as the author of this Epic: Ramcharitmanas. He has been acclaimed as one of the greatest poets in Indian and world literature.

—o—

श्रीरामचरितमानस
śrīrāmacaritamānasa

CONTENTS

I	प्रथम सोपान	**बालकाण्ड**	prathama sopāna	**bālakāṇḍa**	**1**
II	द्वितीय सोपान	**अयोध्याकाण्ड**	dvitīya sopāna	**ayodhyākāṇḍa**	**139**
III	तृतीय सोपान	**अरण्यकाण्ड**	tṛtīya sopāna	**araṇyakāṇḍa**	**253**
IV	चतुर्थ सोपान	**किष्किन्धाकाण्ड**	caturtha sopāna	**kiṣkindhākāṇḍa**	**279**
V	पञ्चम सोपान	**सुन्दरकाण्ड**	pañcama sopāna	**sundarakāṇḍa**	**293**
VI	षष्ठ सोपान	**लंकाकाण्ड**	ṣaṣṭha sopāna	**laṁkākāṇḍa**	**317**
VII	सप्तम सोपान	**उत्तरकाण्ड**	saptama sopāna	**uttarakāṇḍa**	**373**

— OTHER CONTENTS —

- FRONT -

श्री रामायण आरती . śrī rāmāyaṇa āratī
A Brief Note

- BACK -

श्री राम-स्तुति . śrī rāma-stuti
श्री हनुमान-स्तुति . śrī hanumāna-stuti
श्री हनुमान चालीसा . śrī hanumāna cālīsā
श्री हनुमान आरती . śrī hanumāna āratī
Guide to Pronunciation
About Rāmcharitmānas and Tulsīdās

श्री रामायण आरती — śrī rāmāyaṇa ārati

आरति श्रीरामायनजी की । कीरति कलित ललित सिय पी की ॥
ārati śrīrāmāyanajī kī, kīrati kalita lalita siya pī kī.

गावत ब्रह्मादिक मुनि नारद । बालमीक बिग्यान बिसारद ॥
gāvata brahmādika muni nārada, bālamīka bigyāna bisārada.
सुक सनकादि सेष अरु सारद । बरनि पवनसुत कीरति नीकी ॥१॥
suka sanakādi seṣa aru sārada, barani pavanasuta kīrati nīkī. [1]

गावत बेद पुरान अष्टदस । छओ सास्त्र सब ग्रंथन को रस ॥
gāvata beda purāna aṣṭadasa, chao sāstra saba graṁthana ko rasa.
मुनि जन धन संतन को सरबस । सार अंस संमत सबही की ॥२॥
muni jana dhana saṁtana ko sarabasa, sāra aṁsa saṁmata sabahī kī. [2]

गावत संतत संभु भवानी । अरु घटसंभव मुनि बिग्यानी ॥
gāvata saṁtata saṁbhu bhavānī, aru ghaṭasaṁbhava muni bigyānī.
ब्यास आदि कबिबर्ज बखानी । कागभुसुंडि गरुड के ही की ॥३॥
byāsa ādi kabibarja bakhānī, kāgabhusuṁḍi garuḍa ke hī kī. [3]

कलिमल हरनि बिषय रस फीकी । सुभग सिंगार मुक्ति जुबती की ॥
kalimala harani biṣaya rasa phīkī, subhaga siṁgāra mukti jubatī kī.
दलन रोग भव मूरि अमी की । तात मात सब बिधि तुलसी की ॥४॥
dalana roga bhava mūri amī kī, tāta māta saba bidhi tulasī kī. [4]

आरति श्रीरामायनजी की । कीरति कलित ललित सिय पी की ...
ārati śrīrāmāyanajī kī, kīrati kalita lalita siya pī kī ...

जय हनुमान - जय सीताराम

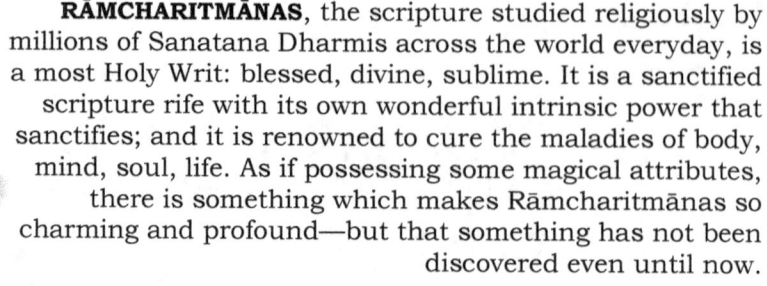

A BRIEF NOTE:

RĀMCHARITMĀNAS, the scripture studied religiously by millions of Sanatana Dharmis across the world everyday, is a most Holy Writ: blessed, divine, sublime. It is a sanctified scripture rife with its own wonderful intrinsic power that sanctifies; and it is renowned to cure the maladies of body, mind, soul, life. As if possessing some magical attributes, there is something which makes Rāmcharitmānas so charming and profound—but that something has not been discovered even until now.

OF course being the Epic of Lord God Rāma, the appeal, enchantment, and profoundness replete herein, should lend itself to no wonderment; but then again, the charm also results because these divine verses come to us through the medium of a remarkable seer and saint, a supreme devotee of Lord Rāma, a true man of God, an empyreal bard: **SANT TULSĪDĀS**.

AS you study this holy scripture—also known as the **TULSĪ RĀMĀYANA**—let it be known: The real substance of this book is the original verses of Tulsīdās. Remove them from the book—or ignore them during the reading—and less than one percent of the book will remain; And that is the reason why we have rendered the original Tulsī text into Transliterated form as well: so that the benefits of reading the Tulsī Rāmāyana can be earned in full by one and all.

AND although we also give English portrayal of the verses to suggest to the reader what is going on but we consider these to be simply merely hints, and deem them as having little import beyond that. The so-called "Translation" is not the real deal, if you will, but just a shadowy clue—which is the best that one can do. Yes; to present the work of a literary giant like Tulsīdās, through the medium of Translation, is a most daunting task and we will not even begin to attempt that. We prefer to call this venture not a Translation but simply a decrepit depiction in English words, of the Tulsī Rāmāyana.

IN the past, numerous great souls have rendered the Rāmcharitmānas into **Hindi, English**, and various other languages, and we are greatly indebted to all of them—for we have copiously made use of the several existing works to cumulate this work here. All the credit goes only to such noble souls who have written and discoursed upon this great Epic over the years, and only the mistakes originate from me: a little bee floundering, who flew to many beautiful flowers, but being incapable, could not gather the nectar well enough.

NOW without further ado, most humbly, sitting at his blessed feet, this book is placed **in the hands of SHRĪ HANUMĀN**—our family deity **&** the most favorite attendant of **SHRĪ RĀMA**—and may he do what he pleases with it.

— Baldev Prasad Saxena (Compiler-Translator-Editor)

— Vidya Wati (Compiler-Translator-Editor)

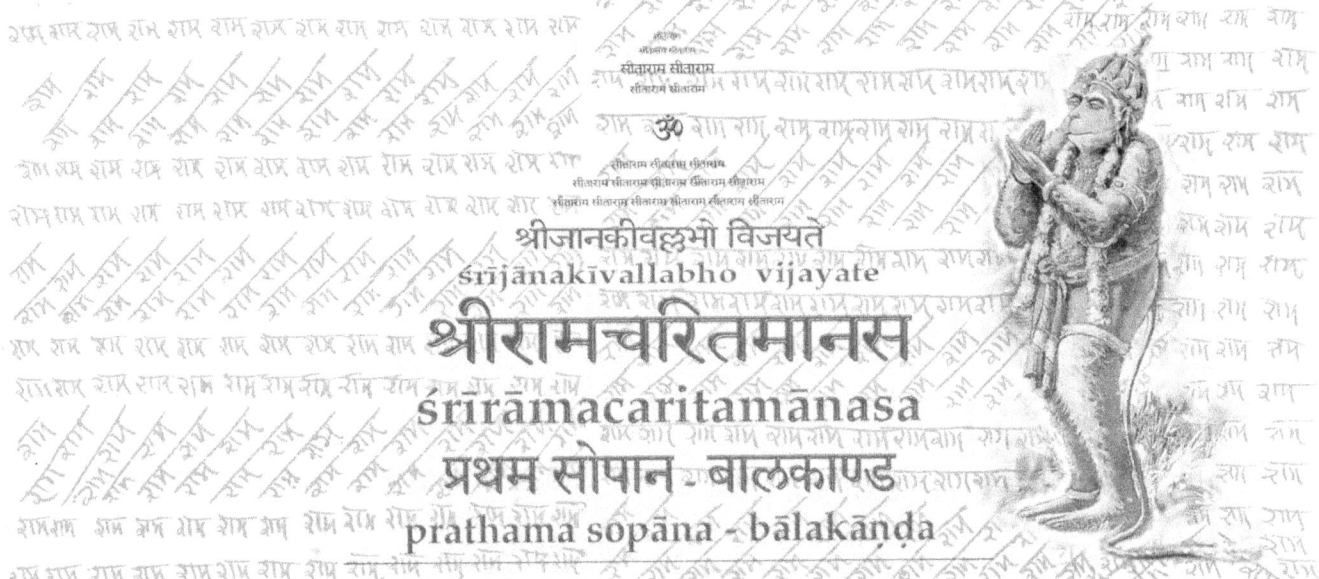

श्रीजानकीवल्लभो विजयते

śrījānakīvallabho vijayate

श्रीरामचरितमानस

śrīrāmacaritamānasa

प्रथम सोपान - बालकाण्ड

prathama sopāna - bālakāṇḍa

श्लोक-śloka:

वर्णानामर्थसंघानां रसानां छन्दसामपि ।
varṇānāmarthasaṁghānāṁ rasānāṁ chandasāmapi,
मङ्गलानां च कर्त्तारौ वन्दे वाणीविनायकौ ॥१॥
maṅgalānāṁ ca karttārau vande vāṇīvināyakau. 1.

Trans:

Venerate I Vānī and Vināyak, the originators of the alphabet and of the multitudinous expressions of those letters; the creators of the poetic styles, of cadence, of metre; and the begetters of all blessings.

भवानीशङ्करौ वन्दे श्रद्धाविश्वासरूपिणौ ।
bhavānīśaṅkarau vande śraddhāviśvāsarūpiṇau,
याभ्यां विना न पश्यन्ति सिद्धाःस्वान्तःस्थमीश्वरम् ॥२॥
yābhyāṁ vinā na paśyanti siddhāḥsvāntaḥsthamīśvaram. 2.

Trans:

I reverence Bhawānī and Shankar, the embodiments of reverence and faith, without whom not even the adept may see the Great Spirit which is enshrined in their very own hearts.

वन्दे बोधमयं नित्यं गुरुं शङ्कररूपिणम् ।
vande bodhamayaṁ nityaṁ guruṁ śaṅkararūpiṇam,
यमाश्रितो हि वक्रोऽपि चन्द्रः सर्वत्र वन्द्यते ॥३॥
yamāśrito hi vakro'pi candraḥ sarvatra vandyate. 3.

Trans:

I make obeisance to the eternal preceptor in the form of Shankar, who is all wisdom, and resting on whose crest the crescent moon, though crooked in shape, is everywhere honored.

सीतारामगुणग्रामपुण्यारण्यविहारिणौ ।
sītārāmaguṇagrāmapuṇyāraṇyavihāriṇau,
वन्दे विशुद्धविज्ञानौ कवीश्वरकपीश्वरौ ॥४॥
vande viśuddhavijñānau kavīśvarakapīśvarau. 4.

Trans:

I reverence the king of bards (Vālmikī) and the king of monkeys (Hanumān), of pure intelligence, who ever linger with delight in the holy woods in the shape of glories of Sītā-Rāma.

उद्भवस्थितिसंहारकारिणीं क्लेशहारिणीम् ।
udbhavasthitisaṁhārakāriṇīṁ kleśahāriṇīm,
सर्वश्रेयस्करीं सीतां नतोऽहं रामवल्लभाम् ॥५॥
sarvaśreyaskarīṁ sītāṁ nato'haṁ rāmavallabhām. 5.

Trans:

I bow to Sītā, the beloved consort of Rāma; the responsible cause of creation, sustenance and dissolution of the universe; who removes afflictions and begets all blessings.

यन्मायावशवर्त्ति विश्वमखिलं ब्रह्मादिदेवासुरा
yanmāyāvaśavartti viśvamakhilaṁ brahmādidevāsurā
यत्सत्त्वादमृषैव भाति सकलं रज्जौ यथाहेर्भ्रमः ।
yatsattvādamṛṣaiva bhāti sakalaṁ rajjau yathāherbhramaḥ,
यत्पादप्लवमेकमेव हि भवाम्भोधेस्तितीर्षावतां
yatpādaplavamekameva hi bhavāmbhodhestitīrṣāvatāṁ
वन्देऽहं तमशेषकारणपरं रामाख्यमीशं हरिम् ॥६॥
vande'haṁ tamaśeṣakāraṇaparaṁ rāmākhyamīśaṁ harim. 6.

Trans:

I reverence Lord Harī, known by the name of Shrī Rāma; the Supreme causative Cause; whose Māyā holds sway over the entire world, upon every being and supernatural beings from Brahmmā downwards; whose presence lends positive reality to the world of appearances—even as the false notion of a serpent is entertained with reference to a rope; and whose feet are the only bark for those eager to cross this ocean of mundane existence.

नानापुराणनिगमागमसम्मतं यद्
nānāpurāṇanigamāgamasammataṁ yad
रामायणे निगदितं क्वचिदन्यतोऽपि ।
rāmāyaṇe nigaditaṁ kvacidanyato'pi,
स्वान्तःसुखाय तुलसी रघुनाथगाथा-
svāntaḥsukhāya tulasī raghunāthagāthā-
भाषानिबन्धमतिमञ्जुलमातनोति ॥७॥
bhāṣānibandhamatimañjulamātanoti. 7.

Trans:

In accord with the various Purānas, Vedas, Agamas, and with what has been recorded in the Rāmāyana and elsewhere, I, Tulsīdās, for the delight of my own heart, have composed these verses of the exquisite saga of Raghunāth in the common parlance.

सोरठा-soraṭhā:

जो सुमिरत सिधि होइ गन नायक करिबर बदन ।
jo sumirata sidhi hoi gana nāyaka karibara badana,
करउ अनुग्रह सोइ बुद्धि रासि सुभ गुन सदन ॥१॥
karau anugraha soi buddhi rāsi subha guna sadana. 1.

Trans:

The mention of whose very name, ensures success, who carries on his shoulders the head of beautiful elephant, who is a repository of wisdom and an abode of blessed qualities, may Ganesh, the leader of Shiva's retinue, shower his grace.

मूक होइ बाचाल पंगु चढइ गिरिबर गहन ।
mūka hoi bācāla paṁgu caḍhai giribara gahana,

जासु कृपाँ सो दयाल द्रवउ सकल कलि मल दहन ॥२॥
jāsu kṛpām̐ so dayāla dravau sakala kali mala dahana. 2.
Trans:

By whose favor the dumb become eloquent and the cripple ascend formidable mountains, who burns all the impurities of the Kali-Yug—may that merciful Harī, be moved to pity.

नील सरोरुह स्याम तरुन अरुन बारिज नयन ।
nīla saroruha syāma taruna aruna bārija nayana,

करउ सो मम उर धाम सदा छीरसागर सयन ॥३॥
karau so mama ura dhāma sadā chīrasāgara sayana. 3.
Trans:

O Harī, thou who ever slumbers on the milky ocean, thou whose body is dark as a blue lotus, thou with eyes bright as budding red water-lilies—do take up thy abode in my heart as well.

कुंद इंदु सम देह उमा रमन करुना अयन ।
kuṁda iṁdu sama deha umā ramana karunā ayana,

जाहि दीन पर नेह करउ कृपा मर्दन मयन ॥४॥
jāhi dīna para neha karau kṛpā mardana mayana. 4.
Trans:

O Hara, Destroyer-of-Kāmdev, whose form resembles in color the jasmine flower and the moon, who is an abode of compassion, who is the refuge of the afflicted, O spouse of Umā, be thou gracious to me.

बंदउँ गुरु पद कंज कृपा सिंधु नररूप हरि ।
baṁdauṁ guru pada kaṁja kṛpā siṁdhu nararūpa hari,

महामोह तम पुंज जासु बचन रबि कर निकर ॥५॥
mahāmoha tama puṁja jāsu bacana rabi kara nikara. 5.
Trans:

I bow to the lotus feet of my Gurū, who is an ocean of mercy and is none other than Harī in human form, and whose words are a deluge of sunshine upon the darkness of Ignorance and Infatuation.

चौपाई-*caupāī:*

बंदउँ गुरु पद पदुम परागा । सुरुचि सुबास सरस अनुरागा ॥
baṁdauṁ guru pada paduma parāgā, suruci subāsa sarasa anurāgā.

अमिअ मूरिमय चूरन चारू । समन सकल भव रुज परिवारू ॥
amia mūrimaya cūrana cārū, samana sakala bhava ruja parivārū.

सुकृति संभु तन बिमल बिभूती । मंजुल मंगल मोद प्रसूती ॥
sukṛti saṁbhu tana bimala bibhūtī, maṁjula maṁgala moda prasūtī.

जन मन मंजु मुकुर मल हरनी । किएँ तिलक गुन गन बस करनी ॥
jana mana maṁju mukura mala haranī, kieṁ tilaka guna gana basa karanī.

श्रीगुर पद नख मनि गन जोती । सुमिरत दिब्य दृष्टि हियँ होती ॥
śrīgura pada nakha mani gana jotī, sumirata dibya dṛṣṭi hiyam̐ hotī.

दलन मोह तम सो सप्रकासू । बड़े भाग उर आवइ जासू ॥
dalana moha tama so saprakāsū, baṛe bhāga ura āvai jāsū.

उघरहिं बिमल बिलोचन ही के । मिटहिं दोष दुख भव रजनी के ॥
ugharahiṁ bimala bilocana hī ke, miṭahiṁ doṣa dukha bhava rajanī ke.

सूझहिं राम चरित मनि मानिक । गुपुत प्रगट जहँ जो जेहि खानिक ॥
sūjhahiṁ rāma carita mani mānika, guputa pragaṭa jaham̐ jo jehi khānika.
Trans:

I reverence the dust—of the lotus-feet of my master—that is like the pollen on a pair of lotuses: a pollen which to my bee-like mind is sweet, refulgent, fragrant and suffused with delight; the dust which is a pure extract of the root of ambrosia, potent to disperse all the attendant ills of life. Beautiful and auspicious, it adorns the body of the fortunate even as white ashes beautify the person of Lord Shiva; and it brings forth sweet blessings, ecstasies, and joys. Applied to the forehead as a *tilak*, it cleanses from defilement the pristine mirror of the human mind; and it gives one a mastery upon all that is auspicious and bright. The splendor of gems in the form of nails—on the feet of the blessed Gurū—unfolds divine vision in the heart by their very thought. That luster disperses all shades of Infatuation; and highly blessed is he in whose heart it glows. With its very appearance the bright eyes of the mind get opened; the attendant evils and sufferings of the night of mundane existence vanish; and gems and rubies in the shape of stories of Shrī Rāma, both patent and potent, wherever and in whatever deep Mines they may be hidden, come to light—

दोहा-*dohā:*

जथा सुअंजन अंजि दृग साधक सिद्ध सुजान ।
jathā suaṁjana aṁji dṛga sādhaka siddha sujāna,

कौतुक देखत सैल बन भूतल भूरि निधान ॥१॥
kautuka dekhata saila bana bhūtala bhūri nidhāna. 1.
Trans:

—as for instance, by applying to the eyes the miraculous salve known by the name of Siddhanjan, all—be they novices, adepts, or men of wisdom—easily discover profusion of precious-mines: even on hill-tops, in the midst of forests, and in the bowels of earth.

चौपाई-*caupāī:*

गुरु पद रज मृदु मंजुल अंजन । नयन अमिअ दृग दोष बिभंजन ॥
guru pada raja mṛdu maṁjula aṁjana, nayana amia dṛga doṣa bibhaṁjana.

तेहिं करि बिमल बिबेक बिलोचन । बरनउँ राम चरित भव मोचन ॥
tehiṁ kari bimala bibeka bilocana, baranauṁ rāma carita bhava mocana.

बंदउँ प्रथम महीसुर चरना । मोह जनित संसय सब हरना ॥
baṁdauṁ prathama mahīsura caranā, moha janita saṁsaya saba haranā.

सुजन समाज सकल गुन खानी । करउँ प्रनाम सप्रेम सुबानी ॥
sujana samāja sakala guna khānī, karauṁ pranāma saprema subānī.

साधु चरित सुभ चरित कपासू । निरस बिसद गुनमय फल जासू ॥
sādhu carita subha carita kapāsū, nirasa bisada gunamaya phala jāsū.

जो सहि दुख परछिद्र दुरावा । बंदनीय जेहिं जग जस पावा ॥
jo sahi dukha parachidra durāvā, baṁdanīya jehiṁ jaga jasa pāvā.

मुद मंगलमय संत समाजू । जो जग जंगम तीरथराजू ॥
muda maṁgalamaya saṁta samājū, jo jaga jaṁgama tīratharājū.

राम भक्ति जहँ सुरसरि धारा । सरसइ ब्रह्म बिचार प्रचारा ॥
rāma bhakti jaham̐ surasari dhārā, sarasai brahma bicāra pracārā.

बिधि निषेधमय कलि मल हरनी । करम कथा रबिनंदनि बरनी ॥
bidhi niṣedhamaya kali mala haranī, karama kathā rabinaṁdani baranī.

हरि हर कथा बिराजति बेनी । सुनत सकल मुद मंगल देनी ॥
hari hara kathā birājati benī, sunata sakala muda maṁgala denī.

बटु बिस्वास अचल निज धरमा । तीरथराज समाज सुकरमा ॥
baṭu bisvāsa acala nija dharamā, tīratharāja samāja sukaramā.

सबहि सुलभ सब दिन सब देसा । सेवत सादर समन कलेसा ॥
sabahi sulabha saba dina saba desā, sevata sādara samana kalesā.

अकथ अलौकिक तीरथराऊ । देइ सद्य फल प्रगट प्रभाऊ ॥
akatha alaukika tīratharāū, dei sadya phala pragaṭa prabhāū.
Trans:

The dust of the Gurū's feet is a soft and agreeable salve—which is ambrosia as it were for the eyes that remedies every defect of vision. Having thus brightened my eyes with understanding and discernment, I proceed to relate the saga of Rāma, which redeems one from the bondage of mundane existence. At first I reverence the feet of the holy saints, the very gods on earth, who are able to dispel all doubts born of Ignorance. Then, with my heart, as with my voice, I make obeisance to the whole body of pious souls: who are Mines of Virtues, whose good deeds resemble the fruit of the cotton plant in austerity, purity, and manifold uses. Even by itself suffering hardship the cotton plant covers others' faults and has thus earned in the world a renown worthy of adoration. The assemblage of saints, replete with joy and felicity, is the moving Prayāg (chief Pilgrimage). Devotion to Shrī Rāma represents, in this moving pilgrimage, the celestial stream Gangā. Contemplation on the formless Brahmm constitutes the Saraswatī; and injunctions and rituals, the precepts and prohibitions of Karma for purification in this Kali-Yug, is the sun-god's daughter—the river Yamunā. And the anecdotes of Vishnu and Shiva stand out as the triple stream known as Trivenī—bringing joy and blessings to all those that listen to them. Unwavering faith in one's own creed constitutes the immortal Banyan tree. And noble actions represent the royal court of that flowing pilgrimage. Easy of access to all, on all days, at all places, curing all the ills of pious devotees, of manifest virtue, and yielding immediate fruit: exists this unspeakable, spiritual chief Tīrtha in the shape of holy men.

दोहा-*dohā:*

सुनि समुझहिं जन मुदित मन मज्जहिं अति अनुराग ।
suni samujhahiṁ jana mudita mana majjahiṁ ati anurāga,
लहहिं चारि फल अछत तनु साधु समाज प्रयाग ॥ २॥
lahahiṁ cāri phala achata tanu sādhu samāja prayāga. 2.

Trans:

At this Prayāg of pious men, whoever hears and understands, and in a spirit of devotion takes a plunge, receives even in this life all the four rewards of life.

चौपाई-*caupāī:*

मज्जन फल पेखिअ ततकाला । काक होहिं पिक बकउ मराला ॥
majjana phala pekhia tatakālā, kāka hohiṁ pika bakau marālā.
सुनि आचरज करै जनि कोई । सतसंगति महिमा नहिं गोई ॥
suni ācaraja karai jani koī, satasaṁgati mahimā nahiṁ goī.
बालमीक नारद घटजोनी । निज निज मुखनि कही निज होनी ॥
bālamīka nārada ghaṭajonī, nija nija mukhani kahī nija honī.
जलचर थलचर नभचर नाना । जे जड़ चेतन जीव जहाना ॥
jalacara thalacara nabhacara nānā, je jaṛa cetana jīva jahānā.
मति कीरति गति भूति भलाई । जब जेहिं जतन जहाँ जेहिं पाई ॥
mati kīrati gati bhūti bhalāī, jaba jehiṁ jatana jahām̐ jehiṁ pāī.
सो जानब सतसंग प्रभाऊ । लोकहुँ बेद न आन उपाऊ ॥
so jānaba satasaṁga prabhāū, lokahum̐ beda na āna upāū.
बिनु सतसंग बिबेक न होई । राम कृपा बिनु सुलभ न सोई ॥
binu satasaṁga bibeka na hoī, rāma kṛpā binu sulabha na soī.
सतसंगत मुद मंगल मूला । सोइ फल सिधि सब साधन फूला ॥
satasaṁgata muda maṁgala mūlā, soi phala sidhi saba sādhana phūlā.
सठ सुधरहिं सतसंगति पाई । पारस परस कुधात सुहाई ॥
saṭha sudharahiṁ satasaṁgati pāī, pārasa parasa kudhāta suhāī.
बिधि बस सुजन कुसंगत परहीं । फनि मनि सम निज गुन अनुसरहीं ॥
bidhi basa sujana kusaṁgata parahīṁ, phani mani sama nija guna anusarahīṁ.
बिधि हरि हर कबि कोबिद बानी । कहत साधु महिमा सकुचानी ॥
bidhi hari hara kabi kobida bānī, kahata sādhu mahimā sakucānī.
सो मो सन कहि जात न कैसें । साक बनिक मनि गुन गन जैसें ॥
so mo sana kahi jāta na kaiseṁ, sāka banika mani guna gana jaiseṁ.

Trans:

In an instant behold the result of immersion into this moving pilgrimage of pious souls: the crow becomes a cuckoo and the heron transforms into a swan. Let no one marvel on hearing this, for the glory of contact with saints is no secret. Vālmikī, Nārad, and the jar-born Agastya have told of its effect upon themselves with their own lips. Whatever moves in the water, or on the earth, or in the air; every creature in the world, whether animate or inanimate, that has attained to knowledge, or glory, or salvation, or power, or virtue, by any work, at any time or place, has triumphed only through the association with the holy—neither the world nor the Veda knows of any other expedient. Without communion with the saintly, wisdom is impossible; and that communion is attainable only by the blessing of Shrī Rāma. Such communion is the root of all joy and felicity; its flowers are good works and its fruit perfection. By it even the wicked are reformed—just as by the touch of the philosopher's stone a base metal becomes gold. If by mischance a good man falls into evil company, like the jewel in a serpent's head, he still retains his character. Brahmmā, Vishnu, Mahādev, wisest of the poets, all have failed to fully describe the supremacy of the saintly people. For me to tell it is like a costermonger expatiating on the excellences of gemstones.

दोहा-*dohā:*

बंदउँ संत समान चित हित अनहित नहिं कोइ ।
baṁdaum̐ saṁta samāna cita hita anahita nahiṁ koi,
अंजलि गत सुभ सुमन जिमि सम सुगंध कर दोइ ॥ ३क॥
aṁjali gata subha sumana jimi sama sugaṁdha kara doi. 3(ka).

संत सरल चित जगत हित जानि सुभाउ सनेहु ।
saṁta sarala cita jagata hita jāni subhāu sanehu,
बालबिनय सुनि करि कृपा रामचरन रति देहु ॥ ३ख॥
bālabinaya suni kari kṛpā rāmacarana rati dehu. 3(kha).

Trans:

I reverence the saints of equable temperament, who regard neither friend nor foe—like a gracious flower which sheds its fragrance alike on both hands: that which cruelly uprooted it and that which tenderly holds. Ye saints, whose upright intention, whose universal charity, and whose ready sympathy I applaud, do hear my child-like prayer: do be gracious to me and inspire me with devotion to the lotus feet of Rāma.

चौपाई-*caupāī:*

बहुरि बंदि खल गन सतिभाएँ । जे बिनु काज दाहिनेहु बाएँ ॥
bahuri baṁdi khala gana satibhāem̐, je binu kāja dāhinehu bāem̐.
पर हित हानि लाभ जिन्ह केरें । उजरें हरष बिषाद बसेरें ॥
para hita hāni lābha jinha kereṁ, ujareṁ haraṣa biṣāda basereṁ.
हरि हर जस राकेस राहु से । पर अकाज भट सहसबाहु से ॥
hari hara jasa rākesa rāhu se, para akāja bhaṭa sahasabāhu se.
जे पर दोष लखहिं सहसाखी । पर हित घृत जिन्ह के मन माखी ॥
je para doṣa lakhahiṁ sahasākhī, para hita ghṛta jinha ke mana mākhī.
तेज कृसानु रोष महिषेसा । अघ अवगुन धन धनी धनेसा ॥
teja kṛsānu roṣa mahiṣesā, agha avaguna dhana dhanī dhanesā.
उदय केत सम हित सबही के । कुंभकरन सम सोवत नीके ॥
udaya keta sama hita sabahī ke, kuṁbhakarana sama sovata nīke.
पर अकाजु लगि तनु परिहरहीं । जिमि हिम उपल कृषी दलि गरहीं ॥
para akāju lagi tanu pariharahīṁ, jimi hima upala kṛṣī dali garahīṁ.
बंदउँ खल जस सेष सरोषा । सहस बदन बरनइ पर दोषा ॥
baṁdaum̐ khala jasa seṣa saroṣā, sahasa badana baranai para doṣā.
पुनि प्रनवउँ पृथुराज समाना । पर अघ सुनइ सहस दस काना ॥
puni pranavaum̐ pṛthurāja samānā, para agha sunai sahasa dasa kānā.
बहुरि सक्र सम बिनवउँ तेही । संतत सुरानीक हित जेही ॥
bahuri sakra sama binavaum̐ tehī, saṁtata surānīka hita jehī.
बचन बज्र जेहि सदा पिआरा । सहस नयन पर दोष निहारा ॥

bacana bajra jehi sadā piārā, sahasa nayana para doṣa nihārā.

Trans:

Again, I greet with a sincere heart the malevolent class, who are hostile without purpose even to the friendly, to whom another's loss is their own gain, who rejoice in calamity and weep in prosperity—of others that is; who are as an eclipse to the full-moon glory of Harī and Hara; who become as a giant with a thousand arms to work woes and with a thousand eyes to detect the faults—of others of course. Like flies on ghee, they settle on one's good points only to spoil them. In splendor they emulate the god of fire, and in anger they vie with the buffalo-riding god of death. Rich as god Kuber, their wealthiness only is in crime and vice. Like the rise of a comet their advancement augurs ill—for others; and like the slumber of Kumbhkaran their quietus alone is propitious for the world. To do injury they are as eager to sacrifice themselves as a hailstone—which perishes after destroying the crop. Expounding others' faults numberless times, the wicked remind me of the thousand-tongued fiery serpent-god Sheshnāg and I bow to them as such; and inasmuch as they hear of others' faults with a thousand ears, I bow to them as king Prithu; and I supplicate to them as Indra—for their fondness of wine and the thunderbolt of harsh language, and their propensity for looking at other's faults with a thousand eyes.

दोहा-dohā:

उदासीन अरि मीत हित सुनत जरहिं खल रीति ।
udāsīna ari mīta hita sunata jarahiṁ khala rīti,
जानि पानि जुग जोरि जन बिनती करइ सप्रीति ॥४॥
jāni pāni juga jori jana binatī karai saprīti. 4.

Trans:

The wicked burn with jealousy as they hear of others' welfare, be they a friend, foe or neutral: such is their very nature. Knowing thus, this humble soul makes loving supplications to them with joined palms.

चौपाई-caupāī:

मैं अपनी दिसि कीन्ह निहोरा । तिन्ह निज ओर न लाउब भोरा ॥
maiṁ apanī disi kīnha nihorā, tinha nija ora na lāuba bhorā.
बायस पलिअहिं अति अनुरागा । होहिं निरामिष कबहुँ कि कागा ॥
bāyasa paliahiṁ ati anurāgā, hohiṁ nirāmiṣa kabahuṁ ki kāgā.
बंदउँ संत असज्जन चरना । दुखप्रद उभय बीच कछु बरना ॥
baṁdauṁ saṁta asajjana caranā, dukhaprada ubhaya bīca kachu baranā.
बिछुरत एक प्रान हरि लेहीं । मिलत एक दुख दारुन देहीं ॥
bichurata eka prāna hari lehīṁ, milata eka dukha dāruna dehīṁ.
उपजहिं एक संग जग माहीं । जलज जोंक जिमि गुन बिलगाहीं ॥
upajahiṁ eka saṁga jaga māhīṁ, jalaja joṁka jimi guna bilagāhīṁ.
सुधा सुरा सम साधु असाधू । जनक एक जग जलधि अगाधू ॥
sudhā surā sama sādhu asādhū, janaka eka jaga jaladhi agādhū.
भल अनभल निज निज करतूती । लहत सुजस अपलोक बिभूती ॥
bhala anabhala nija nija karatūtī, lahata sujasa apaloka bibhūtī.
सुधा सुधाकर सुरसरि साधू । गरल अनल कलिमल सरि ब्याधू ॥
sudhā sudhākara surasari sādhū, garala anala kalimala sari byādhū.
गुन अवगुन जानत सब कोई । जो जेहि भाव नीक तेहि सोई ॥
guna avaguna jānata saba koī, jo jehi bhāva nīka tehi soī.

Trans:

I for my part have made entreaties to them, and they too must reciprocate and not fail to do their part—although one knows that however fondly you may nurture a brood of crows, those ravens will never turn vegans. I propitiate at once the feet of saints and sinners, who each give pain—but with a difference. The former give pain when they leave; the latter bring torment when they meet. They are as opposite as a lotus and a leech, though both alike are produced in water. Good and bad thus resemble nectar and intoxicating drink, which were both begotten by the great ocean. The good and bad each attain to preeminence—the one in glory, the other in disgrace. On the one end, the world has the nectar, the moon, the Gangā, and the vestal pure; and also at the other end there is venom, fire, the unholy river Karmnāshā, and the evil vile. The merits and demerits of good and bad, virtue and vice, are known to all; but whatever is to a man's taste that alone seems to him to be good.

दोहा-dohā:

भलो भलाइहि पै लहइ लहइ निचाइहि नीचु ।
bhalo bhalāihi pai lahai lahai nicāihi nīcu,
सुधा सराहिअ अमरताँ गरल सराहिअ मीचु ॥५॥
sudhā sarāhia amaratāṁ garala sarāhia mīcu. 5.

Trans:

The good take to goodness, and the vile to vileness; and ambrosia is praised for its immortality, and poison is extolled for its deadly effects.

चौपाई-caupāī:

खल अघ अगुन साधु गुन गाहा । उभय अपार उदधि अवगाहा ॥
khala agha aguna sādhu guna gāhā, ubhaya apāra udadhi avagāhā.
तेहि तें कछु गुन दोष बखाने । संग्रह त्याग न बिनु पहिचाने ॥
tehi teṁ kachu guna doṣa bakhāne, saṁgraha tyāga na binu pahicāne.
भलेउ पोच सब बिधि उपजाए । गनि गुन दोष बेद बिलगाए ॥
bhaleu poca saba bidhi upajāe, gani guna doṣa beda bilagāe.
कहहिं बेद इतिहास पुराना । बिधि प्रपंचु गुन अवगुन साना ॥
kahahiṁ beda itihāsa purānā, bidhi prapaṁcu guna avaguna sānā.
दुख सुख पाप पुन्य दिन राती । साधु असाधु सुजाति कुजाती ॥
dukha sukha pāpa punya dina rātī, sādhu asādhu sujāti kujātī.
दानव देव ऊँच अरु नीचू । अमिअ सुजीवनु माहुरु मीचू ॥
dānava deva ūṁca aru nīcū, amia sujīvanu māhuru mīcū.
माया ब्रह्म जीव जगदीसा । लच्छि अलच्छि रंक अवनीसा ॥
māyā brahma jīva jagadīsā, lacchi alacchi raṁka avanīsā.
कासी मग सुरसरि क्रमनासा । मरु मारव महिदेव गवासा ॥
kāsī maga surasari kramanāsā, maru mārava mahideva gavāsā.
सरग नरक अनुराग बिरागा । निगमागम गुन दोष बिभागा ॥
saraga naraka anurāga birāgā, nigamāgama guna doṣa bibhāgā.

Trans:

The tales—of sins and vices of the wicked, and of the goods and merits of the virtuous—are alike boundless, unfathomable oceans. That is why I have counted only a few of virtues and vice. They cannot be acquired or discarded without being duly distinguished. God has created both good and bad—and it is the light of Vedas that differentiates and discerns one from the other. The heroic legends and the Purānas also—no less than the Vedas—declare that the world is an admixture of good and bad. It is characterized by the pairs of opposites such as pleasure and pain, religious merit and sin, day and night, saint and sinner, good birth and vile, high and the low, god and demon, great and small, ambrosia and poison, life and death, Brahmm and Māyā, spirit and matter, God and Jīva, plenty and poverty, king and pauper, Kashī and Magadha, Gangā and the Karmnāshā, rich plains of Mālwā and deserts of Mārwār, Brahmin and butcher, heaven and hell, asceticism and sensual passion. But, the Vedas and other sacred books have sifted through the pairs and separated right from the wrong.

दोहा-dohā:

जड़ चेतन गुन दोषमय बिस्व कीन्ह करतार ।
jaṛa cetana guna doṣamaya bisva kīnha karatāra,
संत हंस गुन गहहिं पय परिहरि बारि बिकार ॥६॥
saṁta haṁsa guna gahahiṁ paya parihari bāri bikāra. 6.

Trans:

The Creator has made the universe to consist of all things, be they animate or inanimate, to be both good and bad. But the saint, like a swan, takes in only the milk of goodness and rejects the remainder as worthless refuse.

चौपाई-caupāī:

असि बिबेक जब देइ बिधाता । तब तजि दोष गुनहिं मनु राता ॥
asa bibeka jaba dei bidhātā, taba taji doṣa gunahiṁ manu rātā.
काल सुभाउ करम बरिआईं । भलेउ प्रकृति बस चुकइ भलाईं ॥
kāla subhāu karama bariāīṁ, bhaleu prakṛti basa cukai bhalāīṁ.
सो सुधारि हरिजन जिमि लेहीं । दलि दुख दोष बिमल जसु देहीं ॥
so sudhāri harijana jimi lehīṁ, dali dukha doṣa bimala jasu dehīṁ.
खलउ करहिं भल पाइ सुसंगू । मिटइ न मलिन सुभाउ अभंगू ॥
khalau karahiṁ bhala pāi susaṁgū, miṭai na malina subhāu abhaṁgū.
लखि सुबेष जग बंचक जेऊ । बेष प्रताप पूजिअहिं तेऊ ॥
lakhi subeṣa jaga baṁcaka jeū, beṣa pratāpa pūjiahiṁ teū.
उधरहिं अंत न होइ निबाहू । कालनेमि जिमि रावन राहू ॥
udharahiṁ aṁta na hoi nibāhū, kālanemi jimi rāvana rāhū.
किएहुँ कुबेषु साधु सनमानू । जिमि जग जामवंत हनुमानू ॥
kiehuṁ kubeṣu sādhu sanamānū, jimi jaga jāmavaṁta hanumānū.
हानि कुसंग सुसंगति लाहू । लोकहुँ बेद बिदित सब काहू ॥
hāni kusaṁga susaṁgati lāhū, lokahuṁ beda bidita saba kāhū.
गगन चढ़इ रज पवन प्रसंगा । कीचहिं मिलइ नीच जल संगा ॥
gagana caṛhai raja pavana prasaṁgā, kīcahiṁ milai nīca jala saṁgā.
साधु असाधु सदन सुक सारीं । सुमिरहिं राम देहिं गनि गारीं ॥
sādhu asādhu sadana suka sārīṁ, sumirahiṁ rāma dehiṁ gani gārīṁ.
धूम कुसंगति कारिख होई । लिखिअ पुरान मंजु मसि सोई ॥
dhūma kusaṁgati kārikha hoī, likhia purāna maṁju masi soī.
सोइ जल अनल अनिल संघाता । होइ जलद जग जीवन दाता ॥
soi jala anala anila saṁghātā, hoi jalada jaga jīvana dātā.

Trans:

When God gives such faculty of discrimination to some, they abandon evil and become enamored of truth. But conquered by time, temperament, or past karma, even the good—under the influence of Māyā—may stray from virtue. But just as servants of Harī rectify their path and removing all sorrow and sin cleanse and glorify themselves, the wicked too occasionally perform good deeds driven by Karma, but their inherent badness is not effaced. An impostor of fair outward show may be honored on account of his garb, but in the end he is exposed and does not succeed—like Kālnemī, or Rāvan, or Rāhu. The good are honored, notwithstanding their measly appearance: like the wise bear Jāmvant or the monkey-god Hanumān. Bad company is loss, and good company is gain—this is a truth recognized both by the world and the Veda. In company with the wind the dust flies heavenwards; but if it joins water then it becomes mud and sinks. According to the character of the house in which a parrot or *maina* is trained, it learns either to repeat the name of Rāma or to curse. With the ignorant, the soot is a mere dross; but for the wise, it can make good ink and even be used for writing a holy book. Again, in conjunction with water, fire and air combine to become earth-refreshing life-giving rain-clouds.

दोहा-dohā:

ग्रह भेषज जल पवन पट पाइ कुजोग सुजोग ।
graha bheṣaja jala pavana paṭa pāi kujoga sujoga,
होहिं कुबस्तु सुबस्तु जग लखहिं सुलच्छन लोग ॥७क॥
hohiṁ kubastu subastu jaga lakhahiṁ sulacchana loga. 7(ka).

सम प्रकास तम पाख दुहुँ नाम भेद बिधि कीन्ह ।
sama prakāsa tama pākha duhuṁ nāma bheda bidhi kīnha,
ससि सोषक पोषक समुझि जग जस अपजस दीन्ह ॥७ख॥
sasi soṣaka poṣaka samujhi jaga jasa apajasa dīnha. 7(kha).

जड़ चेतन जग जीव जत सकल राममय जानि ।
jaṛa cetana jaga jīva jata sakala rāmamaya jāni,
बंदउँ सब के पद कमल सदा जोरि जुग पानि ॥७ग॥
baṁdauṁ saba ke pada kamala sadā jori juga pāni. 7(ga).

देव दनुज नर नाग खग प्रेत पितर गंधर्ब ।
deva danuja nara nāga khaga preta pitara gaṁdharba,
बंदउँ किंनर रजनिचर कृपा करहु अब सर्ब ॥७घ॥
baṁdauṁ kiṁnara rajanicara kṛpā karahu aba sarba. 7(gha).

Trans:

The planets, medicines, water, air, dress, all are good and bad according as their accompaniments are good or bad; and the wise and discriminating observe this distinction. Both lunar fortnights are equal as regards darkness and light, but a difference in name has been wisely made; and as the moon waxes or wanes the fortnight is held in high esteem or low. Now, knowing that the whole universe, whether animate or inanimate, is pervaded by the spirit of Rāma, I reverence with clasped hands the lotus feet of all—gods, giants, men, serpents, birds, ghosts, departed ancestors, Gandharvs, Kinnars, demons of the night: I pray ye all be gracious to me.

चौपाई-caupāī:

आकर चारि लाख चौरासी । जाति जीव जल थल नभ बासी ॥
ākara cāri lākha caurāsī, jāti jīva jala thala nabha bāsī.
सीय राममय सब जग जानी । करउँ प्रनाम जोरि जुग पानी ॥
sīya rāmamaya saba jaga jānī, karauṁ pranāma jori juga pānī.
जानि कृपाकर किंकर मोहू । सब मिलि करहु छाड़ि छल छोहू ॥
jāni kṛpākara kiṁkara mohū, saba mili karahu chāṛi chala chohū.
निज बुधि बल भरोस मोहि नाहीं । तातें बिनय करउँ सब पाहीं ॥
nija budhi bala bharosa mohi nāhīṁ, tāteṁ binaya karauṁ saba pāhīṁ.
करन चहउँ रघुपति गुन गाहा । लघु मति मोरि चरित अवगाहा ॥
karana cahauṁ raghupati guna gāhā, laghu mati mori carita avagāhā.
सूझ न एकउ अंग उपाऊ । मन मति रंक मनोरथ राऊ ॥
sūjha na ekau aṁga upāū, mana mati raṁka manoratha rāū.
मति अति नीच ऊँचि रुचि आछी । चहिअ अमिअ जग जुरइ न छाछी ॥
mati ati nīca ūṁci ruci āchī, cahia amia jaga jurai na chāchī.
छमिहहिं सज्जन मोरि ढिठाई । सुनिहहिं बालबचन मन लाई ॥
chamihahiṁ sajjana mori ḍhiṭhāī, sunihahiṁ bālabacana mana lāī.
जौं बालक कह तोतरि बाता । सुनहिं मुदित मन पितु अरु माता ॥
jauṁ bālaka kaha totari bātā, sunahiṁ mudita mana pitu aru mātā.
हँसिहहिं कूर कुटिल कुबिचारी । जे पर दूषन भूषनधारी ॥
haṁsihahiṁ kūra kuṭila kubicārī, je para dūṣana bhūṣanadhārī.
निज कबित्त केहि लाग न नीका । सरस होउ अथवा अति फीका ॥
nija kabitta kehi lāga na nīkā, sarasa hou athavā ati phīkā.
जे पर भनिति सुनत हरषाहीं । ते बर पुरुष बहुत जग नाहीं ॥
je para bhaniti sunata haraṣāhīṁ, te bara puruṣa bahuta jaga nāhīṁ.
जग बहु नर सर सरि सम भाई । जे निज बाढ़ि बढ़हिं जल पाई ॥
jaga bahu nara sara sari sama bhāī, je nija bāṛhi baṛhahiṁ jala pāī.

सज्जन सकृत सिंधु सम कोई । देखि पूर बिधु बाढ़इ जोई ॥
sajjana sakṛta siṁdhu sama koī, dekhi pūra bidhu bāṛhai joī.

Trans:

By the four modes of birth are produced the eighty-four lakhs of species inhabiting the air, water, and earth. Recognizing the whole world as pervaded by the consciousness of Sītā and Rāma, with clasped hands I perform an act of adoration to all. In your compassion regard me as your servant, and dissembling no longer, be genuinely kind and affectionate. I have no confidence in the strength of my own wisdom, and therefore I supplicate to you all. I would narrate the great deeds of Raghupatī, but my ability is little and His acts unfathomable. I am not conscious of any special qualification or capacity in me. My intellect in short is beggarly, while my ambition is imperial; and I am thirsting for nectar, when not even butter-milk is to be had. Good people all pardon my presumption and listen to my childish babble—even as a father and mother delight to hear the lisping prattle of their little one. Perverse and malignant fools may laugh, who pick out faults in others wherewith to adorn themselves. Everyone is pleased with his own rhymes, whether they be pungent or insipid; but those who praise another's work are good men, of whom there are very few in the world. There are many and plenty like the rivers—which on getting a rainfall swell out in a flood of their own, but few and far between are such noble souls—like the generous ocean—which swells on beholding the fullness of the moon.

दोहा-dohā:

भाग छोट अभिलाषु बड़ करउँ एक बिस्वास ।
bhāga choṭa abhilāṣu baṛa karauṁ eka bisvāsa,
पैहहिं सुख सुनि सुजन सब खल करिहहिं उपहास ॥८॥
paihahiṁ sukha suni sujana saba khala karihahiṁ upahāsa. 8.

Trans:

My lot is low, my ambition lofty; but I am confident of one thing: that the good will be gratified to hear me, though the evil-minded may laugh.

चौपाई-caupāī:

खल परिहास होइ हित मोरा । काक कहहिं कलकंठ कठोरा ॥
khala parihāsa hoi hita morā, kāka kahahiṁ kalakaṁṭha kaṭhorā.
हंसहि बक दादुर चातकही । हँसहिं मलिन खल बिमल बतकही ॥
haṁsahi baka dādura cātakahī, haṁsahiṁ malina khala bimala batakahī.
कबित रसिक न राम पद नेहू । तिन्ह कहँ सुखद हास रस एहू ॥
kabita rasika na rāma pada nehū, tinha kahaṁ sukhada hāsa rasa ehū.
भाषा भनिति भोरि मति मोरी । हँसिबे जोग हँसें नहिं खोरी ॥
bhāṣā bhaniti bhori mati morī, haṁsibe joga haṁseṁ nahiṁ khorī.
प्रभु पद प्रीति न सामुझि नीकी । तिन्हहि कथा सुनि लागिहि फीकी ॥
prabhu pada prīti na sāmujhi nīkī, tinhahi kathā suni lāgihi phīkī.
हरि हर पद रति मति न कुतरकी । तिन्ह कहुँ मधुर कथा रघुबर की ॥
hari hara pada rati mati na kutarakī, tinha kahuṁ madhura kathā raghubara kī.
राम भगति भूषित जियँ जानी । सुनिहहिं सुजन सराहि सुबानी ॥
rāma bhagati bhūṣita jiyaṁ jānī, sunihahiṁ sujana sarāhi subānī.
कबि न होउँ नहिं बचन प्रबीनू । सकल कला सब बिद्या हीनू ॥
kabi na houṁ nahiṁ bacana prabīnū, sakala kalā saba bidyā hīnū.
आखर अरथ अलंकृति नाना । छंद प्रबंध अनेक बिधाना ॥
ākhara aratha alaṁkṛti nānā, chaṁda prabaṁdha aneka bidhānā.
भाव भेद रस भेद अपारा । कबित दोष गुन बिबिध प्रकारा ॥
bhāva bheda rasa bheda apārā, kabita doṣa guna bibidha prakārā.
कबित बिबेक एक नहिं मोरें । सत्य कहउँ लिखि कागद कोरें ॥
kabita bibeka eka nahiṁ moreṁ, satya kahauṁ likhi kāgada koreṁ.

Trans:

The laughter of the evil-minded will benefit me; crows call the cuckoo hoarse; herons ridicule the swan, and frogs the Chātak bird; and malicious rogues deride refined speech. To those who have no taste for poetry, nor devotion to the feet of Shrī Rāma, this undertaking of mine will serve as a subject for delightful mirth. My composition is couched in the crude dialect and my intellect is feeble; hence it is a fit subject for ridicule, and those who laugh shall not incur any blame. To those who cherish no love for the feet of the Lord and have no sound reason either, this story will sound unattractive to ears. To those, however, who possess devotion to the feet of Vishnu and Shiva and whose mind is not perverse, the tale of the Chief of the Raghus will appear sweet of taste. Knowing it in their heart as adorned with devotion to Shrī Rāma, the virtuous will listen to it and appreciate it with kind words. I am no poet nor an adept in the art of speech, and am cipher in all arts and sciences. There are elegant devices of letters, subtleties of meaning, various figures of speech, metrical compositions of different kinds, infinite varieties of emotions and sentiments, and multifarious nuances that distinguish flaws and excellences of poetic verses—of these details and expertise of poesy, I possess critical knowledge of none, alas. And I vouch for it in writing on a blank sheet:

दोहा-dohā:

भनिति मोरि सब गुन रहित बिस्व बिदित गुन एक ।
bhaniti mori saba guna rahita bisva bidita guna eka,
सो बिचारि सुनिहहिं सुमति जिन्ह कें बिमल बिबेक ॥९॥
so bicāri sunihahiṁ sumati jinha keṁ bimala bibeka. 9.

Trans:

that my style has not a single charm of its own. But it does have one charm known throughout the world—which men of discernment will ponder as they read—

चौपाई-caupāī:

एहि महँ रघुपति नाम उदारा । अति पावन पुरान श्रुति सारा ॥
ehi mahaṁ raghupati nāma udārā, ati pāvana purāna śruti sārā.
मंगल भवन अमंगल हारी । उमा सहित जेहि जपत पुरारी ॥
maṁgala bhavana amaṁgala hārī, umā sahita jehi japata purārī.
भनिति बिचित्र सुकबि कृत जोऊ । राम नाम बिनु सोह न सोऊ ॥
bhaniti bicitra sukabi kṛta joū, rāma nāma binu soha na soū.
बिधुबदनी सब भाँति सँवारी । सोह न बसन बिना बर नारी ॥
bidhubadanī saba bhāṁti saṁvārī, soha na basana binā bara nārī.
सब गुन रहित कुकबि कृत बानी । राम नाम जस अंकित जानी ॥
saba guna rahita kukabi kṛta bānī, rāma nāma jasa aṁkita jānī.
सादर कहहिं सुनहिं बुध ताही । मधुकर सरिस संत गुनग्राही ॥
sādara kahahiṁ sunahiṁ budha tāhī, madhukara sarisa saṁta gunagrāhī.
जदपि कबित रस एकउ नाहीं । राम प्रताप प्रकट एहि माहीं ॥
jadapi kabita rasa ekau nāhīṁ, rāma pratāpa prakaṭa ehi māhīṁ.
सोइ भरोस मोरें मन आवा । केहिं न सुसंग बडप्पनु पावा ॥
soi bharosa moreṁ mana āvā, kehiṁ na susaṁga baḍappanu pāvā.
धूमउ तजइ सहज करुआई । अगरु प्रसंग सुगंध बसाई ॥
dhūmau tajai sahaja karuāī, agaru prasaṁga sugaṁdha basāī.
भनिति भदेस बस्तु भलि बरनी । राम कथा जग मंगल करनी ॥
bhaniti bhadesa bastu bhali baranī, rāma kathā jaga maṁgala karanī.

Trans:

—and it is the gracious Name of Rāma: the all-purifying essence of the Purānas and the Vedas, the abode of all that is auspicious, the destroyer of all that is ill, the Mantra ever murmured in prayer by the great Umā and Tripurārī. The most elegant composition of the most talented poet has no real beauty if the name of Raghupati is not in it: in the same way as a lovely woman adorned with the richest jewels appears repugnant if unclothed. But the worthless production of the feeblest versifier, if adorned with the name of Rāma, is heard and repeated with reverence by the wise—like bees gathering honey. Though this poetry has not a single merit, the glory of Rāma is manifest in it. This is the confidence that possesses my soul: is there anything which good company fails to exalt? Even smoke forgets its natural pungency and in contact with incense yields sweet scent. The language I use is crude, but my subject is the highest: the story of Rāma which naturally brings joy to the world.

छंद-chaṁda:

मंगल करनि कलि मल हरनि तुलसी कथा रघुनाथ की ।
maṁgala karani kali mala harani tulasī kathā raghunātha kī,
गति कूर कबिता सरित की ज्यों सरित पावन पाथ की ॥
gati kūra kabitā sarita kī jyoṁ sarita pāvana pātha kī.
प्रभु सुजस संगति भनिति भलि होइहि सुजन मन भावनी ।
prabhu sujasa saṁgati bhaniti bhali hoihi sujana mana bhāvanī,
भव अंग भूति मसान की सुमिरत सुहावनि पावनी ॥
bhava aṁga bhūti masāna kī sumirata suhāvani pāvanī.

Trans:

O Tulsi, the saga of Rāma brings forth every blessing and wipes off all the impurities of Kali-Yug. The course of this rivulet of my rhymes is tortuous—like that of the holy Gangā; but by association with the auspicious glory of Lord Rama, it will get sanctified—even as the ashes of cremation ground, upon the person of Lord Shiva, appear charming, and purify by their very thought.

दोहा-dohā:

प्रिय लागिहि अति सबहि मम भनिति राम जस संग ।
priya lāgihi ati sabahi mama bhaniti rāma jasa saṁga,
दारु बिचारु कि करइ कोउ बंदिअ मलय प्रसंग ॥ १०क॥
dāru bicāru ki karai kou baṁdia malaya prasaṁga. 10(ka).

स्याम सुरभि पय बिसद अति गुनद करहिं सब पान ।
syāma surabhi paya bisada ati gunada karahiṁ saba pāna,
गिरा ग्राम्य सिय राम जस गावहिं सुनहिं सुजान ॥ १०ख॥
girā grāmya siya rāma jasa gāvahiṁ sunahiṁ sujāna. 10(kha).

Trans:

From its connection with the glory of Rāma, my verses will be found most delightful to all. Any wood that comes from the Malaya sandal groves becomes much valued—who then considers what kind of wood it was? Though a cow be black, its milk is white, pure, wholesome, and everyone drinks it; and so, though my speech is rough, it tells the glory of Sītā-Rāma, and will therefore be heard and repeated with pleasure by the wise.

चौपाई-caupāī:

मनि मानिक मुकुता छबि जैसी । अहि गिरि गज सिर सोह न तैसी ॥
mani mānika mukutā chabi jaisī, ahi giri gaja sira soha na taisī.
नृप किरीट तरुनी तनु पाई । लहहिं सकल सोभा अधिकाई ॥
nṛpa kirīṭa tarunī tanu pāī, lahahiṁ sakala sobhā adhikāī.
तैसेहिं सुकबि कबित बुध कहहीं । उपजहिं अनत अनत छबि लहहीं ॥
taisehiṁ sukabi kabita budha kahahīṁ, upajahiṁ anata anata chabi lahahīṁ.
भगति हेतु बिधि भवन बिहाई । सुमिरत सारद आवति धाई ॥
bhagati hetu bidhi bhavana bihāī, sumirata sārada āvati dhāī.
राम चरित सर बिनु अन्हवाएँ । सो श्रम जाइ न कोटि उपाएँ ॥
rāma carita sara binu anhavāeṁ, so śrama jāi na koṭi upāeṁ.
कबि कोबिद अस हृदयँ बिचारी । गावहिं हरि जस कलि मल हारी ॥
kabi kobida asa hṛdayaṁ bicārī, gāvahiṁ hari jasa kali mala hārī.
कीन्हें प्राकृत जन गुन गाना । सिर धुनि गिरा लगत पछिताना ॥
kīnheṁ prākṛta jana guna gānā, sira dhuni girā lagata pachitānā.
हृदय सिंधु मति सीप समाना । स्वाति सारदा कहहिं सुजाना ॥
hṛdaya siṁdhu mati sīpa samānā, svāti sāradā kahahiṁ sujānā.
जौं बरसइ बर बारि बिचारू । होहिं कबित मुकुतामनि चारू ॥
jauṁ barasai bara bāri bicārū, hohiṁ kabita mukutāmani cārū.

Trans:

A diamond in a serpent's head, a ruby on a mountain top, a pearl in an elephant's head, all appear bereft of beauty; but in a king's diadem or on a lovely woman they become lustrous to the extreme. Similarly—as the wise say—the outpourings of a poet originate in one mind and exercise their charm in another. Attracted by a poet's devotion, Saraswatī comes with all speed from the abode of Brahmmā at his invocation. But the fatigue occasioned by her long journey cannot be relieved by millions of devices unless she takes a dip in the lake of glories of Rāma. Realizing this in their heart, wise poets only chant of Harī's glories that wipe away impurities of the Kali-Yug. But finding some bards singing the glories of worldly men and things, the goddess of speech begins to beat her brow and repents why she came. The wise liken the heart of a poet to the sea, his intellect to the shell containing pearls and goddess Saraswatī to the star called Swātī. If there is a shower in the form of beautiful ideas, lovely pearls make their appearance in the form of poetic effusions.

दोहा-dohā:

जुगुति बेधि पुनि पोहिअहिं रामचरित बर ताग ।
juguti bedhi puni pohiahiṁ rāmacarita bara tāga,
पहिरहिं सज्जन बिमल उर सोभा अति अनुराग ॥ ११ ॥
pahirahiṁ sajjana bimala ura sobhā ati anurāga. 11.

Trans:

Then dexterously pierced and strung together on the thread of Rāma's glories, these pearls form a beautiful necklace to be worn on the breast of noble souls.

चौपाई-caupāī:

जे जनमे कलिकाल कराला । करतब बायस बेष मराला ॥
je janame kalikāla karālā, karataba bāyasa beṣa marālā.
चलत कुपंथ बेद मग छाँड़े । कपट कलेवर कलि मल भाँड़े ॥
calata kupaṁtha beda maga chāṁṛe, kapaṭa kalevara kali mala bhāṁṛe.
बंचक भगत कहाइ राम के । किंकर कंचन कोह काम के ॥
baṁcaka bhagata kahāi rāma ke, kiṁkara kaṁcana koha kāma ke.
तिन्ह महँ प्रथम रेख जग मोरी । धींग धरमध्वज धंधक धोरी ॥
tinha mahaṁ prathama rekha jaga morī, dhīṁga dharamadhvaja dhaṁdhaka dhorī.
जौं अपने अवगुन सब कहऊँ । बाढ़इ कथा पार नहिं लहऊँ ॥
jauṁ apane avaguna saba kahaūṁ, bāṛhai kathā pāra nahiṁ lahaūṁ.
ताते मैं अति अलप बखाने । थोरे महुँ जानिहहिं सयाने ॥
tāte maiṁ ati alapa bakhāne, thore mahuṁ jānihahiṁ sayāne.
समुझि बिबिधि बिधि बिनती मोरी । कोउ न कथा सुनि देइहि खोरी ॥
samujhi bibidhi bidhi binatī morī, kou na kathā suni deihi khorī.
एतेहु पर करिहहिं जे असंका । मोहि ते अधिक ते जड़ मति रंका ॥
etehu para karihahiṁ je asaṁkā, mohi te adhika te jaṛa mati raṁkā.
कबि न होउँ नहिं चतुर कहावउँ । मति अनुरूप राम गुन गावउँ ॥
kabi na houṁ nahiṁ catura kahāvauṁ, mati anurūpa rāma guna gāvauṁ.
कहँ रघुपति के चरित अपारा । कहँ मति मोरि निरत संसारा ॥
kahaṁ raghupati ke carita apārā, kahaṁ mati mori nirata saṁsārā.
जेहिं मारुत गिरि मेरु उड़ाहीं । कहहु तूल केहि लेखे माहीं ॥
jehiṁ māruta giri meru uṛāhīṁ, kahahu tūla kehi lekhe māhīṁ.
समुझत अमित राम प्रभुताई । करत कथा मन अति कदराई ॥
samujhata amita rāma prabhutāī, karata kathā mana ati kadarāī.

Trans:

Men born in this grim Kali-Yug are outwardly swans, but inwardly as black as crows, abandoning the Veda, walking in evil paths, embodiments of falsehood, vessels of impurity, hypocrites, professing devotion to Rāma, but actually slaves of gold, of passion, and of lust. Among them I give the first place to myself, a hypocrite, alas, of the very first rank. And were I to tell all my vices, the list would grow so long that it would have no end. I have therefore said very little, but a word is enough for the wise. So therefore, considering my these many prayers and apologies, I hope to be blamed no more for my composition, and those who will still raise objections even then, they are more stupid and deficient in intellect than I am. I am no poet and have no pretensions to ingenuity; I sing the glories of Shrī Rāma according to my own lights. My intellect, which wallows in the world, is a poor match for the unlimited glories of the Lord of Raghus. Of what account is a lightweight cotton like me, in the face of the strong wind before which even mountains like Meru are blown away? Realizing the infinite glories of our Lord God Rāma, my mind feels diffident in proceeding with this story.

दोहा-dohā:

सारद सेस महेस बिधि आगम निगम पुरान ।
sārada sesa mahesa bidhi āgama nigama purāna,
नेति नेति कहि जासु गुन करहिं निरंतर गान ॥१२॥
neti neti kahi jāsu guna karahiṁ niraṁtara gāna. 12.

Trans:

For Saraswatī, Sheshnāg, Shiva and Brahmmā, the Shāstras, the Veda, the Purānas, all are unceasingly singing the glories of Lord God; and yet fail to declare it.

चौपाई-caupāī:

सब जानत प्रभु प्रभुता सोई । तदपि कहें बिनु रहा न कोई ॥
saba jānata prabhu prabhutā soī, tadapi kaheṁ binu rahā na koī.
तहाँ बेद अस कारन राखा । भजन प्रभाउ भाँति बहु भाषा ॥
tahāṁ beda asa kārana rākhā, bhajana prabhāu bhāṁti bahu bhāṣā.
एक अनीह अरूप अनामा । अज सच्चिदानंद पर धामा ॥
eka anīha arūpa anāmā, aja saccidānaṁda para dhāmā.
ब्यापक बिस्वरूप भगवाना । तेहिं धरि देह चरित कृत नाना ॥
byāpaka bisvarūpa bhagavānā, tehiṁ dhari deha carita kṛta nānā.
सो केवल भगतन हित लागी । परम कृपाल प्रनत अनुरागी ॥
so kevala bhagatana hita lāgī, parama kṛpāla pranata anurāgī.
जेहि जन पर ममता अति छोहू । जेहिं करुना करि कीन्ह न कोहू ॥
jehi jana para mamatā ati chohū, jehiṁ karunā kari kīnha na kohū.
गई बहोर गरीब नेवाजू । सरल सबल साहिब रघुराजू ॥
gaī bahora garība nevājū, sarala sabala sāhiba raghurājū.
बुध बरनहिं हरि जस अस जानी । करहिं पुनीत सुफल निज बानी ॥
budha baranahiṁ hari jasa asa jānī, karahiṁ punīta suphala nija bānī.
तेहिं बल मैं रघुपति गुन गाथा । कहिहउँ नाइ राम पद माथा ॥
tehiṁ bala maiṁ raghupati guna gāthā, kahihauṁ nāi rāma pada māthā.
मुनिन्ह प्रथम हरि कीरति गाई । तेहिं मग चलत सुगम मोहि भाई ॥
muninha prathama hari kīrati gāī, tehiṁ maga calata sugama mohi bhāī.

Trans:

All know the greatness of the Lord to be thus unutterable, yet none can refrain from attempting to expound it. For this reason the Veda also has declared many different modes of effectual worship. There is One God: passionless, formless, uncreated, the universal soul, the supreme spirit, the all-pervading, whose shadow is this world; who has become incarnate and done great many things—simply out of love that he bears for his devotees; who is all-gracious and compassionate to the humble; who in his mercy ever refrains from anger against those whom he loves and knows to be his own; who is restorer of the past, protector of the poor, all-good and all-powerful—the Lord Raghurāj. In this belief the wise sing the glory of Harī, and their song thus becomes holy and meritorious. I, too, bowing my head to Rāma's feet, am emboldened to sing his fame following the path which has been made easy by the divine bards who have trodden that path before.

दोहा-dohā:

अति अपार जे सरित बर जौं नृप सेतु कराहिं ।
ati apāra je sarita bara jauṁ nṛpa setu karāhiṁ,
चढि पिपीलिकउ परम लघु बिनु श्रम पारहि जाहिं ॥१३॥
caḍhi pipīlikau parama laghu binu śrama pārahi jāhiṁ. 13.

Trans:

As, when a king has prepared a bridge over a broad stream, an ant, insignificant as it is, is able to get cross without difficulty.

चौपाई-caupāī:

एहि प्रकार बल मनहि देखाई । करिहउँ रघुपति कथा सुहाई ॥
ehi prakāra bala manahi dekhāī, karihauṁ raghupati kathā suhāī.
ब्यास आदि कबि पुंगव नाना । जिन्ह सादर हरि सुजस बखाना ॥
byāsa ādi kabi puṁgava nānā, jinha sādara hari sujasa bakhānā.
चरन कमल बंदउँ तिन्ह केरे । पुरवहुँ सकल मनोरथ मेरे ॥
carana kamala baṁdauṁ tinha kere, puravahuṁ sakala manoratha mere.
कलि के कबिन्ह करउँ परनामा । जिन्ह बरने रघुपति गुन ग्रामा ॥
kali ke kabinha karauṁ paranāmā, jinha barane raghupati guna grāmā.
जे प्राकृत कबि परम सयाने । भाषाँ जिन्ह हरि चरित बखाने ॥
je prākṛta kabi parama sayāne, bhāṣāṁ jinha hari carita bakhāne.
भए जे अहहिं जे होइहहिं आगें । प्रनवउँ सबहि कपट सब त्यागें ॥
bhae je ahahiṁ je hoihahiṁ āgeṁ, pranavauṁ sabahi kapaṭa saba tyāgeṁ.
होहु प्रसन्न देहु बरदानू । साधु समाज भनिति सनमानू ॥
hohu prasanna dehu baradānū, sādhu samāja bhaniti sanamānū.
जो प्रबंध बुध नहिं आदरहीं । सो श्रम बादि बाल कबि करहीं ॥
jo prabaṁdha budha nahiṁ ādarahīṁ, so śrama bādi bāla kabi karahīṁ.
कीरति भनिति भूति भलि सोई । सुरसरि सम सब कहँ हित होई ॥
kīrati bhaniti bhūti bhali soī, surasari sama saba kahaṁ hita hoī.
राम सुकीरति भनिति भदेसा । असमंजस अस मोहि अँदेसा ॥
rāma sukīrati bhaniti bhadesā, asamaṁjasa asa mohi aṁdesā.
तुम्हरी कृपाँ सुलभ सोउ मोरे । सिअनि सुहावनि टाट पटोरे ॥
tumharī kṛpāṁ sulabha sou more, siani suhāvani ṭāṭa paṭore.

Trans:

In this manner re-assuring myself, I undertake to recount Rāma's charming adventures, as they have been reverently told by Vyāsa and the other great poets, whose lotus feet I adore, praying: Fulfill ye my desire—both the Sanskrit poets of these latter days who have sung of Raghupatī, and also those of high intelligence who have written in Prakrit and the popular tongue. All who have been in time past, or who now are, or who hereafter shall be, I bow to all in the utmost good faith and sincerity. Be propitious and grant this boon, that in the assemblies of good men, may this song of mine be honored! If the good and wise will not honor it, the silly poet has had all his labor in vain. The only fame, or poetry, or power that is of any worth is that which, like Gangā water, is beneficent to all. Thought the incongruity between Rāma's glory and my crude speech makes me doubt, yet, by your favor, all will turn out well—for even coarse cloth, if embroidered with silk, becomes beautiful. Be kind enough to think of this, and my style will then become matched with the excellence of my theme.

दोहा-dohā:

सरल कबित कीरति बिमल सोइ आदरहिं सुजान ।
sarala kabita kīrati bimala soi ādarahiṁ sujāna,
सहज बयर बिसराइ रिपु जो सुनि करहिं बखान ॥१४क॥
sahaja bayara bisarāi ripu jo suni karahiṁ bakhāna. 14(ka).

सो न होइ बिनु बिमल मति मोहि मति बल अति थोर ।
so na hoi binu bimala mati mohi mati bala ati thora,
करहु कृपा हरि जस कहउँ पुनि पुनि करउँ निहोर ॥ १४ख॥
karahu kṛpā hari jasa kahauṁ puni puni karauṁ nihora. 14(kha).

कबि कोबिद रघुबर चरित मानस मंजु मराल ।
kabi kobida raghubara carita mānasa maṁju marāla,
बाल बिनय सुनि सुरुचि लखि मो पर होहु कृपाल ॥ १४ग॥
bāla binaya suni suruci lakhi mo para hohu kṛpāla. 14(ga).

Trans:

A clear style and an exalted theme are both commendable; and when they are combined, an enemy even, forgetting his natural hostility, will repeat the strain. But such a combination is not to be acquired without genius; and of genius I have none; so again and again I beg of you to bear with me while I sing the glories of Harī. The great poet are like the swans sporting in the Mānas lake of Harī's deeds. By contrast, look on me as a well-meaning child and make allowances.

सोरठा-sorațhā:

बंदउँ मुनि पद कंजु रामायन जेहिं निरमयउ ।
baṁdauṁ muni pada kaṁju rāmāyana jehiṁ niramayau,
सखर सुकोमल मंजु दोष रहित दूषन सहित ॥ १४घ ॥
sakhara sukomala maṁju doṣa rahita dūṣana sahita. 14(gha).

बंदउँ चारिउ बेद भव बारिधि बोहित सरिस ।
baṁdauṁ cāriu beda bhava bāridhi bohita sarisa,
जिन्हहि न सपनेहुँ खेद बरनत रघुबर बिसद जसु ॥ १४ङ॥
jinhahi na sapanehuṁ kheda baranata raghubara bisada jasu. 14(ṅa).

बंदउँ बिधि पद रेनु भव सागर जेहिं कीन्ह जहँ ।
baṁdauṁ bidhi pada renu bhava sāgara jehiṁ kīnha jahaṁ,
संत सुधा ससि धेनु प्रगटे खल बिष बारुनी ॥ १४च॥
saṁta sudhā sasi dhenu pragaṭe khala biṣa bārunī. 14(ca).

दोहा-dohā:

बिबुध बिप्र बुध ग्रह चरन बंदि कहउँ कर जोरि ।
bibudha bipra budha graha carana baṁdi kahauṁ kara jori,
होइ प्रसन्न पुरवहु सकल मंजु मनोरथ मोरि ॥ १४छ॥
hoi prasanna puravahu sakala maṁju manoratha mori. 14(cha).

Trans:

I reverence the lotus feet of the great sage (Valmiki) who composed the Rāmāyana, which is ever so gentle and charming—even though containing an account of the demon Khar; and is faultless—though full of references to the faulty Dūshan. I reverence the four Vedas which are like the boat in which to cross the ocean of existence recounting Rāma's excellent glories without ever dreaming of weariness. I reverence the dust on the feet of Brahmmā, who has evolved the ocean of worldly existence: the birth-place of nectar, the moon and the cow of plenty in the form of saints on the one hand; and of poison and wine in the form of the wicked, on the other. Reverencing with clasped hands gods, brahmins, philosophers, and sages, I pray—'Be gracious to me and accomplish all my fair desires.'

चौपाई-caupāī:

पुनि बंदउँ सारद सुरसरिता । जुगल पुनीत मनोहर चरिता ॥
puni baṁdauṁ sārada surasaritā, jugala punīta manohara caritā.
मज्जन पान पाप हर एका । कहत सुनत एक हर अबिबेका ॥
majjana pāna pāpa hara ekā, kahata sunata eka hara abibekā.
गुर पितु मातु महेस भवानी । प्रनवउँ दीनबंधु दिन दानी ॥
gura pitu mātu mahesa bhavānī, pranavauṁ dīnabaṁdhu dina dānī.
सेवक स्वामि सखा सिय पी के । हित निरुपधि सब बिधि तुलसी के ॥
sevaka svāmi sakhā siya pī ke, hita nirupadhi saba bidhi tulasī ke.
कलि बिलोकि जग हित हर गिरिजा । साबर मंत्र जाल जिन्ह सिरिजा ॥
kali biloki jaga hita hara girijā, sābara maṁtra jāla jinha sirijā.
अनमिल आखर अरथ न जापू । प्रगट प्रभाउ महेस प्रतापू ॥
anamila ākhara aratha na jāpū, pragaṭa prabhāu mahesa pratāpū.
सो उमेस मोहि पर अनुकूला । करिहिं कथा मुद मंगल मूला ॥
so umesa mohi para anukūlā, karihiṁ kathā muda maṁgala mūlā.
सुमिरि सिवा सिव पाइ पसाऊ । बरनउँ रामचरित चित चाऊ ॥
sumiri sivā siva pāi pasāū, baranauṁ rāmacarita cita cāū.
भनिति मोरि सिव कृपाँ बिभाती । ससि समाज मिलि मनहुँ सुराती ॥
bhaniti mori siva kṛpāṁ bibhātī, sasi samāja mili manahuṁ surātī.
जे एहि कथहि सनेह समेता । कहिहहिं सुनिहहिं समुझि सचेता ॥
je ehi kathahi saneha sametā, kahihahiṁ sunihahiṁ samujhi sacetā.
होइहहिं राम चरन अनुरागी । कलि मल रहित सुमंगल भागी ॥
hoihahiṁ rāma carana anurāgī, kali mala rahita sumaṁgala bhāgī.

Trans:

Again I reverence the Saraswatī and the Gangā, both holy and beautiful streams, cleansing sin by a single draught or immersion, whose name as soon as uttered or heard at once removes sins. I adore as I would my Gurū, or my natural parents, Pārwatī and Shiva, the ever charitable and friend of the forlorn; the servants, masters and friends of Lord of Sītā; and the true benefactors of Tulsīdās in every way. Shiva, out of his benevolence, and considering the degeneracy of the times, has composed many spells in barbarous language, incoherent syllables and unintelligible mutterings that reveal the esoteric essence of his greatness. Meditating on Shiva and Pārwatī, and acquiring their grace, I pray that my story be an agreeable one which imparts great delight to all. It is only by their favor that my verse can be beautified—as a dark night is by the moon and stars. Whoever in a devout spirit, with intelligence and attention, hears or repeats this story of Rama, shall become full of true love for Rāma; and cleansed from worldly stains shall enjoy felicity of the heavens.

दोहा-dohā:

सपनेहुँ साचेहुँ मोहि पर जौं हर गौरि पसाउ ।
sapanehuṁ sācehuṁ mohi para jauṁ hara gauri pasāu,
तौ फुर होउ जो कहेउँ सब भाषा भनिति प्रभाउ ॥ १५॥
tau phura hou jo kaheuṁ saba bhāṣā bhaniti prabhāu. 15.

Trans:

If Hara and Gaurī are really propitious to me even in dream, let all that I have said in glorification of this poetry, written in the popular dialect, come out true.

चौपाई-caupāī:

बंदउँ अवध पुरी अति पावनि । सरजू सरि कलि कलुष नसावनि ॥
baṁdauṁ avadha purī ati pāvani, sarajū sari kali kaluṣa nasāvani.
प्रनवउँ पुर नर नारि बहोरी । ममता जिन्ह पर प्रभुहि न थोरी ॥
pranavauṁ pura nara nāri bahorī, mamatā jinha para prabhuhi na thorī.
सिय निंदक अघ ओघ नसाए । लोक बिसोक बनाइ बसाए ॥
siya niṁdaka agha ogha nasāe, loka bisoka banāi basāe.
बंदउँ कौसल्या दिसि प्राची । कीरति जासु सकल जग माची ॥
baṁdauṁ kausalyā disi prācī, kīrati jāsu sakala jaga mācī.
प्रगटेउ जहँ रघुपति ससि चारू । बिस्व सुखद खल कमल तुसारू ॥
pragaṭeu jahaṁ raghupati sasi cārū, bisva sukhada khala kamala tusārū.
दसरथ राउ सहित सब रानी । सुकृत सुमंगल मूरति मानी ॥
dasaratha rāu sahita saba rānī, sukṛta sumaṁgala mūrati mānī.

करउँ प्रनाम करम मन बानी । करहु कृपा सुत सेवक जानी ॥
karauṁ pranāma karama mana bānī, karahu kṛpā suta sevaka jānī.
जिन्हहि बिरचि बड़ भयउ बिधाता । महिमा अवधि राम पितु माता ॥
jinhahi biraci baṛa bhayau bidhātā, mahimā avadhi rāma pitu mātā.

Trans:

I reverence the holy city of Ajodhyā and the river Sarjū, which cleanse one from all the earthly impurities. I salute also the inhabitants of the city who enjoy the affection of the Lord in no small degree. Even though they were damned as a result of the heap of sins incurred by the calumniators of Sītā, they were lodged in a heavenly abode, having been divested of sorrow. I greet Kausalyā whose glory stands diffused throughout the world. She is the eastern horizon whence arose the lovely moon in the shape of the Lord of Raghus, who affords delight to the entire universe and is a blight of frost to the wicked mushrooming like the lotus. To King Dashrath and all his queens, incarnations of virtue and felicity, I make obeisance in word, deed, and heart saying: 'Be gracious to me as to a servant of your son, O parents of Rāma, that acme of greatness, ye in whose creation the Creator surpassed himself.'

सोरठा-soraṭhā:

बंदउँ अवध भुआल सत्य प्रेम जेहि राम पद ।
baṁdauṁ avadha bhuāla satya prema jehi rāma pada,
बिछुरत दीनदयाल प्रिय तनु तृन इव परिहरेउ ॥ १६ ॥
bichurata dīnadayāla priya tanu tṛna iva parihareu. 16.

Trans:

I reverence the King of Avadh, who had such true love for Rāma's feet that when parted away from his Lord, his life snapped and parted company like a mere straw.

चौपाई-caupāī:

प्रनवउँ परिजन सहित बिदेहू । जाहि राम पद गूढ़ सनेहू ॥
pranavauṁ parijana sahita bidehū, jāhi rāma pada gūṛha sanehū.
जोग भोग महँ राखेउ गोई । राम बिलोकत प्रगटेउ सोई ॥
joga bhoga mahaṁ rākheu goī, rāma bilokata pragaṭeu soī.
प्रनवउँ प्रथम भरत के चरना । जासु नेम ब्रत जाइ न बरना ॥
pranavauṁ prathama bharata ke caranā, jāsu nema brata jāi na baranā.
राम चरन पंकज मन जासू । लुबुध मधुप इव तजइ न पासू ॥
rāma carana paṁkaja mana jāsū, lubudha madhupa iva tajai na pāsū.
बंदउँ लछिमन पद जलजाता । सीतल सुभग भगत सुख दाता ॥
baṁdauṁ lachimana pada jalajātā, sītala subhaga bhagata sukha dātā.
रघुपति कीरति बिमल पताका । दंड समान भयउ जस जाका ॥
raghupati kīrati bimala patākā, daṁḍa samāna bhayau jasa jākā.
सेष सहस्रसीस जग कारन । जो अवतरेउ भूमि भय टारन ॥
seṣa sahasrasīsa jaga kārana, jo avatareu bhūmi bhaya ṭārana.
सदा सो सानुकूल रह मो पर । कृपासिंधु सौमित्रि गुनाकर ॥
sadā so sānukūla raha mo para, kṛpāsiṁdhu saumitri gunākara.
रिपुसूदन पद कमल नमामी । सूर सुसील भरत अनुगामी ॥
ripusūdana pada kamala namāmī, sūra susīla bharata anugāmī.
महाबीर बिनवउँ हनुमाना । राम जासु जस आप बखाना ॥
mahābīra binavauṁ hanumānā, rāma jāsu jasa āpa bakhānā.

Trans:

I salute the King of Videh, with all his court, who had the greatest affection for Rāma. Though he concealed his devotion under royal state, yet it broke as soon as he saw him. Then next I throw myself at the feet of Bharat, whose constancy and devotion surpass description; whose soul, like a bee thirsting for sweets, ever hovered around the lotus feet of Rāma. I reverence too the lotus feet of Lakshman, cool, comely, and source of delight to the worshippers, whose glory is as it were the standard for the display of Rāma's pure emblazonment. He is no other than the thousand-headed serpent-god Shesh, the support of the universe, who came down to dispel the fear of the earth. Be thou ever propitious to me, O son of Sumitrā, ocean of compassion, storehouse of perfection. I bow also to Ripusūdan (Shatrughan), the generous hero, Bharat's constant companion. And I pray to the supremely brave Hanumān whose glory has been told by Rāma himself.

सोरठा-soraṭhā:

प्रनवउँ पवनकुमार खल बन पावक ग्यानधन ।
pranavauṁ pavanakumāra khala bana pāvaka gyānadhana,
जासु हृदय आगार बसहिं राम सर चाप धर ॥ १७ ॥
jāsu hṛdaya āgāra basahiṁ rāma sara cāpa dhara. 17.

Trans:

I bow to the son-of-wind Hanumān, of profound intelligence, like a consuming fire in the forest of vice, in whose heart, Rāma, equipped with bow and arrows, has established his home.

चौपाई-caupāī:

कपिपति रीछ निसाचर राजा । अंगदादि जे कीस समाजा ॥
kapipati rīcha nisācara rājā, aṁgadādi je kīsa samājā.
बंदउँ सब के चरन सुहाए । अधम सरीर राम जिन्ह पाए ॥
baṁdauṁ saba ke carana suhāe, adhama sarīra rāma jinha pāe.
रघुपति चरन उपासक जेते । खग मृग सुर नर असुर समेते ॥
raghupati carana upāsaka jete, khaga mṛga sura nara asura samete.
बंदउँ पद सरोज सब केरे । जे बिनु काम राम के चेरे ॥
baṁdauṁ pada saroja saba kere, je binu kāma rāma ke cere.
सुक सनकादि भगत मुनि नारद । जे मुनिबर बिग्यान बिसारद ॥
suka sanakādi bhagata muni nārada, je munibara bigyāna bisārada.
प्रनवउँ सबहि धरनि धरि सीसा । करहु कृपा जन जानि मुनीसा ॥
pranavauṁ sabahi dharani dhari sīsā, karahu kṛpā jana jāni munīsā.
जनकसुता जग जननि जानकी । अतिसय प्रिय करुना निधान की ॥
janakasutā jaga janani jānakī, atisaya priya karunā nidhāna kī.
ताके जुग पद कमल मनावउँ । जासु कृपाँ निरमल मति पावउँ ॥
tāke juga pada kamala manāvauṁ, jāsu kṛpāṁ niramala mati pāvauṁ.
पुनि मन बचन कर्म रघुनायक । चरन कमल बंदउँ सब लायक ॥
puni mana bacana karma raghunāyaka, carana kamala baṁdauṁ saba lāyaka.
राजिवनयन धरें धनु सायक । भगत बिपति भंजन सुख दायक ॥
rājivanayana dhareṁ dhanu sāyaka, bhagata bipati bhaṁjana sukha dāyaka.

Trans:

The monkey-king Sugrīva, the king of bears Jāmvant, the demon-king Vibhīshan, Angad and all the monkey host, I throw myself at the benign feet of them all, for though abject in appearance they yet found Rāma. I worship all Rāma's faithful servants—whether birds, beasts, gods, men or demons—all his unselfish adherents. I worship Shukdev, Sanat-kumār, Nārad, and the other sages of excellent renown, putting my head to the ground with the cry 'My lords, be gracious to your servant.' I propitiate the lotus feet of Janak's daughter, Jānakī, mother of the world, the best beloved of the fountain of mercy; by whose grace I may attain to unclouded intelligence. Again in heart, word, and deed I worship the all-worthy feet of Raghunāth, the glance of whose lotus eyes, like an arrow from the bow, rejoices his votaries by destroying all their misfortunes.

दोहा-dohā:

गिरा अरथ जल बीचि सम कहिअत भिन्न न भिन्न ।
girā aratha jala bīci sama kahiata bhinna na bhinna,
बंदउँ सीता राम पद जिन्हहि परम प्रिय खिन्न ॥ १८ ॥
baṁdauṁ sītā rāma pada jinhahi parama priya khinna. 18.

Trans:

As a word and its meaning are inseparable, and as a wave cannot be distinguished from the water of which it is composed, the difference being only in the name, so it is with Rāma and Sītā, the refuge of the distressed, whom I adore.

चौपाई-caupāī:

बंदउँ नाम राम रघुबर को । हेतु कृसानु भानु हिमकर को ॥
baṁdauṁ nāma rāma raghubara ko, hetu kṛsānu bhānu himakara ko.
बिधि हरि हरमय बेद प्रान सो । अगुन अनूपम गुन निधान सो ॥
bidhi hari haramaya beda prāna so, aguna anūpama guna nidhāna so.
महामंत्र जोइ जपत महेसू । कासीं मुकुति हेतु उपदेसू ॥
mahāmaṁtra joi japata mahesū, kāsīṁ mukuti hetu upadesū.
महिमा जासु जान गनराऊ । प्रथम पूजिअत नाम प्रभाऊ ॥
mahimā jāsu jāna ganarāū, prathama pūjiata nāma prabhāū.
जान आदिकबि नाम प्रतापू । भयउ सुद्ध करि उलटा जापू ॥
jāna ādikabi nāma pratāpū, bhayau suddha kari ulaṭā jāpū.
सहस नाम सम सुनि सिव बानी । जपि जेईं पिय संग भवानी ॥
sahasa nāma sama suni siva bānī, japi jeīṁ piya saṁga bhavānī.
हरषे हेतु हेरि हर ही को । किय भूषन तिय भूषन ती को ॥
haraṣe hetu heri hara hī ko, kiya bhūṣana tiya bhūṣana tī ko.
नाम प्रभाउ जान सिव नीको । कालकूट फलु दीन्ह अमी को ॥
nāma prabhāu jāna siva nīko, kālakūṭa phalu dīnha amī ko.

Trans:

I adore the Name-of-Rāma chief of Raghus, the source of all light, whether of the fire, or sun, or the moon, the substance of the triune god, the vital breath of the Veda, the passionless, the incomparable, the source of all good, the great spell muttered by Mahādev and enjoined by him as necessary to salvation even at Kashī. By embracing its power, Ganesh obtained the first place among all gods. By its power—though he muttered it backwards—the great poet Vālmikī attained to purity through its repetition. After she had heard from Shiva that it was equal to a thousand names, Bhawānī was able to rejoin her husband. Noticing such partiality of her heart for the name, Hara made that lady, who was the ornament of her sex, the very ornament of his own person. Shiva knows full well the power of the name, due to which deadly poison serves the purpose of nectar to Him.

दोहा-dohā:

बरषा रितु रघुपति भगति तुलसी सालि सुदास ।
baraṣā ritu raghupati bhagati tulasī sāli sudāsa,
राम नाम बर बरन जुग सावन भादव मास ॥१९॥
rāma nāma bara barana juga sāvana bhādava māsa. 19.

Trans:

Devotion to the Lord of Raghus is, as it were, the rainy season and the noble devotees, says Tulsīdās, represent the paddy crop; while the two charming syllables of the name 'Rāma' stand for the two months of Shrāvan and Bhādrapad.

चौपाई-caupāī:

आखर मधुर मनोहर दोऊ । बरन बिलोचन जन जिय जोऊ ॥
ākhara madhura manohara doū, barana bilocana jana jiya joū.
सुमिरत सुलभ सुखद सब काहू । लोक लाहु परलोक निबाहू ॥
sumirata sulabha sukhada saba kāhū, loka lāhu paraloka nibāhū.
कहत सुनत सुमिरत सुठि नीके । राम लखन सम प्रिय तुलसी के ॥
kahata sunata sumirata suṭhi nīke, rāma lakhana sama priya tulasī ke.
बरनत बरन प्रीति बिलगाती । ब्रह्म जीव सम सहज सँघाती ॥
baranata barana prīti bilagātī, brahma jīva sama sahaja saṁghātī.
नर नारायन सरिस सुभ्राता । जग पालक बिसेषि जन त्राता ॥
nara nārāyana sarisa subhrātā, jaga pālaka biseṣi jana trātā.
भगति सुतिय कल करन बिभूषन । जग हित हेतु बिमल बिधु पूषन ॥
bhagati sutiya kala karana bibhūṣana, jaga hita hetu bimala bidhu pūṣana.
स्वाद तोष सम सुगति सुधा के । कमठ सेष सम धर बसुधा के ॥
svāda toṣa sama sugati sudhā ke, kamaṭha seṣa sama dhara basudhā ke.
जन मन मंजु कंज मधुकर से । जीह जसोमति हरि हलधर से ॥
jana mana maṁju kaṁja madhukara se, jīha jasomati hari haladhara se.

Trans:

Two sweet and gracious syllables, the eyes as it were of the soul, easy to remember, satisfying every wish, a gain in this world and felicity in the next; most delightful to utter, to hear, or to remember; as dear to Tulsī as the inseparable Rāma and Lakshman. My love is stirred up as I speak of these two mystic syllables, as intimately connected as the universal soul and the soul of man; twin brothers like Nara and Nārāyan, preservers of the world, redeemers of the elect; bright jewels in the ears of beauteous Devotion; pure and beneficent as the sun and the moon; like sweetness and contentment, the inseparable attributes of ambrosia; like the tortoise and serpent, supporters of the world; like the bee and the lotus of a pious soul; and as sweet to the tongue as Harī and Balrām were sweet to Jasodā.

दोहा-dohā:

एकु छत्रु एकु मुकुटमनि सब बरननि पर जोउ ।
eku chatru eku mukuṭamani saba baranani para jou,
तुलसी रघुबर नाम के बरन बिराजत दोउ ॥२०॥
tulasī raghubara nāma ke barana birājata dou. 20.

Trans:

Like a royal umbrella and jeweled diadem over all the other letters of the alphabet shine the two letters in the name 'Rāma'. [R (written as र and also like the upper curve e.g. in र्स) and M (written as म and also like the upper dot e.g. in सं)]

चौपाई-caupāī:

समुझत सरिस नाम अरु नामी । प्रीति परसपर प्रभु अनुगामी ॥
samujhata sarisa nāma aru nāmī, prīti parasapara prabhu anugāmī.
नाम रूप दुइ ईस उपाधी । अकथ अनादि सुसामुझि साधी ॥
nāma rūpa dui īsa upādhī, akatha anādi susāmujhi sādhī.
को बड़ छोट कहत अपराधू । सुनि गुन भेदु समुझिहहिं साधू ॥
ko baṛa choṭa kahata aparādhū, suni guna bhedu samujhihahiṁ sādhū.
देखिअहिं रूप नाम आधीना । रूप ग्यान नहिं नाम बिहीना ॥
dekhiahiṁ rūpa nāma ādhīnā, rūpa gyāna nahiṁ nāma bihīnā.
रूप बिसेष नाम बिनु जानें । करतल गत न परहिं पहिचानें ॥
rūpa biseṣa nāma binu jāneṁ, karatala gata na parahiṁ pahicāneṁ.
सुमिरिअ नाम रूप बिनु देखें । आवत हृदयँ सनेह बिसेषें ॥
sumiria nāma rūpa binu dekheṁ, āvata hṛdayaṁ saneha biseṣeṁ.
नाम रूप गति अकथ कहानी । समुझत सुखद न परति बखानी ॥
nāma rūpa gati akatha kahānī, samujhata sukhada na parati bakhānī.
अगुन सगुन बिच नाम सुसाखी । उभय प्रबोधक चतुर दुभाषी ॥
aguna saguna bica nāma susākhī, ubhaya prabodhaka catura dubhāṣī.

Trans:

A name may be regarded as equivalent to what is named; the connection being such as subsists between a master and his follower. Both name and form are shadows of the Lord God, who, rightly understood, is unspeakable and uncreated. They are sometimes wrongly distinguished as greater and less, but the wise will understand my explanation of the difference between them. See how the Name dominates Form, for without the Name the knowledge of material does not rise in mind. Even if the very object be in your hand, still, without knowing its name, it is unrecognized. But meditate on Name without seeing its Form, and the Form crystallizes and overwhelms your soul. The mystery of Name and Form is unspeakable and cannot be told, but delightful to those who have intuition of it—with the

Name acting as a attestor between the material and immaterial forms of the deity, and being a guide and interpreter to both.

दोहा-dohā:

राम नाम मनिदीप धरु जीह देहरीं द्वार ।
rāma nāma manidīpa dharu jīha deharīṁ dvāra,
तुलसी भीतर बाहेरहुँ जौं चाहसि उजिआर ॥२१॥
tulasī bhītara bāherahum̐ jauṁ cāhasi ujiāra. 21.

Trans:

Install the luminous gem in the shape of the divine name 'Rāma' on the threshold of the tongue at the doorway of your mouth—and you will have light both inside and outside, O Tulsīdās.

चौपाई-caupāī:

नाम जीहँ जपि जागहिं जोगी । बिरति बिरंचि प्रपंच बियोगी ॥
nāma jīham̐ japi jāgahiṁ jogī, birati biraṁci prapaṁca biyogī.
ब्रह्मसुखहि अनुभवहिं अनूपा । अकथ अनामय नाम न रूपा ॥
brahmasukhahi anubhavahiṁ anūpā, akatha anāmaya nāma na rūpā.
जाना चहहिं गूढ़ गति जेऊ । नाम जीहँ जपि जानहिं तेऊ ॥
jānā cahahiṁ gūṛha gati jeū, nāma jīham̐ japi jānahiṁ teū.
साधक नाम जपहिं लय लाएँ । होहिं सिद्ध अनिमादिक पाएँ ॥
sādhaka nāma japahiṁ laya lāem̐, hohiṁ siddha animādika pāem̐.
जपहिं नामु जन आरत भारी । मिटहिं कुसंकट होहिं सुखारी ॥
japahiṁ nāmu jana ārata bhārī, miṭahiṁ kusaṁkaṭa hohiṁ sukhārī.
राम भगत जग चारि प्रकारा । सुकृती चारिउ अनघ उदारा ॥
rāma bhagata jaga cāri prakārā, sukṛtī cāriu anagha udārā.
चहू चतुर कहुँ नाम अधारा । ग्यानी प्रभुहि बिसेषि पिआरा ॥
cahū catura kahum̐ nāma adhārā, gyānī prabhuhi biseṣi piārā.
चहुँ जुग चहुँ श्रुति नाम प्रभाऊ । कलि बिसेषि नहिं आन उपाऊ ॥
cahum̐ juga cahum̐ śruti nāma prabhāū, kali biseṣi nahiṁ āna upāū.

Trans:

Yogis, who are full of dispassion and detached from the world, keep awake in the daylight of wisdom repeating the Name Rāma and enjoy the incomparable felicity of Brahmm, who is incomparable, unspeakable, unmixed with sorrow and void of name and form. Gyanis, those who aspire for knowledge, are able to understand all mysteries by repeating this Name. Sadhaks (Strivers), who repeat this Name absorbed in contemplation, become workers of miracles and acquire the power of rendering themselves invisible and the like. Those who repeat it when burdened with affliction are freed from their troubles and become happy. In this world there are four kinds of devotees of Shrī Rāma; all the four of them are virtuous, sinless and noble; and all the four, clever as they are, rely upon this Name. Of these the enlightened devotee is especially dear to the Lord. The glory of the Name is supreme in all the four Yugas and all the four Vedas, particularly in the Kali-Yug, in which there is no other means of salvation.

दोहा-dohā:

सकल कामना हीन जे राम भगति रस लीन ।
sakala kāmanā hīna je rāma bhagati rasa līna,
नाम सुप्रेम पियूष ह्रद तिन्हहुँ किए मन मीन ॥२२॥
nāma suprema piyūṣa hrada tinhahum̐ kie mana mīna. 22.

Trans:

Even those who are free from all desires and remain absorbed in the joy of devotion to Shrī Rāma have thrown their heart as fish into the nectarine lake of affection for the Name.

चौपाई-caupāī:

अगुन सगुन दुइ ब्रह्म सरूपा । अकथ अगाध अनादि अनूपा ॥
aguna saguna dui brahma sarūpā, akatha agādha anādi anūpā.
मोरें मत बड़ नामु दुहू तें । किए जेहिं जुग निज बस निज बूतें ॥
moreṁ mata baṛa nāmu duhū teṁ, kie jehiṁ juga nija basa nija būteṁ.
प्रौढ़ि सुजन जनि जानहिं जन की । कहउँ प्रतीति प्रीति रुचि मन की ॥
prauṛhi sujana jani jānahiṁ jana kī, kahaum̐ pratīti prīti ruci mana kī.
एकु दारुगत देखिअ एकू । पावक सम जुग ब्रह्म बिबेकू ॥
eku dārugata dekhia ekū, pāvaka sama juga brahma bibekū.
उभय अगम जुग सुगम नाम तें । कहेउँ नामु बड़ ब्रह्म राम तें ॥
ubhaya agama juga sugama nāma teṁ, kaheum̐ nāmu baṛa brahma rāma teṁ.
ब्यापकु एकु ब्रह्म अबिनासी । सत चेतन घन आनँद रासी ॥
byāpaku eku brahma abināsī, sata cetana dhana ānam̐da rāsī.
अस प्रभु हृदयँ अछत अबिकारी । सकल जीव जग दीन दुखारी ॥
asa prabhu hṛdayam̐ achata abikārī, sakala jīva jaga dīna dukhārī.
नाम निरूपन नाम जतन तें । सोउ प्रगटत जिमि मोल रतन तें ॥
nāma nirūpana nāma jatana teṁ, sou pragaṭata jimi mola ratana teṁ.

Trans:

There are two aspects of God—the one unqualified and the other qualified. Both these aspects are unspeakable, unfathomable, without beginning and without parallels. To my mind the Name is greater than both forms of God, and by its own might it has brought both under its sway. My friends must not take this as an exaggeration on my part, for I say it confidently and with sincere devotion. The knowledge of the supreme is of two kinds—like fire in wood which is either potent or patent—each is in itself incomprehensible, but is comprehended by means of the Name; and therefore I say that the Name is greater than either Brahmm Rāma or Shrī Rāma. For the one immortal, true, sentient, complete, and blissful Brahmm is all-pervading; and yet though such an unchangeable Lord is in our very soul, the whole creation is in slavery and wretchedness, until He is revealed in definite shape, and is energized by the Name—just as a gemstone is not valued until it is identified by its name.

दोहा-dohā:

निरगुन तें एहि भाँति बड़ नाम प्रभाउ अपार ।
niraguna teṁ ehi bhām̐ti baṛa nāma prabhāu apāra,
कहउँ नामु बड़ राम तें निज बिचार अनुसार ॥२३॥
kahaum̐ nāmu baṛa rāma teṁ nija bicāra anusāra. 23.

Trans:

Thus the virtue of the Name of Rāma is infinite and transcends the supreme, and in my judgment is greater than Rāma himself.

चौपाई-caupāī:

राम भगत हित नर तनु धारी । सहि संकट किए साधु सुखारी ॥
rāma bhagata hita nara tanu dhārī, sahi saṁkaṭa kie sādhu sukhārī.
नामु सप्रेम जपत अनयासा । भगत होहिं मुद मंगल बासा ॥
nāmu saprema japata anayāsā, bhagata hohiṁ muda maṁgala bāsā.
राम एक तापस तिय तारी । नाम कोटि खल कुमति सुधारी ॥
rāma eka tāpasa tiya tārī, nāma koṭi khala kumati sudhārī.
रिषि हित राम सुकेतुसुता की । सहित सेन सुत कीन्हि बिबाकी ॥
riṣi hita rāma suketusutā kī, sahita sena suta kīnhi bibākī.
सहित दोष दुख दास दुरासा । दलइ नामु जिमि रबि निसि नासा ॥
sahita doṣa dukha dāsa durāsā, dalai nāmu jimi rabi nisi nāsā.
भंजेउ राम आपु भव चापू । भव भय भंजन नाम प्रतापू ॥
bhaṁjeu rāma āpu bhava cāpū, bhava bhaya bhaṁjana nāma pratāpū.
दंडक बनु प्रभु कीन्ह सुहावन । जन मन अमित नाम किए पावन ॥
daṁḍaka banu prabhu kīnha suhāvana, jana mana amita nāma kie pāvana.
निसिचर निकर दले रघुनंदन । नामु सकल कलि कलुष निकंदन ॥
nisicara nikara dale raghunaṁdana, nāmu sakala kali kaluṣa nikaṁdana.

Trans:

From the love that he bore to his followers, Rāma took a human form and by enduring misery secured the happiness of many; but by incessantly and devoutly repeating his Name, an infinite body of faithfuls now attain to felicity. Then again Rāma himself may have redeemed only one woman—the ascetic's wife—but his Name has corrected the errors of millions of sinners. To gratify Rishī Vishwāmitra, Rāma wrought the destruction of Suketu's daughter Tādakā along with her army, but his Name has been dissipating faults, sorrows, anguish of the world for Ages—in the same way as the Sun puts an end to the night. In his own person Rāma broke the bow of Shiva, but the glory of his Name has been continually breaking the fears of the world for Ages. Again, the Lord himself restored to life only the forest of Dandak, but his Name has sanctified countless generations. The son of Raghu destroyed many demons, but his Name has destroyed all the many evils of the world.

दोहा-dohā:

सबरी गीध सुसेवकनि सुगति दीन्हि रघुनाथ ।
sabarī gīdha susevakani sugati dīnhi raghunātha,
नाम उधारे अमित खल बेद बिदित गुन गाथ ॥२४॥
nāma udhāre amita khala beda bidita guna gātha. 24.

Trans:

Raghunāth conferred immortality on Shabrī and the vulture Jatāyu and his other faithful servants; but his Name, the precious theme of the Vedas, has delivered innumerable hapless Jivas.

चौपाई-caupāī:

राम सुकंठ बिभीषन दोऊ । राखे सरन जान सबु कोऊ ॥
rāma sukaṁṭha bibhīṣana doū, rākhe sarana jāna sabu koū.
नाम गरीब अनेक नेवाजे । लोक बेद बर बिरिद बिराजे ॥
nāma garība aneka nevāje, loka beda bara birida birāje.
राम भालु कपि कटकु बटोरा । सेतु हेतु श्रमु कीन्ह न थोरा ॥
rāma bhālu kapi kaṭaku baṭorā, setu hetu śramu kīnha na thorā.
नामु लेत भवसिंधु सुखाहीं । करहु बिचारु सुजन मन माहीं ॥
nāmu leta bhavasiṁdhu sukhāhīṁ, karahu bicāru sujana mana māhīṁ.
राम सकुल रन रावनु मारा । सीय सहित निज पुर पगु धारा ॥
rāma sakula rana rāvanu mārā, sīya sahita nija pura pagu dhārā.
राजा रामु अवध रजधानी । गावत गुन सुर मुनि बर बानी ॥
rājā rāmu avadha rajadhānī, gāvata guna sura muni bara bānī.
सेवक सुमिरत नामु सप्रीती । बिनु श्रम प्रबल मोह दलु जीती ॥
sevaka sumirata nāmu saprītī, binu śrama prabala moha dalu jītī.
फिरत सनेहँ मगन सुख अपनें । नाम प्रसाद सोच नहिं सपनें ॥
phirata sanehaṁ magana sukha apaneṁ, nāma prasāda soca nahiṁ sapaneṁ.

Trans:

Rāma, as all people know, extended his protection to Sugrīva and Vibhīshan; but his Name, shining forth gloriously in the world and the Vedas, has protected countless supplicants. Rāma assembled a host of bears and monkeys, and had no little trouble to build a bridge; but his Name can dry up the ocean of life—meditate thereon, O ye faithful. Rāma killed in battle Rāvan and his entire clan, and returned with Sītā to his own city, a king to Avadh, his capital, with the gods and saints hymning his praises; but his servants now, if only they affectionately meditate on his Name, vanquish with ease the whole army of sins and more. Remaining immersed in rapture, they get no sorrows even in dream.

दोहा-dohā:

ब्रह्म राम तें नामु बड़ बर दायक बर दानि ।
brahma rāma teṁ nāmu baṛa bara dāyaka bara dāni,
रामचरित सत कोटि महँ लिय महेस जियँ जानि ॥२५॥
rāmacarita sata koṭi mahaṁ liya mahesa jiyaṁ jāni. 25.

Trans:

The Name is greater than either Brahmm Rāma or Shrī Rāma, and even the boon-bestowers have to seek the favor of its grace. This Mahādev knew when he selected these two-letters of Rāma from the hundred crores of verses in the Rāmāyana for himself.

मासपारायण पहला विश्राम
māsapārāyaṇa pahalā viśrāma
(Pause 1 for a Thirty-Day Recitation)

चौपाई-caupāī:

नाम प्रसाद संभु अबिनासी । साजु अमंगल मंगल रासी ॥
nāma prasāda saṁbhu abināsī, sāju amaṁgala maṁgala rāsī.
सुक सनकादि सिद्ध मुनि जोगी । नाम प्रसाद ब्रह्मसुख भोगी ॥
suka sanakādi siddha muni jogī, nāma prasāda brahmasukha bhogī.
नारद जानेउ नाम प्रतापू । जग प्रिय हरि हरि हर प्रिय आपू ॥
nārada jāneu nāma pratāpū, jaga priya hari hari hara priya āpū.
नामु जपत प्रभु कीन्ह प्रसादू । भगत सिरोमनि भे प्रहलादू ॥
nāmu japata prabhu kīnha prasādū, bhagata siromani bhe prahalādū.
ध्रुवँ सगलानि जपेउ हरि नाऊँ । पायउ अचल अनूपम ठाऊँ ॥
dhruvaṁ sagalāni japeu hari nāūṁ, pāyau acala anūpama ṭhāūṁ.
सुमिरि पवनसुत पावन नामू । अपने बस करि राखे रामू ॥
sumiri pavanasuta pāvana nāmū, apane basa kari rākhe rāmū.
अपतु अजामिलु गजु गनिकाऊ । भए मुकुत हरि नाम प्रभाऊ ॥
apatu ajāmilu gaju ganikāū, bhae mukuta hari nāma prabhāū.
कहौं कहाँ लगि नाम बड़ाई । रामु न सकहिं नाम गुन गाई ॥
kahauṁ kahāṁ lagi nāma baṛāī, rāmu na sakahiṁ nāma guna gāī.

Trans:

By the power of this Name Shiva, the immortal god of inauspicious attire was blest and became brightened with auspiciousness. By the power of this Name Shukdev, Sanat-kumār, and all saints, sages, and ascetics have enjoyed heavenly rapture. Nārad, himself as dear to Hara and Harī as Harī is dear to the world, too sang the praises of the power of Name. By repeating this Name Prahlād, through the Lord's grace, became the crown of the faithful. Dhruva in his distress repeated the name of Harī, and was rewarded by a fixed and incomparable station in the heavens. By meditating on this Holy Name Hanumān won and kept the affection of Rāma. By the power of Harī's name Ajāmil and the elephant and the harlot all three obtained salvation. Why farther extend the list? Not even the incarnate Shrī Rāma could exhaust the glories of the Name 'Rāma'.

दोहा-dohā:

नामु राम को कलपतरु कलि कल्यान निवासु ।
nāmu rāma ko kalapataru kali kalyāna nivāsu,
जो सुमिरत भयो भाँग तें तुलसी तुलसीदासु ॥२६॥
jo sumirata bhayo bhāṁga teṁ tulasī tulasīdāsu. 26.

Trans:

The name of Rāma is as the tree of paradise, the centre of all that is good in the world; and whoever meditates upon it too becomes transformed—as if from a vile hemp-stick into the sanctifying Tulsī plant (says Tulsī).

चौपाई-caupāī:

चहुँ जुग तीनि काल तिहुँ लोका । भए नाम जपि जीव बिसोका ॥
cahuṁ juga tīni kāla tihuṁ lokā, bhae nāma japi jīva bisokā.
बेद पुरान संत मत एहू । सकल सुकृत फल राम सनेहू ॥
beda purāna saṁta mata ehū, sakala sukṛta phala rāma sanehū.
ध्यानु प्रथम जुग मखबिधि दूजें । द्वापर परितोषत प्रभु पूजें ॥
dhyānu prathama juga makhabidhi dūjeṁ, dvāpara paritoṣata prabhu pūjeṁ.
कलि केवल मल मूल मलीना । पाप पयोनिधि जन मन मीना ॥
kali kevala mala mūla malīnā, pāpa payonidhi jana mana mīnā.
नाम कामतरु काल कराला । सुमिरत समन सकल जग जाला ॥
nāma kāmataru kāla karālā, sumirata samana sakala jaga jālā.

राम नाम कलि अभिमत दाता । हित परलोक लोक पितु माता ॥
rāma nāma kali abhimata dātā, hita paraloka loka pitu mātā.
नहिं कलि करम न भगति बिबेकू । राम नाम अवलंबन एकू ॥
nahiṁ kali karama na bhagati bibekū, rāma nāma avalaṁbana ekū.
कालनेमि कलि कपट निधानू । नाम सुमति समरथ हनुमानू ॥
kālanemi kali kapaṭa nidhānū, nāma sumati samaratha hanumānū.

Trans:

In all the four ages; in all time, past, present, or future; in the three spheres of earth, heaven and hell; any creature that repeats the name Rāma becomes blessed. The following is the verdict of the Vedas, the Purānas and all the saints—that love of Rāma is the fruit of all virtue. In the first-age, contemplation; in the second-age, sacrifice; in the Dwāpar-Yug temple worship was the appointed propitiation; but in this vile and impure Kali-Yug, where the soul of man floats like a fish in an ocean of sin, in such dreadful times, the Name is the only tree of life, and by meditating on it all vile commotion is stilled. In these evil days neither good deeds, nor piety, nor spiritual wisdom is of any avail, but only the name of Rāma. His name is as it were the wisdom and the might of Hanumān to expose and destroy the Kālnemī-like wiles of the wicked world.

दोहा-dohā:

राम नाम नरकेसरी कनककसिपु कलिकाल ।
rāma nāma narakesarī kanakakasipu kalikāla,
जापक जन प्रहलाद जिमि पालिहि दलि सुरसाल ॥२७॥
jāpaka jana prahalāda jimi pālihi dali surasāla. 27.

Trans:

As Narsingh was manifested to destroy Hiranyā-kashyap, the enemy of heaven—in order to protect Prahlād—so is the Name of Rāma for the destruction of the wicked and the protection of the pious.

चौपाई-caupāī:

भायँ कुभायँ अनख आलसहूँ । नाम जपत मंगल दिसि दसहूँ ॥
bhāyaṁ kubhāyaṁ anakha ālasahūṁ, nāma japata maṁgala disi dasahūṁ.
सुमिरि सो नाम राम गुन गाथा । करउँ नाइ रघुनाथहि माथा ॥
sumiri so nāma rāma guna gāthā, karauṁ nāi raghunāthahi māthā.
मोरि सुधारिहि सो सब भाँती । जासु कृपा नहिं कृपाँ अघाती ॥
mori sudhārihi so saba bhāṁtī, jāsu kṛpā nahiṁ kṛpāṁ aghātī.
राम सुस्वामि कुसेवकु मोसो । निज दिसि देखि दयानिधि पोसो ॥
rāma susvāmi kusevaku moso, nija disi dekhi dayānidhi poso.
लोकहुँ बेद सुसाहिब रीती । बिनय सुनत पहिचानत प्रीती ॥
lokahuṁ beda susāhiba rītī, binaya sunata pahicānata prītī.
गनी गरीब ग्रामनर नागर । पंडित मूढ़ मलीन उजागर ॥
ganī garība grāmanara nāgara, paṁḍita mūṛha malīna ujāgara.
सुकबि कुकबि निज मति अनुहारी । नृपहि सराहत सब नर नारी ॥
sukabi kukabi nija mati anuhārī, nṛpahi sarāhata saba nara nārī.
साधु सुजान सुसील नृपाला । ईस अंस भव परम कृपाला ॥
sādhu sujāna susīla nṛpālā, īsa aṁsa bhava parama kṛpālā.
सुनि सनमानहिं सबहि सुबानी । भनिति भगति नति गति पहिचानी ॥
suni sanamānahiṁ sabahi subānī, bhaniti bhagati nati gati pahicānī.
यह प्राकृत महिपाल सुभाऊ । जान सिरोमनि कोसलराऊ ॥
yaha prākṛta mahipāla subhāū, jāna siromani kosalarāū.
रीझत राम सनेह निसोतें । को जग मंद मलिनमति मोतें ॥
rījhata rāma saneha nisoteṁ, ko jaga maṁda malinamati moteṁ.

Trans:

By repeating this name—whether in joy or in sadness, in activity or in repose—bliss is diffused all around. Remembering that Name and bowing my head to the Lord of Raghus, I proceed to recount the virtues of Shrī Rāma. He, whose grace is never tired of showing its good-will to devotees, will mend my errors in every way. Thou art my good Lord, and I thy poor servant; bear this in mind and graciously protect me. The world and scripture alike declare it to be a characteristic of a good master that he hears prayer and acknowledges affection. Rich or poor, villager or urban, learned or unlearned, pure or impure, good poet or bad, all according to their ability extol their master as being the good, amiable, gracious lord of incomparable compassion; and he hears and accepts their honest attempts, recognizing in their words both devotion and a measure of ability. Such is the way of earthly lords, to say nothing of the Lord of Kaushal Shrī Rāma, who is the crest-jewel of wisdom. Shrī Rāma gets pleased by unalloyed love; but alas, who is duller and more impure of mind in this world than I am?

दोहा-dohā:

सठ सेवक की प्रीति रुचि रखिहहिं राम कृपालु ।
saṭha sevaka kī prīti ruci rakhihahiṁ rāma kṛpālu,
उपल किए जलजान जेहिं सचिव सुमति कपि भालु ॥२८क॥
upala kie jalajāna jehiṁ saciva sumati kapi bhālu. 28(ka).

हौंहु कहावत सबु कहत राम सहत उपहास ।
hauṁhu kahāvata sabu kahata rāma sahata upahāsa,
साहिब सीतानाथ सो सेवक तुलसीदास ॥२८ख॥
sāhiba sītānātha so sevaka tulasīdāsa. 28(kha).

Trans:

The benevolent Shrī Rāma—who made a ship out of a rock and wise ministers out of monkeys and bears—will nonetheless respect the devotion and pleasure of this wicked servant (which I am). Everybody calls me a servant of the Lord and I myself claim to be one; and Shrī Rāma puts up with the scoffing remark that a master like Sītā's Lord has such a servant as Tulsīdās.

चौपाई-caupāī:

अति बड़ि मोरि ढिठाई खोरी । सुनि अघ नरकहुँ नाक सकोरी ॥
ati baṛi mori ḍhiṭhāī khorī, suni agha narakahuṁ nāka sakorī.
समुझि सहम मोहि अपडर अपनें । सो सुधि राम कीन्हि नहिं सपनें ॥
samujhi sahama mohi apaḍara apaneṁ, so sudhi rāma kīnhi nahiṁ sapaneṁ.
सुनि अवलोकि सुचित चख चाही । भगति मोरि मति स्वामि सराही ॥
suni avaloki sucita cakha cāhī, bhagati mori mati svāmi sarāhī.
कहत नसाइ होइ हियँ नीकी । रीझत राम जानि जन जी की ॥
kahata nasāi hoi hiyaṁ nīkī, rījhata rāma jāni jana jī kī.
रहति न प्रभु चित चूक किए की । करत सुरति सय बार हिए की ॥
rahati na prabhu cita cūka kie kī, karata surati saya bāra hie kī.
जेहिं अघ बधेउ ब्याध जिमि बाली । फिरि सुकंठ सोइ कीन्हि कुचाली ॥
jehiṁ agha badheu byādha jimi bālī, phiri sukaṁṭha soi kīnhi kucālī.
सोइ करतूति बिभीषन केरी । सपनेहुँ सो न राम हियँ हेरी ॥
soi karatūti bibhīṣana kerī, sapanehuṁ so na rāma hiyaṁ herī.
ते भरतहि भेंटत सनमाने । राजसभाँ रघुबीर बखाने ॥
te bharatahi bheṁṭata sanamāne, rājasabhāṁ raghubīra bakhāne.

Trans:

My presumption is indeed very sad, as villainous and disgusting as hell; but seeing me alarmed with these terrors of my own, Rāma would not dream of considering them; but hearing, and with his own eyes perceiving my good faith, the Lord will applaud my devout intention. Though this story is spoilt by the retelling, Rāma is satisfied and accounts it as good—since the intent is good. The Lord is not mindful of a chance fault, and on every occasion he considers the heart. Thus the very crime—for which he, like a huntsman, killed Bālī—was in turn the sin of Sugrīva, and again of Vibhīshan, but in their case Rāma did not dream of censure, but honored them both at the meeting with Bharat and commended them in open court.

दोहा-dohā:

प्रभु तरु तर कपि डार पर ते किए आपु समान ।
prabhu taru tara kapi ḍāra para te kie āpu samāna,
तुलसी कहूँ न राम से साहिब सीलनिधान ॥२९क॥
tulasī kahūm̐ na rāma se sāhiba sīlanidhāna. 29(ka).

राम निकाईं रावरी है सबही को नीक ।
rāma nikāīṁ rāvarī hai sabahī ko nīka,
जौं यह साँची है सदा तौ नीको तुलसीक ॥२९ख॥
jauṁ yaha sām̐cī hai sadā tau nīko tulasīka. 29(kha).

एहि बिधि निज गुन दोष कहि सबहि बहुरि सिरु नाइ ।
ehi bidhi nija guna doṣa kahi sabahi bahuri siru nāi,
बरनउँ रघुबर बिसद जसु सुनि कलि कलुष नसाइ ॥२९ग॥
baranaum̐ raghubara bisada jasu suni kali kaluṣa nasāi. 29(ga).

Trans:

The Lord sat under the tree and the monkeys above on the bough, he thus exalted all equal to himself. There is no master so generous as Shrī Rāma, O Tulsīdās! O Rāma, thy goodness is good to all, and if so, then be good to Tulsīdās as well. Thus declaring my merits and defects and again bowing my head to all, I proceed to tell the glorious saga of Raghubar, by the sounds of which all the sins of the world is effaced.

चौपाई-caupāī:

जागबलिक जो कथा सुहाई । भरद्वाज मुनिबरहि सुनाई ॥
jāgabalika jo kathā suhāī, bharadvāja munibarahi sunāī.
कहिहउँ सोइ संबाद बखानी । सुनहुँ सकल सज्जन सुखु मानी ॥
kahihaum̐ soi saṁbāda bakhānī, sunahum̐ sakala sajjana sukhu mānī.
संभु कीन्ह यह चरित सुहावा । बहुरि कृपा करि उमहि सुनावा ॥
saṁbhu kīnha yaha carita suhāvā, bahuri kṛpā kari umahi sunāvā.
सोइ सिव कागभुसुंडिहि दीन्हा । राम भगत अधिकारी चीन्हा ॥
soi siva kāgabhusuṁḍihi dīnhā, rāma bhagata adhikārī cīnhā.
तेहि सन जागबलिक पुनि पावा । तिन्ह पुनि भरद्वाज प्रति गावा ॥
tehi sana jāgabalika puni pāvā, tinha puni bharadvāja prati gāvā.
ते श्रोता बकता समसीला । सवँदरसी जानहिं हरिलीला ॥
te śrotā bakatā samasīlā, savam̐darasī jānahiṁ harilīlā.
जानहिं तीनि काल निज ग्याना । करतल गत आमलक समाना ॥
jānahiṁ tīni kāla nija gyānā, karatala gata āmalaka samānā.
औरउ जे हरिभगत सुजाना । कहहिं सुनहिं समुझहिं बिधि नाना ॥
aurau je haribhagata sujānā, kahahiṁ sunahiṁ samujhahiṁ bidhi nānā.

Trans:

Now listen all in friendly wise while I relate the story as I have heard it, as it was communicated by Yāgyavalk to the great sage Bharadvāja. It was first of all composed by Shiva and graciously revealed to Umā, and again declared to Kāgabhusumdi—known to be chief among the votaries of Rāma. From him Yāgyavalk received it, and he recited it to Bharadvāja. Both these, the listener and the reciter, are equally virtuous; they view all alike and are acquainted with the pastimes of Shrī Harī. Like a plum placed on one's palm, they hold the knowledge of past, present and future within their minds. Besides these, other enlightened devotees of Shrī Harī too recite, hear and understand this story in diverse ways.

दोहा-dohā:

मैं पुनि निज गुर सन सुनी कथा सो सूकरखेत ।
maiṁ puni nija gura sana sunī kathā so sūkarakheta,
समुझी नहिं तसि बालपन तब अति रहेउँ अचेत ॥३०क॥
samujhī nahiṁ tasi bālapana taba ati raheum̐ aceta. 30(ka).

श्रोता बकता ग्याननिधि कथा राम कै गूढ़ ।
śrotā bakatā gyānanidhi kathā rāma kai gūṛha,
किमि समुझौं मैं जीव जड़ कलि मल ग्रसित बिमूढ़ ॥३०ख॥
kimi samujhauṁ maiṁ jīva jaṛa kali mala grasita bimūṛha. 30(kha).

Trans:

I again heard the story from my own master at Sūkar-khet without understanding it, when I was quite a child and had no sense. And how could such a dull creature, being both ignorant and eaten up with worldly impurities, understand so mysterious a legend and dialogue between such sage interlocutors?

चौपाई-caupāī:

तदपि कही गुर बारहिं बारा । समुझि परी कछु मति अनुसारा ॥
tadapi kahī gura bārahiṁ bārā, samujhi parī kachu mati anusārā.
भाषाबद्ध करबि मैं सोई । मोरें मन प्रबोध जेहिं होई ॥
bhāṣābaddha karabi maiṁ soī, moreṁ mana prabodha jehiṁ hoī.
जस कछु बुधि बिबेक बल मेरें । तस कहिहउँ हियँ हरि के प्रेरें ॥
jasa kachu budhi bibeka bala mereṁ, tasa kahihaum̐ hiyam̐ hari ke prereṁ.
निज संदेह मोह भ्रम हरनी । करउँ कथा भव सरिता तरनी ॥
nija saṁdeha moha bhrama haranī, karaum̐ kathā bhava saritā taranī.
बुध बिश्राम सकल जन रंजनि । रामकथा कलि कलुष बिभंजनि ॥
budha biśrāma sakala jana raṁjani, rāmakathā kali kaluṣa bibhaṁjani.
रामकथा कलि पंनग भरनी । पुनि बिबेक पावक कहुँ अरनी ॥
rāmakathā kali paṁnaga bharanī, puni bibeka pāvaka kahum̐ aranī.
रामकथा कलि कामद गाई । सुजन सजीवनि मूरि सुहाई ॥
rāmakathā kali kāmada gāī, sujana sajīvani mūri suhāī.
सोइ बसुधातल सुधा तरंगिनि । भय भंजनि भ्रम भेक भुअंगिनि ॥
soi basudhātala sudhā taraṁgini, bhaya bhaṁjani bhrama bheka bhuaṁgini.
असुर सेन सम नरक निकंदिनि । साधु बिबुध कुल हित गिरिनंदिनि ॥
asura sena sama naraka nikaṁdini, sādhu bibudha kula hita girinaṁdini.
संत समाज पयोधि रमा सी । बिस्व भार भर अचल छमा सी ॥
saṁta samāja payodhi ramā sī, bisva bhāra bhara acala chamā sī.
जम गन मुहँ मसि जग जमुना सी । जीवन मुकुति हेतु जनु कासी ॥
jama gana muham̐ masi jaga jamunā sī, jīvana mukuti hetu janu kāsī.
रामहि प्रिय पावनि तुलसी सी । तुलसिदास हित हियँ हुलसी सी ॥
rāmahi priya pāvani tulasī sī, tulasidāsa hita hiyam̐ hulasī sī.
सिवप्रिय मेकल सैल सुता सी । सकल सिद्धि सुख संपति रासी ॥
sivapriya mekala saila sutā sī, sakala siddhi sukha saṁpati rāsī.
सदगुन सुरगन अंब अदिति सी । रघुबर भगति प्रेम परमिति सी ॥
sadaguna suragana aṁba aditi sī, raghubara bhagati prema paramiti sī.

Trans:

But my master repeated it time after time, till at length I understood as much as could be expected; and I now put it down in the coarse tongue for the better elucidation of my ideas; with my heart inspired by Harī and using all the little sense, judgment, and ability that I possess. The story that I have to tell clears my own doubts as it does every other error and delusion, and is a raft on which to cross the ocean of existence. The story of Rāma is a resting-place for the intellect, a universal delight, a destroyer of worldly impurity, an antidote to the venom of passion, a match to enkindle the fire of wisdom, the cow of plenty of this Kali-Yug. It is the life-giving herb of ambrosia to make good men immortal, a stream of nectar flowing on the earth, destroyer of death, a virtual snake to devour toad-like delusion. It is beneficent to pious souls-even as Goddess Pārwatī is friendly to gods; again, it puts an end to hell even as Pārwatī exterminated the army of demons. It flows from the assemblage of saints even as Lakshmī emerged from the ocean. It is like the immoveable earth that supports all the weight of creation; like the Yamunā to put to shame the angel of death; like Kashī the savior of all living creatures. It is as dear to Rāma as the pure Tulsī; as beneficent to Tulsīdās as his own mother; as dear to Shiva as Narmada, the daughter of Mount Mekal. It is the bestower of all perfection and prosperity; like Aditī, gracious mother of all the gods; the perfect outcome of love and devotion to Raghubar.

दोहा-dohā:

रामकथा मंदाकिनी चित्रकूट चित चारु ।
rāmakathā maṁdākinī citrakūṭa cita cāru,
तुलसी सुभग सनेह बन सिय रघुबीर बिहारु ॥ ३१ ॥
tulasī subhaga saneha bana siya raghubīra bihāru. 31.

Trans:

The story of Rāma is as the river Mandakinī and a good intention like Mount Chitra-kūt, while sincere affection is as it were the forest where Rāma and Sītā love to abide.

चौपाई-caupāī:

रामचरित चिंतामनि चारू । संत सुमति तिय सुभग सिंगारू ॥
rāmacarita ciṁtāmani cārū, saṁta sumati tiya subhaga siṁgārū.
जग मंगल गुनग्राम राम के । दानि मुकुति धन धरम धाम के ॥
jaga maṁgala gunagrāma rāma ke, dāni mukuti dhana dharama dhāma ke.
सदगुर ग्यान बिराग जोग के । बिबुध बैद भव भीम रोग के ॥
sadagura gyāna birāga joga ke, bibudha baida bhava bhīma roga ke.
जननि जनक सिय राम प्रेम के । बीज सकल ब्रत धरम नेम के ॥
janani janaka siya rāma prema ke, bīja sakala brata dharama nema ke.
समन पाप संताप सोक के । प्रिय पालक परलोक लोक के ॥
samana pāpa saṁtāpa soka ke, priya pālaka paraloka loka ke.
सचिव सुभट भूपति बिचार के । कुंभज लोभ उदधि अपार के ॥
saciva subhaṭa bhūpati bicāra ke, kuṁbhaja lobha udadhi apāra ke.
काम कोह कलिमल करिगन के । केहरि सावक जन मन बन के ॥
kāma koha kalimala karigana ke, kehari sāvaka jana mana bana ke.
अतिथि पूज्य प्रियतम पुरारि के । कामद घन दारिद दवारि के ॥
atithi pūjya priyatama purāri ke, kāmada ghana dārida davāri ke.
मंत्र महामनि बिषय ब्याल के । मेटत कठिन कुअंक भाल के ॥
maṁtra mahāmani biṣaya byāla ke, meṭata kaṭhina kuaṁka bhāla ke.
हरन मोह तम दिनकर कर से । सेवक सालि पाल जलधर से ॥
harana moha tama dinakara kara se, sevaka sāli pāla jaladhara se.
अभिमत दानि देवतरु बर से । सेवत सुलभ सुखद हरि हर से ॥
abhimata dāni devataru bara se, sevata sulabha sukhada hari hara se.
सुकबि सरद नभ मन उडगन से । रामभगत जन जीवन धन से ॥
sukabi sarada nabha mana uḍagana se, rāmabhagata jana jīvana dhana se.
सकल सुकृत फल भूरि भोग से । जग हित निरुपधि साधु लोग से ॥
sakala sukṛta phala bhūri bhoga se, jaga hita nirupadhi sādhu loga se.
सेवक मन मानस मराल से । पावक गंग तंरग माल से ॥
sevaka mana mānasa marāla se, pāvaka gaṁga taṁraga māla se.

Trans:

The legend of Rāma is a delectable wish-yielding gem and a graceful adornment of saintly wisdom. Rama's perfections are a joy of the world and bestower of virtue, wealth, and eternal salvation. They are the saintly instructors of wisdom, asceticism, and spiritual contemplation; and like the physician of the gods to heal the fearful diseases of life; and are the very parent of Devotion to Sītā and Rāma. They are the seed of all holy vows and practices; the destroyer of sin, of pain, and of sorrow; our guardian in this world and the next; the Prime Minister and the General of Kingly Counsel; a very Agastya to drink up the illimitable ocean of desire; a young lion in the forest of life to attack the wild elephants of lust, anger, and sensual imparity; as dear to Shiva as the presence of a highly-honored guest; as an abundant shower to quench the fire of meanness; a potent spell against the venom of the world; the effacers from the forehead of the deep brand of evil destiny; the dispeller of the darkness of error like the rays of sun; like a shower on the rice field in the form of devotees; like the tree of paradise granting every desire; like Harī and Hara, accessible and gracious to all servants; like the stars in the clear autumn sky of the poet's mind; like the richness of life enjoyed by Rāma's votaries; like the perfect felicity that is the reward of virtue; like the assembly of the faithful in benevolence and composure; like a swan in the pure lake of the believer's soul; like the abundant flow of the purifying stream Gangā.

दोहा-dohā:

कुपथ कुतरक कुचालि कलि कपट दंभ पाषंड ।
kupatha kutaraka kucāli kali kapaṭa daṁbha pāṣaṁḍa,
दहन राम गुन ग्राम जिमि इंधन अनल प्रचंड ॥ ३२क॥
dahana rāma guna grāma jimi iṁdhana anala pracaṁḍa. 32(ka).

रामचरित राकेस कर सरिस सुखद सब काहु ।
rāmacarita rākesa kara sarisa sukhada saba kāhu,
सज्जन कुमुद चकोर चित हित बिसेषि बड़ लाहु ॥ ३२ख॥
sajjana kumuda cakora cita hita biseṣi baṛa lāhu. 32(kha).

Trans:

Rāma's perfect merit is like a strong fire to consume the dry wood of schism and heresy, evil practices and worldly deceit, hypocrisy and infidelity. His acts are like the rays of the full moon that give pleasure to all, but they are especially consoling to the souls of the pious like the lotus and the *chakor*.

चौपाई-caupāī:

कीन्हि प्रस्न जेहि भाँति भवानी । जेहि बिधि संकर कहा बखानी ॥
kīnhi prasna jehi bhām̐ti bhavānī, jehi bidhi saṁkara kahā bakhānī.
सो सब हेतु कहब मैं गाई । कथाप्रबंध बिचित्र बनाई ॥
so saba hetu kahaba maiṁ gāī, kathāprabaṁdha bicitra banāī.
जेहिं यह कथा सुनी नहिं होई । जनि आचरजु करै सुनि सोई ॥
jehiṁ yaha kathā sunī nahiṁ hoī, jani ācaraju karai suni soī.
कथा अलौकिक सुनहिं जे ग्यानी । नहिं आचरजु करहिं अस जानी ॥
kathā alaukika sunahiṁ je gyānī, nahiṁ ācaraju karahiṁ asa jānī.
रामकथा कै मिति जग नाहीं । असि प्रतीति तिन्ह के मन माहीं ॥
rāmakathā kai miti jaga nāhīṁ, asi pratīti tinha ke mana māhīṁ.
नाना भाँति राम अवतारा । रामायन सत कोटि अपारा ॥
nānā bhām̐ti rāma avatārā, rāmāyana sata koṭi apārā.
कलपभेद हरिचरित सुहाए । भाँति अनेक मुनीसन्ह गाए ॥
kalapabheda haricarita suhāe, bhām̐ti aneka munīsanha gāe.
करिअ न संसय अस उर आनी । सुनिअ कथा सारद रति मानी ॥
karia na saṁsaya asa ura ānī, sunia kathā sārada rati mānī.

Trans:

All the questions that Bhawānī asked, with Shankar's replies thereto, I now proceed to give in substance, with agreeable diversity of style. No one is to be astonished if one should happen not to have heard any particular legend before—for a wise man, on hearing for the first time any marvelous act, will feel no surprise, reasoning thus with himself: 'I know well that there is no limit in the world to the stories about Rāma, for he has in various forms become incarnate, and the verses of the Rāmāyana are some thousand millions in number; his glorious acts are of myriad diversity, and have been sung by sages in countless ways.' So indulge no doubts, but listen reverently and devoutly.

दोहा-dohā:

राम अनंत अनंत गुन अमित कथा बिस्तार ।
rāma anaṁta anaṁta guna amita kathā bistāra,
सुनि आचरजु न मानिहहिं जिन्ह कें बिमल बिचार ॥३३॥
suni ācaraju na mānihahiṁ jinha keṁ bimala bicāra. 33.

Trans:

Rāma is infinite, his perfections infinite, and his legends are of immeasurable extent; men of enlightened understanding will therefore wonder at nothing they hear.

चौपाई-caupāī:

एहि बिधि सब संसय करि दूरी । सिर धरि गुर पद पंकज धूरी ॥
ehi bidhi saba saṁsaya kari dūrī, sira dhari gura pada paṁkaja dhūrī.
पुनि सबही बिनवउँ कर जोरी । करत कथा जेहिं लाग न खोरी ॥
puni sabahī binavauṁ kara jorī, karata kathā jehiṁ lāga na khorī.
सादर सिवहि नाइ अब माथा । बरनउँ बिसद राम गुन गाथा ॥
sādara sivahi nāi aba māthā, baranauṁ bisada rāma guna gāthā.
संबत सोरह सै एकतीसा । करउँ कथा हरि पद धरि सीसा ॥
saṁbata soraha sai ekatīsā, karauṁ kathā hari pada dhari sīsā.
नौमी भौम बार मधु मासा । अवधपुरीं यह चरित प्रकासा ॥
naumī bhauma bāra madhu māsā, avadhapurīṁ yaha carita prakāsā.
जेहि दिन राम जनम श्रुति गावहिं । तीरथ सकल तहाँ चलि आवहिं ॥
jehi dina rāma janama śruti gāvahiṁ, tīratha sakala tahāṁ cali āvahiṁ.
असुर नाग खग नर मुनि देवा । आइ करहिं रघुनायक सेवा ॥
asura nāga khaga nara muni devā, āi karahiṁ raghunāyaka sevā.
जन्म महोत्सव रचहिं सुजाना । करहिं राम कल कीरति गाना ॥
janma mahotsava racahiṁ sujānā, karahiṁ rāma kala kīrati gānā.

Trans:

Having in this manner put away all doubt, I place on my head the dust from the lotus feet of my master, and with folded hands making an obeisance to all with the prayer that no fault may attach to my telling of the story, and bowing my head reverently before Shiva, I proceed to sing the excellent glories of Rāma. In this Samvat year of 1631, I write, with my head at Harī's feet, on Tuesday the 9th of the sweet month of Chaitra, at the city of Avadh; on the day when the scriptures say Rāma was born; when the spirits of all holy places there assemble with demons, serpents, birds, men, saints, and gods; and there they offer homage to Raghunāth, while the enlightened celebrate the great birthday festivities and hymn the high glories of Shrī Rāma.

दोहा-dohā:

मज्जहिं सज्जन बृंद बहु पावन सरजू नीर ।
majjahiṁ sajjana bṛṁda bahu pāvana sarajū nīra,
जपहिं राम धरि ध्यान उर सुंदर स्याम सरीर ॥३४॥
japahiṁ rāma dhari dhyāna ura suṁdara syāma sarīra. 34.

Trans:

Pious crowds bathe in the all-purifying stream of the Sarjū and murmur Rāma's name, while his dark and beautiful form is imprinted on their hearts.

चौपाई-caupāī:

दरस परस मज्जन अरु पाना । हरइ पाप कह बेद पुराना ॥
darasa parasa majjana aru pānā, harai pāpa kaha beda purānā.
नदी पुनीत अमित महिमा अति । कहि न सकइ सारदा बिमलमति ॥
nadī punīta amita mahimā ati, kahi na sakai sāradā bimalamati.
राम धामदा पुरी सुहावनि । लोक समस्त बिदित अति पावनि ॥
rāma dhāmadā purī suhāvani, loka samasta bidita ati pāvani.
चारि खानि जग जीव अपारा । अवध तजें तनु नहिं संसारा ॥
cāri khāni jaga jīva apārā, avadha tajeṁ tanu nahiṁ saṁsārā.
सब बिधि पुरी मनोहर जानी । सकल सिद्धिप्रद मंगल खानी ॥
saba bidhi purī manohara jānī, sakala siddhiprada maṁgala khānī.
बिमल कथा कर कीन्ह अरंभा । सुनत नसाहिं काम मद दंभा ॥
bimala kathā kara kīnha araṁbhā, sunata nasāhiṁ kāma mada daṁbhā.
रामचरितमानस एहि नामा । सुनत श्रवन पाइअ बिश्रामा ॥
rāmacaritamānasa ehi nāmā, sunata śravana pāia biśrāmā.
मन करि बिषय अनल बन जरई । होइ सुखी जौं एहिं सर परई ॥
mana kari biṣaya anala bana jaraī, hoi sukhī jauṁ ehiṁ sara paraī.
रामचरितमानस मुनि भावन । बिरचेउ संभु सुहावन पावन ॥
rāmacaritamānasa muni bhāvana, biraceu saṁbhu suhāvana pāvana.
त्रिबिध दोष दुख दारिद दावन । कलि कुचालि कुलि कलुष नसावन ॥
tribidha doṣa dukha dārida dāvana, kali kucāli kuli kaluṣa nasāvana.
रचि महेस निज मानस राखा । पाइ सुसमउ सिवा सन भाषा ॥
raci mahesa nija mānasa rākhā, pāi susamau sivā sana bhāṣā.
तातें रामचरितमानस बर । धरेउ नाम हियँ हेरि हरषि हर ॥
tāteṁ rāmacaritamānasa bara, dhareu nāma hiyaṁ heri haraṣi hara.
कहउँ कथा सोइ सुखद सुहाई । सादर सुनहु सुजन मन लाई ॥
kahauṁ kathā soi sukhada suhāī, sādara sunahu sujana mana lāī.

Trans:

The Vedas and Purānas declare that sin is cleansed by the mere sight or touch of the holy stream Sarjū, as well as by bathing in or drinking of it. Its immeasurable grandeur is indescribable even by the pure intelligence of Saraswatī. The city, which exalts one to Rāma's own heaven, is beautiful and celebrated through all worlds as all-purifying. A soul goes through countless births in animate species from the four modes of birth, but he becomes freed from every body—once at last having dropped his body at Ajodhyā. Knowing it to be in every way charming, a bestower of success and a mine of auspiciousness, I hereby make a beginning of my sacred song which destroys, in those who hear it, the mad frenzy of lust. Its mere name—the lake of glorious enactments of Rāma—serves to refresh the ear, while the soul itself, like an elephant escaping from a forest afire with lust, gains immense relief upon plunging into it. Holy and beautiful; the delight of the sages; consuming the three ill conditions of sin, sorrow, and want; putting an end to the evil practices and impurities of the wicked world; first composed by Mahādev and buried in the deep lake of his own soul till at an auspicious moment he declared it to Umā, this Epic—which Shiva looking into his own soul joyfully gave the excellent name of Rāmcharitmānas—this is the blessed legend which I repeat. Hear it, ye good people, reverently and with attention.

दोहा-dohā:

जस मानस जेहि बिधि भयउ जग प्रचार जेहि हेतु ।
jasa mānasa jehi bidhi bhayau jaga pracāra jehi hetu,
अब सोइ कहउँ प्रसंग सब सुमिरि उमा बृषकेतु ॥३५॥
aba soi kahauṁ prasaṁga saba sumiri umā bṛṣaketu. 35.

Trans:

Now meditating upon Umā and upon Mahādev, who has a bull emblazoned on his standard, I explain the connection, showing how it is a lake and in what manner it is formed, and for what reason it has spread through the world.

चौपाई-caupāī:

संभु प्रसाद सुमति हियँ हुलसी । रामचरितमानस कबि तुलसी ॥
saṁbhu prasāda sumati hiyaṁ hulasī, rāmacaritamānasa kabi tulasī.
करइ मनोहर मति अनुहारी । सुजन सुचित सुनि लेहु सुधारी ॥

karai manohara mati anuhārī, sujana sucita suni lehu sudhārī.

सुमति भूमि थल हृदय अगाधू । बेद पुरान उदधि घन साधू ॥
sumati bhūmi thala hṛdaya agādhū, beda purāna udadhi ghana sādhū.

बरषहिं राम सुजस बर बारी । मधुर मनोहर मंगलकारी ॥
baraṣahiṁ rāma sujasa bara bārī, madhura manohara maṁgalakārī.

लीला सगुन जो कहहिं बखानी । सोइ स्वच्छता करइ मल हानी ॥
līlā saguna jo kahahiṁ bakhānī, soi svacchatā karai mala hānī.

प्रेम भगति जो बरनि न जाई । सोइ मधुरता सुसीतलताई ॥
prema bhagati jo barani na jāī, soi madhuratā susītalatāī.

सो जल सुकृत सालि हित होई । राम भगत जन जीवन सोई ॥
so jala sukṛta sāli hita hoī, rāma bhagata jana jīvana soī.

मेधा महि गत सो जल पावन । सकिलि श्रवन मग चलेउ सुहावन ॥
medhā mahi gata so jala pāvana, sakili śravana maga caleu suhāvana.

भरेउ सुमानस सुथल थिराना । सुखद सीत रुचि चारु चिराना ॥
bhareu sumānasa suthala thirānā, sukhada sīta ruci cāru cirānā.

Trans:

By the blessing of Shambhu, the heart and mind of Tulsīdās has become sanctified by the blessed theme of Rāmcharitmānas—which composition I will narrate as well as I can, subject to the correction of all good people whose attention I invite. The heart is, as it were, a deep place in the terrain of good thoughts, and the Vedas and Purānas are the sea, and the saints are as clouds which rain down praises of Rāma in sweet, grateful, auspicious showers; the sportive enactments related of Him are like the inherent purity and cleansing power of rain-water; while loving devotion—which is beyond any power of words to describe—is its sweetness and coolness. When such a shower falls on the rice-fields of virtue, it gives new life to the faithful; and as its holy drops fall to the earth they are collected in the channel supplied by the ears; and then flowing down into the lake of the soul they inundate it; and there they settle down permanently—beautiful, refreshing, cool.

दोहा-dohā:

सुठि सुंदर संबाद बर बिरचे बुद्धि बिचारि ।
suṭhi suṁdara saṁbāda bara birace buddhi bicāri,

तेइ एहि पावन सुभग सर घाट मनोहर चारि ॥ ३६ ॥
tei ehi pāvana subhaga sara ghāṭa manohara cāri. 36.

Trans:

The four most beautiful and excellent dialogues—(between Bhusumdi and Garud; Shiva and Pārwatī; Yāgyavalk and Bharadvāja; Tulsīdās and all listeners)—which have been charmingly woven into this narrative are the four lovely Ghāts of this holy and charming lake.

चौपाई-caupāī:

सप्त प्रबंध सुभग सोपाना । ग्यान नयन निरखत मन माना ॥
sapta prabaṁdha subhaga sopānā, gyāna nayana nirakhata mana mānā.

रघुपति महिमा अगुन अबाधा । बरनब सोइ बर बारि अगाधा ॥
raghupati mahimā aguna abādhā, baranaba soi bara bāri agādhā.

राम सीय जस सलिल सुधासम । उपमा बीचि बिलास मनोरम ॥
rāma sīya jasa salila sudhāsama, upamā bīci bilāsa manorama.

पुरइनि सघन चारु चौपाई । जुगुति मंजु मनि सीप सुहाई ॥
puraini saghana cāru caupāī, juguti maṁju mani sīpa suhāī.

छंद सोरठा सुंदर दोहा । सोइ बहुरंग कमल कुल सोहा ॥
chaṁda soraṭhā suṁdara dohā, soi bahuraṁga kamala kula sohā.

अरथ अनूप सुभाव सुभासा । सोइ पराग मकरंद सुबासा ॥
aratha anūpa subhāva subhāsā, soi parāga makaraṁda subāsā.

सुकृत पुंज मंजुल अलि माला । ग्यान बिराग बिचार मराला ॥
sukṛta puṁja maṁjula ali mālā, gyāna birāga bicāra marālā.

धुनि अवरेब कबित गुन जाती । मीन मनोहर ते बहुभाँती ॥
dhuni avareba kabita guna jātī, mīna manohara te bahubhām̐tī.

अरथ धरम कामादिक चारी । कहब ग्यान बिग्यान बिचारी ॥
aratha dharama kāmādika cārī, kahaba gyāna bigyāna bicārī.

नव रस जप तप जोग बिरागा । ते सब जलचर चारु तड़ागा ॥
nava rasa japa tapa joga birāgā, te saba jalacara cāru taṛāgā.

सुकृती साधु नाम गुन गाना । ते बिचित्र जल बिहग समाना ॥
sukṛtī sādhu nāma guna gānā, te bicitra jala bihaga samānā.

संतसभा चहुँ दिसि अवँराई । श्रद्धा रितु बसंत सम गाई ॥
saṁtasabhā cahum̐ disi avam̐rāī, śraddhā ritu basaṁta sama gāī.

भगति निरुपन बिबिध बिधाना । छमा दया दम लता बिताना ॥
bhagati nirupana bibidha bidhānā, chamā dayā dama latā bitānā.

सम जम नियम फूल फल ग्याना । हरि पद रति रस बेद बखाना ॥
sama jama niyama phūla phala gyānā, hari pada rati rasa beda bakhānā.

औरउ कथा अनेक प्रसंगा । तेइ सुक पिक बहुबरन बिहंगा ॥
aurau kathā aneka prasaṁgā, tei suka pika bahubarana bihaṁgā.

Trans:

The Seven Cantos are its beautiful flights of steps, which the eyes of the soul delight to look upon; the unqualified and unsullied greatness of Raghupatī may be described as its clear deep expanse; the glory of Rāma and Sītā are its ambrosial waters; the similes its pretty wavelets; the stanzas its beautiful lotus beds; the elegance of expression are as lovely mother-of-pearl; the chaṁdas, sorthās, and couplets are as many-colored lotus flowers; the incomparable sense, sentiment, and language is the lotus-pollen, filaments, and fragrance; the exalted action are as the beautiful swarms of bees; the sage moral reflections are like swans; the rhythm, involutions, and different poetical artifices are many diverse kinds of graceful fish; the precepts regarding the four ends of life, the wise sayings, the thoughtful judgments, the nine styles of compositions, the prayers, penance, abstraction, and asceticism, of which examples are given—are all the beautiful living creatures in the lake; the eulogies on the faithful, the saints, and the holy name are like flocks of water-birds; the religious audience are like circling mango groves, and their faith as like the season of the spring; the expositions of all the phases of devotion and of tenderness and generosity are like the trees and canopying creepers; virtues and holy vows are as flowers, with the wisdom as the fruit; the love for Harī's feet is the sound of the Vedas; and all other stories and episodes are as parrots and cuckoos and diverse kinds of birds.

दोहा-dohā:

पुलक बाटिका बाग बन सुख सुबिहंग बिहारु ।
pulaka bāṭikā bāga bana sukha subihaṁga bihāru,

माली सुमन सनेह जल सींचत लोचन चारु ॥ ३७ ॥
mālī sumana saneha jala sīṁcata locana cāru. 37.

Trans:

Pleasant is the sporting of the birds in grove, garden, or parterre, where good intention like a gardener bedews the eyes with the water of affection.

चौपाई-caupāī:

जे गावहिं यह चरित सँभारे । तेइ एहि ताल चतुर रखवारे ॥
je gāvahiṁ yaha carita saṁbhāre, tei ehi tāla catura rakhavāre.

सदा सुनहिं सादर नर नारी । तेइ सुरबर मानस अधिकारी ॥
sadā sunahiṁ sādara nara nārī, tei surabara mānasa adhikārī.

अति खल जे बिषई बग कागा । एहि सर निकट न जाहिं अभागा ॥
ati khala je biṣaī baga kāgā, ehi sara nikaṭa na jāhiṁ abhāgā.

संबुक भेक सेवार समाना । इहाँ न बिषय कथा रस नाना ॥
saṁbuka bheka sevāra samānā, ihām̐ na biṣaya kathā rasa nānā.

तेहि कारन आवत हियँ हारे । कामी काक बलाक बिचारे ॥
tehi kārana āvata hiyaṁ hāre, kāmī kāka balāka bicāre.
आवत एहिं सर अति कठिनाई । राम कृपा बिनु आइ न जाई ॥
āvata ehiṁ sara ati kaṭhināī, rāma kṛpā binu āi na jāī.
कठिन कुसंग कुपंथ कराला । तिन्ह के बचन बाघ हरि ब्याला ॥
kaṭhina kusaṁga kupaṁtha karālā, tinha ke bacana bāgha hari byālā.
गृह कारज नाना जंजाला । ते अति दुर्गम सैल बिसाला ॥
gṛha kāraja nānā jaṁjālā, te ati durgama saila bisālā.
बन बहु बिषम मोह मद माना । नदीं कुतर्क भयंकर नाना ॥
bana bahu biṣama moha mada mānā, nadīṁ kutarka bhayaṁkara nānā.

Trans:

Those who accurately recite these cantos are like the diligent guardians of the lake; the men and women who reverently hear them, those excellent people, are like its owners. Sensual wretches are like the cranes and crows that have no part in this pond nor ever come near it; for here are no prurient and seductive stories—which are like the snails, frogs, and scum on the water that attract crows—and therefore the lustful crow and greedy crane, if they do happen to come, are disappointed. It is only by the favor of Rāma that anyone reaches here, for there is much difficulty in getting to this lake. You see, bad company makes much steepness and difficulty to this road; and their evil sayings are like so many tigers, lions, and serpents upon the path; and the various entanglements of domestic affairs are like the vast insurmountable mountains; and sensual desires are like dense forests full of wild delusions on the way; and unsound reasoning is like the raging flood.

दोहा-dohā:

जे श्रद्धा संबल रहित नहिं संतन्ह कर साथ ।
je śraddhā saṁbala rahita nahiṁ saṁtanha kara sātha,
तिन्ह कहुँ मानस अगम अति जिन्हहि न प्रिय रघुनाथ ॥३८॥
tinha kahuṁ mānasa agama ati jinhahi na priya raghunātha. 38.

Trans:

For those who have not the support of faith, nor the company of the saints, nor fervent love for Raghunāth, for them this lake is very hard of access.

चौपाई-caupāī:

जौं करि कष्ट जाइ पुनि कोई । जातहिं नीद जुड़ाई होई ॥
jauṁ kari kaṣṭa jāi puni koī, jātahiṁ nīda juṛāī hoī.
जड़ता जाड़ बिषम उर लागा । गएहुँ न मज्जन पाव अभागा ॥
jaṛatā jāṛa biṣama ura lāgā, gaehuṁ na majjana pāva abhāgā.
करि न जाइ सर मज्जन पाना । फिरि आवइ समेत अभिमाना ॥
kari na jāi sara majjana pānā, phiri āvai sameta abhimānā.
जौं बहोरि कोउ पूछन आवा । सर निंदा करि ताहि बुझावा ॥
jauṁ bahori kou pūchana āvā, sara niṁdā kari tāhi bujhāvā.
सकल बिघ्न ब्यापहिं नहिं तेही । राम सुकृपाँ बिलोकहिं जेही ॥
sakala bighna byāpahiṁ nahiṁ tehī, rāma sukṛpāṁ bilokahiṁ jehī.
सोइ सादर सर मज्जनु करई । महा घोर त्रयताप न जरई ॥
soi sādara sara majjanu karaī, mahā ghora trayatāpa na jaraī.
ते नर यह सर तजहिं न काऊ । जिन्ह कें राम चरन भल भाऊ ॥
te nara yaha sara tajahiṁ na kāū, jinha keṁ rāma carana bhala bhāū.
जो नहाइ चह एहिं सर भाई । सो सतसंग करउ मन लाई ॥
jo nahāi caha ehiṁ sara bhāī, so satasaṁga karau mana lāī.
अस मानस मानस चख चाही । भइ कबि बुद्धि बिमल अवगाही ॥
asa mānasa mānasa cakha cāhī, bhai kabi buddhi bimala avagāhī.
भयउ हृदयँ आनंद उछाहू । उमगेउ प्रेम प्रमोद प्रबाहू ॥
bhayau hṛdayaṁ ānaṁda uchāhū, umageu prema pramoda prabāhū.
चली सुभग कबिता सरिता सो । राम बिमल जस जल भरिता सो ॥
calī subhaga kabitā saritā so, rāma bimala jasa jala bharitā so.
सरजू नाम सुमंगल मूला । लोक बेद मत मंजुल कूला ॥
sarajū nāma sumaṁgala mūlā, loka beda mata maṁjula kūlā.
नदी पुनीत सुमानस नंदिनि । कलिमल तृन तरु मूल निकंदिनि ॥
nadī punīta sumānasa naṁdini, kalimala tṛna taru mūla nikaṁdini.

Trans:

Again, if anyone laboriously makes his way up to it but becomes overpowered by sleep and feverishness, a strange torpor and numbness settle on his soul; and though he is at the very spot, the luckless wretch makes no ablution. Having neither bathed in the lake, nor drunk of it, he goes away in his pride, and when someone comes to enquire of him he abuses it. But no difficulties deter those whom Rāma regards with affection. They reverently bathe here, are relieved from the fierce flames of sin, sorrow, and pain, and being sincerely devoted to Rāma, will never abandon it. If, my friend, you would bathe in this lake, be diligent to keep company with the good. As for myself, having thus with the mind's eye contemplated it, my poetical faculty has become clear and profound, my heart swells with joy and rapture, and it overflows in torrents of ecstatic devotion. My song flows on like a river flooded with Rāma's bright renown—just like the river Sarjū, the fount of bliss, with religion and theology for its two fair banks. This holy stream, issuing as it does from the beautiful Mānas Lake, sweeps away in its course all the impurities of the Kali-Yug, whether in the form of tiny blades of grass or may be like mighty trees tall.

दोहा-dohā:

श्रोता त्रिबिध समाज पुर ग्राम नगर दुहुँ कूल ।
śrotā tribidha samāja pura grāma nagara duhuṁ kūla,
संतसभा अनुपम अवध सकल सुमंगल मूल ॥३९॥
saṁtasabhā anupama avadha sakala sumaṁgala mūla. 39.

Trans:

The three kinds of hearers in the assembly are like the towns, villages, and hamlets on the river side, while the saints are like the incomparable city of Avadh, full of all that is auspicious.

चौपाई-caupāī:

रामभगति सुरसरितहि जाई । मिली सुकीरति सरजु सुहाई ॥
rāmabhagati surasaritahi jāī, milī sukīrati saraju suhāī.
सानुज राम समर जसु पावन । मिलेउ महानदु सोन सुहावन ॥
sānuja rāma samara jasu pāvana, mileu mahānadu sona suhāvana.
जुग बिच भगति देवधुनि धारा । सोहति सहित सुबिरति बिचारा ॥
juga bica bhagati devadhuni dhārā, sohati sahita subirati bicārā.
त्रिबिध ताप त्रासक तिमुहानी । राम सरुप सिंधु समुहानी ॥
tribidha tāpa trāsaka timuhānī, rāma sarupa siṁdhu samuhānī.
मानस मूल मिली सुरसरिही । सुनत सुजन मन पावन करिही ॥
mānasa mūla milī surasarihī, sunata sujana mana pāvana karihī.
बिच बिच कथा बिचित्र बिभागा । जनु सरि तीर तीर बन बागा ॥
bica bica kathā bicitra bibhāgā, janu sari tīra tīra bana bāgā.
उमा महेस बिबाह बराती । ते जलचर अगनित बहुभाँती ॥
umā mahesa bibāha barātī, te jalacara aganita bahubhāṁtī.
रघुबर जनम अनंद बधाई । भवँर तरंग मनोहरताई ॥
raghubara janama anaṁda badhāī, bhavaṁra taraṁga manoharatāī.

Trans:

The beautiful Sarjū, in the form of Shrī Rāma's fair renown, joined the heavenly stream, the Gangā of devotion to Rāma. The latter was joined again by the charming stream of the mighty Sona in the form of the martial glory of Rāma with his younger brother Lakshman. Intervening the two streams of Sarjū and Sona shines the celestial stream of Devotion blended with noble Dispassion and Reason. This triple stream, which scares away the threefold agony referred to above, headed towards the ocean of Shrī Rāma's divine persona. With its source in the Mānas Lake and united with the celestial river Gangā, the Sarjū of Shrī Rāma's fame will purify the mind of such pious souls that listen to it. The various tales and episodes interspersed here and there are the groves and gardens on its opposite banks. The details of the marriage and wedding procession of Umā and Shiva are like the innumerable fish in the water; the joy and gladness that attended Rāma's birth are like beautiful swarms of bees and the ripple of the lake.

दोहा-dohā:

बालचरित चहु बंधु के बनज बिपुल बहुरंग ।
bālacarita cahu baṁdhu ke banaja bipula bahuraṁga,
नृप रानी परिजन सुकृत मधुकर बारिबिहंग ॥४०॥
nṛpa rānī parijana sukṛta madhukara bāribihaṁga. 40.

Trans:

The childish sports of the four brothers are like the goodly lotus flowers; the virtuous king Dashrath and his consorts and their court like the bees and water-birds.

चौपाई-caupāī:

सीय स्वयंबर कथा सुहाई । सरित सुहावनि सो छबि छाई ॥
sīya svayaṁbara kathā suhāī, sarita suhāvani so chabi chāī.
नदी नाव पटु प्रस्न अनेका । केवट कुसल उतर सबिबेका ॥
nadī nāva paṭu prasna anekā, kevaṭa kusala utara sabibekā.
सुनि अनुकथन परस्पर होई । पथिक समाज सोह सरि सोई ॥
suni anukathana paraspara hoī, pathika samāja soha sari soī.
घोर धार भृगुनाथ रिसानी । घाट सुबद्ध राम बर बानी ॥
ghora dhāra bhṛgunātha risānī, ghāṭa subaddha rāma bara bānī.
सानुज राम बिबाह उछाहू । सो सुभ उमग सुखद सब काहू ॥
sānuja rāma bibāha uchāhū, so subha umaga sukhada saba kāhū.
कहत सुनत हरषहिं पुलकाहीं । ते सुकृती मन मुदित नहाहीं ॥
kahata sunata haraṣahiṁ pulakāhīṁ, te sukṛtī mana mudita nahāhīṁ.
राम तिलक हित मंगल साजा । परब जोग जनु जुरे समाजा ॥
rāma tilaka hita maṁgala sājā, paraba joga janu jure samājā.
काई कुमति केकई केरी । परी जासु फल बिपति घनेरी ॥
kāī kumati kekaī kerī, parī jāsu phala bipati ghanerī.

Trans:

The charming story of Sītā's marriage is like the bright gleam of pleasing river; the many formidable question, if it will be bridged, are like the boats on the stream; but the appropriate and judicious resolutions are like the skilled boats-men. Again, the argumentative discussions show like crowding travelers and the wrath of Bhrigunāth is like the rushing torrent that might inundate all; but there is Rāma's soft speech which is like the well-arranged Ghāts; the marriage festivities of Rāma and Lakshman like the grateful swell of the tide; the thrill of pleasure that spreads through the delighted audience is like the ecstatic feelings of the virtuous bathers; the auspicious preparations for marking Rāma's forehead with the *Tilak* are like the crowds assembled on holidays; and Kaekayī's evil counsel, is like the perilous moss on the bank, the cause of many calamities.

दोहा-dohā:

समन अमित उतपात सब भरतचरित जपजाग ।
samana amita utapāta saba bharatacarita japajāga,
कलि अघ खल अवगुन कथन ते जलमल बग काग ॥४१॥
kali agha khala avaguna kathana te jalamala baga kāga. 41.

Trans:

Like prayers and sacrifices, effectual to remove every misfortune, are the virtuous acts of Bharat; while the corruptions of the world and sinful men and slanderers are like the scum on the water and the cranes and crows.

चौपाई-caupāī:

कीरति सरित छहूँ रितु रूरी । समय सुहावनि पावनि भूरी ॥
kīrati sarita chahūṁ ritu rūrī, samaya suhāvani pāvani bhūrī.
हिम हिमसैलसुता सिव ब्याहू । सिसिर सुखद प्रभु जनम उछाहू ॥
hima himasailasutā siva byāhū, sisira sukhada prabhu janama uchāhū.
बरनब राम बिबाह समाजू । सो मुद मंगलमय रितुराजू ॥
baranaba rāma bibāha samājū, so muda maṁgalamaya riturājū.
ग्रीषम दुसह राम बनगवनू । पंथकथा खर आतप पवनू ॥
grīṣama dusaha rāma banagavanū, paṁthakathā khara ātapa pavanū.
बरषा घोर निसाचर रारी । सुरकुल सालि सुमंगलकारी ॥
baraṣā ghora nisācara rārī, surakula sāli sumaṁgalakārī.
राम राज सुख बिनय बड़ाई । बिसद सुखद सोइ सरद सुहाई ॥
rāma rāja sukha binaya baṛāī, bisada sukhada soi sarada suhāī.
सती सिरोमनि सिय गुनगाथा । सोइ गुन अमल अनूपम पाथा ॥
satī siromani siya gunagāthā, soi guna amala anūpama pāthā.
भरत सुभाउ सुसीतलताई । सदा एकरस बरनि न जाई ॥
bharata subhāu susītalatāī, sadā ekarasa barani na jāī.

Trans:

This river of Rāma's glory is beautiful in each of the six seasons—bright and exceedingly holy at all the times. The story of the marriage of Shiva with the daughter of the snowy mountains is like the winter; the glad rejoicings at the Lord's birth are like the dewy season; the account of the preparations for Rāma's wedding are like the delightful and auspicious spring; Rāma's intolerable banishment is like the hot weather, and the story of his rough journeys like the blazing sun and the wind; his encounters with fierce demons, by which he gladdens the hosts of heaven, are like the rains that refresh the fields; the prosperity of his reign, his humility and greatness, are like the clear, bountiful, and lovely autumn; the recital of the virtues of Sītā, that jewel of faithful wives, is as the undefiled and excellent water; the amiability of Bharat is its unvarying coolness.

दोहा-dohā:

अवलोकनि बोलनि मिलनि प्रीति परसपर हास ।
avalokani bolani milani prīti parasapara hāsa,
भायप भलि चहु बंधु की जल माधुरी सुबास ॥४२॥
bhāyapa bhali cahu baṁdhu kī jala mādhurī subāsa. 42.

Trans:

Their looks and words at meeting, their mutual love and laughter, the true fraternal affection of the four brothers, are as the water's sweetness and fragrance.

चौपाई-caupāī:

आरति बिनय दीनता मोरी । लघुता ललित सुबारि न थोरी ॥
ārati binaya dīnatā morī, laghutā lalita subāri na thorī.
अदभुत सलिल सुनत गुनकारी । आस पिआस मनोमल हारी ॥
adabhuta salila sunata gunakārī, āsa piāsa manomala hārī.
राम सुप्रेमहि पोषत पानी । हरत सकल कलि कलुष गलानी ॥
rāma supremahi poṣata pānī, harata sakala kali kaluṣa galānī.
भव श्रम सोषक तोषक तोषा । समन दुरित दुख दारिद दोषा ॥
bhava śrama soṣaka toṣaka toṣā, samana durita dukha dārida doṣā.
काम कोह मद मोह नसावन । बिमल बिबेक बिराग बढ़ावन ॥
kāma koha mada moha nasāvana, bimala bibeka birāga baṛhāvana.
सादर मज्जन पान किए तें । मिटहिं पाप परिताप हिए तें ॥
sādara majjana pāna kie teṁ, miṭahiṁ pāpa paritāpa hie teṁ.
जिन्ह एहिं बारि न मानस धोए । ते कायर कलिकाल बिगोए ॥
jinha ehiṁ bāri na mānasa dhoe, te kāyara kalikāla bigoe.

तृषित निरखि रबि कर भव बारी । फिरिहहिं मृग जिमि जीव दुखारी ॥
tṛṣita nirakhi rabi kara bhava bārī, phirihahiṁ mṛga jimi jīva dukhārī.

Trans:

My intense longing, supplication and humility represent the not inconsiderable lightness of this pure and holy water. This marvelous water heals by the mere hearing, quenches the thirst of desire and washes the dirt of the mind. This water resuscitates true love to Rāma and puts an end to all the sin and sorrows of the world, drawing out weariness from life, consoling with true comfort, destroying sin and pain and error and poverty, dispelling lust and passion and frenzy and infatuation, and promoting pure intelligence and detachment from the world. Those who reverently drink or bathe in this stream—from their soul is effaced all sin and distress; those who do not cleanse their heart in it are wretches whom the world has ruined. Those thirsty souls are like panting deer that, having seen mirage in this worldly desert, wander around lost and hapless.

दोहा-dohā:

मति अनुहारि सुबारि गुन गनि मन अन्हवाइ ।
mati anuhāri subāri guna gani mana anhavāi,
सुमिरि भवानी संकरहि कह कबि कथा सुहाइ ॥४३क ॥
sumiri bhavānī saṁkarahi kaha kabi kathā suhāi. 43(ka).

अब रघुपति पद पंकरुह हियँ धरि पाइ प्रसाद ।
aba raghupati pada paṁkaruha hiyaṁ dhari pāi prasāda,
कहउँ जुगल मुनिबर्ज कर मिलन सुभग संबाद ॥४३ख॥
kahauṁ jugala munibarja kara milana subhaga saṁbāda. 43(kha).

Trans:

Thus have I declared to the best of my ability the virtues of this excellent water, and having plunged my own soul in it, and ever remembering Bhawānī and Shankar, I proceed with my delectable story. I will first repeat in substance the original conversation, with the questions put by Bharadvāja when he found the Muni Yāgyavalk; and laying my soul at the lotus feet of Raghupatī and thus having secured his patronage, I will sing the meeting of the two great saints and their auspicious discourse.

चौपाई-caupāī:

भरद्वाज मुनि बसहिं प्रयागा । तिन्हहि राम पद अति अनुरागा ॥
bharadvāja muni basahiṁ prayāgā, tinhahi rāma pada ati anurāgā.
तापस सम दम दया निधाना । परमारथ पथ परम सुजाना ॥
tāpasa sama dama dayā nidhānā, paramāratha patha parama sujānā.
माघ मकरगत रबि जब होई । तीरथपतिहिं आव सब कोई ॥
māgha makaragata rabi jaba hoī, tīrathapatihiṁ āva saba koī.
देव दनुज किंनर नर श्रेनीं । सादर मज्जहिं सकल त्रिबेनीं ॥
deva danuja kiṁnara nara śrenīṁ, sādara majjahiṁ sakala tribenīṁ.
पूजहिं माधव पद जलजाता । परसि अखय बटु हरषहिं गाता ॥
pūjahiṁ mādhava pada jalajātā, parasi akhaya baṭu haraṣahiṁ gātā.
भरद्वाज आश्रम अति पावन । परम रम्य मुनिबर मन भावन ॥
bharadvāja āśrama ati pāvana, parama ramya munibara mana bhāvana.
तहाँ होइ मुनि रिषय समाजा । जाहिं जे मज्जन तीरथराजा ॥
tahāṁ hoi muni riṣaya samājā, jāhiṁ je majjana tīratharājā.
मज्जहिं प्रात समेत उछाहा । कहहिं परसपर हरि गुन गाहा ॥
majjahiṁ prāta sameta uchāhā, kahahiṁ parasapara hari guna gāhā.

Trans:

At Prayāg lives the saint Bharadvāja, devoted beyond measure to Rāma's feet, a self-restrained ascetic full of sobriety and benevolence, supremely skilled in divine knowledge. In the month of Magh, when the sun enters the sign of Capricorn, everyone visits this chief of holy places. Gods, demigods, Kinnars, and men in troops, all devoutly bathe in the triple flood and worship the lotus feet of Madhav, and they have the happiness of touching the imperishable Banyan. At Bharadvāja's hallowed hermitage—so charming a spot that even the saints loved it—is ever a concourse of seers and sages, come to bathe at the holiest of all holy places; and having with gladness performed their ablutions at break of day, they converse together on the glories of Harī;

दोहा-dohā:

ब्रह्म निरूपन धरम बिधि बरनहिं तत्त्व बिभाग ।
brahma nirūpana dharama bidhi baranahiṁ tattva bibhāga,
कहहिं भगति भगवंत कै संजुत ग्यान बिराग ॥४४॥
kahahiṁ bhagati bhagavaṁta kai saṁjuta gyāna birāga. 44.

Trans:

and they discuss the nature of Brahmm, the precepts of religion and the classification of fundamental entities; and they expatiate on Devotion to the Lord coupled with spiritual enlightenment and dispassion.

चौपाई-caupāī:

एहि प्रकार भरि माघ नहाहीं । पुनि सब निज निज आश्रम जाहीं ॥
ehi prakāra bhari māgha nahāhīṁ, puni saba nija nija āśrama jāhīṁ.
प्रति संबत अति होइ अनंदा । मकर मज्जि गवनहिं मुनिबृंदा ॥
prati saṁbata ati hoi anaṁdā, makara majji gavanahiṁ munibṛṁdā.
एक बार भरि मकर नहाए । सब मुनीस आश्रमन्ह सिधाए ॥
eka bāra bhari makara nahāe, saba munīsa āśramanha sidhāe.
जागबलिक मुनि परम बिबेकी । भरद्वाज राखे पद टेकी ॥
jāgabalika muni parama bibekī, bharadvāja rākhe pada ṭekī.
सादर चरन सरोज पखारे । अति पुनीत आसन बैठारे ॥
sādara carana saroja pakhāre, ati punīta āsana baiṭhāre.
करि पूजा मुनि सुजसु बखानी । बोले अति पुनीत मृदु बानी ॥
kari pūjā muni sujasu bakhānī, bole ati punīta mṛdu bānī.
नाथ एक संसउ बड़ मोरें । करगत बेदतत्व सबु तोरें ॥
nātha eka saṁsau baṛa moreṁ, karagata bedatatva sabu toreṁ.
कहत सो मोहि लागत भय लाजा । जौं न कहउँ बड़ होइ अकाजा ॥
kahata so mohi lāgata bhaya lājā, jauṁ na kahauṁ baṛa hoi akājā.

Trans:

In this manner bathing regularly all through the festival, they again return each to his own hermitage, and every year there is a similar rejoicing when the saints meet for their annual ablution. On one occasion, when the bathing time was over and all the holy men had left, Bharadvāja clasped by the feet and detained the supremely wise saint Yāgyavalk; and having reverently laved his lotus feet and seating him on a most honored seat, and with ritual ceremonies having extolled the saint's glory, he finally addressed him in the mildest of tones thusly: "Sir, I have a great doubt—while in your grasp are all the mysteries of the Vedas. I am afraid and ashamed to speak, but if I speak not, I lose a great opportunity.

दोहा-dohā:

संत कहहि असि नीति प्रभु श्रुति पुरान मुनि गाव ।
saṁta kahahi asi nīti prabhu śruti purāna muni gāva,
होइ न बिमल बिबेक उर गुर सन किएँ दुराव ॥४५॥
hoi na bimala bibeka ura gura sana kieṁ durāva. 45.

Trans:

The saints lay down the rule—and the Vedas as well as the Purānas and sages too loudly proclaim—that pure wisdom cannot dawn in the heart should one keep anything concealed from one's spiritual preceptor.

चौपाई-caupāī:

अस बिचारि प्रगटउँ निज मोहू । हरहु नाथ करि जन पर छोहू ॥
asa bicāri pragaṭauṁ nija mohū, harahu nātha kari jana para chohū.
राम नाम कर अमित प्रभावा । संत पुरान उपनिषद गावा ॥
rāma nāma kara amita prabhāvā, saṁta purāna upaniṣada gāvā.

संतत जपत संभु अबिनासी । सिव भगवान ग्यान गुन रासी ॥
saṁtata japata saṁbhu abināsī, siva bhagavāna gyāna guna rāsī.
आकर चारि जीव जग अहहीं । कासीं मरत परम पद लहहीं ॥
ākara cāri jīva jaga ahahīṁ, kāsīṁ marata parama pada lahahīṁ.
सोपि राम महिमा मुनिराया । सिव उपदेसु करत करि दाया ॥
sopi rāma mahimā munirāyā, siva upadesu karata kari dāyā.
रामु कवन प्रभु पूछउँ तोही । कहिअ बुझाइ कृपानिधि मोही ॥
rāmu kavana prabhu pūchauṁ tohī, kahia bujhāi kṛpānidhi mohī.
एक राम अवधेस कुमारा । तिन्ह कर चरित बिदित संसारा ॥
eka rāma avadhesa kumārā, tinha kara carita bidita saṁsārā.
नारि बिरहँ दुखु लहेउ अपारा । भयहु रोषु रन रावनु मारा ॥
nāri birahaṁ dukhu laheu apārā, bhayahu roṣu rana rāvanu mārā.

Trans:

Remembering this, I lay bare my folly—take pity, my Lord, on your faithful servant and dispel it. The might of the Name-of-Rāma is immeasurable—thus speak the saints, the Purānas and the Vedic commentaries; the immortal Shambhu—who is the Lord Shiva, the perfection of wisdom and goodness—is ever repeating the Name. Though all the four groups of animate beings in the world attain to salvation if they die in his city Kashī, yet, O king of saints, such is the virtue of Rāma's Name that even Shiva in his compassion enjoins it as a charm. I ask of you, my Lord, who is this Rāma? Be gracious enough to instruct me. There is one Rāma, the prince of Avadh, whose acts are known throughout the world, who suffered infinite distress by the loss of his spouse, and waxing wrath slew Rāvan in battle.

दोहा-dohā:

प्रभु सोइ राम कि अपर कोउ जाहि जपत त्रिपुरारि ।
prabhu soi rāma ki apara kou jāhi japata tripurāri,
सत्यधाम सर्बग्य तुम्ह कहहु बिबेकु बिचारि ॥४६॥
satyadhāma sarbagya tumha kahahu bibeku bicāri. 46.

Trans:

Is it this Rāma, my Lord, or another Rāma, whose name Tripurārī is ever repeating? Ponder the matter well and tell me, O wisest and most faithful of men.

चौपाई-caupāī:

जैसें मिटै मोर भ्रम भारी । कहहु सो कथा नाथ बिस्तारी ॥
jaiseṁ miṭai mora bhrama bhārī, kahahu so kathā nātha bistārī.
जागबलिक बोले मुसुकाई । तुम्हहि बिदित रघुपति प्रभुताई ॥
jāgabalika bole musukāī, tumhahi bidita raghupati prabhutāī.
रामभगत तुम्ह मन क्रम बानी । चतुराई तुम्हारि मैं जानी ॥
rāmabhagata tumha mana krama bānī, caturāī tumhāri maiṁ jānī.
चाहहु सुनै राम गुन गूढ़ा । कीन्हिहु प्रस्न मनहुँ अति मूढ़ा ॥
cāhahu sunai rāma guna gūṛhā, kīnhihu prasna manahuṁ ati mūṛhā.
तात सुनहु सादर मनु लाई । कहउँ राम कै कथा सुहाई ॥
tāta sunahu sādara manu lāī, kahauṁ rāma kai kathā suhāī.
महामोहु महिषेसु बिसाला । रामकथा कालिका कराला ॥
mahāmohu mahiṣesu bisālā, rāmakathā kālikā karālā.
रामकथा ससि किरन समाना । संत चकोर करहिं जेहि पाना ॥
rāmakathā sasi kirana samānā, saṁta cakora karahiṁ jehi pānā.
ऐसेइ संसय कीन्ह भवानी । महादेव तब कहा बखानी ॥
aisei saṁsaya kīnha bhavānī, mahādeva taba kahā bakhānī.

Trans:

Tell me the whole history in full, my master, so that my strong delusion may be dissipated." Yāgyavalk answered with a smile: "All the glory of Raghupatī is known to you—you are a votary of His in heart, word, and deed; but I understand your stratagem. Wishing to hear the marvelous stories of Rāma's virtues, you are questioning me with an affectation of bewilderment and ignorance. Listen then, my son, with devout attention as I repeat the fair legend, which vanquishes every monstrous error, just as dread Kalikā vanquished the demon Mahishāsur, but which is drunk in by the saints as the light of the moon by the *chakor*. When a similar doubt was suggested by Bhawānī, Mahādev then expounded the whole matter in detail.

दोहा-dohā:

कहउँ सो मति अनुहारि अब उमा संभु संबाद ।
kahauṁ so mati anuhāri aba umā saṁbhu saṁbāda,
भयउ समय जेहि हेतु जेहि सुनु मुनि मिटिहि बिषाद ॥४७॥
bhayau samaya jehi hetu jehi sunu muni miṭihi biṣāda. 47.

Trans:

And as best I can, I will repeat their conversation, noting both its time and occasion; and upon hearing it, my friend, all difficulties will vanish.

चौपाई-caupāī:

एक बार त्रेता जुग माहीं । संभु गए कुंभज रिषि पाहीं ॥
eka bāra tretā juga māhīṁ, saṁbhu gae kuṁbhaja riṣi pāhīṁ.
संग सती जगजननि भवानी । पूजे रिषि अखिलेस्वर जानी ॥
saṁga satī jagajanani bhavānī, pūje riṣi akhilesvara jānī.
रामकथा मुनीबर्ज बखानी । सुनी महेस परम सुखु मानी ॥
rāmakathā munībarja bakhānī, sunī mahesa parama sukhu mānī.
रिषि पूछी हरिभगति सुहाई । कही संभु अधिकारी पाई ॥
riṣi pūchī haribhagati suhāī, kahī saṁbhu adhikārī pāī.
कहत सुनत रघुपति गुन गाथा । कछु दिन तहाँ रहे गिरिनाथा ॥
kahata sunata raghupati guna gāthā, kachu dina tahāṁ rahe girināthā.
मुनि सन बिदा मागि त्रिपुरारी । चले भवन सँग दच्छकुमारी ॥
muni sana bidā māgi tripurārī, cale bhavana saṁga dacchakumārī.
तेहि अवसर भंजन महिभारा । हरि रघुबंस लीन्ह अवतारा ॥
tehi avasara bhaṁjana mahibhārā, hari raghubaṁsa līnha avatārā.
पिता बचन तजि राजु उदासी । दंडक बन बिचरत अबिनासी ॥
pitā bacana taji rāju udāsī, daṁḍaka bana bicarata abināsī.

Trans:

Once upon a time in Tretā-Yug, the second age of the world, Shambhu went to Rishī Agastya; and with him went the mother of the world, the faithful Bhawānī, his consort. The hermit made obeisance—for he recognized them as the sovereigns of the universe, and recited the story of Rāma, with which Mahādev was delighted. The sage then inquired about Devotion to Harī and Shambhu discoursed upon that finding in the sage a fit recipient. In such converse the mountain Lord Mahādev passed some days there and then took his leave and returned home with the daughter of Daksha. During those very days, with a view to relieving the burden of the earth, Shrī Harī had descended in the line of King Raghu. Renouncing his right to the throne at the word of his father Dashrath, the immortal Lord was wandering in the Dandak forest in the garb of an ascetic.

दोहा-dohā:

हृदयँ बिचारत जात हर केहि बिधि दरसनु होइ ।
hṛdayaṁ bicārata jāta hara kehi bidhi darasanu hoi,
गुप्त रुप अवतरेउ प्रभु गएँ जान सबु कोइ ॥४८क॥
gupta rupa avatareu prabhu gaeṁ jāna sabu koi. 48(ka).

Trans:

Shiva kept pondering as he went: 'How can I obtain a sight of him? The Lord has become incarnate secretly, and if I do then the secret will become known to all.'

सोरठा-soraṭhā:

संकर उर अति छोभु सती न जानहिं मरमु सोइ ।
saṁkara ura ati chobhu satī na jānahiṁ maramu soi,
तुलसी दरसन लोभु मन डरु लोचन लालची ॥४८ख॥
tulasī darasana lobhu mana ḍaru locana lālacī. 48(kha).

Trans:

In Shankar's heart was a great tumult, but Sati did not comprehend the mystery. Says Tulsī: the hope of a meeting with the Lord fills the soul with agitation and the eyes with wistfulness.

चौपाई-caupāī:

रावन मरन मनुज कर जाचा । प्रभु बिधि बचनु कीन्ह चह साचा ॥
rāvana marana manuja kara jācā, prabhu bidhi bacanu kīnha caha sācā.
जौं नहिं जाउँ रहइ पछितावा । करत बिचारु न बनत बनावा ॥
jauṁ nahiṁ jāuṁ rahai pachitāvā, karata bicāru na banata banāvā.
एहि बिधि भए सोचबस ईसा । तेहि समय जाइ दससीसा ॥
ehi bidhi bhae socabasa īsā, tehi samaya jāi dasasīsā.
लीन्ह नीच मारीचहि संगा । भयउ तुरत सोइ कपट कुरंगा ॥
līnha nīca mārīcahi saṁgā, bhayau turata soi kapaṭa kuraṁgā.
करि छलु मूढ़ हरी बैदेही । प्रभु प्रभाउ तस बिदित न तेही ॥
kari chalu mūṛha harī baidehī, prabhu prabhāu tasa bidita na tehī.
मृग बधि बन्धु सहित हरि आए । आश्रमु देखि नयन जल छाए ॥
mṛga badhi bandhu sahita hari āe, āśramu dekhi nayana jala chāe.
बिरह बिकल नर इव रघुराई । खोजत बिपिन फिरत दोउ भाई ॥
biraha bikala nara iva raghurāī, khojata bipina phirata dou bhāī.
कबहूँ जोग बियोग न जाकें । देखा प्रगट बिरह दुखु ताकें ॥
kabahūṁ joga biyoga na jākeṁ, dekhā pragaṭa biraha dukhu tākeṁ.

Trans:

'Rāvan has obtained the boon of death at the hands of man alone; and the Lord has willed Brahmmā's boon to come true. Yet, if I do not go to meet him, I shall ever regret it'. Thought as he would, yet he could not hit upon a plan. At the very time that he was thus lost in thought, the ten-headed Rāvan—taking with him the vile Mārich that had assumed the form of a false deer—in his folly treacherously carried away Sītā: not knowing the Lord's great power. When Rāma returned with his brother from the chase and saw the empty hermitage, his eyes filled with tears; and like a mortal man distressed by the loss of his spouse, he wandered through the forest in search of her—he and his brother; and He, who knows neither union nor separation, manifested all the pangs of parting.

दोहा-dohā:

अति बिचित्र रघुपति चरित जानहिं परम सुजान ।
ati bicitra raghupati carita jānahiṁ parama sujāna,
जे मतिमंद बिमोह बस हृदयँ धरहिं कछु आन ॥४९॥
je matimaṁda bimoha basa hṛdayaṁ dharahiṁ kachu āna. 49.

Trans:

Rāma's ways are most mysterious; only the supremely wise can comprehend them; the dull of soul and the sensual imagine something quite different.

चौपाई-caupāī:

संभु समय तेहि रामहि देखा । उपजा हियँ अति हरषु बिसेषा ॥
saṁbhu samaya tehi rāmahi dekhā, upajā hiyaṁ ati haraṣu biseṣā.
भरि लोचन छबिसिंधु निहारी । कुसमय जानि न कीन्हि चिन्हारी ॥
bhari locana chabisiṁdhu nihārī, kusamaya jāni na kīnhi cinhārī.
जय सच्चिदानंद जग पावन । अस कहि चलेउ मनोज नसावन ॥
jaya saccidānaṁda jaga pāvana, asa kahi caleu manoja nasāvana.
चले जात सिव सती समेता । पुनि पुनि पुलकत कृपानिकेता ॥
cale jāta siva satī sametā, puni puni pulakata kṛpāniketā.
सतीं सो दसा संभु कै देखी । उर उपजा संदेहु बिसेषी ॥
satīṁ so dasā saṁbhu kai dekhī, ura upajā saṁdehu biseṣī.
संकरु जगतबंद्य जगदीसा । सुर नर मुनि सब नावत सीसा ॥
saṁkaru jagatabaṁdya jagadīsā, sura nara muni saba nāvata sīsā.
तिन्ह नृपसुतहि कीन्ह परनामा । कहि सच्चिदानंद परधामा ॥
tinha nṛpasutahi kīnha paranāmā, kahi saccidānaṁda paradhāmā.
भए मगन छबि तासु बिलोकी । अजहुँ प्रीति उर रहति न रोकी ॥
bhae magana chabi tāsu bilokī, ajahuṁ prīti ura rahati na rokī.

Trans:

Then it was that Shambhu saw Rāma; and a great joy arose in his soul. His eyes were filled with the vision of the most beautiful, but it was no fitting time to make himself known, and so he simply passed on exclaiming: 'Hail, Supreme Being, redeemer of the world.' But as he went on his way with Sati, his whole body thrilled with delight; and in Sati's soul, when she observed her Lord's emotion, a great doubt arose: 'To Shankar, the universally adored and sovereign Lord, gods, men, and saints all bow their heads, yet he has made obeisance to this Prince saluting him as the Supreme God; and he so enraptured to behold him; and he feels a great upsurge of emotion which subsides not even now.

दोहा-dohā:

ब्रह्म जो ब्यापक बिरज अज अकल अनीह अभेद ।
brahma jo byāpaka biraja aja akala anīha abheda,
सो कि देह धरि होइ नर जाहि न जानत बेद ॥५०॥
so ki deha dhari hoi nara jāhi na jānata beda. 50.

Trans:

What! The omnipresent and unbegotten God, the creator who has neither parts nor passions, who is beyond all distinctions, beyond Māyā, whom not even the Veda can comprehend, has He taken the form of a man?

चौपाई-caupāī:

बिष्नु जो सुर हित नरतनु धारी । सोउ सर्बग्य जथा त्रिपुरारी ॥
biṣnu jo sura hita naratanu dhārī, sou sarbagya jathā tripurārī.
खोजइ सो कि अग्य इव नारी । ग्यानधाम श्रीपति असुरारी ॥
khojai so ki agya iva nārī, gyānadhāma śrīpati asurārī.
संभुगिरा पुनि मृषा न होई । सिव सर्बग्य जान सबु कोई ॥
saṁbhugirā puni mṛṣā na hoī, siva sarbagya jāna sabu koī.
अस संसय मन भयउ अपारा । होइ न हृदयँ प्रबोध प्रचारा ॥
asa saṁsaya mana bhayau apārā, hoi na hṛdayaṁ prabodha pracārā.
जद्यपि प्रगट न कहेउ भवानी । हर अंतरजामी सब जानी ॥
jadyapi pragaṭa na kaheu bhavānī, hara aṁtarajāmī saba jānī.
सुनहि सती तव नारि सुभाऊ । संसय अस न धरिअ उर काऊ ॥
sunahi satī tava nāri subhāū, saṁsaya asa na dharia ura kāū.
जासु कथा कुंभज रिषि गाई । भगति जासु मैं मुनिहि सुनाई ॥
jāsu kathā kuṁbhaja riṣi gāī, bhagati jāsu maiṁ munihi sunāī.
सोइ मम इष्टदेव रघुबीरा । सेवत जाहि सदा मुनि धीरा ॥
soi mama iṣṭadeva raghubīrā, sevata jāhi sadā muni dhīrā.

Trans:

According to what Shiva says, though Vishnu in heaven assumes a human Avatar, He remains all-wise; yet here like an ignorant man He is hunting about, this fountain of wisdom, this Lord of Lakshmī, this vanquisher of demons! Still Shambhu's words cannot be false, nor can his knowledge be gainsaid. Thus an infinite doubt has come into my mind, and there is no way of solving it.' Although Bhawānī did not speak out, Mahādev can read the heart and knew her thoughts, and he said: "Look here, Sati; the woman is foremost in you; but you should not entertain these doubts; this is that Rāma, my beloved Deity, whose story was sung by the Rishī Agastya; in whom I exhorted the saint to have faith, and who is ever worshipped by seers and sages.

छंद-chamda:

मुनि धीर जोगी सिद्ध संतत बिमल मन जेहि ध्यावहीं ।
muni dhīra jogī siddha saṁtata bimala mana jehi dhyāvahīṁ,
कहि नेति निगम पुरान आगम जासु कीरति गावहीं ॥
kahi neti nigama purāna āgama jāsu kīrati gāvahīṁ.
सोइ रामु ब्यापक ब्रह्म भुवन निकाय पति माया धनी ।
soi rāmu byāpaka brahma bhuvana nikāya pati māyā dhanī,
अवतरेउ अपने भगत हित निजतंत्र नित रघुकुलमनी ॥
avatareu apane bhagata hita nijataṁtra nita raghukulamanī.

Trans:

He who has bodied Himself forth as the Jewel of Raghu's race for the sake of His devotees is no other than the Supreme Eternal, who is all-pervading and ever free, who is the Ruler of all the worlds, the Lord of Māyā, whom illumined sages, Yogi's and Siddhas constantly meditate upon with their sinless mind; and whose glory is sung by the Vedas as well as the Purānas and other scriptures in negative terms as 'Not-This'."

सोरठा-sorathā:

लाग न उर उपदेसु जदपि कहेउ सिवँ बार बहु ।
lāga na ura upadesu jadapi kaheu sivaṁ bāra bahu,
बोले बिहसि महेसु हरिमाया बलु जानि जियँ ॥५१॥
bole bihasi mahesu harimāyā balu jāni jiyaṁ. 51.

Trans:

Though he spoke thus time after time, his words made no impression upon her; and at last Mahādev, recognizing Rāma's deceptive power, smiled and said:

चौपाई-caupāī:

जौं तुम्हरें मन अति संदेहू । तौ किन जाइ परीछा लेहू ॥
jauṁ tumhareṁ mana ati saṁdehū, tau kina jāi parīchā lehū.
तब लगि बैठ अहउँ बटछाहीं । जब लगि तुम्ह ऐहहु मोहि पाहीं ॥
taba lagi baiṭha ahauṁ baṭachāhīṁ, jaba lagi tumha aihahu mohi pāhīṁ.
जैसें जाइ मोह भ्रम भारी । करेहु सो जतनु बिबेक बिचारी ॥
jaiseṁ jāi moha bhrama bhārī, karehu so jatanu bibeka bicārī.
चलीं सती सिव आयसु पाई । करहिं बिचारु करौं का भाई ॥
calīṁ satī siva āyasu pāī, karahiṁ bicāru karauṁ kā bhāī.
इहाँ संभु अस मन अनुमाना । दच्छसुता कहुँ नहिं कल्याना ॥
ihāṁ saṁbhu asa mana anumānā, dacchasutā kahuṁ nahiṁ kalyānā.
मोरेहु कहें न संसय जाहीं । बिधि बिपरीत भलाई नाहीं ॥
morehu kaheṁ na saṁsaya jāhīṁ, bidhi biparīta bhalāī nāhīṁ.
होइहि सोइ जो राम रचि राखा । को करि तर्क बढ़ावै साखा ॥
hoihi soi jo rāma raci rākhā, ko kari tarka baṛhāvai sākhā.
अस कहि लगे जपन हरिनामा । गईं सती जहँ प्रभु सुखधामा ॥
asa kahi lage japana harināmā, gaiṁ satī jahaṁ prabhu sukhadhāmā.

Trans:

"As the doubt in your mind is so great that it will not leave you till you have put the fact to the test, I will stay here in the shade of this Banyan until you come back after having evolved some stratagem by which to satisfy your menacing doubts." So Sati went by Shiva's order, saying to herself: 'Come now, what shall I do?', while Shambhu came to the conclusion that only mischief was in store for Daksha's daughter. "When her doubt did not yield even to my assurances," he said to himself, "it seems the stars are unpropitious to her and no good-will come out of it. Well, whatever Shrī Rāma has ordained will come to pass. Why add to complication by indulging in idle speculation?" Thinking thus he began the repetition of Harī's name, while Sati drew nigh to the Lord of abounding grace.

दोहा-dohā:

पुनि पुनि हृदयँ बिचारु करि धरि सीता कर रुप ।
puni puni hṛdayaṁ bicāru kari dhari sītā kara rupa,
आगें होइ चलि पंथ तेहिं जेहिं आवत नरभूप ॥५२॥
āgeṁ hoi cali paṁtha tehiṁ jehiṁ āvata narabhūpa. 52.

Trans:

After many an anxious thought she finally assumed the form of Sītā and began walking in front on the pathway where the King of heaven was coming.

चौपाई-caupāī:

लछिमन दीख उमाकृत बेषा । चकित भए भ्रम हृदयँ बिसेषा ॥
lachimana dīkha umākṛta beṣā, cakita bhae bhrama hṛdayaṁ biseṣā.
कहि न सकत कछु अति गंभीरा । प्रभु प्रभाउ जानत मतिधीरा ॥
kahi na sakata kachu ati gaṁbhīrā, prabhu prabhāu jānata matidhīrā.
सती कपटु जानेउ सुरस्वामी । सबदरसी सब अंतरजामी ॥
satī kapaṭu jāneu surasvāmī, sabadarasī saba aṁtarajāmī.
सुमिरत जाहि मिटइ अग्याना । सोइ सरबग्य रामु भगवाना ॥
sumirata jāhi miṭai agyānā, soi sarabagya rāmu bhagavānā.
सती कीन्ह चह तहँहुँ दुराऊ । देखहु नारि सुभाव प्रभाऊ ॥
satī kīnha caha tahaṁhuṁ durāū, dekhahu nāri subhāva prabhāū.
निज माया बलु हृदयँ बखानी । बोले बिहसि रामु मृदु बानी ॥
nija māyā balu hṛdayaṁ bakhānī, bole bihasi rāmu mṛdu bānī.
जोरि पानि प्रभु कीन्ह प्रनामू । पिता समेत लीन्ह निज नामू ॥
jori pāni prabhu kīnha pranāmū, pitā sameta līnha nija nāmū.
कहेउ बहोरि कहाँ बृषकेतू । बिपिन अकेलि फिरहु केहि हेतू ॥
kaheu bahori kahāṁ bṛṣaketū, bipina akeli phirahu kehi hetū.

Trans:

When Lakshman saw her in that disguise, he was astonished and much perplexed. Wise as he was, he could say nothing, but discreetly waited for the revelation of the Lord. Shrī Rāma took no time in detecting the deceptive trick of Sati. Rāma was the same omniscient Lord whose very thought wipes out Ignorance; and yet even him Sati attempted to deceive—see how inveterate the woman nature! But Rāma acknowledging the effect of his own delusive power, with a sweet smile and with folded hands saluted her, mentioning both his own name and that of his father, and added: 'Where is Mahādev, and why are you so wandering alone in the forest?'

दोहा-dohā:

राम बचन मृदु गूढ़ सुनि उपजा अति संकोचु ।
rāma bacana mṛdu gūṛha suni upajā ati saṁkocu,
सती सभीत महेस पहिं चलीं हृदयँ बड़ सोचु ॥५३॥
satī sabhīta mahesa pahiṁ calīṁ hṛdayaṁ baṛa socu. 53.

Trans:

When she heard these simple and profound words, a great awe came upon her and she returned to Mahādev full of fear and distress.

चौपाई-caupāī:

मैं संकर कर कहा न माना । निज अग्यानु राम पर आना ॥
maiṁ saṁkara kara kahā na mānā, nija agyānu rāma para ānā.
जाइ उतरु अब देहउँ काहा । उर उपजा अति दारुन दाहा ॥
jāi utaru aba dehauṁ kāhā, ura upajā ati dāruna dāhā.
जाना राम सतीं दुखु पावा । निज प्रभाउ कछु प्रगटि जनावा ॥
jānā rāma satīṁ dukhu pāvā, nija prabhāu kachu pragaṭi janāvā.
सतीं दीख कौतुकु मग जाता । आगें रामु सहित श्री भ्राता ॥
satīṁ dīkha kautuku maga jātā, āgeṁ rāmu sahita śrī bhrātā.
फिरि चितवा पाछें प्रभु देखा । सहित बंधु सिय सुंदर बेषा ॥

phiri citavā pāchem̐ prabhu dekhā, sahita bam̐dhu siya sum̐dara beṣā.

जहँ चितवहिं तहँ प्रभु आसीना । सेवहिं सिद्ध मुनीस प्रबीना ॥
jaham̐ citavahiṁ taham̐ prabhu āsīnā, sevahiṁ siddha munīsa prabīnā.

देखे सिव बिधि बिष्नु अनेका । अमित प्रभाउ एक तें एका ॥
dekhe siva bidhi biṣnu anekā, amita prabhāu eka teṁ ekā.

बंदत चरन करत प्रभु सेवा । बिबिध बेष देखे सब देवा ॥
baṁdata carana karata prabhu sevā, bibidha beṣa dekhe saba devā.

Trans:

"I heeded not the word of Shankar, and imposed my ignorance upon Rāma; now what answer shall I give to my Lord?"—her distress was most grievous. Then Rāma, perceiving her vexation, manifested in part his glory; and as Sati went on her way she beheld a marvelous vision: In front of her were Rāma, Sītā, and Lakshman; when again she looked back, there too she saw the Lord with his brother and Sītā in beauteous apparel. Whichever way she turned her eyes there was the Lord enthroned—with saints and learned pundits ministering to him. Innumerable Shivas, and Brahmmās, and Vishnūs, each excelling in majesty, were there bowing at his feet and doing homage; and likewise all the many lords of heaven in their different attributes.

दोहा-dohā:

सती बिधात्री इंदिरा देखीं अमित अनूप ।
satī bidhātrī iṁdirā dekhīṁ amita anūpa,

जेहिं जेहिं बेष अजादि सुर तेहि तेहि तन अनुरूप ॥५४॥
jehiṁ jehiṁ beṣa ajādi sura tehi tehi tana anurūpa. 54.

Trans:

Further she perceived innumerable Satīs, Vidhatrīs, and Indirās—all peerless in beauty. They conformed in their appearance to the garb in which their respective consorts, Brahmmā, and the other gods appeared.

चौपाई-caupāī:

देखे जहँ तहँ रघुपति जेते । सक्तिन्ह सहित सकल सुर तेते ॥
dekhe jaham̐ taham̐ raghupati jete, saktinha sahita sakala sura tete.

जीव चराचर जो संसारा । देखे सकल अनेक प्रकारा ॥
jīva carācara jo saṁsārā, dekhe sakala aneka prakārā.

पूजहिं प्रभुहि देव बहु बेषा । राम रूप दूसर नहिं देखा ॥
pūjahiṁ prabhuhi deva bahu beṣā, rāma rūpa dūsara nahiṁ dekhā.

अवलोके रघुपति बहुतेरे । सीता सहित न बेष घनेरे ॥
avaloke raghupati bahutere, sītā sahita na beṣa ghanere.

सोइ रघुबर सोइ लछिमनु सीता । देखि सती अति भईं सभीता ॥
soi raghubara soi lachimanu sītā, dekhi satī ati bhaīṁ sabhītā.

हृदय कंप तन सुधि कछु नाहीं । नयन मूदि बैठीं मग माहीं ॥
hṛdaya kaṁpa tana sudhi kachu nāhīṁ, nayana mūdi baiṭhīṁ maga māhīṁ.

बहुरि बिलोकेउ नयन उघारी । कछु न दीख तहँ दच्छकुमारी ॥
bahuri bilokeu nayana ughārī, kachu na dīkha taham̐ dacchakumārī.

पुनि पुनि नाइ राम पद सीसा । चलीं तहाँ जहँ रहे गिरीसा ॥
puni puni nāi rāma pada sīsā, calīṁ tahām̐ jaham̐ rahe girīsā.

Trans:

Each separate vision of Rāma was attended by all the gods and their consorts, and by the whole animate creation with all its multitudinous species. But while the adoring gods appeared in diverse forms there was absolutely no diverseness in the form of Rāma. Though she saw multiple figures of Rāma, and with him the oft-repeated Sītā—but it was always the exact same Rāma, the same Sītā and the same Lakshman. Sati was awestricken as she gazed; and then with fluttering heart and unconscious frame she sank upon the ground, her eyes closed. When again she looked up she saw nothing. Then oft bowing her head at Rāma's feet she returned to the spot where Mahādev awaited her.

दोहा-dohā:

गईं समीप महेस तब हँसि पूछी कुसलात ।
gaīṁ samīpa mahesa taba haṁsi pūchī kusalāta,

लीन्हि परीछा कवन बिधि कहहु सत्य सब बात ॥५५॥
līnhi parīchā kavana bidhi kahahu satya saba bāta. 55.

Trans:

When she drew near he smiled and asked if all were well saying, "Tell me now the whole truth, how did you put him to the test?"

मासपारायण दूसरा विश्राम
māsapārāyaṇa dūsarā viśrāma
(Pause 2 for a Thirty-Day Recitation)

चौपाई-caupāī:

सतीं समुझि रघुबीर प्रभाऊ । भय बस सिव सन कीन्ह दुराऊ ॥
satīṁ samujhi raghubīra prabhāū, bhaya basa siva sana kīnha durāū.

कछु न परीछा लीन्हि गोसाईं । कीन्ह प्रनामु तुम्हारिहि नाईं ॥
kachu na parīchā līnhi gosāīṁ, kīnha pranāmu tumhārihi nāīṁ.

जो तुम्ह कहा सो मृषा न होई । मोरें मन प्रतीति अति सोई ॥
jo tumha kahā so mṛṣā na hoī, moreṁ mana pratīti ati soī.

तब संकर देखेउ धरि ध्याना । सतीं जो कीन्ह चरित सबु जाना ॥
taba saṁkara dekheu dhari dhyānā, satīṁ jo kīnha carita sabu jānā.

बहुरि राममायहि सिरु नावा । प्रेरि सतिहि जेहिं झूँठ कहावा ॥
bahuri rāmamāyahi siru nāvā, preri satihi jehiṁ jhūm̐ṭha kahāvā.

हरि इच्छा भावी बलवाना । हृदयँ बिचारत संभु सुजाना ॥
hari icchā bhāvī balavānā, hṛdayam̐ bicārata saṁbhu sujānā.

सतीं कीन्ह सीता कर बेषा । सिव उर भयउ बिषाद बिसेषा ॥
satīṁ kīnha sītā kara beṣā, siva ura bhayau biṣāda biseṣā.

जौं अब करउँ सती सन प्रीती । मिटइ भगति पथु होइ अनीती ॥
jauṁ aba karaum̐ satī sana prītī, miṭai bhagati pathu hoi anītī.

Trans:

Sati remembered the glory of the Lord, and in her awe concealed the truth from Shiva, saying, "O sir, I tried no test, but like you simply made obeisance. I was confident that what you said could not be false." Then Shankar perceived by contemplation and understood all that Sati had done. He bowed to the might of Rāma's delusive power, which had been sent forth to put a lying speech into Sati's mouth. 'The will of heaven and fate are strong indeed,' thus he reflected, in a great distress of mind. 'As Sati has taken Sītā's form, if now I regard her as my wife, my devotion will be at an end, and it will be a sin to me.

दोहा-dohā:

परम पुनीत न जाइ तजि किएँ प्रेम बड़ पापु ।
parama punīta na jāi taji kiem̐ prema baṛa pāpu,

प्रगटि न कहत महेसु कछु हृदयँ अधिक संतापु ॥५६॥
pragaṭi na kahata mahesu kachu hṛdayam̐ adhika saṁtāpu. 56.

Trans:

Sati is too chaste to be abandoned, and it is a great sin to love her any more as a wife.' The great Lord Shiva uttered not a word aloud, although there was great agony in his heart.

चौपाई-caupāī:

तब संकर प्रभु पद सिरु नावा । सुमिरत रामु हृदयँ अस आवा ॥
taba saṁkara prabhu pada siru nāvā, sumirata rāmu hṛdayam̐ asa āvā.

एहिं तन सतिहि भेट मोहि नाहीं । सिव संकल्पु कीन्ह मन माहीं ॥
ehiṁ tana satihi bheṭa mohi nāhīṁ, siva saṁkalpu kīnha mana māhīṁ.

अस बिचारि संकरु मतिधीरा । चले भवन सुमिरत रघुबीरा ॥
asa bicāri saṁkaru matidhīrā, cale bhavana sumirata raghubīrā.

चलत गगन भै गिरा सुहाई । जय महेस भलि भगति दृढ़ाई ॥

calata gagana bhai girā suhāī, jaya mahesa bhali bhagati dṛṛhāī.
अस पन तुम्ह बिनु करइ को आना । रामभगत समरथ भगवाना ॥
asa pana tumha binu karai ko ānā, rāmabhagata samaratha bhagavānā.
सुनि नभगिरा सती उर सोचा । पूछा सिवहि समेत सकोचा ॥
suni nabhagirā satī ura socā, pūchā sivahi sameta sakocā.
कीन्ह कवन पन कहहु कृपाला । सत्यधाम प्रभु दीनदयाला ॥
kīnha kavana pana kahahu kṛpālā, satyadhāma prabhu dīnadayālā.
जदपि सतीं पूछा बहु भाँती । तदपि न कहेउ त्रिपुर आराती ॥
jadapi satīṁ pūchā bahu bhām̐tī, tadapi na kaheu tripura ārātī.

Trans:

At last having bowed his head at Rāma's feet and meditating on his Name, he thus resolved and made a vow in his mind: 'So long as Sati remains as she is now, I will never touch her.' With this firm determination he turned homewards, with his mind fixed on Raghubar; and as he went there was a jubilant cry in the heaven, "Glory to thee, Mahādev, for thy staunch devotion! Who other but thou, O Lord most strong in faith, would make such a vow." Sati was troubled when she heard the heavenly voice and tremblingly asked Shiva, "Tell me, O true and gracious Lord, what was the vow?" But though she asked once and again he told her not.

दोहा-dohā:

सतीं हृदयँ अनुमान किय सबु जानेउ सर्बग्य ।
satīṁ hṛdayam̐ anumāna kiya sabu jāneu sarbagya,
कीन्ह कपटु मैं संभु सन नारि सहज जड़ अग्य ॥५७क॥
kīnha kapaṭu maiṁ saṁbhu sana nāri sahaja jaṛa agya. 57(ka).

Trans:

Then she guessed of herself: 'The all-wise has discovered it all, though I attempted to deceive him—silly and senseless woman that I am.'

सोरठा-soraṭhā:

जलु पय सरिस बिकाइ देखहु प्रीति कि रीति भलि ।
jalu paya sarisa bikāi dekhahu prīti ki rīti bhali,
बिलग होइ रसु जाइ कपट खटाई परत पुनि ॥५७ख॥
bilaga hoi rasu jāi kapaṭa khaṭāī parata puni. 57(kha).

Trans:

Water and milk if mixed together are both sold as milk—look at the unifying process of love. But the introduction of a drop of lemon, or of a lie, at once causes separation.

चौपाई-caupāī:

हृदयँ सोचु समुझत निज करनी । चिंता अमित जाइ नहिं बरनी ॥
hṛdayam̐ socu samujhata nija karanī, ciṁtā amita jāi nahiṁ baranī.
कृपासिंधु सिव परम अगाधा । प्रगट न कहेउ मोर अपराधा ॥
kṛpāsiṁdhu siva parama agādhā, pragaṭa na kaheu mora aparādhā.
संकर रुख अवलोकि भवानी । प्रभु मोहि तजेउ हृदयँ अकुलानी ॥
saṁkara rukha avaloki bhavānī, prabhu mohi tajeu hṛdayam̐ akulānī.
निज अघ समुझि न कछु कहि जाई । तपइ अवाँ इव उर अधिकाई ॥
nija agha samujhi na kachu kahi jāī, tapai avām̐ iva ura adhikāī.
सतिहि ससोच जानि बृषकेतू । कहीं कथा सुंदर सुख हेतू ॥
satihi sasoca jāni bṛṣaketū, kahīṁ kathā suṁdara sukha hetū.
बरनत पंथ बिबिध इतिहासा । बिस्वनाथ पहुँचे कैलासा ॥
baranata paṁtha bibidha itihāsā, bisvanātha pahum̐ce kailāsā.
तहँ पुनि संभु समुझि पन आपन । बैठे बट तर करि कमलासन ॥
taham̐ puni saṁbhu samujhi pana āpana, baiṭhe baṭa tara kari kamalāsana.
संकर सहज सरुपु सम्हारा । लागि समाधि अखंड अपारा ॥
saṁkara sahaja sarupu samhārā, lāgi samādhi akhaṁḍa apārā.

Trans:

Deep in thought and reflecting on what she had done, no words could express her infinite sorrow, and she kept saying to herself, 'The gracious but impenetrable Shiva has not openly mentioned my offence, but my Lord has abandoned me.' Thus disturbed in soul by Shankar's sternness and thinking of her sin, she could say nothing; but her soul burned within, as if like a smoldering furnace. When Mahādev saw her so sorrowful, he began to amuse her with pleasant tales, relating various legends all the way till they came to Kailāsh. Then recalling his vow, he seated himself under a Banyan in the posture of meditation and by an immediate control of all his senses passed into a long and unbroken trance.

दोहा-dohā:

सती बसहिं कैलास तब अधिक सोचु मन माहिं ।
satī basahiṁ kailāsa taba adhika socu mana māhiṁ,
मरमु न कोऊ जान कछु जुग सम दिवस सिराहिं ॥५८॥
maramu na koū jāna kachu juga sama divasa sirāhiṁ. 58.

Trans:

There Sati dwelt on Kailāsh, sorrowing grievously. Not a soul knew her secret but each day that she lived was like an age.

चौपाई-caupāī:

नित नव सोचु सती उर भारा । कब जैहउँ दुख सागर पारा ॥
nita nava socu satī ura bhārā, kaba jaihaum̐ dukha sāgara pārā.
मैं जो कीन्ह रघुपति अपमाना । पुनि पतिबचनु मृषा करि जाना ॥
maiṁ jo kīnha raghupati apamānā, puni patibacanu mṛṣā kari jānā.
सो फलु मोहि बिधाताँ दीन्हा । जो कछु उचित रहा सोइ कीन्हा ॥
so phalu mohi bidhātām̐ dīnhā, jo kachu ucita rahā soi kīnhā.
अब बिधि अस बूझिअ नहिं तोही । संकर बिमुख जिआवसि मोही ॥
aba bidhi asa būjhia nahiṁ tohī, saṁkara bimukha jiāvasi mohī.
कहि न जाइ कछु हृदय गलानी । मन महुँ रामहि सुमिर सयानी ॥
kahi na jāi kachu hṛdaya galānī, mana mahum̐ rāmahi sumira sayānī.
जौं प्रभु दीनदयालु कहावा । आरति हरन बेद जसु गावा ॥
jauṁ prabhu dīnadayālu kahāvā, ārati harana beda jasu gāvā.
तौ मैं बिनय करउँ कर जोरी । छूटउ बेगि देह यह मोरी ॥
tau maiṁ binaya karaum̐ kara jorī, chūṭau begi deha yaha morī.
जौं मोरें सिव चरन सनेहू । मन क्रम बचन सत्य ब्रतु एहू ॥
jauṁ moreṁ siva carana sanehū, mana krama bacana satya bratu ehū.

Trans:

Growing ever more sick at heart: 'When shall I emerge from this ocean of sorrow? Alas, I put a slight upon Rāma and took my husband's word to be a lie. The creator has repaid me and has done as I deserved. But O fate, do not make me live without Shankar, for I just can not. The anguish of my heart is beyond words, but I take comfort when I remember Rāma, whom men call the Lord of compassion, and whom the Vedas hymn as the remover of distress. Him I supplicate with folded hands. May this body of mine be speedily dissolved? As my love for Shiva is unfeigned in thought, word, and deed, and as his word cannot fail,

दोहा-dohā:

तौ सबदरसी सुनिअ प्रभु करउ सो बेगि उपाइ ।
tau sabadarasī sunia prabhu karau so begi upāi,
होइ मरनु जेहिं बिनहिं श्रम दुसह बिपत्ति बिहाइ ॥५९॥
hoi maranu jehiṁ binahiṁ śrama dusaha bipatti bihāi. 59.

Trans:

do thou, O Impartial Lord, hear my prayer and speedily devise a plan by which I may die without pain and avoid this intolerable calamity.'

चौपाई-caupāī:

एहि बिधि दुखित प्रजेसकुमारी । अकथनीय दारुन दुखु भारी ॥
ehi bidhi dukhita prajesakumārī, akathanīya dāruna dukhu bhārī.

बीतें संबत सहस सतासी । तजी समाधि संभु अबिनासी ॥
bītem sambata sahasa satāsī, tajī samādhi sambhu abināsī.
राम नाम सिव सुमिरन लागे । जानेउ सतीं जगतपति जागे ॥
rāma nāma siva sumirana lāge, jāneu satīṁ jagatapati jāge.
जाइ संभु पद बंदनु कीन्हा । सनमुख संकर आसनु दीन्हा ॥
jāi sambhu pada bamdanu kīnhā, sanamukha samkara āsanu dīnhā.
लगे कहन हरिकथा रसाला । दच्छ प्रजेस भए तेहि काला ॥
lage kahana harikathā rasālā, daccha prajesa bhae tehi kālā.
देखा बिधि बिचारि सब लायक । दच्छहि कीन्ह प्रजापति नायक ॥
dekhā bidhi bicāri saba lāyaka, dacchahi kīnha prajāpati nāyaka.
बड़ अधिकार दच्छ जब पावा । अति अभिमानु हृदयँ तब आवा ॥
bara adhikāra daccha jaba pāvā, ati abhimānu hṛdayaṁ taba āvā.
नहिं कोउ अस जनमा जग माहीं । प्रभुता पाइ जाहि मद नाहीं ॥
nahiṁ kou asa janamā jaga māhīṁ, prabhutā pāi jāhi mada nāhīṁ.

Trans:
The daughter of Daksha was thus very miserable. Her deep agony was terrible beyond words. When eighty-seven thousand years elapsed, the immortal Shambhu emerged from his trance; and he began to repeat the name Rāma. Then Sati perceived that he had returned to consciousness and went and bowed herself at his feet. He gave her a seat in his presence and began reciting the divine praises of the Lord. Now at that time Daksha was king, and the creator seeing him to be thoroughly fit had made him a king of kings. But when he had obtained great dominion he waxed exceeding proud. Never was a man born into the world whom a lordship did not intoxicate.

दोहा-dohā:

दच्छ लिए मुनि बोलि सब करन लगे बड़ जाग ।
daccha lie muni boli saba karana lage bara jāga,
नेवते सादर सकल सुर जे पावत मख भाग ॥६०॥
nevate sādara sakala sura je pāvata makha bhāga. 60.

Trans:
By the priests' suggestion it was decided to prepare a great sacrifice for Daksha, and the gods who accept oblations were all courteously invited to attend.

चौपाई-caupāī:

किंनर नाग सिद्ध गंधर्बा । बधुन्ह समेत चले सुर सर्बा ॥
kiṁnara nāga siddha gaṁdharbā, badhunha sameta cale sura sarbā.
बिष्नु बिरंचि महेसु बिहाई । चले सकल सुर जान बनाई ॥
biṣnu biraṁci mahesu bihāī, cale sakala sura jāna banāī.
सतीं बिलोके ब्योम बिमाना । जात चले सुंदर बिधि नाना ॥
satīṁ biloke byoma bimānā, jāta cale suṁdara bidhi nānā.
सुर सुंदरी करहिं कल गाना । सुनत श्रवन छूटहिं मुनि ध्याना ॥
sura suṁdarī karahiṁ kala gānā, sunata śravana chūṭahiṁ muni dhyānā.
पूछेउ तब सिवँ कहेउ बखानी । पिता जग्य सुनि कछु हरषानी ॥
pūcheu taba sivaṁ kaheu bakhānī, pitā jagya suni kachu haraṣānī.
जौं महेसु मोहि आयसु देहीं । कुछ दिन जाइ रहौं मिस एहीं ॥
jauṁ mahesu mohi āyasu dehīṁ, kucha dina jāi rahauṁ misa ehīṁ.
पति परित्याग हृदयँ दुखु भारी । कहइ न निज अपराध बिचारी ॥
pati parityāga hṛdayaṁ dukhu bhārī, kahai na nija aparādha bicārī.
बोली सती मनोहर बानी । भय संकोच प्रेम रस सानी ॥
bolī satī manohara bānī, bhaya saṁkoca prema rasa sānī.

Trans:
Kinnars, Serpents, Saints, Gandharvs, all the gods and their consorts—except Vishnu, Brahmmā, and Mahādev—proceeded thither in their chariots. Sati saw the strangely beautiful procession going through the sky, with the heavenly nymphs, singing so melodiously that any saint's meditation would be broken by the sound of it; and she asked Shiva its reason; whereupon he explained. Then was she glad when she heard of her father's sacrifice and thought: 'If my Lord will allow me, I will make it an excuse for going to stay a few days there.' It was such sore pain to leave her Lord, that she long dare not speak, remembering her transgression; but at last with a soft and timid voice, overflowing with modesty and affection, she said:

दोहा-dohā:

पिता भवन उत्सव परम जौं प्रभु आयसु होइ ।
pitā bhavana utsava parama jauṁ prabhu āyasu hoi,
तौ मैं जाउँ कृपायतन सादर देखन सोइ ॥६१॥
tau maiṁ jāuṁ kṛpāyatana sādara dekhana soi. 61.

Trans:
"There is great rejoicing at my father's house; with my gracious Lord's permission I will duteously go and see it."

चौपाई-caupāī:

कहेहु नीक मोरेहुँ मन भावा । यह अनुचित नहिं नेवत पठावा ॥
kahehu nīka morehuṁ mana bhāvā, yaha anucita nahiṁ nevata paṭhāvā.
दच्छ सकल निज सुता बोलाईं । हमरें बयर तुम्हउ बिसराईं ॥
daccha sakala nija sutā bolāīṁ, hamareṁ bayara tumhau bisarāīṁ.
ब्रह्मसभाँ हम सन दुखु माना । तेहि तें अजहुँ करहिं अपमाना ॥
brahmasabhāṁ hama sana dukhu mānā, tehi teṁ ajahuṁ karahiṁ apamānā.
जौं बिनु बोलें जाहु भवानी । रहइ न सीलु सनेहु न कानी ॥
jauṁ binu boleṁ jāhu bhavānī, rahai na sīlu sanehu na kānī.
जदपि मित्र प्रभु पितु गुर गेहा । जाइअ बिनु बोलेहुँ न सँदेहा ॥
jadapi mitra prabhu pitu gura gehā, jāia binu bolehuṁ na saṁdehā.
तदपि बिरोध मान जहँ कोई । तहाँ गएँ कल्यानु न होई ॥
tadapi birodha māna jahaṁ koī, tahāṁ gaeṁ kalyānu na hoī.
भाँति अनेक संभु समुझावा । भावी बस न ग्यानु उर आवा ॥
bhāṁti aneka saṁbhu samujhāvā, bhāvī basa na gyānu ura āvā.
कह प्रभु जाहु जो बिनहिं बोलाएँ । नहिं भलि बात हमारे भाएँ ॥
kaha prabhu jāhu jo binahiṁ bolāeṁ, nahiṁ bhali bāta hamāre bhāeṁ.

Trans:
Said he: "It would please me well, but there is this difficulty—that you have not been invited. Daksha has summoned all his other daughters, but has left you out on account of his quarrel with me. For he took offence at my behavior in Brahmmā's court, and that is the reason he slights me even now. If you go without being asked, all decorum, affection and honor will be cast to the winds. One may go, no doubt, without an invitation to the house of a friend, or master, or father, or gurū; but no good can result from going where an enemy is present." Thus Shambhu warned her over and over again, but fate was too strong, she would not be convinced. Said the Lord: "If you go there unasked, no good will come out of it, I tell you now."

दोहा-dohā:

कहि देखा हर जतन बहु रहइ न दच्छकुमारि ।
kahi dekhā hara jatana bahu rahai na dacchakumāri,
दिए मुख्य गन संग तब बिदा कीन्ह त्रिपुरारि ॥६२॥
die mukhya gana saṁga taba bidā kīnha tripurāri. 62.

Trans:
But when Mahādev realized that no amount of talking would make her stay, he detailed a few of his principal attendants as escorts and sent her away.

चौपाई-caupāī:

पिता भवन जब गईं भवानी । दच्छ त्रास काहुँ न सनमानी ॥
pitā bhavana jaba gaīṁ bhavānī, daccha trāsa kāhuṁ na sanamānī.

सादर भलेहि मिली एक माता । भगिनीं मिलीं बहुत मुसुकाता ॥
sādara bhalehi milī eka mātā, bhaginīṁ milīṁ bahuta musukātā.
दच्छ न कछु पूछी कुसलाता । सतिहि बिलोकि जरे सब गाता ॥
daccha na kachu pūchī kusalātā, satihi biloki jare saba gātā.
सतीं जाइ देखेउ तब जागा । कतहुँ न दीख संभु कर भागा ॥
satīṁ jāi dekheu taba jāgā, katahuṁ na dīkha saṁbhu kara bhāgā.
तब चित चढ़ेउ जो संकर कहेऊ । प्रभु अपमानु समुझि उर दहेऊ ॥
taba cita caṛheu jo saṁkara kaheū, prabhu apamānu samujhi ura daheū.
पाछिल दुखु न हृदयँ अस ब्यापा । जस यह भयउ महा परितापा ॥
pāchila dukhu na hṛdayaṁ asa byāpā, jasa yaha bhayau mahā paritāpā.
जद्यपि जग दारुन दुख नाना । सब तें कठिन जाति अवमाना ॥
jadyapi jaga dāruna dukha nānā, saba teṁ kaṭhina jāti avamānā.
समुझि सो सतिहि भयउ अति क्रोधा । बहु बिधि जननीं कीन्ह प्रबोधा ॥
samujhi so satihi bhayau ati krodhā, bahu bidhi jananīṁ kīnha prabodhā.

Trans:

Bhawānī came to her father's house, but from fear of Daksha no one there greeted her. Only her mother met her most affectionately; from her sisters she received smiles. Daksha uttered not a word of salutation and burned with rage upon seeing her. When Sati went to look at the sacrifice, she could nowhere find anything marked for Shambhu. Then Shankar's words came back into her mind and her heart so burned within her at the slight upon her Lord that the former pain she had felt was not to be compared to her present emotion. There are many grievous pains in the world, but nothing so bad as a family slight. The more she thought of it, the more furious she grew, though her mother tried hard to pacify her.

दोहा-dohā:

सिव अपमानु न जाइ सहि हृदयँ न होइ प्रबोध ।
siva apamānu na jāi sahi hṛdayaṁ na hoi prabodha,
सकल सभहि हठि हटकि तब बोलीं बचन सक्रोध ॥६३॥
sakala sabhahi haṭhi haṭaki taba bolīṁ bacana sakrodha. 63.

Trans:

This insult to Shiva could not be borne; her soul refused to be pacified; and thrusting away from her the shrinking crowd, she called out in furious accents:

चौपाई-caupāī:

सुनहु सभासद सकल मुनिंदा । कही सुनी जिन्ह संकर निंदा ॥
sunahu sabhāsada sakala muniṁdā, kahī sunī jinha saṁkara niṁdā.
सो फलु तुरत लहब सब काहूँ । भली भाँति पछिताब पिताहूँ ॥
so phalu turata lahaba saba kāhūṁ, bhalī bhāṁti pachitāba pitāhūṁ.
संत संभु श्रीपति अपबादा । सुनिअ जहाँ तहँ असि मरजादा ॥
saṁta saṁbhu śrīpati apabādā, sunia jahāṁ tahaṁ asi marajādā.
काटिअ तासु जीभ जो बसाई । श्रवन मूदि न त चलिअ पराई ॥
kāṭia tāsu jībha jo basāī, śravana mūdi na ta calia parāī.
जगदातमा महेसु पुरारी । जगत जनक सब के हितकारी ॥
jagadātamā mahesu purārī, jagata janaka saba ke hitakārī.
पिता मंदमति निंदत तेही । दच्छ सुक्र संभव यह देही ॥
pitā maṁdamati niṁdata tehī, daccha sukra saṁbhava yaha dehī.
तजिहउँ तुरत देह तेहि हेतू । उर धरि चंद्रमौलि बृषकेतू ॥
tajihauṁ turata deha tehi hetū, ura dhari caṁdramauli bṛṣaketū.
अस कहि जोग अगिनि तनु जारा । भयउ सकल मख हाहाकारा ॥
asa kahi joga agini tanu jārā, bhayau sakala makha hāhākārā.

Trans:

"Hear, all ye elders of the assembly, all of you who have reviled Shankar or heard Him reviled: speedily shall ye reap your due reward, and dearly shall my father rue it. Whenever blasphemy is spoken against the saints, or Shambhu, or Vishnu, the ordinance is either to cut out the blasphemer's tongue, if it is in your power, or else to close your ears and run away. The universal spirit, the great Lord, Purārī, the father of the world, the friend of all—he it is whom my besotted father has reviled. Therefore this body of mine, begotten of his seed, I hasten to abandon, and impress on my soul the image of him who bears the moon as his crest and a bull as his device." As she thus spoke, Yogic flames flared up and consumed her body! A great cry of lamentation went up from the whole assembly.

दोहा-dohā:

सती मरनु सुनि संभु गन लगे करन मख खीस ।
satī maranu suni saṁbhu gana lage karana makha khīsa,
जग्य बिधंस बिलोकि भृगु रच्छा कीन्हि मुनीस ॥६४॥
jagya bidhaṁsa biloki bhṛgu racchā kīnhi munīsa. 64.

Trans:

When Shambhu's attendants heard of Sati's death, they began to destroy all the sacrificial offerings; but the great saint Bhrigu, seeing the destruction, came and saved it.

चौपाई-caupāī:

समाचार सब संकर पाए । बीरभद्रु करि कोप पठाए ॥
samācāra saba saṁkara pāe, bīrabhadru kari kopa paṭhāe.
जग्य बिधंस जाइ तिन्ह कीन्हा । सकल सुरन्ह बिधिवत फलु दीन्हा ॥
jagya bidhaṁsa jāi tinha kīnhā, sakala suranha bidhivata phalu dīnhā.
भै जगबिदित दच्छ गति सोई । जसि कछु संभु बिमुख कै होई ॥
bhai jagabidita daccha gati soī, jasi kachu saṁbhu bimukha kai hoī.
यह इतिहास सकल जग जानी । ताते मैं संछेप बखानी ॥
yaha itihāsa sakala jaga jānī, tāte maiṁ saṁchepa bakhānī.
सतीं मरत हरि सन बरु मागा । जनम जनम सिव पद अनुरागा ॥
satīṁ marata hari sana baru māgā, janama janama siva pada anurāgā.
तेहि कारन हिमगिरि गृह जाई । जनमीं पारबती तनु पाई ॥
tehi kārana himagiri gṛha jāī, janamīṁ pārabatī tanu pāī.
जब तें उमा सैल गृह जाईं । सकल सिद्धि संपति तहँ छाईं ॥
jaba teṁ umā saila gṛha jāīṁ, sakala siddhi saṁpati tahaṁ chāīṁ.
जहँ तहँ मुनिन्ह सुआश्रम कीन्हे । उचित बास हिम भूधर दीन्हे ॥
jahaṁ tahaṁ muninha suāśrama kīnhe, ucita bāsa hima bhūdhara dīnhe.

Trans:

When Shambhu got the news he, in his wrath, sent Vīr-bhadra who went and scattered the sacrifice and requited all the gods each as they deserved. Daksha's act is famous throughout the world as an example of hostility to Shambhu; and as the story is so well known, I have told it only in brief. Now Sati at her death asked this boon of Harī: that in every successive birth she might show her love to Shiva. On this account she was born now in the form of Pārwatī, the daughter of King Himalaya. From the time that she entered the house of the monarch of mountains, it was pervaded by fortune and prosperity, and hermits made their homes all about it—in fit places assigned them by the king.

दोहा-dohā:

सदा सुमन फल सहित सब द्रुम नव नाना जाति ।
sadā sumana phala sahita saba druma nava nānā jāti,
प्रगटीं सुंदर सैल पर मनि आकर बहु भाँति ॥६५॥
pragaṭīṁ suṁdara saila para mani ākara bahu bhāṁti. 65.

Trans:

Strange trees of various kinds, with never-fading flowers and fruits, appeared on the beautiful hills, and mines of gems were discovered.

चौपाई-caupāī:

सरिता सब पुनीत जलु बहहीं । खग मृग मधुप सुखी सब रहहीं ॥
saritā saba punīta jalu bahahīṁ, khaga mṛga madhupa sukhī saba rahahīṁ.

सहज बयरु सब जीवन्ह त्यागा। गिरि पर सकल करहिं अनुरागा॥
sahaja bayaru saba jīvanha tyāgā, giri para sakala karahiṁ anurāgā.
सोह सैल गिरिजा गृह आएँ। जिमि जनु रामभगति के पाएँ॥
soha saila girijā gṛha āeṁ, jimi janu rāmabhagati ke pāeṁ.
नित नूतन मंगल गृह तासू। ब्रह्मादिक गावहिं जसु जासू॥
nita nūtana maṁgala gṛha tāsū, brahmādika gāvahiṁ jasu jāsū.
नारद समाचार सब पाए। कौतुकहीं गिरि गेह सिधाए॥
nārada samācāra saba pāe, kautukahīṁ giri geha sidhāe.
सैलराज बड़ आदर कीन्हा। पद पखारि बर आसनु दीन्हा॥
sailarāja baṛa ādara kīnhā, pada pakhāri bara āsanu dīnhā.
नारि सहित मुनि पद सिरु नावा। चरन सलिल सबु भवनु सिंचावा॥
nāri sahita muni pada siru nāvā, carana salila sabu bhavanu siṁcāvā.
निज सौभाग्य बहुत गिरि बरना। सुता बोलि मेली मुनि चरना॥
nija saubhāgya bahuta giri baranā, sutā boli melī muni caranā.

Trans:

The rivers flowed with the purest water; birds, deer, and bees were all equally joyous; every animal forgot its instinctive antipathies and dwelt lovingly on the mountain, which was as glorified by the coming of Girijā as a human is glorified by the spirit of faith. Every day was some new delight in the king's palace, and Brahmmā and all the gods vied in singing its praises. On hearing the news Nārad went to visit the mountain king who received him with high honor and bathed his feet and led him to a throne. The queen too bowed her head before him and sprinkled the whole house with the water sanctified by his use. Then the king told all his good fortune and summoned his daughter also to the presence and said:

दोहा-dohā:

त्रिकालग्य सर्बग्य तुम्ह गति सर्बत्र तुम्हारि।
trikālagya sarbagya tumha gati sarbatra tumhāri,
कहहु सुता के दोष गुन मुनिबर हृदयँ बिचारि॥६६॥
kahahu sutā ke doṣa guna munibara hṛdayaṁ bicāri. 66.

Trans:

"Thou who knowest all time, past, present, or future, and who has traversed the whole universe, tell me O best of saints, after well considering the matter—what there is good and what bad about my daughter?"

चौपाई-caupāī:

कह मुनि बिहसि गूढ़ मृदु बानी। सुता तुम्हारि सकल गुन खानी॥
kaha muni bihasi gūṛha mṛdu bānī, sutā tumhāri sakala guna khānī.
सुंदर सहज सुसील सयानी। नाम उमा अंबिका भवानी॥
suṁdara sahaja susīla sayānī, nāma umā aṁbikā bhavānī.
सब लच्छन संपन्न कुमारी। होइहि संतत पियहि पिआरी॥
saba lacchana saṁpanna kumārī, hoihi saṁtata piyahi piārī.
सदा अचल एहि कर अहिवाता। एहि तें जसु पैहहिं पितु माता॥
sadā acala ehi kara ahivātā, ehi teṁ jasu paihahiṁ pitu mātā.
होइहि पूज्य सकल जग माहीं। एहि सेवत कछु दुर्लभ नाहीं॥
hoihi pūjya sakala jaga māhīṁ, ehi sevata kachu durlabha nāhīṁ.
एहि कर नामु सुमिरि संसारा। त्रिय चढ़िहहिं पतिब्रत असिधारा॥
ehi kara nāmu sumiri saṁsārā, triya caṛhihahiṁ patibrata asidhārā.
सैल सुलच्छन सुता तुम्हारी। सुनहु जे अब अवगुन दुइ चारी॥
saila sulacchana sutā tumhārī, sunahu je aba avaguna dui cārī.
अगुन अमान मातु पितु हीना। उदासीन सब संसय छीना॥
aguna amāna mātu pitu hīnā, udāsīna saba saṁsaya chīnā.

Trans:

The saint replied with a smile, in soft but profound words: "Your daughter is a mine of perfection, beautiful, amiable, and intelligent. Umā, Ambikā, Bhawānī are her many names. She is a maiden with every quality that endears a wife to a husband. Firm as a rock is her good fortune, and by her, her parents will be renowned. She shall be worshipped throughout the world, and in her service shall be fruition of every desire. Through her name women shall be enabled to walk the path of wifely duty—which is like the edge of a sword. Such, O king, are thy daughter's merits; but you also have to hear some two or three drawbacks. Devoid of merits, free from pride, without a father or mother, an ascetic with no thought for anyone—

दोहा-dohā:

जोगी जटिल अकाम मन नगन अमंगल बेष।
jogī jaṭila akāma mana nagana amaṁgala beṣa,
अस स्वामी एहि कहँ मिलिहि परी हस्त असि रेख॥६७॥
asa svāmī ehi kahaṁ milihi parī hasta asi rekha. 67.

Trans:

—a mendicant recluse with matted hair, a celibate with naked body and hideous accoutrements: such a one shall be her spouse, as I read by the lines on her palm."

चौपाई-caupāī:

सुनि मुनि गिरा सत्य जियँ जानी। दुख दंपतिहि उमा हरषानी॥
suni muni girā satya jiyaṁ jānī, dukha daṁpatihi umā haraṣānī.
नारदहूँ यह भेदु न जाना। दसा एक समुझब बिलगाना॥
nāradahūṁ yaha bhedu na jānā, dasā eka samujhaba bilagānā.
सकल सखीं गिरिजा गिरि मैना। पुलक सरीर भरे जल नैना॥
sakala sakhīṁ girijā giri mainā, pulaka sarīra bhare jala nainā.
होइ न मृषा देवरिषि भाषा। उमा सो बचनु हृदयँ धरि राखा॥
hoi na mṛṣā devariṣi bhāṣā, umā so bacanu hṛdayaṁ dhari rākhā.
उपजेउ सिव पद कमल सनेहू। मिलन कठिन मन भा संदेहू॥
upajeu siva pada kamala sanehū, milana kaṭhina mana bhā saṁdehū.
जानि कुअवसरु प्रीति दुराई। सखी उछँग बैठी पुनि जाई॥
jāni kuavasaru prīti durāī, sakhī uchaṁga baiṭhī puni jāī.
झूठि न होइ देवरिषि बानी। सोचहिं दंपति सखीं सयानी॥
jhūṭhi na hoi devariṣi bānī, socahiṁ daṁpati sakhīṁ sayānī.
उर धरि धीर कहइ गिरिराऊ। कहहु नाथ का करिअ उपाऊ॥
ura dhari dhīra kahai girirāū, kahahu nātha kā karia upāū.

Trans:

Hearing the words of the sage and believing them to be true, Himalaya and his wife became disconsolate; but Umā rejoiced. Even Nārad could not perceive this difference. Even though their outer expression was the same, their feeling was different. All Girijā's attendants, and she herself and her father and her mother Mainā were trembling and had their eyes full of tears; but for Umā it was tears of joy, and she cherished the saint's words in her heart, thinking, 'They cannot be false' and her love for Shiva's lotus feet revived. She however felt diffident in her mind—for union with Shiva appeared so difficult to her. But as it was no fitting time for a disclosure, she suppressed her emotion and went back to the bosom of her playmates. They and the parents were distrest by the thought of the saint's infallible utterance, and the king, with an effort, cried in dismay, "O sir, tell me what remedy to devise."

दोहा-dohā:

कह मुनीस हिमवंत सुनु जो बिधि लिखा लिलार।
kaha munīsa himavaṁta sunu jo bidhi likhā lilāra,
देव दनुज नर नाग मुनि कोउ न मेटनिहार॥६८॥
deva danuja nara nāga muni kou na meṭanihāra. 68.

Trans:

Said the saint: "Hear, O Himvān; what fate has written on the forehead, not god or demon, nor man or serpent or saint, is able to efface.

चौपाई-caupāī:

तदपि एक मैं कहउँ उपाई । होइ करै जौं दैउ सहाई ॥
tadapi eka maiṁ kahauṁ upāī, hoi karai jauṁ daiu sahāī.
जस बरु मैं बरनेउँ तुम्ह पाहीं । मिलिहि उमहि तस संसय नाहीं ॥
jasa baru maiṁ baraneuṁ tumha pāhīṁ, milihi umahi tasa saṁsaya nāhīṁ.
जे जे बर के दोष बखाने । ते सब सिव पहिं मैं अनुमाने ॥
je je bara ke doṣa bakhāne, te saba siva pahiṁ maiṁ anumāne.
जौं बिबाहु संकर सन होई । दोषउ गुन सम कह सबु कोई ॥
jauṁ bibāhu saṁkara sana hoī, doṣau guna sama kaha sabu koī.
जौं अहि सेज सयन हरि करहीं । बुध कछु तिन्ह कर दोषु न धरहीं ॥
jauṁ ahi seja sayana hari karahīṁ, budha kachu tinha kara doṣu na dharahīṁ.
भानु कृसानु सर्ब रस खाहीं । तिन्ह कहँ मंद कहत कोउ नाहीं ॥
bhānu kṛsānu sarba rasa khāhīṁ, tinha kahaṁ maṁda kahata kou nāhīṁ.
सुभ अरु असुभ सलिल सब बहई । सुरसरि कोउ अपुनीत न कहई ॥
subha aru asubha salila saba bahaī, surasari kou apunīta na kahaī.
समरथ कहुँ नहिं दोषु गोसाईं । रबि पावक सुरसरि की नाईं ॥
samaratha kahuṁ nahiṁ doṣu gosāīṁ, rabi pāvaka surasari kī nāīṁ.

Trans:

Yet one mode of escape I shall tell you, which by the help of heaven may avail. Umā's bridegroom will infallibly be such a one as I have described to you; but all the demerits that I have enumerated, I find to exist in Shiva. If a marriage with him can be brought about, everyone will account his vices as virtues. Though Harī takes a serpent for his couch, the wise account it of no fault to him; and though fire and the sun soak up moistness of all kinds, yet no one calls them names. Though the stream flows in one place pure and in another sullied, no one would call the Gangā impure. The powerful, my friend, are always faultless, like the sun, fire, or the Gangā.

दोहा-dohā:

जौं अस हिसिषा करहिं नर जड़ बिबेक अभिमान ।
jauṁ asa hisiṣā karahiṁ nara jaṛa bibeka abhimāna,
परहिं कलप भरि नरक महुँ जीव कि ईस समान ॥ ६९॥
parahiṁ kalapa bhari naraka mahuṁ jīva ki īsa samāna. 69.

Trans:

If in their pride of wisdom foolish men emulate the great, they are cast into hell for a whole Kalpa or life-time of the universe. Can an embodied soul vie with God?"

चौपाई-caupāī:

सुरसरि जल कृत बारुनि जाना । कबहुँ न संत करहिं तेहि पाना ॥
surasari jala kṛta bāruni jānā, kabahuṁ na saṁta karahiṁ tehi pānā.
सुरसरि मिलें सो पावन जैसें । ईस अनीसहि अंतरु तैसें ॥
surasari mileṁ so pāvana jaiseṁ, īsa anīsahi aṁtaru taiseṁ.
संभु सहज समरथ भगवाना । एहि बिबाहँ सब बिधि कल्याना ॥
saṁbhu sahaja samaratha bhagavānā, ehi bibāhaṁ saba bidhi kalyānā.
दुराराध्य पै अहहिं महेसू । आसुतोष पुनि किएँ कलेसू ॥
durārādhya pai ahahiṁ mahesū, āsutoṣa puni kieṁ kalesū.
जौं तपु करै कुमारि तुम्हारी । भाविउ मेटि सकहिं त्रिपुरारी ॥
jauṁ tapu karai kumāri tumhārī, bhāviu meṭi sakahiṁ tripurārī.
जद्यपि बर अनेक जग माहीं । एहि कहँ सिव तजि दूसर नाहीं ॥
jadyapi bara aneka jaga māhīṁ, ehi kahaṁ siva taji dūsara nāhīṁ.
बर दायक प्रनतारति भंजन । कृपासिंधु सेवक मन रंजन ॥
bara dāyaka pranatārati bhaṁjana, kṛpāsiṁdhu sevaka mana raṁjana.
इच्छित फल बिनु सिव अवराधें । लहिअ न कोटि जोग जप साधें ॥
icchita phala binu siva avarādheṁ, lahia na koṭi joga japa sādheṁ.

Trans:

Holy men would never drink wine even if they came to know that it had been made of water from the Gangā; but the same wine becomes pure when it is poured into the Gangā. The difference between an individual soul and God should be similarly explained. The Lord Shambhu is all-powerful, and an alliance with him is in every way auspicious. But it is hard to propitiate him; yet if penance is undergone he is quickly satisfied. If then your daughter will practice penance, Tripurārī will be able to erase the lines of fate; and though there may be many bridegrooms in the world, the only one for her is Shiva, and none else. He answers prayer, relieves the distress of the faithful, is full of compassion and a delight to his servants; unless he is propitiated, no one attains the heart's desire though they practice infinite penance and austerity."

दोहा-dohā:

अस कहि नारद सुमिरि हरि गिरिजहि दीन्हि असीस ।
asa kahi nārada sumiri hari girijahi dīnhi asīsa,
होइहि यह कल्यान अब संसय तजहु गिरीस ॥ ७०॥
hoihi yaha kalyāna aba saṁsaya tajahu girīsa. 70.

Trans:

So saying, and with his thoughts fixed on Harī, Nārad gave his blessing to the king and added, "Now fear not, all will turn out well."

चौपाई-caupāī:

कहि अस ब्रह्मभवन मुनि गयऊ । आगिल चरित सुनहु जस भयऊ ॥
kahi asa brahmabhavana muni gayaū, āgila carita sunahu jasa bhayaū.
पतिहि एकांत पाइ कह मैना । नाथ न मैं समुझे मुनि बैना ॥
patihi ekāṁta pāi kaha mainā, nātha na maiṁ samujhe muni bainā.
जौं घरु बरु कुलु होइ अनूपा । करिअ बिबाहु सुता अनुरुपा ॥
jauṁ gharu baru kulu hoi anūpā, karia bibāhu sutā anurupā.
न त कन्या बरु रहउ कुआरी । कंत उमा मम प्रानपिआरी ॥
na ta kanyā baru rahau kuārī, kaṁta umā mama prānapiārī.
जौं न मिलिहि बरु गिरिजहि जोगू । गिरि जड़ सहज कहिहि सबु लोगू ॥
jauṁ na milihi baru girijahi jogū, giri jaṛa sahaja kahihi sabu logū.
सोइ बिचारि पति करेहु बिबाहू । जेहिं न बहोरि होइ उर दाहू ॥
soi bicāri pati karehu bibāhū, jehiṁ na bahori hoi ura dāhū.
अस कहि परी चरन धरि सीसा । बोले सहित सनेह गिरीसा ॥
asa kahi parī carana dhari sīsā, bole sahita saneha girīsā.
बरु पावक प्रगटै ससि माहीं । नारद बचनु अन्यथा नाहीं ॥
baru pāvaka pragaṭai sasi māhīṁ, nārada bacanu anyathā nāhīṁ.

Trans:

Having thus spoken, the Munī returned to Brahmmā's court. Hear now the rest of the story how it came about. Mainā, finding her husband alone, said to him, "My Lord, I do not understand the saint's meaning. If the bridegroom and his position and family are unobjectionable and such as befit your daughter then conclude the marriage; but if not, let her remain a maiden. My Lord, Umā is as dear to me as life. If she does not get a husband worthy of her, everyone will say the king of mountain is himself a mere block. Remember this, and so marry her that there may be no heartburning hereafter." With these words she laid her head at his feet. The king affectionately replied, "Sooner shall fire break out in the moon than Nārad's word be gainsaid.

दोहा-dohā:

प्रिया सोचु परिहरहु सबु सुमिरहु श्रीभगवान ।
priyā socu pariharahu sabu sumirahu śrībhagavāna,
पारबतिहि निरमयउ जेहिं सोइ करिहि कल्यान ॥ ७१॥
pārabatihi niramayau jehiṁ soi karihi kalyāna. 71.

Trans:

Put away all anxiety, my dear, and fix your thoughts on the good Lord, who has created Pārwatī and who will protect her.

चौपाई-caupāī:

अब जौं तुम्हहि सुता पर नेहू । तौ अस जाइ सिखावनु देहू ॥
aba jauṁ tumhahi sutā para nehū, tau asa jāi sikhāvanu dehū.
करै सो तपु जेहिं मिलहिं महेसू । आन उपायँ न मिटिहि कलेसू ॥
karai so tapu jehiṁ milahiṁ mahesū, āna upāyaṁ na miṭihi kalesū.
नारद बचन सगर्भ सहेतू । सुंदर सब गुन निधि बृषकेतू ॥
nārada bacana sagarbha sahetū, suṁdara saba guna nidhi bṛṣaketū.
अस बिचारि तुम्ह तजहु असंका । सबहि भाँति संकरु अकलंका ॥
asa bicāri tumha tajahu asaṁkā, sabahi bhāṁti saṁkaru akalaṁkā.
सुनि पति बचन हरषि मन माहीं । गई तुरत उठि गिरिजा पाहीं ॥
suni pati bacana haraṣi mana māhīṁ, gaī turata uṭhi girijā pāhīṁ.
उमहि बिलोकि नयन भरे बारी । सहित सनेह गोद बैठारी ॥
umahi biloki nayana bhare bārī, sahita saneha goda baiṭhārī.
बारहिं बार लेति उर लाई । गदगद कंठ न कछु कहि जाई ॥
bārahiṁ bāra leti ura lāī, gadagada kaṁṭha na kachu kahi jāī.
जगत मातु सर्बग्य भवानी । मातु सुखद बोलीं मृदु बानी ॥
jagata mātu sarbagya bhavānī, mātu sukhada bolīṁ mṛdu bānī.

Trans:

Now, if by dint of your love for your child, go and thus counsel her: Penance is the means of approach to Shiva, and there is no other means of escaping sorrow. Nārad's words are pregnant and full of meaning. Mahādev is in fact beautiful and accomplished; recognize this truth and doubt not; he is in every way irreproachable." When she heard her husband's words she was glad of heart and at once rose and went to where Umā was. On seeing the girl her eyes filled with tears, and she affectionately took her in her lap and again and again pressed her to her bosom; but she could not say a word, for her throat choked with emotion. Then the mother of the universe, the all-wise Bhawānī, to her mother's delight, said softly,

दोहा-dohā:

सुनहि मातु मैं दीख अस सपन सुनावउँ तोहि ।
sunahi mātu maiṁ dīkha asa sapana sunāvauṁ tohi,
सुंदर गौर सुबिप्रबर अस उपदेसेउ मोहि ॥७२॥
suṁdara gaura subiprabara asa upadeseu mohi. 72.

Trans:

"Listen mother to the vision I am about to tell you. A fair and lovely noble Brahmin has thus instructed me in dream:

चौपाई-caupāī:

करहि जाइ तपु सैलकुमारी । नारद कहा सो सत्य बिचारी ॥
karahi jāi tapu sailakumārī, nārada kahā so satya bicārī.
मातु पितहि पुनि यह मत भावा । तपु सुखप्रद दुख दोष नसावा ॥
mātu pitahi puni yaha mata bhāvā, tapu sukhaprada dukha doṣa nasāvā.
तपबल रचइ प्रपंचु बिधाता । तपबल बिष्नु सकल जग त्राता ॥
tapabala racai prapaṁcu bidhātā, tapabala biṣnu sakala jaga trātā.
तपबल संभु करहिं संघारा । तपबल सेषु धरइ महिभारा ॥
tapabala saṁbhu karahiṁ saṁghārā, tapabala seṣu dharai mahibhārā.
तप अधार सब सृष्टि भवानी । करहि जाइ तपु अस जियँ जानी ॥
tapa adhāra saba sṛṣṭi bhavānī, karahi jāi tapu asa jiyaṁ jānī.
सुनत बचन बिसमित महतारी । सपन सुनायउ गिरिहि हँकारी ॥
sunata bacana bisamita mahatārī, sapana sunāyau girihi haṁkārī.
मातु पितहि बहुबिधि समुझाई । चलीं उमा तप हित हरषाई ॥
mātu pitahi bahubidhi samujhāī, calīṁ umā tapa hita haraṣāī.
प्रिय परिवार पिता अरु माता । भए बिकल मुख आव न बाता ॥
priya parivāra pitā aru mātā, bhae bikala mukha āva na bātā.

Trans:

'Recognizing the truth of Nārad's words go and practice austerity, O mountain-maid; the idea has commended itself to your father and mother as well—for *Tapas* (penance) is full of peace and puts an end to sin and pain. By the virtue of penance the creator made the world; by the virtue of penance Vishnu redeems the world; by the virtue of penance Shambhu is able to destroy it. It is by the virtue of penance that the Great Serpent supports the burden of the earth. In short the whole creation, O Bhawānī, depends upon penance; do you then practice it.'" On hearing these words her mother was astounded, and sent for the king and declared to him the vision. Then, after consoling her parents in every possible way, Umā in gladness of heart commenced her penance; while they and all their loving dependents grew sad of face, nor could speak a word.

दोहा-dohā:

बेदसिरा मुनि आइ तब सबहि कहा समुझाइ ।
bedasirā muni āi taba sabahi kahā samujhāi,
पारबती महिमा सुनत रहे प्रबोधहि पाइ ॥७३॥
pārabatī mahimā sunata rahe prabodhahi pāi. 73.

Trans:

Then came sage Vedshīr and instructed them all; and when they had heard of Pārwatī's glory they were comforted.

चौपाई-caupāī:

उर धरि उमा प्रानपति चरना । जाइ बिपिन लागीं तपु करना ॥
ura dhari umā prānapati caranā, jāi bipina lāgīṁ tapu karanā.
अति सुकुमार न तनु तप जोगू । पति पद सुमिरि तजेउ सबु भोगू ॥
ati sukumāra na tanu tapa jogū, pati pada sumiri tajeu sabu bhogū.
नित नव चरन उपज अनुरागा । बिसरी देह तपहिं मनु लागा ॥
nita nava carana upaja anurāgā, bisarī deha tapahiṁ manu lāgā.
संबत सहस मूल फल खाए । सागु खाइ सत बरष गवाँए ॥
saṁbata sahasa mūla phala khāe, sāgu khāi sata baraṣa gavāṁe.
कछु दिन भोजनु बारि बतासा । किए कठिन कछु दिन उपबासा ॥
kachu dina bhojanu bāri batāsā, kie kaṭhina kachu dina upabāsā.
बेल पाती महि परइ सुखाई । तीनि सहस संबत सोइ खाई ॥
bela pātī mahi parai sukhāī, tīni sahasa saṁbata soi khāī.
पुनि परिहरे सुखानेउ परना । उमहि नाम तब भयउ अपरना ॥
puni parihare sukhāneu paranā, umahi nāma taba bhayau aparanā.
देखि उमहि तप खीन सरीरा । ब्रह्मगिरा भै गगन गभीरा ॥
dekhi umahi tapa khīna sarīrā, brahmagirā bhai gagana gabhīrā.

Trans:

And then Umā, cherishing in her heart the feet of her dear Lord, went into the forest and began her *Tapas*. Though her delicate frame was little fit for such austerities, she abandoned all food and became absorbed in prayer; her devotion so growing day by day that all bodily wants were forgotten and her soul was wholly given to penance. For a thousand years she ate only roots and fruit; for a hundred years she lived on vegetables; for some days her only sustenance was water and air, and on some she maintained a yet more absolute fast. For three thousand years she ate only dry leaves of the *bel* tree that had fallen to the ground; and then at last she abstained even from dry leaves, whence she acquired the name of Aparnā ('the leafless'). At the sight of her emaciated frame, Brahmmā's deep voice resounded through the heavens:

दोहा-dohā:

भयउ मनोरथ सुफल तव सुनु गिरिराजकुमारि ।
bhayau manoratha suphala tava sunu girirājakumāri,
परिहरु दुसह कलेस सब अब मिलिहहिं त्रिपुरारि ॥७४॥
pariharu dusaha kalesa saba aba milihahiṁ tripurāri. 74.

Trans:

"Hear, O daughter of the mountain king! Your desire is accomplished; cease all these intolerable afflictions; Tripurārī will be yours very soon.

चौपाई-caupāī:

असु तपु काहुँ न कीन्ह भवानी । भउ अनेक धीर मुनि ग्यानी ॥
asa tapu kāhum̐ na kīnha bhavānī, bhau aneka dhīra muni gyānī.
अब उर धरहु ब्रह्म बर बानी । सत्य सदा संतत सुचि जानी ॥
aba ura dharahu brahma bara bānī, satya sadā saṁtata suci jānī.
आवै पिता बोलावन जबहीं । हठ परिहरि घर जाएहु तबहीं ॥
āvai pitā bolāvana jabahīṁ, haṭha parihari ghara jāehu tabahīṁ.
मिलहिं तुम्हहि जब सप्त रिषीसा । जानेहु तब प्रमान बागीसा ॥
milahiṁ tumhahi jaba sapta riṣīsā, jānehu taba pramāna bāgīsā.
सुनत गिरा बिधि गगन बखानी । पुलक गात गिरिजा हरषानी ॥
sunata girā bidhi gagana bakhānī, pulaka gāta girijā haraṣānī.
उमा चरित सुंदर मैं गावा । सुनहु संभु कर चरित सुहावा ॥
umā carita suṁdara maiṁ gāvā, sunahu saṁbhu kara carita suhāvā.
जब तें सतीं जाइ तनु त्यागा । तब तें सिव मन भयउ बिरागा ॥
jaba teṁ satīṁ jāi tanu tyāgā, taba teṁ siva mana bhayau birāgā.
जपहिं सदा रघुनायक नामा । जहँ तहँ सुनहिं राम गुन ग्रामा ॥
japahiṁ sadā raghunāyaka nāmā, jaham̐ taham̐ sunahiṁ rāma guna grāmā.

Trans:

Though there have been many saints, both resolute and wise, not one, O Bhawānī, has performed such penance as this. Accept now the divine oracle as ever true and ever good. When your father comes to call you, cease to resist and go home with him; and when the seven sages meet you, know this to be the sign of the heavenly prediction." When she heard Brahmmā's voice thus speaking from on high, Girijā thrilled with delight. Now with her we have done for a time while we turn to Shambhu. From the day when Sati's spirit left the body he became a rigid ascetic, ever telling his beads on Rāma's name, and attending recitals narrating glories of Ramā.

दोहा-dohā:

चिदानंद सुखधाम सिव बिगत मोह मद काम ।
cidānaṁda sukhadhāma siva bigata moha mada kāma,
बिचरहिं महि धरि हृदयँ हरि सकल लोक अभिराम ॥७५॥
bicarahiṁ mahi dhari hṛdayam̐ hari sakala loka abhirāma. 75.

Trans:

Even he, Shiva, who is pure intelligence, the abode of bliss, exempt from lust, frenzy, and delusion, wanders about on earth with his heart fixed on Harī, the joy of the whole world,

चौपाई-caupāī:

कतहुँ मुनिन्ह उपदेसहिं ग्याना । कतहुँ राम गुन करहिं बखाना ॥
katahum̐ muninha upadesahiṁ gyānā, katahum̐ rāma guna karahiṁ bakhānā.
जदपि अकाम तदपि भगवाना । भगत बिरह दुख दुखित सुजाना ॥
jadapi akāma tadapi bhagavānā, bhagata biraha dukha dukhita sujānā.
एहि बिधि गयउ कालु बहु बीती । नित नै होइ राम पद प्रीती ॥
ehi bidhi gayau kālu bahu bītī, nita nai hoi rāma pada prītī.
नेमु प्रेमु संकर कर देखा । अबिचल हृदयँ भगति कै रेखा ॥
nemu premu saṁkara kara dekhā, abicala hṛdayam̐ bhagati kai rekhā.
प्रगटे रामु कृतग्य कृपाला । रूप सील निधि तेज बिसाला ॥
pragaṭe rāmu kṛtagya kṛpālā, rūpa sīla nidhi teja bisālā.
बहु प्रकार संकरहि सराहा । तुम्ह बिनु अस ब्रतु को निरबाहा ॥
bahu prakāra saṁkarahi sarāhā, tumha binu asa bratu ko nirabāhā.
बहुबिधि राम सिवहि समुझावा । पारबती कर जन्मु सुनावा ॥
bahubidhi rāma sivahi samujhāvā, pārabatī kara janmu sunāvā.
अति पुनीत गिरिजा कै करनी । बिस्तर सहित कृपानिधि बरनी ॥
ati punīta girijā kai karanī, bistara sahita kṛpānidhi baranī.

Trans:

Now instructing the saints in wisdom, now expounding Rāma's praises, and though himself the all-wise and passionless God, and yet in pain of separation from the Lord like some bereaved devotee. In this way many ages passed, while his love for Rāma increased every day. Then the generous and merciful God, full of grace and benignity, seeing his steadfastness and affection, and the unchangeable stamp of devotion on his soul, became manifest in all his glory and lauded him highly, for none other had over accomplished such a vow. In diverse ways he instructed him; telling him, in his infinite compassion, of Pārwatī's birth and of her virtuous deeds, at full length.

दोहा-dohā:

अब बिनती मम सुनहु सिव जौं मो पर निज नेहु ।
aba binatī mama sunahu siva jauṁ mo para nija nehu,
जाइ बिबाहहु सैलजहि यह मोहि मागें देहु ॥७६॥
jāi bibāhahu sailajahi yaha mohi māgeṁ dehu. 76.

Trans:

"Now, Shiva, if you have any love for me, listen to my request: go and marry the mountain maid at my behest."

चौपाई-caupāī:

कह सिव जदपि उचित अस नाहीं । नाथ बचन पुनि मेटि न जाहीं ॥
kaha siva jadapi ucita asa nāhīṁ, nātha bacana puni meṭi na jāhīṁ.
सिर धरि आयसु करिअ तुम्हारा । परम धरमु यह नाथ हमारा ॥
sira dhari āyasu karia tumhārā, parama dharamu yaha nātha hamārā.
मातु पिता गुर प्रभु कै बानी । बिनहिं बिचार करिअ सुभ जानी ॥
mātu pitā gura prabhu kai bānī, binahiṁ bicāra karia subha jānī.
तुम्ह सब भाँति परम हितकारी । अग्या सिर पर नाथ तुम्हारी ॥
tumha saba bhām̐ti parama hitakārī, agyā sira para nātha tumhārī.
प्रभु तोषेउ सुनि संकर बचना । भक्ति बिबेक धर्म जुत रचना ॥
prabhu toṣeu suni saṁkara bacanā, bhakti bibeka dharma juta racanā.
कह प्रभु हर तुम्हार पन रहेऊ । अब उर राखेहु जो हम कहेऊ ॥
kaha prabhu hara tumhāra pana raheū, aba ura rākhehu jo hama kaheū.
अंतरधान भए अस भाषी । संकर सोइ मूरति उर राखी ॥
aṁtaradhāna bhae asa bhāṣī, saṁkara soi mūrati ura rākhī.
तबहिं सप्तरिषि सिव पहिं आए । बोले प्रभु अति बचन सुहाए ॥
tabahiṁ saptariṣi siva pahiṁ āe, bole prabhu ati bacana suhāe.

Trans:

Said Shiva: "Though it is scarcely seemly, yet when a master speaks he is not to be gainsaid. I must needs bow to your order, for obedience is the highest duty. If a man would prosper, he must do, without thinking, as he is told by his parents, or his gurū, or his superior. You are in every way my benefactor, and I bow to your commands." The Lord was pleased when he heard Shankar's reply so full of faith, knowledge, and religious feeling, and said, "Hara, your vow stands good; take to heart what I have told you." So saying he vanished, but his vision remained impressed on Shankar's soul. Then came the seven Rishis to visit him, and he addressed them thus in charming ascents:

दोहा-dohā:

पारबती पहिं जाइ तुम्ह प्रेम परिच्छा लेहु ।
pārabatī pahiṁ jāi tumha prema paricchā lehu,
गिरिहि प्रेरि पठएहु भवन दूरि करेहु संदेहु ॥७७॥
girihi preri paṭhaehu bhavana dūri karehu saṁdehu. 77.

Trans:

"Go to Pārwatī and make a trial of her love, and then send her father to her to remove all doubts and fetch her home fully assured."

चौपाई-caupāī:

रिषिन्ह गौरि देखी तहँ कैसी । मूरतिमंत तपस्या जैसी ॥

riṣinha gauri dekhī tahaṁ kaisī, mūratimaṁta tapasyā jaisī.

बोले मुनि सुनु सैलकुमारी । करहु कवन कारन तपु भारी ॥
bole muni sunu sailakumārī, karahu kavana kārana tapu bhārī.

केहि अवराधहु का तुम्ह चहहू । हम सन सत्य मरमु किन कहहू ॥
kehi avarādhahu kā tumha cahahū, hama sana satya maramu kina kahahū.

कहत बचत मनु अति सकुचाई । हँसिहहु सुनि हमारि जड़ताई ॥
kahata bacata manu ati sakucāī, haṁsihahu suni hamāri jaṛatāī.

मनु हठ परा न सुनइ सिखावा । चहत बारि पर भीति उठावा ॥
manu haṭha parā na sunai sikhāvā, cahata bāri para bhīti uṭhāvā.

नारद कहा सत्य सोइ जाना । बिनु पंखन्ह हम चहहिं उड़ाना ॥
nārada kahā satya soi jānā, binu paṁkhanha hama cahahiṁ uṛānā.

देखहु मुनि अबिबेकु हमारा । चाहिअ सदा सिवहि भरतारा ॥
dekhahu muni abibeku hamārā, cāhia sadā sivahi bharatārā.

Trans:

When the Rishis saw Gaurī, she appeared to them like Penance personified, and they exclaimed—"Hear, O daughter of the mountain! Why practice such grievous self-mortification? What has been the sin, or what is the aim? Tell us the whole secret truly." When Bhawānī heard their speech, she replied in strangely moving terms: "I greatly shrink from telling my secret, for you will smile at my folly when you hear it; but my soul is obstinately set and refuses to hear instruction, though I am like one building a house upon the water, or as one who would fly without wings, relying only on the truth of Nārad's prophecy. See, O saints, the extent of my madness: I long for the unchangeable Shankar as my husband."

दोहा-dohā:

सुनत बचन बिहसे रिषय गिरिसंभव तव देह ।
sunata bacana bihase riṣaya girisaṁbhava tava deha,

नारद कर उपदेसु सुनि कहहु बसेउ किसु गेह ॥७८॥
nārada kara upadesu suni kahahu baseu kisu geha. 78.

Trans:

The Rishis smiled on hearing her speech, and said: "After all your body owes its existence to a mountain; tell us who has ever listened to Nārad's advice and lived to have a home?

चौपाई-caupāī:

दच्छसुतन्ह उपदेसेन्हि जाई । तिन्ह फिरि भवनु न देखा आई ॥
dacchasutanha upadesenhi jāī, tinha phiri bhavanu na dekhā āī.

चित्रकेतु कर घरु उन घाला । कनककसिपु कर पुनि अस हाला ॥
citraketu kara gharu una ghālā, kanakakasipu kara puni asa hālā.

नारद सिख जे सुनहिं नर नारी । अवसि होहिं तजि भवनु भिखारी ॥
nārada sikha je sunahiṁ nara nārī, avasi hohiṁ taji bhavanu bhikhārī.

मन कपटी तन सज्जन चीन्हा । आपु सरिस सबही चह कीन्हा ॥
mana kapaṭī tana sajjana cīnhā, āpu sarisa sabahī caha kīnhā.

तेहि कें बचन मानि बिस्वासा । तुम्ह चाहहु पति सहज उदासा ॥
tehi keṁ bacana māni bisvāsā, tumha cāhahu pati sahaja udāsā.

निर्गुन निलज कुबेष कपाली । अकुल अगेह दिगंबर ब्याली ॥
nirguna nilaja kubeṣa kapālī, akula ageha digaṁbara byālī.

कहहु कवन सुखु अस बरु पाएँ । भल भूलिहु ठग के बौराएँ ॥
kahahu kavana sukhu asa baru pāeṁ, bhala bhūlihu ṭhaga ke baurāeṁ.

पंच कहें सिवँ सती बिबाही । पुनि अवडेरि मराएन्हि ताही ॥
paṁca kaheṁ sivaṁ satī bibāhī, puni avaḍeri marāenhi tāhī.

Trans:

Did he not advise Daksha's sons—and they never saw their father's house again? It was he too who ruined Chitraketu's family, and also Hiranyākashyap's. Whoever listens to Nārad's advice, be it man or woman, is certain to become a homeless beggar. Seemingly pious, but deceitful at heart, he would make everyone like himself. And now you too are led away by his words, and are longing to marry a very outcast, a worthless, shameless, tattered wretch, with a necklace of serpents and skulls, and without either family, or house, or even clothes. Tell me now—what pleasure is to be had from such a bridegroom as this? Better forget the ravings of the impostor. Shankar married Sati only because other people suggested it, and soon abandoned her and left her to die.

दोहा-dohā:

अब सुख सोवत सोचु नहिं भीख मागि भव खाहिं ।
aba sukha sovata socu nahiṁ bhīkha māgi bhava khāhiṁ,

सहज एकाकिन्ह के भवन कबहुँ कि नारि खटाहिं ॥७९॥
sahaja ekākinha ke bhavana kabahuṁ ki nāri khaṭāhiṁ. 79.

Trans:

And now he never gives her a thought but goes about a begging, and eats and sleeps at his ease. What respectable woman could ever stay with such a confirmed solitary?

चौपाई-caupāī:

अजहूँ मानहु कहा हमारा । हम तुम्ह कहुँ बरु नीक बिचारा ॥
ajahūṁ mānahu kahā hamārā, hama tumha kahuṁ baru nīka bicārā.

अति सुंदर सुचि सुखद सुसीला । गावहिं बेद जासु जस लीला ॥
ati suṁdara suci sukhada susīlā, gāvahiṁ beda jāsu jasa līlā.

दूषन रहित सकल गुन रासी । श्रीपति पुर बैकुंठ निवासी ॥
dūṣana rahita sakala guna rāsī, śrīpati pura baikuṁṭha nivāsī.

अस बरु तुम्हहि मिलाउब आनी । सुनत बिहसि कह बचन भवानी ॥
asa baru tumhahi milāuba ānī, sunata bihasi kaha bacana bhavānī.

सत्य कहेहु गिरिभव तनु एहा । हठ न छूट छूटै बरु देहा ॥
satya kahehu giribhava tanu ehā, haṭha na chūṭa chūṭai baru dehā.

कनकउ पुनि पषान तें होई । जारेहुँ सहजु न परिहर सोई ॥
kanakau puni paṣāna teṁ hoī, jārehuṁ sahaju na parihara soī.

नारद बचन न मैं परिहरऊँ । बसउ भवनु उजरउ नहिं डरऊँ ॥
nārada bacana na maiṁ pariharaūṁ, basau bhavanu ujarau nahiṁ ḍaraūṁ.

गुर कें बचन प्रतीति न जेही । सपनेहुँ सुगम न सुख सिधि तेही ॥
gura keṁ bacana pratīti na jehī, sapanehuṁ sugama na sukha sidhi tehī.

Trans:

Today if you will hear my words, I have thought of an excellent bridegroom for you, so beautiful and honorable, so pleasant and amiable, that even the Veda hymns his praise—the faultless and all-perfect Lord of Lakshmī, who reigns at Vaikūnth. He is the husband that I will bring you." On hearing this Bhawānī smiled and replied "You said true that I inherit a rock-nature, and would sooner die than yield. Gold, again, is another product of the rock that cannot be changed by any amount of burning. Nor will I change my faith in Nārad's word; whether my house be full or desolate, I fear not. Whoever doubts the word of his spiritual adviser must never dream of obtaining either happiness or riches.

दोहा-dohā:

महादेव अवगुन भवन बिष्नु सकल गुन धाम ।
mahādeva avaguna bhavana biṣnu sakala guna dhāma,

जेहि कर मनु रम जाहि सन तेहि तेही सन काम ॥८०॥
jehi kara manu rama jāhi sana tehi tehī sana kāma. 80.

Trans:

Mahādev is full of faults, while Vishnu is all-perfect: but the heart concerns itself only about the things it happens to fancy.

चौपाई-caupāī:

जौं तुम्ह मिलतेहु प्रथम मुनीसा । सुनतिउँ सिख तुम्हारि धरि सीसा ॥
jauṁ tumha milatehu prathama munīsā, sunatiuṁ sikha tumhāri dhari sīsā.

अब मैं जन्मु संभु हित हारा । को गुन दूषन करै बिचारा ॥
aba maiṁ janmu saṁbhu hita hārā, ko guna dūṣana karai bicārā.

जौं तुम्हरे हठ हृदयँ बिसेषी । रहि न जाइ बिनु किएँ बरेषी ॥
jauṁ tumhare haṭha hṛdayaṁ biseṣī, rahi na jāi binu kieṁ bareṣī.
तौ कौतुकिअन्ह आलसु नाहीं । बर कन्या अनेक जग माहीं ॥
tau kautukianha ālasu nāhīṁ, bara kanyā aneka jaga māhīṁ.
जन्म कोटि लगि रगर हमारी । बरउँ संभु न त रहउँ कुआरी ॥
janma koṭi lagi ragara hamārī, barauṁ saṁbhu na ta rahauṁ kuārī.
तजउँ न नारद कर उपदेसू । आपु कहहिं सत बार महेसू ॥
tajauṁ na nārada kara upadesū, āpu kahahiṁ sata bāra mahesū.
मैं पा परउँ कहइ जगदंबा । तुम्ह गृह गवनहु भयउ बिलंबा ॥
maiṁ pā parauṁ kahai jagadaṁbā, tumha gṛha gavanahu bhayau bilaṁbā.
देखि प्रेमु बोले मुनि ग्यानी । जय जय जगदंबिके भवानी ॥
dekhi premu bole muni gyānī, jaya jaya jagadaṁbike bhavānī.

Trans:

If, reverend sirs, I had met you sooner, I would have submitted to your advice; but now that I have given my life for Shambhu, it is too late to weigh his merits and defects. If you are firmly resolved and cannot rest without making a match, there is no dearth of lovers; the world is full of young men and maidens; but as for me, though I hold out for a million lives, I will either wed Shambhu or remain a virgin. I will not forget Nārad's admonition, who told me again and again of Mahādev. I, who am styled the mother of the world, fall at your feet and bid you, return home; for your time is lost here." When the sages beheld her devotion they cried, "Glory, glory, glory to the great mother Bhawānī,

दोहा-dohā:

तुम्ह माया भगवान सिव सकल जगत पितु मातु ।
tumha māyā bhagavāna siva sakala jagata pitu mātu,
नाइ चरन सिर मुनि चले पुनि पुनि हरषत गातु ॥८१॥
nāi carana sira muni cale puni puni haraṣata gātu. 81.

Trans:

You are united as Māyā to the god Shiva, and remain the parents of the universe!" Then bowing their heads at her feet and thrilling with rapture they left.

चौपाई-caupāī:

जाइ मुनिन्ह हिमवंतु पठाए । करि बिनती गिरजहिं गृह ल्याए ॥
jāi muninha himavaṁtu paṭhāe, kari binatī girajahiṁ gṛha lyāe.
बहुरि सप्तरिषि सिव पहिं जाई । कथा उमा कै सकल सुनाई ॥
bahuri saptariṣi siva pahiṁ jāī, kathā umā kai sakala sunāī.
भए मगन सिव सुनत सनेहा । हरषि सप्तरिषि गवने गेहा ॥
bhae magana siva sunata sanehā, haraṣi saptariṣi gavane gehā.
मनु थिर करि तब संभु सुजाना । लगे करन रघुनायक ध्याना ॥
manu thira kari taba saṁbhu sujānā, lage karana raghunāyaka dhyānā.
तारकु असुर भयउ तेहि काला । भुज प्रताप बल तेज बिसाला ॥
tāraku asura bhayau tehi kālā, bhuja pratāpa bala teja bisālā.
तेहिं सब लोक लोकपति जीते । भए देव सुख संपति रीते ॥
tehiṁ saba loka lokapati jīte, bhae deva sukha saṁpati rīte.
अजर अमर सो जीति न जाई । हारे सुर करि बिबिध लराई ॥
ajara amara so jīti na jāī, hāre sura kari bibidha larāī.
तब बिरंचि सन जाइ पुकारे । देखे बिधि सब देव दुखारे ॥
taba biraṁci sana jāi pukāre, dekhe bidhi saba deva dukhāre.

Trans:

And they then sent King Himvān there who, with many entreaties, brought Girijā back. When they returned to Shiva and told him Umā's whole story, he was delighted to hear of her affection, and the seven sages went gladly home. Then the all-wise Shambhu, firmly directing his intention, began a meditation on Rāma. Now at that time was a demon Tārak, of gigantic strength of arm and high renown, who had subdued the sovereigns of every region and despoiled the gods of all their happiness. Knowing neither age nor death, he was invincible and the powers of heaven were vanquished by him in innumerable battles. At last they all went and cried to the Brahmmā, and he, seeing them so dismayed,

दोहा-dohā:

सब सन कहा बुझाइ बिधि दनुज निधन तब होइ ।
saba sana kahā bujhāi bidhi danuja nidhana taba hoi,
संभु सुक्र संभूत सुत एहि जीतइ रन सोइ ॥८२॥
saṁbhu sukra saṁbhūta suta ehi jītai rana soi. 82.

Trans:

reassured them, saying: "The demon shall die when from the seed of Shambhu is born a son, who shall conquer him in fight.

चौपाई-caupāī:

मोर कहा सुनि करहु उपाई । होइहि ईस्वर करिहि सहाई ॥
mora kahā suni karahu upāī, hoihi īsvara karihi sahāī.
सतीं जो तजी दच्छ मख देहा । जनमी जाइ हिमाचल गेहा ॥
satīṁ jo tajī daccha makha dehā, janamī jāi himācala gehā.
तेहिं तपु कीन्ह संभु पति लागी । सिव समाधि बैठे सबु त्यागी ॥
tehiṁ tapu kīnha saṁbhu pati lāgī, siva samādhi baiṭhe sabu tyāgī.
जदपि अहइ असमंजस भारी । तदपि बात एक सुनहु हमारी ॥
jadapi ahai asamaṁjasa bhārī, tadapi bāta eka sunahu hamārī.
पठवहु कामु जाइ सिव पाहीं । करै छोभु संकर मन माहीं ॥
paṭhavahu kāmu jāi siva pāhīṁ, karai chobhu saṁkara mana māhīṁ.
तब हम जाइ सिवहि सिर नाई । करवाउब बिबाहु बरिआई ॥
taba hama jāi sivahi sira nāī, karavāuba bibāhu bariāī.
एहि बिधि भलेहिं देवहित होई । मत अति नीक कहइ सबु कोई ॥
ehi bidhi bhalehiṁ devahita hoī, mata ati nīka kahai sabu koī.
अस्तुति सुरन्ह कीन्हि अति हेतू । प्रगटेउ बिषमबान झषकेतू ॥
astuti suranha kīnhi ati hetū, pragaṭeu biṣamabāna jhaṣaketū.

Trans:

Having heard what I say, devise a plan by which such a lord may arise and assist you. After Sati quitted the body at Daksha's sacrifice, she was born again as the daughter of the Himalaya, and has been practicing penance in the hope of obtaining Shambhu to be her husband. He, on the other hand, has left all, and sits absorbed in contemplation. Though the disparity is great, yet list to what I propose. Send Kāma, the god of love, to Shiva to agitate his soul, and then I will approach with bowed head and arrange the marriage, and in this way your object will be attained." All exclaimed that the plan was good, and heartily applauded it. The gods then prayed with great devotion and the god of love, armed with five arrows and having a fish emblazoned on his standard, appeared on the scene.

दोहा-dohā:

सुरन्ह कही निज बिपति सब सुनि मन कीन्ह बिचार ।
suranha kahī nija bipati saba suni mana kīnha bicāra,
संभु बिरोध न कुसल मोहि बिहसि कहेउ अस मार ॥८३॥
saṁbhu birodha na kusala mohi bihasi kaheu asa māra. 83.

Trans:

And they told him their distress. He heard, and after reflecting a little replied with a smile—"Shambhu's displeasure will work me no good;

चौपाई-caupāī:

तदपि करब मैं काजु तुम्हारा । श्रुति कह परम धरम उपकारा ॥
tadapi karaba maiṁ kāju tumhārā, śruti kaha parama dharama upakārā.
पर हित लागि तजइ जो देही । संतत संत प्रसंसहिं तेही ॥
para hita lāgi tajai jo dehī, saṁtata saṁta prasaṁsahiṁ tehī.
अस कहि चलेउ सबहि सिरु नाई । सुमन धनुष कर सहित सहाई ॥

asa kahi caleu sabahi siru nāī, sumana dhanuṣa kara sahita sahāī.

चलत मार अस हृदयँ बिचारा । सिव बिरोध ध्रुव मरनु हमारा ॥
calata māra asa hṛdayaṁ bicārā, siva birodha dhruva maranu hamārā.

तब आपन प्रभाउ बिस्तारा । निज बस कीन्ह सकल संसारा ॥
taba āpana prabhāu bistārā, nija basa kīnha sakala saṁsārā.

कोपेउ जबहि बारिचरकेतू । छन महुँ मिटे सकल श्रुति सेतू ॥
kopeu jabahi bāricaraketū, chana mahuṁ miṭe sakala śruti setū.

ब्रह्मचर्ज ब्रत संजम नाना । धीरज धरम ग्यान बिग्याना ॥
brahmacarja brata saṁjama nānā, dhīraja dharama gyāna bigyānā.

सदाचार जप जोग बिरागा । सभय बिबेक कटकु सबु भागा ॥
sadācāra japa joga birāgā, sabhaya bibeka kaṭaku sabu bhāgā.

Trans:

Yet I will do you this service. The scriptures say charity is the highest of virtues, and one who gives his life for another is ever the praise of the saints." So saying he bowed and took his leave—he and his attendants, with his bow of flowers in his hand. And as he went he thought with anxiety, 'Shiva's displeasure will surely be my death.' Therefore he hastened to exhibit his power, and for a time reduced to subjection the entire world. If the god of love is agitated, the stepping-stones of the law are swept away in a moment; religious vows and obligations, self-control, ceremonial observances, knowledge and philosophy, virtuous practices, prayer, penance, self-mortification, the whole spiritual army, is panic-stricken and put to flight.

छंद-chaṁda:

भागेउ बिबेकु सहाय सहित सो सुभट संजुग महि मुरे ।
bhāgeu bibeku sahāya sahita so subhaṭa saṁjuga mahi mure,

सदग्रंथ पर्बत कंदरन्हि महुँ जाइ तेहि अवसर दुरे ॥
sadagraṁtha parbata kaṁdaranhi mahuṁ jāi tehi avasara dure.

होनिहार का करतार को रखवार जग खरभरु परा ।
honihāra kā karatāra ko rakhavāra jaga kharabharu parā,

दुइ माथ केहि रतिनाथ जेहि कहुँ कोपि कर धनु सरु धरा ॥
dui mātha kehi ratinātha jehi kahuṁ kopi kara dhanu saru dharā.

Trans:

Discrimination, and his companions, took to flight; his great warriors fled from the fight. At that time, they went and hid themselves in mountain-caves taking the form of holy scriptures. There was agitation throughout the world and said all in dismay, "Goodness gracious, what next! Who now will save us? Is there any being of supreme might to conquer the Lord of Rati who rages on with his bow and arrows lifted?"

दोहा-dohā:

जे सजीव जग अचर चर नारि पुरुष अस नाम ।
je sajīva jaga acara cara nāri puruṣa asa nāma,

ते निज निज मरजाद तजि भए सकल बस काम ॥८४॥
te nija nija marajāda taji bhae sakala basa kāma. 84.

Trans:

Every creature in the world, animate or inanimate, male or female, forgot natural restraint and became completely possessed by desire.

चौपाई-caupāī:

सब के हृदयँ मदन अभिलाषा । लता निहारि नवहिं तरु साखा ॥
saba ke hṛdayaṁ madana abhilāṣā, latā nihāri navahiṁ taru sākhā.

नदीं उमगि अंबुधि कहुँ धाई । संगम करहिं तलाव तलाईं ॥
nadīṁ umagi aṁbudhi kahuṁ dhāīṁ, saṁgama karahiṁ talāva talāīṁ.

जहँ असि दसा जड़न्ह कै बरनी । को कहि सकइ सचेतन करनी ॥
jahaṁ asi dasā jaṛanha kai baranī, ko kahi sakai sacetana karanī.

पसु पच्छी नभ जल थलचारी । भए कामबस समय बिसारी ॥
pasu pacchī nabha jala thalacārī, bhae kāmabasa samaya bisārī.

मदन अंध ब्याकुल सब लोका । निसि दिनु नहिं अवलोकहिं कोका ॥
madana aṁdha byākula saba lokā, nisi dinu nahiṁ avalokahiṁ kokā.

देव दनुज नर किंनर ब्याला । प्रेत पिसाच भूत बेताला ॥
deva danuja nara kiṁnara byālā, preta pisāca bhūta betālā.

इन्ह कै दसा न कहेउँ बखानी । सदा काम के चेरे जानी ॥
inha kai dasā na kaheuṁ bakhānī, sadā kāma ke cere jānī.

सिद्ध बिरक्त महामुनि जोगी । तेपि कामबस भए बियोगी ॥
siddha birakta mahāmuni jogī, tepi kāmabasa bhae biyogī.

Trans:

In every heart was a craving for lust: the tree bent its boughs to kiss the creeper; the overflowing river ran into the arms of ocean; lakes and ponds effected a meeting. And when such was the case with inanimate creation, what need then to speak of the animate? Beasts on land and birds in the air, under the influence of love, were unmindful of time and season; all were agitated and blind with desire, and the swan regarded neither night nor day. Gods, demons, men, Kinnars, serpents, ghosts, witches, goblins, and imps were all at once enslaved by love; even saints and hermits, sages and ascetics, became sensual again under the influence of god of Love.

छंद-chaṁda:

भए कामबस जोगीस तापस पावँरन्हि की को कहै ।
bhae kāmabasa jogīsa tāpasa pāvaṁranhi kī ko kahai,

देखहिं चराचर नारिमय जे ब्रह्ममय देखत रहे ॥
dekhahiṁ carācara nārimaya je brahmamaya dekhata rahe.

अबला बिलोकहिं पुरुषमय जगु पुरुष सब अबलामयं ।
abalā bilokahiṁ puruṣamaya jagu puruṣa saba abalāmayaṁ,

दुइ दंड भरि ब्रह्मांड भीतर कामकृत कौतुक अयं ॥
dui daṁḍa bhari brahmāṁḍa bhītara kāmakṛta kautuka ayaṁ.

Trans:

When even saints and hermits were owned in his sway, what then to say of serf and thrall? Even the most wise, who looked ere upon creation pervaded with Brahmm now saw it full of opposite sex. Each one was like a jocund dame or an amorous swain, who found heaven only in love's embrace; and an hour sped past this way, and love still stood fast, and he reigned unrestrained in the domain of Brahmmā.

सोरठा-sorathā:

धरी न काहूँ धीर सब के मन मनसिज हरे ।
dharī na kāhūṁ dhīra saba ke mana manasija hare,

जे राखे रघुबीर ते उबरे तेहि काल महुँ ॥८५॥
je rākhe raghubīra te ubare tehi kāla mahuṁ. 85.

Trans:

None is so bold but passion steals his heart, and only they whom Rāma protects can escape his onslaught.

चौपाई-caupāī:

उभय घरी अस कौतुक भयऊ । जौ लगि कामु संभु पहिं गयऊ ॥
ubhaya gharī asa kautuka bhayaū, jau lagi kāmu saṁbhu pahiṁ gayaū.

सिवहि बिलोकि ससंकेउ मारू । भयउ जथाथिति सबु संसारू ॥
sivahi biloki sasaṁkeu mārū, bhayau jathāthiti sabu saṁsārū.

भए तुरत सब जीव सुखारे । जिमि मद उतरि गएँ मतवारे ॥
bhae turata saba jīva sukhāre, jimi mada utari gaeṁ matavāre.

रुद्रहि देखि मदन भय माना । दुराधरष दुर्गम भगवाना ॥
rudrahi dekhi madana bhaya mānā, durādharaṣa durgama bhagavānā.

फिरत लाज कछु करि नहिं जाई । मरनु ठानि मन रचेसि उपाई ॥
phirata lāja kachu kari nahiṁ jāī, maranu ṭhāni mana racesi upāī.

प्रगटेसि तुरत रुचिर रितुराजा । कुसुमित नव तरु राजि बिराजा ॥
pragaṭesi turata rucira riturājā, kusumita nava taru rāji birājā.

बन उपबन बापिका तड़ागा । परम सुभग सब दिसा बिभागा ॥
bana upabana bāpikā taṛāgā, parama subhaga saba disā bibhāgā.

जहँ तहँ जनु उमगत अनुरागा । देखि मुएहुँ मन मनसिज जागा ॥
jaham̐ taham̐ janu umagata anurāgā, dekhi muehum̐ mana manasija jāgā.

Trans:
For nearly an hour this triumph lasted. Then as Kāmdev drew nigh to Shambhu, upon seeing him he trembled in fear—and the whole world returned to itself. Every living creature at once grew calm—as when a drunkard recovers from his drunkenness. When Love looked at Shiva—the invincible and unapproachable god, he was overpowered with fright. He felt shy in retreating, but felt incapable of doing anything else; ultimately he resolved upon death and devised a plan. Forthwith lusty Spring stepped forth, and every tree broke into blossom. Wood and grove, lake and pond, every quarter of the heaven, gladdened and overflowed as it were with erotism, and even the deadest soul quickened at the sight.

छंद-*chaṁda:*

जागइ मनोभव मुएहुँ मन बन सुभगता न परै कही ।
jāgai manobhava muehum̐ mana bana subhagatā na parai kahī.

सीतल सुगंध सुमंद मारुत मदन अनल सखा सही ॥
sītala sugaṁdha sumaṁda māruta madana anala sakhā sahī.

बिकसे सरन्हि बहु कंज गुंजत पुंज मंजुल मधुकरा ।
bikase saranhi bahu kaṁja guṁjata puṁja maṁjula madhukarā,

कलहंस पिक सुक सरस रव करि गान नाचहिं अपछरा ॥
kalahaṁsa pika suka sarasa rava kari gāna nācahiṁ apacharā.

Trans:
The beauty of the gardens beggared description; and passion flared up even in dead souls, while a soft, cool, fragrant breeze fanned love-kindled sparks. The lakes sparkled with lotuses in bloom and swarms of charming bees hummed with drowsy sounds. Swans, parrots, cuckoos cooed out their souls in the sweet songs; and celestial damsels sang and danced.

दोहा-*dohā:*

सकल कला करि कोटि बिधि हारेउ सेन समेत ।
sakala kalā kari koṭi bidhi hāreu sena sameta,

चली न अचल समाधि सिव कोपेउ हृदयनिकेत ॥८६॥
calī na acala samādhi siva kopeu hṛdayaniketa. 86.

Trans:
Though he tried every trick and manifold device, yet he and his army were defeated; Shiva's unbroken trance still continued, and Love now became irate.

चौपाई-*caupāī:*

देखि रसाल बिटप बर साखा । तेहि पर चढ़ेउ मदनु मन माखा ॥
dekhi rasāla biṭapa bara sākhā, tehi para caṛheu madanu mana mākhā.

सुमन चाप निज सर संधाने । अति रिस ताकि श्रवन लगि ताने ॥
sumana cāpa nija sara saṁdhāne, ati risa tāki śravana lagi tāne.

छाँड़े बिषम बिसिख उर लागे । छुटि समाधि संभु तब जागे ॥
chām̐ṛe biṣama bisikha ura lāge, chuṭi samādhi saṁbhu taba jāge.

भयउ ईस मन छोभु बिसेषी । नयन उघारि सकल दिसि देखी ॥
bhayau īsa mana chobhu biseṣī, nayana ughāri sakala disi dekhī.

सौरभ पल्लव मदनु बिलोका । भयउ कोपु कंपेउ त्रैलोका ॥
saurabha pallava madanu bilokā, bhayau kopu kaṁpeu trailokā.

तब सिवँ तीसर नयन उघारा । चितवत कामु भयउ जरि छारा ॥
taba sivam̐ tīsara nayana ughārā, citavata kāmu bhayau jari chārā.

हाहाकार भयउ जग भारी । डरपे सुर भए असुर सुखारी ॥
hāhākāra bhayau jaga bhārī, ḍarape sura bhae asura sukhārī.

समुझि कामसुखु सोचहिं भोगी । भए अकंटक साधक जोगी ॥
samujhi kāmasukhu socahiṁ bhogī, bhae akaṁṭaka sādhaka jogī.

Trans:
Seeing a mango tree with spreading boughs, he in his folly climbed up into it, then fitted a shaft to his flowery bow, and then in his great passion taking aim, and drawing the string home to the ear, he let fly and lodged the five arrows in Shiva's chest. Then the trance was broken and Shambhu awoke. In the Lord's soul was great agitation. He opened his eyes and looking all around saw Kāmdev in the mango tree. He was filled with wrath, and with his ire the three worlds trembled. Then Shiva unclosed his third eye—and in its flash Kāmdev was reduced to ashes. A bewildered cry went up through the universe; the gods were in dismay and the demons rejoiced; the voluptuary were sad when they remembered love's delights, while the saints and hermits felt relieved as if of a thorn.

छंद-*chaṁda:*

जोगि अकंटक भए पति गति सुनत रति मुरुछित भई ।
jogi akaṁṭaka bhae pati gati sunata rati muruchita bhaī,

रोदति बदति बहु भाँति करुना करति संकर पहिं गई ॥
rodati badati bahu bhām̐ti karunā karati saṁkara pahiṁ gaī.

अति प्रेम करि बिनती बिबिध बिधि जोरि कर सन्मुख रही ।
ati prema kari binatī bibidha bidhi jori kara sanmukha rahī,

प्रभु आसुतोष कृपाल सिव अबला निरखि बोले सही ॥
prabhu āsutoṣa kṛpāla siva abalā nirakhi bole sahī.

Trans:
The saints were freed from torment; while love's consort Ratī swooned learning of her dear lord's tragic fate. In sad guise and weeping eyes, weeping, mourning, wailing, in every which way, she approached Shankar; and making loving entreaties in divergent forms, she stood low before the Lord with clasped hands. Seeing the hapless woman, the benevolent Shiva, who is so easy to placate, spoke in words compassionate:

दोहा-*dohā:*

अब तें रति तव नाथ कर होइहि नामु अनंगु ।
aba teṁ rati tava nātha kara hoihi nāmu anaṁgu,

बिनु बपु ब्यापिहि सबहि पुनि सुनु निज मिलन प्रसंगु ॥८७॥
binu bapu byāpihi sabahi puni sunu nija milana prasaṁgu. 87.

Trans:
"Henceforth, Ratī, your husband's name shall be called Anang, the bodiless, and thus etherealized he shall pervade all things. But hear how you will again find him hereafter.

चौपाई-*caupāī:*

जब जदुबंस कृष्न अवतारा । होइहि हरन महा महिभारा ॥
jaba jadubaṁsa kṛṣna avatārā, hoihi harana mahā mahibhārā.

कृष्न तनय होइहि पति तोरा । बचनु अन्यथा होइ न मोरा ॥
kṛṣna tanaya hoihi pati torā, bacanu anyathā hoi na morā.

रति गवनी सुनि संकर बानी । कथा अपर अब कहउँ बखानी ॥
rati gavanī suni saṁkara bānī, kathā apara aba kahauṁ bakhānī.

देवन्ह समाचार सब पाए । ब्रह्मादिक बैकुंठ सिधाए ॥
devanha samācāra saba pāe, brahmādika baikuṁṭha sidhāe.

सब सुर बिष्नु बिरंचि समेता । गए जहाँ सिव कृपानिकेता ॥
saba sura biṣnu biraṁci sametā, gae jahām̐ siva kṛpāniketā.

पृथक पृथक तिन्ह कीन्ह प्रसंसा । भए प्रसन्न चंद्र अवतंसा ॥
pṛthaka pṛthaka tinha kīnha prasaṁsā, bhae prasanna caṁdra avataṁsā.

बोले कृपासिंधु बृषकेतू । कहहु अमर आए केहि हेतू ॥
bole kṛpāsiṁdhu bṛṣaketū, kahahu amara āe kehi hetū.

कह बिधि तुम्ह प्रभु अंतरजामी । तदपि भगति बस बिनवउँ स्वामी ॥
kaha bidhi tumha prabhu aṁtarajāmī, tadapi bhagati basa binavauṁ svāmī.

Trans:

When Krishna becomes incarnate in the line of Jadu to relieve the world of its burdens, your husband shall be born again as his son Pradyumna: this, my word, shall not fail." On hearing this prophecy of Shankar's, Ratī retired. Now let's turn to another part of the story. When Brahmmā and the other gods heard these tidings they first went to Vaikūnth, and thence, with Vishnu, Brahmmā, and all the rest, into the presence of the merciful Shiva; and each of them separately sang his praises. Then the gracious power, whose crest is the moon and whose standard a bull said: "Tell me, ye immortals, why ye have come." Said Brahmmā: "My Lord, you can read our hearts, but since you ask, so I say.

दोहा-*dohā:*

सकल सुरन्ह के हृदयँ अस संकर परम उछाहु ।
sakala suranha ke hṛdayam̐ asa saṁkara parama uchāhu,
निज नयनन्हि देखा चहहिं नाथ तुम्हार बिबाहु ॥८८॥
nija nayananhi dekhā cahahiṁ nātha tumhāra bibāhu. 88.

Trans:

The heart of all the immortals is seized with a dominating impulse. They long to witness your wedding with their own eyes, my Lord.

चौपाई-*caupāī:*

यह उत्सव देखिअ भरि लोचन । सोइ कछु करहु मदन मद मोचन ॥
yaha utsava dekhia bhari locana, soi kachu karahu madana mada mocana.
कामु जारि रति कहुँ बरु दीन्हा । कृपासिंधु यह अति भल कीन्हा ॥
kāmu jāri rati kahum̐ baru dīnhā, kṛpāsiṁdhu yaha ati bhala kīnhā.
सासति करि पुनि करहिं पसाऊ । नाथ प्रभुन्ह कर सहज सुभाऊ ॥
sāsati kari puni karahiṁ pasāū, nātha prabhunha kara sahaja subhāū.
पारबतीं तपु कीन्ह अपारा । करहु तासु अब अंगीकारा ॥
pārabatīṁ tapu kīnha apārā, karahu tāsu aba aṁgīkārā.
सुनि बिधि बिनय समुझि प्रभु बानी । ऐसेइ होउ कहा सुखु मानी ॥
suni bidhi binaya samujhi prabhu bānī, aisei hou kahā sukhu mānī.
तब देवन्ह दुंदुभीं बजाईं । बरषि सुमन जय जय सुर साईं ॥
taba devanha duṁdubhīṁ bajāīṁ, baraṣi sumana jaya jaya sura sāīṁ.
अवसरु जानि सप्तरिषि आए । तुरतहिं बिधि गिरिभवन पठाए ॥
avasaru jāni saptariṣi āe, turatahiṁ bidhi giribhavana paṭhāe.
प्रथम गए जहँ रहीं भवानी । बोले मधुर बचन छल सानी ॥
prathama gae jaham̐ rahīṁ bhavānī, bole madhura bacana chala sānī.

Trans:

O destroyer of the pride of love, let us feast our eyes on this glad event. In granting a husband to Ratī after Kāmdev had been consumed you have done well, O sea of compassion, in punishment remembering mercy; the great have ever an easy temper. Accept now the interminable penance that Pārwatī has endured." On hearing Brahmmā's speech and perceiving its purport, he exclaimed joyfully, "So be it!" Then the gods sounded their kettledrums and rained down flowers, and cried "Victory, Victory, to the King of Heaven!" Then, perceiving it was the proper time, the seven sages came and were dispatched by Brahmmā to the Himalaya, where first they sought Bhawānī, and addressed her in mild but deceptive terms:

दोहा-*dohā:*

कहा हमार न सुनेहु तब नारद कें उपदेस ।
kahā hamāra na sunehu taba nārada keṁ upadesa,
अब भा झूठ तुम्हार पन जारेउ कामु महेस ॥८९॥
aba bhā jhūṭha tumhāra pana jāreu kāmu mahesa. 89.

Trans:

"You would not listen to us, but rather took Nārad's advice; now again is your vow proved vain, for the god of love has been consumed by Mahādev."

मासपारायण तीसरा विश्राम
māsapārāyaṇa tīsarā viśrāma
(Pause 3 for a Thirty-Day Recitation)

चौपाई-*caupāī:*

सुनि बोलीं मुसुकाइ भवानी । उचित कहेहु मुनिबर बिग्यानी ॥
suni boliṁ musukāi bhavānī, ucita kahehu munibara bigyānī.
तुम्हरें जान कामु अब जारा । अब लगि संभु रहे सबिकारा ॥
tumhareṁ jāna kāmu aba jārā, aba lagi saṁbhu rahe sabikārā.
हमरें जान सदा सिव जोगी । अज अनवद्य अकाम अभोगी ॥
hamareṁ jāna sadā siva jogī, aja anavadya akāma abhogī.
जौं मैं सिव सेये अस जानी । प्रीति समेत कर्म मन बानी ॥
jauṁ maiṁ siva seye asa jānī, prīti sameta karma mana bānī.
तौ हमार पन सुनहु मुनीसा । करिहहिं सत्य कृपानिधि ईसा ॥
tau hamāra pana sunahu munīsā, karihahiṁ satya kṛpānidhi īsā.
तुम्ह जो कहा हर जारेउ मारा । सोइ अति बड़ अबिबेकु तुम्हारा ॥
tumha jo kahā hara jāreu mārā, soi ati baṛa abibeku tumhārā.
तात अनल कर सहज सुभाऊ । हिम तेहि निकट जाइ नहिं काऊ ॥
tāta anala kara sahaja subhāū, hima tehi nikaṭa jāi nahiṁ kāū.
गएँ समीप सो अवसि नसाई । असि मन्मथ महेस की नाई ॥
gaem̐ samīpa so avasi nasāī, asi manmatha mahesa kī nāī.

Trans:

Bhawānī replied with a smile, "O wisest of sages, you have said well. Your words—'Love has been consumed by Mahādev'—imply a belief that aforetime Shambhu was liable to change. But I know him to be from everlasting an ascetic, faultless, without cravings, passionless; and if, knowing him to be such as he is, I have served him devotedly in heart, word, and deed, so gracious a Lord, be assured O sages, will bring my vow to accomplishment. Your saying that Hara has destroyed love betrays great want of judgment. Fire, my friend, has this unalterable nature whereby frost cannot exist near it; and if brought near, must inevitably perish; and so must Lust in the presence of Mahādev."

दोहा-*dohā:*

हियँ हरषे मुनि बचन सुनि देखि प्रीति बिस्वास ।
hiyam̐ haraṣe muni bacana suni dekhi prīti bisvāsa,
चले भवानिहि नाइ सिर गए हिमाचल पास ॥९०॥
cale bhavānihi nāi sira gae himācala pāsa. 90.

Trans:

On hearing this speech and seeing her love and confidence, the sages were delighted and bowed the head before her, and went to King Himāchal.

चौपाई-*caupāī:*

सबु प्रसंगु गिरिपतिहि सुनावा । मदन दहन सुनि अति दुखु पावा ॥
sabu prasaṁgu giripatihi sunāvā, madana dahana suni ati dukhu pāvā.
बहुरि कहेउ रति कर बरदाना । सुनि हिमवंत बहुत सुखु माना ॥
bahuri kaheu rati kara baradānā, suni himavaṁta bahuta sukhu mānā.
हृदयँ बिचारि संभु प्रभुताई । सादर मुनिबर लिए बोलाई ॥
hṛdayam̐ bicāri saṁbhu prabhutāī, sādara munibara lie bolāī.
सुदिनु सुनखतु सुघरी सोचाई । बेगि बेदबिधि लगन धराई ॥
sudinu sunakhatu sugharī socāī, begi bedabidhi lagana dharāī.
पत्री सप्तरिषिन्ह सोइ दीन्ही । गहि पद बिनय हिमाचल कीन्ही ॥
patrī saptariṣinha soi dīnhī, gahi pada binaya himācala kīnhī.
जाइ बिधिहि तिन्ह दीन्हि सो पाती । बाचत प्रीति न हृदयँ समाती ॥
jāi bidhihi tinha dīnhi so pātī, bācata prīti na hṛdayam̐ samātī.
लगन बाचि अज सबहि सुनाई । हरषे मुनि सब सुर समुदाई ॥
lagana bāci aja sabahi sunāī, haraṣe muni saba sura samudāī.
सुमन बृष्टि नभ बाजन बाजे । मंगल कलस दसहुँ दिसि साजे ॥
sumana bṛṣṭi nabha bājana bāje, maṁgala kalasa dasahum̐ disi sāje.

Trans:

And they told him the whole history. When he heard of Kāmdev's destruction he was much distressed, but was again comforted when told of Ratī's promised husband. After pondering on the majesty of Shambhu he reverently summoned the wise men, and at once had the marriage day fixed according to Vedic prescription, selecting an auspicious date, planet, and hour. Then he gave the letter to the seven sages, humbly falling at their feet, and they took it to Brahmmā, who could not contain himself for joy on reading it, and at once proclaimed it aloud. The whole company of heaven was delighted: there was music and a shower of flowers, and in every quarter festive preparations were commenced.

दोहा-dohā:

लगे सँवारन सकल सुर बाहन बिबिध बिमान ।
lage saṁvārana sakala sura bāhana bibidha bimāna,
होहिं सगुन मंगल सुभद करहिं अपछरा गान ॥९१॥
hohiṁ saguna maṁgala subhada karahiṁ apacharā gāna. 91.

Trans:

All the gods began adorning their vehicles and aerial cars of different kinds; and the celestial dames sang with joy; and all around there was bliss and happiness.

चौपाई-caupāī:

सिवहि संभु गन करहिं सिंगारा । जटा मुकुट अहि मौरु सँवारा ॥
sivahi saṁbhu gana karahiṁ siṁgārā, jaṭā mukuṭa ahi mauru saṁvārā.
कुंडल कंकन पहिरे ब्याला । तन बिभूति पट केहरि छाला ॥
kuṁḍala kaṁkana pahire byālā, tana bibhūti paṭa kehari chālā.
ससि ललाट सुंदर सिर गंगा । नयन तीनि उपबीत भुजंगा ॥
sasi lalāṭa suṁdara sira gaṁgā, nayana tīni upabīta bhujaṁgā.
गरल कंठ उर नर सिर माला । असिव बेष सिवधाम कृपाला ॥
garala kaṁṭha ura nara sira mālā, asiva beṣa sivadhāma kṛpālā.
कर त्रिसूल अरु डमरु बिराजा । चले बसहँ चढ़ि बाजहिं बाजा ॥
kara trisūla aru ḍamaru birājā, cale basahaṁ caṛhi bājahiṁ bājā.
देखि सिवहि सुरत्रिय मुसुकाहीं । बर लायक दुलहिनि जग नाहीं ॥
dekhi sivahi suratriya musukāhīṁ, bara lāyaka dulahini jaga nāhīṁ.
बिष्नु बिरंचि आदि सुरब्राता । चढ़ि चढ़ि बाहन चले बराता ॥
biṣnu biraṁci ādi surabrātā, caṛhi caṛhi bāhana cale barātā.
सुर समाज सब भाँति अनूपा । नहिं बरात दूलह अनुरूपा ॥
sura samāja saba bhāṁti anūpā, nahiṁ barāta dūlaha anurūpā.

Trans:

Shiva's attendants began to dress their Lord, arranging his serpent-crest and crown of matted locks: with snakes for his earrings and bracelets of snakes for his wrists; his body smeared with ashes, and a lion's skin about his loins; the moon on his brow, the lovely Gangā on the crown of his head, his eyes three in number, and a serpent for his *Janeu*; his throat black with poison; a wreath of dead men's skulls about his front. In such ghastly attire was arrayed the great god Shiva. With trident in hand he advanced riding on a bull, while the drums beat and instruments of music were played. The female divinities all smiled to see him, and said, "The world has no bride worthy of such a lover." Vishnu and Brahmmā and all the company of heaven followed in the procession, each on his own carriage; they formed a wondrous sight, but were nothing compared to the bridegroom.

दोहा-dohā:

बिष्नु कहा अस बिहसि तब बोलि सकल दिसिराज ।
biṣnu kahā asa bihasi taba boli sakala disirāja,
बिलग बिलग होइ चलहु सब निज निज सहित समाज ॥९२॥
bilaga bilaga hoi calahu saba nija nija sahita samāja. 92.

Trans:

Then Vishnu with a smile cried to all the heavenly warders and said, "March separately, each one with his own retinue;

चौपाई-caupāī:

बर अनुहारि बरात न भाई । हँसी करैहहु पर पुर जाई ॥
bara anuhāri barāta na bhāī, haṁsī karaihahu para pura jāī.
बिष्नु बचन सुनि सुर मुसुकाने । निज निज सेन सहित बिलगाने ॥
biṣnu bacana suni sura musukāne, nija nija sena sahita bilagāne.
मनहीं मन महेसु मुसुकाहीं । हरि के बिंग्य बचन नहिं जाहीं ॥
manahīṁ mana mahesu musukāhīṁ, hari ke biṁgya bacana nahiṁ jāhīṁ.
अति प्रिय बचन सुनत प्रिय केरे । भृंगिहि प्रेरि सकल गन टेरे ॥
ati priya bacana sunata priya kere, bhṛṁgihi preri sakala gana ṭere.
सिव अनुसासन सुनि सब आए । प्रभु पद जलज सीस तिन्ह नाए ॥
siva anusāsana suni saba āe, prabhu pada jalaja sīsa tinha nāe.
नाना बाहन नाना बेषा । बिहसे सिव समाज निज देखा ॥
nānā bāhana nānā beṣā, bihase siva samāja nija dekhā.
कोउ मुखहीन बिपुल मुख काहू । बिनु पद कर कोउ बहु पद बाहू ॥
kou mukhahīna bipula mukha kāhū, binu pada kara kou bahu pada bāhū.
बिपुल नयन कोउ नयन बिहीना । रिष्टपुष्ट कोउ अति तनखीना ॥
bipula nayana kou nayana bihīnā, riṣṭapuṣṭa kou ati tanakhīnā.

Trans:

otherwise on going into a strange city they will laugh and say what a sorry procession for such a bridegroom." The gods smiled to hear this speech, and marched separately, each at the head of his own followers. Mahādev smiled too; not noting Harī's humor but taking it as a most friendly suggestion; and sent Bhringi to bring all his own company together. On receiving Shiva's order they all came and bowed head at his lotus feet. Then Shiva laughed to see the host in their motley attire: riding every kind of vehicle; some with monstrous heads, some with no head at all; some with many hands and feet and some with none; some with great eyes, some with no eyes; some very stout, some very slim.

छंद-chaṁda:

तन खीन कोउ अति पीन पावन कोउ अपावन गति धरें ।
tana khīna kou ati pīna pāvana kou apāvana gati dhareṁ,
भूषन कराल कपाल कर सब सद्य सोनित तन भरें ॥
bhūṣana karāla kapāla kara saba sadya sonita tana bhareṁ.
खर स्वान सुअर सृकाल मुख गन बेष अगनित को गनै ।
khara svāna suara sṛkāla mukha gana beṣa aganita ko ganai,
बहु जिनस प्रेत पिसाच जोगि जमात बरनत नहिं बनै ॥
bahu jinasa preta pisāca jogi jamāta baranata nahiṁ banai.

Trans:

Some were lean and thin, others blubbery plump; some tidy, others with frightful adornments gross and gruesome. With skulls for wine-cups filled with blood, they staggered and quaffed with glee. With head of dog, or ass, or swine, this was an army of ghosts, goblins, witches, every kind of denizen of hell—which no tongue can tell.

सोरठा-sorațhā:

नाचहिं गावहिं गीत परम तरंगी भूत सब ।
nācahiṁ gāvahiṁ gīta parama taraṁgī bhūta saba,
देखत अति बिपरीत बोलहिं बचन बिचित्र बिधि ॥९३॥
dekhata ati biparīta bolahiṁ bacana bicitra bidhi. 93.

Trans:

All the demons went singing and dancing with wonderful contortions, such as never were seen, and emitting every kind of strange screams.

चौपाई-caupāī:

जस दूलहु तसि बनी बराता । कौतुक बिबिध होहिं मग जाता ॥
jasa dūlahu tasi banī barātā, kautuka bibidha hohiṁ maga jātā.
इहाँ हिमाचल रचेउ बिताना । अति बिचित्र नहिं जाइ बखाना ॥

ihāṁ himācala raceu bitānā, ati bicitra nahiṁ jāi bakhānā.
सैल सकल जहँ लगि जग माहीं । लघु बिसाल नहिं बरनि सिराहीं ॥
saila sakala jahaṁ lagi jaga māhīṁ, laghu bisāla nahiṁ barani sirāhīṁ.
बन सागर सब नदीं तलावा । हिमगिरि सब कहुँ नेवत पठावा ॥
bana sāgara saba nadīṁ talāvā, himagiri saba kahuṁ nevata paṭhāvā.
कामरूप सुंदर तन धारी । सहित समाज सहित बर नारी ॥
kāmarūpa suṁdara tana dhārī, sahita samāja sahita bara nārī.
गए सकल तुहिनाचल गेहा । गावहिं मंगल सहित सनेहा ॥
gae sakala tuhinācala gehā, gāvahiṁ maṁgala sahita sanehā.
प्रथमहिं गिरि बहु गृह सँवराए । जथाजोगु तहँ तहँ सब छाए ॥
prathamahiṁ giri bahu gṛha saṁvarāe, jathājogu tahaṁ tahaṁ saba chāe.
पुर सोभा अवलोकि सुहाई । लागइ लघु बिरंचि निपुनाई ॥
pura sobhā avaloki suhāī, lāgai laghu biraṁci nipunāī.

Trans:

Like bridegroom, like procession—an extraordinary sight as it went along the route. There King Himāchal had erected canopies more splendid then words can tell; and every hill in the world, small and great, more than man can count, and every wood and sea, river, stream, and lake, all were invited to attend; and assuming forms of exquisite beauty, with all their retinue, male and female, they flocked to the palace, singing songs of gladness. First of all the king had built a number of guest houses with tasteful arrangements. After a glance at the beauty of the city, the Creator of the world seemed a contemptible architect in comparison.

छंद-chaṁda:

लघु लाग बिधि की निपुनता अवलोकि पुर सोभा सही ।
laghu lāga bidhi kī nipunatā avaloki pura sobhā sahī,
बन बाग कूप तड़ाग सरिता सुभग सब सक को कही ॥
bana bāga kūpa taṛāga saritā subhaga saba saka ko kahī.
मंगल बिपुल तोरन पताका केतु गृह गृह सोहहीं ।
maṁgala bipula torana patākā ketu gṛha gṛha sohahīṁ,
बनिता पुरुष सुंदर चतुर छबि देखि मुनि मन मोहहीं ॥
banitā puruṣa suṁdara catura chabi dekhi muni mana mohahīṁ.

Trans:

A glance at the beautiful city made the creative art of Brahmmā pale into insignificance. Lakes and fountains, groves and gardens, shone more fair then aught else on earth. Wreaths and arches, flags, and banners, decorated each house. Youths and maidens, gallant and lovely, enraptured the hearts even of saints.

दोहा-dohā:

जगदंबा जहँ अवतरी सो पुरु बरनि कि जाइ ।
jagadaṁbā jahaṁ avatarī so puru barani ki jāi,
रिद्धि सिद्धि संपत्ति सुख नित नूतन अधिकाइ ॥९४॥
riddhi siddhi saṁpatti sukha nita nūtana adhikāi. 94.

Trans:

The city in which the great mother had taken birth surpassed description; joy, prosperity, and abundance were ever on the increase.

चौपाई-caupāī:

नगर निकट बरात सुनि आई । पुर खरभरु सोभा अधिकाई ॥
nagara nikaṭa barāta suni āī, pura kharabharu sobhā adhikāī.
करि बनाव सजि बाहन नाना । चले लेन सादर अगवाना ॥
kari banāva saji bāhana nānā, cale lena sādara agavānā.
हियँ हरषे सुर सेन निहारी । हरिहि देखि अति भए सुखारी ॥
hiyaṁ haraṣe sura sena nihārī, harihi dekhi ati bhae sukhārī.
सिव समाज जब देखन लागे । बिडरि चले बाहन सब भागे ॥
siva samāja jaba dekhana lāge, biḍari cale bāhana saba bhāge.
धरि धीरजु तहँ रहे सयाने । बालक सब लै जीव पराने ॥
dhari dhīraju tahaṁ rahe sayāne, bālaka saba lai jīva parāne.
गएँ भवन पूछहिं पितु माता । कहहिं बचन भय कंपित गाता ॥
gaeṁ bhavana pūchahiṁ pitu mātā, kahahiṁ bacana bhaya kaṁpita gātā.
कहिअ काह कहि जाइ न बाता । जम कर धार किधौं बरिआता ॥
kahia kāha kahi jāi na bātā, jama kara dhāra kidhauṁ bariātā.
बरु बौराह बसहँ असवारा । ब्याल कपाल बिभूषन छारा ॥
baru baurāha basahaṁ asavārā, byāla kapāla bibhūṣana chārā.

Trans:

When it was known that the marriage procession was close at hand, the stir in the city and the brilliancy of the decorations grew more and more. With numerous carriages and all due equipment the heralds started for the formal reception. When they saw the army of gods they were glad of heart, and yet more so when they beheld Harī. But when they perceived Shiva's entourage, every animal they rode upon started back in affright. Grown men summoned up courage to stand, but the children all ran for their lives straight back to their homes; and when their parents questioned them could only reply trembling all over—"What can we say, it is beyond all telling; it is no marriage procession, but the army of Death; and the bridegroom a maniac mounted on a bull, with snakes and skulls and ashes to adorn him.

छंद-chaṁda:

तन छार ब्याल कपाल भूषन नगन जटिल भयंकरा ।
tana chāra byāla kapāla bhūṣana nagana jaṭila bhayaṁkarā,
सँग भूत प्रेत पिसाच जोगिनि बिकट मुख रजनीचरा ॥
saṁga bhūta preta pisāca jogini bikaṭa mukha rajanīcarā.
जो जिअत रहिहि बरात देखत पुन्य बड़ तेहि कर सही ।
jo jiata rahihi barāta dekhata punya baṛa tehi kara sahī,
देखिहि सो उमा बिबाहु घर घर बात असि लरिकन्ह कही ॥
dekhihi so umā bibāhu ghara ghara bāta asi larikanha kahī.

Trans:

With skulls and snakes, and streaks of ashes, and with matted locks, and with his body bare, the groom—with witches, and imps, and frightful goblins, and dreadful ghosts—is here. He, who survives the dreadful spectacle of the bridegroom's procession, is a person of great fortune—for he alone will witness the wedding of Umā." This was the babble from children that rang from house to house.

दोहा-dohā:

समुझि महेस समाज सब जननि जनक मुसुकाहिं ।
samujhi mahesa samāja saba janani janaka musukāhiṁ,
बाल बुझाए बिबिध बिधि निडर होहु डरु नाहिं ॥९५॥
bāla bujhāe bibidha bidhi niḍara hohu ḍaru nāhiṁ. 95.

Trans:

The fathers and mothers smiled, for they recognized Shiva's entourage, and reassured the children in every possible way, saying, "Do not be afraid; there is no cause for fear."

चौपाई-caupāī:

लै अगवान बरातहि आए । दिए सबहि जनवास सुहाए ॥
lai agavāna barātahi āe, die sabahi janavāsa suhāe.
मैनाँ सुभ आरती सँवारी । संग सुमंगल गावहिं नारी ॥
mainām̐ subha āratī saṁvārī, saṁga sumaṁgala gāvahiṁ nārī.
कंचन थार सोह बर पानी । परिछन चली हरहि हरषानी ॥
kaṁcana thāra soha bara pānī, parichana calī harahi haraṣānī.
बिकट बेष रुद्रहि जब देखा । अबलन्ह उर भय भयउ बिसेषा ॥
bikaṭa beṣa rudrahi jaba dekhā, abalanha ura bhaya bhayau biseṣā.
भागि भवन पैठीं अति त्रासा । गए महेसु जहाँ जनवासा ॥
bhāgi bhavana paiṭhīṁ ati trāsā, gae mahesu jahām̐ janavāsā.

मैना हृदयँ भयउ दुखु भारी । लीन्ही बोलि गिरीसकुमारी ॥
mainā hṛdayaṁ bhayau dukhu bhārī, līnhī boli girīsakumārī.
अधिक सनेहँ गोद बैठारी । स्याम सरोज नयन भरे बारी ॥
adhika sanehaṁ goda baiṭhārī, syāma saroja nayana bhare bārī.
जेहिं बिधि तुम्हहि रूपु अस दीन्हा । तेहिं जड़ बरु बाउर कस कीन्हा ॥
jehiṁ bidhi tumhahi rūpu asa dīnhā, tehiṁ jaṛa baru bāura kasa kīnhā.

Trans:

The heralds brought in the procession, and assigned them at pleasant quarters. And Mainā—having prepared an elegant sacrificial lamp, and lustrous water in a golden bowl, to move it round and round over Shiva's head—proceeded with much gladness as her attendants sang festive songs. But when they saw the groom's terrible attire the women trembled in great fear and ran inside the house. Mahādev advanced to the guestroom, and Mainā, sorely grieved at heart, called her daughter; and then in the most loving manner took her into her lap, while her lotus eyes overflowed with tears: "To think that the Creator should have made you so beautiful, and then give you such a raving madman for a bridegroom!

छंद-chaṁda:

कस कीन्ह बरु बौराह बिधि जेहिं तुम्हहि सुंदरता दई ।
kasa kīnha baru baurāha bidhi jehiṁ tumhahi suṁdaratā daī,
जो फलु चहिअ सुरतरुहिं सो बरबस बबूरहिं लागई ॥
jo phalu cahia surataruhiṁ so barabasa babūrahiṁ lāgaī.
तुम्ह सहित गिरि तें गिरौं पावक जरौं जलनिधि महुँ परौं ।
tumha sahita giri teṁ giraum̐ pāvaka jaraum̐ jalanidhi mahuṁ paraum̐,
घरु जाउ अपजसु होउ जग जीवत बिबाहु न हौं करौं ॥
gharu jāu apajasu hou jaga jīvata bibāhu na hauṁ karauṁ.

Trans:

How can God send such a raving groom for such a lovely bride? A fruit that should have adorned the wish-yielding tree is fruitlessly appearing on a thorny bush! Alas!! From mountain-top, in sea or fire, I would rather cast me down along with thee. Let my home be ruined, or my name, I care not; but this wedding shall never be. In no case would I marry you with this maniac so long as there is life in me."

दोहा-dohā:

भईं बिकल अबला सकल दुखित देखि गिरिनारि ।
bhaīṁ bikala abalā sakala dukhita dekhi girināri,
करि बिलापु रोदति बदति सुता सनेहु सँभारि ॥९६॥
kari bilāpu rodati badati sutā sanehu saṁbhāri. 96.

Trans:

All the ladies were distressed when they saw the queen so sad—who in her deep affection for her daughter began to weep and make great lamentations:

चौपाई-caupāī:

नारद कर मैं काह बिगारा । भवनु मोर जिन्ह बसत उजारा ॥
nārada kara maiṁ kāha bigārā, bhavanu mora jinha basata ujārā.
अस उपदेसु उमहि जिन्ह दीन्हा । बौरे बरहि लागि तपु कीन्हा ॥
asa upadesu umahi jinha dīnhā, baure barahi lāgi tapu kīnhā.
साचेहुँ उन्ह कें मोह न माया । उदासीन धनु धामु न जाया ॥
sācehuṁ unha keṁ moha na māyā, udāsīna dhanu dhāmu na jāyā.
पर घर घालक लाज न भीरा । बाझँ कि जान प्रसव कै पीरा ॥
para ghara ghālaka lāja na bhīrā, bājhaṁ ki jāna prasava kai pīrā.
जननिहि बिकल बिलोकि भवानी । बोली जुत बिबेक मृदु बानी ॥
jananihi bikala biloki bhavānī, bolī juta bibeka mṛdu bānī.
अस बिचारि सोचहि मति माता । सो न टरइ जो रचइ बिधाता ॥
asa bicāri socahi mati mātā, so na ṭarai jo racai bidhātā.
करम लिखा जौं बाउर नाहू । तौ कत दोसु लगाइअ काहू ॥
karama likhā jauṁ bāura nāhū, tau kata dosu lagāia kāhū.
तुम्ह सन मिटहिं कि बिधि के अंका । मातु ब्यर्थ जनि लेहु कलंका ॥
tumha sana miṭahiṁ ki bidhi ke aṁkā, mātu byartha jani lehu kalaṁkā.

Trans:

"What harm had I done to Nārad that he should make my home desolate and give Umā such advice, to undergo penance for the sake of a mad bridegroom? In good sooth he is fancy-free and passionless, an ascetic who wants neither money, nor house, not wife, and therefore in destroying another's home he has neither shame nor compunction; for what does a barren woman know of the pangs of childbirth?" When Bhawānī saw her mother's distress, she answered thus placidly and discreetly, "Be not troubled, my mother, with these thoughts—for God's plans is unalterable. If fate decrees me a mad husband, then why should anyone be blamed? Can you blot out the handwriting of the Creator? Then refrain from profitless reproaches.

छंद-chaṁda:

जनि लेहु मातु कलंकु करुना परिहरहु अवसर नहीं ।
jani lehu mātu kalaṁku karunā pariharahu avasara nahīṁ,
दुखु सुखु जो लिखा लिलार हमरें जाब जहँ पाउब तहीं ॥
dukhu sukhu jo likhā lilāra hamareṁ jāba jahaṁ pāuba tahīṁ.
सुनि उमा बचन बिनीत कोमल सकल अबला सोचहीं ।
suni umā bacana binīta komala sakala abalā socahīṁ,
बहु भाँति बिधिहि लगाइ दूषन नयन बारि बिमोचहीं ॥
bahu bhāṁti bidhihi lagāi dūṣana nayana bāri bimocahīṁ.

Trans:

Cease from profitless reproaches, nor in vain bemoan my fate. I must go wheresoever my destined joys and sorrows await. Hearing the soft pious words of Umā, all the ladies became thoughtful and sad. Much they talked of God's injustice, and tears bedewed their eyes.

दोहा-dohā:

तेहि अवसर नारद सहित अरु रिषि सप्त समेत ।
tehi avasara nārada sahita aru riṣi sapta sameta,
समाचार सुनि तुहिनगिरि गवने तुरत निकेत ॥९७॥
samācāra suni tuhinagiri gavane turata niketa. 97.

Trans:

At that time there came Nārad, and with him the sages—for they had heard the news, and at once betook themselves to the king's palace.

चौपाई-caupāī:

तब नारद सबही समुझावा । पूरुब कथाप्रसंगु सुनावा ॥
taba nārada sabahī samujhāvā, pūruba kathāprasaṁgu sunāvā.
मयना सत्य सुनहु मम बानी । जगदंबा तव सुता भवानी ॥
mayanā satya sunahu mama bānī, jagadaṁbā tava sutā bhavānī.
अजा अनादि सक्ति अबिनासिनि । सदा संभु अरधंग निवासिनि ॥
ajā anādi sakti abināsini, sadā saṁbhu aradhaṁga nivāsini.
जग संभव पालन लय कारिनि । निज इच्छा लीला बपु धारिनि ॥
jaga saṁbhava pālana laya kārini, nija icchā līlā bapu dhārini.
जनमीं प्रथम दच्छ गृह जाई । नामु सती सुंदर तनु पाई ॥
janamīṁ prathama daccha gṛha jāī, nāmu satī suṁdara tanu pāī.
तहँहुँ सती संकरहि बिबाहीं । कथा प्रसिद्ध सकल जग माहीं ॥
tahaṁhuṁ satī saṁkarahi bibāhīṁ, kathā prasiddha sakala jaga māhīṁ.
एक बार आवत सिव संगा । देखेउ रघुकुल कमल पतंगा ॥
eka bāra āvata siva saṁgā, dekheu raghukula kamala pataṁgā.
भयउ मोहु सिव कहा न कीन्हा । भ्रम बस बेषु सीय कर लीन्हा ॥
bhayau mohu siva kahā na kīnhā, bhrama basa beṣu sīya kara līnhā.

Trans:

Then Nārad instructed them all, and recited in full the past history, saying: "Hear, Mainā! My words are true; your daughter is Bhawānī, the mother of the world, the everlasting female energy; without birth or beginning; Shambhu's inseparable half; the creator, supporter, and destroyer of the universe; who at will assumes the semblance of human form. First she was born in Daksha's house, Sati by name, of excellent beauty. Then as Sati she married Shankar, and her story is famous throughout the world—how once with Shiva she met Rāma, the sun of Raghu's lotus line, and in her bewilderment was not obedient to Shiva, but was beguiled into assuming the form of Sītā.

छंद-*chamda:*

सिय बेषु सतीं जो कीन्ह तेहिं अपराध संकर परिहरीं ।
siya beṣu satīṁ jo kīnha tehiṁ aparādha saṁkara pariharīṁ,
हर बिरहँ जाइ बहोरि पितु कें जग्य जोगानल जरीं ॥
hara birahaṁ jāi bahori pitu keṁ jagya jogānala jarīṁ.
अब जनमि तुम्हरे भवन निज पति लागि दारुन तपु किया ।
aba janami tumhare bhavana nija pati lāgi dāruna tapu kiyā,
अस जानि संसय तजहु गिरिजा सर्बदा संकर प्रिया ॥
asa jāni saṁsaya tajahu girijā sarbadā saṁkara priyā.

Trans:

For the crime of this assumption she was widowed many a days—till in the fire before her sire her sins were burnt away. Now, born your daughter, for her Lord in penitence she stays. And Shiva aye shall be her Lord; know this, be not dismayed."

दोहा-*dohā:*

सुनि नारद के बचन तब सब कर मिटा बिषाद ।
suni nārada ke bacana taba saba kara miṭā biṣāda,
छन महुँ ब्यापेउ सकल पुर घर घर यह संबाद ॥९८॥
chana mahuṁ byāpeu sakala pura ghara ghara yaha saṁbāda. 98.

Trans:

On bearing Nārad's explanation the sadness of all was dispersed, and in a moment his words were spread from house to house throughout the city.

चौपाई-*caupāī:*

तब मयना हिमवंतु अनंदे । पुनि पुनि पारबती पद बंदे ॥
taba mayanā himavaṁtu anaṁde, puni puni pārabatī pada baṁde.
नारि पुरुष सिसु जुबा सयाने । नगर लोग सब अति हरषाने ॥
nāri puruṣa sisu jubā sayāne, nagara loga saba ati haraṣāne.
लगे होन पुर मंगलगाना । सजे सबहिं हाटक घट नाना ॥
lage hona pura maṁgalagānā, saje sabahiṁ hāṭaka ghaṭa nānā.
भाँति अनेक भई जेवनारा । सूपसास्त्र जस कछु ब्यवहारा ॥
bhāṁti aneka bhaī jevanārā, sūpasāstra jasa kachu byavahārā.
सो जेवनार कि जाइ बखानी । बसहिं भवन जेहिं मातु भवानी ॥
so jevanāra ki jāi bakhānī, basahiṁ bhavana jehiṁ mātu bhavānī.
सादर बोले सकल बराती । बिष्नु बिरंचि देव सब जाती ॥
sādara bole sakala barātī, biṣnu biraṁci deva saba jātī.
बिबिधि पाँति बैठी जेवनारा । लागे परुसन निपुन सुआरा ॥
bibidhi pāṁti baiṭhī jevanārā, lāge parusana nipuna suārā.
नारिबृंद सुर जेवँत जानी । लगीं देन गारीं मृदु बानी ॥
nāribṛṁda sura jevaṁta jānī, lagīṁ dena gārīṁ mṛdu bānī.

Trans:

Then Mainā and Himvān were glad and fell again and again at Pārwatī's feet. All the people of the city, whatever their age, men and women alike, were delighted equal most. Songs of joy began to resound in the streets; golden vases were brought out; dishes were dressed in various ways according to the rules of gastronomic science. The banquet tables in the palace inhabited by the great mother Bhawānī were altogether beyond depiction. The marriage guests—Vishnu, Brahmmā, and all the heavenly orders—were courteously entreated and they took their seats line after line. Then skillful servers began to serve; and the women, when they found the gods were sat down, began to jest and banter in pleasant strain.

छंद-*chamda:*

गारीं मधुर स्वर देहिं सुंदरि बिंग्य बचन सुनावहीं ।
gārīṁ madhura svara dehiṁ suṁdari biṁgya bacana sunāvahīṁ,
भोजनु करहिं सुर अति बिलंबु बिनोदु सुनि सचु पावहीं ॥
bhojanu karahiṁ sura ati bilaṁbu binodu suni sacu pāvahīṁ.
जेवँत जो बढ़्यो अनंदु सो मुख कोटिहूँ न परै कह्यो ।
jevaṁta jo baṛhyo anaṁdu so mukha koṭihūṁ na parai kahyo,
अचवाँइ दीन्हे पान गवने बास जहँ जाको रह्यो ॥
acavāṁi dīnhe pāna gavane bāsa jahaṁ jāko rahyo.

Trans:

Charming women railed in sweet strains and jested and japed. Charmed with the song, the gods sat and dined for long, not heeding the waning night. The joy that welled up at that time cannot be described even with a million tongues. Then with betel-leaves served they rise and bids adieu and leave to rest.

दोहा-*dohā:*

बहुरि मुनिन्ह हिमवंत कहुँ लगन सुनाई आइ ।
bahuri muninha himavaṁta kahuṁ lagana sunāī āi,
समय बिलोकि बिबाह कर पठए देव बोलाइ ॥९९॥
samaya biloki bibāha kara paṭhae deva bolāi. 99.

Trans:

Then the sages came and declared to Himvān the marriage proposal, and seeing the time was fit, summoned all the deities and immortals—

चौपाई-*caupāī:*

बोलि सकल सुर सादर लीन्हे । सबहि जथोचित आसन दीन्हे ॥
boli sakala sura sādara līnhe, sabahi jathocita āsana dīnhe.
बेदी बेद बिधान सँवारी । सुभग सुमंगल गावहिं नारी ॥
bedī beda bidhāna saṁvārī, subhaga sumaṁgala gāvahiṁ nārī.
सिंघासनु अति दिब्य सुहावा । जाइ न बरनि बिरंचि बनावा ॥
siṁghāsanu ati dibya suhāvā, jāi na barani biraṁci banāvā.
बैठे सिव बिप्रन्ह सिरु नाई । हृदयँ सुमिरि निज प्रभु रघुराई ॥
baiṭhe siva bipranha siru nāī, hṛdayaṁ sumiri nija prabhu raghurāī.
बहुरि मुनीसन्ह उमा बोलाईं । करि सिंगारु सखीं लै आईं ॥
bahuri munīsanha umā bolāīṁ, kari siṁgāru sakhīṁ lai āīṁ.
देखत रूपु सकल सुर मोहे । बरनै छबि अस जग कबि को है ॥
dekhata rūpu sakala sura mohe, baranai chabi asa jaga kabi ko hai.
जगदंबिका जानि भव भामा । सुरन्ह मनहिं मन कीन्ह प्रनामा ॥
jagadaṁbikā jāni bhava bhāmā, suranha manahiṁ mana kīnha pranāmā.
सुंदरता मरजाद भवानी । जाइ न कोटिहुँ बदन बखानी ॥
suṁdaratā marajāda bhavānī, jāi na koṭihuṁ badana bakhānī.

Trans:

—whom he courteously addressed, and assigned to each an appropriate seat. An altar was prepared according to Vedic rites; and the women chanted festal strains; and a divinely beautiful throne was erected; and that handiwork of gods was beyond any description. Then Shiva, after bowing to the Brahmins, took his seat, remembering in his heart Rāma, his own Lord. Then the sages sent for Umā, who was brought in by her handmaids, richly adored. All the gods beholding her beauty were charmed. What poet in the world could describe the loveliness of Bhawānī, the crown of beauty, whose praises would be beyond me even though I had a myriad tongues. The divinities recognized in that spouse of Mahādev the universal mother and adored her as such in their inmost soul.

छंद-chaṁda:

कोटिहुँ बदन नहिं बनै बरनत जग जननि सोभा महा ।
koṭihuṁ badana nahiṁ banai baranata jaga janani sobhā mahā,
सकुचहिं कहत श्रुति सेष सारद मंदमति तुलसी कहा ॥
sakucahiṁ kahata śruti seṣa sārada maṁdamati tulasī kahā.
छबिखानि मातु भवानि गवनीं मध्य मंडप सिव जहाँ ।
chabikhāni mātu bhavāni gavanīṁ madhya maṁḍapa siva jahāṁ,
अवलोकि सकहिं न सकुच पति पद कमल मनु मधुकरु तहाँ ॥
avaloki sakahiṁ na sakuca pati pada kamala manu madhukaru tahāṁ.

Trans:

The matchless beauty and grace of the Universal Mother could not be described even with a myriad tongues. When even the Vedas, Shesh, and Shārdā shrink abashed to rhyme her praises, then of what account is this dull-witted Tulsīdās? With downcast eyes Mother Bhawānī walked to the middle of the hall where Shiva was. Out of shyness she could not gaze at her Lord's lotus feet although, like a bee, her heart was fixated only thereupon.

दोहा-dohā:

मुनि अनुसासन गनपतिहि पूजेउ संभु भवानि ।
muni anusāsana ganapatihi pūjeu saṁbhu bhavāni,
कोउ सुनि संसय करै जनि सुर अनादि जियँ जानि ॥ १०० ॥
kou suni saṁsaya karai jani sura anādi jiyaṁ jāni. 100.

Trans:

At the injunction of the priests, both Shambhu and Bhawānī paid divine honors to Ganesh. And let no one be perplexed on hearing this, but know well that these are gods from everlasting times.

चौपाई-caupāī:

जसि बिबाह कै बिधि श्रुति गाई । महामुनिन्ह सो सब करवाई ॥
jasi bibāha kai bidhi śruti gāī, mahāmuninha so saba karavāī.
गहि गिरीस कुस कन्या पानी । भवहि समरपीं जानि भवानी ॥
gahi girīsa kusa kanyā pānī, bhavahi samarapīṁ jāni bhavānī.
पानिग्रहन जब कीन्ह महेसा । हियँ हरषे तब सकल सुरेसा ॥
pānigrahana jaba kīnha mahesā, hiyaṁ haraṣe taba sakala suresā.
बेदमंत्र मुनिबर उच्चरहीं । जय जय जय संकर सुर करहीं ॥
bedamaṁtra munibara uccarahīṁ, jaya jaya jaya saṁkara sura karahīṁ.
बाजहिं बाजन बिबिध बिधाना । सुमनबृष्टि नभ भै बिधि नाना ॥
bājahiṁ bājana bibidha bidhānā, sumanabṛṣṭi nabha bhai bidhi nānā.
हर गिरिजा कर भयउ बिबाहू । सकल भुवन भरि रहा उछाहू ॥
hara girijā kara bhayau bibāhū, sakala bhuvana bhari rahā uchāhū.
दासीं दास तुरग रथ नागा । धेनु बसन मनि बस्तु बिभागा ॥
dāsīṁ dāsa turaga ratha nāgā, dhenu basana mani bastu bibhāgā.
अन्न कनकभाजन भरि जाना । दाइज दीन्ह न जाइ बखाना ॥
anna kanakabhājana bhari jānā, dāija dīnha na jāi bakhānā.

Trans:

The whole marriage ceremony was performed by the priests in accordance with Vedic rituals; and the father, with *Kusha* grass in his hand, took the bride and gave her to Shiva. When the two had joined hands, all the gods were glad of heart; and he chief priests uttered the scriptural rhymes, and the cry went up to the heavens: 'Glory, glory, glory to Lord Shankar!'. All kinds of music began to play; and flowers were rained down from heaven; and thus was accomplished the marriage of Hara and Girijā amidst great rejoicing. The dowry given defied description: men-servants and maid-servants; horses, carriages, cows, elephants; raiment, jewelry, and things of all sorts; and wagonloads of grain and golden vessels.

छंद-chaṁda:

दाइज दियो बहु भाँति पुनि कर जोरि हिमभूधर कह्यो ।
dāija diyo bahu bhāṁti puni kara jori himabhūdhara kahyo,
का देउँ पूरनकाम संकर चरन पंकज गहि रह्यो ॥
kā deuṁ pūranakāma saṁkara carana paṁkaja gahi rahyo.
सिवँ कृपासागर ससुर कर संतोषु सब भाँतिहिं कियो ।
sivaṁ kṛpāsāgara sasura kara saṁtoṣu saba bhāṁtihiṁ kiyo,
पुनि गहे पद पाथोज मयनाँ प्रेम परिपूरन हियो ॥
puni gahe pada pāthoja mayanāṁ prema paripūrana hiyo.

Trans:

King Himāchal brought forth many great presents, and yet falling low at Shiva's feet he cried that all this was naught—for what could he give to one who had his desires sated and thus had it all. Clasping his lotus feet, he became choked and could speak no more. The ocean of mercy that Shiva is, reassured his sire in every possible way. Then came Mainā and with her heart overflowing with love, clasped Shiva's lotus-feet and said:

दोहा-dohā:

नाथ उमा मन प्रान सम गृहकिंकरी करेहु ।
nātha umā mana prāna sama gṛhakiṁkarī karehu,
छमेहु सकल अपराध अब होइ प्रसन्न बरु देहु ॥ १०१ ॥
chamehu sakala aparādha aba hoi prasanna baru dehu. 101.

Trans:

"Umā, my Lord, is dear to me as my own soul; take her as one of your servants, and pardon all her offences: this is the boon I beg of your favor."

चौपाई-caupāī:

बहु बिधि संभु सासु समुझाई । गवनी भवन चरन सिरु नाई ॥
bahu bidhi saṁbhu sāsu samujhāī, gavanī bhavana carana siru nāī.
जननीं उमा बोलि तब लीन्ही । लै उछंग सुंदर सिख दीन्ही ॥
jananīṁ umā boli taba līnhī, lai uchaṁga suṁdara sikha dīnhī.
करेहु सदा संकर पद पूजा । नारिधरमु पति देउ न दूजा ॥
karehu sadā saṁkara pada pūjā, nāridharamu pati deu na dūjā.
बचन कहत भरे लोचन बारी । बहुरि लाइ उर लीन्हि कुमारी ॥
bacana kahata bhare locana bārī, bahuri lāi ura līnhi kumārī.
कत बिधि सृजीं नारि जग माहीं । पराधीन सपनेहुँ सुखु नाहीं ॥
kata bidhi sṛjīṁ nāri jaga māhīṁ, parādhīna sapanehuṁ sukhu nāhīṁ.
भै अति प्रेम बिकल महतारी । धीरजु कीन्ह कुसमय बिचारी ॥
bhai ati prema bikala mahatārī, dhīraju kīnha kusamaya bicārī.
पुनि पुनि मिलति परति गहि चरना । परम प्रेम कछु जाइ न बरना ॥
puni puni milati parati gahi caranā, parama prema kachu jāi na baranā.
सब नारिन्ह मिलि भेटि भवानी । जाइ जननि उर पुनि लपटानी ॥
saba nārinha mili bheṭi bhavānī, jāi janani ura puni lapaṭānī.

Trans:

Shambhu comforted his mother-in-law in ways more than one; and she returned home bowing her head at his feet. The mother then sent for Umā, and taking her into her lap gave her the following excellent advice: "Be ever obedient to Shankar. To say 'My lord and my god' is the sum of all wifely duty." At these words her eyes filled with tears, and again and again she pressed her daughter to her bosom: "Why has God created woman in the world, seeing that she is always in a state of subjection, and can never even dream of happiness?" Though utterly distracted by motherly love, she knew it was no time to display it and restrained herself. Running to her again and again, and falling on the ground to clasp her feet, in a transport of affection beyond all words, Bhawānī then said adieu to all her companions; and then she again went and clung to her mother's bosom.

छंद-chaṁda:

जननिहि बहुरि मिलि चली उचित असीस सब काहूँ दईं ।
jananihi bahuri mili calī ucita asīsa saba kāhūṁ daīṁ,
फिरि फिरि बिलोकति मातु तन तब सखीं लै सिव पहिं गईं ॥

phiri phiri bilokati mātu tana taba sakhīṁ lai siva pahiṁ gaīṁ.

जाचक सकल संतोषि संकरु उमा सहित भवन चले ।
jācaka sakala saṁtoṣi saṁkaru umā sahita bhavana cale,
सब अमर हरषे सुमन बरषि निसान नभ बाजे भले ॥
saba amara harașe sumana barași nisāna nabha bāje bhale.

Trans:

Clinging to her mother once more, and again once more, Bhawānī departed. Everyone showered blessings upon her. She turned back often, to have a look at her mother once again, as her companions led her to Shiva. Having gratified all the beggars Shankar, along with Umā, proceeded towards his home. The glad gods rained down flowers on the royal pair and sounds of music filled the air.

दोहा-dohā:

चले संग हिमवंतु तब पहुँचावन अति हेतु ।
cale saṁga himavaṁtu taba pahuṁcāvana ati hetu,
बिबिध भाँति परितोषु करि बिदा कीन्ह बृषकेतु ॥ १०२॥
bibidha bhāṁti paritoṣu kari bidā kīnha bṛṣaketu. 102.

Trans:

Then went Himvān most lovingly to escort them till with many words of consolation Mahādev bid him return.

चौपाई-caupāī:

तुरत भवन आए गिरिराई । सकल सैल सर लिए बोलाई ॥
turata bhavana āe girirāī, sakala saila sara lie bolāī.
आदर दान बिनय बहुमाना । सब कर बिदा कीन्ह हिमवाना ॥
ādara dāna binaya bahumānā, saba kara bidā kīnha himavānā.
जबहिं संभु कैलासहिं आए । सुर सब निज निज लोक सिधाए ॥
jabahiṁ saṁbhu kailāsahiṁ āe, sura saba nija nija loka sidhāe.
जगत मातु पितु संभु भवानी । तेहिं सिंगारु न कहउँ बखानी ॥
jagata mātu pitu saṁbhu bhavānī, tehiṁ siṁgāru na kahauṁ bakhānī.
करहिं बिबिध बिधि भोग बिलासा । गनन्ह समेत बसहिं कैलासा ॥
karahiṁ bibidha bidhi bhoga bilāsā, gananha sameta basahiṁ kailāsā.
हर गिरिजा बिहार नित नयऊ । एहि बिधि बिपुल काल चलि गयऊ ॥
hara girijā bihāra nita nayaū, ehi bidhi bipula kāla cali gayaū.
तब जनमेउ षटबदन कुमारा । तारकु असुरु समर जेहिं मारा ॥
taba janameu ṣaṭabadana kumārā, tāraku asuru samara jehiṁ mārā.
आगम निगम प्रसिद्ध पुराना । षन्मुख जन्मु सकल जग जाना ॥
āgama nigama prasiddha purānā, ṣanmukha janmu sakala jaga jānā.

Trans:

Then Himvān returned to his palace and called all the hills and lakes, and entreated them courteously with words and gifts, and allowed them to depart; and they preceded each to their realm. Here Shambhu arrived at Kailāsh. Shambhu and Bhawānī are the parents of the universe—hence I refrain from portraying their amorous sports. Indulging in luxuries and enjoyments of various kinds, the divine pair lived on Mount Kailāsh along with their attendants. In this way, a length of time passed and Kārtikay, the six-headed god was born—who vanquished in battle the demon Tārak. His birth is sung by all the sacred books and his deeds are known throughout the world.

छंद-chaṁda:

जगु जान षन्मुख जन्मु कर्मु प्रतापु पुरुषारथु महा ।
jagu jāna ṣanmukha janmu karmu pratāpu puruṣārathu mahā,
तेहि हेतु मैं बृषकेतु सुत कर चरित संछेपहिं कहा ॥
tehi hetu maiṁ bṛṣaketu suta kara carita saṁchepahiṁ kahā.
यह उमा संगु बिबाहु जे नर नारि कहहिं जे गावहीं ।
yaha umā saṁgu bibāhu je nara nāri kahahiṁ je gāvahīṁ,
कल्यान काज बिबाह मंगल सर्बदा सुखु पावहीं ॥
kalyāna kāja bibāha maṁgala sarbadā sukhu pāvahīṁ.

Trans:

The story of the birth, glory, and surpassing strength of Mahādev's six headed son is known to all; that is why I have only briefly touched upon the generous deeds that he has done. Man or maid, who shall tell or sing this story of the wedding of Shiva and Umā shall be happily wed and ever rejoice in all their auspicious undertakings, and live with ease through all the days of their lives.

दोहा-dohā:

चरित सिंधु गिरिजा रमन बेद न पावहिं पारु ।
carita siṁdhu girijā ramana beda na pāvahiṁ pāru,
बरनै तुलसीदासु किमि अति मतिमंद गवाँरु ॥ १०३॥
baranai tulasīdāsu kimi ati matimaṁda gavāṁru. 103.

Trans:

The enactments of Girijā and her beloved are of ocean-like depth which not even the Vedas can sound; how then can an ignorant clown like Tulsīdās succeed in describing them?

चौपाई-caupāī:

संभु चरित सुनि सरस सुहावा । भरद्वाज मुनि अति सुखु पावा ॥
saṁbhu carita suni sarasa suhāvā, bharadvāja muni ati sukhu pāvā.
बहु लालसा कथा पर बाढ़ी । नयनन्हि नीरु रोमावलि ठाढ़ी ॥
bahu lālasā kathā para bāṛhī, nayananhi nīru romāvali ṭhāṛhī.
प्रेम बिबस मुख आव न बानी । दसा देखि हरषे मुनि ग्यानी ॥
prema bibasa mukha āva na bānī, dasā dekhi harașe muni gyānī.
अहो धन्य तव जन्मु मुनीसा । तुम्हहि प्रान सम प्रिय गौरीसा ॥
aho dhanya tava janmu munīsā, tumhahi prāna sama priya gaurīsā.
सिव पद कमल जिन्हहि रति नाहीं । रामहि ते सपनेहुँ न सोहाहीं ॥
siva pada kamala jinhahi rati nāhīṁ, rāmahi te sapanehuṁ na sohāhīṁ.
बिनु छल बिस्वनाथ पद नेहू । राम भगत कर लच्छन एहू ॥
binu chala bisvanātha pada nehū, rāma bhagata kara lacchana ehū.
सिव सम को रघुपति ब्रतधारी । बिनु अघ तजी सती असि नारी ॥
siva sama ko raghupati bratadhārī, binu agha tajī satī asi nārī.
पनु करि रघुपति भगति देखाई । को सिव सम रामहि प्रिय भाई ॥
panu kari raghupati bhagati dekhāī, ko siva sama rāmahi priya bhāī.

Trans:

When the saint Bharadvāja had heard this pleasant and delectable history of Shambhu's doings, he was delighted and longed to hear yet more. With overflowing eyes and every limb thrilling, he was so mastered by love that his tongue could not utter a word. On seeing his condition the great Munī Yāgyavalk was pleased: "Blessed is thy birth to whom Gaurī's Lord is dear as life. He who loves not Shiva's lotus feet can never dream of pleasing Rāma. A guileless love for Shiva's feet is the surest sign of faith in Rāma. For who is so faithful to Rāma as Shiva—who for no fault left his wife Sati and made a stern vow, the very pledge of unswerving fidelity? And whom does Rāma hold more dear then Shiva?

दोहा-dohā:

प्रथमहिं मैं कहि सिव चरित बूझा मरमु तुम्हार ।
prathamahiṁ maiṁ kahi siva carita būjhā maramu tumhāra,
सुचि सेवक तुम्ह राम के रहित समस्त बिकार ॥ १०४॥
suci sevaka tumha rāma ke rahita samasta bikāra. 104.

Trans:

I have begun by telling you of Shiva's deeds, knowing well your secret, that you are a true servant of Rāma, without any variableness.

चौपाई-caupāī:

मैं जाना तुम्हार गुन सीला । कहउँ सुनहु अब रघुपति लीला ॥
maiṁ jānā tumhāra guna sīlā, kahauṁ sunahu aba raghupati līlā.

सुनु मुनि आजु समागम तोरें । कहि न जाइ जस सुखु मन मोरें ॥
sunu muni āju samāgama toreṁ, kahi na jāi jasa sukhu mana moreṁ.
राम चरित अति अमित मुनिसा । कहि न सकहिं सत कोटि अहीसा ॥
rāma carita ati amita munisā, kahi na sakahiṁ sata koṭi ahīsā.
तदपि जथाश्रुत कहउँ बखानी । सुमिरि गिरापति प्रभु धनुपानी ॥
tadapi jathāśruta kahauṁ bakhānī, sumiri girāpati prabhu dhanupānī.
सारद दारुनारि सम स्वामी । रामु सूत्रधर अंतरजामी ॥
sārada dārunāri sama svāmī, rāmu sūtradhara aṁtarajāmī.
जेहि पर कृपा करहिं जनु जानी । कबि उर अजिर नचावहिं बानी ॥
jehi para kṛpā karahiṁ janu jānī, kabi ura ajira nacāvahiṁ bānī.
प्रनवउँ सोइ कृपाल रघुनाथा । बरनउँ बिसद तासु गुन गाथा ॥
pranavauṁ soi kṛpāla raghunāthā, baranauṁ bisada tāsu guna gāthā.
परम रम्य गिरिबरु कैलासू । सदा जहाँ सिव उमा निवासू ॥
parama ramya giribaru kailāsū, sadā jahāṁ siva umā nivāsū.

Trans:

I understand your character and disposition; listen therefore while I proceed to recount Rāma's adventures now. I cannot say how glad I am at this meeting with you today. Though Rāma's deeds are beyond measure, and not a myriad serpent kings could tell them all, yet I repeat the tale as it has been revealed, after fixing my thoughts on the God with bow in hand, who is the Lord of the queen of speech. For Saraswatī is, as it were, but a puppet, and Rāma the conductor who plays the hidden strings. When he finds a true believer, he graciously sets her to dance in the courtyard of the poet's fancy. To Him, the merciful Raghunāth, I humbly bow, before commencing the recitals of his glories. Of all mountains the most beautiful was Kailāsh, since Shiva and Umā had made it their home.

दोहा-dohā:

सिद्ध तपोधन जोगिजन सुर किंनर मुनिबृंद ।
siddha tapodhana jogijana sura kiṁnara munibṛṁda,
बसहिं तहाँ सुकृती सकल सेवहिं सिव सुखकंद ॥ १०५॥
basahiṁ tahāṁ sukṛtī sakala sevahiṁ siva sukhakaṁda. 105.

Trans:

Saints, hermits, ascetics, gods, *kinnars*, sages, and all pious souls came there to dwell and adore Mahādev, the root of all that is good.

चौपाई-caupāī:

हरि हर बिमुख धर्म रति नाहीं । ते नर तहँ सपनेहुँ नहिं जाहीं ॥
hari hara bimukha dharma rati nāhīṁ, te nara tahaṁ sapanehuṁ nahiṁ jāhīṁ.
तेहि गिरि पर बट बिटप बिसाला । नित नूतन सुंदर सब काला ॥
tehi giri para baṭa biṭapa bisālā, nita nūtana suṁdara saba kālā.
त्रिबिध समीर सुसीतलि छाया । सिव बिश्राम बिटप श्रुति गाया ॥
tribidha samīra susītali chāyā, siva biśrāma biṭapa śruti gāyā.
एक बार तेहि तर प्रभु गयऊ । तरु बिलोकि उर अति सुखु भयऊ ॥
eka bāra tehi tara prabhu gayaū, taru biloki ura ati sukhu bhayaū.
निज कर डासि नागरिपु छाला । बैठे सहजहिं संभु कृपाला ॥
nija kara ḍāsi nāgaripu chālā, baiṭhe sahajahiṁ saṁbhu kṛpālā.
कुंद इंदु दर गौर सरीरा । भुज प्रलंब परिधन मुनिचीरा ॥
kuṁda iṁdu dara gaura sarīrā, bhuja pralaṁba paridhana municīrā.
तरुन अरुन अंबुज सम चरना । नख दुति भगत हृदय तम हरना ॥
taruna aruna aṁbuja sama caranā, nakha duti bhagata hṛdaya tama haranā.
भुजग भूति भूषन त्रिपुरारी । आननु सरद चंद छबि हारी ॥
bhujaga bhūti bhūṣana tripurārī, ānanu sarada caṁda chabi hārī.

Trans:

But the enemies of Harī and Hara, who had no love for virtue, could never even in dream find their way to that place. On this mountain was an enormous *Barh* tree, which no time or season could rob of its beauty. Ever stirred by soft, cool, fragrant breezes and a shade from the hottest sun, the *Vitap* tree famous in sacred songs was Mahādev's favorite haunt. Once upon a time the Lord had gone under it, and in an excess of delight spread with his own hands the tiger skin on ground and there sat at ease—his body as fair in hue as the jasmine or the moon, his arms of great length, a hermit's cloth wrapped about his loins, his feet like lotus blossoms, his toe-nails like gleams of light to dispel the darkness of faithful souls, and with his face more splendid than the moon in autumn, and his adornments the serpents and streaks of ashes.

दोहा-dohā:

जटा मुकुट सुरसरित सिर लोचन नलिन बिसाल ।
jaṭā mukuṭa surasarita sira locana nalina bisāla,
नीलकंठ लावन्यनिधि सोह बालबिधु भाल ॥ १०६॥
nīlakaṁṭha lāvanyanidhi soha bālabidhu bhāla. 106.

Trans:

With his twisted coils of hair for a crown, with the Gangā springing from his head, with full-orbed eyes like the lotus, and with the crescent moon on his brow, the dark-throated god shone forth in all his resplendency.

चौपाई-caupāī:

बैठे सोह कामरिपु कैसें । धरें सरीरु सांतरसु जैसें ॥
baiṭhe soha kāmaripu kaiseṁ, dhareṁ sarīru sāṁtarasu jaiseṁ.
पारबती भल अवसरु जानी । गईं संभु पहिं मातु भवानी ॥
pārabatī bhala avasaru jānī, gaīṁ saṁbhu pahiṁ mātu bhavānī.
जानि प्रिया आदरु अति कीन्हा । बाम भाग आसनु हर दीन्हा ॥
jāni priyā ādaru ati kīnhā, bāma bhāga āsanu hara dīnhā.
बैठीं सिव समीप हरषाई । पूरुब जन्म कथा चित आई ॥
baiṭhīṁ siva samīpa haraṣāī, pūruba janma kathā cita āī.
पति हियँ हेतु अधिक अनुमानी । बिहसि उमा बोलीं प्रिय बानी ॥
pati hiyaṁ hetu adhika anumānī, bihasi umā bolīṁ priya bānī.
कथा जो सकल लोक हितकारी । सोइ पूछन चह सैलकुमारी ॥
kathā jo sakala loka hitakārī, soi pūchana caha sailakumārī.
बिस्वनाथ मम नाथ पुरारी । त्रिभुवन महिमा बिदित तुम्हारी ॥
bisvanātha mama nātha purārī, tribhuvana mahimā bidita tumhārī.
चर अरु अचर नाग नर देवा । सकल करहिं पद पंकज सेवा ॥
cara aru acara nāga nara devā, sakala karahiṁ pada paṁkaja sevā.

Trans:

So sat the Destroyer of Lust, as it were Quietism personified. Then Pārwatī, who is the great mother Bhawānī, approached, seeing her time. In recognition of her love he received her most courteously and enthroned her on his left side. Joyously she sat beside him and recalled her former life; and reckoning on his augmented attachment she spoke, being fain to hear the salutary tale: "O Lord of the world, my Lord Purārī, your greatness is known through all the three worlds; things moving or motionless, serpents, men, and gods, all do homage at your lotus feet.

दोहा-dohā:

प्रभु समरथ सर्बग्य सिव सकल कला गुन धाम ।
prabhu samaratha sarbagya siva sakala kalā guna dhāma,
जोग ग्यान बैराग्य निधि प्रनत कलपतरु नाम ॥ १०७॥
joga gyāna bairāgya nidhi pranata kalapataru nāma. 107.

Trans:

You are the Lord of all power and of all knowledge; the very centre of art and science; the great storehouse of meditation, of wisdom and of asceticism; and your name is as the tree of life to the afflicted.

चौपाई-caupāī:

जौं मो पर प्रसन्न सुखरासी । जानिअ सत्य मोहि निज दासी ॥
jauṁ mo para prasanna sukharāsī, jānia satya mohi nija dāsī.

तौ प्रभु हरहु मोर अग्याना । कहि रघुनाथ कथा बिधि नाना ॥
tau prabhu harahu mora agyānā, kahi raghunātha kathā bidhi nānā.
जासु भवनु सुरतरु तर होई । सहि कि दरिद्र जनित दुखु सोई ॥
jāsu bhavanu surataru tara hoī, sahi ki daridra janita dukhu soī.
ससिभूषन अस हृदयँ बिचारी । हरहु नाथ मम मति भ्रम भारी ॥
sasibhūṣana asa hṛdayaṁ bicārī, harahu nātha mama mati bhrama bhārī.
प्रभु जे मुनि परमारथबादी । कहहिं राम कहुँ ब्रह्म अनादी ॥
prabhu je muni paramārathabādī, kahahiṁ rāma kahuṁ brahma anādī.
सेस सारदा बेद पुराना । सकल करहिं रघुपति गुन गाना ॥
sesa sāradā beda purānā, sakala karahiṁ raghupati guna gānā.
तुम्ह पुनि राम राम दिन राती । सादर जपहु अनँग आराती ॥
tumha puni rāma rāma dina rātī, sādara japahu anaṁga ārātī.
रामु सो अवध नृपति सुत सोई । की अज अगुन अलखगति कोई ॥
rāmu so avadha nṛpati suta soī, kī aja aguna alakhagati koī.

Trans:
O blissful being, if I have found favor in your sight, and you know me to be your own devoted slave, then, my Lord, disperse my ignorance by reciting to me the story of Rāma. Why should one, who has her abode beneath a wish-yielding tree, undergo any suffering born of want? Consider, O moon-crowned god, and relieve my mind of this perplexity. The saints, who preach salvation, declare that Rāma is the uncreated God. Sheshnāg, Saraswatī, the Vedas, the Purānas—all sing his praises. You too day and night, O great conqueror of Lust, reverently repeat the Rāma-Rāma name. Is Rāma the son of the King of Avadh, and is that some other—the uncreated, passionless invisible being?

दोहा-dohā:

जौं नृप तनय त ब्रह्म किमि नारि बिरहँ मति भोरि ।
jauṁ nṛpa tanaya ta brahma kimi nāri birahaṁ mati bhori,
देखि चरित महिमा सुनत भ्रमति बुद्धि अति मोरि ॥१०८॥
dekhi carita mahimā sunata bhramati buddhi ati mori. 108.

Trans:
If a king's son, and so distressed by the loss of his wife, then how it is that he is Brahmm? When I compare the acts which I see, with the eulogies which I hear, then my mind becomes completely bewildered.

चौपाई-caupāī:

जौं अनीह ब्यापक बिभु कोऊ । कहहु बुझाइ नाथ मोहि सोऊ ॥
jauṁ anīha byāpaka bibhu koū, kahahu bujhāi nātha mohi soū.
अग्य जानि रिस उर जनि धरहू । जेहि बिधि मोह मिटै सोइ करहू ॥
agya jāni risa ura jani dharahū, jehi bidhi moha miṭai soi karahū.
मैं बन दीखि राम प्रभुताई । अति भय बिकल न तुम्हहि सुनाई ॥
maiṁ bana dīkhi rāma prabhutāī, ati bhaya bikala na tumhahi sunāī.
तदपि मलिन मन बोधु न आवा । सो फलु भली भाँति हम पावा ॥
tadapi malina mana bodhu na āvā, so phalu bhalī bhāṁti hama pāvā.
अजहूँ कछु संसउ मन मोरें । करहु कृपा बिनवउँ कर जोरें ॥
ajahūṁ kachu saṁsau mana moreṁ, karahu kṛpā binavauṁ kara joreṁ.
प्रभु तब मोहि बहु भाँति प्रबोधा । नाथ सो समुझि करहु जनि क्रोधा ॥
prabhu taba mohi bahu bhāṁti prabodhā, nātha so samujhi karahu jani krodhā.
तब कर अस बिमोह अब नाहीं । रामकथा पर रुचि मन माहीं ॥
taba kara asa bimoha aba nāhīṁ, rāmakathā para ruci mana māhīṁ.
कहहु पुनीत राम गुन गाथा । भुजगराज भूषन सुरनाथा ॥
kahahu punīta rāma guna gāthā, bhujagarāja bhūṣana suranāthā.

Trans:
Instruct me, O Lord, with regard to Him who is the passionless all-pervading, omnipresent God. Be not wroth at my ignorance but take steps to remove it. In the woods—though I was too awe-stricken to tell you—I beheld the majesty of Rāma, yet my mind was so dull that I did not understand; and verily I reaped a just reward. Today again a little doubt lingers on, and with clasped hands I beg of you to be compassionate to me: be not angry nor say you have been taught already. The past is past; my delusion is gone, and now I have a hearty longing to hear the sacred story of Rāma's virtuous deeds. Declare that very theme—O glory of the serpent king, O great Lord of heaven.

दोहा-dohā:

बंदउँ पद धरि धरनि सिरु बिनय करउँ कर जोरि ।
baṁdauṁ pada dhari dharani siru binaya karauṁ kara jori,
बरनहु रघुबर बिसद जसु श्रुति सिद्धांत निचोरि ॥१०९॥
baranahu raghubara bisada jasu śruti siddhāṁta nicori. 109.

Trans:
Laying my head in the dust, I worship your feet, and with folded hands entreat you to tell me all Raghubar's excellent glory, as extracted from the scriptures and philosophies.

चौपाई-caupāī:

जदपि जोषिता नहिं अधिकारी । दासी मन क्रम बचन तुम्हारी ॥
jadapi joṣitā nahiṁ adhikārī, dāsī mana krama bacana tumhārī.
गूढ़उ तत्व न साधु दुरावहिं । आरत अधिकारी जहँ पावहिं ॥
gūṛhau tatva na sādhu durāvahiṁ, ārata adhikārī jahaṁ pāvahiṁ.
अति आरति पूछउँ सुरराया । रघुपति कथा कहहु करि दाया ॥
ati ārati pūchauṁ surarāyā, raghupati kathā kahahu kari dāyā.
प्रथम सो कारन कहहु बिचारी । निर्गुन ब्रह्म सगुन बपु धारी ॥
prathama so kārana kahahu bicārī, nirguna brahma saguna bapu dhārī.
पुनि प्रभु कहहु राम अवतारा । बालचरित पुनि कहहु उदारा ॥
puni prabhu kahahu rāma avatārā, bālacarita puni kahahu udārā.
कहहु जथा जानकी बिबाहीं । राज तजा सो दूषन काहीं ॥
kahahu jathā jānakī bibāhīṁ, rāja tajā so dūṣana kāhīṁ.
बन बसि कीन्हे चरित अपारा । कहहु नाथ जिमि रावन मारा ॥
bana basi kīnhe carita apārā, kahahu nātha jimi rāvana mārā.
राज बैठि कीन्हीं बहु लीला । सकल कहहु संकर सुखलीला ॥
rāja baiṭhi kīnhīṁ bahu līlā, sakala kahahu saṁkara sukhalīlā.

Trans:
Though being a woman, not entitled to initiation, yet I am in a special degree your servant. Further, the saints do not forbid mystic instruction to one in great distress—and it is in extreme distress that I call upon you, O heavenly king, to narrate to me Rāma's history. First weigh well and declare to me the cause why the invisible Brahmm assumed a visible body? Then, my Lord, tell me of his Incarnation and his charming actions when a child? And how he wedded Jānakī? And for what fault he left his father's kingdom? And what he did while living in the woods? And how he slew Rāvan? and what all sports did he enact after his coronation? Tell me all about him, O most blissful Shankar.

दोहा-dohā:

बहुरि कहहु करुनायतन कीन्ह जो अचरज राम ।
bahuri kahahu karunāyatana kīnha jo acaraja rāma,
प्रजा सहित रघुबंसमनि किमि गवने निज धाम ॥११०॥
prajā sahita raghubaṁsamani kimi gavane nija dhāma. 110.

Trans:
Then tell me, gracious Lord, of all his marvelous acts, and how with all his subjects the jewel of House of Raghus returned to his own abode.

चौपाई-caupāī:

पुनि प्रभु कहहु सो तत्व बखानी । जेहिं बिग्यान मगन मुनि ग्यानी ॥
puni prabhu kahahu so tatva bakhānī, jehiṁ bigyāna magana muni gyānī.

भगति ग्यान बिग्यान बिरागा । पुनि सब बरनहु सहित बिभागा ॥
bhagati gyāna bigyāna birāgā, puni saba baranahu sahita bibhāgā.
औरउ राम रहस्य अनेका । कहहु नाथ अति बिमल बिबेका ॥
aurau rāma rahasya anekā, kahahu nātha ati bimala bibekā.
जो प्रभु मैं पूछा नहिं होई । सोउ दयाल राखहु जनि गोई ॥
jo prabhu maiṁ pūchā nahiṁ hoī, sou dayāla rākhahu jani goī.
तुम्ह त्रिभुवन गुर बेद बखाना । आन जीव पाँवर का जाना ॥
tumha tribhuvana gura beda bakhānā, āna jīva pāṁvara kā jānā.
प्रस्न उमा कै सहज सुहाई । छल बिहीन सुनि सिव मन भाई ॥
prasna umā kai sahaja suhāī, chala bihīna suni siva mana bhāī.
हर हियँ रामचरित सब आए । प्रेम पुलक लोचन जल छाए ॥
hara hiyaṁ rāmacarita saba āe, prema pulaka locana jala chāe.
श्रीरघुनाथ रूप उर आवा । परमानंद अमित सुख पावा ॥
śrīraghunātha rūpa ura āvā, paramānaṁda amita sukha pāvā.

Trans:

Next tell me, O Lord, what it all means—explaining to me in full detail of the realization which so absorbs the wisest saints. What is Devotion? And Wisdom? And the Supreme Knowledge? And detachment from the world? Tell me also, O Lord of purest understanding, the many other mysteries connected with Rāma. And if there be anything which I have omitted to ask, be kind enough not to suppress it now. You, as the Vedas say, are the great teacher of the three worlds; what can other poor creatures know?" When Shiva heard Umā's winning and guileless speech he was overjoyed, and the whole of enactments of Rāma's glories burst forth upon his soul; and his eyes became bedewed with tears; and his every limb thrilled with rapture—for the vision of Rāma filled his heart, and his ecstatic joy was beyond measure.

दोहा-dohā:

मगन ध्यानरस दंड जुग पुनि मन बाहेर कीन्ह ।
magana dhyānarasa daṁḍa juga puni mana bāhera kīnha,
रघुपति चरित महेस तब हरषित बरनै लीन्ह ॥ १११॥
raghupati carita mahesa taba haraṣita baranai līnha. 111.

Trans:

For a brief space Mahādev was lost in contemplation; then recovering himself and with great joy he began to recount the saga of Rāma.

चौपाई-caupāī:

झूठेउ सत्य जाहि बिनु जानें । जिमि भुजंग बिनु रजु पहिचानें ॥
jhūṭheu satya jāhi binu jāneṁ, jimi bhujaṁga binu raju pahicāneṁ.
जेहि जानें जग जाइ हेराई । जागें जथा सपन भ्रम जाई ॥
jehi jāneṁ jaga jāi herāī, jāgeṁ jathā sapana bhrama jāī.
बंदउँ बालरूप सोइ रामू । सब सिधि सुलभ जपत जिसु नामू ॥
baṁdauṁ bālarūpa soi rāmū, saba sidhi sulabha japata jisu nāmū.
मंगल भवन अमंगल हारी । द्रवउ सो दसरथ अजिर बिहारी ॥
maṁgala bhavana amaṁgala hārī, dravau so dasaratha ajira bihārī.
करि प्रनाम रामहि त्रिपुरारी । हरषि सुधा सम गिरा उचारी ॥
kari pranāma rāmahi tripurārī, haraṣi sudhā sama girā ucārī.
धन्य धन्य गिरिराजकुमारी । तुम्ह समान नहिं कोउ उपकारी ॥
dhanya dhanya girirājakumārī, tumha samāna nahiṁ kou upakārī.
पूँछेहु रघुपति कथा प्रसंगा । सकल लोक जग पावनि गंगा ॥
pūṁchehu raghupati kathā prasaṁgā, sakala loka jaga pāvani gaṁgā.
तुम्ह रघुबीर चरन अनुरागी । कीन्हिहु प्रस्न जगत हित लागी ॥
tumha raghubīra carana anurāgī, kīnhihu prasna jagata hita lāgī.

Trans:

"Not to distinguish between the false and the true is like mistaking a snake for a rope; and this delusion of the world vanishes only upon knowing Him, our Lord God—just as a dream disappears upon wakening up. Now I reverence, in his form as a child, Lord Rāma, most easy of access to those that repeat his holy name. Come appear before me—O home of bliss, O bane of woe—just as thou used to sport in Dashrath's courtyard." In this way paying homage to Rāma, Tripurārī began his mellifluous recital. "All blessings on thee, O daughter of the mountain king, there is no such benefactor as thou art. Thou hast asked for Rāma's history—as potent as the Gangā to sanctify the world; and it is on the people's account that thou hast so asked, being thyself full of love for Rāma's feet.

दोहा-dohā:

राम कृपा तें पारबति सपनेहुँ तव मन माहिं ।
rāma kṛpā teṁ pārabati sapanehuṁ tava mana māhiṁ,
सोक मोह संदेह भ्रम मम बिचार कछु नाहिं ॥ ११२॥
soka moha saṁdeha bhrama mama bicāra kachu nāhiṁ. 112.

Trans:

By the blessing of Rāma, O Pārwatī, not even in sleep can doubt, error, delusion, or distress enter into your mind; this I well know.

चौपाई-caupāī:

तदपि असंका कीन्हिहु सोई । कहत सुनत सब कर हित होई ॥
tadapi asaṁkā kīnhihu soī, kahata sunata saba kara hita hoī.
जिन्ह हरि कथा सुनी नहिं काना । श्रवन रंध्र अहिभवन समाना ॥
jinha hari kathā sunī nahiṁ kānā, śravana raṁdhra ahibhavana samānā.
नयनन्हि संत दरस नहिं देखा । लोचन मोरपंख कर लेखा ॥
nayananhi saṁta darasa nahiṁ dekhā, locana morapaṁkha kara lekhā.
ते सिर कटु तुंबरि समतूला । जे न नमत हरि गुर पद मूला ॥
te sira kaṭu tuṁbari samatūlā, je na namata hari gura pada mūlā.
जिन्ह हरिभगति हृदयँ नहिं आनी । जीवत सव समान तेइ प्रानी ॥
jinha haribhagati hṛdayaṁ nahiṁ ānī, jīvata sava samāna tei prānī.
जो नहिं करइ राम गुन गाना । जीह सो दादुर जीह समाना ॥
jo nahiṁ karai rāma guna gānā, jīha so dādura jīha samānā.
कुलिस कठोर निठुर सोइ छाती । सुनि हरिचरित न जो हरषाती ॥
kulisa kaṭhora niṭhura soi chātī, suni haricarita na jo haraṣātī.
गिरिजा सुनहु राम कै लीला । सुर हित दनुज बिमोहनसीला ॥
girijā sunahu rāma kai līlā, sura hita danuja bimohanasīlā.

Trans:

Yet you have expressed the same old doubts again—so that all those who repeat or hear this account may be benefited thereby. For the ears that hear not Rāma's name are mere snake-holes; the eyes that have not seen his true vision are like the false eyes in a peacock's tail; the heads that have not bowed at the feet of Harī are of no more worth then bitter pumpkins; and they whose heart is not inspired with faith in Harī are mere animated corpses; and those who sing not his praises are like croaking frogs; and hard and impenetrable as a thunderbolt is that heart who hears his deeds and takes no delight in them. Listen, O Girijā, to the enactments of Rāma, which to gods are gems of delight, and to demons germs of bewilderment.

दोहा-dohā:

रामकथा सुरधेनु सम सेवत सब सुख दानि ।
rāmakathā suradhenu sama sevata saba sukha dāni,
सतसमाज सुरलोक सब को न सुनै अस जानि ॥ ११३॥
satasamāja suraloka saba ko na sunai asa jāni. 113.

Trans:

Who is the good man that will not listen to the story of Rāma—which is like the heavenly cow that fulfils every desire of those who tend to it?

चौपाई-caupāī:

रामकथा सुंदर कर तारी । संसय बिहग उड़ावनिहारी ॥

rāmakathā suṁdara kara tārī, saṁsaya bihaga uṛāvanihārī.

रामकथा कलि बिटप कुठारी । सादर सुनु गिरिराजकुमारी ॥

rāmakathā kali biṭapa kuṭhārī, sādara sunu girirājakumārī.

राम नाम गुन चरित सुहाए । जनम करम अगनित श्रुति गाए ॥

rāma nāma guna carita suhāe, janama karama aganita śruti gāe.

जथा अनंत राम भगवाना । तथा कथा कीरति गुन नाना ॥

jathā anaṁta rāma bhagavānā, tathā kathā kīrati guna nānā.

तदपि जथा श्रुत जसि मति मोरी । कहिहउँ देखि प्रीति अति तोरी ॥

tadapi jathā śruta jasi mati morī, kahihauṁ dekhi prīti ati torī.

उमा प्रस्न तव सहज सुहाई । सुखद संतसंमत मोहि भाई ॥

umā prasna tava sahaja suhāī, sukhada saṁtasaṁmata mohi bhāī.

एक बात नहिं मोहि सोहानी । जदपि मोह बस कहेहु भवानी ॥

eka bāta nahiṁ mohi sohānī, jadapi moha basa kahehu bhavānī.

तुम्ह जो कहा राम कोउ आना । जेहि श्रुति गाव धरहिं मुनि ध्याना ॥

tumha jo kahā rāma kou ānā, jehi śruti gāva dharahiṁ muni dhyānā.

Trans:

The story of Rāma is like a fair pair of cymbals to frighten away the birds of doubt, or like an axe at the root of the tree of sin; listen reverently, O daughter of the mountain king. How sweet the name of Rāma, and his ways and his deeds! His lives and his actions are declared by the scriptures to be beyond number. And as there is no end to Rāma, so the legends about him and his glory are endless too; yet seeing the greatness of your love I will attempt to tell them to the best of my ability and as the scriptures have revealed. O Umā, your enquiries are most becoming and profitable, such as the saints approve, and I too am pleased to hear those; but there was one thing, O Bhawānī, which did not please me—although you uttered it under a spell of delusion—when you suggested that the Rāma whom the Vedas extol, and on whom the sages contemplate, is someone else!

दोहा-dohā:

कहहिं सुनहिं अस अधम नर ग्रसे जे मोह पिसाच ।

kahahiṁ sunahiṁ asa adhama nara grase je moha pisāca,

पाषंडी हरि पद बिमुख जानहिं झूठ न साच ॥ ११४॥

pāṣaṁḍī hari pada bimukha jānahiṁ jhūṭha na sāca. 114.

Trans:

This is what is said by the vile wretches whom the demon of delusion has in his clutch—heretics, who are the enemies of Harī and know not the difference between truth and falsehood.

चौपाई-caupāī:

अग्य अकोबिद अंध अभागी । काई बिषय मुकुर मन लागी ॥

agya akobida aṁdha abhāgī, kāī biṣaya mukura mana lāgī.

लंपट कपटी कुटिल बिसेषी । सपनेहुँ संतसभा नहिं देखी ॥

laṁpaṭa kapaṭī kuṭila biseṣī, sapanehuṁ saṁtasabhā nahiṁ dekhī.

कहहिं ते बेद असंमत बानी । जिन्ह कें सूझ लाभु नहिं हानी ॥

kahahiṁ te beda asaṁmata bānī, jinha keṁ sūjha lābhu nahiṁ hānī.

मुकुर मलिन अरु नयन बिहीना । राम रूप देखहिं किमि दीना ॥

mukura malina aru nayana bihīnā, rāma rūpa dekhahiṁ kimi dīnā.

जिन्ह कें अगुन न सगुन बिबेका । जल्पहिं कल्पित बचन अनेका ॥

jinha keṁ aguna na saguna bibekā, jalpahiṁ kalpita bacana anekā.

हरिमाया बस जगत भ्रमाहीं । तिन्हहि कहत कछु अघटित नाहीं ॥

harimāyā basa jagata bhramāhīṁ, tinhahi kahata kachu aghaṭita nāhīṁ.

बातुल भूत बिबस मतवारे । ते नहिं बोलहिं बचन बिचारे ॥

bātula bhūta bibasa matavāre, te nahiṁ bolahiṁ bacana bicāre.

जिन्ह कृत महामोह मद पाना । तिन्ह कर कहा करिअ नहिं काना ॥

jinha kṛta mahāmoha mada pānā, tinha kara kahā karia nahiṁ kānā.

Trans:

Such are ignorant, unlearned, and blind reprobates; the mirror of whose mind is clouded by shroud of sensuality; lustful, treacherous, and desperately perverse, who have never even in a dream attained to the vision of true faith. They utter doctrines repugnant to the Veda, with no understanding of loss or gain; the mirror of their heart is dimmed and their eyes are naught; how then can such hapless wights see the beauty of Rāma? Unable to distinguish between the material and immaterial, they jabber many lying words, and under Harī's delusive influence go utterly astray in the world; for whom no words are too strong. Windy, devilish, drunken, they can utter nothing to the purpose, and are so intoxicated with delusion that no one ought to give ear to their ravings.

सोरठा-soraṭhā:

अस निज हृदयँ बिचारि तजु संसय भजु राम पद ।

asa nija hṛdayaṁ bicāri taju saṁsaya bhaju rāma pada,

सुनु गिरिराज कुमारि भ्रम तम रबि कर बचन मम ॥ ११५॥

sunu girirāja kumāri bhrama tama rabi kara bacana mama. 115.

Trans:

Being thus assured in your heart, discard all doubt and fall in adoration at Rāma's feet. Listen, O daughter of the mountain king, and the luster of these words shall disperse all the mist from your soul, just like the sun.

चौपाई-caupāī:

सगुनहि अगुनहि नहिं कछु भेदा । गावहिं मुनि पुरान बुध बेदा ॥

sagunahi agunahi nahiṁ kachu bhedā, gāvahiṁ muni purāna budha bedā.

अगुन अरुप अलख अज जोई । भगत प्रेम बस सगुन सो होई ॥

aguna arupa alakha aja joī, bhagata prema basa saguna so hoī.

जो गुन रहित सगुन सोइ कैसें । जलु हिम उपल बिलग नहिं जैसें ॥

jo guna rahita saguna soi kaiseṁ, jalu hima upala bilaga nahiṁ jaiseṁ.

जासु नाम भ्रम तिमिर पतंगा । तेहि किमि कहिअ बिमोह प्रसंगा ॥

jāsu nāma bhrama timira pataṁgā, tehi kimi kahia bimoha prasaṁgā.

राम सच्चिदानंद दिनेसा । नहिं तहँ मोह निसा लवलेसा ॥

rāma saccidānaṁda dinesā, nahiṁ tahaṁ moha nisā lavalesā.

सहज प्रकासरुप भगवाना । नहिं तहँ पुनि बिग्यान बिहाना ॥

sahaja prakāsarupa bhagavānā, nahiṁ tahaṁ puni bigyāna bihānā.

हरष बिषाद ग्यान अग्याना । जीव धर्म अहमिति अभिमाना ॥

haraṣa biṣāda gyāna agyānā, jīva dharma ahamiti abhimānā.

राम ब्रह्म ब्यापक जग जाना । परमानंद परेस पुराना ॥

rāma brahma byāpaka jaga jānā, paramānaṁda paresa purānā.

Trans:

There is no difference between the Material and the Immaterial—so declare saints and sages, and the Vedas and Purānas. The formless Supreme—invisible, uncreated, immaterial—becomes materialized, out of love for the faithful. How can the Absolute become qualified? In the same way as water is crystallized into ice. But how can he be subject to sensual delusion, whose very name is like the sun to disperse the darkness of error? In Rāma, the Supreme Being, the sun to the delusional night of the world, error can have whatsoever no part; and in the Lord, who is himself the True Light, there can be no night of delusion or a dawn of understanding; neither a joy nor sorrow, neither knowledge nor ignorance; neither personal piety nor the sins of vanity and pride—for Rāma is the omnipresent God, the most ancient Being, the blissful Lord of all;

दोहा-dohā:

पुरुष प्रसिद्ध प्रकास निधि प्रगट परावर नाथ ।

puruṣa prasiddha prakāsa nidhi pragaṭa parāvara nātha,

रघुकुलमनि मम स्वामि सोइ कहि सिवँ नायउ माथ ॥ ११६॥

raghukulamani mama svāmi soi kahi sivaṁ nāyau mātha. 116.

Trans:

the Great Spirit, the glorious fount of light; the Revealed, the Incomprehensible, the jewel of the family of Raghu, my own Lord," and saying so Shiva bowed his head.

चौपाई-caupāī:

निज भ्रम नहिं समुझहिं अग्यानी । प्रभु पर मोह धरहिं जड़ प्रानी ॥
nija bhrama nahiṁ samujhahiṁ agyānī, prabhu para moha dharahiṁ jaṛa prānī.
जथा गगन घन पटल निहारी । झाँपेउ भानु कहहिं कुबिचारी ॥
jathā gagana ghana paṭala nihārī, jhām̐peu bhānu kahahiṁ kubicārī.
चितव जो लोचन अंगुलि लाएँ । प्रगट जुगल ससि तेहि के भाएँ ॥
citava jo locana aṁguli lāem̐, pragaṭa jugala sasi tehi ke bhāem̐.
उमा राम बिषइक अस मोहा । नभ तम धूम धूरि जिमि सोहा ॥
umā rāma biṣaika asa mohā, nabha tama dhūma dhūri jimi sohā.
बिषय करन सुर जीव समेता । सकल एक तें एक सचेता ॥
biṣaya karana sura jīva sametā, sakala eka teṁ eka sacetā.
सब कर परम प्रकासक जोई । राम अनादि अवधपति सोई ॥
saba kara parama prakāsaka joī, rāma anādi avadhapati soī.
जगत प्रकास्य प्रकासक रामू । मायाधीस ग्यान गुन धामू ॥
jagata prakāsya prakāsaka rāmū, māyādhīsa gyāna guna dhāmū.
जासु सत्यता तें जड माया । भास सत्य इव मोह सहाया ॥
jāsu satyatā teṁ jaḍa māyā, bhāsa satya iva moha sahāyā.

Trans:

"Fools do not perceive their own errors, but senselessly attribute delusion upon the Lord—like simple folks, who seeing a clouded sky say that the sun itself is dim, or who gaze at the moon through their fingers and fancy they see it doubled. O Umā, delusion affects Rāma in the same way as smoke, or a cloud, or dust affects the brightness of the heavens. The five objects of senses and the sense organs, and their presiding deities, as well as the Soul, are all in their degree possessed of Intelligence; but the great enlightener of them all is the eternal Spirit Rāma, Avadh's Lord. The world of matter is the object of illumination, and know that Rāma is its illuminator. He is the Lord of Māyā, the abode of all knowledge and virtue. By the light of his truth shines bright this dullness of material creation which appears real through the sense-organs.

दोहा-dohā:

रजत सीप महुँ भास जिमि जथा भानु कर बारि ।
rajata sīpa mahum̐ bhāsa jimi jathā bhānu kara bāri,
जदपि मृषा तिहुँ काल सोइ भ्रम न सकइ कोउ टारि ॥११७॥
jadapi mṛṣā tihum̐ kāla soi bhrama na sakai kou ṭāri. 117.

Trans:

Though false as the gleam of a polished shell, or as a mirage caused by the sun's rays, yet no one at any time, past, present, or future, can rid himself of that delusion!

चौपाई-caupāī:

एहि बिधि जग हरि आश्रित रहई । जदपि असत्य देत दुख अहई ॥
ehi bidhi jaga hari āśrita rahaī, jadapi asatya deta dukha ahaī.
जौं सपनें सिर काटै कोई । बिनु जागें न दूरि दुख होई ॥
jauṁ sapaneṁ sira kāṭai koī, binu jāgeṁ na dūri dukha hoī.
जासु कृपाँ अस भ्रम मिटि जाई । गिरिजा सोइ कृपाल रघुराई ॥
jāsu kṛpām̐ asa bhrama miṭi jāī, girijā soi kṛpāla raghurāī.
आदि अंत कोउ जासु न पावा । मति अनुमानि निगम अस गावा ॥
ādi aṁta kou jāsu na pāvā, mati anumāni nigama asa gāvā.
बिनु पद चलइ सुनइ बिनु काना । कर बिनु करम करइ बिधि नाना ॥
binu pada calai sunai binu kānā, kara binu karama karai bidhi nānā.
आनन रहित सकल रस भोगी । बिनु बानी बकता बड़ जोगी ॥
ānana rahita sakala rasa bhogī, binu bānī bakatā baṛa jogī.
तन बिनु परस नयन बिनु देखा । ग्रहइ घ्रान बिनु बास असेषा ॥
tana binu parasa nayana binu dekhā, grahai ghrāna binu bāsa aseṣā.
असि सब भाँति अलौकिक करनी । महिमा जासु जाइ नहिं बरनी ॥
asi saba bhām̐ti alaukika karanī, mahimā jāsu jāi nahiṁ baranī.

Trans:

And such is the world in its connection with Harī. Though unreal the world can cause pain—in the same way as a man, who dreams that his head is cut off, is in pain till he awakens. None can declare God's beginning or end, though the holy scripture have hymned Him as best as they could. He moves without feet, He hears without ears, and He works in manifold ways, yet without hands. Without a mouth He enjoys all tastes, and without a voice He is the most apt of speakers. He can see without eyes, touch without limbs, and without a nose catch every scent. His actions are thus in every way supernatural, and His greatness is utterly beyond words.

दोहा-dohā:

जेहि इमि गावहिं बेद बुध जाहि धरहिं मुनि ध्यान ।
jehi imi gāvahiṁ beda budha jāhi dharahiṁ muni dhyāna,
सोइ दसरथ सुत भगत हित कोसलपति भगवान ॥११८॥
soi dasaratha suta bhagata hita kosalapati bhagavāna. 118.

Trans:

He whom the scriptures and philosophy have thus sung, and whom the saints love to contemplate, that son of Dashrath, that beneficent, that King of Kaushal, is none other than the Lord God.

चौपाई-caupāī:

कासीं मरत जंतु अवलोकी । जासु नाम बल करउँ बिसोकी ॥
kāsīṁ marata jaṁtu avalokī, jāsu nāma bala karaum̐ bisokī.
सोइ प्रभु मोर चराचर स्वामी । रघुबर सब उर अंतरजामी ॥
soi prabhu mora carācara svāmī, raghubara saba ura aṁtarajāmī.
बिबसहुँ जासु नाम नर कहहीं । जनम अनेक रचित अघ दहहीं ॥
bibasahum̐ jāsu nāma nara kahahīṁ, janama aneka racita agha dahahīṁ.
सादर सुमिरन जे नर करहीं । भव बारिधि गोपद इव तरहीं ॥
sādara sumirana je nara karahīṁ, bhava bāridhi gopada iva tarahīṁ.
राम सो परमातमा भवानी । तहँ भ्रम अति अबिहित तव बानी ॥
rāma so paramātamā bhavānī, taham̐ bhrama ati abihita tava bānī.
अस संसय आनत उर माहीं । ग्यान बिराग सकल गुन जाहीं ॥
asa saṁsaya ānata ura māhīṁ, gyāna birāga sakala guna jāhīṁ.
सुनि सिव के भ्रम भंजन बचना । मिटि गै सब कुतरक कै रचना ॥
suni siva ke bhrama bhaṁjana bacanā, miṭi gai saba kutaraka kai racanā.
भइ रघुपति पद प्रीति प्रतीती । दारुन असंभावना बीती ॥
bhai raghupati pada prīti pratītī, dāruna asaṁbhāvanā bītī.

Trans:

By the power of his Name I exalt to the regions of the blessed any creature whom I see dying at Kashī. He is the sovereign of all creation, inanimate or animate: my Lord Raghubar, who reads all hearts. By repeating His name the most abandoned of sinners destroys the accumulated sins of many previous existences; and by those who devoutly meditate upon Him the ocean of life is as easily crossed as a puddle on the road. Rāma, O Bhawānī, is the Supreme Spirit, and the error to which you gave utterance on this point was rather improper. Such doubt, when entertained in the heart, destroys knowledge, sobriety, and every virtue." On hearing Shiva's luminous exposition, her whole structure of heresy fell to pieces; her love and devotion to Raghupatī grew strong, and her sore incredulity passed away.

दोहा-dohā:

पुनि पुनि प्रभु पद कमल गहि जोरि पंकरुह पानि ।
puni puni prabhu pada kamala gahi jori paṁkaruha pāni,
बोलीं गिरिजा बचन बर मनहुँ प्रेम रस सानि ॥ ११९॥
bolīṁ girijā bacana bara manahuṁ prema rasa sāni. 119.

Trans:

Again and again clasping her Lord's lotus feet and suppliantly folding her hands, her whole soul overflowing with affection, Girijā spoke in gentle tones:

चौपाई-caupāī:

ससि कर सम सुनि गिरा तुम्हारी । मिटा मोह सरदातप भारी ॥
sasi kara sama suni girā tumhārī, miṭā moha saradātapa bhārī.
तुम्ह कृपाल सबु संसउ हरेऊ । राम स्वरुप जानि मोहि परेऊ ॥
tumha kṛpāla sabu saṁsau hareū, rāma svarupa jāni mohi pareū.
नाथ कृपाँ अब गयउ बिषादा । सुखी भयउँ प्रभु चरन प्रसादा ॥
nātha kṛpāṁ aba gayau biṣādā, sukhī bhayauṁ prabhu carana prasādā.
अब मोहि आपनि किंकरि जानी । जदपि सहज जड़ नारि अयानी ॥
aba mohi āpani kiṁkari jānī, jadapi sahaja jaṛa nāri ayānī.
प्रथम जो मैं पूछा सोइ कहहू । जौं मो पर प्रसन्न प्रभु अहहू ॥
prathama jo maiṁ pūchā soi kahahū, jauṁ mo para prasanna prabhu ahahū.
राम ब्रह्म चिनमय अबिनासी । सर्ब रहित सब उर पुर बासी ॥
rāma brahma cinamaya abināsī, sarba rahita saba ura pura bāsī.
नाथ धरेउ नरतनु केहि हेतू । मोहि समुझाइ कहहु बृषकेतू ॥
nātha dhareu naratanu kehi hetū, mohi samujhāi kahahu bṛṣaketū.
उमा बचन सुनि परम बिनीता । रामकथा पर प्रीति पुनीता ॥
umā bacana suni parama binītā, rāmakathā para prīti punītā.

Trans:

"My grievous delusion, like the feverish heat of autumn, has yielded to the moon-like spell of your voice. In your compassion you have removed all my doubts, and I now understand Rāma's essence. By my Lord's mercy my distress is all gone, and I am made glad by his favor. Now regarding me as your own immediate servant, though I am but a poor ignorant woman, if I have really found grace in your sight, reply to those my former questions. If Rāma is the invisible and immortal God, without parts and passions, and whose temple is the heart, why did he take the form of a human? Declare and explain this to me." On hearing Umā's modest speech, and perceiving her sincere desire to be instructed in Rāma's history,

दोहा-dohā:

हियँ हरषे कामारि तब संकर सहज सुजान ।
hiyaṁ harașe kāmāri taba saṁkara sahaja sujāna,
बहु बिधि उमहि प्रसंसि पुनि बोले कृपानिधान ॥ १२०क॥
bahu bidhi umahi prasaṁsi puni bole kṛpānidhāna. 120(ka).

Trans:

the all-wise Shankar, the destroyer of Kāmdev, was glad of heart, and with many words of praises for Umā then spoke:

मासपारायण चौथा विश्राम

नवाह्नपारायण पहला विश्राम

māsapārāyaṇa cauthā viśrāma
navāhnapārāyaṇa pahalā viśrāma
(Pause 4 for a Thirty-Day Recitation)
(Pause 1 for a Nine-Day Recitation)

सोरठा-soraṭhā:

सुनु सुभ कथा भवानि रामचरितमानस बिमल ।
sunu subha kathā bhavāni rāmacaritamānasa bimala,
कहा भुसुंडि बखानि सुना बिहग नायक गरुड ॥ १२०ख॥
kahā bhusuṁḍi bakhāni sunā bihaga nāyaka garuḍa. 120(kha).

सो संबाद उदार जेहि बिधि भा आगें कहब ।
so saṁbāda udāra jehi bidhi bhā āgeṁ kahaba,
सुनहु राम अवतार चरित परम सुंदर अनघ ॥ १२०ग॥
sunahu rāma avatāra carita parama suṁdara anagha. 120(ga).

हरि गुन नाम अपार कथा रूप अगनित अमित ।
hari guna nāma apāra kathā rūpa aganita amita,
मैं निज मति अनुसार कहउँ उमा सादर सुनहु ॥ १२०घ॥
maiṁ nija mati anusāra kahauṁ umā sādara sunahu. 120(gha.

Trans:

"Listen, O Bhawānī, while I recite in auspicious strains the Rāmcharitmānas, or pure lake of Rāma's glories, as in days of yore Bhusumdi declared it in the hearing of Garud, the king-of-birds. First I will relate the manner of their exalted converse, after which you shall hear of Rāma's incarnation and his all-glorious and sinless deeds. Harī's virtues and names are infinite, and his history and his manifestations beyond number or measure; I tell them as best I can; listen, Umā, with respect.

चौपाई-caupāī:

सुनु गिरिजा हरिचरित सुहाए । बिपुल बिसद निगमागम गाए ॥
sunu girijā haricarita suhāe, bipula bisada nigamāgama gāe.
हरि अवतार हेतु जेहि होई । इदमित्थं कहि जाइ न सोई ॥
hari avatāra hetu jehi hoī, idamitthaṁ kahi jāi na soī.
राम अतर्क्य बुद्धि मन बानी । मत हमार अस सुनहि सयानी ॥
rāma atarkya buddhi mana bānī, mata hamāra asa sunahi sayānī.
तदपि संत मुनि बेद पुराना । जस कछु कहहिं स्वमति अनुमाना ॥
tadapi saṁta muni beda purānā, jasa kachu kahahiṁ svamati anumānā.
तस मैं सुमुखि सुनावउँ तोही । समुझि परइ जस कारन मोही ॥
tasa maiṁ sumukhi sunāvauṁ tohī, samujhi parai jasa kārana mohī.
जब जब होइ धरम कै हानी । बाढहिं असुर अधम अभिमानी ॥
jaba jaba hoi dharama kai hānī, bāḍhahiṁ asura adhama abhimānī.
करहिं अनीति जाइ नहिं बरनी । सीदहिं बिप्र धेनु सुर धरनी ॥
karahiṁ anīti jāi nahiṁ baranī, sīdahiṁ bipra dhenu sura dharanī.
तब तब प्रभु धरि बिबिध सरीरा । हरहिं कृपानिधि सज्जन पीरा ॥
taba taba prabhu dhari bibidha sarīrā, harahiṁ kṛpānidhi sajjana pīrā.

Trans:

Listen, Girijā, to the grateful tale of Harī's great and holy acts, as they have been recorded in the scriptures. The cause of Harī's incarnation is not to be narrowly defined for, to my mind, O Bhawānī, Rāma is beyond the grasp of intellect or soul, or speech. And yet—as saints and sages, the Veda and the Purānas, have partly and to the extent of their capacity explained the matter—so do I, O fair dame, now declare to you the mystery as I understand it. Whenever virtue declines, and vile and haughty demons multiply and work iniquity that cannot be told, and whenever Brahmins, cows, gods and earth itself are in trouble—the gracious Lord assumes some new bodily form and relieves the distress of the faithful;

दोहा-dohā:

असुर मारि थापहिं सुरन्ह राखहिं निज श्रुति सेतु ।
asura māri thāpahiṁ suranha rākhahiṁ nija śruti setu,
जग बिस्तारहिं बिसद जस राम जन्म कर हेतु ॥१२१॥
jaga bistārahiṁ bisada jasa rāma janma kara hetu. 121.

Trans:

And He destroys the evil spirits, and reinstates the gods, and maintains the way of salvation, and diffuses the brightness of his glory throughout the worlds—such are some of the motives of Rāma's incarnations.

चौपाई-caupāī:

सोइ जस गाइ भगत भव तरहीं । कृपासिंधु जन हित तनु धरहीं ॥
soi jasa gāi bhagata bhava tarahīṁ, kṛpāsiṁdhu jana hita tanu dharahīṁ.
राम जनम के हेतु अनेका । परम बिचित्र एक तें एका ॥
rāma janama ke hetu anekā, parama bicitra eka teṁ ekā.
जनम एक दुइ कहउँ बखानी । सावधान सुनु सुमति भवानी ॥
janama eka dui kahauṁ bakhānī, sāvadhāna sunu sumati bhavānī.
द्वारपाल हरि के प्रिय दोऊ । जय अरु बिजय जान सब कोऊ ॥
dvārapāla hari ke priya doū, jaya aru bijaya jāna saba koū.
बिप्र श्राप तें दूनउ भाई । तामस असुर देह तिन्ह पाई ॥
bipra śrāpa teṁ dūnau bhāī, tāmasa asura deha tinha pāī.
कनककसिपु अरु हाटक लोचन । जगत बिदित सुरपति मद मोचन ॥
kanakakasipu aru hāṭaka locana, jagata bidita surapati mada mocana.
बिजई समर बीर बिख्याता । धरि बराह बपु एक निपाता ॥
bijaī samara bīra bikhyātā, dhari barāha bapu eka nipātā.
होइ नरहरि दूसर पुनि मारा । जन प्रहलाद सुजस बिस्तारा ॥
hoi narahari dūsara puni mārā, jana prahalāda sujasa bistārā.

Trans:

Singing his glory, the saints escape the waves of duality of life, and it is for their sake only that the Compassionate assumes a bodily form. The causes of Rāma's incarnations have been many and various—each more wonderful than the other. I will relate one or two of his previous births if, O Bhawānī, you are prepared to give me your devout attention. Harī once had two loving door-keepers, the famous Jaya and Bijaya. Both brothers, in consequence of the Brahmins' curse, were born again in the form of the malignant demons Hiranyā-kashyap and Hiranyaksh—who became celebrated throughout the world as the tamers of the pride of the king of heaven. Incarnate as a Boar, he triumphed in battle over the first illustrious hero and destroyed him; and again in the Narsingh avatar slew the second one; and the story of the faithful Prahlād is widespread.

दोहा-dohā:

भए निसाचर जाइ तेइ महाबीर बलवान ।
bhae nisācara jāi tei mahābīra balavāna,
कुंभकरन रावण सुभट सुर बिजई जग जान ॥१२२॥
kuṁbhakarana rāvaṇa subhaṭa sura bijaī jaga jāna. 122.

Trans:

Then the evil spirits were reborn as the bold and powerful warriors Kumbhkaran and Rāvan, who as all the world knows, subdued even the gods.

चौपाई-caupāī:

मुकुत न भए हते भगवाना । तीनि जनम द्विज बचन प्रवाना ॥
mukuta na bhae hate bhagavānā, tīni janama dvija bacana pravānā.
एक बार तिन्ह के हित लागी । धरेउ सरीर भगत अनुरागी ॥
eka bāra tinha ke hita lāgī, dhareu sarīra bhagata anurāgī.
कस्यप अदिति तहाँ पितु माता । दसरथ कौसल्या बिख्याता ॥
kasyapa aditi tahāṁ pitu mātā, dasaratha kausalyā bikhyātā.
एक कलप एहि बिधि अवतारा । चरित्र पवित्र किए संसारा ॥
eka kalapa ehi bidhi avatārā, caritra pavitra kie saṁsārā.
एक कलप सुर देखि दुखारे । समर जलंधर सन सब हारे ॥
eka kalapa sura dekhi dukhāre, samara jalaṁdhara sana saba hāre.
संभु कीन्ह संग्राम अपारा । दनुज महाबल मरइ न मारा ॥
saṁbhu kīnha saṁgrāma apārā, danuja mahābala marai na mārā.
परम सती असुराधिप नारी । तेहिं बल ताहि न जितहिं पुरारी ॥
parama satī asurādhipa nārī, tehiṁ bala tāhi na jitahiṁ purārī.

Trans:

Though killed by God they did not attain to salvation, for the Brahmins had doomed them to three births. It was on their account that the cherisher of the faithful assumed a body upon one occasion; and in that birth Kashyap and Aditī were his parents known as Dashrath and Kausalyā respectively; and it was how he descended from heaven in that age to perform many deeds to save the virtuous on earth. In another Kalpa all the gods were worsted in their conflict with the demon Jalandhar. Seeing their distress Shambhu waged a war against him which knew no end; but the demon, who possessed a great might, could not be killed in spite of Shambhu's best efforts—for the wife of the demon chief was a most virtuous woman. Armed by her strength of character the demon could not be conquered even by the Vanquisher of Tripura.

दोहा-dohā:

छल करि टारेउ तासु ब्रत प्रभु सुर कारज कीन्ह ।
chala kari ṭāreu tāsu brata prabhu sura kāraja kīnha,
जब तेहिं जानेउ मरम तब श्राप कोप करि दीन्ह ॥१२३॥
jaba tehiṁ jāneu marama taba śrāpa kopa kari dīnha. 123.

Trans:

By a stratagem the Lord broke her vow and affected the will of the gods. When she discovered the deception, then in her wrath she cursed him.

चौपाई-caupāī:

तासु श्राप हरि दीन्ह प्रमाना । कौतुकनिधि कृपाल भगवाना ॥
tāsu śrāpa hari dīnha pramānā, kautukanidhi kṛpāla bhagavānā.
तहाँ जलंधर रावन भयऊ । रन हति राम परम पद दयऊ ॥
tahāṁ jalaṁdhara rāvana bhayaū, rana hati rāma parama pada dayaū.
एक जनम कर कारन एहा । जेहि लागि राम धरी नरदेहा ॥
eka janama kara kārana ehā, jehi lāgi rāma dharī naradehā.
प्रति अवतार कथा प्रभु केरी । सुनु मुनि बरनी कबिन्ह घनेरी ॥
prati avatāra kathā prabhu kerī, sunu muni baranī kabinha ghanerī.
नारद श्राप दीन्ह एक बारा । कलप एक तेहि लगि अवतारा ॥
nārada śrāpa dīnha eka bārā, kalapa eka tehi lagi avatārā.
गिरिजा चकित भई सुनि बानी । नारद बिष्नुभगत पुनि ग्यानी ॥
girijā cakita bhaiṁ suni bānī, nārada biṣnubhagata puni gyānī.
कारन कवन श्राप मुनि दीन्हा । का अपराध रमापति कीन्हा ॥
kārana kavana śrāpa muni dīnhā, kā aparādha ramāpati kīnhā.
यह प्रसंग मोहि कहहु पुरारी । मुनि मन मोह आचरज भारी ॥
yaha prasaṁga mohi kahahu purārī, muni mana moha ācaraja bhārī.

Trans:

And Harī did according to her curse; for though the Lord God, he is full of playfulness and mercy. So Jalandhar was born as Rāvan and being killed in battle by Rāma attained to high glory. This then was the cause of one birth and the reason why Rāma, in that Age, assumed a human form. Each Avatar has its legend, which the poets have sung in various ways and according to tradition. On one occasion it was Nārad's curse that caused him to become incarnate." At this saying Girijā was astounded: "Nārad is a wise saint and a votary of Vishnu's; what was his reason for uttering a curse? What offence had Lakshmī's Lord committed? Tell me the whole story, Purārī; it is passing strange that a saint should be subject to passion."

दोहा-dohā:

बोले बिहसि महेस तब ग्यानी मूढ़ न कोइ ।
bole bihasi mahesa taba gyānī mūṛha na koi,
जेहि जस रघुपति करहिं जब सो तस तेहि छन होइ ॥१२४क॥
jehi jasa raghupati karahiṁ jaba so tasa tehi chana hoi. 124(ka).

Trans:

Then answered Mahādev with a smile: "There is neither wise nor fool O lady; it is just that man becomes such as Raghupatī wills him to be."

सोरठा-soraṭhā:

कहउँ राम गुन गाथ भरद्वाज सादर सुनहु ।
kahauṁ rāma guna gātha bharadvāja sādara sunahu,
भव भंजन रघुनाथ भजु तुलसी तजि मान मद ॥१२४ख॥
bhava bhaṁjana raghunātha bhaju tulasī taji māna mada. 124(kha).

Trans:

[Now said Yāgyavalk] "I sing the glory of Rāma; hearken earnestly, O Bharadvāja." And do thou, O Tulsī and the world—putting away intoxication of pride and worshipping Raghunāth, the destroyer of death—devoutly listen.

चौपाई-caupāī:

हिमगिरि गुहा एक अति पावनि । बह समीप सुरसरी सुहावनि ॥
himagiri guhā eka ati pāvani, baha samīpa surasarī suhāvani.
आश्रम परम पुनीत सुहावा । देखि देवरिषि मन अति भावा ॥
āśrama parama punīta suhāvā, dekhi devariṣi mana ati bhāvā.
निरखि सैल सरि बिपिन बिभागा । भयउ रमापति पद अनुरागा ॥
nirakhi saila sari bipina bibhāgā, bhayau ramāpati pada anurāgā.
सुमिरत हरिहि श्राप गति बाधी । सहज बिमल मन लागि समाधी ॥
sumirata harihi śrāpa gati bādhī, sahaja bimala mana lāgi samādhī.
मुनि गति देखि सुरेस डेराना । कामहि बोलि कीन्ह सनमाना ॥
muni gati dekhi suresa ḍerānā, kāmahi boli kīnha sanamānā.
सहित सहाय जाहु मम हेतू । चकेउ हरषि हियँ जलचरकेतू ॥
sahita sahāya jāhu mama hetū, cakeu haraṣi hiyaṁ jalacaraketū.
सुनासीर मन महुँ असि त्रासा । चहत देवरिषि मम पुर बासा ॥
sunāsīra mana mahuṁ asi trāsā, cahata devariṣi mama pura bāsā.
जे कामी लोलुप जग माहीं । कुटिल काक इव सबहि डेराहीं ॥
je kāmī lolupa jaga māhīṁ, kuṭila kāka iva sabahi ḍerāhīṁ.

Trans:

In the Himālaya mountains is a very sacred cave close to the holy Gangā. Once, seeing this pure and delightful hermitage the divine sage Nārad was greatly pleased; and as he gazed upon the beauty of the rocks and the forest glades he was filled with love for God; and as he thought upon Harī a previous curse upon him was broken and his spotless soul fell all at once into a trance. When the king of heaven saw the sage's high state he feared [lest his throne be lost]; and in terms of high respect addressed himself to Kāmdev: "Go, I beg, with your assistants." He, the god of Love, went very gladly. In Indra's mind was great alarm, for he thought 'The saint would rob me of my kingdom.' All the world over those that are lustful and covetous are much so afraid of interference—just as is a thievish crow.

दोहा-dohā:

सूख हाड़ लै भाग सठ स्वान निरखि मृगराज ।
sūkha hāṛa lai bhāga saṭha svāna nirakhi mṛgarāja,
छीनि लेइ जनि जान जड़ तिमि सुरपतिहि न लाज ॥१२५॥
chīni lei jani jāna jaṛa timi surapatihi na lāja. 125.

Trans:

A wretched dog, on seeing a lion, runs away with the dry bone that's in his mouth—for fear it would be stolen from him by the king-of-beasts. So did Indra, the king of heaven, shamelessly thought—just like such a dog.

चौपाई-caupāī:

तेहि आश्रमहिं मदन जब गयऊ । निज मायाँ बसंत निरमयऊ ॥
tehi āśramahiṁ madana jaba gayaū, nija māyāṁ basaṁta niramayaū.
कुसुमित बिबिध बिटप बहुरंगा । कूजहिं कोकिल गुंजहिं भृंगा ॥
kusumita bibidha biṭapa bahuraṁgā, kūjahiṁ kokila guṁjahiṁ bhṛṁgā.
चली सुहावनि त्रिबिध बयारी । काम कृसानु बढ़ावनिहारी ॥
calī suhāvani tribidha bayārī, kāma kṛsānu baṛhāvanihārī.
रंभादिक सुरनारि नबीना । सकल असमसर कला प्रबीना ॥
raṁbhādika suranāri nabīnā, sakala asamasara kalā prabīnā.
करहिं गान बहु तान तरंगा । बहुबिधि क्रीड़हिं पानि पतंगा ॥
karahiṁ gāna bahu tāna taraṁgā, bahubidhi krīṛahiṁ pāni pataṁgā.
देखि सहाय मदन हरषाना । कीन्हेसि पुनि प्रपंच बिधि नाना ॥
dekhi sahāya madana haraṣānā, kīnhesi puni prapaṁca bidhi nānā.
काम कला कछु मुनिहि न ब्यापी । निज भयँ डरेउ मनोभव पापी ॥
kāma kalā kachu munihi na byāpī, nija bhayaṁ ḍareu manobhava pāpī.
सीम कि चाँपि सकइ कोउ तासू । बड़ रखवार रमापति जासू ॥
sīma ki cāṁpi sakai kou tāsū, baṛa rakhavāra ramāpati jāsū.

Trans:

When Love reached the hermitage his deceptive power created a false spring. All the trees broke out into many-colored blossoms, there was a murmuring of cuckoos and humming of bees. Delightful winds—soft, cool, and fragrant—sprung up fanning the flame of desire as Rambha and the other heavenly nymphs—all well skilled in the art of love—began singing songs in every variety of measure and disporting themselves in dances, undulating their hands. When Love saw himself so well supported he was glad and manifested his creative powers in many diverse ways; but his devices had no effect upon the saint; and so guilty Love began to tremble in fear for himself. Who can dare trespass the bounds of a Devotee who has the Great Ramāpati as his protector?

दोहा-dohā:

सहित सहाय सभीत अति मानि हारि मन मैन ।
sahita sahāya sabhīta ati māni hāri mana maina,
गहेसि जाइ मुनि चरन तब कहि सुठि आरत बैन ॥१२६॥
gahesi jāi muni carana taba kahi suṭhi ārata baina. 126.

Trans:

In dire dismay both Kāmdev and his accomplices confessed themselves defeated; and they went and clasped the holy man's feet, addressing him in accents of the deepest humility.

चौपाई-caupāī:

भयउ न नारद मन कछु रोषा । कहि प्रिय बचन काम परितोषा ॥
bhayau na nārada mana kachu roṣā, kahi priya bacana kāma paritoṣā.
नाइ चरन सिरु आयसु पाई । गयउ मदन तब सहित सहाई ॥
nāi carana siru āyasu pāī, gayau madana taba sahita sahāī.
मुनि सुसीलता आपनि करनी । सुरपति सभाँ जाइ सब बरनी ॥
muni susīlatā āpani karanī, surapati sabhāṁ jāi saba baranī.
सुनि सब कें मन अचरजु आवा । मुनिहि प्रसंसि हरिहि सिरु नावा ॥
suni saba keṁ mana acaraju āvā, munihi prasaṁsi harihi siru nāvā.
तब नारद गवने सिव पाहीं । जिता काम अहमिति मन माहीं ॥
taba nārada gavane siva pāhīṁ, jitā kāma ahamiti mana māhīṁ.
मार चरित संकरहि सुनाए । अतिप्रिय जानि महेस सिखाए ॥
māra carita saṁkarahi sunāe, atipriya jāni mahesa sikhāe.
बार बार बिनवउँ मुनि तोही । जिमि यह कथा सुनायहु मोही ॥
bāra bāra binavauṁ muni tohī, jimi yaha kathā sunāyahu mohī.

तिमि जनि हरिहि सुनावहु कबहूँ । चलेहुँ प्रसंग दुराएहु तबहूँ ॥
timi jani harihi sunāvahu kabahūṁ, calehuṁ prasaṁga durāehu tabahūṁ.

Trans:

There was no anger in Nārad's soul, and he, in friendly terms, replied to Kāmdev and reassured him. Bowing the head at saint's feet, and accepting his commands, they all retired—the god and his companions; and repairing to Indra's court there related all their own doings and the saint's clemency. As they listened to the tale all were astonished, and bowing their heads to Harī extolled the saint. Later went Nārad to Shiva, greatly proud of his victory over Love, and told him all Love's doings. In acknowledgment of his affection Mahādev gave him one sound advice: "O great saint, again and again I beg of you never to repeat to Harī this story that you have now told me. Even should it happen to be brought forward, keep it dark as possible."

दोहा-dohā:

संभु दीन्ह उपदेस हित नहिं नारदहि सोहान ।
saṁbhu dīnha upadesa hita nahiṁ nāradahi sohāna,
भरद्वाज कौतुक सुनहु हरि इच्छा बलवान ॥१२७॥
bharadvāja kautuka sunahu hari icchā balavāna. 127.

Trans:

Good as the advice was, it did not please Nārad. O Bharadvāja, now listen to the strange recital, and see the strength of Harī's will.

चौपाई-caupāī:

राम कीन्ह चाहहिं सोइ होई । करै अन्यथा अस नहिं कोई ॥
rāma kīnha cāhahiṁ soi hoī, karai anyathā asa nahiṁ koī.
संभु बचन मुनि मन नहिं भाए । तब बिरंचि के लोक सिधाए ॥
saṁbhu bacana muni mana nahiṁ bhāe, taba biraṁci ke loka sidhāe.
एक बार करतल बर बीना । गावत हरि गुन गान प्रबीना ॥
eka bāra karatala bara bīnā, gāvata hari guna gāna prabīnā.
छीरसिंधु गवने मुनिनाथा । जहँ बस श्रीनिवास श्रुतिमाथा ॥
chīrasiṁdhu gavane munināthā, jahaṁ basa śrīnivāsa śrutimāthā.
हरषि मिले उठि रमानिकेता । बैठे आसन रिषिहि समेता ॥
haraṣi mile uṭhi ramāniketā, baiṭhe āsana riṣihi sametā.
बोले बिहसि चराचर राया । बहुते दिनन कीन्हि मुनि दाया ॥
bole bihasi carācara rāyā, bahute dinana kīnhi muni dāyā.
काम चरित नारद सब भाषे । जद्यपि प्रथम बरजि सिवँ राखे ॥
kāma carita nārada saba bhāṣe, jadyapi prathama baraji sivaṁ rākhe.
अति प्रचंड रघुपति कै माया । जेहि न मोह अस को जग जाया ॥
ati pracaṁḍa raghupati kai māyā, jehi na moha asa ko jaga jāyā.

Trans:

What Rāma wills to have done—is done, and there is no one who can alter it. As Shambhu's words did not please the saint, he went straight, to Brahmmā's court, and to the accompaniment of the famous lute that he had in his hand sung right through the excellent songs of Harī's praises. Then he passed on to the milky ocean, where abides Vishnu, the glory of revelation. The Lord rushed to meet him in great joy, and side by side they sat together. Said the sovereign of the universe with a smile: 'Reverend sir, 'tis long since you last did me this honor.' Then Nārad declared all of Love's doings—although Shiva had beforehand cautioned him. The deceptive power of Raghupatī is so strong that there is no man living who can resist it!

दोहा-dohā:

रूख बदन करि बचन मृदु बोले श्रीभगवान ।
rūkha badana kari bacana mṛdu bole śrībhagavāna,
तुम्हरे सुमिरन तें मिटहिं मोह मार मद मान ॥१२८॥
tumhare sumirana teṁ miṭahiṁ moha māra mada māna. 128.

Trans:

With an impassive look, yet in coaxing accents, said the Lord, "By your very thought self-delusion, lust, arrogance and pride disappear.

चौपाई-caupāī:

सुनु मुनि मोह होइ मन ताकें । ग्यान बिराग हृदय नहिं जाकें ॥
sunu muni moha hoi mana tākeṁ, gyāna birāga hṛdaya nahiṁ jākeṁ.
ब्रह्मचरज ब्रत रत मतिधीरा । तुम्हहि कि करइ मनोभव पीरा ॥
brahmacaraja brata rata matidhīrā, tumhahi ki karai manobhava pīrā.
नारद कहेउ सहित अभिमाना । कृपा तुम्हारि सकल भगवाना ॥
nārada kaheu sahita abhimānā, kṛpā tumhāri sakala bhagavānā.
करुनानिधि मन दीख बिचारी । उर अंकुरेउ गरब तरु भारी ॥
karunānidhi mana dīkha bicārī, ura aṁkureu garaba taru bhārī.
बेगि सो मैं डारिहउँ उखारी । पन हमार सेवक हितकारी ॥
begi so maiṁ ḍārihauṁ ukhārī, pana hamāra sevaka hitakārī.
मुनि कर हित मम कौतुक होई । अवसि उपाय करबि मैं सोई ॥
muni kara hita mama kautuka hoī, avasi upāya karabi maiṁ soī.
तब नारद हरि पद सिर नाई । चले हृदयँ अहमिति अधिकाई ॥
taba nārada hari pada sira nāī, cale hṛdayaṁ ahamiti adhikāī.
श्रीपति निज माया तब प्रेरी । सुनहु कठिन करनी तेहि केरी ॥
śrīpati nija māyā taba prerī, sunahu kaṭhina karanī tehi kerī.

Trans:

Know, O saint, that infatuation prevails in a soul that is devoid of wisdom and self-control; but what pain can Love cause to one so steadfast in asceticism as yourself?" And Nārad said in his pride "It is all your favor, my Lord." The Compassionate saw into his heart and thought within himself: "Pride, like a huge tree, has sprouted into his soul; I must at once tear it up by the roots—ever to relieve my servants is the vow that I have made. I will surely contrive some sportive device on behalf of the saint." Then Nārad bowed his head at Harī's feet and took his leave, swelling with pride, while Vishnu gave orders to the spirit of delusion. Listen now to her strange doings.

दोहा-dohā:

बिरचेउ मग महुँ नगर तेहिं सत जोजन बिस्तार ।
biraceu maga mahuṁ nagara tehiṁ sata jojana bistāra,
श्रीनिवासपुर तें अधिक रचना बिबिध प्रकार ॥१२९॥
śrīnivāsapura teṁ adhika racanā bibidha prakāra. 129.

Trans:

Māyā constructed on the way a city a hundred leagues in circumference, with everything more perfect then even in Vishnu's own capital;

चौपाई-caupāī:

बसहिं नगर सुंदर नर नारी । जनु बहु मनसिज रति तनुधारी ॥
basahiṁ nagara suṁdara nara nārī, janu bahu manasija rati tanudhārī.
तेहिं पुर बसइ सीलनिधि राजा । अगनित हय गय सेन समाजा ॥
tehiṁ pura basai sīlanidhi rājā, aganita haya gaya sena samājā.
सत सुरेस सम बिभव बिलासा । रूप तेज बल नीति निवासा ॥
sata suresa sama bibhava bilāsā, rūpa teja bala nīti nivāsā.
बिस्वमोहनी तासु कुमारी । श्री बिमोह जिसु रूपु निहारी ॥
bisvamohanī tāsu kumārī, śrī bimoha jisu rūpu nihārī.
सोइ हरिमाया सब गुन खानी । सोभा तासु कि जाइ बखानी ॥
soi harimāyā saba guna khānī, sobhā tāsu ki jāi bakhānī.
करइ स्वयंबर सो नृपबाला । आए तहँ अगनित महिपाला ॥
karai svayaṁbara so nṛpabālā, āe tahaṁ aganita mahipālā.
मुनि कौतुकी नगर तेहिं गयऊ । पुरबासिन्ह सब पूछत भयऊ ॥
muni kautukī nagara tehiṁ gayaū, purabāsinha saba pūchata bhayaū.
सुनि सब चरित भूपगृहँ आए । करि पूजा नृप मुनि बैठाए ॥
suni saba carita bhūpagṛhaṁ āe, kari pūjā nṛpa muni baiṭhāe.

Trans:

and the city was inhabited by such graceful men and women that you would take them all to be incarnations of Kāmdev and Ratī. The king of the city—by the name Shil-nidhi—had horses, elephants, and troops beyond number; his royal pomp was like that of a hundred Indras—himself a centre of power, policy, and magnificence. His daughter Vishwa-mohini was so beautiful that even Lakshmī would be put to the blush, and by Harī's delusive power was in every way so exquisite that no words could describe her. As the princess was selecting a husband, kings beyond number came as suitors. The saint too came to the delusive city and began making enquiries of the people. When he had heard all that was going on, he proceeded to the palace, where the king most respectfully gave him a seat;

दोहा-dohā:

आनि देखाई नारदहि भूपति राजकुमारि ।
āni dekhāī nāradahi bhūpati rājakumāri,
कहहु नाथ गुन दोष सब एहि के हृदयँ बिचारि ॥१३०॥
kahahu nātha guna doṣa saba ehi ke hṛdayam̐ bicāri. 130.

Trans:

and then he brought his daughter for him to see, saying, "Tell me good sir after consideration, all that is good or bad about her."

चौपाई-caupāī:

देखि रूप मुनि बिरति बिसारी । बड़ी बार लगि रहे निहारी ॥
dekhi rūpa muni birati bisārī, baṛī bāra lagi rahe nihārī.
लच्छन तासु बिलोकि भुलाने । हृदयँ हरष नहिं प्रगट बखाने ॥
lacchana tāsu biloki bhulāne, hṛdayam̐ haraṣa nahiṁ pragaṭa bakhāne.
जो एहि बरइ अमर सोइ होई । समरभूमि तेहि जीत न कोई ॥
jo ehi barai amara soi hoī, samarabhūmi tehi jīta na koī.
सेवहिं सकल चराचर ताही । बरइ सीलनिधि कन्या जाही ॥
sevahiṁ sakala carācara tāhī, barai sīlanidhi kanyā jāhī.
लच्छन सब बिचारि उर राखे । कछुक बनाइ भूप सन भाषे ॥
lacchana saba bicāri ura rākhe, kachuka banāi bhūpa sana bhāṣe.
सुता सुलच्छन कहि नृप पाहीं । नारद चले सोच मन माहीं ॥
sutā sulacchana kahi nṛpa pāhīṁ, nārada cale soca mana māhīṁ.
करौं जाइ सोइ जतन बिचारी । जेहि प्रकार मोहि बरै कुमारी ॥
karauṁ jāi soi jatana bicārī, jehi prakāra mohi barai kumārī.
जप तप कछु न होइ तेहि काला । हे बिधि मिलइ कवन बिधि बाला ॥
japa tapa kachu na hoi tehi kālā, he bidhi milai kavana bidhi bālā.

Trans:

When Nārad saw her beauty, he forgot his vow of chastity and continued for long to gaze upon her. Her features quite fascinated him, yet he would not in words express his heart's delight. 'Her bridegroom shall be one of the immortals, invincible in battle, reverenced by all creation; aye, such a one shall Shil-nidhi's daughter wed.'—but though he thought thus, he kept it to himself, and said something or the other to the king, and then, after he had finished speaking, went away full of thought, considering: "What scheme can I devise now so as to make her marry me? No time is this for prayers or penance; good god, how can I to get this girl?

दोहा-dohā:

एहि अवसर चाहिअ परम सोभा रूप बिसाल ।
ehi avasara cāhia parama sobhā rūpa bisāla,
जो बिलोकि रीझै कुअँरि तब मेलै जयमाल ॥१३१॥
jo biloki rījhai kuam̐ri taba melai jayamāla. 131.

Trans:

On this occasion I must make myself such exceedingly charming and beautiful, that the princess will become pleased when she sees me and thus give me the wreath of victory.

चौपाई-caupāī:

हरि सन मागौं सुंदरताई । होइहि जात गहरु अति भाई ॥
hari sana māgauṁ suṁdaratāī, hoihi jāta gaharu ati bhāī.
मोरें हित हरि सम नहिं कोऊ । एहि अवसर सहाय सोइ होऊ ॥
moreṁ hita hari sama nahiṁ koū, ehi avasara sahāya soi hoū.
बहुबिधि बिनय कीन्हि तेहि काला । प्रगटेउ प्रभु कौतुकी कृपाला ॥
bahubidhi binaya kīnhi tehi kālā, pragaṭeu prabhu kautukī kṛpālā.
प्रभु बिलोकि मुनि नयन जुड़ाने । होइहि काजु हिएँ हरषाने ॥
prabhu biloki muni nayana juṛāne, hoihi kāju hiem̐ haraṣāne.
अति आरति कहि कथा सुनाई । करहु कृपा करि होहु सहाई ॥
ati ārati kahi kathā sunāī, karahu kṛpā kari hohu sahāī.
आपन रूप देहु प्रभु मोही । आन भाँति नहिं पावौं ओही ॥
āpana rūpa dehu prabhu mohī, āna bhām̐ti nahiṁ pāvauṁ ohī.
जेहि बिधि नाथ होइ हित मोरा । करहु सो बेगि दास मैं तोरा ॥
jehi bidhi nātha hoi hita morā, karahu so begi dāsa maiṁ torā.
निज माया बल देखि बिसाला । हियँ हँसि बोले दीनदयाला ॥
nija māyā bala dekhi bisālā, hiyam̐ ham̐si bole dīnadayālā.

Trans:

I will ask Harī for the gift of beauty; in going to him there will be much delay; but I have no other such friend, and this is an opportunity for him to help me." So he offered up a fervent prayer and the merciful Lord appeared to him in a vision. The saint's eyes brightened at the sight and he rejoiced in heart, saying: 'My object will be accomplished.' He then with the utmost humility told his tale, and added: "O my Lord, be gracious and assist me. Bestow on me a beauty equal to yours, for in no other way will I be able to get possession of this girl. Make haste to accomplish my success, for lo, I am your slave." When the Compassionate saw the mighty influence of the deception he had wrought, he smiled to himself and then said:

दोहा-dohā:

जेहि बिधि होइहि परम हित नारद सुनहु तुम्हार ।
jehi bidhi hoihi parama hita nārada sunahu tumhāra,
सोइ हम करब न आन कछु बचन न मृषा हमार ॥१३२॥
soi hama karaba na āna kachu bacana na mṛṣā hamāra. 132.

Trans:

"Hear, O Nārad; I will assuredly bring about your highest good—that and naught else; nor shall my words prove vain.

चौपाई-caupāī:

कुपथ माग रुज ब्याकुल रोगी । बैद न देइ सुनहु मुनि जोगी ॥
kupatha māga ruja byākula rogī, baida na dei sunahu muni jogī.
एहि बिधि हित तुम्हार मैं ठयऊ । कहि अस अंतरहित प्रभु भयऊ ॥
ehi bidhi hita tumhāra maiṁ ṭhayaū, kahi asa aṁtarahita prabhu bhayaū.
माया बिबस भए मुनि मूढ़ा । समुझी नहिं हरि गिरा निगूढ़ा ॥
māyā bibasa bhae muni mūṛhā, samujhī nahiṁ hari girā nigūṛhā.
गवने तुरत तहाँ रिषिराई । जहाँ स्वयंबर भूमि बनाई ॥
gavane turata tahām̐ riṣirāī, jahām̐ svayaṁbara bhūmi banāī.
निज निज आसन बैठे राजा । बहु बनाव करि सहित समाजा ॥
nija nija āsana baiṭhe rājā, bahu banāva kari sahita samājā.
मुनि मन हरष रूप अति मोरें । मोहि तजि आनहि बरिहि न भोरें ॥
muni mana haraṣa rūpa ati moreṁ, mohi taji ānahi barihi na bhoreṁ.
मुनि हित कारन कृपानिधाना । दीन्ह कुरूप न जाइ बखाना ॥
muni hita kārana kṛpānidhānā, dīnha kurūpa na jāi bakhānā.
सो चरित्र लखि काहुँ न पावा । नारद जानि सबहिं सिर नावा ॥
so caritra lakhi kāhum̐ na pāvā, nārada jāni sabahiṁ sira nāvā.

Trans:

If a sick man in the weariness of disease ask for what will harm him, mark me, holy ascetic, the physician will not grant it. In the same way will I act, as is best for you." So saying the Lord vanished. The saint was so demented by the power of the delusion that he did not understand Harī's hidden meaning, but hastened at once to the spot where the marriage arena had been prepared. The Rajas were seated rank upon rank, each with his retinue, in grand attire. The saint thought joyfully within himself: 'My beauty is such that she will never leave me to wed another.' In fact the merciful God, the saint's true friend, had made him hideous beyond all description. Everyone recognized him as Nārad and bowed the head, knowing nothing of what had taken place.

दोहा-dohā:

रहे तहाँ दुइ रुद्र गन ते जानहिं सब भेउ ।
rahe tahāṁ dui rudra gana te jānahiṁ saba bheu,
बिप्रबेष देखत फिरहिं परम कौतुकी तेउ ॥ १३३॥
biprabeṣa dekhata phirahiṁ parama kautukī teu. 133.

Trans:

Now there were there two of Shiva's attendants who knew the whole secret. Dressed like Brahmins, they seemed to be spectators of the show, walking here and there and looking about.

चौपाई-caupāī:

जेहिं समाज बैठे मुनि जाई । हृदयँ रूप अहमिति अधिकाई ॥
jehiṁ samāja baiṭhe muni jāī, hṛdayaṁ rūpa ahamiti adhikāī.
तहँ बैठ महेस गन दोऊ । बिप्रबेष गति लखइ न कोऊ ॥
tahaṁ baiṭha mahesa gana doū, biprabeṣa gati lakhai na koū.
करहिं कूटि नारदहि सुनाई । नीकि दीन्हि हरि सुंदरताई ॥
karahiṁ kūṭi nāradahi sunāī, nīki dīnhi hari suṁdaratāī.
रीझिहि राजकुअँरि छबि देखी । इन्हहि बरिहि हरि जानि बिसेषी ॥
rījhihi rājakuaṁri chabi dekhī, inhahi barihi hari jāni biseṣī.
मुनिहि मोह मन हाथ पराएँ । हँसहिं संभु गन अति सचु पाएँ ॥
munihi moha mana hātha parāeṁ, haṁsahiṁ saṁbhu gana ati sacu pāeṁ.
जदपि सुनहिं मुनि अटपटि बानी । समुझि न परइ बुद्धि भ्रम सानी ॥
jadapi sunahiṁ muni aṭapaṭi bānī, samujhi na parai buddhi bhrama sānī.
काहुँ न लखा सो चरित बिसेषा । सो सरूप नृपकन्याँ देखा ॥
kāhuṁ na lakhā so carita biseṣā, so sarūpa nṛpakanyāṁ dekhā.
मर्कट बदन भयंकर देही । देखत हृदयँ क्रोध भा तेही ॥
markaṭa badana bhayaṁkara dehī, dekhata hṛdayaṁ krodha bhā tehī.

Trans:

Both went and sat down in the same group with the saint, so proud of his beauty; and in their Brahminical attire they attracted no notice. They spoke in jest so that Nārad might hear: "Harī has given this man such excellent beauty that the princess will be charmed with his appearance and will certainly wed him, taking him for Harī himself." The saint was so utterly subjugated by passion that Shambhu's servants could laugh and jeer as much as they liked, and though he heard their mockery, his intellect was too bewildered to understand it. No one present saw what was going on save only the princess who, on beholding him just as he was—with his monkey face and deformed body—and was quite disgusted at the sight.

दोहा-dohā:

सखीं संग लै कुअँरि तब चलि जनु राजमराल ।
sakhīṁ saṁga lai kuaṁri taba cali janu rājamarāla,
देखत फिरइ महीप सब कर सरोज जयमाल ॥ १३४॥
dekhata phirai mahīpa saba kara saroja jayamāla. 134.

Trans:

Then with her handmaids she glided like a swan through the long line of kings with the wreath of victory in her lotus hands.

चौपाई-caupāī:

जेहि दिसि बैठे नारद फूली । सो दिसि तेहिं न बिलोकी भूली ॥
jehi disi baiṭhe nārada phūlī, so disi tehiṁ na bilokī bhūlī.
पुनि पुनि मुनि उकसहिं अकुलाहीं । देखि दसा हर गन मुसुकाहीं ॥
puni puni muni ukasahiṁ akulāhīṁ, dekhi dasā hara gana musukāhīṁ.
धरि नृपतनु तहँ गयउ कृपाला । कुअँरि हरषि मेलेउ जयमाला ॥
dhari nṛpatanu tahaṁ gayau kṛpālā, kuaṁri haraṣi meleu jayamālā.
दुलहिनि लै गे लच्छिनिवासा । नृपसमाज सब भयउ निरासा ॥
dulahini lai ge lacchinivāsā, nṛpasamāja saba bhayau nirāsā.
मुनि अति बिकल मोहँ मति नाठी । मनि गिरि गई छूटि जनु गाँठी ॥
muni ati bikala mohaṁ mati nāṭhī, mani giri gaī chūṭi janu gāṁṭhī.
तब हर गन बोले मुसुकाई । निज मुख मुकुर बिलोकहु जाई ॥
taba hara gana bole musukāī, nija mukha mukura bilokahu jāī.
अस कहि दोउ भागे भयँ भारी । बदन दीख मुनि बारि निहारी ॥
asa kahi dou bhāge bhayaṁ bhārī, badana dīkha muni bāri nihārī.
बेषु बिलोकि क्रोध अति बाढ़ा । तिन्हहि सराप दीन्ह अति गाढ़ा ॥
beṣu biloki krodha ati bāṛhā, tinhahi sarāpa dīnha ati gāṛhā.

Trans:

She would not let her eyes rest for a moment on the spot where Nārad was sitting in his pride. The saint in his anxiety kept fidgeting about, and Shiva's attendants smiled to see the state in which he was. Then entered the Compassionate Lord in form as a king, and gladly the princess cast on him the victory garland. And thus Lakshmī's Lord carried off his bride to the despair of the assembled kings. The saint was much disturbed; in his infatuation his reason was quite gone, as if a diamond had dropped out of a hole in his bag. Then Shiva's attendants said with a smile, "Go find a mirror and look at yourself"; and having said so, both ran away in great fright, afraid of the consequence. The saint looked at his reflection in the water. When he saw himself he was furious and condemned those two with a grievous curse:

दोहा-dohā:

होहु निसाचर जाइ तुम्ह कपटी पापी दोउ ।
hohu nisācara jāi tumha kapaṭī pāpī dou,
हँसेहु हमहि सो लेहु फल बहुरि हँसेहु मुनि कोउ ॥ १३५॥
haṁsehu hamahi so lehu phala bahuri haṁsehu muni kou. 135.

Trans:

"Go, false and guilty pair, and take birth as demons of the night. Be this your reward for mocking me; mock again a saint, if you dare."

चौपाई-caupāī:

पुनि जल दीख रूप निज पावा । तदपि हृदयँ संतोष न आवा ॥
puni jala dīkha rūpa nija pāvā, tadapi hṛdayaṁ saṁtoṣa na āvā.
फरकत अधर कोप मन माहीं । सपदी चले कमलापति पाहीं ॥
pharakata adhara kopa mana māhīṁ, sapadī cale kamalāpati pāhīṁ.
देहउँ श्राप कि मरिहउँ जाई । जगत मोरि उपहास कराई ॥
dehauṁ śrāpa ki marihauṁ jāī, jagata mori upahāsa karāī.
बीचहिं पंथ मिले दनुजारी । संग रमा सोइ राजकुमारी ॥
bīcahiṁ paṁtha mile danujārī, saṁga ramā soi rājakumārī.
बोले मधुर बचन सुरसाईं । मुनि कहँ चले बिकल की नाईं ॥
bole madhura bacana surasāīṁ, muni kahaṁ cale bikala kī nāīṁ.
सुनत बचन उपजा अति क्रोधा । माया बस न रहा मन बोधा ॥
sunata bacana upajā ati krodhā, māyā basa na rahā mana bodhā.
पर संपदा सकहु नहिं देखी । तुम्हरें इरिषा कपट बिसेषी ॥
para saṁpadā sakahu nahiṁ dekhī, tumhareṁ iriṣā kapaṭa biseṣī.
मथत सिंधु रुद्रहि बौरायहु । सुरन्ह प्रेरि बिष पान करायहु ॥
mathata siṁdhu rudrahi baurāyahu, suranha preri biṣa pāna karāyahu.

Trans:

Looking again in the water again he saw himself in his proper form. But still he was not content at heart, and his lips quivered with rage, and in haste he went to meet Vishnu thinking, 'Shall I curse him to death or die myself, seeing that he has made mock of me throughout the world?' On the way the Terror of the Demons met him, and with him was Ramā, the princess. With a smile and in gentle tones he asked, "Where goes the saint, like one so distracted?" On hearing these words, his anger rose and infatuation utterly mastered his reason: "You never could bear to look upon another's prosperity; your envy and deceit are notorious. At the churning of the ocean you drove Shiva mad and, inciting him through the gods, made him quaff the poisoned cup.

दोहा-dohā:

असुर सुरा बिष संकरहि आपु रमा मनि चारु ।
asura surā biṣa saṁkarahi āpu ramā mani cāru,
स्वारथ साधक कुटिल तुम्ह सदा कपट ब्यवहारु ॥१३६॥
svāratha sādhaka kuṭila tumha sadā kapaṭa byavahāru. 136.

Trans:

Intoxicating liquor was the demon's share; and the poison was for Mahādev; and yet for yourself you kept Ramā and the Kaustubh jewel! You have ever been so selfish and perverse and treacherous in your dealings.

चौपाई-caupāī:

परम स्वतंत्र न सिर पर कोई । भावइ मनहि करहु तुम्ह सोई ॥
parama svataṁtra na sira para koī, bhāvai manahi karahu tumha soī.
भलेहि मंद मंदेहि भल करहू । बिसमय हरष न हियँ कछु धरहू ॥
bhalehi maṁda maṁdehi bhala karahū, bisamaya haraṣa na hiyaṁ kachu dharahū.
डहकि डहकि परिचेहु सब काहू । अति असंक मन सदा उछाहू ॥
ḍahaki ḍahaki paricehu saba kāhū, ati asaṁka mana sadā uchāhū.
करम सुभासुभ तुम्हहि न बाधा । अब लगि तुम्हहि न काहूँ साधा ॥
karama subhāsubha tumhahi na bādhā, aba lagi tumhahi na kāhūṁ sādhā.
भले भवन अब बायन दीन्हा । पावहुगे फल आपन कीन्हा ॥
bhale bhavana aba bāyana dīnhā, pāvahuge phala āpana kīnhā.
बंचेहु मोहि जवनि धरि देहा । सोइ तनु धरहु श्राप मम एहा ॥
baṁcehu mohi javani dhari dehā, soi tanu dharahu śrāpa mama ehā.
कपि आकृति तुम्ह कीन्हि हमारी । करिहहिं कीस सहाय तुम्हारी ॥
kapi ākṛti tumha kīnhi hamārī, karihahiṁ kīsa sahāya tumhārī.
मम अपकार कीन्ह तुम्ह भारी । नारि बिरहँ तुम्ह होब दुखारी ॥
mama apakāra kīnha tumha bhārī, nāri birahaṁ tumha hoba dukhārī.

Trans:

Utterly self-willed, with no one over you, and bent on doing whatever comes into your mind, confounding the good and exalting the bad, and with a heart incapable either of pleasure or surprise, you ply everyone with your tricks without the slightest consideration and in mere lightness of heart. Neither good deeds nor bad in any way affect you, nor has anyone up to the present ever succeeded in restraining you. Now for this fine treat that you have given me you shall receive a due return. Be born in the form in which you have now imposed upon me—this is my curse. And as you have made me like a monkey, you shall have monkeys for helpmates; and in the same way as you have sorely wronged me, so shall you be in distress for the loss of your wife."

दोहा-dohā:

श्राप सीस धरि हरषि हियँ प्रभु बहु बिनती कीन्हि ।
śrāpa sīsa dhari harași hiyaṁ prabhu bahu binatī kīnhi,
निज माया कै प्रबलता करषि कृपानिधि लीन्हि ॥१३७॥
nija māyā kai prabalatā karași kṛpānidhi līnhi. 137.

Trans:

The Lord gladly accepted the curse, thus working the will of the gods, and in his compassion withdrew the influence of his deceptive power.

चौपाई-caupāī:

जब हरि माया दूरि निवारी । नहिं तहँ रमा न राजकुमारी ॥
jaba hari māyā dūri nivārī, nahiṁ tahaṁ ramā na rājakumārī.
तब मुनि अति सभीत हरि चरना । गहे पाहि प्रनतारति हरना ॥
taba muni ati sabhīta hari caranā, gahe pāhi pranatārati haranā.
मृषा होउ मम श्राप कृपाला । मम इच्छा कह दीनदयाला ॥
mṛṣā hou mama śrāpa kṛpālā, mama icchā kaha dīnadayālā.
मैं दुर्बचन कहे बहुतेरे । कह मुनि पाप मिटिहिं किमि मेरे ॥
maiṁ durbacana kahe bahutere, kaha muni pāpa miṭihiṁ kimi mere.
जपहु जाइ संकर सत नामा । होइहि हृदयँ तुरत बिश्रामा ॥
japahu jāi saṁkara sata nāmā, hoihi hṛdayaṁ turata biśrāmā.
कोउ नहिं सिव समान प्रिय मोरें । असि परतीति तजहु जनि भोरें ॥
kou nahiṁ siva samāna priya moreṁ, asi paratīti tajahu jani bhoreṁ.
जेहि पर कृपा न करहिं पुरारी । सो न पाव मुनि भगति हमारी ॥
jehi para kṛpā na karahiṁ purārī, so na pāva muni bhagati hamārī.
अस उर धरि महि बिचरहु जाई । अब न तुम्हहि माया निअराई ॥
asa ura dhari mahi bicarahu jāī, aba na tumhahi māyā niarāī.

Trans:

With that removed, there appeared neither Ramā nor the princess; and the saint fell in great fear at the feet of Harī—who is ever ready to heal the sorrows of a suppliant—crying: "May my curse be made of no effect." Said the gracious God, "It was my will." Said the saint, "I have spoken many injurious words; how shall my guilt be expiated?" "Go and repeat Shankar's hundred names, and your soul will at once be relieved. There is no one so dear to me as Shiva; never let your faith in this truth be shaken. He on whom Shiva will not show mercy shall never know true love to me. Think on this as you wander over the earth; the delusion haunts you no longer."

दोहा-dohā:

बहुबिधि मुनिहि प्रबोधि प्रभु तब भए अंतरधान ।
bahubidhi munihi prabodhi prabhu taba bhae aṁtaradhāna,
सत्यलोक नारद चले करत राम गुन गान ॥१३८॥
satyaloka nārada cale karata rāma guna gāna. 138.

Trans:

Having thus reassured the saint, the Lord disappeared, and Nārad took his way to Paradise chanting Rāma's praises as he went.

चौपाई-caupāī:

हर गन मुनिहि जात पथ देखी । बिगतमोह मन हरष बिसेषी ॥
hara gana munihi jāta patha dekhī, bigatamoha mana haraṣa biseṣī.
अति सभीत नारद पहिं आए । गहि पद आरत बचन सुनाए ॥
ati sabhīta nārada pahiṁ āe, gahi pada ārata bacana sunāe.
हर गन हम न बिप्र मुनिराया । बड़ अपराध कीन्ह फल पाया ॥
hara gana hama na bipra munirāyā, baṛa aparādha kīnha phala pāyā.
श्राप अनुग्रह करहु कृपाला । बोले नारद दीनदयाला ॥
śrāpa anugraha karahu kṛpālā, bole nārada dīnadayālā.
निसिचर जाइ होहु तुम्ह दोऊ । बैभव बिपुल तेज बल होऊ ॥
nisicara jāi hohu tumha doū, baibhava bipula teja bala hoū.
भुजबल बिस्व जितब तुम्ह जहिआ । धरिहहिं बिष्नु मनुज तनु तहिआ ॥
bhujabala bisva jitaba tumha jahiā, dharihahiṁ biṣnu manuja tanu tahiā,
समर मरन हरि हाथ तुम्हारा । होइहहु मुकुत न पुनि संसारा ॥
samara marana hari hātha tumhārā, hoihahu mukuta na puni saṁsārā.
चले जुगल मुनि पद सिर नाई । भए निसाचर कालहि पाई ॥
cale jugala muni pada sira nāī, bhae nisācara kālahi pāī.

Trans:

Shiva's two followers saw him on the road rejoicing and in his right mind now. In great alarm they drew near and clasping his feet made their supplication: "O great saint, we are not Brahmins, but servants of Mahādev and have reaped the fruit of our great sin; in your mercy please remove our curse." Said the compassionate Nārad: "You must both be born as demons of great power, majesty, and strength; but when you have subdued the universe by the might of your arm, Vishnu shall take upon him a human form, and then dying in battle at his hands you shall attain to salvation and never be born again." After bowing their heads at his feet, both went their way and in due course were born as demons.

दोहा-dohā:

एक कलप एहि हेतु प्रभु लीन्ह मनुज अवतार।
eka kalapa ehi hetu prabhu līnha manuja avatāra,
सुर रंजन सज्जन सुखद हरि भंजन भुबि भार ॥१३९॥
sura raṁjana sajjana sukhada hari bhaṁjana bhubi bhāra. 139.

Trans:

So in one age this was the reason why the Lord became incarnate to gladden the gods, to comfort the saints, and to ease earth of her burdens.

चौपाई-caupāī:

एहि बिधि जनम करम हरि केरे। सुंदर सुखद बिचित्र घनेरे ॥
ehi bidhi janama karama hari kere, suṁdara sukhada bicitra ghanere.
कलप कलप प्रति प्रभु अवतरहीं। चारु चरित नानाबिधि करहीं ॥
kalapa kalapa prati prabhu avatarahīṁ, cāru carita nānābidhi karahīṁ.
तब तब कथा मुनीसन्ह गाई। परम पुनीत प्रबंध बनाई ॥
taba taba kathā munīsanha gāī, parama punīta prabaṁdha banāī.
बिबिध प्रसंग अनूप बखाने। करहिं न सुनि आचरजु सयाने ॥
bibidha prasaṁga anūpa bakhāne, karahiṁ na suni ācaraju sayāne.
हरि अनंत हरिकथा अनंता। कहहिं सुनहिं बहुबिधि सब संता ॥
hari anaṁta harikathā anaṁtā, kahahiṁ sunahiṁ bahubidhi saba saṁtā.
रामचंद्र के चरित सुहाए। कलप कोटि लगि जाहिं न गाए ॥
rāmacaṁdra ke carita suhāe, kalapa koṭi lagi jāhiṁ na gāe.
यह प्रसंग मैं कहा भवानी। हरिमायाँ मोहहिं मुनि ग्यानी ॥
yaha prasaṁga maiṁ kahā bhavānī, harimāyāṁ mohahiṁ muni gyānī.
प्रभु कौतुकी प्रनत हितकारी। सेवत सुलभ सकल दुख हारी ॥
prabhu kautukī pranata hitakārī, sevata sulabha sakala dukha hārī.

Trans:

Thus Harī's births and actions are many and various, but all of them beneficent and glorious. In every Age he has manifested himself and wrought many excellent works; and on each occasion great saints have sung his acts in holy strains of choicest verses, relating marvelous histories of diverse kinds, which the wise hear without any surprise. For as Harī is without end, so are there endless verses about him, which are heard and repeated by scripture and the faithful. The delightful adventures of Rāmachandra could not all be sung in a myriad Ages. This story that I have now told, O Bhawānī, shows how Harī's deceptive power can infatuate even the sages and saints. He, the Lord, is sportive, gracious to suppliants, accessible to his servants, and a remover of all sorrows.

सोरठा-soraṭhā:

सुर नर मुनि कोउ नाहिं जेहि न मोह माया प्रबल।
sura nara muni kou nāhiṁ jehi na moha māyā prabala,
अस बिचारि मन माहिं भजिअ महामाया पतिहि ॥१४०॥
asa bicāri mana māhiṁ bhajia mahāmāyā patihi. 140.

Trans:

There is neither god, man, nor saint who has not become infatuated by Māyā's sway. Reflect upon this dear and worship the great master of Māyā.

चौपाई-caupāī:

अपर हेतु सुनु सैलकुमारी। कहउँ बिचित्र कथा बिस्तारी ॥
apara hetu sunu sailakumārī, kahauṁ bicitra kathā bistārī.
जेहि कारन अज अगुन अरूपा। ब्रह्म भयउ कोसलपुर भूपा ॥
jehi kārana aja aguna arūpā, brahma bhayau kosalapura bhūpā.
जो प्रभु बिपिन फिरत तुम्ह देखा। बंधु समेत धरें मुनिबेषा ॥
jo prabhu bipina phirata tumha dekhā, baṁdhu sameta dhareṁ munibeṣā.
जासु चरित अवलोकि भवानी। सती सरीर रहिहु बौरानी ॥
jāsu carita avaloki bhavānī, satī sarīra rahihu baurānī.
अजहुँ न छाया मिटति तुम्हारी। तासु चरित सुनु भ्रम रुज हारी ॥
ajahuṁ na chāyā miṭati tumhārī, tāsu carita sunu bhrama ruja hārī.
लीला कीन्हि जो तेहिं अवतारा। सो सब कहिहउँ मति अनुसारा ॥
līlā kīnhi jo tehiṁ avatārā, so saba kahihauṁ mati anusārā.
भरद्वाज सुनि संकर बानी। सकुचि सप्रेम उमा मुसुकानी ॥
bharadvāja suni saṁkara bānī, sakuci saprema umā musukānī.
लगे बहुरि बरनै बृषकेतू। सो अवतार भयउ जेहि हेतू ॥
lage bahuri baranai bṛṣaketū, so avatāra bhayau jehi hetū.

Trans:

Hear, O daughter of the Himalaya, a second reason, which I will proceed to relate at full length, why the uncreated, the passionless, the incomparable Brahmm became King of Kaushal. The Lord, whom you saw roaming in the forest with his brother in hermit's attire—at whose doings, O Bhawānī, you in Sati's form lost your senses, and still to this day have a touch of the disease—the recital of his adventures will heal all your malady. All his sportive acts in that incarnation I am now about to tell as best as I can." O Bharadvāja, on hearing Shankar thus speak, the modest and affectionate Umā smiled for joy, while her Lord began to relate the cause of the Lord-God's descent on that occasion.

दोहा-dohā:

सो मैं तुम्ह सन कहउँ सबु सुनु मुनीस मन लाइ।
so maiṁ tumha sana kahauṁ sabu sunu munīsa mana lāi,
राम कथा कलि मल हरनि मंगल करनि सुहाइ ॥१४१॥
rāma kathā kali mala harani maṁgala karani suhāi. 141.

Trans:

I now proceed to tell you all about it, O Bharadvāja; listen with attention to the delightful story of Rāma, which is most charming and cleanses all the worldy stains.

चौपाई-caupāī:

स्वायंभू मनु अरु सतरूपा। जिन्ह तें भै नरसृष्टि अनूपा ॥
svāyaṁbhū manu aru satarūpā, jinha teṁ bhai narasṛṣṭi anūpā.
दंपति धरम आचरन नीका। अजहुँ गाव श्रुति जिन्ह कै लीका ॥
daṁpati dharama ācarana nīkā, ajahuṁ gāva śruti jinha kai līkā.
नृप उत्तानपाद सुत तासू। ध्रुव हरि भगत भयउ सुत जासू ॥
nṛpa uttānapāda suta tāsū, dhruva hari bhagata bhayau suta jāsū.
लघु सुत नाम प्रियब्रत ताही। बेद पुरान प्रसंसहि जाही ॥
laghu suta nāma priyabrata tāhī, beda purāna prasaṁsahi jāhī.
देवहूति पुनि तासु कुमारी। जो मुनि कर्दम कै प्रिय नारी ॥
devahūti puni tāsu kumārī, jo muni kardama kai priya nārī.
आदिदेव प्रभु दीनदयाला। जठर धरेउ जेहिं कपिल कृपाला ॥
ādideva prabhu dīnadayālā, jaṭhara dhareu jehiṁ kapila kṛpālā.
सांख्य सास्त्र जिन्ह प्रगट बखाना। तत्व बिचार निपुन भगवाना ॥
sāṁkhya sāstra jinha pragaṭa bakhānā, tatva bicāra nipuna bhagavānā.
तेहिं मनु राज कीन्ह बहु काला। प्रभु आयसु सब बिधि प्रतिपाला ॥
tehiṁ manu rāja kīnha bahu kālā, prabhu āyasu saba bidhi pratipālā.

Trans:

Swayambhu Manu had Shatrupā as wife—of them was born this human race, peerless in God's creation—and even to this day the fame of their virtue and conjugal fidelity is celebrated in the scriptures. Their son was King Uttān-pād, who begot Harī's faithful client Dhruva. The younger son, by name Priya-vratt, is mentioned with praise both by the Vedas and Purānas. Their daughter, Devahuti, became the devoted wife of Saint Kardam, and in her womb the eternal Lord God, in his mercy and compassion, planted Kapil, the author of the Samkhya philosophy, the divine exponent of the theory of entities. Thus Manu reigned a long while, keeping all god's commandments.

सोरठा-soraṭhā:

होइ न बिषय बिराग भवन बसत भा चौथपन ।
hoi na biṣaya birāga bhavana basata bhā cauthapana,
हृदयँ बहुत दुख लाग जनम गयउ हरिभगति बिनु ॥ १४२॥
hṛdayaṁ bahuta dukha lāga janama gayau haribhagati binu. 142.

Trans:

But in a palace complete detachment from the senses is impracticable. Old age came upon him and he thought with grief, 'Alas, my life has been wasted away with no true devotion to Harī.'

चौपाई-caupāī:

बरबस राज सुतहि तब दीन्हा । नारि समेत गवन बन कीन्हा ॥
barabasa rāja sutahi taba dīnhā, nāri sameta gavana bana kīnhā.
तीरथ बर नैमिष बिख्याता । अति पुनीत साधक सिधि दाता ॥
tīratha bara naimiṣa bikhyātā, ati punīta sādhaka sidhi dātā.
बसहिं तहाँ मुनि सिद्ध समाजा । तहँ हियँ हरषि चलेउ मनु राजा ॥
basahiṁ tahāṁ muni siddha samājā, tahaṁ hiyaṁ haraṣi caleu manu rājā.
पंथ जात सोहहिं मतिधीरा । ग्यान भगति जनु धरें सरीरा ॥
paṁtha jāta sohahiṁ matidhīrā, gyāna bhagati janu dhareṁ sarīrā.
पहुँचे जाइ धेनुमति तीरा । हरषि नहाने निरमल नीरा ॥
pahuṁce jāi dhenumati tīrā, haraṣi nahāne niramala nīrā.
आए मिलन सिद्ध मुनि ग्यानी । धरम धुरंधर नृपरिषि जानी ॥
āe milana siddha muni gyānī, dharama dhuraṁdhara nṛpariṣi jānī.
जहँ जहँ तीरथ रहे सुहाए । मुनिन्ह सकल सादर करवाए ॥
jahaṁ jahaṁ tīratha rahe suhāe, muninha sakala sādara karavāe.
कृस सरीर मुनिपट परिधाना । सत समाज नित सुनहिं पुराना ॥
kṛsa sarīra munipaṭa paridhānā, sata samāja nita sunahiṁ purānā.

Trans:

Then he resigned the throne and thrust it upon his son, and then along with his queen he repaired to the forest, to Naimish, famous among all holy places as specially sacred and bounteous of success. Glad of heart, King Manu sought the spot where dwelt the company of saints and sages; and as the resolute pair passed along the way they seemed incarnations of Wisdom and Faith. On reaching the bank of the Gomati, they bathed with delight in the clear stream; and there the inspired saints and sages came to meet them, recognizing in the king a champion of religion. Devoutly they took them to visit each different shrine, and with emaciated body, clad in hermit's robes, they were ever in the assembly of the faithfuls listening to the holy Purānas.

दोहा-dohā:

द्वादस अच्छर मंत्र पुनि जपहिं सहित अनुराग ।
dvādasa acchara maṁtra puni japahiṁ sahita anurāga,
बासुदेव पद पंकरुह दंपति मन अति लाग ॥ १४३॥
bāsudeva pada paṁkaruha daṁpati mana ati lāga. 143.

Trans:

Devoutly repeating the twelve-lettered Mantra, and with their souls directed to the lotus feet of Vasudeva, the all-pervading Vishnu;

चौपाई-caupāī:

करहिं अहार साक फल कंदा । सुमिरहिं ब्रह्म सच्चिदानंदा ॥
karahiṁ ahāra sāka phala kaṁdā, sumirahiṁ brahma saccidānaṁdā.
पुनि हरि हेतु करन तप लागे । बारि अधार मूल फल त्यागे ॥
puni hari hetu karana tapa lāge, bāri adhāra mūla phala tyāge.
उर अभिलाष निरंतर होई । देखिअ नयन परम प्रभु सोई ॥
ura abhilāṣa niraṁtara hoī, dekhia nayana parama prabhu soī.
अगुन अखंड अनंत अनादी । जेहि चिंतहिं परमारथबादी ॥
aguna akhaṁḍa anaṁta anādī, jehi ciṁtahiṁ paramārathabādī.
नेति नेति जेहि बेद निरूपा । निजानंद निरुपाधि अनूपा ॥
neti neti jehi beda nirūpā, nijānaṁda nirupādhi anūpā.
संभु बिरंचि बिष्नु भगवाना । उपजहिं जासु अंस तें नाना ॥
saṁbhu biraṁci biṣnu bhagavānā, upajahiṁ jāsu aṁsa teṁ nānā.
ऐसेउ प्रभु सेवक बस अहई । भगत हेतु लीलातनु गहई ॥
aiseu prabhu sevaka basa ahaī, bhagata hetu līlātanu gahaī.
जौं यह बचन सत्य श्रुति भाषा । तौ हमार पूजिहि अभिलाषा ॥
jauṁ yaha bacana satya śruti bhāṣā, tau hamāra pūjihi abhilāṣā.

Trans:

meditating on the Supreme Brahmm, they lived on leaves and fruits and roots. Then doing penance for Harī as before they give up even roots and fruits for water alone. In their heart was an endless craving: "O that we might see with our eyes the very God, without parts or passions; without beginning or end; whom the preachers of salvation contemplate; whom the Vedas define as the unutterable, the pure spirit without attributes and beyond all comparisons; as parts of whom are produced in various forms the lords Shambhu, Brahmmā, and Vishnu. Yet, so great a god, submits to his own servants; and for their sake assumes in sport a material body. If this be true—as the scriptures have declared—our desire will of assuredly be accomplished."

दोहा-dohā:

एहि बिधि बीते बरष षट सहस बारि आहार ।
ehi bidhi bīte baraṣa ṣaṭa sahasa bāri āhāra,
संबत सप्त सहस्र पुनि रहे समीर अधार ॥ १४४॥
saṁbata sapta sahasra puni rahe samīra adhāra. 144.

Trans:

In this way they spent six thousand years living just on water; and then seven thousand living on air alone.

चौपाई-caupāī:

बरष सहस दस त्यागेउ सोऊ । ठाढ़े रहे एक पद दोऊ ॥
baraṣa sahasa dasa tyāgeu soū, ṭhāṛhe rahe eka pada doū.
बिधि हरि हर तप देखि अपारा । मनु समीप आए बहु बारा ॥
bidhi hari hara tapa dekhi apārā, manu samīpa āe bahu bārā.
मागहु बर बहु भाँति लोभाए । परम धीर नहिं चलहिं चलाए ॥
māgahu bara bahu bhāṁti lobhāe, parama dhīra nahiṁ calahiṁ calāe.
अस्थिमात्र होइ रहे सरीरा । तदपि मनाग मनहिं नहिं पीरा ॥
asthimātra hoi rahe sarīrā, tadapi manāga manahiṁ nahiṁ pīrā.
प्रभु सर्बग्य दास निज जानी । गति अनन्य तापस नृप रानी ॥
prabhu sarbagya dāsa nija jānī, gati ananya tāpasa nṛpa rānī.
मागु मागु बरु भै नभ बानी । परम गभीर कृपामृत सानी ॥
māgu māgu baru bhai nabha bānī, parama gabhīra kṛpāmṛta sānī.
मृतक जिआवनि गिरा सुहाई । श्रवन रंध्र होइ उर जब आई ॥
mṛtaka jiāvani girā suhāī, śravana raṁdhra hoi ura jaba āī.
हृष्टपुष्ट तन भए सुहाए । मानहुँ अबहिं भवन ते आए ॥

hṛṣṭapuṣṭa tana bhae suhāe, mānahuṁ abahiṁ bhavana te āe.

Trans:

Then for ten thousand years they gave up all and remained both standing on one leg. Now Brahmmā, Harī, and Hara saw this interminable penance and repeatedly came near to Manu and tempted him saying, "Ask your boon," yet for all their persuasion he was too steadfast to move. Though the body was reduced to a skeleton there was not the least pain in their soul. Then the Omniscient Lord knew that the king and queen were his servants and had just a single object in practicing such austerities. A solemn voice full of ambrosial grace sounded in the sky, saying "Ask, Ask"—a voice so enchanting it would wake the dead. As it dropped upon the ears of their soul, their bodies became again as comely and sturdy as if they had only that day left their home.

दोहा-dohā:

श्रवन सुधा सम बचन सुनि पुलक प्रफुल्लित गात ।
śravana sudhā sama bacana suni pulaka praphullita gāta,
बोले मनु करि दंडवत प्रेम न हृदयँ समात ॥ १४५॥
bole manu kari daṁḍavata prema na hṛdayaṁ samāta. 145.

Trans:

As the ambrosial voice rung in their ears, their body quivered, and thrilled; and falling on the ground in an irrepressible transport of love, Manu thusly spoke:

चौपाई-caupāī:

सुनु सेवक सुरतरु सुरधेनू । बिधि हरि हर बंदित पद रेनू ॥
sunu sevaka surataru suradhenū, bidhi hari hara baṁdita pada renū.
सेवत सुलभ सकल सुख दायक । प्रनतपाल सचराचर नायक ॥
sevata sulabha sakala sukha dāyaka, pranatapāla sacarācara nāyaka.
जौं अनाथ हित हम पर नेहू । तौ प्रसन्न होइ यह बर देहू ॥
jauṁ anātha hita hama para nehū, tau prasanna hoi yaha bara dehū.
जो सरूप बस सिव मन माहीं । जेहि कारन मुनि जतन कराहीं ॥
jo sarūpa basa siva mana māhīṁ, jehi kārana muni jatana karāhīṁ.
जो भुसुंडि मन मानस हंसा । सगुन अगुन जेहि निगम प्रसंसा ॥
jo bhusuṁḍi mana mānasa haṁsā, saguna aguna jehi nigama prasaṁsā.
देखहिं हम सो रूप भरि लोचन । कृपा करहु प्रनतारति मोचन ॥
dekhahiṁ hama so rūpa bhari locana, kṛpā karahu pranatārati mocana.
दंपति बचन परम प्रिय लागे । मुदुल बिनीत प्रेम रस पागे ॥
daṁpati bacana parama priya lāge, mudula binīta prema rasa pāge.
भगत बछल प्रभु कृपानिधाना । बिस्वबास प्रगटे भगवाना ॥
bhagata bachala prabhu kṛpānidhānā, bisvabāsa pragaṭe bhagavānā.

Trans:

"Hearken, O thou that art as the tree of paradise or the sacred cow to thy servants; the dust on whose feet is ever worshipped by Brahmmā, Harī, and Hara; accessible to the faithful; bounteous of all good; protector of suppliants; Lord of all creation; if, O friend of the friendless, I have found favor in thy sight, then in thy mercy grant me this boon: Let me with mine own eyes behold thee in that form in which thou dwellest in Shiva's heart, which form the saints crave to see; the swan in the lake of Bhusumdi's soul; the sum and the negation of all attributes; the theme of the Veda; do me this grace, O thou that healest the woes of every suppliant." This gentle, submissive, and affectionate speech of the wedded pair went to the heart of the generous and merciful God; and the sovereign of the universe manifested himself:

दोहा-dohā:

नील सरोरुह नील मनि नील नीरधर स्याम ।
nīla saroruha nīla mani nīla nīradhara syāma,
लाजहिं तन सोभा निरखि कोटि कोटि सत काम ॥ १४६॥
lājahiṁ tana sobhā nirakhi koṭi koṭi sata kāma. 146.

Trans:

In hue as the lotus or the sapphire; dark as a rain-cloud; of such a lustrous form that a myriad Loves could not be compared to it;

चौपाई-caupāī:

सरद मयंक बदन छबि सींवा । चारु कपोल चिबुक दर ग्रीवा ॥
sarada mayaṁka badana chabi sīṁvā, cāru kapola cibuka dara grīvā.
अधर अरुन रद सुंदर नासा । बिधु कर निकर बिनिंदक हासा ॥
adhara aruna rada suṁdara nāsā, bidhu kara nikara biniṁdaka hāsā.
नव अंबुज अंबक छबि नीकी । चितवनि ललित भावँती जी की ॥
nava aṁbuja aṁbaka chabi nīkī, citavani lalita bhāvaṁtī jī kī.
भृकुटि मनोज चाप छबि हारी । तिलक ललाट पटल दुतिकारी ॥
bhṛkuṭi manoja cāpa chabi hārī, tilaka lalāṭa paṭala dutikārī.
कुंडल मकर मुकुट सिर भ्राजा । कुटिल केस जनु मधुप समाजा ॥
kuṁḍala makara mukuṭa sira bhrājā, kuṭila kesa janu madhupa samājā.
उर श्रीबत्स रुचिर बनमाला । पदिक हार भूषन मनिजाला ॥
ura śrībatsa rucira banamālā, padika hāra bhūṣana manijālā.
केहरि कंधर चारु जनेऊ । बाहु बिभूषन सुंदर तेऊ ॥
kehari kaṁdhara cāru janeū, bāhu bibhūṣana suṁdara teū.
करि कर सरिस सुभग भुजदंडा । कटि निषंग कर सर कोदंडा ॥
kari kara sarisa subhaga bhujadaṁḍā, kaṭi niṣaṁga kara sara kodaṁḍā.

Trans:

with a face perfect in beauty like the autumnal moon; with beautiful cheeks and chin, neck resembling a conch-shell in its spiral shape; charming nose, ruddy lips, gleaming teeth and smile more radiant than a moonbeam; eyes bright as a lotus bud and a glance to fascinate the heart; brows surpassing Love's bow; on the forehead a sectarian mark and glistening star; golden fish as his earrings and a bright crown on his head; crisp curling hair like a swarm of bees; on his chest the Srivatsa jewel and a long wreath of sweet wild flowers, and jeweled adornments about his neck; a waist like a lion, a comely Brahminical thread, and exquisite clasps upon his arms, long and round as an elephant's trunk; with a quiver at his side and bow and arrow in his hand;

दोहा-dohā:

तड़ित बिनिंदक पीत पट उदर रेख बर तीनि ।
taṛita biniṁdaka pīta paṭa udara rekha bara tīni,
नाभि मनोहर लेति जनु जमुन भवँर छबि छीनि ॥ १४७॥
nābhi manohara leti janu jamuna bhavaṁra chabi chīni. 147.

Trans:

his yellow apparel more lustrous then the lightning; his body charmingly dimpled, and his navel like a bee hovering over the dark wave of the Yamunā;

चौपाई-caupāī:

पद राजीव बरनि नहिं जाहीं । मुनि मन मधुप बसहिं जेन्ह माहीं ॥
pada rājīva barani nahiṁ jāhiṁ, muni mana madhupa basahiṁ jenha māhiṁ.
बाम भाग सोभति अनुकूला । आदिसक्ति छबिनिधि जगमूला ॥
bāma bhāga sobhati anukūlā, ādisakti chabinidhi jagamūlā.
जासु अंस उपजहिं गुनखानी । अगनित लच्छि उमा ब्रह्मानी ॥
jāsu aṁsa upajahiṁ gunakhānī, aganita lacchi umā brahmānī.
भृकुटि बिलास जासु जग होई । राम बाम दिसि सीता सोई ॥
bhṛkuṭi bilāsa jāsu jaga hoī, rāma bāma disi sītā soī.
छबिसमुद्र हरि रूप बिलोकी । एकटक रहे नयन पट रोकी ॥
chabisamudra hari rūpa bilokī, ekaṭaka rahe nayana paṭa rokī.
चितवहिं सादर रूप अनूपा । तृप्ति न मानहिं मनु सतरूपा ॥
citavahiṁ sādara rūpa anūpā, tṛpti na mānahiṁ manu satarūpā.
हरष बिबस तन दसा भुलानी । परे दंड इव गहि पद पानी ॥

haraṣa bibasa tana dasā bhulānī, pare daṁḍa iva gahi pada pānī.
सिर परसे प्रभु निज कर कंजा । तुरत उठाए करुनापुंजा ॥
sira parase prabhu nija kara kaṁjā, turata uṭhāe karunāpuṁjā.

Trans:

his feet beautiful beyond description, lotus haunt of the bee-like souls of the saints. On his left side shone in equal glory the Primal Energy—queen of beauty, mother of the world; of whose members are born countless Umās and Ramās and Brahmanis, all alike perfect; by the play of whose eyebrows a world flashes into existence—even Sītā, enthroned at Rāma's side. As Manu and Shatrupā beheld this vision of Harī in all his beauty, gazing fixedly with open eyes, they adored his incomparable magnificence, nor could be satiated with the sight. Overcome with delight and transported out of themselves, they fell flat on the ground, clasping his feet in their hands. But the gracious Lord putting his lotus hand upon their heads quickly raised them up;

दोहा-dohā:

बोले कृपानिधान पुनि अति प्रसन्न मोहि जानि ।
bole kṛpānidhāna puni ati prasanna mohi jāni,
मागहु बर जोइ भाव मन महादानि अनुमानि ॥ १४८॥
māgahu bara joi bhāva mana mahādāni anumāni. 148.

Trans:

and again said,—"Be assured that you have found favor with me; ask whatever boon you will, the largest gift you can think of."

चौपाई-caupāī:

सुनि प्रभु बचन जोरि जुग पानी । धरि धीरजु बोली मृदु बानी ॥
suni prabhu bacana jori juga pānī, dhari dhīraju bolī mṛdu bānī.
नाथ देखि पद कमल तुम्हारे । अब पूरे सब काम हमारे ॥
nātha dekhi pada kamala tumhāre, aba pūre saba kāma hamāre.
एक लालसा बड़ि उर माहीं । सुगम अगम कहि जाति सो नाहीं ॥
eka lālasā baṛi ura māhīṁ, sugama agama kahi jāti so nāhīṁ.
तुम्हहि देत अति सुगम गोसाईं । अगम लाग मोहि निज कृपनाईं ॥
tumhahi deta ati sugama gosāīṁ, agama lāga mohi nija kṛpanāīṁ.
जथा दरिद्र बिबुधतरु पाई । बहु संपति मागत सकुचाई ॥
jathā daridra bibudhataru pāī, bahu saṁpati māgata sakucāī.
तासु प्रभाउ जान नहिं सोई । तथा हृदयँ मम संसय होई ॥
tāsu prabhāu jāna nahiṁ soī, tathā hṛdayaṁ mama saṁsaya hoī.
सो तुम्ह जानहु अंतरजामी । पुरवहु मोर मनोरथ स्वामी ॥
so tumha jānahu aṁtarajāmī, puravahu mora manoratha svāmī.
सकुच बिहाइ मागु नृप मोही । मोरें नहिं अदेय कछु तोही ॥
sakuca bihāi māgu nṛpa mohī, moreṁ nahiṁ adeya kachu tohī.

Trans:

On hearing the Lord's words they clasped their hands in prayer, and taking courage thus spoke in humble accents: "O Lord, we have seen your lotus feet, and our every object has been accomplished. Yet one longing remains, and I know not whether to describe it as easy or difficult of attainment. It is easy, my master, for you to give; but so far as my meanness is concerned, it is difficult. Like a beggar who has found the wishing-tree but trembles to ask for too good a fortune, not realizing its full power, so my heart is troubled by doubt. O my God you read all hearts and know what I wish; grant me my desire." "O king, fear not, but ask of me; there is nothing I would not give you."

दोहा-dohā:

दानि सिरोमनि कृपानिधि नाथ कहउँ सतिभाउ ।
dāni siromani kṛpānidhi nātha kahauṁ satibhāu,
चाहउँ तुम्हहि समान सुत प्रभु सन कवन दुराउ ॥ १४९॥
cāhauṁ tumhahi samāna suta prabhu sana kavana durāu. 149.

Trans:

"O gracious Lord, I will declare honestly the crowning boon—for what concealment can there be from you—that I may have a son like you."

चौपाई-caupāī:

देखि प्रीति सुनि बचन अमोले । एवमस्तु करुनानिधि बोले ॥
dekhi prīti suni bacana amole, evamastu karunānidhi bole.
आपु सरिस खोजौं कहँ जाई । नृप तव तनय होब मैं आई ॥
āpu sarisa khojauṁ kahaṁ jāī, nṛpa tava tanaya hoba maiṁ āī.
सतरूपहि बिलोकि कर जोरें । देबि मागु बरु जो रुचि तोरें ॥
satarūpahi biloki kara joreṁ, debi māgu baru jo ruci toreṁ.
जो बरु नाथ चतुर नृप मागा । सोइ कृपाल मोहि अति प्रिय लागा ॥
jo baru nātha catura nṛpa māgā, soi kṛpāla mohi ati priya lāgā.
प्रभु परंतु सुठि होति ढिठाई । जदपि भगत हित तुम्हहि सोहाई ॥
prabhu paraṁtu suṭhi hoti ḍhiṭhāī, jadapi bhagata hita tumhahi sohāī.
तुम्ह ब्रह्मादि जनक जग स्वामी । ब्रह्म सकल उर अंतरजामी ॥
tumha brahmādi janaka jaga svāmī, brahma sakala ura aṁtarajāmī.
अस समुझत मन संसय होई । कहा जो प्रभु प्रवान पुनि सोई ॥
asa samujhata mana saṁsaya hoī, kahā jo prabhu pravāna puni soī.
जे निज भगत नाथ तव अहहीं । जो सुख पावहिं जो गति लहहीं ॥
je nija bhagata nātha tava ahahīṁ, jo sukha pāvahiṁ jo gati lahahīṁ.

Trans:

On seeing his love and hearing his sincere words, said the Compassionate, "So be it. But where can I go to find my equal? I myself, O king, will be born as your son." Then seeing Shatrupā with her hands still clasped said He, "O lady, ask whatever boon you please." "O my Lord, the boon my husband has wisely asked is what I too should most desire. But it is great presumption, though in your clemency you have confirmed it. You are the father of all the gods, the Lord of the world, the supreme spirit, the omniscient; and therefore my mind doubts; and yet the Lord's word cannot fail. O my Lord God: That bliss which is enjoyed, and the future state that is attained by Devotees who are verily Thy very own—

दोहा-dohā:

सोइ सुख सोइ गति सोइ भगति सोइ निज चरन सनेहु ।
soi sukha soi gati soi bhagati soi nija carana sanehu,
सोइ बिबेक सोइ रहनि प्रभु हमहि कृपा करि देहु ॥ १५०॥
soi bibeka soi rahani prabhu hamahi kṛpā kari dehu. 150.

Trans:

—in your mercy grant to me just that: that very bliss, that very state, that very devotion, that very love to your holy feet, and that very knowledge, and that very existence."

चौपाई-caupāī:

सुनि मृदु गूढ़ रुचिर बर रचना । कृपासिंधु बोले मृदु बचना ॥
suni mṛdu gūṛha rucira bara racanā, kṛpāsiṁdhu bole mṛdu bacanā.
जो कछु रुचि तुम्हरे मन माहीं । मैं सो दीन्ह सब संसय नाहीं ॥
jo kachu ruci tumhare mana māhīṁ, maiṁ so dīnha saba saṁsaya nāhīṁ.
मातु बिबेक अलौकिक तोरें । कबहुँ न मिटिहि अनुग्रह मोरें ॥
mātu bibeka alaukika toreṁ, kabahuṁ na miṭihi anugraha moreṁ.
बंदि चरन मनु कहेउ बहोरी । अवर एक बिनती प्रभु मोरी ॥
baṁdi carana manu kaheu bahorī, avara eka binatī prabhu morī.
सुत बिषइक तव पद रति होऊ । मोहि बड़ मूढ़ कहै किन कोऊ ॥
suta biṣaika tava pada rati hoū, mohi baṛa mūṛha kahai kina koū.
मनि बिनु फनि जिमि जल बिनु मीना । मम जीवन तिमि तुम्हहि अधीना ॥
mani binu phani jimi jala binu mīnā, mama jīvana timi tumhahi adhīnā.
अस बरु मागि चरन गहि रहेऊ । एवमस्तु करुनानिधि कहेऊ ॥
asa baru māgi carana gahi raheū, evamastu karunānidhi kaheū.

अब तुम्ह मम अनुसासन मानी । बसहु जाइ सुरपति रजधानी ॥
aba tumha mama anusāsana mānī, basahu jāi surapati rajadhānī.

Trans:

Hearing this modest and deeply touching petition, the Compassionate gently replied: "Fear not; whatever your mind desires that I have granted. O mother, your supernatural wisdom by my favor shall never fail." Then again spoke Manu, bowing at his feet: "I too have another petition, my Lord. Is there anyone who will not call me fool for devoting myself to your feet simply on account of a son? As a snake's hood without a jewel, or a fish without water, even so may my life upon you be utterly dependent." Begging this boon he remained clasping his feet till the All-merciful said: "Be it so; now as I order go and dwell at Indra's capital.

सोरठा-soraṭhā:

तहँ करि भोग बिसाल तात गएँ कछु काल पुनि ।
tahaṁ kari bhoga bisāla tāta gaeṁ kachu kāla puni,
होइहहु अवध भुआल तब मैं होब तुम्हार सुत ॥ १५१ ॥
hoihahu avadha bhuāla taba maiṁ hoba tumhāra suta. 151.

Trans:

There, O father, enjoy yourself freely; and again, when some time has passed, be born as the king of Avadh; and there I will be your son.

चौपाई-caupāī:

इच्छामय नरबेष सँवारें । होइहउँ प्रगट निकेत तुम्हारे ॥
icchāmaya narabeṣa saṁvāreṁ, hoihauṁ pragaṭa niketa tumhāre.
अंसन्ह सहित देह धरि ताता । करिहउँ चरित भगत सुखदाता ॥
aṁsanha sahita deha dhari tātā, karihauṁ carita bhagata sukhadātā.
जे सुनि सादर नर बड़भागी । भव तरिहहिं ममता मद त्यागी ॥
je suni sādara nara baṛabhāgī, bhava tarihahiṁ mamatā mada tyāgī.
आदिसक्ति जेहिं जग उपजाया । सोउ अवतरिहि मोरि यह माया ॥
ādisakti jehiṁ jaga upajāyā, sou avatarihi mori yaha māyā.
पुरउब मैं अभिलाष तुम्हारा । सत्य सत्य पन सत्य हमारा ॥
purauba maiṁ abhilāṣa tumhārā, satya satya pana satya hamārā.
पुनि पुनि अस कहि कृपानिधाना । अंतरधान भए भगवाना ॥
puni puni asa kahi kṛpānidhānā, aṁtaradhāna bhae bhagavānā.
दंपति उर धरि भगत कृपाला । तेहिं आश्रम निवसे कछु काला ॥
daṁpati ura dhari bhagata kṛpālā, tehiṁ āśrama nivase kachu kālā.
समय पाइ तनु तजि अनयासा । जाइ कीन्ह अमरावति बासा ॥
samaya pāi tanu taji anayāsā, jāi kīnha amarāvati bāsā.

Trans:

Willfully assuming human guise, I will manifest myself in your house, O father; and there embodying myself, together with the secondary emanations of my divinity, will do great many deeds for the solacement of my people; and blessed will be those who shall listen reverently to those enactments, and quitting the vain conceits of the self they shall pass over the ocean of life. And my Primal Energy—by whom the visible world was created, that self-same shadow of me here present—shall become incarnate too. Verily I will accomplish your desire; true is my promise—true, aye true." Again and again speaking thusly the compassionate Lord vanished out of sight; and the wedded pair, full of faith in the All-merciful, stayed for a while at the hermitage; and then, when their time was come, eased painlessly out of their bodies and took up their abode in Amaravati—city of the immortals.

दोहा-dohā:

यह इतिहास पुनीत अति उमहि कही बृषकेतु ।
yaha itihāsa punīta ati umahi kahī bṛṣaketu,
भरद्वाज सुनु अपर पुनि राम जनम कर हेतु ॥ १५२ ॥
bharadvāja sunu apara puni rāma janama kara hetu. 152.

Trans:

Such was the pious legend which Shiva related to Umā. Hearken now, O Bharadvāja, to yet another motive for Rāma's incarnation.

मासपारायण पाँचवाँ विश्राम
māsapārāyaṇa pāṁcavāṁ viśrāma
(Pause 5 for a Thirty-Day Recitation)

चौपाई-caupāī:

सुनु मुनि कथा पुनीत पुरानी । जो गिरिजा प्रति संभु बखानी ॥
sunu muni kathā punīta purānī, jo girijā prati saṁbhu bakhānī.
बिस्व बिदित एक कैकय देसू । सत्यकेतु तहँ बसइ नरेसू ॥
bisva bidita eka kaikaya desū, satyaketu tahaṁ basai naresū.
धरम धुरंधर नीति निधाना । तेज प्रताप सील बलवाना ॥
dharama dhuraṁdhara nīti nidhānā, teja pratāpa sīla balavānā.
तेहि कें भए जुगल सुत बीरा । सब गुन धाम महा रनधीरा ॥
tehi keṁ bhae jugala suta bīrā, saba guna dhāma mahā ranadhīrā.
राज धनी जो जेठ सुत आही । नाम प्रतापभानु अस ताही ॥
rāja dhanī jo jeṭha suta āhī, nāma pratāpabhānu asa tāhī.
अपर सुतहि अरिमर्दन नामा । भुजबल अतुल अचल संग्रामा ॥
apara sutahi arimardana nāmā, bhujabala atula acala saṁgrāmā.
भाइहि भाइहि परम समीती । सकल दोष छल बरजित प्रीती ॥
bhāihi bhāihi parama samītī, sakala doṣa chala barajita prītī.
जेठे सुतहि राज नृप दीन्हा । हरि हित आपु गवन बन कीन्हा ॥
jeṭhe sutahi rāja nṛpa dīnhā, hari hita āpu gavana bana kīnhā.

Trans:

Listen, O great saint, to the holy ancient saga as it was repeated by Shambhu to Girijā. There is a world-famous country called Kaikaya, and Satya-ketu was its king. A champion of religion; a storehouse of good policy; great in glory, magnificence, virtue, and power, he had two gallant sons, staunch in fight, endowed with every good quality. The elder and the heir to the kingdom was named Pratap-bhanu, and the other Ari-mardan, of unequalled strength of arm and like a rock to stand the brunt of battle. The sympathy between brother and brother was perfect, and their mutual affection without flaw or disguise. To the elder son the king resigned the throne, and then withdrew into the woods to devote himself to religion.

दोहा-dohā:

जब प्रतापरबि भयउ नृप फिरी दोहाई देस ।
jaba pratāparabi bhayau nṛpa phirī dohāī desa,
प्रजा पाल अति बेदबिधि कतहुँ नहीं अघ लेस ॥ १५३ ॥
prajā pāla ati bedabidhi katahuṁ nahīṁ agha lesa. 153.

Trans:

"When Pratap-bhanu became king that proclamation rang throughout all the lands; and under that sovereign so skilled in sacred lore, not a speck of sin was left anywhere.

चौपाई-caupāī:

नृप हितकारक सचिव सयाना । नाम धरमरुचि सुक्र समाना ॥
nṛpa hitakāraka saciva sayānā, nāma dharamaruci sukra samānā.
सचिव सयान बंधु बलबीरा । आपु प्रतापपुंज रनधीरा ॥
saciva sayāna baṁdhu balabīrā, āpu pratāpapuṁja ranadhīrā.
सेन संग चतुरंग अपारा । अमित सुभट सब समर जुझारा ॥
sena saṁga caturaṁga apārā, amita subhaṭa saba samara jujhārā.
सेन बिलोकि राउ हरषाना । अरु बाजे गहगहे निसाना ॥
sena biloki rāu haraṣānā, aru bāje gahagahe nisānā.
बिजय हेतु कटकई बनाई । सुदिन साधि नृप चलेउ बजाई ॥
bijaya hetu kaṭakaī banāī, sudina sādhi nṛpa caleu bajāī.
जहँ तहँ परीं अनेक लराईं । जीते सकल भूप बरिआईं ॥
jahaṁ tahaṁ parīṁ aneka larāīṁ, jīte sakala bhūpa bariāīṁ.

सप्त दीप भुजबल बस कीन्हे । लै लै दंड छाड़ि नृप दीन्हे ॥
sapta dīpa bhujabala basa kīnhe, lai lai daṁḍa chāṛi nṛpa dīnhe.
सकल अवनि मंडल तेहि काला । एक प्रतापभानु महिपाला ॥
sakala avani maṁḍala tehi kālā, eka pratāpabhānu mahipālā.

Trans:

The Prime Minister Dharm-ruchi, a second Sukra as it were, was ever so wise and devoted to the king. With a prudent counselor and valiant kinsmen, and himself a glorious leader in war, and with a countless host on horse and foot, and chariots and elephants, and fighting men beyond number all eager for a fray, the king rejoiced mightily as he inspected his army amidst the clash of tumultuous music. Then, having selected an auspicious day, he marched forth with that special force bent on universal conquest. In all the numerous battles, wherever they took place, the pride of all the other kings was abased; and all the seven continents were reduced by the might of his arm and their kings could escape only upon the payment of tributes. At that time Pratap-bhanu became the sole monarch of the whole round world.

दोहा-dohā:

स्वबस बिस्व करि बाहुबल निज पुर कीन्ह प्रबेसु ।
svabasa bisva kari bāhubala nija pura kīnha prabesu,
अरथ धरम कामादि सुख सेवइ समयँ नरेसु ॥ १५४॥
aratha dharama kāmādi sukha sevai samayaṁ naresu. 154.

Trans:

Having thus subdued the universe by the might of his arm, he re-entered his capital and devoted himself in turn to business, duty, love, and religion.

चौपाई-caupāī:

भूप प्रतापभानु बल पाई । कामधेनु भै भूमि सुहाई ॥
bhūpa pratāpabhānu bala pāī, kāmadhenu bhai bhūmi suhāī.
सब दुख बरजित प्रजा सुखारी । धरमसील सुंदर नर नारी ॥
saba dukha barajita prajā sukhārī, dharamasīla suṁdara nara nārī.
सचिव धरमरुचि हरि पद प्रीती । नृप हित हेतु सिखव नित नीती ॥
saciva dharamaruci hari pada prītī, nṛpa hita hetu sikhava nita nītī.
गुर सुर संत पितर महिदेवा । करइ सदा नृप सब कै सेवा ॥
gura sura saṁta pitara mahidevā, karai sadā nṛpa saba kai sevā.
भूप धरम जे बेद बखाने । सकल करइ सादर सुख माने ॥
bhūpa dharama je beda bakhāne, sakala karai sādara sukha māne.
दिन प्रति देह बिबिध बिधि दाना । सुनइ सास्त्र बर बेद पुराना ॥
dina prati deha bibidha bidhi dānā, sunai sāstra bara beda purānā.
नाना बापीं कूप तड़ागा । सुमन बाटिका सुंदर बागा ॥
nānā bāpīṁ kūpa taṛāgā, sumana bāṭikā suṁdara bāgā.
बिप्रभवन सुरभवन सुहाए । सब तीरथन्ह बिचित्र बनाए ॥
biprabhavana surabhavana suhāe, saba tīrathanha bicitra banāe.

Trans:

The grateful earth, invigorated by Pratap-bhanu's sway, became the very *Kām-dhenu*; and his subjects—men, women, all—grew in virtue and beauty, and were happy and free from any sorrows,. The minister Dharm-ruchi, a devoted servant of Harī, lovingly instructed his lord in state policy. Nor did the king ever fail in due reverence either to his spiritual teacher, or the gods, or the saints, or his departed ancestors, or the Brahmins. All the duties which are enjoined upon a king in the Vedas, he carefully and gladly performed every day, and he made large offerings; and he heard the scriptures read—both the Vedas and the Purānas; and he constructed many baths, wells and tanks, and numerous flower gardens and beautiful orchards, and many handsome monasteries and temples, and he also restored every ancient shrine.

दोहा-dohā:

जहँ लगि कहे पुरान श्रुति एक एक सब जाग ।
jahaṁ lagi kahe purāna śruti eka eka saba jāga,
बार सहस्र सहस्र नृप किए सहित अनुराग ॥ १५५॥
bāra sahasra sahasra nṛpa kie sahita anurāga. 155.

Trans:

For every single ritual enjoined in the scriptures or the Purānas the king in his zeal performed a thousand.

चौपाई-caupāī:

हृदयँ न कछु फल अनुसंधाना । भूप बिबेकी परम सुजाना ॥
hṛdayaṁ na kachu phala anusaṁdhānā, bhūpa bibekī parama sujānā.
करइ जे धरम करम मन बानी । बासुदेव अर्पित नृप ग्यानी ॥
karai je dharama karama mana bānī, bāsudeva arpita nṛpa gyānī.
चढ़ि बर बाजि बार एक राजा । मृगया कर सब साजि समाजा ॥
caṛhi bara bāji bāra eka rājā, mṛgayā kara saba sāji samājā.
बिंध्याचल गभीर बन गयऊ । मृग पुनीत बहु मारत भयऊ ॥
biṁdhyācala gabhīra bana gayaū, mṛga punīta bahu mārata bhayaū.
फिरत बिपिन नृप दीख बराहू । जनु बन दुरेउ ससिहि ग्रसि राहू ॥
phirata bipina nṛpa dīkha barāhū, janu bana dureu sasihi grasi rāhū.
बड़ बिधु नहिं समात मुख माहीं । मनहुँ क्रोध बस उगिलत नाहीं ॥
baṛa bidhu nahiṁ samāta mukha māhīṁ, manahuṁ krodha basa ugilata nāhīṁ.
कोल कराल दसन छबि गाई । तनु बिसाल पीवर अधिकाई ॥
kola karāla dasana chabi gāī, tanu bisāla pīvara adhikāī.
घुरुघुरात हय आरौ पाएँ । चकित बिलोकत कान उठाएँ ॥
ghurughurāta haya ārau pāeṁ, cakita bilokata kāna uṭhāeṁ.

Trans:

In his heart there was no seeking after a reward of any kind; and such was his high knowledge and intelligence that he dedicated to God the whole merit of all his thoughts, words, and actions. One day be mounted his gallant steed and went along with his retinue equipped for the chase; and into a dense forest of the Vindhyachal mountains he forayed and killed many a fine deer. As he ranged the wood, be spied a wild boar showing amid the foliage like Rāhu with the moon in his clutch, with its orb too vast to be contained in the mouth, though in his rage he would not entirely disgorge it. The monstrous boar, with its remarkable tusks as described, had vast limbs of immeasurable bulk; and it growled when he heard the tramp of the horse; which too, at the sight, started and pricked up its ears.

दोहा-dohā:

नील महीधर सिखर सम देखि बिसाल बराहु ।
nīla mahīdhara sikhara sama dekhi bisāla barāhu,
चपरि चलेउ हय सुटुकि नृप हाँकि न होइ निबाहु ॥ १५६॥
capari caleu haya suṭuki nṛpa hāṁki na hoi nibāhu. 156.

Trans:

On seeing the vast boar resembling some purple mountain-peak the horse started aside, and it was only by much spurring and persuasion that the king could prevent it from breaking away.

चौपाई-caupāī:

आवत देखि अधिक रव बाजी । चलेउ बराह मरुत गति भाजी ॥
āvata dekhi adhika rava bājī, caleu barāha maruta gati bhājī.
तुरत कीन्ह नृप सर संधाना । महि मिलि गयउ बिलोकत बाना ॥
turata kīnha nṛpa sara saṁdhānā, mahi mili gayau bilokata bānā.
तकि तकि तीर महीस चलावा । करि छल सुअर सरीर बचावा ॥
taki taki tīra mahīsa calāvā, kari chala suara sarīra bacāvā.
प्रगटत दुरत जाइ मृग भागा । रिस बस भूप चलेउ सँग लागा ॥
pragaṭata durata jāi mṛga bhāgā, risa basa bhūpa caleu saṁga lāgā.

गयउ दूरि घन गहन बराहू । जहँ नाहिन गज बाजि निबाहू ॥
gayau dūri ghana gahana barāhū, jahaṁ nāhina gaja bāji nibāhū.
अति अकेल बन बिपुल कलेसू । तदपि न मृग मग तजइ नरेसू ॥
ati akela bana bipula kalesū, tadapi na mṛga maga tajai naresū.
कोल बिलोकि भूप बड़ धीरा । भागि पैठ गिरिगुहाँ गभीरा ॥
kola biloki bhūpa baṛa dhīrā, bhāgi paiṭha giriguhāṁ gabhīrā.
अगम देखि नृप अति पछिताई । फिरेउ महाबन परेउ भुलाई ॥
agama dekhi nṛpa ati pachitāī, phireu mahābana pareu bhulāī.

Trans:

When it saw the horse coming on with speed, the beast took to flight swift as the wind, keeping close to the ground as it went, ever careful of the shaft which the king had fitted to his bow. Taking steady aim he let it fly; but the boar saved himself by his wiliness and rushed on—now well in sight, and now altogether hidden. The king in much excitement followed closely on his tracks. At length it reached a dense thicket impenetrable by horse or elephant. Though alone in the wood, and distressed by his exertions, still the king would not abandon the chase; till the boar seeing him so determined slunk away into a deep cave. When the king perceived that there was no getting near him, he was quite sad; and moreover he discovered that he had lost his way in this hunt through so great a forest.

दोहा-dohā:

खेद खिन्न छुद्धित तृषित राजा बाजि समेत ।
kheda khinna chuddhita tṛṣita rājā bāji sameta,
खोजत ब्याकुल सरित सर जल बिनु भयउ अचेत ॥ १५७॥
khojata byākula sarita sara jala binu bhayau aceta. 157.

Trans:

Hungry and thirsty and exhausted with fatigue the king and his horse kept searching in distress for a pond or stream, and now they became half-dead for want of water.

चौपाई-caupāī:

फिरत बिपिन आश्रम एक देखा । तहँ बस नृपति कपट मुनिबेषा ॥
phirata bipina āśrama eka dekhā, tahaṁ basa nṛpati kapaṭa munibeṣā.
जासु देस नृप लीन्ह छड़ाई । समर सेन तजि गयउ पराई ॥
jāsu desa nṛpa līnha chaṛāī, samara sena taji gayau parāī.
समय प्रतापभानु कर जानी । आपन अति असमय अनुमानी ॥
samaya pratāpabhānu kara jānī, āpana ati asamaya anumānī.
गयउ न गृह मन बहुत गलानी । मिला न राजहि नृप अभिमानी ॥
gayau na gṛha mana bahuta galānī, milā na rājahi nṛpa abhimānī.
रिस उर मारि रंक जिमि राजा । बिपिन बसइ तापस कें साजा ॥
risa ura māri raṁka jimi rājā, bipina basai tāpasa keṁ sājā.
तासु समीप गवन नृप कीन्हा । यह प्रतापरबि तेहिं तब चीन्हा ॥
tāsu samīpa gavana nṛpa kīnhā, yaha pratāparabi tehiṁ taba cīnhā.
राउ तृषित नहिं सो पहिचाना । देखि सुबेष महामुनि जाना ॥
rāu tṛṣita nahiṁ so pahicānā, dekhi subeṣa mahāmuni jānā.
उतरि तुरग तें कीन्ह प्रनामा । परम चतुर न कहेउ निज नामा ॥
utari turaga teṁ kīnha pranāmā, parama catura na kaheu nija nāmā.

Trans:

As he wandered through the forest, he spied a hermitage where dwelt a king in the guise of a holy man. He had been despoiled of his kingdom by Pratap-bhanu and had left his army on the field of battle—knowing that his adversary's star was in the ascendant and his own in the decline. Too proud to meet the king, much too mortified to go home, nursing the rage in his heart like a dagger, he, like a beggar though a prince, took up his abode in these woods in the garb of an anchorite. He at once recognized king Pratap-bhanu as he drew near; but the latter was too tired to recognize him, and looking only at his dress took him to be a holy man, and alighting from his horse he saluted him. He was, however, too astute to declare his name.

दोहा-dohā:

भूपति तृषित बिलोकि तेहिं सरबरु दीन्ह देखाइ ।
bhūpati tṛṣita biloki tehiṁ sarabaru dīnha dekhāi,
मज्जन पान समेत हय कीन्ह नृपति हरषाइ ॥ १५८॥
majjana pāna sameta haya kīnha nṛpati haraṣāi. 158.

Trans:

Seeing the king to be faint with thirst, he pointed out to him a fine pond, where he bathed and drank—both he and his horse, with much gladness.

चौपाई-caupāī:

गै श्रम सकल सुखी नृप भयऊ । निज आश्रम तापस लै गयऊ ॥
gai śrama sakala sukhī nṛpa bhayaū, nija āśrama tāpasa lai gayaū.
आसन दीन्ह अस्त रबि जानी । पुनि तापस बोलेउ मृदु बानी ॥
āsana dīnha asta rabi jānī, puni tāpasa boleu mṛdu bānī.
को तुम्ह कस बन फिरहु अकेलें । सुंदर जुबा जीव परहेलें ॥
ko tumha kasa bana phirahu akeleṁ, suṁdara jubā jīva paraheleṁ.
चक्रबर्ति के लच्छन तोरें । देखत दया लागि अति मोरें ॥
cakrabarti ke lacchana toreṁ, dekhata dayā lāgi ati moreṁ.
नाम प्रतापभानु अवनीसा । तासु सचिव मैं सुनहु मुनीसा ॥
nāma pratāpabhānu avanīsā, tāsu saciva maiṁ sunahu munīsā.
फिरत अहेरें परेउँ भुलाई । बड़ें भाग देखउँ पद आई ॥
phirata ahereṁ pareuṁ bhulāī, baṛeṁ bhāga dekhauṁ pada āī.
हम कहँ दुर्लभ दरस तुम्हारा । जानत हौं कछु भल होनिहारा ॥
hama kahaṁ durlabha darasa tumhārā, jānata hauṁ kachu bhala honihārā.
कह मुनि तात भयउ अँधियारा । जोजन सत्तरि नगरु तुम्हारा ॥
kaha muni tāta bhayau aṁdhiyārā, jojana sattari nagaru tumhārā.

Trans:

All his weariness passed away and he was quite happy again. The hermit took him to his hut, and as the sun had now set, showed him where he might rest; and then enquired of him in courteous tones: "Who may you be? And why, so young and handsome, do you risk your life by roaming alone in the forest? You have all the marks of a great sovereign and at the sight of you I am quite moved." "Know then, reverend sir, that I am the minister of King Pratap-bhanu. In pursuit of a chase I have lost my way and by great good fortune have been brought into your presence. To get a sight of you was no easy matter, and I am satisfied that something good is about to befall me." Said the false hermit: "My son, it is now dusk, and your city is seventy leagues away.

दोहा-dohā:

निसा घोर गंभीर बन पंथ न सुनहु सुजान ।
nisā ghora gaṁbhīra bana paṁtha na sunahu sujāna,
बसहु आजु अस जानि तुम्ह जाएहु होत बिहान ॥ १५९क॥
basahu āju asa jāni tumha jāehu hota bihāna. 159(ka).

Trans:

The night is dark, the forest dense, and the road not easy to find. Tarry then here for today and start tomorrow at dawn."

तुलसी जसि भवतब्यता तैसी मिलइ सहाइ ।
tulasī jasi bhavatabyatā taisī milai sahāi,
आपुनु आवइ ताहि पहिं ताहि तहाँ लै जाइ ॥ १५९ख॥
āpunu āvai tāhi pahiṁ tāhi tahāṁ lai jāi. 159(kha).

Trans:

Says Tulsī: Fate is furthered in its own way; either you go to meet it or itself comes and carries you away.

चौपाई-caupāī:

भलेहिं नाथ आयसु धरि सीसा । बाँधि तुरग तरु बैठ महीसा ॥

bhalehiṁ nātha āyasu dhari sīsā, bāṁdhi turaga taru baiṭha mahīsā.

नृप बहु भाँति प्रसंसेउ ताही । चरन बंदि निज भाग्य सराही ॥
nṛpa bahu bhāṁti prasaṁseu tāhī, carana baṁdi nija bhāgya sarāhī.
पुनि बोलेउ मृदु गिरा सुहाई । जानि पिता प्रभु करउँ ढिठाई ॥
puni boleu mṛdu girā suhāī, jāni pitā prabhu karauṁ ḍhiṭhāī.
मोहि मुनिस सुत सेवक जानी । नाथ नाम निज कहहु बखानी ॥
mohi munisa suta sevaka jānī, nātha nāma nija kahahu bakhānī.
तेहि न जान नृप नृपहि सो जाना । भूप सुहृद सो कपट सयाना ॥
tehi na jāna nṛpa nṛpahi so jānā, bhūpa suhṛda so kapaṭa sayānā.
बैरी पुनि छत्री पुनि राजा । छल बल कीन्ह चहइ निज काजा ॥
bairī puni chatrī puni rājā, chala bala kīnha cahai nija kājā.
समुझि राजसुख दुखित अराती । अवाँ अनल इव सुलगइ छाती ॥
samujhi rājasukha dukhita arātī, avāṁ anala iva sulagai chātī.
सरल बचन नृप के सुनि काना । बयर सँभारि हृदयँ हरषाना ॥
sarala bacana nṛpa ke suni kānā, bayara saṁbhāri hṛdayaṁ haraṣānā.

Trans:

"Very well, my lord, I obey your command." And so saying the king tied up his horse to a tree and came and sat down. With many words of praise, the king bowed at his feet, extolling his own good fortune, and at last in modest and winning terms put this question: "Regarding you as a father, my lord, I make bold and beg of you to look upon me as your son and servant, and to declare to me your name." Now the king did not recognize him but the hermit recognized the king, and he was as false and crafty as the king was straight. Moreover being an enemy, and at the same time a warrior by caste and of royal birth, he was bent on accomplishing his own ends, whether by fraud or by right. In his enmity he was grieved to see the king's prosperity, and his heart within burned with revenge just as the furnace fire. However he controlled his resentment and showed himself to appear pleased; and on hearing the king's simple words,

दोहा-dohā:

कपट बोरि बानी मृदुल बोलेउ जुगुति समेत ।
kapaṭa bori bānī mṛdula boleu juguti sameta,
नाम हमार भिखारि अब निर्धन रहित निकेत ॥१६०॥
nāma hamāra bhikhāri aba nirdhana rahita niketa. 160.

Trans:

he uttered yet another smooth and artful speech which was but false: "My name now is *Bhikhāri*, a homeless beggar."

चौपाई-caupāī:

कह नृप जे बिग्यान निधाना । तुम्ह सारिखे गलित अभिमाना ॥
kaha nṛpa je bigyāna nidhānā, tumha sārikhe galita abhimānā.
सदा रहहिं अपनपौ दुराएँ । सब बिधि कुसल कुबेष बनाएँ ॥
sadā rahahiṁ apanapau durāeṁ, saba bidhi kusala kubeṣa banāeṁ.
तेहि तें कहहिं संत श्रुति टेरें । परम अकिंचन प्रिय हरि केरें ॥
tehi teṁ kahahiṁ saṁta śruti ṭereṁ, parama akiṁcana priya hari kereṁ.
तुम्ह सम अधन भिखारि अगेहा । होत बिरंचि सिवहि संदेहा ॥
tumha sama adhana bhikhāri agehā, hota biraṁci sivahi saṁdehā.
जोसि सोसि तव चरन नमामी । मो पर कृपा करिअ अब स्वामी ॥
josi sosi tava carana namāmī, mo para kṛpā karia aba svāmī.
सहज प्रीति भूपति कै देखी । आपु बिषय बिस्वास बिसेषी ॥
sahaja prīti bhūpati kai dekhī, āpu biṣaya bisvāsa biseṣī.
सब प्रकार राजहि अपनाई । बोलेउ अधिक सनेह जनाई ॥
saba prakāra rājahi apanāī, boleu adhika saneha janāī.
सुनु सतिभाउ कहउँ महिपाला । इहाँ बसत बीते बहु काला ॥
sunu satibhāu kahauṁ mahipālā, ihāṁ basata bīte bahu kālā.

Trans:

Said the king: "Philosophers like you—with whom all selfish-consciousness has been extinguished—ever conceal their personality, and though in every way blessed, remain in the outer garb as seeming wretched. Therefore the saints and the Vedas have proclaimed aloud: that it is the poor whom Harī holds most dear. A poor and homeless beggar, such as you are, is an anxiety to Brahmmā and Shiva. Whoever you may be, I prostrate myself at your feet and beg of you to grant me your grace." When he saw the king's simple affection he waxed all the more confident, and won him over in every way, using words with a still greater show of friendliness: "Hearken, O king, while I relate the truth of the matter. I have for a long time dwelt here,

दोहा-dohā:

अब लगि मोहि न मिलेउ कोउ मैं न जनावउँ काहु ।
aba lagi mohi na mileu kou maiṁ na janāvauṁ kāhu,
लोकमान्यता अनल सम कर तप कानन दाहु ॥१६१क॥
lokamānyatā anala sama kara tapa kānana dāhu. 161(ka).

Trans:

and until now neither has anyone come to me, nor have I spoken to anyone; for worldly honor is like a fire, and penance is the forest for it to consume."

सोरठा-soraṭhā:

तुलसी देखि सुबेषु भूलहिं मूढ़ न चतुर नर ।
tulasī dekhi subeṣu bhūlahiṁ mūṛha na catura nara,
सुंदर केकिहि पेखु बचन सुधा सम असन अहि ॥१६१ख॥
suṁdara kekihi pekhu bacana sudhā sama asana ahi. 161(kha).

Trans:

Says Tulsī: Fools are deceived by fair appearances, but not the wise. Though a peacock is fair to look upon and its voice pleasant, it actually devours on snakes.

चौपाई-caupāī:

तातें गुपुत रहउँ जग माहीं । हरि तजि किमपि प्रयोजन नाहीं ॥
tāteṁ guputa rahauṁ jaga māhīṁ, hari taji kimapi prayojana nāhīṁ.
प्रभु जानत सब बिनहिं जनाएँ । कहहु कवनि सिधि लोक रिझाएँ ॥
prabhu jānata saba binahiṁ janāeṁ, kahahu kavani sidhi loka rijhāeṁ.
तुम्ह सुचि सुमति परम प्रिय मोरें । प्रीति प्रतीति मोहि पर तोरें ॥
tumha suci sumati parama priya moreṁ, prīti pratīti mohi para toreṁ.
अब जौं तात दुरावउँ तोही । दारुन दोष घटइ अति मोही ॥
aba jauṁ tāta durāvauṁ tohī, dāruna doṣa ghaṭai ati mohī.
जिमि जिमि तापसु कथइ उदासा । तिमि तिमि नृपहि उपज बिस्वासा ॥
jimi jimi tāpasu kathai udāsā, timi timi nṛpahi upaja bisvāsā.
देखा स्वबस कर्म मन बानी । तब बोला तापस बगध्यानी ॥
dekhā svabasa karma mana bānī, taba bolā tāpasa bagadhyānī.
नाम हमार एकतनु भाई । सुनि नृप बोलेउ पुनि सिरु नाई ॥
nāma hamāra ekatanu bhāī, suni nṛpa boleu puni siru nāī.
कहहु नाम कर अरथ बखानी । मोहि सेवक अति आपन जानी ॥
kahahu nāma kara aratha bakhānī, mohi sevaka ati āpana jānī.

Trans:

"I therefore live retired in the woods, and other than Harī I have no concerns whatever. The lord knows everything without being told; so what is to be gained by conciliating the world. But you are so good and sensible that I cannot but love you in return for the faith and confidence you have placed in me; and if I were to turn you away, my son, it would be very grievous sin on my part." The more the hermit talked of his detachment from the world, the more trustful grew the king, until at last the false anchorite, seeing him completely in his power, said: "My name, brother, is *Ektanu*." The king bowed and asked further: "Knowing me to be your servant, tell me, I pray, the meaning of this name?"

दोहा-dohā:

आदिसृष्टि उपजी जबहिं तब उतपति भै मोरि ।
ādisṛṣṭi upajī jabahiṁ taba utapati bhai mori,
नाम एकतनु हेतु तेहि देह न धरी बहोरि ॥ १६२॥
nāma ekatanu hetu tehi deha na dharī bahori. 162.

Trans:

"It was at the first dawn of creation when my birth took place; and my name is *Ektanu* (one-bodied) for that reason—because I have never taken up another body, other than this.

चौपाई-caupāī:

जनि आचरजु करहु मन माहीं । सुत तप तें दुर्लभ कछु नाहीं ॥
jani ācaraju karahu mana māhīṁ, suta tapa teṁ durlabha kachu nāhīṁ.
तपबल तें जग सृजइ बिधाता । तपबल बिष्नु भए परित्राता ॥
tapabala teṁ jaga sṛjai bidhātā, tapabala biṣnu bhae paritrātā.
तपबल संभु करहिं संघारा । तप तें अगम न कछु संसारा ॥
tapabala saṁbhu karahiṁ saṁghārā, tapa teṁ agama na kachu saṁsārā.
भयउ नृपहि सुनि अति अनुरागा । कथा पुरातन कहै सो लागा ॥
bhayau nṛpahi suni ati anurāgā, kathā purātana kahai so lāgā.
करम धरम इतिहास अनेका । करइ निरूपन बिरति बिबेका ॥
karama dharama itihāsa anekā, karai nirūpana birati bibekā.
उदभव पालन प्रलय कहानी । कहेसि अमित आचरज बखानी ॥
udabhava pālana pralaya kahānī, kahesi amita ācaraja bakhānī.
सुनि महीप तापस बस भयऊ । आपन नाम कहन तब लयऊ ॥
suni mahīpa tāpasa basa bhayaū, āpana nāma kahana taba layaū.
कह तापस नृप जानउँ तोही । कीन्हेहु कपट लाग भल मोही ॥
kaha tāpasa nṛpa jānauṁ tohī, kīnhehu kapaṭa lāga bhala mohī.

Trans:

Marvel not in your mind, my son; for nothing is too difficult by the grace of *Tapa* (penance). By the power of penance the Creator created the world; and by the power of penance Vishnu is the great redeemer; and by the power of penance Shiva works destruction; and through penance there is nothing in the world that's impossible." The king was charmed as he listened to the false hermit who continued relating old-world stories—many legends of pious deeds and holy lives; examples of asceticism and divine wisdom; tales of the birth, preservation, and destruction of the worlds, and innumerable other marvelous narratives. In time the king yielded completely to his influence, and proceeded to reveal his true identity. Said the hermit: "Verily I knew that; and though you tried to practice a trick upon me, I took it quite in good sport.

सोरठा-soraṭhā:

सुनु महीस असि नीति जहँ तहँ नाम न कहहिं नृप ।
sunu mahīsa asi nīti jahaṁ tahaṁ nāma na kahahiṁ nṛpa,
मोहि तोहि पर अति प्रीति सोइ चतुरता बिचारि तव ॥ १६३॥
mohi tohi para ati prīti soi caturatā bicāri tava. 163.

Trans:

Hear, O king; it is a political maxim that on some occasions a king should not declare his true name; moreover when I observe your excellent sagacity I conceive a great affection for you.

चौपाई-caupāī:

नाम तुम्हार प्रताप दिनेसा । सत्यकेतु तव पिता नरेसा ॥
nāma tumhāra pratāpa dinesā, satyaketu tava pitā naresā.
गुर प्रसाद सब जानिअ राजा । कहिअ न आपन जानि अकाजा ॥
gura prasāda saba jānia rājā, kahia na āpana jāni akājā.
देखि तात तव सहज सुधाई । प्रीति प्रतीति नीति निपुनाई ॥
dekhi tāta tava sahaja sudhāī, prīti pratīti nīti nipunāī.
उपजि परी ममता मन मोरें । कहउँ कथा निज पूछे तोरें ॥
upaji parī mamatā mana moreṁ, kahauṁ kathā nija pūche toreṁ.
अब प्रसन्न मैं संसय नाहीं । मागु जो भूप भाव मन माहीं ॥
aba prasanna maiṁ saṁsaya nāhīṁ, māgu jo bhūpa bhāva mana māhīṁ.
सुनि सुबचन भूपति हरषाना । गहि पद बिनय कीन्हि बिधि नाना ॥
suni subacana bhūpati haraṣānā, gahi pada binaya kīnhi bidhi nānā.
कृपासिंधु मुनि दरसन तोरें । चारि पदारथ करतल मोरें ॥
kṛpāsiṁdhu muni darasana toreṁ, cāri padāratha karatala moreṁ.
प्रभुहि तथापि प्रसन्न बिलोकी । मागि अगम बर होउँ असोकी ॥
prabhuhi tathāpi prasanna bilokī, māgi agama bara houṁ asokī.

Trans:

Your name is Pratap-bhanu, and your father is king Satya-ketu. O sir, a spiritual man knows everything and there is no need of another's telling. Ah, my son, when I beheld your natural goodness, your faith and trustfulness, and your knowledge of state-craft, there sprung up great affection for you in my soul, and I told you my own story as you asked of me. Now I am well pleased with you; doubt not, but ask of me whatever you will." On hearing these fair words the king was delighted and clasping his feet entreated him suppliantly: "O merciful saint, by the sight of you the four objects of human desire have all come within my grasp. Yet, as I see my lord so gracious, I will ask an impossible boon and be happy for ever.

दोहा-dohā:

जरा मरन दुख रहित तनु समर जितै जनि कोउ ।
jarā marana dukha rahita tanu samara jitai jani kou,
एकछत्र रिपुहीन महि राज कलप सत होउ ॥ १६४॥
ekachatra ripuhīna mahi rāja kalapa sata hou. 164.

Trans:

May I die of old age, free from bodily pain; may I never be conquered in battle; may the whole earth, rid of every foe, be under my sole sway; and may my empire last for a hundred Ages."

चौपाई-caupāī:

कह तापस नृप ऐसेइ होऊ । कारन एक कठिन सुनु सोऊ ॥
kaha tāpasa nṛpa aisei hoū, kārana eka kaṭhina sunu soū.
कालउ तुअ पद नाइहि सीसा । एक बिप्रकुल छाड़ि महीसा ॥
kālau tua pada nāihi sīsā, eka biprakula chāṛi mahīsā.
तपबल बिप्र सदा बरिआरा । तिन्ह के कोप न कोउ रखवारा ॥
tapabala bipra sadā bariārā, tinha ke kopa na kou rakhavārā.
जौं बिप्रन्ह बस करहु नरेसा । तौ तुअ बस बिधि बिष्नु महेसा ॥
jauṁ bipranha basa karahu naresā, tau tua basa bidhi biṣnu mahesā.
चल न ब्रह्मकुल सन बरिआई । सत्य कहउँ दोउ भुजा उठाई ॥
cala na brahmakula sana bariāī, satya kahauṁ dou bhujā uṭhāī.
बिप्र श्राप बिनु सुनु महिपाला । तोर नास नहिं कवनेहुँ काला ॥
bipra śrāpa binu sunu mahipālā, tora nāsa nahiṁ kavanehuṁ kālā.
हरषेउ राउ बचन सुनि तासू । नाथ न होइ मोर अब नासू ॥
haraṣeu rāu bacana suni tāsū, nātha na hoi mora aba nāsū.
तव प्रसाद प्रभु कृपानिधाना । मो कहुँ सर्ब काल कल्याना ॥
tava prasāda prabhu kṛpānidhānā, mo kahuṁ sarba kāla kalyānā.

Trans:

Said the anchorite: "So be it, O king; however there is one difficulty, so hear of it: All, even Death, shall bow before you—with the sole exception of the Brahmins. By the virtue of penance a Brahmin is ever powerful, and there is none who can deliver from his wrath. If you can reduce them to your will, then Brahmmā, Vishnu, and Mahādev too will be at your command. But against a Brahmin might is of no avail: with both arms raised to heaven I tell you this solemn truth. Hearken, O king, if you can escape a Brahmin's curse, your destruction shall never come to pass." On hearing that promise the king was glad. "Then, my lord, my destruction shall never be; by your favor, O most gracious sir, I shall be prosperous for all times."

दोहा-dohā:

एवमस्तु कहि कपटमुनि बोला कुटिल बहोरि ।
evamastu kahi kapaṭamuni bolā kuṭila bahori,
मिलब हमार भुलाब निज कहहु त हमहि न खोरि ॥ १६५ ॥
milaba hamāra bhulāba nija kahahu ta hamahi na khori. 165.

Trans:

"Amen!" said the false anchorite, and added with crafty intent, "But if you tell anyone about my meeting with you and your straying away, then the fault shall not be mine."

चौपाई-caupāī:

तातें मैं तोहि बरजउँ राजा । कहें कथा तव परम अकाजा ॥
tātem maiṁ tohi barajauṁ rājā, kahem kathā tava parama akājā.
छठें श्रवन यह परत कहानी । नास तुम्हार सत्य मम बानी ॥
chaṭhem śravana yaha parata kahānī, nāsa tumhāra satya mama bānī.
यह प्रगटें अथवा द्विजश्रापा । नास तोर सुनु भानुप्रतापा ॥
yaha pragaṭem athavā dvijaśrāpā, nāsa tora sunu bhānupratāpā.
आन उपायँ निधन तव नाहीं । जौं हरि हर कोपहिं मन माहीं ॥
āna upāyaṁ nidhana tava nāhīṁ, jauṁ hari hara kopahiṁ mana māhīṁ.
सत्य नाथ पद गहि नृप भाषा । द्विज गुर कोप कहहु को राखा ॥
satya nātha pada gahi nṛpa bhāṣā, dvija gura kopa kahahu ko rākhā.
राखइ गुर जौं कोप बिधाता । गुर बिरोध नहिं कोउ जग त्राता ॥
rākhai gura jauṁ kopa bidhātā, gura birodha nahiṁ kou jaga trātā.
जौं न चलब हम कहे तुम्हारें । होउ नास नहिं सोच हमारें ॥
jauṁ na calaba hama kahe tumhārem, hou nāsa nahiṁ soca hamārem.
एकहिं डर डरपत मन मोरा । प्रभु महिदेव श्राप अति घोरा ॥
ekahiṁ ḍara ḍarapata mana morā, prabhu mahideva śrāpa ati ghorā.

Trans:

For I warn you, sir, that it is most inexpedient to repeat the matter; and if it come to a third pair of ears, I tell you, truly it will be your ruin. If you divulge this secret, or if a Brahmin curses you, you are undone, O Pratap-bhanu. When Harī and Hara are wrath, that cursed man has no escape." "True, my lord," said the king, clasping his feet, "who can deliver from the wrath of a Brahmin or Gurū? The Gurū can save from Brahmmā's anger, but if the Gurū himself be against, then there is none in the world that can save. If I do not follow your advice, I have not the slightest doubt that I shall perish. But tell me, for my soul is disturbed by this one fear: the curse of a Brahmin is something most terrible.

दोहा-dohā:

होहिं बिप्र बस कवन बिधि कहहु कृपा करि सोउ ।
hohiṁ bipra basa kavana bidhi kahahu kṛpā kari sou,
तुम्ह तजि दीनदयाल निज हितू न देखउँ कोउ ॥ १६६ ॥
tumha taji dīnadayāla nija hitū na dekhauṁ kou. 166.

Trans:

Of your great goodness, tell me in what way I can win over the Brahmins? Except for you, gracious lord, I have no other friend."

चौपाई-caupāī:

सुनु नृप बिबिध जतन जग माहीं । कष्टसाध्य पुनि होहिं कि नाहीं ॥
sunu nṛpa bibidha jatana jaga māhīṁ, kaṣṭasādhya puni hohiṁ ki nāhīṁ.
अहइ एक अति सुगम उपाई । तहाँ परंतु एक कठिनाई ॥
ahai eka ati sugama upāī, tahāṁ paraṁtu eka kaṭhināī.
मम आधीन जुगुति नृप सोई । मोर जाब तव नगर न होई ॥
mama ādhīna juguti nṛpa soī, mora jāba tava nagara na hoī.
आजु लगें अरु जब तें भयउँ । काहू के गृह ग्राम न गयउँ ॥
āju lagem aru jaba tem bhayauṁ, kāhū ke gṛha grāma na gayauṁ.
जौं न जाउँ तव होइ अकाजू । बना आइ असमंजस आजू ॥
jauṁ na jāuṁ tava hoi akājū, banā āi asamaṁjasa ājū.
सुनि महीस बोलेउ मृदु बानी । नाथ निगम असि नीति बखानी ॥
suni mahīsa boleu mṛdu bānī, nātha nigama asi nīti bakhānī.
बड़े सनेह लघुन्ह पर करहीं । गिरि निज सिरनि सदा तृन धरहीं ॥
baṛe saneha laghunha para karahīṁ, giri nija sirani sadā tṛna dharahīṁ.
जलधि अगाध मौलि बह फेनू । संतत धरनि धरत सिर रेनू ॥
jaladhi agādha mauli baha phenū, saṁtata dharani dharata sira renū.

Trans:

"Hearken, O king, there are diverse expedients among men, but hard to put in practice and of doubtful effect. There is however, one very simple plan—though even this involves a difficulty. Its contrivance depends upon me; and for me to go to your capital is out of the question—for to this day from the time I was born I have never entered a house or a village. But if I do not go, it will be a misfortune for you; so thus I am in a dilemma." The king replied in gentle tones, "It is, my lord, a maxim of scripture that the great show kindness to the small; thus mountains bear even tiny grasses on their head; and the fathomless ocean bears on its bosom the floating foam; and the earth on its head wears the dust."

दोहा-dohā:

अस कहि गहे नरेस पद स्वामी होहु कृपाल ।
asa kahi gahe naresa pada svāmī hohu kṛpāla,
मोहि लागि दुख सहिअ प्रभु सज्जन दीनदयाल ॥ १६७ ॥
mohi lāgi dukha sahia prabhu sajjana dīnadayāla. 167.

Trans:

Saying thusly and embracing his feet, the king cried: "Be gracious, my lord, ever pitiful to the faithful in distress, and take this trouble on my behalf."

चौपाई-caupāī:

जानि नृपहि आपन आधीना । बोला तापस कपट प्रबीना ॥
jāni nṛpahi āpana ādhīnā, bolā tāpasa kapaṭa prabīnā.
सत्य कहउँ भूपति सुनु तोही । जग नाहिन दुर्लभ कछु मोही ॥
satya kahauṁ bhūpati sunu tohī, jaga nāhina durlabha kachu mohī.
अवसि काज मैं करिहउँ तोरा । मन तन बचन भगत तैं मोरा ॥
avasi kāja maiṁ karihauṁ torā, mana tana bacana bhagata taiṁ morā.
जोग जुगुति तप मंत्र प्रभाऊ । फलइ तबहिं जब करिअ दुराऊ ॥
joga juguti tapa maṁtra prabhāū, phalai tabahiṁ jaba karia durāū.
जौं नरेस मैं करौं रसोई । तुम्ह परुसहु मोहि जान न कोई ॥
jauṁ naresa maiṁ karauṁ rasoī, tumha parusahu mohi jāna na koī.
अन्न सो जोइ जोइ भोजन करई । सोइ सोइ तव आयसु अनुसरई ॥
anna so joi joi bhojana karaī, soi soi tava āyasu anusaraī.
पुनि तिन्ह के गृह जेवँइ जोऊ । तव बस होइ भूप सुनु सोऊ ॥
puni tinha ke gṛha jevaṁi joū, tava basa hoi bhūpa sunu soū.
जाइ उपाय रचहु नृप एहू । संबत भरि संकलप करेहू ॥
jāi upāya racahu nṛpa ehū, saṁbata bhari saṁkalapa karehū.

Trans:

Perceiving that the king was altogether under his influence the false hermit, the arch-deceiver, now plunged it in: "Hearken, O king, I tell you truly there is nothing in the world I cannot do; and as you show yourself in thought, word, and action to be devoted to me, I will assuredly accomplish your object for you. The power of magical devices, penance, and spells works only when secrecy is maintained. If, O king, I act as cook and you serve, without anyone knowing me, then whosoever partakes the food so prepared shall become amenable to your edicts; and further anyone who in turn eats at their house too will come under the power of your will. Go now and carry out this stratagem; and make a vow for a whole year;

दोहा-dohā:

नित नूतन द्विज सहस सत बरेहु सहित परिवार ।
nita nūtana dvija sahasa sata barehu sahita parivāra,
मैं तुम्हरे संकलप लगि दिनहिं करबि जेवनार ॥ १६८॥
maiṁ tumhare saṁkalapa lagi dinahiṁ karabi jevanāra. 168.

Trans:

and every day entertain a new set of a hundred thousand Brahmins with their families; while I, as long as the vow lasts, will prepare the daily banquet.

चौपाई-caupāī:

एहि बिधि भूप कष्ट अति थोरें । होइहहिं सकल बिप्र बस तोरें ॥
ehi bidhi bhūpa kaṣṭa ati thoreṁ, hoihahiṁ sakala bipra basa toreṁ.
करिहहिं बिप्र होम मख सेवा । तेहिं प्रसंग सहजेहिं बस देवा ॥
karihahiṁ bipra homa makha sevā, tehiṁ prasaṁga sahajehiṁ basa devā.
और एक तोहि कहउँ लखाऊ । मैं एहिं बेष न आउब काऊ ॥
aura eka tohi kahaūṁ lakhāū, maiṁ ehiṁ beṣa na āuba kāū.
तुम्हरे उपरोहित कहुँ राया । हरि आनब मैं करि निज माया ॥
tumhare uparohita kahuṁ rāyā, hari ānaba maiṁ kari nija māyā.
तपबल तेहि करि आपु समाना । रखिहउँ इहाँ बरष परवाना ॥
tapabala tehi kari āpu samānā, rakhihauṁ ihāṁ baraṣa paravānā.
मैं धरि तासु बेषु सुनु राजा । सब बिधि तोर सँवारब काजा ॥
maiṁ dhari tāsu beṣu sunu rājā, saba bidhi tora saṁvāraba kājā.
गै निसि बहुत सयन अब कीजे । मोहि तोहि भूप भेंट दिन तीजे ॥
gai nisi bahuta sayana aba kīje, mohi tohi bhūpa bheṁṭa dina tīje.
मैं तपबल तोहि तुरग समेता । पहुँचैहउँ सोवतहि निकेता ॥
maiṁ tapabala tohi turaga sametā, pahuṁcaihauṁ sovatahi niketā.

Trans:

In this way, O king, there will be very little trouble, and all the Brahmins will come under the sway of your will. They again will perform sacrificial services, and thus the gods too will be easily won over. Now let me give you one sign: I will not come to you in this form but another. By my delusive power I will bring away your family priest and by the virtue of penance will make him look completely like myself—while I keep him here for a year. Meanwhile I, in his form, will manage everything for you there. Now the night is far gone, so take rest; on the third day we shall meet again. By my penitential power, I will convey you home—both you and your horse—even though you sleep.

दोहा-dohā:

मैं आउब सोइ बेषु धरि पहिचानेहु तब मोहि ।
maiṁ āuba soi beṣu dhari pahicānehu taba mohi,
जब एकांत बोलाइ सब कथा सुनावौं तोहि ॥ १६९॥
jaba ekāṁta bolāi saba kathā sunāvauṁ tohi. 169.

Trans:

Remember I will come in the form I have indicated to you; and you will recognize me when I call you to one side and remind you of all this."

चौपाई-caupāī:

सयन कीन्ह नृप आयसु मानी । आसन जाइ बैठ छलग्यानी ॥
sayana kīnha nṛpa āyasu mānī, āsana jāi baiṭha chalagyānī.
श्रमित भूप निद्रा अति आई । सो किमि सोव सोच अधिकाई ॥
śramita bhūpa nidrā ati āī, so kimi sova soca adhikāī.
कालकेतु निसिचर तहँ आवा । जेहिं सूकर होइ नृपहि भुलावा ॥
kālaketu nisicara tahaṁ āvā, jehiṁ sūkara hoi nṛpahi bhulāvā.
परम मित्र तापस नृप केरा । जानइ सो अति कपट घनेरा ॥
parama mitra tāpasa nṛpa kerā, jānai so ati kapaṭa ghanerā.
तेहि के सत सुत अरु दस भाई । खल अति अजय देव दुखदाई ॥
tehi ke sata suta aru dasa bhāī, khala ati ajaya deva dukhadāī.
प्रथमहिं भूप समर सब मारे । बिप्र संत सुर देखि दुखारे ॥
prathamahiṁ bhūpa samara saba māre, bipra saṁta sura dekhi dukhāre.
तेहिं खल पाछिल बयरु सँभारा । तापस नृप मिलि मंत्र बिचारा ॥
tehiṁ khala pāchila bayaru saṁbhārā, tāpasa nṛpa mili maṁtra bicārā.
जेहिं रिपु छय सोइ रचेन्हि उपाऊ । भावी बस न जान कछु राऊ ॥
jehiṁ ripu chaya soi racenhi upāū, bhāvī basa na jāna kachu rāū.

Trans:

The king, as enjoined, retired to his couch, while the arch-deceiver took his wonted seat. Deep sleep came upon the weary king, but what sleep for the other distraught with care? Then came the demon Kal-ketu—who was the boar that had led the king astray—a great friend of the hermit king, and much skilled in manifold ways of deceit. He had a hundred sons and ten brothers, who were great villains, invincible and annoying to the gods. Seeing the Brahmins, saints and gods in distress the king had already killed them all in battle. That wretch, nursing his old quarrel, combined with the false-hermit in devising a plot for the destruction of their common enemy. The king overmastered by fate knew nothing of it.

दोहा-dohā:

रिपु तेजसी अकेल अपि लघु करि गनिअ न ताहु ।
ripu tejasī akela api laghu kari gania na tāhu,
अजहुँ देत दुख रबि ससिहि सिर अवसेषित राहु ॥ १७०॥
ajahuṁ deta dukha rabi sasihi sira avaseṣita rāhu. 170.

Trans:

A powerful foe, even though surprised alone, is not to be lightly regarded. To this day Rāhu, though he has nothing left but his head, is able to annoy both the sun and the moon.

चौपाई-caupāī:

तापस नृप निज सखहि निहारी । हरषि मिलेउ उठि भयउ सुखारी ॥
tāpasa nṛpa nija sakhahi nihārī, haraṣi mileu uṭhi bhayau sukhārī.
मित्रहि कहि सब कथा सुनाई । जातुधान बोला सुख पाई ॥
mitrahi kahi saba kathā sunāī, jātudhāna bolā sukha pāī.
अब साधेउँ रिपु सुनहु नरेसा । जौं तुम्ह कीन्ह मोर उपदेसा ॥
aba sādheuṁ ripu sunahu naresā, jauṁ tumha kīnha mora upadesā.
परिहरि सोच रहहु तुम्ह सोई । बिनु औषध बिआधि बिधि खोई ॥
parihari soca rahahu tumha soī, binu auṣadha biādhi bidhi khoī.
कुल समेत रिपु मूल बहाई । चौथें दिवस मिलब मैं आई ॥
kula sameta ripu mūla bahāī, cautheṁ divasa milaba maiṁ āī.
तापस नृपहि बहुत परितोषी । चला महाकपटी अतिरोषी ॥
tāpasa nṛpahi bahuta paritoṣī, calā mahākapaṭī atiroṣī.
भानुप्रतापहि बाजि समेता । पहुँचाएसि छन माझ निकेता ॥
bhānupratāpahi bāji sametā, pahuṁcāesi chana mājha niketā.
नृपहि नारि पहिं सयन कराई । हयगृहँ बाँधेसि बाजि बनाई ॥
nṛpahi nāri pahiṁ sayana karāī, hayagṛhaṁ bāṁdhesi bāji banāī.

Trans:

When the hermit-king saw his ally, he rose in great joy to meet him and told his friend the whole story. The demon too was very glad and said, "Listen king, since you have followed my advice, take the enemy as subdued. Free yourself of all anxiety and remain at ease. God has affected a cure without the use of a medicine; and now we will destroy the enemy to the very root. Let me go and see you in four days from now." Fully reassuring the hermit-king, the arch-impostor left in great wrath. In an instant he conveyed Pratap-bhanu to his palace, horse and all. Putting the king to bed besides his queen, he tied up the horse in the stall at its usual spot.

दोहा-dohā:

राजा के उपरोहितहि हरि लै गयउ बहोरि ।
rājā ke uparohitahi hari lai gayau bahori,
लै राखेसि गिरि खोह महुँ मायाँ करि मति भोरि ॥ १७१ ॥
lai rākhesi giri khoha mahuṁ māyāṁ kari mati bhori. 171.

Trans:

Next he carried away the king's family priest, and by dint of his supernatural powers deprived him of all senses, and thus imprisoned him in a cave on the mountain.

चौपाई-caupāī:

आपु बिरचि उपरोहित रूपा । परेउ जाइ तेहि सेज अनूपा ॥
āpu biraci uparohita rūpā, pareu jāi tehi seja anūpā.
जागेउ नृप अनभएँ बिहाना । देखि भवन अति अचरजु माना ॥
jāgeu nṛpa anabhaeṁ bihānā, dekhi bhavana ati acaraju mānā.
मुनि महिमा मन महुँ अनुमानी । उठेउ गवँहिं जेहिं जान न रानी ॥
muni mahimā mana mahuṁ anumānī, uṭheu gavaṁhiṁ jehiṁ jāna na rānī.
कानन गयउ बाजि चढ़ि तेहीं । पुर नर नारि न जानेउ केहीं ॥
kānana gayau bāji caṛhi tehīṁ, pura nara nāri na jāneu kehīṁ.
गएँ जाम जुग भूपति आवा । घर घर उत्सव बाज बधावा ॥
gaeṁ jāma juga bhūpati āvā, ghara ghara utsava bāja badhāvā.
उपरोहितहि देख जब राजा । चकित बिलोक सुमिरि सोइ काजा ॥
uparohitahi dekha jaba rājā, cakita biloka sumiri soi kājā.
जुग सम नृपहि गए दिन तीनी । कपटी मुनि पद रह मति लीनी ॥
juga sama nṛpahi gae dina tīnī, kapaṭī muni pada raha mati līnī.
समय जानि उपरोहित आवा । नृपहि मते सब कहि समुझावा ॥
samaya jāni uparohita āvā, nṛpahi mate saba kahi samujhāvā.

Trans:

Then himself assuming the priest's form the demon went and lay down on the couch in his nice home. At daybreak the king woke and was astonished to find himself at his palace. Much impressed with the hermit's power, he rose and went out unperceived by the queen. Then mounting his horse he rode off to the wood, without any of the people in the city knowing it. When it was noon he returned; and in every house there was rejoicing, with music and singing. When he saw the family priest, he looked at him and he marveled as he remembered the work that was to be accomplished. The three days seemed like an age, so absorbed was he in expectation of the false hermit's coming. At the appointed time the priest approached and reminded him in detail of all that had been agreed upon.

दोहा-dohā:

नृप हरषेउ पहिचानि गुरु भ्रम बस रहा न चेत ।
nṛpa haraṣeu pahicāni guru bhrama basa rahā na ceta,
बरे तुरत सत सहस बर बिप्र कुटुंब समेत ॥ १७२ ॥
bare turata sata sahasa bara bipra kuṭuṁba sameta. 172.

Trans:

The king was delighted to recognize the Gurū, and being too infatuated to have any sense left, at once sent out an invitation for feast to a hundred thousand Brahmins along with their families.

चौपाई-caupāī:

उपरोहित जेवनार बनाई । छरस चारि बिधि जसि श्रुति गाई ॥
uparohita jevanāra banāī, charasa cāri bidhi jasi śruti gāī.
मायामय तेहिं कीन्हि रसोई । बिंजन बहु गनि सकइ न कोई ॥
māyāmaya tehiṁ kīnhi rasoī, biṁjana bahu gani sakai na koī.
बिबिध मृगन्ह कर आमिष राँधा । तेहि महुँ बिप्र माँसु खल साँधा ॥
bibidha mṛganha kara āmiṣa rāṁdhā, tehi mahuṁ bipra māṁsu khala sāṁdhā.
भोजन कहुँ सब बिप्र बोलाए । पद पखारि सादर बैठाए ॥
bhojana kahuṁ saba bipra bolāe, pada pakhāri sādara baiṭhāe.
परुसन जबहिं लाग महिपाला । भै अकासबानी तेहि काला ॥
parusana jabahiṁ lāga mahipālā, bhai akāsabānī tehi kālā.
बिप्रबृंद उठि उठि गृह जाहू । है बड़ि हानि अन्न जनि खाहू ॥
biprabṛṁda uṭhi uṭhi gṛha jāhū, hai baṛi hāni anna jani khāhū.
भयउ रसोईं भूसुर माँसू । सब द्विज उठे मानि बिस्वासू ॥
bhayau rasoīṁ bhūsura māṁsū, saba dvija uṭhe māni bisvāsū.
भूप बिकल मति मोहँ भुलानी । भावी बस न आव मुख बानी ॥
bhūpa bikala mati mohaṁ bhulānī, bhāvī basa na āva mukha bānī.

Trans:

The fake-priest superintended the cooking, and in accordance with sacred prescription concocted the six tastes in the four different ways, preparing a most sumptuous banquet, with sauces and condiments more than anyone could count. After dressing a great variety of dishes, the wretch introduced into the recipe some pieces of Brahmin's flesh. Meanwhile the guests were all ushered, and the king respectfully washed their feet and politely showed them to their seats. But directly as they began to touch the food, a voice came down from the heavens: "Up, up, all ye Brahmins, and return to your homes; though the loss be great, yet touch not the food—for there is Brahmin's flesh in the dish." Up rose all the holy men, believing the heavenly voice, while the king, distracted and out of his senses, could not utter a single word, overmastered by fate.

दोहा-dohā:

बोले बिप्र सकोप तब नहिं कछु कीन्ह बिचार ।
bole bipra sakopa taba nahiṁ kachu kīnha bicāra,
जाइ निसाचर होहु नृप मूढ़ सहित परिवार ॥ १७३ ॥
jāi nisācara hohu nṛpa mūṛha sahita parivāra. 173.

Trans:

Without giving a second thought, the Brahmins in their wrath spelled out this curse: "O foolish king take birth in a demon's form, you and your entire clan.

चौपाई-caupāī:

छत्रबंधु तैं बिप्र बोलाई । घालै लिए सहित समुदाई ॥
chatrabaṁdhu taiṁ bipra bolāī, ghālai lie sahita samudāī.
ईस्वर राखा धरम हमारा । जैहसि तैं समेत परिवारा ॥
īsvara rākhā dharama hamārā, jaihasi taiṁ sameta parivārā.
संबत मध्य नास तव होऊ । जलदाता न रहिहि कुल कोऊ ॥
saṁbata madhya nāsa tava hoū, jaladātā na rahihi kula koū.
नृप सुनि श्राप बिकल अति त्रासा । भै बहोरि बर गिरा अकासा ॥
nṛpa suni śrāpa bikala ati trāsā, bhai bahori bara girā akāsā.
बिप्रहु श्राप बिचारि न दीन्हा । नहिं अपराध भूप कछु कीन्हा ॥
biprahu śrāpa bicāri na dīnhā, nahiṁ aparādha bhūpa kachu kīnhā.
चकित बिप्र सब सुनि नभबानी । भूप गयउ जहँ भोजन खानी ॥
cakita bipra saba suni nabhabānī, bhūpa gayau jahaṁ bhojana khānī.
तहँ न असन नहिं बिप्र सुआरा । फिरेउ राउ मन सोच अपारा ॥
tahaṁ na asana nahiṁ bipra suārā, phireu rāu mana soca apārā.
सब प्रसंग महिसुरन्ह सुनाई । त्रसित परेउ अवनीं अकुलाई ॥
saba prasaṁga mahisuranha sunāī, trasita pareu avanīṁ akulāī.

Trans:

O vile king, inviting all we Brahmins, you were bent to destroy us along with our families? Thankfully God has preserved our honor—but you and your entire race are now completely undone. You shall perish in the course of a year, nor shall there be anyone left to offer libations to your soul." When the king heard the curse he was terror-stricken. Again a voice came from heaven: "The Brahmins have uttered this curse without due consideration, the king has committed no crime." All the Brahmins were astounded when they heard the heavenly voice. The king hastened to the kitchen; there he found neither, food nor the cook; and then turning away in deep thought, he declared the whole history to the Brahmins, and in his terror and distress threw himself upon the ground.

दोहा-dohā:

भूपति भावी मिटइ नहिं जदपि न दूषन तोर ।
bhūpati bhāvī miṭai nahiṁ jadapi na dūṣana tora,
किएँ अन्यथा होइ नहिं बिप्रश्राप अति घोर ॥ १७४॥
kieṁ anyathā hoi nahiṁ bipraśrāpa ati ghora. 174.

Trans:

"Though you, O king, are guiltless, what is fated fails not; the past is unalterable; a Brahmin's curse is a terrible thing."

चौपाई-caupāī:

अस कहि सब महिदेव सिधाए । समाचार पुरलोगन्ह पाए ॥
asa kahi saba mahideva sidhāe, samācāra puraloganha pāe.
सोचहिं दूषन दैवहि देहीं । बिचरत हंस काग किय जेहीं ॥
socahiṁ dūṣana daivahi dehīṁ, bicarata haṁsa kāga kiya jehīṁ.
उपरोहितहि भवन पहुँचाई । असुर तापसहि खबरि जनाई ॥
uparohitahi bhavana pahuṁcāī, asura tāpasahi khabari janāī.
तेहिं खल जहँ तहँ पत्र पठाए । सजि सजि सेन भूप सब धाए ॥
tehiṁ khala jahaṁ tahaṁ patra paṭhāe, saji saji sena bhūpa saba dhāe.
घेरेन्हि नगर निसान बजाई । बिबिध भाँति नित होइ लराई ॥
gherenhi nagara nisāna bajāī, bibidha bhāṁti nita hoi larāī.
जूझे सकल सुभट करि करनी । बंधु समेत परेउ नृप धरनी ॥
jūjhe sakala subhaṭa kari karanī, baṁdhu sameta pareu nṛpa dharanī.
सत्यकेतु कुल कोउ नहिं बाँचा । बिप्रश्राप किमि होइ असाँचा ॥
satyaketu kula kou nahiṁ bāṁcā, bipraśrāpa kimi hoi asāṁcā.
रिपु जिति सब नृप नगर बसाई । निज पुर गवने जय जसु पाई ॥
ripu jiti saba nṛpa nagara basāī, nija pura gavane jaya jasu pāī.

Trans:

So saying, all the Brahmins went their way. When the people of the city heard the news, they were much vexed and abused Fate, who had begun upon a swan and ended making a crow instead. Conveying the family priest back to the palace, the demon told the hermit-king all the tidings. The wretch in turn dispatched letters in all directions and a host of princes hastened with their troops martially arrayed and, beating their kettledrums, beleaguered the city. Day after day there were battles of various kinds; all his champions fell in fight after doing valorously, and the king with his brother bit the dust. Not one of Satyaketu's families escaped: for a Brahmin's curse can never fail of accomplishing. Triumphing over their foe the rival kings re-founded the city, and then, crowned with victory, returned to their own states.

दोहा-dohā:

भरद्वाज सुनु जाहि जब होइ बिधाता बाम ।
bharadvāja sunu jāhi jaba hoi bidhātā bāma,
धूरि मेरुसम जनक जम ताहि ब्यालसम दाम ॥ १७५॥
dhūri merusama janaka jama tāhi byālasama dāma. 175.

Trans:

Hearken, Bharadvāja, whoever incurs the anger of heaven, for him a grain of dust becomes vast as Mount Meru, a feather becomes like the angel of death, and every rope a snake.

चौपाई-caupāī:

काल पाइ मुनि सुनु सोइ राजा । भयउ निसाचर सहित समाजा ॥
kāla pāi muni sunu soi rājā, bhayau nisācara sahita samājā.
दस सिर ताहि बीस भुजदंडा । रावन नाम बीर बरिबंडा ॥
dasa sira tāhi bīsa bhujadaṁḍā, rāvana nāma bīra baribaṁḍā.
भूप अनुज अरिमर्दन नामा । भयउ सो कुंभकरन बलधामा ॥
bhūpa anuja arimardana nāmā, bhayau so kuṁbhakarana baladhāmā.
सचिव जो रहा धरमरुचि जासू । भयउ बिमात्र बंधु लघु तासू ॥
saciva jo rahā dharamaruci jāsū, bhayau bimātra baṁdhu laghu tāsū.
नाम बिभीषन जेहि जग जाना । बिष्नुभगत बिग्यान निधाना ॥
nāma bibhīṣana jehi jaga jānā, biṣnubhagata bigyāna nidhānā.
रहे जे सुत सेवक नृप केरे । भए निसाचर घोर घनेरे ॥
rahe je suta sevaka nṛpa kere, bhae nisācara ghora ghanere.
कामरूप खल जिनस अनेका । कुटिल भयंकर बिगत बिबेका ॥
kāmarūpa khala jinasa anekā, kuṭila bhayaṁkara bigata bibekā.
कृपा रहित हिंसक सब पापी । बरनि न जाहिं बिस्व परितापी ॥
kṛpā rahita hiṁsaka saba pāpī, barani na jāhiṁ bisva paritāpī.

Trans:

Hearken, reverend sir, in due time along with his race, that king was born as a demon—with ten heads and twenty arms, a formidable hero, by the name Rāvan. The king's younger brother, Ari-mardan, became the valiant Kumbh-karan, while the minister Dharm-ruchi became his half-brother, the world-famous Vibhīshan, the all-wise votary of Vishnu. As for the king's sons and servants, they were born a fierce demon crew: wretches taking various shapes at will; wicked, monstrous, and devoid of knowledge, they were merciless, injurious, criminals—a torment to all creation beyond what the words can tell.

दोहा-dohā:

उपजे जदपि पुलस्त्यकुल पावन अमल अनूप ।
upaje jadapi pulastyakula pāvana amala anūpa,
तदपि महीसुर श्राप बस भए सकल अघरूप ॥ १७६॥
tadapi mahīsura śrāpa basa bhae sakala agharūpa. 176.

Trans:

Though born in the incomparably pure and holy family of Pulastya, yet on account of the Brahmin's curse all were of hateful mien.

चौपाई-caupāī:

कीन्ह बिबिध तप तीनिहुँ भाई । परम उग्र नहिं बरनि सो जाई ॥
kīnha bibidha tapa tīnihuṁ bhāī, parama ugra nahiṁ barani so jāī.
गयउ निकट तप देखि बिधाता । मागहु बर प्रसन्न मैं ताता ॥
gayau nikaṭa tapa dekhi bidhātā, māgahu bara prasanna maiṁ tātā.
करि बिनती पद गहि दससीसा । बोलेउ बचन सुनहु जगदीसा ॥
kari binatī pada gahi dasasīsā, boleu bacana sunahu jagadīsā.
हम काहू के मरहिं न मारें । बानर मनुज जाति दुइ बारें ॥
hama kāhū ke marahiṁ na māreṁ, bānara manuja jāti dui bāreṁ.
एवमस्तु तुम्ह बड़ तप कीन्हा । मैं ब्रह्माँ मिलि तेहि बर दीन्हा ॥
evamastu tumha baṛa tapa kīnhā, maiṁ brahmāṁ mili tehi bara dīnhā.
पुनि प्रभु कुंभकरन पहिं गयऊ । तेहि बिलोकि मन बिसमय भयऊ ॥
puni prabhu kuṁbhakarana pahiṁ gayaū, tehi biloki mana bisamaya bhayaū.
जौं एहिं खल नित करब अहारू । होइहि सब उजारि संसारू ॥
jauṁ ehiṁ khala nita karaba ahārū, hoihi saba ujāri saṁsārū.
सारद प्रेरि तासु मति फेरी । मागेसि नीद मास षट केरी ॥
sārada preri tāsu mati pherī, māgesi nīda māsa ṣaṭa kerī.

Trans:

The three brothers practiced manifold penitential observances, severe beyond all descriptions. The Creator drew nigh to witness them, and said: 'Son, I am well pleased, ask a boon.' The ten-headed suppliantly clasped his feet and said: "Hear, O lord of earth, may I die at the hand of none, save men or monkey." Brahmmā and I granted him his boon, saying: 'So be it, you have done great penance.' Then the lord went to Kumbh-karan, and was astounded at his appearance: "If this wretch is always eating, the whole world will be laid to waste." So he sent Saraswatī to turn his head, and so in his confusion he asked for six months of slumber—the very opposite of what he had wished to ask.

दोहा-dohā:

गए बिभीषन पास पुनि कहेउ पुत्र बर मागु।
gae bibhīṣana pāsa puni kaheu putra bara māgu,
तेहिं मागेउ भगवंत पद कमल अमल अनुरागु॥१७७॥
tehiṁ māgeu bhagavaṁta pada kamala amala anurāgu. 177.

Trans:

Then he went to Vibhīshan and said: 'Son, ask a boon' and he asked for perfect love for God.

चौपाई-caupāī:

तिन्हहि देइ बर ब्रह्म सिधाए। हरषित ते अपने गृह आए॥
tinhahi dei bara brahma sidhāe, harașita te apane gṛha āe.
मय तनुजा मंदोदरि नामा। परम सुंदरी नारि ललामा॥
maya tanujā maṁdodari nāmā, parama suṁdarī nāri lalāmā.
सोइ मयँ दीन्हि रावनहि आनी। होइहि जातुधानपति जानी॥
soi mayaṁ dīnhi rāvanahi ānī, hoihi jātudhānapati jānī.
हरषित भयउ नारि भलि पाई। पुनि दोउ बंधु बिआहेसि जाई॥
harașita bhayau nāri bhali pāī, puni dou baṁdhu biāhesi jāī.
गिरि त्रिकूट एक सिंधु मझारी। बिधि निर्मित दुर्गम अति भारी॥
giri trikūṭa eka siṁdhu majhārī, bidhi nirmita durgama ati bhārī.
सोइ मय दानवँ बहुरि सँवारा। कनक रचित मनिभवन अपारा॥
soi maya dānavaṁ bahuri saṁvārā, kanaka racita manibhavana apārā.
भोगावति जसि अहिकुल बासा। अमरावति जसि सक्रनिवासा॥
bhogāvati jasi ahikula bāsā, amarāvati jasi sakranivāsā.
तिन्ह तें अधिक रम्य अति बंका। जग बिख्यात नाम तेहि लंका॥
tinha teṁ adhika ramya ati baṁkā, jaga bikhyāta nāma tehi laṁkā.

Trans:

After granting these boons Brahmmā departed, and the brothers went home rejoicing. Now Māyā had a daughter by name Mandodarī—of exceeding beauty, a jewel of womankind, whom her father brought and made over to Rāvan; and thus she became the demon's head-queen. Delighted at having obtained so good a wife, he went and found suitable brides for his brothers as well. Now, in the middle of the ocean is a three-peaked mountain, by Brahmmā's contrivance most difficult of access; here the demon Māyā had constructed a vast palace of gold and jewels, more beautiful and charming than Bhogwati, the city of the serpent kings, or Indra's capital Amrawati, and it was called Lankā, a name famous throughout the world.

दोहा-dohā:

खाईं सिंधु गभीर अति चारिहुँ दिसि फिरि आव।
khāīṁ siṁdhu gabhīra ati cārihuṁ disi phiri āva,
कनक कोट मनि खचित दृढ़ बरनि न जाइ बनाव॥१७८क॥
kanaka koṭa mani khacita dṛṛha barani na jāi banāva. 178(ka).

हरि प्रेरित जेहिं कलप जोइ जातुधानपति होइ।
hari prerita jehiṁ kalapa joi jātudhānapati hoi,
सूर प्रतापी अतुलबल दल समेत बस सोइ॥१७८ख॥
sūra pratāpī atulabala dala sameta basa soi. 178(kha).

Trans:

The deep ocean was its moat, washing its four sides; and its massive walls were of gold set with jewels in ways that defied description. In every Age a soul, whom Harī predestines, lives there with his army, as a mighty and puissant chief: as the Demon King.

चौपाई-caupāī:

रहे तहाँ निसिचर भट भारे। ते सब सुरन्ह समर संघारे॥
rahe tahāṁ nisicara bhaṭa bhāre, te saba suranha samara saṁghāre.
अब तहँ रहहिं सक्र के प्रेरे। रच्छक कोटि जच्छपति केरे॥
aba tahaṁ rahahiṁ sakra ke prere, racchaka koṭi jacchapati kere.
दसमुख कतहुँ खबरि असि पाई। सेन साजि गढ़ घेरेसि जाई॥
dasamukha katahuṁ khabari asi pāī, sena sāji gaṛha gheresi jāī.
देखि बिकट भट बड़ि कटकाई। जच्छ जीव लै गए पराई॥
dekhi bikaṭa bhaṭa baṛi kaṭakāī, jaccha jīva lai gae parāī.
फिरि सब नगर दसानन देखा। गयउ सोच सुख भयउ बिसेषा॥
phiri saba nagara dasānana dekhā, gayau soca sukha bhayau biseṣā.
सुंदर सहज अगम अनुमानी। कीन्हि तहाँ रावन रजधानी॥
suṁdara sahaja agama anumānī, kīnhi tahāṁ rāvana rajadhānī.
जेहि जस जोग बाँटि गृह दीन्हे। सुखी सकल रजनीचर कीन्हे॥
jehi jasa joga bāṁṭi gṛha dīnhe, sukhī sakala rajanīcara kīnhe.
एक बार कुबेर पर धावा। पुष्पक जान जीति लै आवा॥
eka bāra kubera para dhāvā, puṣpaka jāna jīti lai āvā.

Trans:

There in Lankā, had dwelt great demon warriors once, but all had been slain in battle by the gods; and now by Indra's commission it was occupied by a million guards of Kuber's. Rāvan happened to hear of this, and at once marshaled his army and went and besieged the place. When the Yakshs saw the vast host of fierce warriors, they all fled for their lives. Thereupon Rāvan inspected the whole of the city, and was so highly pleased with it that all his trouble was forgotten. Seeing that it was not only beautiful but also a naturally impregnable site, he fixed his capital there; and assigning quarters to his followers according to their ranks, made them live happily there. Upon one occasion he sallied forth against Kuber and carried away his aerial chariot '*Pushpak*' as a trophy.

दोहा-dohā:

कौतुकहीं कैलास पुनि लीन्हेसि जाइ उठाइ।
kautukahīṁ kailāsa puni līnhesi jāi uṭhāi,
मनहुँ तौलि निज बाहुबल चला बहुत सुख पाइ॥१७९॥
manahuṁ tauli nija bāhubala calā bahuta sukha pāi. 179.

Trans:

At another time, in mere jest and sport he went and overthrew Kailāsh, and after thus testing the prowess of his men of war, waxed yet more jubilant than ever before.

चौपाई-caupāī:

सुख संपति सुत सेन सहाई। जय प्रताप बल बुद्धि बड़ाई॥
sukha saṁpati suta sena sahāī, jaya pratāpa bala buddhi baṛāī.
नित नूतन सब बाढ़त जाई। जिमि प्रतिलाभ लोभ अधिकाई॥
nita nūtana saba bāṛhata jāī, jimi pratilābha lobha adhikāī.
अतिबल कुंभकरन अस भ्राता। जेहि कहुँ नहिं प्रतिभट जग जाता॥
atibala kuṁbhakarana asa bhrātā, jehi kahuṁ nahiṁ pratibhaṭa jaga jātā.
करइ पान सोवइ षट मासा। जागत होइ तिहूँ पुर त्रासा॥
karai pāna sovai ṣaṭa māsā, jāgata hoi tihūṁ pura trāsā.
जौं दिन प्रति अहार कर सोई। बिस्व बेगि सब चौपट होई॥
jauṁ dina prati ahāra kara soī, bisva begi saba caupaṭa hoī.
समर धीर नहिं जाइ बखाना। तेहि सम अमित बीर बलवाना॥
samara dhīra nahiṁ jāi bakhānā, tehi sama amita bīra balavānā.
बारिदनाद जेठ सुत तासू। भट महुँ प्रथम लीक जग जासू॥
bāridanāda jeṭha suta tāsū, bhaṭa mahuṁ prathama līka jaga jāsū.
जेहि न होइ रन सनमुख कोई। सुरपुर नितहिं परावन होई॥
jehi na hoi rana sanamukha koī, surapura nitahiṁ parāvana hoī.

Trans:

His happiness and prosperity, the number of his sons, his army and his allies, his conquests, his might, and his superior wisdom, all grew day by day, more and more, in the same way as avarice grows with gain. Thus too did his brother, the stalwart Kumbh-karan, who was a champion without a match in the world. After drinking his fill he slept for six months, and at his waking the three worlds trembled. If he had taken a meal every day the whole world would soon have been stripped bare: so unspeakably staunch in fight was he that no other hero could be compared to him. Rāvan's eldest son was Meghnad, who held the first place among the world's champions; before whom none could stand in the battle, and who was ever harassing the city of heaven.

दोहा-dohā:

कुमुख अकंपन कुलिसरद धूमकेतु अतिकाय ।
kumukha akaṁpana kulisarada dhūmaketu atikāya,
एक एक जग जीति सक ऐसे सुभट निकाय ॥ १८० ॥
eka eka jaga jīti saka aise subhaṭa nikāya. 180.

Trans:

And many other demons were there, each by himself able to subdue the whole world, such as the hideous Kumukh, the dauntless Akampan, Kulisarad with teeth like thunderbolts, the fiery Dhumr-ketu, and the huge Atikaya—

चौपाई-caupāī:

कामरूप जानहिं सब माया । सपनेहुँ जिन्ह कें धरम न दाया ॥
kāmarūpa jānahiṁ saba māyā, sapanehuṁ jinha keṁ dharama na dāyā.
दसमुख बैठ सभाँ एक बारा । देखि अमित आपन परिवारा ॥
dasamukha baiṭha sabhāṁ eka bārā, dekhi amita āpana parivārā.
सुत समूह जन परिजन नाती । गनै को पार निसाचर जाती ॥
suta samūha jana parijana nātī, ganai ko pāra nisācara jātī.
सेन बिलोकि सहज अभिमानी । बोला बचन क्रोध मद सानी ॥
sena biloki sahaja abhimānī, bolā bacana krodha mada sānī.
सुनहु सकल रजनीचर जूथा । हमरे बैरी बिबुध बरूथा ॥
sunahu sakala rajanīcara jūthā, hamare bairī bibudha barūthā.
ते सनमुख नहिं करहिं लराई । देखि सबल रिपु जाहिं पराई ॥
te sanamukha nahiṁ karahiṁ larāī, dekhi sabala ripu jāhiṁ parāī.
तेन्ह कर मरन एक बिधि होई । कहउँ बुझाइ सुनहु अब सोई ॥
tenha kara marana eka bidhi hoī, kahauṁ bujhāi sunahu aba soī.
द्विजभोजन मख होम सराधा । सब कै जाइ करहु तुम्ह बाधा ॥
dvijabhojana makha homa sarādhā, saba kai jāi karahu tumha bādhā.

Trans:

—all able to take any form at will, skilled in every kind of fraud, and without ever a thought of piety, pity, or goodness of heart. One day the Ten-headed was seated in court and reviewed his innumerable retainers, sons and grandsons, friends and servants, troops of demons, more than anyone could count. On seeing the host, he swelled with pride, and in fierce tones said: "Hearken, all ye demon troops, the host of heaven are my enemies; and they don't dare to stand up in an open fight but flee away at the sight of my great army. There is just one way of effecting their death, which I will declare, now listen to it: Go ye and put a stop to all feasting of Brahmins, to every sacrifice, oblation, and funeral rite;

दोहा-dohā:

छुधा छीन बलहीन सुर सहजेहिं मिलिहहिं आइ ।
chudhā chīna balahīna sura sahajehiṁ milihahiṁ āi,
तब मारिहउँ कि छाड़िहउँ भली भाँति अपनाइ ॥ १८१ ॥
taba mārihauṁ ki chāṛihauṁ bhalī bhāṁti apanāi. 181.

Trans:

then forthwith the faint and hungry gods will come out in the open, and whether I slay them or let them go they will be equally in my prowess.

चौपाई-caupāī:

मेघनाद कहुँ पुनि हँकरावा । दीन्ही सिख बलु बयरु बढ़ावा ॥
meghanāda kahuṁ puni haṁkarāvā, dīnhī sikha balu bayaru baṛhāvā.
जे सुर समर धीर बलवाना । जिन्ह कें लरिबे कर अभिमाना ॥
je sura samara dhīra balavānā, jinha keṁ laribe kara abhimānā.
तिन्हहि जीति रन आनेसु बाँधी । उठि सुत पितु अनुसासन काँधी ॥
tinhahi jīti rana ānesu bāṁdhī, uṭhi suta pitu anusāsana kāṁdhī.
एहि बिधि सबही अग्या दीन्ही । आपुनु चलेउ गदा कर लीन्ही ॥
ehi bidhi sabahī agyā dīnhī, āpunu caleu gadā kara līnhī.
चलत दसानन डोलति अवनी । गर्जत गर्भ स्त्रवहिं सुर रवनी ॥
calata dasānana ḍolati avanī, garjata garbha sravahiṁ sura ravanī.
रावन आवत सुनेउ सकोहा । देवन्ह तके मेरु गिरि खोहा ॥
rāvana āvata suneu sakohā, devanha take meru giri khohā.
दिगपालन्ह के लोक सुहाए । सूने सकल दसानन पाए ॥
digapālanha ke loka suhāe, sūne sakala dasānana pāe.
पुनि पुनि सिंघनाद करि भारी । देइ देवतन्ह गारि पचारी ॥
puni puni siṁghanāda kari bhārī, dei devatanha gāri pacārī.
रन मद मत्त फिरइ जग धावा । प्रतिभट खोजत कतहुँ न पावा ॥
rana mada matta phirai jaga dhāvā, pratibhaṭa khojata katahuṁ na pāvā.
रबि ससि पवन बरुन धनधारी । अगिनि काल जम सब अधिकारी ॥
rabi sasi pavana baruna dhanadhārī, agini kāla jama saba adhikārī.
किंनर सिद्ध मनुज सुर नागा । हठि सबही के पंथहिं लागा ॥
kiṁnara siddha manuja sura nāgā, haṭhi sabahī ke paṁthahiṁ lāgā.
ब्रह्मसृष्टि जहँ लगि तनुधारी । दसमुख बसबर्ती नर नारी ॥
brahmasṛṣṭi jahaṁ lagi tanudhārī, dasamukha basabartī nara nārī.
आयसु करहिं सकल भयभीता । नवहिं आइ नित चरन बिनीता ॥
āyasu karahiṁ sakala bhayabhītā, navahiṁ āi nita carana binītā.

Trans:

Again he called for Meghnad and exhorted him to yet more fury and greater courage: "The strong and warlike gods, who dare to confront you—you must vanquish and bring them here in chains." And up arose the son to perform his father's biddings. In this manner he ordered them all; and then he himself sallied forth, club in hand. As he marched, the earth shook, the heaven thundered, and pains of premature labor overtook the pregnant spouses of the gods. The gods themselves, on hearing of Rāvan's wrathful approach, sought the caves of Mount Meru. As he approached in turn each of the eight quarters of the globe, he found it deserted and abandoned by its guardian. Again and again he vehemently scoffed at the gods and shouted out challenges for a battle. Mad with lust of blood he traversed the whole wide world in search of a foe, but could nowhere discover one. The sun and moon; the wind; Varun and Kuber; fire, time death, and every divine power; *kinnars*, saints, men, gods, and serpents, all were turned out of their course. From one end of earth to the other, every living creature, whether male or female, was made a subject to Rāvan. All in turn did his bidding and crouched suppliantly at his feet.

दोहा-dohā:

भुजबल बिस्व बस्य करि राखेसि कोउ न सुतंत्र ।
bhujabala bisva basya kari rākhesi kou na sutaṁtra,
मंडलीक मनि रावन राज करइ निज मंत्र ॥ १८२क ॥
maṁḍalīka mani rāvana rāja karai nija maṁtra. 182(ka).

देव जच्छ गंधर्व नर किंनर नाग कुमारि ।
deva jaccha gaṁdharva nara kiṁnara nāga kumāri,
जीति बरीं निज बाहुबल बहु सुंदर बर नारि ॥ १८२ख ॥
jīti barīṁ nija bāhubala bahu suṁdara bara nārī. 182kha.

Trans:

By his mighty arm he subdued the whole universe and left not a single soul independent. Acting on his own counsel he exercised dominion over the whole round world. And many were the lovely dames he wedded after his conquests—daughters of gods and Yakshs and Gandharvs and men and Kinnars and Nags.

चौपाई-*caupāī:*

इंद्रजीत सन जो कछु कहेऊ । सो सब जनु पहिलेहिं करि रहेऊ ॥
imdrajīta sana jo kachu kaheū, so saba janu pahilehiṁ kari raheū.
प्रथमहिं जिन्ह कहुँ आयसु दीन्हा । तिन्ह कर चरित सुनहु जो कीन्हा ॥
prathamahiṁ jinha kahuṁ āyasu dīnhā, tinha kara carita sunahu jo kīnhā.
देखत भीमरूप सब पापी । निसिचर निकर देव परितापी ॥
dekhata bhīmarūpa saba pāpī, nisicara nikara deva paritāpī.
करहिं उपद्रव असुर निकाया । नाना रूप धरहिं करि माया ॥
karahiṁ upadrava asura nikāyā, nānā rūpa dharahiṁ kari māyā.
जेहि बिधि होइ धर्म निर्मूला । सो सब करहिं बेद प्रतिकूला ॥
jehi bidhi hoi dharma nirmūlā, so saba karahiṁ beda pratikūlā.
जेहिं जेहिं देस धेनु द्विज पावहिं । नगर गाउँ पुर आगि लगावहिं ॥
jehiṁ jehiṁ desa dhenu dvija pāvahiṁ, nagara gāuṁ pura āgi lagāvahiṁ.
सुभ आचरन कतहुँ नहिं होई । देव बिप्र गुरू मान न कोई ॥
subha ācarana katahuṁ nahiṁ hoī, deva bipra gurū māna na koī.
नहिं हरिभगति जग्य तप ग्याना । सपनेहुँ सुनिअ न बेद पुराना ॥
nahiṁ haribhagati jagya tapa gyānā, sapanehuṁ sunia na beda purānā.

Trans:

Whatever he told Indrajit to do was done in less time then it took to tell. Hear now how the other chiefs acted, to whom he gave orders. The whole demon crew—torments of heaven, villainous at heart, and foul of aspect, disguising themselves by the assumption of various forms, and acting in every way contrary to the Veda—in order to eradicate religion were ever ready for wreaking havocs everywhere. Wherever they found a cow or a Brahmin, they at once set fire to that city, town, or village. Pious observances were no longer anywhere in existence; and no respect was paid either to scripture, or Brahmin, or spiritual instructor; and there was no faith in Harī, or sacrifice, or prayer; nor existed alms-giving, and no one would ever dream of hearing either the Vedas or Purānas.

छंद-*chaṁda:*

जप जोग बिरागा तप मख भागा श्रवन सुनइ दससीसा ।
japa joga birāgā tapa makha bhāgā śravana sunai dasasīsā,
आपुनु उठि धावइ रहै न पावइ धरि सब घालइ खीसा ॥
āpunu uṭhi dhāvai rahai na pāvai dhari saba ghālai khīsā.
अस भ्रष्ट अचारा भा संसारा धर्म सुनिअ नहिं काना ।
asa bhraṣṭa acārā bhā saṁsārā dharma sunia nahiṁ kānā,
तेहि बहुबिधि त्रासइ देस निकासइ जो कह बेद पुराना ॥
tehi bahubidhi trāsai desa nikāsai jo kaha beda purānā.

Trans:

If ever any talk of prayer, penance, sacrifice, vigil, or fasting entered Rāvan's ear he would at once be on vigil and run to stop it. Allowing nothing of these, he destroyed everything with his own hands. The world was sunk in lawlessness; all holy sounds were banned; to read a sacred text was to be death or exile from the land.

सोरठा-*soraṭhā:*

बरनि न जाइ अनीति घोर निसाचर जो करहिं ।
barani na jāi anīti ghora nisācara jo karahiṁ,
हिंसा पर अति प्रीति तिन्ह के पापहि कवनि मिति ॥ १८३॥
hiṁsā para ati prīti tinha ke pāpahi kavani miti. 183.

Trans:

The fearful oppression that the demons wrought is beyond description: bent on total mischief, there was no limit to their evil doings.

मासपारायण छठा विश्राम
māsapārāyaṇa chaṭhā viśrāma
(Pause 6 for a Thirty-Day Recitation)

चौपाई-*caupāī:*

बाढ़े खल बहु चोर जुआरा । जे लंपट परधन परदारा ॥
bāṛhe khala bahu cora juārā, je laṁpaṭa paradhana paradārā.
मानहिं मातु पिता नहिं देवा । साधुन्ह सन करवावहिं सेवा ॥
mānahiṁ mātu pitā nahiṁ devā, sādhunha sana karavāvahiṁ sevā.
जिन्ह के यह आचरन भवानी । ते जानेहु निसिचर सब प्रानी ॥
jinha ke yaha ācarana bhavānī, te jānehu nisicara saba prānī.
अतिसय देखि धर्म कै ग्लानी । परम सभीत धरा अकुलानी ॥
atisaya dekhi dharma kai glānī, parama sabhīta dharā akulānī.
गिरि सरि सिंधु भार नहिं मोही । जस मोहि गरुअ एक पर द्रोही ॥
giri sari siṁdhu bhāra nahiṁ mohī, jasa mohi garua eka para drohī.
सकल धर्म देखइ बिपरीता । कहि न सकइ रावन भय भीता ॥
sakala dharma dekhai biparītā, kahi na sakai rāvana bhaya bhītā.
धेनु रूप धरि हृदयँ बिचारी । गई तहाँ जहँ सुर मुनि झारी ॥
dhenu rūpa dhari hṛdayaṁ bicārī, gaī tahāṁ jahaṁ sura muni jhārī.
निज संताप सुनाएसि रोई । काहू तें कछु काज न होई ॥
nija saṁtāpa sunāesi roī, kāhū teṁ kachu kāja na hoī.

Trans:

The wicked all thrived: thieves and gamblers, those who coveted their neighbor's wife or goods, those who honored neither father and mother nor the gods, and those who exacted service of men better than themselves. People who act in this way, O Bhawānī, resemble demons. Seeing the general persecution of religion, earth was terror-stricken and dismayed: 'The weight of mountains, lakes, and seas is nothing so heavy as this one tyrant.' She saw all faith perverted, and yet for fear of Rāvan could say nothing. After some consideration she took the form of a cow and went to the spot where the gods and saints were gathered together, and with tears in eyes declared to them her distress. But there was no help to be had from anyone of them.

छंद-*chaṁda:*

सुर मुनि गंधर्बा मिलि करि सर्बा गे बिरंचि के लोका ।
sura muni gaṁdharbā mili kari sarbā ge biraṁci ke lokā,
सँग गोतनुधारी भूमि बिचारी परम बिकल भय सोका ॥
saṁga gotanudhārī bhūmi bicārī parama bikala bhaya sokā.
ब्रह्माँ सब जाना मन अनुमाना मोर कछू न बसाई ।
brahmāṁ saba jānā mana anumānā mora kachū na basāī,
जा करि तैं दासी सो अबिनासी हमरेउ तोर सहाई ॥
jā kari taiṁ dāsī so abināsī hamareu tora sahāī.

Trans:

Then gods and saints and heavenly minstrels, repaired all to Brahmmā's throne. With them was earth in the form of cow, stricken grievously with fear, making sad, piteous moans. Brahmmā pondered, and realizing in his heart of heart his inability to help her, said, "The Immortal Lord, whose servant you are, will be my help as well as yours.

सोरठा-*soraṭhā:*

धरनि धरहि मन धीर कह बिरंचि हरिपद सुमिरु ।
dharani dharahi mana dhīra kaha biraṁci haripada sumiru,
जानत जन की पीर प्रभु भंजिहि दारुन बिपति ॥ १८४॥
jānata jana kī pīra prabhu bhaṁjihi dāruna bipati. 184.

Trans:

Take courage, O earth," said Brahmmā, "and remember Harī; the Lord knows the distress of his servants; and He will put an end to this cruel oppression."

चौपाई-caupāī:

बैठे सुर सब करहिं बिचारा । कहँ पाइअ प्रभु करिअ पुकारा ॥
baiṭhe sura saba karahiṁ bicārā, kahaṁ pāia prabhu karia pukārā.
पुर बैकुंठ जान कह कोई । कोउ कह पयनिधि बस प्रभु सोई ॥
pura baikuṁṭha jāna kaha koī, kou kaha payanidhi basa prabhu soī.
जाके हृदयँ भगति जसि प्रीति । प्रभु तहँ प्रगट सदा तेहिं रीती ॥
jāke hṛdayaṁ bhagati jasi prīti, prabhu tahaṁ pragaṭa sadā tehiṁ rītī.
तेहिं समाज गिरिजा मैं रहेऊँ । अवसर पाइ बचन एक कहेऊँ ॥
tehiṁ samāja girijā maiṁ raheūṁ, avasara pāi bacana eka kaheūṁ.
हरि ब्यापक सर्बत्र समाना । प्रेम तें प्रगट होहिं मैं जाना ॥
hari byāpaka sarbatra samānā, prema teṁ pragaṭa hohiṁ maiṁ jānā.
देस काल दिसि बिदिसिहु माहीं । कहहु सो कहाँ जहाँ प्रभु नाहीं ॥
desa kāla disi bidisihu māhīṁ, kahahu so kahāṁ jahāṁ prabhu nāhīṁ.
अग जगमय सब रहित बिरागी । प्रेम तें प्रभु प्रगटइ जिमि आगी ॥
aga jagamaya saba rahita birāgī, prema teṁ prabhu pragaṭai jimi āgī.
मोर बचन सब के मन माना । साधु साधु करि ब्रह्म बखाना ॥
mora bacana saba ke mana mānā, sādhu sādhu kari brahma bakhānā.

Trans:

All the gods sat in counsel: "Where can we find the Lord and make our cry to him?" Said some, "We must go to Vaikūnth"; "His home is in the ocean," said others. "The Lord becomes manifest wheresoever the faithful and loving devotees look for him—this is the way of the Lord." Now, Girijā, I too was in the assembly and took occasion to say briefly: "Harī is omnipresent, everywhere present alike; but, as I well know, He is revealed only by love. Tell me any place, time, or quarter of the heaven where the Lord is not. Present in all creation, animate or inanimate, passionless and unbiased, he is revealed like fire in wood through love." My words were approved by all, and Brahmmā exclaimed: 'Well said, well said.'

दोहा-dohā:

सुनि बिरंचि मन हरष तन पुलकि नयन बह नीर ।
suni biraṁci mana haraṣa tana pulaki nayana baha nīra,
अस्तुति करत जोरि कर सावधान मतिधीर ॥ १८५॥
astuti karata jori kara sāvadhāna matidhīra. 185.

Trans:

The Creator was glad at heart and thrilled with delight, while his eyes filled with tears, and clasping his hands, well-composed in heart, he composed this praise of the Lord:

छंद-chaṁda:

जय जय सुरनायक जन सुखदायक प्रनतपाल भगवंता ।
jaya jaya suranāyaka jana sukhadāyaka pranatapāla bhagavaṁtā,
गो द्विज हितकारी जय असुरारी सिंधुसुता प्रिय कंता ॥
go dvija hitakārī jaya asurārī siṁdhusutā priya kaṁtā.
पालन सुर धरनी अद्भुत करनी मरम न जानइ कोई ।
pālana sura dharanī adbhuta karanī marama na jānai koī,
जो सहज कृपाला दीनदयाला करउ अनुग्रह सोई ॥
jo sahaja kṛpālā dīnadayālā karau anugraha soī.

जय जय अबिनासी सब घट बासी ब्यापक परमानंदा ।
jaya jaya abināsī saba ghaṭa bāsī byāpaka paramānaṁdā,
अबिगत गोतीतं चरित पुनीतं मायारहित मुकुंदा ॥
abigata gotītaṁ carita punītaṁ māyārahita mukuṁdā.
जेहि लागि बिरागी अति अनुरागी बिगतमोह मुनिबृंदा ।
jehi lāgi birāgī ati anurāgī bigatamoha munibṛṁdā,
निसि बासर ध्यावहिं गुन गन गावहिं जयति सच्चिदानंदा ॥
nisi bāsara dhyāvahiṁ guna gana gāvahiṁ jayati saccidānaṁdā.

जेहिं सृष्टि उपाई त्रिबिध बनाई संग सहाय न दूजा ।
jehiṁ sṛṣṭi upāī tribidha banāī saṁga sahāya na dūjā,
सो करउ अघारी चिंत हमारी जानिअ भगति न पूजा ॥
so karau aghārī ciṁta hamārī jānia bhagati na pūjā.
जो भव भय भंजन मुनि मन रंजन गंजन बिपति बरूथा ।
jo bhava bhaya bhaṁjana muni mana raṁjana gaṁjana bipati barūthā,
मन बच क्रम बानी छाडि सयानी सरन सकल सुर जूथा ॥
mana baca krama bānī chāṛi sayānī sarana sakala sura jūthā.

सारद श्रुति सेषा रिषय असेषा जा कहुँ कोउ नहिं जाना ।
sārada śruti seṣā riṣaya aseṣā jā kahuṁ kou nahiṁ jānā,
जेहि दीन पिआरे बेद पुकारे द्रवउ सो श्रीभगवाना ॥
jehi dīna piāre beda pukāre dravau so śrībhagavānā.
भव बारिधि मंदर सब बिधि सुंदर गुनमंदिर सुखपुंजा ।
bhava bāridhi maṁdara saba bidhi suṁdara gunamaṁdira sukhapuṁjā,
मुनि सिद्ध सकल सुर परम भयातुर नमत नाथ पद कंजा ॥
muni siddha sakala sura parama bhayātura namata nātha pada kaṁjā.

Trans:

"Glory, glory to the Lord of gods; All glory to the delight of devotees, protector of the suppliants. O benefactor of cows and twice-born; O slayer of demons; O beloved consort of Lakshmī, glory be unto thee. O upholder of earth and heavens, mysterious are thy ways: their secrets known to none but thee. Ever kind and loving unto the humble, do shower thy grace upon me. Hail Mukund, the all-pervading spirit, ever pure and holy, the immortal-Lord of supreme blissfulness, the unknowable absolute who lies beyond the world-deluding Māyā's veils. Glory to him who is Truth, Consciousness, personified Bliss. Glory, glory, glory, to the theme of endless story, sung in ecstasy of love by saints and sages who from infatuation and passion are ever free. O thou, who brought forth the threefold creation without any aid, the Lord of Heaven, the Slayer of sinful Agha, do hear our piteous cry and bestow thy care upon us—who know neither worship, nor devotion, nor prayer. O thou—who disperses the fear of transmigration and delights the minds of sages and puts an end to all calamities—we gods betake ourselves unto thee—falling low with unfeigned submission of body, soul, and vow—and sincerely implore in thought, word and deed: be our aid, O Lord God. Thou—who is known neither to Shārdā, or the Vedas or to Shesh, nor to all the saintly throng—but who, the Vedas declare, loves the lowly, let thou be moved to pity. O Lord—thou who is the Mount Mandara for churning the ocean of worldly existence, who is charming in every way, who is abode of virtues and embodiment of bliss—we gods, saints and sages, clasp to thy lotus feet, for this tempest rages, and grievously stricken with fear are we."

दोहा-dohā:

जानि सभय सुरभूमि सुनि बचन समेत सनेह ।
jāni sabhaya surabhūmi suni bacana sameta saneha,
गगनगिरा गंभीर भइ हरनि सोक संदेह ॥ १८६॥
gaganagirā gaṁbhīra bhai harani soka saṁdeha. 186.

Trans:

Beholding the alarm of the gods and earth, and hearing this devout speech, a deep voice came down from the heavens—a profound sound to remove all doubts and anxiety:

चौपाई-caupāī:

जनि डरपहु मुनि सिद्ध सुरेसा । तुम्हहि लागि धरिहउँ नर बेसा ॥
jani ḍarapahu muni siddha suresā, tumhahi lāgi dharihauṁ nara besā.

अंसन्ह सहित मनुज अवतारा । लेहउँ दिनकर बंस उदारा ॥
aṁsanha sahita manuja avatārā, lehauṁ dinakara baṁsa udārā.
कस्यप अदिति महातप कीन्हा । तिन्ह कहुँ मैं पूरब बर दीन्हा ॥
kasyapa aditi mahātapa kīnhā, tinha kahuṁ maiṁ pūraba bara dīnhā.
ते दसरथ कौसल्या रूपा । कोसलपुरीं प्रगट नरभूपा ॥
te dasaratha kausalyā rūpā, kosalapurīṁ pragaṭa narabhūpā.
तिन्ह कें गृह अवतरिहउँ जाई । रघुकुल तिलक सो चारिउ भाई ॥
tinha keṁ gṛha avatarihauṁ jāī, raghukula tilaka so cāriu bhāī.
नारद बचन सत्य सब करिहउँ । परम सक्ति समेत अवतरिहउँ ॥
nārada bacana satya saba karihauṁ, parama sakti sameta avatarihauṁ.
हरिहउँ सकल भूमि गरुआई । निर्भय होहु देव समुदाई ॥
harihauṁ sakala bhūmi garuāī, nirbhaya hohu deva samudāī.
गगन ब्रह्मबानी सुनी काना । तुरत फिरे सुर हृदय जुड़ाना ॥
gagana brahmabānī sunī kānā, turata phire sura hṛdaya juṛānā.
तब ब्रह्माँ धरनिहि समुझावा । अभय भई भरोस जियँ आवा ॥
taba brahmāṁ dharanihi samujhāvā, abhaya bhaī bharosa jiyaṁ āvā.

Trans:

"Fear not gods, and ye sages and saints; for your sake I am about to assume the form of human, and with part manifestation will take birth in the glorious solar race. For the severe penance practiced by Kashyap and Aditī I granted them the full boon they asked. In the form of Dashrath and Kausalyā they shall take royal birth in the city of Kaushal. In their house shall become incarnate the four brothers, the pride of the family of Raghu. I will fulfill all that Nārad predicted—by myself descending from heaven with my eternal spouse, and I shall remove the burden of the whole earth." On hearing that heavenly voice the gods returned, their hearts consoled; and Brahmmā cheered Mother Earth, who forgot her fears in hopefulness.

दोहा-dohā:

निज लोकहि बिरंचि गे देवन्ह इहइ सिखाइ ।
nija lokahi biraṁci ge devanha ihai sikhāi,
बानर तनु धरि धरि महि हरि पद सेवहु जाइ ॥ १८७॥
bānara tanu dhari dhari mahi hari pada sevahu jāi. 187.

Trans:

Then Brahmmā proceeded to his own realm after instructing the gods thusly: "Go take form as monkeys upon earth, and there worship Harī."

चौपाई-caupāī:

गए देव सब निज निज धामा । भूमि सहित मन कहुँ बिश्रामा ॥
gae deva saba nija nija dhāmā, bhūmi sahita mana kahuṁ biśrāmā.
जो कछु आयसु ब्रह्माँ दीन्हा । हरषे देव बिलंब न कीन्हा ॥
jo kachu āyasu brahmāṁ dīnhā, harașe deva bilaṁba na kīnhā.
बनचर देह धरी छिति माहीं । अतुलित बल प्रताप तिन्ह पाहीं ॥
banacara deha dharī chiti māhīṁ, atulita bala pratāpa tinha pāhīṁ.
गिरि तरु नख आयुध सब बीरा । हरि मारग चितवहिं मतिधीरा ॥
giri taru nakha āyudha saba bīrā, hari māraga citavahiṁ matidhīrā.
गिरि कानन जहँ तहँ भरि पूरी । रहे निज निज अनीक रचि रूरी ॥
giri kānana jahaṁ tahaṁ bhari pūrī, rahe nija nija anīka raci rūrī.
यह सब रुचिर चरित मैं भाषा । अब सो सुनहु जो बीचहिं राखा ॥
yaha saba rucira carita maiṁ bhāṣā, aba so sunahu jo bīcahiṁ rākhā.
अवधपुरीं रघुकुलमनि राऊ । बेद बिदित तेहि दसरथ नाऊँ ॥
avadhapurīṁ raghukulamani rāū, beda bidita tehi dasaratha nāūṁ.
धरम धुरंधर गुननिधि ग्यानी । हृदयँ भगति मति सारँगपानी ॥
dharama dhuraṁdhara gunanidhi gyānī, hṛdayaṁ bhagati mati sāraṁgapānī.

Trans:

All the gods went to their several abodes. Along with the Earth they felt relieved in their hearts. All the dictates that Brahmmā had given they executed gladly and without delay. Taking birth on earth as monkeys of incomparable strength and dignity, warriors with rocks and trees and claws for weapons, they patiently awaited Harī's coming—swarming into all the mountains and forests, dividing themselves into orderly troops. I have told you of their noble acts, and now you must hear of what occurred meanwhile elsewhere. The king of Avadh was named Dashrath, the jewel of the line of Raghu, well skilled in the Vedas, virtuous and wise, a staunch defender of faith and a sincere votary of Vishnu.

दोहा-dohā:

कौसल्यादि नारि प्रिय सब आचरन पुनीत ।
kausalyādi nāri priya saba ācarana punīta,
पति अनुकूल प्रेम दृढ़ हरि पद कमल बिनीत ॥ १८८॥
pati anukūla prema dṛṛha hari pada kamala binīta. 188.

Trans:

Kausalyā and his other loving queens were all of holy life, faithful and affectionate to their lord, and full of humble devotion to Harī's lotus feet.

चौपाई-caupāī:

एक बार भूपति मन माहीं । भै गलानि मोरें सुत नाहीं ॥
eka bāra bhūpati mana māhīṁ, bhai galāni moreṁ suta nāhīṁ.
गुर गृह गयउ तुरत महिपाला । चरन लागि करि बिनय बिसाला ॥
gura gṛha gayau turata mahipālā, carana lāgi kari binaya bisālā.
निज दुख सुख सब गुरहि सुनायउ । कहि बसिष्ठ बहुबिधि समुझायउ ॥
nija dukha sukha saba gurahi sunāyau, kahi basiṣṭha bahubidhi samujhāyau.
धरहु धीर होइहहिं सुत चारी । त्रिभुवन बिदित भगत भय हारी ॥
dharahu dhīra hoihahiṁ suta cārī, tribhuvana bidita bhagata bhaya hārī.
सृंगी रिषिहि बसिष्ठ बोलावा । पुत्रकाम सुभ जग्य करावा ॥
sṛṁgī riṣihi basiṣṭha bolāvā, putrakāma subha jagya karāvā.
भगति सहित मुनि आहुति दीन्हें । प्रगटे अगिनि चरू कर लीन्हें ॥
bhagati sahita muni āhuti dīnheṁ, pragaṭe agini carū kara līnheṁ.
जो बसिष्ठ कछु हृदयँ बिचारा । सकल काजु भा सिद्ध तुम्हारा ॥
jo basiṣṭha kachu hṛdayaṁ bicārā, sakala kāju bhā siddha tumhārā.
यह हबि बाँटि देहु नृप जाई । जथा जोग जेहि भाग बनाई ॥
yaha habi bāṁṭi dehu nṛpa jāī, jathā joga jehi bhāga banāī.

Trans:

One day the king was sad that he had no son, and directly he rushed to his Gurū's abode and fell at his feet with many entreaties; and there he shared with him all the joys and sorrows of his being. Vasishtha in reply comforted him in many way, "Take courage, for you will have four sons who will be renowned throughout the Ages, and they will rid the faithful of all their fears." Thereupon Vasishtha summoned Saint Shringi to perform a *Yajna* ceremony for the birth of a progeny. The saint devoutly offered the oblation, and the Fire-god himself appeared with the offering in his hand and spoke in gracious tones: "I am pleased more than I can say; and whatever Vasishtha has imagined in his heart is granted and will come out true. Take this oblation, O king, and divide it in such proportions as you deem it proper."

दोहा-dohā:

तब अदृस्य भए पावक सकल सभहि समुझाइ ।
taba adṛsya bhae pāvaka sakala sabhahi samujhāi,
परमानंद मगन नृप हरष न हृदयँ समाइ ॥ १८९॥
paramānaṁda magana nṛpa harașa na hṛdayaṁ samāi. 189.

Trans:

The Fire-god then vanished after telling them all of all that had to be done. The king was transported with ecstasy and could not contain himself for joy.

चौपाई-caupāī:

तबहिं रायँ प्रिय नारि बोलाईं । कौसल्यादि तहाँ चलि आईं ॥
tabahiṁ rāyaṁ priya nāri bolāīṁ, kausalyādi tahāṁ cali āīṁ.
अर्ध भाग कौसल्यहि दीन्हा । उभय भाग आधे कर कीन्हा ॥
ardha bhāga kausalyahi dīnhā, ubhaya bhāga ādhe kara kīnhā.
कैकेई कहँ नृप सो दयऊ । रह्यो सो उभय भाग पुनि भयऊ ॥
kaikeī kahaṁ nṛpa so dayaū, rahyo so ubhaya bhāga puni bhayaū.
कौसल्या कैकेई हाथ धरि । दीन्ह सुमित्रहि मन प्रसन्न करि ॥
kausalyā kaikeī hātha dhari, dīnha sumitrahi mana prasanna kari.
एहि बिधि गर्भसहित सब नारी । भईं हृदयँ हरषित सुख भारी ॥
ehi bidhi garbhasahita saba nārī, bhaīṁ hṛdayaṁ haraṣita sukha bhārī.
जा दिन तें हरि गर्भहिं आए । सकल लोक सुख संपति छाए ॥
jā dina teṁ hari garbhahiṁ āe, sakala loka sukha saṁpati chāe.
मंदिर महँ सब राजहिं रानीं । सोभा सील तेज की खानीं ॥
maṁdira mahaṁ saba rājahiṁ rānīṁ, sobhā sīla teja kī khānīṁ.
सुख जुत कछुक काल चलि गयऊ । जेहिं प्रभु प्रगट सो अवसर भयऊ ॥
sukha juta kachuka kāla cali gayaū, jehiṁ prabhu pragaṭa so avasara bhayaū.

Trans:

He at once sent for his loving wives; and Kausalyā and the others came. To Kausalyā he gave the half-share of offering, and of the remaining half he made two portions, one of which he offered to Kaekayī; and of what remained he again divided into two, which he placed in the hands of Kausalyā and Kaekayī, which they then gave to Sumitrā, to her great delight. In this manner all the queens became pregnant, and they grew glad of heart with exceeding joy. From the day that Harī was conceived in their womb the whole world was fulfilled with happiness and prosperity, and the queens shone resplendent in the palace, full of beauty, virtue, and glory. A little time was thus happily spent, until the day arrived for the Lord God to be revealed.

दोहा-dohā:

जोग लगन ग्रह बार तिथि सकल भए अनुकूल ।
joga lagana graha bāra tithi sakala bhae anukūla,
चर अरु अचर हर्षजुत राम जनम सुखमूल ॥ १९० ॥
cara aru acara harṣajuta rāma janama sukhamūla. 190.

Trans:

Auspicious was the conjunction of planets in the auspicious house; auspicious was the moment; auspicious the day of the week and month; and full of delight was all creation, animate and inanimate, when Rāma, the fount of Bliss, was born.

चौपाई-caupāī:

नौमी तिथि मधु मास पुनीता । सुकल पच्छ अभिजित हरिप्रीता ॥
naumī tithi madhu māsa punītā, sukala paccha abhijita haripritā.
मध्यदिवस अति सीत न घामा । पावन काल लोक बिश्रामा ॥
madhyadivasa ati sīta na ghāmā, pāvana kāla loka biśrāmā.
सीतल मंद सुरभि बह बाऊ । हरषित सुर संतन मन चाऊ ॥
sītala maṁda surabhi baha bāū, haraṣita sura saṁtana mana cāū.
बन कुसुमित गिरिगन मनिआरा । स्रवहिं सकल सरिताऽमृतधारा ॥
bana kusumita girigana maniārā, sravahiṁ sakala saritā'mṛtadhārā.
सो अवसर बिरंचि जब जाना । चले सकल सुर साजि बिमाना ॥
so avasara biraṁci jaba jānā, cale sakala sura sāji bimānā.
गगन बिमल संकुल सुर जूथा । गावहिं गुन गंधर्ब बरूथा ॥
gagana bimala saṁkula sura jūthā, gāvahiṁ guna gaṁdharba barūthā.
बरषहिं सुमन सुअंजुलि साजी । गहगहि गगन दुंदुभी बाजी ॥
baraṣahiṁ sumana suaṁjuli sājī, gahagahi gagana duṁdubhī bājī.
अस्तुति करहिं नाग मुनि देवा । बहुबिधि लावहिं निज निज सेवा ॥
astuti karahiṁ nāga muni devā, bahubidhi lāvahiṁ nija nija sevā.

Trans:

It was the Ninth-Day of the sweet and holy month of *Chaitra*; in the bright lunar fortnight; under *Abhijit*, Lord's favorite constellation; on a most seasonable day, neither hot nor cold; at a holy time of rest for all; with soft, cool, fragrant breezes blowing, amidst the delight of gods; and heartfelt was the rapture of sages and saints—with the woods full of blossoms and the hills overflowing with gems, and with every river streaming with ambrosial flow. When the creator saw the time so fit, all the gods had their chariots equipped and they all came forth. The bright heaven was crowded with the hosts of gods; and troops of Gandharvs chanted epic verses; and flowers were rained down by handfuls; and the sky resounded with the beats of kettledrums; and serpents, saints, and gods hymned a myriad praises; and everyone and everything in their own fashion tendered their humble service—

दोहा-dohā:

सुर समूह बिनती करि पहुँचे निज निज धाम ।
sura samūha binatī kari pahuṁce nija nija dhāma,
जगनिवास प्रभु प्रगटे अखिल लोक बिश्राम ॥ १९१ ॥
jaganivāsa prabhu pragaṭe akhila loka biśrāma. 191.

Trans:

—when the Lord God, the abode of the universe and the solace of all creation, manifested Himself. With much jubilations the gods offered their praises to the Lord—finally returning to their respective regions.

छंद-chaṁda:

भए प्रगट कृपाला दीनदयाला कौसल्या हितकारी ।
bhae pragaṭa kṛpālā dīnadayālā kausalyā hitakārī,
हरषित महतारी मुनि मन हारी अद्भुत रूप बिचारी ॥
haraṣita mahatārī muni mana hārī adbhuta rūpa bicārī.
लोचन अभिरामा तनु घनस्यामा निज आयुध भुज चारी ।
locana abhirāmā tanu ghanasyāmā nija āyudha bhuja cārī,
भूषन बनमाला नयन बिसाला सोभासिंधु खरारी ॥
bhūṣana banamālā nayana bisālā sobhāsiṁdhu kharārī.

कह दुइ कर जोरी अस्तुति तोरी केहि बिधि करौं अनंता ।
kaha dui kara jorī astuti torī kehi bidhi karauṁ anaṁtā,
माया गुन ग्यानातीत अमाना बेद पुरान भनंता ॥
māyā guna gyānātīta amānā beda purāna bhanaṁtā.
करुना सुख सागर सब गुन आगर जेहि गावहिं श्रुति संता ।
karunā sukha sāgara saba guna āgara jehi gāvahiṁ śruti saṁtā,
सो मम हित लागी जन अनुरागी भयउ प्रगट श्रीकंता ॥
so mama hita lāgī jana anurāgī bhayau pragaṭa śrīkaṁtā.

ब्रह्मांड निकाया निर्मित माया रोम रोम प्रति बेद कहै ।
brahmāṁḍa nikāyā nirmita māyā roma roma prati beda kahai,
मम उर सो बासी यह उपहासी सुनत धीर मति थिर न रहै ॥
mama ura so bāsī yaha upahāsī sunata dhīra mati thira na rahai.
उपजा जब ग्याना प्रभु मुसुकाना चरित बहुत बिधि कीन्ह चहै ।
upajā jaba gyānā prabhu musukānā carita bahuta bidhi kīnha cahai,
कहि कथा सुहाई मातु बुझाई जेहि प्रकार सुत प्रेम लहै ॥
kahi kathā suhāī mātu bujhāī jehi prakāra suta prema lahai.

माता पुनि बोली सो मति डोली तजहु तात यह रूपा ।
mātā puni bolī so mati ḍolī tajahu tāta yaha rūpā,

कीजै सिसुलीला अति प्रियसीला यह सुख परम अनूपा ॥
kījai sisulīlā ati priyasīlā yaha sukha parama anūpā.
सुनि बचन सुजाना रोदन ठाना होइ बालक सुरभूपा ।
suni bacana sujānā rodana ṭhānā hoi bālaka surabhūpā,
यह चरित जे गावहिं हरिपद पावहिं ते न परहिं भवकूपा ॥
yaha carita je gāvahiṁ haripada pāvahiṁ te na parahiṁ bhavakūpā.

Trans:

The gracious Lord God, compassionate to the lowly, the benefactor of Kausalyā appeared in human form; and she gazed with great delight on the face of her dear boy—the very thought of whose marvelous form enraptures the hearts of sages and saints, filling them with joy supreme. The delight of all eyes, with his eyes big and bright, his body shone like the darkly clouds dense and grand. In his four arms, he bore weapon in each hand. Adorned with jewels and a garland of sylvan flowers, endowed with large eyes, the slayer of the demon Khara was like a beauteous ocean. Then with fingers locked in prayer the mother cried, "O Lord God Immortal, how can I, thy boundless praises, tell? Transcending Māyā, above knowledge and beyond attributes, the Vedas and Puranas fail to tell of thee. The fount of compassion, the source of every grace, whom the scriptures and holy sages have hymned through all the ages, the same Lord of Lakshmī, the repository of all virtues, the lover of His devotees, has revealed himself for my sake. The Vedas declare that each pore of his body contains heavens and earths and a myriad creations, and the same Lord God is in my arms now in sweetly dreams—and this is a mystery supreme, far beyond the comprehension of sages most profound." Thus, when this revelation came upon the mother, the Lord smiled; and so as to perform his many human enactments, and so that she might love him as her child and not God, he told her of the charming accounts of her previous birth. And now the mother's mind was changed, and then hurriedly she said, "Give up this superhuman form and let me see you as a child, disporting free and wild, indulging in childish sports that are so dear to a mother's heart." She spoke and he obeyed; and he at once made as an infant and began to cry. O world, know that all who sing these verses, they will never again fall into the well of mundane existence, but instead will attain to Rāma's abode.

दोहा-dohā:

बिप्र धेनु सुर संत हित लीन्ह मनुज अवतार ।
bipra dhenu sura saṁta hita līnha manuja avatāra,
निज इच्छा निर्मित तनु माया गुन गो पार ॥ १९२ ॥
nija icchā nirmita tanu māyā guna go pāra. 192.

Trans:

For the sake of Brahmins, cows and gods and saints, He took birth as a human, in a body formed of His own will—He the Lord God, who is beyond all quality or form, or perception of the sense-organs.

चौपाई-caupāī:

सुनि सिसु रुदन परम प्रिय बानी । संभ्रम चलि आईं सब रानी ॥
suni sisu rudana parama priya bānī, saṁbhrama cali āīṁ saba rānī.
हरषित जहँ तहँ धाईं दासी । आनँद मगन सकल पुरबासी ॥
haraṣita jahaṁ tahaṁ dhāīṁ dāsī, ānaṁda magana sakala purabāsī.
दसरथ पुत्रजन्म सुनि काना । मानहुँ ब्रह्मानंद समाना ॥
dasaratha putrajanma suni kānā, mānahuṁ brahmānaṁda samānā.
परम प्रेम मन पुलक सरीरा । चाहत उठत करत मति धीरा ॥
parama prema mana pulaka sarīrā, cāhata uṭhata karata mati dhīrā.
जाकर नाम सुनत सुभ होई । मोरें गृह आवा प्रभु सोई ॥
jākara nāma sunata subha hoī, moreṁ gṛha āvā prabhu soī.
परमानंद पूरि मन राजा । कहा बोलाइ बजावहु बाजा ॥
paramānaṁda pūri mana rājā, kahā bolāi bajāvahu bājā.
गुर बसिष्ठ कहँ गयउ हँकारा । आए द्विजन सहित नृपद्वारा ॥
gura basiṣṭha kahaṁ gayau haṁkārā, āe dvijana sahita nṛpadvārā.
अनुपम बालक देखेन्हि जाई । रूप रासि गुन कहि न सिराई ॥
anupama bālaka dekhenhi jāī, rūpa rāsi guna kahi na sirāī.

Trans:

On hearing the delightful sound of the baby's cries, all the queens came forward greatly excited; their glad handmaids ran excitedly hither and thither and all the people of the city were drowned in joy. Especially, when Dashrath knew he had a son born, his joy was like that of the blest in heaven. With his soul full of love and his body quivering with delight he sought to rise, but could not till he had collected himself, "The Lord, whose very name it is bliss to hear, has come to my house." Thus rejoicing at heart the king sent for minstrels to play, and next summoned the Gurū Vasishtha, who came to the court with a train of Brahmins. He went and gazed upon the peerless babe, whose beauty and grace were beyond any words to tell.

दोहा-dohā:

नंदीमुख सराध करि जातकरम सब कीन्ह ।
naṁdīmukha sarādha kari jātakarama saba kīnha,
हाटक धेनु बसन मनि नृप बिप्रन्ह कहँ दीन्ह ॥ १९३ ॥
hāṭaka dhenu basana mani nṛpa bipranha kahaṁ dīnha. 193.

Trans:

Then after performing the Nandi-mukh Shrādh, the king completed every caste observance; and he made great many offerings to the Brahmins of gold, cows, vessels, and jewels.

चौपाई-caupāī:

ध्वज पताक तोरन पुर छावा । कहि न जाइ जेहि भाँति बनावा ॥
dhvaja patāka torana pura chāvā, kahi na jāi jehi bhāṁti banāvā.
सुमनबृष्टि अकास तें होई । ब्रह्मानंद मगन सब लोई ॥
sumanabṛṣṭi akāsa teṁ hoī, brahmānaṁda magana saba loī.
बृंद बृंद मिलि चलीं लोगाईं । सहज सिंगार किएँ उठि धाईं ॥
bṛṁda bṛṁda mili calīṁ logāīṁ, sahaja siṁgāra kieṁ uṭhi dhāīṁ.
कनक कलस मंगल भरि थारा । गावत पैठहिं भूप दुआरा ॥
kanaka kalasa maṁgala bhari thārā, gāvata paiṭhahiṁ bhūpa duārā.
करि आरति नेवछावरि करहीं । बार बार सिसु चरनन्हि परहीं ॥
kari ārati nevachāvari karahīṁ, bāra bāra sisu carananhi parahīṁ.
मागध सूत बंदिगन गायक । पावन गुन गावहिं रघुनायक ॥
māgadha sūta baṁdigana gāyaka, pāvana guna gāvahiṁ raghunāyaka.
सर्बस दान दीन्ह सब काहू । जेहिं पावा राखा नहिं ताहू ॥
sarbasa dāna dīnha saba kāhū, jehiṁ pāvā rākhā nahiṁ tāhū.
मृगमद चंदन कुंकुम कीचा । मची सकल बीथिन्ह बिच बीचा ॥
mṛgamada caṁdana kuṁkuma kīcā, macī sakala bīthinha bica bīcā.

Trans:

The city was full of flags and banners and festal wreaths arranged in a fashion that defied all description. Showers of flowers fell from heaven and every soul was rapt in bliss. There was a concourse of troops of women, who had come running in their ordinary dress just as they were at that time, with golden vases and salvers laden with things of good omen, singing as they entered the court of King Dashrath. After passing their offerings round and round over the child's head they strew them on the ground; and again and again they throw themselves at his feet; and bards and minstrels, and singing men and choristers chanted the solemn praises of Raghunāth. Everyone made an offering of all that they had, and those who received did not keep but in turn gave away with joy; while musk, sandal, and saffron were thrown about in such profusion that the streets were muddy with perfumes.

दोहा-dohā:

गृह गृह बाज बधाव सुभ प्रगटे सुषमा कंद ।

gṛha gṛha bāja badhāva subha pragaṭe suṣamā kaṁda,

हरषवंत सब जहँ तहँ नगर नारि नर बृंद ॥१९४॥

haraṣavaṁta saba jahaṁ tahaṁ nagara nāri nara bṛṁda. 194.

Trans:

In every house there was music and the jubilant shouts, "Verily the fount of joy has been revealed to us." In this way all the men and women in the city were rejoicing everywhere.

चौपाई-caupāī:

कैकयसुता सुमित्रा दोऊ । सुंदर सुत जनमत भैं ओऊ ॥

kaikayasutā sumitrā doū, suṁdara suta janamata bhaiṁ oū.

वह सुख संपति समय समाजा । कहि न सकइ सारद अहिराजा ॥

vaha sukha saṁpati samaya samājā, kahi na sakai sārada ahirājā.

अवधपुरी सोहइ एहि भाँती । प्रभुहि मिलन आई जनु राती ॥

avadhapurī sohai ehi bhāṁtī, prabhuhi milana āī janu rātī.

देखि भानु जनु मन सकुचानी । तदपि बनी संध्या अनुमानी ॥

dekhi bhānu janu mana sakucānī, tadapi banī saṁdhyā anumānī.

अगर धूप बहु जनु अँधिआरी । उड़इ अबीर मनहुँ अरुनारी ॥

agara dhūpa bahu janu aṁdhiārī, uṛai abīra manahuṁ arunārī.

मंदिर मनि समूह जनु तारा । नृप गृह कलस सो इंदु उदारा ॥

maṁdira mani samūha janu tārā, nṛpa gṛha kalasa so iṁdu udārā.

भवन बेदधुनि अति मृदु बानी । जनु खग मुखर समयँ जनु सानी ॥

bhavana bedadhuni ati mṛdu bānī, janu khaga mukhara samayaṁ janu sānī.

कौतुक देखि पतंग भुलाना । एक मास तेइँ जात न जाना ॥

kautuka dekhi pataṁga bhulānā, eka māsa teiṁ jāta na jānā.

Trans:

Then soon Kaekayī and Sumitrā too gave birth to lovely boys. At that time the joy, the auspiciousness, the grandeur, and the crowds was more than Saraswatī or the serpent king could describe. The city of Ajodhyā wore a most gala look; and it looked as if Night had come to see the Lord and, feeling abashed as it were at the sight of the Sun—her own lord—had deliberately stayed over in the form of twilight. Clouds of celebratory incense represented the dusk; and the red *Abir* tossed up in festivity that wafted in the air represented the reddish light of sunset. The hosts of jewels that gleamed on house tops looked like so many stars; while the round pinnacle on the top of the royal palace corresponded to the beautiful moon. The murmuring sound of the chanting of Veda in the palace resembled the chirping of birds appropriate to the occasion. Gazing upon this spectacle, the Sun forgot himself, and a whole month passed without his knowing of it.

दोहा-dohā:

मास दिवस कर दिवस भा मरम न जानइ कोइ ।

māsa divasa kara divasa bhā marama na jānai koi,

रथ समेत रबि थाकेउ निसा कवन बिधि होइ ॥१९५॥

ratha sameta rabi thākeu nisā kavana bidhi hoi. 195.

Trans:

The day was a month long, but the marvel was noticed by none. The Sun in his chariot stood still to gaze below; how then could there be night?

चौपाई-caupāī:

यह रहस्य काहूँ नहिं जाना । दिनमनि चले करत गुनगाना ॥

yaha rahasya kāhūṁ nahiṁ jānā, dinamani cale karata gunagānā.

देखि महोत्सव सुर मुनि नागा । चले भवन बरनत निज भागा ॥

dekhi mahotsava sura muni nāgā, cale bhavana baranata nija bhāgā.

औरउ एक कहउँ निज चोरी । सुनु गिरिजा अति दृढ़ मति तोरी ॥

aurau eka kahauṁ nija corī, sunu girijā ati dṛṛha mati torī.

काकभुसुंडि संग हम दोऊ । मनुजरूप जानइ नहिं कोऊ ॥

kākabhusuṁḍi saṁga hama doū, manujarūpa jānai nahiṁ koū.

परमानंद प्रेमसुख फूले । बीथिन्ह फिरहिं मगन मन भूले ॥

paramānaṁda premasukha phūle, bīthinha phirahiṁ magana mana bhūle.

यह सुभ चरित जान पै सोई । कृपा राम कै जापर होई ॥

yaha subha carita jāna pai soī, kṛpā rāma kai jāpara hoī.

तेहि अवसर जो जेहि बिधि आवा । दीन्ह भूप जो जेहि मन भावा ॥

tehi avasara jo jehi bidhi āvā, dīnha bhūpa jo jehi mana bhāvā.

गज रथ तुरग हेम गो हीरा । दीन्हे नृप नानाबिधि चीरा ॥

gaja ratha turaga hema go hīrā, dīnhe nṛpa nānābidhi cīrā.

Trans:

There was not one who observed the strange event, and at last the Sun set—still chanting of Rāma's praises. The gods, saints, and Nagas, who had witnessed the spectacle, returned home congratulating themselves on their good fate. And I will even tell you of a deception I practiced myself, hearken, O Girijā, for I know you of steadfast faith. Kāgabhusumdi and I were there together in a human form, without anyone knowing it. Full of rapture, love, and delight, we roamed about the streets in ecstatic unconsciousness. Only one upon whom rests the mercy of Rāma can attain to the knowledge of these acts of ours. At that time the king granted everyone his heart's desire, whatever it might be that he had come for, bestowing on them elephants, carriages, horses, gold, cows, jewels, and all sorts of apparels.

दोहा-dohā:

मन संतोषे सबन्हि के जहँ तहँ देहिं असीस ।

mana saṁtoṣe sabanhi ke jahaṁ tahaṁ dehiṁ asīsa,

सकल तनय चिर जीवहुँ तुलसिदास के ईस ॥१९६॥

sakala tanaya cira jīvahuṁ tulasidāsa ke īsa. 196.

Trans:

All were satisfied from their very hearts and invoked blessings upon him, saying: 'May all the boys live long—these Lords of Tulsīdās.'

चौपाई-caupāī:

कछुक दिवस बीते एहि भाँती । जात न जानिअ दिन अरु राती ॥

kachuka divasa bīte ehi bhāṁtī, jāta na jānia dina aru rātī.

नामकरन कर अवसरु जानी । भूप बोलि पठए मुनि ग्यानी ॥

nāmakarana kara avasaru jānī, bhūpa boli paṭhae muni gyānī.

करि पूजा भूपति अस भाषा । धरिअ नाम जो मुनि गुनि राखा ॥

kari pūjā bhūpati asa bhāṣā, dharia nāma jo muni guni rākhā.

इन्ह के नाम अनेक अनूपा । मैं नृप कहब स्वमति अनुरूपा ॥

inha ke nāma aneka anūpā, maiṁ nṛpa kahaba svamati anurūpā.

जो आनंद सिंधु सुखरासी । सीकर तें त्रैलोक सुपासी ॥

jo ānaṁda siṁdhu sukharāsī, sīkara teṁ trailoka supāsī.

सो सुख धाम राम अस नामा । अखिल लोक दायक बिश्रामा ॥

so sukha dhāma rāma asa nāmā, akhila loka dāyaka biśrāmā.

बिस्व भरन पोषन कर जोई । ताकर नाम भरत अस होई ॥

bisva bharana poṣana kara joī, tākara nāma bharata asa hoī.

जाके सुमिरन तें रिपु नासा । नाम सत्रुहन बेद प्रकासा ॥

jāke sumirana teṁ ripu nāsā, nāma satruhana beda prakāsā.

Trans:

In this manner some days were spent, without anyone taking thought of noon or night, till the king, knowing the time had come for naming the children, sent and called the wise Vasishtha, and after reverently greeting him thusly said: "O holy father, be pleased to declare the names upon which you have secretly determined." "Their names are many and wonderful; I will tell them, O king, to the best of my ability. The storehouse of delights, the ocean of joy, by whose spray the three worlds are gladdened, the very home of bliss, the comforter of the universe, has for his name RĀMA (all-abiding/delight). The bearer and supporter of the world is named Bharat (supporter); while he whose very thought brings victory over the foe is celebrated in the Veda by his name Shatrughan (destroyer of enemies)."

दोहा-dohā:

लच्छन धाम राम प्रिय सकल जगत आधार ।
lacchana dhāma rāma priya sakala jagata ādhāra,
गुरु बसिष्ट तेहि राखा लछिमन नाम उदार ॥ १९७॥
guru basiṣṭa tehi rākhā lachimana nāma udāra. 197.

Trans:

And for the auspicious, the very beloved of Rāma, the fundament of the whole world, was reserved by saint Vasishtha the noble name of Lakshman (of auspicious signs).

चौपाई-caupāī:

धरे नाम गुर हृदयँ बिचारी । बेद तत्व नृप तव सुत चारी ॥
dhare nāma gura hṛdayaṁ bicārī, beda tatva nṛpa tava suta cārī.
मुनि धन जन सरबस सिव प्राना । बाल केलि रस तेहिं सुख माना ॥
muni dhana jana sarabasa siva prānā, bāla keli rasa tehiṁ sukha mānā.
बारेहि ते निज हित पति जानी । लछिमन राम चरन रति मानी ॥
bārehi te nija hita pati jānī, lachimana rāma carana rati mānī.
भरत सत्रुहन दूनउ भाई । प्रभु सेवक जसि प्रीति बड़ाई ॥
bharata satruhana dūnau bhāī, prabhu sevaka jasi prīti baṛāī.
स्याम गौर सुंदर दोउ जोरी । निरखहिं छबि जननीं तृन तोरी ॥
syāma gaura suṁdara dou jorī, nirakhahiṁ chabi jananīṁ tṛna torī.
चारिउ सील रूप गुन धामा । तदपि अधिक सुखसागर रामा ॥
cāriu sīla rūpa guna dhāmā, tadapi adhika sukhasāgara rāmā.
हृदयँ अनुग्रह इंदु प्रकासा । सूचत किरन मनोहर हासा ॥
hṛdayaṁ anugraha iṁdu prakāsā, sūcata kirana manohara hāsā.
कबहुँ उछंग कबहुँ बर पलना । मातु दुलारइ कहि प्रिय ललना ॥
kabahuṁ uchaṁga kabahuṁ bara palanā, mātu dulārai kahi priya lalanā.

Trans:

The saint, who had assigned these names after profound consideration, then said, "O king, your four sons are the very Vedas themselves, treasure of a saint's heart, a believer's all in all, the darlings of Shiva, who is ever delighted with their childish sports." Even from his earliest days Lakshman knew his dear Lord and devoted himself to Rāma; while the affection of the two other brothers, Bharat and Shatrughan, grew also as between a master and devotee. Of both pairs one was dark, the other fair. Their mothers, as they gazed upon their loveliness, would break a straw to avert the evil eye. Though all four were full of amiability, beauty, and intellect, yet Rāma was a higher joy. His kindliness of heart was like the bright moon which manifested itself in the radiance of a most winning smile. Now in the cradle, now on her lap, his mother fondled him and called him her very darling dear.

दोहा-dohā:

ब्यापक ब्रह्म निरंजन निर्गुन बिगत बिनोद ।
byāpaka brahma niraṁjana nirguna bigata binoda,
सो अज प्रेम भगति बस कौसल्या कें गोद ॥ १९८॥
so aja prema bhagati basa kausalyā keṁ goda. 198.

Trans:

Behold the unborn and all-pervading Brahmm—who has neither passion nor quality, nor sensation of pleasure, and who is untainted by Māyā—how He lies as babe in Kausalyā's arms, conquered by her love and devotion.

चौपाई-caupāī:

काम कोटि छबि स्याम सरीरा । नील कंज बारिद गंभीरा ॥
kāma koṭi chabi syāma sarīrā, nīla kaṁja bārida gaṁbhīrā.
अरुन चरन पकंज नख जोती । कमल दलन्हि बैठे जनु मोती ॥
aruna carana pakaṁja nakha jotī, kamala dalanhi baiṭhe janu motī.
रेख कुलिस ध्वज अंकुस सोहे । नूपुर धुनि सुनि मुनि मन मोहे ॥
rekha kulisa dhvaja aṁkusa sohe, nūpura dhuni suni muni mana mohe.
कटि किंकिनी उदर त्रय रेखा । नाभि गभीर जान जेहिं देखा ॥
kaṭi kiṁkinī udara traya rekhā, nābhi gabhīra jāna jehiṁ dekhā.
भुज बिसाल भूषन जुत भूरी । हियँ हरि नख अति सोभा रूरी ॥
bhuja bisāla bhūṣana juta bhūrī, hiyaṁ hari nakha ati sobhā rūrī.
उर मनिहार पदिक की सोभा । बिप्र चरन देखत मन लोभा ॥
ura manihāra padika kī sobhā, bipra carana dekhata mana lobhā.
कंबु कंठ अति चिबुक सुहाई । आनन अमित मदन छबि छाई ॥
kaṁbu kaṁṭha ati cibuka suhāī, ānana amita madana chabi chāī.
दुइ दुइ दसन अधर अरुनारे । नासा तिलक को बरनै पारे ॥
dui dui dasana adhara arunāre, nāsā tilaka ko baranai pāre.
सुंदर श्रवन सुचारु कपोला । अति प्रिय मधुर तोतरे बोला ॥
suṁdara śravana sucāru kapolā, ati priya madhura totare bolā.
चिक्कन कच कुंचित गभुआरे । बहु प्रकार रचि मातु सँवारे ॥
cikkana kaca kuṁcita gabhuāre, bahu prakāra raci mātu saṁvāre.
पीत झगुलिआ तनु पहिराई । जानु पानि बिचरनि मोहि भाई ॥
pīta jhaguliā tanu pahirāī, jānu pāni bicarani mohi bhāī.
रूप सकहिं नहिं कहि श्रुति सेषा । सो जानइ सपनेहुँ जेहिं देखा ॥
rūpa sakahiṁ nahiṁ kahi śruti seṣā, so jānai sapanehuṁ jehiṁ dekhā.

Trans:

With all the beauty of a myriad Loves; dark of hue as a lotus or a heavy rain-cloud; the glistening nails on his rosy feet like clustered pearls set on the petals of pink lotus; the marks of the thunderbolt, the flag, and the elephant-goad to be seen distinctly on the sole; the tinkling of his anklets enough to charm any saint's soul; with girdled waist and dimpled body and deep navel, such as no one could believe who had not seen; with long arms covered with many jewels and a lovely set of tiger's claws hanging upon his chest—along with necklace of gems and sparkling amulet, and soul-ravishing mark of the Brahmin's feet; with shell-marked neck and exquisite chin, and a face flushed with the beauty of many Loves; with well-matched teeth and ruddy lips, and nose and forehead-mark beyond description; with beautiful ears and charming cheeks and lisping prattle most delightful to hear; with eyes dark and full as the lotus, and heavy brows and a fair pendant on his forehead; with lustrous curling hair that his mother was ever delighting to stroke; with his body clothed in little yellow drawers, crawling on knees and hands upon the ground—neither Scripture nor Sheshnāg could do justice to his beauty, nor without a vision could anyone imagine it.

दोहा-dohā:

सुख संदोह मोहपर ग्यान गिरा गोतीत ।
sukha saṁdoha mohapara gyāna girā gotīta,
दंपति परम प्रेम बस कर सिसुचरित पुनीत ॥ १९९॥
daṁpati parama prema basa kara sisucarita punīta. 199.

Trans:

The All-blissful God, who is above the reach of delusion and transcends all intellect, speech, and perception of the senses, became subject to the strong love of his parents and sported like an innocent babe.

चौपाई-caupāī:

एहि बिधि राम जगत पितु माता । कोसलपुर बासिन्ह सुखदाता ॥
ehi bidhi rāma jagata pitu mātā, kosalapura bāsinha sukhadātā.
जिन्ह रघुनाथ चरन रति मानी । तिन्ह की यह गति प्रगट भवानी ॥
jinha raghunātha carana rati mānī, tinha kī yaha gati pragaṭa bhavānī.
रघुपति बिमुख जतन कर कोरी । कवन सकइ भव बंधन छोरी ॥

raghupati bimukha jatana kara korī, kavana sakai bhava baṁdhana chorī.

जीव चराचर बस कै राखे । सो माया प्रभु सों भय भाखे ॥

jīva carācara basa kai rākhe, so māyā prabhu soṁ bhaya bhākhe.

भृकुटि बिलास नचावइ ताही । अस प्रभु छाड़ि भजिअ कहु काही ॥

bhṛkuṭi bilāsa nacāvai tāhī, asa prabhu chāṛi bhajia kahu kāhī.

मन क्रम बचन छाड़ि चतुराई । भजत कृपा करिहहिं रघुराई ॥

mana krama bacana chāṛi caturāī, bhajata kṛpā karihahiṁ raghurāī.

एहि बिधि सिसुबिनोद प्रभु कीन्हा । सकल नगरबासिन्ह सुख दीन्हा ॥

ehi bidhi sisubinoda prabhu kīnhā, sakala nagarabāsinha sukha dīnhā.

लै उछंग कबहुँक हलरावै । कबहुँ पालनें घालि झुलावै ॥

lai uchaṁga kabahuṁka halarāvai, kabahuṁ pālaneṁ ghāli jhulāvai.

Trans:

In this way Rāma, the father and mother of the universe, showed himself the delight of the people of Kaushal. O Bhawānī, this demonstrates how those, who have conceived devotion to the feet of the Lord of Raghus, are repaid by Him. But those who are averse to the Lord of Raghus, though they struggle for ever, will never extricate themselves from the bonds of existence. The delusive power that has subdued all life—whether in animate or inanimate creation—trembles before the Lord who, with the play of his eyebrows, forces it to dance like a puppet. If we leave such a Lord, whom else can we supplicate? God is merciful to those who pray and surrender to the Lord in thoughts, words, deeds—giving up all craftiness. Thus the Lord sported as a child to the delight of all the people of the city; and now his mother would take and dandle him in her arms, and now put him down and rock him in his cradle;

दोहा-dohā:

प्रेम मगन कौसल्या निसि दिन जात न जान ।

prema magana kausalyā nisi dina jāta na jāna,

सुत सनेह बस माता बालचरित कर गान ॥२००॥

suta saneha basa mātā bālacarita kara gāna. 200.

Trans:

—so lost in love that day and night succeeded one another unobserved, while in her fondness for her boy she kept singing to him nursery rhymes.

चौपाई-caupāī:

एक बार जननीं अन्हवाए । करि सिंगार पलनाँ पौढ़ाए ॥

eka bāra jananīṁ anhavāe, kari siṁgāra palanāṁ pauṛhāe.

निज कुल इष्टदेव भगवाना । पूजा हेतु कीन्ह अस्नाना ॥

nija kula iṣṭadeva bhagavānā, pūjā hetu kīnha asnānā.

करि पूजा नैबेद्य चढ़ावा । आपु गई जहँ पाक बनावा ॥

kari pūjā naibedya caṛhāvā, āpu gaī jahaṁ pāka banāvā.

बहुरि मातु तहवाँ चलि आई । भोजन करत देख सुत जाई ॥

bahuri mātu tahavāṁ cali āī, bhojana karata dekha suta jāī.

गै जननी सिसु पहिं भयभीता । देखा बाल तहाँ पुनि सूता ॥

gai jananī sisu pahiṁ bhayabhītā, dekhā bāla tahāṁ puni sūtā.

बहुरि आइ देखा सुत सोई । हृदयँ कंप मन धीर न होई ॥

bahuri āi dekhā suta soī, hṛdayaṁ kaṁpa mana dhīra na hoī.

इहाँ उहाँ दुइ बालक देखा । मतिभ्रम मोर कि आन बिसेषा ॥

ihāṁ uhāṁ dui bālaka dekhā, matibhrama mora ki āna biseṣā.

देखि राम जननी अकुलानी । प्रभु हँसि दीन्ह मधुर मुसुकानी ॥

dekhi rāma jananī akulānī, prabhu haṁsi dīnha madhura musukānī.

Trans:

One day his mother, after washing and dressing him, put him to sleep in the cradle and prepared an offering for presentation to her patron divinity. When the service was over and she had made her oblation, she came to the place where she was dressing up the food; and when she returned she beheld Rāma in the act of eating the *Prasād* there. In great alarm she ran to the nursery but she found the child sleeping blissfully there. Coming back once more to the Temple she saw the boy partaking of the food here. Then she trembled and was much disturbed in mind, for she saw two children, one here and one there, and she was utterly bewildered saying, "Are my own senses at fault? Or is something else the matter?" When Rāma saw his mother's distress, he broke out into a merry laugh;

दोहा-dohā:

देखरावा मातहि निज अद्भुत रुप अखंड ।

dekharāvā mātahi nija adbhuta rupa akhaṁḍa,

रोम रोम प्रति लागे कोटि कोटि ब्रह्मंड ॥२०१॥

roma roma prati lāge koṭi koṭi brahmaṁḍa. 201.

Trans:

and He then exhibited to her His whole marvelous form—with a myriad worlds gleaming on each individual pore of His skin—

चौपाई-caupāī:

अगनित रबि ससि सिव चतुरानन । बहु गिरि सरित सिंधु महि कानन ॥

aganita rabi sasi siva caturānana, bahu giri sarita siṁdhu mahi kānana.

काल कर्म गुन ग्यान सुभाऊ । सोउ देखा जो सुना न काऊ ॥

kāla karma guna gyāna subhāū, sou dekhā jo sunā na kāū.

देखी माया सब बिधि गाढ़ी । अति सभीत जोरें कर ठाढ़ी ॥

dekhī māyā saba bidhi gāṛhī, ati sabhīta joreṁ kara ṭhāṛhī.

देखा जीव नचावइ जाही । देखी भगति जो छोरइ ताही ॥

dekhā jīva nacāvai jāhī, dekhī bhagati jo chorai tāhī.

तन पुलकित मुख बचन न आवा । नयन मूदि चरननि सिरु नावा ॥

tana pulakita mukha bacana na āvā, nayana mūdi caranani siru nāvā.

बिसमयवंत देखि महतारी । भए बहुरि सिसुरूप खरारी ॥

bisamayavaṁta dekhi mahatārī, bhae bahuri sisurūpa kharārī.

अस्तुति करि न जाइ भय माना । जगत पिता मैं सुत करि जाना ॥

astuti kari na jāi bhaya mānā, jagata pitā maiṁ suta kari jānā.

हरि जननि बहुबिधि समुझाई । यह जनि कतहुँ कहसि सुनु माई ॥

hari janani bahubidhi samujhāī, yaha jani katahuṁ kahasi sunu māī.

Trans:

—with unnumbered Suns and Moons, many Shivas and Brahmmās; with countless mountains, rivers, oceans, lands, and forests; with time, fate, merit, demerit, nature, and every power there manifested, even though unknown by name. As she beheld the marvelous vision she stood terror-stricken—with hands clasped in prayer; and she saw both the Jīva which Māyā forces into motion and the Devotion which sets him free. With quivering body and speechless mouth she closed her eyes and bowed her head at His feet. Seeing his mother thus overpowered with amazement, Rāma again assumed the form of a child. But her terror left her not, while she hymned his praises, saying, "I have regarded the great father as my own offspring!" Again and again Harī exhorted his mother, "See, my mother, that you reveal this to none."

दोहा-dohā:

बार बार कौसल्या बिनय करइ कर जोरि ।

bāra bāra kausalyā binaya karai kara jori,

अब जनि कबहूँ ब्यापै प्रभु मोहि माया तोरि ॥२०२॥

aba jani kabahūṁ byāpai prabhu mohi māyā tori. 202.

Trans:

Joining her palms Kausalyā prayed again and again, "You too see, my Lord, that this delusive power of yours visits me never again."

चौपाई-caupāī:

बालचरित हरि बहुबिधि कीन्हा । अति अनंद दासन्ह कहँ दीन्हा ॥

bālacarita hari bahubidhi kīnhā, ati anaṁda dāsanha kahaṁ dīnhā.

कछुक काल बीतें सब भाई । बड़े भए परिजन सुखदाई ॥

kachuka kāla bīteṁ saba bhāī, baṛe bhae parijana sukhadāī.

चूड़ाकरन कीन्ह गुरु जाई । बिप्रन्ह पुनि दछिना बहु पाई ॥
cūṛākarana kīnha guru jāī, bipranha puni dachinā bahu pāī.
परम मनोहर चरित अपारा । करत फिरत चारिउ सुकुमारा ॥
parama manohara carita apārā, karata phirata cāriu sukumārā.
मन क्रम बचन अगोचर जोई । दसरथ अजिर बिचर प्रभु सोई ॥
mana krama bacana agocara joī, dasaratha ajira bicara prabhu soī.
भोजन करत बोल जब राजा । नहिं आवत तजि बाल समाजा ॥
bhojana karata bola jaba rājā, nahiṁ āvata taji bāla samājā.
कौसल्या जब बोलन जाई । ठुमुकु ठुमुकु प्रभु चलहिं पराई ॥
kausalyā jaba bolana jāī, ṭhumuku ṭhumuku prabhu calahiṁ parāī.
निगम नेति सिव अंत न पावा । ताहि धरै जननी हठि धावा ॥
nigama neti siva aṁta na pāvā, tāhi dharai jananī haṭhi dhāvā.
धूसर धूरि भरें तनु आए । भूपति बिहसि गोद बैठाए ॥
dhūsara dhūri bhareṁ tanu āe, bhūpati bihasi goda baiṭhāe.

Trans:
Harī indulged in every kind of childish amusement, to the great delight of his attendants. After a time all the brothers grew to be big boys—gladdening everyone about them. Then the Gurū came to perform the tonsure, and again the Brahmins received large offerings. The four lads run about and divert themselves in all sorts of pretty ways; and the Lord—whose thoughts, words, and acts transcend every human sense—plays in the yard of Dashrath's court. If the king, when at dinner, called him he would not leave his playmates and come till Kausalyā herself went for him—when he would toddle along with her as fast as he could. He—whom the scripture declares to be incomprehensible, of whom Shiva could find no end—is picked up by his mother and carried off in a pet, and his father, with a smile, takes him into his lap, though grimy all over with dust.

दोहा-dohā:

भोजन करत चपल चित इत उत अवसरु पाइ ।
bhojana karata capala cita ita uta avasaru pāi,
भाजि चले किलकत मुख दधि ओदन लपटाइ ॥२०३॥
bhāji cale kilakata mukha dadhi odana lapaṭāi. 203.

Trans:
Quickly glancing here and there during the meal, as soon as he gets a chance, he would run away with a scream of delight, his mouth daubed with curds and rice.

चौपाई-caupāī:

बालचरित अति सरल सुहाए । सारद सेष संभु श्रुति गाए ॥
bālacarita ati sarala suhāe, sārada seṣa saṁbhu śruti gāe.
जिन्ह कर मन इन्ह सन नहिं राता । ते जन बंचित किए बिधाता ॥
jinha kara mana inha sana nahiṁ rātā, te jana baṁcita kie bidhātā.
भए कुमार जबहिं सब भ्राता । दीन्ह जनेऊ गुरु पितु माता ॥
bhae kumāra jabahiṁ saba bhrātā, dīnha janeū guru pitu mātā.
गुरगृहँ गए पढ़न रघुराई । अलप काल बिद्या सब आई ॥
guragṛhaṁ gae paṛhana raghurāī, alapa kāla bidyā saba āī.
जाकी सहज स्वास श्रुति चारी । सो हरि पढ़ यह कौतुक भारी ॥
jākī sahaja svāsa śruti cārī, so hari paṛha yaha kautuka bhārī.
बिद्या बिनय निपुन गुन सीला । खेलहिं खेल सकल नृपलीला ॥
bidyā binaya nipuna guna sīlā, khelahiṁ khela sakala nṛpalīlā.
करतल बान धनुष अति सोहा । देखत रूप चराचर मोहा ॥
karatala bāna dhanuṣa ati sohā, dekhata rūpa carācara mohā.
जिन्ह बीथिन्ह बिहरहिं सब भाई । थकित होहिं सब लोग लुगाई ॥
jinha bīthinha biharahiṁ saba bhāī, thakita hohiṁ saba loga lugāī.

Trans:
His pretty innocent childish sports have been sung by Saraswatī, Sheshnāg, Shambhu, and the Vedas; and he, whose soul does not warm to them, has been brought into the world by God to no purpose. When the brothers were all grown up, the Gurū and their father and mother invested them with the sacred thread; and then Rāma went to his Gurū's house to study. In a short time he mastered all knowledge. What a great sport that Shrī Harī—whose natural breath stands crystallized in the form of the four Vedas—should go to a school to learn! When they were proficient in scholarship and politeness and morality, they began to practice all princely sports. With bow and arrow in hand they showed so fair that all creation was ravished at the sight; and as the brothers passed along the road every man and woman stopped to gaze at them.

दोहा-dohā:

कोसलपुर बासी नर नारि बृद्ध अरु बाल ।
kosalapura bāsī nara nāri bṛddha aru bāla,
प्रानहु ते प्रिय लागत सब कहुँ राम कृपाल ॥२०४॥
prānahu te priya lāgata saba kahuṁ rāma kṛpāla. 204.

Trans:
Rāma was gracious to all; and was not a soul in Kaushal, man or woman, young or old, but held him dearer than life itself.

चौपाई-caupāī:

बंधु सखा संग लेहिं बोलाई । बन मृगया नित खेलहिं जाई ॥
baṁdhu sakhā saṁga lehiṁ bolāī, bana mṛgayā nita khelahiṁ jāī.
पावन मृग मारहिं जियँ जानी । दिन प्रति नृपहि देखावहिं आनी ॥
pāvana mṛga mārahiṁ jiyaṁ jānī, dina prati nṛpahi dekhāvahiṁ ānī.
जे मृग राम बान के मारे । ते तनु तजि सुरलोक सिधारे ॥
je mṛga rāma bāna ke māre, te tanu taji suraloka sidhāre.
अनुज सखा सँग भोजन करहीं । मातु पिता अग्या अनुसरहीं ॥
anuja sakhā saṁga bhojana karahīṁ, mātu pitā agyā anusarahīṁ.
जेहि बिधि सुखी होहिं पुर लोगा । करहिं कृपानिधि सोइ संजोगा ॥
jehi bidhi sukhī hohiṁ pura logā, karahiṁ kṛpānidhi soi saṁjogā.
बेद पुरान सुनहिं मन लाई । आपु कहहिं अनुजन्ह समुझाई ॥
beda purāna sunahiṁ mana lāī, āpu kahahiṁ anujanha samujhāī.
प्रातकाल उठि कै रघुनाथा । मातु पिता गुरु नावहिं माथा ॥
prātakāla uṭhi kai raghunāthā, mātu pitā guru nāvahiṁ māthā.
आयसु मागि करहिं पुर काजा । देखि चरित हरषइ मन राजा ॥
āyasu māgi karahiṁ pura kājā, dekhi carita haraṣai mana rājā.

Trans:
Taking his brother with him as a companion, he would go to the forest to hunt; there selecting for death the noblest game, he brought and showed it to the king; and each beast slain by his shaft, after death, went straight to the heaven. He took his meals in the company of his younger brothers, and was ever obedient to his parents' commands. That which would bring happiness to the citizens, the gracious God contrived many such means for the benefit of his people. He gave his mind to hear the Vedas and Purānas, and then he himself taught his brothers. Rising at the break of day, he first saluted his parents and the priest; and then, after obtaining their sanction, busied himself with work in the city. The king was glad of heart when he saw his mode of life.

दोहा-dohā:

ब्यापक अकल अनीह अज निर्गुन नाम न रूप ।
byāpaka akala anīha aja nirguna nāma na rūpa,
भगत हेतु नाना बिधि करत चरित्र अनूप ॥२०५॥
bhagata hetu nānā bidhi karata caritra anūpa. 205.

Trans:
The all-pervading, indivisible, passionless, eternal God, who is without attributes, or name, or form, performs many wonders for the sake of his faithful people.

चौपाई-caupāī:

यह सब चरित कहा मैं गाई । आगिलि कथा सुनहु मन लाई ॥
yaha saba carita kahā maiṁ gāī, āgili kathā sunahu mana lāī.
बिस्वामित्र महामुनि ग्यानी । बसहिं बिपिन सुभ आश्रम जानी ॥
bisvāmitra mahāmuni gyānī, basahiṁ bipina subha āśrama jānī.
जहँ जप जग्य जोग मुनि करहीं । अति मारीच सुबाहुहि डरहीं ॥
jahaṁ japa jagya joga muni karahīṁ, ati mārīca subāhuhi ḍarahīṁ.
देखत जग्य निसाचर धावहिं । करहिं उपद्रव मुनि दुख पावहिं ॥
dekhata jagya nisācara dhāvahiṁ, karahiṁ upadrava muni dukha pāvahiṁ.
गाधितनय मन चिंता ब्यापी । हरि बिनु मरहि न निसिचर पापी ॥
gādhitanaya mana ciṁtā byāpī, hari binu marahi na nisicara pāpī.
तब मुनिबर मन कीन्ह बिचारा । प्रभु अवतरेउ हरन महि भारा ॥
taba munibara mana kīnha bicārā, prabhu avatareu harana mahi bhārā.
एहूँ मिस देखौं पद जाई । करि बिनती आनौं दोउ भाई ॥
ehūṁ misa dekhauṁ pada jāī, kari binatī ānauṁ dou bhāī.
ग्यान बिराग सकल गुन अयना । सो प्रभु मैं देखब भरि नयना ॥
gyāna birāga sakala guna ayanā, so prabhu maiṁ dekhaba bhari nayanā.

Trans:

All these of his many doings I have sung; and hearken attentively now to the remainder of the saga. Elsewhere, the great and wise saint Vishwāmitra had chosen a fair hermitage in the forest, where he gave himself up to prayer, sacrifice, meditation. The demons Mārich and Subahu, on beholding the preparations for religious rituals became greatly excited—and hastened to disrupt them. The saintly son of Gādhi was pained and full of thought, 'There is no killing of these accursed demons without Harī's help.' He further reflected: "The Lord has become incarnate to relieve the earth of her burdens; and I now have an excuse for going to visit him; and after making entreaty will bring back with me the two brothers. Ah, now I will feast my eyes with the sight of him who is the abode of all knowledge, piety, and goodness!"

दोहा-dohā:

बहुबिधि करत मनोरथ जात लागि नहिं बार ।
bahubidhi karata manoratha jāta lāgi nahiṁ bāra,
करि मज्जन सरऊ जल गए भूप दरबार ॥२०६॥
kari majjana saraū jala gae bhūpa darabāra. 206.

Trans:

His manifold longing brooked no delay on the road; and after bathing in the stream of the Sarjū he proceeded to the king's court.

चौपाई-caupāī:

मुनि आगमन सुना जब राजा । मिलन गयऊ लै बिप्र समाजा ॥
muni āgamana sunā jaba rājā, milana gayaū lai bipra samājā.
करि दंडवत मुनिहि सनमानी । निज आसन बैठारेन्हि आनी ॥
kari daṁḍavata munihi sanamānī, nija āsana baiṭhārenhi ānī.
चरन पखारि कीन्हि अति पूजा । मो सम आजु धन्य नहिं दूजा ॥
carana pakhāri kīnhi ati pūjā, mo sama āju dhanya nahiṁ dūjā.
बिबिध भाँति भोजन करवावा । मुनिबर हृदयँ हरष अति पावा ॥
bibidha bhāṁti bhojana karavāvā, munibara hṛdayaṁ haraṣa ati pāvā.
पुनि चरननि मेले सुत चारी । राम देखि मुनि देह बिसारी ॥
puni caranani mele suta cārī, rāma dekhi muni deha bisārī.
भए मगन देखत मुख सोभा । जनु चकोर पूरन ससि लोभा ॥
bhae magana dekhata mukha sobhā, janu cakora pūrana sasi lobhā.
तब मन हरषि बचन कह राऊ । मुनि अस कृपा न कीन्हिहु काऊ ॥
taba mana haraṣi bacana kaha rāū, muni asa kṛpā na kīnhihu kāū.
केहि कारन आगमन तुम्हारा । कहहु सो करत न लावउँ बारा ॥
kehi kārana āgamana tumhārā, kahahu so karata na lāvauṁ bārā.
असुर समूह सतावहिं मोही । मैं जाचन आयउँ नृप तोही ॥
asura samūha satāvahiṁ mohī, maiṁ jācana āyauṁ nṛpa tohī.
अनुज समेत देहु रघुनाथा । निसिचर बध मैं होब सनाथा ॥
anuja sameta dehu raghunāthā, nisicara badha maiṁ hoba sanāthā.

Trans:

When the Raja heard of the saint's arrival, he went to meet him with a retinue of Brahmins, and prostrating himself reverently on the ground before him, guided and seated him on his very own throne. He then laved his feet and offered him religious honors, saying, "There is none so blessed as I am today"; and he had various kinds of food prepared for him. The great saint was highly pleased. Next, the king brought his four sons into his presence. On seeing Rāma the saint forgot his detachment from the world and was as enraptured with his lovely face as is the *chakor* of the full moon. Then said the glad king, "Reverend sir, this favor is unparalleled; what is the cause of your coming? Tell me, and I will not delay to accomplish it." "There is a crew of demons that trouble me much, and so I have come to you with a request: Let me have Raghunāth and his brother. The demons' death, sire, is all I desire.

दोहा-dohā:

देहु भूप मन हरषित तजहु मोह अग्यान ।
dehu bhūpa mana haraṣita tajahu moha agyāna,
धर्म सुजस प्रभु तुम्ह कौं इन्ह कहँ अति कल्यान ॥२०७॥
dharma sujasa prabhu tumha kauṁ inha kahaṁ ati kalyāna. 207.

Trans:

Give them gladly, O king, without any selfish folly; for you it will be a meritorious and honorable act; and it also will turn out well for them."

चौपाई-caupāī:

सुनि राजा अति अप्रिय बानी । हृदय कंप मुख दुति कुमुलानी ॥
suni rājā ati apriya bānī, hṛdaya kaṁpa mukha duti kumulānī.
चौथेंपन पायउँ सुत चारी । बिप्र बचन नहिं कहेहु बिचारी ॥
cautheṁpana pāyauṁ suta cārī, bipra bacana nahiṁ kahehu bicārī.
मागहु भूमि धेनु धन कोसा । सर्बस देउँ आजु सहरोसा ॥
māgahu bhūmi dhenu dhana kosā, sarbasa deuṁ āju saharosā.
देह प्रान तें प्रिय कछु नाहीं । सोउ मुनि देउँ निमिष एक माहीं ॥
deha prāna teṁ priya kachu nāhīṁ, sou muni deuṁ nimiṣa eka māhīṁ.
सब सुत प्रिय मोहि प्रान कि नाईं । राम देत नहिं बनइ गोसाईं ॥
saba suta priya mohi prāna ki nāīṁ, rāma deta nahiṁ banai gosāīṁ.
कहँ निसिचर अति घोर कठोरा । कहँ सुंदर सुत परम किसोरा ॥
kahaṁ nisicara ati ghora kaṭhorā, kahaṁ suṁdara suta parama kisorā.
सुनि नृप गिरा प्रेम रस सानी । हृदयँ हरष माना मुनि ग्यानी ॥
suni nṛpa girā prema rasa sānī, hṛdayaṁ haraṣa mānā muni gyānī.
तब बसिष्ठ बहुबिधि समुझावा । नृप संदेह नास कहँ पावा ॥
taba basiṣṭha bahubidhi samujhāvā, nṛpa saṁdeha nāsa kahaṁ pāvā.
अति आदर दोउ तनय बोलाए । हृदयँ लाइ बहु भाँति सिखाए ॥
ati ādara dou tanaya bolāe, hṛdayaṁ lāi bahu bhāṁti sikhāe.
मेरे प्रान नाथ सुत दोऊ । तुम्ह मुनि पिता आन नहिं कोऊ ॥
mere prāna nātha suta doū, tumha muni pitā āna nahiṁ koū.

Trans:

When the king heard this cruel request, his heart beat fast and all the brightness of his face grew dim, "In my old age I have begotten four sons; O sir, you have spoken without consideration. Ask me of land, cattle, goods, and treasure, and I will gladly give you all I have at once. Nothing is dearer than one's life, but even my life I would give to you in a minute. All my sons are dear to me as my own soul; O sir, I cannot spare Rāma to you. What is this pretty little boy of mine against fierce and terrible demons?" On hearing the king's words so fraught with love, the wise saint was glad of heart within, though remaining outwardly cold. Then Vasishtha, the king's Gurū, exhorted the king in several ways and his doubts were dispelled. Obediently he sent for the two boys and pressed them to his heart and fervently exclaimed: "My two boys are my very life; but you, holy sir, are their father now."

दोहा-*dohā:*

सौंपे भूप रिषिहि सुत बहुबिधि देइ असीस।
saumpe bhūpa riṣihi suta bahubidhi dei asīsa,
जननी भवन गए प्रभु चले नाइ पद सीस ॥२०८क॥
jananī bhavana gae prabhu cale nāi pada sīsa. 208(ka).

Trans:

The king consigned the boys to the saint—again and again blessing them. Then they went to their mother's apartment and bowed their head to her feet.

सोरठा-*soraṭhā:*

पुरुषसिंह दोउ बीर हरषि चले मुनि भय हरन।
puruṣasiṁha dou bīra harași cale muni bhaya harana.
कृपासिंधु मतिधीर अखिल बिस्व कारन करन ॥२०८ख॥
kṛpāsiṁdhu matidhīra akhila bisva kārana karana. 208(kha).

Trans:

Glad to relieve the saint of his alarm, the two lion-hearted heroes then sallied forth—oceans of compassion, resolute of purpose, the whole world's champions.

चौपाई-*caupāī:*

अरुन नयन उर बाहु बिसाला। नील जलज तनु स्याम तमाला ॥
aruna nayana ura bāhu bisālā, nīla jalaja tanu syāma tamālā.
कटि पट पीत कसें बर भाथा। रुचिर चाप सायक दुहुँ हाथा ॥
kaṭi paṭa pīta kaseṁ bara bhāthā, rucira cāpa sāyaka duhuṁ hāthā.
स्याम गौर सुंदर दोउ भाई। बिस्बामित्र महानिधि पाई ॥
syāma gaura suṁdara dou bhāī, bisbāmitra mahānidhi pāī.
प्रभु ब्रह्मन्यदेव मैं जाना। मोहि निति पिता तजेउ भगवाना ॥
prabhu brahmanyadeva maiṁ jānā, mohi niti pitā tajeu bhagavānā.
चले जात मुनि दीन्हि दिखाई। सुनि ताड़का क्रोध करि धाई ॥
cale jāta muni dīnhi dikhāī, suni tāṛakā krodha kari dhāī.
एकहिं बान प्रान हरि लीन्हा। दीन जानि तेहि निज पद दीन्हा ॥
ekahiṁ bāna prāna hari līnhā, dīna jāni tehi nija pada dīnhā.
तब रिषि निज नाथहि जियँ चीन्ही। बिद्यानिधि कहुँ बिद्या दीन्ही ॥
taba riṣi nija nāthahi jiyaṁ cīnhī, bidyānidhi kahuṁ bidyā dīnhī.
जाते लाग न छुधा पिपासा। अतुलित बल तनु तेज प्रकासा ॥
jāte lāga na chudhā pipāsā, atulita bala tanu teja prakāsā.

Trans:

Bright-eyed, broad-chested, long of arms, dark of hue as the lotus or the *tamal* tree; with quiver at side, pendent from a yellow sash, and in either hand arrows and a comely bow—so marched the two brothers, one dark, the other fair, the treasure that Vishwāmitra had acquired. 'I have now realized that the Lord is a votary of the Brahmins; on my account He has left His own father', so thought the saint; and as he went he pointed out the demon *Tādakā*, who on hearing their presence rushed up in a fury. With a single arrow Harī took her life, but recognizing her submission gave her a place in his own heaven. Then the saint knew he had found his Lord, but yet instructed him, the all-wise. As they traveled they felt neither hunger nor thirst; such was the incomparable strength of their body and glorious vigor.

दोहा-*dohā:*

आयुध सर्ब समर्पि कै प्रभु निज आश्रम आनि।
āyudha sarba samarpi kai prabhu nija āśrama āni,
कंद मूल फल भोजन दीन्ह भगति हित जानि ॥२०९॥
kaṁda mūla phala bhojana dīnha bhagati hita jāni. 209.

Trans:

After taking the Lord to his own hermitage, he made over to him every kind of weapon, and devoutedly gave him herbs and roots and fruit to eat—perceiving in him a friend, ever gracious to men of holy life.

चौपाई-*caupāī:*

प्रात कहा मुनि सन रघुराई। निर्भय जग्य करहु तुम्ह जाई ॥
prāta kahā muni sana raghurāī, nirbhaya jagya karahu tumha jāī.
होम करन लागे मुनि झारी। आपु रहे मख कीं रखवारी ॥
homa karana lāge muni jhārī, āpu rahe makha kīṁ rakhavārī.
सुनि मारीच निसाचर क्रोही। लै सहाय धावा मुनिद्रोही ॥
suni mārīca nisācara krohī, lai sahāya dhāvā munidrohī.
बिनु फर बान राम तेहि मारा। सत जोजन गा सागर पारा ॥
binu phara bāna rāma tehi mārā, sata jojana gā sāgara pārā.
पावक सर सुबाहु पुनि मारा। अनुज निसाचर कटकु सँघारा ॥
pāvaka sara subāhu puni mārā, anuja nisācara kaṭaku saṁghārā.
मारि असुर द्विज निर्भयकारी। अस्तुति करहिं देव मुनि झारी ॥
māri asura dvija nirbhayakārī, astuti karahiṁ deva muni jhārī.
तहँ पुनि कछुक दिवस रघुराया। रहे कीन्हि बिप्रन्ह पर दाया ॥
tahaṁ puni kachuka divasa raghurāyā, rahe kīnhi bipranha para dāyā.
भगति हेतु बहु कथा पुराना। कहे बिप्र जद्यपि प्रभु जाना ॥
bhagati hetu bahu kathā purānā, kahe bipra jadyapi prabhu jānā.
तब मुनि सादर कहा बुझाई। चरित एक प्रभु देखिअ जाई ॥
taba muni sādara kahā bujhāī, carita eka prabhu dekhia jāī.
धनुषजग्य सुनि रघुकुल नाथा। हरषि चले मुनिबर के साथा ॥
dhanuṣajagya suni raghukula nāthā, harași cale munibara ke sāthā.
आश्रम एक दीख मग माहीं। खग मृग जीव जंतु तहँ नाहीं ॥
āśrama eka dīkha maga māhīṁ, khaga mṛga jīva jaṁtu tahaṁ nāhīṁ.
पूछा मुनिहि सिला प्रभु देखी। सकल कथा मुनि कहा बिसेषी ॥
pūchā munihi silā prabhu dekhī, sakala kathā muni kahā biseṣī.

Trans:

At daybreak Raghurāī said to the sage, "Go and make ready the yajna; have no fear." The saints began preparing the oblation; while Rāma himself guarded the sacrificial fire. On hearing of this, the demon Mārich rushed up in a fury with his army to disrupt the ritual. Rāma smote him with a headless shaft, and he fell a hundred leagues on the other side of ocean. Then he slew Subahu with an arrow of fire, while his brother routed the whole demon host. When they had thus slain the demons and restored peace to the Brahmins, the whole company of gods and saints began to hymn their praises. There Raghurāī then stayed a few days and showed kindness to the hermits, who devoutly repeated to him many legends of the Purānas, although he knew them all before. Then the saint respectfully informed him, "There is a sight, O Lord, which is worth going to behold." Hearing of a Bow-Sacrifice ceremony, the Lord of Raghus gladly accompanied the noble sage. On the way he spied a hermitage without bird, deer, or any living creature near it, and observing a remarkable stone enquired of the saint about it, who in reply gave him the whole history.

दोहा-dohā:

गौतम नारि श्राप बस उपल देह धरि धीर ।
gautama nāri śrāpa basa upala deha dhari dhīra,
चरन कमल रज चाहति कृपा करहु रघुबीर ॥२१०॥
carana kamala raja cāhati kṛpā karahu raghubīra. 210.

Trans:

"Gautam's wife was by a curse turned into a rock, and is now longing for the dust of your lotus feet, O Raghubīr, show mercy upon her."

छंद-chaṁda:

परसत पद पावन सोक नसावन प्रगट भई तपपुंज सही ।
parasata pada pāvana soka nasāvana pragaṭa bhaī tapapuṁja sahī,
देखत रघुनायक जन सुखदायक सनमुख होइ कर जोरि रही ॥
dekhata raghunāyaka jana sukhadāyaka sanamukha hoi kara jori rahī.
अति प्रेम अधीरा पुलक सरीरा मुख नहिं आवइ बचन कही ।
ati prema adhīrā pulaka sarīrā mukha nahiṁ āvai bacana kahī,
अतिसय बड़भागी चरनन्हि लागी जुगल नयन जलधार बही ॥
atisaya baṛabhāgī carananhi lāgī jugala nayana jaladhāra bahī.

धीरजु मन कीन्हा प्रभु कहुँ चीन्हा रघुपति कृपाँ भगति पाई ।
dhīraju mana kīnhā prabhu kahuṁ cīnhā raghupati kṛpāṁ bhagati pāī,
अति निर्मल बानीं अस्तुति ठानी ग्यानगम्य जय रघुराई ॥
ati nirmala bānīṁ astuti ṭhānī gyānagamya jaya raghurāī.
मैं नारि अपावन प्रभु जग पावन रावन रिपु जन सुखदाई ।
maiṁ nāri apāvana prabhu jaga pāvana rāvana ripu jana sukhadāī,
राजीव बिलोचन भव भय मोचन पाहि पाहि सरनहिं आई ॥
rājīva bilocana bhava bhaya mocana pāhi pāhi saranahiṁ āī.

मुनि श्राप जो दीन्हा अति भल कीन्हा परम अनुग्रह मैं माना ।
muni śrāpa jo dīnhā ati bhala kīnhā parama anugraha maiṁ mānā,
देखेउँ भरि लोचन हरि भवमोचन इहइ लाभ संकर जाना ॥
dekheuṁ bhari locana hari bhavamocana ihai lābha saṁkara jānā.
बिनती प्रभु मोरी मैं मति भोरी नाथ न मागउँ बर आना ।
binatī prabhu morī maiṁ mati bhorī nātha na māgauṁ bara ānā,
पद कमल परागा रस अनुरागा मम मन मधुप करै पाना ॥
pada kamala parāgā rasa anurāgā mama mana madhupa karai pānā.

जेहिं पद सुरसरिता परम पुनीता प्रगट भई सिव सीस धरी ।
jehiṁ pada surasaritā parama punītā pragaṭa bhaī siva sīsa dharī,
सोइ पद पंकज जेहि पूजत अज मम सिर धरेउ कृपाल हरी ॥
soi pada paṁkaja jehi pūjata aja mama sira dhareu kṛpāla harī.
एहि भाँति सिधारी गौतम नारी बार बार हरि चरन परी ।
ehi bhāṁti sidhārī gautama nārī bāra bāra hari carana parī,
जो अति मन भावा सो बरु पावा गै पतिलोक अनंद भरी ॥
jo ati mana bhāvā so baru pāvā gai patiloka anaṁda bharī.

Trans:

And at the touch so sweet of those hallowed feet which drive away sorrows, Ahalyā, the embodiment of austerity, awoke from her long unrest. Beholding Raghu-nāyak, the delight of his servants, she stood before Him with joined palms. And then with speechless tongue, limbs all unstrung, she fell before him in rapture, unable to utter a word. Like one most-blessed, she cleaved to his feet, with tears streaming from her eyes. Then composing herself, and hailing the Lord God before her, and by his grace attaining devotion to his holy feet, she began to raise hymns of praises for the Lord in most lucid tones: "Glory to the Lord of Raghus, accessible through spiritual knowledge most high. Sinful wretch though I be, you are the Great Spirit, the Lord of heavens, who is able to sanctify the whole world. O lotus-eyed vanquisher of Rāvan, the delight of your servants, you rid your devotees tossing upon life's troubled seas from the fears of births and deaths. Pray save me, save me O Holy God, I have taken refuge in Thee. The saint cursed me sore in days of yore, but now I hold it as a blessing most sweet—for with my own eyes today, I feast my eyes upon Thee, the Redeemer who liberates one from bondages of every worldly existence; whose sight, Shankara counts, as the only blessing worth its name. Lord, I am simple and innocent of heart; and there is only one boon that I seek: may my mind ever take delight in the dust of your feet—even as a bee ever hovers over the lotus-pollen. Blessed am I, that those very feet—from where effused the divine stream Gangā which Shiva placed upon his head, the same lotus feet that are adored by Brahmmā—has the merciful Harī placed upon me." Thus full of jubilation, and with oft-renewed prostrations, did Gautam's long lost bride—and with the boon she most had craved hereby graciously vouchsafed—returned to her husband's side.

दोहा-dohā:

अस प्रभु दीनबंधु हरि कारन रहित दयाल ।
asa prabhu dīnabaṁdhu hari kārana rahita dayāla,
तुलसिदास सठ तेहि भजु छाड़ि कपट जंजाल ॥२११॥
tulasidāsa saṭha tehi bhaju chāṛi kapaṭa jaṁjāla. 211.

Trans:

He, Lord Harī, benevolent to the lowly, compassionate without a cause, worship Him, O fool Tulsīdās, and cease from these wily wranglings, vain hypocrisies of the world.

मासपारायण सातवाँ विश्राम
māsapārāyaṇa sātavāṁ viśrāma
(Pause 7 for a Thirty-Day Recitation)

चौपाई-caupāī:

चले राम लछिमन मुनि संगा । गए जहाँ जग पावनि गंगा ॥
cale rāma lachimana muni saṁgā, gae jahāṁ jaga pāvani gaṁgā.
गाधिसूनु सब कथा सुनाई । जेहि प्रकार सुरसरि महि आई ॥
gādhisūnu saba kathā sunāī, jehi prakāra surasari mahi āī.
तब प्रभु रिषिन्ह समेत नहाए । बिबिध दान महिदेवन्हि पाए ॥
taba prabhu riṣinha sameta nahāe, bibidha dāna mahidevanhi pāe.
हरषि चले मुनि बृंद सहाया । बेगि बिदेह नगर निअराया ॥
haraṣi cale muni bṛṁda sahāyā, begi bideha nagara niarāyā.
पुर रम्यता राम जब देखी । हरषे अनुज समेत बिसेषी ॥
pura ramyatā rāma jaba dekhī, haraṣe anuja sameta biseṣī.
बापीं कूप सरित सर नाना । सलिल सुधासम मनि सोपाना ॥
bāpīṁ kūpa sarita sara nānā, salila sudhāsama mani sopānā.
गुंजत मंजु मत्त रस भृंगा । कूजत कल बहुबरन बिहंगा ॥
guṁjata maṁju matta rasa bhṛṁgā, kūjata kala bahubarana bihaṁgā.
बरन बरन बिकसे बन जाता । त्रिबिध समीर सदा सुखदाता ॥
barana barana bikase bana jātā, tribidha samīra sadā sukhadātā.

Trans:

Rāma and Lakshman accompanied the saint to the world-purifying Gangā. Both the Lord and his younger brother reverently saluted it, and Rāma was delighted beyond measure, as the son of Gādhi told him of the ancient legend how the heavenly stream had come down upon earth. Then the Lord and the hermits performed their ablutions and the Brahmins received manifold gifts. The hermits' champion went on his way rejoicing, and quickly they drew near to the capital of Videh. When Rāma beheld the beauty of the city, he and his brother were delighted at the sight—numerous ponds and wells, and rivers and streams, with water of ambrosial purity and jeweled flights of steps; where the humm of bees—drunk on nectar—made delicious sounds; where birds of all kinds were cooing softly; where the lilies expanded their many-colored petals, and cool, soft, fragrant breezes blew ever so delightfully.

दोहा-dohā:

सुमन बाटिका बाग बन बिपुल बिहंग निवास ।
sumana bāṭikā bāga bana bipula bihaṁga nivāsa,
फूलत फलत सुपल्लवत सोहत पुर चहुँ पास ॥२१२॥
phūlata phalata supallavata sohata pura cahum̐ pāsa. 212.

Trans:

On all four sides the city was bright with flower-gardens, orchards, and groves, the resort of innumerable birds, and full of fruit and flowers and verdure.

चौपाई-caupāī:

बनइ न बरनत नगर निकाई । जहाँ जाइ मन तहँइँ लोभाई ॥
banai na baranata nagara nikāī, jahām̐ jāi mana taham̐im̐ lobhāī.
चारु बजारु बिचित्र अँबारी । मनिमय बिधि जनु स्वकर सँवारी ॥
cāru bajāru bicitra am̐bārī, manimaya bidhi janu svakara sam̐vārī.
धनिक बनिक बर धनद समाना । बैठे सकल बस्तु लै नाना ॥
dhanika banika bara dhanada samānā, baiṭhe sakala bastu lai nānā.
चौहट सुंदर गलीं सुहाई । संतत रहहिं सुगंध सिंचाई ॥
cauhaṭa suṁdara galīṁ suhāī, saṁtata rahahiṁ sugaṁdha siṁcāī.
मंगलमय मंदिर सब केरें । चित्रित जनु रतिनाथ चितेरें ॥
maṁgalamaya maṁdira saba kereṁ, citrita janu ratinātha citereṁ.
पुर नर नारि सुभग सुचि संता । धरमसील ग्यानी गुनवंता ॥
pura nara nāri subhaga suci saṁtā, dharamasīla gyānī gunavaṁtā.
अति अनूप जहँ जनक निवासू । बिथकहिं बिबुध बिलोकि बिलासू ॥
ati anūpa jaham̐ janaka nivāsū, bithakahiṁ bibudha biloki bilāsū.
होत चकित चित कोट बिलोकी । सकल भुवन सोभा जनु रोकी ॥
hota cakita cita koṭa bilokī, sakala bhuvana sobhā janu rokī.

Trans:

The beauty of the city is not to be told; wherever one went there was something to charm the soul: Handsome bazars and gorgeous balconies all studded with jewels, as though the Creator had fashioned them with his own hands. Thriving bankers and traders, very Kubers of wealth, sat in shops with their various goods displayed. There were fine squares and beautiful streets, which were constantly sprinkled with fragrant sprays. Many were the magnificent temples to the many gods—as bright as if they had been painted by Kāmdev himself. All the people of the city, both men and women, were prosperous, well-dressed, virtuous, pious, intelligent, and accomplished. Above all, Janak's palace was such a masterpiece that the gods tired themselves just looking at its splendor; and the mind was quite overcome by the sight of that fort—for it seemed to have reserved for itself all that was the most beautiful in the world.

दोहा-dohā:

धवल धाम मनि पुरट पट सुघटित नाना भाँति ।
dhavala dhāma mani puraṭa paṭa sughaṭita nānā bhām̐ti,
सिय निवास सुंदर सदन सोभा किमि कहि जाति ॥२१३॥
siya nivāsa suṁdara sadana sobhā kimi kahi jāti. 213.

Trans:

With glistening white walls and doors of gold, with gems set in different designs and folds, the exquisite mansion where Sītā herself lived was far too lovely for words to extol.

चौपाई-caupāī:

सुभग द्वार सब कुलिस कपाटा । भूप भीर नट मागध भाटा ॥
subhaga dvāra saba kulisa kapāṭā, bhūpa bhīra naṭa māgadha bhāṭā.
बनी बिसाल बाजि गज साला । हय गय रथ संकुल सब काला ॥
banī bisāla bāji gaja sālā, haya gaya ratha saṁkula saba kālā.
सूर सचिव सेनप बहुतेरे । नृपगृह सरिस सदन सब केरे ॥
sūra saciva senapa bahutere, nṛpagṛha sarisa sadana saba kere.
पुर बाहेर सर सरित समीपा । उतरे जहँ तहँ बिपुल महीपा ॥
pura bāhera sara sarita samīpā, utare jaham̐ taham̐ bipula mahīpā.
देखि अनूप एक अँवराई । सब सुपास सब भाँति सुहाई ॥
dekhi anūpa eka am̐varāī, saba supāsa saba bhām̐ti suhāī.
कौसिक कहेउ मोर मनु माना । इहाँ रहिअ रघुबीर सुजाना ॥
kausika kaheu mora manu mānā, ihām̐ rahia raghubīra sujānā.
भलेहिं नाथ कहि कृपानिकेता । उतरे तहँ मुनिबृंद समेता ॥
bhalehiṁ nātha kahi kṛpāniketā, utare taham̐ munibṛṁda sametā.
बिस्वामित्र महामुनि आए । समाचार मिथिलापति पाए ॥
bisvāmitra mahāmuni āe, samācāra mithilāpati pāe.

Trans:

All the city gates were most massive with panels of adamant, and they were thronged with princes and their retinues of mimists, bards, and heralds. The vast and well-built stables were at all hours of the day crowded with elephants, chariots, horses; and the many ministers, generals, and warriors all had their residences on the same style as the king's. Outside the city, by pools and streams, the multitudinous princes had pitched their various camps. Upon beholding a fine mango grove, a most agreeable and convenient spot, sage Kaushik said: "This is the spot I like; let us just camp here, Raghubīr." "Very well, my lord," answered the gracious God; and there they alighted with all the hermit train. When the king of Mithilā heard the news that the great saint Vishwāmitra had come,

दोहा-dohā:

संग सचिव सुचि भूरि भट भूसुर बर गुर ग्याति ।
saṁga saciva suci bhūri bhaṭa bhūsura bara gura gyāti,
चले मिलन मुनिनायकहि मुदित राउ एहि भाँति ॥२१४॥
cale milana munināyakahi mudita rāu ehi bhām̐ti. 214.

Trans:

he took with him his ministers and many gallant fighting men and noble Brahmins and the chief of his kinsmen, and in this fashion the king went forth rejoicing, to meet the king of saints.

चौपाई-caupāī:

कीन्ह प्रनामु चरन धरि माथा । दीन्हि असीस मुदित मुनिनाथा ॥
kīnha pranāmu carana dhari māthā, dīnhi asīsa mudita muninathā.
बिप्रबृंद सब सादर बंदे । जानि भाग्य बड़ राउ अनंदे ॥
biprabṛṁda saba sādara baṁde, jāni bhāgya baṛa rāu anaṁde.
कुसल प्रस्न कहि बारहिं बारा । बिस्वामित्र नृपहि बैठारा ॥
kusala prasna kahi bārahiṁ bārā, bisvāmitra nṛpahi baiṭhārā.
तेहि अवसर आए दोउ भाई । गए रहे देखन फुलवाई ॥
tehi avasara āe dou bhāī, gae rahe dekhana phulavāī.
स्याम गौर मृदु बयस किसोरा । लोचन सुखद बिस्व चित चोरा ॥
syāma gaura mṛdu bayasa kisorā, locana sukhada bisva cita corā.
उठे सकल जब रघुपति आए । बिस्वामित्र निकट बैठाए ॥
uṭhe sakala jaba raghupati āe, bisvāmitra nikaṭa baiṭhāe.
भए सब सुखी देखि दोउ भ्राता । बारि बिलोचन पुलकित गाता ॥
bhae saba sukhī dekhi dou bhrātā, bāri bilocana pulakita gātā.
मूरति मधुर मनोहर देखी । भयउ बिदेहु बिदेहु बिसेषी ॥
mūrati madhura manohara dekhī, bhayau bidehu bidehu biseṣī.

Trans:

Bowing to the ground, he made many obeisance, and the saint gave him his glad blessings. Then the king respectfully saluted all the hermit train and congratulated himself on his good fortune. After making many enquiries as to his health and welfare, Vishwāmitra led the king to a seat—when at that very moment arrived the two brothers who had gone to see the garden, one dark, the other fair, in childhood's tender bloom, the joy of all beholders, ravishing the senses of the whole world. When Raghupatī came, all rose and Vishwāmitra seated him by his side. Everyone was charmed at the sight of the two brothers: their eyes filled with tears and their body thrilled with rapture, and the king especially was beside himself with joy on beholding their sweet and lovely appearance.

दोहा-dohā:

प्रेम मगन मनु जानि नृपु करि बिबेकु धरि धीर।
prema magana manu jāni nṛpu kari bibeku dhari dhīra,
बोलेउ मुनि पद नाइ सिरु गदगद गिरा गभीर ॥२१५॥
boleu muni pada nāi siru gadagada girā gabhīra. 215.

Trans:

Though feeling himself overpowered with love, the king discreetly restrained himself, and, bowing his head at the saint's feet, said in suppressed accents choking with emotion:

चौपाई-caupāī:

कहहु नाथ सुंदर दोउ बालक। मुनिकुल तिलक कि नृपकुल पालक॥
kahahu nātha suṁdara dou bālaka, munikula tilaka ki nṛpakula pālaka.
ब्रह्म जो निगम नेति कहि गावा। उभय बेष धरि की सोइ आवा॥
brahma jo nigama neti kahi gāvā, ubhaya beṣa dhari kī soi āvā.
सहज बिरागरुप मनु मोरा। थकित होत जिमि चंद चकोरा॥
sahaja birāgarupa manu morā, thakita hota jimi caṁda cakorā.
ताते प्रभु पूछउँ सतिभाऊ। कहहु नाथ जनि करहु दुराऊ॥
tāte prabhu pūchauṁ satibhāū, kahahu nātha jani karahu durāū.
इन्हहि बिलोकत अति अनुरागा। बरबस ब्रह्मसुखहि मन त्यागा॥
inhahi bilokata ati anurāgā, barabasa brahmasukhahi mana tyāgā.
कह मुनि बिहसि कहेहु नृप नीका। बचन तुम्हार न होइ अलीका॥
kaha muni bihasi kahehu nṛpa nīkā, bacana tumhāra na hoi alīkā.
ये प्रिय सबहि जहाँ लगि प्रानी। मन मुसुकाहिं रामु सुनि बानी॥
ye priya sabahi jahāṁ lagi prānī, mana musukāhiṁ rāmu suni bānī.
रघुकुल मनि दसरथ के जाए। मम हित लागि नरेस पठाए॥
raghukula mani dasaratha ke jāe, mama hita lāgi naresa paṭhāe.

Trans:

"Tell me, my lord, who are these two lovely youths? Are they the glory of a saintly family, or the bulwarks of a kingly line? Or are they the double impersonation of the Supreme Spirit, whom scripture declares to be unutterable. My mind, ordinarily free from worldly attachment, does not weary itself gazing upon them, just as the *chakor* gazing upon the moon. Therefore, sir, I beg you to tell me the truth, and to conceal nothing. My love grows just by looking, and my soul perforce is withdrawn from divine contemplation within the Self." Said the saint with a smile, "You have spoken well, O king; your word is always true; there is not a living creature that does not love these boys." Rāma smiled to himself on hearing this. "They are the sons of Dashrath, the glory of the line of Raghu, and the king has sent them to help me.

दोहा-dohā:

रामु लखनु दोउ बंधुबर रूप सील बल धाम।
rāmu lakhanu dou baṁdhubara rūpa sīla bala dhāma,
मख राखेउ सबु साखि जगु जिते असुर संग्राम ॥२१६॥
makha rākheu sabu sākhi jagu jite asura saṁgrāma. 216.

Trans:

Rāma and Lakshman by name, these two brothers are as valiant as they are good and beautiful. The whole world knows that these two only protected my sacrifice and vanquished all the demons in battle."

चौपाई-caupāī:

मुनि तव चरन देखि कह राऊ। कहि न सकउँ निज पुन्य प्रभाऊ॥
muni tava carana dekhi kaha rāū, kahi na sakauṁ nija punya prabhāū.
सुंदर स्याम गौर दोउ भ्राता। आनँदहू के आनँद दाता॥
suṁdara syāma gaura dou bhrātā, ānaṁdahū ke ānaṁda dātā.
इन्ह कै प्रीति परसपर पावनि। कहि न जाइ मन भाव सुहावनि॥
inha kai prīti parasapara pāvani, kahi na jāi mana bhāva suhāvani.
सुनहु नाथ कह मुदित बिदेहू। ब्रह्म जीव इव सहज सनेहू॥
sunahu nātha kaha mudita bidehū, brahma jīva iva sahaja sanehū.
पुनि पुनि प्रभुहि चितव नरनाहू। पुलक गात उर अधिक उछाहू॥
puni puni prabhuhi citava naranāhū, pulaka gāta ura adhika uchāhū.
मुनिहि प्रसंसि नाइ पद सीसू। चलेउ लवाइ नगर अवनीसू॥
munihi prasaṁsi nāi pada sīsū, caleu lavāi nagara avanīsū.
सुंदर सदनु सुखद सब काला। तहाँ बासु लै दीन्ह भुआला॥
suṁdara sadanu sukhada saba kālā, tahāṁ bāsu lai dīnha bhuālā.
करि पूजा सब बिधि सेवकाई। गयउ राउ गृह बिदा कराई॥
kari pūjā saba bidhi sevakāī, gayau rāu gṛha bidā karāī.

Trans:

Said the king: "O saint, when I behold your feet I cannot tell how richly I am rewarded for my former good deeds. These two brothers, of hue dark and fair, verily confer bliss upon Bliss herself. Their innocent mutual affection is indescribable in words; a delight to the inmost soul. Hear to me sir," continued the king in his rapture, "it is like the natural union between the universal soul and the soul of man." Again and again the king gazed upon the Lord, with quivering body and a heart bursting with emotion. Then with courteous phrases and bowed head he escorted the saint and his companions to the city, and there assigned quarters which were bright, cheerful, comfortable at all times; and finally, after further homage and proffering of service, the king took his leave and returned to his palace.

दोहा-dohā:

रिषय संग रघुबंस मनि करि भोजनु बिश्रामु।
riṣaya saṁga raghubaṁsa mani kari bhojanu biśrāmu,
बैठे प्रभु भ्राता सहित दिवसु रहा भरि जामु ॥२१७॥
baiṭhe prabhu bhrātā sahita divasu rahā bhari jāmu. 217.

Trans:

Having dined with the seers and having rested awhile, Lord Shrī Rāma, the Jewel of Raghu's race, sat down by his brother's side. A quarter of the day still remained.

चौपाई-caupāī:

लखन हृदयँ लालसा बिसेषी। जाइ जनकपुर आइअ देखी॥
lakhana hṛdayaṁ lālasā biseṣī, jāi janakapura āia dekhī.
प्रभु भय बहुरि मुनिहि सकुचाहीं। प्रगट न कहहिं मनहिं मुसुकाहीं॥
prabhu bhaya bahuri munihi sakucāhiṁ, pragaṭa na kahahiṁ manahiṁ musukāhiṁ.
राम अनुज मन की गति जानी। भगत बछलता हियँ हुलसानी॥
rāma anuja mana kī gati jānī, bhagata bachalatā hiyaṁ hulasānī.
परम बिनीत सकुचि मुसुकाई। बोले गुर अनुसासन पाई॥
parama binīta sakuci musukāī, bole gura anusāsana pāī.
नाथ लखनु पुरु देखन चहहीं। प्रभु सकोच डर प्रगट न कहहीं॥
nātha lakhanu puru dekhana cahahiṁ, prabhu sakoca ḍara pragaṭa na kahahiṁ.
जौं राउर आयसु मैं पावौं। नगर देखाइ तुरत लै आवौं॥
jauṁ rāura āyasu maiṁ pāvauṁ, nagara dekhāi turata lai āvauṁ.
सुनि मुनीसु कह बचन सप्रीती। कस न राम तुम्ह राखहु नीती॥
suni munīsu kaha bacana saprītī, kasa na rāma tumha rākhahu nītī.
धरम सेतु पालक तुम्ह ताता। प्रेम बिबस सेवक सुखदाता॥
dharama setu pālaka tumha tātā, prema bibasa sevaka sukhadātā.

Trans:

Lakshman felt in his heart a great longing to go see the city; however in awe of his brother and respect for the saint, he said nothing out loud, but merely smiled to himself. Rāma understood what was passing in his mind—being ever considerate to his devotees; and then with a most modest and submissive smile, after gaining permission of his Gurū to speak, said, "Sir, Lakshman wishes to see the city, but out of respect for you is afraid to ask. If you will please allow, I will show him the place and quickly bring him back again." The saint replied most affectionately, "O Rāma, how can you do aught but good! You are the guardian of the bridge of religion, the very loving benefactor of your faithful servants.

दोहा-dohā:

जाइ देखी आवहु नगरु सुख निधान दोउ भाइ ।
jāi dekhī āvahu nagaru sukha nidhāna dou bhāi,
करहु सुफल सब के नयन सुंदर बदन देखाइ ॥२१८॥
karahu suphala saba ke nayana suṁdara badana dekhāi. 218.

Trans:

Go, blessed pair, and see the city, and gladden the eyes of all the people by the sight of your beauty."

चौपाई-caupāī:

मुनि पद कमल बंदि दोउ भ्राता । चले लोक लोचन सुख दाता ॥
muni pada kamala baṁdi dou bhrātā, cale loka locana sukha dātā.
बालक बृंद देखि अति सोभा । लगे संग लोचन मनु लोभा ॥
bālaka bṛṁda dekhi ati sobhā, lage saṁga locana manu lobhā.
पीत बसन परिकर कटि भाथा । चारु चाप सर सोहत हाथा ॥
pīta basana parikara kaṭi bhāthā, cāru cāpa sara sohata hāthā.
तन अनुहरत सुचंदन खोरी । स्यामल गौर मनोहर जोरी ॥
tana anuharata sucaṁdana khorī, syāmala gaura manohara jorī.
केहरि कंधर बाहु बिसाला । उर अति रुचिर नागमनि माला ॥
kehari kaṁdhara bāhu bisālā, ura ati rucira nāgamani mālā.
सुभग सोन सरसीरुह लोचन । बदन मयंक तापत्रय मोचन ॥
subhaga sona sarasīruha locana, badana mayaṁka tāpatraya mocana.
कानन्हि कनक फूल छबि देहीं । चितवत चितहि चोरि जनु लेहीं ॥
kānanhi kanaka phūla chabi dehīṁ, citavata citahi cori janu lehīṁ.
चितवनि चारु भृकुटि बर बाँकी । तिलक रेख सोभा जनु चाँकी ॥
citavani cāru bhṛkuṭi bara bāṁkī, tilaka rekha sobhā janu cāṁkī.

Trans:

After bowing at the saint's feet they went—those two brothers, the delight of eyes of whole world. When the children in the market place saw their exceeding beauty, their eyes and their very soul fastened greedily upon them. Clad in yellow apparel, with belt and quiver at their side, with graceful bow and arrows in hand, a lovely pair, one dark, the other fair of hue, with sandalwood *tilak* to match their complexion; with lion-like waist and long arms, and chest adorned with strings of elephant pearls, with shapely ears and lotus eyes, and moonlike face to assuage the three kinds of pain; with golden flowers for earrings, so beautiful as to steal the heart of every beholder; with a bewitching glance and fair arched eyebrows, and a star on the forehead that seemed beauty's own stamp;

दोहा-dohā:

रुचिर चौतनीं सुभग सिर मेचक कुंचित केस ।
rucira cautanīṁ subhaga sira mecaka kuṁcita kesa,
नख सिख सुंदर बंधु दोउ सोभा सकल सुदेस ॥२१९॥
nakha sikha suṁdara baṁdhu dou sobhā sakala sudesa. 219.

Trans:

with jaunty cap on comely head, with black curly locks, the two brothers were all-beautiful from head to foot and exquisite in every part.

चौपाई-caupāī:

देखन नगरु भूपसुत आए । समाचार पुरबासिन्ह पाए ॥
dekhana nagaru bhūpasuta āe, samācāra purabāsinha pāe.
धाए धाम काम सब त्यागी । मनहुँ रंक निधि लूटन लागी ॥
dhāe dhāma kāma saba tyāgī, manahuṁ raṁka nidhi lūṭana lāgī.
निरखि सहज सुंदर दोउ भाई । होहिं सुखी लोचन फल पाई ॥
nirakhi sahaja suṁdara dou bhāī, hohiṁ sukhī locana phala pāī.
जुबतीं भवन झरोखन्हि लागीं । निरखहिं राम रूप अनुरागीं ॥
jubatīṁ bhavana jharokhanhi lāgīṁ, nirakhahiṁ rāma rūpa anurāgīṁ.
कहहिं परसपर बचन सप्रीती । सखि इन्ह कोटि काम छबि जीती ॥
kahahiṁ parasapara bacana saprītī, sakhi inha koṭi kāma chabi jītī.
सुर नर असुर नाग मुनि माहीं । सोभा असि कहुँ सुनिअति नाहीं ॥
sura nara asura nāga muni māhīṁ, sobhā asi kahuṁ suniati nāhīṁ.
बिष्नु चारि भुज बिघि मुख चारी । बिकट बेष मुख पंच पुरारी ॥
biṣnu cāri bhuja bighi mukha cārī, bikaṭa beṣa mukha paṁca purārī.
अपर देउ अस कोउ न आही । यह छबि सखि पटतरिअ जाही ॥
apara deu asa kou na āhī, yaha chabi sakhi paṭataria jāhī.

Trans:

When the citizens heard that the princes were come to see the town, they all left their own business and started off like beggars to pillage a treasure-house. When they beheld the easy grace of the two brothers they were glad indeed and their eyes were rewarded. The maidens peeping from the windows of the houses at once fell in love with Rāma's beauty and in loving strain addressed one another: "They surpass in beauty a thousand Loves. Neither among gods, nor men, nor demons, nor serpents, nor deified saints has beauty such as theirs ever been heard of. As for Vishnu with his four arms, Brahmmā with his four heads, and Purārī with his five faces and wondrous attire, and all the other gods, there is not one in the whole universe whose beauty, my friend, can be compared to theirs.

दोहा-dohā:

बय किसोर सुषमा सदन स्याम गौर सुख घाम ।
baya kisora suṣamā sadana syāma gaura sukha ghāma,
अंग अंग पर वारिअहिं कोटि कोटि सत काम ॥२२०॥
aṁga aṁga para vāriahiṁ koṭi koṭi sata kāma. 220.

Trans:

Of tender age, the very abode of beauty, equally lovely whether dark or fair, as though a myriad, myriad Loves had been lavished on each individual limb of their bodies.

चौपाई-caupāī:

कहहु सखी अस को तनुधारी । जो न मोह यह रूप निहारी ॥
kahahu sakhī asa ko tanudhārī, jo na moha yaha rūpa nihārī.
कोउ सप्रेम बोली मृदु बानी । जो मैं सुना सो सुनहु सयानी ॥
kou saprema bolī mṛdu bānī, jo maiṁ sunā so sunahu sayānī.
ए दोऊ दसरथ के ढोटा । बाल मरालन्हि के कल जोटा ॥
e doū dasaratha ke ḍhoṭā, bāla marālanhi ke kala joṭā.
मुनि कौसिक मख के रखवारे । जिन्ह रन अजिर निसाचर मारे ॥
muni kausika makha ke rakhavāre, jinha rana ajira nisācara māre.
स्याम गात कल कंज बिलोचन । जो मारीच सुभुज मदु मोचन ॥
syāma gāta kala kaṁja bilocana, jo mārīca subhuja madu mocana.
कौसल्या सुत सो सुख खानी । नामु रामु धनु सायक पानी ॥
kausalyā suta so sukha khānī, nāmu rāmu dhanu sāyaka pānī.
गौर किसोर बेषु बर काछें । कर सर चाप राम के पाछें ॥
gaura kisora beṣu bara kācheṁ, kara sara cāpa rāma ke pācheṁ.
लछिमनु नामु राम लघु भ्राता । सुनु सखि तासु सुमित्रा माता ॥
lachimanu nāmu rāma laghu bhrātā, sunu sakhi tāsu sumitrā mātā.

Trans:

Tell me, O friend, is there anyone in human form who would not be charmed at the sight of such beauty?" Said one in gentle loving tones: "Hear, my dear, what I have been told. This pretty pair of young cygnets are the two sons of king Dashrath. They have protected the sacrifice of saint Vishwāmitra and slain in battle the invincible demons. The lovely youth with dark complexion and lotus eyes, who quelled the pride of Mārich and Subahu and bears the bow and arrows in his hand, is the charming son of Kausalyā—Rāma his name. The fair youth in gallant attire, who also has bow and arrows in hand and everywhere follows Rāma, is named Lakshman, his younger brother; and Sumitrā, you must know, is his mother.

दोहा-dohā:

बिप्रकाजु करि बंधु दोउ मग मुनिबधू उधारि ।
biprakāju kari baṁdhu dou maga munibadhū udhāri,
आए देखन चापमख सुनि हरषीं सब नारि ॥२२१॥
āe dekhana cāpamakha suni haraṣīṁ saba nāri. 221.

Trans:

After befriending the Brahmins, and on the road setting free the sage's wife, the two brothers have come here to see the tournament." On hearing this all the ladies were delighted.

चौपाई-caupāī:

देखि राम छबि कोउ एक कहई । जोगु जानकिहि यह बरु अहई ॥
dekhi rāma chabi kou eka kahaī, jogu jānakihi yaha baru ahaī.
जौं सखि इन्हहि देख नरनाहू । पन परिहरि हठि करइ बिबाहू ॥
jauṁ sakhi inhahi dekha naranāhū, pana parihari haṭhi karai bibāhū.
कोउ कह ए भूपति पहिचाने । मुनि समेत सादर सनमाने ॥
kou kaha e bhūpati pahicāne, muni sameta sādara sanamāne.
सखि परंतु पनु राउ न तजई । बिधि बस हठि अबिबेकहि भजई ॥
sakhi paraṁtu panu rāu na tajaī, bidhi basa haṭhi abibekahi bhajaī.
कोउ कह जौं भल अहइ बिधाता । सब कहँ सुनिअ उचित फलदाता ॥
kou kaha jauṁ bhala ahai bidhātā, saba kahaṁ sunia ucita phaladātā.
तौ जानकिहि मिलिहि बरु एहू । नाहिन आलि इहाँ संदेहू ॥
tau jānakihi milihi baru ehū, nāhina āli ihāṁ saṁdehū.
जौं बिधि बस अस बनै सँजोगू । तौ कृतकृत्य होइ सब लोगू ॥
jauṁ bidhi basa asa banai saṁjogū, tau kṛtakṛtya hoi saba logū.
सखि हमरें आरति अति तातें । कबहुँक ए आवहिं एहि नातें ॥
sakhi hamareṁ ārati ati tāteṁ, kabahuṁka e āvahiṁ ehi nāteṁ.

Trans:

Said one, after regarding Rāma's beauty: "Here is a bridegroom worthy of our Jānakī. If the king does but see them, he will abjure his vow and insist only upon a marriage with them." Said another: "The king knows who they are and has received both them and the saint with high honors. He hasn't however gone back on his vow, and persists in his folly—mastered by fate." Said another: "If God is good, and is certain to reward every man according to his deserve, then here is the bridegroom Jānakī will wed. About this, my dear, there can be no doubt. When such a union is brought about by destiny, everyone will be satisfied. O friend, I am deeply moved by the thought that when married he may at some time come here,

दोहा-dohā:

नाहिं त हम कहुँ सुनहु सखि इन्ह कर दरसनु दूरि ।
nāhiṁ ta hama kahuṁ sunahu sakhi inha kara darasanu dūri,
यह संघटु तब होइ जब पुन्य पुराकृत भूरि ॥२२२॥
yaha saṁghaṭu taba hoi jaba punya purākṛta bhūri. 222.

Trans:

otherwise there is no chance of our seeing him; but if I have accumulated sufficient merits in my previous existences, the union will surely take place."

चौपाई-caupāī:

बोली अपर कहेहु सखि नीका । एहिं बिआह अति हित सबही का ॥
bolī apara kahehu sakhi nīkā, ehiṁ biāha ati hita sabahī kā.
कोउ कह संकर चाप कठोरा । ए स्यामल मृदुगात किसोरा ॥
kou kaha saṁkara cāpa kaṭhorā, e syāmala mṛdugāta kisorā.
सबु असमंजस अहइ सयानी । यह सुनि अपर कहइ मृदु बानी ॥
sabu asamaṁjasa ahai sayānī, yaha suni apara kahai mṛdu bānī.
सखि इन्ह कहँ कोउ कोउ अस कहहीं । बड़ प्रभाउ देखत लघु अहहीं ॥
sakhi inha kahaṁ kou kou asa kahahīṁ, baṛa prabhāu dekhata laghu ahahīṁ.
परसि जासु पद पंकज धूरी । तरी अहल्या कृत अघ भूरी ॥
parasi jāsu pada paṁkaja dhūrī, tarī ahalyā kṛta agha bhūrī.
सो कि रहिहि बिनु सिवधनु तोरें । यह प्रतीति परिहरिअ न भोरें ॥
so ki rahihi binu sivadhanu toreṁ, yaha pratīti pariharia na bhoreṁ.
जेहिं बिरंचि रचि सीय सँवारी । तेहिं स्यामल बरु रचेउ बिचारी ॥
jehiṁ biraṁci raci sīya saṁvārī, tehiṁ syāmala baru raceu bicārī.
तासु बचन सुनि सब हरषानीं । ऐसेइ होउ कहहिं मृदु बानीं ॥
tāsu bacana suni saba haraṣānīṁ, aisei hou kahahiṁ mṛdu bānīṁ.

Trans:

Said another: "Friend, you have spoken well, for this is a marriage that will please everyone," Said another: "Shiva's bow is hard to bend, and for this dark lad of delicate frame, it is really a most unfair test." Hearing this, another soft-voiced maiden said: "I have once and again heard say of them that though slight in appearance their strength is great. Touched by the dust of his lotus feet, the guilty Ahalyā attained salvation. He will, therefore, surely break Shiva's bow; one should never commit the mistake of giving up faith. When the Creator fashioned Sītā, he predestined for her this dark-complexioned bridegroom." On hearing these words all were glad and softly exclaimed: "May it indeed prove so."

दोहा-dohā:

हियँ हरषहिं बरषहिं सुमन सुमुखि सुलोचनि बृंद ।
hiyaṁ haraṣahiṁ baraṣahiṁ sumana sumukhi sulocani bṛṁda,
जाहिं जहाँ जहँ बंधु दोउ तहँ तहँ परमानंद ॥२२३॥
jāhiṁ jahāṁ jahaṁ baṁdhu dou tahaṁ tahaṁ paramānaṁda. 223.

Trans:

In their gladness of heart the bevy of bright-eyed fair-faced dames shower down petals, and wherever the two brothers went there was just the complete joy of heaven.

चौपाई-caupāī:

पुर पूरब दिसि गे दोउ भाई । जहँ धनुमख हित भूमि बनाई ॥
pura pūraba disi ge dou bhāī, jahaṁ dhanumakha hita bhūmi banāī.
अति बिस्तार चारु गच ढारी । बिमल बेदिका रुचिर सँवारी ॥
ati bistāra cāru gaca ḍhārī, bimala bedikā rucira saṁvārī.
चहुँ दिसि कंचन मंच बिसाला । रचे जहाँ बैठहिं महिपाला ॥
cahuṁ disi kaṁcana maṁca bisālā, race jahāṁ baiṭhahiṁ mahipālā.
तेहि पाछें समीप चहुँ पासा । अपर मंच मंडली बिलासा ॥
tehi pācheṁ samīpa cahuṁ pāsā, apara maṁca maṁḍalī bilāsā.
कछुक ऊँचि सब भाँति सुहाई । बैठहिं नगर लोग जहँ जाई ॥
kachuka ūṁci saba bhāṁti suhāī, baiṭhahiṁ nagara loga jahaṁ jāī.
तिन्ह के निकट बिसाल सुहाए । धवल धाम बहुबरन बनाए ॥
tinha ke nikaṭa bisāla suhāe, dhavala dhāma bahubarana banāe.
जहँ बैठें देखहिं सब नारी । जथा जोगु निज कुल अनुहारी ॥
jahaṁ baiṭheṁ dekhahiṁ saba nārī, jathā jogu nija kula anuhārī.
पुर बालक कहि कहि मृदु बचना । सादर प्रभुहि देखावहिं रचना ॥
pura bālaka kahi kahi mṛdu bacanā, sādara prabhuhi dekhāvahiṁ racanā.

Trans:

Now they reached the eastern quarter of the city where the lists had been prepared for the wedding tournament. In the midst of a fair and spacious paved area, a spotless altar had been gorgeously adorned, with a broad golden platform all round for the reception of the princes; and close behind was another circular tier for the spectators—of somewhat greater height and elegantly decorated—where all people of the city might come, sit, watch. Close to this was another large and beautiful gallery—glistening white, painted in diverse hues, whence ladies might view the spectacle with due decorum according to their family rank. The children politely showed the two lords all the preparations, and with pleasant voices keep telling them what this is and what is that;

दोहा-*dohā:*

सब सिसु एहि मिस प्रेमबस परसि मनोहर गात ।
saba sisu ehi misa premabasa parasi manohara gāta,
तन पुलकहिं अति हरषु हियँ देखि देखि दोउ भ्रात ॥२२४॥
tana pulakahiṁ ati haraṣu hiyaṁ dekhi dekhi dou bhrāta. 224.

Trans:

and thereby, in their affection finding a pretext for frequently touching their lovely person. They all thrill over with delight as again and again they gaze upon the twosome brothers.

चौपाई-*caupāī:*

सिसु सब राम प्रेमबस जाने । प्रीति समेत निकेत बखाने ॥
sisu saba rāma premabasa jāne, prīti sameta niketa bakhāne.
निज निज रुचि सब लेहिं बोलाई । सहित सनेह जाहिं दोउ भाई ॥
nija nija ruci saba lehiṁ bolāī, sahita saneha jāhiṁ dou bhāī.
राम देखावहिं अनुजहि रचना । कहि मृदु मधुर मनोहर बचना ॥
rāma dekhāvahiṁ anujahi racanā, kahi mṛdu madhura manohara bacanā.
लव निमेष महुँ भुवन निकाया । रचइ जासु अनुसासन माया ॥
lava nimeṣa mahuṁ bhuvana nikāyā, racai jāsu anusāsana māyā.
भगति हेतु सोइ दीनदयाला । चितवत चकित धनुष मखसाला ॥
bhagati hetu soi dīnadayālā, citavata cakita dhanuṣa makhasālā.
कौतुक देखि चले गुरु पाहीं । जानि बिलंबु त्रास मन माहीं ॥
kautuka dekhi cale guru pāhīṁ, jāni bilaṁbu trāsa mana māhīṁ.
जासु त्रास डर कहुँ डर होई । भजन प्रभाउ देखावत सोई ॥
jāsu trāsa ḍara kahuṁ ḍara hoī, bhajana prabhāu dekhāvata soī.
कहि बातें मृदु मधुर सुहाईं । किए बिदा बालक बरिआईं ॥
kahi bāteṁ mṛdu madhura suhāīṁ, kie bidā bālaka bariāīṁ.

Trans:

When they perceived that Rāma was won by their devotion, they lovingly described the different places, each according to his own fancy, excitedly pulling away the two brothers, who in their kindness are ever ready to follow. Rāma shows Lakshman everything, still talking in light and merry tone; and he—in obedience to whose fiat, Māyā in a moment of time created the entire universe—out of compassion to his faithful people, feigns amazement at the sight of the tourney-ground. When they had seen all the show, they begin to go back to their Gurū in alarm at being so late; and he, by whose awe Terror itself is dismayed, thus manifests the transcendent virtue of devotion. With many kind and courteous phrases they take leave of the children—much to their reluctance.

दोहा-*dohā:*

सभय सप्रेम बिनीत अति सकुच सहित दोउ भाइ ।
sabhaya saprema binīta ati sakuca sahita dou bhāi,
गुर पद पंकज नाइ सिर बैठे आयसु पाइ ॥२२५॥
gura pada paṁkaja nāi sira baiṭhe āyasu pāi. 225.

Trans:

Returning—meekly and submissively, with mingled awe and love—they bow their heads at the Gurū's feet; nor sit down till they obtain his permission.

चौपाई-*caupāī:*

निसि प्रबेस मुनि आयसु दीन्हा । सबहीं संध्याबंदनु कीन्हा ॥
nisi prabesa muni āyasu dīnhā, sabahīṁ saṁdhyābaṁdanu kīnhā.
कहत कथा इतिहास पुरानी । रुचिर रजनि जुग जाम सिरानी ॥
kahata kathā itihāsa purānī, rucira rajani juga jāma sirānī.
मुनिबर सयन कीन्हि तब जाई । लगे चरन चापन दोउ भाई ॥
munibara sayana kīnhi taba jāī, lage carana cāpana dou bhāī.
जिन्ह के चरन सरोरुह लागी । करत बिबिध जप जोग बिरागी ॥
jinha ke carana saroruha lāgī, karata bibidha japa joga birāgī.
तेइ दोउ बंधु प्रेम जनु जीते । गुर पद कमल पलोटत प्रीते ॥
tei dou baṁdhu prema janu jīte, gura pada kamala paloṭata prīte.
बार बार मुनि अग्या दीन्ही । रघुबर जाइ सयन तब कीन्ही ॥
bāra bāra muni agyā dīnhī, raghubara jāi sayana taba kīnhī.
चापत चरन लखनु उर लाएँ । सभय सप्रेम परम सचु पाएँ ॥
cāpata carana lakhanu ura lāeṁ, sabhaya saprema parama sacu pāeṁ.
पुनि पुनि प्रभु कह सोवहु ताता । पौढ़े धरि उर पद जलजाता ॥
puni puni prabhu kaha sovahu tātā, pauṛhe dhari ura pada jalajātā.

Trans:

When came dusk, the saint gave the word, and all performed their evening worship; and then, in the recital of sacred legends, were spent two watches of the solemn night. Now the saint retired to his couch, and the two brothers began to massage his feet. They—to behold whose lotus feet the holiest of men practice all kinds of penance and meditations—even they, these two brothers—mastered by love—affectionately rubbed their master's lotus feet. At last, when the saint had so ordered again and again, Rāma himself retired to rest, while Lakshman pressed his feet to his heart, and reverently caressed them with emotions of exquisite delight. Again and again the Lord said, "Sleep now, my brother"; and at last he laid himself down, but treasuring the divine feet still in his heart.

दोहा-*dohā:*

उठे लखनु निसि बिगत सुनि अरुनसिखा धुनि कान ।
uṭhe lakhanu nisi bigata suni arunasikhā dhuni kāna,
गुर तें पहिलेहिं जगतपति जागे रामु सुजान ॥२२६॥
gura teṁ pahilehiṁ jagatapati jāge rāmu sujāna. 226.

Trans:

When the night was spent, at the first sound of cock-crow, Lakshman arose; and next, before the saint did, awoke the Lord of the universe, the all-wise Rāma.

चौपाई-*caupāī:*

सकल सौच करि जाइ नहाए । नित्य निबाहि मुनिहि सिर नाए ॥
sakala sauca kari jāi nahāe, nitya nibāhi munihi sira nāe.
समय जानि गुर आयसु पाई । लेन प्रसून चले दोउ भाई ॥
samaya jāni gura āyasu pāī, lena prasūna cale dou bhāī.
भूप बागु बर देखेउ जाई । जहँ बसंत रितु रही लोभाई ॥
bhūpa bāgu bara dekheu jāī, jahaṁ basaṁta ritu rahī lobhāī.
लागे बिटप मनोहर नाना । बरन बरन बर बेलि बिताना ॥
lāge biṭapa manohara nānā, barana barana bara beli bitānā.
नव पल्लव फल सुमन सुहाए । निज संपति सुर रूख लजाए ॥
nava pallava phala sumana suhāe, nija saṁpati sura rūkha lajāe.
चातक कोकिल कीर चकोरा । कूजत बिहग नटत कल मोरा ॥
cātaka kokila kīra cakorā, kūjata bihaga naṭata kala morā.
मध्य बाग सरु सोह सुहावा । मनि सोपान बिचित्र बनावा ॥
madhya bāga saru soha suhāvā, mani sopāna bicitra banāvā.

बिमल सलिलु सरसिज बहुरंगा । जलखग कूजत गुंजत भृंगा ॥
bimala salilu sarasija bahuraṁgā, jalakhaga kūjata guṁjata bhṛṁgā.

Trans:

After performing all the customary acts of purification and going to bathe, they bowed before the Gurū, and by his permission went out to gather worship-flowers, as befitted the time. As they went they espied a beautiful garden of the king's, where reigned perpetual Spring, planted with ornamental trees of every kind; trees overhung with many-colored creepers, and so rich in bud and fruit and flower that in its abundance it put to shame even the tree of paradise. Here and there danced the peacocks, responsive to the music made by the feathered choir of *chātak*, *koel*, parrot, and *chakor*. In the midst of the garden there was a lovely lake that shone bright with jeweled steps of every design. Its pure expanse was gladdened with many-colored lotuses and the cooing of water-birds and the hum of bees.

दोहा-dohā:

बागु तड़ागु बिलोकि प्रभु हरषे बंधु समेत ।
bāgu taṛāgu biloki prabhu haraṣe baṁdhu sameta,
परम रम्य आरामु यहु जो रामहि सुख देत ॥२२७॥
parama ramya ārāmu yahu jo rāmahi sukha deta. 227.

Trans:

Both the Lord and his brother were delighted at the sight of the lake and the garden. What charming sweetness must that have been—that which pleased even Rāma.

चौपाई-caupāī:

चहुँ दिसि चितइ पूँछि मालीगन । लगे लेन दल फूल मुदित मन ॥
cahuṁ disi citai pūṁchi mālīgana, lage lena dala phūla mudita mana.
तेहि अवसर सीता तहँ आई । गिरिजा पूजन जननि पठाई ॥
tehi avasara sītā tahaṁ āī, girijā pūjana janani paṭhāī.
संग सखीं सब सुभग सयानीं । गावहिं गीत मनोहर बानीं ॥
saṁga sakhīṁ saba subhaga sayānīṁ, gāvahiṁ gīta manohara bānīṁ.
सर समीप गिरिजा गृह सोहा । बरनि न जाइ देखि मनु मोहा ॥
sara samīpa girijā gṛha sohā, barani na jāi dekhi manu mohā.
मज्जनु करि सर सखिन्ह समेता । गई मुदित मन गौरि निकेता ॥
majjanu kari sara sakhinha sametā, gaī mudita mana gauri niketā.
पूजा कीन्हि अधिक अनुरागा । निज अनुरूप सुभग बरु मागा ॥
pūjā kīnhi adhika anurāgā, nija anurūpa subhaga baru māgā.
एक सखी सिय संगु बिहाई । गई रही देखन फुलवाई ॥
eka sakhī siya saṁgu bihāī, gaī rahī dekhana phulavāī.
तेहिं दोउ बंधु बिलोके जाई । प्रेम बिबस सीता पहिं आई ॥
tehiṁ dou baṁdhu biloke jāī, prema bibasa sītā pahiṁ āī.

Trans:

After looking all about and asking permission of the gardeners they began joyfully to gather leaves and flowers for worship. At that very time Sītā too came there, having been sent by her mother to visit the shrine of Girijā. With her came all her young and lovely companions, joyfully singing happy songs. Now Girijā's shrine was close to the lake, beautiful beyond description, the delight of all beholders. When she and her attendants had bathed in the pool, she approached the goddess with glad heart, and after adoration, she prayed with much devotion, and begged of her a handsome well-matched bridegroom. One of her attendant damsels, who had strayed away to look at the garden, chanced to see the two brothers, and returned to Sītā quite love-smitten.

दोहा-dohā:

तासु दसा देखि सखिन्ह पुलक गात जलु नैन ।
tāsu dasā dekhi sakhinha pulaka gāta jalu naina,
कहु कारनु निज हरष कर पूछहिं सब मृदु बैन ॥२२८॥
kahu kāranu nija haraṣa kara pūchahiṁ saba mṛdu baina. 228.

Trans:

When her companions observed what state she was in—her body all in a tremble and her eyes full of tears—they asked in gentle tones, "Declare the cause of this rapture."

चौपाई-caupāī:

देखन बागु कुअँर दुइ आए । बय किसोर सब भाँति सुहाए ॥
dekhana bāgu kuaṁra dui āe, baya kisora saba bhāṁti suhāe.
स्याम गौर किमि कहौं बखानी । गिरा अनयन नयन बिनु बानी ॥
syāma gaura kimi kahauṁ bakhānī, girā anayana nayana binu bānī.
सुनि हरषीं सब सखीं सयानी । सिय हियँ अति उतकंठा जानी ॥
suni haraṣīṁ saba sakhīṁ sayānī, siya hiyaṁ ati utakaṁṭhā jānī.
एक कहइ नृपसुत तेइ आली । सुने जे मुनि सँग आए काली ॥
eka kahai nṛpasuta tei ālī, sune je muni saṁga āe kālī.
जिन्ह निज रूप मोहनी डारी । कीन्हे स्वबस नगर नर नारी ॥
jinha nija rūpa mohanī ḍārī, kīnhe svabasa nagara nara nārī.
बरनत छबि जहँ तहँ सब लोगू । अवसि देखिअहिं देखन जोगू ॥
baranata chabi jahaṁ tahaṁ saba logū, avasi dekhiahiṁ dekhana jogū.
तासु बचन अति सियहि सोहाने । दरस लागि लोचन अकुलाने ॥
tāsu bacana ati siyahi sohāne, darasa lāgi locana akulāne.
चली अग्र करि प्रिय सखि सोई । प्रीति पुरातन लखइ न कोई ॥
calī agra kari priya sakhi soī, prīti purātana lakhai na koī.

Trans:

"There have come to see the garden two princes—of tender age and charming in every way, one dark of hue, the other fair, but how can I describe them? Alas the voice is sightless and the eyes are dumb." All the damsels were delighted at her speech, and perceiving the intense longing in Sītā's bosom, one of them exclaimed: "My dear, these must be the king's sons, who, as I hear, along with the saint arrived yesterday; and who have completely fascinated everybody with their beauty, and have stolen the hearts of all the men and women in the city. Everyone is talking of their loveliness; we really must go see them; they are every worth seeing." These words were most grateful to Sītā, whose eyes were restless with longing. With her kind friends to lead the way, she followed; nor did anyone know that it was the case of old love.

दोहा-dohā:

सुमिरि सीय नारद बचन उपजी प्रीति पुनीत ।
sumiri sīya nārada bacana upajī prīti punīta,
चकित बिलोकति सकल दिसि जनु सिसु मृगी सभीत ॥२२९॥
cakita bilokati sakala disi janu sisu mṛgī sabhīta. 229.

Trans:

Remembering Nārad's words, she was filled with holy love, and she anxiously turned her gaze on every side, like a startled fawn.

चौपाई-caupāī:

कंकन किंकिनि नूपुर धुनि सुनि । कहत लखन सन रामु हृदयँ गुनि ॥
kaṁkana kiṁkini nūpura dhuni suni, kahata lakhana sana rāmu hṛdayaṁ guni.
मानहुँ मदन दुंदुभी दीन्ही । मनसा बिस्व बिजय कहँ कीन्ही ॥
mānahuṁ madana duṁdubhī dīnhī. manasā bisva bijaya kahaṁ kīnhī.
अस कहि फिरि चितए तेहि ओरा । सिय मुख ससि भए नयन चकोरा ॥
asa kahi phiri citae tehi orā, siya mukha sasi bhae nayana cakorā.
भए बिलोचन चारु अचंचल । मनहुँ सकुचि निमि तजे दिगंचल ॥

bhae bilocana cāru acaṁcala, manahuṁ sakuci nimi taje digaṁcala.

देखि सीय सोभा सुखु पावा । हृदयँ सराहत बचनु न आवा ॥
dekhi sīya sobhā sukhu pāvā, hṛdayaṁ sarāhata bacanu na āvā.

जनु बिरंचि सब निज निपुनाई । बिरचि बिस्व कहँ प्रगटि देखाई ॥
janu biraṁci saba nija nipunāī, biraci bisva kahaṁ pragaṭi dekhāī.

सुंदरता कहुँ सुंदर करई । छबिगृहँ दीपसिखा जनु बरई ॥
suṁdaratā kahuṁ suṁdara karaī, chabigṛhaṁ dīpasikhā janu baraī.

सब उपमा कबि रहे जुठारी । केहिं पटतरौं बिदेहकुमारी ॥
saba upamā kabi rahe juṭhārī, kehiṁ paṭataraum bidehakumārī.

Trans:

When he heard the sound of the golden bangles on her hands and feet, Rāma thought within himself, and then said to Lakshman: "Imagine Love, triumphant over the whole world, is now sounding the kettledrums of victory." So saying he again looked in her direction, and like the moon on the *chakor*, flashed Sītā's face upon his sight His beautiful eyes became motionless—as though Nimi, the god who presides over eyelids, had fled in shyness from his wonted post. Beholding her beauty he was enraptured; but his admiration was all within, and utterance failed him. 'Twas as though the great Architect, after creating the whole world, had put forth his highest skills eventually to showcase the Loveliest in visible form; or it was as if 'Beautiful' herself had been beautified into a temple of beauty and illuminated by a sudden flash of light. Alas, all the similes of the poets are stale and hackneyed—for where can one find any likeness to Jānakī!

दोहा-dohā:

सिय सोभा हियँ बरनि प्रभु आपनि दसा बिचारि ।
siya sobhā hiyaṁ barani prabhu āpani dasā bicāri,

बोले सुचि मन अनुज सन बचन समय अनुहारि ॥२३०॥
bole suci mana anuja sana bacana samaya anuhāri. 230.

Trans:

Dwelling in heart on Sītā's beauty and reflecting on his own state of mind, the pure-souled god thus addressed his brother in terms appropriate to the occasion:

चौपाई-caupāī:

तात जनकतनया यह सोई । धनुषजग्य जेहि कारन होई ॥
tāta janakatanayā yaha soī, dhanuṣajagya jehi kārana hoī.

पूजन गौरि सखीं लै आईं । करत प्रकासु फिरइ फुलवाईं ॥
pūjana gauri sakhīṁ lai āīṁ, karata prakāsu phirai phulavāīṁ.

जासु बिलोकि अलौकिक सोभा । सहज पुनीत मोर मनु छोभा ॥
jāsu biloki alaukika sobhā, sahaja punīta mora manu chobhā.

सो सबु कारन जान बिधाता । फरकहिं सुभद अंग सुनु भ्राता ॥
so sabu kārana jāna bidhātā, pharakahiṁ subhada aṁga sunu bhrātā.

रघुबंसिन्ह कर सहज सुभाऊ । मनु कुपंथ पगु धरइ न काऊ ॥
raghubaṁsinha kara sahaja subhāū, manu kupaṁtha pagu dharai na kāū.

मोहि अतिसय प्रतीति मन केरी । जेहिं सपनेहुँ परनारि न हेरी ॥
mohi atisaya pratīti mana kerī, jehiṁ sapanehuṁ paranāri na herī.

जिन्ह कै लहहिं न रिपु रन पीठी । नहिं पावहिं परतिय मनु डीठी ॥
jinha kai lahahiṁ na ripu rana pīṭhī, nahiṁ pāvahiṁ paratiya manu ḍīṭhī.

मंगन लहहिं न जिन्ह कै नाहीं । ते नरबर थोरे जग माहीं ॥
maṁgana lahahiṁ na jinha kai nāhīṁ, te narabara thore jaga māhīṁ.

Trans:

"Brother, this is the very daughter of king Janak, for whom the tournament has been set up. She has come with her attendants to worship Gaurī, and a train of light marks her path through the garden. My heart, which is naturally pure, is agitated by the sight of her transcendent beauty. The reason of all this is known to god alone; but I tell you, brother, my right limbs are throbbing, which is an index of coming good fortune. It is a natural trait with the race of Raghu that they never set their heart on evil courses; and thus I am confidently assured that all will be well; for I have never even in a dream looked upon another's man's wife, or to long after her. Rare in this world are those noble men who never turn their back on the foe in battle, nor give their heart to, or cast an amorous glance, on another's wife, and from whom no beggar meets with rebuff.

दोहा-dohā:

करत बतकही अनुज सन मन सिय रूप लोभान ।
karata batakahī anuja sana mana siya rūpa lobhāna,

मुख सरोज मकरंद छबि करइ मधुप इव पान ॥२३१॥
mukha saroja makaraṁda chabi karai madhupa iva pāna. 231.

Trans:

Thus discoursing to his brother, and with his soul enamored of Sītā's beauty, like a bee soaking up honey from a flower, he imbibed the loveliness of her face.

चौपाई-caupāī:

चितवति चकित चहूँ दिसि सीता । कहँ गए नृपकिसोर मनु चिंता ॥
citavati cakita cahūṁ disi sītā, kahaṁ gae nṛpakisora manu ciṁtā.

जहँ बिलोक मृग सावक नैनी । जनु तहँ बरिस कमल सित श्रेनी ॥
jahaṁ biloka mṛga sāvaka nainī, janu tahaṁ barisa kamala sita śrenī.

लता ओट तब सखिन्ह लखाए । स्यामल गौर किसोर सुहाए ॥
latā oṭa taba sakhinha lakhāe, syāmala gaura kisora suhāe.

देखि रूप लोचन ललचाने । हरषे जनु निज निधि पहिचाने ॥
dekhi rūpa locana lalacāne, haraṣe janu nija nidhi pahicāne.

थके नयन रघुपति छबि देखें । पलकन्हिहूँ परिहरीं निमेषें ॥
thake nayana raghupati chabi dekheṁ, palakanhihūṁ pariharīṁ nimeṣeṁ.

अधिक सनेहँ देह भै भोरी । सरद ससिहि जनु चितव चकोरी ॥
adhika sanehaṁ deha bhai bhorī, sarada sasihi janu citava cakorī.

लोचन मग रामहि उर आनी । दीन्हे पलक कपाट सयानी ॥
locana maga rāmahi ura ānī, dīnhe palaka kapāṭa sayānī.

जब सिय सखिन्ह प्रेमबस जानी । कहि न सकहिं कछु मन सकुचानी ॥
jaba siya sakhinha premabasa jānī, kahi na sakahiṁ kachu mana sakucānī.

Trans:

Sītā kept looking anxiously all around in doubt as to where the princes had gone. Wherever fell her fawn-like glance, it seemed there was a rain of glistening lotus flowers. Then her companions pointed out to her under the shade of the creepers the two lovely youths, the one dark, the other fair of hue. Her eyes, on beholding that beauty, were filled with longing and with the gladness of one who has found a long-lost treasure. Wearied with gazing upon Rāma's charms, her eyelids forgot to blink, and her whole frame was fulfilled with excess of love, as is the partridge when it sees the autumnal moon. Receiving Rāma into her heart by the pathway of vision, she cleverly closed upon him the doors of her eyelids. When her companions saw her thus overcome they were much too abashed to utter a single word.

दोहा-dohā:

लताभवन तें प्रगट भे तेहि अवसर दोउ भाइ ।
latābhavana teṁ pragaṭa bhe tehi avasara dou bhāi,

निकसे जनु जुग बिमल बिधु जलद पटल बिलगाइ ॥२३२॥
nikase janu juga bimala bidhu jalada paṭala bilagāi. 232.

Trans:

Then emerged the twin brothers from the shade of the arbor, like two spotless moons from a riven cloud:

चौपाई-caupāī:

सोभा सीवँ सुभग दोउ बीरा । नील पीत जलजाभ सरीरा ॥
sobhā sīvaṁ subhaga dou bīrā, nīla pīta jalajābha sarīrā.

मोरपंख सिर सोहत नीके । गुच्छ बीच बिच कुसुम कली के ॥
morapaṁkha sira sohata nīke, guccha bīca bica kusuma kalī ke.
भाल तिलक श्रमबिंदु सुहाए । श्रवन सुभग भूषन छबि छाए ॥
bhāla tilaka śramabiṁdu suhāe, śravana subhaga bhūṣana chabi chāe.
बिकट भृकुटि कच घूघरवारे । नव सरोज लोचन रतनारे ॥
bikaṭa bhṛkuṭi kaca ghūgharavāre, nava saroja locana ratanāre.
चारु चिबुक नासिका कपोला । हास बिलास लेत मनु मोला ॥
cāru cibuka nāsikā kapolā, hāsa bilāsa leta manu molā.
मुखछबि कहि न जाइ मोहि पाहीं । जो बिलोकि बहु काम लजाहीं ॥
mukhachabi kahi na jāi mohi pāhīṁ, jo biloki bahu kāma lajāhīṁ.
उर मनि माल कंबु कल गीवा । काम कलभ कर भुज बलसींवा ॥
ura mani māla kaṁbu kala gīvā, kāma kalabha kara bhuja balasīṁvā.
सुमन समेत बाम कर दोना । सावँर कुअँर सखी सुठि लोना ॥
sumana sameta bāma kara donā, sāvaṁra kuaṁra sakhī suṭhi lonā.

Trans:

Two gallant champions, the perfection of beauty, like a pair of lotus bright and a dark, with their hair parted like a raven's wing on their comely head, and here and there bedecked with bunches of flower-buds; their forehead bright with the *tilak* and beads of perspiration, and their graceful ears adorned with ornaments, with arched eyebrows and curly locks, and eyes bright as lotus buds, with lovely chin and nose and cheeks, and a gracious smile enslaving every soul—such beauteous features as one could never describe—they would put to shame a myriad Loves. With a string of jewels on his chest, an exquisite neck like a conch-shell in spiral shape, and powerful arms, like the trunk of some young elephant in whom Kāmdev had become incarnate. With the flowers and cup of leaves in his left hand, the dark prince, O my friend, is beautiful exceedingly.

दोहा-dohā:

केहरि कटि पट पीत धर सुषमा सील निधान ।
kehari kaṭi paṭa pīta dhara suṣamā sīla nidhāna,
देखि भानुकुलभूषनहि बिसरा सखिन्ह अपान ॥२३३॥
dekhi bhānukulabhūṣanahi bisarā sakhinha apāna. 233.

Trans:

As her companions gazed upon the two glories of the Solar race, with their lion-like waist and bright yellow attire, very abodes of bliss and amiability, they lost all consciousness of their self.

चौपाई-caupāī:

धरि धीरजु एक आलि सयानी । सीता सन बोली गहि पानी ॥
dhari dhīraju eka āli sayānī, sītā sana bolī gahi pānī.
बहुरि गौरि कर ध्यान करेहू । भूपकिसोर देखि किन लेहू ॥
bahuri gauri kara dhyāna karehū, bhūpakisora dekhi kina lehū.
सकुचि सीयँ तब नयन उघारे । सनमुख दोउ रघुसिंघ निहारे ॥
sakuci sīyaṁ taba nayana ughāre, sanamukha dou raghusiṁgha nihāre.
नख सिख देखि राम कै सोभा । सुमिरि पिता पनु मनु अति छोभा ॥
nakha sikha dekhi rāma kai sobhā, sumiri pitā panu manu ati chobhā.
परबस सखिन्ह लखी जब सीता । भयउ गहरु सब कहहिं सभीता ॥
parabasa sakhinha lakhī jaba sītā, bhayau gaharu saba kahahiṁ sabhītā.
पुनि आउब एहि बेरिआँ काली । अस कहि मन बिहसी एक आली ॥
puni āuba ehi beriāṁ kālī, asa kahi mana bihasī eka ālī.
गूढ़ गिरा सुनि सिय सकुचानी । भयउ बिलंबु मातु भय मानी ॥
gūṛha girā suni siya sakucānī, bhayau bilaṁbu mātu bhaya mānī.
धरि बड़ि धीर रामु उर आने । फिरी अपनपउ पितुबस जाने ॥
dhari baṛi dhīra rāmu ura āne, phirī apanapau pitubasa jāne.

Trans:

Yet one summoning up courage grasped Sītā by the hand and said: "You can at any time meditate upon Gaurī; why not now look at the prince?" Then the modest Sītā unclosed her eyes and saw before her the two scions of Raghu. As she gazed on Rāma, all beautiful from head to foot, and remembered her father's vow, she was greatly agitated. When her companions saw her thus overcome they all cried as if in alarm, "It is getting late," and one added with an inward smile, "We will come again at this time tomorrow." On hearing these meaningful words Sītā was abashed and said, as if in fear of her mother, "It is late, indeed." Then summoning up resolution she turned to go, having fixed the image of Rāma in her heart. Then she thought how entirely it all depended upon her sire.

दोहा-dohā:

देखन मिस मृग बिहग तरु फिरइ बहोरि बहोरि ।
dekhana misa mṛga bihaga taru phirai bahori bahori,
निरखि निरखि रघुबीर छबि बाढ़इ प्रीति न थोरि ॥२३४॥
nirakhi nirakhi raghubīra chabi bāṛhai prīti na thori. 234.

Trans:

Under pretense of looking at a deer, or bird, or tree, again and again she turned her head, and each time that she beheld the beauteous Raghubīr her love was augmented not little, but in leaps.

चौपाई-caupāī:

जानि कठिन सिवचाप बिसूरति । चली राखि उर स्यामल मूरति ॥
jāni kaṭhina sivacāpa bisūrati, calī rākhi ura syāmala mūrati.
प्रभु जब जात जानकी जानी । सुख सनेह सोभा गुन खानी ॥
prabhu jaba jāta jānakī jānī, sukha saneha sobhā guna khānī.
परम प्रेममय मृदु मसि कीन्ही । चारु चित्त भीतीं लिखि लीन्ही ॥
parama premamaya mṛdu masi kīnhī, cāru citta bhītīṁ likhi līnhī.
गई भवानी भवन बहोरी । बंदि चरन बोली कर जोरी ॥
gaī bhavānī bhavana bahorī, baṁdi carana bolī kara jorī.
जय जय गिरिबरराज किसोरी । जय महेस मुख चंद चकोरी ॥
jaya jaya giribararāja kisorī, jaya mahesa mukha caṁda cakorī.
जय गजबदन षडानन माता । जगत जननि दामिनि दुति गाता ॥
jaya gajabadana ṣaḍānana mātā, jagata janani dāmini duti gātā.
नहिं तव आदि मध्य अवसाना । अमित प्रभाउ बेदु नहिं जाना ॥
nahiṁ tava ādi madhya avasānā, amita prabhāu bedu nahiṁ jānā.
भव भव बिभव पराभव कारिनि । बिस्व बिमोहनि स्वबस बिहारिनि ॥
bhava bhava bibhava parābhava kārini, bisva bimohani svabasa bihārini.

Trans:

As she went she kept in her heart the image of the dark-hued swain; but the thought of Shiva's unyielding bow made her wilt. When the Lord perceived that she was going, he drew in his heart—with the indelible ink of love—a charming sketch of her infinite beauty, virtue and blissful devotion. Again she sought Bhawānī's shrine, and after embracing her feet, thus prayed with clasped hands: "Glory, glory, glory to thee, O daughter of the mountain king, as fixed in thy gaze on Shiva's face as is the partridge to the moon; O mother of Ganesh and Kartikey; great mother of the world; whose body is lustrous as the lightning; of whom there is neither beginning nor middle nor end; whose infinite majesty is a mystery even to the Veda; cause of the birth, continuance, and ultimate destruction of all beings; enchantress of the universe; delighting in thy own supremacy;

दोहा-dohā:

पतिदेवता सुतीय महुँ मातु प्रथम तव रेख ।
patidevatā sutīya mahuṁ mātu prathama tava rekha,
महिमा अमित न सकहिं कहि सहस सारदा सेष ॥२३५॥
mahimā amita na sakahiṁ kahi sahasa sāradā seṣa. 235.

Trans:

Among all faithful wives and true women, thy name, O mother, holds the first place; thy immeasurable grandeur is more than a thousand Shārdās and Sheshnāgs could ever tell.

चौपाई-caupāī:

सेवत तोहि सुलभ फल चारी । बरदायनी पुरारि पिआरी ॥
sevata tohi sulabha phala cārī, baradāyanī purāri piārī.
देबि पूजि पद कमल तुम्हारे । सुर नर मुनि सब होहिं सुखारे ॥
debi pūji pada kamala tumhāre, sura nara muni saba hohiṁ sukhāre.
मोर मनोरथु जानहु नीकें । बसहु सदा उर पुर सबही कें ॥
mora manorathu jānahu nīkeṁ, basahu sadā ura pura sabahī keṁ.
कीन्हेउँ प्रगट न कारन तेहीं । अस कहि चरन गहे बैदेहीं ॥
kīnheuṁ pragaṭa na kārana tehīṁ, asa kahi carana gahe baidehīṁ.
बिनय प्रेम बस भई भवानी । खसी माल मूरति मुसुकानी ॥
binaya prema basa bhaī bhavānī, khasī māla mūrati musukānī.
सादर सियँ प्रसादु सिर धरेऊ । बोली गौरि हरषु हियँ भरेऊ ॥
sādara siyaṁ prasādu sira dhareū, bolī gauri haraṣu hiyaṁ bhareū.
सुनु सिय सत्य असीस हमारी । पूजिहि मन कामना तुम्हारी ॥
sunu siya satya asīsa hamārī, pūjihi mana kāmanā tumhārī.
नारद बचन सदा सुचि साचा । सो बरु मिलिहि जाहिं मनु राचा ॥
nārada bacana sadā suci sācā, so baru milihi jāhiṁ manu rācā.

Trans:

The fourfold rewards of life are easy of attainment by thy servants, O granter of boons, beloved of Tripurārī. All, O goddess, who adore thy lotus feet, are made happy—whether they be gods, or men, or saints. Thou knowest well my heart's desire, for in the heart of all thou ever dwellest; there is no need that I may declare it aloud to thee." So saying, Sītā embraced her feet. Bhawānī was moved by her humility and devotion; the effigy smiled and the garland on her neck slipped below. Reverently Sītā clasped to her bosom the divine gift, and Gaurī herself with a heart full of joy spoke thusly: "Hearken Sītā, my blessing will come true; your heart's desire shall be accomplished. Nārad's words are ever truth itself; the bridegroom upon whom your soul is set, shall indeed be yours.

छंद-chaṁda:

मनु जाहिं राचेउ मिलिहि सो बरु सहज सुंदर साँवरो ।
manu jāhiṁ rāceu milihi so baru sahaja suṁdara sāṁvaro,
करुना निधान सुजान सीलु सनेहु जानत रावरो ॥
karunā nidhāna sujāna sīlu sanehu jānata rāvaro.
एहि भाँति गौरि असीस सुनि सिय सहित हियँ हरषीं अली ।
ehi bhāṁti gauri asīsa suni siya sahita hiyaṁ haraṣīṁ alī,
तुलसी भवानिहि पूजि पुनि पुनि मुदित मन मंदिर चली ॥
tulasī bhavānihi pūji puni puni mudita mana maṁdira calī.

Trans:

The dark-complexioned youth, upon whose simple beauty your soul is set, shall be yours. The All-merciful in his wisdom knows your loving disposition." On hearing Gaurī pronounce this blessing, Sītā and her companions were overjoyed, and in their delight (says Tulsī) turned again and again to the temple to adore the goddess.

सोरठा-sorathā:

जानि गौरि अनुकूल सिय हिय हरषु न जाइ कहि ।
jāni gauri anukūla siya hiya haraṣu na jāi kahi,
मंजुल मंगल मूल बाम अंग फरकन लगे ॥२३६॥
maṁjula maṁgala mūla bāma aṁga pharakana lage. 236.

Trans:

Finding Gaurī so gracious, Sītā was more glad of heart than words can tell; and as a propitious omen, her left side, the seat of good fortune for women, began to throb.

चौपाई-caupāī:

हृदयँ सराहत सीय लोनाई । गुर समीप गवने दोउ भाई ॥
hṛdayaṁ sarāhata sīya lonāī, gura samīpa gavane dou bhāī.
राम कहा सबु कौसिक पाहीं । सरल सुभाउ छुअत छल नाहीं ॥
rāma kahā sabu kausika pāhīṁ, sarala subhāu chuata chala nāhīṁ.
सुमन पाइ मुनि पूजा कीन्ही । पुनि असीस दुहु भाइन्ह दीन्ही ॥
sumana pāi muni pūjā kīnhī, puni asīsa duhu bhāinha dīnhī.
सुफल मनोरथ होहुँ तुम्हारे । रामु लखनु सुनि भए सुखारे ॥
suphala manoratha hohuṁ tumhāre, rāmu lakhanu suni bhae sukhāre.
करि भोजनु मुनिबर बिग्यानी । लगे कहन कछु कथा पुरानी ॥
kari bhojanu munibara bigyānī, lage kahana kachu kathā purānī.
बिगत दिवसु गुरु आयसु पाई । संध्या करन चले दोउ भाई ॥
bigata divasu guru āyasu pāī, saṁdhyā karana cale dou bhāī.
प्राची दिसि ससि उयउ सुहावा । सिय मुख सरिस देखि सुखु पावा ॥
prācī disi sasi uyau suhāvā, siya mukha sarisa dekhi sukhu pāvā.
बहुरि बिचारु कीन्ह मन माहीं । सीय बदन सम हिमकर नाहीं ॥
bahuri bicāru kīnha mana māhīṁ, sīya badana sama himakara nāhīṁ.

Trans:

Here, with Rama inwardly praising Sītā's loveliness, the two brothers returned to their Gurū; and Rāma related to him all that had taken place—being simplicity itself and utterly devoid of guile. The saint took the flowers and performed his devotions, and then imparted his blessings to the two brothers, saying: "May your desire be accomplished." Rāma and Lakshman gladdened at the words. Then, after taking food, the saintly sage began the recital of sacred legends. When the day was spent, they first asked his permission and then went out to perform their evening duties. In the meantime the charming moon rose in the eastern horizon; perceiving that her orb resembled Sītā's face Shrī Rāma felt elated. The Lord then reasoned within himself: 'The queen of night bears no resemblance to Sītā;

दोहा-dohā:

जनमु सिंधु पुनि बंधु बिषु दिन मलीन सकलंक ।
janamu siṁdhu puni baṁdhu biṣu dina malīna sakalaṁka,
सिय मुख समता पाव किमि चंदु बापुरो रंक ॥२३७॥
siya mukha samatā pāva kimi caṁdu bāpuro raṁka. 237.

Trans:

for she was born of the restless Ocean, with poison for a brother, and by day she is dim and obscure; how then can such a poor feeble creature be likened to the lovely Sītā?

चौपाई-caupāī:

घटइ बढ़इ बिरहिनि दुखदाई । ग्रसइ राहु निज संधिहिं पाई ॥
ghaṭai baṛhai birahini dukhadāī, grasai rāhu nija saṁdhihiṁ pāī.
कोक सोकप्रद पंकज द्रोही । अवगुन बहुत चंद्रमा तोही ॥
koka sokaprada paṁkaja drohī, avaguna bahuta caṁdramā tohī.
बैदेही मुख पटतर दीन्हे । होइ दोष बड़ अनुचित कीन्हे ॥
baidehī mukha paṭatara dīnhe, hoi doṣa baṛa anucita kīnhe.
सिय मुख छबि बिधु ब्याज बखानी । गुरु पहिं चले निसा बड़ि जानी ॥
siya mukha chabi bidhu byāja bakhānī, guru pahiṁ cale nisā baṛi jānī.
करि मुनि चरन सरोज प्रनामा । आयसु पाइ कीन्ह बिश्रामा ॥
kari muni carana saroja pranāmā, āyasu pāi kīnha biśrāmā.
बिगत निसा रघुनायक जागे । बंधु बिलोकि कहन अस लागे ॥
bigata nisā raghunāyaka jāge, baṁdhu biloki kahana asa lāge.
उयउ अरुन अवलोकहु ताता । पंकज कोक लोक सुखदाता ॥
uyau aruna avalokahu tātā, paṁkaja koka loka sukhadātā.

बोले लखनु जोरि जुग पानी । प्रभु प्रभाउ सूचक मृदु बानी ॥
bole lakhanu jori juga pānī, prabhu prabhāu sūcaka mṛdu bānī.

Trans:

The moon waxes and wanes, is the curse of love-sick maidens, and is devoured by Rāhu whenever his appointed time comes round; she causes anguish to the *chakwā* and withers the lotus. O moon, thou art full of faults; it is a great sin and highly improper to compare Janak's daughter to thee.' Thus, Rāma found in the moon a pretext for extolling the beauty of Sītā. Then they returned to their Gurū, the night being now far advanced; and after bowing themselves at his feet and obtaining his permission they retired to rest. When the night was over Raghunāyak arose, and looking towards his brother, thus began to speak: "See, brother, the day has dawned to the delight of the lotus, the *chakwā*, and all mankind." Then said Lakshman in gentle tones and with folded hands, declaring the glory of the Lord:

दोहा-*dohā:*

अरुनोदयँ सकुचे कुमुद उडगन जोति मलीन ।
arunodayaṁ sakuce kumuda uḍagana joti malīna,
जिमि तुम्हार आगमन सुनि भए नृपति बलहीन ॥२३८॥
jimi tumhāra āgamana suni bhae nṛpati balahīna. 238.

Trans:

"At the dawn of day the lily fades and the brightness of the stars is dimmed, likewise at the news of your coming all other princes have waned faint;

चौपाई-*caupāī:*

नृप सब नखत करहिं उजिआरी । टारि न सकहिं चाप तम भारी ॥
nṛpa saba nakhata karahiṁ ujiārī, ṭāri na sakahiṁ cāpa tama bhārī.
कमल कोक मधुकर खग नाना । हरषे सकल निसा अवसाना ॥
kamala koka madhukara khaga nānā, haraṣe sakala nisā avasānā.
ऐसेहिं प्रभु सब भगत तुम्हारे । होइहहिं टूटें धनुष सुखारे ॥
aisehiṁ prabhu saba bhagata tumhāre, hoihahiṁ ṭūṭeṁ dhanuṣa sukhāre.
उयउ भानु बिनु श्रम तम नासा । दुरे नखत जग तेजु प्रकासा ॥
uyau bhānu binu śrama tama nāsā, dure nakhata jaga teju prakāsā.
रबि निज उदय ब्याज रघुराया । प्रभु प्रतापु सब नृपन्ह दिखाया ॥
rabi nija udaya byāja raghurāyā, prabhu pratāpu saba nṛpanha dikhāyā.
तव भुज बल महिमा उदघाटी । प्रगटी धनु बिघटन परिपाटी ॥
tava bhuja bala mahimā udaghāṭī, pragaṭī dhanu bighaṭana paripāṭī.
बंधु बचन सुनि प्रभु मुसुकाने । होइ सुचि सहज पुनीत नहाने ॥
baṁdhu bacana suni prabhu musukāne, hoi suci sahaja punīta nahāne.
नित्यक्रिया करि गुरु पहिं आए । चरन सरोज सुभग सिर नाए ॥
nityakriyā kari guru pahiṁ āe, carana saroja subhaga sira nāe.
सतानंदु तब जनक बोलाए । कौसिक मुनि पहिं तुरत पठाए ॥
satānaṁdu taba janaka bolāe, kausika muni pahiṁ turata paṭhāe.
जनक बिनय तिन्ह आइ सुनाई । हरषे बोलि लिए दोउ भाई ॥
janaka binaya tinha āi sunāī, haraṣe boli lie dou bhāī.

Trans:

—for bright though they be as the planets, they cannot master the black-bow of the Night, which is left only up to the Sun. The lotus, the *chakwā*, the bee, and every bird—all rejoice in the night's defeat; and so, O Lord, all your votaries will be glad when the bow is broken. Sunrise is a painless triumph over darkness; the constellations flee away and light flashes upon the world. Under the pretext of rising, the Sun demonstrates to these princes, the majesty of you, Raghurāī, my Lord. Verily it is to reveal the might of your arms, that this ceremony of breaking of the bow is ordained." The Lord smiled to hear his brother's speech. The All-pure then performed the daily rites of purification and bathed, and after observance of the prescribed ceremonies, presented himself before the Gurū and bowed his comely head at his feet. Then Janak summoned Shatānand and sent him in haste to Vishwāmitra. He came and declared his sovereign's message, and also called for the two brothers.

दोहा-*dohā:*

सतानंद पद बंदि प्रभु बैठे गुर पहिं जाइ ।
satānaṁda pada baṁdi prabhu baiṭhe gura pahiṁ jāi,
चलहु तात मुनि कहेउ तब पठवा जनक बोलाइ ॥२३९॥
calahu tāta muni kaheu taba paṭhavā janaka bolāi. 239.

Trans:

After reverently saluting Shatānand, the Lord went and sat down by his Gurū, who said: "Come, my son, Janak has sent for us.

मासपारायण आठवाँ विश्राम

नवाह्नपारायण दूसरा विश्राम

māsapārāyaṇa āṭhavāṁ viśrāma
navāhnapārāyaṇa dūsarā viśrāma
(Pause 8 for a Thirty-Day Recitation)
(Pause 2 for a Nine-Day Recitation)

चौपाई-*caupāī:*

सीय स्वयंबरु देखिअ जाई । ईसु काहि धौं देइ बड़ाई ॥
sīya svayaṁbaru dekhia jāī, īsu kāhi dhauṁ dei baṛāī.
लखन कहा जस भाजनु सोई । नाथ कृपा तव जापर होई ॥
lakhana kahā jasa bhājanu soī, nātha kṛpā tava jāpara hoī.
हरषे मुनि सब सुनि बर बानी । दीन्हि असीस सबहिं सुखु मानी ॥
haraṣe muni saba suni bara bānī, dīnhi asīsa sabahiṁ sukhu mānī.
पुनि मुनिबृंद समेत कृपाला । देखन चले धनुषमख साला ॥
puni munibṛṁda sameta kṛpālā, dekhana cale dhanuṣamakha sālā.
रंगभूमि आए दोउ भाई । असि सुधि सब पुरबासिन्ह पाई ॥
raṁgabhūmi āe dou bhāī, asi sudhi saba purabāsinha pāī.
चले सकल गृह काज बिसारी । बाल जुबान जरठ नर नारी ॥
cale sakala gṛha kāja bisārī, bāla jubāna jaraṭha nara nārī.
देखी जनक भीर भै भारी । सुचि सेवक सब लिए हँकारी ॥
dekhī janaka bhīra bhai bhārī, suci sevaka saba lie haṁkārī.
तुरत सकल लोगन्ह पहिं जाहू । आसन उचित देहू सब काहू ॥
turata sakala loganha pahiṁ jāhū, āsana ucita dehū saba kāhū.

Trans:

Let us go see Sītā's nuptials, and discover who is the happy man whom heaven will honor." Said Lakshman: "His will be the glory, my lord, upon whom your favor rests." The saints were glad to hear this seemly speech, and all with much effusion gave their blessings. Then the Gracious God, attended by all the saintly throng, sallied forth to witness the tournament. No sooner had they reached the arena than the news spread all over the city, and everyone put away his work and came pouring in—men and women, young and old, and even children in arms. When Janak saw the enormous crowd he gave orders to his practiced servitors: "Go round at once to all the people and marshal them to their appropriate seats."

दोहा-*dohā:*

कहि मृदु बचन बिनीत तिन्ह बैठारे नर नारि ।
kahi mṛdu bacana binīta tinha baiṭhāre nara nāri,
उत्तम मध्यम नीच लघु निज निज थल अनुहारि ॥२४०॥
uttama madhyama nīca laghu nija nija thala anuhāri. 240.

Trans:

With courteous phrase they respectfully seated them all, both men and women, according to their respective rank, whether noble or middling, humble or low.

चौपाई-*caupāī:*

राजकुअँर तेहि अवसर आए । मनहुँ मनोहरता तन छाए ॥
rājakuaṁra tehi avasara āe, manahuṁ manoharatā tana chāe.

गुन सागर नागर बर बीरा । सुंदर स्यामल गौर सरीरा ॥
guna sāgara nāgara bara bīrā, suṁdara syāmala gaura sarīrā.
राज समाज बिराजत रूरे । उडगन महुँ जनु जुग बिधु पूरे ॥
rāja samāja birājata rūre, uḍagana mahuṁ janu juga bidhu pūre.
जिन्ह कें रही भावना जैसी । प्रभु मूरति तिन्ह देखी तैसी ॥
jinha keṁ rahī bhāvanā jaisī, prabhu mūrati tinha dekhī taisī.
देखहिं रूप महा रनधीरा । मनहुँ बीर रसु धरें सरीरा ॥
dekhahiṁ rūpa mahā ranadhīrā, manahuṁ bīra rasu dhareṁ sarīrā.
डरे कुटिल नृप प्रभुहि निहारी । मनहुँ भयानक मूरति भारी ॥
ḍare kuṭila nṛpa prabhuhi nihārī, manahuṁ bhayānaka mūrati bhārī.
रहे असुर छल छोनिप बेषा । तिन्ह प्रभु प्रगट कालसम देखा ॥
rahe asura chala chonipa beṣā, tinha prabhu pragaṭa kālasama dekhā.
पुरबासिन्ह देखे दोउ भाई । नरभूषन लोचन सुखदाई ॥
purabāsinha dekhe dou bhāī, narabhūṣana locana sukhadāī.

Trans:

Then stepped forth the two princes, like beauty beautified, graceful and accomplished champions, one dark, the other fair, and both charming; resplendent in the assembly of princes like two full moons in a circle of stars. Every spectator seemed to see in them the embodiment of his own ideal: the princes beheld a gallant warrior, as it were the Heroism incarnate; the wicked kings trembled at the sight of the Lord, as an incarnation of the Terrible; the demons in princely disguise thought they saw the image of Death; while the citizens regarded the twin brothers as the glory of humanity, the delight of all eyes.

दोहा-dohā:

नारि बिलोकहिं हरषि हियँ निज निज रुचि अनुरूप ।
nāri bilokahiṁ haraṣi hiyaṁ nija nija ruci anurūpa,
जनु सोहत सिंगार धरि मूरति परम अनूप ॥२४१॥
janu sohata siṁgāra dhari mūrati parama anūpa. 241.

Trans:

The women gazed with rapture, however different their tastes, as though the intense sentiment had itself been manifested in incomparable form.

चौपाई-caupāī:

बिदुषन्ह प्रभु बिराटमय दीसा । बहु मुख कर पग लोचन सीसा ॥
biduṣanha prabhu birāṭamaya dīsā, bahu mukha kara paga locana sīsā.
जनक जाति अवलोकहिं कैसें । सजन सगे प्रिय लागहिं जैसें ॥
janaka jāti avalokahiṁ kaiseṁ, sajana sage priya lāgahiṁ jaiseṁ.
सहित बिदेह बिलोकहिं रानी । सिसु सम प्रीति न जाति बखानी ॥
sahita bideha bilokahiṁ rānī, sisu sama prīti na jāti bakhānī.
जोगिन्ह परम तत्वमय भासा । सांत सुद्ध सम सहज प्रकासा ॥
joginha parama tatvamaya bhāsā, sāṁta suddha sama sahaja prakāsā.
हरिभगतन्ह देखे दोउ भ्राता । इष्टदेव इव सब सुख दाता ॥
haribhagatanha dekhe dou bhrātā, iṣṭadeva iva saba sukha dātā.
रामहि चितव भायँ जेहि सीया । सो सनेहु सुखु नहिं कथनीया ॥
rāmahi citava bhāyaṁ jehi sīyā, so sanehu sukhu nahiṁ kathanīyā.
उर अनुभवति न कहि सक सोऊ । कवन प्रकार कहै कबि कोऊ ॥
ura anubhavati na kahi saka soū, kavana prakāra kahai kabi koū.
एहि बिधि रहा जाहि जस भाऊ । तेहिं तस देखेउ कोसलराऊ ॥
ehi bidhi rahā jāhi jasa bhāū, tehiṁ tasa dekheu kosalarāū.

Trans:

By sages the Lord was seen in his divine majesty with many faces and hands and feet and eyes and heads. And how did he appear to Janak's family group? Like a noble kinsman and a beloved friend. The queen, no less than the king, regarded him with unspeakable love like a dear child; to mystics he shone forth as eternal Truth, the placid radiance of unruffled Quietism; while to the pious the two brothers appeared as their own benignant patron saint. But as for Sītā, when she gazed on Rāma, her love and joy were unspeakable. If she could not utter the emotion of her heart, how can any poet declare it? In this way everyone regarded the Lord of Ajodhyā according to the attitude of mind each had towards him.

दोहा-dohā:

राजत राज समाज महुँ कोसलराज किसोर ।
rājata rāja samāja mahuṁ kosalarāja kisora,
सुंदर स्यामल गौर तन बिस्व बिलोचन चोर ॥२४२॥
suṁdara syāmala gaura tana bisva bilocana cora. 242.

Trans:

Thus shone in the assembly of kings the two lovely princes of Ajodhyā, the one dark and the other fair of form, catching the eyes of the whole universe.

चौपाई-caupāī:

सहज मनोहर मूरति दोऊ । कोटि काम उपमा लघु सोऊ ॥
sahaja manohara mūrati doū, koṭi kāma upamā laghu soū.
सरद चंद निंदक मुख नीके । नीरज नयन भावते जी के ॥
sarada caṁda niṁdaka mukha nīke, nīraja nayana bhāvate jī ke.
चितवनि चारु मार मनु हरनी । भावति हृदय जाति नहीं बरनी ॥
citavani cāru māra manu haranī, bhāvati hṛdaya jāti nahīṁ baranī.
कल कपोल श्रुति कुंडल लोला । चिबुक अधर सुंदर मृदु बोला ॥
kala kapola śruti kuṁḍala lolā, cibuka adhara suṁdara mṛdu bolā.
कुमुदबंधु कर निंदक हाँसा । भृकुटी बिकट मनोहर नासा ॥
kumudabaṁdhu kara niṁdaka hāṁsā, bhṛkuṭī bikaṭa manohara nāsā.
भाल बिसाल तिलक झलकाहीं । कच बिलोकि अलि अवलि लजाहीं ॥
bhāla bisāla tilaka jhalakāhīṁ, kaca biloki ali avali lajāhīṁ.
पीत चौतनीं सिरन्हि सुहाईं । कुसुम कलीं बिच बीच बनाईं ॥
pīta cautanīṁ siranhi suhāīṁ, kusuma kalīṁ bica bīca banāīṁ.
रेखें रुचिर कंबु कल गीवाँ । जनु त्रिभुवन सुषमा की सीवाँ ॥
rekheṁ rucira kaṁbu kala gīvāṁ, janu tribhuvana suṣamā kī sīvāṁ.

Trans:

Both with such facile grace of form that a myriad Loves were all too mean a comparison: with beaming face, that would put to shame the autumnal moon, and irresistibly charming lotus eyes; with a glance so unspeakably winning that it would rob Love of all his pride; with rounded cheeks and ears adorned with pendulous gems; with beautiful chin and lips and sweet voice; with a smile more radiant than the light of the moon, and arched eyebrows and delicate nose, and broad forehead with glittering *tilak*, and clustering locks with which no swarm of bees could vie; with yellow turban on their shapely head, dotted here and there with flower-buds; with exquisite neck, marked with a triple line, enclosing as it were the bliss of the three spheres of creation.

दोहा-dohā:

कुंजर मनि कंठा कलित उरन्हि तुलसिका माल ।
kuṁjara mani kaṁṭhā kalita uranhi tulasikā māla,
बृषभ कंध केहरि ठवनि बल निधि बाहु बिसाल ॥२४३॥
bṛṣabha kaṁdha kehari ṭhavani bala nidhi bāhu bisāla. 243.

Trans:

Adorned with a necklace of elephant pearls and a Tulsī garland on their chest; with the shoulders of a bull and the gait of a lion, and long arms, they were the very embodiments of Strength.

चौपाई-caupāī:

कटि तूनीर पीत पट बाँधें । कर सर धनुष बाम बर काँधें ॥
kaṭi tūnīra pīta paṭa bāṁdheṁ, kara sara dhanuṣa bāma bara kāṁdheṁ.
पीत जग्य उपबीत सुहाए । नख सिख मंजु महाछबि छाए ॥
pīta jagya upabīta suhāe, nakha sikha maṁju mahāchabi chāe.

देखि लोग सब भए सुखारे । एकटक लोचन चलत न तारे ॥
dekhi loga saba bhae sukhāre, ekaṭaka locana calata na tāre.
हरषे जनकु देखि दोउ भाई । मुनि पद कमल गहे तब जाई ॥
harașe janaku dekhi dou bhāī, muni pada kamala gahe taba jāī.
करि बिनती निज कथा सुनाई । रंग अवनि सब मुनिहि देखाई ॥
kari binatī nija kathā sunāī, raṁga avani saba munihi dekhāī.
जहँ जहँ जाहिं कुअँर बर दोऊ । तहँ तहँ चकित चितव सबु कोऊ ॥
jahaṁ jahaṁ jāhiṁ kuaṁra bara doū, tahaṁ tahaṁ cakita citava sabu koū.
निज निज रुख रामहि सबु देखा । कोउ न जान कछु मरमु बिसेषा ॥
nija nija rukha rāmahi sabu dekhā, kou na jāna kachu maramu biseṣā.
भलि रचना मुनि नृप सन कहेऊ । राजाँ मुदित महासुख लहेऊ ॥
bhali racanā muni nṛpa sana kaheū, rājāṁ mudita mahāsukha laheū.

Trans:

By their side a quiver slung from a yellow brace; with arrows in hand and bow on their left shoulder; with a charming Brahminical cord, also of yellow tint—in short, beautiful from head to foot, resplendent all over. Everyone who saw them was made happy, nor could for a minute take his eyes off of them. Janak too rejoiced to behold the two brothers. Then went he to the saint and embraced his feet, and deferentially related to him all his past history, and showed the hermits the place marked out for the ceremony. Wherever the two gallant princes turned, all men's eyes were dazzled; each saw in Rāma what he himself most admired, nor did anyone comprehend in the least the special mystery. The saint told the king the arrangements were perfect, and the king was thereby highly gratified.

दोहा-dohā:

सब मंचन्ह तें मंचु एक सुंदर बिसद बिसाल ।
saba maṁcanha teṁ maṁcu eka suṁdara bisada bisāla,
मुनि समेत दोउ बंधु तहँ बैठारे महिपाल ॥२४४॥
muni sameta dou baṁdhu tahaṁ baiṭhāre mahipāla. 244.

Trans:

There was one tier of seats bright, spacious, and beautiful above all the rest; and here the Raja seated the saint and the two brothers.

चौपाई-caupāī:

प्रभुहि देखि सब नृप हियँ हारे । जनु राकेस उदय भएँ तारे ॥
prabhuhi dekhi saba nṛpa hiyaṁ hāre, janu rākesa udaya bhaeṁ tāre.
असि प्रतीति सब के मन माहीं । राम चाप तोरब सक नाहीं ॥
asi pratīti saba ke mana māhīṁ, rāma cāpa toraba saka nāhīṁ.
बिनु भंजेहुँ भव धनुषु बिसाला । मेलिहि सीय राम उर माला ॥
binu bhaṁjehuṁ bhava dhanuṣu bisālā, melihi sīya rāma ura mālā.
अस बिचारि गवनहु घर भाई । जसु प्रतापु बलु तेजु गवाँई ॥
asa bicāri gavanahu ghara bhāī, jasu pratāpu balu teju gavāṁī.
बिहसे अपर भूप सुनि बानी । जे अबिबेक अंध अभिमानी ॥
bihase apara bhūpa suni bānī, je abibeka aṁdha abhimānī.
तोरेहुँ धनुषु ब्याहु अवगाहा । बिनु तोरें को कुअँरि बिआहा ॥
torehuṁ dhanuṣu byāhu avagāhā, binu toreṁ ko kuaṁri biāhā.
एक बार कालउ किन होऊ । सिय हित समर जितब हम सोऊ ॥
eka bāra kālau kina hoū, siya hita samara jitaba hama soū.
यह सुनि अवर महिप मुसुकाने । धरमसील हरिभगत सयाने ॥
yaha suni avara mahipa musukāne, dharamasīla haribhagata sayāne.

Trans:

At the sight of the Lord all the chiefs grew dim in heart, like the stars at the rising of the full moon: for they felt inwardly certain that beyond all doubt Rāma alone would succeed in bending the bow; or even if he did not break the massy beam, then Sītā would still bestow upon him the garland of victory. And so thinking, sir, some turned homewards, abandoning all glory of victory and pride of strength. There were other kings, blind and insolent fools, who mocked at such words and cried: "To break the bow and win the bride is difficult, but unless it is broken how can the bride be won? Should Death himself for once come forth against us, him too would we conquer in battle for Sītā's sake." Hearing this, there were other kings who smiled—good, pious, and sensible men—and spoke:

सोरठा-sorațhā:

सीय बिआहबि राम गरब दूरि करि नृपन्ह के ।
sīya biāhabi rāma garaba dūri kari nṛpanha ke,
जीति को सक संग्राम दसरथ के रन बाँकुरे ॥२४५॥
jīti ko saka saṁgrāma dasaratha ke rana bāṁkure. 245.

Trans:

"Rāma will certainly marry Sītā, to the discomfiture of those proud princes; for who can conquer in battle Dashrath's gallant sons?

चौपाई-caupāī:

ब्यर्थ मरहु जनि गाल बजाई । मन मोदकन्हि कि भूख बुताई ॥
byartha marahu jani gāla bajāī, mana modakanhi ki bhūkha butāī.
सिख हमारि सुनि परम पुनीता । जगदंबा जानहु जियँ सीता ॥
sikha hamāri suni parama punītā, jagadaṁbā jānahu jiyaṁ sītā.
जगत पिता रघुपतिहि बिचारी । भरि लोचन छबि लेहु निहारी ॥
jagata pitā raghupatihi bicārī, bhari locana chabi lehu nihārī.
सुंदर सुखद सकल गुन रासी । ए दोउ बंधु संभु उर बासी ॥
suṁdara sukhada sakala guna rāsī, e dou baṁdhu saṁbhu ura bāsī.
सुधा समुद्र समीप बिहाई । मृगजलु निरखि मरहु कत धाई ॥
sudhā samudra samīpa bihāī, mṛgajalu nirakhi marahu kata dhāī.
करहु जाइ जा कहुँ जोइ भावा । हम तौ आजु जनम फलु पावा ॥
karahu jāi jā kahuṁ joi bhāvā, hama tau āju janama phalu pāvā.
अस कहि भले भूप अनुरागे । रूप अनूप बिलोकन लागे ॥
asa kahi bhale bhūpa anurāge, rūpa anūpa bilokana lāge.
देखहिं सुर नभ चढ़े बिमाना । बरषहिं सुमन करहिं कल गाना ॥
dekhahiṁ sura nabha caṛhe bimānā, baraṣahiṁ sumana karahiṁ kala gānā.

Trans:

Why thus scoff and throw away your lives to no purpose? Imagined sweets do not stop man's hunger. Listen to this our solemn warning: be inwardly assured that Sītā is the mother, and Rāma the father of the universe. Feast your eyes to the full upon their beauty: these two brothers, so lovely, so gracious, so full of every excellence, who have their home in Shambhu's heart. Why—when you have a sea of ambrosia at hand—should you leave it to run upon your death in pursuit of mirage? But do ye what seemeth to you good—for we have today reaped our life's reward." So saying the good kings turned to gaze with affection upon the picture of incomparable beauty; while in heavens the gods mounted their chariots to behold the spectacle, and showered down flowers, and versified songs of joy.

दोहा-dohā:

जानि सुअवसरु सीय तब पठई जनक बोलाइ ।
jāni suavasaru sīya taba paṭhaī janaka bolāi,
चतुर सखीं सुंदर सकल सादर चलीं लवाइ ॥२४६॥
catura sakhīṁ suṁdara sakala sādara calīṁ lavāi. 246.

Trans:

Then seeing the fitness of the time, Janak sent and summoned Sītā; and obediently she came, with all her lovely and accomplished attendants.

चौपाई-caupāī:

सिय सोभा नहिं जाइ बखानी । जगदंबिका रूप गुन खानी ॥
siya sobhā nahiṁ jāi bakhānī, jagadaṁbikā rūpa guna khānī.
उपमा सकल मोहि लघु लागीं । प्राकृत नारि अंग अनुरागीं ॥
upamā sakala mohi laghu lāgīṁ, prākṛta nāri aṁga anurāgīṁ.

सिय बरनिअ तेइ उपमा देई । कुकबि कहाइ अजसु को लेई ॥
siya barania tei upamā deī, kukabi kahāi ajasu ko leī.
जौं पटतरिअ तीय सम सीया । जग असि जुबति कहाँ कमनीया ॥
jauṁ paṭataria tīya sama sīyā, jaga asi jubati kahāṁ kamanīyā.
गिरा मुखर तन अरध भवानी । रति अति दुखित अतनु पति जानी ॥
girā mukhara tana aradha bhavānī, rati ati dukhita atanu pati jānī.
बिष बारुनी बंधु प्रिय जेही । कहिअ रमासम किमि बैदेही ॥
biṣa bārunī baṁdhu priya jehī, kahia ramāsama kimi baidehī.
जौं छबि सुधा पयोनिधि होई । परम रूपमय कच्छपु सोई ॥
jauṁ chabi sudhā payonidhi hoī, parama rūpamaya kacchapu soī.
सोभा रजु मंदरु सिंगारू । मथै पानि पंकज निज मारू ॥
sobhā raju maṁdaru siṁgārū, mathai pāni paṁkaja nija mārū.

Trans:

Her beauty is not to be told: seeing that she is the mother of the world, the perfection of all grace and goodness, every comparison seems to me unworthy of her and appropriate only to mortal woman. In describing Sītā, to what can she be likened, or what can the poet name that will not rather do her dishonor? If we should liken her to another women, where is there on earth a nymph so swell? Or, if we look to the denizens of heaven: Saraswatī is a chatterer, Bhawānī has only half a body, Ratī is in sore distress on account of her dis-embodied lord; and as for Lakshmī—who has poison and spirituous drink for her dear brothers—how can to her Sītā be compared? Supposing there was an ocean of nectar in the form of loveliness, and the tortoise, serving as a base for churning, was an embodiment of consummate beauty, and if splendor itself were to take the form of a cord, and the sensual sentiment should crystallize and assume the shape of Mount Mandara, and the god of Love himself were to churn this ocean with his own hands;

दोहा-dohā:

एहि बिधि उपजै लच्छि जब सुंदरता सुख मूल ।
ehi bidhi upajai lacchi jaba suṁdaratā sukha mūla,
तदपि सकोच समेत कबि कहहिं सीय समतूल ॥ २४७॥
tadapi sakoca sameta kabi kahahiṁ sīya samatūla. 247.

Trans:

even then, though Lakshmī, the source of all beauty and bliss, had thus been born, still the poet would shrink from saying that she could be compared to Sītā.

चौपाई-caupāī:

चलीं संग लै सखीं सयानी । गावत गीत मनोहर बानी ॥
calīṁ saṁga lai sakhīṁ sayānī, gāvata gīta manohara bānī.
सोह नवल तनु सुंदर सारी । जगत जननि अतुलित छबि भारी ॥
soha navala tanu suṁdara sārī, jagata janani atulita chabi bhārī.
भूषन सकल सुदेस सुहाए । अंग अंग रचि सखिन्ह बनाए ॥
bhūṣana sakala sudesa suhāe, aṁga aṁga raci sakhinha banāe.
रंगभूमि जब सिय पगु धारी । देखि रूप मोहे नर नारी ॥
raṁgabhūmi jaba siya pagu dhārī, dekhi rūpa mohe nara nārī.
हरषि सुरन्ह दुंदुभीं बजाईं । बरषि प्रसून अपछरा गाईं ॥
haraṣi suranha duṁdubhīṁ bajāīṁ, baraṣi prasūna apacharā gāīṁ.
पानि सरोज सोह जयमाला । अवचट चितए सकल भुआला ॥
pāni saroja soha jayamālā, avacaṭa citae sakala bhuālā.
सीय चकित चित रामहि चाहा । भए मोहबस सब नरनाहा ॥
sīya cakita cita rāmahi cāhā, bhae mohabasa saba naranāhā.
मुनि समीप देखे दोउ भाई । लगे ललकि लोचन निधि पाई ॥
muni samīpa dekhe dou bhāī, lage lalaki locana nidhi pāī.

Trans:

She came, and with her, her attendant maids, singing sweet-voiced songs: the mother of creation, of incomparable beauty; her delicate frame veiled in a beautiful Sari, and with a profusion of brilliant and tasteful ornaments—with which her maidens had bedecked her every limb. When she set her foot within the arena, all beholders, men and women alike, were fascinated by her charms; the gods in their delight sounded their kettledrums, and rained down flowers amidst the singing of celestial dames. The wreath of victory sparkled in her hands as she casts a hurried glance on the assembled kings, with anxious heart looking for Rāma. Not a king but was love-smitten. By the saint sat the two brothers, and on them she fell with her avid eyes as upon a rich treasure.

दोहा-dohā:

गुरजन लाज समाजु बड़ देखि सीय सकुचानि ।
gurajana lāja samāju baṛa dekhi sīya sakucāni,
लागि बिलोकन सखिन्ह तन रघुबीरहि उर आनि ॥ २४८॥
lāgi bilokana sakhinha tana raghubīrahi ura āni. 248.

Trans:

Shrinking into herself—from awe of the reverend elders, and at the sight of the vast assemblage—she turned her eyes upon her attendants, though at the same time she drew Rāma into her soul.

चौपाई-caupāī:

राम रूपु अरु सिय छबि देखें । नर नारिन्ह परिहरीं निमेषें ॥
rāma rūpu aru siya chabi dekheṁ, nara nārinha pariharīṁ nimeṣeṁ.
सोचहिं सकल कहत सकुचाहीं । बिधि सन बिनय करहिं मन माहीं ॥
socahiṁ sakala kahata sakucāhīṁ, bidhi sana binaya karahiṁ mana māhīṁ.
हरु बिधि बेगि जनक जड़ताई । मति हमारि असि देहि सुहाई ॥
haru bidhi begi janaka jaṛatāī, mati hamāri asi dehi suhāī.
बिनु बिचार पनु तजि नरनाहू । सीय राम कर करै बिबाहू ॥
binu bicāra panu taji naranāhū, sīya rāma kara karai bibāhū.
जगु भल कहिहि भाव सब काहू । हठ कीन्हें अंतहुँ उर दाहू ॥
jagu bhala kahihi bhāva saba kāhū, haṭha kīnheṁ aṁtahuṁ ura dāhū.
एहिं लालसाँ मगन सब लोगू । बरु साँवरो जानकी जोगू ॥
ehiṁ lālasāṁ magana saba logū, baru sāṁvaro jānakī jogū.
तब बंदीजन जनक बोलाए । बिरिदावली कहत चलि आए ॥
taba baṁdījana janaka bolāe, biridāvalī kahata cali āe.
कह नृपु जाइ कहहु पन मोरा । चले भाट हियँ हरषु न थोरा ॥
kaha nṛpu jāi kahahu pana morā, cale bhāṭa hiyaṁ haraṣu na thorā.

Trans:

Not a man or woman, who beheld the beauty of Rāma and the loveliness of Sītā, could close his eyes for one second. But then all thought with dismay of the king's vow, and in their hearts made supplication to Brahmmā: "O God, quickly remove Janak's obstinacy and make him right-minded as ourselves. Let the king have no hesitation about breaking his vow and giving Sītā in marriage to Rāma; the world will approve, and we all shall be pleased; but obstinacy, if persisted in, will to the last be as a containing fire in his bosom." All were absorbed in the same ardent desire, saying: "This dark youth alone is the match for Sītā." Then Janak summoned the heralds, who stepped forward and eulogized the king and his race, and proclaimed his dignity and state, and as bade they declared his vow; there was not a little joy in their heart.

दोहा-dohā:

बोले बंदी बचन बर सुनहु सकल महिपाल ।
bole baṁdī bacana bara sunahu sakala mahipāla,
पन बिदेह कर कहहिं हम भुजा उठाइ बिसाल ॥ २४९॥
pana bideha kara kahahiṁ hama bhujā uṭhāi bisāla. 249.

Trans:

The heralds cried aloud: "Hearken, all ye princes, we announce to you our sovereign's vow, and with upraised hands call heaven to witness it.

चौपाई-caupāī:

नृप भुजबलु बिधु सिवधनु राहू । गरुअ कठोर बिदित सब काहू ॥
nṛpa bhujabalu bidhu sivadhanu rāhū, garua kaṭhora bidita saba kāhū.
रावनु बानु महाभट भारे । देखि सरासन गवँहिं सिधारे ॥
rāvanu bānu mahābhaṭa bhāre, dekhi sarāsana gavam̐him̐ sidhāre.
सोइ पुरारि कोदंडु कठोरा । राज समाज आजु जोइ तोरा ॥
soi purāri kodaṁḍu kaṭhorā, rāja samāja āju joi torā.
त्रिभुवन जय समेत बैदेही । बिनहिं बिचार बरइ हठि तेही ॥
tribhuvana jaya sameta baidehī, binahiṁ bicāra barai haṭhi tehī.
सुनि पन सकल भूप अभिलाषे । भटमानी अतिसय मन माखे ॥
suni pana sakala bhūpa abhilāṣe, bhaṭamānī atisaya mana mākhe.
परिकर बाँधि उठे अकुलाई । चले इष्टदेवन्ह सिर नाई ॥
parikara bām̐dhi uṭhe akulāī, cale iṣṭadevanha sira nāī.
तमकि ताकि तकि सिवधनु धरहीं । उठइ न कोटि भाँति बलु करहीं ॥
tamaki tāki taki sivadhanu dharahīṁ, uṭhai na koṭi bhām̐ti balu karahīṁ.
जिन्ह के कछु बिचारु मन माहीं । चाप समीप महीप न जाहीं ॥
jinha ke kachu bicāru mana māhīṁ, cāpa samīpa mahīpa na jāhīṁ.

Trans:

Though your arms be mighty, yet Shiva's famous bow is as terrible and unyielding as Rāhu to the moon. When Rāvan and Bānāsur saw it—albeit sturdy champions—they left it and went their way. Here is now the great god's massy beam, and whoever in this royal assembly shall today bend it, shall be renowned in all the three worlds, and at once without hesitation shall receive in marriage the hand of the king's daughter." When they heard the vow, all the kings were full of eagerness—insolent warriors, savage of soul—and girding up their loins they rose in haste, bowing their heads, ere they commenced, before their patron god. With flushed faces and angry looks at it, they grapple with the divine bow; but though they put forth all their strength in a thousand different ways, they cannot move it. Those, indeed, who had any sense at all, did not even go near it.

दोहा-dohā:

तमकि धरहिं धनु मूढ़ नृप उठइ न चलहिं लजाइ ।
tamaki dharahiṁ dhanu mūṛha nṛpa uṭhai na calahiṁ lajāi,
मनहुँ पाइ भट बाहुबलु अधिकु अधिकु गरुआइ ॥२५०॥
manahum̐ pāi bhaṭa bāhubalu adhiku adhiku garuāi. 250.

Trans:

After straining at the bow, those foolish kings, without being able to stir it, retire in confusion—as though it had gathered strength by in turn absorbing the force of each successive warrior.

चौपाई-caupāī:

भूप सहस दस एकहि बारा । लगे उठावन टरइ न टारा ॥
bhūpa sahasa dasa ekahi bārā, lage uṭhāvana ṭarai na ṭārā.
डगइ न संभु सरासनु कैसें । कामी बचन सती मनु जैसें ॥
ḍagai na saṁbhu sarāsanu kaiseṁ, kāmī bacana satī manu jaiseṁ.
सब नृप भए जोगु उपहासी । जैसें बिनु बिराग संन्यासी ॥
saba nṛpa bhae jogu upahāsī, jaiseṁ binu birāga saṁnyāsī.
कीरति बिजय बीरता भारी । चले चाप कर बरबस हारी ॥
kīrati bijaya bīratā bhārī, cale cāpa kara barabasa hārī.
श्रीहत भए हारि हियँ राजा । बैठे निज निज जाइ समाजा ॥
śrīhata bhae hāri hiyaṁ rājā, baiṭhe nija nija jāi samājā.
नृपन्ह बिलोकि जनकु अकुलाने । बोले बचन रोष जनु साने ॥
nṛpanha biloki janaku akulāne, bole bacana roṣa janu sāne.
दीप दीप के भूपति नाना । आए सुनि हम जो पनु ठाना ॥
dīpa dīpa ke bhūpati nānā, āe suni hama jo panu ṭhānā.
देव दनुज धरि मनुज सरीरा । बिपुल बीर आए रनधीरा ॥
deva danuja dhari manuja sarīrā, bipula bīra āe ranadhīrā.

Trans:

Ten thousand kings all at once attempted to raise it, but the bow was not to be moved, and yielded as little as a virtuous wife at the words of a debaucherer. All the princes appeared as ridiculous as a hermit that has no religion. Their mighty glory and renown and heroism were utterly worsted by the bow, and with much confusion of face and sadness of heart, they went and took again each to his own place is the assembly. When Janak saw the kings thus dejected, he cried aloud as in anger: "Hearing the vow that I made, many kings have come from diverse realms, many gods and demons in human form, many stalwart heroes, staunch in fight.

दोहा-dohā:

कुअँरि मनोहर बिजय बड़ि कीरति अति कमनीय ।
kuam̐ri manohara bijaya baṛi kīrati ati kamanīya,
पावनिहार बिरंचि जनु रचेउ न धनु दमनीय ॥२५१॥
pāvanihāra biraṁci janu raceu na dhanu damanīya. 251.

Trans:

And though a lovely bride, a grand triumph and splendid renown are the prize—but God it seems has not created the man who can break the bow and win it.

चौपाई-caupāī:

कहहु काहि यहु लाभु न भावा । काहुँ न संकर चाप चढ़ावा ॥
kahahu kāhi yahu lābhu na bhāvā, kāhum̐ na saṁkara cāpa caṛhāvā.
रहउ चढ़ाउब तोरब भाई । तिलु भरि भूमि न सके छड़ाई ॥
rahau caṛhāuba toraba bhāī, tilu bhari bhūmi na sake chaṛāī.
अब जनि कोउ माखै भट मानी । बीर बिहीन मही मैं जानी ॥
aba jani kou mākhai bhaṭa mānī, bīra bihīna mahī maiṁ jānī.
तजहु आस निज निज गृह जाहू । लिखा न बिधि बैदेहि बिबाहू ॥
tajahu āsa nija nija gṛha jāhū, likhā na bidhi baidehi bibāhū.
सुकृतु जाइ जौं पनु परिहरऊँ । कुअँरि कुआरि रहउ का करऊँ ॥
sukṛtu jāi jauṁ panu pariharaūm̐, kuam̐ri kuāri rahau kā karaūm̐.
जौं जनतेउँ बिनु भट भुबि भाई । तौ पनु करि होतेउँ न हँसाई ॥
jauṁ janateum̐ binu bhaṭa bhubi bhāī, tau panu kari hoteum̐ na ham̐sāī.
जनक बचन सुनि सब नर नारी । देखि जानकिहि भए दुखारी ॥
janaka bacana suni saba nara nārī, dekhi jānakihi bhae dukhārī.
माखे लखनु कुटिल भइँ भौंहें । रदपट फरकत नयन रिसौंहें ॥
mākhe lakhanu kuṭila bhaiṁ bhauṁheṁ, radapaṭa pharakata nayana risauṁheṁ.

Trans:

Tell me now who was dissatisfied with the guerdon, or refused to try his strength on Shiva's bow? But let alone lifting and breaking it, sirs, there was not one of you who could stir it even a grain's breadth from the ground! Now let no proud warrior wax wrath if I assert there is not a man left on this earth. Give up all hope and go back to your homes. Perhaps it is God's will that Sītā is not to be married. If I break my vow, all my religious merit is gone. Alas, the girl must remain a maid; what can I do? Had I known, sirs, that there were no men in the world, I would not have made myself a laughing-stock by recording such a vow." Every man and woman who heard Janak's words and looked at Jānakī were sad; but Lakshman was furious; his eyes flashed, his lips quivered, and his brows were knit.

दोहा-dohā:

कहि न सकत रघुबीर डर लगे बचन जनु बान ।
kahi na sakata raghubīra ḍara lage bacana janu bāna,
नाइ राम पद कमल सिरु बोले गिरा प्रमान ॥२५२॥
nāi rāma pada kamala siru bole girā pramāna. 252.

Trans:

But for fear of his brother he could not speak, though the taunt pierced his heart like an arrow. Yet at last, bowing his head at Rāma's lotus feet, he thundered in imposing tone:

चौपाई-caupāī:

रघुबंसिन्ह महुँ जहँ कोउ होई । तेहिं समाज अस कहइ न कोई ॥
raghubaṁsinha mahuṁ jahaṁ kou hoī, tehiṁ samāja asa kahai na koī.
कही जनक जसि अनुचित बानी । बिद्यमान रघुकुल मनि जानी ॥
kahī janaka jasi anucita bānī, bidyamāna raghukula mani jānī.
सुनहु भानुकुल पंकज भानू । कहउँ सुभाउ न कछु अभिमानू ॥
sunahu bhānukula paṁkaja bhānū, kahauṁ subhāu na kachu abhimānū.
जौं तुम्हारि अनुसासन पावौं । कंदुक इव ब्रह्मांड उठावौं ॥
jauṁ tumhāri anusāsana pāvauṁ, kaṁduka iva brahmāṁḍa uṭhāvauṁ.
काचे घट जिमि डारौं फोरी । सकउँ मेरु मूलक जिमि तोरी ॥
kāce ghaṭa jimi ḍārauṁ phorī, sakauṁ meru mūlaka jimi torī.
तव प्रताप महिमा भगवाना । को बापुरो पिनाक पुराना ॥
tava pratāpa mahimā bhagavānā, ko bāpuro pināka purānā.
नाथ जानि अस आयसु होऊ । कौतुकु करौं बिलोकिअ सोऊ ॥
nātha jāni asa āyasu hoū, kautuku karauṁ bilokia soū.
कमल नाल जिमि चाप चढ़ावौं । जोजन सत प्रमान लै धावौं ॥
kamala nāla jimi cāp caṛhāvauṁ, jojana sata pramāna lai dhāvauṁ.

Trans:

"In an assembly where anyone of Raghu's race is present no one would dare speak such disgraceful words as Janak has just done—even though he knew of the presence of Shrī Rāma, the Jewel of Raghu's race." Turning towards his brother, Lakshman added: "Hearken thou sun of the lotus-like solar race; and I state the truth simply, without a vain boast: if but I have your permission, I will lift the round world with as much ease as a ball, and break it into pieces like an ill-baked potter's jar; and will tear up Mount Meru as if it were a radish. Before thy infinite majesty, O my Lord God, what is this pathetic old bow? Only give me an order, and see what a exhibit I will make of it. I will take up the bow as though it were a lotus stalk, and will run a hundred leagues with it to show.

दोहा-dohā:

तोरौं छत्रक दंड जिमि तव प्रताप बल नाथ ।
torauṁ chatraka daṁḍa jimi tava pratāpa bala nātha,
जौं न करौं प्रभु पद सपथ कर न धरौं धनु भाथ ॥ २५३ ॥
jauṁ na karauṁ prabhu pada sapatha kara na dharauṁ dhanu bhātha. 253.

Trans:

Inspired by thy presence, my Lord, I will snap it like the stick of an umbrella; or if I fail, I swear by thy holy feet never to take a bow in my hand ever again."

चौपाई-caupāī:

लखन सकोप बचन जे बोले । डगमगानि महि दिग्गज डोले ॥
lakhana sakopa bacana je bole, ḍagamagāni mahi diggaja ḍole.
सकल लोग सब भूप डेराने । सिय हियँ हरषु जनकु सकुचाने ॥
sakala loga saba bhūpa ḍerāne, siya hiyaṁ haraṣu janaku sakucāne.
गुर रघुपति सब मुनि मन माहीं । मुदित भए पुनि पुनि पुलकाहीं ॥
gura raghupati saba muni mana māhīṁ, mudita bhae puni puni pulakāhīṁ.
सयनहिं रघुपति लखनु नेवारे । प्रेम समेत निकट बैठारे ॥
sayanahiṁ raghupati lakhanu nevāre, prema sameta nikaṭa baiṭhāre.
बिस्वामित्र समय सुभ जानी । बोले अति सनेहमय बानी ॥
bisvāmitra samaya subha jānī, bole ati sanehamaya bānī.
उठहु राम भंजहु भवचापा । मेटहु तात जनक परितापा ॥
uṭhahu rāma bhaṁjahu bhavacāpā, meṭahu tāta janaka paritāpā.
सुनि गुरु बचन चरन सिरु नावा । हरषु बिषादु न कछु उर आवा ॥
suni guru bacana carana siru nāvā, haraṣu biṣādu na kachu ura āvā.
ठाढ़े भए उठि सहज सुभाएँ । ठवनि जुबा मृगराजु लजाएँ ॥
ṭhāṛhe bhae uṭhi sahaja subhāeṁ, ṭhavani jubā mṛgarāju lajāeṁ.

Trans:

As Lakshman thus spoke in his wrath, the earth shook and its supporting elephants trembled. The entire assembly and all kings were struck with terror. Sītā was glad of heart and Janak was ashamed; while the saint and Rāma and all the hermits were enraptured and quivered all over with excitement. Then Rāma with a sign checked Lakshman, and lovingly made him sit beside him; while Vishwāmitra, perceiving the fitness of the time, spoke in gentle and affectionate tones: "Up, Rāma; break this bow of Shiva and relieve Janak of his distress, my son." On hearing the Gurū's command, Rāma bowed his head at his feet, and without joy or sorrow in his mind, rose and stood upright in all his native grace; and lordly in gait as a young lion, he stepped forth.

दोहा-dohā:

उदित उदयगिरि मंच पर रघुबर बालपतंग ।
udita udayagiri maṁca para raghubara bālapataṁga,
बिकसे संत सरोज सब हरषे लोचन भृंग ॥ २५४ ॥
bikase saṁta saroja saba haraṣe locana bhṛṁga. 254.

Trans:

As Raghubar ascended the stage, like the sun climbing the mountains of the east, the hearts of the saints expanded like the lotus, and their eyes were glad as bees at the return of day.

चौपाई-caupāī:

नृपन्ह केरि आसा निसि नासी । बचन नखत अवली न प्रकासी ॥
nṛpanha keri āsā nisi nāsī, bacana nakhata avalī na prakāsī.
मानी महिप कुमुद सकुचाने । कपटी भूप उलूक लुकाने ॥
mānī mahipa kumuda sakucāne, kapaṭī bhūpa ulūka lukāne.
भए बिसोक कोक मुनि देवा । बरिसहिं सुमन जनावहिं सेवा ॥
bhae bisoka koka muni devā, barisahiṁ sumana janāvahiṁ sevā.
गुर पद बंदि सहित अनुरागा । राम मुनिन्ह सन आयसु मागा ॥
gura pada baṁdi sahita anurāgā, rāma muninha sana āyasu māgā.
सहजहिं चले सकल जग स्वामी । मत्त मंजु बर कुंजर गामी ॥
sahajahiṁ cale sakala jaga svāmī, matta maṁju bara kuṁjara gāmī.
चलत राम सब पुर नर नारी । पुलक पूरि तन भए सुखारी ॥
calata rāma saba pura nara nārī, pulaka pūri tana bhae sukhārī.
बंदि पितर सुर सुकृत सँभारे । जौं कछु पुन्य प्रभाउ हमारे ॥
baṁdi pitara sura sukṛta saṁbhāre, jauṁ kachu punya prabhāu hamāre.
तौ सिवधनु मृनाल की नाईं । तोरहुँ राम गनेस गोसाईं ॥
tau sivadhanu mṛnāla kī nāīṁ, torahuṁ rāma ganesa gosāīṁ.

Trans:

The dark hopes of the kings vanished like the night, and like the serried stars their vaunts waxed feeble; the arrogant shriveled up like the lilies, and the false slunk away like the owls; saints and gods, like the *chakwā*, were relieved of their distress and rained down flowers in acts of homage. After affectionately reverencing the Gurū's feet and asking permission of the holy fathers, the Lord of all creation quickly stepped forth with the stride of a majestic elephant that is inflamed with love. As he moved, every man and woman in the city quivered all over their body with delight; and worshipping the spirits of their ancestors and the gods, and recalling their own past good deeds, they prayed, "If my virtuous acts be of any avail, O father Ganesh, may Rāma snap the bow as it were a lotus-stalk."

दोहा-dohā:

रामहि प्रेम समेत लखि सखिन्ह समीप बोलाइ ।
rāmahi prema sameta lakhi sakhinha samīpa bolāi,
सीता मातु सनेह बस बचन कहइ बिलखाइ ॥२५५॥
sītā mātu saneha basa bacana kahai bilakhāi. 255.

Trans:

After lovingly gazing upon Rāma, Sītā's mother bid her attendants draw near, and spoke with much affectionate anxiety:

चौपाई-caupāī:

सखि सब कौतुकु देखनिहारे । जेउ कहावत हितू हमारे ॥
sakhi saba kautuku dekhanihāre, jeu kahāvata hitū hamāre.
कोउ न बुझाइ कहइ गुर पाहीं । ए बालक असि हठ भलि नाहीं ॥
kou na bujhāi kahai gura pāhīṁ, e bālaka asi haṭha bhali nāhīṁ.
रावन बान छुआ नहिं चापा । हारे सकल भूप करि दापा ॥
rāvana bāna chuā nahiṁ cāpā, hāre sakala bhūpa kari dāpā.
सो धनु राजकुअँर कर देहीं । बाल मराल कि मंदर लेहीं ॥
so dhanu rājakuaṁra kara dehīṁ, bāla marāla ki maṁdara lehīṁ.
भूप सयानप सकल सिरानी । सखि बिधि गति कछु जाति न जानी ॥
bhūpa sayānapa sakala sirānī, sakhi bidhi gati kachu jāti na jānī.
बोली चतुर सखी मृदु बानी । तेजवंत लघु गनिअ न रानी ॥
bolī catura sakhī mṛdu bānī, tejavaṁta laghu gania na rānī.
कहँ कुंभज कहँ सिंधु अपारा । सोषेउ सुजसु सकल संसारा ॥
kahaṁ kuṁbhaja kahaṁ siṁdhu apārā, soṣeu sujasu sakala saṁsārā.
रबि मंडल देखत लघु लागा । उदयँ तासु तिभुवन तम भागा ॥
rabi maṁḍala dekhata laghu lāgā, udayaṁ tāsu tibhuvana tama bhāgā.

Trans:

"Girls, everyone is bent on seeing this spectacle; and as for saying what would be for my own good, alas, there is no one who will tell the king plainly: 'These are two mere boys; this excessive obstinacy of yours is wrong. Rāvan and Bānāsur could not touch the bow, and the kings with all their pride were conquered by it. Why then give it into the hands of this young prince?' As well might a cygnet carry off Mount Meru. All the king's good sense is clearly gone! Ah girls, god's ways are inscrutable." An intelligent maiden gently answered, "O queen, the great are never to be lightly regarded. Look at Agastya—how small—and the boundlessness of ocean, yet he drained it dry, and his fame has spread through the world. Again, the orb of the sun is small to look at, but at its rising darkness is expelled from heaven and hell and earth.

दोहा-dohā:

मंत्र परम लघु जासु बस बिधि हरि हर सुर सर्ब ।
maṁtra parama laghu jāsu basa bidhi hari hara sura sarba,
महामत्त गजराज कहुँ बस कर अंकुस खर्ब ॥२५६॥
mahāmatta gajarāja kahuṁ basa kara aṁkusa kharba. 256.

Trans:

A charm is a very little thing, yet it overpowers Brahmmā, Vishnu, Mahādev and all the gods; and a mere goad governs the mightiest and most furious of elephants.

चौपाई-caupāī:

काम कुसुम धनु सायक लीन्हे । सकल भुवन अपनें बस कीन्हे ॥
kāma kusuma dhanu sāyaka līnhe, sakala bhuvana apaneṁ basa kīnhe.
देबि तजिअ संसउ अस जानी । भंजब धनुषु राम सुनु रानी ॥
debi tajia saṁsau asa jānī, bhaṁjaba dhanuṣu rāma sunu rānī.
सखी बचन सुनि भै परतीती । मिटा बिषादु बढ़ी अति प्रीती ॥
sakhī bacana suni bhai paratītī, miṭā biṣādu baṛhī ati prītī.
तब रामहि बिलोकि बैदेही । सभय हृदयँ बिनवति जेहि तेही ॥
taba rāmahi biloki baidehī, sabhaya hṛdayaṁ binavati jehi tehī.
मनहीं मन मनाव अकुलानी । होहु प्रसन्न महेस भवानी ॥
manahīṁ mana manāva akulānī, hohu prasanna mahesa bhavānī.
करहु सफल आपनि सेवकाई । करि हितु हरहु चाप गरुआई ॥
karahu saphala āpani sevakāī, kari hitu harahu cāpa garuāī.
गननायक बरदायक देवा । आजु लगें कीन्हिउँ तुअ सेवा ॥
gananāyaka baradāyaka devā, āju lageṁ kīnhiuṁ tua sevā.
बार बार बिनती सुनि मोरी । करहु चाप गुरुता अति थोरी ॥
bāra bāra binatī suni morī, karahu cāpa gurutā ati thorī.

Trans:

Love too—though his bow and arrow are but of flowers—has brought the whole world under subjection. Fear not then, O lady, but hearken to me: Rāma will assuredly break the bow." The Queen took heart at these words of her attendant, her despondency ceased, and her hope was magnified. Then Sītā, with her eyes fixed on Rāma, implored with anxious heart each god in turn, praying to them in her inward soul, "Be gracious to me, O Mahādev and Bhawānī, and reward my service by kindly lightening the weight of this bow. O divine Ganesh, granter of boons, it is with a view to today that I have done you service. Hearken to my oft-repeated supplication, and reduce the weight of the bow to a mere trifle."

दोहा-dohā:

देखि देखि रघुबीर तन सुर मनाव धरि धीर ।
dekhi dekhi raghubīra tana sura manāva dhari dhīra,
भरे बिलोचन प्रेम जल पुलकावली सरीर ॥२५७॥
bhare bilocana prema jala pulakāvalī sarīra. 257.

Trans:

Oft glancing at Raghubīr's form, and taking courage from her heavenward prayers, her eyes were filled with tears of love, and her whole body was in tremor.

चौपाई-caupāī:

नीकें निरखि नयन भरि सोभा । पितु पनु सुमिरि बहुरि मनु छोभा ॥
nīkeṁ nirakhi nayana bhari sobhā, pitu panu sumiri bahuri manu chobhā.
अहह तात दारुनि हठ ठानी । समुझत नहिं कछु लाभु न हानी ॥
ahaha tāta dāruni haṭha ṭhānī, samujhata nahiṁ kachu lābhu na hānī.
सचिव सभय सिख देइ न कोई । बुध समाज बड़ अनुचित होई ॥
saciva sabhaya sikha dei na koī, budha samāja baṛa anucita hoī.
कहँ धनु कुलिसहु चाहि कठोरा । कहँ स्यामल मृदुगात किसोरा ॥
kahaṁ dhanu kulisahu cāhi kaṭhorā, kahaṁ syāmala mṛdugāta kisorā.
बिधि केहि भाँति धरौं उर धीरा । सिरस सुमन कन बेधिअ हीरा ॥
bidhi kehi bhāṁti dharauṁ ura dhīrā, sirasa sumana kana bedhia hīrā.
सकल सभा कै मति भै भोरी । अब मोहि संभुचाप गति तोरी ॥
sakala sabhā kai mati bhai bhorī, aba mohi saṁbhucāpa gati torī.
निज जड़ता लोगन्ह पर डारी । होहि हरुअ रघुपतिहि निहारी ॥
nija jaṛatā loganha para ḍārī, hohi harua raghupatihi nihārī.
अति परिताप सीय मन माहीं । लव निमेष जुग सय सम जाहीं ॥
ati paritāpa sīya mana māhīṁ, lava nimeṣa juga saya sama jāhīṁ.

Trans:

With fixed gaze she devoured his beauty, and then as she remembered her father's vow, her soul was troubled, "Alas, my father has made a terrible resolve, made without any regard to good or evil consequences; and not a minister, out of fear, gave him good advice—the more the pity considering he has a great conclave of counselors. Here is a bow as firm as adamant, and here a little dark-hued prince of tender frame. O God, how can I maintain my faith? Is it possible for a delicate *siris*-flower to transpierce a diamond? The judgment of the whole assembly has gone astray. Now, O bow of Shambhu, thou art the only hope left to me; impart thy own heaviness to the crowd, and grow light thyself at once at the sight of Rāma."

So great was the agitation of Sītā's soul that an instant of time passed to her as slowly as an age.

दोहा-dohā:

प्रभुहि चितइ पुनि चितव महि राजत लोचन लोल ।
prabhuhi citai puni citava mahi rājata locana lola,
खेलत मनसिज मीन जुग जनु बिधु मंडल डोल ॥२५८॥
khelata manasija mīna juga janu bidhu maṁḍala ḍola. 258.

Trans:

As she looks, now at the Lord, and now at the ground, her tremulous eyes glisten so, as it were Love's two fish disporting themselves in the orb of the moon.

चौपाई-caupāī:

गिरा अलिनि मुख पंकज रोकी । प्रगट न लाज निसा अवलोकी ॥
girā alini mukha paṁkaja rokī, pragaṭa na lāja nisā avalokī.
लोचन जलु रह लोचन कोना । जैसें परम कृपन कर सोना ॥
locana jalu raha locana konā, jaiseṁ parama kṛpana kara sonā.
सकुची ब्याकुलता बड़ि जानी । धरि धीरजु प्रतीति उर आनी ॥
sakucī byākulatā baṛi jānī, dhari dhīraju pratīti ura ānī.
तन मन बचन मोर पनु साचा । रघुपति पद सरोज चितु राचा ॥
tana mana bacana mora panu sācā, raghupati pada saroja citu rācā.
तौ भगवानु सकल उर बासी । करिहि मोहि रघुबर कै दासी ॥
tau bhagavānu sakala ura bāsī, karihi mohi raghubara kai dāsī.
जेहि कें जेहि पर सत्य सनेहू । सो तेहि मिलइ न कछु संदेहू ॥
jehi keṁ jehi para satya sanehū, so tehi milai na kachu saṁdehū.
प्रभु तन चितइ प्रेम तन ठाना । कृपानिधान राम सबु जाना ॥
prabhu tana citai prema tana ṭhānā, kṛpānidhāna rāma sabu jānā.
सियहि बिलोकि तकेउ धनु कैसें । चितव गरुरु लघु ब्यालहि जैसें ॥
siyahi biloki takeu dhanu kaiseṁ, citava garuru laghu byālahi jaiseṁ.

Trans:

In her lotus mouth her bee-like speech lay bound; it did not stir for modesty, like a night, allowed it not. In the corner of her eye stood a tear-drop, which was like a gold in a miser's buried hoard. Abashed by the consciousness of extreme excitement, she yet summoned up courage and confidence and said to herself, "If there is any truth in me at all, and I am really enamored of Raghupatī's lotus feet, then the Lord God, who knoweth the hearts of all, will make me Rāma's handmaid; for wherever there is true affection of soul to soul, union will follow beyond a doubt." With her eyes fixed upon the Lord she recorded this loving vow; and he, the most merciful, comprehended it all. After looking at Sītā, he cast a glance at the bow, as Garud might glance at a poor little snake.

दोहा-dohā:

लखन लखेउ रघुबंसमनि ताकेउ हर कोदंडु ।
lakhana lakheu raghubaṁsamani tākeu hara kodaṁḍu,
पुलकि गात बोले बचन चरन चापि ब्रह्मांडु ॥२५९॥
pulaki gāta bole bacana carana cāpi brahmāṁḍu. 259.

Trans:

When Lakshman perceived that the glory of his race had his eye fixed upon the bow he thrilled with emotion; and pressing the crust of the earth under his foot he spoke out:

चौपाई-caupāī:

दिसिकुंजरहु कमठ अहि कोला । धरहु धरनि धरि धीर न डोला ॥
disikuṁjarahu kamaṭha ahi kolā, dharahu dharani dhari dhīra na ḍolā.
रामु चहहिं संकर धनु तोरा । होहु सजग सुनि आयसु मोरा ॥
rāmu cahahiṁ saṁkara dhanu torā, hohu sajaga suni āyasu morā.
चाप समीप रामु जब आए । नर नारिन्ह सुर सुकृत मनाए ॥
cāpa samīpa rāmu jaba āe, nara nārinha sura sukṛta manāe.
सब कर संसउ अरु अग्यानू । मंद महीपन्ह कर अभिमानू ॥
saba kara saṁsau aru agyānū, maṁda mahīpanha kara abhimānū.
भृगुपति केरि गरब गरुआई । सुर मुनिबरन्ह केरि कदराई ॥
bhṛgupati keri garaba garuāī, sura munibaranha keri kadarāī.
सिय कर सोचु जनक पछितावा । रानिन्ह कर दारुन दुख दावा ॥
siya kara socu janaka pachitāvā, rāninha kara dāruna dukha dāvā.
संभुचाप बड बोहितु पाई । चढे जाइ सब संगु बनाई ॥
saṁbhucāpa baḍa bohitu pāī, caḍhe jāi saba saṁgu banāī.
राम बाहुबल सिंधु अपारू । चहत पारु नहिं कोउ कड़हारू ॥
rāma bāhubala siṁdhu apārū, cahata pāru nahiṁ kou kaṛahārū.

Trans:

"Ye elephant warders of the cardinal points, ye tortoise, serpent, and boar, hold fast the earth steadfastly that it shakes not—for Rāma is about to break the great bow; hearken to my order and be prepared." When Rāma drew near to the bow, the people all supplicated the gods by their past good deeds. The doubts and errors of the crowd, the arrogance of the foolish kings, the proud pretensions of Parshurām, the apprehensions of the gods and saints, the distress of Sītā, the regrets of Janak, the burning anguish of the queens—all these seemed to have boarded together on the great bark of Shambhu's Bow—with whose help they sought to cross the boundless ocean of Shrī Rāma's strength of arms; but there being no helmsman to essay it.

दोहा-dohā:

राम बिलोके लोग सब चित्र लिखे से देखि ।
rāma biloke loga saba citra likhe se dekhi,
चितई सीय कृपायतन जानी बिकल बिसेषि ॥२६०॥
citaī sīya kṛpāyatana jānī bikala biseṣi. 260.

Trans:

Rāma looked at the crowd, who all stood still as statues as if drawn on a painting; then the gracious Lord turned from them to Sītā, and perceived her yet deeper distress.

चौपाई-caupāī:

देखी बिपुल बिकल बैदेही । निमिष बिहात कलप सम तेही ॥
dekhī bipula bikala baidehī, nimiṣa bihāta kalapa sama tehī.
तृषित बारि बिनु जो तनु त्यागा । मुएँ करइ का सुधा तड़ागा ॥
tṛṣita bāri binu jo tanu tyāgā, mueṁ karai kā sudhā taṛāgā.
का बरषा सब कृषी सुखानें । समय चुकें पुनि का पछितानें ॥
kā baraṣā saba kṛṣī sukhāneṁ, samaya cukeṁ puni kā pachitāneṁ.
अस जियँ जानि जानकी देखी । प्रभु पुलके लखि प्रीति बिसेषी ॥
asa jiyaṁ jāni jānakī dekhī, prabhu pulake lakhi prīti biseṣī.
गुरहि प्रनामु मनहिं मन कीन्हा । अति लाघवँ उठाइ धनु लीन्हा ॥
gurahi pranāmu manahiṁ mana kīnhā, ati lāghavaṁ uṭhāi dhanu līnhā.
दमकेउ दामिनि जिमि जब लयऊ । पुनि नभ धनु मंडल सम भयऊ ॥
damakeu dāmini jimi jaba layaū, puni nabha dhanu maṁḍala sama bhayaū.
लेत चढ़ावत खैंचत गाढ़ें । काहुँ न लखा देख सबु ठाढ़ें ॥
leta caṛhāvata khaiṁcata gāṛheṁ, kāhuṁ na lakhā dekha sabu ṭhāṛheṁ.
तेहि छन राम मध्य धनु तोरा । भरे भुवन धुनि घोर कठोरा ॥
tehi chana rāma madhya dhanu torā, bhare bhuvana dhuni ghora kaṭhorā.

Trans:

He found her to be so terribly agitated that a moment of time seemed an age in passing. If a man dies of thirst for want of water, of what use to him is a lake full of nectar later? What good is the rain when the crop is dead? Or what avails regret when the one chance has been lost? Thinking thus to himself as he gazed at Jānakī, the Lord was enraptured at the sight of her singular devotion. And after making a reverential obeisance to his Gurū, he took up the bow with most superlative ease. As he grasped it in his hand, it gleamed like a bolt of lightning; and again as he bent it, it seemed like a circle flashed in heaven. Though all stood looking on, before anyone could see—he had lifted it from the ground and raised it aloft and drawn it tight, and in a moment broken it in halves. The awful crash echoed throughout the worlds.

छंद-chamda:

भरे भुवन घोर कठोर रव रबि बाजि तजि मारगु चले ।
bhare bhuvana ghora kaṭhora rava rabi bāji taji māragu cale,
चिक्करहिं दिग्गज डोल महि अहि कोल कूरुम कलमले ॥
cikkarahiṁ diggaja ḍola mahi ahi kola kūruma kalamale.
सुर असुर मुनि कर कान दीन्हें सकल बिकल बिचारहीं ।
sura asura muni kara kāna dīnheṁ sakala bikala bicārahīṁ,
कोदंड खंडेउ राम तुलसी जयति बचन उचारहीं ॥
kodaṁḍa khaṁḍeu rāma tulasī jayati bacana ucārahīṁ.

Trans:

So frightening a sound re-echoed through the world that the horses of the sun started from their course; the elephants of the four quarters groaned; the earth shook, and the great serpent, the boar, and the tortoise tottered. Across the world, gods, demons, and saints put their hands to their ears, and began anxiously to consider the cause—but when they learnt that Rāma had broken the bow, they uttered shouts of Victory.

सोरठा-soraṭhā:

संकर चापु जहाजु सागरु रघुबर बाहुबलु ।
saṁkara cāpu jahāju sāgaru raghubara bāhubalu,
बूड सो सकल समाजु चढ़ा जो प्रथमहिं मोह बस ॥२६१॥
būṛa so sakala samāju caṛhā jo prathamahiṁ moha basa. 261.

Trans:

Shankar's bow was the bark, and Rāma's strength of arm was the ocean to be crossed with its aid, and the deluded crowd who had gone on board that were drowned in the waves of Rāma's might.

चौपाई-caupāī:

प्रभु दोउ चापखंड महि डारे । देखि लोग सब भए सुखारे ॥
prabhu dou cāpakhaṁḍa mahi ḍāre, dekhi loga saba bhae sukhāre.
कौसिकरुप पयोनिधि पावन । प्रेम बारि अवगाहु सुहावन ॥
kausikarupa payonidhi pāvana, prema bāri avagāhu suhāvana.
रामरूप राकेसु निहारी । बढ़त बीचि पुलकावलि भारी ॥
rāmarūpa rākesu nihārī, baṛhata bīci pulakāvali bhārī.
बाजे नभ गहगहे निसाना । देवबधू नाचहिं करि गाना ॥
bāje nabha gahagahe nisānā, devabadhū nācahiṁ kari gānā.
ब्रह्मादिक सुर सिद्ध मुनीसा । प्रभुहि प्रसंसहिं देहिं असीसा ॥
brahmādika sura siddha munīsā, prabhuhi prasaṁsahiṁ dehiṁ asīsā.
बरिसहिं सुमन रंग बहु माला । गावहिं किंनर गीत रसाला ॥
barisahiṁ sumana raṁga bahu mālā, gāvahiṁ kiṁnara gīta rasālā.
रही भुवन भरि जय जय बानी । धनुषभंग धुनि जात न जानी ॥
rahī bhuvana bhari jaya jaya bānī, dhanuṣabhaṁga dhuni jāta na jānī.
मुदित कहहिं जहँ तहँ नर नारी । भंजेउ राम संभुधनु भारी ॥
mudita kahahiṁ jahaṁ tahaṁ nara nārī, bhaṁjeu rāma saṁbhudhanu bhārī.

Trans:

The Lord tossed upon the ground the two broken pieces of the bow, and at that sight the multitudes rejoiced. Vishwāmitra's love, like the clear unfathomed depth of ocean, swelled to the highest tide of ecstasy under the full-moon influence of Rāma's presence. There was a jubilant noise of music in the sky; the heavenly nymphs danced and sang; Brahmmā and all the gods and deified saints and sages praised and blessed the hero, and they rained down wreaths of many-colored flowers; the Kinnars sung melodious strains; and the shout of 'Victory, Victory' re-echoed throughout the world. The sound that followed the breaking of the bow defies description. Everywhere the people in their joy keep saying "Rāma has broken the great bow."

दोहा-dohā:

बंदी मागध सूतगन बिरुद बदहिं मतिधीर ।
baṁdī māgadha sūtagana biruda badahiṁ matidhīra,
करहिं निछावरि लोग सब हय गय धन मनि चीर ॥२६२॥
karahiṁ nichāvari loga saba haya gaya dhana mani cīra. 262.

Trans:

Bards, minstrels, and rhapsodists raise their loud-voiced paeans, and all the people lavish gifts of horse, elephants, money, jewels, and raiment.

चौपाई-caupāī:

झाँझि मृदंग संख सहनाई । भेरि ढोल दुंदुभी सुहाई ॥
jhāṁjhi mṛdaṁga saṁkha sahanāī, bheri ḍhola duṁdubhī suhāī.
बाजहिं बहु बाजने सुहाए । जहँ तहँ जुबतिन्ह मंगल गाए ॥
bājahiṁ bahu bājane suhāe, jahaṁ tahaṁ jubatinha maṁgala gāe.
सखिन्ह सहित हरषी अति रानी । सूखत धान परा जनु पानी ॥
sakhinha sahita haraṣī ati rānī, sūkhata dhāna parā janu pānī.
जनक लहेउ सुखु सोचु बिहाई । पैरत थकें थाह जनु पाई ॥
janaka laheu sukhu socu bihāī, pairata thakeṁ thāha janu pāī.
श्रीहत भए भूप धनु टूटे । जैसें दिवस दीप छबि छूटे ॥
śrīhata bhae bhūpa dhanu ṭūṭe, jaiseṁ divasa dīpa chabi chūṭe.
सीय सुखहि बरनिअ केहि भाँती । जनु चातकी पाइ जलु स्वाती ॥
sīya sukhahi barania kehi bhāṁtī, janu cātakī pāi jalu svātī.
रामहि लखनु बिलोकत कैसें । ससिहि चकोर किसोरकु जैसें ॥
rāmahi lakhanu bilokata kaiseṁ, sasihi cakora kisoraku jaiseṁ.
सतानंद तब आयसु दीन्हा । सीताँ गमनु राम पहिं कीन्हा ॥
satānaṁda taba āyasu dīnhā, sītāṁ gamanu rāma pahiṁ kīnhā.

Trans:

There was a clash of cymbals, tabors, drums, conches, clarions, sackbuts, kettledrums, with all kinds of music; and in every place were choirs of women singing auspicious strains. The queen with her attendants was as glad as a parched rice-field at the fall of rain; Janak was as pleased and free of care as a tired swimmer on reaching the shallow; the kings were as confounded at the breaking of the bow as a lamp is dimmed at the dawn of day. But Sītā's gladness can only be compared to that of the chātaki on finding a rain-drop in constellation *svātī*; while Lakshman fixed his eyes on Rāma as the *chakor* on the moon. Then Shatānand gave the word and Sītā advanced towards Rāma.

दोहा-dohā:

संग सखीं सुंदर चतुर गावहिं मंगलचार ।
saṁga sakhīṁ suṁdara catura gāvahiṁ maṁgalacāra,
गवनी बाल मराल गति सुषमा अंग अपार ॥२६३॥
gavanī bāla marāla gati suṣamā aṁga apāra. 263.

Trans:

Graceful in motion as a swan, and of infinite beauty in every limb, and with her, her fair and sprightly companions who raised the glad marriage songs.

चौपाई-caupāī:

सखिन्ह मध्य सिय सोहति कैसें । छबिगन मध्य महाछबि जैसें ॥
sakhinha madhya siya sohati kaiseṁ, chabigana madhya mahāchabi jaiseṁ.
कर सरोज जयमाल सुहाई । बिस्व बिजय सोभा जेहिं छाई ॥
kara saroja jayamāla suhāī, bisva bijaya sobhā jehiṁ chāī.
तन सकोचु मन परम उछाहू । गूढ़ प्रेमु लखि परइ न काहू ॥
tana sakocu mana parama uchāhū, gūṛha premu lakhi parai na kāhū.
जाइ समीप राम छबि देखी । रहि जनु कुअँरि चित्र अवरेखी ॥
jāi samīpa rāma chabi dekhī, rahi janu kuaṁri citra avarekhī.

चतुर सखीं लखि कहा बुझाई । पहिरावहु जयमाल सुहाई ॥
catura sakhīṁ lakhi kahā bujhāī, pahirāvahu jayamāla suhāī.
सुनत जुगल कर माल उठाई । प्रेम बिबस पहिराइ न जाई ॥
sunata jugala kara māla uṭhāī, prema bibasa pahirāi na jāī.
सोहत जनु जुग जलज सनाला । ससिहि सभीत देत जयमाला ॥
sohata janu juga jalaja sanālā, sasihi sabhīta deta jayamālā.
गावहिं छबि अवलोकि सहेली । सियँ जयमाल राम उर मेली ॥
gāvahiṁ chabi avaloki sahelī, siyaṁ jayamāla rāma ura melī.

Trans:

Resplendent in their midst as the Queen of Love among the loves, she held in her lotus hand the fair wreath of victory, enriched as it were with the glory of triumph upon the whole world. With modest air she moved, and with rapture in her soul, but her inner devotion was withdrawn from the sight of all. As she drew near and beheld Rāma's beauty, she stood motionless like a figure on the wall, till a watchful attendant bestirred her saying, "Now invest him with the ennobling wreath." At the word she raised the garland with both her hands, but was much too overcome by emotion to drop it—as if two lotus flowers, stalk and all, were tremulously offering wreath to the moon. At this charming sight her handmaids break into a song; and Sītā places the garland around his neck, upon his chest.

सोरठा-soraṭhā:

रघुबर उर जयमाल देखि देव बरिसहिं सुमन ।
raghubara ura jayamāla dekhi deva barisahiṁ sumana,
सकुचे सकल भुआल जनु बिलोकि रबि कुमुदगन ॥२६४॥
sakuce sakala bhuāla janu biloki rabi kumudagana. 264.

Trans:

When the gods see the wreath resting upon his heart, they rain showers of flowers; and the other kings all shrunk into nothing, like lilies at the rising of the Sun.

चौपाई-caupāī:

पुर अरु ब्योम बाजने बाजे । खल भए मलिन साधु सब राजे ॥
pura aru byoma bājane bāje, khala bhae malina sādhu saba rāje.
सुर किंनर नर नाग मुनीसा । जय जय जय कहि देहिं असीसा ॥
sura kiṁnara nara nāga munīsā, jaya jaya jaya kahi dehiṁ asīsā.
नाचहिं गावहिं बिबुध बधूटीं । बार बार कुसुमांजलि छूटीं ॥
nācahiṁ gāvahiṁ bibudha badhūṭīṁ, bāra bāra kusumāṁjali chūṭīṁ.
जहँ तहँ बिप्र बेदधुनि करहीं । बंदी बिरिदावलि उच्चरहीं ॥
jahaṁ tahaṁ bipra bedadhuni karahīṁ, baṁdī biridāvali uccarahīṁ.
महि पाताल नाक जसु ब्यापा । राम बरी सिय भंजेउ चापा ॥
mahi pātāla nāka jasu byāpā, rāma barī siya bhaṁjeu cāpā.
करहिं आरती पुर नर नारी । देहिं निछावरि बित्त बिसारी ॥
karahiṁ āratī pura nara nārī, dehiṁ nichāvari bitta bisārī.
सोहति सीय राम कै जोरी । छबि सिंगारु मनहुँ एक ठोरी ॥
sohati sīya rāma kai jorī, chabi siṁgāru manahuṁ eka ṭhorī.
सखीं कहहिं प्रभुपद गहु सीता । करति न चरन परस अति भीता ॥
sakhīṁ kahahiṁ prabhupada gahu sītā, karati na carana parasa ati bhītā.

Trans:

Both in the city and in the heaven there were sounds of music; the bad were sad and the good were glad. Gods, Kinnars, men, serpents, and saints uttered blessings and shouts of victory; the heavenly nymphs danced and sang; and flowers fell in constant showers. In every place were Brahmins muttering Vedic texts, and rhapsodists reciting lays of praise. Earth, hell, and heaven were pervaded with the glad news: 'Rāma has broken the bow and weds Sītā.' The men and women of the city light votive lamps, and, regardless of their means, scatter gifts in profusion. Sītā by Rāma's side was as resplendent as if Beauty and Love had met together. Her companions whisper, 'Embrace your Lord's feet'; but in excess of revere she dares not touch them.

दोहा-dohā:

गौतम तिय गति सुरति करि नहिं परसति पग पानि ।
gautama tiya gati surati kari nahiṁ parasati paga pāni,
मन बिहसे रघुबंसमनि प्रीति अलौकिक जानि ॥२६५॥
mana bihase raghubaṁsamani prīti alaukika jāni. 265.

Trans:

She touches them not with her hands, remembering the fate of Gautam's wife; and Rāma smiles inwardly at this proof of her supernatural devotion.

चौपाई-caupāī:

तब सिय देखि भूप अभिलाषे । कूर कपूत मूढ़ मन माखे ॥
taba siya dekhi bhūpa abhilāṣe, kūra kapūta mūṛha mana mākhe.
उठि उठि पहिरि सनाह अभागे । जहँ तहँ गाल बजावन लागे ॥
uṭhi uṭhi pahiri sanāha abhāge, jahaṁ tahaṁ gāla bajāvana lāge.
लेहु छड़ाइ सीय कह कोऊ । धरि बाँधहु नृप बालक दोऊ ॥
lehu chaṛāi sīya kaha koū, dhari bāṁdhahu nṛpa bālaka doū.
तोरें धनुषु चाड़ नहिं सरई । जीवत हमहि कुअँरि को बरई ॥
toreṁ dhanuṣu cāṛa nahiṁ saraī, jīvata hamahi kuaṁri ko baraī.
जौं बिदेहु कछु करै सहाई । जीतहु समर सहित दोउ भाई ॥
jauṁ bidehu kachu karai sahāī, jītahu samara sahita dou bhāī.
साधु भूप बोले सुनि बानी । राजसमाजहि लाज लजानी ॥
sādhu bhūpa bole suni bānī, rājasamājahi lāja lajānī.
बलु प्रतापु बीरता बड़ाई । नाक पिनाकहि संग सिधाई ॥
balu pratāpu bīratā baṛāī, nāka pinākahi saṁga sidhāī.
सोइ सूरता कि अब कहुँ पाई । असि बुधि तौ बिधि मुहँ मसि लाई ॥
soi sūratā ki aba kahuṁ pāī, asi budhi tau bidhi muhaṁ masi lāī.

Trans:

Then, as they looked on Sītā, some kings were inflamed with desire, and waxed wrath of soul—frantic, degenerate fools—and sprung up—wretches most foul—and donned their armor and began a general chorus of abuse: "Come now, let us carry off Sītā, and overthrow and bind fast these two princes. Though he has broken the bow, he has not yet gained his end; for who dare marry Sītā while we are still alive? If the monarch give them any assistance, we will conquer him in battle along with the two brothers." When the good kings heard these words, they answered, and put the whole assembly to shame, "The glory of your might and greatness of your strength were disgraced forever at the breaking of the bow. Is that the might of which ye now boast? Or have ye since acquired something new? Was it not thus that ye reckoned afore, when gods so blackened your faces?

दोहा-dohā:

देखहु रामहि नयन भरि तजि इरिषा मदु कोहु ।
dekhahu rāmahi nayana bhari taji iriṣā madu kohu,
लखन रोषु पावकु प्रबल जानि सलभ जनि होहु ॥२६६॥
lakhana roṣu pāvaku prabala jāni salabha jani hohu. 266.

Trans:

Cease from envy and arrogance and folly; feast your eyes upon Rāma; and be not like a moth in the fierce flames of Lakshman's wrath.

चौपाई-caupāī:

बैनतेय बलि जिमि चह कागू । जिमि ससु चहै नाग अरि भागू ॥
bainateya bali jimi caha kāgū, jimi sasu cahai nāga ari bhāgū.
जिमि चह कुसल अकारन कोही । सब संपदा चहै सिवद्रोही ॥
jimi caha kusala akārana kohī, saba saṁpadā cahai sivadrohī.
लोभी लोलुप कल कीरति चहई । अकलंकता कि कामी लहई ॥
lobhī lolupa kala kīrati cahaī, akalaṁkatā ki kāmī lahaī.

हरि पद बिमुख परम गति चाहा । तस तुम्हार लालचु नरनाहा ॥
hari pada bimukha parama gati cāhā, tasa tumhāra lālacu naranāhā.
कोलाहलु सुनि सीय सकानी । सखीं लवाइ गईं जहँ रानी ॥
kolāhalu suni sīya sakānī, sakhīṁ lavāi gaīṁ jahaṁ rānī.
रामु सुभायँ चले गुरु पाहीं । सिय सनेहु बरनत मन माहीं ॥
rāmu subhāyaṁ cale guru pāhīṁ, siya sanehu baranata mana māhīṁ.
रानिन्ह सहित सोचबस सीया । अब धौं बिधिहि काह करनीया ॥
rāninha sahita socabasa sīyā, aba dhauṁ bidhihi kāha karanīyā.
भूप बचन सुनि इत उत तकहीं । लखनु राम डर बोलि न सकहीं ॥
bhūpa bacana suni ita uta takahīṁ, lakhanu rāma ḍara boli na sakahīṁ.

Trans:

Like a crow who would rob offering meant for Garud, king-of-birds; or a rat who should covet spoils of a lion; or as a man who is angry without cause, yet wishes for peace of mind; or as a reviler of Shiva who wishes for prosperity and happiness; or as a greedy and covetous man who wishes for fair fame; or as a gallant man who wishes to have no scandal; or as an enemy of God who wishes for supreme destiny—such is your own desire, ye foolish kings." When Sītā heard the tumult, she was afraid, and with her companions went away to the queen; while Rāma composedly joined the Gurū, inwardly praising Sītā's affection. Sītā and the queens were in much distress thinking: "What has providence in store for us now?" At the sound of the voices of kings they looked helplessly up and down. Meanwhile, for revere of Rāma, Lakshman could not speak.

दोहा-dohā:

अरुन नयन भृकुटी कुटिल चितवत नृपन्ह सकोप ।
aruna nayana bhṛkuṭī kuṭila citavata nṛpanha sakopa,
मनहुँ मत्त गजगन निरखि सिंघकिसोरहि चोप ॥२६७॥
manahuṁ matta gajagana nirakhi siṁghakisorahi copa. 267.

Trans:

With fiery eyes and knitted brows he cast a furious look at the kings—like a lion's whelp watching to spring on a herd of wild elephants.

चौपाई-caupāī:

खरभरु देखि बिकल पुर नारीं । सब मिलि देहिं महीपन्ह गारीं ॥
kharabharu dekhi bikala pura nārīṁ, saba mili dehiṁ mahīpanha gārīṁ.
तेहिं अवसर सुनि सिवधनु भंगा । आयउ भृगुकुल कमल पतंगा ॥
tehiṁ avasara suni sivadhanu bhaṁgā, āyau bhṛgukula kamala pataṁgā.
देखि महीप सकल सकुचाने । बाज झपट जनु लवा लुकाने ॥
dekhi mahīpa sakala sakucāne, bāja jhapaṭa janu lavā lukāne.
गौरि सरीर भूति भल भ्राजा । भाल बिसाल त्रिपुंड बिराजा ॥
gauri sarīra bhūti bhala bhrājā, bhāla bisāla tripuṁḍa birājā.
सीस जटा ससिबदनु सुहावा । रिसबस कछुक अरुन होइ आवा ॥
sīsa jaṭā sasibadanu suhāvā, risabasa kachuka aruna hoi āvā.
भृकुटी कुटिल नयन रिस राते । सहजहुँ चितवत मनहुँ रिसाते ॥
bhṛkuṭī kuṭila nayana risa rāte, sahajahuṁ citavata manahuṁ risāte.
बृषभ कंध उर बाहु बिसाला । चारु जनेउ माल मृगछाला ॥
bṛṣabha kaṁdha ura bāhu bisālā, cāru janeu māla mṛgachālā.
कटि मुनिबसन तून दुइ बाँधें । धनु सर कर कुठारु कल काँधें ॥
kaṭi munibasana tūna dui bāṁdheṁ, dhanu sara kara kuṭhāru kala kāṁdheṁ.

Trans:

Seeing the tumult, the people were all distressed and joined in reproaching the kings. Then it was that the sun of the lotus race of Bhrigu (Parshurām) arrived there—for he had heard of the breaking of the bow. At the sight of him the kings all cowered down, like as partridge shrinking beneath the swoop of a hawk. Of pallid hue and well bestreaked with ashes; with the three horizontal lines sacred to Shiva conspicuous on his broad forehead; with the hair on his head bound in a knot; and his moon-like face flushed with the furnace fire of smoldering wrath; with frowning brows and eyes inflamed with passion; he cast a quick and furious glance all around. With bull-like shoulders and mighty chest and arms; with fair sacrificial cord and string of beads and deerskin; with an anchorite's dress about his loins and two quivers slung by his side; with bow and arrows in hand, and his sharp axe upon his shoulder;

दोहा-dohā:

सांत बेषु करनी कठिन बरनि न जाइ सरुप ।
sāṁta beṣu karanī kaṭhina barani na jāi sarupa,
धरि मुनितनु जनु बीर रसु आयउ जहँ सब भूप ॥२६८॥
dhari munitanu janu bīra rasu āyau jahaṁ saba bhūpa. 268.

Trans:

in his saintly attire and savage mien, a figure beyond description, as though the Heroic had taken the form of a hermit—so he drew fiercely near to the kings.

चौपाई-caupāī:

देखत भृगुपति बेषु कराला । उठे सकल भय बिकल भुआला ॥
dekhata bhṛgupati beṣu karālā, uṭhe sakala bhaya bikala bhuālā.
पितु समेत कहि कहि निज नामा । लगे करन सब दंड प्रनामा ॥
pitu sameta kahi kahi nija nāmā, lage karana saba daṁḍa pranāmā.
जेहि सुभायँ चितवहिं हितु जानी । सो जानइ जनु आइ खुटानी ॥
jehi subhāyaṁ citavahiṁ hitu jānī, so jānai janu āi khuṭānī.
जनक बहोरि आइ सिरु नावा । सीय बोलाइ प्रनामु करावा ॥
janaka bahori āi siru nāvā, sīya bolāi pranāmu karāvā.
आसिष दीन्हि सखीं हरषानीं । निज समाज लै गईं सयानीं ॥
āsiṣa dīnhi sakhīṁ haraṣānīṁ, nija samāja lai gaīṁ sayānīṁ.
बिस्वामित्रु मिले पुनि आई । पद सरोज मेले दोउ भाई ॥
bisvāmitru mile puni āī, pada saroja mele dou bhāī.
रामु लखनु दसरथ के ढोटा । दीन्हि असीस देखि भल जोटा ॥
rāmu lakhanu dasaratha ke ḍhoṭā, dīnhi asīsa dekhi bhala joṭā.
रामहि चितइ रहे थकि लोचन । रूप अपार मार मद मोचन ॥
rāmahi citai rahe thaki locana, rūpa apāra māra mada mocana.

Trans:

When they beheld his ghastly attire, they all rose in consternation, each mentioning his own and his father's name and fell prostrate on the ground before him; and even those on whom he cast a kindly glance thought that his life had come to an end. Then came Janak and bowed his head and called for Sītā also to pay homage to him. He bestowed upon her his blessing, and her glad companions escorted her back to her own place. Next came Vishwāmitra to salute him and he placed the two boys at his feet saying: "These are Rāma and Lakshman, Dashrath's sons." He admired the well matched pair and blessed them with his eyes long fixed upon Rāma's incomparable beauty, which would humble the pride even of Love himself.

दोहा-dohā:

बहुरि बिलोकि बिदेह सन कहहु काह अति भीर ।
bahuri biloki bideha sana kahahu kāha ati bhīra,
पूछत जानि अजान जिमि ब्यापेउ कोपु सरीर ॥२६९॥
pūchata jāni ajāna jimi byāpeu kopu sarīra. 269.

Trans:

Then he turned and said to Videh: "Why all this crowd?" Asking as though he did not know, while his whole body was bursting with ire.

चौपाई-caupāī:

समाचार कहि जनक सुनाए । जेहि कारन महीप सब आए ॥
samācāra kahi janaka sunāe, jehi kārana mahīpa saba āe.
सुनत बचन फिरि अनत निहारे । देखे चापखंड महि डारे ॥
sunata bacana phiri anata nihāre, dekhe cāpakhaṁḍa mahi ḍāre.

अति रिस बोले बचन कठोरा । कहु जड़ जनक धनुष कै तोरा ॥
ati risa bole bacana kaṭhorā, kahu jaṛa janaka dhanuṣa kai torā.
बेगि देखाउ मूढ़ न त आजू । उलटउँ महि जहँ लहि तव राजू ॥
begi dekhāu mūṛha na ta ājū, ulaṭauṁ mahi jahaṁ lahi tava rājū.
अति डरु उतरु देत नृपु नाहीं । कुटिल भूप हरषे मन माहीं ॥
ati ḍaru utaru deta nṛpu nāhīṁ, kuṭila bhūpa haraṣe mana māhīṁ.
सुर मुनि नाग नगर नर नारी । सोचहिं सकल त्रास उर भारी ॥
sura muni nāga nagara nara nārī, socahiṁ sakala trāsa ura bhārī.
मन पछिताति सीय महतारी । बिधि अब सँवरी बात बिगारी ॥
mana pachitāti sīya mahatārī, bidhi aba saṁvarī bāta bigārī.
भृगुपति कर सुभाउ सुनि सीता । अरध निमेष कलप सम बीता ॥
bhṛgupati kara subhāu suni sītā, aradha nimeṣa kalapa sama bītā.

Trans:

Janak told him the whole history and the reason why the kings had assembled. After hearing his reply he again looked away and spied the fragments of the bow lying on the ground. In a mighty passion he cried in furious tones: "Tell me now Janak, you fool, who has broken this bow? Show him to me at once, or this very day I will overthrow the whole of your dominion." In his excess of fear the king could give no answer; the wicked suitors were glad of heart; gods, saints, serpents, and all the people of the city were full of anxiety and profound alarm. Sītā's mother was lamenting, "God has now undone all that had just been done so well"; and Sītā when she heard of Bhrigupati's character felt half a minute pass like an age.

दोहा-dohā:

सभय बिलोके लोग सब जानि जानकी भीरु ।
sabhaya biloke loga saba jāni jānakī bhīru,
हृदयँ न हरषु बिषादु कछु बोले श्रीरघुबीरु ॥२७०॥
hṛdayaṁ na haraṣu biṣādu kachu bole śrīraghubīru. 270.

Trans:

Seeing the people's consternation and Jānakī's anxiety, the imperturbable Raghubīr spoke, with neither joy nor sorrow in his heart:

मासपारायण नवाँ विश्राम

māsapārāyaṇa navāṁ viśrāma
(Pause 9 for a Thirty-Day Recitation)

चौपाई-caupāī:

नाथ संभुधनु भंजनिहारा । होइहि केउ एक दास तुम्हारा ॥
nātha saṁbhudhanu bhaṁjanihārā, hoihi keu eka dāsa tumhārā.
आयसु काह कहिअ किन मोही । सुनि रिसाइ बोले मुनि कोही ॥
āyasu kāha kahia kina mohī, suni risāi bole muni kohī.
सेवकु सो जो करै सेवकाई । अरि करनी करि करिअ लराई ॥
sevaku so jo karai sevakāī, ari karanī kari karia larāī.
सुनहु राम जेहिं सिवधनु तोरा । सहसबाहु सम सो रिपु मोरा ॥
sunahu rāma jehiṁ sivadhanu torā, sahasabāhu sama so ripu morā.
सो बिलगाउ बिहाइ समाजा । न त मारे जैहहिं सब राजा ॥
so bilagāu bihāi samājā, na ta māre jaihahiṁ saba rājā.
सुनि मुनि बचन लखन मुसुकाने । बोले परसुधरहि अपमाने ॥
suni muni bacana lakhana musukāne, bole parasudharahi apamāne.
बहु धनुहीं तोरीं लरिकाईं । कबहुँ न असि रिस कीन्हि गोसाईं ॥
bahu dhanuhīṁ torīṁ larikāīṁ, kabahuṁ na asi risa kīnhi gosāīṁ.
एहि धनु पर ममता केहि हेतू । सुनि रिसाइ कह भृगुकुलकेतू ॥
ehi dhanu para mamatā kehi hetū, suni risāi kaha bhṛgukulaketū.

Trans:

"My lord, the bow must have been broken by someone who is your servant. Now what are your orders? Pray tell me?" At this the furious saint was yet more incensed and cried: "A servant is one who does service, but he who does the deeds of an enemy must be fought. Hearken, Rāma, whoever it was who broke Shiva's bow is as much my enemy as was Sahastr-bahu. Separate him from among the assembly, or else every one of these kings shall be killed." When Lakshman heard the saint's words, he smiled and said to him in a tone of contempt: "O sir, I have broken many a bow as a child, and you were never before thus angry; is there a reason why you are so fond of this bow in particular?" And Parshurām flew into a fury:

दोहा-dohā:

रे नृप बालक काल बस बोलत तोहि न सँभार ।
re nṛpa bālaka kāla basa bolata tohi na saṁbhāra,
धनुही सम तिपुरारि धनु बिदित सकल संसार ॥२७१॥
dhanuhī sama tipurāri dhanu bidita sakala saṁsāra. 271.

Trans:

"Ah! death-doomed prince, is there no stopping your tongue? Would you compare to a common bow the great bow of Shiva which is famous throughout the world?"

चौपाई-caupāī:

लखन कहा हँसि हमरें जाना । सुनहु देव सब धनुष समाना ॥
lakhana kahā haṁsi hamareṁ jānā, sunahu deva saba dhanuṣa samānā.
का छति लाभु जून धनु तोरें । देखा राम नयन के भोरें ॥
kā chati lābhu jūna dhanu toreṁ, dekhā rāma nayana ke bhoreṁ.
छुअत टूट रघुपतिहु न दोसू । मुनि बिनु काज करिअ कत रोसू ॥
chuata ṭūṭa raghupatihu na dosū, muni binu kāja karia kata rosū.
बोले चितइ परसु की ओरा । रे सठ सुनेहि सुभाउ न मोरा ॥
bole citai parasu kī orā, re saṭha sunehi subhāu na morā.
बालकु बोलि बधउँ नहिं तोही । केवल मुनि जड़ जानहि मोही ॥
bālaku boli badhauṁ nahiṁ tohī, kevala muni jaṛa jānahi mohī.
बाल ब्रह्मचारी अति कोही । बिस्व बिदित छत्रियकुल द्रोही ॥
bāla brahmacārī ati kohī, bisva bidita chatriyakula drohī.
भुजबल भूमि भूप बिनु कीन्ही । बिपुल बार महिदेवन्ह दीन्ही ॥
bhujabala bhūmi bhūpa binu kīnhī, bipula bāra mahidevanha dīnhī.
सहसबाहु भुज छेदनिहारा । परसु बिलोकु महीपकुमारा ॥
sahasabāhu bhuja chedanihārā, parasu biloku mahīpakumārā.

Trans:

Said Lakshman with a smile: "I thought, holy sir, that all bows are alike. What gain or what loss can there be in the breaking of a worn-out bow? Rāma by mistake took it for a new one, and directly he touched it, it snapped into two; It was no fault of his; why then, reverend sir, be so angry for no cause?" He answered, with a glance at his axe: "Fool, have you never heard of my temper? I do not slay you because, as I say, you are but a child. You in your folly take me for a mere recluse; and from my childhood an ascetic I am, but a fiery one, and the terror of the whole Kshatriya race, as is known throughout the world. By the might of my arm I have made earth void of kings, and time after time have bestowed her upon the Brahmins. See here, you king's son, the axe with which I lopped off Sahastr-bahu's thousand arms.

दोहा-dohā:

मातु पितहि जनि सोचबस करसि महीसकिसोर ।
mātu pitahi jani socabasa karasi mahīsakisora,
गर्भन्ह के अर्भक दलन परसु मोर अति घोर ॥२७२॥
garbhanha ke arbhaka dalana parasu mora ati ghora. 272.

Trans:

Do not bring distress upon your father and mother; my cruel axe has ripped up even unborn infants in the womb."

चौपाई-caupāī:

बिहसि लखनु बोले मृदु बानी । अहो मुनीसु महा भटमानी ॥
bihasi lakhanu bole mṛdu bānī, aho munīsu mahā bhaṭamānī.

पुनि पुनि मोहि देखाव कुठारू । चहत उड़ावन फूँकि पहारू ॥
puni puni mohi dekhāva kuṭhārū, cahata uṛāvana phūm̐ki pahārū.
इहाँ कुम्हड़बतिया कोउ नाहीं । जे तरजनी देखि मरि जाहीं ॥
ihām̐ kumhaṛabatiyā kou nāhīṁ, je tarajanī dekhi mari jāhīṁ.
देखि कुठारु सरासन बाना । मैं कछु कहा सहित अभिमाना ॥
dekhi kuṭhāru sarāsana bānā, maiṁ kachu kahā sahita abhimānā.
भृगुसुत समुझि जनेउ बिलोकी । जो कछु कहहु सहउँ रिस रोकी ॥
bhṛgusuta samujhi janeu bilokī, jo kachu kahahu sahaum̐ risa rokī.
सुर महिसुर हरिजन अरु गाई । हमरें कुल इन्ह पर न सुराई ॥
sura mahisura harijana aru gāī, hamareṁ kula inha para na surāī.
बधें पापु अपकीरति हारें । मारतहूँ पा परिअ तुम्हारें ॥
badheṁ pāpu apakīrati hāreṁ, māratahūm̐ pā paria tumhāreṁ.
कोटि कुलिस सम बचनु तुम्हारा । ब्यर्थ धरहु धनु बान कुठारा ॥
koṭi kulisa sama bacanu tumhārā, byartha dharahu dhanu bāna kuṭhārā.

Trans:

Lakshman replied with a quiet smile: "Ah holy sir! You think yourself a great warrior indeed, and keep brandishing your axe before me, as if with a mere puff of breath you could blow away a mountain. But I am not a *kumhar* blossom that drops as soon as it sees a finger raised against it. When I perceived your axe and quiver and arrows, I spoke a little haughtily; but now that I see by your Brahminical thread that you are of Bhrigu's line, say what you like, and I will bear it patiently. In my family there is no waging battle against gods, or Brahmins, or devotees, or cows; for to kill them is a crime, and to be overcome by them a disgrace; and therefore I must throw myself at your feet even though you strike me. Your tongue itself is as awful as a million thunderbolts, and your axe and bow and arrows are unnecessary.

दोहा-dohā:

जो बिलोकि अनुचित कहेउँ छमहु महामुनि धीर ।
jo biloki anucita kaheum̐ chamahu mahāmuni dhīra,
सुनि सरोष भृगुबंसमनि बोले गिरा गभीर ॥ २७३ ॥
suni saroṣa bhṛgubaṁsamani bole girā gabhīra. 273.

Trans:

Pardon me, great and reverend sage, for anything improper that I said when I first saw you." The glory of Bhrigu's race then thundered furiously in his deep-toned voice:

चौपाई-caupāī:

कौसिक सुनहु मंद यहु बालकु । कुटिल कालबस निज कुल घालकु ॥
kausika sunahu maṁda yahu bālaku, kuṭila kālabasa nija kula ghālaku.
भानु बंस राकेस कलंकू । निपट निरंकुस अबुध असंकू ॥
bhānu baṁsa rākesa kalaṁkū, nipaṭa niraṁkusa abudha asaṁkū.
काल कवलु होइहि छन माहीं । कहउँ पुकारि खोरि मोहि नाहीं ॥
kāla kavalu hoihi chana māhīṁ, kahaum̐ pukāri khori mohi nāhīṁ.
तुम्ह हटकहु जौं चहहु उबारा । कहि प्रतापु बलु रोषु हमारा ॥
tumha haṭakahu jauṁ cahahu ubārā, kahi pratāpu balu roṣu hamārā.
लखन कहेउ मुनि सुजसु तुम्हारा । तुम्हहि अछत को बरनै पारा ॥
lakhana kaheu muni sujasu tumhārā, tumhahi achata ko baranai pārā.
अपने मुँह तुम्ह आपनि करनी । बार अनेक भाँति बहु बरनी ॥
apane mum̐ha tumha āpani karanī, bāra aneka bhām̐ti bahu baranī.
नहिं संतोषु त पुनि कछु कहहू । जनि रिस रोकि दुसह दुख सहहू ॥
nahiṁ saṁtoṣu ta puni kachu kahahū, jani risa roki dusaha dukha sahahū.
बीरब्रती तुम्ह धीर अछोभा । गारी देत न पावहु सोभा ॥
bīrabratī tumha dhīra achobhā, gārī deta na pāvahu sobhā.

Trans:

"Hearken Kaushik, this child is demented; a perverse and death-doomed destroyer of his own house; a dark spot on the moon-like brightness of the solar race; utterly ungovernable, senseless and reckless. Another moment and he shall be a mouthful in the jaws of death, and I loudly declare it will be no fault of mine. Take him away, if you would save him, and teach him my glory and might and the fierceness of my temper." Said Lakshman: "So long as you live, father, who else can tell your fame so well? With your own mouth you have so many times and in so many ways declared your own doings. If you are not yet satisfied tell them over again; and do not distress yourself beyond endurance by putting any restraint upon your passion. But if you are really a resolute and dauntless warrior, there is no honor to be got by abuse.

दोहा-dohā:

सूर समर करनी करहिं कहि न जनावहिं आपु ।
sūra samara karanī karahiṁ kahi na janāvahiṁ āpu,
बिद्यमान रन पाइ रिपु कायर कथहिं प्रतापु ॥ २७४ ॥
bidyamāna rana pāi ripu kāyara kathahiṁ pratāpu. 274.

Trans:

Heroes perform valiant deeds in fight, but do not themselves publish them; cowards finding a foe before them in the battle talk very large,

चौपाई-caupāī:

तुम्ह तौ कालु हाँक जनु लावा । बार बार मोहि लागि बोलावा ॥
tumha tau kālu hām̐ka janu lāvā, bāra bāra mohi lāgi bolāvā.
सुनत लखन के बचन कठोरा । परसु सुधारि धरेउ कर घोरा ॥
sunata lakhana ke bacana kaṭhorā, parasu sudhāri dhareu kara ghorā.
अब जनि देइ दोसु मोहि लोगू । कटुबादी बालकु बधजोगू ॥
aba jani dei dosu mohi logū, kaṭubādī bālaku badhajogū.
बाल बिलोकि बहुत मैं बाँचा । अब यहु मरनिहार भा साँचा ॥
bāla biloki bahuta maiṁ bām̐cā, aba yahu maranihāra bhā sām̐cā.
कौसिक कहा छमिअ अपराधू । बाल दोष गुन गनहिं न साधू ॥
kausika kahā chamia aparādhū, bāla doṣa guna ganahiṁ na sādhū.
खर कुठार मैं अकरुन कोही । आगें अपराधी गुरुद्रोही ॥
khara kuṭhāra maiṁ akaruna kohī, āgeṁ aparādhī gurudrohī.
उतर देत छोड़उँ बिनु मारें । केवल कौसिक सील तुम्हारें ॥
utara deta choṛaum̐ binu māreṁ, kevala kausika sīla tumhāreṁ.
न त एहि काटि कुठार कठोरें । गुरहि उरिन होतेउँ श्रम थोरें ॥
na ta ehi kāṭi kuṭhāra kaṭhoreṁ, gurahi urina hoteum̐ śrama thoreṁ.

Trans:

as you now try to terrify me with your repeated cries of Death." On hearing Lakshman's rude speech he closed his hand upon his terrible axe: "After this let no man blame me; this sharp-tongued boy deserves his death. I have spared him long on account of his being a child, but now of a truth he is as good as dead." Said Vishwāmitra: "Pardon his offence; the wise regard not the faults or merits of children." "I have axe in hand and am pitiless in my wrath; he is moreover guilty, and has injured my Gurū. Yet though this be my answer, I will still spare his life, just solely out of regard for you, Vishwāmitra. But for you, I would have cut him in pieces with my terrible axe, and thus easily paid my Gurū his due."

दोहा-dohā:

गाधिसूनु कह हृदयँ हँसि मुनिहि हरिअरइ सूझ ।
gādhisūnu kaha hṛdayam̐ ham̐si munihi hariarai sūjha,
अयमय खाँड न ऊखमय अजहुँ न बूझ अबूझ ॥ २७५ ॥
ayamaya khām̐ḍa na ūkhamaya ajahum̐ na būjha abūjha. 275.

Trans:

Said the son of Gādhi, smiling to himself, 'Everything looks green to the saint's eyes; though Rāma has today broken the bow as though it were a stick of sugarcane, still he has not the sense to understand.'

चौपाई-caupāī:

कहेउ लखन मुनि सीलु तुम्हारा । को नहिं जान बिदित संसारा ॥
kaheu lakhana muni sīlu tumhārā, ko nahiṁ jāna bidita saṁsārā.
माता पितहि उरिन भए नीकें । गुर रिनु रहा सोचु बड़ जीकें ॥
mātā pitahi urina bhae nīkeṁ, gura rinu rahā socu baṛa jīkeṁ.
सो जनु हमरेहि माथे काढ़ा । दिन चलि गए ब्याज बड़ बाढ़ा ॥
so janu hamarehi māthe kāṛhā, dina cali gae byāja baṛa bāṛhā.
अब आनिअ ब्यवहरिआ बोली । तुरत देउँ मैं थैली खोली ॥
aba ānia byavahariā bolī, turata deuṁ maiṁ thailī kholī.
सुनि कटु बचन कुठार सुधारा । हाय हाय सब सभा पुकारा ॥
suni kaṭu bacana kuṭhāra sudhārā, hāya hāya saba sabhā pukārā.
भृगुबर परसु देखावहु मोही । बिप्र बिचारि बचउँ नृपद्रोही ॥
bhṛgubara parasu dekhāvahu mohī, bipra bicāri bacauṁ nṛpadrohī.
मिले न कबहुँ सुभट रन गाढ़े । द्विज देवता घरहि के बाढ़े ॥
mile na kabahuṁ subhaṭa rana gāṛhe, dvija devatā gharahi ke bāṛhe.
अनुचित कहि सब लोग पुकारे । रघुपति सयनहिं लखनु नेवारे ॥
anucita kahi saba loga pukāre, raghupati sayanahiṁ lakhanu nevāre.

Trans:

Said Lakshman: "Is there anyone in the world, father, ignorant of your gentle disposition? It is notorious throughout the world. You have well paid the debt you owed to your father and mother; but it was a great distress to you to be still in debt to your Gurū. It looks like you incurred that debt on our account; and the interest by lapse of time has become very heavy now. So please bring forward the original creditor, and then, sir, I will at once open my purse." When he heard these sarcastic words he grasped his axe, and all the people cried—'Alack, alack'. "O Bhrigubar, you still keep showing me your axe, but, regicide as you are, I only spare you on account of your being a Brahmin. You have never yet met a real staunch fighting man. O most reverend sir, you are a great man in your own little house." To which everyone exclaimed in shock: 'How very wrong'; and Rāma gave Lakshman a sign to be quiet.

दोहा-dohā:

लखन उतर आहुति सरिस भृगुबर कोपु कृसानु ।
lakhana utara āhuti sarisa bhṛgubara kopu kṛsānu,
बढ़त देखि जल सम बचन बोले रघुकुलभानु ॥ २७६ ॥
baṛhata dekhi jala sama bacana bole raghukulabhānu. 276.

Trans:

Perceiving the flames of Parshurām's passion grow with the pouring of oblation in the form of Lakshman's rejoinders, the Sun of Raghu's race spoke words that were like quenching water:

चौपाई-caupāī:

नाथ करहु बालक पर छोहू । सूध दूधमुख करिअ न कोहू ॥
nātha karahu bālaka para chohū, sūdha dūdhamukha karia na kohū.
जौं पै प्रभु प्रभाउ कछु जाना । तौ कि बराबरि करत अयाना ॥
jauṁ pai prabhu prabhāu kachu jānā, tau ki barābari karata ayānā.
जौं लरिका कछु अचगरि करहीं । गुर पितु मातु मोद मन भरहीं ॥
jauṁ larikā kachu acagari karahīṁ, gura pitu mātu moda mana bharahīṁ.
करिअ कृपा सिसु सेवक जानी । तुम्ह सम सील धीर मुनि ग्यानी ॥
karia kṛpā sisu sevaka jānī, tumha sama sīla dhīra muni gyānī.
राम बचन सुनि कछुक जुड़ाने । कहि कछु लखनु बहुरि मुसुकाने ॥
rāma bacana suni kachuka juṛāne, kahi kachu lakhanu bahuri musukāne.
हँसत देखि नख सिख रिस ब्यापी । राम तोर भ्राता बड़ पापी ॥
haṁsata dekhi nakha sikha risa byāpī, rāma tora bhrātā baṛa pāpī.
गौर सरीर स्याम मन माहीं । कालकूटमुख पयमुख नाहीं ॥
gaura sarīra syāma mana māhīṁ, kālakūṭamukha payamukha nāhīṁ.
सहज टेढ़ अनुहरइ न तोही । नीचु मीचु सम देख न मोही ॥
sahaja ṭeṛha anuharai na tohī, nīcu mīcu sama dekha na mohī.

Trans:

"My lord, have compassion on a child, and wreak not your wrath on such an unweaned infant. If he had any idea of your glorious power, how could he be so foolish as to put himself on an equality with you? When a child commits any naughtiness, its Gurū and father and mother are in raptures at it. Have pity then on the boy, who is really one of your servants; for thus it becometh a saint—patient and wise that you are." On hearing Rāma's words he cooled down a little; but again Lakshman said something with a smile, and seeing him smile he flushed all over again with rage: "Rāma, your brother is too wicked. Though fair in outward hue, he is black at heart; and it is not mother's milk but poison that his lips have sucked. Perverse by nature, he neither takes after you, nor regards me."

दोहा-dohā:

लखन कहेउ हँसि सुनहु मुनि क्रोधु पाप कर मूल ।
lakhana kaheu haṁsi sunahu muni krodhu pāpa kara mūla,
जेहि बस जन अनुचित करहिं चरहिं बिस्व प्रतिकूल ॥ २७७ ॥
jehi basa jana anucita karahiṁ carahiṁ bisva pratikūla. 277.

Trans:

Said Lakshman with a smile: "Hearken, O saint, passion is the root of sin; those who are under its influence do wrong and set themselves against the world.

चौपाई-caupāī:

मैं तुम्हार अनुचर मुनिराया । परिहरि कोपु करिअ अब दाया ॥
maiṁ tumhāra anucara munirāyā, parihari kopu karia aba dāyā.
टूट चाप नहिं जुरिहि रिसाने । बैठिअ होइहिं पाय पिराने ॥
ṭūṭa cāpa nahiṁ jurihi risāne, baiṭhia hoihiṁ pāya pirāne.
जौं अति प्रिय तौ करिअ उपाई । जोरिअ कोउ बड़ गुनी बोलाई ॥
jauṁ ati priya tau karia upāī, joria kou baṛa gunī bolāī.
बोलत लखनहिं जनकु डेराहीं । मष्ट करहु अनुचित भल नाहीं ॥
bolata lakhanahiṁ janaku ḍerāhīṁ, maṣṭa karahu anucita bhala nāhīṁ.
थर थर काँपहिं पुर नर नारी । छोट कुमार खोट बड़ भारी ॥
thara thara kāṁpahiṁ pura nara nārī, choṭa kumāra khoṭa baṛa bhārī.
भृगुपति सुनि सुनि निरभय बानी । रिस तन जरइ होइ बल हानी ॥
bhṛgupati suni suni nirabhaya bānī, risa tana jarai hoi bala hānī.
बोले रामहि देइ निहोरा । बचउँ बिचारि बंधु लघु तोरा ॥
bole rāmahi dei nihorā, bacauṁ bicāri baṁdhu laghu torā.
मनु मलीन तनु सुंदर कैसें । बिष रस भरा कनक घटु जैसें ॥
manu malīna tanu suṁdara kaiseṁ, biṣa rasa bharā kanaka ghaṭu jaiseṁ.

Trans:

I am one of your followers, reverend sir; put away your wrath and show mercy upon me. Anger will not mend the broken bow; pray sit down, you must be tired of standing. If you were so very fond of it, devise a plan for getting it mended and call in some skillful workman." Janak was frightened at Lakshman's words: "Be quiet; such forwardness is not right." The citizens all shook and trembled: to think so small a boy could be so naughty. As Bhrigupati heard his fearless words, his whole body was aflame with rage, and he became quite powerless, and in a tone of entreaty cried to Rāma: "See if you can manage this little brother of yours; so fair outside and foul within; verily he resembles a golden jar full of poison."

दोहा-dohā:

सुनि लछिमन बिहसे बहुरि नयन तरेरे राम ।
suni lachimana bihase bahuri nayana tarere rāma,
गुर समीप गवने सकुचि परिहरि बानी बाम ॥ २७८ ॥
gura samīpa gavane sakuci parihari bānī bāma. 278.

Trans:

At this Lakshman smiled, but Rāma gave him a look of reproof; at which putting away all forwardness of speech, he submissively went up to his Gurū.

चौपाई-caupāī:

अति बिनीत मृदु सीतल बानी । बोले रामु जोरि जुग पानी ॥
ati binīta mṛdu sītala bānī, bole rāmu jori juga pānī.
सुनहु नाथ तुम्ह सहज सुजाना । बालक बचनु करिअ नहिं काना ॥
sunahu nātha tumha sahaja sujānā, bālaka bacanu karia nahiṁ kānā.
बररै बालकु एकु सुभाऊ । इन्हहि न संत बिदूषहिं काऊ ॥
bararai bālaku eku subhāū, inhahi na saṁta bidūṣahiṁ kāū.
तेहिं नाहीं कछु काज बिगारा । अपराधी मैं नाथ तुम्हारा ॥
tehiṁ nāhīṁ kachu kāja bigārā, aparādhī maiṁ nātha tumhārā.
कृपा कोपु बधु बँधब गोसाईं । मो पर करिअ दास की नाईं ॥
kṛpā kopu badhu baṁdhaba gosāīṁ, mo para karia dāsa kī nāīṁ.
कहिअ बेगि जेहि बिधि रिस जाई । मुनिनायक सोइ करौं उपाई ॥
kahia begi jehi bidhi risa jāī, munināyaka soi karauṁ upāī.
कह मुनि राम जाइ रिस कैसें । अजहुँ अनुज तव चितव अनैसें ॥
kaha muni rāma jāi risa kaiseṁ, ajahuṁ anuja tava citava anaiseṁ.
एहि कें कंठ कुठारु न दीन्हा । तौ मैं काह कोपु करि कीन्हा ॥
ehi keṁ kaṁṭha kuṭhāru na dīnhā, tau maiṁ kāha kopu kari kīnhā.

Trans:

Than, clasping his two hands together and speaking in most modest, gentle, and placid tones, Rāma said: "Hearken, my lord, you were born a sage; pay no heed then to the words of a child. Boys are like gnats; no wise man will ever trouble himself about them. Nor is it he who has done the mischief; I, my lord, am your offender. Be pleased, your Reverence, to visit everything on me, your servant, whether it be favor or anger, or death or bonds. Tell me quickly the means, O king of saints, by which your anger may be appeased." Said the saint: "O Rāma, how can my passion be assuaged? Your brother has today set me at naught, and yet I have not struck off his head with my axe; what then have I done in anger?

दोहा-dohā:

गर्भ स्त्रवहिं अवनिप रवनि सुनि कुठार गति घोर ।
garbha sravahiṁ avanipa ravani suni kuṭhāra gati ghora,
परसु अछत देखउँ जिअत बैरी भूपकिसोर ॥ २७९ ॥
parasu achata dekhauṁ jiata bairī bhūpakisora. 279.

Trans:

When they heard of the fierce doings of my axe, the proudest queens were seized with untimely pains of labor; my axe is still here, and yet I see this princeling, my enemy, alive.

चौपाई-caupāī:

बहइ न हाथु दहइ रिस छाती । भा कुठारु कुंठित नृपघाती ॥
bahai na hāthu dahai risa chātī, bhā kuṭhāru kuṁṭhita nṛpaghātī.
भयउ बाम बिधि फिरेउ सुभाऊ । मोरे हृदयँ कृपा कसि काऊ ॥
bhayau bāma bidhi phireu subhāū, more hṛdayaṁ kṛpā kasi kāū.
आजु दया दुखु दुसह सहावा । सुनि सौमित्रि बिहसि सिरु नावा ॥
āju dayā dukhu dusaha sahāvā, suni saumitri bihasi siru nāvā.
बाउ कृपा मूरति अनुकूला । बोलत बचन झरत जनु फूला ॥
bāu kṛpā mūrati anukūlā, bolata bacana jharata janu phūlā.
जौं पै कृपाँ जरिहिं मुनि गाता । क्रोध भएँ तनु राख बिधाता ॥
jauṁ pai kṛpāṁ jarihiṁ muni gātā, krodha bhaeṁ tanu rākha bidhātā.
देखु जनक हठि बालकु एहू । कीन्ह चहत जड़ जमपुर गेहू ॥
dekhu janaka haṭhi bālaku ehū, kīnha cahata jaṛa jamapura gehū.
बेगि करहु किन आँखिन्ह ओटा । देखत छोट खोट नृप ढोटा ॥
begi karahu kina āṁkhinha oṭā, dekhata choṭa khoṭa nṛpa ḍhoṭā.
बिहसे लखनु कहा मन माहीं । मूदें आँखि कतहुँ कोउ नाहीं ॥
bihase lakhanu kahā mana māhīṁ, mūdeṁ āṁkhi katahuṁ kou nāhīṁ.

Trans:

My hand moves not, though passion consumes my heart. My regicide axe has become blunted. Fate is against me; my nature is changed; for when was I ever pitiful before? Today by heaven's will I have suffered intolerable pain." On hearing this, the son of Sumitrā smiled and bowed his head: "Your pity is like the wind, and the words you speak scatter blossoms. If a saint's body is consumed even by pity, how can God preserve him when he is angry?" "See now, Janak, keep this child away; he is bent in his folly on visiting the realms of death. Why do you not at once take him out of my sight, this little prince; so small to look at and yet so wicked?" Lakshman laughed as he muttered to himself, 'Shut the eyes and everything disappears.'

दोहा-dohā:

परसुरामु तब राम प्रति बोले उर अति क्रोधु ।
parasurāmu taba rāma prati bole ura ati krodhu,
संभु सरासनु तोरि सठ करसि हमार प्रबोधु ॥ २८० ॥
saṁbhu sarāsanu tori saṭha karasi hamāra prabodhu. 280.

Trans:

Then said Parshurām in tones of fury to Rāma: "Wretch, after breaking Shiva's bow do you now teach me?

चौपाई-caupāī:

बंधु कहइ कटु संमत तोरें । तू छल बिनय करसि कर जोरें ॥
baṁdhu kahai kaṭu saṁmata toreṁ, tū chala binaya karasi kara joreṁ.
करु परितोषु मोर संग्रामा । नाहिं त छाड़ कहाउब रामा ॥
karu paritoṣu mora saṁgrāmā, nāhiṁ ta chāṛa kahāuba rāmā.
छलु तजि करहि समरु सिवद्रोही । बंधु सहित न त मारउँ तोही ॥
chalu taji karahi samaru sivadrohī, baṁdhu sahita na ta mārauṁ tohī.
भृगुपति बकहिं कुठार उठाएँ । मन मुसुकाहिं रामु सिर नाएँ ॥
bhṛgupati bakahiṁ kuṭhāra uṭhāeṁ, mana musukāhiṁ rāmu sira nāeṁ.
गुनह लखन कर हम पर रोषू । कतहुँ सुधाइहु ते बड़ दोषू ॥
gunaha lakhana kara hama para roṣū, katahuṁ sudhāihu te baṛa doṣū.
टेढ़ जानि सब बंदइ काहू । बक्र चंद्रमहि ग्रसइ न राहू ॥
ṭeṛha jāni saba baṁdai kāhū, bakra caṁdramahi grasai na rāhū.
राम कहेउ रिस तजिअ मुनीसा । कर कुठारु आगें यह सीसा ॥
rāma kaheu risa tajia munīsā, kara kuṭhāru āgeṁ yaha sīsā.
जेहिं रिस जाइ करिअ सोइ स्वामी । मोहि जानिअ आपन अनुगामी ॥
jehiṁ risa jāi karia soi svāmī, mohi jānia āpana anugāmī.

Trans:

It is at your suggestion that your brother utters these sarcasms, and your humility and folded hands are a mockery. Give me my satisfaction in combat, or forswear your name of Rāma. You enemy of Shiva, have done with your tricks and meet me in battle, or I will slay both you and your brother too." Flushed with passion he raised his axe on high, but Rāma only smiled and bowed: "Though the fault is Lakshman's, your wrath is against me. At times, being much too virtuous is counted a negative, whereas a crooked man will be reverence by all—in the same way as Rāhu does not attack the crescent moon. Cease, O great saint, from your wrath." Said Rāma: "Your axe is in your hand and my head is in front of you; do anything, sir, that will tend to pacify you, for I am your servant.

दोहा-dohā:

प्रभुहि सेवकहि समरु कस तजहु बिप्रबर रोसु ।
prabhuhi sevakahi samaru kasa tajahu biprabara rosu,
बेषु बिलोकें कहेसि कछु बालकहू नहिं दोसु ॥ २८१ ॥
beṣu bilokeṁ kahesi kachu bālakahū nahiṁ dosu. 281.

Trans:

And how can a servant fight his master? O holy Brahmin, stop your wrath; if the boy said anything after looking at your attire he meant no harm.

चौपाई-caupāī:

देखि कुठार बान धनु धारी । भै लरिकहि रिस बीरु बिचारी ॥
dekhi kuṭhāra bāna dhanu dhārī, bhai larikahi risa bīru bicārī.
नामु जान पै तुम्हहि न चीन्हा । बंस सुभायँ उतरु तेहिं दीन्हा ॥
nāmu jāna pai tumhahi na cīnhā, baṁsa subhāyaṁ utaru tehiṁ dīnhā.
जौं तुम्ह औतेहु मुनि की नाईं । पद रज सिर सिसु धरत गोसाईं ॥
jauṁ tumha autehu muni kī nāīṁ, pada raja sira sisu dharata gosāīṁ.
छमहु चूक अनजानत केरी । चहिअ बिप्र उर कृपा घनेरी ॥
chamahu cūka anajānata kerī, cahia bipra ura kṛpā ghanerī.
हमहि तुम्हहि सरिबरि कसि नाथा । कहहु न कहाँ चरन कहँ माथा ॥
hamahi tumhahi saribari kasi nāthā, kahahu na kahāṁ carana kahaṁ māthā.
राम मात्र लघु नाम हमारा । परसु सहित बड़ नाम तोहारा ॥
rāma mātra laghu nāma hamārā, parasu sahita baṛa nāma tohārā.
देव एकु गुनु धनुष हमारें । नव गुन परम पुनीत तुम्हारें ॥
deva eku gunu dhanuṣa hamāreṁ, nava guna parama punīta tumhāreṁ.
सब प्रकार हम तुम्ह सन हारे । छमहु बिप्र अपराध हमारे ॥
saba prakāra hama tumha sana hāre, chamahu bipra aparādha hamāre.

Trans:

For seeing you equipped with axe and bow and arrows, the child took you for a knight and challenged you; for though he knew your name, he did not recognize your person, and answered you according to his lineage. If you had come as a Spiritual-Master, he would have put the dust of your holiness' feet upon his head. Forgive the mistake of one who did not know you; a Brahmin's heart should be all mercy. What equality, my lord, can there be between you and me? We are as far apart as head and feet. I am called simply Rāma. You have the long name of 'Rāma with the axe.' I have only one string to my bow, while you have all the holy nine. In every way I am your inferior. Being a Brahmin, please pardon my offence."

दोहा-dohā:

बार बार मुनि बिप्रबर कहा राम सन राम ।
bāra bāra muni biprabara kahā rāma sana rāma,
बोले भृगुपति सरुष हसि तहूँ बंधु सम बाम ॥२८२॥
bole bhṛgupati saruṣa hasi tahūṁ baṁdhu sama bāma. 282.

Trans:

Again and again did Rāma entreat his namesake, addressing him by his titles of 'Saint' and 'Holy Brahmin', till Bhrigupati exclaimed in his rage: "You are as perverse as your brother.

चौपाई-caupāī:

निपटहिं द्विज करि जानहि मोही । मैं जस बिप्र सुनावउँ तोही ॥
nipaṭahiṁ dvija kari jānahi mohī, maiṁ jasa bipra sunāvauṁ tohī.
चाप स्रुवा सर आहुति जानू । कोपु मोर अति घोर कृसानू ॥
cāpa sruvā sara āhuti jānū, kopu mora ati ghora kṛsānū.
समिधि सेन चतुरंग सुहाई । महा महीप भए पसु आई ॥
samidhi sena caturaṁga suhāī, mahā mahīpa bhae pasu āī.
मैं एहिं परसु काटि बलि दीन्हे । समर जग्य जप कोटिन्ह कीन्हे ॥
maiṁ ehiṁ parasu kāṭi bali dīnhe, samara jagya japa koṭinha kīnhe.
मोर प्रभाउ बिदित नहिं तोरें । बोलसि निदरि बिप्र के भोरें ॥
mora prabhāu bidita nahiṁ toreṁ, bolasi nidari bipra ke bhoreṁ.
भंजेउ चापु दापु बड़ बाढ़ा । अहमिति मनहुँ जीति जगु ठाढ़ा ॥
bhaṁjeu cāpu dāpu baṛa bāṛhā, ahamiti manahuṁ jīti jagu ṭhāṛhā.
राम कहा मुनि कहहु बिचारी । रिस अति बड़ि लघु चूक हमारी ॥
rāma kahā muni kahahu bicārī, risa ati baṛi laghu cūka hamārī.
छुअतहिं टूट पिनाक पुराना । मैं केहि हेतु करौं अभिमाना ॥
chuatahiṁ ṭūṭa pināka purānā, maiṁ kehi hetu karauṁ abhimānā.

Trans:

You persist in taking me for a Brahmin; I will tell you now what kind of a Brahmin I am. My bow is my sacrificial ladle, my arrow the oblation, and my wrath the blazing fire; armies fully equipt with horses and chariots and elephants and footmen are the fuel, and mighty kings are the victims for oblation, whom I have cut in pieces with this axe; thus have I celebrated countless sacrifices of war all over the world. To you my glory is unknown, and you address me contemptuously, taking me for a mere Brahmin. Now that you have broken the bow, your pride has increased enormously, and you put yourself forward in your arrogance as a universal conqueror." Said Rāma: "O saint, think before you speak; your anger is excessive, my fault is a trifling one. The old bow broke at a touch. What reason have I to be proud?

दोहा-dohā:

जौं हम निदरहिं बिप्र बदि सत्य सुनहु भृगुनाथ ।
jauṁ hama nidarahiṁ bipra badi satya sunahu bhṛgunātha,
तौ अस को जग सुभटु जेहि भय बस नावहिं माथ ॥२८३॥
tau asa ko jaga subhaṭu jehi bhaya basa nāvahiṁ mātha. 283.

Trans:

Hear the truth, O Bhrigunāth; you say I set you at naught when I treat you with the respect due to a Brahmin; but is there any warrior to whom I would bow my head in fear?

चौपाई-caupāī:

देव दनुज भूपति भट नाना । समबल अधिक होउ बलवाना ॥
deva danuja bhūpati bhaṭa nānā, samabala adhika hou balavānā.
जौं रन हमहि पचारै कोऊ । लरहिं सुखेन कालु किन होऊ ॥
jauṁ rana hamahi pacārai koū, larahiṁ sukhena kālu kina hoū.
छत्रिय तनु धरि समर सकाना । कुल कलंकु तेहि पावँर आना ॥
chatriya tanu dhari samara sakānā, kula kalaṁku tehi pāvaṁra ānā.
कहउँ सुभाउ न कुलहि प्रसंसी । कालहु डरहिं न रन रघुबंसी ॥
kahauṁ subhāu na kulahi prasaṁsī, kālahu ḍarahiṁ na rana raghubaṁsī.
बिप्रबंस कै असि प्रभुताई । अभय होइ जो तुम्हहि डेराई ॥
biprabaṁsa kai asi prabhutāī, abhaya hoi jo tumhahi ḍerāī.
सुनि मृदु गूढ़ बचन रघुपति के । उघरे पटल परसुधर मति के ॥
suni mṛdu gūṛha bacana raghupati ke, ughare paṭala parasudhara mati ke.
राम रमापति कर धनु लेहू । खैंचहु मिटै मोर संदेहू ॥
rāma ramāpati kara dhanu lehū, khaiṁcahu miṭai mora saṁdehū.
देत चापु आपुहिं चलि गयऊ । परसुराम मन बिसमय भयऊ ॥
deta cāpu āpuhiṁ cali gayaū, parasurāma mana bisamaya bhayaū.

Trans:

Any god, demon, king, or warrior, whether my equal in strength or my superior, who will challenge me to combat, him would I gladly meet—even Death himself. For one who is born of warrior caste and yet shirks the battle is a disgrace to his lineage and is a contemptible wretch. I state what is only a characteristic of my race and make no idle boast: there is not a descendant of Raghu who would fear to meet in battle even Death himself; but so great is the power of Brahminical descent that he fears you who fears naught else." On hearing this calm and profound speech of Rāma's, the eyes of the soul of the axe-bearer were opened: "O Rāma, take and draw this bow of Vishnu's and let my doubts be ended." As he offered his bow it simply glided into Rāma's hands out of its own accord, and Parshurām felt amazed at this.

दोहा-dohā:

जाना राम प्रभाउ तब पुलक प्रफुल्लित गात ।
jānā rāma prabhāu taba pulaka praphullita gāta,
जोरि पानि बोले बचन हृदयँ न प्रेमु अमात ॥२८४॥
jori pāni bole bacana hṛdayaṁ na premu amāta. 284.

Trans:

He acknowledged the power of Rāma; his whole frame quivered with excitement; and, his heart bursting with love, he thus spoke with clasped hands:

चौपाई-caupāī:

जय रघुबंस बनज बन भानू । गहन दनुज कुल दहन कृसानू ॥
jaya raghubaṁsa banaja bana bhānū, gahana danuja kula dahana kṛsānū.
जय सुर बिप्र धेनु हितकारी । जय मद मोह कोह भ्रम हारी ॥
jaya sura bipra dhenu hitakārī, jaya mada moha koha bhrama hārī.
बिनय सील करुना गुन सागर । जयति बचन रचना अति नागर ॥
binaya sīla karunā guna sāgara, jayati bacana racanā ati nāgara.
सेवक सुखद सुभग सब अंगा । जय सरीर छबि कोटि अनंगा ॥
sevaka sukhada subhaga saba aṁgā, jaya sarīra chabi koṭi anaṁgā.
करौं काह मुख एक प्रसंसा । जय महेस मन मानस हंसा ॥
karauṁ kāha mukha eka prasaṁsā, jaya mahesa mana mānasa haṁsā.
अनुचित बहुत कहेउँ अग्याता । छमहु छमामंदिर दोउ भ्राता ॥
anucita bahuta kaheuṁ agyātā, chamahu chamāmaṁdira dou bhrātā.
कहि जय जय जय रघुकुलकेतू । भृगुपति गए बनहि तप हेतू ॥
kahi jaya jaya jaya raghukulaketū, bhṛgupati gae banahi tapa hetū.
अपभयँ कुटिल महीप डेराने । जहँ तहँ कायर गवँहिं पराने ॥
apabhayaṁ kuṭila mahīpa ḍerāne, jahaṁ tahaṁ kāyara gavaṁhiṁ parāne.

Trans:

"Glory to the sun of the lotus race of Raghu, to the fire that consumes the serried ranks of the demons; glory to the friend of gods, Brahmins, and kine; glory to the dispeller of the delusions induced by pride, ignorance, and passion; glory to him whose piety, amiability, and compassion are fathomless as ocean; glory to him who is unrivalled in the art of speech, the rewarder of service, the all-beautiful of form, more gracious of person than a myriad Loves. How can I with one tongue declare his praise, who is as it were the divine swan in the hyperborean lake of Mahādev's soul? In my ignorance I have said much that was unseemly: but pardon me, ye twin brothers, shrines of mercy." Still repeating as he went, 'Glory, glory, glory to the mighty Rāma,' Bhrigupati withdrew to the forest to practice penance. The wicked kings were self-dismayed and trembled, and fled—the cowards—in all directions without a word.

दोहा-dohā:

देवन्ह दीन्हीं दुंदुभीं प्रभु पर बरषहिं फूल ।
devanha dīnhīṁ duṁdubhīṁ prabhu para baraṣahiṁ phūla,
हरषे पुर नर नारि सब मिटी मोहमय सूल ॥२८५॥
haraṣe pura nara nāri saba miṭī mohamaya sūla. 285.

Trans:

The gods sounded their kettledrums and rained down flowers on the Lord; and all the people of the city rejoiced, now that the thorn of fear and error had been extracted from their hearts.

चौपाई-caupāī:

अति गहगहे बाजने बाजे । सबहिं मनोहर मंगल साजे ॥
ati gahagahe bājane bāje, sabahiṁ manohara maṁgala sāje.
जूथ जूथ मिलि सुमुखि सुनयनीं । करहिं गान कल कोकिलबयनीं ॥
jūtha jūtha mili sumukhi sunayanīṁ, karahiṁ gāna kala kokilabayanīṁ.
सुखु बिदेह कर बरनि न जाई । जन्मदरिद्र मनहुँ निधि पाई ॥
sukhu bideha kara barani na jāī, janmadaridra manahuṁ nidhi pāī.
बिगत त्रास भइ सीय सुखारी । जनु बिधु उदयँ चकोरकुमारी ॥
bigata trāsa bhai sīya sukhārī, janu bidhu udayaṁ cakorakumārī.
जनक कीन्ह कौसिकहि प्रनामा । प्रभु प्रसाद धनु भंजेउ रामा ॥
janaka kīnha kausikahi pranāmā, prabhu prasāda dhanu bhaṁjeu rāmā.
मोहि कृतकृत्य कीन्ह दुहुँ भाईं । अब जो उचित सो कहिअ गोसाईं ॥
mohi kṛtakṛtya kīnha duhuṁ bhāīṁ, aba jo ucita so kahia gosāīṁ.
कह मुनि सुनु नरनाथ प्रबीना । रहा बिबाहु चाप आधीना ॥
kaha muni sunu naranātha prabīnā, rahā bibāhu cāpa ādhīnā.
टूटतहीं धनु भयउ बिबाहू । सुर नर नाग बिदित सब काहू ॥
ṭūṭatahīṁ dhanu bhayau bibāhū, sura nara nāga bidita saba kāhū.

Trans:

There was a tumultuous clash of instruments of music and a display of all things pleasant and auspicious. Troops of fair-faced bright-eyed maidens joined in song with voices of exquisite melody. Janak's delight was beyond description, as that of a born beggar who has found a treasure; and Sītā, relieved of her fears, was as glad as a young partridge at the rising of the moon. The king made obeisance before Vishwāmitra, saying: "It is by my lord's favor that Rāma has broken the bow. These two brothers have gained me my purpose: tell me now, reverend sir, what it becomes me to do." Said the saint : "Hearken, wise king, the marriage was dependent on the bow, and took effect directly the bow broke; this is well known to everyone, whether god, man, or Naga.

दोहा-dohā:

तदपि जाइ तुम्ह करहु अब जथा बंस ब्यवहारु ।
tadapi jāi tumha karahu aba jathā baṁsa byavahāru,
बूझि बिप्र कुलबृद्ध गुर बेद बिदित आचारु ॥२८६॥
būjhi bipra kulabṛddha gura beda bidita ācāru. 286.

Trans:

Still, go and perform, according to family usage, whatever practices are prescribed in the Veda, after consultation with the Brahmins and elders and your own Gurū;

चौपाई-caupāī:

दूत अवधपुर पठवहु जाई । आनहिं नृप दसरथहि बोलाई ॥
dūta avadhapura paṭhavahu jāī, ānahiṁ nṛpa dasarathahi bolāī.
मुदित राउ कहि भलेहिं कृपाला । पठए दूत बोलि तेहि काला ॥
mudita rāu kahi bhalehiṁ kṛpālā, paṭhae dūta boli tehi kālā.
बहुरि महाजन सकल बोलाए । आइ सबन्हि सादर सिर नाए ॥
bahuri mahājana sakala bolāe, āi sabanhi sādara sira nāe.
हाट बाट मंदिर सुरबासा । नगरु सँवारहु चारिहुँ पासा ॥
hāṭa bāṭa maṁdira surabāsā, nagaru saṁvārahu cārihuṁ pāsā.
हरषि चले निज निज गृह आए । पुनि परिचारक बोलि पठाए ॥
haraṣi cale nija nija gṛha āe, puni paricāraka boli paṭhāe.
रचहु बिचित्र बितान बनाई । सिर धरि बचन चले सचु पाई ॥
racahu bicitra bitāna banāī, sira dhari bacana cale sacu pāī.
पठए बोलि गुनी तिन्ह नाना । जे बितान बिधि कुसल सुजाना ॥
paṭhae boli gunī tinha nānā, je bitāna bidhi kusala sujānā.
बिधिहि बंदि तिन्ह कीन्ह अरंभा । बिरचे कनक कदलि के खंभा ॥
bidhihi baṁdi tinha kīnha araṁbhā, birace kanaka kadali ke khaṁbhā.

Trans:

and dispatch heralds to Avadh to invite king Dashrath." The king responded gladly: "Very well, gracious sir," and sent messengers to Avadh that very moment. Then he summoned all the burghers, who came, every one of them, and humbly bowing before him received the order: "Decorate all the markets and streets and temples and shrines in all four quarters of the city." They returned in joy, each to his own house. Then he called up his own servants and instructed them: "Have all kinds of pavilions made and erected." They obeyed in all gladness and sent word to the different artificers who were skillful in the construction of canopies and triumphal arches; and they, after invoking Brahmmā, set to work and made pillars of gold in the shape of plantain trees;

दोहा-dohā:

हरित मनिन्ह के पत्र फल पदुमराग के फूल ।
harita maninha ke patra phala padumarāga ke phūla,
रचना देखि बिचित्र अति मनु बिरंचि कर भूल ॥२८७॥
racanā dekhi bicitra ati manu biraṁci kara bhūla. 287.

Trans:

with leaves and fruit of emeralds, and ruby flowers; such a gorgeous show that the Creator himself was lost in bewilderment.

चौपाई-caupāī:

बेनु हरित मनिमय सब कीन्हे । सरल सपरब परहिं नहिं चीन्हे ॥
benu harita manimaya saba kīnhe, sarala saparaba parahiṁ nahiṁ cīnhe.
कनक कलित अहिबेलि बनाई । लखि नहिं परइ सपरन सुहाई ॥
kanaka kalita ahibeli banāī, lakhi nahiṁ parai saparana suhāī.
तेहि के रचि पचि बंध बनाए । बिच बिच मुकुता दाम सुहाए ॥
tehi ke raci paci baṁdha banāe, bica bica mukutā dāma suhāe.
मानिक मरकत कुलिस पिरोजा । चीरि कोरि पचि रचे सरोजा ॥
mānika marakata kulisa pirojā, cīri kori paci race sarojā.
किए भृंग बहुरंग बिहंगा । गुंजहिं कूजहिं पवन प्रसंगा ॥
kie bhṛṁga bahuraṁga bihaṁgā, guṁjahiṁ kūjahiṁ pavana prasaṁgā.
सुर प्रतिमा खंभन गढ़ि काढ़ीं । मंगल द्रब्य लिएँ सब ठाढ़ीं ॥
sura pratimā khaṁbhana gaṛhi kāṛhīṁ, maṁgala drabya lieṁ saba ṭhāṛhīṁ.
चौकें भाँति अनेक पुराईं । सिंधुर मनिमय सहज सुहाईं ॥
caukeṁ bhām̐ti aneka purāīṁ, siṁdhura manimaya sahaja suhāīṁ.

Trans:

The columns all encrusted with emeralds, and so like in form and color that no one could tell them from real, with betel leaves fashioned in gold so bright and glistening that no one could look at their dazzle. Then they worked up the leaves into wreaths, with strings of beautiful pearls inserted here and there, and after much cutting and graving and inlaying made lotuses of mosaic with rubies, emeralds, diamonds, and turquoises. Bees too they made, and birds of varied plumage, which buzzed and whistled in the rustling breeze; and on the pillars they sculptured figures of the gods, all standing tall with things of good omen in their hands. Squares were drawn on the ground and filled in with diverse devices made of elephant pearls of exquisite beauty.

दोहा-dohā:

सौरभ पल्लव सुभग सुठि किए नीलमनि कोरि ।
saurabha pallava subhaga suṭhi kie nīlamani kori,
हेम बौर मरकत घवरि लसत पाटमय डोरि ॥२८८॥
hema baura marakata ghavari lasata pāṭamaya ḍori. 288.

Trans:

There were also made most lovely mango-boughs of graven sapphires with blossoms of gold, while clusters of emerald fruit glistened on silken cords.

चौपाई-caupāī:

रचे रुचिर बर बंदनिवारे । मनहुँ मनोभवँ फंद सँवारे ॥
race rucira bara baṁdanivāre, manahum̐ manobhavam̐ phaṁda sam̐vāre.
मंगल कलस अनेक बनाए । ध्वज पताक पट चमर सुहाए ॥
maṁgala kalasa aneka banāe, dhvaja patāka paṭa camara suhāe.
दीप मनोहर मनिमय नाना । जाइ न बरनि बिचित्र बिताना ॥
dīpa manohara manimaya nānā, jāi na barani bicitra bitānā.
जेहिं मंडप दुलहिनि बैदेही । सो बरनै असि मति कबि केही ॥
jehiṁ maṁḍapa dulahini baidehī, so baranai asi mati kabi kehī.
दूलहु रामु रूप गुन सागर । सो बितानु तिहुँ लोक उजागर ॥
dūlahu rāmu rūpa guna sāgara, so bitānu tihum̐ loka ujāgara.
जनक भवन कै सोभा जैसी । गृह गृह प्रति पुर देखिअ तैसी ॥
janaka bhavana kai sobhā jaisī, gṛha gṛha prati pura dekhia taisī.
जेहिं तेरहुति तेहि समय निहारी । तेहि लघु लगहिं भुवन दस चारी ॥
jehiṁ terahuti tehi samaya nihārī, tehi laghu lagahiṁ bhuvana dasa cārī.
जो संपदा नीच गृह सोहा । सो बिलोकि सुरनायक मोहा ॥
jo saṁpadā nīca gṛha sohā, so biloki suranāyaka mohā.

Trans:

And they made charming festoons as it were Love's own nooses, and many golden vases with silken flags and banners and waving fans, and elegant lamps all studded with gems. It is impossible to describe the various pavilions, and in particular the one intended for the royal bride—for what poet would have the hardihood to attempt its description? The canopy meant for Rāma, the bridegroom, the centre of all beauty and perfection, flashed its splendor through all three worlds. In every house throughout the city there was the same splendor as in Janak's palace; anyone who then saw Trihut thought there was nothing in the fourteen spheres to compare with it; and the prosperous appearance of even the very meanest house was enough to fascinate the king of heaven.

दोहा-dohā:

बसइ नगर जेहिं लच्छि करि कपट नारि बर बेषु ।
basai nagara jehiṁ lacchi kari kapaṭa nāri bara beṣu,
तेहि पुर कै सोभा कहत सकुचहिं सारद सेषु ॥२८९॥
tehi pura kai sobhā kahata sakucahiṁ sārada seṣu. 289.

Trans:

The splendor of the city inhabited by goddess Lakshmī—in the guise of a woman—was more than even Shārdā or Sheshnāg could tell.

चौपाई-caupāī:

पहुँचे दूत राम पुर पावन । हरषे नगर बिलोकि सुहावन ॥
pahum̐ce dūta rāma pura pāvana, haraṣe nagara biloki suhāvana.
भूप द्वार तिन्ह खबरि जनाई । दसरथ नृप सुनि लिए बोलाई ॥
bhūpa dvāra tinha khabari janāī, dasaratha nṛpa suni lie bolāī.
करि प्रनामु तिन्ह पाती दीन्ही । मुदित महीप आपु उठि लीन्ही ॥
kari pranāmu tinha pātī dīnhī, mudita mahīpa āpu uṭhi līnhī.
बारि बिलोचन बाँचत पाती । पुलक गात आई भरि छाती ॥
bāri bilocana bām̐cata pātī, pulaka gāta āī bhari chātī.
रामु लखनु उर कर बर चीठी । रहि गए कहत न खाटी मीठी ॥
rāmu lakhanu ura kara bara cīṭhī, rahi gae kahata na khāṭī mīṭhī.
पुनि धरि धीर पत्रिका बाँची । हरषी सभा बात सुनि साँची ॥
puni dhari dhīra patrikā bām̐cī, haraṣī sabhā bāta suni sām̐cī.
खेलत रहे तहाँ सुधि पाई । आए भरतु सहित हित भाई ॥
khelata rahe tahām̐ sudhi pāī, āe bharatu sahita hita bhāī.
पूछत अति सनेहँ सकुचाई । तात कहाँ तें पाती आई ॥
pūchata ati saneham̐ sakucāī, tāta kahām̐ teṁ pātī āī.

Trans:

Meanwhile when Janak's heralds arrived at Rāma's sacred birthplace they rejoiced to see the beauty of the city. At the royal gate they sent in the word, and king Dashrath at once summoned them in his presence. With a profound salutation they delivered the letter, and the king himself in his joy rose to receive it. As he read it, tears rushed to his eyes, his body quivered all over, and his heart seemed full. With Rāma and Lakshman in his soul, and the precious letter in his hand, he could not utter a single word this way or that. At last, composing himself, he read aloud the letter, and all the court rejoiced to hear the grand news. Now Bharat was playing about, and on hearing the tidings he came there with his brother and playmates, and with the utmost modesty and affection asked, "Father, where has the letter come from?

दोहा-dohā:

कुसल प्रानप्रिय बंधु दोउ अहहिं कहहु केहिं देस ।
kusala prānapriya baṁdhu dou ahahiṁ kahahu kehiṁ desa,
सुनि सनेह साने बचन बाची बहुरि नरेस ॥२९०॥
suni saneha sāne bacana bācī bahuri naresa. 290.

Trans:

Is all well with my two dear brothers? Tell me what country they are in?" On hearing these loving words the king again read the letter.

चौपाई-caupāī:

सुनि पाती पुलके दोउ भ्राता । अधिक सनेहु समात न गाता ॥
suni pātī pulake dou bhrātā, adhika sanehu samāta na gātā.
प्रीति पुनीत भरत कै देखी । सकल सभाँ सुखु लहेउ बिसेषी ॥
prīti punīta bharata kai dekhī, sakala sabhāṁ sukhu laheu biseṣī.
तब नृप दूत निकट बैठारे । मधुर मनोहर बचन उचारे ॥
taba nṛpa dūta nikaṭa baiṭhāre, madhura manohara bacana ucāre.
भैया कहहु कुसल दोउ बारे । तुम्ह नीकें निज नयन निहारे ॥
bhaiyā kahahu kusala dou bāre, tumha nīkeṁ nija nayana nihāre.
स्यामल गौर धरें धनु भाथा । बय किसोर कौसिक मुनि साथा ॥
syāmala gaura dhareṁ dhanu bhāthā, baya kisora kausika muni sāthā.
पहिचानहु तुम्ह कहहु सुभाऊ । प्रेम बिबस पुनि पुनि कह राऊ ॥
pahicānahu tumha kahahu subhāū, prema bibasa puni puni kaha rāū.
जा दिन तें मुनि गए लवाई । तब तें आजु साँचि सुधि पाई ॥
jā dina teṁ muni gae lavāī, taba teṁ āju sāṁci sudhi pāī.
कहहु बिदेह कवन बिधि जाने । सुनि प्रिय बचन दूत मुसुकाने ॥
kahahu bideha kavana bidhi jāne, suni priya bacana dūta musukāne.

Trans:

On hearing it the two brothers trembled all over with irrepressible joy, and the whole court was charmed to see Bharat's holy devotion. Then the king seated the messengers close by him and said in sweet and winning tones: "Tell me, friend, are the two boys well? Have you really seen them with your own eyes?" "One is dark, the other fair; both are equipt with bow and quiver, and are of tender age, and with them is saint Vishwāmitra." Said the king again and again in his overpowering love: "You do know them—right? To be sure, describe them to me. From the day that the saint took them away till now I have had no definite news of them. Tell me how Janak knew about them." At these fond words the messengers smiled,

दोहा-dohā:

सुनहु महीपति मुकुट मनि तुम्ह सम धन्य न कोउ ।
sunahu mahīpati mukuṭa mani tumha sama dhanya na kou,
रामु लखनु जिन्ह के तनय बिस्व बिभूषन दोउ ॥२९१॥
rāmu lakhanu jinha ke tanaya bisva bibhūṣana dou. 291.

Trans:

"Hearken, O jewel and crown of kings; there is no man so blessed as you, who have for sons Rāma and Lakshman, who are the glory of the whole world.

चौपाई-caupāī:

पूछन जोगु न तनय तुम्हारे । पुरुषसिंघ तिहु पुर उजिआरे ॥
pūchana jogu na tanaya tumhāre, puruṣasiṁgha tihu pura ujiāre.
जिन्ह के जस प्रताप कें आगे । ससि मलीन रबि सीतल लागे ॥
jinha ke jasa pratāpa keṁ āge, sasi malīna rabi sītala lāge.
तिन्ह कहँ कहिअ नाथ किमि चीन्हे । देखिअ रबि कि दीप कर लीन्हे ॥
tinha kahaṁ kahia nātha kimi cīnhe, dekhia rabi ki dīpa kara līnhe.
सीय स्वयंबर भूप अनेका । समिटे सुभट एक तें एका ॥
sīya svayaṁbara bhūpa anekā, samiṭe subhaṭa eka teṁ ekā.
संभु सरासनु काहुँ न टारा । हारे सकल बीर बरिआरा ॥
saṁbhu sarāsanu kāhuṁ na ṭārā, hāre sakala bīra bariārā.
तीनि लोक महँ जे भटमानी । सभ कै सकति संभु धनु भानी ॥
tīni loka mahaṁ je bhaṭamānī, sabha kai sakati saṁbhu dhanu bhānī.
सकइ उठाइ सरासुर मेरू । सोउ हियँ हारि गयउ करि फेरू ॥
sakai uṭhāi sarāsura merū, sou hiyaṁ hāri gayau kari pherū.
जेहिं कौतुक सिवसैलु उठावा । सोउ तेहि सभाँ पराभउ पावा ॥
jehiṁ kautuka sivasailu uṭhāvā, sou tehi sabhāṁ parābhau pāvā.

Trans:

There is no need to ask who are your sons, for they are the lion-hearted heroes who irradiate the three spheres. Before their glory and renown the moon is dim and the sun is cold. Why say, my lord, how they were recognized? Does one take a lamp in his hand in order to see the sun? The countless kings at Sītā's marriage, great warriors as they were, all shrunk away one after the other; for not one of them could stir Shambhu's bow; they all failed, all those mighty princes. The power of the haughtiest champions in the three worlds was crushed by it. Though Bānāsur could uproot Mount Meru, even he confessed himself beaten, and retired after pacing around it; and Rāvan, who in sport uplifted Kailāsh was worsted in the assembly and left.

दोहा-dohā:

तहाँ राम रघुबंस मनि सुनिअ महा महिपाल ।
tahāṁ rāma raghubaṁsa mani sunia mahā mahipāla,
भंजेउ चाप प्रयास बिनु जिमि गज पंकज नाल ॥२९२॥
bhaṁjeu cāpa prayāsa binu jimi gaja paṁkaja nāla. 292.

Trans:

Hearken O sovereign lord, it was Rāma, the jewel of Raghu's line, who snapped the bow with as little effort as an elephant would put forth in breaking the stalk of a lotus.

चौपाई-caupāī:

सुनि सरोष भृगुनायकु आए । बहुत भाँति तिन्ह आँखि देखाए ॥
suni saroṣa bhṛgunāyaku āe, bahuta bhāṁti tinha āṁkhi dekhāe.
देखि राम बलु निज धनु दीन्हा । करि बहु बिनय गवनु बन कीन्हा ॥
dekhi rāma balu nija dhanu dīnhā, kari bahu binaya gavanu bana kīnhā.
राजन रामु अतुलबल जैसें । तेज निधान लखनु पुनि तैसें ॥
rājana rāmu atulabala jaiseṁ, teja nidhāna lakhanu puni taiseṁ.
कंपहिं भूप बिलोकत जाकें । जिमि गज हरि किसोर के ताकें ॥
kaṁpahiṁ bhūpa bilokata jākeṁ, jimi gaja hari kisora ke tākeṁ.
देव देखि तव बालक दोऊ । अब न आँखि तर आवत कोऊ ॥
deva dekhi tava bālaka doū, aba na āṁkhi tara āvata koū.
दूत बचन रचना प्रिय लागी । प्रेम प्रताप बीर रस पागी ॥
dūta bacana racanā priya lāgī, prema pratāpa bīra rasa pāgī.
सभा समेत राउ अनुरागे । दूतन्ह देन निछावरि लागे ॥
sabhā sameta rāu anurāge, dūtanha dena nichāvari lāge.
कहि अनीति ते मूदहिं काना । धरमु बिचारि सबहिं सुखु माना ॥
kahi anīti te mūdahiṁ kānā, dharamu bicāri sabahiṁ sukhu mānā.

Trans:

At these tidings Parshurām came in a fury, and after much browbeating gave Rāma his own bow to test his strength, then suppliantly withdrew to the woods. Even as Rāma, O king, is unequalled in strength, Lakshman too is a mine of glory, at whose very sight the kings trembled as elephants at the gaze of a young lion. No one who sees your two sons, sir, can regard anything else on earth." At this eloquent and affectionate speech of the heralds, so loving, grand, and heroic, the king and his court were much moved, and began to offer them lavish gifts; but they closed their ears in protest, crying, "No, no, that's not right, we can't accept." All were charmed to see their integrity.

दोहा-dohā:

तब उठि भूप बसिष्ट कहुँ दीन्हि पत्रिका जाइ ।
taba uṭhi bhūpa basiṣṭa kahuṁ dīnhi patrikā jāi,
कथा सुनाई गुरहि सब सादर दूत बोलाइ ॥२९३॥
kathā sunāī gurahi saba sādara dūta bolāi. 293.

Trans:

The king then left and went straight to Guru Vasishtha to give him the letter, and sending courteously for the envoys, again related all the circumstance.

चौपाई-caupāī:

सुनि बोले गुर अति सुखु पाई । पुन्य पुरुष कहुँ महि सुख छाई ॥
suni bole gura ati sukhu pāī, punya puruṣa kahuṁ mahi sukha chāī.
जिमि सरिता सागर महुँ जाहीं । जद्यपि ताहि कामना नाहीं ॥
jimi saritā sāgara mahuṁ jāhīṁ, jadyapi tāhi kāmanā nāhīṁ.
तिमि सुख संपति बिनहिं बोलाएँ । धरमसील पहिं जाहिं सुभाएँ ॥
timi sukha saṁpati binahiṁ bolāeṁ, dharamasīla pahiṁ jāhiṁ subhāeṁ.
तुम्ह गुर बिप्र धेनु सुर सेबी । तसि पुनीत कौसल्या देबी ॥
tumha gura bipra dhenu sura sebī, tasi punīta kausalyā debī.
सुकृती तुम्ह समान जग माहीं । भयउ न है कोउ होनेउ नाहीं ॥
sukṛtī tumha samāna jaga māhīṁ, bhayau na hai kou honeu nāhīṁ.
तुम्ह ते अधिक पुन्य बड़ कार्कें । राजन राम सरिस सुत जार्कें ॥
tumha te adhika punya baṛa kākeṁ, rājana rāma sarisa suta jākeṁ.
बीर बिनीत धरम ब्रत धारी । गुन सागर बर बालक चारी ॥
bīra binīta dharama brata dhārī, guna sāgara bara bālaka cārī.
तुम्ह कहुँ सर्ब काल कल्याना । सजहु बरात बजाइ निसाना ॥
tumha kahuṁ sarba kāla kalyānā, sajahu barāta bajāi nisānā.

Trans:

After hearing them the saint was highly pleased and said: "To a good man the world is full of happiness. As rivers run into the sea, though it has no greed for them, so joy and prosperity come unasked and of their own accord to a virtuous soul. Strict in the performance of your duties to your Gurū and to Brahmins, and kine and gods—and your queen Kausalyā no less devout than yourself—you have no equals for piety in the whole world—either now, or in past, nor hereafter. Who, O king, can be more blessed than you, who has a son like Rāma; nay, four heroic sons, all equally obedient, religious, and amiable. Happy, indeed, are you for all time. Now go ahead, prepare the marriage procession to the sounds of music;

दोहा-dohā:

चलहु बेगि सुनि गुर बचन भलेहिं नाथ सिरु नाइ ।
calahu begi suni gura bacana bhalehiṁ nātha siru nāi,
भूपति गवने भवन तब दूतन्ह बासु देवाइ ॥२९४॥
bhūpati gavane bhavana taba dūtanha bāsu devāi. 294.

Trans:

and proceed quickly!" On hearing the saint's commands the king bowed in assent, and hastened to the palace, after assigning quarters to the heralds.

चौपाई-caupāī:

राजा सबु रनिवास बोलाई । जनक पत्रिका बाचि सुनाई ॥
rājā sabu ranivāsa bolāī, janaka patrikā bāci sunāī.
सुनि संदेसु सकल हरषानीं । अपर कथा सब भूप बखानीं ॥
suni saṁdesu sakala haraṣānīṁ, apara kathā saba bhūpa bakhānīṁ.
प्रेम प्रफुल्लित राजहिं रानी । मनहुँ सिखिनि सुनि बारिद बानी ॥
prema praphullita rājahiṁ rānī, manahuṁ sikhini suni bārida bānī.
मुदित असीस देहिं गुर नारीं । अति आनंद मगन महतारीं ॥
mudita asīsa dehiṁ gura nārīṁ, ati ānaṁda magana mahatārīṁ.
लेहिं परस्पर अति प्रिय पाती । हृदयँ लगाइ जुड़ावहिं छाती ॥
lehiṁ paraspara ati priya pātī, hṛdayaṁ lagāi juṛāvahiṁ chātī.
राम लखन कै कीरति करनी । बारहिं बार भूपबर बरनी ॥
rāma lakhana kai kīrati karanī, bārahiṁ bāra bhūpabara baranī.
मुनि प्रसादु कहि द्वार सिधाए । रानिन्ह तब महिदेव बोलाए ॥
muni prasādu kahi dvāra sidhāe, rāninha taba mahideva bolāe.
दिए दान आनंद समेता । चले बिप्रबर आसिष देता ॥
die dāna ānaṁda sametā, cale biprabara āsiṣa detā.

Trans:

Then the King called all the ladies of the gynoecium and himself read aloud to them Janak's letter. All rejoiced greatly at the news, and the King told them all the verbal messages as well. The queens were as ecstatic with delight as a peacock at the sound of approaching rain. The Gurū's wife and other elders, in their joy, invoked the blessings of heaven, while the queen-mothers were completely overwhelmed with rapture. They take the precious letter from one to another, and press it to their bosom to cool as it were their burning heart. The great king recounted again and again the glory and exploits of both Rāma and Lakshman; and saying that it was all due to the sage's grace, he went out the door. Then the ladies sent for the Brahmins and joyfully made them offerings; and giving their blessings, the holy men returned.

सोरठा-soraṭhā:

जाचक लिए हँकारि दीन्हि निछावरि कोटि बिधि ।
jācaka lie haṁkāri dīnhi nichāvari koṭi bidhi,
चिरु जीवहुँ सुत चारि चक्रबर्ति दसरत्थ के ॥२९५॥
ciru jīvahuṁ suta cāri cakrabarti dasarattha ke. 295.

Trans:

Next they called together the mendicants and seekers and lavished every kind of gift upon them. "May the four sons of the Emperor Dashrath live forever"—

चौपाई-caupāī:

कहत चले पहिरें पट नाना । हरषि हने गहगहे निसाना ॥
kahata cale pahireṁ paṭa nānā, haraṣi hane gahagahe nisānā.
समाचार सब लोगन्ह पाए । लागे घर घर होन बधाए ॥
samācāra saba loganha pāe, lāge ghara ghara hona badhāe.
भुवन चारि दस भरा उछाहू । जनकसुता रघुबीर बिआहू ॥
bhuvana cāri dasa bharā uchāhū, janakasutā raghubīra biāhū.
सुनि सुभ कथा लोग अनुरागे । मग गृह गलीं सँवारन लागे ॥
suni subha kathā loga anurāge, maga gṛha galīṁ saṁvārana lāge.
जद्यपि अवध सदैव सुहावनि । राम पुरी मंगलमय पावनि ॥
jadyapi avadha sadaiva suhāvani, rāma purī maṁgalamaya pāvani.
तदपि प्रीति कै प्रीति सुहाई । मंगल रचना रची बनाई ॥
tadapi prīti kai prīti suhāī, maṁgala racanā racī banāī.
ध्वज पताक पट चामर चारु । छावा परम बिचित्र बजारू ॥
dhvaja patāka paṭa cāmara cāru, chāvā parama bicitra bajārū.
कनक कलस तोरन मनि जाला । हरद दूब दधि अच्छत माला ॥
kanaka kalasa torana mani jālā, harada dūba dadhi acchata mālā.

Trans:

—thus they shouted as they left, attired in raiments of many colors. There was a jubilant clamor of music and in every house, as the news spread among the people, there were joyous congratulations. The fourteen spheres, were fulfilled with delight at the marriage of Raghubīr with the daughter of Janak. When they heard the glad tidings, the citizens were enraptured and began decorating the roads and houses and streets; for although Avadh in itself was a charming place, and clean and pure—being Rāma's home, yet as the natural outcome of its love, it garnished and adorned itself still more with festal decorations. Silken flags and banners and graceful chauries crested the gay bazaar; and at every turn were golden jars and festoons of netted pearls and heaps of turmeric, *dūba* grass, curds, rice, and garlands of flowers.

दोहा-*dohā:*

मंगलमय निज निज भवन लोगन्ह रचे बनाइ ।
maṁgalamaya nija nija bhavana loganha race banāi,
बीथीं सींचीं चतुरसम चौकें चारु पुराइ ॥२९६॥
bīthīṁ sīṁcīṁ caturasama caukeṁ cāru purāi. 296.

Trans:

Everyone decorated their house; the streets were duly watered, and every square was filled in with some tasteful design.

चौपाई-*caupāī:*

जहँ तहँ जूथ जूथ मिलि भामिनि । सजि नव सप्त सकल दुति दामिनि ॥
jahaṁ tahaṁ jūtha jūtha mili bhāmini, saji nava sapta sakala duti dāmini.
बिधुबदनीं मृग सावक लोचनि । निज सरुप रति मानु बिमोचनि ॥
bidhubadanīṁ mṛga sāvaka locani, nija sarupa rati mānu bimocani.
गावहिं मंगल मंजुल बानीं । सुनि कल रव कलकंठि लजानीं ॥
gāvahiṁ maṁgala maṁjula bānīṁ, suni kala rava kalakaṁṭhi lajānīṁ.
भूप भवन किमि जाइ बखाना । बिस्व बिमोहन रचेउ बिताना ॥
bhūpa bhavana kimi jāi bakhānā, bisva bimohana raceu bitānā.
मंगल द्रब्य मनोहर नाना । राजत बाजत बिपुल निसाना ॥
maṁgala drabya manohara nānā, rājata bājata bipula nisānā.
कतहुँ बिरिद बंदी उच्चरहीं । कतहुँ बेद धुनि भूसुर करहीं ॥
katahuṁ birida baṁdī uccarahīṁ, katahuṁ beda dhuni bhūsura karahīṁ.
गावहिं सुंदरि मंगल गीता । लै लै नामु रामु अरु सीता ॥
gāvahiṁ suṁdari maṁgala gītā, lai lai nāmu rāmu aru sītā.
बहुत उछाहु भवनु अति थोरा । मानहुँ उमगि चला चहु ओरा ॥
bahuta uchāhu bhavanu ati thorā, mānahuṁ umagi calā cahu orā.

Trans:

Collected here and there, troops of ladies, all brilliant as the lightning, with moon-like face and eyes resembling those of a fawn and beauty enough to rob Love's consort of her pride, and who had practiced all the sixteen kinds of female adornments, sang auspicious strains with voices so melodious that the female cuckoo was put to shame on hearing their sweet sound! How is the king's palace to be described? The pavilion they set up would dazzle the world. Everything beautiful and of fair omen was displayed, and every kind of music was heard. Here were rhapsodists chanting songs of praise; and there Brahmins muttering Vedic spells; and elsewhere were lovely women that caroled joyous songs, ever dwelling on the names of Sītā-Rāma. The joy was so great that the palace was too small for it, and it overflowed on all four sides.

दोहा-*dohā:*

सोभा दसरथ भवन कइ को कबि बरनै पार ।
sobhā dasaratha bhavana kai ko kabi baranai pāra,
जहाँ सकल सुर सीस मनि राम लीन्ह अवतार ॥२९७॥
jahāṁ sakala sura sīsa mani rāma līnha avatāra. 297.

Trans:

What poet can describe in full the magnificence of the palace of Dashrath, in which Rāma, the glory of highest heaven, took Avatār?

चौपाई-*caupāī:*

भूप भरत पुनि लिए बोलाई । हय गय स्यंदन साजहु जाई ॥
bhūpa bharata puni lie bolāī, haya gaya syaṁdana sājahu jāī.
चलहु बेगि रघुबीर बराता । सुनत पुलक पूरे दोउ भ्राता ॥
calahu begi raghubīra barātā, sunata pulaka pūre dou bhrātā.
भरत सकल साहनी बोलाए । आयसु दीन्ह मुदित उठि धाए ॥
bharata sakala sāhanī bolāe, āyasu dīnha mudita uṭhi dhāe.
रचि रुचि जीन तुरग तिन्ह साजे । बरन बरन बर बाजि बिराजे ॥
raci ruci jīna turaga tinha sāje, barana barana bara bāji birāje.
सुभग सकल सुठि चंचल करनी । अय इव जरत धरत पग धरनी ॥
subhaga sakala suṭhi caṁcala karanī, aya iva jarata dharata paga dharanī.
नाना जाति न जाहिं बखाने । निदरि पवनु जनु चहत उड़ाने ॥
nānā jāti na jāhiṁ bakhāne, nidari pavanu janu cahata uṛāne.
तिन्ह सब छयल भए असवारा । भरत सरिस बय राजकुमारा ॥
tinha saba chayala bhae asavārā, bharata sarisa baya rājakumārā.
सब सुंदर सब भूषनधारी । कर सर चाप तून कटि भारी ॥
saba suṁdara saba bhūṣanadhārī, kara sara cāpa tūna kaṭi bhārī.

Trans:

Next the king called Bharat, "Go and prepare horses and elephants and chariots and commence with speed for Raghubīr's marriage procession." When they heard this order, both brothers were full of excitement. Bharat sent for all the chief officers and issued his commands, and they rose in joy and haste to perform them. First they made gorgeous trappings for the horses. Of different colors were the gallant steeds, all well-proportioned and mettlesome, touching the ground with their feet as lightly as though it were red-hot iron. All the various breeds cannot be told, but they could race the wind and outstrip it. The princes who mounted them were all like Bharat—graceful, beautiful, and gorgeously attired, with bow and arrows in hand, and well-filled quiver fastened at their side.

दोहा-*dohā:*

छरे छबीले छयल सब सूर सुजान नबीन ।
chare chabīle chayala saba sūra sujāna nabīna,
जुग पदचर असवार प्रति जे असिकला प्रबीन ॥२९८॥
juga padacara asavāra prati je asikalā prabīna. 298.

Trans:

Slim, elegant, and lithesome youths, and expert warriors all; and with each knight were two footmen, well skilled in the sport of sword.

चौपाई-*caupāī:*

बाँधें बिरद बीर रन गाढ़े । निकसि भए पुर बाहेर ठाढ़े ॥
bāṁdheṁ birada bīra rana gāṛhe, nikasi bhae pura bāhera ṭhāṛhe.
फेरहिं चतुर तुरग गति नाना । हरषहिं सुनि सुनि पनव निसाना ॥
pherahiṁ catura turaga gati nānā, haraṣahiṁ suni suni panava nisānā.
रथ सारथिन्ह बिचित्र बनाए । ध्वज पताक मनि भूषन लाए ॥
ratha sārathinha bicitra banāe, dhvaja patāka mani bhūṣana lāe.
चवँर चारु किंकिनि धुनि करहीं । भानु जान सोभा अपहरहीं ॥
cavaṁra cāru kiṁkini dhuni karahīṁ, bhānu jāna sobhā apaharahīṁ.
सावँकरन अगनित हय होते । ते तिन्ह रथन्ह सारथिन्ह जोते ॥
sāvaṁkarana aganita haya hote, te tinha rathanha sārathinha jote.
सुंदर सकल अलंकृत सोहे । जिन्हहि बिलोकत मुनि मन मोहे ॥
suṁdara sakala alaṁkṛta sohe, jinhahi bilokata muni mana mohe.
जे जल चलहिं थलहि की नाईं । टाप न बूड़ बेग अधिकाईं ॥
je jala calahiṁ thalahi kī nāīṁ, ṭāpa na būṛa bega adhikāīṁ.
अस्त्र सस्त्र सबु साजु बनाई । रथी सारथिन्ह लिए बोलाई ॥
astra sastra sabu sāju banāī, rathī sārathinha lie bolāī.

Trans:

Full of high resolve the warriors, staunch in fight, sallied forth and halted outside the city, putting their well-trained steeds through all their paces and rejoicing in the clash of tabor and drums. The charioteers had made their cars equally gorgeous with flags and banners and jeweled adornments, with elegant chauries and tinkling bells, so as to outdo in splendor the chariot of the Sun. Innumerable were the black-eared horses which the grooms yoked to the chariots, and all were so beautiful and richly caparisoned that even a saint would be enraptured at the sight. Skimming the surface of the water like dry land, nor sinking even hoof-deep, so marvelous was their speed. After completing their equipment of armor and weapons, the charioteers gave word to their masters,

दोहा-*dohā:*

चढ़ि चढ़ि रथ बाहेर नगर लागी जुरन बरात ।
caṛhi caṛhi ratha bāhera nagara lāgī jurana barāta,
होत सगुन सुंदर सबहि जो जेहि कारज जात ॥२९९॥
hota saguna suṁdara sabahi jo jehi kāraja jāta. 299.

Trans:

who all mounted in turn, and the procession began to form outside the city. All, whatever the object on which they were bent, were met by auspicious omens.

चौपाई-*caupāī:*

कलित करिबरन्हि परीं अँबारीं । कहि न जाहिं जेहि भाँति सँवारीं ॥
kalita karibaranhi parīṁ aṁbārīṁ, kahi na jāhiṁ jehi bhāṁti saṁvārīṁ.
चले मत्त गज घंट बिराजी । मनहुँ सुभग सावन घन राजी ॥
cale matta gaja ghaṁṭa birājī, manahuṁ subhaga sāvana ghana rājī.
बाहन अपर अनेक बिधाना । सिबिका सुभग सुखासन जाना ॥
bāhana apara aneka bidhānā, sibikā subhaga sukhāsana jānā.
तिन्ह चढ़ि चले बिप्रबर बृंदा । जनु तनु धरें सकल श्रुति छंदा ॥
tinha caṛhi cale biprabara bṛṁdā, janu tanu dhareṁ sakala śruti chaṁdā.
मागध सूत बंदि गुनगायक । चले जान चढ़ि जो जेहि लायक ॥
māgadha sūta baṁdi gunagāyaka, cale jāna caṛhi jo jehi lāyaka.
बेसर ऊँट बृषभ बहु जाती । चले बस्तु भरि अगनित भाँती ॥
besara ūṁṭa bṛṣabha bahu jātī, cale bastu bhari aganita bhāṁtī.
कोटिन्ह काँवरि चले कहारा । बिबिध बस्तु को बरनै पारा ॥
koṭinha kāṁvari cale kahārā, bibidha bastu ko baranai pārā.
चले सकल सेवक समुदाई । निज निज साजु समाजु बनाई ॥
cale sakala sevaka samudāī, nija nija sāju samāju banāī.

Trans:

On the magnificent elephants were splendid canopies, wrought in a manner beyond all words. As the mighty elephants moved, the bells clanged like the thunder from the clouds in the grateful month of *Sāwan*. And other vehicles were there of many kinds: elegant *Pālkīs* and sedans and coaches, wherein were seated companies of noble Brahmins, incarnations as it were of all the hymns of the Vedas. The genealogists and bards and minstrels and rhapsodists were mounted on other cars according to their rank; while mules and camels and oxen of every breed were laden with all sorts of baggage; there were also innumerous *kahars* with burdens slung across their shoulders; and who could enumerate such endless list of things and the crowd of servants, each with his own set of appliances?

दोहा-*dohā:*

सब कें उर निर्भर हरषु पूरित पुलक सरीर ।
saba keṁ ura nirbhara haraṣu pūrita pulaka sarīra,
कबहिं देखिबे नयन भरि रामु लखनु दोउ बीर ॥३००॥
kabahiṁ dekhibe nayana bhari rāmu lakhanu dou bīra. 300.

Trans:

All were glad and fearless of heart, and were quivering with excitement in every limb, saying: "When shall we feast our eyes with the sight of the two heroes, Rāma and Lakshman?"

चौपाई-*caupāī:*

गरजहिं गज घंटा धुनि घोरा । रथ रव बाजि हिंस चहु ओरा ॥
garajahiṁ gaja ghaṁṭā dhuni ghorā, ratha rava bāji hiṁsa cahu orā.
निदरि घनहि घुर्म्मरहिं निसाना । निज पराइ कछु सुनिअ न काना ॥
nidari ghanahi ghurmmarahiṁ nisānā, nija parāi kachu sunia na kānā.
महा भीर भूपति के द्वारें । रज होइ जाइ पषान पबारें ॥
mahā bhīra bhūpati ke dvāreṁ, raja hoi jāi paṣāna pabāreṁ.
चढ़ी अटारिन्ह देखहिं नारीं । लिएँ आरती मंगल थारीं ॥
caṛhī aṭārinha dekhahiṁ nārīṁ, lieṁ āratī maṁgala thārīṁ.
गावहिं गीत मनोहर नाना । अति आनंदु न जाइ बखाना ॥
gāvahiṁ gīta manohara nānā, ati ānaṁdu na jāi bakhānā.
तब सुमंत्र दुइ स्यंदन साजी । जोते रबि हय निंदक बाजी ॥
taba sumaṁtra dui syaṁdana sājī, jote rabi haya niṁdaka bājī.
दोउ रथ रुचिर भूप पहिं आने । नहिं सारद पहिं जाहिं बखाने ॥
dou ratha rucira bhūpa pahiṁ āne, nahiṁ sārada pahiṁ jāhiṁ bakhāne.
राज समाजु एक रथ साजा । दूसर तेज पुंज अति भ्राजा ॥
rāja samāju eka ratha sājā, dūsara teja puṁja ati bhrājā.

Trans:

The elephants' bells clanged with a fearful din; on all sides there was a creaking of wheels and a neighing of horses; the drums would drown a tempest's roar, and no one could hear himself speak nor anyone else. At the king's gate was such an enormous crowd that the stone pavement was all trodden into dust. Women mounted on the upper story viewed the sight with festal torches and salvers in their hands, and they caroled melodious songs in an ecstasy of joy beyond description. Then Sumant made ready two chariots and yoked them with steeds that would outrun the horses of the Sun, and brought them in all their beauty before the king—not Shārdā herself could do them justice—the one was for the royal retinue, but the other was still more splendid;

दोहा-*dohā:*

तेहिं रथ रुचिर बसिष्ठ कहुँ हरषि चढ़ाइ नरेसु ।
tehiṁ ratha rucira basiṣṭha kahuṁ haraṣi caṛhāi naresu,
आपु चढ़ेउ स्यंदन सुमिरि हर गुर गौरि गनेसु ॥३०१॥
āpu caṛheu syaṁdana sumiri hara gura gauri ganesu. 301.

Trans:

and upon that the king caused Vasishtha to mount, and then himself ascended the other—with his thoughts fixed upon Hara, his Gurū, Gaurī, and Ganesh.

चौपाई-*caupāī:*

सहित बसिष्ठ सोह नृप कैसें । सुर गुर संग पुरंदर जैसें ॥
sahita basiṣṭha soha nṛpa kaiseṁ, sura gura saṁga puraṁdara jaiseṁ.
करि कुल रीति बेद बिधि राऊ । देखि सबहि सब भाँति बनाऊ ॥
kari kula rīti beda bidhi rāū, dekhi sabahi saba bhāṁti banāū.
सुमिरि रामु गुर आयसु पाई । चले महीपति संख बजाई ॥
sumiri rāmu gura āyasu pāī, cale mahīpati saṁkha bajāī.
हरषे बिबुध बिलोकि बराता । बरषहिं सुमन सुमंगल दाता ॥
haraṣe bibudha biloki barātā, baraṣahiṁ sumana sumaṁgala dātā.
भयउ कोलाहल हय गय गाजे । ब्योम बरात बाजने बाजे ॥
bhayau kolāhala haya gaya gāje, byoma barāta bājane bāje.
सुर नर नारि सुमंगल गाईं । सरस राग बाजहिं सहनाईं ॥
sura nara nāri sumaṁgala gāīṁ, sarasa rāga bājahiṁ sahanāīṁ.
घंट घंटि धुनि बरनि न जाहीं । सरव करहिं पाइक फहराहीं ॥
ghaṁṭa ghaṁṭi dhuni barani na jāhīṁ, sarava karahiṁ pāika phaharāhīṁ.
करहिं बिदूषक कौतुक नाना । हास कुसल कल गान सुजाना ॥
karahiṁ bidūṣaka kautuka nānā, hāsa kusala kala gāna sujānā.

Trans:

By Vasishtha's side the king shone forth as Purandar beside Brihaspati. After performing every ceremony prescribed either by family usage or by the Veda, and inspecting whatever had been done, he set forth to the boom of the conch-shells—after obtaining the permission of his Gurū, and with his thoughts fixed upon Rāma. The beneficent gods rejoiced to see the procession and rained down flowers. There was a bleary uproar—horses neighing, elephants trumpeting, and drums beating, both in the sky and on the line of march. Women and goddesses alike broke out in songs of joy, while tuneful clarions played in sweet accord. There was an indescribable clamor of bells, both great and small. The foot soldiers leaped and danced as if challenging attack; the jesters practiced all kinds of buffoonery, provoking laughter with facetious songs.

दोहा-dohā:

तुरग नचावहिं कुअँर बर अकनि मृदंग निसान ।
turaga nacāvahiṁ kuaṁra bara akani mṛdaṁga nisāna,
नागर नट चितवहिं चकित डगहिं न ताल बँधान ॥३०२॥
nāgara naṭa citavahiṁ cakita ḍagahiṁ na tāla baṁdhāna. 302.

Trans:

Gallant youths make their steeds curvet to the measured beat of tabors and kettledrums, and accomplished dancers note with surprise that they never make a step out of time.

चौपाई-caupāī:

बनइ न बरनत बनी बराता । होहिं सगुन सुंदर सुभदाता ॥
banai na baranata banī barātā, hohiṁ saguna suṁdara subhadātā.
चारा चाषु बाम दिसि लेई । मनहुँ सकल मंगल कहि देई ॥
cārā cāṣu bāma disi leī, manahuṁ sakala maṁgala kahi deī.
दाहिन काग सुखेत सुहावा । नकुल दरसु सब काहूँ पावा ॥
dāhina kāga sukheta suhāvā, nakula darasu saba kāhūṁ pāvā.
सानुकूल बह त्रिबिध बयारी । सघट सबाल आव बर नारी ॥
sānukūla baha tribidha bayārī, saghaṭa sabāla āva bara nārī.
लोवा फिरि फिरि दरसु देखावा । सुरभी सनमुख सिसुहि पिआवा ॥
lovā phiri phiri darasu dekhāvā, surabhī sanamukha sisuhi piāvā.
मृगमाला फिरि दाहिनि आई । मंगल गन जनु दीन्हि देखाई ॥
mṛgamālā phiri dāhini āī, maṁgala gana janu dīnhi dekhāī.
छेमकरी कह छेम बिसेषी । स्यामा बाम सुतरु पर देखी ॥
chemakarī kaha chema biseṣī, syāmā bāma sutaru para dekhī.
सनमुख आयउ दधि अरु मीना । कर पुस्तक दुइ बिप्र प्रबीना ॥
sanamukha āyau dadhi aru mīnā, kara pustaka dui bipra prabīnā.

Trans:

The splendor of the marriage procession is more than can be described in words; every omen that occurred was fair and auspicious. On the left side a blue-necked jay was picking up food, as if to announce the very highest good fortune; on a fair field on the right were a crow and a mongoose in the sight of all; a grateful breeze breathed soft and cool and fragrant; a woman was seen with a pitcher and a child in her arm; a fox showed himself winding about; and in front a cow was suckling its calf; a herd of deer came out on the right, an indication of everything good; a Brahmani-kite promised all success; and a *shyama* bird was perched on a tree to the left. A man bearing curds and fish and two learned Brahmins each with a book in his hand came from the opposite direction.

दोहा-dohā:

मंगलमय कल्यानमय अभिमत फल दातार ।
maṁgalamaya kalyānamaya abhimata phala dātāra,
जनु सब साचे होन हित भए सगुन एक बार ॥३०३॥
janu saba sāce hona hita bhae saguna eka bāra. 303.

Trans:

All kinds of blessed and auspicious omens, and those conducive of desired results, occurred all at once as if to fulfill themselves.

चौपाई-caupāī:

मंगल सगुन सुगम सब ताकें । सगुन ब्रह्म सुंदर सुत जाकें ॥
maṁgala saguna sugama saba tākeṁ, saguna brahma suṁdara suta jākeṁ.
राम सरिस बरु दुलहिनि सीता । समधी दसरथु जनकु पुनीता ॥
rāma sarisa baru dulahini sītā, samadhī dasarathu janaku punītā.
सुनि अस ब्याहु सगुन सब नाचे । अब कीन्हे बिरंचि हम साँचे ॥
suni asa byāhu saguna saba nāce, aba kīnhe biraṁci hama sāṁce.
एहि बिधि कीन्ह बरात पयाना । हय गय गाजहिं हने निसाना ॥
ehi bidhi kīnha barāta payānā, haya gaya gājahiṁ hane nisānā.
आवत जानि भानुकुल केतू । सरितन्हि जनक बँधाए सेतू ॥
āvata jāni bhānukula ketū, saritanhi janaka baṁdhāe setū.
बीच बीच बर बास बनाए । सुरपुर सरिस संपदा छाए ॥
bīca bīca bara bāsa banāe, surapura sarisa saṁpadā chāe.
असन सयन बर बसन सुहाए । पावहिं सब निज निज मन भाए ॥
asana sayana bara basana suhāe, pāvahiṁ saba nija nija mana bhāe.
नित नूतन सुख लखि अनुकूले । सकल बरातिन्ह मंदिर भूले ॥
nita nūtana sukha lakhi anukūle, sakala barātinha maṁdira bhūle.

Trans:

Auspicious omens easily occur to him who has God with form as his own son. In the marriage which was going to take place, the bridegroom was no other than Shrī Rāma; and Sītā herself was the bride; while the pious Dashrath and Janak were the parents of the bridegroom and the bride. When they heard of the marriage, all the good omens began to dance and say: "Now at last the Creator has really made us to be what our names denote." In this manner the procession set forth with sounds of horses and elephants and beat of drums. When Janak, the glory of the Solar race, heard of its approach, he had all the rivers bridged, and at different stages had convenient rest-houses erected, which vied in splendor with the city of heaven, and were supplied with beds, food, linen and everything that one could desire. Ever discovering some new charm, all the travelers forgot their own homes.

दोहा-dohā:

आवत जानि बरात बर सुनि गहगहे निसान ।
āvata jāni barāta bara suni gahagahe nisāna,
सजि गज रथ पदचर तुरग लेन चले अगवान ॥३०४॥
saji gaja ratha padacara turaga lena cale agavāna. 304.

Trans:

When it was known that the procession was close at hand and the beating of the drums was heard, a deputation went out to meet it with elephants and chariots and on foot and horses.

मासपारायण दसवाँ विश्राम
māsapārāyaṇa dasavāṁ viśrāma
(Pause 10 for a Thirty-Day Recitation)

चौपाई-caupāī:

कनक कलस भरि कोपर थारा । भाजन ललित अनेक प्रकारा ॥
kanaka kalasa bhari kopara thārā, bhājana lalita aneka prakārā.
भरे सुधासम सब पकवाने । नाना भाँति न जाहिं बखाने ॥
bhare sudhāsama saba pakavāne, nānā bhāṁti na jāhiṁ bakhāne.
फल अनेक बर बस्तु सुहाईं । हरषि भेंट हित भूप पठाईं ॥
phala aneka bara bastu suhāīṁ, haraṣi bheṁṭa hita bhūpa paṭhāīṁ.
भूषन बसन महामनि नाना । खग मृग हय गय बहु बिधि जाना ॥
bhūṣana basana mahāmani nānā, khaga mṛga haya gaya bahu bidhi jānā.
मंगल सगुन सुगंध सुहाए । बहुत भाँति महिपाल पठाए ॥
maṁgala saguna sugaṁdha suhāe, bahuta bhāṁti mahipāla paṭhāe.
दधि चिउरा उपहार अपारा । भरि भरि काँवरि चले कहारा ॥
dadhi ciurā upahāra apārā, bhari bhari kāṁvari cale kahārā.
अगवानन्ह जब दीखि बराता । उर आनंदु पुलक भर गाता ॥
agavānanha jaba dīkhi barātā, ura ānaṁdu pulaka bhara gātā.

देखि बनाव सहित अगवाना । मुदित बरातिन्ह हने निसाना ॥
dekhi banāva sahita agavānā, mudita barātinha hane nisānā.

Trans:

Beautiful golden vases and trays and salvers and costly dishes of every kind, laden with cakes as sweet as nectar and of indescribable variety, with much luscious fruit—in short everything of the best—did the king in his gladness send as offerings. Ornaments, wearing-apparels, jewels of all kinds, birds, deer, horses, elephants, carriages of every description, well-omened spices, delicious perfumes, these too, did the king send; and there was a train of porters with their baskets full of curds and parched rice and other light entremets. When the deputation saw the wedding guests, their soul was fall of rapture and their body quivered with excitement; while the guests were no less charmed by the preparations made for their reception and had their drummer beat drums more loud.

दोहा-dohā:

हरषि परसपर मिलन हित कछुक चले बगमेल ।
haraṣi parasapara milana hita kachuka cale bagamela,
जनु आनंद समुद्र दुइ मिलत बिहाइ सुबेल ॥३०५॥
janu ānaṁda samudra dui milata bihāi subela. 305.

Trans:

For a little while they joined their ranks and marched in their joy as one body for the sake of company; like two oceans of bliss that had burst their bounds and come together.

चौपाई-caupāī:

बरषि सुमन सुर सुंदरि गावहिं । मुदित देव दुंदुभीं बजावहिं ॥
baraṣi sumana sura suṁdari gāvahiṁ, mudita deva duṁdubhīṁ bajāvahiṁ.
बस्तु सकल राखीं नृप आगें । बिनय कीन्हि तिन्ह अति अनुरागें ॥
bastu sakala rākhīṁ nṛpa āgeṁ, binaya kīnhi tinha ati anurāgeṁ.
प्रेम समेत रायँ सबु लीन्हा । भै बकसीस जाचकन्हि दीन्हा ॥
prema sameta rāyaṁ sabu līnhā, bhai bakasīsa jācakanhi dīnhā.
करि पूजा मान्यता बड़ाई । जनवासे कहुँ चले लवाई ॥
kari pūjā mānyatā baṛāī, janavāse kahuṁ cale lavāī.
बसन बिचित्र पाँवड़े परहीं । देखि धनहु धन मदु परिहरहीं ॥
basana bicitra pāṁvaṛe parahīṁ, dekhi dhanahu dhana madu pariharahīṁ.
अति सुंदर दीन्हेउ जनवासा । जहँ सब कहुँ सब भाँति सुपासा ॥
ati suṁdara dīnheu janavāsā, jahaṁ saba kahuṁ saba bhāṁti supāsā.
जानी सियँ बरात पुर आई । कछु निज महिमा प्रगटि जनाई ॥
jānī siyaṁ barāta pura āī, kachu nija mahimā pragaṭi janāī.
हृदयँ सुमिरि सब सिद्धि बोलाईं । भूप पहुनई करन पठाईं ॥
hṛdayaṁ sumiri saba siddhi bolāīṁ, bhūpa pahunaī karana paṭhāīṁ.

Trans:

The nymphs of heaven rained down flowers and sang, the glad gods sounded kettle-drums. The offerings were all set out before the king with a humble and affectionate address. The king graciously accepted them and bestowed them in charity on the poor. Then with religious honors and hymns of praise they conducted him to the guest-chambers. The cloths spread as carpets for king Dashrath to tread upon were so gorgeous that the god of wealth on seeing them could boast no longer. The gods rained down flowers and shouted 'Victory, Victory'. The apartments assigned were magnificent and supplied with every kind of comfort. When Sītā knew that the procession had arrived in the city, she manifested her glory to a slight extent, and with thoughtful heart called up the eight Siddhis, or wonder-working spirits, and sent them to arrange for the king's reception.

दोहा-dohā:

सिधि सब सिय आयसु अकनि गईं जहाँ जनवास ।
sidhi saba siya āyasu akani gaīṁ jahāṁ janavāsa,
लिएँ संपदा सकल सुख सुरपुर भोग बिलास ॥३०६॥
lieṁ saṁpadā sakala sukha surapura bhoga bilāsa. 306.

Trans:

Obedient to her command, they repaired to the reception-hall, taking with them every kind of luxury and comfort and all the joys and delights of heaven.

चौपाई-caupāī:

निज निज बास बिलोकि बराती । सुर सुख सकल सुलभ सब भाँती ॥
nija nija bāsa biloki barātī, sura sukha sakala sulabha saba bhāṁtī.
बिभव भेद कछु कोउ न जाना । सकल जनक कर करहिं बखाना ॥
bibhava bheda kachu kou na jānā, sakala janaka kara karahiṁ bakhānā.
सिय महिमा रघुनायक जानी । हरषे हृदयँ हेतु पहिचानी ॥
siya mahimā raghunāyaka jānī, haraṣe hṛdayaṁ hetu pahicānī.
पितु आगमनु सुनत दोउ भाई । हृदयँ न अति आनंदु अमाई ॥
pitu āgamanu sunata dou bhāī, hṛdayaṁ na ati ānaṁdu amāī.
सकुचन्ह कहि न सकत गुरु पाहीं । पितु दरसन लालचु मन माहीं ॥
sakucanha kahi na sakata guru pāhīṁ, pitu darasana lālacu mana māhīṁ.
बिस्वामित्र बिनय बड़ि देखी । उपजा उर संतोषु बिसेषी ॥
bisvāmitra binaya baṛi dekhī, upajā ura saṁtoṣu biseṣī.
हरषि बंधु दोउ हृदयँ लगाए । पुलक अंग अंबक जल छाए ॥
haraṣi baṁdhu dou hṛdayaṁ lagāe, pulaka aṁga aṁbaka jala chāe.
चले जहाँ दसरथु जनवासे । मनहुँ सरोबर तकेउ पिआसे ॥
cale jahāṁ dasarathu janavāse, manahuṁ sarobara takeu piāse.

Trans:

Each guest on going to see his apartment found it a veritable paradise; no one, however, had an inkling of the mysterious power that had been exerted, but took it all as Janak's doing. Rāma alone recognized the influence of Sītā and rejoiced at this proof of her love. When the two brothers heard of their father's arrival they could not contain themselves for joy, but were too modest to speak to their Gurū, though they longed greatly to see their sire again. Vishwāmitra perceived their humility, which filled his soul with contentment, and took the two brothers to his bosom, with quivering body and eyes bedewed with tears. Then went they to Dashrath's mansion, like thirsting travelers who have spied a pool.

दोहा-dohā:

भूप बिलोके जबहिं मुनि आवत सुतन्ह समेत ।
bhūpa biloke jabahiṁ muni āvata sutanha sameta,
उठे हरषि सुखसिंधु महुँ चले थाह सी लेत ॥३०७॥
uṭhe haraṣi sukhasiṁdhu mahuṁ cale thāha sī leta. 307.

Trans:

When the king saw the saint coming with the two boys, he rose in joy and advanced to meet them, like one who feels his footing in a deep flood of bliss.

चौपाई-caupāī:

मुनिहि दंडवत कीन्ह महीसा । बार बार पद रज धरि सीसा ॥
munihi daṁḍavata kīnha mahīsā, bāra bāra pada raja dhari sīsā.
कौसिक राउ लिये उर लाई । कहि असीस पूछी कुसलाई ॥
kausika rāu liye ura lāī, kahi asīsa pūchī kusalāī.
पुनि दंडवत करत दोउ भाई । देखि नृपति उर सुखु न समाई ॥
puni daṁḍavata karata dou bhāī, dekhi nṛpati ura sukhu na samāī.
सुत हियँ लाइ दुसह दुख मेटे । मृतक सरीर प्रान जनु भेंटे ॥
suta hiyaṁ lāi dusaha dukha meṭe, mṛtaka sarīra prāna janu bheṁṭe.

पुनि बसिष्ठ पद सिर तिन्ह नाए । प्रेम मुदित मुनिबर उर लाए ॥
puni basiṣṭha pada sira tinha nāe, prema mudita munibara ura lāe.
बिप्र बृंद बंदे दुहुँ भाईं । मनभावती असीसें पाईं ॥
bipra bṛṁda baṁde duhuṁ bhāīṁ, manabhāvatī asīseṁ pāīṁ.
भरत सहानुज कीन्ह प्रनामा । लिए उठाइ लाइ उर रामा ॥
bharata sahānuja kīnha pranāmā, lie uṭhāi lāi ura rāmā.
हरषे लखन देखि दोउ भ्राता । मिले प्रेम परिपूरित गाता ॥
harașe lakhana dekhi dou bhrātā, mile prema paripūrita gātā.

Trans:

He prostrated himself before the saint, again and again sprinkling on his head the dust of his feet. Vishwāmitra took him to his bosom and blessed him and enquired after his welfare. Then the two brothers prostrated themselves. The king on seeing them could not contain himself for joy, but took his boys to his heart, and forgetting the intolerable pain of the past seemed like a dead man restored to life. Then they bowed their head at Vasishtha's feet, who also embraced them most affectionately; and in turn they saluted all the Brahmins and received their welcome blessings. Bharat and his younger brother Shatrughan greeted Rāma, who at once lifted and embraced them. Lakshman too rejoiced to see the two brothers again. Thus they all met together with a display of the utmost affection.

दोहा-dohā:

पुरजन परिजन जातिजन जाचक मंत्री मीत ।
purajana parijana jātijana jācaka maṁtrī mīta,
मिले जथाबिधि सबहि प्रभु परम कृपाल बिनीत ॥३०८॥
mile jathābidhi sabahi prabhu parama kṛpāla binīta. 308.

Trans:

The all-merciful and gracious Lord had an appropriate greeting for all, whether citizens, or attendants, or kinsmen, beggars, or ministers, or friends.

चौपाई-caupāī:

रामहि देखि बरात जुड़ानी । प्रीति कि रीति न जाति बखानी ॥
rāmahi dekhi barāta juṛānī, prīti ki rīti na jāti bakhānī.
नृप समीप सोहहिं सुत चारी । जनु धन धरमादिक तनुधारी ॥
nṛpa samīpa sohahiṁ suta cārī, janu dhana dharamādika tanudhārī.
सुतन्ह समेत दसरथहि देखी । मुदित नगर नर नारि बिसेषी ॥
sutanha sameta dasarathahi dekhī, mudita nagara nara nāri biseṣī.
सुमन बरिसि सुर हनहिं निसाना । नाकनटीं नाचहिं करि गाना ॥
sumana barisi sura hanahiṁ nisānā, nākanaṭīṁ nācahiṁ kari gānā.
सतानंद अरु बिप्र सचिव गन । मागध सूत बिदुष बंदीजन ॥
satānaṁda aru bipra saciva gana, māgadha sūta biduṣa baṁdījana.
सहित बरात राउ सनमाना । आयसु मागि फिरे अगवाना ॥
sahita barāta rāu sanamānā, āyasu māgi phire agavānā.
प्रथम बरात लगन तें आई । तातें पुर प्रमोदु अधिकाई ॥
prathama barāta lagana teṁ āī, tāteṁ pura pramodu adhikāī.
ब्रह्मानंदु लोग सब लहहीं । बढ़हुँ दिवस निसि बिधि सन कहहीं ॥
brahmānaṁdu loga saba lahahīṁ, baṛhahuṁ divasa nisi bidhi sana kahahīṁ.

Trans:

At the sight of Rāma the wedding guests were repaid for their toilsome journey, and their demonstrations of love were beyond all telling. Beside their royal father the four boys seemed as incarnations of the four great ends of life. All the people of the city were delighted beyond measure at the sight of Dashrath and his sons; the gods rained down flowers and beat their drums; the nymphs of heaven danced and sang. Shatānand with the Brahmins and ministers of state, and the rhapsodists and bards, and players and minstrels who had come in deputation paid due honor to the king and his party and returned with their permission. The whole city was exceedingly delighted that the procession had come before the day fixed for the wedding, and was supremely happy, praying to God to lengthen the days and nights.

दोहा-dohā:

रामु सीय सोभा अवधि सुकृत अवधि दोउ राज ।
rāmu sīya sobhā avadhi sukṛta avadhi dou rāja,
जहँ जहँ पुरजन कहहिं अस मिलि नर नारि समाज ॥३०९॥
jahaṁ jahaṁ purajana kahahiṁ asa mili nara nāri samāja.,309.

Trans:

"Rāma and Sītā are the perfection of beauty, and the two kings the perfection of virtue," thus would say all the people of the city whenever they happened to meet:

चौपाई-caupāī:

जनक सुकृत मूरति बैदेही । दसरथ सुकृत रामु धरें देही ॥
janaka sukṛta mūrati baidehī, dasaratha sukṛta rāmu dhareṁ dehī.
इन्ह सम काहुँ न सिव अवराधे । काहुँ न इन्ह समान फल लाधे ॥
inha sama kāhuṁ na siva avarādhe, kāhuṁ na inha samāna phala lādhe.
इन्ह सम कोउ न भयउ जग माहीं । है नहिं कतहूँ होनेउ नाहीं ॥
inha sama kou na bhayau jaga māhīṁ, hai nahiṁ katahūṁ honeu nāhīṁ.
हम सब सकल सुकृत कै रासी । भए जग जनमि जनकपुर बासी ॥
hama saba sakala sukṛta kai rāsī, bhae jaga janami janakapura bāsī.
जिन्ह जानकी राम छबि देखी । को सुकृती हम सरिस बिसेषी ॥
jinha jānakī rāma chabi dekhī, ko sukṛtī hama sarisa biseṣī.
पुनि देखब रघुबीर बिआहू । लेब भली बिधि लोचन लाहू ॥
puni dekhaba raghubīra biāhū, leba bhalī bidhi locana lāhū.
कहहिं परसपर कोकिलबयनीं । एहि बिआहँ बड़ लाभु सुनयनीं ॥
kahahiṁ parasapara kokilabayanīṁ, ehi biāhaṁ baṛa lābhu sunayanīṁ.
बड़ें भाग बिधि बात बनाई । नयन अतिथि होइहहिं दोउ भाई ॥
baṛeṁ bhāga bidhi bāta banāī, nayana atithi hoihahiṁ dou bhāī.

Trans:

"Sītā is the incarnation of Janak's merit and Rāma of Dashrath's: no one has equaled these kings in devotion to Shiva, nor has anyone obtained a reward such as they have. We too must have had many good merits from past—seeing that we have been born into the world as Janak's citizens and have beheld the beauty of Jānakī and Rāma. Who is so superlatively blessed as we are? And we have yet to see Rāma's wedding—of all sights the best worth seeing." So too, sweet-voiced maidens whispered to one another, "This marriage, my dear, will be a great treat. God has brought about an event of such high felicity—in lodging these two brothers in the guest-chambers of our eyes.

दोहा-dohā:

बारहिं बार सनेह बस जनक बोलाउब सीय ।
bārahiṁ bāra saneha basa janaka bolāuba sīya,
लेन आइहहिं बंधु दोउ कोटि काम कमनीय ॥३१०॥
lena āihahiṁ baṁdhu dou koṭi kāma kamanīya. 310.

Trans:

Many and many a time will Janak lovingly send for Sītā, and the two brothers, beautiful as a myriad Loves, will come to fetch her.

चौपाई-caupāī:

बिबिध भाँति होइहि पहुनाई । प्रिय न काहि अस सासुर माई ॥
bibidha bhāṁti hoihi pahunāī, priya na kāhi asa sāsura māī.
तब तब राम लखनहि निहारी । होइहहिं सब पुर लोग सुखारी ॥
taba taba rāma lakhanahi nihārī, hoihahiṁ saba pura loga sukhārī.
सखि जस राम लखन कर जोटा । तैसेइ भूप संग दुइ ढोटा ॥
sakhi jasa rāma lakhana kara joṭā, taisei bhūpa saṁga dui ḍhoṭā.

स्याम गौर सब अंग सुहाए । ते सब कहहिं देखि जे आए ॥
syāma gaura saba aṁga suhāe, te saba kahahiṁ dekhi je āe.
कहा एक मैं आजु निहारे । जनु बिरंचि निज हाथ सँवारे ॥
kahā eka maiṁ āju nihāre, janu biraṁci nija hātha saṁvāre.
भरतु रामही की अनुहारी । सहसा लखि न सकहिं नर नारी ॥
bharatu rāmahī kī anuhārī, sahasā lakhi na sakahiṁ nara nārī.
लखनु सत्रुसूदनु एकरूपा । नख सिख ते सब अंग अनूपा ॥
lakhanu satrusūdanu ekarūpā, nakha sikha te saba aṁga anūpā.
मन भावहिं मुख बरनि न जाहीं । उपमा कहुँ त्रिभुवन कोउ नाहीं ॥
mana bhāvahiṁ mukha barani na jāhīṁ, upamā kahuṁ tribhuvana kou nāhīṁ.

Trans:

There will be all kinds of hospitable entertainments; who, dear girl, would not rejoice to stay at such a father-in-law? Everyone in the place will be delighted at the sight of Rāma and Lakshman; and now two other lads, my friends, have come with the king, who are a match even for them; one dark, the other fair, and beautiful in every limb, so says everyone who has seen them." Said one in reply, "I saw them today, and thought God must have made them with his own hands. Rāma and Bharat are so much alike that neither man nor woman could without looking close tell one from the other; while again Lakshman and Shatrughan are also one in appearance, perfectly beautiful in every limb from head to foot; the soul would fain express its rapture, but language fails it, for there is nothing comparable to them in all the three spheres of creation."

छँद-chaṁda:

उपमा न कोउ कह दास तुलसी कतहुँ कबि कोबिद कहैं ।
upamā na kou kaha dāsa tulasī katahuṁ kabi kobida kahaiṁ,
बल बिनय बिद्या सील सोभा सिंधु इन्ह से एइ अहैं ॥
bala binaya bidyā sīla sobhā siṁdhu inha se ei ahaiṁ.
पुर नारि सकल पसारि अंचल बिधिहि बचन सुनावहीं ।
pura nāri sakala pasāri aṁcala bidhihi bacana sunāvahīṁ,
ब्याहिअहुँ चारिउ भाइ एहिं पुर हम सुमंगल गावहीं ॥
byāhiahuṁ cāriu bhāi ehiṁ pura hama sumaṁgala gāvahīṁ.

Trans:

No poet, however ingenious, says Tulsīdās, could find aught comparable to them; for so unbounded is their strength, their courtesy, their knowledge, their amiability, and their beauty, that they have no peers but themselves. All the women in the city, spreading out their garments, made prayer to Brahmmā: "May all four brothers be married here, and may we sing their wedding songs."

सोरठा-soraṭhā:

कहहिं परस्पर नारि बारि बिलोचन पुलक तन ।
kahahiṁ paraspara nāri bāri bilocana pulaka tana,
सखि सबु करब पुरारि पुन्य पयोनिधि भूप दोउ ॥३११॥
sakhi sabu karaba purāri punya payonidhi bhūpa dou. 311.

Trans:

Said the damsels to one another with streaming eyes and quivering body: "Friends, the two kings are of such boundless religious merit that for their sake Mahādev will bring it all about."

चौपाई-caupāī:

एहि बिधि सकल मनोरथ करहीं । आनँद उमगि उमगि उर भरहीं ॥
ehi bidhi sakala manoratha karahīṁ, ānaṁda umagi umagi ura bharahīṁ.
जे नृप सीय स्वयंबर आए । देखि बंधु सब तिन्ह सुख पाए ॥
je nṛpa sīya svayaṁbara āe, dekhi baṁdhu saba tinha sukha pāe.
कहत राम जसु बिसद बिसाला । निज निज भवन गए महिपाला ॥
kahata rāma jasu bisada bisālā, nija nija bhavana gae mahipālā.
गए बीति कुछ दिन एहि भाँती । प्रमुदित पुरजन सकल बराती ॥
gae bīti kucha dina ehi bhāṁtī, pramudita purajana sakala barātī.
मंगल मूल लगन दिनु आवा । हिम रितु अगहनु मासु सुहावा ॥
maṁgala mūla lagana dinu āvā, hima ritu agahanu māsu suhāvā.
ग्रह तिथि नखतु जोगु बर बारू । लगन सोधि बिधि कीन्ह बिचारू ॥
graha tithi nakhatu jogu bara bārū, lagana sodhi bidhi kīnha bicārū.
पठै दीन्हि नारद सन सोई । गनी जनक के गनकन्ह जोई ॥
paṭhai dīnhi nārada sana soī, ganī janaka ke ganakanha joī.
सुनी सकल लोगन्ह यह बाता । कहहिं जोतिषी आहिं बिधाता ॥
sunī sakala loganha yaha bātā, kahahiṁ jotiṣī āhiṁ bidhātā.

Trans:

In like manner they all expressed their desire, while their full heart overflowed with rapture. The princes who had come as Sītā's suitors rejoiced to see the four brothers and returned each to his own home extolling Shrī Rāma's widespread and spotless fame. In this fashion several days were spent, to the joy alike of citizens and guests. At length the auspicious day arrived, in the cold season, in the pleasant month of *Agahn*. The Creator himself had carefully fixed the date, when the signs of the zodiac, the age of the moon, the conjunction of the stars, and the day of the week, were one and all propitious. Of this he sent word through Nārad, and it was the very same that Janak's wise men had calculated. All the people on hearing this fact declared their astrologers to be very gods.

दोहा-dohā:

धेनुधूरि बेला बिमल सकल सुमंगल मूल ।
dhenudhūri belā bimala sakala sumaṁgala mūla,
बिप्रन्ह कहेउ बिदेह सन जानि सगुन अनुकूल ॥३१२॥
bipranha kaheu bideha sana jāni saguna anukūla. 312.

Trans:

It was towards sunset, the clearest and most delightful hour of the day, that the Brahmins apprised Videh's king that the auspicious time had arrived.

चौपाई-caupāī:

उपरोहितहि कहेउ नरनाहा । अब बिलंब कर कारनु काहा ॥
uparohitahi kaheu naranāhā, aba bilaṁba kara kāranu kāhā.
सतानंद तब सचिव बोलाए । मंगल सकल साजि सब ल्याए ॥
satānaṁda taba saciva bolāe, maṁgala sakala sāji saba lyāe.
संख निसान पनव बहु बाजे । मंगल कलस सगुन सुभ साजे ॥
saṁkha nisāna panava bahu bāje, maṁgala kalasa saguna subha sāje.
सुभग सुआसिनि गावहिं गीता । करहिं बेद धुनि बिप्र पुनीता ॥
subhaga suāsini gāvahiṁ gītā, karahiṁ beda dhuni bipra punītā.
लेन चले सादर एहि भाँती । गए जहाँ जनवास बराती ॥
lena cale sādara ehi bhāṁtī, gae jahāṁ janavāsa barātī.
कोसलपति कर देखि समाजू । अति लघु लाग तिन्हहि सुरराजू ॥
kosalapati kara dekhi samājū, ati laghu lāga tinhahi surarājū.
भयउ समउ अब धारिअ पाऊ । यह सुनि परा निसानहिं घाऊ ॥
bhayau samau aba dhāria pāū, yaha suni parā nisānahiṁ ghāū.
गुरहि पूछि करि कुल बिधि राजा । चले संग मुनि साधु समाजा ॥
gurahi pūchi kari kula bidhi rājā, cale saṁga muni sādhu samājā.

Trans:

The monarch said to the family priest: "What now the cause of delay?" At once Shatānand summoned the ministers, who all came bearing festal vases. Conches, drums, and tabors sounded; all decked their vases in auspicious ways; graceful damsels sang songs, and holy Brahmins chanted Vedic texts. In this manner they went with all ceremony to the visitors' camp, and on beholding the king of Kaushal's retinue, it seemed to them that Indra was of much less glory. "The hour has come, be pleased to start." At this the drums gave a thundering beat. After consulting his Gurū and performing the family rites, the king and the saint sallied forth with all their host.

दोहा-dohā:

भाग्य बिभव अवधेस कर देखि देव ब्रह्मादि ।
bhāgya bibhava avadhesa kara dekhi deva brahmādi,
लगे सराहन सहस मुख जानि जनम निज बादि ॥ ३१३॥
lage sarāhana sahasa mukha jāni janama nija bādi. 313.

Trans:

Brahmmā and all the other gods, on beholding the pomp and magnificence of Avadh's king, declare their own lives to be nothing, and extol him with a thousand tongues.

चौपाई-caupāī:

सुरन्ह सुमंगल अवसरु जाना । बरषहिं सुमन बजाइ निसाना ॥
suranha sumaṁgala avasaru jānā, baraṣahiṁ sumana bajāi nisānā.
सिव ब्रह्मादिक बिबुध बरूथा । चढ़े बिमानन्हि नाना जूथा ॥
siva brahmādika bibudha barūthā, caṛhe bimānanhi nānā jūthā.
प्रेम पुलक तन हृदयँ उछाहू । चले बिलोकन राम बिआहू ॥
prema pulaka tana hṛdayaṁ uchāhū, cale bilokana rāma biāhū.
देखि जनकपुरु सुर अनुरागे । निज निज लोक सबहिं लघु लागे ॥
dekhi janakapuru sura anurāge, nija nija loka sabahiṁ laghu lāge.
चितवहिं चकित बिचित्र बिताना । रचना सकल अलौकिक नाना ॥
citavahiṁ cakita bicitra bitānā, racanā sakala alaukika nānā.
नगर नारि नर रूप निधाना । सुघर सुधरम सुसील सुजाना ॥
nagara nāri nara rūpa nidhānā, sughara sudharama susīla sujānā.
तिन्हहि देखि सब सुर सुरनारीं । भए नखत जनु बिधु उजिआरीं ॥
tinhahi dekhi saba sura suranārīṁ, bhae nakhata janu bidhu ujiārīṁ.
बिधिहि भयउ आचरजु बिसेषी । निज करनी कछु कतहुँ न देखी ॥
bidhihi bhayau ācaraju biseṣī, nija karanī kachu katahuṁ na dekhī.

Trans:

Seeing the auspiciousness of the time, the deities rained down flowers and sounded drums. Shiva and Brahmmā and all the host of heaven mounted their chariots and came in crowds to see Rāma's wedding, their heart and every limb throbbing and quivering with excess of love. They were so charmed with Janak's capital that their own realms seemed to them as nothing worth. They gaze with astonishment at the pavilions and all the marvelous decorations; at the men and women so beautiful and well-formed, so good and amiable and intelligent, before whom all the gods and goddesses seemed like the stars at the rising of the full moon. Above all was Brahmmā astounded at finding his own handiwork nowhere.

दोहा-dohā:

सिवँ समुझाए देव सब जनि आचरज भुलाहु ।
sivaṁ samujhāe deva saba jani ācaraja bhulāhu,
हृदयँ बिचारहु धीर धरि सिय रघुबीर बिआहु ॥ ३१४॥
hṛdayaṁ bicārahu dhīra dhari siya raghubīra biāhu. 314.

Trans:

But Shiva admonished them all, "Do not give way to such surprise; recover yourselves and reflect that this is the marriage of Sītā and Raghubīr—

चौपाई-caupāī:

जिन्ह कर नामु लेत जग माहीं । सकल अमंगल मूल नसाहीं ॥
jinha kara nāmu leta jaga māhīṁ, sakala amaṁgala mūla nasāhīṁ.
करतल होहिं पदारथ चारी । तेइ सिय रामु कहेउ कामारी ॥
karatala hohiṁ padāratha cārī, tei siya rāmu kaheu kāmārī.
एहि बिधि संभु सुरन्ह समुझावा । पुनि आगें बर बसह चलावा ॥
ehi bidhi saṁbhu suranha samujhāvā, puni āgeṁ bara basaha calāvā.
देवन्ह देखे दसरथु जाता । महामोद मन पुलकित गाता ॥
devanha dekhe dasarathu jātā, mahāmoda mana pulakita gātā.
साधु समाज संग महिदेवा । जनु तनु धरें करहिं सुख सेवा ॥
sādhu samāja saṁga mahidevā, janu tanu dhareṁ karahiṁ sukha sevā.
सोहत साथ सुभग सुत चारी । जनु अपबरग सकल तनुधारी ॥
sohata sātha subhaga suta cārī, janu apabaraga sakala tanudhārī.
मरकत कनक बरन बर जोरी । देखि सुरन्ह भै प्रीति न थोरी ॥
marakata kanaka barana bara jorī, dekhi suranha bhai prīti na thorī.
पुनि रामहि बिलोकि हियँ हरषे । नृपहि सराहि सुमन तिन्ह बरषे ॥
puni rāmahi biloki hiyaṁ haraṣe, nṛpahi sarāhi sumana tinha baraṣe.

Trans:

—the mere mention of whose name destroys all that is evil in the world, in whose hand are the four great ends of human life, such are Sītā and Rāma, says Lust's destroyer." When Shambhu had thus admonished the gods, he again urged on his noble bull. Beholding Dashrath march forth, their soul was full of joy and their limbs trembled. The crowd of saints and Brahmins who accompanied him seemed like incarnate gods ministering to him. In the midst shone forth the beautiful boys as it were final Beatitude manifested in its four phases. As they gazed on the two pairs, of golden and sapphire hues, the gods were moved with intense love, and still more were they delighted at the sight of Rāma; and they glorified the king, and rained down flowers.

दोहा-dohā:

राम रूपु नख सिख सुभग बारहिं बार निहारि ।
rāma rūpu nakha sikha subhaga bārahiṁ bāra nihāri,
पुलक गात लोचन सजल उमा समेत पुरारि ॥ ३१५॥
pulaka gāta locana sajala umā sameta purāri. 315.

Trans:

Again and again as Umā and Mahādev fixed their gaze upon Rāma, all-perfect in beauty from head to foot, their body trembled and their eyes filled with tears.

चौपाई-caupāī:

केकि कंठ दुति स्यामल अंगा । तड़ित बिनिंदक बसन सुरंगा ॥
keki kaṁṭha duti syāmala aṁgā, taṛita biniṁdaka basana suraṁgā.
ब्याह बिभूषन बिबिध बनाए । मंगल सब सब भाँति सुहाए ॥
byāha bibhūṣana bibidha banāe, maṁgala saba saba bhāṁti suhāe.
सरद बिमल बिधु बदनु सुहावन । नयन नवल राजीव लजावन ॥
sarada bimala bidhu badanu suhāvana, nayana navala rājīva lajāvana.
सकल अलौकिक सुंदरताई । कहि न जाइ मनहीं मन भाई ॥
sakala alaukika suṁdaratāī, kahi na jāi manahīṁ mana bhāī.
बंधु मनोहर सोहहिं संगा । जात नचावत चपल तुरंगा ॥
baṁdhu manohara sohahiṁ saṁgā, jāta nacāvata capala turaṁgā.
राजकुअँर बर बाजि देखावहिं । बंस प्रसंसक बिरिद सुनावहिं ॥
rājakuaṁra bara bāji dekhāvahiṁ, baṁsa prasaṁsaka birida sunāvahiṁ.
जेहि तुरंग पर रामु बिराजे । गति बिलोकि खगनायकु लाजे ॥
jehi turaṁga para rāmu birāje, gati biloki khaganāyaku lāje.
कहि न जाइ सब भाँति सुहावा । बाजि बेषु जनु काम बनावा ॥
kahi na jāi saba bhāṁti suhāvā, bāji beṣu janu kāma banāvā.

Trans:

On his body, dark as a peacock's glistening neck, his bright raiment outshone the lightning; his wedding adornments of every kind were most exquisitely fashioned; his face more lustrous than a cloudless autumn moon; his eyes more brilliant than the lotus; his beauty, in short, so marvelous that no words can describe how it moved the soul. By his side shone forth his charming brothers, making the mettlesome steed dip and bound on the way, as also did all the attendant princes; while the family bards recited the glories of their line. As the king-of-birds noted the action of the horse that Rāma bestrode, he blushed for shame; for its beauty was beyond all telling, as it might be Kāmdev himself in guise of a majestic steed.

छंद-chaṁda:

जनु बाजि बेषु बनाइ मनसिजु राम हित अति सोहई ।
janu bāji beṣu banāi manasiju rāma hita ati sohaī,
आपनें बय बल रूप गुन गति सकल भुवन बिमोहई ॥
āpaneṁ baya bala rūpa guna gati sakala bhuvana bimohaī.
जगमगत जीनु जराव जोति सुमोति मनि मानिक लगे ।
jagamagata jīnu jarāva joti sumoti mani mānika lage,
किंकिनि ललाम लगामु ललित बिलोकि सुर नर मुनि ठगे ॥
kiṁkini lalāma lagāmu lalita biloki sura nara muni ṭhage.

Trans:

As though Kāmdev himself in his love for Rāma had assumed an equine disguise, of such resplendent beauty as to charm all creation with his youth and vigor and form and points and paces. A saddle flashed its splendors on his back, thick set with pearls and rubies; bridle too and band gleamed bright with jewels that dazzled the eyes of men, saints, gods.

दोहा-dohā:

प्रभु मनसहिं लयलीन मनु चलत बाजि छबि पाव ।
prabhu manasahiṁ layalīna manu calata bāji chabi pāva,
भूषित उड़गन तड़ित घनु जनु बर बरहि नचाव ॥ ३१६ ॥
bhūṣita uṛagana taṛita ghanu janu bara barahi nacāva. 316.

Trans:

Obedient in every movement to the will of its lord, the gallant steed was as beautiful as a peacock, that dances in response to a thunder-cloud, whose dark mass is irradiated by the stars of heaven and the fitful lightning.

चौपाई-caupāī:

जेहिं बर बाजि रामु असवारा । तेहि सारदउ न बरनै पारा ॥
jehiṁ bara bāji rāmu asavārā, tehi sāradau na baranai pārā.
संकरु राम रूप अनुरागे । नयन पंचदस अति प्रिय लागे ॥
saṁkaru rāma rūpa anurāge, nayana paṁcadasa ati priya lāge.
हरि हित सहित रामु जब जोहे । रमा समेत रमापति मोहे ॥
hari hita sahita rāmu jaba johe, ramā sameta ramāpati mohe.
निरखि राम छबि बिधि हरषाने । आठइ नयन जानि पछिताने ॥
nirakhi rāma chabi bidhi haraṣāne, āṭhai nayana jāni pachitāne.
सुर सेनप उर बहुत उछाहू । बिधि ते डेवढ़ लोचन लाहू ॥
sura senapa ura bahuta uchāhū, bidhi te ḍevaṛha locana lāhū.
रामहि चितव सुरेस सुजाना । गौतम श्रापु परम हित माना ॥
rāmahi citava suresa sujānā, gautama śrāpu parama hita mānā.
देव सकल सुरपतिहि सिहाहीं । आजु पुरंदर सम कोउ नाहीं ॥
deva sakala surapatihi sihāhīṁ, āju puraṁdara sama kou nāhīṁ.
मुदित देवगन रामहि देखी । नृपसमाज दुहुँ हरषु बिसेषी ॥
mudita devagana rāmahi dekhī, nṛpasamāja duhuṁ haraṣu biseṣī.

Trans:

Not Shārdā herself could do justice to the noble steed on which Rāma rode. Shankar was enchanted with Rama's beauty, and congratulated himself on having fifteen eyes. When Harī affectionately gazed on Rāma, he and Lakshmī were both equally charmed; while four-faced Brahmmā rejoiced to behold his beauty, and regretted that he had only eight eyes. Six-faced Kartikeya exulted greatly that in the matter of eyes he was times and a half as well off as Brahmmā. When wise Indra, of a thousand eyes, looked at Rāma he thought Gautam's curse a great blessing; and all the gods broke out in Indra's praise, saying: 'Today there is no one like him.' All heaven was delighted at the sight of Rāma, and there was joy above measure in the court of both the kings.

छंद-chaṁda:

अति हरषु राजसमाज दुहु दिसि दुंदुभीं बाजहिं घनी ।
ati haraṣu rājasamāja duhu disi duṁdubhīṁ bājahiṁ ghanī,
बरषहिं सुमन सुर हरषि कहि जय जयति जय रघुकुलमनी ॥
baraṣahiṁ sumana sura haraṣi kahi jaya jayati jaya raghukulamanī.
एहि भाँति जानि बरात आवत बाजने बहु बाजहीं ।
ehi bhāṁti jāni barāta āvata bājane bahu bājahīṁ,
रानी सुआसिनि बोलि परिछनि हेतु मंगल साजहीं ॥
rānī suāsini boli parichani hetu maṁgala sājahīṁ.

Trans:

There was great rejoicing in both royal courts; all ten-quarters resounded with multitudinous kettledrums; the gods rained down flowers and shouted in their joy: 'Glory, glory, glory to Raghu's noble son.' In this manner when they learnt that the procession was approaching, all sorts of music began to play, and the queen gave orders to her handmaids to prepare the auspicious materials for the lustral rite.

दोहा-dohā:

सजि आरती अनेक बिधि मंगल सकल सँवारि ।
saji āratī aneka bidhi maṁgala sakala saṁvāri,
चलीं मुदित परिछनि करन गजगामिनि बर नारि ॥ ३१७ ॥
calīṁ mudita parichani karana gajagāmini bara nāri. 317.

Trans:

With many lights and torches and festal preparations of every kind, a body of graceful dames proceeded joyously to perform the lustral rite.

चौपाई-caupāī:

बिधुबदनीं सब सब मृगलोचनि । सब निज तन छबि रति मदु मोचनि ॥
bidhubadanīṁ saba saba mṛgalocani, saba nija tana chabi rati madu mocani.
पहिरें बरन बरन बर चीरा । सकल बिभूषन सजें सरीरा ॥
pahireṁ barana barana bara cīrā, sakala bibhūṣana sajeṁ sarīrā.
सकल सुमंगल अंग बनाएँ । करहिं गान कलकंठि लजाएँ ॥
sakala sumaṁgala aṁga banāeṁ, karahiṁ gāna kalakaṁṭhi lajāeṁ.
कंकन किंकिनि नूपुर बाजहिं । चालि बिलोकि काम गज लाजहिं ॥
kaṁkana kiṁkini nūpura bājahiṁ, cāli biloki kāma gaja lājahiṁ.
बाजहिं बाजने बिबिध प्रकारा । नभ अरु नगर सुमंगलचारा ॥
bājahiṁ bājane bibidha prakārā, nabha aru nagara sumaṁgalacārā.
सची सारदा रमा भवानी । जे सुरतिय सुचि सहज सयानी ॥
sacī sāradā ramā bhavānī, je suratiya suci sahaja sayānī.
कपट नारि बर बेष बनाई । मिलीं सकल रनिवासहिं जाई ॥
kapaṭa nāri bara beṣa banāī, milīṁ sakala ranivāsahiṁ jāī.
करहिं गान कल मंगल बानीं । हरष बिबस सब काहुँ न जानीं ॥
karahiṁ gāna kala maṁgala bānīṁ, haraṣa bibasa saba kāhuṁ na jānīṁ.

Trans:

With fawn-like eyes and face of moon-like brightness, each one was beautiful enough to rob Ratī of all self-conceit. Attired in costly garments of different colors, covered all over with ornaments, and rendered beautiful in every limb, they sang more melodiously than the *koel* to the music of the bells on their wrists and waist and feet, as they moved with all the undulating grace of a wild elephant. All kinds of music played, and there were rejoicings both in heaven and in the city. Indranī, Shārdā, Lakshmī, and Bhawānī, the wisest of all the queens of heaven, assumed the disguise of lovely women, and flocked to the king's gynoecium, singing delightfully with divine voice; and for joy there was no one who recognized them.

छंद-chaṁda:

को जान केहि आनंद बस सब ब्रह्मु बर परिछन चली ।
ko jāna kehi ānaṁda basa saba brahmu bara parichana calī,

कल गान मधुर निसान बरषहिं सुमन सुर सोभा भली ॥
kala gāna madhura nisāna baraṣahiṁ sumana sura sobhā bhalī.
आनंदकंदु बिलोकि दूलहु सकल हियँ हरषित भई ।
ānaṁdakaṁdu biloki dūlahu sakala hiyaṁ haraṣita bhaī,
अंभोज अंबक अंबु उमगि सुअंग पुलकावलि छई ॥
aṁbhoja aṁbaka aṁbu umagi suaṁga pulakāvali chaī.

Trans:
In their ecstatic joy as they went to receive the bridegroom, with melodious song and sweet music, who could tell who was who; the gods showered down flowers and everything was delightful. As they gazed upon the bridegroom, the source of bliss, they were all glad of heart, their lotus eyes overflowed with tears and their every limb quivered with rapture.

दोहा-dohā:

जो सुखु भा सिय मातु मन देखि राम बर बेषु ।
jo sukhu bhā siya mātu mana dekhi rāma bara beṣu,
सो न सकहिं कहि कलप सत सहस सारदा सेषु ॥३१८॥
so na sakahiṁ kahi kalapa sata sahasa sāradā seṣu. 318.

Trans:
The joy of Sītā's mother on beholding Rāma's gallant appearance was more than a thousand Shārdās and Sheshnāgs could tell in a hundred ages.

चौपाई-caupāī:

नयन नीरु हटि मंगल जानी । परिछनि करहिं मुदित मन रानी ॥
nayana nīru haṭi maṁgala jānī, parichani karahiṁ mudita mana rānī.
बेद बिहित अरु कुल आचारू । कीन्ह भली बिधि सब ब्यवहारू ॥
beda bihita aru kula ācārū, kīnha bhalī bidhi saba byavahārū.
पंच सबद धुनि मंगल गाना । पट पाँवड़े परहिं बिधि नाना ॥
paṁca sabada dhuni maṁgala gānā, paṭa pāṁvaṛe parahiṁ bidhi nānā.
करि आरती अरघु तिन्ह दीन्हा । राम गमनु मंडप तब कीन्हा ॥
kari āratī araghu tinha dīnhā, rāma gamanu maṁḍapa taba kīnhā.
दसरथु सहित समाज बिराजे । बिभव बिलोकि लोकपति लाजे ॥
dasarathu sahita samāja birāje, bibhava biloki lokapati lāje.
समयँ समयँ सुर बरषहिं फूला । सांति पढ़हिं महिसुर अनुकूला ॥
samayaṁ samayaṁ sura baraṣahiṁ phūlā, sāṁti paṛhahiṁ mahisura anukūlā.
नभ अरु नगर कोलाहल होई । आपनि पर कछु सुनइ न कोई ॥
nabha aru nagara kolāhala hoī, āpani para kachu sunai na koī.
एहि बिधि रामु मंडपहिं आए । अरघु देइ आसन बैठाए ॥
ehi bidhi rāmu maṁḍapahiṁ āe, araghu dei āsana baiṭhāe.

Trans:
Restraining her tears out of regard for the auspiciousness of the event, the queen with gladness of heart performed the lustral rite, and diligently completed the entire ceremony in accordance with Vedic prescription and family usage. The five instruments of music were accompanied by festal chanting, and rich carpets of different kinds were spread upon the ground. After the lustral rite and the oblation Rāma proceeded to the pavilion. So great was the splendor and magnificence of Dashrath and his retinue that Indra was put to shame by it. From time to time the gods rained down flowers, while the Brahmins repeated the appropriate propitiatory texts. There was such jubilation on the earth and in heaven that no one could hear himself speak, much less anyone else. In this manner Rāma entered the pavilion, where the libation was offered, and he was conducted to his throne.

छंद-chaṁda:

बैठारि आसन आरती करि निरखि बरु सुखु पावहीं ।
baiṭhāri āsana āratī kari nirakhi baru sukhu pāvahīṁ,
मनि बसन भूषन भूरि वारहिं नारि मंगल गावहीं ॥
mani basana bhūṣana bhūri vārahiṁ nāri maṁgala gāvahīṁ.
ब्रह्मादि सुरबर बिप्र बेष बनाइ कौतुक देखहीं ।
brahmādi surabara bipra beṣa banāi kautuka dekhahīṁ,
अवलोकि रघुकुल कमल रबि छबि सुफल जीवन लेखहीं ॥
avaloki raghukula kamala rabi chabi suphala jīvana lekhahīṁ.

Trans:
When the bridegroom was seated on the throne and the lustral rite was performed, all rejoiced at the sight, scattering around him jewels and raiment and ornaments in profusion, while women sang festal songs. Brahmmā and all the other gods disguised as noble Brahmins witnessed the spectacle, and as they gazed on the glorious son of the lotus race of Raghu, reckoned it the happiest moment of their life.

दोहा-dohā:

नाऊ बारी भाट नट राम निछावरि पाइ ।
nāū bārī bhāṭa naṭa rāma nichāvari pāi,
मुदित असीसहिं नाइ सिर हरषु न हृदयँ समाइ ॥३१९॥
mudita asīsahiṁ nāi sira haraṣu na hṛdayaṁ samāi. 319.

Trans:
The barbers and torch-bearers and singers and dancers, who gathered up the offerings that had been scattered about Rāma, bowed their head and invoked blessings upon him from a heart that was bursting with joy.

चौपाई-caupāī:

मिले जनकु दसरथु अति प्रीतीं । करि बैदिक लौकिक सब रीतीं ॥
mile janaku dasarathu ati prītīṁ, kari baidika laukika saba rītīṁ.
मिलत महा दोउ राज बिराजे । उपमा खोजि खोजि कबि लाजे ॥
milata mahā dou rāja birāje, upamā khoji khoji kabi lāje.
लही न कतहुँ हारि हियँ मानी । इन्ह सम एइ उपमा उर आनी ॥
lahī na katahuṁ hāri hiyaṁ mānī, inha sama ei upamā ura ānī.
सामध देखि देव अनुरागे । सुमन बरषि जसु गावन लागे ॥
sāmadha dekhi deva anurāge, sumana baraṣi jasu gāvana lāge.
जगु बिरंचि उपजावा जब तें । देखे सुने ब्याह बहु तब तें ॥
jagu biraṁci upajāvā jaba teṁ, dekhe sune byāha bahu taba teṁ.
सकल भाँति सम साजु समाजू । सम समधी देखे हम आजू ॥
sakala bhāṁti sama sāju samājū, sama samadhī dekhe hama ājū.
देव गिरा सुनि सुंदर साँची । प्रीति अलौकिक दुहु दिसि माची ॥
deva girā suni suṁdara sāṁcī, prīti alaukika duhu disi mācī.
देत पाँवड़े अरघु सुहाए । सादर जनकु मंडपहिं ल्याए ॥
deta pāṁvaṛe araghu suhāe, sādara janaku maṁḍapahiṁ lyāe.

Trans:
Janak and Dashrath joined most affectionately in the observance of every custom, whether religions or secular; and the royal pair were so glorious a sight that the poet, searching where to liken them and finding nothing, must acknowledge himself defeated and admit that they were comparable only to themselves. The gods were enraptured to see the tie of love between the two kings united by marriage alliance; raining down flowers they began to sing the glories of both: "Since Brahmmā first created the world, we have seen and heard of many marriages, but never till this day have we seen a match so perfect in all respects, and two such well-matched fathers." At the sound of this voice from heaven, so gracious and yet so true, there was on both sides a marvelous access of love. Janak led the way with due honors to the pavilion, offering libations and unrolling a carpet as he went.

छंद-chaṁda:

मंडपु बिलोकि बिचित्र रचनाँ रुचिरताँ मुनि मन हरे ।
maṁḍapu biloki bicitra racanāṁ ruciratāṁ muni mana hare,
निज पानि जनक सुजान सब कहुँ आनि सिंघासन धरे ॥
nija pāni janaka sujāna saba kahuṁ āni siṁghāsana dhare.
कुल इष्ट सरिस बसिष्ट पूजे बिनय करि आसिष लही ।

kula iṣṭa sarisa basiṣṭa pūje binaya kari āsiṣa lahī,
कौसिकहि पूजत परम प्रीति कि रीति तौ न परै कही ॥
kausikahi pūjata parama prīti ki rīti tau na parai kahī.

Trans:

Beholding the beauty of the manifold decorations of the pavilion, even the saints were astonished; but the wise Janak with his own hands conducted them all to their seats. Paying the same honor and respect to Vasishtha as to his own patron divinity, he received his blessing; but the supreme devotion with which he greeted Vishwāmitra was of a kind that surpasses description.

दोहा-dohā:

बामदेव आदिक रिषय पूजे मुदित महीस ।
bāmadeva ādika riṣaya pūje mudita mahīsa,
दिए दिब्य आसन सबहि सब सन लही असीस ॥ ३२० ॥
die dibya āsana sabahi saba sana lahī asīsa. 320.

Trans:

With great joy the king did homage to Vāmdev too and the other saints, and gave them all exalted seats and received their blessings.

चौपाई-caupāī:

बहुरि कीन्हि कोसलपति पूजा । जानि ईस सम भाउ न दूजा ॥
bahuri kīnhi kosalapati pūjā, jāni īsa sama bhāu na dūjā.
कीन्हि जोरि कर बिनय बड़ाई । कहि निज भाग्य बिभव बहुताई ॥
kīnhi jori kara binaya baṛāī, kahi nija bhāgya bibhava bahutāī.
पूजे भूपति सकल बराती । समधी सम सादर सब भाँती ॥
pūje bhūpati sakala barātī, samadhī sama sādara saba bhām̐tī.
आसन उचित दिए सब काहू । कहौं काह मुख एक उछाहू ॥
āsana ucita die saba kāhū, kahaum̐ kāha mukha eka uchāhū.
सकल बरात जनक सनमानी । दान मान बिनती बर बानी ॥
sakala barāta janaka sanamānī, dāna māna binatī bara bānī.
बिधि हरि हरु दिसिपति दिनराऊ । जे जानहिं रघुबीर प्रभाऊ ॥
bidhi hari haru disipati dinarāū, je jānahiṁ raghubīra prabhāū.
कपट बिप्र बर बेष बनाएँ । कौतुक देखहिं अति सचु पाएँ ॥
kapaṭa bipra bara beṣa banāem̐, kautuka dekhahiṁ ati sacu pāem̐.
पूजे जनक देव सम जानें । दिए सुआसन बिनु पहिचानें ॥
pūje janaka deva sama jāneṁ, die suāsana binu pahicāneṁ.

Trans:

Again he did homage to the Lord of Kaushal, taking him to be the peer of Mahādev, yea, none other; with clasped hands and in humble phrase extolling him and enlarging on his own marvelous good fortune. Then to all the wedding guests he paid the same homage in every respect as to the bridegroom's father, and assigned them all appropriate seats. How can I with one tongue describe all the pageant? With gifts and compliments and profuse apologies Janak did the honors to all his guests. Brahmmā, Vishnu, Mahādev, the eight guardians of the world and the god of day, who knew Raghubīr's glory, disguised themselves as learned Brahmins and were delighted spectators of the festivities. Janak, though he recognized them not, paid them homage as gods, and led them to exalted seats.

छंद-chaṁda:

पहिचान को केहि जान सबहि अपान सुधि भोरी भई ।
pahicāna ko kehi jāna sabahi apāna sudhi bhorī bhaī,
आनंद कंदु बिलोकि दूलहु उभय दिसि आनँद मई ॥
ānaṁda kaṁdu biloki dūlahu ubhaya disi ānam̐da maī.
सुर लखे राम सुजान पूजे मानसिक आसन दए ।
sura lakhe rāma sujāna pūje mānasika āsana dae,
अवलोकि सीलु सुभाउ प्रभु को बिबुध मन प्रमुदित भए ॥
avaloki sīlu subhāu prabhu ko bibudha mana pramudita bhae.

Trans:

Who could tell who was who, when there was no one who could answer even for himself. As they gazed on the bridegroom, the root of joy, joy was diffused on all sides. When he saw the gods, the all-wise Rāma worshipped them mentally and assigned them what seats they fancied; and the heavenly powers were delighted to behold the gracious manner of their Lord.

दोहा-dohā:

रामचंद्र मुख चंद्र छबि लोचन चारु चकोर ।
rāmacaṁdra mukha caṁdra chabi locana cāru cakora,
करत पान सादर सकल प्रेमु प्रमोदु न थोर ॥ ३२१ ॥
karata pāna sādara sakala premu pramodu na thora. 321.

Trans:

As the partridge drinks in the light of the moon, so their eyes reverently drank in the beauty of Rāma's face with the utmost rapture.

चौपाई-caupāī:

समउ बिलोकि बसिष्ठ बोलाए । सादर सतानंदु सुनि आए ॥
samau biloki basiṣṭha bolāe, sādara satānaṁdu suni āe.
बेगि कुअँरि अब आनहु जाई । चले मुदित मुनि आयसु पाई ॥
begi kuam̐ri aba ānahu jāī, cale mudita muni āyasu pāī.
रानी सुनि उपरोहित बानी । प्रमुदित सखिन्ह समेत सयानी ॥
rānī suni uparohita bānī, pramudita sakhinha sameta sayānī.
बिप्र बधू कुलबृद्ध बोलाईं । करि कुल रीति सुमंगल गाईं ॥
bipra badhū kulabṛddha bolāīṁ, kari kula rīti sumaṁgala gāīṁ.
नारि बेष जे सुर बर बामा । सकल सुभायँ सुंदरी स्यामा ॥
nāri beṣa je sura bara bāmā, sakala subhāyam̐ suṁdarī syāmā.
तिन्हहि देखि सुखु पावहिं नारीं । बिनु पहिचानि प्रानहु ते प्यारीं ॥
tinhahi dekhi sukhu pāvahiṁ nārīṁ, binu pahicāni prānahu te pyārīṁ.
बार बार सनमानहिं रानी । उमा रमा सारद सम जानी ॥
bāra bāra sanamānahiṁ rānī, umā ramā sārada sama jānī.
सीय सँवारि समाजु बनाई । मुदित मंडपहिं चलीं लवाई ॥
sīya sam̐vāri samāju banāī, mudita maṁḍapahiṁ calīṁ lavāī.

Trans:

Perceiving that the time had arrived, Vasishtha called, and Shatānand came with ready obedience. "Go now and quickly bring the bride." On receiving this order, the saint went gladly, and on hearing his message the queen with her attendants was delighted, and she sent for the Brahmin ladies and the elders of the family, and with songs of joy performed all the family rites. The goddesses, who were disguised as women, were all so amiable and lovely, in the first bloom of their youth, that the ladies were charmed to see them; and though not recognizing them, held them dearer than life. Again and again the queen did them honor, accounting them the equals of Umā, Rāma, and Shārdā. After dressing Sītā and forming in procession they joyously conducted her to the pavilion.

छंद-chaṁda:

चलि ल्याइ सीतहि सखीं सादर सजि सुमंगल भामिनीं ।
cali lyāi sītahi sakhīṁ sādara saji sumaṁgala bhāminīṁ,
नवसप्त साजें सुंदरी सब मत्त कुंजर गामिनीं ॥
navasapta sājeṁ suṁdarī saba matta kuṁjara gāminīṁ.
कल गान सुनि मुनि ध्यान त्यागहिं काम कोकिल लाजहीं ।
kala gāna suni muni dhyāna tyāgahiṁ kāma kokila lājahīṁ,
मंजीर नूपुर कलित कंकन ताल गती बर बाजहीं ॥
maṁjīra nūpura kalita kaṁkana tāla gatī bara bājahīṁ.

Trans:

Reverently and with auspicious pomp her attendant ladies conducted Sītā, each of them of lovely form and superbly adorned, moving with the voluptuous grace of young elephant. At the sound of their melodious strains the saints forgot their meditations, the god of love and the *koel* were abashed; while the bells on their anklets and gleaming girdles rang out with the cymbals a delightful accompaniment as they moved.

दोहा-dohā:

सोहति बनिता बृंद महुँ सहज सुहावनि सीय ।
sohati banitā bṛṁda mahuṁ sahaja suhāvani sīya,
छबि ललना गन मध्य जनु सुषमा तिय कमनीय ॥ ३२२ ॥
chabi lalanā gana madhya janu suṣamā tiya kamanīya. 322.

Trans:

Among her maidens Sītā shines forth in native loveliness, like Bliss personified among the Graces.

चौपाई-caupāī:

सिय सुंदरता बरनि न जाई । लघु मति बहुत मनोहरताई ॥
siya suṁdaratā barani na jāī, laghu mati bahuta manoharatāī.
आवत दीखि बरातिन्ह सीता । रूप रासि सब भाँति पुनीता ॥
āvata dīkhi barātinha sītā, rūpa rāsi saba bhāṁti punītā.
सबहि मनहिं मन किए प्रनामा । देखि राम भए पूरनकामा ॥
sabahi manahiṁ mana kie pranāmā, dekhi rāma bhae pūranakāmā.
हरषे दसरथ सुतन्ह समेता । कहि न जाइ उर आनँदु जेता ॥
harașe dasaratha sutanha sametā, kahi na jāi ura ānaṁdu jetā.
सुर प्रनामु करि बरिसहिं फूला । मुनि असीस धुनि मंगल मूला ॥
sura pranāmu kari barisahiṁ phūlā, muni asīsa dhuni maṁgala mūlā.
गान निसान कोलाहलु भारी । प्रेम प्रमोद मगन नर नारी ॥
gāna nisāna kolāhalu bhārī, prema pramoda magana nara nārī.
एहि बिधि सीय मंडपहिं आई । प्रमुदित सांति पढ़हिं मुनिराई ॥
ehi bidhi sīya maṁḍapahiṁ āī, pramudita sāṁti paṛhahiṁ munirāī.
तेहि अवसर कर बिधि ब्यवहारू । दुहुँ कुलगुर सब कीन्ह अचारू ॥
tehi avasara kara bidhi byavahārū, duhuṁ kulagura saba kīnha acārū.

Trans:

Her beauty is indescribable, so great is it and so little my wit. When the wedding guests saw her approach, so exquisitely charming and every way divine, they all did homage to her from their inmost soul. At the sight of her Rāma was filled with love, and Dashrath and his sons were glad of heart beyond all telling. The gods did homage and rained down flowers; the saints gave their blessings in auspicious wise; there was a mingled noise of singing and playing and general rejoicing throughout the city. In this manner Sītā arrived at the pavilion, while the great saints joyously recited the set forms of prayer, and the two family Gurūs performed all the due rites and ceremonies.

छंद-chaṁda:

आचारु करि गुर गौरि गनपति मुदित बिप्र पुजावहीं ।
ācāru kari gura gauri ganapati mudita bipra pujāvahīṁ,
सुर प्रगटि पूजा लेहिं देहिं असीस अति सुखु पावहीं ॥
sura pragaṭi pūjā lehiṁ dehiṁ asīsa ati sukhu pāvahīṁ.
मधुपर्क मंगल द्रब्य जो जेहि समय मुनि मन महुँ चहैं ।
madhuparka maṁgala drabya jo jehi samaya muni mana mahuṁ cahaiṁ,
भरे कनक कोपर कलस सो तब लिएहिं परिचारक रहैं ॥ १ ॥
bhare kanaka kopara kalasa so taba liehiṁ paricāraka rahaiṁ. 1.

कुल रीति प्रीति समेत रबि कहि देत सबु सादर कियो ।
kula rīti prīti sameta rabi kahi deta sabu sādara kiyo,
एहि भाँति देव पुजाइ सीतहि सुभग सिंघासनु दियो ॥
ehi bhāṁti deva pujāi sītahi subhaga siṁghāsanu diyo.
सिय राम अवलोकनि परसपर प्रेम काहु न लखि परै ।
siya rāma avalokani parasapara prema kāhu na lakhi parai,
मन बुद्धि बर बानी अगोचर प्रगट कबि कैसें करै ॥ २ ॥
mana buddhi bara bānī agocara pragaṭa kabi kaiseṁ karai. 2.

Trans:

After the ceremonies the Gurūs directed the glad Brahmins to worship Gaurī and Ganesh; the gods in visible form accepted the homage, and gave their blessing, which they received with joy. Whatever auspicious article or condiment the holy men sought at any time was at once supplied, in plates and bowls of gold, by the ever ready attendants. The sun-god himself lovingly pointed out the family traditions; and having reverently and dutifully performed all family rites in accordance with that, and having offered homage to the gods, they conducted Sītā to her glorious throne. The mutual love with which Sītā and Rāma regarded each other was too much for words; it exceeds all senses, or intelligence, or speech, or perception; how then can the poet express it?

दोहा-dohā:

होम समय तनु धरि अनलु अति सुख आहुति लेहिं ।
homa samaya tanu dhari analu ati sukha āhuti lehiṁ,
बिप्र बेष धरि बेद सब कहि बिबाह बिधि देहिं ॥ ३२३ ॥
bipra beṣa dhari beda saba kahi bibāha bidhi dehiṁ. 323.

Trans:

While oblations were offered to the sacred fire, the fire-god in person accepted the offerings with great delight; and the Vedas in the guise of Brahmins directed the procedure of the nuptial ceremony.

चौपाई-caupāī:

जनक पाटमहिषी जग जानी । सीय मातु किमि जाइ बखानी ॥
janaka pāṭamahiṣī jaga jānī, sīya mātu kimi jāi bakhānī.
सुजसु सुकृत सुख सुंदरताई । सब समेटि बिधि रची बनाई ॥
sujasu sukṛta sukha suṁdaratāī, saba sameṭi bidhi racī banāī.
समउ जानि मुनिबरन्ह बोलाईं । सुनत सुआसिनि सादर ल्याईं ॥
samau jāni munibaranha bolāīṁ, sunata suāsini sādara lyāīṁ.
जनक बाम दिसि सोह सुनयना । हिमगिरि संग बनि जनु मयना ॥
janaka bāma disi soha sunayanā, himagiri saṁga bani janu mayanā.
कनक कलस मनि कोपर रूरे । सुचि सुगंध मंगल जल पूरे ॥
kanaka kalasa mani kopara rūre, suci sugaṁdha maṁgala jala pūre.
निज कर मुदित रायँ अरु रानी । धरे राम के आगें आनी ॥
nija kara mudita rāyaṁ aru rānī, dhare rāma ke āgeṁ ānī.
पढ़हिं बेद मुनि मंगल बानी । गगन सुमन झरि अवसरु जानी ॥
paṛhahiṁ beda muni maṁgala bānī, gagana sumana jhari avasaru jānī.
बरु बिलोकि दंपति अनुरागे । पाय पुनीत पखारन लागे ॥
baru biloki daṁpati anurāge, pāya punīta pakhārana lāge.

Trans:

What words can describe Janak's illustrious queen-consort, the mother of Sītā—in whose composition the Creator had combined the perfection of glory, piety, happiness, and beauty. At the due time the saints called her, and she came responsive to the summons along with other wedded ladies. Then shone forth Sunayanā at Janak's left hand, just as Mainā beside Himalaya. With their own hands the glad king and queen take and place before Rāma golden vases and costly jeweled trays full of holy water and delicious perfumes. The saints with auspicious voice recite the Veda, and at the proper time the heaven rains flowers, while the father and mother of the bride look on in rapture and begin to wash his holy feet.

छंद-chaṁda:

लागे पखारन पाय पंकज प्रेम तन पुलकावली ।
lāge pakhārana pāya paṁkaja prema tana pulakāvalī,
नभ नगर गान निसान जय धुनि उमगि जनु चहुँ दिसि चली ॥

nabha nagara gāna nisāna jaya dhuni umagi janu cahuṁ disi calī.

जे पद सरोज मनोज अरि उर सर सदैव बिराजहीं ।
je pada saroja manoja ari ura sara sadaiva birājahīṁ,
जे सकृत सुमिरत बिमलता मन सकल कलि मल भाजहीं ॥ १ ॥
je sakṛta sumirata bimalatā mana sakala kali mala bhājahīṁ. 1.

जे परसि मुनिबनिता लही गति रही जो पातकमई ।
je parasi munibanitā lahī gati rahī jo pātakamaī,
मकरंदु जिन्ह को संभु सिर सुचिता अवधि सुर बरनई ॥
makaraṁdu jinha ko saṁbhu sira sucitā avadhi sura baranaī.
करि मधुप मन मुनि जोगिजन जे सेइ अभिमत गति लहैं ।
kari madhupa mana muni jogijana je sei abhimata gati lahaiṁ,
ते पद पखारत भाग्यभाजनु जनकु जय जय सब कहैं ॥ २ ॥
te pada pakhārata bhāgyabhājanu janaku jaya jaya saba kahaiṁ. 2.

बर कुअँरि करतल जोरि साखोचारु दोउ कुलगुर करैं ।
bara kuaṁri karatala jori sākhocāru dou kulagura karaiṁ,
भयो पानिगहनु बिलोकि बिधि सुर मनुज मुनि आँनद भरैं ॥
bhayo pānigahanu biloki bidhi sura manuja muni āṁnada bharaiṁ.
सुखमूल दूलहु देखि दंपति पुलक तन हुलस्यो हियो ।
sukhamūla dūlahu dekhi daṁpati pulaka tana hulasyo hiyo,
करि लोक बेद बिधानु कन्यादानु नृपभूषन कियो ॥ ३ ॥
kari loka beda bidhānu kanyādānu nṛpabhūṣana kiyo. 3.

हिमवंत जिमि गिरिजा महेसहि हरिहि श्री सागर दई ।
himavaṁta jimi girijā mahesahi harihi śrī sāgara daī,
तिमि जनक रामहि सिय समरपी बिस्व कल कीरति नई ॥
timi janaka rāmahi siya samarapī bisva kala kīrati naī.
क्यों करै बिनय बिदेहु कियो बिदेहु मूरति सावँरीं ।
kyoṁ karai binaya bidehu kiyo bidehu mūrati sāvaṁrīṁ,
करि होमु बिधिवत गाँठि जोरी होन लागीं भावँरीं ॥ ४ ॥
kari homu bidhivata gāṁṭhi jorī hona lāgīṁ bhāvaṁrīṁ. 4.

Trans:

Their whole frame quivering with excess of love they began to lave the lotus feet; while both in heaven and in the city there was singing and music and shouts of victory bursting forth and overflowing in all directions. The lotus feet that ever gleam in the lake of Shiva's bosom; by meditating upon which for a single moment every impurity of the soul and defilement of this wicked world is removed; by whose touch the sage's guilty wife attained salvation; whose honeyed fragrance, as the gods declare, is ever present on Shambhu's head; on which the bee-like soul of saints and ascetics ever dwells ere they reach the heaven of their desire; these holy feet are bathed by Janak, amidst the glad acclaim of all. The two family priests join the hands of the bride and bridegroom and recite their genealogy descent. The mystic union is completed, and at the sight Brahmmā and all gods and men and saints are full of joy. As the bride's parents gazed on the gracious bridegroom, both their soul and body are raptured with delight; and having completed every family and scriptural observance, the glorious monarch gives his daughter to her Lord. As Himalaya gave Girijā to Mahādev, and as Ocean gave Lakshmī to Vishnu, in like manner did Janak bestow Sītā on Rāma; and creation was glorified anew. King Videh was unable to make any supplication, since Rāma, that Prince of swarthy complexion had justified his name by making him forget everything about his body. When oblations had been offered to the sacred fire with due rites, the ends of garments of the Bride and the Bridegroom were tied together and the couple began to circumambulate the fire.

दोहा-dohā:

जय धुनि बंदी बेद धुनि मंगल गान निसान ।
jaya dhuni baṁdī beda dhuni maṁgala gāna nisāna,
सुनि हरषहिं बरषहिं बिबुध सुरतरु सुमन सुजान ॥ ३२४ ॥
suni haraṣahiṁ baraṣahiṁ bibudha surataru sumana sujāna. 324.

Trans:

At the sound of the huzzas and the minstrelsy and the recitation of the Veda and the auspicious chanting and the music, the all-wise gods were delighted and rained down flowers from the tree of paradise.

चौपाई-caupāī:

कुअँरु कुअँरि कल भावँरि देहीं । नयन लाभु सब सादर लेहीं ॥
kuaṁru kuaṁri kala bhāvaṁri dehīṁ, nayana lābhu saba sādara lehīṁ.
जाइ न बरनि मनोहर जोरी । जो उपमा कछु कहौं सो थोरी ॥
jāi na barani manohara jorī, jo upamā kachu kahauṁ so thorī.
राम सीय सुंदर प्रतिछाहीं । जगमगात मनि खंभन माहीं ॥
rāma sīya suṁdara pratichāhīṁ, jagamagāta mani khaṁbhana māhīṁ.
मनहुँ मदन रति धरि बहु रूपा । देखत राम बिआहु अनूपा ॥
manahuṁ madana rati dhari bahu rūpā, dekhata rāma biāhu anūpā.
दरस लालसा सकुच न थोरी । प्रगटत दुरत बहोरि बहोरी ॥
darasa lālasā sakuca na thorī, pragaṭata durata bahori bahorī.
भए मगन सब देखनिहारे । जनक समान अपान बिसारे ॥
bhae magana saba dekhanihāre, janaka samāna apāna bisāre.
प्रमुदित मुनिन्ह भाँवरीं फेरीं । नेगसहित सब रीति निबेरीं ॥
pramudita muninha bhāṁvarīṁ pherīṁ, negasahita saba rīti niberīṁ.
राम सीय सिर सेंदुर देहीं । सोभा कहि न जाति बिधि केहीं ॥
rāma sīya sira seṁdura dehīṁ, sobhā kahi na jāti bidhi kehīṁ.
अरुन पराग जलजु भरि नीकें । ससिहि भूष अहि लोभ अमी कें ॥
aruna parāga jalaju bhari nīkeṁ, sasihi bhūṣa ahi lobha amī keṁ.
बहुरि बसिष्ठ दीन्हि अनुसासन । बरु दुलहिनि बैठे एक आसन ॥
bahuri basiṣṭha dīnhi anusāsana, baru dulahini baiṭhe eka āsana.

Trans:

The bride and bridegroom with measured paces performed the circumambulation, while all present feasted their adoring gaze on the lovely display. The beauty of the happy pair is not to be described; whatever comparison might be suggested would fall short of the reality. The beauteous images of Rāma and Sītā were reflected in the jeweled pillars and sparkled like incarnations of Kāmdev and Ratī, who themselves had come to witness Rāma's glorious wedding and, from mingled curiosity and bashfulness, at one moment showed themselves openly and at another retired out of sight. All the spectators were enraptured and like Janak forgot all about themselves. Joyously the saints bade them pace the circles around; the rite was accomplished and the marriage offerings made. Rāma applied the vermilion to Sītā's forehead, brilliant beyond all description; and it seemed like a serpent thirsting for ambrosia, as he decorated her moonlike face with the red pollen of his lotus hand. Then by Vasishtha's direction the bride and bridegroom took their seat together.

छंद-chaṁda:

बैठे बरासन रामु जानकि मुदित मन दसरथु भए ।
baiṭhe barāsana rāmu jānaki mudita mana dasarathu bhae,
तनु पुलक पुनि पुनि देखि अपनें सुकृत सुरतरु फल नए ॥
tanu pulaka puni puni dekhi apaneṁ sukṛta surataru phala nae.
भरि भुवन रहा उछाहु राम बिबाहु भा सबहीं कहा ।
bhari bhuvana rahā uchāhu rāma bibāhu bhā sabahīṁ kahā,
केहि भाँति बरनि सिरात रसना एक यहु मंगलु महा ॥ १ ॥

kehi bhām̐ti barani sirāta rasanā eka yahu mam̐galu mahā. 1.

तब जनक पाइ बसिष्ठ आयसु ब्याह साज सँवारि कै ।
taba janaka pāi basiṣṭha āyasu byāha sāja sam̐vāri kai,
माँडवी श्रुतिकीरति उरमिला कुअँरि लईं हँकारि कै ॥
mām̐ḍavī śrutikīrati uramilā kuam̐ri laīṁ ham̐kāri kai.
कुसकेतु कन्या प्रथम जो गुन सील सुख सोभामई ।
kusaketu kanyā prathama jo guna sīla sukha sobhāmaī,
सब रीति प्रीति समेत करि सो ब्याहि नृप भरतहि दई ॥२॥
saba rīti prīti sameta kari so byāhi nṛpa bharatahi daī. 2.

जानकी लघु भगिनी सकल सुंदरि सिरोमनि जानि कै ।
jānakī laghu bhaginī sakala suṁdari siromani jāni kai,
सो तनय दीन्ही ब्याहि लखनहि सकल बिधि सनमानि कै ॥
so tanaya dīnhī byāhi lakhanahi sakala bidhi sanamāni kai.
जेहि नामु श्रुतकीरति सुलोचनि सुमुखि सब गुन आगरी ।
jehi nāmu śrutakīrati sulocani sumukhi saba guna āgarī,
सो दई रिपुसूदनहि भूपति रूप सील उजागरी ॥३॥
so daī ripusūdanahi bhūpati rūpa sīla ujāgarī. 3.

अनुरुप बर दुलहिनि परस्पर लखि सकुच हियँ हरषहीं ।
anurupa bara dulahini paraspara lakhi sakuca hiyam̐ haraṣahīṁ,
सब मुदित सुंदरता सराहहिं सुमन सुर गन बरषहीं ॥
saba mudita suṁdaratā sarāhahiṁ sumana sura gana baraṣahīṁ.
सुंदरी सुंदर बरन्ह सह सब एक मंडप राजहीं ।
suṁdarī suṁdara baranha saha saba eka maṁḍapa rājahīṁ,
जनु जीव उर चारिउ अवस्था बिभुन सहित बिराजहीं ॥४॥
janu jīva ura cāriu avasthā bibhuna sahita birājahīṁ. 4.

Trans:

When Rāma and Jānakī took their seat, Dashrath's soul rejoiced and his frame quivered with emotion, as again and again he fixed his gaze upon them and saw as it were his own virtue, like the tree of paradise, blossoming anew. There was such rejoicing all over the world at the news of Rāma's wedding, how can it be described? With but one tongue how can anybody delineate that infinite joy that had no bounds? Then Janak, having received Vasishtha's order summoned the other three princesses, Māndvī, Urmilā, and Shruti-kīrtī, and made all arrangements necessary for their marriage ceremonies. After affectionately performing every rite, the king at first gave to Bharat Māndvī, the beautiful and accomplished daughter of Kush-ketu. Then next with all honor Janak bestowed upon Lakshman Urmilā, Jānakī's lovely younger sister; and finally gave away to Ripusūdan Shruti-kīrtī, most bright-eyed and charming, and no less amiable than beautiful. As bride and bridegroom modestly gazed on each other and noticed the contrast, they were glad of heart; while everyone delightedly applauded the beauty of the scene, and the gods rained down flowers. All equally beautiful, though diverse in hue, they shone resplendent in the pavilion, as though the four states of life with their several lords had met in one living soul.

दोहा-dohā:

मुदित अवधपति सकल सुत बधुन्ह समेत निहारि ।
mudita avadhapati sakala suta badhunha sameta nihāri,
जनु पाए महिपाल मनि क्रियन्ह सहित फल चारि ॥३२५॥
janu pāe mahipāla mani kriyanha sahita phala cāri. 325.

Trans:

The king of Avadh gazed with delight on his four sons and their brides; as though that jewel of monarchs had, in them, realized the four methods of religion and the four cognate aims of life.

चौपाई-caupāī:

जसि रघुबीर ब्याह बिधि बरनी । सकल कुअँर ब्याहे तेहिं करनी ॥
jasi raghubīra byāha bidhi baranī, sakala kuam̐ra byāhe tehiṁ karanī.
कहि न जाइ कछु दाइज भूरी । रहा कनक मनि मंडपु पूरी ॥
kahi na jāi kachu dāija bhūrī, rahā kanaka mani maṁḍapu pūrī.
कंबल बसन बिचित्र पटोरे । भाँति भाँति बहु मोल न थोरे ॥
kaṁbala basana bicitra paṭore, bhām̐ti bhām̐ti bahu mola na thore.
गज रथ तुरग दास अरु दासी । धेनु अलंकृत कामदुहा सी ॥
gaja ratha turaga dāsa aru dāsī, dhenu alaṁkṛta kāmaduhā sī.
बस्तु अनेक करिअ किमि लेखा । कहि न जाइ जानहिं जिन्ह देखा ॥
bastu aneka karia kimi lekhā, kahi na jāi jānahiṁ jinha dekhā.
लोकपाल अवलोकि सिहाने । लीन्ह अवधपति सबु सुखु माने ॥
lokapāla avaloki sihāne, līnha avadhapati sabu sukhu māne.
दीन्ह जाचकन्हि जो जेहि भावा । उबरा सो जनवासेहिं आवा ॥
dīnha jācakanhi jo jehi bhāvā, ubarā so janavāsehiṁ āvā.
तब कर जोरि जनकु मृदु बानी । बोले सब बरात सनमानी ॥
taba kara jori janaku mṛdu bānī, bole saba barāta sanamānī.

Trans:

All the princes were married with the same rites as have been described for Rāma. The enormous bestowment was beyond description; the whole pavilion was full of gold and jewels. Shawls, robes and silks of all kinds in the greatest profusion and of immense value, elephants, chariots, horses, men-servants and maid-servants, and cows with gilded horns and hoofs, as beautiful as the cow of plenty; things so many that no one could count them, nor credit their number if he had not seen them. At the sight the guardians of the world broke out into praises of the bestowal, and Avadh's king received it all most graciously. To everyone who asked was given whatever he desired, and what remained over was taken to the guests' quarters. Then with folded hands and bated breath Janak courteously entreated all the bridegroom's party.

छंद-chaṁda:

सनमानि सकल बरात आदर दान बिनय बड़ाइ कै ।
sanamāni sakala barāta ādara dāna binaya baṛāi kai,
प्रमुदित महा मुनि बृंद बंदे पूजि प्रेम लड़ाइ कै ॥
pramudita mahā muni bṛṁda baṁde pūji prema laṛāi kai.
सिरु नाइ देव मनाइ सब सन कहत कर संपुट किएँ ।
siru nāi deva manāi saba sana kahata kara saṁpuṭa kieṁ,
सुर साधु चाहत भाउ सिंधु कि तोष जल अंजलि दिएँ ॥१॥
sura sādhu cāhata bhāu siṁdhu ki toṣa jala aṁjali dieṁ. 1.

कर जोरि जनकु बहोरि बंधु समेत कोसलराय सों ।
kara jori janaku bahori baṁdhu sameta kosalarāya soṁ,
बोले मनोहर बयन सानि सनेह सील सुभाय सों ॥
bole manohara bayana sāni saneha sīla subhāya soṁ.
संबंध राजन रावरें हम बड़े अब सब बिधि भए ।
saṁbaṁdha rājana rāvareṁ hama baṛe aba saba bidhi bhae,
एहि राज साज समेत सेवक जानिबे बिनु गथ लए ॥२॥
ehi rāja sāja sameta sevaka jānibe binu gatha lae. 2.

ए दारिका परिचारिका करि पालिबीं करुना नई ।
e dārikā paricārikā kari pālibīṁ karunā naī,
अपराधु छमिबो बोलि पठए बहुत हौं ढीट्यो कई ॥
aparādhu chamibo boli paṭhae bahuta hauṁ ḍhīṭyo kaī.

पुनि भानुकुलभूषन सकल सनमान निधि समधी किए ।
puni bhānukulabhūṣana sakala sanamāna nidhi samadhī kie,
कहि जाति नहिं बिनती परस्पर प्रेम परिपूरन हिए ॥ ३ ॥
kahi jāti nahiṁ binatī paraspara prema paripūrana hie. 3.

बृंदारका गन सुमन बरिसहिं राउ जनवासेहि चले ।
bṛṁdārakā gana sumana barisahiṁ rāu janavāsehi cale,
दुंदुभी जय धुनि बेद धुनि नभ नगर कौतूहल भले ॥
duṁdubhī jaya dhuni beda dhuni nabha nagara kautūhala bhale.
तब सखीं मंगल गान करत मुनीस आयसु पाइ कै ।
taba sakhīṁ maṁgala gāna karata munīsa āyasu pāi kai,
दूलह दुलहिनिन्ह सहित सुंदरि चलीं कोहबर ल्याइ कै ॥ ४ ॥
dūlaha dulahininha sahita suṁdari calīṁ kohabara lyāi kai. 4.

Trans:

After courteously entreating all the marriage guests with high ceremony, gifts, apologies and compliments, he joyfully proceeded with much devotion to do his humble homage to the saintly throng. With bowed head he propitiated the gods, and thus, with hands clasped in prayer, addressed them all: "Gods and saints seek only one's love alone; can the ocean's wants be satisfied by libation of few drops?" Again with clasped hands Janak and his brother spoke to the king of Kaushal, with winning words full of love and amiability: "O king, I am greatly ennobled by your alliance; know that my realm and all that I have is freely yours to command. Take these girls as your hand-maidens and graciously protect them, and pardon me my sin and presumption in calling you here." The glory of the Solar race in turn addressed his royal cousin in terms of highest honor; their courtesy was past all telling, and also the love that overflowed their hearts. The deities rained down flowers as the monarch proceeded to the guest-chamber amidst the crash of kettledrums, the muttered recitation of the Veda, and glad rejoicings both on earth and in heaven. Then by the saint's command and singing auspicious strains as they went, the fair ladies of the court conducted to the marriage pavilion the bridegrooms and their brides.

दोहा-dohā:

पुनि पुनि रामहि चितव सिय सकुचति मनु सकुचै न ।
puni puni rāmahi citava siya sakucati manu sakucai na,
हरत मनोहर मीन छबि प्रेम पिआसे नैन ॥ ३२६ ॥
harata manohara mīna chabi prema piāse naina. 326.

Trans:

Again and again did Sītā gaze upon Rāma with modest mien, but full of confidence at heart; and her eyes athirst with love outshone the fish in Kāmdev's blazon.

मासपारायण ग्यारहवाँ विश्राम
māsapārāyaṇa gyārahavām̐ viśrāma
(Pause 11 for a Thirty-Day Recitation)

चौपाई-caupāī:

स्याम सरीरु सुभायँ सुहावन । सोभा कोटि मनोज लजावन ॥
syāma sarīru subhāyam̐ suhāvana, sobhā koṭi manoja lajāvana.
जावक जुत पद कमल सुहाए । मुनि मन मधुप रहत जिन्ह छाए ॥
jāvaka juta pada kamala suhāe, muni mana madhupa rahata jinha chāe.
पीत पुनीत मनोहर धोती । हरति बाल रबि दामिनि जोती ॥
pīta punīta manohara dhotī, harati bāla rabi dāmini jotī.
कल किंकिनि कटि सूत्र मनोहर । बाहु बिसाल बिभूषन सुंदर ॥
kala kiṁkini kaṭi sūtra manohara, bāhu bisāla bibhūṣana suṁdara.
पीत जनेउ महाछबि देई । कर मुद्रिका चोरि चितु लेई ॥
pīta janeu mahāchabi deī, kara mudrikā cori citu leī.
सोहत ब्याह साज सब साजे । उर आयत उरभूषन राजे ॥
sohata byāha sāja saba sāje, ura āyata urabhūṣana rāje.
पिअर उपरना काखासोती । दुहुँ आँचरन्हि लगे मनि मोती ॥
piara uparanā kākhāsotī, duhum̐ ām̐caranhi lage mani motī.
नयन कमल कल कुंडल काना । बदनु सकल सौंदर्ज निधाना ॥
nayana kamala kala kuṁḍala kānā, badanu sakala sauṁdarja nidhānā.
सुंदर भृकुटि मनोहर नासा । भाल तिलकु रुचिरता निवासा ॥
suṁdara bhṛkuṭi manohara nāsā, bhāla tilaku ruciratā nivāsā.
सोहत मौरु मनोहर माथे । मंगलमय मुकुता मनि गाथे ॥
sohata mauru manohara māthe, maṁgalamaya mukutā mani gāthe.

Trans:

Dark in hue and full of untaught grace, his beauty put to shame a myriad Loves; his lac-stained feet gleamed like some lotus, the haunt of bee-like saintly souls; his pure and lustrous yellow robe outshone the rising sun or lightning-flash; the little bells on his waist-belt made a delicious tinkling; long were his arms, clasped with glittering bracelets; his yellow *janeu* set him off to perfection; his signet ring ravishing; lustrous were all his many wedding adornments and the stars and collars on his broad chest; across his shoulders draped a yellow serape with fringe of gems and pearls; with lotus eyes and bright pendants from his ears and a face the very storehouse of beauty; with lovely brows and charming nose, and on his forehead a most bewitching spot, while on his head the auspicious marriage-crown shone glorious with knotted pearls and gems.

छंद-chaṁda:

गाथे महामनि मौर मंजुल अंग सब चित चोरहीं ।
gāthe mahāmani maura maṁjula aṁga saba cita corahīṁ,
पुर नारि सुर सुंदरीं बरहि बिलोकि सब तिन तोरहीं ॥
pura nāri sura suṁdarīṁ barahi biloki saba tina torahīṁ.
मनि बसन भूषन वारि आरति करहिं मंगल गावहिं ।
mani basana bhūṣana vāri ārati karahiṁ maṁgala gāvahiṁ,
सुर सुमन बरिसहिं सूत मागध बंदि सुजसु सुनावहीं ॥ १ ॥
sura sumana barisahiṁ sūta māgadha baṁdi sujasu sunāvahīṁ. 1.

कोहबरहिं आने कुअँरु कुअँरि सुआसिनिन्ह सुख पाइ कै ।
kohabarahiṁ āne kuam̐ra kuam̐ri suāsininha sukha pāi kai,
अति प्रीति लौकिक रीति लागीं करन मंगल गाइ कै ॥
ati prīti laukika rīti lāgīṁ karana maṁgala gāi kai.
लहकौरि गौरि सिखाव रामहि सीय सन सारद कहैं ।
lahakauri gauri sikhāva rāmahi sīya sana sārada kahaiṁ,
रनिवासु हास बिलास रस बस जन्म को फलु सब लहैं ॥ २ ॥
ranivāsu hāsa bilāsa rasa basa janma ko phalu saba lahaiṁ. 2.

निज पानि मनि महुँ देखिअति मूरति सुरूपनिधान की ।
nija pāni mani mahum̐ dekhiati mūrati surūpanidhāna kī,
चालति न भुजबल्ली बिलोकनि बिरह भय बस जानकी ॥
cālati na bhujaballī bilokani biraha bhaya basa jānakī.
कौतुक बिनोद प्रमोदु प्रेमु न जाइ कहि जानहिं अलीं ।
kautuka binoda pramodu premu na jāi kahi jānahiṁ alīṁ,
बर कुअँरि सुंदर सकल सखीं लवाइ जनवासेहि चलीं ॥ ३ ॥
bara kuam̐ri suṁdara sakala sakhīṁ lavāi janavāsehi calīṁ. 3.

तेहि समय सुनिअ असीस जहँ तहँ नगर नभ आनँदु महा ।
tehi samaya sunia asīsa jaham̐ taham̐ nagara nabha ānam̐du mahā,
चिरु जिअहुँ जोरीं चारु चारयो मुदित मन सबहीं कहा ॥
ciru jiahum̐ jorīṁ cāru cārayo mudita mana sabahīṁ kahā.

जोगींद्र सिद्ध मुनीस देव बिलोकि प्रभु दुंदुभि हनी ।
jogīṁdra siddha munīsa deva biloki prabhu duṁdubhi hanī,
चले हरषि बरषि प्रसून निज निज लोक जय जय जय भनी ॥४॥
cale haraṣi baraṣi prasūna nija nija loka jaya jaya jaya bhanī. 4.

Trans:

The knotted gems and the crown and his comely person ravished all hearts; and not a woman or goddess was there in heaven or earth, who did not, at the sight of his beauty, break a straw. After scattering round about him jewels and raiment and adornments they perform the lustral rite, singing auspicious songs, while the gods rain down flowers, and bards, minstrels, and rhapsodists announce his glories. When the bride and bridegroom entered the marriage pavilion, great was the joy of the attendants, who with festive songs and in most loving ways began to perform the accustomed observances. Gaurī herself taught Rāma, and Shārdā told Sītā how to give each other the rice-milk; and all the ladies of the seraglio were so taken with the merry sport that they reckoned it the happiest moment of their lives. When Jānakī saw in the gems on her fingers the reflection of the all-beautiful, she dared not move her eyes or lithesome arm for fear of losing his presence. The rapture of delight, the ecstasy of love surpassed all telling; only those happy dames could comprehend it who escorted the bride and bridegroom to the guesthouse. Then might be heard on all sides blessings and great exultation in heaven and on earth and a universal shout of joy, "Long life to the four happy couples." Hermits, saints and sages, the gods too on beholding their Lord, sounded their kettledrums and returned in gladness, each to his own realm, raining down flowers and crying "Victory, Victory."

दोहा-dohā:

सहित बधूटिन्ह कुअँर सब तब आए पितु पास ।
sahita badhūṭinha kuaṁra saba taba āe pitu pāsa,
सोभा मंगल मोद भरि उमगेउ जनु जनवास ॥३२७॥
sobhā maṁgala moda bhari umageu janu janavāsa. 327.

Trans:

Then the four princes with their brides approached their father and such was the glory, the felicity, and the rapture that it seemed to overflow the court like a torrent.

चौपाई-caupāī:

पुनि जेवनार भई बहु भाँती । पठए जनक बोलाइ बराती ॥
puni jevanāra bhaī bahu bhāṁtī, paṭhae janaka bolāi barātī.
परत पाँवड़े बसन अनूपा । सुतन्ह समेत गवन कियो भूपा ॥
parata pāṁvaṛe basana anūpā, sutanha sameta gavana kiyo bhūpā.
सादर सब के पाय पखारे । जथाजोगु पीढ़न्ह बैठारे ॥
sādara saba ke pāya pakhāre, jathājogu pīṛhanha baiṭhāre.
धोए जनक अवधपति चरना । सीलु सनेहु जाइ नहिं बरना ॥
dhoe janaka avadhapati caranā, sīlu sanehu jāi nahiṁ baranā.
बहुरि राम पद पंकज धोए । जे हर हृदय कमल महुँ गोए ॥
bahuri rāma pada paṁkaja dhoe, je hara hṛdaya kamala mahuṁ goe.
तीनिउ भाई राम सम जानी । धोए चरन जनक निज पानी ॥
tīniu bhāī rāma sama jānī, dhoe carana janaka nija pānī.
आसन उचित सबहि नृप दीन्हे । बोलि सूपकारी सब लीन्हे ॥
āsana ucita sabahi nṛpa dīnhe, boli sūpakārī saba līnhe.
सादर लगे परन पनवारे । कनक कील मनि पान सँवारे ॥
sādara lage parana panavāre, kanaka kīla mani pāna saṁvāre.

Trans:

Again there was a magnificent banquet, to which Janak sent and invited all the visitors. Carpets of richest stuff were spread as the king sallied forth with his sons. After reverently washing his guests' feet, he seated them all according to their rank. First Janak bathed the feet of Avadh's lord with a loving devotion past all telling; then he bathed Rāma's lotus feet, feet ever enshrined in Mahādev's heart; and, also with his own hands, bathed the feet of the three brothers, regarding them as Rāma's peers. To all the others the king assigned appropriate seats, and then gave orders to the cooks, who with due ceremony set out the plates, made all of jewels instead of leaves, and stitched with golden pins.

दोहा-dohā:

सूपोदन सुरभी सरपि सुंदर स्वादु पुनीत ।
sūpodana surabhī sarapi suṁdara svādu punīta,
छन महुँ सब कें परुसि गे चतुर सुआर बिनीत ॥३२८॥
chana mahuṁ saba keṁ parusi ge catura suāra binīta. 328.

Trans:

The quick and clever waiting-men passed round, and in a moment every guest was supplied with rice and condiments and fragrant butter, and everything luscious and savory and nice.

चौपाई-caupāī:

पंच कवल करि जेवन लागे । गारि गान सुनि अति अनुरागे ॥
paṁca kavala kari jevana lāge, gāri gāna suni ati anurāge.
भाँति अनेक परे पकवाने । सुधा सरिस नहिं जाहिं बखाने ॥
bhāṁti aneka pare pakavāne, sudhā sarisa nahiṁ jāhiṁ bakhāne.
परुसन लगे सुआर सुजाना । बिंजन बिबिध नाम को जाना ॥
parusana lage suāra sujānā, biṁjana bibidha nāma ko jānā.
चारि भाँति भोजन बिधि गाई । एक एक बिधि बरनि न जाई ॥
cāri bhāṁti bhojana bidhi gāī, eka eka bidhi barani na jāī.
छरस रुचिर बिंजन बहु जाती । एक एक रस अगनित भाँती ॥
charasa rucira biṁjana bahu jātī, eka eka rasa aganita bhāṁtī.
जेवँत देहिं मधुर धुनि गारी । लै लै नाम पुरुष अरु नारी ॥
jevaṁta dehiṁ madhura dhuni gārī, lai lai nāma puruṣa aru nārī.
समय सुहावनि गारि बिराजा । हँसत राउ सुनि सहित समाजा ॥
samaya suhāvani gāri birājā, haṁsata rāu suni sahita samājā.
एहि बिधि सबहीं भोजनु कीन्हा । आदर सहित आचमनु दीन्हा ॥
ehi bidhi sabahīṁ bhojanu kīnhā, ādara sahita ācamanu dīnhā.

Trans:

After making the five oblations they began to eat, listening with delight all the while to allusive songs. There were confections of many kinds, sweeter than nectar or that words can tell, which the well-trained waiters handed rounds, and such an infinite variety of dishes that no one could recount all their names, with food of the four kinds mentioned in the sacred books and an indescribable variety of each kind, and seasonings of the six flavors, and each flavor exhibited in a countless number of dishes. As the dinner was in progress, women railed in melodious strains at men and women both, mentioning each by name. Even raillery at an opportune time is agreeable and welcome. The king and the whole assembly were moved to laughter as they listened to it. In this manner they were all feasted, and in the end reverently given water to rinse the mouth.

दोहा-dohā:

देइ पान पूजे जनक दसरथु सहित समाज ।
dei pāna pūje janaka dasarathu sahita samāja,
जनवासेहि गवने मुदित सकल भूप सिरताज ॥३२९॥
janavāsehi gavane mudita sakala bhūpa siratāja. 329.

Trans:

Offering betel-leaves in due form, Janak paid his homage to Dashrath and all his guests; and the glorious king then retired to his own apartment with a cheerful heart.

चौपाई-caupāī:

नित नूतन मंगल पुर माहीं । निमिष सरिस दिन जामिनि जाहीं ॥
nita nūtana maṁgala pura māhīṁ, nimiṣa sarisa dina jāmini jāhīṁ.

बड़े भोर भूपतिमनि जागे । जाचक गुन गन गावन लागे ॥
baṛe bhora bhūpatimani jāge, jācaka guna gana gāvana lāge.

देखि कुअँर बर बधुन्ह समेता । किमि कहि जात मोदु मन जेता ॥
dekhi kuam̐ra bara badhunha sametā, kimi kahi jāta modu mana jetā.

प्रातक्रिया करि गे गुरु पाहीं । महाप्रमोदु प्रेमु मन माहीं ॥
prātakriyā kari ge guru pāhīṁ, mahāpramodu premu mana māhīṁ.

करि प्रनामु पूजा कर जोरी । बोले गिरा अमिअँ जनु बोरी ॥
kari pranāmu pūjā kara jorī, bole girā amiam̐ janu borī.

तुम्हरी कृपाँ सुनहु मुनिराजा । भयउँ आजु मैं पूरनकाजा ॥
tumharī kṛpām̐ sunahu munirājā, bhayaum̐ āju maiṁ pūranakājā.

अब सब बिप्र बोलाइ गोसाईं । देहु धेनु सब भाँति बनाईं ॥
aba saba bipra bolāi gosāīṁ, dehu dhenu saba bhām̐ti banāīṁ.

सुनि गुर करि महिपाल बड़ाई । पुनि पठए मुनि बृंद बोलाई ॥
suni gura kari mahipāla baṛāī, puni paṭhae muni bṛṁda bolāī.

Trans:

There was ever some new rejoicing in the city, and the whole day and night seemed gone like minutes. At early dawn the best of monarchs woke, and mendicants began to chant his praises. As he gazed upon the gallant princes and their brides, the rapture of his soul was beyond all telling. After performing his morning devotions he went to his Gurū, with his heart full of love and exultation, and clasping his hands in prayer bowed before him and said with a voice of mellifluous sweetness: "Hearken, king of saints; it is by your favor that today my toils have been rewarded. Now, holy father, summon the Brahmins and present them all with cows with costly adornments." On hearing these words the Gurū much applauded the king, and sent to summon the whole saintly throng.

दोहा-dohā:

बामदेउ अरु देवरिषि बालमीकि जाबालि ।
bāmadeu aru devariṣi bālamīki jābāli,

आए मुनिबर निकर तब कौसिकादि तपसाली ॥३३०॥
āe munibara nikara taba kausikādi tapasālī. 330.

Trans:

Then came Vāmdev and Nārad and Vālmīkī and Jabālī and Vishwāmitra and all the other great saints and ascetics.

चौपाई-caupāī:

दंड प्रनाम सबहि नृप कीन्हे । पूजि सप्रेम बरासन दीन्हे ॥
daṁḍa pranāma sabahi nṛpa kīnhe, pūji saprema barāsana dīnhe.

चारि लच्छ बर धेनु मगाईं । कामसुरभि सम सील सुहाईं ॥
cāri laccha bara dhenu magāīṁ, kāmasurabhi sama sīla suhāīṁ.

सब बिधि सकल अलंकृत कीन्हीं । मुदित महिप महिदेवन्ह दीन्हीं ॥
saba bidhi sakala alaṁkṛta kīnhīṁ, mudita mahipa mahidevanha dīnhīṁ.

करत बिनय बहु बिधि नरनाहू । लहेउँ आजु जग जीवन लाहू ॥
karata binaya bahu bidhi naranāhū, laheum̐ āju jaga jīvana lāhū.

पाइ असीस महिसु अनंदा । लिए बोलि पुनि जाचक बृंदा ॥
pāi asīsa mahisu anaṁdā, lie boli puni jācaka bṛṁdā.

कनक बसन मनि हय गय स्यंदन । दिए बूझि रुचि रबिकुलनंदन ॥
kanaka basana mani haya gaya syaṁdana, die būjhi ruci rabikulanaṁdana.

चले पढ़त गावत गुन गाथा । जय जय जय दिनकर कुल नाथा ॥
cale paṛhata gāvata guna gāthā, jaya jaya jaya dinakara kula nāthā.

एहि बिधि राम बिआह उछाहू । सकइ न बरनि सहस मुख जाहू ॥
ehi bidhi rāma biāha uchāhū, sakai na barani sahasa mukha jāhū.

Trans:

The king threw himself upon the ground before them all and worshipped them, and then conducted them to seats of honor. Next he sent for four *lakh* cows, all as gentle and beautiful as the cow of paradise, and after decorating them in every possible way, bestowed them with great joy upon the saints. The king supplicated them in many ways and said, "It is only today that I have attained the fruit of my existence." On receiving their blessing the king, the pride of the Solar-Dynasty, rejoiced, and next sent for all the begging fraternity and gave them, according as each desired, gold, or apparel, or jewels, or horse, or elephants, or chariots. They all left loudly telling and singing his praises, "Glory, glory, glory to the Lord of the Solar-Race.' Such were the rejoicings at Rāma's wedding, beyond all that could be told, even had I a thousand tongues.

दोहा-dohā:

बार बार कौसिक चरन सीसु नाइ कह राउ ।
bāra bāra kausika carana sīsu nāi kaha rāu,

यह सबु सुखु मुनिराज तव कृपा कटाच्छ पसाउ ॥३३१॥
yaha sabu sukhu munirāja tava kṛpā kaṭāccha pasāu. 331.

Trans:

Again and again the king bowed his head at Vishwāmitra's feet: "All this happiness, O king of saints, is the result of your benign grace."

चौपाई-caupāī:

जनक सनेहु सीलु करतूती । नृपु सब भाँति सराह बिभूती ॥
janaka sanehu sīlu karatūtī, nṛpu saba bhām̐ti sarāha bibhūtī.

दिन उठि बिदा अवधपति मागा । राखहिं जनकु सहित अनुरागा ॥
dina uṭhi bidā avadhapati māgā, rākhahiṁ janaku sahita anurāgā.

नित नूतन आदरु अधिकाई । दिन प्रति सहस भाँति पहुनाई ॥
nita nūtana ādaru adhikāī, dina prati sahasa bhām̐ti pahunāī.

नित नव नगर अनंद उछाहू । दसरथ गवनु सोहाइ न काहू ॥
nita nava nagara anaṁda uchāhū, dasaratha gavanu sohāi na kāhū.

बहुत दिवस बीते एहि भाँती । जनु सनेह रजु बँधे बराती ॥
bahuta divasa bīte ehi bhām̐tī, janu saneha raju bam̐dhe barātī.

कौसिक सतानंद तब जाई । कहा बिदेह नृपहि समुझाई ॥
kausika satānaṁda taba jāī, kahā bideha nṛpahi samujhāī.

अब दसरथ कहँ आयसु देहू । जद्यपि छाड़ि न सकहु सनेहू ॥
aba dasaratha kaham̐ āyasu dehū, jadyapi chāṛi na sakahu sanehū.

भलेहिं नाथ कहि सचिव बोलाए । कहि जय जीव सीस तिन्ह नाए ॥
bhalehiṁ nātha kahi saciva bolāe, kahi jaya jīva sīsa tinha nāe.

Trans:

King Dashrath extolled in every way Janak's affection, amiability, affluence and doings. Every morning the King of Ajodhyā asked leave to return home; but each time Janak would lovingly detain him. There was constantly some new fete in his honor, and every day a thousand different kinds of entertainment. The rejoicings in the city never flagged, and no one liked to think of Dashrath's departure. In this manner many days were spent, and the guests were fast bound by the cords of love, until Vishwāmitra and Shatānand went and told Videh's lord: "You must now let Dashrath take his leave, even though you cannot part with your love for him." The king replied: "It is well," and summoned his ministers, who came and bowed the head crying, "All hail!"

दोहा-dohā:

अवधनाथु चाहत चलन भीतर करहु जनाउ ।
avadhanāthu cāhata calana bhītara karahu janāu,

भए प्रेमबस सचिव सुनि बिप्र सभासद राउ ॥३३२॥
bhae premabasa saciva suni bipra sabhāsada rāu. 332.

Trans:

"Make it known in the palace that Avadh's lord wishes to depart." At these words the ministers, Brahmins, counselors, and princes, were greatly moved.

चौपाई-caupāī:

पुरबासी सुनि चलिहि बराता । बूझत बिकल परस्पर बाता ॥
purabāsī suni calihi barātā, būjhata bikala paraspara bātā.
सत्य गवनु सुनि सब बिलखाने । मनहुँ साँझ सरसिज सकुचाने ॥
satya gavanu suni saba bilakhāne, manahuṁ sāṁjha sarasija sakucāne.
जहँ जहँ आवत बसे बराती । तहँ तहँ सिद्ध चला बहु भाँती ॥
jahaṁ jahaṁ āvata base barātī, tahaṁ tahaṁ siddha calā bahu bhāṁtī.
बिबिध भाँति मेवा पकवाना । भोजन साजु न जाइ बखाना ॥
bibidha bhāṁti mevā pakavānā, bhojana sāju na jāi bakhānā.
भरि भरि बसहँ अपार कहारा । पठई जनक अनेक सुसारा ॥
bhari bhari basahaṁ apāra kahārā, paṭhaī janaka aneka susārā.
तुरग लाख रथ सहस पचीसा । सकल सँवारे नख अरु सीसा ॥
turaga lākha ratha sahasa pacīsā, sakala saṁvāre nakha aru sīsā.
मत्त सहस दस सिंधुर साजे । जिन्हहि देखि दिसिकुंजर लाजे ॥
matta sahasa dasa siṁdhura sāje, jinhahi dekhi disikuṁjara lāje.
कनक बसन मनि भरि भरि जाना । महिषीं धेनु बस्तु बिधि नाना ॥
kanaka basana mani bhari bhari jānā, mahiṣīṁ dhenu bastu bidhi nānā.

Trans:

When it was heard in the city that the guests were leaving, everyone anxiously asked his neighbor if it was true. When they heard they were actually going, all were as unhappy as a lotus that fades in the evening. Every place where the visitors had put up on their arrival was crowded with parting presents, fruits and confections of every kind, and dishes, too various for description. A multitude of porters laden with wearing apparel and cooks beyond number were sent by Janak with a hundred-thousand horses and twenty-five thousand chariots, all exquisitely finished throughout, with ten thousand powerful elephants duly caparisoned, at sight of which earth's guardian elephants would feel ashamed of themselves; besides wagons full of gold and raiment and jewels; buffaloes too and cows, and things of all kinds.

दोहा-dohā:

दाइज अमित न सकिअ कहि दीन्ह बिदेहँ बहोरि ।
dāija amita na sakia kahi dīnha bidehaṁ bahori,
जो अवलोकत लोकपति लोक संपदा थोरि ॥३३३॥
jo avalokata lokapati loka saṁpadā thori. 333.

Trans:

The gifts given by Videh's king were immeasurable and beyond all telling; and Indra, had he seen it, would have thought the riches of the universe as nothing in comparison.

चौपाई-caupāī:

सबु समाजु एहि भाँति बनाई । जनक अवधपुर दीन्ह पठाई ॥
sabu samāju ehi bhāṁti banāī, janaka avadhapura dīnha paṭhāī.
चलिहि बरात सुनत सब रानीं । बिकल मीनगन जनु लघु पानीं ॥
calihi barāta sunata saba rānīṁ, bikala mīnagana janu laghu pānīṁ.
पुनि पुनि सीय गोद करि लेहीं । देइ असीस सिखावनु देहीं ॥
puni puni sīya goda kari lehīṁ, dei asīsa sikhāvanu dehīṁ.
होएहु संतत पियहि पिआरी । चिरु अहिबात असीस हमारी ॥
hoehu saṁtata piyahi piārī, ciru ahibāta asīsa hamārī.
सासु ससुर गुर सेवा करेहू । पति रुख लखि आयसु अनुसरेहू ॥
sāsu sasura gura sevā karehū, pati rukha lakhi āyasu anusarehū.
अति सनेह बस सखीं सयानी । नारि धरम सिखवहिं मृदु बानी ॥
ati saneha basa sakhīṁ sayānī, nāri dharama sikhavahiṁ mṛdu bānī.
सादर सकल कुअँरि समुझाईं । रानिन्ह बार बार उर लाईं ॥
sādara sakala kuaṁri samujhāīṁ, rāninha bāra bāra ura lāīṁ.
बहुरि बहुरि भेटहिं महतारीं । कहहिं बिरंचि रचीं कत नारीं ॥
bahuri bahuri bheṭahiṁ mahatārīṁ, kahahiṁ biraṁci racīṁ kata nārīṁ.

Trans:

When the whole equipage had been thus arranged, Janak dispatched it to Avadh. On hearing that the guests were about to start, all the queens were as unhappy as fish when water fails. Again and again they clasped Sītā to their bosom and blessed and exhorted her, saying; "May you ever be beloved by your husband and with him live a long and happy life: this is our blessing. Be obedient to your new father and mother and Gurū; and be mindful of your Lord's inclinations, and do as he bids." Her sweet-voiced companions too in their overpowering affection reminded her of woman's crowning duty. Again and again after thus duly admonishing them the queens clasped the four brides to their bosom, and time after time, in the midst of their maternal embraces, exclaimed, 'Why has God made women?'

दोहा-dohā:

तेहि अवसर भाइन्ह सहित रामु भानु कुल केतु ।
tehi avasara bhāinha sahita rāmu bhānu kula ketu,
चले जनक मंदिर मुदित बिदा करावन हेतु ॥३३४॥
cale janaka maṁdira mudita bidā karāvana hetu. 334.

Trans:

Then, along with his brothers, the joyous prince Rāma, the glory of the Solar race, came to Janak's palace, to take leave.

चौपाई-caupāī:

चारिउ भाइ सुभायँ सुहाए । नगर नारि नर देखन धाए ॥
cāriu bhāi subhāyaṁ suhāe, nagara nāri nara dekhana dhāe.
कोउ कह चलन चहत हहिं आजू । कीन्ह बिदेह बिदा कर साजू ॥
kou kaha calana cahata hahiṁ ājū, kīnha bideha bidā kara sājū.
लेहु नयन भरि रूप निहारी । प्रिय पाहुने भूप सुत चारी ॥
lehu nayana bhari rūpa nihārī, priya pāhune bhūpa suta cārī.
को जानै केहिं सुकृत सयानी । नयन अतिथि कीन्हे बिधि आनी ॥
ko jānai kehiṁ sukṛta sayānī, nayana atithi kīnhe bidhi ānī.
मरनसीलु जिमि पाव पिऊषा । सुरतरु लहै जनम कर भूखा ॥
maranasīlu jimi pāva piūṣā, surataru lahai janama kara bhūkhā.
पाव नारकी हरिपदु जैसें । इन्ह कर दरसनु हम कहँ तैसें ॥
pāva nārakī haripadu jaiseṁ, inha kara darasanu hama kahaṁ taiseṁ.
निरखि राम सोभा उर धरहू । निज मन फनि मूरति मनि करहू ॥
nirakhi rāma sobhā ura dharahū, nija mana phani mūrati mani karahū.
एहि बिधि सबहि नयन फलु देता । गए कुअँर सब राज निकेता ॥
ehi bidhi sabahi nayana phalu detā, gae kuaṁra saba rāja niketā.

Trans:

All the people of the city, whether men or women, ran to see the four brothers, who were so naturally charming. Said one: "Today they have made up their mind to go, and Janak has completed all the preparations for their departure; so feast your eyes on their beauty for one last time. All four princes have been most welcome visitors; who can say, friends, what we have done to deserve—that gods should bring such guests for our eyes to behold! Like a man at the point of death who is given ambrosia; or as one who has been hungry all life discovers tree of paradise; or like one damned in hell should get Harī's abode—so feel I after seeing them. Gaze upon Rāma's beauty and treasure his image in your heart—even as a serpent treasures the jewel on his hood." Gladdening the eyes of all the princes proceeded towards the palace.

दोहा-dohā:

रूप सिंधु सब बंधु लखि हरषि उठा रनिवासु ।
rūpa siṁdhu saba baṁdhu lakhi haraṣi uṭhā ranivāsu,
करहिं निछावरि आरती महा मुदित मन सासु ॥३३५॥
karahiṁ nichāvari āratī mahā mudita mana sāsu. 335.

Trans:

The ladies all rose in their joy as they beheld their exquisite beauty; and the mothers of the brides, in token of their delight, pass the lustral lamp around their heads and scatter gifts.

चौपाई-caupāī:

देखि राम छबि अति अनुरागीं । प्रेमबिबस पुनि पुनि पद लागीं ॥
dekhi rāma chabi ati anurāgīṁ, premabibasa puni puni pada lāgīṁ.
रही न लाज प्रीति उर छाई । सहज सनेहु बरनि किमि जाई ॥
rahī na lāja prīti ura chāī, sahaja sanehu barani kimi jāī.
भाइन्ह सहित उबटि अन्हवाए । छरस असन अति हेतु जेवाँए ॥
bhāinha sahita ubaṭi anhavāe, charasa asana ati hetu jevāṁe.
बोले रामु सुअवसरु जानी । सील सनेह सकुचमय बानी ॥
bole rāmu suavasaru jānī, sīla saneha sakucamaya bānī.
राउ अवधपुर चहत सिधाए । बिदा होन हम इहाँ पठाए ॥
rāu avadhapura cahata sidhāe, bidā hona hama ihāṁ paṭhāe.
मातु मुदित मन आयसु देहू । बालक जानि करब नित नेहू ॥
mātu mudita mana āyasu dehū, bālaka jāni karaba nita nehū.
सुनत बचन बिलखेउ रनिवासू । बोलि न सकहिं प्रेमबस सासू ॥
sunata bacana bilakheu ranivāsū, boli na sakahiṁ premabasa sāsū.
हृदयँ लगाइ कुअँरि सब लीन्ही । पतिन्ह सौंपि बिनती अति कीन्ही ॥
hṛdayaṁ lagāi kuaṁri saba līnhī, patinha sauṁpi binatī ati kīnhī.

Trans:

Full of love at the vision of Rāma's beauty, they affectionately fall at his feet again and again, nor are they conscious of shame—so rapt is their soul in devotion and an involuntary attachment beyond all description. After bathing him and his brothers and decanting them with perfumes, they lovingly entertain them at a banquet of the six flavors. Then seeing that the time had come, Rāma said to them in the most amiable, loving, and modest tone, "The king is desirous of starting for Avadh and has sent us to take leave of you. O mother, be pleased to give me your order and ever regard me with affection as your own child." At these words the queens grieved sore, and were too overcome by love to speak a word, but then clasped their daughters to their bosom and humbly gave them to their lords.

छंद-chaṁda:

करि बिनय सिय रामहि समरपी जोरि कर पुनि पुनि कहै ।
kari binaya siya rāmahi samarapī jori kara puni puni kahai,
बलि जाँउ तात सुजान तुम्ह कहुँ बिदित गति सब की अहै ॥
bali jāṁu tāta sujāna tumha kahuṁ bidita gati saba kī ahai.
परिवार पुरजन मोहि राजहि प्रानप्रिय सिय जानिबी ।
parivāra purajana mohi rājahi prānapriya siya jānibī,
तुलसीस सीलु सनेहु लखि निज किंकरी करि मानिबी ॥
tulasīsa sīlu sanehu lakhi nija kiṁkarī kari mānibī.

Trans:

With humble submission Queen Sunayanā committed Sītā to Rāma, and with joined palms prayed again and again, "Ah my son, I sacrifice myself over you, my all-wise darling. You know the thoughts of all; you know well that Sītā is dear as life to the king and myself—nay, to all her kinsfolk and all the people of the city; consider her amiability and her affection and accept her as your very own servant, O Lord of Tulsī.

सोरठा-soraṭhā:

तुम्ह परिपूरन काम जान सिरोमनि भावप्रिय ।
tumha paripūrana kāma jāna siromani bhāvapriya,
जन गुन गाहक राम दोष दलन करुनायतन ॥३३६॥
jana guna gāhaka rāma doṣa dalana karunāyatana. 336.

Trans:

Beyond desires, you are the fullness of desire, the crown of wisdom, who is attracted by love alone, quick to recognize merit in your votaries, the destroyer of evil, O Rāma the all-merciful."

चौपाई-caupāī:

अस कहि रही चरन गहि रानी । प्रेम पंक जनु गिरा समानी ॥
asa kahi rahī carana gahi rānī, prema paṁka janu girā samānī.
सुनि सनेहसानी बर बानी । बहुबिधि राम सासु सनमानी ॥
suni sanehasānī bara bānī, bahubidhi rāma sāsu sanamānī.
राम बिदा मागत कर जोरी । कीन्ह प्रनामु बहोरि बहोरी ॥
rāma bidā māgata kara jorī, kīnha pranāmu bahori bahorī.
पाइ असीस बहुरि सिरु नाई । भाइन्ह सहित चले रघुराई ॥
pāi asīsa bahuri siru nāī, bhāinha sahita cale raghurāī.
मंजु मधुर मूरति उर आनी । भईं सनेह सिथिल सब रानी ॥
maṁju madhura mūrati ura ānī, bhaīṁ saneha sithila saba rānī.
पुनि धीरजु धरि कुअँरि हँकारी । बार बार भेटहिं महतारीं ॥
puni dhīraju dhari kuaṁri haṁkārī, bāra bāra bheṭahiṁ mahatārīṁ.
पहुँचावहिं फिरि मिलहिं बहोरी । बढ़ी परस्पर प्रीति न थोरी ॥
pahuṁcāvahiṁ phiri milahiṁ bahorī, baṛhī paraspara prīti na thorī.
पुनि पुनि मिलत सखिन्ह बिलगाई । बाल बच्छ जिमि धेनु लवाई ॥
puni puni milata sakhinha bilagāī, bāla baccha jimi dhenu lavāī.

Trans:

So saying the queens clung to his feet and their voice seemed lost as it were in the quicksand of love. On hearing their most affectionate address, Rāma showed them the highest honor, and with clasped hands begged his conge, again and again making them obeisance. When he had received their blessing, he bowed once more and then with his brothers took his leave. Treasuring up his sweet and gracious image in their heart, the queens at first seemed paralyzed by excess of love; but summoning up courage they called their daughters and again and again gave them maternal embrace; then leading them a few steps would take them to their arms yet again with ever growing mutual love. Time after time they left their attendants for yet one more last embrace, just as would a heifer not yet weaned from the cow.

दोहा-dohā:

प्रेमबिबस नर नारि सब सखिन्ह सहित रनिवासु ।
premabibasa nara nāri saba sakhinha sahita ranivāsu,
मानहुँ कीन्ह बिदेहपुर करुनाँ बिरहँ निवासु ॥३३७॥
mānahuṁ kīnha bidehapura karunāṁ birahaṁ nivāsu. 337.

Trans:

Everyone in the palace, attendants and all, were so overpowered by emotion that it seemed as though poignancy, pathos, and parting had made the city of Videh their very home.

चौपाई-caupāī:

सुक सारिका जानकी ज्याए । कनक पिंजरन्हि राखि पढ़ाए ॥
suka sārikā jānakī jyāe, kanaka piṁjaranhi rākhi paṛhāe.
ब्याकुल कहहिं कहाँ बैदेही । सुनि धीरजु परिहरइ न केही ॥
byākula kahahiṁ kahāṁ baidehī, suni dhīraju pariharai na kehī.
भए बिकल खग मृग एहि भाँति । मनुज दसा कैसें कहि जाती ॥
bhae bikala khaga mṛga ehi bhāṁti, manuja dasā kaiseṁ kahi jātī.

बंधु समेत जनकु तब आए । प्रेम उमगि लोचन जल छाए ॥
baṁdhu sameta janaku taba āe, prema umagi locana jala chāe.
सीय बिलोकि धीरता भागी । रहे कहावत परम बिरागी ॥
sīya biloki dhīratā bhāgī, rahe kahāvata parama birāgī.
लीन्हि रायँ उर लाइ जानकी । मिटी महामरजाद ग्यान की ॥
līnhi rāyam̐ ura lāi jānakī, miṭī mahāmarajāda gyāna kī.
समुझावत सब सचिव सयाने । कीन्ह बिचारु न अवसर जाने ॥
samujhāvata saba saciva sayāne, kīnha bicāru na avasara jāne.
बारहिं बार सुता उर लाईं । सजि सुंदर पालकीं मगाईं ॥
bārahiṁ bāra sutā ura lāīṁ, saji suṁdara pālakīṁ magāīṁ.

Trans:

The pet parrots and *maina*s, that Jānakī had brought up, and kept in golden cages and taught to speak, cry in their agitation, 'Where is the princess?'; and on hearing that which of them was not robbed of all peace of mind? When birds and beasts were thus distressed, how then can the feelings of the people be told? Then came Janak with his brother Kush-ketu, overflowing with love and his eyes full of tears. As he gazed upon Sītā, all his courage deserted him and his eminent asceticism lasted but in name. As he clasped Jānakī to his bosom, the stronghold of his stern philosophy was broken down. All his wise counselors consoled him; and seeing the unfitness of the time he recovered himself, and again taking his daughter to his heart, he ordered a gorgeous *Palkī* to be brought.

दोहा-dohā:

प्रेमबिबस परिवारु सबु जानि सुलगन नरेस ।
premabibasa parivāru sabu jāni sulagana naresa,
कुअँरि चढ़ाईं पालकिन्ह सुमिरे सिद्धि गनेस ॥३३८॥
kuam̐ri caṛhāīṁ pālakinha sumire siddhi ganesa. 338.

Trans:

The whole court was overpowered with emotion, when the king, perceiving that the auspicious moment had arrived, seated the maiden in the *Pālkī*, with his thoughts intent upon Ganesh, the source of success.

चौपाई-caupāī:

बहुबिधि भूप सुता समुझाईं । नारिधरमु कुलरीति सिखाईं ॥
bahubidhi bhūpa sutā samujhāīṁ, nāridharamu kularīti sikhāīṁ.
दासीं दास दिए बहुतेरे । सुचि सेवक जे प्रिय सिय केरे ॥
dāsīṁ dāsa die bahutere, suci sevaka je priya siya kere.
सीय चलत ब्याकुल पुरबासी । होहिं सगुन सुभ मंगल रासी ॥
sīya calata byākula purabāsī, hohiṁ saguna subha maṁgala rāsī.
भूसुर सचिव समेत समाजा । संग चले पहुँचावन राजा ॥
bhūsura saciva sameta samājā, saṁga cale pahum̐cāvana rājā.
समय बिलोकि बाजने बाजे । रथ गज बाजि बरातिन्ह साजे ॥
samaya biloki bājane bāje, ratha gaja bāji barātinha sāje.
दसरथ बिप्र बोलि सब लीन्हे । दान मान परिपूरन कीन्हे ॥
dasaratha bipra boli saba līnhe, dāna māna paripūrana kīnhe.
चरन सरोज धूरि धरि सीसा । मुदित महीपति पाइ असीसा ॥
carana saroja dhūri dhari sīsā, mudita mahīpati pāi asīsā.
सुमिरि गजाननु कीन्ह पयाना । मंगलमूल सगुन भए नाना ॥
sumiri gajānanu kīnha payānā, maṁgalamūla saguna bhae nānā.

Trans:

The monarch gave his daughter much advice and instructed her in the whole duty of women and in family customs. He bestowed upon her many men-servants and maid-servants and all her own favorite attendants. As she went on her way the citizens were in distress, but all good signs and auspicious omens were forthcoming. Brahmins and ministers with all their retinue joined company to escort the king. The wedding guests made ready their chariots and elephants and horses, and there was a tumultuous sound of music. Then Dashrath called up all the Brahmins and gratified them with gifts and compliments, and putting the dust of their lotus feet upon his head rejoiced—great king as he was—to obtain their blessing. As he set forth on his way with his thoughts on Ganesh, every omen of good came about.

दोहा-dohā:

सुर प्रसून बरषहिं हरषि करहिं अपछरा गान ।
sura prasūna baraṣahiṁ haraṣi karahiṁ apacharā gāna,
चले अवधपति अवधपुर मुदित बजाइ निसान ॥३३९॥
cale avadhapati avadhapura mudita bajāi nisāna. 339.

Trans:

The gods rained down flowers, the heavenly nymphs sang for joy as the king of Avadh set forth for his capital amidst the clash of jubilant music.

चौपाई-caupāī:

नृप करि बिनय महाजन फेरे । सादर सकल मागने टेरे ॥
nṛpa kari binaya mahājana phere, sādara sakala māgane ṭere.
भूषन बसन बाजि गज दीन्हे । प्रेम पोषि ठाढ़े सब कीन्हे ॥
bhūṣana basana bāji gaja dīnhe, prema poṣi ṭhāṛhe saba kīnhe.
बार बार बिरिदावलि भाषी । फिरे सकल रामहि उर राखी ॥
bāra bāra biridāvali bhāṣī, phire sakala rāmahi ura rākhī.
बहुरि बहुरि कोसलपति कहहीं । जनकु प्रेमबस फिरै न चहहीं ॥
bahuri bahuri kosalapati kahahīṁ, janaku premabasa phirai na cahahīṁ.
पुनि कह भूपति बचन सुहाए । फिरिअ महीस दूरि बड़ि आए ॥
puni kaha bhūpati bacana suhāe, phiria mahīsa dūri baṛi āe.
राउ बहोरि उतरि भए ठाढ़े । प्रेम प्रबाह बिलोचन बाढ़े ॥
rāu bahori utari bhae ṭhāṛhe, prema prabāha bilocana bāṛhe.
तब बिदेह बोले कर जोरी । बचन सनेह सुधाँ जनु बोरी ॥
taba bideha bole kara jorī, bacana saneha sudhām̐ janu borī.
करौं कवन बिधि बिनय बनाई । महाराज मोहि दीन्हि बड़ाई ॥
karauṁ kavana bidhi binaya banāī, mahārāja mohi dīnhi baṛāī.

Trans:

Courteously the king dismissed the burghers and reverently bade all the mendicants approach; and he bestowed upon them many ornaments and clothes and horses and elephants; and cherishing them affectionately, bade them stand before. After again and again reciting the king's praises they all returned home—with Rāma in their heart. Though Kaushal's lord spoke time after time, Janak, in his exceeding love, would not turn back. Once again said the king in gracious tones, "I beg you to turn back, sir; you have come a great distance." At last he dismounted and remained standing, his eyes overflowing with love's torrent. Then said Videh's lord with folded hands and in a voice fraught with the ambrosia of affection, "How can I fitly express my unworthiness upon whom my lord has conferred such high honor?"

दोहा-dohā:

कोसलपति समधी सजन सनमाने सब भाँति ।
kosalapati samadhī sajana sanamāne saba bhām̐ti,
मिलनि परसपर बिनय अति प्रीति न हृदयँ समाति ॥३४०॥
milani parasapara binaya ati prīti na hṛdayam̐ samāti. 340.

Trans:

Kaushal's king in return showed the profoundest respect to the father of the bride and his retinue; and as they embraced with mutual courtesy their heart could not contain the love they felt.

चौपाई-caupāī:

मुनि मंडलिहि जनक सिरु नावा । आसिरबादु सबहि सन पावा ॥
muni maṁḍalihi janaka siru nāvā, āsirabādu sabahi sana pāvā.
सादर पुनि भेंटे जामाता । रूप सील गुन निधि सब भ्राता ॥
sādara puni bheṁṭe jāmātā, rūpa sīla guna nidhi saba bhrātā.

जोरि पंकरुह पानि सुहाए । बोले बचन प्रेम जनु जाए ॥
jori paṁkaruha pāni suhāe, bole bacana prema janu jāe.
राम करौं केहि भाँति प्रसंसा । मुनि महेस मन मानस हंसा ॥
rāma karauṁ kehi bhām̐ti prasaṁsā, muni mahesa mana mānasa haṁsā.
करहिं जोग जोगी जेहि लागी । कोहु मोहु ममता मदु त्यागी ॥
karahiṁ joga jogī jehi lāgī, kohu mohu mamatā madu tyāgī.
ब्यापकु ब्रह्मु अलखु अबिनासी । चिदानंदु निरगुन गुनरासी ॥
byāpaku brahmu alakhu abināsī, cidānaṁdu niraguna gunarāsī.
मन समेत जेहि जान न बानी । तरकि न सकहिं सकल अनुमानी ॥
mana sameta jehi jāna na bānī, taraki na sakahiṁ sakala anumānī.
महिमा निगमु नेति कहि कहई । जो तिहुँ काल एकरस रहई ॥
mahimā nigamu neti kahi kahaī, jo tihum̐ kāla ekarasa rahaī.

Trans:

Janak bowed his head to the throng of saints and received a blessing from them all. Next he reverently saluted his sons-in-law—the four brothers—each a treasure of beauty, amiability, and accomplishments; and clasping the gracious lotus hands he cried in accents begotten of love: "O Rāma, how can I tell thy praises! O swan of the Mānas lake of the saints' and Mahādev's soul! O thou, for whose sake ascetics practice their asceticism! O thou, void of ire, infatuation, selfishness, pride; the all-pervading Brahmm, the invisible, the immortal, the supreme spirit, at once the sum and negation of all qualities; whom neither words nor fancy can ever portray; whom all philosophy fails to expound; whose greatness the divine oracles declare unutterable, and who remains the selfsame in all times, past, present, and future—how can thy praises be told!

दोहा-dohā:

नयन बिषय मो कहुँ भयउ सो समस्त सुख मूल ।
nayana biṣaya mo kahum̐ bhayau so samasta sukha mūla,
सबइ लाभु जग जीव कहँ भएँ ईसु अनुकूल ॥ ३४१ ॥
sabai lābhu jaga jīva kaham̐ bhaem̐ īsu anukūla. 341.

Trans:

Source of every joy, thou hast revealed thyself to my material vision—for nothing in the world is beyond the reach of him to whom God is propitious.

चौपाई-caupāī:

सबहि भाँति मोहि दीन्हि बड़ाई । निज जन जानि लीन्ह अपनाई ॥
sabahi bhām̐ti mohi dīnhi baṛāī, nija jana jāni līnha apanāī.
होहिं सहस दस सारद सेषा । करहिं कलप कोटिक भरि लेखा ॥
hohiṁ sahasa dasa sārada seṣā, karahiṁ kalapa koṭika bhari lekhā.
मोर भाग्य राउर गुन गाथा । कहि न सिराहिं सुनहु रघुनाथा ॥
mora bhāgya rāura guna gāthā, kahi na sirāhiṁ sunahu raghunāthā.
मैं कछु कहउँ एक बल मोरें । तुम्ह रीझहु सनेह सुठि थोरें ॥
maiṁ kachu kahaum̐ eka bala moreṁ, tumha rījhahu saneha suṭhi thoreṁ.
बार बार मागउँ कर जोरें । मनु परिहरै चरन जनि भोरें ॥
bāra bāra māgaum̐ kara joreṁ, manu pariharai carana jani bhoreṁ.
सुनि बर बचन प्रेम जनु पोषे । पूरनकाम रामु परितोषे ॥
suni bara bacana prema janu poṣe, pūranakāma rāmu paritoṣe.
करि बर बिनय ससुर सनमाने । पितु कौसिक बसिष्ठ सम जाने ॥
kari bara binaya sasura sanamāne, pitu kausika basiṣṭha sama jāne.
बिनती बहुरि भरत सन कीन्ही । मिलि सप्रेमु पुनि आसिष दीन्ही ॥
binatī bahuri bharata sana kīnhī, mili sapremu puni āsiṣa dīnhī.

Trans:

Thou hast magnified me in every way, and recognizing me as one of thy servants hast made me thy very own. Not ten thousand Shārdās and Sheshnāgs, though they kept up their count for a myriad ages, could tell all my good fortune or thy perfections; know this, O Raghunāth. Yet I have somewhat to say—for I have this ground of confidence that thou art easily appeased by the slightest evidence of affection—and therefore time after time I implore with clasped hands that never may my soul be deluded into deserting thy holy feet." On hearing these profound sentiments, the true birth of devotion, even Rāma, in whom all hapinesses ever dwell, was pleased and with much courtesy saluted his father-in-law, holding him equal to his own sire, or Vishwāmitra or Vasishtha. The king then humbly approached Bharat and embracing him with affection gave him his blessings.

दोहा-dohā:

मिले लखन रिपुसूदनहि दीन्हि असीस महीस ।
mile lakhana ripusūdanahi dīnhi asīsa mahīsa,
भए परसपर प्रेमबस फिरि फिरि नावहिं सीस ॥ ३४२ ॥
bhae parasapara premabasa phiri phiri nāvahiṁ sīsa. 342.

Trans:

Then the king embraced and blessed both Lakshman and Shatrughan, and all again and again bowed the head, being overpowered with mutual love.

चौपाई-caupāī:

बार बार करि बिनय बड़ाई । रघुपति चले संग सब भाई ॥
bāra bāra kari binaya baṛāī, raghupati cale saṁga saba bhāī.
जनक गहे कौसिक पद जाई । चरन रेनु सिर नयनन्ह लाई ॥
janaka gahe kausika pada jāī, carana renu sira nayananha lāī.
सुनु मुनीस बर दरसन तोरें । अगमु न कछु प्रतीति मन मोरें ॥
sunu munīsa bara darasana toreṁ, agamu na kachu pratīti mana moreṁ.
जो सुखु सुजसु लोकपति चहहीं । करत मनोरथ सकुचत अहहीं ॥
jo sukhu sujasu lokapati cahahīṁ, karata manoratha sakucata ahahīṁ.
सो सुखु सुजसु सुलभ मोहि स्वामी । सब सिधि तव दरसन अनुगामी ॥
so sukhu sujasu sulabha mohi svāmī, saba sidhi tava darasana anugāmī.
कीन्हि बिनय पुनि पुनि सिरु नाई । फिरे महीसु आसिषा पाई ॥
kīnhi binaya puni puni siru nāī, phire mahīsu āsiṣā pāī.
चली बरात निसान बजाई । मुदित छोट बड़ सब समुदाई ॥
calī barāta nisāna bajāī, mudita choṭa baṛa saba samudāī.
रामहि निरखि ग्राम नर नारी । पाइ नयन फलु होहिं सुखारी ॥
rāmahi nirakhi grāma nara nārī, pāi nayana phalu hohiṁ sukhārī.

Trans:

Paying his respectful compliments to Janak again and again the Lord of Raghus, along with his brothers, started out. Next Janak approached Kaushik, clasped his feet and put the dust of the same on his head and eyes. He said, "Hearken, O greatest of saints; now that I have seen you, I am persuaded that nothing is beyond my attainment. Such bliss and glory as the sovereigns of the universe might desire, though they would be ashamed to express their longing, has all, my lord, been brought within my reach, for all prosperity follows upon seeing you." After again and again humbly bowing the head, the king received his blessing and took leave. The marriage procession set forth to the sound of music, and the whole populace, great and small, were all enraptured and, as they gazed upon Rāma and feasted their eyes upon him, were happy for being born on earth.

दोहा-dohā:

बीच बीच बर बास करि मग लोगन्ह सुख देत ।
bīca bīca bara bāsa kari maga loganha sukha deta,
अवध समीप पुनीत दिन पहुँची आइ जनेत ॥ ३४३ ॥
avadha samīpa punīta dina pahum̐cī āi janeta. 343.

Trans:

Halting at convenient stages on the road, to the great delight of the people there, the procession on an auspicious day drew near to Avadh.

चौपाई-caupāī:

हने निसान पनव बर बाजे । भेरि संख धुनि हय गय गाजे ॥

hane nisāna panava bara bāje, bheri saṁkha dhuni haya gaya gāje.

झाँझि बिरव डिंडिमीं सुहाई । सरस राग बाजहिं सहनाई ॥
jhāṁjhi birava ḍiṁḍimīṁ suhāī, sarasa rāga bājahiṁ sahanāī.

पुर जन आवत अकनि बराता । मुदित सकल पुलकावलि गाता ॥
pura jana āvata akani barātā, mudita sakala pulakāvali gātā.

निज निज सुंदर सदन सँवारे । हाट बाट चौहट पुर द्वारे ॥
nija nija suṁdara sadana saṁvāre, hāṭa bāṭa cauhaṭa pura dvāre.

गलीं सकल अरगजाँ सिंचाईं । जहँ तहँ चौकें चारु पुराईं ॥
galīṁ sakala aragajāṁ siṁcāīṁ, jahaṁ tahaṁ caukeṁ cāru purāīṁ.

बना बजारु न जाइ बखाना । तोरन केतु पताक बिताना ॥
banā bajāru na jāi bakhānā, torana ketu patāka bitānā.

सफल पूगफल कदलि रसाला । रोपे बकुल कदंब तमाला ॥
saphala pūgaphala kadali rasālā, rope bakula kadaṁba tamālā.

लगे सुभग तरु परसत धरनी । मनिमय आलबाल कल करनी ॥
lage subhaga taru parasata dharanī, manimaya ālabāla kala karanī.

Trans:

Amidst beat of kettledrums and noise of many tabors and sackbuts and conches, and a din of horses and elephants, and clash of cymbals and drums and sweet-tuned clarions, when the citizens knew of the procession coming, they were all aquiver with delight, and everyone began to decorate their house and the markets and streets and squares and gates of the city. The whole roadway was watered with perfumes; on every side were festal squares filled in with elegant devices. The show in the bazaar was beyond all telling, with wreaths and flags and banners and canopies. Trees of the areca-nut, and the plantain and the mango, the *malsuri*, the *kadamb* and the *tamala*, were transplanted all laden with fruit, and they grew into fine trees as soon as they touched the soil, being set in jeweled screens of exquisite workmanship.

दोहा-*dohā:*

बिबिध भाँति मंगल कलस गृह गृह रचे सँवारि ।
bibidha bhāṁti maṁgala kalasa gṛha gṛha race saṁvāri,

सुर ब्रह्मादि सिहाहिं सब रघुबर पुरी निहारि ॥ ३४४ ॥
sura brahmādi sihāhiṁ saba raghubara purī nihāri. 344.

Trans:

In houses after houses festal vases of every kind were set out in order, and Brahmmā and all the gods were delighted as they gazed upon the city of Rāma.

चौपाई-*caupāī:*

भूप भवनु तेहि अवसर सोहा । रचना देखि मदन मनु मोहा ॥
bhūpa bhavanu tehi avasara sohā, racanā dekhi madana manu mohā.

मंगल सगुन मनोहरताई । रिधि सिधि सुख संपदा सुहाई ॥
maṁgala saguna manoharatāī, ridhi sidhi sukha saṁpadā suhāī.

जनु उछाह सब सहज सुहाए । तनु धरि धरि दसरथ गृहँ छाए ॥
janu uchāha saba sahaja suhāe, tanu dhari dhari dasaratha gṛhaṁ chāe.

देखन हेतु राम बैदेही । कहहु लालसा होहि न केही ॥
dekhana hetu rāma baidehī, kahahu lālasā hohi na kehī.

जूथ जूथ मिलि चलीं सुआसिनि । निज छबि निदरहिं मदन बिलासिनि ॥
jūtha jūtha mili calīṁ suāsini, nija chabi nidarahiṁ madana bilāsini.

सकल सुमंगल सजें आरती । गावहिं जनु बहु बेष भारती ॥
sakala sumaṁgala sajeṁ āratī, gāvahiṁ janu bahu beṣa bhāratī.

भूपति भवन कोलाहलु होई । जाइ न बरनि समउ सुखु सोई ॥
bhūpati bhavana kolāhalu hoī, jāi na barani samau sukhu soī.

कौसल्यादि राम महतारीं । प्रेमबिबस तन दसा बिसारीं ॥
kausalyādi rāma mahatārīṁ, premabibasa tana dasā bisārīṁ.

Trans:

At that time the king's palace was so resplendent that the god of love was distracted by the sight of such magnificence. It was as though everything auspicious and of good omen, and all beauty, all plenteousness and prosperity and joy and felicity and gladness had come in bodily form to visit king Dashrath. There was a universal longing to get a sight of Rāma and Jānakī. Troops of fair women were crowding together, each exceeding in loveliness the love-god's queen, all with festal offerings and lamps, and singing, as if so many Saraswatīs. The rejoicings in the palace at that glad time were beyond any description. Rāma's mother Kausalyā and the other queens were too overcome with love to think about themselves.

दोहा-*dohā:*

दिए दान बिप्रन्ह बिपुल पूजि गनेस पुरारि ।
die dāna bipranha bipula pūji ganesa purāri,

प्रमुदित परम दरिद्र जनु पाइ पदारथ चारि ॥ ३४५ ॥
pramudita parama daridra janu pāi padāratha cāri. 345.

Trans:

After worshipping Ganesh and Mahādev they bestowed large gifts upon the Brahmins, and were as jubilant as Poverty would be on finding the four great prizes of life.

चौपाई-*caupāī:*

मोद प्रमोद बिबस सब माता । चलहिं न चरन सिथिल भए गाता ॥
moda pramoda bibasa saba mātā, calahiṁ na carana sithila bhae gātā.

राम दरस हित अति अनुरागीं । परिछनि साजु सजन सब लागीं ॥
rāma darasa hita ati anurāgīṁ, parichani sāju sajana saba lāgīṁ.

बिबिध बिधान बाजने बाजे । मंगल मुदित सुमित्राँ साजे ॥
bibidha bidhāna bājane bāje, maṁgala mudita sumitrāṁ sāje.

हरद दूब दधि पल्लव फूला । पान पूगफल मंगल मूला ॥
harada dūba dadhi pallava phūlā, pāna pūgaphala maṁgala mūlā.

अच्छत अंकुर लोचन लाजा । मंजुल मंजरि तुलसि बिराजा ॥
acchata aṁkura locana lājā, maṁjula maṁjari tulasi birājā.

छुहे पुरट घट सहज सुहाए । मदन सकुन जनु नीड़ बनाए ॥
chuhe puraṭa ghaṭa sahaja suhāe, madana sakuna janu nīṛa banāe.

सगुन सुगंध न जाहिं बखानी । मंगल सकल सजहिं सब रानी ॥
saguna sugaṁdha na jāhiṁ bakhānī, maṁgala sakala sajahiṁ saba rānī.

रचीं आरतीं बहुत बिधाना । मुदित करहिं कल मंगल गाना ॥
racīṁ āratīṁ bahuta bidhānā, mudita karahiṁ kala maṁgala gānā.

Trans:

Each royal mother was so overcome with love and delight that her feet refused to walk—the whole body benumbed. Greatly longing for a sight of Rāma, they all began preparing the lustral lamps. Instruments of music were played in various modes, as the glad Sumitrā arranged her auspicious offering of turmeric, *dūba* grass, curds, sprigs and flowers, *pān*, betel-nut and well-flavored roots, rice, blades of wheat, yellow pigment, parched grain, and bunches of the graceful Tulsī plant in embossed golden vases, so exquisitely beautiful that they seemed like nests made for Love's own birdlings. Auspicious perfumes defied all description. In this way all the queens prepared all sorts of auspicious articles. With lustral lights arranged in various devices they sing in joy in melodious festal strains.

दोहा-*dohā:*

कनक थार भरि मंगलन्हि कमल करन्हि लिएँ मात ।
kanaka thāra bhari maṁgalanhi kamala karanhi lieṁ māta,

चलीं मुदित परिछनि करन पुलक पल्लवित गात ॥ ३४६ ॥
calīṁ mudita parichani karana pulaka pallavita gāta. 346.

Trans:

With golden salvers in their lotus hands, laden with their offerings, and their body quivering with emotion, the queens go forth with joy to perform the lustration.

चौपाई-*caupāī:*

धूप धूम नभु मेचक भयऊ । सावन घन घमंडु जनु ठयऊ ॥
dhūpa dhūma nabhu mecaka bhayaū, sāvana ghana ghamaṁḍu janu ṭhayaū.
सुरतरु सुमन माल सुर बरषहिं । मनहुँ बलाक अवलि मनु करषहिं ॥
surataru sumana māla sura baraṣahiṁ, manahuṁ balāka avali manu karaṣahiṁ.
मंजुल मनिमय बंदनिवारे । मनहुँ पाकरिपु चाप सँवारे ॥
maṁjula manimaya baṁdanivāre, manahuṁ pākaripu cāpa saṁvāre.
प्रगटहिं दुरहिं अटन्ह पर भामिनि । चारु चपल जनु दमकहिं दामिनि ॥
pragaṭahiṁ durahiṁ aṭanha para bhāmini, cāru capala janu damakahiṁ dāmini.
दुंदुभि धुनि घन गरजनि घोरा । जाचक चातक दादुर मोरा ॥
duṁdubhi dhuni ghana garajani ghorā, jācaka cātaka dādura morā.
सुर सुगंध सुचि बरषहिं बारी । सुखी सकल ससि पुर नर नारी ॥
sura sugaṁdha suci baraṣahiṁ bārī, sukhī sakala sasi pura nara nārī.
समउ जानी गुर आयसु दीन्हा । पुर प्रबेसु रघुकुलमनि कीन्हा ॥
samau jānī gura āyasu dīnhā, pura prabesu raghukulamani kīnhā.
सुमिरि संभु गिरिजा गनराजा । मुदित महीपति सहित समाजा ॥
sumiri saṁbhu girijā ganarājā, mudita mahīpati sahita samājā.

Trans:

The heaven was darkened with the fumes of burning incense, as though overhung with *Sāvan*'s densest thunderclouds. The gods rained down garlands of flowers from the tree of paradise, which seemed to the beholders as cranes in graceful flight. The lustrous jeweled festoons resembled the rainbow; the maidens on the housetops, now in sight and now behind, were like the fitful flashes of lightning; the beat of the drums was as the crash of thunder; the beggars as clamorous as the cuckoos and the frogs and peacocks. The sweet perfumes poured down by celestial was as a copious showers of rain upon the people of the city which was like a gladdening thirsty crop. Seeing that the time had arrived, the Gurū gave the word, and the glory of Raghu's line made his entry into the city, remembering in his heart Shambhu and Girijā and Ganesh, and rejoicing greatly—he and all his retinue.

दोहा-*dohā:*

होहिं सगुन बरषहिं सुमन सुर दुंदुभीं बजाइ ।
hohiṁ saguna baraṣahiṁ sumana sura duṁdubhīṁ bajāi,
बिबुध बधू नाचहिं मुदित मंजुल मंगल गाइ ॥ ३४७ ॥
bibudha badhū nācahiṁ mudita maṁjula maṁgala gāi. 347.

Trans:

Every omen was auspicious; the gods rained down flowers to the beat of drums; and all the while heavenly nymphs danced for joy and sang jubilant songs of triumph.

चौपाई-*caupāī:*

मागध सूत बंदि नट नागर । गावहिं जसु तिहु लोक उजागर ॥
māgadha sūta baṁdi naṭa nāgara, gāvahiṁ jasu tihu loka ujāgara.
जय धुनि बिमल बेद बर बानी । दस दिसि सुनिअ सुमंगल सानी ॥
jaya dhuni bimala beda bara bānī, dasa disi sunia sumaṁgala sānī.
बिपुल बाजने बाजन लागे । नभ सुर नगर लोग अनुरागे ॥
bipula bājane bājana lāge, nabha sura nagara loga anurāge.
बने बराती बरनि न जाहीं । महा मुदित मन सुख न समाहीं ॥
bane barātī barani na jāhīṁ, mahā mudita mana sukha na samāhīṁ.
पुरबासिन्ह तब राय जोहारे । देखत रामहि भए सुखारे ॥
purabāsinha taba rāya johāre, dekhata rāmahi bhae sukhāre.
करहिं निछावरि मनिगन चीरा । बारि बिलोचन पुलक सरीरा ॥
karahiṁ nichāvari manigana cīrā, bāri bilocana pulaka sarīrā.
आरति करहिं मुदित पुर नारी । हरषहिं निरखि कुअँर बर चारी ॥
ārati karahiṁ mudita pura nārī, haraṣahiṁ nirakhi kuaṁra bara cārī.
सिबिका सुभग ओहार उघारी । देखि दुलहिनिन्ह होहिं सुखारी ॥
sibikā subhaga ohāra ughārī, dekhi dulahininha hohiṁ sukhārī.

Trans:

Bards, minstrels, rhapsodists, mimes and players chanted the glory of the Lord—who illumines all the three worlds. In all ten regions of the heaven might be heard loud shouts of victory intermingled with the religious intoning of the Vedas. All varieties of music played, and gods in heaven and men on earth were alike enraptured. The magnificence of the procession was past all telling, and the joy was more than heart could contain. The citizens made many an obeisance to the king, and then were gladdened by the sight of Shrī Rāma. They scatter around him jewels and vestments—with their eyes full of tears and their body all tremulous with excitement. The ladies move over his head the lustral lights and rejoice greatly to behold the four noble princes; but then when they lift the curtain of the well-appointed *Pālkī* and see the brides, they are still all the more glad.

दोहा-*dohā:*

एहि बिधि सबही देत सुखु आए राजदुआर ।
ehi bidhi sabahī deta sukhu āe rājaduāra,
मुदित मातु परिछनि करहिं बधुन्ह समेत कुमार ॥ ३४८ ॥
mudita mātu parichani karahiṁ badhunha sameta kumāra. 348.

Trans:

In this manner, to the delight of all, they arrive at the gate of the palace, where the glad queens waved the lustral lights over the princes and their brides.

चौपाई-*caupāī:*

करहिं आरती बारहिं बारा । प्रेमु प्रमोदु कहै को पारा ॥
karahiṁ āratī bārahiṁ bārā, premu pramodu kahai ko pārā.
भूषन मनि पट नाना जाती । करहिं निछावरि अगनित भाँती ॥
bhūṣana mani paṭa nānā jātī, karahiṁ nichāvari aganita bhāṁtī.
बधुन्ह समेत देखि सुत चारी । परमानंद मगन महतारी ॥
badhunha sameta dekhi suta cārī, paramānaṁda magana mahatārī.
पुनि पुनि सीय राम छबि देखी । मुदित सफल जग जीवन लेखी ॥
puni puni sīya rāma chabi dekhī, mudita saphala jaga jīvana lekhī.
सखीं सीय मुख पुनि पुनि चाही । गान करहिं निज सुकृत सराही ॥
sakhīṁ sīya mukha puni puni cāhī, gāna karahiṁ nija sukṛta sarāhī.
बरषहिं सुमन छनहिं छन देवा । नाचहिं गावहिं लावहिं सेवा ॥
baraṣahiṁ sumana chanahiṁ chana devā, nācahiṁ gāvahiṁ lāvahiṁ sevā.
देखि मनोहर चारिउ जोरीं । सारद उपमा सकल ढँढोरीं ॥
dekhi manohara cāriu jorīṁ, sārada upamā sakala ḍhaṁḍhorīṁ.
देत न बनहिं निपट लघु लागीं । एकटक रहीं रूप अनुरागीं ॥
deta na banahiṁ nipaṭa laghu lāgīṁ, ekaṭaka rahīṁ rūpa anurāgīṁ.

Trans:

Time after time they perform the ceremony in a rapture of love that is beyond all words. They scatter around in boundless profusion gold and silver ornaments and gems and silks of every kind, and as they gaze on their four sons and their brides, they are overwhelmed with the bliss of heaven. Again and again as they regard the beauty of Rāma and Sītā, they think with joy that this is the happiest moment of their life. As her companions look again and again into Sītā's face they sing and exult over their good fortune. All the while the gods rain down flowers, amidst dancing and singing and obsequious homage. Seeing four such charming couples, Shārdā looks up all her similes but not one would do; all seemed unworthy; and she could only stand and gaze, enchanted with that supreme loveliness.

दोहा-dohā:

निगम नीति कुल रीति करि अरघ पाँवड़े देत ।
nigama nīti kula rīti kari aragha pāṁvaṛe deta,
बधुन्ह सहित सुत परिछि सब चलीं लवाइ निकेत ॥ ३४९॥
badhunha sahita suta parichi saba calīṁ lavāi niketa. 349.

Trans:

After performing all the rites prescribed by the Veda and family usage, they conduct the sons and their brides to the palace; sprinkling lustral water, spreading carpets in the way, and waving lights.

चौपाई-caupāī:

चारि सिंघासन सहज सुहाए । जनु मनोज निज हाथ बनाए ॥
cāri siṁghāsana sahaja suhāe, janu manoja nija hātha banāe.
तिन्ह पर कुअँरि कुअँर बैठारे । सादर पाय पुनीत पखारे ॥
tinha para kuaṁri kuaṁra baiṭhāre, sādara pāya punīta pakhāre.
धूप दीप नैबेद बेद बिधि । पूजे बर दुलहिनि मंगलनिधि ॥
dhūpa dīpa naibeda beda bidhi, pūje bara dulahini maṁgalanidhi.
बारहिं बार आरती करहीं । ब्यजन चारु चामर सिर ढरहीं ॥
bārahiṁ bāra āratī karahīṁ, byajana cāru cāmara sira ḍharahīṁ.
बस्तु अनेक निछावरि होहीं । भरीं प्रमोद मातु सब सोहीं ॥
bastu aneka nichāvari hohīṁ, bharīṁ pramoda mātu saba sohīṁ.
पावा परम तत्व जनु जोगीं । अमृतु लहेउ जनु संतत रोगीं ॥
pāvā parama tatva janu jogīṁ, amṛtu laheu janu saṁtata rogīṁ.
जनम रंक जनु पारस पावा । अंधहि लोचन लाभु सुहावा ॥
janama raṁka janu pārasa pāvā, aṁdhahi locana lābhu suhāvā.
मूक बदन जनु सारद छाई । मानहुँ समर सूर जय पाई ॥
mūka badana janu sārada chāī, mānahuṁ samara sūra jaya pāī.

Trans:

After seating the brides and their grooms on four thrones so magnificent that they seemed as if made by Love's own hands, they proceeded reverently to lave their sacred feet, and to do them homage—all holy as they were—with incense and lights and oblations, in accordance with Vedic ritual. Time after time they pass the lights around, and wave over their head gorgeous fans and *chouries*, and scatter profuse gifts—for each royal mother was as full of exultation as a devotee who has obtained beatitude; or a man sick all his life who has gotten an elixir; or a born beggar who has found the philosopher's stone; or a blind man is suddenly restored to sight; or a dumb man now endued with eloquence; or a warrior who has triumphed in the battle.

दोहा-dohā:

एहि सुख ते सत कोटि गुन पावहिं मातु अनंदु ।
ehi sukha te sata koṭi guna pāvahiṁ mātu anaṁdu,
भाइन्ह सहित बिआहि घर आए रघुकुलचंदु ॥ ३५०क॥
bhāinha sahita biāhi ghara āe raghukulacaṁdu. 350(ka).

लोक रीति जननीं करहिं बर दुलहिनि सकुचाहिं ।
loka rīti jananīṁ karahiṁ bara dulahini sakucāhiṁ,
मोदु बिनोदु बिलोकि बड़ रामु मनहिं मुसुकाहिं ॥ ३५०ख॥
modu binodu biloki baṛa rāmu manahiṁ musukāhiṁ. 350(kha).

Trans:

In truth the rapture of the queens was greater by a hundred millions times the joy described above—for it was the very Delighter of Raghu's race who had returned with all his brothers duly married. As the royal matrons performed the accustomed ceremonies the brides and their grooms were much shy, while Rāma smiled to himself on beholding their joy and delight.

चौपाई-caupāī:

देव पितर पूजे बिधि नीकी । पूजीं सकल बासना जी की ॥
deva pitara pūje bidhi nīkī, pūjīṁ sakala bāsanā jī kī.
सबहि बंदि मागहिं बरदाना । भाइन्ह सहित राम कल्याना ॥
sabahi baṁdi māgahiṁ baradānā, bhāinha sahita rāma kalyānā.
अंतरहित सुर आसिष देहीं । मुदित मातु अंचल भरि लेहीं ॥
aṁtarahita sura āsiṣa dehīṁ, mudita mātu aṁcala bhari lehīṁ.
भूपति बोलि बराती लीन्हे । जान बसन मनि भूषन दीन्हे ॥
bhūpati boli barātī līnhe, jāna basana mani bhūṣana dīnhe.
आयसु पाइ राखि उर रामहि । मुदित गए सब निज निज धामहि ॥
āyasu pāi rākhi ura rāmahi, mudita gae saba nija nija dhāmahi.
पुर नर नारि सकल पहिराए । घर घर बाजन लगे बधाए ॥
pura nara nāri sakala pahirāe, ghara ghara bājana lage badhāe.
जाचक जन जाचहिं जोइ जोई । प्रमुदित राउ देहिं सोइ सोई ॥
jācaka jana jācahiṁ joi joī, pramudita rāu dehiṁ soi soī.
सेवक सकल बजनिआ नाना । पूरन किए दान सनमाना ॥
sevaka sakala bajaniā nānā, pūrana kie dāna sanamānā.

Trans:

In due fashion all made their homage to the gods and the spirits of their ancestors, and every imagination of the heart was satisfied. Humbly they begged from all the highest boon: namely, the prosperity of Rāma and his brothers; and the gods unseen conferred their blessings. The matrons in their joy took them to their bosom; while the king sent for all who had joined in procession and gave them carriages and raiment and jewels and ornaments. Then, on receiving permission, and still cherishing the image of Rāma in their heart, they returned in joy each to his own home. All the people of the city, both men and women, were clad in festal dress, and in every home was the sound of jubilant dance. Anything that a seeker sought was at once bestowed upon him by the glad king, and every attendant and every minstrel band was overwhelmed with gifts and compliments.

दोहा-dohā:

देहिं असीस जोहारि सब गावहिं गुन गन गाथ ।
dehiṁ asīsa johāri saba gāvahiṁ guna gana gātha,
तब गुर भूसुर सहित गृहँ गवनु कीन्ह नरनाथ ॥ ३५१॥
taba gura bhūsura sahita gṛhaṁ gavanu kīnha naranātha. 351.

Trans:

All profoundly bowing invoke blessings upon him and sing his praises, as the king with his Gurū and the Brahmins proceeded to the palace.

चौपाई-caupāī:

जो बसिष्ट अनुसासन दीन्ही । लोक बेद बिधि सादर कीन्ही ॥
jo basiṣṭa anusāsana dīnhī, loka beda bidhi sādara kīnhī.
भूसुर भीर देखि सब रानी । सादर उठीं भाग्य बड़ जानी ॥
bhūsura bhīra dekhi saba rānī, sādara uṭhīṁ bhāgya baṛa jānī.
पाय पखारि सकल अन्हवाए । पूजि भली बिधि भूप जेवाँए ॥
pāya pakhāri sakala anhavāe, pūji bhalī bidhi bhūpa jevāṁe.
आदर दान प्रेम परिपोषे । देत असीस चले मन तोषे ॥
ādara dāna prema paripoṣe, deta asīsa cale mana toṣe.
बहु बिधि कीन्हि गाधिसुत पूजा । नाथ मोहि सम धन्य न दूजा ॥
bahu bidhi kīnhi gādhisuta pūjā, nātha mohi sama dhanya na dūjā.
कीन्हि प्रसंसा भूपति भूरी । रानिन्ह सहित लीन्हि पग धूरी ॥
kīnhi prasaṁsā bhūpati bhūrī, rāninha sahita līnhi paga dhūrī.
भीतर भवन दीन्ह बर बासू । मन जोगवत रह नृपु रनिवासू ॥
bhītara bhavana dīnha bara bāsū, mana jogavata raha nṛpu ranivāsū.
पूजे गुर पद कमल बहोरी । कीन्हि बिनय उर प्रीति न थोरी ॥
pūje gura pada kamala bahorī, kīnhi binaya ura prīti na thorī.

Trans:

Under Vasishtha's directions he reverently performed every ceremony prescribed either by usage or by the Vedas. The queens, on seeing the throng of Brahmins, rose to greet them and thought themselves most highly favored. After bathing their feet and doing them all due homage, the king feasted them at a banquet and loaded them with gifts and affectionate civilities. Grateful at heart, they blessed him at parting. To the son of Gādhi the king paid special homage, saying, "My lord, there is no man in the world as blessed as I am"; and with many supplicant speeches both he and his queens took of the dust of his feet. Next he assigned him a splendid apartment within the palace; the king and his royal consorts alike awaiting his every wish. Again he adored his lotus feet with the greatest humility and devotion.

दोहा-dohā:

बधुन्ह समेत कुमार सब रानिन्ह सहित महीसु ।
badhunha sameta kumāra saba rāninha sahita mahīsu,
पुनि पुनि बंदत गुर चरन देत असीस मुनीसु ॥ ३५२॥
puni puni baṁdata gura carana deta asīsa munīsu. 352.

Trans:

The princes and their brides, the king and his royal consorts again and again did reverence to the Gurū's feet and received the holy man's blessing.

चौपाई-caupāī:

बिनय कीन्हि उर अति अनुरागें । सुत संपदा राखि सब आगें ॥
binaya kīnhi ura ati anurāgeṁ, suta saṁpadā rākhi saba āgeṁ.
नेगु मागि मुनिनायक लीन्हा । आसिरबादु बहुत बिधि दीन्हा ॥
negu māgi munināyaka līnhā, āsirabādu bahuta bidhi dīnhā.
उर धरि रामहि सीय समेता । हरषि कीन्ह गुर गवनु निकेता ॥
ura dhari rāmahi sīya sametā, haraṣi kīnha gura gavanu niketā.
बिप्रबधू सब भूप बोलाईं । चैल चारु भूषन पहिराईं ॥
biprabadhū saba bhūpa bolāīṁ, caila cāru bhūṣana pahirāīṁ.
बहुरि बोलाइ सुआसिनि लीन्हीं । रुचि बिचारि पहिरावनि दीन्हीं ॥
bahuri bolāi suāsini līnhīṁ, ruci bicāri pahirāvani dīnhīṁ.
नेगी नेग जोग सब लेहीं । रुचि अनुरुप भूपमनि देहीं ॥
negī nega joga saba lehīṁ, ruci anurupa bhūpamani dehīṁ.
प्रिय पाहुने पूज्य जे जाने । भूपति भली भाँति सनमाने ॥
priya pāhune pūjya je jāne, bhūpati bhalī bhāṁti sanamāne.
देव देखि रघुबीर बिबाहू । बरषि प्रसून प्रसंसि उछाहू ॥
deva dekhi raghubīra bibāhū, baraṣi prasūna prasaṁsi uchāhū.

Trans:

With humility of heart and deep devotion he placed before him his sons and everything that he possessed. But the great saint asked only for the accustomed offering and invoking upon him every blessing set out with joy on his homeward way—with the image of Rāma and Sītā impressed upon his heart. Then were summoned the Brahmin ladies and others and invested with fair robes and ornaments; and next the younger ladies of the city, who too were presented with dresses such as each most fancied. Everyone with entitlement to claims on ceremonial occasions received from the jewel of kings suitable remembrance according to their taste; while more dear and honored friends were overwhelmed with courtesies. The gods, who witnessed Raghubīr's marriage, rained down flowers as they applauded the spectacle.

दोहा-dohā:

चले निसान बजाइ सुर निज निज पुर सुख पाइ ।
cale nisāna bajāi sura nija nija pura sukha pāi,
कहत परसपर राम जसु प्रेम न हृदयँ समाइ ॥ ३५३॥
kahata parasapara rāma jasu prema na hṛdayaṁ samāi. 353.

Trans:

With beat of drums each returned to his own realm, all highly delighted, and talking to one another of Rāma's glory with irrepressible rapture.

चौपाई-caupāī:

सब बिधि सबहि समदि नरनाहू । रहा हृदयँ भरि पूरि उछाहू ॥
saba bidhi sabahi samadi naranāhū, rahā hṛdayaṁ bhari pūri uchāhū.
जहँ रनिवासु तहाँ पगु धारे । सहित बहूटिन्ह कुअँर निहारे ॥
jahaṁ ranivāsu tahāṁ pagu dhāre, sahita bahūṭinha kuaṁra nihāre.
लिए गोद करि मोद समेता । को कहि सकइ भयउ सुखु जेता ॥
lie goda kari moda sametā, ko kahi sakai bhayau sukhu jetā.
बधू सप्रेम गोद बैठारीं । बार बार हियँ हरषि दुलारीं ॥
badhū saprema goda baiṭhārīṁ, bāra bāra hiyaṁ haraṣi dulārīṁ.
देखि समाजु मुदित रनिवासू । सब कें उर अनंद कियो बासू ॥
dekhi samāju mudita ranivāsū, saba keṁ ura anaṁda kiyo bāsū.
कहेउ भूप जिमि भयउ बिबाहू । सुनि सुनि हरषु होत सब काहू ॥
kaheu bhūpa jimi bhayau bibāhū, suni suni haraṣu hota saba kāhū.
जनक राज गुन सीलु बड़ाई । प्रीति रीति संपदा सुहाई ॥
janaka rāja guna sīlu baṛāī, prīti rīti saṁpadā suhāī.
बहुबिधि भूप भाट जिमि बरनी । रानीं सब प्रमुदित सुनि करनी ॥
bahubidhi bhūpa bhāṭa jimi baranī, rānīṁ saba pramudita suni karanī.

Trans:

The king showed everyone all possible honor, and with a heart full to overflowing with gladness proceeded to the private apartments, and there beheld the princes and their brides. He gladly took the boys in his arms and experienced a thrill of joy which nobody could tell. Similarly he tenderly seated the brides near him and fondly showered affections upon them again and again with a heart full of rapture. The ladies of the gynoecium were delighted to behold this spectacle; the heart of everyone became an abode of joy. The king related how the wedding had taken place and everyone was delighted to hear the account. The goodness, amiability, nobility, loving nature and the splendid wealth of King Janak were extolled by King Dashrath in a variety of ways even as a rhapsodist would do; and the queens were enraptured to hear the record of his doings.

दोहा-dohā:

सुतन्ह समेत नहाइ नृप बोलि बिप्र गुर ग्याति ।
sutanha sameta nahāi nṛpa boli bipra gura gyāti,
भोजन कीन्ह अनेक बिधि घरी पंच गइ राति ॥ ३५४॥
bhojana kīnha aneka bidhi gharī paṁca gai rāti. 354.

Trans:

After bathing with his sons the king called the Brahmins, the preceptor, and his own kinsmen and, having entertained them at meal with a variety of dishes, himself feasted too; and this way a few hours of the night passed.

चौपाई-caupāī:

मंगलगान करहिं बर भामिनि । भै सुखमूल मनोहर जामिनि ॥
maṁgalagāna karahiṁ bara bhāmini, bhai sukhamūla manohara jāmini.
अँचइ पान सब काहूँ पाए । स्रग सुगंध भूषित छबि छाए ॥
aṁcai pāna saba kāhūṁ pāe, sraga sugaṁdha bhūṣita chabi chāe.
रामहि देखि रजायसु पाई । निज निज भवन चले सिर नाई ॥
rāmahi dekhi rajāyasu pāī, nija nija bhavana cale sira nāī.
प्रेमु प्रमोदु बिनोदु बढ़ाई । समउ समाजु मनोहरताई ॥
premu pramodu binodu baṛhāī, samau samāju manoharatāī.
कहि न सकहिं सत सारद सेसू । बेद बिरंचि महेस गनेसू ॥
kahi na sakahiṁ sata sārada sesū, beda biraṁci mahesa ganesū.
सो मैं कहौं कवन बिधि बरनी । भूमिनागु सिर धरइ कि धरनी ॥
so maiṁ kahauṁ kavana bidhi baranī, bhūmināgu sira dharai ki dharanī.

नृप सब भाँति सबहि सनमानी । कहि मृदु बचन बोलाईं रानी ॥
nṛpa saba bhām̐ti sabahi sanamānī, kahi mṛdu bacana bolāīṁ rānī.
बधू लरिकनीं पर घर आईं । राखेहु नयन पलक की नाईं ॥
badhū larikanīṁ para ghara āīṁ, rākhehu nayana palaka kī nāīṁ.

Trans:

Lovely women sang joyous songs, and the night was one of exquisite happiness. As they rose from their seats, having rinsed, all were presented with *Pān*, and decorated with beautiful and sweet-scented garlands; then after one more look at Rāma and bowing their head they received the royal permission to retire, each to his abode. The display of love and rapturous delight and the beauty of the court at that time was more than could be told by a hundred Shārdās, or Sheshnāgs, or by the Vedas, or Brahmmā, or Mahādev, or Ganesh—how then can I tell it, any more than an earthly serpent can support the globe on its head? After showing everyone the highest honor, the king in gentle tones addressed the queens, "The brides are but youngsters and they have come to a strange house; watch over them as closely as the eyelid guards the eye.

दोहा-dohā:

लरिका श्रमित उनीद बस सयन करावहु जाइ ।
larikā śramita unīda basa sayana karāvahu jāi,
अस कहि गे बिश्रामगृहँ राम चरन चितु लाइ ॥ ३५५॥
asa kahi ge biśrāmagṛham̐ rāma carana citu lāi. 355.

Trans:

Go and put them to bed, for they are tired and sleepy." And so saying the king retired to his own couch with his thoughts intent on Rāma's feet.

चौपाई-caupāī:

भूप बचन सुनि सहज सुहाए । जरित कनक मनि पलँग डसाए ॥
bhūpa bacana suni sahaja suhāe, jarita kanaka mani palam̐ga ḍasāe.
सुभग सुरभि पय फेन समाना । कोमल कलित सुपेतीं नाना ॥
subhaga surabhi paya phena samānā, komala kalita supetīṁ nānā.
उपबरहन बर बरनि न जाहीं । स्रग सुगंध मनिमंदिर माहीं ॥
upabarahana bara barani na jāhīṁ, sraga sugaṁdha manimaṁdira māhīṁ.
रतनदीप सुठि चारु चँदोवा । कहत न बनइ जान जेहिं जोवा ॥
ratanadīpa suṭhi cāru caṁdovā, kahata na banai jāna jehiṁ jovā.
सेज रुचिर रचि रामु उठाए । प्रेम समेत पलँग पौढ़ाए ॥
seja rucira raci rāmu uṭhāe, prema sameta palam̐ga pauṛhāe.
अग्या पुनि पुनि भाइन्ह दीन्ही । निज निज सेज सयन तिन्ह कीन्ही ॥
agyā puni puni bhāinha dīnhī, nija nija seja sayana tinha kīnhī.
देखि स्याम मृदु मंजुल गाता । कहहिं सप्रेम बचन सब माता ॥
dekhi syāma mṛdu maṁjula gātā, kahahiṁ saprema bacana saba mātā.
मारग जात भयावनि भारी । केहि बिधि तात ताड़का मारी ॥
māraga jāta bhayāvani bhārī, kehi bidhi tāta tāṛakā mārī.

Trans:

On hearing the king's kind words, they made ready the bed which was of gold and set with gems, with various rich coverings as soft and white as the froth of milk, and pillows finer than words can tell. In the jeweled chamber were sweet-scented garlands, and a beautiful canopy flashing with lustrous gems that defied description; no one who had not seen it could imagine it. Having thus prepared a number of fine beds, the queens took up Shrī Rāma and lovingly directed him upon one of them. On being repeatedly asked by Shrī Rāma, his brothers too retired each to his own bed. On seeing his dark little body, so soft and delicate, the adoring mothers cried: "O my son, how could you kill on the way the terrible monster Taraka?

दोहा-dohā:

घोर निसाचर बिकट भट समर गनहिं नहिं काहु ।
ghora nisācara bikaṭa bhaṭa samara ganahiṁ nahiṁ kāhu,
मारे सहित सहाय किमि खल मारीच सुबाहु ॥ ३५६॥
māre sahita sahāya kimi khala mārīca subāhu. 356.

Trans:

How were you able to slay those savage demons, those ferocious warriors who in battle held no man of any account, the vile Mārich and Subahu and all their army?

चौपाई-caupāī:

मुनि प्रसाद बलि तात तुम्हारी । ईस अनेक करवरें टारी ॥
muni prasāda bali tāta tumhārī, īsa aneka karavareṁ ṭārī.
मख रखवारी करि दुहुँ भाईं । गुरु प्रसाद सब बिद्या पाईं ॥
makha rakhavārī kari duhum̐ bhāīṁ, guru prasāda saba bidyā pāīṁ.
मुनितिय तरी लगत पग धूरी । कीरति रही भुवन भरि पूरी ॥
munitiya tarī lagata paga dhūrī, kīrati rahī bhuvana bhari pūrī.
कमठ पीठि पबि कूट कठोरा । नृप समाज महुँ सिव धनु तोरा ॥
kamaṭha pīṭhi pabi kūṭa kaṭhorā, nṛpa samāja mahum̐ siva dhanu torā.
बिस्व बिजय जसु जानकि पाई । आए भवन ब्याहि सब भाई ॥
bisva bijaya jasu jānaki pāī, āe bhavana byāhi saba bhāī.
सकल अमानुष करम तुम्हारे । केवल कौसिक कृपाँ सुधारे ॥
sakala amānuṣa karama tumhāre, kevala kausika kṛpām̐ sudhāre.
आजु सुफल जग जनमु हमारा । देखि तात बिधुबदन तुम्हारा ॥
āju suphala jaga janamu hamārā, dekhi tāta bidhubadana tumhārā.
जे दिन गए तुम्हहि बिनु देखें । ते बिरंचि जनि पारहिं लेखें ॥
je dina gae tumhahi binu dekheṁ, te biraṁci jani pārahiṁ lekheṁ.

Trans:

It was by the saint's (Vishwāmitra) favor, I vow, my son, that God averted from you countless calamities, while you and your brother guarded the sacrifice; and by your Gurū's blessing you acquired all knowledge. At the touch of the dust of your feet the hermit's wife attained to salvation. The whole world is filled with your glory; in the assembly of princes you broke Shiva's bow, though hard as a tortoise-shell or a thunderbolt; you have won universal glory and renown and Jānakī for your bride, and have now with your brothers returned home married. All your actions are more than human; it is only by Vishwāmitra's good favor that you have prospered. Today my birth into the world has borne fruit, now that I see your moon-like face, my son. The days that were spent without seeing you God ought not to take into account at all."

दोहा-dohā:

राम प्रतोषीं मातु सब कहि बिनीत बर बैन ।
rāma pratoṣīṁ mātu saba kahi binīta bara baina,
सुमिरि संभु गुर बिप्र पद किए नीदबस नैन ॥ ३५७॥
sumiri saṁbhu gura bipra pada kie nīdabasa naina. 357.

Trans:

Rāma in most modest phrase reassured the mothers, and meditating on the feet of Shambhu and his Gurū and all Brahmins, he closed his eyes in sleep.

चौपाई-caupāī:

नीदउँ बदन सोह सुठि लोना । मनहुँ साँझ सरसीरुह सोना ॥
nīdaum̐ badana soha suṭhi lonā, manahum̐ sām̐jha sarasīruha sonā.
घर घर करहिं जागरन नारीं । देहिं परसपर मंगल गारीं ॥
ghara ghara karahiṁ jāgarana nārīṁ, dehiṁ parasapara maṁgala gārīṁ.
पुरी बिराजति राजति रजनी । रानीं कहहिं बिलोकहु सजनी ॥
purī birājati rājati rajanī, rānīṁ kahahiṁ bilokahu sajanī.

सुंदर बधुन्ह सासु लै सोईं । फनिकन्ह जनु सिरमनि उर गोईं ॥
suṁdara badhunha sāsu lai soīṁ, phanikanha janu siramani ura goīṁ.
प्रात पुनीत काल प्रभु जागे । अरुनचूड़ बर बोलन लागे ॥
prāta punīta kāla prabhu jāge, arunacūṛa bara bolana lāge.
बंदि मागधन्हि गुनगन गाए । पुरजन द्वार जोहारन आए ॥
baṁdi māgadhanhi gunagana gāe, purajana dvāra johārana āe.
बंदि बिप्र सुर गुर पितु माता । पाइ असीस मुदित सब भ्राता ॥
baṁdi bipra sura gura pitu mātā, pāi asīsa mudita saba bhrātā.
जननिन्ह सादर बदन निहारे । भूपति संग द्वार पगु धारे ॥
jananinha sādara badana nihāre, bhūpati saṁga dvāra pagu dhāre.

Trans:

Even during sleep Rāma's most charming countenance gleamed as a red lotus, half closed at eventide. In every house women kept vigil and jested with one another in auspicious wise. The city was so resplendent, nay, so splendid the night itself that the queens cried "See, girls, see." The mothers-in-law then slept with the lovely brides enfolded in their arms even as serpents would clasp to their bosom the gems from their hood. At the holy hour of dawn the Lord awoke ere the chanticleer had begun to crow. Minstrels and bards proclaimed his praises and the citizens flocked to the gate to do him homage. The four brothers saluted the Brahmins, the gods, their Gurū, and their father and mother, and gladly received their blessing, and while the queens reverentially gazed upon their faces, advanced with the king to the door.

दोहा-dohā:

कीन्हि सौच सब सहज सुचि सरित पुनीत नहाइ ।
kīnhi sauca saba sahaja suci sarita punīta nahāi,
प्रातक्रिया करि तात पहिं आए चारिउ भाइ ॥३५८॥
prātakriyā kari tāta pahiṁ āe cāriu bhāi. 358.

Trans:

Pure though they were in themselves, they performed all the customary ablutions and bathed in the holy river and completed their morning devotions, ere they returned to their sire.

नवाह्नपारायण तीसरा विश्राम

navāhnapārāyaṇa tīsarā viśrāma
(Pause 3 for a Nine-Day Recitation)

चौपाई-caupāī:

भूप बिलोकि लिए उर लाई । बैठे हरषि रजायसु पाई ॥
bhūpa biloki lie ura lāī, baiṭhe haraṣi rajāyasu pāī.
देखि रामु सब सभा जुड़ानी । लोचन लाभ अवधि अनुमानी ॥
dekhi rāmu saba sabhā juṛānī, locana lābha avadhi anumānī.
पुनि बसिष्टु मुनि कौसिकु आए । सुभग आसनन्हि मुनि बैठाए ॥
puni basiṣṭu muni kausiku āe, subhaga āsananhi muni baiṭhāe.
सुतन्ह समेत पूजि पद लागे । निरखि रामु दोउ गुर अनुरागे ॥
sutanha sameta pūji pada lāge, nirakhi rāmu dou gura anurāge.
कहहिं बसिष्टु धरम इतिहासा । सुनहिं महीसु सहित रनिवासा ॥
kahahiṁ basiṣṭu dharama itihāsā, sunahiṁ mahīsu sahita ranivāsā.
मुनि मन अगम गाधिसुत करनी । मुदित बसिष्ट बिपुल बिधि बरनी ॥
muni mana agama gādhisuta karanī, mudita basiṣṭa bipula bidhi baranī.
बोले बामदेउ सब साँची । कीरति कलित लोक तिहुँ माची ॥
bole bāmadeu saba sāṁcī, kīrati kalita loka tihuṁ mācī.
सुनि आनंदु भयउ सब काहू । राम लखन उर अधिक उछाहू ॥
suni ānaṁdu bhayau saba kāhū, rāma lakhana ura adhika uchāhū.

Trans:

The king on seeing them took them to his bosom. Then at his command they gladly seated themselves. The whole court rejoiced at the sight of Rāma, and accounted their eyes supremely blest. Then came saint Vasishtha and Vishwāmitra and were conducted to exalted thrones. Father and sons reverently adored their feet, and both the holy men rejoiced as they gazed on Rāma. Vasishtha recited sacred legends while the monarch and his queens listened. He told with joy in diffuse strain of all the doings of Gādhi's son, which surpass even the imagination of the saints. Averred Vāmdev, "That is true; Vishwāmitra's fame has become renowned through the three worlds." All who heard were glad; and in Rāma and Lakshman's heart there was exceeding joy.

दोहा-dohā:

मंगल मोद उछाह नित जाहिं दिवस एहि भाँति ।
maṁgala moda uchāha nita jāhiṁ divasa ehi bhāṁti,
उमगी अवध अनंद भरि अधिक अधिक अधिकाति ॥३५९॥
umagī avadha anaṁda bhari adhika adhika adhikāti. 359.

Trans:

Thus passed the days in perpetual delight, happiness, and festivity; and the whole of Avadh was full to overflowing with bliss that was ever on the increase.

चौपाई-caupāī:

सुदिन सोधि कल कंकन छोरे । मंगल मोद बिनोद न थोरे ॥
sudina sodhi kala kaṁkana chore, maṁgala moda binoda na thore.
नित नव सुखु सुर देखि सिहाहीं । अवध जन्म जाचहिं बिधि पाहीं ॥
nita nava sukhu sura dekhi sihāhīṁ, avadha janma jācahiṁ bidhi pāhīṁ.
बिस्वामित्रु चलन नित चहहीं । राम सप्रेम बिनय बस रहहीं ॥
bisvāmitru calana nita cahahīṁ, rāma saprema binaya basa rahahīṁ.
दिन दिन सयगुन भूपति भाऊ । देखि सराह महामुनिराऊ ॥
dina dina sayaguna bhūpati bhāū, dekhi sarāha mahāmunirāū.
मागत बिदा राउ अनुरागे । सुतन्ह समेत ठाढ़ भे आगे ॥
māgata bidā rāu anurāge, sutanha sameta ṭhāṛha bhe āge.
नाथ सकल संपदा तुम्हारी । मैं सेवकु समेत सुत नारी ॥
nātha sakala saṁpadā tumhārī, maiṁ sevaku sameta suta nārī.
करब सदा लरिकन्ह पर छोहू । दरसनु देत रहब मुनि मोहू ॥
karaba sadā larikanha para chohū, darasanu deta rahaba muni mohū.
अस कहि राउ सहित सुत रानी । परेउ चरन मुख आव न बानी ॥
asa kahi rāu sahita suta rānī, pareu carana mukha āva na bānī.
दीन्हि असीस बिप्र बहु भाँती । चले न प्रीति रीति कहि जाती ॥
dīnhi asīsa bipra bahu bhāṁtī, cale na prīti rīti kahi jātī.
रामु सप्रेम संग सब भाई । आयसु पाइ फिरे पहुँचाई ॥
rāmu saprema saṁga saba bhāī, āyasu pāi phire pahuṁcāī.

Trans:

After calculating an auspicious day, they loosened the string on the wrist with no little solemnity and rejoicing. The gods, beholding the constant succession of delights, were in raptures and begged of Brahmmā that they might be born at Avadh. Vishwāmitra was always wishing to take leave, but was persuaded by Rāma's affectionate entreaties to stay on. Day after day, seeing the king's devotion and the excellence of his nature, the great saint was loud in his praises. When he asked permission to go, the king was greatly moved and with his sons stood before him in the way, saying, "My lord, all that I have is yours, and I, my sons, and my wives are your servants; be ever gracious to these boys and allow me to see you." So saying, the king with his sons and his queens fell at his feet, and speech failed his tongue. The Brahmin invoked upon him every kind of blessing and set forth amidst a display of affection that is past all telling, Rāma and his brothers lovingly escorting him till they received orders to return.

दोहा-dohā:

राम रूपु भूपति भगति ब्याहु उछाहु अनंदु ।
rāma rūpu bhūpati bhagati byāhu uchāhu anaṁdu,
जात सराहत मनहिं मन मुदित गाधिकुलचंदु ॥३६०॥
jāta sarāhata manahiṁ mana mudita gādhikulacaṁdu. 360.

Trans:

The moon of Gādhi's race went on his way rejoicing and praising to himself Rāma's beauty, the piety of the king, and the magnificence of the marriage festivities.

चौपाई-caupāī:

बामदेव रघुकुल गुर ग्यानी । बहुरि गाधिसुत कथा बखानी ॥
bāmadeva raghukula gura gyānī, bahuri gādhisuta kathā bakhānī.
सुनि मुनि सुजसु मनहिं मन राऊ । बरनत आपन पुन्य प्रभाऊ ॥
suni muni sujasu manahiṁ mana rāū, baranata āpana punya prabhāū.
बहुरे लोग रजायसु भयऊ । सुतन्ह समेत नृपति गृहँ गयऊ ॥
bahure loga rajāyasu bhayaū, sutanha sameta nṛpati gṛhaṁ gayaū.
जहँ तहँ राम ब्याहु सबु गावा । सुजसु पुनीत लोक तिहुँ छावा ॥
jahaṁ tahaṁ rāma byāhu sabu gāvā, sujasu punīta loka tihuṁ chāvā.
आए ब्याहि रामु घर जब तें । बसइ अनंद अवध सब तब तें ॥
āe byāhi rāmu ghara jaba teṁ, basai anaṁda avadha saba taba teṁ.
प्रभु बिबाहँ जस भयउ उछाहू । सकहिं न बरनि गिरा अहिनाहू ॥
prabhu bibāhaṁ jasa bhayau uchāhū, sakahiṁ na barani girā ahināhū.
कबिकुल जीवनु पावन जानी । राम सीय जसु मंगल खानी ॥
kabikula jīvanu pāvana jānī, rāma sīya jasu maṁgala khānī.
तेहि ते मैं कछु कहा बखानी । करन पुनीत हेतु निज बानी ॥
tehi te maiṁ kachu kahā bakhānī, karana punīta hetu nija bānī.

Trans:

Then Vāmdev and the learned Gurū of the house of Raghus, again told the story of Gādhi's son. As he listened to the saint's high fame, the king thought to himself how efficacious his own good deeds had been. At his command the crowd dispersed, while the king and his sons entered the palace. Everywhere the glory of Rāma's wedding was sung, and his holy fame was diffused through the three worlds. From the day Shrī Rāma came home having married, every kind of joy took its abode in Ajodhyā. The rejoicings attendant on the Lord's marriage were more than the tongue of serpent-king could tell, but knowing the praises of Rāma and Sītā to be a mine of auspiciousness, and the very life and salvation of the race of poets, I too have tried to sing them to some extent, in the hope of thus sanctifying my poesy.

छंद-chaṁda:

निज गिरा पावनि करन कारन राम जसु तुलसीं कह्यो ।
nija girā pāvani karana kārana rāma jasu tulasīṁ kahyo,
रघुबीर चरित अपार बारिधि पारु कबि कौनें लह्यो ॥
raghubīra carita apāra bāridhi pāru kabi kauneṁ lahyo.
उपबीत ब्याह उछाह मंगल सुनि जे सादर गावहीं ।
upabīta byāha uchāha maṁgala suni je sādara gāvahīṁ,
बैदेहि राम प्रसाद ते जन सर्बदा सुखु पावहीं ॥
baidehi rāma prasāda te jana sarbadā sukhu pāvahīṁ.

Trans:

For the purpose of sanctifying his song has Tulsī recountged the glories of Rāma; but the acts of Raghubīr are a boundless ocean that no poet can traverse. All pious souls that devoutly hear or recite the auspicious festivities which accompanied Rāma's investiture with the sacred thread and his marriage shall—by his and Vaidehi's favor—attain to everlasting felicity.

सोरठा-soraṭhā:

सिय रघुबीर बिबाहु जे सप्रेम गावहिं सुनहिं ।
siya raghubīra bibāhu je saprema gāvahiṁ sunahiṁ,
तिन्ह कहुँ सदा उछाहु मंगलायतन राम जसु ॥३६१॥
tinha kahuṁ sadā uchāhu maṁgalāyatana rāma jasu. 361.

Trans:

Whoever with love and reverence listens to or sings the accounts of the marriage of Rāma and Sītā shall be ever happy—for Rāma's praises are an unfailing joy.

मासपारायण बारहवाँ विश्राम
māsapārāyaṇa bārahavāṁ viśrāma
(Pause 12 for a Thirty-Day Recitation)

इति श्रीमद्रामचरितमानसे सकलकलिकलुषविध्वंसने प्रथमः सोपानः समाप्तः
iti śrīmadrāmacaritamānase sakalakalikaluṣavidhvaṁsane prathamaḥ sopānaḥ samāptaḥ
(Now ends the First-Ascent into the Manasa Lake of Shrī Rāma's Charita which eradicates all the impurities of the Kali-Yug)

सीताराम सीताराम

ॐ

श्रीजानकीवल्लभो विजयते

śrījānakīvallabho vijayate

श्रीरामचरितमानस

śrīrāmacaritamānasa

द्वितीय सोपान - अयोध्याकाण्ड

dvitīya sopāna - ayodhyākāṇḍa

श्लोक-śloka:

यस्याङ्के च विभाति भूधरसुता देवापगा मस्तके

yasyāṅke ca vibhāti bhūdharasutā devāpagā mastake

भाले बालविधुर्गले च गरलं यस्योरसि व्यालराट् ।

bhāle bālavidhurgale ca garalaṁ yasyorasi vyālarāṭ,

सोऽयं भूतिविभूषणः सुरवरः सर्वाधिपः सर्वदा

so'yaṁ bhūtivibhūṣaṇaḥ suravaraḥ sarvādhipaḥ sarvadā

शर्वः सर्वगतः शिवः शशिनिभः श्रीशङ्करः पातु माम् ॥ १ ॥

śarvaḥ sarvagataḥ śivaḥ śaśinibhaḥ śrīśaṅkaraḥ pātu mām. 1.

Trans:

May he—on whose left side shines resplendent the daughter of the mountain, on whose head is the river of the gods, on whose brow the crescent moon, on whose throat the poison-stain, on whose chest a huge serpent, and whose adornments are streaks of ashes—the chief of divinities Shiva, the destroyer of worlds, the omnipresent eternal Lord of all, of a moon-like hue—may he, holy Shankar protect me.

प्रसन्नतां या न गताभिषेकतस्तथा न मम्ले वनवासदुःखतः ।

prasannatāṁ yā na gatābhiṣekatastathā na mamle vanavāsaduḥkhataḥ,

मुखाम्बुजश्री रघुनन्दनस्य मे सदास्तु सा मञ्जुलमङ्गलप्रदा ॥ २ ॥

mukhāmbujaśrī raghunandanasya me sadāstu sā mañjulamaṅgalapradā. 2.

Trans:

May he—who neither rejoiced when anointed to become king, nor was saddened by his painful exile to the woods—that holy son of Raghu of the lotus face, may he ever remain the conferrer of felicity and of everything that is good, auspicious, redeeming in my life.

नीलाम्बुजश्यामलकोमलाङ्गं सीतासमारोपितवामभागम् ।

nīlāmbujaśyāmalakomalāṅgaṁ sītāsamāropitavāmabhāgam,

पाणौ महासायकचारुचापं नमामि रामं रघुवंशनाथम् ॥ ३ ॥

pāṇau mahāsāyakacārucāpaṁ namāmi rāmaṁ raghuvaṁśanātham. 3.

Trans:

Him I adore, with his body dark and soft as the lotus, with Sītā enthroned on his left side, with a graceful bow and arrows in hand—Shrī Rāma, the Lord, the glory of Raghu's lineage.

दोहा-dohā:

श्रीगुरु चरन सरोज रज निज मनु मुकुरु सुधारि ।

śrīguru carana saroja raja nija manu mukuru sudhāri,

बरनउँ रघुबर बिमल जसु जो दायकु फल चारि ॥

baranauṁ raghubara bimala jasu jo dāyaku phala cāri.

Trans:

Cleansing the mirror of my soul with the dust from the lotus feet of the holy Gurū, I sing Rāma's spotless fame, the bestower of four fruits of endeavors.

चौपाई-caupāī:

जब तें रामु ब्याहि घर आए । नित नव मंगल मोद बधाए ॥

jaba teṁ rāmu byāhi ghara āe, nita nava maṁgala moda badhāe.

भुवन चारिदस भूधर भारी । सुकृत मेघ बरषहिं सुख बारी ॥

bhuvana cāridasa bhūdhara bhārī, sukṛta megha baraṣahiṁ sukha bārī.

रिधि सिधि संपति नदीं सुहाई । उमगि अवध अंबुधि कहुँ आई ॥

ridhi sidhi saṁpati nadīṁ suhāī, umagi avadha aṁbudhi kahuṁ āī.

मनिगन पुर नर नारि सुजाती । सुचि अमोल सुंदर सब भाँती ॥

manigana pura nara nāri sujātī, suci amola suṁdara saba bhāṁtī.

कहि न जाइ कछु नगर बिभूती । जनु एतनिअ बिरंचि करतूती ॥

kahi na jāi kachu nagara bibhūtī, janu etania biraṁci karatūtī.

सब बिधि सब पुर लोग सुखारी । रामचंद मुख चंदु निहारी ॥

saba bidhi saba pura loga sukhārī, rāmacaṁda mukha caṁdu nihārī.

मुदित मातु सब सखीं सहेली । फलित बिलोकि मनोरथ बेली ॥

mudita mātu saba sakhīṁ sahelī, phalita biloki manoratha belī.

राम रूपु गुन सीलु सुभाऊ । प्रमुदित होइ देखि सुनि राऊ ॥

rāma rūpu guna sīlu subhāū, pramudita hoi dekhi suni rāū.

Trans:

From the time that Rāma returned home after matrimony, there was a constant succession of joys and delights. The fourteen spheres were like the great mountains where clouds of virtue fall in showers of happiness. Wealth, affluence, and prosperity were like bounteous streams that overflowed into Avadh as rivers into the ocean; while the noble citizens, men and women alike, were its brilliant pearls, all precious and of perfect beauty. The splendor of the capital was beyond description; it seemed as if the Creator's workmanship had been exhausted there. Gazing on Rāmachandra's moon-like face, the people were perfectly happy; the queens and their attendants were enraptured to see their heart's desire bear fruit; and still more enraptured was the king, as he heard and saw for himself Rāma's charming form, accomplishments, and amiability.

दोहा-dohā:

सब कें उर अभिलाषु अस कहहिं मनाइ महेसु ।

saba keṁ ura abhilāṣu asa kahahiṁ manāi mahesu,

आप अछत जुबराज पद रामहि देउ नरेसु ॥ १ ॥

āpa achata jubarāja pada rāmahi deu naresu. 1.

Trans:

In every heart was one desire, which they expressed in their prayers to Mahādev: "O that the king in his own lifetime would entrust Rāma with the regency."

चौपाई-caupāī:

एक समय सब सहित समाजा । राजसभाँ रघुराजु बिराजा ॥
eka samaya saba sahita samājā, rājasabhāṁ raghurāju birājā.
सकल सुकृत मूरति नरनाहू । राम सुजसु सुनि अतिहि उछाहू ॥
sakala sukṛta mūrati naranāhū, rāma sujasu suni atihi uchāhū.
नृप सब रहहिं कृपा अभिलाषें । लोकप करहिं प्रीति रुख राखें ॥
nṛpa saba rahahiṁ kṛpā abhilāṣeṁ, lokapa karahiṁ prīti rukha rākheṁ.
तिभुवन तीनि काल जग माहीं । भूरि भाग दसरथ सम नाहीं ॥
tibhuvana tīni kāla jaga māhīṁ, bhūri bhāga dasaratha sama nāhīṁ.
मंगलमूल रामु सुत जासू । जो कछु कहिअ थोर सबु तासू ॥
maṁgalamūla rāmu suta jāsū, jo kachu kahia thora sabu tāsū.
रायँ सुभायँ मुकुरु कर लीन्हा । बदनु बिलोकि मुकुटु सम कीन्हा ॥
rāyaṁ subhāyaṁ mukuru kara līnhā, badanu biloki mukuṭu sama kīnhā.
श्रवन समीप भए सित केसा । मनहुँ जरठपनु अस उपदेसा ॥
śravana samīpa bhae sita kesā, manahuṁ jaraṭhapanu asa upadesā.
नृप जुबराजु राम कहुँ देहू । जीवन जनम लाहु किन लेहू ॥
nṛpa jubarāju rāma kahuṁ dehū, jīvana janama lāhu kina lehū.

Trans:

One day the monarch sat enthroned in court with all his nobles. Himself the incarnation of every virtue, he was delighted beyond measure to hear of Rāma's renown. All kings were solicitous for his patronage, and the very gods desired his friendship. In the three spheres of the universe, and in all of Time—past, present, or to come, none is so blessed as Dashrath. Words fail to describe his blessedness, who has for his son Rāma, the source of every happiness. Once, the king happened to take a mirror in his hand, and looking at his face in it, set his crown straight. Close to his ear was a white hair, like old-age whispering, "O king, make Rāma regent and thereby accomplish the purpose of thy life."

दोहा-dohā:

यह बिचारु उर आनि नृप सुदिनु सुअवसरु पाइ ।
yaha bicāru ura āni nṛpa sudinu suavasaru pāi,
प्रेम पुलकि तन मुदित मन गुरहि सुनायउ जाइ ॥ २ ॥
prema pulaki tana mudita mana gurahi sunāyau jāi. 2.

Trans:

Having thus considered and settled it in his mind, the king on an auspicious day and at a fitting time, his body quivering with emotion and his soul full of joy, went and declared his purpose to his Gurū.

चौपाई-caupāī:

कहइ भुआलु सुनिअ मुनिनायक । भए राम सब बिधि सब लायक ॥
kahai bhuālu sunia munināyaka, bhae rāma saba bidhi saba lāyaka.
सेवक सचिव सकल पुरबासी । जे हमारे अरि मित्र उदासी ॥
sevaka saciva sakala purabāsī, je hamāre ari mitra udāsī.
सबहि रामु प्रिय जेहि बिधि मोही । प्रभु असीस जनु तनु धरि सोही ॥
sabahi rāmu priya jehi bidhi mohī, prabhu asīsa janu tanu dhari sohī.
बिप्र सहित परिवार गोसाईं । करहिं छोहु सब रौरिहि नाईं ॥
bipra sahita parivāra gosāīṁ, karahiṁ chohu saba raurihi nāīṁ.
जे गुर चरन रेनु सिर धरहीं । ते जनु सकल बिभव बस करहीं ॥
je gura carana renu sira dharahīṁ, te janu sakala bibhava basa karahīṁ.
मोहि सम यहु अनुभयउ न दूजें । सबु पायउँ रज पावनि पूजें ॥
mohi sama yahu anubhayau na dūjeṁ, sabu pāyauṁ raja pāvani pūjeṁ.
अब अभिलाषु एकु मन मोरें । पूजिहि नाथ अनुग्रह तोरें ॥
aba abhilāṣu eku mana moreṁ, pūjihi nātha anugraha toreṁ.
मुनि प्रसन्न लखि सहज सनेहू । कहेउ नरेस रजायसु देहू ॥
muni prasanna lakhi sahaja sanehū, kaheu naresa rajāyasu dehū.

Trans:

Said the king, "Hearken, O great saint; Rāma is now perfect in every accomplishment. Servants, ministers, all of the citizens, and many others—whether my enemies, or friends, or indifferent—all hold Rāma as dear even as I do and regard him as god's blessing incarnate. The Brahmins and their families, reverend sir, have the same love for him as you have. They, who put on their head the dust from the feet of their spiritual father, obtain as it were the mastery over all dominion There is no man my equal, but all that I have flows from the worship of your holy feet. I have now a desire at heart; it can only be accomplished, my lord, by your good favor." The saint was pleased to witness his sincere devotion and said, "O king, give me your command.

दोहा-dohā:

राजन राउर नामु जसु सब अभिमत दातार ।
rājana rāura nāmu jasu saba abhimata dātāra,
फल अनुगामी महिप मनि मन अभिलाषु तुम्हार ॥ ३ ॥
phala anugāmī mahipa mani mana abhilāṣu tumhāra. 3.

Trans:

Your name and glory, sire, provide for every wish. On every desire of your soul, O jewel of kings, success follows naturally."

चौपाई-caupāī:

सब बिधि गुरु प्रसन्न जियँ जानी । बोलेउ राउ रहँसि मृदु बानी ॥
saba bidhi guru prasanna jiyaṁ jānī, boleu rāu rahaṁsi mṛdu bānī.
नाथ रामु करिअहिं जुबराजू । कहिअ कृपा करि करिअ समाजू ॥
nātha rāmu kariahiṁ jubarājū, kahia kṛpā kari karia samājū.
मोहि अछत यहु होइ उछाहू । लहहिं लोग सब लोचन लाहू ॥
mohi achata yahu hoi uchāhū, lahahiṁ loga saba locana lāhū.
प्रभु प्रसाद सिव सबइ निबाहीं । यह लालसा एक मन माहीं ॥
prabhu prasāda siva sabai nibāhīṁ, yaha lālasā eka mana māhīṁ.
पुनि न सोच तनु रहउ कि जाऊ । जेहिं न होइ पाछें पछिताऊ ॥
puni na soca tanu rahau ki jāū, jehiṁ na hoi pācheṁ pachitāū.
सुनि मुनि दसरथ बचन सुहाए । मंगल मोद मूल मन भाए ॥
suni muni dasaratha bacana suhāe, maṁgala moda mūla mana bhāe.
सुनु नृप जासु बिमुख पछिताहीं । जासु भजन बिनु जरनि न जाहीं ॥
sunu nṛpa jāsu bimukha pachitāhīṁ, jāsu bhajana binu jarani na jāhīṁ.
भयउ तुम्हार तनय सोइ स्वामी । रामु पुनीत प्रेम अनुगामी ॥
bhayau tumhāra tanaya soi svāmī, rāmu punīta prema anugāmī.

Trans:

Perceiving that the Gurū was thoroughly pleased at heart, the king spoke smilingly and in gentle tones, "My lord, invest Rāma with regal powers; be pleased to direct that the council be convened. Let this happy event take place in my lifetime—that the eyes of all people are gladdened by that sight. By my lord's blessing Shiva has brought everything happily to pass, but I have still this one desire at heart; once fulfilled, it will then be a matter of no concern whether I remain in the body or depart; for then I will have nothing on this score whereof to repent." When the saint heard Dashrath's noble words, he experienced the greatest delight, "Hearken, O king; the Lord whose averted face all creatures lament, and to whom one must pray for removal of all distress, himself has been born your son— Rāma, most holy and compassionate.

दोहा-dohā:

बेगि बिलंबु न करिअ नृप साजिअ सबुइ समाजु ।

begi bilaṁbu na karia nṛpa sājia sabui samāju,

सुदिन सुमंगलु तबहिं जब रामु होहिं जुबराजु ॥४॥

sudina sumaṁgalu tabahiṁ jaba rāmu hohiṁ jubarāju. 4.

Trans:

Quick then, O king, let there be no delay; gather together all your council; happy and auspicious indeed the day when Rāma is proclaimed regent."

चौपाई-caupāī:

मुदित महीपति मंदिर आए । सेवक सचिव सुमंत्रु बोलाए ॥

mudita mahīpati maṁdira āe, sevaka saciva sumaṁtru bolāe.

कहि जयजीव सीस तिन्ह नाए । भूप सुमंगल बचन सुनाए ॥

kahi jayajīva sīsa tinha nāe, bhūpa sumaṁgala bacana sunāe.

जौं पाँचहि मत लागै नीका । करहु हरषि हियँ रामहि टीका ॥

jauṁ pāṁcahi mata lāgai nīkā, karahu haraṣi hiyaṁ rāmahi ṭīkā.

मंत्री मुदित सुनत प्रिय बानी । अभिमत बिरवँ परेउ जनु पानी ॥

maṁtrī mudita sunata priya bānī, abhimata biravaṁ pareu janu pānī.

बिनती सचिव करहिं कर जोरी । जिअहु जगतपति बरिस करोरी ॥

binatī saciva karahiṁ kara jorī, jiahu jagatapati barisa karorī.

जग मंगल भल काजु बिचारा । बेगिअ नाथ न लाइअ बारा ॥

jaga maṁgala bhala kāju bicārā, begia nātha na lāia bārā.

नृपहि मोदु सुनि सचिव सुभाषा । बढ़त बौंड़ जनु लही सुसाखा ॥

nṛpahi modu suni saciva subhāṣā, baṛhata bauṁṛa janu lahī susākhā.

Trans:

The glad king proceeded to the palace and summoned his retainers, ministers and the chief councilor Sumant. They came and bowed their heads proclaiming "Victory to you O king; long may you live." The king declared to them the glad news, "Today, to my great joy, the Gurū has charged me to install Rāma as heir to the throne. If the proposal seems good to the council, prepare with gladness, to impress the royal mark on Rāma's forehead." The ministers rejoiced to hear these gracious words, which fell like a shower of rain on the young plant of their desire. With clasped hands Sumant made his petition, "Live forever, O lord of the world; the deed you propose is good and beneficent; haste my lord, let us have no delay." The king was delighted by his minister's assent—like a creeper that spreads apace when it has once clasped a strong bough.

दोहा-dohā:

कहेउ भूप मुनिराज कर जोइ जोइ आयसु होइ ।

kaheu bhūpa munirāja kara joi joi āyasu hoi,

राम राज अभिषेक हित बेगि करहु सोइ सोइ ॥५॥

rāma rāja abhiṣeka hita begi karahu soi soi. 5.

Trans:

Said the king: "Whatever orders the saint may give with regard to Rāma's coronation, see to it that you perform it with all speed."

चौपाई-caupāī:

हरषि मुनीस कहेउ मृदु बानी । आनहु सकल सुतीरथ पानी ॥

haraṣi munīsa kaheu mṛdu bānī, ānahu sakala sutīratha pānī.

औषध मूल फूल फल पाना । कहे नाम गनि मंगल नाना ॥

auṣadha mūla phūla phala pānā, kahe nāma gani maṁgala nānā.

चामर चरम बसन बहु भाँती । रोम पाट पट अगनित जाती ॥

cāmara carama basana bahu bhāṁtī, roma pāṭa paṭa aganita jātī.

मनिगन मंगल बस्तु अनेका । जो जग जोगु भूप अभिषेका ॥

manigana maṁgala bastu anekā, jo jaga jogu bhūpa abhiṣekā.

बेद बिदित कहि सकल बिधाना । कहेउ रचहु पुर बिबिध बिताना ॥

beda bidita kahi sakala bidhānā, kaheu racahu pura bibidha bitānā.

सफल रसाल पूगफल केरा । रोपहु बीथिन्ह पुर चहुँ फेरा ॥

saphala rasāla pūgaphala kerā, ropahu bīthinha pura cahuṁ pherā.

रचहु मंजु मनि चौकें चारू । कहहु बनावन बेगि बजारू ॥

racahu maṁju mani caukeṁ cārū, kahahu banāvana begi bajārū.

पूजहु गनपति गुर कुलदेवा । सब बिधि करहु भूमिसुर सेवा ॥

pūjahu ganapati gura kuladevā, saba bidhi karahu bhūmisura sevā.

Trans:

In gentle accents the glad saint then began imparting instructions, "Bring water from all holy places," and he enumerated by name a number of auspicious objects such as herbs, roots, flowers, fruits, leaves, *chouries*, deerskins, and draperies of various kinds including countless varieties of woolen and silken textiles, jewels and numerous other articles of good omen which are considered essential during the ceremony of a King's coronation. Detailing all the procedure laid down in the Vedas he said: "Erect in the city a number of pavilions; and plant the streets in every quarter with fruit-bearing mangoes and trees of betel-nut and plantains; and fashion bright and beautiful jeweled squares; and have all the bazaars speedily decorated; and do reverence to Ganesh and your Gurū and your family god, and diligently serve the Brahmins.

दोहा-dohā:

ध्वज पताक तोरन कलस सजहु तुरग रथ नाग ।

dhvaja patāka torana kalasa sajahu turaga ratha nāga,

सिर धरि मुनिबर बचन सबु निज निज काजहिं लाग ॥६॥

sira dhari munibara bacana sabu nija nija kājahiṁ lāga. 6.

Trans:

Make ready flags and banners and wreaths and vases, horses too, and chariots and elephants." All were obedient to the holy sage's words and busied themselves each in his own special task.

चौपाई-caupāī:

जो मुनीस जेहि आयसु दीन्हा । सो तेहिं काजु प्रथम जनु कीन्हा ॥

jo munīsa jehi āyasu dīnhā, so tehiṁ kāju prathama janu kīnhā.

बिप्र साधु सुर पूजत राजा । करत राम हित मंगल काजा ॥

bipra sādhu sura pūjata rājā, karata rāma hita maṁgala kājā.

सुनत राम अभिषेक सुहावा । बाज गहागह अवध बधावा ॥

sunata rāma abhiṣeka suhāvā, bāja gahāgaha avadha badhāvā.

राम सीय तन सगुन जनाए । फरकहिं मंगल अंग सुहाए ॥

rāma sīya tana saguna janāe, pharakahiṁ maṁgala aṁga suhāe.

पुलकि सप्रेम परसपर कहहीं । भरत आगमनु सूचक अहहीं ॥

pulaki saprema parasapara kahahīṁ, bharata āgamanu sūcaka ahahīṁ.

भए बहुत दिन अति अवसेरी । सगुन प्रतीति भेंट प्रिय केरी ॥

bhae bahuta dina ati avaserī, saguna pratīti bheṁṭa priya kerī.

भरत सरिस प्रिय को जग माहीं । इहइ सगुन फलु दूसर नाहीं ॥

bharata sarisa priya ko jaga māhīṁ, ihai saguna phalu dūsara nāhīṁ.

रामहि बंधु सोच दिन राती । अंडन्हि कमठ हृदउ जेहि भाँती ॥

rāmahi baṁdhu soca dina rātī, aṁḍanhi kamaṭha hṛdau jehi bhāṁtī.

Trans:

Whatever the order that anyone had been given by the saint, that he regarded as the very first thing to be undertaken. The king worshipped Brahmins, saints and gods, and did everything to promote Rāma's prosperity. On hearing the glad news of Rāma's installation, all Avadh resounded with songs of jubilation. Good omens declared themselves in the body, both of Rāma and Sītā, by a sudden quiver of their lucky side, and they said affectionately to one another: "This betokens Bharat's return. We have greatly missed him for many a long days. This good sign assures us of a friend's approach, and in the whole world there is no friend so dear to us as Bharat; this good omen can have but one meaning." Every day Rāma had been as lovingly anxious about his brother as a turtle for its eggs in the sand far away.

दोहा-dohā:

एहि अवसर मंगलु परम सुनि रहँसेउ रनिवासु।
ehi avasara maṁgalu parama suni rahaṁseu ranivāsu,
सोभत लखि बिधु बढ़त जनु बारिधि बीचि बिलासु ॥७॥
sobhata lakhi bidhu baṛhata janu bāridhi bīci bilāsu. 7.

Trans:

At that time the ladies of the court were as delighted to hear these most glad tidings, as the waves of ocean swell with joy on beholding the moon in its glory.

चौपाई-caupāī:

प्रथम जाइ जिन्ह बचन सुनाए। भूषन बसन भूरि तिन्ह पाए ॥
prathama jāi jinha bacana sunāe, bhūṣana basana bhūri tinha pāe.
प्रेम पुलकि तन मन अनुरागीं। मंगल कलस सजन सब लागीं ॥
prema pulaki tana mana anurāgīṁ, maṁgala kalasa sajana saba lāgīṁ.
चौकें चारु सुमित्राँ पुरी। मनिमय बिबिध भाँति अति रुरी ॥
caukeṁ cāru sumitrāṁ purī, manimaya bibidha bhāṁti ati rurī.
आनँद मगन राम महतारी। दिए दान बहु बिप्र हँकारी ॥
ānaṁda magana rāma mahatārī, die dāna bahu bipra haṁkārī.
पूजीं ग्रामदेबि सुर नागा। कहेउ बहोरि देन बलिभागा ॥
pūjīṁ grāmadebi sura nāgā, kaheu bahori dena balibhāgā.
जेहि बिधि होइ राम कल्यानू। देहु दया करि सो बरदानू ॥
jehi bidhi hoi rāma kalyānū, dehu dayā kari so baradānū.
गावहिं मंगल कोकिलबयनीं। बिधुबदनीं मृगसावकनयनीं ॥
gāvahiṁ maṁgala kokilabayanīṁ, bidhubadanīṁ mṛgasāvakanayanīṁ.

Trans:

First they took care that those who brought the news were richly guerdoned with jewels and robes; then with body all quivering with emotion and soul full of love, they proceeded to make all festal preparations. Sumitrā filled in a lovely square with exquisite gems of every kind; Rāma's mothers drowned in joy, sent for a crowd of Brahmins and loaded them with gifts; then worshipped the local divinity and the gods and the serpents, and vowed them future sacrifices, praying: "In your mercy, grant me this boon, that Rāma ever prosper." Auspicious strains are chanted by moon-faced, fawn-eyed damsels, with voice sweet as that of the *koel*.

दोहा-dohā:

राम राज अभिषेकु सुनि हियँ हरषे नर नारि।
rāma rāja abhiṣeku suni hiyaṁ haraṣe nara nāri,
लगे सुमंगल सजन सब बिधि अनुकूल बिचारि ॥८॥
lage sumaṁgala sajana saba bidhi anukūla bicāri. 8.

Trans:

On hearing of Rāma's installation, all good women were glad of heart and began diligently to make festal preparations, thinking god to be gracious to them.

चौपाई-caupāī:

तब नरनाहँ बसिष्ठु बोलाए। रामधाम सिख देन पठाए ॥
taba naranāhaṁ basiṣṭhu bolāe, rāmadhāma sikha dena paṭhāe.
गुर आगमनु सुनत रघुनाथा। द्वार आइ पद नायउ माथा ॥
gura āgamanu sunata raghunāthā, dvāra āi pada nāyau māthā.
सादर अरघ देइ घर आने। सोरह भाँति पूजि सनमाने ॥
sādara aragha dei ghara āne, soraha bhāṁti pūji sanamāne.
गहे चरन सिय सहित बहोरी। बोले रामु कमल कर जोरी ॥
gahe carana siya sahita bahorī, bole rāmu kamala kara jorī.
सेवक सदन स्वामि आगमनू। मंगल मूल अमंगल दमनू ॥
sevaka sadana svāmi āgamanū, maṁgala mūla amaṁgala damanū.
तदपि उचित जनु बोलि सप्रीती। पठइअ काज नाथ असि नीती ॥
tadapi ucita janu boli saprītī, paṭhaia kāja nātha asi nītī.
प्रभुता तजि प्रभु कीन्ह सनेहू। भयउ पुनीत आजु यहु गेहू ॥
prabhutā taji prabhu kīnha sanehū, bhayau punīta āju yahu gehū.
आयसु होइ सो करौं गोसाईं। सेवकु लहइ स्वामि सेवकाईं ॥
āyasu hoi so karauṁ gosāīṁ, sevaku lahai svāmi sevakāīṁ.

Trans:

Then the monarch summoned Vasishtha and sent him to Rāma's apartments to inform him of the coming event. When Raghunāth heard of the Gurū's approach, he came to the door and bowed his head at his feet, and after reverently sprinkling lustral water, conducted him in, and paid him honor in the sixteen prescribed modes. Then along with Sītā again clasping his Gurū's feet, and with his lotus hands folded in prayer, Rāma thusly spake: "For a lord to visit his servant's house is a source of great joy, a cure for all distress; yet it had been more fitting, sir, and more in accordance with custom, had you kindly sent to say you wanted me. Since my lord has graciously waived his prerogative, my house has today become highly blessed. Let me know, O holy father, what are your orders; it is for a servant to do his master's bidding."

दोहा-dohā:

सुनि सनेह साने बचन मुनि रघुबरहि प्रसंस।
suni saneha sāne bacana muni raghubarahi prasaṁsa,
राम कस न तुम्ह कहहु अस हंस बंस अवतंस ॥९॥
rāma kasa na tumha kahahu asa haṁsa baṁsa avataṁsa. 9.

Trans:

On hearing these affectionate words the saint extolled Raghubīr, "O Rāma, glory of the solar race that you are, it is like you to speak thusly."

चौपाई-caupāī:

बरनि राम गुन सीलु सुभाऊ। बोले प्रेम पुलकि मुनिराऊ ॥
barani rāma guna sīlu subhāū, bole prema pulaki munirāū.
भूप सजेउ अभिषेक समाजू। चाहत देन तुम्हहि जुबराजू ॥
bhūpa sajeu abhiṣeka samājū, cāhata dena tumhahi jubarājū.
राम करहु सब संजम आजू। जौं बिधि कुसल निबाहै काजू ॥
rāma karahu saba saṁjama ājū, jauṁ bidhi kusala nibāhai kājū.
गुरु सिख देइ राय पहिं गयउ। राम हृदयँ अस बिसमउ भयऊ ॥
guru sikha dei rāya pahiṁ gayau, rāma hṛdayaṁ asa bisamau bhayaū.
जनमे एक संग सब भाई। भोजन सयन केलि लरिकाई ॥
janame eka saṁga saba bhāī, bhojana sayana keli larikāī.
करनबेध उपबीत बिआहा। संग संग सब भए उछाहा ॥
karanabedha upabīta biāhā, saṁga saṁga saba bhae uchāhā.
बिमल बंस यहु अनुचित एकू। बंधु बिहाइ बड़ेहि अभिषेकू ॥
bimala baṁsa yahu anucita ekū, baṁdhu bihāi baṛehi abhiṣekū.
प्रभु सप्रेम पछितानि सुहाई। हरउ भगत मन कै कुटिलाई ॥
prabhu saprema pachitāni suhāī, harau bhagata mana kai kuṭilāī.

Trans:

After eulogizing Rāma's high qualifications and amiable character, the great saint with much emotion explained: "The king has prepared for a royal installation, and wishes to confer upon you the dignity of regent. Rāma, today you two should devote yourself to religious austerity—that gods may bring the matter to a happy conclusion." Having thus instructed him, the Gurū returned to the king; while Rāma's heart was full of astonishment: "My brothers and I were all born together, and together have we ate and slept and played in childhood; the piercing of our ears, the investiture with the sacred thread, our marriage, in short all our rejoicings have taken place together. This is the one flaw in this spotless line: that the eldest alone should be enthroned without his younger brothers." This loving and gracious expression of regret on the part of Lord removes any unworthy suspicion from the mind of his votaries.

दोहा-dohā:

तेहि अवसर आए लखन मगन प्रेम आनंद ।
tehi avasara āe lakhana magana prema ānaṁda,
सनमाने प्रिय बचन कहि रघुकुल कैरव चंद ॥ १० ॥
sanamāne priya bacana kahi raghukula kairava caṁda. 10.

Trans:

Then came Lakshman, full of love and joy, and with many affectionate speeches did homage to the moon of the lily-like solar race.

चौपाई-caupāī:

बाजहिं बाजने बिबिध बिधाना । पुर प्रमोदु नहिं जाइ बखाना ॥
bājahiṁ bājane bibidha bidhānā, pura pramodu nahiṁ jāi bakhānā.
भरत आगमनु सकल मनावहिं । आवहुँ बेगि नयन फलु पावहिं ॥
bharata āgamanu sakala manāvahiṁ, āvahuṁ begi nayana phalu pāvahiṁ.
हाट बाट घर गलीं अथाईं । कहहिं परसपर लोग लोगाईं ॥
hāṭa bāṭa ghara galīṁ athāīṁ, kahahiṁ parasapara loga logāīṁ.
कालि लगन भलि केतिक बारा । पूजिहि बिधि अभिलाषु हमारा ॥
kāli lagana bhali ketika bārā, pūjihi bidhi abhilāṣu hamārā.
कनक सिंघासन सीय समेता । बैठहिं रामु होइ चित चेता ॥
kanaka siṁghāsana sīya sametā, baiṭhahiṁ rāmu hoi cita cetā.
सकल कहहिं कब होइहि काली । बिघन मनावहिं देव कुचाली ॥
sakala kahahiṁ kaba hoihi kālī, bighana manāvahiṁ deva kucālī.
तिन्हहि सोहाइ न अवध बधावा । चोरहि चंदिनि राति न भावा ॥
tinhahi sohāi na avadha badhāvā, corahi caṁdini rāti na bhāvā.
सारद बोलि बिनय सुर करहीं । बारहिं बार पाय लै परहीं ॥
sārada boli binaya sura karahīṁ, bārahiṁ bāra pāya lai parahīṁ.

Trans:

There were sounds of music of every kind, and the delight of the city was beyond description. All prayed for Bharat's return, that he too might come quickly and like them enjoy the spectacle. In every street and lane and house and market and place of resort, men and women were saying to one another: "When will tomorrow come? When will that auspicious moment arrive in which God will accomplish our desire—when, with Sītā by his side, Rāma will take his seat on the regal throne? May our wishes be gratified now." They were all saying "When will tomorrow come?" But the envious gods prayed that difficulties might arise; the rejoicings at Avadh pleased them as little as a full-moon night pleases a thief. So they humbly called in Shārdā and again and again threw themselves at her feet:

दोहा-dohā:

बिपति हमारि बिलोकि बड़ि मातु करिअ सोइ आजु ।
bipati hamāri biloki baṛi mātu karia soi āju,
रामु जाहिं बन राजु तजि होइ सकल सुरकाजु ॥ ११ ॥
rāmu jāhiṁ bana rāju taji hoi sakala surakāju. 11.

Trans:

"Perceiving our grave calamity, O Mother, manipulate things in such a way today that Shrī Rāma may retire into the forest relinquishing His throne—so that our objective may be completely accomplished."

चौपाई-caupāī:

सुनि सुर बिनय ठाढ़ि पछिताती । भइउँ सरोज बिपिन हिमराती ॥
suni sura binaya ṭhāṛhi pachitātī, bhaiuṁ saroja bipina himarātī.
देखि देव पुनि कहहिं निहोरी । मातु तोहि नहिं थोरिउ खोरी ॥
dekhi deva puni kahahiṁ nihorī, mātu tohi nahiṁ thoriu khorī.
बिसमय हरष रहित रघुराऊ । तुम्ह जानहु सब राम प्रभाऊ ॥
bisamaya haraṣa rahita raghurāū, tumha jānahu saba rāma prabhāū.
जीव करम बस सुख दुख भागी । जाइअ अवध देव हित लागी ॥
jīva karama basa sukha dukha bhāgī, jāia avadha deva hita lāgī.
बार बार गहि चरन सँकोची । चली बिचारि बिबुध मति पोची ॥
bāra bāra gahi carana saṁkocī, calī bicāri bibudha mati pocī.
ऊँच निवासु नीचि करतूती । देखि न सकहिं पराइ बिभूती ॥
ūṁca nivāsu nīci karatūtī, dekhi na sakahiṁ parāi bibhūtī.
आगिल काजु बिचारि बहोरी । करिहहिं चाह कुसल कबि मोरी ॥
āgila kāju bicāri bahorī, karihahiṁ cāha kusala kabi morī.
हरषि हृदयँ दसरथ पुर आई । जनु ग्रह दसा दुसह दुखदाई ॥
haraṣi hṛdayaṁ dasaratha pura āī, janu graha dasā dusaha dukhadāī.

Trans:

On hearing this prayer of the gods, she stood still, thinking sadly, "Am I to be like a winter's night to a bed of lotuses?" The gods, seeing her hesitate, pleaded yet once again, "Mother, not the least blame will attach to you; for the Lord of Raghus is above sorrow and joy alike. You are fully acquainted with Rāma's glory. As for the people, every embodied soul is subject to pleasure and pain according to its fate. Therefore, you should go to Ajodhyā for the good of the celestials." Time after time they clasped her feet till she yielded and went, though still thinking to herself, "These gods are a mean-spirited crew. Though they dwell on so high, yet their acts are so low, and they cannot endure to see another's prosperity." Again, reflecting on the role she will play in future—when the ablest poets would invoke her to seek her favor, she became more cheerful and flew to the city of Dashrath, which seemed smitten by inauspicious turn of stars most terrible.

दोहा-dohā:

नामु मंथरा मंदमति चेरी कैकइ केरि ।
nāmu maṁtharā maṁdamati cerī kaikai keri,
अजस पेटारी ताहि करि गई गिरा मति फेरि ॥ १२ ॥
ajasa peṭārī tāhi kari gaī girā mati pheri. 12.

Trans:

Now Kaekayī had a wicked handmaid—by name Manthrā. Having perverted her reason, and making her a receptacle of meanness, Shārdā returned to her abode.

चौपाई-caupāī:

दीख मंथरा नगरु बनावा । मंजुल मंगल बाज बधावा ॥
dīkha maṁtharā nagaru banāvā, maṁjula maṁgala bāja badhāvā.
पूछेसि लोगन्ह काह उछाहू । राम तिलकु सुनि भा उर दाहू ॥
pūchesi loganha kāha uchāhū, rāma tilaku suni bhā ura dāhū.
करइ बिचारु कुबुद्धि कुजाती । होइ अकाजु कवनि बिधि राती ॥
karai bicāru kubuddhi kujātī, hoi akāju kavani bidhi rātī.
देखि लागि मधु कुटिल किराती । जिमि गवँ तकइ लेउँ केहि भाँती ॥
dekhi lāgi madhu kuṭila kirātī, jimi gavaṁ takai leuṁ kehi bhāṁtī.
भरत मातु पहिं गइ बिलखानी । का अनमनि हसि कह हँसि रानी ॥
bharata mātu pahiṁ gai bilakhānī, kā anamani hasi kaha haṁsi rānī.
ऊतरु देइ न लेइ उसासू । नारि चरित करि ढारइ आँसू ॥
ūtaru dei na lei usāsū, nāri carita kari ḍhārai āṁsū.
हँसि कह रानि गालु बड़ तोरें । दीन्ह लखन सिख अस मन मोरें ॥
haṁsi kaha rāni gālu baṛa toreṁ, dīnha lakhana sikha asa mana moreṁ.
तबहुँ न बोल चेरि बड़ि पापिनि । छाड़इ स्वास कारि जनु साँपिनि ॥
tabahuṁ na bola ceri baṛi pāpini, chāṛai svāsa kāri janu sāṁpini.

Trans:

When Manthrā saw the preparations in the city, the joyous festivities, the music and the singing, she asked the people "What mean these rejoicings?" When she heard of Rāma's inauguration, her soul was afire and she plotted, wicked wretch that she was, how that very night to defeat it—like a crafty hill-woman, who has spied a honeycomb hanging from a tree and schemes how to get hold of the honey. So she went crying to Bharat's mother. "What is wrong now?," the queen smiled and said. She gave no answer, but drew a deep sigh and like a crafty woman began shedding flood of tears. Said the queen laughing, "O girl, since you are most devious and impudent, I guess Lakshman took you to task for it—seemingly." Still the wicked handmaid said not a word, but breathed hard like some venomous serpent.

दोहा-dohā:

सभय रानि कह कहसि किन कुसल रामु महिपालु ।
sabhaya rāni kaha kahasi kina kusala rāmu mahipālu,
लखनु भरतु रिपुदमनु सुनि भा कुबरी उर सालु ॥ १३ ॥
lakhanu bharatu ripudamanu suni bhā kubarī ura sālu. 13.

Trans:

Then said the queen with a nervous smile: "Is Rāma un-well? Or the King, or Bharat, or Lakshman, or Shatrughan?" These words further tortured the heart of the humpbacked girl.

चौपाई-caupāī:

कत सिख देइ हमहि कोउ माई । गालु करब केहि कर बलु पाई ॥
kata sikha dei hamahi kou māī, gālu karaba kehi kara balu pāī.
रामहि छाड़ि कुसल केहि आजू । जेहि जनेसु देइ जुबराजू ॥
rāmahi chāṛi kusala kehi ājū, jehi janesu dei jubarājū.
भयउ कौसिलहि बिधि अति दाहिन । देखत गरब रहत उर नाहिन ॥
bhayau kausilahi bidhi ati dāhina, dekhata garaba rahata ura nāhina.
देखहु कस न जाइ सब सोभा । जो अवलोकि मोर मनु छोभा ॥
dekhahu kasa na jāi saba sobhā, jo avaloki mora manu chobhā.
पूतु बिदेस न सोचु तुम्हारें । जानति हहु बस नाहु हमारें ॥
pūtu bidesa na socu tumhāreṁ, jānati hahu basa nāhu hamāreṁ.
नीद बहुत प्रिय सेज तुराई । लखहु न भूप कपट चतुराई ॥
nīda bahuta priya seja turāī, lakhahu na bhūpa kapaṭa caturāī.
सुनि प्रिय बचन मलिन मनु जानी । झुकी रानि अब रहु अरगानी ॥
suni priya bacana malina manu jānī, jhukī rāni aba rahu aragānī.
पुनि अस कबहुँ कहसि घरफोरी । तब धरि जीभ कढ़ावउँ तोरी ॥
puni asa kabahuṁ kahasi gharaphorī, taba dhari jībha kaṛhāvauṁ torī.

Trans:

"Why, O lady, should anyone give me a lesson, and who is there to encourage me in any impudence? With whom again is it well today if not with Rāma, upon whom the king is now conferring the throne? God has been very gracious to Kausalyā; and after seeing her, who else can have any pride left? Why not go and see all the magnificence, the sight of which has so agitated me? Your son is away and you take no heed. You remain complacent under the false notion of your influence with the king—not realizing his treachery and wiliness; so drowsy you are and so content with just for your pillow and bed. On hearing this fancy speech dripping with affection, the queen—who knew well her malicious mind—cried, "Quiet, and be done! If ever you speak to me again this way, you mischief-maker, I will have your tongue pulled out."

दोहा-dohā:

काने खोरे कूबरे कुटिल कुचाली जानि ।
kāne khore kūbare kuṭila kucālī jāni,
तिय बिसेषि पुनि चेरि कहि भरतमातु मुसुकानि ॥ १४ ॥
tiya biseṣi puni ceri kahi bharatamātu musukāni. 14.

Trans:

"There's a saying—the one-eyed, the lame, the humpbacked are vicious and vile, more so if they be of the menial class," added the queen as she smiled.

चौपाई-caupāī:

प्रियबादिनि सिख दीन्हिउँ तोही । सपनेहुँ तो पर कोपु न मोही ॥
priyabādini sikha dīnhiuṁ tohī, sapanehuṁ to para kopu na mohī.
सुदिनु सुमंगल दायकु सोई । तोर कहा फुर जेहि दिन होई ॥
sudinu sumaṁgala dāyaku soī, tora kahā phura jehi dina hoī.
जेठ स्वामि सेवक लघु भाई । यह दिनकर कुल रीति सुहाई ॥
jeṭha svāmi sevaka laghu bhāī, yaha dinakara kula rīti suhāī.
राम तिलकु जौं साँचेहुँ काली । देउँ मागु मन भावत आली ॥
rāma tilaku jauṁ sāṁcehuṁ kālī, deuṁ māgu mana bhāvata ālī.
कौसल्या सम सब महतारी । रामहि सहज सुभायँ पिआरी ॥
kausalyā sama saba mahatārī, rāmahi sahaja subhāyaṁ piārī.
मो पर करहिं सनेहु बिसेषी । मैं करि प्रीति परीछा देखी ॥
mo para karahiṁ sanehu biseṣī, maiṁ kari prīti parīchā dekhī.
जौं बिधि जनमु देइ करि छोहू । होहुँ राम सिय पूत पुतोहू ॥
jauṁ bidhi janamu dei kari chohū, hohuṁ rāma siya pūta putohū.
प्रान तें अधिक रामु प्रिय मोरें । तिन्ह कें तिलक छोभु कस तोरें ॥
prāna teṁ adhika rāmu priya moreṁ, tinha keṁ tilaka chobhu kasa toreṁ.

Trans:

Than said the queen, "O sweet-tongued one, I spoke to you like that by way of advice; I can't even dream of being angry at you. If what you say is true, it is the best and happiest of days. It has ever been the custom in the solar race that the eldest-born should be the lord, and the younger brothers his servants. If Rāma is really to be crowned tomorrow, ask of me, girl, what you will and I will give it you. There is no difference between Kausalyā and the other royal mothers. Rāma is equally fond of all; in fact he has a special affection for me, as I have often tested. If I am born again, may god in his goodness grant that Rāma and Sītā be again my son and daughter! Rāma is dearer to me than life; why then should you be troubled at his being crowned king?

दोहा-dohā:

भरत सपथ तोहि सत्य कहु परिहरि कपट दुराउ ।
bharata sapatha tohi satya kahu parihari kapaṭa durāu,
हरष समय बिसमउ करसि कारन मोहि सुनाउ ॥ १५ ॥
haraṣa samaya bisamau karasi kārana mohi sunāu. 15.

Trans:

I abjure you in Bharat's name, tell me the truth without any fraud or concealment. Declare to me the reason why you are in distress at such a time of gladness."

चौपाई-caupāī:

एकहिं बार आस सब पूजी । अब कछु कहब जीभ करि दूजी ॥
ekahiṁ bāra āsa saba pūjī, aba kachu kahaba jībha kari dūjī.
फोरै जोगु कपारु अभागा । भलेउ कहत दुख रउरेहि लागा ॥
phorai jogu kapāru abhāgā, bhaleu kahata dukha raurehi lāgā.
कहहिं झूठि फुरि बात बनाई । ते प्रिय तुम्हहि करुइ मैं माई ॥
kahahiṁ jhūṭhi phuri bāta banāī, te priya tumhahi karui maiṁ māī.
हमहुँ कहबि अब ठकुरसोहाती । नाहिं त मौन रहब दिनु राती ॥
hamahuṁ kahabi aba ṭhakurasohātī, nāhiṁ ta mauna rahaba dinu rātī.
करि कुरूप बिधि परबस कीन्हा । बवा सो लुनिअ लहिअ जो दीन्हा ॥
kari kurūpa bidhi parabasa kīnhā, bavā so lunia lahia jo dīnhā.
कोउ नृप होउ हमहि का हानी । चेरि छाड़ि अब होब कि रानी ॥
kou nṛpa hou hamahi kā hānī, ceri chāṛi aba hoba ki rānī.
जारै जोगु सुभाउ हमारा । अनभल देखि न जाइ तुम्हारा ॥
jārai jogu subhāu hamārā, anabhala dekhi na jāi tumhārā.
तातें कछुक बात अनुसारी । छमिअ देबि बड़ि चूक हमारी ॥
tāteṁ kachuka bāta anusārī, chamia debi baṛi cūka hamārī.

Trans:

"I have been satisfied once already speaking my mind out; have I a second tongue that I should speak again? I deserve to have my head broken on the funeral pile, wretch that I am, since I pain you by my well-meaning words. Those who make the false appear true are the people who please you, my lady; while I offend you. Henceforth I too will speak only as my mistress pleases, or else will remain silent day and night. God has given me a deformed body and made me dependent on others; we must all reap as we have sown and take as we are given. Whoever be the king, what have I to lose? Shall I cease to be a servant and become a queen? Damn me and my nature which cannot bear to see your disgrace—and hence I give utterance to a word or two here and there! Do pardon me, mistress; it was a great fault on my part."

दोहा-*dohā:*

गूढ़ कपट प्रिय बचन सुनि तीय अधरबुधि रानि ।
gūṛha kapaṭa priya bacana suni tīya adharabudhi rāni,
सुरमाया बस बैरिनिहि सुहृद जानि पतिआनि ॥ १६ ॥
suramāyā basa bairinihi suhṛda jāni patiāni. 16.

Trans:

On hearing these affectionate words, so deep and crafty, the queen, being only a weak-minded woman, and under the influence of a divine delusion, really believed her enemy to be a friend.

चौपाई-*caupāī:*

सादर पुनि पुनि पूँछति ओही । सबरी गान मृगी जनु मोही ॥
sādara puni puni pūm̐chati ohī, sabarī gāna mṛgī janu mohī.
तसि मति फिरी अहइ जसि भाबी । रहसी चेरि घात जनु फाबी ॥
tasi mati phirī ahai jasi bhābī, rahasī ceri ghāta janu phābī.
तुम्ह पूँछहु मैं कहत डेराऊँ । धरेहु मोर घरफोरी नाऊँ ॥
tumha pūm̐chahu maiṁ kahata ḍerāūm̐, dharehu mora gharaphorī nāūm̐.
सजि प्रतीति बहुबिधि गढ़ि छोली । अवध साढ़साती तब बोली ॥
saji pratīti bahubidhi gaṛhi cholī, avadha sāṛhasātī taba bolī.
प्रिय सिय रामु कहा तुम्ह रानी । रामहि तुम्ह प्रिय सो फुरि बानी ॥
priya siya rāmu kahā tumha rānī, rāmahi tumha priya so phuri bānī.
रहा प्रथम अब ते दिन बीते । समउ फिरें रिपु होहिं पिरीते ॥
rahā prathama aba te dina bīte, samau phireṁ ripu hohiṁ pirīte.
भानु कमल कुल पोषनिहारा । बिनु जल जारि करइ सोइ छारा ॥
bhānu kamala kula poṣanihārā, binu jala jāri karai soi chārā.
जरि तुम्हारि चह सवति उखारी । रूँधहु करि उपाउ बर बारी ॥
jari tumhāri caha savati ukhārī, rūm̐dhahu kari upāu bara bārī.

Trans:

Again and again in kindly terms she questioned her, like a fawn bewitched by the song of a huntress. Her reason veered—as fate would have it ; and the servant-girl rejoiced at the success of her scheme. "You persist in asking, but I am afraid to reply since you have given me the name of mischief-maker"; thus spoke the malignant star of Avadh by trimming and fashioning her speech in every way to win confidence, "O queen, you spoke of Sītā and Rāma as your friends; and true enough Rāma did love you once, but now all those days are past. In time friends become foes; the sun invigorates the lotus, but burns it to ashes if it has no water. The rival queen will tear you up by the root; so better take care of your garden and hedge it about now.

दोहा-*dohā:*

तुम्हहि न सोचु सोहाग बल निज बस जानहु राउ ।
tumhahi na socu sohāga bala nija basa jānahu rāu,
मन मलीन मुह मीठ नृपु राउर सरल सुभाउ ॥ १७ ॥
mana malīna muha mīṭha nṛpu rāura sarala subhāu. 17.

Trans:

Thinking yourself the king's favorite and assuming that he is quite in your power, you notice nothing. Though sweet of tongue the king—but his heart is black; and you are such a guileless one.

चौपाई-*caupāī:*

चतुर गँभीर राम महतारी । बीचु पाइ निज बात सँवारी ॥
catura gam̐bhīra rāma mahatārī, bīcu pāi nija bāta sam̐vārī.
पठए भरतु भूप ननिअउरें । राम मातु मत जानव रउरें ॥
paṭhae bharatu bhūpa naniaureṁ, rāma mātu mata jānava raureṁ.
सेवहिं सकल सवति मोहि नीकें । गरबित भरत मातु बल पी कें ॥
sevahiṁ sakala savati mohi nīkeṁ, garabita bharata mātu bala pī keṁ.
सालु तुम्हार कौसिलहि माई । कपट चतुर नहिं होइ जनाई ॥
sālu tumhāra kausilahi māī, kapaṭa catura nahiṁ hoi janāī.
राजहि तुम्ह पर प्रेमु बिसेषी । सवति सुभाउ सकइ नहिं देखी ॥
rājahi tumha para premu biseṣī, savati subhāu sakai nahiṁ dekhī.
रचि प्रपंचु भूपहि अपनाई । राम तिलक हित लगन धराई ॥
raci prapaṁcu bhūpahi apanāī, rāma tilaka hita lagana dharāī.
यह कुल उचित राम कहुँ टीका । सबहि सोहाइ मोहि सुठि नीका ॥
yaha kula ucita rāma kahum̐ ṭīkā, sabahi sohāi mohi suṭhi nīkā.
आगिलि बात समुझि डरु मोही । देउ दैउ फिरि सो फलु ओही ॥
āgili bāta samujhi ḍaru mohī, deu daiu phiri so phalu ohī.

Trans:

Rāma's mother on the contrary is deep and crafty and having found the means has played her own game. The king has sent away Bharat to his grandfather's by her suggestion—simply because he is your son; and now thinks she—'All the other queens are well disposed to me, but Bharat's mother is proud, for she presumes her influence with the king'. You, lady, are the thorn in Kausalyā's side; she is too deep and crafty for you to fathom; the king has greater love for you than for anyone else, and like a rival she cannot bear to see it. For her own ends she has worked upon the king and got him to fix a day for Rāma's inauguration. Now Rāma's promotion is a good thing for the family, all are pleased at it, and I too like it well. However I shudder to think of the consequences. May heaven so ordain that the mischief may recoil on its own head."

दोहा-*dohā:*

रचि पचि कोटिक कुटिलपन कीन्हेसि कपट प्रबोधु ।
raci paci koṭika kuṭilapana kīnhesi kapaṭa prabodhu,
कहिसि कथा सत सवति कै जेहि बिधि बाढ़ बिरोधु ॥ १८ ॥
kahisi kathā sata savati kai jehi bidhi bāṛha birodhu. 18.

Trans:

With innumerable crafty devices she planned her cunning tale, telling story after story of jealous wives, whereby to increase her resentment.

चौपाई-*caupāī:*

भावी बस प्रतीति उर आई । पूँछ रानि पुनि सपथ देवाई ॥
bhāvī basa pratīti ura āī, pūm̐cha rāni puni sapatha devāī.
का पूँछहु तुम्ह अबहुँ न जाना । निज हित अनहित पसु पहिचाना ॥
kā pūm̐chahu tumha abahum̐ na jānā, nija hita anahita pasu pahicānā.
भयउ पाखु दिन सजत समाजू । तुम्ह पाई सुधि मोहि सन आजू ॥
bhayau pākhu dina sajata samājū, tumha pāī sudhi mohi sana ājū.
खाइअ पहिरिअ राज तुम्हारें । सत्य कहें नहिं दोषु हमारें ॥
khāia pahiria rāja tumhāreṁ, satya kaheṁ nahiṁ doṣu hamāreṁ.
जौं असत्य कछु कहब बनाई । तौ बिधि देइहि हमहि सजाई ॥
jauṁ asatya kachu kahaba banāī, tau bidhi deihi hamahi sajāī.
रामहि तिलक कालि जौं भयऊ । तुम्ह कहुँ बिपति बीजु बिधि बयऊ ॥
rāmahi tilaka kāli jauṁ bhayaū, tumha kahum̐ bipati bīju bidhi bayaū.
रेख खँचाइ कहउँ बलु भाषी । भामिनि भइहु दूध कइ माखी ॥
rekha kham̐cāi kahaum̐ balu bhāṣī, bhāmini bhaihu dūdha kai mākhī.
जौं सुत सहित करहु सेवकाई । तौ घर रहहु न आन उपाई ॥

jauṁ suta sahita karahu sevakāī, tau ghara rahahu na āna upāī.

Trans:

Overmastered by fate, the queen was persuaded at heart, and adjured her, by the love she bore her, to speak out, "What is it you would ask?" "Still you do not understand? Even the brute beasts know what is good or bad for them! For the last fortnight the preparations have been going on, and it is only today that you learn the news from me. I am clothed and fed in your service, and I must therefore speak the truth at any cost. If I invent a word of falsehood, may God repay me for that! Should Rāma be crowned tomorrow, God will have sown you a crop of misfortunes. I draw this line on the ground, O lady, and declare most emphatically that you will be like a fly in a milk-bowl. If you and your son will submit to be servants, you will be able to stay, but on no other condition.

दोहा-dohā:

कद्रूँ बिनतहि दीन्ह दुखु तुम्हहि कौसिलाँ देब ।
kadrūm̐ binatahi dīnha dukhu tumhahi kausilām̐ deba,
भरतु बंदिगृह सेइहहिं लखनु राम के नेब ॥१९॥
bharatu baṁdigṛha seihahiṁ lakhanu rāma ke neba. 19.

Trans:

As Kadru tormented Binātā so will Kausalyā treat you. Bharat will be a slave in bonds under Rāma and Lakshman."

चौपाई-caupāī:

कैकयसुता सुनत कटु बानी । कहि न सकइ कछु सहमि सुखानी ॥
kaikayasutā sunata kaṭu bānī, kahi na sakai kachu sahami sukhānī.
तन पसेउ कदली जिमि काँपी । कुबरीं दसन जीभ तब चाँपी ॥
tana paseu kadalī jimi kām̐pī, kubarīṁ dasana jībha taba cām̐pī.
कहि कहि कोटिक कपट कहानी । धीरजु धरहु प्रबोधिसि रानी ॥
kahi kahi koṭika kapaṭa kahānī, dhīraju dharahu prabodhisi rānī.
फिरा करमु प्रिय लागि कुचाली । बकिहि सराहइ मानि मराली ॥
phirā karamu priya lāgi kucālī, bakihi sarāhai māni marālī.
सुनु मंथरा बात फुरि तोरी । दहिनि आँखि नित फरकइ मोरी ॥
sunu maṁtharā bāta phuri torī, dahini ām̐khi nita pharakai morī.
दिन प्रति देखउँ राति कुसपने । कहउँ न तोहि मोह बस अपने ॥
dina prati dekhaum̐ rāti kusapane, kahaum̐ na tohi moha basa apane.
काह करौं सखि सूध सुभाऊ । दाहिन बाम न जानउँ काऊ ॥
kāha karauṁ sakhi sūdha subhāū, dāhina bāma na jānaum̐ kāū.

Trans:

When she heard these cutting words Kekaya's daughter could say nothing; she was all in a fever for fear; her limbs were bathed with perspiration; and she trembled like a plantain stalk. The Humpback bit her tongue and with innumerable crafty speeches kept consoling the queen saying 'courage, courage,' till with her ill-teaching she warped her like a seasoned plank—of which there is no bending straight. By a turn of fate the vile became a favorite, as though a beautiful flamingo should flatter an ugly crane. "Hearken, Manthrā, your words are true; my right eye is always throbbing, and every night I have some ill dream—but in my folly I did not tell you. What can I do, friend? I am such a simpleton that by myself I cannot tell the right from the left.

दोहा-dohā:

अपनें चलत न आजु लगि अनभल काहुक कीन्ह ।
apaneṁ calata na āju lagi anabhala kāhuka kīnha,
केहिं अघ एकहि बार मोहि दैअँ दुसह दुखु दीन्ह ॥२०॥
kehiṁ agha ekahi bāra mohi daiam̐ dusaha dukhu dīnha. 20.

Trans:

Up to this day I have never of my own accord done an unkindness to anyone: for what offence has heaven all at once put me to such intolerable distress?

चौपाई-caupāī:

नैहर जनमु भरब बरु जाई । जिअत न करबि सवति सेवकाई ॥
naihara janamu bharaba baru jāī, jiata na karabi savati sevakāī.
अरि बस दैउ जिआवत जाही । मरनु नीक तेहि जीवन चाही ॥
ari basa daiu jiāvata jāhī, maranu nīka tehi jīvana cāhī.
दीन बचन कह बहुबिधि रानी । सुनि कुबरीं तियमाया ठानी ॥
dīna bacana kaha bahubidhi rānī, suni kubarīṁ tiyamāyā ṭhānī.
अस कस कहहु मानि मन ऊना । सुखु सोहागु तुम्ह कहुँ दिन दूना ॥
asa kasa kahahu māni mana ūnā, sukhu sohāgu tumha kahum̐ dina dūnā.
जेहिं राउर अति अनभल ताका । सोइ पाइहि यहु फलु परिपाका ॥
jehiṁ rāura ati anabhala tākā, soi pāihi yahu phalu paripākā.
जब तें कुमत सुना मैं स्वामिनि । भूख न बासर नींद न जामिनि ॥
jaba teṁ kumata sunā maiṁ svāmini, bhūkha na bāsara nīṁda na jāmini.
पूँछेउँ गुनिन्ह रेख तिन्ह खाँची । भरत भुआल होहिं यह साँची ॥
pūm̐cheum̐ guninha rekha tinha khām̐cī, bharata bhuāla hohiṁ yaha sām̐cī.
भामिनि करहु त कहौं उपाऊ । है तुम्हरीं सेवा बस राऊ ॥
bhāmini karahu ta kahauṁ upāū, hai tumharīṁ sevā basa rāū.

Trans:

Rather would I go and spend all my days in my father's house than live a servant of a rival wife. Whomever god creates the dependent of an enemy, it is good for her to die rather than live." Many such lamentable speeches did the queen utter, and the Humpback, on hearing them, resorted to the devices of wily women: "Why speak thus, as though a casualty of disgrace? Your honor and wedded joy shall yet increase daily; and may she, who has plotted you this misfortune, in the end reap the fruit of it herself! Since your unworthy servant, my lady, first heard the news, I could neither eat by day nor sleep at night. I consulted the astrologers and they declared positively—"Bharat shall be king, this much is certain." If, O good lady, you will only act upon it, I can tell you a way; for the king is under an obligation to you."

दोहा-dohā:

परउँ कूप तुअ बचन पर सकउँ पूत पति त्यागि ।
paraum̐ kūpa tua bacana para sakaum̐ pūta pati tyāgi,
कहसि मोर दुखु देखि बड़ कस न करब हित लागि ॥२१॥
kahasi mora dukhu dekhi baṛa kasa na karaba hita lāgi. 21.

Trans:

"I would throw myself into a well if you told me, or even abandon my husband and son. Speak, then; you see how great is my distress. Why should I not do what will be for my own good?"

चौपाई-caupāī:

कुबरीं करि कबुली कैकेई । कपट छुरी उर पाहन टेई ॥
kubarīṁ kari kabulī kaikeī, kapaṭa churī ura pāhana ṭeī.
लखइ न रानि निकट दुखु कैसें । चरइ हरित तिन बलिपसु जैसें ॥
lakhai na rāni nikaṭa dukhu kaiseṁ, carai harita tina balipasu jaiseṁ.
सुनत बात मृदु अंत कठोरी । देति मनहुँ मधु माहुर घोरी ॥
sunata bāta mṛdu aṁta kaṭhorī, deti manahum̐ madhu māhura ghorī.
कहइ चेरि सुधि अहइ कि नाही । स्वामिनि कहिहु कथा मोहि पाहीं ॥
kahai ceri sudhi ahai ki nāhī, svāmini kahihu kathā mohi pāhīṁ.
दुइ बरदान भूप सन थाती । मागहु आजु जुड़ावहु छाती ॥
dui baradāna bhūpa sana thātī, māgahu āju juṛāvahu chātī.
सुतहि राजु रामहि बनबासू । देहु लेहु सब सवति हुलासू ॥
sutahi rāju rāmahi banabāsū, dehu lehu saba savati hulāsū.
भूपति राम सपथ जब करई । तब मागेहु जेहिं बचनु न टरई ॥
bhūpati rāma sapatha jaba karaī, taba māgehu jehiṁ bacanu na ṭaraī.
होइ अकाजु आजु निसि बीतें । बचनु मोर प्रिय मानेहु जी तें ॥
hoi akāju āju nisi bīteṁ, bacanu mora priya mānehu jī teṁ.

Trans:

Taking Kaekayī as a victim for the slaughter, the Humpback whetted the knife of treachery on her heart of stone; and the queen, like a sacrificial beast that nibbles the greensward, saw not the approaching danger. Pleasant to hear, but disastrous in their results, her words were like honey mingled with deadly poison. Said the handmaid: "Do you or do you not, my lady, remember the story you once told me of the two boons promised you by the king. Ask for them now and relieve your soul—the kingdom for your son, and for Rāma banishment to the woods. Thus shall you triumph over all your rivals. But ask not till the king has sworn upon Rāma, so that he may not go back from his word. If you let this night pass it will be too late; give heed to my words with all your heart."

दोहा-dohā:

बड़ कुघातु करि पातकिनि कहेसि कोपगृहँ जाहु ।
baṛa kughātu kari pātakini kahesi kopagṛhaṁ jāhu,
काजु सँवारेहु सजग सबु सहसा जनि पतिआहु ॥ २२ ॥
kāju saṁvārehu sajaga sabu sahasā jani patiāhu. 22.

Trans:

Said the wretch, having fully contrived her abominable design: "Go to the chamber-of-ire; make all your arrangements circumspectly, and do not yield too readily."

चौपाई-caupāī:

कुबरिहि रानि प्रानप्रिय जानी । बार बार बड़ि बुद्धि बखानी ॥
kubarihi rāni prānapriya jānī, bāra bāra baṛi buddhi bakhānī.
तोहि सम हित न मोर संसारा । बहे जात कइ भइसि अधारा ॥
tohi sama hita na mora saṁsārā, bahe jāta kai bhaisi adhārā.
जौं बिधि पुरब मनोरथु काली । करौं तोहि चख पूतरि आली ॥
jauṁ bidhi puraba manorathu kālī, karauṁ tohi cakha pūtari ālī.
बहुबिधि चेरिहि आदरु देई । कोपभवन गवनि कैकेई ॥
bahubidhi cerihi ādaru deī, kopabhavana gavani kaikeī.
बिपति बीजु बरषा रितु चेरी । भुइँ भइ कुमति कैकई केरी ॥
bipati bīju baraṣā ritu cerī, bhuiṁ bhai kumati kaikaī kerī.
पाइ कपट जलु अंकुर जामा । बर दोउ दल दुख फल परिनामा ॥
pāi kapaṭa jalu aṁkura jāmā, bara dou dala dukha phala parināmā.
कोप समाजु साजि सबु सोई । राजु करत निज कुमति बिगोई ॥
kopa samāju sāji sabu soī, rāju karata nija kumati bigoī.
राउर नगर कोलाहलु होई । यह कुचालि कछु जान न कोई ॥
rāura nagara kolāhalu hoī, yaha kucāli kachu jāna na koī.

Trans:

The queen considered Humpback her best friend, and again and again extolled her cleverness, saying, "I have no such friend as you in the whole world! I had been swept away by the flood but for your support. Tomorrow if god will fulfill my desire I will cherish you, my dear, as the apple of my eye." Thus lavishing every term of endearment on her handmaid, Kaekayī went to the chamber-of-wrath: her evil temper like the soil in which the servant-girl, like the rains, had sown the seed of Calamity, which, watered by Treachery, took root and sprouted with the two Boons as its leaves, and in the end would have Ruin as its fruit. Gathering about her every token of resentment, she undid her reign by her evil counsel. Meanwhile the city and the palace were given over to rejoicing, for no one knew of these wicked plans.

दोहा-dohā:

प्रमुदित पुर नर नारि सब सजहिं सुमंगलचार ।
pramudita pura nara nāri saba sajahiṁ sumaṁgalacāra,
एक प्रबिसहिं एक निर्गमहिं भीर भूप दरबार ॥ २३ ॥
eka prabisahiṁ eka nirgamahiṁ bhīra bhūpa darabāra. 23.

Trans:

All the citizens in their delight were busied with festive preparations and the royal hall of audience was crowded with a continuous stream of people passing in and out.

चौपाई-caupāī:

बाल सखा सुन हियँ हरषाहीं । मिलि दस पाँच राम पहिं जाहीं ॥
bāla sakhā suna hiyaṁ haraṣāhīṁ, mili dasa pāṁca rāma pahiṁ jāhīṁ.
प्रभु आदरहिं प्रेमु पहिचानी । पूँछहिं कुसल खेम मृदु बानी ॥
prabhu ādarahiṁ premu pahicānī, pūṁchahiṁ kusala khema mṛdu bānī.
फिरहिं भवन प्रिय आयसु पाई । करत परसपर राम बड़ाई ॥
phirahiṁ bhavana priya āyasu pāī, karata parasapara rāma baṛāī.
को रघुबीर सरिस संसारा । सीलु सनेह निबाहनिहारा ॥
ko raghubīra sarisa saṁsārā, sīlu saneha nibāhanihārā.
जेहिं जेहिं जोनि करम बस भ्रमहीं । तहँ तहँ ईसु देउ यह हमहीं ॥
jehiṁ jehiṁ joni karama basa bhramahīṁ, tahaṁ tahaṁ īsu deu yaha hamahīṁ.
सेवक हम स्वामी सियनाहू । होउ नात यह ओर निबाहू ॥
sevaka hama svāmī siyanāhū, hou nāta yaha ora nibāhū.
अस अभिलाषु नगर सब काहू । कैकयसुता हृदयँ अति दाहू ॥
asa abhilāṣu nagara saba kāhū, kaikayasutā hṛdayaṁ ati dāhū.
को न कुसंगति पाइ नसाई । रहइ न नीच मतें चतुराई ॥
ko na kusaṁgati pāi nasāī, rahai na nīca mateṁ caturāī.

Trans:

Delighted at the news, a few five-ten of Rāma's boyhood friends went up to congratulate him; and the Lord, sensible of their affection, received them graciously and warmly asked of their welfare. Then, after taking permission of their beloved friend, they returned home speaking highly of him to one another, "Is there anyone in the whole world so kind and amiable as Raghubīr? Whatever future births fate has in store for us, god only grant us this: that we may always be the servants of Sītā's lordly spouse; and we ask for nothing else." Such was the wish of everyone in the city; only Kaekayī's heart was in a flame—for who is not spoiled by evil communications? There is no profit in taking counsel with the vile.

दोहा-dohā:

साँझ समय सानंद नृपु गयउ कैकई गेहँ ।
sāṁjha samaya sānaṁda nṛpu gayau kaikaī gehaṁ,
गवनु निठुरता निकट किय जनु धरि देह सनेहँ ॥ २४ ॥
gavanu niṭhuratā nikaṭa kiya janu dhari deha sanehaṁ. 24.

Trans:

At eventide the happy king repaired to Kaekayī's apartments, as it were Love incarnate visiting Obduracy.

चौपाई-caupāī:

कोपभवन सुनि सकुचेउ राऊ । भय बस अगहुड़ परइ न पाऊ ॥
kopabhavana suni sakuceu rāū, bhaya basa agahuṛa parai na pāū.
सुरपति बसइ बाहँबल जाकें । नरपति सकल रहहिं रुख ताकें ॥
surapati basai bāhaṁbala jākeṁ, narapati sakala rahahiṁ rukha tākeṁ.
सो सुनि तिय रिस गयउ सुखाई । देखहु काम प्रताप बड़ाई ॥
so suni tiya risa gayau sukhāī, dekhahu kāma pratāpa baṛāī.
सूल कुलिस असि अँगवनिहारे । ते रतिनाथ सुमन सर मारे ॥
sūla kulisa asi aṁgavanihāre, te ratinātha sumana sara māre.
सभय नरेसु प्रिया पहिं गयऊ । देखि दसा दुखु दारुन भयऊ ॥
sabhaya naresu priyā pahiṁ gayaū, dekhi dasā dukhu dāruna bhayaū.
भूमि सयन पटु मोट पुराना । दिए डारि तन भूषन नाना ॥
bhūmi sayana paṭu moṭa purānā, die ḍāri tana bhūṣana nānā.
कुमतिहि कसि कुबेषता फाबी । अन अहिवातु सूच जनु भाबी ॥
kumatihi kasi kubeṣatā phābī, ana ahivātu sūca janu bhābī.
जाइ निकट नृपु कह मृदु बानी । प्रानप्रिया केहि हेतु रिसानी ॥
jāi nikaṭa nṛpu kaha mṛdu bānī, prānapriyā kehi hetu risānī.

Trans:

He was dismayed when he heard of the sulking-chamber and could scarcely put his feet to the ground for fear. He—under whose mighty arm the Lord of heaven dwells secure, and upon whose favor waited all the many kings—was in a fever at hearing of an angry woman: see how great is the power of love. The bearers of trident, thunderbolt, and sword are slain by the flowery shafts of Ratī's spouse. Anxiously the king approached his beloved and was terribly distressed to see her condition: lying on the ground in old and coarse attire, with all her personal adornments cast away—her wretched appearance in accordance with her wretched design, as if in mourning for her instant widowhood. The king drew near and asked in gentle tones, "Why are you angry, my dear, my heart's delight?"

छंद-chaṁda:

केहि हेतु रानि रिसानि परसत पानि पतिहि नेवारई ।
kehi hetu rāni risāni parasata pāni patihi nevārai,
मानहुँ सरोष भुअंग भामिनि बिषम भाँति निहारई ॥
mānahuṁ saroṣa bhuaṁga bhāmini biṣama bhāṁti nihārai.
दोउ बासना रसना दसन बर मरम ठाहरु देखई ।
dou bāsanā rasanā dasana bara marama ṭhāharu dekhaī,
तुलसी नृपति भवतब्यता बस काम कौतुक लेखई ॥
tulasī nṛpati bhavatabyatā basa kāma kautuka lekhaī.

Trans:

"Why so angry, my queen?" and touched her with his hands. She flung it aside and flashed upon him a furious glance—like an enraged serpent with her two desires for its double tongue, and with the Boons for fangs spying out like vulnerable points. Under the influence of fate, says Tulsī, the king took it all as one of Love's amorous devices.

सोरठा-soraṭhā:

बार बार कह राउ सुमुखि सुलोचनि पिकबचनि ।
bāra bāra kaha rāu sumukhi sulocani pikabacani,
कारन मोहि सुनाउ गजगामिनि निज कोप कर ॥२५॥
kārana mohi sunāu gajagāmini nija kopa kara. 25.

Trans:

Again and again the king said, "Tell me the cause of your anger, O beautiful, bright-eyed dame, with voice as melodious as the *koel*, and gait as voluptuous as the elephant.

चौपाई-caupāī:

अनहित तोर प्रिया केइँ कीन्हा । केहि दुइ सिर केहि जमु चह लीन्हा ॥
anahita tora priyā keiṁ kīnhā, kehi dui sira kehi jamu caha līnhā.
कहु केहि रंकहि करौं नरेसू । कहु केहि नृपहि निकासौं देसू ॥
kahu kehi raṁkahi karauṁ naresū, kahu kehi nṛpahi nikāsauṁ desū.
सकउँ तोर अरि अमरउ मारी । काह कीट बपुरे नर नारी ॥
sakauṁ tora ari amarau mārī, kāha kīṭa bapure nara nārī.
जानसि मोर सुभाउ बरोरू । मनु तव आनन चंद चकोरू ॥
jānasi mora subhāu barorū, manu tava ānana caṁda cakorū.
प्रिया प्रान सुत सरबसु मोरें । परिजन प्रजा सकल बस तोरें ॥
priyā prāna suta sarabasu moreṁ, parijana prajā sakala basa toreṁ.
जौं कछु कहौं कपटु करि तोही । भामिनि राम सपथ सत मोही ॥
jauṁ kachu kahauṁ kapaṭu kari tohī, bhāmini rāma sapatha sata mohī.
बिहसि मागु मनभावति बाता । भूषन सजहि मनोहर गाता ॥
bihasi māgu manabhāvati bātā, bhūṣana sajahi manohara gātā.
घरी कुघरी समुझि जियँ देखू । बेगि प्रिया परिहरहि कुबेषू ॥
gharī kugharī samujhi jiyaṁ dekhū, begi priyā pariharahi kubeṣū.

Trans:

Who is it, my dear, who has vexed you? Who is it with a head to spare and so enamored of death? Tell me what beggar I should make a king, or what king I should banish from his realm. I could slay even an immortal, were he your enemy—of what account then are any poor worms of men and women? O my love, you know my sentiments and how my eyes ever turn to your face as the partridge to the moon. O my beloved: my life, my sons, and everything that I own, my palace, my subjects are all at your disposal. Could I tell you a word of untruth, lady, at least an oath by Rāma must be binding. Ask with a smile whatever you desire. Now, adorn your lovely person with jewels; consider within yourself what an hour of torture this is for me, and at once, my darling, put away this unseemly attire."

दोहा-dohā:

यह सुनि मन गुनि सपथ बड़ि बिहसि उठी मतिमंद ।
yaha suni mana guni sapatha baṛi bihasi uṭhī matimaṁda,
भूषन सजति बिलोकि मृगु मनहुँ किरातिनि फंद ॥२६॥
bhūṣana sajati biloki mṛgu manahuṁ kirātini phaṁda. 26.

Trans:

On hearing this and considering the greatness of the oath the king took, the wicked queen arose with a smile and resumed her royal attire—like a huntress who sets the snare upon marking the chase.

चौपाई-caupāī:

पुनि कह राउ सुहृद जियँ जानी । प्रेम पुलकि मृदु मंजुल बानी ॥
puni kaha rāu suhṛda jiyaṁ jānī, prema pulaki mṛdu maṁjula bānī.
भामिनि भयउ तोर मनभावा । घर घर नगर अनंद बधावा ॥
bhāmini bhayau tora manabhāvā, ghara ghara nagara anaṁda badhāvā.
रामहि देउँ कालि जुबराजू । सजहि सुलोचनि मंगल साजू ॥
rāmahi deuṁ kāli jubarājū, sajahi sulocani maṁgala sājū.
दलकि उठेउ सुनि हृदउ कठोरू । जनु छुइ गयउ पाक बरतोरू ॥
dalaki uṭheu suni hṛdau kaṭhorū, janu chui gayau pāka baratorū.
ऐसिउ पीर बिहसि तेहिं गोई । चोर नारि जिमि प्रगटि न रोई ॥
aisiu pīra bihasi tehiṁ goī, cora nāri jimi pragaṭi na roī.
लखहिं न भूप कपट चतुराई । कोटि कुटिल मनि गुरू पढ़ाई ॥
lakhahiṁ na bhūpa kapaṭa caturāī, koṭi kuṭila mani gurū paṛhāī.
जद्यपि नीति निपुन नरनाहू । नारिचरित जलनिधि अवगाहू ॥
jadyapi nīti nipuna naranāhū, nāricarita jalanidhi avagāhū.
कपट सनेहु बढ़ाइ बहोरी । बोली बिहसि नयन मुहु मोरी ॥
kapaṭa sanehu baṛhāi bahorī, bolī bihasi nayana muhu morī.

Trans:

Thinking her reconciled, the king spoke again in soft and winning tones, his whole body quivering with love, "Your heart's desire, my lady, has come to pass. In the city there is joy and gladness in every house, every heart—for tomorrow I give Rāma the rank of Regent. So, my love, make ready for the festival." At the sound of these untoward words she sprung up with a bound, like an over ripe gourd that bursts at a touch. With a smile on her lips, but with such secret pain at heart as an accused thief's wife who dare not openly cry. The king could not penetrate her crafty schemes, for she had been tutored in every villainy by a crafty master; and skilled as he was in statesmanship, the abyss of a woman's ways was more than he could fathom. Again she spoke with a further show of hypocritical affection and a forced smile in her eyes and her lips:

दोहा-dohā:

मागु मागु पै कहहु पिय कबहुँ न देहु न लेहु ।
māgu māgu pai kahahu piya kabahuṁ na dehu na lehu,
देन कहेहु बरदान दुइ तेउ पावत संदेहु ॥२७॥
dena kahehu baradāna dui teu pāvata saṁdehu. 27.

Trans:

"Ask-ask, indeed! But tell me, sir, when has it really come to giving and taking? You once promised me two boons, and yet I have my doubts of ever getting them."

चौपाई-caupāī:

जानेउँ मरमु राउ हँसि कहई । तुम्हहि कोहाब परम प्रिय अहई ॥
jāneuṁ maramu rāu haṁsi kahaī, tumhahi kohāba parama priya ahaī.

थाती राखि न मागिहु काऊ । बिसरि गयउ मोहि भोर सुभाऊ ॥
thātī rākhi na māgihu kāū, bisari gayau mohi bhora subhāū.
झूठेहुँ हमहि दोषु जनि देहू । दुइ कै चारि मागि मकु लेहू ॥
jhūṭhehuṁ hamahi doṣu jani dehū, dui kai cāri māgi maku lehū.
रघुकुल रीति सदा चलि आई । प्रान जाहुँ बरु बचनु न जाई ॥
raghukula rīti sadā cali āī, prāna jāhuṁ baru bacanu na jāī.
नहिं असत्य सम पातक पुंजा । गिरि सम होहिं कि कोटिक गुंजा ॥
nahiṁ asatya sama pātaka puṁjā, giri sama hohiṁ ki koṭika guṁjā.
सत्यमूल सब सुकृत सुहाए । बेद पुरान बिदित मनु गाए ॥
satyamūla saba sukṛta suhāe, beda purāna bidita manu gāe.
तेहि पर राम सपथ करि आई । सुकृत सनेह अवधि रघुराई ॥
tehi para rāma sapatha kari āī, sukṛta saneha avadhi raghurāī.
बात दृढ़ाइ कुमति हँसि बोली । कुमत कुबिहग कुलह जनु खोली ॥
bāta dṛṛhāi kumati haṁsi bolī, kumata kubihaga kulaha janu kholī.

Trans:

The king replied with a smile, "O, I see what you mean; you are very fond of a little quarrel. You kept my promise in reserve and asked for nothing, and, as my way is, I forgot all about it. Do not tax me with the guilt of a lie, but for two requests make four and today you shall have them. It is an immemorial rule in the Raghu family to cast off life rather than break a promise. No number of sins is equal to a lie; in the same way as myriads of *ghunchi* seeds will not make a mountain. Truth is the foundation of all merit and virtue, as the Vedas and Purānas declare and as Manu has expounded. Moreover I have sworn by Rāma, the chief of our house, the perfection of all that is good and amiable." When she had thus bound him to his word, the wicked queen smiled and said—removing as it were the caps from the eyes of her hawk-like plot.

दोहा-*dohā:*

भूप मनोरथ सुभग बनु सुख सुबिहंग समाजु ।
bhūpa manoratha subhaga banu sukha subihaṁga samāju,
भिल्लिनि जिमि छाड़न चहति बचनु भयंकरु बाजु ॥२८॥
bhillini jimi chāṛana cahati bacanu bhayaṁkaru bāju. 28.

Trans:

The king's desire for Rāma's coronation was like a lovely grove, and his joy was like the happiness of a flock of birds dwelling therein—at which, like a cruel huntress, she sent forth the savage falcon of her speech:

मासपारायण तेरहवाँ विश्राम
māsapārāyaṇa terahavāṁ viśrāma
(Pause 13 for a Thirty-Day Recitation)

चौपाई-*caupāī:*

सुनहु प्रानप्रिय भावत जी का । देहु एक बर भरतहि टीका ॥
sunahu prānapriya bhāvata jī kā, dehu eka bara bharatahi ṭīkā.
मागउँ दूसर बर कर जोरी । पुरवहु नाथ मनोरथ मोरी ॥
māgauṁ dūsara bara kara jorī, puravahu nātha manoratha morī.
तापस बेष बिसेषि उदासी । चौदह बरिस रामु बनबासी ॥
tāpasa beṣa biseṣi udāsī, caudaha barisa rāmu banabāsī.
सुनि मृदु बचन भूप हियँ सोकू । ससि कर छुअत बिकल जिमि कोकू ॥
suni mṛdu bacana bhūpa hiyaṁ sokū, sasi kara chuata bikala jimi kokū.
गयउ सहमि नहिं कछु कहि आवा । जनु सचान बन झपटेउ लावा ॥
gayau sahami nahiṁ kachu kahi āvā, janu sacāna bana jhapaṭeu lāvā.
बिबरन भयउ निपट नरपालू । दामिनि हनेउ मनहुँ तरु तालू ॥
bibarana bhayau nipaṭa narapālū, dāmini haneu manahuṁ taru tālū.
माथें हाथ मूदि दोउ लोचन । तनु धरि सोचु लाग जनु सोचन ॥
māthem hātha mūdi dou locana, tanu dhari socu lāga janu socana.
मोर मनोरथु सुरतरु फूला । फरत करिनि जिमि हतेउ समूला ॥
mora manorathu surataru phūlā, pharata karini jimi hateu samūlā.
अवध उजारि कीन्हि कैकेईं । दीन्हिसि अचल बिपति कै नेईं ॥
avadha ujāri kīnhi kaikeīṁ, dīnhisi acala bipati kai neīṁ.

Trans:

"Hear, my beloved, what is the desire of my heart: Grant me for one boon Bharat's installation; and for the second—I beg with clasped hands, O my lord, accomplish my desire—may Rāma be banished to the woods for fourteen years, there to dwell in the penitential garb of a hermit" At these words of the queen the king's heart grew faint—as the *chakwā* is troubled by the rays of the moon; he trembled all over, nor could utter a single sound—like a partridge in the wood at the swoop of a falcon. The mighty monarch was as crestfallen as a palm-tree struck by lightning. With his hands to his forehead and closing both his eyes, as if it was Grief personified, he moaned, "Ah my fair wish—which had blossomed like the tree of paradise—has been stricken and uprooted by an elephant at the time of bearing fruit. Alas, Kaekayī has desolated Avadh and laid the foundation of everlasting calamity.

दोहा-*dohā:*

कवनें अवसर का भयउ गयउँ नारि बिस्वास ।
kavaneṁ avasara kā bhayau gayauṁ nāri bisvāsa,
जोग सिद्धि फल समय जिमि जतिहि अबिद्या नास ॥२९॥
joga siddhi phala samaya jimi jatihi abidyā nāsa. 29.

Trans:

What a thing to happen at such a time! I am undone by putting trust in a woman—like, as at the time of heavenly reward for penance, an ascetic is destroyed by nescience."

चौपाई-*caupāī:*

एहि बिधि राउ मनहिं मन झाँखा । देखि कुभाँति कुमति मन माखा ॥
ehi bidhi rāu manahiṁ mana jhāṁkhā, dekhi kubhāṁti kumati mana mākhā.
भरतु कि राउर पूत न होंही । आनेहु मोल बेसाहि कि मोही ॥
bharatu ki rāura pūta na hoṁhī, ānehu mola besāhi ki mohī.
जो सुनि सरु अस लाग तुम्हारें । काहे न बोलहु बचनु सँभारें ॥
jo suni saru asa lāga tumhāreṁ, kāhe na bolahu bacanu saṁbhāreṁ.
देहु उतरु अनु करहु कि नाहीं । सत्यसंध तुम्ह रघुकुल माहीं ॥
dehu utaru anu karahu ki nāhīṁ, satyasaṁdha tumha raghukula māhīṁ.
देन कहेहु अब जनि बरु देहू । तजहु सत्य जग अपजसु लेहू ॥
dena kahehu aba jani baru dehū, tajahu satya jaga apajasu lehū.
सत्य सराहि कहेहु बरु देना । जानेहु लेइहि मागि चबेना ॥
satya sarāhi kahehu baru denā, jānehu leihi māgi cabenā.
सिबि दधीचि बलि जो कछु भाषा । तनु धनु तजेउ बचन पनु राखा ॥
sibi dadhīci bali jo kachu bhāṣā, tanu dhanu tajeu bacana panu rākhā.
अति कटु बचन कहति कैकेई । मानहुँ लोन जरे पर देई ॥
ati kaṭu bacana kahati kaikeī, mānahuṁ lona jare para deī.

Trans:

In this manner the king burned within himself, and the wicked woman, seeing his evil plight, then began: "What? Then is Bharat not your son too? Is he but a slave even as I am? Bought for price? If my words, thus like arrows, pierce you to the heart, why did you not think before you spoke? Answer now, say either yes or no, most truthful lord of Raghu's truthful line. Refuse me the boon you erst promised, break your word and be publicly disgraced. When you engaged to grant the boon, you were loud in your praises of truth, imagining no doubt that I should ask for a handful of parched grain. When Sivi, Dadhichi and Bālī made a promise, they gave life and wealth to keep their word." Kaekayī's speech was as stinging as salt applied to a burn.

दोहा-dohā:

धरम धुरंधर धीर धरि नयन उघारे रायँ ।
dharama dhuraṁdhara dhīra dhari nayana ughāre rāyaṁ,
सिरु धुनि लीन्हि उसास असि मारेसि मोहि कुठायँ ॥३०॥
siru dhuni līnhi usāsa asi māresi mohi kuṭhāyaṁ. 30.

Trans:

The righteous king took courage and opened his eyes, and beating his head gasped out, "Ah, she has pierced me in the most vital part!"

चौपाई-caupāī:

आगें दीखि जरत रिस भारी । मनहुँ रोष तरवारि उघारी ॥
āgeṁ dīkhi jarata risa bhārī, manahuṁ roṣa taravāri ughārī.
मूठि कुबुद्धि धार निठुराई । धरी कूबरीं सान बनाई ॥
mūṭhi kubuddhi dhārā niṭhurāī, dharī kūbarīṁ sāna banāī.
लखी महीप कराल कठोरा । सत्य कि जीवनु लेइहि मोरा ॥
lakhī mahīpa karāla kaṭhorā, satya ki jīvanu leihi morā.
बोले राउ कठिन करि छाती । बानी सबिनय तासु सोहाती ॥
bole rāu kaṭhina kari chātī, bānī sabinaya tāsu sohātī.
प्रिया बचन कस कहसि कुभाँती । भीर प्रतीति प्रीति करि हाँती ॥
priyā bacana kasa kahasi kubhāṁtī, bhīra pratīti prīti kari hāṁtī.
मोरें भरतु रामु दुइ आँखी । सत्य कहउँ करि संकरू साखी ॥
moreṁ bharatu rāmu dui āṁkhī, satya kahauṁ kari saṁkarū sākhī.
अवसि दूतु मैं पठइब प्राता । ऐहहिं बेगि सुनत दोउ भ्राता ॥
avasi dūtu maiṁ paṭhaiba prātā, aihahiṁ begi sunata dou bhrātā.
सुदिन सोधि सबु साजु सजाई । देउँ भरत कहुँ राजु बजाई ॥
sudina sodhi sabu sāju sajāī, deuṁ bharata kahuṁ rāju bajāī.

Trans:

He saw her standing before him burning with passion, as it were Fury's own sword drawn from the sheath, with ill-counsel for its hilt and cruelty for its sharp edge whetted on the Humpback grindstone. The monarch saw her like a sword terrible and stern, 'She will rob me either of life or honor', he thought. Then steeling his heart he spoke in suppliant tones and endearing terms, "O my beloved, what is this ill word that you have uttered, destructive of all order, confidence, and affection? Bharat and Rāma are my two eyes; I tell you truly and call Shiva as my witness. First thing tomorrow, I will immediately dispatch a messenger at daybreak, and soon as they hear the news both brothers will come back. Then after fixing an auspicious day and making all due preparations I will solemnly confer the kingdom on Bharat.

दोहा-dohā:

लोभु न रामहि राजु कर बहुत भरत पर प्रीति ।
lobhu na rāmahi rāju kara bahuta bharata para prīti,
मैं बड़ छोट बिचारि जियँ करत रहेउँ नृपनीति ॥३१॥
maiṁ baṛa choṭa bicāri jiyaṁ karata raheuṁ nṛpanīti. 31.

Trans:

"Rāma has no greed of empire and is devotedly attached to Bharat; I made my plans according to royal usage, thinking only of their respective ages.

चौपाई-caupāī:

राम सपथ सत कहउँ सुभाऊ । राममातु कछु कहेउ न काऊ ॥
rāma sapatha sata kahauṁ subhāū, rāmamātu kachu kaheu na kāū.
मैं सबु कीन्ह तोहि बिनु पूँछें । तेहि तें परेउ मनोरथु छूछें ॥
maiṁ sabu kīnha tohi binu pūṁcheṁ, tehi teṁ pareu manorathu chūcheṁ.
रिस परिहरू अब मंगल साजू । कछु दिन गएँ भरत जुबराजू ॥
risa pariharū aba maṁgala sājū, kachu dina gaeṁ bharata jubarājū.
एकहि बात मोहि दुखु लागा । बर दूसर असमंजस मागा ॥
ekahi bāta mohi dukhu lāgā, bara dūsara asamaṁjasa māgā.
अजहुँ हृदय जरत तेहि आँचा । रिस परिहास कि साँचेहुँ साँचा ॥
ajahūṁ hṛdaya jarata tehi āṁcā, risa parihāsa ki sāṁcehuṁ sāṁcā.
कहु तजि रोषु राम अपराधू । सबु कोउ कहइ रामु सुठि साधू ॥
kahu taji roṣu rāma aparādhū, sabu kou kahai rāmu suṭhi sādhū.
तुहूँ सराहसि करसि सनेहू । अब सुनि मोहि भयउ संदेहू ॥
tuhūṁ sarāhasi karasi sanehū, aba suni mohi bhayau saṁdehū.
जासु सुभाउ अरिहि अनुकूला । सो किमि करिहि मातु प्रतिकूला ॥
jāsu subhāu arihi anukūlā, so kimi karihi mātu pratikūlā.

Trans:

"I swear by Rāma a hundred times, that his mother never said a word to me on this subject. I arranged it all without asking you, and this is how my scheme has failed. Put away your displeasure, assume a festal garb; yet a few days and Bharat shall be Regent. There was only one thing that pained me, your second petition, really an unreasonable request. Today your bosom burns with unwonted fire; is it anger, or do you jest, or is it all really true? Tell me calmly of Rāma's offence. Everyone says that he is Amiability itself. Even you used to praise and caress him, and I am quite perplexed at what I now hear. His pleasant ways would charm even an enemy; how then can he have vexed his own mother?

दोहा-dohā:

प्रिया हास रिस परिहरहि मागु बिचारि बिबेकु ।
priyā hāsa risa pariharahi māgu bicāri bibeku,
जेहिं देखौं अब नयन भरि भरत राज अभिषेकु ॥३२॥
jehiṁ dekhauṁ aba nayana bhari bharata rāja abhiṣeku. 32.

Trans:

Have done my beloved with this—be it raillery or displeasure; make a just and reasonable request, that I may rejoice in the sight of Bharat's installation.

चौपाई-caupāī:

जिऐ मीन बरू बारि बिहीना । मनि बिनु फनिकु जिऐ दुख दीना ॥
jiai mīna barū bāri bihīnā, mani binu phaniku jiai dukha dīnā.
कहउँ सुभाउ न छलु मन माहीं । जीवनु मोर राम बिनु नाहीं ॥
kahauṁ subhāu na chalu mana māhīṁ, jīvanu mora rāma binu nāhīṁ.
समुझि देखु जियँ प्रिया प्रबीना । जीवनु राम दरस आधीना ॥
samujhi dekhu jiyaṁ priyā prabīnā, jīvanu rāma darasa ādhīnā.
सुनि मृदु बचन कुमति अति जरई । मनहुँ अनल आहुति घृत परई ॥
suni mṛdu bacana kumati ati jaraī, manahuṁ anala āhuti ghṛta paraī.
कहइ करहु किन कोटि उपाया । इहाँ न लागिहि राउरि माया ॥
kahai karahu kina koṭi upāyā, ihāṁ na lāgihi rāuri māyā.
देहु कि लेहु अजसु करि नाहीं । मोहि न बहुत प्रपंच सोहाहीं ॥
dehu ki lehu ajasu kari nāhīṁ, mohi na bahuta prapaṁca sohāhīṁ.
रामु साधु तुम्ह साधु सयाने । राममातु भलि सब पहिचाने ॥
rāmu sādhu tumha sādhu sayāne, rāmamātu bhali saba pahicāne.
जस कौसिलाँ मोर भल ताका । तस फलु उन्हहि देउँ करि साका ॥
jasa kausilāṁ mora bhala tākā, tasa phalu unhahi deuṁ kari sākā.

Trans:

Rather might a fish live out of the water, or a wretched serpent live without its head-jewel—I tell you my true case without any deception—but there is no life for me without Rāma. Consider well, my dear, my prudent wife, my very existence depends upon my seeing Rāma." On hearing this soft speech the wicked woman blazed up like the fire on which has fallen an oblation of butter, "You may devise and carry out any number of plans, but your subterfuges will not avail with me. Either grant my request, or refuse me and be disgraced; I do not want any long discussions. Rāma is good, you too are good and wise, and Rāma's mother, as you have discovered, is also good. The benefit that Kausalyā devised for me is the only fruit that I now in turn give her.

दोहा-dohā:

होत प्रातु मुनिबेष धरि जौं न रामु बन जाहिं ।
hota prātu munibeṣa dhari jauṁ na rāmu bana jāhiṁ,
मोर मरनु राउर अजस नृप समुझिअ मन माहिं ॥ ३३ ॥
mora maranu rāura ajasa nṛpa samujhia mana māhiṁ. 33.

Trans:

At daybreak if Rāma does not assume the hermit's dress and go out into the woods, my death will ensue, O king, and so will your disgrace—be well assured of this."

चौपाई-caupāī:

अस कहि कुटिल भई उठि ठाढ़ी । मानहुँ रोष तरंगिनि बाढ़ी ॥
asa kahi kuṭila bhaī uṭhi ṭhāṛhī, mānahuṁ roṣa taraṁgini bāṛhī.
पाप पहार प्रगट भइ सोई । भरी क्रोध जल जाइ न जोई ॥
pāpa pahāra pragaṭa bhai soī, bharī krodha jala jāi na joī.
दोउ बर कूल कठिन हठ धारा । भवँर कूबरी बचन प्रचारा ॥
dou bara kūla kaṭhina haṭha dhārā, bhavaṁra kūbarī bacana pracārā.
ढाहत भूपरूप तरु मूला । चली बिपति बारिधि अनुकूला ॥
ḍhāhata bhūparūpa taru mūlā, calī bipati bāridhi anukūlā.
लखी नरेस बात फुरि साँची । तिय मिस मीचु सीस पर नाची ॥
lakhī naresa bāta phuri sāṁcī, tiya misa mīcu sīsa para nācī.
गहि पद बिनय कीन्ह बैठारी । जनि दिनकर कुल होसि कुठारी ॥
gahi pada binaya kīnha baiṭhārī, jani dinakara kula hosi kuṭhārī.
मागु माथ अबहीं देउँ तोही । राम बिरहँ जनि मारसि मोही ॥
māgu mātha abahīṁ deuṁ tohī, rāma birahaṁ jani mārasi mohī.
राखु राम कहुँ जेहि तेहि भाँती । नाहिं त जरिहि जनम भरि छाती ॥
rākhu rāma kahuṁ jehi tehi bhāṁtī, nāhiṁ ta jarihi janama bhari chātī.

Trans:

So saying the wretch rose and stood erect, as it were a swollen flood of wrath that had risen in the mountains of sin, turgid with streams of passion, terrible to behold, with the two boons for its banks, her stern obduracy for its currents, with her voluble speech for its eddies—overthrowing the king like some tree torn up by the roots, as it rushed on to the ocean of calamity. The king perceived that it was all true, and that Death, in the garb of a woman, was dancing in triumph upon his head. Humbly he clasped her by the feet and begged her to be seated crying, "Be not the axe to the root of the Solar-Dynasty. Demand of me my head and I will give it at once, but do not kill me by the loss of Rāma. Keep Rāma, be it in any way you will, or your heart will be ill at ease all life long."

दोहा-dohā:

देखी ब्याधि असाध नृपु परेउ धरनि धुनि माथ ।
dekhī byādhi asādha nṛpu pareu dharani dhuni mātha,
कहत परम आरत बचन राम राम रघुनाथ ॥ ३४ ॥
kahata parama ārata bacana rāma rāma raghunātha. 34.

Trans:

Seeing that his disease was incurable, the king fell upon the ground and beat his head, sobbing out in most lamentable tones "O Rāma, Rāma."

चौपाई-caupāī:

ब्याकुल राउ सिथिल सब गाता । करिनि कलपतरु मनहुँ निपाता ॥
byākula rāu sithila saba gātā, karini kalapataru manahuṁ nipātā.
कंठु सूख मुख आव न बानी । जनु पाठीनु दीन बिनु पानी ॥
kaṁṭhu sūkha mukha āva na bānī, janu pāṭhīnu dīna binu pānī.
पुनि कह कटु कठोर कैकेई । मनहुँ घाय महुँ माहुर देई ॥
puni kaha kaṭu kaṭhora kaikeī, manahuṁ ghāya mahuṁ māhura deī.
जौं अंतहुँ अस करतबु रहेऊ । मागु मागु तुम्ह केहिं बल कहेऊ ॥
jauṁ aṁtahuṁ asa karatabu raheū, māgu māgu tumha kehiṁ bala kaheū.
दुइ कि होइ एक समय भुआला । हँसब ठठाइ फुलाउब गाला ॥
dui ki hoi eka samaya bhuālā, haṁsaba ṭhaṭhāi phulāuba gālā.
दानि कहाउब अरु कृपनाई । होइ कि खेम कुसल रौताई ॥
dāni kahāuba aru kṛpanāī, hoi ki khema kusala rautāī.
छाड़हु बचनु कि धीरजु धरहू । जनि अबला जिमि करुना करहू ॥
chāṛahu bacanu ki dhīraju dharahū, jani abalā jimi karunā karahū.
तनु तिय तनय धामु धनु धरनी । सत्यसंध कहुँ तृन सम बरनी ॥
tanu tiya tanaya dhāmu dhanu dharanī, satyasaṁdha kahuṁ tṛna sama baranī.

Trans:

The king's whole body was so broken down by distress that he seemed like the tree of paradise that an elephant had uprooted. His throat was dry, speech failed his lips, like some poor fish deprived of water. Again Kaekayī plied him with biting taunts, infusing as it were poison into his wounds: "If you meant to act thus in the end, what compulsion was there to say 'Ask, ask'? Is it possible, sire, to be two things at once? To laugh and jest—and at the same time mourn; to be called the munificent—and yet be miserly; to live without anxiety—and yet be a king? Either break your word or show more fortitude; be not, like a woman, appeal to compassion. It is said that life, wife, sons, home, wealth, nay the whole world, all is but as a straw compared to the ocean of truth."

दोहा-dohā:

मरम बचन सुनि राउ कह कहु कछु दोषु न तोर ।
marama bacana suni rāu kaha kahu kachu doṣu na tora,
लागेउ तोहि पिसाच जिमि कालु कहावत मोर ॥ ३५ ॥
lāgeu tohi pisāca jimi kālu kahāvata mora. 35.

Trans:

On hearing these fatal words the king exclaimed, "It is no fault of yours; my evil destiny, like some demoniacal delusion, has possessed you and bids you speak.

चौपाई-caupāī:

चहत न भरत भूपतहि भोरें । बिधि बस कुमति बसी जिय तोरें ॥
cahata na bharata bhūpatahi bhoreṁ, bidhi basa kumati basī jiya toreṁ.
सो सबु मोर पाप परिनामू । भयउ कुठाहर जेहिं बिधि बामू ॥
so sabu mora pāpa parināmū, bhayau kuṭhāhara jehiṁ bidhi bāmū.
सुबस बसिहि फिरि अवध सुहाई । सब गुन धाम राम प्रभुताई ॥
subasa basihi phiri avadha suhāī, saba guna dhāma rāma prabhutāī.
करिहहिं भाइ सकल सेवकाई । होइहि तिहुँ पुर राम बड़ाई ॥
karihahiṁ bhāi sakala sevakāī, hoihi tihuṁ pura rāma baṛāī.
तोर कलंकु मोर पछिताऊ । मुएहुँ न मिटिहि न जाइहि काऊ ॥
tora kalaṁku mora pachitāū, muehuṁ na miṭihi na jāihi kāū.
अब तोहि नीक लाग करु सोई । लोचन ओट बैठु मुहु गोई ॥
aba tohi nīka lāga karu soī, locana oṭa baiṭhu muhu goī.
जब लगि जिऔं कहउँ कर जोरी । तब लगि जनि कछु कहसि बहोरी ॥
jaba lagi jiauṁ kahauṁ kara jorī, taba lagi jani kachu kahasi bahorī.
फिरि पछितैहसि अंत अभागी । मारसि गाइ नहारु लागी ॥
phiri pachitaihasi aṁta abhāgī, mārasi gāi nahāru lāgī.

Trans:

Bharat has never dreamed of desiring the royal dignity; but by the decree of fate evil counsel has lodged in your breast. All this is the result of my sins; due to which the tide has turned against me at an inopportune moment. Hereafter beautiful Avadh shall flourish again under the sway of the all-perfect Rāma; all his brethren shall do him service, and his glory shall spread through the three spheres of creation; and your disgrace and my remorse, though we die, shall never be effaced or forgotten. Now do whatever that seemeth to you good, only stay out of my sight and let your face be veiled. With clasped hands I ask but this: speak not to me again so long as I live. You too will repent at the last, O miserable woman, who, for the sake of gut, killed the cow."

दोहा-dohā:

परेउ राउ कहि कोटि बिधि काहे करसि निदानु ।
pareu rāu kahi koṭi bidhi kāhe karasi nidānu,
कपट सयानि न कहति कछु जागति मनहुँ मसानु ॥३६॥
kapaṭa sayāni na kahati kachu jāgati manahuṁ masānu. 36.

Trans:

The king fell to the ground crying again and again, "Why has she wrought this ruin on all?" But the perfidious queen spoke not a word, as though a witch scheming on funeral grounds.

चौपाई-caupāī:

राम राम रट बिकल भुआलू । जनु बिनु पंख बिहंग बेहालू ॥
rāma rāma raṭa bikala bhuālū, janu binu paṁkha bihaṁga behālū.
हृदयँ मनाव भोरु जनि होई । रामहि जाइ कहै जनि कोई ॥
hṛdayaṁ manāva bhoru jani hoī, rāmahi jāi kahai jani koī.
उदउ करहु जनि रबि रघुकुल गुर । अवध बिलोकि सूल होइहि उर ॥
udau karahu jani rabi raghukula gura, avadha biloki sūla hoihi ura.
भूप प्रीति कैकइ कठिनाई । उभय अवधि बिधि रची बनाई ॥
bhūpa prīti kaikai kaṭhināī, ubhaya avadhi bidhi racī banāī.
बिलपत नृपहि भयउ भिनुसारा । बीना बेनु संख धुनि द्वारा ॥
bilapata nṛpahi bhayau bhinusārā, bīnā benu saṁkha dhuni dvārā.
पढ़हिं भाट गुन गावहिं गायक । सुनत नृपहि जनु लागहिं सायक ॥
paṛhahiṁ bhāṭa guna gāvahiṁ gāyaka, sunata nṛpahi janu lāgahiṁ sāyaka.
मंगल सकल सोहाहिं न कैसें । सहगामिनिहि बिभूषन जैसें ॥
maṁgala sakala sohāhiṁ na kaiseṁ, sahagāminihi bibhūṣana jaiseṁ.
तेहिं निसि नीद परी नहिं काहू । राम दरस लालसा उछाहू ॥
tehiṁ nisi nīda parī nahiṁ kāhū, rāma darasa lālasā uchāhū.

Trans:

The king in his distress sobbed out "Rāma, Rāma." He was like some luckless bird clipped of its wings. In his heart he was praying: "May the day never break nor anyone go and tell Rāma. Rise not, great patriarch of the solar race, for at the sight of Avadh your heart will be consumed with anguish." The king's affection and Kaekayī's cruelty were both the most extreme that God could make. While the monarch was yet lamenting, day broke and the music of lute and pipe and conch resounded at his gate. Bards recited his titles, minstrels sung his praises; but like arrows they wounded the king, as he heard them. All tokens of rejoicing pleased him as little as the adornments of a widow who ascends the funeral pile. Meanwhile that night no one had slept from the joyous anticipation of beholding Rāma.

दोहा-dohā:

द्वार भीर सेवक सचिव कहहिं उदित रबि देखि ।
dvāra bhīra sevaka saciva kahahiṁ udita rabi dekhi,
जागेउ अजहुँ न अवधपति कारनु कवनु बिसेषि ॥३७॥
jāgeu ajahuṁ na avadhapati kāranu kavanu biseṣi. 37.

Trans:

At the gate was a crowd of servants and ministers, who exclaimed as they beheld the risen sun, "What can be the reason why today of all days our lord awaketh not?

चौपाई-caupāī:

पछिले पहर भूपु नित जागा । आजु हमहि बड़ अचरजु लागा ॥
pachile pahara bhūpu nita jāgā, āju hamahi baṛa acaraju lāgā.
जाहु सुमंत्र जगावहु जाई । कीजिअ काजु रजायसु पाई ॥
jāhu sumaṁtra jagāvahu jāī, kījia kāju rajāyasu pāī.
गए सुमंत्रु तब राउर माहीं । देखि भयावन जात डेराहीं ॥
gae sumaṁtru taba rāura māhīṁ, dekhi bhayāvana jāta ḍerāhīṁ.
धाइ खाइ जनु जाइ न हेरा । मानहुँ बिपति बिषाद बसेरा ॥
dhāi khāi janu jāi na herā, mānahuṁ bipati biṣāda baserā.
पूछें कोउ न ऊतरु देई । गए जेहिं भवन भूप कैकेई ॥
pūcheṁ kou na ūtaru deī, gae jehiṁ bhavana bhūpa kaikeī.
कहि जयजीव बैठ सिरु नाई । देखि भूप गति गयउ सुखाई ॥
kahi jayajīva baiṭha siru nāī, dekhi bhūpa gati gayau sukhāī.
सोच बिकल बिबरन महि परेऊ । मानहुँ कमल मूलु परिहरेऊ ॥
soca bikala bibarana mahi pareū, mānahuṁ kamala mūlu parihareū.
सचिउ सभीत सकइ नहिं पूछी । बोली असुभ भरी सुभ छूछी ॥
saciu sabhīta sakai nahiṁ pūchī, bolī asubha bharī subha chūchī.

Trans:

He was always wont to wake at the last watch; today it strikes us as very strange. Go Sumant and rouse him and obtain the royal order to commence the work." Sumant entered the palace, but as he passed on he was struck with fear and dismay at its appearance, as though some terrible monster were about to spring and devour him. It seemed the very home of calamity and distress. Asking, but with no one to answer him, he came to the apartment where were the king and Kaekayī. With the salutation "Live forever" he bowed the head and sat down. On beholding the king's condition he was much distressed, for he was fallen on the ground crushed and colorless, like a lotus broken off from its root. The terrified minister could ask no question; but she, full of evil and void of all good, answered and said:

दोहा-dohā:

परी न राजहि नीद निसि हेतु जान जगदीसु ।
parī na rājahi nīda nisi hetu jāna jagadīsu,
रामु रामु रटि भोरु किय कहइ न मरमु महीसु ॥३८॥
rāmu rāmu raṭi bhoru kiya kahai na maramu mahīsu. 38.

Trans:

"The king has not slept all night; god knows why. He has done nothing but mutter 'Rāma, Rāma,' even till daybreak; but he has not told me the reason.

चौपाई-caupāī:

आनहु रामहि बेगि बोलाई । समाचार तब पूँछेहु आई ॥
ānahu rāmahi begi bolāī, samācāra taba pūṁchehu āī.
चलेउ सुमंत्रु राय रूख जानी । लखी कुचालि कीन्हि कछु रानी ॥
caleu sumaṁtru rāya rūkha jānī, lakhī kucāli kīnhi kachu rānī.
सोच बिकल मग परइ न पाऊ । रामहि बोलि कहिहि का राऊ ॥
soca bikala maga parai na pāū, rāmahi boli kahihi kā rāū.
उर धरि धीरजु गयउ दुआरें । पूँछहिं सकल देखि मनु मारें ॥
ura dhari dhīraju gayau duāreṁ, pūṁchahiṁ sakala dekhi manu māreṁ.
समाधानु करि सो सबही का । गयउ जहाँ दिनकर कुल टीका ॥
samādhānu kari so sabahī kā, gayau jahāṁ dinakara kula ṭīkā.
राम सुमंत्रहि आवत देखा । आदरु कीन्ह पिता सम लेखा ॥
rāma sumaṁtrahi āvata dekhā, ādaru kīnha pitā sama lekhā.
निरखि बदनु कहि भूप रजाई । रघुकुलदीपहि चलेउ लेवाई ॥
nirakhi badanu kahi bhūpa rajāī, raghukuladīpahi caleu levāī.
रामु कुभाँति सचिव सँग जाहीं । देखि लोग जहँ तहँ बिलखाहीं ॥
rāmu kubhāṁti saciva saṁga jāhīṁ, dekhi loga jahaṁ tahaṁ bilakhāhīṁ.

Trans:

Go at once and send Rāma here; and when you come back you can ask what the matter is." Perceiving it to be the king's wish, Sumant went; but he saw that the queen had formed some evil design. So anxious was he that his feet scarcely touched the ground as he wondered to himself, "What can the king have to say to Rāma?" Composing himself, he reached the gate. When all observed his sadness and asked the cause, he reassured them and proceeded to the prince's abode. When Rāma saw Sumant coming he received him with the same honor that he would have shown to his own father. Looking him in the face, he declared the king's commands and returned with him. Remarking at the state of disorder in which Rāma accompanied the minister, the people began to be a little anxious.

दोहा-dohā:

जाइ दीख रघुबंसमनि नरपति निपट कुसाजु ।
jāi dīkha raghubaṁsamani narapati nipaṭa kusāju,
सहमि परेउ लखि सिंघिनिहि मनहुँ बृद्ध गजराजु ॥३९॥
sahami pareu lakhi siṁghinihi manahuṁ bṛddha gajarāju. 39.

Trans:

When the jewel of Raghu's race came, he beheld the king's miserable condition—like some aged and pain-stricken elephant in the power of a tigress.

चौपाई-caupāī:

सूखहिं अधर जरइ सबु अंगू । मनहुँ दीन मनिहीन भुअंगू ॥
sūkhahiṁ adhara jarai sabu aṁgū, manahuṁ dīna manihīna bhuaṁgū.
सरुष समीप दीखि कैकेई । मानहुँ मीचु घरीं गनि लेई ॥
saruṣa samīpa dīkhi kaikeī, mānahuṁ mīcu gharīṁ gani leī.
करुनामय मृदु राम सुभाऊ । प्रथम दीख दुखु सुना न काऊ ॥
karunāmaya mṛdu rāma subhāū, prathama dīkha dukhu sunā na kāū.
तदपि धीर धरि समउ बिचारी । पूँछी मधुर बचन महतारी ॥
tadapi dhīra dhari samau bicārī, pūṁchī madhura bacana mahatārī.
मोहि कहु मातु तात दुख कारन । करिअ जतन जेहिं होइ निवारन ॥
mohi kahu mātu tāta dukha kārana, karia jatana jehiṁ hoi nivārana.
सुनहु राम सबु कारन एहू । राजहि तुम्ह पर बहुत सनेहू ॥
sunahu rāma sabu kārana ehū, rājahi tumha para bahuta sanehū.
देन कहेन्हि मोहि दुइ बरदाना । मागेउँ जो कछु मोहि सोहाना ॥
dena kahenhi mohi dui baradānā, māgeuṁ jo kachu mohi sohānā.
सो सुनि भयउ भूप उर सोचू । छाड़ि न सकहिं तुम्हार सँकोचू ॥
so suni bhayau bhūpa ura socū, chāṛi na sakahiṁ tumhāra saṁkocū.

Trans:

His lips were parched and his body all aflame, like a poor snake that has been robbed of the jewel in its head. The furious Kaekayī was near him—like death waiting and counting the minutes. Raghunāth, who was compassionate and amiable by nature, for the first time saw sorrow; he had never before even heard of its name. He then composed himself, as the occasion required, and in pleasant tones asked his mother, "Tell me, mother, the cause of my father's distress, that I may endeavor to put an end to it." "Listen, Rāma; the sole cause is this: the king is very fond of you; he has promised to grant me two boons, and I have asked for what I wanted; but he is disturbed on hearing them and cannot get rid of a scruple on your account.

दोहा-dohā:

सुत सनेहु इत बचनु उत संकट परेउ नरेसु ।
suta sanehu ita bacanu uta saṁkaṭa pareu naresu,
सकहु न आयसु धरहु सिर मेटहु कठिन कलेसु ॥४०॥
sakahu na āyasu dharahu sira meṭahu kaṭhina kalesu. 40.

Trans:

"On the one side is his love for his son; on the other his promise; he is thus in a strait. If it lies in your power, be obedient to his commands and thereby terminate his misery."

चौपाई-caupāī:

निधरक बैठि कहइ कटु बानी । सुनत कठिनता अति अकुलानी ॥
nidharaka baiṭhi kahai kaṭu bānī, sunata kaṭhinatā ati akulānī.
जीभ कमान बचन सर नाना । मनहुँ महिप मृदु लच्छ समाना ॥
jībha kamāna bacana sara nānā, manahuṁ mahipa mṛdu laccha samānā.
जनु कठोरपनु धरें सरीरू । सिखइ धनुषबिद्या बर बीरू ॥
janu kaṭhorapanu dhareṁ sarīrū, sikhai dhanuṣabidyā bara bīrū.
सबु प्रसंगु रघुपतिहि सुनाई । बैठि मनहुँ तनु धरि निठुराई ॥
sabu prasaṁgu raghupatihi sunāī, baiṭhi manahuṁ tanu dhari niṭhurāī.
मन मुसुकाइ भानुकुल भानू । रामु सहज आनंद निधानू ॥
mana musukāi bhānukula bhānū, rāmu sahaja ānaṁda nidhānū.
बोले बचन बिगत सब दूषन । मृदु मंजुल जनु बाग बिभूषन ॥
bole bacana bigata saba dūṣana, mṛdu maṁjula janu bāga bibhūṣana.
सुनु जननी सोइ सुतु बड़भागी । जो पितु मातु बचन अनुरागी ॥
sunu jananī soi sutu baṛabhāgī, jo pitu mātu bacana anurāgī.
तनय मातु पितु तोषनिहारा । दुर्लभ जननि सकल संसारा ॥
tanaya mātu pitu toṣanihārā, durlabha janani sakala saṁsārā.

Trans:

She sat and spoke these stinging words so composedly that Cruelty itself was disturbed to hear her. From the bow of her tongue she shot forth the arrows of her speech against the king as it were some yielding target; as though Obduracy had taken form and become a bold and practiced archer. Sitting like the very incarnation of heartlessness, she expounded to Raghupatī the whole incident. Rāma, the sun of the solar race, the fountain of every joy, smiled inwardly and replied in guileless terms, so soft and gracious that they seemed the very jewels of the goddess of speech, "Hearken, mother; blessed is the son who obeys his parent's commands. A son who cherishes his father and mother is not often found in the world.

दोहा-dohā:

मुनिगन मिलनु बिसेषि बन सबहि भाँति हित मोर ।
munigana milanu biseṣi bana sabahi bhāṁti hita mora,
तेहि महँ पितु आयसु बहुरि संमत जननी तोर ॥४१॥
tehi mahaṁ pitu āyasu bahuri saṁmata jananī tora. 41.

Trans:

I have a particular wish to join the hermits is the woods, and now there is also my father's order and your approval, O mother.

चौपाई-caupāī:

भरतु प्रानप्रिय पावहिं राजू । बिधि सब बिधि मोहि सनमुख आजू ॥
bharatu prānapriya pāvahiṁ rājū, bidhi saba bidhi mohi sanamukha ājū.
जौं न जाउँ बन ऐसेहु काजा । प्रथम गनिअ मोहि मूढ़ समाजा ॥
jauṁ na jāuṁ bana aisehu kājā, prathama gania mohi mūṛha samājā.
सेवहिं अरँडु कलपतरु त्यागी । परिहरि अमृत लेहिं बिषु मागी ॥
sevahiṁ araṁḍu kalapataru tyāgī, parihari amṛta lehiṁ biṣu māgī.
तेउ न पाइ अस समउ चुकाहीं । देखु बिचारि मातु मन माहीं ॥
teu na pāi asa samau cukāhīṁ, dekhu bicāri mātu mana māhīṁ.
अंब एक दुखु मोहि बिसेषी । निपट बिकल नरनायकु देखी ॥
aṁba eka dukhu mohi biseṣī, nipaṭa bikala naranāyaku dekhī.
थोरिहिं बात पितहि दुख भारी । होति प्रतीति न मोहि महतारी ॥
thorihiṁ bāta pitahi dukha bhārī, hoti pratīti na mohi mahatārī.
राउ धीर गुन उदधि अगाधू । भा मोहि तें कछु बड़ अपराधू ॥
rāu dhīra guna udadhi agādhū, bhā mohi teṁ kachu baṛa aparādhū.
जातें मोहि न कहत कछु राऊ । मोरि सपथ तोहि कहु सतिभाऊ ॥
jāteṁ mohi na kahata kachu rāū, mori sapatha tohi kahu satibhāū.

Trans:

Bharat, moreover, whom I love as myself, will obtain the kingdom. In every which way God favors me today. If I go not to the woods under these circumstances, then reckon me first in any gathering of fools. They who desert the tree of paradise to tend a castor-oil plant, or refuse ambrosia to ask for poison, having once lost their chance, will never get it again; see, mother, and ponder this in your heart. One special anxiety still remains, when I see the king so exceedingly disturbed: I cannot understand, mother, how my father can be so much pained by such a trifling matter. He is stout-hearted and a fathomless ocean of piety: there must have been some great offence on my part, that he will not say a word to me: I adjure you to tell me the truth."

दोहा-dohā:

सहज सरल रघुबर बचन कुमति कुटिल करि जान ।
sahaja sarala raghubara bacana kumati kuṭila kari jāna,
चलइ जोंक जल बक्रगति जद्यपि सलिलु समान ॥४२॥
calai joṁka jala bakragati jadyapi salilu samāna. 42.

Trans:

Though Raghubar's words were as straightforward as possible the wicked queen gave them a perverse twist; like a leech, which must always move crookedly, however smooth the water be.

चौपाई-caupāī:

रहसी रानि राम रुख पाई । बोली कपट सनेहु जनाई ॥
rahasī rāni rāma rukha pāī, bolī kapaṭa sanehu janāī.
सपथ तुम्हार भरत कै आना । हेतु न दूसर मैं कछु जाना ॥
sapatha tumhāra bharata kai ānā, hetu na dūsara maiṁ kachu jānā.
तुम्ह अपराध जोगु नहिं ताता । जननी जनक बंधु सुखदाता ॥
tumha aparādha jogu nahiṁ tātā, jananī janaka baṁdhu sukhadātā.
राम सत्य सबु जो कछु कहहू । तुम्ह पितु मातु बचन रत अहहू ॥
rāma satya sabu jo kachu kahahū, tumha pitu mātu bacana rata ahahū.
पितहि बुझाइ कहहु बलि सोई । चौथेंपन जेहिं अजसु न होई ॥
pitahi bujhāi kahahu bali soī, cauthempana jehiṁ ajasu na hoī.
तुम्ह सम सुअन सुकृत जेहिं दीन्हे । उचित न तासु निरादरु कीन्हे ॥
tumha sama suana sukṛta jehiṁ dīnhe, ucita na tāsu nirādaru kīnhe.
लागहिं कुमुख बचन सुभ कैसे । मगहँ गयादिक तीरथ जैसे ॥
lāgahiṁ kumukha bacana subha kaise, magahaṁ gayādika tīratha jaise.
रामहि मातु बचन सब भाए । जिमि सुरसरि गत सलिल सुहाए ॥
rāmahi mātu bacana saba bhāe, jimi surasari gata salila suhāe.

Trans:

Seeing Rāma's readiness, the queen smiled and said with much show of false affection, "I swear by yourself and Bharat, there is no other cause that I know of. There is no room for fault in you, my son, who confer such happiness both on your parents and your brothers. All that you say, Rāma, is true; you are devoted to the wishes of your father and mother. Remonstrate then solemnly with your sire that he incur not sin and disgrace in his old age. Having been blessed with a son like you, he cannot properly disregard your advice." These polite words adorned her detestable mouth, even as sacred spots like Gayā beautify the accursed land of Magadha. All these words from His stepmother sounded pleasant to Rāma in the same way as waters of all kinds are hallowed through their confluence with the holy Gangā.

दोहा-dohā:

गइ मुरुछा रामहि सुमिरि नृप फिरि करवट लीन्ह ।
gai muruchā rāmahi sumiri nṛpa phiri karavaṭa līnha,
सचिव राम आगमन कहि बिनय समय सम कीन्ह ॥४३॥
saciva rāma āgamana kahi binaya samaya sama kīnha. 43.

Trans:

At the remembrance of Rāma, the king's swoon left him and he turned on his side. Taking advantage of the opportunity, the minister humbly informed him of Rāma's arrival.

चौपाई-caupāī:

अवनिप अकनि रामु पगु धारे । धरि धीरजु तब नयन उघारे ॥
avanipa akani rāmu pagu dhāre, dhari dhīraju taba nayana ughāre.
सचिवँ सँभारि राउ बैठारे । चरन परत नृप रामु निहारे ॥
sacivaṁ saṁbhāri rāu baiṭhāre, carana parata nṛpa rāmu nihāre.
लिए सनेह बिकल उर लाई । गै मनि मनहुँ फनिक फिरि पाई ॥
lie saneha bikala ura lāī, gai mani manahuṁ phanika phiri pāī.
रामहि चितइ रहेउ नरनाहू । चला बिलोचन बारि प्रबाहू ॥
rāmahi citai raheu naranāhū, calā bilocana bāri prabāhū.
सोक बिबस कछु कहै न पारा । हृदयँ लगावत बारहिं बारा ॥
soka bibasa kachu kahai na pārā, hṛdayaṁ lagāvata bārahiṁ bārā.
बिधिहि मनाव राउ मन माहीं । जेहिं रघुनाथ न कानन जाहीं ॥
bidhihi manāva rāu mana māhīṁ, jehiṁ raghunātha na kānana jāhīṁ.
सुमिरि महेसहि कहइ निहोरी । बिनती सुनहु सदासिव मोरी ॥
sumiri mahesahi kahai nihorī, binatī sunahu sadāsiva morī.
आसुतोष तुम्ह अवढर दानी । आरति हरहु दीन जनु जानी ॥
āsutoṣa tumha avaḍhara dānī, ārati harahu dīna janu jānī.

Trans:

When the king heard that Rāma had come he summoned up courage and opened his eyes. The minister supported his king to a seat; and the king saw Rāma falling at his feet. In an agony of affection, he clasped him to his bosom, like a snake that has recovered the jewel it had lost. As the monarch continued gazing upon Rāma, a flood of tears came into his eyes; but in his sore distress he couldn't utter any words—only again and again he pressed him to his heart. Inwardly he was praying: may God that Raghunāth is not banished to the woods; and remembering Mahādev humbly begged: "Immortal Shiva, hear my petition; thou art easily satisfied, O compassionate and generous; recognize then in me a poor suppliant and remove my distress.

दोहा-dohā:

तुम्ह प्रेरक सब के हृदयँ सो मति रामहि देहु ।
tumha preraka saba ke hṛdayaṁ so mati rāmahi dehu,
बचनु मोर तजि रहहिं घर परिहरि सीलु सनेहु ॥४४॥
bacanu mora taji rahahiṁ ghara parihari sīlu sanehu. 44.

Trans:

As thou directest the hearts of all, give Rāma the sense to disregard my words and stay at home, forgetful for once of his filial affection.

चौपाई-caupāī:

अजसु होउ जग सुजसु नसाऊ । नरक परौं बरु सुरपुरु जाऊ ॥
ajasu hou jaga sujasu nasāū, naraka paraum̐ baru surapuru jāū.
सब दुख दुसह सहावहु मोही । लोचन ओट रामु जनि होंही ॥
saba dukha dusaha sahāvahu mohī, locana oṭa rāmu jani hoṁhī.
अस मन गुनइ राउ नहिं बोला । पीपर पात सरिस मनु डोला ॥
asa mana gunai rāu nahiṁ bolā, pīpara pāta sarisa manu ḍolā.
रघुपति पितहि प्रेमबस जानी । पुनि कछु कहिहि मातु अनुमानी ॥
raghupati pitahi premabasa jānī, puni kachu kahihi mātu anumānī.
देस काल अवसर अनुसारी । बोले बचन बिनीत बिचारी ॥
desa kāla avasara anusārī, bole bacana binīta bicārī.
तात कहउँ कछु करउँ ढिठाई । अनुचितु छमब जानि लरिकाई ॥
tāta kahauṁ kachu karauṁ ḍhiṭhāī, anucitu chamaba jāni larikāī.
अति लघु बात लागि दुखु पावा । काहुँ न मोहि कहि प्रथम जनावा ॥
ati laghu bāta lāgi dukhu pāvā, kāhuṁ na mohi kahi prathama janāvā.
देखि गोसाइँहि पूँछिउँ माता । सुनि प्रसंगु भए सीतल गाता ॥
dekhi gosāiṁhi pūṁchiuṁ mātā, suni prasaṁgu bhae sītala gātā.

Trans:

Welcome is disgrace, and let perish my good name; may I sink into Hell rather than mount to Heaven; let me support the most intolerable pain, but let not Rāma be taken away from my sight." Thinking thus to himself, the king spoke not a word, while his soul quivered like a *Peepul* leaf. Perceiving his father to be thus overpowered with love, Raghupatī spoke again with a view to his mother, in modest and thoughtful phrase, as the place, the time, and the circumstance demanded, "Father, if I speak a little willfully, forgive the offence by reason of my childish years. You are troubled about a very little matter; why did you not speak and let me know of this at the very first? After seeing you, sire, I questioned my mother, and on hearing her account my fear subsided.

दोहा-dohā:

मंगल समय सनेह बस सोच परिहरिअ तात ।
maṁgala samaya saneha basa soca parihariа tāta,
आयसु देइअ हरषि हियँ कहि पुलके प्रभु गात ॥ ४५ ॥
āyasu deia haraṣi hiyaṁ kahi pulake prabhu gāta. 45.

Trans:

Put away, O father, the anxiety which at this time of rejoicing your affection has caused you, and give me your commands," so spoke the Lord with heartfelt joy and a body quivering with emotion.

चौपाई-caupāī:

धन्य जनमु जगतीतल तासू । पितहि प्रमोदु चरित सुनि जासू ॥
dhanya janamu jagatītala tāsū, pitahi pramodu carita suni jāsū.
चारि पदारथ करतल ताकें । प्रिय पितु मातु प्रान सम जाकें ॥
cāri padāratha karatala tākeṁ, priya pitu mātu prāna sama jākeṁ.
आयसु पालि जनम फलु पाई । ऐहउँ बेगिहिं होउ रजाई ॥
āyasu pāli janama phalu pāī, aihauṁ begihiṁ hou rajāī.
बिदा मातु सन आवउँ मागी । चलिहउँ बनहि बहुरि पग लागी ॥
bidā mātu sana āvauṁ māgī, calihauṁ banahi bahuri paga lāgī.
अस कहि राम गवनु तब कीन्हा । भूप सोक बस उतरु न दीन्हा ॥
asa kahi rāma gavanu taba kīnhā, bhūpa soka basa utaru na dīnhā.
नगर ब्यापि गइ बात सुतीछी । छुअत चढ़ी जनु सब तन बीछी ॥
nagara byāpi gai bāta sutīchī, chuata caṛhī janu saba tana bīchī.
सुनि भए बिकल सकल नर नारी । बेलि बिटप जिमि देखि दवारी ॥
suni bhae bikala sakala nara nārī, beli biṭapa jimi dekhi davārī.
जो जहँ सुनइ धुनइ सिरु सोई । बड़ बिषादु नहिं धीरजु होई ॥
jo jahaṁ sunai dhunai siru soī, baṛa biṣādu nahiṁ dhīraju hoī.

Trans:

"Blessed is that birth into the world—whose father rejoices to hear his deeds. He has in his hand all the four rewards of life, who holds his parents dear as his own life. By obeying your orders, I attain to the aim of my existence. With your permission let me return after taking leave of my mother, and then I will throw myself once more at your feet and start for the woods," Having thus spoken, Rāma departed, while the king in his anguish answered not a word. The bitter news spread through the city, like the sting of a scorpion which at once affects the entire body. Every man and woman that heard it was as wretched as the creeper and bush when the forest is on fire. Wherever this was told, everyone beat their head; the grief was too great to be endured.

दोहा-dohā:

मुख सुखाहिं लोचन स्रवहिं सोकु न हृदयँ समाइ ।
mukha sukhāhiṁ locana sravahiṁ soku na hṛdayaṁ samāi,
मनहुँ करुन रस कटकई उतरी अवध बजाइ ॥ ४६ ॥
manahuṁ karuna rasa kaṭakaī utarī avadha bajāi. 46.

Trans:

Their lips were parched, their eyes streamed, their heart could not contain their sorrow. It seemed as though the Pathos, in battle array and with beats of drum, had marched into Avadh and taken up abode there.

चौपाई-caupāī:

मिलेहि माझ बिधि बात बेगारी । जहँ तहँ देहिं कैकइहि गारी ॥
milehi mājha bidhi bāta begārī, jahaṁ tahaṁ dehiṁ kaikahi gārī.
एहि पापिनिहि बूझि का परेऊ । छाइ भवन पर पावकु धरेऊ ॥
ehi pāpinihi būjhi kā pareū, chāi bhavana para pāvaku dhareū.
निज कर नयन काढ़ि चह दीखा । डारि सुधा बिषु चाहत चीखा ॥
nija kara nayana kāṛhi caha dīkhā, ḍāri sudhā biṣu cāhata cīkhā.
कुटिल कठोर कुबुद्धि अभागी । भइ रघुबंस बेनु बन आगी ॥
kuṭila kaṭhora kubuddhi abhāgī, bhai raghubaṁsa benu bana āgī.
पालव बैठि पेड़ु एहिं काटा । सुख महुँ सोक ठाटु धरि ठाटा ॥
pālava baiṭhi peṛu ehiṁ kāṭā, sukha mahuṁ soka ṭhāṭu dhari ṭhāṭā.
सदा रामु एहि प्रान समाना । कारन कवन कुटिलपनु ठाना ॥
sadā rāmu ehi prāna samānā, kārana kavana kuṭilapanu ṭhānā.
सत्य कहहिं कबि नारि सुभाऊ । सब बिधि अगहु अगाध दुराऊ ॥
satya kahahiṁ kabi nāri subhāū, saba bidhi agahu agādha durāū.
निज प्रतिबिंबु बरुकु गहि जाई । जानि न जाइ नारि गति भाई ॥
nija pratibiṁbu baruku gahi jāī, jāni na jāi nāri gati bhāī.

Trans:

"It was a well-contrived plan, but god has spoilt it." In this fashion they kept abusing Kaekayī. "What could this wicked woman mean by thus setting fire to a new-thatched house? Who tears out her eyes with own hands, and yet wishes to see? Who throws away ambrosia and prefers the taste of poison—cruel, stubborn, demented wretch, the very fire among the reeds of Raghu's line? Who sitting on a branch of the tree has hacked down the stem; and in the midst of joy has introduced this tragedy? Rāma used ever to be dear to her as life; for what reason has she now taken to such perversity? The poets say truly that a woman's mind is altogether inscrutable, unfathomable, and beyond comprehension. Sooner may a man catch his own reflection than know the ways of a woman.

दोहा-dohā:

काह न पावकु जारि सक का न समुद्र समाइ ।
kāha na pāvaku jāri saka kā na samudra samāi,
का न करै अबला प्रबल केहि जग कालु न खाइ ॥ ४७ ॥
kā na karai abalā prabala kehi jaga kālu na khāi. 47.

Trans:

What is there that fire will not burn? What is there that ocean cannot hold? What cannot a woman do in her strength? What is there in the world that death does not devour?'

चौपाई-caupāī:

का सुनाइ बिधि काह सुनावा । का देखाइ चह काह देखावा ॥
kā sunāi bidhi kāha sunāvā, kā dekhāi caha kāha dekhāvā.
एक कहहिं भल भूप न कीन्हा । बरु बिचारि नहिं कुमतिहि दीन्हा ॥
eka kahahiṁ bhala bhūpa na kīnhā, baru bicāri nahiṁ kumatihi dīnhā.
जो हठि भयउ सकल दुख भाजनु । अबला बिबस ग्यानु गुनु गा जनु ॥
jo haṭhi bhayau sakala dukha bhājanu, abalā bibasa gyānu gunu gā janu.
एक धरम परमिति पहिचाने । नृपहि दोसु नहिं देहिं सयाने ॥
eka dharama paramiti pahicāne, nṛpahi dosu nahiṁ dehiṁ sayāne.
सिबि दधीचि हरिचंद कहानी । एक एक सन कहहिं बखानी ॥
sibi dadhīci haricaṁda kahānī, eka eka sana kahahiṁ bakhānī.
एक भरत कर संमत कहहीं । एक उदास भायँ सुनि रहहीं ॥
eka bharata kara saṁmata kahahīṁ, eka udāsa bhāyaṁ suni rahahīṁ.
कान मूदि कर रद गहि जीहा । एक कहहिं यह बात अलीहा ॥
kāna mūdi kara rada gahi jīhā, eka kahahiṁ yaha bāta alīhā.
सुकृत जाहिं अस कहत तुम्हारे । रामु भरत कहुँ प्रानपिआरे ॥
sukṛta jāhiṁ asa kahata tumhāre, rāmu bharata kahuṁ prānapiāre.

Trans:

"God first ordained one thing, but now ordains something quite different, and what he would show us now is the very reverse of what he showed us then." Said another, "The king has not done well, and without consideration has granted the wicked woman her request. He has willfully brought all this misery upon himself, and by yielding to a woman has lost all good sense and discretion." Another wisely recognized the king's supreme virtue and would not blame him, as they repeated to one another the legends of Sivi, Dadhichi, and Harish-chandra. One suggested Bharat's connivance, another was distressed at the mention of such a thing; while a third stopping his ears with his hands and biting his tongue exclaimed, "Such words are false; you damn yourself by saying such things. Bharat is Rāma's dearest, very own.

दोहा-dohā:

चंदु चवै बरु अनल कन सुधा होइ बिषतूल ।
caṁdu cavai baru anala kana sudhā hoi biṣatūla,
सपनेहुँ कबहुँ न करहिं किछु भरतु राम प्रतिकूल ॥४८॥
sapanehum̐ kabahum̐ na karahiṁ kichu bharatu rāma pratikūla. 48.

Trans:

Sooner shall the moon rain sparks of fire, or ambrosia have the same effect as poison, than Bharat ever dream of doing anything opposed to Rāma."

चौपाई-caupāī:

एक बिधातहि दूषनु देहीं । सुधा देखाइ दीन्ह बिषु जेहीं ॥
eka bidhātahi dūṣanu dehīṁ, sudhā dekhāi dīnha biṣu jehīṁ.
खरभरु नगर सोचु सब काहू । दुसह दाहु उर मिटा उछाहू ॥
kharabharu nagara socu saba kāhū, dusaha dāhu ura miṭā uchāhū.
बिप्रबधू कुलमान्य जठेरी । जे प्रिय परम कैकई केरी ॥
biprabadhū kulamānya jaṭherī, je priya parama kaikaī kerī.
लगीं देन सिख सीलु सराही । बचन बानसम लागहिं ताही ॥
lagīṁ dena sikha sīlu sarāhī, bacana bānasama lāgahiṁ tāhī.
भरतु न मोहि प्रिय राम समाना । सदा कहहु यहु सबु जगु जाना ॥
bharatu na mohi priya rāma samānā, sadā kahahu yahu sabu jagu jānā.
करहु राम पर सहज सनेहू । केहिं अपराध आजु बनु देहू ॥
karahu rāma para sahaja sanehū, kehiṁ aparādha āju banu dehū.
कबहुँ न कियहु सवति आरेसू । प्रीति प्रतीति जान सबु देसू ॥
kabahum̐ na kiyahu savati āresū, prīti pratīti jāna sabu desū.
कौसल्याँ अब काह बिगारा । तुम्ह जेहि लागि बज्र पुर पारा ॥
kausalyām̐ aba kāha bigārā, tumha jehi lāgi bajra pura pārā.

Trans:

Some reproached the Creator, who had promised ambrosia but given poison. The whole city was agitated and everyone so sad that the intolerable pain in their heart utterly effaced all the previous rejoicings. The venerable and high-born Brahmin matrons, who were Kaekayī's chief friends, began to give her advice, and to praise her good disposition; though their words pierced her heart like arrows, "You have always said, as everyone knows, that Bharat was not so dear to you as Rāma; show him then your wonted affection. For what offence do you now banish him to the woods? You have never shown any jealousy of the rival queens; your love and confidence in them were known throughout the land. What has Kausalyā done wrong now that you should launch this thunderbolt against the kingdom?

दोहा-dohā:

सीय कि पिय सँगु परिहरिहि लखनु कि रहिहहिं धाम ।
sīya ki piya saṁgu pariharihi lakhanu ki rahihahiṁ dhāma,
राजु कि भूँजब भरत पुर नृपु कि जिइहि बिनु राम ॥४९॥
rāju ki bhūm̐jaba bharata pura nṛpu ki jiihi binu rāma. 49.

Trans:

What! Will Sītā desert her spouse? Or Lakshman remain here at home? Will Bharat enjoy the dominion of the state? Or the king survive without Rāma?

चौपाई-caupāī:

अस बिचारि उर छाड़हु कोहू । सोक कलंक कोठि जनि होहू ॥
asa bicāri ura chāṛahu kohū, soka kalaṁka koṭhi jani hohū.
भरतहि अवसि देहु जुबराजू । कानन काह राम कर काजू ॥
bharatahi avasi dehu jubarājū, kānana kāha rāma kara kājū.
नाहिन रामु राज के भूखे । धरम धुरीन बिषय रस रूखे ॥
nāhina rāmu rāja ke bhūkhe, dharama dhurīna biṣaya rasa rūkhe.
गुर गृह बसहुँ रामु तजि गेहू । नृप सन अस बरु दूसर लेहू ॥
gura gṛha basahum̐ rāmu taji gehū, nṛpa sana asa baru dūsara lehū.
जौं नहिं लगिहहु कहें हमारे । नहिं लागिहि कछु हाथ तुम्हारे ॥
jauṁ nahiṁ lagihahu kaheṁ hamāre, nahiṁ lāgihi kachu hātha tumhāre.
जौं परिहास कीन्हि कछु होई । तौ कहि प्रगट जनावहु सोई ॥
jauṁ parihāsa kīnhi kachu hoī, tau kahi pragaṭa janāvahu soī.
राम सरिस सुत कानन जोगू । काह कहिहि सुनि तुम्ह कहुँ लोगू ॥
rāma sarisa suta kānana jogū, kāha kahihi suni tumha kahum̐ logū.
उठहु बेगि सोइ करहु उपाई । जेहि बिधि सोकु कलंकु नसाई ॥
uṭhahu begi soi karahu upāī, jehi bidhi soku kalaṁku nasāī.

Trans:

Reflect upon this and expunge passion from your breast, nor make yourself a stronghold of remorse and disgrace. By all means make Bharat the king's coadjutor; but what need is there for Rāma to be banished to the woods? Rāma is not greedy of royal power; he is righteous and averse to sensual pleasures. Let him leave the palace and go and live with his Gurū; ask this of the king as your second petition. A son like Rāma does not deserve banishment; what will people say to you when they hear of it? If you do not agree to what we tell you, nothing will prosper in your hands. If this is only some jest of yours, speak out clearly and let it be known. Up quickly and devise a plan to avert grief and obloquy.

छंद-chaṁda:

जेहि भाँति सोकु कलंकु जाइ उपाय करि कुल पालही ।
jehi bhām̐ti soku kalaṁku jāi upāya kari kula pālahī,
हठि फेरु रामहि जात बन जनि बात दूसरि चालही ॥
haṭhi pheru rāmahi jāta bana jani bāta dūsari cālahī.
जिमि भानु बिनु दिनु प्रान बिनु तनु चंद बिनु जिमि जामिनी ।
jimi bhānu binu dinu prāna binu tanu caṁda binu jimi jāminī,
तिमि अवध तुलसीदास प्रभु बिनु समुझि धौं जियँ भामिनी ॥
timi avadha tulasīdāsa prabhu binu samujhi dhauṁ jiyam̐ bhāminī.

Trans:

Devise a plan to avert remorse and disgrace and save your family. Forcibly dissuade Rāma from going to the woods, and labor for nothing else. As the day without the sun, as the body without life, as the night without the moon, so is Avadh without the Lord of Tulsīdās; I beg you, lady, to weigh all this."

सोरठा-sorathā:

सखिन्ह सिखावनु दीन्ह सुनत मधुर परिनाम हित ।
sakhinha sikhāvanu dīnha sunata madhura parināma hita,
तेइँ कछु कान न कीन्ह कुटिल प्रबोधी कूबरी ॥५०॥
teim̐ kachu kāna na kīnha kuṭila prabodhī kūbarī. 50.

Trans:

Pleasant to hear and beneficial in its outcome was the advice her friends gave; but she paid no heed to it, having been tutored in villainy by the Humpback.

चौपाई-caupāī:

उतरु न देइ दुसह रिस रूखी । मृगिन्ह चितव जनु बाघिनि भूखी ॥
utaru na dei dusaha risa rūkhī, mṛginha citava janu bāghini bhūkhī.
ब्याधि असाधि जानि तिन्ह त्यागी । चलीं कहत मतिमंद अभागी ॥
byādhi asādhi jāni tinha tyāgī, calīṁ kahata matimaṁda abhāgī.

राजु करत यह दैअँ बिगोई । कीन्हेसि अस जस करइ न कोई ॥
rāju karata yaha daiaṁ bigoī, kīnhesi asa jasa karai na koī.
एहि बिधि बिलपहिं पुर नर नारीं । देहिं कुचालिहि कोटिक गारीं ॥
ehi bidhi bilapahiṁ pura nara nārīṁ, dehiṁ kucālihi koṭika gārīṁ.
जरहिं बिषम जर लेहिं उसासा । कवनि राम बिनु जीवन आसा ॥
jarahiṁ biṣama jara lehiṁ usāsā, kavani rāma binu jīvana āsā.
बिपुल बियोग प्रजा अकुलानी । जनु जलचर गन सूखत पानी ॥
bipula biyoga prajā akulānī, janu jalacara gana sūkhata pānī.
अति बिषाद बस लोग लोगाईं । गए मातु पहिं रामु गोसाईं ॥
ati biṣāda basa loga logāīṁ, gae mātu pahiṁ rāmu gosāīṁ.
मुख प्रसन्न चित चौगुन चाऊ । मिटा सोचु जनि राखै राऊ ॥
mukha prasanna cita cauguna cāū, miṭā socu jani rākhai rāū.

Trans:

She answered not a word but raged with irrepressible fury like a hungry tigress that has spied a deer. Perceiving her disease to be incurable, they left her, saying as they went "Demented wretch! Fate has destroyed her in her pride; she has acted in such a way as no one has ever acted before." Thus all the men and women of the city were lamenting and heaping countless abuse on the wicked queen. Burning with intolerable fever they sob out, 'What hope of life is there without Rāma?' Agonized by his loss, the people were as miserable as creatures of the deep when water fails. Great was the distress of all, be they men or women. Meanwhile, the saintly Rāma went to his mother, with joy on his face and fourfold joy in his soul. The apprehension that the king might detain him was gone.

दोहा-dohā:

नव गयंदु रघुबीर मनु राजु अलान समान ।
nava gayaṁdu raghubīra manu rāju alāna samāna,
छूट जानि बन गवनु सुनि उर अनंदु अधिकान ॥५१॥
chūṭa jāni bana gavanu suni ura anaṁdu adhikāna. 51.

Trans:

The glory of Raghu's line resembled a young elephant that had been fettered with the chains of dominion of kingdom; and the news of banishment was alike the breaking of the chains—at which he rejoices exceedingly.

चौपाई-caupāī:

रघुकुलतिलक जोरि दोउ हाथा । मुदित मातु पद नायउ माथा ॥
raghukulatilaka jori dou hāthā, mudita mātu pada nāyau māthā.
दीन्हि असीस लाइ उर लीन्हे । भूषन बसन निछावरि कीन्हे ॥
dīnhi asīsa lāi ura līnhe, bhūṣana basana nichāvari kīnhe.
बार बार मुख चुंबति माता । नयन नेह जलु पुलकित गाता ॥
bāra bāra mukha cuṁbati mātā, nayana neha jalu pulakita gātā.
गोद राखि पुनि हृदयँ लगाए । स्त्रवत प्रेमरस पयद सुहाए ॥
goda rākhi puni hṛdayaṁ lagāe, sravata premarasa payada suhāe.
प्रेमु प्रमोदु न कछु कहि जाई । रंक धनद पदबी जनु पाई ॥
premu pramodu na kachu kahi jāī, raṁka dhanada padabī janu pāī.
सादर सुंदर बदनु निहारी । बोली मधुर बचन महतारी ॥
sādara suṁdara badanu nihārī, bolī madhura bacana mahatārī.
कहहु तात जननी बलिहारी । कबहिं लगन मुद मंगलकारी ॥
kahahu tāta jananī balihārī, kabahiṁ lagana muda maṁgalakārī.
सुकृत सील सुख सीवँ सुहाई । जनम लाभ कइ अवधि अघाई ॥
sukṛta sīla sukha sīvaṁ suhāī, janama lābha kai avadhi aghāī.

Trans:

With folded hands the crown of Raghu's line bowed his head blithely at his mother's feet. Unaware of the turn of event, Kausalyā gave him her blessing and clasped him to her bosom, and scattered around him gifts of jewels and raiment. Again and again she kissed his face, with tears of joy in her eyes and her body all quivering with emotion. Then seating him near her she pressed him once more to her heart, while drops of affection trickled from her breasts. Her rapture of love was past all telling, like that of a beggar made all at once rich as Kuber. Tenderly regarding his lovely features, his mother thus addressed him in sweetest tones, "Tell me, my son, I adjure you as your mother, at what time is the happy moment to be? —the hour which is the beautiful culmination of piety, amiability, and good fortune, the highest fruition of our human existence?

दोहा-dohā:

जेहि चाहत नर नारि सब अति आरत एहि भाँति ।
jehi cāhata nara nāri saba ati ārata ehi bhāṁti,
जिमि चातक चातकि तृषित बृष्टि सरद रितु स्वाति ॥५२॥
jimi cātaka cātaki tṛṣita bṛṣṭi sarada ritu svāti. 52.

Trans:

The hour for which people have so long been hungry and anxious—just like a pair of thirsting chātaks, in the season of autumn, for the rainfall of Arcturus?

चौपाई-caupāī:

तात जाउँ बलि बेगि नहाहू । जो मन भाव मधुर कछु खाहू ॥
tāta jāuṁ bali begi nahāhū, jo mana bhāva madhura kachu khāhū.
पितु समीप तब जाएहु भैआ । भइ बड़ि बार जाइ बलि मैआ ॥
pitu samīpa taba jāehu bhaiā, bhai baṛi bāra jāi bali maiā.
मातु बचन सुनि अति अनुकूला । जनु सनेह सुरतरु के फूला ॥
mātu bacana suni ati anukūlā, janu saneha surataru ke phūlā.
सुख मकरंद भरे श्रियमूला । निरखि राम मनु भवरुँ न भूला ॥
sukha makaraṁda bhare śriyamūlā, nirakhi rāma manu bhavaruṁ na bhūlā.
धरम धुरीन धरम गति जानी । कहेउ मातु सन अति मृदु बानी ॥
dharama dhurīna dharama gati jānī, kaheu mātu sana ati mṛdu bānī.
पिताँ दीन्ह मोहि कानन राजू । जहँ सब भाँति मोर बड़ काजू ॥
pitāṁ dīnha mohi kānana rājū, jahaṁ saba bhāṁti mora baṛa kājū.
आयसु देहि मुदित मन माता । जेहिं मुद मंगल कानन जाता ॥
āyasu dehi mudita mana mātā, jehiṁ muda maṁgala kānana jātā.
जनि सनेह बस डरपसि भोरें । आनँदु अंब अनुग्रह तोरें ॥
jani saneha basa ḍarapasi bhoreṁ, ānaṁdu aṁba anugraha toreṁ.

Trans:

Go at once, my darling, I beg of you; and bathe quickly and take something nice to eat, and then, dear boy, approach your father. I protest there has been too much delay already." On hearing his mother's most loving speech, which seemed as the flower of the paradisal tree of affection, laden with the fragrance of delight and produced from the stem of prosperity, Rāma's beelike soul was not distracted by the sight, but in his righteousness he discerned the path of virtue, and thus in honeyed tones addressed his mother, "My father has assigned me the forests for my realm, where I shall have much in every way to do. Give me your orders, mother, with a cheerful heart, that I too may cheerfully and in auspicious wise set out for the forest. Do not in your affection give way to causeless alarm. My happiness, O mother, depends on your consent.

दोहा-dohā:

बरष चारिदस बिपिन बसि करि पितु बचन प्रमान ।
baraṣa cāridasa bipina basi kari pitu bacana pramāna,
आइ पाय पुनि देखिहउँ मनु जनि करसि मलान ॥५३॥
āi pāya puni dekhihauṁ manu jani karasi malāna. 53.

Trans:

After staying four years and ten in the woods, in obedience to my sire's command, I will come back and again behold your feet; make not your mind uneasy."

चौपाई-caupāī:

बचन बिनीत मधुर रघुबर के । सर सम लगे मातु उर करके ॥
bacana binīta madhura raghubara ke, sara sama lage mātu ura karake.
सहमि सूखि सुनि सीतलि बानी । जिमि जवास परें पावस पानी ॥
sahami sūkhi suni sītali bānī, jimi javāsa pareṁ pāvasa pānī.
कहि न जाइ कछु हृदय बिषादू । मनहुँ मृगी सुनि केहरि नादू ॥
kahi na jāi kachu hṛdaya biṣādū, manahuṁ mṛgī suni kehari nādū.
नयन सजल तन थर थर काँपी । माजहि खाइ मीन जनु मापी ॥
nayana sajala tana thara thara kāṁpī, mājahi khāi mīna janu māpī.
धरि धीरजु सुत बदनु निहारी । गदगद बचन कहति महतारी ॥
dhari dhīraju suta badanu nihārī, gadagada bacana kahati mahatārī.
तात पितहि तुम्ह प्रानपिआरे । देखि मुदित नित चरित तुम्हारे ॥
tāta pitahi tumha prānapiāre, dekhi mudita nita carita tumhāre.
राजु देन कहुँ सुभ दिन साधा । कहेउ जान बन केहिं अपराधा ॥
rāju dena kahuṁ subha dina sādhā, kaheu jāna bana kehiṁ aparādhā.
तात सुनावहु मोहि निदानू । को दिनकर कुल भयउ कृसानू ॥
tāta sunāvahu mohi nidānū, ko dinakara kula bhayau kṛsānū.

Trans:

Raghubar's sweet and dutiful words pierced like arrows through his mother's heart. At the sound of his chilling speech she withered and drooped like the *jawāsā* at a shower in the rains. The anguish of her soul was past telling, as when an elephant shrinks at the roar of a tiger. Her eyes filled with tears and her body trembled all over—like a fish overtaken by the scour of a flooded river. Summing up courage, she looked her son in the face and spoke in faltering accents, "My son, you are your father's darling and it is a constant delight to him to watch your doings. He had fixed an auspicious day for giving you the scepter; for what offence does he now banish you to the woods? Tell me, my boy, the upshot of it all; who is the destroying fire of the Sun-god's line?"

दोहा-dohā:

निरखि राम रुख सचिवसुत कारनु कहेउ बुझाइ ।
nirakhi rāma rukha sacivasuta kāranu kaheu bujhāi,
सुनि प्रसंगु रहि मूक जिमि दसा बरनि नहिं जाइ ॥५४॥
suni prasaṁgu rahi mūka jimi dasā barani nahiṁ jāi. 54.

Trans:

After a look at Rāma's face the minister's son, who had accompanied, explained to her the reason. On hearing his account she was struck dumb; words failed to describe her condition.

चौपाई-caupāī:

राखि न सकइ न कहि सक जाहू । दुहूँ भाँति उर दारुन दाहू ॥
rākhi na sakai na kahi saka jāhū, duhūṁ bhāṁti ura dāruna dāhū.
लिखत सुधाकर गा लिखि राहू । बिधि गति बाम सदा सब काहू ॥
likhata sudhākara gā likhi rāhū, bidhi gati bāma sadā saba kāhū.
धरम सनेह उभयँ मति घेरी । भइ गति साँप छुछुंदरि केरी ॥
dharama saneha ubhayaṁ mati gherī, bhai gati sāṁpa chuchuṁdari kerī.
राखउँ सुतहि करउँ अनुरोधू । धरमु जाइ अरु बंधु बिरोधू ॥
rākhauṁ sutahi karauṁ anurodhū, dharamu jāi aru baṁdhu birodhū.
कहउँ जान बन तौ बड़ि हानी । संकट सोच बिबस भइ रानी ॥
kahauṁ jāna bana tau baṛi hānī, saṁkaṭa soca bibasa bhai rānī.
बहुरि समुझि तिय धरमु सयानी । रामु भरतु दोउ सुत सम जानी ॥
bahuri samujhi tiya dharamu sayānī, rāmu bharatu dou suta sama jānī.
सरल सुभाउ राम महतारी । बोली बचन धीर धरि भारी ॥
sarala subhāu rāma mahatārī, bolī bacana dhīra dhari bhārī.
तात जाउँ बलि कीन्हेहु नीका । पितु आयसु सब धरमक टीका ॥
tāta jāuṁ bali kīnhehu nīkā, pitu āyasu saba dharamaka ṭīkā.

Trans:

She could neither detain Rāma, nor yet say Go; either way her heart was distraught with cruel pain: as though for 'moon' one had written 'eclipse'. God's hand is ever against us all, she thought. Duty and affection both laid siege to her soul; her dilemma was like that of a snake with a muskrat. 'If I keep my son, it will be a sin; my past virtue will go for nothing and my kinfolks will abhor me. If I order him into exile, it will be a sad loss', she thought. In this distressing strait the queen was sore tried. Again reflecting discreetly on her wifely duty and remembering that Rāma and Bharat were both equally her sons, the queen in the sweetness of her disposition summoned up courage and spoke these woeful words: "May I die, my son, but you have done well; a father's command is the most paramount duty.

दोहा-dohā:

राजु देन कहि दीन्ह बनु मोहि न सो दुख लेसु ।
rāju dena kahi dīnha banu mohi na so dukha lesu,
तुम्ह बिनु भरतहि भूपतिहि प्रजहि प्रचंड कलेसु ॥५५॥
tumha binu bharatahi bhūpatihi prajahi pracaṁḍa kalesu. 55.

Trans:

Though he promised you the kingdom, and now banishes you to the woods, I am not the least sad or sorry. But without you, Bharat and the king and the people will all be put to terrible distress.

चौपाई-caupāī:

जौं केवल पितु आयसु ताता । तौ जनि जाहु जानि बड़ि माता ॥
jauṁ kevala pitu āyasu tātā, tau jani jāhu jāni baṛi mātā.
जौं पितु मातु कहेउ बन जाना । तौ कानन सत अवध समाना ॥
jauṁ pitu mātu kaheu bana jānā, tau kānana sata avadha samānā.
पितु बनदेव मातु बनदेवी । खग मृग चरन सरोरुह सेवी ॥
pitu banadeva mātu banadevī, khaga mṛga carana saroruha sevī.
अंतहुँ उचित नृपहिं बनबासू । बय बिलोकि हियँ होइ हराँसू ॥
aṁtahuṁ ucita nṛpahiṁ banabāsū, baya biloki hiyaṁ hoi harāṁsū.
बड़भागी बनु अवध अभागी । जो रघुबंसतिलक तुम्ह त्यागी ॥
baṛabhāgī banu avadha abhāgī, jo raghubaṁsatilaka tumha tyāgī.
जौं सुत कहौं संग मोहि लेहू । तुम्हरे हृदयँ होइ संदेहू ॥
jauṁ suta kahauṁ saṁga mohi lehū, tumhare hṛdayaṁ hoi saṁdehū.
पूत परम प्रिय तुम्ह सबही के । प्रान प्रान के जीवन जी के ॥
pūta parama priya tumha sabahī ke, prāna prāna ke jīvana jī ke.
ते तुम्ह कहहु मातु बन जाऊँ । मैं सुनि बचन बैठि पछिताऊँ ॥
te tumha kahahu mātu bana jāūṁ, maiṁ suni bacana baiṭhi pachitāūṁ.

Trans:

Yet, boy, if it is only your father's order, then go not; hold your mother still greater. If both father and mother bid you go, the forest will be a hundred times better than Avadh, with its god for your father, its goddess for your mother, and its birds and deer to wait upon your lotus feet. At the end of life, retirement to the woods is the proper thing for a king, but I am troubled at heart when I consider your tender age. How blessed the forests and how wretched Avadh if you abandon it, you, the crown of Raghu's line. If, O child, I say 'take me with you,' there may be some hesitation in your mind. O my son, all hold you most dear, breath of our breaths, life of our life. If you say 'mother, I go alone to the woods' on hearing your words I sink down in despair.

दोहा-dohā:

यह बिचारि नहिं करउँ हठ झूठ सनेहु बढ़ाइ ।
yaha bicāri nahiṁ karauṁ haṭha jhūṭha sanehu baṛhāi,
मानि मातु कर नात बलि सुरति बिसरि जनि जाइ ॥५६॥
māni mātu kara nāta bali surati bisari jani jāi. 56.

Trans:

Being thus minded I do not press my cause with a show of love beyond what I really feel; agree to your mother's request; or if you go alone, at least I pray you not to forget me.

चौपाई-caupāī:

देव पितर सब तुम्हहि गोसाईं । राखहुँ पलक नयन की नाईं ॥
deva pitara saba tumhahi gosāīṁ, rākhahuṁ palaka nayana kī nāīṁ.
अवधि अंबु प्रिय परिजन मीना । तुम्ह करुनाकर धरम धुरीना ॥
avadhi aṁbu priya parijana mīnā, tumha karunākara dharama dhurīnā.
अस बिचारि सोइ करहु उपाई । सबहि जिअत जेहिं भेंटहु आई ॥
asa bicāri soi karahu upāī, sabahi jiata jehiṁ bhemṭahu āī.
जाहु सुखेन बनहि बलि जाऊँ । करि अनाथ जन परिजन गाऊँ ॥
jāhu sukhena banahi bali jāūṁ, kari anātha jana parijana gāūṁ.
सब कर आजु सुकृत फल बीता । भयउ कराल कालु बिपरीता ॥
saba kara āju sukṛta phala bītā, bhayau karāla kālu biparītā.
बहुबिधि बिलपि चरन लपटानी । परम अभागिनि आपुहि जानी ॥
bahubidhi bilapi carana lapaṭānī, parama abhāgini āpuhi jānī.
दारुन दुसह दाहु उर ब्यापा । बरनि न जाहिं बिलाप कलापा ॥
dāruna dusaha dāhu ura byāpā, barani na jāhiṁ bilāpa kalāpā.
राम उठाइ मातु उर लाई । कहि मृदु बचन बहुरि समुझाई ॥
rāma uṭhāi mātu ura lāī, kahi mṛdu bacana bahuri samujhāī.

Trans:

May all the gods and the spirits of your ancestors guard you, noble boy—as closely as the eyelids guard the eyes. The term of exile is like the water of lake, and your relatives and friends are the fish that live in it. You are all-merciful and righteous; remember then to make your plans so that you may find them all alive when you come again. Go in peace to the woods—ah! woe is me!—leaving your servants, your relatives, the whole city in bereavement! Today the fruit of all their past good deeds has gone and awful death confronts them." Then with many mournful words she clung to his feet, accounting herself the most hapless of women. Cruel and intolerable pangs pierced her heart through and through; the burden of her misery was past all telling. Rāma raised his mother and took her to his heart and consoled her with words most soothing.

दोहा-dohā:

समाचार तेहि समय सुनि सीय उठी अकुलाइ ।
samācāra tehi samaya suni sīya uṭhī akulāi,
जाइ सासु पद कमल जुग बंदि बैठि सिरु नाइ ॥५७॥
jāi sāsu pada kamala juga baṁdi baiṭhi siru nāi. 57.

Trans:

At that moment Sītā, who had heard the news, arrived in great agitation, and having reverenced her mother's lotus feet, bowed her head and sat down.

चौपाई-caupāī:

दीन्हि असीस सासु मृदु बानी । अति सुकुमारि देखि अकुलानी ॥
dīnhi asīsa sāsu mṛdu bānī, ati sukumāri dekhi akulānī.
बैठि नमितमुख सोचति सीता । रूप रासि पति प्रेम पुनीता ॥
baiṭhi namitamukha socati sītā, rūpa rāsi pati prema punītā.
चलन चहत बन जीवननाथू । केहि सुकृती सन होइहि साथू ॥
calana cahata bana jīvananāthū, kehi sukṛtī sana hoihi sāthū.
की तनु प्रान कि केवल प्राना । बिधि करतबु कछु जाइ न जाना ॥
kī tanu prāna ki kevala prānā, bidhi karatabu kachu jāi na jānā.
चारु चरन नख लेखति धरनी । नूपुर मुखर मधुर कबि बरनी ॥
cāru carana nakha lekhati dharanī, nūpura mukhara madhura kabi baranī.
मनहुँ प्रेम बस बिनती करहीं । हमहि सीय पद जनि परिहरहीं ॥
manahuṁ prema basa binatī karahīṁ, hamahi sīya pada jani pariharahīṁ.
मंजु बिलोचन मोचति बारी । बोली देखि राम महतारी ॥
maṁju bilocana mocati bārī, bolī dekhi rāma mahatārī.
तात सुनहु सिय अति सुकुमारी । सासु ससुर परिजनहि पिआरी ॥
tāta sunahu siya ati sukumārī, sāsu sasura parijanahi piārī.

Trans:

In tender accents her mother gave her blessing, and at the sight of her delicate frame was more distressed than ever. With drooping eyes Sītā, the perfection of beauty, the model of wifely devotion, sat and thought, "The Lord of my life would go in exile to the forests. It is yet to be seen who will have the good fortune to accompany him—my body and soul together, or just my soul alone, with body dropt away. What gods intend to do cannot be foreseen even partly." With her lovely toenails she wrote upon the ground, while the music of her anklets, like the poet's honeyed song, rang out this passionate prayer: "Never may we be torn from your feet." Seeing that a flood of tears flowed from her lovely eyes, Rāma's mother said, "Hearken, my son; Sītā is very delicate; she is the darling of your father and mother and entire family.

दोहा-dohā:

पिता जनक भूपाल मनि ससुर भानुकुल भानु ।
pitā janaka bhūpāla mani sasura bhānukula bhānu,
पति रबिकुल कैरव बिपिन बिधु गुन रूप निधानु ॥५८॥
pati rabikula kairava bipina bidhu guna rūpa nidhānu. 58.

Trans:

She has for her father Janak, the jewel among kings, while her father-in-law is none other than the sun of the solar race; and her Lord is a veritable moon for the lily-like progeny of the sun-god and a repository of goodness and beauty.

चौपाई-caupāī:

मैं पुनि पुत्रबधू प्रिय पाई । रूप रासि गुन सील सुहाई ॥
maiṁ puni putrabadhū priya pāī, rūpa rāsi guna sīla suhāī.
नयन पुतरि करि प्रीति बढ़ाई । राखेउँ प्रान जानकिहिं लाई ॥
nayana putari kari prīti baṛhāī, rākheuṁ prāna jānakihiṁ lāī.
कलपबेलि जिमि बहुबिधि लाली । सींचि सनेह सलिल प्रतिपाली ॥
kalapabeli jimi bahubidhi lālī, sīṁci saneha salila pratipālī.
फूलत फलत भयउ बिधि बामा । जानि न जाइ काह परिनामा ॥
phūlata phalata bhayau bidhi bāmā, jāni na jāi kāha parināmā.
पलँग पीठ तजि गोद हिंडोरा । सियँ न दीन्ह पगु अवनि कठोरा ॥
palaṁga pīṭha taji goda hiṁḍorā, siyaṁ na dīnha pagu avani kaṭhorā.
जिअनमूरि जिमि जोगवत रहऊँ । दीप बाति नहिं टारन कहऊँ ॥
jianamūri jimi jogavata rahaūṁ, dīpa bāti nahiṁ ṭārana kahaūṁ.
सोइ सिय चलन चहति बन साथा । आयसु काह होइ रघुनाथा ॥
soi siya calana cahati bana sāthā, āyasu kāha hoi raghunāthā.
चंद किरन रस रसिक चकोरी । रबि रुख नयन सकइ किमि जोरी ॥
caṁda kirana rasa rasika cakorī, rabi rukha nayana sakai kimi jorī.

Trans:

I again have found in her a dear daughter, amiable, beautiful, and accomplished. She is like the apple of my eye, and my affection has so grown that it is only in Jānakī that I have my being. I have tended her as carefully as the tree of paradise and nourished her with streams of affection. When she should have blossomed and borne fruit, god has turned against me, and there is no knowing what will be the end. If ever she left her bed or seat, I cradled her in my lap; and never has Sītā set her foot on a hard ground. I cherished her as the very source of my life, and I never bade her so much as even to trim the wick of a lamp. And the same Sītā wishes to accompany you to the woods and awaits your orders, Raghunāth. How will the partridge, that drinks in with delight the rays of the moon, endure to fix its gaze on the orb of sun?

दोहा-dohā:

करि केहरि निसिचर चरहिं दुष्ट जंतु बन भूरि ।
kari kehari nisicara carahiṁ duṣṭa jaṁtu bana bhūri,
बिष बाटिकाँ कि सोह सुत सुभग सजीवनि मूरि ॥५९॥
biṣa bāṭikām̐ ki soha suta subhaga sajīvani mūri. 59.

Trans:

Elephants, lions, fiends, demons, and many fierce animals roam the woods: ah, my son, is a charming Tree-of-Life fit to endure such deadly pastures?

चौपाई-caupāī:

बन हित कोल किरात किसोरी । रचीं बिरंचि बिषय सुख भोरी ॥
bana hita kola kirāta kisorī, racīṁ biraṁci biṣaya sukha bhorī.
पाहनकृमि जिमि कठिन सुभाऊ । तिन्हहि कलेसु न कानन काऊ ॥
pāhanakṛmi jimi kaṭhina subhāū, tinhahi kalesu na kānana kāū.
कै तापस तिय कानन जोगू । जिन्ह तप हेतु तजा सब भोगू ॥
kai tāpasa tiya kānana jogū, jinha tapa hetu tajā saba bhogū.
सिय बन बसिहि तात केहि भाँती । चित्रलिखित कपि देखि डेराती ॥
siya bana basihi tāta kehi bhām̐tī, citralikhita kapi dekhi ḍerātī.
सुरसर सुभग बनज बन चारी । डाबर जोगु कि हंसकुमारी ॥
surasara subhaga banaja bana cārī, ḍābara jogu ki haṁsakumārī.
अस बिचारि जस आयसु होई । मैं सिख देउँ जानकिहि सोई ॥
asa bicāri jasa āyasu hoī, maiṁ sikha deum̐ jānakihi soī.
जौं सिय भवन रहै कह अंबा । मोहि कहँ होइ बहुत अवलंबा ॥
jauṁ siya bhavana rahai kaha aṁbā, mohi kaham̐ hoi bahuta avalaṁbā.
सुनि रघुबीर मातु प्रिय बानी । सील सनेह सुधाँ जनु सानी ॥
suni raghubīra mātu priya bānī, sīla saneha sudhām̐ janu sānī.

Trans:

God has created for the forest *Kol* and *Kirāt* women, who care not for bodily delights. Of nature hard as adamantine, the woods are no trial to them. A hermit's wife again is fit for the woods, who for the sake of penance has renounced all pleasures. But how, my son, can Sītā live in the woods—she who would be frightened even by the picture of monkey? Can the cygnet that has sported in the lovely lotus-beds of the Gangā find a fit abode in a muddy puddle? Ponder it well and then, as you order, I will instruct Jānakī. If she remains at home," continued the mother "she will be the support of my life." Raghubīr—on hearing his mother's speech, which was drenched as it were with the ambrosia of grace and affection—

दोहा-dohā:

कहि प्रिय बचन बिबेकमय कीन्हि मातु परितोष ।
kahi priya bacana bibekamaya kīnhi mātu paritoṣa,
लगे प्रबोधन जानकिहि प्रगटि बिपिन गुन दोष ॥६०॥
lage prabodhana jānakihi pragaṭi bipina guna doṣa. 60.

Trans:

—replied in tender and discreet terms for his mother's consolation, and began to set clearly before Jānakī all the all the pros and cons of the forest life.

मासपारायण चौदहवाँ विश्राम
māsapārāyaṇa caudahavām̐ viśrāma
(Pause 14 for a Thirty-Day Recitation)

चौपाई-caupāī:

मातु समीप कहत सकुचाहीं । बोले समउ समुझि मन माहीं ॥
mātu samīpa kahata sakucāhīṁ, bole samau samujhi mana māhīṁ.
राजकुमारि सिखावनु सुनहू । आन भाँति जियँ जनि कछु गुनहू ॥
rājakumāri sikhāvanu sunahū, āna bhām̐ti jiyam̐ jani kachu gunahū.
आपन मोर नीक जौं चहहू । बचनु हमार मानि गृह रहहू ॥
āpana mora nīka jauṁ cahahū, bacanu hamāra māni gṛha rahahū.
आयसु मोर सासु सेवकाई । सब बिधि भामिनि भवन भलाई ॥
āyasu mora sāsu sevakāī, saba bidhi bhāmini bhavana bhalāī.
एहि ते अधिक धरमु नहिं दूजा । सादर सासु ससुर पद पूजा ॥
ehi te adhika dharamu nahiṁ dūjā, sādara sāsu sasura pada pūjā.
जब जब मातु करिहि सुधि मोरी । होइहि प्रेम बिकल मति भोरी ॥
jaba jaba mātu karihi sudhi morī, hoihi prema bikala mati bhorī.
तब तब तुम्ह कहि कथा पुरानी । सुंदरि समुझाएहु मृदु बानी ॥
taba taba tumha kahi kathā purānī, suṁdari samujhāehu mṛdu bānī.
कहउँ सुभायँ सपथ सत मोही । सुमुखि मातु हित राखउँ तोही ॥
kahaum̐ subhāyam̐ sapatha sata mohī, sumukhi mātu hita rākhaum̐ tohī.

Trans:

Even though he hesitated in speaking to her in the presence of his mother, yet, considering the exigency of the time and deliberating within himself, he spoke, "Hearken princess to my advice, and do not misunderstand me. If you desire your own good and mine, agree to what I say and remain here. You will be obeying me and rendering service to your mother-in-law by remaining at home, good lady. You will be benefited in every way. There is no other duty so paramount as reverential submission to a husband's parents. Whenever my mother recalls me to mind and is distracted by affectionate solicitude, do you, my love, console her with old-world tales and tender speech. I speak from my heart and confirm it with a hundred oaths: it is for my mother's sake, my beloved, that I leave you here.

दोहा-dohā:

गुर श्रुति संमत धरम फलु पाइअ बिनहिं कलेस ।
gura śruti saṁmata dharama phalu pāia binahiṁ kalesa,
हठ बस सब संकट सहे गालव नहुष नरेस ॥६१॥
haṭha basa saba saṁkaṭa sahe gālava nahuṣa naresa. 61.

Trans:

The reward of virtue can be obtained without trouble by submission to the scripture and the elderly and the wise; whereas by giving oneself over to obstinacy one is subjected to all sorts of trouble, as was the case of Galav and king Nahush.

चौपाई-caupāī:

मैं पुनि करि प्रवान पितु बानी । बेगि फिरब सुनु सुमुखि सयानी ॥
maiṁ puni kari pravāna pitu bānī, begi phiraba sunu sumukhi sayānī.
दिवस जात नहिं लागिहि बारा । सुंदरि सिखवनु सुनहु हमारा ॥
divasa jāta nahiṁ lāgihi bārā, suṁdari sikhavanu sunahu hamārā.
जौं हठ करहु प्रेम बस बामा । तौ तुम्ह दुखु पाउब परिनामा ॥
jauṁ haṭha karahu prema basa bāmā, tau tumha dukhu pāuba parināmā.
काननु कठिन भयंकरु भारी । घोर घामु हिम बारि बयारी ॥
kānanu kaṭhina bhayaṁkaru bhārī, ghora ghāmu hima bāri bayārī.
कुस कंटक मग काँकर नाना । चलब पयादेहिं बिनु पदत्राना ॥
kusa kaṁṭaka maga kām̐kara nānā, calaba payādehiṁ binu padatrānā.
चरन कमल मृदु मंजु तुम्हारे । मारग अगम भूमिधर भारे ॥
carana kamala mṛdu maṁju tumhāre, māraga agama bhūmidhara bhāre.
कंदर खोह नदीं नद नारे । अगम अगाध न जाहिं निहारे ॥
kaṁdara khoha nadīṁ nada nāre, agama agādha na jāhiṁ nihāre.
भालु बाघ बृक केहरि नागा । करहिं नाद सुनि धीरजु भागा ॥
bhālu bāgha bṛka kehari nāgā, karahiṁ nāda suni dhīraju bhāgā.

Trans:

As for me, I shall soon fulfill my father's words and come back before long—hearken, O fair sensible dame. These days will quickly pass away; listen dear to my advice. If you persist in your obstinacy, due to excessive affection for me, you will rue it in the end, O fair one. The forest is exceedingly toilsome and terrible, with horrific heat and cold and rains and winds. The path is beset with prickly grass and stones, and you will have to walk without protection to your feet. Your lotus feet are so soft and pretty, while the path will be extremely harsh. There will be huge mountains, chasms and precipices; streams, rivers and torrents; deep and impassable, terrible to behold. And bears and tigers, wolves, lions and elephants make such a roar that even the boldest is dismayed.

दोहा-dohā:

भूमि सयन बलकल बसन असनु कंद फल मूल ।
bhūmi sayana balakala basana asanu kaṁda phala mūla,
ते कि सदा सब दिन मिलहिं सबुइ समय अनुकूल ॥६२॥
te ki sadā saba dina milahiṁ sabui samaya anukūla. 62.

Trans:

The ground will be your only couch, the bark of trees your raiment, and your food the bulbs, wild fruits, and roots; nor think that even these will be always forthcoming every day, but only when they are in season.

चौपाई-caupāī:

नर अहार रजनीचर चरहीं । कपट बेष बिधि कोटिक करहीं ॥
nara ahāra rajanīcara carahīṁ, kapaṭa beṣa bidhi koṭika karahīṁ.
लागइ अति पहार कर पानी । बिपिन बिपति नहिं जाइ बखानी ॥
lāgai ati pahāra kara pānī, bipina bipati nahiṁ jāi bakhānī.
ब्याल कराल बिहग बन घोरा । निसिचर निकर नारि नर चोरा ॥
byāla karāla bihaga bana ghorā, nisicara nikara nāri nara corā.
डरपहिं धीर गहन सुधि आएँ । मृगलोचनि तुम्ह भीरु सुभाएँ ॥
ḍarapahiṁ dhīra gahana sudhi āeṁ, mṛgalocani tumha bhīru subhāeṁ.
हंसगवनि तुम्ह नहिं बन जोगू । सुनि अपजसु मोहि देइहि लोगू ॥
haṁsagavani tumha nahiṁ bana jogū, suni apajasu mohi deihi logū.
मानस सलिल सुधाँ प्रतिपाली । जिअइ कि लवन पयोधि मराली ॥
mānasa salila sudhāṁ pratipālī, jiai ki lavana payodhi marālī.
नव रसाल बन बिहरनसीला । सोह कि कोकिल बिपिन करीला ॥
nava rasāla bana biharanasīlā, soha ki kokila bipina karīlā.
रहहु भवन अस हृदयँ बिचारी । चंदबदनि दुखु कानन भारी ॥
rahahu bhavana asa hṛdayaṁ bicārī, caṁdabadani dukhu kānana bhārī.

Trans:

There are man-eating monsters who assume all sorts of deceptive forms; the rainfall on the hills is to the extreme. Truly, the hardships of the forest are past all telling. There are terrible serpents and fierce wild birds and packs of demons that steal both men and women. The bravest shudders at the thought of dense forests; while you, my fawn-eyed wife, are timid by nature. Ah! delicate dame, you are not fit for the woods; people will revile me on hearing of such a thing. Can a swan, that has been nurtured in the ambrosial flood of the Mānas lake, survive on salty waters of sea? Can the *koel*—that roves with delight through the luxuriant mango groves—take pleasure in jungles of *karil* bush? Ponder this, my fair bride, and stay at home; the hardships of the forest are too great.

दोहा-dohā:

सहज सुहृद गुर स्वामि सिख जो न करइ सिर मानि ।
sahaja suhṛda suhda gura svāmi sikha jo na karai sira māni,
सो पछिताइ अघाइ उर अवसि होइ हित हानि ॥६३॥
so pachitāi aghāi ura avasi hoi hita hāni. 63.

Trans:

Whoever with a view to her own good does not at once accept the advice given by a friend, or Gurū, or her husband, shall assuredly have a surfeit of repentance and gain no good."

चौपाई-caupāī:

सुनि मृदु बचन मनोहर पिय के । लोचन ललित भरे जल सिय के ॥
suni mṛdu bacana manohara piya ke, locana lalita bhare jala siya ke.
सीतल सिख दाहक भइ कैसें । चकइहि सरद चंद निसि जैसें ॥
sītala sikha dāhaka bhai kaiseṁ, cakaihi sarada caṁda nisi jaiseṁ.
उतरु न आव बिकल बैदेही । तजन चहत सुचि स्वामि सनेही ॥
utaru na āva bikala baidehī, tajana cahata suci svāmi sanehī.
बरबस रोकि बिलोचन बारी । धरि धीरजु उर अवनिकुमारी ॥
barabasa roki bilocana bārī, dhari dhīraju ura avanikumārī.
लागि सासु पग कह कर जोरी । छमबि देबि बड़ि अबिनय मोरी ॥
lāgi sāsu paga kaha kara jorī, chamabi debi baṛi abinaya morī.
दीन्हि प्रानपति मोहि सिख सोई । जेहि बिधि मोर परम हित होई ॥
dīnhi prānapati mohi sikha soī, jehi bidhi mora parama hita hoī.
मैं पुनि समुझि दीखि मन माहीं । पिय बियोग सम दुखु जग नाहीं ॥
maiṁ puni samujhi dīkhi mana māhīṁ, piya biyoga sama dukhu jaga nāhīṁ.

Trans:

On hearing the tender and winning words of her husband, Sītā's lotus eyes filled with tears, and his soothing advice caused her as burning a pain as the autumn moon causes to the chakwi. In her distress no answer came to her lips; she was filled with agony that her love would leave her behind. Perforce restraining her tears and summing up courage, Earth's daughter embraced her mother's feet, and with folded hands thus spake, "Pardon me mother of my great presumption. My dear Lord has taught me what is all for my own good; but I look to my feelings and conclude that no sorrow in the world is so great as separation from one's beloved.

दोहा-dohā:

प्राननाथ करुनायतन सुंदर सुखद सुजान ।
prānanātha karunāyatana suṁdara sukhada sujāna,
तुम्ह बिनु रघुकुल कुमुद बिधु सुरपुर नरक समान ॥६४॥
tumha binu raghukula kumuda bidhu surapura naraka samāna. 64.

Trans:

O my dear Lord, most compassionate, beautiful, bounteous and wise, the moon of the lilies of the Raghu race, even heaven without you would be a very hell.

चौपाई-caupāī:

मातु पिता भगिनी प्रिय भाई । प्रिय परिवारु सुहृद समुदाई ॥
mātu pitā bhaginī priya bhāī, priya parivāru suhṛda samudāī.
सासु ससुर गुर सजन सहाई । सुत सुंदर सुसील सुखदाई ॥
sāsu sasura gura sajana sahāī, suta suṁdara susīla sukhadāī.
जहँ लगि नाथ नेह अरु नाते । पिय बिनु तियहि तरनिहु ते ताते ॥
jahaṁ lagi nātha neha aru nāte, piya binu tiyahi taranihu te tāte.
तनु धनु धामु धरनि पुर राजू । पति बिहीन सबु सोक समाजू ॥
tanu dhanu dhāmu dharani pura rājū, pati bihīna sabu soka samājū.
भोग रोगसम भूषन भारू । जम जातना सरिस संसारू ॥
bhoga rogasama bhūṣana bhārū, jama jātanā sarisa saṁsārū.
प्राननाथ तुम्ह बिनु जग माहीं । मो कहुँ सुखद कतहुँ कछु नाहीं ॥
prānanātha tumha binu jaga māhīṁ, mo kahuṁ sukhada katahuṁ kachu nāhīṁ.
जिय बिनु देह नदी बिनु बारी । तैसिअ नाथ पुरुष बिनु नारी ॥
jiya binu deha nadī binu bārī, taisia nātha puruṣa binu nārī.
नाथ सकल सुख साथ तुम्हारें । सरद बिमल बिधु बदनु निहारें ॥
nātha sakala sukha sātha tumhāreṁ, sarada bimala bidhu badanu nihāreṁ.

Trans:

Dear are the father and mother, sisters and brothers; dear are my companions and my many friends; but they all—father-in-law and mother-in-law, spiritual advisors, generous associates, and even sons, however beautiful, amiable, and affectionate—nay, my Lord, all love and every tie of kindred—to a woman without her husband, are a greater distress than the sun's most burning heat. Life, wealth, house, land, city and empire are but accumulated misery to a woman bereft of her lord; for then, ease is a disease, her jewels a burden, and the world like the torments of hell. Without you, O Lord of my soul, there is nothing in the whole world that could give me any comfort. As the body without its soul, as a river without water, so, my Lord, is a woman without her husband. With you, my Lord, are all delights—so long as I can behold your face which vies in brightness with the autumn moon.

दोहा-dohā:

खग मृग परिजन नगरु बनु बलकल बिमल दुकूल ।
khaga mṛga parijana nagaru banu balakala bimala dukūla,
नाथ साथ सुरसदन सम परनसाल सुख मूल ॥६५॥
nātha sātha surasadana sama paranasāla sukha mūla. 65.

Trans:

The birds and deer will be my attendants, the forest my city, and strips of bark my glistening robes; with my Lord, a hut of grass will be as the palace of the gods, and all will be well.

चौपाई-caupāī:

बनदेबीं बनदेव उदारा । करिहहिं सासु ससुर सम सारा ॥
banadebīṁ banadeva udārā, karihahiṁ sāsu sasura sama sārā.
कुस किसलय साथरी सुहाई । प्रभु सँग मंजु मनोज तुराई ॥
kusa kisalaya sātharī suhāī, prabhu saṁga maṁju manoja turāī.
कंद मूल फल अमिअ अहारू । अवध सौध सत सरिस पहारू ॥
kaṁda mūla phala amia ahārū, avadha saudha sata sarisa pahārū.
छिनु छिनु प्रभु पद कमल बिलोकी । रहिहउँ मुदित दिवस जिमि कोकी ॥
chinu chinu prabhu pada kamala bilokī, rahihauṁ mudita divasa jimi kokī.
बन दुख नाथ कहे बहुतेरे । भय बिषाद परिताप घनेरे ॥
bana dukha nātha kahe bahutere, bhaya biṣāda paritāpa ghanere.
प्रभु बियोग लवलेस समाना । सब मिलि होहिं न कृपानिधाना ॥
prabhu biyoga lavalesa samānā, saba mili hohiṁ na kṛpānidhānā.
अस जियँ जानि सुजान सिरोमनि । लेइअ संग मोहि छाड़िअ जनि ॥
asa jiyaṁ jāni sujāna siromani, leia saṁga mohi chāṛia jani.
बिनती बहुत करौं का स्वामी । करुनामय उर अंतरजामी ॥
binatī bahuta karauṁ kā svāmī, karunāmaya ura aṁtarajāmī.

Trans:

The sylvan nymphs and gods will of their grace protect me like my own Lord's parents; my simple litter of grass and twigs will, with my Lord, become a luxurious marriage-couch; bulbs, roots, and fruits will form an ambrosial repast; and the mountains will resemble the stately halls of Avadh. Every moment that I gaze on my Lord's lotus feet, I shall be as glad as the chakwi at the dawn. You have recounted, my Lord, the numerous hardships of the forest, its terrors, annoyances, and many discomforts; but, O fountain of mercy, all those united will not be comparable to the Pain of Bereavement. Consider that, O jewel of wisdom, and take me with you; please abandon me not. Why make long supplications? My Lord is full of compassion and knoweth the heart.

दोहा-dohā:

राखिअ अवध जो अवधि लगि रहत न जनिअहिं प्रान ।
rākhia avadha jo avadhi lagi rahata na janiahiṁ prāna,
दीनबंधु सुंदर सुखद सील सनेह निधान ॥६६॥
dīnabaṁdhu suṁdara sukhada sīla saneha nidhāna. 66.

Trans:

Do you think, if you keep me at Avadh, that I will survive till the end of your exile? O most beautiful, most bountiful helper of the helpless, fountain of grace and of love;

चौपाई-caupāī:

मोहि मग चलत न होइहि हारी । छिनु छिनु चरन सरोज निहारी ॥
mohi maga calata na hoihi hārī, chinu chinu carana saroja nihārī.
सबहि भाँति पिय सेवा करिहौं । मारग जनित सकल श्रम हरिहौं ॥
sabahi bhāṁti piya sevā karihauṁ, māraga janita sakala śrama harihauṁ.
पाय पखारि बैठि तरु छाहीं । करिहउँ बाउ मुदित मन माहीं ॥
pāya pakhāri baiṭhi taru chāhīṁ, karihauṁ bāu mudita mana māhīṁ.
श्रम कन सहित स्याम तनु देखें । कहँ दुख समउ प्रानपति पेखें ॥
śrama kana sahita syāma tanu dekheṁ, kahaṁ dukha samau prānapati pekheṁ.
सम महि तृन तरुपल्लव डासी । पाय पलोटिहि सब निसि दासी ॥
sama mahi tṛna tarupallava ḍāsī, pāya paloṭihi saba nisi dāsī.
बार बार मृदु मूरति जोही । लागिहि तात बयारि न मोही ॥
bāra bāra mṛdu mūrati johī, lāgihi tāta bayāri na mohī.
को प्रभु सँग मोहि चितवनिहारा । सिंघबधुहि जिमि ससक सिआरा ॥
ko prabhu saṁga mohi citavanihārā, siṁghabadhuhi jimi sasaka siārā.
मैं सुकुमारि नाथ बन जोगू । तुम्हहि उचित तप मो कहुँ भोगू ॥
maiṁ sukumāri nātha bana jogū, tumhahi ucita tapa mo kahuṁ bhogū.

Trans:

as I go along the road I shall never weary—every moment beholding thy lotus feet. In every way I shall minister to my beloved, and relieve him of all the toils of the march. Seated in the shade of some tree, I shall lave your feet and rapturously fan you. And gazing upon your body stained with sweat and blackened by the sun, what thought, my dearest Lord, shall I have for my own hard times? Spreading grass and leaves on a level ground, your handmaid will all night knead your feet, and ever gazing on your gracious form, nor heat nor wind will ever vex me. Who will dare look at me when I am with my Lord, except as a hare or jackal furtively regards a lioness? Am I to be dainty and delicate, while my Lord roams the forest? Is penance to be your lot and enjoyment mine?

दोहा-dohā:

ऐसेउ बचन कठोर सुनि जौं न हृदउ बिलगान ।
aiseu bacana kaṭhora suni jauṁ na hṛdau bilagāna,
तौ प्रभु बिषम बियोग दुख सहिहहिं पावँर प्रान ॥६७॥
tau prabhu biṣama biyoga dukha sahihahiṁ pāvaṁra prāna. 67.

Trans:

My heart will burst at the mere sound of so cruel a sentence, and never will my miserable existence survive the anguish and torture of bereavement."

चौपाई-caupāī:

अस कहि सीय बिकल भइ भारी । बचन बियोगु न सकी सँभारी ॥
asa kahi sīya bikala bhai bhārī, bacana biyogu na sakī saṁbhārī.
देखि दसा रघुपति जियँ जाना । हठि राखें नहिं राखिहि प्राना ॥
dekhi dasā raghupati jiyaṁ jānā, haṭhi rākheṁ nahiṁ rākhihi prānā.
कहेउ कृपाल भानुकुलनाथा । परिहरि सोचु चलहु बन साथा ॥
kaheu kṛpāla bhānukulanāthā, parihari socu calahu bana sāthā.
नहिं बिषाद कर अवसरु आजू । बेगि करहु बन गवन समाजू ॥
nahiṁ biṣāda kara avasaru ājū, begi karahu bana gavana samājū.
कहि प्रिय बचन प्रिया समुझाई । लगे मातु पद आसिष पाई ॥
kahi priya bacana priyā samujhāī, lage mātu pada āsiṣa pāī.
बेगि प्रजा दुख मेटब आई । जननी निठुर बिसरि जनि जाई ॥
begi prajā dukha meṭaba āī, jananī niṭhura bisari jani jāī.
फिरिहि दसा बिधि बहुरि कि मोरी । देखिहउँ नयन मनोहर जोरी ॥
phirihi dasā bidhi bahuri ki morī, dekhihauṁ nayana manohara jorī.
सुदिन सुघरी तात कब होइहि । जननी जिअत बदन बिधु जोइहि ॥
sudina sugharī tāta kaba hoihi, jananī jiata badana bidhu joihi.

Trans:

So saying, Sītā was overwhelmed with distress, nor could endure the word 'separation.' On seeing her condition, Rāma deliberated: 'If I insist on leaving her, then I leave her dead.' Then said the compassionate Lord of the solar race, "Have done with lamentation and come with me to the woods. There is no time now for weeping; at once make your preparations for the journey." Having consoled his beloved with these tender words, he embraced his mother's feet and received her blessing. "Return quickly and relieve your subjects' distress, nor forget me, your hard-hearted mother. Who knows but God may change my lot, and my eye may see you both again. Ah! my son, when will arrive the happy day and moment that I shall live to see your moon-like face once more?

दोहा-*dohā:*

बहुरि बच्छ कहि लालु कहि रघुपति रघुबर तात ।
bahuri baccha kahi lālu kahi raghupati raghubara tāta,
कबहिं बोलाइ लगाइ हियँ हरषि निरखिहउँ गात ॥६८॥
kabahiṁ bolāi lagāi hiyam̐ haraṣi nirakhihaum̐ gāta. 68.

Trans:

When again I shall call you 'my child,' 'my darling,' 'noblest and best of Raghu's line,' 'my very son,' and fondly bid you come to my arms so that I may gaze upon your features?"

चौपाई-*caupāī:*

लखि सनेह कातरि महतारी । बचनु न आव बिकल भइ भारी ॥
lakhi saneha kātari mahatārī, bacanu na āva bikala bhai bhārī.
राम प्रबोधु कीन्ह बिधि नाना । समउ सनेहु न जाइ बखाना ॥
rāma prabodhu kīnha bidhi nānā, samau sanehu na jāi bakhānā.
तब जानकी सासु पग लागी । सुनिअ माय मैं परम अभागी ॥
taba jānakī sāsu paga lāgī, sunia māya maiṁ parama abhāgī.
सेवा समय दैअँ बनु दीन्हा । मोर मनोरथु सफल न कीन्हा ॥
sevā samaya daiam̐ banu dīnhā, mora manorathu saphala na kīnhā.
तजब छोभु जनि छाड़िअ छोहू । करमु कठिन कछु दोसु न मोहू ॥
tajaba chobhu jani chāṛia chohū, karamu kaṭhina kachu dosu na mohū.
सुनि सिय बचन सासु अकुलानी । दसा कवनि बिधि कहौं बखानी ॥
suni siya bacana sāsu akulānī, dasā kavani bidhi kahauṁ bakhānī.
बारहिं बार लाइ उर लीन्ही । धरि धीरजु सिख आसिष दीन्ही ॥
bārahiṁ bāra lāi ura līnhī, dhari dhīraju sikha āsiṣa dīnhī.
अचल होउ अहिवातु तुम्हारा । जब लगि गंग जमुन जल धारा ॥
acala hou ahivātu tumhārā, jaba lagi gaṁga jamuna jala dhārā.

Trans:

Seeing that his mother was so agitated by affection for him that she could not speak, and was utterly overwhelmed with distress, Rāma did everything to console her. The pathos of the scene defied description. Then Jānakī embraced her mother's feet: "Hearken mother, I am, of all women, most miserable. At the time when I should have been doing you service, fate has banished me to the woods and has denied me my desire. Cease to sorrow, but cease not to love me. Fate is cruel, I am blameless." On hearing Sītā's words her mother was deeply afflicted; her state past all telling. Again and again she took her to her bosom and summing up courage blessed her, "May your prosperity be as enduring as the streams of Gangā and Yamunā!"

दोहा-*dohā:*

सीतहि सासु असीस सिख दीन्हि अनेक प्रकार ।
sītahi sāsu asīsa sikha dīnhi aneka prakāra,
चली नाइ पद पदुम सिरु अति हित बारहिं बार ॥६९॥
calī nāi pada paduma siru ati hita bārahiṁ bāra. 69.

Trans:

When her mother had repeatedly blessed and imparted parting advice, Sītā took her leave, after again and again affectionately bowing her head at her lotus feet.

चौपाई-*caupāī:*

समाचार जब लछिमन पाए । ब्याकुल बिलख बदन उठि धाए ॥
samācāra jaba lachimana pāe, byākula bilakha badana uṭhi dhāe.
कंप पुलक तन नयन सनीरा । गहे चरन अति प्रेम अधीरा ॥
kaṁpa pulaka tana nayana sanīrā, gahe carana ati prema adhīrā.
कहि न सकत कछु चितवत ठाढ़े । मीनु दीन जनु जल तें काढ़े ॥
kahi na sakata kachu citavata ṭhāṛhe, mīnu dīna janu jala teṁ kāṛhe.
सोचु हृदयँ बिधि का होनिहारा । सबु सुखु सुकृतु सिरान हमारा ॥
socu hṛdayam̐ bidhi kā honihārā, sabu sukhu sukṛtu sirāna hamārā.
मो कहुँ काह कहब रघुनाथा । रखिहहिं भवन कि लेहहिं साथा ॥
mo kahum̐ kāha kahaba raghunāthā, rakhihahiṁ bhavana ki lehahiṁ sāthā.
राम बिलोकि बंधु कर जोरें । देह गेह सब सन तृनु तोरें ॥
rāma biloki baṁdhu kara joreṁ, deha geha saba sana tṛnu toreṁ.
बोले बचनु राम नय नागर । सील सनेह सरल सुख सागर ॥
bole bacanu rāma naya nāgara, sīla saneha sarala sukha sāgara.
तात प्रेम बस जनि कदराहू । समुझि हृदयँ परिनाम उछाहू ॥
tāta prema basa jani kadarāhū, samujhi hṛdayam̐ parināma uchāhū.

Trans:

When Lakshman heard the news, he started up in dismay with a doleful face, his body all atremble and his eyes full of tears; and he ran and clasped Rāma's feet in an agony of affection. He could not speak but stood aghast and stared—like some poor fish drawn out of the water—thinking within himself, "Good god, what will happen now? All my happiness and past good deeds are gone forever. What will Raghunāth tell me to do? Will he keep me here, or take me with him?" When Rāma saw his brother with folded hands, renouncing life and home and all, he addressed him in the following words—the all-righteous, fountain of grace, love, and perfect bliss that Rāma was, "Brother, do not afflict yourself with love, but reflect that all will be well in the end.

दोहा-*dohā:*

मातु पिता गुरु स्वामि सिख सिर धरि करहिं सुभायँ ।
mātu pitā guru svāmi sikha sira dhari karahiṁ subhāyam̐,
लहेउ लाभु तिन्ह जनम कर नतरु जनमु जग जायँ ॥७०॥
laheu lābhu tinha janama kara nataru janamu jaga jāyam̐. 70.

Trans:

They who submit without reserve to the commands of their father and mother, their spiritual advisor, and their Lord, are born into the world to some purpose; otherwise their birth is in vain.

चौपाई-*caupāī:*

अस जियँ जानि सुनहु सिख भाई । करहु मातु पितु पद सेवकाई ॥
asa jiyam̐ jāni sunahu sikha bhāī, karahu mātu pitu pada sevakāī.
भवन भरतु रिपुसूदनु नाहीं । राउ बृद्ध मम दुखु मन माहीं ॥
bhavana bharatu ripusūdanu nāhīṁ, rāu bṛddha mama dukhu mana māhīṁ.
मैं बन जाउँ तुम्हहि लेइ साथा । होइ सबहि बिधि अवध अनाथा ॥
maiṁ bana jāum̐ tumhahi lei sāthā, hoi sabahi bidhi avadha anāthā.
गुरु पितु मातु प्रजा परिवारू । सब कहुँ परइ दुसह दुख भारू ॥
guru pitu mātu prajā parivārū, saba kahum̐ parai dusaha dukha bhārū.
रहहु करहु सब कर परितोषू । नतरु तात होइहि बड़ दोषू ॥
rahahu karahu saba kara paritoṣū, nataru tāta hoihi baṛa doṣū.
जासु राज प्रिय प्रजा दुखारी । सो नृपु अवसि नरक अधिकारी ॥
jāsu rāja priya prajā dukhārī, so nṛpu avasi naraka adhikārī.
रहहु तात असि नीति बिचारी । सुनत लखनु भए ब्याकुल भारी ॥
rahahu tāta asi nīti bicārī, sunata lakhanu bhae byākula bhārī.
सिअरें बचन सूखि गए कैसें । परसत तुहिन तामरसु जैसें ॥
siareṁ bacana sūkhi gae kaiseṁ, parasata tuhina tāmarasu jaiseṁ.

Trans:

Consider this, O brother, and hearken to my advice: wait upon the feet of your father and mother. Neither Bharat is at home nor Ripusūdan; the king is old and sorrowing for me. If I go to the woods and take you with me

Avadh will be completely master-less, and an intolerable weight of affliction will fall upon priests and parents, subjects, family and all. Stay then to comfort them, brother, if not then it will be a great sin. The king, whose faithful subjects endure distress, is in truth a prince of hell. This is sound doctrine, O brother. Ponder it well and stay." Lakshman was in grievous distress upon hearing this; and his body became as dead and shriveled as a lotus that has been touched by the frost.

दोहा-dohā:

उतरु न आवत प्रेम बस गहे चरन अकुलाइ ।
utaru na āvata prema basa gahe carana akulāi,
नाथ दासु मैं स्वामि तुम्ह तजहु त काह बसाइ ॥७१॥
nātha dāsu maiṁ svāmi tumha tajahu ta kāha basāi. 71.

Trans:

Overmastered by love, he could not answer, but clung in anguish to his Lord's feet: "O my Lord, I am your slave and you my master; leave me and then what will I do?

चौपाई-caupāī:

दीन्हि मोहि सिख नीकि गोसाईं । लागि अगम अपनी कदराईं ॥
dīnhi mohi sikha nīki gosāīṁ, lāgi agama apanī kadarāīṁ.
नरबर धीर धरम धुर धारी । निगम नीति कहुँ ते अधिकारी ॥
narabara dhīra dharama dhura dhārī, nigama nīti kahuṁ te adhikārī.
मैं सिसु प्रभु सनेहँ प्रतिपाला । मंदरु मेरु कि लेहिं मराला ॥
maiṁ sisu prabhu sanehaṁ pratipālā, maṁdaru meru ki lehiṁ marālā.
गुर पितु मातु न जानउँ काहू । कहउँ सुभाउ नाथ पतिआहू ॥
gura pitu mātu na jānauṁ kāhū, kahauṁ subhāu nātha patiāhū.
जहँ लगि जगत सनेह सगाई । प्रीति प्रतीति निगम निजु गाई ॥
jahaṁ lagi jagata saneha sagāī, prīti pratīti nigama niju gāī.
मोरे सबइ एक तुम्ह स्वामी । दीनबंधु उर अंतरजामी ॥
more sabai eka tumha svāmī, dīnabaṁdhu ura aṁtarajāmī.
धरम नीति उपदेसिअ ताही । कीरति भूति सुगति प्रिय जाही ॥
dharama nīti upadesia tāhī, kīrati bhūti sugati priya jāhī.
मन क्रम बचन चरन रत होई । कृपासिंधु परिहरिअ कि सोई ॥
mana krama bacana carana rata hoī, kṛpāsiṁdhu pariharia ki soī.

Trans:

You have given me, good sir, an excellent advice; but in my confusion I find it impracticable. Valiant leaders of men and champions of the faith can master such abstruse doctrine, but I am a mere child, nurtured by your affection. Can a cygnet uplift Mount Mandar or Meru? I know no Gurū, nor father, nor mother; believe me, my Lord, I speak from my heart: all the love in the world, all claims of kin, all affection, sympathy, wisdom, and skill are for me centered only in you, my Lord—the protector of the humble, the reader of the heart. Expound questions of theology to one who aims at fame and glory and high estate. I am in heart, word, and deed devoted only to your feet. Am I, O gracious Lord, to be abandoned?"

दोहा-dohā:

करुनासिंधु सुबंधु के सुनि मृदु बचन बिनीत ।
karunāsiṁdhu subaṁdhu ke suni mṛdu bacana binīta,
समुझाए उर लाइ प्रभु जानि सनेहँ सभीत ॥७२॥
samujhāe ura lāi prabhu jāni sanehaṁ sabhīta. 72.

Trans:

The compassionate Lord, on hearing the tender and modest words of his good brother, took him to his bosom, and seeing him so dejected affectionately consoled him saying:

चौपाई-caupāī:

मागहु बिदा मातु सन जाई । आवहु बेगि चलहु बन भाई ॥
māgahu bidā mātu sana jāī, āvahu begi calahu bana bhāī.
मुदित भए सुनि रघुबर बानी । भयउ लाभ बड़ गइ बड़ि हानी ॥
mudita bhae suni raghubara bānī, bhayau lābha baṛa gai baṛi hānī.
हरषित हृदयँ मातु पहिं आए । मनहुँ अंध फिरि लोचन पाए ॥
haraṣita hṛdayaṁ mātu pahiṁ āe, manahuṁ aṁdha phiri locana pāe.
जाइ जननि पग नायउ माथा । मनु रघुनंदन जानकि साथा ॥
jāi janani paga nāyau māthā, manu raghunaṁdana jānaki sāthā.
पूँछे मातु मलिन मन देखी । लखन कही सब कथा बिसेषी ॥
pūṁche mātu malina mana dekhī, lakhana kahī saba kathā biseṣī.
गई सहमि सुनि बचन कठोरा । मृगी देखि दव जनु चहु ओरा ॥
gaī sahami suni bacana kaṭhorā, mṛgī dekhi dava janu cahu orā.
लखन लखेउ भा अनरथ आजू । एहिं सनेह बस करब अकाजू ॥
lakhana lakheu bhā anaratha ājū, ehiṁ saneha basa karaba akājū.
मागत बिदा सभय सकुचाहीं । जाइ संग बिधि कहिहि कि नाहीं ॥
māgata bidā sabhaya sakucāhīṁ, jāi saṁga bidhi kahihi ki nāhīṁ.

Trans:

"Go, brother and take leave of your mother; come fast, let's set out for the woods." On hearing Raghubar thus speak, Lakshman was overjoyed. His triumph was great, his sorrow all gone. He approached his mother as glad of heart as a blind man who has recovered his sight, and while he bowed his head at her feet, his heart was away with Raghunandan and Jānakī. Seeing his agitation, his mother enquired the cause, and Lakshman told her the whole story. On hearing of the cruel events she trembled like a fawn that sees the forest on fire all around. Lakshman reflected, "Everything goes wrong today; her very love will work me harm." Timidly and hesitatingly he asked her permission to go, thinking "Good god, will she let me go or not?"

दोहा-dohā:

समुझि सुमित्राँ राम सिय रूपु सुसीलु सुभाउ ।
samujhi sumitrāṁ rāma siya rūpu susīlu subhāu,
नृप सनेहु लखि धुनेउ सिरु पापिनि दीन्ह कुदाउ ॥७३॥
nṛpa sanehu lakhi dhuneu siru pāpini dīnha kudāu. 73.

Trans:

After reflecting on the beauty and amiable disposition of Rāma and Sītā, and considering the king's affection, Sumitrā beat her head and exclaimed: "That wicked woman is at the bottom of this bad business."

चौपाई-caupāī:

धीरजु धरेउ कुअवसर जानी । सहज सुहृद बोली मृदु बानी ॥
dhīraju dhareu kuavasara jānī, sahaja suhṛda bolī mṛdu bānī.
तात तुम्हारि मातु बैदेही । पिता रामु सब भाँति सनेही ॥
tāta tumhāri mātu baidehī, pitā rāmu saba bhāṁti sanehī.
अवध तहाँ जहँ राम निवासू । तहँइँ दिवसु जहँ भानु प्रकासू ॥
avadha tahāṁ jahaṁ rāma nivāsū, tahaṁiṁ divasu jahaṁ bhānu prakāsū.
जौं पै सीय रामु बन जाहीं । अवध तुम्हार काजु कछु नाहीं ॥
jauṁ pai sīya rāmu bana jāhīṁ, avadha tumhāra kāju kachu nāhīṁ.
गुर पितु मातु बंधु सुर साईं । सेइअहिं सकल प्रान की नाईं ॥
gura pitu mātu baṁdhu sura sāīṁ, seiahiṁ sakala prāna kī nāīṁ.
रामु प्रानप्रिय जीवन जी के । स्वारथ रहित सखा सबही के ॥
rāmu prānapriya jīvana jī ke, svāratha rahita sakhā sabahī ke.
पूजनीय प्रिय परम जहाँ तें । सब मानिअहिं राम के नातें ॥
pūjanīya priya parama jahāṁ teṁ, saba māniahiṁ rāma ke nāteṁ.
अस जियँ जानि संग बन जाहू । लेहु तात जग जीवन लाहू ॥
asa jiyaṁ jāni saṁga bana jāhū, lehu tāta jaga jīvana lāhū.

Trans:

But perceiving the time to be untoward, she took patience and in her kindness of heart answered gently, "Your mother, my child, is Vaidehi; and Rāma, who loves you dearly, is your father. Where Rāma dwells, that is Avadh; wherever is the light of the sun, that is considered the day. If Rāma and Sītā go to the woods, you have no business staying here. A Gurū, a father and mother, brethren, the gods and our masters are all to be tended as our own life; but Rāma is dearer even than life; he is the soul of our soul, the disinterested friend of all. Our dearest and most honored friends are to be accounted only as far as they are related to Rāma. Thinking thus to yourself go with them to the woods and receive, my son, the fruition of your existence.

दोहा-dohā:

भूरि भाग भाजनु भयहु मोहि समेत बलि जाउँ ।
bhūri bhāga bhājanu bhayahu mohi sameta bali jāuṁ,
जौं तुम्हरें मन छाड़ि छलु कीन्ह राम पद ठाउँ ॥७४॥
jauṁ tumhareṁ mana chāṛi chalu kīnha rāma pada ṭhāuṁ. 74.

Trans:

It is your great good fortune as well as mine, I solemnly declare, that abandoning untruth, your mind has taken up true refuge at Rāma's feet.

चौपाई-caupāī:

पुत्रवती जुबती जग सोई । रघुपति भगतु जासु सुतु होई ॥
putravatī jubatī jaga soī, raghupati bhagatu jāsu sutu hoī.
नतरु बाँझ भलि बादि बिआनी । राम बिमुख सुत तें हित जानी ॥
nataru bām̐jha bhali bādi biānī, rāma bimukha suta teṁ hita jānī.
तुम्हरेहिं भाग रामु बन जाहीं । दूसर हेतु तात कछु नाहीं ॥
tumharehiṁ bhāga rāmu bana jāhīṁ, dūsara hetu tāta kachu nāhīṁ.
सकल सुकृत कर बड़ फलु एहू । राम सीय पद सहज सनेहू ॥
sakala sukṛta kara baṛa phalu ehū, rāma sīya pada sahaja sanehū.
राग रोषु इरिषा मदु मोहू । जनि सपनेहुँ इन्ह के बस होहू ॥
rāga roṣu iriṣā madu mohū, jani sapanehuṁ inha ke basa hohū.
सकल प्रकार बिकार बिहाई । मन क्रम बचन करेहु सेवकाई ॥
sakala prakāra bikāra bihāī, mana krama bacana karehu sevakāī.
तुम्ह कहुँ बन सब भाँति सुपासू । सँग पितु मातु रामु सिय जासू ॥
tumha kahuṁ bana saba bhām̐ti supāsū, sam̐ga pitu mātu rāmu siya jāsū.
जेहिं न रामु बन लहहिं कलेसू । सुत सोइ करेहु इहइ उपदेसू ॥
jehiṁ na rāmu bana lahahiṁ kalesū, suta soi karehu ihai upadesū.

Trans:

A mother indeed is she who has a son devoted to Raghubar; if not, it is better to be barren, for she has given birth in vain. A son who is hostile to Rāma is a curse. It is due to your good fortune that Rāma goes to the woods; and of any other reason there is none. The highest reward of all meritorious acts is verily this: to have spontaneous love for the holy feet of Sītā and Rāma. Never give way even in thought to lust, or passion, or envy, or pride, or delusion. Put aside all shiftiness and serve Sītā-Rāma in heart, word, and deed. For you the forest is a place of joy, for Rāma—your father, and Sītā—your mother, will be there with you. Take heed, my son, that Rāma is never put to any trouble: that is my admonition.

छंद-chaṁda:

उपदेसु यहु जेहिं तात तुम्हरे राम सिय सुख पावहीं ।
upadesu yahu jehiṁ tāta tumhare rāma siya sukha pāvahīṁ,
पितु मातु प्रिय परिवार पुर सुख सुरति बन बिसरावहीं ॥
pitu mātu priya parivāra pura sukha surati bana bisarāvahīṁ,
तुलसी प्रभुहि सिख देइ आयसु दीन्ह पुनि आसिष दई ।
tulasī prabhuhi sikha dei āyasu dīnha puni āsiṣa daī,
रति होउ अबिरल अमल सिय रघुबीर पद नित नित नई ॥
rati hou abirala amala siya raghubīra pada nita nita naī.

Trans:

This is my instruction, my son: see that Rāma and Sītā live at ease, and in the woods forget to remember their father and mother, their friends and relations, and all the pleasures of the city." Having given her son such advice and commands she again invoked upon the Lord of Tulsīdās her choicest blessings: "May your love for Sītā and Raghubīr be constant and unsullied and ever renewed!"

सोरठा-soraṭhā:

मातु चरन सिरु नाइ चले तुरत संकित हृदयँ ।
mātu carana siru nāi cale turata saṁkita hṛdayaṁ,
बागुर बिषम तोराइ मनहुँ भाग मृगु भाग बस ॥७५॥
bāgura biṣama torāi manahuṁ bhāga mṛgu bhāga basa. 75.

Trans:

Having bowed his head at his mother's feet, Lakshman left in haste with anxious heart—as flies a hapless deer that has burst a strong net.

चौपाई-caupāī:

गए लखनु जहँ जानकिनाथू । भे मन मुदित पाइ प्रिय साथू ॥
gae lakhanu jahaṁ jānakināthū, bhe mana mudita pāi priya sāthū.
बंदि राम सिय चरन सुहाए । चले संग नृपमंदिर आए ॥
baṁdi rāma siya carana suhāe, cale saṁga nṛpamaṁdira āe.
कहहिं परसपर पुर नर नारी । भलि बनाइ बिधि बात बिगारी ॥
kahahiṁ parasapara pura nara nārī, bhali banāi bidhi bāta bigārī.
तन कृस मन दुखु बदन मलीने । बिकल मनहुँ माखी मधु छीने ॥
tana kṛsa mana dukhu badana malīne, bikala manahuṁ mākhī madhu chīne.
कर मीजहिं सिरु धुनि पछिताहीं । जनु बिन पंख बिहग अकुलाहीं ॥
kara mījahiṁ siru dhuni pachitāhīṁ, janu bina paṁkha bihaga akulāhīṁ.
भइ बड़ि भीर भूप दरबारा । बरनि न जाइ बिषादु अपारा ॥
bhai baṛi bhīra bhūpa darabārā, barani na jāi biṣādu apārā.
सचिवँ उठाइ राउ बैठारे । कहि प्रिय बचन रामु पगु धारे ॥
sacivaṁ uṭhāi rāu baiṭhāre, kahi priya bacana rāmu pagu dhāre.
सिय समेत दोउ तनय निहारी । ब्याकुल भयउ भूमिपति भारी ॥
siya sameta dou tanaya nihārī, byākula bhayau bhūmipati bhārī.

Trans:

He went to Jānakī's Lord, and his soul rejoiced to again reclaim his dear companionship. After reverencing Rāma and Sītā's gracious feet, he proceeded with them to the king's palace. The citizens say to one another: "How goodly a plan did god make, and now so sadly marred!" With wasted frame, sad soul and doleful face, they were in great distress—as bees robbed of their honey. Wringing their hands, beating their heads and lamenting, they were like wretched birds that have been clipped of their wings. There was a great crowd in the royal hall but replete with a grief immeasurable, past all telling. The minister raised the king and seated him, and told him of the glad coming of Rāma. When he saw Sītā and his two sons the king's agitation was profound.

दोहा-dohā:

सीय सहित सुत सुभग दोउ देखि देखि अकुलाइ ।
sīya sahita suta subhaga dou dekhi dekhi akulāi,
बारहिं बार सनेह बस राउ लेइ उर लाइ ॥७६॥
bārahiṁ bāra saneha basa rāu lei ura lāi. 76.

Trans:

The king felt much disturbed as he gazed on his two sons and Sītā. Overwhelmed with emotion he pressed them to his heart again and again.

चौपाई-caupāī:

सकइ न बोलि बिकल नरनाहू । सोक जनित उर दारुन दाहू ॥
sakai na boli bikala naranāhū, soka janita ura dāruna dāhū.
नाइ सीसु पद अति अनुरागा । उठि रघुबीर बिदा तब मागा ॥
nāi sīsu pada ati anurāgā, uṭhi raghubīra bidā taba māgā.
पितु असीस आयसु मोहि दीजै । हरष समय बिसमउ कत कीजै ॥
pitu asīsa āyasu mohi dījai, haraṣa samaya bisamau kata kījai.
तात किएँ प्रिय प्रेम प्रमादू । जसु जग जाइ होइ अपबादू ॥

tāta kiem̐ priya prema pramādū, jasu jaga jāi hoi apabādū.

सुनि सनेह बस उठि नरनाहाँ । बैठारे रघुपति गहि बाहाँ ॥
suni saneha basa uṭhi naranāhām̐, baiṭhāre raghupati gahi bāhām̐.

सुनहु तात तुम्ह कहुँ मुनि कहहीं । रामु चराचर नायक अहहीं ॥
sunahu tāta tumha kahum̐ muni kahahīṁ, rāmu carācara nāyaka ahahīṁ.

सुभ अरु असुभ करम अनुहारी । ईसु देइ फलु हृदयँ बिचारी ॥
subha aru asubha karama anuhārī, īsu dei phalu hṛdayam̐ bicārī.

करइ जो करम पाव फल सोई । निगम नीति असि कह सबु कोई ॥
karai jo karama pāva phala soī, nigama nīti asi kaha sabu koī.

Trans:

In his agitation he could not speak; grief overmastered him amidst wild anguish of heart. After most affectionately bowing head to his feet, Raghunāth arose and begged permission to depart, "Father, give me your blessing and commands. Why be so dismayed at this time of rejoicing? Swerving from the path, sire, through excessive attachment to beloved things, leads to loss of honor, and incurs disgrace." At this the lovesick king arose, and taking Raghupatī by the arm made him sit down: "Hearken, my son: the sages say that Rāma is the Lord of all creation, animate and inanimate—the very God who, after weighing good and bad actions and mentally considering them, apportions their fruit as an act of judgment upon all. This is the doctrine of the Scriptures and the opinion of all.

दोहा-dohā:

औरु करै अपराधु कोउ और पाव फल भोगु ।
auru karai aparādhu kou aura pāva phala bhogu,

अति बिचित्र भगवंत गति को जग जानै जोगु ॥७७॥
ati bicitra bhagavaṁta gati ko jaga jānai jogu. 77.

Trans:

But in this case, for one to sin and for another to reap its reward, is an enigma most mysterious. The ways of God are inscrutable; and who is there in the world that can comprehend them?"

चौपाई-caupāī:

रायँ राम राखन हित लागी । बहुत उपाय किए छलु त्यागी ॥
rāyam̐ rāma rākhana hita lāgī, bahuta upāya kie chalu tyāgī.

लखी राम रुख रहत न जाने । धरम धुरंधर धीर सयाने ॥
lakhī rāma rukha rahata na jāne, dharama dhuraṁdhara dhīra sayāne.

तब नृप सीय लाइ उर लीन्ही । अति हित बहुत भाँति सिख दीन्ही ॥
taba nṛpa sīya lāi ura līnhī, ati hita bahuta bhām̐ti sikha dīnhī.

कहि बन के दुख दुसह सुनाए । सासु ससुर पितु सुख समुझाए ॥
kahi bana ke dukha dusaha sunāe, sāsu sasura pitu sukha samujhāe.

सिय मनु राम चरन अनुरागा । घरु न सुगमु बनु बिषमु न लागा ॥
siya manu rāma carana anurāgā, gharu na sugamu banu biṣamu na lāgā.

औरउ सबहिं सीय समुझाई । कहि कहि बिपिन बिपति अधिकाई ॥
aurau sabahiṁ sīya samujhāī, kahi kahi bipina bipati adhikāī.

सचिव नारि गुर नारि सयानी । सहित सनेह कहहिं मृदु बानी ॥
saciva nāri gura nāri sayānī, sahita saneha kahahiṁ mṛdu bānī.

तुम्ह कहुँ तौ न दीन्ह बनबासू । करहु जो कहहिं ससुर गुर सासू ॥
tumha kahum̐ tau na dīnha banabāsū, karahu jo kahahiṁ sasura gura sāsū.

Trans:

The king in his anxiety to detain Rāma tried every honest expedient, but when he saw that Rāma was bent on going—righteous, brave, and wise as he was—he took and pressed Sītā to his heart and gave her a most affectionate advice, telling her of all the intolerable hardships of the forest, and reminding her of the happiness she might enjoy with her parents-in-law or at her own father's house. But Sītā's heart was set on Rāma's feet, and neither home seemed to her attractive, nor the woods repulsive. Everyone else too warned her with stories of all the many miseries of the exile. The wives of the ministers and the Gurūs—prudent dames all—affectionately urged her in gentle tones: "He has not sent you into exile. You should do as you are told by your parents and your Gurū."

दोहा-dohā:

सिख सीतलि हित मधुर मृदु सुनि सीतहि न सोहानि ।
sikha sītali hita madhura mṛdu suni sītahi na sohāni,

सरद चंद चंदिनि लगत जनु चकई अकुलानि ॥७८॥
sarada caṁda caṁdini lagata janu cakaī akulāni. 78.

Trans:

This advice, friendly and kind and tender and judicious as it was, was not pleasing to Sītā's ear; in the same way as the chakwi is distressed by the rays of the autumn moon.

चौपाई-caupāī:

सीय सकुच बस उतरु न देई । सो सुनि तमकि उठी कैकेई ॥
sīya sakuca basa utaru na deī, so suni tamaki uṭhī kaikeī.

मुनि पट भूषन भाजन आनी । आगें धरि बोली मृदु बानी ॥
muni paṭa bhūṣana bhājana ānī, āgeṁ dhari bolī mṛdu bānī.

नृपहि प्रानप्रिय तुम्ह रघुबीरा । सील सनेह न छाड़िहि भीरा ॥
nṛpahi prānapriya tumha raghubīrā, sīla saneha na chāṛihi bhīrā.

सुकृतु सुजसु परलोकु नसाऊ । तुम्हहि जान बन कहिहि न काऊ ॥
sukṛtu sujasu paraloku nasāū, tumhahi jāna bana kahihi na kāū.

अस बिचारि सोइ करहु जो भावा । राम जननि सिख सुनि सुखु पावा ॥
asa bicāri soi karahu jo bhāvā, rāma janani sikha suni sukhu pāvā.

भूपहि बचन बानसम लागे । करहिं न प्रान पयान अभागे ॥
bhūpahi bacana bānasama lāge, karahiṁ na prāna payāna abhāge.

लोग बिकल मुरुछित नरनाहू । काह करिअ कछु सूझ न काहू ॥
loga bikala muruchita naranāhū, kāha karia kachu sūjha na kāhū.

रामु तुरत मुनि बेषु बनाई । चले जनक जननिहि सिरु नाई ॥
rāmu turata muni beṣu banāī, cale janaka jananihi siru nāī.

Trans:

She was, however, too modest to reply; but Kaekayī on hearing them started up in excitement and, bringing a box of anchorites' dresses and ornaments, placed them before her and said in whispered tones, "Raghubīr, you are dearer than life to the king; he cannot rid himself of his too great kindness and love, and will never tell you to go, though he forfeit his virtue, his honor, and his hope of heaven. Think of this and act as seems to you good." Rāma was glad to hear his mother's suggestion, but her words pierced the king like arrows, "Will my miserable life never leave me?" In his distress he fainted outright, and no one knew what to do. But Rāma quickly assumed the hermit's dress and bowing his head to his father and mother left.

दोहा-dohā:

सजि बन साजु समाजु सबु बनिता बंधु समेत ।
saji bana sāju samāju sabu banitā baṁdhu sameta,

बंदि बिप्र गुर चरन प्रभु चले करि सबहि अचेत ॥७९॥
baṁdi bipra gura carana prabhu cale kari sabahi aceta. 79.

Trans:

Ready for journey to the woods, the Lord set forth with his wife and brother, after reverencing the feet of the Brahmins and his Gurū, and leaving them all in bewilderment.

चौपाई-caupāī:

निकसि बसिष्ठ द्वार भए ठाढ़े । देखे लोग बिरह दव दाढ़े ॥
nikasi basiṣṭha dvāra bhae ṭhāṛhe, dekhe loga biraha dava dāṛhe.

कहि प्रिय बचन सकल समुझाए । बिप्र बृंद रघुबीर बोलाए ॥
kahi priya bacana sakala samujhāe, bipra bṛṁda raghubīra bolāe.

गुर सन कहि बरषासन दीन्हे । आदर दान बिनय बस कीन्हे ॥
gura sana kahi baraṣāsana dīnhe, ādara dāna binaya basa kīnhe.

जाचक दान मान संतोषे । मीत पुनीत प्रेम परितोषे ॥
jācaka dāna māna saṁtoṣe, mīta punīta prema paritoṣe.

दासी दास बोलाइ बहोरी । गुरहि सौंपि बोले कर जोरी ॥
dāsīṁ dāsa bolāi bahorī, gurahi saumpi bole kara jorī.

सब कै सार सँभार गोसाईं । करबि जनक जननी की नाईं ॥
saba kai sāra sam̐bhāra gosāīṁ, karabi janaka jananī kī nāīṁ.

बारहिं बार जोरि जुग पानी । कहत रामु सब सन मृदु बानी ॥
bārahiṁ bāra jori juga pānī, kahata rāmu saba sana mṛdu bānī.

सोइ सब भाँति मोर हितकारी । जेहि तें रहै भुआल सुखारी ॥
soi saba bhām̐ti mora hitakārī, jehi teṁ rahai bhuāla sukhārī.

Trans:
Leaving the palace, he halted at Gurū Vasishtha's door; and he found all the people consumed with the fire of anguish that comes from parting. With kindly words Raghubīr consoled them all, and then summoning the Brahmins, begged his Gurū to give them a year's maintenance. Many gifts he bestowed with respectful courtesy, satisfying the mendicants with largesse and civilities; and upon his personal friends showered many demonstrations of affection. Next he called his men-servants and maids and made them over to his Gurū, saying with clasped hands, "O sir, be to them as their own father and mother, and cherish them all." Again and again did Rāma with clasped hands and in gentle tones address each one of them, "He is my best friend through whom the king, my father, derives solace.

दोहा-doha:

मातु सकल मोरे बिरहँ जेहिं न होहिं दुख दीन ।
mātu sakala more birahaṁ jehiṁ na hohiṁ dukha dīna,

सोइ उपाउ तुम्ह करेहु सब पुर जन परम प्रबीन ॥८०॥
soi upāu tumha karehu saba pura jana parama prabīna. 80.

Trans:
So take care you all, my thoughtful considerate citizens; and see to it that that none of my mothers is distressed by my absence."

चौपाई-caupāī:

एहि बिधि राम सबहि समुझावा । गुर पद पदुम हरषि सिरु नावा ॥
ehi bidhi rāma sabahi samujhāvā, gura pada paduma haraṣi siru nāvā.

गनपती गौरि गिरीसु मनाई । चले असीस पाइ रघुराई ॥
ganapatī gauri girīsu manāī, cale asīsa pāi raghurāī.

राम चलत अति भयउ बिषादू । सुनि न जाइ पुर आरत नादू ॥
rāma calata ati bhayau biṣādū, suni na jāi pura ārata nādū.

कुसगुन लंक अवध अति सोकू । हरष बिषाद बिबस सुरलोकू ॥
kusaguna laṁka avadha ati sokū, haraṣa biṣāda bibasa suralokū.

गइ मुरुछा तब भूपति जागे । बोलि सुमंत्रु कहन अस लागे ॥
gai muruchā taba bhūpati jāge, boli sumaṁtru kahana asa lāge.

रामु चले बन प्रान न जाहीं । केहि सुख लागि रहत तन माहीं ॥
rāmu cale bana prāna na jāhīṁ, kehi sukha lāgi rahata tana māhīṁ.

एहि तें कवन ब्यथा बलवाना । जो दुखु पाइ तजहिं तनु प्राना ॥
ehi teṁ kavana byathā balavānā, jo dukhu pāi tajahiṁ tanu prānā.

पुनि धरि धीर कहइ नरनाहू । लै रथु संग सखा तुम्ह जाहू ॥
puni dhari dhīra kahai naranāhū, lai rathu saṁga sakhā tumha jāhū.

Trans:
When Rāma had thus exhorted them all, he cheerfully bowed his head at his Gurū's lotus feet, and invoking Ganesh, Gaurī, and Mahādev, and receiving their blessing sallied forth. As he went, there was great lamentation and a mournful wailing throughout the city, terrible to hear. In Laṅkā omens of ill, in Avadh exceeding distress; while mingled joy and sorrow possessed the hosts of heaven. When his swoon had passed, the king awoke and sent for Sumant and thus began, "Rāma has gone to the woods, and yet my life flits not; what good does it hope to get by still remaining in this body? What more grievous torture can there be—to force life away from my frame?" Again taking patience, he added, "Friend, take you the chariot and go.

दोहा-doha:

सुठि सुकुमार कुमार दोउ जनकसुता सुकुमारि ।
suṭhi sukumāra kumāra dou janakasutā sukumāri,

रथ चढ़ाइ देखराइ बनु फिरेहु गएँ दिन चारि ॥८१॥
ratha caṛhāi dekharāi banu phirehu gaem̐ dina cāri. 81.

Trans:
The two boys are young and delicate, and Janak's daughter, but a girl so frail. Take them up into the chariot and show them the forest, and come back in a day or two.

चौपाई-caupāī:

जौं नहिं फिरहिं धीर दोउ भाई । सत्यसंध दृढ़ब्रत रघुराई ॥
jauṁ nahiṁ phirahiṁ dhīra dou bhāī, satyasaṁdha dṛṛhabrata raghurāī.

तौ तुम्ह बिनय करेहु कर जोरी । फेरिअ प्रभु मिथिलेसकिसोरी ॥
tau tumha binaya karehu kara jorī, pheria prabhu mithilesakisorī.

जब सिय कानन देखि डेराई । कहेहु मोरि सिख अवसरु पाई ॥
jaba siya kānana dekhi ḍerāī, kahehu mori sikha avasaru pāī.

सासु ससुर अस कहेउ सँदेसू । पुत्रि फिरिअ बन बहुत कलेसू ॥
sāsu sasura asa kaheu sam̐desū, putri phiria bana bahuta kalesū.

पितुगृह कबहुँ कबहुँ ससुरारी । रहेहु जहाँ रुचि होइ तुम्हारी ॥
pitugṛha kabahum̐ kabahum̐ sasurārī, rahehu jahām̐ ruci hoi tumhārī.

एहि बिधि करेहु उपाय कदंबा । फिरइ त होइ प्रान अवलंबा ॥
ehi bidhi karehu upāya kadaṁbā, phirai ta hoi prāna avalaṁbā.

नाहिं त मोर मरनु परिनामा । कछु न बसाइ भएँ बिधि बामा ॥
nāhiṁ ta mora maranu parināmā, kachu na basāi bhaeṁ bidhi bāmā.

अस कहि मुरुछि परा महि राऊ । रामु लखनु सिय आनि देखाऊ ॥
asa kahi muruchi parā mahi rāū, rāmu lakhanu siya āni dekhāū.

Trans:
Both brothers are brave, and Raghurāī the very ocean of truth and staunch to his word. If they will not turn, do you, with clasped hands, humbly entreat him, 'Send back, my Lord, the daughter of Mithilā's king.' When Sītā is alarmed by the sight of the forest, take the opportunity of telling her my instructions, saying: 'This is the message sent by your father-in-law and mother-in-law; come back, daughter; there are many perils in the wilderness. You can stay at your pleasure now with your own father, now with your husband's parents.' In this manner try every which way you can. If she comes back it will be the ministration of my life; if not, it will end in my death. What can I do? God is against me." So saying, the king fainted and fell to the ground, crying: "O that you could bring them back to me, Rāma, Lakshman, and Sītā!"

दोहा-doha:

पाइ रजायसु नाइ सिरु रथु अति बेग बनाइ ।
pāi rajāyasu nāi siru rathu ati bega banāi,

गयउ जहाँ बाहर नगर सीय सहित दोउ भाइ ॥८२॥
gayau jahām̐ bāhera nagara sīya sahita dou bhāi. 82.

Trans:
Having received the king's commands, he bowed his head and in haste made ready the chariot and went to the place outside the city, where walked the two brothers with Sītā.

चौपाई-caupāī:

तब सुमंत्र नृप बचन सुनाए । करि बिनती रथ रामु चढ़ाए ॥
taba sumaṁtra nṛpa bacana sunāe, kari binatī ratha rāmu caṛhāe.

चढ़ि रथ सीय सहित दोउ भाई । चले हृदयँ अवधहि सिरु नाई ॥
caṛhi ratha sīya sahita dou bhāī, cale hṛdayam̐ avadhahi siru nāī.

चलत रामु लखि अवध अनाथा । बिकल लोग सब लागे साथा ॥
calata rāmu lakhi avadha anāthā, bikala loga saba lāge sāthā.
कृपासिंधु बहुबिधि समुझावहिं । फिरहिं प्रेम बस पुनि फिरि आवहिं ॥
kṛpāsiṁdhu bahubidhi samujhāvahiṁ, phirahiṁ prema basa puni phiri āvahiṁ.
लागति अवध भयावनि भारी । मानहुँ कालराति अँधिआरी ॥
lāgati avadha bhayāvani bhārī, mānahum̐ kālarāti am̐dhiārī.
घोर जंतु सम पुर नर नारी । डरपहिं एकहि एक निहारी ॥
ghora jaṁtu sama pura nara nārī, ḍarapahiṁ ekahi eka nihārī.
घर मसान परिजन जनु भूता । सुत हित मीत मनहुँ जमदूता ॥
ghara masāna parijana janu bhūtā, suta hita mīta manahum̐ jamadūtā.
बागन्ह बिटप बेलि कुम्हिलाहीं । सरित सरोवर देखि न जाहीं ॥
bāganha biṭapa beli kumhilāhīṁ, sarita sarovara dekhi na jāhīṁ.

Trans:

Then Sumant declared to them the king's message and respectfully made Rāma ascend the chariot. Having mounted, the two brothers with Sītā drove away, and they mentally bowed their heads towards Avadh. As the bereaved city saw Rāma depart, all the people began in disarray to follow behind. The gracious Lord said many words to console them, and they turned homewards, but then again came back overmastered by their affection. Avadh appeared to them as gloomy and oppressive as the dark night of death; the citizens themselves looked like ghastly creatures and were frightened to see one another, like so many wild beasts; their home seemed to them like graveyard, their retainers like ghosts, and their sons, friends, and neighbors as the angels of death—because bereft of Rāma all was naught. The trees and creepers in the gardens began to wither; the erst lovely streams and ponds were now fearful to behold.

दोहा-dohā:

हय गय कोटिन्ह केलिमृग पुरपसु चातक मोर ।
haya gaya koṭinha kelimṛga purapasu cātaka mora,
पिक रथांग सुक सारिका सारस हंस चकोर ॥८३॥
pika rathāṁga suka sārikā sārasa haṁsa cakora. 83.

Trans:

All the horses, elephants, and tame deer; the town-cattle, the cuckoos, and the peacocks; the *koels*, swans, parrots, *mainas*, herons, flamingoes, and partridges—

चौपाई-caupāī:

राम बियोग बिकल सब ठाढ़े । जहँ तहँ मनहुँ चित्र लिखि काढ़े ॥
rāma biyoga bikala saba ṭhāṛhe, jaham̐ taham̐ manahum̐ citra likhi kāṛhe.
नगरु सफल बनु गहबर भारी । खग मृग बिपुल सकल नर नारी ॥
nagaru saphala banu gahabara bhārī, khaga mṛga bipula sakala nara nārī.
बिधि कैकई किरातिनि कीन्ही । जेहिं दव दुसह दसहुँ दिसि दीन्ही ॥
bidhi kaikaī kirātini kīnhī, jehiṁ dava dusaha dasahum̐ disi dīnhī.
सहि न सके रघुबर बिरहागी । चले लोग सब ब्याकुल भागी ॥
sahi na sake raghubara birahāgī, cale loga saba byākula bhāgī.
सबहिं बिचारु कीन्ह मन माहीं । राम लखन सिय बिनु सुखु नाहीं ॥
sabahiṁ bicāru kīnha mana māhīṁ, rāma lakhana siya binu sukhu nāhīṁ.
जहाँ रामु तहँ सबुइ समाजू । बिनु रघुबीर अवध नहिं काजू ॥
jahām̐ rāmu taham̐ sabui samājū, binu raghubīra avadha nahiṁ kājū.
चले साथ अस मंत्रु दृढ़ाई । सुर दुर्लभ सुख सदन बिहाई ॥
cale sātha asa maṁtru dṛṛhāī, sura durlabha sukha sadana bihāī.
राम चरन पंकज प्रिय जिन्हही । बिषय भोग बस करहिं कि तिन्हही ॥
rāma carana paṁkaja priya jinhahī, biṣaya bhoga basa karahiṁ ki tinhahī.

Trans:

—all stood aghast at Rāma's departure, dumb and motionless as statues. The whole city resembled some dense forest, in which the agitated people were as the birds and deer, while Kaekayī had been fashioned by God as some wild woman of the woods who had set everything into a fierce blaze. Unable to endure the burning pain of Rāma's departure, the people all flocked after him in their bewilderment, each one thinking to himself, "There is no happiness apart from Rāma, Sītā, Lakshman. Everything can be had where Rāma is, and Avadh without Raghubīr is absolutely of no account." With this settled idea they bore him company abandoning halls of delight that the gods might envy. For what influence can the pleasures of senses have upon people who are devoted to Rāma's lotus feet?

दोहा-dohā:

बालक बृद्ध बिहाइ गृहँ लगे लोग सब साथ ।
bālaka bṛddha bihāi gṛham̐ lage loga saba sātha,
तमसा तीर निवासु किय प्रथम दिवस रघुनाथ ॥८४॥
tamasā tīra nivāsu kiya prathama divasa raghunātha. 84.

Trans:

Young and old, all left their homes and followed him; and on the bank of the Tamasa, Rāma made his first day's halt.

चौपाई-caupāī:

रघुपति प्रजा प्रेमबस देखी । सदय हृदयँ दुखु भयउ बिसेषी ॥
raghupati prajā premabasa dekhī, sadaya hṛdayam̐ dukhu bhayau biseṣī.
करुनामय रघुनाथ गोसाँई । बेगि पाइअहिं पीर पराई ॥
karunāmaya raghunātha gosām̐ī, begi pāiahiṁ pīra parāī.
कहि सप्रेम मृदु बचन सुहाए । बहुबिधि राम लोग समुझाए ॥
kahi saprema mṛdu bacana suhāe, bahubidhi rāma loga samujhāe.
किए धरम उपदेस घनेरे । लोग प्रेम बस फिरहिं न फेरे ॥
kie dharama upadesa ghanere, loga prema basa phirahiṁ na phere.
सीलु सनेहु छाड़ि नहिं जाई । असमंजस बस भे रघुराई ॥
sīlu sanehu chāṛi nahiṁ jāī, asamaṁjasa basa bhe raghurāī.
लोग सोग श्रम बस गए सोई । कछुक देवमायाँ मति मोई ॥
loga soga śrama basa gae soī, kachuka devamāyām̐ mati moī.
जबहिं जाम जुग जामिनि बीती । राम सचिव सन कहेउ सप्रीती ॥
jabahiṁ jāma juga jāmini bītī, rāma saciva sana kaheu saprītī.
खोज मारि रथु हाँकहु ताता । आन उपायँ बनिहि नहिं बाता ॥
khoja māri rathu hām̐kahu tātā, āna upāyam̐ banihi nahiṁ bātā.

Trans:

When Raghupatī saw his people overpowered with love, his kind heart was greatly troubled. The merciful Lord Raghunāth, being quickly touched by the grief of others, spoke to them many words of affection and tenderness; and he did his best to comfort them, admonishing them much of their religious duties. But in their fondness they could not tear themselves away. As there was no way of overcoming their innate affection, Raghurāī was reduced to perplexity. Worn out with grief and toil the people fell asleep—a divine delusion helping to beguile them—and when two watches of the night were spent Rāma affectionately addressed his minister, "Father, drive the chariot so as to efface the tracks of the wheels; there is no other way of settling this business."

दोहा-dohā:

राम लखन सिय जान चढ़ि संभु चरन सिरु नाइ ।
rāma lakhana siya jāna caṛhi saṁbhu carana siru nāi,
सचिवँ चलायउ तुरत रथु इत उत खोज दुराइ ॥८५॥
sacivam̐ calāyau turata rathu ita uta khoja durāi. 85.

Trans:

Rāma, Lakshman, and Sītā then mounted the car, after bowing the head to Shambhu's feet, and the minister drove it hither and thither confusing the tracks, and then speedily left.

चौपाई-caupāī:

जागे सकल लोग भएँ भोरू । गे रघुनाथ भयउ अति सोरू ॥
jāge sakala loga bhaem̐ bhorū, ge raghunātha bhayau ati sorū.

रथ कर खोज कतहुँ नहिं पावहिं । राम राम कहि चहुँ दिसि धावहिं ॥
ratha kara khoja katahuṁ nahiṁ pāvahiṁ, rāma rāma kahi cahuṁ disi dhāvahiṁ.
मनहुँ बारिनिधि बूड़ जहाजू । भयउ बिकल बड़ बनिक समाजू ॥
manahuṁ bārinidhi būṛa jahājū, bhayau bikala baṛa banika samājū.
एकहि एक देहिं उपदेसू । तजे राम हम जानि कलेसू ॥
ekahi eka dehiṁ upadesū, taje rāma hama jāni kalesū.
निंदहिं आपु सराहहिं मीना । धिग जीवनु रघुबीर बिहीना ॥
niṁdahiṁ āpu sarāhahiṁ mīnā, dhiga jīvanu raghubīra bihīnā.
जौं पै प्रिय बियोगु बिधि कीन्हा । तौ कस मरनु न मागें दीन्हा ॥
jauṁ pai priya biyogu bidhi kīnhā, tau kasa maranu na māgeṁ dīnhā.
एहि बिधि करत प्रलाप कलापा । आए अवध भरे परितापा ॥
ehi bidhi karata pralāpa kalāpā, āe avadha bhare paritāpā.
बिषम बियोगु न जाइ बखाना । अवधि आस सब राखहिं प्राना ॥
biṣama biyogu na jāi bakhānā, avadhi āsa saba rākhahiṁ prānā.

Trans:

At daybreak the people all woke, and there was a cry of dismay that Raghubīr had left. They could in no way distinguish the tracks of the chariot, though they ran in all directions, crying 'Rāma, Rāma'—like as when a ship is sinking at sea and all the merchants are in terror. One suggested to another, "Rāma left us on seeing our distress." They revile themselves and envy the fish, crying, "A curse on our life away from Raghubīr! As God has robbed us of our beloved, why has he not granted us our prayer to die?" With many such lamentations they returned to Avadh full of heaviness; the anguish of parting was beyond description, and it was only the hope of Rāma's return that kept them alive.

दोहा-dohā:

राम दरस हित नेम ब्रत लगे करन नर नारि ।
rāma darasa hita nema brata lage karana nara nāri,
मनहुँ कोक कोकी कमल दीन बिहीन तमारि ॥८६॥
manahuṁ koka kokī kamala dīna bihīna tamāri. 86.

Trans:

Men and women alike began to fast and make vows to secure Rāma's safe return. They were as miserable as a pair of *chakwā* birds and the lotus flowers are without the sun.

चौपाई-caupāī:

सीता सचिव सहित दोउ भाई । सृंगबेरपुर पहुँचे जाई ॥
sītā saciva sahita dou bhāī, sṛṁgaberapura pahuṁce jāī.
उतरे राम देवसरि देखी । कीन्ह दंडवत हरषु बिसेषी ॥
utare rāma devasari dekhī, kīnha daṁḍavata haraṣu biseṣī.
लखन सचिवँ सियँ किए प्रनामा । सबहि सहित सुखु पायउ रामा ॥
lakhana sacivaṁ siyaṁ kie pranāmā, sabahi sahita sukhu pāyau rāmā.
गंग सकल मुद मंगल मूला । सब सुख करनि हरनि सब सूला ॥
gaṁga sakala muda maṁgala mūlā, saba sukha karani harani saba sūlā.
कहि कहि कोटिक कथा प्रसंगा । रामु बिलोकहिं गंग तरंगा ॥
kahi kahi koṭika kathā prasaṁgā, rāmu bilokahiṁ gaṁga taraṁgā.
सचिवहि अनुजहि प्रियहि सुनाई । बिबुध नदी महिमा अधिकाई ॥
sacivahi anujahi priyahi sunāī, bibudha nadī mahimā adhikāī.
मज्जनु कीन्ह पंथ श्रम गयऊ । सुचि जलु पिअत मुदित मन भयऊ ॥
majjanu kīnha paṁtha śrama gayaū, suci jalu piata mudita mana bhayaū.
सुमिरत जाहि मिटइ श्रम भारू । तेहि श्रम यह लौकिक ब्यवहारू ॥
sumirata jāhi miṭai śrama bhārū, tehi śrama yaha laukika byavahārū.

Trans:

Meanwhile the two brothers with Sītā and the minister arrive near the city of Sringavera. On beholding the river of the gods, Rāma alighted and with much joy made his obeisance; and so did Lakshman, Sītā, and Sumant as well. Rāma was glad, with all of them—for the Gangā is the source of all bliss and beatitude, the generator of all happiness, the destroyer of every sorrow. Many were the stories and legends that Rāma repeated as he gazed upon the heavenly torrents, telling the minister, his younger brother, and his bride of the majesty and grandeur of the celestial stream. They bathed and the fatigue of their march was removed; they drank of the holy water and their soul abounded with exhilaration. And yes, it is only in rustic phrase that fatigue is ascribed to Him, the Lord God, by whose very remembrance all the burdens of the world are lightened.

दोहा-dohā:

सुद्ध सचिदानंदमय कंद भानुकुल केतु ।
suddha sacidānaṁdamaya kaṁda bhānukula ketu,
चरित करत नर अनुहरत संसृति सागर सेतु ॥८७॥
carita karata nara anuharata saṁsṛti sāgara setu. 87.

Trans:

Rāma, the champion of the solar race, is the holy God, of supreme wisdom and bliss, the bridge over the ocean of existence—though He acts like an ordinary human.

चौपाई-caupāī:

यह सुधि गुहँ निषाद जब पाई । मुदित लिए प्रिय बंधु बोलाई ॥
yaha sudhi guhaṁ niṣāda jaba pāī, mudita lie priya baṁdhu bolāī.
लिए फल मूल भेंट भरि भारा । मिलन चलेउ हियँ हरषु अपारा ॥
lie phala mūla bheṁṭa bhari bhārā, milana caleu hiyaṁ haraṣu apārā.
करि दंडवत भेंट धरि आगें । प्रभुहि बिलोकत अति अनुरागें ॥
kari daṁḍavata bheṁṭa dhari āgeṁ, prabhuhi bilokata ati anurāgeṁ.
सहज सनेह बिबस रघुराई । पूँछी कुसल निकट बैठाई ॥
sahaja saneha bibasa raghurāī, pūṁchī kusala nikaṭa baiṭhāī.
नाथ कुसल पद पंकज देखें । भयउँ भागभाजन जन लेखें ॥
nātha kusala pada paṁkaja dekheṁ, bhayauṁ bhāgabhājana jana lekheṁ.
देव धरनि धनु धामु तुम्हारा । मैं जनु नीचु सहित परिवारा ॥
deva dharani dhanu dhāmu tumhārā, maiṁ janu nīcu sahita parivārā.
कृपा करिअ पुर धारिअ पाऊ । थापिय जनु सबु लोगु सिहाऊ ॥
kṛpā karia pura dhāria pāū, thāpiya janu sabu logu sihāū.
कहेहु सत्य सबु सखा सुजाना । मोहि दीन्ह पितु आयसु आना ॥
kahehu satya sabu sakhā sujānā, mohi dīnha pitu āyasu ānā.

Trans:

When Gūha, the Nishād, heard the news he was glad and called together his friends and relations, and taking a great quantity of fruits and vegetables as presents, went out to meet them with infinite joy. With a profound obeisance he put down his offering before them and gazed upon the Lord with an utmost devotion. Raghurāī with his natural kindliness asked him of his health and seated him by his side. "The sight of your lotus feet, sire, is health indeed. I am most highly favored, as all will admit. My land, my house, my fortune are yours, my Lord; I and all that are mine are your poor vassals. Do me the favor of entering my abode; treat me as one of your own servants and I shall be the envy of all men." "All that you say, my good friend, is very true; but my father has given me other commands.

दोहा-dohā:

बरष चारिदस बासु बन मुनि ब्रत बेषु अहारु ।
baraṣa cāridasa bāsu bana muni brata beṣu ahāru,
ग्राम बासु नहिं उचित सुनि गुहहि भयउ दुखु भारु ॥८८॥
grāma bāsu nahiṁ ucita suni guhahi bhayau dukhu bhāru. 88.

Trans:

For fourteen years I most dwell in the woods and adopt the rules, the dress, and the diet of a hermit. To stay in a village is forbidden." On hearing this Gūha was much grieved.

चौपाई-caupāī:

राम लखन सिय रूप निहारी । कहहिं सप्रेम ग्राम नर नारी ॥
rāma lakhana siya rūpa nihārī, kahahiṁ saprema grāma nara nārī.
ते पितु मातु कहहु सखि कैसे । जिन्ह पठए बन बालक ऐसे ॥
te pitu mātu kahahu sakhi kaise, jinha paṭhae bana bālaka aise.
एक कहहिं भल भूपति कीन्हा । लोयन लाहु हमहि बिधि दीन्हा ॥
eka kahahiṁ bhala bhūpati kīnhā, loyana lāhu hamahi bidhi dīnhā.
तब निषादपति उर अनुमाना । तरु सिंसुपा मनोहर जाना ॥
taba niṣādapati ura anumānā, taru siṁsupā manohara jānā.
लै रघुनाथहि ठाउँ देखावा । कहेउ राम सब भाँति सुहावा ॥
lai raghunāthahi ṭhāuṁ dekhāvā, kaheu rāma saba bhāṁti suhāvā.
पुरजन करि जोहारु घर आए । रघुबर संध्या करन सिधाए ॥
purajana kari johāru ghara āe, raghubara saṁdhyā karana sidhāe.
गुहँ सँवारि साँथरी डसाई । कुस किसलयमय मृदुल सुहाई ॥
guhaṁ saṁvāri sāṁtharī ḍasāī, kusa kisalayamaya mṛdula suhāī.
सुचि फल मूल मधुर मृदु जानी । दोना भरि भरि राखेसि पानी ॥
suci phala mūla madhura mṛdu jānī, donā bhari bhari rākhesi pānī.

Trans:

Seeing Rāma, Lakshman, and Sītā to be so beautiful, the citizens affectionately protested, "What kind of parents can they be, friend, who have banished such children to the woods?" Said another, "The king has done well to give our eyes such a treat." Then the Nishād chief on reflection decided upon a beautiful *sinsapa* tree, and took Raghunāth and showed him the place, who declared it to be most excellent. The citizens after paying him their respects went home, and Rāma proceeded to the performance of his evening devotions. Gūha made and spread for him a charming bed of grass and soft leaves, and brought him leaf-made bowls filled with all such fruits and vegetables as he knew to be sweet and wholesome and good.

दोहा-dohā:

सिय सुमंत्र भ्राता सहित कंद मूल फल खाइ ।
siya sumaṁtra bhrātā sahita kaṁda mūla phala khāi,
सयन कीन्ह रघुबंसमनि पाय पलोटत भाइ ॥८९॥
sayana kīnha raghubaṁsamani pāya paloṭata bhāi. 89.

Trans:

After he had partaken of the fruits and herbs with the minister and Sītā and his brother, the jewel of Raghu's line lay down to sleep, while Lakshman rubbed his feet.

चौपाई-caupāī:

उठे लखनु प्रभु सोवत जानी । कहि सचिवहि सोवन मृदु बानी ॥
uṭhe lakhanu prabhu sovata jānī, kahi sacivahi sovana mṛdu bānī.
कछुक दूरि सजि बान सरासन । जागन लगे बैठि बीरासन ॥
kachuka dūri saji bāna sarāsana, jāgana lage baiṭhi bīrāsana.
गुँह बोलाइ पाहरू प्रतीती । ठावँ ठावँ राखे अति प्रीती ॥
guṁha bolāi pāharū pratītī, ṭhāvaṁ ṭhāvaṁ rākhe ati prītī.
आपु लखन पहिं बैठेउ जाई । कटि भाथी सर चाप चढ़ाई ॥
āpu lakhana pahiṁ baiṭheu jāī, kaṭi bhāthī sara cāpa caṛhāī.
सोवत प्रभुहि निहारि निषादू । भयउ प्रेम बस हृदयँ बिषादू ॥
sovata prabhuhi nihāri niṣādū, bhayau prema basa hṛdayaṁ biṣādū.
तनु पुलकित जलु लोचन बहई । बचन सप्रेम लखन सन कहई ॥
tanu pulakita jalu locana bahaī, bacana saprema lakhana sana kahaī.
भूपति भवन सुभायँ सुहावा । सुरपति सदनु न पटतर पावा ॥
bhūpati bhavana subhāyaṁ suhāvā, surapati sadanu na paṭatara pāvā.
मनिमय रचित चारु चौबारे । जनु रतिपति निज हाथ सँवारे ॥
manimaya racita cāru caubāre, janu ratipati nija hātha saṁvāre.

Trans:

When he knew his Lord to be asleep, he arose and softly bade Sumant take rest, while he himself fitted an arrow to his bow and took up the position of a marksman at a little distance there, keeping watch. The affectionate Gūha, having summoned trusty sentinels and stationed them round-about, went himself and sat down by Lakshman, with quivers fastened to the waist and arrow fitted to the bow. When the Nishād saw Rāma asleep his soul was troubled from an excess of love, his body thrilled with emotion, his eyes awed with tears, and he thus in tender accents addressed Lakshman, "The king's palace is altogether beautiful, nor can the courts of heaven be compared to it. Its charming pavilions, inlaid with precious stones, seem to have been adorned by Love's own hands.

दोहा-dohā:

सुचि सुबिचित्र सुभोगमय सुमन सुगंध सुबास ।
suci subicitra subhogamaya sumana sugaṁdha subāsa,
पलँग मंजु मनिदीप जहँ सब बिधि सकल सुपास ॥९०॥
palaṁga maṁju manidīpa jahaṁ saba bidhi sakala supāsa. 90.

Trans:

Rich and luxurious are its beds, sweet with odorous flowers and perfumes, with jeweled lamps and appliances of every description;

चौपाई-caupāī:

बिबिध बसन उपधान तुराईं । छीर फेन मृदु बिसद सुहाईं ॥
bibidha basana upadhāna turāīṁ, chīra phena mṛdu bisada suhāīṁ.
तहँ सिय रामु सयन निसि करहीं । निज छबि रति मनोज मदु हरहीं ॥
tahaṁ siya rāmu sayana nisi karahīṁ, nija chabi rati manoja madu harahīṁ.
ते सिय रामु साथरीं सोए । श्रमित बसन बिनु जाहिं न जोए ॥
te siya rāmu sātharīṁ soe, śramita basana binu jāhiṁ na joe.
मातु पिता परिजन पुरबासी । सखा सुसील दास अरु दासी ॥
mātu pitā parijana purabāsī, sakhā susīla dāsa aru dāsī.
जोगवहिं जिन्हहि प्रान की नाईं । महि सोवत तेइ राम गोसाईं ॥
jogavahiṁ jinhahi prāna kī nāī, mahi sovata tei rāma gosāīṁ.
पिता जनक जग बिदित प्रभाऊ । ससुर सुरेस सखा रघुराऊ ॥
pitā janaka jaga bidita prabhāū, sasura suresa sakhā raghurāū.
रामचंदु पति सो बैदेही । सोवत महि बिधि बाम न केही ॥
rāmacaṁdu pati so baidehī, sovata mahi bidhi bāma na kehī.
सिय रघुबीर कि कानन जोगू । करम प्रधान सत्य कह लोगू ॥
siya raghubīra ki kānana jogū, karama pradhāna satya kaha logū.

Trans:

with all kinds of coverlets and pillows, and mattresses as soft and white as the froth of milk, where Sītā and Rāma reposed at night and put to shame with their beauty both Ratī and Kāmdev. And now they sleep on a pallet, weary and uncovered, pitiful to behold. That Rāma—whom his father and mother, his own family and all the people of the city, his companions and associates, his menservants and maidservants, all cherished as tenderly as their own life—is now sleeping on the bare ground! And Sītā—whose father is Janak of worldwide fame; whose father-in-law is Dashrath, the friend of the king of heaven; whose spouse is Rāmachandra—is now sleeping on the ground! Is not God against us all? Are Sītā and Rāma fit to be exiled to the woods? Well do men say, 'Fate is supreme'.

दोहा-dohā:

कैकयनंदिनि मंदमति कठिन कुटिलपनु कीन्ह ।
kaikayanaṁdini maṁdamati kaṭhina kuṭilapanu kīnha,
जेहिं रघुनंदन जानकिहि सुख अवसर दुखु दीन्ह ॥९१॥
jehiṁ raghunaṁdana jānakihi sukha avasara dukhu dīnha. 91.

Trans:

The foolish daughter of Kekaya has wrought sad mischief by bringing this trouble upon Rāma and Jānakī on their day of rejoicing.

चौपाई-caupāī:

भइ दिनकर कुल बिटप कुठारी । कुमति कीन्ह सब बिस्व दुखारी ॥
bhai dinakara kula biṭapa kuṭhārī, kumati kīnha saba bisva dukhārī.
भयउ बिषादु निषादहि भारी । राम सीय महि सयन निहारी ॥
bhayau biṣādu niṣādahi bhārī, rāma sīya mahi sayana nihārī.
बोले लखन मधुर मृदु बानी । ग्यान बिराग भगति रस सानी ॥
bole lakhana madhura mṛdu bānī, gyāna birāga bhagati rasa sānī.
काहु न कोउ सुख दुख कर दाता । निज कृत करम भोग सबु भ्राता ॥
kāhu na kou sukha dukha kara dātā, nija kṛta karama bhoga sabu bhrātā.
जोग बियोग भोग भल मंदा । हित अनहित मध्यम भ्रम फंदा ॥
joga biyoga bhoga bhala maṁdā, hita anahita madhyama bhrama phaṁdā.
जनमु मरनु जहँ लगि जग जालू । संपती बिपति करमु अरु कालू ॥
janamu maranu jahaṁ lagi jaga jālū, saṁpatī bipati karamu aru kālū.
धरनि धामु धनु पुर परिवारू । सरगु नरकु जहँ लगि ब्यवहारू ॥
dharani dhāmu dhanu pura parivārū, saragu naraku jahaṁ lagi byavahārū.
देखिअ सुनिअ गुनिअ मन माहीं । मोह मूल परमारथु नाहीं ॥
dekhia sunia gunia mana māhīṁ, moha mūla paramārathu nāhīṁ.

Trans:

She has become the axe at the root of the tree of the solar race, and through her wickedness has plunged the whole world in misery." Seeing Rāma and Sītā asleep upon the ground, the Nishād had become exceedingly sad; but Lakshman addressed him in sweet and gentle tones that were full of the essence of wisdom, sobriety, and faith: "No person is the cause of another's sorrows or joys. All is the fruit of one's own actions, brother. Union and separation, pleasure and pain, good and evil, friendship, hostility and neutrality are all the snares of Māyā. Birth and death, all the entanglements of the world, prosperity and adversity, fortune and destiny, earth, home, wealth, city and family, heaven and hell, and all human affairs—all that you can see, or hear, or imagine in your mind, all this is the delusional Māyā, the façade that hides the Truth.

दोहा-dohā:

सपनें होइ भिखारि नृपु रंकु नाकपति होइ ।
sapaneṁ hoi bhikhāri nṛpu raṁku nākapati hoi,
जागें लाभु न हानि कछु तिमि प्रपंच जियँ जोइ ॥९२॥
jāgeṁ lābhu na hāni kachu timi prapaṁca jiyaṁ joi. 92.

Trans:

In a dream a beggar becomes a king, and the lord of heaven becomes a pauper; but upon waking the one is no gainer nor the other a loser; this is the way in which you should regard affairs of the world.

चौपाई-caupāī:

अस बिचारि नहिं कीजिअ रोसू । काहुहि बादि न देइअ दोसू ॥
asa bicāri nahiṁ kījia rosū, kāhuhi bādi na deia dosū.
मोह निसाँ सबु सोवनिहारा । देखिअ सपन अनेक प्रकारा ॥
moha nisāṁ sabu sovanihārā, dekhia sapana aneka prakārā.
एहिं जग जामिनि जागहिं जोगी । परमारथी प्रपंच बियोगी ॥
ehiṁ jaga jāmini jāgahiṁ jogī, paramārathī prapaṁca biyogī.
जानिअ तबहिं जीव जग जागा । जब जब बिषय बिलास बिरागा ॥
jānia tabahiṁ jīva jaga jāgā, jaba jaba biṣaya bilāsa birāgā.
होइ बिबेकु मोह भ्रम भागा । तब रघुनाथ चरन अनुरागा ॥
hoi bibeku moha bhrama bhāgā, taba raghunātha carana anurāgā.
सखा परम परमारथु एहू । मन क्रम बचन राम पद नेहू ॥
sakhā parama paramārathu ehū, mana krama bacana rāma pada nehū.
राम ब्रह्म परमारथ रूपा । अबिगत अलख अनादि अनूपा ॥
rāma brahma paramāratha rūpā, abigata alakha anādi anūpā.
सकल बिकार रहित गतभेदा । कहि नित नेति निरूपहिं बेदा ॥
sakala bikāra rahita gatabhedā, kahi nita neti nirūpahiṁ bedā.

Trans:

Reasoning thus, be not angry with anyone, nor vainly attribute blame to any. All of us are sleepers in a night of delusion, and see the many kinds of dreams. In this world of darkness they alone are awake who detach themselves from the material, and are absorbed in contemplation upon the Supreme. Nor can any soul be regarded as roused from slumber till he has renounced every sensual enjoyment. Then alone ensues spiritual enlightenment and escape from the errors of delusion; and finally there comes to one that pinnacle: Devotion to Rāma. This, my friend, is man's highest good: to be devoted to Rāma in thought, word, and deed. Rāma is God, the totality of good, imperishable, invisible, uncreated, incomparable, void of all change, indivisible, whom the Veda declares that it cannot define.

दोहा-dohā:

भगत भूमि भूसुर सुरभि सुर हित लागि कृपाल ।
bhagata bhūmi bhūsura surabhi sura hita lāgi kṛpāla,
करत चरित धरि मनुज तनु सुनत मिटहिं जग जाल ॥९३॥
karata carita dhari manuja tanu sunata miṭahiṁ jaga jāla. 93.

Trans:

In his mercy he has taken the form of a human and performs human actions—out of a love which he bears towards his faithful people and the earth, the Brahmins, and cows, and gods—hearing of which the snares of the world are rent asunder.

मासपारायण पंद्रहवा विश्राम
māsapārāyaṇa paṁdrahavā viśrāma
(Pause 15 for a Thirty-Day Recitation)

चौपाई-caupāī:

सखा समुझि अस परिहरि मोहू । सिय रघुबीर चरन रत होहू ॥
sakhā samujhi asa parihari mohū, siya raghubīra carana rata hohū.
कहत राम गुन भा भिनुसारा । जागे जग मंगल सुखदारा ॥
kahata rāma guna bhā bhinusārā, jāge jaga maṁgala sukhadārā.
सकल सौच करि राम नहावा । सुचि सुजान बट छीर मगावा ॥
sakala sauca kari rāma nahāvā, suci sujāna baṭa chīra magāvā.
अनुज सहित सिर जटा बनाए । देखि सुमंत्र नयन जल छाए ॥
anuja sahita sira jaṭā banāe, dekhi sumaṁtra nayana jala chāe.
हृदयँ दाहु अति बदन मलीना । कह कर जोरि बचन अति दीना ॥
hṛdayaṁ dāhu ati badana malīnā, kaha kara jori bacana ati dīnā.
नाथ कहेउ अस कोसलनाथा । लै रथु जाहु राम कें साथा ॥
nātha kaheu asa kosalanāthā, lai rathu jāhu rāma keṁ sāthā.
बनु देखाइ सुरसरि अन्हवाई । आनेहु फेरि बेगि दोउ भाई ॥
banu dekhāi surasari anhavāī, ānehu pheri begi dou bhāī.
लखनु रामु सिय आनेहु फेरी । संसय सकल सँकोच निबेरी ॥
lakhanu rāmu siya ānehu pherī, saṁsaya sakala saṁkoca niberī.

Trans:

Having thus reflected, O friend, give no place to infatuations and perplexities but fix your affections on Sītā-Rāma's lotus feet." While he was yet speaking of Rāma's virtues, the day broke and the joy of the world awoke. After performing the purificatory rites he bathed, the all-pure and wise; and then called for some milk of the bar tree, and with that bound up the hair of his head into a knot—like an ascetic; and so also did his brother. On seeing this, Sumant's eyes were filled with tears. Sore pained at heart, with doleful face and clasped hands he made this humble speech, "The king of Kaushal, my lord, thus enjoined me: 'Take the chariot and go with Rāma; let them see the forest and bathe in the Gangā, and then speedily bring them home again, both the brothers, Lakshman, Rāma and Sītā too; bring them back, settling all their doubts and scruples.'

दोहा-dohā:

नृप अस कहेउ गोसाइँ जस कहइ करौं बलि सोइ ।
nṛpa asa kaheu gosāiṁ jasa kahai karauṁ bali soi,
करि बिनती पायन्ह परेउ दीन्ह बाल जिमि रोइ ॥९४॥
kari binatī pāyanha pareu dīnha bāla jimi roi. 94.

Trans:

Thus spoke the king, sire; but, woe is me! I can do only as you tell me." He fell in supplication at his feet weeping helplessly as a child.

चौपाई-caupāī:

तात कृपा करि कीजिअ सोई । जातें अवध अनाथ न होई ॥
tāta kṛpā kari kījia soī, jāteṁ avadha anātha na hoī.
मंत्रिहि राम उठाइ प्रबोधा । तात धरम मतु तुम्ह सबु सोधा ॥
maṁtrihi rāma uṭhāi prabodhā, tāta dharama matu tumha sabu sodhā.
सिबि दधीच हरिचंद नरेसा । सहे धरम हित कोटि कलेसा ॥
sibi dadhīca haricaṁda naresā, sahe dharama hita koṭi kalesā.
रंतिदेव बलि भूप सुजाना । धरमु धरेउ सहि संकट नाना ॥
raṁtideva bali bhūpa sujānā, dharamu dhareu sahi saṁkaṭa nānā.
धरमु न दूसर सत्य समाना । आगम निगम पुरान बखाना ॥
dharamu na dūsara satya samānā, āgama nigama purāna bakhānā.
मैं सोइ धरमु सुलभ करि पावा । तजें तिहूँ पुर अपजसु छावा ॥
maiṁ soi dharamu sulabha kari pāvā, tajeṁ tihūṁ pura apajasu chāvā.
संभावित कहुँ अपजस लाहू । मरन कोटि सम दारुन दाहू ॥
saṁbhāvita kahuṁ apajasa lāhū, marana koṭi sama dāruna dāhū.
तुम्ह सन तात बहुत का कहऊँ । दिएँ उतरु फिरि पातकु लहऊँ ॥
tumha sana tāta bahuta kā kahaūṁ, dieṁ utaru phiri pātaku lahaūṁ.

Trans:

"Have pity, my son, and so act that Avadh be not left destitute." Rāma raised the minister and urged him kindly: "Father, you know the path of virtue. Sivi, Dadhichi, and king Harish-chandra, for the sake of their Dharma, endured countless afflictions. Rantidev and wise king Bālī kept their faith through many trials and tribulations. There is no virtue equal to Truth—as the Vedas, Shāstras, and Purānas declare. I have reached this virtue by an easy road; if I abandon it, my disgrace will be published in earth, heaven, and hell. And disgrace to a man of honor is a pain as grievous as a million deaths. But why say all this to you, father? I only incur sin by answering you.

दोहा-dohā:

पितु पद गहि कहि कोटि नति बिनय करब कर जोरि ।
pitu pada gahi kahi koṭi nati binaya karaba kara jori,
चिंता कवनिहु बात कै तात करिअ जनि मोरि ॥९५॥
ciṁtā kavanihu bāta kai tāta karia jani mori. 95.

Trans:

Fall humbly at my father's feet and with clasped hands beg of him not to distress himself in any way on account of me.

चौपाई-caupāī:

तुम्ह पुनि पितु सम अति हित मोरें । बिनती करउँ तात कर जोरें ॥
tumha puni pitu sama ati hita moreṁ, binatī karauṁ tāta kara joreṁ.
सब बिधि सोइ करतब्य तुम्हारें । दुख न पाव पितु सोच हमारें ॥
saba bidhi soi karatabya tumhāreṁ, dukha na pāva pitu soca hamāreṁ.
सुनि रघुनाथ सचिव संबादू । भयउ सपरिजन बिकल निषादू ॥
suni raghunātha saciva saṁbādū, bhayau saparijana bikala niṣādū.
पुनि कछु लखन कही कटु बानी । प्रभु बरजे बड़ अनुचित जानी ॥
puni kachu lakhana kahī kaṭu bānī, prabhu baraje baṛa anucita jānī.
सकुचि राम निज सपथ देवाई । लखन सँदेसु कहिअ जनि जाई ॥
sakuci rāma nija sapatha devāī, lakhana saṁdesu kahia jani jāī.
कह सुमंत्रु पुनि भूप सँदेसू । सहि न सकिहि सिय बिपिन कलेसू ॥
kaha sumaṁtru puni bhūpa saṁdesū, sahi na sakihi siya bipina kalesū.
जेहि बिधि अवध आव फिरि सीया । सोइ रघुबरहि तुम्हहि करनीया ॥
jehi bidhi avadha āva phiri sīyā, soi raghubarahi tumhahi karanīyā.
नतरु निपट अवलंब बिहीना । मैं न जिअब जिमि जल बिनु मीना ॥
nataru nipaṭa avalaṁba bihīnā, maiṁ na jiaba jimi jala binu mīnā.

Trans:

You again are equally dear to me as my father, and I implore you, sire, to do everything that will prevent the king from grieving about me." On hearing this conversation between Raghunāth and the minister, the Nishād and his people were saddened and Lakshman spoke a little angrily. But the Lord stopped him, knowing it to be altogether out of place, and adjured Sumant, by the love he bore him, not to repeat Lakshman's words. Sumant then proceeded with the king's message: "Sītā is not able to bear the hardships of the exile; you should try and persuade her to return to Avadh; otherwise I shall have no prop left, and must die as inevitably as a fish out of water.

दोहा-dohā:

मइकें ससुरें सकल सुख जबहिं जहाँ मनु मान ।
maikeṁ sasureṁ sakala sukha jabahiṁ jahāṁ manu māna,
तँह तब रहिहि सुखेन सिय जब लगि बिपति बिहान ॥९६॥
taṁha taba rahihi sukhena siya jaba lagi bipati bihāna. 96.

Trans:

She has a happy home both with her own mother and with her husband's parents, and she can live when she pleases at either, until these troubles are overpast.

चौपाई-caupāī:

बिनती भूप कीन्ह जेहि भाँती । आरति प्रीति न सो कहि जाती ॥
binatī bhūpa kīnha jehi bhāṁtī, ārati prīti na so kahi jātī.
पितु सँदेसु सुनि कृपानिधाना । सियहि दीन्ह सिख कोटि बिधाना ॥
pitu saṁdesu suni kṛpānidhānā, siyahi dīnha sikha koṭi bidhānā.
सासु ससुर गुर प्रिय परिवारू । फिरहु त सब कर मिटै खभारू ॥
sāsu sasura gura priya parivārū, phirahu ta saba kara miṭai khabhārū.
सुनि पति बचन कहति बैदेही । सुनहु प्रानपति परम सनेही ॥
suni pati bacana kahati baidehī, sunahu prānapati parama sanehī.
प्रभु करुनामय परम बिबेकी । तनु तजि रहति छाँह किमि छेंकी ॥
prabhu karunāmaya parama bibekī, tanu taji rahati chāṁha kimi cheṁkī.
प्रभा जाइ कहँ भानु बिहाई । कहँ चंद्रिका चंदु तजि जाई ॥
prabhā jāi kahaṁ bhānu bihāī, kahaṁ caṁdrikā caṁdu taji jāī.
पतिहि प्रेममय बिनय सुनाई । कहति सचिव सन गिरा सुहाई ॥
patihi premamaya binaya sunāī, kahati saciva sana girā suhāī.
तुम्ह पितु ससुर सरिस हितकारी । उतरु देउँ फिरि अनुचित भारी ॥
tumha pitu sasura sarisa hitakārī, utaru deuṁ phiri anucita bhārī.

Trans:

The piteousness of the king's entreaties and the earnestness of his affection are more than I can express." On hearing his father's message, the All-merciful in every way tried to persuade Sītā: "Only return; and the affliction of your parents, your Gurū, and all your friends and relations will be at an end." Replied Vaidehi to her husband's words, "Hearken most dear and loving lord, full of compassion and of infinite wisdom; can a shadow exist apart from its substance? Where is the sunlight without the sun, or the radiance of the moon when the moon is not?" Having uttered this affectionate prayer to her husband, she turned to the minister with these winning words, "You are as much my benefactor as my own father or my father-in-law, and if I answer you, it is the height of impropriety.

दोहा-dohā:

आरति बस सनमुख भइउँ बिलगु न मानब तात ।
ārati basa sanamukha bhaium̐ bilagu na mānaba tāta,
आरजसुत पद कमल बिनु बादि जहाँ लगि नात ॥९७॥
ārajasuta pada kamala binu bādi jahām̐ lagi nāta. 97.

Trans:

Yet, sire, take it not ill of me if in my grief I withstand you. Away from the lotus feet of my Lord, all other ties of kinship are of little account.

चौपाई-caupāī:

पितु बैभव बिलास मैं डीठा । नृप मनि मुकुट मिलित पद पीठा ॥
pitu baibhava bilāsa maiṁ ḍīṭhā, nṛpa mani mukuṭa milita pada pīṭhā.
सुखनिधान अस पितु गृह मोरें । पिय बिहीन मन भाव न भोरें ॥
sukhanidhāna asa pitu gṛha moreṁ, piya bihīna mana bhāva na bhoreṁ.
ससुर चक्कवइ कोसलराऊ । भुवन चारिदस प्रगट प्रभाऊ ॥
sasura cakkavai kosalarāū, bhuvana cāridasa pragaṭa prabhāū.
आगें होइ जेहि सुरपति लेई । अरध सिंघासन आसनु देई ॥
āgeṁ hoi jehi surapati leī, aradha siṁghāsana āsanu deī.
ससुर एतादृस अवध निवासू । प्रिय परिवारु मातु सम सासू ॥
sasura etādṛsa avadha nivāsū, priya parivāru mātu sama sāsū.
बिनु रघुपति पद पदुम परागा । मोहि केउ सपनेहुँ सुखद न लागा ॥
binu raghupati pada paduma parāgā, mohi keu sapanehum̐ sukhada na lāgā.
अगम पंथ बनभूमि पहारा । करि केहरि सर सरित अपारा ॥
agama paṁtha banabhūmi pahārā, kari kehari sara sarita apārā.
कोल किरात कुरंग बिहंगा । मोहि सब सुखद प्रानपति संगा ॥
kola kirāta kuraṁga bihaṁgā, mohi saba sukhada prānapati saṁgā.

Trans:

I have seen my father's luxury and magnificence and his footstool thronged with the jeweled crowns of kings, yet though his palace be such a blissful abode, I have no pleasure there without my spouse. My Imperial father-in-law, the sovereign of Kaushal, is of such glorious renown throughout the fourteen spheres that the king of heaven would advance to meet him and cede him half his throne; yet though he be so great and Avadh his home, and though the whole of his family be dear to me, and with my mother-in-law as my own mother, I could not find pleasure in a single thing for a moment, away from the lotus flowers of Ragupati's feet. Though the forest road be rough, and the country mountainous, full of dangerous elephants and tigers, boundless lakes and streams, untamed tribes of *Kol*s and *Kirāt*s, and wild beasts and birds; all is delightful if my dear Lord be with me.

दोहा-dohā:

सासु ससुर सन मोरि हुँति बिनय करबि परि पायँ ।
sāsu sasura sana mori hum̐ti binaya karabi pari pāyam̐,
मोर सोचु जनि करिअ कछु मैं बन सुखी सुभायँ ॥९८॥
mora socu jani karia kachu maiṁ bana sukhī subhāyam̐. 98.

Trans:

Fall at the feet of my father-in-law and my mother-in-law and tell them humbly from me not to grieve on my account, for I am perfectly happy in the woods.

चौपाई-caupāī:

प्राननाथ प्रिय देवर साथा । बीर धुरीन धरें धनु भाथा ॥
prānanātha priya devara sāthā, bīra dhurīna dhareṁ dhanu bhāthā.
नहिं मग श्रमु भ्रमु दुख मन मोरें । मोहि लगि सोचु करिअ जनि भोरें ॥
nahiṁ maga śramu bhramu dukha mana moreṁ, mohi lagi socu karia jani bhoreṁ.
सुनि सुमंत्रु सिय सीतलि बानी । भयउ बिकल जनु फनि मनि हानी ॥
suni sumaṁtru siya sītali bānī, bhayau bikala janu phani mani hānī.
नयन सूझ नहिं सुनइ न काना । कहि न सकइ कछु अति अकुलाना ॥
nayana sūjha nahiṁ sunai na kānā, kahi na sakai kachu ati akulānā.
राम प्रबोधु कीन्ह बहु भाँती । तदपि होति नहिं सीतलि छाती ॥
rāma prabodhu kīnha bahu bhām̐tī, tadapi hoti nahiṁ sītali chātī.
जतन अनेक साथ हित कीन्हे । उचित उतर रघुनंदन दीन्हे ॥
jatana aneka sātha hita kīnhe, ucita utara raghunaṁdana dīnhe.
मेटि जाइ नहिं राम रजाई । कठिन करम गति कछु न बसाई ॥
meṭi jāi nahiṁ rāma rajāī, kaṭhina karama gati kachu na basāī.
राम लखन सिय पद सिरु नाई । फिरेउ बनिक जिमि मूर गवाँई ॥
rāma lakhana siya pada siru nāī, phireu banika jimi mūra gavām̐ī.

Trans:

With the sovereign of my soul and my dear brother, stoutest of champions, bearing bow and quiver, the toilsome wanderings of the march will not trouble me at all; be not, anxious for me in the least." On hearing Sītā's chilling speech, Sumant became as distressed as a serpent at the loss of its head-jewel. Bedazed, his eyes saw not, and the ears heard not; and unable to utter a word he stood completely confounded. Rāma said everything to console him, but his heart refused to be comforted. Earnestly he begged that he too might accompany them; but Raghunandan returned appropriate answers to all he urged. "Rāma's commands cannot be withstood; Fate is against me, I can do nothing." Bowing his head at the feet of Rāma, Lakshman, and Sītā, he turned away like a merchant who has lost his everything.

दोहा-dohā:

रथु हाँकेउ हय राम तन हेरि हेरि हिहिनाहिं ।
rathu hām̐keu haya rāma tana heri heri hihināhiṁ,
देखि निषाद बिषादबस धुनहिं सीस पछिताहिं ॥९९॥
dekhi niṣāda biṣādabasa dhunahiṁ sīsa pachitāhiṁ. 99.

Trans:

The very horses of his chariot, as he drove, continued whinnying and looking back upon Rāma; and the Nishād at the sight gave way to grief and beat his head and moaned.

चौपाई-caupāī:

जासु बियोग बिकल पसु ऐसें । प्रजा मातु पितु जिइहहिं कैसें ॥
jāsu biyoga bikala pasu aiseṁ, prajā mātu pitu jiihahiṁ kaiseṁ.
बरबस राम सुमंत्रु पठाए । सुरसरि तीर आपु तब आए ॥
barabasa rāma sumaṁtru paṭhāe, surasari tīra āpu taba āe.
मागी नाव न केवटु आना । कहइ तुम्हार मरमु मैं जाना ॥
māgī nāva na kevaṭu ānā, kahai tumhāra maramu maiṁ jānā.
चरन कमल रज कहुँ सबु कहई । मानुष करनि मूरि कछु अहई ॥
carana kamala raja kahum̐ sabu kahaī, mānuṣa karani mūri kachu ahaī.
छुअत सिला भइ नारि सुहाई । पाहन तें न काठ कठिनाई ॥
chuata silā bhai nāri suhāī, pāhana teṁ na kāṭha kaṭhināī.
तरनिउ मुनि घरिनी होइ जाई । बाट परइ मोरि नाव उड़ाई ॥
taraniu muni gharinī hoi jāī, bāṭa parai mori nāva uṛāī.
एहिं प्रतिपालउँ सबु परिवारू । नहिं जानउँ कछु अउर कबारू ॥
ehiṁ pratipālaum̐ sabu parivārū, nahiṁ jānaum̐ kachu aura kabārū.
जौं प्रभु पार अवसि गा चहहू । मोहि पद पदुम पखारन कहहू ॥
jauṁ prabhu pāra avasi gā cahahū, mohi pada paduma pakhārana kahahū.

Trans:

"When even brute beasts are so distressed at his loss, how can his subjects and his father and mother exist without him?" Having thus perforce dismissed Sumant, Rāma went on his way and came to the bank of the Gangā. When he called for the boat, the ferryman would not bring it, saying: "I know the import of your being; everyone pays that the dust of your lotus feet is a charm that turns stone to human. A rock on which it fell became a beautiful woman; and wood is not so hard as stone; and should my boat in like manner be turned into a saint's wife, the ferry will be closed and the boat lost—which is the only support of my family. I have no other means of living. If, my Lord, you are bent on crossing, you must allow me first to wash your feet.

छंद-chaṁda:

पद कमल धोइ चढ़ाइ नाव न नाथ उतराई चहौं ।
pada kamala dhoi caṛhāi nāva na nātha utarāī cahauṁ,
मोहि राम राउरि आन दसरथ सपथ सब साची कहौं ॥
mohi rāma rāuri āna dasaratha sapatha saba sācī kahauṁ.
बरु तीर मारहुँ लखनु पै जब लगि न पाय पखारिहौं ।
baru tīra mārahuṁ lakhanu pai jaba lagi na pāya pakhārihauṁ,
तब लगि न तुलसीदास नाथ कृपाल पारु उतारिहौं ॥
taba lagi na tulasīdāsa nātha kṛpāla pāru utārihauṁ.

Trans:

I will take you on board only after bathing your lotus feet. I seek no toll from you. I tell you the truth, O Rāma, swearing by yourself and Dashrath—Lakshman may shoot me with his arrows, but I will not take you across, gracious Lord, until I have bathed your feet."

सोरठा-soraṭhā:

सुनि केवट के बैन प्रेम लपेटे अटपटे ।
suni kevaṭa ke baina prema lapeṭe aṭapaṭe,
बिहसे करुनाऐन चितइ जानकी लखन तन ॥ १०० ॥
bihase karunāaina citai jānakī lakhana tana. 100.

Trans:

On hearing the ferryman's crude but loving speech, the All-merciful laughed as he looked at Jānakī and Lakshman;

चौपाई-caupāī:

कृपासिंधु बोले मुसुकाई । सोइ करु जेहिं तव नाव न जाई ॥
kṛpāsiṁdhu bole musukāī, soi karu jehiṁ tava nāva na jāī.
बेगि आनु जल पाय पखारू । होत बिलंबु उतारहि पारू ॥
begi ānu jala pāya pakhārū, hota bilaṁbu utārahi pārū.
जासु नाम सुमिरत एक बारा । उतरहिं नर भवसिंधु अपारा ॥
jāsu nāma sumirata eka bārā, utarahiṁ nara bhavasiṁdhu apārā.
सोइ कृपालु केवटहि निहोरा । जेहिं जगु किय तिहु पगहु ते थोरा ॥
soi kṛpālu kevaṭahi nihorā, jehiṁ jagu kiya tihu pagahu te thorā.
पद नख निरखि देवसरि हरषी । सुनि प्रभु बचन मोहँ मति करषी ॥
pada nakha nirakhi devasari haraṣī, suni prabhu bacana mohaṁ mati karaṣī.
केवट राम रजायसु पावा । पानि कठवता भरि लेइ आवा ॥
kevaṭa rāma rajāyasu pāvā, pāni kaṭhavatā bhari lei āvā.
अति आनंद उमगि अनुरागा । चरन सरोज पखारन लागा ॥
ati ānaṁda umagi anurāgā, carana saroja pakhārana lāgā.
बरषि सुमन सुर सकल सिहाहीं । एहि सम पुन्यपुंज कोउ नाहीं ॥
baraṣi sumana sura sakala sihāhīṁ, ehi sama punyapuṁja kou nāhīṁ.

Trans:

and then smilingly he said, "Do anything to save your boat. Bring water at once and bathe my feet; much time has already been lost; do take us across." The gracious Lord thus made request to a boatman—even he by one thought on whose name, mankind is transported across the boundless ocean of existence, and for whose three strides the whole universe did not suffice! The Gangā rejoiced on beholding his toenails, and at the sound of his words was relieved of all anxiety. On receiving Rāma's commands, the ferryman brought a basin full of water, and in an ecstasy of joy and love proceeded to bathe his lotus feet. All the gods rained down flowers and uttered their congratulations: "Never was anyone so meritorious!"

दोहा-dohā:

पद पखारि जलु पान करि आपु सहित परिवार ।
pada pakhāri jalu pāna kari āpu sahita parivāra,
पितर पारु करि प्रभुहि पुनि मुदित गयउ लेइ पार ॥ १०१ ॥
pitara pāru kari prabhuhi puni mudita gayau lei pāra. 101.

Trans:

After laving his feet, and partaking of that water, along his family, and thus redeeming the souls of his ancestors and forefathers, he joyfully conveyed his lords across to the other side.

चौपाई-caupāī:

उतरि ठाढ़ भए सुरसरि रेता । सीय रामु गुह लखन समेता ॥
utari ṭhāṛa bhae surasari retā, sīya rāmu guha lakhana sametā.
केवट उतरि दंडवत कीन्हा । प्रभुहि सकुच एहि नहिं कछु दीन्हा ॥
kevaṭa utari daṁḍavata kīnhā, prabhuhi sakuca ehi nahiṁ kachu dīnhā.
पिय हिय की सिय जाननिहारी । मनि मुदरी मन मुदित उतारी ॥
piya hiya kī siya jānanihārī, mani mudarī mana mudita utārī.
कहेउ कृपाल लेहि उतराई । केवट चरन गहे अकुलाई ॥
kaheu kṛpāla lehi utarāī, kevaṭa carana gahe akulāī.
नाथ आजु मैं काह न पावा । मिटे दोष दुख दारिद दावा ॥
nātha āju maiṁ kāha na pāvā, miṭe doṣa dukha dārida dāvā.
बहुत काल मैं कीन्हि मजूरी । आजु दीन्ह बिधि बनि भलि भूरी ॥
bahuta kāla maiṁ kīnhi majūrī, āju dīnha bidhi bani bhali bhūrī.
अब कछु नाथ न चाहिअ मोरें । दीनदयाल अनुग्रह तोरें ॥
aba kachu nātha na cāhia moreṁ, dīnadayāla anugraha toreṁ.
फिरती बार मोहि जो देबा । सो प्रसादु मैं सिर धरि लेबा ॥
phiratī bāra mohi jo debā, so prasādu maiṁ sira dhari lebā.

Trans:

They landed and stood on the sands of the Gangā, Sītā, Rāma, Lakshman, and Gūha. The ferryman landed too and made his obeisance. The Lord was embarrassed that he had nothing to give him. Sītā knew what was passing in the mind of her beloved and cheerfully drew a jeweled ring from off her finger. Said the All-merciful, "Take your toll." The ferryman in distress clasped Rāma's feet, "What have I not already received, my Lord? Sin, sorrow, poverty, and all their attendant ills, all have been removed. I have labored for many a years, but today God has given me my wages in full. Now, gracious Lord, I ask for nothing but your favor. At the time of your return, whatever you bestow upon me I will thankfully accept."

दोहा-dohā:

बहुत कीन्ह प्रभु लखन सियँ नहिं कछु केवटु लेइ ।
bahuta kīnha prabhu lakhana siyaṁ nahiṁ kachu kevaṭu lei,
बिदा कीन्ह करुनायतन भगति बिमल बरु देइ ॥ १०२ ॥
bidā kīnha karunāyatana bhagati bimala baru dei. 102.

Trans:

Lakshman, Sītā and the Lord all pressed him to the utmost, but the Kevat would take nothing; the All-merciful then let him go with the gift of unclouded Devotion, the best of all boons.

चौपाई-caupāī:

तब मज्जनु करि रघुकुलनाथा । पूजि पारथिव नायउ माथा ॥
taba majjanu kari raghukulanāthā, pūji pārathiva nāyau māthā.
सियँ सुरसरिहि कहेउ कर जोरी । मातु मनोरथ पुरउबि मोरी ॥
siyaṁ surasarihi kaheu kara jorī, mātu manoratha puraubi morī.
पति देवर संग कुसल बहोरी । आइ करौं जेहिं पूजा तोरी ॥
pati devara saṁga kusala bahorī, āi karauṁ jehiṁ pūjā torī.
सुनि सिय बिनय प्रेम रस सानी । भइ तब बिमल बारि बर बानी ॥
suni siya binaya prema rasa sānī, bhai taba bimala bāri bara bānī.

सुनु रघुबीर प्रिया बैदेही । तव प्रभाउ जग बिदित न केही ॥
sunu raghubīra priyā baidehī, tava prabhāu jaga bidita na kehī.
लोकप होहिं बिलोकत तोरें । तोहि सेवहिं सब सिधि कर जोरें ॥
lokapa hohiṁ bilokata toreṁ, tohi sevahiṁ saba sidhi kara joreṁ.
तुम्ह जो हमहि बड़ि बिनय सुनाई । कृपा कीन्हि मोहि दीन्हि बड़ाई ॥
tumha jo hamahi baṛi binaya sunāī, kṛpā kīnhi mohi dīnhi baṛāī.
तदपि देबि मैं देबि असीसा । सफल होन हित निज बागीसा ॥
tadapi debi maiṁ debi asīsā, saphala hona hita nija bāgīsā.

Trans:

Next the Lord of Raghu's line bathed in Gangā and then bowed his head in adoration to Mahādev; while Sītā with clasped hands thus addressed the sacred stream, "O mother, accomplish my desire that I may return in safety with my husband and his brother and then venerate you again." On hearing Sītā's humble and affectionate speech, a favorable response came from the celestial river, "Hearken, Vaidehi, best beloved of Raghubīr; who is there in the world who knows not your glory? They upon whom you cast thy glance, become as the sovereigns of heavens. All supernatural powers meekly do you service. In the petition that you have deigned to address to me, you have graciously paid me all too high an honor; yet, lady, unworthy as I am, I bestow upon you my blessing in order to prove my utterances true.

दोहा-dohā:

प्राननाथ देवर सहित कुसल कोसला आइ ।
prānanātha devara sahita kusala kosalā āi,
पूजिहि सब मनकामना सुजसु रहिहि जग छाइ ॥ १०३ ॥
pūjihi saba manakāmanā sujasu rahihi jaga chāi. 103.

Trans:

You shall return in safety to Kaushal with your beloved and his brother. Your every wish shall be accomplished. And your fair renown shall spread throughout the world, for all times."

चौपाई-caupāī:

गंग बचन सुनि मंगल मूला । मुदित सीय सुरसरि अनुकूला ॥
gaṁga bacana suni maṁgala mūlā, mudita sīya surasari anukūlā.
तब प्रभु गुहहि कहेउ घर जाहू । सुनत सूख मुखु भा उर दाहू ॥
taba prabhu guhahi kaheu ghara jāhū, sunata sūkha mukhu bhā ura dāhū.
दीन बचन गुह कह कर जोरी । बिनय सुनहु रघुकुलमनि मोरी ॥
dīna bacana guha kaha kara jorī, binaya sunahu raghukulamani morī.
नाथ साथ रहि पंथु देखाई । करि दिन चारि चरन सेवकाई ॥
nātha sātha rahi paṁthu dekhāī, kari dina cāri carana sevakāī.
जेहिं बन जाइ रहब रघुराई । परनकुटी मैं करबि सुहाई ॥
jehiṁ bana jāi rahaba raghurāī, paranakuṭī maiṁ karabi suhāī.
तब मोहि कहँ जसि देब रजाई । सोइ करिहउँ रघुबीर दोहाई ॥
taba mohi kahaṁ jasi deba rajāī, soi karihauṁ raghubīra dohāī.
सहज सनेह राम लखि तासू । संग लीन्ह गुह हृदयँ हुलासू ॥
sahaja saneha rāma lakhi tāsū, saṁga līnha guha hṛdayaṁ hulāsū.
पुनि गुहँ ग्याति बोलि सब लीन्हे । करि परितोषु बिदा तब कीन्हे ॥
puni guhaṁ gyāti boli saba līnhe, kari paritoṣu bidā taba kīnhe.

Trans:

On hearing Gangā's gracious speech, Sītā was delighted to find it so propitious. Then said the Lord to Gūha: 'Return home.' At this his face grew wan and his bosom burned, and with clasped hands and in suppliant tones he cried: "Noblest of the sons of Raghu, hearken to my prayer. Let me remain with my Lord to show the road and do him service for a day or two, and make a shapely hut of twigs for him in the wood where he goes to stay. After that I swear by Raghubīr to do as he shall command me." Seeing his unfeigned affection, he took him along—to Gūha's great delight, who thereupon called all his kinsmen and dismissed them with kind assurances.

दोहा-dohā:

तब गनपति सिव सुमिरि प्रभु नाइ सुरसरिहि माथ ।
taba ganapati siva sumiri prabhu nāi surasarihi mātha,
सखा अनुज सिय सहित बन गवनु कीन्ह रघुनाथ ॥ १०४ ॥
sakhā anuja siya sahita bana gavanu kīnha radhunātha. 104.

Trans:

Then directing his intention to Ganesh and Shiva, and bowing his head to the Gangā, the Lord with his friend Gūha and his brother and Sītā took his way to the woods.

चौपाई-caupāī:

तेहि दिन भयउ बिटप तर बासू । लखन सखाँ सब कीन्ह सुपासू ॥
tehi dina bhayau biṭapa tara bāsū, lakhana sakhāṁ saba kīnha supāsū.
प्रात प्रातकृत करि रघुराई । तीरथराजु दीख प्रभु जाई ॥
prāta prātakṛta kari raghurāī, tīratharāju dīkha prabhu jāī.
सचिव सत्य श्रद्धा प्रिय नारी । माधव सरिस मीतु हितकारी ॥
saciva satya śraddhā priya nārī, mādhava sarisa mītu hitakārī.
चारि पदारथ भरा भँडारु । पुन्य प्रदेस देस अति चारु ॥
cāri padāratha bharā bhaṁḍāru, punya pradesa desa ati cāru.
छेत्रु अगम गढ़ु गाढ़ सुहावा । सपनेहुँ नहिं प्रतिपच्छिन्ह पावा ॥
chetru agama gaṛhu gāṛha suhāvā, sapanehuṁ nahiṁ pratipacchinha pāvā.
सेन सकल तीरथ बर बीरा । कलुष अनीक दलन रनधीरा ॥
sena sakala tīratha bara bīrā, kaluṣa anīka dalana ranadhīrā.
संगमु सिंहासनु सुठि सोहा । छत्रु अखयबटु मुनि मनु मोहा ॥
saṁgamu siṁhāsanu suṭhi sohā, chatru akhayabaṭu muni manu mohā.
चवँर जमुन अरु गंग तरंगा । देखि होहिं दुख दारिद भंगा ॥
cavaṁra jamuna aru gaṁga taraṁgā, dekhi hohiṁ dukha dārida bhaṁgā.

Trans:

That day he halted under a tree, and Lakshman and friend Gūha supplied all the necessities. At dawn, having performed his morning ablutions, he proceeded to visit Prayāg, the king of holy places: A king with truth for his minister, faith for his cherished consort, the god Madhav for his friend and favorite, his treasury stored with the four great prizes of life, and all holy places for his fair dominion; with an impregnable domain and magnificent forts, so strong that no enemy could ever dream of taking them; with an army of shrines of such virtue and power as to rout the whole army of Sin; with the meeting of the rivers for his glorious throne and the Immortal-Banyan for his royal umbrella, dazzling even the soul of a saints; with the waves of the Gangā and Yamunā for his chauries, a vision to disperse all distress and sorrows;

दोहा-dohā:

सेवहिं सुकृति साधु सुचि पावहिं सब मनकाम ।
sevahiṁ sukṛti sādhu suci pāvahiṁ saba manakāma,
बंदी बेद पुरान गन कहहिं बिमल गुन ग्राम ॥ १०५ ॥
baṁdī beda purāna gana kahahiṁ bimala guna grāma. 105.

Trans:

his attendants pure and holy anchorites, guerdoned with all they desire; his heralds, the Vedas and Purānas to declare his immaculate virtue.

चौपाई-caupāī:

को कहि सकइ प्रयाग प्रभाऊ । कलुष पुंज कुंजर मृगराऊ ॥
ko kahi sakai prayāga prabhāū, kaluṣa puṁja kuṁjara mṛgarāū.
अस तीरथपति देखि सुहावा । सुख सागर रघुबर सुखु पावा ॥
asa tīrathapati dekhi suhāvā, sukha sāgara raghubara sukhu pāvā.
कहि सिय लखनहि सखहि सुनाई । श्रीमुख तीरथराज बड़ाई ॥
kahi siya lakhanahi sakhahi sunāī, śrīmukha tīratharāja baṛāī.
करि प्रनामु देखत बन बागा । कहत महातम अति अनुरागा ॥

kari pranāmu dekhata bana bāgā, kahata mahātama ati anurāgā.

एहि बिधि आइ बिलोकी बेनी । सुमिरत सकल सुमंगल देनी ॥
ehi bidhi āi bilokī benī, sumirata sakala sumaṁgala denī.

मुदित नहाइ कीन्हि सिव सेवा । पूजि जथाबिधि तीरथ देवा ॥
mudita nahāi kīnhi siva sevā, pūji jathābidhi tīratha devā.

तब प्रभु भरद्वाज पहिं आए । करत दंडवत मुनि उर लाए ॥
taba prabhu bharadvāja pahiṁ āe, karata daṁḍavata muni ura lāe.

मुनि मन मोद न कछु कहि जाई । ब्रह्मानंद रासि जनु पाई ॥
muni mana moda na kachu kahi jāī, brahmānaṁda rāsi janu pāī.

Trans:

Who can tell the power of that chief Tīrtha Prayāg, a lion to destroy the elephantine monster Sin? On beholding the beauty of this king of sanctuaries, Raghubar, the ocean of delight, was himself delighted, and with his holy lips he discoursed on its greatness to Sītā, his brother and his companion. After making obeisance to it, he visited the woods and groves, expatiating on their virtue with the utmost devotion. This way he arrived at the confluence of rivers Trivenī—the mere thought of which confers all happiness— and after gazing upon it, rapturously bathed and paid homage to Shiva and to the divinity of the spot, in all due form. Then came the Lord to Bharadvāja. As he prostrated himself at his feet, the saint took him to his heart in an ecstasy of joy past all telling, as though he had realized the perfect bliss of heaven.

दोहा-dohā:

दीन्हि असीस मुनीस उर अति अनंदु अस जानि ।
dīnhi asīsa munīsa ura ati anaṁdu asa jāni,

लोचन गोचर सुकृत फल मनहुँ किए बिधि आनि ॥१०६॥
locana gocara sukṛta phala manahuṁ kie bidhi āni. 106.

Trans:

The patriarch gave him his blessing with as much joy of heart as though God had set before him in visible form the reward of his virtues.

चौपाई-caupāī:

कुसल प्रस्न करि आसन दीन्हे । पूजि प्रेम परिपूरन कीन्हे ॥
kusala prasna kari āsana dīnhe, pūji prema paripūrana kīnhe.

कंद मूल फल अंकुर नीके । दिए आनि मुनि मनहुँ अमी के ॥
kaṁda mūla phala aṁkura nīke, die āni muni manahuṁ amī ke.

सीय लखन जन सहित सुहाए । अति रुचि राम मूल फल खाए ॥
sīya lakhana jana sahita suhāe, ati ruci rāma mūla phala khāe.

भए बिगतश्रम रामु सुखारे । भरद्वाज मृदु बचन उचारे ॥
bhae bigataśrama rāmu sukhāre, bharadvāja mṛdu bacana ucāre.

आजु सुफल तपु तीरथ त्यागू । आजु सुफल जप जोग बिरागू ॥
āju suphala tapu tīratha tyāgū, āju suphala japa joga birāgū.

सफल सकल सुभ साधन साजू । राम तुम्हहि अवलोकत आजू ॥
saphala sakala subha sādhana sājū, rāma tumhahi avalokata ājū.

लाभ अवधि सुख अवधि न दूजी । तुम्हरें दरस आस सब पूजी ॥
lābha avadhi sukha avadhi na dūjī, tumhareṁ darasa āsa saba pūjī.

अब करि कृपा देहु बर एहू । निज पद सरसिज सहज सनेहू ॥
aba kari kṛpā dehu bara ehū, nija pada sarasija sahaja sanehū.

Trans:

After enquiring of his welfare, he conducted him to a seat and indulged his affection in doing him honor. Then he brought and presented roots, fruits, and herbs, all sweet as ambrosia, of which Rāma, with Sītā, Lakshman, and their attendant, partook with much delight and content. Rāma was refreshed and all their fatigue forgotten. Then spoke Bharadvāja in a complacent tones, "This day my penance, my pilgrimages, and my vigils have been rewarded; my prayers, my meditations, and my detachment from the world have today borne fruit; yea, all my pious practices have today, O Rāma, been rewarded by the sight of you. This and naught else is the height of gain, the height of happiness; in beholding you my every desire is satisfied. Now of your favor grant me this one boon, a lifelong devotion to your lotus feet.

दोहा-dohā:

करम बचन मन छाड़ि छलु जब लगि जनु न तुम्हार ।
karama bacana mana chāṛi chalu jaba lagi janu na tumhāra,

तब लगि सुखु सपनेहुँ नहीं किएँ कोटि उपचार ॥१०७॥
taba lagi sukhu sapanehuṁ nahīṁ kieṁ koṭi upacāra. 107.

Trans:

Until a man in heart, word, and deed, and without reserve becomes wholly yours, he cannot even dream of happiness, despite all that he may do."

चौपाई-caupāī:

सुनि मुनि बचन रामु सकुचाने । भाव भगति आनंद अघाने ॥
suni muni bacana rāmu sakucāne, bhāva bhagati ānaṁda aghāne.

तब रघुबर मुनि सुजसु सुहावा । कोटि भाँति कहि सबहि सुनावा ॥
taba raghubara muni sujasu suhāvā, koṭi bhāṁti kahi sabahi sunāvā.

सो बड सो सब गुन गन गेहू । जेहि मुनीस तुम्ह आदर देहू ॥
so baḍa so saba guna gana gehū, jehi munīsa tumha ādara dehū.

मुनि रघुबीर परसपर नवहीं । बचन अगोचर सुखु अनुभवहीं ॥
muni raghubīra parasapara navahīṁ, bacana agocara sukhu anubhavahīṁ.

यह सुधि पाइ प्रयाग निवासी । बटु तापस मुनि सिद्ध उदासी ॥
yaha sudhi pāi prayāga nivāsī, baṭu tāpasa muni siddha udāsī.

भरद्वाज आश्रम सब आए । देखन दसरथ सुअन सुहाए ॥
bharadvāja āśrama saba āe, dekhana dasaratha suana suhāe.

राम प्रनाम कीन्ह सब काहू । मुदित भए लहि लोयन लाहू ॥
rāma pranāma kīnha saba kāhū, mudita bhae lahi loyana lāhū.

देहिं असीस परम सुखु पाई । फिरे सराहत सुंदरताई ॥
dehiṁ asīsa parama sukhu pāī, phire sarāhata suṁdaratāī.

Trans:

On hearing the saint's words Rāma was abashed, yet reveled with delight in so exquisite a display of faith. Then proceeded he, to declare unto them all in countless ways, the saint's illustrious renown: "Great indeed and highly endowed is he, O chief of sages, whom you are pleased to honor." Thus they bowed to one another, the saint and Raghubīr, and were filled as they conversed with indescribable happiness. When the people of Prayāg heard the news, all the religious students, ascetics, monks, hermits, and anchorites flocked to Bhardwaj's Ashram to see the glorious son of Dashrath. All made their obeisance and rejoiced that their eyes had been so highly favored. They blessed him and returned with exceeding joy, extolling his beauty.

दोहा-dohā:

राम कीन्ह बिश्राम निसि प्रात प्रयाग नहाइ ।
rāma kīnha biśrāma nisi prāta prayāga nahāi,

चले सहित सिय लखन जन मुदित मुनिहि सिरु नाइ ॥१०८॥
cale sahita siya lakhana jana mudita munihi siru nāi. 108.

Trans:

Rāma rested for the night. At daybreak he bathed at Prayāg, and then, after bowing his head to the sage, resumed joyfully on his journey with Sītā, Lakshman, and others alongside.

चौपाई-caupāī:

राम सप्रेम कहेउ मुनि पाहीं । नाथ कहिअ हम केहि मग जाहीं ॥
rāma saprema kaheu muni pāhīṁ, nātha kahia hama kehi maga jāhīṁ.

मुनि मन बिहसि राम सन कहहीं । सुगम सकल मग तुम्ह कहुँ अहहीं ॥
muni mana bihasi rāma sana kahahīṁ, sugama sakala maga tumha kahuṁ ahahīṁ.

साथ लागि मुनि सिष्य बोलाए । सुनि मन मुदित पचासक आए ॥
sātha lāgi muni siṣya bolāe, suni mana mudita pacāsaka āe.

सबन्हि राम पर प्रेम अपारा । सकल कहहिं मगु दीख हमारा ॥
sabanhi rāma para prema apārā, sakala kahahiṁ magu dīkha hamārā.
मुनि बटु चारि संग तब दीन्हे । जिन्ह बहु जनम सुकृत सब कीन्हे ॥
muni baṭu cāri saṁga taba dīnhe, jinha bahu janama sukṛta saba kīnhe.
करि प्रनामु रिषि आयसु पाई । प्रमुदित हृदयँ चले रघुराई ॥
kari pranāmu riṣi āyasu pāī, pramudita hṛdayaṁ cale raghurāī.
ग्राम निकट जब निकसहि जाई । देखहि दरसु नारि नर धाई ॥
grāma nikaṭa jaba nikasahi jāī, dekhahi darasu nāri nara dhāī.
होहिं सनाथ जनम फलु पाई । फिरहिं दुखित मनु संग पठाई ॥
hohiṁ sanātha janama phalu pāī, phirahiṁ dukhita manu saṁga paṭhāī.

Trans:

Rāma first affectionately asked the sage: "Tell me, my lord, by what road should we go?" The sage replied with a smile: "All ways are easy to you," but called his disciples to go with him. They came with joy some fifty in number, all in their boundless lore for Rāma declaring that they well knew the road. The saint selected four students, who in many previous existences had done many good deeds. Then having bowed to the saint and received his permission to depart, Raghurāī went forth rejoicing. When they had come out near to the village the men and women, who all flocked to see them, found in the sight of their Lord the fruition of their life; and then sadly turning home, sent their hearts after him.

दोहा-dohā:

बिदा किए बटु बिनय करि फिरे पाइ मन काम ।
bidā kie baṭu binaya kari phire pāi mana kāma,
उतरि नहाए जमुन जल जो सरीर सम स्याम ॥ १०९ ॥
utari nahāe jamuna jala jo sarīra sama syāma. 109.

Trans:

Courteously Rāma dismissed the disciples, who returned with their heart's desire obtained; and then alighted and bathed in the stream of Yamunā, dark as his own body.

चौपाई-caupāī:

सुनत तीरबासी नर नारी । धाए निज निज काज बिसारी ॥
sunata tīrabāsī nara nārī, dhāe nija nija kāja bisārī.
लखन राम सिय सुंदरताई । देखि करहिं निज भाग्य बड़ाई ॥
lakhana rāma siya suṁdaratāī, dekhi karahiṁ nija bhāgya baṛāī.
अति लालसा बसहिं मन माहीं । नाउँ गाउँ बूझत सकुचाहीं ॥
ati lālasā basahiṁ mana māhīṁ, nāuṁ gāuṁ būjhata sakucāhīṁ.
जे तिन्ह महुँ बयबिरिध सयाने । तिन्ह करि जुगुति रामु पहिचाने ॥
je tinha mahuṁ bayabiridha sayāne, tinha kari juguti rāmu pahicāne.
सकल कथा तिन्ह सबहि सुनाई । बनहि चले पितु आयसु पाई ॥
sakala kathā tinha sabahi sunāī, banahi cale pitu āyasu pāī.
सुनि सबिषाद सकल पछिताहीं । रानी रायँ कीन्ह भल नाहीं ॥
suni sabiṣāda sakala pachitāhīṁ, rānī rāyaṁ kīnha bhala nāhīṁ.
तेहि अवसर एक तापसु आवा । तेजपुंज लघुबयस सुहावा ॥
tehi avasara eka tāpasu āvā, tejapuṁja laghubayasa suhāvā.
कबि अलखित गति बेषु बिरागी । मन क्रम बचन राम अनुरागी ॥
kabi alakhita gati beṣu birāgī, mana krama bacana rāma anurāgī.

Trans:

The dwellers on the bank, when they heard of his arrival, left whatever they were doing and ran to see him. On beholding the beauty of Lakshman, Rāma, and Sītā, they congratulated themselves on their good fortune, and all with longing heart began diffidently to ask their name and home. The sage elders of the party had wit enough to recognize Rāma, and related his whole history, and how he had come into exile by his father's order. At this, they were all sad and complained, 'The king and queen have acted badly.' Men and women alike, on beholding the beauty of Rāma, Lakshman, and Sītā, were charged up with love and pity, 'What kind of father and mother must they be, friends, who have sent such nestlings into the woods?' In the meantime there arrived an ascetic who was an embodiment of spiritual glow, young in years and charming in appearance. His ways were unknown to the poet; he was attired in the garb of a recluse and was devoted to Rāma in thought, word and deed.

दोहा-dohā:

सजल नयन तन पुलकि निज इष्टदेउ पहिचानि ।
sajala nayana tana pulaki nija iṣṭadeu pahicāni,
परेउ दंड जिमि धरनितल दसा न जाइ बखानि ॥ ११० ॥
pareu daṁḍa jimi dharanitala dasā na jāi bakhāni. 110.

Trans:

His eyes were wet with tears and a thrill ran through his body when he came to recognize his beloved Deity, Shrī Rāma. He fell prostrate on the ground and the state of his body and mind could not be described in words.

चौपाई-caupāī:

राम सप्रेम पुलकि उर लावा । परम रंक जनु पारसु पावा ॥
rāma saprema pulaki ura lāvā, parama raṁka janu pārasu pāvā.
मनहुँ प्रेमु परमारथु दोऊ । मिलत धरें तन कह सबु कोऊ ॥
manahuṁ premu paramārathu doū, milata dhareṁ tana kaha sabu koū.
बहुरि लखन पायन्ह सोइ लागा । लीन्ह उठाइ उमगि अनुरागा ॥
bahuri lakhana pāyanha soi lāgā, līnha uṭhāi umagi anurāgā.
पुनि सिय चरन धूरि धरि सीसा । जननि जानि सिसु दीन्हि असीसा ॥
puni siya carana dhūri dhari sīsā, janani jāni sisu dīnhi asīsā.
कीन्ह निषाद दंडवत तेही । मिलेउ मुदित लखि राम सनेही ॥
kīnha niṣāda daṁḍavata tehī, mileu mudita lakhi rāma sanehī.
पिअत नयन पुट रूपु पियूषा । मुदित सुअसनु पाइ जिमि भूखा ॥
piata nayana puṭa rūpu piyūṣā, mudita suasanu pāi jimi bhūkhā.
ते पितु मातु कहहु सखि कैसे । जिन्ह पठए बन बालक ऐसे ॥
te pitu mātu kahahu sakhi kaise, jinha paṭhae bana bālaka aise.
राम लखन सिय रूपु निहारी । होहिं सनेह बिकल नर नारी ॥
rāma lakhana siya rūpu nihārī, hohiṁ saneha bikala nara nārī.

Trans:

He was pressed to the bosom by Shrī Rāma, and he thrilled all over with emotion—as though a pauper had found a philosopher's stone. Everyone who saw them suggested as though Love, on the one hand, and the supreme Reality, on the other, embraced each other in bodily forms. Next he threw himself at the feet of Lakshman, who lifted him with a heart overflowing with love. Again he placed on his head the dust of Sītā's feet and the Mother Sītā gave him her blessing, knowing him to be her own child. The Nishād chief in his turn fell prostrate before the hermit, who gladly embraced him recognizing him to be a friend of Shrī Rāma. With the cup of his eyes he drank the nectar of Shrī Rāma's beauty and was delighted as a hungry soul who had secured sumptuous food. "Tell me, friend, what are those father and mother like—that have exiled to the woods children such as these?" Beholding the beauty of Shrī Rāma, Lakshman and Sītā, all—men and women alike—were stirred up on account of love.

दोहा-dohā:

तब रघुबीर अनेक बिधि सखहि सिखावनु दीन्ह ।
taba raghubīra aneka bidhi sakhahi sikhāvanu dīnha,
राम रजायसु सीस धरि भवन गवनु तेइँ कीन्ह ॥ १११ ॥
rāma rajāyasu sīsa dhari bhavana gavanu teiṁ kīnha. 111.

Trans:

Then Raghubīr urged his friend Gūha in many ways, who in submission to his commands took the way towards his house.

चौपाई-caupāī:

पुनि सियँ राम लखन कर जोरी । जमुनहि कीन्ह प्रनामु बहोरी ॥
puni siyaṁ rāma lakhana kara jorī, jamunahi kīnha pranāmu bahorī.

चले ससीय मुदित दोउ भाई । रबितनुजा कइ करत बड़ाई ॥
cale sasīya mudita dou bhāī, rabitanujā kai karata baṛāī.
पथिक अनेक मिलहिं मग जाता । कहहिं सप्रेम देखि दोउ भ्राता ॥
pathika aneka milahiṁ maga jātā, kahahiṁ saprema dekhi dou bhrātā.
राज लखन सब अंग तुम्हारें । देखि सोचु अति हृदय हमारें ॥
rāja lakhana saba aṁga tumhāreṁ, dekhi socu ati hṛdaya hamāreṁ.
मारग चलहु पयादेहि पाएँ । ज्योतिषु झूठ हमारें भाएँ ॥
māraga calahu payādehi pāeṁ, jyotiṣu jhūṭha hamāreṁ bhāeṁ.
अगमु पंथ गिरि कानन भारी । तेहि महँ साथ नारि सुकुमारी ॥
agamu paṁtha giri kānana bhārī, tehi mahaṁ sātha nāri sukumārī.
करि केहरि बन जाइ न जोई । हम सँग चलहि जो आयसु होई ॥
kari kehari bana jāi na joī, hama saṁga calahi jo āyasu hoī.
जाब जहाँ लगि तहँ पहुँचाई । फिरब बहोरि तुम्हहि सिरु नाई ॥
jāba jahāṁ lagi tahaṁ pahuṁcāī, phiraba bahori tumhahi siru nāī.

Trans:

Again with clasped hands Sītā, Rāma, and Lakshman made renewed obeisance to the Yamunā, and as they went on their way their talk was all of the daughter of the Sun and her glory. Many travelers met them on the way, and exclaimed, after gazing with affection at the two brothers, 'You have all the marks of royalty on your person; on seeing them we are troubled at heart, for you go your way on foot, and the astrologers methinks are false. The road is difficult; the mountains and forests are very great; yet you have with you a delicate girl. Elephants and tigers make the woods too terrible to contemplate; with your permission, we will accompany you, will escort you as far as you please, and then make our bow and return.'

दोहा-dohā:

एहि बिधि पूँछहिं प्रेम बस पुलक गात जलु नैन ।
ehi bidhi pūṁchahiṁ prema basa pulaka gāta jalu naina,
कृपासिंधु फेरहिं तिन्हहि कहि बिनीत मृदु बैन ॥११२॥
kṛpāsiṁdhu pherahiṁ tinhahi kahi binīta mṛdu baina. 112.

Trans:

As they proffered this petition, their body trembled all over with excess of love, and their eyes were filled with tears; but the All-merciful gently and courteously dismissed them.

चौपाई-caupāī:

जे पुर गाँव बसहिं मग माहीं । तिन्हहि नाग सुर नगर सिहाहीं ॥
je pura gāṁva basahiṁ maga māhīṁ, tinhahi nāga sura nagara sihāhīṁ.
केहि सुकृतीं केहि घरीं बसाए । धन्य पुन्यमय परम सुहाए ॥
kehi sukṛtīṁ kehi gharīṁ basāe, dhanya punyamaya parama suhāe.
जहँ जहँ राम चरन चलि जाहीं । तिन्ह समान अमरावति नाहीं ॥
jahaṁ jahaṁ rāma carana cali jāhīṁ, tinha samāna amarāvati nāhīṁ.
पुन्यपुंज मग निकट निवासी । तिन्हहि सराहहिं सुरपुरबासी ॥
punyapuṁja maga nikaṭa nivāsī, tinhahi sarāhahiṁ surapurabāsī.
जे भरि नयन बिलोकहिं रामहि । सीता लखन सहित घनस्यामहि ॥
je bhari nayana bilokahiṁ rāmahi, sītā lakhana sahita ghanasyāmahi.
जे सर सरित राम अवगाहहिं । तिन्हहि देव सर सरित सराहहिं ॥
je sara sarita rāma avagāhahiṁ, tinhahi deva sara sarita sarāhahiṁ.
जेहि तरु तर प्रभु बैठहिं जाई । करहिं कलपतरु तासु बड़ाई ॥
jehi taru tara prabhu baiṭhahiṁ jāī, karahiṁ kalapataru tāsu baṛāī.
परसि राम पद पदुम परागा । मानति भूमि भूरि निज भागा ॥
parasi rāma pada paduma parāgā, mānati bhūmi bhūri nija bhāgā.

Trans:

All the towns and villages along the road were the envy of the cities of the *Nāgas* and the gods: 'At what an auspicious moment and by what a holy man must they have been founded, to be so happy and blessed, and altogether highly favored!' Whatever spot was trodden by Rāma's feet, Paradise was not to be compared to it. The dwellers by the wayside, were all embodiments of virtue; and they invoked the praises of the denizens of heaven; for they feasted their eyes on Sītā and Lakshman and Rāma dark of hue as a storm-cloud. The lakes and rivers in which Rāma bathed were the envy of the lake and river of Heaven; the trees under which the Lord sat were lauded by the Tree of Paradise. Nay, the very earth, touched by the dust of Rāma's lotus feet, thought her blessings completed, and made wholesome.

दोहा-dohā:

छाँह करहिं घन बिबुधगन बरषहिं सुमन सिहाहिं ।
chāṁha karahiṁ ghana bibudhagana barasahiṁ sumana sihāhiṁ,
देखत गिरि बन बिहग मृग रामु चले मग जाहिं ॥११३॥
dekhata giri bana bihaga mṛga rāmu cale maga jāhiṁ. 113.

Trans:

The clouds gave him shade, the exultant hosts of heaven rained down flowers, as Rāma went on his way—walking, looking at the hills and woods and birds and deer.

चौपाई-caupāī:

सीता लखन सहित रघुराई । गाँव निकट जब निकसहिं जाई ॥
sītā lakhana sahita raghurāī, gāṁva nikaṭa jaba nikasahiṁ jāī.
सुनि सब बाल बृद्ध नर नारी । चलहिं तुरत गृहकाजु बिसारी ॥
suni saba bāla bṛddha nara nārī, calahiṁ turata gṛhakāju bisārī.
राम लखन सिय रूप निहारी । पाइ नयनफलु होहिं सुखारी ॥
rāma lakhana siya rūpa nihārī, pāi nayanaphalu hohiṁ sukhārī.
सजल बिलोचन पुलक सरीरा । सब भए मगन देखि दोउ बीरा ॥
sajala bilocana pulaka sarīrā, saba bhae magana dekhi dou bīrā.
बरनि न जाइ दसा तिन्ह केरी । लहि जनु रंकन्ह सुरमनि ढेरी ॥
barani na jāi dasā tinha kerī, lahi janu raṁkanha suramani ḍherī.
एकन्ह एक बोलि सिख देहीं । लोचन लाहु लेहु छन एहीं ॥
ekanha eka boli sikha dehīṁ, locana lāhu lehu chana ehīṁ.
रामहि देखि एक अनुरागे । चितवत चले जाहिं सँग लागे ॥
rāmahi dekhi eka anurāge, citavata cale jāhiṁ saṁga lāge.
एक नयन मग छबि उर आनी । होहिं सिथिल तन मन बर बानी ॥
eka nayana maga chabi ura ānī, hohiṁ sithila tana mana bara bānī.

Trans:

Whenever Sītā, Lakshman, and Raghurāī swept past near a village on the way, everyone—young and old, men and women—came directly when they heard the news, forgetting their own private affairs; and as they gazed upon their beauty, obtained the fruition of their eyes and were made happy for ever. At the sight of the two heroes their eyes filled with tears, their body quivered with emotion and they became all enraptured—their state of mind as indescribable as though a beggar had discovered a pile of heavenly jewels. Everyone was telling his neighbor, "Now is the time to prove the value of vision." One, in his delight to see Rāma, would go with him, gazing as he went; another, drawing his beautiful image into his heart by the way of his eyes, was utterly overpowered in body, soul, speech.

दोहा-dohā:

एक देखि बट छाँह भलि डासि मृदुल तृन पात ।
eka dekhi baṭa chāṁha bhali ḍāsi mṛdula tṛna pāta,
कहहिं गवाँइअ छिनुकु श्रमु गवनब अबहिं कि प्रात ॥११४॥
kahahiṁ gavāṁia chinuku śramu gavanaba abahiṁ ki prāta. 114.

Trans:

One, seeing a fine shady Banyan, spread under it soft grass and leaves and said, "Pray rest awhile and you may then depart, either now or preferably next morning."

चौपाई-caupāī:

एक कलस भरि आनहिं पानी । अँचइअ नाथ कहहिं मृदु बानी ॥
eka kalasa bhari ānahiṁ pānī, aṁcaia nātha kahahiṁ mṛdu bānī.
सुनि प्रिय बचन प्रीति अति देखी । राम कृपाल सुसील बिसेषी ॥
suni priya bacana prīti ati dekhī, rāma kṛpāla susīla biseṣī.
जानी श्रमित सीय मन माहीं । घरिक बिलंबु कीन्ह बट छाहीं ॥
jānī śramita sīya mana māhīṁ, gharika bilaṁbu kīnha baṭa chāhīṁ.
मुदित नारि नर देखहिं सोभा । रूप अनूप नयन मनु लोभा ॥
mudita nāri nara dekhahiṁ sobhā, rūpa anūpa nayana manu lobhā.
एकटक सब सोहहिं चहुँ ओरा । रामचंद्र मुख चंद चकोरा ॥
ekaṭaka saba sohahiṁ cahuṁ orā, rāmacaṁdra mukha caṁda cakorā.
तरुन तमाल बरन तनु सोहा । देखत कोटि मदन मनु मोहा ॥
taruna tamāla barana tanu sohā, dekhata koṭi madana manu mohā.
दामिनि बरन लखन सुठि नीके । नख सिख सुभग भावते जी के ॥
dāmini barana lakhana suṭhi nīke, nakha sikha subhaga bhāvate jī ke.
मुनिपट कटिन्ह कसें तूनीरा । सोहहिं कर कमलनि धनु तीरा ॥
munipaṭa kaṭinha kaseṁ tūnīrā, sohahiṁ kara kamalani dhanu tīrā.

Trans:

Another brought a jar full of water and tenderly besought, "Have a drink, my lords." On hearing their affectionate speech and seeing their great devotion, the compassionate and most amiable Rāma who, having perceived that Sītā was wearied, rested for a while in the shade of the fig-tree. All were enraptured with his beauty—men and women alike—and their soul was enamored of his incomparable loveliness. Like a circle of partridges about his moon-like face, so fixed was their gaze. At the sight of his body, dark in hue as a young tamal tree, a myriad Loves were fascinated; while Lakshman, all comely from head to foot, charmed the souls with his fair limbs, bright as the lightning—in his anchorite's dress, with his tightly-fitted quiver and bow, and arrows gleaming in his lotus hand.

दोहा-dohā:

जटा मुकुट सीसनि सुभग उर भुज नयन बिसाल ।
jaṭā mukuṭa sīsani subhaga ura bhuja nayana bisāla,
सरद परब बिधु बदन बर लसत स्वेद कन जाल ॥ ११५॥
sarada paraba bidhu badana bara lasata sveda kana jāla. 115.

Trans:

With their hair done up in a knot as a crown upon their graceful heads, with broad chest, strong arms, and large deep eyes, with face like the autumnal full moon, glistening with beads of perspiration;

चौपाई-caupāī:

बरनि न जाइ मनोहर जोरी । सोभा बहुत थोरि मति मोरी ॥
barani na jāi manohara jorī, sobhā bahuta thori mati morī.
राम लखन सिय सुंदरताई । सब चितवहिं चित मन मति लाई ॥
rāma lakhana siya suṁdaratāī, saba citavahiṁ cita mana mati lāī.
थके नारि नर प्रेम पिआसे । मनहुँ मृगी मृग देखि दिआ से ॥
thake nāri nara prema piāse, manahuṁ mṛgī mṛga dekhi diā se.
सीय समीप ग्रामतिय जाहीं । पूँछत अति सनेहँ सकुचाहीं ॥
sīya samīpa grāmatiya jāhīṁ, pūṁchata ati sanehaṁ sakucāhīṁ.
बार बार सब लागहिं पाएँ । कहहिं बचन मृदु सरल सुभाएँ ॥
bāra bāra saba lāgahiṁ pāeṁ, kahahiṁ bacana mṛdu sarala subhāeṁ.
राजकुमारि बिनय हम करहीं । तिय सुभायँ कछु पूँछत डरहीं ॥
rājakumāri binaya hama karahīṁ, tiya subhāyaṁ kachu pūṁchata ḍarahīṁ.
स्वामिनि अबिनय छमबि हमारी । बिलगु न मानब जानि गवाँरी ॥
svāmini abinaya chamabi hamārī, bilagu na mānaba jāni gavāṁrī.
राजकुअँर दोउ सहज सलोने । इन्ह तें लही दुति मरकत सोने ॥
rājakuaṁra dou sahaja salone, inha teṁ lahī duti marakata sone.

Trans:

the loveliness of the two brothers is past all telling; it is boundless, and my wit is scant. With every faculty of mind and soul, they all gaze upon the beauteous trio; man and woman thirsting and faint with love, like deer dazed by a light. The village women drew near to Sītā with tender and bashful enquiries, and, again and again embracing her feet, in their simplicity whispered the question, "Noble lady, we have a petition, but like women are afraid to make it. Pardon our presumption, O princess, and be not offended by our coarse manners. These two charming young princes, from whom emerald and gold might borrow splendor,

दोहा-dohā:

स्यामल गौर किसोर बर सुंदर सुषमा ऐन ।
syāmala gaura kisora bara suṁdara suṣamā aina,
सरद सर्बरीनाथ मुखु सरद सरोरुह नैन ॥ ११६॥
sarada sarbarīnātha mukhu sarada saroruha naina. 116.

Trans:

the one dark, the other fair, but both beautiful and abodes of delight, with face like the autumn moon, and eyes like the lotuses of autumn,

मासपारायण सोलहवाँ विश्राम

नवाह्नपारायण चौथा विश्राम

māsapārāyaṇa solahavāṁ viśrāma
navāhnapārāyaṇa cauthā viśrāma
(Pause 16 for a Thirty-Day Recitation)
(Pause 4 for a Nine-Day Recitation)

चौपाई-caupāī:

कोटि मनोज लजावनिहारे । सुमुखि कहहु को आहिं तुम्हारे ॥
koṭi manoja lajāvanihāre, sumukhi kahahu ko āhiṁ tumhāre.
सुनि सनेहमय मंजुल बानी । सकुची सिय मन महुँ मुसुकानी ॥
suni sanehamaya maṁjula bānī, sakucī siya mana mahuṁ musukānī.
तिन्हहि बिलोकि बिलोकति धरनी । दुहुँ सकोच सकुचित बरबरनी ॥
tinhahi biloki bilokati dharanī, duhuṁ sakoca sakucita barabaranī.
सकुचि सप्रेम बाल मृग नयनी । बोली मधुर बचन पिकबयनी ॥
sakuci saprema bāla mṛga nayanī, bolī madhura bacana pikabayanī.
सहज सुभाय सुभग तन गोरे । नामु लखनु लघु देवर मोरे ॥
sahaja subhāya subhaga tana gore, nāmu lakhanu laghu devara more.
बहुरि बदनु बिधु अंचल ढाँकी । पिय तन चितइ भौंह करि बाँकी ॥
bahuri badanu bidhu aṁcala ḍhāṁkī, piya tana citai bhauṁha kari bāṁkī.
खंजन मंजु तिरीछे नयननि । निज पति कहेउ तिन्हहि सियँ सयननि ॥
khaṁjana maṁju tirīche nayanani, nija pati kaheu tinhahi siyaṁ sayanani.
भईं मुदित सब ग्रामबधूटीं । रंकन्ह राय रासि जनु लूटीं ॥
bhaiṁ mudita saba grāmabadhūṭīṁ, raṁkanha rāya rāsi janu lūṭīṁ.

Trans:

which would put to shame a myriad Loves, say, O fair lady, how stand they to you?" Hearing their loving and sweet words Sītā felt abashed and smiled within herself. Looking at them in the first instance she then cast her eyes towards the earth; the fair-complexioned lady felt a dual delicacy. With a voice sweet as the notes of a *koel* the fawn-eyed princess bashfully replied in loving and sweet accents, "The one who is artless in manners and has a fair and graceful form is called Lakshman, and is my younger brother-in-law." Again veiling her moon-like face with an end of her sari she looked at her beloved Lord, and then bending her eyebrows and casting a sidelong glance with her beautiful eyes that resembled the *Khanjan* bird in their quick movements, she indicated to them by signs that that was her husband. All the village women were as delighted as beggars who have plucked piles of jewels.

दोहा-dohā:

अति सप्रेम सिय पायँ परि बहुबिधि देहिं असीस ।
ati saprema siya pāyam̐ pari bahubidhi dehiṁ asīsa,
सदा सोहागिनि होहु तुम्ह जब लगि महि अहि सीस ॥११७॥
sadā sohāgini hohu tumha jaba lagi mahi ahi sīsa. 117.

Trans:

Falling at Sītā's feet in their great affection, they invoked upon her every blessing, "May your happy wedded life last as long as the Earth rests upon the serpent's head.

चौपाई-caupāī:

पारबती सम पतिप्रिय होहू । देबि न हम पर छाड़ब छोहू ॥
pārabatī sama patipriya hohū, debi na hama para chāṛaba chohū.
पुनि पुनि बिनय करिअ कर जोरी । जौं एहि मारग फिरिअ बहोरी ॥
puni puni binaya karia kara jorī, jauṁ ehi māraga phiria bahorī.
दरसनु देब जानि निज दासी । लखीं सीयँ सब प्रेम पिआसी ॥
darasanu deba jāni nija dāsī, lakhīṁ sīyam̐ saba prema piāsī.
मधुर बचन कहि कहि परितोषीं । जनु कुमुदिनीं कौमुदीं पोषीं ॥
madhura bacana kahi kahi paritoṣīṁ, janu kumudinīṁ kaumudīṁ poṣīṁ.
तबहिं लखन रघुबर रुख जानी । पूँछेउ मगु लोगन्हि मृदु बानी ॥
tabahiṁ lakhana raghubara rukha jānī, pūm̐cheu magu loganhi mṛdu bānī.
सुनत नारि नर भए दुखारी । पुलकित गात बिलोचन बारी ॥
sunata nāri nara bhae dukhārī, pulakita gāta bilocana bārī.
मिटा मोदु मन भए मलीने । बिधि निधि दीन्ह लेत जनु छीने ॥
miṭā modu mana bhae malīne, bidhi nidhi dīnha leta janu chīne.
समुझि करम गति धीरजु कीन्हा । सोधि सुगम मगु तिन्ह कहि दीन्हा ॥
samujhi karama gati dhīraju kīnhā, sodhi sugama magu tinha kahi dīnhā.

Trans:

May you be as dear to your Lord as Pārwatī to Shiva. Yet, O princess, cease not to have some regard for us; again and again with clasped hands we beseech you, if you return by this road, remember us, your servants, and allow us to see you again." Finding them all so athirst with love, Sītā comforted them with many soothing words, as the lily is cheered by the moonlight. Then Lakshman, perceiving Raghubar's wish, gently asked the people the way. At his words they became sad, their limbs trembled, their eyes filled with tears, their joy was extinguished, and they were troubled at heart. "God has given us a treasure only to take it away again!" Then reflecting on the ways of Fate and taking courage, they fixed upon the easiest road and explained it to them.

दोहा-dohā:

लखन जानकी सहित तब गवनु कीन्ह रघुनाथ ।
lakhana jānakī sahita taba gavanu kīnha raghunātha,
फेरे सब प्रिय बचन कहि लिए लाइ मन साथ ॥११८॥
phere saba priya bacana kahi lie lāi mana sātha. 118.

Trans:

Raghunāth again took his way to the woods—with him Lakshman and Jānakī. With soothing words he sent back the others who tried to follow—though their hearts went along with the trio.

चौपाई-caupāī:

फिरत नारि नर अति पछिताहीं । दैअहि दोषु देहिं मन माहीं ॥
phirata nāri nara ati pachitāhīṁ, daiahi doṣu dehiṁ mana māhīṁ.
सहित बिषाद परसपर कहहीं । बिधि करतब उलटे सब अहहीं ॥
sahita biṣāda parasapara kahahīṁ, bidhi karataba ulaṭe saba ahahīṁ.
निपट निरंकुस निठुर निसंकू । जेहिं ससि कीन्ह सरुज सकलंकू ॥
nipaṭa niraṁkusa niṭhura nisaṁkū, jehiṁ sasi kīnha saruja sakalaṁkū.
रूख कलपतरु सागरु खारा । तेहिं पठए बन राजकुमारा ॥
rūkha kalapataru sāgaru khārā, tehiṁ paṭhae bana rājakumārā.
जौं पै इन्हहि दीन्ह बनबासू । कीन्ह बादि बिधि भोग बिलासू ॥
jauṁ pai inhahi dīnha banabāsū, kīnha bādi bidhi bhoga bilāsū.
ए बिचरहिं मग बिनु पदत्राना । रचे बादि बिधि बाहन नाना ॥
e bicarahiṁ maga binu padatrānā, race bādi bidhi bāhana nānā.
ए महि परहिं डासि कुस पाता । सुभग सेज कत सृजत बिधाता ॥
e mahi parahiṁ ḍāsi kusa pātā, subhaga seja kata sṛjata bidhātā.
तरुबर बास इन्हहि बिधि दीन्हा । धवल धाम रचि रचि श्रमु कीन्हा ॥
tarubara bāsa inhahi bidhi dīnhā, dhavala dhāma raci raci śramu kīnhā.

Trans:

Men and women alike on their way back lamented exceedingly and imputed blame to Destiny, saying sadly to one another, "God's doings are all perverse. He is utterly uncontrollable, cruel, and remorseless—who has made the moon sickly and spotted, the tree of paradise a lifeless block, and the ocean all salty, and—who now has sent these princely boys into the wilderness. If the woods are their proper abode, then for whom has God intended ease and pleasure? If they are to wander on their way barefooted, it is to no purpose that he has invented so many kinds of carriages. If they are to lie on the ground littered only with grass and leaves, for whom has he created couches of comfort? If he makes them live under the trees, why has he taken such pains to erect splendid palaces?

दोहा-dohā:

जौं ए मुनि पट धर जटिल सुंदर सुठि सुकुमार ।
jauṁ e muni paṭa dhara jaṭila suṁdara suṭhi sukumāra,
बिबिध भाँति भूषन बसन बादि किए करतार ॥११९॥
bibidha bhām̐ti bhūṣana basana bādi kie karatāra. 119.

Trans:

If such lovely and delicate souls wear the rough dress and matted locks of anchorites, it is to no purpose that the great artificer has made so many kinds of dresses and ornaments.

चौपाई-caupāī:

जौं ए कंद मूल फल खाहीं । बादि सुधादि असन जग माहीं ॥
jauṁ e kaṁda mūla phala khāhīṁ, bādi sudhādi asana jaga māhīṁ.
एक कहहिं ए सहज सुहाए । आपु प्रगट भए बिधि न बनाए ॥
eka kahahiṁ e sahaja suhāe, āpu pragaṭa bhae bidhi na banāe.
जहँ लगि बेद कही बिधि करनी । श्रवन नयन मन गोचर बरनी ॥
jaham̐ lagi beda kahī bidhi karanī, śravana nayana mana gocara baranī.
देखहु खोजि भुअन दस चारी । कहँ अस पुरुष कहाँ असि नारी ॥
dekhahu khoji bhuana dasa cārī, kaham̐ asa puruṣa kahām̐ asi nārī.
इन्हहि देखि बिधि मनु अनुरागा । पटतर जोग बनावै लागा ॥
inhahi dekhi bidhi manu anurāgā, paṭatara joga banāvai lāgā.
कीन्ह बहुत श्रम ऐक न आए । तेहिं इरिषा बन आनि दुराए ॥
kīnha bahuta śrama aika na āe, tehiṁ iriṣā bana āni durāe.
एक कहहिं हम बहुत न जानहिं । आपुहि परम धन्य करि मानहिं ॥
eka kahahiṁ hama bahuta na jānahiṁ, āpuhi parama dhanya kari mānahiṁ.
ते पुनि पुन्यपुंज हम लेखे । जे देखहिं देखिहहिं जिन्ह देखे ॥
te puni punyapuṁja hama lekhe, je dekhahiṁ dekhihahiṁ jinha dekhe.

Trans:

If they are to eat only fruits and herbs, then all the delicacies of the world have been created in vain." Said another, "Beautiful as they are, they must have come upon earth of their own accord, and could not have been created by God at all. In all the works of God of which the Vedas tell—that either the ears can hear, or the eyes see, or the mind imagine, or the tongue speak—search and examine the whole fourteen spheres—where is there such a man, and where a woman like this? When he saw them, God was so pleased that he essayed to make their match; but after much labor nothing came of it, and thus in malice he has sent and shrouded them within the woods." Said yet another, "I am no great a scholar, but I account myself supremely happy; nay blessed are all, in my opinion, who see him, or have seen him, or shall see him."

दोहा-dohā:

एहि बिधि कहि कहि बचन प्रिय लेहिं नयन भरि नीर ।
ehi bidhi kahi kahi bacana priya lehiṁ nayana bhari nīra,
किमि चलिहहिं मारग अगम सुठि सुकुमार सरीर ॥ १२० ॥
kimi calihahiṁ māraga agama suṭhi sukumāra sarīra. 120.

Trans:

With such affectionate discourse their eyes filled with tears: "How can they, who are so delicate, traverse so difficult a road?"

चौपाई-caupāī:

नारि सनेह बिकल बस होहीं । चकईं साँझ समय जनु सोहीं ॥
nāri saneha bikala basa hohīṁ, cakaīṁ sām̐jha samaya janu sohīṁ.
मृदु पद कमल कठिन मगु जानी । गहबरि हृदयँ कहहिं बर बानी ॥
mṛdu pada kamala kaṭhina magu jānī, gahabari hṛdayam̐ kahahiṁ bara bānī.
परसत मृदुल चरन अरुनारे । सकुचति महि जिमि हृदय हमारे ॥
parasata mṛdula carana arunāre, sakucati mahi jimi hṛdaya hamāre.
जौं जगदीस इन्हहि बनु दीन्हा । कस न सुमनमय मारगु कीन्हा ॥
jauṁ jagadīsa inhahi banu dīnhā, kasa na sumanamaya māragu kīnhā.
जौं मागा पाइअ बिधि पाहीं । ए रखिअहिं सखि आँखिन्ह माहीं ॥
jauṁ māgā pāia bidhi pāhīṁ, e rakhiahiṁ sakhi ām̐khinha māhīṁ.
जे नर नारि न अवसर आए । तिन्ह सिय रामु न देखन पाए ॥
je nara nāri na avasara āe, tinha siya rāmu na dekhana pāe.
सुनि सुरुपु बूझहिं अकुलाई । अब लगि गए कहाँ लगि भाई ॥
suni surupu būjhahiṁ akulāī, aba lagi gae kahām̐ lagi bhāī.
समरथ धाइ बिलोकहिं जाई । प्रमुदित फिरहिं जनमफलु पाई ॥
samaratha dhāi bilokahiṁ jāī, pramudita phirahiṁ janamaphalu pāī.

Trans:

All the women were made as uneasy by their love, as is the chakwi at the evening time. As they thought upon their tender lotus feet, and the hardness of the road, they were distressed in heart and cried in plaintive tones, "At the touch of their soft and rosy feet, the very earth shrinks—as shrinks our heart. If the great God must send them to the woods, why did he not strew their path with flowers? If there be one boon that we may ask of Heaven and obtain, O friends, let it be that we may keep them ever in our eyes." All the people who had not come in time—and thus had missed seeing Sītā and Rāma—when they heard of their beauty, asked anxiously, "How far, brother, will they have got by this time?" Those who were strong ran on, and saw them, and returned with joy—having obtained the fruition of their eyes.

दोहा-dohā:

अबला बालक बृद्ध जन कर मीजहिं पछिताहिं ।
abalā bālaka bṛddha jana kara mījahiṁ pachitāhiṁ,
होहिं प्रेमबस लोग इमि रामु जहाँ जहँ जाहिं ॥ १२१ ॥
hohiṁ premabasa loga imi rāmu jahām̐ jaham̐ jāhiṁ. 121.

Trans:

The women and children and the aged wrung their hands and lamented. In this manner, wherever Rāma went, the people were smitten with love.

चौपाई-caupāī:

गावँ गावँ अस होइ अनंदू । देखि भानुकुल कैरव चंदू ॥
gāvam̐ gāvam̐ asa hoi anaṁdū, dekhi bhānukula kairava caṁdū.
जे कछु समाचार सुनि पावहिं । ते नृप रानिहि दोसु लगावहिं ॥
je kachu samācāra suni pāvahiṁ, te nṛpa rānihi dosu lagāvahiṁ.
कहहिं एक अति भल नरनाहू । दीन्ह हमहि जोइ लोचन लाहू ॥
kahahiṁ eka ati bhala naranāhū, dīnha hamahi joi locana lāhū.
कहहिं परसपर लोग लोगाईं । बातें सरल सनेह सुहाईं ॥
kahahiṁ parasapara loga logāīṁ, bāteṁ sarala saneha suhāīṁ.
ते पितु मातु धन्य जिन्ह जाए । धन्य सो नगरु जहाँ तें आए ॥
te pitu mātu dhanya jinha jāe, dhanya so nagaru jahām̐ teṁ āe.
धन्य सो देसु सैलु बन गाऊँ । जहँ जहँ जाहिं धन्य सोइ ठाऊँ ॥
dhanya so desu sailu bana gāūm̐, jaham̐ jaham̐ jāhiṁ dhanya soi ṭhāūm̐.
सुखु पायउ बिरंचि रचि तेही । ए जेहि के सब भाँति सनेही ॥
sukhu pāyau biraṁci raci tehī, e jehi ke saba bhām̐ti sanehī.
राम लखन पथि कथा सुहाई । रही सकल मग कानन छाई ॥
rāma lakhana pathi kathā suhāī, rahī sakala maga kānana chāī.

Trans:

In every village was similar rejoicing at the sight of the moon of the lily-like solar race. Some who had learnt by hearsay of what had been going on, imputed blame to the king and queen. One said, "It was very good of the king to give our eyes such a treat." Said others among themselves in simple and loving phrase, "Happy the father and mother who gave them birth, and happy the city from whence they came! Happy the hills and plains and woods and towns, and every place which they ever touched. Even the Creator who made them is pleased, nay, is absolutely in love with them." The delightful history of Rāma, Lakshman, and Sītā thus spread across every road and forest.

दोहा-dohā:

एहि बिधि रघुकुल कमल रबि मग लोगन्ह सुख देत ।
ehi bidhi raghukula kamala rabi maga loganha sukha deta,
जाहिं चले देखत बिपिन सिय सौमित्रि समेत ॥ १२२ ॥
jāhiṁ cale dekhata bipina siya saumitri sameta. 122.

Trans:

In this manner the sun of the lotus-like solar race gladdened the people on the road as he—with Sītā and the son of Sumitrā along—proceeded on his travels through the woods.

चौपाई-caupāī:

आगें रामु लखनु बने पाछें । तापस बेष बिराजत काछें ॥
āgeṁ rāmu lakhanu bane pācheṁ, tāpasa beṣa birājata kācheṁ.
उभय बीच सिय सोहति कैसें । ब्रह्म जीव बिच माया जैसें ॥
ubhaya bīca siya sohati kaiseṁ, brahma jīva bica māyā jaiseṁ.
बहुरि कहउँ छबि जसि मन बसई । जनु मधु मदन मध्य रति लसई ॥
bahuri kahaum̐ chabi jasi mana basaī, janu madhu madana madhya rati lasaī.
उपमा बहुरि कहउँ जियँ जोही । जनु बुध बिधु बिच रोहिनि सोही ॥
upamā bahuri kahaum̐ jiyam̐ johī, janu budha bidhu bica rohini sohī.
प्रभु पद रेख बीच बिच सीता । धरति चरन मग चलति सभीता ॥
prabhu pada rekha bīca bica sītā, dharati carana maga calati sabhītā.
सीय राम पद अंक बराएँ । लखन चलहिं मगु दाहिन लाएँ ॥
sīya rāma pada aṁka barāem̐, lakhana calahiṁ magu dāhina lāem̐.
राम लखन सिय प्रीति सुहाई । बचन अगोचर किमि कहि जाई ॥
rāma lakhana siya prīti suhāī, bacana agocara kimi kahi jāī.
खग मृग मगन देखि छबि होहीं । लिए चोरि चित राम बटोहीं ॥
khaga mṛga magana dekhi chabi hohīṁ, lie cori cita rāma baṭohīṁ.

Trans:

Rāma walked in front, and Lakshman behind, conspicuous in the hermit's dress they wore; and between them both, Sītā shone resplendent, as Māyā—which stands in between the Supreme-Soul and the Soul. Or, to describe her beauty by another fancy, she seemed like Ratī between Spring and Love; or, to ransack my mind for yet another simile, like the constellation *Rohini* between *Budh* and the Moon. As she went along the way Sītā carefully planted her feet between the footprints of her Lord; while avoiding the footprints both of Sītā and Rāma, Lakshman traversed the road always keeping theirs to his right. The charming affection of all three was beyond all telling; how then can I declare it? Birds and deer were fascinated at the sight of their beauty. Rāma the wayfarer stole all hearts.

दोहा-dohā:

जिन्ह जिन्ह देखे पथिक प्रिय सिय समेत दोउ भाइ ।
jinha jinha dekhe pathika priya siya sameta dou bhāi,
भव मगु अगमु अनंदु तेइ बिनु श्रम रहे सिराइ ॥ १२३॥
bhava magu agamu anaṁdu tei binu śrama rahe sirāi. 123.

Trans:

All who beheld the dear travelers, Sītā and the two brothers, joyously and without fatigue arrived at once at the end of their toilsome journey of life.

चौपाई-caupāī:

अजहुँ जासु उर सपनेहुँ काऊ । बसहुँ लखनु सिय रामु बटाऊ ॥
ajahuṁ jāsu ura sapanehuṁ kāū, basahuṁ lakhanu siya rāmu baṭāū.
राम धाम पथ पाइहि सोई । जो पथ पाव कबहुँ मुनि कोई ॥
rāma dhāma patha pāihi soī, jo patha pāva kabahuṁ muni koī.
तब रघुबीर श्रमित सिय जानी । देखि निकट बटु सीतल पानी ॥
taba raghubīra śramita siya jānī, dekhi nikaṭa baṭu sītala pānī.
तहँ बसि कंद मूल फल खाई । प्रात नहाइ चले रघुराई ॥
tahaṁ basi kaṁda mūla phala khāī, prāta nahāi cale raghurāī.
देखत बन सर सैल सुहाए । बालमीकि आश्रम प्रभु आए ॥
dekhata bana sara saila suhāe, bālamīki āśrama prabhu āe.
राम दीख मुनि बासु सुहावन । सुंदर गिरि काननु जलु पावन ॥
rāma dīkha muni bāsu suhāvana, suṁdara giri kānanu jalu pāvana.
सरनि सरोज बिटप बन फूले । गुंजत मंजु मधुप रस भूले ॥
sarani saroja biṭapa bana phūle, guṁjata maṁju madhupa rasa bhūle.
खग मृग बिपुल कोलाहल करहीं । बिरहित बैर मुदित मन चरहीं ॥
khaga mṛga bipula kolāhala karahīṁ, birahita baira mudita mana carahīṁ.

Trans:

And to this day any soul in whom the vision of the wayfarers, Rāma, Sītā, and Lakshman abides, finds the path which leads to Rāma's divine abode—a path that scarce a saint may find. Then Raghubīr, knowing that Sītā was tired, and observing a Banyan closeby and also cool water, rested there and took some roots and fruits to eat. After bathing at dawn, they again went on their way. Admiring the beauty of the woods and lakes and rocks, finally Rāma arrived at Vālmikī's hermitage. He found the saint's dwelling a charming spot—a lovely wooded hill with a spring of clear water, lotuses in the pond, the forest trees all in flower, with a delightful hum of bees drunk on honey, and a joyous clamor of birds and beasts feeding happily and in peace together.

दोहा-dohā:

सुचि सुंदर आश्रमु निरखि हरषे राजिवनेन ।
suci suṁdara āśramu nirakhi harașe rājivanena,
सुनि रघुबर आगमनु मुनि आगें आयउ लेन ॥ १२४॥
suni raghubara āgamanu muni āgeṁ āyau lena. 124.

Trans:

The Lotus-eyed was glad as he gazed upon the bright and fair retreat, and the saint on hearing of his arrival came forth to meet him.

चौपाई-caupāī:

मुनि कहुँ राम दंडवत कीन्हा । आसिरबादु बिप्रबर दीन्हा ॥
muni kahuṁ rāma daṁḍavata kīnhā, āsirabādu biprabara dīnhā.
देखि राम छबि नयन जुड़ाने । करि सनमानु आश्रमहिं आने ॥
dekhi rāma chabi nayana juṛāne, kari sanamānu āśramahiṁ āne.
मुनिबर अतिथि प्रानप्रिय पाए । कंद मूल फल मधुर मगाए ॥
munibara atithi prānapriya pāe, kaṁda mūla phala madhura magāe.
सिय सौमित्रि राम फल खाए । तब मुनि आश्रम दिए सुहाए ॥
siya saumitri rāma phala khāe, taba muni āśrama die suhāe.
बालमीकि मन आनँदु भारी । मंगल मूरति नयन निहारी ॥
bālamīki mana ānaṁdu bhārī, maṁgala mūrati nayana nihārī.
तब कर कमल जोरि रघुराई । बोले बचन श्रवन सुखदाई ॥
taba kara kamala jori raghurāī, bole bacana śravana sukhadāī.
तुम्ह त्रिकाल दरसी मुनिनाथा । बिस्व बदर जिमि तुम्हरें हाथा ॥
tumha trikāla darasī munināthā, bisva badara jimi tumhareṁ hāthā.
अस कहि प्रभु सब कथा बखानी । जेहि जेहि भाँति दीन्ह बनु रानी ॥
asa kahi prabhu saba kathā bakhānī, jehi jehi bhāṁti dīnha banu rānī.

Trans:

Rāma prostrated himself before him, and the holy man gave him his blessing. At the sight of Rāma's beauty his eyes beamed and he conducted him with all honor to his hut. There he gave him a choice seat, like to a guest dear to him as his own life; and then sent for herbs and sweet fruits—which Sītā, Lakshman, and Rāma partook. Great was the joy of Vālmikī's soul as his eyes beheld the Epitome-of-Bliss. Then folding his lotus hands Rāma spoke—words that were like charm to his ears: "O king of sages; all time—past, present, and future—is in your ken; and the universe is like a little plum in the palm of your hand." Then the Lord related to him the whole episode and how the his exile had come about at the behest of the queen.

दोहा-dohā:

तात बचन पुनि मातु हित भाइ भरत अस राउ ।
tāta bacana puni mātu hita bhāi bharata asa rāu,
मो कहुँ दरस तुम्हार प्रभु सबु मम पुन्य प्रभाउ ॥ १२५॥
mo kahuṁ darasa tumhāra prabhu sabu mama punya prabhāu. 125.

Trans:

"My father's promise, my mother's order, my brother Bharat's coronation, and my own meeting with you, my Lord—are all blessings that only my past merits could have won for me.

चौपाई-caupāī:

देखि पाय मुनिराय तुम्हारे । भए सुकृत सब सुफल हमारे ॥
dekhi pāya munirāya tumhāre, bhae sukṛta saba suphala hamāre.
अब जहँ राउर आयसु होई । मुनि उदबेगु न पावै कोई ॥
aba jahaṁ rāura āyasu hoī, muni udabegu na pāvai koī.
मुनि तापस जिन्ह तें दुखु लहहीं । ते नरेस बिनु पावक दहहीं ॥
muni tāpasa jinha teṁ dukhu lahahīṁ, te naresa binu pāvaka dahahīṁ.
मंगल मूल बिप्र परितोषू । दहइ कोटि कुल भूसुर रोषू ॥
maṁgala mūla bipra paritoṣū, dahai koṭi kula bhūsura roṣū.
अस जियँ जानि कहिअ सोइ ठाऊँ । सिय सौमित्रि सहित जहँ जाऊँ ॥
asa jiyaṁ jāni kahia soi ṭhāūṁ, siya saumitri sahita jahaṁ jāūṁ.
तहँ रचि रुचिर परन तृन साला । बासु करौं कछु काल कृपाला ॥
tahaṁ raci rucira parana tṛna sālā, bāsu karauṁ kachu kāla kṛpālā.
सहज सरल सुनि रघुबर बानी । साधु साधु बोले मुनि ग्यानी ॥
sahaja sarala suni raghubara bānī, sādhu sādhu bole muni gyānī.
कस न कहहु अस रघुकुलकेतू । तुम्ह पालक संतत श्रुति सेतू ॥
kasa na kahahu asa raghukulaketū, tumha pālaka saṁtata śruti setū.

Trans:

In beholding your feet, holy sir, all my good deeds are rewarded. Now, wherever you command me to go—where no anchorite may be disturbed—there I will proceed—for those kings are consumed without fire, who vex either saints or ascetics. Satisfaction of the virtuous is the root of all happiness, while their wrath consumes a thousand generations. Bearing that in mind, tell me of some place to which I can go with Sītā and Sumitrā's son; and there build a pretty hut of grass and twigs and rest awhile, kind sir." On hearing his ingenuous speech, the all-wise seer exclaimed, "True,

true! It is only natural for you to so speak, pride of the Raghu's line, O guardian of the eternal bridge of revelation.

छंद-chamda:

श्रुति सेतु पालक राम तुम्ह जगदीस माया जानकी ।
śruti setu pālaka rāma tumha jagadīsa māyā jānakī,
जो सृजति जगु पालति हरति रूख पाइ कृपानिधान की ॥
jo sṛjati jagu pālati harati rūkha pāi kṛpānidhāna kī.
जो सहससीसु अहीसु महिधरु लखनु सचराचर धनी ।
jo sahasasīsu ahīsu mahidharu lakhanu sacarācara dhanī,
सुर काज धरि नरराज तनु चले दलन खल निसिचर अनी ॥
sura kāja dhari nararāja tanu cale dalana khala nisicara anī.

Trans:

Custodian of the Vedas, embodiment of Scriptures, you, O Rāma, are the Lord of the universe; and Jānakī is Māyā, who with your gracious volition creates, preserves, and destroys the universe; and Lakshman the thousand-headed serpent lord, the supporter of the world, with all that it contains, living or lifeless. On behalf of the gods you have taken a kingly form and go forth to rout the demons.

सोरठा-soraṭhā:

राम सरुप तुम्हार बचन अगोचर बुद्धिपर ।
rāma sarupa tumhāra bacana agocara buddhipara,
अबिगत अकथ अपार नेति नेति नित निगम कह ॥ १२६ ॥
abigata akatha apāra neti neti nita nigama kaha. 126.

Trans:

Your being, O Rāma, transcends speech and is beyond conception: the all-pervading, unutterable, illimitable existence which the Vedas speak of as 'Not-this', 'Not-this'.

चौपाई-caupāī:

जगु पेखन तुम्ह देखनिहारे । बिधि हरि संभु नचावनिहारे ॥
jagu pekhana tumha dekhanihāre, bidhi hari sambhu nacāvanihāre.
तेउ न जानहिं मरमु तुम्हारा । औरु तुम्हहि को जाननिहारा ॥
teu na jānahiṁ maramu tumhārā, auru tumhahi ko jānanihārā.
सोइ जानइ जेहि देहु जनाई । जानत तुम्हहि तुम्हइ होइ जाई ॥
soi jānai jehi dehu janāī, jānata tumhahi tumhai hoi jāī.
तुम्हरिहि कृपाँ तुम्हहि रघुनंदन । जानहिं भगत भगत उर चंदन ॥
tumharihi kṛpāṁ tumhahi raghunaṁdana, jānahiṁ bhagata bhagata ura caṁdana.
चिदानंदमय देह तुम्हारी । बिगत बिकार जान अधिकारी ॥
cidānaṁdamaya deha tumhārī, bigata bikāra jāna adhikārī.
नर तनु धरेहु संत सुर काजा । कहहु करहु जस प्राकृत राजा ॥
nara tanu dharehu saṁta sura kājā, kahahu karahu jasa prākṛta rājā.
राम देखि सुनि चरित तुम्हारे । जड़ मोहहिं बुध होहिं सुखारे ॥
rāma dekhi suni carita tumhāre, jaṛa mohahiṁ budha hohiṁ sukhāre.
तुम्ह जो कहहु करहु सबु साँचा । जस काछिअ तस चाहिअ नाचा ॥
tumha jo kahahu karahu sabu sāṁcā, jasa kāchia tasa cāhia nācā.

Trans:

The world is a stage and you are the witness watching the drama in play. Nay, you make even Brahmmā, Harī, and Shambhu dance to your orchestration—for even they know not your secret. Verily who else could ever discover you? He only knows you—to whom you have vouchsafed knowledge—and he who knows you becomes one with you. It is by your very grace, Raghunandan, that your votaries learn to know you, O thou soothing sandalwood salve unto the devout soul. Your body is pure intelligence and bliss, void of change—as they know, who have found your essence. On behalf of the saints and the gods you have taken a human form and speak and act like an ordinary king. Fools are bewildered, but the wise rejoice, as they see or hear of your deeds; whatever you say or do is true, and we can only play such parts as you set us to do.

दोहा-dohā:

पूँछेहु मोहि कि रहौं कहँ मैं पूँछत सकुचाउँ ।
pūṁchehu mohi ki rahauṁ kahaṁ maiṁ pūṁchata sakucāuṁ,
जहँ न होहु तहँ देहु कहि तुम्हहि देखावौं ठाउँ ॥ १२७ ॥
jahaṁ na hohu tahaṁ dehu kahi tumhahi dekhāvauṁ ṭhāuṁ. 127.

Trans:

You ask of me 'Where can I dwell?' but I ask with diffidence, tell me where are you not, for then alone can I determine for you some place."

चौपाई-caupāī:

सुनि मुनि बचन प्रेम रस साने । सकुचि राम मन महुँ मुसुकाने ॥
suni muni bacana prema rasa sāne, sakuci rāma mana mahuṁ musukāne.
बालमीकि हँसि कहहिं बहोरी । बानी मधुर अमिअ रस बोरी ॥
bālamīki haṁsi kahahiṁ bahorī, bānī madhura amia rasa borī.
सुनहु राम अब कहउँ निकेता । जहाँ बसहु सिय लखन समेता ॥
sunahu rāma aba kahauṁ niketā, jahāṁ basahu siya lakhana sametā.
जिन्ह के श्रवन समुद्र समाना । कथा तुम्हारि सुभग सरि नाना ॥
jinha ke śravana samudra samānā, kathā tumhāri subhaga sari nānā.
भरहिं निरंतर होहिं न पूरे । तिन्ह के हिय तुम्ह कहुँ गृह रूरे ॥
bharahiṁ niraṁtara hohiṁ na pūre, tinha ke hiya tumha kahuṁ gṛha rūre.
लोचन चातक जिन्ह करि राखे । रहहिं दरस जलधर अभिलाषे ॥
locana cātaka jinha kari rākhe, rahahiṁ darasa jaladhara abhilāṣe.
निदरहिं सरित सिंधु सर भारी । रूप बिंदु जल होहिं सुखारी ॥
nidarahiṁ sarita siṁdhu sara bhārī, rūpa biṁdu jala hohiṁ sukhārī.
तिन्ह कें हृदय सदन सुखदायक । बसहु बंधु सिय सह रघुनायक ॥
tinha keṁ hṛdaya sadana sukhadāyaka, basahu baṁdhu siya saha raghunāyaka.

Trans:

On hearing the sage's affectionate words, Rāma was abashed and smiled to himself. Vālmikī smiled too and spoke again in tones of honeyed accents, "Hearken O Rāma; I will tell you the places where you, with Sītā and Lakshman, ought to abide: They whose ears are like the ocean to catch the blessed streams of your traditions, and though ever replenished are never filled to the full, their hearts shall be your chosen abode. They whose eyes long for your presence, as passionately as the Chātak for the rain-cloud—which scorning the water of river, lake, or sea quench their thirst only in the rain-cloud of your beauty, their hearts are your glorious mansion; there abide, O Raghunāyak, with Lakshman and Sītā.

दोहा-dohā:

जसु तुम्हार मानस बिमल हंसिनि जीहा जासु ।
jasu tumhāra mānasa bimala haṁsini jīhā jāsu,
मुकुताहल गुन गन चुनइ राम बसहु हियँ तासु ॥ १२८ ॥
mukutāhala guna gana cunai rāma basahu hiyaṁ tāsu. 128.

Trans:

Whose tongue—like the swan in the clear hyperborean lake of your renown—gathers up the pearls of your perfections, in his heart, O Rāma, fix your home.

चौपाई-caupāī:

प्रभु प्रसाद सुचि सुभग सुबासा । सादर जासु लहइ नित नासा ॥
prabhu prasāda suci subhaga subāsā, sādara jāsu lahai nita nāsā.
तुम्हहि निबेदित भोजन करहीं । प्रभु प्रसाद पट भूषन धरहीं ॥
tumhahi nibedita bhojana karahīṁ, prabhu prasāda paṭa bhūṣana dharahīṁ.
सीस नवहिं सुर गुरु द्विज देखी । प्रीति सहित करि बिनय बिसेषी ॥
sīsa navahiṁ sura guru dvija dekhī, prīti sahita kari binaya biseṣī.
कर नित करहिं राम पद पूजा । राम भरोस हृदयँ नहिं दूजा ॥
kara nita karahiṁ rāma pada pūjā, rāma bharosa hṛdayaṁ nahiṁ dūjā.

चरन राम तीरथ चलि जाहीं । राम बसहु तिन्ह के मन माहीं ॥
carana rāma tīratha cali jāhīṁ, rāma basahu tinha ke mana māhīṁ.
मंत्रराजु नित जपहिं तुम्हारा । पूजहिं तुम्हहि सहित परिवारा ॥
maṁtrarāju nita japahiṁ tumhārā, pūjahiṁ tumhahi sahita parivārā.
तरपन होम करहिं बिधि नाना । बिप्र जेवाँइ देहिं बहु दाना ॥
tarapana homa karahiṁ bidhi nānā, bipra jevāṁi dehiṁ bahu dānā.
तुम्ह तें अधिक गुरहि जियँ जानी । सकल भायँ सेवहिं सनमानी ॥
tumha teṁ adhika gurahi jiyaṁ jānī, sakala bhāyaṁ sevahiṁ sanamānī.

Trans:

They who ever reverently inhale the sweet and blessed odor of the offerings to their Lord; who feed upon what has been offered to you; who wear only raiment and adornments first offered to you; who bow their heads when they see a god, a Gurū, or a Brahmin, and treat them with all honor and affection; whose hands are ever engaged in adoring the feet of Rāma; who have no other hope but only of Rāma in their heart; and whose feet ever bear them to your shrine—let their souls, O Rāma, be your dwelling-home. They who are ever repeating your holy name, and are worshiping you alongside their family; who perform the varied rites of oblation and sacrifice; who feast Brahmins and bestow them with gifts; who regard their own Gurū even more than you, and serve him with honor and high affection,

दोहा-dohā:

सबु करि मागहिं एक फलु राम चरन रति होउ ।
sabu kari māgahiṁ eka phalu rāma carana rati hou,
तिन्ह कें मन मंदिर बसहु सिय रघुनंदन दोउ ॥१२९॥
tinha keṁ mana maṁdira basahu siya raghunaṁdana dou. 129.

Trans:

who ask of all one only boon: devotion to Rāma's holy feet—choose their hearts as your temple wherein to abide, both Sītā and you two brothers.

चौपाई-caupāī:

काम कोह मद मान न मोहा । लोभ न छोभ न राग न द्रोहा ॥
kāma koha mada māna na mohā, lobha na chobha na rāga na drohā.
जिन्ह कें कपट दंभ नहिं माया । तिन्ह कें हृदय बसहु रघुराया ॥
jinha keṁ kapaṭa daṁbha nahiṁ māyā, tinha keṁ hṛdaya basahu raghurāyā.
सब के प्रिय सब के हितकारी । दुख सुख सरिस प्रसंसा गारी ॥
saba ke priya saba ke hitakārī, dukha sukha sarisa prasaṁsā gārī.
कहहिं सत्य प्रिय बचन बिचारी । जागत सोवत सरन तुम्हारी ॥
kahahiṁ satya priya bacana bicārī, jāgata sovata sarana tumhārī.
तुम्हहि छाड़ि गति दूसरि नाहीं । राम बसहु तिन्ह के मन माहीं ॥
tumhahi chāṛi gati dūsari nāhīṁ, rāma basahu tinha ke mana māhīṁ.
जननी सम जानहिं परनारी । धनु पराव बिष तें बिष भारी ॥
jananī sama jānahiṁ paranārī, dhanu parāva biṣa teṁ biṣa bhārī.
जे हरषहिं पर संपति देखी । दुखित होहिं पर बिपति बिसेषी ॥
je haraṣahiṁ para saṁpati dekhī, dukhita hohiṁ para bipati biseṣī.
जिन्हहि राम तुम्ह प्रानपिआरे । तिन्ह के मन सुभ सदन तुम्हारे ॥
jinhahi rāma tumha prānapiāre, tinha ke mana subha sadana tumhāre.

Trans:

Whoso is unmoved by lust, anger, pride, or arrogance; and whoso is without covetousness, excitement, partiality, or malice; and is without fraud, hypocrisy, or heretical delusions—there in his heart dwell, O Raghurāī. They who are friends to all beings and are well-disposed to all; to whom pleasure and pain, praise and abuse are alike; who are careful to say what is both true and kind; who, whether sleeping or waking, place themselves under your protection and have no other means of redemption but in you—do in their hearts O Rāma ever abide. They who look upon another man's wife as their own mother, and another's wealth as the deadliest poison, who rejoice to see a neighbor's prosperity and are grieved for his misfortunes; and to whom, you, O Rāma, are dear as their own life—let their hearts forever be your auspicious home.

दोहा-dohā:

स्वामि सखा पितु मातु गुर जिन्ह के सब तुम्ह तात ।
svāmi sakhā pitu mātu gura jinha ke saba tumha tāta,
मन मंदिर तिन्ह कें बसहु सीय सहित दोउ भ्रात ॥१३०॥
mana maṁdira tinha keṁ basahu sīya sahita dou bhrāta. 130.

Trans:

To whom, my son, you are at once the master and companion, and father, mother, and spiritual guide—let their hearts be your temples wherein to stay, ye brothers twain, along with Sītā.

चौपाई-caupāī:

अवगुन तजि सब के गुन गहहीं । बिप्र धेनु हित संकट सहहीं ॥
avaguna taji saba ke guna gahahīṁ, bipra dhenu hita saṁkaṭa sahahīṁ.
नीति निपुन जिन्ह कइ जग लीका । घर तुम्हार तिन्ह कर मनु नीका ॥
nīti nipuna jinha kai jaga līkā, ghara tumhāra tinha kara manu nīkā.
गुन तुम्हार समुझइ निज दोसा । जेहि सब भाँति तुम्हार भरोसा ॥
guna tumhāra samujhai nija dosā, jehi saba bhāṁti tumhāra bharosā.
राम भगत प्रिय लागहिं जेही । तेहि उर बसहु सहित बैदेही ॥
rāma bhagata priya lāgahiṁ jehī, tehi ura basahu sahita baidehī.
जाति पाँति धनु धरमु बड़ाई । प्रिय परिवार सदन सुखदाई ॥
jāti pāṁti dhanu dharamu baṛāī, priya parivāra sadana sukhadāī.
सब तजि तुम्हहि रहइ उर लाई । तेहि के हृदयँ रहहु रघुराई ॥
saba taji tumhahi rahai ura lāī, tehi ke hṛdayaṁ rahahu raghurāī.
सरगु नरकु अपबरगु समाना । जहँ तहँ देख धरें धनु बाना ॥
saragu naraku apabaragu samānā, jahaṁ tahaṁ dekha dhareṁ dhanu bānā.
करम बचन मन राउर चेरा । राम करहु तेहि कें उर डेरा ॥
karama bacana mana rāura cerā, rāma karahu tehi keṁ ura ḍerā.

Trans:

They who pick out all men's good points and leave the bad; who endure troubles on behalf of Brahmins and kine; and who are of note in the world for soundness of doctrine—let their hearts be your chosen abode. They who understand thy righteousness and their own defects and fix all their hopes just upon thee, and who have an affection for all thy worshippers—in their hearts dwell, O thou with Sītā. He who has left all—kin, sect, wealth, hereditary religion, worldly advancement, friends, relations, home and all—and given himself wholly unto you—in his heart do abide, O Raghurāī. To whom heaven and hell and release from transmigration are all alike—if only they can behold the God with his bow and arrows; and who in heart, words, and deeds, are your faithful slaves—be their hearts your tabernacle, O Shrī Rāma.

दोहा-dohā:

जाहि न चाहिअ कबहुँ कछु तुम्ह सन सहज सनेहु ।
jāhi na cāhia kabahuṁ kachu tumha sana sahaja sanehu,
बसहु निरंतर तासु मन सो राउर निज गेहु ॥१३१॥
basahu niraṁtara tāsu mana so rāura nija gehu. 131.

Trans:

They who never ask for anything but simply love you; in their hearts abide forever—for that is your natural abode."

चौपाई-caupāī:

एहि बिधि मुनिबर भवन देखाए । बचन सप्रेम राम मन भाए ॥
ehi bidhi munibara bhavana dekhāe, bacana saprema rāma mana bhāe.
कह मुनि सुनहु भानुकुलनायक । आश्रम कहउँ समय सुखदायक ॥
kaha muni sunahu bhānukulanāyaka, āśrama kahauṁ samaya sukhadāyaka.
चित्रकूट गिरि करहु निवासू । तहँ तुम्हार सब भाँति सुपासू ॥
citrakūṭa giri karahu nivāsū, tahaṁ tumhāra saba bhāṁti supāsū.

सैलु सुहावन कानन चारू। करि केहरि मृग बिहग बिहारू॥
sailu suhāvana kānana cārū, kari kehari mṛga bihaga bihārū.
नदी पुनीत पुरान बखानी। अत्रिप्रिया निज तपबल आनी॥
nadī punīta purāna bakhānī, atripriyā nija tapabala ānī.
सुरसरि धार नाउँ मंदाकिनि। जो सब पातक पोतक डाकिनि॥
surasari dhāra nāuṁ maṁdākini, jo saba pātaka potaka ḍākini.
अत्रि आदि मुनिबर बहु बसहीं। करहिं जोग जप तप तन कसहीं॥
atri ādi munibara bahu basahīṁ, karahiṁ joga japa tapa tana kasahīṁ.
चलहु सफल श्रम सब कर करहू। राम देहु गौरव गिरिबरहू॥
calahu saphala śrama saba kara karahū, rāma dehu gaurava giribarahū.

Trans:

The eminent sage thus showed him many a dwelling places and these loving words gladdened Rāma's soul. The saint continued, "Hearken, O Lord of the solar race; I will tell you a hermitage suitable for your present wants. Take up your abode on the hill of Chitra-kūt; there you will have every convenience. It is a beautiful hill finely wooded, the haunt of elephants, tigers, deer, and birds. It has a sacred river mentioned in the Purānas, which the wife of Atri brought there by the power of penance. It is called the Mandakinī, a branch of the Gangā, as quick to drown sin as a witch to strangle an infant. Atri and other sages live there engaged in meditation and prayer and wasting their bodies with penance. Go and bless their labors, O Rāma, and confer dignity upon the mountain."

दोहा-dohā:

चित्रकूट महिमा अमित कही महामुनि गाइ।
citrakūṭa mahimā amita kahī mahāmuni gāi,
आए नहाए सरित बर सिय समेत दोउ भाइ॥१३२॥
āe nahāe sarita bara siya sameta dou bhāi. 132.

Trans:

The great sage Vālmikī then described at length the infinite glory of Chitra-kūt and the two brothers proceeded there along with Sītā; and then all bathed in the sacred stream.

चौपाई-caupāī:

रघुबर कहेउ लखन भल घाटू। करहु कतहुँ अब ठाहर ठाटू॥
raghubara kaheu lakhana bhala ghāṭū, karahu katahuṁ aba ṭhāhara ṭhāṭū.
लखन दीख पय उतर करारा। चहुँ दिसि फिरेउ धनुष जिमि नारा॥
lakhana dīkha paya utara karārā, cahuṁ disi phireu dhanuṣa jimi nārā.
नदी पनच सर सम दम दाना। सकल कलुष कलि साउज नाना॥
nadī panaca sara sama dama dānā, sakala kaluṣa kali sāuja nānā.
चित्रकूट जनु अचल अहेरी। चुकइ न घात मार मुठभेरी॥
citrakūṭa janu acala aherī, cukai na ghāta māra muṭhabherī.
अस कहि लखन ठाउँ देखरावा। थलु बिलोकि रघुबर सुखु पावा॥
asa kahi lakhana ṭhāuṁ dekharāvā, thalu biloki raghubara sukhu pāvā.
रमेउ राम मनु देवन्ह जाना। चले सहित सुर थपति प्रधाना॥
rameu rāma manu devanha jānā, cale sahita sura thapati pradhānā.
कोल किरात बेष सब आए। रचे परन तृन सदन सुहाए॥
kola kirāta beṣa saba āe, race parana tṛna sadana suhāe.
बरनि न जाहिं मंजु दुइ साला। एक ललित लघु एक बिसाला॥
barani na jāhiṁ maṁju dui sālā, eka lalita laghu eka bisālā.

Trans:

Said Raghubar, "It is a good place, Lakshman; now make arrangements for our stopping somewhere here." Lakshman spied out a spot on the northern bank, "The ravine bends round it like a bow, with the river for its string, asceticism and charity for its arrows, and all the sins of this evil age for its quarry, while Mount Chitra-kūt is the huntsman of unerring aim, striking at close quarters." So saying, Lakshman showed the spot. When he had seen it, Raghupatī was pleased. The gods learnt that Rāma was well content, and they came with Indra at their head. In the garb of *Kols* and *Kirāts* they arrived and put up neat huts of boughs and grass—two of them, both prettier than the words can tell, one a nifty little cottage, and the other of larger size;

दोहा-dohā:

लखन जानकी सहित प्रभु राजत रुचिर निकेत।
lakhana jānakī sahita prabhu rājata rucira niketa,
सोह मदनु मुनि बेष जनु रति रितुराज समेत॥१३३॥
soha madanu muni beṣa janu rati riturāja sameta. 133.

Trans:

And in those rustic cells the Lord, attended by Lakshman and Jānakī, shone forth as beautiful as Love in the dress of a hermit between Ratī and Spring.

मासपारायण सत्रहँवा विश्राम

māsapārāyaṇa satrahaṁvā viśrāma

(Pause 17 for a Thirty-Day Recitation)

चौपाई-caupāī:

अमर नाग किंनर दिसिपाला। चित्रकूट आए तेहि काला॥
amara nāga kiṁnara disipālā, citrakūṭa āe tehi kālā.
राम प्रनामु कीन्ह सब काहू। मुदित देव लहि लोचन लाहू॥
rāma pranāmu kīnha saba kāhū, mudita deva lahi locana lāhū.
बरषि सुमन कह देव समाजू। नाथ सनाथ भए हम आजू॥
baraṣi sumana kaha deva samājū, nātha sanātha bhae hama ājū.
करि बिनती दुख दुसह सुनाए। हरषित निज निज सदन सिधाए॥
kari binatī dukha dusaha sunāe, haraṣita nija nija sadana sidhāe.
चित्रकूट रघुनंदनु छाए। समाचार सुनि सुनि मुनि आए॥
citrakūṭa raghunaṁdanu chāe, samācāra suni suni muni āe.
आवत देखि मुदित मुनिबृंदा। कीन्ह दंडवत रघुकुल चंदा॥
āvata dekhi mudita munibṛṁdā, kīnha daṁḍavata raghukula caṁdā.
मुनि रघुबरहि लाइ उर लेहीं। सुफल होन हित आसिष देहीं॥
muni raghubarahi lāi ura lehīṁ, suphala hona hita āsiṣa dehīṁ.
सिय सौमित्रि राम छबि देखहिं। साधन सकल सफल करि लेखहिं॥
siya saumitri rāma chabi dekhahiṁ, sādhana sakala saphala kari lekhahiṁ.

Trans:

Then flocked to Chitra-kūt gods, serpents, *Kinnars*, and *Dig-pāls*. All the immortals bowed low before Rāma and gazed with joy on that most longed-for vision. Showering down flowers and exclaiming, "At length, O God, we have found our Lord," the heavenly host in piteous wise declared their intolerable distress, and joyfully started for their several homes. As soon as they heard the news of Raghu-nandan's stay at Chitra-kūt, many a saints sallied forth to that place. Seeing the holy company draw near, Rāma prostrated himself before them; but they all took him to their bosom and invoked upon him many blessings—just to affirm their own speech become true. As they beheld the beauty of Rāma and Sītā and Sumitrā's son, they accounted all their good deeds as well rewarded.

दोहा-dohā:

जथाजोग सनमानि प्रभु बिदा किए मुनिबृंद।
jathājoga sanamāni prabhu bidā kie munibṛṁda,
करहिं जोग जप जाग तप निज आश्रमन्हि सुछंद॥१३४॥
karahiṁ joga japa jāga tapa nija āśramanhi suchaṁda. 134.

Trans:

After all due honors paid, the Lord dismissed the saintly throng to practice contemplation, prayer, sacrifice and penance at pleasure in their own retreats.

चौपाई-caupāī:

यह सुधि कोल किरातन्ह पाई। हरषे जनु नव निधि घर आई॥
yaha sudhi kola kirātanha pāī, haraṣe janu nava nidhi ghara āī.
कंद मूल फल भरि भरि दोना। चले रंक जनु लूटन सोना॥

kaṁda mūla phala bhari bhari donā, cale raṁka janu lūṭana sonā.

तिन्ह महँ जिन्ह देखे दोउ भ्राता । अपर तिन्हहि पूँछहिं मगु जाता ॥
tinha mahaṁ jinha dekhe dou bhrātā, apara tinhahi pūm̐chahiṁ magu jātā.

कहत सुनत रघुबीर निकाई । आइ सबन्हि देखे रघुराई ॥
kahata sunata raghubīra nikāī, āi sabanhi dekhe raghurāī.

करहिं जोहारु भेंट धरि आगे । प्रभुहि बिलोकहिं अति अनुरागे ॥
karahiṁ johāru bheṁṭa dhari āge, prabhuhi bilokahiṁ ati anurāge.

चित्र लिखे जनु जहँ तहँ ठाढ़े । पुलक सरीर नयन जल बाढ़े ॥
citra likhe janu jahaṁ tahaṁ ṭhāṛhe, pulaka sarīra nayana jala bāṛhe.

राम सनेह मगन सब जाने । कहि प्रिय बचन सकल सनमाने ॥
rāma saneha magana saba jāne, kahi priya bacana sakala sanamāne.

प्रभुहि जोहारि बहोरि बहोरी । बचन बिनीत कहहिं कर जोरी ॥
prabhuhi johāri bahori bahorī, bacana binīta kahahiṁ kara jorī.

Trans:

When the *Kols* and *Kirāts* got the tidings they were as glad as if the nine treasures had come to their house. Filling leaf platters full of herbs, roots, and fruits they ran—like beggars scrambling for gold—to offer them to their guests. Those among them who had already seen the two brothers were questioned about them by the others on the road. Telling and hearing Rāma's perfections, all came and saw him. Laying their offerings before him and making obeisance, their love increased exceedingly as they gazed upon their Lord. Motionless as figures in a picture, they stood about anyhow, their body thrilling with emotion and their eyes filled with tears. Rāma, perceiving that they were overwhelmed with affection, spoke to them words of kindness and received them with honor. Again and again bowing low before the Lord, they addressed him in humble strain with folded hands:

दोहा-dohā:

अब हम नाथ सनाथ सब भए देखि प्रभु पाय ।
aba hama nātha sanātha saba bhae dekhi prabhu pāya,

भाग हमारें आगमनु राउर कोसलराय ॥ १३५॥
bhāga hamāreṁ āgamanu rāura kosalarāya. 135.

Trans:

"Now at length that we have seen our Lord's feet, we have all found a protector; O prince of Kaushal, what a blessing for us is your arrival.

चौपाई-caupāī:

धन्य भूमि बन पंथ पहारा । जहँ जहँ नाथ पाउ तुम्ह धारा ॥
dhanya bhūmi bana paṁtha pahārā, jahaṁ jahaṁ nātha pāu tumha dhārā.

धन्य बिहग मृग काननचारी । सफल जनम भए तुम्हहि निहारी ॥
dhanya bihaga mṛga kānanacārī, saphala janama bhae tumhahi nihārī.

हम सब धन्य सहित परिवारा । दीख दरसु भरि नयन तुम्हारा ॥
hama saba dhanya sahita parivārā, dīkha darasu bhari nayana tumhārā.

कीन्ह बासु भल ठाउँ बिचारी । इहाँ सकल रितु रहब सुखारी ॥
kīnha bāsu bhala ṭhāuṁ bicārī, ihāṁ sakala ritu rahaba sukhārī.

हम सब भाँति करब सेवकाई । करि केहरि अहि बाघ बराई ॥
hama saba bhām̐ti karaba sevakāī, kari kehari ahi bāgha barāī.

बन बेहड़ गिरि कंदर खोहा । सब हमार प्रभु पग पग जोहा ॥
bana behaṛa giri kaṁdara khohā, saba hamāra prabhu paga paga johā.

तहँ तहँ तुम्हहि अहेर खेलाउब । सर निरझर जलठाउँ देखाउब ॥
tahaṁ tahaṁ tumhahi ahera khelāuba, sara nirajhara jalaṭhāuṁ dekhāuba.

हम सेवक परिवार समेता । नाथ न सकुचब आयसु देता ॥
hama sevaka parivāra sametā, nātha na sakucaba āyasu detā.

Trans:

Happy the land and forest and road and hill, where thou, my Lord, has planted thy foot; happy the birds and deer and beasts of the forest, whose life has been crowned by thy sight; happy we and all our kin, who have filled our eyes with thy vision. Thou hast chosen an excellent spot whereon to take up thy abode; here at all seasons of the year thou wilt live at ease. We shall do thee service in every way, by driving away elephants, lions, tigers, snakes. The thickets, ravines, mountains, chasms and caves have all, my Lord, been explored by us foot by foot; we will take you to the different haunts of game, and point out to you the lakes and waterfalls and many other places. We and our people are thy servants; do not hesitate to command us."

दोहा-dohā:

बेद बचन मुनि मन अगम ते प्रभु करुना ऐन ।
beda bacana muni mana agama te prabhu karunā aina,

बचन किरातन्ह के सुनत जिमि पितु बालक बैन ॥ १३६॥
bacana kirātanha ke sunata jimi pitu bālaka baina. 136.

Trans:

The Lord, whom the Veda cannot utter nor the saints comprehend, in his infinite compassion listened to the words of the Kirāts, as a father to the voice of a child.

चौपाई-caupāī:

रामहि केवल प्रेमु पिआरा । जानि लेउ जो जाननिहारा ॥
rāmahi kevala premu piārā, jāni leu jo jānanihārā.

राम सकल बनचर तब तोषे । कहि मृदु बचन प्रेम परिपोषे ॥
rāma sakala banacara taba toṣe, kahi mṛdu bacana prema paripoṣe.

बिदा किए सिर नाइ सिधाए । प्रभु गुन कहत सुनत घर आए ॥
bidā kie sira nāi sidhāe, prabhu guna kahata sunata ghara āe.

एहि बिधि सिय समेत दोउ भाई । बसहिं बिपिन सुर मुनि सुखदाई ॥
ehi bidhi siya sameta dou bhāī, basahiṁ bipina sura muni sukhadāī.

जब तें आइ रहे रघुनायकु । तब तें भयउ बनु मंगलदायकु ॥
jaba teṁ āi rahe raghunāyaku, taba teṁ bhayau banu maṁgaladāyaku.

फूलहिं फलहिं बिटप बिधि नाना । मंजु बलित बर बेलि बिताना ॥
phūlahiṁ phalahiṁ biṭapa bidhi nānā, maṁju balita bara beli bitānā.

सुरतरु सरिस सुभायँ सुहाए । मनहुँ बिबुध बन परिहरि आए ॥
surataru sarisa subhāyaṁ suhāe, manahuṁ bibudha bana parihari āe.

गंज मंजुतर मधुकर श्रेनी । त्रिबिध बयारि बहइ सुख देनी ॥
gaṁja maṁjutara madhukara śrenī, tribidha bayāri bahai sukha denī.

Trans:

It is only love that Rāma loves; understand this, ye who are men of understanding. He charmed all the foresters by his tender loving speeches. Having taken leave and bowed the heads, they set forth, and discoursing on the way of their Lord's perfections, they reached their respective homes. And in this fashion, delighting gods and saints and all, the two brothers and Sītā dwelt in the forest. From the time that Raghunāyak took up his abode there, the wood became bounteous in blessings; every kind of tree blossomed and bore fruit; luxuriant creepers formed pleasant and beautiful canopies—as though the tree of paradise in all its native loveliness had abandoned the groves of heaven. Strings of bees made a grateful buzzing, and a delicious air breezed: soft, cool, and fragrant.

दोहा-dohā:

नीलकंठ कलकंठ सुक चातक चक्क चकोर ।
nīlakaṁṭha kalakaṁṭha suka cātaka cakka cakora,

भाँति भाँति बोलहिं बिहग श्रवन सुखद चित चोर ॥ १३७॥
bhām̐ti bhām̐ti bolahiṁ bihaga śravana sukhada cita cora. 137.

Trans:

Jays, cuckoos, parrots, *chātaks*, *chakwās*, *chakors*, and birds of every description charmed the ear and ravished the soul with their notes.

चौपाई-caupāī:

करि केहरि कपि कोल कुरंगा । बिगतबैर बिचरहिं सब संगा ॥
kari kehari kapi kola kuraṁgā, bigatabaira bicarahiṁ saba saṁgā.

फिरत अहेर राम छबि देखी । होहिं मुदित मृगबृंद बिसेषी ॥
phirata ahera rāma chabi dekhī, hohiṁ mudita mṛgabṛṁda biseṣī.
बिबुध बिपिन जहँ लगि जग माहीं । देखि राम बनु सकल सिहाहीं ॥
bibudha bipina jahaṁ lagi jaga māhīṁ, dekhi rāma banu sakala sihāhīṁ.
सुरसरि सरसइ दिनकर कन्या । मेकलसुता गोदावरि धन्या ॥
surasari sarasai dinakara kanyā, mekalasutā godāvari dhanyā.
सब सर सिंधु नदीं नद नाना । मंदाकिनि कर करहिं बखाना ॥
saba sara siṁdhu nadīṁ nada nānā, maṁdākini kara karahiṁ bakhānā.
उदय अस्त गिरि अरु कैलासू । मंदर मेरु सकल सुरबासू ॥
udaya asta giri aru kailāsū, maṁdara meru sakala surabāsū.
सैल हिमाचल आदिक जेते । चित्रकूट जसु गावहिं तेते ॥
saila himācala ādika jete, citrakūṭa jasu gāvahiṁ tete.
बिंधि मुदित मन सुखु न समाई । श्रम बिनु बिपुल बड़ाई पाई ॥
biṁdhi mudita mana sukhu na samāī, śrama binu bipula baṛāī pāī.

Trans:
Elephants, lions, monkeys, boars, and deer forgot their animosity and sported together. Enraptured above all were the herds of deer who beheld the beauty of Rāma as he tracked the chase. All the forests of the gods that there are in the world were envious at the sight of Rāma's wood. The Gangā, the Saraswatī, the sun born Yamunā, the Narmadā, daughter of Mount Mekal and the sacred Godāvarī, every river, stream, and torrent praised Mandakinī's good fortune. The mountains of the rising and the setting sun, Kailāsh, Mandar, Meru, home of all the gods, the crags of Himalaya, and all the hills there be, sang the glory of Chitra-kūt—and the delight of that hill-range was more than its soul could contain, thinking it had won so much renown without any effort.

दोहा-dohā:

चित्रकूट के बिहग मृग बेलि बिटप तृन जाति ।
citrakūṭa ke bihaga mṛga beli biṭapa tṛna jāti,
पुन्य पुंज सब धन्य अस कहहिं देव दिन राति ॥ १३८ ॥
punya puṁja saba dhanya asa kahahiṁ deva dina rāti. 138.

Trans:
"Of highest merit and blessed indeed are all the birds, deer, creepers, trees and grasses of Chitra-kūt," so day and night cried the gods.

चौपाई-caupāī:

नयनवंत रघुबरहि बिलोकी । पाइ जनम फल होहिं बिसोकी ॥
nayanavaṁta raghubarahi bilokī, pāi janama phala hohiṁ bisokī.
परसि चरन रज अचर सुखारी । भए परम पद के अधिकारी ॥
parasi carana raja acara sukhārī, bhae parama pada ke adhikārī.
सो बनु सैलु सुभायँ सुहावन । मंगलमय अति पावन पावन ॥
so banu sailu subhāyaṁ suhāvana, maṁgalamaya ati pāvana pāvana.
महिमा कहिअ कवनि बिधि तासू । सुखसागर जहँ कीन्ह निवासू ॥
mahimā kahia kavani bidhi tāsū, sukhasāgara jahaṁ kīnha nivāsū.
पय पयोधि तजि अवध बिहाई । जहँ सिय लखनु रामु रहे आई ॥
paya payodhi taji avadha bihāī, jahaṁ siya lakhanu rāmu rahe āī.
कहि न सकहिं सुषमा जसि कानन । जौं सत सहस होहिं सहसानन ॥
kahi na sakahiṁ suṣamā jasi kānana, jauṁ sata sahasa hohiṁ sahasānana.
सो मैं बरनि कहौं बिधि केहीं । डाबर कमठ कि मंदर लेहीं ॥
so maiṁ barani kahauṁ bidhi kehīṁ, ḍābara kamaṭha ki maṁdara lehīṁ.
सेवहिं लखनु करम मन बानी । जाइ न सीलु सनेहु बखानी ॥
sevahiṁ lakhanu karama mana bānī, jāi na sīlu sanehu bakhānī.

Trans:
All creatures with eyes, who looked on Rāma, today felt with joy that now they had lived to some purpose. Things without life, touched by the dust of his feet, were gladdened by promotion to the highest sphere. The woods and rocks, all charming in themselves, were so blissful, so entirely the holiest of the holy, how would it be possible to glorify them further? The exquisite beauty of the forest where Sītā, Lakshman and Shrī Rāma came and settled—taking leave of the ocean of milk, and bidding adieu to Ajodhyā—could be described not even by a hundred thousand Sheshas. How then can I describe them, any more than a common tortoise living in a puddle uplift Mount Mandar? Lakshman waited upon Shrī Rāma in thought, word and deed with an amiability and devotion more than can be said.

दोहा-dohā:

छिनु छिनु लखि सिय राम पद जानि आपु पर नेहु ।
chinu chinu lakhi siya rāma pada jāni āpu para nehu,
करत न सपनेहुँ लखनु चितु बंधु मातु पितु गेहु ॥ १३९ ॥
karata na sapanehuṁ lakhanu citu baṁdhu mātu pitu gehu. 139.

Trans:
Forever gazing on the feet of Sītā and Rāma and conscious of their love for him, not even in dream did Lakshman think of his own, or father, or mother, or his home.

चौपाई-caupāī:

राम संग सिय रहति सुखारी । पुर परिजन गृह सुरति बिसारी ॥
rāma saṁga siya rahati sukhārī, pura parijana gṛha surati bisārī.
छिनु छिनु पिय बिधु बदनु निहारी । प्रमुदित मनहुँ चकोरकुमारी ॥
chinu chinu piya bidhu badanu nihārī, pramudita manahuṁ cakorakumārī.
नाह नेहु नित बढ़त बिलोकी । हरषित रहति दिवस जिमि कोकी ॥
nāha nehu nita baṛhata bilokī, harașita rahati divasa jimi kokī.
सिय मनु राम चरन अनुरागा । अवध सहस सम बनु प्रिय लागा ॥
siya manu rāma carana anurāgā, avadha sahasa sama banu priya lāgā.
परनकुटी प्रिय प्रियतम संगा । प्रिय परिवारु कुरंग बिहंगा ॥
paranakuṭī priya priyatama saṁgā, priya parivāru kuraṁga bihaṁgā.
सासु ससुर सम मुनितिय मुनिबर । असनु अमिअ सम कंद मूल फर ॥
sāsu sasura sama munitiya munibara, asanu amia sama kaṁda mūla phara.
नाथ साथ साँथरी सुहाई । मयन सयन सय सम सुखदाई ॥
nātha sātha sāṁtharī suhāī, mayana sayana saya sama sukhadāī.
लोकप होहिं बिलोकत जासू । तेहि कि मोहि सक बिषय बिलासू ॥
lokapa hohiṁ bilokata jāsū, tehi ki mohi saka biṣaya bilāsū.

Trans:
In Rāma's company Sītā lived so happy that she forgot all memory of city, family, home. Ever watching the moon-like face of her beloved, she rejoiced like the partridge at night; and seeing her Lord's affection daily increase, she was as happy as the cuckoo by the day. Her heart was so enamored of him that the forest was a thousand times as dear to her as Avadh. Dear was the cottage with her beloved's nearness, dear the fawns and birds—now her only attendants; and like her husband's father and mother were the hermits and their wives; and sweet as ambrosia the wild fruits and roots. Shared with her Lord, a bed of leaves was a hundredfold more delightful than Cupid's own couch. Can the charm of sensuous enjoyments ever enchant her whose very look confers the sovereignty of heavens.

दोहा-dohā:

सुमिरत रामहि तजहिं जन तृन सम बिषय बिलासु ।
sumirata rāmahi tajahiṁ jana tṛna sama biṣaya bilāsu,
रामप्रिया जग जननि सिय कछु न आचरजु तासु ॥ १४० ॥
rāmapriyā jaga janani siya kachu na ācaraju tāsu. 140.

Trans:
Remembering Rāma, men discard as no more worth than a blade of grass all the pleasures of sense; no wonder then in the case of Sītā, who is Rāma's own beloved, the mother of the world.

चौपाई-caupāī:

सीय लखन जेहि बिधि सुखु लहहीं । सोइ रघुनाथ करहिं सोइ कहहीं ॥
sīya lakhana jehi bidhi sukhu lahahīṁ, soi raghunātha karahiṁ soi kahahīṁ.

कहहिं पुरातन कथा कहानी । सुनहिं लखनु सिय अति सुखु मानी ॥
kahahiṁ purātana kathā kahānī, sunahiṁ lakhanu siya ati sukhu mānī.
जब जब रामु अवध सुधि करहीं । तब तब बारि बिलोचन भरहीं ॥
jaba jaba rāmu avadha sudhi karahīṁ, taba taba bāri bilocana bharahīṁ.
सुमिरि मातु पितु परिजन भाई । भरत सनेहु सीलु सेवकाई ॥
sumiri mātu pitu parijana bhāī, bharata sanehu sīlu sevakāī.
कृपासिंधु प्रभु होहिं दुखारी । धीरजु धरहिं कुसमउ बिचारी ॥
kṛpāsiṁdhu prabhu hohiṁ dukhārī, dhīraju dharahiṁ kusamau bicārī.
लखि सिय लखनु बिकल होइ जाहीं । जिमि पुरुषहि अनुसर परिछाहीं ॥
lakhi siya lakhanu bikala hoi jāhīṁ, jimi puruṣahi anusara parichāhīṁ.
प्रिया बंधु गति लखि रघुनंदनु । धीर कृपाल भगत उर चंदनु ॥
priyā baṁdhu gati lakhi raghunaṁdanu, dhīra kṛpāla bhagata ura caṁdanu.
लगे कहन कछु कथा पुनीता । सुनि सुखु लहहिं लखनु अरु सीता ॥
lage kahana kachu kathā punītā, suni sukhu lahahiṁ lakhanu aru sītā.

Trans:

Anything that would please Sītā and Lakshman, that would Raghunāth do, exactly as they suggested. He would recite legends and tales of olden times, on the hearing of which Lakshman and Sītā took great delight. If ever a mention of Avadh came, his eyes filled with tears as he recalled to mind his mother and father, his family and his brothers, with all of Bharat's affection and amiable attentions. At such times, the compassionate Lord grew most sad, but restrained himself knowing that the time was not propitious. At that sight Sītā and Lakshman became distressed as well—just like a shadow behaves which follows a man. When Raghu-nandan noticed the emotion of his spouse and his brother—and being self-restrained and tender and as soothing to his votaries as sandalwood when applied to the chest—he would begin to relate some sacred story to divert them.

दोहा-dohā:

रामु लखन सीता सहित सोहत परन निकेत ।
rāmu lakhana sītā sahita sohata parana niketa,
जिमि बासव बस अमरपुर सची जयंत समेत ॥ १४१ ॥
jimi bāsava basa amarapura sacī jayaṁta sameta. 141.

Trans:

Rāma and Lakshman with Sītā in their leafy hut were as resplendent as Indra in the city of heaven with his spouse Sachi and their son Jayant.

चौपाई-caupāī:

जोगवहिं प्रभु सिय लखनहिं कैसें । पलक बिलोचन गोलक जैसें ॥
jogavahiṁ prabhu siya lakhanahiṁ kaiseṁ, palaka bilocana golaka jaiseṁ.
सेवहिं लखनु सीय रघुबीरहि । जिमि अबिबेकी पुरुष सरीरहि ॥
sevahiṁ lakhanu sīya raghubīrahi, jimi abibekī puruṣa sarīrahi.
एहि बिधि प्रभु बन बसहिं सुखारी । खग मृग सुर तापस हितकारी ॥
ehi bidhi prabhu bana basahiṁ sukhārī, khaga mṛga sura tāpasa hitakārī.
कहेउँ राम बन गवनु सुहावा । सुनहु सुमंत्र अवध जिमि आवा ॥
kaheuṁ rāma bana gavanu suhāvā, sunahu sumaṁtra avadha jimi āvā.
फिरेउ निषादु प्रभुहि पहुँचाई । सचिव सहित रथ देखेसि आई ॥
phireu niṣādu prabhuhi pahuṁcāī, saciva sahita ratha dekhesi āī.
मंत्री बिकल बिलोकि निषादू । कहि न जाइ जस भयउ बिषादू ॥
maṁtrī bikala biloki niṣādū, kahi na jāi jasa bhayau biṣādū.
राम राम सिय लखन पुकारी । परेउ धरनितल ब्याकुल भारी ॥
rāma rāma siya lakhana pukārī, pareu dharanitala byākula bhārī.
देखि दखिन दिसि हय हिहिनाहीं । जनु बिनु पंख बिहग अकुलाहीं ॥
dekhi dakhina disi haya hihinahīṁ, janu binu paṁkha bihaga akulāhīṁ.

Trans:

The Lord was as watchful over Sītā and his younger brother as the eyelids over the pupil of the eye; while Lakshman was as careful of Sītā and Raghubīr, just as a deluded carefully tends to his own body. Thus happily the Lord lived in the woods, gratifying alike birds, beasts, and pious ascetics. I have now told the story of Rāma's exile to the woods; hear now how Sumant reached Avadh. The Nishād returned after escorting his Lord, and came in sight of the minister and the chariot. No words can tell the distress with which he found the minister full of agony. Crying out "Rāma, Rāma, Sītā, Lakshman," he had fallen to the ground utterly overpowered, while the horses kept on looking to the south and neighing, as piteously as a bird that has lost its wings.

दोहा-dohā:

नहिं तृन चरहिं पिअहिं जलु मोचहिं लोचन बारि ।
nahiṁ tṛna carahiṁ piahiṁ jalu mocahiṁ locana bāri,
ब्याकुल भए निषाद सब रघुबर बाजि निहारि ॥ १४२ ॥
byākula bhae niṣāda saba raghubara bāji nihāri. 142.

Trans:

They would neither eat grass nor drink water, and their eyes shed tears. At the plight of the horses all the Nishāds were deeply grieved.

चौपाई-caupāī:

धरि धीरजु तब कहइ निषादू । अब सुमंत्र परिहरहु बिषादू ॥
dhari dhīraju taba kahai niṣādū, aba sumaṁtra pariharahu biṣādū.
तुम्ह पंडित परमारथ ग्याता । धरहु धीर लखि बिमुख बिधाता ॥
tumha paṁḍita paramāratha gyātā, dharahu dhīra lakhi bimukha bidhātā.
बिबिध कथा कहि कहि मृदु बानी । रथ बैठारेउ बरबस आनी ॥
bibidha kathā kahi kahi mṛdu bānī, ratha baiṭhāreu barabasa ānī.
सोक सिथिल रथ सकइ न हाँकी । रघुबर बिरह पीर उर बाँकी ॥
soka sithila ratha sakai na hāṁkī, raghubara biraha pīra ura bāṁkī.
चरफराहिं मग चलहिं न घोरे । बन मृग मनहुँ आनि रथ जोरे ॥
carapharāhiṁ maga calahiṁ na ghore, bana mṛga manahuṁ āni ratha jore.
अढ़ुकि परहिं फिरि हेरहिं पीछें । राम बियोगि बिकल दुख तीछें ॥
aṛhuki parahiṁ phiri herahiṁ pīcheṁ, rāma biyogi bikala dukha tīcheṁ.
जो कह रामु लखनु बैदेही । हिंकरि हिंकरि हित हेरहिं तेही ॥
jo kaha rāmu lakhanu baidehī, hiṁkari hiṁkari hita herahiṁ tehī.
बाजि बिरह गति कहि किमि जाती । बिनु मनि फनिक बिकल जेहि भाँती ॥
bāji biraha gati kahi kimi jātī, binu mani phanika bikala jehi bhāṁtī.

Trans:

At length summoning up courage the Nishād said, "Now Sumant, cease mourning; you are a learned man and a philosopher. Please submit patiently to adverse fortune." With such kindly expostulations he made him mount the chariot, whether he would or not; but he was so unstrung by grief that he could not drive, his heart ached so grievously at Rāma's loss. The horses reared and would not go; you would think they were wild deer put in harness, jibbing, lying down, and turning to look behind them, being overcome by sore pain at Rāma's going. If anyone mentioned the name of Rāma, Lakshman, or Sītā, the horses would at once neigh and look at him; the way in which they declared their grief is not to be described, like a snake that has lost its head-jewel.

दोहा-dohā:

भयउ निषादु बिषादबस देखत सचिव तुरंग ।
bhayau niṣādu biṣādabasa dekhata saciva turaṁga,
बोलि सुसेवक चारि तब दिए सारथी संग ॥ १४३ ॥
boli susevaka cāri taba die sārathī saṁga. 143.

Trans:

The sight of the minister and the horses made the Nishād very sad. He told off four trusty grooms and with them a charioteer to accompany him.

चौपाई-caupāī:

गुह सारथिहि फिरेउ पहुँचाई । बिरहु बिषादु बरनि नहिं जाई ॥
guha sārathihi phireu pahuṁcāī, birahu biṣādu barani nahiṁ jāī.

चले अवध लेइ रथहि निषादा । होहिं छनहिं छन मगन बिषादा ॥
cale avadha lei rathahi niṣādā, hohiṁ chanahiṁ chana magana biṣādā.
सोच सुमंत्र बिकल दुख दीना । धिग जीवन रघुबीर बिहीना ॥
soca sumaṁtra bikala dukha dīnā, dhiga jīvana raghubīra bihīnā.
रहिहि न अंतहुँ अधम सरीरू । जसु न लहेउ बिछुरत रघुबीरू ॥
rahihi na aṁtahuṁ adhama sarīrū, jasu na laheu bichurata raghubīrū.
भए अजस अघ भाजन प्राना । कवन हेतु नहिं करत पयाना ॥
bhae ajasa agha bhājana prānā, kavana hetu nahiṁ karata payānā.
अहह मंद मनु अवसर चूका । अजहुँ न हृदय होत दुइ टूका ॥
ahaha maṁda manu avasara cūkā, ajahuṁ na hṛdaya hota dui ṭūkā.
मीजि हाथ सिरु धुनि पछिताई । मनहुँ कृपन धन रासि गवाँई ॥
mīji hātha siru dhuni pachitāī, manahuṁ kṛpana dhana rāsi gavāṁī.
बिरिद बाँधि बर बीरु कहाई । चलेउ समर जनु सुभट पराई ॥
birida bāṁdhi bara bīru kahāī, caleu samara janu subhaṭa parāī.

Trans:

After making over the charioteer, Gūha returned home, more sorry at leaving than words can tell. The Nishāds drove off to Avadh, sunk every moment in deeper distress. Sumant, tortured by regrets, a prey to woe, cried, "A curse for life without Raghubīr! This vile body must perish at last; it lost all glory when bereft of Raghubīr and became a sink of infamy and crime; why does it not take its departure? Ah! fool that it is, it missed its opportunity, seeing that today my heart has not broken in twain." Wringing his hands and beating his head in his remorse he went his way like a miser robbed of his pelf, or like a warrior of high renown, or some famous champion who has had to flee from the battlefield.

दोहा-dohā:

बिप्र बिबेकी बेदबिद संमत साधु सुजाति ।
bipra bibekī bedabida saṁmata sādhu sujāti,
जिमि धोखें मदपान कर सचिव सोच तेहि भाँति ॥ १४४॥
jimi dhokheṁ madapāna kara saciva soca tehi bhāṁti. 144.

Trans:

The minister's grief was like that of some learned Brahmin well read in the Vedas, a man of good repute, of integrity and birth—who has been entrapped into consuming wine through deceit.

चौपाई-caupāī:

जिमि कुलीन तिय साधु सयानी । पतिदेवता करम मन बानी ॥
jimi kulīna tiya sādhu sayānī, patidevatā karama mana bānī.
रहै करम बस परिहरि नाहू । सचिव हृदयँ तिमि दारुन दाहू ॥
rahai karama basa parihari nāhū, saciva hṛdayaṁ timi dāruna dāhū.
लोचन सजल डीठि भइ थोरी । सुनइ न श्रवन बिकल मति भोरी ॥
locana sajala ḍīṭhi bhai thorī, sunai na śravana bikala mati bhorī.
सूखहिं अधर लागि मुँह लाटी । जिउ न जाइ उर अवधि कपाटी ॥
sūkhahiṁ adhara lāgi muṁha lāṭī, jiu na jāi ura avadhi kapāṭī.
बिबरन भयउ न जाइ निहारी । मारेसि मनहुँ पिता महतारी ॥
bibarana bhayau na jāi nihārī, māresi manahuṁ pitā mahatārī.
हानि गलानि बिपुल मन ब्यापी । जमपुर पंथ सोच जिमि पापी ॥
hāni galāni bipula mana byāpī, jamapura paṁtha soca jimi pāpī.
बचनु न आव हृदयँ पछिताई । अवध काह मैं देखब जाई ॥
bacanu na āva hṛdayaṁ pachitāī, avadha kāha maiṁ dekhaba jāī.
राम रहित रथ देखिहि जोई । सकुचिहि मोहि बिलोकत सोई ॥
rāma rahita ratha dekhihi joī, sakucihi mohi bilokata soī.

Trans:

Or like some well-born, virtuous, discreet lady, entirely devoted to her lord, but whom Fate has forced to desert him—such was the cruel torture that racked the minister's heart. His eyes so full of tears that he could scarcely see; his ears deaf, his senses all confused, his lips dry, his tongue cleaving to his palate, the breath of life only restrained by the bar of Rāma's promise to return; all the color gone from his face, he looked like one who had murdered his parents. His soul was so possessed with the greatness of his loss and remorse, that he might be some grievous sinner standing trembling at the gates of death. Words would not come, but to himself he moaned, "How can I look Avadh in the face? When they see the chariot with no Rāma besides, they will turn to me in bewilderment.

दोहा-dohā:

धाइ पूँछिहहिं मोहि जब बिकल नगर नर नारि ।
dhāi pūṁchihahiṁ mohi jaba bikala nagara nara nāri,
उतरु देब मैं सबहि तब हृदयँ बज्रु बैठारि ॥ १४५॥
utaru deba maiṁ sabahi taba hṛdayaṁ bajru baiṭhāri. 145.

Trans:

When the agitated citizens run to question me and I have to answer them, my heart will be cleft asunder as by a thunder bolt.

चौपाई-caupāī:

पुछिहहिं दीन दुखित सब माता । कहब काह मैं तिन्हहि बिधाता ॥
puchihahiṁ dīna dukhita saba mātā, kahaba kāha maiṁ tinhahi bidhātā.
पूछिहि जबहिं लखन महतारी । कहिहउँ कवन सँदेस सुखारी ॥
pūchihi jabahiṁ lakhana mahatārī, kahihauṁ kavana saṁdesa sukhārī.
राम जननि जब आइहि धाई । सुमिरि बच्छु जिमि धेनु लवाई ॥
rāma janani jaba āihi dhāī, sumiri bacchu jimi dhenu lavāī.
पूँछत उतरु देब मैं तेही । गे बनु राम लखनु बैदेही ॥
pūṁchata utaru deba maiṁ tehī, ge banu rāma lakhanu baidehī.
जोइ पूँछिहि तेहि ऊतरु देबा । जाइ अवध अब यहु सुखु लेबा ॥
joi pūṁchihi tehi ūtaru debā, jāi avadha aba yahu sukhu lebā.
पूँछिहि जबहिं राउ दुख दीना । जिवनु जासु रघुनाथ अधीना ॥
pūṁchihi jabahiṁ rāu dukha dīnā, jivanu jāsu raghunātha adhīnā.
देहउँ उतरु कौनु मुहु लाई । आयउँ कुसल कुअँर पहुँचाई ॥
dehauṁ utaru kaunu muhu lāī, āyauṁ kusala kuaṁra pahuṁcāī.
सुनत लखन सिय राम सँदेसू । तृन जिमि तनु परिहरिहि नरेसू ॥
sunata lakhana siya rāma saṁdesū, tṛna jimi tanu pariharihi naresū.

Trans:

When the piteous queen-mothers ask of me, good god, to them what shall I say? When Lakshman's mother questions me, what good news can I give her? When Rāma's mother comes running, like a cow mindful of its new-weaned calf, and questions me, I can only answer: 'Rāma, Lakshman, and Sītā have gone into the forest'. Whoever asks, I must answer so; this is the fate in store for me at Avadh. When the sorrowful king, whose very life hangs upon Rāma, questions me, with what face will I answer him? —That I have seen the princes safe to their journey's end and returned? When the king hears the news of Lakshman, Sītā, and Rāma, he will discard his life as worthless as a straw.

दोहा-dohā:

हृदउ न बिदरेउ पंक जिमि बिछुरत प्रीतमु नीरु ।
hṛdau na bidareu paṁka jimi bichurata prītamu nīru,
जानत हौं मोहि दीन्ह बिधि यहु जातना सरीरु ॥ १४६॥
jānata hauṁ mohi dīnha bidhi yahu jātanā sarīru. 146.

Trans:

My heart bereft of its beloved is like clay drained of water, but it cracks not; now I know how capable of torture is this body that god has given me."

चौपाई-caupāī:

एहि बिधि करत पंथ पछितावा । तमसा तीर तुरत रथु आवा ॥
ehi bidhi karata paṁtha pachitāvā, tamasā tīra turata rathu āvā.
बिदा किए करि बिनय निषादा । फिरे पायँ परि बिकल बिषादा ॥
bidā kie kari binaya niṣādā, phire pāyaṁ pari bikala biṣādā.

पैठत नगर सचिव सकुचाई । जनु मारेसि गुर बाँभन गाई ॥
paiṭhata nagara saciva sakucāī, janu māresi gura bāṁbhana gāī.
बैठि बिटप तर दिवसु गवाँवा । साँझ समय तब अवसरु पावा ॥
baiṭhi biṭapa tara divasu gavāṁvā, sāṁjha samaya taba avasaru pāvā.
अवध प्रबेसु कीन्ह अँधिआरें । पैठ भवन रथु राखि दुआरें ॥
avadha prabesu kīnha aṁdhiāreṁ, paiṭha bhavana rathu rākhi duāreṁ.
जिन्ह जिन्ह समाचार सुनि पाए । भूप द्वार रथु देखन आए ॥
jinha jinha samācāra suni pāe, bhūpa dvāra rathu dekhana āe.
रथु पहिचानि बिकल लखि घोरे । गरहिं गात जिमि आतप ओरे ॥
rathu pahicāni bikala lakhi ghore, garahiṁ gāta jimi ātapa ore.
नगर नारि नर ब्याकुल कैसें । निघटत नीर मीनगन जैसें ॥
nagara nāri nara byākula kaiseṁ, nighaṭata nīra mīnagana jaiseṁ.

Trans:

Thus bemoaning within as he went, he quickly arrived in his chariot at the bank of the Tamas. There he courteously dismissed the Nishāds—who after falling at his feet turned sorrowfully away. The minister was as downcast on entering the city as one who had killed his own spiritual guide, or a Brahmin or cow. He passed the day sitting under a tree, and at eventide took the opportunity to enter Avadh in the dark. He slunk into his house, leaving the chariot at the gate. All who heard the tidings came to the king's door to see the chariot, and having recognized it and observed the distress of the horses, their bodies melted away like hail in the sun. All the citizens were as woebegone as fish when the waters are dried up.

दोहा-dohā:

सचिव आगमनु सुनत सबु बिकल भयउ रनिवासु ।
saciva āgamanu sunata sabu bikala bhayau ranivāsu,
भवन भयंकरु लाग तेहि मानहुँ प्रेत निवासु ॥ १४७॥
bhavana bhayaṁkaru lāga tehi mānahuṁ preta nivāsu. 147.

Trans:

When they heard of the minister's arrival, all the ladies of the court were agitated. The palace struck him with as much dread as a haunted chamber.

चौपाई-caupāī:

अति आरति सब पूँछहिं रानी । उतरु न आव बिकल भइ बानी ॥
ati ārati saba pūṁchahiṁ rānī, utaru na āva bikala bhai bānī.
सुनइ न श्रवन नयन नहिं सूझा । कहहु कहाँ नृपु तेहि तेहि बूझा ॥
sunai na śravana nayana nahiṁ sūjhā, kahahu kahāṁ nṛpu tehi tehi būjhā.
दासिन्ह दीख सचिव बिकलाई । कौसल्या गृहँ गईं लवाई ॥
dāsinha dīkha saciva bikalāī, kausalyā gṛhaṁ gaīṁ lavāī.
जाइ सुमंत्र दीख कस राजा । अमिअ रहित जनु चंदु बिराजा ॥
jāi sumaṁtra dīkha kasa rājā, amia rahita janu caṁdu birājā.
आसन सयन बिभूषन हीना । परेउ भूमितल निपट मलीना ॥
āsana sayana bibhūṣana hīnā, pareu bhūmitala nipaṭa malīnā.
लेइ उसासु सोच एहि भाँती । सुरपुर तें जनु खँसेउ जजाती ॥
lei usāsu soca ehi bhāṁtī, surapura teṁ janu khaṁseu jajātī.
लेत सोच भरि छिनु छिनु छाती । जनु जरि पंख परेउ संपाती ॥
leta soca bhari chinu chinu chātī, janu jari paṁkha pareu saṁpātī.
राम राम कह राम सनेही । पुनि कह राम लखन बैदेही ॥
rāma rāma kaha rāma sanehī, puni kaha rāma lakhana baidehī.

Trans:

All the queens questioned him in great excitement, but his voice was all broken, no answer came. With no ears to hear nor eyes to see, he could only ask everyone he met, "Tell me where the king is." Seeing his confusion, the handmaidens conducted him to Kausalyā's apartments. On entering, Sumant found the king in such state as the moon shows when all its luster has waned. Fasting, sleepless, stript of every adornment, he lay on the ground in utter wretchedness, sighing as piteously as Yayāti after he had been hurled from heaven, his heart every moment bursting with grief, like Sampāti falling with singed wings, crying fondly, "O Rāma, Rāma, Rāma," and again "O Rāma, Lakshman, Sītā."

दोहा-dohā:

देखि सचिवँ जय जीव कहि कीन्हेउ दंड प्रनामु ।
dekhi sacivaṁ jaya jīva kahi kīnheu daṁḍa pranāmu,
सुनत उठेउ ब्याकुल नृपति कहु सुमंत्र कहँ रामु ॥ १४८॥
sunata uṭheu byākula nṛpati kahu sumaṁtra kahaṁ rāmu. 148.

Trans:

The minister on seeing him cried "All hail!" and bowed to the ground. At the sound of his voice the king started up hurriedly and exclaimed "O Sumant, where is Rāma?"

चौपाई-caupāī:

भूप सुमंत्रु लीन्ह उर लाई । बूड़त कछु अधार जनु पाई ॥
bhūpa sumaṁtru līnha ura lāī, būṛata kachu adhāra janu pāī.
सहित सनेह निकट बैठारी । पूँछत राउ नयन भरि बारी ॥
sahita saneha nikaṭa baiṭhārī, pūṁchata rāu nayana bhari bārī.
राम कुसल कहु सखा सनेही । कहँ रघुनाथु लखनु बैदेही ॥
rāma kusala kahu sakhā sanehī, kahaṁ raghunāthu lakhanu baidehī.
आने फेरि कि बनहि सिधाए । सुनत सचिव लोचन जल छाए ॥
āne pheri ki banahi sidhāe, sunata saciva locana jala chāe.
सोक बिकल पुनि पूँछ नरेसू । कहु सिय राम लखन संदेसू ॥
soka bikala puni pūṁcha naresū, kahu siya rāma lakhana saṁdesū.
राम रूप गुन सील सुभाऊ । सुमिरि सुमिरि उर सोचत राऊ ॥
rāma rūpa guna sīla subhāū, sumiri sumiri ura socata rāū.
राउ सुनाइ दीन्ह बनबासू । सुनि मन भयउ न हरषु हराँसू ॥
rāu sunāi dīnha banabāsū, suni mana bhayau na haraṣu harāṁsū.
सो सुत बिछुरत गए न प्राना । को पापी बड़ मोहि समाना ॥
so suta bichurata gae na prānā, ko pāpī baṛa mohi samānā.

Trans:

The king clasped Sumant to his bosom, like a drowning man who has caught hold of some support. He seated him affectionately by his side, and with his eyes full of tears asked, "Tell me, kind friend, of Rāma's welfare. Where are Raghunāth, Lakshman, and Sītā? Have you brought them back, or have they sought the forest?" At these words the minister's eyes streamed with tears. Overpowered by anxiety, the king asked again, "Give me tidings of Sītā, Rāma, and Lakshman." Calling to mind Rāma's beauty and talents and amiability, he sorrowed yet more, "I promised him the kingdom and then imposed exile; he obeyed with soul unmoved either by joy or sorrow. Bereft of such a son, yet I can live—who is so guilty a monster as I?

दोहा-dohā:

सखा रामु सिय लखनु जहँ तहाँ मोहि पहुँचाउ ।
sakhā rāmu siya lakhanu jahaṁ tahāṁ mohi pahuṁcāu,
नाहिं त चाहत चलन अब प्रान कहउँ सतिभाउ ॥ १४९॥
nāhiṁ ta cāhata calana aba prāna kahauṁ satibhāu. 149.

Trans:

Take me, my friend, to the place where Rāma, Sītā, and Lakshman are. If not, I tell you the very truth, my soul will at once take flight."

चौपाई-caupāī:

पुनि पुनि पूँछत मंत्रिहि राऊ । प्रियतम सुअन सँदेस सुनाऊ ॥
puni puni pūṁchata maṁtrihi rāū, priyatama suana saṁdesa sunāū.
करहि सखा सोइ बेगि उपाऊ । रामु लखनु सिय नयन देखाऊ ॥
karahi sakhā soi begi upāū, rāmu lakhanu siya nayana dekhāū.
सचिव धीर धरि कह मृदु बानी । महाराज तुम्ह पंडित ग्यानी ॥

saciva dhīra dhari kaha mṛdu bānī, mahārāja tumha paṁḍita gyānī.
बीर सुधीर धुरंधर देवा । साधु समाजु सदा तुम्ह सेवा ॥
bīra sudhīra dhuraṁdhara devā, sādhu samāju sadā tumha sevā.
जनम मरन सब दुख सुख भोगा । हानि लाभु प्रिय मिलन बियोगा ॥
janama marana saba dukha sukha bhogā, hāni lābhu priya milana biyogā.
काल करम बस होहिं गोसाईं । बरबस राति दिवस की नाईं ॥
kāla karama basa hohiṁ gosāīṁ, barabasa rāti divasa kī nāīṁ.
सुख हरषहिं जड़ दुख बिलखाहीं । दोउ सम धीर धरहिं मन माहीं ॥
sukha haraṣahiṁ jaṛa dukha bilakhāhīṁ, dou sama dhīra dharahiṁ mana māhīṁ.
धीरज धरहु बिबेकु बिचारी । छाड़िअ सोच सकल हितकारी ॥
dhīraja dharahu bibeku bicārī, chāṛia soca sakala hitakārī.

Trans:
Again and again he implored him, "Friend, tell me of my son. Hearken comrade, contrive some means for speedily showing me Rāma, Sītā, Lakshman." Summoning up courage the minister gently replied, "Sire, your majesty is a scholar and philosopher, a model of courage and endurance, and a constant attendant of holy assemblies. Life and death; pleasure, pain, and all enjoyments; loss and gain; the society of friends and their loss; all, sir, are governed by time and fate as unalterably as the succession of night and day. Fools triumph in prosperity, are downcast in adversity—but the wise account both alike. Consider the matter wisely and take courage; the good of all depends upon you now; cease vain regret.

दोहा-dohā:

प्रथम बासु तमसा भयउ दूसर सुरसरि तीर ।
prathama bāsu tamasā bhayau dūsara surasari tīra,
न्हाइ रहे जलपानु करि सिय समेत दोउ बीर ॥ १५० ॥
nhāi rahe jalapānu kari siya sameta dou bīra. 150.

Trans:
Their first halt was at the Tamas; their second on the bank of the Gangā, where the two heroes and Sītā bathed, took water and stayed.

चौपाई-caupāī:

केवट कीन्हि बहुत सेवकाई । सो जामिनि सिंगरौर गवाँई ॥
kevaṭa kīnhi bahuta sevakāī, so jāmini siṁgaraura gavāṁī.
होत प्रात बट छीरु मगावा । जटा मुकुट निज सीस बनावा ॥
hota prāta baṭa chīru magāvā, jaṭā mukuṭa nija sīsa banāvā.
राम सखाँ तब नाव मगाई । प्रिया चढाइ चढे रघुराई ॥
rāma sakhāṁ taba nāva magāī, priyā caṛhāi caṛhe raghurāī.
लखन बान धनु धरे बनाई । आपु चढे प्रभु आयसु पाई ॥
lakhana bāna dhanu dhare banāī, āpu caṛhe prabhu āyasu pāī.
बिकल बिलोकि मोहि रघुबीरा । बोले मधुर बचन धरि धीरा ॥
bikala biloki mohi raghubīrā, bole madhura bacana dhari dhīrā.
तात प्रनामु तात सन कहेहू । बार बार पद पंकज गहेहू ॥
tāta pranāmu tāta sana kahehū, bāra bāra pada paṁkaja gahehū.
करबि पायँ परि बिनय बहोरी । तात करिअ जनि चिंता मोरी ॥
karabi pāyaṁ pari binaya bahorī, tāta karia jani ciṁtā morī.
बन मग मंगल कुसल हमारें । कृपा अनुग्रह पुन्य तुम्हारें ॥
bana maga maṁgala kusala hamāreṁ, kṛpā anugraha punya tumhāreṁ.

Trans:
The boatmen showed them great courtesy and they passed the night at Sringavera. At daybreak they called for milk of the fig-tree and fastened up the hair of their head into a crown-like topknot. Then Rāma's friend called for the boat, and after putting his beloved on board, Rāma himself followed, and after him, by his Lord's permission, Lakshman too climbed the boat, equipt with bow and arrows. Seeing my distress, Raghubīr restrained his emotion and addressed me thus kindly, 'Father, give my salutation to my father, and again and again embrace his lotus feet.' There at his feet entreat him with all humility, saying, 'Father, mourn not for me; my banishment to the forest is pleasant and profitable to myself, and on your part it's a grace, a favor, and a meritorious deed.

छंद-chaṁda:

तुम्हरें अनुग्रह तात कानन जात सब सुखु पाइहौं ।
tumhareṁ anugraha tāta kānana jāta saba sukhu pāihauṁ,
प्रतिपालि आयसु कुसल देखन पाय पुनि फिरि आइहौं ॥
pratipāli āyasu kusala dekhana pāya puni phiri āihauṁ.
जननीं सकल परितोषि परि परि पायँ करि बिनती घनी ।
jananīṁ sakala paritoṣi pari pari pāyaṁ kari binatī ghanī,
तुलसी करेहु सोइ जतनु जेहिं कुसली रहहिं कोसलधनी ॥
tulasī karehu soi jatanu jehiṁ kusalī rahahiṁ kosaladhanī.

Trans:
By your favor, father, I go to the forest, there to enjoy complete happiness. After fulfilling your command, I shall return again in safety to behold your feet.' Next falling at the feet of each of the queen-mothers, console and implore them to make every effort that Kaushal's king may live happy.

सोरठा-soraṭhā:

गुर सन कहब सँदेसु बार बार पद पदुम गहि ।
gura sana kahaba saṁdesu bāra bāra pada paduma gahi,
करब सोइ उपदेसु जेहिं न सोच मोहि अवधपति ॥ १५१ ॥
karaba soi upadesu jehiṁ na soca mohi avadhapati. 151.

Trans:
Again and again clasping the lotus feet of my Guru, give him this my message, 'So exhort the king that he may cease to sorrow on my account.'

चौपाई-caupāī:

पुरजन परिजन सकल निहोरी । तात सुनाएहु बिनती मोरी ॥
purajana parijana sakala nihorī, tāta sunāehu binatī morī.
सोइ सब भाँति मोर हितकारी । जातें रह नरनाहु सुखारी ॥
soi saba bhāṁti mora hitakārī, jāteṁ raha naranāhu sukhārī.
कहब सँदेसु भरत के आएँ । नीति न तजिअ राजपदु पाएँ ॥
kahaba saṁdesu bharata ke āeṁ, nīti na tajia rājapadu pāeṁ.
पालेहु प्रजहि करम मन बानी । सेएहु मातु सकल सम जानी ॥
pālehu prajahi karama mana bānī, seehu mātu sakala sama jānī.
ओर निबाहेहु भायप भाई । करि पितु मातु सुजन सेवकाई ॥
ora nibāhehu bhāyapa bhāī, kari pitu mātu sujana sevakāī.
तात भाँति तेहि राखब राऊ । सोच मोर जेहिं करै न काऊ ॥
tāta bhāṁti tehi rākhaba rāū, soca mora jehiṁ karai na kāū.
लखन कहे कछु बचन कठोरा । बरजि राम पुनि मोहि निहोरा ॥
lakhana kahe kachu bacana kaṭhorā, baraji rāma puni mohi nihorā.
बार बार निज सपथ देवाई । कहबि न तात लखन लरिकाई ॥
bāra bāra nija sapatha devāī, kahabi na tāta lakhana larikāī.

Trans:
Bowing down before all the citizens and the people of the court make known to them, sir, this my petition: 'He is my best friend who ensures the king's happiness.' Say to Bharat too when he comes: 'Now that you have obtained the royal dignity, forget not sound polity. Cherish your subjects in word, thought, and deed, and be obedient to all the queen-mothers without partiality. Fulfill your duty brother as a brother, and in dutifulness to father, mother, and kindred; and take such care of the king, sir, that he may never regret for me.' Lakshman gave vent to some angry words, but Rāma checked him and begged of me again and again, adjuring me by himself, not to mention his childishness.

दोहा-dohā:

कहि प्रनामु कछु कहन लिय सिय भइ सिथिल सनेह ।
kahi pranāmu kachu kahana liya siya bhai sithila saneha,
थकित बचन लोचन सजल पुलक पल्लवित देह ॥ १५२॥
thakita bacana locana sajala pulaka pallavita deha. 152.

Trans:

Sītā sent her reverence, and would have said more but was unable; her voice faltered, her eyes filled with tears, and her body quivered with emotion.

चौपाई-caupāī:

तेहि अवसर रघुबर रूख पाई । केवट पारहि नाव चलाई ॥
tehi avasara raghubara rūkha pāī, kevaṭa pārahi nāva calāī.
रघुकुलतिलक चले एहि भाँती । देखउँ ठाढ़ कुलिस धरि छाती ॥
raghukulatilaka cale ehi bhām̐tī, dekhaum̐ ṭhāṛha kulisa dhari chātī.
मैं आपन किमि कहौं कलेसू । जिअत फिरेउँ लेइ राम सँदेसू ॥
maiṁ āpana kimi kahauṁ kalesū, jiata phireum̐ lei rāma sam̐desū.
अस कहि सचिव बचन रहि गयऊ । हानि गलानि सोच बस भयऊ ॥
asa kahi saciva bacana rahi gayaū, hāni galāni soca basa bhayaū.
सूत बचन सुनतहिं नरनाहू । परेउ धरनि उर दारुन दाहू ॥
sūta bacana sunatahiṁ naranāhū, pareu dharani ura dāruna dāhū.
तलफत बिषम मोह मन मापा । माजा मनहुँ मीन कहुँ ब्यापा ॥
talaphata biṣama moha mana māpā, mājā manahum̐ mīna kahum̐ byāpā.
करि बिलाप सब रोवहिं रानी । महा बिपति किमि जाइ बखानी ॥
kari bilāpa saba rovahiṁ rānī, mahā bipati kimi jāi bakhānī.
सुनि बिलाप दुखहू दुखु लागा । धीरजहू कर धीरजु भागा ॥
suni bilāpa dukhahū dukhu lāgā, dhīrajahū kara dhīraju bhāgā.

Trans:

Then it was that at a sign from Raghubar the boatman propelled the boat to the opposite side. In this manner the glory of Raghu's line went his way, and I stood looking on with a heart as of adamant. How can I describe my own anguish, who have come back alive, bearing Rāma's message?" With these words the minister stopped speaking, being overpowered by affliction, remorse, and distress. When he had heard Sumant's speech, the king fell to the ground, heart-broken with grief, and in a wild frenzy of soul writhed like a fish in the scour of a turbid stream. All the queens wept and made lamentation; how can I describe so great a calamity? At the sound of their wailings sorrow itself grew sorrowful and endurance could no more endure.

दोहा-dohā:

भयउ कोलाहलु अवध अति सुनि नृप राउर सोरु ।
bhayau kolāhalu avadha ati suni nṛpa rāura soru,
बिपुल बिहग बन परेउ निसि मानहुँ कुलिस कठोरु ॥ १५३॥
bipula bihaga bana pareu nisi mānahum̐ kulisa kaṭhoru. 153.

Trans:

Avadh was in a tumult at the sound of the outcry in the king's palace—as when a cruel thunderbolt has fallen at night in some dense forest full of birds.

चौपाई-caupāī:

प्रान कंठगत भयउ भुआलू । मनि बिहीन जनु ब्याकुल ब्यालू ॥
prāna kaṁṭhagata bhayau bhuālū, mani bihīna janu byākula byālū.
इंद्रीं सकल बिकल भइँ भारी । जनु सर सरसिज बनु बिनु बारी ॥
iṁdrīṁ sakala bikala bhaim̐ bhārī, janu sara sarasija banu binu bārī.
कौसल्याँ नृपु दीख मलाना । रबिकुल रबि अँथयउ जियँ जाना ॥
kausalyām̐ nṛpu dīkha malānā, rabikula rabi am̐thayau jiyam̐ jānā.
उर धरि धीर राम महतारी । बोली बचन समय अनुसारी ॥
ura dhari dhīra rāma mahatārī, bolī bacana samaya anusārī.
नाथ समुझि मन करिअ बिचारू । राम बियोग पयोधि अपारू ॥
nātha samujhi mana karia bicārū, rāma biyoga payodhi apārū.
करनधार तुम्ह अवध जहाजू । चढ़ेउ सकल प्रिय पथिक समाजू ॥
karanadhāra tumha avadha jahājū, caṛheu sakala priya pathika samājū.
धीरजु धरिअ त पाइअ पारू । नाहिं त बूड़िहि सबु परिवारू ॥
dhīraju dharia ta pāia pārū, nāhiṁ ta būṛihi sabu parivārū.
जौं जियँ धरिअ बिनय पिय मोरी । रामु लखनु सिय मिलहिं बहोरी ॥
jauṁ jiyam̐ dharia binaya piya morī, rāmu lakhanu siya milahiṁ bahorī.

Trans:

The breath of life flickered at the king's mouth, forlorn as a snake robbed of its jewel; all his senses as heavy smitten as the lotuses in a lake that has been drained of its water. When Kausalyā saw the king's misery—the sun of the solar race setting as it were at noon—Rāma's mother summoned up courage and spoke in words befitting the occasion, "Consider, my lord, and reflect that Rāma's exile is like the vast ocean, you are the helmsman of the good ship Avadh, and your friends are the merchants, its passengers; if you have courage you will get across; if not, the whole family will be drowned. Take to heart this entreaty of mine, my husband, and you will yet again see Rāma, Lakshman, and Sītā."

दोहा-dohā:

प्रिया बचन मृदु सुनत नृपु चितयउ आँखि उघारि ।
priyā bacana mṛdu sunata nṛpu citayau ām̐khi ughāri,
तलफत मीन मलीन जनु सींचत सीतल बारि ॥ १५४॥
talaphata mīna malīna janu sīṁcata sītala bāri. 154.

Trans:

Hearing these tender words from his beloved, the king opened his eyes and looked up, writhing like some hapless fish when sprinkled with cold water.

चौपाई-caupāī:

धरि धीरजु उठि बैठ भुआलू । कहु सुमंत्र कहँ राम कृपालू ॥
dhari dhīraju uṭhi baiṭha bhuālū, kahu sumaṁtra kaham̐ rāma kṛpālū.
कहाँ लखनु कहँ रामु सनेही । कहँ प्रिय पुत्रबधू बैदेही ॥
kahām̐ lakhanu kaham̐ rāmu sanehī, kaham̐ priya putrabadhū baidehī.
बिलपत राउ बिकल बहु भाँती । भइ जुग सरिस सिराति न राती ॥
bilapata rāu bikala bahu bhām̐tī, bhai juga sarisa sirāti na rātī.
तापस अंध साप सुधि आई । कौसल्यहि सब कथा सुनाई ॥
tāpasa aṁdha sāpa sudhi āī, kausalyahi saba kathā sunāī.
भयउ बिकल बरनत इतिहासा । राम रहित धिग जीवन आसा ॥
bhayau bikala baranata itihāsā, rāma rahita dhiga jīvana āsā.
सो तनु राखि करब मैं काहा । जेहिं न प्रेम पनु मोर निबाहा ॥
so tanu rākhi karaba maiṁ kāhā, jehiṁ na prema panu mora nibāhā.
हा रघुनंदन प्रान पिरीते । तुम्ह बिनु जिअत बहुत दिन बीते ॥
hā raghunaṁdana prāna pirīte, tumha binu jiata bahuta dina bīte.
हा जानकी लखन हा रघुबर । हा पितु हित चित चातक जलधर ॥
hā jānakī lakhana hā raghubara, hā pitu hita cita cātaka jaladhara.

Trans:

The king with an effort sat up, "Tell me, Sumant, where is my generous Rāma? Where is Lakshman? Where my loving Rāma? Where my dear daughter-in-law, the princess of Videh?" Thus miserably moaning, the night seemed an age long and as though it never would end. The blind hermit's curse came back to his mind, and he told the whole story to Kausalyā. As he related the circumstances his agitation increased: "Bereft as I am of Rāma, I am done with life and hope. Why should I cherish a body that has failed to fulfill my love's engagement? Ah, Raghu-nandan, dearer to me than life, already I have lived too long without you. Ah, Jānakī and Lakshman! Ah, Raghubar! the rain cloud of your fond father's Chātak-like heart."

दोहा-dohā:

राम राम कहि राम कहि राम राम कहि राम ।
rāma rāma kahi rāma kahi rāma rāma kahi rāma,
तनु परिहरि रघुबर बिरहँ राउ गयउ सुरधाम ॥ १५५ ॥
tanu parihari raghubara birahaṁ rāu gayau suradhāma. 155.

Trans:

Crying "Rāma, Rāma!" and again "Rāma!" and yet once more "Rāma, Rāma, Rāma!" the king's soul, bereft of Raghubar, quitted his body and entered heaven.

चौपाई-caupāī:

जिअन मरन फलु दसरथ पावा । अंड अनेक अमल जसु छावा ॥
jiana marana phalu dasaratha pāvā, aṁḍa aneka amala jasu chāvā.
जिअत राम बिधु बदनु निहारा । राम बिरह करि मरनु सँवारा ॥
jiata rāma bidhu badanu nihārā, rāma biraha kari maranu saṁvārā.
सोक बिकल सब रोवहिं रानी । रूपु सीलु बलु तेजु बखानी ॥
soka bikala saba rovahiṁ rānī, rūpu sīlu balu teju bakhānī.
करहिं बिलाप अनेक प्रकारा । परहिं भूमितल बारहिं बारा ॥
karahiṁ bilāpa aneka prakārā, parahiṁ bhūmitala bārahiṁ bārā.
बिलपहिं बिकल दास अरु दासी । घर घर रुदनु करहिं पुरबासी ॥
bilapahiṁ bikala dāsa aru dāsī, ghara ghara rudanu karahiṁ purabāsī.
अँथयउ आजु भानुकुल भानू । धरम अवधि गुन रूप निधानू ॥
aṁthayau āju bhānukula bhānū, dharama avadhi guna rūpa nidhānū.
गारीं सकल कैकइहि देहीं । नयन बिहीन कीन्ह जग जेहीं ॥
gārīṁ sakala kaikaihi dehīṁ, nayana bihīna kīnha jaga jehīṁ.
एहि बिधि बिलपत रैनि बिहानी । आए सकल महामुनि ग्यानी ॥
ehi bidhi bilapata raini bihānī, āe sakala mahāmuni gyānī.

Trans:

Thus Dashrath reaped his reward both in life and death, and his spotless fame has spread through countless cycles of creation. In life he saw Rāma's moon-like face, and dying for his loss had a glorious death. All the queens bewept him in an agony of grief, and spoke of his beauty, his amiability, his power and majesty. They made manifold lamentation, throwing themselves upon the ground again and again. Men-servants and maid-servants sadly bemoaned him; and there was weeping in every house throughout the city: "Today has set the sun of the solar race, the perfection of justice, the treasury of all good qualities." All reviled Kaekayī, who had robbed the world of its very eyes. In this manner the night was spent in lamentations till all the great and learned sages arrived.

दोहा-dohā:

तब बसिष्ठ मुनि समय सम कहि अनेक इतिहास ।
taba basiṣṭha muni samaya sama kahi aneka itihāsa,
सोक नेवारेउ सबहि कर निज बिग्यान प्रकास ॥ १५६ ॥
soka nevāreu sabahi kara nija bigyāna prakāsa. 156.

Trans:

Then the holy Vasishtha recited many legends befitting the time, and checked their grief by the wisdom that he displayed.

चौपाई-caupāī:

तेल नावँ भरि नृप तनु राखा । दूत बोलाइ बहुरि अस भाषा ॥
tela nāvaṁ bhari nṛpa tanu rākhā, dūta bolāi bahuri asa bhāṣā.
धावहु बेगि भरत पहिं जाहू । नृप सुधि कतहुँ कहहु जनि काहू ॥
dhāvahu begi bharata pahiṁ jāhū, nṛpa sudhi katahuṁ kahahu jani kāhū.
एतनेइ कहेहु भरत सन जाई । गुर बोलाई पठयउ दोउ भाई ॥
etanei kahehu bharata sana jāī, gura bolāī paṭhayau dou bhāī.
सुनि मुनि आयसु धावन धाए । चले बेग बर बाजि लजाए ॥
suni muni āyasu dhāvana dhāe, cale bega bara bāji lajāe.
अनरथु अवध अरंभेउ जब तें । कुसगुन होहिं भरत कहुँ तब तें ॥
anarathu avadha araṁbheu jaba teṁ, kusaguna hohiṁ bharata kahuṁ taba teṁ.
देखहिं राति भयानक सपना । जागि करहिं कटु कोटि कलपना ॥
dekhahiṁ rāti bhayānaka sapanā, jāgi karahiṁ kaṭu koṭi kalapanā.
बिप्र जेवाँइ देहिं दिन दाना । सिव अभिषेक करहिं बिधि नाना ॥
bipra jevāṁi dehiṁ dina dānā, siva abhiṣeka karahiṁ bidhi nānā.
मागहिं हृदयँ महेस मनाई । कुसल मातु पितु परिजन भाई ॥
māgahiṁ hṛdayaṁ mahesa manāī, kusala mātu pitu parijana bhāī.

Trans:

After filling a boat with oil and putting the king's body in it, he summoned messengers and thus addressed them: "Hasten with all speed to Bharat, and say nothing to anybody about the king; only this much you tell Bharat when you arrive: 'The Gurū has sent for you two brothers.'" Hearing the sage's orders the couriers rushed along with a speed that would put an excellent steed to shame. Meanwhile ever since these troubles began at Avadh, Bharat was visited with evil omens; he saw fearful visions in his sleep by night, and on awaking formed all sorts of ill conjectures. He daily feasted Brahmins and gave alms, and with elaborate ritual poured water over the emblem of Mahādev, and with heartfelt prayers implored the god for the prosperity of his parents, his family, and his brethren.

दोहा-dohā:

एहि बिधि सोचत भरत मन धावन पहुँचे आइ ।
ehi bidhi socata bharata mana dhāvana pahuṁce āi,
गुर अनुसासन श्रवन सुनि चले गनेसु मनाइ ॥ १५७ ॥
gura anusāsana śravana suni cale ganesu manāi. 157.

Trans:

In this state of anxiety was Bharat found by the heralds on their arrival. As soon as he had heard his Gurū's commands he offered up a prayer to Ganesh and started immediately along with Shatrughan.

चौपाई-caupāī:

चले समीर बेग हय हाँके । नाघत सरित सैल बन बाँके ॥
cale samīra bega haya hāṁke, nāghata sarita saila bana bāṁke.
हृदयँ सोचु बड़ कछु न सोहाई । अस जानहिं जियँ जाउँ उड़ाई ॥
hṛdayaṁ socu baṛa kachu na sohāī, asa jānahiṁ jiyaṁ jāuṁ uṛāī.
एक निमेष बरस सम जाई । एहि बिधि भरत नगर निअराई ॥
eka nimeṣa barasa sama jāī, ehi bidhi bharata nagara niarāī.
असगुन होहिं नगर पैठारा । रटहिं कुभाँति कुखेत करारा ॥
asaguna hohiṁ nagara paiṭhārā, raṭahiṁ kubhāṁti kukheta karārā.
खर सिआर बोलहिं प्रतिकूला । सुनि सुनि होइ भरत मन सूला ॥
khara siāra bolahiṁ pratikūlā, suni suni hoi bharata mana sūlā.
श्रीहत सर सरिता बन बागा । नगरु बिसेषि भयावनु लागा ॥
śrīhata sara saritā bana bāgā, nagaru biseṣi bhayāvanu lāgā.
खग मृग हय गय जाहिं न जोए । राम बियोग कुरोग बिगोए ॥
khaga mṛga haya gaya jāhiṁ na joe, rāma biyoga kuroga bigoe.
नगर नारि नर निपट दुखारी । मनहुँ सबन्हि सब संपति हारी ॥
nagara nāri nara nipaṭa dukhārī, manahuṁ sabanhi saba saṁpati hārī.

Trans:

They went surging with the speed of the wind, urging their horses onwards—over rivers, rocks, trackless forests. So great was his distress of mind that nothing pleased him; and he thought to himself, 'O that I had wings to fly!' A moment seemed like a year. In this manner Bharat drew near to the city. On entering, he was met by evil omens. Gruesome noises sounded in uncanny places; asses and jackals uttered presages of ill that pierced him to the heart as he listened. Even the lakes and rivers, groves and gardens seemed forlorn; and the city struck him as more melancholy still. Birds, deer, horses, and elephants were painful to look at, as though the loss of Rāma were some dreadful disease that had destroyed them. The citizens were as downcast as if they had all lost everything they had in the world.

दोहा-dohā:

पुरजन मिलहिं न कहहिं कछु गवँहिं जोहारहिं जाहिं ।
purajana milahiṁ na kahahiṁ kachu gavaṁhiṁ johārahiṁ jāhiṁ,
भरत कुसल पूँछि न सकहिं भय बिषाद मन माहिं ॥१५८॥
bharata kusala pūṁchi na sakahiṁ bhaya biṣāda mana māhiṁ. 158.

Trans:

The people who met him did not speak, but bowed and passed on. For the fear and dismay in his mind Bharat could not ask 'Is all well?'

चौपाई-caupāī:

हाट बाट नहिं जाइ निहारी । जनु पुर दहँ दिसि लागि दवारी ॥
hāṭa bāṭa nahiṁ jāi nihārī, janu pura dahaṁ disi lāgi davārī.
आवत सुत सुनि कैकयनंदिनि । हरषी रबिकुल जलरुह चंदिनि ॥
āvata suta suni kaikayanaṁdini, haraṣī rabikula jalaruha caṁdini.
सजि आरती मुदित उठि धाई । द्वारेहिं भेंटि भवन लेइ आई ॥
saji āratī mudita uṭhi dhāī, dvārehiṁ bheṁṭi bhavana lei āī.
भरत दुखित परिवारु निहारा । मानहुँ तुहिन बनज बनु मारा ॥
bharata dukhita parivāru nihārā, mānahuṁ tuhina banaja banu mārā.
कैकेई हरषित एहि भाँति । मनहुँ मुदित दव लाइ किराती ॥
kaikeī haraṣita ehi bhāṁti, manahuṁ mudita dava lāi kirātī.
सुतहि ससोच देखि मनु मारें । पूँछति नैहर कुसल हमारें ॥
sutahi sasoca dekhi manu māreṁ, pūṁchati naihara kusala hamāreṁ.
सकल कुसल कहि भरत सुनाई । पूँछी निज कुल कुसल भलाई ॥
sakala kusala kahi bharata sunāī, pūṁchī nija kula kusala bhalāī.
कहु कहँ तात कहाँ सब माता । कहँ सिय राम लखन प्रिय भ्राता ॥
kahu kahaṁ tāta kahāṁ saba mātā, kahaṁ siya rāma lakhana priya bhrātā.

Trans:

The market-places and streets were as dreary as though the city had been the prey of a general conflagration. Kaekayī, who was to the solar race what the moon is to the lotuses, was rejoiced to hear of her son's approach. She sprang up gladly and ran with lamp in hand and met him at the door and brought him in. Bharat saw all the household as woebegone as a bed of lotus when smitten by the frost, his mother as jubilant as a wild hill-woman who has set the forest in a blaze. Seeing her son sad and distressed, she asked, "Is all well at my mother's house?" Bharat assured her that all was well, and then asked after the welfare of his own family, "Say, where is father and where the other queen-mothers? Where is Sītā and my dear brothers, Rāma and Lakshman?"

दोहा-dohā:

सुनि सुत बचन सनेहमय कपट नीर भरि नैन ।
suni suta bacana sanehamaya kapaṭa nīra bhari naina,
भरत श्रवन मन सूल सम पापिनि बोली बैन ॥१५९॥
bharata śravana mana sūla sama pāpini bolī baina. 159.

Trans:

On hearing her son's loving speech the guilty woman's eyes filled with false tears, and she replied in words that pierced Bharat's soul and ears:

चौपाई-caupāī:

तात बात मैं सकल सँवारी । भै मंथरा सहाय बिचारी ॥
tāta bāta maiṁ sakala saṁvārī, bhai maṁtharā sahāya bicārī.
कछुक काज बिधि बीच बिगारेउ । भूपति सुरपति पुर पगु धारेउ ॥
kachuka kāja bidhi bīca bigāreu, bhūpati surapati pura pagu dhāreu.
सुनत भरतु भए बिबस बिषादा । जनु सहमेउ करि केहरि नादा ॥
sunata bharatu bhae bibasa biṣādā, janu sahameu kari kehari nādā.
तात तात हा तात पुकारी । परे भूमितल ब्याकुल भारी ॥
tāta tāta hā tāta pukārī, pare bhūmitala byākula bhārī.
चलत न देखन पायउँ तोही । तात न रामहि सौंपेहु मोही ॥
calata na dekhana pāyauṁ tohī, tāta na rāmahi sauṁpehu mohī.
बहुरि धीर धरि उठे सँभारी । कहु पितु मरन हेतु महतारी ॥
bahuri dhīra dhari uṭhe saṁbhārī, kahu pitu marana hetu mahatārī.
सुनि सुत बचन कहति कैकेई । मरमु पाँछि जनु माहुर देई ॥
suni suta bacana kahati kaikeī, maramu pāṁchi janu māhura deī.
आदिहु तें सब आपनि करनी । कुटिल कठोर मुदित मन बरनी ॥
ādihu teṁ saba āpani karanī, kuṭila kaṭhora mudita mana baranī.

Trans:

"My son, I had arranged everything with the help of poor Manthrā, but god somehow spoilt my plans half-way. The king has gone to heaven." On hearing that Bharat was struck shocked—like an elephant at the sudden roar of lion. Crying "My father, my father, alas, my father!" he fell upon the ground in grievous affliction. "I could not see you at leaving, O father, nor did you commend me to Rāma." Again, with an effort, he collected himself and got up, "Tell me, mother, the cause of my father's death." On hearing her son's words Kaekayī replied, as one who drops poison into a wound, and with a glad heart—the vile wretch that she was—recounted all that she had done from the very beginning.

दोहा-dohā:

भरतहि बिसरेउ पितु मरन सुनत राम बन गौनु ।
bharatahi bisareu pitu marana sunata rāma bana gaunu,
हेतु अपनपउ जानि जियँ थकित रहे धरि मौनु ॥१६०॥
hetu apanapau jāni jiyaṁ thakita rahe dhari maunu. 160.

Trans:

Bharat forgot his father's death when he heard of Rāma's banishment, and knowing himself to be the cause he was completely staggered and remained speechless.

चौपाई-caupāī:

बिकल बिलोकि सुतहि समुझावति । मनहुँ जरे पर लोनु लगावति ॥
bikala biloki sutahi samujhāvati, manahuṁ jare para lonu lagāvati.
तात राउ नहिं सोचै जोगू । बिढ़इ सुकृत जसु कीन्हेउ भोगू ॥
tāta rāu nahiṁ socai jogū, biṛhai sukṛta jasu kīnheu bhogū.
जीवत सकल जनम फल पाए । अंत अमरपति सदन सिधाए ॥
jīvata sakala janama phala pāe, aṁta amarapati sadana sidhāe.
अस अनुमानि सोच परिहरहू । सहित समाज राज पुर करहू ॥
asa anumāni soca pariharahū, sahita samāja rāja pura karahū.
सुनि सुठि सहमेउ राजकुमारू । पाकें छत जनु लाग अँगारू ॥
suni suṭhi sahameu rājakumārū, pākeṁ chata janu lāga aṁgārū.
धीरज धरि भरि लेहिं उसासा । पापिनि सबहि भाँति कुल नासा ॥
dhīraja dhari bhari lehiṁ usāsā, pāpini sabahi bhāṁti kula nāsā.
जौं पै कुरुचि रही अति तोही । जनमत काहे न मारे मोही ॥
jauṁ pai kuruci rahī ati tohī, janamata kāhe na māre mohī.
पेड़ काटि तैं पालउ सींचा । मीन जिअन निति बारि उलीचा ॥
peṛa kāṭi taiṁ pālau sīṁcā, mīna jiana niti bāri ulīcā.

Trans:

Seeing her son's distress she comforted him, in such manner as when one applies salt to a burn, "The king, my boy, is no fit subject for lamentation; he won glory and renown and lived happily. In his life he reaped all life's rewards, and in the end has entered the court of heaven. Regard the matter in this light, banish grief and rule the kingdom with all the subjects." The prince shrunk exceedingly at her words, as though cautery had been applied to a festered wound; then collecting himself he gave a deep sigh, "Wretched woman, the ruin of us all! If this was your vile desire, why did you not kill me at birth? After cutting down a tree you water the branches? And you drain a pond to keep the fish alive?

दोहा-dohā:

हंसबंसु दसरथु जनकु राम लखन से भाइ ।
hamsabamsu dasarathu janaku rāma lakhana se bhāi,
जननी तूँ जननी भई बिधि सन कछु न बसाइ ॥ १६१ ॥
jananī tūm̐ jananī bhaī bidhi sana kachu na basāi. 161.

Trans:

Born of the solar race, with Dashrath for my father and Rāma and Lakshman for my brothers—that I should have *you*, for a mother! Ah, what cruel fate!

चौपाई-caupāī:

जब तैं कुमति कुमत जियँ ठयऊ । खंड खंड होइ हृदउ न गयऊ ॥
jaba taiṁ kumati kumata jiyam̐ ṭhayaū, khaṁḍa khaṁḍa hoi hṛdau na gayaū.
बर मागत मन भइ नहिं पीरा । गरि न जीह मुहँ परेउ न कीरा ॥
bara māgata mana bhai nahiṁ pīrā, gari na jīha muham̐ pareu na kīrā.
भूपँ प्रतीति तोरि किमि कीन्ही । मरन काल बिधि मति हरि लीन्ही ॥
bhūpam̐ pratīti tori kimi kīnhī, marana kāla bidhi mati hari līnhī.
बिधिहुँ न नारि हृदय गति जानी । सकल कपट अघ अवगुन खानी ॥
bidhihum̐ na nāri hṛdaya gati jānī, sakala kapaṭa agha avaguna khānī.
सरल सुसील धरम रत राऊ । सो किमि जानै तीय सुभाऊ ॥
sarala susīla dharama rata rāū, so kimi jānai tīya subhāū.
अस को जीव जंतु जग माहीं । जेहि रघुनाथ प्रानप्रिय नाहीं ॥
asa ko jīva jaṁtu jaga māhīṁ, jehi raghunātha prānapriya nāhīṁ.
भे अति अहित रामु तेउ तोही । को तू अहसि सत्य कहु मोही ॥
bhe ati ahita rāmu teu tohī, ko tū ahasi satya kahu mohī.
जो हसि सो हसि मुहँ मसि लाई । आँखि ओट उठि बैठहि जाई ॥
jo hasi so hasi muham̐ masi lāī, ām̐khi oṭa uṭhi baiṭhahi jāī.

Trans:

You wretch! When you formed such an evil design in your mind, how was it your heart did not break into pieces? When you asked the boon, your soul felt no pain? Your tongue did not burn? Your mouth did not fester? How could the king trust you? His hour of death had come and god robbed him of his senses! Even gods don't know the way of hearts of woman such as you—mines of deceits, sins, crimes. The king was so simple, good, and pious; what did he know of woman's nature? Is there any living creature in the world who loves not Raghunāth like himself? Yet even he appeared to you as a great enemy? Tell me the truth, what are you? Whatever you may be, you have blackened your own face; up and out of my sight.

दोहा-dohā:

राम बिरोधी हृदय तें प्रगट कीन्ह बिधि मोहि ।
rāma birodhī hṛdaya teṁ pragaṭa kīnha bidhi mohi,
मो समान को पातकी बादि कहउँ कछु तोहि ॥ १६२ ॥
mo samāna ko pātakī bādi kahaum̐ kachu tohi. 162.

Trans:

God has created me out of a women hostile to Rāma! Who is so sinful a wretch as I myself? Why then blame you, the sinful one is I."

चौपाई-caupāī:

सुनि सत्रुघुन मातु कुटिलाई । जरहिं गात रिस कछु न बसाई ॥
suni satrughuna mātu kuṭilāī, jarahiṁ gāta risa kachu na basāī.
तेहि अवसर कुबरी तहँ आई । बसन बिभूषन बिबिध बनाई ॥
tehi avasara kubarī taham̐ āī, basana bibhūṣana bibidha banāī.
लखि रिस भरेउ लखन लघु भाई । बरत अनल घृत आहुति पाई ॥
lakhi risa bhareu lakhana laghu bhāī, barata anala ghṛta āhuti pāī.
हुमगि लात तकि कूबर मारा । परि मुह भर महि करत पुकारा ॥
humagi lāta taki kūbara mārā, pari muha bhara mahi karata pukārā.
कूबर टूटेउ फूट कपारू । दलित दसन मुख रुधिर प्रचारू ॥
kūbara ṭūṭeu phūṭa kapārū, dalita dasana mukha rudhira pracārū.
आह दइअ मैं काह नसावा । करत नीक फलु अनइस पावा ॥
āha daia maiṁ kāha nasāvā, karata nīka phalu anaisa pāvā.
सुनि रिपुहन लखि नख सिख खोटी । लगे घसीटन धरि धरि झोंटी ॥
suni ripuhana lakhi nakha sikha khoṭī, lage ghasīṭana dhari dhari jhoṁṭī.
भरत दयानिधि दीन्हि छड़ाई । कौसल्या पहिं गे दोउ भाई ॥
bharata dayānidhi dīnhi chaṛāī, kausalyā pahiṁ ge dou bhāī.

Trans:

When Shatrughan heard of mother Kaekayī's wickedness he burned all over, his anger was beyond control. At that very moment the Humpback came up, dressed out in fine attire and many jewels. On seeing her Lakshman's young brother was filled with passion, like fire upon which oil has been poured. He sprung forward and struck her such a blow on her hump that she fell flat on her face and screamed aloud. Her hump was smashed, her head split, her teeth broken, and her mouth streamed blood. "Oh mother! What harm have I done? This is an ill reward for all my services!" Then Shatrughan, seeing her so all vile from head to foot, seized her by the hair of the head and began dragging her about, till the merciful Bharat rescued her. Both brothers then went to Kausalyā.

दोहा-dohā:

मलिन बसन बिबरन बिकल कृस सरीर दुख भार ।
malina basana bibarana bikala kṛsa sarīra dukha bhāra,
कनक कलप बर बेलि बन मानहुँ हनी तुसार ॥ १६३ ॥
kanaka kalapa bara beli bana mānahum̐ hanī tusāra. 163.

Trans:

In sordid attire, pale, agitated, with wasted frame and soul oppressed with woe, she seemed like some lovely celestial creeper of golden hue blasted by the frost in the forest.

चौपाई-caupāī:

भरतहि देखि मातु उठि धाई । मुरुछित अवनि परी झइँ आई ॥
bharatahi dekhi mātu uṭhi dhāī, muruchita avani parī jhaim̐ āī.
देखत भरतु बिकल भए भारी । परे चरन तन दसा बिसारी ॥
dekhata bharatu bikala bhae bhārī, pare carana tana dasā bisārī.
मातु तात कहँ देहि देखाई । कहँ सिय रामु लखनु दोउ भाई ॥
mātu tāta kaham̐ dehi dekhāī, kaham̐ siya rāmu lakhanu dou bhāī.
कैकइ कत जनमी जग माझा । जौं जनमि त भइ काहे न बाँझा ॥
kaikai kata janamī jaga mājhā, jauṁ janami ta bhai kāhe na bām̐jhā.
कुल कलंकु जेहिं जनमेउ मोही । अपजस भाजन प्रियजन द्रोही ॥
kula kalaṁku jehiṁ janameu mohī, apajasa bhājana priyajana drohī.
को तिभुवन मोहि सरिस अभागी । गति असि तोरि मातु जेहि लागी ॥
ko tibhuvana mohi sarisa abhāgī, gati asi tori mātu jehi lāgī.
पितु सुरपुर बन रघुबर केतू । मैं केवल सब अनरथ हेतू ॥
pitu surapura bana raghubara ketū, maiṁ kevala saba anaratha hetū.
धिग मोहि भयउँ बेनु बन आगी । दुसह दाह दुख दूषन भागी ॥
dhiga mohi bhayaum̐ benu bana āgī, dusaha dāha dukha dūṣana bhāgī.

Trans:

When the queen saw Bharat she sprang up in haste but fell swooning to the ground overtaken by giddiness. At this sight Bharat was grievously distressed, and threw himself at her feet, forgetting his own condition, "Mother let me see my father; where is Sītā, and where Rāma and Lakshman my two brothers? Why was Kaekayī born into the world? Or if born, why was she not barren instead of bearing me to disgrace the family, a very sink of infamy, the curse of my home? Who in the three spheres is so wretched as I am, on whose account, mother, you have been brought to this condition? My father dead, Rāma banished, and I alone the calamity that caused it all! Woe is me, a very fire amongst the reeds, fraught with intolerable torment, censure, anguish."

दोहा-dohā:

मातु भरत के बचन मृदु सुनि सुनि उठी सँभारि ।
mātu bharata ke bacana mṛdu suni suni uṭhī saṁbhāri,
लिए उठाइ लगाइ उर लोचन मोचति बारी ॥१६४॥
lie uṭhāi lagāi ura locana mocati bārī. 164.

Trans:

Hearing Bharat speak so tenderly, his mother again took courage and rose and lifted him up too and clasped him to her bosom, as she wiped the tears from his eyes.

चौपाई-caupāī:

सरल सुभाय मायँ हियँ लाए । अति हित मनहुँ राम फिरि आए ॥
sarala subhāya māyaṁ hiyaṁ lāe, ati hita manahuṁ rāma phiri āe.
भेंटेउ बहुरि लखन लघु भाई । सोकु सनेहु न हृदयँ समाई ॥
bheṁṭeu bahuri lakhana laghu bhāī, soku sanehu na hṛdayaṁ samāī.
देखि सुभाउ कहत सबु कोई । राम मातु अस काहे न होई ॥
dekhi subhāu kahata sabu koī, rāma mātu asa kāhe na hoī.
माताँ भरतु गोद बैठारे । आँसु पोंछि मृदु बचन उचारे ॥
mātāṁ bharatu goda baiṭhāre, āṁsu poṁchi mṛdu bacana ucāre.
अजहुँ बच्छ बलि धीरज धरहू । कुसमउ समुझि सोक परिहरहू ॥
ajahuṁ baccha bali dhīraja dharahū, kusamau samujhi soka pariharahū.
जनि मानहु हियँ हानि गलानी । काल करम गति अघटित जानी ॥
jani mānahu hiyaṁ hāni galānī, kāla karama gati aghaṭita jānī.
काहुहि दोसु देहु जनि ताता । भा मोहि सब बिधि बाम बिधाता ॥
kāhuhi dosu dehu jani tātā, bhā mohi saba bidhi bāma bidhātā.
जो एतेहुँ दुख मोहि जिआवा । अजहुँ को जानै का तेहि भावा ॥
jo etehuṁ dukha mohi jiāvā, ajahuṁ ko jānai kā tehi bhāvā.

Trans:

Simple and kind, she took him to her heart as lovingly as though Rāma himself had come back. Then Lakshman's young brother was also embraced, while her soul overflowed with sorrow and affection. All who witnessed her kindness said, "She is Rāma's mother, it is natural for her to be so." Seating Bharat in her lap, she wiped away his tears and said soothingly, "Now, my child, I adjure you to compose yourself; reflect that the times are evil and cease to lament. Think no more of your loss and vexation; remember that the course of time and fate is unalterable. Do not attach blame to anyone, my son; it is providence that has turned hostile to me. He has made me live through such distress; who knows what may be his choice with regard to me even now?"

दोहा-dohā:

पितु आयसु भूषन बसन तात तजे रघुबीर ।
pitu āyasa bhūṣana basana tāta taje raghubīra,
बिसमउ हरषु न हृदयँ कछु पहिरे बलकल चीर ॥१६५॥
bisamau haraṣu na hṛdayaṁ kachu pahire balakala cīra. 165.

Trans:

At his father's command Raghubīr put aside his ornaments and ordinary attire and assumed the bark dress without exultation or dismay.

चौपाई-caupāī:

मुख प्रसन्न मन रंग न रोषू । सब कर सब बिधि करि परितोषू ॥
mukha prasanna mana raṁga na roṣū, saba kara saba bidhi kari paritoṣū.
चले बिपिन सुनि सिय सँग लागी । रहइ न राम चरन अनुरागी ॥
cale bipina suni siya saṁga lāgī, rahai na rāma carana anurāgī.
सुनतहिं लखनु चले उठि साथा । रहहिं न जतन किए रघुनाथा ॥
sunatahiṁ lakhanu cale uṭhi sāthā, rahahiṁ na jatana kie raghunāthā.
तब रघुपति सबही सिरु नाई । चले संग सिय अरु लघु भाई ॥
taba raghupati sabahī siru nāī, cale saṁga siya aru laghu bhāī.
रामु लखनु सिय बनहि सिधाए । गइउँ न संग न प्रान पठाए ॥
rāmu lakhanu siya banahi sidhāe, gaiuṁ na saṁga na prāna paṭhāe.
यह सबु भा इन्ह आँखिन्ह आगें । तउ न तजा तनु जीव अभागें ॥
yahu sabu bhā inha āṁkhinha āgeṁ, tau na tajā tanu jīva abhāgeṁ.
मोहि न लाज निज नेहु निहारी । राम सरिस सुत मैं महतारी ॥
mohi na lāja nija nehu nihārī, rāma sarisa suta maiṁ mahatārī.
जिऐ मरै भल भूपति जाना । मोर हृदय सत कुलिस समाना ॥
jiai marai bhala bhūpati jānā, mora hṛdaya sata kulisa samānā.

Trans:

With a cheerful countenance and a soul unmoved by anger or attachment, he did all in his power to comfort us. Sītā, hearing he was off to the forest, went too. In her devotion to Rāma's feet she could not stay. Lakshman also, when he heard the news rose up to accompany him; and for all Rāma's persuasions would not remain behind. Then Raghupatī bowed his head to all in turn and set out accompanied by Sītā and his younger brother. Rāma, Lakshman, and Sītā went thus into exile. I neither joined them, nor sent my spirit after them. All this took place before my eyes, and yet this wretched soul did not leave the body. Alas, to think that a son like Rāma should have a mother such as me. The king well knew how to live, and how to die; but my heart is a hundredfold harder than adamantine."

दोहा-dohā:

कौसल्या के बचन सुनि भरत सहित रनिवासु ।
kausalyā ke bacana suni bharata sahita ranivāsu,
ब्याकुल बिलपत राजगृह मानहुँ सोक नेवासु ॥१६६॥
byākula bilapata rājagṛha mānahuṁ soka nevāsu. 166.

Trans:

Hearing Kausalyā's words, Bharat and all the seraglio made woeful lamentation; the palace seemed the very home of affliction.

चौपाई-caupāī:

बिलपहिं बिकल भरत दोउ भाई । कौसल्याँ लिए हृदयँ लगाई ॥
bilapahiṁ bikala bharata dou bhāī, kausalyāṁ lie hṛdayaṁ lagāī.
भाँति अनेक भरतु समुझाए । कहि बिबेकमय बचन सुनाए ॥
bhāṁti aneka bharatu samujhāe, kahi bibekamaya bacana sunāe.
भरतहुँ मातु सकल समुझाईं । कहि पुरान श्रुति कथा सुहाईं ॥
bharatahuṁ mātu sakala samujhāīṁ, kahi purāna śruti kathā suhāīṁ.
छल बिहीन सुचि सरल सुबानी । बोले भरत जोरि जुग पानी ॥
chala bihīna suci sarala subānī, bole bharata jori juga pānī.
जे अघ मातु पिता सुत मारें । गाइ गोठ महिसुर पुर जारें ॥
je agha mātu pitā suta māreṁ, gāi goṭha mahisura pura jāreṁ.
जे अघ तिय बालक बध कीन्हें । मीत महीपति माहुर दीन्हें ॥
je agha tiya bālaka badha kīnheṁ, mīta mahīpati māhura dīnheṁ.
जे पातक उपपातक अहहीं । करम बचन मन भव कबि कहहीं ॥
je pātaka upapātaka ahahīṁ, karama bacana mana bhava kabi kahahīṁ.
ते पातक मोहि होहुँ बिधाता । जौं यह होइ मोर मत माता ॥
te pātaka mohi hohuṁ bidhātā, jauṁ yahu hoi mora mata mātā.

Trans:

Bharat, nay, both brothers wept piteously. Kausalyā clasped them to her bosom, and comforted Bharat in every way with words of excellent wisdom. With appropriate maxims from the Purāṇas and Vedas all the queens consoled Bharat. And Bharat too—pure, guileless, and sincere—in turn consoled others, and said he with clasped hands, "The crime of slaying one's father, mother, or Guru; and of burning cows in their stalls, or a village full of Brahmins; and the crime of murdering wife or child; and of poisoning a friend or monarch; and every mortal or venial sin, of thought, word, and deed, as have been enumerated by the seers—may all these sins accrue to me, by god, if this was in any way a plot of mine, my mother.

दोहा-dohā:

जे परिहरि हरि हर चरन भजहिं भूतगन घोर ।
je parihari hari hara carana bhajahiṁ bhūtagana ghora,
तेहि कइ गति मोहि देउ बिधि जौं जननी मत मोर ॥ १६७॥
tehi kai gati mohi deu bidhi jauṁ jananī mata mora. 167.

Trans:

May god award me the fate of those who forsake the feet of Harī and Hara and worship abominable demons, if, O mother, any of this had my concurrence.

चौपाई-caupāī:

बेचहिं बेदु धरमु दुहि लेहीं । पिसुन पराय पाप कहि देहीं ॥
becahiṁ bedu dharamu duhi lehīṁ, pisuna parāya pāpa kahi dehīṁ.
कपटी कुटिल कलहप्रिय क्रोधी । बेद बिदूषक बिस्व बिरोधी ॥
kapaṭī kuṭila kalahapriya krodhī, beda bidūṣaka bisva birodhī.
लोभी लंपट लोलुपचारा । जे ताकहिं परधनु परदारा ॥
lobhī laṁpaṭa lolupacārā, je tākahiṁ paradhanu paradārā.
पावौं मैं तिन्ह कै गति घोरा । जौं जननी यहु संमत मोरा ॥
pāvauṁ maiṁ tinha kai gati ghorā, jauṁ jananī yahu saṁmata morā.
जे नहिं साधुसंग अनुरागे । परमारथ पथ बिमुख अभागे ॥
je nahiṁ sādhusaṁga anurāge, paramāratha patha bimukha abhāge.
जे न भजहिं हरि नरतनु पाई । जिन्हहि न हरि हर सुजसु सोहाई ॥
je na bhajahiṁ hari naratanu pāī, jinhahi na hari hara sujasu sohāī.
तजि श्रुतिपंथु बाम पथ चलहीं । बंचक बिरचि बेष जगु छलहीं ॥
taji śrutipaṁthu bāma patha calahīṁ, baṁcaka biraci beṣa jagu chalahīṁ.
तिन्ह कै गति मोहि संकर देऊ । जननी जौं यहु जानौं भेऊ ॥
tinha kai gati mohi saṁkara deū, jananī jauṁ yahu jānauṁ bheū.

Trans:

Those who sell the Vedas and trade on piety; backbiters, who talk of other's faults; the treacherous, the perverse, the litigious, the violent; the revilers of the Vedas and enemies of creation; the covetous, the lecherous, the fickle, the boastful, who covet their neighbor's wealth or wife—may I come to an ill end like them if, O mother, this plot had any conniving of me. The wretches who have no regard for the example of the good, who reject the way of salvation, who worship not the incarnation of Harī, and take no delight in the glory of Harī and Hara, who abandon the path of Scripture and follow a contrary road, who by knavish disguise impose upon the world—may Shankar allot me a fate like theirs if, mother, I knew of this scheme.

दोहा-dohā:

मातु भरत के बचन सुनि साँचे सरल सुभायँ ।
mātu bharata ke bacana suni sāṁce sarala subhāyaṁ,
कहति राम प्रिय तात तुम्ह सदा बचन मन कायँ ॥ १६८॥
kahati rāma priya tāta tumha sadā bacana mana kāyaṁ. 168.

Trans:

Hearing Bharat's true and honest and generous words, mother Kausalyā exclaimed: "Son, you have ever and ever in thought, word, and deed been the dearest of Rāma.

चौपाई-caupāī:

राम प्रानहु तें प्रान तुम्हारे । तुम्ह रघुपतिहि प्रानहु तें प्यारे ॥
rāma prānahu teṁ prāna tumhāre, tumha raghupatihi prānahu teṁ pyāre.
बिधु बिष चवै स्रवै हिमु आगी । होइ बारिचर बारि बिरागी ॥
bidhu biṣa cavai sravai himu āgī, hoi bāricara bāri birāgī.
भएँ ग्यानु बरु मिटै न मोहू । तुम्ह रामहि प्रतिकूल न होहू ॥
bhaeṁ gyānu baru miṭai na mohū, tumha rāmahi pratikūla na hohū.
मत तुम्हार यहु जो जग कहहीं । सो सपनेहुँ सुख सुगति न लहहीं ॥
mata tumhāra yahu jo jaga kahahiṁ, so sapanehuṁ sukha sugati na lahahiṁ.
अस कहि मातु भरतु हियँ लाए । थन पय स्रवहिं नयन जल छाए ॥
asa kahi mātu bharatu hiyaṁ lāe, thana paya sravahiṁ nayana jala chāe.
करत बिलाप बहुत यहि भाँती । बैठेहिं बीति गई सब राती ॥
karata bilāpa bahuta yahi bhāṁtī, baiṭhehiṁ bīti gaī saba rātī.
बामदेउ बसिष्ठ तब आए । सचिव महाजन सकल बोलाए ॥
bāmadeu basiṣṭha taba āe, saciva mahājana sakala bolāe.
मुनि बहु भाँति भरत उपदेसे । कहि परमारथ बचन सुदेसे ॥
muni bahu bhāṁti bharata upadese, kahi paramāratha bacana sudese.

Trans:

Rāma is the very life of your life, and you are dearer than life to him. The moon may drop poison, ice distil fire, fish avoid water, or spiritual enlightenment may fail to eradicate error, but you could never become Rāma's enemy. If anyone in the world says this was of your contriving, he shall never even in his sleep have any happiness or peace." With these words mother Kausalyā took Bharat to her arms, and her bosom dripped milk and her eyes dripped tears. As they sat she made long lamentations, and the whole night was thus spent. Saints Vāmdev and Vasishtha came and summoned all the ministers and nobles, and did everything to console Bharat by appropriate discourse on religion

दोहा-dohā:

तात हृदयँ धीरजु धरहु करहु जो अवसर आजु ।
tāta hṛdayaṁ dhīraju dharahu karahu jo avasara āju,
उठे भरत गुर बचन सुनि करन कहेउ सबु साजु ॥ १६९॥
uṭhe bharata gura bacana suni karana kaheu sabu sāju. 169.

Trans:

"Son, take heart and perform the duties of the day." Bharat arose at the Gurū's command and ordered everything to be done.

चौपाई-caupāī:

नृपतनु बेद बिदित अन्हवावा । परम बिचित्र बिमानु बनावा ॥
nṛpatanu beda bidita anhavāvā, parama bicitra bimānu banāvā.
गहि पद भरत मातु सब राखी । रहीं रानि दरसन अभिलाषी ॥
gahi pada bharata mātu saba rākhī, rahīṁ rāni darasana abhilāṣī.
चंदन अगर भार बहु आए । अमित अनेक सुगंध सुहाए ॥
caṁdana agara bhāra bahu āe, amita aneka sugaṁdha suhāe.
सरजु तीर रचि चिता बनाई । जनु सुरपुर सोपान सुहाई ॥
saraju tīra raci citā banāī, janu surapura sopāna suhāī.
एहि बिधि दाह क्रिया सब कीन्ही । बिधिवत न्हाइ तिलांजुलि दीन्ही ॥
ehi bidhi dāha kriyā saba kīnhī, bidhivata nhāi tilāṁjuli dīnhī.
सोधि सुमृति सब बेद पुराना । कीन्ह भरत दसगात बिधाना ॥
sodhi sumṛti saba beda purānā, kīnha bharata dasagāta bidhānā.
जहँ जस मुनिबर आयसु दीन्हा । तहँ तस सहस भाँति सबु कीन्हा ॥
jahaṁ jasa munibara āyasu dīnhā, tahaṁ tasa sahasa bhāṁti sabu kīnhā.
भए बिसुद्ध दिए सब दाना । धेनु बाजि गज बाहन नाना ॥
bhae bisuddha die saba dānā, dhenu bāji gaja bāhana nānā.

Trans:

As directed in the Veda, he had the body of the king washed and a splendid funeral bier prepared. Then clasping the feet of each of the queens he bid them stay. They stayed in the hope of seeing Rāma. Many loads of sandalwood and aloes were brought, and also immense quantities of sweet-scented spices. The pile was raised on the bank of the Sarjū like a fair ladder reaching up to heaven. So all the rites of cremation were accomplished: the prescribed bathing, the oblation of sesame seeds, the ceremony of the ten balls of rice. After ascertaining the views of all the Smriti texts, the Vedas and the Purānas, Bharat performed the ceremony of

Dasagatra. Whatever order was given at any time by the great sage was thereupon executed accordingly a thousand times over. He bestowed all sorts of gifts on attaining purity. He gave away cows, horses, elephants and conveyances of various sorts;

दोहा-dohā:

सिंघासन भूषन बसन अन्न धरनि धन धाम ।
siṁghāsana bhūṣana basana anna dharani dhana dhāma,
दिए भरत लहि भूमिसुर भे परिपूरन काम ॥ १७० ॥
die bharata lahi bhūmisura bhe paripūrana kāma. 170.

Trans:

and even so thrones, ornaments and costumes, food-grains, lands, money and houses; and the Brahmins had all their desires fulfilled on receiving them.

चौपाई-caupāī:

पितु हित भरत कीन्हि जसि करनी । सो मुख लाख जाइ नहिं बरनी ॥
pitu hita bharata kīnhi jasi karanī, so mukha lākha jāi nahiṁ baranī.
सुदिनु सोधि मुनिबर तब आए । सचिव महाजन सकल बोलाए ॥
sudinu sodhi munibara taba āe, saciva mahājana sakala bolāe.
बैठे राजसभाँ सब जाई । पठए बोलि भरत दोउ भाई ॥
baiṭhe rājasabhāṁ saba jāī, paṭhae boli bharata dou bhāī.
भरतु बसिष्ठ निकट बैठारे । नीति धरममय बचन उचारे ॥
bharatu basiṣṭha nikaṭa baiṭhāre, nīti dharamamaya bacana ucāre.
प्रथम कथा सब मुनिबर बरनी । कैकइ कुटिल कीन्हि जसि करनी ॥
prathama kathā saba munibara baranī, kaikai kuṭila kīnhi jasi karanī.
भूप धरमब्रतु सत्य सराहा । जेहिं तनु परिहरि प्रेमु निबाहा ॥
bhūpa dharamabratu satya sarāhā, jehiṁ tanu parihari premu nibāhā.
कहत राम गुन सील सुभाऊ । सजल नयन पुलकेउ मुनिराऊ ॥
kahata rāma guna sīla subhāū, sajala nayana pulakeu munirāū.
बहुरि लखन सिय प्रीति बखानी । सोक सनेह मगन मुनि ग्यानी ॥
bahuri lakhana siya prīti bakhānī, soka saneha magana muni gyānī.

Trans:

All the ceremonies that Bharat performed on his father's account were more than a million tongues could tell. Then came the great sages, after determining an auspicious day, and summoned all the nobles and ministers, who went and sat down in the royal council chamber, where they sent and summoned Bharat and his brother. Vasishtha seated Bharat by his side and addressed him in words full of wisdom and piety. First the holy man repeated the whole history of Kaekayī's monstrous doings and extolled the king for his piety and faithfulness to his promise—who by his death had manifested his love. As he spoke of Rāma's good qualities and amiable disposition, the saint's eyes filled with tears and his body quivered with emotion. As he went on to tell of the affection shown by Lakshman and Sītā, the ascetic sage was drowned in love and grief.

दोहा-dohā:

सुनहु भरत भावी प्रबल बिलखि कहेउ मुनिनाथ ।
sunahu bharata bhāvī prabala bilakhi kaheu muninātha,
हानि लाभु जीवनु मरनु जसु अपजसु बिधि हाथ ॥ १७१ ॥
hāni lābhu jīvanu maranu jasu apajasu bidhi hātha. 171.

Trans:

"Hearken, Bharat," thus sadly spoke the prince of sages, "Fate is over-strong; loss and gain, life and death, honor and dishonor are all in God's hands.

चौपाई-caupāī:

अस बिचारि केहि देइअ दोसू । ब्यरथ काहि पर कीजिअ रोसू ॥
asa bicāri kehi deia dosū, byaratha kāhi para kījia rosū.
तात बिचारु करहु मन माहीं । सोच जोगु दसरथु नृपु नाहीं ॥
tāta bicāru karahu mana māhīṁ, soca jogu dasarathu nṛpu nāhīṁ.
सोचिअ बिप्र जो बेद बिहीना । तजि निज धरमु बिषय लयलीना ॥
socia bipra jo beda bihīnā, taji nija dharamu biṣaya layalīnā.
सोचिअ नृपति जो नीति न जाना । जेहि न प्रजा प्रिय प्रान समाना ॥
socia nṛpati jo nīti na jānā, jehi na prajā priya prāna samānā.
सोचिअ बयसु कृपन धनवानू । जो न अतिथि सिव भगति सुजानू ॥
socia bayasu kṛpana dhanavānū, jo na atithi siva bhagati sujānū.
सोचिअ सूद्रु बिप्र अवमानी । मुखर मानप्रिय ग्यान गुमानी ॥
socia sūdru bipra avamānī, mukhara mānapriya gyāna gumānī.
सोचिअ पुनि पति बंचक नारी । कुटिल कलहप्रिय इच्छाचारी ॥
socia puni pati baṁcaka nārī, kuṭila kalahapriya icchācārī.
सोचिअ बटु निज ब्रतु परिहरई । जो नहिं गुर आयसु अनुसरई ॥
socia baṭu nija bratu pariharaī, jo nahiṁ gura āyasu anusaraī.

Trans:

Having so considered, why blame anyone, or why be angry with, or without, cause? Ponder this in your heart, my son; king Dashrath is not to be pitied. Pitiable the Brahmin who is ignorant of the Veda and has abandoned his faith and become absorbed in the delights of sense; pitiable the king who knows not the principles of government, and to whom his subjects are not as dear as his own life; pitiable the merchant, miserly and rich, who regards not the duties of hospitality nor the service of Mahādev; pitiable the unlearned who insults a learned, and is boastful, ambitious, and proud of his knowledge; pitiable again the wife who deceives her own husband, who is perverse, quarrelsome, self-willed; pitiable the religious student who breaks his vows and obeys not the commands of his Gurū;

दोहा-dohā:

सोचिअ गृही जो मोह बस करइ करम पथ त्याग ।
socia gṛhī jo moha basa karai karama patha tyāga,
सोचिअ जती प्रपंच रत बिगत बिबेक बिराग ॥ १७२ ॥
socia jatī prapaṁca rata bigata bibeka birāga. 172.

Trans:

pitiable the householder who, overcome by delusion, forsakes the path of religion; pitiable the ascetic who is enamored of the world and has lost his judgment and self-governance.

चौपाई-caupāī:

बैखानस सोइ सोचै जोगू । तपु बिहाइ जेहि भावइ भोगू ॥
baikhānasa soi socai jogū, tapu bihāi jehi bhāvai bhogū.
सोचिअ पिसुन अकारन क्रोधी । जननि जनक गुर बंधु बिरोधी ॥
socia pisuna akārana krodhī, janani janaka gura baṁdhu birodhī.
सब बिधि सोचिअ पर अपकारी । निज तनु पोषक निरदय भारी ॥
saba bidhi socia para apakārī, nija tanu poṣaka niradaya bhārī.
सोचनीय सबहीं बिधि सोई । जो न छाड़ि छलु हरि जन होई ॥
socanīya sabahīṁ bidhi soī, jo na chāṛi chalu hari jana hoī.
सोचनीय नहिं कोसलराऊ । भुवन चारिदस प्रगट प्रभाऊ ॥
socanīya nahiṁ kosalarāū, bhuvana cāridasa pragaṭa prabhāū.
भयउ न अहइ न अब होनिहारा । भूप भरत जस पिता तुम्हारा ॥
bhayau na ahai na aba honihārā, bhūpa bharata jasa pitā tumhārā.
बिधि हरि हरु सुरपति दिसिनाथा । बरनहिं सब दसरथ गुन गाथा ॥
bidhi hari haru surapati disināthā, baranahiṁ saba dasaratha guna gāthā.

Trans:

Pitiable the anchorite who has given up penance and takes delight in pleasures; pitiable the backbiter and those angry without a cause; or the enemy of their own parents, spiritual guide, and their kinsmen; pitiable in every way is the malevolent who cherishes only himself and is utterly merciless; pitiable in every way is he who does not eschew guile and becomes Harī's follower—but the king of Kaushal is not to be pitied; his glory is spread abroad through the fourteen spheres. There neither has been, nor is now, nor shall be hereafter—a king like your father, Bharat. Brahmmā, Vishnu, Shiva, Indra, and all the Regents of the air sing the virtues of Dashrath.

दोहा-dohā:

कहहु तात केहि भाँति कोउ करिहि बड़ाई तासु ।
kahahu tāta kehi bhām̐ti kou karihi baṛāī tāsu,
राम लखन तुम्ह सत्रुहन सरिस सुअन सुचि जासु ॥ १७३ ॥
rāma lakhana tumha satruhana sarisa suana suci jāsu. 173.

Trans:

Tell me, my son, in what way can anyone magnify him, who has such noble sons as Rāma, Lakshman, you, and Shatrughan?

चौपाई-caupāī:

सब प्रकार भूपति बड़भागी । बादि बिषादु करिअ तेहि लागी ॥
saba prakāra bhūpati baṛabhāgī, bādi biṣādu karia tehi lāgī.
यहु सुनि समुझि सोचु परिहरहू । सिर धरि राज रजायसु करहू ॥
yahu suni samujhi socu pariharahū, sira dhari rāja rajāyasu karahū.
रायँ राजपदु तुम्ह कहुँ दीन्हा । पिता बचनु फुर चाहिअ कीन्हा ॥
rāyam̐ rājapadu tumha kahum̐ dīnhā, pitā bacanu phura cāhia kīnhā.
तजे रामु जेहिं बचनहि लागी । तनु परिहरेउ राम बिरहागी ॥
taje rāmu jehiṁ bacanahi lāgī, tanu parihareu rāma birahāgī.
नृपहि बचन प्रिय नहिं प्रिय प्राना । करहु तात पितु बचन प्रवाना ॥
nṛpahi bacana priya nahiṁ priya prānā, karahu tāta pitu bacana pravānā.
करहु सीस धरि भूप रजाई । हइ तुम्ह कहँ सब भाँति भलाई ॥
karahu sīsa dhari bhūpa rajāī, hai tumha kaham̐ saba bhām̐ti bhalāī.
परसुराम पितु अग्या राखी । मारी मातु लोक सब साखी ॥
parasurāma pitu agyā rākhī, mārī mātu loka saba sākhī.
तनय जजातिहि जौबनु दयऊ । पितु अग्याँ अघ अजसु न भयऊ ॥
tanaya jajātihi jaubanu dayaū, pitu agyām̐ agha ajasu na bhayaū.

Trans:

The king is altogether fortunate; it is vain to lament on his account. Thus hearing and considering, cease from grief; obediently submit to the royal commands. The king has given you the throne, and you must need fulfill your father's word. The monarch who for the sake of his word abandoned Rāma, though in the anguish of separation from Rāma he lost his life, and who thus held his word dearer than life, is a father, my son, whose word must be obeyed. Bow your head to the royal command; it will be in every way for your good. The world knows the story how Parshurām cut his own mother to obey his father's command. Yayāti's son gave him his own youth in exchange for old-age. In a father's order there can be no sin nor disgrace.

दोहा-dohā:

अनुचित उचित बिचारु तजि जे पालहिं पितु बैन ।
anucita ucita bicāru taji je pālahiṁ pitu baina,
ते भाजन सुख सुजस के बसहिं अमरपति ऐन ॥ १७४ ॥
te bhājana sukha sujasa ke basahiṁ amarapati aina. 174.

Trans:

They who cherish their father's words, without discussing right or wrong, they are receptacles of honor and glory and dwell in the palace of the king of heaven.

चौपाई-caupāī:

अवसि नरेस बचन फुर करहू । पालहु प्रजा सोकु परिहरहू ॥
avasi naresa bacana phura karahū, pālahu prajā soku pariharahū.
सुरपुर नृपु पाइहि परितोषू । तुम्ह कहुँ सुकृतु सुजसु नहिं दोषू ॥
surapura nṛpu pāihi paritoṣū, tumha kahum̐ sukṛtu sujasu nahiṁ doṣū.
बेद बिदित संमत सबही का । जेहि पितु देइ सो पावइ टीका ॥
beda bidita saṁmata sabahī kā, jehi pitu dei so pāvai ṭīkā.
करहु राजु परिहरहु गलानी । मानहु मोर बचन हित जानी ॥
karahu rāju pariharahu galānī, mānahu mora bacana hita jānī.
सुनि सुखु लहब राम बैदेहीं । अनुचित कहब न पंडित केहीं ॥
suni sukhu lahaba rāma baidehīṁ, anucita kahaba na paṁḍita kehīṁ.
कौसल्यादि सकल महतारीं । तेउ प्रजा सुख होहिं सुखारीं ॥
kausalyādi sakala mahatārīṁ, teu prajā sukha hohiṁ sukhārīṁ.
परम तुम्हार राम कर जानिहि । सो सब बिधि तुम्ह सन भल मानिहि ॥
parama tumhāra rāma kara jānihi, so saba bidhi tumha sana bhala mānihi.
सौंपेहु राजु राम के आएँ । सेवा करेहु सनेह सुहाएँ ॥
sauṁpehu rāju rāma ke āem̐, sevā karehu saneha suhāem̐.

Trans:

You must certainly make good the king's word; cherish your subjects and cease to grieve. He will receive comfort in heaven; for you, it will be a merit and an honor, and bring no fault. It is laid down in the Veda, and approved by all men, that he takes the crown to whom the father gives it. Reign then, nor further distress yourself, but accept my advice as the best for you. Rāma and Sītā will rejoice when they hear of it, and no wise man will call it wrong. Kausalyā and all the queens will be happy in the happiness of the people. Rāma knows your secret thoughts and will take it quite in good part; on his return you can deliver up the throne and serve him with cheerful affection."

दोहा-dohā:

कीजिअ गुर आयसु अवसि कहहिं सचिव कर जोरि ।
kījia gura āyasu avasi kahahiṁ saciva kara jori,
रघुपति आएँ उचित जस तस तब करब बहोरि ॥ १७५ ॥
raghupati āem̐ ucita jasa tasa taba karaba bahori. 175.

Trans:

The ministers with clasped hands exclaimed, "You must need obey your Gurū's command. When Raghupatī returns you can then do as seems to you good."

चौपाई-caupāī:

कौसल्या धरि धीरजु कहई । पूत पथ्य गुर आयसु अहई ॥
kausalyā dhari dhīraju kahaī, pūta pathya gura āyasu ahaī.
सो आदरिअ करिअ हित मानी । तजिअ बिषादु काल गति जानी ॥
so ādaria karia hita mānī, tajia biṣādu kāla gati jānī.
बन रघुपति सुरपुर नरनाहू । तुम्ह एहि भाँति तात कदराहू ॥
bana raghupati surapura naranāhū, tumha ehi bhām̐ti tāta kadarāhū.
परिजन प्रजा सचिव सब अंबा । तुम्हही सुत सब कहँ अवलंबा ॥
parijana prajā saciva saba aṁbā, tumhahī suta saba kaham̐ avalaṁbā.
लखि बिधि बाम कालु कठिनाई । धीरजु धरहु मातु बलि जाई ॥
lakhi bidhi bāma kālu kaṭhināī, dhīraju dharahu mātu bali jāī.
सिर धरि गुर आयसु अनुसरहू । प्रजा पालि परिजन दुखु हरहू ॥
sira dhari gura āyasu anusarahū, prajā pāli parijana dukhu harahū.
गुर के बचन सचिव अभिनंदनु । सुने भरत हिय हित जनु चंदनु ॥
gura ke bacana saciva abhinaṁdanu, sune bharata hiya hita janu caṁdanu.
सुनी बहोरि मातु मृदु बानी । सील सनेह सरल रस सानी ॥
sunī bahori mātu mṛdu bānī, sīla saneha sarala rasa sānī.

Trans:

Kausalyā took courage and spoke, 'Yes my son, you have your father's and your Gurū's commands, which you must respect and affectionately carry out. Cease to lament, knowing it to be the will of providence that Rāma is in banishment, the king in heaven, and you in such perplexity. You, my son," continued his mother, "are the sole refuge of your family, your people, and the ministers of state. Seeing gods against us and the fates untoward, summon up resolution. I, your mother, adjure you, obediently comply with your Gurū's commands; cherish your people, relieve the affliction of your family." Bharat listened to the Gurū's speech and the ministers' approval—words that to the ear are soothing as sandal paste. And he heard his mother's tender appeal fraught with the pathos of sincere affection;

छँद-chamda:

सानी सरल रस मातु बानी सुनि भरतु ब्याकुल भए।
sānī sarala rasa mātu bānī suni bharatu byākula bhae,
लोचन सरोरुह स्रवत सींचत बिरह उर अंकुर नए॥
locana saroruha sravata sīṁcata biraha ura aṁkura nae.
सो दसा देखत समय तेहि बिसरी सबहि सुधि देह की।
so dasā dekhata samaya tehi bisarī sabahi sudhi deha kī,
तुलसी सराहत सकल सादर सीवँ सहज सनेह की॥
tulasī sarāhata sakala sādara sīvaṁ sahaja saneha kī.

Trans:

but when he heard his mother's pathetic appeal, Bharat was overcome; his lotus eyes rained with tears that bedewed the fresh shoots of desolation in his soul. All those who saw his condition at that time forgot their own existence. Everyone, says Tulsīdās, reverently extolled him as the perfection of artless love.

सोरठा-sorathā:

भरतु कमल कर जोरि धीर धुरंधर धीर धरि।
bharatu kamala kara jori dhīra dhuraṁdhara dhīra dhari,
बचन अमिअँ जनु बोरि देत उचित उत्तर सबहि॥१७६॥
bacana amiaṁ janu bori deta ucita uttara sabahi. 176.

Trans:

Clasping his lotus hands, Bharat, the champion of honor, stoutly made answer to them all in noble words that seemed as if dipped in nectar.

मासपारायण अठारहवाँ विश्राम
māsapārāyaṇa aṭhārahavāṁ viśrāma
(Pause 18 for a Thirty-Day Recitation)

चौपाई-caupāī:

मोहि उपदेसु दीन्ह गुर नीका। प्रजा सचिव संमत सबही का॥
mohi upadesu dīnha gura nīkā, prajā saciva saṁmata sabahī kā.
मातु उचित धरि आयसु दीन्हा। अवसि सीस धरि चाहउँ कीन्हा॥
mātu ucita dhari āyasu dīnhā, avasi sīsa dhari cāhauṁ kīnhā.
गुर पितु मातु स्वामि हित बानी। सुनि मन मुदित करिअ भलि जानी॥
gura pitu mātu svāmi hita bānī, suni mana mudita karia bhali jānī.
उचित कि अनुचित किएँ बिचारू। धरमु जाइ सिर पातक भारू॥
ucita ki anucita kieṁ bicārū, dharamu jāi sira pātaka bhārū.
तुम्ह तौ देहु सरल सिख सोई। जो आचरत मोर भल होई॥
tumha tau dehu sarala sikha soī, jo ācarata mora bhala hoī.
जद्यपि यह समुझत हउँ नीकें। तदपि होत परितोषु न जी कें॥
jadyapi yaha samujhata hauṁ nīkeṁ, tadapi hota paritoṣu na jī keṁ.
अब तुम्ह बिनय मोरि सुनि लेहू। मोहि अनुहरत सिखावनु देहू॥
aba tumha binaya mori suni lehū, mohi anuharata sikhāvanu dehū.
ऊतरु देउँ छमब अपराधू। दुखित दोष गुन गनहिं न साधू॥
ūtaru deuṁ chamaba aparādhū, dukhita doṣa guna ganahiṁ na sādhū.

Trans:

"The Gurū has given me good advice, which has been approved by ministers, people, and all. My mother, too, has given me proper commands, and I must needs bow and obey. The injunctions of a Gurū, a father or mother, or master, or friend, should be cheerfully performed as soon as heard, presumed for the best; to deliberate whether they are right or wrong is a failure of duty and involves grievous sin. You have now given me honest advice, which it will be good for me to follow; yet, though I understand this clearly, my soul is still discontent. Hearken then to my prayer, and according to my circumstances so instruct me, forgiving my presumption in answering you: when a man is in distress good people do not reckon up his demerits or merits.

दोहा-dohā:

पितु सुरपुर सिय रामु बन करन कहहु मोहि राजु।
pitu surapura siya rāmu bana karana kahahu mohi rāju,
एहि तें जानहु मोर हित कै आपन बड़ काजु॥१७७॥
ehi teṁ jānahu mora hita kai āpana baṛa kāju. 177.

Trans:

My father is in heaven, and Sītā and Rāma in exile, and you tell me to be king? Is it my gain or your own advantage that you expect to result from this?

चौपाई-caupāī:

हित हमार सियपति सेवकाईं। सो हरि लीन्ह मातु कुटिलाईं॥
hita hamāra siyapati sevakāīṁ, so hari līnha mātu kuṭilāīṁ.
मैं अनुमानि दीख मन माहीं। आन उपायँ मोर हित नाहीं॥
maiṁ anumāni dīkha mana māhīṁ, āna upāyaṁ mora hita nāhīṁ.
सोक समाजु राजु केहि लेखें। लखन राम सिय बिनु पद देखें॥
soka samāju rāju kehi lekheṁ, lakhana rāma siya binu pada dekheṁ.
बादि बसन बिनु भूषन भारू। बादि बिरति बिनु ब्रह्म बिचारू॥
bādi basana binu bhūṣana bhārū, bādi birati binu brahma bicārū.
सरुज सरीर बादि बहु भोगा। बिनु हरिभगति जायँ जप जोगा॥
saruja sarīra bādi bahu bhogā, binu haribhagati jāyaṁ japa jogā.
जायँ जीव बिनु देह सुहाई। बादि मोर सबु बिनु रघुराई॥
jāyaṁ jīva binu deha suhāī, bādi mora sabu binu raghurāī.
जाउँ राम पहिं आयसु देहू। एकहिं आँक मोर हित एहू॥
jāuṁ rāma pahiṁ āyasu dehū, ekahiṁ āṁka mora hita ehū.
मोहि नृप करि भल आपन चहहू। सोउ सनेह जड़ता बस कहहू॥
mohi nṛpa kari bhala āpana cahahū, sou saneha jaṛatā basa kahahū.

Trans:

My gain is only to serve Sītā's Lord; and of that I have been robbed by my mother's wickedness. But after reflecting and searching my thoughts I find no other way of happiness other than that. Of what account is a throne with all its cares if I cannot see the feet of Lakshman, Rāma, Sītā? Without clothes a mass of jewels is of no use; of no use is asceticism without divine meditation; of no use is any enjoyment to a diseased body; prayer and penance go for naught without faith in Harī; without life, beauty of body is naught; and all is naught to me without Rāma. Permit me to join Rāma: this in one word is my only happiness. Again, in making me king, it is your own advantage that you seek; and you speak so only through ignorance caused by affection.

दोहा-dohā:

कैकेई सुअ कुटिलमति राम बिमुख गतलाज।
kaikeī sua kuṭilamati rāma bimukha gatalāja,
तुम्ह चाहत सुखु मोहबस मोहि से अधम कें राज॥१७८॥
tumha cāhata sukhu mohabasa mohi se adhama keṁ rāja. 178.

Trans:

In your infatuation you hope for happiness from the reign of such a wretched soul as I—Kaekayī's son, of wicked nature, Rāma's enemy, and lost to shame.

चौपाई-caupāī:

कहउँ साँचु सब सुनि पतिआहू। चाहिअ धरमसील नरनाहू॥
kahauṁ sāṁcu saba suni patiāhū, cāhia dharamasīla naranāhū.
मोहि राजु हठि देइहहु जबहीं। रसा रसातल जाइहि तबहीं॥
mohi rāju haṭhi deihahu jabahīṁ, rasā rasātala jāihi tabahīṁ.
मोहि समान को पाप निवासू। जेहि लगि सीय राम बनबासू॥
mohi samāna ko pāpa nivāsū, jehi lagi sīya rāma banabāsū.

रायँ राम कहुँ काननु दीन्हा । बिछुरत गमनु अमरपुर कीन्हा ॥
rāyaṁ rāma kahuṁ kānanu dīnhā, bichurata gamanu amarapura kīnhā.
मैं सठु सब अनरथ कर हेतू । बैठ बात सब सुनउँ सचेतू ॥
maiṁ saṭhu saba anaratha kara hetū, baiṭha bāta saba sunauṁ sacetū.
बिनु रघुबीर बिलोकि अबासू । रहे प्रान सहि जग उपहासू ॥
binu raghubīra biloki abāsū, rahe prāna sahi jaga upahāsū.
राम पुनीत बिषय रस रूखे । लोलुप भूमि भोग के भूखे ॥
rāma punīta biṣaya rasa rūkhe, lolupa bhūmi bhoga ke bhūkhe.
कहँ लगि कहौं हृदय कठिनाई । निदरि कुलिसु जेहिं लही बड़ाई ॥
kahaṁ lagi kahauṁ hṛdaya kaṭhināī, nidari kulisu jehiṁ lahī baṛāī.

Trans:

I speak the truth; hearken all and believe: In a king is required a righteous disposition. If you persist in giving the crown to me, earth will sink into hell. What guilty wretch is equal to me—for whose sake Sītā-Rāma were forced into the woods? The king banished Rāma, but died in losing him. I, the miserable cause of all this wrong-doing, sit and listen to it unmoved. I see the palace with no Rāma here, and yet live to endure the world's jeers. Holy Rāma eschews all pleasures of sense, and I, a greedy king, am hungering after enjoyment? In what words can I tell the hardness of my heart, which surpasses even adamant?

दोहा-dohā:

कारन तें कारजु कठिन होइ दोसु नहिं मोर ।
kārana teṁ kāraju kaṭhina hoi dosu nahiṁ mora,
कुलिस अस्थि तें उपल तें लोह कराल कठोर ॥ १७९ ॥
kulisa asthi teṁ upala teṁ loha karāla kaṭhora. 179.

Trans:

That every issue is harder than its origin is nature's law—is no fault of mine. Thunderbolt is harder than bone, and iron more stiff and unbending than the rock from which quarried.

चौपाई-caupāī:

कैकेई भव तनु अनुरागे । पावँर प्रान अघाइ अभागे ॥
kaikeī bhava tanu anurāge, pāvaṁra prāna aghāi abhāge.
जौं प्रिय बिरहँ प्रान प्रिय लागे । देखब सुनब बहुत अब आगे ॥
jauṁ priya birahaṁ prāna priya lāge, dekhaba sunaba bahuta aba āge.
लखन राम सिय कहुँ बनु दीन्हा । पठइ अमरपुर पति हित कीन्हा ॥
lakhana rāma siya kahuṁ banu dīnhā, paṭhai amarapura pati hita kīnhā.
लीन्ह बिधवपन अपजसु आपू । दीन्हेउ प्रजहि सोकु संतापू ॥
līnha bidhavapana apajasu āpū, dīnheu prajahi soku saṁtāpū.
मोहि दीन्ह सुखु सुजसु सुराजू । कीन्ह कैकईं सब कर काजू ॥
mohi dīnha sukhu sujasu surājū, kīnha kaikaīṁ saba kara kājū.
एहि तें मोर काह अब नीका । तेहि पर देन कहहु तुम्ह टीका ॥
ehi teṁ mora kāha aba nīkā, tehi para dena kahahu tumha ṭīkā.
कैकइ जठर जनमि जग माहीं । यह मोहि कहँ कछु अनुचित नाहीं ॥
kaikai jaṭhara janami jaga māhīṁ, yaha mohi kahaṁ kachu anucita nāhīṁ.
मोरि बात सब बिधिहिं बनाई । प्रजा पाँच कत करहु सहाई ॥
mori bāta saba bidhihiṁ banāī, prajā pāṁca kata karahu sahāī.

Trans:

Clinging to this body borne of Kaekayī, my worthless life is miserable indeed. If, bereaved of my beloved, life is still dear to me—much misery I have yet left—to see, hear, bear. Kaekayī has banished Lakshman, Rāma, Sītā, and for her own advantage has caused the death of the king. She has taken upon herself widowhood and disgrace, and has caused the people sorrow and afflictions; and to me she has allotted glory, honor and dominion, and thus has served the interests of all. I cannot expect greater good than this now, and yet you now cry out to make me king! True. Since I have been born into the world from Kaekayī's womb, I suppose this is all my just due. God himself has accomplished everything for me; and now you all combine to help my cause as well!

दोहा-dohā:

ग्रह ग्रहीत पुनि बात बस तेहि पुनि बीछी मार ।
graha grahīta puni bāta basa tehi puni bīchī māra,
तेहि पिआइअ बारुनी कहहु काह उपचार ॥ १८० ॥
tehi piāia bārunī kahahu kāha upacāra. 180.

Trans:

Stricken as I am by Fate; and then overcome by hysteria as well; and further stung by poisonous scorpion—and if all that delirium is not enough, you now give me some wine to drink! Tell me, sirs, what kind of treatment is all this?

चौपाई-caupāī:

कैकइ सुअन जोगु जग जोई । चतुर बिरंचि दीन्ह मोहि सोई ॥
kaikai suana jogu jaga joī, catura biraṁci dīnha mohi soī.
दसरथ तनय राम लघु भाई । दीन्हि मोहि बिधि बादि बड़ाई ॥
dasaratha tanaya rāma laghu bhāī, dīnhi mohi bidhi bādi baṛāī.
तुम्ह सब कहहु कढ़ावन टीका । राय रजायसु सब कहँ नीका ॥
tumha saba kahahu kaṛhāvana ṭīkā, rāya rajāyasu saba kahaṁ nīkā.
उतरु देउँ केहि बिधि केहि केही । कहहु सुखेन जथा रुचि जेही ॥
utaru deuṁ kehi bidhi kehi kehī, kahahu sukhena jathā ruci jehī.
मोहि कुमातु समेत बिहाई । कहहु कहिहि के कीन्ह भलाई ॥
mohi kumātu sameta bihāī, kahahu kahihi ke kīnha bhalāī.
मो बिनु को सचराचर माहीं । जेहि सिय रामु प्रानप्रिय नाहीं ॥
mo binu ko sacarācara māhīṁ, jehi siya rāmu prānapriya nāhīṁ.
परम हानि सब कहँ बड़ लाहू । अदिनु मोर नहि दूषन काहू ॥
parama hāni saba kahaṁ baṛa lāhū, adinu mora nahi dūṣana kāhū.
संसय सील प्रेम बस अहहू । सबुइ उचित सब जो कछु कहहू ॥
saṁsaya sīla prema basa ahahū, sabui ucita saba jo kachu kahahū.

Trans:

Truly, the wise Creator has ordained for me everything that befits a son of Kaekayī! That I am also Dashrath's son and Rāma's younger brother is an honor which god has wasted upon me in vain. You all tell me to allow myself to be crowned—for kingly power is desired by all men. How and whom shall I answer? You talk at random as the fancy takes you. Apart from myself and my unhappy mother, tell me who will say that I have acted rightly? Excepting myself, who else is there in the whole animate or inanimate creation that does not love Sītā and Rāma as their own life? That a universal calamity should be my great gain—alas this is my ill-fortune; I blame no one. You are moved by anxiety, kindness, and affection, and anything you say is all for the best.

दोहा-dohā:

राम मातु सुठि सरलचित मो पर प्रेमु बिसेषि ।
rāma mātu suṭhi saralacita mo para premu biseṣi,
कहइ सुभाय सनेह बस मोरि दीनता देखि ॥ १८१ ॥
kahai subhāya saneha basa mori dīnatā dekhi. 181.

Trans:

Rāma's mother is so utterly guileless and bears me such great affection that she speaks from natural amiability, after seeing my remorse.

चौपाई-caupāī:

गुर बिबेक सागर जगु जाना । जिन्हहि बिस्व कर बदर समाना ॥
gura bibeka sāgara jagu jānā, jinhahi bisva kara badara samānā.
मो कहँ तिलक साज सज सोऊ । भएँ बिधि बिमुख बिमुख सबु कोऊ ॥
mo kahaṁ tilaka sāja saja soū, bhaeṁ bidhi bimukha bimukha sabu koū.
परिहरि रामु सीय जग माहीं । कोउ न कहिहि मोर मत नाहीं ॥
parihari rāmu sīya jaga māhīṁ, kou na kahihi mora mata nāhīṁ.

सो मैं सुनब सहब सुखु मानी । अंतहुँ कीच तहाँ जहँ पानी ॥
so maiṁ sunaba sahaba sukhu mānī, aṁtahuṁ kīca tahāṁ jahaṁ pānī.
डरु न मोहि जग कहिहि कि पोचू । परलोकहु कर नाहिन सोचू ॥
ḍaru na mohi jaga kahihi ki pocū, paralokahu kara nāhina socū.
एकइ उर बस दुसह दवारी । मोहि लगि भे सिय रामु दुखारी ॥
ekai ura basa dusaha davārī, mohi lagi bhe siya rāmu dukhārī.
जीवन लाहु लखन भल पावा । सबु तजि राम चरन मनु लावा ॥
jīvana lāhu lakhana bhala pāvā, sabu taji rāma carana manu lāvā.
मोर जनम रघुबर बन लागी । झूठ काह पछिताउँ अभागी ॥
mora janama raghubara bana lāgī, jhūṭha kāha pachitāuṁ abhāgī.

Trans:

The Gurū, as all the world knows, is an ocean of wisdom, and the universe is like a plum in the palm of his hand. He too is making ready for my coronation! When God is against me, everyone is against me. Except Rāma and Sītā there is not anyone in the whole world who will not say this was a scheme of mine, and I must listen and bear it patiently. Wherever there is water, mud will be there eventually. But, I am not afraid of the world calling me vile; I have no thought for heaven: the one great intolerable anguish of soul is this: that it is through me that Sītā and Rāma have been rendered unhappy. Well has Lakshman reaped his life's reward—who left all and cleaved to Rāma's feet; while my birth has been the cause of Rāma's banishment. Wretch that I am, why thus lament in vain?

दोहा-dohā:

आपनि दारुन दीनता कहउँ सबहि सिरु नाइ ।
āpani dāruna dīnatā kahauṁ sabahi siru nāi,
देखें बिनु रघुनाथ पद जिय कै जरनि न जाइ ॥ १८२॥
dekheṁ binu raghunātha pada jiya kai jarani na jāi. 182.

Trans:

I declare before you all my grievous distress, unless I see Rāma's feet, the fire in my soul cannot be extinguished.

चौपाई-caupāī:

आन उपाउ मोहि नहिं सूझा । को जिय कै रघुबर बिनु बूझा ॥
āna upāu mohi nahiṁ sūjhā, ko jiya kai raghubara binu būjhā.
एकहिं आँक इहइ मन माहीं । प्रातकाल चलिहउँ प्रभु पाहीं ॥
ekahiṁ āṁka ihai mana māhīṁ, prātakāla calihauṁ prabhu pāhīṁ.
जद्यपि मैं अनभल अपराधी । भै मोहि कारन सकल उपाधी ॥
jadyapi maiṁ anabhala aparādhī, bhai mohi kārana sakala upādhī.
तदपि सरन सनमुख मोहि देखी । छमि सब करिहहिं कृपा बिसेषी ॥
tadapi sarana sanamukha mohi dekhī, chami saba karihahiṁ kṛpā biseṣī.
सील सकुच सुठि सरल सुभाऊ । कृपा सनेह सदन रघुराऊ ॥
sīla sakuca suṭhi sarala subhāū, kṛpā saneha sadana raghurāū.
अरिहुक अनभल कीन्ह न रामा । मैं सिसु सेवक जद्यपि बामा ॥
arihuka anabhala kīnha na rāmā, maiṁ sisu sevaka jadyapi bāmā.
तुम्ह पै पाँच मोर भल मानी । आयसु आसिष देहु सुबानी ॥
tumha pai pāṁca mora bhala mānī, āyasu āsiṣa dehu subānī.
जेहिं सुनि बिनय मोहि जनु जानी । आवहिं बहुरि रामु रजधानी ॥
jehiṁ suni binaya mohi janu jānī, āvahiṁ bahuri rāmu rajadhānī.

Trans:

No other remedy can be seen by me; without Raghubar what care I for life? This wish alone is stamped upon my soul: at daybreak let me follow my Lord. Although I am a guilty wretch, and all this trouble is on my account, still when he sees my suppliant mien he will in his great mercy forgive me—for Raghurāī is so modest and utterly guileless of disposition; and such a home of mercy and tenderness, that he would never injure even an enemy; while I, bad as I am, am his son and his servant. Be pleased, sirs, then to give me your blessing and permit me to depart, knowing it to be for my good; so Rāma will come again to his kingdom, after hearing my prayers and considering my devotion.

दोहा-dohā:

जद्यपि जनमु कुमातु तें मैं सठु सदा सदोस ।
jadyapi janamu kumātu teṁ maiṁ saṭhu sadā sadosa,
आपन जानि न त्यागिहहिं मोहि रघुबीर भरोस ॥ १८३॥
āpana jāni na tyāgihahiṁ mohi raghubīra bharosa. 183.

Trans:

Though born of a wicked mother, and myself evil and ever doing wrong, still I am confident of Raghubar that he will know me for his own, and not abandon me."

चौपाई-caupāī:

भरत बचन सब कहँ प्रिय लागे । राम सनेह सुधाँ जनु पागे ॥
bharata bacana saba kahaṁ priya lāge, rāma saneha sudhāṁ janu pāge.
लोग बियोग बिषम बिष दागे । मंत्र सबीज सुनत जनु जागे ॥
loga biyoga biṣama biṣa dāge, maṁtra sabīja sunata janu jāge.
मातु सचिव गुर पुर नर नारी । सकल सनेहँ बिकल भए भारी ॥
mātu saciva gura pura nara nārī, sakala sanehaṁ bikala bhae bhārī.
भरतहि कहहिं सराहि सराही । राम प्रेम मूरति तनु आही ॥
bharatahi kahahi sarāhi sarāhī, rāma prema mūrati tanu āhī.
तात भरत अस काहे न कहहू । प्रान समान राम प्रिय अहहू ॥
tāta bharata asa kāhe na kahahū, prāna samāna rāma priya ahahū.
जो पावँरु अपनी जड़ताईं । तुम्हहि सुगाइ मातु कुटिलाईं ॥
jo pāvaṁru apanī jaṛatāīṁ, tumhahi sugāi mātu kuṭilāīṁ.
सो सठु कोटिक पुरुष समेता । बसिहि कलप सत नरक निकेता ॥
so saṭhu koṭika puruṣa sametā, basihi kalapa sata naraka niketā.
अहि अघ अवगुन नहिं मनि गहई । हरइ गरल दुख दारिद दहई ॥
ahi agha avaguna nahiṁ mani gahaī, harai garala dukha dārida dahaī.

Trans:

Bharat's words pleased all, imbued as they were with the nectar of piety. The people suffering from the baneful poison of separation revived as if at the sound of a healing charm. The queen-mothers, the ministers, the Gurū, and all the men and women in the city were agitated by the vehemence of their affection and kept on telling Bharat's praises: "Your body is the personification of devotion to Rāma. It is no wonder you should speak thus, since you are as precious to Rāma as his own life. If any churl in his folly ascribe to you your mother's sin, the wretch—along with all who are his own from generation to generation—shall have their abode in hell for hundreds of ages. The jewel is not infected with the guilt and villainy of the serpent—on whose head it was found; on the other hand, it is an antidote to poison and subdues pain and poverty.

दोहा-dohā:

अवसि चलिअ बन रामु जहँ भरत मंत्रु भल कीन्ह ।
avasi calia bana rāmu jahaṁ bharata maṁtru bhala kīnha,
सोक सिंधु बूडत सबहि तुम्ह अवलंबनु दीन्ह ॥ १८४॥
soka siṁdhu būṛata sabahi tumha avalaṁbanu dīnha. 184.

Trans:

"By all means let us follow Rāma to the woods. Bharat, you have given us good advice; sinking as we all were in an ocean of despair, you have held out help to all of us."

चौपाई-caupāī:

भा सब कें मन मोदु न थोरा । जनु घन धुनि सुनि चातक मोरा ॥
bhā saba keṁ mana modu na thorā, janu ghana dhuni suni cātaka morā.
चलत प्रात लखि निरनउ नीके । भरतु प्रानप्रिय भे सबही के ॥
calata prāta lakhi niranau nīke, bharatu prānapriya bhe sabahī ke.
मुनिहि बंदि भरतहि सिरु नाई । चले सकल घर बिदा कराई ॥

munihi baṁdi bharatahi siru nāī, cale sakala ghara bidā karāī.

धन्य भरत जीवनु जग माहीं । सीलु सनेहु सराहत जाहीं ॥

dhanya bharata jīvanu jaga māhīṁ, sīlu sanehu sarāhata jāhīṁ.

कहहिं परसपर भा बड़ काजू । सकल चलै कर साजहिं साजू ॥

kahahiṁ parasapara bhā baṛa kājū, sakala calai kara sājahiṁ sājū.

जेहि राखहिं रहु घर रखवारी । सो जानइ जनु गरदनि मारी ॥

jehi rākhahiṁ rahu ghara rakhavārī, so jānai janu garadani mārī.

कोउ कह रहन कहिअ नहिं काहू । को न चहइ जग जीवन लाहू ॥

kou kaha rahana kahia nahiṁ kāhū, ko na cahai jaga jīvana lāhū.

Trans:

There was as great joy in the hearts of all, as when the Chātak and peacock hear the sound of thunder. To start tomorrow seemed an excellent resolution, and Bharat was to everyone dear as their own life. After reverencing the sage and bowing their heads to Bharat, they took leave and went to their several homes, praising as they went his affectionate disposition, and how his life was a blessing to the whole world. Exclaiming to one another, "What a glorious idea!" they began to make hurried preparations. Whoever was left with orders to keep watch at home, felt it like his death-stroke, and one would cry "No one ought to be told to stay. Who does not desire life's best reward?

दोहा-dohā:

जरउ सो संपति सदन सुखु सुहृद मातु पितु भाइ ।

jarau so saṁpati sadana sukhu suhṛda mātu pitu bhāi,

सनमुख होत जो राम पद करै न सहस सहाइ ॥ १८५॥

sanamukha hota jo rāma pada karai na sahasa sahāi. 185.

Trans:

Perish that property, and vacate the house, and woe to that fortune, and abandon those friends, parents, kinsmen, all—who do not help to bring one closer up to Rāma."

चौपाई-caupāī:

घर घर साजहिं बाहन नाना । हरषु हृदयँ परभात पयाना ॥

ghara ghara sājahiṁ bāhana nānā, haraṣu hṛdayaṁ parabhāta payānā.

भरत जाइ घर कीन्ह बिचारू । नगरु बाजि गज भवन भँडारू ॥

bharata jāi ghara kīnha bicārū, nagaru bāji gaja bhavana bhaṁḍārū.

संपति सब रघुपति कै आही । जौं बिनु जतन चलौं तजि ताही ॥

saṁpati saba raghupati kai āhī, jau binu jatana calauṁ taji tāhī.

तौ परिनाम न मोरि भलाई । पाप सिरोमनि साइँ दोहाई ॥

tau parināma na mori bhalāī, pāpa siromani sāiṁ dohāī.

करइ स्वामि हित सेवकु सोई । दूषन कोटि देइ किन कोई ॥

karai svāmi hita sevaku soī, dūṣana koṭi dei kina koī.

अस बिचारि सुचि सेवक बोले । जे सपनेहुँ निज धरम न डोले ॥

asa bicāri suci sevaka bole, je sapanehuṁ nija dharama na ḍole.

कहि सबु मरमु धरमु भल भाषा । जो जेहि लायक सो तेहिं राखा ॥

kahi sabu maramu dharamu bhala bhāṣā, jo jehi lāyaka so tehiṁ rākhā.

करि सबु जतनु राखि रखवारे । राम मातु पहिं भरतु सिधारे ॥

kari sabu jatanu rākhi rakhavāre, rāma mātu pahiṁ bharatu sidhāre.

Trans:

In every house carriages of all kinds were making ready, and the start tomorrow was a heartfelt joy. Bharat pondered upon reaching home, "The city, with its horses, elephants, palaces and treasuries, and all its wealth is Rāma's. If I recklessly go and leave it, in the end it will not be good for me; for to cause injury to one's own lord is a crowning sin. A good servant acts for his master's interests, however much others may abuse him." Thinking thusly he called such faithful servants as would never dream of failing in their duty, and after declaring to them his intention, and instructing them in their work, he told them off for the post for which they were severally fit. When he had thus diligently posted the guards, he proceeded to visit Rāma's mother.

दोहा-dohā:

आरत जननी जानि सब भरत सनेह सुजान ।

ārata jananī jāni saba bharata saneha sujāna,

कहेउ बनावन पालकीं सजन सुखासन जान ॥ १८६॥

kaheu banāvana pālakīṁ sajana sukhāsana jāna. 186.

Trans:

Knowing all the mothers in distress, Bharat, who understood the ways of love, ordered palanquins to be got ready and sedan-chairs to be equipped.

चौपाई-caupāī:

चक्क चक्कि जिमि पुर नर नारी । चहत प्रात उर आरत भारी ॥

cakka cakki jimi pura nara nārī, cahata prāta ura ārata bhārī.

जागत सब निसि भयउ बिहाना । भरत बोलाए सचिव सुजाना ॥

jāgata saba nisi bhayau bihānā, bharata bolāe saciva sujānā.

कहेउ लेहु सबु तिलक समाजू । बनहिं देब मुनि रामहि राजू ॥

kaheu lehu sabu tilaka samājū, banahiṁ deba muni rāmahi rājū.

बेगि चलहु सुनि सचिव जोहारे । तुरत तुरग रथ नाग सँवारे ॥

begi calahu suni saciva johāre, turata turaga ratha nāga saṁvāre.

अरुंधती अरु अगिनि समाऊ । रथ चढ़ि चले प्रथम मुनिराऊ ॥

aruṁdhatī aru agini samāū, ratha caṛhi cale prathama munirāū.

बिप्र बृंद चढ़ि बाहन नाना । चले सकल तप तेज निधाना ॥

bipra bṛṁda caṛhi bāhana nānā, cale sakala tapa teja nidhānā.

नगर लोग सब सजि सजि जाना । चित्रकूट कहँ कीन्ह पयाना ॥

nagara loga saba saji saji jānā, citrakūṭa kahaṁ kīnha payānā.

सिबिका सुभग न जाहिं बखानी । चढ़ि चढ़ि चलत भईं सब रानी ॥

sibikā subhaga na jāhiṁ bakhānī, caṛhi caṛhi calata bhaīṁ saba rānī.

Trans:

The men and women of the city, like the *chakwā* and *chakwi*, were anxious at heart for the dawn—when they could start. The whole night had been spent in watching, when Bharat summoned his wise counselors and said to them, "Make ready all materials for the coronation and there in the forest, sirs, invest Rāma with the sovereignty; do start at once." At his word they bowed and speedily made ready horses, carriages, and elephants. The king of sages, Vasishtha, first mounted his chariot and led the way with his spouse Arundhati, and all the materials for *Agnīhotra*. A host of Brahmins, renowned for their asceticism, followed in vehicles of different kinds, and next the citizens on their own conveyances all set forth for Chitra-kūt. The elegance of the palanquins in which the different *Rānī*s were seated was lovely beyond words.

दोहा-dohā:

सौंपि नगर सुचि सेवकनि सादर सकल चलाइ ।

sauṁpi nagara suci sevakani sādara sakala calāi,

सुमिरि राम सिय चरन तब चले भरत दोउ भाइ ॥ १८७॥

sumiri rāma siya carana taba cale bharata dou bhāi. 187.

Trans:

After making over the city to his faithful servants and ceremoniously starting the procession, Bharat himself with his brother started too, his thoughts fixed on the holy feet of Rāma and Sītā.

चौपाई-caupāī:

राम दरस बस सब नर नारी । जनु करि करिनि चले तकि बारी ॥

rāma darasa basa saba nara nārī, janu kari karini cale taki bārī.

बन सिय रामु समुझि मन माहीं । सानुज भरत पयादेहिं जाहीं ॥

bana siya rāmu samujhi mana māhīṁ, sānuja bharata payādehiṁ jāhīṁ.

देखि सनेहु लोग अनुरागे । उतरि चले हय गय रथ त्यागे ॥

dekhi sanehu loga anurāge, utari cale haya gaya ratha tyāge.

जाइ समीप राखि निज डोली । राम मातु मृदु बानी बोली ॥
jāi samīpa rākhi nija ḍolī, rāma mātu mṛdu bānī bolī.
तात चढ़हु रथ बलि महतारी । होइहि प्रिय परिवारु दुखारी ॥
tāta caṛhahu ratha bali mahatārī, hoihi priya parivāru dukhārī.
तुम्हरें चलत चलिहि सबु लोगू । सकल सोक कृस नहिं मग जोगू ॥
tumhareṁ calata calihi sabu logū, sakala soka kṛsa nahiṁ maga jogū.
सिर धरि बचन चरन सिरु नाई । रथ चढ़ि चलत भए दोउ भाई ॥
sira dhari bacana carana siru nāī, ratha caṛhi calata bhae dou bhāī.
तमसा प्रथम दिवस करि बासू । दूसर गोमति तीर निवासू ॥
tamasā prathama divasa kari bāsū, dūsara gomati tīra nivāsū.

Trans:

All the people were as eager for a sight of Rāma as when a herd of elephants makes a rush for a stream. Reflecting within themselves that Sītā and Rāma were in exile, Bharat and his brother went on foot. The people were moved by their affection and themselves dismounted and left horses, elephants and carriages. But Rāma's mother stopped her palanquin by his side and softly said, "My son, I entreat you to mount your chariot, or all your people will be sufferers; if you walk, they will all walk, and they are so wasted with sorrow that they are not fit for the journey." Obedient to her commands, he bowed his head to her feet, and with his brother mounted the chariot. They halted the first day at the Tamas, and the second on the bank of the Gomati.

दोहा-dohā:

पय अहार फल असन एक निसि भोजन एक लोग ।
paya ahāra phala asana eka nisi bhojana eka loga,
करत राम हित नेम ब्रत परिहरि भूषन भोग ॥ १८८ ॥
karata rāma hita nema brata parihari bhūṣana bhoga. 188.

Trans:

Out of devotion to Rāma, some vowed to drink only water, some to eat nothing but fruit, others to make only one meal at night and they forswore all luxuries of dress and food.

चौपाई-caupāī:

सई तीर बसि चले बिहाने । सृंगबेरपुर सब निअराने ॥
saī tīra basi cale bihāne, sṛṁgaberapura saba niarāne.
समाचार सब सुने निषादा । हृदयँ बिचार करइ सबिषादा ॥
samācāra saba sune niṣādā, hṛdayaṁ bicāra karai sabiṣādā.
कारन कवन भरतु बन जाहीं । है कछु कपट भाउ मन माहीं ॥
kārana kavana bharatu bana jāhīṁ, hai kachu kapaṭa bhāu mana māhīṁ.
जौं पै जियँ न होति कुटिलाई । तौ कत लीन्ह संग कटकाई ॥
jauṁ pai jiyaṁ na hoti kuṭilāī, tau kata līnha saṁga kaṭakāī.
जानहिं सानुज रामहि मारी । करउँ अकंटक राजु सुखारी ॥
jānahiṁ sānuja rāmahi mārī, karauṁ akaṁṭaka rāju sukhārī.
भरत न राजनीति उर आनी । तब कलंकु अब जीवन हानी ॥
bharata na rājanīti ura ānī, taba kalaṁku aba jīvana hānī.
सकल सुरासुर जुरहिं जुझारा । रामहि समर न जीतनिहारा ॥
sakala surāsura jurahiṁ jujhārā, rāmahi samara na jītanihārā.
का आचरजु भरतु अस करहीं । नहिं बिष बेलि अमिअ फल फरहीं ॥
kā ācaraju bharatu asa karahīṁ, nahiṁ biṣa beli amia phala pharahīṁ.

Trans:

After resting on the banks of Sai river, they started at dawn and drew near to the city of Shring-vera. When the Nishād heard the news he thought sadly to himself: "For what reason is Bharat going to the forest? He has some evil design at heart. If he had no wrong intention why should he bring an army with him? He thinks to kill Rāma and his brother, and then to reign in ease and security. Bharat has not taken to heart the maxims of sound polity; there was disgrace already, and now there will be loss of life. If all the gods and demons were to combine to fight, they could never conquer Rāma in battle. What wonder that Bharat should act thusly; fruits of ambrosia do not grow from a poison stock."

दोहा-dohā:

अस बिचारि गुहँ ग्याति सन कहेउ सजग सब होहु ।
asa bicāri guhaṁ gyāti sana kaheu sajaga saba hohu,
हथवाँसहु बोरहु तरनि कीजिअ घाटारोहु ॥ १८९ ॥
hathavāṁsahu borahu tarani kījia ghāṭārohu. 189.

Trans:

Having thus reflected, Gūha cried to his kinsmen: "Be on the alert, up and sink the boats, and blockade the *ghāts*.

चौपाई-caupāī:

होहु सँजोइल रोकहु घाटा । ठाटहु सकल मरै के ठाटा ॥
hohu saṁjoila rokahu ghāṭā, ṭhāṭahu sakala marai ke ṭhāṭā.
सनमुख लोह भरत सन लेऊँ । जिअत न सुरसरि उतरन देऊँ ॥
sanamukha loha bharata sana leūṁ, jiata na surasari utarana deūṁ.
समर मरनु पुनि सुरसरि तीरा । राम काजु छनभंगु सरीरा ॥
samara maranu puni surasari tīrā, rāma kāju chanabhaṁgu sarīrā.
भरत भाइ नृपु मैं जन नीचू । बड़ें भाग असि पाइअ मीचू ॥
bharata bhāi nṛpu maiṁ jana nīcū, baṛeṁ bhāga asi pāia mīcū.
स्वामि काज करिहउँ रन रारी । जस धवलिहउँ भुवन दस चारी ॥
svāmi kāja karihauṁ rana rārī, jasa dhavalihauṁ bhuvana dasa cārī.
तजउँ प्रान रघुनाथ निहोरें । दुहूँ हाथ मुद मोदक मोरें ॥
tajauṁ prāna raghunātha nihoreṁ, duhūṁ hātha muda modaka moreṁ.
साधु समाज न जाकर लेखा । राम भगत महुँ जासु न रेखा ॥
sādhu samāja na jākara lekhā, rāma bhagata mahuṁ jāsu na rekhā.
जायँ जिअत जग सो महि भारू । जननी जौबन बिटप कुठारू ॥
jāyaṁ jiata jaga so mahi bhārū, jananī jaubana biṭapa kuṭhārū.

Trans:

Make ready and barricade every pass, equip yourselves with every instrument of death. Take up arms against Bharat, and never let him cross alive the Gangā. To die in battle and on the Gangā bank, and in Rāma's cause to lay down this frail body—that too for one so mean as I, to join battle with a king like Bharat—indeed it is great gain for me if I meet my death this way. If I war and fight on my Lord's behalf, I reap brilliant renown throughout the fourteen spheres. If I lose my life for Raghunāth I shall have both hands full of luscious sweets. Whoever is not numbered among the just, nor counted among Rāma's votaries, is all the time that he lives only a burden to earth—a very axe to the foot of the tree of his mother's youth."

दोहा-dohā:

बिगत बिषाद निषादपति सबहि बढ़ाइ उछाहु ।
bigata biṣāda niṣādapati sabahi baṛhāi uchāhu,
सुमिरि राम मागेउ तुरत तरकस धनुष सनाहु ॥ १९० ॥
sumiri rāma māgeu turata tarakasa dhanuṣa sanāhu. 190.

Trans:

The Nishād king thus fearlessly excited the ardor of his followers, and remembering Lord Rāma called in haste for quiver, bow, and coat of mail.

चौपाई-caupāī:

बेगहु भाइहु सजहु सँजोऊ । सुनि रजाइ कदराइ न कोऊ ॥
begahu bhāihu sajahu saṁjoū, suni rajāi kadarāi na koū.
भलेहिं नाथ सब कहहिं सहरषा । एकहिं एक बढ़ावइ करषा ॥
bhalehiṁ nātha saba kahahiṁ saharaṣā, ekahiṁ eka baṛhāvai karaṣā.
चले निषाद जोहारि जोहारी । सूर सकल रन रूचइ रारी ॥
cale niṣāda johāri johārī, sūra sakala rana rūcai rārī.
सुमिरि राम पद पंकज पनहीं । भाथीं बाँधि चढ़ाइन्हि धनहीं ॥

sumiri rāma pada paṁkaja panahīṁ, bhāthīṁ bāṁdhi caṛhāinhi dhanahīṁ.

अँगरी पहिरि कूँड़ि सिर धरहीं । फरसा बाँस सेल सम करहीं ॥
aṁgarī pahiri kūṁṛi sira dharahīṁ, pharasā bāṁsa sela sama karahīṁ.

एक कुसल अति ओड़न खाँड़े । कूदहिं गगन मनहुँ छिति छाँड़े ॥
eka kusala ati oṛana khāṁṛe, kūdahiṁ gagana manahuṁ chiti chāṁṛe.

निज निज साजु समाजु बनाई । गुह राउतहि जोहारे जाई ॥
nija nija sāju samāju banāī, guha rāutahi johāre jāī.

देखि सुभट सब लायक जाने । लै लै नाम सकल सनमाने ॥
dekhi subhaṭa saba lāyaka jāne, lai lai nāma sakala sanamāne.

Trans:

"Hasten, brethren, to complete your equipment, and after hearing my command let no one hesitate." All cheerfully responded "'tis well, my lord," and mutually encouraged each other's ardor. Bowing again and again before the Nishād, all the gallant warriors, eager for the fray, invoking the thought of Rāma's lotus feet, girt themselves with quiver, slung on the bow, donned their coats of mail, put helmets on head, and furbished up axe and bludgeon and spear—some so expert in the use of shield and sword that they seemed when they sprung into the air as though they had left the earth for good. When each and all had prepared their full arrangements they went and bowed before chief Gūha. Seeing his gallant warriors so fit and ready, he addressed them each by name with honoring phrases.

दोहा-dohā:

भाइहु लावहु धोख जनि आजु काज बड़ मोहि ।
bhāihu lāvahu dhokha jani āju kāja baṛa mohi,
सुनि सरोष बोले सुभट बीर अधीर न होहि ॥ १९१ ॥
suni saroṣa bole subhaṭa bīra adhīra na hohi. 191.

Trans:

"Do not play me false, my brethren; this is a great day's work for me." At this they cried with vehemence, "Fear not, captain;

चौपाई-caupāī:

राम प्रताप नाथ बल तोरे । करहिं कटकु बिनु भट बिनु घोरे ॥
rāma pratāpa nātha bala tore, karahiṁ kaṭaku binu bhaṭa binu ghore.

जीवत पाउ न पाछें धरहीं । रुंड मुंडमय मेदिनि करहीं ॥
jīvata pāu na pācheṁ dharahīṁ, ruṁḍa muṁḍamaya medini karahīṁ.

दीख निषादनाथ भल टोलू । कहेउ बजाउ जुझाऊ ढोलू ॥
dīkha niṣādanātha bhala ṭolū, kaheu bajāu jujhāū ḍholū.

एतना कहत छींक भइ बाँए । कहेउ सगुनिअन्ह खेत सुहाए ॥
etanā kahata chīṁka bhai bāṁe, kaheu sagunianha kheta suhāe.

बूढ़ु एकु कह सगुन बिचारी । भरतहि मिलिअ न होइहि रारी ॥
būṛhu eku kaha saguna bicārī, bharatahi milia na hoihi rārī.

रामहि भरतु मनावन जाहीं । सगुन कहइ अस बिग्रहु नाहीं ॥
rāmahi bharatu manāvana jāhīṁ, saguna kahai asa bigrahu nāhīṁ.

सुनि गुह कहइ नीक कह बूढ़ा । सहसा करि पछिताहिं बिमूढ़ा ॥
suni guha kahai nīka kaha būṛhā, sahasā kari pachitāhiṁ bimūṛhā.

भरत सुभाउ सीलु बिनु बूझें । बड़ि हित हानि जानि बिनु जूझें ॥
bharata subhāu sīlu binu būjheṁ, baṛi hita hāni jāni binu jūjheṁ.

Trans:

by Rāma's favor and your might, my lord, we will leave the host without a single fighting-man or horse. While life lasts we will never draw back our foot, and will make the earth a heap of corpses and skulls." When the Nishād lord had inspected his gallant band he cried, "Beat the drum for the onset." When he had so said, someone sneezed on the left. The soothsayers exclaimed, "A prosperous issue to the battle!" One old man thought over the omen and said, "The omen tells us that there will be no discord. There will be no conflict. Bharat is out to persuade Shrī Rāma to return. So first let's meet Bharat." On hearing this Gūha said, "The elder has spoken well; fools act in haste and repent. Unless we ascertain Bharat's temper and disposition, we may do ourselves harm by fighting without knowing.

दोहा-dohā:

गहहु घाट भट समिटि सब लेउँ मरम मिलि जाइ ।
gahahu ghāṭa bhaṭa samiṭi saba leuṁ marama mili jāi,
बूझि मित्र अरि मध्य गति तस तब करिहउँ आइ ॥ १९२ ॥
būjhi mitra ari madhya gati tasa taba karihauṁ āi. 192.

Trans:

Close up, my warriors, and blockade the pass—until I meet Bharat and get insight to his heart. When we know whether he is a friend, an enemy, or a neutral, we can then lay our plans accordingly.

चौपाई-caupāī:

लखब सनेहु सुभायँ सुहाएँ । बैरु प्रीति नहिं दुरइँ दुराएँ ॥
lakhaba sanehu subhāyaṁ suhāeṁ, bairu prīti nahiṁ duraiṁ durāeṁ.

अस कहि भेंट सँजोवन लागे । कंद मूल फल खग मृग मागे ॥
asa kahi bheṁṭa saṁjovana lāge, kaṁda mūla phala khaga mṛga māge.

मीन पीन पाठीन पुराने । भरि भरि भार कहारन्ह आने ॥
mīna pīna pāṭhīna purāne, bhari bhari bhāra kahāranha āne.

मिलन साजु सजि मिलन सिधाए । मंगल मूल सगुन सुभ पाए ॥
milana sāju saji milana sidhāe, maṁgala mūla saguna subha pāe.

देखि दूरि तें कहि निज नामू । कीन्ह मुनीसहि दंड प्रनामू ॥
dekhi dūri teṁ kahi nija nāmū, kīnha munīsahi daṁḍa pranāmū.

जानि रामप्रिय दीन्हि असीसा । भरतहि कहेउ बुझाइ मुनीसा ॥
jāni rāmapriya dīnhi asīsā, bharatahi kaheu bujhāi munīsā.

राम सखा सुनि संदनु त्यागा । चले उतरि उमगत अनुरागा ॥
rāma sakhā suni saṁdanu tyāgā, cale utari umagata anurāgā.

गाउँ जाति गुहँ नाउँ सुनाई । कीन्ह जोहारु माथ महि लाई ॥
gāuṁ jāti guhaṁ nāuṁ sunāī, kīnha johāru mātha mahi lāī.

Trans:

We shall soon test his devotion and honest intent; hatred and love cannot be concealed." So saying, he began to make ready a present, and sent for bulbs, roots and fruit, birds and beasts, with large *pathinas*—the finest of fish, all brought by *kahars* by the baskets full. When everything was arranged they went out to meet the train, and had the most auspicious omens of good fortune. As soon as he saw the great sage Vasishtha, from afar Gūha declared his name and prostrated himself before him. Knowing him to be a friend of Rāma's, the saint gave him his blessing and told Bharat about him—who, on learning that he was Rāma's friend, left his chariot and advanced on foot to meet him full of affection. Gūha declared his home and race and name, and making obeisance laid his forehead to the ground.

दोहा-dohā:

करत दंडवत देखि तेहि भरत लीन्ह उर लाइ ।
karata daṁḍavata dekhi tehi bharata līnha ura lāi,
मनहुँ लखन सन भेंट भइ प्रेम न हृदयँ समाइ ॥ १९३ ॥
manahuṁ lakhana sana bheṁṭa bhai prema na hṛdayaṁ samāi. 193.

Trans:

But Bharat seeing him prostrate, immediately took him to his bosom with as much incontrollable affection as though he had met Lakshman.

चौपाई-caupāī:

भेंटत भरतु ताहि अति प्रीती । लोग सिहाहिं प्रेम कै रीती ॥
bheṁṭata bharatu tāhi ati prītī, loga sihāhiṁ prema kai rītī.

धन्य धन्य धुनि मंगल मूला । सुर सराहि तेहि बरिसहिं फूला ॥
dhanya dhanya dhuni maṁgala mūlā, sura sarāhi tehi barisahiṁ phūlā.

लोक बेद सब भाँतिहिं नीचा । जासु छाँह छुइ लेइअ सींचा ॥
loka beda saba bhāṁtihiṁ nīcā, jāsu chāṁha chui leia sīṁcā.

तेहि भरि अंक राम लघु भ्राता । मिलत पुलक परिपूरित गाता ॥
tehi bhari aṁka rāma laghu bhrātā, milata pulaka paripūrita gātā.
राम राम कहि जे जमुहाहीं । तिन्हहि न पाप पुंज समुहाहीं ॥
rāma rāma kahi je jamuhāhīṁ, tinhahi na pāpa puṁja samuhāhīṁ.
यह तौ राम लाइ उर लीन्हा । कुल समेत जगु पावन कीन्हा ॥
yaha tau rāma lāi ura līnhā, kula sameta jagu pāvana kīnhā.
करमनास जलु सुरसरि परई । तेहि को कहहु सीस नहिं धरई ॥
karamanāsa jalu surasari paraī, tehi ko kahahu sīsa nahiṁ dharaī.
उलटा नामु जपत जगु जाना । बालमीकि भए ब्रह्म समाना ॥
ulaṭā nāmu japata jagu jānā, bālamīki bhae brahma samānā.

Trans:

Bharat received him with the greatest tenderness, and the people extolled the manner of his affection. There was a jubilant cry of 'Glory, Glory', as the gods applauded and rained down flowers upon him. "This man is low in the customs of the world and scriptural prescriptions—so much so that even contact with his shadow requires ablution; and yet Rāma's brother embraces him in his arms and thrills all over with delight at meeting him. A multitude of sins turn away if one is fond of saying 'Rāma', Rāma' even while yawning. Here is one whom Rāma had clasped to his bosom and thereby purified him and all his family. If water of the Karmnāshā falls into the Gangā, tell me who will refuse to reverence it? And it is known throughout the world that Vālmikī was made equal to Brahmmā simply for repeating Rāma's name backwards.

दोहा-dohā:

स्वपच सबर खस जमन जड़ पावँर कोल किरात ।
svapaca sabara khasa jamana jaṛa pāvaṁra kola kirāta,
रामु कहत पावन परम होत भुवन बिख्यात ॥ १९४॥
rāmu kahata pāvana parama hota bhuvana bikhyāta. 194.

Trans:

Even a *Chandāl*, a *Savara*, a *Khasiyā*, a cloddish barbarian, an outcast, a *Kol*, or a *Kirāt*, by repeating the name of Rāma becomes most holy and renowned throughout the world.

चौपाई-caupāī:

नहिं अचिरिजु जुग जुग चलि आई । केहि न दीन्हि रघुबीर बड़ाई ॥
nahiṁ aciriju juga juga cali āī, kehi na dīnhi raghubīra baṛāī.
राम नाम महिमा सुर कहहीं । सुनि सुनि अवध लोग सुखु लहहीं ॥
rāma nāma mahimā sura kahahīṁ, suni suni avadha loga sukhu lahahīṁ.
रामसखहि मिलि भरत सप्रेमा । पूँछी कुसल सुमंगल खेमा ॥
rāmasakhahi mili bharata sapremā, pūṁchī kusala sumaṁgala khemā.
देखि भरत कर सीलु सनेहू । भा निषाद तेहि समय बिदेहू ॥
dekhi bharata kara sīlu sanehū, bhā niṣāda tehi samaya bidehū.
सकुच सनेहु मोदु मन बाढ़ा । भरतहि चितवत एकटक ठाढ़ा ॥
sakuca sanehu modu mana bāṛhā, bharatahi citavata ekaṭaka ṭhāṛhā.
धरि धीरजु पद बंदि बहोरी । बिनय सप्रेम करत कर जोरी ॥
dhari dhīraju pada baṁdi bahorī, binaya saprema karata kara jorī.
कुसल मूल पद पंकज पेखी । मैं तिहुँ काल कुसल निज लेखी ॥
kusala mūla pada paṁkaja pekhī, maiṁ tihuṁ kāla kusala nija lekhī.
अब प्रभु परम अनुग्रह तोरें । सहित कोटि कुल मंगल मोरें ॥
aba prabhu parama anugraha toreṁ, sahita koṭi kula maṁgala moreṁ.

Trans:

It is no wonder, and it has been so for ages: who is there whom Raghubīr cannot exalt?" As the gods told the greatness of Rāma's name, and the people of Avadh listened and were glad. Bharat affectionately greeted Rāma's friend and asked him of his health and welfare. At the sight of Bharat's warm disposition, the Nishād was at once utterly overpowered; so great was his diffidence, his love and his delight, that he could only stand and gaze at Bharat. Collecting himself, he again embraced his feet and with clasped hands made this loving speech, "Having beheld your blessed lotus feet I account myself forever blessed. By your high favor my welfare is now secured for thousands of generations.

दोहा-dohā:

समुझि मोरि करतूति कुलु प्रभु महिमा जियँ जोइ ।
samujhi mori karatūti kulu prabhu mahimā jiyaṁ joi,
जो न भजइ रघुबीर पद जग बिधि बंचित सोइ ॥ १९५॥
jo na bhajai raghubīra pada jaga bidhi baṁcita soi. 195.

Trans:

Reflecting on my past deeds and my descent, and again considering the greatness of the Lord in adopting the lowly me, any man in the world who adores not the feet of Raghubīr suffers from a supreme delusion.

चौपाई-caupāī:

कपटी कायर कुमति कुजाती । लोक बेद बाहेर सब भाँती ॥
kapaṭī kāyara kumati kujātī, loka beda bāhera saba bhāṁtī.
राम कीन्ह आपन जबही तें । भयउँ भुवन भूषन तबही तें ॥
rāma kīnha āpana jabahī teṁ, bhayauṁ bhuvana bhūṣana tabahī teṁ.
देखि प्रीति सुनि बिनय सुहाई । मिलेउ बहोरि भरत लघु भाई ॥
dekhi prīti suni binaya suhāī, mileu bahori bharata laghu bhāī.
कहि निषाद निज नाम सुबानीं । सादर सकल जोहारीं रानीं ॥
kahi niṣāda nija nāma subānīṁ, sādara sakala johārīṁ rānīṁ.
जानि लखन सम देहिं असीसा । जिअहु सुखी सय लाख बरीसा ॥
jāni lakhana sama dehiṁ asīsā, jiahu sukhī saya lākha barīsā.
निरखि निषादु नगर नर नारी । भए सुखी जनु लखनु निहारी ॥
nirakhi niṣādu nagara nara nārī, bhae sukhī janu lakhanu nihārī.
कहहिं लहेउ एहिं जीवन लाहू । भेंटेउ रामभद्र भरि बाहू ॥
kahahiṁ laheu ehiṁ jīvana lāhū, bheṁṭeu rāmabhadra bhari bāhū.
सुनि निषादु निज भाग बड़ाई । प्रमुदित मन लइ चलेउ लेवाई ॥
suni niṣādu nija bhāga baṛāī, pramudita mana lai caleu levāī.

Trans:

False, cowardly, low-minded and low-born as I am, an utter outcast by the law both of gods and men, since the time that Rāma took me for his own, see how I have become a jewel of the world." After witnessing his devotion and hearing his graceful humility Lakshman's younger brother next embraced him. Then the Nishād introduced himself by name and respectfully saluted the loyal dames, who received him even as they would Lakshman and gave him their blessing, "May you live happily for millions of years." The citizens too were as glad to see him as if he had been Lakshman and cried, "Here is one who has loved to some purpose; whom Rāma's own brother has taken to his arms and embraced." When the Nishād heard them thus magnify his good fortune, he was glad at heart as he showed them the way.

दोहा-dohā:

सनकारे सेवक सकल चले स्वामि रुख पाइ ।
sanakāre sevaka sakala cale svāmi rukha pāi,
घर तरु तर सर बाग बन बास बनाएन्हि जाइ ॥ १९६॥
ghara taru tara sara bāga bana bāsa banāenhi jāi. 196.

Trans:

At a signal all his attendants, having learnt their master's will, went on and made ready tents under the trees and rest-houses by the ponds, gardens, groves.

चौपाई-caupāī:

सृंगबेरपुर भरत दीख जब । भे सनेहँ सब अंग सिथिल तब ॥
sṛṁgaberapura bharata dīkha jaba, bhe sanehaṁ saba aṁga sithila taba.
सोहत दिएँ निषादहि लागू । जनु तनु धरें बिनय अनुरागू ॥
sohata dieṁ niṣādahi lāgū, janu tanu dhareṁ binaya anurāgū.

एहि बिधि भरत सेनु सबु संगा । दीखि जाइ जग पावनि गंगा ॥
ehi bidhi bharata senu sabu saṁgā, dīkhi jāi jaga pāvani gaṁgā.
रामघाट कहँ कीन्ह प्रनामू । भा मनु मगनु मिले जनु रामू ॥
rāmaghāṭa kahaṁ kīnha pranāmū, bhā manu maganu mile janu rāmū.
करहिं प्रनाम नगर नर नारी । मुदित ब्रह्ममय बारि निहारी ॥
karahiṁ pranāma nagara nara nārī, mudita brahmamaya bāri nihārī.
करि मज्जनु मागहिं कर जोरी । रामचंद्र पद प्रीति न थोरी ॥
kari majjanu māgahiṁ kara jorī, rāmacaṁdra pada prīti na thorī.
भरत कहेउ सुरसरि तव रेनू । सकल सुखद सेवक सुरधेनू ॥
bharata kaheu surasari tava renū, sakala sukhada sevaka suradhenū.
जोरि पानि बर मागउँ एहू । सीय राम पद सहज सनेहू ॥
jori pāni bara māgauṁ ehū, sīya rāma pada sahaja sanehū.

Trans:

When Bharat beheld the city of Sringvera he was overcome by emotion and was unnerved in every limb. As he leaned upon the Nishād chief, it was as goodly a sight as though embodied Humility and Love had met together. In this manner Bharat with all his army went to see the earth-purifying stream of the Gangā. As he made his obeisance to the ford where Rāma had crossed, he was as entranced as though he had met Rāma himself. The citizens bowing low gazed upon the divine stream with rapture, and after bathing, prayed with clasped hands, "May our love to Rāmachandra's feet never grow less." Bharat exclaimed, "Thy sands, O Gangā, are the bestower of all happiness, the very cow of plenty to thy votaries: with folded hands I beg this high boon: a spontaneous love for the holy feet of Sītā and Rāma."

दोहा-dohā:

एहि बिधि मज्जनु भरतु करि गुर अनुसासन पाइ ।
ehi bidhi majjanu bharatu kari gura anusāsana pāi,
मातु नहानीं जानि सब डेरा चले लवाइ ॥ १९७॥
mātu nahānīṁ jāni saba ḍerā cale lavāi. 197.

Trans:

When Bharat had thus bathed and knew that all his mothers had bathed too, he received the Gurū's permission and took them to their tents.

चौपाई-caupāī:

जहँ तहँ लोगन्ह डेरा कीन्हा । भरत सोधु सबही कर लीन्हा ॥
jahaṁ tahaṁ loganha ḍerā kīnhā, bharata sodhu sabahī kara līnhā.
सुर सेवा करि आयसु पाई । राम मातु पहिं गे दोउ भाई ॥
sura sevā kari āyasu pāī, rāma mātu pahiṁ ge dou bhāī.
चरन चाँपि कहि कहि मृदु बानी । जननीं सकल भरत सनमानी ॥
carana cāṁpi kahi kahi mṛdu bānī, jananīṁ sakala bharata sanamānī.
भाइहि सौंपि मातु सेवकाई । आपु निषादहि लीन्ह बोलाई ॥
bhāihi sauṁpi mātu sevakāī, āpu niṣādahi līnha bolāī.
चले सखा कर सों कर जोरें । सिथिल सरीरु सनेह न थोरें ॥
cale sakhā kara soṁ kara joreṁ, sithila sarīru saneha na thoreṁ.
पूँछत सखहि सो ठाउँ देखाऊ । नेकु नयन मन जरनि जुड़ाऊ ॥
pūṁchata sakhahi so ṭhāuṁ dekhāū, neku nayana mana jarani juṛāū.
जहँ सिय रामु लखनु निसि सोए । कहत भरे जल लोचन कोए ॥
jahaṁ siya rāmu lakhanu nisi soe, kahata bhare jala locana koe.
भरत बचन सुनि भयउ बिषादू । तुरत तहाँ लइ गयउ निषादू ॥
bharata bacana suni bhayau biṣādū, turata tahāṁ lai gayau niṣādū.

Trans:

Wherever the people had pitched their tents, Bharat took every care of them all. After paying homage to the Gurū and obtaining his permission, the two brothers went to Rāma's mother. Then Bharat, after touching their feet with many tender phrases, did reverence to all the queens, and having left them to the dutiful care of his brother, went away with the Nishād. Hand-in-hand they went, his body fainting with excess of love, as he begged his companion to show him the spot—so that the fierce longing of his eyes and soul might be assuaged a little bit—where Sītā, Rāma, Lakshman had spent the night. As he spoke, his eyes overflowed with tears, and the Nishād in great distress at his speech, led him at once to the place—

दोहा-dohā:

जहँ सिंसुपा पुनीत तर रघुबर किय बिश्रामु ।
jahaṁ siṁsupā punīta tara raghubara kiya biśrāmu,
अति सनेहँ सादर भरत कीन्हेउ दंड प्रनामु ॥ १९८॥
ati sanehaṁ sādara bharata kīnheu daṁḍa pranāmu. 198.

Trans:

—the place where Raghubar had rested under the sacred *sinsapa* tree. With great reverence and devotion Bharat prostrated himself.

चौपाई-caupāī:

कुस साँथरी निहारि सुहाई । कीन्ह प्रनामु प्रदच्छिन जाई ॥
kusa sāṁtharī nihāri suhāī, kīnha pranāmu pradacchina jāī.
चरन रेख रज आँखिन्ह लाई । बनइ न कहत प्रीति अधिकाई ॥
carana rekha raja āṁkhinha lāī, banai na kahata prīti adhikāī.
कनक बिंदु दुइ चारिक देखे । राखे सीस सीय सम लेखे ॥
kanaka biṁdu dui cārika dekhe, rākhe sīsa sīya sama lekhe.
सजल बिलोचन हृदयँ गलानी । कहत सखा सन बचन सुबानी ॥
sajala bilocana hṛdayaṁ galānī, kahata sakhā sana bacana subānī.
श्रीहत सीय बिरहँ दुतिहीना । जथा अवध नर नारि बिलीना ॥
śrīhata sīya birahaṁ dutihīnā, jathā avadha nara nāri bilīnā.
पिता जनक देउँ पटतर केही । करतल भोगु जोगु जग जेही ॥
pitā janaka deuṁ paṭatara kehī, karatala bhogu jogu jaga jehī.
ससुर भानुकुल भानु भुआलू । जेहि सिहात अमरावतिपालू ॥
sasura bhānukula bhānu bhuālū, jehi sihāta amarāvatipālū.
प्राननाथु रघुनाथ गोसाईं । जो बड़ होत सो राम बड़ाईं ॥
prānanāthu raghunātha gosāīṁ, jo baṛa hota so rāma baṛāīṁ.

Trans:

When he spied the delectable grassy couch, he again made obeisance and reverently paced round it. He put upon his eyes the dust of the footprints with an enthusiasm of devotion beyond all telling. And seeing two or three golden spangles, he placed them upon his head as relics of Sītā. With streaming eyes and aching heart he thus in gentle tones addressed his companion: "They are dim and lusterless through Sītā's absence, and all the people of Avadh are equally woebegone. To whom can I compare her father Janak, who was conversant at once with all life's pleasures and all philosophy? Her father-in-law, the sun like monarch of the solar race, was the envy of even the lord of heaven; her husband is the beloved Raghunāth by whose greatness alone it is that anyone is great;

दोहा-dohā:

पति देवता सुतीय मनि सीय साँथरी देखि ।
pati devatā sutīya mani sīya sāṁtharī dekhi,
बिहरत हृदउ न हहरि हर पबि तें कठिन बिसेषि ॥ १९९॥
biharata hṛdau na hahari hara pabi teṁ kaṭhina biseṣi. 199.

Trans:

and as I gaze on the pitiful couch where rested Sītā—that devoted wife, that jewel of good women—and my heart breaks not with agitation, surely it is harder than a thunderbolt.

चौपाई-caupāī:

लालन जोगु लखन लघु लोने । भे न भाइ अस अहहिं न होने ॥
lālana jogu lakhana laghu lone, bhe na bhāi asa ahahiṁ na hone.
पुरजन प्रिय पितु मातु दुलारे । सिय रघुबीरहि प्रानपिआरे ॥
purajana priya pitu mātu dulāre, siya raghubīrahi prānapiāre.

मृदु मूरति सुकुमार सुभाऊ । तात बाउ तन लाग न काऊ ॥
mṛdu mūrati sukumāra subhāū, tāta bāu tana lāga na kāū.
ते बन सहहिं बिपति सब भाँती । निदरे कोटि कुलिस एहिं छाती ॥
te bana sahahiṁ bipati saba bhām̐tī, nidare koṭi kulisa ehiṁ chātī.
राम जनमि जगु कीन्ह उजागर । रूप सील सुख सब गुन सागर ॥
rāma janami jagu kīnha ujāgara, rūpa sīla sukha saba guna sāgara.
पुरजन परिजन गुर पितु माता । राम सुभाउ सबहि सुखदाता ॥
purajana parijana gura pitu mātā, rāma subhāu sabahi sukhadātā.
बैरिउ राम बड़ाई करहीं । बोलनि मिलनि बिनय मन हरहीं ॥
bairiu rāma baṛāī karahīṁ, bolani milani binaya mana harahīṁ.
सारद कोटि कोटि सत सेषा । करि न सकहिं प्रभु गुन गन लेखा ॥
sārada koṭi koṭi sata seṣā, kari na sakahiṁ prabhu guna gana lekhā.

Trans:

Lakshman is so young and comely and made to be fondled—never was there such a brother, nor is there, nor will be; so beloved by the people, the darling of his father and mother, and dear as their own life to Rāma and Sītā—the picture of delicacy, the daintiest of striplings, whose body has never been exposed to the hot wind—how can he bear the hardships of the forest? O my heart would shame for hardness a million thunderbolts! Rāma from his birth has been the light of the world, an ocean of beauty, of virtue, and all good qualities. Rāma's amiability is the delight of his subjects, his household, his Gurū, his father and mother, and all. Even enemies would praise Rāma; his courtesy of speech and manner stole every heart; not a million Saraswatīs, not a hundred million Sheshnāgs could reckon up all of my Lord's virtues.

दोहा-dohā:

सुखस्वरुप रघुबंसमनि मंगल मोद निधान ।
sukhasvarupa raghubaṁsamani maṁgala moda nidhāna,
ते सोवत कुस डासि महि बिधि गति अति बलवान ॥२००॥
te sovata kusa ḍāsi mahi bidhi gati ati balavāna. 200.

Trans:

The image of bliss, jewel of the family of Raghu, the storehouse of all auspicious delights, slept on the ground on this littered grass! Indeed, how strange are the ways of Providence.

चौपाई-caupāī:

राम सुना दुखु कान न काऊ । जीवनतरु जिमि जोगवइ राऊ ॥
rāma sunā dukhu kāna na kāū, jīvanataru jimi jogavai rāū.
पलक नयन फनि मनि जेहि भाँती । जोगवहिं जननि सकल दिन राती ॥
palaka nayana phani mani jehi bhām̐tī, jogavahiṁ janani sakala dina rātī.
ते अब फिरत बिपिन पदचारी । कंद मूल फल फूल अहारी ॥
te aba phirata bipina padacārī, kaṁda mūla phala phūla ahārī.
धिग कैकई अमंगल मूला । भइसि प्रान प्रियतम प्रतिकूला ॥
dhiga kaikaī amaṁgala mūlā, bhaisi prāna priyatama pratikūlā.
मैं धिग धिग अघ उदधि अभागी । सबु उतपातु भयउ जेहि लागी ॥
maiṁ dhiga dhiga agha udadhi abhāgī, sabu utapātu bhayau jehi lāgī.
कुल कलंकु करि सृजेउ बिधाताँ । साइँदोह मोहि कीन्ह कुमाताँ ॥
kula kalaṁku kari sṛjeu bidhātām̐, sāim̐doha mohi kīnha kumātām̐.
सुनि सप्रेम समुझाव निषादू । नाथ करिअ कत बादि बिषादू ॥
suni saprema samujhāva niṣādū, nātha karia kata bādi biṣādū.
राम तुम्हहि प्रिय तुम्ह प्रिय रामहि । यह निरजोसु दोसु बिधि बामहि ॥
rāma tumhahi priya tumha priya rāmahi, yaha nirajosu dosu bidhi bāmahi.

Trans:

Rāma had never even heard a mention of pain, the king cherished him like the tree of life, and day and night all his mothers guarded him as the eyelids guard the eye, and as a serpent guards the jewel in its head. And now he is roaming on foot through the woods, with nothing to eat but wild roots and fruits. A curse on thee, Kaekayī, root of all evil, thou hast undone my best beloved; cursed be my wretched self, that ocean of iniquity, on whose account all these calamities have come to pass. God created me to disgrace my family, and my wicked mother has made me the ruin of my Lord." Hearing these words the Nishād affectionately implored him, "Why, my lord, make these vain laments? Rāma is dear to you, and you are dear to Rāma; even she is blameless; the blame rests with untoward fate.

छंद-chaṁda:

बिधि बाम की करनी कठिन जेहिं मातु कीन्ही बावरी ।
bidhi bāma kī karanī kaṭhina jehiṁ mātu kīnhī bāvarī,
तेहि राति पुनि पुनि करहिं प्रभु सादर सरहना रावरी ॥
tehi rāti puni puni karahiṁ prabhu sādara sarahanā rāvarī.
तुलसी न तुम्ह सो राम प्रीतमु कहतु हौं सौंहें किएँ ।
tulasī na tumha so rāma prītamu kahatu hauṁ sauṁheṁ kiem̐,
परिनाम मंगल जानि अपने आनिए धीरजु हिएँ ॥
parināma maṁgala jāni apane ānie dhīraju hiem̐.

Trans:

The ways of adverse fate are cruel; it was what made your mother crazed. That very night Rāma again and again broke out into respectful praises of you. There is no one so dearly beloved by Rāma as you; I declare this on oath. Be assured that all will be well in the end; so take comfort in your soul.

सोरठा-soraṭhā:

अंतरजामी रामु सकुच सप्रेम कृपायतन ।
aṁtarajāmī rāmu sakuca saprema kṛpāyatana,
चलिअ करिअ बिश्रामु यह बिचारि दृढ आनि मन ॥२०१॥
calia karia biśrāmu yaha bicāri dṛṛha āni mana. 201.

Trans:

Rāma is omniscient, full of modesty, tenderness, and compassion; consider that be assured in your heart. Now come please take some rest."

चौपाई-caupāī:

सखा बचन सुनि उर धरि धीरा । बास चले सुमिरत रघुबीरा ॥
sakhā bacana suni ura dhari dhīrā, bāsa cale sumirata raghubīrā.
यह सुधि पाइ नगर नर नारी । चले बिलोकन आरत भारी ॥
yaha sudhi pāi nagara nara nārī, cale bilokana ārata bhārī.
परदखिना करि करहिं प्रनामा । देहिं कैकइहि खोरि निकामा ॥
paradakhinā kari karahiṁ pranāmā, dehiṁ kaikaihi khori nikāmā.
भरि भरि बारि बिलोचन लेहीं । बाम बिधातहि दूषन देहीं ॥
bhari bhari bāri bilocana lehīṁ, bāma bidhātahi dūṣana dehīṁ.
एक सराहहिं भरत सनेहू । कोउ कह नृपति निबाहेउ नेहू ॥
eka sarāhahiṁ bharata sanehū, kou kaha nṛpati nibāheu nehū.
निंदहिं आपु सराहि निषादहि । को कहि सकइ बिमोह बिषादहि ॥
niṁdahiṁ āpu sarāhi niṣādahi, ko kahi sakai bimoha biṣādahi.
एहि बिधि राति लोगु सबु जागा । भा भिनुसार गुदारा लागा ॥
ehi bidhi rāti logu sabu jāgā, bhā bhinusāra gudārā lāgā.
गुरहि सुनावँ चढ़ाइ सुहाईं । नईं नाव सब मातु चढ़ाईं ॥
gurahi sunāvam̐ caṛhāi suhāīṁ, naīṁ nāva saba mātu caṛhāīṁ.
दंड चारि महँ भा सबु पारा । उतरि भरत तब सबहि सँभारा ॥
daṁḍa cāri maham̐ bhā sabu pārā, utari bharata taba sabahi sam̐bhārā.

Trans:

Hearing his friend's words, he took some comfort, and with his thoughts directed to Raghubīr went to his tent. When the citizens came to know of that spot, they too came to see, and then became sad at heart. Having reverently paced around they made obeisance, and also cursed Kaekayī to their heart's content. Their eyes streamed with tears as they reproached fate and her cruelty. One would praise Bharat for his devotion, another would say the king had shown the greatest love; they reproached themselves and praised the Nishād—who can describe their agitation and distress? In this manner they all kept watch throughout the night and at daybreak began their passage. First the Gurū was put on a fine handsome boat, and then all the queens on another boat newly built. In an hour and a half all had crossed over. As they came to land Bharat took count of them.

दोहा-dohā:

प्रातक्रिया करि मातु पद बंदि गुरहि सिरु नाइ ।
prātakriyā kari mātu pada baṁdi gurahi siru nāi,
आगें किए निषाद गन दीन्हेउ कटकु चलाइ ॥२०२॥
āgeṁ kie niṣāda gana dīnheu kaṭaku calāi. 202.

Trans:

After performing his morning rites and reverencing his mother's feet and bowing the head to the Gurū, he sent the Nishāds on ahead and then started the rest all.

चौपाई-caupāī:

कियउ निषादनाथु अगुआईं । मातु पालकीं सकल चलाईं ॥
kiyau niṣādanāthu aguāīṁ, mātu pālakīṁ sakala calāīṁ.
साथ बोलाइ भाइ लघु दीन्हा । बिप्रन्ह सहित गवनु गुर कीन्हा ॥
sātha bolāi bhāi laghu dīnhā, bipranha sahita gavanu gura kīnhā.
आपु सुरसरिहि कीन्ह प्रनामू । सुमिरे लखन सहित सिय रामू ॥
āpu surasarihi kīnha pranāmū, sumire lakhana sahita siya rāmū.
गवने भरत पयादेहिं पाए । कोतल संग जाहिं डोरिआए ॥
gavane bharata payadehiṁ pāe, kotala saṁga jāhiṁ ḍoriāe.
कहहिं सुसेवक बारहिं बारा । होइअ नाथ अस्व असवारा ॥
kahahiṁ susevaka bārahiṁ bārā, hoia nātha asva asavārā.
रामु पयादेहि पायँ सिधाए । हम कहँ रथ गज बाजि बनाए ॥
rāmu payadehi pāyaँ sidhāe, hama kahaँ ratha gaja bāji banāe.
सिर भर जाउँ उचित अस मोरा । सब तें सेवक धरमु कठोरा ॥
sira bhara jāuँ ucita asa morā, saba teṁ sevaka dharamu kaṭhorā.
देखि भरत गति सुनि मृदु बानी । सब सेवक गन गरहिं गलानी ॥
dekhi bharata gati suni mṛdu bānī, saba sevaka gana garahiṁ galānī.

Trans:

He made the Nishād chief lead the van and started all the queens in their palanquins—charging his younger brother as their escort; the Gurū, accompanied by Brahmins, followed. He himself bowed reverently to the Gangā, and invoking Rāma, Sītā, and Lakshman, set forth on foot, while his horse was led by the bridle. Again and again his faithful servants cried, "Be pleased lord, to mount the horse." "Rāma," he answered, "has gone on foot, and are chariots, elephants, and horses made for me? It would be right for me to walk on my head; a servant's work is always the hardest." When they saw his behavior and heard his tender speech, all his servants melted away for pity.

दोहा-dohā:

भरत तीसरे पहर कहँ कीन्ह प्रबेसु प्रयाग ।
bharata tīsare pahara kahaँ kīnha prabesu prayāga,
कहत राम सिय राम सिय उमगि उमगि अनुराग ॥२०३॥
kahata rāma siya rāma siya umagi umagi anurāga. 203.

Trans:

At the third watch of the day Bharat entered Prayāg. His heart overflowing with love, he cried, "O Rāma, Sītā; Rāma, Sītā!"

चौपाई-caupāī:

झलका झलकत पायन्ह कैसें । पंकज कोस ओस कन जैसें ॥
jhalakā jhalakata pāyanha kaiseṁ, paṁkaja kosa osa kana jaiseṁ.
भरत पयादेहिं आए आजू । भयउ दुखित सुनि सकल समाजू ॥
bharata payādehiṁ āe ājū, bhayau dukhita suni sakala samājū.
खबरि लीन्ह सब लोग नहाए । कीन्ह प्रनामु त्रिबेनिहिं आए ॥
khabari līnha saba loga nahāe, kīnha pranāmu tribenihiṁ āe.
सबिधि सितासित नीर नहाने । दिए दान महिसुर सनमाने ॥
sabidhi sitāsita nīra nahāne, die dāna mahisura sanamāne.
देखत स्यामल धवल हलोरे । पुलकि सरीर भरत कर जोरे ॥
dekhata syāmala dhavala halore, pulaki sarīra bharata kara jore.
सकल काम प्रद तीरथराऊ । बेद बिदित जग प्रगट प्रभाऊ ॥
sakala kāma prada tīratharāū, beda bidita jaga pragaṭa prabhāū.
मागउँ भीख त्यागि निज धरमू । आरत काह न करइ कुकरमू ॥
māgauँ bhīkha tyāgi nija dharamū, ārata kāha na karai kukaramū.
अस जियँ जानि सुजान सुदानी । सफल करहिं जग जाचक बानी ॥
asa jiyaँ jāni sujāna sudānī, saphala karahiṁ jaga jācaka bānī.

Trans:

The blisters on his feet glistened like drops of dew on a lotus bud. The whole company were distressed when they heard that Bharat had made the day's march on foot. After ascertaining that the people had bathed, he went and did homage to the threefold stream. They, who had dipped in the parti-colored stream, gave alms and did honor to the Brahmins. As Bharat gazed on the commingling of the dark and white waves, his body throbbed with emotion and he clasped his hands in prayer, "O queen of all holy places, bounteous of every blessing, whose power is declared in the Vedas and renowned throughout the world, I abandon my proper calling as a warrior and beg alms of you. What vile act is there that an afflicted soul will not stoop to do? I know you to be all-wise and beneficent, do please accomplish the prayer of this suppliant.

दोहा-dohā:

अरथ न धरम न काम रुचि गति न चहउँ निरबान ।
aratha na dharama na kāma ruci gati na cahauँ nirabāna,
जनम जनम रति राम पद यह बरदानु न आन ॥२०४॥
janama janama rati rāma pada yaha baradānu na āna. 204.

Trans:

I crave not wealth, nor religious merit, nor voluptuous delights, nor deliverance from transmigration—but only that in every new birth I may persevere in my love for Rāma: this is the boon I beg, and naught else.

चौपाई-caupāī:

जानहुँ राम कुटिल करि मोही । लोग कहउ गुर साहिब द्रोही ॥
jānahuँ rāma kuṭila kari mohī, loga kahau gura sāhiba drohī.
सीता राम चरन रति मोरें । अनुदिन बढ़उ अनुग्रह तोरें ॥
sītā rāma carana rati moreṁ, anudina baṛhau anugraha toreṁ.
जलदु जनम भरि सुरति बिसारउ । जाचत जलु पबि पाहन डारउ ॥
jaladu janama bhari surati bisārau, jācata jalu pabi pāhana ḍārau.
चातकु रटनि घटें घटि जाई । बढ़ें प्रेमु सब भाँति भलाई ॥
cātaku raṭani ghaṭeṁ ghaṭi jāī, baṛheṁ premu saba bhāँti bhalāī.
कनकहिं बान चढ़इ जिमि दाहें । तिमि प्रियतम पद नेम निबाहें ॥
kanakahiṁ bāna caṛhai jimi dāheṁ, timi priyatama pada nema nibāheṁ.
भरत बचन सुनि माझ त्रिबेनी । भइ मृदु बानि सुमंगल देनी ॥
bharata bacana suni mājha tribenī, bhai mṛdu bāni sumaṁgala denī.
तात भरत तुम्ह सब बिधि साधू । राम चरन अनुराग अगाधू ॥
tāta bharata tumha saba bidhi sādhū, rāma carana anurāga agādhū.
बादि गलानि करहु मन माहीं । तुम्ह सम रामहि कोउ प्रिय नाहीं ॥
bādi galāni karahu mana māhīṁ, tumha sama rāmahi kou priya nāhīṁ.

Trans:

Rāma knows my wickedness; the people call me the ruin of my Lord and master; through your favor may my devotion to the feet of Sītā and Rāma increase more and more every day like the *Chātak*. Though the cloud forgets her all her life, and while she begs for rain, casts down upon her thunder and hail, yet if the *Chātak* bird cease her importunity, she is despised, and if she persevere in her affection, is much honored. As the quality of gold is refined by the fire, so may my vow to the feet of my beloved endure through all tribulation." In answer to Bharat's speech there came a soft and auspicious voice from the midst of the Trivenī, "Son Bharat, you are altogether upright; your love to Rāma's feet is unfathomable; you distress yourself without cause; there is no one so dear to Rāma as you are."

दोहा-*dohā:*

तनु पुलकेउ हियँ हरषु सुनि बेनि बचन अनुकूल ।
tanu pulakeu hiyaṁ harașu suni beni bacana anukūla,
भरत धन्य कहि धन्य सुर हरषित बरषहिं फूल ॥२०५॥
bharata dhanya kahi dhanya sura harașita barașahiṁ phūla. 205.

Trans:

As he heard the river's gracious speech Bharat's body quivered with heartfelt gladness; the heaven resounded with shouts of applause, and the gods rained down flowers.

चौपाई-*caupāī:*

प्रमुदित तीरथराज निवासी । बैखानस बटु गृही उदासी ॥
pramudita tīratharāja nivāsī, baikhānasa baṭu gṛhī udāsī.
कहहिं परसपर मिलि दस पाँचा । भरत सनेहु सीलु सुचि साँचा ॥
kahahiṁ parasapara mili dasa pāṁcā, bharata sanehu sīlu suci sāṁcā.
सुनत राम गुन ग्राम सुहाए । भरद्वाज मुनिबर पहिं आए ॥
sunata rāma guna grāma suhāe, bharadvāja munibara pahiṁ āe.
दंड प्रनामु करत मुनि देखे । मूरतिमंत भाग्य निज लेखे ॥
daṁḍa pranāmu karata muni dekhe, mūratimaṁta bhāgya nija lekhe.
धाइ उठाइ लाइ उर लीन्हे । दीन्हि असीस कृतारथ कीन्हे ॥
dhāi uṭhāi lāi ura līnhe, dīnhi asīsa kṛtāratha kīnhe.
आसनु दीन्ह नाइ सिरु बैठे । चहत सकुच गृहँ जनु भजि पैठे ॥
āsanu dīnha nāi siru baiṭhe, cahata sakuca gṛhaṁ janu bhaji paiṭhe.
मुनि पूँछब कछु यह बड़ सोचू । बोले रिषि लखि सीलु सँकोचू ॥
muni pūṁchaba kachu yaha baṛa socū, bole riṣi lakhi sīlu saṁkocū.
सुनहु भरत हम सब सुधि पाई । बिधि करतब पर किछु न बसाई ॥
sunahu bharata hama saba sudhi pāī, bidhi karataba para kichu na basāī.

Trans:

The inhabitants of Prayāg, aged anchorites and boy students, householders and celibates, were all enraptured and said to one another as they met in groups, "Bharat's affection and amiability are so thoroughly genuine." Still hearing of Rāma's many charming qualities, Bharat approached the great saint Bharadvāja. When the saint saw him prostrate himself upon the ground, he looked upon him as his own good-luck personified, and ran and raised him up and took him to his arms, and gave him the blessing he desired, and made him sit down. He bowed his head and sat, shrinking into the inmost recesses of shamefacedness—in great distress lest the saint should ask any question. Seeing his confusion the saint said, "Hearken, Bharat; I have heard everything. The doings of fate are beyond our power.

दोहा-*dohā:*

तुम्ह गलानि जियँ जनि करहु समुझि मातु करतूति ।
tumha galāni jiyaṁ jani karahu samujhi mātu karatūti,
तात कैकइहि दोसु नहिं गई गिरा मति धूति ॥२०६॥
tāta kaikaihi dosu nahiṁ gaī girā mati dhūti. 206.

Trans:

Be not distressed at heart by the thought of what your mother has done. Son, it is no fault of Kaekayī's; it was Saraswatī who stole away her senses.

चौपाई-*caupāī:*

यहउ कहत भल कहिहि न कोऊ । लोकु बेदु बुध संमत दोऊ ॥
yahau kahata bhala kahihi na koū, loku bedu budha saṁmata doū.
तात तुम्हार बिमल जसु गाई । पाइहि लोकउ बेदु बड़ाई ॥
tāta tumhāra bimala jasu gāī, pāihi lokau bedu baṛāī.
लोक बेद संमत सबु कहई । जेहि पितु देइ राजु सो लहई ॥
loka beda saṁmata sabu kahaī, jehi pitu dei rāju so lahaī.
राउ सत्यब्रत तुम्हहि बोलाई । देत राजु सुखु धरमु बड़ाई ॥
rāu satyabrata tumhahi bolāī, deta rāju sukhu dharamu baṛāī.
राम गवनु बन अनरथ मूला । जो सुनि सकल बिस्व भइ सूला ॥
rāma gavanu bana anaratha mūlā, jo suni sakala bisva bhai sūlā.
सो भावी बस रानि अयानी । करि कुचालि अंतहुँ पछितानी ॥
so bhāvī basa rāni ayānī, kari kucāli aṁtahuṁ pachitānī.
तहँउँ तुम्हार अलप अपराधू । कहै सो अधम अयान असाधू ॥
tahaṁuṁ tumhāra alapa aparādhū, kahai so adhama ayāna asādhū.
करतेहु राजु त तुम्हहि न दोषू । रामहि होत सुनत संतोषू ॥
karatehu rāju ta tumhahi na doșū, rāmahi hota sunata saṁtoșū.

Trans:

But even knowing so, none would excuse her act, because only scriptural proof and the worldy customs are accepted as authorities by the wise, and none goes against those. But by singing your unsullied glory, my son, both the Vedas and the traditions are forever elevated. According both by custom and the Vedas, he takes the throne to whom the father gives it. The truthful king would have summoned you to confer upon you the throne, and this would have brought him joy, glory, religious merit. What was wrong was Rāma's banishment, which the whole world is grieved to hear of. But the queen was demented by the power of fate; and in the end she has repented of the evil she has done. You are not the least in fault; whoever says you are, is a vile ignorant wretch. Had you reigned, it would have been no sin, and Rāma would have been pleased to hear of it.

दोहा-*dohā:*

अब अति कीन्हेहु भरत भल तुम्हहि उचित मत एहु ।
aba ati kīnhehu bharata bhala tumhahi ucita mata ehu,
सकल सुमंगल मूल जग रघुबर चरन सनेहु ॥२०७॥
sakala sumaṁgala mūla jaga raghubara carana sanehu. 207.

Trans:

But now, Bharat, you have done still better; your present purpose is excellent: devotion to the feet of Raghubar is the root of every blessing in the world.

चौपाई-*caupāī:*

सो तुम्हार धनु जीवनु प्राना । भूरिभाग को तुम्हहि समाना ॥
so tumhāra dhanu jīvanu prānā, bhūribhāga ko tumhahi samānā.
यह तुम्हार आचरजु न ताता । दसरथ सुअन राम प्रिय भ्राता ॥
yaha tumhāra ācaraju na tātā, dasaratha suana rāma priya bhrātā.
सुनहु भरत रघुबर मन माहीं । पेम पात्रु तुम्ह सम कोउ नाहीं ॥
sunahu bharata raghubara mana māhīṁ, pema pātru tumha sama kou nāhīṁ.
लखन राम सीतहि अति प्रीती । निसि सब तुम्हहि सराहत बीती ॥
lakhana rāma sītahi ati prītī, nisi saba tumhahi sarāhata bītī.
जाना मरमु नहात प्रयागा । मगन होहिं तुम्हरें अनुरागा ॥
jānā maramu nahāta prayāgā, magana hohiṁ tumhareṁ anurāgā.
तुम्ह पर अस सनेहु रघुबर कें । सुख जीवन जग जस जड़ नर कें ॥
tumha para asa sanehu raghubara keṁ, sukha jīvana jaga jasa jaṛa nara keṁ.
यह न अधिक रघुबीर बड़ाई । प्रनत कुटुंब पाल रघुराई ॥
yaha na adhika raghubīra baṛāī, pranata kuṭuṁba pāla raghurāī.
तुम्ह तौ भरत मोर मत एहू । धरें देह जनु राम सनेहू ॥
tumha tau bharata mora mata ehū, dhareṁ deha janu rāma sanehū.

Trans:

And that is your wealth and the very breath of your life; is there anyone with good fortune equal to yours? Nor, my son, is it strange that you should act thus; you are a son of Dashrath's and Rāma's very own brother. Hearken Bharat: in Raghupatī's heart there is no one upon whom so much love is lavished as upon you. Lakshman, Rāma, and Sītā are all most fond of you; they spent the whole night in your praises. I learnt their secret when they came here to Prayāg to bathe; they were overwhelmed with love for you. Raghubar has as great affection for you as a fool has for a life of pleasure. And this is no credit to Raghurāī, who cherishes all his suppliants and their kin; while you, Bharat, as it seems to me, are the very incarnation of love.

दोहा-dohā:

तुम्ह कहँ भरत कलंक यह हम सब कहँ उपदेसु ।
tumha kahaṁ bharata kalaṁka yaha hama saba kahaṁ upadesu,
राम भगति रस सिद्धि हित भा यह समउ गनेसु ॥२०८॥
rāma bhagati rasa siddhi hita bhā yaha samau ganesu. 208.

Trans:

That which seems a reproach to you, Bharat, is a lesson to all of us; it is an event which inaugurates a new flood of passionate devotion.

चौपाई-caupāī:

नव बिधु बिमल तात जसु तोरा । रघुबर किंकर कुमुद चकोरा ॥
nava bidhu bimala tāta jasu torā, raghubara kiṁkara kumuda cakorā.
उदित सदा अँथइहि कबहूँ ना । घटिहि न जग नभ दिन दिन दूना ॥
udita sadā aṁthaihi kabahūṁ nā, ghaṭihi na jaga nabha dina dina dūnā.
कोक तिलोक प्रीति अति करिही । प्रभु प्रताप रबि छबिहि न हरिही ॥
koka tiloka prīti ati karihī, prabhu pratāpa rabi chabihi na harihī.
निसि दिन सुखद सदा सब काहू । ग्रसिहि न कैकइ करतबु राहू ॥
nisi dina sukhada sadā saba kāhū, grasihi na kaikai karatabu rāhū.
पूरन राम सुपेम पियूषा । गुर अवमान दोष नहिं दूषा ॥
pūrana rāma supema piyūṣā, gura avamāna doṣa nahiṁ dūṣā.
राम भगत अब अमिअँ अघाहूँ । कीन्हेहु सुलभ सुधा बसुधाहूँ ॥
rāma bhagata aba amiaṁ aghāhūṁ, kīnhehu sulabha sudhā basudhāhūṁ.
भूप भगीरथ सुरसरि आनी । सुमिरत सकल सुंमगल खानी ॥
bhūpa bhagīratha surasari ānī, sumirata sakala suṁmagala khānī.
दसरथ गुन गन बरनि न जाहीं । अधिकु कहा जेहि सम जग नाहीं ॥
dasaratha guna gana barani na jāhīṁ, adhiku kahā jehi sama jaga nāhīṁ.

Trans:

Your glory, my son, is a newly created spotless moon; Rāma's devotees are its lotuses and partridges; it will be seen ever rising, never set; nor ever wane in the heavens of the world, but increase day by day. The three spheres, like the *chakwā* are exceedingly enamored of it; and the sun of Rāma's majesty never robs it of splendor; and by day as well as night it is ever bountiful to all, and Kaekayī's evil deeds cannot eclipse it. Full of the nectar of devotion to Rāma, and unsullied by any stain for wrong done to the Gurū, you are saturated with the nectar of faith, and have brought this nectar within the reach of the whole world. Of your forefathers, King Bhagirathi brought down the Gangā, whose invocation is a mine of all prosperity. As for Dashrath's virtues, they are past all telling; why say more? He has no equal in the world.

दोहा-dohā:

जासु सनेह सकोच बस राम प्रगट भए आइ ।
jāsu saneha sakoca basa rāma pragaṭa bhae āi,
जे हर हिय नयननि कबहुँ निरखे नहीं अघाइ ॥२०९॥
je hara hiya nayanani kabahuṁ nirakhe nahīṁ aghāi. 209.

Trans:

Through Dashrath's devotion and humility, Rāma was made manifest—He, whom the eyes of Shiva's heart are never wearied of beholding.

चौपाई-caupāī:

कीरति बिधु तुम्ह कीन्ह अनूपा । जहँ बस राम पेम मृगरूपा ॥
kīrati bidhu tumha kīnha anūpā, jahaṁ basa rāma pema mṛgarūpā.
तात गलानि करहु जियँ जाएँ । डरहु दरिद्रहि पारसु पाएँ ॥
tāta galāni karahu jiyaṁ jāeṁ, ḍarahu daridrahi pārasu pāeṁ.
सुनहु भरत हम झूठ न कहहीं । उदासीन तापस बन रहहीं ॥
sunahu bharata hama jhūṭha na kahahīṁ, udāsīna tāpasa bana rahahīṁ.
सब साधन कर सुफल सुहावा । लखन राम सिय दरसनु पावा ॥
saba sādhana kara suphala suhāvā, lakhana rāma siya darasanu pāvā.
तेहि फल कर फलु दरस तुम्हारा । सहित पयाग सुभाग हमारा ॥
tehi phala kara phalu darasa tumhārā, sahita payāga subhāga hamārā.
भरत धन्य तुम्ह जसु जगु जयऊ । कहि अस पेम मगन पुनि भयऊ ॥
bharata dhanya tumha jasu jagu jayaū, kahi asa pema magana puni bhayaū.
सुनि मुनि बचन सभासद हरषे । साधु सराहि सुमन सुर बरषे ॥
suni muni bacana sabhāsada harașe, sādhu sarāhi sumana sura barașe.
धन्य धन्य धुनि गगन पयागा । सुनि सुनि भरतु मगन अनुरागा ॥
dhanya dhanya dhuni gagana payāgā, suni suni bharatu magana anurāgā.

Trans:

In you has been created the peerless moon of glory, which bears on it the figure of a deer in the shape of love for Rāma. Cease, my son, from lamentation; you have found the philosopher's stone and yet fear poverty! Hearken Bharat, I tell no falsehood: I—a hermit and ascetic dwelling in the forest—obtained a glorious reward for all my good deeds when I beheld Rāma, Sītā, and Lakshman. And the fruit of that fruit is the sight of you! Prayāg and I are both highly favored, O Bharat, I congratulate you; you have achieved universal renown." So saying the saint was overwhelmed with emotion. As they hearkened to his words, the whole assembly rejoiced; the gods applauded his goodness and rained down flowers. Shouts of 'Glory, Glory' resounded in heaven and in Prayāg; Bharat was lost in rapture at the sound.

दोहा-dohā:

पुलक गात हियँ रामु सिय सजल सरोरुह नैन ।
pulaka gāta hiyaṁ rāmu siya sajala saroruha naina,
करि प्रनामु मुनि मंडलिहि बोले गदगद बैन ॥२१०॥
kari pranāmu muni maṁḍalihi bole gadagada baina. 210.

Trans:

With quivering body, with his heart full of Rāma and Sītā, and his lotus eyes flowing with tears, he bowed to the saintly assembly and thus spoke in faltering accents:

चौपाई-caupāī:

मुनि समाजु अरु तीरथराजू । साँचिहुँ सपथ अघाइ अकाजू ॥
muni samāju aru tīratharājū, sāṁcihuṁ sapatha aghāi akājū.
एहिं थल जौं किछु कहिअ बनाई । एहि सम अधिक न अघ अधमाई ॥
ehiṁ thala jauṁ kichu kahia banāī, ehi sama adhika na agha adhamāī.
तुम्ह सर्बग्य कहउँ सतिभाऊ । उर अंतरजामी रघुराऊ ॥
tumha sarbagya kahauṁ satibhāū, ura aṁtarajāmī raghurāū.
मोहि न मातु करतब कर सोचू । नहिं दुखु जियँ जगु जानिहि पोचू ॥
mohi na mātu karataba kara socū, nahiṁ dukhu jiyaṁ jagu jānihi pocū.
नाहिन डरु बिगरिहि परलोकू । पितहु मरन कर मोहि न सोकू ॥
nāhina ḍaru bigarihi paralokū, pitahu marana kara mohi na sokū.
सुकृत सुजस भरि भुअन सुहाए । लछिमन राम सरिस सुत पाए ॥
sukṛta sujasa bhari bhuana suhāe, lachimana rāma sarisa suta pāe.
राम बिरहँ तजि तनु छनभंगू । भूप सोच कर कवन प्रसंगू ॥
rāma birahaṁ taji tanu chanabhaṁgū, bhūpa soca kara kavana prasaṁgū.

राम लखन सिय बिनु पग पनहीं। करि मुनि बेष फिरहिं बन बनहीं॥
rāma lakhana siya binu paga panahīṁ, kari muni beṣa phirahiṁ bana banahīṁ.

Trans:

"In a conclave of saints and in this so holy a place, truth must needs be spoken; any oath is superfluous and vain. If in such a spot I were to say anything false, no sin or vileness would equal mine. You are all-wise, and therefore I speak honestly; Rāma, too, knows the secrets of the heart. I am not grieved for what my mother has done, nor pained at heart lest the world deem me caitiff; I have no dread of the loss of heaven, no sorrow for my father's death, whose good deeds and renown are glorious all the world over, who had such sons as Lakshman and Rāma, and who, as soon as he lost Rāma, dropped his body away. Why make long mourning for the king? But Rāma, Lakshman, and Sītā, without shoes to their feet, in hermit's dress, are wandering from wood to wood—

दोहा-dohā:

अजिन बसन फल असन महि सयन डासि कुस पात।
ajina basana phala asana mahi sayana ḍāsi kusa pāta,
बसि तरु तर नित सहत हिम आतप बरषा बात॥२११॥
basi taru tara nita sahata hima ātapa baraṣā bāta. 211.

Trans:

—wandering clad in deer-skins, feeding on wild fruits, sleeping on the ground on a litter of grass and leaves, living under trees, ever exposed to the inclemency of cold and heat and rain and wind.

चौपाई-caupāī:

एहि दुख दाहँ दहइ दिन छाती। भूख न बासर नीद न राती॥
ehi dukha dāhaṁ dahai dina chātī, bhūkha na bāsara nīda na rātī.
एहि कुरोग कर औषधु नाहीं। सोधेउँ सकल बिस्व मन माहीं॥
ehi kuroga kara auṣadhu nāhīṁ, sodheuṁ sakala bisva mana māhīṁ.
मातु कुमत बढ़ई अघ मूला। तेहिं हमार हित कीन्ह बँसूला॥
mātu kumata baṛhaī agha mūlā, tehiṁ hamāra hita kīnha baṁsūlā.
कलि कुकाठ कर कीन्ह कुजंत्रू। गाड़ि अवधि पढ़ि कठिन कुमंत्रू॥
kali kukāṭha kara kīnha kujaṁtrū, gāṛi avadhi paṛhi kaṭhina kumaṁtrū.
मोहि लगि यहु कुठाटु तेहिं ठाटा। घालेसि सब जगु बारहबाटा॥
mohi lagi yahu kuṭhāṭu tehiṁ ṭhāṭā, ghālesi saba jagu bārahabāṭā.
मिटइ कुजोगु राम फिरि आएँ। बसइ अवध नहिं आन उपाएँ॥
miṭai kujogu rāma phiri āeṁ, basai avadha nahiṁ āna upāeṁ.
भरत बचन सुनि मुनि सुखु पाई। सबहिं कीन्हि बहु भाँति बड़ाई॥
bharata bacana suni muni sukhu pāī, sabahiṁ kīnhi bahu bhāṁti baṛāī.
तात करहु जनि सोचु बिसेषी। सब दुखु मिटिहि राम पग देखी॥
tāta karahu jani socu biseṣī, saba dukhu miṭihi rāma paga dekhī.

Trans:

This is the burning pain that is ever consuming my heart, such that I cannot eat by day, nor sleep by night. For this sore disease there is no remedy; I have searched in mind and the whole world over. My mother's evil counsel—the root of all calamity—was like a carpenter who used my perceived welfare as an adze, and fashioned out of the ill wood of Discord a destructive magical contraption and muttering the horrible spell of Banishment planted it in soil. To me she applied this infamous contrivance and has burled me down in wide-spreading ruin. These disasters will cease when Rāma returns to live in Avadh; there is no other remedy." When the saints heard Bharat's speech, they were glad and all gave him high praise, "Son, grieve not so sorely; at the sight of Rāma's feet all sorrow will pass away."

दोहा-dohā:

करि प्रबोधु मुनिबर कहेउ अतिथि पेमप्रिय होहु।
kari prabodhu munibara kaheu atithi pemapriya hohu,
कंद मूल फल फूल हम देहिं लेहु करि छोहु॥२१२॥
kaṁda mūla phala phūla hama dehiṁ lehu kari chohu. 212.

Trans:

The great saints comforted him and said, "Be our welcome guest; accept such herbs and roots and fruits as we can offer, and be content."

चौपाई-caupāī:

सुनि मुनि बचन भरत हियँ सोचू। भयउ कुअवसर कठिन सँकोचू॥
suni muni bacana bharata hiyaṁ socū, bhayau kuavasara kaṭhina saṁkocū.
जानि गरुइ गुर गिरा बहोरी। चरन बंदि बोले कर जोरी॥
jāni garui gura girā bahorī, carana baṁdi bole kara jorī.
सिर धरि आयसु करिअ तुम्हारा। परम धरम यहु नाथ हमारा॥
sira dhari āyasu karia tumhārā, parama dharama yahu nātha hamārā.
भरत बचन मुनिबर मन भाए। सुचि सेवक सिष निकट बोलाए॥
bharata bacana munibara mana bhāe, suci sevaka siṣa nikaṭa bolāe.
चाहिअ कीन्हि भरत पहुनाई। कंद मूल फल आनहु जाई॥
cāhia kīnhi bharata pahunāī, kaṁda mūla phala ānahu jāī.
भलेहीं नाथ कहि तिन्ह सिर नाए। प्रमुदित निज निज काज सिधाए॥
bhalehīṁ nātha kahi tinha sira nāe, pramudita nija nija kāja sidhāe.
मुनिहि सोच पाहुन बड़ नेवता। तसि पूजा चाहिअ जस देवता॥
munihi soca pāhuna baṛa nevatā, tasi pūjā cāhia jasa devatā.
सुनि रिधि सिधि अनिमादिक आईं। आयसु होइ सो करहिं गोसाईं॥
suni ridhi sidhi animādika āīṁ, āyasu hoi so karahiṁ gosāīṁ.

Trans:

On hearing the saints' words Bharat was troubled at heart; the time was not one for feasting, and yet he was very loth to decline. At last, reflecting that a Gurū's command is imperative, he held his feet and replied with clasped hands, "I must needs bow to your behest, for this, my Lord, is my highest duty." The great saint was pleased at Bharat's words and called up all his trusty servants and pupils, "A welcome must be provided for Bharat: go and gather herbs, roots, and fruits." They bowed the head and said, "Very well, sir," and gladly set about each his own work. But the saint thought to himself, "I have invited a distinguished guest, who should be treated like a god." At his command the Supreme-Powers—*Riddhi*s and *Siddhi*s like *Anima*—came, "What are your orders, master; we stand to obey."

दोहा-dohā:

राम बिरह ब्याकुल भरतु सानुज सहित समाज।
rāma biraha byākula bharatu sānuja sahita samāja,
पहुनाई करि हरहु श्रम कहा मुदित मुनिराज॥२१३॥
pahunāī kari harahu śrama kahā mudita munirāja. 213.

Trans:

"Bharat and his brother and all their host are distressed by the loss of Rāma; show them hospitality and ease them of their toil," thus cheerily spoke the great saint.

चौपाई-caupāī:

रिधि सिधि सिर धरि मुनिबर बानी। बड़भागिनि आपुहि अनुमानी॥
ridhi sidhi sira dhari munibara bānī, baṛabhāgini āpuhi anumānī.
कहहिं परसपर सिधि समुदाई। अतुलित अतिथि राम लघु भाई॥
kahahiṁ parasapara sidhi samudāī, atulita atithi rāma laghu bhāī.
मुनि पद बंदि करिअ सोइ आजू। होइ सुखी सब राज समाजू॥
muni pada baṁdi karia soi ājū, hoi sukhī saba rāja samājū.
अस कहि रचेउ रुचिर गृह नाना। जेहि बिलोकि बिलखाहिं बिमाना॥
asa kahi raceu rucira gṛha nānā, jehi biloki bilakhāhiṁ bimānā.

भोग बिभूति भूरि भरि राखे । देखत जिन्हहि अमर अभिलाषे ॥
bhoga bibhūti bhūri bhari rākhe, dekhata jinhahi amara abhilāṣe.
दासीं दास साजु सब लीन्हें । जोगवत रहहिं मनहि मनु दीन्हें ॥
dāsīṁ dāsa sāju saba līnheṁ, jogavata rahahiṁ manahi manu dīnheṁ.
सब समाजु सजि सिधि पल माहीं । जे सुख सुरपुर सपनेहुँ नाहीं ॥
saba samāju saji sidhi pala māhīṁ, je sukha surapura sapanehum̐ nāhīṁ.
प्रथमहिं बास दिए सब केही । सुंदर सुखद जथा रुचि जेही ॥
prathamahiṁ bāsa die saba kehī, suṁdara sukhada jathā ruci jehī.

Trans:

The riches and supernatural powers in their embodied forms bowed to the command of the great sage and deemed themselves highly favored, saying one to another, "Rāma's brother is indeed a guest beyond compare, brothers." Then holding the saint's feet, "Today we shall do such things that the whole of the king's entourage will be pleased," so saying, a number of charming pavilions were erected—so lovely that the equipages of the gods were put out of countenance at the sight of them. They were furnished with so much luxury and magnificence that even the immortals beheld them longingly. Men-servants and maid-servants with every appliance were in attendance, and they gave their whole mind to the pleasure of the guests. In an instant of time the Siddhis completed all their arrangements, even though no dream of heaven was ever so beautiful as this. First they assigned to the people their quarters, all bright and pleasant, and in accordance with their individual tastes.

दोहा-dohā:

बहुरि सपरिजन भरत कहुँ रिषि अस आयसु दीन्ह ।
bahuri saparijana bharata kahum̐ riṣi asa āyasu dīnha,
बिधि बिसमय दायकु बिभव मुनिबर तपबल कीन्ह ॥२१४॥
bidhi bisamaya dāyaku bibhava munibara tapabala kīnha. 214.

Trans:

Thereafter Bharat and his family were assigned quarters—for such were the instructions given by the sage. By dint of his penance the great sage produced such wealth that astonished Brahmmā, the Creator himself.

चौपाई-caupāī:

मुनि प्रभाउ जब भरत बिलोका । सब लघु लगे लोकपति लोका ॥
muni prabhāu jaba bharata bilokā, saba laghu lage lokapati lokā.
सुख समाजु नहिं जाइ बखानी । देखत बिरति बिसारहिं ग्यानी ॥
sukha samāju nahiṁ jāi bakhānī, dekhata birati bisārahiṁ gyānī.
आसन सयन सुबसन बिताना । बन बाटिका बिहग मृग नाना ॥
āsana sayana subasana bitānā, bana bāṭikā bihaga mṛga nānā.
सुरभि फूल फल अमिअ समाना । बिमल जलासय बिबिध बिधाना ॥
surabhi phūla phala amia samānā, bimala jalāsaya bibidha bidhānā.
असन पान सुचि अमिअ अमी से । देखि लोग सकुचात जमी से ॥
asana pāna suci amia amī se, dekhi loga sakucāta jamī se.
सुर सुरभी सुरतरु सबही कें । लखि अभिलाषु सुरेस सची कें ॥
sura surabhī surataru sabahī keṁ, lakhi abhilāṣu suresa sacī keṁ.
रितु बसंत बह त्रिबिध बयारी । सब कहँ सुलभ पदारथ चारी ॥
ritu basaṁta baha tribidha bayārī, saba kaham̐ sulabha padāratha cārī.
स्रक चंदन बनितादिक भोगा । देखि हरष बिसमय बस लोगा ॥
sraka caṁdana banitādika bhogā, dekhi harasa bisamaya basa logā.

Trans:

Bharat beheld the saint's power—the realms of rulers of all spheres seemed trifles in comparison. The luxuries that had been prepared cannot be described; any philosopher would forget his self-restraint on seeing them. Thrones, couches, drapery and canopies; groves and gardens; birds and beasts; sweet-scented flowers, nectar-like fruits, and many a lake of limpid water; with luscious food and drinks of innumerable kinds—which the guests would hesitate to accept, as if they were ascetics. Each dwelling had as it were his own cow of plenty and tree of paradise; Indra and Sachi grew covetous at the sight. It was the vernal season and a cool, fragrant and gentle breeze was blowing. Everyone had all the four prizes of life within one's easy reach. At the sight of luxuries like garlands, sandal-paste and women the guests were overcome by a mixed feeling of joy and sorrow.

दोहा-dohā:

संपति चकई भरतु चक मुनि आयस खेलवार ।
saṁpati cakaī bharatu caka muni āyasa khelavāra,
तेहि निसि आश्रम पिंजराँ राखे भा भिनुसार ॥२१५॥
tehi nisi āśrama piṁjarām̐ rākhe bhā bhinusāra. 215.

Trans:

Affluence—as the chakwi, and Bharat—as her mate, by compulsion of the orders of the saint—who was like a playful child—were prisoners together that night in the cage of the hermitage until the dawn broke.

मासपारायण उन्नीसवाँ विश्राम
māsapārāyaṇa unnīsavām̐ viśrāma
(Pause 19 for a Thirty-Day Recitation)

चौपाई-caupāī:

कीन्ह निमज्जनु तीरथराजा । नाइ मुनिहि सिरु सहित समाजा ॥
kīnha nimajjanu tīratharājā, nāi munihi siru sahita samājā.
रिषि आयसु असीस सिर राखी । करि दंडवत बिनय बहु भाषी ॥
riṣi āyasu asīsa sira rākhī, kari daṁḍavata binaya bahu bhāṣī.
पथ गति कुसल साथ सब लीन्हें । चले चित्रकूटहिं चितु दीन्हें ॥
patha gati kusala sātha saba līnheṁ, cale citrakūṭahiṁ citu dīnheṁ.
रामसखा कर दीन्हें लागू । चलत देह धरि जनु अनुरागू ॥
rāmasakhā kara dīnheṁ lāgū, calata deha dhari janu anurāgū.
नहिं पद त्रान सीस नहिं छाया । पेमु नेमु ब्रतु धरमु अमाया ॥
nahiṁ pada trāna sīsa nahiṁ chāyā, pemu nemu bratu dharamu amāyā.
लखन राम सिय पंथ कहानी । पूँछत सखहि कहत मृदु बानी ॥
lakhana rāma siya paṁtha kahānī, pūm̐chata sakhahi kahata mṛdu bānī.
राम बास थल बिटप बिलोकें । उर अनुराग रहत नहिं रोकें ॥
rāma bāsa thala biṭapa bilokeṁ, ura anurāga rahata nahiṁ rokeṁ.
देखि दसा सुर बरिसहिं फूला । भइ मृदु महि मगु मंगल मूला ॥
dekhi dasā sura barisahiṁ phūlā, bhai mṛdu mahi magu maṁgala mūlā.

Trans:

At daybreak all bathed at the holy place and came bowed their heads to the sage. Having submissively received his commands and blessing, Bharat prostrated himself and made much supplication. Then taking guides well acquainted with the road, resolutely he set out for Chitra-kūt. Supported on the arm of Rāma's friend, he seemed, as he went, the very incarnation of Love. With no shoes and no shelter for his head, in the fulfillment of his loving vow and his unfeigned integrity, he asked his companion for a history of the wanderings of Rāma, Sītā, and Lakshman, who gently narrated it. When he saw the tree where Rāma had rested, his heart could not contain its emotion. At the sight of his condition, the gods rained down flowers, and the path that he trod grew smooth and pleasant.

दोहा-dohā:

किएँ जाहिं छाया जलद सुखद बहइ बर बात ।
kiem̐ jāhiṁ chāyā jalada sukhada bahai bara bāta,
तस मगु भयउ न राम कहँ जस भा भरतहि जात ॥२१६॥
tasa magu bhayau na rāma kaham̐ jasa bhā bharatahi jāta. 216.

Trans:

The clouds afforded him shade and the air breathed soft and refreshing. Even Rāma's journey was not so agreeable, as it now was for Bharat.

चौपाई-caupāī:

जड़ चेतन मग जीव घनेरे । जे चितए प्रभु जिन्ह प्रभु हेरे ॥
jaṛa cetana maga jīva ghanere, je citae prabhu jinha prabhu here.

ते सब भए परम पद जोगू । भरत दरस मेटा भव रोगू ॥
te saba bhae parama pada jogū, bharata darasa meṭā bhava rogū.
यह बड़ि बात भरत कइ नाहीं । सुमिरत जिनहि रामु मन माहीं ॥
yaha baṛi bāta bharata kai nāhīṁ, sumirata jinahi rāmu mana māhīṁ.
बारक राम कहत जग जेऊ । होत तरन तारन नर तेऊ ॥
bāraka rāma kahata jaga jeū, hota tarana tārana nara teū.
भरतु राम प्रिय पुनि लघु भ्राता । कस न होइ मगु मंगलदाता ॥
bharatu rāma priya puni laghu bhrātā, kasa na hoi magu maṁgaladātā.
सिद्ध साधु मुनिबर अस कहहीं । भरतहि निरखि हरषु हियँ लहहीं ॥
siddha sādhu munibara asa kahahīṁ, bharatahi nirakhi haraṣu hiyaṁ lahahīṁ.
देखि प्रभाउ सुरेसहि सोचू । जगु भल भलेहि पोच कहुँ पोचू ॥
dekhi prabhāu suresahi socū, jagu bhala bhalehi poca kahuṁ pocū.
गुर सन कहेउ करिअ प्रभु सोई । रामहि भरतहि भेट न होई ॥
gura sana kaheu karia prabhu soī, rāmahi bharatahi bheṭa na hoī.

Trans:

All created things, whether living or lifeless, that had seen Lord Rāma, or were seen by him, were rendered fit for the highest state; and now the sight of Bharat had finally healed them of the disease of transmigration. This is no great thing for Bharat, whom Rāma ever cherishes in his heart. "Even they who utter the name of Rāma only once in this world not only reach the other shore themselves but are also able to take others across. As for Bharat, he is the dearly beloved of Rāma and a younger brother to boot. No wonder, then, that the journey should be so delightful for him."—this way saints, sages, and hermits thus reasoned amongst themselves as they gazed upon Bharat and rejoiced at heart. Indra was troubled by the sight of his powers; verily the world appears good to the good and vile to the vile. Then turning to his Gurū Brihaspati said Indra, "Something must be done, sir, to prevent the meeting between Rāma and Bharat.

दोहा-dohā:

रामु सँकोची प्रेम बस भरत सपेम पयोधि ।
rāmu saṁkocī prema basa bharata sapema payodhi,
बनी बात बेगरन चहति करिअ जतनु छलु सोधि ॥२१७॥
banī bāta begarana cahati karia jatanu chalu sodhi. 217.

Trans:

Rāma is so modest and sympathetic, and Bharat such an ocean of affection; our scheme threatens to be spoilt; we must bestir ourselves and devise some new stratagem."

चौपाई-caupāī:

बचन सुनत सुरगुरु मुसुकाने । सहसनयन बिनु लोचन जाने ॥
bacana sunata suraguru musukāne, sahasanayana binu locana jāne.
मायापति सेवक सन माया । करइ त उलटि परइ सुरराया ॥
māyāpati sevaka sana māyā, karai ta ulaṭi parai surarāyā.
तब किछु कीन्ह राम रुख जानी । अब कुचालि करि होइहि हानी ॥
taba kichu kīnha rāma rukha jānī, aba kucāli kari hoihi hānī.
सुनु सुरेस रघुनाथ सुभाऊ । निज अपराध रिसाहिं न काऊ ॥
sunu suresa raghunātha subhāū, nija aparādha risāhiṁ na kāū.
जो अपराधु भगत कर करई । राम रोष पावक सो जरई ॥
jo aparādhu bhagata kara karaī, rāma roṣa pāvaka so jaraī.
लोकहुँ बेद बिदित इतिहासा । यह महिमा जानहिं दुरबासा ॥
lokahuṁ beda bidita itihāsā, yaha mahimā jānahiṁ durabāsā.
भरत सरिस को राम सनेही । जगु जप राम रामु जप जेही ॥
bharata sarisa ko rāma sanehī, jagu japa rāma rāmu japa jehī.

Trans:

Hearing this speech and finding the thousand-eyed so blind, the teacher of the gods smiled and said, "Leave tricks alone; it will be all trouble in vain; any deception here would be absurd. O king of heaven, any delusion practiced on a servant of the Lord of delusion must recoil on the contriver. I interfered once, knowing it was Rāma's wish, but any underhand work now would only do harm. Listen, O king; it is Rāma's nature never to be angry at any sin against himself; but whoever sins against one of his servants is consumed in the fire of his wrath. Popular tradition and the Vedas abound in such legends; Durvāsā knows well this great trait in his character. And is there anyone so faithful to Rāma as Bharat—who is ever repeating Rāma's name and Rāma his?

दोहा-dohā:

मनहुँ न आनिअ अमरपति रघुबर भगत अकाजु ।
manahuṁ na ānia amarapati raghubara bhagata akāju,
अजसु लोक परलोक दुख दिन दिन सोक समाजु ॥२१८॥
ajasu loka paraloka dukha dina dina soka samāju. 218.

Trans:

Think not, lord of the immortals, to injure any servant of Raghubar's, unless you would suffer the pain of disgrace in this world, sorrow in the next, and a daily increasing burden of regret.

चौपाई-caupāī:

सुनु सुरेस उपदेसु हमारा । रामहि सेवकु परम पिआरा ॥
sunu suresa upadesu hamārā, rāmahi sevaku parama piārā.
मानत सुखु सेवक सेवकाईं । सेवक बैर बैरु अधिकाईं ॥
mānata sukhu sevaka sevakāīṁ, sevaka baira bairu adhikāīṁ.
जद्यपि सम नहिं राग न रोषू । गहहिं न पाप पूनु गुन दोषू ॥
jadyapi sama nahiṁ rāga na roṣū, gahahiṁ na pāpa pūnu guna doṣū.
करम प्रधान बिस्व करि राखा । जो जस करइ सो तस फलु चाखा ॥
karama pradhāna bisva kari rākhā, jo jasa karai so tasa phalu cākhā.
तदपि करहिं सम बिषम बिहारा । भगत अभगत हृदय अनुसारा ॥
tadapi karahiṁ sama biṣama bihārā, bhagata abhagata hṛdaya anusārā.
अगुन अलेप अमान एकरस । रामु सगुन भए भगत पेम बस ॥
aguna alepa amāna ekarasa, rāmu saguna bhae bhagata pema basa.
राम सदा सेवक रुचि राखी । बेद पुरान साधु सुर साखी ॥
rāma sadā sevaka ruci rākhī, beda purāna sādhu sura sākhī.
अस जियँ जानि तजहु कुटिलाई । करहु भरत पद प्रीति सुहाई ॥
asa jiyaṁ jāni tajahu kuṭilāī, karahu bharata pada prīti suhāī.

Trans:

Hearken to my advice, king of the gods: Rāma has the greatest love for his servants; he is pleased at any service done to a servant, while enmity to a servant is the height of enmity to himself. Although he is ever the same, without either passion or anger, and contracts neither sin nor merit, virtue nor defect; and though he has made fate the sovereign of the universe, and everyone has to taste the fruit of his own karma, still he plays at variations according as hearts are faithful or unfaithful. Though without attributes or form, illimitable and impassible, Rāma has yielded to the love of his followers and taken a material form. He has always regarded the wishes of his devotees the highest—as the Vedas and Purānas and gods and saints bear witness. Knowing this, refrain from mischief and show Bharat fitting devotion.

दोहा-dohā:

राम भगत परहित निरत पर दुख दुखी दयाल ।
rāma bhagata parahita nirata para dukha dukhī dayāla,
भगत सिरोमनि भरत तें जनि डरपहु सुरपाल ॥२१९॥
bhagata siromani bharata teṁ jani ḍarapahu surapāla. 219.

Trans:

Any worshipper of Rāma is zealous for the good of others, sorrows with the sorrowful, and is full of compassion. Thus, O king, remain untroubled on account of Bharat, who is the crown of worshippers.

चौपाई-caupāī:

सत्यसंध प्रभु सुर हितकारी । भरत राम आयस अनुसारी ॥
satyasaṁdha prabhu sura hitakārī, bharata rāma āyasa anusārī.
स्वारथ बिबस बिकल तुम्ह होहू । भरत दोसु नहिं राउर मोहू ॥
svāratha bibasa bikala tumha hohū, bharata dosu nahiṁ rāura mohū.
सुनि सुरबर सुरगुर बर बानी । भा प्रमोदु मन मिटी गलानी ॥
suni surabara suragura bara bānī, bhā pramodu mana miṭī galānī.
बरषि प्रसून हरषि सुरराऊ । लगे सराहन भरत सुभाऊ ॥
baraṣi prasūna haraṣi surarāū, lage sarāhana bharata subhāū.
एहि बिधि भरत चले मग जाहीं । दसा देखि मुनि सिद्ध सिहाहीं ॥
ehi bidhi bharata cale maga jāhīṁ, dasā dekhi muni siddha sihāhīṁ.
जबहिं रामु कहि लेहिं उसासा । उमगत पेमु मनहँ चहु पासा ॥
jabahiṁ rāmu kahi lehiṁ usāsā, umagata pemu manahaṁ cahu pāsā.
द्रवहिं बचन सुनि कुलिस पषाना । पुरजन पेमु न जाइ बखाना ॥
dravahiṁ bacana suni kulisa paṣānā, purajana pemu na jāi bakhānā.
बीच बास करि जमुनहिं आए । निरखि नीरु लोचन जल छाए ॥
bīca bāsa kari jamunahiṁ āe, nirakhi nīru locana jala chāe.

Trans:

The Lord is an ocean of truth and a well-wisher of the gods, and Bharat obeys his orders. You are troubled by your own selfishness. There is no fault in Bharat; it is all delusion on your part." When the great god heard the words of the heavenly preceptor he got understanding and his anxiety passed away. In his joy he rained down flowers and began to extol Bharat's good qualities. In this manner Bharat went on his way, while saints and sages looked on and praised. Whenever he sighed and uttered Rāma's name, it seemed like the bubbling over of love. Thunderbolts and stones melted at his words; as for the people, their emotion was beyond description. Encamping halfway, he came to the Yamunā; and as he gazed on its water his eyes filled with tears.

दोहा-dohā:

रघुबर बरन बिलोकि बर बारि समेत समाज ।
raghubara barana biloki bara bāri sameta samāja,
होत मगन बारिधि बिरह चढ़े बिबेक जहाज ॥२२०॥
hota magana bāridhi biraha caṛhe bibeka jahāja. 220.

Trans:

As he and his retinue gazed on the lovely stream, the color of Rāma's body, he was plunged into a sea of desolation, till he climbed the boat of discretion.

चौपाई-caupāī:

जमुन तीर तेहि दिन करि बासू । भयउ समय सम सबहि सुपासू ॥
jamuna tīra tehi dina kari bāsū, bhayau samaya sama sabahi supāsū.
रातिहिं घाट घाट की तरनी । आईं अगनित जाहिं न बरनी ॥
rātihiṁ ghāṭa ghāṭa kī taranī, āīṁ aganita jāhiṁ na baranī.
प्रात पार भए एकहि खेवाँ । तोषे रामसखा की सेवाँ ॥
prāta pāra bhae ekahi khevāṁ, toṣe rāmasakhā kī sevāṁ.
चले नहाइ नदिहि सिर नाई । साथ निषादनाथ दोउ भाई ॥
cale nahāi nadihi sira nāī, sātha niṣādanātha dou bhāī.
आगें मुनिबर बाहन आछें । राजसमाज जाइ सबु पाछें ॥
āgeṁ munibara bāhana ācheṁ, rājasamāja jāi sabu pācheṁ.
तेहि पाछें दोउ बंधु पयादें । भूषन बसन बेष सुठि सादें ॥
tehi pācheṁ dou baṁdhu payādeṁ, bhūṣana basana beṣa suṭhi sādeṁ.
सेवक सुहृद सचिवसुत साथा । सुमिरत लखनु सीय रघुनाथा ॥
sevaka suhṛda sacivasuta sāthā, sumirata lakhanu sīya raghunāthā.
जहँ जहँ राम बास बिश्रामा । तहँ तहँ करहिं सप्रेम प्रनामा ॥
jahaṁ jahaṁ rāma bāsa biśrāmā, tahaṁ tahaṁ karahiṁ saprema pranāmā.

Trans:

That day they halted on the bank of the Yamunā, giving everyone time for what they had to do. In the night many boats came from many a Ghāts, in numbers greater than what could be counted. At daybreak all crossed in a single trip. Everyone was pleased with the services rendered by the Nishād chief. After bathing and bowing to the river, the two brothers set forth with the Nishād chief. First of all in his glorious car went the great saint, followed by all the royal host; after them the two brothers on foot—their dress, apparel, and ornaments, all of the very simplest; and with them their servants and friends and the minister's son, all the while invoking names of Lakshman, Sītā, Rāma. Any spot wherever Rāma had encamped or rested they lovingly saluted.

दोहा-dohā:

मगबासी नर नारि सुनि धाम काम तजि धाइ ।
magabāsī nara nāri suni dhāma kāma taji dhāi,
देखि सरूप सनेह सब मुदित जनम फलु पाइ ॥२२१॥
dekhi sarūpa saneha saba mudita janama phalu pāi. 221.

Trans:

At the news, the dwellers by the roadside left their household work and ran after them; seeing his form, they were overcome with love and joy and had their life's reward.

चौपाई-caupāī:

कहहिं सपेम एक एक पाहीं । रामु लखनु सखि होहिं कि नाहीं ॥
kahahiṁ sapema eka eka pāhīṁ, rāmu lakhanu sakhi hohiṁ ki nāhīṁ.
बय बपु बरन रूपु सोइ आली । सीलु सनेहु सरिस सम चाली ॥
baya bapu barana rūpu soi ālī, sīlu sanehu sarisa sama cālī.
बेषु न सो सखि सीय न संगा । आगें अनी चली चतुरंगा ॥
beṣu na so sakhi sīya na saṁgā, āgeṁ anī calī caturaṁgā.
नहिं प्रसन्न मुख मानस खेदा । सखि संदेहु होइ एहिं भेदा ॥
nahiṁ prasanna mukha mānasa khedā, sakhi saṁdehu hoi ehiṁ bhedā.
तासु तरक तियगन मन मानी । कहहिं सकल तेहि सम न सयानी ॥
tāsu taraka tiyagana mana mānī, kahahiṁ sakala tehi sama na sayānī.
तेहि सराहि बानी फुरि पूजी । बोली मधुर बचन तिय दूजी ॥
tehi sarāhi bānī phuri pūjī, bolī madhura bacana tiya dūjī.
कहि सपेम सब कथाप्रसंगू । जेहि बिधि राम राज रस भंगू ॥
kahi sapema saba kathāprasaṁgū, jehi bidhi rāma rāja rasa bhaṁgū.
भरतहि बहुरि सराहन लागी । सील सनेह सुभाय सुभागी ॥
bharatahi bahuri sarāhana lāgī, sīla saneha subhāya subhāgī.

Trans:

Lovingly one spoke to others, "Friend, are they Rāma and Lakshman—or not? In age, figure, complexion, and beauty they are the same, dear girl, and also resemble them every bit in affectionate disposition. But their dress is not the same, friend, nor is Sītā with them, and before them marches a vast host of horses and foot-soldiers, elephants and chariots. Nor are they glad of countenance, but have some sorrow at heart. From this difference, O friend, a doubt arises." The women were persuaded by her arguments and said, "There is no one so clever as you." After praising her and admiring the truth of her remarks, another woman spoke in winning tones, and lovingly related the whole history—how Rāma had lost the delights of empire; and again set to praising Bharat for his affectionate disposition and happy nature.

दोहा-dohā:

चलत पयादें खात फल पिता दीन्ह तजि राजु ।
calata payādeṁ khāta phala pitā dīnha taji rāju,
जात मनावन रघुबरहि भरत सरिस को आजु ॥२२२॥
jāta manāvana raghubarahi bharata sarisa ko āju. 222.

Trans:

"He travels on foot, feeding only on wild fruits, and abandoning the crown given him by his father, and is going to Rāma to persuade him to return. Is there anyone at the present day like Bharat?

चौपाई-caupāī:

भायप भगति भरत आचरनू । कहत सुनत दुख दूषन हरनू ॥
bhāyapa bhagati bharata ācaranū, kahata sunata dukha dūṣana haranū.
जो किछु कहब थोर सखि सोई । राम बंधु अस काहे न होई ॥
jo kichu kahaba thora sakhi soī, rāma baṁdhu asa kāhe na hoī.
हम सब सानुज भरतहि देखें । भइन्ह धन्य जुबती जन लेखें ॥
hama saba sānuja bharatahi dekheṁ, bhainha dhanya jubatī jana lekheṁ.
सुनि गुन देखि दसा पछिताहीं । कैकइ जननि जोगु सुतु नाहीं ॥
suni guna dekhi dasā pachitāhīṁ, kaikai janani jogu sutu nāhīṁ.
कोउ कह दूषनु रानिहि नाहिन । बिधि सबु कीन्ह हमहि जो दाहिन ॥
kou kaha dūṣanu rānihi nāhina, bidhi sabu kīnha hamahi jo dāhina.
कहँ हम लोक बेद बिधि हीनी । लघु तिय कुल करतूति मलीनी ॥
kahaṁ hama loka beda bidhi hīnī, laghu tiya kula karatūti malīnī.
बसहिं कुदेस कुगाँव कुबामा । कहँ यह दरसु पुन्य परिनामा ॥
basahiṁ kudesa kugāṁva kubāmā, kahaṁ yaha darasu punya parināmā.
अस अनंदु अचिरिजु प्रति ग्रामा । जनु मरुभूमि कलपतरु जामा ॥
asa anaṁdu aciriju prati grāmā, janu marubhūmi kalapataru jāmā.

Trans:

To tell and hear of Bharat's brotherly devotion and his course of action dispels all sin and sorrow. Anything that I can say, friend, is all too little. He is Rāma's brother; how could he be different from him? All of us, who have seen him and Shatrughan, have truly become blessed among women." Hearing his virtues and seeing his forlorn state someone lamented, "Surely he is not a fit son for such a vile mother as Kaekayī." Another said, "It is no blame to the queen that god has been so kind to us. What are we—outcasts from the world and Vedas, women of low birth and mean livelihood, whose home is a wretched hovel in some poor village of a paltry county—that we should have such a vision, a sufficient reward for the highest religious merit?" There was the same delight and wonder in every town, as though the tree of paradise had sprung up in the desert.

दोहा-dohā:

भरत दरसु देखत खुलेउ मग लोगन्ह कर भागु ।
bharata darasu dekhata khuleu maga loganha kara bhāgu,
जनु सिंघलबासिन्ह भयउ बिधि बस सुलभ प्रयागु ॥२२३॥
janu siṁghalabāsinha bhayau bidhi basa sulabha prayāgu. 223.

Trans:

At the sight of Bharat, the good fortune of the people by the wayside manifested itself in like manner, as though by the will of providence Prayāg had been made accessible to the people of Lankā.

चौपाई-caupāī:

निज गुन सहित राम गुन गाथा । सुनत जाहिं सुमिरत रघुनाथा ॥
nija guna sahita rāma guna gāthā, sunata jāhiṁ sumirata raghunāthā.
तीरथ मुनि आश्रम सुरधामा । निरखि निमज्जहिं करहिं प्रनामा ॥
tīratha muni āśrama suradhāmā, nirakhi nimajjahiṁ karahiṁ pranāmā.
मनहीं मन मागहिं बरु एहू । सीय राम पद पदुम सनेहू ॥
manahīṁ mana māgahiṁ baru ehū, sīya rāma pada paduma sanehū.
मिलहिं किरात कोल बनबासी । बैखानस बटु जती उदासी ॥
milahiṁ kirāta kola banabāsī, baikhānasa baṭu jatī udāsī.
करि प्रनामु पूँछहिं जेहि तेही । केहि बन लखनु रामु बैदेही ॥
kari pranāmu pūṁchahiṁ jehi tehī, kehi bana lakhanu rāmu baidehī.
ते प्रभु समाचार सब कहहीं । भरतहि देखि जनम फलु लहहीं ॥
te prabhu samācāra saba kahahīṁ, bharatahi dekhi janama phalu lahahīṁ.
जे जन कहहिं कुसल हम देखे । ते प्रिय राम लखन सम लेखे ॥
je jana kahahiṁ kusala hama dekhe, te priya rāma lakhana sama lekhe.
एहि बिधि बूझत सबहि सुबानी । सुनत राम बनबास कहानी ॥
ehi bidhi būjhata sabahi subānī, sunata rāma banabāsa kahānī.

Trans:

Hearing such praises and Rāma's many virtues, he went on his way, ever mindful of Raghunāth. Whenever he spied any holy place, or hermitage, or temple, he bathed and reverently saluted it, praying in his heart of hearts for this one boon: perseverance in devotion to the feet of Sītā and Rāma. If there met him a *Kirāt* or *Kol*, or other dweller in the woods, anchorite or student, hermit or ascetic, whoever he might be, he saluted him and asked in what part of the forest were Lakshman, Rāma, and the Videhan princess. They told him all the news of the Lord, and at the sight of Bharat reaped their life's reward. If any person said, "We have seen them well," they were counted as dear as Rāma and Lakshman themselves. In this manner asking courteously of everyone, he heard the whole story of Rāma's forest life.

दोहा-dohā:

तेहि बासर बसि प्रातहीं चले सुमिरि रघुनाथ ।
tehi bāsara basi prātahīṁ cale sumiri raghunātha,
राम दरस की लालसा भरत सरिस सब साथ ॥२२४॥
rāma darasa kī lālasā bharata sarisa saba sātha. 224.

Trans:

Halting that day, Bharat started again at dawn invoking Raghunāth; all who were with him being equally desirous like himself for a sight of Rāma.

चौपाई-caupāī:

मंगल सगुन होहिं सब काहू । फरकहिं सुखद बिलोचन बाहू ॥
maṁgala saguna hohiṁ saba kāhū, pharakahiṁ sukhada bilocana bāhū.
भरतहि सहित समाज उछाहू । मिलिहहिं रामु मिटिहि दुख दाहू ॥
bharatahi sahita samāja uchāhū, milihahiṁ rāmu miṭihi dukha dāhū.
करत मनोरथ जस जियँ जाके । जाहिं सनेह सुराँ सब छाके ॥
karata manoratha jasa jiyaṁ jāke, jāhiṁ saneha surāṁ saba chāke.
सिथिल अंग पग मग डगि डोलहिं । बिहबल बचन पेम बस बोलहिं ॥
sithila aṁga paga maga ḍagi ḍolahiṁ, bihabala bacana pema basa bolahiṁ.
रामसखाँ तेहि समय देखावा । सैल सिरोमनि सहज सुहावा ॥
rāmasakhāṁ tehi samaya dekhāvā, saila siromani sahaja suhāvā.
जासु समीप सरित पय तीरा । सीय समेत बसहिं दोउ बीरा ॥
jāsu samīpa sarita paya tīrā, sīya sameta basahiṁ dou bīrā.
देखि करहिं सब दंड प्रनामा । कहि जय जानकि जीवन रामा ॥
dekhi karahiṁ saba daṁḍa pranāmā, kahi jaya jānaki jīvana rāmā.
प्रेम मगन अस राज समाजू । जनु फिरि अवध चले रघुराजू ॥
prema magana asa rāja samājū, janu phiri avadha cale raghurājū.

Trans:

Everyone had auspicious omens, lucky throbbings in the eyes and arms; Bharat and the host rejoiced, "Rāma will be found and our sore distress will be at an end." Each indulged in his own fancy; and as they marched all seemed intoxicated with the wine of love, their limbs relaxed, their feet unsteady on the ground, and the accents of their voice inarticulate from excess of emotion. Then came the time when from afar Rāma's guide pointed out the crest-jewel of the hills in all its beauty, near which, on the river's bank, the two heroes and Sītā dwelt. All at the sight fell to the ground with cries of "Glory to Rāma, the life of Jānakī!" The royal host was as overwhelmed with emotion as though Rāma had come back to Avadh.

दोहा-dohā:

भरत प्रेमु तेहि समय जस तस कहि सकइ न सेषु ।
bharata premu tehi samaya jasa tasa kahi sakai na seṣu,
कबिहि अगम जिमि ब्रह्मसुखु अह मम मलिन जनेषु ॥२२५॥
kabihi agama jimi brahmasukhu aha mama malina janeṣu. 225,

Trans:

Bharat's love at that time was such that not Sheshnāg could describe it; it is as far beyond the poet as the bliss of heaven is beyond a man stained of selfishness and sensuality.

चौपाई-caupāī:

सकल सनेह सिथिल रघुबर कें । गए कोस दुइ दिनकर ढरकें ॥
sakala saneha sithila raghubara keṁ, gae kosa dui dinakara ḍharakeṁ.
जलु थलु देखि बसे निसि बीतें । कीन्ह गवन रघुनाथ पिरीतें ॥
jalu thalu dekhi base nisi bīteṁ, kīnha gavana raghunātha pirīteṁ.
उहाँ रामु रजनी अवसेषा । जागे सीयँ सपन अस देखा ॥
uhāṁ rāmu rajanī avaseṣā, jāge sīyaṁ sapana asa dekhā.
सहित समाज भरत जनु आए । नाथ बियोग ताप तन ताए ॥
sahita samāja bharata janu āe, nātha biyoga tāpa tana tāe.
सकल मलिन मन दीन दुखारी । देखीं सासु आन अनुहारी ॥
sakala malina mana dīna dukhārī, dekhīṁ sāsu āna anuhārī.
सुनि सिय सपन भरे जल लोचन । भए सोचबस सोच बिमोचन ॥
suni siya sapana bhare jala locana, bhae socabasa soca bimocana.
लखन सपन यह नीक न होई । कठिन कुचाह सुनाइहि कोई ॥
lakhana sapana yaha nīka na hoī, kaṭhina kucāha sunāihi koī.
अस कहि बंधु समेत नहाने । पूजि पुरारि साधु सनमाने ॥
asa kahi baṁdhu sameta nahāne, pūji purāri sādhu sanamāne.

Trans:

Being all overpowered by their love for Raghubar, they had covered but four miles by the close of the day; then scanning land and water they halted. When the night was past, the beloved of Raghunāth sallied forth again. Out there while it was as yet dark, Rāma awoke. Sītā told him what she had seen in a dream, "Me-thought Bharat had come with an entourage, being tortured in body by the fever of separation from his Lord; all were sad, wretched, downcast; and the queen's appearance appeared greatly altered." On hearing Sītā's dream, the healer of sorrows grew sorrowful, and his eyes filled with tears, "This dream, O Lakshman, augurs no good. We shall hear of something that we by no means wished." So saying, he and his brother bathed, worshipped Purārī, and propitiated the saints.

छंद-chaṁda:

सनमानि सुर मुनि बंदि बैठे उतर दिसि देखत भए ।
sanamāni sura muni baṁdi baiṭhe utara disi dekhata bhae,
नभ धूरि खग मृग भूरि भागे बिकल प्रभु आश्रम गए ॥
nabha dhūri khaga mṛga bhūri bhāge bikala prabhu āśrama gae.
तुलसी उठे अवलोकि कारनु काह चित सचकित रहे ।
tulasī uṭhe avaloki kāranu kāha cita sacakita rahe,
सब समाचार किरात कोलन्हि आइ तेहि अवसर कहे ॥
saba samācāra kirāta kolanhi āi tehi avasara kahe.

Trans:

After placating the gods and reverencing the saints, the Lord went and sat down with his gaze to the north. The dust in the air and the many birds and deer taking to flight disquieted him and he returned to the hermitage. He stood up and looked, anxious in mind as to the cause. Then came some *Kirāt*s and *Kol*s and told him all the news.

दोहा-dohā:

सुनत सुमंगल बैन मन प्रमोद तन पुलक भर ।
sunata sumaṁgala baina mana pramoda tana pulaka bhara,
सरद सरोरुह नैन तुलसी भरे सनेह जल ॥२२६॥
sarada saroruha naina tulasī bhare saneha jala. 226.

Trans:

When he heard the glad tidings his heart was full of joy, and his body quivered all over; while his eyes, like the autumnal lotus, were filled with the tears of affection.

चौपाई-caupāī:

बहुरि सोचबस भे सियरवनू । कारन कवन भरत आगवनू ॥
bahuri socabasa bhe siyaravanū, kārana kavana bharata āgavanū.
एक आइ अस कहा बहोरी । सेन संग चतुरंग न थोरी ॥
eka āi asa kahā bahorī, sena saṁga caturaṁga na thorī.
सो सुनि रामहि भा अति सोचू । इत पितु बच इत बंधु सकोचू ॥
so suni rāmahi bhā ati socū, ita pitu baca ita baṁdhu sakocū.
भरत सुभाउ समुझि मन माहीं । प्रभु चित हित थिति पावत नाहीं ॥
bharata subhāu samujhi mana māhīṁ, prabhu cita hita thiti pāvata nāhīṁ.
समाधान तब भा यह जाने । भरतु कहे महुँ साधु सयाने ॥
samādhāna taba bhā yaha jāne, bharatu kahe mahuṁ sādhu sayāne.
लखन लखेउ प्रभु हृदयँ खभारू । कहत समय सम नीति बिचारू ॥
lakhana lakheu prabhu hṛdayaṁ khabhārū, kahata samaya sama nīti bicārū.
बिनु पूछें कछु कहउँ गोसाईं । सेवकु समयँ न ढीठ ढिठाईं ॥
binu pūcheṁ kachu kahauṁ gosāīṁ, sevaku samayaṁ na ḍhīṭha ḍhiṭhāīṁ.
तुम्ह सर्बग्य सिरोमनि स्वामी । आपनि समुझि कहउँ अनुगामी ॥
tumha sarbagya siromani svāmī, āpani samujhi kahauṁ anugāmī.

Trans:

Again Sītā's Lord became anxious, "What can be the cause of Bharat's coming?" Then came one and said, "There is with him no small army in full equipment." Hearing this Rāma was greatly disturbed; on the one hand was his father's injunction, on the other his regard for his brother. Thinking to himself over Bharat's disposition, the Lord's mind found no sure standing-point; but at last he calmed himself with the reflection, "Bharat is said to be good and sensible." Lakshman saw that his Lord was troubled at heart, and spoke out as he thought the occasion demanded, "I speak, sire, before I am asked; but sometimes impertinence in a servant is not irreverent. You, master, are the crown of the wise; I a mere retainer, but I say what I think.

दोहा-dohā:

नाथ सुहृद सुठि सरल चित सील सनेह निधान ।
nātha suhṛda suṭhi sarala cita sīla saneha nidhāna,
सब पर प्रीति प्रतीति जियँ जानिअ आपु समान ॥२२७॥
saba para prīti pratīti jiyaṁ jānia āpu samāna. 227.

Trans:

You, my Lord, are kind and easy, a storehouse of amiability; you love and trust everyone, and think of them like you yourself are.

चौपाई-caupāī:

बिषई जीव पाइ प्रभुताई । मूढ़ मोह बस होहिं जनाई ॥
biṣaī jīva pāi prabhutāī, mūṛha moha basa hohiṁ janāī.
भरतु नीति रत साधु सुजाना । प्रभु पद प्रेमु सकल जगु जाना ॥
bharatu nīti rata sādhu sujānā, prabhu pada premu sakala jagu jānā.
तेऊ आजु राम पदु पाई । चले धरम मरजाद मेटाई ॥
teū āju rāma padu pāī, cale dharama marajāda meṭāī.
कुटिल कुबंधु कुअवसरु ताकी । जानि राम बनबास एकाकी ॥
kuṭila kubaṁdhu kuavasaru tākī, jāni rāma banabāsa ekākī.

करि कुमंत्रु मन साजि समाजू । आए करै अकंटक राजू ॥
kari kumaṁtru mana sāji samājū, āe karai akaṁṭaka rājū.
कोटि प्रकार कलपि कुटलाई । आए दल बटोरि दोउ भाई ॥
koṭi prakāra kalapi kuṭalāī, āe dala baṭori dou bhāī.
जौं जियँ होति न कपट कुचाली । केहि सोहाति रथ बाजि गजाली ॥
jauṁ jiyaṁ hoti na kapaṭa kucālī, kehi sohāti ratha bāji gajālī.
भरतहि दोसु देइ को जाएँ । जग बौराइ राज पदु पाएँ ॥
bharatahi dosu dei ko jāeṁ, jaga baurāi rāja padu pāeṁ.

Trans:

A worldly man who gets lordship becomes mad and infatuated and soon is lead astray. Bharat was well taught, good, and clever, and, as everyone knew, was devoted to his Lord's feet; but now that he has become king, he breaks down in his course all the bounds of duty. A wicked and ill-disposed brother having spied out his time, and knowing that Rāma is alone in the forest, he has taken evil counsel, and equipped an army, and has come to make his sovereignty secure. After plotting all sorts of wicked schemes the two brothers have assembled their army and come. If he had no treacherous malpractice at heart, why should he affect chariots and horses and elephants? But why reproach Bharat? All in the world go mad on getting dominion.

दोहा-dohā:

ससि गुर तिय गामी नघुषु चढ़ेउ भूमिसुर जान ।
sasi gura tiya gāmī naghuṣu caṛheu bhūmisura jāna,
लोक बेद तें बिमुख भा अधम न बेन समान ॥२२८॥
loka beda teṁ bimukha bhā adhama na bena samāna. 228.

Trans:

The Moon-god debauched his Gurū's wife; Nahush mounted a palanquin borne by Brahmins; and who fell down so low as King Vena, the enemy of established usage and the Vedas?

चौपाई-caupāī:

सहसबाहु सुरनाथु त्रिसंकू । केहि न राजमद दीन्ह कलंकू ॥
sahasabāhu suranāthu trisaṁkū, kehi na rājamada dīnha kalaṁkū.
भरत कीन्ह यह उचित उपाऊ । रिपु रिन रंच न राखब काऊ ॥
bharata kīnha yaha ucita upāū, ripu rina raṁca na rākhaba kāū.
एक कीन्हि नहिं भरत भलाई । निदरे रामु जानि असहाई ॥
eka kīnhi nahiṁ bharata bhalāī, nidare rāmu jāni asahāī.
समुझि परिहि सोउ आजु बिसेषी । समर सरोष राम मुखु पेखी ॥
samujhi parihi sou āju biseṣī, samara saroṣa rāma mukhu pekhī.
एतना कहत नीति रस भूला । रन रस बिटपु पुलक मिस फूला ॥
etanā kahata nīti rasa bhūlā, rana rasa biṭapu pulaka misa phūlā.
प्रभु पद बंदि सीस रज राखी । बोले सत्य सहज बलु भाषी ॥
prabhu pada baṁdi sīsa raja rākhī, bole satya sahaja balu bhāṣī.
अनुचित नाथ न मानब मोरा । भरत हमहि उपचार न थोरा ॥
anucita nātha na mānaba morā, bharata hamahi upacāra na thorā.
कहँ लगि सहिअ रहिअ मनु मारें । नाथ साथ धनु हाथ हमारें ॥
kahaṁ lagi sahia rahia manu māreṁ, nātha sātha dhanu hātha hamāreṁ.

Trans:

Sahastr-bahu, Indra, Trishanku—all were brought to disgrace by the intoxication of kingly powers. Bharat has planned this clever scheme so as not to leave himself a single enemy in the field; but in one point he has made a mistake: in being hostile to Rāma assuming him forlorn; he will discover this today with a vengeance, when he sees Rāma's indignant face in the battle." So saying, he forgot all prudence, and his whole body, so to speak, bristled with belligerence. Falling at his Lord's feet and putting the dust of them upon his head, he thundered with innate honest ferocity, "My Lord, think it not wrong of me; Bharat has tried me not a little; now, how long shall I endure to remain quiet, with my Lord being with me and my bow in my hand?

दोहा-dohā:

छत्रि जाति रघुकुल जनमु राम अनुग जगु जान ।
chatri jāti raghukula janamu rāma anuga jagu jāna,
लातहुँ मारें चढ़ति सिर नीच को धूरि समान ॥२२९॥
lātahuṁ māreṁ caṛhati sira nīca ko dhūri samāna. 229.

Trans:

Am I not of warrior descent, a scion of the house of Raghu, and known throughout the world as Rāma's brother? What is so low as the dust? Yet if stirred by a kick it rises and falls upon the head."

चौपाई-caupāī:

उठि कर जोरि रजायसु मागा । मनहुँ बीर रस सोवत जागा ॥
uṭhi kara jori rajāyasu māgā, manahuṁ bīra rasa sovata jāgā.
बाँधि जटा सिर कसि कटि भाथा । साजि सरासनु सायकु हाथा ॥
bāṁdhi jaṭā sira kasi kaṭi bhāthā, sāji sarāsanu sāyaku hāthā.
आजु राम सेवक जसु लेऊँ । भरतहि समर सिखावन देऊँ ॥
āju rāma sevaka jasu leūṁ, bharatahi samara sikhāvana deūṁ.
राम निरादर कर फलु पाई । सोवहुँ समर सेज दोउ भाई ॥
rāma nirādara kara phalu pāī, sovahuṁ samara seja dou bhāī.
आइ बना भल सकल समाजू । प्रगट करउँ रिस पाछिल आजू ॥
āi banā bhala sakala samājū, pragaṭa karauṁ risa pāchila ājū.
जिमि करि निकर दलइ मृगराजू । लेइ लपेटि लवा जिमि बाजू ॥
jimi kari nikara dalai mṛgarājū, lei lapeṭi lavā jimi bājū.
तैसेहिं भरतहि सेन समेता । सानुज निदरि निपातउँ खेता ॥
taisehiṁ bharatahi sena sametā, sānuja nidari nipātauṁ khetā.
जौं सहाय कर संकरु आई । तौ मारउँ रन राम दोहाई ॥
jauṁ sahāya kara saṁkaru āī, tau mārauṁ rana rāma dohāī.

Trans:

As he stood with clasped hands and sought permission, he seemed like heroism itself aroused from slumber. Binding up his hair in a knot, girding on his quiver by his side, trimming his bow, and taking arrows in hand he spoke, "Today I shall distinguish myself as Rāma's servant and will give Bharat a lesson in fight. Reaping the fruit of their contempt for Rāma, both brothers shall sleep on the couch of battle. It is so well that the whole host has come; today I shall manifest my wrath and have done with it. As a lion tears to pieces a herd of elephants, or as a hawk clutches and carries off a quail, so will I lightly overthrow upon the field Bharat and his brother and all their host. If Shiva himself should come to their aid, in Rāma's name, I would worst him in battle."

दोहा-dohā:

अति सरोष माखे लखनु लखि सुनि सपथ प्रवान ।
ati saroṣa mākhe lakhanu lakhi suni sapatha pravāna,
सभय लोक सब लोकपति चाहत भभरि भगान ॥२३०॥
sabhaya loka saba lokapati cāhata bhabhari bhagāna. 230.

Trans:

Lakshman spoke so furiously that the regents of the spheres, beholding and hearing his solemn oath, looked on in terror and longed to flee away.

चौपाई-caupāī:

जगु भय मगन गगन भइ बानी । लखन बाहुबलु बिपुल बखानी ॥
jagu bhaya magana gagana bhai bānī, lakhana bāhubalu bipula bakhānī.
तात प्रताप प्रभाउ तुम्हारा । को कहि सकइ को जाननिहारा ॥
tāta pratāpa prabhāu tumhārā, ko kahi sakai ko jānanihārā.
अनुचित उचित काजु किछु होऊ । समुझि करिअ भल कह सबु कोऊ ॥
anucita ucita kāju kichu hoū, samujhi karia bhala kaha sabu koū.

सहसा करि पाछें पछिताहीं । कहहिं बेद बुध ते बुध नाहीं ॥
sahasā kari pāchem̐ pachitāhīm̐, kahahim̐ beda budha te budha nāhīm̐.
सुनि सुर बचन लखन सकुचाने । राम सीयँ सादर सनमाने ॥
suni sura bacana lakhana sakucāne, rāma sīyam̐ sādara sanamāne.
कही तात तुम्ह नीति सुहाई । सब तें कठिन राजमदु भाई ॥
kahī tāta tumha nīti suhāī, saba tem̐ kaṭhina rājamadu bhāī.
जो अचवँत नृप मातहिं तेई । नाहिन साधुसभा जेहिं सेई ॥
jo acavam̐ta nṛpa mātahim̐ teī, nāhina sādhusabhā jehim̐ seī.
सुनहु लखन भल भरत सरीसा । बिधि प्रपंच महँ सुना न दीसा ॥
sunahu lakhana bhala bharata sarīsā, bidhi prapam̐ca maham̐ sunā na dīsā.

Trans:

The world was entranced. Then a voice was heard in the air, declaring the mighty power of Lakshman's arm, "Son, who can tell, or who can understand your might and majesty? But any business, should be done after deliberate thought, weighing right and wrong—so that it meets approval. They who act rashly and afterwards repent, the Vedas say are anything but wise." On hearing this voice from heaven Lakshman was abashed; and both Rāma and Sītā addressed him courteously, "What you have said, brother, is sound wisdom; the intoxication of power is the worst of all; the merest taste of it maddens any king who has not been trained in the school of good philosophy. But hearken Lakshman: in the whole of god's creation I have never seen nor heard of anyone so good as Bharat.

दोहा-dohā:

भरतहि होइ न राजमदु बिधि हरि हर पद पाइ ।
bharatahi hoi na rājamadu bidhi hari hara pada pāi,
कबहुँ कि काँजी सीकरनि छीरसिंधु बिनसाइ ॥ २३१ ॥
kabahum̐ ki kām̐jī sīkarani chīrasim̐dhu binasāi. 231.

Trans:

He would never be intoxicated with power, even though he sat upon the throne of Brahmmā, Vishnu, and Shiva. What! Can a few drops of sour *kanjī* curdle the milky ocean?

चौपाई-caupāī:

तिमिरु तरुन तरनिहि मकु गिलई । गगनु मगन मकु मेघहिं मिलई ॥
timiru taruna taranihi maku gilaī, gaganu magana maku meghahim̐ milaī.
गोपद जल बूड़हिं घटजोनी । सहज छमा बरु छाड़ै छोनी ॥
gopada jala būṛahim̐ ghaṭajonī, sahaja chamā baru chāṛai chonī.
मसक फूँक मकु मेरु उड़ाई । होइ न नृपमदु भरतहि भाई ॥
masaka phūm̐ka maku meru uṛāī, hoi na nṛpamadu bharatahi bhāī.
लखन तुम्हार सपथ पितु आना । सुचि सुबंधु नहिं भरत समाना ॥
lakhana tumhāra sapatha pitu ānā, suci subam̐dhu nahim̐ bharata samānā.
सगुनु खीरु अवगुन जलु ताता । मिलइ रचइ परपंचु बिधाता ॥
sagunu khīru avaguna jalu tātā, milai racai parapam̐cu bidhātā.
भरतु हंस रबिबंस तड़ागा । जनमि कीन्ह गुन दोष बिभागा ॥
bharatu ham̐sa rabibam̐sa taṛāgā, janami kīnha guna doṣa bibhāgā.
गहि गुन पय तजि अवगुन बारी । निज जस जगत कीन्हि उजिआरी ॥
gahi guna paya taji avaguna bārī, nija jasa jagata kīnhi ujiārī.
कहत भरत गुन सीलु सुभाऊ । पेम पयोधि मगन रघुराऊ ॥
kahata bharata guna sīlu subhāū, pema payodhi magana raghurāū.

Trans:

The sun may grow dim at midday; yea, sooner may the sky be absorbed into the clouds; sooner may Agastya be drowned in the puddle of a cow's footprint, or earth forget its natural forbearance; sooner may the buzz of a mosquito blow away Mount Meru—than kingly pride touch Bharat, O brother. I swear by you and by our father, there is no so true a brother as Bharat. The Creator has fashioned the world by mixing the milk of goodness with the water of evil. Bharat is the swan in the lake of the solar race, who from the day of his birth has known to distinguish between the good and the evil; choosing the milk of goodness and discarding the water of evil, he has illumined the whole world with his glory." As Raghurāī thus recited Bharat's virtues and amiable disposition, he became drowned in a sea of love.

दोहा-dohā:

सुनि रघुबर बानी बिबुध देखि भरत पर हेतु ।
suni raghubara bānī bibudha dekhi bharata para hetu,
सकल सराहत राम सो प्रभु को कृपानिकेतु ॥ २३२ ॥
sakala sarāhata rāma so prabhu ko kṛpāniketu. 232.

Trans:

The gods, hearing his speech and seeing his affection for Bharat, all applauded Rāma, saying, "Who is so compassionate as the Lord?

चौपाई-caupāī:

जौं न होत जग जनम भरत को । सकल धरम धुर धरनि धरत को ॥
jaum̐ na hota jaga janama bharata ko, sakala dharama dhura dharani dharata ko.
कबि कुल अगम भरत गुन गाथा । को जानइ तुम्ह बिनु रघुनाथा ॥
kabi kula agama bharata guna gāthā, ko jānai tumha binu raghunāthā.
लखन राम सियँ सुनि सुर बानी । अति सुखु लहेउ न जाइ बखानी ॥
lakhana rāma siyam̐ suni sura bānī, ati sukhu laheu na jāi bakhānī.
इहाँ भरतु सब सहित सहाए । मंदाकिनीं पुनीत नहाए ॥
ihām̐ bharatu saba sahita sahāe, mam̐dākinīm̐ punīta nahāe.
सरित समीप राखि सब लोगा । मागि मातु गुर सचिव नियोगा ॥
sarita samīpa rākhi saba logā, māgi mātu gura saciva niyogā.
चले भरतु जहँ सिय रघुराई । साथ निषादनाथु लघु भाई ॥
cale bharatu jaham̐ siya raghurāī, sātha niṣādanāthu laghu bhāī.
समुझि मातु करतब सकुचाहीं । करत कुतरक कोटि मन माहीं ॥
samujhi mātu karataba sakucāhīm̐, karata kutaraka koṭi mana māhīm̐.
रामु लखनु सिय सुनि मम नाऊँ । उठि जनि अनत जाहिं तजि ठाऊँ ॥
rāmu lakhanu siya suni mama nāūm̐, uṭhi jani anata jāhim̐ taji ṭhāūm̐.

Trans:

Had Bharat not been born into the world, who on this earth would have championed the cause of virtue in its entirety? Bharat's good qualities are more than all the poets could describe; who save you, Raghunāth, could comprehend them?" When Lakshman, Rāma, and Sītā heard these words of the gods they were more glad than can be told. Meanwhile Bharat and all his host bathed in the sacred Mandakinī. Then leaving the people on the bank and having asked permission from his mother, his Gurū, and the minister, he set out to visit Sītā and Raghurāī with the Nishād king and his brother. As he thought upon his mother's deeds he was abashed and formed a thousand ill-conjectures in his mind, "What if Rāma, Lakshman, and Sītā, on hearing my name, should leave the place and go elsewhere?

दोहा-dohā:

मातु मते महुँ मानि मोहि जो कछु करहिं सो थोर ।
mātu mate mahum̐ māni mohi jo kachu karahim̐ so thora,
अघ अवगुन छमि आदरहिं समुझि आपनी ओर ॥ २३३ ॥
agha avaguna chami ādarahim̐ samujhi āpanī ora. 233.

Trans:

Taking me to be my mother's accomplice, nothing that he might do can be deemed excessive. But knowing of him, I know he will overlook my sin and folly, and receives me kindly—being such a well-wisher that he is.

चौपाई-caupāī:

जौं परिहरहिं मलिन मनु जानी । जौं सनमानहिं सेवकु मानी ॥
jaum̐ pariharahim̐ malina manu jānī, jaum̐ sanamānahim̐ sevaku mānī.
मोरें सरन रामहि की पनही । राम सुस्वामि दोसु सब जनही ॥
morem̐ sarana rāmahi kī panahī, rāma susvāmi dosu saba janahī.
जग जस भाजन चातक मीना । नेम पेम निज निपुन नबीना ॥

jaga jasa bhājana cātaka mīnā, nema pema nija nipuna nabīnā.

अस मन गुनत चले मग जाता । सकुच सनेहँ सिथिल सब गाता ॥
asa mana gunata cale maga jātā, sakuca saneham̐ sithila saba gātā.

फेरति मनहुँ मातु कृत खोरी । चलत भगति बल धीरज धोरी ॥
pherati manahum̐ mātu kṛta khorī, calata bhagati bala dhīraja dhorī.

जब समुझत रघुनाथ सुभाऊ । तब पथ परत उताइल पाऊ ॥
jaba samujhata raghunātha subhāū, taba patha parata utāila pāū.

भरत दसा तेहि अवसर कैसी । जल प्रबाहँ जल अलि गति जैसी ॥
bharata dasā tehi avasara kaisī, jala prabāham̐ jala ali gati jaisī.

देखि भरत कर सोचु सनेहू । भा निषाद तेहि समयँ बिदेहू ॥
dekhi bharata kara socu sanehū, bhā niṣāda tehi samayam̐ bidehū.

Trans:

Whether he spurns me as a black-hearted wretch, or welcomes me as his servant—my only refuge is at Rāma's feet; he is the best of masters, the fault is all this servant's. The Chātak and the fish are celebrated throughout the world for the thoroughness and constancy of their vows of love." With these thoughts in his mind he went on his way, his whole body rendered powerless by excessive love and trepidation; his mother's sin, as it were, dragged him back, while his strong faith, like some sturdy bull, pulled him forward. Whenever he thought of Rāma's good nature, his feet moved swiftly along the way; his course was like that of a water-fly carried along by the stream. Seeing Bharat's anxiety and affection, the Nishād was transported out of himself.

दोहा-dohā:

लगे होन मंगल सगुन सुनि गुनि कहत निषादु ।
lage hona mamgala saguna suni guni kahata niṣādu,

मिटिहि सोचु होइहि हरषु पुनि परिनाम बिषादु ॥२३४॥
miṭihi socu hoihi haraṣu puni parināma biṣādu. 234.

Trans:

Auspicious omens began to occur, and the Nishād after hearing them and making a calculation said, "Sorrow will pass away, joy will succeed; but in the end there will be distress again."

चौपाई-caupāī:

सेवक बचन सत्य सब जाने । आश्रम निकट जाइ निअराने ॥
sevaka bacana satya saba jāne, āśrama nikaṭa jāi niarāne.

भरत दीख बन सैल समाजू । मुदित छुधित जनु पाइ सुनाजू ॥
bharata dīkha bana saila samājū, mudita chudhita janu pāi sunājū.

ईति भीति जनु प्रजा दुखारी । त्रिबिध ताप पीड़ित ग्रह मारी ॥
īti bhīti janu prajā dukhārī, tribidha tāpa pīṛita graha mārī.

जाइ सुराज सुदेस सुखारी । होहिं भरत गति तेहि अनुहारी ॥
jāi surāja sudesa sukhārī, hohiṁ bharata gati tehi anuhārī.

राम बास बन संपति भ्राजा । सुखी प्रजा जनु पाइ सुराजा ॥
rāma bāsa bana sampati bhrājā, sukhī prajā janu pāi surājā.

सचिव बिरागु बिबेकु नरेसू । बिपिन सुहावन पावन देसू ॥
saciva birāgu bibeku naresū, bipina suhāvana pāvana desū.

भट जम नियम सैल रजधानी । सांति सुमति सुचि सुंदर रानी ॥
bhaṭa jama niyama saila rajadhānī, sāmti sumati suci sumdara rānī.

सकल अंग संपन्न सुराऊ । राम चरन आश्रित चित चाऊ ॥
sakala amga sampanna surāū, rāma carana āśrita cita cāū.

Trans:

Knowing his servant's words to be all true, he went on and drew near to the hermitage. When Bharat saw the vast woods and rocks, he was as glad as a hungry wretch on getting a good meal. Like people afflicted by every calamity, worn out with troubles, ill fortune, and pestilence, who rejoice on escaping to a prosperous and well-governed country, such were the feelings of Bharat. The forest where Rāma dwelt was as bright and happy as people are happy who have got a good ruler. That beautiful sacred grove appeared as a realm with Asceticism for king and Wisdom for minister. *Yama*s and *Niyama*s were its champions; with the mountain for its capital; and with Peace and Goodwill for his virtuous lovely queens. In this way the good king was perfect at all points, and further being dependent on Rāma's feet, was therefore perfectly easy in mind.

दोहा-dohā:

जीति मोह महिपालु दल सहित बिबेक भुआलु ।
jīti moha mahipālu dala sahita bibeka bhuālu,

करत अकंटक राजु पुरँ सुख संपदा सुकालु ॥२३५॥
karata akamṭaka rāju puram̐ sukha sampadā sukālu. 235.

Trans:

Royal Wisdom—having conquered king Delusion with all his host—held undisputed sway in this realm. Joy, happiness, prosperity reigned everywhere.

चौपाई-caupāī:

बन प्रदेस मुनि बास घनेरे । जनु पुर नगर गाउँ गन खेरे ॥
bana pradesa muni bāsa ghanere, janu pura nagara gāum̐ gana khere.

बिपुल बिचित्र बिहग मृग नाना । प्रजा समाजु न जाइ बखाना ॥
bipula bicitra bihaga mṛga nānā, prajā samāju na jāi bakhānā.

खगहा करि हरि बाघ बराहा । देखि महिष बृष साजु सराहा ॥
khagahā kari hari bāgha barāhā, dekhi mahiṣa bṛṣa sāju sarāhā.

बयरु बिहाइ चरहिं एक संगा । जहँ तहँ मनहुँ सेन चतुरंगा ॥
bayaru bihāi carahiṁ eka samgā, jaham̐ taham̐ manahum̐ sena caturamgā.

झरना झरहिं मत्त गज गाजहिं । मनहुँ निसान बिबिधि बिधि बाजहिं ॥
jharanā jharahiṁ matta gaja gājahiṁ, manahum̐ nisāna bibidhi bidhi bājahiṁ.

चक चकोर चातक सुक पिक गन । कूजत मंजु मराल मुदित मन ॥
caka cakora cātaka suka pika gana, kūjata mamju marāla mudita mana.

अलिगन गावत नाचत मोरा । जनु सुराज मंगल चहु ओरा ॥
aligana gāvata nācata morā, janu surāja mamgala cahu orā.

बेलि बिटप तृन सफल सफूला । सब समाजु मुद मंगल मूला ॥
beli biṭapa tṛna saphala saphūlā, saba samāju muda mamgala mūlā.

Trans:

The frequent hermits' cells about the woods were his cities, towns, villages, and hamlets; the people, birds and beasts of all descriptions, were his innumerable subjects. The hares, elephants, lions, tigers, boars, buffaloes, and wolves, a wonder to behold, forgetting their antipathies, grazed together, like a duly marshaled army complete in all its parts. The roar of the mountain torrents and the cries of mad elephants were like the din of kettledrums; the *chakwās*, *chakor*s, *chātak*s, parrots, and cuckoos made a delightful concert; the swans were in their glory; the bees buzzed and the peacocks danced like the festive entourage of some Rajah, while the creepers, trees, and grasses, with the flowers and fruits, formed his brilliant court.

दोहा-dohā:

राम सैल सोभा निरखि भरत हृदयँ अति पेमु ।
rāma saila sobhā nirakhi bharata hṛdayam̐ ati pemu,

तापस तप फलु पाइ जिमि सुखी सिरानें नेमु ॥२३६॥
tāpasa tapa phalu pāi jimi sukhī sirāneṁ nemu. 236.

Trans:

Beholding the beauty of Rāma's hill, Bharat's heart was overpowered with love, like as an ascetic is overjoyed when he completes his vow and reaps the fruit of penance.

मासपारायण बीसवाँ विश्राम

नवाह्नपारायण पाँचवाँ विश्राम

māsapārāyaṇa bīsavāṁ viśrāma
navāhnapārāyaṇa pāṁcavāṁ viśrāma
(Pause 20 for a Thirty-Day Recitation)
(Pause 5 for a Nine-Day Recitation)

चौपाई-*caupāī:*

तब केवट ऊँचें चढ़ि धाई । कहेउ भरत सन भुजा उठाई ॥
taba kevaṭa ūṁceṁ caṛhi dhāī, kaheu bharata sana bhujā uṭhāī.
नाथ देखिअहिं बिटप बिसाला । पाकरि जंबु रसाल तमाला ॥
nātha dekhiahiṁ biṭapa bisālā, pākari jaṁbu rasāla tamālā.
जिन्ह तरुबरन्ह मध्य बटु सोहा । मंजु बिसाल देखि मनु मोहा ॥
jinha tarubaranha madhya baṭu sohā, maṁju bisāla dekhi manu mohā.
नील सघन पल्लव फल लाला । अबिरल छाहँ सुखद सब काला ॥
nīla saghana pallava phala lālā, abirala chāhaṁ sukhada saba kālā.
मानहुँ तिमिर अरुनमय रासी । बिरची बिधि सँकेलि सुषमा सी ॥
mānahuṁ timira arunamaya rāsī, biracī bidhi saṁkeli suṣamā sī.
ए तरु सरित समीप गोसाँई । रघुबर परनकुटी जहँ छाई ॥
e taru sarita samīpa gosāṁī, raghubara paranakuṭī jahaṁ chāī.
तुलसी तरुबर बिबिध सुहाए । कहुँ कहुँ सियँ कहुँ लखन लगाए ॥
tulasī tarubara bibidha suhāe, kahuṁ kahuṁ siyaṁ kahuṁ lakhana lagāe.
बट छायाँ बेदिका बनाई । सियँ निज पानि सरोज सुहाई ॥
baṭa chāyāṁ bedikā banāī, siyaṁ nija pāni saroja suhāī.

Trans:

Then the guide mounted a height and reaching out his hand cried to Bharat, "See my lord those huge trees, *pakar*, *jamun*, mango, and *tamala*, in the midst of which is conspicuous a Banyan, so beautiful and grand that the soul is charmed at the sight, with dense dark shoots and red fruit, affording a pleasant shade in all seasons of the year, a mass of black and purple, as if god had brought together all that was lovely to make it. This tree, which is near the riverside, is where Rāma has roofed in his sylvan hut; and there are many a graceful shrubs of Tulsī all around, planted some by Sītā, some by Lakshman; and in the shade of the Banyan Sītā with her own lotus hands has reared a charming altar.

दोहा-*dohā:*

जहाँ बैठि मुनिगन सहित नित सिय रामु सुजान ।
jahāṁ baiṭhi munigana sahita nita siya rāmu sujāna,
सुनहिं कथा इतिहास सब आगम निगम पुरान ॥२३७॥
sunahiṁ kathā itihāsa saba āgama nigama purāna. 237.

Trans:

And there, the all-wise Sītā and Rāma, are ever wont to sit in the midst of hermits, listening as sacred legends are read and all the Vedas, Shāstras, and Purānas recited."

चौपाई-*caupāī:*

सखा बचन सुनि बिटप निहारी । उमगे भरत बिलोचन बारी ॥
sakhā bacana suni biṭapa nihārī, umage bharata bilocana bārī.
करत प्रनाम चले दोउ भाई । कहत प्रीति सारद सकुचाई ॥
karata pranāma cale dou bhāī, kahata prīti sārada sakucāī.
हरषहिं निरखि राम पद अंका । मानहुँ पारसु पायउ रंका ॥
haraṣahiṁ nirakhi rāma pada aṁkā, mānahuṁ pārasu pāyau raṁkā.
रज सिर धरि हियँ नयनन्हि लावहिं । रघुबर मिलन सरिस सुख पावहिं ॥
raja sira dhari hiyaṁ nayananhi lāvahiṁ, raghubara milana sarisa sukha pāvahiṁ.
देखि भरत गति अकथ अतीवा । प्रेम मगन मृग खग जड़ जीवा ॥
dekhi bharata gati akatha atīvā, prema magana mṛga khaga jaṛa jīvā.
सखहि सनेह बिबस मग भूला । कहि सुपंथ सुर बरषहिं फूला ॥
sakhahi saneha bibasa maga bhūlā, kahi supaṁtha sura baraṣahiṁ phūlā.
निरखि सिद्ध साधक अनुरागे । सहज सनेहु सराहन लागे ॥
nirakhi siddha sādhaka anurāge, sahaja sanehu sarāhana lāge.
होत न भूतल भाउ भरत को । अचर सचर चर अचर करत को ॥
hota na bhūtala bhāu bharata ko, acara sacara cara acara karata ko.

Trans:

As he listened to his friend's speech and gazed upon the tree, Bharat's eyes overflowed with tears. The two brothers advanced reverently; Shārdā would fail to do justice to their love. When they saw the prints of Rāma's feet they rejoiced like some beggar on finding the philosopher's stone, and applied the dust to their head, heart, and eyes—with as much delight as if they had found Rāma himself. Seeing Bharat's utterly indescribable condition, birds, beasts, and all created things, whether animate or inanimate, were absorbed in devotion. The guide in his excitement lost the way, but the gods showed it to him by raining down flowers. Saints and sages gazed in rapture and burst out into praises of his sincere affection. "Who in all the world is like Bharat, who makes the animate look inanimate, and the inanimate animate?"

दोहा-*dohā:*

पेम अमिअ मंदरु बिरहु भरतु पयोधि गँभीर ।
pema amia maṁdaru birahu bharatu payodhi gaṁbhīra,
मथि प्रगटेउ सुर साधु हित कृपासिंधु रघुबीर ॥२३८॥
mathi pragaṭeu sura sādhu hita kṛpāsiṁdhu raghubīra. 238.

Trans:

Raghubīr, the ocean of compassion, after churning the depths of Bharat's soul with the Mount Meru of bereavement, brought out from it the nectar of love.

चौपाई-*caupāī:*

सखा समेत मनोहर जोटा । लखेउ न लखन सघन बन ओटा ॥
sakhā sameta manohara joṭā, lakheu na lakhana saghana bana oṭā.
भरत दीख प्रभु आश्रमु पावन । सकल सुमंगल सदनु सुहावन ॥
bharata dīkha prabhu āśramu pāvana, sakala sumaṁgala sadanu suhāvana.
करत प्रबेस मिटे दुख दावा । जनु जोगीं परमारथु पावा ॥
karata prabesa miṭe dukha dāvā, janu jogīṁ paramārathu pāvā.
देखे भरत लखन प्रभु आगे । पूँछे बचन कहत अनुरागे ॥
dekhe bharata lakhana prabhu āge, pūṁche bacana kahata anurāge.
सीस जटा कटि मुनि पट बाँधें । तून कसें कर सरु धनु काँधें ॥
sīsa jaṭā kaṭi muni paṭa bāṁdheṁ, tūna kaseṁ kara saru dhanu kāṁdheṁ.
बेदी पर मुनि साधु समाजू । सीय सहित राजत रघुराजू ॥
bedī para muni sādhu samājū, sīya sahita rājata raghurājū.
बलकल बसन जटिल तनु स्यामा । जनु मुनि बेष कीन्ह रति कामा ॥
balakala basana jaṭila tanu syāmā, janu muni beṣa kīnha rati kāmā.
कर कमलनि धनु सायकु फेरत । जिय की जरनि हरत हँसि हेरत ॥
kara kamalani dhanu sāyaku pherata, jiya kī jarani harata haṁsi herata.

Trans:

The two charming brothers and their guide were not visible to Lakshman, by reason of the dense shade of the forest; but Bharat could see his Lord's sacred hermitage, the charming home of everything delightful. As he entered it his burning grief was assuaged, as when an ascetic is awarded with salvation. He saw before him Lakshman affectionately serving the Lord, his hair fastened in a knot, a hermit's robe girt about his loins, his quiver slung, arrows in his hand, and his bow on his shoulder. By the altar were an assembly of saints and sages, among whom Sītā and Rāma were conspicuous in hermit's attire, with matted hair and body darkened by exposure, like Ratī and Kāmdev in saint's disguise. He, who with one smiling glance can dispel every anguish of soul, had bow and arrows ready in his lotus hands.

दोहा-dohā:

लसत मंजु मुनि मंडली मध्य सीय रघुचंदु ।
lasata maṁju muni maṁḍalī madhya sīya raghucaṁdu,
ग्यान सभाँ जनु तनु धरें भगति सच्चिदानंदु ॥२३९॥
gyāna sabhāṁ janu tanu dhareṁ bhagati saccidānaṁdu. 239.

Trans:

In the midst of the circle of saints Sītā and Rāma shone forth as fair as Faith and the Supreme Spirit incarnate in the council chamber of Wisdom.

चौपाई-caupāī:

सानुज सखा समेत मगन मन । बिसरे हरष सोक सुख दुख गन ॥
sānuja sakhā sameta magana mana, bisare haraṣa soka sukha dukha gana.
पाहि नाथ कहि पाहि गोसाईं । भूतल परे लकुट की नाईं ॥
pāhi nātha kahi pāhi gosāīṁ, bhūtala pare lakuṭa kī nāīṁ.
बचन सपेम लखन पहिचाने । करत प्रनामु भरत जियँ जाने ॥
bacana sapema lakhana pahicāne, karata pranāmu bharata jiyaṁ jāne.
बंधु सनेह सरस एहि ओरा । उत साहिब सेवा बस जोरा ॥
baṁdhu saneha sarasa ehi orā, uta sāhiba sevā basa jorā.
मिलि न जाइ नहिं गुदरत बनई । सुकबि लखन मन की गति भनई ॥
mili na jāi nahiṁ gudarata banaī, sukabi lakhana mana kī gati bhanaī.
रहे राखि सेवा पर भारू । चढ़ी चंग जनु खैंच खेलारू ॥
rahe rākhi sevā para bhārū, caṛhī caṁga janu khaiṁca khelārū.
कहत सप्रेम नाइ महि माथा । भरत प्रनाम करत रघुनाथा ॥
kahata saprema nāi mahi māthā, bharata pranāma karata raghunāthā.
उठे रामु सुनि पेम अधीरा । कहुँ पट कहुँ निषंग धनु तीरा ॥
uṭhe rāmu suni pema adhīrā, kahuṁ paṭa kahuṁ niṣaṁga dhanu tīrā.

Trans:

He, his brother, and their guide were so absorbed that joy and sorrow, pleasure and pain were all forgotten. Crying "Mercy, mercy, O Lord and master!" he fell flat on the ground like a log. Lakshman recognized his loving speech and concluded in his mind that it was Bharat making obeisance. On the one hand there was the loving affection of an elder brother, while, on the other, there was the stronger claim of service to his master. He was, therefore, neither able to meet Bharat nor ignore him; some good poet alone could describe Lakshman's state of mind. Though obedience was the weightier, and therefore he stayed; he was like a child pulling against a kite high in the air. Bowing his head to the ground, he said affectionately, "It is Bharat, O Raghunāth, who greets you." On hearing this, Rāma started up in loving agitation, his robe flying in one direction and his quiver and bow and arrows in another.

दोहा-dohā:

बरबस लिए उठाइ उर लाए कृपानिधान ।
barabasa lie uṭhāi ura lāe kṛpānidhāna,
भरत राम की मिलनि लखि बिसरे सबहि अपान ॥२४०॥
bharata rāma kī milani lakhi bisare sabahi apāna. 240.

Trans:

Whether he would or no, the All-compassionate forcibly took and raised him up and clasped him to his bosom. Those who witnessed the meeting of Bharat and Rāma lost all self-consciousness.

चौपाई-caupāī:

मिलनि प्रीति किमि जाइ बखानी । कबिकुल अगम करम मन बानी ॥
milani prīti kimi jāi bakhānī, kabikula agama karama mana bānī.
परम पेम पूरन दोउ भाई । मन बुधि चित अहमिति बिसराई ॥
parama pema pūrana dou bhāī, mana budhi cita ahamiti bisarāī.
कहहु सुपेम प्रगट को करई । केहि छाया कबि मति अनुसरई ॥
kahahu supema pragaṭa ko karaī, kehi chāyā kabi mati anusaraī.
कबिहि अरथ आखर बलु साँचा । अनुहरि ताल गतिहि नटु नाचा ॥
kabihi aratha ākhara balu sāṁcā, anuhari tāla gatihi naṭu nācā.
अगम सनेह भरत रघुबर को । जहँ न जाइ मनु बिधि हरि हर को ॥
agama saneha bharata raghubara ko, jahaṁ na jāi manu bidhi hari hara ko.
सो मैं कुमति कहौं केहि भाँती । बाज सुराग कि गाँडर ताँती ॥
so maiṁ kumati kahauṁ kehi bhāṁtī, bāja surāga ki gāṁḍara tāṁtī.
मिलनि बिलोकि भरत रघुबर की । सुरगन सभय धकधकी धरकी ॥
milani biloki bharata raghubara kī, suragana sabhaya dhakadhakī dharakī.
समुझाए सुरगुरु जड़ जागे । बरषि प्रसून प्रसंसन लागे ॥
samujhāe suraguru jaṛa jāge, baraṣi prasūna prasaṁsana lāge.

Trans:

How can such an affectionate meeting be described? Their thoughts, words, and actions were beyond any poet's. Both brothers were filled with the utmost love; self, reason, knowledge, and understanding were all forgotten. Tell me who can portray such perfect love? By what shadow can the poet's mind attain to it? A poet works with themes and expressions, and dancers work to the music of accompanying beats; but the love of Rāma and Bharat is unapproachable, beyond the conception even of Brahmmā, Vishnu, and Shiva; how then can I describe it? If an instrument is only strung with grass can it make sweet music? When the gods saw the meeting of Bharat and Raghubar they were alarmed and trembled all over; but when Brihaspati had spoken to them, they awoke from their folly and rained down flowers and applauded.

दोहा-dohā:

मिलि सपेम रिपुसूदनहि केवटु भेंटेउ राम ।
mili sapema ripusūdanahi kevaṭu bheṁṭeu rāma,
भूरि भायँ भेंटे भरत लछिमन करत प्रनाम ॥२४१॥
bhūri bhāyaṁ bheṁṭe bharata lachimana karata pranāma. 241.

Trans:

After affectionately embracing Shatrughan, Rāma met the Nishād chief; even so with profuse love Bharat embraced Lakshman.

चौपाई-caupāī:

भेंटेउ लखन ललकि लघु भाई । बहुरि निषादु लीन्ह उर लाई ॥
bheṁṭeu lakhana lalaki laghu bhāī, bahuri niṣādu līnha ura lāī.
पुनि मुनिगन दुहुँ भाइन्ह बंदे । अभिमत आसिष पाइ अनंदे ॥
puni munigana duhuṁ bhāinha baṁde, abhimata āsiṣa pāi anaṁde.
सानुज भरत उमगि अनुरागा । धरि सिर सिय पद पदुम परागा ॥
sānuja bharata umagi anurāgā, dhari sira siya pada paduma parāgā.
पुनि पुनि करत प्रनाम उठाए । सिर कर कमल परसि बैठाए ॥
puni puni karata pranāma uṭhāe, sira kara kamala parasi baiṭhāe.
सीयँ असीस दीन्हि मन माहीं । मगन सनेहँ देह सुधि नाहीं ॥
sīyaṁ asīsa dīnhi mana māhīṁ, magana sanehaṁ deha sudhi nāhīṁ.
सब बिधि सानुकूल लखि सीता । भे निसोच उर अपडर बीता ॥
saba bidhi sānukūla lakhi sītā, bhe nisoca ura apaḍara bītā.
कोउ किछु कहइ न कोउ किछु पूँछा । प्रेम भरा मन निज गति छूँछा ॥
kou kichu kahai na kou kichu pūṁchā, prema bharā mana nija gati chūṁchā.
तेहि अवसर केवटु धीरजु धरि । जोरि पानि बिनवत प्रनामु करि ॥
tehi avasara kevaṭu dhīraju dhari, jori pāni binavata pranāmu kari.

Trans:

When he had fondly embraced his younger brother, Lakshman next took the Nishād to his bosom. Then the two brothers, Bharat and Shatrughan—after reverencing all the saints and joyfully receiving from them the desired blessing—in a rapture of love placed on their head the dust of Sītā's lotus feet. As they again and again prostrated themselves, she raised them up, and with a touch of her lotus hands motioned them to be seated, in her heart invoking a blessing upon them, and was so absorbed in affection as to lose all self-consciousness. When he saw Sītā so thoroughly propitious, Bharat became free from anxiety and all fear passed away. No one made any remark nor asked any question; the soul was so full of love that it ceased to act. Then the Nishād chief took courage and bowing with clasped hands made this humble petition,

दोहा-dohā:

नाथ साथ मुनिनाथ के मातु सकल पुर लोग ।
nātha sātha muninātha ke mātu sakala pura loga,
सेवक सेनप सचिव सब आए बिकल बियोग ॥ २४२ ॥
sevaka senapa saciva saba āe bikala biyoga. 242.

Trans:

"Distressed by your absence, my Lord, there have come with the great sage your mothers and all the people of the city, your servants, captains, and ministers."

चौपाई-caupāī:

सीलसिंधु सुनि गुर आगवनू । सिय समीप राखे रिपुदवनू ॥
sīlasiṁdhu suni gura āgavanū, siya samīpa rākhe ripudavanū.
चले सबेग रामु तेहि काला । धीर धरम धुर दीनदयाला ॥
cale sabega rāmu tehi kālā, dhīra dharama dhura dīnadayālā.
गुरहि देखि सानुज अनुरागे । दंड प्रनाम करन प्रभु लागे ॥
gurahi dekhi sānuja anurāge, daṁḍa pranāma karana prabhu lāge.
मुनिबर धाइ लिए उर लाई । प्रेम उमगि भेंटे दोउ भाई ॥
munibara dhāi lie ura lāī, prema umagi bheṁṭe dou bhāī.
प्रेम पुलकि केवट कहि नामू । कीन्ह दूरि तें दंड प्रनामू ॥
prema pulaki kevaṭa kahi nāmū, kīnha dūri teṁ daṁḍa pranāmū.
रामसखा रिषि बरबस भेंटा । जनु महि लुठत सनेह समेटा ॥
rāmasakhā riṣi barabasa bheṁṭā, janu mahi luṭhata saneha sameṭā.
रघुपति भगति सुमंगल मूला । नभ सराहि सुर बरिसहिं फूला ॥
raghupati bhagati sumaṁgala mūlā, nabha sarāhi sura barisahiṁ phūlā.
एहि सम निपट नीच कोउ नाहीं । बड़ बसिष्ठ सम को जग माहीं ॥
ehi sama nipaṭa nīca kou nāhīṁ, baṛa basiṣṭha sama ko jaga māhīṁ.

Trans:

When the Ocean of amiability heard that the Gurū had come, he left Shatrughan with Sītā and went off in haste that very minute—he, Rāma, the steadfast, the righteous, the all-merciful. On seeing the Gurū, Rāma and his brother were delighted and fell on their faces to the ground; but the holy man ran and raised them up and embraced them, and greeted both brothers with the utmost affection. Kevat, quivering with emotion, gave his name and prostrated himself afar off; but the Rishī forcibly embraced him as a friend of Rāma's—as though love had been spilt upon the ground and he stooped to pick it up. Faith in Rāma is the root of all good; in heaven the gods applauding rained down flowers, "There is no one so utterly low as this man, nor anyone in the world so exalted as the great Vasishtha;

दोहा-dohā:

जेहि लखि लखनहु तें अधिक मिले मुदित मुनिराउ ।
jehi lakhi lakhanahu teṁ adhika mile mudita munirāu,
सो सीतापति भजन को प्रगट प्रताप प्रभाउ ॥ २४३ ॥
so sītāpati bhajana ko pragaṭa pratāpa prabhāu. 243.

Trans:

And yet, on seeing him, the king of saints was overjoyed and embraced him with greater joy than he would have Lakshman; so glorious in their manifestation are the effects of faith in Sītā's Lord."

चौपाई-caupāī:

आरत लोग राम सबु जाना । करुनाकर सुजान भगवाना ॥
ārata loga rāma sabu jānā, karunākara sujāna bhagavānā.
जो जेहि भायँ रहा अभिलाषी । तेहि तेहि कै तसि तसि रुख राखी ॥
jo jehi bhāyaṁ rahā abhilāṣī, tehi tehi kai tasi tasi rukha rākhī.
सानुज मिलि पल महुँ सब काहू । कीन्ह दूरि दुखु दारुन दाहू ॥
sānuja mili pala mahuṁ saba kāhū, kīnha dūri dukhu dāruna dāhū.
यह बड़ि बात राम कै नाहीं । जिमि घट कोटि एक रबि छाहीं ॥
yaha baṛi bāta rāma kai nāhīṁ, jimi ghaṭa koṭi eka rabi chāhīṁ.
मिलि केवटहि उमगि अनुरागा । पुरजन सकल सराहहिं भागा ॥
mili kevaṭahi umagi anurāgā, purajana sakala sarāhahiṁ bhāgā.
देखीं राम दुखित महतारीं । जनु सुबेलि अवलीं हिम मारीं ॥
dekhīṁ rāma dukhita mahatārīṁ, janu subeli avalīṁ hima mārīṁ.
प्रथम राम भेंटी कैकेई । सरल सुभायँ भगति मति भेई ॥
prathama rāma bheṁṭī kaikeī, sarala subhāyaṁ bhagati mati bheī.
पग परि कीन्ह प्रबोधु बहोरी । काल करम बिधि सिर धरि खोरी ॥
paga pari kīnha prabodhu bahorī, kāla karama bidhi sira dhari khorī.

Trans:

Finding all the people sad, Rāma, the all-merciful and all-wise God, gave everyone his wish in the way he most desired: in an instant he and his brother embraced them all and at once removed the sore anguish of their pain. This was no such great thing for Rāma to do—for He is akin to the sun reflected in a thousand water-jars. All the citizens with rapturous affection embraced the Nishād chief and praised his good fortune. Seeing his mothers as woebegone as the sprays of some delicate creeper smitten by the frost, Rāma first of all saluted Kaekayī, softening her will by his gentleness and piety. Falling at her feet, he soothed her with many words, attributing all the blame to Time, Karma, Providence.

दोहा-dohā:

भेटीं रघुबर मातु सब करि प्रबोधु परितोषु ।
bheṭīṁ raghubara mātu saba kari prabodhu paritoṣu,
अंब ईस आधीन जगु काहु न देइअ दोषु ॥ २४४ ॥
aṁba īsa ādhīna jagu kāhu na deia doṣu. 244.

Trans:

Raghubar embraced all his mothers and consoled them saying, "Mother, the world is subject to God; there is no one to blame."

चौपाई-caupāī:

गुरतिय पद बंदे दुहु भाईं । सहित बिप्रतिय जे सँग आईं ॥
guratiya pada baṁde duhu bhāīṁ, sahita bipratiya je saṁga āīṁ.
गंग गौरि सम सब सनमानीं । देहिं असीस मुदित मृदु बानीं ॥
gaṁga gauri sama saba sanamānīṁ, dehiṁ asīsa mudita mṛdu bānīṁ.
गहि पद लगे सुमित्रा अंका । जनु भेंटी संपति अति रंका ॥
gahi pada lage sumitrā aṁkā, janu bheṁṭī saṁpati ati raṁkā.
पुनि जननी चरननि दोउ भ्राता । परे पेम ब्याकुल सब गाता ॥
puni jananī caranani dou bhrātā, pare pema byākula saba gātā.
अति अनुराग अंब उर लाए । नयन सनेह सलिल अन्हवाए ॥
ati anurāga aṁba ura lāe, nayana saneha salila anhavāe.
तेहि अवसर कर हरष बिषादू । किमि कबि कहै मूक जिमि स्वादू ॥
tehi avasara kara haraṣa biṣādū, kimi kabi kahai mūka jimi svādū.
मिलि जननिहि सानुज रघुराऊ । गुर सन कहेउ कि धारिअ पाऊ ॥
mili jananihi sānuja raghurāū, gura sana kaheu ki dhāria pāū.
पुरजन पाइ मुनीस नियोगू । जल थल तकि तकि उतरेउ लोगू ॥
purajana pāi munīsa niyogū, jala thala taki taki utareu logū.

Trans:

The two brothers bowed at the feet of their Gurū's wife, as also of the Brahmin ladies who had accompanied her, paying the same honor to them as to Gangā and Gaurī; and they with gentle voice gladly gave them their blessing. When he embraced Sumitrā, after clasping her feet, he was like a beggar who has picked up a fortune. Then both brothers fell at the feet of queen Kausalyā and their whole body was convulsed with love; the mother took them tenderly to her bosom and bathed them with tears of affection. How can any poet describe the mingled joy and grief of such a time— anymore than a dumb man can express the sweetness that he tastes. After embracing their mother, Rāma and his brother requested the Gurū to accompany them; while at the Gurū's command the citizens encamped themselves, finding suitable places with water nearby.

दोहा-dohā:

महिसुर मंत्री मातु गुर गने लोग लिए साथ ।
mahisura maṁtrī mātu gura gane loga lie sātha,
पावन आश्रम गवनु किय भरत लखन रघुनाथ ॥२४५॥
pāvana āśrama gavanu kiya bharata lakhana raghunātha. 245.

Trans:

Taking with them the Brahmins, the minister, the queens, the Gurū, and a few others, Bharat, Lakshman, and Raghunāth proceeded to the holy hermitage.

चौपाई-caupāī:

सीय आइ मुनिबर पग लागी । उचित असीस लही मन मागी ॥
sīya āi munibara paga lāgī, ucita asīsa lahī mana māgī.
गुरपतिनिहि मुनितियन्ह समेता । मिली पेमु कहि जाइ न जेता ॥
gurapatinihi munitiyanha sametā, milī pemu kahi jāi na jetā.
बंदि बंदि पग सिय सबही के । आसिरबचन लहे प्रिय जी के ॥
baṁdi baṁdi paga siya sabahī ke, āsirabacana lahe priya jī ke.
सासु सकल जब सीयँ निहारीं । मूदे नयन सहमि सुकुमारीं ॥
sāsu sakala jaba sīyaṁ nihārīṁ, mūde nayana sahami sukumārīṁ.
परीं बधिक बस मनहुँ मरालीं । काह कीन्ह करतार कुचालीं ॥
parīṁ badhika basa manahuṁ marālīṁ, kāha kīnha karatāra kucālīṁ.
तिन्ह सिय निरखि निपट दुखु पावा । सो सबु सहिअ जो दैउ सहावा ॥
tinha siya nirakhi nipaṭa dukhu pāvā, so sabu sahia jo daiu sahāvā.
जनकसुता तब उर धरि धीरा । नील नलिन लोयन भरि नीरा ॥
janakasutā taba ura dhari dhīrā, nīla nalina loyana bhari nīrā.
मिली सकल सासुन्ह सिय जाई । तेहि अवसर करुना महि छाई ॥
milī sakala sāsunha siya jāī, tehi avasara karunā mahi chāī.

Trans:

Sītā came and embraced the saint's feet and received the precious blessing her soul desired. The affectionate manner in which she greeted the Gurū's wife and the Brahmin ladies cannot be portrayed. Again and again she bowed at all their feet and received the benedictions craved in her heart. Looking at the condition of queen-mothers, the tender-hearted Sītā closed her eyes and shivered inside—they looked like cygnet fallen into the clutches of fowler. "What cruel thing fate has done?" she thought. In turn, as they gazed at Sītā, they became distressed beyond measure—that she should have to bear all which destiny has put upon her. Then summoning courage Janak's daughter, with her dark lotus eyes suffused with tears, went and embraced all her mothers-in-law; at that moment poignancy pervaded everywhere.

दोहा-dohā:

लागि लागि पग सबनि सिय भेंटति अति अनुराग ।
lāgi lāgi paga sabani siya bheṁṭati ati anurāga,
हृदयँ असीसहिं पेम बस रहिअहु भरी सोहाग ॥२४६॥
hṛdayaṁ asīsahiṁ pema basa rahiahu bharī sohāga. 246.

Trans:

Again and again holding to their feet, Sītā embraced them most tenderly; and from their heart came the loving benediction, "May you live long a happy wife, with always your husband by your side!"

चौपाई-caupāī:

बिकल सनेहँ सीय सब रानीं । बैठन सबहि कहेउ गुर ग्यानीं ॥
bikala sanehaṁ sīya saba rānīṁ, baiṭhana sabahi kaheu gura gyānīṁ.
कहि जग गति मायिक मुनिनाथा । कहे कछुक परमारथ गाथा ॥
kahi jaga gati māyika muninātha, kahe kachuka paramāratha gāthā.
नृप कर सुरपुर गवनु सुनावा । सुनि रघुनाथ दुसह दुखु पावा ॥
nṛpa kara surapura gavanu sunāvā, suni raghunātha dusaha dukhu pāvā.
मरन हेतु निज नेहु बिचारी । भे अति बिकल धीर धुर धारी ॥
marana hetu nija nehu bicārī, bhe ati bikala dhīra dhura dhārī.
कुलिस कठोर सुनत कटु बानी । बिलपत लखन सीय सब रानी ॥
kulisa kaṭhora sunata kaṭu bānī, bilapata lakhana sīya saba rānī.
सोक बिकल अति सकल समाजू । मानहुँ राजु अकाजेउ आजू ॥
soka bikala ati sakala samājū, mānahuṁ rāju akājeu ājū.
मुनिबर बहुरि राम समुझाए । सहित समाज सुसरित नहाए ॥
munibara bahuri rāma samujhāe, sahita samāja susarita nahāe.
ब्रतु निरंबु तेहि दिन प्रभु कीन्हा । मुनिहु कहें जलु काहुँ न लीन्हा ॥
bratu niraṁbu tehi dina prabhu kīnhā, munihu kaheṁ jalu kāhuṁ na līnhā.

Trans:

Sītā and the queens being thus agitated by emotions, the learned Gurū bade them all be seated. First he expounded to them the instability of the world and spoke a little of the joys of heaven, and then announced the king's death. Raghunāth was grievously pained at heart; and all the more distressed when he found that the king died out of love for him. The firmest of the firm was sore shaken. On hearing the sad tidings, which fell upon them like a thunderbolt, Lakshman, Sītā, and all the queens broke out into lamentations, and the whole assembly was as much agitated as if the king had died only that very day. Then the great sage exhorted Rāma and directed him and all the people to bathe in the sacred stream. All that day the Lord fasted even from water; and though the saint allowed them, no one else would drink either.

दोहा-dohā:

भोरु भएँ रघुनंदनहि जो मुनि आयसु दीन्ह ।
bhoru bhaeṁ raghunaṁdanahi jo muni āyasu dīnha.
श्रद्धा भगति समेत प्रभु सो सबु सादरु कीन्ह ॥२४७॥
śraddhā bhagati sameta prabhu so sabu sādaru kīnha. 247.

Trans:

At daybreak, according to the order given him by the saint, the Lord Raghunandan reverently and devoutly performed his father's funeral obsequies.

चौपाई-caupāī:

करि पितु क्रिया बेद जसि बरनी । भे पुनीत पातक तम तरनी ॥
kari pitu kriyā beda jasi baranī, bhe punīta pātaka tama taranī.
जासु नाम पावक अघ तूला । सुमिरत सकल सुमंगल मूला ॥
jāsu nāma pāvaka agha tūlā, sumirata sakala sumaṁgala mūlā.
सुद्ध सो भयउ साधु संमत अस । तीरथ आवाहन सुरसरि जस ॥
suddha so bhayau sādhu saṁmata asa, tīratha āvāhana surasari jasa.
सुद्ध भएँ दुइ बासर बीते । बोले गुर सन राम पिरीते ॥
suddha bhaeṁ dui bāsara bīte, bole gura sana rāma pirīte.
नाथ लोग सब निपट दुखारी । कंद मूल फल अंबु अहारी ॥
nātha loga saba nipaṭa dukhārī, kaṁda mūla phala aṁbu ahārī.
सानुज भरतु सचिव सब माता । देखि मोहि पल जिमि जुग जाता ॥
sānuja bharatu saciva saba mātā, dekhi mohi pala jimi juga jātā.
सब समेत पुर धारिअ पाऊ । आपु इहाँ अमरावति राऊ ॥
saba sameta pura dhāria pāū, āpu ihāṁ amarāvati rāū.
बहुत कहेउँ सब कियउँ ढिठाई । उचित होइ तस करिअ गोसाँई ॥
bahuta kaheuṁ saba kiyauṁ ḍhiṭhāī, ucita hoi tasa karia gosāṁī.

Trans:

Having celebrated every rite as prescribed in the Veda, he became pure, even he, the Sun to annihilate the night of sin, whose name is a fire that consumes the cotton of wickedness, and which if merely invoked is the source of all prosperity. He became pure in like manner, as Pundits say, a bather in the Gangā who invokes other *Tīrtha*s is purified. After his purification, when two days had passed, Rāma said affectionately to the Gurū, "My lord, all the people are much inconvenienced by having nothing to take but water and the wild produce of the woods. When I look at Bharat and his brother, the minister, and all the queens, a minute seems to me like an age. Return, I pray, with all of them to the city: for you are here, the king is in heaven, and there is no one left at Ajodhyā. I have said too much and have presumed greatly, but do, sir, as you think best."

दोहा-*dohā:*

धर्म सेतु करुनायतन कस न कहहु अस राम ।
dharma setu karunāyatana kasa na kahahu asa rāma,
लोग दुखित दिन दुइ दरस देखि लहहुँ बिश्राम ॥२४८॥
loga dukhita dina dui darasa dekhi lahahuṁ biśrāma. 248.

Trans:

"O Rāma, bulwark of righteousness, home of compassion, it is but natural for you to speak thus: the people are wearied, let them rest for two days and delight in your presence."

चौपाई-*caupāī:*

राम बचन सुनि सभय समाजू । जनु जलनिधि महुँ बिकल जहाजू ॥
rāma bacana suni sabhaya samājū, janu jalanidhi mahuṁ bikala jahājū.
सुनि गुर गिरा सुमंगल मूला । भयउ मनहुँ मारुत अनुकूला ॥
suni gura girā sumaṁgala mūlā, bhayau manahuṁ māruta anukūlā.
पावन पयँ तिहुँ काल नहाहीं । जो बिलोकि अघ ओघ नसाहीं ॥
pāvana payaṁ tihuṁ kāla nahāhīṁ, jo biloki agha ogha nasāhīṁ.
मंगलमूरति लोचन भरि भरि । निरखहिं हरषि दंडवत करि करि ॥
maṁgalamūrati locana bhari bhari, nirakhahiṁ haraṣi daṁḍavata kari kari.
राम सैल बन देखन जाहीं । जहँ सुख सकल सकल दुख नाहीं ॥
rāma saila bana dekhana jāhīṁ, jahaṁ sukha sakala sakala dukha nāhīṁ.
झरना झरहिं सुधासम बारी । त्रिबिध तापहर त्रिबिध बयारी ॥
jharanā jharahiṁ sudhāsama bārī, tribidha tāpahara tribidha bayārī.
बिटप बेलि तृन अगनित जाती । फल प्रसून पल्लव बहु भाँती ॥
biṭapa beli tṛna aganita jātī, phala prasūna pallava bahu bhāṁtī.
सुंदर सिला सुखद तरु छाहीं । जाइ बरनि बन छबि केहि पाहीं ॥
suṁdara silā sukhada taru chāhīṁ, jāi barani bana chabi kehi pāhīṁ.

Trans:

On hearing Rāma's words, the assembly was in dismay, like a ship tossed on the ocean; but when they heard the saint's auspicious speech, it was as if the wind had turned in their favor. At the three set times they bathed in the sacred stream, the mere sight of which destroys any multitude of sins; and ever feasting their eyes on the incarnation of blessedness, and again and again prostrating themselves before him, they look and rejoice. Then they went to see Rāma's hill and wood, where all was good, and evil none: the torrents flowing with streams of nectar; the air so soft, cool, and fragrant that it soothed every pain of mind or body; the trees, creepers, and grasses of infinite variety; the many kinds of fruits, flowers, leaves; the magnificent rocks and the pleasant shade under the trees—all made the forest beautiful beyond description.

दोहा-*dohā:*

सरनि सरोरुह जल बिहग कूजत गुंजत भृंग ।
sarani saroruha jala bihaga kūjata guṁjata bhṛṁga,
बैर बिगत बिहरत बिपिन मृग बिहंग बहुरंग ॥२४९॥
baira bigata biharata bipina mṛga bihaṁga bahuraṁga. 249.

Trans:

The ponds were festive with lotuses—the haunt of cooing waterfowl and buzzing bees; and forgetful of mutual animosity, beasts roamed in the forest; and many were the birds of varied plumage.

चौपाई-*caupāī:*

कोल किरात भिल्ल बनबासी । मधु सुचि सुंदर स्वादु सुधा सी ॥
kola kirāta bhilla banabāsī, madhu suci suṁdara svādu sudhā sī.
भरि भरि परन पुटीं रचि रुरी । कंद मूल फल अंकुर जूरी ॥
bhari bhari parana puṭīṁ raci rurī, kaṁda mūla phala aṁkura jūrī.
सबहि देहिं करि बिनय प्रनामा । कहि कहि स्वाद भेद गुन नामा ॥
sabahi dehiṁ kari binaya pranāmā, kahi kahi svāda bheda guna nāmā.
देहिं लोग बहु मोल न लेहीं । फेरत राम दोहाई देहीं ॥
dehiṁ loga bahu mola na lehīṁ, pherata rāma dohāī dehīṁ.
कहहिं सनेह मगन मृदु बानी । मानत साधु पेम पहिचानी ॥
kahahiṁ saneha magana mṛdu bānī, mānata sādhu pema pahicānī.
तुम्ह सुकृती हम नीच निषादा । पावा दरसनु राम प्रसादा ॥
tumha sukṛtī hama nīca niṣādā, pāvā darasanu rāma prasādā.
हमहि अगम अति दरसु तुम्हारा । जस मरु धरनि देवधुनि धारा ॥
hamahi agama ati darasu tumhārā, jasa maru dharani devadhuni dhārā.
राम कृपाल निषाद नेवाजा । परिजन प्रजउ चहिअ जस राजा ॥
rāma kṛpāla niṣāda nevājā, parijana prajau cahia jasa rājā.

Trans:

The inhabitants of the woods—*Kol*s, *Kirāt*s, and *Bhīl*s—brought delicious honey sweet as nectar, and piled up leafy bowls with herbs, roots, fruits, sprouts daintily arranged. With humble salutations they offered them to all, telling the taste, character, quality, and name of each. The people offered a liberal price, but they would not accept it, and begged them in Rāma's name to take it back, saying in gentle tones in the depth of their affection, "Good people respect true love once they know of it. You are holy, and we Nishāds are lowly; by Rāma's favor we have been admitted into your presence, an honor as difficult of attainment for us as for the desert of Maru to be watered by the Gangā. The all-merciful Rāma has showered his grace on the Nishāds' chief. Let his family and subjects too share Rāma's disposition.

दोहा-*dohā:*

यह जियँ जानि सँकोचु तजि करिअ छोहु लखि नेहु ।
yaha jiyaṁ jāni saṁkocu taji karia chohu lakhi nehu,
हमहि कृतारथ करन लगि फल तृन अंकुर लेहु ॥२५०॥
hamahi kṛtāratha karana lagi phala tṛna aṁkura lehu. 250.

Trans:

Bear this in mind, and without any more demur, recognize our affection and shower your grace upon us. Do please accept these fruits and herbs and sprouts and render us happy.

चौपाई-*caupāī:*

तुम्ह प्रिय पाहुने बन पगु धारे । सेवा जोगु न भाग हमारे ॥
tumha priya pāhune bana pagu dhāre, sevā jogu na bhāga hamāre.
देब काह हम तुम्हहि गोसाँई । ईंधनु पात किरात मिताई ॥
deba kāha hama tumhahi gosāṁī, īṁdhanu pāta kirāta mitāī.
यह हमारि अति बड़ि सेवकाई । लेहिं न बासन बसन चोराई ॥
yaha hamāri ati baṛi sevakāī, lehiṁ na bāsana basana corāī.
हम जड़ जीव जीव गन घाती । कुटिल कुचाली कुमति कुजाती ॥
hama jaṛa jīva jīva gana ghātī, kuṭila kucālī kumati kujātī.
पाप करत निसि बासर जाहीं । नहिं पट कटि नहिं पेट अघाहीं ॥
pāpa karata nisi bāsara jāhīṁ, nahiṁ paṭa kaṭi nahiṁ peṭa aghāhīṁ.
सपनेहुँ धरम बुद्धि कस काऊ । यह रघुनंदन दरस प्रभाऊ ॥
sapanehuṁ dharama buddhi kasa kāū, yaha raghunaṁdana darasa prabhāū.
जब तें प्रभु पद पदुम निहारे । मिटे दुसह दुख दोष हमारे ॥
jaba teṁ prabhu pada paduma nihāre, miṭe dusaha dukha doṣa hamāre.
बचन सुनत पुरजन अनुरागे । तिन्ह के भाग सराहन लागे ॥

bacana sunata purajana anurāge, tinha ke bhāga sarāhana lāge.

Trans:

You have come to the forest as our welcome guests, though we are all unworthy to do you any service. And what is it, sirs, that we offer you? Fuel and fodder are a Kirāt's tokens of friendship, and our greatest service is not to steal and run off with your clothes and dishes. We are a rude people, low-minded and lowly-born, who day and night commit sins; we are of vile nature and vile pursuits, often taking life. Barely getting clothes for the body, or food for the belly—let alone anything higher—how could we possibly have dreamt of entertaining any pious sentiment, except by the virtue of having seen Shrī Rāma? Since we beheld our Lord's lotus feet, our sore distress and sins have all been removed." On hearing this speech, the citizens were much affected and broke out into praises of their good fortune.

छंद-chamda:

लागे सराहन भाग सब अनुराग बचन सुनावहीं ।
lāge sarāhana bhāga saba anurāga bacana sunāvahīṁ,
बोलनि मिलनि सिय राम चरन सनेहु लखि सुखु पावहीं ॥
bolani milani siya rāma carana sanehu lakhi sukhu pāvahīṁ.
नर नारि निदरहिं नेहु निज सुनि कोल भिल्लनि की गिरा ।
nara nāri nidarahiṁ nehu nija suni kola bhillani kī girā,
तुलसी कृपा रघुबंसमनि की लोह लै लौका तिरा ॥
tulasī kṛpā raghubaṁsamani kī loha lai laukā tirā.

Trans:

All began to praise their good fortune and addressed them in loving terms—being delighted to find in their speech and attitude such high degree of devotion to the feet of Sītā and Rāma; everyone, man or woman, thought little of his own devotion, on hearing the language of the *Kol*s and *Bhīls*. Through the mercy of the jewel of Raghu's line, says Tulsīdās, a boat floats even though laden with iron.

सोरठा-sorathā:

बिहरहिं बन चहु ओर प्रतिदिन प्रमुदित लोग सब ।
biharahiṁ bana cahu ora pratidina pramudita loga saba,
जल ज्यों दादुर मोर भए पीन पावस प्रथम ॥ २५१ ॥
jala jyoṁ dādura mora bhae pīna pāvasa prathama. 251.

Trans:

Each day people roamed through every part of the forest in as great a delight as frogs and peacocks invigorated by the first shower of rains.

चौपाई-caupāī:

पुर जन नारि मगन अति प्रीती । बासर जाहिं पलक सम बीती ॥
pura jana nāri magana ati prītī, bāsara jāhiṁ palaka sama bītī.
सीय सासु प्रति बेष बनाई । सादर करइ सरिस सेवकाई ॥
sīya sāsu prati beṣa banāī, sādara karai sarisa sevakāī.
लखा न मरमु राम बिनु काहूँ । माया सब सिय माया माहूँ ॥
lakhā na maramu rāma binu kāhūṁ, māyā saba siya māyā māhūṁ.
सीयँ सासु सेवा बस कीन्हीं । तिन्ह लहि सुख सिख आसिष दीन्हीं ॥
sīyaṁ sāsu sevā basa kīnhīṁ, tinha lahi sukha sikha āsiṣa dīnhīṁ.
लखि सिय सहित सरल दोउ भाई । कुटिल रानि पछितानि अघाई ॥
lakhi siya sahita sarala dou bhāī, kuṭila rāni pachitāni aghāī.
अवनि जमहि जाचति कैकेई । महि न बीचु बिधि मीचु न देई ॥
avani jamahi jācati kaikeī, mahi na bīcu bidhi mīcu na deī.
लोकहुँ बेद बिदित कबि कहहीं । राम बिमुख थलु नरक न लहहीं ॥
lokahuṁ beda bidita kabi kahahīṁ, rāma bimukha thalu naraka na lahahīṁ.
यहु संसउ सब के मन माहीं । राम गवनु बिधि अवध कि नाहीं ॥
yahu saṁsau saba ke mana māhīṁ, rāma gavanu bidhi avadha ki nāhīṁ.

Trans:

So absorbed in excess of love were the citizens of Ajodhyā that a day went by as in a minute. Sītā, assuming as many forms as she had mothers-in-law, waited reverently upon them all with equal attention. No one but Rāma noticed the miracle; for Sītā is the very power of Māyā, and he the Māyā's Lord. Sītā won over all the queens by her services, and they being pleased gave her both instruction and benediction. Looking at Sītā and the two noble brothers, the wicked queen Kaekayī repented bitterly, and now she prays in her heart, "Is there no escape for me? Does God refuse me even death? As it is declared in the Vedas and by popular tradition, and as the poets also have sung—if Rāma be against you, not even in hell you will find shelter." Meanwhile this was the question in everyone's mind, "Good God, will Rāma return to Avadh or not?"

दोहा-dohā:

निसि न नीद नहिं भूख दिन भरतु बिकल सुचि सोच ।
nisi na nīda nahiṁ bhūkha dina bharatu bikala suci soca,
नीच कीच बिच मगन जस मीनहि सलिल सँकोच ॥ २५२ ॥
nīca kīca bica magana jasa mīnahi salila saṁkoca. 252.

Trans:

Bharat was so anxious and disquieted that he could neither sleep by night nor eat by day, like as a fish sunk in the last of the mud is in trouble without water.

चौपाई-caupāī:

कीन्हि मातु मिस काल कुचाली । ईति भीति जस पाकत साली ॥
kīnhi mātu misa kāla kucālī, īti bhīti jasa pākata sālī.
केहि बिधि होइ राम अभिषेकू । मोहि अवकलत उपाउ न एकू ॥
kehi bidhi hoi rāma abhiṣekū, mohi avakalata upāu na ekū.
अवसि फिरहिं गुर आयसु मानी । मुनि पुनि कहब राम रुचि जानी ॥
avasi phirahiṁ gura āyasu mānī, muni puni kahaba rāma ruci jānī.
मातु कहेहुँ बहुरहिं रघुराऊ । राम जननि हठ करबि कि काऊ ॥
mātu kahehuṁ bahurahiṁ raghurāū, rāma janani haṭha karabi ki kāū.
मोहि अनुचर कर केतिक बाता । तेहि महँ कुसमउ बाम बिधाता ॥
mohi anucara kara ketika bātā, tehi mahaṁ kusamau bāma bidhātā.
जौं हठ करउँ त निपट कुकरमू । हरगिरि तें गुरु सेवक धरमू ॥
jauṁ haṭha karauṁ ta nipaṭa kukaramū, haragiri teṁ guru sevaka dharamū.
एकउ जुगुति न मन ठहरानी । सोचत भरतहि रैनि बिहानी ॥
ekau juguti na mana ṭhaharānī, socata bharatahi raini bihānī.
प्रात नहाइ प्रभुहि सिर नाई । बैठत पठए रिषयँ बोलाई ॥
prāta nahāi prabhuhi sira nāī, baiṭhata paṭhae riṣayaṁ bolāī.

Trans:

"It was Fate, in the form of my mother, that did me this injury, just like when a rice field ripening for harvest is smitten by hail. In what manner can Rāma's coronation be secured? There is nothing now left for me to do. He would certainly return in obedience to an order of the Gurū; but then the saint will only order what he knows Rāma to wish. At his mother's bidding too, he would return, but Kausalyā would never insist upon anything. Of what account am I, who am only his vassal? Moreover, I am fallen upon evil times with gods against me? If I resist him, it would be a grievous sin—for the duty of a servant to his master is weightier than Kailāsh." Without being able to settle a single plan in his mind, Bharat spent the whole night in thought. At daybreak he bathed, bowed his head to his Lord, and was sitting down when he was sent for by the Rishī.

दोहा-dohā:

गुर पद कमल प्रनामु करि बैठे आयसु पाइ ।
gura pada kamala pranāmu kari baiṭhe āyasu pāi,
बिप्र महाजन सचिव सब जुरे सभासद आइ ॥ २५३ ॥
bipra mahājana saciva saba jure sabhāsada āi. 253.

Trans:

After saluting the Gurū's lotus feet and receiving his permission, he took his seat; while all the Brahmins, nobles, and ministers of state came and assembled in the council.

चौपाई-caupāī:

बोले मुनिबरु समय समाना । सुनहु सभासद भरत सुजाना ॥
bole munibaru samaya samānā, sunahu sabhāsada bharata sujānā.
धरम धुरीन भानुकुल भानू । राजा रामु स्वबस भगवानू ॥
dharama dhurīna bhānukula bhānū, rājā rāmu svabasa bhagavānū.
सत्यसंध पालक श्रुति सेतू । राम जनमु जग मंगल हेतू ॥
satyasaṁdha pālaka śruti setū, rāma janamu jaga maṁgala hetū.
गुर पितु मातु बचन अनुसारी । खल दलु दलन देव हितकारी ॥
gura pitu mātu bacana anusārī, khala dalu dalana deva hitakārī.
नीति प्रीति परमारथ स्वारथु । कोउ न राम सम जान जथारथु ॥
nīti prīti paramāratha svārathu, kou na rāma sama jāna jathārathu.
बिधि हरि हरु ससि रबि दिसिपाला । माया जीव करम कुलि काला ॥
bidhi hari haru sasi rabi disipālā, māyā jīva karama kuli kālā.
अहिप महिप जहँ लगि प्रभुताई । जोग सिद्धि निगमागम गाई ॥
ahipa mahipa jahaṁ lagi prabhutāī, joga siddhi nigamāgama gāī.
करि बिचार जियँ देखहु नीकें । राम रजाइ सीस सबही कें ॥
kari bicāra jiyaṁ dekhahu nīkeṁ, rāma rajāi sīsa sabahī keṁ.

Trans:

The great sage addressed them in words appropriate to the occasion, "Hearken, ye counselors, and you, wise Bharat. The champion of righteousness, the sun of the solar race, king Rāma, the autocratic, the Lord God, the ocean of truth, the protector, the bulwark of scripture, has taken birth for the benefit of the whole world. Obedient to the word of his Gurū and his father and mother; destroying the armies of the wicked and befriending the gods; in policy and devotion, in all things that pertain to this life or the next, there is no one equal to Rāma in the knowledge of what is right. Brahmmā, Vishnu, and Shiva; the sun, the moon, the guardians of the spheres; Delusion, Life, Fate, and this Kali-Yug; the sovereigns of hell, the sovereigns of earth, and all the powers that be; magic and sorcery, and every spell in the Vedas and the Tantras—ponder it in your heart and consider well—are all obedient to Rāma's commands.

दोहा-dohā:

राखें राम रजाइ रुख हम सब कर हित होइ ।
rākheṁ rāma rajāi rukha hama saba kara hita hoi,
समुझि सयाने करहु अब सब मिलि संमत सोइ ॥२५४॥
samujhi sayāne karahu aba saba mili saṁmata soi. 254.

Trans:

If we observe Rāma's pleasure and commands, it will be all well for us all. Now, wise sirs, think it over, and implement a plan upon which you unanimously resolve.

चौपाई-caupāī:

सब कहुँ सुखद राम अभिषेकू । मंगल मोद मूल मग एकू ॥
saba kahuṁ sukhada rāma abhiṣekū, maṁgala moda mūla maga ekū.
केहि बिधि अवध चलहिं रघुराऊ । कहहु समुझि सोइ करिअ उपाऊ ॥
kehi bidhi avadha calahiṁ raghurāū, kahahu samujhi soi karia upāū.
सब सादर सुनि मुनिबर बानी । नय परमारथ स्वारथ सानी ॥
saba sādara suni munibara bānī, naya paramāratha svāratha sānī.
उतरु न आव लोग भए भोरे । तब सिरु नाइ भरत कर जोरे ॥
utaru na āva loga bhae bhore, taba siru nāi bharata kara jore.
भानुबंस भए भूप घनेरे । अधिक एक तें एक बड़ेरे ॥
bhānubaṁsa bhae bhūpa ghanere, adhika eka teṁ eka baṛere.
जनम हेतु सब कहँ पितु माता । करम सुभासुभ देइ बिधाता ॥
janam hetu saba kahaṁ pitu mātā, karama subhāsubha dei bidhātā.
दलि दुख सजइ सकल कल्याना । अस असीस राउरि जगु जाना ॥
dali dukha sajai sakala kalyānā, asa asīsa rāuri jagu jānā.
सो गोसाइँ बिधि गति जेहिं छेंकी । सकइ को टारि टेक जो टेकी ॥
so gosāiṁ bidhi gati jehiṁ cheṁkī, sakai ko ṭāri ṭeka jo ṭekī.

Trans:

Rāma's coronation will be agreeable to all, as a sure source of happiness and the one way to felicity. But how is he to be prevailed upon to return to Avadh? Think before you speak, and upon that plan we will act." All listened respectfully to Vasishtha's speech, full as it was of justice, unworldly, and secular wisdom, but no answer was forthcoming; everyone was dumb-founded, till with bowed head and clasped hands Bharat spoke, "In the solar race there have been many kings, each one greater than the other; all owe their birth to their parents, but the good and ill fruits one gets is dispensed by God. However, your benediction, as all the world knows, confers prosperity and a triumph over sorrows; and you have thwarted the course of destiny; and none could alter what you resolve upon.

दोहा-dohā:

बूझिअ मोहि उपाउ अब सो सब मोर अभागु ।
būjhia mohi upāu aba so saba mora abhāgu,
सुनि सनेहमय बचन गुर उर उमगा अनुरागु ॥२५५॥
suni sanehamaya bacana gura ura umagā anurāgu. 255.

Trans:

And yet now you ask advice of me: such is my ill fate." When the Gurū heard this affectionate speech, love sprung up in his heart.

चौपाई-caupāī:

तात बात फुरि राम कृपाहीं । राम बिमुख सिधि सपनेहुँ नाहीं ॥
tāta bāta phuri rāma kṛpāhīṁ, rāma bimukha sidhi sapanehuṁ nāhīṁ.
सकुचउँ तात कहत एक बाता । अरध तजहिं बुध सरबस जाता ॥
sakucauṁ tāta kahata eka bātā, aradha tajahiṁ budha sarabasa jātā.
तुम्ह कानन गवनहु दोउ भाई । फेरिअहिं लखन सीय रघुराई ॥
tumha kānana gavanahu dou bhāī, pheriahiṁ lakhana sīya raghurāī.
सुनि सुबचन हरषे दोउ भ्राता । भे प्रमोद परिपूरन गाता ॥
suni subacana harașe dou bhrātā, bhe pramoda paripūrana gātā.
मन प्रसन्न तन तेजु बिराजा । जनु जिय राउ रामु भए राजा ॥
mana prasanna tana teju birājā, janu jiya rāu rāmu bhae rājā.
बहुत लाभ लोगन्ह लघु हानी । सम दुख सुख सब रोवहिं रानी ॥
bahuta lābha loganha laghu hānī, sama dukha sukha saba rovahiṁ rānī.
कहहिं भरतु मुनि कहा सो कीन्हे । फलु जग जीवन्ह अभिमत दीन्हे ॥
kahahiṁ bharatu muni kahā so kīnhe, phalu jaga jīvanha abhimata dīnhe.
कानन करउँ जनम भरि बासू । एहिं तें अधिक न मोर सुपासू ॥
kānana karauṁ janama bhari bāsū, ehiṁ teṁ adhika na mora supāsū.

Trans:

"My son this is a true saying: it is all Rāma's mercy; without Rāma no one can even dream of felicity. There is one way my son, though I am ashamed to propose it; but a wise man will sacrifice one half when he sees the entire going. Do you two brothers go into exile; then Lakshman, Sītā, Rāma may be sent back." On hearing this favorable speech, the two brothers rejoiced and their whole body thrilled with excitement; they were as pleased at heart and as radiant all over as if King Dashrath had been restored to life, and Rāma enthroned already; while the people thought that this way their gain would be higher than their loss; and the queens all wept for their pain was equal to their joy. Said Bharat, "What the saint has proposed is already as good as done; he has granted me the one thing above all others that I most desired. I will stay all my life in the forest; there is nothing I, should like better.

दोहा-dohā:

अंतरजामी रामु सिय तुम्ह सरबग्य सुजान ।
aṁtarajāmī rāmu siya tumha sarabagya sujāna,
जौं फुर कहहु त नाथ निज कीजिअ बचनु प्रवान ॥२५६॥
jauṁ phura kahahu ta nātha nija kījia bacanu pravāna. 256.

Trans:

Rāma and Sītā know my heart and you are full of knowledge and wisdom; if my lord you mean what you say, please make good your word."

चौपाई-caupāī:

भरत बचन सुनि देखि सनेहू । सभा सहित मुनि भए बिदेहू ॥
bharata bacana suni dekhi sanehū, sabhā sahita muni bhae bidehū.
भरत महा महिमा जलरासी । मुनि मति ठाढ़ि तीर अबला सी ॥
bharata mahā mahimā jalarāsī, muni mati ṭhāṛhi tīra abalā sī.
गा चह पार जतनु हियँ हेरा । पावति नाव न बोहितु बेरा ॥
gā caha pāra jatanu hiyaṁ herā, pāvati nāva na bohitu berā.
औरु करिहि को भरत बड़ाई । सरसी सीपि कि सिंधु समाई ॥
auru karihi ko bharata baṛāī, sarasī sīpi ki siṁdhu samāī.
भरतु मुनिहि मन भीतर भाए । सहित समाज राम पहिं आए ॥
bharatu munihi mana bhītara bhāe, sahita samāja rāma pahiṁ āe.
प्रभु प्रनामु करि दीन्ह सुआसनु । बैठे सब सुनि मुनि अनुसासनु ॥
prabhu pranāmu kari dīnha suāsanu, baiṭhe saba suni muni anusāsanu.
बोले मुनिबरु बचन बिचारी । देस काल अवसर अनुहारी ॥
bole munibaru bacana bicārī, desa kāla avasara anuhārī.
सुनहु राम सरबग्य सुजाना । धरम नीति गुन ग्यान निधाना ॥
sunahu rāma sarabagya sujānā, dharama nīti guna gyāna nidhānā.

Trans:

Hearing Bharat's words and seeing his love, the saint and the whole assembly were transported out of themselves. Bharat's vast generosity was like a sheet of water and the saint's proposal like a woman standing on its brink, anxious to cross and trying different ways, but unable to find either ship, boat, or raft. Who can describe Bharat's magnanimity? Can the ocean be contained in a river-shell? The saint was inwardly at heart charmed with Bharat, and accompanied by the assembly went to Rāma. The Lord saluted him and led him to a seat of honor; and on receiving the saint's permission all sat down. Then spoke Vasishtha in well considered words, according to the circumstance of the place and time, "Hearken Rāma: you are omniscient and wise, a store-house of piety, prudence, virtue, and intelligence;

दोहा-dohā:

सब के उर अंतर बसहु जानहु भाउ कुभाउ ।
saba ke ura aṁtara basahu jānahu bhāu kubhāu,
पुरजन जननी भरत हित होइ सो कहिअ उपाउ ॥२५७॥
purajana jananī bharata hita hoi so kahia upāu. 257.

Trans:

you dwell in the hearts of all and know all thoughts—good or spoiled; now advise what will be best for your subjects your mothers, and Bharat.

चौपाई-caupāī:

आरत कहहिं बिचारि न काऊ । सूझ जूआरिहि आपन दाऊ ॥
ārata kahahiṁ bicāri na kāū, sūjha jūārihi āpana dāū.
सुनि मुनि बचन कहत रघुराऊ । नाथ तुम्हारेहि हाथ उपाऊ ॥
suni muni bacana kahata raghurāū, nātha tumhārehi hātha upāū.
सब कर हित रुख राउरि राखें । आयसु किएँ मुदित फुर भाषें ॥
saba kara hita rukha rāuri rākheṁ, āyasu kieṁ mudita phura bhāṣeṁ.
प्रथम जो आयसु मो कहुँ होई । माथें मानि करौं सिख सोई ॥
prathama jo āyasu mo kahuṁ hoī, mātheṁ māni karauṁ sikha soī.
पुनि जेहि कहँ जस कहब गोसाईं । सो सब भाँति घटिहि सेवकाईं ॥
puni jehi kahaṁ jasa kahaba gosāīṁ, so saba bhāṁti ghaṭihi sevakāīṁ.
कह मुनि राम सत्य तुम्ह भाषा । भरत सनेहँ बिचारु न राखा ॥
kaha muni rāma satya tumha bhāṣā, bharata sanehaṁ bicāru na rākhā.
तेहि तें कहउँ बहोरि बहोरी । भरत भगति बस भइ मति मोरी ॥
tehi teṁ kahauṁ bahori bahorī, bharata bhagati basa bhai mati morī.
मोरें जान भरत रुचि राखि । जो कीजिअ सो सुभ सिव साखी ॥
moreṁ jāna bharata ruci rākhi, jo kījia so subha siva sākhī.

Trans:

A man in pain talks wildly without forethought, and a gambler watches only his own play." On hearing the saint's speech, Raghurāī replied, "My lord, the remedy is in your own hands. To attend to your wishes will be best for us all. Only give the order, and cheerfully, I assure you, whatever your commands may be for me, those instructions firstly I will dutifully obey; and after me, as each has his orders, so will they do you service." Said the saint, "Rāma, you speak truly; but Bharat's affection has robbed me of my wits; therefore I say again and again my judgment is overcome by Bharat's devotion. To me now—and may Shiva be my witness—whatever pleases Bharat is the best thing to be done.

दोहा-dohā:

भरत बिनय सादर सुनिअ करिअ बिचारु बहोरि ।
bharata binaya sādara sunia karia bicāru bahori,
करब साधुमत लोकमत नृपनय निगम निचोरि ॥२५८॥
karaba sādhumata lokamata nṛpanaya nigama nicori. 258.

Trans:

Listen respectfully to Bharat's prayer; reconsider the matter; and after weighing well the duties of a king and the texts of Scripture, take the advice given you both by the sages and the worldly-wise."

चौपाई-caupāī:

गुर अनुरागु भरत पर देखी । राम हृदयँ आनंदु बिसेषी ॥
gura anurāgu bharata para dekhī, rāma hṛdayaṁ ānaṁdu biseṣī.
भरतहि धरम धुरंधर जानी । निज सेवक तन मानस बानी ॥
bharatahi dharama dhuraṁdhara jānī, nija sevaka tana mānasa bānī.
बोले गुर आयस अनुकूला । बचन मंजु मृदु मंगलमूला ॥
bole gura āyasa anukūlā, bacana maṁju mṛdu maṁgalamūlā.
नाथ सपथ पितु चरन दोहाई । भयउ न भुअन भरत सम भाई ॥
nātha sapatha pitu carana dohāī, bhayau na bhuana bharata sama bhāī.
जे गुर पद अंबुज अनुरागी । ते लोकहुँ बेदहुँ बड़भागी ॥
je gura pada aṁbuja anurāgī, te lokahuṁ bedahuṁ baṛabhāgī.
राउर जा पर अस अनुरागू । को कहि सकइ भरत कर भागू ॥
rāura jā para asa anurāgū, ko kahi sakai bharata kara bhāgū.
लखि लघु बंधु बुद्धि सकुचाई । करत बदन पर भरत बड़ाई ॥
lakhi laghu baṁdhu buddhi sakucāī, karata badana para bharata baṛāī.
भरतु कहहिं सोइ किएँ भलाई । अस कहि राम रहे अरगाई ॥
bharatu kahahiṁ soi kieṁ bhalāī, asa kahi rāma rahe aragāī.

Trans:

Seeing the Gurū's love for Bharat, Rāma's heart rejoiced exceedingly, for he knew Bharat to be a champion of righteousness, and in thought, word, and deed his own faithful servant. In obedience to the Gurū's commands, he made this sweet, gentle, and excellent reply, "I swear by you, my lord, and by my father's feet, that in all the world there has been no brother like Bharat. All who love the lotus feet of their Gurū are highly blessed; so say both the world and the Veda. But who can tell Bharat's blessedness, to whom such love has been shown by you? Knowing him to be my younger brother, my senses are abashed when I thus praise him to his face. Of course, whatever Bharat says, that will be good for us to do." Having said so, Rāma remained silent.

दोहा-dohā:

तब मुनि बोले भरत सन सब सँकोचु तजि तात ।
taba muni bole bharata sana saba saṁkocu taji tāta,
कृपासिंधु प्रिय बंधु सन कहहु हृदय कै बात ॥२५९॥
kṛpāsiṁdhu priya baṁdhu sana kahahu hṛdaya kai bāta. 259.

Trans:

Then the saint said to Bharat, "Put aside all diffidence, my son, and tell the ocean of mercy, your own dear brother, what you really have at heart."

चौपाई-caupāī:

सुनि मुनि बचन राम रुख पाई । गुरु साहिब अनुकूल अघाई ॥
suni muni bacana rāma rukha pāī, guru sāhiba anukūla aghāī.
लखि अपनें सिर सबु छरु भारू । कहि न सकहिं कछु करहिं बिचारू ॥
lakhi apaneṁ sira sabu charu bhārū, kahi na sakahiṁ kachu karahiṁ bicārū.
पुलकि सरीर सभाँ भए ठाढे । नीरज नयन नेह जल बाढे ॥
pulaki sarīra sabhām̐ bhae ṭhāḍhe, nīraja nayana neha jala bāṛhe.
कहब मोर मुनिनाथ निबाहा । एहि तें अधिक कहौं मैं काहा ॥
kahaba mora muninātha nibāhā, ehi teṁ adhika kahauṁ maiṁ kāhā.
मैं जानउँ निज नाथ सुभाऊ । अपराधिहु पर कोह न काऊ ॥
maiṁ jānaum̐ nija nātha subhāū, aparādhihu para koha na kāū.
मो पर कृपा सनेहु बिसेषी । खेलत खुनिस न कबहूँ देखी ॥
mo para kṛpā sanehu biseṣī, khelata khunisa na kabahūm̐ dekhī.
सिसुपन तें परिहरेउँ न संगू । कबहुँ न कीन्ह मोर मन भंगू ॥
sisupana teṁ parihareum̐ na saṁgū, kabahum̐ na kīnha mora mana bhaṁgū.
मैं प्रभु कृपा रीति जियँ जोही । हारेहुँ खेल जितावहिं मोही ॥
maiṁ prabhu kṛpā rīti jiyam̐ johī, hārehum̐ khela jitāvahiṁ mohī.

Trans:

Hearing the saint's address, and having already received Rāma's consent, he was satisfied of the goodwill both of his Gurū and his master; but seeing the weight of the whole business put upon his own head, he could say nothing and remained lost in thought, as he stood in the assembly, quivering all over his body, and his lotus eyes filled wet with affection, "The king of saints has already spoken for me, what more is there for me to say? I know my Lord's amiable disposition, that he never shows displeasure even to the guilty; and for me he has a special love and tenderness; even in play he has never frowned at me. From childhood I have never left him, and never at any time has he wounded my feelings. I have observed my Lord's gracious ways; and even when beating me in game he would let me win.

दोहा-dohā:

महूँ सनेह सकोच बस सनमुख कही न बैन ।
mahūm̐ saneha sakoca basa sanamukha kahī na baina,
दरसन तृपित न आजु लगि पेम पिआसे नैन ॥२६०॥
darasana tṛpita na āju lagi pema piāse naina. 260.

Trans:

I am much too overcome by affection and modesty to say a word before him; to this day my eyes—thirsting for his love—have not been satiated with the sight of him.

चौपाई-caupāī:

बिधि न सकेउ सहि मोर दुलारा । नीच बीचु जननी मिस पारा ॥
bidhi na sakeu sahi mora dulārā, nīca bīcu jananī misa pārā.
यहउ कहत मोहि आजु न सोभा । अपनी समुझि साधु सुचि को भा ॥
yahau kahata mohi āju na sobhā, apanī samujhi sādhu suci ko bhā.
मातु मंदि मैं साधु सुचाली । उर अस आनत कोटि कुचाली ॥
mātu maṁdi maiṁ sādhu sucālī, ura asa ānata koṭi kucālī.
फरइ कि कोदव बालि सुसाली । मुकता प्रसव कि संबुक काली ॥
pharai ki kodava bāli susālī, mukatā prasava ki saṁbuka kālī.
सपनेहुँ दोसक लेसु न काहू । मोर अभाग उदधि अवगाहू ॥
sapanehum̐ dosaka lesu na kāhū, mora abhāga udadhi avagāhū.
बिनु समुझें निज अघ परिपाकू । जारिउँ जायँ जननि कहि काकू ॥
binu samujheṁ nija agha paripākū, jārium̐ jāyam̐ janani kahi kākū.
हृदयँ हेरि हारेउँ सब ओरा । एकहि भाँति भलेहिं भल मोरा ॥
hṛdayam̐ heri hāreum̐ saba orā, ekahi bhām̐ti bhalehiṁ bhala morā.
गुर गोसाइँ साहिब सिय रामू । लागत मोहि नीक परिनामू ॥
gura gosāim̐ sāhiba siya rāmū, lāgata mohi nīka parināmū.

Trans:

But Fate could not endure my fondness, and has cruelly interposed an obstacle through the agency of my mother. In saying this now I do myself no honor; for who is made good by his own good estimation? To entertain the thought that my mother is a wretch and I am good, upright is a thousand times worse. Can rice be produced from stalks of *kodu*, or the shells of a pond sweat pearls? Not a shadow of blame or wrongdoing attaches to anyone: it is my ill-luck, which is like some fathomless ocean. Not perceiving that it is the fruit of my own sins, I revile my mother, to my own undoing. I search my heart, but am beaten all round. In one matter only am I really fortunate; with Vasishtha for my Gurū and Sītā and Rāma for my masters, and so things must come right in the end.

दोहा-dohā:

साधु सभाँ गुर प्रभु निकट कहउँ सुथल सतिभाउ ।
sādhu sabhām̐ gura prabhu nikaṭa kahaum̐ suthala satibhāu,
प्रेम प्रपंचु कि झूठ फुर जानहिं मुनि रघुराउ ॥२६१॥
prema prapaṁcu ki jhūṭha phura jānahiṁ muni raghurāu. 261.

Trans:

In this honorable assemblage, in the presence of my Lord and my Gurū, and in this holy place, I speak my true sentiments; the saint and Rāma know whether my affection is sincere or feigned, my words, true or false.

चौपाई-caupāī:

भूपति मरन पेम पनु राखी । जननी कुमति जगतु सबु साखी ॥
bhūpati marana pema panu rākhī, jananī kumati jagatu sabu sākhī.
देखि न जाहिं बिकल महतारीं । जरहिं दुसह जर पुर नर नारीं ॥
dekhi na jāhiṁ bikala mahatārīṁ, jarahiṁ dusaha jara pura nara nārīṁ.
महीं सकल अनरथ कर मूला । सो सुनि समुझि सहिउँ सब सूला ॥
mahīṁ sakala anaratha kara mūlā, so suni samujhi sahium̐ saba sūlā.
सुनि बन गवनु कीन्ह रघुनाथा । करि मुनि बेष लखन सिय साथा ॥
suni bana gavanu kīnha raghunāthā, kari muni beṣa lakhana siya sāthā.
बिनु पानहिन्ह पयादेहि पाएँ । संकरु साखि रहेउँ एहि घाएँ ॥
binu pānahinha payādehi pāem̐, saṁkaru sākhi raheum̐ ehi ghāem̐.
बहुरि निहार निषाद सनेहू । कुलिस कठिन उर भयउ न बेहू ॥
bahuri nihāra niṣāda sanehū, kulisa kaṭhina ura bhayau na behū.
अब सबु आँखिन्ह देखेउँ आई । जिअत जीव जड़ सबइ सहाई ॥
aba sabu ām̐khinha dekheum̐ āī, jiata jīva jaṛa sabai sahāī.
जिन्हहि निरखि मग साँपिनि बीछी । तजहिं बिषम बिषु तामस तीछी ॥
jinhahi nirakhi maga sām̐pini bīchī, tajahiṁ biṣama biṣu tāmasa tīchī.

Trans:

The whole world is witness to the king's death, the result of his uncompromising love, and of my mother's wickedness. The queens are so woebegone that one cannot bear to look at them; the citizens are consumed by intolerable anguish; and I am the cause of all their troubles; and yet, though I hear and feel all this, I can still endure the torment. When I heard that Raghunāth had taken with him Lakshman and Sītā and in pilgrim's garb set out for the woods, without shoes and walking on foot, be Shankar my witness, I survived even that blow. Again when I saw the Nishāds devotion, my heart must have been harder than adamant not to break. And now I have come and with my own eyes have seen everything; surely in this life my wretched soul has borne all that can be borne. The serpents and scorpions on the road—at the sight of Rāma, Lakshman, Sītā—forget their virulent venom and savage viciousness;

दोहा-dohā:

तेइ रघुनंदनु लखनु सिय अनहित लागे जाहि ।
tei raghunaṁdanu lakhanu siya anahita lāge jāhi,
तासु तनय तजि दुसह दुख दैउ सहावइ काहि ॥२६२॥
tāsu tanaya taji dusaha dukha daiu sahāvai kāhi. 262.

Trans:

on whom else then, should Providence inflict severe pain if not on the son of that woman who looked upon Rāma, Lakshman, and Sītā as her enemies!"

चौपाई-caupāī:

सुनि अति बिकल भरत बर बानी । आरति प्रीति बिनय नय सानी ॥
suni ati bikala bharata bara bānī, ārati prīti binaya naya sānī.
सोक मगन सब सभाँ खभारू । मनहुँ कमल बन परेउ तुसारू ॥
soka magana saba sabhāṁ khabhārū, manahuṁ kamala bana pareu tusārū.
कहि अनेक बिधि कथा पुरानी । भरत प्रबोधु कीन्ह मुनि ग्यानी ॥
kahi aneka bidhi kathā purānī, bharata prabodhu kīnha muni gyānī.
बोले उचित बचन रघुनंदू । दिनकर कुल कैरव बन चंदू ॥
bole ucita bacana raghunaṁdū, dinakara kula kairava bana caṁdū.
तात जायँ जियँ करहु गलानी । ईस अधीन जीव गति जानी ॥
tāta jāyaṁ jiyaṁ karahu galānī, īsa adhīna jīva gati jānī.
तीनि काल तिभुअन मत मोरें । पुन्यसिलोक तात तर तोरें ॥
tīni kāla tibhuana mata moreṁ, punyasiloka tāta tara toreṁ.
उर आनत तुम्ह पर कुटिलाई । जाइ लोकु परलोकु नसाई ॥
ura ānata tumha para kuṭilāī, jāi loku paraloku nasāī.
दोसु देहिं जननिहि जड़ तेई । जिन्ह गुर साधु सभा नहिं सेई ॥
dosu dehiṁ jananihi jaṛa teī, jinha gura sādhu sabhā nahiṁ seī.

Trans:

On hearing these lamentable words of Bharat's, fraught with distress and love, humility and discretion, the whole assembly was lost in sorrow and anxiety, as when the frost smites a bed of lotuses. The learned sage comforted Bharat by reference to various ancient legends, and Rāma, the moon of the lilies of the solar race, spoke thus in seemly wise, "Brother grieve not your heart in vain; know that the ways of life are in God's hands. To my mind, O brother, all the men of the highest renown in virtue, in all time, past, present, or future, and in the three spheres of creation, fall short of you. Whoever even imagines wickedness in you, shall perish both in this life and in the next. It is only fools, who have never studied in the school of philosophy and religion, who ascribe blame to your mother.

दोहा-dohā:

मिटिहहिं पाप प्रपंच सब अखिल अमंगल भार ।
miṭihahiṁ pāpa prapaṁca saba akhila amaṁgala bhāra,
लोक सुजसु परलोक सुखु सुमिरत नामु तुम्हार ॥२६३॥
loka sujasu paraloka sukhu sumirata nāmu tumhāra. 263.

Trans:

By the invocation of your name, sin, delusion, and the burden of every ill are destroyed; and glory is won in this world and eternal happiness in the world to come.

चौपाई-caupāī:

कहउँ सुभाउ सत्य सिव साखी । भरत भूमि रह राउरि राखी ॥
kahauṁ subhāu satya siva sākhī, bharata bhūmi raha rāuri rākhī.
तात कुतरक करहु जनि जाएँ । बैर पेम नहिं दुरइ दुराएँ ॥
tāta kutaraka karahu jani jāeṁ, baira pema nahiṁ durai durāeṁ.
मुनि गन निकट बिहग मृग जाहीं । बाधक बधिक बिलोकि पराहीं ॥
muni gana nikaṭa bihaga mṛga jāhīṁ, bādhaka badhika biloki parāhīṁ.
हित अनहित पसु पच्छिउ जाना । मानुष तनु गुन ग्यान निधाना ॥
hita anahita pasu pacchiu jānā, mānuṣa tanu guna gyāna nidhānā.
तात तुम्हहि मैं जानउँ नीकें । करौं काह असमंजस जीकें ॥
tāta tumhahi maiṁ jānauṁ nīkeṁ, karauṁ kāha asamaṁjasa jīkeṁ.
राखेउ रायँ सत्य मोहि त्यागी । तनु परिहरेउ पेम पन लागी ॥
rākheu rāyaṁ satya mohi tyāgī, tanu parihareu pema pana lāgī.
तासु बचन मेटत मन सोचू । तेहि तें अधिक तुम्हार सँकोचू ॥
tāsu bacana meṭata mana socū, tehi teṁ adhika tumhāra saṁkocū.
ता पर गुर मोहि आयसु दीन्हा । अवसि जो कहहु चहउँ सोइ कीन्हा ॥
tā para gura mohi āyasu dīnhā, avasi jo kahahu cahauṁ soi kīnhā.

Trans:

Be Shiva my witness, and I state the fact truly: the world, O Bharat, exists by virtue of your support. Do not, my brother, entertain evil surmises to no purpose; neither love nor hatred can be hid; birds and beasts come up close to a saint, but flee at the sight of a fowler, though he tries to stop them. If beasts and birds can distinguish between friends and enemies, how much more a man, in whose mind is virtue and intelligence. I know you thoroughly, brother; how can I do anything that would be discordant with your spirit? The king, to keep his word, abandoned me, and to keep his vow of love, discarded his life. If I now break his word, I shall be heartily grieved; and yet my respect for you is greater. Moreover the Gurū has given me his commands; in short, whatever you say, that I am ready to do.

दोहा-dohā:

मनु प्रसन्न करि सकुच तजि कहहु करौं सोइ आजु ।
manu prasanna kari sakuca taji kahahu karauṁ soi āju,
सत्यसंध रघुबर बचन सुनि भा सुखी समाजु ॥२६४॥
satyasaṁdha raghubara bacana suni bhā sukhī samāju. 264.

Trans:

Set your mind at ease; cease this timidity and speak out, and I will do it at once." When they heard Rāma, the ocean of truth, speak thus, the assembly rejoiced.

चौपाई-caupāī:

सुर गन सहित सभय सुरराजू । सोचहिं चाहत होन अकाजू ॥
sura gana sahita sabhaya surarājū, socahiṁ cāhata hona akājū.
बनत उपाउ करत कछु नाहीं । राम सरन सब गे मन माहीं ॥
banata upāu karata kachu nāhīṁ, rāma sarana saba ge mana māhīṁ.
बहुरि बिचारि परस्पर कहहीं । रघुपति भगत भगति बस अहहीं ॥
bahuri bicāri paraspara kahahīṁ, raghupati bhagata bhagati basa ahahīṁ.
सुधि करि अंबरीष दुरबासा । भे सुर सुरपति निपट निरासा ॥
sudhi kari aṁbarīṣa durabāsā, bhe sura surapati nipaṭa nirāsā.
सहे सुरन्ह बहु काल बिषादा । नरहरि किए प्रगट प्रहलादा ॥
sahe suranha bahu kāla biṣādā, narahari kie pragaṭa prahalādā.
लगि लगि कान कहहिं धुनि माथा । अब सुर काज भरत के हाथा ॥
lagi lagi kāna kahahiṁ dhuni māthā, aba sura kāja bharata ke hāthā.
आन उपाउ न देखिअ देवा । मानत रामु सुसेवक सेवा ॥
āna upāu na dekhia devā, mānata rāmu susevaka sevā.
हियँ सपेम सुमिरहु सब भरतहि । निज गुन सील राम बस करतहि ॥
hiyaṁ sapema sumirahu saba bharatahi, nija guna sīla rāma basa karatahi.

Trans:

But the king of heaven and all the gods were alarmed and began to think, "Things will all go wrong." Though they took counsel together, nothing came of it. At last they mentally took recourse to Rāma's protection. After considering, they said to one anther, "Rāma is moved by the faith of the faithful." Remembering the story of Ambarish and Durvāsā, Indra and the gods were greatly dejected. In the past too for long time the gods endured distress, until it was the devotee Prahlād who revealed Lord Narsingh. They beat their heads and whispered in the ear, "Now our only chance lies with Bharat; there is no other plan, sir, that I can see. Rāma accepts service done to one of his servants. Do you all now, with loving heart, do service to Bharat, who has subdued Rāma by his disposition."

दोहा-dohā:

सुनि सुर मत सुरगुर कहेउ भल तुम्हार बड़ भागु ।
suni sura mata suragura kaheu bhala tumhāra baṛa bhāgu,
सकल सुमंगल मूल जग भरत चरन अनुरागु ॥२६५॥
sakala sumaṁgala mūla jaga bharata carana anurāgu. 265.

Trans:

When the Gurū of the gods heard this their plan he said, "Well done, you are in great good fortune; devotion to Bharat's feet is the source of every good in the world.

चौपाई-caupāī:

सीतापति सेवक सेवकाई । कामधेनु सय सरिस सुहाई ॥
sītāpati sevaka sevakāī, kāmadhenu saya sarisa suhāī.
भरत भगति तुम्हरें मन आई । तजहु सोचु बिधि बात बनाई ॥
bharata bhagati tumhareṁ mana āī, tajahu socu bidhi bāta banāī.
देखु देवपति भरत प्रभाऊ । सहज सुभायँ बिबस रघुराऊ ॥
dekhu devapati bharata prabhāū, sahaja subhāyaṁ bibasa raghurāū.
मन थिर करहु देव डरु नाहीं । भरतहि जानि राम परिछाहीं ॥
mana thira karahu deva ḍaru nāhīṁ, bharatahi jāni rāma parichāhīṁ.
सुनि सुरगुर सुर संमत सोचू । अंतरजामी प्रभुहि सकोचू ॥
suni suragura sura saṁmata socū, aṁtarajāmī prabhuhi sakocū.
निज सिर भारु भरत जियँ जाना । करत कोटि बिधि उर अनुमाना ॥
nija sira bhāru bharata jiyaṁ jānā, karata koṭi bidhi ura anumānā.
करि बिचारु मन दीन्ही ठीका । राम रजायस आपन नीका ॥
kari bicāru mana dīnhī ṭhīkā, rāma rajāyasa āpana nīkā.
निज पन तजि राखेउ पनु मोरा । छोहु सनेहु कीन्ह नहिं थोरा ॥
nija pana taji rākheu panu morā, chohu sanehu kīnha nahiṁ thorā.

Trans:

The service of the servant of Sītā's Lord is as good as a thousand *Kāmdhenus*. Now that you are resolved to put faith in Bharat, cease to have any anxiety: God has provided a way. See O Indra the extent of Bharat's power: he has subdued Rāma with the greatest ease. Make your mind easy, sir, never fear, knowing that Bharat is Rāma's shadow." The Lord, who knows the heart, was uncomfortable when he heard the plans and fears of Brihaspati and the other gods. Bharat, knowing that the whole responsibility rested upon him, was raising a thousand different arguments in his mind. After much deliberation, he came to the conclusion that his happiness consisted in obeying Rāma. "He is breaking his own vow in order to satisfy me, and in this is showing me no little love and affection.

दोहा-dohā:

कीन्ह अनुग्रह अमित अति सब बिधि सीतानाथ ।
kīnha anugraha amita ati saba bidhi sītānātha,
करि प्रनामु बोले भरतु जोरि जलज जुग हाथ ॥२६६॥
kari pranāmu bole bharatu jori jalaja juga hātha. 266.

Trans:

Sītā's Lord has in every way done me great and unbounded favor." Then bowing low, and with his lotus hands clasped in supplication, Bharat thus spoke:

चौपाई-caupāī:

कहौं कहावौं का अब स्वामी । कृपा अंबुनिधि अंतरजामी ॥
kahauṁ kahāvauṁ kā aba svāmī, kṛpā aṁbunidhi aṁtarajāmī.
गुर प्रसन्न साहिब अनुकूला । मिटी मलिन मन कलपित सूला ॥
gura prasanna sāhiba anukūlā, miṭī malina mana kalapita sūlā.
अपडर डरेउँ न सोच समूलें । रबिहि न दोसु देव दिसि भूलें ॥
apaḍara ḍareuṁ na soca samūleṁ, rabihi na dosu deva disi bhūleṁ.
मोर अभागु मातु कुटिलाई । बिधि गति बिषम काल कठिनाई ॥
mora abhāgu mātu kuṭilāī, bidhi gati biṣama kāla kaṭhināī.
पाउ रोपि सब मिलि मोहि घाला । प्रनतपाल पन आपन पाला ॥
pāu ropi saba mili mohi ghālā, pranatapāla pana āpana pālā.
यह नइ रीति न राउरि होई । लोकहुँ बेद बिदित नहिं गोई ॥
yaha nai rīti na rāuri hoī, lokahuṁ beda bidita nahiṁ goī.
जगु अनभल भल एकु गोसाईं । कहिअ होइ भल कासु भलाईं ॥
jagu anabhala bhala eku gosāīṁ, kahia hoi bhala kāsu bhalāīṁ.
देउ देवतरु सरिस सुभाऊ । सनमुख बिमुख न काहुहि काऊ ॥
deu devataru sarisa subhāū, sanamukha bimukha na kāhuhi kāū.

Trans:

"O All-merciful and omniscient Lord, what now can I say myself—you know the hearts of all. My Gurū is pleased and my master kind. The imaginary torments of my troubled soul are all over. I feared disgrace, but my fear was unreasonable; it is no fault of the sun, sir, if a man may mistake the quarters. My ill-luck, my mother's wickedness, god's aversion action, and the malignity of fate set themselves firm and combined to overthrow me; but the protector of the suppliants has maintained his character. This is no strange procedure of his; it is declared both by Vedas and tradition, and is no secret. If the whole world be against, and you Lord are kindly disposed, that is enough. By whose goodness, but by yours, does one get saved? Your attributes, sire, are those of the tree of paradise, which is never either for or against anyone in particular.

दोहा-dohā:

जाइ निकट पहिचानि तरु छाहँ समनि सब सोच ।
jāi nikaṭa pahicāni taru chāhaṁ samani saba soca,
मागत अभिमत पाव जग राउ रंकु भल पोच ॥२६७॥
māgata abhimata pāva jaga rāu raṁku bhala poca. 267.

Trans:

But recognizing it to be the Tree of Paradise, those who draw near it are relieved of every sorrow; and they obtain the fruit of their desires under its shade be they rich or poor, high or low.

चौपाई-caupāī:

लखि सब बिधि गुर स्वामि सनेहू । मिटेउ छोभु नहिं मन संदेहू ॥
lakhi saba bidhi gura svāmi sanehū, miṭeu chobhu nahiṁ mana saṁdehū.
अब करुनाकर कीजिअ सोई । जन हित प्रभु चित छोभु न होई ॥
aba karunākara kījia soī, jana hita prabhu cita chobhu na hoī.
जो सेवकु साहिबहि सँकोची । निज हित चहइ तासु मति पोची ॥
jo sevaku sāhibahi saṁkocī, nija hita cahai tāsu mati pocī.
सेवक हित साहिब सेवकाई । करै सकल सुख लोभ बिहाई ॥
sevaka hita sāhiba sevakāī, karai sakala sukha lobha bihāī.
स्वारथु नाथ फिरें सबही का । किएँ रजाइ कोटि बिधि नीका ॥
svārathu nātha phireṁ sabahī kā, kieṁ rajāi koṭi bidhi nīkā.
यह स्वारथ परमारथ सारु । सकल सुकृत फल सुगति सिंगारु ॥
yaha svāratha paramāratha sāru, sakala sukṛta phala sugati siṁgāru.
देव एक बिनती सुनि मोरी । उचित होइ तस करब बहोरी ॥
deva eka binatī suni morī, ucita hoi tasa karaba bahorī.
तिलक समाजु साजि सबु आना । करिअ सुफल प्रभु जौं मनु माना ॥
tilaka samāju sāji sabu ānā, karia suphala prabhu jauṁ manu mānā.

Trans:

Now that I have seen the affection of my Gurū and my master, my anxiety is gone. My mind is freed from doubt. Now, O mine of compassion, do whatever you will for the good of your servant so it causes no distress to my

Lord's heart. The servant who worries his master and seeks only his own advantage is a base-minded varlet. A servant's gain is to do his master's service, to get him every comfort, and not be greedy. If my Lord returns to Ajodhyā, everyone will be a gainer; but obedience to orders will be a thousand times greater gain: it is the highest good in this world, and in the next, the fruit of all well-doing and the ornament of beatitude. Listen, sire, to this my one request, and then do as you think proper. I have brought with me all the requisites for the coronation; if you approve, my Lord, have them brought into use.

दोहा-dohā:

सानुज पठइअ मोहि बन कीजिअ सबहि सनाथ ।
sānuja paṭhaia mohi bana kījia sabahi sanātha,
नतरु फेरिअहिं बंधु दोउ नाथ चलौं मैं साथ ॥२६८॥
nataru pheriahiṁ baṁdhu dou nātha calauṁ maiṁ sātha. 268.

Trans:

Send me and my brother into the woods and give the people back their king; or else let Lakshman and Shatrughan return and let me accompany you;

चौपाई-caupāī:

नतरु जाहिं बन तीनिउ भाई । बहुरिअ सीय सहित रघुराई ॥
nataru jāhiṁ bana tīniu bhāī, bahuria sīya sahita raghurāī.
जेहि बिधि प्रभु प्रसन्न मन होई । करुना सागर कीजिअ सोई ॥
jehi bidhi prabhu prasanna mana hoī, karunā sāgara kījia soī.
देवँ दीन्ह सबु मोहि अभारु । मोरें नीति न धरम बिचारु ॥
devaṁ dīnha sabu mohi abhāru, moreṁ nīti na dharama bicāru.
कहउँ बचन सब स्वारथ हेतू । रहत न आरत कें चित चेतू ॥
kahauṁ bacana saba svāratha hetū, rahata na ārata keṁ cita cetū.
उतरु देइ सुनि स्वामि रजाई । सो सेवकु लखि लाज लजाई ॥
utaru dei suni svāmi rajāī, so sevaku lakhi lāja lajāī.
अस मैं अवगुन उदधि अगाधू । स्वामि सनेहँ सराहत साधू ॥
asa maiṁ avaguna udadhi agādhū, svāmi sanehaṁ sarāhata sādhū.
अब कृपाल मोहि सो मत भावा । सकुच स्वामि मन जाइँ न पावा ॥
aba kṛpāla mohi so mata bhāvā, sakuca svāmi mana jāiṁ na pāvā.
प्रभु पद सपथ कहउँ सति भाऊ । जग मंगल हित एक उपाऊ ॥
prabhu pada sapatha kahauṁ sati bhāū, jaga maṁgala hita eka upāū.

Trans:

or let all three brothers go into the woods, and only you and Sītā return. O most merciful Lord, do whatever is most pleasing to you. You have cast the whole burden upon me, sire, who am unversed both in politics and theology; I make all my proposals on the ground of worldly interest; but when a man is in distress he cannot reason. A servant who hears his master's orders and answers him is one that Shame herself would be ashamed to look at: and yet, though I do this and am a fathomless ocean of faultiness, still my master in his kindness praises me as good. Now, O merciful one, that plan best pleases me which will cause my Lord's soul the least vexation. By my Lord's feet I swear that I speak the truth: there is only one scheme for securing the world's happiness;

दोहा-dohā:

प्रभु प्रसन्न मन सकुच तजि जो जेहि आयसु देब ।
prabhu prasanna mana sakuca taji jo jehi āyasu deba,
सो सिर धरि धरि करिहि सबु मिटिहि अनट अवरेब ॥२६९॥
so sira dhari dhari karihi sabu miṭihi anaṭa avareba. 269.

Trans:

if my Lord cheerfully and without reserve will only give each one of us his orders, they will be reverently obeyed, and all this trouble and perplexity will be at an end."

चौपाई-caupāī:

भरत बचन सुचि सुनि सुर हरषे । साधु सराहि सुमन सुर बरषे ॥
bharata bacana suci suni sura haraṣe, sādhu sarāhi sumana sura baraṣe.
असमंजस बस अवध नेवासी । प्रमुदित मन तापस बनबासी ॥
asamaṁjasa basa avadha nevāsī, pramudita mana tāpasa banabāsī.
चुपहिं रहे रघुनाथ सँकोची । प्रभु गति देखि सभा सब सोची ॥
cupahiṁ rahe raghunātha saṁkocī, prabhu gati dekhi sabhā saba socī.
जनक दूत तेहि अवसर आए । मुनि बसिष्ठँ सुनि बेगि बोलाए ॥
janaka dūta tehi avasara āe, muni basiṣṭhaṁ suni begi bolāe.
करि प्रनाम तिन्ह रामु निहारे । बेषु देखि भए निपट दुखारे ॥
kari pranāma tinha rāmu nihāre, beṣu dekhi bhae nipaṭa dukhāre.
दूतन्ह मुनिबर बूझी बाता । कहहु बिदेह भूप कुसलाता ॥
dūtanha munibara būjhī bātā, kahahu bideha bhūpa kusalātā.
सुनि सकुचाइ नाइ महि माथा । बोले चर बर जोरें हाथा ॥
suni sakucāi nāi mahi māthā, bole cara bara joreṁ hāthā.
बूझब राउर सादर साईं । कुसल हेतु सो भयउ गोसाईं ॥
būjhaba rāura sādara sāīṁ, kusala hetu so bhayau gosāīṁ.

Trans:

On hearing Bharat's guileless speech the gods were glad of heart and extolled his generosity and rained down flowers; the people of Avadh were much confounded, and the hermits and all the dwellers in the woods greatly rejoiced. Raghunāth maintained an anxious silence; and seeing his state the whole assembly became perturbed. At that very moment arrived messengers from Janak. Saint Vasishtha on hearing of it sent for them at once. They made obeisance and looked towards Rāma. At the sight of his attire they were exceedingly grieved. The great saint asked the embassy the news, "Tell me, is all well with the king of Videh?" At this question the noble herald with a deprecating air bowed their heads to the ground and with clasped hands replied, "Your courteous enquiry, sire, makes all well;

दोहा-dohā:

नाहिं त कोसल नाथ कें साथ कुसल गइ नाथ ।
nāhiṁ ta kosala nātha keṁ sātha kusala gai nātha,
मिथिला अवध बिसेष तें जगु सब भयउ अनाथ ॥२७०॥
mithilā avadha biseṣa teṁ jagu saba bhayau anātha. 270.

Trans:

otherwise, my lord, welfare died with the king of Kaushal; the whole world is in bereavement, but especially Mithilā and Avadh.

चौपाई-caupāī:

कोसलपति गति सुनि जनकौरा । भे सब लोक सोक बस बौरा ॥
kosalapati gati suni janakaurā, bhe saba loka soka basa baurā.
जेहिं देखे तेहि समय बिदेहू । नामु सत्य अस लाग न केहू ॥
jehiṁ dekhe tehi samaya bidehū, nāmu satya asa lāga na kehū.
रानि कुचालि सुनत नरपालहि । सूझ न कछु जस मनि बिनु ब्यालहि ॥
rāni kucāli sunata narapālahi, sūjha na kachu jasa mani binu byālahi.
भरत राज रघुबर बनबासू । भा मिथिलेसहि हृदयँ हराँसू ॥
bharata rāja raghubara banabāsū, bhā mithilesahi hṛdayaṁ harāṁsū.
नृप बूझे बुध सचिव समाजू । कहहु बिचारि उचित का आजू ॥
nṛpa būjhe budha saciva samājū, kahahu bicāri ucita kā ājū.
समुझि अवध असमंजस दोऊ । चलिअ कि रहिअ न कह कछु कोऊ ॥
samujhi avadha asamaṁjasa doū, calia ki rahia na kaha kachu koū.
नृपहि धीर धरि हृदयँ बिचारी । पठए अवध चतुर चर चारी ॥
nṛpahi dhīra dhari hṛdayaṁ bicārī, paṭhae avadha catura cara cārī.
बूझि भरत सति भाउ कुभाऊ । आएहु बेगि न होइ लखाऊ ॥

būjhi bharata sati bhāu kubhāū, āehu begi na hoi lakhāū.

Trans:

When Janak and his court heard of king Dashrath's death everyone was mad with excess of grief. No one, who at that time saw Videh (body-less), could think of that name being truly appropriate. As he listened to the tale of the queen's wickedness, the monarch became as helpless as a serpent without its head-jewel. Bharat king, and Rāma in exile! Janak's soul was sorely distressed. He enquired of all his wise men and ministers, "Consider and tell me what ought to be done now." Reflecting on the state of Avadh and the double difficulty, if he went or if he stayed, no one gave any answer. After reasoning with himself, the king resolved to send four clever spies to Avadh to discover whether Bharat meant well or ill, and return in haste without being seen.

दोहा-dohā:

गए अवध चर भरत गति बूझि देखि करतूति ।
gae avadha cara bharata gati būjhi dekhi karatūti,
चले चित्रकूटहि भरतु चार चले तेरहूति ॥ २७१ ॥
cale citrakūṭahi bharatu cāra cale terahūti. 271.

Trans:

The spies went to Avadh, ascertained Bharat's movements and saw what he was doing: that he had started for Chitra-kūt. Immediately they returned to Terhūt.

चौपाई-caupāī:

दूतन्ह आइ भरत कइ करनी । जनक समाज जथामति बरनी ॥
dūtanha āi bharata kai karanī, janaka samāja jathāmati baranī.
सुनि गुर परिजन सचिव महीपति । भे सब सोच सनेहँ बिकल अति ॥
suni gura parijana saciva mahīpati, bhe saba soca sanehaṁ bikala ati.
धरि धीरजु करि भरत बड़ाई । लिए सुभट साहनी बोलाई ॥
dhari dhīraju kari bharata baṛāī, lie subhaṭa sāhanī bolāī.
घर पुर देस राखि रखवारे । हय गय रथ बहु जान सँवारे ॥
ghara pura desa rākhi rakhavāre, haya gaya ratha bahu jāna saṁvāre.
दुघरी साधि चले ततकाला । किए बिश्रामु न मग महीपाला ॥
dugharī sādhi cale tatakālā, kie biśrāmu na maga mahīpālā.
भोरहिं आजु नहाइ प्रयागा । चले जमुन उतरन सबु लागा ॥
bhorahiṁ āju nahāi prayāgā, cale jamuna utarana sabu lāgā.
खबरि लेन हम पठए नाथा । तिन्ह कहि अस महि नायउ माथा ॥
khabari lena hama paṭhae nāthā, tinha kahi asa mahi nāyau māthā.
साथ किरात छ सातक दीन्हे । मुनिबर तुरत बिदा चर कीन्हे ॥
sātha kirāta cha sātaka dīnhe, munibara turata bidā cara kīnhe.

Trans:

Upon their arrival, they announced in Janak's court to the best of their ability all of Bharat's doings. The Gurū, the citizens, the ministers, and the king were all overwhelmed with grief and love at the report. Restraining his emotion and glorifying Bharat, he summoned his warriors and captains, and having stationed guards for the palace, city, and kingdom, and made ready horses, elephants, chariots and conveyances of every description, all in less than an hour, the king set out and has halted nowhere on the road, but this morning at daybreak bathed at Prayāg. The host have begun to cross the Yamunā, and we, my lord, have been sent on ahead with news." So saying, they bowed their heads to the ground. The saint at once gave them an escort of six or seven Kirāts and bid them adieu.

दोहा-dohā:

सुनत जनक आगवनु सबु हरषेउ अवध समाजु ।
sunata janaka āgavanu sabu haraṣeu avadha samāju,
रघुनंदनहि सकोचु बड़ सोच बिबस सुरराजु ॥ २७२ ॥
raghunaṁdanahi sakocu baṛa soca bibasa surarāju. 272.

Trans:

The people of Avadh were all delighted to hear of Janak's arrival; but Raghu-nandan was greatly disquieted, and Indra overwhelmed with alarm;

चौपाई-caupāī:

गरइ गलानि कुटिल कैकेई । काहि कहै केहि दूषनु देई ॥
garai galāni kuṭila kaikeī, kāhi kahai kehi dūṣanu deī.
अस मन आनि मुदित नर नारी । भयउ बहोरि रहब दिन चारी ॥
asa mana āni mudita nara nārī, bhayau bahori rahaba dina cārī.
एहि प्रकार गत बासर सोऊ । प्रात नहान लाग सबु कोऊ ॥
ehi prakāra gata bāsara soū, prāta nahāna lāga sabu koū.
करि मज्जनु पूजहिं नर नारी । गनप गौरि तिपुरारि तमारी ॥
kari majjanu pūjahiṁ nara nārī, ganapa gauri tipurāri tamārī.
रमा रमन पद बंदि बहोरी । बिनवहिं अंजुलि अंचल जोरी ॥
ramā ramana pada baṁdi bahorī, binavahiṁ aṁjuli aṁcala jorī.
राजा रामु जानकी रानी । आनँद अवधि अवध रजधानी ॥
rājā rāmu jānakī rānī, ānaṁda avadhi avadha rajadhānī.
सुबस बसउ फिरि सहित समाजा । भरतहि रामु करहुँ जुबराजा ॥
subasa basau phiri sahita samājā, bharatahi rāmu karahuṁ jubarājā.
एहि सुख सुधाँ सींचि सब काहू । देव देहु जग जीवन लाहू ॥
ehi sukha sudhāṁ sīṁci saba kāhū, deva dehu jaga jīvana lāhū.

Trans:

the wicked Kaekayī was sinking with remorse, "What can I say? And whom can I blame?" while the people were delighted with the thought that now they had got another day or two to stay. In this manner the day was spent. On the morrow all bathed and after their ablutions worshipped Ganesh, Gaurī, Shiva, and the Sun; then reverenced the feet of Lakshman's Lord, and offered up their prayers, the men raising their joined hands, the women holding out the skirt of their garment: "With Rāma our King and Jānakī our Queen, may Avadh, our capital, the centre of all delights, be gloriously re-peopled, court and all, and Rāma install Bharat as heir-apparent. Revive us all, O Lord, with this ambrosial bliss and grant the world its life's desire.

दोहा-dohā:

गुर समाज भाइन्ह सहित राम राजु पुर होउ ।
gura samāja bhāinha sahita rāma rāju pura hou,
अछत राम राजा अवध मरिअ माग सबु कोउ ॥ २७३ ॥
achata rāma rājā avadha maria māga sabu kou. 273.

Trans:

May Rāma reign over the state, assisted by his Gurū, the council, and his brothers; and may we die with Rāma still Avadh's King." This was the universal prayer.

चौपाई-caupāī:

सुनि सनेहमय पुरजन बानी । निंदहिं जोग बिरति मुनि ग्यानी ॥
suni sanehamaya purajana bānī, niṁdahiṁ joga birati muni gyānī.
एहि बिधि नित्यकरम करि पुरजन । रामहि करहिं प्रनाम पुलकि तन ॥
ehi bidhi nityakarama kari purajana, rāmahi karahiṁ pranāma pulaki tana.
ऊँच नीच मध्यम नर नारी । लहहिं दरसु निज निज अनुहारी ॥
ūṁca nīca madhyama nara nārī, lahahiṁ darasu nija nija anuhārī.
सावधान सबही सनमानहिं । सकल सराहत कृपानिधानहिं ॥
sāvadhāna sabahī sanamānahiṁ, sakala sarāhata kṛpānidhānahiṁ.
लरिकाइहि तें रघुबर बानी । पालत नीति प्रीति पहिचानी ॥
larikāihi teṁ raghubara bānī, pālata nīti prīti pahicānī.
सील सकोच सिंधु रघुराऊ । सुमुख सुलोचन सरल सुभाऊ ॥
sīla sakoca siṁdhu raghurāū, sumukha sulocana sarala subhāū.
कहत राम गुन गन अनुरागे । सब निज भाग सराहन लागे ॥
kahata rāma guna gana anurāge, saba nija bhāga sarāhana lāge.
हम सम पुन्य पुंज जग थोरे । जिन्हहि रामु जानत करि मोरे ॥

hama sama punya puṁja jaga thore, jinhahi rāmu jānata kari more.

Trans:

When they heard the citizens' loving words, the wisest saints thought little of their own penance and austerities. Having in this manner performed their daily devotions, the people, with much joy, went and saluted Rāma. High or low or middling, men and women, all looked up to him as their own special patron; and he discreetly reciprocated their devotion. Everyone extolled his inexhaustible generosity, "From a child it was said of Raghubar that he cherishes all in whom he recognizes sincerity and affection. With his bright face, bright eyes, and guileless ways, he is the very ocean of amiability and gentleness." Thus affectionately telling Rāma's virtues, all began to extol their own good fortune. "There are few people in the world, who can have been so meritorious as we, whom Rāma has thus accepted as his own."

दोहा-dohā:

प्रेम मगन तेहि समय सब सुनि आवत मिथिलेसु ।
prema magana tehi samaya saba suni āvata mithilesu,
सहित सभा संभ्रम उठेउ रबिकुल कमल दिनेसु ॥२७४॥
sahita sabhā saṁbhrama uṭheu rabikula kamala dinesu. 274.

Trans:

At the time when all were thus absorbed in love, they heard of the approach of the king of Maithal. The sun of the lotus of solar race rose in haste—he and the whole assembly.

चौपाई-caupāī:

भाइ सचिव गुर पुरजन साथा । आगें गवनु कीन्ह रघुनाथा ॥
bhāi saciva gura purajana sāthā, āgeṁ gavanu kīnha raghunāthā.
गिरिबरु दीख जनकपति जबहीं । करि प्रनामु रथ त्यागेउ तबहीं ॥
giribaru dīkha janakapati jabahīṁ, kari pranāmu ratha tyāgeu tabahīṁ.
राम दरस लालसा उछाहू । पथ श्रम लेसु कलेसु न काहू ॥
rāma darasa lālasā uchāhū, patha śrama lesu kalesu na kāhū.
मन तहँ जहँ रघुबर बैदेही । बिनु मन तन दुख सुख सुधि केही ॥
mana tahaṁ jahaṁ raghubara baidehī, binu mana tana dukha sukha sudhi kehī.
आवत जनकु चले एहि भाँती । सहित समाज प्रेम मति माती ॥
āvata janaku cale ehi bhāṁtī, sahita samāja prema mati mātī.
आए निकट देखि अनुरागे । सादर मिलन परसपर लागे ॥
āe nikaṭa dekhi anurāge, sādara milana parasapara lāge.
लगे जनक मुनिजन पद बंदन । रिषिन्ह प्रनामु कीन्ह रघुनंदन ॥
lage janaka munijana pada baṁdana, riṣinha pranāmu kīnha raghunaṁdana.
भाइन्ह सहित रामु मिलि राजहि । चले लवाइ समेत समाजहि ॥
bhāinha sahita rāmu mili rājahi, cale lavāi sameta samājahi.

Trans:

Raghunāth led the way, accompanied by his brothers, the Gurū, the minister, and the people. As soon as king Janak saw the holy hill he dismounted from his chariot and saluted it. In their eagerness and excitement to see Rāma, no one felt the slightest fatigue from the toilsome journey, for their soul was with Rāma and Sītā; and who without a soul can be conscious of bodily pain or pleasure? In this manner Janak and his host advanced, drunken with the drunkenness of love. When they came near and in sight, they lovingly and reverentially began mutual salutations. Janak bowed at the feet of the hermits, and Rāma with his brothers having first reverenced the king's spiritual advisers, embraced him, and led the way for him and his companions.

दोहा-dohā:

आश्रम सागर सांत रस पूरन पावन पाथु ।
āśrama sāgara sāṁta rasa pūrana pāvana pāthu,
सेन मनहुँ करुना सरित लिएँ जाहिं रघुनाथु ॥२७५॥
sena manahuṁ karunā sarita lieṁ jāhiṁ raghunāthu. 275.

Trans:

Rāma conducted the host to the hermitage, as it were a river of serenity flowing into an ocean full of the pure waters of tranquility—

चौपाई-caupāī:

बोरति ग्यान बिराग करारे । बचन ससोक मिलत नद नारे ॥
borati gyāna birāga karāre, bacana sasoka milata nada nāre.
सोच उसास समीर तंरगा । धीरज तट तरुबर कर भंगा ॥
soca usāsa samīra taṁragā, dhīraja taṭa tarubara kara bhaṁgā.
बिषम बिषाद तोरावति धारा । भय भ्रम भवँर अबर्त अपारा ॥
biṣama biṣāda torāvati dhārā, bhaya bhrama bhavaṁra abarta apārā.
केवट बुध बिद्या बड़ि नावा । सकहिं न खेइ ऐक नहिं आवा ॥
kevaṭa budha bidyā baṛi nāvā, sakahiṁ na khei aika nahiṁ āvā.
बनचर कोल किरात बिचारे । थके बिलोकि पथिक हियँ हारे ॥
banacara kola kirāta bicāre, thake biloki pathika hiyaṁ hāre.
आश्रम उदधि मिली जब जाई । मनहुँ उठेउ अंबुधि अकुलाई ॥
āśrama udadhi milī jaba jāī, manahuṁ uṭheu aṁbudhi akulāī.
सोक बिकल दोउ राज समाजा । रहा न ग्यानु न धीरजु लाजा ॥
soka bikala dou rāja samājā, rahā na gyānu na dhīraju lājā.
भूप रूप गुन सील सराही । रोवहिं सोक सिंधु अवगाही ॥
bhūpa rūpa guna sīla sarāhī, rovahiṁ soka siṁdhu avagāhī.

Trans:

—waters flooding the banks of Wisdom and Asceticism; with sorrowful speeches for its tributary streams and torrents; with sighs and lamentations for the wind and waves that break the stout trees of Resolution on its bank; with grievous anguish for its rapid current, and terror and delusion for its many eddies and whirlpools; with sages for ferrymen and Learning for the huge boat, which can no how be got across; while the poor *Kols* and *Kirāts* of the woods are the forlorn travelers wearied with waiting. When it reached the hermitage, it was as though ocean had been agitated with a sudden rush of waters. The two royal hosts were so overcome with grief that they had no sense, fortitude, or shame left. Extolling king Dashrath's majesty, virtue, and amiability, they sorrowed like men drowned in a sea of sorrow.

छंद-chaṁda:

अवगाहि सोक समुद्र सोचहिं नारि नर ब्याकुल महा ।
avagāhi soka samudra socahiṁ nāri nara byākula mahā,
दै दोष सकल सरोष बोलहिं बाम बिधि कीन्हो कहा ॥
dai doṣa sakala saroṣa bolahiṁ bāma bidhi kīnho kahā.
सुर सिद्ध तापस जोगिजन मुनि देखि दसा बिदेह की ।
sura siddha tāpasa jogijana muni dekhi dasā bideha kī,
तुलसी न समरथु कोउ जो तरि सकै सरित सनेह की ॥
tulasī na samarathu kou jo tari sakai sarita saneha kī.

Trans:

Drowned in a sea of sorrow, they sorrowed—men and women alike, in utter bewilderment, all exasperatedly and reproachfully exclaiming "What is this that cruel fate has done?" Gods, saints, anchorites, ascetics, and sages witnessed Janak's condition, but his love—says Tulsī—was like a broad river that no one could span.

सोरठा-soraṭhā:

किए अमित उपदेस जहँ तहँ लोगन्ह मुनिबरन्ह ।
kie amita upadesa jahaṁ tahaṁ loganha munibaranha,
धीरजु धरिअ नरेस कहेउ बसिष्ठ बिदेह सन ॥२७६॥
dhīraju dharia naresa kaheu basiṣṭha bideha sana. 276.

Trans:

When all the people and the great sages had exhausted every topic of consolation, Vasishtha thus addressed Videh: "King of men, be comforted.

चौपाई-caupāī:

जासु ग्यानु रबि भव निसि नासा । बचन किरन मुनि कमल बिकासा ॥
jāsu gyānu rabi bhava nisi nāsā, bacana kirana muni kamala bikāsā.

तेहि कि मोह ममता निअराई । यह सिय राम सनेह बड़ाई ॥
tehi ki moha mamatā niarāī, yaha siya rāma saneha baṛāī.
बिषई साधक सिद्ध सयाने । त्रिबिध जीव जग बेद बखाने ॥
biṣaī sādhaka siddha sayāne, tribidha jīva jaga beda bakhāne.
राम सनेह सरस मन जासू । साधु सभाँ बड़ आदर तासू ॥
rāma saneha sarasa mana jāsū, sādhu sabhām̐ baṛa ādara tāsū.
सोह न राम पेम बिनु ग्यानू । करनधार बिनु जिमि जलजानू ॥
soha na rāma pema binu gyānū, karanadhāra binu jimi jalajānū.
मुनि बहुबिधि बिदेहु समुझाए । रामघाट सब लोग नहाए ॥
muni bahubidhi bidehu samujhāe, rāmaghāṭa saba loga nahāe.
सकल सोक संकुल नर नारी । सो बासरु बीतेउ बिनु बारी ॥
sakala soka saṁkula nara nārī, so bāsaru bīteu binu bārī.
पसु खग मृगन्ह न कीन्ह अहारू । प्रिय परिजन कर कौन बिचारू ॥
pasu khaga mṛganha na kīnha ahārū, priya parijana kara kauna bicārū.

Trans:

By the sun of your wisdom the darkness of the world is dispelled, and in the light of your speech, saints expand like the lotus; how then can the power of Māyā affect you? This is the marvelous result of love for Sītā and Rāma. There are three classes of beings, who are talked of by the Scriptures and the world: the sensual, the seeker, the wise. Amongst the pious the highest honor is for him whose soul is full of love for Rāma; but without knowledge love for Rāma is imperfect, like a boat without a helmsman." When the saint had finished his exhortation to the king, all the people bathed at the Rām-ghāt. Everyone, men and women alike, were so overwhelmed with grief. that they spent the day without drinking water; even the cattle, birds, and deer would eat nothing; much less would his own kindred think of doing so.

दोहा-dohā:

दोउ समाज निमिराजु रघुराजु नहाने प्रात ।
dou samāja nimirāju raghurāju nahāne prāta,
बैठे सब बट बिटप तर मन मलीन कृस गात ॥ २७७॥
baiṭhe saba baṭa biṭapa tara mana malīna kṛsa gāta. 277.

Trans:

At daybreak the royal son of Nimi and the royal son of Raghu, having bathed with all their retinue, went and sat under the Banyan, sad at heart, their bodies wasted.

चौपाई-caupāī:

जे महिसुर दसरथ पुर बासी । जे मिथिलापति नगर निवासी ॥
je mahisura dasaratha pura bāsī, je mithilāpati nagara nivāsī.
हंस बंस गुर जनक पुरोधा । जिन्ह जग मगु परमारथु सोधा ॥
haṁsa baṁsa gura janaka purodhā, jinha jaga magu paramārathu sodhā.
लगे कहन उपदेस अनेका । सहित धरम नय बिरति बिबेका ॥
lage kahana upadesa anekā, sahita dharama naya birati bibekā.
कौसिक कहि कहि कथा पुरानीं । समुझाई सब सभा सुबानीं ॥
kausika kahi kahi kathā purānīṁ, samujhāī saba sabhā subānīṁ.
तब रघुनाथ कौसिकहि कहेऊ । नाथ कालि जल बिनु सबु रहेऊ ॥
taba raghunātha kausikahi kaheū, nātha kāli jala binu sabu raheū.
मुनि कह उचित कहत रघुराई । गयउ बीति दिन पहर अढ़ाई ॥
muni kaha ucita kahata raghurāī, gayau bīti dina pahara aṛhāī.
रिषि रुख लखि कह तेरहुतिराजू । इहाँ उचित नहिं असन अनाजू ॥
riṣi rukha lakhi kaha terahutirājū, ihām̐ ucita nahiṁ asana anājū.
कहा भूप भल सबहि सोहाना । पाइ रजायसु चले नहाना ॥
kahā bhūpa bhala sabahi sohānā, pāi rajāyasu cale nahānā.

Trans:

The Brahmins from Ajodhyā, as also those from the capital of the king of Mithilā; Vasishtha, the Gurū of the solar race, and Shatānand Janak's family priest, who while on earth had explored the path of heaven, began long exhortations full of religion, morality asceticism, and philosophy. Then Vishwāmitra eloquently instructed the assembly with many a reference to ancient legend. Now Raghunāth suggested to him, "Sire, everyone since yesterday has gone without water." Said the saint, "Rāma has spoken reasonably; two and a half watches of the day are now spent." Understanding the saint's disposition the king of Tirhut replied, "It is not proper to take cereal here." The king's word pleased everyone, and having obtained his permission they went to bathe.

दोहा-dohā:

तेहि अवसर फल फूल दल मूल अनेक प्रकार ।
tehi avasara phala phūla dala mūla aneka prakāra,
लइ आए बनचर बिपुल भरि भरि काँवरि भार ॥ २७८॥
lai āe banacara bipula bhari bhari kām̐vari bhāra. 278.

Trans:

At that very moment arrived the people of the woods, bringing large baskets laden with fruits, flowers, leaves and roots of every description.

चौपाई-caupāī:

कामद भे गिरि राम प्रसादा । अवलोकत अपहरत बिषादा ॥
kāmada bhe giri rāma prasādā, avalokata apaharata biṣādā.
सर सरिता बन भूमि बिभागा । जनु उमगत आनँद अनुरागा ॥
sara saritā bana bhūmi bibhāgā, janu umagata ānam̐da anurāgā.
बेलि बिटप सब सफल सफूला । बोलत खग मृग अलि अनुकूला ॥
beli biṭapa saba saphala saphūlā, bolata khaga mṛga ali anukūlā.
तेहि अवसर बन अधिक उछाहू । त्रिबिध समीर सुखद सब काहू ॥
tehi avasara bana adhika uchāhū, tribidha samīra sukhada saba kāhū.
जाइ न बरनि मनोहरताई । जनु महि करति जनक पहुनाई ॥
jāi na barani manoharatāī, janu mahi karati janaka pahunāī.
तब सब लोग नहाइ नहाई । राम जनक मुनि आयसु पाई ॥
taba saba loga nahāi nahāī, rāma janaka muni āyasu pāī.
देखि देखि तरुबर अनुरागे । जहँ तहँ पुरजन उतरन लागे ॥
dekhi dekhi tarubara anurāge, jaham̐ taham̐ purajana utarana lāge.
दल फल मूल कंद बिधि नाना । पावन सुंदर सुधा समाना ॥
dala phala mūla kaṁda bidhi nānā, pāvana suṁdara sudhā samānā.

Trans:

By Rāma's favor the mountain had become a grantor of desires; merely to look at it removed sorrow. The ponds, streams, and glades were bursting as it were with joy and love; all the creepers and trees broke out into blossom and fruit; the birds and beasts made a most melodious concert. In short, the gladsomeness of the forest was surpassing. The air, soft, cool, and fragrant, was delightful to everyone, and the beauty of the scene was beyond description—as though Earth herself had prepared Janak's reception. When each and all of the people had finished bathing and had received permission from Rāma, Janak, and saint Vasishtha, they gazed with rapture on the magnificent trees and sat themselves down here and there; while leaves and fruits, flowers and roots of every kind, fresh and fair, and sweet as nectar,

दोहा-dohā:

सादर सब कहँ रामगुर पठए भरि भरि भार ।
sādara saba kaham̐ rāmagura paṭhae bhari bhari bhāra,
पूजि पितर सुर अतिथि गुर लगे करन फरहार ॥ २७९॥
pūji pitara sura atithi gura lage karana pharahāra. 279.

Trans:

were courteously sent to all in baskets full by Rāma's Gurū—on which they made their repast after reverencing their ancestors, the gods, their guests, and the Gurū.

चौपाई-caupāī:

एहि बिधि बासर बीते चारी । रामु निरखि नर नारि सुखारी ॥
ehi bidhi bāsara bīte cārī, rāmu nirakhi nara nāri sukhārī.
दुहु समाज असि रुचि मन माहीं । बिनु सिय राम फिरब भल नाहीं ॥
duhu samāja asi ruci mana māhīṁ, binu siya rāma phiraba bhala nāhīṁ.
सीता राम संग बनबासू । कोटि अमरपुर सरिस सुपासू ॥
sītā rāma saṁga banabāsū, koṭi amarapura sarisa supāsū.
परिहरि लखन रामु बैदेही । जेहि घरु भाव बाम बिधि तेही ॥
parihari lakhana rāmu baidehī, jehi gharu bhāva bāma bidhi tehī.
दाहिन दइउ होइ जब सबही । राम समीप बसिअ बन तबही ॥
dāhina daiu hoi jaba sabahī, rāma samīpa basia bana tabahī.
मंदाकिनि मज्जनु तिहु काला । राम दरसु मुद मंगल माला ॥
maṁdākini majjanu tihu kālā, rāma darasu muda maṁgala mālā.
अटनु राम गिरि बन तापस थल । असनु अमिअ सम कंद मूल फल ॥
aṭanu rāma giri bana tāpasa thala, asanu amia sama kaṁda mūla phala.
सुख समेत संबत दुइ साता । पल सम होहिं न जनिअहिं जाता ॥
sukha sameta saṁbata dui sātā, pala sama hohiṁ na janiahiṁ jātā.

Trans:

In this manner four days were spent, in which the people saw Rāma and were happy. In both camps there was this desire at heart, "It is not good for us to return without Sītā and Rāma. Life in the woods in their society is a thousand times better than heaven. If anyone in his longing for home would desert Lakshman, Rāma, and Sītā, his fate is an unlucky one. It is the height of good fortune for us all to dwell in the forest near Rāma, bathing three times a day in the Mandakinī, seeing Rāma the constant delight, rambling about on the sacred hill and among the hermitages in the wood, and feeding on sweet herbs and roots and fruits, so contentedly that the fourteen years will pass like a minute, without our knowing how they go.

दोहा-dohā:

एहि सुख जोग न लोग सब कहहिं कहाँ अस भागु ।
ehi sukha joga na loga saba kahahiṁ kahāṁ asa bhāgu,
सहज सुभायँ समाज दुहु राम चरन अनुरागु ॥२८०॥
sahaja subhāyaṁ samāja duhu rāma carana anurāgu. 280.

Trans:

We are not worthy to deserve so great a happiness," they all exclaimed. "What fate can be like this?" Such was the spontaneous devotion to Rāma's feet in both camps.

चौपाई-caupāī:

एहि बिधि सकल मनोरथ करहीं । बचन सप्रेम सुनत मन हरहीं ॥
ehi bidhi sakala manoratha karahīṁ, bacana saprema sunata mana harahīṁ.
सीय मातु तेहि समय पठाईं । दासीं देखि सुअवसरु आईं ॥
sīya mātu tehi samaya paṭhāīṁ, dāsīṁ dekhi suavasaru āīṁ.
सावकास सुनि सब सिय सासू । आयउ जनकराज रनिवासू ॥
sāvakāsa suni saba siya sāsū, āyau janakarāja ranivāsū.
कौसल्याँ सादर सनमानी । आसन दिए समय सम आनी ॥
kausalyāṁ sādara sanamānī, āsana die samaya sama ānī.
सीलु सनेह सकल दुहु ओरा । द्रवहिं देखि सुनि कुलिस कठोरा ॥
sīlu saneha sakala duhu orā, dravahiṁ dekhi suni kulisa kaṭhorā.
पुलक सिथिल तन बारि बिलोचन । महि नख लिखन लगीं सब सोचन ॥
pulaka sithila tana bāri bilocana, mahi nakha likhana lagīṁ saba socana.
सब सिय राम प्रीति कि सि मूरती । जनु करुना बहु बेष बिसूरति ॥
saba siya rāma prīti ki si mūratī, janu karunā bahu beṣa bisūrati.
सीय मातु कह बिधि बुधि बाँकी । जो पय फेनु फोर पबि टाँकी ॥
sīya mātu kaha bidhi budhi bāṁkī, jo paya phenu phora pabi ṭāṁkī.

Trans:

In this way all were expressing their heart's desire in affectionate words which ravished the soul to hear. Sītā's mother then sent a handmaid who ascertained that it was a convenient time and returned. On learning that Sītā's mothers-in-law were at leisure, Janak's queen and her attendants came to visit them. Kausalyā received them with due honor, and gave them such seats as circumstance allowed. On both sides there was such love and tenderness, that the most rigid thunderbolt would have melted, could it have seen and heard. Their body quivering and unnerved, their eyes full of tears, and all lost in grief, they drew lines with their toes on the ground, each a separate incarnation of love to Sītā and Rāma, or as it were tearful tenderness repeated in many forms. Said Sītā's mother, "God's judgment has gone astray—using the thunderbolt as a chisel to break up foam!

दोहा-dohā:

सुनिअ सुधा देखिअहिं गरल सब करतूति कराल ।
sunia sudhā dekhiahiṁ garala saba karatūti karāla,
जहँ तहँ काक उलूक बक मानस सकृत मराल ॥२८१॥
jahaṁ tahaṁ kāka ulūka baka mānasa sakṛta marāla. 281.

Trans:

We hear of ambrosia, but see only venom; all His doings are hard. Crows, owls, and cranes are everywhere, but swans can be found only in the inaccessible Mānas lake."

चौपाई-caupāī:

सुनि ससोच कह देबि सुमित्रा । बिधि गति बड़ि बिपरीत बिचित्रा ॥
suni sasoca kaha debi sumitrā, bidhi gati baṛi biparīta bicitrā.
जो सृजि पालइ हरइ बहोरी । बाल केलि सम बिधि मति भोरी ॥
jo sṛji pālai harai bahorī, bāla keli sama bidhi mati bhorī.
कौसल्या कह दोसु न काहू । करम बिबस दुख सुख छति लाहू ॥
kausalyā kaha dosu na kāhū, karama bibasa dukha sukha chati lāhū.
कठिन करम गति जान बिधाता । जो सुभ असुभ सकल फल दाता ॥
kaṭhina karama gati jāna bidhātā, jo subha asubha sakala phala dātā.
ईस रजाइ सीस सबही कें । उतपति थिति लय बिषहु अमी कें ॥
īsa rajāi sīsa sabahī keṁ, utapati thiti laya biṣahu amī keṁ.
देबि मोह बस सोचिअ बादी । बिधि प्रपंचु अस अचल अनादी ॥
debi moha basa socia bādī, bidhi prapaṁcu asa acala anādī.
भूपति जिअब मरब उर आनी । सोचिअ सखि लखि निज हित हानी ॥
bhūpati jiaba maraba ura ānī, socia sakhi lakhi nija hita hānī.
सीय मातु कह सत्य सुबानी । सुकृती अवधि अवधपति रानी ॥
sīya mātu kaha satya subānī, sukṛtī avadhi avadhapati rānī.

Trans:

Upon this, queen Sumitrā said sadly: "God's ways are contrary and unaccountable. He creates and cherishes and then destroys: his purposes as idle as a child's play." Said Kausalyā, "It is no one's fault; pain and pleasures, loss and gain are governed by actions; the effects of Karma are inscrutable; only God knows them, who awards its own fruit to every act, whether it be good or bad. The Lord's decree dominates over all, whether for raising, staying, or falling, whether for poison or ambrosia. It is vain, O good lady, to give way to sorrow; God's schemes are, as I have said, unchangeable and from everlasting. If we mourn over the contrast between the king's lifetime and his death, it is because we see that our own interests have suffered on account of his demise. Sītā's mother replied, "Your noble words are quite true, a spouse that you are of Avadh's king, who was the most noble amongst virtuous souls."

दोहा-dohā:

लखनु रामु सिय जाहुँ बन भल परिनाम न पोचु ।
lakhanu rāmu siya jāhuṁ bana bhala parināma na pocu,
गहबरि हियँ कह कौसिला मोहि भरत कर सोचु ॥२८२॥
gahabari hiyaṁ kaha kausilā mohi bharata kara socu. 282.

Trans:

"If Lakshman, Rāma, and Sītā stay in exile, all will be right in the end and no harm done, for I am anxious about Bharat," said Kausalyā with a troubled heart.

चौपाई-caupāī:

ईस प्रसाद असीस तुम्हारी । सुत सुतबधू देवसरि बारी ॥
īsa prasāda asīsa tumhārī, suta sutabadhū devasari bārī.
राम सपथ मैं कीन्हि न काऊ । सो करि कहउँ सखी सति भाऊ ॥
rāma sapatha maiṁ kīnhi na kāū, so kari kahauṁ sakhī sati bhāū.
भरत सील गुन बिनय बड़ाई । भायप भगति भरोस भलाई ॥
bharata sīla guna binaya baṛāī, bhāyapa bhagati bharosa bhalāī.
कहत सारदहु कर मति हीचे । सागर सीप कि जाहिं उलीचे ॥
kahata sāradahu kara mati hīce, sāgara sīpa ki jāhiṁ ulīce.
जानउँ सदा भरत कुलदीपा । बार बार मोहि कहेउ महीपा ॥
jānauṁ sadā bharata kuladīpā, bāra bāra mohi kaheu mahīpā.
कसें कनकु मनि पारिखि पाएँ । पुरुष परिखिअहिं समयँ सुभाएँ ॥
kaseṁ kanaku mani pārikhi pāeṁ, puruṣa parikhiahiṁ samayaṁ subhāeṁ.
अनुचित आजु कहब अस मोरा । सोक सनेहँ सयानप थोरा ॥
anucita āju kahaba asa morā, soka sanehaṁ sayānapa thorā.
सुनि सुरसरि सम पावनि बानी । भईं सनेह बिकल सब रानी ॥
suni surasari sama pāvani bānī, bhaīṁ saneha bikala saba rānī.

Trans:

"By God's favor and your blessing, my son and daughter-in-law are both pure as Gangā water. Though I have never yet sworn by Rāma, I now invoke him as my witness that I speak truly, friends. The greatness of Bharat's generosity, goodness, and humility, his brotherly affection, faith, hope, and charity—even Saraswatī's eloquence would fail to declare. Can the ocean be ladled out with a shell? I have always known that Bharat was the glory of his house, and the king repeatedly told me so. Gold is known by assay and precious stones by the test; a man's temper is tried by fortune. It is not right for me now to have spoken thus; but sorrow and love have left me little reason." On hearing these words as pure as Gangā stream, the queens were overcome with emotion.

दोहा-dohā:

कौसल्या कह धीर धरि सुनहु देबि मिथिलेसि ।
kausalyā kaha dhīra dhari sunahu debi mithilesi,
को बिबेकनिधि बल्लभहि तुम्हहि सकइ उपदेसि ॥२८३॥
ko bibekanidhi ballabhahi tumhahi sakai upadesi. 283.

Trans:

Kausalyā continued: "Listen to me, O queen of Mithilā, take courage. Who is able to advise you, the consort of the wisest of men?

चौपाई-caupāī:

रानि राय सन अवसरु पाई । अपनी भाँति कहब समुझाई ॥
rāni rāya sana avasaru pāī, apanī bhāṁti kahaba samujhāī.
रखिअहिं लखनु भरतु गवनहिं बन । जौं यह मत मानै महीप मन ॥
rakhiahiṁ lakhanu bharatu gavanahiṁ bana, jauṁ yaha mata mānai mahīpa mana.
तौ भल जतनु करब सुबिचारी । मोरें सोचु भरत कर भारी ॥
tau bhala jatanu karaba subicārī, moreṁ socu bharata kara bhārī.
गूढ़ सनेह भरत मन माहीं । रहें नीक मोहि लागत नाहीं ॥
gūṛha saneha bharata mana māhī, raheṁ nīka mohi lāgata nāhiṁ.
लखि सुभाउ सुनि सरल सुबानी । सब भइ मगन करुन रस रानी ॥
lakhi subhāu suni sarala subānī, saba bhai magana karuna rasa rānī.
नभ प्रसून झरि धन्य धन्य धुनि । सिथिल सनेहँ सिद्ध जोगी मुनि ॥
nabha prasūna jhari dhanya dhanya dhuni, sithila sanehaṁ siddha jogī muni.
सबु रनिवासु बिथकि लखि रहेऊ । तब धरि धीर सुमित्राँ कहेऊ ॥
sabu ranivāsu bithaki lakhi raheū, taba dhari dhīra sumitrāṁ kaheū.
देबि दंड जुग जामिनि बीती । राम मातु सुनी उठी सप्रीती ॥
debi daṁḍa juga jāmini bītī, rāma mātu sunī uṭhī saprītī.

Trans:

But when you find a fitting opportunity speak to the king, O queen, and in your own way suggest to him that he should stop Lakshman and let Bharat go to the forest instead. If the king agrees to this proposal, I will then devise and carry out some proper plan. I feel much concerned about Bharat, for the love in his heart is so profound that if he stays at home I fear something untoward might happen to him." When they saw her generosity and heard her frank appeal, they were all overpowered with sympathy. There was a shower of flowers from heaven with cries of 'Glory, Glory'; saints, ascetics, and sages grew faint with love. The queens, despite their fatigue, still looked and waited, till Sumitrā made bold to say, "O good lady, nearly an hour of the night is gone." At this Kausalyā rose and

दोहा-dohā:

बेगि पाउ धारिअ थलहि कह सनेहँ सतिभाय ।
begi pāu dhāria thalahi kaha sanehaṁ satibhāya,
हमरें तौ अब ईस गति के मिथिलेस सहाय ॥२८४॥
hamareṁ tau aba īsa gati ke mithilesa sahāya. 284.

Trans:

spoke out of affection and good will, "Pray return speedily to your tent; of a truth now our only help is in God and the king of Mithilā."

चौपाई-caupāī:

लखि सनेह सुनि बचन बिनीता । जनकप्रिया गह पाय पुनीता ॥
lakhi saneha suni bacana binītā, janakapriyā gaha pāya punītā.
देबि उचित असि बिनय तुम्हारी । दसरथ घरिनि राम महतारी ॥
debi ucita asi binaya tumhārī, dasaratha gharini rāma mahatārī.
प्रभु अपने नीचहु आदरहीं । अगिनि धूम गिरि सिर तिनु धरहीं ॥
prabhu apane nīcahu ādarahīṁ, agini dhūma giri sira tinu dharahīṁ.
सेवकु राउ करम मन बानी । सदा सहाय महेसु भवानी ॥
sevaku rāu karama mana bānī, sadā sahāya mahesu bhavānī.
रउरे अंग जोगु जग को है । दीप सहाय कि दिनकर सोहै ॥
raure aṁga jogu jaga ko hai, dīpa sahāya ki dinakara sohai.
रामु जाइ बनु करि सुर काजू । अचल अवधपुर करिहहिं राजू ॥
rāmu jāi banu kari sura kājū, acala avadhapura karihahiṁ rājū.
अमर नाग नर राम बाहुबल । सुख बसिहहिं अपनें अपनें थल ॥
amara nāga nara rāma bāhubala, sukha basihahiṁ apaneṁ apaneṁ thala.
यह सब जागबलिक कहि राखा । देबि न होइ मुधा मुनि भाषा ॥
yaha saba jāgabalika kahi rākhā, debi na hoi mudhā muni bhāṣā.

Trans:

Seeing her affection and hearing her modest speech, Janak's queen clasped her holy feet, "Venerable lady, this modesty on your part is only natural, since you are Dashrath's wife and Rāma's mother. Monarchs give honor to the lowest of their servants; in the same way as fire tops itself with smoke and the hill with grass. King Janak is your servant in thought, word, and deed; and Mahādev and Bhawānī are your constant auxiliaries. Who is there on earth who can act as your supplement? Does the sun shine by the help of a torch? After going into exile and assisting the gods, Rāma will hold undisputed sway at Ajodhyā. Through the might of his arm, gods serpents, and men will all dwell in peace, each in his own sphere. This has all been foretold by Yāgyavalk; and the words of a saint, madam, can never be false."

दोहा-dohā:

अस कहि पग परि पेम अति सिय हित बिनय सुनाइ ।
asa kahi paga pari pema ati siya hita binaya sunāi,
सिय समेत सियमातु तब चली सुआयसु पाइ ॥२८५॥
siya sameta siyamātu taba calī suāyasu pāi. 285.

Trans:

So saying, she fell at her feet and affectionately made request for Sītā. Permission was accorded and Sītā set out with her mother.

चौपाई-caupāī:

प्रिय परिजनहि मिली बैदेही । जो जेहि जोगु भाँति तेहि तेही ॥
priya parijanahi milī baidehī, jo jehi jogu bhāṁti tehi tehī.
तापस बेष जानकी देखी । भा सबु बिकल बिषाद बिसेषी ॥
tāpasa beṣa jānakī dekhī, bhā sabu bikala biṣāda biseṣī.
जनक राम गुर आयसु पाई । चले थलहि सिय देखी आई ॥
janaka rāma gura āyasu pāī, cale thalahi siya dekhī āī.
लीन्हि लाइ उर जनक जानकी । पाहुन पावन पेम प्रान की ॥
līnhi lāi ura janaka jānakī, pāhuna pāvana pema prāna kī.
उर उमगेउ अंबुधि अनुरागू । भयउ भूप मनु मनहुँ पयागू ॥
ura umageu aṁbudhi anurāgū, bhayau bhūpa manu manahuṁ payāgū.
सिय सनेह बटु बाढ़त जोहा । ता पर राम पेम सिसु सोहा ॥
siya saneha baṭu bāṛhata johā, tā para rāma pema sisu sohā.
चिरजीवी मुनि ग्यान बिकल जनु । बूड़त लहेउ बाल अवलंबनु ॥
cirajīvī muni gyāna bikala janu, būṛata laheu bāla avalaṁbanu.
मोह मगन मति नहिं बिदेह की । महिमा सिय रघुबर सनेह की ॥
moha magana mati nahiṁ bideha kī, mahimā siya raghubara saneha kī.

Trans:

Arriving, Sītā embraced all her old domestics in such manner as in each case was most befitting. When they saw her in hermit's dress, they were all distressed with exceeding sorrow. Janak, on receiving the permission of Rāma and the Gurū, came to the tent to see his daughter and clasped her to his bosom—the sanctifying guest of the soul of love. His bosom swelled with a flood of affection and his royal soul resembled Prayāg, with his love for Sītā conspicuous as the spreading *Barh*-tree, on which devotion to Rāma appeared like the child—clutched for support by the king's bewildered senses as by the sage Chiranjeev when on the point of drowning. Videh was so overwhelmed by his feelings that he had no sense left—such is the power of love for Sītā and Raghubar.

दोहा-dohā:

सिय पितु मातु सनेह बस बिकल न सकी सँभारि ।
siya pitu mātu saneha basa bikala na sakī saṁbhāri,
धरनिसुताँ धीरजु धरेउ समउ सुधरमु बिचारि ॥२८६॥
dharanisutāṁ dhīraju dhareu samau sudharamu bicāri. 286.

Trans:

Sītā could not bear to see her father and mother so overcome by affection, but calling to mind both the time and her own duty, Earth's daughter summoned up courage.

चौपाई-caupāī:

तापस बेष जनक सिय देखी । भयउ पेमु परितोषु बिसेषी ॥
tāpasa beṣa janaka siya dekhī, bhayau pemu paritoṣu biseṣī.
पुत्रि पबित्र किए कुल दोऊ । सुजस धवल जगु कह सबु कोऊ ॥
putri pabitra kie kula doū, sujasa dhavala jagu kaha sabu koū.
जिति सुरसरि कीरति सरि तोरी । गवनु कीन्ह बिधि अंड करोरी ॥
jiti surasari kīrati sari torī, gavanu kīnha bidhi aṁḍa karorī.
गंग अवनि थल तीनि बड़ेरे । एहिं किए साधु समाज घनेरे ॥
gaṁga avani thala tīni baṛere, ehiṁ kie sādhu samāja ghanere.
पितु कह सत्य सनेहँ सुबानी । सीय सकुच महुँ मनहुँ समानी ॥
pitu kaha satya sanehaṁ subānī, sīya sakuca mahuṁ manahuṁ samānī.
पुनि पितु मातु लीन्हि उर लाई । सिख आसिष हित दीन्हि सुहाई ॥
puni pitu mātu līnhi ura lāī, sikha āsiṣa hita dīnhi suhāī.
कहति न सीय सकुचि मन माहीं । इहाँ बसब रजनीं भल नाहीं ॥
kahati na sīya sakuci mana māhīṁ, ihāṁ basaba rajanīṁ bhala nāhīṁ.
लखि रुख रानि जनायउ राऊ । हृदयँ सराहत सीलु सुभाऊ ॥
lakhi rukha rāni janāyau rāū, hṛdayaṁ sarāhata sīlu subhāū.

Trans:

When Janak looked at her in her anchorite's dress, he was filled with love and consolation, "Daughter, you have sanctified both families; everybody in the world proclaims your brilliant renown. The stream of your fame excels the Gangā and has spread over millions of universes. The Gangā has only three great sites on earth, but the congregations of saints that have been made by you are innumerable." At her father's sincere and loving eloquence Sītā was abashed and shrank into herself. Again her father and mother took her to their arms and gave her kind instructions and invoked rich blessings upon her. Sītā could not speak out, but was anxious at heart, "It is not well for me to spend the night here." The queen saw her wish and explained it to the king—inwardly praising the excellence of her disposition.

दोहा-dohā:

बार बार मिलि भेंटि सिय बिदा कीन्हि सनमानि ।
bāra bāra mili bheṁṭi siya bidā kīnhi sanamāni,
कही समय सिर भरत गति रानि सुबानि सयानि ॥२८७॥
kahī samaya sira bharata gati rāni subāni sayāni. 287.

Trans:

After again and again embracing her, they graciously gave her leave to depart. Having now an excellent opportunity, the discreet queen adroitly mentioned Bharat's going.

चौपाई-caupāī:

सुनि भूपाल भरत ब्यवहारू । सोन सुगंध सुधा ससि सारू ॥
suni bhūpāla bharata byavahārū, sona sugaṁdha sudhā sasi sārū.
मूदे सजल नयन पुलके तन । सुजसु सराहन लगे मुदित मन ॥
mūde sajala nayana pulake tana, sujasu sarāhana lage mudita mana.
सावधान सुनु सुमुखि सुलोचनि । भरत कथा भव बंध बिमोचनि ॥
sāvadhāna sunu sumukhi sulocani, bharata kathā bhava baṁdha bimocani.
धरम राजनय ब्रह्मबिचारू । इहाँ जथामति मोर प्रचारू ॥
dharama rājanaya brahmabicārū, ihāṁ jathāmati mora pracārū.
सो मति मोरि भरत महिमाही । कहै काह छलि छुअति न छाँही ॥
so mati mori bharata mahimāhī, kahai kāha chali chuati na chāṁhī.
बिधि गनपति अहिपति सिव सारद । कबि कोबिद बुध बुद्धि बिसारद ॥
bidhi ganapati ahipati siva sārada, kabi kobida budha buddhi bisārada.
भरत चरित कीरति करतूती । धरम सील गुन बिमल बिभूती ॥
bharata carita kīrati karatūtī, dharama sīla guna bimala bibhūtī.
समुझत सुनत सुखद सब काहू । सुचि सुरसरि रुचि निदर सुधाहू ॥
samujhata sunata sukhada saba kāhū, suci surasari ruci nidara sudhāhū.

Trans:

When the king heard of Bharat's conduct, brilliant as gold, refreshing as angelic perfumes, consolatory as ambrosia or the soft light of the moon, he closed his tearful eyes and his body thrilled with rapture, as he broke out into ecstatic praises of his glory. "Mark me well, fair-faced and bright-eyed dame, the legend of Bharat is effectual to loosen the bands of existence. According to my ability, I too have mastered somewhat of theology, state-craft, and spiritual meditation; but whatever my ability, I could not tell

Bharat's greatness, I cannot make a pretence of reaching even its shadow. Brahmmā, Ganesh, Sheshnāg, Shiva, Saraswatī, the inspired poets and the sages most renowned for wisdom, when they hear or meditate upon Bharat's doings, his glory, his vigor, his piety, his temper, his virtues, and his spotless dignity—all are enraptured; it has a flavor of purity like the Gangā, surpassing ambrosia.

दोहा-dohā:

निरवधि गुन निरुपम पुरुषु भरतु भरत सम जानि ।
niravadhi guna nirupama puruṣu bharatu bharata sama jāni,
कहिअ सुमेरु कि सेर सम कबिकुल मति सकुचानि ॥२८८॥
kahia sumeru ki sera sama kabikula mati sakucāni. 288.

Trans:

Possessed of infinite virtues and a man above comparison, know Bharat alone to be the like of Bharat. Can Mount Meru be weighed in any balance? The wit of whole races of poets is at end.

चौपाई-caupāī:

अगम सबहि बरनत बरबरनी । जिमि जलहीन मीन गमु धरनी ॥
agama sabahi baranata barabaranī, jimi jalahīna mīna gamu dharanī.
भरत अमित महिमा सुनु रानी । जानहिं रामु न सकहिं बखानी ॥
bharata amita mahimā sunu rānī, jānahiṁ rāmu na sakahiṁ bakhānī.
बरनि सप्रेम भरत अनुभाऊ । तिय जिय की रुचि लखि कह राऊ ॥
barani saprema bharata anubhāū, tiya jiya kī ruci lakhi kaha rāū.
बहुरहिं लखनु भरतु बन जाहीं । सब कर भल सब के मन माहीं ॥
bahurahiṁ lakhanu bharatu bana jāhīṁ, saba kara bhala saba ke mana māhīṁ.
देबि परंतु भरत रघुबर की । प्रीति प्रतीति जाइ नहिं तरकी ॥
debi paraṁtu bharata raghubara kī, prīti pratīti jāi nahiṁ tarakī.
भरतु अवधि सनेह ममता की । जद्यपि रामु सीम समता की ॥
bharatu avadhi saneha mamatā kī, jadyapi rāmu sīma samatā kī.
परमारथ स्वारथ सुख सारे । भरत न सपनेहुँ मनहुँ निहारे ॥
paramāratha svāratha sukha sāre, bharata na sapanehum̐ manahum̐ nihāre.
साधन सिद्धि राम पग नेहू । मोहि लखि परत भरत मत एहू ॥
sādhana siddhi rāma paga nehū, mohi lakhi parata bharata mata ehū.

Trans:

He is, O fair dame, as impossible to describe as it is impossible for a fish to walk on dry land. Hearken lady: Rāma knows, but even he cannot describe Bharat's illimitable greatness. If Lakshman returns and Bharat goes to the forest, everyone will imagine it to be good for all; but, O gracious lady, Bharat's love and confidence in Rāma are past all telling. Bharat is the perfection of love and devoted attachment, but Rāma is the Lord of impartiality. Bharat's mind has never even dreamt of any of the felicities of this world or the next; only the love for Rāma's feet is his beginning and his end. This, as I consider, is Bharat's belief.

दोहा-dohā:

भोरेहुँ भरत न पेलिहहिं मनसहुँ राम रजाइ ।
bhorehum̐ bharata na pelihahiṁ manasahum̐ rāma rajāi,
करिअ न सोचु सनेह बस कहेउ भूप बिलखाइ ॥२८९॥
karia na socu saneha basa kaheu bhūpa bilakhāi. 289.

Trans:

He would never be beguiled into thwarting an order of Rāma's; do not then in your affection give way to sorrow," said the king, and sighed he as he spoke.

चौपाई-caupāī:

राम भरत गुन गनत सप्रीती । निसि दंपतिहि पलक सम बीती ॥
rāma bharata guna ganata saprītī, nisi daṁpatihi palaka sama bītī.
राज समाज प्रात जुग जागे । न्हाइ न्हाइ सुर पूजन लागे ॥
rāja samāja prāta juga jāge, nhāi nhāi sura pūjana lāge.
गे नहाइ गुर पहीं रघुराई । बंदि चरन बोले रुख पाई ॥
ge nahāi gura pahīṁ raghurāī, baṁdi carana bole rukha pāī.
नाथ भरतु पुरजन महतारी । सोक बिकल बनबास दुखारी ॥
nātha bharatu purajana mahatārī, soka bikala banabāsa dukhārī.
सहित समाज राउ मिथिलेसू । बहुत दिवस भए सहत कलेसू ॥
sahita samāja rāu mithilesū, bahuta divasa bhae sahata kalesū.
उचित होइ सोइ कीजिअ नाथा । हित सबही कर रौरें हाथा ॥
ucita hoi soi kījia nāthā, hita sabahī kara raureṁ hāthā.
अस कहि अति सकुचे रघुराऊ । मुनि पुलके लखि सीलु सुभाऊ ॥
asa kahi ati sakuce raghurāū, muni pulake lakhi sīlu subhāū.
तुम्ह बिनु राम सकल सुख साजा । नरक सरिस दुहु राज समाजा ॥
tumha binu rāma sakala sukha sājā, naraka sarisa duhu rāja samājā.

Trans:

With the wedded pair affectionately discoursing on Bharat's excellences, the night passed away like a minute. At daybreak both the royal camps awoke and bathed and worshipped the gods. After bathing Rāma approached his Gurū, embraced his feet; and on receiving permission spoke thusly: "My lord, Bharat and the people and my mothers are distressed and inconvenienced by this sojourn in the woods. The king of Mithilā too, and his retinue, have been enduring hardships for many days; be pleased to do, my lord, as seems to you good; the happiness of all is in your hands." So saying, Rāma was greatly abashed. The saint thrilled with delight on seeing his amiable disposition. "Without you, O Rāma, the greatest bliss would seem like hell to people in both camps.

दोहा-dohā:

प्रान प्रान के जीव के जिव सुख के सुख राम ।
prāna prāna ke jīva ke jiva sukha ke sukha rāma,
तुम्ह तजि तात सोहात गृह जिन्हहि तिन्हहि बिधि बाम ॥२९०॥
tumha taji tāta sohāta gṛha jinhahi tinhahi bidhi bāma. 290.

Trans:

O Rāma, you are the soul of their soul, the life of their life, the joy of their joy. Anyone, my son, who would desert you for the sake of the pleasures of home has destiny set against him.

चौपाई-caupāī:

सो सुखु करमु धरमु जरि जाऊ । जहँ न राम पद पंकज भाऊ ॥
so sukhu karamu dharamu jari jāū, jaham̐ na rāma pada paṁkaja bhāū.
जोगु कुजोगु ग्यानु अग्यानू । जहँ नहिं राम पेम परधानू ॥
jogu kujogu gyānu agyānū, jaham̐ nahiṁ rāma pema paradhānū.
तुम्ह बिनु दुखी सुखी तुम्ह तेहीं । तुम्ह जानहु जिय जो जेहि केहीं ॥
tumha binu dukhī sukhī tumha tehīṁ, tumha jānahu jiya jo jehi kehīṁ.
राउर आयसु सिर सबही कें । बिदित कृपालहि गति सब नीकें ॥
rāura āyasu sira sabahī keṁ, bidita kṛpālahi gati saba nīkeṁ.
आपु आश्रमहि धारिअ पाऊ । भयउ सनेह सिथिल मुनिराऊ ॥
āpu āśramahi dhāria pāū, bhayau saneha sithila munirāū.
करि प्रनामु तब रामु सिधाए । रिषि धरि धीर जनक पहिं आए ॥
kari pranāmu taba rāmu sidhāe, riṣi dhari dhīra janaka pahiṁ āe.
राम बचन गुरु नृपहि सुनाए । सील सनेह सुभायँ सुहाए ॥
rāma bacana guru nṛpahi sunāe, sīla saneha subhāyam̐ suhāe.
महाराज अब कीजिअ सोई । सब कर धरम सहित हित होई ॥
mahārāja aba kījia soī, saba kara dharama sahita hita hoī.

Trans:

Perish that happiness, life, and religion in which there is no love for Rāma's lotus feet! That piety is impiety, and that wisdom unwisdom, in which love for Rāma is not supreme! Through you people are made happy, and without you they are unhappy; you know the hearts of everyone. Your commands rule all; and every motion is thoroughly manifest to your benignity. You may now return to the hermitage." The king of saints was overpowered with love. With Rāma having bowed and retired, the Gurū composed himself and went to Janak, and repeated to him what Rāma had said, enlarging upon his amiability, affection, and excellent disposition: "Now, sire, do whatever will be for the advantage of all, without prejudice to religion.

दोहा-dohā:

ग्यान निधान सुजान सुचि धरम धीर नरपाल ।
gyāna nidhāna sujāna suci dharama dhīra narapāla,
तुम्ह बिनु असमंजस समन को समरथ एहि काल ॥२९१॥
tumha binu asamaṁjasa samana ko samaratha ehi kāla. 291.

Trans:

O king of men, you are the wisest among the most wise, the champion of true piety; who, save you, can at this time end these troubles?"

चौपाई-caupāī:

सुनि मुनि बचन जनक अनुरागे । लखि गति ग्यानु बिरागु बिरागे ॥
suni muni bacana janaka anurāge, lakhi gati gyānu birāgu birāge.
सिथिल सनेहँ गुनत मन माहीं । आए इहाँ कीन्ह भल नाहीं ॥
sithila sanehaṁ gunata mana māhīṁ, āe ihāṁ kīnha bhala nāhīṁ.
रामहि रायँ कहेउ बन जाना । कीन्ह आपु प्रिय प्रेम प्रवाना ॥
rāmahi rāyaṁ kaheu bana jānā, kīnha āpu priya prema pravānā.
हम अब बन तें बनहि पठाई । प्रमुदित फिरब बिबेक बड़ाई ॥
hama aba bana teṁ banahi paṭhāī, pramudita phiraba bibeka baṛāī.
तापस मुनि महिसुर सुनि देखी । भए प्रेम बस बिकल बिसेषी ॥
tāpasa muni mahisura suni dekhī, bhae prema basa bikala biseṣī.
समउ समुझि धरि धीरजु राजा । चले भरत पहिं सहित समाजा ॥
samau samujhi dhari dhīraju rājā, cale bharata pahiṁ sahita samājā.
भरत आइ आगें भइ लीन्हे । अवसर सरिस सुआसन दीन्हे ॥
bharata āi āgeṁ bhai līnhe, avasara sarisa suāsana dīnhe.
तात भरत कह तेरहुति राऊ । तुम्हहि बिदित रघुबीर सुभाऊ ॥
tāta bharata kaha terahuti rāū, tumhahi bidita raghubīra subhāū.

Trans:

Janak was so moved by the saint's address and by the sight of his agitation, that all his philosophy and asceticism were forgotten. Faint with love, he reasoned to himself, "I have not done well in coming here. Dashrath ordered Rāma into exile, but himself gave the best proof of his affection. As for us, we shall just send him from this forest to another and return in triumph forsooth with increased reputation for wisdom." Seeing the agitation of the anchorites, saints, and Brahmins, the king was still more overcome with emotion; but considering the circumstances he made an effort, and with his retinue set forth to visit Bharat. Bharat advanced to meet him and gave him the best seat the times allowed. "Son Bharat," said the king of Tirhut, "you are well acquainted with Rāma's character.

दोहा-dohā:

राम सत्यब्रत धरम रत सब कर सीलु सनेहु ।
rāma satyabrata dharama rata saba kara sīlu sanehu,
संकट सहत सकोच बस कहिअ जो आयसु देहु ॥२९२॥
saṁkaṭa sahata sakoca basa kahia jo āyasu dehu. 292.

Trans:

He is devoted to truth and replete with Dharma; out of kindness, he endures inconvenience without murmuring; but if you have any orders to give, speak so."

चौपाई-caupāī:

सुनि तन पुलकि नयन भरि बारी । बोले भरतु धीर धरि भारी ॥
suni tana pulaki nayana bhari bārī, bole bharatu dhīra dhari bhārī.
प्रभु प्रिय पूज्य पिता सम आपू । कुलगुरु सम हित माय न बापू ॥
prabhu priya pūjya pitā sama āpū, kulaguru sama hita māya na bāpū.
कौसिकादि मुनि सचिव समाजू । ग्यान अंबुनिधि आपुनु आजू ॥
kausikādi muni saciva samājū, gyāna aṁbunidhi āpunu ājū.
सिसु सेवकु आयसु अनुगामी । जानि मोहि सिख देइअ स्वामी ॥
sisu sevaku āyasu anugāmī, jāni mohi sikha deia svāmī.
एहिं समाज थल बूझब राउर । मौन मलिन मैं बोलब बाउर ॥
ehiṁ samāja thala būjhaba rāura, mauna malina maiṁ bolaba bāura.
छोटे बदन कहउँ बड़ि बाता । छमब तात लखि बाम बिधाता ॥
choṭe badana kahauṁ baṛi bātā, chamaba tāta lakhi bāma bidhātā.
आगम निगम प्रसिद्ध पुराना । सेवाधरमु कठिन जगु जाना ॥
āgama nigama prasiddha purānā, sevādharamu kaṭhina jagu jānā.
स्वामि धरम स्वारथहि बिरोधू । बैरु अंध प्रेमहि न प्रबोधू ॥
svāmi dharama svārathahi birodhū, bairu aṁdha premahi na prabodhū.

Trans:

At this Bharat's whole frame quivered and his eyes filled with tears; but putting a strong restraint upon himself he replied, "My lord, I love and revere you as my father; and as to our family Gurū, even my own parents were not so benevolent as him. Here are Vishwāmitra and the other sages, and all this assembly; you too yourself, an ocean of wisdom; I am your obedient son and servant; regard me in this light, my lord, and instruct me. In this assembly and at this holy place you enquire of me, and I am to answer, though besmirched of soul and demented? Can I speak great words out of my little mouth? Pardon me, father; the fates are against me. It is declared in the Vedas, Tantras, and Purānas, and all the world knows, that loyal service is difficult indeed. Duty towards a master and selfishness always conflict. Hatred is blind; and love is not discreet.

दोहा-dohā:

राखि राम रुख धरमु ब्रतु पराधीन मोहि जानि ।
rākhi rāma rukha dharamu bratu parādhīna mohi jāni,
सब कें संमत सर्ब हित करिअ पेमु पहिचानि ॥२९३॥
saba keṁ saṁmata sarba hita karia pemu pahicāni. 293.

Trans:

Have regard to Rāma's wishes, so pious as he is, and remember that I am but a servant of his. Do as all approve and as will be best for all, and forget not their love for him."

चौपाई-caupāī:

भरत बचन सुनि देखि सुभाऊ । सहित समाज सराहत राऊ ॥
bharata bacana suni dekhi subhāū, sahita samāja sarāhata rāū.
सुगम अगम मृदु मंजु कठोरे । अरथु अमित अति आखर थोरे ॥
sugama agama mṛdu maṁju kaṭhore, arathu amita ati ākhara thore.
ज्यों मुखु मुकुर मुकुरु निज पानी । गहि न जाइ अस अद्भुत बानी ॥
jyoṁ mukhu mukura mukuru nija pānī, gahi na jāi asa adbhuta bānī.
भूप भरतु मुनि सहित समाजू । गे जहँ बिबुध कुमुद द्विजराजू ॥
bhūpa bharatu muni sahita samājū, ge jahaṁ bibudha kumuda dvijarājū.
सुनि सुधि सोच बिकल सब लोगा । मनहुँ मीनगन नव जल जोगा ॥
suni sudhi soca bikala saba logā, manahuṁ mīnagana nava jala jogā.
देवँ प्रथम कुलगुर गति देखी । निरखि बिदेह सनेह बिसेषी ॥
devaṁ prathama kulagura gati dekhī, nirakhi bideha saneha biseṣī.
राम भगतिमय भरतु निहारे । सुर स्वारथी हहरि हियँ हारे ॥
rāma bhagatimaya bharatu nihāre, sura svārathī hahari hiyaṁ hāre.
सब कोउ राम पेममय पेखा । भउ अलेख सोच बस लेखा ॥
saba kou rāma pemamaya pekhā, bhau alekha soca basa lekhā.

Trans:

When the king heard Bharat's speech and witnessed his generosity, he and his court burst into praises. Simple but profound, soft and delicate but severe, pregnant with meaning in a small compass, his speech was as mysterious as the shadow of a face in a glass, which no hand can grasp. The king, Bharat, the saint, and all the venerable assembly went to Rāma, by whom the gods were made as glad as the lilies by the moon. On hearing the news, the people were as distrest as fish in unaccustomed waters. The gods—seeing first the emotion of the family Gurū, and then Janak's exceeding affection, and Bharat so full of devotion to Rāma—were sorely anxious and began to despond in their selfishness. The sight of Rāma's kindness made the company of heaven unspeakably dismayed.

दोहा-dohā:

रामु सनेह सकोच बस कह ससोच सुरराजु ।
rāmu saneha sakoca basa kaha sasoca surarāju,
रचहु प्रपंचहि पंच मिलि नाहिं त भयउ अकाजु ॥२९४॥
racahu prapaṁcahi paṁca mili nāhiṁ ta bhayau akāju. 294.

Trans:

Indra cried sadly, "Rāma is overcome by love and modesty; we must combine to devise some scheme, or else we shall be undone."

चौपाई-caupāī:

सुरन्ह सुमिरि सारदा सराही । देबि देव सरनागत पाही ॥
suranha sumiri sāradā sarāhī, debi deva saranāgata pāhī.
फेरि भरत मति करि निज माया । पालु बिबुध कुल करि छल छाया ॥
pheri bharata mati kari nija māyā, pālu bibudha kula kari chala chāyā.
बिबुध बिनय सुनि देबि सयानी । बोली सुर स्वारथ जड़ जानी ॥
bibudha binaya suni debi sayānī, bolī sura svāratha jaṛa jānī.
मो सन कहहु भरत मति फेरू । लोचन सहस न सूझ सुमेरू ॥
mo sana kahahu bharata mati pherū, locana sahasa na sūjha sumerū.
बिधि हरि हर माया बड़ि भारी । सोउ न भरत मति सकइ निहारी ॥
bidhi hari hara māyā baṛi bhārī, sou na bharata mati sakai nihārī.
सो मति मोहि कहत करु भोरी । चंदिनि कर कि चंडकर चोरी ॥
so mati mohi kahata karu bhorī, caṁdini kara ki caṁḍakara corī.
भरत हृदयँ सिय राम निवासू । तहँ कि तिमिर जहँ तरनि प्रकासू ॥
bharata hṛdayaṁ siya rāma nivāsū, tahaṁ ki timira jahaṁ tarani prakāsū.
अस कहि सारद गइ बिधि लोका । बिबुध बिकल निसि मानहुँ कोका ॥
asa kahi sārada gai bidhi lokā, bibudha bikala nisi mānahuṁ kokā.

Trans:

The gods invoked Shārdā in flattering terms, "Protect, O goddess, we gods, your suppliants. Exert your power of delusion and change Bharat's purpose; by some deceptive artifice rescue the host of heaven." When the wise goddess heard their prayer, she understood their stupid selfishness and said, "You tell me to change Bharat's purpose; you have a thousand eyes and yet cannot see Mount Meru! The delusive power of Brahmmā, Vishnu, and Shiva is exceeding great, but it cannot see through Bharat's purpose; and yet you tell me to pervert it. What! Can the moonlight rob the moon? Bharat's heart is inhabited by Sītā and Rāma; can darkness invade the splendor of the sun?" So saying, Shārdā withdrew to Brahmmā's heaven, and the gods were as downcast as the *koka* bird at the approach of night.

दोहा-dohā:

सुर स्वारथी मलीन मन कीन्ह कुमंत्र कुठाटु ।
sura svārathī malīna mana kīnha kumaṁtra kuṭhāṭu,
रचि प्रपंच माया प्रबल भय भ्रम अरति उचाटु ॥२९५॥
raci prapaṁca māyā prabala bhaya bhrama arati ucāṭu. 295.

Trans:

The self-seeking gods were troubled at heart and devised evil projects and schemes, creating by strong delusion artifices of fear, error, sorrow, and vexation.

चौपाई-caupāī:

करि कुचालि सोचत सुरराजू । भरत हाथ सबु काजु अकाजू ॥
kari kucāli socata surarājū, bharata hātha sabu kāju akājū.
गए जनकु रघुनाथ समीपा । सनमाने सब रबिकुल दीपा ॥
gae janaku raghunātha samīpā, sanamāne saba rabikula dīpā.
समय समाज धरम अबिरोधा । बोले तब रघुबंस पुरोधा ॥
samaya samāja dharama abirodhā, bole taba raghubaṁsa purodhā.
जनक भरत संबादु सुनाई । भरत कहाउति कही सुहाई ॥
janaka bharata saṁbādu sunāī, bharata kahāuti kahī suhāī.
तात राम जस आयसु देहू । सो सबु करै मोर मत एहू ॥
tāta rāma jasa āyasu dehū, so sabu karai mora mata ehū.
सुनि रघुनाथ जोरि जुग पानी । बोले सत्य सरल मृदु बानी ॥
suni raghunātha jori juga pānī, bole satya sarala mṛdu bānī.
बिद्यमान आपुनि मिथिलेसू । मोर कहब सब भाँति भदेसू ॥
bidyamāna āpuni mithilesū, mora kahaba saba bhāṁti bhadesū.
राउर राय रजायसु होई । राउरि सपथ सही सिर सोई ॥
rāura rāya rajāyasu hoī, rāuri sapatha sahī sira soī.

Trans:

Indra practiced this villainy, thinking "Success or defeat is all in Bharat's hands." When Janak approached Rāma, the glory of Raghu's line received them all with honor. Then Vasishtha spoke words that were appropriate to the occasion as well as the gathering and consistent with the principles of Dharma. He iterated the conversation between Janak and Bharat, and eloquently repeated all that Bharat had urged and added, "Son Rāma, any order that you may give, all will obey; this is my conclusion." Upon this Raghunāth, clasping his hands, made truthful and guileless reply in gentle tones: "In the presence of yourself, sir, and the king of Mithilā, for me to speak is altogether out of place. Whatever command you may be pleased to give, I swear by yourself, I am ready to comply."

दोहा-dohā:

राम सपथ सुनि मुनि जनकु सकुचे सभा समेत ।
rāma sapatha suni muni janaku sakuce sabhā sameta,
सकल बिलोकत भरत मुखु बनइ न ऊतरु देत ॥२९६॥
sakala bilokata bharata mukhu banai na ūtaru deta. 296.

Trans:

On hearing Rāma's oath, the saint and Janak and the whole assembly were confounded; all fixed their eyes on Bharat's face helplessly and without power to answer.

चौपाई-caupāī:

सभा सकुच बस भरत निहारी । रामबंधु धरि धीरजु भारी ॥
sabhā sakuca basa bharata nihārī, rāmabaṁdhu dhari dhīraju bhārī.
कुसमउ देखि सनेहु सँभारा । बढ़त बिंधि जिमि घटज निवारा ॥
kusamau dekhi sanehu saṁbhārā, baṛhata biṁdhi jimi ghaṭaja nivārā.
सोक कनकलोचन मति छोनी । हरी बिमल गुन गन जगजोनी ॥
soka kanakalocana mati chonī, harī bimala guna gana jagajonī.
भरत बिबेक बराहँ बिसाला । अनायास उधरी तेहि काला ॥
bharata bibeka barāhaṁ bisālā, anāyāsa udharī tehi kālā.
करि प्रनामु सब कहँ कर जोरे । रामु राउ गुर साधु निहोरे ॥
kari pranāmu saba kahaṁ kara jore, rāmu rāu gura sādhu nihore.
छमब आजु अति अनुचित मोरा । कहउँ बदन मृदु बचन कठोरा ॥
chamaba āju ati anucita morā, kahauṁ badana mṛdu bacana kaṭhorā.
हियँ सुमिरी सारदा सुहाई । मानस तें मुख पंकज आई ॥
hiyaṁ sumirī sāradā suhāī, mānasa teṁ mukha paṁkaja āī.
बिमल बिबेक धरम नय साली । भरत भारती मंजु मराली ॥
bimala bibeka dharama naya sālī, bharata bhāratī maṁju marālī.

Trans:

Bharat saw the distress of the assembly, and being Rāma's brother, put a strong restraint upon himself. Seeing the unfitness of the time, he subdued his emotion, in the same way as Agastya bowed down the Vindhyā mountains. Grief like Hiranyaksh carried away his soul as it were the Earth; but at once from his spotless perfection like the womb of the universe came forth the mighty Boar of Discretion and wrought immediate deliverance. Clasping his hands, he bowed reverentially to all, to Rāma, the king, the Gurū, and the saints, "Pardon me if today I act most unbecomingly and with the tongue of a child speak stubborn words." As he mentally invoked the gracious Shārdā, from the depths of his soul there came to his lotus mouth a swan-like strain fraught with pure intelligence, piety, and justice.

दोहा-dohā:

निरखि बिबेक बिलोचनन्हि सिथिल सनेहँ समाजु ।
nirakhi bibeka bilocananhi sithila saneham̐ samāju,
करि प्रनामु बोले भरतु सुमिरि सीय रघुराजु ॥२९७॥
kari pranāmu bole bharatu sumiri sīya raghurāju. 297.

Trans:

With the eyes of his mind, Bharat saw that the assembly was faint with love; bowing low and invoking Sītā and Rāma, he thusly spoke:

चौपाई-caupāī:

प्रभु पितु मातु सुहृद गुर स्वामी । पूज्य परम हित अंतरजामी ॥
prabhu pitu mātu suhṛda gura svāmī, pūjya parama hita aṁtarajāmī.
सरल सुसाहिबु सील निधानू । प्रनतपाल सर्बग्य सुजानू ॥
sarala susāhibu sīla nidhānū, pranatapāla sarbagya sujānū.
समरथ सरनागत हितकारी । गुनगाहकु अवगुन अघ हारी ॥
samaratha saranāgata hitakārī, gunagāhaku avaguna agha hārī.
स्वामि गोसाँइहि सरिस गोसाईं । मोहि समान मैं साइँ दोहाईं ॥
svāmi gosām̐ihi sarisa gosāīṁ, mohi samāna maiṁ sāim̐ dohāīṁ.
प्रभु पितु बचन मोह बस पेली । आयउँ इहाँ समाजु सकेली ॥
prabhu pitu bacana moha basa pelī, āyaum̐ ihām̐ samāju sakelī.
जग भल पोच ऊँच अरु नीचू । अमिअ अमरपद माहुरु मीचू ॥
jaga bhala poca ūm̐ca aru nīcū, amia amarapada māhuru mīcū.
राम रजाइ मेट मन माहीं । देखा सुना कतहुँ कोउ नाहीं ॥
rāma rajāi meṭa mana māhīṁ, dekhā sunā katahum̐ kou nāhīṁ.
सो मैं सब बिधि कीन्हि ढिठाई । प्रभु मानी सनेह सेवकाई ॥
so maiṁ saba bidhi kīnhi ḍhiṭhāī, prabhu mānī saneha sevakāī.

Trans:

"My Lord is my father and mother, my friend, my Gurū, and my master; object of my adoration, my best benefactor, the reader of my heart; the kindest of patrons, the perfection of amiability, the protector of the humble; the all-learned, the all-wise; the powerful befriender of suppliants; quick to appreciate merit and to ignore demerit and wickedness; my sovereign, my god-like God—even though no servant can be so bad as I am. In my infatuation I have come here at the head of an army, in defiance of the commands of my Lord and my father. In the world there are good and vile, high and low, ambrosia and heaven, poison and death; but never have I seen or heard of anyone, who even in thought could violate an order of Rāma's. Yet I have been thus contumacious; and my Lord in his kindness has taken this presumption on my part as a token of affection and an act of service.

दोहा-dohā:

कृपाँ भलाईं आपनी नाथ कीन्ह भल मोर ।
kṛpām̐ bhalāīṁ āpanī nātha kīnha bhala mora,
दूषन भे भूषन सरिस सुजसु चारु चहु ओर ॥२९८॥
dūṣana bhe bhūṣana sarisa sujasu cāru cahu ora. 298.

Trans:

Out of his own mercy and goodness my Lord has made me good; my errors have become adornments, and my fair fame has been spread all around.

चौपाई-caupāī:

राउरि रीति सुबानि बड़ाई । जगत बिदित निगमागम गाई ॥
rāuri rīti subāni baṛāī, jagata bidita nigamāgama gāī.
कूर कुटिल खल कुमति कलंकी । नीच निसील निरीस निसंकी ॥
kūra kuṭila khala kumati kalaṁkī, nīca nisīla nirīsa nisaṁkī.
तेउ सुनि सरन सामुहें आए । सकृत प्रनामु किहें अपनाए ॥
teu suni sarana sāmuheṁ āe, sakṛta pranāmu kiheṁ apanāe.
देखि दोष कबहुँ न उर आने । सुनि गुन साधु समाज बखाने ॥
dekhi doṣa kabahum̐ na ura āne, suni guna sādhu samāja bakhāne.
को साहिब सेवकहि नेवाजी । आपु समाज साज सब साजी ॥
ko sāhiba sevakahi nevājī, āpu samāja sāja saba sājī.
निज करतूति न समुझिअ सपनें । सेवक सकुच सोचु उर अपनें ॥
nija karatūti na samujhia sapaneṁ, sevaka sakuca socu ura apaneṁ.
सो गोसाइँ नहिं दूसर कोपी । भुजा उठाइ कहउँ पन रोपी ॥
so gosāim̐ nahiṁ dūsara kopī, bhujā uṭhāi kahaum̐ pana ropī.
पसु नाचत सुक पाठ प्रबीना । गुन गति नट पाठक आधीना ॥
pasu nācata suka pāṭha prabīnā, guna gati naṭa pāṭhaka ādhīnā.

Trans:

My Lord, your ways, your gracious speech, and generosity are known throughout the world; they are sung in the Vedas and Tantras. The cruel, the perverse, the vile, the low minded, the outcast, the base, the ill-conditioned, the godless, the reckless—as soon as you hear that they have come before you as suppliants and have made a single prostration, are all reckoned as friends. Though you see faults, you never take them to heart; and if you but hear of virtues, you proclaim them in the assembly of the saints. What other master is there so kind to his servants, so perfect in all points, who never dreams of reckoning up what he has done himself, and is heartily vexed at any embarrassment of his servants. He is my sovereign Lord, and there is none other, with arms upraised I declare this on oath. A beast would dance and a parrot may attain proficiency in repeating what it is taught, but the proficiency of the bird and the rhythmic movements of the beast depend on the teacher and the dance-master.

दोहा-dohā:

यों सुधारि सनमानि जन किए साधु सिरमोर ।
yoṁ sudhāri sanamāni jana kie sādhu siramora,
को कृपाल बिनु पालिहै बिरिदावलि बरजोर ॥२९९॥
ko kṛpāla binu pālihai biridāvali barajora. 299.

Trans:

Thus by reforming your servants and treating them with honour you have made them the crest-jewels of holy men. Is there anyone save you, the All-merciful, who will rigidly maintain his high reputation as a kind and generous master?"

चौपाई-caupāī:

सोक सनेहँ कि बाल सुभाएँ । आयउँ लाइ रजायसु बाएँ ॥
soka saneham̐ ki bāla subhāem̐, āyaum̐ lāi rajāyasu bāem̐.
तबहुँ कृपाल हेरि निज ओरा । सबहि भाँति भल मानेउ मोरा ॥
tabahum̐ kṛpāla heri nija orā, sabahi bhām̐ti bhala māneu morā.
देखेउँ पाय सुमंगल मूला । जानेउँ स्वामि सहज अनुकूला ॥
dekheum̐ pāya sumaṁgala mūlā, jāneum̐ svāmi sahaja anukūlā.
बड़े समाज बिलोकेउँ भागू । बड़ीं चूक साहिब अनुरागू ॥
baṛe samāja bilokeum̐ bhāgū, baṛīṁ cūka sāhiba anurāgū.
कृपा अनुग्रहु अंगु अघाई । कीन्हि कृपानिधि सब अधिकाई ॥
kṛpā anugrahu aṁgu aghāī, kīnhi kṛpānidhi saba adhikāī.
राखा मोर दुलार गोसाईं । अपनें सील सुभायँ भलाईं ॥
rākhā mora dulāra gosāīṁ, apaneṁ sīla subhāyam̐ bhalāīṁ.

नाथ निपट मैं कीन्हि ढिठाई । स्वामि समाज सकोच बिहाई ॥
nātha nipaṭa maiṁ kīnhi ḍhiṭhāī, svāmi samāja sakoca bihāī.
अबिनय बिनय जथारुचि बानी । छमिहि देउ अति आरति जानी ॥
abinaya binaya jathāruci bānī, chamihi deu ati ārati jānī.

Trans:

Whether it was from grief and affection or from mere childishness that I came here in despite of your commands, you in your compassion have looked upon me as a friend and in every way taken it in good part. I have seen my Lord's blessed feet and have experienced his natural benignity. In this august assembly I have ascertained my good fortune in that I continue to enjoy my master's affection despite my many sins. My all-gracious lord has been extremely kind and compassionate to me in everyway, and all this is more than I have ever deserved. Out of the goodness of his own disposition my good Lord has made sure of my fidelity. I have now displayed great audacity in discarding respect for this august assembly and speaking boldly or humbly, just as the fancy moved me; but pardon me, sire, for I am in grievous perplexity.

दोहा-dohā:

सुहृद सुजान सुसाहिबहि बहुत कहब बड़ि खोरि ।
suhṛda sujāna susāhibahi bahuta kahaba baṛi khori,
आयसु देइअ देव अब सबइ सुधारी मोरि ॥ ३००॥
āyasu deia deva aba sabai sudhārī mori. 300.

Trans:

It is a great mistake to say too much to a true friend or really wise man or good master. Be pleased, sire, to give your commands and set me all right.

चौपाई-caupāī:

प्रभु पद पदुम पराग दोहाई । सत्य सुकृत सुख सीवँ सुहाई ॥
prabhu pada paduma parāga dohāī, satya sukṛta sukha sīvaṁ suhāī.
सो करि कहउँ हिए अपने की । रुचि जागत सोवत सपने की ॥
so kari kahauṁ hie apane kī, ruci jāgata sovata sapane kī.
सहज सनेहँ स्वामि सेवकाई । स्वारथ छल फल चारि बिहाई ॥
sahaja sanehaṁ svāmi sevakāī, svāratha chala phala cāri bihāī.
अग्या सम न सुसाहिब सेवा । सो प्रसादु जन पावै देवा ॥
agyā sama na susāhiba sevā, so prasādu jana pāvai devā.
अस कहि प्रेम बिबस भए भारी । पुलक सरीर बिलोचन बारी ॥
asa kahi prema bibasa bhae bhārī, pulaka sarīra bilocana bārī.
प्रभु पद कमल गहे अकुलाई । समउ सनेहु न सो कहि जाई ॥
prabhu pada kamala gahe akulāī, samau sanehu na so kahi jāī.
कृपासिंधु सनमानि सुबानी । बैठाए समीप गहि पानी ॥
kṛpāsiṁdhu sanamāni subānī, baiṭhāe samīpa gahi pānī.
भरत बिनय सुनि देखि सुभाऊ । सिथिल सनेहँ सभा रघुराऊ ॥
bharata binaya suni dekhi subhāū, sithila sanehaṁ sabhā raghurāū.

Trans:

I swear by the dust of my Lord's lotus feet—the glorious consummation of truth, virtue, and happiness, and with an oath I declare that the desire of my soul, whether waking, sleeping, or dreaming, is to serve my Lord with spontaneous devotion, without any regard to self-interest, fraud, or my own ends in this life or the next. There is no duty so imperative as submission; let your servant, sire, obtain this favor." So saying, he was utterly overwhelmed with emotion; his body quivered, his eyes filled with tears, and is great agitation he clasped his Lord's lotus feet. So poignant a scene defies description. The Ocean of compassion honored him with gracious words and took him by the hand and seated him by his side; while himself and all the assembly were faint with love, after hearing Bharat's prayer and seeing his noble nature.

छंद-chaṁda:

रघुराउ सिथिल सनेहँ साधु समाज मुनि मिथिला धनी ।
raghurāu sithila sanehaṁ sādhu samāja muni mithilā dhanī,
मन महुँ सराहत भरत भायप भगति की महिमा घनी ॥
mana mahuṁ sarāhata bharata bhāyapa bhagati kī mahimā ghanī.
भरतहि प्रसंसत बिबुध बरषत सुमन मानस मलिन से ।
bharatahi prasaṁsata bibudha baraṣata sumana mānasa malina se,
तुलसी बिकल सब लोग सुनि सकुचे निसागम नलिन से ॥
tulasī bikala saba loga suni sakuce nisāgama nalina se.

Trans:

Raghurāī himself, the august assembly, the saint, the king of Mithilā, all were faint with love, and mentally applauded the exceeding greatness of Bharat's brotherly affection and devotedness. The gods too commended Bharat and rained down flowers, though with a heavy heart. Everyone, says Tulsī, was distrest by what he had heard—like the lotus that withers at the approach of night.

सोरठा-sorathā:

देखि दुखारी दीन दुहु समाज नर नारि सब ।
dekhi dukhārī dīna duhu samāja nara nāri saba,
मघवा महा मलीन मुए मारि मंगल चहत ॥ ३०१ ॥
maghavā mahā malīna mue māri maṁgala cahata. 301.

Trans:

Seeing every man and woman in both assemblies so grieved and downcast, Indra, vile wretch, still sought his own happiness, killing as it were the already dead.

चौपाई-caupāī:

कपट कुचालि सीवँ सुरराजू । पर अकाज प्रिय आपन काजू ॥
kapaṭa kucāli sīvaṁ surarājū, para akāja priya āpana kājū.
काक समान पाकरिपु रीती । छली मलीन कतहुँ न प्रतीती ॥
kāka samāna pākaripu rītī, chalī malīna katahuṁ na pratītī.
प्रथम कुमत करि कपटु सँकेला । सो उचाटु सब कें सिर मेला ॥
prathama kumata kari kapaṭu saṁkelā, so ucāṭu saba keṁ sira melā.
सुरमायाँ सब लोग बिमोहे । राम प्रेम अतिसय न बिछोहे ॥
suramāyāṁ saba loga bimohe, rāma prema atisaya na bichohe.
भय उचाट बस मन थिर नाहीं । छन बन रुचि छन सदन सोहाहीं ॥
bhaya ucāṭa basa mana thira nāhīṁ, chana bana ruci chana sadana sohāhīṁ.
दुबिध मनोगति प्रजा दुखारी । सरित सिंधु संगम जनु बारी ॥
dubidha manogati prajā dukhārī, sarita siṁdhu saṁgama janu bārī.
दुचित कतहुँ परितोषु न लहहीं । एक एक सन मरमु न कहहीं ॥
ducita katahuṁ paritoṣu na lahahīṁ, eka eka sana maramu na kahahīṁ.
लखि हियँ हँसि कह कृपानिधानू । सरिस स्वान मघवान जुबानू ॥
lakhi hiyaṁ haṁsi kaha kṛpānidhānū, sarisa svāna maghavāna jubānū.

Trans:

Though king of the gods, there is no limit to his deceitfulness and villainy; he loves another's loss and his own gain; Indra's ways are like those of a crow—crafty, disreputable, and with no faith in anyone. Having in the first instance formed an evil design and accumulated deceits, he piled up trouble on the heads of all. Everyone was infatuated by the god's delusive power; their love for Rāma was so violent that they would not be separated from him. They were all distracted, with nothing settled in their mind, at one moment longing for the woods, at another anxious to return home. The people in their distress had the current of their ideas as divided as the water at the confluence of a river with the sea. Thus wavering in mind they got no comfort in any quarter; no one told another his secret thoughts. Seeing this, the Ocean of compassion smiled to himself and said: "The canines, reckless youth, and Indra are alike in many ways."

दोहा-dohā:

भरतु जनकु मुनिजन सचिव साधु सचेत बिहाइ ।
bharatu janaku munijana saciva sādhu saceta bihāi,
लागि देवमाया सबहि जथाजोगु जनु पाइ ॥३०२॥
lāgi devamāyā sabahi jathājogu janu pāi. 302.

Trans:

Excepting Bharat, Janak, the saints, the ministers, and the more intelligent nobles, the heaven-sent Delusion took effect upon all, according to the circumstances of the individual.

चौपाई-caupāī:

कृपासिंधु लखि लोग दुखारे । निज सनेहँ सुरपति छल भारे ॥
kṛpāsiṁdhu lakhi loga dukhāre, nija sanehaṁ surapati chala bhāre.
सभा राउ गुर महिसुर मंत्री । भरत भगति सब कै मति जंत्री ॥
sabhā rāu gura mahisura maṁtrī, bharata bhagati saba kai mati jaṁtrī.
रामहि चितवत चित्र लिखे से । सकुचत बोलत बचन सिखे से ॥
rāmahi citavata citra likhe se, sakucata bolata bacana sikhe se.
भरत प्रीति नति बिनय बड़ाई । सुनत सुखद बरनत कठिनाई ॥
bharata prīti nati binaya baṛāī, sunata sukhada baranata kaṭhināī.
जासु बिलोकि भगति लवलेसू । प्रेम मगन मुनिगन मिथिलेसू ॥
jāsu biloki bhagati lavalesū, prema magana munigana mithilesū.
महिमा तासु कहै किमि तुलसी । भगति सुभायँ सुमति हियँ हुलसी ॥
mahimā tāsu kahai kimi tulasī, bhagati subhāyaṁ sumati hiyaṁ hulasī.
आपु छोटि महिमा बड़ि जानी । कबिकुल कानि मानि सकुचानी ॥
āpu choṭi mahimā baṛi jānī, kabikula kāni māni sakucānī.
कहि न सकति गुन रुचि अधिकाई । मति गति बाल बचन की नाईं ॥
kahi na sakati guna ruci adhikāī, mati gati bāla bacana kī nāīṁ.

Trans:

The Ocean of compassion saw the people distressed by their love and by Indra's potent deception. The assembly, the king, the Gurū, the Brahmins and the ministers, all with their hearts under the spell of Bharat's devotion; motionless as pictures, gazed upon Rāma, nervously uttering words which they seemed to have learnt by rote. The eulogy of Bharat's affection, and constant humility is delightful to hear, but difficult to pronounce. Seeing only the tiniest morsel of his devotion, the saints and the king of Mithilā were absorbed in love; how then can I, Tulsī, tell all its greatness? It is only by the blessing of faith that the ambitious design of my heart has prospered. I am little; I know the enormous greatness of my subject, and I shrink in confusion before a crowd of other poets, unable to utter the vehemence of my passionate love for his perfections, the motions of my fancy are like the stammerings of a child.

दोहा-dohā:

भरत बिमल जसु बिमल बिधु सुमति चकोरकुमारि ।
bharata bimala jasu bimala bidhu sumati cakorakumāri,
उदित बिमल जन हृदय नभ एकटक रही निहारि ॥३०३॥
udita bimala jana hṛdaya nabha ekaṭaka rahī nihāri. 303.

Trans:

Bharat's bright fame is as the bright moon rising in the bright sky of a faithful heart, ever intently watched by my daring fancy as by an unfledged partridge.

चौपाई-caupāī:

भरत सुभाउ न सुगम निगमहूँ । लघु मति चापलता कबि छमहूँ ॥
bharata subhāu na sugama nigamahūṁ, laghu mati cāpalatā kabi chamahūṁ.
कहत सुनत सति भाउ भरत को । सीय राम पद होइ न रत को ॥
kahata sunata sati bhāu bharata ko, sīya rāma pada hoi na rata ko.
सुमिरत भरतहि प्रेमु राम को । जेहि न सुलभु तेहि सरिस बाम को ॥
sumirata bharatahi premu rāma ko, jehi na sulabhu tehi sarisa bāma ko.
देखि दयाल दसा सबही की । राम सुजान जानि जन जी की ॥
dekhi dayāla dasā sabahī kī, rāma sujāna jāni jana jī kī.
धरम धुरीन धीर नय नागर । सत्य सनेह सील सुख सागर ॥
dharama dhurīna dhīra naya nāgara, satya saneha sīla sukha sāgara.
देसु कालु लखि समउ समाजू । नीति प्रीति पालक रघुराजू ॥
desu kālu lakhi samau samājū, nīti prīti pālaka raghurājū.
बोले बचन बानि सरबसु से । हित परिनाम सुनत ससि रसु से ॥
bole bacana bāni sarabasu se, hita parināma sunata sasi rasu se.
तात भरत तुम्ह धरम धुरीना । लोक बेद बिद प्रेम प्रबीना ॥
tāta bharata tumha dharama dhurīnā, loka beda bida prema prabīnā.

Trans:

Bharat's generosity is scarce fathomable by the Vedas; pardon, ye poets, the frivolities of my poor wit. Who, that hears or tells of Bharat's perfect nature, does he not become enamored of the feet of Sītā and Rāma? Whoever invokes Bharat and still finds love for Rāma a difficult matter is a monster without a parallel. Seeing the state that everyone was in, the merciful and all-wise Rāma, who knew their devotion to him, being the staunch, champion of religion, a master of policy, an ocean of truth and love and amiability and everything good, having considered the place and circumstances, the time and assembly, Raghurāī, the maintainer of justice and affection, delivered a speech, the quintessence of eloquence, grateful as ambrosia at the time of hearing, and salutary, also in the end, "Brother Bharat, you are the champion of righteousness, perfectly conversant with all the laws of the world and the Vedas;

दोहा-dohā:

करम बचन मानस बिमल तुम्ह समान तुम्ह तात ।
karama bacana mānasa bimala tumha samāna tumha tāta,
गुर समाज लघु बंधु गुन कुसमयँ किमि कहि जात ॥३०४॥
gura samāja laghu baṁdhu guna kusamayaṁ kimi kahi jāta. 304.

Trans:

for purity of thought, word, and act, your only equal, brother, is you yourself. In this venerable assembly and in such distressing circumstances how can all the virtues of my younger brother be told?

चौपाई-caupāī:

जानहु तात तरनि कुल रीती । सत्यसंध पितु कीरति प्रीती ॥
jānahu tāta tarani kula rītī, satyasaṁdha pitu kīrati prītī.
समउ समाजु लाज गुरजन की । उदासीन हित अनहित मन की ॥
samau samāju lāja gurajana kī, udāsīna hita anahita mana kī.
तुम्हहि बिदित सबही कर करमू । आपन मोर परम हित धरमू ॥
tumhahi bidita sabahī kara karamū, āpana mora parama hita dharamū.
मोहि सब भाँति भरोस तुम्हारा । तदपि कहउँ अवसर अनुसारा ॥
mohi saba bhāṁti bharosa tumhārā, tadapi kahauṁ avasara anusārā.
तात तात बिनु बात हमारी । केवल गुरकुल कृपाँ सँभारी ॥
tāta tāta binu bāta hamārī, kevala gurakula kṛpāṁ saṁbhārī.
नतरु प्रजा परिजन परिवारू । हमहि सहित सबु होत खुआरू ॥
nataru prajā parijana parivārū, hamahi sahita sabu hota khuārū.
जौं बिनु अवसर अथवँ दिनेसू । जग केहि कहहु न होइ कलेसू ॥
jauṁ binu avasara athavaṁ dinesū, jaga kehi kahahu na hoi kalesū.
तस उतपातु तात बिधि कीन्हा । मुनि मिथिलेस राखि सबु लीन्हा ॥
tasa utapātu tāta bidhi kīnhā, muni mithilesa rākhi sabu līnhā.

Trans:

Brother, you know the custom of the solar race and the renown and the affection of our father—that ocean of truth. The circumstances of the time and of this assembly, the reverence due to these venerable personages, and the secret thoughts of all men, whether they be indifferent, or friends or unfriends, are understood by you, as also your own highest gain and mine, and the requirements of religion. I have entire confidence in you, and yet I speak as the circumstances suggest. My words, brother, in the absence of our father, have been kept straight only by the favor of our Gurū; otherwise all my subjects, together with the citizens, the people of the palace, and myself, would have been undone. If the Sun sets at the wrong time, tell me, will not the whole world be in confusion? Such trouble, brother, fate had ordained; but sage and the king of Mithilā have averted it.

दोहा-dohā:

राज काज सब लाज पति धरम धरनि धन धाम ।
rāja kāja saba lāja pati dharama dharani dhana dhāma,
गुर प्रभाउ पालिहि सबहि भल होइहि परिनाम ॥ ३०५ ॥
gura prabhāu pālihi sabahi bhala hoihi parināma. 305.

Trans:

The affairs of the State, our honor and fair name, Religion, our land, wealth, and homes—all have been defended by the power of the Gurū; and everything will be well in the end as well.

चौपाई-caupāī:

सहित समाज तुम्हार हमारा । घर बन गुर प्रसाद रखवारा ॥
sahita samāja tumhāra hamārā, ghara bana gura prasāda rakhavārā.
मातु पिता गुर स्वामि निदेसू । सकल धरम धरनीधर सेसू ॥
mātu pitā gura svāmi nidesū, sakala dharama dharanīdhara sesū.
सो तुम्ह करहु करावहु मोहू । तात तरनिकुल पालक होहू ॥
so tumha karahu karāvahu mohū, tāta taranikula pālaka hohū.
साधक एक सकल सिधि देनी । कीरति सुगति भूतिमय बेनी ॥
sādhaka eka sakala sidhi denī, kīrati sugati bhūtimaya benī.
सो बिचारि सहि संकटु भारी । करहु प्रजा परिवारु सुखारी ॥
so bicāri sahi saṁkaṭu bhārī, karahu prajā parivāru sukhārī.
बाँटी बिपति सबहिं मोहि भाई । तुम्हहि अवधि भरि बड़ि कठिनाई ॥
bām̐ṭī bipati sabahiṁ mohi bhāī, tumhahi avadhi bhari baṛi kaṭhināī.
जानि तुम्हहि मृदु कहउँ कठोरा । कुसमयँ तात न अनुचित मोरा ॥
jāni tumhahi mṛdu kahaum̐ kaṭhorā, kusamayam̐ tāta na anucita morā.
होहिं कुठायँ सुबंधु सहाए । ओड़िअहिं हाथ असनिहु के घाए ॥
hohiṁ kuṭhāyam̐ subaṁdhu sahāe, oṛiahiṁ hātha asanihu ke ghāe.

Trans:

My followers and yours, the palace and the forest, are both protected by his favor. The order of a father or mother, a Gurū or a master, is like Sheshnāg, the supporter of a whole world of righteousness. Obey it yourself, brother, and let me obey it, and thus become the protector of all the solar race. Obedience is the one means for the attainment of every success, a triple flood of Glory, Salvation, and Power. Having thus reflected, endure the grievous burden and make your people and family happy. I have distributed my afflictions amongst you all; but upon you is the full weight of the greatest difficulty, I know your tenderness, though I speak so harshly. The times, brother, are unpropitious; the fault is not mine. In an emergency a brother is used as a shield in the same way as the stroke of a sword is parried by the hand."

दोहा-dohā:

सेवक कर पद नयन से मुख सो साहिबु होइ ।
sevaka kara pada nayana se mukha so sāhibu hoi,
तुलसी प्रीति कि रीति सुनि सुकबि सराहहिं सोइ ॥ ३०६ ॥
tulasī prīti ki rīti suni sukabi sarāhahiṁ soi. 306.

Trans:

A servant is like a hand, or foot, or eye; a master is like the head. Hearing this description of love, says Tulsī, the greatest poets are full of admiration.

चौपाई-caupāī:

सभा सकल सुनि रघुबर बानी । प्रेम पयोधि अमिअँ जनु सानी ॥
sabhā sakala suni raghubara bānī, prema payodhi amia janu sānī.
सिथिल समाज सनेह समाधी । देखि दसा चुप सारद साधी ॥
sithila samāja saneha samādhī, dekhi dasā cupa sārada sādhī.
भरतहि भयउ परम संतोषू । सनमुख स्वामि बिमुख दुख दोषू ॥
bharatahi bhayau parama saṁtoṣū, sanamukha svāmi bimukha dukha doṣū.
मुख प्रसन्न मन मिटा बिषादू । भा जनु गूँगेहि गिरा प्रसादू ॥
mukha prasanna mana miṭā biṣādū, bhā janu gūm̐gehi girā prasādū.
कीन्ह सप्रेम प्रनामु बहोरी । बोले पानि पंकरुह जोरी ॥
kīnha saprema pranāmu bahorī, bole pāni paṁkaruha jorī.
नाथ भयउ सुखु साथ गए को । लहेउँ लाहु जग जनमु भए को ॥
nātha bhayau sukhu sātha gae ko, laheum̐ lāhu jaga janamu bhae ko.
अब कृपाल जस आयसु होई । करौं सीस धरि सादर सोई ॥
aba kṛpāla jasa āyasu hoī, karauṁ sīsa dhari sādara soī.
सो अवलंब देव मोहि देई । अवधि पारु पावौं जेहि सेई ॥
so avalaṁba deva mohi deī, avadhi pāru pāvauṁ jehi seī.

Trans:

When they heard Raghubar's speech, imbued as it were with the nectar of an ocean of tenderness, the whole assembly became lost in an overpowering trance of love. Shārdā herself was struck dumb at the sight of them. Bharat was immensely consoled by the graciousness of his Lord and his putting away of every trouble and wrong-doing. Cheerful of aspect and with the grief of his soul effaced, he seemed like a dumb man who has received the gift of speech. Affectionately bowing again and again and folding his lotus hands, he thus spoke, "My Lord, I am as happy as if I had gone with you; I have reaped the reward of being born into the world. Now, O merciful sire, whatever may be your order, that will I dutifully and reverently obey. But, sire, grant me some support, by the help of which I may struggle on to the end of the time.

दोहा-dohā:

देव देव अभिषेक हित गुर अनुसासनु पाइ ।
deva deva abhiṣeka hita gura anusāsanu pāi,
आनेउँ सब तीरथ सलिलु तेहि कहँ काह रजाइ ॥ ३०७ ॥
āneum̐ saba tīratha salilu tehi kaham̐ kāha rajāi. 307.

Trans:

In compliance with the Gurū's commands, sire, I have brought here water from all holy places for the purpose of your royal inauguration: what are your orders concerning it?

चौपाई-caupāī:

एकु मनोरथु बड़ मन माहीं । सभयँ सकोच जात कहि नाहीं ॥
eku manorathu baṛa mana māhīṁ, sabhayam̐ sakoca jāta kahi nāhīṁ.
कहहु तात प्रभु आयसु पाई । बोले बानि सनेह सुहाई ॥
kahahu tāta prabhu āyasu pāī, bole bāni saneha suhāī.
चित्रकूट सुचि थल तीरथ बन । खग मृग सर सरि निर्झर गिरिगन ॥
citrakūṭa suci thala tīratha bana, khaga mṛga sara sari nirjhara girigana.
प्रभु पद अंकित अवनि बिसेषी । आयसु होइ त आवौं देखी ॥
prabhu pada aṁkita avani biseṣī, āyasu hoi ta āvauṁ dekhī.
अवसि अत्रि आयसु सिर धरहू । तात बिगतभय कानन चरहू ॥
avasi atri āyasu sira dharahū, tāta bigatabhaya kānana carahū.
मुनि प्रसाद बनु मंगल दाता । पावन परम सुहावन भ्राता ॥
muni prasāda banu maṁgala dātā, pāvana parama suhāvana bhrātā.
रिषिनायकु जहँ आयसु देहीं । राखेहु तीरथ जलु थल तेहीं ॥
riṣināyaku jaham̐ āyasu dehīṁ, rākhehu tīratha jalu thala tehīṁ.
सुनि प्रभु बचन भरत सुखु पावा । मुनि पद कमल मुदित सिरु नावा ॥
suni prabhu bacana bharata sukhu pāvā, muni pada kamala mudita siru nāvā.

Trans:

Also I have one great desire at heart, but for fear and shame I cannot tell it." "Tell me what it is, brother." Upon this his Lord's command, he replied in affectionate and winning terms, "With your permission I would go and see Chitra-kūt with all its hermitages, shrines and woods, its birds and beasts, its ponds and streams, its waterfalls and rocks, and the spot so specially marked with the prints of my Lord's feet." "Certainly brother; only obtain Atri's permission, and then wander without fear through the woods. It is the saint's blessing, brother, that makes the forest so auspicious, holy, and exquisitely beautiful. And whatever the place that the king of sages may direct, there deposit the holy water." On hearing his Lord's words, Bharat was glad and joyfully bowed his head to the saint's lotus feet.

दोहा-dohā:

भरत राम संबादु सुनि सकल सुमंगल मूल ।
bharata rāma saṁbādu suni sakala sumaṁgala mūla,
सुर स्वारथी सराहि कुल बरषत सुरतरु फूल ॥ ३०८॥
sura svārathī sarāhi kula baraṣata surataru phūla. 308.

Trans:

The selfish gods, when they heard this most delightful conversation between Bharat and Rāma, praised the whole family, and rapturously showered down flowers upon them.

चौपाई-caupāī:

धन्य भरत जय राम गोसाईं । कहत देव हरषत बरिआईं ॥
dhanya bharata jaya rāma gosāīṁ, kahata deva haraṣata bariāīṁ.
मुनि मिथिलेस सभाँ सब काहू । भरत बचन सुनि भयउ उछाहू ॥
muni mithilesa sabhām̐ saba kāhū, bharata bacana suni bhayau uchāhū.
भरत राम गुन ग्राम सनेहू । पुलकि प्रसंसत राउ बिदेहू ॥
bharata rāma guna grāma sanehū, pulaki prasaṁsata rāu bidehū.
सेवक स्वामि सुभाउ सुहावन । नेमु पेमु अति पावन पावन ॥
sevaka svāmi subhāu suhāvana, nemu pemu ati pāvana pāvana.
मति अनुसार सराहन लागे । सचिव सभासद सब अनुरागे ॥
mati anusāra sarāhana lāge, saciva sabhāsada saba anurāge.
सुनि सुनि राम भरत संबादू । दुहु समाज हियँ हरषु बिषादू ॥
suni suni rāma bharata saṁbādū, duhu samāja hiyam̐ haraṣu biṣādū.
राम मातु दुखु सुखु सम जानी । कहि गुन राम प्रबोधीं रानी ॥
rāma mātu dukhu sukhu sama jānī, kahi guna rāma prabodhīṁ rānī.
एक कहहिं रघुबीर बड़ाई । एक सराहत भरत भलाई ॥
eka kahahiṁ raghubīra baṛāī, eka sarāhata bharata bhalāī.

Trans:

"Blessed be Bharat and glory to our Lord Rāma," cried the gods in their irrepressible delight. The saint, the king of Maithal, and everyone in the assembly rejoiced on hearing Bharat's speech. King Videh broke out into ecstatic praises of the many virtues and the affection both of Bharat and Rāma; master and servant of equally charming disposition, their fidelity and love the purest of the pure. The ministers too and all the spectators affectionately extolled them, as each best could. In both camps there was blended joy and sorrow, when they heard the conversation between Rāma, Bharat, and the saint. Rāma's mother, feeling pleasure and pain equally balanced, exhorted the queens, reckoning up both good and evil. One would magnify Rāma, another would praise Bharat's amiability.

दोहा-dohā:

अत्रि कहेउ तब भरत सन सैल समीप सुकूप ।
atri kaheu taba bharata sana saila samīpa sukūpa,
राखिअ तीरथ तोय तहँ पावन अमिअ अनूप ॥ ३०९॥
rākhia tīratha toya taham̐ pāvana amia anūpa. 309.

Trans:

Then said Atri to Bharat, "There is a fine well near the hill; there deposit the holy water, pure, unsullied, incomparable."

चौपाई-caupāī:

भरत अत्रि अनुसासन पाई । जल भाजन सब दिए चलाई ॥
bharata atri anusāsana pāī, jala bhājana saba die calāī.
सानुज आपु अत्रि मुनि साधू । सहित गए जहँ कूप अगाधू ॥
sānuja āpu atri muni sādhū, sahita gae jahaṁ̐ kūpa agādhū.
पावन पाथ पुन्यथल राखा । प्रमुदित प्रेम अत्रि अस भाषा ॥
pāvana pātha punyathala rākhā, pramudita prema atri asa bhāṣā.
तात अनादि सिद्ध थल एहू । लोपेउ काल बिदित नहिं केहू ॥
tāta anādi siddha thala ehū, lopeu kāla bidita nahiṁ kehū.
तब सेवकन्ह सरस थलु देखा । कीन्ह सुजल हित कूप बिसेषा ॥
taba sevakanha sarasa thalu dekhā, kīnha sujala hita kūpa biseṣā.
बिधि बस भयउ बिस्व उपकारू । सुगम अगम अति धरम बिचारू ॥
bidhi basa bhayau bisva upakārū, sugama agama ati dharama bicārū.
भरतकूप अब कहिहहिं लोगा । अति पावन तीरथ जल जोगा ॥
bharatakūpa aba kahihahiṁ logā, ati pāvana tīratha jala jogā.
प्रेम सनेम निमज्जत प्रानी । होइहहिं बिमल करम मन बानी ॥
prema sanema nimajjata prānī, hoihahiṁ bimala karama mana bānī.

Trans:

On receiving Atri's command, Bharat dispatched all the water vessels, and himself with Shatrughan, the saint and the elders, went to the deep well. There he poured out the holy waters of inauguration on that sacred spot; and Atri in a rapture of affection thus spoke, "Son, this has been a holy place from all eternity; but time had obscured it, and it was known to no one, till my servants, seeing the spot to be a desirable one, made this great well for the sake of a good supply of water. By the decree of fate the whole universe has been benefited, and a merit most difficult to compass has been rendered easy. People will now call this well the Bharat-Koop, hallowed in a special degree by the combination in it of the water of all holy places. Everyone, who lovingly and religiously bathes in it, will be made pure in thought, word, and deed."

दोहा-dohā:

कहत कूप महिमा सकल गए जहाँ रघुराउ ।
kahata kūpa mahimā sakala gae jahām̐ raghurāu,
अत्रि सुनायउ रघुबरहि तीरथ पुन्य प्रभाउ ॥ ३१०॥
atri sunāyau raghubarahi tīratha punya prabhāu. 310.

Trans:

All then went to Raghunāth, telling the virtue of the well; and Atri further explained to him the blessed efficacy of holy places.

चौपाई-caupāī:

कहत धरम इतिहास सप्रीती । भयउ भोरु निसि सो सुख बीती ॥
kahata dharama itihāsa saprītī, bhayau bhoru nisi so sukha bītī.
नित्य निबाहि भरत दोउ भाई । राम अत्रि गुर आयसु पाई ॥
nitya nibāhi bharata dou bhāī, rāma atri gura āyasu pāī.
सहित समाज साज सब सादें । चले राम बन अटन पयादें ॥
sahita samāja sāja saba sādeṁ, cale rāma bana aṭana payādeṁ.
कोमल चरन चलत बिनु पनहीं । भइ मृदु भूमि सकुचि मन मनहीं ॥
komala carana calata binu panahīṁ, bhai mṛdu bhūmi sakuci mana manahīṁ.
कुस कंटक काँकरीं कुराईं । कटुक कठोर कुबस्तु दुराईं ॥
kusa kaṁṭaka kām̐karīṁ kurāīṁ, kaṭuka kaṭhora kubastu durāīṁ.
महि मंजुल मृदु मारग कीन्हे । बहत समीर त्रिबिध सुख लीन्हे ॥
mahi maṁjula mṛdu māraga kīnhe, bahata samīra tribidha sukha līnhe.
सुमन बरषि सुर घन करि छाहीं । बिटप फूलि फलि तृन मृदुताहीं ॥
sumana baraṣi sura ghana kari chāhīṁ, biṭapa phūli phali tṛna mṛdutāhīṁ.
मृग बिलोकि खग बोलि सुबानी । सेवहिं सकल राम प्रिय जानी ॥

mṛga biloki khaga boli subānī, sevahiṁ sakala rāma priya jānī.

Trans:

The night was pleasantly spent in loving discourse on matters of religion and sacred legends until it was dawn. After performing their daily duties, Bharat and his brother, having received permission from Rāma and Saint Atri, attended by all their retinue in simple attire, proceeded on foot to visit the Woods-of-Rāma. Earth, in confusion of heart at being trodden by their delicate and unshod feet, smoothened herself, and cleared away all the spiky grass and thorns and stones and ruts, and everything rough and unpleasant. Earth made the way delightfully easy for them; they were refreshed by soft, cool, and fragrant breezes; the gods rained down flowers; the clouds offered shade; the trees gave blossom and fruit; the grass made a soft carpet; the deer with their timid glances, and the birds with their sweet song, all recognized Rāma's friends and did them homage.

दोहा-dohā:

सुलभ सिद्धि सब प्राकृतहु राम कहत जमुहात ।
sulabha siddhi saba prākṛtahu rāma kahata jamuhāta,
राम प्रानप्रिय भरत कहुँ यह न होइ बड़ि बात ॥ ३११ ॥
rāma prānapriya bharata kahuṁ yaha na hoi baṛi bāta. 311.

Trans:

And what great matter is this for Bharat, Rāma's dearest friend?—when even an ordinary person finds the highest success easy of attainment, if he only repeats Rāma's name even while yawning.

चौपाई-caupāī:

एहि बिधि भरतु फिरत बन माहीं । नेमु प्रेमु लखि मुनि सकुचाहीं ॥
ehi bidhi bharatu phirata bana māhīṁ, nemu premu lakhi muni sakucāhīṁ.
पुन्य जलाश्रय भूमि बिभागा । खग मृग तरु तृन गिरि बन बागा ॥
punya jalāśraya bhūmi bibhāgā, khaga mṛga taru tṛna giri bana bāgā.
चारु बिचित्र पबित्र बिसेषी । बूझत भरतु दिब्य सब देखी ॥
cāru bicitra pabitra biseṣī, būjhata bharatu dibya saba dekhī.
सुनि मन मुदित कहत रिषिराऊ । हेतु नाम गुन पुन्य प्रभाऊ ॥
suni mana mudita kahata riṣirāū, hetu nāma guna punya prabhāū.
कतहुँ निमज्जन कतहुँ प्रनामा । कतहुँ बिलोकत मन अभिरामा ॥
katahuṁ nimajjana katahuṁ pranāmā, katahuṁ bilokata mana abhirāmā.
कतहुँ बैठि मुनि आयसु पाई । सुमिरत सीय सहित दोउ भाई ॥
katahuṁ baiṭhi muni āyasu pāī, sumirata sīya sahita dou bhāī.
देखि सुभाउ सनेहु सुसेवा । देहिं असीस मुदित बनदेवा ॥
dekhi subhāu sanehu susevā, dehiṁ asīsa mudita banadevā.
फिरहिं गएँ दिनु पहर अढ़ाई । प्रभु पद कमल बिलोकहिं आई ॥
phirahiṁ gaeṁ dinu pahara aṛhāī, prabhu pada kamala bilokahiṁ āī.

Trans:

In this manner Bharat roamed the woods, and the saints, who saw his faith and love, were abashed. Seeing all so divine, he asked about the sacred ponds and various localities, the birds and deer, the trees and grasses, the hills, woods and orchards, beautiful and varied, and pre-eminently holy; and in reply the great saint with gladness of heart gave him the history of each—with its name, virtue, and spiritual efficacy. Bathing at one place, prostrating himself at another; here admiring the beauty of the wood, there sitting down to rest as the saint directed, he meditated on Rāma with Sītā and Lakshman. Seeing the goodness of his disposition, his love and faithfulness in service, the gods of the wood were charmed and gave him their blessing. The third watch of the day was half spent when he returned to gaze upon the lotus feet of his Lord.

दोहा-dohā:

देखे थल तीरथ सकल भरत पाँच दिन माझ ।
dekhe thala tīratha sakala bharata pāṁca dina mājha,
कहत सुनत हरि हर सुजसु गयउ दिवसु भइ साँझ ॥ ३१२ ॥
kahata sunata hari hara sujasu gayau divasu bhai sāṁjha. 312.

Trans:

In five days Bharat visited every shrine and holy place there. The day was spent in discourse on the glory of Harī and Hara until the evening.

चौपाई-caupāī:

भोर न्हाइ सबु जुरा समाजू । भरत भूमिसुर तेरहुति राजू ॥
bhora nhāi sabu jurā samājū, bharata bhūmisura terahuti rājū.
भल दिन आजु जानि मन माहीं । रामु कृपाल कहत सकुचाहीं ॥
bhala dina āju jāni mana māhīṁ, rāmu kṛpāla kahata sakucāhīṁ.
गुर नृप भरत सभा अवलोकी । सकुचि राम फिरि अवनि बिलोकी ॥
gura nṛpa bharata sabhā avalokī, sakuci rāma phiri avani bilokī.
सील सराहि सभा सब सोची । कहुँ न राम सम स्वामि सँकोची ॥
sīla sarāhi sabhā saba socī, kahuṁ na rāma sama svāmi saṁkocī.
भरत सुजान राम रुख देखी । उठि सप्रेम धरि धीर बिसेषी ॥
bharata sujāna rāma rukha dekhī, uṭhi saprema dhari dhīra biseṣī.
करि दंडवत कहत कर जोरी । राखीं नाथ सकल रुचि मोरी ॥
kari daṁḍavata kahata kara jorī, rākhīṁ nātha sakala ruci morī.
मोहि लगि सहेउ सबहिं संतापू । बहुत भाँति दुखु पावा आपू ॥
mohi lagi saheu sabahiṁ saṁtāpū, bahuta bhāṁti dukhu pāvā āpū.
अब गोसाइँ मोहि देउ रजाई । सेवौं अवध अवधि भरि जाई ॥
aba gosāiṁ mohi deu rajāī, sevauṁ avadha avadhi bhari jāī.

Trans:

On the morrow, after bathing, the whole assembly was gathered together with Bharat, the Brahmins, and the king of Tirhut. Rāma knew at heart that the day was an auspicious one, but in his kindness hesitated to say so. He looked at the Gurū, the king, Bharat and the assembly, and then in diffidence turned his eyes to the ground. All the spectators admired his generosity, thinking, "Never was there a master so considerate as Rāma is!" Bharat in his wisdom understood Rāma's wish. He stood up and, lovingly putting the greatest restraint upon himself, bowed low, and with clasped hands thus spoke, "My Lord has granted my every desire. For me he has borne every affliction, and has himself experienced every kind of trouble. Now, sire, give me your royal permission to go and serve at Avadh till the appointed time.

दोहा-dohā:

जेहिं उपाय पुनि पाय जनु देखै दीनदयाल ।
jehiṁ upāya puni pāya janu dekhai dīnadayāla,
सो सिख देइअ अवधि लगि कोसलपाल कृपाल ॥ ३१३ ॥
so sikha deia avadhi lagi kosalapāla kṛpāla. 313.

Trans:

But, O merciful and compassionate king of Kaushal, teach me some way by which your servant may live to see your feet again when the time is over.

चौपाई-caupāī:

पुरजन परिजन प्रजा गोसाईं । सब सुचि सरस सनेहँ सगाईं ॥
purajana parijana prajā gosāīṁ, saba suci sarasa sanehaṁ sagāīṁ.
राउर बदि भल भव दुख दाहू । प्रभु बिनु बादि परम पद लाहू ॥
rāura badi bhala bhava dukha dāhū, prabhu binu bādi parama pada lāhū.
स्वामि सुजानु जानि सब ही की । रुचि लालसा रहनि जन जी की ॥
svāmi sujānu jāni saba hī kī, ruci lālasā rahani jana jī kī.
प्रनतपालु पालिहि सब काहू । देउ दुहू दिसि ओर निबाहू ॥
pranatapālu pālihi saba kāhū, deu duhū disi ora nibāhū.
अस मोहि सब बिधि भूरि भरोसो । किएँ बिचारु न सोचु खरो सो ॥
asa mohi saba bidhi bhūri bharoso, kieṁ bicāru na socu kharo so.
आरति मोर नाथ कर छोहू । दुहुँ मिलि कीन्ह ढीठु हठि मोहू ॥
ārati mora nātha kara chohū, duhuṁ mili kīnha ḍhīṭhu haṭhi mohū.
यह बड़ दोषु दूरि करि स्वामी । तजि सकोच सिखइअ अनुगामी ॥

yaha baṛa dosu dūri kari svāmī, taji sakoca sikhaia anugāmī.

भरत बिनय सुनि सबहिं प्रसंसी । खीर नीर बिबरन गति हंसी ॥

bharata binaya suni sabahiṁ prasaṁsī, khīra nīra bibarana gati haṁsī.

Trans:

Your citizens, your kinsmen, and all your subjects, sire, are true and leal, and bound to you by ties of affection. The sorrows of this miserable life, borne by your command, are a delight; and without my Lord, the highest heaven is a worthless gain. The all-wise master knows the fancies, the desires, the habit of mind of all his servants; the protector of suppliants will be our protector, and both in this world and the next will secure our deliverance. I have thus the most perfect confidence; not a particle of anxiety disturbs my calculations. My own distress and my Lord's forbearance have combined to make me thus presumptuous. Pardon, my Lord, this my great offence, and shrink not from instructing your servant what to do." All who heard Bharat's prayer applauded it—like a swan it had separated the milk of truth from the water of error.

दोहा-dohā:

दीनबंधु सुनि बंधु के बचन दीन छलहीन ।

dīnabaṁdhu suni baṁdhu ke bacana dīna chalahīna,

देस काल अवसर सरिस बोले रामु प्रबीन ॥३१४॥

desa kāla avasara sarisa bole rāmu prabīna. 314.

Trans:

The all-wise Rāma, the brother of the meek, on hearing his brother's humble and guileless speech, replied in terms appropriate to the place, the circumstances, and the time:

चौपाई-caupāī:

तात तुम्हारि मोरि परिजन की । चिंता गुरहि नृपहि घर बन की ॥

tāta tumhāri mori parijana kī, ciṁtā gurahi nṛpahi ghara bana kī.

माथे पर गुर मुनि मिथिलेसू । हमहि तुम्हहि सपनेहुँ न कलेसू ॥

māthe para gura muni mithilesū, hamahi tumhahi sapanehuṁ na kalesū.

मोर तुम्हार परम पुरुषारथु । स्वारथु सुजसु धरमु परमारथु ॥

mora tumhāra parama puruṣārathu, svārathu sujasu dharamu paramārathu.

पितु आयसु पालिहिं दुहु भाईं । लोक बेद भल भूप भलाईं ॥

pitu āyasu pālihiṁ duhu bhāīṁ, loka beda bhala bhūpa bhalāīṁ.

गुरु पितु मातु स्वामि सिख पालें । चलेहुँ कुमग पग परहिं न खालें ॥

guru pitu mātu svāmi sikha pāleṁ, calehuṁ kumaga paga parahiṁ na khāleṁ.

अस बिचारि सब सोच बिहाई । पालहु अवध अवधि भरि जाई ॥

asa bicāri saba soca bihāī, pālahu avadha avadhi bhari jāī.

देसु कोसु परिजन परिवारू । गुर पद रजहिं लाग छरुभारू ॥

desu kosu parijana parivārū, gura pada rajahiṁ lāga charubhārū.

तुम्ह मुनि मातु सचिव सिख मानी । पालेहु पुहुमि प्रजा रजधानी ॥

tumha muni mātu saciva sikha mānī, pālehu puhumi prajā rajadhānī.

Trans:

"The Gurū and the king, O brother, take thought for you, for me, and our people, whether at home or in the forest. So long as Vishwāmitra, Vasishtha, and Janak direct us, neither you nor I can dream of trouble. For us two brothers, both for me and you, obedience to our father's command is the highest object we can have: our greatest gain, our glory, our duty, and our salvation. A king's good is a good thing both in the Veda and in the estimation of the world. Whoever observes the injunctions of Gurū, or father and mother, or master, treads an easy path and never stumbles. Remember this, and putting aside all regrets, go and reign at Avadh for the appointed time. The responsibility for the protection of our land, treasury, kinsmen and our own people rests on the dust of our preceptor's feet. As for yourself you should protect the earth, your subjects and your capital in accordance with the advice of your preceptor, mothers and the minister."

दोहा-dohā:

मुखिआ मुखु सो चाहिऐ खान पान कहुँ एक ।

mukhiā mukhu so cāhiai khāna pāna kahuṁ eka,

पालइ पोषइ सकल अँग तुलसी सहित बिबेक ॥३१५॥

pālai poṣai sakala aṁga tulasī sahita bibeka. 315.

Trans:

A chief should be like the mouth, which alone, says Tulsīdās, does all the eating and drinking, and yet supports and nourishes to a nicety each separate member of the body.

चौपाई-caupāī:

राजधरम सरबसु एतनोई । जिमि मन माहँ मनोरथ गोई ॥

rājadharama sarabasu etanoī, jimi mana māhaṁ manoratha goī.

बंधु प्रबोधु कीन्ह बहु भाँती । बिनु अधार मन तोषु न साँती ॥

baṁdhu prabodhu kīnha bahu bhāṁtī, binu adhāra mana toṣu na sāṁtī.

भरत सील गुर सचिव समाजू । सकुच सनेह बिबस रघुराजू ॥

bharata sīla gura saciva samājū, sakuca saneha bibasa raghurājū.

प्रभु करि कृपा पाँवरीं दीन्हीं । सादर भरत सीस धरि लीन्हीं ॥

prabhu kari kṛpā pāṁvarīṁ dīnhīṁ, sādara bharata sīsa dhari līnhīṁ.

चरनपीठ करुनानिधान के । जनु जुग जामिक प्रजा प्रान के ॥

caranapīṭha karunānidhāna ke, janu juga jāmika prajā prāna ke.

संपुट भरत सनेह रतन के । आखर जुग जनु जीव जतन के ॥

saṁpuṭa bharata saneha ratana ke, ākhara juga janu jīva jatana ke.

कुल कपाट कर कुसल करम के । बिमल नयन सेवा सुधरम के ॥

kula kapāṭa kara kusala karama ke, bimala nayana sevā sudharama ke.

भरत मुदित अवलंब लहे तें । अस सुख जस सिय रामु रहे तें ॥

bharata mudita avalaṁba lahe teṁ, asa sukha jasa siya rāmu rahe teṁ.

Trans:

"A king's duty includes everything, in the same way as every latent desire exists potentially in the mind." In various ways he consoled his brother; but without some memento his mind would not be satisfied nor rest. The Gurū, the minister, and the whole assembly were like-minded with Bharat; and Rāma, overpowered with modesty and affection, took compassion upon him and gave him his wooden sandals, which Bharat reverently received and placed upon his head. Not were these the mere footgear of the All-merciful, but rather twin guardians of his people's life; a casket to contain the jewel of Bharat's love—the two letters of the alphabet for which the soul struggles; the folding-doors that guard the house; the hands for holy work; the pure eyes of service and righteousness. Bharat was as glad to receive this memento as if Rāma and Sītā had themselves stayed.

दोहा-dohā:

मागेउ बिदा प्रनामु करि राम लिए उर लाइ ।

māgeu bidā pranāmu kari rāma lie ura lāi,

लोग उचाटे अमरपति कुटिल कुअवसरु पाइ ॥३१६॥

loga ucāṭe amarapati kuṭila kuavasaru pāi. 316.

Trans:

As he bowed and begged permission to depart, Rāma took and clasped him to his bosom; while the malevolent lord of celestials, taking advantage of this adverse situation made the people weary.

चौपाई-caupāī:

सो कुचालि सब कहँ भइ नीकी । अवधि आस सम जीवनि जी की ॥

so kucāli saba kahaṁ bhai nīkī, avadhi āsa sama jīvani jī kī.

नतरु लखन सिय सम बियोगा । हहरि मरत सब लोग कुरोगा ॥

nataru lakhana siya sama biyogā, hahari marata saba loga kurogā.

रामकृपाँ अवरेब सुधारी । बिबुध धारि भइ गुनद गोहारी ॥

rāmakṛpāṁ avareba sudhārī, bibudha dhāri bhai gunada gohārī.

भेंटत भुज भरि भाइ भरत सो । राम प्रेम रसु कहि न परत सो ॥
bhemṭata bhuja bhari bhāi bharata so, rāma prema rasu kahi na parata so.
तन मन बचन उमग अनुरागा । धीर धुरंधर धीरजु त्यागा ॥
tana mana bacana umaga anurāgā, dhīra dhuraṁdhara dhīraju tyāgā.
बारिज लोचन मोचत बारी । देखि दसा सुर सभा दुखारी ॥
bārija locana mocata bārī, dekhi dasā sura sabhā dukhārī.
मुनिगन गुर धुर धीर जनक से । ग्यान अनल मन कसें कनक से ॥
munigana gura dhura dhīra janaka se, gyāna anala mana kasem kanaka se.
जे बिरंचि निरलेप उपाए । पदुम पत्र जिमि जग जल जाए ॥
je biraṁci niralepa upāe, paduma patra jimi jaga jala jāe.

Trans:

But his villainy was a good thing for all; the hope that the time of exile would soon be over was the life of their life. Otherwise the separation from Lakshman, Sītā, and Rāma would have been such a blow that all would have died of it. The mercy of Rāma solved this difficulty, and the hostile gods became serviceable allies. Rāma closed his arms around Bharat with a burst of affection that cannot be described. Body, soul, and speech overflowed with love; the firmest of the firm lost all firmness, and his lotus eyes streamed with tears; even the assembled gods were grieved to see his condition. The saints, the Gurūs, the stalwarts of firmness such as Janak—the gold of whose soul had been tested in the fire of wisdom, nay, they whom the Creator had created as unimpressionable by the world as the leaves of the lotus by the water—

दोहा-dohā:

तेउ बिलोकि रघुबर भरत प्रीति अनूप अपार ।
teu biloki raghubara bharata prīti anūpa apāra,
भए मगन मन तन बचन सहित बिराग बिचार ॥३१७॥
bhae magana mana tana bacana sahita birāga bicāra. 317.

Trans:

—even they, seeing the unparalleled and boundless affection of Rāma and Bharat, were overwhelmed in body, soul, and speech, and lost all reason and restraint.

चौपाई-caupāī:

जहाँ जनक गुर गति मति भोरी । प्राकृत प्रीति कहत बड़ि खोरी ॥
jahāṁ janaka gura gati mati bhorī, prākṛta prīti kahata baṛi khorī.
बरनत रघुबर भरत बियोगू । सुनि कठोर कबि जानिहि लोगू ॥
baranata raghubara bharata biyogū, suni kaṭhora kabi jānihi logū.
सो सकोच रसु अकथ सुबानी । समउ सनेहु सुमिरि सकुचानी ॥
so sakoca rasu akatha subānī, samau sanehu sumiri sakucānī.
भेंटि भरतु रघुबर समुझाए । पुनि रिपुदवनु हरषि हियँ लाए ॥
bhemṭi bharatu raghubara samujhāe, puni ripudavanu haraṣi hiyaṁ lāe.
सेवक सचिव भरत रुख पाई । निज निज काज लगे सब जाई ॥
sevaka saciva bharata rukha pāī, nija nija kāja lage saba jāī.
सुनि दारुन दुखु दुहूँ समाजा । लगे चलन के साजन साजा ॥
suni dāruna dukhu duhūṁ samājā, lage calana ke sājana sājā.
प्रभु पद पदुम बंदि दोउ भाई । चले सीस धरि राम रजाई ॥
prabhu pada paduma baṁdi dou bhāī, cale sīsa dhari rāma rajāī.
मुनि तापस बनदेव निहोरी । सब सनमानि बहोरि बहोरी ॥
muni tāpasa banadeva nihorī, saba sanamāni bahori bahorī.

Trans:

If Janak and Vasishtha were dumb-founded the emotion of ordinary persons is not worth speaking about. People would think any poet harsh when they hear him describe the parting of Rāma and Bharat. Eloquence herself, remembering the unspeakable pathos of the scene, would be struck dumb with confusion. Raghubar first embraced and consoled Bharat and then rejoiced to take Shatrughan to his arms. Knowing Bharat's wishes, his servants and ministers began each to set about their work. In both camps there was sore distress at the news, as they commenced their preparations for the march. The two brothers, after reverencing their Lord's lotus feet and submissively receiving his commands, set out on the way, bowing to the saints, the hermits, and forest gods, and again and again showing them respect.

दोहा-dohā:

लखनहि भेंटि प्रनामु करि सिर धरि सिय पद धूरि ।
lakhanahi bhemṭi pranāmu kari sira dhari siya pada dhūri,
चले सप्रेम असीस सुनि सकल सुमंगल मूरि ॥३१८॥
cale saprema asīsa suni sakala sumaṁgala mūri. 318.

Trans:

Lakshman too, they embraced, and making obeisance, placed on their head the dust of Sītā's feet, and received her affectionate blessing, the source of every happiness.

चौपाई-caupāī:

सानुज राम नृपहि सिर नाई । कीन्हि बहुत बिधि बिनय बड़ाई ॥
sānuja rāma nṛpahi sira nāī, kīnhi bahuta bidhi binaya baṛāī.
देव दया बस बड दुखु पायउ । सहित समाज काननहिं आयउ ॥
deva dayā basa baṛa dukhu pāyau, sahita samāja kānanahiṁ āyau.
पुर पगु धारिअ देइ असीसा । कीन्ह धीर धरि गवनु महीसा ॥
pura pagu dhāria dei asīsā, kīnha dhīra dhari gavanu mahīsā.
मुनि महिदेव साधु सनमाने । बिदा किए हरि हर सम जाने ॥
muni mahideva sādhu sanamāne, bidā kie hari hara sama jāne.
सासु समीप गए दोउ भाई । फिरे बंदि पग आसिष पाई ॥
sāsu samīpa gae dou bhāī, phire baṁdi paga āsiṣa pāī.
कौसिक बामदेव जाबाली । पुरजन परिजन सचिव सुचाली ॥
kausika bāmadeva jābālī, purajana parijana saciva sucālī.
जथा जोगु करि बिनय प्रनामा । बिदा किए सब सानुज रामा ॥
jathā jogu kari binaya pranāmā, bidā kie saba sānuja rāmā.
नारि पुरुष लघु मध्य बड़ेरे । सब सनमानि कृपानिधि फेरे ॥
nāri puruṣa laghu madhya baṛere, saba sanamāni kṛpānidhi phere.

Trans:

Rāma and his brother bowed the head to the king with many expressions of modesty and praise, "In your kindness, sire, you have suffered great inconvenience, you and your retinue, by coming to the forest; now grant me your blessing and return to the city." The monarch mastered his emotion and went. After reverencing the saints, Brahmins and nobles, and taking leave of them as though they were the equals of Harī and Hara, the two brothers approached their mother-in-law, and came back after bowing at her feet and obtaining her blessing. Then they took leave of Vishwāmitra, Vāmdev, and Jabālī, the people of the court, the citizens, the good ministers and all, with courteous speech and address, as was most befitting. The Ocean of compassion sent back all most respectfully—men and women, high, middle-class, and low.

दोहा-dohā:

भरत मातु पद बंदि प्रभु सुचि सनेहँ मिलि भेंटि ।
bharata mātu pada baṁdi prabhu suci sanehaṁ mili bhemṭi,
बिदा कीन्ह सजि पालकी सकुच सोच सब मेटि ॥३१९॥
bidā kīnha saji pālakī sakuca soca saba meṭi. 319.

Trans:

With sincere affection the Lord bowed at the feet of Bharat's mother and embraced her, and escorting her to the *Pālkī* that he had in readiness, effaced all her alarm and distress.

चौपाई-caupāī:

परिजन मातु पितहि मिलि सीता । फिरी प्रानप्रिय प्रेम पुनीता ॥
parijana mātu pitahi mili sītā, phirī prānapriya prema punītā.

करि प्रनामु भेंटीं सब सासू । प्रीति कहत कबि हियँ न हुलासू ॥
kari pranāmu bheṁṭīṁ saba sāsū, prīti kahata kabi hiyaṁ na hulāsū.
सुनि सिख अभिमत आसिष पाई । रही सीय दुहु प्रीति समाई ॥
suni sikha abhimata āsiṣa pāī, rahī sīya duhu prīti samāī.
रघुपति पटु पालकीं मगाईं । करि प्रबोधु सब मातु चढ़ाईं ॥
raghupati paṭu pālakīṁ magāīṁ, kari prabodhu saba mātu caṛhāīṁ.
बार बार हिलि मिलि दुहु भाईं । सम सनेहँ जननी पहुँचाईं ॥
bāra bāra hili mili duhu bhāīṁ, sama sanehaṁ janaṇī pahuṁcāīṁ.
साजि बाजि गज बाहन नाना । भरत भूप दल कीन्ह पयाना ॥
sāji bāji gaja bāhana nānā, bharata bhūpa dala kīnha payānā.
हृदयँ रामु सिय लखन समेता । चले जाहिं सब लोग अचेता ॥
hṛdayaṁ rāmu siya lakhana sametā, cale jāhiṁ saba loga acetā.
बसह बाजि गज पसु हियँ हारें । चले जाहिं परबस मन मारें ॥
basaha bāji gaja pasu hiyaṁ hāreṁ, cale jāhiṁ parabasa mana māreṁ.

Trans:

After saluting her father and mother and the court, Sītā came back purified by the love of her beloved. Reverently she embraced all her mothers-in-law with an affection which the poet soul shrinks from describing. Hearkening to their instructions and receiving the blessing she desired of them, Sītā stood burdened with conflicting love. Having sent for elegant *Pālkī*s, Rāma, with words of consolation, escorted each of his mothers to their carriage. Again and again both brothers embraced them and led each by the hand with equal affection. Equipping the horses, elephants and vehicles of every description the hosts of Bharat and King Janak set out on their journey. Their hearts full of Rāma, Sītā, and Lakshman, all the people went disconsolate; even the bullocks, horses, elephants, and cattle were out of heart, and went only by force and against their will.

दोहा-dohā:

गुर गुरतिय पद बंदि प्रभु सीता लखन समेत ।
gura guratiya pada baṁdi prabhu sītā lakhana sameta,
फिरे हरष बिसमय सहित आए परन निकेत ॥ ३२० ॥
phire haraṣa bisamaya sahita āe parana niketa. 320.

Trans:

The Lord with Sītā and Lakshman bowed at the feet of the Gurū and the Gurū's wife, and turned and came back to their leafy hut with mingled pleasure and amazement.

चौपाई-caupāī:

बिदा कीन्ह सनमानि निषादू । चलेउ हृदयँ बड़ बिरह बिषादू ॥
bidā kīnha sanamāni niṣādū, caleu hṛdayaṁ baṛa biraha biṣādū.
कोल किरात भिल्ल बनचारी । फेरे फिरे जोहारि जोहारी ॥
kola kirāta bhilla banacārī, phere phire johāri johārī.
प्रभु सिय लखन बैठि बट छाहीं । प्रिय परिजन बियोग बिलखाहीं ॥
prabhu siya lakhana baiṭhi baṭa chāhīṁ, priya parijana biyoga bilakhāhīṁ.
भरत सनेह सुभाउ सुबानी । प्रिया अनुज सन कहत बखानी ॥
bharata saneha subhāu subānī, priyā anuja sana kahata bakhānī.
प्रीति प्रतीति बचन मन करनी । श्रीमुख राम प्रेम बस बरनी ॥
prīti pratīti bacana mana karanī, śrīmukha rāma prema basa baranī.
तेहि अवसर खग मृग जल मीना । चित्रकूट चर अचर मलीना ॥
tehi avasara khaga mṛga jala mīnā, citrakūṭa cara acara malīnā.
बिबुध बिलोकि दसा रघुबर की । बरषि सुमन कहि गति घर घर की ॥
bibudha biloki dasā raghubara kī, baraṣi sumana kahi gati ghara ghara kī.
प्रभु प्रनामु करि दीन्ह भरोसो । चले मुदित मन डर न खरो सो ॥
prabhu pranāmu kari dīnha bharoso, cale mudita mana ḍara na kharo so.

Trans:

The Nishād was dismissed with honor and departed, sorely grieved at heart to leave. The *Kol*s, *Kirāt*s, and *Bhīl*s, the people of the woods, turned again and again, after they had departed, to make yet one more obeisance. The Lord with Sītā and Lakshman sat under the shade of the Banyan tree and felt sorrow of separation from their near and dear ones. Rāma, overpowered with affection, discoursed to his spouse and brother in eloquent terms on Bharat's love and generosity, and with his own blessed mouth declared that faith and devotion were in his every thought, word, and deed. At that time the birds, deer, and fish, every creature at Chitra-kūt, whether animate or inanimate, were all woebegone. The gods, seeing Raghubar's state, rained down flowers and told him of what was doing in their several spheres. The Lord bowed and reassured them; they went away glad without a particle of anxiety in their mind.

दोहा-dohā:

सानुज सीय समेत प्रभु राजत परन कुटीर ।
sānuja sīya sameta prabhu rājata parana kuṭīra,
भगति ग्यानु बैराग्य जनु सोहत धरें सरीर ॥ ३२१ ॥
bhagati gyānu bairāgya janu sohata dhareṁ sarīra. 321.

Trans:

With Sītā, and his brother, the Lord shone forth in the leafy hut as resplendent as Faith, Wisdom, and Asceticism incarnate.

चौपाई-caupāī:

मुनि महिसुर गुर भरत भुआलू । राम बिरहँ सबु साजु बिहालू ॥
muni mahisura gura bharata bhuālū, rāma birahaṁ sabu sāju bihālū.
प्रभु गुन ग्राम गनत मन माहीं । सब चुपचाप चले मग जाहीं ॥
prabhu guna grāma ganata mana māhīṁ, saba cupacāpa cale maga jāhīṁ.
जमुना उतरि पार सबु भयऊ । सो बासरु बिनु भोजन गयऊ ॥
jamunā utari pāra sabu bhayaū, so bāsaru binu bhojana gayaū.
उतरि देवसरि दूसर बासू । रामसखाँ सब कीन्ह सुपासू ॥
utari devasari dūsara bāsū, rāmasakhāṁ saba kīnha supāsū.
सई उतरि गोमतीं नहाए । चौथें दिवस अवधपुर आए ॥
saī utari gomatīṁ nahāe, cautheṁ divasa avadhapura āe.
जनकु रहे पुर बासर चारी । राज काज सब साज सँभारी ॥
janaku rahe pura bāsara cārī, rāja kāja saba sāja saṁbhārī.
सौंपि सचिव गुर भरतहि राजू । तेरहुति चले साजि सबु साजू ॥
sauṁpi saciva gura bharatahi rājū, terahuti cale sāji sabu sājū.
नगर नारि नर गुर सिख मानी । बसे सुखेन राम रजधानी ॥
nagara nāri nara gura sikha mānī, base sukhena rāma rajadhānī.

Trans:

Vasishtha, the Brahmins and Vishwāmitra, Bharat and the king were all in distress at leaving Rāma; and they paced the road in silence, counting up in their mind all of Rāma's virtues. After crossing the Yamunā they passed the whole day without food. The next day they crossed the Gangā, where Rāma's friend made every arrangement for them. Then they crossed the Sai, bathed in the Gomati, and on the fourth day reached Ajodhyā. Janak stayed four days in the city, settled the entire administration of the state, committed the government to the ministers, the Gurū, and Bharat, and then with all his retinue set out for Tirhut. All the people, in compliance with the Gurū's directions, settled down quietly in Rāma's capital—

दोहा-dohā:

राम दरस लगि लोग सब करत नेम उपबास ।
rāma darasa lagi loga saba karata nema upabāsa,
तजि तजि भूषन भोग सुख जिअत अवधि कीं आस ॥ ३२२ ॥
taji taji bhūṣana bhoga sukha jiata avadhi kīṁ āsa. 322.

Trans:

—all the time fasting, and praying to see him once again, discarding all personal adornments, pleasure and enjoyment, and living only in the hope of his return.

चौपाई-caupāī:

सचिव सुसेवक भरत प्रबोधे । निज निज काज पाइ सिख ओधे ॥
saciva susevaka bharata prabodhe, nija nija kāja pāi sikha odhe.
पुनि सिख दीन्हि बोलि लघु भाई । सौंपी सकल मातु सेवकाई ॥
puni sikha dīnhi boli laghu bhāī, sauṁpī sakala mātu sevakāī.
भूसुर बोलि भरत कर जोरे । करि प्रनाम बय बिनय निहोरे ॥
bhūsura boli bharata kara jore, kari pranāma baya binaya nihore.
ऊँच नीच कारजु भल पोचू । आयसु देब न करब सँकोचू ॥
ūṁca nīca kāraju bhala pocū, āyasu deba na karaba saṁkocū.
परिजन पुरजन प्रजा बोलाए । समाधानु करि सुबस बसाए ॥
parijana purajana prajā bolāe, samādhānu kari subasa basāe.
सानुज गे गुर गेहँ बहोरी । करि दंडवत कहत कर जोरी ॥
sānuja ge gura gehaṁ bahorī, kari daṁḍavata kahata kara jorī.
आयसु होइ त रहौं सनेमा । बोले मुनि तन पुलकि सपेमा ॥
āyasu hoi ta rahauṁ sanemā, bole muni tana pulaki sapemā.
समुझव कहब करब तुम्ह जोई । धरम सारु जग होइहि सोई ॥
samujhava kahaba karaba tumha joī, dharama sāru jaga hoihi soī.

Trans:

Bharat exhorted his ministers and trusty servants, and they executed his orders, each in their appointed sphere. Then he spoke and gave instructions to his younger brother, and entrusted to him the care of the dowager queens. He also, with folded hands, spoke to the Brahmins, bowing low and using humble supplication, "Give your orders and hesitate not, to high or to low, in great matters or in small." Next he summoned the people of the palace, of the city, and all his subjects, and set their minds at rest and appointed them places to live in. After this he, with his brother, went to the Gurū's house, and after prostrating himself and joining his hands in prayer said thus, "With your permission I will now live a life of penance." The saint thrilled with rapturous affection and replied, "Whatever you think, or say, or do, is always best."

दोहा-dohā:

सुनि सिख पाइ असीस बड़ि गनक बोलि दिनु साधि ।
suni sikha pāi asīsa baṛi ganaka boli dinu sādhi,
सिंघासन प्रभु पादुका बैठारे निरुपाधि ॥ ३२३ ॥
siṁghāsana prabhu pādukā baiṭhāre nirupādhi. 323.

Trans:

On receiving his commands and his blessing he sent for astrologers and fixed the day, and then devoutly placed upon the throne his Lord's sandals.

चौपाई-caupāī:

राम मातु गुर पद सिरु नाई । प्रभु पद पीठ रजायसु पाई ॥
rāma mātu gura pada siru nāī, prabhu pada pīṭha rajāyasu pāī.
नंदिगावँ करि परन कुटीरा । कीन्ह निवासु धरम धुर धीरा ॥
naṁdigāvaṁ kari parana kuṭīrā, kīnha nivāsu dharama dhura dhīrā.
जटाजूट सिर मुनिपट धारी । महि खनि कुस साँथरी सँवारी ॥
jaṭājūṭa sira munipaṭa dhārī, mahi khani kusa sāṁtharī saṁvārī.
असन बसन बासन ब्रत नेमा । करत कठिन रिषि धरम सप्रेमा ॥
asana basana bāsana brata nemā, karata kaṭhina riṣi dharama sapremā.
भूषन बसन भोग सुख भूरी । मन तन बचन तजे तिन तूरी ॥
bhūṣana basana bhoga sukha bhūrī, mana tana bacana taje tina tūrī.
अवध राजु सुर राजु सिहाई । दसरथ धनु सुनि धनदु लजाई ॥
avadha rāju sura rāju sihāī, dasaratha dhanu suni dhanadu lajāī.
तेहिं पुर बसत भरत बिनु रागा । चंचरीक जिमि चंपक बागा ॥
tehiṁ pura basata bharata binu rāgā, caṁcarīka jimi caṁpaka bāgā.
रमा बिलासु राम अनुरागी । तजत बमन जिमि जन बड़भागी ॥
ramā bilāsu rāma anurāgī, tajata bamana jimi jana baṛabhāgī.

Trans:

After bowing his head at the feet of Rāma's mother and the Gurū, and receiving the commands of his Lord's sandals, the champion of righteousness made for himself a hut of leaves at Nandi-grām, and dwelt there—with his hair gathered up into a knot on his head, attired in hermit's dress, and his couch of grass spread in a hole in the ground, lovingly practicing the austerities of religious life in food, dress, posture, fasting and prayer; discarding all finery and adornments and every luxury and enjoyment in thought, word, and deed, as of no more value than a broken blade of grass. The city of heaven envied the capital of Avadh, and the god of riches was confounded at the sight of Dashrath's wealth; yet in that city Bharat dwelt as indifferent as a bee in a garden of *champā* trees. The blessed souls, who are devoted to Rāma, spurn like spue all of Lakshmī's delights.

दोहा-dohā:

राम पेम भाजन भरतु बड़े न एहिं करतूति ।
rāma pema bhājana bharatu baṛe na ehiṁ karatūti,
चातक हंस सराहिअत टेंक बिबेक बिभूति ॥ ३२४ ॥
cātaka haṁsa sarāhiata ṭeṁka bibeka bibhūti. 324.

Trans:

As for Bharat, he was the beloved of Rāma and did not owe his greatness to this achievement. The Chātak and the swan are models in their own way, the one of marvelous constancy, the other of discrimination.

चौपाई-caupāī:

देह दिनहुँ दिन दूबरि होई । घटइ तेजु बलु मुख छबि सोई ॥
deha dinahuṁ dina dūbari hoī, ghaṭai teju balu mukha chabi soī.
नित नव राम प्रेम पनु पीना । बढ़त धरम दलु मनु न मलीना ॥
nita nava rāma prema panu pīnā, baṛhata dharama dalu manu na malīnā.
जिमि जलु निघटत सरद प्रकासे । बिलसत बेतस बनज बिकासे ॥
jimi jalu nighaṭata sarada prakāse, bilasata betasa banaja bikāse.
सम दम संजम नियम उपासा । नखत भरत हिय बिमल अकासा ॥
sama dama saṁjama niyama upāsā, nakhata bharata hiya bimala akāsā.
ध्रुव बिस्वासु अवधि राका सी । स्वामि सुरति सुरबीथि बिकासी ॥
dhruva bisvāsu avadhi rākā sī, svāmi surati surabīthi bikāsī.
राम पेम बिधु अचल अदोषा । सहित समाज सोह नित चोखा ॥
rāma pema bidhu acala adoṣā, sahita samāja soha nita cokhā.
भरत रहनि समुझनि करतूती । भगति बिरति गुन बिमल बिभूती ॥
bharata rahani samujhani karatūtī, bhagati birati guna bimala bibhūtī.
बरनत सकल सुकबि सकुचाहीं । सेस गनेस गिरा गमु नाहीं ॥
baranata sakala sukabi sakucāhīṁ, sesa ganesa girā gamu nāhīṁ.

Trans:

Day by day Bharat's body grew thinner, but his luster and vigor were not diminished, and the beauty of his face remained the same. Nourished by an ever-increasing devotion, his virtue waxed stronger, and his soul was unclouded: as the waters decrease in the brightness of the autumn, but the reeds spring up and the lotuses blossom. His tranquility, self-control, piety, fasting and prayer were like stars in the pure heaven of Bharat's soul; his faith like the pole-star, the return from exile of Rāma as the full moon, his constant remembrance of the Lord as the glistening milky way, his devotion a fixed and unsullied moon shining ever clear amidst a galaxy of stars. All the greatest of poets would fail to describe Bharat's composure, wisdom and magnanimity, his faith, his impassability, and the perfect splendor of his virtues. Not even Sheshnāg, Ganesh, and Saraswatī could attain to them.

दोहा-dohā:

नित पूजत प्रभु पाँवरी प्रीति न हृदयँ समाति ।
nita pūjata prabhu pām̐varī prīti na hṛdayam̐ samāti.
मागि मागि आयसु करत राज काज बहु भाँति ॥३२५॥
māgi māgi āyasu karata rāja kāja bahu bhām̐ti. 325.

Trans:

Paying daily homage to his Lord's sandals, his affection for them was greater than his heart could contain; and he constantly referred to them in the disposal of all matters of state;

चौपाई-caupāī:

पुलक गात हियँ सिय रघुबीरू । जीह नामु जप लोचन नीरू ॥
pulaka gāta hiyam̐ siya raghubīrū, jīha nāmu japa locana nīrū.
लखन राम सिय कानन बसहीं । भरतु भवन बसि तप तनु कसहीं ॥
lakhana rāma siya kānana basahīṁ, bharatu bhavana basi tapa tanu kasahīṁ.
दोउ दिसि समुझि कहत सबु लोगू । सब बिधि भरत सराहन जोगू ॥
dou disi samujhi kahata sabu logū, saba bidhi bharata sarāhana jogū.
सुनि ब्रत नेम साधु सकुचाहीं । देखि दसा मुनिराज लजाहीं ॥
suni brata nema sādhu sakucāhīṁ, dekhi dasā munirāja lajāhīṁ.
परम पुनीत भरत आचरनू । मधुर मंजु मुद मंगल करनू ॥
parama punīta bharata ācaranū, madhura maṁju muda maṁgala karanū.
हरन कठिन कलि कलुष कलेसू । महामोह निसि दलन दिनेसू ॥
harana kaṭhina kali kaluṣa kalesū, mahāmoha nisi dalana dinesū.
पाप पुंज कुंजर मृगराजू । समन सकल संताप समाजू ॥
pāpa puṁja kuṁjara mṛgarājū, samana sakala saṁtāpa samājū.
जन रंजन भंजन भव भारू । राम सनेह सुधाकर सारू ॥
jana raṁjana bhaṁjana bhava bhārū, rāma saneha sudhākara sārū.

Trans:

His body quivering with emotion, Sītā and Rāma dwelt in his heart—with their names upon his tongue, and tears in his eyes. Rāma, Lakshman, and Sītā roamed the forest, but Bharat, though dwelling in the palace, too endured same bodily penance. Everyone after considering both sides said that Bharat was in every way praiseworthy. The religious were abashed who heard of his fasting and penance. The king of saints, who saw his condition, was put to shame. Bharat's mode of life is utterly holy, sweet and charming, and the cause of every blessing; it removes the grievous distresses of this sinful age; and it is the sun to disperse the darkness of Māyā, the great delusion; the lion to quell the elephant host of sin; the pacifier of every kind of affliction; the joy of the faithful; the liberator from the burden of existence; the essence of the nectar of love for Rāma.

छंद-chaṁda:

सिय राम प्रेम पियूष पूरन होत जनमु न भरत को ।
siya rāma prema piyūṣa pūrana hota janamu na bharata ko,
मुनि मन अगम जम नियम सम दम बिषम ब्रत आचरत को ॥
muni mana agama jama niyama sama dama biṣama brata ācarata ko.
दुख दाह दारिद दंभ दूषन सुजस मिस अपहरत को ।
dukha dāha dārida daṁbha dūṣana sujasa misa apaharata ko,
कलिकाल तुलसी से सठन्हि हठि राम सनमुख करत को ॥
kalikāla tulasī se saṭhanhi haṭhi rāma sanamukha karata ko.

Trans:

If Bharat had never been born, full of the ambrosia of devotion to Rāma and Sītā, who would have practiced such self-restraint and penance, such composure, patience, and rigorous fasting, transcending every imagination of the saints? Who else would have removed our burning sorrows and poverty, our arrogance and sin—except he, by dint of his fair renown? And who in this Kali-age would have forcibly diverted the mind of villains like Tulsīdās towards Shrī Rāma?

सोरठा-sorathā:

भरत चरित करि नेमु तुलसी जो सादर सुनहिं ।
bharata carita kari nemu tulasī jo sādara sunahiṁ,
सीय राम पद पेमु अवसि होइ भव रस बिरति ॥३२६॥
sīya rāma pada pemu avasi hoi bhava rasa birati. 326.

Trans:

All, says Tulsī, who make a vow and listen with reverence to Bharat's acts, shall assuredly acquire a great devotion to the feet of Sītā and Rāma and a distaste for the mundane pleasures of life.

मासपारायण इक्कीसवाँ विश्राम
māsapārāyaṇa ikkīsavām̐ viśrāma
(Pause 21 for a Thirty-Day Recitation)

इति श्रीमद्रामचरितमानसे सकलकलिकलुषविध्वंसने द्वितीयः सोपानः समाप्तः

iti śrīmadrāmacaritamānase sakalakalikaluṣavidhvaṁsane dvitīyaḥ sopānaḥ samāptaḥ

(Now ends the Second-Ascent into the Manasa Lake of Shrī Rāma's Charita which eradicates all the impurities of the Kali-Yug)

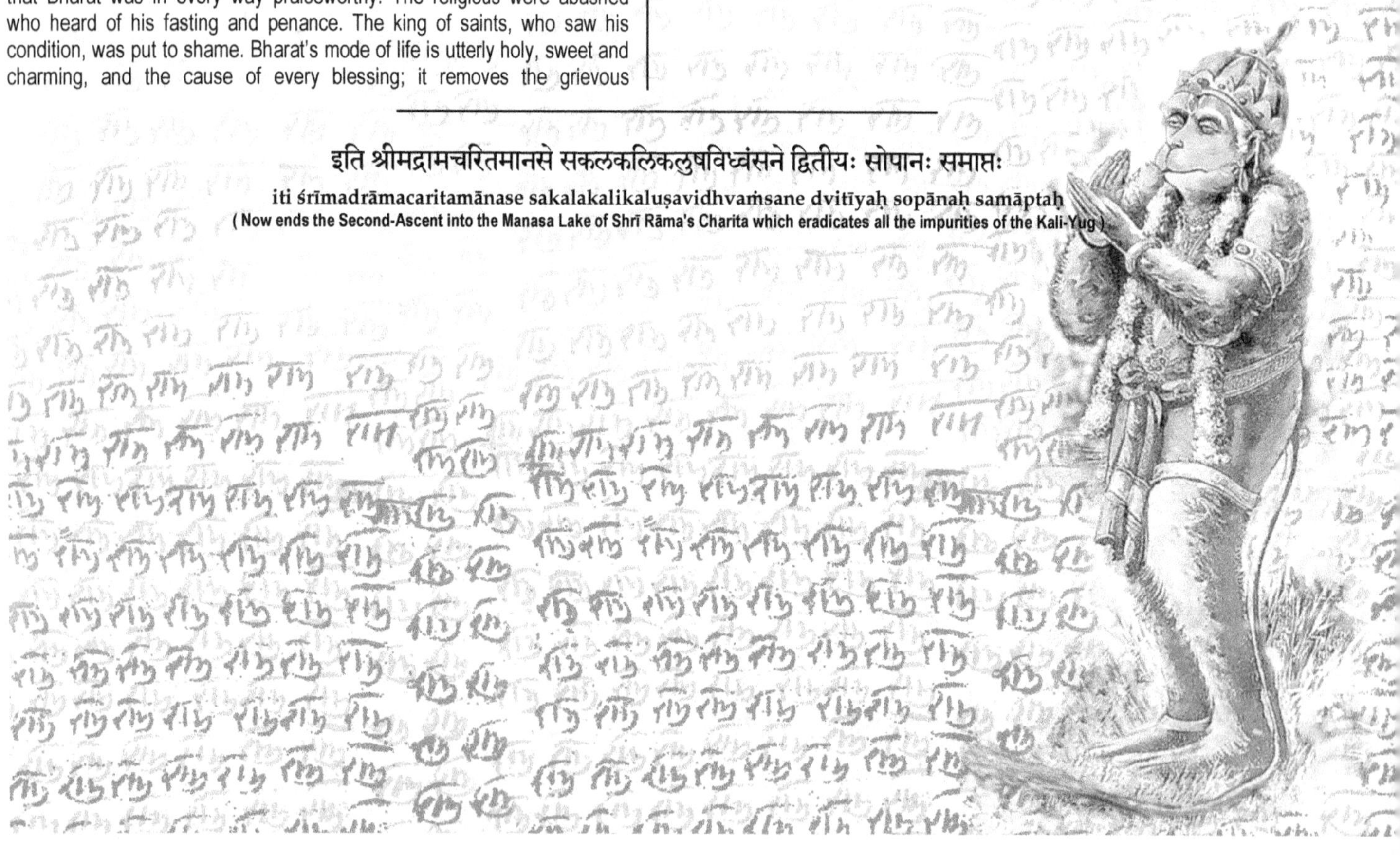

श्रीजानकीवल्लभो विजयते

śrījānakīvallabho vijayate

श्रीरामचरितमानस

śrīrāmacaritamānasa

तृतीय सोपान - अरण्यकाण्ड

tṛtīya sopāna - araṇyakāṇḍa

श्लोक-śloka:

मूलं धर्मतरोर्विवेकजलधेः पूर्णेन्दुमानन्ददं

mūlaṁ dharmatarorvivekajaladheḥ pūrṇendumānandadaṁ

वैराग्याम्बुजभास्करं ह्यघघनध्वान्तापहं तापहम् ।

vairāgyāmbujabhāskaraṁ hyaghaghanadhvāntāpahaṁ tāpaham,

मोहाम्भोधरपूगपाटनविधौ स्वःसम्भवं शङ्करं

mohāmbhodharapūgapāṭanavidhau svaḥsambhavaṁ śaṅkaraṁ

वन्दे ब्रह्मकुलं कलङ्कशमनं श्रीरामभूपप्रियम् ॥ १ ॥

vande brahmakulaṁ kalaṁkaśamanaṁ śrīrāmabhūpapriyam. 1.

Trans:

I reverence him—the progeny of Brahmmā; the very root of the tree of piety, the full moon that brings joy to the sea of wisdom, the healer of distress, who dispels the thick darkness of sin; the sun that opens the lotus of dispassion, and the wind which disperses clouds of ignorance; who wipes off calumny—him, Bhagwān Shankar, the beloved devotee of Shrī Rāma.

सान्द्रानन्दपयोदसौभगतनुं पीताम्बरं सुन्दरं

sāndrānandapayodasaubhagatanuṁ pītāmbaraṁ sundaraṁ

पाणौ बाणशरासनं कटिलसत्तूणीरभारं वरम् ।

pāṇau bāṇaśarāsanaṁ kaṭilasattūṇīrabhāraṁ varam,

राजीवायतलोचनं धृतजटाजूटेन संशोभितं

rājīvāyatalocanaṁ dhṛtajaṭājūṭena saṁśobhitaṁ

सीतालक्ष्मणसंयुतं पथिगतं रामाभिरामं भजे ॥ २ ॥

sītālakṣmaṇasaṁyutaṁ pathigataṁ rāmābhirāmaṁ bhaje. 2.

Trans:

I worship him, whose body resembles a cloud teeming with abundant delights; the yellow appareled, the beautiful, the hero with bow and arrows in hand and a well-fitted quiver gleaming by his aide; the long tresses of whose hair are bound into a knot on his head, with large lotus eyes, all glorious to behold, the charmer of charmers, the wayfarer accompanied by Sītā and Lakshman: Shrī Rāma.

सोरठा-soraṭhā:

उमा राम गुन गूढ़ पंडित मुनि पावहिं बिरति ।

umā rāma guna gūṛha paṁḍita muni pāvahiṁ birati,

पावहिं मोह बिमूढ़ जे हरि बिमुख न धर्म रति ॥

pāvahiṁ moha bimūṛha je hari bimukha na dharma rati.

Trans:

O Umā, the saintly, who are learned in Rāma's mysterious lore, savor peace and emancipation; but fools, who are Harī's enemies and have no love for Dharma, reap delusion alone.

चौपाई-caupāī:

पुर नर भरत प्रीति मैं गाई । मति अनुरूप अनूप सुहाई ॥

pura nara bharata prīti maiṁ gāī, mati anurūpa anūpa suhāī.

अब प्रभु चरित सुनहु अति पावन । करत जे बन सुर नर मुनि भावन ॥

aba prabhu carita sunahu ati pāvana, karata je bana sura nara muni bhāvana.

एक बार चुनि कुसुम सुहाए । निज कर भूषन राम बनाए ॥

eka bāra cuni kusuma suhāe, nija kara bhūṣana rāma banāe.

सीतहि पहिराए प्रभु सादर । बैठे फटिक सिला पर सुंदर ॥

sītahi pahirāe prabhu sādara, baiṭhe phaṭika silā para suṁdara.

सुरपति सुत धरि बायस बेषा । सठ चाहत रघुपति बल देखा ॥

surapati suta dhari bāyasa beṣā, saṭha cāhata raghupati bala dekhā.

जिमि पिपीलिका सागर थाहा । महा मंदमति पावन चाहा ॥

jimi pipīlikā sāgara thāhā, mahā maṁdamati pāvana cāhā.

सीता चरन चोंच हति भागा । मूढ़ मंदमति कारन कागा ॥

sītā carana coṁca hati bhāgā, mūṛha maṁdamati kārana kāgā.

चला रुधिर रघुनायक जाना । सींक धनुष सायक संधाना ॥

calā rudhira raghunāyaka jānā, sīṁka dhanuṣa sāyaka saṁdhānā.

Trans:

I have sung to the best of my ability the incomparable and charming affection shown by the citizens and Bharat; hearken now to the all-holy acts of the Lord which he enacted in the forest to the delight of gods, men and saints. Once upon a time, Rāma picked some lovely flowers and with his own hands made garlands with which he reverently bedecked Sītā. As she sat in her glory on the crystal rock, the son of Indra took the form of a crow and in his wickedness sought to make trial of Rāma's might—like an ant so imbecile of mind as to attempt to sound the depths of ocean. With its beak it bit Sītā in the foot and fled—the foolish crow, in its utter stupidity. The blood flowed; Raghunāyak saw it, and fitted a shaft of reed to his bow.

दोहा-dohā:

अति कृपाल रघुनायक सदा दीन पर नेह ।

ati kṛpāla raghunāyaka sadā dīna para neha,

ता सन आइ कीन्ह छलु मूरख अवगुन गेह ॥ १ ॥

tā sana āi kīnha chalu mūrakha avaguna geha. 1.

Trans:

The All-merciful Rāma, ever full of compassion for the poor, even he it was, upon whom the wicked wretch came and played his tricks.

चौपाई-caupāī:

प्रेरित मंत्र ब्रह्मसर धावा । चला भाजि बायस भय पावा ॥
prerita maṁtra brahmasara dhāvā, calā bhāji bāyasa bhaya pāvā.

धरि निज रुप गयउ पितु पाहीं । राम बिमुख राखा तेहि नाहीं ॥
dhari nija rupa gayau pitu pāhīṁ, rāma bimukha rākhā tehi nāhīṁ.

भा निरास उपजी मन त्रासा । जथा चक्र भय रिषि दुर्बासा ॥
bhā nirāsa upajī mana trāsā, jathā cakra bhaya riṣi durbāsā.

ब्रह्मधाम सिवपुर सब लोका । फिरा श्रमित ब्याकुल भय सोका ॥
brahmadhāma sivapura saba lokā, phirā śramita byākula bhaya sokā.

काहूँ बैठन कहा न ओही । राखि को सकइ राम कर द्रोही ॥
kāhūṁ baiṭhana kahā na ohī, rākhi ko sakai rāma kara drohī.

मातु मृत्यु पितु समन समाना । सुधा होइ बिष सुनु हरिजाना ॥
mātu mṛtyu pitu samana samānā, sudhā hoi biṣa sunu harijānā.

मित्र करइ सत रिपु कै करनी । ता कहँ बिबुधनदी बैतरनी ॥
mitra karai sata ripu kai karanī, tā kahaṁ bibudhanadī baitaranī.

सब जगु ताहि अनलहु ते ताता । जो रघुबीर बिमुख सुनु भ्राता ॥
saba jagu tāhi analahu te tātā, jo raghubīra bimukha sunu bhrātā.

नारद देखा बिकल जयंता । लागि दया कोमल चित संता ॥
nārada dekhā bikala jayaṁtā, lāgi dayā komala cita saṁtā.

पठवा तुरत राम पहिं ताही । कहेसि पुकारि प्रनत हित पाही ॥
paṭhavā turata rāma pahiṁ tāhī, kahesi pukāri pranata hita pāhī.

आतुर सभय गहेसि पद जाई । त्राहि त्राहि दयाल रघुराई ॥
ātura sabhaya gahesi pada jāī, trāhi trāhi dayāla raghurāī.

अतुलित बल अतुलित प्रभुताई । मैं मतिमंद जानि नहिं पाई ॥
atulita bala atulita prabhutāī, maiṁ matimaṁda jāni nahiṁ pāī.

निज कृत कर्म जनित फल पायउँ । अब प्रभु पाहि सरन तकि आयउँ ॥
nija kṛta karma janita phala pāyauṁ, aba prabhu pāhi sarana taki āyauṁ.

सुनि कृपाल अति आरत बानी । एकनयन करि तजा भवानी ॥
suni kṛpāla ati ārata bānī, ekanayana kari tajā bhavānī.

Trans:
The divine arrow, winged with a charm, sped forth; the crow in terror took to flight and assuming his proper form went to his father—who did not shelter him knowing him as Rāma's enemy. He was in despair, and as panic-stricken in soul as was the Rishī Durvāsā by the terror of Vishnu's discus. Weary and worn with fear and remorse, he traversed the realm of Brahmmā, the city of Shiva and every other sphere; but no one even asked him to sit down: who can befriend an enemy of Rāma's? Hearken O Garud: his own mother becomes his death; his father becomes, as it were, the king of infernal regions; ambrosia turns to poison; a friend does him all the harm of a hundred enemies; the Gangā is converted into the Vaitaranī, and all the world burns hotter than fire—mark me, brother—when a man opposes Rāma. When Nārad saw Jayanta's distress, being tender hearted and good, he took pity on him and sent him straight to Rāma. There he cried "Save me, O thou that art the suppliant's friend!" In terror and confusion he went and clasped his feet, crying "Quarter, quarter, O merciful Raghurāī! Thy might is immeasurable, and immeasurable thy majesty; in ignorance of mind, I knew thee not. I have reaped the fruit of my own actions; now my Lord, succor me, for unto thee I have come for refuge." When the Merciful heard this most piteous appeal, he dismissed him, O Bhawānī, merely with the loss of one eye.

सोरठा-soraṭhā:

कीन्ह मोह बस द्रोह जद्यपि तेहि कर बध उचित ।
kīnha moha basa droha jadyapi tehi kara badha ucita,

प्रभु छाड़ेउ करि छोह को कृपाल रघुबीर सम ॥२॥
prabhu chāṛeu kari choha ko kṛpāla raghubīra sama. 2.

Trans:
Although in his infatuation he had committed such an offence that death was his due, the Lord had compassion upon him and set him free; who is so merciful as Raghubīr!

चौपाई-caupāī:

रघुपति चित्रकूट बसि नाना । चरित किए श्रुति सुधा समाना ॥
raghupati citrakūṭa basi nānā, carita kie śruti sudhā samānā.

बहुरि राम अस मन अनुमाना । होइहि भीर सबहिं मोहि जाना ॥
bahuri rāma asa mana anumānā, hoihi bhīra sabahiṁ mohi jānā.

सकल मुनिन्ह सन बिदा कराई । सीता सहित चले द्वौ भाई ॥
sakala muninha sana bidā karāī, sītā sahita cale dvau bhāī.

अत्रि के आश्रम जब प्रभु गयऊ । सुनत महामुनि हरषित भयऊ ॥
atri ke āśrama jaba prabhu gayaū, sunata mahāmuni haraṣita bhayaū.

पुलकित गात अत्रि उठि धाए । देखि रामु आतुर चलि आए ॥
pulakita gāta atri uṭhi dhāe, dekhi rāmu ātura cali āe.

करत दंडवत मुनि उर लाए । प्रेम बारि द्वौ जन अन्हवाए ॥
karata daṁḍavata muni ura lāe, prema bāri dvau jana anhavāe.

देखि राम छबि नयन जुड़ाने । सादर निज आश्रम तब आने ॥
dekhi rāma chabi nayana juṛāne, sādara nija āśrama taba āne.

करि पूजा कहि बचन सुहाए । दिए मूल फल प्रभु मन भाए ॥
kari pūjā kahi bacana suhāe, die mūla phala prabhu mana bhāe.

Trans:
Rāma stayed on at Chitrakūṭ and performed many acts that were excellent and ambrosia for the ear. At last, he thought to himself, "There will be a crowd here, now that everyone knows of me." So the two brothers with Sītā took leave of all the saints and went on their way. When the Lord drew near to Atri's hermitage, the holy man was rejoiced at the news and quivering in every limb he sprang up and ran to meet him. On seeing him, Rāma advanced hurriedly and was falling to the ground before him, but the saint took him to his bosom, and also Lakshman, and bathed them with tears of love. At the sight of Rāma's beauty his eyes were gladdened and he reverently conducted them to his Ashram where, doing him every honor, he addressed him in gracious terms and offered roots and fruits such as the Lord would relish.

सोरठा-soraṭhā:

प्रभु आसन आसीन भरि लोचन सोभा निरखि ।
prabhu āsana āsīna bhari locana sobhā nirakhi,

मुनिबर परम प्रबीन जोरि पानि अस्तुति करत ॥३॥
munibara parama prabīna jori pāni astuti karata. 3.

Trans:
As the Lord took his seat, the great saint, supremely wise, gazed with streaming eyes upon his beauty; and joining his hands in supplication thus hymned the Lord's praise.

छंद-chaṁda:

नमामि भक्त वत्सलं । कृपालु शील कोमलं ॥
namāmi bhakta vatsalaṁ, kṛpālu śīla komalaṁ.

भजामि ते पदांबुजं । अकामिनां स्वधामदं ॥
bhajāmi te padāṁbujaṁ, akāmināṁ svadhāmadaṁ.

निकाम श्याम सुंदरं । भवाम्बुनाथ मंदरं ॥

nikāma śyāma suṁdaraṁ, bhavāmbunātha maṁdaraṁ.

प्रफुल्ल कंज लोचनं । मदादि दोष मोचनं ॥
praphulla kaṁja locanaṁ, madādi doṣa mocanaṁ.

प्रलंब बाहु विक्रमं । प्रभोऽप्रमेय वैभवं ॥
pralaṁba bāhu vikramaṁ, prabho'prameya vaibhavaṁ.

निषंग चाप सायकं । धरं त्रिलोक नायकं ॥
niṣaṁga cāpa sāyakaṁ, dharaṁ triloka nāyakaṁ.

दिनेश वंश मंडनं । महेश चाप खंडनं ॥
dineśa vaṁśa maṁḍanaṁ, maheśa cāpa khaṁḍanaṁ.

मुनींद्र संत रंजनं । सुरारि बृंद भंजनं ॥
munīṁdra saṁta raṁjanaṁ, surāri bṛṁda bhaṁjanaṁ.

मनोज वैरि वंदितं । अजादि देव सेवितं ॥
manoja vairi vaṁditaṁ, ajādi deva sevitaṁ.

विशुद्ध बोध विग्रहं । समस्त दूषणापहं ॥
viśuddha bodha vigrahaṁ, samasta dūṣaṇāpahaṁ.

नमामि इंदिरा पतिं । सुखाकरं सतां गतिं ॥
namāmi iṁdirā patiṁ, sukhākaraṁ satāṁ gatiṁ.

भजे सशक्ति सानुजं । शची पति प्रियानुजं ॥
bhaje saśakti sānujaṁ, śacī pati priyānujaṁ.

त्वदंघ्रि मूल ये नराः । भजंति हीन मत्सराः ॥
tvadaṁghri mūla ye narāḥ, bhajaṁti hīna matsarāḥ.

पतंति नो भवार्णवे । वितर्क वीचि संकुले ॥
pataṁti no bhavārṇave, vitarka vīci saṁkule.

विविक्त वासिनः सदा । भजंति मुक्तये मुदा ॥
vivikta vāsinaḥ sadā, bhajaṁti muktaye mudā.

निरस्य इंद्रियादिकं । प्रयांति ते गतिं स्वकं ॥
nirasya iṁdriyādikaṁ, prayāṁti te gatiṁ svakaṁ.

तमेकमद्भुतं प्रभुं । निरीहमीश्वरं विभुं ॥
tamekamadbhutaṁ prabhuṁ, nirīhamīśvaraṁ vibhuṁ.

जगद्गुरुं च शाश्वतं । तुरीयमेव केवलं ॥
jagadguruṁ ca śāśvataṁ, turīyameva kevalaṁ.

भजामि भाव वल्लभं । कुयोगिनां सुदुर्लभं ॥
bhajāmi bhāva vallabhaṁ, kuyogināṁ sudurlabhaṁ.

स्वभक्त कल्प पादपं । समं सुसेव्यमन्वहं ॥
svabhakta kalpa pādapaṁ, samaṁ susevyamanvahaṁ.

अनूप रूप भूपतिं । नतोऽहमुर्विजा पतिं ॥
anūpa rūpa bhūpatiṁ, nato'hamurvijā patiṁ.

प्रसीद मे नमामि ते । पदाब्ज भक्ति देहि मे ॥
prasīda me namāmi te, padābja bhakti dehi me.

पठंति ये स्तवं इदं । नरादरेण ते पदं ॥
paṭhaṁti ye stavaṁ idaṁ, narādareṇa te padaṁ.

व्रजंति नात्र संशयं । त्वदीय भक्ति संयुताः ॥
vrajaṁti nātra saṁśayaṁ, tvadīya bhakti saṁyutāḥ.

Trans:

"I reverence thee, the lover of the devout; the merciful, the tenderhearted; I worship thy lotus feet, which bestow upon the unsensual, thine own abode in heaven. I adore thee, the wondrously dark and beautiful, the mount Mandar to churn the ocean of existence; with eyes like the full-blown lotus. I adore thee, the dispeller of pride and every other vice; the long-armed hero of immeasurable power and glory; the mighty Lord of the three spheres, equipped with quiver and bow and arrows; the ornament of the solar race; the breaker of Shiva's bow; the delight of the greatest sages and saints; the destroyer of all the enemies of gods; the adored of Kāmdev's foe Shiva, the reverenced of Brahmmā and the other divinities; the home of enlightened intelligence; the dispeller of all error; Lakshmī's Lord; the mine of felicity; the salvation of the saints. I worship thee with thy spouse and thy brother—O thou beloved younger brother of Sachi's lord. Men, who unselfishly worship thy holy feet, do not sink in the ocean of transmigration, tossing upon the billows of wranglings. They, who in the hope of salvation, with subdued passions, ever delightedly worship thee, having discarded every object of sense, are advanced to thy own sphere in heaven. I worship thee, the one alone, the mysterious Lord, the unchangeable and omnipresent energy, the eternal governor of the world, the one absolute and universal spirit; the joy of all living creatures, far beyond the reach of false believers, but the very tree of paradise to thy own followers; adorable, of easy worship, day after day. I reverently adore thee, the king of incomparable beauty, the Lord of the earth-born Sītā; be gracious to me and grant me devotion to thy lotus feet." They who reverently repeat this hymn, full of faith in thee, will undoubtedly attain to thy heaven.

दोहा-*dohā:*

बिनती करि मुनि नाइ सिरु कह कर जोरि बहोरि ।
binatī kari muni nāi siru kaha kara jori bahori,

चरन सरोरुह नाथ जनि कबहुँ तजै मति मोरि ॥४॥
carana saroruha nātha jani kabahuṁ tajai mati mori. 4.

Trans:

Again with bowed head and folded hands the saint made supplication and cried, "Never, O Lord, may my soul abandon thy lotus feet."

चौपाई-*caupāī:*

अनुसुइया के पद गहि सीता । मिली बहोरि सुसील बिनीता ॥
anusuiyā ke pada gahi sītā, milī bahori susīla binītā.

रिषिपतिनी मन सुख अधिकाई । आसिष देइ निकट बैठाई ॥
riṣipatinī mana sukha adhikāī, āsiṣa dei nikaṭa baiṭhāī.

दिब्य बसन भूषन पहिराए । जे नित नूतन अमल सुहाए ॥
dibya basana bhūṣana pahirāe, je nita nūtana amala suhāe.

कह रिषिबधू सरस मृदु बानी । नारिधर्म कछु ब्याज बखानी ॥
kaha riṣibadhū sarasa mṛdu bānī, nāridharma kachu byāja bakhānī.

मातु पिता भ्राता हितकारी । मितप्रद सब सुनु राजकुमारी ॥
mātu pitā bhrātā hitakārī, mitaprada saba sunu rājakumārī.

अमित दानि भर्ता बयदेही । अधम सो नारि जो सेव न तेही ॥
amita dāni bhartā bayadehī, adhama so nāri jo seva na tehī.

धीरज धर्म मित्र अरु नारी । आपद काल परिखिअहिं चारी ॥
dhīraja dharma mitra aru nārī, āpada kāla parikhiahiṁ cārī.

बृद्ध रोगबस जड़ धनहीना । अंध बधिर क्रोधी अति दीना ॥
bṛddha rogabasa jaṛa dhanahīnā, aṁdha badhira krodhī ati dīnā.

ऐसेहु पति कर किएँ अपमाना । नारि पाव जमपुर दुख नाना ॥
aisehu pati kara kieṁ apamānā, nāri pāva jamapura dukha nānā.

एकइ धर्म एक ब्रत नेमा । कायँ बचन मन पति पद प्रेमा ॥
ekai dharma eka brata nemā, kāyaṁ bacana mana pati pada premā.

जग पतिब्रता चारि बिधि अहहीं । बेद पुरान संत सब कहहीं ॥
jaga patibratā cāri bidhi ahahīṁ, beda purāna saṁta saba kahahīṁ.

उत्तम के अस बस मन माहीं । सपनेहुँ आन पुरुष जग नाहीं ॥
uttama ke asa basa mana māhīṁ, sapanehuṁ āna puruṣa jaga nāhīṁ.

मध्यम परपति देखइ कैसें । भ्राता पिता पुत्र निज जैसें ॥
madhyama parapati dekhai kaiseṁ, bhrātā pitā putra nija jaiseṁ.
धर्म बिचारि समुझि कुल रहई । सो निकिष्ट त्रिय श्रुति अस कहई ॥
dharma bicāri samujhi kula rahaī, so nikiṣṭa triya śruti asa kahaī.
बिनु अवसर भय तें रह जोई । जानेहु अधम नारि जग सोई ॥
binu avasara bhaya teṁ raha joī, jānehu adhama nāri jaga soī.
पति बंचक परपति रति करई । रौरव नरक कल्प सत परई ॥
pati baṁcaka parapati rati karaī, raurava naraka kalpa sata paraī.
छन सुख लागि जनम सत कोटी । दुख न समुझ तेहि सम को खोटी ॥
chana sukha lāgi janama sata koṭī, dukha na samujha tehi sama ko khoṭī.
बिनु श्रम नारि परम गति लहई । पतिब्रत धर्म छाड़ि छल गहई ॥
binu śrama nāri parama gati lahaī, patibrata dharma chāṛi chala gahaī.
पति प्रतिकूल जनम जहँ जाई । बिधवा होइ पाइ तरुनाई ॥
pati pratikūla janama jahaṁ jāī, bidhavā hoi pāi tarunāī.

Trans:

The amiable and modest Sītā clasped Atri's wife Anusuiyā by the feet with frequent embraces. The soul of the Rishī's wife was filled with joy; she gave her her blessing and seated her by her side. Then she arrayed her in heavenly robes and jewels which retained their beauty and freshness at all times. Then, in simple and affectionate phrase the saintly dame spoke and instructed her in matters of wifely duty. "Hearken royal lady: mother, father, brethren and friends are all good in a limited degree; but a husband, Vaidehi, is an unlimited blessing; and vile is the woman who worships him not. Courage, virtue, a friend, and a woman: are four things that are tried in the time of adversity. Though her lord be old, diseased, impotent and poor, blind, deaf, passionate and utterly vile, yet even so the wife who treats him with disrespect shall suffer many torments in hell. Her one duty, her one fast and penance, consists of devotion in body, word and thought to her husband's feet. There are four kinds of faithful wife in the world, as the Vedas, Purānas and saints, all say. The best is so firmly settled in mind that she could not even dream of there being any other man living. The next regards another's husband as her own brother, or father, or son. She who is restrained only by thought of duty and consideration for her family is said in the scriptures to be a woman of lower character; but reckon her the very lowest of all, who is restrained only by fear and want of opportunity. She who deceives her husband and carries on an intrigue with another man shall be cast for a hundred ages into the hell called the Terrible. Who is such a wretch as she, who for a moment's pleasure considers not the torment that shall endure through a hundred million lives? Without any difficulty a woman attains to salvation, if only without guile she adhere to her duty as a faithful wife; while she, who lives disloyal to her spouse, becomes a widow while still young.

सोरठा-soraṭhā:

सहज अपावनि नारि पति सेवत सुभ गति लहइ ।
sahaja apāvani nāri pati sevata subha gati lahai,
जसु गावत श्रुति चारि अजहुँ तुलसिका हरिहि प्रिय ॥५क॥
jasu gāvata śruti cāri ajahuṁ tulasikā harihi priya. 5ka.
सुनु सीता तव नाम सुमिरि नारि पतिब्रत करहिं ।
sunu sītā tava nāma sumiri nāri patibrata karahiṁ,
तोहि प्रानप्रिय राम कहिउँ कथा संसार हित ॥५ख॥
tohi prānapriya rāma kahiuṁ kathā saṁsāra hita. 5kha.

Trans:

An utterly wicked woman who is faithful to her husband has a happy fate. It is due to her loyalty to her husband that Tulsī is loved by Shrī Harī even to this day and her glory is sung by all the four Vedas. Listen Sītā: women all over will maintain their vow of fidelity to their husbands by invoking your very name, for you love Rāma like your own life. Those words of admonition that I spoke are only for the sake of the world."

चौपाई-caupāī:

सुनि जानकीं परम सुखु पावा । सादर तासु चरन सिरु नावा ॥
suni jānakīṁ parama sukhu pāvā, sādara tāsu carana siru nāvā.
तब मुनि सन कह कृपानिधाना । आयसु होइ जाउँ बन आना ॥
taba muni sana kaha kṛpānidhānā, āyasu hoi jāuṁ bana ānā.
संतत मो पर कृपा करेहू । सेवक जानि तजेहु जनि नेहू ॥
saṁtata mo para kṛpā karehū, sevaka jāni tajehu jani nehū.
धर्म धुरंधर प्रभु कै बानी । सुनि सप्रेम बोले मुनि ग्यानी ॥
dharma dhuraṁdhara prabhu kai bānī, suni saprema bole muni gyānī.
जासु कृपा अज सिव सनकादी । चहत सकल परमारथ बादी ॥
jāsu kṛpā aja siva sanakādī, cahata sakala paramāratha bādī.
ते तुम्ह राम अकाम पिआरे । दीन बंधु मृदु बचन उचारे ॥
te tumha rāma akāma piāre, dīna baṁdhu mṛdu bacana ucāre.
अब जानी मैं श्री चतुराई । भजी तुम्हहि सब देव बिहाई ॥
aba jānī maiṁ śrī caturāī, bhajī tumhahi saba deva bihāī.
जेहि समान अतिसय नहिं कोई । ता कर सील कस न अस होई ॥
jehi samāna atisaya nahiṁ koī, tā kara sīla kasa na asa hoī.
केहि बिधि कहौं जाहु अब स्वामी । कहहु नाथ तुम्ह अंतरजामी ॥
kehi bidhi kahauṁ jāhu aba svāmī, kahahu nātha tumha aṁtarajāmī.
अस कहि प्रभु बिलोकि मुनि धीरा । लोचन जल बह पुलक सरीरा ॥
asa kahi prabhu biloki muni dhīrā, locana jala baha pulaka sarīrā.

Trans:

On hearing this Jānakī was overjoyed and reverently bowed at her feet. Then the All-merciful said to the saint, "With your permission I would go to some other forest. Continue to be ever gracious to me, and knowing me to be your servant, cease not your kindness." On hearing this speech of the Lord, the champion of righteousness, the wise saint affectionately replied, "O Rāma, you are he, whose favor is desired by Brahmmā, Shiva, Sanat-kumār, and the other gods and by all the preachers of salvation. You, the passionless, the kindly, the friend of the helpless, bespeak to me so modestly. Now I understand the cleverness of Lakshmī, who has left every other god and worships you alone. Of a truth there is none your equal; how then could your goodness be other than it is? Now, how can I, my lord, tell you to go? Tell me, my master, for you know the hearts of all." Having thus spoken, the saint strong-minded as he was, thrilled in every limb and his eyes streamed with tears as he gazed upon the Lord.

छंद-chaṁda:

तन पुलक निर्भर प्रेम पूरन नयन मुख पंकज दिए ।
tana pulaka nirbhara prema pūrana nayana mukha paṁkaja die,
मन ग्यान गुन गोतीत प्रभु मैं दीख जप तप का किए ॥
mana gyāna guna gotīta prabhu maiṁ dīkha japa tapa kā kie.
जप जोग धर्म समूह तें नर भगति अनुपम पावई ।
japa joga dharma samūha teṁ nara bhagati anupama pāvaī,
रघुबीर चरित पुनीत निसि दिन दास तुलसी गावई ॥
radhubīra carita punīta nisi dina dāsa tulasī gāvaī.

Trans:

Atremble exceedingly in every limb he fixed his loving eyes upon his lotus face, "It is the reward of prayer and penance that I have beheld the Lord, who transcends the senses and every faculty of thought and reason." By prayer and meditation and religious observances men attain to the crowning virtue of faith; therefore day and night Tulsīdās sings the holy acts of Raghubīr.

दोहा-dohā:

कलिमल समन दमन मन राम सुजस सुखमूल ।
kalimala samana damana mana rāma sujasa sukhamūla,
सादर सुनहिं जे तिन्ह पर राम रहहिं अनुकूल ॥६क॥
sādara sunahiṁ je tinha para rāma rahahiṁ anukūla. 6(ka).

Trans:

Rāma's praises remove the pollution of this wicked age, subdue the soul, and are a constant source of beatitude; Rāma continues gracious to all who reverently hear them.

सोरठा-sorathā:

कठिन काल मल कोस धर्म न ग्यान न जोग जप ।
kaṭhina kāla mala kosa dharma na gyāna na joga japa,
परिहरि सकल भरोस रामहि भजहिं ते चतुर नर ॥६ख॥
parihari sakala bharosa rāmahi bhajahiṁ te catura nara. 6(kha).

Trans:

Grievous is the burden of the sin of the world—not religion, nor knowledge, nor meditation, nor penance avails against it. They alone are wise who discard trust in all else and worship Rāma only.

चौपाई-caupāī:

मुनि पद कमल नाइ करि सीसा । चले बनहि सुर नर मुनि ईसा ॥
muni pada kamala nāi kari sīsā, cale banahi sura nara muni īsā.
आगें राम अनुज पुनि पाछें । मुनि बर बेष बने अति काछें ॥
āgeṁ rāma anuja puni pācheṁ, muni bara beṣa bane ati kācheṁ.
उभय बीच श्री सोहइ कैसी । ब्रह्म जीव बिच माया जैसी ॥
ubhaya bīca śrī sohai kaisī, brahma jīva bica māyā jaisī.
सरिता बन गिरि अवघट घाटा । पति पहिचानि देहिं बर बाटा ॥
saritā bana giri avaghaṭa ghāṭā, pati pahicāni dehiṁ bara bāṭā.
जहँ जहँ जाहिं देव रघुराया । करहिं मेध तहँ तहँ नभ छाया ॥
jahaṁ jahaṁ jāhiṁ deva raghurāyā, karahiṁ medha tahaṁ tahaṁ nabha chāyā.
मिला असुर बिराध मग जाता । आवतहीं रघुबीर निपाता ॥
milā asura birādha maga jātā, āvatahīṁ raghubīra nipātā.
तुरतहिं रुचिर रूप तेहिं पावा । देखि दुखी निज धाम पठावा ॥
turatahiṁ rucira rūpa tehiṁ pāvā, dekhi dukhī nija dhāma paṭhāvā.
पुनि आए जहँ मुनि सरभंगा । सुंदर अनुज जानकी संगा ॥
puni āe jahaṁ muni sarabhaṁgā, suṁdara anuja jānakī saṁgā.

Trans:

The Lord of gods and men and saints, after bowing his head at the lotus feet of the sage, proceeded to the woods. Rāma ahead and after him his brother, in the garb of hermits appeared most lovely; between the two, the incarnation of Lakshmī shone forth, like Māyā between Supreme-Soul and the Soul. The rivers and thickets and precipitous mountain-passes all recognized their Lord and made the way smooth for him. Wherever the divine Raghurāī passed, the clouds made a canopy in the heaven. As they went along the road the demon Viradha met them. While he was yet coming Raghubīr overthrew him; then at once he assumed a beauteous form; and Rāma, seeing him sorrowful, dismissed him to his own sphere. Then the All-beautiful with his brother and Jānakī visited the sage Sarabhangā.

दोहा-dohā:

देखि राम मुख पंकज मुनिबर लोचन भृंग ।
dekhi rāma mukha paṁkaja munibara locana bhṛṁga,
सादर पान करत अति धन्य जन्म सरभंग ॥७॥
sādara pāna karata ati dhanya janma sarabhaṁga. 7.

Trans:

At the sight of Rāma's lotus face, the bee-like eyes of the saint reverently drank thereof; blessed indeed was Sarabhangā to have been born.

चौपाई-caupāī:

कह मुनि सुनु रघुबीर कृपाला । संकर मानस राजमराला ॥
kaha muni sunu raghubīra kṛpālā, saṁkara mānasa rājamarālā.
जात रहेउँ बिरंचि के धामा । सुनेउँ श्रवन बन ऐहहिं रामा ॥
jāta raheuṁ biraṁci ke dhāmā, suneuṁ śravana bana aihahiṁ rāmā.
चितवत पंथ रहेउँ दिन राती । अब प्रभु देखि जुड़ानी छाती ॥
citavata paṁtha raheuṁ dina rātī, aba prabhu dekhi juṛānī chātī.
नाथ सकल साधन मैं हीना । कीन्ही कृपा जानि जन दीना ॥
nātha sakala sādhana maiṁ hīnā, kīnhī kṛpā jāni jana dīnā.
सो कछु देव न मोहि निहोरा । निज पन राखेउ जन मन चोरा ॥
so kachu deva na mohi nihorā, nija pana rākheu jana mana corā.
तब लगि रहहु दीन हित लागी । जब लगि मिलौं तुम्हहि तनु त्यागी ॥
taba lagi rahahu dīna hita lāgī, jaba lagi milauṁ tumhahi tanu tyāgī.
जोग जग्य जप तप ब्रत कीन्हा । प्रभु कहँ देइ भगति बर लीन्हा ॥
joga jagya japa tapa brata kīnhā, prabhu kahaṁ dei bhagati bara līnhā.
एहि बिधि सर रचि मुनि सरभंगा । बैठे हृदयँ छाड़ि सब संगा ॥
ehi bidhi sara raci muni sarabhaṁgā, baiṭhe hṛdayaṁ chāṛi saba saṁgā.

Trans:

Said the saint, "Hearken gracious Raghubīr, the swan of Shankar's lake. I had taken my departure to the halls of the Creator, but I heard mentioned that Rāma is coming into the forest. Day and night I have been watching the road; now I have seen my Lord and my heart is at rest. I am deficient, my Lord, in all that is good, but you have graciously acknowledged me as your humble servant. Really speaking, however, this is no favour to my credit, O Lord; for you have only redeemed your vow, O Stealer of your Devotee's hearts! Now, for the sake of this humble servant remain here till I discard this body and meet you in your own divine abode." So saying the sage offered to the Lord whatever practices of meditation, sacrifice, prayers, penance and fastings, he had done; and received in return the boon of Devotion. Having thus acquired the rare gift of Devotion the sage Sarabhanga prepared a pyre and, discarding all attachment from his heart, ascended it.

दोहा-dohā:

सीता अनुज समेत प्रभु नील जलद तनु स्याम ।
sītā anuja sameta prabhu nīla jalada tanu syāma,
मम हियँ बसहु निरंतर सगुनरुप श्रीराम ॥८॥
mama hiyaṁ basahu niraṁtara sagunarupa śrīrāma. 8.

Trans:

"May the Lord, whose body is dark of hue as a somber rain-cloud, incarnate in form as the divine Rāma, dwell for ever in my soul together with Sītā, and his brother!"

चौपाई-caupāī:

अस कहि जोग अगिनि तनु जारा । राम कृपाँ बैकुंठ सिधारा ॥
asa kahi joga agini tanu jārā, rāma kṛpāṁ baikuṁṭha sidhārā.
ताते मुनि हरि लीन न भयऊ । प्रथमहिं भेद भगति बर लयऊ ॥
tāte muni hari līna na bhayaū, prathamahiṁ bheda bhagati bara layaū.
रिषि निकाय मुनि बर गति देखी । सुखी भए निज हृदयँ बिसेषी ॥
riṣi nikāya muni bara gati dekhī, sukhī bhae nija hṛdayaṁ biseṣī.
अस्तुति करहिं सकल मुनि बृंदा । जयति प्रनत हित करुना कंदा ॥
astuti karahiṁ sakala muni bṛṁdā, jayati pranata hita karunā kaṁdā.
पुनि रघुनाथ चले बन आगे । मुनिबर बृंद बिपुल सँग लागे ॥
puni raghunātha cale bana āge, munibara bṛṁda bipula saṁga lāge.
अस्थि समूह देखि रघुराया । पूछी मुनिन्ह लागि अति दाया ॥

asthi samūha dekhi raghurāyā, pūchī muninha lāgi ati dāyā.

जानतहूँ पूछिअ कस स्वामी । सबदरसी तुम्ह अंतरजामी ॥
jānatahūṁ pūchia kasa svāmī, sabadarasī tumha aṁtarajāmī.

निसिचर निकर सकल मुनि खाए । सुनि रघुबीर नयन जल छाए ॥
nisicara nikara sakala muni khāe, suni raghubīra nayana jala chāe.

Trans:

Having said so he burnt his body in the fire of Yoga and by the grace of Shrī Rāma ascended to Vaikūnth. The saint was not assimilated within the Divine-Ocean for the simple reason that he had received the boon of Devotion. When the assembled Rishis saw the great saint's transformation, they were mightily rejoiced at heart and all broke forth into hymns of praise: "Glory to the champion of the humble, the fountain of mercy." Then Raghunāth went on further into the forest—with a great company of holy men with him. Seeing a heap of bones, he was moved with much compassion and asked the saints about it. "Though knowing everything, how is it that you ask us, O Master? You have seen all and know even our inmost thoughts. These are all the saints whom the host of demons devoured." On hearing this, Raghubīr's eyes filled with tears.

दोहा-dohā:

निसिचर हीन करउँ महि भुज उठाइ पन कीन्ह ।
nisicara hīna karauṁ mahi bhuja uṭhāi pana kīnha,

सकल मुनिन्ह के आश्रमन्हि जाइ जाइ सुख दीन्ह ॥९॥
sakala muninha ke āśramanhi jāi jāi sukha dīnha. 9.

Trans:

He raised his arms and vowed to rid the earth of demons. Then he gladdened the saints by visiting them all in turn at their hermitages.

चौपाई-caupāī:

मुनि अगस्ति कर सिष्य सुजाना । नाम सुतीछन रति भगवाना ॥
muni agasti kara siṣya sujānā, nāma sutīchana rati bhagavānā.

मन क्रम बचन राम पद सेवक । सपनेहु आन भरोस न देवक ॥
mana krama bacana rāma pada sevaka, sapanehu āna bharosa na devaka.

प्रभु आगवनु श्रवन सुनि पावा । करत मनोरथ आतुर धावा ॥
prabhu āgavanu śravana suni pāvā, karata manoratha ātura dhāvā.

हे बिधि दीनबंधु रघुराया । मो से सठ पर करिहहिं दाया ॥
he bidhi dīnabaṁdhu raghurāyā, mo se saṭha para karihahiṁ dāyā.

सहित अनुज मोहि राम गोसाईं । मिलिहहिं निज सेवक की नाईं ॥
sahita anuja mohi rāma gosāīṁ, milihahiṁ nija sevaka kī nāīṁ.

मोरे जियँ भरोस दृढ़ नाहीं । भगति बिरति न ग्यान मन माहीं ॥
more jiyaṁ bharosa dṛṛha nāhīṁ, bhagati birati na gyāna mana māhīṁ.

नहिं सतसंग जोग जप जागा । नहिं दृढ़ चरन कमल अनुरागा ॥
nahiṁ satasaṁga joga japa jāgā, nahiṁ dṛṛha carana kamala anurāgā.

एक बानि करुनानिधान की । सो प्रिय जाकें गति न आन की ॥
eka bāni karunānidhāna kī, so priya jākeṁ gati na āna kī.

होइहैं सुफल आजु मम लोचन । देखि बदन पंकज भव मोचन ॥
hoihaiṁ suphala āju mama locana, dekhi badana paṁkaja bhava mocana.

निर्भर प्रेम मगन मुनि ग्यानी । कहि न जाइ सो दसा भवानी ॥
nirbhara prema magana muni gyānī, kahi na jāi so dasā bhavānī.

दिसि अरु बिदिसि पंथ नहिं सूझा । को मैं चलेउँ कहाँ नहिं बूझा ॥
disi aru bidisi paṁtha nahiṁ sūjhā, ko maiṁ caleuṁ kahāṁ nahiṁ būjhā.

कबहुँक फिरि पाछें पुनि जाई । कबहुँक नृत्य करइ गुन गाई ॥
kabahuṁka phiri pācheṁ puni jāī, kabahuṁka nṛtya karai guna gāī.

अबिरल प्रेम भगति मुनि पाई । प्रभु देखैं तरु ओट लुकाई ॥
abirala prema bhagati muni pāī, prabhu dekhaiṁ taru oṭa lukāī.

अतिसय प्रीति देखि रघुबीरा । प्रगटे हृदयँ हरन भव भीरा ॥
atisaya prīti dekhi raghubīrā, pragaṭe hṛdayaṁ harana bhava bhīrā.

मुनि मग माझ अचल होइ बैसा । पुलक सरीर पनस फल जैसा ॥
muni maga mājha acala hoi baisā, pulaka sarīra panasa phala jaisā.

तब रघुनाथ निकट चलि आए । देखि दसा निज जन मन भाए ॥
taba raghunātha nikaṭa cali āe, dekhi dasā nija jana mana bhāe.

मुनिहि राम बहु भाँति जगावा । जाग न ध्यान जनित सुख पावा ॥
munihi rāma bahu bhāṁti jagāvā, jāga na dhyāna janita sukha pāvā.

भूप रूप तब राम दुरावा । हृदयँ चतुर्भुज रूप देखावा ॥
bhūpa rūpa taba rāma durāvā, hṛdayaṁ caturbhuja rūpa dekhāvā.

मुनि अकुलाइ उठा तब कैसें । बिकल हीन मनि फनि बर जैसें ॥
muni akulāi uṭhā taba kaiseṁ, bikala hīna mani phani bara jaiseṁ.

आगें देखि राम तन स्यामा । सीता अनुज सहित सुख धामा ॥
āgeṁ dekhi rāma tana syāmā, sītā anuja sahita sukha dhāmā.

परेउ लकुट इव चरनन्हि लागी । प्रेम मगन मुनिबर बड़भागी ॥
pareu lakuṭa iva carananhi lāgī, prema magana munibara baṛabhāgī.

भुज बिसाल गहि लिए उठाई । परम प्रीति राखे उर लाई ॥
bhuja bisāla gahi lie uṭhāī, parama prīti rākhe ura lāī.

मुनिहि मिलत अस सोह कृपाला । कनक तरुहि जनु भेंट तमाला ॥
munihi milata asa soha kṛpālā, kanaka taruhi janu bheṁṭa tamālā.

राम बदनु बिलोक मुनि ठाढ़ा । मानहुँ चित्र माझ लिखि काढ़ा ॥
rāma badanu biloka muni ṭhāṛhā, mānahuṁ citra mājha likhi kāṛhā.

Trans:

Saint Agastya had a learned disciple, by name Sutīkshan, devoted to God in thought, word and deed, one of Rāma's very faithful servants who had never even dreamt of any other hope or divinity. When he heard of the Lord's approach, he rushed out hurriedly, full of longing desire, "Ah God! the compassionate Raghurāī will be gracious to even a wretch like me. The holy Rāma and his brother will receive me as their own servant. I have no assured confidence of heart, no faith, nor command over self, nor wisdom of intellect; no communion with saints, no practice in meditation, prayer, or vigil, and no steadfast devotion to his lotus feet—only this promise of the All-merciful: 'He is my own who goeth to no other.' Today my eyes will be blest with the sight of the lotus-faced, the deliverer from the bondage of existence." The saint, philosopher as he was, was so utterly overwhelmed with love that his state, O Bhawānī, was beyond all description. He could not see his way either in this direction or in that, nor remember who he was, or where he was going; at one time he would turn and go back, at another would dance and sing songs of praise. The saint's love and faith waxed yet more vehement as the Lord watched him stealthily from behind a tree. Then Raghubīr, who removes all the troubles of the world, after witnessing his exceeding devotion, manifested himself in his soul. The saint was struck motionless in the middle of the road, and his body bristled like the jackfruit with every hair on end. Then Raghunāth drew near, rejoicing to witness the emotion of his servant. Though he tried many ways to rouse him, the sage would not wake, lost as he was in the ecstasy of his vision—until Rāma doffed his human guise and mentally revealed himself as the four-armed God. The saint thereupon started up in alarm, like a poor snake that has been robbed of its head jewel, and seeing before him the dark-hued Rāma with Sītā and his younger brother, the abode of delight, he fell like a log at his feet, drowned in love and supremely happy. With his strong arms, Rāma took and lifted him up and clasped him to his bosom with the utmost affection. As he embraced the saint, the All-merciful showed forth like a *Tamālā* tree clasped by a tree of gold; and the saint, as he gazed in Rāma's face, stood so still that you would take him for a figure painted in a picture.

दोहा-dohā:

तब मुनि हृदयँ धीर धरि गहि पद बारहिं बार ।
taba muni hṛdayaṁ dhīra dhari gahi pada bārahiṁ bāra,
निज आश्रम प्रभु आनि करि पूजा बिबिध प्रकार ॥ १० ॥
nija āśrama prabhu āni kari pūjā bibidha prakāra. 10.

Trans:

At last the saint, growing bolder at heart, after again and again clasping the Lord's feet, conducted him to his hermitage and did everything in his honor.

चौपाई-caupāī:

कह मुनि प्रभु सुनु बिनती मोरी । अस्तुति करौं कवन बिधि तोरी ॥
kaha muni prabhu sunu binatī morī, astuti karauṁ kavana bidhi torī.
महिमा अमित मोरि मति थोरी । रबि सन्मुख खद्योत अँजोरी ॥
mahimā amita mori mati thorī, rabi sanmukha khadyota aṁjorī.
श्याम तामरस दाम शरीरं । जटा मुकुट परिधन मुनिचीरं ॥
śyāma tāmarasa dāma śarīraṁ, jaṭā mukuṭa paridhana municīraṁ.
पाणि चाप शर कटि तूणीरं । नौमि निरंतर श्रीरघुवीरं ॥
pāṇi cāpa śara kaṭi tūṇīraṁ, naumi niraṁtara śrīraghuvīraṁ.
मोह विपिन घन दहन कृशानुः । संत सरोरुह कानन भानुः ॥
moha vipina ghana dahana kṛśānuḥ, saṁta saroruha kānana bhānuḥ.
निशिचर करि वरूथ मृगराजः । त्रातु सदा नो भव खग बाजः ॥
niśicara kari varūtha mṛgarājaḥ, trātu sadā no bhava khaga bājaḥ.
अरुण नयन राजीव सुवेशं । सीता नयन चकोर निशेशं ॥
aruṇa nayana rājīva suveśaṁ, sītā nayana cakora niśeśaṁ.
हर हृदि मानस बाल मरालं । नौमि राम उर बाहु विशालं ॥
hara hṛdi mānasa bāla marālaṁ, naumi rāma ura bāhu viśālaṁ.
संशय सर्प ग्रसन उरगादः । शमन सुकर्कश तर्क विषादः ॥
saṁśaya sarpa grasana uragādaḥ, śamana sukarkaśa tarka viṣādaḥ.
भव भंजन रंजन सुर यूथः । त्रातु सदा नो कृपा वरूथः ॥
bhava bhaṁjana raṁjana sura yūthaḥ, trātu sadā no kṛpā varūthaḥ.
निर्गुण सगुण विषम सम रूपं । ज्ञान गिरा गोतीतमनूपं ॥
nirguṇa saguṇa viṣama sama rūpaṁ, jñāna girā gotītamanūpaṁ.
अमलमखिलमनवद्यमपारं । नौमि राम भंजन महि भारं ॥
amalamakhilamanavadyamapāraṁ, naumi rāma bhaṁjana mahi bhāraṁ.
भक्त कल्पपादप आरामः । तर्जन क्रोध लोभ मद कामः ॥
bhakta kalpapādapa ārāmaḥ, tarjana krodha lobha mada kāmaḥ.
अति नागर भव सागर सेतुः । त्रातु सदा दिनकर कुल केतुः ॥
ati nāgara bhava sāgara setuḥ, trātu sadā dinakara kula ketuḥ.
अतुलित भुज प्रताप बल धामः । कलि मल विपुल विभंजन नामः ॥
atulita bhuja pratāpa bala dhāmaḥ, kali mala vipula vibhaṁjana nāmaḥ.
धर्म वर्म नर्मद गुण ग्रामः । संतत शं तनोतु मम रामः ॥
dharma varma narmada guṇa grāmaḥ, saṁtata śaṁ tanotu mama rāmaḥ.
जदपि बिरज ब्यापक अबिनासी । सब के हृदयँ निरंतर बासी ॥
jadapi biraja byāpaka abināsī, saba ke hṛdayaṁ niraṁtara bāsī.
तदपि अनुज श्री सहित खरारी । बसतु मनसि मम काननचारी ॥
tadapi anuja śrī sahita kharārī, basatu manasi mama kānanacārī.
जे जानहिं ते जानहुँ स्वामी । सगुन अगुन उर अंतरजामी ॥
je jānahiṁ te jānahuṁ svāmī, saguna aguna ura aṁtarajāmī.
जो कोसल पति राजिव नयना । करउ सो राम हृदय मम अयना ॥
jo kosala pati rājiva nayanā, karau so rāma hṛdaya mama ayanā,
अस अभिमान जाइ जनि भोरे । मैं सेवक रघुपति पति मोरे ॥
asa abhimāna jāi jani bhore, maiṁ sevaka raghupati pati more.
सुनि मुनि बचन राम मन भाए । बहुरि हरषि मुनिबर उर लाए ॥
suni muni bacana rāma mana bhāe, bahuri haraṣi munibara ura lāe.
परम प्रसन्न जानु मुनि मोही । जो बर मागहु देउँ सो तोही ॥
parama prasanna jānu muni mohī, jo bara māgahu deuṁ so tohī.
मुनि कह मैं बर कबहुँ न जाचा । समुझि न परइ झूठ का साचा ॥
muni kaha maiṁ bara kabahuṁ na jācā, samujhi na parai jhūṭha kā sācā.
तुम्हहि नीक लागै रघुराई । सो मोहि देहु दास सुखदाई ॥
tumhahi nīka lāgai raghurāī, so mohi dehu dāsa sukhadāī.
अबिरल भगति बिरति बिग्याना । होहु सकल गुन ग्यान निधाना ॥
abirala bhagati birati bigyānā, hohu sakala guna gyāna nidhānā.
प्रभु जो दीन्ह सो बरु मैं पावा । अब सो देहु मोहि जो भावा ॥
prabhu jo dīnha so baru maiṁ pāvā, aba so dehu mohi jo bhāvā.

Trans:

Said the Saint, "Hearken O Lord to my supplication; but how can I hymn thy praises? Thy greatness is immeasurable and my wit is scant: as ineffectual as a firefly in the presence of the Sun. I adore without ceasing the divine Raghubīr, with body dark of hue as a string of lotuses, with his knotted hair for a crown and an anchorite's dress for his robe, with bow and arrows in hand and quiver by his side. A fire to consume the dense forest of delusion, a sun to animate the lotus growth of the saints, a lion against the elephant herd of demons, a hawk to scatter the birds of transmigrations—may he, with eyes bright as the lotus, ever protect me. Suffused with glory, the moon of Sītā's partridge-like eyes, the swan in the lake of Shiva's soul, the broad-chested, strong-armed Rāma—him I adore. A Garud to devour the serpents of doubt; the queller of violence, wrangling and pain; the conqueror of death; the delight of the company of heaven; the home of compassion, may he ever protect me. At once bodiless and embodied, like and unlike, endowed with form and also formless; transcending all thought, speech and perception; pure, all-pervading, faultless, illimitable, Rāma, the reliever of earth's burdens—him I adore. A forest of trees of Paradise for his faithful people; the dispeller of passion, avarice, pride and lust; the All-beautiful; the bridge to cross the ocean of life, the champion of the solar race—may he ever protect us. With unlimited might of arm, the home of strength; the true disperser of the manifold impurity of this iron age; the shield of righteousness; the giver of delights, the assemblage of all good qualities—may he, my Rāma, ever grant us prosperity. Though he be passionless, all-pervading, eternal, and ever dwelleth in the hearts of all; yet in his character of the wood roaming conqueror of Khar, with his brother and bride, may he abide in my thoughts. They who understand, know him to be the Lord, though embodied, the bodiless ruler of the soul, the lotus eyed sovereign of Kaushal. Do make thy abode in my heart, O Rāma. May never be this sentiment forgotten: that I am his servant and Raghupatī my Lord." Rāma was pleased at heart on hearing the saint's speech, and in his delight pressed him again to his bosom, "Know, O Saint, that I am highly gratified; ask any boon and I will grant it to you." Said the saint, "I have never begged a boon nor can I discern between true and false. Whatever seems good to you, O Raghurāī, that bestow upon me, for you are your servant's benefactor." "I give you steadfast faith, self-control, and wisdom, and make you a storehouse of all virtue and knowledge." "I have received, my lord, the boon that you have given, now grant me my own wish.

दोहा-dohā:

अनुज जानकी सहित प्रभु चाप बान धर राम ।
anuja jānakī sahita prabhu cāpa bāna dhara rāma,
मम हिय गगन इंदु इव बसहु सदा निहकाम ॥ ११ ॥
mama hiya gagana iṁdu iva basahu sadā nihakāma. 11.

Trans:

O my lord Rāma, with your brother and Jānakī, yourself equipt with bow and arrows, for ever and ever abide like the moon in the heaven of my soul."

चौपाई-caupāī:

एवमस्तु करि रमानिवासा । हरषि चले कुंभज रिषि पासा ॥
evamastu kari ramānivāsā, haraṣi cale kuṁbhaja riṣi pāsā.
बहुत दिवस गुर दरसनु पाएँ । भए मोहि एहिं आश्रम आएँ ॥
bahuta divasa gura darasanu pāeṁ, bhae mohi ehiṁ āśrama āeṁ.
अब प्रभु संग जाउँ गुर पाहीं । तुम्ह कहँ नाथ निहोरा नाहीं ॥
aba prabhu saṁga jāuṁ gura pāhīṁ, tumha kahaṁ nātha nihorā nāhīṁ.
देखि कृपानिधि मुनि चतुराई । लिए संग बिहसे द्वौ भाई ॥
dekhi kṛpānidhi muni caturāī, lie saṁga bihase dvau bhāī.
पंथ कहत निज भगति अनूपा । मुनि आश्रम पहुँचे सुरभूपा ॥
paṁtha kahata nija bhagati anūpā, muni āśrama pahuṁce surabhūpā.
तुरत सुतीछन गुर पहिं गयऊ । करि दंडवत कहत अस भयऊ ॥
turata sutīchana gura pahiṁ gayaū, kari daṁḍavata kahata asa bhayaū.
नाथ कोसलाधीस कुमारा । आए मिलन जगत आधारा ॥
nātha kosalādhīsa kumārā, āe milana jagata ādhārā.
राम अनुज समेत बैदेही । निसि दिनु देव जपत हहु जेही ॥
rāma anuja sameta baidehī, nisi dinu deva japata hahu jehī.
सुनत अगस्ति तुरत उठि धाए । हरि बिलोकि लोचन जल छाए ॥
sunata agasti turata uṭhi dhāe, hari biloki locana jala chāe.
मुनि पद कमल परे द्वौ भाई । रिषि अति प्रीति लिए उर लाई ॥
muni pada kamala pare dvau bhāī, riṣi ati prīti lie ura lāī.
सादर कुसल पूछि मुनि ग्यानी । आसन बर बैठारे आनी ॥
sādara kusala pūchi muni gyānī, āsana bara baiṭhāre ānī.
पुनि करि बहु प्रकार प्रभु पूजा । मोहि सम भाग्यवंत नहिं दूजा ॥
puni kari bahu prakāra prabhu pūjā, mohi sama bhāgyavaṁta nahiṁ dūjā.
जहँ लगि रहे अपर मुनि बृंदा । हरषे सब बिलोकि सुखकंदा ॥
jahaṁ lagi rahe apara muni bṛṁdā, haraṣe saba biloki sukhakaṁdā.

Trans:

"So be it," said Lakshmī's Lord, as he joyously started on his visit to the jar-born sage, Agastya. "It is a long time since I last saw my Gurū and since I came to live in this hermitage; now, my lord, I will go and see him with you; I am not putting you under any obligation." The Fountain of Mercy saw through the sage's cleverness and both the brothers smiled as they took him with them. Discoursing on the way on the excellence of faith in himself, the king of the gods arrived at the saint's hermitage. Sutīkshan at once went to the Gurū and after prostrating himself thus addressed him: "My lord, the two sons of the kingdom of Kaushal, the support of the world, have come to see you. Shrī Rāma—accompanied by his younger brother and Videh's Daughter—whose name you repeat night and day, venerable sir, are here." As soon as he heard this, Agastya started up and ran; and at the sight of Harī, his eyes filled with tears. The two brothers fell at the saint's holy feet, but he took and clasped them to his bosom with the utmost affection. After courteously enquiring of their welfare, the holy sage conducted them to a seat and then again did all homage to his lord, saying, "There is no other man so blessed as I am." All the other hermits assembled there were all delighted to gaze upon the fount of joy.

दोहा-dohā:

मुनि समूह महँ बैठे सन्मुख सब की ओर ।
muni samūha mahaṁ baiṭhe sanmukha saba kī ora,
सरद इंदु तन चितवत मानहुँ निकर चकोर ॥ १२ ॥
sarada iṁdu tana citavata mānahuṁ nikara cakora. 12.

Trans:

As he sat in their midst with their eyes all fastened upon his person, they seemed like a bevy of partridges gazing on the autumnal moon.

चौपाई-caupāī:

तब रघुबीर कहा मुनि पाहीं । तुम्ह सन प्रभु दुराव कछु नाहीं ॥
taba raghubīra kahā muni pāhīṁ, tumha sana prabhu durāva kachu nāhīṁ.
तुम्ह जानहु जेहि कारन आयउँ । ताते तात न कहि समुझायउँ ॥
tumha jānahu jehi kārana āyauṁ, tāte tāta na kahi samujhāyauṁ.
अब सो मंत्र देहु प्रभु मोही । जेहि प्रकार मारौं मुनिद्रोही ॥
aba so maṁtra dehu prabhu mohī, jehi prakāra mārauṁ munidrohī.
मुनि मुसुकाने सुनि प्रभु बानी । पूछेहु नाथ मोहि का जानी ॥
muni musukāne suni prabhu bānī, pūchehu nātha mohi kā jānī.
तुम्हरेइँ भजन प्रभाव अघारी । जानउँ महिमा कछुक तुम्हारी ॥
tumhareiṁ bhajana prabhāva aghārī, jānauṁ mahimā kachuka tumhārī.
ऊमरि तरु बिसाल तव माया । फल ब्रह्मांड अनेक निकाया ॥
ūmari taru bisāla tava māyā, phala brahmāṁḍa aneka nikāyā.
जीव चराचर जंतु समाना । भीतर बसहिं न जानहिं आना ॥
jīva carācara jaṁtu samānā, bhītara basahiṁ na jānahiṁ ānā.
ते फल भच्छक कठिन कराला । तव भयँ डरत सदा सोउ काला ॥
te phala bhacchaka kaṭhina karālā, tava bhayaṁ ḍarata sadā sou kālā.
ते तुम्ह सकल लोकपति साईं । पूँछिहु मोहि मनुज की नाईं ॥
te tumha sakala lokapati sāīṁ, pūṁchehu mohi manuja kī nāīṁ.
यह बर मागउँ कृपानिकेता । बसहु हृदयँ श्री अनुज समेता ॥
yaha bara māgauṁ kṛpāniketā, basahu hṛdayaṁ śrī anuja sametā.
अबिरल भगति बिरति सतसंगा । चरन सरोरुह प्रीति अभंगा ॥
abirala bhagati birati satasaṁgā, carana saroruha prīti abhaṁgā.
जद्यपि ब्रह्म अखंड अनंता । अनुभव गम्य भजहिं जेहि संता ॥
jadyapi brahma akhaṁḍa anaṁtā, anubhava gamya bhajahiṁ jehi saṁtā.
अस तव रूप बखानउँ जानउँ । फिरि फिरि सगुन ब्रह्म रति मानउँ ॥
asa tava rūpa bakhānauṁ jānauṁ, phiri phiri saguna brahma rati mānauṁ.
संतत दासन्ह देहु बड़ाई । तातें मोहि पूँछेहु रघुराई ॥
saṁtata dāsanha dehu baṛāī, tāteṁ mohi pūṁchehu raghurāī.
है प्रभु परम मनोहर ठाऊँ । पावन पंचबटी तेहि नाऊँ ॥
hai prabhu parama manohara ṭhāūṁ, pāvana paṁcabaṭī tehi nāūṁ.
दंडक बन पुनीत प्रभु करहू । उग्र साप मुनिबर कर हरहू ॥
daṁḍaka bana punīta prabhu karahū, ugra sāpa munibara kara harahū.
बास करहु तहँ रघुकुल राया । कीजे सकल मुनिन्ह पर दाया ॥
bāsa karahu tahaṁ raghukula rāyā, kīje sakala muninha para dāyā.
चले राम मुनि आयसु पाई । तुरतहिं पंचबटी निअराई ॥
cale rāma muni āyasu pāī, turatahiṁ paṁcabaṭī niarāī.

Trans:

Then said Raghubīr to the saint, "My lord, nothing is hid from you; you know why I have come, and therefore, sire, there is no need to inform you. Give me now some advice by which I may destroy the persecutors of saints." The sage smiled when he heard the Lord's speech, "You ask me, sire, but what do I know? Though by virtue of my devotion to you, O destroyer of sin, I understand a little of your greatness, your delusive power is a vast fig tree, its clustering fruit the countless multitude of worlds; and all things animate and inanimate are like the insects that dwell inside which think their own particular fig the only one in existence. This fruit is devoured by harsh and inexorable Time, but even that Time trembles in fear of you. You, sire, are the sovereign of all the spheres, and you ask of me, as though you were only a human. O fountain of mercy, I beg this boon: dwell in my heart with Lakshmī and your brother, and grant me steadfast faith, piety, fellowship with the saints, and unbroken love for your lotus feet. Though you are the supreme spirit, indivisible and eternal, beyond the reach of perception, the adoration of the saints, yet I am enamored of your qualified form, and declare and recognize your incarnation, and again and again adore you, the personification of Brahmm. You always exalt your own servants, and this, O Raghurāī, is the reason why you consult me. There is, my Lord, a very charming and holy spot called Panchvatī. Sanctify the whole Dandak forest, in which it is, and relieve it of the saint's grievous curse by taking up your abode there, O Rāma, and thus show mercy to all the saints." On receiving his permission, Rāma set out and soon arrived at Panchvatī.

दोहा-dohā:

गीधराज सैं भेंट भइ बहु बिधि प्रीति बढ़ाइ ।
gīdharāja saiṁ bheṁṭa bhai bahu bidhi prīti baṛhāi,
गोदावरी निकट प्रभु रहे परन गृह छाइ ॥ १३ ॥
godāvarī nikaṭa prabhu rahe parana gṛha chāi. 13.

Trans:

After meeting the king of the vultures and warmly renewing old friendship, Rāma stayed near the Godāvari, where he made himself a thatched cottage.

चौपाई-caupāī:

जब ते राम कीन्ह तहँ बासा । सुखी भए मुनि बीती त्रासा ॥
jaba te rāma kīnha tahaṁ bāsā, sukhī bhae muni bītī trāsā.
गिरि बन नदीं ताल छबि छाए । दिन दिन प्रति अति होहिं सुहाए ॥
giri bana nadīṁ tāla chabi chāe, dina dina prati ati hohiṁ suhāe.
खग मृग बृंद अनंदित रहहीं । मधुप मधुर गुंजत छबि लहहीं ॥
khaga mṛga bṛṁda anaṁdita rahahīṁ, madhupa madhura guṁjata chabi lahahīṁ.
सो बन बरनि न सक अहिराजा । जहाँ प्रगट रघुबीर बिराजा ॥
so bana barani na saka ahirājā, jahāṁ pragaṭa raghubīra birājā.
एक बार प्रभु सुख आसीना । लछिमन बचन कहे छलहीना ॥
eka bāra prabhu sukha āsīnā, lachimana bacana kahe chalahīnā.
सुर नर मुनि सचराचर साईं । मैं पूछउँ निज प्रभु की नाईं ॥
sura nara muni sacarācara sāiṁ, maiṁ pūchauṁ nija prabhu kī nāiṁ.
मोहि समुझाइ कहहु सोइ देवा । सब तजि करौं चरन रज सेवा ॥
mohi samujhāi kahahu soi devā, saba taji karauṁ carana raja sevā.
कहहु ग्यान बिराग अरु माया । कहहु सो भगति करहु जेहिं दाया ॥
kahahu gyāna birāga aru māyā, kahahu so bhagati karahu jehiṁ dāyā.

Trans:

From the time that Rāma took up his abode there, the saints lived happily and without fear. The mountains, woods, rivers and lakes were suffused with beauty, and day by day grew yet more exceedingly lovely. The many birds and deer were full of joy and the bees added a charm by their sweet buzzing. Not even the serpent-king would be able to describe the forest in which the glorious Rāma had manifested himself. One day, as the Lord was sitting relaxed, Lakshman most humbly addressed him thus, "O Sovereign of gods, men and saints, and of all animate and inanimate creation, I have a question to ask of you as of my own special master. Speak, sire, and answer it for me, for I have left all to serve the dust of your feet. Explain to me knowledge, self-governance, and the delusion of Māyā; tell me what is that faith, to which you extend mercy.

दोहा-dohā:

ईस्वर जीव भेद प्रभु सकल कहौ समुझाइ ।
īsvara jīva bheda prabhu sakala kahau samujhāi,
जातें होइ चरन रति सोक मोह भ्रम जाइ ॥ १४ ॥
jāteṁ hoi carana rati soka moha bhrama jāi. 14.

Trans:

Instruct me, my lord, in all the difference between Bhagwān and the Jīva, so that I may be entirely devoted to your feet and be free from grief, ignorance and error."

चौपाई-caupāī:

थोरेहि महँ सब कहउँ बुझाई । सुनहु तात मति मन चित लाई ॥
thorehi mahaṁ saba kahauṁ bujhāī, sunahu tāta mati mana cita lāī.
मैं अरु मोर तोर तैं माया । जेहिं बस कीन्हे जीव निकाया ॥
maiṁ aru mora tora taiṁ māyā, jehiṁ basa kīnhe jīva nikāyā.
गो गोचर जहँ लगि मन जाई । सो सब माया जानेहु भाई ॥
go gocara jahaṁ lagi mana jāī, so saba māyā jānehu bhāī.
तेहि कर भेद सुनहु तुम्ह सोऊ । बिद्या अपर अबिद्या दोऊ ॥
tehi kara bheda sunahu tumha soū, bidyā apara abidyā doū.
एक दुष्ट अतिसय दुखरूपा । जा बस जीव परा भवकूपा ॥
eka dusṭa atisaya dukharūpā, jā basa jīva parā bhavakūpā.
एक रचइ जग गुन बस जाकें । प्रभु प्रेरित नहिं निज बल ताकें ॥
eka racai jaga guna basa jākeṁ, prabhu prerita nahiṁ nija bala tākeṁ.
ग्यान मान जहँ एकउ नाहीं । देख ब्रह्म समान सब माहीं ॥
gyāna māna jahaṁ ekau nāhīṁ, dekha brahma samāna saba māhīṁ.
कहिअ तात सो परम बिरागी । तृन सम सिद्धि तीनि गुन त्यागी ॥
kahia tāta so parama birāgī, tṛna sama siddhi tīni guna tyāgī.

Trans:

"I will explain the whole matter in brief; hearken brother, with attention of mind and soul. It is from egoism and distinctions between mine and thine that the illusion is produced which has subjugated all classes of existence. The senses and the objects of the senses, so far as the mind can reach, are all Māyā, brother; understand that. Now learn its divisions too. They are two: Knowledge and Ignorance. Ignorance is vile and extremely painful, and has cast the ego into the sink of worldly existence. The other, Knowledge, which brings forth the creation and which holds sway over the three Gunas is directed by the Lord and has no strength of its own. Spiritual wisdom is that which is free from all blemishes in the shape of pride etc., and which sees the Supreme Spirit equally in all; and he, brother, is to be reckoned chief of stoics, who abandons all supernatural powers and the three elements of which the universe is composed, as if of no more account than a blade of grass.

दोहा-dohā:

माया ईस न आपु कहुँ जान कहिअ सो जीव ।
māyā īsa na āpu kahuṁ jāna kahia so jīva,
बंध मोच्छ प्रद सर्बपर माया प्रेरक सीव ॥ १५ ॥
baṁdha moccha prada sarbapara māyā preraka sīva. 15.

Trans:

That alone deserves to be called a Jīva, which knows not Māyā nor God nor one's own Self. And God is He who is the giver of bondage and of deliverance, who transcends all this, and is the controller of Māyā.

चौपाई-caupāī:

धर्म तें बिरति जोग तें ग्याना । ग्यान मोच्छप्रद बेद बखाना ॥
dharma teṁ birati joga teṁ gyānā, gyāna mocchaprada beda bakhānā.

जातें बेगि द्रवउँ मैं भाई । सो मम भगति भगत सुखदाई ॥
jātem̐ begi dravaum̐ maim̐ bhāī, so mama bhagati bhagata sukhadāī.
सो सुतंत्र अवलंब न आना । तेहि आधीन ग्यान बिग्याना ॥
so sutam̐tra avalam̐ba na ānā, tehi ādhīna gyāna bigyānā.
भगति तात अनुपम सुखमूला । मिलइ जो संत होइँ अनुकूला ॥
bhagati tāta anupama sukhamūlā, milai jo sam̐ta hoim̐ anukūlā.
भगति कि साधन कहउँ बखानी । सुगम पंथ मोहि पावहिं प्रानी ॥
bhagati ki sādhana kahaum̐ bakhānī, sugama pam̐tha mohi pāvahim̐ prānī.
प्रथमहिं बिप्र चरन अति प्रीती । निज निज कर्म निरत श्रुति रीती ॥
prathamahim̐ bipra carana ati prītī, nija nija karma nirata śruti rītī.
एहि कर फल पुनि बिषय बिरागा । तब मम धर्म उपज अनुरागा ॥
ehi kara phala puni biṣaya birāgā, taba mama dharma upaja anurāgā.
श्रवनादिक नव भक्ति दृढाहीं । मम लीला रति अति मन माहीं ॥
śravanādika nava bhakti dṛṛhāhīm̐, mama līlā rati ati mana māhīm̐.
संत चरन पंकज अति प्रेमा । मन क्रम बचन भजन दृढ नेमा ॥
sam̐ta carana pam̐kaja ati premā, mana krama bacana bhajana dṛṛha nemā.
गुरु पितु मातु बंधु पति देवा । सब मोहि कहँ जानै दृढ सेवा ॥
guru pitu mātu bam̐dhu pati devā, saba mohi kaham̐ jānai dṛṛha sevā.
मम गुन गावत पुलक सरीरा । गदगद गिरा नयन बह नीरा ॥
mama guna gāvata pulaka sarīrā, gadagada girā nayana baha nīrā.
काम आदि मद दंभ न जाकें । तात निरंतर बस मैं ताकें ॥
kāma ādi mada dam̐bha na jākem̐, tāta niram̐tara basa maim̐ tākem̐.

Trans:

From piety arises asceticism; and from ascetic-meditation—knowledge; and knowledge, as the Vedas declare, is the giver of salvation. But that at which I melt more quickly, O brother, is Devotion, which is the blessing of my votaries. It stands by itself without other support, and is above all knowledge whether spiritual or worldly. Devotion, brother, is an incomparable source of happiness, and only to be acquired by the favor of saints. But I will explain the means towards it, the easy path by which men may find me. In the first place, an exceeding devotion to Brahmins and in every action a close adherence to scriptural prescription. Secondly, the fruit of this will be detachment from the world, and then will spring up delight towards worship. The nine kinds of faith as exercised by the ears, etc., will become strengthened; there will be an exceeding love in the soul for my manifestations, a great affection for the lotus feet of the saints, a persistency in prayer—in deed and in heart as well as in tongue—and faithfulness in service done to one's Gurū, or parents, or family, or lords and masters: knowing it to be really done to me. When while singing the Lord's praises the body quivers, the voice trembles, the eyes flow with tears; and neither lust, pride nor deceit finds a place in the soul—then I am ever, brother, at the command of such ones as those.

दोहा-dohā:

बचन कर्म मन मोरि गति भजनु करहिं निःकाम ।
bacana karma mana mori gati bhajanu karahim̐ niḥkāma,
तिन्ह के हृदय कमल महुँ करउँ सदा बिश्राम ॥१६॥
tinha ke hṛdaya kamala mahum̐ karaum̐ sadā biśrāma. 16.

Trans:

I take up my abode forever in the lotus heart of those who—in thought, word and deed—make their fervent prayer to my incarnation."

चौपाई-caupāī:

भगति जोग सुनि अति सुख पावा । लछिमन प्रभु चरनन्हि सिरु नावा ॥
bhagati joga suni ati sukha pāvā, lachimana prabhu carananhi siru nāvā.
एहि बिधि गए कछुक दिन बीती । कहत बिराग ग्यान गुन नीती ॥
ehi bidhi gae kachuka dina bītī, kahata birāga gyāna guna nītī.
सूपनखा रावन कै बहिनी । दुष्ट हृदय दारुन जस अहिनी ॥
sūpanakhā rāvana kai bahinī, duṣṭa hṛdaya dāruna jasa ahinī.
पंचबटी सो गइ एक बारा । देखि बिकल भइ जुगल कुमारा ॥
pam̐cabaṭī so gai eka bārā, dekhi bikala bhai jugala kumārā.
भ्राता पिता पुत्र उरगारी । पुरुष मनोहर निरखत नारी ॥
bhrātā pitā putra uragārī, puruṣa manohara nirakhata nārī.
होइ बिकल सक मनहि न रोकी । जिमि रबिमनि द्रव रबिहि बिलोकी ॥
hoi bikala saka manahi na rokī, jimi rabimani drava rabihi bilokī.
रुचिर रुप धरि प्रभु पहिं जाई । बोली बचन बहुत मुसुकाई ॥
rucira rupa dhari prabhu pahim̐ jāī, bolī bacana bahuta musukāī.
तुम्ह सम पुरुष न मो सम नारी । यह सँजोग बिधि रचा बिचारी ॥
tumha sama puruṣa na mo sama nārī, yaha sam̐joga bidhi racā bicārī.
मम अनुरूप पुरुष जग माहीं । देखेउँ खोजि लोक तिहु नाहीं ॥
mama anurūpa puruṣa jaga māhīm̐, dekheum̐ khoji loka tihu nāhīm̐.
तातें अब लगि रहिउँ कुमारी । मनु माना कछु तुम्हहि निहारी ॥
tātem̐ aba lagi rahium̐ kumārī, manu mānā kachu tumhahi nihārī.
सीतहि चितइ कही प्रभु बाता । अहइ कुआर मोर लघु भ्राता ॥
sītahi citai kahī prabhu bātā, ahai kuāra mora laghu bhrātā.
गइ लछिमन रिपु भगिनी जानी । प्रभु बिलोकि बोले मृदु बानी ॥
gai lachimana ripu bhaginī jānī, prabhu biloki bole mṛdu bānī.
सुंदरि सुनु मैं उन्ह कर दासा । पराधीन नहिं तोर सुपासा ॥
sum̐dari sunu maim̐ unha kara dāsā, parādhīna nahim̐ tora supāsā.
प्रभु समर्थ कोसलपुर राजा । जो कछु करहिं उनहि सब छाजा ॥
prabhu samartha kosalapura rājā, jo kachu karahim̐ unahi saba chājā.
सेवक सुख चह मान भिखारी । ब्यसनी धन सुभ गति बिभिचारी ॥
sevaka sukha caha māna bhikhārī, byasanī dhana subha gati bibhicārī.
लोभी जसु चह चार गुमानी । नभ दुहि दूध चहत ए प्रानी ॥
lobhī jasu caha cāra gumānī, nabha duhi dūdha cahata e prānī.
पुनि फिरि राम निकट सो आई । प्रभु लछिमन पहिं बहुरि पठाई ॥
puni phiri rāma nikaṭa so āī, prabhu lachimana pahim̐ bahuri paṭhāī.
लछिमन कहा तोहि सो बरई । जो तृन तोरि लाज परिहरई ॥
lachimana kahā tohi so baraī, jo tṛna tori lāja pariharaī.
तब खिसिआनि राम पहिं गई । रूप भयंकर प्रगटत भई ॥
taba khisiāni rāma pahim̐ gaī, rūpa bhayam̐kara pragaṭata bhaī.
सीतहि सभय देखि रघुराई । कहा अनुज सन सयन बुझाई ॥
sītahi sabhaya dekhi raghurāī, kahā anuja sana sayana bujhāī.

Trans:

On hearing the doctrine of faith and devotion thus expounded, Lakshman greatly rejoiced and bowed his head at his Lord's feet. In this manner several days were spent in discourses on asceticism, wisdom, virtue and morality. One day Rāvan's sister Surpa-nakhā, foul-hearted and venomous as a serpent, came to Panchvatī and was excited by the sight of the two princes. Wanton woman, O Garud, is wont to delightedly admire every man who is handsome—even though he be brother, father or son. But she in her excitement could not contain herself, like the sun-stone that melts at the sight of the sun. Having assumed a beautiful form, she went to the Lord and with many smiles thus addressed him, "There is no other man like you, nor a woman like me; ours is a match that gods have taken some pains to make. I have searched the three spheres, but have not found anywhere in the world a man worthy of me. And for this reason I have till now remained a virgin; but now that I have seen you I am fairly satisfied." The Lord looked towards Sītā and declined saying, "My younger brother sits there single." The demon's sister took the hint and went to Lakshman. He looked to his Lord and said in gentle tones, "Hearken, fair lady, I am his servant, and so therefore you too would remain in subjection—which will not be right. By contrast, my Lord is the mighty master of Kaushal, and whatever he does is all done at his own pleasure. A servant who expects to take it easy, a beggar who expects honor, a spendthrift who hopes for wealth, a profligate who hopes for heaven, or an avaricious man who expects renown, these are four dreamers, men who would expect milk from milking the air." Again she turned and came to Rāma, but he sent her back once more to Lakshman. Said Lakshman, "The bridegroom for you must be a man lost to all sense of shame." Then in a fury she went to Rāma, revealing herself in a shape of terror. Raghurāī, seeing that Sītā was frightened, made a sign to his brother;

दोहा-dohā:

लछिमन अति लाघवँ सो नाक कान बिनु कीन्हि ।
lachimana ati lāghavaṁ so nāka kāna binu kīnhi,
ताके कर रावन कहँ मनौ चुनौती दीन्हि ॥ १७॥
tāke kara rāvana kahaṁ manau cunautī dīnhi. 17.

Trans:

and Lakshman with the greatest of ease struck off her nose and ears; thereby inviting Rāvan, through her, to a contest as it were.

चौपाई-caupāī:

नाक कान बिनु भइ बिकरारा । जनु स्रव सैल गेरु कै धारा ॥
nāka kāna binu bhai bikarārā, janu srava saila geru kai dhārā.
खर दूषन पहिं गइ बिलपाता । धिग धिग तव पौरुष बल भ्राता ॥
khara dūṣana pahiṁ gai bilapātā, dhiga dhiga tava pauruṣa bala bhrātā.
तेहिं पूछा सब कहेसि बुझाई । जातुधान सुनि सेन बनाई ॥
tehiṁ pūchā saba kahesi bujhāī, jātudhāna suni sena banāī.
धाए निसिचर निकर बरूथा । जनु सपच्छ कज्जल गिरि जूथा ॥
dhāe nisicara nikara barūthā, janu sapaccha kajjala giri jūthā.
नाना बाहन नानाकारा । नानायुध धर घोर अपारा ॥
nānā bāhana nānākārā, nānāyudha dhara ghora apārā.
सुपनखा आगें करि लीनी । असुभ रूप श्रुति नासा हीनी ॥
supanakhā āgeṁ kari līnī, asubha rūpa śruti nāsā hīnī.
असगुन अमित होहिं भयकारी । गनहिं न मृत्यु बिबस सब झारी ॥
asaguna amita hohiṁ bhayakārī, ganahiṁ na mṛtyu bibasa saba jhārī.
गर्जहिं तर्जहिं गगन उड़ाहीं । देखि कटकु भट अति हरषाहीं ॥
garjahiṁ tarjahiṁ gagana uṛāhīṁ, dekhi kaṭaku bhaṭa ati haraṣāhīṁ.
कोउ कह जिअत धरहु द्वौ भाई । धरि मारहु तिय लेहु छड़ाई ॥
kou kaha jiata dharahu dvau bhāī, dhari mārahu tiya lehu chaṛāī.
धूरि पूरि नभ मंडल रहा । राम बोलाइ अनुज सन कहा ॥
dhūri pūri nabha maṁḍala rahā, rāma bolāi anuja sana kahā.
लै जानकिहि जाहु गिरि कंदर । आवा निसिचर कटकु भयंकर ॥
lai jānakihi jāhu giri kaṁdara, āvā nisicara kaṭaku bhayaṁkara.
रहेहु सजग सुनि प्रभु कै बानी । चले सहित श्री सर धनु पानी ॥
rahehu sajaga suni prabhu kai bānī, cale sahita śrī sara dhanu pānī.
देखि राम रिपुदल चलि आवा । बिहसि कठिन कोदंड चढ़ावा ॥
dekhi rāma ripudala cali āvā, bihasi kaṭhina kodaṁḍa caṛhāvā.

Trans:

Without nose and ears she was as hideous to look upon as a mountain flowing with torrents of red ochre. She went moaning to Khar and Dūshan; "A curse, a curse, I say, on your manhood and strength, O brothers." They questioned her and she told them all. When they had heard, the demons gathered an army and a swarming multitude of fiends rushed forth like so many winged mountains of darkness, on diverse vehicles, of diverse shapes, armed with various weapons, terrible and beyond number. At the head went Surpa-nakhā in hideous guise, without ears and nose. Many fearful omens of ill occurred, but the host heeded them not, being all death-doomed. They shouted, they dared, and they leaped in the air, their captains inspected the ranks and rejoiced exceedingly. Said one, "Take the two brothers alive and then bind and kill them and carry off the bride." The vault of heaven was filled with the dust of them. Rāma called his brother and said, "Take Jānakī away to a mountain-cave; a terrible array of demons has come; remain on your guard." Obedient to his Lord's command he took his bow and arrows in hand and led Sītā away. When Rāma saw that the hostile force had drawn near, he smiled as he strung his massive bow.

छंद-chaṁda:

कोदंड कठिन चढ़ाइ सिर जट जूट बाँधत सोह क्यों ।
kodaṁḍa kaṭhina caṛhāi sira jaṭa jūṭa bāṁdhata soha kyoṁ,
मरकत सयल पर लरत दामिनि कोटि सों जुग भुजग ज्यों ॥
marakata sayala para larata dāmini koṭi soṁ juga bhujaga jyoṁ.
कटि कसि निषंग बिसाल भुज गहि चाप बिसिख सुधारि कै ।
kaṭi kasi niṣaṁga bisāla bhuja gahi cāpa bisikha sudhāri kai,
चितवत मनहुँ मृगराज प्रभु गजराज घटा निहारि कै ॥
citavata manahuṁ mṛgarāja prabhu gajarāja ghaṭā nihāri kai.

Trans:

As he strung his massive bow and bound up his long hair in a knot on his head, he seemed as it were a sapphire rock encircled with flashes of lightning and with two snakes entwining its summit. As the Lord girded up his quiver by his side and clasped the bow in his mighty arm and fitted the arrow to the string, he looked as if with the glance of a lion on a herd of elephants.

सोरठा-soraṭhā:

आइ गए बगमेल धरहु धरहु धावत सुभट ।
āi gae bagamela dharahu dharahu dhāvata subhaṭa,
जथा बिलोकि अकेल बाल रबिहि घेरत दनुज ॥ १८॥
jathā biloki akela bāla rabihi gherata danuja. 18.

Trans:

The warriors came on with a rush, shouting 'seize him, seize him,' for they saw that he was alone. The demons closed round upon him, but he stood as the rising sun.

चौपाई-caupāī:

प्रभु बिलोकि सर सकहिं न डारी । थकित भई रजनीचर धारी ॥
prabhu biloki sara sakahiṁ na ḍārī, thakita bhaī rajanīcara dhārī.
सचिव बोलि बोले खर दूषन । यह कोउ नृपबालक नर भूषन ॥
saciva boli bole khara dūṣana, yaha kou nṛpabālaka nara bhūṣana.
नाग असुर सुर नर मुनि जेते । देखे जिते हते हम केते ॥
nāga asura sura nara muni jete, dekhe jite hate hama kete.
हम भरि जन्म सुनहु सब भाई । देखी नहिं असि सुंदरताई ॥
hama bhari janma sunahu saba bhāī, dekhī nahiṁ asi suṁdaratāī.
जद्यपि भगिनी कीन्हि कुरूपा । बध लायक नहिं पुरुष अनूपा ॥
jadyapi bhaginī kīnhi kurūpā, badha lāyaka nahiṁ puruṣa anūpā.
देहु तुरत निज नारि दुराई । जीअत भवन जाहु द्वौ भाई ॥
dehu turata nija nāri durāī, jīata bhavana jāhu dvau bhāī.

मोर कहा तुम्ह ताहि सुनावहु । तासु बचन सुनि आतुर आवहु ॥
mora kahā tumha tāhi sunāvahu, tāsu bacana suni ātura āvahu.
दूतन्ह कहा राम सन जाई । सुनत राम बोले मुसुकाई ॥
dūtanha kahā rāma sana jāī, sunata rāma bole musukāī.
हम छत्री मृगया बन करहीं । तुम्ह से खल मृग खोजत फिरहीं ॥
hama chatrī mṛgayā bana karahīṁ, tumha se khala mṛga khojata phirahīṁ.
रिपु बलवंत देखि नहिं डरहीं । एक बार कालहु सन लरहीं ॥
ripu balavaṁta dekhi nahiṁ ḍarahīṁ, eka bāra kālahu sana larahīṁ.
जद्यपि मनुज दनुज कुल घालक । मुनि पालक खल सालक बालक ॥
jadyapi manuja danuja kula ghālaka, muni pālaka khala sālaka bālaka.
जौं न होइ बल घर फिरि जाहू । समर बिमुख मैं हतउँ न काहू ॥
jauṁ na hoi bala ghara phiri jāhū, samara bimukha maiṁ hatauṁ na kāhū.
रन चढ़ि करिअ कपट चतुराई । रिपु पर कृपा परम कदराई ॥
rana caṛhi karia kapaṭa caturāī, ripu para kṛpā parama kadarāī.
दूतन्ह जाइ तुरत सब कहेऊ । सुनि खर दूषन उर अति दहेऊ ॥
dūtanha jāi turata saba kaheū, suni khara dūṣana ura ati daheū.

Trans:

And at the sight of his majesty they could not discharge their arrows; the whole demon host became powerless. Khar and Dūshan summoned their ministers and said, "These king's sons are verily the ornament of human race. *Nagas*, demons, gods, men and saints of all sorts I have seen, conquered and slain; but in the whole of my life—mark me, my brethren all—I have never seen such beauty. Though he has disfigured my sister, so incomparable a hero is not worthy of death. 'At once put away and surrender your bride and return home alive, you and your brother', declare to him this that I have said and quickly come back with his answer." The heralds went and told Rāma. He smiled to hear them and said, "I am a warrior by caste and am hunting in these woods. Wretches like you are the game that I am tracking. I am not dismayed at the sight of the enemy's strength, but am ready to do combat with Death himself. Though a human, I am the exterminator of the race of demons; and though youthful in appearance, I am the protector of the saints and the destroyer of the wicked. If there is no strength in you, turn and go home; I will never kill an enemy who has turned his back upon the field of battle. If you have come up to fight, show now your might and dexterity; mercy to an enemy is the height of weakness." The heralds immediately went and repeated this all. Khar and Dūshan's heart was on fire when they heard it.

छंद-chaṁda:

उर दहेउ कहेउ कि धरहु धाए बिकट भट रजनीचरा ।
ura daheu kaheu ki dharahu dhāe bikaṭa bhaṭa rajanīcarā,
सर चाप तोमर सक्ति सूल कृपान परिघ परसु धरा ॥
sara cāpa tomara sakti sūla kṛpāna parigha parasu dharā.
प्रभु कीन्हि धनुष टकोर प्रथम कठोर घोर भयावहा ।
prabhu kīnhi dhanuṣa ṭakora prathama kaṭhora ghora bhayāvahā,
भए बधिर ब्याकुल जातुधान न ग्यान तेहि अवसर रहा ॥
bhae badhira byākula jātudhāna na gyāna tehi avasara rahā.

Trans:

Their heart on fire, they cried, "Rush upon him and seize him, ye mighty demon warriors; go fight with your bows and arrows, clubs, pikes, spears, scimitars, maces and axes." The Lord gave his bow one twang; in a moment at the awful and terrible sound the demons were deafened and dismayed; they had no sense left in them.

दोहा-dohā:

सावधान होइ धाए जानि सबल आराति ।
sāvadhāna hoi dhāe jāni sabala ārāti,
लागे बरषन राम पर अस्त्र सस्त्र बहुभाँति ॥ १९क ॥
lāge baraṣana rāma para astra sastra bahubhāṁti. 19(ka).
तिन्ह के आयुध तिल सम करि काटे रघुबीर ।
tinha ke āyudha tila sama kari kāṭe raghubīra,
तानि सरासन श्रवन लगि पुनि छाँड़े निज तीर ॥ १९ख ॥
tāni sarāsana śravana lagi puni chāṁṛe nija tīra. 19(kha).

Trans:

When they had recovered themselves they made a rush, for they knew the strength of their foe; and shafts and weapons of all kinds began to rain upon Rāma. But Raghubīr cleft them in twain making them of no more account than so many sesame seeds; and then drawing the bowstring to his ear he let fly his own arrows.

छंद-chaṁda:

तब चले बान कराल । फुंकरत जनु बहु ब्याल ॥
taba cale bāna karāla, phuṁkarata janu bahu byāla.
कोपेउ समर श्रीराम । चले बिसिख निसित निकाम ॥
kopeu samara śrīrāma, cale bisikha nisita nikāma.
अवलोकि खर तर तीर । मुरि चले निसिचर बीर ॥
avaloki khara tara tīra, muri cale nisicara bīra.
भए क्रुद्ध तीनिउ भाइ । जो भागि रन ते जाइ ॥
bhae kruddha tīniu bhāi, jo bhāgi rana te jāi.
तेहि बधब हम निज पानि । फिरे मरन मन महुँ ठानि ॥
tehi badhaba hama nija pāni, phire marana mana mahuṁ ṭhāni.
आयुध अनेक प्रकार । सनमुख ते करहिं प्रहार ॥
āyudha aneka prakāra, sanamukha te karahiṁ prahāra.
रिपु परम कोपे जानि । प्रभु धनुष सर संधानि ॥
ripu parama kope jāni, prabhu dhanuṣa sara saṁdhāni.
छाँड़े बिपुल नाराच । लगे कटन बिकट पिसाच ॥
chāṁṛe bipula nārāca, lage kaṭana bikaṭa pisāca.
उर सीस भुज कर चरन । जहँ तहँ लगे महि परन ॥
ura sīsa bhuja kara carana, jahaṁ tahaṁ lage mahi parana.
चिक्करत लागत बान । धर परत कुधर समान ॥
cikkarata lāgata bāna, dhara parata kudhara samāna.
भट कटत तन सत खंड । पुनि उठत करि पाषंड ॥
bhaṭa kaṭata tana sata khaṁḍa, puni uṭhata kari pāṣaṁḍa.
नभ उड़त बहु भुज मुंड । बिनु मौलि धावत रुंड ॥
nabha uṛata bahu bhuja muṁḍa, binu mauli dhāvata ruṁḍa.
खग कंक काक सृगाल । कटकटहिं कठिन कराल ॥
khaga kaṁka kāka sṛgāla, kaṭakaṭahiṁ kaṭhina karāla.

Trans:

Then the terrible arrows sped forth, hissing like so many serpents. The holy Rāma waxed wrath in battle; his arrows flew with exceeding sharpness. When they saw his shafts so keen, the demon turned to flee, but the demon brothers became furious, "Whoever runs from the field we will slay with our own hands; let him stay then and make up his mind to die." Weapons of diverse kinds beat upon him from the front, and the Lord perceiving that the foe was exceedingly furious fitted an arrow to his bow. He let fly the huge bolts; the hideous demons were cut to pieces; bodies, heads, arms, hands and feet were scattered about all over the ground. Pierced by shafts, they yelled and their trunks fell like mountains. The leaders had their bodies cut into a hundred pieces, yet they stood up again by the power of magic. Many arms and heads flew through the air and headless trunks ran to and fro. Kites, crows and jackals made an awful and horrible brawling.

छंद-*chaṁda:*

कटकटहिं जंबुक भूत प्रेत पिसाच खर्पर संचहीं ।
kaṭakaṭahiṁ zaṁbuka bhūta preta pisāca kharpara saṁcahīṁ,
बेताल बीर कपाल ताल बजाइ जोगिनि नंचहीं ॥
betāla bīra kapāla tāla bajāi jogini naṁcahīṁ.
रघुबीर बान प्रचंड खंडहिं भटन्ह के उर भुज सिरा ।
raghubīra bāna pracaṁḍa khaṁḍahiṁ bhaṭanha ke ura bhuja sirā,
जहँ तहँ परहिं उठि लरहिं धर धरु धरु करहिं भयकर गिरा ॥
jahaṁ tahaṁ parahiṁ uṭhi larahiṁ dhara dharu dharu karahiṁ bhayakara girā.
अंतावरीं गहि उड़त गीध पिसाच कर गहि धावहीं ।
aṁtāvarīṁ gahi uṛata gīdha pisāca kara gahi dhāvahīṁ.
संग्राम पुर बासी मनहुँ बहु बाल गुडी उड़ावहीं ॥
saṁgrāma pura bāsī manahuṁ bahu bāla guṛī uṛāvahīṁ.
मारे पछारे उर बिदारे बिपुल भट कहँरत परे ।
māre pachāre ura bidāre bipula bhaṭa kahaṁrata pare,
अवलोकि निज दल बिकल भट तिसिरादि खर दूषन फिरे ॥
avaloki nija dala bikala bhaṭa tisirādi khara dūṣana phire.
सर सक्ति तोमर परसु सूल कृपान एकहि बारहीं ।
sara sakti tomara parasu sūla kṛpāna ekahi bārahīṁ,
करि कोप श्रीरघुबीर पर अगनित निसाचर डारहीं ॥
kari kopa śrīraghubīra para aganita nisācara ḍārahīṁ.
प्रभु निमिष महुँ रिपु सर निवारि पचारि डारे सायका ।
prabhu nimiṣa mahuṁ ripu sara nivāri pacāri ḍāre sāyakā,
दस दस बिसिख उर माझ मारे सकल निसिचर नायका ॥
dasa dasa bisikha ura mājha māre sakala nisicara nāyakā.
महि परत उठि भट भिरत मरत न करत माया अति घनी ।
mahi parata uṭhi bhaṭa bhirata marata na karata māyā ati ghanī,
सुर डरत चौदह सहस प्रेत बिलोकि एक अवध धनी ॥
sura ḍarata caudaha sahasa preta biloki eka avadha dhanī.
सुर मुनि सभय प्रभु देखि मायानाथ अति कौतुक करयो ।
sura muni sabhaya prabhu dekhi māyānātha ati kautuka karayo,
देखहिं परसपर राम करि संग्राम रिपुदल लरि मरयो ॥
dekhahiṁ parasapara rāma kari saṁgrāma ripudala lari marayo.

Trans:

Jackals wrangled; ghosts, goblins and demons made caps of the skulls; more warlike devils clasped skulls together for music, and witches danced. Raghubīr's mighty arrows smote off the leaders' bodies, arms and heads; they fell on every side, but stood up again to fight with terrible cries of 'strike, strike'. Vultures flew away with men's entrails in their claws, goblins scampered off with hands that they had seized; one might fancy countless children in the town of the battle-field were flying kites. The mighty champions lay dead and vanquished, with mangled bodies. Seeing their army routed, Khar and Dūshan, with Trisirā and the other champions, stood at bay, and all at once demons innumerable furiously hurled arrows and spears, clubs, axes, javelins, and daggers against Raghubīr. In the twinkling of an eye the Lord had warded off all his enemies' missiles and sent forth his own arrows, slaying all the demon leaders with ten shafts planted in the chest of each of them. Though they fell to the ground, they rose again in their valor and joined in the fray, and would not die, and that made the strangest sight. The gods feared, when they saw the demons fourteen thousand in number, and the king of Avadh alone; till the Lord, perceiving the alarm of gods and saints, and having power over all illusion, wrought a prodigy, and while they were yet looking at one another he finished the battle, and the army of the enemy all perished in the fight.

दोहा-*dohā:*

राम राम कहि तनु तजहिं पावहिं पद निर्बान ।
rāma rāma kahi tanu tajahiṁ pāvahiṁ pada nirbāna,
करि उपाय रिपु मारे छन महुँ कृपानिधान ॥ २०क॥
kari upāya ripu māre chana mahuṁ kṛpānidhāna. 20(ka).
हरषित बरषहिं सुमन सुर बाजहिं गगन निसान ।
haraṣita baraṣahiṁ sumana sura bājahiṁ gagana nisāna,
अस्तुति करि करि सब चले सोभित बिबिध बिमान ॥ २०ख॥
astuti kari kari saba cale sobhita bibidha bimāna. 20(kha).

Trans:

Crying 'Rāma, Rāma', their soul left their body; they thus attained beatitude. In a moment the fountain of mercy slew all his enemies by some device. The gods in their joy rained down flowers, instruments of music sounded in the air, and with cries of 'Glory, glory', they all departed, each in his own splendid carriage.

चौपाई-*caupāī:*

जब रघुनाथ समर रिपु जीते । सुर नर मुनि सब के भय बीते ॥
jaba raghunātha samara ripu jīte, sura nara muni saba ke bhaya bīte.
तब लछिमन सीतहि लै आए । प्रभु पद परत हरषि उर लाए ॥
taba lachimana sītahi lai āe, prabhu pada parata haraṣi ura lāe,
सीता चितव स्याम मृदु गाता । परम प्रेम लोचन न अघाता ॥
sītā citava syāma mṛdu gātā, parama prema locana na aghātā.
पंचवटीं बसि श्रीरघुनायक । करत चरित सुर मुनि सुखदायक ॥
paṁcavaṭīṁ basi śrīraghunāyaka, karata carita sura muni sukhadāyaka.
धुआँ देखि खरदूषन केरा । जाइ सुपनखाँ रावन प्रेरा ॥
dhuāṁ dekhi kharadūṣana kerā, jāi supanakhāṁ rāvana prerā.
बोली बचन क्रोध करि भारी । देस कोस कै सुरति बिसारी ॥
bolī bacana krodha kari bhārī, desa kosa kai surati bisārī.
करसि पान सोवसि दिनु राती । सुधि नहिं तव सिर पर आराती ॥
karasi pāna sovasi dinu rātī, sudhi nahiṁ tava sira para ārātī.
राज नीति बिनु धन बिनु धर्मा । हरिहि समर्पे बिनु सतकर्मा ॥
rāja nīti binu dhana binu dharmā, harihi samarpe binu satakarmā.
बिद्या बिनु बिबेक उपजाएँ । श्रम फल पढ़े किएँ अरु पाएँ ॥
bidyā binu bibeka upajāeṁ, śrama phala paṛhe kieṁ aru pāeṁ.
संग ते जती कुमंत्र ते राजा । मान ते ग्यान पान तें लाजा ॥
saṁga te jatī kumaṁtra te rājā, māna te gyāna pāna teṁ lājā.
प्रीति प्रनय बिनु मद ते गुनी । नासहिं बेगि नीति अस सुनी ॥
prīti pranaya binu mada te gunī, nāsahiṁ begi nīti asa sunī.

Trans:

When Raghunāth had vanquished his foes in the battle, gods, men, saints were relieved from fear. Lakshman then brought Sītā back. As she fell at her Lord's feet, he took and rapturously clasped her to his bosom, and she fixed her gaze upon his dark and delicate form, but so vehement was her love that her eyes could not be satisfied. Thus the blessed Rāma stayed at Panchvatī, delighting gods and saints by his enactments. But Surpa-nakhā, when she saw the defeat of Khar and Dūshan, went and called Rāvan. In tones full of fury she cried, "You have lost all thought of your kingdom and treasure; you drink and sleep day and night, and do not consider that the enemy is at your door. A kingdom without policy, wealth without religion, consecration to Harī without good works, knowledge without discretion—these all bring no fruit save trouble to the possessor, the doer, the student. An ascetic is quickly undone by attachment, a king by ill-counsel, wisdom by conceit, modesty by drinking, friendship by want of consideration, and good sense by pride: so goes the saying.

सोरठा-sorathā:

रिपु रुज पावक पाप प्रभु अहि गनिअ न छोट करि ।

ripu ruja pāvaka pāpa prabhu ahi gania na choṭa kari,

अस कहि बिबिध बिलाप करि लागी रोदन करन ॥२१क॥

asa kahi bibidha bilāpa kari lāgī rodana karana. 21(ka).

Trans:

An enemy, sickness, fire, sin, a master, and a serpent are never to be accounted as trifles." Saying so with many lamentation, she set to weeping.

दोहा-dohā:

सभा माझ परि ब्याकुल बहु प्रकार कह रोइ ।

sabhā mājha pari byākula bahu prakāra kaha roi,

तोहि जिअत दसकंधर मोरि कि असि गति होइ ॥२१ख॥

tohi jiata dasakaṁdhara mori ki asi gati hoi. 21(kha).

Trans:

In her distress she threw herself down in the midst of the assembly with much tears and cries, "O Rāvan, to think that you should live and see me thus treated!"

चौपाई-caupāī:

सुनत सभासद उठे अकुलाई । समुझाई गहि बाँह उठाई ॥

sunata sabhāsada uṭhe akulāī, samujhāī gahi bām̐ha uṭhāī.

कह लंकेस कहसि निज बाता । केइँ तव नासा कान निपाता ॥

kaha laṁkesa kahasi nija bātā, keim̐ tava nāsā kāna nipātā.

अवध नृपति दसरथ के जाए । पुरुष सिंघ बन खेलन आए ॥

avadha nṛpati dasaratha ke jāe, puruṣa siṁgha bana khelana āe.

समुझि परी मोहि उन्ह कै करनी । रहित निसाचर करिहहिं धरनी ॥

samujhi parī mohi unha kai karanī, rahita nisācara karihahiṁ dharanī.

जिन्ह कर भुजबल पाइ दसानन । अभय भए बिचरत मुनि कानन ॥

jinha kara bhujabala pāi dasānana, abhaya bhae bicarata muni kānana.

देखत बालक काल समाना । परम धीर धन्वी गुन नाना ॥

dekhata bālaka kāla samānā, parama dhīra dhanvī guna nānā.

अतुलित बल प्रताप द्वौ भ्राता । खल बध रत सुर मुनि सुखदाता ॥

atulita bala pratāpa dvau bhrātā, khala badha rata sura muni sukhadātā.

सोभा धाम राम अस नामा । तिन्ह के संग नारि एक स्यामा ॥

sobhā dhāma rāma asa nāmā, tinha ke saṁga nāri eka syāmā.

रुप रासि बिधि नारि सँवारी । रति सत कोटि तासु बलिहारी ॥

rupa rāsi bidhi nāri sam̐vārī, rati sata koṭi tāsu balihārī.

तासु अनुज काटे श्रुति नासा । सुनि तव भगिनि करहिं परिहासा ॥

tāsu anuja kāṭe śruti nāsā, suni tava bhagini karahiṁ parihāsā.

खर दूषन सुनि लगे पुकारा । छन महुँ सकल कटक उन्ह मारा ॥

khara dūṣana suni lage pukārā, chana mahum̐ sakala kaṭaka unha mārā.

खर दूषन तिसिरा कर घाता । सुनि दससीस जरे सब गाता ॥

khara dūṣana tisirā kara ghātā, suni dasasīsa jare saba gātā.

Trans:

When they heard this, the assembly rose in confusion; they took her by the hand and lifting her up, consoled her. Said the king of Lankā, "Why do you not tell me what has happened? Who has cut off your nose and ears?" "Sons of Dashrath, the Lords of Avadh, the very lions amongst men, have come to hunt in the forest. I understood what they were about—to rid the earth of us demons. Relying on the might of their arm, O Rāvan, the saints now roam the woods without any fear. These are very young to look at, but in fact are irresistible—like Death himself; for they are most formidable archers, accomplished in many ways. Both brothers are glorious with incomparable might and have vowed themselves to the extermination of the wicked and the relief of gods and saints. Rāma—for such is his name—is the very perfection of beauty, and with him is a beautiful complexioned girl, whom the Creator has made the loveliest of the sex: a hundred million *Ratīs* would be no match for her. It is his younger brother, who cut off my ears and nose and made a mock of me, when he heard I was your sister. When Khar and Dūshan were told of this, they gave him challenge; but in an instant their whole of army was slain." When he heard of the defeat of Khar, Dūshan, and Trisirā, the Ten-headed was on fire all over.

दोहा-dohā:

सुपनखहि समुझाइ करि बल बोलेसि बहु भाँति ।

supanakhahi samujhāi kari bala bolesi bahu bhām̐ti,

गयउ भवन अति सोचबस नीद परइ नहिं राति ॥२२॥

gayau bhavana ati socabasa nīda parai nahiṁ rāti. 22.

Trans:

After consoling Surpa-nakhā and boasting of his strength, he went to his palace; but in a great state of anxiety he could not sleep that night.

चौपाई-caupāī:

सुर नर असुर नाग खग माहीं । मोरे अनुचर कहँ कोउ नाहीं ॥

sura nara asura nāga khaga māhīṁ, more anucara kaham̐ kou nāhīṁ.

खर दूषन मोहि सम बलवंता । तिन्हहि को मारइ बिनु भगवंता ॥

khara dūṣana mohi sama balavaṁtā, tinhahi ko mārai binu bhagavaṁtā.

सुर रंजन भंजन महि भारा । जौं भगवंत लीन्ह अवतारा ॥

sura raṁjana bhaṁjana mahi bhārā, jauṁ bhagavaṁta līnha avatārā.

तौ मैं जाइ बैरु हठि करऊँ । प्रभु सर प्रान तजें भव तरऊँ ॥

tau maiṁ jāi bairu haṭhi karaūm̐, prabhu sara prāna tajeṁ bhava taraūm̐.

होइहि भजनु न तामस देहा । मन क्रम बचन मंत्र दृढ एहा ॥

hoihi bhajanu na tāmasa dehā, mana krama bacana maṁtra dṛṛha ehā.

जौं नररुप भूपसुत कोऊ । हरिहउँ नारि जीति रन दोऊ ॥

jauṁ nararupa bhūpasuta koū, harihaum̐ nāri jīti rana doū.

चला अकेल जान चढि तहवाँ । बस मारीच सिंधु तट जहवाँ ॥

calā akela jāna caḍhi tahavām̐, basa mārīca siṁdhu taṭa jahavām̐.

इहाँ राम जसि जुगुति बनाई । सुनहु उमा सो कथा सुहाई ॥

ihām̐ rāma jasi juguti banāī, sunahu umā so kathā suhāī.

Trans:

"Among gods, men and demons, serpents and birds, there is none who can withstand my servants. Khar and Dūshan were my own equals in strength; now who could have killed them, unless it be God himself? If God has become incarnate in order to rejoice the saints and relieve the earth of its burden, then if I go and fight against him and lose my life by an arrow of the Lord's, I shall escape further transmigration. Prayer will not do for one like me of demonic form; and so this is the plan upon which I am absolutely determined. If he is only some earthly king's son, I shall conquer them both in battle and carry off the bride." He mounted his chariot and went off alone to the spot where Mārich was living by the seashore. Hearken now, Umā, to the delectable account of a device that Rāma invented.

दोहा-dohā:

लछिमन गए बनहिं जब लेन मूल फल कंद ।
lachimana gae banahiṁ jaba lena mūla phala kaṁda,
जनकसुता सन बोले बिहसि कृपा सुख बृंद ॥२३॥
janakasutā sana bole bihasi kṛpā sukha bṛṁda. 23.

Trans:

When Lakshman had gone into the wood to gather roots, fruits and herbs, the gentle and joyous God said with a smile to Janak's daughter,

चौपाई-caupāī:

सुनहु प्रिया ब्रत रुचिर सुसीला । मैं कछु करबि ललित नरलीला ॥
sunahu priyā brata rucira susīlā, maiṁ kachu karabi lalita naralīlā.
तुम्ह पावक महुँ करहु निवासा । जौ लगि करौं निसाचर नासा ॥
tumha pāvaka mahuṁ karahu nivāsā, jau lagi karauṁ nisācara nāsā.
जबहिं राम सब कहा बखानी । प्रभु पद धरि हियँ अनल समानी ॥
jabahiṁ rāma saba kahā bakhānī, prabhu pada dhari hiyaṁ anala samānī.
निज प्रतिबिंब राखि तहँ सीता । तैसइ सील रुप सुबिनीता ॥
nija pratibiṁba rākhi tahaṁ sītā, taisai sīla rupa subinītā.
लछिमनहूँ यह मरमु न जाना । जो कछु चरित रचा भगवाना ॥
lachimanahūṁ yaha maramu na jānā, jo kachu carita racā bhagavānā.
दसमुख गयउ जहाँ मारीचा । नाइ माथ स्वारथ रत नीचा ॥
dasamukha gayau jahāṁ mārīcā, nāi mātha svāratha rata nīcā.
नवनि नीच कै अति दुखदाई । जिमि अंकुस धनु उरग बिलाई ॥
navani nīca kai ati dukhadāī, jimi aṁkusa dhanu uraga bilāī.
भयदायक खल कै प्रिय बानी । जिमि अकाल के कुसुम भवानी ॥
bhayadāyaka khala kai priya bānī, jimi akāla ke kusuma bhavānī.

Trans:

"Hearken, most lovely and amiable of faithful wives, I am going to enact a fantastic human part. Be you absorbed into fire until I have completed the destruction of the demons." As soon as Rāma had finished speaking, she pressed her Lord's feet to her heart and entered into the fire, leaving only an image of herself—of exactly the same appearance and the same amiable and gentle disposition. Lakshman did not know this mystery or that the Lord God had taken any action. Meanwhile the Ten-headed approached Mārich and bowed his head—the selfish and contemptible wretch. When a mean thing stoops, it is only to inflict some pain, like an elephant goad, a bow, a snake, and a cat. The friendly speech of a churl is as portentous, O Bhawānī, as flowers that blossom out of season.

दोहा-dohā:

करि पूजा मारीच तब सादर पूछी बात ।
kari pūjā mārīca taba sādara pūchī bāta,
कवन हेतु मन ब्यग्र अति अकसर आयहु तात ॥२४॥
kavana hetu mana byagra ati akasara āyahu tāta. 24.

Trans:

After doing him homage, Mārich respectfully enquired of him his business, "What is the cause, my son, that you have come so disturbed in mind and all alone?

चौपाई-caupāī:

दसमुख सकल कथा तेहि आगें । कही सहित अभिमान अभागें ॥
dasamukha sakala kathā tehi āgeṁ, kahī sahita abhimāna abhāgeṁ.
होहु कपट मृग तुम्ह छलकारी । जेहि बिधि हरि आनौं नृपनारी ॥
hohu kapaṭa mṛga tumha chalakārī, jehi bidhi hari ānauṁ nṛpanārī.
तेहिं पुनि कहा सुनहु दससीसा । ते नररुप चराचर ईसा ॥
tehiṁ puni kahā sunahu dasasīsā, te nararupa carācara īsā.
तासों तात बयरु नहिं कीजै । मारें मरिअ जिआएँ जीजै ॥
tāsoṁ tāta bayaru nahiṁ kījai, māreṁ maria jiāeṁ jījai.
मुनि मख राखन गयउ कुमारा । बिनु फर सर रघुपति मोहि मारा ॥
muni makha rākhana gayau kumārā, binu phara sara raghupati mohi mārā.
सत जोजन आयउँ छन माहीं । तिन्ह सन बयरु किएँ भल नाहीं ॥
sata jojana āyauṁ chana māhīṁ, tinha sana bayaru kieṁ bhala nāhīṁ.
भइ मम कीट भृंग की नाई । जहँ तहँ मैं देखउँ दोउ भाई ॥
bhai mama kīṭa bhṛṁga kī nāī, jahaṁ tahaṁ maiṁ dekhauṁ dou bhāī.
जौं नर तात तदपि अति सूरा । तिन्हहि बिरोधि न आइहि पूरा ॥
jauṁ nara tāta tadapi ati sūrā, tinhahi birodhi na āihi pūrā.

Trans:

Rāvan put the whole matter before him and added presumptuously—that wretch—"Do you, for the purpose of deception, assume the form of a deer, and by this means, I shall be able to carry off the princess." He replied, "Hearken Rāvan: though in form of a human, this is the Lord of all animate and inanimate creation; there is no fighting against him, my son; if he kills, you die, and if you live, it is he who gives you life. He is the prince Raghupatī who, when he went to protect the saint's sacrifice, smote me with a pointless-arrow, and in an instant I was driven a distance of a hundred leagues. It is not well to quarrel with him. Now wherever I look, I see these two brothers everywhere, and my senses are utterly bewildered—like a fly fascinated by a spider. Even if he be only a man, my son, he is a remarkable hero, and opposition to him will do you no good.

दोहा-dohā:

जेहिं ताड़का सुबाहु हति खंडेउ हर कोदंड ।
jehiṁ tāṛakā subāhu hati khaṁḍeu hara kodaṁḍa.
खर दूषन तिसिरा बधेउ मनुज कि अस बरिबंड ॥२५॥
khara dūṣana tisirā badheu manuja ki asa baribaṁḍa. 25.

Trans:

Can he possibly be a man—who was strong enough to vanquish Tādakā and Subāhu and broke Shiva's bow and slew Khar, Dūshan and Trisirā?

चौपाई-caupāī:

जाहु भवन कुल कुसल बिचारी । सुनत जरा दीन्हिसि बहु गारी ॥
jāhu bhavana kula kusala bicārī, sunata jarā dīnhisi bahu gārī.
गुरु जिमि मूढ़ करसि मम बोधा । कहु जग मोहि समान को जोधा ॥
guru jimi mūṛha karasi mama bodhā, kahu jaga mohi samāna ko jodhā.
तब मारीच हृदयँ अनुमाना । नवहि बिरोधें नहिं कल्याना ॥
taba mārīca hṛdayaṁ anumānā, navahi birodheṁ nahiṁ kalyānā.
सस्त्री मर्मी प्रभु सठ धनी । बैद बंदि कबि भानस गुनी ॥
sastrī marmī prabhu saṭha dhanī, baida baṁdi kabi bhānasa gunī.
उभय भाँति देखा निज मरना । तब ताकिसि रघुनायक सरना ॥
ubhaya bhāṁti dekhā nija maranā, taba tākisi raghunāyaka saranā.
उतरु देत मोहि बधब अभागें । कस न मरौं रघुपति सर लागें ॥
utaru deta mohi badhaba abhāgeṁ, kasa na marauṁ raghupati sara lāgeṁ.
अस जियँ जानि दसानन संगा । चला राम पद प्रेम अभंगा ॥
asa jiyaṁ jāni dasānana saṁgā, calā rāma pada prema abhaṁgā.
मन अति हरष जनाव न तेही । आजु देखिहउँ परम सनेही ॥
mana ati haraṣa janāva na tehī, āju dekhihauṁ parama sanehī.

Trans:

So consider the welfare of your family and go home." Hearing that Rāvan was much infuriated, and lashed out abusingly, "You fool, you take upon yourself to teach me, as if you were my master! Tell me where in the world is there a warrior my equal?" Mārich then thought to himself, 'There are nine whom it is not good to make enemies: an armed man, a confidant, a king, a villain, a rich man, a physician, a panegyrist, a poet, and a man of special ability.' Either way he saw it, he must die; but he reflected that in Rāma would be his sanctuary. So he answered, "You will be the death of me, poor wretch; for how can I escape when smitten by Raghupatī's shaft?" With these thoughts at heart, he accompanied Rāvan, staunch in his devotion to Rāma's feet and with an exceeding gladness of heart that he would not show, "Today I shall behold my best beloved.

छंद-chaṁda:

निज परम प्रीतम देखि लोचन सुफल करि सुख पाइहौं।
nija parama prītama dekhi locana suphala kari sukha pāihauṁ,
श्री सहित अनुज समेत कृपानिकेत पद मन लाइहौं॥
śrī sahita anuja sameta kṛpāniketa pada mana lāihauṁ.
निर्बान दायक क्रोध जा कर भगति अबसहि बसकरी।
nirbāna dāyaka krodha jā kara bhagati abasahi basakarī,
निज पानि सर संधानि सो मोहि बधिहि सुखसागर हरी॥
nija pāni sara saṁdhāni so mohi badhihi sukhasāgara harī.

Trans:

My eyes will be rewarded with the sight of my beloved, and I shall be happy. I shall imprint upon my soul the feet of the All-merciful with Sītā too and his brother. Harī, the ocean of beatitude, even whose wrath confers salvation, who gives himself up entirely to the will of his worshippers, will, with his own hands, fit an arrow to the string and slay me.

दोहा-dohā:

मम पाछें धर धावत धरें सरासन बान।
mama pācheṁ dhara dhāvata dhareṁ sarāsana bāna,
फिरि फिरि प्रभुहि बिलोकिहउँ धन्य न मो सम आन॥२६॥
phiri phiri prabhuhi bilokihauṁ dhanya na mo sama āna. 26.

Trans:

As he runs after me to seize me with his bow and arrows, I shall ever and again turn and get a sight of my Lord: there is none else so blessed as I am."

चौपाई-caupāī:

तेहि बन निकट दसानन गयऊ। तब मारीच कपटमृग भयऊ॥
tehi bana nikaṭa dasānana gayaū, taba mārīca kapaṭamṛga bhayaū.
अति बिचित्र कछु बरनि न जाई। कनक देह मनि रचित बनाई॥
ati bicitra kachu barani na jāī, kanaka deha mani racita banāī.
सीता परम रुचिर मृग देखा। अंग अंग सुमनोहर बेषा॥
sītā parama rucira mṛga dekhā, aṁga aṁga sumanohara beṣā.
सुनहु देव रघुबीर कृपाला। एहि मृग कर अति सुंदर छाला॥
sunahu deva raghubīra kṛpālā, ehi mṛga kara ati suṁdara chālā.
सत्यसंध प्रभु बधि करि एही। आनहु चर्म कहति बैदेही॥
satyasaṁdha prabhu badhi kari ehī, ānahu carma kahati baidehī.
तब रघुपति जानत सब कारन। उठे हरषि सुर काजु सँवारन॥
taba raghupati jānata saba kārana, uṭhe haraṣi sura kāju saṁvārana.
मृग बिलोकि कटि परिकर बाँधा। करतल चाप रुचिर सर साँधा॥
mṛga biloki kaṭi parikara bāṁdhā, karatala cāpa rucira sara sāṁdhā.
प्रभु लछिमनहि कहा समुझाई। फिरत बिपिन निसिचर बहु भाई॥
prabhu lachimanahi kahā samujhāī, phirata bipina nisicara bahu bhāī.
सीता केरि करेहु रखवारी। बुधि बिबेक बल समय बिचारी॥
sītā keri karehu rakhavārī, budhi bibeka bala samaya bicārī.
प्रभुहि बिलोकि चला मृग भाजी। धाए रामु सरासन साजी॥
prabhuhi biloki calā mṛga bhājī, dhāe rāmu sarāsana sājī.
निगम नेति सिव ध्यान न पावा। मायामृग पाछें सो धावा॥
nigama neti siva dhyāna na pāvā, māyāmṛga pācheṁ so dhāvā.
कबहुँ निकट पुनि दूरि पराई। कबहुँक प्रगटइ कबहुँ छपाई॥
kabahuṁ nikaṭa puni dūri parāī, kabahuṁka pragaṭai kabahuṁ chapāī.
प्रगटत दुरत करत छल भूरी। एहि बिधि प्रभुहि गयउ लै दूरी॥
pragaṭata durata karata chala bhūrī, ehi bidhi prabhuhi gayau lai dūrī.
तब तकि राम कठिन सर मारा। धरनि परेउ करि घोर पुकारा॥
taba taki rāma kaṭhina sara mārā, dharani pareu kari ghora pukārā.
लछिमन कर प्रथमहिं लै नामा। पाछें सुमिरेसि मन महुँ रामा॥
lachimana kara prathamahiṁ lai nāmā, pācheṁ sumiresi mana mahuṁ rāmā.
प्रान तजत प्रगटेसि निज देहा। सुमिरेसि रामु समेत सनेहा॥
prāna tajata pragaṭesi nija dehā, sumiresi rāmu sameta sanehā.
अंतर प्रेम तासु पहिचाना। मुनि दुर्लभ गति दीन्हि सुजाना॥
aṁtara prema tāsu pahicānā, muni durlabha gati dīnhi sujānā.

Trans:

According to the plan, when the Ten-headed drew near to the wood, Mārich took the form of a deer—spotted so beautifully as to defy description, with a body of gold, all bespangled with jewels. When Sītā saw this wondrously beautiful creature clothed with loveliness in its every limb, she cried, "O Raghubīr hearken kind sir, this deer has a most charming skin; remove it then, most truthful Lord, and bring me the hide." Thereupon Rāma, who understood the meaning of it all, arose with joy to execute the purpose of the gods. Having marked the deer, he girded up his waist-belt, took his bow in his hand and trimmed his shapely arrows. Then the Lord cautioned Lakshman, "Many demons, my brother, roam the forest; take care of Sītā with all thought and consideration and with force too, if occasion requires so." The deer, seeing the Lord, took to flight. Rāma pursued with a ready bow: even he, to whom the Veda cannot attain, nor Shiva is able to contemplate, hastened in pursuit of a mimic deer. Now close at hand, now fleeing at a distance, at one time in sight, at another hid, alternately showing and concealing himself and practicing every kind of wile, in this manner the deer look the Lord far away. At last Rāma aimed and let fly the fatal shaft, and he fell to the ground with a terrible cry, taking first of all Lakshman's name, but afterwards mentally invoking Rāma. As his life ebbed he appeared in his natural form and affectionately invoked Rāma's name; who in his wisdom recognizing his inward love, gave him such a place in heaven such as saints can scarcely attain to.

दोहा-dohā:

बिपुल सुमन सुर बरषहिं गावहिं प्रभु गुन गाथ।
bipula sumana sura baraṣahiṁ gāvahiṁ prabhu guna gātha,
निज पद दीन्ह असुर कहुँ दीनबंधु रघुनाथ॥२७॥
nija pada dīnha asura kahuṁ dīnabaṁdhu raghunātha. 27.

Trans:

The gods rained down abundant flowers and hymned the Lord's high virtue, "Raghunāth, the suppliant's friend, raises to his own sphere even a demon!"

चौपाई-caupāī:

खल बधि तुरत फिरे रघुबीरा। सोह चाप कर कटि तूनीरा॥
khala badhi turata phire raghubīrā, soha cāpa kara kaṭi tūnīrā.
आरत गिरा सुनी जब सीता। कह लछिमन सन परम सभीता॥
ārata girā sunī jaba sītā, kaha lachimana sana parama sabhītā.
जाहु बेगि संकट अति भ्राता। लछिमन बिहसि कहा सुनु माता॥
jāhu begi saṁkaṭa ati bhrātā, lachimana bihasi kahā sunu mātā.
भृकुटि बिलास सृष्टि लय होई। सपनेहुँ संकट परइ कि सोई॥
bhṛkuṭi bilāsa sṛṣṭi laya hoī, sapanehuṁ saṁkaṭa parai ki soī.

मरम बचन जब सीता बोला । हरि प्रेरित लछिमन मन डोला ॥
marama bacana jaba sītā bolā, hari prerita lachimana mana ḍolā.
बन दिसि देव सौंपि सब काहू । चले जहाँ रावन ससि राहू ॥
bana disi deva saumpi saba kāhū, cale jahāṁ rāvana sasi rāhū.
सून बीच दसकंधर देखा । आवा निकट जती कें बेषा ॥
sūna bīca dasakaṁdhara dekhā, āvā nikaṭa jatī keṁ beṣā.
जाकें डर सुर असुर डेराहीं । निसि न नीद दिन अन्न न खाहीं ॥
jākeṁ ḍara sura asura ḍerāhīṁ, nisi na nīda dina anna na khāhīṁ.
सो दससीस स्वान की नाईं । इत उत चितइ चला भड़िहाईं ॥
so dasasīsa svāna kī nāīṁ, ita uta citai calā bhaṛihāīṁ.
इमि कुपंथ पग देत खगेसा । रह न तेज तन बुधि बल लेसा ॥
imi kupaṁtha paga deta khagesā, raha na teja tana budhi bala lesā.
नाना बिधि करि कथा सुहाई । राजनीति भय प्रीति देखाई ॥
nānā bidhi kari kathā suhāī, rājanīti bhaya prīti dekhāī.
कह सीता सुनु जती गोसाईं । बोलेहु बचन दुष्ट की नाईं ॥
kaha sītā sunu jatī gosāīṁ, bolehu bacana duṣṭa kī nāīṁ.
तब रावन निज रूप देखावा । भई सभय जब नाम सुनावा ॥
taba rāvana nija rūpa dekhāvā, bhaī sabhaya jaba nāma sunāvā.
कह सीता धरि धीरजु गाढ़ा । आइ गयउ प्रभु रहु खल ठाढ़ा ॥
kaha sītā dhari dhīraju gāṛhā, āi gayau prabhu rahu khala ṭhāṛhā.
जिमि हरिबधुहि छुद्र सस चाहा । भएसि कालबस निसिचर नाहा ॥
jimi haribadhuhi chudra sasa cāhā, bhaesi kālabasa nisicara nāhā.
सुनत बचन दससीस रिसाना । मन महुँ चरन बंदि सुख माना ॥
sunata bacana dasasīsa risānā, mana mahuṁ carana baṁdi sukha mānā.

Trans:

As soon as he had slain the monster, Raghubīr returned; the bow gleaming in his hand and the quiver by his side. Meanwhile when Sītā heard the agonizing cry, she called to Lakshman in the greatest alarm, "Go in haste, your brother is in some sad strait." Lakshman answered with a smile, "Hearken mother: he, by the play of whose eyebrows the world is annihilated, cannot be imagined to having fallen into any difficulty." But when Sītā urged him with derisive words, Lakshman's resolution—for such was Harī's will—was shaken; he made over charge of everything to the forest and its gods, and went towards Rāma, the Rāhu of the moon-like Rāvan. As soon as the Ten-headed saw the ground vacant, he drew near in the guise of an anchorite. He—for fear of whom gods and demons trembled and could neither sleep by night nor eat food by day—even that Rāvan came looking this side and that, as furtively as a cur, bent on thieving. O Garud, after a man has turned his steps towards the path of vice, not a particle of majesty, or intellect, or strength of body is left in him. At first repeating a variety of legends and moral sentiments, the false hermit then took recourse to threats and blandishments. Said Sītā, "Hearken, reverend father, what you speak is very offensive." Then Rāvan showed himself in his proper form; and she was terror-stricken when he declared his name. But plucking up all her courage she said, "Wretch, stay as you are; my Lord is at hand. Like a hare pursuing a lioness you have wooed your own destruction, and now you will die, demon king." On hearing this speech the Ten-headed was furious, though in his heart he delighted to adore her feet.

दोहा-dohā:

क्रोधवंत तब रावन लीन्हिसि रथ बैठाइ ।
krodhavaṁta taba rāvana līnhisi ratha baiṭhāi,
चला गगनपथ आतुर भयँ रथ हाँकि न जाइ ॥२८॥
calā gaganapatha ātura bhayaṁ ratha hāṁki na jāi. 28.

Trans:

Rāvan angrily seized her and seated her in his chariot. As he took his way through the air, he was so agitated with fear that he could scarcely steer.

चौपाई-caupāī:

हा जग एक बीर रघुराया । केहिं अपराध बिसारेहु दाया ॥
hā jaga eka bīra raghurāyā, kehiṁ aparādha bisārehu dāyā.
आरति हरन सरन सुखदायक । हा रघुकुल सरोज दिननायक ॥
ārati harana sarana sukhadāyaka, hā raghukula saroja dinanāyaka.
हा लछिमन तुम्हार नहिं दोसा । सो फलु पायउँ कीन्हेउँ रोसा ॥
hā lachimana tumhāra nahiṁ dosā, so phalu pāyauṁ kīnheuṁ rosā.
बिबिध बिलाप करति बैदेही । भूरि कृपा प्रभु दूरि सनेही ॥
bibidha bilāpa karati baidehī, bhūri kṛpā prabhu dūri sanehī.
बिपति मोरि को प्रभुहि सुनावा । पुरोडास चह रासभ खावा ॥
bipati mori ko prabhuhi sunāvā, puroḍāsa caha rāsabha khāvā.
सीता कै बिलाप सुनि भारी । भए चराचर जीव दुखारी ॥
sītā kai bilāpa suni bhārī, bhae carācara jīva dukhārī.
गीधराज सुनि आरत बानी । रघुकुलतिलक नारि पहिचानी ॥
gīdharāja suni ārata bānī, raghukulatilaka nāri pahicānī.
अधम निसाचर लीन्हें जाई । जिमि मलेछ बस कपिला गाई ॥
adhama nisācara līnheṁ jāī, jimi malecha basa kapilā gāī.
सीते पुत्रि करसि जनि त्रासा । करिहउँ जातुधान कर नासा ॥
sīte putri karasi jani trāsā, karihauṁ jātudhāna kara nāsā.
धावा क्रोधवंत खग कैसें । छूटइ पबि परबत कहुँ जैसें ॥
dhāvā krodhavaṁta khaga kaiseṁ, chūṭai pabi parabata kahuṁ jaiseṁ.
रे रे दुष्ट ठाढ़ किन होही । निर्भय चलेसि न जानेहि मोही ॥
re re duṣṭa ṭhāṛha kina hohī, nirbhaya calesi na jānehi mohī.
आवत देखि कृतांत समाना । फिरि दसकंधर कर अनुमाना ॥
āvata dekhi kṛtāṁta samānā, phiri dasakaṁdhara kara anumānā.
की मैनाक कि खगपति होई । मम बल जान सहित पति सोई ॥
kī maināka ki khagapati hoī, mama bala jāna sahita pati soī.
जाना जरठ जटायू एहा । मम कर तीरथ छाँड़िहि देहा ॥
jānā jaraṭha jaṭāyū ehā, mama kara tīratha chāṁṛihi dehā.
सुनत गीध क्रोधातुर धावा । कह सुनु रावन मोर सिखावा ॥
sunata gīdha krodhātura dhāvā, kaha sunu rāvana mora sikhāvā.
तजि जानकिहि कुसल गृह जाहू । नाहिं त अस होइहि बहुबाहू ॥
taji jānakihi kusala gṛha jāhū, nāhiṁ ta asa hoihi bahubāhū.
राम रोष पावक अति घोरा । होइहि सकल सलभ कुल तोरा ॥
rāma roṣa pāvaka ati ghorā, hoihi sakala salabha kula torā.
उतरु न देत दसानन जोधा । तबहिं गीध धावा करि क्रोधा ॥
utaru na deta dasānana jodhā, tabahiṁ gīdha dhāvā kari krodhā.
धरि कच बिरथ कीन्ह महि गिरा । सीतहि राखि गीध पुनि फिरा ॥
dhari kaca biratha kīnha mahi girā, sītahi rākhi gīdha puni phirā.
चोचन्ह मारि बिदारेसि देही । दंड एक भइ मुरुछा तेही ॥
cocanha māri bidāresi dehī, daṁḍa eka bhai muruchā tehī.
तब सक्रोध निसिचर खिसिआना । काढ़ेसि परम कराल कृपाना ॥
taba sakrodha nisicara khisiānā, kāṛhesi parama karāla kṛpānā.
काटेसि पंख परा खग धरनी । सुमिरि राम करि अदभुत करनी ॥
kāṭesi paṁkha parā khaga dharanī, sumiri rāma kari adabhuta karanī.

सीतहि जानि चढ़ाइ बहोरी । चला उताइल त्रास न थोरी ॥
sītahi jāni caṛhāi bahorī, calā utāila trāsa na thorī.
करति बिलाप जाति नभ सीता । ब्याध बिबस जनु मृगी सभीता ॥
karati bilāpa jāti nabha sītā, byādha bibasa janu mṛgī sabhītā.
गिरि पर बैठे कपिन्ह निहारी । कहि हरि नाम दीन्ह पट डारी ॥
giri para baiṭhe kapinha nihārī, kahi hari nāma dīnha paṭa ḍārī.
एहि बिधि सीतहि सो लै गयऊ । बन असोक महँ राखत भयऊ ॥
ehi bidhi sītahi so lai gayaū, bana asoka mahaṁ rākhata bhayaū.

Trans:

"Ah! Gallant Raghurāī, sovereign of the universe, for what fault of mine have you forgotten mercy? Ah! reliever of distress, life-giving sanctuary, sun of the lotuses of the Raghu race. Ah! Lakshman! this is no fault of yours; I reap the fruit of the temper I showed." Manifold were the lamentations that Sītā uttered. "My affectionate and loving Lord is far away; who will tell him of my calamity; would a donkey devour the oblation intended for gods!" At the sound of Sītā's woeful lament every created being, whether animate or inanimate, was made sad. The vulture-king too heard her piteous cry and recognized the spouse of the glory of Raghu's line, whom the vile demon was carrying away—as it were the *Kapila* cow that had fallen into the hands of some barbarian. "Fear not, Sītā, my daughter, I will annihilate this monster." The bird darted forth in his fury, like a thunderbolt launched against a mountain. "Stop, you villain, how dare you go on and take no heed of me." Seeing him bearing down upon him like the angel of death, Rāvan paused and considered, "Is it mount Maināk or the king-of-birds! Anyhow they both know my might, as also do their lords." When he perceived that it was poor old Jatāyu, he cried, "He shall leave his body at the shrine of my hands." At this, the vulture rushed on in a fury, crying, "Hearken Rāvan to my advice; surrender Jānakī and go home in peace; if not, despite your many arms it will turn out thus: Rāma's wrath is like a fierce flame, and your whole clan will be consumed in it like a moth." The warrior demon gave no answer. The vulture rushed on in a fury and clutched him by the hair and dragged him from his chariot so that he fell to the ground; then, having sheltered Sītā, the vulture turned and with his beak tore and rent his body. For nearly half an hour the demon was in a swoon, then gnashed his teeth with rage and drew his monstrous sword and cut off Jatāyu's wings. Having accomplished a marvelous feat of courage, the bird alas fell to the ground crying 'Rāma'. Then Rāvan put Sītā back into the chariot and drove off in haste much alarmed. Sītā was borne through the air lamenting, like a frightened fawn in the power of huntsman. Seeing the monkeys sitting on the rocks, she cried out Harī's name and dropped her scarf. In this manner he went off with Sītā and put her down in the Asoka grove in Lankā.

दोहा-dohā:

हारि परा खल बहु बिधि भय अरु प्रीति देखाइ ।
hāri parā khala bahu bidhi bhaya aru prīti dekhāi,
तब असोक पादप तर राखिसि जतन कराइ ॥ २९क॥
taba asoka pādapa tara rākhisi jatana karāi. 29(ka).

Trans:

Though be tried every kind of threat and blandishment, the monster could not succeed, and at last after exhausting all his devices he left her under the Asoka tree.

नवाह्नपारायण छठा विश्राम
navāhnapārāyaṇa chaṭhā viśrāma
(Pause 6 for a Nine-Day Recitation)

दोहा-dohā:

जेहि बिधि कपट कुरंग सँग धाइ चले श्रीराम ।
jehi bidhi kapaṭa kuraṁga saṁga dhāi cale śrīrāma,
सो छबि सीता राखि उर रटति रहति हरिनाम ॥ २९ख॥
so chabi sītā rākhi ura raṭati rahati harināma. 29(kha).

Trans:

With Rāma's beauteous form impressed upon her heart—as he appeared when he left in pursuit of the mimic deer—Sītā was incessantly invoking his name, "O Harī, Harī!"

चौपाई-caupāī:

रघुपति अनुजहि आवत देखी । बाहिज चिंता कीन्हि बिसेषी ॥
raghupati anujahi āvata dekhī, bāhija ciṁtā kīnhi biseṣī.
जनकसुता परिहरिहु अकेली । आयहु तात बचन मम पेली ॥
janakasutā pariharihu akelī, āyahu tāta bacana mama pelī.
निसिचर निकर फिरहिं बन माहीं । मम मन सीता आश्रम नाहीं ॥
nisicara nikara phirahiṁ bana māhīṁ, mama mana sītā āśrama nāhīṁ.
गहि पद कमल अनुज कर जोरी । कहेउ नाथ कछु मोहि न खोरी ॥
gahi pada kamala anuja kara jorī, kaheu nātha kachu mohi na khorī.
अनुज समेत गए प्रभु तहवाँ । गोदावरि तट आश्रम जहवाँ ॥
anuja sameta gae prabhu tahavāṁ, godāvari taṭa āśrama jahavāṁ.
आश्रम देखि जानकी हीना । भए बिकल जस प्राकृत दीना ॥
āśrama dekhi jānakī hīnā, bhae bikala jasa prākṛta dīnā.
हा गुन खानि जानकी सीता । रूप सील ब्रत नेम पुनीता ॥
hā guna khāni jānakī sītā, rūpa sīla brata nema punītā.
लछिमन समुझाए बहु भाँती । पूछत चले लता तरु पाँती ॥
lachimana samujhāe bahu bhāṁtī, pūchata cale latā taru pāṁtī.
हे खग मृग हे मधुकर श्रेनी । तुम्ह देखी सीता मृगनैनी ॥
he khaga mṛga he madhukara śrenī, tumha dekhī sītā mṛganainī.
खंजन सुक कपोत मृग मीना । मधुप निकर कोकिला प्रबीना ॥
khaṁjana suka kapota mṛga mīnā, madhupa nikara kokilā prabīnā.
कुंद कली दाड़िम दामिनी । कमल सरद ससि अहिभामिनी ॥
kuṁda kalī dāṛima dāminī, kamala sarada sasi ahibhāminī.
बरुन पास मनोज धनु हंसा । गज केहरि निज सुनत प्रसंसा ॥
baruna pāsa manoja dhanu haṁsā, gaja kehari nija sunata prasaṁsā.
श्रीफल कनक कदलि हरषाहीं । नेकु न संक सकुच मन माहीं ॥
śrīphala kanaka kadali haraṣāhīṁ, neku na saṁka sakuca mana māhīṁ.
सुनु जानकी तोहि बिनु आजू । हरषे सकल पाइ जनु राजू ॥
sunu jānakī tohi binu ājū, haraṣe sakala pāi janu rājū.
किमि सहि जात अनख तोहि पाहीं । प्रिया बेगि प्रगटसि कस नाहीं ॥
kimi sahi jāta anakha tohi pāhīṁ, priyā begi pragaṭasi kasa nāhīṁ.
एहि बिधि खोजत बिलपत स्वामी । मनहुँ महा बिरही अति कामी ॥
ehi bidhi khojata bilapata svāmī, manahuṁ mahā birahī ati kāmī.
पूरनकाम राम सुख रासी । मनुज चरित कर अज अबिनासी ॥
pūranakāma rāma sukha rāsī, manuja carita kara aja abināsī.
आगें परा गीधपति देखा । सुमिरत राम चरन जिन्ह रेखा ॥
āgeṁ parā gīdhapati dekhā, sumirata rāma carana jinha rekhā.

Trans:

Here, when Raghupatī saw his brother coming, outwardly expressed much concern, "O brother, have you left Sītā alone and come here against my order, though so many demons roam the forest? My mind tells me that Sītā is not at the hermitage." Lakshman clasped his lotus feet and cried with folded hands, "Hearken my Lord, it is no fault of mine." When he saw the hermitage bereft of Sītā, he was as agitated as an ordinary mortal. "Alas! Jānakī, my precious Sītā, so beautiful and amiable, so divinely pious and devoted!" Lakshman did all he could to comfort him. As he went along, he questioned all the trees and flowers by the way, "O ye birds and deer, O ye swarms of bees, have you seen the fawn-eyed Sītā? The wagtails, parrots, and pigeons; the deer and fish; the swarming bees and clever cuckoos; the jasmine and pomegranate flowers; the lightning, the lotus, the autumn moon; the gliding serpent, the meshes of Varun, the bow of Kāmdev; the swan, the elephant, and the lion—can now hear themselves praised; the cocoanut, the champs, and the plantain—can now rejoice, without any doubt or misgiving at heart. Hearken, Jānakī, now that you are away, they are all as glad as if they have gotten a unrivaled kingdom. How can you bear such rivalry? Why do you not at once disclose yourself, my beloved?" In this manner the Lord searched and lamented—like a fond lover distressed by separation. Rāma, who has no wish unsatisfied, the perfection of bliss, the uncreated and the everlasting, acted the part of a man. Further on he saw the vulture-king lying, with his thoughts fixed on the prints of Rāma's feet.

दोहा-dohā:

कर सरोज सिर परसेउ कृपासिंधु रघुबीर ।

kara saroja sira paraseu kṛpāsiṁdhu raghubīra.

निरखि राम छबि धाम मुख बिगत भई सब पीर ॥३०॥

nirakhi rāma chabi dhāma mukha bigata bhaī saba pīra. 30.

Trans:

The compassionate Raghubīr laid his lotus hands upon his head. At the sight of Rāma's lovely face all his pain was forgotten.

चौपाई-caupāī:

तब कह गीध बचन धरि धीरा । सुनहु राम भंजन भव भीरा ॥

taba kaha gīdha bacana dhari dhīrā, sunahu rāma bhaṁjana bhava bhīrā.

नाथ दसानन यह गति कीन्ही । तेहिं खल जनकसुता हरि लीन्ही ॥

nātha dasānana yaha gati kīnhī, tehiṁ khala janakasutā hari līnhī.

लै दच्छिन दिसि गयउ गोसाईं । बिलपति अति कुररी की नाईं ॥

lai dacchina disi gayau gosāīṁ, bilapati ati kurarī kī nāīṁ.

दरस लागी प्रभु राखेउँ प्राना । चलन चहत अब कृपानिधाना ॥

darasa lāgī prabhu rākheuṁ prānā, calana cahata aba kṛpānidhānā.

राम कहा तनु राखहु ताता । मुख मुसुकाइ कही तेहिं बाता ॥

rāma kahā tanu rākhahu tātā, mukha musukāi kahī tehiṁ bātā.

जा कर नाम मरत मुख आवा । अधमउ मुकुत होई श्रुति गावा ॥

jā kara nāma marata mukha āvā, adhamau mukuta hoī śruti gāvā.

सो मम लोचन गोचर आगें । राखौं देह नाथ केहि खाँगें ॥

so mama locana gocara āgeṁ, rākhauṁ deha nātha kehi khāṁgeṁ.

जल भरि नयन कहहिं रघुराई । तात कर्म निज तें गति पाई ॥

jala bhari nayana kahahiṁ raghurāī, tāta karma nija teṁ gati pāī.

परहित बस जिन्ह के मन माहीं । तिन्ह कहुँ जग दुर्लभ कछु नाहीं ॥

parahita basa jinha ke mana māhīṁ, tinha kahuṁ jaga durlabha kachu nāhīṁ.

तनु तजि तात जाहु मम धामा । देउँ काह तुम्ह पूरनकामा ॥

tanu taji tāta jāhu mama dhāmā, deuṁ kāha tumha pūranakāmā.

Trans:

And the vulture recovered himself and spoke as follows, "Hearken Rāma, remover of life's troubles: My Lord, this is Rāvan's doing; he is the wretch, who has carried off Janak's daughter. He took her away, sire, to the south, crying as piteously as an osprey. I have kept alive, my Lord, only to see you; now, O most merciful, I will depart." Said Rāma, "Remain alive, father." He smiled and answered, "He—by the repetition of whose name at the hour of death the vilest sinner, as the scriptures declare, attains salvation—has come in bodily form before my eyes; what need is there, sire, for me to live any longer?" Raghurāī's eyes filled with tears as he spoke, "Father, it is your own good deeds that have saved you. There is nothing in the world beyond the reach of those who devote their soul to the good of others. When you pass out of the body, father, ascend to my sphere in heaven. What more can I give you. Your every wish is gratified.

दोहा-dohā:

सीता हरन तात जनि कहहु पिता सन जाइ ।

sītā harana tāta jani kahahu pitā sana jāi,

जौं मैं राम त कुल सहित कहिहि दसानन आइ ॥३१॥

jauṁ maiṁ rāma ta kula sahita kahihi dasānana āi. 31.

Trans:

But on reaching there, sire, tell not my father about Sītā's abduction. If I be Rāma—if I am what I am—then the ten-headed Rāvan, along with his kin, will himself go and say everything to him."

चौपाई-caupāī:

गीध देह तजि धरि हरि रुपा । भूषन बहु पट पीत अनूपा ॥

gīdha deha taji dhari hari rupā, bhūṣana bahu paṭa pīta anūpā.

स्याम गात बिसाल भुज चारी । अस्तुति करत नयन भरि बारी ॥

syāma gāta bisāla bhuja cārī, astuti karata nayana bhari bārī.

Trans:

Dropping the form of a vulture, he appeared in all the beauty of Harī, bedecked with jewels and in gorgeous yellow attire, with dark-hued body and four mighty arms, and with his eyes full of tears he chanted this hymn of praise:

छंद-chaṁda:

जय राम रूप अनूप निर्गुन सगुन गुन प्रेरक सही ।

jaya rāma rūpa anūpa nirguna saguna guna preraka sahī,

दससीस बाहु प्रचंड खंडन चंड सर मंडन मही ॥

dasasīsa bāhu pracaṁḍa khaṁḍana caṁḍa sara maṁḍana mahī.

पाथोद गात सरोज मुख राजीव आयत लोचनं ।

pāthoda gāta saroja mukha rājīva āyata locanaṁ,

नित नौमि रामु कृपाल बाहु बिसाल भव भय मोचनं ॥१॥

nita naumi rāmu kṛpāla bāhu bisāla bhava bhaya mocanaṁ. 1.

बलमप्रमेयमनादिमजमब्यक्तमेकमगोचरं ।

balamaprameyamanādimajamabyaktamekamagocaraṁ,

गोबिंद गोपर द्वंद्वहर बिग्यानघन धरनीधरं ॥

gobiṁda gopara dvaṁdvahara bigyānaghana dharanīdharaṁ.

जे राम मंत्र जपंत संत अनंत जन मन रंजनं ।

je rāma maṁtra japaṁta saṁta anaṁta jana mana raṁjanaṁ,

नित नौमि राम अकाम प्रिय कामादि खल दल गंजनं ॥२॥

nita naumi rāma akāma priya kāmādi khala dala gaṁjanaṁ. 2.

जेहि श्रुति निरंजन ब्रह्म ब्यापक बिरज अज कहि गावहीं ।

jehi śruti niraṁjana brahma byāpaka biraja aja kahi gāvahīṁ,

करि ध्यान ग्यान बिराग जोग अनेक मुनि जेहि पावहीं ॥

kari dhyāna gyāna birāga joga aneka muni jehi pāvahīṁ.

सो प्रगट करुना कंद सोभा बृंद अग जग मोहई ।

so pragaṭa karunā kaṁda sobhā bṛṁda aga jaga mohaī,

मम हृदय पंकज भृंग अंग अनंग बहु छबि सोहई ॥३॥

mama hṛdaya paṁkaja bhṛṁga aṁga anaṁga bahu chabi sohaī. 3.

जो अगम सुगम सुभाव निर्मल असम सम सीतल सदा ।

jo agama sugama subhāva nirmala asama sama sītala sadā,

पस्यंति जं जोगी जतन करि करत मन गो बस सदा ॥

pasyaṁti jaṁ jogī jatana kari karata mana go basa sadā.

सो राम रमा निवास संतत दास बस त्रिभुवन धनी ।

so rāma ramā nivāsa saṁtata dāsa basa tribhuvana dhanī,

मम उर बसउ सो समन संसृति जासु कीरति पावनी ॥४॥

mama ura basau so samana saṁsṛti jāsu kīrati pāvanī. 4.

Trans:

"Glory to Rāma of incomparable beauty; the bodiless, the embodied, the veritable source of every bodily element; the arrows from whose mighty arms are potent to cut off the terrible arms of the ten-headed demon; the ornament of the earth. I unceasingly worship Rāma, with his body dark as a rain-cloud, with his face like blue-lotus and his eyes large as red-lotus; the merciful, the mighty-armed, the dispeller of all life's terrors; of immeasurable strength; unborn, without a beginning and end; the indivisible, the one; beyond the reach of senses, the incarnate Govind; the annihilator of duality, profound in wisdom; the supporter of the earth; an everlasting delight to the soul of the saints who practice the spell of Rāma's name. I unceasingly worship Rāma, the friend of the unsensual, the destroyer of lust and every other wickedness. He, whom the scriptures hymn under the name of the passionless Brahmm the all-pervading, the supreme spirit, the unbegotten; to whom the saints attain after infinite study, contemplation, penance and abstraction; he the all-merciful, the all-radiant, the un-approachable, has now become manifest for the delight of the world. He who is at once inaccessible and accessible, like and unlike, the essentially pure, the unfailing comforter, whom ascetics behold only when they have laboriously subdued their mind and senses—that Rāma, the terminator of transmigration; whose praises make pure; the spouse of Lakshmī; who is ever at the command of his servants, though the Lord of the three spheres—may he ever abide in my heart."

दोहा-dohā:

अबिरल भगति मागि बर गीध गयउ हरिधाम ।

abirala bhagati māgi bara gīdha gayau haridhāma,

तेहि की क्रिया जथोचित निज कर कीन्ही राम ॥३२॥

tehi kī kriyā jathocita nija kara kīnhī rāma. 32.

Trans:

After asking the boon of perfect *Bhakti*, the vulture departed to Harī's sphere. Rāma with his own hands performed his funeral rites with all due ceremony.

चौपाई-caupāī:

कोमल चित अति दीनदयाला । कारन बिनु रघुनाथ कृपाला ॥

komala cita ati dīnadayālā, kārana binu raghunātha kṛpālā.

गीध अधम खग आमिष भोगी । गति दीन्हि जो जाचत जोगी ॥

gīdha adhama khaga āmiṣa bhogī, gati dīnhi jo jācata jogī.

सुनहु उमा ते लोग अभागी । हरि तजि होहिं बिषय अनुरागी ॥

sunahu umā te loga abhāgī, hari taji hohiṁ biṣaya anurāgī.

पुनि सीतहि खोजत द्वौ भाई । चले बिलोकत बन बहुताई ॥

puni sītahi khojata dvau bhāī, cale bilokata bana bahutāī.

संकुल लता बिटप घन कानन । बहु खग मृग तहँ गज पंचानन ॥

saṁkula latā biṭapa ghana kānana, bahu khaga mṛga tahaṁ gaja paṁcānana.

आवत पंथ कबंध निपाता । तेहिं सब कही साप कै बाता ॥

āvata paṁtha kabaṁdha nipātā, tehiṁ saba kahī sāpa kai bātā.

दुरबासा मोहि दीन्ही सापा । प्रभु पद पेखि मिटा सो पापा ॥

durabāsā mohi dīnhī sāpā, prabhu pada pekhi miṭā so pāpā.

सुनु गंधर्ब कहउँ मैं तोही । मोहि न सोहाइ ब्रह्मकुल द्रोही ॥

sunu gaṁdharba kahauṁ maiṁ tohī, mohi na sohāi brahmakula drohī.

Trans:

The tender-hearted and compassionate Raghunāth, who shows mercy even on the undeserving, bestowed upon a vulture—an unclean, flesh-eating bird—such a place in heaven as the greatest ascetics desire. Hearken O Umā, the most miserable of men are they who abandon Harī and become attached to objects of senses. The two brothers in their search for Sītā visited and examined many woods, tangled with creepers, dense with trees, and swarming with birds, deer, elephants and lions. As they went on their way they overthrew Kabandh, who declared the whole history of the curse. "Durvāsā cursed me, but now that I have seen my Lord's feet, my sin has been blotted out." "Hearken, Gandharv; those who trouble the learned and wise—are displeasing to me.

दोहा-dohā:

मन क्रम बचन कपट तजि जो कर भूसुर सेव ।

mana krama bacana kapaṭa taji jo kara bhūsura seva,

मोहि समेत बिरंचि सिव बस ताकें सब देव ॥३३॥

mohi sameta biraṁci siva basa tākeṁ saba deva. 33.

Trans:

They who without guile in thought, word, and deed do service to the gods of earth—subdue unto themselves Brahmmā, Shiva, myself and every other divinity.

चौपाई-caupāī:

सापत ताड़त परुष कहंता । बिप्र पूज्य अस गावहिं संता ॥

sāpata tāṛata paruṣa kahaṁtā, bipra pūjya asa gāvahiṁ saṁtā.

पूजिअ बिप्र सील गुन हीना । सूद्र न गुन गन ग्यान प्रबीना ॥

pūjia bipra sīla guna hīnā, sūdra na guna gana gyāna prabīnā.

कहि निज धर्म ताहि समुझावा । निज पद प्रीति देखि मन भावा ॥

kahi nija dharma tāhi samujhāvā, nija pada prīti dekhi mana bhāvā.

रघुपति चरन कमल सिरु नाई । गयउ गगन आपनि गति पाई ॥

raghupati carana kamala siru nāī, gayau gagana āpani gati pāī.

ताहि देइ गति राम उदारा । सबरी कें आश्रम पगु धारा ॥

tāhi dei gati rāma udārā, sabarī keṁ āśrama pagu dhārā.

सबरी देखि राम गृहँ आए । मुनि के बचन समुझि जियँ भाए ॥

sabarī dekhi rāma gṛhaṁ āe, muni ke bacana samujhi jiyaṁ bhāe.

सरसिज लोचन बाहु बिसाला । जटा मुकुट सिर उर बनमाला ॥

sarasija locana bāhu bisālā, jaṭā mukuṭa sira ura banamālā.

स्याम गौर सुंदर दोउ भाई । सबरी परी चरन लपटाई ॥

syāma gaura suṁdara dou bhāī, sabarī parī carana lapaṭāī.

प्रेम मगन मुख बचन न आवा । पुनि पुनि पद सरोज सिर नावा ॥

prema magana mukha bacana na āvā, puni puni pada saroja sira nāvā.

सादर जल लै चरन पखारे । पुनि सुंदर आसन बैठारे ॥

sādara jala lai carana pakhāre, puni suṁdara āsana baiṭhāre.

Trans:

The holy and wise of the learned class—though he may beat, abuse, curse—is still an object of reverence: so declare the saints; and they are approved for respect, despite their outward lack of amiability; but not so the menial class though they display visible signs of merit and wisdom." So saying, he instructed him in his doctrine and was pleased to see his devotion to his feet. When the beneficent Rāma had given him beatitude, he next went on to the hermitage of Shabrī. When she saw that Rāma had come to her abode she remembered the saint's promise and was glad of heart. With lotus eyes, mighty arms, hair fastened up in knots on their heads, and a garland of wild flowers upon their chest, one dark of hue the other fair—there stood the two brothers. Shabrī fell and embraced their feet. She was so drowned in love that no speech came to her lips. Again and again she bowed her head at their lotus feet; then she reverently brought water and laved their feet and finally conducted them to a honored seat.

दोहा-dohā:

कंद मूल फल सुरस अति दिए राम कहुँ आनि ।
kaṁda mūla phala surasa ati die rāma kahuṁ āni,
प्रेम सहित प्रभु खाए बारंबार बखानि ॥३४॥
prema sahita prabhu khāe bāraṁbāra bakhāni. 34.

Trans:

She brought and presented to Rāma the most delicious fruits and herbs and roots, and the Lord graciously partook of them, appreciating again and again.

चौपाई-caupāī:

पानि जोरि आगें भइ ठाढ़ी । प्रभुहि बिलोकि प्रीति अति बाढ़ी ॥
pāni jori āgeṁ bhai ṭhāṛhī, prabhuhi biloki prīti ati bāṛhī.
केहि बिधि अस्तुति करौं तुम्हारी । अधम जाति मैं जड़मति भारी ॥
kehi bidhi astuti karauṁ tumhārī, adhama jāti maiṁ jaṛamati bhārī.
अधम ते अधम अधम अति नारी । तिन्ह महँ मैं मतिमंद अघारी ॥
adhama te adhama adhama ati nārī, tinha mahaṁ maiṁ matimaṁda aghārī.
कह रघुपति सुनु भामिनि बाता । मानउँ एक भगति कर नाता ॥
kaha raghupati sunu bhāmini bātā, mānauṁ eka bhagati kara nātā.
जाति पाँति कुल धर्म बड़ाई । धन बल परिजन गुन चतुराई ॥
jāti pāṁti kula dharma baṛāī, dhana bala parijana guna caturāī.
भगति हीन नर सोहइ कैसा । बिनु जल बारिद देखिअ जैसा ॥
bhagati hīna nara sohai kaisā, binu jala bārida dekhia jaisā.
नवधा भगति कहउँ तोहि पाहीं । सावधान सुनु धरु मन माहीं ॥
navadhā bhagati kahauṁ tohi pāhīṁ, sāvadhāna sunu dharu mana māhīṁ.
प्रथम भगति संतन्ह कर संगा । दूसरि रति मम कथा प्रसंगा ॥
prathama bhagati saṁtanha kara saṁgā, dūsari rati mama kathā prasaṁgā.

Trans:

She stood before him with folded hands and as she gazed upon the Lord, her love waxed yet more eloquent. "How can I hymn thy praises, seeing that I am of meanest descent and of dullest wit; the lowest of the low and a woman to boot; nay among the lowest of women the one who is of all most ignorant, O sinless God." Said Raghupatī, "Hearken O beautiful lady, to my words: I recognize no kinsmanship except that of Devotion—neither lineage, family, religion, rank, wealth, power, connections, virtue, nor ability. A man without Devotion is of no more account than a cloud without water. I will explain to you the nine kinds of Devotion; hearken attentively and lay them up in your mind. The first step in Devotion is communion with the saints; the second a love for the legends relating to me;

दोहा-dohā:

गुर पद पंकज सेवा तीसरि भगति अमान ।
gura pada paṁkaja sevā tīsari bhagati amāna,
चौथि भगति मम गुन गन करइ कपट तजि गान ॥३५॥
cauthi bhagati mama guna gana karai kapaṭa taji gāna. 35.

Trans:

The third, an incalculable step—devotion to the lotus feet of the Gurū; the fourth, singing my praises with a guileless purpose.

चौपाई-caupāī:

मंत्र जाप मम दृढ़ बिस्वासा । पंचम भजन सो बेद प्रकासा ॥
maṁtra jāpa mama dṛṛha bisvāsā, paṁcama bhajana so beda prakāsā.
छठ दम सील बिरति बहु करमा । निरत निरंतर सज्जन धरमा ॥
chaṭha dama sīla birati bahu karamā, nirata niraṁtara sajjana dharamā.
सातवँ सम मोहि मय जग देखा । मोतें संत अधिक करि लेखा ॥
sātavaṁ sama mohi maya jaga dekhā, moteṁ saṁta adhika kari lekhā.
आठवँ जथालाभ संतोषा । सपनेहुँ नहिं देखइ परदोषा ॥
āṭhavaṁ jathālābha saṁtoṣā, sapanehuṁ nahiṁ dekhai paradoṣā.
नवम सरल सब सन छलहीना । मम भरोस हियँ हरष न दीना ॥
navama sarala saba sana chalahīnā, mama bharosa hiyaṁ haraṣa na dīnā.
नव महुँ एकउ जिन्ह कें होई । नारि पुरुष सचराचर कोई ॥
nava mahuṁ ekau jinha keṁ hoī, nāri puruṣa sacarācara koī.
सोइ अतिसय प्रिय भामिनि मोरें । सकल प्रकार भगति दृढ़ तोरें ॥
soi atisaya priya bhāmini moreṁ, sakala prakāra bhagati dṛṛha toreṁ.
जोगि बृंद दुरलभ गति जोई । तो कहुँ आजु सुलभ भइ सोई ॥
jogi bṛṁda duralabha gati joī, to kahuṁ āju sulabha bhai soī.
मम दरसन फल परम अनूपा । जीव पाव निज सहज सरूपा ॥
mama darasana phala parama anūpā, jīva pāva nija sahaja sarūpā.
जनकसुता कइ सुधि भामिनी । जानहि कहु करिबरगामिनी ॥
janakasutā kai sudhi bhāminī, jānahi kahu karibaragāminī.
पंपा सरहि जाहु रघुराई । तहँ होइहि सुग्रीव मिताई ॥
paṁpā sarahi jāhu raghurāī, tahaṁ hoihi sugrīva mitāī.
सो सब कहिहि देव रघुबीरा । जानतहूँ पूछहु मतिधीरा ॥
so saba kahihi deva raghubīrā, jānatahūṁ pūchahu matidhīrā.
बार बार प्रभु पद सिरु नाई । प्रेम सहित सब कथा सुनाई ॥
bāra bāra prabhu pada siru nāī, prema sahita saba kathā sunāī.

Trans:

The fifth, as the Vedas have expounded, prayer and the repetition, with an assured confidence, of my mystic name; the sixth, self-governance, kindness, detachment from the world and in every action a loving and persevering piety; the seventh, seeing the whole world full of me, and holding the saints in yet greater account than myself; the eighth, contentment with what one has, without ever a thought of spying out fault in others; the ninth, a guileless simplicity towards all, and a hearty confidence in me without either exultation or dejection. Verily, O lady, whoever possesses anyone of these, whether he be man or woman, sentient or insentient, is my friend; and you have all these to the highest degree. The heavenly prize, which the greatest ascetics scarcely win, is today within your easy grasp. The result of seeing me is something most marvelous: every creature at once attains its proper consummation. But lady, have you any tidings of Jānakī? Tell me, O fair dame, all that you know." "Go, Raghurāī, to the river Pampā; there make friends with Sugrīva; he will tell you all. You know it already my god Raghubīr, yet have the patience to ask me." After again and again bowing her head at the Lord's feet, she lovingly repeated the whole history.

छंद-chaṁda:

कहि कथा सकल बिलोकि हरि मुख हृदयँ पद पंकज धरे ।
kahi kathā sakala biloki hari mukha hṛdayaṁ pada paṁkaja dhare,
तजि जोग पावक देह हरि पद लीन भइ जहँ नहिं फिरे ॥
taji joga pāvaka deha hari pada līna bhai jahaṁ nahiṁ phire.
नर बिबिध कर्म अधर्म बहु मत सोकप्रद सब त्यागहू ।
nara bibidha karma adharma bahu mata sokaprada saba tyāgahū,
बिस्वास करि कह दास तुलसी राम पद अनुरागहू ॥
bisvāsa kari kaha dāsa tulasī rāma pada anurāgahū.

Trans:

After repeating the whole story, as she gazed on Harī's feet and imprinted his lotus feet on her heart, she left her body through the Yogic fire and became absorbed in Harī's feet, the realm beyond return. O men, abandon your varied activities, sins and diverse creeds, which all give birth to sorrows, and with genuine faith, lovingly embrace the feet of Rāma—says Tulsīdās.

दोहा-dohā:

जाति हीन अघ जन्म महि मुक्त कीन्हि असि नारि ।
jāti hīna agha janma mahi mukta kīnhi asi nāri,
महामंद मन सुख चहसि ऐसे प्रभुहि बिसारि ॥ ३६ ॥
mahāmaṁda mana sukha cahasi aise prabhuhi bisāri. 36.

Trans:

The Lord gave salvation to a woman of such low descent and so altogether born in sin as even this Shabrī was. Foolish indeed are they who desire peace of mind after forgetting such a Lord.

चौपाई-caupāī:

चले राम त्यागा बन सोऊ । अतुलित बल नर केहरि दोऊ ॥
cale rāma tyāgā bana soū, atulita bala nara kehari doū.
बिरही इव प्रभु करत बिषादा । कहत कथा अनेक संबादा ॥
birahī iva prabhu karata biṣādā, kahata kathā aneka saṁbādā.
लछिमन देखु बिपिन कइ सोभा । देखत केहि कर मन नहिं छोभा ॥
lachimana dekhu bipina kai sobhā, dekhata kehi kara mana nahiṁ chobhā.
नारि सहित सब खग मृग बृंदा । मानहुँ मोरि करत हहिं निंदा ॥
nāri sahita saba khaga mṛga bṛṁdā, mānahuṁ mori karata hahiṁ niṁdā.
हमहि देखि मृग निकर पराहीं । मृगीं कहहिं तुम्ह कहँ भय नाहीं ॥
hamahi dekhi mṛga nikara parāhīṁ, mṛgīṁ kahahiṁ tumha kahaṁ bhaya nāhīṁ.
तुम्ह आनंद करहु मृग जाए । कंचन मृग खोजन ए आए ॥
tumha ānaṁda karahu mṛga jāe, kaṁcana mṛga khojana e āe.
संग लाइ करिनीं करि लेहीं । मानहुँ मोहि सिखावनु देहीं ॥
saṁga lāi karinīṁ kari lehīṁ, mānahuṁ mohi sikhāvanu dehīṁ.
सास्त्र सुचिंतित पुनि पुनि देखिअ । भूप सुसेवित बस नहिं लेखिअ ॥
sāstra suciṁtita puni puni dekhia, bhūpa susevita basa nahiṁ lekhia.
राखिअ नारि जदपि उर माहीं । जुबती सास्त्र नृपति बस नाहीं ॥
rākhia nāri jadapi ura māhīṁ, jubatī sāstra nṛpati basa nāhīṁ.
देखहु तात बसंत सुहावा । प्रिया हीन मोहि भय उपजावा ॥
dekhahu tāta basaṁta suhāvā, priyā hīna mohi bhaya upajāvā.

Trans:

When they left that forest, they went on further—Rāma and his brother, two lions among men, of immeasurable strength. The Lord lamented, like a bereaved lover; and spoke and discussed many subjects: "Observe, Lakshman, the beauty of the forest: whose heart is not moved to see it? The birds and deer, all accompanied by their mates, seem to laugh and jeer at me. When the deer see me and scamper away, they cry, 'Have no fear, enjoy yourselves, for we are genuine deer; and it is only a golden deer that these people have come to look for'. The female elephants, as they take aside their lords, seem to be giving me this caution, 'The scriptures, however well studied, must be read over and over again; a king, however well served, is never to be depended upon; and a woman, like the scriptures and the king, though you cherish her in your bosom, is never thoroughly mastered'. See, my brother, how beautiful the spring is; and yet to me, without my beloved, it looks frightful.

दोहा-dohā:

बिरह बिकल बलहीन मोहि जानेसि निपट अकेल ।
biraha bikala balahīna mohi jānesi nipaṭa akela,
सहित बिपिन मधुकर खग मदन कीन्ह बगमेल ॥ ३७क ॥
sahita bipina madhukara khaga madana kīnha bagamela. 37(ka).

देखि गयउ भ्राता सहित तासु दूत सुनि बात ।
dekhi gayau bhrātā sahita tāsu dūta suni bāta,
डेरा कीन्हेउ मनहुँ तब कटकु हटकि मनजात ॥ ३७ख ॥
ḍerā kīnheu manahuṁ taba kaṭaku haṭaki manajāta. 37(kha).

Trans:

Love, finding me tortured by separation, powerless and absolutely alone, has made a raid upon me with the bees and birds of the forest. After hearing his spy's report, 'He has looked and gone on with his brother,' the amorous god has, as it were, resolutely encamped against me with his army.

चौपाई-caupāī:

बिटप बिसाल लता अरुझानी । बिबिध बितान दिए जनु तानी ॥
biṭapa bisāla latā arujhānī, bibidha bitāna die janu tānī.
कदलि ताल बर धुजा पताका । देखि न मोह धीर मन जाका ॥
kadali tāla bara dhujā patākā, dekhi na moha dhīra mana jākā.
बिबिध भाँति फूले तरु नाना । जनु बानैत बने बहु बाना ॥
bibidha bhāṁti phūle taru nānā, janu bānaita bane bahu bānā.
कहुँ कहुँ सुन्दर बिटप सुहाए । जनु भट बिलग बिलग होइ छाए ॥
kahuṁ kahuṁ sundara biṭapa suhāe, janu bhaṭa bilaga bilaga hoi chāe.
कूजत पिक मानहुँ गज माते । ढेक महोख ऊँट बिसराते ॥
kūjata pika mānahuṁ gaja māte, ḍheka mahokha ūṁṭa bisarāte.
मोर चकोर कीर बर बाजी । पारावत मराल सब ताजी ॥
mora cakora kīra bara bājī, pārāvata marāla saba tājī.
तीतिर लावक पदचर जूथा । बरनि न जाइ मनोज बरुथा ॥
tītira lāvaka padacara jūthā, barani na jāi manoja baruthā.
रथ गिरि सिला दुंदुभीं झरना । चातक बंदी गुन गन बरना ॥
ratha giri silā duṁdubhīṁ jharanā, cātaka baṁdī guna gana baranā.
मधुकर मुखर भेरि सहनाई । त्रिबिध बयारि बसीठीं आई ॥
madhukara mukhara bheri sahanāī, tribidha bayāri basīṭhīṁ āī.
चतुरंगिनी सेन सँग लीन्हें । बिचरत सबहि चुनौती दीन्हें ॥
caturaṁginī sena saṁga līnheṁ, bicarata sabahi cunautī dīnheṁ.
लछिमन देखत काम अनीका । रहहिं धीर तिन्ह कै जग लीका ॥
lachimana dekhata kāma anīkā, rahahiṁ dhīra tinha kai jaga līkā.
एहि कें एक परम बल नारी । तेहि तें उबर सुभट सोइ भारी ॥
ehi keṁ eka parama bala nārī, tehi teṁ ubara subhaṭa soi bhārī.

Trans:

These trees and tangled creepers are like the diverse pavilions that the love-god has spread; the plantains and stately palms his pennons and standards that none but the stoutest can see without being possessed; these different flowering shrubs are his warriors, arrayed in all their various type panoply; the magnificent forest-trees, which stand here and there, are the separate encampments of warrior chiefs; the murmuring cuckoos are his infuriated elephants, and the herons and rooks his camels and mules; the peacocks, *chakor*s and parrots are his war horses, the pigeons and swans his steed; the partridges and quails his foot soldiers; Ah, there is no describing the whole of army of Love's. The mountains and rocks are his chariots, the waterfalls his kettledrums, the *chātaks* the bards that sing his praises, the garrulous bees are his trumpets and clarions, and the three kind of winds his scouts. With an army complete in all its four branches, he goes about and exhorts everyone. O Lakshman, they who can see Love's battle array and stand firm, they truly are men of mark in this world. His greatest capability lies in woman, anyone who can escape her is indeed a mighty champion.

दोहा-dohā:

तात तीनि अति प्रबल खल काम क्रोध अरु लोभ ।
tāta tīni ati prabala khala kāma krodha aru lobha,
मुनि बिग्यान धाम मन करहिं निमिष महुँ छोभ ॥३८क॥
muni bigyāna dhāma mana karahiṁ nimiṣa mahuṁ chobha. 38(ka).

लोभ कें इच्छा दंभ बल काम कें केवल नारि ।
lobha keṁ icchā daṁbha bala kāma keṁ kevala nāri,
क्रोध कें परुष बचन बल मुनिबर कहहिं बिचारि ॥३८ख॥
krodha keṁ paruṣa bacana bala munibara kahahiṁ bicāri. 38(kha).

Trans:

Brother, there are three evils of surpassing strength: love, anger, greed. In an instant they upset the souls of the wisest philosopher. The weapons of greed are desire and pride; of love nothing else but woman; while anger's weapon is harsh speech. All this the thoughtful sages have declared to us."

चौपाई-caupāī:

गुनातीत सचराचर स्वामी । राम उमा सब अंतरजामी ॥
gunātīta sacarācara svāmī, rāma umā saba aṁtarajāmī.
कामिन्ह कै दीनता देखाई । धीरन्ह कें मन बिरति दृढ़ाई ॥
kāminha kai dīnatā dekhāī, dhīranha keṁ mana birati dṛṛhāī.
क्रोध मनोज लोभ मद माया । छूटहिं सकल राम कीं दाया ॥
krodha manoja lobha mada māyā, chūṭahiṁ sakala rāma kīṁ dāyā.
सो नर इंद्रजाल नहिं भूला । जा पर होइ सो नट अनुकूला ॥
so nara iṁdrajāla nahiṁ bhūlā, jā para hoi so naṭa anukūlā.
उमा कहउँ मैं अनुभव अपना । सत हरि भजनु जगत सब सपना ॥
umā kahauṁ maiṁ anubhava apanā, sata hari bhajanu jagata saba sapanā.
पुनि प्रभु गए सरोबर तीरा । पंपा नाम सुभग गंभीरा ॥
puni prabhu gae sarobara tīrā, paṁpā nāma subhaga gaṁbhīrā.
संत हृदय जस निर्मल बारी । बाँधे घाट मनोहर चारी ॥
saṁta hṛdaya jasa nirmala bārī, bāṁdhe ghāṭa manohara cārī.
जहँ तहँ पिअहिं बिबिध मृग नीरा । जनु उदार गृह जाचक भीरा ॥
jahaṁ tahaṁ piahiṁ bibidha mṛga nīrā, janu udāra gṛha jācaka bhīrā.

Trans:

O Umā, Rāma is without attributes, the Lord of all animate and inanimate creation, and he knows all secrets; yet he exhibited all the distress of a lover no less than the detachment and steadfastness of a philosopher. Anger, love, greed, pride, delusion, all are dissipated by the grace of Rāma; and the only man superior to all his jugglery is he upon whom the great conjuror has himself shown favor. I tell you, O Umā, what my conclusion is: Harī and the worship of Him alone is real; the world and all else is a dream. Then the Lord went on from there to the shore of the deep and beautiful lake called Pampā; its water as clear as the soul of the saints; with charming flights of steps on each of its four aides; where beasts of different kinds came as they listed, to drink of the deluge, like crowds of beggars at a good man's home.

दोहा-dohā:

पुरइनि सघन ओट जल बेगि न पाइअ मर्म ।
puraini sadhana oṭa jala begi na pāia marma,
मायाछन्न न देखिऐ जैसें निर्गुन ब्रह्म ॥३९क॥
māyāchanna na dekhiai jaiseṁ nirguna brahma. 39(ka).

सुखी मीन सब एकरस अति अगाध जल माहिं ।
sukhī mīna saba ekarasa ati agādha jala māhiṁ,
जथा धर्मसीलन्ह के दिन सुख संजुत जाहिं ॥३९ख॥
jathā dharmasīlanha ke dina sukha saṁjuta jāhiṁ. 39(kha).

Trans:

Under its cover of dense lotus-leaves the water was as difficult to distinguish as is the un-embodied supreme spirit under the veil of delusive Māyā. The happy fish were all in placid repose at the bottom of the deep pool, like the days of the righteous that are passed in peace.

चौपाई-caupāī:

बिकसे सरसिज नाना रंगा । मधुर मुखर गुंजत बहु भृंगा ॥
bikase sarasija nānā raṁgā, madhura mukhara guṁjata bahu bhṛṁgā.
बोलत जलकुक्कुट कलहंसा । प्रभु बिलोकि जनु करत प्रसंसा ॥
bolata jalakukkuṭa kalahaṁsā, prabhu biloki janu karata prasaṁsā.
चक्रबाक बक खग समुदाई । देखत बनइ बरनि नहिं जाई ॥
cakrabāka baka khaga samudāī, dekhata banai barani nahiṁ jāī.
सुंदर खग गन गिरा सुहाई । जात पथिक जनु लेत बोलाई ॥
suṁdara khaga gana girā suhāī, jāta pathika janu leta bolāī.
ताल समीप मुनिन्ह गृह छाए । चहु दिसि कानन बिटप सुहाए ॥
tāla samīpa muninha gṛha chāe, cahu disi kānana biṭapa suhāe.
चंपक बकुल कदंब तमाला । पाटल पनस परास रसाला ॥
caṁpaka bakula kadaṁba tamālā, pāṭala panasa parāsa rasālā.
नव पल्लव कुसुमित तरु नाना । चंचरीक पटली कर गाना ॥
nava pallava kusumita taru nānā, caṁcarīka paṭalī kara gānā.
सीतल मंद सुगंध सुभाऊ । संतत बहइ मनोहर बाऊ ॥
sītala maṁda sugaṁdha subhāū, saṁtata bahai manohara bāū.
कुहू कुहू कोकिल धुनि करहीं । सुनि रव सरस ध्यान मुनि टरहीं ॥
kuhū kuhū kokila dhuni karahīṁ, suni rava sarasa dhyāna muni ṭarahīṁ.

Trans:

Lotuses of many colors displayed their flowers; there was a buzzing of garrulous bees, both honey-makers and bumble bees; while swans and waterfowl were so noisy, you would think they had seen the Lord and were telling his praises. The geese and cranes and other birds were so numerous that only seeing them would be believing—what words could describe them? Delightful voice of so many beautiful birds seemed as an invitation to the wayfarer. Many saints had built themselves huts near the lake with magnificent forest-trees all around—the *champāk*, the *mālsāri*, the *kadamb*, and *tamālā*, the *pātala*, the *kathal*, the *dhāk* and the mango. Every tree had put forth its new leaves and flowers and was resonant with swarms of bees. A delightful air, soft, cool and fragrant, was ever in delicious motion, and the cooing of the cuckoos was so pleasant to hear that a saint's meditation would be broken by it.

दोहा-dohā:

फल भारन नमि बिटप सब रहे भूमि निअराइ ।
phala bhārana nami biṭapa saba rahe bhūmi niarāi,
पर उपकारी पुरुष जिमि नवहिं सुसंपति पाइ ॥४०॥
para upakārī puruṣa jimi navahiṁ susaṁpati pāi. 40.

Trans:

The trees laden with fruit bowed low to the ground—like a generous soul whom every increase of fortune renders only more humble than before.

चौपाई-caupāī:

देखि राम अति रुचिर तलावा । मज्जनु कीन्ह परम सुख पावा ॥
dekhi rāma ati rucira talāvā, majjanu kīnha parama sukha pāvā.
देखी सुंदर तरुबर छाया । बैठे अनुज सहित रघुराया ॥

dekhī suṁdara tarubara chāyā, baiṭhe anuja sahita raghurāyā.

तहँ पुनि सकल देव मुनि आए । अस्तुति करि निज धाम सिधाए ॥
tahaṁ puni sakala deva muni āe, astuti kari nija dhāma sidhāe.

बैठे परम प्रसन्न कृपाला । कहत अनुज सन कथा रसाला ॥
baiṭhe parama prasanna kṛpālā, kahata anuja sana kathā rasālā.

बिरहवंत भगवंतहि देखी । नारद मन भा सोच बिसेषी ॥
birahavaṁta bhagavaṁtahi dekhī, nārada mana bhā soca biseṣī.

मोर साप करि अंगीकारा । सहत राम नाना दुख भारा ॥
mora sāpa kari aṁgīkārā, sahata rāma nānā dukha bhārā.

ऐसे प्रभुहि बिलोकउँ जाई । पुनि न बनिहि अस अवसरु आई ॥
aise prabhuhi bilokauṁ jāī, puni na banihi asa avasaru āī.

यह बिचारि नारद कर बीना । गए जहाँ प्रभु सुख आसीना ॥
yaha bicāri nārada kara bīnā, gae jahāṁ prabhu sukha āsīnā.

गावत राम चरित मृदु बानी । प्रेम सहित बहु भाँति बखानी ॥
gāvata rāma carita mṛdu bānī, prema sahita bahu bhāṁti bakhānī.

करत दंडवत लिए उठाई । राखे बहुत बार उर लाई ॥
karata daṁḍavata lie uṭhāī, rākhe bahuta bāra ura lāī.

स्वागत पूँछि निकट बैठारे । लछिमन सादर चरन पखारे ॥
svāgata pūṁchi nikaṭa baiṭhāre, lachimana sādara carana pakhāre.

Trans:

When Rāma saw this most beautiful lake, he bathed in it with great delight and then with his brother sat down in the shade of magnificent trees. There all the gods and saints came once more to hymn his praises and then returned each to his own realm. The All-merciful rested in supreme content and addressed his brother in an edifying discourse. When Nārad saw the Lord God thus sorrowing for the loss of his beloved, his soul was much disturbed. "In submission to my curse Rāma endures all this weight of woe. I must go and visit so noble a Lord, for I may never have such an opportunity again." Having thus reflected, Nārad, with his lute in hand, approached the spot where the Lord was sitting in comfort. In dulcet tones he sang his acts, affectionately dwelling upon them in all detail. As he prostrated himself, Rāma took and lifted him up, and again and again clasped him to his bosom, then asked him of his welfare and seated him by his side; while Lakshman reverently held his feet.

दोहा-dohā:

नाना बिधि बिनती करि प्रभु प्रसन्न जियँ जानि ।
nānā bidhi binatī kari prabhu prasanna jiyaṁ jāni,

नारद बोले बचन तब जोरि सरोरुह पानि ॥४१॥
nārada bole bacana taba jori saroruha pāni. 41.

Trans:

Perceiving that his Lord was well pleased, Nārad made much supplication and clasping his lotus hands addressed him in these words:

चौपाई-caupāī:

सुनहु उदार सहज रघुनायक । सुंदर अगम सुगम बर दायक ॥
sunahu udāra sahaja raghunāyaka, suṁdara agama sugama bara dāyaka.

देहु एक बर मागउँ स्वामी । जद्यपि जानत अंतरजामी ॥
dehu eka bara māgauṁ svāmī, jadyapi jānata aṁtarajāmī.

जानहु मुनि तुम्ह मोर सुभाऊ । जन सन कबहुँ कि करउँ दुराऊ ॥
jānahu muni tumha mora subhāū, jana sana kabahuṁ ki karauṁ durāū.

कवन बस्तु असि प्रिय मोहि लागी । जो मुनिबर न सकहु तुम्ह मागी ॥
kavana bastu asi priya mohi lāgī, jo munibara na sakahu tumha māgī.

जन कहुँ कछु अदेय नहिं मोरें । अस बिस्वास तजहु जनि भोरें ॥
jana kahuṁ kachu adeya nahiṁ moreṁ, asa bisvāsa tajahu jani bhoreṁ.

तब नारद बोले हरषाई । अस बर मागउँ करउँ ढिठाई ॥
taba nārada bole haraṣāī, asa bara māgauṁ karauṁ ḍhiṭhāī.

जद्यपि प्रभु के नाम अनेका । श्रुति कह अधिक एक तें एका ॥
jadyapi prabhu ke nāma anekā, śruti kaha adhika eka teṁ ekā.

राम सकल नामन्ह ते अधिका । होउ नाथ अघ खग गन बधिका ॥
rāma sakala nāmanha te adhikā, hou nātha agha khaga gana badhikā.

Trans:

"Hearken, most generous Raghunāyak, beautiful and beneficent, at once unapproachable and easy of approach, grant me, my Lord, the one boon that I ask: though you know it without my asking, since you know the secrets of all hearts." "O sage, you understand my disposition; can I ever turn away my face from anyone of my worshippers? There is nothing I hold so dear that you, most excellent of saints, may not ask it of me. There is nothing of mine that I would refuse to my votary; never allow yourself to abandon this confidence in me." Then Nārad was glad and said, "This is the boon that I presume to ask. Though my Lord has many names, each more glorious than the other, as declared in the scriptures, may the name RĀMA, sire, surpass all names, exterminating the whole brood of sin as when a fowler ensnares an entire flock of birds.

दोहा-dohā:

राका रजनी भगति तव राम नाम सोइ सोम ।
rākā rajanī bhagati tava rāma nāma soi soma,

अपर नाम उडगन बिमल बसहुँ भगत उर ब्योम ॥४२क॥
apara nāma uḍagana bimala basahuṁ bhagata ura byoma. 42(ka).

एवमस्तु मुनि सन कहेउ कृपासिंधु रघुनाथ ।
evamastu muni sana kaheu kṛpāsiṁdhu raghunātha,

तब नारद मन हरष अति प्रभु पद नायउ माथ ॥४२ख॥
taba nārada mana haraṣa ati prabhu pada nāyau mātha. 42(kha).

Trans:

May your one name, 'RĀMA', be as the moon in the bright night of cloudless faith; and may your all other names be as brilliant stars in the heaven of the believer's soul." Raghunāth, the ocean of mercy, said to the saint, "Let that come to pass." Then was Nārad's soul rejoiced exceedingly and he bowed his head at his Lord's feet.

चौपाई-caupāī:

अति प्रसन्न रघुनाथहि जानी । पुनि नारद बोले मृदु बानी ॥
ati prasanna raghunāthahi jānī, puni nārada bole mṛdu bānī.

राम जबहिं प्रेरेउ निज माया । मोहेहु मोहि सुनहु रघुराया ॥
rāma jabahiṁ prereu nija māyā, mohehu mohi sunahu raghurāyā.

तब बिबाह मैं चाहउँ कीन्हा । प्रभु केहि कारन करै न दीन्हा ॥
taba bibāha maiṁ cāhauṁ kīnhā, prabhu kehi kārana karai na dīnhā.

सुनु मुनि तोहि कहउँ सहरोसा । भजहिं जे मोहि तजि सकल भरोसा ॥
sunu muni tohi kahauṁ saharosā, bhajahiṁ je mohi taji sakala bharosā.

करउँ सदा तिन्ह कै रखवारी । जिमि बालक राखइ महतारी ॥
karauṁ sadā tinha kai rakhavārī, jimi bālaka rākhai mahatārī.

गह सिसु बच्छ अनल अहि धाई । तहँ राखइ जननी अरगाई ॥
gaha sisu baccha anala ahi dhāī, tahaṁ rākhai jananī aragāī.

प्रौढ़ भएँ तेहि सुत पर माता । प्रीति करइ नहिं पाछिलि बाता ॥
prauṛha bhaeṁ tehi suta para mātā, prīti karai nahiṁ pāchili bātā.

मोरे प्रौढ़ तनय सम ग्यानी । बालक सुत सम दास अमानी ॥
more prauṛha tanaya sama gyānī, bālaka suta sama dāsa amānī.

जनहि मोर बल निज बल ताही । दुहु कहँ काम क्रोध रिपु आही ॥
janahi mora bala nija bala tāhī, duhu kahaṁ kāma krodha ripu āhī.

यह बिचारि पंडित मोहि भजहीं । पाएहुँ ग्यान भगति नहिं तजहीं ॥
yaha bicāri paṁḍita mohi bhajahīṁ, pāehuṁ gyāna bhagati nahiṁ tajahīṁ.

Trans:

Seeing Raghunāth so gracious, Nārad spoke again in winning tones, "O Rāma, when you sent forth your delusive power and infatuated me—hearken, O Raghurāī—I was anxious to accomplish a marriage. Why was it, my Lord, that you did not allow me to do so?" "Hearken, O saint, and I tell you with all earnestness: that I always take care of those who worship me with undivided faith, even as a mother tends to her child. If a child or a calf runs to lay hold of the fire or a snake, the mother or the cow at once rescues it; when her son has grown up, the mother does not show her affection to him in the same way as before. The wise are, as it were, my grown up sons, and humble worshippers my infant children. The latter are protected by my strength, the former by their own, and both have to fight against love and anger. Philosophers know this and worship me, and though they have acquired wisdom, still they do not discard Devotion.

दोहा-dohā:

काम क्रोध लोभादि मद प्रबल मोह कै धारि ।
kāma krodha lobhādi mada prabala moha kai dhāri,
तिन्ह महँ अति दारुन दुखद मायारूपी नारि ॥४३॥
tinha mahaṁ ati dāruna dukhada māyārūpī nāri. 43.

Trans:

Lust, anger, greed and all other violent passions form the rushing torrents of Ignorance; but among them all the most formidable and the most calamitous is that incarnation of Māyā called woman.

चौपाई-caupāī:

सुनु मुनि कह पुरान श्रुति संता । मोह बिपिन कहुँ नारि बसंता ॥
sunu muni kaha purāna śruti saṁtā, moha bipina kahuṁ nāri basaṁtā.
जप तप नेम जलाश्रय झारी । होइ ग्रीषम सोषइ सब नारी ॥
japa tapa nema jalāśraya jhārī, hoi grīṣama soṣai saba nārī.
काम क्रोध मद मत्सर भेका । इन्हहि हरषप्रद बरषा एका ॥
kāma krodha mada matsara bhekā, inhahi haraṣaprada baraṣā ekā.
दुर्बासना कुमुद समुदाई । तिन्ह कहँ सरद सदा सुखदाई ॥
durbāsanā kumuda samudāī, tinha kahaṁ sarada sadā sukhadāī.
धर्म सकल सरसीरुह बृंदा । होइ हिम तिन्हहि दहइ सुख मंदा ॥
dharma sakala sarasīruha bṛṁdā, hoi hima tinhahi dahai sukha maṁdā.
पुनि ममता जवास बहुताई । पलुहइ नारि सिसिर रितु पाई ॥
puni mamatā javāsa bahutāī, paluhai nāri sisira ritu pāī.
पाप उलूक निकर सुखकारी । नारि निबिड़ रजनी अँधिआरी ॥
pāpa ulūka nikara sukhakārī, nāri nibiṛa rajanī aṁdhiārī.
बुधि बल सील सत्य सब मीना । बनसी सम त्रिय कहहिं प्रबीना ॥
budhi bala sīla satya saba mīnā, banasī sama triya kahahiṁ prabīnā.

Trans:

Hearken, O saint, to the teaching of the Purānas, the Vedas and the saints: A woman is like the season of spring to the forest of infatuation; like the heat of summer to dry up the pools and waterfalls of prayer, penance and devotional exercises; like the rains to rejoice the gnats and frogs of lust, anger and pride; like the autumn to revive the lily-like growth of evil propensities; like the winter to distress and deaden all the lotus beds of piety; and like the dewy season to foster the *jawāsā* weeds of selfishness. Woman, again, is like a dark and murky night, in which owls and deeds of darkness take delight; or like a hook to catch the fish of sense and strength and honor and truth—thus have spoken the wise.

दोहा-dohā:

अवगुन मूल सूलप्रद प्रमदा सब दुख खानि ।
avaguna mūla sūlaprada pramadā saba dukha khāni,
ताते कीन्ह निवारन मुनि मैं यह जियँ जानि ॥४४॥
tāte kīnha nivārana muni maiṁ yaha jiyaṁ jāni. 44.

Trans:

Young woman is a source of torment, root of ill, mine of sorrow; therefore, O saint, know this, I prevented your marriage."

चौपाई-caupāī:

सुनि रघुपति के बचन सुहाए । मुनि तन पुलक नयन भरि आए ॥
suni raghupati ke bacana suhāe, muni tana pulaka nayana bhari āe.
कहहु कवन प्रभु कै असि रीती । सेवक पर ममता अरु प्रीती ॥
kahahu kavana prabhu kai asi rītī, sevaka para mamatā aru prītī.
जे न भजहिं अस प्रभु भ्रम त्यागी । ग्यान रंक नर मंद अभागी ॥
je na bhajahiṁ asa prabhu bhrama tyāgī, gyāna raṁka nara maṁda abhāgī.
पुनि सादर बोले मुनि नारद । सुनहु राम बिग्यान बिसारद ॥
puni sādara bole muni nārada, sunahu rāma bigyāna bisārada.
संतन्ह के लच्छन रघुबीरा । कहहु नाथ भव भंजन भीरा ॥
saṁtanha ke lacchana raghubīrā, kahahu nātha bhava bhaṁjana bhīrā.
सुनु मुनि संतन्ह के गुन कहऊँ । जिन्ह ते मैं उन्ह कें बस रहऊँ ॥
sunu muni saṁtanha ke guna kahaūṁ, jinha te maiṁ unha keṁ basa rahaūṁ.
षट बिकार जित अनघ अकामा । अचल अकिंचन सुचि सुखधामा ॥
ṣaṭa bikāra jita anagha akāmā, acala akiṁcana suci sukhadhāmā.
अमितबोध अनीह मितभोगी । सत्यसार कबि कोबिद जोगी ॥
amitabodha anīha mitabhogī, satyasāra kabi kobida jogī.
सावधान मानद मदहीना । धीर धर्म गति परम प्रबीना ॥
sāvadhāna mānada madahīnā, dhīra dharma gati parama prabīnā.

Trans:

As the saint listened to Raghupatī's delightful discourse, his body quivered with emotion and his eyes filled with tears. "Tell me, is there any other Lord, whose wont it is to be so kind and considerate to his servants. All, who will not abandon their errors, nor worship such a Lord as this, are indeed dull and witless fools." Nārad the sage reverentially enquired further, "Hearken, O Rāma, versed in all wisdom; tell me, my Lord Raghubīr, lightener of earth's burdens: what are the marks of a saint?" "Listen, reverend Sir, and I will tell you what are the qualities of the saints, by virtue of which they hold me in their power. They are masters of the six passions (lust, anger, greed, infatuation, pride, jealousy), sinless, disinterested, firm, possessing nothing, pure within and without, full of bliss, of boundless wisdom, desireless, moderate in diet, truthful, inspired, learned and united with God, circumspect, bestowing honour on others, free from pride, strong-minded and highly conversant with the course of Dharma.

दोहा-dohā:

गुनागार संसार दुख रहित बिगत संदेह ।
gunāgāra saṁsāra dukha rahita bigata saṁdeha.
तजि मम चरन सरोज प्रिय तिन्ह कहुँ देह न गेह ॥४५॥
taji mama carana saroja priya tinha kahuṁ deha na geha. 45.

Trans:

Saints are mines of virtue, free from the troubles of the world, and with their doubts all resolved; who, rather than abandon my lotus feet, account neither life nor home of any account;

चौपाई-caupāī:

निज गुन श्रवन सुनत सकुचाहीं । पर गुन सुनत अधिक हरषाहीं ॥
nija guna śravana sunata sakucāhīṁ, para guna sunata adhika haraṣāhīṁ.

सम सीतल नहिं त्यागहिं नीती । सरल सुभाउ सबहि सन प्रीती ॥
sama sītala nahiṁ tyāgahiṁ nītī, sarala subhāu sabahi sana prītī.
जप तप ब्रत दम संजम नेमा । गुरु गोबिंद बिप्र पद प्रेमा ॥
japa tapa brata dama saṁjama nemā, guru gobiṁda bipra pada premā.
श्रद्धा छमा मयत्री दाया । मुदिता मम पद प्रीति अमाया ॥
śraddhā chamā mayatrī dāyā, muditā mama pada prīti amāyā.
बिरति बिबेक बिनय बिग्याना । बोध जथारथ बेद पुराना ॥
birati bibeka binaya bigyānā, bodha jathāratha beda purānā.
दंभ मान मद करहिं न काऊ । भूलि न देहिं कुमारग पाऊ ॥
daṁbha māna mada karahiṁ na kāū, bhūli na dehiṁ kumāraga pāū.
गावहिं सुनहिं सदा मम लीला । हेतु रहित परहित रत सीला ॥
gāvahiṁ sunahiṁ sadā mama līlā, hetu rahita parahita rata sīlā.
मुनि सुनु साधुन्ह के गुन जेते । कहि न सकहिं सारद श्रुति तेते ॥
muni sunu sādhunha ke guna jete, kahi na sakahiṁ sārada śruti tete.

Trans:

who are abashed, when they hear themselves praised and exceedingly glad to hear the praises of others; who are always equable and calm, consistent in virtuous practice, honest and kindly disposed to all; and who are distinguished for—prayer, penance, religious observances, temperance, self-denial, and performance of pious vows, for their devotion to Gurū, Govinda and the virtuous; and for faith, forbearance, charitableness and compassion; and for a rapturous love of my feet, and having arisen above all the materialistic delusions, an absolute composure, discrimination, humility and knowledge; and for doctrine in strict accordance with the Vedas and Purānas; who never display ostentation, arrogance, or pride, nor ever by any chance set their foot on the way of wickedness; who are always either hearing or singing my enactments and have no selfish object, but are devoted to the good of others. In short, O good sage, the characteristics of the saints are so numerous that even Shārdā or the scriptures could not tell them all.

छंद-chaṁda:

कहि सक न सारद सेष नारद सुनत पद पंकज गहे ।
kahi saka na sārada seṣa nārada sunata pada paṁkaja gahe,
अस दीनबंधु कृपाल अपने भगत गुन निज मुख कहे ॥
asa dīnabaṁdhu kr̥pāla apane bhagata guna nija mukha kahe.
सिरु नाइ बारहिं बार चरनन्हि ब्रह्मपुर नारद गए ।
siru nāi bārahiṁ bāra carananhi brahmapura nārada gae.
ते धन्य तुलसीदास आस बिहाइ जे हरि रँग रँए ॥
te dhanya tulasīdāsa āsa bihāi je hari raṁga raṁe.

Trans:

Yes, not Shārdā nor Sheshnāg could tell them." Hearing this, Nārad clasped the Lord's lotus feet, crying, "Thus the friend of the suppliant, the all-merciful, has with his own lips declared the characteristics of his devotees." After again and again bowing his head at Rāma's feet, Nārad returned to the city of Brahmmā. Blessed, says Tulsīdās, are all they who abandon all other hope and attach themselves only to Harī.

दोहा-dohā:

रावनारि जसु पावन गावहिं सुनहिं जे लोग ।
rāvanāri jasu pāvana gāvahiṁ sunahiṁ je loga,
राम भगति दृढ़ पावहिं बिनु बिराग जप जोग ॥४६क॥
rāma bhagati dr̥ṛha pāvahiṁ binu birāga japa joga. 46(ka).
दीप सिखा सम जुबति तन मन जनि होसि पतंग ।
dīpa sikhā sama jubati tana mana jani hosi pataṁga,
भजहि राम तजि काम मद करहि सदा सतसंग ॥४६ख॥
bhajahi rāma taji kāma mada karahi sadā satasaṁga. 46(kha).

Trans:

People who hear or recite the sanctifying praises of Rāvan's Destroyer, even without asceticism, prayer and meditation, are rewarded with steadfast faith in Rāma. The body of a young woman is like the flame of a lamp; be not a moth to it, O mind. Abandoning lust and intoxication, worship Shrī Rāma and hold communion with the saints.

मासपारायण बाईसवाँ विश्राम
māsapārāyaṇa bāīsavāṁ viśrāma
(Pause 22 for a Thirty-Day Recitation)

इति श्रीमद्रामचरितमानसे सकलकलिकलुषविध्वंसने तृतीयः सोपानः समाप्तः

iti śrīmadrāmacaritamānase sakalakalikaluṣavidhvaṁsane tr̥tīyaḥ sopānaḥ samāptaḥ

(Now ends the Third-Ascent into the Manasa Lake of Shrī Rāma's Charita which eradicates all the impurities of the Kali-Yug)

सीताराम
सीताराम सीताराम
सीताराम सीताराम
सीताराम सीताराम

ॐ

सीताराम सीताराम सीताराम
सीताराम सीताराम सीताराम सीताराम सीताराम
सीताराम सीताराम सीताराम सीताराम सीताराम सीताराम

श्रीजानकीवल्लभो विजयते
śrījānakīvallabho vijayate

श्रीरामचरितमानस
śrīrāmacaritamānasa

चतुर्थ सोपान - किष्किन्धाकाण्ड
caturtha sopāna - kiṣkindhākāṇḍa

सीताराम

श्लोक-śloka:

कुन्देन्दीवरसुन्दरावतिबलौ विज्ञानधामावुभौ
kundendīvarasundarāvatibalau vijñānadhāmāvubhau
शोभाढ्यौ वरधन्विनौ श्रुतिनुतौ गोविप्रवृन्दप्रियौ ।
śobhāḍhyau varadhanvinau śrutinutau govipravṛndapriyau,
मायामानुषरूपिणौ रघुवरौ सद्धर्मवर्मौं हितौ
māyāmānuṣarūpiṇau raghuvarau saddharmavarmauṁ hitau
सीतान्वेषणतत्परौ पथिगतौ भक्तिप्रदौ तौ हि नः ॥१॥
sītānveṣaṇatatparau pathigatau bhaktipradau tau hi naḥ. 1.

Trans:

As like a beautiful jasmine and blue-lotus together, of surpassing strength, repositories of wisdom, all glorious excellent archers, hymned of by the Vedas, benefactors of cows and Virtuous; who, through their own Māyā, appeared in the form of mortal humans as the two noble scions of Raghu; the armors of true religion, favorable to all, the wayfarers intent on their search for Sītā: may they both grant us Bhakti.

ब्रह्माम्भोधिसमुद्भवं कलिमलप्रध्वंसनं चाव्ययं
brahmāmbhodhisamudbhavaṁ kalimalapradhvaṁsanaṁ cāvyayaṁ
श्रीमच्छम्भुमुखेन्दुसुन्दरवरे संशोभितं सर्वदा ।
śrīmacchambhumukhendusundaravare saṁśobhitaṁ sarvadā,
संसारामयभेषजं सुखकरं श्रीजानकीजीवनं
saṁsārāmayabheṣajaṁ sukhakaraṁ śrījānakījīvanaṁ
धन्यास्ते कृतिनः पिबन्ति सततं श्रीरामनामामृतम् ॥२॥
dhanyāste kṛtinaḥ pibanti satataṁ śrīrāmanāmāmṛtam. 2.

Trans:

Blessed are the pious souls who ever imbibe the nectar churned from the ocean of Vedas: the holy word Rāma—which is imperishable and the utter exterminator of all impurities of this Kali-age; which shines ever bright in the beauty of blessed Shambhu's moon-like face. Ever glorious and a palatable remedy for the disease of transmigration is the name Rāma, which is exquisitely sweet and the very life of blessed Jānakī.

सोरठा-soraṭhā:

मुक्ति जन्म महि जानि ग्यान खानि अघ हानि कर ।
mukti janma mahi jāni gyāna khāni agha hāni kara
जहँ बस संभु भवानि सो कासी सेइअ कस न ॥
jahaṁ basa saṁbhu bhavāni so kāsī seia kasa na.
जरत सकल सुर बृंद बिषम गरल जेहिं पान किय ।
jarata sakala sura bṛṁda biṣama garala jehiṁ pāna kiya,
तेहि न भजसि मन मंद को कृपाल संकर सरिस ॥
tehi na bhajasi mana maṁda ko kṛpāla saṁkara sarisa.

Trans:

Why not dwell in Kashī, the home of Shambhu and Bhawānī, knowing it to be a destroyer of sins, a treasure-house of wisdom, and the provenience of salvation? O stupid mind, how is it that you worship him not—who drank off the deadly venom: the very presence of which was scorching the legions of gods—him Shankar, the most merciful?

चौपाई-caupāī:

आगें चले बहुरि रघुराया । रिष्यमूक पर्बत निअराया ॥
āgeṁ cale bahuri raghurāyā, riṣyamūka parbata niarāyā.
तहँ रह सचिव सहित सुग्रीवा । आवत देखि अतुल बल सींवा ॥
tahaṁ raha saciva sahita sugrīvā, āvata dekhi atula bala sīṁvā.
अति सभीत कह सुनु हनुमाना । पुरुष जुगल बल रूप निधाना ॥
ati sabhīta kaha sunu hanumānā, puruṣa jugala bala rūpa nidhānā.
धरि बटु रूप देखु तैं जाई । कहेसु जानि जियँ सयन बुझाई ॥
dhari baṭu rūpa dekhu taiṁ jāī, kahesu jāni jiyaṁ sayana bujhāī.
पठए बालि होहिं मन मैला । भागौं तुरत तजौं यह सैला ॥
paṭhae bāli hohiṁ mana mailā, bhāgauṁ turata tajauṁ yaha sailā.
बिप्र रूप धरि कपि तहँ गयऊ । माथ नाइ पूछत अस भयऊ ॥
bipra rūpa dhari kapi tahaṁ gayaū, mātha nāi pūchata asa bhayaū.
को तुम्ह स्यामल गौर सरीरा । छत्री रूप फिरहु बन बीरा ॥
ko tumha syāmala gaura sarīrā, chatrī rūpa phirahu bana bīrā.
कठिन भूमि कोमल पद गामी । कवन हेतु बिचरहु बन स्वामी ॥
kaṭhina bhūmi komala pada gāmī, kavana hetu bicarahu bana svāmī.
मृदुल मनोहर सुंदर गाता । सहत दुसह बन आतप बाता ॥
mṛdula manohara suṁdara gātā, sahata dusaha bana ātapa bātā.
की तुम्ह तीनि देव महँ कोऊ । नर नारायन की तुम्ह दोऊ ॥

kī tumha tīni deva mahaṁ koū, nara nārāyana kī tumha doū.

Trans:

Proceeding further, Rāma, Lord of Raghus, drew near to the mountain Rishyamuka. There, with his counselors, dwelt Sugrīva. Seeing them—of such immeasurable strength—approach, he was exceedingly alarmed and said, "Hearken Hanumān: take the form of a Brahmin ascetic and go see who these two heroes are—of such remarkable strength and beauty; and when you have so ascertained, do make some sign by which means I may also know. If that wretch Bālī has sent them then we must flee at once and relinquish this hill." The monkey assumed the form of a Brahmin and went up to the two brothers, and then, having bowed his head to them, asked thus, "Who are you two knights of warrior mien that roam this wood, one of dark hue, the other fair? The ground is rough for your soft feet to tread—wherefore are you wandering in the forest thus, my masters? Your body is too delicate and exquisitely beautiful to be thusly exposed to the intolerable sun and winds of such wilderness. Who are you, pray say? Do you count amongst the Holy-Trinity? Or are you the two divine sages Nara and Nārāyan?

दोहा-dohā:

जग कारन तारन भव भंजन धरनी भार ।
jaga kārana tārana bhava bhaṁjana dharanī bhāra,
की तुम्ह अखिल भुवन पति लीन्ह मनुज अवतार ॥ १ ॥
kī tumha akhila bhuvana pati līnha manuja avatāra. 1.

Trans:

Or has the prime-cause of Creation, the Lord of all spheres, become incarnate in a human form—for the good of the world, to bridge the ocean of worldly-existence, and relieve the earth of her burdens?"

चौपाई-caupāī:

कोसलेस दसरथ के जाए । हम पितु बचन मानि बन आए ॥
kosalesa dasaratha ke jāe, hama pitu bacana māni bana āe.
नाम राम लछिमन दोउ भाई । संग नारि सुकुमारि सुहाई ॥
nāma rāma lachimana dou bhāī, saṁga nāri sukumāri suhāī.
इहाँ हरी निसिचर बैदेही । बिप्र फिरहिं हम खोजत तेही ॥
ihāṁ harī nisicara baidehī, bipra phirahiṁ hama khojata tehī.
आपन चरित कहा हम गाई । कहहु बिप्र निज कथा बुझाई ॥
āpana carita kahā hama gāī, kahahu bipra nija kathā bujhāī.
प्रभु पहिचानि परेउ गहि चरना । सो सुख उमा जाइ नहिं बरना ॥
prabhu pahicāni pareu gahi caranā, so sukha umā jāi nahiṁ baranā.
पुलकित तन मुख आव न बचना । देखत रुचिर बेष कै रचना ॥
pulakita tana mukha āva na bacanā, dekhata rucira beṣa kai racanā.
पुनि धीरजु धरि अस्तुति कीन्ही । हरष हृदयँ निज नाथहि चीन्ही ॥
puni dhīraju dhari astuti kīnhī, haraṣa hṛdayaṁ nija nāthahi cīnhī.
मोर न्याउ मैं पूछा साईं । तुम्ह पूछहु कस नर की नाईं ॥
mora nyāu maiṁ pūchā sāīṁ, tumha pūchahu kasa nara kī nāīṁ.
तव माया बस फिरउँ भुलाना । ता ते मैं नहिं प्रभु पहिचाना ॥
tava māyā basa phirauṁ bhulānā, tā te maiṁ nahiṁ prabhu pahicānā.

Trans:

"We are sons of Dashrath, the King of Kaushal, and have come into the forest in compliance of our father's bid. We are two brothers Rāma and Lakshman by name; and also there was with me my bride delicate—the daughter of the King of Videh, and who has been carried away by some demon here; and it is she whom we are trying to find. We have recounted our account; now tell us your own story, O Brahmin." Now then Hanumān recognized his Lord and falling to the ground clasped his feet. That joy, O Umā, is beyond all descriptions. His body thrilled all over and words failed his tongue—as he gazed upon the fashion of their bewitching disguise. At last he collected himself and burst forth into hymns of praise with great joy of heart, for he had found his Lord. "It was in the fitness of things that I questioned you, sire, due to my ignorance; but why should you—feigning like a mere mortal—so inquire? Under the influence of Māyā, your delusive power, I was roving in error, and so did not at once recognize my Lord.

दोहा-dohā:

एकु मैं मंद मोहबस कुटिल हृदय अग्यान ।
eku maiṁ maṁda mohabasa kuṭila hṛdaya agyāna,
पुनि प्रभु मोहि बिसारेउ दीनबंधु भगवान ॥ २ ॥
puni prabhu mohi bisāreu dīnabaṁdhu bhagavāna. 2.

Trans:

In the first place I am dull-witted and deluded, wicked at heart and ignorant; and to crown it, you my Lord—who is the befriender of humble and the gracious Lord God—forgot me and let go.

चौपाई-caupāī:

जदपि नाथ बहु अवगुन मोरें । सेवक प्रभुहि परै जनि भोरें ॥
jadapi nātha bahu avaguna moreṁ, sevaka prabhuhi parai jani bhoreṁ.
नाथ जीव तव मायाँ मोहा । सो निस्तरइ तुम्हारेहिं छोहा ॥
nātha jīva tava māyāṁ mohā, so nistarai tumhārehiṁ chohā.
ता पर मैं रघुबीर दोहाई । जानउँ नहिं कछु भजन उपाई ॥
tā para maiṁ raghubīra dohāī, jānauṁ nahiṁ kachu bhajana upāī.
सेवक सुत पति मातु भरोसें । रहइ असोच बनइ प्रभु पोसें ॥
sevaka suta pati mātu bharoseṁ, rahai asoca banai prabhu poseṁ.
अस कहि परेउ चरन अकुलाई । निज तनु प्रगटि प्रीति उर छाई ॥
asa kahi pareu carana akulāī, nija tanu pragaṭi prīti ura chāī.
तब रघुपति उठाइ उर लावा । निज लोचन जल सींचि जुड़ावा ॥
taba raghupati uṭhāi ura lāvā, nija locana jala sīṁci juṛāvā.
सुनु कपि जियँ मानसि जनि ऊना । तैं मम प्रिय लछिमन ते दूना ॥
sunu kapi jiyaṁ mānasi jani ūnā, taiṁ mama priya lachimana te dūnā.
समदरसी मोहि कह सब कोऊ । सेवक प्रिय अनन्यगति सोऊ ॥
samadarasī mohi kaha saba koū, sevaka priya ananyagati soū.

Trans:

Although master my faults are many, but please let not this servant be cast away into oblivion, O Lord. The Jīva is fettered by your Māyā, and can be freed only by your grace. I make my cry to you O Raghubīr, for I know no other saving mode of prayer. As a servant has confidence in his master, and a child in the mother, so does the Lord's Devotee dwell secure under the protection of his Lord God." Saying so, with utter fervor, Hanumān fell at Rāma's feet. He manifested his own monkey form and became overwhelmed with love. Then Raghupatī raised him up and took him to his bosom and then nourished him with tears of love that flowed from his eyes. "Hearken, O monkey; be not distressed—for you are twice as dear to me as Lakshman. Everyone states that I look upon all with equal eyes; but a Devotee is especially dear to me—for he depends on me, else on none.

दोहा-dohā:

सो अनन्य जाकें असि मति न टरइ हनुमंत ।
so ananya jākeṁ asi mati na ṭarai hanumaṁta,
मैं सेवक सचराचर रूप स्वामि भगवंत ॥ ३ ॥
maiṁ sevaka sacarācara rūpa svāmi bhagavaṁta. 3.

Trans:

And he alone, Hanumān, is exclusively devoted to me, who never wavers in this faith: 'I am the servant of my Lord God who is manifested as this entire Creation.'

चौपाई-caupāī:

देखि पवनसुत पति अनुकूला । हृदयँ हरष बीती सब सूला ॥
dekhi pavanasuta pati anukūlā, hṛdayaṁ haraṣa bītī saba sūlā.
नाथ सैल पर कपिपति रहई । सो सुग्रीव दास तव अहई ॥

nātha saila para kapipati rahaī, so sugrīva dāsa tava ahaī.
तेहि सन नाथ मयत्री कीजे । दीन जानि तेहि अभय करीजे ॥
tehi sana nātha mayatrī kīje, dīna jāni tehi abhaya karīje.
सो सीता कर खोज कराइहि । जहँ तहँ मरकट कोटि पठाइहि ॥
so sītā kara khoja karāihi, jahaṁ tahaṁ marakaṭa koṭi paṭhāihi.
एहि बिधि सकल कथा समुझाई । लिए दुऔ जन पीठि चढ़ाई ॥
ehi bidhi sakala kathā samujhāī, lie duau jana pīṭhi caṛhāī.
जब सुग्रीवँ राम कहुँ देखा । अतिसय जन्म धन्य करि लेखा ॥
jaba sugrīvaṁ rāma kahuṁ dekhā, atisaya janma dhanya kari lekhā.
सादर मिलेउ नाइ पद माथा । भेंटिउ अनुज सहित रघुनाथा ॥
sādara mileu nāi pada māthā, bheiṁṭeu anuja sahita raghunāthā.
कपि कर मन बिचार एहि रीती । करिहहिं बिधि मो सन ए प्रीती ॥
kapi kara mana bicāra ehi rītī, karihahiṁ bidhi mo sana e prītī.

Trans:

When Hanumān, the son of wind-god, found his Lord so gracious, he rejoiced in his heart; and his agony disappeared. "My Lord, on the summit of this hill dwells the chief of the monkeys, Sugrīva, a servant of yours. Make friends with him, O Lord; and knowing him to be in affliction rid him of all fear. He will have Sītā tracked by dispatching millions of monkeys in all directions." Having thus explained to them all the particulars Hanumān took them both with him on his back. When Sugrīva saw Rāma he fructified his birth as the greatest blessing. Reverentially he met them, bowing his head at the feet; and Raghunāth and his brother embraced him in return. The monkey's mind was occupied with this thought, 'If heavens would only give me such ones as my allies!'

दोहा-dohā:

तब हनुमंत उभय दिसि की सब कथा सुनाइ ।
taba hanumaṁta ubhaya disi kī saba kathā sunāi,
पावक साखी देइ करि जोरी प्रीति दृढाइ ॥४॥
pāvaka sākhī dei kari jorī prīti dṛṛhāi. 4.

Trans:

Hanumān then related the circumstance on both sides, and having installed the sacred fire as Witness, a firm alliance was concluded between them.

चौपाई-caupāī:

कीन्हि प्रीति कछु बीच न राखा । लछमिन राम चरित सब भाषा ॥
kīnhi prīti kachu bīca na rākhā, lachamina rāma carita saba bhāṣā.
कह सुग्रीव नयन भरि बारी । मिलिहि नाथ मिथिलेसकुमारी ॥
kaha sugrīva nayana bhari bārī, milihi nātha mithilesakumārī.
मंत्रिन्ह सहित इहाँ एक बारा । बैठ रहेउँ मैं करत बिचारा ॥
maṁtrinha sahita ihāṁ eka bārā, baiṭha raheuṁ maiṁ karata bicārā.
गगन पंथ देखी मैं जाता । परबस परी बहुत बिलपाता ॥
gagana paṁtha dekhī maiṁ jātā, parabasa parī bahuta bilapātā.
राम राम हा राम पुकारी । हमहि देखि दीन्हेउ पट डारी ॥
rāma rāma hā rāma pukārī, hamahi dekhi dīnheu paṭa ḍārī.
मागा राम तुरत तेहिं दीन्हा । पट उर लाइ सोच अति कीन्हा ॥
māgā rāma turata tehiṁ dīnhā, paṭa ura lāi soca ati kīnhā.
कह सुग्रीव सुनहु रघुबीरा । तजहु सोच मन आनहु धीरा ॥
kaha sugrīva sunahu raghubīrā, tajahu soca mana ānahu dhīrā.
सब प्रकार करिहउँ सेवकाई । जेहि बिधि मिलिहि जानकी आई ॥
saba prakāra karihauṁ sevakāī, jehi bidhi milihi jānakī āī.

Trans:

When the alliance had been concluded, nothing was kept in reserve; Rāma and Lakshman told all their adventures. Said Sugrīva, his eyes full of tears, "The daughter of King of Mithilā will surely be recovered. On one occasion, when I was deliberating with my counselors, I saw someone borne through the air with a woman in his power, who wept piteously and cried 'Rāma, Rāma, O my Rāma!' When she saw us, she dropped her scarf." When Rāma asked for it, it was brought to him at once. He pressed the scarf to his bosom in the deep distress. Said Sugrīva: "Hearken Raghubīr; be not so distressed, take heart. I will render service to you in every possible way so that Jānakī is recovered."

दोहा-dohā:

सखा बचन सुनि हरषे कृपासिंधु बलसींव ।
sakhā bacana suni harașe kṛpāsiṁdhu balasīṁva,
कारन कवन बसहु बन मोहि कहहु सुग्रीव ॥५॥
kārana kavana basahu bana mohi kahahu sugrīva. 5.

Trans:

The All-mighty, Ocean of Mercy, rejoiced to hear his friend's speech. "Tell me, O Sugrīva, the reason why you are living in this forest."

चौपाई-caupāī:

नाथ बालि अरु मैं द्वौ भाई । प्रीति रही कछु बरनि न जाई ॥
nātha bāli aru maiṁ dvau bhāī, prīti rahī kachu barani na jāī.
मय सुत मायावी तेहि नाऊँ । आवा सो प्रभु हमरें गाऊँ ॥
maya suta māyāvī tehi nāūṁ, āvā so prabhu hamareṁ gāūṁ.
अर्ध राति पुर द्वार पुकारा । बाली रिपु बल सहै न पारा ॥
ardha rāti pura dvāra pukārā, bālī ripu bala sahai na pārā.
धावा बालि देखि सो भागा । मैं पुनि गयउँ बंधु सँग लागा ॥
dhāvā bāli dekhi so bhāgā, maiṁ puni gayauṁ baṁdhu saṁga lāgā.
गिरिबर गुहाँ पैठ सो जाई । तब बालीं मोहि कहा बुझाई ॥
giribara guhāṁ paiṭha so jāī, taba bālīṁ mohi kahā bujhāī.
परिखेसु मोहि एक पखवारा । नहिं आवौं तब जानेसु मारा ॥
parikhesu mohi eka pakhavārā, nahiṁ āvauṁ taba jānesu mārā.
मास दिवस तहँ रहेउँ खरारी । निसरी रुधिर धार तहँ भारी ॥
māsa divasa tahaṁ raheuṁ kharārī, nisarī rudhira dhāra tahaṁ bhārī.
बाली हतेसि मोहि मारिहि आई । सिला देइ तहँ चलेउँ पराई ॥
bālī hatesi mohi mārihi āī, silā dei tahaṁ caleuṁ parāī.
मंत्रिन्ह पुर देखा बिनु साईं । दीन्हेउ मोहि राज बरिआईं ॥
maṁtrinha pura dekhā binu sāīṁ, dīnheu mohi rāja bariāīṁ.
बालि ताहि मारि गृह आवा । देखि मोहि जियँ भेद बढ़ावा ॥
bāli tāhi māri gṛha āvā, dekhi mohi jiyaṁ bheda baṛhāvā.
रिपु सम मोहि मारेसि अति भारी । हरि लीन्हेसि सर्बसु अरु नारी ॥
ripu sama mohi māresi ati bhārī, hari līnhesi sarbasu aru nārī.
ताकें भय रघुबीर कृपाला । सकल भुवन मैं फिरेउँ बिहाला ॥
tākeṁ bhaya raghubīra kṛpālā, sakala bhuvana maiṁ phireuṁ bihālā.
इहाँ साप बस आवत नाहीं । तदपि सभीत रहउँ मन माहीं ॥
ihāṁ sāpa basa āvata nāhīṁ, tadapi sabhīta rahauṁ mana māhīṁ.
सुनि सेवक दुख दीनदयाला । फरकि उठीं द्वै भुजा बिसाला ॥
suni sevaka dukha dīnadayālā, pharaki uṭhīṁ dvai bhujā bisālā.

Trans:

"My Lord, Bālī and I are two brothers; our mutual love was past all telling. Once, Māyāvi, the son of demon Māyā, came to our town, and at the dead of night he hollered at the city-gate. Bālī would not brook any enemy's challenge to bout, and so he stormed out. Seeing Bālī come, the demon fled; and Bālī, with me besides, offered him chase. Seeing that he had entered a mountain cave, Bālī instructed me: 'Await here my return for a fortnight; and if I haven't returned by then, then take me as slain.' When I had stayed there a whole month, O Kharārī, a copious stream of blood flowed forth from the cave. Concluding that Bālī had been killed and that the enemy would now come kill me as well, I closed the cave-mouth with a rock and fled home. When the ministers saw the town without a chief, they forced me upon the throne, whether I would or not. Meanwhile it was Bālī who had slew the foe and he came home. Then seeing what had happened it tore his heart apart. He severely thrashed me, as one would an enemy, and took from me everything, including my wife. For fear of him, O merciful Raghubīr, I wander forlorn all over the world. A curse prevents Bālī from coming to this hill; still I remain here ill at ease in mind." When the friend of the suppliant heard of his devotee's distress, his two mighty arms began to throb.

दोहा-dohā:

सुनु सुग्रीव मारिहउँ बालिहि एकहिं बान ।
sunu sugrīva mārihaum̐ bālihi ekahiṁ bāna,
ब्रह्म रुद्र सरनागत गएँ न उबरिहिं प्रान ॥ ६ ॥
brahma rudra saranāgata gaem̐ na ubarihiṁ prāna. 6.

Trans:

"Hearken, Sugrīva: I will slay Bālī with a single arrow; he shall not escape with his life, though he may take refuge with Brahmmā, or Rudra.

चौपाई-caupāī:

जे न मित्र दुख होहिं दुखारी । तिन्हहि बिलोकत पातक भारी ॥
je na mitra dukha hohiṁ dukhārī, tinhahi bilokata pātaka bhārī.
निज दुख गिरि सम रज करि जाना । मित्रक दुख रज मेरु समाना ॥
nija dukha giri sama raja kari jānā, mitraka dukha raja meru samānā.
जिन्ह कें असि मति सहज न आई । ते सठ कत हठि करत मिताई ॥
jinha keṁ asi mati sahaja na āī, te saṭha kata haṭhi karata mitāī.
कुपथ निवारि सुपंथ चलावा । गुन प्रगटै अवगुनन्हि दुरावा ॥
kupatha nivāri supaṁtha calāvā, guna pragaṭai avagunanhi durāvā.
देत लेत मन संक न धरई । बल अनुमान सदा हित करई ॥
deta leta mana saṁka na dharaī, bala anumāna sadā hita karaī.
बिपति काल कर सतगुन नेहा । श्रुति कह संत मित्र गुन एहा ॥
bipati kāla kara sataguna nehā, śruti kaha saṁta mitra guna ehā.
आगें कह मृदु बचन बनाई । पाछें अनहित मन कुटिलाई ॥
āgeṁ kaha mṛdu bacana banāī, pācheṁ anahita mana kuṭilāī.
जा कर चित अहि गति सम भाई । अस कुमित्र परिहरेहिं भलाई ॥
jā kara cita ahi gati sama bhāī, asa kumitra pariharehiṁ bhalāī.
सेवक सठ नृप कृपन कुनारी । कपटी मित्र सूल सम चारी ॥
sevaka saṭha nṛpa kṛpana kunārī, kapaṭī mitra sūla sama cārī.
सखा सोच त्यागहु बल मोरें । सब बिधि घटब काज मैं तोरें ॥
sakhā soca tyāgahu bala moreṁ, saba bidhi ghaṭaba kāja maiṁ toreṁ.
कह सुग्रीव सुनहु रघुबीरा । बालि महाबल अति रनधीरा ॥
kaha sugrīva sunahu raghubīrā, bāli mahābala ati ranadhīrā.
दुंदुभि अस्थि ताल देखराए । बिनु प्रयास रघुनाथ ढहाए ॥
duṁdubhi asthi tāla dekharāe, binu prayāsa raghunātha ḍhahāe.
देखि अमित बल बाढ़ी प्रीती । बालि बधब इन्ह भइ परतीती ॥
dekhi amita bala bāṛhī prītī, bāli badhaba inha bhai paratīti.
बार बार नावइ पद सीसा । प्रभुहि जानि मन हरष कपीसा ॥
bāra bāra nāvai pada sīsā, prabhuhi jāni mana haraṣa kapīsā.
उपजा ग्यान बचन तब बोला । नाथ कृपाँ मन भयउ अलोला ॥
upajā gyāna bacana taba bolā, nātha kṛpām̐ mana bhayau alolā.
सुख संपति परिवार बड़ाई । सब परिहरि करिहउँ सेवकाई ॥
sukha saṁpati parivāra baṛāī, saba parihari karihaum̐ sevakāī.
ए सब राम भगति के बाधक । कहहिं संत तव पद अवराधक ॥
e saba rāma bhagati ke bādhaka, kahahiṁ saṁta tava pada avarādhaka.
सत्रु मित्र सुख दुख जग माहीं । माया कृत परमारथ नाहीं ॥
satru mitra sukha dukha jaga māhīṁ, māyā kṛta paramāratha nāhīṁ.
बालि परम हित जासु प्रसादा । मिलेहु राम तुम्ह समन बिषादा ॥
bāli parama hita jāsu prasādā, milehu rāma tumha samana biṣādā.
सपनें जेहि सन होइ लराई । जागें समुझत मन सकुचाई ॥
sapaneṁ jehi sana hoi larāī, jāgeṁ samujhata mana sakucāī.
अब प्रभु कृपा करहु एहि भाँती । सब तजि भजनु करौं दिन राती ॥
aba prabhu kṛpā karahu ehi bhām̐tī, saba taji bhajanu karauṁ dina rātī.
सुनि बिराग संजुत कपि बानी । बोले बिहँसि रामु धनुपानी ॥
suni birāga saṁjuta kapi bānī, bole biham̐si rāmu dhanupānī.
जो कछु कहेहु सत्य सब सोई । सखा बचन मम मृषा न होई ॥
jo kachu kahehu satya saba soī, sakhā bacana mama mṛṣā na hoī.
नट मरकट इव सबहि नचावत । रामु खगेस बेद अस गावत ॥
naṭa marakaṭa iva sabahi nacāvata, rāmu khagesa beda asa gāvata.
लै सुग्रीव संग रघुनाथा । चले चाप सायक गहि हाथा ॥
lai sugrīva saṁga raghunāthā, cale cāpa sāyaka gahi hāthā.
तब रघुपति सुग्रीव पठावा । गर्जेसि जाइ निकट बल पावा ॥
taba raghupati sugrīva paṭhāvā, garjesi jāi nikaṭa bala pāvā.
सुनत बालि क्रोधातुर धावा । गहि कर चरन नारि समुझावा ॥
sunata bāli krodhātura dhāvā, gahi kara carana nāri samujhāvā.
सुनु पति जिन्हहि मिलेउ सुग्रीवा । ते द्वौ बंधु तेज बल सींवा ॥
sunu pati jinhahi mileu sugrīvā, te dvau baṁdhu teja bala sīṁvā.
कोसलेस सुत लछिमन रामा । कालहु जीति सकहिं संग्रामा ॥
kosalesa suta lachimana rāmā, kālahu jīti sakahiṁ saṁgrāmā.

Trans:

Those, who are not distressed at their friend's distress, even to look at them, incurs grievous sin. One should regard as a mere grain of sand their own mountain-like troubles, while a friend's trouble, though really no bigger than a grain of sand, should seem weighty as mount Meru. Churls, to whom this isn't the natural stance, in vain do they make friends. To restrain from evil path and to direct on the path of virtue; to publish all good qualities and conceal the bad; to give and take without any distrust of mind; to be always ready to assist with all one's power, and in times of misfortune to be a hundred times more affectionate than ever—such, the scriptures declare, are the characteristics of a true friend. But one who speaks fairly to your face, but behind your back is an enemy in the viciousness of his soul; whose mind, brother, is as tortuous as the movements of a snake—such a one is a bad friend whom it is well to let alone. A dishonest servant, a miserly king, a false wife, and a treacherous friend, are four things as bad as a stake. Cease to distress yourself, O friend; I will put forth all my strength to serve your cause in every way possible." Said Sugrīva, "Hearken Raghubīr: Bālī is very strong and most resolute in battle," and he showed him Dundubhi's bones and the seven palm-trees. Without an effort, Raghubīr tossed them away. At this display of enormous strength the affection of the monkey-king grew all the more and he felt assured Bālī will be killed. Again and again he bowed his head at his feet in the greatest delight, knowing Rāma to be the Lord God. Light of understanding had downed upon him, and he spoke, "O Lord, by your grace my mind is now set at rest. I will abandon pleasure, fortune, home, grandeur, and all, to do you service; for all these things are hindrances to devotion to Lord God, so declare saints who are given to the worship of your holy feet. Dualities of the world—like friends and enemies, joys and sorrows—are not eternal realities but the effects of your delusional Māyā. Bālī is my greatest benefactor, by whose favor I have met you, O Rāma, destroyer of all sorrows. A man dreams that he has been fighting someone, and then, upon waking and coming to his senses, is ashamed of his illusion. Now, my Lord, do me this favor: may I leave all and worship you day and night." When Rāma heard the monkey's devout speech, he smiled and said, with his bow in his hand, "Whatever you have said is all true; but my words, O friend, cannot fail." O Garud, Rāma, as the Vedas say, makes everything move, even as a juggler makes the monkey dance. Taking Sugrīva away with him, Raghunāth then proceeded with bow and arrows in hand. Then he sent Sugrīva ahead, who, strengthened by Shrī Rāma, thundered under the very nose of Bālī. Bālī, on hearing him, sprang up in a fury, but his wife clasped his feet in her hands and warned him thus, "Hearken my Lord: Sugrīva's allies are two brothers of untold majesty and might, the sons of the King of Kaushal, Lakshman and Rāma, who would conquer in battle even Death himself."

दोहा-dohā:

कह बाली सुनु भीरु प्रिय समदरसी रघुनाथ ।
kaha bālī sunu bhīru priya samadarasī raghunātha,
जौं कदाचि मोहि मारहिं तौ पुनि होउँ सनाथ ॥७॥
jauṁ kadāci mohi mārahiṁ tau puni houṁ sanātha. 7.

Trans:

Said Bālī, "Listen, you coward, Raghunāth is kind and the same to all; even if he kills me, I will attain His divine abode and have Him as my eternal Lord."

चौपाई-caupāī:

अस कहि चला महा अभिमानी । तृन समान सुग्रीवहि जानी ॥
asa kahi calā mahā abhimānī, tṛna samāna sugrīvahi jānī.
भिरे उभौ बाली अति तर्जा । मुठिका मारि महाधुनि गर्जा ॥
bhire ubhau bālī ati tarjā, muṭhikā māri mahādhuni garjā.
तब सुग्रीव बिकल होइ भागा । मुष्टि प्रहार बज्र सम लागा ॥
taba sugrīva bikala hoi bhāgā, muṣṭi prahāra bajra sama lāgā.
मैं जो कहा रघुबीर कृपाला । बंधु न होइ मोर यह काला ॥
maiṁ jo kahā raghubīra kṛpālā, baṁdhu na hoi mora yaha kālā.
एकरूप तुम्ह भ्राता दोऊ । तेहि भ्रम तें नहिं मारेउँ सोऊ ॥
ekarūpa tumha bhrātā doū, tehi bhrama teṁ nahiṁ māreuṁ soū.
कर परसा सुग्रीव सरीरा । तनु भा कुलिस गई सब पीरा ॥
kara parasā sugrīva sarīrā, tanu bhā kulisa gaī saba pīrā.
मेली कंठ सुमन कै माला । पठवा पुनि बल देइ बिसाला ॥
melī kaṁṭha sumana kai mālā, paṭhavā puni bala dei bisālā.
पुनि नाना बिधि भई लराई । बिटप ओट देखहिं रघुराई ॥
puni nānā bidhi bhaī larāī, biṭapa oṭa dekhahiṁ raghurāī.

Trans:

So saying, he sallied forth in all his pride, thinking no more of Sugrīva than of a mere blade of grass. The two joined combat; and Bālī with a furious leap struck him a blow with his fist, and he roared like a clap of thunder. The stroke of clenched fists rained down upon him like bolts from heaven, until Sugrīva fled in dismay. "Did I not say, O merciful Raghubīr? This is no brother of mine but Death himself." "You two brothers are so much alike that for fear of mistake I did not kill him." He then stroked Sugrīva's body with his fist and his frame was healed and his pain was gone and he became hard as adamant. Then placing around his neck a wreath of flowers and granting enormous strength, Rāma sent him back again. Once more they fought in every kind of way, while Rāma watched them from behind a tree.

दोहा-dohā:

बहु छल बल सुग्रीव कर हियँ हारा भय मानि ।
bahu chala bala sugrīva kara hiyaṁ hārā bhaya māni,
मारा बालि राम तब हृदय माझ सर तानि ॥८॥
mārā bāli rāma taba hṛdaya mājha sara tāni. 8.

Trans:

When Sugrīva had tried every trick and put forth all his strength and had given up in despair, then Rāma drew an arrow and struck Bālī in the heart.

चौपाई-caupāī:

परा बिकल महि सर के लागें । पुनि उठि बैठ देखि प्रभु आगें ॥
parā bikala mahi sara ke lāgeṁ, puni uṭhi baiṭha dekhi prabhu āgeṁ.
स्याम गात सिर जटा बनाएँ । अरुन नयन सर चाप चढ़ाएँ ॥
syāma gāta sira jaṭā banāeṁ, aruna nayana sara cāpa caṛhāeṁ.
पुनि पुनि चितइ चरन चित दीन्हा । सुफल जन्म माना प्रभु चीन्हा ॥
puni puni citai carana cita dīnhā, suphala janma mānā prabhu cīnhā.
हृदयँ प्रीति मुख बचन कठोरा । बोला चितइ राम की ओरा ॥
hṛdayaṁ prīti mukha bacana kaṭhorā, bolā citai rāma kī orā.
धर्म हेतु अवतरेहु गोसाईं । मारेहु मोहि ब्याध की नाईं ॥
dharma hetu avatarehu gosāīṁ, mārehu mohi byādha kī nāīṁ.
मैं बैरी सुग्रीव पिआरा । अवगुन कवन नाथ मोहि मारा ॥
maiṁ bairī sugrīva piārā, avaguna kavana nātha mohi mārā.
अनुज बधू भगिनी सुत नारी । सुनु सठ कन्या सम ए चारी ॥
anuja badhū bhaginī suta nārī, sunu saṭha kanyā sama e cārī.
इन्हहि कुदृष्टि बिलोकइ जोई । ताहि बधें कछु पाप न होई ॥
inhahi kudraṣṭi bilokai joī, tāhi badheṁ kachu pāpa na hoī.
मूढ़ तोहि अतिसय अभिमाना । नारि सिखावन करसि न काना ॥
mūṛha tohi atisaya abhimānā, nāri sikhāvana karasi na kānā.
मम भुज बल आश्रित तेहि जानी । मारा चहसि अधम अभिमानी ॥
mama bhuja bala āśrita tehi jānī, mārā cahasi adhama abhimānī.

Trans:

Struck by the arrow, Bālī fell in agony on the ground. Again he sat up and saw the Lord standing before him, dark of hue, with his hair fastened up in a knot on his head, with flaming eyes and an arrow fitted to his bow-string. Again and again as he gazed upon him, he laid his soul at his feet and accounted his life blessed: for he recognized his Lord. Though his heart was full of affection, the words from his mouth were harsh, as he looked towards Rāma and said, "You became Incarnate, sire, for the upholding of righteousness; and yet you take my life as a huntsman would hunt a wild beast? I am the enemy and Sugrīva a friend? But why? For what fault you took my life, O Lord?" "Listen wretch; a brother's wife, a sister, a daughter-in-law and an unwedded maid are all alike: whoever looks upon one of them with an evil eye may be slain without any sin. Fool, in your extravagant pride you paid no heed to your wife's warning. You knew that your brother had taken refuge under the might of my arm, and yet in your vile arrogance you sought to kill him!"

दोहा-dohā:

सुनहु राम स्वामी सन चल न चातुरी मोरि ।
sunahu rāma svāmī sana cala na cāturī mori,
प्रभु अजहूँ मैं पापी अंतकाल गति तोरि ॥९॥
prabhu ajahūṁ maiṁ pāpī aṁtakāla gati tori. 9.

Trans:

"Hearken Rāma; my craftiness cannot prevail over you, master. But Lord, am I a sinner still? Even though I have found shelter in you at the hour of my death?"

चौपाई-caupāī:

सुनत राम अति कोमल बानी । बालि सीस परसेउ निज पानी ॥
sunata rāma ati komala bānī, bāli sīsa paraseu nija pānī.
अचल करौं तनु राखहु प्राना । बालि कहा सुनु कृपानिधाना ॥
acala karauṁ tanu rākhahu prānā, bāli kahā sunu kṛpānidhānā.
जन्म जन्म मुनि जतनु कराहीं । अंत राम कहि आवत नाहीं ॥
janma janma muni jatanu karāhīṁ, aṁta rāma kahi āvata nāhīṁ.
जासु नाम बल संकर कासी । देत सबहि सम गति अबिनासी ॥
jāsu nāma bala saṁkara kāsī, deta sabahi sama gati abināsī.
मम लोचन गोचर सोइ आवा । बहुरि कि प्रभु अस बनिहि बनावा ॥
mama locana gocara soi āvā, bahuri ki prabhu asa banihi banāvā.

Trans:

When Rāma heard this most tender speech, he touched Bālī's head with his hands, "I will restore you; retain your life." Said Bālī, "Hearken O All-merciful: Born repeatedly, sages labor throughout their life, life after life; and yet, at the end, even the name Rāma does not come to them. But Rāma himself—the everlasting, by the virtue of whose name Shankar at Kashī bestows heaven upon all alike—has come in visible form before my very eyes! Can I ever, my Lord, have such opportunity again?

छंद-chaṁda:

सो नयन गोचर जासु गुन नित नेति कहि श्रुति गावहीं ।
so nayana gocara jāsu guna nita neti kahi śruti gāvahīṁ,
जिति पवन मन गो निरस करि मुनि ध्यान कबहुँक पावहीं ॥
jiti pavana mana go nirasa kari muni dhyāna kabahuṁka pāvahīṁ.
मोहि जानि अति अभिमान बस प्रभु कहेउ राखु सरीरही ।
mohi jāni ati abhimāna basa prabhu kaheu rākhu sarīrahī,
अस कवन सठ हठि काटि सुरतरु बारि करिहि बबूरही ॥ १ ॥
asa kavana saṭha haṭhi kāṭi surataru bāri karihi babūrahī. 1.

अब नाथ करि करुना बिलोकहु देहु जो बर मागऊँ ।
aba nātha kari karunā bilokahu dehu jo bara māgaūṁ,
जेहिं जोनि जन्मौं कर्म बस तहँ राम पद अनुरागऊँ ॥
jehiṁ joni janmauṁ karma basa tahaṁ rāma pada anurāgaūṁ.
यह तनय मम सम बिनय बल कल्यानप्रद प्रभु लीजिऐ ।
yaha tanaya mama sama binaya bala kalyānaprada prabhu lījiai,
गहि बाहँ सुर नर नाह आपन दास अंगद कीजिऐ ॥ २ ॥
gahi bāhaṁ sura nara nāha āpana dāsa aṁgada kījiai. 2.

Trans:

He has become visible to my eyes: He, whose praises the scriptures are all unable to declare, the Lord God to whom the saints scarcely attain even after profound contemplation accompanied by laborious control of the breath, mind, and control of the senses. Seeing me, the victim of excessive pride, the Lord has told me to retain this body. But who would be such a fool as to insist upon cutting down a celestial-tree to fence a wild babul tree? Now, my Lord, look upon me with compassion and grant me the boon I beg: whatever the species, in which it be my fate to be born, may I ever cherish a special devotion to your holy-feet Rāma. O Bestower of Blessedness, this here is my son Angad who equals me in service and valour; please deign to accept him Lord. Grasp him by hand and make him your servant, O king of gods and men."

दोहा-dohā:

राम चरन दृढ़ प्रीति करि बालि कीन्ह तनु त्याग ।
rāma carana dṛṛha prīti kari bāli kīnha tanu tyāga,
सुमन माल जिमि कंठ ते गिरत न जानइ नाग ॥ १० ॥
sumana māla jimi kaṁṭha te girata na jānai nāga. 10.

Trans:

After making a fervent act of devotion to Rāma's feet, Bālī's soul left the body; as placidly as when a wreath of flowers drops from an elephant's neck without his knowing of it.

चौपाई-caupāī:

राम बालि निज धाम पठावा । नगर लोग सब ब्याकुल धावा ॥
rāma bāli nija dhāma paṭhāvā, nagara loga saba byākula dhāvā.
नाना बिधि बिलाप कर तारा । छूटे केस न देह सँभारा ॥
nānā bidhi bilāpa kara tārā, chūṭe kesa na deha saṁbhārā.
तारा बिकल देखि रघुराया । दीन्ह ग्यान हरि लीन्ही माया ॥
tārā bikala dekhi raghurāyā, dīnha gyāna hari līnhī māyā.
छिति जल पावक गगन समीरा । पंच रचित अति अधम सरीरा ॥
chiti jala pāvaka gagana samīrā, paṁca racita ati adhama sarīrā.
प्रगट सो तनु तव आगें सोवा । जीव नित्य केहि लगि तुम्ह रोवा ॥
pragaṭa so tanu tava āgeṁ sovā, jīva nitya kehi lagi tumha rovā.
उपजा ग्यान चरन तब लागी । लीन्हेसि परम भगति बर मागी ॥
upajā gyāna carana taba lāgī, līnhesi parama bhagati bara māgī.
उमा दारु जोषित की नाईं । सबहि नचावत रामु गोसाईं ॥
umā dāru joṣita kī nāīṁ, sabahi nacāvata rāmu gosāīṁ.
तब सुग्रीवहि आयसु दीन्हा । मृतक कर्म बिधिवत सब कीन्हा ॥
taba sugrīvahi āyasu dīnhā, mṛtaka karma bidhivata saba kīnhā.
राम कहा अनुजहि समुझाई । राज देहु सुग्रीवहि जाई ॥
rāma kahā anujahi samujhāī, rāja dehu sugrīvahi jāī.
रघुपति चरन नाइ करि माथा । चले सकल प्रेरित रघुनाथा ॥
raghupati carana nāi kari māthā, cale sakala prerita raghunāthā.

Trans:

And Rāma dismissed him to his own heavenly mansion. All the people of the city came running in dismay; and Tara with disheveled hair and tottering frame broke out in wild lamentation. When Raghurāī saw her distress, he imparted her wisdom and dispersed her delusion. "The body, which is composed of the five elements—earth, water, fire, air and ether—is of no measure. The mortal frame, which you see before you, sleeps—but the soul is eternal; why then do you weep?" True understanding arose in her mind; and she embraced his feet and received the boon which she asked: boon of Supreme Devotion. O Umā, Lord Rāma makes the whole world dance like puppets on strings. Then Rāma gave orders to Sugrīva, who performed all the funeral rites with due ceremony. Rāma next directed his brother to bestow the crown upon Sugrīva and make him king. He bowed his head at Raghupatī's feet and went forth—he and all whom Rāma had commissioned to accompany him.

दोहा-dohā:

लछिमन तुरत बोलाए पुरजन बिप्र समाज ।
lachimana turata bolāe purajana bipra samāja,
राजु दीन्ह सुग्रीव कहँ अंगद कहँ जुबराज ॥ ११ ॥
rāju dīnha sugrīva kahaṁ aṁgada kahaṁ jubarāja. 11.

Trans:

Lakshman immediately summoned the citizens and the council of Brahmins, and invested Sugrīva with the sovereignty and appointed Angad the Prince Imperial.

चौपाई-caupāī:

उमा राम सम हित जग माहीं । गुरु पितु मातु बंधु प्रभु नाहीं ॥
umā rāma sama hita jaga māhīṁ, guru pitu mātu baṁdhu prabhu nāhīṁ.
सुर नर मुनि सब कै यह रीती । स्वारथ लागि करहिं सब प्रीती ॥
sura nara muni saba kai yaha rītī, svāratha lāgi karahiṁ saba prītī.
बालि त्रास ब्याकुल दिन राती । तन बहु ब्रन चिंताँ जर छाती ॥
bāli trāsa byākula dina rātī, tana bahu brana ciṁtāṁ jara chātī.
सोइ सुग्रीव कीन्ह कपिराऊ । अति कृपाल रघुबीर सुभाऊ ॥
soi sugrīva kīnha kapirāū, ati kṛpāla raghubīra subhāū.
जानतहूँ अस प्रभु परिहरहीं । काहे न बिपति जाल नर परहीं ॥
jānatahūṁ asa prabhu pariharahīṁ, kāhe na bipati jāla nara parahīṁ.
पुनि सुग्रीवहि लीन्ह बोलाई । बहु प्रकार नृपनीति सिखाई ॥
puni sugrīvahi līnha bolāī, bahu prakāra nṛpanīti sikhāī.
कह प्रभु सुनु सुग्रीव हरीसा । पुर न जाउँ दस चारि बरीसा ॥
kaha prabhu sunu sugrīva harīsā, pura na jāuṁ dasa cāri barīsā.
गत ग्रीषम बरषा रितु आई । रहिहउँ निकट सैल पर छाई ॥
gata grīṣama baraṣā ritu āī, rahihauṁ nikaṭa saila para chāī.
अंगद सहित करहु तुम्ह राजू । संतत हृदयँ धरेहु मम काजू ॥
aṁgada sahita karahu tumha rājū, saṁtata hṛdayaṁ dharehu mama kājū.
जब सुग्रीव भवन फिरि आए । रामु प्रबरषन गिरि पर छाए ॥
jaba sugrīva bhavana phiri āe, rāmu prabaraṣana giri para chāe.

Trans:

O Umā, there is no such friend as Rāma in the whole world, neither Gurū, nor father, nor mother, nor kinsman, nor master. It is the way with all else—be they gods, men or saints—to proffer kinship for some motive or the other; but the generous Raghubīr, from his natural self kindness, made Sugrīva king of the monkeys—who ere trembled day and night in such fear of Bālī that there was no color left in his face and his heart was burnt up with anxiety. I know this: that any man, who deserts such a Lord, is fated to be caught in the meshes of calamity. Rāma then sent for Sugrīva and instructed him in all the principles of statecraft, and added, "Hearken Sugrīva, lord of the monkey race; I may not enter a city for four years and ten. The hot season is now over and the rains have set in. I will encamp on the hills close by. Do you, with Angad, reign in the royal state; but remain ever mindful of my interest." Sugrīva then returned to the palace, and Rāma remained in camp on mount Pravarshana.

दोहा-dohā:

प्रथमहिं देवन्ह गिरि गुहा राखेउ रुचिर बनाइ ।
prathamahiṁ devanha giri guhā rākheu rucira banāi,
राम कृपानिधि कछु दिन बास करहिंगे आइ ॥ १२ ॥
rāma kṛpānidhi kachu dina bāsa karahiṁge āi. 12.

Trans:

The gods had beforehand made and kept a charming cave in readiness in the mountain—knowing that the All-merciful Rāma would come and stay there for a few days.

चौपाई-caupāī:

सुंदर बन कुसुमित अति सोभा । गुंजत मधुप निकर मधु लोभा ॥
suṁdara bana kusumita ati sobhā, guṁjata madhupa nikara madhu lobhā.
कंद मूल फल पत्र सुहाए । भए बहुत जब ते प्रभु आए ॥
kaṁda mūla phala patra suhāe, bhae bahuta jaba te prabhu āe.
देखि मनोहर सैल अनूपा । रहे तहँ अनुज सहित सुरभूपा ॥
dekhi manohara saila anūpā, rahe tahaṁ anuja sahita surabhūpā.
मधुकर खग मृग तनु धरि देवा । करहिं सिद्ध मुनि प्रभु कै सेवा ॥
madhukara khaga mṛga tanu dhari devā, karahiṁ siddha muni prabhu kai sevā.
मंगलरुप भयउ बन तब ते । कीन्ह निवास रमापति जब ते ॥
maṁgalarupa bhayau bana taba te, kīnha nivāsa ramāpati jaba te.
फटिक सिला अति सुभ्र सुहाई । सुख आसीन तहाँ द्वौ भाई ॥
phaṭika silā ati subhra suhāī, sukha āsīna tahāṁ dvau bhāī.
कहत अनुज सन कथा अनेका । भगति बिरति नृपनीति बिबेका ॥
kahata anuja sana kathā anekā, bhagati birati nṛpanīti bibekā.
बरषा काल मेघ नभ छाए । गरजत लागत परम सुहाए ॥
baraṣā kāla megha nabha chāe, garajata lāgata parama suhāe.

Trans:

The magnificent forest was a most charming sight, with the trees all in flower and the swarms of buzzing bees gathering honey. From the time that the Lord came, every plant and fruit and every kind of agreeable foliage was forthcoming in profusion. Seeing the incomparable beauty of the hill, the Lord and his brother rested there. In the form of bees, birds and deer, the gods, saints and seers came and did service to their Lord. Now that Lakshmī's spouse took up his abode there, the forest became a picture of perfect felicity. There the two brothers sat at ease on the bright glistening crystal rock, and the younger was told many a narrative inculcating faith, self-governance, wisdom and statecraft. What, with the clouds that ever canopied the heavens and the frequent thunder, the season of the rains seemed a most delightful time.

दोहा-dohā:

लछिमन देखु मोर गन नाचत बारिद पेखि ।
lachimana dekhu mora gana nācata bārida pekhi,
गृही बिरति रत हरष जस बिष्नु भगत कहुँ देखि ॥ १३ ॥
gṛhī birati rata haraṣa jasa biṣnu bhagata kahuṁ dekhi. 13.

Trans:

"See, Lakshman, how dance the peacocks at the sight of clouds: like a householder with a leaning towards dispassion, rejoices when he finds a Devotee of Vishnu.

चौपाई-caupāī:

घन घमंड नभ गरजत घोरा । प्रिया हीन डरपत मन मोरा ॥
ghana ghamaṁḍa nabha garajata ghorā, priyā hīna ḍarapata mana morā.
दामिनि दमक रह न घन माहीं । खल कै प्रीति जथा थिर नाहीं ॥
dāmini damaka raha na ghana māhīṁ, khala kai prīti jathā thira nāhīṁ.
बरषहिं जलद भूमि निअराएँ । जथा नवहिं बुध बिद्या पाएँ ॥
baraṣahiṁ jalada bhūmi niarāeṁ, jathā navahiṁ budha bidyā pāeṁ.
बूँद अघात सहहिं गिरि कैसें । खल के बचन संत सह जैसें ॥
būṁda aghāta sahahiṁ giri kaiseṁ, khala ke bacana saṁta saha jaiseṁ.
छुद्र नदीं भरि चलीं तोराई । जस थोरेहुँ धन खल इतराई ॥
chudra nadīṁ bhari calīṁ torāī, jasa thorehuṁ dhana khala itarāī.
भूमि परत भा ढाबर पानी । जनु जीवहि माया लपटानी ॥
bhūmi parata bhā ḍhābara pānī, janu jīvahi māyā lapaṭānī.
समिटि समिटि जल भरहिं तलावा । जिमि सदगुन सज्जन पहिं आवा ॥
samiṭi samiṭi jala bharahiṁ talāvā, jimi sadaguna sajjana pahiṁ āvā.
सरिता जल जलनिधि महुँ जाई । होई अचल जिमि जिव हरि पाई ॥
saritā jala jalanidhi mahuṁ jāī, hoī acala jimi jiva hari pāī.

Trans:

Clouds gather in the sky and thunders roar; but my darling is gone and my soul is sore. The lightning flashes fitfully amid the darkness: like the friendship of the vile which is never lasting. The clouds heavy with rain cleave close to the ground: even as the learned stoop down upon accumulating wisdom. The mountain endures the buffeting of the storm: as a saint would put up with taunts of wicked. The flooded streamlets rush proudly along: like mean men puffed up with a little wealth. The water by its contact with the earth becomes muddy: as the soul is soiled when hemmed in by delusion. The lakes swell gradually and imperceptibly: like as when the quality of goodness develop in a good man; and the rivers flow into the bosom of the ocean: like the soul that has found Harī comes for ever to repose.

दोहा-dohā:

हरित भूमि तृन संकुल समुझि परहिं नहिं पंथ ।
harita bhūmi tṛna saṁkula samujhi parahiṁ nahiṁ paṁtha,
जिमि पाखंड बाद तें गुप्त होहिं सदग्रंथ ॥१४॥
jimi pākhaṁḍa bāda teṁ gupta hohiṁ sadagraṁtha. 14.

Trans:

The green earth is so choked with grass that the paths can no longer be distinguished: like the holy books obscured by the wrangling of heretics.

चौपाई-caupāī:

दादुर धुनि चहु दिसा सुहाई । बेद पढ़हिं जनु बटु समुदाई ॥
dādura dhuni cahu disā suhāī, beda paṛhahiṁ janu baṭu samudāī.
नव पल्लव भए बिटप अनेका । साधक मन जस मिलें बिबेका ॥
nava pallava bhae biṭapa anekā, sādhaka mana jasa mileṁ bibekā.
अर्क जवास पात बिनु भयऊ । जस सुराज खल उद्यम गयऊ ॥
arka javāsa pāta binu bhayaū, jasa surāja khala udyama gayaū.
खोजत कतहुँ मिलइ नहिं धूरी । करइ क्रोध जिमि धरमहि दूरी ॥
khojata katahuṁ milai nahiṁ dhūrī, karai krodha jimi dharamahi dūrī.
ससि संपन्न सोह महि कैसी । उपकारी कै संपति जैसी ॥
sasi saṁpanna soha mahi kaisī, upakārī kai saṁpati jaisī.
निसि तम घन खद्योत बिराजा । जनु दंभिन्ह कर मिला समाजा ॥
nisi tama ghana khadyota birājā, janu daṁbhinha kara milā samājā.
महाबृष्टि चलि फूटि किआरीं । जिमि सुतंत्र भएँ बिगरहिं नारीं ॥
mahābṛṣṭi cali phūṭi kiārīṁ, jimi sutaṁtra bhaeṁ bigarahiṁ nārīṁ.
कृषी निरावहिं चतुर किसाना । जिमि बुध तजहिं मोह मद माना ॥
kṛṣī nirāvahiṁ catura kisānā, jimi budha tajahiṁ moha mada mānā.
देखिअत चक्रबाक खग नाहीं । कलिहि पाइ जिमि धर्म पराहीं ॥
dekhiata cakrabāka khaga nāhīṁ, kalihi pāi jimi dharma parāhīṁ.
ऊषर बरषइ तृन नहिं जामा । जिमि हरिजन हियँ उपज न कामा ॥
ūṣara baraṣai tṛna nahiṁ jāmā, jimi harijana hiyaṁ upaja na kāmā.
बिबिध जंतु संकुल महि भ्राजा । प्रजा बाढ़ जिमि पाइ सुराजा ॥
bibidha jaṁtu saṁkula mahi bhrājā, prajā bāṛha jimi pāi surājā.
जहँ तहँ रहे पथिक थकि नाना । जिमि इंद्रिय गन उपजें ग्याना ॥
jahaṁ tahaṁ rahe pathika thaki nānā, jimi iṁdriya gana upajeṁ gyānā.

Trans:

On all sides there is a lively croaking of frogs: like a group of Brahmin students chanting the Vedas. All the trees put forth their new leaves: like pious souls that have come to maturity with wisdom. The *āk* and *jawāsā* plants lose their leaves: as in a well governed kingdom the schemes of the wicked come to naught. Search as you like, there is no dust to be seen on the road: like as when religion is put out of sight by lust and passion. The earth rich with crops appears delightful: like the wealth of a generous man. The fireflies glitter in the darkness of the cloudy night: like a mustered band of hypocritical pretenders. The ridges of the fields are broken down by the heavy rains: like women ruined by too much license. The diligent cultivators weed their lands: like philosophers who root up vanity, pride, ignorance. The *chakwā* and other birds are not to be seen: like virtue that has fled at the coming of the Kali-Yug. However much it may rain, no grass springs up on barren ground: just as lust takes no root in the heart of Harī's worshippers. The earth gleams with swarms of living creatures of every kind: just as people multiply under good government. Here and there weary wayfarers stay and rest: like a man's bodily senses after the attainment of wisdom.

दोहा-dohā:

कबहुँ प्रबल बह मारुत जहँ तहँ मेघ बिलाहिं ।
kabahuṁ prabala baha māruta jahaṁ tahaṁ megha bilāhiṁ,
जिमि कपूत के उपजें कुल सद्धर्म नसाहिं ॥१५क॥
jimi kapūta ke upajeṁ kula saddharma nasāhiṁ. 15(ka).
कबहुँ दिवस महँ निबिड़ तम कबहुँक प्रगट पतंग ।
kabahuṁ divasa mahaṁ nibiṛa tama kabahuṁka pragaṭa pataṁga,
बिनसइ उपजइ ग्यान जिमि पाइ कुसंग सुसंग ॥१५ख॥
binasai upajai gyāna jimi pāi kusaṁga susaṁga. 15(kha).

Trans:

At times a strong wind disperses the clouds in all directions: like the birth of a bad son, who destroys all the pious practices of his lineage. Now it becomes pitch dark even during the day, while at other times the sun would shine brightly: just as the light of wisdom is obscured in the company of the vile and manifests itself in the company of virtuous.

चौपाई-caupāī:

बरषा बिगत सरद रितु आई । लछिमन देखहु परम सुहाई ॥
baraṣā bigata sarada ritu āī, lachimana dekhahu parama suhāī.
फूलें कास सकल महि छाई । जनु बरषाँ कृत प्रगट बुढ़ाई ॥
phūleṁ kāsa sakala mahi chāī, janu baraṣāṁ kṛta pragaṭa buṛhāī.
उदित अगस्ति पंथ जल सोषा । जिमि लोभहि सोषइ संतोषा ॥
udita agasti paṁtha jala soṣā, jimi lobhahi soṣai saṁtoṣā.
सरिता सर निर्मल जल सोहा । संत हृदय जस गत मद मोहा ॥
saritā sara nirmala jala sohā, saṁta hṛdaya jasa gata mada mohā.
रस रस सूख सरित सर पानी । ममता त्याग करहिं जिमि ग्यानी ॥
rasa rasa sūkha sarita sara pānī, mamatā tyāga karahiṁ jimi gyānī.
जानि सरद रितु खंजन आए । पाइ समय जिमि सुकृत सुहाए ॥
jāni sarada ritu khaṁjana āe, pāi samaya jimi sukṛta suhāe.
पंक न रेनु सोह असि धरनी । नीति निपुन नृप कै जसि करनी ॥
paṁka na renu soha asi dharanī, nīti nipuna nṛpa kai jasi karanī.
जल संकोच बिकल भइँ मीना । अबुध कुटुंबी जिमि धनहीना ॥
jala saṁkoca bikala bhaiṁ mīnā, abudha kuṭuṁbī jimi dhanahīnā.
बिनु धन निर्मल सोह अकासा । हरिजन इव परिहरि सब आसा ॥
binu dhana nirmala soha akāsā, harijana iva parihari saba āsā.
कहुँ कहुँ बृष्टि सारदी थोरी । कोउ एक पाव भगति जिमि मोरी ॥
kahuṁ kahuṁ bṛṣṭi sāradī thorī, kou eka pāva bhagati jimi morī.

Trans:

Now the rains are over and the season of autumn has returned; see, Lakshman, how exquisitely beautiful everything is. The whole earth is covered with the *kusha* grass and its white flowers: as though the rains have exposed its old age. The rising of Agastya (Canopus) has dried up the water on the roads: like as greed is dried up by contentment. The surface of every river and lake is pure and bright: as the soul of saints void of delusion and pride; drop by drop now their depths are diminished: like as the enlightened gradually lose all notions of selfishness. The wagtails know the autumn season and come out once more: like virtuous deeds sprung up in auspicious time. There is neither mud nor dust: the earth is as brilliant as the administration of a king who is well versed in state policy. The fish are distressed by the shrinking of the water: like improvident men of family by the loss of money. The unclouded sky shines so bright: as a worshipper of Harī who has discarded every other hope. Here and there is a slight autumn shower: like the faith of one who is not yet fully persuaded.

दोहा-dohā:

चले हरषि तजि नगर नृप तापस बनिक भिखारि ।
cale haraṣi taji nagara nṛpa tāpasa banika bhikhāri,
जिमि हरि भगति पाइ श्रम तजहिं आश्रमी चारि ॥१६॥
jimi hari bhagati pāi śrama tajahiṁ āśramī cāri. 16.

Trans:

Kings and ascetics, merchants and mendicants, leave the city and go about with enjoyment: like men in any of the four stages of life, who cease to labor when they have once attained to faith in Harī.

चौपाई-caupāī:

सुखी मीन जे नीर अगाधा । जिमि हरि सरन न एकउ बाधा ॥
sukhī mīna je nīra agādhā, jimi hari sarana na ekau bādhā.
फूलें कमल सोह सर कैसा । निर्गुन ब्रह्म सगुन भएँ जैसा ॥
phūleṁ kamala soha sara kaisā, nirguna brahma saguna bhaeṁ jaisā.
गुंजत मधुकर मुखर अनूपा । सुंदर खग रव नाना रूपा ॥
guṁjata madhukara mukhara anūpā, suṁdara khaga rava nānā rūpā.
चक्रबाक मन दुख निसि पेखी । जिमि दुर्जन पर संपति देखी ॥
cakrabāka mana dukha nisi pekhī, jimi durjana para saṁpati dekhī.
चातक रटत तृषा अति ओही । जिमि सुख लहइ न संकरद्रोही ॥
cātaka raṭata tṛṣā ati ohī, jimi sukha lahai na saṁkaradrohī.
सरदातप निसि ससि अपहरई । संत दरस जिमि पातक टरई ॥
saradātapa nisi sasi apaharaī, saṁta darasa jimi pātaka ṭaraī.
देखि इंदु चकोर समुदाई । चितवहिं जिमि हरिजन हरि पाई ॥
dekhi iṁdu cakora samudāī, citavahiṁ jimi harijana hari pāī.
मसक दंस बीते हिम त्रासा । जिमि द्विज द्रोह किएँ कुल नासा ॥
masaka daṁsa bīte hima trāsā, jimi dvija droha kieṁ kula nāsā.

Trans:

Where the water is deep, the fish are so glad: as are men who have taken refuge with Harī and have not one single trouble. The lakes, with their flowering lotuses, are so beautiful: as the immaterial Supreme Spirit when clothed with a material form. The garrulous bees make a wonderful buzzing, and the birds a charming concert of diverse sounds, but the *chakwā* is sad of soul to see the night: like a bad man at the sight of another's prosperity. The *Chātak* cries out from excess of thirst: like a rebel against Mahādev who knows no rest. The moon by night subdues the autumnal heat of sun: like at the sight of saints expelled are all sins. Flocks of partridges fix their gaze upon the moon: as Harī's worshippers look only up to their Lord. Mosquitoes and gadflies are driven away by the terrors of winter: like as a family is destroyed by the sin of persecuting the Virtuous.

दोहा-dohā:

भूमि जीव संकुल रहे गए सरद रितु पाइ ।
bhūmi jīva saṁkula rahe gae sarada ritu pāi,
सदगुर मिलें जाहिं जिमि संसय भ्रम समुदाइ ॥१७॥
sadagura mileṁ jāhiṁ jimi saṁsaya bhrama samudāi. 17.

Trans:

Under the influence of the autumn, earth is rid of its insect swarms: as a man, who has found a good teacher, is relieved from all error and doubt.

चौपाई-caupāī:

बरषा गत निर्मल रितु आई । सुधि न तात सीता कै पाई ॥
baraṣā gata nirmala ritu āī, sudhi na tāta sītā kai pāī.
एक बार कैसेहुँ सुधि जानौं । कालहु जीति निमिष महुँ आनौं ॥
eka bāra kaisehuṁ sudhi jānauṁ, kālahu jīti nimiṣa mahuṁ ānauṁ.
कतहुँ रहउ जौं जीवति होई । तात जतन करि आनउँ सोई ॥
katahuṁ rahau jauṁ jīvati hoī, tāta jatana kari ānauṁ soī.
सुग्रीवहुँ सुधि मोरि बिसारी । पावा राज कोस पुर नारी ॥
sugrīvahuṁ sudhi mori bisārī, pāvā rāja kosa pura nārī.
जेहिं सायक मारा मैं बाली । तेहिं सर हतौं मूढ़ कहँ काली ॥
jehiṁ sāyaka mārā maiṁ bālī, tehiṁ sara hatauṁ mūṛha kahaṁ kālī.
जासु कृपाँ छूटहिं मद मोहा । ता कहुँ उमा कि सपनेहुँ कोहा ॥
jāsu kṛpāṁ chūṭahiṁ mada mohā, tā kahuṁ umā ki sapanehuṁ kohā.
जानहिं यह चरित्र मुनि ग्यानी । जिन्ह रघुबीर चरन रति मानी ॥
jānahiṁ yaha caritra muni gyānī, jinha raghubīra carana rati mānī.
लछिमन क्रोधवंत प्रभु जाना । धनुष चढ़ाइ गहे कर बाना ॥
lachimana krodhavaṁta prabhu jānā, dhanuṣa caṛhāi gahe kara bānā.

Trans:

The rains are over and the clear season has come, but I have had no news, brother, of Sītā. If I could only once anyhow get tidings of her, I would in an instant recover her out of the hands of even Death himself. Wherever she may be, if only she still lives, brother, I would spare no effort to rescue her. Sugrīva has forgotten all about me, now that he has got back his treasure and kingdom, his city and his queen. Fool that he is, I will tomorrow slay him with the self-same arrow with which I slew Bālī." He, by whose favor, Umā, pride and delusion are dissipated, could never even dream of being angry. Only enlightened saints can understand these actions of his, who have a hearty devotion to the feet of Raghubīr. Lakshman thought his Lord was angry, and strung his bow and took arrows into his hands.

दोहा-dohā:

तब अनुजहि समुझावा रघुपति करुना सींव ।
taba anujahi samujhāvā raghupati karunā sīṁva,
भय देखाइ लै आवहु तात सखा सुग्रीव ॥१८॥
bhaya dekhāi lai āvahu tāta sakhā sugrīva. 18.

Trans:

Then the All-merciful Raghupatī instructed his brother, saying, "Just frighten our friend Sugrīva, and bring him."

चौपाई-caupāī:

इहाँ पवनसुत हृदयँ बिचारा । राम काजु सुग्रीवँ बिसारा ॥
ihāṁ pavanasuta hṛdayaṁ bicārā, rāma kāju sugrīvaṁ bisārā.
निकट जाइ चरनन्हि सिरु नावा । चारिहु बिधि तेहि कहि समुझावा ॥
nikaṭa jāi caranaṇhi siru nāvā, cārihu bidhi tehi kahi samujhāvā.
सुनि सुग्रीवँ परम भय माना । बिषयँ मोर हरि लीन्हेउ ग्याना ॥
suni sugrīvaṁ parama bhaya mānā, biṣayaṁ mora hari līnheu gyānā.
अब मारुतसुत दूत समूहा । पठवहु जहँ तहँ बानर जूहा ॥
aba mārutasuta dūta samūhā, paṭhavahu jahaṁ tahaṁ bānara jūhā.
कहहु पाख महुँ आव न जोई । मोरें कर ता कर बध होई ॥
kahahu pākha mahuṁ āva na joī, moreṁ kara tā kara badha hoī.
तब हनुमंत बोलाए दूता । सब कर करि सनमान बहूता ॥
taba hanumaṁta bolāe dūtā, saba kara kari sanamāna bahūtā.
भय अरु प्रीति नीति देखराई । चले सकल चरनन्हि सिर नाई ॥
bhaya aru prīti nīti dekhrāī, cale sakala carananhi sira nāī.
एहि अवसर लछिमन पुर आए । क्रोध देखि जहँ तहँ कपि धाए ॥
ehi avasara lachimana pura āe, krodha dekhi jahaṁ tahaṁ kapi dhāe.

Trans:

Meanwhile the Son-of-wind was thinking to himself, 'Sugrīva has forgotten all about Rāma.' So approaching Sugrīva, he bowed his head to his feet and tried to bring him round by employing all the four methods of persuasion. As Sugrīva listened, he became much alarmed, "Sensual pleasures have robbed me of all my understanding. Now, O Hanumān, dispatch multitude of spies and legions of monkeys in every direction; and tell them that anyone who is not back in a fortnight, shall meet his death at my very hands." Thereupon Hanumān sent for envoys and receiving them most politely charged them with their duties making use of threats, blandishments and persuasion. They all bowed their heads at his feet and set forth. At that very time Lakshman entered the city. Seeing him to be angry the monkeys ran helter-skelter.

दोहा-dohā:

धनुष चढ़ाइ कहा तब जारि करउँ पुर छार ।
dhanuṣa caṛhāi kahā taba jāri karauṁ pura chāra,
ब्याकुल नगर देखि तब आयउ बालिकुमार ॥ १९॥
byākula nagara dekhi taba āyau bālikumāra. 19.

Trans:

Lakshman twanged his bow and cried, "I will burn the city to ashes." Then came Bālī's son, seeing the distress of the people.

चौपाई-caupāī:

चरन नाइ सिरु बिनती कीन्ही । लछिमन अभय बाँह तेहि दीन्ही ॥
carana nāi siru binatī kīnhī, lachimana abhaya bāṁha tehi dīnhī.
क्रोधवंत लछिमन सुनि काना । कह कपीस अति भयँ अकुलाना ॥
krodhavaṁta lachimana suni kānā, kaha kapīsa ati bhayaṁ akulānā.
सुनु हनुमंत संग लै तारा । करि बिनती समुझाउ कुमारा ॥
sunu hanumaṁta saṁga lai tārā, kari binatī samujhāu kumārā.
तारा सहित जाइ हनुमाना । चरन बंदि प्रभु सुजस बखाना ॥
tārā sahita jāi hanumānā, carana baṁdi prabhu sujasa bakhānā.
करि बिनती मंदिर लै आए । चरन पखारि पलँग बैठाए ॥
kari binatī maṁdira lai āe, carana pakhāri palaṁga baiṭhāe.
तब कपीस चरनन्हि सिरु नावा । गहि भुज लछिमन कंठ लगावा ॥
taba kapīsa caranaṇhi siru nāvā, gahi bhuja lachimana kaṁṭha lagāvā.
नाथ बिषय सम मद कछु नाहीं । मुनि मन मोह करइ छन माहीं ॥
nātha biṣaya sama mada kachu nāhīṁ, muni mana moha karai chana māhīṁ.
सुनत बिनीत बचन सुख पावा । लछिमन तेहि बहु बिधि समुझावा ॥
sunata binīta bacana sukha pāvā, lachimana tehi bahu bidhi samujhāvā.
पवन तनय सब कथा सुनाई । जेहि बिधि गए दूत समुदाई ॥
pavana tanaya saba kathā sunāī, jehi bidhi gae dūta samudāī.

Trans:

He bowed his head at his feet and made humble petition until Lakshman assured him he had naught to fear. When the reports of Lakshman's wrath reached the monkey-king he was terribly alarmed, "Hearken Hanumān; take Tara with you and with suppliant prayers appease the prince." Hanumān went with Tara and fell at his feet, and hymned his Lord's praises; then respectfully conducted him to the palace and bathed his feet and seated him on a couch. The monkey king then came bowed his head at his feet and Lakshman took him by the hand and embraced him. "There is nothing, my Lord, so intoxicating as pleasure; in a single moment it infatuates even the soul of a saint." On hearing this humble speech, Lakshman was glad and said everything to reassure him; while Hanumān told him all that had been done and how a multitude of spies had already started.

दोहा-dohā:

हरषि चले सुग्रीव तब अंगदादि कपि साथ ।
haraṣi cale sugrīva taba aṁgadādi kapi sātha,
रामानुज आगें करि आए जहँ रघुनाथ ॥ २०॥
rāmānuja āgeṁ kari āe jahaṁ raghunātha. 20.

Trans:

Then Sugrīva with Angad and the other monkeys went forth with joy, preceded by Lakshman, and arrived in Rāma's presence.

चौपाई-caupāī:

नाइ चरन सिरु कह कर जोरी । नाथ मोहि कछु नाहिन खोरी ॥
nāi carana siru kaha kara jorī, nātha mohi kachu nāhina khorī.
अतिसय प्रबल देव तव माया । छूटइ राम करहु जौं दाया ॥
atisaya prabala deva tava māyā, chūṭai rāma karahu jauṁ dāyā.
बिषय बस्य सुर नर मुनि स्वामी । मैं पावँर पसु कपि अति कामी ॥
biṣaya basya sura nara muni svāmī, maiṁ pāvaṁra pasu kapi ati kāmī.
नारि नयन सर जाहि न लागा । घोर क्रोध तम निसि जो जागा ॥
nāri nayana sara jāhi na lāgā, ghora krodha tama nisi jo jāgā.
लोभ पाँस जेहिं गर न बँधाया । सो नर तुम्ह समान रघुराया ॥
lobha pāṁsa jehiṁ gara na baṁdhāyā, so nara tumha samāna raghurāyā.
यह गुन साधन तें नहिं होई । तुम्हरी कृपाँ पाव कोइ कोई ॥
yaha guna sādhana teṁ nahiṁ hoī, tumharī kṛpāṁ pāva koi koī.
तब रघुपति बोले मुसुकाई । तुम्ह प्रिय मोहि भरत जिमि भाई ॥
taba raghupati bole musukāī, tumha priya mohi bharata jimi bhāī.
अब सोइ जतनु करहु मन लाई । जेहि बिधि सीता कै सुधि पाई ॥
aba soi jatanu karahu mana lāī, jehi bidhi sītā kai sudhi pāī.

Trans:

With folded hands he bowed his head at his feet and cried, "My Lord, it has been no fault of mine. Your delusive power, sire, is so strong that only Rāma's favor can disperse it. Gods and men, saints and kings are mastered by their senses; and I am but a poor brute beast, a monkey, one of the most libidinous of animals. A man who is invulnerable by the arrow of a woman's eye, who remains wakeful through the dark night of angry passion, and whose neck has never been bound by the halter of covetousness—that can only be you, the Lord God, O Raghurāī! It is a virtue not attainable by any religious observances; it is only by your grace that one here and there might accomplish it." Then Raghupatī smiled and said, "You are as dear to me as my own brother Bharat. Now take thought and make an effort to get tidings of Sītā."

दोहा-dohā:

एहि बिधि होत बतकही आए बानर जूथ ।
ehi bidhi hota batakahī āe bānara jūtha,
नाना बरन सकल दिसि देखिअ कीस बरुथ ॥ २१॥
nānā barana sakala disi dekhia kīsa barutha. 21.

Trans:

While they were yet thus speaking, the troops of monkeys arrived, of all colors and from all parts of the earth, host of monkeys all marvelous to behold.

चौपाई-caupāī:

बानर कटक उमा मैं देखा । सो मूरुख जो करन चह लेखा ॥
bānara kaṭaka umā maiṁ dekhā, so mūrukha jo karana caha lekhā.
आइ राम पद नावहिं माथा । निरखि बदनु सब होहिं सनाथा ॥
āi rāma pada nāvahiṁ māthā, nirakhi badanu saba hohiṁ sanāthā.
अस कपि एक न सेना माहीं । राम कुसल जेहि पूछी नाहीं ॥
asa kapi eka na senā māhīṁ, rāma kusala jehi pūchī nāhīṁ.
यह कछु नहिं प्रभु कइ अधिकाई । बिस्वरूप ब्यापक रघुराई ॥
yaha kachu nahiṁ prabhu kai adhikāī, bisvarūpa byāpaka raghurāī.
ठाढ़े जहँ तहँ आयसु पाई । कह सुग्रीव सबहि समुझाई ॥
ṭhāṛhe jahaṁ tahaṁ āyasu pāī, kaha sugrīva sabahi samujhāī.
राम काजु अरु मोर निहोरा । बानर जूथ जाहु चहुँ ओरा ॥
rāma kāju aru mora nihorā, bānara jūtha jāhu cahuṁ orā.
जनकसुता कहुँ खोजहु जाई । मास दिवस महँ आएहु भाई ॥
janakasutā kahuṁ khojahu jāī, māsa divasa mahaṁ āehu bhāī.
अवधि मेटि जो बिनु सुधि पाएँ । आवइ बनिहि सो मोहि मराएँ ॥

avadhi meṭi jo binu sudhi pāeṁ, āvai banihi so mohi marāeṁ.

Trans:

I, O Umā, saw this army of monkeys; and only a fool would try to count them. They came and bowed the head at Rāma's feet and gazing upon his face found in him their true Lord. In the whole host there was not a single monkey to whom Rāma did not give separate greeting. This was no great miracle for Lord Raghurāī—who is omnipresent and all-pervading. They all stood as they were told, rank after rank, while Sugrīva spoke and thus instructed them, "In Rāma's behoof and at my request go forth ye monkey hosts in every direction. Make search for Janak's daughter, brethren, and return within a month. Whoever comes back at the end of the time without any news shall die at my hands."

दोहा-dohā:

बचन सुनत सब बानर जहँ तहँ चले तुरंत ।

bacana sunata saba bānara jahaṁ tahaṁ cale turaṁta,

तब सुग्रीवँ बोलाए अंगद नल हनुमंत ॥२२॥

taba sugrīvaṁ bolāe aṁgada nala hanumaṁta. 22.

Trans:

No sooner had they heard this command then all the monkeys started at once in every direction. Sugrīva then called Angad, Nīl and Hanumān:

चौपाई-caupāī:

सुनहु नील अंगद हनुमाना । जामवंत मतिधीर सुजाना ॥

sunahu nīla aṁgada hanumānā, jāmavaṁta matidhīra sujānā.

सकल सुभट मिलि दच्छिन जाहू । सीता सुधि पूँछेउ सब काहू ॥

sakala subhaṭa mili dacchina jāhū, sītā sudhi pūm̐cheu saba kāhū.

मन क्रम बचन सो जतन बिचारेहु । रामचंद्र कर काजु सँवारेहु ॥

mana krama bacana so jatana bicārehu, rāmacaṁdra kara kāju saṁvārehu.

भानु पीठि सेइअ उर आगी । स्वामिहि सर्ब भाव छल त्यागी ॥

bhānu pīṭhi seia ura āgī, svāmihi sarba bhāva chala tyāgī.

तजि माया सेइअ परलोका । मिटहिं सकल भवसंभव सोका ॥

taji māyā seia paralokā, miṭahiṁ sakala bhavasaṁbhava sokā.

देह धरे कर यह फलु भाई । भजिअ राम सब काम बिहाई ॥

deha dhare kara yaha phalu bhāī, bhajia rāma saba kāma bihāī.

सोइ गुनग्य सोई बड़भागी । जो रघुबीर चरन अनुरागी ॥

soi gunagya soī baṛabhāgī, jo raghubīra carana anurāgī.

आयसु मागि चरन सिरु नाई । चले हरषि सुमिरत रघुराई ॥

āyasu māgi carana siru nāī, cale haraṣi sumirata raghurāī.

पाछें पवन तनय सिरु नावा । जानि काज प्रभु निकट बोलावा ॥

pācheṁ pavana tanaya siru nāvā, jāni kāja prabhu nikaṭa bolāvā.

परसा सीस सरोरुह पानी । करमुद्रिका दीन्हि जन जानी ॥

parasā sīsa saroruha pānī, karamudrikā dīnhi jana jānī.

बहु प्रकार सीतहि समुझाएहु । कहि बल बिरह बेगि तुम्ह आएहु ॥

bahu prakāra sītahi samujhāehu, kahi bala biraha begi tumha āehu.

हनुमत जन्म सुफल करि माना । चलेउ हृदयँ धरि कृपानिधाना ॥

hanumata janma suphala kari mānā, caleu hṛdayaṁ dhari kṛpānidhānā.

जद्यपि प्रभु जानत सब बाता । राजनीति राखत सुरत्राता ॥

jadyapi prabhu jānata saba bātā, rājanīti rākhata suratrātā.

Trans:

"Hearken, Nīl, Angad and Hanumān, and you, O staunch and sagacious Jāmvant; go ye together, all ye gallant warriors, to the south and ask everyone for news of Sītā. Strain every faculty to devise some scheme by which to accomplish Rāma's purpose. The heat from sun is served from back, and heat of fire served from front, but a master must be served with one's entire being, without any subterfuges. Discard the unrealities of the world and consider the future; so shall all troubles connected with mundane existence be destroyed. This is the purpose, brother, for which we were born: to serve Rāma without any desire for self. He only is truly discriminative, he only greatly blessed—he who is enamored of the feet of Raghubīr." After begging permission to depart and bowing the head at his feet all set out with joy, invoking Raghurāī. The last to make obeisance was Hanumān. The Lord, knowing what would happen, called him near and with his lotus hands touched his head and gave him his ring off his finger, for he knew his devotion, "Say everything to comfort Sītā, telling her of my might and my constancy, and come quickly." Hanumān thought himself happy to have been born, and set forth with the image of the All-merciful impressed upon his heart. Although the Lord knows everything, he observes the rules of statecraft in his character as the champion of the gods.

दोहा-dohā:

चले सकल बन खोजत सरिता सर गिरि खोह ।

cale sakala bana khojata saritā sara giri khoha,

राम काज लयलीन मन बिसरा तन कर छोह ॥२३॥

rāma kāja layalīna mana bisarā tana kara choha. 23.

Trans:

They went forth searching every wood, river, lake, and mountain cave, with their soul so absorbed in Rāma's concern that they forgot about their own bodily wants.

चौपाई-caupāī:

कतहुँ होइ निसिचर सैं भेटा । प्रान लेहिं एक एक चपेटा ॥

katahuṁ hoi nisicara saiṁ bheṭā, prāna lehiṁ eka eka capeṭā.

बहु प्रकार गिरि कानन हेरहिं । कोउ मुनि मिलइ ताहि सब घेरहिं ॥

bahu prakāra giri kānana herahiṁ, kou muni milai tāhi saba gherahiṁ.

लागि तृषा अतिसय अकुलाने । मिलइ न जल घन गहन भुलाने ॥

lāgi tṛṣā atisaya akulāne, milai na jala ghana gahana bhulāne.

मन हनुमान कीन्ह अनुमाना । मरन चहत सब बिनु जल पाना ॥

mana hanumāna kīnha anumānā, marana cahata saba binu jala pānā.

चढ़ि गिरि सिखर चहूँ दिसि देखा । भूमि बिबर एक कौतुक पेखा ॥

caṛhi giri sikhara cahūṁ disi dekhā, bhūmi bibara eka kautuka pekhā.

चक्रबाक बक हंस उड़ाहीं । बहुतक खग प्रबिसहिं तेहि माहीं ॥

cakrabāka baka haṁsa uṛāhīṁ, bahutaka khaga prabisahiṁ tehi māhīṁ.

गिरि ते उतरि पवनसुत आवा । सब कहुँ लै सोइ बिबर देखावा ॥

giri te utari pavanasuta āvā, saba kahuṁ lai soi bibara dekhāvā.

आगें कै हनुमंतहि लीन्हा । पैठे बिबर बिलंबु न कीन्हा ॥

āgeṁ kai hanumaṁtahi līnhā, paiṭhe bibara bilaṁbu na kīnhā.

Trans:

Wherever it might be that they came across a demon, they took his life with a single blow. They looked into every recess of forest and hill, and if they met any hermit they eagerly surrounded him for some news. Once, overcome by thirst they were dreadfully distressed; having lost their way in the dense jungles, they could find no water anywhere. Hanumān thought to himself, "with no water to be had, it seems we might die here." He climbed a mountain peak, and looking around about, spied a strange opening down below: with geese, herons, and swans on wing, and all kinds of birds making their way into it. Hanumān came down from the mountain and took them all there and showed them the cave. With him to lead the way, they lost no time, and entered the chasm.

दोहा-dohā:

दीख जाइ उपवन बर सर बिगसित बहु कंज ।

dīkha jāi upavana bara sara bigasita bahu kaṁja,

मंदिर एक रुचिर तहँ बैठि नारि तप पुंज ॥२४॥

maṁdira eka rucira tahaṁ baiṭhi nāri tapa puṁja. 24.

Trans:

A grove and beautiful lake came in sight with many flowering lotuses and a magnificent temple where a holy woman was sitting by.

चौपाई-caupāī:

दूरि ते ताहि सबन्हि सिर नावा । पूछें निज बृत्तांत सुनावा ॥
dūri te tāhi sabanhi sira nāvā, pūcheṁ nija bṛttāṁta sunāvā.
तेहिं तब कहा करहु जल पाना । खाहु सुरस सुंदर फल नाना ॥
tehiṁ taba kahā karahu jala pānā, khāhu surasa suṁdara phala nānā.
मज्जनु कीन्ह मधुर फल खाए । तासु निकट पुनि सब चलि आए ॥
majjanu kīnha madhura phala khāe, tāsu nikaṭa puni saba cali āe.
तेहिं सब आपनि कथा सुनाई । मैं अब जाब जहाँ रघुराई ॥
tehiṁ saba āpani kathā sunāī, maiṁ aba jāba jahāṁ raghurāī.
मूदहु नयन बिबर तजि जाहू । पैहहु सीतहि जनि पछिताहू ॥
mūdahu nayana bibara taji jāhū, paihahu sītahi jani pachitāhū.
नयन मूदि पुनि देखहिं बीरा । ठाढ़े सकल सिंधु कें तीरा ॥
nayana mūdi puni dekhahiṁ bīrā, ṭhāṛhe sakala siṁdhu keṁ tīrā.
सो पुनि गई जहाँ रघुनाथा । जाइ कमल पद नाएसि माथा ॥
so puni gaī jahāṁ raghunāthā, jāi kamala pada nāesi māthā.
नाना भाँति बिनय तेहिं कीन्ही । अनपायनी भगति प्रभु दीन्ही ॥
nānā bhāṁti binaya tehiṁ kīnhī, anapāyanī bhagati prabhu dīnhī.

Trans:

From a distance they all bowed the head before her and made enquiry and also declared their own circumstance. She then said, "Take water to drink and eat at will of these delicious beautiful fruits." They bathed and ate the sweet fruits, and then all came and drew near to her and told her all their adventures. "I will now go to Raghurāī; close your eyes and you will find yourself outside the cavern; you will recover Sītā, do not fear." The warriors closed their eyes, and when they again opened them, they were all standing on the shore of the ocean. But she herself went to Raghunāth and came and bowed her head at his lotus feet, and made much supplication. The Lord bestowed upon her imperishable faith.

दोहा-dohā:

बदरीबन कहुँ सो गई प्रभु अग्या धरि सीस ।
badarībana kahuṁ so gaī prabhu agyā dhari sīsa,
उर धरि राम चरन जुग जे बंदत अज ईस ॥२५॥
ura dhari rāma carana juga je baṁdata aja īsa. 25.

Trans:

In obedience to the Lord's commands she went to the Badri forest, cherishing in her heart Rāma's feet, the adoration of the eternal Shiva.

चौपाई-caupāī:

इहाँ बिचारहिं कपि मन माहीं । बीती अवधि काजु कछु नाहीं ॥
ihāṁ bicārahiṁ kapi mana māhīṁ, bītī avadhi kāju kachu nāhīṁ.
सब मिलि कहहिं परस्पर बाता । बिनु सुधि लएँ करब का भ्राता ॥
saba mili kahahiṁ paraspara bātā, binu sudhi laeṁ karaba kā bhrātā.
कह अंगद लोचन भरि बारी । दुहुँ प्रकार भइ मृत्यु हमारी ॥
kaha aṁgada locana bhari bārī, duhuṁ prakāra bhai mṛtyu hamārī.
इहाँ न सुधि सीता कै पाई । उहाँ गएँ मारिहि कपिराई ॥
ihāṁ na sudhi sītā kai pāī, uhāṁ gaeṁ mārihi kapirāī.
पिता बधे पर मारत मोही । राखा राम निहोर न ओही ॥
pitā badhe para mārata mohī, rākhā rāma nihora na ohī.
पुनि पुनि अंगद कह सब पाहीं । मरन भयउ कछु संसय नाहीं ॥
puni puni aṁgada kaha saba pāhīṁ, marana bhayau kachu saṁsaya nāhīṁ.
अंगद बचन सुनत कपि बीरा । बोलि न सकहिं नयन बह नीरा ॥
aṁgada bacana sunata kapi bīrā, boli na sakahiṁ nayana baha nīrā.
छन एक सोच मगन होइ रहे । पुनि अस बचन कहत सब भए ॥
chana eka soca magana hoi rahe, puni asa bacana kahata saba bhae.
हम सीता कै सुधि लीन्हें बिना । नहिं जैहैं जुबराज प्रबीना ॥
hama sītā kai sudhi līnheṁ binā, nahiṁ jaihaiṁ jubarāja prabīnā.
अस कहि लवन सिंधु तट जाई । बैठे कपि सब दर्भ डसाई ॥
asa kahi lavana siṁdhu taṭa jāī, baiṭhe kapi saba darbha ḍasāī.
जामवंत अंगद दुख देखी । कहिं कथा उपदेस बिसेषी ॥
jāmavaṁta aṁgada dukha dekhī, kahiṁ kathā upadesa biseṣī.
तात राम कहुँ नर जनि मानहु । निर्गुन ब्रह्म अजित अज जानहु ॥
tāta rāma kahuṁ nara jani mānahu, nirguna brahma ajita aja jānahu.
हम सब सेवक अति बड़भागी । संतत सगुन ब्रह्म अनुरागी ॥
hama saba sevaka ati baṛabhāgī, saṁtata saguna brahma anurāgī.

Trans:

Now the monkeys were thinking to themselves, "The appointed time has passed and nothing has been accomplished." They gathered together and asked one another, "There is no news, brother; what are we to do?" Angad's eyes were full of tears as he replied, "It's death for us either way. Here we have failed to get tidings of Sītā; and if we go home our king will slay us. After my father's death he would have killed me; but I live, no thanks to him—for it was Shrī Rāma who protected me." Again and again Angad said to them, "Surely it's our death now, without a doubt." When the monkey chiefs heard Angad's words, they could make no answer, tears streamed from their eyes. For a moment they were overwhelmed with despair, but at last they all spoke and said, "Unless we get news of Sītā we will not return, O sagacious prince." So saying the monkeys all went to the sea-shore and there sat down spreading Kush grass. Then Jāmvant seeing Angad's distress, addressed him with words of appropriate admonition: "My son, do not imagine Rāma to be a man; know that he is the invisible supreme spirit without attributes, invincible, the unborn. All we who are his servants are most highly blessed in our love for the formless eternal Brahmm thus made incarnate.

दोहा-dohā:

निज इच्छाँ प्रभु अवतरइ सुर महि गो द्विज लागि ।
nija icchāṁ prabhu avatarai sura mahi go dvija lāgi,
सगुन उपासक संग तहँ रहहिं मोच्छ सब त्यागि ॥२६॥
saguna upāsaka saṁga tahaṁ rahahiṁ moccha saba tyāgi. 26.

Trans:

Of his own free will the Lord has manifested himself on behalf of the gods, the virtuous, the cows and the earth; he remains in bodily form amongst his worshippers, having abandoned all the joys of heaven."

चौपाई-caupāī:

एहि बिधि कथा कहहिं बहु भाँती । गिरि कंदराँ सुनी संपाती ॥
ehi bidhi kathā kahahiṁ bahu bhāṁtī giri kaṁdarāṁ sunī saṁpātī.
बाहेर होइ देखि बहु कीसा । मोहि अहार दीन्ह जगदीसा ॥
bāhera hoi dekhi bahu kīsā, mohi ahāra dīnha jagadīsā.
आजु सबहि कहँ भच्छन करउँ । दिन बहु चले अहार बिनु मरउँ ॥
āju sabahi kahaṁ bhacchana karaūṁ, dina bahu cale ahāra binu maraūṁ.
कबहुँ न मिल भरि उदर अहारा । आजु दीन्ह बिधि एकहिं बारा ॥
kabahuṁ na mila bhari udara ahārā, āju dīnha bidhi ekahiṁ bārā.
डरपे गीध बचन सुनि काना । अब भा मरन सत्य हम जाना ॥
ḍarape gīdha bacana suni kānā, aba bhā marana satya hama jānā.
कपि सब उठे गीध कहँ देखी । जामवंत मन सोच बिसेषी ॥
kapi saba uṭhe gīdha kahaṁ dekhī, jāmavaṁta mana soca biseṣī.
कह अंगद बिचारि मन माहीं । धन्य जटायू सम कोउ नाहीं ॥

kaha aṁgada bicāri mana māhīṁ, dhanya jaṭāyū sama kou nāhīṁ.
राम काज कारन तनु त्यागी । हरि पुर गयउ परम बड़ भागी ॥
rāma kāja kārana tanu tyāgī, hari pura gayau parama baṛa bhāgī.
सुनि खग हरष सोक जुत बानी । आवा निकट कपिन्ह भय मानी ॥
suni khaga haraṣa soka juta bānī, āvā nikaṭa kapinha bhaya mānī.
तिन्हहि अभय करि पूछेसि जाई । कथा सकल तिन्ह ताहि सुनाई ॥
tinhahi abhaya kari pūchesi jāī, kathā sakala tinha tāhi sunāī.
सुनि संपाति बंधु कै करनी । रघुपति महिमा बधुबिधि बरनी ॥
suni saṁpāti baṁdhu kai karanī, raghupati mahimā badhubidhi baranī.

Trans:

Thus they discoursed amongst themselves in this vein at great length—when the vulture Sampāti from his cave in the mountain heard them. He came out and saw a multitude of monkeys, and he rejoiced, "God has provided me with a feast. I will eat them up all at once; I was dying for want of real meal for so many days past. I haven't had a good belly-full, but today gods have supplied me once and for good." The monkeys trembled to hear the vulture's words, "Right we were in saying that today we will die." At the sight of him they all rose up; Jāmvant too was mightily disturbed; but then Angad, after thinking to himself, exclaimed: "Glory to Jatāyu, blessed beyond measure; there is none like him—who gave up his life in Rāma's service and has been translated to Harī's sphere in heaven." When the bird heard these words—of a mingled joy and sadness—he drew near to the monkeys in alarm, and after assuring them of safety, began to question them. They told him the whole history. When Sampāti heard of his brother's doing, he gave great glory to Raghupatī.

दोहा-dohā:

मोहि लै जाहु सिंधुतट देउँ तिलांजलि ताहि ।
mohi lai jāhu siṁdhutaṭa deuṁ tilāṁjali tāhi,
बचन सहाइ करबि मैं पैहहु खोजहु जाहि ॥२७॥
bacana sahāi karabi maiṁ paihahu khojahu jāhi. 27.

Trans:

"Take me to the sea shore that I may make oblation of sesame seeds to my dead brother. And then I will give you instructions so you may find she, whom you seek."

चौपाई-caupāī:

अनुज क्रिया करि सागर तीरा । कहि निज कथा सुनहु कपि बीरा ॥
anuja kriyā kari sāgara tīrā, kahi nija kathā sunahu kapi bīrā.
हम द्वौ बंधु प्रथम तरुनाई । गगन गए रबि निकट उड़ाई ॥
hama dvau baṁdhu prathama tarunāī, gagana gae rabi nikaṭa uṛāī.
तेज न सहि सक सो फिरि आवा । मैं अभिमानी रबि निअरावा ॥
teja na sahi saka so phiri āvā, maiṁ abhimānī rabi niarāvā.
जरे पंख अति तेज अपारा । परेउँ भूमि करि घोर चिकारा ॥
jare paṁkha ati teja apārā, pareuṁ bhūmi kari ghora cikārā.
मुनि एक नाम चंद्रमा ओही । लागी दया देखि करि मोही ॥
muni eka nāma caṁdramā ohī, lāgī dayā dekhi kari mohī.
बहु प्रकार तेहिं ग्यान सुनावा । देह जनित अभिमान छड़ावा ॥
bahu prakāra tehiṁ gyāna sunāvā, deha janita abhimāna chaṛāvā.
त्रेताँ ब्रह्म मनुज तनु धरिही । तासु नारि निसिचर पति हरिही ॥
tretāṁ brahma manuja tanu dharihī, tāsu nāri nisicara pati harihī.
तासु खोज पठइहि प्रभु दूता । तिन्हहि मिलें तैं होब पुनीता ॥
tāsu khoja paṭhaihi prabhu dūtā, tinhahi mileṁ taiṁ hoba punītā.
जमिहहिं पंख करसि जनि चिंता । तिन्हहि देखाइ देहेसु तैं सीता ॥
jamihahiṁ paṁkha karasi jani ciṁtā, tinhahi dekhāi dehesu taiṁ sītā.
मुनि कइ गिरा सत्य भइ आजू । सुनि मम बचन करहु प्रभु काजू ॥
muni kai girā satya bhai ājū, suni mama bacana karahu prabhu kājū.
गिरि त्रिकूट ऊपर बस लंका । तहँ रह रावन सहज असंका ॥
giri trikūṭa ūpara basa laṁkā, tahaṁ raha rāvana sahaja asaṁkā.
तहँ असोक उपबन जहँ रहई । सीता बैठि सोच रत अहई ॥
tahaṁ asoka upabana jahaṁ rahaī, sītā baiṭhi soca rata ahaī.

Trans:

When he had completed the funeral rites for his brother on the sea shore, he told them his own history. "Hearken, monkey chiefs: in the prime of our youth, we two brothers mounted into the heaven, winging our way towards the sun. My brother could not endure that splendor and turned back, but I, in my pride, went closer. My wings were scorched by the excessive heat, and I fell to the earth uttering fearful cries. A saint, by name Chandramā, was moved with compassion when he saw me, and he instructed me in all the ways of wisdom and to rid me of my inveterate pride. "In the Tretā-Yug, God will take the form of human, and his spouse will be carried off by the king of demons. The Lord will send out messengers in search for her, and by joining them you will be purified. Your wings will sprout again when you have shown them Sītā; fear not." The saint's prophecy has come true today. Hearken to my words and set about your Lord's business. On the top of mount Trikūt is the city of Lankā; there lives Rāvan in absolute security; and there, in a grove of Asoka trees, sits Sītā, a prey to grief.

दोहा-dohā:

मैं देखउँ तुम्ह नाहीं गीघहि दृष्टि अपार ।
maiṁ dekhauṁ tumha nāhi gīghahi dṛṣṭi apāra,
बूढ भयउँ न त करतेउँ कछुक सहाय तुम्हार ॥२८॥
būḍha bhayauṁ na ta karateuṁ kachuka sahāya tumhāra. 28.

Trans:

I see her, though you cannot; a vulture's sight has no bounds. I am now old, or else I would have given you some assistance.

चौपाई-caupāī:

जो नाघइ सत जोजन सागर । करइ सो राम काज मति आगर ॥
jo nāghai sata jojana sāgara, karai so rāma kāja mati āgara.
मोहि बिलोकि धरहु मन धीरा । राम कृपाँ कस भयउ सरीरा ॥
mohi biloki dharahu mana dhīrā, rāma kṛpāṁ kasa bhayau sarīrā.
पापिउ जा कर नाम सुमिरहीं । अति अपार भवसागर तरहीं ॥
pāpiu jā kara nāma sumirahīṁ, ati apāra bhavasāgara tarahīṁ.
तासु दूत तुम्ह तजि कदराई । राम हृदयँ धरि करहु उपाई ॥
tāsu dūta tumha taji kadarāī, rāma hṛdayaṁ dhari karahu upāī.
अस कहि गरुड़ गीध जब गयऊ । तिन्ह कें मन अति बिसमय भयऊ ॥
asa kahi garuṛa gīdha jaba gayaū, tinha keṁ mana ati bisamaya bhayaū.
निज निज बल सब काहूँ भाषा । पार जाइ कर संसय राखा ॥
nija nija bala saba kāhūṁ bhāṣā, pāra jāi kara saṁsaya rākhā.
जरठ भयउँ अब कहइ रिछेसा । नहिं तन रहा प्रथम बल लेसा ॥
jaraṭha bhayauṁ aba kahai richesā, nahiṁ tana rahā prathama bala lesā.
जबहिं त्रिबिक्रम भए खरारी । तब मैं तरुन रहेउँ बल भारी ॥
jabahiṁ tribikrama bhae kharārī, taba maiṁ taruna raheuṁ bala bhārī.

Trans:

He—who can leap over a hundred leagues of sea, and is a repository of intelligence—will be able to perform Rāma's work. Look at me and reassure yourselves; see how my body has been restored now by Rāma's favor. Even a wretch, who invokes his name, is able to cross the deep, boundless ocean of existence—what then of you, who are his very messengers. Have then no fear, but with Rāma's image impressed upon your soul, execute your plan." Saying so, O Garud, the vulture then left, and their souls were sole amazed. Then all declared of their respective strengths but none was confident to leap across the ocean. Said the king of the bears, "I am now too old, and not a particle of my former strength is left in this body. When Khararī took his three strides, then I was young and full of vigor.

दोहा-dohā:

बलि बाँधत प्रभु बाढ़ेउ सो तनु बरनि न जाइ ।
bali bām̐dhata prabhu bāṛheu so tanu barani na jāi,
उभय घरी महँ दीन्हीं सात प्रदच्छिन धाइ ॥२९॥
ubhaya gharī maham̐ dīnhīṁ sāta pradacchina dhāi. 29.

Trans:

As he bound Vali, the Lord increased in stature to an indescribable size, but in less than an hour I ran around him seven times."

चौपाई-caupāī:

अंगद कहइ जाउँ मैं पारा । जियँ संसय कछु फिरती बारा ॥
aṁgada kahai jāum̐ maiṁ pārā, jiyam̐ saṁsaya kachu phiratī bārā.
जामवंत कह तुम्ह सब लायक । पठइअ किमि सब ही कर नायक ॥
jāmavaṁta kaha tumha saba lāyaka, paṭhaia kimi saba hī kara nāyaka.
कहइ रीछपति सुनु हनुमाना । का चुप साधि रहेहु बलवाना ॥
kahai rīkṣapati sunu hanumānā, kā cupa sādhi rahehu balavānā.
पवन तनय बल पवन समाना । बुधि बिबेक बिग्यान निधाना ॥
pavana tanaya bala pavana samānā, budhi bibeka bigyāna nidhānā.
कवन सो काज कठिन जग माहीं । जो नहिं होइ तात तुम्ह पाहीं ॥
kavana so kāja kaṭhina jaga māhīṁ, jo nahiṁ hoi tāta tumha pāhīṁ.
राम काज लगि तव अवतारा । सुनतहिं भयउ पर्बताकारा ॥
rāma kāja lagi tava avatārā, sunatahiṁ bhayau parbatākārā.
कनक बरन तन तेज बिराजा । मानहुँ अपर गिरिन्ह कर राजा ॥
kanaka barana tana teja birājā, mānahum̐ apara girinha kara rājā.
सिंहनाद करि बारहिं बारा । लीलहिं नाघउँ जलनिधि खारा ॥
siṁhanāda kari bārahiṁ bārā, līlahiṁ nāghaum̐ jalanidhi khārā.
सहित सहाय रावनहि मारी । आनउँ इहाँ त्रिकूट उपारी ॥
sahita sahāya rāvanahi mārī, ānaum̐ ihām̐ trikūṭa upārī.
जामवंत मैं पूँछउँ तोही । उचित सिखावनु दीजहु मोही ॥
jāmavaṁta maiṁ pūm̐chaum̐ tohī, ucita sikhāvanu dījahu mohī.
एतना करहु तात तुम्ह जाई । सीतहि देखि कहहु सुधि आई ॥
etanā karahu tāta tumha jāī, sītahi dekhi kahahu sudhi āī.
तब निज भुज बल राजिवनैना । कौतुक लागि संग कपि सेना ॥
taba nija bhuja bala rājivanainā, kautuka lāgi saṁga kapi senā.

Trans:

Angad said, "I can leap across; but I am rather doubtful of getting back." And Jāmvant said, "You are quite competent; but why should we send our leader? Hearken O Hanumān," added the king of the bears, "why is our champion so silent? You are the son of wind-god and strong as your sire, a storehouse of good sense, discretion and knowledge; in all the world what undertaking is there so difficult that you, my son, cannot accomplish it? It is on Rāma's account that you have come down upon earth." Upon hearing this Hanumān swelled to the size of a mountain, with a body of golden hue and dazzling splendor—as though a very monarch of mountains; and roaring again and again as it were a lion, he cried, "I will lightly spring across this salty abyss, and having slain Rāvan with all his army, I will uproot Trikut and bring it here. Now I ask you, Jāmvant, what I am to do; give me proper counsel." "Only do this my son: go and see Sītā and come back with news of her. Then the lotus-eyed, by the might of his own arm will recover her, taking with him a host of monkeys merely for show.

छंद-chaṁda:

कपि सेन संग सँघारि निसिचर रामु सीतहि आनिहैं ।
kapi sena saṁga saṁghāri nisicara rāmu sītahi ānihaiṁ,
त्रैलोक पावन सुजसु सुर मुनि नारदादि बखानिहैं ॥
trailoka pāvana sujasu sura muni nāradādi bakhānihaiṁ.
जो सुनत गावत कहत समुझत परम पद नर पावई ।
jo sunata gāvata kahata samujhata parama pada nara pāvaī,
रघुबीर पद पाथोज मधुकर दास तुलसी गावई ॥
raghubīra pada pāthoja madhukara dāsa tulasī gāvaī.

Trans:

Taking with him an army of monkeys, Shrī Rāma will destroy the demons and recover Sītā; and gods and saints and Nārad and all will declare his glory, that sanctifies the three spheres; and whosoever hears, sings, tells or studies them will attain to the highest beatitude; and Tulsīdās, who is devoted to the lotus feet of Shrī Rāma like a bee, will always sing of them.

दोहा-dohā:

भव भेषज रघुनाथ जसु सुनहिं जे नर अरु नारि ।
bhava bheṣaja raghunātha jasu sunahiṁ je nara aru nāri,
तिन्ह कर सकल मनोरथ सिद्ध करहिं त्रिसिरारि ॥३०क॥
tinha kara sakala manoratha siddha karahiṁ trisirāri. 30(ka).

Trans:

Let all men and women hear and sing the glories of Raghunāth—the panacea for all the ills of life—and Shrī Rāma, the slayer of the demon Trisirā, will grant all their heart desires.

सोरठा-soraṭhā:

नीलोत्पल तन स्याम काम कोटि सोभा अधिक ।
nīlotpala tana syāma kāma koṭi sobhā adhika,
सुनिअ तासु गुन ग्राम जासु नाम अघ खग बधिक ॥३०ख॥
sunia tāsu guna grāma jāsu nāma agha khaga badhika. 30(kha).

Trans:

Hearken then to the praises of Shrī Rāma—with his body dark of hue as the lotus, having more than all the beauty of a myriad Loves, whose name is the veritable fowler for birds in the shape of sins.

मासपारायण तेईसवाँ विश्राम
māsapārāyaṇa teīsavām̐ viśrāma
(Pause 23 for a Thirty-Day Recitation)

इति श्रीमद्रामचरितमानसे सकलकलिकलुषविध्वंसने चतुर्थः सोपानः समाप्तः
iti śrīmadrāmacaritamānase sakalakalikaluṣavidhvaṁsane caturthaḥ sopānaḥ samāptaḥ
(Now ends the Fourth-Ascent into the Manasa Lake of Shrī Rāma's Charita which eradicates all the impurities of the Kali-Yug)

ॐ

श्रीजानकीवल्लभो विजयते

śrījānakīvallabho vijayate

श्रीरामचरितमानस

śrīrāmacaritamānasa

पञ्चम सोपान - सुन्दरकाण्ड

pañcama sopāna - sundarakāṇḍa

श्लोक-śloka:

शान्तं शाश्वतमप्रमेयमनघं निर्वाणशान्तिप्रदं
śāntaṁ śāśvatamaprameyamanaghaṁ nirvāṇaśāntipradaṁ
ब्रह्माशम्भुफणीन्द्रसेव्यमनिशं वेदान्तवेद्यं विभुम् ।
brahmāśambhuphaṇīndrasevyamaniśaṁ vedāntavedyaṁ vibhum,
रामाख्यं जगदीश्वरं सुरगुरुं मायामनुष्यं हरिं
rāmākhyaṁ jagadīśvaraṁ suraguruṁ māyāmanuṣyaṁ hariṁ
वन्देऽहं करुणाकरं रघुवरं भूपालचूडामणिम् ॥ १ ॥
vande'haṁ karuṇākaraṁ raghuvaraṁ bhūpālacūrāmaṇim. 1.

Trans:

I adore the Lord of the universe bearing the name Rāma—the passionless, the eternal, the immeasurable, the sinless; bestower of the peace of final emancipation; the theme of the Vedanta whom Brahmmā, Shambhu, and the Serpent-king unceasingly worship; the preceptor of the gods, the All-merciful Harī in the delusive form of man, the jewel of kings—the princely son of Raghu, Shrī Rāma.

नान्या स्पृहा रघुपते हृदयेऽस्मदीये
nānyā spṛhā raghupate hṛdaye'smadīye
सत्यं वदामि च भवानखिलान्तरात्मा ।
satyaṁ vadāmi ca bhavānakhilāntarātmā,
भक्तिं प्रयच्छ रघुपुङ्गव निर्भरां मे
bhaktiṁ prayaccha raghupuṅgava nirbharāṁ me
कामादिदोषरहितं कुरु मानसं च ॥ २ ॥
kāmādidoṣarahitaṁ kuru mānasaṁ ca. 2.

Trans:

O Raghupatī, there is no other desire in my soul—I speak the truth and you know all my inmost thoughts: do grant me the intense-most Devotion to your holy feet, O Raghu King; and make my heart clean of lust and of every other sin.

अतुलितबलधामं हेमशैलाभदेहं
atulitabaladhāmaṁ hemaśailābhadehaṁ
दनुजवनकृशानुं ज्ञानिनामग्रगण्यम् ।
danujavanakṛśānuṁ jñānināmagragaṇyam,
सकलगुणनिधानं वानराणामधीशं
sakalaguṇanidhānaṁ vānarāṇāmadhīśaṁ
रघुपतिप्रियभक्तं वातजातं नमामि ॥ ३ ॥
raghupatipriyabhaktaṁ vātajātaṁ namāmi. 3.

Trans:

I reverence Hanumān, the abode of immeasurable strength with his body resembling a mountain of gold; who is the flame which consumes demons as if trees in forest fire. The store-house of all good qualities, who is the first name in the list of truly wise, the son-of-wind, the noble most messenger of Raghupatī, the chief of monkeys—him I venerate.

चौपाई-caupāī:

जामवंत के बचन सुहाए । सुनि हनुमंत हृदय अति भाए ॥
jāmavaṁta ke bacana suhāe, suni hanumaṁta hṛdaya ati bhāe.
तब लगि मोहि परिखेहु तुम्ह भाई । सहि दुख कंद मूल फल खाई ॥
taba lagi mohi parikhehu tumha bhāī, sahi dukha kaṁda mūla phala khāī.
जब लगि आवौं सीतहि देखी । होइहि काजु मोहि हरष बिसेषी ॥
jaba lagi āvauṁ sītahi dekhī, hoihi kāju mohi haraṣa biseṣī.
यह कहि नाइ सबन्हि कहुँ माथा । चलेउ हरषि हियँ धरि रघुनाथा ॥
yaha kahi nāi sabanhi kahuṁ māthā, caleu haraṣi hiyaṁ dhari raghunāthā.
सिंधु तीर एक भूधर सुंदर । कौतुक कूदि चढ़ेउ ता ऊपर ॥
siṁdhu tīra eka bhūdhara suṁdara, kautuka kūdi caṛheu tā ūpara.
बार बार रघुबीर सँभारी । तरकेउ पवनतनय बल भारी ॥
bāra bāra raghubīra saṁbhārī, tarakeu pavanatanaya bala bhārī.
जेहिं गिरि चरन देइ हनुमंता । चलेउ सो गा पाताल तुरंता ॥
jehiṁ giri carana dei hanumaṁtā, caleu so gā pātāla turaṁtā.
जिमि अमोघ रघुपति कर बाना । एही भाँति चलेउ हनुमाना ॥
jimi amogha raghupati kara bānā, ehī bhāṁti caleu hanumānā.
जलनिधि रघुपति दूत बिचारी । तैं मैनाक होहि श्रमहारी ॥
jalanidhi raghupati dūta bicārī, taiṁ maināka hohi śramahārī.

Trans:

On hearing Jāmvant's delightful speech, Hanumān rejoiced greatly at heart. "Enduring these hardships and with roots, herbs, and fruits for your food wait for me here friends until I have returned after seeing Sītā. There is joy in my heart and I know my task will be done." So saying, he bowed his head to them all and sallied forth joyously, with the image of Raghunāth impressed upon his heart. There was a majestic rock by the sea shore; he lightly sprung on to the top of it; then, again and again invoking Raghubīr, the son-of-wind leaped with all his might. The mountain on which he had planted his foot sank down immediately into the depths of hell; and like an unerring arrow fired by Rāma, Hanumān sped forth on his way. Now Ocean had great regard for Rāma and knowing Hanumān to be his envoy, he told Mount Maināk to go ease Hanumān's toil.

दोहा-dohā:

हनूमान तेहि परसा कर पुनि कीन्ह प्रनाम ।
hanūmāna tehi parasā kara puni kīnha pranāma,
राम काजु कीन्हें बिनु मोहि कहाँ बिश्राम ॥ १ ॥
rāma kāju kīnheṁ binu mohi kahāṁ biśrāma. 1.

Trans:

But Hanumān merely touched him with his hand, then bowed and said, "I can stop nowhere till I have done Rāma's work."

चौपाई-caupāī:

जात पवनसुत देवन्ह देखा । जानैं कहुँ बल बुद्धि बिसेषा ॥
jāta pavanasuta devanha dekhā, jānaiṁ kahuṁ bala buddhi biseṣā.
सुरसा नाम अहिन्ह कै माता । पठइन्हि आइ कही तेहिं बाता ॥
surasā nāma ahinha kai mātā, paṭhainhi āi kahī tehiṁ bātā.
आजु सुरन्ह मोहि दीन्ह अहारा । सुनत बचन कह पवनकुमारा ॥
āju suranha mohi dīnha ahārā, sunata bacana kaha pavanakumārā.
राम काजु करि फिरि मैं आवौं । सीता कइ सुधि प्रभुहि सुनावौं ॥
rāma kāju kari phiri maiṁ āvauṁ, sītā kai sudhi prabhuhi sunāvauṁ.
तब तव बदन पैठिहउँ आई । सत्य कहउँ मोहि जान दे माई ॥
taba tava badana paiṭhihauṁ āī, satya kahauṁ mohi jāna de māī.
कवनेहुँ जतन देइ नहिं जाना । ग्रससि न मोहि कहेउ हनुमाना ॥
kavanehuṁ jatana dei nahiṁ jānā, grasasi na mohi kaheu hanumānā.
जोजन भरि तेहिं बदनु पसारा । कपि तनु कीन्ह दुगुन बिस्तारा ॥
jojana bhari tehiṁ badanu pasārā, kapi tanu kīnha duguna bistārā.
सोरह जोजन मुख तेहिं ठयऊ । तुरत पवनसुत बत्तिस भयऊ ॥
soraha jojana mukha tehiṁ ṭhayaū, turata pavanasuta battisa bhayaū.
जस जस सुरसा बदनु बढ़ावा । तासु दून कपि रूप देखावा ॥
jasa jasa surasā badanu baṛhāvā, tāsu dūna kapi rūpa dekhāvā.
सत जोजन तेहिं आनन कीन्हा । अति लघु रूप पवनसुत लीन्हा ॥
sata jojana tehiṁ ānana kīnhā, ati laghu rūpa pavanasuta līnhā.
बदन पइठि पुनि बाहेर आवा । मागा बिदा ताहि सिरु नावा ॥
badana paiṭhi puni bāhera āvā, māgā bidā tāhi siru nāvā.
मोहि सुरन्ह जेहि लागि पठावा । बुधि बल मरमु तोर मै पावा ॥
mohi suranha jehi lāgi paṭhāvā, budhi bala maramu tora mai pāvā.

Trans:

The gods saw Hanumān on his way and wished to make a special trial of his strength and sagacity. So they sent the mother of the serpents, Sursā by name, who came and cried, "Ah, today the gods have provided me with a meal." On hearing these words the son-of-wind said, "When I have performed Rāma's commission and come back; and when I have given my Lord the news about Sītā, then I will myself enter into your mouth; I tell you the truth, mother, only let me go now." However when she would not let him go on any account, Hanumān said, "Then why not devour me?" She opened her jaws a league wide; the monkey made his body twice that size. Then she stretched her mouth sixteen leagues. Hanumān at once became thirty-two. However much Sursā expanded her jaws, the monkey made his body twice as large again. When she had made her mouth a hundred leagues wide, he reduced himself into a minute form and went into her mouth; and came out again. Then bowing he asked for permission to proceed. "The purpose for which the gods sent me, namely, to make trial of your wisdom and strength, I have now accomplished.

दोहा-dohā:

राम काजु सबु करिहहु तुम्ह बल बुद्धि निधान ।
rāma kāju sabu karihahu tumha bala buddhi nidhāna,
आसिष देह गई सो हरषि चलेउ हनुमान ॥ २ ॥
āsiṣa deha gaī so haraṣi caleu hanumāna. 2.

Trans:

Your wisdom and strength are perfect; you will do all that Rāma requires of you." She then gave him her blessings and left, and Hanumān went on his way rejoicing.

चौपाई-caupāī:

निसिचरि एक सिंधु महुँ रहई । करि माया नभु के खग गहई ॥
nisicari eka siṁdhu mahuṁ rahaī, kari māyā nabhu ke khaga gahaī.
जीव जंतु जे गगन उड़ाहीं । जल बिलोकि तिन्ह कै परिछाहीं ॥
jīva jaṁtu je gagana uṛāhīṁ, jala biloki tinha kai parichāhīṁ.
गहइ छाहँ सक सो न उड़ाई । एहि बिधि सदा गगनचर खाई ॥
gahai chāhaṁ saka so na uṛāī, ehi bidhi sadā gaganacara khāī.
सोइ छल हनूमान कहँ कीन्हा । तासु कपटु कपि तुरतहिं चीन्हा ॥
soi chala hanūmāna kahaṁ kīnhā, tāsu kapaṭu kapi turatahiṁ cīnhā.
ताहि मारि मारुतसुत बीरा । बारिधि पार गयउ मतिधीरा ॥
tāhi māri mārutasuta bīrā, bāridhi pāra gayau matidhīrā.
तहाँ जाइ देखी बन सोभा । गुंजत चंचरीक मधु लोभा ॥
tahāṁ jāi dekhī bana sobhā, guṁjata caṁcarīka madhu lobhā.
नाना तरु फल फूल सुहाए । खग मृग बृंद देखि मन भाए ॥
nānā taru phala phūla suhāe, khaga mṛga bṛṁda dekhi mana bhāe.
सैल बिसाल देखि एक आगें । ता पर धाइ चढेउ भय त्यागें ॥
saila bisāla dekhi eka āgeṁ, tā para dhāi caḍheu bhaya tyāgeṁ.
उमा न कछु कपि कै अधिकाई । प्रभु प्रताप जो कालहि खाई ॥
umā na kachu kapi kai adhikāī, prabhu pratāpa jo kālahi khāī.
गिरि पर चढि लंका तेहिं देखी । कहि न जाइ अति दुर्ग बिसेषी ॥
giri para caḍhi laṁkā tehiṁ dekhī, kahi na jāi ati durga biseṣī.
अति उतंग जलनिधि चहु पासा । कनक कोट कर परम प्रकासा ॥
ati utaṁga jalanidhi cahu pāsā, kanaka koṭa kara parama prakāsā.

Trans:

A female demon dwelt in the ocean who, by magic, caught the birds of air. All living creatures that fly cast their shadow upon the waters below, and she was able to catch their shadows and they could not fly away; and in this manner she always had many creatures to eat. She played the same trick on Hanumān; but the monkey at once saw through her craft and slew her. And thus overcoming obstacles, the hero, all undismayed, crossed over to the opposite shore. Arriving there, he marked the beauty of the wood: with the bees buzzing in their search for honey, the diverse trees all resplendent with plenty of flowers and fruits, and multitudes of birds and deer delightful to behold. Seeing a huge rock farther on, Hanumān fearlessly sprang on to the top of it. The monkey had arrived, but listen Umā, this was not at all by dint of the monkey's own strength. Verily he had arrived by the grace of the Lord, who devours even Death himself. Mounted on the height, he surveyed Lankā, a magnificent fortress that defied description—with the deep sea on all four sides around its golden walls of dazzling splendor.

छंद-chaṁda:

कनक कोट बिचित्र मनि कृत सुंदरायतना घना ।
kanaka koṭa bicitra mani kṛta suṁdarāyatanā ghanā,
चउहट्ट हट्ट सुबट्ट बीथीं चारु पुर बहु बिधि बना ॥
cauhaṭṭa haṭṭa subaṭṭa bīthīṁ cāru pura bahu bidhi banā.

गज बाजि खच्चर निकर पदचर रथ बरूथन्हि को गनै ।
gaja bāji khaccara nikara padacara ratha barūthanhi ko ganai.
बहुरूप निसिचर जूथ अतिबल सेन बरनत नहिं बनै ॥ १ ॥
bahurūpa nisicara jūtha atibala sena baranata nahiṁ banai. 1.

बन बाग उपबन बाटिका सर कूप बापीं सोहहीं ।
bana bāga upabana bāṭikā sara kūpa bāpīṁ sohahīṁ,
नर नाग सुर गंधर्ब कन्या रूप मुनि मन मोहहीं ॥
nara nāga sura gaṁdharba kanyā rūpa muni mana mohahīṁ.
कहुँ माल देह बिसाल सैल समान अतिबल गर्जहीं ।
kahuṁ māla deha bisāla saila samāna atibala garjahīṁ,
नाना अखारेन्ह भिरहिं बहु बिधि एक एकन्ह तर्जहीं ॥ २ ॥
nānā akhārenha bhirahiṁ bahu bidhi eka ekanha tarjahīṁ. 2.

करि जतन भट कोटिन्ह बिकट तन नगर चहुँ दिसि रच्छहीं ।
kari jatana bhaṭa koṭinha bikaṭa tana nagara cahuṁ disi racchahīṁ,
कहुँ महिष मानषु धेनु खर अज खल निसाचर भच्छहीं ॥
kahuṁ mahiṣa mānaṣu dhenu khara aja khala nisācara bhacchahīṁ.
एहि लागि तुलसीदास इन्ह की कथा कछु एक है कही ।
ehi lāgi tulasīdāsa inha kī kathā kachu eka hai kahī,
रघुबीर सर तीरथ सरीरन्हि त्यागि गति पैहहिं सही ॥ ३ ॥
raghubīra sara tīratha sarīranhi tyāgi gati paihahiṁ sahī. 3.

Trans:

The city had golden walls studded with all kinds of jewels, a marvelously beautiful sight, with marketplaces, bazars, quays, and streets, and all the many accessories of a fine city. Who could count the multitude of elephants, horses, and mules, the crowds of footmen and chariots, and the troops of demons of every shape, a formidable host beyond all description. The woods, gardens, groves, and pastures, the ponds, wells, and tanks were all superb; and the soul of even a saint would be ravished at the sight of the fair damsels there, both of men and *nagas*, and of gods and *gandharvs*. Here wrestlers, of monstrous stature like mountains, were thundering with mighty voices and grappling with one another in various courts, with shouts of defiance and challenge. Thousands of warriors of huge bulk were sedulously guarding the city on all four sides. Elsewhere horrid demons were banqueting on buffaloes, men, oxen, asses, and goats. Because they eventually lost their life to Rāma's hallowed shafts, and were granted access into his abode, it is for this reason that Tulsīdās gives them a few words of mention here.

दोहा-dohā:

पुर रखवारे देखि बहु कपि मन कीन्ह बिचार ।
pura rakhavāre dekhi bahu kapi mana kīnha bicāra,
अति लघु रूप धरौं निसि नगर करौं पइसार ॥ ३ ॥
ati laghu rūpa dharauṁ nisi nagara karauṁ paisāra. 3.

Trans:

Seeing the large number of the city guards, the monkey thought to himself, "I must make myself very small and slip into the city by night."

चौपाई-caupāī:

मसक समान रूप कपि धरी । लंकहि चलेउ सुमिरि नरहरी ॥
masaka samāna rūpa kapi dharī, laṁkahi caleu sumiri naraharī.
नाम लंकिनी एक निसिचरी । सो कह चलेसि मोहि निंदरी ॥
nāma laṁkinī eka nisicarī, so kaha calesi mohi niṁdarī.
जानेहि नहीं मरमु सठ मोरा । मोर अहार जहाँ लगि चोरा ॥
jānehi nahīṁ maramu saṭha morā, mora ahāra jahāṁ lagi corā.
मुठिका एक महा कपि हनी । रुधिर बमत धरनीं ढनमनी ॥
muṭhikā eka mahā kapi hanī, rudhira bamata dharanīṁ ḍhanamanī.
पुनि संभारि उठि सो लंका । जोरि पानि कर बिनय संसका ॥
puni saṁbhāri uṭhi so laṁkā, jori pāni kara binaya saṁsakā.
जब रावनहि ब्रह्म बर दीन्हा । चलत बिरंचि कहा मोहि चीन्हा ॥
jaba rāvanahi brahma bara dīnhā, calata biraṁci kahā mohi cīnhā.
बिकल होसि तैं कपि कें मारे । तब जानेसु निसिचर संघारे ॥
bikala hosi taiṁ kapi keṁ māre, taba jānesu nisicara saṁghāre.
तात मोर अति पुन्य बहूता । देखेउँ नयन राम कर दूता ॥
tāta mora ati punya bahūtā, dekheuṁ nayana rāma kara dūtā.

Trans:

When the time came he assumed a form as small as a gnat and entered Lankā after invoking Vishnu. A female demon, by the name Lankini, accosted him, "How dare you come here in contempt of me? Fool, do you not know my practice, that every thief in Lankā is my prey?" The monkey struck her one such a blow with his fist that she fell to the ground spewing blood. Recovering herself she then stood up and with clasped hands made this humble petition, "When Brahmmā, the Creator, granted Rāvan's prayer, he also gave me a sign before he left: 'When worsted by a monkey, know then that it will be soon over with the demons.' My meritorious deeds, my son, must have been very many that I have been rewarded today with the sight of Rāma's envoy.

दोहा-dohā:

तात स्वर्ग अपबर्ग सुख धरिअ तुला एक अंग ।
tāta svarga apabarga sukha dharia tulā eka aṁga,
तूल न ताहि सकल मिलि जो सुख लव सतसंग ॥ ४ ॥
tūla na tāhi sakala mili jo sukha lava satasaṁga. 4.

Trans:

In one scale of the balance put the bliss of heaven and final emancipation of the soul from the body, still it is altogether outweighed by a fraction of the joy which results from communion with the saints.

चौपाई-caupāī:

प्रबिसि नगर कीजे सब काजा । हृदयँ राखि कोसलपुर राजा ॥
prabisi nagara kīje saba kājā, hṛdayaṁ rākhi kosalapura rājā.
गरल सुधा रिपु करहिं मिताई । गोपद सिंधु अनल सितलाई ॥
garala sudhā ripu karahiṁ mitāī, gopada siṁdhu anala sitalāī.
गरुड़ सुमेरु रेनु सम ताही । राम कृपा करि चितवा जाही ॥
garuṛa sumeru renu sama tāhī, rāma kṛpā kari citavā jāhī.
अति लघु रूप धरेउ हनुमाना । पैठा नगर सुमिरि भगवाना ॥
ati laghu rūpa dhareu hanumānā, paiṭhā nagara sumiri bhagavānā.
मंदिर मंदिर प्रति करि सोधा । देखे जहँ तहँ अगनित जोधा ॥
maṁdira maṁdira prati kari sodhā, dekhe jahaṁ tahaṁ aganita jodhā.
गयउ दसानन मंदिर माहीं । अति बिचित्र कहि जात सो नाहीं ॥
gayau dasānana maṁdira māhīṁ, ati bicitra kahi jāta so nāhīṁ.
सयन किएँ देखा कपि तेही । मंदिर महुँ न दीखि बैदेही ॥
sayana kieṁ dekhā kapi tehī, maṁdira mahuṁ na dīkhi baidehī.
भवन एक पुनि दीख सुहावा । हरि मंदिर तहँ भिन्न बनावा ॥
bhavana eka puni dīkha suhāvā, hari maṁdira tahaṁ bhinna banāvā.

Trans:

Go, enter the city and accomplish your task, ever mindful at heart of the Lord of Kaushal." Deadly poison becomes as ambrosia, foes turn into friends, an ocean becomes like puddle, fire gives out cold and the bulk of Sumeru weighs no heavier than a grain of sand—to him whom Rāma deigns to regard with favor. In the tiny form that he had assumed, Hanumān entered the city with a prayer to his Lord. Carefully inspecting every separate palace, he found everywhere warriors innumerable. When he came to Rāvan's palace, its magnificence was past all telling. The monkey saw him in a bed, sound asleep. There was no trace of Sītā in the palace. A splendid home was nearby, with a temple of Harī standing apart, its walls brilliantly illuminated with Rāma's name, too beautiful to describe, it fascinated every beholder.

दोहा-dohā:

रामायुध अंकित गृह सोभा बरनि न जाइ ।
rāmāyudha aṁkita gṛha sobhā barani na jāi,
नव तुलसिका बृंद तहँ देखि हरष कपिराइ ॥५॥
nava tulasikā bṛṁda tahaṁ dekhi haraṣa kapirāi. 5.

Trans:

The beauty of the home emblazoned with signs of Rāma's arms was indescribable. At the sight of fresh sprigs of Tulsī plants, the monkey chief was enraptured.

चौपाई-caupāī:

लंका निसिचर निकर निवासा । इहाँ कहाँ सज्जन कर बासा ॥
laṁkā nisicara nikara nivāsā, ihāṁ kahāṁ sajjana kara bāsā.
मन महुँ तरक करैं कपि लागा । तेहीं समय बिभीषनु जागा ॥
mana mahuṁ taraka karaiṁ kapi lāgā, tehīṁ samaya bibhīṣanu jāgā.
राम राम तेहिं सुमिरन कीन्हा । हृदयँ हरष कपि सज्जन चीन्हा ॥
rāma rāma tehiṁ sumirana kīnhā, hṛdayaṁ haraṣa kapi sajjana cīnhā.
एहि सन हठि करिहउँ पहिचानी । साधु ते होइ न कारज हानी ॥
ehi sana haṭhi karihauṁ pahicānī, sādhu te hoi na kāraja hānī.
बिप्र रुप धरि बचन सुनाए । सुनत बिभीषन उठि तहँ आए ॥
bipra rupa dhari bacana sunāe, sunata bibhīṣana uṭhi tahaṁ āe.
करि प्रनाम पूँछी कुसलाई । बिप्र कहहु निज कथा बुझाई ॥
kari pranāma pūṁchī kusalāī, bipra kahahu nija kathā bujhāī.
की तुम्ह हरि दासन्ह महँ कोई । मोरें हृदय प्रीति अति होई ॥
kī tumha hari dāsanha mahaṁ koī, moreṁ hṛdaya prīti ati hoī.
की तुम्ह रामु दीन अनुरागी । आयहु मोहि करन बड़भागी ॥
kī tumha rāmu dīna anurāgī, āyahu mohi karana baṛabhāgī.

Trans:

"Lankā is the abode of a gang of demons, how can any pious soul have a home here?" While the monkey was thus reasoning within himself, Vibhīshan awoke and began to repeat Rāma's name in prayer. The monkey was delighted to find a devotee of Rāma. "Shall I not at once make myself known to him? A good man will never spoil one's undertaking." Assuming the form of a Brahmin, he raised his voice and hailed. As soon as Vibhīshan heard that he rose to meet him, and bowed low, asking after his welfare, "Tell me, reverend Sir, who may you be! If a servant of Harī, you have my hearty affection; if a loving follower of Rāma, your visit is a great honor for me."

दोहा-dohā:

तब हनुमंत कही सब राम कथा निज नाम ।
taba hanumaṁta kahī saba rāma kathā nija nāma,
सुनत जुगल तन पुलक मन मगन सुमिरि गुन ग्राम ॥६॥
sunata jugala tana pulaka mana magana sumiri guna grāma. 6.

Trans:

Hanumān then told him Rāma's whole history and his own name. At the recital and the recollection of Rāma's infinite virtues, both quivered all over the body, while their souls were drowned in joy.

चौपाई-caupāī:

सुनहु पवनसुत रहनि हमारी । जिमि दसनन्हि महुँ जीभ बिचारी ॥
sunahu pavanasuta rahani hamārī, jimi dasananhi mahuṁ jībha bicārī.
तात कबहुँ मोहि जानि अनाथा । करिहहिं कृपा भानुकुल नाथा ॥
tāta kabahuṁ mohi jāni anāthā, karihahiṁ kṛpā bhānukula nāthā.
तामस तनु कछु साधन नाहीं । प्रीति न पद सरोज मन माहीं ॥
tāmasa tanu kachu sādhana nāhīṁ, prīti na pada saroja mana māhīṁ.
अब मोहि भा भरोस हनुमंता । बिनु हरिकृपा मिलहिं नहिं संता ॥
aba mohi bhā bharosa hanumaṁtā, binu harikṛpā milahiṁ nahiṁ saṁtā.
जौं रघुबीर अनुग्रह कीन्हा । तौ तुम्ह मोहि दरसु हठि दीन्हा ॥
jauṁ raghubīra anugraha kīnhā, tau tumha mohi darasu haṭhi dīnhā.
सुनहु बिभीषन प्रभु कै रीती । करहिं सदा सेवक पर प्रीती ॥
sunahu bibhīṣana prabhu kai rītī, karahiṁ sadā sevaka para prītī.
कहहु कवन मैं परम कुलीना । कपि चंचल सबहीं बिधि हीना ॥
kahahu kavana maiṁ parama kulīnā, kapi caṁcala sabahīṁ bidhi hīnā.
प्रात लेइ जो नाम हमारा । तेहि दिन ताहि न मिलै अहारा ॥
prāta lei jo nāma hamārā, tehi dina tāhi na milai ahārā.

Trans:

"Hearken, Son-of-wind; my condition here is like that of the poor tongue which dwells between the teeth. Will the Lord of the solar race, dear friend, ever show his grace to me, knowing me to be masterless? Alas my sinful body is of no avail, and my heart cherishes no love for the Lord's lotus-feet. Yet I am hopeful—for it is only by Harī's favor that one meets a good man, and it is the result of his kindness that you have so readily revealed yourself to me." "Listen Vibhīshan to my own experience of the Lord; he is ever and ever affectionate to his servants. Tell me what superior birth can I lay claim to—a frivolous monkey vile in every way? A creature, the mention of whose name in the early morning, makes a man go fasting for the whole day.

दोहा-dohā:

अस मैं अधम सखा सुनु मोहू पर रघुबीर ।
asa maiṁ adhama sakhā sunu mohū para raghubīra,
कीन्ही कृपा सुमिरि गुन भरे बिलोचन नीर ॥७॥
kīnhī kṛpā sumiri guna bhare bilocana nīra. 7.

Trans:

So mean am I; yet hearken, O friend, Raghubīr has shown favor even to me." His eyes filled with tears as he recalled the Lord's many virtues.

चौपाई-caupāī:

जानतहूँ अस स्वामि बिसारी । फिरहिं ते काहे न होहिं दुखारी ॥
jānatahūṁ asa svāmi bisārī, phirahiṁ te kāhe na hohiṁ dukhārī.
एहि बिधि कहत राम गुन ग्रामा । पावा अनिर्बाच्य बिश्रामा ॥
ehi bidhi kahata rāma guna grāmā, pāvā anirbācya biśrāmā.
पुनि सब कथा बिभीषन कही । जेहि बिधि जनकसुता तहँ रही ॥
puni saba kathā bibhīṣana kahī, jehi bidhi janakasutā tahaṁ rahī.
तब हनुमंत कहा सुनु भ्राता । देखी चहउँ जानकी माता ॥
taba hanumaṁta kahā sunu bhrātā, dekhī cahauṁ jānakī mātā.
जुगुति बिभीषन सकल सुनाई । चलेउ पवनसुत बिदा कराई ॥
juguti bibhīṣana sakala sunāī, caleu pavanasuta bidā karāī.
करि सोइ रूप गयउ पुनि तहवाँ । बन असोक सीता रह जहवाँ ॥
kari soi rūpa gayau puni tahavāṁ, bana asoka sītā raha jahavāṁ.
देखि मनहि महुँ कीन्ह प्रनामा । बैठेहिं बीति जात निसि जामा ॥
dekhi manahi mahuṁ kīnha pranāmā, baiṭhehiṁ bīti jāta nisi jāmā.
कृस तनु सीस जटा एक बेनी । जपति हृदयँ रघुपति गुन श्रेनी ॥
kṛsa tanu sīsa jaṭā eka benī, japati hṛdayaṁ raghupati guna śrenī.

Trans:

"I know for a truth that any who turn aside in forgetfulness of such a Lord might as well remain miserable." As they thus discoursed on Rāma's excellences, they felt an unspeakable calm descend. Vibhīshan then told him of all that had been going on and of Sītā's mode of life, and said Hanumān, "Hearken brother, I would fain see the august Sītā." Vibhīshan explained to him the entire strategy and plan, and the Son-of-wind then took his leave and proceeded on his way. Again assuming the same form as before, he went to the Asoka grove, where dwelt Sītā. As soon as he saw her, he mentally prostrated himself in her presence. It was obvious she had spent the hours of the long night sitting up—haggard in appearance, her hair knotted in a single braid on her head, repeating to herself the list of Raghupatī's perfections.

दोहा-dohā:

निज पद नयन दिएँ मन राम पद कमल लीन ।
nija pada nayana dieṁ mana rāma pada kamala līna,
परम दुखी भा पवनसुत देखि जानकी दीन ॥८॥
parama dukhī bhā pavanasuta dekhi jānakī dīna. 8.

Trans:

Her eyes were fastened on her own feet, but her soul was absorbed in contemplation of the feet of her Lord. Hanumān was mightily distressed to see her so sad.

चौपाई-caupāī:

तरु पल्लव महुँ रहा लुकाई । करइ बिचार करौं का भाई ॥
taru pallava mahuṁ rahā lukāī, karai bicāra karauṁ kā bhāī.
तेहि अवसर रावनु तहँ आवा । संग नारि बहु किएँ बनावा ॥
tehi avasara rāvanu tahaṁ āvā, saṁga nāri bahu kieṁ banāvā.
बहु बिधि खल सीतहि समुझावा । साम दान भय भेद देखावा ॥
bahu bidhi khala sītahi samujhāvā, sāma dāna bhaya bheda dekhāvā.
कह रावनु सुनु सुमुखि सयानी । मंदोदरी आदि सब रानी ॥
kaha rāvanu sunu sumukhi sayānī, maṁdodarī ādi saba rānī.
तव अनुचरीं करउँ पन मोरा । एक बार बिलोकु मम ओरा ॥
tava anucarīṁ karauṁ pana morā, eka bāra biloku mama orā.
तृन धरि ओट कहति बैदेही । सुमिरि अवधपति परम सनेही ॥
tṛna dhari oṭa kahati baidehī, sumiri avadhapati parama sanehī.
सुनु दसमुख खद्योत प्रकासा । कबहुँ कि नलिनी करइ बिकासा ॥
sunu dasamukha khadyota prakāsā, kabahuṁ ki nalinī karai bikāsā.
अस मन समुझु कहति जानकी । खल सुधि नहिं रघुबीर बान की ॥
asa mana samujhu kahati jānakī, khala sudhi nahiṁ raghubīra bāna kī.
सठ सूनें हरि आनेहि मोही । अधम निलज्ज लाज नहिं तोही ॥
saṭha sūneṁ hari ānehi mohī, adhama nilajja lāja nahiṁ tohī.

Trans:

Concealing himself behind the branches of a tree, he deliberated, "Come sir, what ought I to do?" At that very moment Rāvan drew near, with a troop of women in glad attire. The wretch tried in every way to talk Sītā over—by blandishments, bribes, threats and misrepresentations. "Hearken, fair dame," he said, "I will make Mandodarī and all my other queens your handmaids, I swear to it, if only you give me one look." Sītā plucked a blade of grass, and with averted face, fondly remembering her own dear Lord, replied, "Hearken, Rāvan: will the lotus expand at the light of a glow-worm? Ponder this at heart." Jānakī further cried, "Wretch, have you no fear of Rāma's shafts? You carried me away when there was no one by my side, you shameless monster, have you no honor?

दोहा-dohā:

आपुहि सुनि खद्योत सम रामहि भानु समान ।
āpuhi suni khadyota sama rāmahi bhānu samāna,
परुष बचन सुनि काढ़ि असि बोला अति खिसिआन ॥९॥
paruṣa bacana suni kāṛhi asi bolā ati khisiāna. 9.

Trans:

Hearing himself likened to a glow-worm, and Rāma to the sun, and incensed at her bold speech, Rāvan drew his sword and cried in utter humiliation:

चौपाई-caupāī:

सीता तैं मम कृत अपमाना । कटिहउँ तव सिर कठिन कृपाना ॥
sītā taiṁ mama kṛta apamānā, kaṭihauṁ tava sira kaṭhina kṛpānā.
नाहिं त सपदि मानु मम बानी । सुमुखि होति न त जीवन हानी ॥
nāhiṁ ta sapadi mānu mama bānī, sumukhi hoti na ta jīvana hānī.
स्याम सरोज दाम सम सुंदर । प्रभु भुज करि कर सम दसकंधर ॥
syāma saroja dāma sama suṁdara, prabhu bhuja kari kara sama dasakaṁdhara.
सो भुज कंठ कि तव असि घोरा । सुनु सठ अस प्रवान पन मोरा ॥
so bhuja kaṁṭha ki tava asi ghorā, sunu saṭha asa pravāna pana morā.
चंद्रहास हरु मम परितापं । रघुपति बिरह अनल संजातं ॥
caṁdrahāsa haru mama paritāpaṁ, raghupati biraha anala saṁjātaṁ.
सीतल निसित बहसि बर धारा । कह सीता हरु मम दुख भारा ॥
sītala nisita bahasi bara dhārā, kaha sītā haru mama dukha bhārā.
सुनत बचन पुनि मारन धावा । मयतनयाँ कहि नीति बुझावा ॥
sunata bacana puni mārana dhāvā, mayatanayāṁ kahi nīti bujhāvā.
कहेसि सकल निसिचरिन्ह बोलाई । सीतहि बहु बिधि त्रासहु जाई ॥
kahesi sakala nisicarinha bolāī, sītahi bahu bidhi trāsahu jāī.
मास दिवस महुँ कहा न माना । तौ मैं मारबि काढ़ि कृपाना ॥
māsa divasa mahuṁ kahā na mānā, tau maiṁ mārabi kāṛhi kṛpānā.

Trans:

"Sītā, you have outraged me; and I will cut off your head with this sharp sword. Now if you do not at once obey my words, you will lose your life, lady." "My Lord's arms, Rāvan, are beautiful as a string of dark lotuses and mighty as an elephant's trunk; either they shall have my neck, or if not, then your cruel sword—hearken, wretch, to this my solemn vow. With your gleaming scimitar put an end to my distress, and let the fiery anguish that I endure for Rāma's loss be quenched in night by the sharp blade of your sword," cried Sītā, "Rid me of my burden of pains O scimitar." On hearing these words he again rushed forward to kill her; but his wife, the daughter of Māyā, restrained him with words of admonition. He then summoned all the female attendants and ordered them to go intimidate Sītā: "if she does not obey to what I say in a month's time, with this very sword I will slay her."

दोहा-dohā:

भवन गयउ दसकंधर इहाँ पिसाचिनि बृंद ।
bhavana gayau dasakaṁdhara ihāṁ pisācini bṛṁda,
सीतहि त्रास देखावहिं धरहिं रूप बहु मंद ॥१०॥
sītahi trāsa dekhāvahiṁ dharahiṁ rūpa bahu maṁda. 10.

Trans:

Rāvan then returned to the palace; while the demon crew, assuming every kind of hideous forms, proceeded to terrify Sītā.

चौपाई-caupāī:

त्रिजटा नाम राच्छसी एका । राम चरन रति निपुन बिबेका ॥
trijaṭā nāma rācchasī ekā, rāma carana rati nipuna bibekā.
सबन्हौ बोलि सुनाएसि सपना । सीतहि सेइ करहु हित अपना ॥
sabanhau boli sunāesi sapanā, sītahi sei karahu hita apanā.
सपनें बानर लंका जारी । जातुधान सेना सब मारी ॥
sapaneṁ bānara laṁkā jārī, jātudhāna senā saba mārī.
खर आरूढ़ नगन दससीसा । मुंडित सिर खंडित भुज बीसा ॥
khara ārūṛha nagana dasasīsā, muṁḍita sira khaṁḍita bhuja bīsā.
एहि बिधि सो दच्छिन दिसि जाई । लंका मनहुँ बिभीषन पाई ॥
ehi bidhi so dacchina disi jāī, laṁkā manahuṁ bibhīṣana pāī.
नगर फिरी रघुबीर दोहाई । तब प्रभु सीता बोलि पठाई ॥
nagara phirī raghubīra dohāī, taba prabhu sītā boli paṭhāī.
यह सपना मैं कहउँ पुकारी । होइहि सत्य गएँ दिन चारी ॥
yaha sapanā maiṁ kahauṁ pukārī, hoihi satya gaeṁ dina cārī.
तासु बचन सुनि ते सब डरीं । जनकसुता के चरनन्हि परीं ॥
tāsu bacana suni te saba ḍarīṁ, janakasutā ke caranani parīṁ.

Trans:

But one of them there, by name Trijatā, was devoted to Rāma's service, and much prudent and wise. She declared to them of her dream; and how they, for their own sake, ought to show Sītā reverence. "In my dream a monkey set fire to Lankā and put to death a whole host of demon. As for the ten-headed Rāvan, I saw him mounted on a donkey, all naked, with his heads shorn and his twenty arms chopped. In this fashion he went away riding towards the south; and then it seemed that Vibhīshan got the throne of Lankā. The city resounded with cries for mercy in Rāma's name; and the Lord then sent for Sītā. This dream, I hereby proclaim, will come true a few days hence." Upon hearing her words, they all were dismayed and went and threw themselves at Sītā's feet.

दोहा-dohā:

जहँ तहँ गईं सकल तब सीता कर मन सोच ।
jahaṁ tahaṁ gaiṁ sakala taba sītā kara mana soca,
मास दिवस बीतें मोहि मारिहि निसिचर पोच ॥ ११ ॥
māsa divasa bīteṁ mohi mārihi nisicara poca. 11.

Trans:

Then they dispersed in every direction; and Sītā anxiously thought within herself, "At the end of a long month this vile monster will slay me."

चौपाई-caupāī:

त्रिजटा सन बोलीं कर जोरी । मातु बिपति संगिनि तैं मोरी ॥
trijaṭā sana boliṁ kara jorī, mātu bipati saṁgini taiṁ morī.
तजौं देह करु बेगि उपाई । दुसहु बिरहु अब नहिं सहि जाई ॥
tajauṁ deha karu begi upāī, dusahu birahu aba nahiṁ sahi jāī.
आनि काठ रचु चिता बनाई । मातु अनल पुनि देहि लगाई ॥
āni kāṭha racu citā banāī, mātu anala puni dehi lagāī.
सत्य करहि मम प्रीति सयानी । सुनै को श्रवन सूल सम बानी ॥
satya karahi mama prīti sayānī, sunai ko śravana sūla sama bānī.
सुनत बचन पद गहि समुझाएसि । प्रभु प्रताप बल सुजसु सुनाएसि ॥
sunata bacana pada gahi samujhāesi, prabhu pratāpa bala sujasu sunāesi.
निसि न अनल मिल सुनु सुकुमारी । अस कहि सो निज भवन सिधारी ॥
nisi na anala mila sunu sukumārī, asa kahi so nija bhavana sidhārī.
कह सीता बिधि भा प्रतिकूला । मिलिहि न पावक मिटिहि न सूला ॥
kaha sītā bidhi bhā pratikūlā, milihi na pāvaka miṭihi na sūlā.
देखिअत प्रगट गगन अंगारा । अवनि न आवत एकउ तारा ॥
dekhiata pragaṭa gagana aṁgārā, avani na āvata ekau tārā.
पावकमय ससि स्रवत न आगी । मानहुँ मोहि जानि हत भागी ॥
pāvakamaya sasi sravata na āgī, mānahuṁ mohi jāni hata bhāgī.
सुनहि बिनय मम बिटप असोका । सत्य नाम करु हरु मम सोका ॥
sunahi binaya mama biṭapa asokā, satya nāma karu haru mama sokā.
नूतन किसलय अनल समाना । देहि अगिनि जनि करहि निदाना ॥
nūtana kisalaya anala samānā, dehi agini jani karahi nidānā.
देखि परम बिरहाकुल सीता । सो छन कपिहि कलप सम बीता ॥
dekhi parama birahākula sītā, so chana kapihi kalapa sama bītā.

Trans:

With clasped hands Sītā cried to Trijatā: "Mother, you are my helper in distress; quickly devise some plan that I may be rid of this life; this intolerable bereavement can no longer be endured. Make my funeral pyre from this wood, bring fire and set it aflame; prove the genuineness of my love for my Lord, wise lady. Who can withstand Rāvan's words, that pierce the ear like a shaft?" On hearing these words she clasped Sītā's by the feet and comforted her; and she recounting the majesty, might and glory of Lord Rāma. Then, "Hearken, fair dame; there is no fire to be had at night," saying so, she left for her home. Sītā exclaimed: "Heaven is unkind; without fire my pain cannot be cured. I see the heaven all bright with sparks, but not a single star drops to the earth. The moon is all ablaze, but no fire comes from it, as if it knows what poor wretch I am. Ye Asoka trees, hear my prayer, answer to your name and rid me of my pain; and let you flame colored buds, supply me with the fire to consume my body." A single moment seemed like an age to the monkey, as he beheld Sītā piteously lamenting in her bereavement this way.

सोरठा-soraṭhā:

कपि करि हृदयँ बिचार दीन्हि मुद्रिका डारि तब ।
kapi kari hṛdayaṁ bicāra dīnhi mudrikā ḍāri taba,
जनु असोक अंगार दीन्ह हरषि उठि कर गहेउ ॥ १२ ॥
janu asoka aṁgāra dīnha haraṣi uṭhi kara gaheu. 12.

Trans:

After taking thought Hanumān then threw down the signet ring. It looked as though a spark had fallen from the Asoka; and Sītā started up with joy and clasped it in her hands.

चौपाई-caupāī:

तब देखी मुद्रिका मनोहर । राम नाम अंकित अति सुंदर ॥
taba dekhī mudrikā manohara, rāma nāma aṁkita ati suṁdara.
चकित चितव मुदरी पहिचानी । हरष बिषाद हृदयँ अकुलानी ॥
cakita citava mudarī pahicānī, haraṣa biṣāda hṛdayaṁ akulānī.
जीति को सकइ अजय रघुराई । माया तें असि रचि नहिं जाई ॥
jīti ko sakai ajaya raghurāī, māyā teṁ asi raci nahiṁ jāī.
सीता मन बिचार कर नाना । मधुर बचन बोलेउ हनुमाना ॥
sītā mana bicāra kara nānā, madhura bacana boleu hanumānā.
रामचंद्र गुन बरनैं लागा । सुनतहिं सीता कर दुख भागा ॥
rāmacaṁdra guna baranaiṁ lāgā, sunatahiṁ sītā kara dukha bhāgā.
लागीं सुनैं श्रवन मन लाई । आदिहु तें सब कथा सुनाई ॥
lāgīṁ sunaiṁ śravana mana lāī, ādihu teṁ saba kathā sunāī.
श्रवनामृत जेहिं कथा सुहाई । कही सो प्रगट होति किन भाई ॥
śravanāmṛta jehiṁ kathā suhāī, kahī so pragaṭa hoti kina bhāī.
तब हनुमंत निकट चलि गयऊ । फिरि बैठीं मन बिसमय भयऊ ॥
taba hanumaṁta nikaṭa cali gayaū, phiri baiṭhīṁ mana bisamaya bhayaū.
राम दूत मैं मातु जानकी । सत्य सपथ करुनानिधान की ॥
rāma dūta maiṁ mātu jānakī, satya sapatha karunānidhāna kī.
यह मुद्रिका मातु मैं आनी । दीन्हि राम तुम्ह कहँ सहिदानी ॥
yaha mudrikā mātu maiṁ ānī, dīnhi rāma tumha kahaṁ sahidānī.
नर बानरहि संग कहु कैसें । कही कथा भइ संगति जैसें ॥
nara bānarahi saṁga kahu kaiseṁ, kahī kathā bhai saṁgati jaiseṁ.

Trans:

When she had looked at the lovely ring, beautifully engraved with Rāma's name, she was all astonishment, for she recognized it, and her heart fluttered with mingled joy and sorrow. "This cannot be any trickery of Māyā, but then who can conquer the unconquerable Raghurāī?"—all sorts of fancies passed through her mind, until Hanumān spoke in honeyed accents and began to recount Rāmachandra's praises. As Sītā listened, her grief took flight. Intently she hearkened with all her soul and her ears while the voice narrated the whole story from the very beginning. "The tale you tell is so grateful to my ears; why do you not show yourself, my friend?" Then Hanumān advanced and drew near. Seeing it was a monkey, she turned and sank to the ground in bewilderment. "O mother Jānakī, I am the messenger of Rāma, and the Fountain of Mercy himself attests to that truth—for it is I who brings you this ring, mother, which Rāma gave to me for you as a token." "But how can monkeys consort with men?" He then explained how they had come together.

दोहा-dohā:

कपि के बचन सप्रेम सुनि उपजा मन बिस्वास ।
kapi ke bacana saprema suni upajā mana bisvāsa,
जाना मन क्रम बचन यह कृपासिंधु कर दास ॥ १३ ॥
jānā mana krama bacana yaha kṛpāsiṁdhu kara dāsa. 13.

Trans:

On hearing the monkey's affectionate speech, her soul began to trust him, and she recognized him to be a faithful follower of the All-Merciful.

चौपाई-caupāī:

हरिजन जानि प्रीति अति गाढ़ी । सजल नयन पुलकावलि बाढ़ी ॥
harijana jāni prīti ati gāṛhī, sajala nayana pulakāvali bāṛhī.
बूड़त बिरह जलधि हनुमाना । भयहु तात मो कहुँ जलजाना ॥
būṛata biraha jaladhi hanumānā, bhayahu tāta mo kahuṁ jalajānā.
अब कहु कुसल जाउँ बलिहारी । अनुज सहित सुख भवन खरारी ॥
aba kahu kusala jāuṁ balihārī, anuja sahita sukha bhavana kharārī.
कोमलचित कृपाल रघुराई । कपि केहि हेतु धरी निठुराई ॥
komalacita kṛpāla raghurāī, kapi kehi hetu dharī niṭhurāī.
सहज बानि सेवक सुख दायक । कबहुँक सुरति करत रघुनायक ॥
sahaja bāni sevaka sukha dāyaka, kabahuṁka surati karata raghunāyaka.
कबहुँ नयन मम सीतल ताता । होइहहिं निरखि स्याम मृदु गाता ॥
kabahuṁ nayana mama sītala tātā, hoihahiṁ nirakhi syāma mṛdu gātā.
बचनु न आव नयन भरे बारी । अहह नाथ हौं निपट बिसारी ॥
bacanu na āva nayana bhare bārī, ahaha nātha hauṁ nipaṭa bisārī.
देखि परम बिरहाकुल सीता । बोला कपि मृदु बचन बिनीता ॥
dekhi parama birahākula sītā, bolā kapi mṛdu bacana binītā.
मातु कुसल प्रभु अनुज समेता । तव दुख दुखी सुकृपा निकेता ॥
mātu kusala prabhu anuja sametā, tava dukha dukhī sukṛpā niketā.
जनि जननी मानहु जियँ ऊना । तुम्ह ते प्रेमु राम कें दूना ॥
jani jananī mānahu jiyaṁ ūnā, tumha te premu rāma keṁ dūnā.

Trans:

On perceiving him to be one of Harī's worshippers, she felt much affection for him; her eyes filled with tears, her body quivered with emotion. "O son, I was sinking in the ocean of bereavement; but in you, friend, I have now found a ship. Tell me now of their welfare, I adjure you; how is the blessed Kharārī, and how his brother? Raghurāī is tender-hearted and merciful; so why, O monkey, should he affect such cruelty? He who by his very nature is a source of delight to his devotees—does he even remember me ever? Will my eyes, O son, be ever gladdened by the sight of his dark, delicate body?" Words failed and her eyes swam with tears, "Alas! my Lord has entirely forgotten me!" Seeing Sītā thus distracted by her bereavement, the monkey spoke in gentle respectful tones, "Mother, your Lord and his brother are both well—except that the All-merciful sorrows much in your sorrow. Do not imagine, O mother, that Rāma's affection is a whit less than your own—in fact it is twice.

दोहा-dohā:

रघुपति कर संदेसु अब सुनु जननी धरि धीर ।
raghupati kara saṁdesu aba sunu jananī dhari dhīra,
अस कहि कपि गदगद भयउ भरे बिलोचन नीर ॥ १४ ॥
asa kahi kapi gadagada bhayau bhare bilocana nīra. 14.

Trans:

Take courage now and listen to Rāma's message." Even as he spoke, the monkey's voice choked and his eyes filled with tears.

चौपाई-caupāī:

कहेउ राम बियोग तव सीता । मो कहुँ सकल भए बिपरीता ॥
kaheu rāma biyoga tava sītā, mo kahuṁ sakala bhae biparītā.
नव तरु किसलय मनहुँ कृसानू । काल निसा सम निसि ससि भानू ॥
nava taru kisalaya manahuṁ kṛsānū, kāla nisā sama nisi sasi bhānū.
कुबलय बिपिन कुंत बन सरिसा । बारिद तपत तेल जनु बरिसा ॥
kubalaya bipina kuṁta bana sarisā, bārida tapata tela janu barisā.
जे हित रहे करत तेइ पीरा । उरग स्वास सम त्रिबिध समीरा ॥
je hita rahe karata tei pīrā, uraga svāsa sama tribidha samīrā.
कहेहू तें कछु दुख घटि होई । काहि कहौं यह जान न कोई ॥
kahehū teṁ kachu dukha ghaṭi hoī, kāhi kahauṁ yaha jāna na koī.
तत्व प्रेम कर मम अरु तोरा । जानत प्रिया एकु मनु मोरा ॥
tatva prema kara mama aru torā, jānata priyā eku manu morā.
सो मनु सदा रहत तोहि पाहीं । जानु प्रीति रसु एतनेहि माहीं ॥
so manu sadā rahata tohi pāhīṁ, jānu prīti rasu etanehi māhīṁ.
प्रभु संदेसु सुनत बैदेही । मगन प्रेम तन सुधि नहिं तेही ॥
prabhu saṁdesu sunata baidehī, magana prema tana sudhi nahiṁ tehī.
कह कपि हृदयँ धीर धरु माता । सुमिरु राम सेवक सुखदाता ॥
kaha kapi hṛdayaṁ dhīra dharu mātā, sumiru rāma sevaka sukhadātā.
उर आनहु रघुपति प्रभुताई । सुनि मम बचन तजहु कदराई ॥
ura ānahu raghupati prabhutāī, suni mama bacana tajahu kadarāī.

Trans:

"Shrī Rāma said: Ever since I have been separated from you, Sītā, everything to me has become its very reverse. The fresh buds upon the trees burn like fire; night seems as the night of death, and the moon scorches like the sun. A bed of lotuses seems a prickly brake, and the rain clouds drop boiling oil. That which ere comforted now torments; and the softest most fragrant breeze is like the breath of a serpent. Nothing relieves my torture, but to whom can I declare it? There is no one who will understand. The essence of such love as yours and mine, my beloved, only my own soul can comprehend; this my soul always abides with you. From afar, know this to be the measure of my love through such words alone.'" As the Videhan princess listened to Rāma's message, she became so absorbed in love as to have no thought for herself. Said the monkey, "Mother, compose yourself, remembering that Rāma is a benefactor to all who serve him. Reflect upon his might, and, as you listen to my speech, discard all anxiety.

दोहा-dohā:

निसिचर निकर पतंग सम रघुपति बान कृसानु ।
nisicara nikara pataṁga sama raghupati bāna kṛsānu,
जननी हृदयँ धीर धरु जरे निसाचर जानु ॥ १५ ॥
jananī hṛdayaṁ dhīra dharu jare nisācara jānu. 15.

Trans:

The demon crew are like moths and Raghupatī's arrows are like flames; be stout of heart, mother, and rest assured that they will all be consumed.

चौपाई-caupāī:

जौं रघुबीर होति सुधि पाई । करते नहिं बिलंबु रघुराई ॥
jauṁ raghubīra hoti sudhi pāī, karate nahiṁ bilaṁbu raghurāī.
राम बान रबि उएँ जानकी । तम बरूथ कहँ जातुधान की ॥
rāma bāna rabi ueṁ jānakī, tama barūtha kahaṁ jātudhāna kī.
अबहिं मातु मैं जाउँ लवाई । प्रभु आयसु नहिं राम दोहाई ॥
abahiṁ mātu maiṁ jāuṁ lavāī, prabhu āyasu nahiṁ rāma dohāī.
कछुक दिवस जननी धरु धीरा । कपिन्ह सहित अइहहिं रघुबीरा ॥
kachuka divasa jananī dharu dhīrā, kapinha sahita aihahiṁ raghubīrā.
निसिचर मारि तोहि लै जैहहिं । तिहुँ पुर नारदादि जसु गैहहिं ॥
nisicara māri tohi lai jaihahiṁ, tihuṁ pura nāradādi jasu gaihahiṁ.
हैं सुत कपि सब तुम्हहि समाना । जातुधान अति भट बलवाना ॥

haiṁ suta kapi saba tumhahi samānā, jātudhāna ati bhaṭa balavānā.

मोरें हृदय परम संदेहा । सुनि कपि प्रगट कीन्हि निज देहा ॥

moreṁ hṛdaya parama saṁdehā, suni kapi pragaṭa kīnhi nija dehā.

कनक भूधराकार सरीरा । समर भयंकर अतिबल बीरा ॥

kanaka bhūdharākāra sarīrā, samara bhayaṁkara atibala bīrā.

सीता मन भरोस तब भयऊ । पुनि लघु रूप पवनसुत लयऊ ॥

sītā mana bharosa taba bhayaū, puni laghu rūpa pavanasuta layaū.

Trans:

Had Raghubīr known your whereabouts, he wouldn't have delayed. But now, like the rays of the rising sun, the shafts of Shri Rāma are about to appear and scatter the darkling demon host. I myself would have carried you at once, but I swear to you by Rāma, that I have not received his order to do so. Wait patiently my mother for a few days and he will arrive with the monkeys, slaughter the demons, and take you home; and then Nārad and the other seers will glorify him in all the three spheres of creation." "Are all the monkeys, my son, like you? The demon warriors are very powerful, and my soul is sorely disquieted." On hearing this, the monkey showed himself in his natural form, his body massive like a mountain of gold, terrible in battle, and of vast strength. Then Sītā took comfort at heart, and he at once resumed his diminutive appearance.

दोहा-dohā:

सुनु माता साखामृग नहिं बल बुद्धि बिसाल ।

sunu mātā sākhāmṛga nahiṁ bala buddhi bisāla,

प्रभु प्रताप तें गरुड़हि खाइ परम लघु ब्याल ॥ १६ ॥

prabhu pratāpa teṁ garuṛahi khāi parama laghu byāla. 16.

Trans:

"Listen mother, the monkeys have no great strength or wit of their own, but by the Lord's favor even a snake, small as it is, might swallow a Garud."

चौपाई-caupāī:

मन संतोष सुनत कपि बानी । भगति प्रताप तेज बल सानी ॥

mana saṁtoṣa sunata kapi bānī, bhagati pratāpa teja bala sānī.

आसिष दीन्हि रामप्रिय जाना । होहु तात बल सील निधाना ॥

āsiṣa dīnhi rāmapriya jānā, hohu tāta bala sīla nidhānā.

अजर अमर गुननिधि सुत होहू । करहुँ बहुत रघुनायक छोहू ॥

ajara amara gunanidhi suta hohū, karahuṁ bahuta raghunāyaka chohū.

करहुँ कृपा प्रभु अस सुनि काना । निर्भर प्रेम मगन हनुमाना ॥

karahuṁ kṛpā prabhu asa suni kānā, nirbhara prema magana hanumānā.

बार बार नाएसि पद सीसा । बोला बचन जोरि कर कीसा ॥

bāra bāra nāesi pada sīsā, bolā bacana jori kara kīsā.

अब कृतकृत्य भयउँ मैं माता । आसिष तव अमोघ बिख्याता ॥

aba kṛtakṛtya bhayauṁ maiṁ mātā, āsiṣa tava amogha bikhyātā.

सुनहु मातु मोहि अतिसय भूखा । लागि देखि सुंदर फल रूखा ॥

sunahu mātu mohi atisaya bhūkhā, lāgi dekhi suṁdara phala rūkhā.

सुनु सुत करहिं बिपिन रखवारी । परम सुभट रजनीचर भारी ॥

sunu suta karahiṁ bipina rakhavārī, parama subhaṭa rajanīcara bhārī.

तिन्ह कर भय माता मोहि नाहीं । जौं तुम्ह सुख मानहु मन माहीं ॥

tinha kara bhaya mātā mohi nāhīṁ, jauṁ tumha sukha mānahu mana māhīṁ.

Trans:

As she hearkened to the monkey's speech, so full of glorious faith and noble confidence, her mind became easy; she recognized his love for Rāma and gave him her blessings, "May you abound, my son, in all strength and virtue; may neither age nor death affect your good qualities, and may you be ever constant in your devotion to Rāma, and may the Lord be gracious to you." Hearing these words, Hanumān became utterly overwhelmed with emotion; again and again he bowed his head at her feet, and with clasped hands said, "I have now received all I need in life mother, for your blessing, everyone knows, is unfailing." Adding, "Now listen mother, I am frightfully hungry and I see the trees laden with delicious fruit." "Know, my son, that this grove is guarded by most valiant formidable demons." "I am not afraid of them, O mother, if you feel good in your heart."

दोहा-dohā:

देखि बुद्धि बल निपुन कपि कहेउ जानकीं जाहु ।

dekhi buddhi bala nipuna kapi kaheu jānakīṁ jāhu,

रघुपति चरन हृदयँ धरि तात मधुर फल खाहु ॥ १७ ॥

raghupati carana hṛdayaṁ dhari tāta madhura phala khāhu. 17.

Trans:

Seeing the monkey so strong and sagacious, Jānakī said, "Go son; partake of these delicious fruits—with your heart fixed on the feet of Raghupati."

चौपाई-caupāī:

चलेउ नाइ सिरु पैठेउ बागा । फल खाएसि तरु तोरैं लागा ॥

caleu nāi siru paiṭheu bāgā, phala khāesi taru toraiṁ lāgā.

रहे तहाँ बहु भट रखवारे । कछु मारेसि कछु जाइ पुकारे ॥

rahe tahāṁ bahu bhaṭa rakhavāre, kachu māresi kachu jāi pukāre.

नाथ एक आवा कपि भारी । तेहिं असोक बाटिका उजारी ॥

nātha eka āvā kapi bhārī, tehiṁ asoka bāṭikā ujārī.

खाएसि फल अरु बिटप उपारे । रच्छक मर्दि मर्दि महि डारे ॥

khāesi phala aru biṭapa upāre, racchaka mardi mardi mahi ḍāre.

सुनि रावन पठए भट नाना । तिन्हहि देखि गर्जेउ हनुमाना ॥

suni rāvana paṭhae bhaṭa nānā, tinhahi dekhi garjeu hanumānā.

सब रजनीचर कपि संघारे । गए पुकारत कछु अधमारे ॥

saba rajanīcara kapi saṁghāre, gae pukārata kachu adhamāre.

पुनि पठयउ तेहिं अच्छकुमारा । चला संग लै सुभट अपारा ॥

puni paṭhayau tehiṁ acchakumārā, calā saṁga lai subhaṭa apārā.

आवत देखि बिटप गहि तर्जा । ताहि निपाति महाधुनि गर्जा ॥

āvata dekhi biṭapa gahi tarjā, tāhi nipāti mahādhuni garjā.

Trans:

He bowed his head and went and entered the grove; and there having eaten of the fruits began breaking down the boughs. A number of stalwart watchmen were posted there; some got killed, and the others went and called for help: "My lord, an enormous monkey has come and rooted up the Asoka grove; he has eaten the fruit and broken down the trees, and with many a blow laid down the watchmen on the ground." On hearing this, Rāvan dispatched a number of his champions. At the sight of them Hanumān roared like thunder and overthrew the whole demon host; a few, more dead than alive, ran away shrieking. He then sent the young prince Aksha, who took with him an immense number of his best warriors. Seeing them approach Hanumān seized a tree, which he brandished and with an awful roar dispatched the prince to heaven.

दोहा-dohā:

कछु मारेसि कछु मर्देसि कछु मिलएसि धरि धूरि ।

kachu māresi kachu mardesi kachu milaesi dhari dhūri,

कछु पुनि जाइ पुकारे प्रभु मर्कट बल भूरि ॥ १८ ॥

kachu puni jāi pukāre prabhu markaṭa bala bhūri. 18.

Trans:

Of the soldiers, some he hacked, some he crushed, some he laid low in the dust; some got back and cried "My lord, this monkey is too strong for us."

चौपाई-caupāī:

सुनि सुत बध लंकेस रिसाना । पठएसि मेघनाद बलवाना ॥

suni suta badha laṁkesa risānā, paṭhaesi meghanāda balavānā.

मारसि जनि सुत बांधेसु ताही । देखिअ कपिहि कहाँ कर आही ॥

mārasi jani suta bāṁdhesu tāhī, dekhia kapihi kahāṁ kara āhī.

चला इंद्रजित अतुलित जोधा । बंधु निधन सुनि उपजा क्रोधा ॥

calā iṁdrajita atulita jodhā, baṁdhu nidhana suni upajā krodhā.

कपि देखा दारुन भट आवा । कटकटाइ गर्जा अरु धावा ॥
kapi dekhā dāruna bhaṭa āvā, kaṭakaṭāi garjā aru dhāvā.
अति बिसाल तरु एक उपारा । बिरथ कीन्ह लंकेस कुमारा ॥
ati bisāla taru eka upārā, biratha kīnha laṁkesa kumārā.
रहे महाभट ताके संगा । गहि गहि कपि मर्दइ निज अंगा ॥
rahe mahābhaṭa tāke saṁgā, gahi gahi kapi mardai nija aṁgā.
तिन्हहि निपाति ताहि सन बाजा । भिरे जुगल मानहुँ गजराजा ॥
tinhahi nipāti tāhi sana bājā, bhire jugala mānahuṁ gajarājā.
मुठिका मारि चढ़ा तरु जाई । ताहि एक छन मुरुछा आई ॥
muṭhikā māri caṛhā taru jāī, tāhi eka chana muruchā āī.
उठि बहोरि कीन्हिसि बहु माया । जीति न जाइ प्रभंजन जाया ॥
uṭhi bahori kīnhisi bahu māyā, jīti na jāi prabhaṁjana jāyā.

Trans:

When he heard of his son's death, the king of Lankā was furious, and he sent the valiant Meghnād. "Do not kill him, my son, but bind him; I would fain see this monkey and where he comes from." Indrajit sallied forth, a peerless champion, full of fury at the tidings of his brother's death. When the monkey saw this formidable warrior draw near, he ground his teeth, and with a roar rushed forward and tore up a tree of enormous size—with which he swept the prince of Lankā away from the car. As for the mighty men of war that accompanied him, he seized them one by one and crushed them under his weight. Having finished them off, he closed again with their leader. It was like the encounter of two elephants. After striking him a blow with his fist, Hanumān climbed up a tree—seeing that the antagonist had momentarily swooned. Again the prince arose and practiced many enchantments; but the son of wind-god was not to be vanquished.

दोहा-dohā:

ब्रह्म अस्त्र तेहिं साँधा कपि मन कीन्ह बिचार ।
brahma astra tehiṁ sāṁdhā kapi mana kīnha bicāra,
जौं न ब्रह्मसर मानउँ महिमा मिटइ अपार ॥ १९ ॥
jauṁ na brahmasara mānauṁ mahimā miṭai apāra. 19.

Trans:

Upon the prince making ready the infallible Brahmmā's-weapon, the monkey thought to himself, "If I do not submit to Brahmmā's shaft, its infinite virtue will have failed."

चौपाई-caupāī:

ब्रह्मबान कपि कहुँ तेहिं मारा । परतिहुँ बार कटकु संघारा ॥
brahmabāna kapi kahuṁ tehiṁ mārā, paratihuṁ bāra kaṭaku saṁghārā.
तेहिं देखा कपि मुरुछित भयऊ । नागपास बाँधेसि लै गयऊ ॥
tehiṁ dekhā kapi muruchita bhayaū, nāgapāsa bāṁdhesi lai gayaū.
जासु नाम जपि सुनहु भवानी । भव बंधन काटहिं नर ग्यानी ॥
jāsu nāma japi sunahu bhavānī, bhava baṁdhana kāṭahiṁ nara gyānī.
तासु दूत कि बंध तरु आवा । प्रभु कारज लगि कपिहिं बँधावा ॥
tāsu dūta ki baṁdha taru āvā, prabhu kāraja lagi kapihiṁ baṁdhāvā.
कपि बंधन सुनि निसिचर धाए । कौतुक लागि सभाँ सब आए ॥
kapi baṁdhana suni nisicara dhāe, kautuka lāgi sabhāṁ saba āe.
दसमुख सभा दीखि कपि जाई । कहि न जाइ कछु अति प्रभुताई ॥
dasamukha sabhā dīkhi kapi jāī, kahi na jāi kachu ati prabhutāī.
कर जोरें सुर दिसिप बिनीता । भृकुटि बिलोकत सकल सभीता ॥
kara joreṁ sura disipa binītā, bhṛkuṭi bilokata sakala sabhītā.
देखि प्रताप न कपि मन संका । जिमि अहिगन महुँ गरुड़ असंका ॥
dekhi pratāpa na kapi mana saṁkā, jimi ahigana mahuṁ garuṛa asaṁkā.

Trans:

Meghnād launched the deadly weapon against the monkey, who crushed many host as he fell down. When he saw that the monkey was unconscious, he bound him with a serpent-noose and carried him off. Observe, Bhawānī: the messenger of Lord-God—by the repetition of whose very name, wise men cut the bonds of existence—himself came under bondage, or rather in his Lord's service he submitted himself to be thus bound. When the demons heard that the monkey had been captured, they all rushed to the palace to watch the fun. The monkey arrived and saw the stateliness of Rāvan's court—majestic beyond description. Even gods and regents of the quarters stood meek with joined palms, all watching the movement of his eyebrows in great fear. But the monkey's soul was no more disturbed at the sight of his power than Garud would be frightened by any number of snakes.

दोहा-dohā:

कपिहि बिलोकि दसानन बिहसा कहि दुर्बाद ।
kapihi biloki dasānana bihasā kahi durbāda,
सुत बध सुरति कीन्हि पुनि उपजा हृदयँ बिषाद ॥ २० ॥
suta badha surati kīnhi puni upajā hṛdayaṁ biṣāda. 20.

Trans:

When Rāvan saw the monkey he laughed aloud and mocked him; then he remembered his son's death and his soul grew sad.

चौपाई-caupāī:

कह लंकेस कवन तैं कीसा । केहि कें बल घालेहि बन खीसा ॥
kaha laṁkesa kavana taiṁ kīsā, kehi keṁ bala ghālehi bana khīsā.
की धौं श्रवन सुनेहि नहिं मोही । देखउँ अति असंक सठ तोही ॥
kī dhauṁ śravana sunehi nahiṁ mohī, dekhauṁ ati asaṁka saṭha tohī.
मारे निसिचर केहिं अपराधा । कहु सठ तोहि न प्रान कइ बाधा ॥
māre nisicara kehiṁ aparādhā, kahu saṭha tohi na prāna kai bādhā.
सुनु रावन ब्रह्मांड निकाया । पाइ जासु बल बिरचति माया ॥
sunu rāvana brahmāṁḍa nikāyā, pāi jāsu bala biracati māyā.
जाकें बल बिरंचि हरि ईसा । पालत सृजत हरत दससीसा ॥
jākeṁ bala biraṁci hari īsā, pālata sṛjata harata dasasīsā.
जा बल सीस धरत सहसानन । अंडकोस समेत गिरि कानन ॥
jā bala sīsa dharata sahasānana, aṁḍakosa sameta giri kānana.
धरइ जो बिबिध देह सुरत्राता । तुम्ह ते सठन्ह सिखावनु दाता ॥
dharai jo bibidha deha suratrātā, tumha te saṭhanha sikhāvanu dātā.
हर कोदंड कठिन जेहिं भंजा । तेहि समेत नृप दल मद गंजा ॥
hara kodaṁḍa kaṭhina jehiṁ bhaṁjā, tehi sameta nṛpa dala mada gaṁjā.
खर दूषन त्रिसिरा अरु बाली । बधे सकल अतुलित बलसाली ॥
khara dūṣana trisirā aru bālī, badhe sakala atulita balasālī.

Trans:

Said the King of Lankā, "Who are you, monkey, and by whose might have you wrought the destruction of the grove? What? Don't you hear me? I see you are an exceptionally bold wretch. For what offence did you put the demons to death? Speak, wretch; or you have no hope of life left." "Hearken, Rāvan; He by whose might Māyā creates this universal sphere; by whose might Brahmmā, Vishnu, and Shiva produce, maintain, and destroy the world; by whose might the thousand-headed serpent supports on his pate the entire globe with its mountains and forests; who assumes various forms in order to protect the gods and to teach lessons to wretches like you; who broke Shiva's stubborn bow and crushed your pride and that of the assembled kings; who slew Khar and Dūshan and Trisirā and Bālī, in spite of their matchless strength;

दोहा-dohā:

जाके बल लवलेस तें जितेहु चराचर झारि ।
jāke bala lavalesa teṁ jitehu carācara jhāri,
तासु दूत मैं जा करि हरि आनेहु प्रिय नारि ॥ २१ ॥
tāsu dūta maiṁ jā kari hari ānehu priya nāri. 21.

Trans:

by the slightest exercise of whose might the entire mass of creation, animate and inanimate, exists—he it is whose messenger I am, and it is his beloved spouse whom you have stolen away.

चौपाई-*caupāī:*

जानउँ मैं तुम्हारि प्रभुताई । सहसबाहु सन परी लराई ॥
jānaum̐ maiṁ tumhāri prabhutāī, sahasabāhu sana parī larāī.
समर बालि सन करि जसु पावा । सुनि कपि बचन बिहसि बिहरावा ॥
samara bāli sana kari jasu pāvā, suni kapi bacana bihasi biharāvā.
खायउँ फल प्रभु लागी भूँखा । कपि सुभाव तें तोरेउँ रूखा ॥
khāyaum̐ phala prabhu lāgī bhūm̐khā, kapi subhāva teṁ toreum̐ rūkhā.
सब कें देह परम प्रिय स्वामी । मारहिं मोहि कुमारग गामी ॥
saba keṁ deha parama priya svāmī, mārahiṁ mohi kumāraga gāmī.
जिन्ह मोहि मारा ते मैं मारे । तेहि पर बाँधेउँ तनयँ तुम्हारे ॥
jinha mohi mārā te maiṁ māre, tehi para bām̐dhem̐ tanayam̐ tumhāre.
मोहि न कछु बाँधे कइ लाजा । कीन्ह चहउँ निज प्रभु कर काजा ॥
mohi na kachu bām̐dhe kai lājā, kīnha cahaum̐ nija prabhu kara kājā.
बिनती करउँ जोरि कर रावन । सुनहु मान तजि मोर सिखावन ॥
binatī karaum̐ jori kara rāvana, sunahu māna taji mora sikhāvana.
देखहु तुम्ह निज कुलहि बिचारी । भ्रम तजि भजहु भगत भय हारी ॥
dekhahu tumha nija kulahi bicārī, bhrama taji bhajahu bhagata bhaya hārī.
जाकें डर अति काल डेराई । जो सुर असुर चराचर खाई ॥
jākeṁ ḍara ati kāla ḍerāī, jo sura asura carācara khāī.
तासों बयरु कबहुँ नहिं कीजै । मोरे कहें जानकी दीजै ॥
tāsoṁ bayaru kabahum̐ nahiṁ kījai, more kaheṁ jānakī dījai.

Trans:

I know your power; you had a fight with Sahatsr-bhuj, and gained renown in your conflict with Bālī." Rāvan heard the monkey's sarcasm but had to laugh it away. "I ate the fruit because I felt hungry and broke the boughs as a monkey is wont to do. Everyone, O master, loves his life more than aught else; those wicked fellows fell upon me, and I gave them blow for a blow. Thereupon your son put me in bonds—bonds that I am in no way ashamed of—for my only object is to accomplish my master's task. Rāvan, I implore you with folded hands: abandon pride and attend to my advice. In delusion you go astray, give that up. Have some consideration for your family, and adore him who relieves his worshippers from every anxiety. Do not fight against him, from fear of whom even Death trembles—yes even Death, which devours all else: gods and demons, animate and inanimate creation alike. Give up Sītā, I say to you.

दोहा-*dohā:*

प्रनतपाल रघुनायक करुना सिंधु खरारि ।
pranatapāla raghunāyaka karunā siṁdhu kharāri,
गएँ सरन प्रभु राखिहैं तव अपराध बिसारि ॥२२॥
gaem̐ sarana prabhu rākhihaiṁ tava aparādha bisāri. 22.

Trans:

Rāma is the protector of suppliants; Kharārī is the very ocean of compassion; turn to him for protection and the Lord will forgive your offences and shelter you.

चौपाई-*caupāī:*

राम चरन पंकज उर धरहू । लंका अचल राजु तुम्ह करहू ॥
rāma carana paṁkaja ura dharahū, laṁkā acala rāju tumha karahū.
रिषि पुलस्ति जसु बिमल मंयका । तेहि ससि महुँ जनि होहु कलंका ॥
riṣi pulasti jasu bimala maṁyakā, tehi sasi mahum̐ jani hohu kalaṁkā.
राम नाम बिनु गिरा न सोहा । देखु बिचारि त्यागि मद मोहा ॥
rāma nāma binu girā na sohā, dekhu bicāri tyāgi mada mohā.
बसन हीन नहिं सोह सुरारी । सब भूषन भूषित बर नारी ॥
basana hīna nahiṁ soha surārī, saba bhūṣana bhūṣita bara nārī.
राम बिमुख संपति प्रभुताई । जाइ रही पाई बिनु पाई ॥
rāma bimukha saṁpati prabhutāī, jāi rahī pāī binu pāī.
सजल मूल जिन्ह सरितन्ह नाहीं । बरषि गए पुनि तबहिं सुखाहीं ॥
sajala mūla jinha saritanha nāhīṁ, baraṣi gae puni tabahiṁ sukhāhīṁ.
सुनु दसकंठ कहउँ पन रोपी । बिमुख राम त्राता नहिं कोपी ॥
sunu dasakaṁṭha kahaum̐ pana ropī, bimukha rāma trātā nahiṁ kopī.
संकर सहस बिष्नु अज तोही । सकहिं न राखि राम कर द्रोही ॥
saṁkara sahasa biṣnu aja tohī, sakahiṁ na rākhi rāma kara drohī.

Trans:

Take Rāma's lotus feet to your heart and reign for ever in Lankā. The glory of your grandsire saint Pulastya is stainless as the moon; do not make yourself a dark spot in its brightness. Without Rāma's name in it, even speech has no charm: Think and see for yourself, setting aside pride and vanity. Without her clothes, O Rāvan, a modest woman, however richly adorned with jewels, is a shameful sight; and so is wealth, and dominion, without Rāma—gone soon, or gotten as if not gotten at all. Those rivers, that have no perennial source, flow only after rain and then soon dry out. Hearken Rāvan, I tell you on my oath, if Rāma be against you, there is none who can save you. Shiva, Sheshnāg, Vishnu and Brahmmā cannot protect you, if you are Rāma's enemy.

दोहा-*dohā:*

मोहमूल बहु सूल प्रद त्यागहु तम अभिमान ।
mohamūla bahu sūla prada tyāgahu tama abhimāna,
भजहु राम रघुनायक कृपा सिंधु भगवान ॥२३॥
bhajahu rāma raghunāyaka kṛpā siṁdhu bhagavāna. 23.

Trans:

Arrogance is a root fruitful of many thorns; abandon violence and pride and worship Rāma, the prince of Raghu's race, the Ocean of Compassion, the very Lord God."

चौपाई-*caupāī:*

जदपि कही कपि अति हित बानी । भगति बिबेक बिरति नय सानी ॥
jadapi kahī kapi ati hita bānī, bhagati bibeka birati naya sānī.
बोला बिहसि महा अभिमानी । मिला हमहि कपि गुर बड़ ग्यानी ॥
bolā bihasi mahā abhimānī, milā hamahi kapi gura baṛa gyānī.
मृत्यु निकट आई खल तोही । लागेसि अधम सिखावन मोही ॥
mṛtyu nikaṭa āī khala tohī, lāgesi adhama sikhāvana mohī.
उलटा होइहि कह हनुमाना । मतिभ्रम तोर प्रगट मैं जाना ॥
ulaṭā hoihi kaha hanumānā, matibhrama tora pragaṭa maiṁ jānā.
सुनि कपि बचन बहुत खिसिआना । बेगि न हरहु मूढ़ कर प्राना ॥
suni kapi bacana bahuta khisiānā, begi na harahu mūṛha kara prānā.
सुनत निसाचर मारन धाए । सचिवन्ह सहित बिभीषनु आए ॥
sunata nisācara mārana dhāe, sacivanha sahita bibhīṣanu āe.
नाइ सीस करि बिनय बहूता । नीति बिरोध न मारिअ दूता ॥
nāi sīsa kari binaya bahūtā, nīti birodha na māria dūtā.
आन दंड कछु करिअ गोसाँई । सबहीं कहा मंत्र भल भाई ॥
āna daṁḍa kachu karia gosām̐ī, sabahīṁ kahā maṁtra bhala bhāī.
सुनत बिहसि बोला दसकंधर । अंग भंग करि पठइअ बंदर ॥
sunata bihasi bolā dasakaṁdhara, aṁga bhaṁga kari paṭhaia baṁdara.

Trans:

Though the monkey bespoke to him in such friendly wise, in words full of faith and discretion, piety and sound judgment, Rāvan laughed and replied with the highest disdain, "What a sage adviser we have found today, and that too in a monkey! Wretch, for daring to give me such vile counsel, you have come within an inch of death." "Just the contrary is going to happen" retorted Hanumān, "I clearly perceive that you are laboring under mental illusion dark." On hearing the monkey's words, he ground his teeth in fury. "Quick someone; put an end to this fool's life." The demons rushed forward in obeyance to slay him, but Vibhīshan with his ministers then stepped forward and bowing his head made this humble petition, "It is against all state craft; an ambassador must never be killed. Punish him in some other way, sir." All exclaimed to one another, "That is sound counsel, friends." Rāvan upon hearing that, laughingly said, "Let the monkey go then, but first mutilate him.

दोहा-dohā:

कपि कें ममता पूँछ पर सबहि कहउँ समुझाइ ।
kapi kem̐ mamatā pūm̐cha para sabahi kahaum̐ samujhāi,
तेल बोरि पट बाँधि पुनि पावक देहु लगाइ ॥२४॥
tela bori paṭa bām̐dhi puni pāvaka dehu lagāi. 24.

Trans:

A monkey is very fond of his tail: I tell you this secret. Therefore, swathe his tail with rags soaked in oil and set fire to it.

चौपाई-caupāī:

पूँछहीन बानर तहँ जाइहि । तब सठ निज नाथहि लइ आइहि ॥
pūm̐chahīna bānara taham̐ jāihi, taba saṭha nija nāthahi lai āihi.
जिन्ह कै कीन्हिसि बहुत बड़ाई । देखउँ मैं तिन्ह कै प्रभुताई ॥
jinha kai kīnhisi bahuta baṛāī, dekhaum̐ maiṁ tinha kai prabhutāī.
बचन सुनत कपि मन मुसुकाना । भइ सहाय सारद मैं जाना ॥
bacana sunata kapi mana musukānā, bhai sahāya sārada maiṁ jānā.
जातुधान सुनि रावन बचना । लागे रचैं मूढ़ सोइ रचना ॥
jātudhāna suni rāvana bacanā, lāge racaiṁ mūṛha soi racanā.
रहा न नगर बसन घृत तेला । बाढ़ी पूँछ कीन्ह कपि खेला ॥
rahā na nagara basana ghṛta telā, bāṛhī pūm̐cha kīnha kapi khelā.
कौतुक कहँ आए पुरबासी । मारहिं चरन करहिं बहु हाँसी ॥
kautuka kaham̐ āe purabāsī, mārahiṁ carana karahiṁ bahu hām̐sī.
बाजहिं ढोल देहिं सब तारी । नगर फेरि पुनि पूँछ प्रजारी ॥
bājahiṁ ḍhola dehiṁ saba tārī, nagara pheri puni pūm̐cha prajārī.
पावक जरत देखि हनुमंता । भयउ परम लघुरुप तुरंता ॥
pāvaka jarata dekhi hanumaṁtā, bhayau parama laghurupa turaṁtā.
निबुकि चढ़ेउ कपि कनक अटारीं । भईं सभीत निसाचर नारीं ॥
nibuki caṛheu kapi kanaka aṭārīṁ, bhaīṁ sabhīta nisācara nārīṁ.

Trans:

The poor tail-less wretch can then go back and fetch his master; and I shall have an opportunity of seeing his might, whom he has so extravagantly extols." The monkey smiled to himself upon hearing that, "Shārdā, I think, helps me." Obedient to Rāvan's command the demons began making their foolish preparations. Not a rag was left in the city nor a drop of ghee or oil—to such a length had Hanumān grown his tail. Then they made sport of the monkey; the citizens crowded to see the sight, and struck him with their feet and jeered at him exceedingly; and with clapping of hands and beating of drums they took him throughout the city and set fire to his tail. When Hanumān saw the fire blazing, he at once reduced himself to a diminutive size, and slipping out of his bonds sprang on to the upper levels of the gilded palaces, to the dismay of the demons' wives.

दोहा-dohā:

हरि प्रेरित तेहि अवसर चले मरुत उनचास ।
hari prerita tehi avasara cale maruta unacāsa,
अट्टहास करि गर्जा कपि बढ़ि लाग अकास ॥२५॥
aṭṭahāsa kari garjā kapi baṛhi lāga akāsa. 25.

Trans:

That very instant the forty-nine winds, whom Harī had sent, began to rage; the monkey bellowed and roared and swelled so big that he touched the skies, it seemed.

चौपाई-caupāī:

देह बिसाल परम हरुआई । मंदिर तें मंदिर चढ़ धाई ॥
deha bisāla parama haruāī, maṁdira teṁ maṁdira caṛha dhāī.
जरइ नगर भा लोग बिहाला । झपट लपट बहु कोटि कराला ॥
jarai nagara bhā loga bihālā, jhapaṭa lapaṭa bahu koṭi karālā.
तात मातु हा सुनिअ पुकारा । एहिं अवसर को हमहि उबारा ॥
tāta mātu hā sunia pukārā, ehiṁ avasara ko hamahi ubārā.
हम जो कहा यह कपि नहिं होई । बानर रूप धरें सुर कोई ॥
hama jo kahā yaha kapi nahiṁ hoī, bānara rūpa dhareṁ sura koī.
साधु अवग्या कर फलु ऐसा । जरइ नगर अनाथ कर जैसा ॥
sādhu avagyā kara phalu aisā, jarai nagara anātha kara jaisā.
जारा नगरु निमिष एक माहीं । एक बिभीषन कर गृह नाहीं ॥
jārā nagaru nimiṣa eka māhīṁ, eka bibhīṣana kara gṛha nāhīṁ.
ता कर दूत अनल जेहिं सिरिजा । जरा न सो तेहि कारन गिरिजा ॥
tā kara dūta anala jehiṁ sirijā, jarā na so tehi kārana girijā.
उलटि पलटि लंका सब जारी । कूदि परा पुनि सिंधु मझारी ॥
ulaṭi palaṭi laṁkā saba jārī, kūdi parā puni siṁdhu majhārī.

Trans:

Of enormous stature and yet marvelous agility, Hanumān leapt and ran from one palace to another. As the city was thus set on fire, the people were at their wits end—for the terrible flames burst forth in a countless million places. "Alas! O father, O mother, hearken to my cry. Who it is that is destroying us! As I said, this is no monkey, but some god in a monkey's form. This is the result of not taking a good man's advice; our city is burning as though it has been orphaned." In short order the city was consumed in flames except for Vibhīshan's house. Hanumān escaped unscathed, O Bhawānī; and it's because he was the messenger of He, Lord God—the Creator of fire. After the whole of Lankā had been turned upside down and given over to the flames, Hanumān threw himself into the ocean.

दोहा-dohā:

पूँछ बुझाइ खोइ श्रम धरि लघु रूप बहोरि ।
pūm̐cha bujhāi khoi śrama dhari laghu rūpa bahori,
जनकसुता कें आगें ठाढ़ भयउ कर जोरि ॥२६॥
janakasutā keṁ āgeṁ ṭhāṛha bhayau kara jori. 26.

Trans:

After extinguishing his tail and recovering from his fatigue, he reassumed the diminutive form and went and stood before mother Jānakī, with hands clasped in prayer:

चौपाई-caupāī:

मातु मोहि दीजे कछु चीन्हा । जैसें रघुनायक मोहि दीन्हा ॥
mātu mohi dīje kachu cīnhā, jaiseṁ raghunāyaka mohi dīnhā.
चूड़ामनि उतारि तब दयऊ । हरष समेत पवनसुत लयऊ ॥
cūṛāmani utāri taba dayaū, haraṣa sameta pavanasuta layaū.
कहेहु तात अस मोर प्रनामा । सब प्रकार प्रभु पूरनकामा ॥
kahehu tāta asa mora pranāmā, saba prakāra prabhu pūranakāmā.
दीन दयाल बिरिदु संभारी । हरहु नाथ मम संकट भारी ॥
dīna dayāla biridu saṁbhārī, harahu nātha mama saṁkaṭa bhārī.
तात सक्रसुत कथा सुनाएहु । बान प्रताप प्रभुहि समुझाएहु ॥
tāta sakrasuta kathā sunāehu, bāna pratāpa prabhuhi samujhāehu.
मास दिवस महुँ नाथु न आवा । तौ पुनि मोहि जिअत नहिं पावा ॥
māsa divasa mahum̐ nāthu na āvā, tau puni mohi jiata nahiṁ pāvā.
कहु कपि केहि बिधि राखौं प्राना । तुम्हहू तात कहत अब जाना ॥
kahu kapi kehi bidhi rākhauṁ prānā, tumhahū tāta kahata aba jānā.
तोहि देखि सीतलि भइ छाती । पुनि मो कहुँ सोइ दिनु सो राती ॥

tohi dekhi sītali bhai chātī, puni mo kahum̐ soi dinu so rātī.

Trans:

"Be pleased, O mother, to give me some token, such as Rāma gave me." She unfastened the jewel in her hair and gave it to him. The son-of-wind received it gladly. "Salute him respectfully for me, my son, with these words: 'My Lord, you never fail to fulfill desire, and you support the reputation of being the suppliant's friend; relieve me then from my grievous distress. Repeat to him my son, the story of Indra's son, and remind my Lord of the might of his arrows. If he does not come within a month, he will not find me alive. Tell me, Hanumān, how can I keep myself alive; for you too now, my son, speak of going. It is only the sight of you that gave me some comfort; henceforth day and night will seem to me both alike."

दोहा-dohā:

जनकसुतहि समुझाइ करि बहु बिधि धीरजु दीन्ह ।

janakasutahi samujhāi kari bahu bidhi dhīraju dīnha,

चरन कमल सिरु नाइ कपि गवनु राम पहिं कीन्ह ॥२७॥

carana kamala siru nāi kapi gavanu rāma pahiṁ kīnha. 27.

Trans:

He did everything he could to console Sītā and inspire her with confidence; and then bowing his head at her lotus feet, set forth to rejoin Rāma.

चौपाई-caupāī:

चलत महाधुनि गर्जेसि भारी । गर्भ स्रवहिं सुनि निसिचर नारी ॥

calata mahādhuni garjesi bhārī, garbha sravahiṁ suni nisicara nārī.

नाघि सिंधु एहि पारहि आवा । सबद किलिकिला कपिन्ह सुनावा ॥

nāghi siṁdhu ehi pārahi āvā, sabada kilikilā kapinha sunāvā.

हरषे सब बिलोकि हनुमाना । नूतन जन्म कपिन्ह तब जाना ॥

haraṣe saba biloki hanumānā, nūtana janma kapinha taba jānā.

मुख प्रसन्न तन तेज बिराजा । कीन्हेसि रामचन्द्र कर काजा ॥

mukha prasanna tana teja birājā, kīnhesi rāmacandra kara kājā.

मिले सकल अति भए सुखारी । तलफत मीन पाव जिमि बारी ॥

mile sakala ati bhae sukhārī, talaphata mīna pāva jimi bārī.

चले हरषि रघुनायक पासा । पूँछत कहत नवल इतिहासा ॥

cale haraṣi raghunāyaka pāsā, pūm̐chata kahata navala itihāsā.

तब मधुबन भीतर सब आए । अंगद संमत मधु फल खाए ॥

taba madhubana bhītara saba āe, aṁgada saṁmata madhu phala khāe.

रखवारे जब बरजन लागे । मुष्टि प्रहार हनत सब भागे ॥

rakhavāre jaba barajana lāge, muṣṭi prahāra hanata saba bhāge.

Trans:

As he left, he let aloud such a dreadful roar that the pregnant demon-wives upon hearing it were overcome by childbirth premature. Crossing the sea with a leap, he arrived on this side and uttered a cry of joy for all the monkeys to hear. At the sight of Hanumān, they were as delighted as if given a now spell of life. "Your face is so glad and your whole body so radiant that you cannot but have accomplished Rāma's work." They greeted him with as much delight as a dying fish in dry feels when it gets back into the water. On their way back to Rāma it was a pleasure for them to ask Hanumān again and again—to relate all that had happened at Lankā. Soon they reached the Madhuban, and with Angad's consent began eating the luscious fruit from the garden; the watchman tried to stop, but were beaten off with fisticuffs; who then fled to Sugrīva,

दोहा-dohā:

जाइ पुकारे ते सब बन उजार जुबराज ।

jāi pukāre te saba bana ujāra jubarāja,

सुनि सुग्रीव हरष कपि करि आए प्रभु काज ॥२८॥

suni sugrīva haraṣa kapi kari āe prabhu kāja. 28.

Trans:

crying out that the prince had laid waste to the garden. Sugrīva rejoiced at the news, "The monkey must have returned after successfully completing the Lord's business.

चौपाई-caupāī:

जौं न होति सीता सुधि पाई । मधुबन के फल सकहिं कि खाई ॥

jauṁ na hoti sītā sudhi pāī, madhubana ke phala sakahiṁ ki khāī.

एहि बिधि मन बिचार कर राजा । आइ गए कपि सहित समाजा ॥

ehi bidhi mana bicāra kara rājā, āi gae kapi sahita samājā.

आइ सबन्हि नावा पद सीसा । मिलेउ सबन्हि अति प्रेम कपीसा ॥

āi sabanhi nāvā pada sīsā, mileu sabanhi ati prema kapīsā.

पूँछी कुसल कुसल पद देखी । राम कृपाँ भा काजु बिसेषी ॥

pūm̐chī kusala kusala pada dekhī, rāma kr̥pām̐ bhā kāju biseṣī.

नाथ काजु कीन्हेउ हनुमाना । राखे सकल कपिन्ह के प्राना ॥

nātha kāju kīnheu hanumānā, rākhe sakala kapinha ke prānā.

सुनि सुग्रीव बहुरि तेहि मिलेऊ । कपिन्ह सहित रघुपति पहिं चलेऊ ॥

suni sugrīva bahuri tehi mileū, kapinha sahita raghupati pahiṁ caleū.

राम कपिन्ह जब आवत देखा । किएँ काजु मन हरष बिसेषा ॥

rāma kapinha jaba āvata dekhā, kiem̐ kāju mana haraṣa biseṣā.

फटिक सिला बैठे द्वौ भाई । परे सकल कपि चरनन्हि जाई ॥

phaṭika silā baiṭhe dvau bhāī, pare sakala kapi carananhi jāī.

Trans:

If they had not got news of Sītā, they could not have eaten the fruits of the Madhuban like that." While the king was thus reasoning within himself, Hanumān and his party arrived. They bowed their heads at his feet, and he received them with all possible cordiality and asked them of their welfare. "It is well with us now that we have seen your feet. By Rāma's favor the business has turned out excellently. Hanumān has accomplished our Lord's purpose and has saved the life of us all." On hearing this, Sugrīva again embraced Hanumān; and then left immediately with the monkeys to where Rāma was. When Rāma saw them coming, he was greatly delighted; the two brothers were seated on a crystal rock and the monkeys went and fell at their feet.

दोहा-dohā:

प्रीति सहित सब भेटे रघुपति करुना पुंज ।

prīti sahita saba bheṭe raghupati karunā puṁja,

पूँछी कुसल नाथ अब कुसल देखि पद कंज ॥२९॥

pūm̐chī kusala nātha aba kusala dekhi pada kaṁja. 29.

Trans:

Raghupatī in his infinite tenderness greeted them all with much affection and asked of their welfare. "All is well with us my Lord, now that we have seen your lotus feet."

चौपाई-caupāī:

जामवंत कह सुनु रघुराया । जा पर नाथ करहु तुम्ह दाया ॥

jāmavaṁta kaha sunu raghurāyā, jā para nātha karahu tumha dāyā.

ताहि सदा सुभ कुसल निरंतर । सुर नर मुनि प्रसन्न ता ऊपर ॥

tāhi sadā subha kusala niraṁtara, sura nara muni prasanna tā ūpara.

सोइ बिजई बिनई गुन सागर । तासु सुजसु त्रैलोक उजागर ॥

soi bijaī binaī guna sāgara, tāsu sujasu trailoka ujāgara.

प्रभु कीं कृपा भयउ सबु काजू । जन्म हमार सुफल भा आजू ॥

prabhu kīṁ kr̥pā bhayau sabu kājū, janma hamāra suphala bhā ājū.

नाथ पवनसुत कीन्हि जो करनी । सहसहुँ मुख न जाइ सो बरनी ॥

nātha pavanasuta kīnhi jo karanī, sahasahum̐ mukha na jāi so baranī.

पवनतनय के चरित सुहाए । जामवंत रघुपतिहि सुनाए ॥

pavanatanaya ke carita suhāe, jāmavaṁta raghupatihi sunāe.

सुनत कृपानिधि मन अति भाए । पुनि हनुमान हरषि हियँ लाए ॥

sunata kr̥pānidhi mana ati bhāe, puni hanumāna haraṣi hiyam̐ lāe.

कहहु तात केहि भाँति जानकी । रहति करति रच्छा स्वप्रान की ॥

kahahu tāta kehi bhām̐ti jānakī, rahati karati racchā svaprāna kī.

Trans:

Then said Jāmvant, "Hearken Raghurāī: anyone, my Lord, on whom you show favor, will be ever prosperous; gods, men, and saints will be gracious to him; though victorious he will still remain modest and amiable; and his glory will irradiate through all the three spheres of creation. By my Lord's favor the task has been accomplished, and today we may well say that our life has been worth living. My Lord, to tell the entirety of Hanumān's doings would be too much for a thousand tongues." Jāmvant then proceeded to inform Rāma of Hanumān's principal exploits. The All-merciful was charmed by the recital and again in his joy clasped Hanumān to his bosom. "Tell me, my son, how abides Jānakī? And how she protects her life?"

दोहा-dohā:

नाम पाहरु दिवस निसि ध्यान तुम्हार कपाट ।
nāma pāharu divasa nisi dhyāna tumhāra kapāṭa,
लोचन निज पद जंत्रित जाहिं प्रान केहिं बाट ॥३०॥
locana nija pada jaṁtrita jāhiṁ prāna kehiṁ bāṭa. 30.

Trans:

"Your name is the sentinel over her by night and day; contemplation upon you is as a prison-gate; her own eyes are the fetters for her feet; how then is it possible for her life to flee?

चौपाई-caupāī:

चलत मोहि चूड़ामनि दीन्ही । रघुपति हृदयँ लाइ सोइ लीन्ही ॥
calata mohi cūṛāmani dīnhī, raghupati hṛdayam̐ lāi soi līnhī.
नाथ जुगल लोचन भरि बारी । बचन कहे कछु जनककुमारी ॥
nātha jugala locana bhari bārī, bacana kahe kachu janakakumārī.
अनुज समेत गहेहु प्रभु चरना । दीन बंधु प्रनतारति हरना ॥
anuja sameta gahehu prabhu caranā, dīna baṁdhu pranatārati haranā.
मन क्रम बचन चरन अनुरागी । केहिं अपराध नाथ हौं त्यागी ॥
mana krama bacana carana anurāgī, kehiṁ aparādha nātha hauṁ tyāgī.
अवगुन एक मोर मैं माना । बिछुरत प्रान न कीन्ह पयाना ॥
avaguna eka mora maiṁ mānā, bichurata prāna na kīnha payānā.
नाथ सो नयनन्हि को अपराधा । निसरत प्रान करहिं हठि बाधा ॥
nātha so nayananhi ko aparādhā, nisarata prāna karahiṁ haṭhi bādhā.
बिरह अगिनि तनु तूल समीरा । स्वास जरइ छन माहिं सरीरा ॥
biraha agini tanu tūla samīrā, svāsa jarai chana māhiṁ sarīrā.
नयन स्रवहिं जलु निज हित लागी । जरैं न पाव देह बिरहागी ॥
nayana sravahiṁ jalu nija hita lāgī, jaraiṁ na pāva deha birahāgī.
सीता कै अति बिपति बिसाला । बिनहिं कहें भलि दीनदयाला ॥
sītā kai ati bipati bisālā, binahiṁ kaheṁ bhali dīnadayālā.

Trans:

When I was leaving, she gave me this jewel from her hair." Raghupatī took and clasped it to his heart. "And my Lord, with tears in her eyes, Sītā spoke these few words for you: 'Embrace the feet of my Lord and his brother, crying, O friend of the poor, reliever of the suppliant's distress, in heart, word, and deed, I am devoted to your service; for what offence, my Lord, have you deserted me? Of one fault I am myself conscious, in that I still continue to live, though separated from you. But this, my Lord, is the fault of my eyes, which prevent my soul from taking flight. The fire of bereavement has rendered my body as light as the air, and in a moment my frame would burn itself out in sighs; but my eyes drop such a flood in self-commiseration, that my vile body gets not consumed in flames. Sītā's distress is so utterly overwhelming, and you are so compassionate, that it is better not to describe further.

दोहा-dohā:

निमिष निमिष करुनानिधि जाहिं कलप सम बीति ।
nimiṣa nimiṣa karunānidhi jāhiṁ kalapa sama bīti,
बेगि चलिय प्रभु आनिअ भुज बल खल दल जीति ॥३१॥
begi caliya prabhu ānia bhuja bala khala dala jīti. 31.

Trans:

O fountain of mercy, each single moment seems an age in passing to her. Set out at once, my Lord, and with the might of your arm, vanquish the miscreant crew and redeem her."

चौपाई-caupāī:

सुनि सीता दुख प्रभु सुख अयना । भरि आए जल राजिव नयना ॥
suni sītā dukha prabhu sukha ayanā, bhari āe jala rājiva nayanā.
बचन कायँ मन मम गति जाही । सपनेहुँ बूझिअ बिपति कि ताही ॥
bacana kāyam̐ mana mama gati jāhī, sapanehum̐ būjhia bipati ki tāhī.
कह हनुमंत बिपति प्रभु सोई । जब तव सुमिरन भजन न होई ॥
kaha hanumaṁta bipati prabhu soī, jaba tava sumirana bhajana na hoī.
केतिक बात प्रभु जातुधान की । रिपुहि जीति आनिबी जानकी ॥
ketika bāta prabhu jātudhāna kī, ripuhi jīti ānibī jānakī.
सुनु कपि तोहि समान उपकारी । नहिं कोउ सुर नर मुनि तनुधारी ॥
sunu kapi tohi samāna upakārī, nahiṁ kou sura nara muni tanudhārī.
प्रति उपकार करौं का तोरा । सनमुख होइ न सकत मन मोरा ॥
prati upakāra karauṁ kā torā, sanamukha hoi na sakata mana morā.
सुनु सुत तोहि उरिन मैं नाहीं । देखेउँ करि बिचार मन माहीं ॥
sunu suta tohi urina maiṁ nāhīṁ, dekheum̐ kari bicāra mana māhīṁ.
पुनि पुनि कपिहि चितव सुरत्राता । लोचन नीर पुलक अति गाता ॥
puni puni kapihi citava suratrātā, locana nīra pulaka ati gātā.

Trans:

On hearing of Sītā's distress, the lotus eyes of the Lord, the abode of bliss, overflowed with tears. "When in thought, word and deed, a believer follows in my steps, what ought he to know of misfortune?" Said Hanumān: "There is no misfortune, my Lord, except to forget you and your worship. Of what account are the demons to my Lord, who can rout them at once and recover Sītā." "Hearken, O monkey: neither god, nor man, nor saint has ever been born into this world, who has been such a benefactor to me as you. What return can I make to you? There is none that occurs to my mind. Listen, my son: I have thought over the question and concluded that the debt which I owe you cannot be repaid." Again and again as the deliverer of the gods gazed upon the monkey, his eyes filled with tears and his whole body quivered with emotion.

दोहा-dohā:

सुनि प्रभु बचन बिलोकि मुख गात हरषि हनुमंत ।
suni prabhu bacana biloki mukha gāta haraṣi hanumaṁta,
चरन परेउ प्रेमाकुल त्राहि त्राहि भगवंत ॥३२॥
carana pareu premākula trāhi trāhi bhagavaṁta. 32.

Trans:

As he listened to his Lord's words and looked upon his face, Hanumān was enraptured, and in an ecstasy of love fell at his feet, crying, "save me, save me, O my Lord God, lest I become conceited."

चौपाई-caupāī:

बार बार प्रभु चहइ उठावा । प्रेम मगन तेहि उठब न भावा ॥
bāra bāra prabhu cahai uṭhāvā, prema magana tehi uṭhaba na bhāvā.
प्रभु कर पंकज कपि कें सीसा । सुमिरि सो दसा मगन गौरीसा ॥
prabhu kara paṁkaja kapi keṁ sīsā, sumiri so dasā magana gaurīsā.
सावधान मन करि पुनि संकर । लागे कहन कथा अति सुंदर ॥
sāvadhāna mana kari puni saṁkara, lāge kahana kathā ati suṁdara.

कपि उठाइ प्रभु हृदयँ लगावा । कर गहि परम निकट बैठावा ॥
kapi uṭhāi prabhu hṛdayam̐ lagāvā, kara gahi parama nikaṭa baiṭhāvā.

कहु कपि रावन पालित लंका । केहि बिधि दहेउ दुर्ग अति बंका ॥
kahu kapi rāvana pālita laṁkā, kehi bidhi daheu durga ati baṁkā.

प्रभु प्रसन्न जाना हनुमाना । बोला बचन बिगत अभिमाना ॥
prabhu prasanna jānā hanumānā, bolā bacana bigata abhimānā.

साखामृग कै बड़ि मनुसाई । साखा तें साखा पर जाई ॥
sākhāmṛga kai baṛi manusāī, sākhā tem̐ sākhā para jāī.

नाघि सिंधु हाटकपुर जारा । निसिचर गन बधि बिपिन उजारा ॥
nāghi siṁdhu hāṭakapura jārā, nisicara gana badhi bipina ujārā.

सो सब तव प्रताप रघुराई । नाथ न कछू मोरि प्रभुताई ॥
so saba tava pratāpa raghurāī, nātha na kachū mori prabhutāī.

Trans:
Again and again his Lord sought to raise him up, but he was so absorbed in devotion that he would not rise. As he called to mind the Lord with his lotus hands placed on the monkey's head, Shiva himself was overcome with emotion. But then restraining his feelings, he proceeded with the charming narrative. After raising the monkey, the Lord embraced him and took him by the hand and seated him close to his side, "Tell me, O Kapi, about Rāvan's stronghold of Lankā, and how you were able in such an offhand way to burn down his fort." Seeing his Lord so gracious, Hanumān replied in terms of singular modesty, "A monkey forsooth is a creature of singular prowess: to skip about as he does from bough to bough. When I leaped across the sea, burnt down the golden city, routed the demon host and laid waste to the grove, it was all done through your power, my Lord; it was no strength of my own, Raghurāī.

दोहा-dohā:

ता कहुँ प्रभु कछु अगम नहिं जा पर तुम्ह अनुकूल ।
tā kahum̐ prabhu kachu agama nahiṁ jā para tumha anukūla,

तव प्रभावँ बड़वानलहि जारि सकइ खलु तूल ॥३३॥
tava prabhāvam̐ baṛavānalahi jāri sakai khalu tūla. 33.

Trans:
Nothing is difficult for him upon whom you are propitious; a mere flock of cotton, were it your pleasure, would burn up the whole submarine fire.

चौपाई-caupāī:

नाथ भगति अति सुखदायनी । देहु कृपा करि अनपायनी ॥
nātha bhagati ati sukhadāyanī, dehu kṛpā kari anapāyanī.

सुनि प्रभु परम सरल कपि बानी । एवमस्तु तब कहेउ भवानी ॥
suni prabhu parama sarala kapi bānī, evamastu taba kaheu bhavānī.

उमा राम सुभाउ जेहिं जाना । ताहि भजनु तजि भाव न आना ॥
umā rāma subhāu jehiṁ jānā, tāhi bhajanu taji bhāva na ānā.

यह संबाद जासु उर आवा । रघुपति चरन भगति सोइ पावा ॥
yaha saṁbāda jāsu ura āvā, raghupati carana bhagati soi pāvā.

सुनि प्रभु बचन कहहिं कपिबृंदा । जय जय जय कृपाल सुखकंदा ॥
suni prabhu bacana kahahiṁ kapibṛṁdā, jaya jaya jaya kṛpāla sukhakaṁdā.

तब रघुपति कपिपतिहि बोलावा । कहा चलैं कर करहु बनावा ॥
taba raghupati kapipatihi bolāvā, kahā calaiṁ kara karahu banāvā.

अब बिलंबु केहि कारन कीजे । तुरत कपिन्ह कहुँ आयसु दीजे ॥
aba bilaṁbu kehi kārana kīje, turata kapinha kahum̐ āyasu dīje.

कौतुक देखि सुमन बहु बरषी । नभ तें भवन चले सुर हरषी ॥
kautuka dekhi sumana bahu baraṣī, nabha tem̐ bhavana cale sura haraṣī.

Trans:
Therefore, be pleased, to grant me the only source of supreme bliss: an unceasing Devotion for you, my Lord." When the Lord, O Pārwatī, heard the most artless speech of Hanumān He ordained: "Be that so!" Umā, he who has come to know the true nature of Rāma can have no relish for anything other than His worship. Even he who takes this dialogue to heart is blessed with devotion to Shrī Rāma's feet. On hearing the words of the Lord the whole host of monkeys cried, "Glory, glory, all glory to the gracious Lord, the fountain of bliss!" Raghupatī then summoned the monkey chief and told him to make preparations for the march, "What need now for any delay? At once issue orders to the troops." The gods, who had witnessed the spectacle, rained down countless flowers and returned with joy from the air to their own celestial spheres.

दोहा-dohā:

कपिपति बेगि बोलाए आए जूथप जूथ ।
kapipati begi bolāe āe jūthapa jūtha,

नाना बरन अतुल बल बानर भालु बरूथ ॥३४॥
nānā barana atula bala bānara bhālu barūtha. 34.

Trans:
In obedience to Sugrīva's summons the captains came with troops of youths: of many different colors, all unequalled in strength, countless monkeys and bears in abundance.

चौपाई-caupāī:

प्रभु पद पंकज नावहिं सीसा । गर्जहिं भालु महाबल कीसा ॥
prabhu pada paṁkaja nāvahiṁ sīsā, garjahiṁ bhālu mahābala kīsā.

देखी राम सकल कपि सेना । चितइ कृपा करि राजिव नैना ॥
dekhī rāma sakala kapi senā, citai kṛpā kari rājiva nainā.

राम कृपा बल पाइ कपिंदा । भए पच्छजुत मनहुँ गिरिंदा ॥
rāma kṛpā bala pāi kapiṁdā, bhae pacchajuta manahum̐ giriṁdā.

हरषि राम तब कीन्ह पयाना । सगुन भए सुंदर सुभ नाना ॥
haraṣi rāma taba kīnha payānā, saguna bhae suṁdara subha nānā.

जासु सकल मंगलमय कीती । तासु पयान सगुन यह नीती ॥
jāsu sakala maṁgalamaya kītī, tāsu payāna saguna yaha nītī.

प्रभु पयान जाना बैदेहीं । फरकि बाम अँग जनु कहि देहीं ॥
prabhu payāna jānā baidehīṁ, pharaki bāma am̐ga janu kahi dehīṁ.

जोइ जोइ सगुन जानकिहि होई । असगुन भयउ रावनहि सोई ॥
joi joi saguna jānakihi hoī, asaguna bhayau rāvanahi soī.

चला कटकु को बरनै पारा । गर्जहिं बानर भालु अपारा ॥
calā kaṭaku ko baranaiṁ pārā, garjahiṁ bānara bhālu apārā.

नख आयुध गिरि पादपधारी । चले गगन महि इच्छाचारी ॥
nakha āyudha giri pādapadhārī, cale gagana mahi icchācārī.

केहरिनाद भालु कपि करहीं । डगमगाहिं दिग्गज चिक्करहीं ॥
keharināda bhālu kapi karahīṁ, ḍagamagāhiṁ diggaja cikkarahīṁ.

Trans:
They bowed the head at the Lord's lotus feet—those roaring bears and gigantic monkeys. Rāma beheld the host, and swept upon them the gracious glance of his lotus eyes. Each monkey chief was as much emboldened by his favor as Sumera would be by the recovery of his wings. Rāma then sallied forth exulting, and many were the glad and auspicious omens that came to pass at that time. It was only befitting that his march should be attended by favorable omens, since in him abide all glory and auspiciousness. Jānakī knew of his departure, for her left side throbbed as if to tell her; and every good omen that happened to Sītā was converted into an omen of ill which befell Rāvan. Who could adequately describe the army on the road: with the terrible roaring of the monkeys and the bears; and how they marched—brandishing rocks and trees and with their talons for weapons, now in the sky and now on earth, as the fancy moved them. They bellowed as if with voices of tigers; and the earth shook and the elephants of the eight quarters trembled.

छंद-chaṁda:

चिक्करहिं दिग्गज डोल महि गिरि लोल सागर खरभरे ।

cikkarahiṁ diggaja ḍola mahi giri lola sāgara kharabhare,
मन हरष सभ गंधर्ब सुर मुनि नाग किंनर दुख टरे ॥
mana haraṣa sabha gaṁdharba sura muni nāga kiṁnara dukha ṭare.
कटकटहिं मर्कट बिकट भट बहु कोटि कोटिन्ह धावहीं ।
kaṭakaṭahiṁ markaṭa bikaṭa bhaṭa bahu koṭi koṭinha dhāvahīṁ,
जय राम प्रबल प्रताप कोसलनाथ गुन गन गावहीं ॥ १ ॥
jaya rāma prabala pratāpa kosalanātha guna gana gāvahīṁ. 1.

सहि सक न भार उदार अहिपति बार बारहिं मोहई ।
sahi saka na bhāra udāra ahipati bāra bārahiṁ mohaī,
गह दसन पुनि पुनि कमठ पृष्ट कठोर सो किमि सोहई ॥
gaha dasana puni puni kamaṭha pṛṣṭa kaṭhora so kimi sohaī.
रघुबीर रुचिर प्रयान प्रस्थिति जानि परम सुहावनी ।
raghubīra rucira prayāna prasthiti jāni parama suhāvanī,
जनु कमठ खर्पर सर्पराज सो लिखत अबिचल पावनी ॥ २ ॥
janu kamaṭha kharpara sarparāja so likhata abicala pāvanī. 2.

Trans:

The elephants of the eight quarters thrilled, the earth reeled, file mountains tottered, and the oceans were agitated; the sun and the moon, gods, saints, Nagas, and Kinnars, all rejoiced to know that their troubles will be over soon. Myriads upon myriads of enormous fighting monkeys pressed onwards, snapping and snarling, singing glory to Rāma's conquering might, and hymning the praises of the Kaushal's Lord. The huge serpent king could not support the burden; he staggered again and again, but each time saved himself by clutching in his jaws the hard shell of the tortoise—as though to mark the stupendous theme of Raghubīr's glorious expedition, and inscribing it on the tortoise's back as the most imperishable material to be had.

दोहा-dohā:

एहि बिधि जाइ कृपानिधि उतरे सागर तीर ।
ehi bidhi jāi kṛpānidhi utare sāgara tīra,
जहँ तहँ लागे खान फल भालु बिपुल कपि बीर ॥ ३५ ॥
jahaṁ tahaṁ lāge khāna phala bhālu bipula kapi bīra. 35.

Trans:

In such way the All-merciful marched onwards till he arrived at the sea shore where the host of bears and fighting monkeys began to eat fruits that could be found here and there.

चौपाई-caupāī:

उहाँ निसाचर रहहिं ससंका । जब तें जारि गयउ कपि लंका ॥
uhāṁ nisācara rahahiṁ sasaṁkā, jaba teṁ jāri gayau kapi laṁkā.
निज निज गृहँ सब करहिं बिचारा । नहिं निसिचर कुल केर उबारा ॥
nija nija gṛhaṁ saba karahiṁ bicārā, nahiṁ nisicara kula kera ubārā.
जासु दूत बल बरनि न जाई । तेहि आएँ पुर कवन भलाई ॥
jāsu dūta bala barani na jāī, tehi āeṁ pura kavana bhalāī.
दूतिन्ह सन सुनि पुरजन बानी । मंदोदरी अधिक अकुलानी ॥
dūtinha sana suni purajana bānī, maṁdodarī adhika akulānī.
रहसि जोरि कर पति पग लागी । बोली बचन नीति रस पागी ॥
rahasi jori kara pati paga lāgī, bolī bacana nīti rasa pāgī.
कंत करष हरि सन परिहरहू । मोर कहा अति हित हियँ धरहू ॥
kaṁta karaṣa hari sana pariharahū, mora kahā ati hita hiyaṁ dharahū.
समुझत जासु दूत कइ करनी । स्त्रवहिं गर्भ रजनीचर धरनी ॥
samujhata jāsu dūta kai karanī, sravahiṁ garbha rajanīcara dharanī.
तासु नारि निज सचिव बोलाई । पठवहु कंत जो चहहु भलाई ॥
tāsu nāri nija saciva bolāī, paṭhavahu kaṁta jo cahahu bhalāī.
तव कुल कमल बिपिन दुखदाई । सीता सीत निसा सम आई ॥
tava kula kamala bipina dukhadāī, sītā sīta nisā sama āī.
सुनहु नाथ सीता बिनु दीन्हें । हित न तुम्हार संभु अज कीन्हें ॥
sunahu nātha sītā binu dīnheṁ, hita na tumhāra saṁbhu aja kīnheṁ.

Trans:

On the other side the demons had been living in great fear ever since the monkey left after burning the city down. Everyone kept at home thinking to himself, "There is no hope of safety for the demon race now. If his messenger was so unspeakably powerful, how can the city escape when the master himself comes." When Mandodarī was informed of what the people were saying, she was all the more distressed; and beseeching her lord, with clasped hands she fell at his feet and prayed in words full of sound judgment, "O my husband, cease to contend against Harī. Take my words to your heart as a most wholesome advice. His mere messenger did such deeds that our matrons, on hearing of them, were overtaken by premature labor. If you desire your welfare, then call your ministers and send him back his wife. As a frosty night comes upon a bed of lotuses, so has Sītā come for the ruin of our race. Hearken, my lord; unless you give up Sītā, neither Shambhu nor Brahmmā will be able to help you.

दोहा-dohā:

राम बान अहि गन सरिस निकर निसाचर भेक ।
rāma bāna ahi gana sarisa nikara nisācara bheka,
जब लगि ग्रसत न तब लगि जतनु करहु तजि टेक ॥ ३६ ॥
jaba lagi grasata na taba lagi jatanu karahu taji ṭeka. 36.

Trans:

Rāma's arrows are like serpents, and the demons host so many frogs; delay not, but do the best you can before they have snapped you up."

चौपाई-caupāī:

श्रवन सुनी सठ ता करि बानी । बिहसा जगत बिदित अभिमानी ॥
śravana sunī saṭha tā kari bānī, bihasā jagata bidita abhimānī.
सभय सुभाउ नारि कर साचा । मंगल महुँ भय मन अति काचा ॥
sabhaya subhāu nāri kara sācā, maṁgala mahuṁ bhaya mana ati kācā.
जौं आवइ मर्कट कटकाई । जिअहिं बिचारे निसिचर खाई ॥
jauṁ āvai markaṭa kaṭakāī, jiahiṁ bicāre nisicara khāī.
कंपहिं लोकप जाकीं त्रासा । तासु नारि सभीत बड़ि हासा ॥
kaṁpahiṁ lokapa jākīṁ trāsā, tāsu nāri sabhīta baṛi hāsā.
अस कहि बिहसि ताहि उर लाई । चलेउ सभाँ ममता अधिकाई ॥
asa kahi bihasi tāhi ura lāī, caleu sabhāṁ mamatā adhikāī.
मंदोदरी हृदयँ कर चिंता । भयउ कंत पर बिधि बिपरीता ॥
maṁdodarī hṛdayaṁ kara ciṁtā, bhayau kaṁta para bidhi biparītā.
बैठेउ सभाँ खबरि असि पाई । सिंधु पार सेना सब आई ॥
baiṭheu sabhāṁ khabari asi pāī, siṁdhu pāra senā saba āī.
बूझेसि सचिव उचित मत कहहू । ते सब हँसे मष्ट करि रहहू ॥
būjhesi saciva ucita mata kahahū, te saba haṁse maṣṭa kari rahahū.
जितेहु सुरासुर तब श्रम नाहीं । नर बानर केहि लेखे माहीं ॥
jitehu surāsura taba śrama nāhīṁ, nara bānara kehi lekhe māhīṁ.

Trans:

The monster heard her prayer and laughed aloud—his arrogance is well-known throughout the world. "A woman is naturally cast in a timorous mould, and even in prosperity will have a mind ill at ease. If the monkey army comes, the poor wretches will be eaten up by the demons. The very guardians of the spheres tremble in fear of me, so it is quite absurd for my wife to be so afraid." Saying so he laughed and embraced her; and then, full of inordinate conceit, proceeded to the council-chamber. But Mandodarī was troubled at heart, thinking, 'The heavens are against my lord.' While he was sitting in court, Rāvan received intelligence that the whole army had arrived and waited across the ocean. Then he enquired of his ministers,

"Tell me what you think is best to be done here." They all laughed and said, "Relax! You have conquered gods and demons without any trouble; of what account can men and monkeys be?"

दोहा-dohā:

सचिव बैद गुर तीनि जौं प्रिय बोलहिं भय आस ।
saciva baida gura tīni jauṁ priya bolahiṁ bhaya āsa,
राज धर्म तन तीनि कर होइ बेगिहीं नास ॥३७॥
rāja dharma tana tīni kara hoi begihīṁ nāsa. 37.

Trans:

When these three—a minister, physician, and spiritual adviser—use flattering words, either from fear or hope of reward, then know that dominion, religion, and health, all three, will be destroyed quickly.

चौपाई-caupāī:

सोइ रावन कहुँ बनी सहाई । अस्तुति करहिं सुनाइ सुनाई ॥
soi rāvana kahuṁ banī sahāī, astuti karahiṁ sunāi sunāī.
अवसर जानि बिभीषनु आवा । भ्राता चरन सीसु तेहिं नावा ॥
avasara jāni bibhīṣanu āvā, bhrātā carana sīsu tehiṁ nāvā.
पुनि सिरु नाइ बैठ निज आसन । बोला बचन पाइ अनुसासन ॥
puni siru nāi baiṭha nija āsana, bolā bacana pāi anusāsana.
जौ कृपाल पूँछिहु मोहि बाता । मति अनुरुप कहउँ हित ताता ॥
jau kṛpāla pūṁchihu mohi bātā, mati anurupa kahauṁ hita tātā.
जो आपन चाहै कल्याना । सुजसु सुमति सुभ गति सुख नाना ॥
jo āpana cāhai kalyānā, sujasu sumati subha gati sukha nānā.
सो परनारि लिलार गोसाईं । तजउ चउथि के चंद कि नाईं ॥
so paranāri lilāra gosāīṁ, tajau cauthi ke caṁda ki nāīṁ.
चौदह भुवन एक पति होई । भूतद्रोह तिष्टइ नहिं सोई ॥
caudaha bhuvana eka pati hoī, bhūtadroha tiṣṭai nahiṁ soī.
गुन सागर नागर नर जोऊ । अलप लोभ भल कहइ न कोऊ ॥
guna sāgara nāgara nara joū, alapa lobha bhala kahai na koū.

Trans:

This was all the help that Rāvan got; they did nothing but sound his praise. Perceiving his opportunity, Vibhīshan came and bowed his head at his brother's feet, then again bowing took his seat on his own throne and after obtaining permission spoke thus: "As you graciously ask of advice, I declare it, sire, to the best of my ability. If you desire your own welfare and glory, wisdom, a good fate after death, and every other happiness in life, then turn away from the face of another man's wife as from the moon on its fourth day. Though a man be the lord of the fourteen spheres, he cannot set himself to oppose the living force. However amiable and accomplished a person may be, no one will speak well of him if he shows even the slightest covetousness.

दोहा-dohā:

काम क्रोध मद लोभ सब नाथ नरक के पंथ ।
kāma krodha mada lobha saba nātha naraka ke paṁtha,
सब परिहरि रघुबीरहि भजहु भजहिं जेहि संत ॥३८॥
saba parihari raghubīrahi bhajahu bhajahiṁ jehi saṁta. 38.

Trans:

Lust, passion, vanity, and covetousness are all paths that lead to hell; abjure them and worship Raghubīr, whom all saints worship.

चौपाई-caupāī:

तात राम नहिं नर भूपाला । भुवनेस्वर कालहु कर काला ॥
tāta rāma nahiṁ nara bhūpālā, bhuvanesvara kālahu kara kālā.
ब्रह्म अनामय अज भगवंता । ब्यापक अजित अनादि अनंता ॥
brahma anāmaya aja bhagavaṁtā, byāpaka ajita anādi anaṁtā.
गो द्विज धेनु देव हितकारी । कृपा सिंधु मानुष तनुधारी ॥
go dvija dhenu deva hitakārī, kṛpā siṁdhu mānuṣa tanudhārī.
जन रंजन भंजन खल ब्राता । बेद धर्म रच्छक सुनु भ्राता ॥
jana raṁjana bhaṁjana khala brātā, beda dharma racchaka sunu bhrātā.
ताहि बयरु तजि नाइअ माथा । प्रनतारति भंजन रघुनाथा ॥
tāhi bayaru taji nāia māthā, pranatārati bhaṁjana raghunāthā.
देहु नाथ प्रभु कहुँ बैदेही । भजहु राम बिनु हेतु सनेही ॥
dehu nātha prabhu kahuṁ baidehī, bhajahu rāma binu hetu sanehī.
सरन गएँ प्रभु ताहु न त्यागा । बिस्व द्रोह कृत अघ जेहि लागा ॥
sarana gaeṁ prabhu tāhu na tyāgā, bisva droha kṛta agha jehi lāgā.
जासु नाम त्रय ताप नसावन । सोइ प्रभु प्रगट समुझु जियँ रावन ॥
jāsu nāma traya tāpa nasāvana, soi prabhu pragaṭa samujhu jiyaṁ rāvana.

Trans:

Shrī Rāma, O my brother, is no mortal king, but the sovereign of the universe, the Fate of Fate itself, the Supreme Spirit, the imperishable and uncreated God, the benefactor of cows and of Brahmins, of the earth and of the gods: who in his infinite mercy has assumed the form of human to rejoice his votaries and to break the ranks of the impious, the champion of the Veda and true religion, the savior of the immortals. Cease to fight against him and humbly bow your head. Raghunāth relieves the distress of every suppliant. O my lord, give him back Sītā and worship him with disinterested affection. The Lord has never abandoned anyone who has fled to him for protection, though he were guilty of having ruined the whole world. Know of a truth, Rāvan, that it is the Lord, he who has for his name 'the savior from every calamity,' who has now appeared among us as Rāma.

दोहा-dohā:

बार बार पद लागउँ बिनय करउँ दससीस ।
bāra bāra pada lāgauṁ binaya karauṁ dasasīsa,
परिहरि मान मोह मद भजहु कोसलाधीस ॥३९क ॥
parihari māna moha mada bhajahu kosalādhīsa. 39(ka).

मुनि पुलस्ति निज सिष्य सन कहि पठई यह बात ।
muni pulasti nija siṣya sana kahi paṭhaī yaha bāta,
तुरत सो मैं प्रभु सन कही पाइ सुअवसरु तात ॥३९ख ॥
turata so maiṁ prabhu sana kahī pāi suavasaru tāta. 39(kha).

Trans:

Again and again I lay my head at your feet and utter this my prayer: have done with pride, arrogance, and conceit and worship Rāma. These are the words which Saint Pulastya sent in a message to me, and I have at once taken this opportunity of conveying them to you, sir."

चौपाई-caupāī:

माल्यवंत अति सचिव सयाना । तासु बचन सुनि अति सुख माना ॥
mālyavaṁta ati saciva sayānā, tāsu bacana suni ati sukha mānā.
तात अनुज तव नीति बिभूषन । सो उर धरहु जो कहत बिभीषन ॥
tāta anuja tava nīti bibhūṣana, so ura dharahu jo kahata bibhīṣana.
रिपु उतकरष कहत सठ दोऊ । दूरि न करहु इहाँ हइ कोऊ ॥
ripu utakaraṣa kahata saṭha doū, dūri na karahu ihāṁ hai koū.
माल्यवंत गृह गयउ बहोरी । कहइ बिभीषनु पुनि कर जोरी ॥
mālyavaṁta gṛha gayau bahorī, kahai bibhīṣanu puni kara jorī.
सुमति कुमति सब कें उर रहहीं । नाथ पुरान निगम अस कहहीं ॥
sumati kumati saba keṁ ura rahahīṁ, nātha purāna nigama asa kahahīṁ.
जहाँ सुमति तहँ संपति नाना । जहाँ कुमति तहँ बिपति निदाना ॥
jahāṁ sumati tahaṁ saṁpati nānā, jahāṁ kumati tahaṁ bipati nidānā.
तव उर कुमति बसी बिपरीता । हित अनहित मानहु रिपु प्रीता ॥
tava ura kumati basī biparītā, hita anahita mānahu ripu prītā.

कालराति निसिचर कुल केरी । तेहि सीता पर प्रीति घनेरी ॥
kālarāti nisicara kula kerī, tehi sītā para prīti ghanerī.

Trans:

One of his wisest counselors, Malyavan, greatly rejoiced to hear this speech, "Take to heart, my son, this admirable counsel which your brother Vibhīshan gives." "These two villains magnify my enemy! Is there no one here who will rid me of them?" Malyavan thereupon returned home, but Vibhīshan with clasped hands spoke yet again, "In everyone's heart, my Lord, so the Vedas and Purānas declare, either wisdom or unwisdom finds a place. Where wisdom dwells, there dwells every kind of prosperity; and where rules unwisdom, there is complete destruction. In your heart malignant unwisdom has established herself; you take your friends for enemies and your enemies for friends; and thus are being so exceedingly enamored of Sītā—who is the very night of Death for our entire race.

दोहा-dohā:

तात चरन गहि मागउँ राखहु मोर दुलार ।
tāta carana gahi māgaum̐ rākhahu mora dulāra,
सीता देहु राम कहुँ अहित न होइ तुम्हार ॥४०॥
sītā dehu rāma kahum̐ ahita na hoi tumhāra. 40.

Trans:

My brother, I clasp your feet and implore you to lake my words in good spirit; by dint of your love for me, restore Sītā to Rāma; and it will be much to your welfare."

चौपाई-caupāī:

बुध पुरान श्रुति संमत बानी । कही बिभीषन नीति बखानी ॥
budha purāna śruti saṁmata bānī, kahī bibhīṣana nīti bakhānī.
सुनत दसानन उठा रिसाई । खल तोहि निकट मुत्यु अब आई ॥
sunata dasānana uṭhā risāī, khala tohi nikaṭa mutyu aba āī.
जिअसि सदा सठ मोर जिआवा । रिपु कर पच्छ मूढ़ तोहि भावा ॥
jiasi sadā saṭha mora jiāvā, ripu kara paccha mūṛha tohi bhāvā.
कहसि न खल अस को जग माहीं । भुज बल जाहि जिता मैं नाहीं ॥
kahasi na khala asa ko jaga māhīṁ, bhuja bala jāhi jitā maiṁ nāhīṁ.
मम पुर बसि तपसिन्ह पर प्रीती । सठ मिलु जाइ तिन्हहि कहु नीती ॥
mama pura basi tapasinha para prītī, saṭha milu jāi tinhahi kahu nītī.
अस कहि कीन्हेसि चरन प्रहारा । अनुज गहे पद बारहिं बारा ॥
asa kahi kīnhesi carana prahārā, anuja gahe pada bārahiṁ bārā.
उमा संत कइ इहइ बड़ाई । मंद करत जो करइ भलाई ॥
umā saṁta kai ihai baṛāī, maṁda karata jo karai bhalāī.
तुम्ह पितु सरिस भलेहिं मोहि मारा । रामु भजें हित नाथ तुम्हारा ॥
tumha pitu sarisa bhalehiṁ mohi mārā, rāmu bhajeṁ hita nātha tumhārā.
सचिव संग लै नभ पथ गयऊ । सबहि सुनाइ कहत अस भयऊ ॥
saciva saṁga lai nabha patha gayaū, sabahi sunāi kahata asa bhayaū.

Trans:

Though the words that Vibhīshan spoke were wise and prudent, and supported by the authority of the Vedas and Purānas, the Ten-headed rose in fury at hearing them: "Wretch, you are within an inch of your death. It is all owing to me, you rascal, that you have been able to live at all; and yet, fool as you are, you take the side of my enemy? Can you tell me, you wretch, of anyone in the entire world, whom I have not conquered by the might of my arms. You live in my capital, but are in love with those hermits? You had better go to them if you want to preach." Saying so he spurned him with a kick, but who still continued to clasp him by the feet. "You are as it were my father; kill me, if you think proper; but, O my lord, to worship Rāma alone would be best for you." This, is the virtue of the saints, Umā, that they return good for evil. Eventually taking his ministers with him, he went his way through the air, proclaiming aloud to all:

दोहा-dohā:

रामु सत्यसंकल्प प्रभु सभा कालबस तोरि ।
rāmu satyasaṁkalpa prabhu sabhā kālabasa tori,
मैं रघुबीर सरन अब जाउँ देहु जनि खोरि ॥४१॥
maiṁ raghubīra sarana aba jāum̐ dehu jani khori. 41.

Trans:

"Rāma is the very soul of truth; your courtiers, my lord, are overpowered by fate; I will now take refuge with Raghubīr; lay no blame to me."

चौपाई-caupāī:

अस कहि चला बिभीषनु जबहीं । आयूहीन भए सब तबहीं ॥
asa kahi calā bibhīṣanu jabahīṁ, āyūhīna bhae saba tabahīṁ.
साधु अवग्या तुरत भवानी । कर कल्यान अखिल कै हानी ॥
sādhu avagyā turata bhavānī, kara kalyāna akhila kai hānī.
रावन जबहिं बिभीषन त्यागा । भयउ बिभव बिनु तबहिं अभागा ॥
rāvana jabahiṁ bibhīṣana tyāgā, bhayau bibhava binu tabahiṁ abhāgā.
चलेउ हरषि रघुनायक पाहीं । करत मनोरथ बहु मन माहीं ॥
caleu haraṣi raghunāyaka pāhīṁ, karata manoratha bahu mana māhīṁ.
देखिहउँ जाइ चरन जलजाता । अरुन मृदुल सेवक सुखदाता ॥
dekhihaum̐ jāi carana jalajātā, aruna mṛdula sevaka sukhadātā.
जे पद परसि तरी रिषिनारी । दंडक कानन पावनकारी ॥
je pada parasi tarī riṣinārī, daṁḍaka kānana pāvanakārī.
जे पद जनकसुताँ उर लाए । कपट कुरंग संग धर धाए ॥
je pada janakasutām̐ ura lāe, kapaṭa kuraṁga saṁga dhara dhāe.
हर उर सर सरोज पद जेई । अहोभाग्य मैं देखिहउँ तेई ॥
hara ura sara saroja pada jeī, ahobhāgya maiṁ dekhihaum̐ teī.

Trans:

No sooner had Vibhīshan left with these words it was all over with everyone of them. Disrespect to a saint, O Bhawānī, brings speedy ruin to even the most prosperous. When Vibhīshan left Rāvan, all his glory and good fortune went with him. Meanwhile indulging in many expectations, Vibhīshan gladly proceeded to the Lord of the Raghus, "I am about to behold his lotus feet, so roseate, so soft, so beneficent to all who wait upon them; at whose touch the Rishī's wife was delivered from the curse and the Dandak forest was sanctified; feet that Sītā cherished in her bosom, even while they ran to seize the delusive deer; lotus feet in Shiva's lake-like heart; how blessed am I who am now about to see them!

दोहा-dohā:

जिन्ह पायन्ह के पादुकन्हि भरतु रहे मन लाइ ।
jinha pāyanha ke pādukanhi bharatu rahe mana lāi,
ते पद आजु बिलोकिहउँ इन्ह नयनन्हि अब जाइ ॥४२॥
te pada āju bilokihaum̐ inha nayananhi aba jāi. 42.

Trans:

With these very eyes shall I this day behold the feet, even whose wooden sandals Bharat keeps clasped to his heart."

चौपाई-caupāī:

एहि बिधि करत सप्रेम बिचारा । आयउ सपदि सिंधु एहिं पारा ॥
ehi bidhi karata saprema bicārā, āyau sapadi siṁdhu ehiṁ pārā.
कपिन्ह बिभीषनु आवत देखा । जाना कोउ रिपु दूत बिसेषा ॥
kapinha bibhīṣanu āvata dekhā, jānā kou ripu dūta biseṣā.
ताहि राखि कपीस पहिं आए । समाचार सब ताहि सुनाए ॥
tāhi rākhi kapīsa pahiṁ āe, samācāra saba tāhi sunāe.
कह सुग्रीव सुनहु रघुराई । आवा मिलन दसानन भाई ॥
kaha sugrīva sunahu raghurāī, āvā milana dasānana bhāī.
कह प्रभु सखा बूझिऐ काहा । कहइ कपीस सुनहु नरनाहा ॥
kaha prabhu sakhā būjhiai kāhā, kahai kapīsa sunahu naranāhā.

जानि न जाइ निसाचर माया । कामरूप केहि कारन आया ॥
jāni na jāi nisācara māyā, kāmarūpa kehi kārana āyā.
भेद हमार लेन सठ आवा । राखिअ बाँधि मोहि अस भावा ॥
bheda hamāra lena saṭha āvā, rākhia bāṁdhi mohi asa bhāvā.
सखा नीति तुम्ह नीकि बिचारी । मम पन सरनागत भयहारी ॥
sakhā nīti tumha nīki bicārī, mama pana saranāgata bhayahārī.
सुनि प्रभु बचन हरष हनुमाना । सरनागत बच्छल भगवाना ॥
suni prabhu bacana haraṣa hanumānā, saranāgata bacchala bhagavānā.

Trans:

With such loving fancies to occupy his mind, he quickly arrived on this side of the ocean. When the monkeys saw Vibhīshan coming, they took him to be some special envoy. So they stopped him and went to their chief and told him all the circumstances. Said Sugrīva, "Hearken Raghurāī: Rāvan's brother has come to see you." The Lord asked, "What do you advise, friend?" The monkey king rejoined, "Mark my words sire, the craft of these demons is past all telling. Why should he come thus of his own accord? The villain's object is to spy out our secrets. Me thinks we ought to keep him prisoner." "Friend, you have reasoned with much worldly wisdom; but I have a vow to befriend all suppliants." Hanumān was delighted to hear these words from the Lord, the God who shows compassion on all who flee to him.

दोहा-dohā:

सरनागत कहुँ जे तजहिं निज अनहित अनुमानि ।
saranāgata kahuṁ je tajahiṁ nija anahita anumāni,
ते नर पावँर पापमय तिन्हहि बिलोकत हानि ॥४३॥
te nara pāvaṁra pāpamaya tinhahi bilokata hāni. 43.

Trans:

"Those people who forsake a suppliant, apprehending evil from him are vile and sinful; even their sight is abominable.

चौपाई-caupāī:

कोटि बिप्र बध लागहिं जाहू । आएँ सरन तजउँ नहिं ताहू ॥
koṭi bipra badha lāgahiṁ jāhū, āeṁ sarana tajauṁ nahiṁ tāhū.
सनमुख होइ जीव मोहि जबहीं । जन्म कोटि अघ नासहिं तबहीं ॥
sanamukha hoi jīva mohi jabahīṁ, janma koṭi agha nāsahiṁ tabahīṁ.
पापवंत कर सहज सुभाऊ । भजनु मोर तेहि भाव न काऊ ॥
pāpavaṁta kara sahaja subhāū, bhajanu mora tehi bhāva na kāū.
जौं पै दुष्टहदय सोइ होई । मोरें सनमुख आव कि सोई ॥
jauṁ pai duṣṭahadaya soi hoī, moreṁ sanamukha āva ki soī.
निर्मल मन जन सो मोहि पावा । मोहि कपट छल छिद्र न भावा ॥
nirmala mana jana so mohi pāvā, mohi kapaṭa chala chidra na bhāvā.
भेद लेन पठवा दससीसा । तबहुँ न कछु भय हानि कपीसा ॥
bheda lena paṭhavā dasasīsā, tabahuṁ na kachu bhaya hāni kapīsā.
जग महुँ सखा निसाचर जेते । लछिमनु हनइ निमिष महुँ तेते ॥
jaga mahuṁ sakhā nisācara jete, lachimanu hanai nimiṣa mahuṁ tete.
जौं सभीत आवा सरनाई । रखिहउँ ताहि प्रान की नाई ॥
jauṁ sabhīta āvā saranāīṁ, rakhihauṁ tāhi prāna kī nāīṁ.

Trans:

I will not abandon even the murderer of myriads of Brahmins, if he seeks refuge in me. Directly any creature appears before me, I blot out the sins of all his past lives. No one who is essentially wicked can delight in my service. If he were really bad at heart, how could he come into my presence? Only a man of pure soul can find me; I take no pleasure in hypocrisy, deceit, and vice. Rāvan may have sent him to spy; but even so, O king, we need not fear any loss. All the demons that the whole world contains, my friend, Lakshman could rout in a single moment. If he has come out of fear, to seek clemency, I will protect him as I would my own life.

दोहा-dohā:

उभय भाँति तेहि आनहु हँसि कह कृपानिकेत ।
ubhaya bhāṁti tehi ānahu haṁsi kaha kṛpāniketa,
जय कृपाल कहि कपि चले अंगद हनू समेत ॥४४॥
jaya kṛpāla kahi kapi cale aṁgada hanū sameta. 44.

Trans:

In either case bring him here," thus spake the All-Merciful with a smile. "Glory to the Lord of mercy" cried the monkeys as they went, taking with them Hanumān and Angad.

चौपाई-caupāī:

सादर तेहि आगें करि बानर । चले जहाँ रघुपति करुनाकर ॥
sādara tehi āgeṁ kari bānara, cale jahāṁ raghupati karunākara.
दूरिहि ते देखे द्वौ भ्राता । नयनानंद दान के दाता ॥
dūrihi te dekhe dvau bhrātā, nayanānaṁda dāna ke dātā.
बहुरि राम छबिधाम बिलोकी । रहेउ ठटुकि एकटक पल रोकी ॥
bahuri rāma chabidhāma bilokī, raheu ṭhaṭuki ekaṭaka pala rokī.
भुज प्रलंब कंजारुन लोचन । स्यामल गात प्रनत भय मोचन ॥
bhuja pralaṁba kaṁjāruna locana, syāmala gāta pranata bhaya mocana.
सिंघ कंध आयत उर सोहा । आनन अमित मदन मन मोहा ॥
siṁgha kaṁdha āyata ura sohā, ānana amita madana mana mohā.
नयन नीर पुलकित अति गाता । मन धरि धीर कही मृदु बाता ॥
nayana nīra pulakita ati gātā, mana dhari dhīra kahī mṛdu bātā.
नाथ दसानन कर मैं भ्राता । निसिचर बंस जनम सुरत्राता ॥
nātha dasānana kara maiṁ bhrātā, nisicara baṁsa janama suratrātā.
सहज पापप्रिय तामस देहा । जथा उलूकहि तम पर नेहा ॥
sahaja pāpapriya tāmasa dehā, jathā ulūkahi tama para nehā.

Trans:

The monkeys respectfully escorted Vibhīshan into the presence of Rāma, the All-Merciful. He beheld from a distance the two brothers, the delight of all eyes, the givers of every blessing; then looking again upon Rāma's perfect beauty, he stood frozen still, with all his gaze intently fixed upon Him: the long arms, the lotus eyes, the dark-hued body of suppliant's friend, lion-like shoulders and magnificent broad chest and a beautiful charming face which would ravish the soul of Kāmdev himself. With streaming eyes and trembling limbs he at last made bold to speak in mild accents, "My Lord, I am Rāvan's brother. O Champion of heaven, I am born of demon race, with a savage temperament; and am as naturally prone to evil as an owl is partial to the dark night.

दोहा-dohā:

श्रवन सुजसु सुनि आयउँ प्रभु भंजन भव भीर ।
śravana sujasu suni āyauṁ prabhu bhaṁjana bhava bhīra,
त्राहि त्राहि आरति हरन सरन सुखद रघुबीर ॥४५॥
trāhi trāhi ārati harana sarana sukhada raghubīra. 45.

Trans:

I have heard with my ears of your glory and have come; O my Lord, save me, save me, save me—for you who are the deliverer from all of life's troubles, the remover of distress, the only true friend of every suppliant, O Raghubīr."

चौपाई-caupāī:

अस कहि करत दंडवत देखा । तुरत उठे प्रभु हरष बिसेषा ॥
asa kahi karata daṁḍavata dekhā, turata uṭhe prabhu haraṣa biseṣā.
दीन बचन सुनि प्रभु मन भावा । भुज बिसाल गहि हृदयँ लगावा ॥
dīna bacana suni prabhu mana bhāvā, bhuja bisāla gahi hṛdayaṁ lagāvā.
अनुज सहित मिलि ढिग बैठारी । बोले बचन भगत भयहारी ॥
anuja sahita mili ḍhiga baiṭhārī, bole bacana bhagata bhayahārī.

कहु लंकेस सहित परिवारा । कुसल कुठाहर बास तुम्हारा ॥
kahu laṁkesa sahita parivārā, kusala kuṭhāhara bāsa tumhārā.
खल मंडलीं बसहु दिनु राती । सखा धरम निबहइ केहि भाँती ॥
khala maṁḍalīṁ basahu dinu rātī, sakhā dharama nibahai kehi bhāṁtī.
मैं जानउँ तुम्हारि सब रीती । अति नय निपुन न भाव अनीती ॥
maiṁ jānauṁ tumhāri saba rītī, ati naya nipuna na bhāva anītī.
बरु भल बास नरक कर ताता । दुष्ट संग जनि देइ बिधाता ॥
baru bhala bāsa naraka kara tātā, duṣṭa saṁga jani dei bidhātā.
अब पद देखि कुसल रघुराया । जौं तुम्ह कीन्हि जानि जन दाया ॥
aba pada dekhi kusala raghurāyā, jauṁ tumha kīnhi jāni jana dāyā.

Trans:

So saying he prostrated himself, but at the sight the Lord arose in haste and with much delight—being pleased to hear his humble address—took him in his mighty arms and clasped him to his heart; and along with his brother seated him by his side, and to calm his votary's fears spake tenderly, "Tell me O prince of Lankā, is all well with you and your family? Your home is at an ill place. How, my friend, can you practice the duties of religion, when shrouded day and night by the wicked? I know all your circumstance, your proficiency in virtue, your aversion to evil. May providence keep us from evil people, 'twere better, my friend, to live in hell." "Now that I have seen your feet, O Rāma, it is all well with me—since you have recognized me as one of your worshippers and have shown mercy upon me.

दोहा-dohā:

तब लगि कुसल न जीव कहुँ सपनेहुँ मन बिश्राम ।
taba lagi kusala na jīva kahuṁ sapanehuṁ mana biśrāma,
जब लगि भजत न राम कहुँ सोक धाम तजि काम ॥४६॥
jaba lagi bhajata na rāma kahuṁ soka dhāma taji kāma. 46.

Trans:

No creature can be happy, or even dream of rest to his soul, till he worships Rāma after forswearing lust—that fountain of remorse.

चौपाई-caupāī:

तब लगि हृदयँ बसत खल नाना । लोभ मोह मच्छर मद माना ॥
taba lagi hṛdayaṁ basata khala nānā, lobha moha macchara mada mānā.
जब लगि उर न बसत रघुनाथा । धरें चाप सायक कटि भाथा ॥
jaba lagi ura na basata raghunāthā, dhareṁ cāpa sāyaka kaṭi bhāthā.
ममता तरुन तमी अँधिआरी । राग द्वेष उलूक सुखकारी ॥
mamatā taruna tamī aṁdhiārī, rāga dveṣa ulūka sukhakārī.
तब लगि बसति जीव मन माहीं । जब लगि प्रभु प्रताप रबि नाहीं ॥
taba lagi basati jīva mana māhīṁ, jaba lagi prabhu pratāpa rabi nāhīṁ.
अब मैं कुसल मिटे भय भारे । देखि राम पद कमल तुम्हारे ॥
aba maiṁ kusala miṭe bhaya bhāre, dekhi rāma pada kamala tumhāre.
तुम्ह कृपाल जा पर अनुकूला । ताहि न ब्याप त्रिबिध भव सूला ॥
tumha kṛpāla jā para anukūlā, tāhi na byāpa tribidha bhava sūlā.
मैं निसिचर अति अधम सुभाऊ । सुभ आचरनु कीन्ह नहिं काऊ ॥
maiṁ nisicara ati adhama subhāū, subha ācaranu kīnha nahiṁ kāū.
जासु रूप मुनि ध्यान न आवा । तेहिं प्रभु हरषि हृदयँ मोहि लावा ॥
jāsu rūpa muni dhyāna na āvā, tehiṁ prabhu haraṣi hṛdayaṁ mohi lāvā.

Trans:

So long as the heart is peopled by the villainous crew—avarice, sensuality, selfishness, arrogance, pride—there is no room there for Raghunāth, with his bow and arrows and quiver by the side. The intensely dark night of selfishness—so agreeable to the owl-like passions of love and hate—abides in the soul only until the rising of our sun-like Lord. Now I am well Lord, and all my fears are over—in that I have beheld your lotus holy feet. None of the threefold torments of life has any effect upon him, to whom you in your mercy show favor. I am a demon, utterly vile of nature, who has never observed any pious practices, and yet the Lord—whose vision even the saints scarce attain for all their profound meditations—has been pleased to take me to his heart.

दोहा-dohā:

अहोभाग्य मम अमित अति राम कृपा सुख पुंज ।
ahobhāgya mama amita ati rāma kṛpā sukha puṁja,
देखेउँ नयन बिरंचि सिव सेब्य जुगल पद कंज ॥४७॥
dekheuṁ nayana biraṁci siva sebya jugala pada kaṁja. 47.

Trans:

Surely I am blessed beyond measure, and your grace, O Rāma, is most beneficent—in that I behold with my eyes those lotus feet, which even Brahmmā and Shiva love to adore."

चौपाई-caupāī:

सुनहु सखा निज कहउँ सुभाऊ । जान भुसुंडि संभु गिरिजाऊ ॥
sunahu sakhā nija kahauṁ subhāū, jāna bhusuṁḍi saṁbhu girijāū.
जौं नर होइ चराचर द्रोही । आवे सभय सरन तकि मोही ॥
jauṁ nara hoi carācara drohī, āve sabhaya sarana taki mohī.
तजि मद मोह कपट छल नाना । करउँ सद्य तेहि साधु समाना ॥
taji mada moha kapaṭa chala nānā, karauṁ sadya tehi sādhu samānā.
जननी जनक बंधु सुत दारा । तनु धनु भवन सुहृद परिवारा ॥
jananī janaka baṁdhu suta dārā, tanu dhanu bhavana suhrada parivārā.
सब कै ममता ताग बटोरी । मम पद मनहि बाँध बरि डोरी ॥
saba kai mamatā tāga baṭorī, mama pada manahi bāṁdha bari ḍorī.
समदरसी इच्छा कछु नाहीं । हरष सोक भय नहिं मन माहीं ॥
samadarasī icchā kachu nāhīṁ, haraṣa soka bhaya nahiṁ mana māhīṁ.
अस सज्जन मम उर बस कैसें । लोभी हृदयँ बसइ धनु जैसें ॥
asa sajjana mama ura basa kaiseṁ, lobhī hṛdayaṁ basai dhanu jaiseṁ.
तुम्ह सारिखे संत प्रिय मोरें । धरउँ देह नहिं आन निहोरें ॥
tumha sārikhe saṁta priya moreṁ, dharauṁ deha nahiṁ āna nihoreṁ.

Trans:

"Hearken, friend; I will declare to you my nature, as known by Bhusumdi, Shambhu, Umā too. Even if a man who has been the curse of whole world, comes in fear and looks to me for protection, if he abjures all his pride and sensuality without guile or subterfuge, then I make him at once like one of the saints. The ties of affection that bind a man to his mother, father, brother, son, wife, body, wealth, house, friends and relations are like so many threads which that pious soul then gathers up and twists into a string wherewith he binds his soul to my feet. And then he looks upon all with the same eye and has no craving, and his mind becomes free from joy, fear, grief. A saint like such is as fixed in my soul as money in the heart of miser. The saintly, like you, are very dear to me, and it is only for their benefit that I become incarnate.

दोहा-dohā:

सगुन उपासक परहित निरत नीति दृढ़ नेम ।
saguna upāsaka parahita nirata nīti dṛṛha nema,
ते नर प्रान समान मम जिन्ह कें द्विज पद प्रेम ॥४८॥
te nara prāna samāna mama jinha keṁ dvija pada prema. 48.

Trans:

Virtuous and devoted believers, who are steadfast in uprightness, strict in pious observance, and who love and revere Brahmins, are the men whom I regard as my own soul.

चौपाई-caupāī:

सुनु लंकेस सकल गुन तोरें । तातें तुम्ह अतिसय प्रिय मोरें ॥
sunu laṁkesa sakala guna toreṁ, tāteṁ tumha atisaya priya moreṁ.
राम बचन सुनि बानर जूथा । सकल कहहिं जय कृपा बरूथा ॥
rāma bacana suni bānara jūthā, sakala kahahiṁ jaya kṛpā barūthā.

सुनत बिभीषनु प्रभु कै बानी । नहिं अघात श्रवनामृत जानी ॥
sunata bibhīṣanu prabhu kai bānī, nahiṁ aghāta śravanāmṛta jānī.
पद अंबुज गहि बारहिं बारा । हृदयँ समात न प्रेमु अपारा ॥
pada aṁbuja gahi bārahiṁ bārā, hṛdayam̐ samāta na premu apārā.
सुनहु देव सचराचर स्वामी । प्रनतपाल उर अंतरजामी ॥
sunahu deva sacarācara svāmī, pranatapāla ura aṁtarajāmī.
उर कछु प्रथम बासना रही । प्रभु पद प्रीति सरित सो बही ॥
ura kachu prathama bāsanā rahī, prabhu pada prīti sarita so bahī.
अब कृपाल निज भगति पावनी । देहु सदा सिव मन भावनी ॥
aba kṛpāla nija bhagati pāvanī, dehu sadā siva mana bhāvanī.
एवमस्तु कहि प्रभु रनधीरा । मागा तुरत सिंधु कर नीरा ॥
evamastu kahi prabhu ranadhīrā, māgā turata siṁdhu kara nīrā.
जदपि सखा तव इच्छा नाहीं । मोर दरसु अमोघ जग माहीं ॥
jadapi sakhā tava icchā nāhīṁ, mora darasu amogha jaga māhīṁ.
अस कहि राम तिलक तेहि सारा । सुमन बृष्टि नभ भई अपारा ॥
asa kahi rāma tilaka tehi sārā, sumana bṛṣṭi nabha bhaī apārā.

Trans:

Hearken, Prince of Lankā; all these good qualities are already yours, and you are therefore very dear to me." On hearing Rāma's speech, all the assembled monkeys exclaimed, "Glory, glory, to the all-merciful!" Vibhīshan, on hearing such ambrosial words, could not contain himself; and again and again he clasped Rāma's lotus feet, his heart bursting with boundless felicity. "Hearken my God, Lord of all creation, friend of the suppliant, reader of man's thoughts: Erst I had some desires in my heart, but now, in the presence of my Lord's feet, they are all washed away—like a river in flood. Now in your infinite mercy please grant me such pure faith as that which ever gladdens Shiva's heart." "So be it," ordained the Lord; and the Valiant-Lord then asked for some sea-water be brought. "Even though you have no craving my friend, but the sight of me nevertheless brings reward all its own, as known throughout the world." So saying Rāma marked his forehead with the *Tilak*, the sacred mark of sovereignty, and a shower of flowers rained from the sky.

दोहा-dohā:

रावन क्रोध अनल निज स्वास समीर प्रचंड ।
rāvana krodha anala nija svāsa samīra pracaṁḍa,
जरत बिभीषनु राखेउ दीन्हेउ राजु अखंड ॥४९क॥
jarata bibhīṣanu rākheu dīnheu rāju akhaṁḍa. 49(ka).

जो संपति सिव रावनहि दीन्हि दिएँ दस माथ ।
jo saṁpati siva rāvanahi dīnhi diem̐ dasa mātha,
सोइ संपदा बिभीषनहि सकुचि दीन्ह रघुनाथ ॥४९ख॥
soi saṁpadā bibhīṣanahi sakuci dīnha raghunātha. 49(kha).

Trans:

Thus did Raghunāth protect the humble Vibhīshan from Rāvan's fiery wrath, fanned by the strong blast of his own breath, and gave him secure dominion and all the good fortune which Shiva had formerly bestowed upon the ten-headed Rāvan.

चौपाई-caupāī:

अस प्रभु छाड़ि भजहिं जे आना । ते नर पसु बिनु पूँछ बिषाना ॥
asa prabhu chāṛi bhajahiṁ je ānā, te nara pasu binu pūm̐cha biṣānā.
निज जन जानि ताहि अपनावा । प्रभु सुभाव कपि कुल मन भावा ॥
nija jana jāni tāhi apanāvā, prabhu subhāva kapi kula mana bhāvā.
पुनि सर्बग्य सर्ब उर बासी । सर्बरूप सब रहित उदासी ॥
puni sarbagya sarba ura bāsī, sarbarūpa saba rahita udāsī.
बोले बचन नीति प्रतिपालक । कारन मनुज दनुज कुल घालक ॥
bole bacana nīti pratipālaka, kārana manuja danuja kula ghālaka.
सुनु कपीस लंकापति बीरा । केहि बिधि तरिअ जलधि गंभीरा ॥
sunu kapīsa laṁkāpati bīrā, kehi bidhi taria jaladhi gaṁbhīrā.
संकुल मकर उरग झष जाती । अति अगाध दुस्तर सब भाँती ॥
saṁkula makara uraga jhaṣa jātī, ati agādha dustara saba bhām̐tī.
कह लंकेस सुनहु रघुनायक । कोटि सिंधु सोषक तव सायक ॥
kaha laṁkesa sunahu raghunāyaka, koṭi siṁdhu soṣaka tava sāyaka.
जद्यपि तदपि नीति असि गाई । बिनय करिअ सागर सन जाई ॥
jadyapi tadapi nīti asi gāī, binaya karia sāgara sana jāī.

Trans:

Men, who forsake such a Lord to worship any other, are mere beasts without tails and horns. Recognising Vibhīshan as his own, the Lord accepted him in his service; and the monkeys were all charmed with the Lord's amiability. Then the All-wise—who dwells in the hearts of all, assuming any form at will, though himself formless and passionless, the champion of religion, the friend of men, and the destroyer of all demons—spoke these words observing the rules of decorum, "Listen, lord of monkeys, and O valiant king of Lankā: how are we to cross this deep ocean, full of alligators, serpents and different kinds of sea-monsters, of fathomless profundity and seemingly impassable?" Vibhīshan replied, "Hearken Raghunāyak; your arrows could burn up a thousand seas, but still it would be better policy to go and make petition to the god of ocean.

दोहा-dohā:

प्रभु तुम्हार कुलगुर जलधि कहिहि उपाय बिचारि ।
prabhu tumhāra kulagura jaladhi kahihi upāya bicāri,
बिनु प्रयास सागर तरिहि सकल भालु कपि धारि ॥५०॥
binu prayāsa sāgara tarihi sakala bhālu kapi dhāri. 50.

Trans:

The deity presiding over the ocean is an ancestor of yours, my Lord, and can suggest of some means by which the host of bears and monkeys may cross the deeps without any trouble."

चौपाई-caupāī:

सखा कही तुम्ह नीकि उपाई । करिअ दैव जौं होइ सहाई ॥
sakhā kahī tumha nīki upāī, karia daiva jauṁ hoi sahāī.
मंत्र न यह लछिमन मन भावा । राम बचन सुनि अति दुख पावा ॥
maṁtra na yaha lachimana mana bhāvā, rāma bacana suni ati dukha pāvā.
नाथ दैव कर कवन भरोसा । सोषिअ सिंधु करिअ मन रोसा ॥
nātha daiva kara kavana bharosā, soṣia siṁdhu karia mana rosā.
कादर मन कहुँ एक अधारा । दैव दैव आलसी पुकारा ॥
kādara mana kahum̐ eka adhārā, daiva daiva ālasī pukārā.
सुनत बिहसि बोले रघुबीरा । ऐसेहिं करब धरहु मन धीरा ॥
sunata bihasi bole raghubīrā, aisehiṁ karaba dharahu mana dhīrā.
अस कहि प्रभु अनुजहि समुझाई । सिंधु समीप गए रघुराई ॥
asa kahi prabhu anujahi samujhāī, siṁdhu samīpa gae raghurāī.
प्रथम प्रनाम कीन्ह सिरु नाई । बैठे पुनि तट दर्भ डसाई ॥
prathama pranāma kīnha siru nāī, baiṭhe puni taṭa darbha ḍasāī.
जबहिं बिभीषन प्रभु पहिं आए । पाछें रावन दूत पठाए ॥
jabahiṁ bibhīṣana prabhu pahiṁ āe, pācheṁ rāvana dūta paṭhāe.

Trans:

"Friend, you have made a good suggestion; let's try that and see how providence is of help." This advice did not please Lakshman; he was much pained at Rāma's words. "Give vent to your indignation and dry up the ocean at once. Why trust on fate, my Lord? That is the resort of the timorous and sluggards—to be always crying out for luck." Raghubīr smiled to hear that and said, "Yes we shall do that, but pray be at ease for now." Saying so he went to the sea-shore and there placing Kush grass took his seat. Now after Vibhīshan left to join Rāma, Rāvan sent some spies behind.

दोहा-dohā:

सकल चरित तिन्ह देखे धरें कपट कपि देह ।
sakala carita tinha dekhe dhareṁ kapaṭa kapi deha,
प्रभु गुन हृदयँ सराहहिं सरनागत पर नेह ॥५१॥
prabhu guna hṛdayam̐ sarāhahiṁ saranāgata para neha. 51.

Trans:

They disguised themselves as monkeys and saw all that was going on; and they couldn't help but gain profound admiration for the Lord's generosity and his tenderness to suppliants.

चौपाई-caupāī:

प्रगट बखानहिं राम सुभाऊ । अति सप्रेम गा बिसरि दुराऊ ॥
pragaṭa bakhānahiṁ rāma subhāū, ati saprema gā bisari durāū.
रिपु के दूत कपिन्ह तब जाने । सकल बाँधि कपीस पहिं आने ॥
ripu ke dūta kapinha taba jāne, sakala bām̐dhi kapīsa pahiṁ āne.
कह सुग्रीव सुनहु सब बानर । अंग भंग करि पठवहु निसिचर ॥
kaha sugrīva sunahu saba bānara, aṁga bhaṁga kari paṭhavahu nisicara.
सुनि सुग्रीव बचन कपि धाए । बाँधि कटक चहु पास फिराए ॥
suni sugrīva bacana kapi dhāe, bām̐dhi kaṭaka cahu pāsa phirāe.
बहु प्रकार मारन कपि लागे । दीन पुकारत तदपि न त्यागे ॥
bahu prakāra mārana kapi lāge, dīna pukārata tadapi na tyāge.
जो हमार हर नासा काना । तेहि कोसलाधीस कै आना ॥
jo hamāra hara nāsā kānā, tehi kosalādhīsa kai ānā.
सुनि लछिमन सब निकट बोलाए । दया लागि हँसि तुरत छोड़ाए ॥
suni lachimana saba nikaṭa bolāe, dayā lāgi ham̐si turata choṛāe.
रावन कर दीजहु यह पाती । लछिमन बचन बाचु कुलघाती ॥
rāvana kara dījahu yaha pātī, lachimana bacana bācu kulaghātī.

Trans:

And in the intensity of their devotion, they forgot their disguise and loudly extolled the Lord's magnanimity. When the monkeys perceived them to be spies from the enemy, they seized them and took them to their chief. Said Sugrīva, "Hearken monkeys: just mutilate these demons and let them go." On receiving his command, the monkeys ran and paraded them in bonds all through the camp, ill-treating them in every possible way and refusing to let them go for all their prayers for mercy, until they cried, "We adjure you in the name of Rāma, please do not rob us of our ears and nose." When Lakshman heard the commotion he called them all to him, and, being moved with compassion, smiled and had them at once set free, "Now give this missive into Rāvan's hands and say 'Read, destroyer of your race, to what Lakshman has to say.'

दोहा-dohā:

कहेहु मुखागर मूढ़ सन मम संदेसु उदार ।
kahehu mukhāgara mūṛha sana mama saṁdesu udāra,
सीता देइ मिलेहु न त आवा कालु तुम्हार ॥५२॥
sītā dei milehu na ta āvā kālu tumhāra. 52.

Trans:

Further, tell the fool by word of mouth my emphatic command—'Surrender Sītā and submit yourself, or it will be your very death.'"

चौपाई-caupāī:

तुरत नाइ लछिमन पद माथा । चले दूत बरनत गुन गाथा ॥
turata nāi lachimana pada māthā, cale dūta baranata guna gāthā.
कहत राम जसु लंकाँ आए । रावन चरन सीस तिन्ह नाए ॥
kahata rāma jasu laṁkām̐ āe, rāvana carana sīsa tinha nāe.
बिहसि दसानन पूँछी बाता । कहसि न सुक आपनि कुसलाता ॥
bihasi dasānana pūm̐chī bātā, kahasi na suka āpani kusalātā.
पुनि कहु खबरि बिभीषन केरी । जाहि मृत्यु आई अति नेरी ॥
puni kahu khabari bibhīṣana kerī, jāhi mṛtyu āī ati nerī.
करत राज लंका सठ त्यागी । होइहि जव कर कीट अभागी ॥
karata rāja laṁkā saṭha tyāgī, hoihi java kara kīṭa abhāgī.
पुनि कहु भालु कीस कटकाई । कठिन काल प्रेरित चलि आई ॥
puni kahu bhālu kīsa kaṭakāī, kaṭhina kāla prerita cali āī.
जिन्ह के जीवन कर रखवारा । भयउ मृदुल चित सिंधु बिचारा ॥
jinha ke jīvana kara rakhavārā, bhayau mṛdula cita siṁdhu bicārā.
कहु तपसिन्ह कै बात बहोरी । जिन्ह के हृदयँ त्रास अति मोरी ॥
kahu tapasinha kai bāta bahorī, jinha ke hṛdayam̐ trāsa ati morī.

Trans:

The spies bowed their head at Lakshman's feet and left at once, praising his generosity. Still repeating Rāma's praises, they arrived at Lankā and prostrated themselves before Rāvan. The Ten-headed with a smile asked them the news, "Tell me O Suka of your own welfare, and then let me hear about Vibhīshan, to whom death has drawn very nigh. The fool left Lankā where he was a ruling; but now the wretched weevil must be crushed along with the wheat. Next, tell me what forces these bears and monkeys muster, who have come here by command of their evil destiny; although the softhearted poor old sea, protects their lives for now. Tell me finally about those hermits whose souls I bet trembles in fear of me.

दोहा-dohā:

की भइ भेंट कि फिरि गए श्रवन सुजसु सुनि मोर ।
kī bhai bheṁṭa ki phiri gae śravana sujasu suni mora,
कहसि न रिपु दल तेज बल बहुत चकित चित तोर ॥५३॥
kahasi na ripu dala teja bala bahuta cakita cita tora. 53.

Trans:

Did they meet you as suppliants, or did they take to flight on hearing report of my great renown? Will you tell me nothing about the enemy's might and magnificence? Your wits seem utterly dazed."

चौपाई-caupāī:

नाथ कृपा करि पूँछेहु जैसें । मानहु कहा क्रोध तजि तैसें ॥
nātha kṛpā kari pūm̐chehu jaiseṁ, mānahu kahā krodha taji taiseṁ.
मिला जाइ जब अनुज तुम्हारा । जातहिं राम तिलक तेहि सारा ॥
milā jāi jaba anuja tumhārā, jātahiṁ rāma tilaka tehi sārā.
रावन दूत हमहि सुनि काना । कपिन्ह बाँधि दीन्हे दुख नाना ॥
rāvana dūta hamahi suni kānā, kapinha bām̐dhi dīnhe dukha nānā.
श्रवन नासिका काटैं लागे । राम सपथ दीन्हें हम त्यागे ॥
śravana nāsikā kāṭaiṁ lāge, rāma sapatha dīnheṁ hama tyāge.
पूँछिहु नाथ राम कटकाई । बदन कोटि सत बरनि न जाई ॥
pūm̐chihu nātha rāma kaṭakāī, badana koṭi sata barani na jāī.
नाना बरन भालु कपि धारी । बिकटानन बिसाल भयकारी ॥
nānā barana bhālu kapi dhārī, bikaṭānana bisāla bhayakārī.
जेहिं पुर दहेउ हतेउ सुत तोरा । सकल कपिन्ह महँ तेहि बलु थोरा ॥
jehiṁ pura daheu hateu suta torā, sakala kapinha maham̐ tehi balu thorā.
अमित नाम भट कठिन कराला । अमित नाग बल बिपुल बिसाला ॥
amita nāma bhaṭa kaṭhina karālā, amita nāga bala bipula bisālā.

Trans:

"O your grace, my lord, be not wrath but accept a frank reply to your blunt question. Soon as your brother joined him Rāma bestowed upon him the mark of sovereignty. The monkeys, who had heard that we were your spies, put us in bonds and abused us shamefully. They were about to cut off our ears and nose, but when we invoked the name of Rāma they let us go. You ask, my lord, of Rāma's army; a myriad tongues would fail to tell of it: such a host of bears and monkeys of diverse hue and gruesome visage, huge and terrible—the one who set fire to the city and slew your son is the very weakest of them all. There are champions with innumerable names, fierce and unyielding monsters of vast bulk, with the strength of unnumbered elephants.

दोहा-dohā:

द्विबिद मयंद नील नल अंगद गद बिकटासि ।
dvibida mayaṁda nīla nala aṁgada gada bikaṭāsi,
दधिमुख केहरि निसठ सठ जामवंत बलरासि ॥५४॥
dadhimukha kehari nisaṭha saṭha jāmavaṁta balarāsi. 54.

Trans:

Dwivid and Mayand, Nīl and Nala, Angad and Gada of the mighty sword, Dadhi-mukh and Kehari, the malignant Nisatha and the powerful Jāmvant.

चौपाई-caupāī:

ए कपि सब सुग्रीव समाना । इन्ह सम कोटिन्ह गनइ को नाना ॥
e kapi saba sugrīva samānā, inha sama koṭinha ganai ko nānā.
राम कृपाँ अतुलित बल तिन्हहीं । तृन समान त्रैलोकहि गनहीं ॥
rāma kṛpāṁ atulita bala tinhahīṁ, tṛna samāna trailokahi ganahīṁ.
अस मैं सुना श्रवन दसकंधर । पदुम अठारह जूथप बंदर ॥
asa maiṁ sunā śravana dasakaṁdhara, paduma aṭhāraha jūthapa baṁdara.
नाथ कटक महँ सो कपि नाहीं । जो न तुम्हहि जीतै रन माहीं ॥
nātha kaṭaka mahaṁ so kapi nāhīṁ, jo na tumhahi jītai rana māhīṁ.
परम क्रोध मीजहिं सब हाथा । आयसु पै न देहिं रघुनाथा ॥
parama krodha mījahiṁ saba hāthā, āyasu pai na dehiṁ raghunāthā.
सोषहिं सिंधु सहित झष ब्याला । पूरहिं न त भरि कुधर बिसाला ॥
soṣahiṁ siṁdhu sahita jhaṣa byālā, pūrahiṁ na ta bhari kudhara bisālā.
मर्दि गर्द मिलवहिं दससीसा । ऐसेइ बचन कहहिं सब कीसा ॥
mardi garda milavahiṁ dasasīsā, aisei bacana kahahiṁ saba kīsā.
गर्जहिं तर्जहिं सहज असंका । मानहुँ ग्रसन चहत हहिं लंका ॥
garjahiṁ tarjahiṁ sahaja asaṁkā, mānahuṁ grasana cahata hahiṁ laṁkā.

Trans:

Each of these monkeys is equal to Sugrīva in strength; and who could count all the myriads like them? By Rāma's favor their strength is unbounded; they reckon the three spheres of creation as of no more account than a blade of grass. I have heard said, O Rāvan, that the monkey chiefs number eighteen thousand billions; and in the whole of the army, my lord, there is not a single monkey who could not conquer you in battle. They are all wringing their hands in excess of passion: "Why does not Rāma give us an order; and we shall swallow up the ocean with all its fish and serpents; if not then fill it up with piles of trees and mighty mountains; and then we will crush Rāvan and lay him low in the dust."—This is the belligerent language which the monkeys bellow. Utterly void of fear, they shout and leap about as if they would make Lankā a mere mouthful.

दोहा-dohā:

सहज सूर कपि भालु सब पुनि सिर पर प्रभु राम ।
sahaja sūra kapi bhālu saba puni sira para prabhu rāma,
रावन काल कोटि कहुँ जीति सकहिं संग्राम ॥५५॥
rāvana kāla koṭi kahuṁ jīti sakahiṁ saṁgrāma. 55.

Trans:

All the bears and monkeys are born warriors; and moreover, they have Lord Rāma's favor upon their head. O Rāvan, they could conquer in battle even Death himself a myriad times over.

चौपाई-caupāī:

राम तेज बल बुधि बिपुलाई । सेष सहस सत सकहिं न गाई ॥
rāma teja bala budhi bipulāī, seṣa sahasa sata sakahiṁ na gāī.
सक सर एक सोषि सत सागर । तव भ्रातहि पूँछेउ नय नागर ॥
saka sara eka soṣi sata sāgara, tava bhrātahi pūṁcheu naya nāgara.
तासु बचन सुनि सागर पाहीं । मागत पंथ कृपा मन माहीं ॥
tāsu bacana suni sāgara pāhīṁ, māgata paṁtha kṛpā mana māhīṁ.
सुनत बचन बिहसा दससीसा । जौं असि मति सहाय कृत कीसा ॥
sunata bacana bihasā dasasīsā, jauṁ asi mati sahāya kṛta kīsā.
सहज भीरु कर बचन दृढ़ाई । सागर सन ठानी मचलाई ॥
sahaja bhīru kara bacana dṛṛhāī, sāgara sana ṭhānī macalāī.
मूढ़ मृषा का करसि बड़ाई । रिपु बल बुद्धि थाह मैं पाई ॥
mūṛha mṛṣā kā karasi baṛāī, ripu bala buddhi thāha maiṁ pāī.
सचिव सभीत बिभीषन जाकें । बिजय बिभूति कहाँ जग ताकें ॥
saciva sabhīta bibhīṣana jākeṁ, bijaya bibhūti kahāṁ jaga tākeṁ.
सुनि खल बचन दूत रिस बाढ़ी । समय बिचारि पत्रिका काढ़ी ॥
suni khala bacana dūta risa bāṛhī, samaya bicāri patrikā kāṛhī.
रामानुज दीन्ही यह पाती । नाथ बचाइ जुड़ावहु छाती ॥
rāmānuja dīnhī yaha pātī, nātha bacāi juṛāvahu chātī.
बिहसि बाम कर लीन्ही रावन । सचिव बोलि सठ लाग बचावन ॥
bihasi bāma kara līnhī rāvana, saciva boli saṭha lāga bacāvana.

Trans:

A hundred thousand Sheshnāgs would fail to declare all of Rāma's glory, power, wisdom. With a single shaft he could burn up a hundred seas, yet so prudent is he that he took advice of your brother and, on hearing his advice, went to the sea and humbly asks the favor of passage." On hearing that, the Ten-headed roared with laughter, "Truly he shows as much sense as when he took the monkeys for his allies. He has put faith in the words of my brother, who is a born coward; and like a child now begs the ocean of something he will never get. Fool, you have been extolling a mere impostor. I have sounded the depth of my enemy's strength and skill. Where in the world could anyone achieve glory of triumph, who has such a cowardly counselor as Vibhīshan." The envoy waxed wrath at the wretch's speech, and thought it a good time to produce the letter. "Rāma's brother gave us this missive; have it read, my lord, and much good may it do you." Rāvan laughed and took it with his left hand and the wretch then asked his minister to read that out aloud.

दोहा-dohā:

बातन्ह मनहि रिझाइ सठ जनि घालसि कुल खीस ।
bātanha manahi rijhāi saṭha jani ghālasi kula khīsa,
राम बिरोध न उबरसि सरन बिष्नु अज ईस ॥५६क॥
rāma birodha na ubarasi sarana biṣnu aja īsa. 56(ka).
की तजि मान अनुज इव प्रभु पद पंकज भृंग ।
kī taji māna anuja iva prabhu pada paṁkaja bhṛṁga,
होहि कि राम सरानल खल कुल सहित पतंग ॥५६ख॥
hohi ki rāma sarānala khala kula sahita pataṁga. 56(kha).

Trans:

And it read: "Fool, stop living merely on words, and be not the one who destroyed his entire race; opposed to Rāma, you cannot escape from death, even though Vishnu, Brahmmā, and Shiva be your protectors. Abandon pride and, like your younger brother, flee like a bee to the lotus feet of the Lord; or like a moth you will be consumed in all your wickedness, you and your entire clan—in the fiery flames of Rāma's shafts."

चौपाई-caupāī:

सुनत सभय मन मुख मुसुकाई । कहत दसानन सबहि सुनाई ॥
sunata sabhaya mana mukha musukāī, kahata dasānana sabahi sunāī.
भूमि परा कर गहत अकासा । लघु तापस कर बाग बिलासा ॥
bhūmi parā kara gahata akāsā, laghu tāpasa kara bāga bilāsā.
कह सुक नाथ सत्य सब बानी । समुझहु छाड़ि प्रकृति अभिमानी ॥
kaha suka nātha satya saba bānī, samujhahu chāṛi prakṛti abhimānī.
सुनहु बचन मम परिहरि क्रोधा । नाथ राम सन तजहु बिरोधा ॥
sunahu bacana mama parihari krodhā, nātha rāma sana tajahu birodhā.

अति कोमल रघुबीर सुभाऊ । जद्यपि अखिल लोक कर राऊ ॥
ati komala raghubīra subhāū, jadyapi akhila loka kara rāū.
मिलत कृपा तुम्ह पर प्रभु करिही । उर अपराध न एकउ धरिही ॥
milata kṛpā tumha para prabhu karihī, ura aparādha na ekau dharihī.
जनकसुता रघुनाथहि दीजे । एतना कहा मोर प्रभु कीजे ॥
janakasutā raghunāthahi dīje, etanā kahā mora prabhu kīje.
जब तेहिं कहा देन बैदेही । चरन प्रहार कीन्ह सठ तेही ॥
jaba tehiṁ kahā dena baidehī, carana prahāra kīnha saṭha tehī.
नाइ चरन सिरु चला सो तहाँ । कृपासिंधु रघुनायक जहाँ ॥
nāi carana siru calā so tahām̐, kṛpāsiṁdhu raghunāyaka jahām̐.
करि प्रनामु निज कथा सुनाई । राम कृपाँ आपनि गति पाई ॥
kari pranāmu nija kathā sunāī, rāma kṛpām̐ āpani gati pāī.
रिषि अगस्ति कीं साप भवानी । राछस भयउ रहा मुनि ग्यानी ॥
riṣi agasti kīṁ sāpa bhavānī, rāchasa bhayau rahā muni gyānī.
बंदि राम पद बारहिं बारा । मुनि निज आश्रम कहुँ पगु धारा ॥
baṁdi rāma pada bārahiṁ bārā, muni nija āśrama kahum̐ pagu dhārā.

Trans:

The ten-headed, as he listened, was terror-stricken at heart; but then outwardly smiled and spoke aloud for all to hearken: "The young hermit's grand eloquence is like attempt of a man lying on the ground to clutch the vaults of heaven with his hands." Then said Suka, "My lord, take every word of this missive to be true; be wise and abandon your innate arrogance. Cease from wrath and hearken to our advice: make an end, sire, of your feud with Rāma. Raghubīr is exceedingly mild in disposition—even though he is the sovereign of all worlds. The Lord will be gracious to you directly as you approach him, and he will not remember even one of your offences. Restore to him Janak's daughter; this, sire, is all we ask of you; please do so." When he spoke to him of giving up Sītā, the wretch kicked him with his foot; but he bowed his head to the ground before him and then went to join the All-merciful Rāma; and after due obeisance told him all that had happened. By Rāma's grace, he recovered his original state—for it was by the Rishī Agastya's curse, O Bhawānī, that he had become a demon, although still retaining the disposition of a saint. Now, once more in the form of a saint, after again and again prostrating himself at Rāma's feet, he went his way to his own hermitage.

दोहा-dohā:

बिनय न मानत जलधि जड़ गए तीनि दिन बीति ।
binaya na mānata jaladhi jaṛa gae tīni dina bīti,
बोले राम सकोप तब भय बिनु होइ न प्रीति ॥५७॥
bole rāma sakopa taba bhaya binu hoi na prīti. 57.

Trans:

Meanwhile, the immovable ocean made no answer to prayer, though three days went past. Then spoke Rāma in fury, "Love, without some awe and dread as the backdrop, is futile."

चौपाई-caupāī:

लछिमन बान सरासन आनू । सोषौं बारिधि बिसिख कृसानू ॥
lachimana bāna sarāsana ānū, soṣauṁ bāridhi bisikha kṛsānū.
सठ सन बिनय कुटिल सन प्रीती । सहज कृपन सन सुंदर नीती ॥
saṭha sana binaya kuṭila sana prītī, sahaja kṛpana sana suṁdara nītī.
ममता रत सन ग्यान कहानी । अति लोभी सन बिरति बखानी ॥
mamatā rata sana gyāna kahānī, ati lobhī sana birati bakhānī.
क्रोधिहि सम कामिहि हरि कथा । ऊसर बीज बएँ फल जथा ॥
krodhihi sama kāmihi hari kathā, ūsara bīja baem̐ phala jathā.
अस कहि रघुपति चाप चढ़ावा । यह मत लछिमन के मन भावा ॥
asa kahi raghupati cāpa caṛhāvā, yaha mata lachimana ke mana bhāvā.
संघानेउ प्रभु बिसिख कराला । उठी उदधि उर अंतर ज्वाला ॥
saṁghāneu prabhu bisikha karālā, uṭhī udadhi ura aṁtara jvālā.
मकर उरग झष गन अकुलाने । जरत जंतु जलनिधि जब जाने ॥
makara uraga jhaṣa gana akulāne, jarata jaṁtu jalanidhi jaba jāne.
कनक थार भरि मनि गन नाना । बिप्र रूप आयउ तजि माना ॥
kanaka thāra bhari mani gana nānā, bipra rūpa āyau taji mānā.

Trans:

"Lakshman, bring my bow and arrow, and with a fiery dart I will dry up the deeps. To use entreaties upon a churl, to lavish affection on a rogue, to deal liberally with a born miser, to discourse on divine wisdom to a man full of worldliness, to speak of detachment from world to a covetous, to teach mind-control to one quick-tempered, and to tell of Harī to someone libidinous—is all the same as sowing seeds in sand in harvest's hope." Saying so Rāma strung his bow, an act which pleased Lakshman mightily. When the Lord fitted the terrible arrow to his bow a burning pain ensued in the bosom of ocean; the crocodiles, serpents, and fish were all sore distressed. When ocean perceived that the creatures were burning, he filled a golden dish with many kinds of jewels and humbly presented himself taking the form of a Brahmin.

दोहा-dohā:

काटेहिं पइ कदरी फरइ कोटि जतन कोउ सींच ।
kāṭehiṁ pai kadarī pharai koṭi jatana kou sīṁca,
बिनय न मान खगेस सुनु डाटेहिं पइ नव नीच ॥५८॥
binaya na māna khagesa sunu ḍāṭehiṁ pai nava nīca. 58.

Trans:

Though you may take infinite trouble in watering it, a plantain will not bear fruit, until hewed; similarly, mark me, O Garud, a mean upstart, heeds neither prayers nor compliments, but requires reprimanding.

चौपाई-caupāī:

सभय सिंधु गहि पद प्रभु केरे । छमहु नाथ सब अवगुन मेरे ॥
sabhaya siṁdhu gahi pada prabhu kere, chamahu nātha saba avaguna mere.
गगन समीर अनल जल धरनी । इन्ह कइ नाथ सहज जड़ करनी ॥
gagana samīra anala jala dharanī, inha kai nātha sahaja jaṛa karanī.
तव प्रेरित मायाँ उपजाए । सृष्टि हेतु सब ग्रंथनि गाए ॥
tava prerita māyām̐ upajāe, sṛṣṭi hetu saba graṁthani gāe.
प्रभु आयसु जेहि कहँ जस अहई । सो तेहि भाँति रहें सुख लहई ॥
prabhu āyasu jehi kaham̐ jasa ahaī, so tehi bhām̐ti raheṁ sukha lahaī.
प्रभु भल कीन्ह मोहि सिख दीन्ही । मरजादा पुनि तुम्हरी कीन्ही ॥
prabhu bhala kīnha mohi sikha dīnhī, marajādā puni tumharī kīnhī.
ढोल गवाँर सूद्र पसु नारी । सकल ताड़ना के अधिकारी ॥
ḍhola gavām̐ra sūdra pasu nārī, sakala tāṛanā ke adhikārī.
प्रभु प्रताप मैं जाब सुखाई । उतरिहि कटकु न मोरि बड़ाई ॥
prabhu pratāpa maiṁ jāba sukhāī, utarihi kaṭaku na mori baṛāī.
प्रभु अग्या अपेल श्रुति गाई । करौं सो बेगि जो तुम्हहि सोहाई ॥
prabhu agyā apela śruti gāī, karauṁ so begi jo tumhahi sohāī.

Trans:

The terrified ocean clasped the Lord's feet: "Pardon me, sire, of all my offences. Air, wind, fire, water, and earth are all, my Lord, naturally dull and slow to change. They have been produced by the delusive power Māyā that you sent forth with the purpose of raising your Creation—so all the scriptures declare—and as each has been fixed by the Lord's ordain, so it must remain, to secure its own happy state. My Lord has done well in giving me this lesson; but still it was you who first fixed my bounds. Drum, rustic, worker, beast, woman—deserve to be enjoined. By the Lord's glory I shall be dried up and the army will cross over; but that will bring no credit to me. Your command however is inviolable: thus declare the Vedas; I shall do at once what pleases you."

दोहा-dohā:

सुनत बिनीत बचन अति कह कृपाल मुसुकाइ ।
sunata binīta bacana ati kaha kṛpāla musukāi,
जेहि बिधि उतरै कपि कटकु तात सो कहहु उपाइ ॥५९॥
jehi bidhi utarai kapi kaṭaku tāta so kahahu upāi. 59.

Trans:

The Lord smiled to hear this exceedingly humble speech, and said "Tell me, sire, of some device, whereby the monkey host may cross over?"

चौपाई-caupāī:

नाथ नील नल कपि द्वौ भाई । लरिकाईं रिषि आसिष पाई ॥
nātha nīla nala kapi dvau bhāī, larikāīṁ riṣi āsiṣa pāī.
तिन्ह कें परस किएँ गिरि भारे । तरिहहिं जलधि प्रताप तुम्हारे ॥
tinha keṁ parasa kieṁ giri bhāre, tarihahiṁ jaladhi pratāpa tumhāre.
मैं पुनि उर धरि प्रभु प्रभुताई । करिहउँ बल अनुमान सहाई ॥
maiṁ puni ura dhari prabhu prabhutāī, karihauṁ bala anumāna sahāī.
एहि बिधि नाथ पयोधि बँधाइअ । जेहिं यह सुजसु लोक तिहुँ गाइअ ॥
ehi bidhi nātha payodhi baṁdhāia, jehiṁ yaha sujasu loka tihuṁ gāia.
एहिं सर मम उत्तर तट बासी । हतहु नाथ खल नर अघ रासी ॥
ehiṁ sara mama uttara taṭa bāsī, hatahu nātha khala nara agha rāsī.
सुनि कृपाल सागर मन पीरा । तुरतहिं हरी राम रनधीरा ॥
suni kṛpāla sāgara mana pīrā, turatahiṁ harī rāma ranadhīrā.
देखि राम बल पौरुष भारी । हरषि पयोनिधि भयउ सुखारी ॥
dekhi rāma bala pauruṣa bhārī, harași payonidhi bhayau sukhārī.
सकल चरित कहि प्रभुहि सुनावा । चरन बंदि पाथोधि सिधावा ॥
sakala carita kahi prabhuhi sunāvā, carana baṁdi pāthodhi sidhāvā.

Trans:

"My Lord, there are two monkey brothers, Nīl and Nala, who from childhood were instructed by a sage. Even the mightiest rocks touched by them float upon water by the favor of your grace. I too, holding in my heart your majesty and prowess, will assist to the best of my ability. In this manner, my Lord, you will bridge the sea and this glorious deed will be sung forever in the three sphere. Now Lord, with this drawn arrow, please slay the vile criminals that dwell on my northern shore." The all-merciful, the valiant Rāma, on hearing its grievance, immediately removed the ocean's agony. At the sight of his might and vigor the ocean rejoiced and became easy of mind; and after telling him all that had transpired, bowed at his feet and took his leave.

छंद-chaṁda:

निज भवन गवनेउ सिंधु श्रीरघुपतिहि यह मत भायऊ ।
nija bhavana gavaneu siṁdhu śrīraghupatihi yaha mata bhāyaū,
यह चरित कलि मलहर जथामति दास तुलसी गायऊ ॥
yaha carita kali malahara jathāmati dāsa tulasī gāyaū.
सुख भवन संसय समन दवन बिषाद रघुपति गुन गना ।
sukha bhavana saṁsaya samana davana biṣāda raghupati guna ganā,
तजि सकल आस भरोस गावहि सुनहि संतत सठ मना ॥
taji sakala āsa bharosa gāvahi sunahi saṁtata saṭha manā.

Trans:

And thus the Ocean returned to his abode, with Rāma having approved of his counsel. These acts of Rāma, which remove all the impurities of this sinful age, has Tulsīdās sung to the best of his ability. The excellencies of Raghupatī are a treasure of delight, a panacea for all doubts, a purge for every sorrow, and they who are wise of heart will abandon every other hope and assurance and be ever singing them or hear them sung.

दोहा-dohā:

सकल सुमंगल दायक रघुनायक गुन गान ।
sakala sumaṁgala dāyaka raghunāyaka guna gāna,
सादर सुनहिं ते तरहिं भव सिंधु बिना जलजान ॥६०॥
sādara sunahiṁ te tarahiṁ bhava siṁdhu binā jalajāna. 60.

Trans:

The virtues of Raghunāyak are the source of every blessing, and those who reverently hear these recital, cross the ocean of existence without need for another boat.

मासपारायण चौबीसवाँ विश्राम
māsapārāyaṇa caubīsavāṁ viśrāma
(Pause 24 for a Thirty-Day Recitation)

इति श्रीमद्रामचरितमानसे सकलकलिकलुषविध्वंसने पञ्चमः सोपानः समाप्तः
iti śrīmadrāmacaritamānase sakalakalikaluṣavidhvaṁsane pañcamaḥ sopānaḥ samāptaḥ
(Now ends the Fifth-Ascent into the Manasa Lake of Shrī Rāma's Charita which eradicates all the impurities of the Kali-Yug)

श्रीजानकीवल्लभो विजयते

śrījānakīvallabho vijayate

श्रीरामचरितमानस

śrīrāmacaritamānasa

षष्ठ सोपान - लंकाकाण्ड

ṣaṣṭha sopāna - laṁkākāṇḍa

श्लोक-śloka:

रामं कामारिसेव्यं भवभयहरणं कालमत्तेभसिंहं

rāmaṁ kāmārisevyaṁ bhavabhayaharaṇaṁ kālamattebha siṁhaṁ

योगीन्द्रं ज्ञानगम्यं गुणनिधिमजितं निर्गुणं निर्विकारम् ।

yogīndraṁ jñānagamyaṁ guṇanidhimajitaṁ nirguṇaṁ nirvikāram,

मायातीतं सुरेशं खलवधनिरतं ब्रह्मवृन्दैकदेवं

māyātītaṁ sureśaṁ khalavadhaniratam brahmavṛndaikadevaṁ

वन्दे कन्दावदातं सरसिजनयनं देवमुर्वीशरूपम् ॥ १ ॥

vande kandāvadātaṁ sarasijanayanaṁ devamurvīśarūpam. 1.

Trans:

I worship Rāma; the adored of the destroyer of Cupid—Shiva; the dispeller of all terrors of existence; the lion to demolish the mad elephant Death; the Lord of ascetics accessible only by contemplation; the store-house of all good qualities; the invincible, the passionless, the unchangeable; above the influence of Māyā; the Lord of the gods; the implacable destroyer of the wicked; the one God over Brahmmā and all his fellows; beautiful as a rain-bearing cloud, the lotus-eyed God incarnate in the form of an earthly king.

शङ्खेन्द्वाभमतीवसुन्दरतनुं शार्दूलचर्माम्बरं

śaṅkhendvābhamatīvasundaratanuṁ śārdūlacarmāmbaraṁ

कालव्यालकरालभूषणधरं गङ्गाशशाङ्कप्रियम् ।

kālavyālakarālabhūṣaṇadharaṁ gaṅgāśaśāṅkapriyam,

काशीशं कलिकल्मषौघशमनं कल्याणकल्पद्रुमं

kāśīśaṁ kalikalmaṣaughaśamanaṁ kalyāṇakalpadrumaṁ

नौमीड्यं गिरिजापतिं गुणनिधिं कन्दर्पहं शङ्करम् ॥ २ ॥

naumīḍyaṁ girijāpatiṁ guṇanidhiṁ kandarpahaṁ śaṅkaram. 2.

Trans:

I glorify the divine Shankar: as glistening in hue as the conch shell or the moon; the all-beautiful in person, robed in tiger's skin; bedecked with dreadful black snakes as ornaments, attended by the Gangā and the moon; the Lord of Kashī; the allayer of the sins of the Kali-Yug; the celestial tree yielding the fruit of Blessedness for mere asking; the ever adorable Lord of Pārwatī; the store-house of good qualities; the vanquisher of Lust.

यो ददाति सतां शम्भुः कैवल्यमपि दुर्लभम् ।

yo dadāti satāṁ śambhuḥ kaivalyamapi durlabham,

खलानां दण्डकृद्योऽसौ शङ्करः शं तनोतु मे ॥ ३ ॥

khalānāṁ daṇḍakṛdyo'sau śaṅkaraḥ śaṁ tanotu me. 3.

Trans:

May Shambhu—who rewards the saints with eternal beatitude that's most difficult for anyone to obtain, and who punishes the evil-doers—may that self-same Shankar have mercy and grant me prosperity.

दोहा-dohā:

लव निमेष परमानु जुग बरष कलप सर चंड ।

lava nimeṣa paramānu juga baraṣa kalapa sara caṁḍa,

भजसि न मन तेहि राम को कालु जासु कोदंड ॥

bhajasi na mana tehi rāma ko kālu jāsu kodaṁḍa.

Trans:

O my soul, why dost thou not worship Rāma: whose has for his bow the indivisible Time, and whose fierce arrows are sharp as a *Paramānu*, a Twinkling, a Moment, and mighty as Years, Ages, Cycles.

सोरठा-sorathā:

सिंधु बचन सुनि राम सचिव बोलि प्रभु अस कहेउ ।

siṁdhu bacana suni rāma saciva boli prabhu asa kaheu,

अब बिलंबु केहि काम करहु सेतु उतरै कटकु ॥

aba bilaṁbu kehi kāma karahu setu utarai kaṭaku.

सुनहु भानुकुल केतु जामवंत कर जोरि कह ।

sunahu bhānukula ketu jāmavaṁta kara jori kaha,

नाथ नाम तव सेतु नर चढ़ि भव सागर तरहिं ॥

nātha nāma tava setu nara caṛhi bhava sāgara tarahiṁ.

Trans:

After hearing ocean's speech, Lord Rāma spoke and said to his ministers, "Why delay now? Make the bridge that the army may cross across." Jāmvant clasped his hands and said, "Hearken O pride of the solar race: your very name is the bridge, by aid of which men cross the ocean of life, Lord.

चौपाई-caupāī:

यह लघु जलधि तरत कति बारा । अस सुनि पुनि कह पवनकुमारा ॥

yaha laghu jaladhi tarata kati bārā, asa suni puni kaha pavanakumārā.

प्रभु प्रताप बड़वानल भारी । सोषेउ प्रथम पयोनिधि बारी ॥

prabhu pratāpa baṛavānala bhārī, soṣeu prathama payonidhi bārī.

तव रिपु नारि रुदन जल धारा । भरेउ बहोरि भयउ तेहिं खारा ॥

tava ripu nāri rudana jala dhārā, bhareu bahori bhayau tehiṁ khārā.

सुनि अति उकुति पवनसुत केरी । हरषे कपि रघुपति तन हेरी ॥

suni ati ukuti pavanasuta kerī, harașe kapi raghupati tana herī.

जामवंत बोले दोउ भाई । नल नीलहि सब कथा सुनाई ॥

jāmavaṁta bole dou bhāī, nala nīlahi saba kathā sunāī.

राम प्रताप सुमिरि मन माहीं । करहु सेतु प्रयास कछु नाहीं ॥
rāma pratāpa sumiri mana māhīṁ, karahu setu prayāsa kachu nāhīṁ.
बोलि लिए कपि निकर बहोरी । सकल सुनहु बिनती कछु मोरी ॥
boli lie kapi nikara bahorī, sakala sunahu binatī kachu morī.
राम चरन पंकज उर धरहू । कौतुक एक भालु कपि करहू ॥
rāma carana paṁkaja ura dharahū, kautuka eka bhālu kapi karahū.
धावहु मर्कट बिकट बरूथा । आनहु बिटप गिरिन्ह के जूथा ॥
dhāvahu markaṭa bikaṭa barūthā, ānahu biṭapa girinha ke jūthā.
सुनि कपि भालु चले करि हूहा । जय रघुबीर प्रताप समूहा ॥
suni kapi bhālu cale kari hūhā, jaya raghubīra pratāpa samūhā.

Trans:

What trouble then can there be about crossing this little stream?" Hearing this, the son-of-wind added, "By my Lord's favor a fierce subterranean fire had ere dried up the depths of the sea, but it has filled up subsequently—by the floods of tears shed by the widows of his foes—and that's what makes the sea so salty." On hearing Hanumān's adroit speech, the monkeys gazed with rapture on Rāma's person. Then Jāmvant spoke to the two brothers Nala and Nīl, and explained to them all the circumstance, "Keep your thoughts fixed on Rāma's might and begin building the bridge; you will find no difficulty." Then he addressed the whole monkey host, "Hearken, all of you; I have one request to make: only impress upon your soul Rāma's lotus feet and then you bears and monkeys will find this task a mere play. Go forth my sturdy troops and bring hither heaps of rocks and trees." On hearing this, the monkeys and bears went forth hurrahing, "Glory, Glory to Rāma and his might!'

दोहा-dohā:

अति उतंग गिरि पादप लीलहिं लेहिं उठाइ ।
ati utaṁga giri pādapa līlahiṁ lehiṁ uṭhāi,
आनि देहिं नल नीलहि रचहिं ते सेतु बनाइ ॥ १ ॥
āni dehiṁ nala nīlahi racahiṁ te setu banāi. 1.

Trans:

They plucked up and carried off in mere sport the biggest rocks and trees and brought them to Nala and Nīl, who set to work building the bridge.

चौपाई-caupāī:

सैल बिसाल आनि कपि देहीं । कंदुक इव नल नील ते लेहीं ॥
saila bisāla āni kapi dehīṁ, kaṁduka iva nala nīla te lehīṁ.
देखि सेतु अति सुंदर रचना । बिहसि कृपानिधि बोले बचना ॥
dekhi setu ati suṁdara racanā, bihasi kṛpānidhi bole bacanā.
परम रम्य उत्तम यह धरनी । महिमा अमित जाइ नहिं बरनी ॥
parama ramya uttama yaha dharanī, mahimā amita jāi nahiṁ baranī.
करिहउँ इहाँ संभु थापना । मोरे हृदयँ परम कलपना ॥
karihauṁ ihāṁ saṁbhu thāpanā, more hṛdayaṁ parama kalapanā.
सुनि कपीस बहु दूत पठाए । मुनिबर सकल बोलि लै आए ॥
suni kapīsa bahu dūta paṭhāe, munibara sakala boli lai āe.
लिंग थापि बिधिवत करि पूजा । सिव समान प्रिय मोहि न दूजा ॥
liṁga thāpi bidhivata kari pūjā, siva samāna priya mohi na dūjā.
सिव द्रोही मम भगत कहावा । सो नर सपनेहुँ मोहि न पावा ॥
siva drohī mama bhagata kahāvā, so nara sapanehuṁ mohi na pāvā.
संकर बिमुख भगति चह मोरी । सो नारकी मूढ़ मति थोरी ॥
saṁkara bimukha bhagati caha morī, so nārakī mūṛha mati thorī.

Trans:

The enormous rocks, which the monkeys brought and handed them, were handled by Nala and Nīl like mere pellets. When the All-Merciful saw the charming construction of the bridge, he smiled and said, "This is a most exceedingly delightful spot; no words can tell its immeasurable dignity. I will set up here an image of Shambhu, for I have a great desire in heart to do just that." On hearing that, the monkey king sent a number of messengers to summon and fetch all the great saints. After molding a lingam in the prescribed manner and worshipping it, Rāma said, "There is none other so dear to me as Shiva. No man, though he calls himself a votary of mine, if he offends Shiva, can ever dream of really finding me. He who is opposed to Shiva and yet aspires for devotion to me is doomed to perdition—stupid and dull-witted as he is.

दोहा-dohā:

संकरप्रिय मम द्रोही सिव द्रोही मम दास ।
saṁkarapriya mama drohī siva drohī mama dāsa,
ते नर करहिं कलप भरि धोर नरक महुँ बास ॥ २ ॥
te nara karahiṁ kalapa bhari dhora naraka mahuṁ bāsa. 2.

Trans:

They who either out of attachment to Shiva dishonor me, or who serve me, but dishonor Shiva, shall have their abode in the deepest hell till the end of the world.

चौपाई-caupāī:

जे रामेस्वर दरसनु करिहहिं । ते तनु तजि मम लोक सिधरिहहिं ॥
je rāmesvara darasanu karihahiṁ, te tanu taji mama loka sidharihahiṁ.
जो गंगाजलु आनि चढ़ाइहि । सो साजुज्य मुक्ति नर पाइहि ॥
jo gaṁgājalu āni caṛhāihi, so sājujya mukti nara pāihi.
होइ अकाम जो छल तजि सेइहि । भगति मोरि तेहि संकर देइहि ॥
hoi akāma jo chala taji seihi, bhagati mori tehi saṁkara deihi.
मम कृत सेतु जो दरसनु करिही । सो बिनु श्रम भवसागर तरिही ॥
mama kṛta setu jo darasanu karihī, so binu śrama bhavasāgara tarihī.
राम बचन सब के जिय भाए । मुनिबर निज निज आश्रम आए ॥
rāma bacana saba ke jiya bhāe, munibara nija nija āśrama āe.
गिरिजा रघुपति कै यह रीती । संतत करहिं प्रनत पर प्रीती ॥
girijā raghupati kai yaha rītī, saṁtata karahiṁ pranata para prītī.
बाँधा सेतु नील नल नागर । राम कृपाँ जसु भयउ उजागर ॥
bāṁdhā setu nīla nala nāgara, rāma kṛpāṁ jasu bhayau ujāgara.
बूड़हिं आनहि बोरहिं जेई । भए उपल बोहित सम तेई ॥
būṛahiṁ ānahi borahiṁ jeī, bhae upala bohita sama teī.
महिमा यह न जलधि कइ बरनी । पाहन गुन न कपिन्ह कइ करनी ॥
mahimā yaha na jaladhi kai baranī, pāhana guna na kapinha kai karanī.

Trans:

All who make a pilgrimage to Rameshwar on quitting the body will go direct to my sphere in heaven. Anyone who brings and offers Gangā water here, will, by the strength of his faith, be absorbed into the divine essence. To all who serve me unselfishly and without guile Shiva will grant the boon of devotion. Whoever makes a pilgrimage to this bridge that I have built will without any trouble cross the ocean of life." Rāma's words gladdened the hearts of all, and the saints thereupon returned to their hermitages. This, Pārwatī, is Rāma's way: always gracious he is to the humble. Nīl and Nala built the bridge so cleverly that by Rāma's favor they acquired brilliant renown. Those very rocks that not only sink themselves but cause even other things to sink along with them floated like so many rafts. This is, however, not ascribed to any miraculous power of the ocean, nor to a virtue of the rocks themselves, nor again to any skill of the monkeys.

दोहा-dohā:

श्री रघुबीर प्रताप ते सिंधु तरे पाषान ।
śrī raghubīra pratāpa te siṁdhu tare pāṣāna,
ते मतिमंद जे राम तजि भजहिं जाइ प्रभु आन ॥ ३ ॥
te matimaṁda je rāma taji bhajahiṁ jāi prabhu āna. 3.

Trans:

It was by the might of the blessed Rāma that the rocks made a way across the sea. How dull of soul then are they who leave Rāma to worship any other Lord.

चौपाई-caupāī:

बाँधि सेतु अति सुदृढ़ बनावा । देखि कृपानिधि के मन भावा ॥
bāṁdhi setu ati sudṛṛha banāvā, dekhi kṛpānidhi ke mana bhāvā.
चली सेन कछु बरनि न जाई । गर्जहिं मर्कट भट समुदाई ॥
calī sena kachu barani na jāī, garjahiṁ markaṭa bhaṭa samudāī.
सेतुबंध ढिग चढ़ि रघुराई । चितव कृपाल सिंधु बहुताई ॥
setubaṁdha ḍhiga caṛhi raghurāī, citava kṛpāla siṁdhu bahutāī.
देखन कहुँ प्रभु करुना कंदा । प्रगट भए सब जलचर बृंदा ॥
dekhana kahuṁ prabhu karunā kaṁdā, pragaṭa bhae saba jalacara bṛṁdā.
मकर नक्र नाना झष ब्याला । सत जोजन तन परम बिसाला ॥
makara nakra nānā jhaṣa byālā, sata jojana tana parama bisālā.
अइसेउ एक तिन्हहि जे खाहीं । एकन्ह कें डर तेपि डेराहीं ॥
aiseu eka tinhahi je khāhīṁ, ekanha keṁ ḍara tepi ḍerāhīṁ.
प्रभुहि बिलोकहिं टरहिं न टारे । मन हरषित सब भए सुखारे ॥
prabhuhi bilokahiṁ ṭarahiṁ na ṭāre, mana haraṣita saba bhae sukhāre.
तिन्ह की ओट न देखिअ बारी । मगन भए हरि रूप निहारी ॥
tinha kī oṭa na dekhia bārī, magana bhae hari rūpa nihārī.
चला कटकु प्रभु आयसु पाई । को कहि सक कपि दल बिपुलाई ॥
calā kaṭaku prabhu āyasu pāī, ko kahi saka kapi dala bipulāī.

Trans:

When they had completed the bridge and made it thoroughly secure, the All-merciful was glad of heart at the sight. The passage of the host was beyond all telling, with the clamor of the multitude of warlike monkeys. The gracious Rāma mounted a spot near the bridge and gazed upon the mighty deep. Then all the creatures of the sea showed themselves in their anxiety to behold the Lord of compassion—every kind of crocodile, alligator, fish, and serpent, with bodies a hundred leagues in length and of enormous size. After them were others, such that a single one could devour all the fish-swarm, while they again trembled no less before one of the swarms that followed them. They could not take their eyes off the Lord, and in the general gladness of heart all were happy together. You could not see the water, so thickly they covered it, as they gazed in delight on the vision of Harī. At their Lord's command the army marched on, and who can describe the magnitude of the monkey host?

दोहा-dohā:

सेतुबंध भइ भीर अति कपि नभ पंथ उड़ाहिं ।
setubaṁdha bhai bhīra ati kapi nabha paṁtha uṛāhiṁ,
अपर जलचरन्हि ऊपर चढ़ि चढ़ि पारहि जाहिं ॥४॥
apara jalacaranhi ūpara caṛhi caṛhi pārahi jāhiṁ. 4.

Trans:

The bridge was thronged with the crowd; then some of the monkeys took to flying through the air, while others crossed over on the backs of sea monsters.

चौपाई-caupāī:

अस कौतुक बिलोकि द्वौ भाई । बिहँसि चले कृपाल रघुराई ॥
asa kautuka biloki dvau bhāī, bihaṁsi cale kṛpāla raghurāī.
सेन सहित उतरे रघुबीरा । कहि न जाइ कपि जूथप भीरा ॥
sena sahita utare raghubīrā, kahi na jāi kapi jūthapa bhīrā.
सिंधु पार प्रभु डेरा कीन्हा । सकल कपिन्ह कहुँ आयसु दीन्हा ॥
siṁdhu pāra prabhu ḍerā kīnhā, sakala kapinha kahuṁ āyasu dīnhā.
खाहु जाइ फल मूल सुहाए । सुनत भालु कपि जहँ तहँ धाए ॥
khāhu jāi phala mūla suhāe, sunata bhālu kapi jahaṁ tahaṁ dhāe.
सब तरु फरे राम हित लागी । रितु अरु कुरितु काल गति त्यागी ॥
saba taru phare rāma hita lāgī, ritu aru kuritu kāla gati tyāgī.
खाहिं मधुर फल बटप हलावहिं । लंका सन्मुख सिखर चलावहिं ॥
khāhiṁ madhura phala baṭapa halāvahiṁ, laṁkā sanmukha sikhara calāvahiṁ.
जहँ कहुँ फिरत निसाचर पावहिं । घेरि सकल बहु नाच नचावहिं ॥
jahaṁ kahuṁ phirata nisācara pāvahiṁ, gheri sakala bahu nāca nacāvahiṁ.
दसनन्हि काटि नासिका काना । कहि प्रभु सुजसु देहिं तब जाना ॥
dasananhi kāṭi nāsikā kānā, kahi prabhu sujasu dehiṁ taba jānā.
जिन्ह कर नासा कान निपाता । तिन्ह रावनहि कही सब बाता ॥
jinha kara nāsā kāna nipātā, tinha rāvanahi kahī saba bātā.
सुनत श्रवन बारिधि बंधाना । दस मुख बोलि उठा अकुलाना ॥
sunata śravana bāridhi baṁdhānā, dasa mukha boli uṭhā akulānā.

Trans:

The two brothers gazed a while at the spectacle, and then the gracious Lord God smilingly advanced too, to cross over alongside the others. The throng of monkey chiefs was more than can be described. Reaching the opposite shore the tents were pitched, and the monkeys were told that they may go and feast on the goodly fruits and roots. On hearing that the bears and monkeys ran off in every directions. To please the Lord every tree became laden with fruit, whether it was in season or not, with no regard to the time of year. They devoured the sweet fruits and shook the trees, and hurled masses of rock into the city of Lankā. If ever they found a straggling demon, they all hemmed him in and led him a pretty dance; and they finally bit off his nose and ears with their teeth and then let him go—after making him hear their Lord God's great deeds. Those who had lost their nose and ears went and told all to Rāvan. When he heard of the bridging of the sea, the Ten-headed started up and cried in consternation:

दोहा-dohā:

बांध्यो बननिधि नीरनिधि जलधि सिंधु बारीस ।
bāṁdhyo bananidhi nīranidhi jaladhi siṁdhu bārīsa,
सत्य तोयनिधि कंपति उदधि पयोधि नदीस ॥५॥
satya toyanidhi kaṁpati udadhi payodhi nadīsa. 5.

Trans:

"What! Has He really bridged the waves, the billows, the sea, the ocean, the main, the deep, the brine, the tide, the hyaline, the lord of rivers?"

चौपाई-caupāī:

निज बिकलता बिचारि बहोरी । बिहँसि गयउ गृह करि भय भोरी ॥
nija bikalatā bicāri bahorī, bihaṁsi gayau gṛha kari bhaya bhorī.
मंदोदरीं सुन्यो प्रभु आयो । कौतुकहीं पाथोधि बँधायो ॥
maṁdodarīṁ sunyo prabhu āyo, kautukahīṁ pāthodhi baṁdhāyo.
कर गहि पतिहि भवन निज आनी । बोली परम मनोहर बानी ॥
kara gahi patihi bhavana nija ānī, bolī parama manohara bānī.
चरन नाइ सिरु अंचलु रोपा । सुनहु बचन पिय परिहरि कोपा ॥
carana nāi siru aṁcalu ropā, sunahu bacana piya parihari kopā.
नाथ बयरु कीजे ताही सों । बुधि बल सकिअ जीति जाही सों ॥
nātha bayaru kīje tāhī soṁ, budhi bala sakia jīti jāhī soṁ.
तुम्हहि रघुपतिहि अंतर कैसा । खलु खद्योत दिनकरहि जैसा ॥
tumhahi raghupatihi aṁtara kaisā, khalu khadyota dinakarahi jaisā.
अतिबल मधु कैटभ जेहिं मारे । महाबीर दितिसुत संघारे ॥
atibala madhu kaiṭabha jehiṁ māre, mahābīra ditisuta saṁghāre.
जेहिं बलि बाँधि सहजभुज मारा । सोइ अवतरेउ हरन महि भारा ॥
jehiṁ bali bāṁdhi sahajabhuja mārā, soi avatareu harana mahi bhārā.
तासु बिरोध न कीजिअ नाथा । काल करम जिव जाकें हाथा ॥
tāsu birodha na kījia nāthā, kāla karama jiva jākeṁ hāthā.

Trans:

Then becoming conscious of the nervousness he had thus displayed, he turned with a smile to the palace, full of frantic imaginations. When Mandodarī heard that the Lord had arrived, and had made nothing of bridging the sea, she took her spouse by the hand and led him to her own apartment, and besought him with these humble and winning words, bowing her head at his feet and holding up the hem of her mantle, "Be not angry, my beloved, but hearken to my speech: You should fight, my lord, with one whom you may be able to subdue either by wit or strength. But the difference between you and Rāma is like that between a poor little firefly and the sun. He who slew the monsters Madhu and Kaitabh, who worsted Diti's valiant son, Hiranyaksh, who put Bālī in bonds, and slew Sahastr-bahu, he it is who has now become incarnate to relieve the earth of her burdens. O my lord, do not fight against him—in whose hands are Death and Fate and our very Life.

दोहा-dohā:

रामहि सौंपि जानकी नाइ कमल पद माथ ।
rāmahi sauṁpi jānakī nāi kamala pada mātha,
सुत कहुँ राज समर्पि बन जाइ भजिअ रघुनाथ ॥६॥
suta kahuṁ rāja samarpi bana jāi bhajia raghunātha. 6.

Trans:

Bow your head at Rāma's lotus feet and give him back Sītā; then resign your throne to your son and retire to the woods and there worship Raghunāth.

चौपाई-caupāī:

नाथ दीनदयाल रघुराई । बाघउ सनमुख गएँ न खाई ॥
nātha dīnadayāla raghurāī, bāghau sanamukha gaeṁ na khāī.
चाहिअ करन सो सब करि बीते । तुम्ह सुर असुर चराचर जीते ॥
cāhia karana so saba kari bīte, tumha sura asura carācara jīte.
संत कहहिं असि नीति दसानन । चौथेंपन जाइहि नृप कानन ॥
saṁta kahahiṁ asi nīti dasānana, cautheṁpana jāihi nṛpa kānana.
तासु भजन कीजिअ तहँ भर्ता । जो कर्ता पालक संहर्ता ॥
tāsu bhajana kījia tahaṁ bhartā, jo kartā pālaka saṁhartā.
सोइ रघुवीर प्रनत अनुरागी । भजहु नाथ ममता सब त्यागी ॥
soi raghuvīra pranata anurāgī, bhajahu nātha mamatā saba tyāgī.
मुनिबर जतनु करहिं जेहि लागी । भूप राजु तजि होहिं बिरागी ॥
munibara jatanu karahiṁ jehi lāgī, bhūpa rāju taji hohiṁ birāgī.
सोइ कोसलधीस रघुराया । आयउ करन तोहि पर दाया ॥
soi kosaladhīsa raghurāyā, āyau karana tohi para dāyā.
जौं पिय मानहु मोर सिखावन । सुजसु होइ तिहुँ पुर अति पावन ॥
jauṁ piya mānahu mora sikhāvana, sujasu hoi tihuṁ pura ati pāvana.

Trans:

Rāma is pitiful to the humble, like a tiger which will not devour a man who comes to meet him. All that you had to do, you have done long ago; you have vanquished gods and demons and all creation. The saints, O Rāvan, have laid down this rule, that a king in his old age should retire to the forest. There, O my spouse, make your prayers to him, who is the creator, preserver, and destroyer: Shrī Rāma, ever gracious to the humble. Put away your self-love and pride, my lord, and worship him. He for whom the greatest saints perform all their labors, for whom kings leave their throne to become hermits, is this very king of Kaushal, this Rāma, who has come here to show mercy upon you. Only submit to my advice, my spouse, and the glory of your renown shall spread through the three spheres."

दोहा-dohā:

अस कहि नयन नीर भरि गहि पद कंपित गात ।
asa kahi nayana nīra bhari gahi pada kaṁpita gāta,
नाथ भजहु रघुनाथहि अचल होइ अहिवात ॥७॥
nātha bhajahu raghunāthahi acala hoi ahivāta. 7.

Trans:

So saying she clasped him by the feet, her eyes full of tears and trembling in every limb. "O my lord, worship Rāma, and your prosperity shall never be shaken."

चौपाई-caupāī:

तब रावन मयसुता उठाई । कहै लाग खल निज प्रभुताई ॥
taba rāvana mayasutā uṭhāī, kahai lāga khala nija prabhutāī.
सुनु तैं प्रिया बृथा भय माना । जग जोधा को मोहि समाना ॥
sunu taiṁ priyā bṛthā bhaya mānā, jaga jodhā ko mohi samānā.
बरुन कुबेर पवन जम काला । भुज बल जितेउँ सकल दिगपाला ॥
baruna kubera pavana jama kālā, bhuja bala jiteuṁ sakala digapālā.
देव दनुज नर सब बस मोरें । कवन हेतु उपजा भय तोरें ॥
deva danuja nara saba basa moreṁ, kavana hetu upajā bhaya toreṁ.
नाना बिधि तेहि कहेसि बुझाई । सभाँ बहोरि बैठ सो जाई ॥
nānā bidhi tehi kahesi bujhāī, sabhāṁ bahori baiṭha so jāī.
मंदोदरीं हृदयँ अस जाना । काल बस्य उपजा अभिमाना ॥
maṁdodarīṁ hṛdayaṁ asa jānā, kāla basya upajā abhimānā.
सभाँ आइ मंत्रिन्ह तेहिं बूझा । करब कवन बिधि रिपु सैं जूझा ॥
sabhāṁ āi maṁtrinha tehiṁ būjhā, karaba kavana bidhi ripu saiṁ jūjhā.
कहहिं सचिव सुनु निसिचर नाहा । बार बार प्रभु पूछहु काहा ॥
kahahiṁ saciva sunu nisicara nāhā, bāra bāra prabhu pūchahu kāhā.
कहहु कवन भय करिअ बिचारा । नर कपि भालु अहार हमारा ॥
kahahu kavana bhaya karia bicārā, nara kapi bhālu ahāra hamārā.

Trans:

Rāvan then raised the daughter of Māyā from the ground and began—the fool—to boast of his own might, "Hearken, my beloved, you are disturbed by idle fears; is there any warrior in the world my equal? Varun, Kuber, the Wind-god, Yama, and Fate, and all the regents of the eight quarters, have been subdued by the might of my arm. Gods, demons, and Kinnars are all in my power: what cause can have arisen for these fears of yours?" Having thusly said many things that he could to comfort her, he went and took his seat in the Council. But Mandodarī knew at heart that his arrogance was doomed to destroy him. In the council he enquired of his ministers, "In what way shall we fight the enemy?" They replied, "Hearken demon-king, why question us thus, again and again? Consider now and say what is there to be afraid of? Man, monkeys, and bears are our natural food."

दोहा-dohā:

सब के बचन श्रवन सुनि कह प्रहस्त कर जोरि ।
saba ke bacana śravana suni kaha prahasta kara jori,
नीति बिरोध न करिअ प्रभु मंत्रिन्ह मति अति थोरि ॥८॥
nīti birodha na karia prabhu maṁtrinha mati ati thori. 8.

Trans:

But Prahasth, after listening to all they said, clasped his hands and cried, "Do not, my lord, act contrary to sound judgment; your counselors have mighty little sense.

चौपाई-caupāī:

कहहिं सचिव सठ ठकुरसोहाती । नाथ न पूर आव एहि भाँती ॥
kahahiṁ saciva saṭha ṭhakurasohātī, nātha na pūra āva ehi bhāṁtī.
बारिधि नाघि एक कपि आवा । तासु चरित मन महुँ सबु गावा ॥
bāridhi nāghi eka kapi āvā, tāsu carita mana mahuṁ sabu gāvā.
छुधा न रही तुम्हहि तब काहू । जारत नगरु कस न धरि खाहू ॥
chudhā na rahī tumhahi taba kāhū, jārata nagaru kasa na dhari khāhū.
सुनत नीक आगें दुख पावा । सचिवन अस मत प्रभुहि सुनावा ॥
sunata nīka āgeṁ dukha pāvā, sacivana asa mata prabhuhi sunāvā.
जेहिं बारीस बँधायउ हेला । उतरेउ सेन समेत सुबेला ॥
jehiṁ bārīsa baṁdhāyau helā, utareu sena sameta subelā.
सो भनु मनुज खाब हम भाई । बचन कहहिं सब गाल फुलाई ॥
so bhanu manuja khāba hama bhāī, bacana kahahiṁ saba gāla phulāī.
तात बचन मम सुनु अति आदर । जनि मन गुनहु मोहि करि कादर ॥
tāta bacana mama sunu ati ādara, jani mana gunahu mohi kari kādara.
प्रिय बानी जे सुनहिं जे कहहीं । ऐसे नर निकाय जग अहहीं ॥
priya bānī je sunahiṁ je kahahīṁ, aise nara nikāya jaga ahahīṁ.

बचन परम हित सुनत कठोरे । सुनहिं जे कहहिं ते नर प्रभु थोरे ॥
bacana parama hita sunata kaṭhore, sunahiṁ je kahahiṁ te nara prabhu thore.
प्रथम बसीठ पठउ सुनु नीती । सीता देइ करहु पुनि प्रीती ॥
prathama basīṭha paṭhau sunu nītī, sītā dei karahu puni prītī.
Trans:
They have all spoken simply to please their master; but good results do not come in that way. A single monkey leapt across the ocean and came hither; and what he did—you all know by heart. What! Were none of you hungry then, that you did not seize and devour him, when he set fire to the city? Pleasant to hear but fraught with future trouble is the advice which your counselors have given their lord. Come, sir, tell me now, is he a mere man that we can devour, who has bridged the sea without any trouble, and has crossed over to Suvel with all his army? What they say is all idle boast. Hearken sire with due respect to my prayer, and do not in your arrogance account me a coward. There are plenty of people in the world who are ready to make or listen to pleasant speeches; but few, my lord, who care either to hear or to give wholesome advice, if it sounds unpleasant. Hearken now to wise counsel: first send an envoy, and when you have restored Sītā, do your best to make friends with him.

दोहा-dohā:

नारि पाइ फिरि जाहिं जौं तौ न बढ़ाइअ रारि ।
nāri pāi phiri jāhiṁ jauṁ tau na baṛhāia rāri,
नाहिं त सन्मुख समर महि तात करिअ हठि मारि ॥९॥
nāhiṁ ta sanmukha samara mahi tāta karia haṭhi māri. 9.
Trans:
If he withdraws after recovering his wife, there will be no need of any further dispute; if otherwise, then sir, prepare for a resolute encounter face to face in battle.

चौपाई-caupāī:

यह मत जौं मानहु प्रभु मोरा । उभय प्रकार सुजसु जग तोरा ॥
yaha mata jauṁ mānahu prabhu morā, ubhaya prakāra sujasu jaga torā.
सुत सन कह दसकंठ रिसाई । असि मति सठ केहिं तोहि सिखाई ॥
suta sana kaha dasakaṁṭha risāī, asi mati saṭha kehiṁ tohi sikhāī.
अबहीं ते उर संसय होई । बेनुमूल सुत भयहु घमोई ॥
abahīṁ te ura saṁsaya hoī, benumūla suta bhayahu ghamoī.
सुनि पितु गिरा परुष अति घोरा । चला भवन कहि बचन कठोरा ॥
suni pitu girā paruṣa ati ghorā, calā bhavana kahi bacana kaṭhorā.
हित मत तोहि न लागत कैसें । काल बिबस कहुँ भेषज जैसें ॥
hita mata tohi na lāgata kaiseṁ, kāla bibasa kahuṁ bheṣaja jaiseṁ.
संध्या समय जानि दससीसा । भवन चलेउ निरखत भुज बीसा ॥
saṁdhyā samaya jāni dasasīsā, bhavana caleu nirakhata bhuja bīsā.
लंका सिखर उपर आगारा । अति बिचित्र तहँ होइ अखारा ॥
laṁkā sikhara upara āgārā, ati bicitra tahaṁ hoi akhārā.
बैठ जाइ तेहिं मंदिर रावन । लागे किंनर गुन गन गावन ॥
baiṭha jāi tehiṁ maṁdira rāvana, lāge kiṁnara guna gana gāvana.
बाजहिं ताल पखाउज बीना । नृत्य करहिं अपछरा प्रबीना ॥
bājahiṁ tāla pakhāuja bīnā, nṛtya karahiṁ apacharā prabīnā.
Trans:
In either case my lord, if you accept my advice, you will have glory in the world." The Ten-headed answered his son in a fury. "Wretch, who has taught you to give such advice as this? From this time I have a doubt in my mind about you. Can a bamboo root have produced such a mere reed." On hearing his father's savage and violent speech, he turned home saying these bitter words, "Good advice is as much thrown away upon him as medicine on a man doomed to die." Seeing that it was now evening, Rāvan proceeded to the palace, glancing with pride at his twenty arms. On the top of the Lankā rock was a hall with a handsome courtyard, where he went and took his seat. A number of Kinnars began to sing to the accompaniment of cymbals, drums and lute, while beauteous nymphs danced before him.

दोहा-dohā:

सुनासीर सत सरिस सो संतत करइ बिलास ।
sunāsīra sata sarisa so saṁtata karai bilāsa,
परम प्रबल रिपु सीस पर तद्यपि सोच न त्रास ॥१०॥
parama prabala ripu sīsa para tadyapi soca na trāsa. 10.
Trans:
The delights that he enjoyed there exceeded a hundred-fold those of the king of heaven. The most powerful enemy might threaten, but no fear nor anxiety could disturb his repose.

चौपाई-caupāī:

इहाँ सुबेल सैल रघुबीरा । उतरे सेन सहित अति भीरा ॥
ihāṁ subela saila raghubīrā, utare sena sahita ati bhīrā.
सिखर एक उतंग अति देखी । परम रम्य सम सुभ्र बिसेषी ॥
sikhara eka utaṁga ati dekhī, parama ramya sama subhra biseṣī.
तहँ तरु किसलय सुमन सुहाए । लछिमन रचि निज हाथ डसाए ॥
tahaṁ taru kisalaya sumana suhāe, lachimana raci nija hātha ḍasāe.
ता पर रूचिर मृदुल मृगछाला । तेहिं आसन आसीन कृपाला ॥
tā para rūcira mṛdula mṛgachālā, tehiṁ āsana āsīna kṛpālā.
प्रभु कृत सीस कपीस उछंगा । बाम दहिन दिसि चाप निषंगा ॥
prabhu kṛta sīsa kapīsa uchaṁgā, bāma dahina disi cāpa niṣaṁgā.
दुहुँ कर कमल सुधारत बाना । कह लंकेस मंत्र लगि काना ॥
duhuṁ kara kamala sudhārata bānā, kaha laṁkesa maṁtra lagi kānā.
बड़भागी अंगद हनुमाना । चरन कमल चापत बिधि नाना ॥
baṛabhāgī aṁgada hanumānā, carana kamala cāpata bidhi nānā.
प्रभु पाछें लछिमन बीरासन । कटि निषंग कर बान सरासन ॥
prabhu pācheṁ lachimana bīrāsana, kaṭi niṣaṁga kara bāna sarāsana.
Trans:
Now the valiant Rāma had crossed over with his army to mount Suvel. There, having noted one particular lofty peak, beautiful and bright above all others, Lakshman, with his own hands, spread a couch of lovely flowers and fresh twigs, which he covered with a fine soft deer's skin; and here the All-merciful took his seat. The Lord's head rested in the lap of the monkey king; to right and left of him were his bow and quiver; with his lotus hands he trimmed his arrows, while the prince of Lankā whispered some secret in his ear. The highly favored Angad and Hanumān massaged his lotus feet, while from behind Lakshman kept watch as a sentinel, with quiver by his side and bow and arrows in his hands.

दोहा-dohā:

एहि बिधि कृपा रूप गुन धाम रामु आसीन ।
ehi bidhi kṛpā rūpa guna dhāma rāmu āsīna,
धन्य ते नर एहिं ध्यान जे रहत सदा लयलीन ॥११क॥
dhanya te nara ehiṁ dhyāna je rahata sadā layalīna. 11(ka).

पूरब दिसा बिलोकि प्रभु देखा उदित मंयक ।
pūraba disā biloki prabhu dekhā udita maṁyaka,
कहत सबहि देखहु ससिहि मृगपति सरिस असंक ॥११ख॥
kahata sabahi dekhahu sasihi mṛgapati sarisa asaṁka. 11(kha).
Trans:
Thus rested Rāma—the very store-house of benignity, beauty, and all perfection. Blessed are they who, with profound devotion, contemplate upon him in this form. As he looked towards the east the Lord observed the risen moon and said to them all, "See the moon, like some dauntless lion,

चौपाई-caupāī:

पूरब दिसि गिरिगुहा निवासी । परम प्रताप तेज बल रासी ॥
pūraba disi giriguhā nivāsī, parama pratāpa teja bala rāsī.
मत्त नाग तम कुंभ बिदारी । ससि केसरी गगन बन चारी ॥
matta nāga tama kuṁbha bidārī, sasi kesarī gagana bana cārī.

बिथुरे नभ मुकुताहल तारा । निसि सुंदरी केर सिंगारा ॥
bithure nabha mukutāhala tārā, nisi suṁdarī kera siṁgārā.
कह प्रभु ससि महुँ मेचकताई । कहहु काह निज निज मति भाई ॥
kaha prabhu sasi mahuṁ mecakatāī, kahahu kāha nija nija mati bhāī.
कह सुग्रीव सुनहु रघुराई । ससि महुँ प्रगट भूमि कै झाँई ॥
kaha sugrīva sunahu raghurāī, sasi mahuṁ pragaṭa bhūmi kai jhāṁī.
मारेउ राहु ससिहि कह कोई । उर महँ परी स्यामता सोई ॥
māreu rāhu sasihi kaha koī, ura mahaṁ parī syāmatā soī.
कोउ कह जब बिधि रति मुख कीन्हा । सार भाग ससि कर हरि लीन्हा ॥
kou kaha jaba bidhi rati mukha kīnhā, sāra bhāga sasi kara hari līnhā.
छिद्र सो प्रगट इंदु उर माहीं । तेहि मग देखिअ नभ परिछाहीं ॥
chidra so pragaṭa iṁdu ura māhīṁ, tehi maga dekhia nabha parichāhīṁ.
प्रभु कह गरल बंधु ससि केरा । अति प्रिय निज उर दीन्ह बसेरा ॥
prabhu kaha garala baṁdhu sasi kerā, ati priya nija ura dīnha baserā.
बिष संजुत कर निकर पसारी । जारत बिरहवंत नर नारी ॥
biṣa saṁjuta kara nikara pasārī, jārata birahavaṁta nara nārī.

Trans:

dwelling in the eastern quarter, which may be compared to a mountain-cave. This lion of a moon, an embodiment of supreme grandeur, glory and strength, struts through the forest of the sky having rent asunder the crown of that mad elephant in the form of darkness. The stars appear like so many pearls strewn all over the sky, which serve to adorn the lovely dame of the night." "But," said the Lord again, "tell me, my friends, each one of you, your opinion as to the stains on the moon." Said Sugrīva, "Hearken Rāma; it is only the shadow of the earth that is seen in the moon." Another said, "When Rāhu attacked the moon, its bosom was made thus discolored. A third suggested, "When Brahmmā fashioned Ratī's face, he stole from the moon a part of its essence; and this is the crater that you see in the moon's surface showing the shadow of the sky." Said the Lord, "The moon has a great liking for poison and has given it a home in its very heart; then darting abroad innumerable empoisoned rays, it tortures parted lovers."

दोहा-dohā:

कह हनुमंत सुनहु प्रभु ससि तुम्हार प्रिय दास ।
kaha hanumaṁta sunahu prabhu sasi tumhāra priya dāsa,
तव मूरति बिधु उर बसति सोइ स्यामता अभास ॥ १२क॥
tava mūrati bidhu ura basati soi syāmatā abhāsa. 12(ka).

Trans:

But Hanumān said: "Hear me, my Lord; the moon is your devoted slave, and it is your image enshrined in the moon's bosom that causes the darkness."

नवाह्नपारायण सातवाँ विश्राम
navāhnapārāyaṇa sātavāṁ viśrāma
(Pause 7 for a Nine-Day Recitation)

पवन तनय के बचन सुनि बिहँसे रामु सुजान ।
pavana tanaya ke bacana suni bihaṁse rāmu sujāna,
दच्छिन दिसि अवलोकि प्रभु बोले कृपानिधान ॥ १२ख॥
dacchina disi avaloki prabhu bole kṛpānidhāna. 12(kha).

Trans:

The All-wise Rāma smiled to hear the speech of the Son-of-wind; then, turning towards the south, the All-merciful spoke again,

चौपाई-caupāī:

देखु बिभीषन दच्छिन आसा । घन घंमड दामिनि बिलासा ॥
dekhu bibhīṣana dacchina āsā, ghana ghaṁmaḍa dāmini bilāsā.
मधुर मधुर गरजइ घन घोरा । होइ बृष्टि जनि उपल कठोरा ॥
madhura madhura garajai ghana ghorā, hoi bṛṣṭi jani upala kaṭhorā.
कहत बिभीषन सुनहु कृपाला । होइ न तड़ित न बारिद माला ॥
kahata bibhīṣana sunahu kṛpālā, hoi na taṛita na bārida mālā.
लंका सिखर उपर आगारा । तहँ दसकंघर देख अखारा ॥
laṁkā sikhara upara āgārā, tahaṁ dasakaṁghara dekha akhārā.
छत्र मेघडंबर सिर धारी । सोइ जनु जलद घटा अति कारी ॥
chatra meghaḍaṁbara sira dhārī, soi janu jalada ghaṭā ati kārī.
मंदोदरी श्रवन ताटंका । सोइ प्रभु जनु दामिनी दमंका ॥
maṁdodarī śravana tāṭaṁkā, soi prabhu janu dāminī damaṁkā.
बाजहिं ताल मृदंग अनूपा । सोइ रव मधुर सुनहु सुरभूपा ॥
bājahiṁ tāla mṛdaṁga anūpā, soi rava madhura sunahu surabhūpā.
प्रभु मुसुकान समुझि अभिमाना । चाप चढ़ाइ बान संधाना ॥
prabhu musukāna samujhi abhimānā, cāpa caṛhāi bāna saṁdhānā.

Trans:

"Look, Vibhīshan, to the southern quarter, to the gathering clouds and the flashes of lightning. A pleasant sound of distant thunder is heard amidst the gloom; there will be some rain, think you, or a storm of hail?" Vibhīshan replied: "Mark me, sire, there is neither lightning nor the gathered clouds. On the top of the Lankā hill there is a palace, where Rāvan witnesses the sports of the arena; the royal umbrella held above his head presents the appearance of a mighty mass of cloud, the jeweled ornament in Mandodarī's ears emits the flashes, my Lord, that you take for lightning; while the incomparable music of the cymbals and drums is the pleasant sound that you hear, O king of the gods." The Lord smiled, and perceiving Rāvan's arrogance strung his bow and fitted an arrow to the string.

दोहा-dohā:

छत्र मुकुट ताटंक तब हते एकहीं बान ।
chatra mukuṭa tāṭaṁka taba hate ekahīṁ bāna,
सब कें देखत महि परे मरमु न कोऊ जान ॥ १३क॥
saba keṁ dekhata mahi pare maramu na koū jāna. 13(ka).

अस कौतुक करि राम सर प्रबिसेउ आइ निषंग ।
asa kautuka kari rāma sara prabiseu āi niṣaṁga,
रावन सभा ससंक सब देखि महा रसभंग ॥ १३ख॥
rāvana sabhā sasaṁka saba dekhi mahā rasabhaṁga. 13(kha).

Trans:

A single shaft struck umbrella, crown, and eardrop; in the sight of all they fell to the ground, and none could explain the mystery. Having performed this startling feat, Rāma's arrow returned and dropped into the quiver. But Rāvan and the whole assembly were much disturbed when they saw this interruption to their revelry.

चौपाई-caupāī:

कंप न भूमि न मरुत बिसेषा । अस्त्र सस्त्र कछु नयन न देखा ॥
kaṁpa na bhūmi na maruta biseṣā, astra sastra kachu nayana na dekhā.
सोचहिं सब निज हृदय मझारी । असगुन भयउ भयंकर भारी ॥
socahiṁ saba nija hṛdaya majhārī, asaguna bhayau bhayaṁkara bhārī.
दसमुख देखि सभा भय पाई । बिहसि बचन कह जुगुति बनाई ॥
dasamukha dekhi sabhā bhaya pāī, bihasi bacana kaha juguti banāī.
सिरउ गिरे संतत सुभ जाही । मुकुट परे कस असगुन ताही ॥
sirau gire saṁtata subha jāhī, mukuṭa pare kasa asaguna tāhī.
सयन करहु निज निज गृह जाई । गवने भवन सकल सिर नाई ॥
sayana karahu nija nija gṛha jāī, gavane bhavana sakala sira nāī.
मंदोदरी सोच उर बसेऊ । जब ते श्रवनपूर महि खसेऊ ॥
maṁdodarī soca ura baseū, jaba te śravanapūra mahi khaseū.
सजल नयन कह जुग कर जोरी । सुनहु प्रानपति बिनती मोरी ॥
sajala nayana kaha juga kara jorī, sunahu prānapati binatī morī.
कंत राम बिरोध परिहरहू । जानि मनुज जनि हठ मन धरहू ॥
kaṁta rāma birodha pariharahū, jāni manuja jani haṭha mana dharahū.

Trans:

"There was no earthquake, nor wind to speak of, nor did we see a weapon of any kind," thus they pondered each to himself, "It is certainly a most alarming ill omen." When Rāvan perceived that the assembly had taken fright, he smiled and invented an ingenious answer, "When a man's head falls, it is all up with him; but what is the harm if only his crown falls? Go home all of you and go to sleep." They bowed and took their leave. But anxiety had settled in Mandodarī's bosom the moment the jewel had dropt from her ear to the ground. With streaming eyes and hands clasped in prayer, she cried: "O lord of my life, hearken to my petition. O my husband, give over fighting against Rāma, and do not indulge your pride with the idea that he is a mere man.

दोहा-dohā:

बिस्वरुप रघुबंस मनि करहु बचन बिस्वासु ।
bisvarupa raghubaṁsa mani karahu bacana bisvāsu,
लोक कल्पना बेद कर अंग अंग प्रति जासु ॥ १४॥
loka kalpanā beda kara aṁga aṁga prati jāsu. 14.

Trans:

The jewel of the line of Raghu, believe what I say, is the omnipresent God, in whose every limb, as the Vedas declare, is the fabric of a universe.

चौपाई-caupāī:

पद पाताल सीस अज धामा । अपर लोक अँग अँग बिश्रामा ॥
pada pātāla sīsa aja dhāmā, apara loka am̐ga am̐ga biśrāmā.
भृकुटि बिलास भयंकर काला । नयन दिवाकर कच घन माला ॥
bhṛkuṭi bilāsa bhayaṁkara kālā, nayana divākara kaca ghana mālā.
जासु घ्रान अस्विनीकुमारा । निसि अरु दिवस निमेष अपारा ॥
jāsu ghrāna asvinīkumārā, nisi aru divasa nimeṣa apārā.
श्रवन दिसा दस बेद बखानी । मारुत स्वास निगम निज बानी ॥
śravana disā dasa beda bakhānī, māruta svāsa nigama nija bānī.
अधर लोभ जम दसन कराला । माया हास बाहु दिगपाला ॥
adhara lobha jama dasana karālā, māyā hāsa bāhu digapālā.
आनन अनल अंबुपति जीहा । उतपति पालन प्रलय समीहा ॥
ānana anala aṁbupati jīhā, utapati pālana pralaya samīhā.
रोम राजि अष्टादस भारा । अस्थि सैल सरिता नस जारा ॥
roma rāji aṣṭādasa bhārā, asthi saila saritā nasa jārā.
उदर उदधि अधगो जातना । जगमय प्रभु का बहु कलपना ॥
udara udadhi adhago jātanā, jagamaya prabhu kā bahu kalapanā.

Trans:

The subterranean regions are his feet, his head the abode of Brahmmā, and in every limb subsists some separate sphere; the play of his brows is the doom of fate, his eyes are the sun, his hair the dark thundercloud, his nostrils the twin suns of Ashvini, and the constant winking of his eyes the cause of night and day. His ears, as the Vedas declare, are the ten quarters of the heaven, his breath the wind, and his articulate voice the scriptures. His lower lips is covetousness and his teeth the terror of death; his smile is Māyā; his arms the regents of the quarters; his face the element of fire; his tongue, water; and his movements the creation, preservation, and destruction of the universe. The hairs on his body are the trees and bushes that grow on the earth; his bones the mountains, and the network of his veins the rivers; his belly the sea, and his hinder parts hell. Everything may be called a manifestation of the omnipresent Lord—

दोहा-dohā:

अहंकार सिव बुद्धि अज मन ससि चित्त महान ।
ahaṁkāra siva buddhi aja mana sasi citta mahāna,
मनुज बास सचराचर रुप राम भगवान ॥ १५ क॥
manuja bāsa sacarācara rupa rāma bhagavāna. 15 ka.
अस बिचारि सुनु प्रानपति प्रभु सन बयरु बिहाइ ।
asa bicāri sunu prānapati prabhu sana bayaru bihāi,
प्रीति करहु रघुबीर पद मम अहिवात न जाइ ॥ १५ ख॥
prīti karahu raghubīra pada mama ahivāta na jāi. 15 kha.

Trans:

—who has Shiva for his self-consciousness, Brahmmā for his intelligence, the moon for his mind, and the great First Principle for his soul; who not only indwells in man, but also assumes the form of any animate or inanimate creature—He is the Lord God. Hearken, my beloved, ponder upon this and cease hostility with the Lord and cultivate devotion to the feet of Shrī Rāma so that my good-luck may not desert me."

चौपाई-caupāī:

बिहँसा नारि बचन सुनि काना । अहो मोह महिमा बलवाना ॥
bihaṁsā nāri bacana suni kānā, aho moha mahimā balavānā.
नारि सुभाउ सत्य सब कहहीं । अवगुन आठ सदा उर रहहीं ॥
nāri subhāu satya saba kahahīṁ, avaguna āṭha sadā ura rahahīṁ.
साहस अनृत चपलता माया । भय अबिबेक असौच अदाया ॥
sāhasa anṛta capalatā māyā, bhaya abibeka asauca adāyā.
रिपु कर रुप सकल तैं गावा । अति बिसाल भय मोहि सुनावा ॥
ripu kara rupa sakala taiṁ gāvā, ati bisāla bhaya mohi sunāvā.
सो सब प्रिया सहज बस मोरें । समुझि परा प्रसाद अब तोरें ॥
so saba priyā sahaja basa moreṁ, samujhi parā prasāda aba toreṁ.
जानिउँ प्रिया तोरि चतुराई । एहि बिधि कहहु मोरि प्रभुताई ॥
jānium̐ priyā tori caturāī, ehi bidhi kahahu mori prabhutāī.
तव बतकही गूढ़ मृगलोचनि । समुझत सुखद सुनत भय मोचनि ॥
tava batakahī gūṛha mṛgalocani, samujhata sukhada sunata bhaya mocani.
मंदोदरि मन महुँ अस ठयऊ । पियहि काल बस मतिभ्रम भयऊ ॥
maṁdodari mana mahum̐ asa ṭhayaū, piyahi kāla basa matibhrama bhayaū.

Trans:

He laughed when he heard his wife's speech. "Wonderful, indeed, is the power of infatuation. The poets have truly described a woman's nature. There are eight faults from which she is never free at heart: imprudence, falsehood, fickleness, infatuation, timidity, want of judgment, impurity, and illiberality. You have described all the manifestations of the enemy and told me a most alarming story; but my dear lady, I see through it at once and perfectly understand your kindness. I recognize your cleverness, my dear, for in this way you have exalted my own power. Your words, fair dame, are obscure; but they are auspicious when understood, though they sound alarming." Then Mandodarī perceived that her husband's infatuation was the fated forerunner of his ruin.

दोहा-dohā:

एहि बिधि करत बिनोद बहु प्रात प्रगट दसकंध ।
ehi bidhi karata binoda bahu prāta pragaṭa dasakaṁdha,
सहज असंक लंकपति सभाँ गयउ मद अंध ॥ १६क॥
sahaja asaṁka laṁkapati sabhām̐ gayau mada aṁdha. 16(ka).

Trans:

In such diverse ways did Rāvan amuse himself until the dawn appeared, when the lord of Lankā, fearless by nature and further blinded by pride, entered the council chamber.

सोरठा-sorațhā:

फूलइ फरइ न बेत जदपि सुधा बरषहिं जलद ।
phūlai pharai na beta jadapi sudhā baraṣahiṁ jalada,
मूरुख हृदयँ न चेत जौं गुर मिलहिं बिरंचि सम ॥ १६ख॥
mūrukha hṛdayam̐ na ceta jauṁ gura milahiṁ biraṁci sama. 16(kha).

Trans:

Though the clouds rain ambrosia upon it, the bamboo neither flowers nor fruits; so is the soul of a fool who never learns, though he may have Brahmmā and Shiva for his teachers.

चौपाई-caupāī:

इहाँ प्रात जागे रघुराई । पूछा मत सब सचिव बोलाई ॥
ihām̐ prāta jāge raghurāī, pūchā mata saba saciva bolāī.
कहहु बेगि का करिअ उपाई । जामवंत कह पद सिरु नाई ॥
kahahu begi kā karia upāī, jāmavaṁta kaha pada siru nāī.
सुनु सर्बग्य सकल उर बासी । बुधि बल तेज धर्म गुन रासी ॥
sunu sarbagya sakala ura bāsī, budhi bala teja dharma guna rāsī.
मंत्र कहउँ निज मति अनुसारा । दूत पठाइअ बालिकुमारा ॥
maṁtra kahaum̐ nija mati anusārā, dūta paṭhāia bālikumārā.
नीक मंत्र सब के मन माना । अंगद सन कह कृपानिधाना ॥
nīka maṁtra saba ke mana mānā, aṁgada sana kaha kṛpānidhānā.
बालितनय बुधि बल गुन धामा । लंका जाहु तात मम कामा ॥
bālitanaya budhi bala guna dhāmā, laṁkā jāhu tāta mama kāmā.
बहुत बुझाइ तुम्हहि का कहऊँ । परम चतुर मैं जानत अहऊँ ॥
bahuta bujhāi tumhahi kā kahaūm̐, parama catura maiṁ jānata ahaūm̐.
काजु हमार तासु हित होई । रिपु सन करेहु बतकही सोई ॥
kāju hamāra tāsu hita hoī, ripu sana karehu batakahī soī.

Trans:

Now Rāma awoke at the break of day and summoned his ministers to take counsel of them. "Quick, tell me what course should be adopted." Jāmvant bowed his head at his feet and said, "Hearken, omniscient observer of all men's hearts, perfection of wisdom, power, majesty, justice and every good quality. I thus advise you to the best of my ability: send the son of Bālī as an ambassador." Everyone heartily approved this good suggestion, and the All-merciful said to Angad, "Son of Bālī, wise, strong and virtuous, go to Lankā my son, in my service. What need is there to give you any lengthy instructions, I am aware of your distinguished ability. Frame your address to the enemy in such a way that he will agree to my terms."

सोरठा-sorațhā:

प्रभु अग्या धरि सीस चरन बंदि अंगद उठेउ ।
prabhu agyā dhari sīsa carana baṁdi aṁgada uṭheu,
सोइ गुन सागर ईस राम कृपा जा पर करहु ॥ १७क॥
soi guna sāgara īsa rāma kṛpā jā para karahu. 17(ka).

स्वयंसिद्ध सब काज नाथ मोहि आदरु दियउ ।
svayaṁsiddha saba kāja nātha mohi ādaru diyau,
अस बिचारि जुबराज तन पुलकित हरषित हियउ ॥ १७ख॥
asa bicāri jubarāja tana pulakita haraṣita hiyau. 17(kha).

Trans:

Obedient to his Lord's command and bowing at his feet Angad arose, crying, "O Rāma, anyone upon whom you show favor becomes possessed of every virtue. All your objectives are self-accomplished. You have graciously granted me an honor, my Lord—for any task of yours abides already completed." At this thought the young prince exulted at heart and his whole body quivered with excitement.

चौपाई-caupāī:

बंदि चरन उर धरि प्रभुताई । अंगद चलेउ सबहि सिरु नाई ॥
baṁdi carana ura dhari prabhutāī, aṁgada caleu sabahi siru nāī.
प्रभु प्रताप उर सहज असंका । रन बाँकुरा बालिसुत बंका ॥
prabhu pratāpa ura sahaja asaṁkā, rana bām̐kurā bālisuta baṁkā.
पुर पैठत रावन कर बेटा । खेलत रहा सो होइ गै भेटा ॥
pura paiṭhata rāvana kara beṭā, khelata rahā so hoi gai bheṭā.
बातहिं बात करष बढ़ि आई । जुगल अतुल बल पुनि तरुनाई ॥
bātahiṁ bāta karaṣa baṛhi āī, jugala atula bala puni tarunāī.
तेहिं अंगद कहुँ लात उठाई । गहि पद पटकेउ भूमि भवाँई ॥
tehiṁ aṁgada kahum̐ lāta uṭhāī, gahi pada paṭakeu bhūmi bhavām̐ī.
निसिचर निकर देखि भट भारी । जहँ तहँ चले न सकहिं पुकारी ॥
nisicara nikara dekhi bhaṭa bhārī, jaham̐ taham̐ cale na sakahiṁ pukārī.
एक एक सन मरमु न कहहीं । समुझि तासु बध चुप करि रहहीं ॥
eka eka sana maramu na kahahīṁ, samujhi tāsu badha cupa kari rahahīṁ.
भयउ कोलाहल नगर मझारी । आवा कपि लंका जेहिं जारी ॥
bhayau kolāhala nagara majhārī, āvā kapi laṁkā jehiṁ jārī.
अब धौं कहा करिहि करतारा । अति सभीत सब करहिं बिचारा ॥
aba dhauṁ kahā karihi karatārā, ati sabhīta saba karahiṁ bicārā.
बिनु पूछें मगु देहिं दिखाई । जेहि बिलोक सोइ जाइ सुखाई ॥
binu pūcheṁ magu dehiṁ dikhāī, jehi biloka soi jāi sukhāī.

Trans:

After prostrating himself at his feet and imprinting the image of his majesty on his soul, Angad bowed to the assembly and went forth, dauntless by nature and his heart all aglow with the might of his Lord. The delighter in battle, the gallant son of Bālī sallied forth; and as he entered the city, he came across Rāvan's son, who was sporting there. From words they came to blows—both of unequalled strength and in the prime of their youth to boot. He raised his foot to kick Angad, who at once seized him by it and swung him round and dashed him to the ground. All the demons, even the stoutest warriors among them, who saw this deed, dispersed hither and thither, daring not to give the alarm. They did not even whisper to one another, but remained silent, when they remembered the death of Rāvan's son. A rumor, however, spread throughout the city: "The monkey who set Lankā on fire has come again; what has God in store for us now?" Thus they all pondered in excessive dismay. Without being asked they showed him the way; and if he but looked at anyone they withered away.

दोहा-dohā:

गयउ सभा दरबार तब सुमिरि राम पद कंज ।
gayau sabhā darabāra taba sumiri rāma pada kaṁja,
सिंह ठवनि इत उत चितव धीर बीर बल पुंज ॥ १८॥
siṁha ṭhavani ita uta citava dhīra bīra bala puṁja. 18.

Trans:

Then, with his thoughts fixed on Rāma's lotus feet, he entered the Council Hall with the gait of a lion, glancing on this side and that, a bold and stalwart hero.

चौपाई-caupāī:

तुरत निसाचर एक पठावा । समाचार रावनहि जनावा ॥
turata nisācara eka paṭhāvā, samācāra rāvanahi janāvā.
सुनत बिहँसि बोला दससीसा । आनहु बोलि कहाँ कर कीसा ॥
sunata bihaṁsi bolā dasasīsā, ānahu boli kahām̐ kara kīsā.
आयसु पाइ दूत बहु धाए । कपिकुंजरहि बोलि लै आए ॥
āyasu pāi dūta bahu dhāe, kapikuṁjarahi boli lai āe.
अंगद दीख दसानन बैसें । सहित प्रान कज्जलगिरि जैसें ॥
aṁgada dīkha dasānana baiseṁ, sahita prāna kajjalagiri jaiseṁ.
भुजा बिटप सिर सृंग समाना । रोमावली लता जनु नाना ॥
bhujā biṭapa sira sṛṁga samānā, romāvalī latā janu nānā.
मुख नासिका नयन अरु काना । गिरि कंदरा खोह अनुमाना ॥
mukha nāsikā nayana aru kānā, giri kaṁdarā khoha anumānā.

गयउ सभाँ मन नेकु न मुरा । बालितनय अतिबल बाँकुरा ॥
gayau sabhāṁ mana neku na murā, bālitanaya atibala bāṁkurā.
उठे सभासद कपि कहुँ देखी । रावन उर भा क्रोध बिसेषी ॥
uṭhe sabhāsada kapi kahuṁ dekhī, rāvana ura bhā krodha biseṣī.

Trans:

One of the guards was immediately dispatched to report the news to Rāvan. On hearing it, the Ten-headed cried with a laugh, "Go, bring this strange monkey here." On receiving this order, a number of his messengers ran and fetched the monkey-chief. In Angad's eyes the Ten-headed appeared like a mountain of dark mass endued with life—his arms like trees, his head a rocky peak, the hair on his body as it were all kinds of creepers, and his mouth, nose, eyes and ears like caves and chasms in the rock. Without the slightest trepidation of heart he entered the Court—that son of Bālī, the most dauntless of heroes. The assembly rose at the sight of the monkey; but in Rāvan's heart was ungovernable fury.

दोहा-dohā:

जथा मत्त गज जूथ महुँ पंचानन चलि जाइ ।
jathā matta gaja jūtha mahuṁ paṁcānana cali jāi,
राम प्रताप सुमिरि मन बैठ सभाँ सिरु नाइ ॥ १९ ॥
rāma pratāpa sumiri mana baiṭha sabhāṁ siru nāi. 19.

Trans:

As when a lion enters among a herd of mad elephants, so after bowing to the assembly he took his seat, his thoughts ever fixed on Rāma's might.

चौपाई-caupāī:

कह दसकंठ कवन तैं बंदर । मैं रघुबीर दूत दसकंधर ॥
kaha dasakaṁṭha kavana taiṁ baṁdara, maiṁ raghubīra dūta dasakaṁdhara.
मम जनकहि तोहि रही मिताई । तव हित कारन आयउँ भाई ॥
mama janakahi tohi rahī mitāī, tava hita kārana āyauṁ bhāī.
उत्तम कुल पुलस्ति कर नाती । सिव बिरंचि पूजेहु बहु भाँती ॥
uttama kula pulasti kara nātī, siva biraṁci pūjehu bahu bhāṁtī.
बर पायहु कीन्हेहु सब काजा । जीतेहु लोकपाल सब राजा ॥
bara pāyahu kīnhehu saba kājā, jītehu lokapāla saba rājā.
नृप अभिमान मोह बस किंबा । हरि आनिहु सीता जगदंबा ॥
nṛpa abhimāna moha basa kiṁbā, hari ānihu sītā jagadaṁbā.
अब सुभ कहा सुनहु तुम्ह मोरा । सब अपराध छमिहि प्रभु तोरा ॥
aba subha kahā sunahu tumha morā, saba aparādha chamihi prabhu torā.
दसन गहहु तृन कंठ कुठारी । परिजन सहित संग निज नारी ॥
dasana gahahu tṛna kaṁṭha kuṭhārī, parijana sahita saṁga nija nārī.
सादर जनकसुता करि आगें । एहि बिधि चलहु सकल भय त्यागें ॥
sādara janakasutā kari āgeṁ, ehi bidhi calahu sakala bhaya tyāgeṁ.

Trans:

Rāvan asked: "Monkey, who are you?" "I am an ambassador of Rāma, Rāvan. There was friendship between you and my father; and on that account, brother, I have come to you to do you a service. Of a high descent you, the grandson of Pulastya, duly worshipped Shiva and Brahmmā, and obtained your boons through them, accomplished many undertakings and conquered the guardians of the eight quarters and many earthly sovereign. Now under the influence of royal arrogance, or some delusion, you have carried off Sītā, the mother of the world. Yet hearken to my friendly advice and the Lord will still pardon you. Put a straw between your teeth and an axe to your throat, and with all your family and your wives, and with Janak's daughter placed respectfully in front, go all of you in this way without any alarm,

दोहा-dohā:

प्रनतपाल रघुबंसमनि त्राहि त्राहि अब मोहि ।
pranatapāla raghubaṁsamani trāhi trāhi aba mohi,
आरत गिरा सुनत प्रभु अभय करैगो तोहि ॥ २० ॥
ārata girā sunata prabhu abhaya karaigo tohi. 20.

Trans:

crying, 'O jewel of the race of Raghu, defender of the suppliant, save us, save us', and when he hears your piteous cry the Lord will set your minds at rest."

चौपाई-caupāī:

रे कपिपोत बोलु संभारी । मूढ़ न जानेहि मोहि सुरारी ॥
re kapipota bolu saṁbhārī, mūṛha na jānehi mohi surārī.
कहु निज नाम जनक कर भाई । केहि नातें मानिऐ मिताई ॥
kahu nija nāma janaka kara bhāī, kehi nāteṁ māniai mitāī.
अंगद नाम बालि कर बेटा । तासों कबहुँ भई ही भेटा ॥
aṁgada nāma bāli kara beṭā, tāsoṁ kabahuṁ bhaī hī bheṭā.
अंगद बचन सुनत सकुचाना । रहा बालि बानर मैं जाना ॥
aṁgada bacana sunata sakucānā, rahā bāli bānara maiṁ jānā.
अंगद तहीं बालि कर बालक । उपजेहु बंस अनल कुल घालक ॥
aṁgada tahīṁ bāli kara bālaka, upajehu baṁsa anala kula ghālaka.
गर्भ न गयहु ब्यर्थ तुम्ह जायहु । निज मुख तापस दूत कहायहु ॥
garbha na gayahu byartha tumha jāyahu, nija mukha tāpasa dūta kahāyahu.
अब कहु कुसल बालि कहँ अहई । बिहँसि बचन तब अंगद कहई ॥
aba kahu kusala bāli kahaṁ ahaī, bihaṁsi bacana taba aṁgada kahaī.
दिन दस गएँ बालि पहिं जाई । बूझेहु कुसल सखा उर लाई ॥
dina dasa gaeṁ bāli pahiṁ jāī, būjhehu kusala sakhā ura lāī.
राम बिरोध कुसल जसि होई । सो सब तोहि सुनाइहि सोई ॥
rāma birodha kusala jasi hoī, so saba tohi sunāihi soī.
सुनु सठ भेद होइ मन ताकें । श्रीरघुबीर हृदय नहिं जाकें ॥
sunu saṭha bheda hoi mana tākeṁ, śrīraghubīra hṛdaya nahiṁ jākeṁ.

Trans:

"Ah, you wretched monkey, take care what you say. Fool, do you not know that I am the declared enemy of the gods? Tell me your own name and your father's, my friend, and through what relation you claim an alliance." "My name is Angad; I am the son of Bālī, with whom you once were on terms of friendship." On hearing Angad's reply, he was uncomfortable. "I admit, monkey, that it was so with Bālī; but if Angad is that Bālī's son, then he has been born as a firebrand for the destruction of his race. The womb that bears you, forsooth, was pregnant for nothing—when with your own mouth confess yourself as the hermit's envoy. Tell me now, is all well with Bālī?" Angad laughed and replied: "Ten days hence go to Bālī and embrace your old friend and ask him yourself of his welfare. He will tell you the kind of welfare that results from fighting against Rāma. Hearken fool: the seeds of dissension can be sown in the mind of him alone whose heart is closed to the divine Raghubīr.

दोहा-dohā:

हम कुल घालक सत्य तुम्ह कुल पालक दससीस ।
hama kula ghālaka satya tumha kula pālaka dasasīsa,
अंधउ बधिर न अस कहहिं नयन कान तव बीस ॥ २१ ॥
aṁdhau badhira na asa kahahiṁ nayana kāna tava bīsa. 21,

Trans:

I, forsooth, am the destroyer of my race, while you, Rāvan, are the preserver of yours! Who will not say that you are blind and deaf even with your twenty eyes and twenty ears?

चौपाई-caupāī:

सिव बिरंचि सुर मुनि समुदाई । चाहत जासु चरन सेवकाई ॥
siva biraṁci sura muni samudāī, cāhata jāsu carana sevakāī.

तासु दूत होइ हम कुल बोरा । अइसिहुँ मति उर बिहर न तोरा ॥
tāsu dūta hoi hama kula borā, aisihuṁ mati ura bihara na torā.
सुनि कठोर बानी कपि केरी । कहत दसानन नयन तरेरी ॥
suni kaṭhora bānī kapi kerī, kahata dasānana nayana tarerī.
खल तव कठिन बचन सब सहऊँ । नीति धर्म मैं जानत अहऊँ ॥
khala tava kaṭhina bacana saba sahaūṁ, nīti dharma maiṁ jānata ahaūṁ.
कह कपि धर्मसीलता तोरी । हमहुँ सुनी कृत पर त्रिय चोरी ॥
kaha kapi dharmasīlatā torī, hamahuṁ sunī kṛta para triya corī.
देखी नयन दूत रखवारी । बूड़ि न मरहु धर्म ब्रतधारी ॥
dekhī nayana dūta rakhavārī, būṛi na marahu dharma bratadhārī.
कान नाक बिनु भगिनि निहारी । छमा कीन्हि तुम्ह धर्म बिचारी ॥
kāna nāka binu bhagini nihārī, chamā kīnhi tumha dharma bicārī.
धर्मसीलता तव जग जागी । पावा दरसु हमहुँ बड़भागी ॥
dharmasīlatā tava jaga jāgī, pāvā darasu hamahuṁ baṛabhāgī.

Trans:

What! It is I who disgrace my family by acting as his ambassador, whose feet Shiva and Brahmmā and all the gods and saints desire to serve? Your heart should burst asunder for even entertaining such a thought." When he heard the monkey's fierce rejoinder, Rāvan glared at him and cried, "Wretch, I suffer all your abuse because I know the bounds of decorum and righteousness." Said the monkey, "I too have heard of your piety, which is evident from the fact that you abducted another man's wife. And I have witnessed with my own eyes the protection you vouchsafed to an envoy. An upholder of piety, why do you not drown yourself and thus end your life? When you saw your sister with her ears and nose cut off, evidently it was from considerations of piety that you forgave the wrong! Your piety is famed throughout the world; I too am very fortunate in having been able to see that."

दोहा-dohā:

जनि जल्पसि जड़ जंतु कपि सठ बिलोकु मम बाहु ।
jani jalpasi jaṛa jaṁtu kapi saṭha biloku mama bāhu,
लोकपाल बल बिपुल ससि ग्रसन हेतु सब राहु ॥ २२क॥
lokapāla bala bipula sasi grasana hetu saba rāhu. 22(ka).

पुनि नभ सर मम कर निकर कमलन्हि पर करि बास ।
puni nabha sara mama kara nikara kamalanhi para kari bāsa,
सोभत भयउ मराल इव संभु सहित कैलास ॥ २२ख॥
sobhata bhayau marāla iva saṁbhu sahita kailāsa. 22(kha).

Trans:

"Prate no more, you stupid brute, you impudent monkey, but look at my arms that are the very Rāhus to eclipse the full-moon-like might of the Lokpāls. Shambhu and Kailāsh, in the palm of my lotus hand, were but as the stately swan in the heavenly lake once.

चौपाई-caupāī:

तुम्हरे कटक माझ सुनु अंगद । मो सन भिरिहि कवन जोधा बद ॥
tumhare kaṭaka mājha sunu aṁgada, mo sana bhirihi kavana jodhā bada.
तव प्रभु नारि बिरहँ बलहीना । अनुज तासु दुख दुखी मलीना ॥
tava prabhu nāri birahaṁ balahīnā, anuja tāsu dukha dukhī malīnā.
तुम्ह सुग्रीव कूलद्रुम दोऊ । अनुज हमार भीरु अति सोऊ ॥
tumha sugrīva kūladruma doū, anuja hamāra bhīru ati soū.
जामवंत मंत्री अति बूढ़ा । सो कि होइ अब समरारूढ़ा ॥
jāmavaṁta maṁtrī ati būṛhā, so ki hoi aba samarārūṛhā.
सिल्पि कर्म जानहिं नल नीला । है कपि एक महा बलसीला ॥
silpi karma jānahiṁ nala nīlā, hai kapi eka mahā balasīlā.
आवा प्रथम नगरु जेहिं जारा । सुनत बचन कह बालिकुमारा ॥
āvā prathama nagaru jehiṁ jārā, sunata bacana kaha bālikumārā.
सत्य बचन कहु निसिचर नाहा । साँचेहुँ कीस कीन्ह पुर दाहा ॥
satya bacana kahu nisicara nāhā, sāṁcehuṁ kīsa kīnha pura dāhā.
रावन नगर अल्प कपि दहई । सुनि अस बचन सत्य को कहई ॥
rāvana nagara alpa kapi dahaī, suni asa bacana satya ko kahaī.
जो अति सुभट सराहेहु रावन । सो सुग्रीव केर लघु धावन ॥
jo ati subhaṭa sarāhehu rāvana, so sugrīva kera laghu dhāvana.
चलइ बहुत सो बीर न होई । पठवा खबरि लेन हम सोई ॥
calai bahuta so bīra na hoī, paṭhavā khabari lena hama soī.

Trans:

Hearken Angad, tell me what champion there is in all your army who is a match for me. Your Lord has lost strength through pining for his bride; his younger brother too is all sad and forlorn; you and Sugrīva are each the curse of your family; while my brother is an utter coward. Your counselor, Jāmvant, is so stricken in years that he can no longer enter the field of battle. Nala and Nīl are good architects, and there is one monkey, no doubt, of exceptional strength—he who came first and set fire to the city." On hearing that Angad said, "Tell me the truth now, O demon king: is it a fact that a monkey burnt down your city? A poor little monkey set Rāvan's capital on fire? Who, on hearing this said, could believe it true? He, O Rāvan, whom you extol as so distinguished a champion, is only one of Sugrīva's inferior runners. He is a good one to go but no fighter: we only sent him here to get news.

दोहा-dohā:

सत्य नगरु कपि जारेउ बिनु प्रभु आयसु पाइ ।
satya nagaru kapi jāreu binu prabhu āyasu pāi,
फिरि न गयउ सुग्रीव पहिं तेहिं भय रहा लुकाइ ॥ २३क॥
phiri na gayau sugrīva pahiṁ tehiṁ bhaya rahā lukāi. 23(ka).

सत्य कहहि दसकंठ सब मोहि न सुनि कछु कोह ।
satya kahahi dasakaṁṭha saba mohi na suni kachu koha,
कोउ न हमारें कटक अस तो सन लरत जो सोह ॥ २३ख॥
kou na hamāreṁ kaṭaka asa to sana larata jo soha. 23(kha).

प्रीति बिरोध समान सन करिअ नीति असि आहि ।
prīti birodha samāna sana karia nīti asi āhi,
जौं मृगपति बध मेड़ुकन्हि भल कि कहइ कोउ ताहि ॥ २३ग॥
jauṁ mṛgapati badha meḍukanhi bhala ki kahai kou tāhi. 23(ga).

जद्यपि लघुता राम कहुँ तोहि बधें बड़ दोष ।
jadyapi laghutā rāma kahuṁ tohi badheṁ baṛa doṣa,
तदपि कठिन दसकंठ सुनु छत्र जाति कर रोष ॥ २३घ॥
tadapi kaṭhina dasakaṁṭha sunu chatra jāti kara roṣa. 23(gha).

बक्र उक्ति धनु बचन सर हृदय दहेउ रिपु कीस ।
bakra ukti dhanu bacana sara hṛdaya daheu ripu kīsa,
प्रतिउत्तर सड़सिन्ह मनहुँ काढ़त भट दससीस ॥ २३ङ॥
pratiuttara saṛasinha manahuṁ kāṛhata bhaṭa dasasīsa. 23(ṅa).

हँसि बोलेउ दसमौलि तब कपि कर बड़ गुन एक ।
haṁsi boleu dasamauli taba kapi kara baṛa guna eka,
जो प्रतिपालइ तासु हित करइ उपाय अनेक ॥ २३च॥
jo pratipālai tāsu hita karai upāya aneka. 23(ca).

Trans:

Is it true that a monkey set fire to this city without any orders from our Lord? This is why he did not go back to Sugrīva, but kept himself out of sight for fear. All that you have said, Rāvan, is quite true, and I am not in the least angry at hearing it; there is not anyone in our army who would be a fair match for you. Take your friends and enemies from among your equals is a good sound maxim: if a lion kills frogs who thinks it a fine deed? Though it is no glory for Rāma to kill you, however great your offence, still, mark me, O Rāvan, the fury of the Kshatriya clan is hard to withstand." The monkey foe set his heart on fire with the arrows of speech shot forth from the bow of sarcastic eloquence, and it was, so to speak, only with a pair of pincers that the dauntless Rāvan could get out a rejoinder. At last he laughed and cried, "A monkey has at all events one good quality; he will do anything to serve the man who feeds him.

चौपाई-caupāī:

धन्य कीस जो निज प्रभु काजा । जहँ तहँ नाचइ परिहरि लाजा ॥
dhanya kīsa jo nija prabhu kājā, jahaṁ tahaṁ nācai parihari lājā.
नाचि कूदि करि लोग रिझाई । पति हित करइ धर्म निपुनाई ॥
nāci kūdi kari loga rijhāī, pati hita karai dharma nipunāī.
अंगद स्वामिभक्त तव जाती । प्रभु गुन कस न कहसि एहि भाँती ॥
aṁgada svāmibhakta tava jātī, prabhu guna kasa na kahasi ehi bhāṁtī.
मैं गुन गाहक परम सुजाना । तव कटु रटनि करउँ नहिं काना ॥
maiṁ guna gāhaka parama sujānā, tava kaṭu raṭani karauṁ nahiṁ kānā.
कह कपि तव गुन गाहकताई । सत्य पवनसुत मोहि सुनाई ॥
kaha kapi tava guna gāhakatāī, satya pavanasuta mohi sunāī.
बन बिधंसि सुत बधि पुर जारा । तदपि न तेहिं कछु कृत अपकारा ॥
bana bidhaṁsi suta badhi pura jārā, tadapi na tehiṁ kachu kṛta apakārā.
सोइ बिचारि तव प्रकृति सुहाई । दसकंधर मैं कीन्हि ढिठाई ॥
soi bicāri tava prakṛti suhāī, dasakaṁdhara maiṁ kīnhi ḍhiṭhāī.
देखेउँ आइ जो कछु कपि भाषा । तुम्हरें लाज न रोष न माखा ॥
dekheuṁ āi jo kachu kapi bhāṣā, tumhareṁ lāja na roṣa na mākhā.
जौं असि मति पितु खाए कीसा । कहि अस बचन हँसा दससीसा ॥
jauṁ asi mati pitu khāe kīsā, kahi asa bacana haṁsā dasasīsā.
पितहि खाइ खातेउँ पुनि तोही । अबहीं समुझि परा कछु मोही ॥
pitahi khāi khāteuṁ puni tohī, abahīṁ samujhi parā kachu mohī.
बालि बिमल जस भाजन जानी । हतउँ न तोहि अधम अभिमानी ॥
bāli bimala jasa bhājana jānī, hatauṁ na tohi adhama abhimānī.
कहु रावन रावन जग केते । मैं निज श्रवन सुने सुनु जेते ॥
kahu rāvana rāvana jaga kete, maiṁ nija śravana sune sunu jete.
बलिहि जितन एक गयउ पताला । राखेउ बाँधि सिसुन्ह हयसाला ॥
balihi jitana eka gayau patālā, rākheu bāṁdhi sisunha hayasālā.
खेलहिं बालक मारहिं जाई । दया लागि बलि दीन्ह छोड़ाई ॥
khelahiṁ bālaka mārahiṁ jāī, dayā lāgi bali dīnha choṛāī.
एक बहोरि सहसभुज देखा । धाइ धरा जिमि जंतु बिसेषा ॥
eka bahori sahasabhuja dekhā, dhāi dharā jimi jaṁtu biseṣā.
कौतुक लागि भवन लै आवा । सो पुलस्ति मुनि जाइ छोड़ावा ॥
kautuka lāgi bhavana lai āvā, so pulasti muni jāi choṛāvā.

Trans:

Bravo for a monkey who regardless of shame dances up and down in his master's service; dancing and jumping about to amuse the people, he does his duty for his master quite well. Your entire race, Angad, is devoted to their Lord; it is quite natural for you to speak of your master's good qualities in the way you do. I am very sagacious in appreciating merit, and therefore I pay no attention to your insolent tirade." Said the monkey, "Hanumān gave me a very true account of your generosity. Though he had laid waste your garden, killed your son and set fire to your city, still you would not do him any harm. It was in reliance upon your magnanimity, Rāvan, that I have been thus outspoken. Now that I am here, I see that whatever a monkey may say will neither put you to shame nor excite you to anger or resentment." "It is because you possess such a mentality that you have proved to be the death of your own father," uttering so, the Ten-headed burst into a laugh. "Having been the death of my father I would have next claimed you as my victim; but a thought has come to me just now. Knowing you to be a living memorial of Bālī's unsullied fame, I desist from killing you, you wretched braggart. Come, Rāvan, tell me how many Rāvans there are in the world, or listen while I tell you how many I have heard of: One went down into hell to conquer Bālī, where the children tied him up in the stable and made sport of him and buffeted him, until Bālī took pity on him and let him go. Another again was discovered by Sahastr-bahu, who ran and secured him as a curiosity and took him home for a show, till saint Pulastya came and rescued him.

दोहा-dohā:

एक कहत मोहि सकुच अति रहा बालि कीं काँख ।
eka kahata mohi sakuca ati rahā bāli kīṁ kāṁkha,
इन्ह महुँ रावन तैं कवन सत्य बदहि तजि माख ॥ २४॥
inha mahuṁ rāvana taiṁ kavana satya badahi taji mākha. 24.

Trans:

Another, as I am ashamed to say, was held tight under Bālī's armpit for months. Do not be angry, Rāvan, but tell me the truth, which of all these are you?"

चौपाई-caupāī:

सुनु सठ सोइ रावन बलसीला । हरगिरि जान जासु भुज लीला ॥
sunu saṭha soi rāvana balasīlā, haragiri jāna jāsu bhuja līlā.
जान उमापति जासु सुराई । पूजेउँ जेहि सिर सुमन चढ़ाई ॥
jāna umāpati jāsu surāī, pūjeuṁ jehi sira sumana caṛhāī.
सिर सरोज निज करन्हि उतारी । पूजेउँ अमित बार त्रिपुरारी ॥
sira saroja nija karanhi utārī, pūjeuṁ amita bāra tripurārī.
भुज बिक्रम जानहिं दिगपाला । सठ अजहूँ जिन्ह कें उर साला ॥
bhuja bikrama jānahiṁ digapālā, saṭha ajahūṁ jinha keṁ ura sālā.
जानहिं दिग्गज उर कठिनाई । जब जब भिरउँ जाइ बरिआई ॥
jānahiṁ diggaja ura kaṭhināī, jaba jaba bhirauṁ jāi bariāī.
जिन्ह के दसन कराल न फूटे । उर लागत मूलक इव टूटे ॥
jinha ke dasana karāla na phūṭe, ura lāgata mūlaka iva ṭūṭe.
जासु चलत डोलति इमि धरनी । चढ़त मत्त गज जिमि लघु तरनी ॥
jāsu calata ḍolati imi dharanī, caṛhata matta gaja jimi laghu taranī.
सोइ रावन जग बिदित प्रतापी । सुनेहि न श्रवन अलीक प्रलापी ॥
soi rāvana jaga bidita pratāpī, sunehi na śravana alīka pralāpī.

Trans:

"Hearken O fool, I am that mighty Rāvan, the action of whose arms is well-known by Kailāsh and whose valor known by Shiva, for him I worshipped not with flowers but with my own lotus-like heads, which I took off with my own hands innumerable times when I worshipped Tripurārī. The guardians of the eight quarters know the might of my arms; in their heart, you fool, is sore distress today. The toughness of my chest is familiar to the elephants supporting the eight quarters, whose fierce tusks, whenever I impetuously grappled with them, failed to make any impression on it and snapped off like radishes the moment they struck against it. When I move, the earth quivers like a small boat when a wild elephant steps into it. I am that glorious and renowned Rāvan; have you no ears to hear, you lying prattler?

दोहा-dohā:

तेहि रावन कहँ लघु कहसि नर कर करसि बखान ।
tehi rāvana kahaṁ laghu kahasi nara kara karasi bakhāna,
रे कपि बर्बर खर्ब खल अब जाना तव ग्यान ॥ २५॥
re kapi barbara kharba khala aba jānā tava gyāna. 25.

Trans:

This is the Rāvan of whom you make light, while you exalt a mere man? Ah vile monkey, infamous wretch, are you at last beginning to understand?"

चौपाई-caupāī:

सुनि अंगद सकोप कह बानी । बोलु सँभारि अधम अभिमानी ॥
suni aṁgada sakopa kaha bānī, bolu saṁbhāri adhama abhimānī.
सहसबाहु भुज गहन अपारा । दहन अनल सम जासु कुठारा ॥
sahasabāhu bhuja gahana apārā, dahana anala sama jāsu kuṭhārā.
जासु परसु सागर खर धारा । बूड़े नृप अगनित बहु बारा ॥
jāsu parasu sāgara khara dhārā, būṛe nṛpa aganita bahu bārā.
तासु गर्ब जेहि देखत भागा । सो नर क्यों दससीस अभागा ॥
tāsu garba jehi dekhata bhāgā, so nara kyoṁ dasasīsa abhāgā.
राम मनुज कस रे सठ बंगा । धन्वी कामु नदी पुनि गंगा ॥
rāma manuja kasa re saṭha baṁgā, dhanvī kāmu nadī puni gaṁgā.
पसु सुरधेनु कल्पतरु रूखा । अन्न दान अरु रस पीयूषा ॥
pasu suradhenu kalpataru rūkhā, anna dāna aru rasa pīyūṣā.
बैनतेय खग अहि सहसानन । चिंतामनि पुनि उपल दसानन ॥
bainateya khaga ahi sahasānana, ciṁtāmani puni upala dasānana.
सुनु मतिमंद लोक बैकुंठा । लाभ कि रघुपति भगति अकुंठा ॥
sunu matimaṁda loka baikuṁṭhā, lābha ki raghupati bhagati akuṁṭhā.

Trans:

On hearing this, Angad replied indignantly: "Give up talking, you pitiful boaster. He, whose axe was like a fire to consume Sahastr-bahu's mighty forest of arms; whose sword was like the tide of the salt sea in which kings innumerable have been drowned time after time; and at the sight of whose majesty everyone took to flight, how can he be a mere man, you wretched Rāvan? How can Rāma be a mere man, you arrogant fool? Is Kāmdev an ordinary archer? Is the Gangā merely a river? The cow of plenty merely an animal? The tree of Paradise only a tree? Is charity only so much gain? Is ambrosia merely liquid? Garud simply a bird? Sheshnāg a serpent? And the philosopher's stone, just a trifle stone, O Rāvan? Hearken O dull of understanding, is Vaikūnth an ordinary sphere? Is an unflinching devotion to Rāma an ordinary gain?

दोहा-dohā:

सेन सहित तव मान मथि बन उजारि पुर जारि ।
sena sahita tava māna mathi bana ujāri pura jāri,
कस रे सठ हनुमान कपि गयउ जो तव सुत मारि ॥२६॥
kasa re saṭha hanumāna kapi gayau jo tava suta māri. 26.

Trans:

Fool, how was it that the monkey Hanumān escaped, after trampling on the pride of you and your army, laying waste your garden, setting fire to your city and slaying your son?

चौपाई-caupāī:

सुनु रावन परिहरि चतुराई । भजसि न कृपासिंधु रघुराई ॥
sunu rāvana parihari caturāī, bhajasi na kṛpāsiṁdhu raghurāī.
जौं खल भएसि राम कर द्रोही । ब्रह्म रुद्र सक राखि न तोही ॥
jauṁ khala bhaesi rāma kara drohī, brahma rudra saka rākhi na tohī.
मूढ़ बृथा जनि मारसि गाला । राम बयर अस होइहि हाला ॥
mūṛha bṛthā jani mārasi gālā, rāma bayara asa hoihi hālā.
तव सिर निकर कपिन्ह के आगें । परिहहिं धरनि राम सर लागें ॥
tava sira nikara kapinha ke āgeṁ, parihahiṁ dharani rāma sara lāgeṁ.
ते तव सिर कंदुक सम नाना । खेलिहहिं भालु कीस चौगाना ॥
te tava sira kaṁduka sama nānā, khelihahiṁ bhālu kīsa caugānā.
जबहिं समर कोपिहि रघुनायक । छुटिहहिं अति कराल बहु सायक ॥
jabahiṁ samara kopihi raghunāyaka, chuṭihahiṁ ati karāla bahu sāyaka.
तब कि चलिहि अस गाल तुम्हारा । अस बिचारि भजु राम उदारा ॥
taba ki calihi asa gāla tumhārā, asa bicāri bhaju rāma udārā.
सुनत बचन रावन परजरा । जरत महानल जनु घृत परा ॥
sunata bacana rāvana parajarā, jarata mahānala janu ghṛta parā.

Trans:

Hearken Rāvan: be done with your conceit and go worship Rāma, the All-merciful. If you are foolish enough to provoke Rāma, neither Brahmmā nor Rudra has the power to protect you. Do not puff yourself out with vain delusions; if you fight against Rāma, this will be your fate: smitten by Rāma's arrows, your many heads will roll on the ground in front of the monkeys, and they and the bears will play game with them, like so many balls. When Rāma waxes wroth in battle, his arrows fly quick and terrible. Will you then persist in your vain boasting and be a little wise and adore him and seek clemency?" On hearing these words Rāvan flared up afresh, like a blazing fire upon which oil has been thrown.

दोहा-dohā:

कुंभकरन अस बंधु मम सुत प्रसिद्ध सक्रारि ।
kuṁbhakarana asa baṁdhu mama suta prasiddha sakrāri,
मोर पराक्रम नहिं सुनेहि जितेउँ चराचर झारि ॥२७॥
mora parākrama nahiṁ sunehi jiteuṁ carācara jhāri. 27.

Trans:

"Have you never heard of my brother Kumbh-karan, and my renowned son Indrajit, and of my own valor—by which I have conquered the whole universe?

चौपाई-caupāī:

सठ साखामृग जोरि सहाई । बाँधा सिंधु इहइ प्रभुताई ॥
saṭha sākhāmṛga jori sahāī, bāṁdhā siṁdhu ihai prabhutāī.
नाघहिं खग अनेक बारीसा । सूर न होहिं ते सुनु सब कीसा ॥
nāghahiṁ khaga aneka bārīsā, sūra na hohiṁ te sunu saba kīsā.
मम भुज सागर बल जल पूरा । जहँ बूड़े बहु सुर नर सूरा ॥
mama bhuja sāgara bala jala pūrā, jahaṁ būṛe bahu sura nara sūrā.
बीस पयोधि अगाध अपारा । को अस बीर जो पाइहि पारा ॥
bīsa payodhi agādha apārā, ko asa bīra jo pāihi pārā.
दिगपालन्ह मैं नीर भरावा । भूप सुजस खल मोहि सुनावा ॥
digapālanha maiṁ nīra bharāvā, bhūpa sujasa khala mohi sunāvā.
जौं पै समर सुभट तव नाथा । पुनि पुनि कहसि जासु गुन गाथा ॥
jauṁ pai samara subhaṭa tava nāthā, puni puni kahasi jāsu guna gāthā.
तौ बसीठ पठवत केहि काजा । रिपु सन प्रीति करत नहिं लाजा ॥
tau basīṭha paṭhavata kehi kājā, ripu sana prīti karata nahiṁ lājā.
हरगिरि मथन निरखु मम बाहू । पुनि सठ कपि निज प्रभुहि सराहू ॥
haragiri mathana nirakhu mama bāhū, puni saṭha kapi nija prabhuhi sarāhū.

Trans:

Fool, with the help of his monkey friends he has bridged the sea, but what is that to be proud of? Birds innumerable traverse the ocean, yet they are no heroes. Now mark me, monkey: my arms are like a sea filled with a flood of strength, beneath which many gods, men and heroes have been drowned. Who is there so strong that he can overcome these twenty unfathomable, boundless oceans? I make even the *Digpāls* draw water for me. You have told me, poor wretch, of your king's renown, but if your Lord is really so valiant in battle, as one would judge from the way in which you harp upon his achievements, then why does he send an envoy? Is he not ashamed to make terms with an enemy? Look at my arms, which could treat mount Kailāsh as a mere churning-stick, and then, foolish monkey, sing, if you like, the praises of your Lord.

दोहा-dohā:

सूर कवन रावन सरिस स्वकर काटि जेहिं सीस ।
sūra kavana rāvana sarisa svakara kāṭi jehiṁ sīsa,
हुने अनल अति हरष बहु बार साखि गौरीस ॥२८॥
hune anala ati haraṣa bahu bāra sākhi gaurīsa. 28.

Trans:

What hero is there equal to Rāvan, who, with his own hands, cut off his own heads, and delighted to cast them into the fire, time after time—with Shiva as the witness?

चौपाई-caupāī:

जरत बिलोकेउँ जबहिं कपाला । बिधि के लिखे अंक निज भाला ॥
jarata bilokeuṁ jabahiṁ kapālā, bidhi ke likhe aṁka nija bhālā.
नर कें कर आपन बध बाँची । हसेउँ जानि बिधि गिरा असाँची ॥
nara keṁ kara āpana badha bāṁcī, haseuṁ jāni bidhi girā asāṁcī.
सोउ मन समुझि त्रास नहिं मोरें । लिखा बिरंचि जरठ मति भोरें ॥
sou mana samujhi trāsa nahiṁ moreṁ, likhā biraṁci jaraṭha mati bhoreṁ.
आन बीर बल सठ मम आगें । पुनि पुनि कहसि लाज पति त्यागें ॥
āna bīra bala saṭha mama āgeṁ, puni puni kahasi lāja pati tyāgeṁ.
कह अंगद सलज्ज जग माहीं । रावन तोहि समान कोउ नाहीं ॥
kaha aṁgada salajja jaga māhīṁ, rāvana tohi samāna kou nāhīṁ.
लाजवंत तव सहज सुभाऊ । निज मुख निज गुन कहसि न काऊ ॥
lājavaṁta tava sahaja subhāū, nija mukha nija guna kahasi na kāū.
सिर अरु सैल कथा चित रही । ताते बार बीस तैं कही ॥
sira aru saila kathā cita rahī, tāte bāra bīsa taiṁ kahī.
सो भुजबल राखेउ उर घाली । जीतेहु सहसबाहु बलि बाली ॥
so bhujabala rākheu ura ghālī, jītehu sahasabāhu bali bālī.
सुनु मतिमंद देहि अब पूरा । काटें सीस कि होइअ सूरा ॥
sunu matimaṁda dehi aba pūrā, kāṭeṁ sīsa ki hoia sūrā.
इंद्रजालि कहु कहिअ न बीरा । काटइ निज कर सकल सरीरा ॥
iṁdrajāli kahu kahia na bīrā, kāṭai nija kara sakala sarīrā.

Trans:

When, as my skulls began to burn, I saw the decree of Providence traced on my brow and read that I was going to die at the hands of a mortal, I laughed—for I knew Brahmmā's prophecy to be false. When I remember this, I have no fear: Brahmmā must have written that when he was old and stupid. Are you not ashamed, you fool, to keep boasting of any warrior's strength as compared with mine?" Angad replied, "There is no one in the whole world, Rāvan, so shamefaced as you. Your modesty is so innate that you never yourself speak of your own merits. You are always thinking of the old story of your heads and the mountain, and that is the reason why you tell it to me twenty times over. But that very so-called strength of arm by which you couldn't overcame Sahastr-bahu and Bālī—that you bury deep in your heart. Now hearken, O dull of soul, brag no more; if a man who cuts off his head is a hero, what a hero then must a magician be—who with his own hands cuts his whole body to pieces?

दोहा-dohā:

जरहिं पतंग मोह बस भार बहहिं खर बृंद ।
jarahiṁ pataṁga moha basa bhāra bahahiṁ khara bṛṁda,
ते नहिं सूर कहावहिं समुझि देखु मतिमंद ॥२९॥
te nahiṁ sūra kahāvahiṁ samujhi dekhu matimaṁda. 29.

Trans:

Ponder, O fool, and see for yourself: a moth is infatuated enough to burn itself to death [like your head sacrifice]; and an ass bears much burden [O mountain bearing ass]; but such are not called heroes.

चौपाई-caupāī:

अब जनि बतबढ़ाव खल करही । सुनु मम बचन मान परिहरही ॥
aba jani batabaṛhāva khala karahī, sunu mama bacana māna pariharahī.
दसमुख मैं न बसीठीं आयउँ । अस बिचारि रघुबीर पठायउँ ॥
dasamukha maiṁ na basīṭhīṁ āyauṁ, asa bicāri raghubīra paṭhāyauṁ.
बार बार अस कहइ कृपाला । नहिं गजारि जसु बधें सृकाला ॥
bāra bāra asa kahai kṛpālā, nahiṁ gajāri jasu badheṁ sṛkālā.
मन महुँ समुझि बचन प्रभु केरे । सहेउँ कठोर बचन सठ तेरे ॥
mana mahuṁ samujhi bacana prabhu kere, saheuṁ kaṭhora bacana saṭha tere.
नाहिं त करि मुख भंजन तोरा । लै जातेउँ सीतहि बरजोरा ॥
nāhiṁ ta kari mukha bhaṁjana torā, lai jāteuṁ sītahi barajorā.
जानेउँ तव बल अधम सुरारी । सूनें हरि आनिहि परनारी ॥
jāneuṁ tava bala adhama surārī, sūneṁ hari ānihi paranārī.
तैं निसिचरपति गर्ब बहूता । मैं रघुपति सेवक कर दूता ॥
taiṁ nisicarapati garba bahūtā, maiṁ raghupati sevaka kara dūtā.
जौं न राम अपमानहि डरउँ । तोहि देखत अस कौतुक करऊँ ॥
jauṁ na rāma apamānahi ḍarauṁ, tohi dekhata asa kautuka karaūṁ.

Trans:

Boast no more in arrogant wise, but listen modestly to my advice. I have not come, O Rāvan, as an envoy to propose terms, but Raghubīr has sent me with another motive. In his mercy he has said again and again, 'It is no honor for a lion to kill a jackal.' Pondering at heart to my Lord's words, I have submitted to your injurious speech, wretch, otherwise, I would have broken your head and carried off Sītā by force. I know of your strength, O vile enemy of heaven, just from the fact that you robbed someone's wife when no one else was about. You are a haughty demon king, and I am the messenger of one of Rāma's servants; I would be disrespectful to Rama if I disobey him, else I myself would make a perfect spectacle of you right now.

दोहा-dohā:

तोहि पटकि महि सेन हति चौपट करि तव गाउँ ।
tohi paṭaki mahi sena hati caupaṭa kari tava gāuṁ,
तव जुबतिन्ह समेत सठ जनकसुतहि लै जाउँ ॥३०॥
tava jubatinha sameta saṭha janakasutahi lai jāuṁ. 30.

Trans:

Dashing you to the ground, destroying your army and laying waste to your city, O fool, I would have taken away Janak's daughter along with all the ladies of your house.

चौपाई-caupāī:

जौं अस करौं तदपि न बड़ाई । मुएहि बधें नहिं कछु मनुसाई ॥
jauṁ asa karauṁ tadapi na baṛāī, muehi badheṁ nahiṁ kachu manusāī.
कौल कामबस कृपिन बिमूढ़ा । अति दरिद्र अजसी अति बूढ़ा ॥
kaula kāmabasa kṛpina bimūṛhā, ati daridra ajasī ati būṛhā.
सदा रोगबस संतत क्रोधी । बिष्नु बिमुख श्रुति संत बिरोधी ॥
sadā rogabasa saṁtata krodhī, biṣnu bimukha śruti saṁta birodhī.
तनु पोषक निंदक अघ खानी । जीवत सव सम चौदह प्रानी ॥
tanu poṣaka niṁdaka agha khānī, jīvata sava sama caudaha prānī.
अस बिचारि खल बधउँ न तोही । अब जनि रिस उपजावसि मोही ॥
asa bicāri khala badhauṁ na tohī, aba jani risa upajāvasi mohī.
सुनि सकोप कह निसिचर नाथा । अधर दसन दसि मीजत हाथा ॥
suni sakopa kaha nisicara nāthā, adhara dasana dasi mījata hāthā.
रे कपि अधम मरन अब चहसी । छोटे बदन बात बड़ि कहसी ॥
re kapi adhama marana aba cahasī, choṭe badana bāta baṛi kahasī.
कटु जल्पसि जड़ कपि बल जाकें । बल प्रताप बुधि तेज न ताकें ॥
kaṭu jalpasi jaṛa kapi bala jākeṁ, bala pratāpa budhi teja na tākeṁ.

Trans:

Even if I did so, it would still be no great matter; there is no valor shown in slaying the slain. An outcast, a man mad with lust, a miser, a destitute beggar, a man in disgrace, a man in extreme old age, one who is always ill or always in a passion, a rebel against Vishnu, a hater of religion and the saints, a man who thinks only of his own body, a scandal-monger and a man thoroughly vicious—these twelve even while they live are no better than corpses. On this account, wretch, I do not slay you, but do provoke me no further." On hearing this, the demon king cried in fury, "Though small of stature, you have spoken big words. O foolish monkey, he, whose might you so fiercely vaunt, has no might, or sense, or glory at all.

दोहा-dohā:

अगुन अमान जानि तेहि दीन्ह पिता बनबास ।
aguna amāna jāni tehi dīnha pitā banabāsa,
सो दुख अरु जुबती बिरह पुनि निसि दिन मम त्रास ॥३१क॥
so dukha aru jubatī biraha puni nisi dina mama trāsa. 31(ka).

जिन्ह के बल कर गर्ब तोहि अइसे मनुज अनेक ।
jinha ke bala kara garba tohi aise manuja aneka,
खाहिं निसाचर दिवस निसि मूढ़ समुझु तजि टेक ॥३१ख॥
khāhiṁ nisācara divasa nisi mūṛha samujhu taji ṭeka. 31(kha).

Trans:

Seeing him to be of no worth or dignity, his father banished him, which is a sorrow to him as also the loss of his wife; and his terror of me, oppresses him day and night. Proud as you are of his might, there are thousands of men like him, whom my demons devour all day and night. Cease your perverseness, O fool, and come to your sense."

चौपाई-caupāī:

जब तेहिं कीन्हि राम कै निंदा । क्रोधवंत अति भयउ कपिंदा ॥
jaba tehiṁ kīnhi rāma kai niṁdā, krodhavaṁta ati bhayau kapiṁdā.
हरि हर निंदा सुनइ जो काना । होइ पाप गोघात समाना ॥
hari hara niṁdā sunai jo kānā, hoi pāpa goghāta samānā.
कटकटान कपिकुंजर भारी । दुहु भुजदंड तमकि महि मारी ॥
kaṭakaṭāna kapikuṁjara bhārī, duhu bhujadaṁḍa tamaki mahi mārī.
डोलत धरनि सभासद खसे । चले भाजि भय मारुत ग्रसे ॥
ḍolata dharani sabhāsada khase, cale bhāji bhaya māruta grase.
गिरत सँभारि उठा दसकंधर । भूतल परे मुकुट अति सुंदर ॥
girata saṁbhāri uṭhā dasakaṁdhara, bhūtala pare mukuṭa ati suṁdara.
कछु तेहिं लै निज सिरन्हि सँवारे । कछु अंगद प्रभु पास पबारे ॥
kachu tehiṁ lai nija siranhi saṁvāre, kachu aṁgada prabhu pāsa pabāre.
आवत मुकुट देखि कपि भागे । दिनहीं लूक परन बिधि लागे ॥
āvata mukuṭa dekhi kapi bhāge, dinahīṁ lūka parana bidhi lāge.
की रावन करि कोप चलाए । कुलिस चारि आवत अति धाए ॥
kī rāvana kari kopa calāe, kulisa cāri āvata ati dhāe.
कह प्रभु हँसि जनि हृदयँ डेराहू । लूक न असनि केतु नहिं राहू ॥
kaha prabhu haṁsi jani hṛdayaṁ ḍerāhū, lūka na asani ketu nahiṁ rāhū.
ए किरीट दसकंधर केरे । आवत बालितनय के प्रेरे ॥
e kirīṭa dasakaṁdhara kere, āvata bālitanaya ke prere.

Trans:

When he thus abused Rāma, the monkey prince waxed wroth. Those who open their ears to attacks upon Harī and Hara are guilty as if they had killed a cow. The huge monkey gave a loud yell and furiously struck both his mighty arms against the ground. The earth shook, the assembly quaked and took to flight as if driven by a hurricane of terror. The ten-headed monster too was about to topple down but recovered himself and stood up; but his magnificent diadems had fallen to the ground; part he took and re-arranged on his heads, and part Angad dispatched to his Lord. When the monkeys saw the crowns coming, they ran away, crying, "Good God, here are stars falling in the day time, or Rāvan in his fury has sent forth four thunderbolts that come with rushing speed." The Lord smiled and said, "Fear not at heart; here is no star, nor sword, nor either Ketu or Rāhu; those are Rāvan's crowns, which come as dispatched by the son of Bālī."

दोहा-dohā:

तरकि पवनसुत कर गहे आनि धरे प्रभु पास ।
taraki pavanasuta kara gahe āni dhare prabhu pāsa,
कौतुक देखहिं भालु कपि दिनकर सरिस प्रकास ॥३२क॥
kautuka dekhahiṁ bhālu kapi dinakara sarisa prakāsa. 32(ka).

उहाँ सकोपि दसानन सब सन कहत रिसाइ ।
uhāṁ sakopi dasānana saba sana kahata risāi,
धरहु कपिहि धरि मारहु सुनि अंगद मुसुकाइ ॥३२ख॥
dharahu kapihi dhari mārahu suni aṁgada musukāi. 32(kha).

Trans:

The son-of-wind sprang forward and caught them in his hand and brought and laid them at his Lord's feet; the bears and monkeys gazed in astonishment at the sight, for their brilliancy was like that of the sun. On the other hand, Rāvan in his wrath cried furiously to one and all: "seize the monkey, seize him and kill him." Angad heard and simply smiled.

चौपाई-caupāī:

एहि बधि बेगि सुभट सब धावहु । खाहु भालु कपि जहँ जहँ पावहु ॥
ehi badhi begi subhaṭa saba dhāvahu, khāhu bhālu kapi jahaṁ jahaṁ pāvahu.
मर्कटहीन करहु महि जाई । जिअत धरहु तापस द्वौ भाई ॥
markaṭahīna karahu mahi jāī, jiata dharahu tāpasa dvau bhāī.
पुनि सकोप बोलेउ जुबराजा । गाल बजावत तोहि न लाजा ॥
puni sakopa boleu jubarājā, gāla bajāvata tohi na lājā.
मरु गर काटि निलज कुलघाती । बल बिलोकि बिहरति नहिं छाती ॥
maru gara kāṭi nilaja kulaghātī, bala biloki biharati nahiṁ chātī.
रे त्रिय चोर कुमारग गामी । खल मल रासि मंदमति कामी ॥
re triya cora kumāraga gāmī, khala mala rāsi maṁdamati kāmī.
सन्यपात जल्पसि दुर्बादा । भएसि कालबस खल मनुजादा ॥
sanyapāta jalpasi durbādā, bhaesi kālabasa khala manujādā.
याको फलु पावहिगो आगें । बानर भालु चपेटन्हि लागें ॥
yāko phalu pāvahigo āgeṁ, bānara bhālu capeṭanhi lāgeṁ.
रामु मनुज बोलत असि बानी । गिरहिं न तव रसना अभिमानी ॥
rāmu manuja bolata asi bānī, girahiṁ na tava rasanā abhimānī.
गिरिहहिं रसना संसय नाहीं । सिरन्हि समेत समर महि माहीं ॥
girihahiṁ rasanā saṁsaya nāhīṁ, siranhi sameta samara mahi māhīṁ.

Trans:

"Further, in like manner sally forth in haste, all ye mighty men, and devour every bear and monkey wherever ye find one. Go and leave not a single monkey in the whole world, but take alive the two hermit brothers." The prince replied indignantly, "Are you not ashamed to bluster like this. Cut your throat and die, you reckless destroyer of your race. Does not your heart crack at the sight of his power? Ah! villainous woman-stealer, a storehouse of all that is mean and impure, you sensual dullard—you still babble abuse though at the doorstep of death? Fate has you in his toils, wretched cannibal. Hereafter you shall reap the fruit of this, when the bears and monkeys belabor you, but when you thus speak of Rāma as a man, I wonder your proud tongue does not drop off; and beyond a doubt it will drop off to the ground, head and all, in the battle.

सोरठा-sorațhā:

सो नर क्यों दसकंध बालि बध्यो जेहिं एक सर ।
so nara kyoṁ dasakaṁdha bāli badhyo jehiṁ eka sara,
बीसहुँ लोचन अंध धिग तव जन्म कुजाति जड़ ॥३३क॥
bīsahuṁ locana aṁdha dhiga tava janma kujāti jaṛa. 33(ka).

तव सोनित कीं प्यास तृषित राम सायक निकर ।

tava sonita kīṁ pyāsa tṛṣita rāma sāyaka nikara,

तजउँ तोहि तेहि त्रास कटु जल्पक निसिचर अधम ॥३३ख॥

tajauṁ tohi tehi trāsa kaṭu jalpaka nisicara adhama. 33(kha).

Trans:

How can he be a mere man, O Rāvan, who slew Bālī with a single arrow? You are blind with all your twenty eyes. Fie upon your birth, O dullard of ignoble womb! Rāma's arrows are all athirst to drink your blood; for fear of him I spare you, insolent boaster, contemptible demon.

चौपाई-caupāī:

मैं तव दसन तोरिबे लायक । आयसु मोहि न दीन्ह रघुनायक ॥

maiṁ tava dasana toribe lāyaka, āyasu mohi na dīnha raghunāyaka.

असि रिस होति दसउ मुख तोरौं । लंका गहि समुद्र महँ बोरौं ॥

asi risa hoti dasau mukha toraum̐, laṁkā gahi samudra maham̐ boraum̐.

गूलरि फल समान तव लंका । बसहु मध्य तुम्ह जंतु असंका ॥

gūlari phala samāna tava laṁkā, basahu madhya tumha jaṁtu asaṁkā.

मैं बानर फल खात न बारा । आयसु दीन्ह न राम उदारा ॥

maiṁ bānara phala khāta na bārā, āyasu dīnha na rāma udārā.

जुगुति सुनत रावन मुसुकाई । मूढ़ सिखिहि कहँ बहुत झुठाई ॥

juguti sunata rāvana musukāī, mūṛha sikhihi kaham̐ bahuta jhuṭhāī.

बालि न कबहुँ गाल अस मारा । मिलि तपसिन्ह तैं भएसि लबारा ॥

bāli na kabahum̐ gāla asa mārā, mili tapasinha taiṁ bhaesi labārā.

साँचेहुँ मैं लबार भुज बीहा । जौं न उपारिउँ तव दस जीहा ॥

sām̐cehum̐ maiṁ labāra bhuja bīhā, jauṁ na upārium̐ tava dasa jīhā.

समुझि राम प्रताप कपि कोपा । सभा माझ पन करि पद रोपा ॥

samujhi rāma pratāpa kapi kopā, sabhā mājha pana kari pada ropā.

जौं मम चरन सकसि सठ टारी । फिरहिं रामु सीता मैं हारी ॥

jauṁ mama carana sakasi saṭha ṭārī, phirahiṁ rāmu sītā maiṁ hārī.

सुनहु सुभट सब कह दससीसा । पद गहि धरनि पछारहु कीसा ॥

sunahu subhaṭa saba kaha dasasīsā, pada gahi dharani pachārahu kīsā.

इंद्रजीत आदिक बलवाना । हरषि उठे जहँ तहँ भट नाना ॥

iṁdrajīta ādika balavānā, haraṣi uṭhe jaham̐ taham̐ bhaṭa nānā.

झपटहिं करि बल बिपुल उपाई । पद न टरइ बैठहिं सिरु नाई ॥

jhapaṭahiṁ kari bala bipula upāī, pada na ṭarai baiṭhahiṁ siru nāī.

पुनि उठि झपटहीं सुर आराती । टरइ न कीस चरन एहि भाँती ॥

puni uṭhi jhapaṭahīṁ sura ārātī, ṭarai na kīsa carana ehi bhām̐tī.

पुरुष कुजोगी जिमि उरगारी । मोह बिटप नहिं सकहिं उपारी ॥

puruṣa kujogī jimi uragārī, moha biṭapa nahiṁ sakahiṁ upārī.

Trans:

I am quite able to smash your jaws, but Rāma has given me no order, otherwise I am so enraged that I would cleave asunder your ten heads and take up Lankā and drop it in the ocean. Your Lankā is like a fig on a gular tree, and you the unsuspecting insect that lives in it. I, like a monkey, would lose no time in eating the fruit, but the gracious Rāma has given me no order." On hearing this simile, Rāvan smiled, "Fool, where did you learn to tell such lies? Bālī never blustered like this; communion with the hermits has made you such a boaster." "Well, if I do not tear out your ten tongues and twenty arms, then truly I am a mere boaster." As he thought on Rāma's power, the monkey waxed wroth; and he planted his foot firmly on ground and offered the assembly this wager: "If you can stir my foot, you wretch, Rāma will return home, and I shall lose the wager and forgo Sītā." "Hearken, champions all," cried Rāvan, "seize this monkey by the leg and throw him to the ground." Indrajit and the other men of valor in their different ranks all rose with joy, but though they fell upon him with their full strength and with many a trick, his foot did not budge; and they bowed their heads and sat down. The enemies of heaven again stood up and dashed forward, but the monkey's foot moved no more than a sensually-minded striver is able to uproot the tree of error implanted in his heart, O Garud.

दोहा-dohā:

कोटिन्ह मेघनाद सम सुभट उठे हरषाइ ।

koṭinha meghanāda sama subhaṭa uṭhe haraṣāi,

झपटहिं टरै न कपि चरन पुनि बैठहिं सिर नाइ ॥३४क॥

jhapaṭahiṁ ṭarai na kapi carana puni baiṭhahiṁ sira nāi. 34(ka).

भूमि न छाँडत कपि चरन देखत रिपु मद भाग ।

bhūmi na chām̐ḍata kapi carana dekhata ripu mada bhāga.

कोटि बिघ्न ते संत कर मन जिमि नीति न त्याग ॥३४ख॥

koṭi bighna te saṁta kara mana jimi nīti na tyāga. 34(kha).

Trans:

Myriads of warriors, Meghnād's peers, arose with joy and essayed the wrestle; but the monkey's foot did not stir, and they were forced to bow their heads and back down. The pride of the enemy was broken when they found that the monkey's foot was moved from the ground as little as the soul of a saint abandons the maxims of morality, though assailed by thousands of difficulties.

चौपाई-caupāī:

कपि बल देखि सकल हियँ हारे । उठा आपु कपि कें परचारे ॥

kapi bala dekhi sakala hiyam̐ hāre, uṭhā āpu kapi keṁ paracāre.

गहत चरन कह बालिकुमारा । मम पद गहें न तोर उबारा ॥

gahata carana kaha bālikumārā, mama pada gaheṁ na tora ubārā.

गहसि न राम चरन सठ जाई । सुनत फिरा मन अति सकुचाई ॥

gahasi na rāma carana saṭha jāī, sunata phirā mana ati sakucāī.

भयउ तेजहत श्री सब गई । मध्य दिवस जिमि ससि सोहई ॥

bhayau tejahata śrī saba gaī, madhya divasa jimi sasi sohaī.

सिंघासन बैठेउ सिर नाई । मानहुँ संपति सकल गँवाई ॥

siṁghāsana baiṭheu sira nāī, mānahum̐ saṁpati sakala gam̐vāī.

जगदातमा प्रानपति रामा । तासु बिमुख किमि लह बिश्रामा ॥

jagadātamā prānapati rāmā, tāsu bimukha kimi laha biśrāmā.

उमा राम की भृकुटि बिलासा । होइ बिस्व पुनि पावइ नासा ॥

umā rāma kī bhṛkuṭi bilāsā, hoi bisva puni pāvai nāsā.

तृन ते कुलिस कुलिस तृन करई । तासु दूत पन कहु किमि टरई ॥

tṛna te kulisa kulisa tṛna karaī, tāsu dūta pana kahu kimi ṭaraī.

पुनि कपि कही नीति बिधि नाना । मान न ताहि कालु निअराना ॥

puni kapi kahī nīti bidhi nānā, māna na tāhi kālu niarānā.

रिपु मद मथि प्रभु सुजसु सुनायो । यह कहि चल्यो बालि नृप जायो ॥

ripu mada mathi prabhu sujasu sunāyo, yaha kahi calyo bāli nṛpa jāyo.

हतौं न खेत खेलाइ खेलाई । तोहि अबहिं का करौं बड़ाई ॥

hataum̐ na kheta khelāi khelāī, tohi abahiṁ kā karaum̐ baṛāī.

प्रथमहिं तासु तनय कपि मारा । सो सुनि रावन भयउ दुखारा ॥

prathamahiṁ tāsu tanaya kapi mārā, so suni rāvana bhayau dukhārā.

जातुधान अंगद पन देखी । भय ब्याकुल सब भए बिसेषी ॥

jātudhāna aṁgada pana dekhī, bhaya byākula saba bhae biseṣī.

Trans:

When they saw the monkey's strength, they all were discomforted at heart, until Rāvan himself arose to try the test. Even as he moved to grasp his feet, Bālī's son spoke, "There is no safety in clinging to my feet, you fool. Why don't you go and clasp Rāma's feet instead?" On hearing that, Rāvan turned away much abashed, robbed of all his dignity, and his majesty clean gone from him—as when the moon shows faintly in the daytime. With bowed head he took his seat on his throne, like one despoiled of all his possessions. How can there be any rest for an enemy of Rāma, the soul of the world, the Lord of life? O Umā, the play of Rāma's eyebrows now creates a universe and now destroys it again. He makes a blade of grass into a thunderbolt and again a thunderbolt into a blade of grass. How could his messenger fail is his challenge? Again the monkey urged upon Rāvan sound advice in every possible way; but he would not listen—for his time had drawn near. After thus trampling on the pride of the enemy and exalting his master's fame, the son of king Bālī left with this taunt, "Shall I not slay you on the field after sporting with you? It is no use my indulging in self-praise just now." When Rāvan heard that the monkey on his first arrival had killed his son, he was sore distrest at heart. The demons too, who had witnessed Angad's challenge, were all greatly disturbed.

दोहा-dohā:

रिपु बल धरषि हरषि कपि बालितनय बल पुंज ।
ripu bala dharaṣi haraṣi kapi bālitanaya bala puṁja,
पुलक सरीर नयन जल गहे राम पद कंज ॥ ३५क॥
pulaka sarīra nayana jala gahe rāma pada kaṁja. 35(ka).

साँझ जानि दसकंधर भवन गयउ बिलखाइ ।
sām̐jha jāni dasakaṁdhara bhavana gayau bilakhāi,
मंदोदरीं रावनहि बहुरि कहा समुझाइ ॥ ३५ख॥
maṁdodarīṁ rāvanahi bahuri kahā samujhāi. 35(kha).

Trans:

Having crushed the power of the enemy, the mighty monkey, son of Bālī, his body quivering with emotion, and his eyes full of tears, returned and clasped in delight Rāma's lotus feet. Finding it was evening, Rāvan returned sadly to the palace, where Mandodarī again spoke and advised him.

चौपाई-caupāī:

कंत समुझि मन तजहु कुमतिही । सोह न समर तुम्हहि रघुपतिही ॥
kaṁta samujhi mana tajahu kumatihī, soha na samara tumhahi raghupatihī.
रामानुज लघु रेख खचाई । सोउ नहिं नाघेहु असि मनुसाई ॥
rāmānuja laghu rekha khacāī, sou nahiṁ nāghehu asi manusāī.
पिय तुम्ह ताहि जितब संग्रामा । जाके दूत केर यह कामा ॥
piya tumha tāhi jitaba saṁgrāmā, jāke dūta kera yaha kāmā.
कौतुक सिंधु नाघि तव लंका । आयउ कपि केहरी असंका ॥
kautuka siṁdhu nāghi tava laṁkā, āyau kapi keharī asaṁkā.
रखवारे हति बिपिन उजारा । देखत तोहि अच्छ तेहिं मारा ॥
rakhavāre hati bipina ujārā, dekhata tohi accha tehiṁ mārā.
जारि सकल पुर कीन्हेसि छारा । कहाँ रहा बल गर्ब तुम्हारा ॥
jāri sakala pura kīnhesi chārā, kahām̐ rahā bala garba tumhārā.
अब पति मृषा गाल जनि मारहु । मोर कहा कछु हृदयँ बिचारहु ॥
aba pati mṛṣā gāla jani mārahu, mora kahā kachu hṛdayam̐ bicārahu.
पति रघुपतिहि नृपति जनि मानहु । अग जग नाथ अतुल बल जानहु ॥
pati raghupatihi nṛpati jani mānahu, aga jaga nātha atula bala jānahu.
बान प्रताप जान मारीचा । तासु कहा नहिं मानेहि नीचा ॥
bāna pratāpa jāna mārīcā, tāsu kahā nahiṁ mānehi nīcā.
जनक सभाँ अगनित भूपाला । रहे तुम्हउ बल अतुल बिसाला ॥
janaka sabhām̐ aganita bhūpālā, rahe tumhau bala atula bisālā.
भंजि धनुष जानकी बिआही । तब संग्राम जितेहु किन ताही ॥
bhaṁji dhanuṣa jānakī biāhī, taba saṁgrāma jitehu kina tāhī.
सुरपति सुत जानइ बल थोरा । राखा जिअत आँखि गहि फोरा ॥
surapati suta jānai bala thorā, rākhā jiata ām̐khi gahi phorā.
सूपनखा कै गति तुम्ह देखी । तदपि हृदयँ नहिं लाज बिसेषी ॥
sūpanakhā kai gati tumha dekhī, tadapi hṛdayam̐ nahiṁ lāja biseṣī.

Trans:

"Reflect, my husband, and abandon ill counsel; it is not well for you to fight against Rāma. His younger brother drew a little line, which you could not cross; such is your strength? My beloved, you can never conquer him in battle, whose simple messenger has done such great acts. Having lightly leaped across the sea, the monkey, like a dauntless lion, entered your Lankā, killed your watchmen, laid waste to your garden, slew Aksha as soon as he looked at him, and then set fire to the whole of the city reducing it to ashes. What place is left now for your pride of power? Cease, my spouse, from idle vaunts and take my words a little to your heart. Do not suppose that Rāma is a mere earthly king, but recognize him to be the Lord of all animate and inanimate creation, of infinite power. The might of his arrows is known to Mārich; but you did not heed his words, taking him to be a lowly human. Janak's court was crowded with kings, you too were there in all your might, but he broke the bow and wedded Sītā; why did you not conquer him in battle then? The son of Indra felt his strength a little, whose life he spared after putting out one of his eyes, and you have certainly seen Surpa-nakhā's condition; yet still you do not feel abashed at heart?

दोहा-dohā:

बधि बिराध खर दूषनहि लीलाँ हत्यो कबंध ।
badhi birādha khara dūṣanahi līlām̐ hatyo kabaṁdha,
बालि एक सर मारयो तेहि जानहु दसकंध ॥ ३६॥
bāli eka sara mārayo tehi jānahu dasakaṁdha. 36.

Trans:

Know my lord of Him—who slew Viradha and Khar and Dūshan, and with the greatest ease killed Kabandha and disposed off Bālī with a single arrow.

चौपाई-caupāī:

जेहिं जलनाथ बँधायउ हेला । उतरे प्रभु दल सहित सुबेला ॥
jehiṁ jalanātha bam̐dhāyau helā, utare prabhu dala sahita subelā.
कारुनीक दिनकर कुल केतू । दूत पठायउ तव हित हेतू ॥
kārunīka dinakara kula ketū, dūta paṭhāyau tava hita hetū.
सभा माझ जेहिं तव बल मथा । करि बरूथ महुँ मृगपति जथा ॥
sabhā mājha jehiṁ tava bala mathā, kari barūtha mahum̐ mṛgapati jathā.
अंगद हनुमत अनुचर जाके । रन बाँकुरे बीर अति बाँके ॥
aṁgada hanumata anucara jāke, rana bām̐kure bīra ati bām̐ke.
तेहि कहँ पिय पुनि पुनि नर कहहू । मुधा मान ममता मद बहहू ॥
tehi kaham̐ piya puni puni nara kahahū, mudhā māna mamatā mada bahahū.
अहह कंत कृत राम बिरोधा । काल बिबस मन उपज न बोधा ॥
ahaha kaṁta kṛta rāma birodhā, kāla bibasa mana upaja na bodhā.
काल दंड गहि काहु न मारा । हरइ धर्म बल बुद्धि बिचारा ॥
kāla daṁḍa gahi kāhu na mārā, harai dharma bala buddhi bicārā.
निकट काल जेहि आवत साईं । तेहि भ्रम होइ तुम्हारिहि नाईं ॥
nikaṭa kāla jehi āvata sāīṁ, tehi bhrama hoi tumhārihi nāīṁ.

Trans:

He bridged the ocean as a mere pastime and with all his army crossed over to Suvel. But the glory of the solar race is full of compassion, and out of regard to you dispatched an envoy, who in the midst of your court, trampled on your power, like a lion let loose upon a herd of elephants. Seeing that Angad and Hanumān are his servants—such brave and dauntless leaders of the fray—how can you, my husband, persist in calling him a mere man? You are bewildered in the intoxication of pride and self-conceit. O my lord, overtaken by fate, you wage this quarrel with Rāma, and wisdom has left you it seems. It is not with uplifted club that fate strikes, but by robbing a man of his religion, his strength, and his faculty of reason. Whenever, sir, a man's doom is near at hand he becomes infatuated just like you.

दोहा-dohā:

दुइ सुत मरे दहेउ पुर अजहुँ पूर पिय देहु ।
dui suta mare daheu pura ajahuṁ pūra piya dehu,
कृपासिंधु रघुनाथ भजि नाथ बिमल जसु लेहु ॥३७॥
kṛpāsiṁdhu raghunātha bhaji nātha bimala jasu lehu. 37.

Trans:

He has slain your two sons and set your city on fire; mend your ways even now, my husband. O lord, adore the All-merciful Rāma and thereby win for yourself the highest renown."

चौपाई-caupāī:

नारि बचन सुनि बिसिख समाना । सभाँ गयउ उठि होत बिहाना ॥
nāri bacana suni bisikha samānā, sabhāṁ gayau uṭhi hota bihānā.
बैठ जाइ सिंघासन फूली । अति अभिमान त्रास सब भूली ॥
baiṭha jāi siṁghāsana phūlī, ati abhimāna trāsa saba bhūlī.
इहाँ राम अंगदहि बोलावा । आइ चरन पंकज सिरु नावा ॥
ihāṁ rāma aṁgadahi bolāvā, āi carana paṁkaja siru nāvā.
अति आदर समीप बैठारी । बोले बिहँसि कृपाल खरारी ॥
ati ādara samīpa baiṭhārī, bole bihaṁsi kṛpāla kharārī.
बालितनय कौतुक अति मोही । तात सत्य कहु पूछउँ तोही ॥
bālitanaya kautuka ati mohī, tāta satya kahu pūchauṁ tohī.
रावनु जातुधान कुल टीका । भुज बल अतुल जासु जग लीका ॥
rāvanu jātudhāna kula ṭīkā, bhuja bala atula jāsu jaga līkā.
तासु मुकुट तुम्ह चारि चलाए । कहहु तात कवनी बिधि पाए ॥
tāsu mukuṭa tumha cāri calāe, kahahu tāta kavanī bidhi pāe.
सुनु सर्बग्य प्रनत सुखकारी । मुकुट न होहिं भूप गुन चारी ॥
sunu sarbagya pranata sukhakārī, mukuṭa na hohiṁ bhūpa guna cārī.
साम दान अरु दंड बिभेदा । नृप उर बसहिं नाथ कह बेदा ॥
sāma dāna aru daṁḍa bibhedā, nṛpa ura basahiṁ nātha kaha bedā.
नीति धर्म के चरन सुहाए । अस जियँ जानि नाथ पहिं आए ॥
nīti dharma ke carana suhāe, asa jiyaṁ jāni nātha pahiṁ āe.

Trans:

He heard his wife's speech which pierced him like an arrow; then he rose and left for the council-chamber, for it was now dawn. Forgetting all his fears he went and occupied his throne bloated with excess of pride. On the other side Rāma summoned Angad, who came and bowed his head at his lotus feet; but he, with the utmost courtesy, seated him by his side and then said, with a smile, the gracious Kharārī, "O son of Bālī, I am full of curiosity, answer truly, my son, to what I ask you. Rāvan is the chief of the entire demon race, and the unbounded might of his arm is famous throughout the world—how then did you send me four of his crowns? Tell me son, by what device did you secure them?" "Hearken, All-wise protector of the humble, they were not crowns, but the four prerogatives of a king—conciliation, concession, subjugation, and division, which, as the Vedas say, abide in a king's soul. Having recognized your gracious feet of kingly polity and religion, they came of themselves to their true Lord.

दोहा-dohā:

धर्महीन प्रभु पद बिमुख काल बिबस दससीस ।
dharmahīna prabhu pada bimukha kāla bibasa dasasīsa,
तेहि परिहरि गुन आए सुनहु कोसलाधीस ॥३८क॥
tehi parihari guna āe sunahu kosalādhīsa. 38(((ka).

परम चतुरता श्रवन सुनि बिहँसे रामु उदार ।
parama caturatā śravana suni bihaṁse rāmu udāra,
समाचार पुनि सब कहे गढ़ के बालिकुमार ॥३८ख॥
samācāra puni saba kahe gaṛha ke bālikumāra. 38(kha).

Trans:

Leaving the impious Rāvan, the death-doomed, the rebel against his Lord, his kingly prerogatives—mark me, O Monarch of Kaushal—have come to you." On hearing this most ingenious fancy, the gracious Rāma smiled, and the son of Bālī then proceeded to give him all the news from the fort.

चौपाई-caupāī:

रिपु के समाचार जब पाए । राम सचिव सब निकट बोलाए ॥
ripu ke samācāra jaba pāe, rāma saciva saba nikaṭa bolāe.
लंका बाँके चारि दुआरा । केहि बिधि लागिअ करहु बिचारा ॥
laṁkā bāṁke cāri duārā, kehi bidhi lāgia karahu bicārā.
तब कपीस रिच्छेस बिभीषन । सुमिरि हृदयँ दिनकर कुल भूषन ॥
taba kapīsa ricchesa bibhīṣana, sumiri hṛdayaṁ dinakara kula bhūṣana.
करि बिचार तिन्ह मंत्र दृढ़ावा । चारि अनी कपि कटकु बनावा ॥
kari bicāra tinha maṁtra dṛṛhāvā, cāri anī kapi kaṭaku banāvā.
जथाजोग सेनापति कीन्हे । जूथप सकल बोलि तब लीन्हे ॥
jathājoga senāpati kīnhe, jūthapa sakala boli taba līnhe.
प्रभु प्रताप कहि सब समुझाए । सुनि कपि सिंघनाद करि धाए ॥
prabhu pratāpa kahi saba samujhāe, suni kapi siṁghanāda kari dhāe.
हरषित राम चरन सिर नावहिं । गहि गिरि सिखर बीर सब धावहिं ॥
haraṣita rāma carana sira nāvahiṁ, gahi giri sikhara bīra saba dhāvahiṁ.
गर्जहिं तर्जहिं भालु कपीसा । जय रघुबीर कोसलाधीसा ॥
garjahiṁ tarjahiṁ bhālu kapīsā, jaya raghubīra kosalādhīsā.
जानत परम दुर्ग अति लंका । प्रभु प्रताप कपि चले असंका ॥
jānata parama durga ati laṁkā, prabhu pratāpa kapi cale asaṁkā.
घटाटोप करि चहुँ दिसि घेरी । मुखहिं निसान बजावहीं भेरी ॥
ghaṭāṭopa kari cahuṁ disi gherī, mukhahiṁ nisāna bajāvahīṁ bherī.

Trans:

Having heard this report of Lankā, Rāma next called all his ministers and said, "Let's take counsel as to how we should attack the four great gates of Lankā." Then the king of the monkeys and the king of the bears, and Vibhīshan, mindful at heart of the glory of the solar race, took counsel and settled upon a plan which divided the monkey army into four companies. After exalting their Lord's power, they issued the orders; and the monkeys no sooner heard them when they rushed forward, roaring like lions. First, they bowed their heads with joy at Rāma's feet and then the heroes sallied forth, with mighty rocks in their hands, roaring and leaping, bears and monkeys alike, shouting "Glory to Raghubīr, the Monarch of Kaushal!" Though they knew that Lankā was a most formidable stronghold, they pressed on undismayed, secure in the strength of their Lord, spreading like clouds over the whole horizon, with loud trumpets making calls of war.

दोहा-dohā:

जयति राम जय लछिमन जय कपीस सुग्रीव ।
jayati rāma jaya lachimana jaya kapīsa sugrīva,
गर्जहिं सिंघनाद कपि भालु महा बल सींव ॥३९॥
garjahiṁ siṁghanāda kapi bhālu mahā bala sīṁva. 39.

Trans:

"Glory to Rāma, glory to Lakshman, glory to the monkey chief, Sugrīva!" such was the leonine roar of the great and valiant bears and monkeys.

चौपाई-caupāī:

लंकाँ भयउ कोलाहल भारी । सुना दसानन अति अहँकारी ॥
laṁkāṁ bhayau kolāhala bhārī, sunā dasānana ati ahaṁkārī.
देखहु बनरन्ह केरि ढिठाई । बिहँसि निसाचर सेन बोलाई ॥
dekhahu banaranha keri ḍhiṭhāī, bihaṁsi nisācara sena bolāī.
आए कीस काल के प्रेरे । छुधावंत सब निसिचर मेरे ॥
āe kīsa kāla ke prere, chudhāvaṁta saba nisicara mere.
अस कहि अट्टहास सठ कीन्हा । गृह बैठें अहार बिधि दीन्हा ॥
asa kahi aṭṭahāsa saṭha kīnhā, gṛha baiṭheṁ ahāra bidhi dīnhā.

सुभट सकल चारिहुँ दिसि जाहू । धरि धरि भालु कीस सब खाहू ॥
subhaṭa sakala cārihuṁ disi jāhū, dhari dhari bhālu kīsa saba khāhū.
उमा रावनहि अस अभिमाना । जिमि टिट्टिभ खग सूत उताना ॥
umā rāvanahi asa abhimānā, jimi ṭiṭṭibha khaga sūta utānā.
चले निसाचर आयसु मागी । गहि कर भिंडिपाल बर साँगी ॥
cale nisācara āyasu māgī, gahi kara bhiṁḍipāla bara sāṁgī.
तोमर मुद्गर परसु प्रचंडा । सूल कृपान परिघ गिरिखंडा ॥
tomara mudgara parasu pracaṁḍā, sūla kṛpāna parigha girikhaṁḍā.
जिमि अरुनोपल निकर निहारी । धावहिं सठ खग मांस अहारी ॥
jimi arunopala nikara nihārī, dhāvahiṁ saṭha khaga māṁsa ahārī.
चोंच भंग दुख तिन्हहि न सूझा । तिमि धाए मनुजाद अबूझा ॥
coṁca bhaṁga dukha tinhahi na sūjhā, timi dhāe manujāda abūjhā.

Trans:

Lankā was full of the utmost confusion; but Rāvan heard the news with his wonted arrogance. "See the impudence of these monkeys," he said with a smile and summoned his demon hosts, "These monkeys have come by the decree of fate; you see, my demons wanted a hearty meal," so saying the wretch burst into loud laughter, "and gods have provided them with one without their going abroad to seek it. Sally forth in every direction, my warriors all, and seize these bears and monkeys and devour them." O Umā, Rāvan's conceit was as great as that of the sandpiper—when it goes to sleep with its legs in the air, imagining supporting the heavens. On receiving their orders, the demons sallied forth, armed with slings and mighty javelins, clubs, maces, and trenchant axes, pikes, swords, bludgeons, and masses of rock. Like foul carnivorous birds that mistakenly swoop down upon a heap of rubies which they have espied, and after breaking their beaks upon them discover their error, so these man-eating monsters rushed forth in their folly.

दोहा-dohā:

नानायुध सर चाप धर जातुधान बल बीर ।
nānāyudha sara cāpa dhara jātudhāna bala bīra,
कोट कँगूरन्हि चढ़ि गए कोटि कोटि रनधीर ॥४०॥
koṭa kaṁgūranhi caṛhi gae koṭi koṭi ranadhīra. 40.

Trans:

Taking bow and arrows and weapons of every description, myriads upon myriads of the stoutest and most valiant demons climbed up to the battlements of the fort.

चौपाई-caupāī:

कोट कँगूरन्हि सोहहिं कैसे । मेरु के सृंगनि जनु घन बैसे ॥
koṭa kaṁgūranhi sohahiṁ kaise, meru ke sṛṁgani janu ghana baise.
बाजहिं ढोल निसान जुझाऊ । सुनि धुनि होइ भटन्हि मन चाऊ ॥
bājahiṁ ḍhola nisāna jujhāū, suni dhuni hoi bhaṭanhi mana cāū.
बाजहिं भेरि नफीरि अपारा । सुनि कादर उर जाहिं दरारा ॥
bājahiṁ bheri naphīri apārā, suni kādara ura jāhiṁ darārā.
देखिन्ह जाइ कपिन्ह के ठट्टा । अति बिसाल तनु भालु सुभट्टा ॥
dekhinha jāi kapinha ke ṭhaṭṭā, ati bisāla tanu bhālu subhaṭṭā.
धावहिं गनहिं न अवघट घाटा । पर्बत फोरि करहिं गहि बाटा ॥
dhāvahiṁ ganahiṁ na avaghaṭa ghāṭā, parbata phori karahiṁ gahi bāṭā.
कटकटाहिं कोटिन्ह भट गर्जहिं । दसन ओठ काटहिं अति तर्जहिं ॥
kaṭakaṭāhiṁ koṭinha bhaṭa garjahiṁ, dasana oṭha kāṭahiṁ ati tarjahiṁ.
उत रावन इत राम दोहाई । जयति जयति जय परी लराई ॥
uta rāvana ita rāma dohāī, jayati jayati jaya parī larāī.
निसिचर सिखर समूह ढहावहिं । कूदि धरहिं कपि फेरि चलावहिं ॥
nisicara sikhara samūha ḍhahāvahiṁ, kūdi dharahiṁ kapi pheri calāvahiṁ.

Trans:

The battlements of the fort looked like the peaks of Meru amidst dense clouds. Drums and other instruments of music sounded for the battle, and the soul of the warriors was stirred by their crash. The trumpets and clarions brayed so fiercely that even a coward on hearing them would forget his fear. The throng of monkeys could not be seen for the mighty stature of the warrior bears. They rush on, taking no account of the most precipitous passes, but tearing down the rocks and thus clearing a way for themselves. Grinding their teeth and biting their lips in their excess of fury, myriads of warriors on both sides wildly shout—there calling upon Rāvan, and here upon Rāma, "Glory and victory, the combat has begun." If the demons cast down any mountain crag, the monkeys with a bound would seize it and hurl it right back.

छंद-chaṁda:

धरि कुधर खंड प्रचंड मर्कट भालु गढ़ पर डारहीं ।
dhari kudhara khaṁḍa pracaṁḍa markaṭa bhālu gaṛha para ḍārahīṁ,
झपटहिं चरन गहि पटकि महि भजि चलत बहुरि पचारहीं ॥
jhapaṭahiṁ carana gahi paṭaki mahi bhaji calata bahuri pacārahīṁ.
अति तरल तरुन प्रताप तरपहिं तमकि गढ़ चढ़ि चढ़ि गए ।
ati tarala taruna pratāpa tarapahiṁ tamaki gaṛha caṛhi caṛhi gae,
कपि भालु चढ़ि मंदिरन्ह जहँ तहँ राम जसु गावत भए ॥
kapi bhālu caṛhi maṁdiranha jahaṁ tahaṁ rāma jasu gāvata bhae.

Trans:

The furious monkeys and bears lay hold of the mountain crags and hurl them against the fort; and they grapple in close encounters, seizing antagonists by legs and dashing them to the ground; and if one takes to flight challenging him again to the combat. With a bold dash and a vigorous spring they bound up the heights of the fort; and every palace, into which the bears and monkeys penetrate, resounds with songs of Rāma's praise.

दोहा-dohā:

एकु एकु निसिचर गहि पुनि कपि चले पराइ ।
eku eku nisicara gahi puni kapi cale parāi,
ऊपर आपु हेठ भट गिरहिं धरनि पर आइ ॥४१॥
ūpara āpu heṭha bhaṭa girahiṁ dharani para āi. 41.

Trans:

Taking each demon in his clutch, the monkeys run off again and again; and they drop them to the ground, and crush their prey beneath them.

चौपाई-caupāī:

राम प्रताप प्रबल कपिजूथा । मर्दहिं निसिचर सुभट बरूथा ॥
rāma pratāpa prabala kapijūthā, mardahiṁ nisicara subhaṭa barūthā.
चढ़े दुर्ग पुनि जहँ तहँ बानर । जय रघुबीर प्रताप दिवाकर ॥
caṛhe durga puni jahaṁ tahaṁ bānara, jaya raghubīra pratāpa divākara.
चले निसाचर निकर पराई । प्रबल पवन जिमि घन समुदाई ॥
cale nisācara nikara parāī, prabala pavana jimi ghana samudāī.
हाहाकार भयउ पुर भारी । रोवहिं बालक आतुर नारी ॥
hāhākāra bhayau pura bhārī, rovahiṁ bālaka ātura nārī.
सब मिलि देहिं रावनहिं गारी । राज करत एहिं मृत्यु हँकारी ॥
saba mili dehiṁ rāvanahiṁ gārī, rāja karata ehiṁ mṛtyu haṁkārī.
निज दल बिचल सुनी तेहिं काना । फेरि सुभट लंकेस रिसाना ॥
nija dala bicala sunī tehiṁ kānā, pheri subhaṭa laṁkesa risānā.
जो रन बिमुख सुना मैं काना । सो मैं हतब कराल कृपाना ॥
jo rana bimukha sunā maiṁ kānā, so maiṁ hataba karāla kṛpānā.
सर्बसु खाइ भोग करि नाना । समर भूमि भए बल्लभ प्राना ॥
sarbasu khāi bhoga kari nānā, samara bhūmi bhae ballabha prānā.
उग्र बचन सुनि सकल डेराने । चले क्रोध करि सुभट लजाने ॥
ugra bacana suni sakala ḍerāne, cale krodha kari subhaṭa lajāne.
सन्मुख मरन बीर कै सोभा । तब तिन्ह तजा प्रान कर लोभा ॥
sanmukha marana bīra kai sobhā, taba tinha tajā prāna kara lobhā.

Trans:

Strong in the power of Rāma, the monkey host overcame the throng of demon warriors; and having climbed the fort, made it ring all over with shouts of glory to Raghubīr, the sun of majesty! The demons fled headlong, like thunderclouds driven by strong winds. There was a grievous wailing throughout the city, with children crying and women in dire distress. All agreed in abusing Rāvan the king, who had thus invited ruin. When he heard that his forces had been routed, the lord of Lankā indignantly rallied his captains, "If I hear of anyone turning his back in battle, I will slay him myself with my terrible sword. After devouring all my substance and feasting as you pleased, now on the field of battle you think of nothing but your own safety?" On hearing these stern words, the chiefs became frightened and ashamed. Working themselves into fury they sallied forth again, crying "It is the glory of a warrior to die with his face to the foe"; and all desire to live entirely left them.

दोहा-dohā:

बहु आयुध धर सुभट सब भिरहिं पचारि पचारि ।
bahu āyudha dhara subhaṭa saba bhirahiṁ pacāri pacāri,
ब्याकुल किए भालु कपि परिघ त्रिसूलन्हि मारि ॥४२॥
byākula kie bhālu kapi parigha trisūlanhi māri. 42.

Trans:

Armed with weapons of various kinds, all the champions grappled with their foes, challenging them again and again. Striking the bears and monkeys with iron bludgeons and tridents, they deprived them of their nerve.

चौपाई-caupāī:

भय आतुर कपि भागन लागे । जद्यपि उमा जीतिहहिं आगे ॥
bhaya ātura kapi bhāgana lāge, jadyapi umā jītihahiṁ āge.
कोउ कह कहँ अंगद हनुमंता । कहँ नल नील दुबिद बलवंता ॥
kou kaha kahaṁ aṁgada hanumaṁtā, kahaṁ nala nīla dubida balavaṁtā.
निज दल बिकल सुना हनुमाना । पच्छिम द्वार रहा बलवाना ॥
nija dala bikala sunā hanumānā, pacchima dvāra rahā balavānā.
मेघनाद तहँ करइ लराई । टूट न द्वार परम कठिनाई ॥
meghanāda tahaṁ karai larāī, ṭūṭa na dvāra parama kaṭhināī.
पवनतनय मन भा अति क्रोधा । गर्जेउ प्रबल काल सम जोधा ॥
pavanatanaya mana bhā ati krodhā, garjeu prabala kāla sama jodhā.
कूदि लंक गढ़ ऊपर आवा । गहि गिरि मेघनाद कहुँ धावा ॥
kūdi laṁka gaṛha ūpara āvā, gahi giri meghanāda kahuṁ dhāvā.
भंजेउ रथ सारथी निपाता । ताहि हृदय महुँ मारेसि लाता ॥
bhaṁjeu ratha sārathī nipātā, tāhi hṛdaya mahuṁ māresi lātā.
दुसरें सूत बिकल तेहि जाना । स्यंदन घालि तुरत गृह आना ॥
dusareṁ sūta bikala tehi jānā, syaṁdana ghāli turata gṛha ānā.

Trans:

Overcome with terror, the monkeys began to flee, although, Umā, they had already won the victory. Said one, "Where are Angad and Hanumān? Where Nala and Nīl and the stalwart Dwivid?" Hanumān heard that his troops were in distress, but the hero was holding the position at the western gate. There Meghnād led the defense, nor was it possible to force the gate, so great was its strength. Then the son-of-wind waxed exceeding wrath of soul; and with a terrible roar, as though the end of the world had come, the hero made a bound and sprang upon the top of Lankā fort, and then seizing a rock he rushed upon Meghnād. He shattered the chariot, hurled the driver to the ground, and struck the prince himself with his foot to his chest. Another charioteer, seeing him senseless, somehow threw him upon another chariot and brought him home with speed.

दोहा-dohā:

अंगद सुना पवनसुत गढ़ पर गयउ अकेल ।
aṁgada sunā pavanasuta gaṛha para gayau akela,
रन बाँकुरा बालिसुत तरकि चढ़ेउ कपि खेल ॥४३॥
rana bāṁkurā bālisuta taraki caṛheu kapi khela. 43.

Trans:

When Angad heard that Hanumān had made his way into the fort alone, he too, the adventurous warrior, bounded forward to join in the monkey sports.

चौपाई-caupāī:

जुद्ध बिरुद्ध क्रुद्ध द्वौ बंदर । राम प्रताप सुमिरि उर अंतर ॥
juddha biruddha kruddha dvau baṁdara, rāma pratāpa sumiri ura aṁtara.
रावन भवन चढ़े द्वौ धाई । करहिं कोसलाधीस दोहाई ॥
rāvana bhavana caṛhe dvau dhāī, karahiṁ kosalādhīsa dohāī.
कलस सहित गहि भवनु ढहावा । देखि निसाचरपति भय पावा ॥
kalasa sahita gahi bhavanu ḍhahāvā, dekhi nisācarapati bhaya pāvā.
नारि बृंद कर पीटहिं छाती । अब दुइ कपि आए उतपाती ॥
nāri bṛṁda kara pīṭahiṁ chātī, aba dui kapi āe utapātī.
कपिलीला करि तिन्हहि डेरावहिं । रामचंद्र कर सुजसु सुनावहिं ॥
kapilīlā kari tinhahi ḍerāvahiṁ, rāmacaṁdra kara sujasu sunāvahiṁ.
पुनि कर गहि कंचन के खंभा । कहेन्हि करिअ उतपात अरंभा ॥
puni kara gahi kaṁcana ke khaṁbhā, kahenhi karia utapāta araṁbhā.
गर्जि परे रिपु कटक मझारी । लागे मर्दै भुज बल भारी ॥
garji pare ripu kaṭaka majhārī, lāge mardai bhuja bala bhārī.
काहुहि लात चपेटन्हि केहू । भजहु न रामहि सो फल लेहू ॥
kāhuhi lāta capeṭanhi kehū, bhajahu na rāmahi so phala lehū.

Trans:

Maddened by the battle and full of fury, the two monkeys, mindful at heart of Rāma's glory, rushed upon Rāvan's palace shouting "The king of Kaushal to the fore"; and the overthrew the whole building, so that not a pinnacle was left standing. When the demon chief saw this, he was dismayed; while the women all struck their breasts crying, "Now two of these pestilent monkeys have come." After terrifying them with their monkey tricks, and proclaiming the praises of Rāmachandra, they grasped each a golden pillar in their hand and cried, "Now, let's begin making some destruction in earnest.' With a roar, they rushed into the midst of the enemy's army and began laying them low with their mighty strength of arms, and here a kick and there a blow; crying "You worship not Rāma, and here is the outcome."

दोहा-dohā:

एक एक सों मर्दहिं तोरि चलावहिं मुंड ।
eka eka soṁ mardahiṁ tori calāvahiṁ muṁḍa,
रावन आगें परहिं ते जनु फूटहिं दधि कुंड ॥४४॥
rāvana āgeṁ parahiṁ te janu phūṭahiṁ dadhi kuṁḍa. 44.

Trans:

Overthrowing one after another, they strike off their heads and hurl them away, so that they fall at Rāvan's feet smashed into pieces like so many earthen pots.

चौपाई-caupāī:

महा महा मुखिआ जे पावहिं । ते पद गहि प्रभु पास चलावहिं ॥
mahā mahā mukhiā je pāvahiṁ, te pada gahi prabhu pāsa calāvahiṁ.
कहइ बिभीषनु तिन्ह के नामा । देहिं राम तिन्हहू निज धामा ॥
kahai bibhīṣanu tinha ke nāmā, dehiṁ rāma tinhahū nija dhāmā.
खल मनुजाद द्विजामिष भोगी । पावहिं गति जो जाचत जोगी ॥
khala manujāda dvijāmiṣa bhogī, pāvahiṁ gati jo jācata jogī.
उमा राम मृदुचित करुनाकर । बयर भाव सुमिरत मोहि निसिचर ॥
umā rāma mṛducita karunākara, bayara bhāva sumirata mohi nisicara.
देहिं परम गति सो जियँ जानी । अस कृपाल को कहहु भवानी ॥
dehiṁ parama gati so jiyaṁ jānī, asa kṛpāla ko kahahu bhavānī.
अस प्रभु सुनि न भजहिं भ्रम त्यागी । नर मतिमंद ते परम अभागी ॥
asa prabhu suni na bhajahiṁ bhrama tyāgī, nara matimaṁda te parama abhāgī.
अंगद अरु हनुमंत प्रबेसा । कीन्ह दुर्ग अस कह अवधेसा ॥
aṁgada aru hanumaṁta prabesā, kīnha durga asa kaha avadhesā.

लंकाँ द्वौ कपि सोहहिं कैसें । मथहिं सिंधु दुइ मंदर जैसें ॥
laṁkāṁ dvau kapi sohahiṁ kaisem̐, mathahiṁ siṁdhu dui maṁdara jaisem̐.

Trans:

Whenever they caught any big chief, they seized him by the leg and threw him to their Lord. Vibhīshan mentioned their names and Rāma assigned them his own sphere in heaven. Thus, man-eating monsters, who had devoured even the flesh of a Brahmin, obtained a destiny such as even devotees desire. O Umā, Rāma is tender-hearted and full of compassion, and bestowed salvation upon them for this reason: that the demons had spoken his Holy-Name, albeit in a spirit of enmity. Tell me, O Bhawānī, who else would be so merciful. Dull of heart indeed and utterly wretched are those men who, on hearing of such a Lord, do not abandon their errors and worship him. "Angad and Hanumān have forced their way into the fort and Lankā," observed Shri Rāma. As the two monkeys rampaged in Lankā, it appeared to sight like the sea churned by two Mount Merus.

दोहा-dohā:

भुज बल रिपु दल दलमलि देखि दिवस कर अंत ।
bhuja bala ripu dala dalamali dekhi divasa kara aṁta,
कूदे जुगल बिगत श्रम आए जहँ भगवंत ॥४५॥
kūde jugala bigata śrama āe jahaṁ bhagavaṁta. 45.

Trans:

After crushing the host of enemy with the might of their arms, they perceived that it was now the close of day; and forgetting all their tiredness they both came bounding into the presence of their Lord.

चौपाई-caupāī:

प्रभु पद कमल सीस तिन्ह नाए । देखि सुभट रघुपति मन भाए ॥
prabhu pada kamala sīsa tinha nāe, dekhi subhaṭa raghupati mana bhāe.
राम कृपा करि जुगल निहारे । भए बिगतश्रम परम सुखारे ॥
rāma kṛpā kari jugala nihāre, bhae bigataśrama parama sukhāre.
गए जानि अंगद हनुमाना । फिरे भालु मर्कट भट नाना ॥
gae jāni aṁgada hanumānā, phire bhālu markaṭa bhaṭa nānā.
जातुधान प्रदोष बल पाई । धाए करि दससीस दोहाई ॥
jātudhāna pradoṣa bala pāī, dhāe kari dasasīsa dohāī.
निसिचर अनी देखि कपि फिरे । जहँ तहँ कटकटाइ भट भिरे ॥
nisicara anī dekhi kapi phire, jahaṁ tahaṁ kaṭakaṭāi bhaṭa bhire.
द्वौ दल प्रबल पचारि पचारी । लरत सुभट नहिं मानहिं हारी ॥
dvau dala prabala pacāri pacārī, larata subhaṭa nahiṁ mānahiṁ hārī.
महाबीर निसिचर सब कारे । नाना बरन बलीमुख भारे ॥
mahābīra nisicara saba kāre, nānā barana balīmukha bhāre.
सबल जुगल दल समबल जोधा । कौतुक करत लरत करि क्रोधा ॥
sabala jugala dala samabala jodhā, kautuka karata larata kari krodhā.
प्राबिट सरद पयोद घनेरे । लरत मनहुँ मारुत के प्रेरे ॥
prābiṭa sarada payoda ghanere, larata manahuṁ māruta ke prere.
अनिप अकंपन अरु अतिकाया । बिचलत सेन कीन्हि इन्ह माया ॥
anipa akaṁpana aru atikāyā, bicalata sena kīnhi inha māyā.
भयउ निमिष महँ अति अँधियारा । बृष्टि होइ रुधिरोपल छारा ॥
bhayau nimiṣa mahaṁ ati aṁdhiyārā, bṛṣṭi hoi rudhiropala chārā.

Trans:

They bowed their heads at the Lord's lotus feet, and he was glad at heart to see his champions again. Graciously he looked upon them both, and at once their fatigue passed away and they became completely renewed. On learning that Angad and Hanumān had gone, many warriors among the bears and monkeys too retired from the field; while the demons, recovering their strength at nightfall, made a fresh onset, crying 'Rāvan to the rescue!' At the sight of the demon army, the monkeys turned again; there was everywhere gnashing of teeth as the heroes closed in the fray. In both gallant armies, the leaders impatiently challenged the foe, and fought as those who will not hear of defeat. The valiant demons were all black of hue; the huge monkeys of many different colors. Both armies were equal in strength, with equally matched champions, and the passion with which they fought was a sight to see—as when in the rains, or the autumn, masses of cloud are driven against one another by the force of the wind. When the line began to break, the chiefs Akampan and Atikaya took recourse to wizardly warfare, and within a minute it became pitch dark, and there was shower of blood, stones, and dust everywhere.

दोहा-dohā:

देखि निबिड़ तम दसहुँ दिसि कपिदल भयउ खभार ।
dekhi nibiṛa tama dasahuṁ disi kapidala bhayau khabhāra,
एकहि एक न देखई जहँ तहँ करहिं पुकार ॥४६॥
ekahi eka na dekhaī jahaṁ tahaṁ karahiṁ pukāra. 46.

Trans:

Seeing the dense darkness all around, the monkey host became perplexed; it was impossible to see one another; and there was an outcry everywhere.

चौपाई-caupāī:

सकल मरमु रघुनायक जाना । लिए बोलि अंगद हनुमाना ॥
sakala maramu raghunāyaka jānā, lie boli aṁgada hanumānā.
समाचार सब कहि समुझाए । सुनत कोपि कपिकुंजर धाए ॥
samācāra saba kahi samujhāe, sunata kopi kapikuṁjara dhāe.
पुनि कृपाल हँसि चाप चढ़ावा । पावक सायक सपदि चलावा ॥
puni kṛpāla haṁsi cāpa caṛhāvā, pāvaka sāyaka sapadi calāvā.
भयउ प्रकास कतहुँ तम नाहीं । ग्यान उदयँ जिमि संसय जाहीं ॥
bhayau prakāsa katahuṁ tama nāhīṁ, gyāna udayaṁ jimi saṁsaya jāhīṁ.
भालु बलीमुख पाइ प्रकासा । धाए हरष बिगत श्रम त्रासा ॥
bhālu balīmukha pāi prakāsā, dhāe haraṣa bigata śrama trāsā.
हनूमान अंगद रन गाजे । हाँक सुनत रजनीचर भाजे ॥
hanūmāna aṁgada rana gāje, hāṁka sunata rajanīcara bhāje.
भागत पट पटकहिं धरि धरनी । करहिं भालु कपि अद्भुत करनी ॥
bhāgata paṭa paṭakahiṁ dhari dharanī, karahiṁ bhālu kapi adbhuta karanī.
गहि पद डारहिं सागर माहीं । मकर उरग झष धरि धरि खाहीं ॥
gahi pada ḍārahiṁ sāgara māhīṁ, makara uraga jhaṣa dhari dhari khāhīṁ.

Trans:

Rāma understood the secret of it all and called Angad and Hanumān and explained to them what was going on. The mighty monkeys had no sooner heard that immediately rushed forth in fury. And the All-merciful, with a smile, drew his bow and at once let fly a fiery arrow. Light shone forth, and there was no darkness anymore—as when at the dawn of intelligence all doubts disappear. Having recovered the light, the bears and monkeys forgot their fatigue and alarm, and pressed on exultingly. Hanumān and Angad thundered aloud on the field of battle, and at the sound of their roaring the demons fled; but the bears and monkeys, seizing them in their flight, dashed them to the ground, performing many prodigies of valor; or catching them by the leg hurled them into the sea, where alligators, serpents, and fish snapped them up and devoured them.

दोहा-dohā:

कछु मारे कछु घायल कछु गढ़ चढ़े पराइ ।
kachu māre kachu ghāyala kachu gaṛha caṛhe parāi,
गर्जहिं भालु बलीमुख रिपु दल बल बिचलाइ ॥४७॥
garjahiṁ bhālu balīmukha ripu dala bala bicalāi. 47.

Trans:

Some were killed outright, some were wounded, some fled back to the fort; the bears and monkeys shouted for joy over the rout of the enemy's strong force.

चौपाई-caupāī:

निसा जानि कपि चारिउ अनी । आए जहाँ कोसला धनी ॥
nisā jāni kapi cāriu anī, āe jahāṁ kosalā dhanī.
राम कृपा करि चितवा सबही । भए बिगतश्रम बानर तबही ॥

rāma kṛpā kari citavā sabahī, bhae bigataśrama bānara tabahī.

उहाँ दसानन सचिव हँकारे । सब सन कहेसि सुभट जे मारे ॥
uhām̐ dasānana saciva ham̐kāre, saba sana kahesi subhaṭa je māre.
आधा कटकु कपिन्ह संघारा । कहहु बेगि का करिअ बिचारा ॥
ādhā kaṭaku kapinha saṁghārā, kahahu begi kā karia bicārā.
माल्यवंत अति जरठ निसाचर । रावन मातु पिता मंत्री बर ॥
mālyavaṁta ati jaraṭha nisācara, rāvana mātu pitā maṁtrī bara.
बोला बचन नीति अति पावन । सुनहु तात कछु मोर सिखावन ॥
bolā bacana nīti ati pāvana, sunahu tāta kachu mora sikhāvana.
जब ते तुम्ह सीता हरि आनी । असगुन होहिं न जाहिं बखानी ॥
jaba te tumha sītā hari ānī, asaguna hohiṁ na jāhiṁ bakhānī.
बेद पुरान जासु जसु गायो । राम बिमुख काहुँ न सुख पायो ॥
beda purāna jāsu jasu gāyo, rāma bimukha kāhum̐ na sukha pāyo.

Trans:

Seeing that it was now night, the four divisions of the monkey host returned to the Lord of Kaushal. As soon as Rāma cast his gracious glance upon them, all their fatigue was at once forgotten. On the other hand, Rāvan summoned his ministers and told them how his many champions had been killed, "The monkeys have destroyed half my army; tell me at once what counsel should be adopted." Thereupon Malyavan, a very elderly demon, who had been the sagacious adviser of Rāvan's father and mother, delivered a speech of the soundest policy, "Hearken, my son, to a few words of instruction from me. Ever since you carried off Sītā and brought her here, there have been omens of ill, more than I can tell. No advantage can be gained by opposing him, whose glory is the theme both of Vedas and Purānas.

दोहा-dohā:

हिरन्याच्छ भ्राता सहित मधु कैटभ बलवान ।
hiranyāccha bhrātā sahita madhu kaiṭabha balavāna,
जेहिं मारे सोइ अवतरेउ कृपासिंधु भगवान ॥४८क॥
jehiṁ māre soi avatareu kṛpāsiṁdhu bhagavāna. 48(ka).

Trans:

He is the incarnation of the compassionate Lord God, who slew Hiranyaksh, with his brother Hiranyā-kashyap, and Madhu and the monster Kaitabh.

मासपारायण पचीसवाँ विश्राम
māsapārāyaṇa pacīsavām̐ viśrāma
(Pause 25 for a Thirty-Day Recitation)

कालरूप खल बन दहन गुनागार घनबोध ।
kālarūpa khala bana dahana gunāgāra ghanabodha,
सिव बिरंचि जेहि सेवहिं तासों कवन बिरोध ॥४८ख॥
siva biraṁci jehi sevahiṁ tāsoṁ kavana birodha. 48(kha).

Trans:

Who can fight against him, who is the embodiment of Time—angel of Death, the very fire to consume the forest of wickedness, who is the repository of virtues and embodiment of wisdom, whom Shiva and Brahmmā ever adore.

चौपाई-caupāī:

परिहरि बयरु देहु बैदेही । भजहु कृपानिधि परम सनेही ॥
parihari bayaru dehu baidehī, bhajahu kṛpānidhi parama sanehī.
ताके बचन बान सम लागे । करिआ मुह करि जाहि अभागे ॥
tāke bacana bāna sama lāge, kariā muha kari jāhi abhāge.
बूढ़ भएसि न त मरतेउँ तोही । अब जनि नयन देखावसि मोही ॥
būṛha bhaesi na ta marateum̐ tohī, aba jani nayana dekhāvasi mohī.
तेहिं अपने मन अस अनुमाना । बध्यो चहत एहि कृपानिधाना ॥
tehi apane mana asa anumānā, badhyo cahata ehi kṛpānidhānā.
सो उठि गयउ कहत दुर्बादा । तब सकोप बोलेउ घननादा ॥
so uṭhi gayau kahata durbādā, taba sakopa boleu ghananādā.
कौतुक प्रात देखिअहु मोरा । करिहउँ बहुत कहौं का थोरा ॥
kautuka prāta dekhiahu morā, karihaum̐ bahuta kahauṁ kā thorā.
सुनि सुत बचन भरोसा आवा । प्रीति समेत अंक बैठावा ॥
suni suta bacana bharosā āvā, prīti sameta aṁka baiṭhāvā.
करत बिचार भयउ भिनुसारा । लागे कपि पुनि चहूँ दुआरा ॥
karata bicāra bhayau bhinusārā, lāge kapi puni cahūm̐ duārā.
कोपि कपिन्ह दुर्घट गढ़ु घेरा । नगर कोलाहलु भयउ घनेरा ॥
kopi kapinha durghaṭa gaṛhu gherā, nagara kolāhalu bhayau ghanerā.
बिबिधायुध धर निसिचर धाए । गढ़ ते पर्बत सिखर ढहाए ॥
bibidhāyudha dhara nisicara dhāe, gaṛha te parbata sikhara ḍhahāe.

Trans:

Have done with your quarrelling; give back Sītā and worship the All-merciful with loving devotion." His words stung like arrows, "Away, wretch, with your abominable suggestions; if it were not for your age, I would have killed you; now do not appear in my sight again." He thought within himself 'He wishes to be killed by the All-merciful,' and so arose and departed, uttering words of reproof. Then Meghnād cried in a fury, "See what a sight I will show you tomorrow; though I do not say much, I do a great deal." On hearing his son's speech, Rāvan's confidence returned and he took him lovingly into his embrace. While they were still consulting, the day broke; the monkeys again assailed the four gates and ferociously lay seize upon the precipitous citadel. There was a confused noise in every part of the town, as the demons snatched up their weapons of every description and hurried forward and began hurling down masses of rock from the ramparts.

छंद-chaṁda:

ढाहे महीधर सिखर कोटिन्ह बिबिध बिधि गोला चले ।
ḍhāhe mahīdhara sikhara koṭinha bibidha bidhi golā cale,
घहरात जिमि पबिपात गर्जत जनु प्रलय के बादले ॥
ghaharāta jimi pabipāta garjata janu pralaya ke bādale.
मर्कट बिकट भट जुटत कटत न लटत तन जर्जर भए ।
markaṭa bikaṭa bhaṭa juṭata kaṭata na laṭata tana jarjara bhae,
गहि सैल तेहि गढ़ पर चलावहिं जहँ सो तहँ निसिचर हए ॥
gahi saila tehi gaṛha para calāvahiṁ jaham̐ so taham̐ nisicara hae.

Trans:

Thousands of them hurl down masses of rock; missiles of every kind are sent flying; bomb-shells come roaring like crash of thunder; the warriors roar with thunderous noise like that of clouds on universal night of destruction. The monstrous monkeys join in close combat; their bodies are hacked to pieces, but though mangled they faint not; they seize the rocks and hurl them against the fort wherever the demons are.

दोहा-dohā:

मेघनाद सुनि श्रवन अस गढ़ु पुनि छेंका आइ ।
meghanāda suni śravana asa gaṛhu puni cheṁkā āi,
उतरयो बीर दुर्ग तें सन्मुख चल्यो बजाइ ॥४९॥
utarayo bīra durga teṁ sanmukha calyo bajāi. 49.

Trans:

When Meghnād heard that they had again come and seized the fort, he gallantly left his stronghold and sallied forth with beat of drum to meet the enemy face to face.

चौपाई-caupāī:

कहँ कोसलाधीस द्वौ भ्राता । धन्वी सकल लोक बिख्याता ॥
kaham̐ kosalādhīsa dvau bhrātā, dhanvī sakala loka bikhyātā.
कहँ नल नील दुबिद सुग्रीवा । अंगद हनूमंत बल सींवा ॥
kaham̐ nala nīla dubida sugrīvā, aṁgada hanūmaṁta bala sīṁvā.
कहाँ बिभीषनु भ्राताद्रोही । आजु सबहि हठि मारउँ ओही ॥
kahām̐ bibhīṣanu bhrātādrohī, āju sabahi haṭhi māraum̐ ohī.
अस कहि कठिन बान संधाने । अतिसय क्रोध श्रवन लगि ताने ॥
asa kahi kaṭhina bāna saṁdhāne, atisaya krodha śravana lagi tāne.

सर समूह सो छाड़ै लागा । जनु सपच्छ धावहिं बहु नागा ॥
sara samūha so chāṛai lāgā, janu sapaccha dhāvahiṁ bahu nāgā.
जहँ तहँ परत देखिअहिं बानर । सन्मुख होइ न सके तेहि अवसर ॥
jahaṁ tahaṁ parata dekhiahiṁ bānara, sanmukha hoi na sake tehi avasara.
जहँ तहँ भागि चले कपि रीछा । बिसरी सबहि जुद्ध कै ईछा ॥
jahaṁ tahaṁ bhāgi cale kapi rīchā, bisarī sabahi juddha kai īchā.
सो कपि भालु न रन महँ देखा । कीन्हेसि जेहि न प्रान अवसेषा ॥
so kapi bhālu na rana mahaṁ dekhā, kīnhesi jehi na prāna avaseṣā.

Trans:

"Where are the two brother princes of Kaushal, those archers so famous throughout the universe? Where are Nala and Nīl, Dwivid and Sugrīva, Angad and Hanumān, the most powerful of all? Where is Vibhīshan, his brother's curse, that I may slay the wretch at once, this very day." So saying, he made ready his terrible arrows, and in a vehemence of passion drew the string to his ear. The multitudinous shafts that he left fly sped forth like so many winged serpents. Everywhere you might see monkeys falling to the ground. At that time there was not one that dared to face him. Everywhere bears and monkeys were taking to flight, and every wish to fight was clean forgotten. Not a bear or a monkey was to be seen on the field but those who had left their bodies there.

दोहा-dohā:

दस दस सर सब मारेसि परे भूमि कपि बीर ।
dasa dasa sara saba māresi pare bhūmi kapi bīra,
सिंहनाद करि गर्जा मेघनाद बल धीर ॥५०॥
siṁhanāda kari garjā meghanāda bala dhīra. 50.

Trans:

At each sight he sent forth ten arrows; and the warriors struck all dropped dead to the ground; and Meghnād shouted furiously in the strength of his might, with the roar of a terrible lion.

चौपाई-caupāī:

देखि पवनसुत कटक बिहाला । क्रोधवंत जनु धायउ काला ॥
dekhi pavanasuta kaṭaka bihālā, krodhavaṁta janu dhāyau kālā.
महासैल एक तुरत उपारा । अति रिस मेघनाद पर डारा ॥
mahāsaila eka turata upārā, ati risa meghanāda para ḍārā.
आवत देखि गयउ नभ सोई । रथ सारथी तुरग सब खोई ॥
āvata dekhi gayau nabha soī, ratha sārathī turaga saba khoī.
बार बार पचार हनुमाना । निकट न आव मरमु सो जाना ॥
bāra bāra pacāra hanumānā, nikaṭa na āva maramu so jānā.
रघुपति निकट गयउ घननादा । नाना भाँति करेसि दुर्बादा ॥
raghupati nikaṭa gayau ghananādā, nānā bhāṁti karesi durbādā.
अस्त्र सस्त्र आयुध सब डारे । कौतुकहीं प्रभु काटि निवारे ॥
astra sastra āyudha saba ḍāre, kautukahīṁ prabhu kāṭi nivāre.
देखि प्रताप मूढ़ खिसिआना । करै लाग माया बिधि नाना ॥
dekhi pratāpa mūṛha khisiānā, karai lāga māyā bidhi nānā.
जिमि कोउ करै गरुड़ सैं खेला । डरपावै गहि स्वल्प सपेला ॥
jimi kou karai garuṛa saiṁ khelā, ḍarapāvai gahi svalpa sapelā.

Trans:

When Hanumān saw the distress of the troops, he rushed forth terrible as death; and quickly tearing up an enormous rook, hurled it at Meghnād with the utmost fury. Seeing it coming, he ascended into the air—chariot, driver, and horses were all lost to sight. Again and again Hanumān dared him to combat; but he would not come near, for he knew the monkey's real essence. And Meghnād approached Rāma, and assailed him with every kind of abuse; and he threw at him many weapons and missiles of every description; but the Lord with the utmost ease cut them asunder and blocked them. On seeing this display of power, the fool was sore vexed and began to put into practice many kinds of magic—as if a poor little snakeling would mock Garud and frighten him by snapping at him.

दोहा-dohā:

जासु प्रबल माया बल सिव बिरंचि बड़ छोट ।
jāsu prabala māyā bala siva biraṁci baṛa choṭa,
ताहि दिखावइ निसिचर निज माया मति खोट ॥५१॥
tāhi dikhāvai nisicara nija māyā mati khoṭa. 51.

Trans:

The demon in the foolishness of his soul displayed his supernatural powers before the Lord—He whose mighty Māyā subdues even Shiva and Brahmmā, let alone all great and small.

चौपाई-caupāī:

नभ चढ़ि बरष बिपुल अंगारा । महि ते प्रगट होहिं जलधारा ॥
nabha caṛhi baraṣa bipula aṁgārā, mahi te pragaṭa hohiṁ jaladhārā.
नाना भाँति पिसाच पिसाची । मारु काटु धुनि बोलहिं नाची ॥
nānā bhāṁti pisāca pisācī, māru kāṭu dhuni bolahiṁ nācī.
बिष्टा पूय रुधिर कच हाड़ा । बरषइ कबहुँ उपल बहु छाड़ा ॥
biṣṭā pūya rudhira kaca hāṛā, baraṣai kabahuṁ upala bahu chāṛā.
बरषि धूरि कीन्हेसि अँधिआरा । सूझ न आपन हाथ पसारा ॥
baraṣi dhūri kīnhesi aṁdhiārā, sūjha na āpana hātha pasārā.
कपि अकुलाने माया देखें । सब कर मरन बना एहि लेखें ॥
kapi akulāne māyā dekheṁ, saba kara marana banā ehi lekheṁ.
कौतुक देखि राम मुसुकाने । भए सभीत सकल कपि जाने ॥
kautuka dekhi rāma musukāne, bhae sabhīta sakala kapi jāne.
एक बान काटी सब माया । जिमि दिनकर हर तिमिर निकाया ॥
eka bāna kāṭī saba māyā, jimi dinakara hara timira nikāyā.
कृपादृष्टि कपि भालु बिलोके । भए प्रबल रन रहहिं न रोके ॥
kṛpādṛṣṭi kapi bhālu biloke, bhae prabala rana rahahiṁ na roke.

Trans:

Mounted up in the air, Meghnād rained down showers of firebrands, and floods of water broke out from the earth. Fiends, goblins, witches of diverse forms danced with uproarious shouts of 'kill, kill; tear them to pieces.' Now a shower of excrement, pus, blood, hair, and bones, and now an overwhelming downfall of ashes and stones. The dust storm made it so dark that if you held out your own arm before, you could see it not. The monkeys were dismayed at the sight of these apparitions and thought "looks like we are doomed now." Rāma smiled when he looked at the mock show. Then seeing that the monkeys were alarmed he, with a single arrow, cleft asunder the delusion—just as the sun dispels the thick darkness. With a glance of compassion, he looked upon the bears and monkeys; at once they waxed so strong that there was no holding them back from the field of battle.

दोहा-dohā:

आयसु मागि राम पहिं अंगदादि कपि साथ ।
āyasu māgi rāma pahiṁ aṁgadādi kapi sātha,
लछिमन चले क्रुद्ध होइ बान सरासन हाथ ॥५२॥
lachimana cale kruddha hoi bāna sarāsana hātha. 52.

Trans:

Having obtained Rāma's permission, Lakshman, taking with him Angad and the other monkeys, marched forth in fury, with bow and arrows in hand.

चौपाई-caupāī:

छतज नयन उर बाहु बिसाला । हिमगिरि निभ तनु कछु एक लाला ॥
chataja nayana ura bāhu bisālā, himagiri nibha tanu kachu eka lālā.
इहाँ दसानन सुभट पठाए । नाना अस्त्र सस्त्र गहि धाए ॥
ihāṁ dasānana subhaṭa paṭhāe, nānā astra sastra gahi dhāe.
भूधर नख बिटपायुध धारी । धाए कपि जय राम पुकारी ॥
bhūdhara nakha biṭapāyudha dhārī, dhāe kapi jaya rāma pukārī.
भिरे सकल जोरिहि सन जोरी । इत उत जय इच्छा नहिं थोरी ॥
bhire sakala jorihi sana jorī, ita uta jaya icchā nahiṁ thorī.

मुठिकन्ह लातन्ह दातन्ह काटहिं । कपि जयसील मारि पुनि डाटहिं ॥
muṭhikanha lātanha dātanha kāṭahiṁ, kapi jayasīla māri puni ḍāṭahiṁ.
मारु मारु धरु धरु धरु मारू । सीस तोरि गहि भुजा उपारू ॥
māru māru dharu dharu dharu mārū, sīsa tori gahi bhujā upārū.
असि रव पूरि रही नव खंडा । धावहिं जहँ तहँ रुंड प्रचंडा ॥
asi rava pūri rahī nava khaṁḍā, dhāvahiṁ jahaṁ tahaṁ ruṁḍa pracaṁḍā.
देखहिं कौतुक नभ सुर बृंदा । कबहुँक बिसमय कबहुँ अनंदा ॥
dekhahiṁ kautuka nabha sura bṛṁdā, kabahuṁka bisamaya kabahuṁ anaṁdā.

Trans:

With bloodshot eyes and mighty chest and arms and his body of reddish hue like Mount Himalaya, he sallied forth. On the other side Rāvan sent out his champions, who took up their armor and their weapons and hastened forth. With mountains and huge trees for missiles, the monkeys rushed to meet them, shouting, "Victory to Rāma." They all closed in the fray, equally matched one with the other; both equally confident of success. After hurling the rocks and mountains at the foe, the monkeys next fell upon them with blows of fist and kicks and rending of teeths; "seize, seize, seize, kill, kill, kill, strike off his head, rend off his arm," such were the cries which filled the nine continents of the world, while headless bodies still full of fury kept running to and fro. From the heaven above, the gods beheld the spectacle, now in dismay and now in rapture.

दोहा-dohā:

रुधिर गाड़ भरि भरि जम्यो ऊपर धूरि उड़ाइ ।
rudhira gāṛa bhari bhari jamyo ūpara dhūri uṛāi,
जनु अँगार रासिन्ह पर मृतक धूम रह्यो छाइ ॥५३॥
janu aṁgāra rāsinha para mṛtaka dhūma rahyo chāi. 53.

Trans:

Every hollow in the ground was filled full of blood, drying up there; and the dust that had risen into overhead clouds gathered thick over it—like ashes spread over heaps of burning funeral piles;

चौपाई-caupāī:

घायल बीर बिराजहिं कैसे । कुसुमित किंसुक के तरु जैसे ॥
ghāyala bīra birājahiṁ kaise, kusumita kiṁsuka ke taru jaise.
लछिमन मेघनाद द्वौ जोधा । भिरहिं परसपर करि अति क्रोधा ॥
lachimana meghanāda dvau jodhā, bhirahiṁ parasapara kari ati krodhā.
एकहि एक सकइ नहिं जीती । निसिचर छल बल करइ अनीती ॥
ekahi eka sakai nahiṁ jītī, nisicara chala bala karai anītī.
क्रोधवंत तब भयउ अनंता । भंजेउ रथ सारथी तुरंता ॥
krodhavaṁta taba bhayau anaṁtā, bhaṁjeu ratha sārathī turaṁtā.
नाना बिधि प्रहार कर सेषा । राच्छस भयउ प्रान अवसेषा ॥
nānā bidhi prahāra kara seṣā, rācchasa bhayau prāna avaseṣā.
रावन सुत निज मन अनुमाना । संकठ भयउ हरिहि मम प्राना ॥
rāvana suta nija mana anumānā, saṁkaṭha bhayau harihi mama prānā.
बीरघातिनी छाड़िसि साँगी । तेज पुंज लछिमन उर लागी ॥
bīraghātinī chāṛisi sāṁgī, teja puṁja lachimana ura lāgī.
मुरुछा भई सक्ति के लागें । तब चलि गयउ निकट भय त्यागें ॥
muruchā bhaī sakti ke lāgeṁ, taba cali gayau nikaṭa bhaya tyāgeṁ.

Trans:

and the wounded warriors shone like so many dhak trees in flower. The two champions Lakshman and Meghnād grappled with one another in excessive fury; neither could get the better of the other. The wicked demon now resorted to wily tricks and unfair means. At last the incarnation of Sheshnāg waxed furious, and in rage with a single blow, he crashed both the chariot and the charioteer. Then he smote the demon prince in such various ways that he was left barely alive. Then the son of Rāvan thought to himself, "I am in deep straits, and he will surely take my life'; and then he let fly his notorious spear, the destroyer of heroes, which struck Lakshman in the chest with full force. So great was the shock that he swooned away. Then Meghnād went and drew near, no longer afraid.

दोहा-dohā:

मेघनाद सम कोटि सत जोधा रहे उठाइ ।
meghanāda sama koṭi sata jodhā rahe uṭhāi,
जगदाधार सेष किमि उठै चले खिसिआइ ॥५४॥
jagadādhāra seṣa kimi uṭhai cale khisiāi. 54.

Trans:

A hundred myriad warriors like Meghnād essayed to lift him; but how could Sheshnāg, the supporter of the world, be thus lifted? He had to return empty handed, smarting with shame.

चौपाई-caupāī:

सुनु गिरिजा क्रोधानल जासू । जारइ भुवन चारिदस आसू ॥
sunu girijā krodhānala jāsū, jārai bhuvana cāridasa āsū.
सक संग्राम जीति को ताही । सेवहिं सुर नर अग जग जाही ॥
saka saṁgrāma jīti ko tāhī, sevahiṁ sura nara aga jaga jāhī.
यह कौतूहल जानइ सोई । जा पर कृपा राम कै होई ॥
yaha kautūhala jānai soī, jā para kṛpā rāma kai hoī.
संध्या भइ फिरि द्वौ बाहनी । लगे सँभारन निज निज अनी ॥
saṁdhyā bhai phiri dvau bāhanī, lage saṁbhārana nija nija anī.
ब्यापक ब्रह्म अजित भुवनेस्वर । लछिमन कहाँ बूझ करुनाकर ॥
byāpaka brahma ajita bhuvanesvara, lachimana kahāṁ būjha karunākara.
तब लगि लै आयउ हनुमाना । अनुज देखि प्रभु अति दुख माना ॥
taba lagi lai āyau hanumānā, anuja dekhi prabhu ati dukha mānā.
जामवंत कह बैद सुषेना । लंकाँ रहइ को पठई लेना ॥
jāmavaṁta kaha baida suṣenā, laṁkāṁ rahai ko paṭhaī lenā.
धरि लघु रूप गयउ हनुमंता । आनेउ भवन समेत तुरंता ॥
dhari laghu rūpa gayau hanumaṁtā, āneu bhavana sameta turaṁtā.

Trans:

Hearken O Bhawānī: who can conquer him in battle, the fire of whose wrath would consume in a moment the fourteen spheres of creation, whom gods and men and all things animate and inanimate adore? Only he can understand this mystery, on whom rests the favor of Rāma. It was already evening and both armies left the field and began to muster their forces. The All-merciful, the ubiquitous Supreme Spirit, the invincible Lord of the universe, asked "Where is Lakshman?" Hanumān then brought him forward. When the Lord saw his younger brother, he was much distressed. Jāmvant said, "The physician Sushen is at Lankā, send someone to fetch him." Hanumān at once assumed a diminutive form and went and brought him, including house and all.

दोहा-dohā:

राम पदारबिंद सिर नायउ आइ सुषेन ।
rāma padārabiṁda sira nāyau āi suṣena,
कहा नाम गिरि औषधी जाहु पवनसुत लेन ॥५५॥
kahā nāma giri auṣadhī jāhu pavanasuta lena. 55.

Trans:

Sushen, the physician bowed his head at Rāma's lotus feet. Next he mentioned a certain herb and on which mountain it could be had, and told Hanumān to go fetch it.

चौपाई-caupāī:

राम चरन सरसिज उर राखी । चला प्रभंजन सुत बल भाषी ॥
rāma carana sarasija ura rākhī, calā prabhaṁjana suta bala bhāṣī.
उहाँ दूत एक मरमु जनावा । रावन कालनेमि गृह आवा ॥
uhāṁ dūta eka maramu janāvā, rāvana kālanemi gṛha āvā.
दसमुख कहा मरमु तेहिं सुना । पुनि पुनि कालनेमि सिरु धुना ॥
dasamukha kahā maramu tehiṁ sunā, puni puni kālanemi siru dhunā.
देखत तुम्हहि नगरु जेहिं जारा । तासु पंथ को रोकन पारा ॥

dekhata tumhahi nagaru jehiṁ jārā, tāsu paṁtha ko rokana pārā.

भजि रघुपति करु हित आपना । छाँड़हु नाथ मृषा जल्पना ॥

bhaji raghupati karu hita āpanā, chām̐ṛahu nātha mṛṣā jalpanā.

नील कंज तनु सुंदर स्यामा । हृदयँ राखु लोचनाभिरामा ॥

nīla kaṁja tanu suṁdara syāmā, hṛdayam̐ rākhu locanābhirāmā.

मैं तैं मोर मूढ़ता त्यागू । महा मोह निसि सूतत जागू ॥

maiṁ taiṁ mora mūṛhatā tyāgū, mahā moha nisi sūtata jāgū.

काल ब्याल कर भच्छक जोई । सपनेहुँ समर कि जीतिअ सोई ॥

kāla byāla kara bhacchaka joī, sapanehum̐ samara ki jītia soī.

Trans:

With Rāma's lotus feet impressed upon his heart, the son-of-wind started in confident assurance. On the other side, a spy gave information; and so Rāvan went to the house of Kālnemī and instructed him. When he had heard the news, Kālnemī beat his head again and again crying, "Who can stop his path who burnt your city before your very eyes. Have some regard for your own welfare and worship Rāma and desist, sire, from these vain endeavors. Cherish in your heart the delight of all eyes, whose body is dark and beautiful as the blue lotus. Be done with pride, conceit, arrogance; and rouse yourself from this slumber of delusional night. Can anyone even dream of conquering Him in battle who devours even the serpent Time that is seen to devour all else?"

दोहा-dohā:

सुनि दसकंठ रिसान अति तेहिं मन कीन्ह बिचार ।

suni dasakaṁṭha risāna ati tehiṁ mana kīnha bicāra,

राम दूत कर मरौं बरु यह खल रत मल भार ॥५६॥

rāma dūta kara maraum̐ baru yaha khala rata mala bhāra. 56.

Trans:

When the Ten-headed heard this, he was exceedingly wrath and Kālnemī therefore reasoned to himself, "It will be better for me to die at the hands of Rāma's messenger, and not for this wretch to kill me."

चौपाई-caupāī:

अस कहि चला रचिसि मग माया । सर मंदिर बर बाग बनाया ॥

asa kahi calā racisi maga māyā, sara maṁdira bara bāga banāyā.

मारुतसुत देखा सुभ आश्रम । मुनिहि बूझि जल पियौं जाइ श्रम ॥

mārutasuta dekhā subha āśrama, munihi būjhi jala piyauṁ jāi śrama.

राच्छस कपट बेष तहँ सोहा । मायापति दूतहि चह मोहा ॥

rācchasa kapaṭa beṣa taham̐ sohā, māyāpati dūtahi caha mohā.

जाइ पवनसुत नायउ माथा । लाग सो कहै राम गुन गाथा ॥

jāi pavanasuta nāyau māthā, lāga so kahai rāma guna gāthā.

होत महा रन रावन रामहिं । जितिहहिं राम न संसय या महिं ॥

hota mahā rana rāvana rāmahiṁ, jitihahiṁ rāma na saṁsaya yā mahiṁ.

इहाँ भएँ मैं देखउँ भाई । ग्यान दृष्टि बल मोहि अधिकाई ॥

ihām̐ bhaem̐ maiṁ dekhaum̐ bhāī, gyāna dṛṣṭi bala mohi adhikāī.

मागा जल तेहिं दीन्ह कमंडल । कह कपि नहिं अघाउँ थोरें जल ॥

māgā jala tehiṁ dīnha kamaṁḍala, kaha kapi nahiṁ aghāum̐ thoreṁ jala.

सर मज्जन करि आतुर आवहु । दिच्छा देउँ ग्यान जेहिं पावहु ॥

sara majjana kari ātura āvahu, dicchā deum̐ gyāna jehiṁ pāvahu.

Trans:

So saying he went, and by the power of magic constructed on the way-side a lake and a temple with fine garden. Hanumān saw the charming spot and thought to himself, "After asking the holy man's permission, I will drink of the water and remove my fatigue." The demon had ensconced himself there in the deceitful garb of a hermit and sought to delude even the messenger of the King-of-Delusion. The son-of-wind went and bowed his head; and the demon in turn began to recite Rāma's praises saying, "A great battle is raging between Rāvan and Rāma, but Rāma will win the day; of this there is no doubt. Though I have not moved from here, I have seen it all, my friend; my intelligence is remarkably clear-sighted." On his asking for water, he gave some in a water-pot; to which the monkey said, "That is not enough to quench my thirst." "Go then and bathe in the tank and quickly come back, and I will then bestow upon you a charm, by which you will attain all wisdom."

दोहा-dohā:

सर पैठत कपि पद गहा मकरीं तब अकुलान ।

sara paiṭhata kapi pada gahā makarīṁ taba akulāna,

मारी सो धरि दिब्य तनु चली गगन चढ़ि जान ॥५७॥

mārī so dhari dibya tanu calī gagana caṛhi jāna. 57.

Trans:

No sooner had Hanumān stepped into the lake than a she-alligator seized him by the foot in great agitation; then slain by Hanumān, she assumed a celestial form and mounted an aerial car, to soar into the heavens.

चौपाई-caupāī:

कपि तव दरस भइउँ निष्पापा । मिटा तात मुनिबर कर सापा ॥

kapi tava darasa bhaium̐ niṣpāpā, miṭā tāta munibara kara sāpā.

मुनि न होइ यह निसिचर घोरा । मानहु सत्य बचन कपि मोरा ॥

muni na hoi yaha nisicara ghorā, mānahu satya bacana kapi morā.

अस कहि गई अपछरा जबहीं । निसिचर निकट गयउ कपि तबहीं ॥

asa kahi gaī apacharā jabahīṁ, nisicara nikaṭa gayau kapi tabahīṁ.

कह कपि मुनि गुरदछिना लेहू । पाछें हमहि मंत्र तुम्ह देहू ॥

kaha kapi muni guradachinā lehū, pācheṁ hamahi maṁtra tumha dehū.

सिर लंगूर लपेटि पछारा । निज तनु प्रगटेसि मरती बारा ॥

sira laṁgūra lapeṭi pachārā, nija tanu pragaṭesi maratī bārā.

राम राम कहि छाड़ेसि प्राना । सुनि मन हरषि चलेउ हनुमाना ॥

rāma rāma kahi chāṛesi prānā, suni mana haraṣi caleu hanumānā.

देखा सैल न औषध चीन्हा । सहसा कपि उपारि गिरि लीन्हा ॥

dekhā saila na auṣadha cīnhā, sahasā kapi upāri giri līnhā.

गहि गिरि निसि नभ धावत भयऊ । अवधपुरी ऊपर कपि गयऊ ॥

gahi giri nisi nabha dhāvata bhayaū, avadhapurī ūpara kapi gayaū.

Trans:

"By the sight of you, O monkey, I have become freed from all sins, and the curse of the great saint has been removed. This is no hermit here but a fierce demon; doubt not the truth of my words." So saying, the heavenly nymph went her way, and the monkey at once returned to the demon. Said the monkey, "Holy Sir, first receive my offering and after that tell me of the charm." He then twisted his tail round his head and threw him down. At the moment of his death the demon appeared in his proper form, and with a cry of "Rāma-Rāma" breathed his last; and Hanumān went on his way, glad of heart. He found the mountain, but could not recognize the herbs; so without any hesitation he tore up the entire hill by the root and went off with it. As he rushed through the night air with the mountain in his grasp, he passed over the city of Avadh.

दोहा-dohā:

देखा भरत बिसाल अति निसिचर मन अनुमानि ।

dekhā bharata bisāla ati nisicara mana anumāni,

बिनु फर सायक मारेउ चाप श्रवन लगि तानि ॥५८॥

binu phara sāyaka māreu cāpa śravana lagi tāni. 58.

Trans:

Bharat saw him, and taking him to be some most monstrous demon, drew his bow to his ear and shot him with a headless shaft.

चौपाई-caupāī:

परेउ मुरुछि महि लागत सायक । सुमिरत राम राम रघुनायक ॥

pareu muruchi mahi lāgata sāyaka, sumirata rāma rāma raghunāyaka.

सुनि प्रिय बचन भरत तब धाए । कपि समीप अति आतुर आए ॥

suni priya bacana bharata taba dhāe, kapi samīpa ati ātura āe.

बिकल बिलोकि कीस उर लावा । जागत नहिं बहु भाँति जगावा ॥

bikala biloki kīsa ura lāvā, jāgata nahiṁ bahu bhāṁti jagāvā.
मुख मलीन मन भए दुखारी । कहत बचन भरि लोचन बारी ॥
mukha malīna mana bhae dukhārī, kahata bacana bhari locana bārī.
जेहिं बिधि राम बिमुख मोहि कीन्हा । तेहिं पुनि यह दारुन दुख दीन्हा ॥
jehiṁ bidhi rāma bimukha mohi kīnhā, tehiṁ puni yaha dāruna dukha dīnhā.
जौं मोरें मन बच अरु काया । प्रीति राम पद कमल अमाया ॥
jauṁ moreṁ mana baca aru kāyā, prīti rāma pada kamala amāyā.
तौ कपि होउ बिगत श्रम सूला । जौं मो पर रघुपति अनुकूला ॥
tau kapi hou bigata śrama sūlā, jauṁ mo para raghupati anukūlā.
सुनत बचन उठि बैठ कपीसा । कहि जय जयति कोसलाधीसा ॥
sunata bacana uṭhi baiṭha kapīsā, kahi jaya jayati kosalādhīsā.

Trans:

Struck by the dart he fell in a swoon to the earth, crying "O Rāma, Rāma, Raghu-Nāyak" On hearing these endearing words, Bharat started up and ran, and in the utmost haste drew nigh to the monkey. Seeing him wounded, he clasped him to his bosom and tried in every way to revive him—but with no success. With a disconsolate face and sore grief at heart, he made this prayer, while his eyes streamed with tears, "Gods, who made me Rāma's enemy, have now caused me this additional distress. If in thought, word and deed, I have a sincere affection for Rāma's lotus feet, and if Rāma is kindly disposed to me, may your pain and fatigue, O monkey, all pass away." At the sound of these words, the monkey chief arose and sat up, crying "Glory, Glory to the King of Kaushal."

सोरठा-soraṭhā:

लीन्ह कपिहि उर लाइ पुलकित तनु लोचन सजल ।
līnha kapihi ura lāi pulakita tanu locana sajala,
प्रीति न हृदयँ समाइ सुमिरि राम रघुकुल तिलक ॥५९॥
prīti na hṛdayaṁ samāi sumiri rāma raghukula tilaka. 59.

Trans:

With quivering limbs and eyes full of tears, Bharat took and clasped the monkey to his bosom in a transport of affection. His heart overflowed with love at the very thought of Shrī Rāma, the crown of the line of Raghus.

चौपाई-caupāī:

तात कुसल कहु सुखनिधान की । सहित अनुज अरु मातु जानकी ॥
tāta kusala kahu sukhanidhāna kī, sahita anuja aru mātu jānakī.
कपि सब चरित समास बखाने । भए दुखी मन महुँ पछिताने ॥
kapi saba carita samāsa bakhāne, bhae dukhī mana mahuṁ pachitāne.
अहह दैव मैं कत जग जायउँ । प्रभु के एकहु काज न आयउँ ॥
ahaha daiva maiṁ kata jaga jāyauṁ, prabhu ke ekahu kāja na āyauṁ.
जानि कुअवसरु मन धरि धीरा । पुनि कपि सन बोले बलबीरा ॥
jāni kuavasaru mana dhari dhīrā, puni kapi sana bole balabīrā.
तात गहरु होइहि तोहि जाता । काजु नसाइहि होत प्रभाता ॥
tāta gaharu hoihi tohi jātā, kāju nasāihi hota prabhātā.
चढ़ु मम सायक सैल समेता । पठवौं तोहि जहँ कृपानिकेता ॥
caṛhu mama sāyaka saila sametā, paṭhavauṁ tohi jahaṁ kṛpāniketā.
सुनि कपि मन उपजा अभिमाना । मोरें भार चलिहि किमि बाना ॥
suni kapi mana upajā abhimānā, moreṁ bhāra calihi kimi bānā.
राम प्रभाव बिचारि बहोरी । बंदि चरन कह कपि कर जोरी ॥
rāma prabhāva bicāri bahorī, baṁdi carana kaha kapi kara jorī.

Trans:

"Tell me friend, is all well with the Fountain of Joy, and with his brother, and the revered Jānakī." The monkey told him in brief all that had taken place. He became sad of heart and began to lament, "Alas, my fate, why was I born into the world, if in nothing I could help my Lord." But seeing the unfitness of the time he mastered his feelings, the gallant prince, and again addressed the monkey, "Sir, you will be delayed in your journey and your task will come to naught, for the day is now breaking. Mount my arrow, mountain and all, and I will send you straight into the presence of the All-merciful." On hearing this, the monkey's ego stirred up for a moment, "How can his arrow fly with my weight?" But again reflecting on Rāma's power and glory, he bowed at his feet and cried with clasped hands,

दोहा-dohā:

तव प्रताप उर राखि प्रभु जैहउँ नाथ तुरंत ।
tava pratāpa ura rākhi prabhu jaihauṁ nātha turaṁta,
अस कहि आयसु पाइ पद बंदि चलेउ हनुमंत ॥६०क॥
asa kahi āyasu pāi pada baṁdi caleu hanumaṁta. 60(ka).

भरत बाहु बल सील गुन प्रभु पद प्रीति अपार ।
bharata bāhu bala sīla guna prabhu pada prīti apāra,
मन महुँ जात सराहत पुनि पुनि पवनकुमार ॥६०ख॥
mana mahuṁ jāta sarāhata puni puni pavanakumāra. 60(kha).

Trans:

"O my Lord, I have only to cherish the thought of your majesty in my soul in order to travel quickly." So saying, Hanumān took leave and after bowing at his feet set forth. As he went, the son-of-wind again and again extolled to himself the mighty strength and amiable disposition of Bharat and his boundless devotion to the Lord's feet.

चौपाई-caupāī:

उहाँ राम लछिमनहि निहारी । बोले बचन मनुज अनुसारी ॥
uhāṁ rāma lachimanahi nihārī, bole bacana manuja anusārī.
अर्ध राति गइ कपि नहिं आयउ । राम उठाइ अनुज उर लायउ ॥
ardha rāti gai kapi nahiṁ āyau, rāma uṭhāi anuja ura lāyau.
सकहु न दुखित देखि मोहि काऊ । बंधु सदा तव मृदुल सुभाऊ ॥
sakahu na dukhita dekhi mohi kāū, baṁdhu sadā tava mṛdula subhāū.
मम हित लागि तजेहु पितु माता । सहेहु बिपिन हिम आतप बाता ॥
mama hita lāgi tajehu pitu mātā, sahehu bipina hima ātapa bātā.
सो अनुराग कहाँ अब भाई । उठहु न सुनि मम बच बिकलाई ॥
so anurāga kahāṁ aba bhāī, uṭhahu na suni mama baca bikalāī.
जौं जनतेउँ बन बंधु बिछोहू । पिता बचन मनतेउँ नहिं ओहू ॥
jauṁ janateuṁ bana baṁdhu bichohū, pitā bacana manateuṁ nahiṁ ohū.
सुत बित नारि भवन परिवारा । होहिं जाहिं जग बारहिं बारा ॥
suta bita nāri bhavana parivārā, hohiṁ jāhiṁ jaga bārahiṁ bārā.
अस बिचारि जियँ जागहु ताता । मिलइ न जगत सहोदर भ्राता ॥
asa bicāri jiyaṁ jāgahu tātā, milai na jagata sahodara bhrātā.
जथा पंख बिनु खग अति दीना । मनि बिनु फनि करिबर कर हीना ॥
jathā paṁkha binu khaga ati dīnā, mani binu phani karibara kara hīnā.
अस मम जिवन बंधु बिनु तोही । जौं जड़ दैव जिआवै मोही ॥
asa mama jivana baṁdhu binu tohī, jauṁ jaṛa daiva jiāvai mohī.
जैहउँ अवध कवन मुहु लाई । नारि हेतु प्रिय भाइ गँवाई ॥
jaihauṁ avadha kavana muhu lāī, nāri hetu priya bhāi gaṁvāī.
बरु अपजस सहतेउँ जग माहीं । नारि हानि बिसेष छति नाहीं ॥
baru apajasa sahateuṁ jaga māhīṁ, nāri hāni biseṣa chati nāhīṁ.
अब अपलोकु सोकु सुत तोरा । सहिहि निठुर कठोर उर मोरा ॥
aba apaloku soku suta torā, sahihi niṭhura kaṭhora ura morā.
निज जननी के एक कुमारा । तात तासु तुम्ह प्रान अधारा ॥
nija jananī ke eka kumārā, tāta tāsu tumha prāna adhārā.
सौंपेसि मोहि तुम्हहि गहि पानी । सब बिधि सुखद परम हित जानी ॥
sauṁpesi mohi tumhahi gahi pānī, saba bidhi sukhada parama hita jānī.
उतरु काह दैहउँ तेहि जाई । उठि किन मोहि सिखावहु भाई ॥
utaru kāha daihauṁ tehi jāī, uṭhi kina mohi sikhāvahu bhāī.

बहु बिधि सोचत सोच बिमोचन । स्रवत सलिल राजिव दल लोचन ॥
bahu bidhi socata soca bimocana, sravata salila rājiva dala locana.
उमा एक अखंड रघुराई । नर गति भगत कृपाल देखाई ॥
umā eka akhaṁḍa raghurāī, nara gati bhagata kṛpāla dekhāī.

Trans:

Meanwhile Rāma, as he sat watching over Lakshman, uttered words in the manner of mortals. When half the night was spent, and still the monkey had not returned, Rāma raised his brother and clasped him to his heart, "O my brother, once you could not endure to see me in sorrow; your disposition was ever so full of affection. On my account, you left father and mother and exposed yourself to the forest; the cold, the heat, and the wind. But where now is your old love, my brother, that you do not stir in response to my distress? If I had known that exile involved the loss of my brother, I would never have obeyed my father's commands. Sons, riches, wives, house, and kinsfolk come again time after time in life, but a real brother is not so to be had; remember this, brother, and awaken to life. As a bird is utterly wretched without wings, a serpent without its head-jewel, and an elephant without its trunk, so is Rāma's life without Lakshman. If cruel fate preserves me alive, with what face can I show myself at Avadh after sacrificing a dear brother for the sake of a woman? I would rather have endured the social disgrace; for, after all, the loss of a wife is not such serious as this. Now however, my unfeeling and stony heart will have to endure both that obloquy and the deep anguish of your loss, son. Your mother's only son, you are the sole prop of her life. Yet she took you by the hand and entrusted you to me, knowing that I would make you happy in everyway and that I am your greatest well-wisher. What answer can I go give her? Why do you not arise and advise me, brother?" Thus grievously sorrowed the healer of sorrow and his lotus eyes streamed with tears. O Umā, Rāma is the One-God, unchangeable, and it was only in compassion to his worshippers that he exhibited such manners of a human.

सोरठा-soraṭhā:

प्रभु प्रलाप सुनि कान बिकल भए बानर निकर ।
prabhu pralāpa suni kāna bikala bhae bānara nikara,
आइ गयउ हनुमान जिमि करुना महँ बीर रस ॥ ६१ ॥
āi gayau hanumāna jimi karunā mahaṁ bīra rasa. 61.

Trans:

All the monkeys were in distress on hearing their Lord's lamentation, until arrived there Hanumān—like a heroic tenor in the midst of elegy.

चौपाई-caupāī:

हरषि राम भेंटेउ हनुमाना । अति कृतग्य प्रभु परम सुजाना ॥
haraṣi rāma bheṁṭeu hanumānā, ati kṛtagya prabhu parama sujānā.
तुरत बैद तब कीन्हि उपाई । उठि बैठे लछिमन हरषाई ॥
turata baida taba kīnhi upāī, uṭhi baiṭhe lachimana haraṣāī.
हृदयँ लाइ प्रभु भेटेउ भ्राता । हरषे सकल भालु कपि ब्राता ॥
hṛdayaṁ lāi prabhu bheṭeu bhrātā, haraṣe sakala bhālu kapi brātā.
कपि पुनि बैद तहाँ पहुँचावा । जेहि बिधि तबहिं ताहि लइ आवा ॥
kapi puni baida tahāṁ pahuṁcāvā, jehi bidhi tabahiṁ tāhi lai āvā.
यह बृत्तांत दसानन सुनेऊ । अति बिषाद पुनि पुनि सिर धुनेऊ ॥
yaha bṛttāṁta dasānana suneū, ati biṣāda puni puni sira dhuneū.
ब्याकुल कुंभकरन पहिं आवा । बिबिध जतन करि ताहि जगावा ॥
byākula kuṁbhakarana pahiṁ āvā, bibidha jatana kari tāhi jagāvā.
जागा निसिचर देखिअ कैसा । मानहुँ कालु देह धरि बैसा ॥
jāgā nisicara dekhia kaisā, mānahuṁ kālu deha dhari baisā.
कुंभकरन बूझा कहु भाई । काहे तव मुख रहे सुखाई ॥
kuṁbhakarana būjhā kahu bhāī, kāhe tava mukha rahe sukhāī.
कथा कही सब तेहिं अभिमानी । जेहि प्रकार सीता हरि आनी ॥
kathā kahī saba tehiṁ abhimānī, jehi prakāra sītā hari ānī.
तात कपिन्ह सब निसिचर मारे । महा महा जोधा संघारे ॥
tāta kapinha saba nisicara māre, mahā mahā jodhā saṁghāre.
दुर्मुख सुररिपु मनुज अहारी । भट अतिकाय अकंपन भारी ॥
durmukha suraripu manuja ahārī, bhaṭa atikāya akaṁpana bhārī.
अपर महोदर आदिक बीरा । परे समर महि सब रनधीरा ॥
apara mahodara ādika bīrā, pare samara mahi saba ranadhīrā.

Trans:

Rāma received him with exceeding joy, for the Lord is most grateful by nature and supremely wise. Quickly the physician concocted his remedies, and Lakshman cheerfully rose up and sat. The Lord affectionately clasped his brother to his heart and all the bears and monkeys rejoiced. The physician was then conveyed back in the same manner as he had been brought—home and all. When Rāvan heard of these proceedings, he was greatly disturbed and began beating himself on the head. In his agitation, he went to Kumbh-karan and with much trouble succeeded in waking him. When the monster was roused, he showed like Death itself in visible form. He asked, "Tell me, brother, why is your face so sad." He told him the whole history of how in his pride he had carried off Sītā. "Dear brother, the monkeys have killed all the demons and extirpated the greatest warriors. Durmukha, Devantak (the enemy of gods), Narantak (the devourer of men), the mighty champions Atikaya (of enormous size) and Akampan (who never trembles in fear) and other heroes like Mahodar (the big-bellied), so staunch in battle, have all fallen on the field of battle."

दोहा-dohā:

सुनि दसकंधर बचन तब कुंभकरन बिलखान ।
suni dasakaṁdhara bacana taba kuṁbhakarana bilakhāna,
जगदंबा हरि आनि अब सठ चाहत कल्यान ॥ ६२ ॥
jagadaṁbā hari āni aba saṭha cāhata kalyāna. 62.

Trans:

Upon hearing Rāvan's report, Kumbh-karan cried out, "Wretch, you have carried off the mother of the universe and yet expect to prosper!

चौपाई-caupāī:

भल न कीन्ह तैं निसिचर नाहा । अब मोहि आइ जगाएहि काहा ॥
bhala na kīnha taiṁ nisicara nāhā, aba mohi āi jagāehi kāhā.
अजहूँ तात त्यागि अभिमाना । भजहु राम होइहि कल्याना ॥
ajahūṁ tāta tyāgi abhimānā, bhajahu rāma hoihi kalyānā.
हैं दससीस मनुज रघुनायक । जाके हनूमान से पायक ॥
haiṁ dasasīsa manuja raghunāyaka, jāke hanūmāna se pāyaka.
अहह बंधु तैं कीन्हि खोटाई । प्रथमहिं मोहि न सुनाएहि आई ॥
ahaha baṁdhu taiṁ kīnhi khoṭāī, prathamahiṁ mohi na sunāehi āī.
कीन्हेहु प्रभु बिरोध तेहि देवक । सिव बिरंचि सुर जाके सेवक ॥
kīnhehu prabhu birodha tehi devaka, siva biraṁci sura jāke sevaka.
नारद मुनि मोहि ग्यान जो कहा । कहतेउँ तोहि समय निरबहा ॥
nārada muni mohi gyāna jo kahā, kahateuṁ tohi samaya nirabahā.
अब भरि अंक भेंटु मोहि भाई । लोचन सुफल करौं मैं जाई ॥
aba bhari aṁka bheṁṭu mohi bhāī, locana suphala karauṁ maiṁ jāī.
स्याम गात सरसीरुह लोचन । देखौं जाइ ताप त्रय मोचन ॥
syāma gāta sarasīruha locana, dekhauṁ jāi tāpa traya mocana.

Trans:

You have done great wrong, demon king; and now why have you come and awakened me? At once, my brother, abandon pride and worship Rāma—so you may prosper. How, O Ten-headed, can Rāma be a man, who has such a servant as Hanumān? Alas brother, you have acted foolishly; why did you not come and wake me before? You have rebelled against the One-God who is adored by Shiva and Brahmmā and every other divinity. The knowledge which sage Nārad once imparted to me, I would have declared to you; but the time has passed. Embrace me, my brother, for I go to rejoice my eyes with the sight of the dark-hued, the lotus-eyed, the healer of every sorrow."

दोहा-dohā:

राम रूप गुन सुमिरत मगन भयउ छन एक।

rāma rūpa guna sumirata magana bhayau chana eka,

रावन मागेउ कोटि घट मद अरु महिष अनेक ॥६३॥

rāvana māgeu koṭi ghaṭa mada aru mahiṣa aneka. 63.

Trans:

As he contemplated Rāma's beauty and perfection, he was for a moment lost. In the meantime Rāvan requisitioned, for his consumption, myriads of jars full of wine and whole herds of buffaloes.

चौपाई-caupāī:

महिष खाइ करि मदिरा पाना। गर्जा बज्राघात समाना॥

mahiṣa khāi kari madirā pānā, garjā bajrāghāta samānā.

कुंभकरन दुर्मद रन रंगा। चला दुर्ग तजि सेन न संगा॥

kuṁbhakarana durmada rana raṁgā, calā durga taji sena na saṁgā.

देखि बिभीषनु आगें आयउ। परेउ चरन निज नाम सुनायउ॥

dekhi bibhīṣanu āgeṁ āyau, pareu carana nija nāma sunāyau.

अनुज उठाइ हृदयँ तेहि लायो। रघुपति भक्त जानि मन भायो॥

anuja uṭhāi hṛdayaṁ tehi lāyo, raghupati bhakta jāni mana bhāyo.

तात लात रावन मोहि मारा। कहत परम हित मंत्र बिचारा॥

tāta lāta rāvana mohi mārā, kahata parama hita maṁtra bicārā.

तेहिं गलानि रघुपति पहिं आयउँ। देखि दीन प्रभु के मन भायउँ॥

tehiṁ galāni raghupati pahiṁ āyauṁ, dekhi dīna prabhu ke mana bhāyauṁ.

सुनु सुत भयउ कालबस रावन। सो कि मान अब परम सिखावन॥

sunu suta bhayau kālabasa rāvana, so ki māna aba parama sikhāvana.

धन्य धन्य तैं धन्य बिभीषन। भयहु तात निसिचर कुल भूषन॥

dhanya dhanya taiṁ dhanya bibhīṣana, bhayahu tāta nisicara kula bhūṣana.

बंधु बंस तैं कीन्ह उजागर। भजेहु राम सोभा सुख सागर॥

baṁdhu baṁsa taiṁ kīnha ujāgara, bhajehu rāma sobhā sukha sāgara.

Trans:

After he had eaten the buffaloes and drank the wine, he roared aloud with a voice of thunder and sallied forth from the fort without any escort, maddened with drink—the war-loving Kumbh-karan. Vibhīshan, on seeing him, came forward and fell at his feet and said who he was. He raised his brother and took him to his heart, delighted to find him a worshipper of Rāma. "Brother, that wretch Rāvan struck me with his foot for giving him the best possible advice. Resenting such treatment, I came to Rāma, and the Lord was glad at heart to see me his servant." "Mark me brother, Rāvan is under the influence of fate and will listen to any advice, however good it be. Thrice blessed are you, Vibhīshan, the glory of all the demon race; you have shed a luster on all your kinsfolk by your worship of Rāma—that ocean of beauty and felicity.

दोहा-dohā:

बचन कर्म मन कपट तजि भजेहु राम रनधीर।

bacana karma mana kapaṭa taji bhajehu rāma ranadhīra,

जाहु न निज पर सूझ मोहि भयउँ कालबस बीर ॥६४॥

jāhu na nija para sūjha mohi bhayauṁ kālabasa bīra. 64.

Trans:

Brother, in thought, word and deed, without any guile, you should always worship Shrī Rāma, the gallant in battle. But go now, for I cannot distinguish anymore between friend and foe—doomed to death am I, it seems.

चौपाई-caupāī:

बंधु बचन सुनि चला बिभीषन। आयउ जहँ त्रैलोक बिभूषन॥

baṁdhu bacana suni calā bibhīṣana, āyau jahaṁ trailoka bibhūṣana.

नाथ भूधराकार सरीरा। कुंभकरन आवत रनधीरा॥

nātha bhūdharākāra sarīrā, kuṁbhakarana āvata ranadhīrā.

एतना कपिन्ह सुना जब काना। किलकिलाइ धाए बलवाना॥

etanā kapinha sunā jaba kānā, kilakilāi dhāe balavānā.

लिए उठाइ बिटप अरु भूधर। कटकटाइ डारहिं ता ऊपर॥

lie uṭhāi biṭapa aru bhūdhara, kaṭakaṭāi ḍārahiṁ tā ūpara.

कोटि कोटि गिरि सिखर प्रहारा। करहिं भालु कपि एक एक बारा॥

koṭi koṭi giri sikhara prahārā, karahiṁ bhālu kapi eka eka bārā.

मुरयो न मनु तनु टरयो न टारयो। जिमि गज अर्क फलनि को मारयो॥

mur yo na mana tanu ṭar yo na ṭār yo, jimi gaja arka phalani ko mārayo.

तब मारुतसुत मुठिका हन्यो। परयो धरनि ब्याकुल सिर धुन्यो॥

taba mārutasuta muṭhikā hanyo, parayo dharani byākula sira dhunyo.

पुनि उठि तेहिं मारेउ हनुमंता। घुर्मित भूतल परेउ तुरंता॥

puni uṭhi tehiṁ māreu hanumaṁtā, ghurmita bhūtala pareu turaṁtā.

पुनि नल नीलहि अवनि पछारेसि। जहँ तहँ पटकि पटकि भट डारेसि॥

puni nala nīlahi avani pachāresi, jahaṁ tahaṁ paṭaki paṭaki bhaṭa ḍāresi.

चली बलीमुख सेन पराई। अति भय त्रसित न कोउ समुहाई॥

calī balīmukha sena parāī, ati bhaya trasita na kou samuhāī.

Trans:

On hearing his brother's words, Vibhīshan turned and presented himself before the Glory of the three spheres. "My Lord, here comes Kumbh-karan, a huge warrior, large as a mountain." The monkeys waited to hear no more, and ran off jabbering, the stoutest of them, and plucked up trees and rocks, which they hurled against him, gnashing their teeth the while. Millions upon millions of mountain peaks did the bears and monkeys hurl upon him one after another; but neither did his courage fail, nor did he retreat from his position—like an elephant being pelted with flower-seeds. At last the son-of-wind struck him with his fist; and he fell to the ground and beat his head in dismay. Rising again, he gave Hanumān such a blow that he spun round and fell at once to the earth. Next he overthrew Nala and Nīl upon the ground and dashed down other warriors, hurtling them this side and that. The monkey host scattered and fled in an utter panic, nor were there any to rally.

दोहा-dohā:

अंगदादि कपि मुरुछित करि समेत सुग्रीव।

aṁgadādi kapi muruchita kari sameta sugrīva,

काँख दाबि कपिराज कहुँ चला अमित बल सींव ॥६५॥

kāṁkha dābi kapirāja kahuṁ calā amita bala sīṁva. 65.

Trans:

Having rendered insensible Angad and the other monkeys and Sugrīva as well, he clapped the king of the monkeys under his armpit and went off, the very perfection of strength.

चौपाई-caupāī:

उमा करत रघुपति नरलीला। खेलत गरुड़ जिमि अहिगन मीला॥

umā karata raghupati naralīlā, khelata garuṛa jimi ahigana mīlā.

भृकुटि भंग जो कालहि खाई। ताहि कि सोहइ ऐसि लराई॥

bhṛkuṭi bhaṁga jo kālahi khāī, tāhi ki sohai aisi larāī.

जग पावनि कीरति बिस्तरिहहिं। गाइ गाइ भवनिधि नर तरिहहिं॥

jaga pāvani kīrati bistarihahiṁ, gāi gāi bhavanidhi nara tarihahiṁ.

मुरुछा गइ मारुतसुत जागा। सुग्रीवहि तब खोजन लागा॥

muruchā gai mārutasuta jāgā, sugrīvahi taba khojana lāgā.

सुग्रीवहु कै मुरुछा बीती। निबुक गयउ तेहि मृतक प्रतीती॥

sugrīvahu kai muruchā bītī, nibuka gayau tehi mṛtaka pratītī.

काटेसि दसन नासिका काना। गरजि अकास चलेउ तेहिं जाना॥

kāṭesi dasana nāsikā kānā, garaji akāsa caleu tehiṁ jānā.

गहेउ चरन गहि भूमि पछारा। अति लाघवँ उठि पुनि तेहि मारा॥

gaheu carana gahi bhūmi pachārā, ati lāghavaṁ uṭhi puni tehi mārā.

पुनि आयउ प्रभु पहिं बलवाना। जयति जयति जय कृपानिधाना॥

puni āyau prabhu pahiṁ balavānā, jayati jayati jaya kṛpānidhānā.

नाक कान काटे जियँ जानी । फिरा क्रोध करि भइ मन ग्लानी ॥
nāka kāna kāṭe jiyaṁ jānī, phirā krodha kari bhai mana glānī.
सहज भीम पुनि बिनु श्रुति नासा । देखत कपि दल उपजी त्रासा ॥
sahaja bhīma puni binu śruti nāsā, dekhata kapi dala upajī trāsā.

Trans:

O Umā, when Rāma plays the part of human, it is akin to how Garud would sport in company of snakes. If He but knit His brows, He annihilates Death himself—so then why does He condescend to combats such as these? The answer is that the glory of it, when it spreads, tends to the redemption of the world, and mortals then make it their anthem, singing which they emerge safely from the ocean of existence. When his swoon had passed off, the son-of-wind awoke and began at once to look for Sugrīva. But he, on recovering from his swoon, slipped out of Kumbh-karan's clutches—who had taken him for dead. Having bitten off his nose and ears he, with a shout, ascended into the air; but the giant saw him and caught him by the foot and dashed him to the ground. With wonderful agility he rose and struck him back and then betook himself—the hero—to the presence of his Lord, crying, "Glory, glory, glory to the Fountain of Mercy." When he became sensible of his mutilated nose and ears, Kumbh-karan turned in fury and with sore distress of soul. The monkey host were horror-stricken, when they saw the terrible warrior noseless and earless.

दोहा-dohā:

जय जय जय रघुबंस मनि धाए कपि दै हूह ।
jaya jaya jaya raghubaṁsa mani dhāe kapi dai hūha,
एकहि बार तासु पर छाड़ेन्हि गिरि तरु जूह ॥६६॥
ekahi bāra tāsu para chāṛenhi giri taru jūha. 66.

Trans:

But then raising a shout of "Victory to Rāma," the monkeys rushed forward, and all at once hurled upon him a volley of tree and rocks.

चौपाई-caupāī:

कुंभकरन रन रंग बिरुद्धा । सन्मुख चला काल जनु क्रुद्धा ॥
kuṁbhakarana rana raṁga biruddhā, sanmukha calā kāla janu kruddhā.
कोटि कोटि कपि धरि धरि खाई । जनु टीड़ी गिरि गुहाँ समाई ॥
koṭi koṭi kapi dhari dhari khāī, janu ṭīṛī giri guhāṁ samāī.
कोटिन्ह गहि सरीर सन मर्दा । कोटिन्ह मीजि मिलव महि गर्दा ॥
koṭinha gahi sarīra sana mardā, koṭinha mīji milava mahi gardā.
मुख नासा श्रवनन्हि कीं बाटा । निसरि पराहिं भालु कपि ठाटा ॥
mukha nāsā śravananhi kīṁ bāṭā, nisari parāhiṁ bhālu kapi ṭhāṭā.
रन मद मत्त निसाचर दर्पा । बिस्व ग्रसिहि जनु एहि बिधि अर्पा ॥
rana mada matta nisācara darpā, bisva grasihi janu ehi bidhi arpā.
मुरे सुभट सब फिरहिं न फेरे । सूझ न नयन सुनहिं नहिं टेरे ॥
mure subhaṭa saba phirahiṁ na phere, sūjha na nayana sunahiṁ nahiṁ ṭere.
कुंभकरन कपि फौज बिडारी । सुनि धाई रजनीचर धारी ॥
kuṁbhakarana kapi phauja biḍārī, suni dhāī rajanīcara dhārī.
देखि राम बिकल कटकाई । रिपु अनीक नाना बिधि आई ॥
dekhi rāma bikala kaṭakāī, ripu anīka nānā bidhi āī.

Trans:

Maddened with a lust for battle Kumbh-karan advanced, awful as Death, and seized and devoured myriads of monkeys, like locusts being sucked up into a mountain cave; myriads others he crushed with his body, and countless others he ground into dust between his hands. But many of the bears and monkeys escaped, by the passage of his mouth, nostrils, and ears. Drunk with the madness of battle the demon was as boastful as though the whole universe had been made over to him to ravage. Every champion took to flight, and there was no turning them back; they could neither see with their eyes nor hear any cry. When they learnt that Kumbh-karan had routed the monkey host the demons again rallied together. Rāma saw his army in distress, and the forces of enemy rushing on in full fury.

दोहा-dohā:

सुनु सुग्रीव बिभीषन अनुज सँभारेहु सैन ।
sunu sugrīva bibhīṣana anuja saṁbhārehu saina,
मैं देखउँ खल बल दलहि बोले राजिवनैन ॥६७॥
maiṁ dekhauṁ khala bala dalahi bole rājivanaina. 67.

Trans:

"Hearken Sugrīva, Vibhīshan and you my brother: collect your troops and let me test the might of these rogues," thus said the lotus-eyed.

चौपाई-caupāī:

कर सारंग साजि कटि भाथा । अरि दल दलन चले रघुनाथा ॥
kara sāraṁga sāji kaṭi bhāthā, ari dala dalana cale raghunāthā.
प्रथम कीन्हि प्रभु धनुष टँकोरा । रिपु दल बधिर भयउ सुनि सोरा ॥
prathama kīnhi prabhu dhanuṣa ṭaṁkorā, ripu dala badhira bhayau suni sorā.
सत्यसंध छाँड़े सर लच्छा । कालसर्प जनु चले सपच्छा ॥
satyasaṁdha chāṁṛe sara lacchā, kālasarpa janu cale sapacchā.
जहँ तहँ चले बिपुल नाराचा । लगे कटन भट बिकट पिसाचा ॥
jahaṁ tahaṁ cale bipula nārācā, lage kaṭana bhaṭa bikaṭa pisācā.
कटहिं चरन उर सिर भुजदंडा । बहुतक बीर होहिं सत खंडा ॥
kaṭahiṁ carana ura sira bhujadaṁḍā, bahutaka bīra hohiṁ sata khaṁḍā.
घुर्मि घुर्मि घायल महि परहीं । उठि संभारि सुभट पुनि लरहीं ॥
ghurmi ghurmi ghāyala mahi parahīṁ, uṭhi saṁbhāri subhaṭa puni larahīṁ.
लागत बान जलद जिमि गाजहिं । बहुतक देखी कठिन सर भाजहिं ॥
lāgata bāna jalada jimi gājahiṁ, bahutaka dekhī kaṭhina sara bhājahiṁ.
रुंड प्रचंड मुंड बिनु धावहिं । धरु धरु मारू मारु धुनि गावहिं ॥
ruṁḍa pracaṁḍa muṁḍa binu dhāvahiṁ, dharu dharu mārū māru dhuni gāvahiṁ.

Trans:

With bow in hand and quiver fitted to his side, Raghunāth went forth to scatter the ranks of the enemy. The Lord gave his bow a preliminary twang; and the hosts of the foe were deafened by its din. Then he let fly a million arrows—he, the god ever faithful to his promise; and his winged shafts hissed like serpents of death. The terrible bolts flew in all directions, and the mighty demon warriors were cut to pieces. Feet, trunk, head, and arms were shorn away; many a hero was cut into hundred of pieces. The wounded reel and fall to the ground, but the gallant recover themselves and rise again to renew their fight. The arrows as they strike give a thud like thunder; many fled when they saw how terrible they were. Headless bodies rush madly on; and the skies resound with cries of, "seize, seize; kill, kill."

दोहा-dohā:

छन महुँ प्रभु के सायकन्हि काटे बिकट पिसाच ।
chana mahuṁ prabhu ke sāyakanhi kāṭe bikaṭa pisāca,
पुनि रघुबीर निषंग महुँ प्रबिसे सब नाराच ॥६८॥
puni raghubīra niṣaṁga mahuṁ prabise saba nārāca. 68.

Trans:

In a moment Lord Raghubīr's arrows cut to pieces the terrible demons; and then his shafts all came back into the quiver.

चौपाई-caupāī:

कुंभकरन मन दीख बिचारी । हति छन माझ निसाचर धारी ॥
kuṁbhakarana mana dīkha bicārī, hati chana mājha nisācara dhārī.
भा अति क्रुद्ध महाबल बीरा । कियो मृगनायक नाद गँभीरा ॥
bhā ati kruddha mahābala bīrā, kiyo mṛganāyaka nāda gaṁbhīrā.
कोपि महीधर लेइ उपारी । डारइ जहँ मर्कट भट भारी ॥
kopi mahīdhara lei upārī, ḍārai jahaṁ markaṭa bhaṭa bhārī.
आवत देखि सैल प्रभु भारे । सरन्हि काटि रज सम करि डारे ॥
āvata dekhi saila prabhu bhāre, saranhi kāṭi raja sama kari ḍāre.
पुनि धनु तानि कोपि रघुनायक । छाँड़े अति कराल बहु सायक ॥
puni dhanu tāni kopi raghunāyaka, chāṁṛe ati karāla bahu sāyaka.

तनु महुँ प्रबिसि निसरि सर जाहीं । जिमि दामिनि घन माझ समाहीं ॥
tanu mahuṁ prabisi nisari sara jāhīṁ, jimi dāmini ghana mājha samāhīṁ.
सोनित स्रवत सोह तन कारे । जनु कज्जल गिरि गेरु पनारे ॥
sonita sravata soha tana kāre, janu kajjala giri geru panāre.
बिकल बिलोकि भालु कपि धाए । बिहँसा जबहिं निकट कपि आए ॥
bikala biloki bhālu kapi dhāe, bihaṁsā jabahiṁ nikaṭa kapi āe.

Trans:

When Kumbh-karan perceived and realized that the demon host had been routed in a minute, the mighty warrior waxed exceeding wrath; and he roared aloud with the voice of lion. In his fury he tore up crags by the root and hurled them upon the throng of monkey chiefs. The Lord saw the monstrous rocks coming and with his arrows tattered them into dust. Again Raghunāyak indignantly strung his bow and let fly a volley of his terrible shafts. As they entered and passed through the demon's body, they seemed like flashes of lightning stored in a dense thundercloud. The streams of blood on his black frame resembled rivers of red ochre on a mountain of soot. Perceiving his distress, the bears and monkeys rushed forward for a kill; but he laughed when he saw them draw near.

दोहा-dohā:

महानाद करि गर्जा कोटि कोटि गहि कीस ।
mahānāda kari garjā koṭi koṭi gahi kīsa,
महि पटकइ गजराज इव सपथ करइ दससीस ॥६९॥
mahi paṭakai gajarāja iva sapatha karai dasasīsa. 69.

Trans:

Roaring with a terrible sound, he seized myriads upon myriads of monkeys, and dashed them to the ground like a mad elephant, invoking the name of Rāvan all the while.

चौपाई-caupāī:

भागे भालु बलीमुख जूथा । बृकु बिलोकि जिमि मेष बरूथा ॥
bhāge bhālu balīmukha jūthā, bṛku biloki jimi meṣa barūthā.
चले भागि कपि भालु भवानी । बिकल पुकारत आरत बानी ॥
cale bhāgi kapi bhālu bhavānī, bikala pukārata ārata bānī.
यह निसिचर दुकाल सम अहई । कपिकुल देस परन अब चहई ॥
yaha nisicara dukāla sama ahaī, kapikula desa parana aba cahaī.
कृपा बारिधर राम खरारी । पाहि पाहि प्रनतारति हारी ॥
kṛpā bāridhara rāma kharārī, pāhi pāhi pranatārati hārī.
सकरुन बचन सुनत भगवाना । चले सुधारि सरासन बाना ॥
sakaruna bacana sunata bhagavānā, cale sudhāri sarāsana bānā.
राम सेन निज पाछें घाली । चले सकोप महा बलसाली ॥
rāma sena nija pācheṁ ghālī, cale sakopa mahā balasālī.
खैंचि धनुष सर सत संधाने । छूटे तीर सरीर समाने ॥
khaiṁci dhanuṣa sara sata saṁdhāne, chūṭe tīra sarīra samāne.
लागत सर धावा रिस भरा । कुधर डगमगत डोलति धरा ॥
lāgata sara dhāvā risa bharā, kudhara ḍagamagata ḍolati dharā.
लीन्ह एक तेहिं सैल उपाटी । रघुकुल तिलक भुजा सोइ काटी ॥
līnha eka tehiṁ saila upāṭī, raghukula tilaka bhujā soi kāṭī.
धावा बाम बाहु गिरि धारी । प्रभु सोउ भुजा काटि महि पारी ॥
dhāvā bāma bāhu giri dhārī, prabhu sou bhujā kāṭi mahi pārī.
काटें भुजा सोह खल कैसा । पच्छहीन मंदर गिरि जैसा ॥
kāṭeṁ bhujā soha khala kaisā, pacchahīna maṁdara giri jaisā.
उग्र बिलोकनि प्रभुहि बिलोका । ग्रसन चहत मानहुँ त्रैलोका ॥
ugra bilokani prabhuhi bilokā, grasana cahata mānahuṁ trailokā.

Trans:

The bears and monkeys all fled, like a flock of sheep at the sight of wolf; and in their flight, Bhawānī, they cried in distress with a piteous voice, "This demon, for the monkey race, is like a sore famine that threatens to devastate a whole land. O Rāma, Kharārī, rain-cloud of mercy, ever ready to relieve the distress of the suppliant, have mercy upon us, have mercy." When the Lord God heard their piteous cry, he took his bow and arrows and sallied forth. His army he checked in the rear and went forth in all his might, full of indignation. He drew his bow and fitted a hundred arrows to the string; furiously they winged and entered the enemy's body. Even as they struck him, the demon rushed forth in full fury—the mountains reeled, the earth staggered—as he tore up a rock; but Rāma shot his arm off. Again he rushed on with a rook in his left hand; but that arm too Rāma cut away, and it fell to the ground. The monster, thus robbed of his arms, resembled Mount Mandara without its wings. With savage eyes he glared upon the Lord, as though ready to devour the whole universe.

दोहा-dohā:

करि चिक्कार घोर अति धावा बदनु पसारि ।
kari cikkāra ghora ati dhāvā badanu pasāri,
गगन सिद्ध सुर त्रासित हा हा हेति पुकारि ॥७०॥
gagana siddha sura trāsita hā hā heti pukāri. 70.

Trans:

With a most terrible shriek he rushed forward with open mouth. The saints and gods above cried out in their terror, "Oh, alas, alas, alas!"

चौपाई-caupāī:

सभय देव करुनानिधि जान्यो । श्रवन प्रजंत सरासनु तान्यो ॥
sabhaya deva karunānidhi jānyo, śravana prajaṁta sarāsanu tānyo.
बिसिख निकर निसिचर मुख भरेऊ । तदपि महाबल भूमि न परेऊ ॥
bisikha nikara nisicara mukha bhareū, tadapi mahābala bhūmi na pareū.
सरन्हि भरा मुख सन्मुख धावा । काल त्रोन सजीव जनु आवा ॥
saranhi bharā mukha sanmukha dhāvā, kāla trona sajīva janu āvā.
तब प्रभु कोपि तीब्र सर लीन्हा । धर ते भिन्न तासु सिर कीन्हा ॥
taba prabhu kopi tībra sara līnhā, dhara te bhinna tāsu sira kīnhā.
सो सिर परेउ दसानन आगें । बिकल भयउ जिमि फनि मनि त्यागें ॥
so sira pareu dasānana āgeṁ, bikala bhayau jimi phani mani tyāgeṁ.
धरनि धसइ धर धाव प्रचंडा । तब प्रभु काटि कीन्ह दुइ खंडा ॥
dharani dhasai dhara dhāva pracaṁḍā, taba prabhu kāṭi kīnha dui khaṁḍā.
परे भूमि जिमि नभ तें भूधर । हेठ दाबि कपि भालु निसाचर ॥
pare bhūmi jimi nabha teṁ bhūdhara, heṭha dābi kapi bhālu nisācara.
तासु तेज प्रभु बदन समाना । सुर मुनि सबहिं अचंभव माना ॥
tāsu teja prabhu badana samānā, sura muni sabahiṁ acaṁbhava mānā.
सुर दुंदुभीं बजावहिं हरषहिं । अस्तुति करहिं सुमन बहु बरषहिं ॥
sura duṁdubhīṁ bajāvahiṁ haraṣahiṁ, astuti karahiṁ sumana bahu baraṣahiṁ.
करि बिनती सुर सकल सिधाए । तेही समय देवरिषि आए ॥
kari binatī sura sakala sidhāe, tehī samaya devariṣi āe.
गगनोपरि हरि गुन गन गाए । रुचिर बीररस प्रभु मन भाए ॥
gaganopari hari guna gana gāe, rucira bīrarasa prabhu mana bhāe.
बेगि हतहु खल कहि मुनि गए । राम समर महि सोभत भए ॥
begi hatahu khala kahi muni gae, rāma samara mahi sobhata bhae.

Trans:

When the All-merciful saw the alarm of the gods, he drew his bow with its string right up to his ear and shot a volley of arrows right into his gaping mouth; and though they filled the demon's mouth, yet he was so strong that he did not fall to the ground. With mouth full of arrows he still rushed upon his foe, like a living quiver of death. Then the Lord in his wrath took his sharpest arrow, and struck his head right off the body. And the head went and fell right at the feet of Rāvan, who was devastated and dismayed—like a snake that has lost its crest jewel. The ground sank beneath the weight of the trunk as it still ran madly on, until the Lord again cut it into two. Then it fell to the earth like a mountain from the sky, crushing beneath its weight countless monkeys, bears, and demons. His soul entered the Lord's mouth, to the astonishment of gods, saints, and everyone. The gods in their delight sound the kettle-drum, and hymn his praises, and rain down flowers in abundance. After paying homage, all the gods went their way. At that time came also the divine sage, Nārad; and from up above the heavens, he extolled Harī's infinite perfections. The Lord's soul was pleased by his stirring heroic strain. "Make haste to destroy all these miscreants" were the saint's words as he left. Rāma shone forth in all his glory on the field of battle.

छंद-chaṁda:

संग्राम भूमि बिराज रघुपति अतुल बल कोसल धनी ।
saṁgrāma bhūmi birāja raghupati atula bala kosala dhanī,
श्रम बिंदु मुख राजीव लोचन अरुन तन सोनित कनी ॥
śrama biṁdu mukha rājīva locana aruna tana sonita kanī.
भुज जुगल फेरत सर सरासन भालु कपि चहु दिसि बने ।
bhuja jugala pherata sara sarāsana bhālu kapi cahu disi bane,
कह दास तुलसी कहि न सक छबि सेष जेहि आनन घने ॥
kaha dāsa tulasī kahi na saka chabi seṣa jehi ānana ghane.

Trans:

The All-glorious Raghupatī shone forth on the field of battle in his immeasurable might and manifold beauty, with the drops of toil on his lotus face, with his lovely eyes and his body specked with blood, while in both hands he brandished his bow and arrows, with the bears and monkeys grouped all around him. Not Sheshnāg with his many tongues could tell all his beauty, so says Tulsīdās.

दोहा-dohā:

निसिचर अधम मलाकर ताहि दीन्ह निज धाम ।
nisicara adhama malākara tāhi dīnha nija dhāma,
गिरिजा ते नर मंदमति जे न भजहिं श्रीराम ॥७१॥
girijā te nara maṁdamati je na bhajahiṁ śrīrāma. 71.

Trans:

Though the demons were so vile and very mines of impurity, yet Rāma transported them to his own sphere. O Umā, how dull of understanding are those who do not worship such a divine Shrī Rāma.

चौपाई-caupāī:

दिन कें अंत फिरीं द्वौ अनी । समर भई सुभटन्ह श्रम घनी ॥
dina keṁ aṁta phirīṁ dvou anī, samara bhaī subhaṭanha śrama ghanī.
राम कृपाँ कपि दल बल बाढ़ा । जिमि तृन पाइ लाग अति डाढ़ा ॥
rāma kṛpāṁ kapi dala bala bāṛhā, jimi tṛna pāi lāga ati ḍāṛhā.
छीजहिं निसिचर दिनु अरु राती । निज मुख कहें सुकृत जेहि भाँती ॥
chījahiṁ nisicara dinu aru rātī, nija mukha kaheṁ sukṛta jehi bhāṁtī.
बहु बिलाप दसकंधर करई । बंधु सीस पुनि पुनि उर धरई ॥
bahu bilāpa dasakaṁdhara karaī, baṁdhu sīsa puni puni ura dharaī.
रोवहिं नारि हृदय हति पानी । तासु तेज बल बिपुल बखानी ॥
rovahiṁ nāri hṛdaya hati pānī, tāsu teja bala bipula bakhānī.
मेघनाद तेहि अवसर आयउ । कहि बहु कथा पिता समुझायउ ॥
meghanāda tehi avasara āyau, kahi bahu kathā pitā samujhāyau.
देखेहु कालि मोरि मनुसाई । अबहिं बहुत का करौं बड़ाई ॥
dekhehu kāli mori manusāī, abahiṁ bahuta kā karauṁ baṛāī.
इष्टदेव सैं बल रथ पायउँ । सो बल तात न तोहि देखायउँ ॥
iṣṭadeva saiṁ bala ratha pāyauṁ, so bala tāta na tohi dekhāyauṁ.
एहि बिधि जल्पत भयउ बिहाना । चहुँ दुआर लागे कपि नाना ॥
ehi bidhi jalpata bhayau bihānā, cahuṁ duāra lāge kapi nānā.
इत कपि भालु काल सम बीरा । उत रजनीचर अति रनधीरा ॥
ita kapi bhālu kāla sama bīrā, uta rajanīcara ati ranadhīrā.
लरहिं सुभट निज निज जय हेतू । बरनि न जाइ समर खगकेतू ॥
larahiṁ subhaṭa nija nija jaya hetū, barani na jāi samara khagaketū.

Trans:

At the close of the day both armies retired; the battle had thoroughly exhausted the stoutest warriors. But by Rāma's favor the monkey host gathered fresh strength, like as a fire blazes up when fed with straw; while the demons wasted away day and night, like the merit of a man's good deeds when he tells them himself. Rāvan made great lamentation, again and again taking his brother's head in his lap. His wives also wept and beat their chest with their hands as they told of his pre-eminent majesty and strength. Meghnād arrived there and with many words consoled his father, "Be witness tomorrow of my prowess; what need now of boastful speeches. I have received from my patron divinity a chariot of strength, the virtue of which I have never yet shown you, father." While they were thus talking, the day broke and swarms of monkey assailed the four gates. On the one side were the bears and monkeys terrible as death; on the other the demons, fiercest of warriors. Valiantly they fight, each thirsting for their victory; the battle, O Garud, baffles all description.

दोहा-dohā:

मेघनाद मायामय रथ चढ़ि गयउ अकास ।
meghanāda māyāmaya ratha caṛhi gayau akāsa,
गर्जेउ अट्टहास करि भइ कपि कटकहि त्रास ॥७२॥
garjeu aṭṭahāsa kari bhai kapi kaṭakahi trāsa. 72.

Trans:

Meghnād mounted his wizardly chariot and ascended into the air with a cackle like the roar of thunder, which struck terror in the monkey's hearts.

चौपाई-caupāī:

सक्ति सूल तरवारि कृपाना । अस्त्र सस्त्र कुलिसायुध नाना ॥
sakti sūla taravāri kṛpānā, astra sastra kulisāyudha nānā.
डारइ परसु परिघ पाषाना । लागेउ बृष्टि करै बहु बाना ॥
ḍārai parasu parigha pāṣānā, lāgeu bṛṣṭi karai bahu bānā.
दस दिसि रहे बान नभ छाई । मानहुँ मघा मेघ झरि लाई ॥
dasa disi rahe bāna nabha chāī, mānahuṁ maghā megha jhari lāī.
धरु धरु मारु सुनिअ धुनि काना । जो मारइ तेहि कोउ न जाना ॥
dharu dharu māru sunia dhuni kānā, jo mārai tehi kou na jānā.
गहि गिरि तरु अकास कपि धावहिं । देखहिं तेहि न दुखित फिरि आवहिं ॥
gahi giri taru akāsa kapi dhāvahiṁ, dekhahiṁ tehi na dukhita phiri āvahiṁ.
अवघट घाट बाट गिरि कंदर । माया बल कीन्हेसि सर पंजर ॥
avaghaṭa ghāṭa bāṭa giri kaṁdara, māyā bala kīnhesi sara paṁjara.
जाहिं कहाँ ब्याकुल भए बंदर । सुरपति बंदि परे जनु मंदर ॥
jāhiṁ kahāṁ byākula bhae baṁdara, surapati baṁdi pare janu maṁdara.
मारुतसुत अंगद नल नीला । कीन्हेसि बिकल सकल बलसीला ॥
mārutasuta aṁgada nala nīlā, kīnhesi bikala sakala balasīlā.
पुनि लछिमन सुग्रीव बिभीषन । सरन्हि मारि कीन्हेसि जर्जर तन ॥
puni lachimana sugrīva bibhīṣana, saranhi māri kīnhesi jarjara tana.
पुनि रघुपति सैं जूझै लागा । सर छाँड़इ होइ लागहिं नागा ॥
puni raghupati saiṁ jūjhai lāgā, sara chāṁṛai hoi lāgahiṁ nāgā.
ब्याल पास बस भए खरारी । स्वबस अनंत एक अबिकारी ॥
byāla pāsa basa bhae kharārī, svabasa anaṁta eka abikārī.
नट इव कपट चरित कर नाना । सदा स्वतंत्र एक भगवाना ॥
naṭa iva kapaṭa carita kara nānā, sadā svataṁtra eka bhagavānā.
रन सोभा लगि प्रभुहिं बँधायो । नागपास देवन्ह भय पायो ॥
rana sobhā lagi prabhuhiṁ baṁdhāyo, nāgapāsa devanha bhaya pāyo.

Trans:

Spears, lances, swords, and scimitars were plied, with weapons and missiles of every description, axes, hatchets, clubs, and stones, and there were showers of innumerable arrows. The heaven was as dark with arrows as when the constellation Magha pours down its torrents. "Seize, seize, kill, kill," were the cries that rent the air; none could tell who it was that struck them. Snatching up rocks and trees the monkeys sprang into the air; but they could not see the demon and returned disappointed. Ravines, gorges, roads, and mountain-caves were turned by his magic power into arrowy cages; the monkeys were confounded and knew not where to turn; they felt helpless like so many mount Mandras thrown into prison by Indra. Hanumān, Angad, Nala, Nīl, and every other warrior, he distressed sorely; then he assailed with his shafts Lakshman, Sugrīva, and Vibhīshan, piercing their bodies through and through again. Lastly he joined in combat with Rāma himself and let fly his arrows, which as they struck turned to snakes. Kharārī was rendered powerless by the serpents' coils—he the great free agent, the everlasting, the one unchangeable, who like a juggler performs all sorts of delusive actions, but is ever his own master—even he Rāma, the Lord-God. It was only to enhance the glory of the battle that he allowed himself to be bound by the serpents' coils; but the gods were in panic at the sight.

दोहा-dohā:

गिरिजा जासु नाम जपि मुनि काटहिं भव पास ।
girijā jāsu nāma japi muni kāṭahiṁ bhava pāsa,
सो कि बंध तर आवइ ब्यापक बिस्व निवास ॥७३॥
so ki baṁdha tara āvai byāpaka bisva nivāsa. 73.

Trans:

O Umā, is it possible for him to be brought into bondage—by whose name, repeating in prayers, the saints free themselves from the bonds of existence—who is the omnipresent centre of the universe?

चौपाई-caupāī:

चरित राम के सगुन भवानी । तर्कि न जाहिं बुद्धि बल बानी ॥
carita rāma ke saguna bhavānī, tarki na jāhiṁ buddhi bala bānī.
अस बिचारि जे तग्य बिरागी । रामहि भजहिं तर्क सब त्यागी ॥
asa bicāri je tagya birāgī, rāmahi bhajahiṁ tarka saba tyāgī.
ब्याकुल कटकु कीन्ह घननादा । पुनि भा प्रगट कहइ दुर्बादा ॥
byākula kaṭaku kīnha ghananādā, puni bhā pragaṭa kahai durbādā.
जामवंत कह खल रहु ठाढ़ा । सुनि करि ताहि क्रोध अति बाढ़ा ॥
jāmavaṁta kaha khala rahu ṭhāṛhā, suni kari tāhi krodha ati bāṛhā.
बूढ़ जानि सठ छाँड़िउँ तोही । लागेसि अधम पचारै मोही ॥
būṛha jāni saṭha chāṁṛeuṁ tohī, lāgesi adhama pacārai mohī.
अस कहि तरल त्रिसूल चलायो । जामवंत कर गहि सोइ धायो ॥
asa kahi tarala trisūla calāyo, jāmavaṁta kara gahi soi dhāyo.
मारिसि मेघनाद कै छाती । परा भूमि घुर्मित सुरघाती ॥
mārisi meghanāda kai chātī, parā bhūmi ghurmita suraghātī.
पुनि रिसान गहि चरन फिरायो । महि पछारि निज बल देखरायो ॥
puni risāna gahi carana phirāyo, mahi pachāri nija bala dekharāyo.
बर प्रसाद सो मरइ न मारा । तब गहि पद लंका पर डारा ॥
bara prasāda so marai na mārā, taba gahi pada laṁkā para ḍārā.
इहाँ देवरिषि गरुड़ पठायो । राम समीप सपदि सो आयो ॥
ihāṁ devariṣi garuṛa paṭhāyo, rāma samīpa sapadi so āyo.

Trans:

O Bhawānī, the enactments of Lord God Rāma are beyond the range of human actions, thought, speech. This is the reason why the wisest ascetics discard theological speculations and simply adore. Having thus thrown the army into confusion, Meghnād at last manifested himself visible and began to abuse and deride. To which Jāmvant said, "Wretch, keep your place." On hearing this, his fury waxed still more, "Fool, I only spared you on account of your age; and yet you dare challenge me?" So saying, he let fly his terrible trident; Jāmvant caught it in his hand and then rushed in such fury and gave Meghnād so severe a blow to his chest that he, the scourge of heaven, fell swooning to the ground. Then in his wrath he caught him by the foot and swung him round and dashed him on the earth as a display of his strength. But he, by virtue of the divine boon, died not despite such blows; so he took him by the foot and tossed him into Lankā. Meanwhile the gods and saints sent for Garud, who came in haste to Rāma;

दोहा-dohā:

खगपति सब धरि खाए माया नाग बरूथ ।
khagapati saba dhari khāe māyā nāga barūtha,
माया बिगत भए सब हरषे बानर जूथ ॥७४क॥
māyā bigata bhae saba haraṣe bānara jūtha, 74(ka).

गहि गिरि पादप उपल नख धाए कीस रिसाइ ।
gahi giri pādapa upala nakha dhāe kīsa risāi,
चले तमीचर बिकलतर गढ़ पर चढ़े पराइ ॥७४ख॥
cale tamīcara bikalatara gaṛha para caṛhe parāi. 74(kha).

Trans:

and he seized and devoured the whole swarm of serpents created by Meghnād's delusive powers. The delusion was dispelled, and all the monkey host rejoiced again. Tearing up with their claws the trees and rocks of the mountain, they rushed forward, while the demons fled in utter confusion and climbed up into the fort.

चौपाई-caupāī:

मेघनाद कै मुरछा जागी । पितहि बिलोकि लाज अति लागी ॥
meghanāda kai murachā jāgī, pitahi biloki lāja ati lāgī.
तुरत गयउ गिरिबर कंदरा । करौं अजय मख अस मन धरा ॥
turata gayau giribara kaṁdarā, karauṁ ajaya makha asa mana dharā.
इहाँ बिभीषन मंत्र बिचारा । सुनहु नाथ बल अतुल उदारा ॥
ihāṁ bibhīṣana maṁtra bicārā, sunahu nātha bala atula udārā.
मेघनाद मख करइ अपावन । खल मायावी देव सतावन ॥
meghanāda makha karai apāvana, khala māyāvī deva satāvana.
जौं प्रभु सिद्ध होइ सो पाइहि । नाथ बेगि पुनि जीति न जाइहि ॥
jauṁ prabhu siddha hoi so pāihi, nātha begi puni jīti na jāihi.
सुनि रघुपति अतिसय सुख माना । बोले अंगदादि कपि नाना ॥
suni raghupati atisaya sukha mānā, bole aṁgadādi kapi nānā.
लछिमन संग जाहु सब भाई । करहु बिधंस जग्य कर जाई ॥
lachimana saṁga jāhu saba bhāī, karahu bidhaṁsa jagya kara jāī.
तुम्ह लछिमन मारेहु रन ओही । देखि सभय सुर दुख अति मोही ॥
tumha lachimana mārehu rana ohī, dekhi sabhaya sura dukha ati mohī.
मारेहु तेहि बल बुद्धि उपाई । जेहिं छीजै निसिचर सुनु भाई ॥
mārehu tehi bala buddhi upāī, jehiṁ chījai nisicara sunu bhāī.
जामवंत सुग्रीव बिभीषन । सेन समेत रहेहु तीनिउ जन ॥
jāmavaṁta sugrīva bibhīṣana, sena sameta rahehu tīniu jana.
जब रघुबीर दीन्हि अनुसासन । कटि निषंग कसि साजि सरासन ॥
jaba raghubīra dīnhi anusāsana, kaṭi niṣaṁga kasi sāji sarāsana.
प्रभु प्रताप उर धरि रनधीरा । बोले घन इव गिरा गँभीरा ॥
prabhu pratāpa ura dhari ranadhīrā, bole ghana iva girā gaṁbhīrā.
जौं तेहि आजु बधें बिनु आवौं । तौ रघुपति सेवक न कहावौं ॥
jauṁ tehi āju badheṁ binu āvauṁ, tau raghupati sevaka na kahāvauṁ.
जौं सत संकर करहिं सहाई । तदपि हतउँ रघुबीर दोहाई ॥
jauṁ sata saṁkara karahiṁ sahāī, tadapi hatauṁ raghubīra dohāī.

Trans:

When Meghnād recovered from his swoon, he was greatly ashamed to look his father in the face; and he arose in haste to go to a mountain cave, intending to perform a sacrifice that would ensure victory. Here, Vibhīshan gave the caution, "Hearken, O king of unbounded might and generosity, Meghnād is preparing an unholy sacrifice—wretched sorcerer and scourge of heaven as he is—and if he bring it to completion, sire, it will not be easy to conquer him." On hearing this, Raghupatī was pleased and said to Angad and the other monkeys. "Go, my brothers, you and Lakshman, and put a stop to his sacrifice. It is ordained for you, O Lakshman, to fight and slay him. I am distressed to see the terror of the gods; kill him, either by open force, or by stratagem; one way or another—mark me, brother—this demon must be got rid of. And you three Jāmvant, Sugrīva, and Vibhīshan remain with the army." When Raghubīr had finished his commands, the hero girt his quiver by his side and took his bow, and with the glory of his Lord impressed upon his heart Lakshman cried aloud with a mighty voice as of thunder, "If I return today without slaying him, may I be no longer called Rāma's servant; though a hundred Shivas give him help, I will slay him yet—in the name of Rāma."

दोहा-dohā:

रघुपति चरन नाइ सिरु चलेउ तुरंत अनंत ।
raghupati carana nāi siru caleu turaṁta anaṁta,
अंगद नील मयंद नल संग सुभट हनुमंत ॥७५॥
aṁgada nīla mayaṁda nala saṁga subhaṭa hanumaṁta. 75.

Trans:

After bowing his head at Rāma's feet, the incarnation of Sheshnāg went forth at once; and with him went Angad, Nīl, Mayanda, Nala, and the valiant Hanumān.

चौपाई-caupāī:

जाइ कपिन्ह सो देखा बैसा । आहुति देत रुधिर अरु भैंसा ॥
jāi kapinha so dekhā baisā, āhuti deta rudhira aru bhaiṁsā.
कीन्ह कपिन्ह सब जग्य बिधंसा । जब न उठइ तब करहिं प्रसंसा ॥
kīnha kapinha saba jagya bidhaṁsā, jaba na uṭhai taba karahiṁ prasaṁsā.
तदपि न उठइ धरेन्हि कच जाई । लातन्हि हति हति चले पराई ॥
tadapi na uṭhai dharenhi kaca jāī, lātanhi hati hati cale parāī.
लै त्रिसूल धावा कपि भागे । आए जहँ रामानुज आगे ॥
lai trisūla dhāvā kapi bhāge, āe jahaṁ rāmānuja āge.
आवा परम क्रोध कर मारा । गर्ज घोर रव बारहिं बारा ॥
āvā parama krodha kara mārā, garja ghora rava bārahiṁ bārā.
कोपि मरुतसुत अंगद धाए । हति त्रिसूल उर धरनि गिराए ॥
kopi marutasuta aṁgada dhāe, hati trisūla ura dharani girāe.
प्रभु कहँ छाँड़ेसि सूल प्रचंडा । सर हति कृत अनंत जुग खंडा ॥
prabhu kahaṁ chāṁṛesi sūla pracaṁḍā, sara hati kṛta anaṁta juga khaṁḍā.
उठि बहोरि मारुति जुबराजा । हतहिं कोपि तेहि घाउ न बाजा ॥
uṭhi bahori māruti jubarājā, hatahiṁ kopi tehi ghāu na bājā.
फिरे बीर रिपु मरइ न मारा । तब धावा करि घोर चिकारा ॥
phire bīra ripu marai na mārā, taba dhāvā kari ghora cikārā.
आवत देखि क्रुद्ध जनु काला । लछिमन छाड़े बिसिख कराला ॥
āvata dekhi kruddha janu kālā, lachimana chāṛe bisikha karālā.
देखेसि आवत पबि सम बाना । तुरत भयउ खल अंतरधाना ॥
dekhesi āvata pabi sama bānā, turata bhayau khala aṁtaradhānā.
बिबिध बेष धरि करइ लराई । कबहुँक प्रगट कबहुँ दुरि जाई ॥
bibidha beṣa dhari karai larāī, kabahuṁka pragaṭa kabahuṁ duri jāī.
देखि अजय रिपु डरपे कीसा । परम क्रुद्ध तब भयउ अहीसा ॥
dekhi ajaya ripu ḍarape kīsā, parama kruddha taba bhayau ahīsā.
लछिमन मन अस मंत्र दृढावा । एहि पापिहि मैं बहुत खेलावा ॥
lachimana mana asa maṁtra dṛṛhāvā, ehi pāpihi maiṁ bahuta khelāvā.
सुमिरि कोसलाधीस प्रतापा । सर संधान कीन्ह करि दापा ॥
sumiri kosalādhīsa pratāpā, sara saṁdhāna kīnha kari dāpā.
छाड़ा बान माझ उर लागा । मरती बार कपटु सब त्यागा ॥
chāṛā bāna mājha ura lāgā, maratī bāra kapaṭu saba tyāgā.

Trans:

When the monkeys arrived at the cave, they found the demon prince making oblations of blood and buffalo's flesh. They tried to interrupt the voodoo, but he would not stir; they then took to praising him; still he would not rise; they then went and pulled him by the hair, upon which he kicked out so fiercely that they had to fall back. He pursued them with his trident as they fled, till they joined Lakshman. He came on in the wildest fury striking out again and again, roaring terribly. Hanumān and Angad rushed fiercely forward, but he struck them on the chest with his trident and beat them to the ground. Then he shot forth his mighty spear against Lakshman, but he warded it off and broke it in two. Meanwhile the son-of-wind and the prince had risen anew and smote him furiously; but those wounds had no effect upon him. The heroes fell upon him once more, but their enemy was not to be killed; again he came on with a terrible shriek. Then Lakshman made up his mind, "I have played with this miscreant long enough," and seeing him advance, furious as hell, he let fly his terrible shaft. When he saw the arrow coming on like a thunderbolt, the wretch at once disappeared from sight and continued fighting under various disguises, now visible and now not. The monkeys thought him invincible and trembled. Then the incarnation of the serpent-king became exceeding wrath, and directing his intention to the glory of the Lord of Kaushal fitted an arrow to the string and with all his might let it fly. It struck Meghnād full in the chest. In the moment of death, he abandoned all falsehood;

दोहा-dohā:

रामानुज कहँ रामु कहँ अस कहि छाँड़ेसि प्रान ।
rāmānuja kahaṁ rāmu kahaṁ asa kahi chāṁṛesi prāna,
धन्य धन्य तव जननी कह अंगद हनुमान ॥७६॥
dhanya dhanya tava jananī kaha aṁgada hanumāna. 76.

Trans:

and invoking the names of Lakshman and Rāma drew his last breath. "Blessed indeed is thy mother," exclaimed Angad and Hanumān.

चौपाई-caupāī:

बिनु प्रयास हनुमान उठायो । लंका द्वार राखि पुनि आयो ॥
binu prayāsa hanumāna uṭhāyo, laṁkā dvāra rākhi puni āyo.
तासु मरन सुनि सुर गंधर्बा । चढ़ि बिमान आए नभ सर्बा ॥
tāsu marana suni sura gaṁdharbā, caṛhi bimāna āe nabha sarbā.
बरषि सुमन दुंदुभीं बजावहिं । श्रीरघुनाथ बिमल जसु गावहिं ॥
baraṣi sumana duṁdubhīṁ bajāvahiṁ, śrīraghunātha bimala jasu gāvahiṁ.
जय अनंत जय जगदाधारा । तुम्ह प्रभु सब देवन्हि निस्तारा ॥
jaya anaṁta jaya jagadādhārā, tumha prabhu saba devanhi nistārā.
अस्तुति करि सुर सिद्ध सिधाए । लछिमन कृपासिंधु पहिं आए ॥
astuti kari sura siddha sidhāe, lachimana kṛpāsiṁdhu pahiṁ āe.
सुत बध सुना दसानन जबहीं । मुरुछित भयउ परेउ महि तबहीं ॥
suta badha sunā dasānana jabahīṁ, muruchita bhayau pareu mahi tabahīṁ.
मंदोदरी रुदन कर भारी । उर ताड़न बहु भाँति पुकारी ॥
maṁdodarī rudana kara bhārī, ura tāṛana bahu bhāṁti pukārī.
नगर लोग सब ब्याकुल सोचा । सकल कहहिं दसकंधर पोचा ॥
nagara loga saba byākula socā, sakala kahahiṁ dasakaṁdhara pocā.

Trans:

Without an effort Hanumān took up his body and put it at the gate of the city and returned. When they heard of his death, the gods and Gandharvs mounted their chariots and came thronging the heaven, showering down flowers and beating drums and hymning the spotless renown of the divine Raghubīr. "Glory to Sheshnāg, glory to the world-supporter; You, O Lord, are the Savior of all the gods." Having thus hymned his praises, the gods and saints withdrew, while Lakshman went and presented himself before the All-merciful. When the Ten-headed heard of his son's death, he swooned and fell to the ground; Mandodarī made grievous lamentation, beating her breast and ever calling upon his name; the citizens too were all sorrowful and dismayed, and with one voice reviled Rāvan.

दोहा-dohā:

तब दसकंठ बिबिधि बिधि समुझाईं सब नारि ।
taba dasakaṁṭha bibidhi bidhi samujhāīṁ saba nāri,
नस्वर रूप जगत सब देखहु हृदयँ बिचारि ॥७७॥
nasvara rūpa jagata saba dekhahu hṛdayaṁ bicāri. 77.

Trans:

Then the Ten-headed set to comforting his wives in every way he could: "See and consider at heart how transitory is everything in this world."

चौपाई-caupāī:

तिन्हहि ग्यान उपदेसा रावन । आपुन मंद कथा सुभ पावन ॥
tinhahi gyāna upadesā rāvana, āpuna maṁda kathā subha pāvana.
पर उपदेस कुसल बहुतेरे । जे आचरहिं ते नर न घनेरे ॥
para upadesa kusala bahutere, je ācarahiṁ te nara na ghanere.
निसा सिरानि भयउ भिनुसारा । लगे भालु कपि चारिहुँ द्वारा ॥
nisā sirāni bhayau bhinusārā, lage bhālu kapi cārihuṁ dvārā.
सुभट बोलाइ दसानन बोला । रन सन्मुख जा कर मन डोला ॥
subhaṭa bolāi dasānana bolā, rana sanmukha jā kara mana ḍolā.
सो अबहीं बरु जाउ पराई । संजुग बिमुख भएँ न भलाई ॥
so abahīṁ baru jāu parāī, saṁjuga bimukha bhaeṁ na bhalāī.
निज भुज बल मैं बयरु बढ़ावा । देहउँ उतरु जो रिपु चढ़ि आवा ॥
nija bhuja bala maiṁ bayaru baṛhāvā, dehauṁ utaru jo ripu caṛhi āvā.
अस कहि मरुत बेग रथ साजा । बाजे सकल जुझाऊ बाजा ॥
asa kahi maruta bega ratha sājā, bāje sakala jujhāū bājā.
चले बीर सब अतुलित बली । जनु कज्जल कै आँधी चली ॥
cale bīra saba atulita balī, janu kajjala kai āṁdhī calī.
असगुन अमित होहिं तेहि काला । गनइ न भुजबल गर्ब बिसाला ॥
asaguna amita hohiṁ tehi kālā, ganai na bhujabala garba bisālā.

Trans:

Rāvan gave them sound advice; though a dullard himself, his counsel was good and wholesome. There are countless men who are excellent in giving advices, but those who actually put them into practice are not plentiful at all. When the night had passed and the day broke, the bears and monkeys again beset the four gates. Rāvan summoned his captains and addressed them thus: "If anyone's heart fail him in facing the battle, he had better withdraw now and not incur disgrace by running away in the midst of fray. Relying on the strength of my own arm, I have continued the struggle, and can give an answer to any enemy who may challenge me." So saying he made ready his chariot, swift as the wind, while every instrument of music sounded forth a strain of deadly combat. His champions marched on in their peerless might, like the march of a whirlwind of blackness. At that time occurred numberless omens of ill, but be heeded them not, in the overweening pride of the strength of his arm.

छंद-chaṁda:

अति गर्ब गनइ न सगुन असगुन स्रवहिं आयुध हाथ ते ।
ati garba ganai na saguna asaguna sravahiṁ āyudha hātha te,
भट गिरत रथ ते बाजि गज चिक्करत भाजहिं साथ ते ॥
bhaṭa girata ratha te bāji gaja cikkarata bhājahiṁ sātha te.
गोमाय गीध कराल खर रव स्वान बोलहिं अति घने ।
gomāya gīdha karāla khara rava svāna bolahiṁ ati ghane,
जनु कालदूत उलूक बोलहिं बचन परम भयावने ॥
janu kāladūta ulūka bolahiṁ bacana parama bhayāvane.

Trans:

In his overweening pride he took no heed of omens, good or bad: weapons dropped from the hand; warriors fell from their cars; horses, frightened by the trumpeting of the elephants, ran out of the line; jackals, vultures, and huge packs of dogs made a frightful clamor, and owls, like messengers of death, uttered their most lugubrious notes.

दोहा-dohā:

ताहि कि संपति सगुन सुभ सपनेहुँ मन बिश्राम ।
tāhi ki saṁpati saguna subha sapanehuṁ mana biśrāma,
भूत द्रोह रत मोहबस राम बिमुख रति काम ॥७८॥
bhūta droha rata mohabasa rāma bimukha rati kāma. 78.

Trans:

How was it possible for him to have prosperous omens of good fortune, or even to dream of peace of mind, when he was so infatuated that he desired the ruin of the whole world, and was set upon opposing Rāma.

चौपाई-caupāī:

चलेउ निसाचर कटकु अपारा । चतुरंगिनी अनी बहु धारा ॥
caleu nisācara kaṭaku apārā, caturaṁginī anī bahu dhārā.
बिबिधि भाँति बाहन रथ जाना । बिपुल बरन पताक ध्वज नाना ॥
bibidhi bhāṁti bāhana ratha jānā, bipula barana patāka dhvaja nānā.
चले मत्त गज जूथ घनेरे । प्राबिट जलद मरुत जनु प्रेरे ॥
cale matta gaja jūtha ghanere, prābiṭa jalada maruta janu prere.
बरन बरन बिरदैत निकाया । समर सूर जानहिं बहु माया ॥
barana barana biradaita nikāyā, samara sūra jānahiṁ bahu māyā.
अति बिचित्र बाहिनी बिराजी । बीर बसंत सेन जनु साजी ॥
ati bicitra bāhinī birājī, bīra basaṁta sena janu sājī.
चलत कटक दिगसिंधुर डगहीं । छुभित पयोधि कुधर डगमगहीं ॥
calata kaṭaka digasiṁdhura ḍagahīṁ, chubhita payodhi kudhara ḍagamagahīṁ.
उठी रेनु रबि गयउ छपाई । मरुत थकित बसुधा अकुलाई ॥
uṭhī renu rabi gayau chapāī, maruta thakita basudhā akulāī.
पनव निसान घोर रव बाजहिं । प्रलय समय के घन जनु गाजहिं ॥
panava nisāna ghora rava bājahiṁ, pralaya samaya ke ghana janu gājahiṁ.
भेरि नफीरि बाज सहनाई । मारू राग सुभट सुखदाई ॥
bheri naphīri bāja sahanāī, mārū rāga subhaṭa sukhadāī.
केहरि नाद बीर सब करहीं । निज निज बल पौरुष उच्चरहीं ॥
kehari nāda bīra saba karahīṁ, nija nija bala pauruṣa uccarahīṁ.
कहइ दसानन सुनहु सुभट्टा । मर्दहु भालु कपिन्ह के ठट्टा ॥
kahai dasānana sunahu subhaṭṭā, mardahu bhālu kapinha ke ṭhaṭṭā.
हौं मारिहउँ भूप द्वौ भाई । अस कहि सन्मुख फौज रेंगाई ॥
hauṁ mārihauṁ bhūpa dvau bhāī, asa kahi sanmukha phauja reṁgāī.
यह सुधि सकल कपिन्ह जब पाई । धाए करि रघुबीर दोहाई ॥
yaha sudhi sakala kapinha jaba pāī, dhāe kari raghubīra dohāī.

Trans:

The demon host marched on in countless numbers; elephants and chariots, foot and horse, line after line; equipages of every description, wagons and rigs, with banners and standards of diverse color; innumerable troops of infuriated elephants like autumn clouds driven by winds; battalions of savage demons of different color, martial heroes adept in magical warfare—an army magnificent in every respect, like the mustered array of the gallant god of spring. As the host marched, the elephants of the eight quarters reeled, the ocean was stirred from its depths, and the mountains shook. The dust that rose to the clouds obscured the sun; the winds became still, the earth perturbed. Drums and other instruments of music made an awful din, like a crash of thunderclouds on the final day of dissolution. Clarions, trumpets, and hautboys sounded martial strains to gladden the souls of heroes. With one accord they shouted as with the voice of a lion, each extolling his own strength and manhood. Rāvan cried, "Hearken my warriors: do you attack the common herd of bears and monkeys; I myself will slay the two brother princes." So saying, he ordered the army to advance to the front. When the monkeys all heard this news, they rushed on crying "Rāma to the rescue."

छंद-chaṁda:

धाए बिसाल कराल मर्कट भालु काल समान ते ।
dhāe bisāla karāla markaṭa bhālu kāla samāna te,
मानहुँ सपच्छ उड़ाहिं भूधर बृंद नाना बान ते ॥
mānahuṁ sapaccha uṛāhiṁ bhūdhara bṛṁda nānā bāna te.
नख दसन सैल महाद्रुमायुध सबल संक न मानहीं ।
nakha dasana saila mahādrumāyudha sabala saṁka na mānahīṁ,
जय राम रावन मत्त गज मृगराज सुजसु बखानहीं ॥
jaya rāma rāvana matta gaja mṛgarāja sujasu bakhānahīṁ.

Trans:

Here, the gigantic and terrible bears and monkeys rushed on like Death: flying through the air like so many winged mountains of diverse hues. With talons and teeth and rocks and enormous trees for weapons they feel no fear, and they sing the glories of Shri Rāma, the lion-like vanquisher of wild elephant Rāvan.

दोहा-dohā:

दुहु दिसि जय जयकार करि निज निज जोरी जानि ।
duhu disi jaya jayakāra kari nija nija jorī jāni,
भिरे बीर इत रामहि उत रावनहि बखानि ॥७९॥
bhire bīra ita rāmahi uta rāvanahi bakhāni. 79.

Trans:

With a shout of "Victory, Victory," raised from both sides, the heroes selected each his match and closed in combat, here calling on Rāma and there on Rāvan.

चौपाई-caupāī:

रावनु रथी बिरथ रघुबीरा । देखि बिभीषन भयउ अधीरा ॥
rāvanu rathī biratha raghubīrā, dekhi bibhīṣana bhayau adhīrā.
अधिक प्रीति मन भा संदेहा । बंदि चरन कह सहित सनेहा ॥
adhika prīti mana bhā saṁdehā, baṁdi carana kaha sahita sanehā.
नाथ न रथ नहिं तन पद त्राना । केहि बिधि जितब बीर बलवाना ॥
nātha na ratha nahiṁ tana pada trānā, kehi bidhi jitaba bīra balavānā.
सुनहु सखा कह कृपानिधाना । जेहिं जय होइ सो स्यंदन आना ॥
sunahu sakhā kaha kṛpānidhānā, jehiṁ jaya hoi so syaṁdana ānā.
सौरज धीरज तेहि रथ चाका । सत्य सील दृढ़ ध्वजा पताका ॥
sauraja dhīraja tehi ratha cākā, satya sīla dṛṛha dhvajā patākā.
बल बिबेक दम परहित घोरे । छमा कृपा समता रजु जोरे ॥
bala bibeka dama parahita ghore, chamā kṛpā samatā raju jore.
ईस भजनु सारथी सुजाना । बिरति चर्म संतोष कृपाना ॥
īsa bhajanu sārathī sujānā, birati carma saṁtoṣa kṛpānā.
दान परसु बुधि सक्ति प्रचंडा । बर बिग्यान कठिन कोदंडा ॥
dāna parasu budhi sakti pracaṁṛā, bara bigyāna kaṭhina kodaṁḍā.
अमल अचल मन त्रोन समाना । सम जम नियम सिलीमुख नाना ॥
amala acala mana trona samānā, sama jama niyama silīmukha nānā.
कवच अभेद बिप्र गुर पूजा । एहि सम बिजय उपाय न दूजा ॥
kavaca abheda bipra gura pūjā, ehi sama bijaya upāya na dūjā.
सखा धर्ममय अस रथ जाकें । जीतन कहँ न कतहुँ रिपु ताकें ॥
sakhā dharmamaya asa ratha jākeṁ, jītana kahaṁ na katahuṁ ripu tākeṁ.

Trans:

When Vibhīshan observed that Rāvan was in a chariot and Rāma on foot he became anxious; his extreme affection made him doubtful of mind, and falling at his feet he cried tenderly, "My Lord, you have neither a chariot nor shoes on your feet, how can you conquer so powerful a warrior?" "Hearken, friend," replied the All-merciful, "the chariot, riding which one attains to victory, is a different kind of chariot. Valor and fortitude are the wheels of that chariot; unflinching truthfulness and morality—the banners and standards; strength, discretion, self-control, and benevolence are the horses; with grace, mercy, and equanimity for their harness. Prayer to Mahādev is the unerring charioteer of that Victor; continence his shield, contentment his sword, alms-giving his axe, reason his fierce lance, and perfect wisdom his stout bow. His pure and constant soul stands for a quiver, his pious practices of devotion for the sheaf of arrows, and the reverence he pays to Brahmins and his Gurū is his impenetrable coat of mail. There is no equipment for victory that can be compared to this, nor is there any enemy, my friend, who can conquer the man who takes his stand on the chariot of Dharma.

दोहा-dohā:

महा अजय संसार रिपु जीति सकइ सो बीर ।
mahā ajaya saṁsāra ripu jīti sakai so bīra,
जाकें अस रथ होइ दृढ़ सुनहु सखा मतिधीर ॥८०क॥
jākeṁ asa ratha hoi dṛṛha sunahu sakhā matidhīra. 80(ka).

सुनि प्रभु बचन बिभीषन हरषि गहे पद कंज ।
suni prabhu bacana bibhīṣana harași gahe pada kaṁja,
एहि मिस मोहि उपदेसेहु राम कृपा सुख पुंज ॥८०ख॥
ehi misa mohi upadesehu rāma kṛpā sukha puṁja. 80(kha).

उत पचार दसकंधर इत अंगद हनुमान ।
uta pacāra dasakaṁdhara ita aṁgada hanumāna,
लरत निसाचर भालु कपि करि निज निज प्रभु आन ॥८०ग॥
larata nisācara bhālu kapi kari nija nija prabhu āna. 80(ga).

Trans:

One, who happens to be in possession of such impregnable chariot, can overcome anything—even that great and terrible enemy: attachment to the world. Hearken my friend of resolute mind and fear not." When he had heard his Lord's exhortation, Vibhīshan clasped his feet in his joy and cried, "O Rāma, full of mercy and kindness, you have used this parable to give me a lesson." Now on the one side was Rāvan's rabble; and on the other side Angad and Hanumān—the demons against the bears and monkeys. They had joined in battle, each swearing by their lord.

चौपाई-caupāī:

सुर ब्रह्मादि सिद्ध मुनि नाना । देखत रन नभ चढ़े बिमाना ॥
sura brahmādi siddha muni nānā, dekhata rana nabha caṛhe bimānā.
हमहू उमा रहे तेहिं संगा । देखत राम चरित रन रंगा ॥
hamahū umā rahe tehiṁ saṁgā, dekhata rāma carita rana raṁgā.
सुभट समर रस दुहु दिसि माते । कपि जयसील राम बल ताते ॥
subhaṭa samara rasa duhu disi māte, kapi jayasīla rāma bala tāte.
एक एक सन भिरहिं पचारहिं । एकन्ह एक मर्दि महि पारहिं ॥
eka eka sana bhirahiṁ pacārahiṁ, ekanha eka mardi mahi pārahiṁ.
मारहिं काटहिं धरहिं पछारहिं । सीस तोरि सीसन्ह सन मारहिं ॥
mārahiṁ kāṭahiṁ dharahiṁ pachārahiṁ, sīsa tori sīsanha sana mārahiṁ.
उदर बिदारहिं भुजा उपारहिं । गहि पद अवनि पटकि भट डारहिं ॥
udara bidārahiṁ bhujā upārahiṁ, gahi pada avani paṭaki bhaṭa ḍārahiṁ.
निसिचर भट महि गाड़हिं भालू । ऊपर ढारि देहिं बहु बालू ॥
nisicara bhaṭa mahi gāṛahiṁ bhālū, ūpara ḍhāri dehiṁ bahu bālū.
बीर बलिमुख जुद्ध बिरुद्धे । देखिअत बिपुल काल जनु क्रुद्धे ॥
bīra balimukha juddha biruddhe, dekhiata bipula kāla janu kruddhe.

Trans:

Brahmmā and the other gods, with all the saints and sages, mounted their chariots to watch the combat from the heaven above. I too, O Umā, was with them, beholding Rāma's exploits on the field of battle. On both sides the leaders were maddened with martial frenzy, but the monkeys were triumphant through the might of Rāma. With shouts of defiance they close in single combat, each mauling his foe and beating him to the ground. They strike, they bite, they clutch, they fell; they tear off heads and use them for weapons; they rip up bodies, wrench off arms, and seizing by the leg dash them to the ground. The bears bury the demon warriors in the earth and pile over them heaps of sand; the sturdy monkeys raging in the fight were like so many monstrous images of raven-death to look upon.

छंद-*chaṁda:*

क्रुद्धे कृतांत समान कपि तन स्रवत सोनित राजहीं ।
kruddhe kṛtāṁta samāna kapi tana sravata sonita rājahīṁ,
मर्दहिं निसाचर कटक भट बलवंत घन जिमि गाजहीं ॥
mardahiṁ nisācara kaṭaka bhaṭa balavaṁta ghana jimi gājahīṁ.
मारहिं चपेटन्हि डाटि दातन्ह काटि लातन्ह मीजहीं ।
mārahiṁ capeṭanhi ḍāṭi dātanha kāṭi lātanha mījahīṁ,
चिक्करहिं मर्कट भालु छल बल करहिं जेहिं खल छीजहीं ॥
cikkarahiṁ markaṭa bhālu chala bala karahiṁ jehiṁ khala chījahīṁ.
धरि गाल फारहिं उर बिदारहिं गल अँतावरि मेलहीं ।
dhari gāla phārahiṁ ura bidārahiṁ gala aṁtāvari melahīṁ,
प्रह्लादपति जनु बिबिध तनु धरि समर अंगन खेलहीं ॥
prahlādapati janu bibidha tanu dhari samara aṁgana khelahīṁ.
धरु मारु काटु पछारु घोर गिरा गगन महि भरि रही ।
dharu māru kāṭu pachāru ghora girā gagana mahi bhari rahī,
जय राम जो तृन ते कुलिस कर कुलिस ते कर तृन सही ॥
jaya rāma jo tṛna te kulisa kara kulisa te kara tṛna sahī.

Trans:

The monkeys, their bodies all streaming with gore, stood forth like multiplied images of the god of death, crushing the mightiest warriors of the demon host, and roaring with voices of thunder. They strike, they buffet, they tear with the teeth, they crush beneath the feet, uttering furious cries, both bears and monkeys, and employing strength and stratagem alike, by which to reduce the enemy. They seize and tear open their cheeks, they rip up the belly and take the entrails and hang them round their own necks, as though the Lord of Prahlād (Narsingh) had assumed a multiplicity of forms, and were disporting himself on the field of battle. "Seize, strike, tear, overthrow," were the savage cries with which earth and heaven resounded. Glory to Rāma, who can make a straw into a thunderbolt; and again reduce a thunderbolt to a straw.

दोहा-*dohā:*

निज दल बिचलत देखेसि बीस भुजाँ दस चाप ।
nija dala bicalata dekhesi bīsa bhujāṁ dasa cāpa,
रथ चढ़ि चलेउ दसानन फिरहु फिरहु करि दाप ॥८१॥
ratha caṛhi caleu dasānana phirahu phirahu kari dāpa. 81.

Trans:

When Rāvan saw his troops in confusion, he mounted his chariot, with his twenty arms and ten bows, and essayed to rally the troops crying "turn around, turn around.'

चौपाई-*caupāī:*

धायउ परम क्रुद्ध दसकंधर । सन्मुख चले हूह दै बंदर ॥
dhāyau parama kruddha dasakaṁdhara, sanmukha cale hūha dai baṁdara.
गहि कर पादप उपल पहारा । डारेन्हि ता पर एकहिं बारा ॥
gahi kara pādapa upala pahārā, ḍārenhi tā para ekahiṁ bārā.
लागहिं सैल बज्र तन तासू । खंड खंड होइ फूटहिं आसू ॥
lāgahiṁ saila bajra tana tāsū, khaṁḍa khaṁḍa hoi phūṭahiṁ āsū.
चला न अचल रहा रथ रोपी । रन दुर्मद रावन अति कोपी ॥
calā na acala rahā ratha ropī, rana durmada rāvana ati kopī.
इत उत झपटि दपटि कपि जोधा । मर्दै लाग भयउ अति क्रोधा ॥
ita uta jhapaṭi dapaṭi kapi jodhā, mardai lāga bhayau ati krodhā.
चले पराइ भालु कपि नाना । त्राहि त्राहि अंगद हनुमाना ॥
cale parāi bhālu kapi nānā, trāhi trāhi aṁgada hanumānā.
पाहि पाहि रघुबीर गोसाईं । यह खल खाइ काल की नाईं ॥
pāhi pāhi raghubīra gosāīṁ, yaha khala khāi kāla kī nāīṁ.
तेहिं देखे कपि सकल पराने । दसहुँ चाप सायक संधाने ॥
tehiṁ dekhe kapi sakala parāne, dasahuṁ cāpa sāyaka saṁdhāne.

Trans:

The Ten-headed rushed forth in wild fury, and the monkeys with a whoop advanced to meet him. Taking in their hands trees, crags, and mountains, together they all hurled them upon him. The masses of stone no sooner struck on his adamantine frame than they were at once shattered in pieces, while he flinched not, but stood firm as a rock and stayed in his chariot—he, Rāvan, maddened with the battle and terrible in his fury. In the fierceness of his wrath, he scattered and battered the monkey chiefs this way and that. Bears and monkeys all took to flight, crying, "Help, help, Angad, Hanumān; save, save, O Lord Raghubīr; this monster, as sure as death, will devour us all." When he saw the monkeys in flight, the demon fitted an arrow to each of his ten bows.

छंद-*chaṁda:*

संधानि धनु सर निकर छाड़ेसि उरग जिमि उड़ि लागहीं ।
saṁdhāni dhanu sara nikara chāṛesi uraga jimi uṛi lāgahīṁ,
रहे पूरि सर धरनी गगन दिसि बिदिसि कहँ कपि भागहीं ॥
rahe pūri sara dharanī gagana disi bidisi kahaṁ kapi bhāgahīṁ.
भयो अति कोलाहल बिकल कपि दल भालु बोलहिं आतुरे ।
bhayo ati kolāhala bikala kapi dala bhālu bolahiṁ āture,
रघुबीर करुना सिंधु आरत बंधु जन रच्छक हरे ॥
raghubīra karunā siṁdhu ārata baṁdhu jana racchaka hare.

Trans:

He strung his bow and let fly a volley of arrows; they flew and lodged like serpents; the heaven and the earth were full of arrows; the monkeys fled in all directions; there was a terrible uproar; the monkey host and the bears were panic-stricken and cried in dismay: "O Raghubīr, fountain of mercy; O Harī, friend of the forlorn, savior of mankind, help!"

दोहा-*dohā:*

निज दल बिकल देखि कटि कसि निषंग धनु हाथ ।
nija dala bikala dekhi kaṭi kasi niṣaṁga dhanu hātha,
लछिमन चले क्रुद्ध होइ नाइ राम पद माथ ॥८२॥
lachimana cale kruddha hoi nāi rāma pada mātha. 82.

Trans:

Seeing the distress of his troops, Lakshman slung his quiver by his side, took his bow in his hand, and after bowing his head at Rāma's feet, sallied forth ferociously.

चौपाई-*caupāī:*

रे खल का मारसि कपि भालू । मोहि बिलोकु तोर मैं कालू ॥
re khala kā mārasi kapi bhālū, mohi biloku tora maiṁ kālū.
खोजत रहेउँ तोहि सुतघाती । आजु निपाति जुड़ावउँ छाती ॥
khojata raheuṁ tohi sutaghātī, āju nipāti juṛāvauṁ chātī.
अस कहि छाड़ेसि बान प्रचंडा । लछिमन किए सकल सत खंडा ॥
asa kahi chāṛesi bāna pracaṁḍā, lachimana kie sakala sata khaṁḍā.
कोटिन्ह आयुध रावन डारे । तिल प्रवान करि काटि निवारे ॥
koṭinha āyudha rāvana ḍāre, tila pravāna kari kāṭi nivāre.
पुनि निज बानन्ह कीन्ह प्रहारा । स्यंदनु भंजि सारथी मारा ॥
puni nija bānanha kīnha prahārā, syaṁdanu bhaṁji sārathī mārā.
सत सत सर मारे दस भाला । गिरि सृंगन्ह जनु प्रबिसहिं ब्याला ॥
sata sata sara māre dasa bhālā, giri sṛṁganha janu prabisahiṁ byālā.
पुनि सत सर मारा उर माहीं । परेउ धरनि तल सुधि कछु नाहीं ॥
puni sata sara mārā ura māhīṁ, pareu dharani tala sudhi kachu nāhīṁ.
उठा प्रबल पुनि मुरुछा जागी । छाड़िसि ब्रह्म दीन्हि जो साँगी ॥

uṭhā prabala puni muruchā jāgī, chāṛisi brahma dīnhi jo sāṁgī.

Trans:

"Ah! vile wretch, you kill bears and monkeys; but now look at me, I am your Death." "I have been searching for you, you murderer of my son, and today I will gladden my soul by your destruction." Thus he cried and let fly a storm of arrows; but Lakshman slivered them all into a hundred pieces. Then Rāvan hurled upon him myriads of missiles, but he warded them off as though they had been tiny sesame seeds; and then he in turn assailed him with his own shafts, smashing his chariot and killing his charioteer. Each of his ten heads he transfixed with a hundred arrows, which seemed like serpents boring their way into the peaks of mountains. With a hundred arrows more he struck him full in the chest, and he fell senseless to the ground. When the swoon had passed off, he rose again in his strength and let fly the bolt given to him by Brahmmā.

छंद-chaṁda:

सो ब्रह्म दत्त प्रचंड सक्ति अनंत उर लागी सही ।

so brahma datta pracaṁḍa sakti anaṁta ura lāgī sahī,

परयो बीर बिकल उठाव दसमुख अतुल बल महिमा रही ॥

parayo bīra bikala uṭhāva dasamukha atula bala mahimā rahī.

ब्रह्मांड भवन बिराज जाकें एक सिर जिमि रज कनी ।

brahmāṁḍa bhavana birāja jākeṁ eka sira jimi raja kanī,

तेहि चह उठावन मूढ़ रावन जान नहिं त्रिभुअन धनी ॥

tehi caha uṭhāvana mūṛha rāvana jāna nahiṁ tribhuana dhanī.

Trans:

The mighty bolt, the gift of Brahmmā, smote the incarnate Sheshnāg full in the chest; the hero fell fainting; the Ten-headed essayed to lift his body, but his immeasurable bulk stirred not. In his folly Rāvan thought to carry him off, not knowing him to be the Lord of the three spheres who supports on one of his heads the whole created universe as though it were a mere grain of sand.

दोहा-dohā:

देखि पवनसुत धायउ बोलत बचन कठोर ।

dekhi pavanasuta dhāyau bolata bacana kaṭhora,

आवत कपिहि हन्यो तेहिं मुष्टि प्रहार प्रघोर ॥८३॥

āvata kapihi hanyo tehiṁ muṣṭi prahāra praghora. 83.

Trans:

When the son-of-wind saw this he rushed forward with a furious cry; but as the monkey came on, the demon struck him a violent blow with his fist.

चौपाई-caupāī:

जानु टेकि कपि भूमि न गिरा । उठा सँभारि बहुत रिस भरा ॥

jānu ṭeki kapi bhūmi na girā, uṭhā saṁbhāri bahuta risa bharā.

मुठिका एक ताहि कपि मारा । परेउ सैल जनु बज्र प्रहारा ॥

muṭhikā eka tāhi kapi mārā, pareu saila janu bajra prahārā.

मुरुछा गै बहोरि सो जागा । कपि बल बिपुल सराहन लागा ॥

muruchā gai bahori so jāgā, kapi bala bipula sarāhana lāgā.

धिग धिग मम पौरुष धिग मोही । जौं तैं जिअत रहेसि सुरद्रोही ॥

dhiga dhiga mama pauruṣa dhiga mohī, jauṁ taiṁ jiata rahesi suradrohī.

अस कहि लछिमन कहुँ कपि ल्यायो । देखि दसानन बिसमय पायो ॥

asa kahi lachimana kahuṁ kapi lyāyo, dekhi dasānana bisamaya pāyo.

कह रघुबीर समुझु जियँ भ्राता । तुम्ह कृतांत भच्छक सुर त्राता ॥

kaha raghubīra samujhu jiyaṁ bhrātā, tumha kṛtāṁta bhacchaka sura trātā.

सुनत बचन उठि बैठ कृपाला । गई गगन सो सकति कराला ॥

sunata bacana uṭhi baiṭha kṛpālā, gaī gagana so sakati karālā.

पुनि कोदंड बान गहि धाए । रिपु सन्मुख अति आतुर आए ॥

puni kodaṁḍa bāna gahi dhāe, ripu sanmukha ati ātura āe.

Trans:

The monkey dropped to one knee but did not fall to the ground; and, on recovering himself, arose full of exceeding wrath, and smote him one blow; and Rāvan fell like a mountain struck by a thunderbolt. When he recovered from the swoon he marveled greatly at the monkey's might and strength. "Shame on my valour, and shame on myself—if you remain alive, you plague of heaven," cried Hanumān as he carried Lakshman off to Shrī Rāma. At this sight, the Ten-headed monster was sore amazed. Seeing his brother Raghubīr spoke, "Bear in mind, O brother, that you are the devourer of Death and the savior of gods." On hearing these words, the gracious prince arose and sat up, while the terrible lance vanished into the heavens. Then again picking his bows and arrows Lakshman rushed forward with the utmost impetuosity to meet the enemy.

छंद-chaṁda:

आतुर बहोरि बिभंजि स्यंदन सूत हति ब्याकुल कियो ।

ātura bahori bibhaṁji syaṁdana sūta hati byākula kiyo,

गिरयो धरनि दसकंधर बिकलतर बान सत बेध्यो हियो ॥

girayo dharani dasakaṁdhara bikalatara bāna sata bedhyo hiyo.

सारथी दूसर घालि रथ तेहि तुरत लंका लै गयो ।

sārathī dūsara ghāli ratha tehi turata laṁkā lai gayo,

रघुबीर बंधु प्रताप पुंज बहोरि प्रभु चरनन्हि नयो ॥

raghubīra baṁdhu pratāpa puṁja bahori prabhu carananhi nayo.

Trans:

Again, by his brazen attack, Lakshman smashed Rāvan's chariot and struck down the charioteer. Rāvan fell fainting to the ground, his heart transfixed by a hundred arrows. Another charioteer came and threw him on a chariot, carrying him off to Lankā; while Lakshman in all his glory went and prostrated himself at Rāma's feet.

दोहा-dohā:

उहाँ दसानन जागि करि करै लाग कछु जग्य ।

uhāṁ dasānana jāgi kari karai lāga kachu jagya,

राम बिरोध बिजय चह सठ हठ बस अति अग्य ॥८४॥

rāma birodha bijaya caha saṭha haṭha basa ati agya. 84.

Trans:

There Rāvan, on recovering, began to make preparations for a sacrifice. In his perversity and ignorance he sought to prosper and gain victory even by antagonizing Rāma—the fool that Rāvan was.

चौपाई-caupāī:

इहाँ बिभीषन सब सुधि पाई । सपदि जाइ रघुपतिहि सुनाई ॥

ihāṁ bibhīṣana saba sudhi pāī, sapadi jāi raghupatihi sunāī.

नाथ करइ रावन एक जागा । सिद्ध भएँ नहिं मरिहि अभागा ॥

nātha karai rāvana eka jāgā, siddha bhaeṁ nahiṁ marihi abhāgā.

पठवहु नाथ बेगि भट बंदर । करहिं बिधंस आव दसकंधर ॥

paṭhavahu nātha begi bhaṭa baṁdara, karahiṁ bidhaṁsa āva dasakaṁdhara.

प्रात होत प्रभु सुभट पठाए । हनुमदादि अंगद सब धाए ॥

prāta hota prabhu subhaṭa paṭhāe, hanumadādi aṁgada saba dhāe.

कौतुक कूदि चढ़े कपि लंका । पैठे रावन भवन असंका ॥

kautuka kūdi caṛhe kapi laṁkā, paiṭhe rāvana bhavana asaṁkā.

जग्य करत जबहीं सो देखा । सकल कपिन्ह भा क्रोध बिसेषा ॥

jagya karata jabahīṁ so dekhā, sakala kapinha bhā krodha biseṣā.

रन ते निलज भाजि गृह आवा । इहाँ आइ बक ध्यान लगावा ॥

rana te nilaja bhāji gṛha āvā, ihāṁ āi baka dhyāna lagāvā.

अस कहि अंगद मारा लाता । चितव न सठ स्वारथ मन राता ॥

asa kahi aṁgada mārā lātā, citava na saṭha svāratha mana rātā.

Trans:

Here Vibhīshan, on learning of the news, went at once and told Raghupatī, "My Lord, Rāvan is engaged in performing a sacrifice; if he completes it, the wretch will never die. Dispatch your valiant monkeys, sire, in all speed, to cut short the proceedings." As soon as it was day, the Lord sent out his warriors: Hanumān, Angad, and other, who all rushed forward. Bounding with glee, the monkeys climbed Lankā and boldly entered Rāvan's palace. Finding him engaged in the sacrifice, they became very furious, "Without shame you run away home from the battlefield and are sitting here practicing this hypocrisy!" Saying so, Angad gave him a kick, but the wretch took no notice, so absorbed was he in his own purpose.

छंद-chamda:

नहिं चितव जब करि कोप कपि गहि दसन लातन्ह मारहीं ।
nahiṁ citava jaba kari kopa kapi gahi dasana lātanha mārahīṁ,
धरि केस नारि निकारि बाहेर तेऽतिदीन पुकारहीं ॥
dhari kesa nāri nikāri bāhera te'tidīna pukārahīṁ.
तब उठेउ क्रुद्ध कृतांत सम गहि चरन बानर डारई ।
taba uṭheu kruddha kṛtāṁta sama gahi carana bānara ḍāraī,
एहि बीच कपिन्ह बिधंस कृत मख देखि मन महुँ हारई ॥
ehi bīca kapinha bidhaṁsa kṛta makha dekhi mana mahuṁ hāraī.

Trans:

As he took no notice, the monkeys in a fury tore him with their teeth and kicked him with their feet; his wives too they seized, dragging them by hair out the doors, even as they screamed most piteously. Then at last Rāvan rose, terrible as death, and caught the monkeys by leg and hurled them away. But seeing that the monkeys had thereby succeeded in interrupting his sacrifice, his heart sank.

दोहा-dohā:

जग्य बिधंसि कुसल कपि आए रघुपति पास ।
jagya bidhaṁsi kusala kapi āe raghupati pāsa,
चलेउ निसाचर क्रुद्ध होइ त्यागि जिवन कै आस ॥८५॥
caleu nisācara kruddha hoi tyāgi jivana kai āsa. 85.

Trans:

Rejoicing at having spoilt the sacrifice, the monkeys returned to Raghupatī; while the demon-king went off in fury, abandoning all hopes of life.

चौपाई-caupāī:

चलत होहिं अति असुभ भयंकर । बैठहिं गीध उड़ाइ सिरन्ह पर ॥
calata hohiṁ ati asubha bhayaṁkara, baiṭhahiṁ gīdha uṛāi siranha para.
भयउ कालबस काहु न माना । कहेसि बजावहु जुद्ध निसाना ॥
bhayau kālabasa kāhu na mānā, kahesi bajāvahu juddha nisānā.
चली तमीचर अनी अपारा । बहु गज रथ पदाति असवारा ॥
calī tamīcara anī apārā, bahu gaja ratha padāti asavārā.
प्रभु सन्मुख धाए खल कैसें । सलभ समूह अनल कहँ जैसें ॥
prabhu sanmukha dhāe khala kaiseṁ, salabha samūha anala kahaṁ jaiseṁ.
इहाँ देवतन्ह अस्तुति कीन्ही । दारुन बिपति हमहि एहिं दीन्ही ॥
ihāṁ devatanha astuti kīnhī, dāruna bipati hamahi ehiṁ dīnhī.
अब जनि राम खेलावहु एही । अतिसय दुखित होति बैदेही ॥
aba jani rāma khelāvahu ehī, atisaya dukhita hoti baidehī.
देव बचन सुनि प्रभु मुसुकाना । उठि रघुबीर सुधारे बाना ॥
deva bacana suni prabhu musukānā, uṭhi raghubīra sudhāre bānā.
जटा जूट दृढ़ बाँधें माथे । सोहहिं सुमन बीच बिच गाथे ॥
jaṭā jūṭa dṛṛha bāṁdheṁ māthe, sohahiṁ sumana bīca bica gāthe.
अरुन नयन बारिद तनु स्यामा । अखिल लोक लोचनाभिरामा ॥
aruna nayana bārida tanu syāmā, akhila loka locanābhirāmā.
कटितट परिकर कस्यो निषंगा । कर कोदंड कठिन सारंगा ॥
kaṭitaṭa parikara kasyo niṣaṁgā, kara kodaṁḍa kaṭhina sāraṁgā.

Trans:

Fearful omens of ill befell him as he went. Vultures flew and settled on his heads. Fated to die, he paid no heed, but gave the order to sound the onset. The demon host appeared endless as it marched on with its myriads of elephants, chariots, soldiers and knights. The wicked demons hastened to confront the Lord, like a swarm of gnats when they fly into a fire. On the other hand, the gods raised songs of praise, "He has caused us grievous trouble; play with him no longer, O Rāma, for Sītā is in sore distress." On hearing the prayer of the gods, Rāma smiled and rose and trimmed his arrows. His hair was tightly bound in a knot on his forehead, beautiful with the flowers that had here and there been caught as they fell upon him from heaven. With his bright eyes and his body dark of hue as a rain-cloud, rejoicing the sight of every created sphere, he girded on his quiver with its belt about his loins, and took in his hand his bow—the mighty bow of Vishnu.

छंद-chamda:

सारंग कर सुंदर निषंग सिलीमुखाकर कटि कस्यो ।
sāraṁga kara suṁdara niṣaṁga silīmukhākara kaṭi kasyo,
भुजदंड पीन मनोहरायत उर धरासुर पद लस्यो ॥
bhujadaṁḍa pīna manoharāyata ura dharāsura pada lasyo.
कह दास तुलसी जबहिं प्रभु सर चाप कर फेरन लगे ।
kaha dāsa tulasī jabahiṁ prabhu sara cāpa kara pherana lage,
ब्रह्मांड दिग्गज कमठ अहि महि सिंधु भूधर डगमगे ॥
brahmāṁḍa diggaja kamaṭha ahi mahi siṁdhu bhūdhara ḍagamage.

Trans:

With his bow Sarang in his hand and his beautiful quiver full of arrows slung by his side, with his muscular arms and fine broad chest, adorned with the print of the Brahmin's foot, when the Lord—says Tulsīdās—began to handle his bow and arrows, the elephants that support the world, the tortoise, the serpent, and the earth itself, with its mountains and seas, all reeled.

दोहा-dohā:

सोभा देखि हरषि सुर बरषहिं सुमन अपार ।
sobhā dekhi haraṣi sura baraṣahiṁ sumana apāra,
जय जय जय करुनानिधि छबि बल गुन आगार ॥८६॥
jaya jaya jaya karunānidhi chabi bala guna āgāra. 86.

Trans:

The gods rejoiced at the sight of his splendor and rained down flowers in abundance, singing "Glory, Glory, Glory to the All-merciful, the storehouse of beauty, strength, and perfection."

चौपाई-caupāī:

एहीं बीच निसाचर अनी । कसमसात आई अति घनी ॥
ehīṁ bīca nisācara anī, kasamasāta āī ati ghanī.
देखि चले सन्मुख कपि भट्टा । प्रलयकाल के जनु घन घट्टा ॥
dekhi cale sanmukha kapi bhaṭṭā, pralayakāla ke janu ghana ghaṭṭā.
बहु कृपान तरवारि चमंकहिं । जनु दहँ दिसि दामिनीं दमंकहिं ॥
bahu kṛpāna taravāri camaṁkahiṁ, janu dahaṁ disi dāminīṁ damaṁkahiṁ.
गज रथ तुरग चिकार कठोरा । गर्जहिं मनहुँ बलाहक घोरा ॥
gaja ratha turaga cikāra kaṭhorā, garjahiṁ manahuṁ balāhaka ghorā.
कपि लंगूर बिपुल नभ छाए । मनहुँ इंद्रधनु उए सुहाए ॥
kapi laṁgūra bipula nabha chāe, manahuṁ iṁdradhanu ue suhāe.
उठइ धूरि मानहुँ जलधारा । बान बुंद भै बृष्टि अपारा ॥
uṭhai dhūri mānahuṁ jaladhārā, bāna buṁda bhai bṛṣṭi apārā.
दुहुँ दिसि पर्बत करहिं प्रहारा । बज्रपात जनु बारहिं बारा ॥
duhuṁ disi parbata karahiṁ prahārā, bajrapāta janu bārahiṁ bārā.
रघुपति कोपि बान झरि लाई । घायल भै निसिचर समुदाई ॥
raghupati kopi bāna jhari lāī, ghāyala bhai nisicara samudāī.
लागत बान बीर चिक्करहीं । घुर्मि घुर्मि जहँ तहँ महि परहीं ॥
lāgata bāna bīra cikkarahīṁ, ghurmi ghurmi jahaṁ tahaṁ mahi parahīṁ.
स्रवहिं सैल जनु निर्झर भारी । सोनित सरि कादर भयकारी ॥
sravahiṁ saila janu nirjhara bhārī, sonita sari kādara bhayakārī.

Trans:

Meanwhile the demon hosts came rolling on in infinite number. The monkey warriors at the sight advanced to meet them, like the thunder clouds gathered at the final day of dissolution. Spears, lances, and swords flashed again like gleams of lightning from every quarter of the heaven. The awful din of elephants, chariots, and horses was like the thundering of frightful tempest. The monkeys' huge tails as they spread over the sky were like the uprising of a splendid rainbow. The dust was borne aloft like a cloud, and the arrows fell like a copious shower. The mountains hurled from either side were like the crash of repeated thunderbolts. When Rāma in his wrath poured forth his arrows, the demon crew were sore smitten. At the smart of his shafts the warriors screamed with pain and everywhere reeled and fell upon the ground. The rocks streamed as it were with cascades in a river of blood, a sight to strike terror in the hearts of cowards.

छंद-*chaṁda:*

कादर भयंकर रुधिर सरिता चली परम अपावनी ।
kādara bhayaṁkara rudhira saritā calī parama apāvanī,
दोउ कूल दल रथ रेत चक्र अबर्त बहति भयावनी ॥
dou kūla dala ratha reta cakra abarta bahati bhayāvanī.
जलजंतु गज पदचर तुरग खर बिबिध बाहन को गने ।
jalajaṁtu gaja padacara turaga khara bibidha bāhana ko gane,
सर सक्ति तोमर सर्प चाप तरंग चर्म कमठ घने ॥
sara sakti tomara sarpa cāpa taraṁga carma kamaṭha ghane.

Trans:

A most loathsome river of blood, striking the faint-hearted with terror, rolls on between the two armies for its banks, with chariots for sand and wheels for eddies—a frightful flood: with elephants, foot soldiers, and horses for its aquatic birds, and vehicles of every kind—more than one can count—for its reeds and grasses; with arrows, spears, and lances for its snakes; bows for its waves; and shields for its shoals of tortoises.

दोहा-*dohā:*

बीर परहिं जनु तीर तरु मज्जा बहु बह फेन ।
bīra parahiṁ janu tīra taru majjā bahu baha phena,
कादर देखि डरहिं तहँ सुभटन्ह के मन चेन ॥८७॥
kādara dekhi ḍarahiṁ tahaṁ subhaṭanha ke mana cena. 87.

Trans:

The fallen heroes are the trees on its bank, the marrow of their bones its scum. The timid tremble at the sight, but the gallant are dauntless of soul.

चौपाई-*caupāī:*

मज्जहिं भूत पिसाच बेताला । प्रमथ महा झोटिंग कराला ॥
majjahiṁ bhūta pisāca betālā, pramatha mahā jhoṭiṁga karālā.
काक कंक लै भुजा उड़ाहीं । एक ते छीनि एक लै खाहीं ॥
kāka kaṁka lai bhujā uṛāhīṁ, eka te chīni eka lai khāhīṁ.
एक कहहिं ऐसिउ सौंघाई । सठहु तुम्हार दरिद्र न जाई ॥
eka kahahiṁ aisiu sauṁghāī, saṭhahu tumhāra daridra na jāī.
कहँरत भट घायल तट गिरे । जहँ तहँ मनहुँ अर्धजल परे ॥
kahaṁrata bhaṭa ghāyala taṭa gire, jahaṁ tahaṁ manahuṁ ardhajala pare.
खैंचहिं गीध आँत तट भए । जनु बंसी खेलत चित दए ॥
khaiṁcahiṁ gīdha āṁta taṭa bhae, janu baṁsī khelata cita dae.
बहु भट बहहिं चढ़े खग जाहीं । जनु नावरि खेलहिं सरि माहीं ॥
bahu bhaṭa bahahiṁ caṛhe khaga jāhīṁ, janu nāvari khelahiṁ sari māhīṁ.
जोगिनि भरि भरि खप्पर संचहिं । भूत पिसाच बधू नभ नंचहिं ॥
jogini bhari bhari khappara saṁcahiṁ, bhūta pisāca badhū nabha naṁcahiṁ.
भट कपाल करताल बजावहिं । चामुंडा नाना बिधि गावहिं ॥
bhaṭa kapāla karatāla bajāvahiṁ, cāmuṁḍā nānā bidhi gāvahiṁ.
जंबुक निकर कटक्कट कट्टहिं । खाहिं हुआहिं अघाहिं दपट्टहिं ॥
jaṁbuka nikara kaṭakkaṭa kaṭṭahiṁ, khāhiṁ huāhiṁ aghāhiṁ dapaṭṭahiṁ.
कोटिन्ह रुंड मुंड बिनु डोल्लहिं । सीस परे महि जय जय बोल्लहिं ॥
koṭinha ruṁḍa muṁḍa binu ḍollahiṁ, sīsa pare mahi jaya jaya bollahiṁ.

Trans:

Those who bathe in it are imps, demons, and goblins, monstrous ghouls and horrible vampires. Crows and vultures fly off with human arms, which they tear from one another and seize and devour; at which some said, "You wretch, at such a time of plenty, is your hunger still unsatisfied?' Wounded warriors, fallen on the edge of the field, utter groans like the dying left half in and half out of the water. Vultures sit on the bank and tear the entrails of the dead, as keenly as fishermen intent on their rods. Many bodies float down with birds upon them, as if they were boating in a river. Witches draw water in skulls; other female demons and goblins dance in the air, clashing the skulls of warriors for cymbals, while the infernal goddesses sing songs after songs. Herds of jackals snarl and growl and scamper about devouring till they are gorged. Thousands of headless bodies roam the plain, while the heads fallen to the ground still shout "Victory, Victory."

छंद-*chaṁda:*

बोल्लहिं जो जय जय मुंड रुंड प्रचंड सिर बिनु धावहीं ।
bollahiṁ jo jaya jaya muṁḍa ruṁḍa pracaṁḍa sira binu dhāvahīṁ,
खप्परिन्ह खग्ग अलुज्झि जुज्झहिं सुभट भटन्ह ढहावहीं ॥
khapparinha khagga alujjhi jujjhahiṁ subhaṭa bhaṭanha ḍhahāvahīṁ.
बानर निसाचर निकर मर्दहिं राम बल दर्पित भए ।
bānara nisācara nikara mardahiṁ rāma bala darpita bhae,
संग्राम अंगन सुभट सोवहिं राम सर निकरन्हि हए ॥
saṁgrāma aṁgana subhaṭa sovahiṁ rāma sara nikaranhi hae.

Trans:

The heads cry "Victory, Victory," while the headless trunks rush wildly about. Swords and skulls are inextricably involved, hero against hero, fighting and overthrowing each other. The monkeys crush the demon crew and prevail triumphant through the power of Rāma's grace. Smitten by Rāma's arrows the demon champions lay in eternal sleep on the battle field.

दोहा-*dohā:*

रावन हृदयँ बिचारा भा निसिचर संघार ।
rāvana hṛdayaṁ bicārā bhā nisicara saṁghāra,
मैं अकेल कपि भालु बहु माया करौं अपार ॥८८॥
maiṁ akela kapi bhālu bahu māyā karauṁ apāra. 88.

Trans:

Rāvan thought to himself, "The demons are routed; I am alone; the bears and monkeys are so many; I must put forth all my magic power."

चौपाई-*caupāī:*

देवन्ह प्रभुहि पयादें देखा । उपजा उर अति छोभ बिसेषा ॥
devanha prabhuhi payādeṁ dekhā, upajā ura ati chobha biseṣā.
सुरपति निज रथ तुरत पठावा । हरष सहित मातलि लै आवा ॥
surapati nija ratha turata paṭhāvā, haraṣa sahita mātali lai āvā.
तेज पुंज रथ दिब्य अनूपा । हरषि चढ़े कोसलपुर भूपा ॥
teja puṁja ratha dibya anūpā, haraṣi caṛhe kosalapura bhūpā.
चंचल तुरग मनोहर चारी । अजर अमर मन सम गतिकारी ॥
caṁcala turaga manohara cārī, ajara amara mana sama gatikārī.
रथारूढ़ रघुनाथहि देखी । धाए कपि बलु पाइ बिसेषी ॥
rathārūṛha raghunāthahi dekhī, dhāe kapi balu pāi biseṣī.
सही न जाइ कपिन्ह कै मारी । तब रावन माया बिस्तारी ॥
sahī na jāi kapinha kai mārī, taba rāvana māyā bistārī.
सो माया रघुबीरहि बाँची । लछिमन कपिन्ह सो मानी साँची ॥
so māyā raghubīrahi bāṁcī, lachimana kapinha so mānī sāṁcī.
देखी कपिन्ह निसाचर अनी । अनुज सहित बहु कोसलधनी ॥
dekhī kapinha nisācara anī, anuja sahita bahu kosaladhanī.

Trans:

When the gods saw that the Lord was on foot, they were exceedingly disturbed in mind, and Indra at once dispatched his own chariot. Matali brought it gladly: a splendid chariot, divine, incomparable; the king of Kaushal cheerfully mounted it. Its four beautiful and high mettled steeds, deathless and ever young, flew swift as thought. When they saw Raghunāth mounted on a car, the monkeys rushed forward with renewed vigor. Their onset was irresistible. Then Rāvan exerted his magic power. Raghubīr knew it to be a mere delusion, but Lakshman and the monkeys took it for real. They saw among the demon host, so many Rāmas and as many Lakshmans due to the sorcery.

छंद-chaṁda:

बहु राम लछिमन देखि मर्कट भालु मन अति अपडरे ।
bahu rāma lachimana dekhi markaṭa bhālu mana ati apaḍare,
जनु चित्र लिखित समेत लछिमन जहँ सो तहँ चितवहिं खरे ॥
janu citra likhita sameta lachimana jahaṁ so tahaṁ citavahiṁ khare.
निज सेन चकित बिलोकि हँसि सर चाप सजि कोसल धनी ।
nija sena cakita biloki haṁsi sara cāpa saji kosala dhanī,
माया हरी हरि निमिष महुँ हरषी सकल मर्कट अनी ॥
māyā harī hari nimiṣa mahuṁ haraṣī sakala markaṭa anī.

Trans:

Seeing these multiple forms of Rāmas and Lakshmans, the monkeys and bears were greatly dismayed; wherever they looked, they saw him standing, as in a picture, and Lakshman with him. The Lord of Kaushal smiled to see the perplexity of his troops. Then Harī made ready his bow and in a moment scattered the delusion. The monkey host rejoiced again.

दोहा-dohā:

बहुरि राम सब तन चितइ बोले बचन गँभीर ।
bahuri rāma saba tana citai bole bacana gaṁbhīra,
द्वंदजुद्ध देखहु सकल श्रमित भए अति बीर ॥८९॥
dvaṁdajuddha dekhahu sakala śramita bhae ati bīra. 89.

Trans:

Then Rāma looked round about him and spoke in profound tones, "Watch now the combat between us two—for you all, my heroes, are much wearied."

चौपाई-caupāī:

अस कहि रथ रघुनाथ चलावा । बिप्र चरन पंकज सिरु नावा ॥
asa kahi ratha raghunātha calāvā, bipra carana paṁkaja siru nāvā.
तब लंकेस क्रोध उर छावा । गर्जत तर्जत सन्मुख धावा ॥
taba laṁkesa krodha ura chāvā, garjata tarjata sanmukha dhāvā.
जीतेहु जे भट संजुग माहीं । सुनु तापस मैं तिन्ह सम नाहीं ॥
jītehu je bhaṭa saṁjuga māhīṁ, sunu tāpasa maiṁ tinha sama nāhīṁ.
रावन नाम जगत जस जाना । लोकप जाकें बंदीखाना ॥
rāvana nāma jagata jasa jānā, lokapa jākeṁ baṁdīkhānā.
खर दूषन बिराध तुम्ह मारा । बधेहु ब्याध इव बालि बिचारा ॥
khara dūṣana birādha tumha mārā, badhehu byādha iva bāli bicārā.
निसिचर निकर सुभट संघारेहु । कुंभकरन घननादहि मारेहु ॥
nisicara nikara subhaṭa saṁghārehu, kuṁbhakarana ghananādahi mārehu.
आजु बयरु सबु लेउँ निबाही । जौं रन भूप भाजि नहिं जाही ॥
āju bayaru sabu leuṁ nibāhī, jauṁ rana bhūpa bhāji nahiṁ jāhī.
आजु करउँ खलु काल हवाले । परेहु कठिन रावन के पाले ॥
āju karauṁ khalu kāla havāle, parehu kaṭhina rāvana ke pāle.
सुनि दुर्बचन कालबस जाना । बिहँसि बचन कह कृपानिधाना ॥
suni durbacana kālabasa jānā, bihaṁsi bacana kaha kṛpānidhānā.
सत्य सत्य सब तव प्रभुताई । जल्पसि जनि देखाउ मनुसाई ॥
satya satya saba tava prabhutāī, jalpasi jani dekhāu manusāī.

Trans:

So saying Raghunāth urged forward his chariot, after bowing his head at the Brahmin's lotus feet. Then the king of Lankā, full of fury, rushed to meet him, challenging him with a voice of thunder, "The warriors you have defeated in battle, mark me, hermit, I am not like them. The glory of Rāvan's name is known throughout the world; and how he cast into prison the regents of the spheres. You forsooth have slain Khar and Dūshan and Viradha and killed poor Bālī, lying in ambush for him like a huntsman; you have routed the leaders of the demon host, and put to death Kumbh-karan and Meghnād; but today I will make an end of all this fighting, unless indeed you save yourself by flight from the field. Today, wretch, I will give you in charge to Death; you have now to deal with the mighty Rāvan." On hearing this abusive speech, the All-merciful, knowing him to be death-doomed, smiled and answered, "True, true, I have heard all about your greatness; but no more boasting words, let me see your strength.

छंद-chaṁda:

जनि जल्पना करि सुजसु नासहि नीति सुनहि करहि छमा ।
jani jalpanā kari sujasu nāsahi nīti sunahi karahi chamā,
संसार महँ पूरुष त्रिबिध पाटल रसाल पनस समा ॥
saṁsāra mahaṁ pūruṣa tribidha pāṭala rasāla panasa samā.
एक सुमनप्रद एक सुमन फल एक फलइ केवल लागहीं ।
eka sumanaprada eka sumana phala eka phalai kevala lāgahīṁ,
एक कहहिं कहहिं करहिं अपर एक करहिं कहत न बागहीं ॥
eka kahahiṁ kahahiṁ karahiṁ apara eka karahiṁ kahata na bāgahīṁ.

Trans:

Do not destroy your reputation by boasting, pray excuse me if I give you this maxim: In this world there are three kinds of men resembling the rose, the mango, and the bread-fruit tree: the one has flowers, the second flowers and fruit, and the third fruit only. Even so, the one kind talks; the second talks and does; the third does, but says not a word."

दोहा-dohā:

राम बचन सुनि बिहँसा मोहि सिखावत ग्यान ।
rāma bacana suni bihaṁsā mohi sikhāvata gyāna,
बयरु करत नहिं तब डरे अब लागे प्रिय प्रान ॥९०॥
bayaru karata nahiṁ taba ḍare aba lāge priya prāna. 90.

Trans:

On hearing Rāma's speech, he laughed and said, "Ah, for you to teach me wisdom! You did not fear to wage war against me; but at last you have begun to hold your life dear."

चौपाई-caupāī:

कहि दुर्बचन क्रुद्ध दसकंधर । कुलिस समान लाग छाँडै सर ॥
kahi durbacana kruddha dasakaṁdhara, kulisa samāna lāga chāṁṛai sara.
नानाकार सिलीमुख धाए । दिसि अरु बिदिसि गगन महि छाए ॥
nānākāra silīmukha dhāe, disi aru bidisi gagana mahi chāe.
पावक सर छाँडेउ रघुबीरा । छन महुँ जरे निसाचर तीरा ॥
pāvaka sara chāṁṛeu raghubīrā, chana mahuṁ jare nisācara tīrā.
छाडिसि तीब्र सक्ति खिसिआई । बान संग प्रभु फेरि चलाई ॥
chāṛisi tībra sakti khisiāī, bāna saṁga prabhu pheri calāī.
कोटिन्ह चक्र त्रिसूल पबारै । बिनु प्रयास प्रभु काटि निवारै ॥
koṭinha cakra trisūla pabārai, binu prayāsa prabhu kāṭi nivārai.
निफल होहिं रावन सर कैसें । खल के सकल मनोरथ जैसें ॥
niphala hohiṁ rāvana sara kaiseṁ, khala ke sakala manoratha jaiseṁ.
तब सत बान सारथी मारेसि । परेउ भूमि जय राम पुकारेसि ॥
taba sata bāna sārathī māresi, pareu bhūmi jaya rāma pukāresi.
राम कृपा करि सूत उठावा । तब प्रभु परम क्रोध कहुँ पावा ॥
rāma kṛpā kari sūta uṭhāvā, taba prabhu parama krodha kahuṁ pāvā.

Trans:

Having uttered this taunt, Rāvan in a fury began to let fly his arrows like so many thunderbolts. The shafts sped forth, of many shapes; and all quarters around the heaven and earth were filled with the clouds of them. Raghubīr discharged an arrow of fire, and in a moment the demon's bolts were all consumed. He ground his teeth and hurled forth his mighty spear; the Lord turned it with an arrow and sent it back. Then he cast against him thousands of discs and tridents; but the Lord without an effort snapped and turned them aside. Rāvan's artillery was as unavailing as are always the schemes of the wicked. Then with a hundred arrows at once he struck Rāma's charioteer, who fell to the ground, crying 'Glory to Rāma.' The Lord had compassion upon him and raised him up again. Then a terrible fury possessed Rāma.

छंद-chaṁda:

भए क्रुद्ध जुद्ध बिरुद्ध रघुपति त्रोन सायक कसमसे ।
bhae kruddha juddha biruddha raghupati trona sāyaka kasamase,
कोदंड धुनि अति चंड सुनि मनुजाद सब मारुत ग्रसे ॥
kodaṁḍa dhuni ati caṁḍa suni manujāda saba māruta grase.
मंदोदरी उर कंप कंपति कमठ भू भूधर त्रसे ।
maṁdodarī ura kaṁpa kaṁpati kamaṭha bhū bhūdhara trase,
चिक्करहिं दिग्गज दसन गहि महि देखि कौतुक सुर हँसे ॥
cikkarahiṁ diggaja dasana gahi mahi dekhi kautuka sura haṁse.

Trans:

Full of fury and raging in the battle, Raghupatī's very arrows were ready to jump out of his quiver. At the sound of the awful twang of his bow, all creation was seized with terror. Mandodarī's heart quaked; the sea, the great tortoise, the earth and its supporter trembled; the elephants of the eight quarters squealed and grasped the world tight in their jaws, while the gods laughed to see the sport.

दोहा-dohā:

तानेउ चाप श्रवन लगि छाँड़े बिसिख कराल ।
tāneu cāpa śravana lagi chāṁṛe bisikha karāla,
राम मारगन गन चले लहलहात जनु ब्याल ॥९१॥
rāma māragana gana cale lahalahāta janu byāla. 91.

Trans:

He drew the bow-string to his ear and let fly his terrible shafts; and they cleft the sky, quivering like so many serpents.

चौपाई-caupāī:

चले बान सपच्छ जनु उरगा । प्रथमहिं हतेउ सारथी तुरगा ॥
cale bāna sapaccha janu uragā, prathamahiṁ hateu sārathī turagā.
रथ बिभंजि हति केतु पताका । गर्जा अति अंतर बल थाका ॥
ratha bibhaṁji hati ketu patākā, garjā ati aṁtara bala thākā.
तुरत आन रथ चढ़ि खिसिआना । अस्त्र सस्त्र छाँड़ेसि बिधि नाना ॥
turata āna ratha caṛhi khisiānā, astra sastra chāṁṛesi bidhi nānā.
बिफल होहिं सब उद्यम ताके । जिमि परद्रोह निरत मनसा के ॥
biphala hohiṁ saba udyama tāke, jimi paradroha nirata manasā ke.
तब रावन दस सूल चलावा । बाजि चारि महि मारि गिरावा ॥
taba rāvana dasa sūla calāvā, bāji cāri mahi māri girāvā.
तुरग उठाइ कोपि रघुनायक । खैंचि सरासन छाँड़े सायक ॥
turaga uṭhāi kopi raghunāyaka, khaiṁci sarāsana chāṁṛe sāyaka.
रावन सिर सरोज बनचारी । चलि रघुबीर सिलीमुख धारी ॥
rāvana sira saroja banacārī, cali raghubīra silīmukha dhārī.
दस दस बान भाल दस मारे । निसरि गए चले रुधिर पनारे ॥
dasa dasa bāna bhāla dasa māre, nisari gae cale rudhira panāre.
स्रवत रुधिर धायउ बलवाना । प्रभु पुनि कृत धनु सर संधाना ॥
sravata rudhira dhāyau balavānā, prabhu puni kṛta dhanu sara saṁdhānā.
तीस तीर रघुबीर पबारे । भुजन्हि समेत सीस महि पारे ॥
tīsa tīra raghubīra pabāre, bhujanhi sameta sīsa mahi pāre.
काटतहीं पुनि भए नबीने । राम बहोरि भुजा सिर छीने ॥
kāṭatahīṁ puni bhae nabīne, rāma bahori bhujā sira chīne.
प्रभु बहु बार बाहु सिर हए । कटत झटिति पुनि नूतन भए ॥
prabhu bahu bāra bāhu sira hae, kaṭata jhaṭiti puni nūtana bhae.
पुनि पुनि प्रभु काटत भुज सीसा । अति कौतुकी कोसलाधीसा ॥
puni puni prabhu kāṭata bhuja sīsā, ati kautukī kosalādhīsā.
रहे छाइ नभ सिर अरु बाहू । मानहुँ अमित केतु अरु राहू ॥
rahe chāi nabha sira aru bāhū, mānahuṁ amita ketu aru rāhū.

Trans:

The arrows sped forth like winged serpents and at once laid low Rāvan's charioteer and his horses, breaking the car and snapping the flagstaff. Though inwardly Rāvan's courage failed him, he roared aloud and quickly mounted another car, and grinding his teeth let fly weapons and missiles of every description. But all his efforts had as little reward as those of a man bent only on injuring others. Then Rāvan hurled forth ten spears, which struck the four horses and brought them to the ground. Rāma was furious; he raised the horses and then drew his bow and let fly his arrows. The edge of Raghubīr's shafts swept off Rāvan's heads as though they had been lotuses. He smote each of his ten heads with ten arrows: the blood gushed forth in torrents. Streaming with gore, he rushed on in his strength; but the Lord again fitted arrows to his bow and let fly thirty shafts; his heads and arms all fell to the ground. But they grew again after being cut off. Again Rāma smote away his arms and heads, but they grew back afresh. Time after time the Lord struck off his arms and heads, but they were no sooner smitten off than they were again renewed. Again and again the Lord shred off his heads and arms; for the king of Kaushal takes delight in sporting this way. The whole heaven was full of heads and arms, like an infinite number of Ketus and Rāhus—

छंद-chaṁda:

जनु राहु केतु अनेक नभ पथ स्रवत सोनित धावहीं ।
janu rāhu ketu aneka nabha patha sravata sonita dhāvahīṁ,
रघुबीर तीर प्रचंड लागहिं भूमि गिरन न पावहीं ॥
raghubīra tīra pracaṁḍa lāgahiṁ bhūmi girana na pāvahīṁ.
एक एक सर सिर निकर छेदे नभ उड़त इमि सोहहीं ।
eka eka sara sira nikara chede nabha uṛata imi sohahīṁ,
जनु कोपि दिनकर कर निकर जहँ तहँ बिधुंतुद पोहहीं ॥
janu kopi dinakara kara nikara jahaṁ tahaṁ bidhuṁtuda pohahīṁ.

Trans:

—as though a multitude of Rāhus and Ketus streaming with gore were rushing through the air. Raghubīr's arrows had such force, that after hitting their mark they would not fall to the ground. And as it flew through the sky, each arrow impaling a head, it appeared like rays emanating from an angry sun, strung all over with the moon-troubler Rāhus.

दोहा-dohā:

जिमि जिमि प्रभु हर तासु सिर तिमि तिमि होहिं अपार ।
jimi jimi prabhu hara tāsu sira timi timi hohiṁ apāra,
सेवत बिषय बिबर्ध जिमि नित नित नूतन मार ॥९२॥
sevata biṣaya bibardha jimi nita nita nūtana māra. 92.

Trans:

As quickly as the Lord struck off his heads, they were renewed again without an end in sight; like the passions of a man devoted to the world, which increase ever more and more with every gratification.

चौपाई-caupāī:

दसमुख देखि सिरन्ह कै बाढ़ी । बिसरा मरन भई रिस गाढ़ी ॥
dasamukha dekhi siranha kai bāṛhī, bisarā marana bhaī risa gāṛhī.
गर्जेउ मूढ़ महा अभिमानी । धायउ दसहु सरासन तानी ॥
garjeu mūṛha mahā abhimānī, dhāyau dasahu sarāsana tānī.
समर भूमि दसकंधर कोप्यो । बरषि बान रघुपति रथ तोप्यो ॥
samara bhūmi dasakaṁdhara kopyo, baraṣi bāna raghupati ratha topyo.
दंड एक रथ देखि न परेऊ । जनु निहार महुँ दिनकर दुरेऊ ॥
daṁḍa eka ratha dekhi na pareū, janu nihāra mahuṁ dinakara dureū.
हाहाकार सुरन्ह जब कीन्हा । तब प्रभु कोपि कारमुक लीन्हा ॥
hāhākāra suranha jaba kīnhā, taba prabhu kopi kāramuka līnhā.
सर निवारि रिपु के सिर काटे । ते दिसि बिदिसि गगन महि पाटे ॥
sara nivāri ripu ke sira kāṭe, te disi bidisi gagana mahi pāṭe.

काटे सिर नभ मारग धावहिं । जय जय धुनि करि भय उपजावहिं ॥
kāṭe sira nabha māraga dhāvahiṁ, jaya jaya dhuni kari bhaya upajāvahiṁ.
कहँ लछिमन सुग्रीव कपीसा । कहँ रघुबीर कोसलाधीसा ॥
kahaṁ lachimana sugrīva kapīsā, kahaṁ raghubīra kosalādhīsā.

Trans:

Rāvan saw this multiplication of his heads, and he thought no more of death, and he waxed still more furious. He thundered aloud in his insane pride, and rushed forward with his ten bows all strung at once, raging wildly on the field of battle; and he overwhelmed Rāma's chariot with such a shower of arrows that for a moment it was quite lost to sight, as when the sun is obscured by mist. The gods cried 'alack, alack'; but the Lord wrathfully grasped his bow and parrying the arrows smote off his enemy's heads, which flew in all directions, covering heaven and earth. Severed as they were, they flew through the sky, uttering hideous cries of "Victory! Victory! Where is Lakshman, where Sugrīva and Angad; where Rāma the prince of Kaushal?

छंद-chaṁda:

कहँ रामु कहि सिर निकर धाए देखि मर्कट भजि चले ।
kahaṁ rāmu kahi sira nikara dhāe dekhi markaṭa bhaji cale,
संधानि धनु रघुबंसमनि हँसि सरन्हि सिर बेधे भले ॥
saṁdhāni dhanu raghubaṁsamani haṁsi saranhi sira bedhe bhale.
सिर मालिका कर कालिका गहि बृंद बृंदन्हि बहु मिलीं ।
sira mālikā kara kālikā gahi bṛṁda bṛṁdanhi bahu milīṁ,
करि रुधिर सरि मज्जनु मनहुँ संग्राम बट पूजन चलीं ॥
kari rudhira sari majjanu manahuṁ saṁgrāma baṭa pūjana calīṁ.

Trans:

Where now is Rāma?" cried the multitude of heads as they sped through the air. The monkeys saw and turned to flight; but the Jewel of the race of Raghu with a smile made ready his bow and with his arrows shot the heads through and through; as though the goddess Kali, with a rosary of skulls in her hand, and accompanied by all her attendants, had bathed in the terrible River Blood and come to worship at the shrine of Battle.

दोहा-dohā:

पुनि दसकंठ क्रुद्ध होइ छाँडी सक्ति प्रचंड ।
puni dasakaṁṭha kruddha hoi chāṁṛī sakti pracaṁḍa,
चली बिभीषन सन्मुख मनहुँ काल कर दंड ॥९३॥
calī bibhīṣana sanmukha manahuṁ kāla kara daṁḍa. 93.

Trans:

Again Rāvan in his fury hurled forth his mightiest spear; and like a bolt of death it flew straight for Vibhīshan.

चौपाई-caupāī:

आवत देखि सक्ति अति घोरा । प्रनतारति भंजन पन मोरा ॥
āvata dekhi sakti ati ghorā, pranatārati bhaṁjana pana morā.
तुरत बिभीषन पाछें मेला । सन्मुख राम सहेउ सोइ सेला ॥
turata bibhīṣana pācheṁ melā, sanmukha rāma saheu soi selā.
लागि सक्ति मुरुछा कछु भई । प्रभु कृत खेल सुरन्ह बिकलई ॥
lāgi sakti muruchā kachu bhaī, prabhu kṛta khela suranha bikalaī.
देखि बिभीषन प्रभु श्रम पायो । गहि कर गदा क्रुद्ध होइ धायो ॥
dekhi bibhīṣana prabhu śrama pāyo, gahi kara gadā kruddha hoi dhāyo.
रे कुभाग्य सठ मंद कुबुद्धे । तैं सुर नर मुनि नाग बिरुद्धे ॥
re kubhāgya saṭha maṁda kubuddhe, taiṁ sura nara muni nāga biruddhe.
सादर सिव कहुँ सीस चढ़ाए । एक एक के कोटिन्ह पाए ॥
sādara siva kahuṁ sīsa caṛhāe, eka eka ke koṭinha pāe.
तेहि कारन खल अब लगि बाँच्यो । अब तव कालु सीस पर नाच्यो ॥
tehi kārana khala aba lagi bāṁcyo, aba tava kālu sīsa para nācyo.
राम बिमुख सठ चहसि संपदा । अस कहि हनेसि माझ उर गदा ॥
rāma bimukha saṭha cahasi saṁpadā, asa kahi hanesi mājha ura gadā.

Trans:

When he saw the awful spear coming, he cried, "My trust is in him who ever relieves the distress of the destitute," and Rāma at once put Vibhīshan behind him and exposed himself to the full force of the missile. When it struck, the Lord swooned for a while—a mimicry which filled the gods with dismay. When Vibhīshan saw his Lord fainting, he seized his club in his hand and rushed on in a fury, "Ah, ill-starred wretch, fool, dull of understanding, enemy alike of gods, men, saints, and nagas; inasmuch as you devoutly offered your head to Shiva, you have received a thousand for one in return. This is the only reason why as yet you have escaped; but now death dances on your pate, fool. To oppose Rāma and yet hope to triumph, you fool?" So saying he struck him on the chest with his club.

छंद-chaṁda:

उर माझ गदा प्रहार घोर कठोर लागत महि परयो ।
ura mājha gadā prahāra ghora kaṭhora lāgata mahi parayo,
दस बदन सोनित स्रवत पुनि संभारि धायो रिस भरयो ॥
dasa badana sonita sravata puni saṁbhāri dhāyo risa bharayo.
द्वौ भिरे अतिबल मल्लजुद्ध बिरुद्ध एकु एकहि हनै ।
dvau bhire atibala mallajuddha biruddha eku ekahi hanai,
रघुबीर बल दर्पित बिभीषनु घालि नहिं ता कहुँ गनै ॥
raghubīra bala darpita bibhīṣanu ghāli nahiṁ tā kahuṁ ganai.

Trans:

At the terrible stroke of the mighty club on his chest he fell to the ground; but he again picked himself up and with his ten heads all streaming with blood, he came on in full fury. The two closed with all their might in savage wrestle, each mauling the other; but Vibhīshan was inspired with the strength of Rāma, and fell upon him as though he were of no account whatever.

दोहा-dohā:

उमा बिभीषनु रावनहि सन्मुख चितव कि काउ ।
umā bibhīṣanu rāvanahi sanmukha citava ki kāu,
सो अब भिरत काल ज्यों श्रीरघुबीर प्रभाउ ॥९४॥
so aba bhirata kāla jyoṁ śrīraghubīra prabhāu. 94.

Trans:

O Umā, Vibhīshan, by himself, would not have dared to even look Rāvan in the face; but now in the might of Rāma, he closed with him like the very death.

चौपाई-caupāī:

देखा श्रमित बिभीषनु भारी । धायउ हनूमान गिरि धारी ॥
dekhā śramita bibhīṣanu bhārī, dhāyau hanūmāna giri dhārī.
रथ तुरंग सारथी निपाता । हृदय माझ तेहि मारेसि लाता ॥
ratha turaṁga sārathī nipātā, hṛdaya mājha tehi māresi lātā.
ठाढ़ रहा अति कंपित गाता । गयउ बिभीषनु जहँ जनत्राता ॥
ṭhāṛha rahā ati kaṁpita gātā, gayau bibhīṣanu jahaṁ janatrātā.
पुनि रावन कपि हतेउ पचारी । चलेउ गगन कपि पूँछ पसारी ॥
puni rāvana kapi hateu pacārī, caleu gagana kapi pūṁcha pasārī.
गहिसि पूँछ कपि सहित उड़ाना । पुनि फिरि भिरेउ प्रबल हनुमाना ॥
gahisi pūṁcha kapi sahita uṛānā, puni phiri bhireu prabala hanumānā.
लरत अकास जुगल सम जोधा । एकहि एकु हनत करि क्रोधा ॥
larata akāsa jugala sama jodhā, ekahi eku hanata kari krodhā.
सोहहिं नभ छल बल बहु करहीं । कज्जल गिरि सुमेरु जनु लरहीं ॥
sohahiṁ nabha chala bala bahu karahīṁ, kajjala giri sumeru janu larahīṁ.
बुधि बल निसिचर परइ न पारयो । तब मारुत सुत प्रभु संभारयो ॥
budhi bala nisicara parai na pārayo, taba māruta suta prabhu saṁbhārayo.

Trans:

Now Hanumān saw that Vibhīshan was sorely exhausted and rushed forward with a rock in his hand, with which he crushed chariot, horses, and driver, and then gave the demon himself a kick in the ribs. He stood erect but trembled all over, and Vibhīshan escaped into the presence of the Savior of the world. Then Rāvan fell upon the monkey, who spread his tail and flew into the air. He laid hold of the tail and so was borne aloft with the monkey, the mighty Hanumān, who again turned and closed with him. The well-matched pair continued fighting overhead, each furiously bruising the other, and putting forth all his strength and skill; as though mounts Anjan and Sumeru had come into collision in the heaven. The demon was so astute that there was no throwing him, till the Lord came to the support of the son of wind-god.

छंद-chaṁda:

संभारि श्रीरघुबीर धीर पचारि कपि रावनु हन्यो ।
saṁbhāri śrīraghubīra dhīra pacāri kapi rāvanu hanyo,
महि परत पुनि उठि लरत देवन्ह जुगल कहुँ जय जय भन्यो ॥
mahi parata puni uṭhi larata devanha jugala kahuṁ jaya jaya bhanyo.
हनुमंत संकट देखि मर्कट भालु क्रोधातुर चले ।
hanumaṁta saṁkaṭa dekhi markaṭa bhālu krodhātura cale,
रन मत्त रावन सकल सुभट प्रचंड भुज बल दलमले ॥
rana matta rāvana sakala subhaṭa pracaṁḍa bhuja bala dalamale.

Trans:

Supported by Raghubīr, the valiant monkey struck Rāvan a violent blow. He fell to the ground, but rose again to fight, so that the gods shouted "glory, glory" to both. Seeing Hanumān in such a strait, the monkeys and bears advanced in furious passion; but Rāvan, battle-mad, crushed all their stoutest champions with full might of his terrible arm.

दोहा-dohā:

तब रघुबीर पचारे धाए कीस प्रचंड ।
taba raghubīra pacāre dhāe kīsa pracaṁḍa,
कपि बल प्रबल देखि तेहिं कीन्ह प्रगट पाषंड ॥९५॥
kapi bala prabala dekhi tehiṁ kīnha pragaṭa pāṣaṁḍa. 95.

Trans:

Then, rallied by the Hero of Raghu's line, the fierce monkeys rushed forward. Seeing the overwhelming monkey host, Rāvan, however, displayed his wizardy.

चौपाई-caupāī:

अंतरधान भयउ छन एका । पुनि प्रगटे खल रूप अनेका ॥
aṁtaradhāna bhayau chana ekā, puni pragaṭe khala rūpa anekā.
रघुपति कटक भालु कपि जेते । जहँ तहँ प्रगट दसानन तेते ॥
raghupati kaṭaka bhālu kapi jete, jahaṁ tahaṁ pragaṭa dasānana tete.
देखे कपिन्ह अमित दससीसा । जहँ तहँ भजे भालु अरु कीसा ॥
dekhe kapinha amita dasasīsā, jahaṁ tahaṁ bhaje bhālu aru kīsā.
भागे बानर धरहिं न धीरा । त्राहि त्राहि लछिमन रघुबीरा ॥
bhāge bānara dharahiṁ na dhīrā, trāhi trāhi lachimana raghubīrā.
दहँ दिसि धावहिं कोटिन्ह रावन । गर्जहिं घोर कठोर भयावन ॥
dahaṁ disi dhāvahiṁ koṭinha rāvana, garjahiṁ ghora kaṭhora bhayāvana.
डरे सकल सुर चले पराई । जय कै आस तजहु अब भाई ॥
ḍare sakala sura cale parāī, jaya kai āsa tajahu aba bhāī.
सब सुर जिते एक दसकंधर । अब बहु भए तकहु गिरि कंदर ॥
saba sura jite eka dasakaṁdhara, aba bahu bhae takahu giri kaṁdara.
रहे बिरंचि संभु मुनि ग्यानी । जिन्ह जिन्ह प्रभु महिमा कछु जानी ॥
rahe biraṁci saṁbhu muni gyānī, jinha jinha prabhu mahimā kachu jānī.

Trans:

In a moment he became invisible and then showed himself again in diverse forms. Every bear and monkey in Rāma's army saw a separate Rāvan confronting him. At the sight of such an infinity of Rāvans, the bears and monkeys fled in every direction. Not one of them had the courage to stay; all fled crying "Help, Lakshman; help, Raghubīr." Myriads of Rāvans pursued them on all sides, thundering aloud with dire, shrill, terrible sounds. The gods were all panic-stricken and betook themselves to flight, saying, "Now, brother, abandon all hope of victory. A single Rāvan subdued the whole heavenly host, and now there are so many of them—make for the caves in the mountain." Only Brahmmā and Shambhu, and the wisest of the saints stood fast—those who had some understanding of their Lord's might.

छंद-chaṁda:

जाना प्रताप ते रहे निर्भय कपिन्ह रिपु माने फुरे ।
jānā pratāpa te rahe nirbhaya kapinha ripu māne phure,
चले बिचलि मर्कट भालु सकल कृपाल पाहि भयातुरे ॥
cale bicali markaṭa bhālu sakala kṛpāla pāhi bhayāture.
हनुमंत अंगद नील नल अतिबल लरत रन बाँकुरे ।
hanumaṁta aṁgada nīla nala atibala larata rana bāṁkure,
मर्दहिं दसानन कोटि कोटिन्ह कपट भू भट अंकुरे ॥
mardahiṁ dasānana koṭi koṭinha kapaṭa bhū bhaṭa aṁkure.

Trans:

They who understood the Lord's power remained fearless; but some monkeys took the apparitions for real enemies and fled, monkeys and bears alike, crying in their terror "Help, Lord of mercy." The most powerful Hanumān, Angada, Nīl and Nala, all valiant in battle, fought and crushed the myriads of lofty Rāvans that had sprouted on the soil of deception.

दोहा-dohā:

सुर बानर देखे बिकल हँस्यो कोसलाधीस ।
sura bānara dekhe bikala haṁsyo kosalādhīsa,
सजि सारंग एक सर हते सकल दससीस ॥९६॥
saji sāraṁga eka sara hate sakala dasasīsa. 96.

Trans:

The king of Kaushal smiled to see the panic of the gods and monkeys, and then stringing his bow, dispersed with a single arrow the whole host of Rāvans.

चौपाई-caupāī:

प्रभु छन महुँ माया सब काटी । जिमि रबि उएँ जाहिं तम फाटी ॥
prabhu chana mahuṁ māyā saba kāṭī, jimi rabi ueṁ jāhiṁ tama phāṭī.
रावनु एकु देखि सुर हरषे । फिरे सुमन बहु प्रभु पर बरषे ॥
rāvanu eku dekhi sura harașe, phire sumana bahu prabhu para barașe.
भुज उठाइ रघुपति कपि फेरे । फिरे एक एकन्ह तब टेरे ॥
bhuja uṭhāi raghupati kapi phere, phire eka ekanha taba ṭere.
प्रभु बलु पाइ भालु कपि धाए । तरल तमकि संजुग महि आए ॥
prabhu balu pāi bhālu kapi dhāe, tarala tamaki saṁjuga mahi āe.
अस्तुति करत देवतन्हि देखें । भयउँ एक मैं इन्ह के लेखें ॥
astuti karata devatanhi dekheṁ, bhayauṁ eka maiṁ inha ke lekheṁ.
सठहु सदा तुम्ह मोर मरायल । अस कहि कोपि गगन पर धायल ॥
saṭhahu sadā tumha mora marāyala, asa kahi kopi gagana para dhāyala.
हाहाकार करत सुर भागे । खलहु जाहु कहँ मोरें आगे ॥
hāhākāra karata sura bhāge, khalahu jāhu kahaṁ moreṁ āge.
देखि बिकल सुर अंगद धायो । कूदि चरन गहि भूमि गिरायो ॥
dekhi bikala sura aṁgada dhāyo, kūdi carana gahi bhūmi girāyo.

Trans:

In a moment the Lord dispersed the whole phantom scene, as when the darkness is scattered at the rising of the Sun. Seeing only the one Rāvan, the gods turned back with joy and showered down flowers upon the Lord. Rāma then raised his arms aloft and rallied the monkeys, who turned again, each shouting to his neighbor. Inspired by the might of their Lord, the bears and monkeys went forth and with renewed vigor re-entered the arena. When Rāvan saw the gods exulting, he muttered, "They think I am now reduced to one; fools, you have ever been my game." So saying, he made a savage spring into the air, and the gods fled screaming, and he cried, "Wretches, whither can you escape from my presence?" Seeing their dismay, Angad rushed forward and with a bound seized him by the foot and threw him to the ground.

छंद-chaṁda:

गहि भूमि पारयो लात मारयो बालिसुत प्रभु पहिं गयो ।
gahi bhūmi pārayo lāta mārayo bālisuta prabhu pahiṁ gayo,
संभारि उठि दसकंठ घोर कठोर रव गर्जत भयो ॥
saṁbhāri uṭhi dasakaṁṭha ghora kaṭhora rava garjata bhayo.
करि दाप चाप चढ़ाइ दस संधानि सर बहु बरषई ।
kari dāpa cāpa caṛhāi dasa saṁdhāni sara bahu baraṣaī,
किए सकल भट घायल भयाकुल देखि निज बल हरषई ॥
kie sakala bhaṭa ghāyala bhayākula dekhi nija bala haraṣaī.

Trans:

Having seized and hurled him to the ground, the son of Bālī gave him a kick and then rejoined his Lord. The Ten-headed, on recovering himself, rose again and shouted terribly with a thunderous sound; then proudly he strung his bow, and fitting ten arrows to the string, he let fly many volleys, wounding all his enemies; and at the sight of their confusion he rejoiced in his might.

दोहा-dohā:

तब रघुपति रावन के सीस भुजा सर चाप ।
taba raghupati rāvana ke sīsa bhujā sara cāpa,
काटे बहुत बढ़े पुनि जिमि तीरथ कर पाप ॥९७॥
kāṭe bahuta baṛhe puni jimi tīratha kara pāpa. 97.

Trans:

Raghupatī then, along with his arrows and bows, cut off Rāvan's heads and arms—but they sprouted back again, like sins committed at a holy place.

चौपाई-caupāī:

सिर भुज बाढ़ि देखि रिपु केरी । भालु कपिन्ह रिस भई घनेरी ॥
sira bhuja bāṛhi dekhi ripu kerī, bhālu kapinha risa bhaī ghanerī.
मरत न मूढ़ कटेहुँ भुज सीसा । धाए कोपि भालु भट कीसा ॥
marata na mūṛha kaṭehuṁ bhuja sīsā, dhāe kopi bhālu bhaṭa kīsā.
बालितनय मारुति नल नीला । बानरराज दुबिद बलसीला ॥
bālitanaya māruti nala nīlā, bānararāja dubida balasīlā.
बिटप महीधर करहिं प्रहारा । सोइ गिरि तरु गहि कपिन्ह सो मारा ॥
biṭapa mahīdhara karahiṁ prahārā, soi giri taru gahi kapinha so mārā.
एक नखन्हि रिपु बपुष बिदारी । भागि चलहिं एक लातन्ह मारी ॥
eka nakhanhi ripu bapuṣa bidārī, bhāgi calahiṁ eka lātanha mārī.
तब नल नील सिरन्हि चढ़ि गयऊ । नखन्हि लिलार बिदारत भयऊ ॥
taba nala nīla siranhi caṛhi gayaū, nakhanhi lilāra bidārata bhayaū.
रुधिर देखि बिषाद उर भारी । तिन्हहि धरन कहुँ भुजा पसारी ॥
rudhira dekhi biṣāda ura bhārī, tinhahi dharana kahuṁ bhujā pasārī.
गहे न जाहिं करन्हि पर फिरहीं । जनु जुग मधुप कमल बन चरहीं ॥
gahe na jāhiṁ karanhi para phirahīṁ, janu juga madhupa kamala bana carahīṁ.
कोपि कूदि द्वौ धरेसि बहोरी । महि पटकत भजे भुजा मरोरी ॥
kopi kūdi dvau dharesi bahorī, mahi paṭakata bhaje bhujā marorī.
पुनि सकोप दस धनु कर लीन्हे । सरन्हि मारि घायल कपि कीन्हे ॥
puni sakopa dasa dhanu kara līnhe, saranhi māri ghāyala kapi kīnhe.
हनुमदादि मुरुछित करि बंदर । पाइ प्रदोष हरष दसकंधर ॥
hanumadādi muruchita kari baṁdara, pāi pradoṣa haraṣa dasakaṁdhara.
मुरुछित देखि सकल कपि बीरा । जामवंत धायउ रनधीरा ॥
muruchita dekhi sakala kapi bīrā, jāmavaṁta dhāyau ranadhīrā.
संग भालु भूधर तरु धारी । मारन लगे पचारि पचारी ॥
saṁga bhālu bhūdhara taru dhārī, mārana lage pacāri pacārī.
भयउ क्रुद्ध रावन बलवाना । गहि पद महि पटकइ भट नाना ॥
bhayau kruddha rāvana balavānā, gahi pada mahi paṭakai bhaṭa nānā.
देखि भालुपति निज दल घाता । कोपि माझ उर मारेसि लाता ॥
dekhi bhālupati nija dala ghātā, kopi mājha ura māresi lātā.

Trans:

Seeing their enemy's heads and arms multiply thus, the bears and monkeys were mightily indignant and frustrated "Will the wretch never die, even with his heads and arms all cut off?" and they rushed against him in fury. The son of Bālī, with Hanumān, Nala, and Nīl, the monkey king Sugrīva, and the valiant Dwivid, hurled upon him trees and mountains; but he caught each mountain and tree and threw them back upon the monkeys. One tore the enemy's body with his claws, another would rush past and kick him. Nala and Nīl clambered up on to his heads and set to tearing his face with their talons. When he saw the blood, he was sore troubled in his soul and put out his arms to catch them; but they were not to be caught and sprang about over his hands—like two bees over a bed of lotuses. At last with a savage bound he managed to grasp them, but before he could dash them to the ground, they twisted his arm and broke free. Then in his fury he took his ten bows and let fly his arrows and he struck and wounded many a monkeys. Having thus rendered Hanumān and the other senseless he rejoiced to see the night approaching. Seeing all the monkey chiefs in a swoon, the valiant Jāmvant rushed forward, and with him many bears, armed with mountains and trees, which they began hurling upon him. The mighty Rāvan was enraged, and many of the heroes he seized by the foot and dashed to the ground. Jāmvant, the king of bears, was wrath to see such havoc among his troops and gave Rāvan a savage kick on the chest.

छंद-chaṁda:

उर लात घात प्रचंड लागत बिकल रथ ते महि परा ।
ura lāta ghāta pracaṁḍa lāgata bikala ratha te mahi parā,
गहि भालु बीसहुँ कर मनहुँ कमलन्हि बसे निसि मधुकरा ॥
gahi bhālu bīsahuṁ kara manahuṁ kamalanhi base nisi madhukarā.
मुरुछित बिलोकि बहोरि पद हति भालुपति प्रभु पहिं गयो ।
muruchita biloki bahori pada hati bhālupati prabhu pahiṁ gayo,
निसि जानि स्यंदन घालि तेहि तब सूत जतनु करत भयो ॥
nisi jāni syaṁdana ghāli tehi taba sūta jatanu karata bhayo.

Trans:

The blow on the chest smote him so heavily that Rāvan fell fainting from his chariot to the ground, grasping a bear in each of his twenty hands, like bees hiding by night in the folds of the lotus. Seeing him senseless, the king of the bears again struck him with his foot and then rejoined the Lord. As night had now come, the charioteer lifted Rāvan on to the car and made off as best he could.

दोहा-dohā:

मुरुछा बिगत भालु कपि सब आए प्रभु पास ।
muruchā bigata bhālu kapi saba āe prabhu pāsa,
निसिचर सकल रावनहि घेरि रहे अति त्रास ॥९८॥
nisicara sakala rāvanahi gheri rahe ati trāsa. 98.

Trans:

On recovering from their swoon, the bears and monkeys all appeared before Rāma; while there all the demons crowded around Rāvan in the utmost consternation.

मासपारायण छब्बीसवाँ विश्राम
māsapārāyaṇa chabbīsavāṁ viśrāma
(Pause 26 for a Thirty-Day Recitation)

चौपाई-caupāī:

तेहीं निसि सीता पहिं जाई । त्रिजटा कहि सब कथा सुनाई ॥
tehīṁ nisi sītā pahiṁ jāī, trijaṭā kahi saba kathā sunāī.
सिर भुज बाढ़ि सुनत रिपु केरी । सीता उर भइ त्रास घनेरी ॥
sira bhuja bāṛhi sunata ripu kerī, sītā ura bhai trāsa ghanerī.
मुख मलीन उपजी मन चिंता । त्रिजटा सन बोली तब सीता ॥
mukha malīna upajī mana ciṁtā, trijaṭā sana bolī taba sītā.
होइहि कहा कहसि किन माता । केहि बिधि मरिहि बिस्व दुखदाता ॥

hoihi kahā kahasi kina mātā, kehi bidhi marihi bisva dukhadātā.

रघुपति सर सिर कटेहुँ न मरई । बिधि बिपरीत चरित सब करई ॥
raghupati sara sira kaṭehum̐ na maraī, bidhi biparīta carita saba karaī.

मोर अभाग्य जिआवत ओही । जेहिं हौं हरि पद कमल बिछोही ॥
mora abhāgya jiāvata ohī, jehiṁ hauṁ hari pada kamala bichohī.

जेहिं कृत कपट कनक मृग झूठा । अजहुँ सो दैव मोहि पर रूठा ॥
jehiṁ kṛta kapaṭa kanaka mṛga jhūṭhā, ajahum̐ so daiva mohi para rūṭhā.

जेहिं बिधि मोहि दुख दुसह सहाए । लछिमन कहुँ कटु बचन कहाए ॥
jehiṁ bidhi mohi dukha dusaha sahāe, lachimana kahum̐ kaṭu bacana kahāe.

रघुपति बिरह सबिष सर भारी । तकि तकि मार बार बहु मारी ॥
raghupati biraha sabiṣa sara bhārī, taki taki māra bāra bahu mārī.

ऐसेहुँ दुख जो राख मम प्राना । सोइ बिधि ताहि जिआव न आना ॥
aisehum̐ dukha jo rākha mama prānā, soi bidhi tāhi jiāva na ānā.

बहु बिधि कर बिलाप जानकी । करि करि सुरति कृपानिधान की ॥
bahu bidhi kara bilāpa jānakī, kari kari surati kṛpānidhāna kī.

कह त्रिजटा सुनु राजकुमारी । उर सर लागत मरइ सुरारी ॥
kaha trijaṭā sunu rājakumārī, ura sara lāgata marai surārī.

प्रभु ताते उर हतइ न तेही । एहि के हृदयँ बसति बैदेही ॥
prabhu tāte ura hatai na tehī, ehi ke hṛdayam̐ basati baidehī.

Trans:

During the night Trijatā went to Sītā and told her the whole story. When Sītā heard of the regeneration of the enemy's heads and arms, she was sorely dismayed and thus addressed Trijatā with downcast face and much anxiety of soul, "Why do you not tell me, mother, what is to be done, and how this plague of the universe can be put to death? He does not die even though the arrows of Raghupatī have struck off his heads. It is Heaven who is disposing of things perversely. Nay, it is my ill luck that sustains him, the same misfortune which separated me from Shrī Harī's lotus-feet. The same fate that created the false phantom of the golden deer is still cruel to me. The god that enables me to support such insupportable anguish; which made me speak crossly to Lakshman; which keeps me alive under such pain—pierced through and through as I am with the poisoned arrows of Rāma's loss, arrows with which Love has smitten me: it is the same god, I swear, that keeps him alive." With many such words did Jānakī make piteous lamentation, as she recalled to mind the All-merciful. Trijatā replied, "Hearken, royal princess, the enemy of the gods will die if an arrow strike him in the chest. But the Lord will not smite him there, because the image of Sītā is imprinted on his heart.

छंद-chaṁda:

एहि के हृदयँ बस जानकी जानकी उर मम बास है ।
ehi ke hṛdayam̐ basa jānakī jānakī ura mama bāsa hai,

मम उदर भुअन अनेक लागत बान सब कर नास है ॥
mama udara bhuana aneka lāgata bāna saba kara nāsa hai.

सुनि बचन हरष बिषाद मन अति देखि पुनि त्रिजटाँ कहा ।
suni bacana haraṣa biṣāda mana ati dekhi puni trijaṭām̐ kahā,

अब मरिहि रिपु एहि बिधि सुनहि सुंदरि तजहि संसय महा ॥
aba marihi ripu ehi bidhi sunahi suṁdari tajahi saṁsaya mahā.

Trans:

He is held back by the thought 'Jānakī dwells in his heart and in Jānakī's heart is my home; and in my heart are all the spheres of creation; if an arrow lodges there, then all will be undone'." On hearing this explanation, she was somewhat comforted; but seeing her still uneasy in mind, Trijatā continued, "Now this is the way the monster will be killed, hearken, fair lady, and cease to be so greatly disquieted:

दोहा-dohā:

काटत सिर होइहि बिकल छुटि जाइहि तव ध्यान ।
kāṭata sira hoihi bikala chuṭi jāihi tava dhyāna,

तब रावनहि हृदय महुँ मरिहहिं रामु सुजान ॥९९॥
taba rāvanahi hṛdaya mahum̐ marihahiṁ rāmu sujāna. 99.

Trans:

When in the pain of having his heads cut off, your image will be forgotten, then the sagacious Rāma will smite him in the heart."

चौपाई-caupāī:

अस कहि बहुत भाँति समुझाई । पुनि त्रिजटा निज भवन सिधाई ॥
asa kahi bahuta bhām̐ti samujhāī, puni trijaṭā nija bhavana sidhāī.

राम सुभाउ सुमिरि बैदेही । उपजी बिरह बिथा अति तेही ॥
rāma subhāu sumiri baidehī, upajī biraha bithā ati tehī.

निसिहि ससिहि निंदति बहु भाँती । जुग सम भई सिराति न राती ॥
nisihi sasihi niṁdati bahu bhām̐tī, juga sama bhaī sirāti na rātī.

करति बिलाप मनहिं मन भारी । राम बिरहँ जानकी दुखारी ॥
karati bilāpa manahiṁ mana bhārī, rāma biraham̐ jānakī dukhārī.

जब अति भयउ बिरह उर दाहू । फरकेउ बाम नयन अरु बाहू ॥
jaba ati bhayau biraha ura dāhū, pharakeu bāma nayana aru bāhū.

सगुन बिचारि धरी मन धीरा । अब मिलिहहिं कृपाल रघुबीरा ॥
saguna bicāri dharī mana dhīrā, aba milihahiṁ kṛpāla raghubīrā.

इहाँ अर्धनिसि रावनु जागा । निज सारथि सन खीझन लागा ॥
ihām̐ ardhanisi rāvanu jāgā, nija sārathi sana khījhana lāgā.

सठ रनभूमि छड़ाइसि मोही । धिग धिग अधम मंदमति तोही ॥
saṭha ranabhūmi chaṛāisi mohī, dhiga dhiga adhama maṁdamati tohī.

तेहिं पद गहि बहु बिधि समुझावा । भोरु भएँ रथ चढ़ि पुनि धावा ॥
tehiṁ pada gahi bahu bidhi samujhāvā, bhoru bhaem̐ ratha caṛhi puni dhāvā.

सुनि आगवनु दसानन केरा । कपिदल खरभर भयउ घनेरा ॥
suni āgavanu dasānana kerā, kapidala kharabhara bhayau ghanerā.

जहँ तहँ भूधर बिटप उपारी । धाए कटकटाइ भट भारी ॥
jaham̐ taham̐ bhūdhara biṭapa upārī, dhāe kaṭakaṭāi bhaṭa bhārī.

Trans:

With such words having done all she could to comfort her, Trijatā returned home. But Sītā, reflecting on Rāma's amiability, was a prey to all the anguish of bereavement, and broke out into reproaches of the night and the moon, "This night will never be over, though it seems an Age long already." In her heart of hearts she made sore lamentation, sorrowing from separation from Rāma. When the pangs of bereavement were at their very height, her left eye and arm throbbed. Considering this to be a good omen for women, she took courage, "I shall now see again the gracious Raghubīr." Meanwhile Rāvan awoke at midnight and began abusing his charioteer, "Fool, to bring me away from the field of battle; a curse on you for being a vile dullard." He laid hold of his feet and placated him. As soon as it was dawn, Rāvan mounted his chariot and sallied forth again. When they heard of Rāvan's approach, the monkey army was greatly excited, and tearing up mountains and trees on every side the terrible warriors rushed to the onset, gnashing their teeth.

छंद-chaṁda:

धाए जो मर्कट बिकट भालु कराल कर भूधर धरा ।
dhāe jo markaṭa bikaṭa bhālu karāla kara bhūdhara dharā,

अति कोप करहिं प्रहार मारत भजि चले रजनीचरा ॥
ati kopa karahiṁ prahāra mārata bhaji cale rajanīcarā.

बिचलाइ दल बलवंत कीसन्ह घेरि पुनि रावनु लियो ।
bicalāi dala balavaṁta kīsanha gheri puni rāvanu liyo,

चहुँ दिसि चपेटन्हि मारि नखन्हि बिदारि तनु ब्याकुल कियो ॥

cahuṁ disi capeṭanhi māri nakhanhi bidāri tanu byākula kiyo.

Trans:

The huge monkeys and terrible bears rushed on with mountains in their hands, which they hurled forth with the utmost fury; the demons turned and fled. When they had thus scattered the ranks, the valiant monkeys next closed around Rāvan, buffeting him on every side and tearing him with their claws, so that his whole body was mangled.

दोहा-dohā:

देखि महा मर्कट प्रबल रावन कीन्ह बिचार ।
dekhi mahā markaṭa prabala rāvana kīnha bicāra,
अंतरहित होइ निमिष महुँ कृत माया बिस्तार ॥१००॥
aṁtarahita hoi nimiṣa mahuṁ kṛta māyā bistāra. 100.

Trans:

Seeing the monkeys so powerful, Rāvan took thought, and in a moment became invisible and created a magic illusion.

छंद-chaṁda:

जब कीन्ह तेहिं पाषंड । भए प्रगट जंतु प्रचंड ॥
jaba kīnha tehiṁ pāṣaṁḍa, bhae pragaṭa jaṁtu pracaṁḍa.
बेताल भूत पिसाच । कर धरें धनु नाराच ॥१॥
betāla bhūta pisāca, kara dhareṁ dhanu nārāca. 1.
जोगिनि गहें करबाल । एक हाथ मनुज कपाल ॥
jogini gaheṁ karabāla, eka hātha manuja kapāla.
करि सद्य सोनित पान । नाचहिं करहिं बहु गान ॥२॥
kari sadya sonita pāna, nācahiṁ karahiṁ bahu gāna. 2.
धरु मारु बोलहिं घोर । रहि पूरि धुनि चहुँ ओर ॥
dharu māru bolahiṁ ghora, rahi pūri dhuni cahuṁ ora.
मुख बाइ धावहिं खान । तब लगे कीस परान ॥३॥
mukha bāi dhāvahiṁ khāna, taba lage kīsa parāna. 3.
जहँ जाहिं मर्कट भागि । तहँ बरत देखहिं आगि ॥
jahaṁ jāhiṁ markaṭa bhāgi, tahaṁ barata dekhahiṁ āgi.
भए बिकल बानर भालु । पुनि लाग बरषै बालु ॥४॥
bhae bikala bānara bhālu, puni lāga baraṣai bālu. 4.
जहँ तहँ थकित करि कीस । गर्जेउ बहुरि दससीस ॥
jahaṁ tahaṁ thakita kari kīsa, garjeu bahuri dasasīsa.
लछिमन कपीस समेत । भए सकल बीर अचेत ॥५॥
lachimana kapīsa sameta, bhae sakala bīra aceta. 5.
हा राम हा रघुनाथ । कहि सुभट मीजहिं हाथ ॥
hā rāma hā raghunātha, kahi subhaṭa mījahiṁ hātha.
एहि बिधि सकल बल तोरि । तेहिं कीन्ह कपट बहोरि ॥६॥
ehi bidhi sakala bala tori, tehiṁ kīnha kapaṭa bahori. 6.
प्रगटेसि बिपुल हनुमान । धाए गहे पाषान ॥
pragaṭesi bipula hanumāna, dhāe gahe pāṣāna.
तिन्ह रामु घेरे जाइ । चहुँ दिसि बरूथ बनाइ ॥७॥
tinha rāmu ghere jāi, cahuṁ disi barūtha banāi. 7.
मारहु धरहु जनि जाइ । कटकटहिं पूँछ उठाइ ॥
mārahu dharahu jani jāi, kaṭakaṭahiṁ pūṁcha uṭhāi.
दहँ दिसि लँगूर बिराज । तेहिं मध्य कोसलराज ॥८॥
dahaṁ disi laṁgūra birāja, tehiṁ madhya kosalarāja. 8.

Trans:

By the magic that he wrought terrible beings were manifested: imps, demons, goblins, ghouls, with bows and arrows in their hands, witches clutching swords and in one hand a human skull, from which they quaff draughts of blood, dancing madly and howling songs. Their horrible cries of 'seize and kill' echo all around; with wide open mouths they run to and fro to devour monkeys all. Then began the monkeys to flee; but wherever they turn in flight, they see blazing fires. Monkeys and bears were both in dismay. Then there fell upon them showers of sand. They were routed on all sides and the Ten-headed roared terribly. Lakshman, the monkey-king, and all the chiefs were at their wits' end. The bravest of them wrung their hands, crying "O Rāma, O Raghunāth." Having thus crushed the might of all, Rāvan wrought another delusion. He manifested hosts of Hanumans, who rushed forward with rocks in their hands and encircled Rāma in a dense mass on every side. With gnashing teeth and up-turned tail, they shouted "Kill, hold fast, never let him go"; their tails making a complete circle all round with the king of Kaushal in the midst.

छंद-chaṁda:

तेहिं मध्य कोसलराज सुंदर स्याम तन सोभा लही ।
tehiṁ madhya kosalarāja suṁdara syāma tana sobhā lahī,
जनु इंद्रधनुष अनेक की बर बारि तुंग तमालही ॥
janu iṁdradhanuṣa aneka kī bara bāri tuṁga tamālahī.
प्रभु देखि हरष बिषाद उर सुर बदत जय जय जय करी ।
prabhu dekhi haraṣa biṣāda ura sura badata jaya jaya jaya karī,
रघुबीर एकहिं तीर कोपि निमेष महुँ माया हरी ॥१॥
raghubīra ekahiṁ tīra kopi nimeṣa mahuṁ māyā harī. 1.
माया बिगत कपि भालु हरषे बिटप गिरि गहि सब फिरे ।
māyā bigata kapi bhālu haraṣe biṭapa giri gahi saba phire,
सर निकर छाड़े राम रावन बाहु सिर पुनि महि गिरे ॥
sara nikara chāṛe rāma rāvana bāhu sira puni mahi gire.
श्रीराम रावन समर चरित अनेक कल्प जो गावहीं ।
śrīrāma rāvana samara carita aneka kalpa jo gāvahīṁ,
सत सेष सारद निगम कबि तेउ तदपि पार न पावहीं ॥२॥
sata seṣa sārada nigama kabi teu tadapi pāra na pāvahīṁ. 2.

Trans:

In their midst the dark-hued king of Kaushal shone forth as resplendent in beauty as a lofty tamal tree encircled by a hedge of gleaming rainbows. As they gazed upon the Lord, the heart of the gods was moved with mingled joy and grief, even as they raised the cry of "Victory, Victory." In a moment and with a single arrow Raghubīr, incensed, dispelled the delusion. As the phantoms vanished, the monkeys and bears rejoiced and turned again, with trees and rocks in their hands. Rāma shot forth a flight of arrows and Rāvan's heads and arms again fell to the ground. Though a hundred Sheshnāgs, Shārdās, and Vedic bards were to spend many ages in singing the various achievements of Rāma in his battle with Rāvan, they would never come to the end of them.

दोहा-dohā:

ताके गुन गन कछु कहे जड़मति तुलसीदास ।
tāke guna gana kachu kahe jaṛamati tulasīdāsa,
जिमि निज बल अनुरूप ते माछी उड़इ अकास ॥१०१क॥
jimi nija bala anurūpa te māchī uṛai akāsa. 101(ka).

काटे सिर भुज बार बहु मरत न भट लंकेस ।
kāṭe sira bhuja bāra bahu marata na bhaṭa laṁkesa,
प्रभु क्रीड़त सुर सिद्ध मुनि ब्याकुल देखि कलेस ॥१०१ख॥
prabhu krīṛata sura siddha muni byākula dekhi kalesa. 101(kha).

Trans:

Tulsīdās, poor clown, who would tell even the least part of his glory, is like a gnat who thinks himself strong enough to fly up into heaven. Though his heads and arms were cut off again and again, the mighty king of Lankā was not killed. This was merely a sport for the Lord, but the sages, saints, and gods were confounded and fidgeted at the agonizing sight before.

चौपाई-caupāī:

काटत बढ़हिं सीस समुदाई । जिमि प्रति लाभ लोभ अधिकाई ॥
kāṭata baṛhahiṁ sīsa samudāī, jimi prati lābha lobha adhikāī.

मरइ न रिपु श्रम भयउ बिसेषा । राम बिभीषन तन तब देखा ॥
marai na ripu śrama bhayau biseṣā, rāma bibhīṣana tana taba dekhā.
उमा काल मर जाकीं ईछा । सो प्रभु जन कर प्रीति परीछा ॥
umā kāla mara jākīṁ īchā, so prabhu jana kara prīti parīchā.
सुनु सरबग्य चराचर नायक । प्रनतपाल सुर मुनि सुखदायक ॥
sunu sarabagya carācara nāyaka, pranatapāla sura muni sukhadāyaka.
नाभिकुंड पियूष बस याकें । नाथ जिअत रावनु बल ताकें ॥
nābhikuṁḍa piyūṣa basa yākeṁ, nātha jiata rāvanu bala tākeṁ.
सुनत बिभीषन बचन कृपाला । हरषि गहे कर बान कराला ॥
sunata bibhīṣana bacana kṛpālā, haraṣi gahe kara bāna karālā.
असुभ होन लागे तब नाना । रोवहिं खर सृकाल बहु स्वाना ॥
asubha hona lāge taba nānā, rovahiṁ khara sṛkāla bahu svānā.
बोलहिं खग जग आरति हेतू । प्रगट भए नभ जहँ तहँ केतू ॥
bolahiṁ khaga jaga ārati hetū, pragaṭa bhae nabha jahaṁ tahaṁ ketū.
दस दिसि दाह होन अति लागा । भयउ परब बिनु रबि उपरागा ॥
dasa disi dāha hona ati lāgā, bhayau paraba binu rabi uparāgā.
मंदोदरि उर कंपति भारी । प्रतिमा स्रवहिं नयन मग बारी ॥
maṁdodari ura kaṁpati bhārī, pratimā sravahiṁ nayana maga bārī.

Trans:

No sooner were his heads cut off then a fresh crop grew—like covetousness increased by gain. For all his toil the monster died not and Rāma then turned and looked at Vibhīshan. O Umā, the Lord, whom fate and death obey, thus tested the devotion of one of his servants. "Hearken, omniscient sovereign of all things animate and inanimate, defender of the suppliant, delight of gods and saints, it is only, sire, by virtue of the nectar that abides in the depth of his navel that Rāvan lives." On hearing Vibhīshan's speech the All-merciful was pleased and took his terrible arrows is his hand. Many omens of ill then began to present themselves: asses, jackals, and packs of dogs set up a howling; birds screamed over the distress of the world and comets appeared in every quarter of the heaven; fierce flames broke out on every side, and though there was no new moon, the sun was eclipsed. Mandodarī's heart beat wildly and from the statues flowed tears from the eyes.

छंद-chaṁda:

प्रतिमा रुदहिं पबिपात नभ अति बात बह डोलति मही ।
pratimā rudahiṁ pabipāta nabha ati bāta baha ḍolati mahī,
बरषहिं बलाहक रुधिर कच रज असुभ अति सक को कही ॥
baraṣahiṁ balāhaka rudhira kaca raja asubha ati saka ko kahī.
उतपात अमित बिलोकि नभ सुर बिकल बोलहिं जय जए ।
utapāta amita biloki nabha sura bikala bolahiṁ jaya jae,
सुर सभय जानि कृपाल रघुपति चाप सर जोरत भए ॥
sura sabhaya jāni kṛpāla raghupati cāpa sara jorata bhae.

Trans:

Statues wept, thunder crashed in the air, a mighty wind blew, the earth quaked, the clouds rained blood, hair, dust: who could recount all the ill portents? At the sight of such unspeakable confusion the gods of heaven in utter dismay uttered prayers for victory. Perceiving their distress, the merciful Raghupatī set arrows to his bow;

दोहा-dohā:

खैंचि सरासन श्रवन लगि छाड़े सर एकतीस ।
khaiṁci sarāsana śravana lagi chāṛe sara ekatīsa,
रघुनायक सायक चले मानहुँ काल फनीस ॥ १०२॥
raghunāyaka sāyaka cale mānahuṁ kāla phanīsa. 102.

Trans:

and drawing the string to his ear he let fly at once thirty-one shafts. The bolts of Raghunāyak flew forth like the serpents of death.

चौपाई-caupāī:

सायक एक नाभि सर सोषा । अपर लगे भुज सिर करि रोषा ॥
sāyaka eka nābhi sara soṣā, apara lage bhuja sira kari roṣā.
लै सिर बाहु चले नाराचा । सिर भुज हीन रुंड महि नाचा ॥
lai sira bāhu cale nārācā, sira bhuja hīna ruṁḍa mahi nācā.
धरनि धसइ धर धाव प्रचंडा । तब सर हति प्रभु कृत दुइ खंडा ॥
dharani dhasai dhara dhāva pracaṁḍā, taba sara hati prabhu kṛta dui khaṁḍā.
गर्जेउ मरत घोर रव भारी । कहाँ रामु रन हतौं पचारी ॥
garjeu marata ghora rava bhārī, kahāṁ rāmu rana hatauṁ pacārī.
डोली भूमि गिरत दसकंधर । छुभित सिंधु सरि दिग्गज भूधर ॥
ḍolī bhūmi girata dasakaṁdhara, chubhita siṁdhu sari diggaja bhūdhara.
धरनि परेउ द्वौ खंड बढ़ाई । चापि भालु मर्कट समुदाई ॥
dharani pareu dvau khaṁḍa baṛhāī, cāpi bhālu markaṭa samudāī.
मंदोदरि आगें भुज सीसा । धरि सर चले जहाँ जगदीसा ॥
maṁdodari āgeṁ bhuja sīsā, dhari sara cale jahāṁ jagadīsā.
प्रबिसे सब निषंग महु जाई । देखि सुरन्ह दुंदुभीं बजाई ॥
prabise saba niṣaṁga mahu jāī, dekhi suranha duṁdubhīṁ bajāī.
तासु तेज समान प्रभु आनन । हरषे देखि संभु चतुरानन ॥
tāsu teja samāna prabhu ānana, haraṣe dekhi saṁbhu caturānana.
जय जय धुनि पूरी ब्रह्मंडा । जय रघुबीर प्रबल भुजदंडा ॥
jaya jaya dhuni pūrī brahmaṁḍā, jaya raghubīra prabala bhujadaṁḍā.
बरषहिं सुमन देव मुनि बृंदा । जय कृपाल जय जयति मुकुंदा ॥
baraṣahiṁ sumana deva muni bṛṁdā, jaya kṛpāla jaya jayati mukuṁdā.

Trans:

One arrow dried up the depth of his navel, the others struck off his heads and arms—and with such violence that they carried head and arms away with them. The headless and armless trunk still danced upon the plain. The earth sunk beneath the weight of the body as it rushed wildly on, till the Lord with his arrows smote it in twain. At the moment of his death he thundered aloud with a fierce terrible yell, "Where is Rāma, that I may challenge and slay him?" The earth reeled as Rāvan fell; the sea, the rivers, the elephants of the eight quarters and the mountains were all shaken. The two halves lay full length upon the ground, thronged by a crowd of bears and monkeys. But the arrows deposited the heads and arms before Mandodarī and then returned to the Lord of the universe and dropt again into his quiver. Seeing this, the gods sounded the kettle-drums. His soul entered the Lord's mouth; Shiva and Brahmmā rejoiced to see the sight. The whole universe resounded with cries of "Victory, Victory: glory to Raghubīr, the mighty of arm; glory to the All-merciful; glory to Mukunda"; while throngs of gods and saints rained down flowers.

छंद-chaṁda:

जय कृपा कंद मुकंद द्वंद हरन सरन सुखप्रद प्रभो ।
jaya kṛpā kaṁda mukaṁda dvaṁda harana sarana sukhaprada prabho,
खल दल बिदारन परम कारन कारुनीक सदा बिभो ॥
khala dala bidārana parama kārana kārunīka sadā bibho.
सुर सुमन बरषहिं हरष संकुल बाज दुंदुभि गहगही ।
sura sumana baraṣahiṁ haraṣa saṁkula bāja duṁdubhi gahagahī,
संग्राम अंगन राम अंग अनंग बहु सोभा लही ॥
saṁgrāma aṁgana rāma aṁga anaṁga bahu sobhā lahī.
सिर जटा मुकुट प्रसून बिच बिच अति मनोहर राजहीं ।
sira jaṭā mukuṭa prasūna bica bica ati manohara rājahīṁ,
जनु नीलगिरि पर तड़ित पटल समेत उडुगन भ्राजहीं ॥
janu nīlagiri para taṛita paṭala sameta uḍugana bhrājahīṁ.
भुजदंड सर कोदंड फेरत रुधिर कन तन अति बने ।
bhujadaṁḍa sara kodaṁḍa pherata rudhira kana tana ati bane,

जनु रायमुनीं तमाल पर बैठीं बिपुल सुख आपने ॥
janu rāyamunīṁ tamāla para baiṭhīṁ bipula sukha āpane.

Trans:

"Glory to Mukunda, the fountain of mercy, the subduer of rebellion, our refuge, our health-giving Lord; the scatterer of the ranks of the impious, the great First Cause, the compassionate, the ever Supreme." All the gods in their joy showered down flowers and the kettledrums sounded aloud, as on the field of battle, Rāma's every limb displayed the beauty of a myriad Loves. The crown on his coil of hair all besprinkled with blossoms shone forth in exquisite splendor like flashes of lightning gleaming amidst the star-lit peaks of a dark mountain. With the bow and arrows that he brandished in his arms, his body, spangled with specks of blood, seemed like some spotted *Raimuni* birds that had perched on a *tamal* tree in a rapture of delight.

दोहा-dohā:

कृपादृष्टि करि बृष्टि प्रभु अभय किए सुर बृंद ।
kṛpādṛṣṭi kari bṛṣṭi prabhu abhaya kie sura bṛṁda,
भालु कीस सब हरषे जय सुख धाम मुकंद ॥१०३॥
bhālu kīsa saba haraṣe jaya sukha dhāma mukaṁda. 103.

Trans:

With a shower of his gracious glance the Lord dispelled the fears of all the gods; and bears and monkeys shouted in their joy "glory to Mukund, the abode of bliss."

चौपाई-caupāī:

पति सिर देखत मंदोदरी । मुरुछित बिकल धरनि खसि परी ॥
pati sira dekhata maṁdodarī, muruchita bikala dharani khasi parī.
जुबति बृंद रोवत उठि धाईं । तेहि उठाइ रावन पहिं आईं ॥
jubati bṛṁda rovata uṭhi dhāīṁ, tehi uṭhāi rāvana pahiṁ āīṁ.
पति गति देखि ते करहिं पुकारा । छूटे कच नहिं बपुष सँभारा ॥
pati gati dekhi te karahiṁ pukārā, chūṭe kaca nahiṁ bapuṣa saṁbhārā.
उर ताड़ना करहिं बिधि नाना । रोवत करहिं प्रताप बखाना ॥
ura tāṛanā karahiṁ bidhi nānā, rovata karahiṁ pratāpa bakhānā.
तव बल नाथ डोल नित धरनी । तेज हीन पावक ससि तरनी ॥
tava bala nātha ḍola nita dharanī, teja hīna pāvaka sasi taranī.
सेष कमठ सहि सकहिं न भारा । सो तनु भूमि परेउ भरि छारा ॥
seṣa kamaṭha sahi sakahiṁ na bhārā, so tanu bhūmi pareu bhari chārā.
बरुन कुबेर सुरेस समीरा । रन सन्मुख धरि काहुँ न धीरा ॥
baruna kubera suresa samīrā, rana sanmukha dhari kāhuṁ na dhīrā.
भुजबल जितेहु काल जम साईं । आजु परेहु अनाथ की नाईं ॥
bhujabala jitehu kāla jama sāīṁ, āju parehu anātha kī nāīṁ.
जगत बिदित तुम्हारि प्रभुताई । सुत परिजन बल बरनि न जाई ॥
jagata bidita tumhāri prabhutāī, suta parijana bala barani na jāī.
राम बिमुख अस हाल तुम्हारा । रहा न कोउ कुल रोवनिहारा ॥
rāma bimukha asa hāla tumhārā, rahā na kou kula rovanihārā.
तव बस बिधि प्रपंच सब नाथा । सभय दिसिप नित नावहिं माथा ॥
tava basa bidhi prapaṁca saba nāthā, sabhaya disipa nita nāvahiṁ māthā.
अब तव सिर भुज जंबुक खाहीं । राम बिमुख यह अनुचित नाहीं ॥
aba tava sira bhuja jaṁbuka khāhīṁ, rāma bimukha yaha anucita nāhīṁ.
काल बिबस पति कहा न माना । अग जग नाथु मनुज करि जाना ॥
kāla bibasa pati kahā na mānā, aga jaga nāthu manuja kari jānā.

Trans:

When Mandodarī saw her lord's heads, she fainted in her grief and fell to the ground. Her bevy of weeping maidens sprang up in haste and supported her and brought her to Rāvan's body. When she saw the state in which her lord was, she set up a shriek, her hair flew loose, and there was no strength left in her body. Wildly beating her bosom and weeping, she recounted all his glory, "At your might, my lord, the earth ever trembled; fire, moon, and sun were bereft of splendor; the great serpent and tortoise could not bear the weight of your body, which now lies on the ground, a mere heap of ash. Varun, Kuber, Indra, and the god of the wind had never the courage to face you in battle. By the might of your arm, O my lord, you conquered death and fate; and today you have fallen like the poorest creature. Your magnificence was renowned throughout the world; while the strength of your son and your kinsmen surpassed description. You opposed Rāma and this is now your condition: not one of your stock is left even to make lamentation. The whole sphere of creation was in your power, my lord, and the frightened regents of the eight quarters ever bowed their heads before you; but now jackals devour your heads and arms, and rightly so, seeing that you opposed Rāma. Death-doomed, my lord, you heeded not my words, and took the sovereign of all things, animate and inanimate, for a mere man.

छंद-chaṁda:

जान्यो मनुज करि दनुज कानन दहन पावक हरि स्वयं ।
jānyo manuja kari danuja kānana dahana pāvaka hari svayaṁ,
जेहि नमत सिव ब्रह्मादि सुर पिय भजेहु नहिं करुनामयं ॥
jehi namata siva brahmādi sura piya bhajehu nahiṁ karunāmayaṁ.
आजन्म ते परद्रोह रत पापौघमय तव तनु अयं ।
ājanma te paradroha rata pāpaughamaya tava tanu ayaṁ,
तुम्हहू दियो निज धाम राम नमामि ब्रह्म निरामयं ॥
tumhahū diyo nija dhāma rāma namāmi brahma nirāmayaṁ.

Trans:

You took for a mere man Harī, the self-existent, a veritable fire to consume the forest of the demon race; and you worshipped not, O my spouse, the All-merciful, to whom Shiva and Brahmmā and all the gods do reverence. From your birth you have delighted to injure others, and this, your body, has been a very sink of sin, and yet Rāma has now raised you to his own abode. I bow before the blameless God.

दोहा-dohā:

अहह नाथ रघुनाथ सम कृपासिंधु नहिं आन ।
ahaha nātha raghunātha sama kṛpāsiṁdhu nahiṁ āna,
जोगि बृंद दुर्लभ गति तोहि दीन्हि भगवान ॥१०४॥
jogi bṛṁda durlabha gati tohi dīnhi bhagavāna. 104.

Trans:

Ah, my lord, there is none other so gracious as Raghunāth, the great God, who has given you a rank, to which the company of saints attain with great difficulty."

चौपाई-caupāī:

मंदोदरी बचन सुनि काना । सुर मुनि सिद्ध सबन्हि सुख माना ॥
maṁdodarī bacana suni kānā, sura muni siddha sabanhi sukha mānā.
अज महेस नारद सनकादी । जे मुनिबर परमारथबादी ॥
aja mahesa nārada sanakādī, je munibara paramārathabādī.
भरि लोचन रघुपतिहि निहारी । प्रेम मगन सब भए सुखारी ॥
bhari locana raghupatihi nihārī, prema magana saba bhae sukhārī.
रुदन करत देखीं सब नारी । गयउ बिभीषनु मन दुख भारी ॥
rudana karata dekhīṁ saba nārī, gayau bibhīṣanu mana dukha bhārī.
बंधु दसा बिलोकि दुख कीन्हा । तब प्रभु अनुजहि आयसु दीन्हा ॥
baṁdhu dasā biloki dukha kīnhā, taba prabhu anujahi āyasu dīnhā.
लछिमन तेहि बहु बिधि समुझायो । बहुरि बिभीषन प्रभु पहिं आयो ॥
lachimana tehi bahu bidhi samujhāyo, bahuri bibhīṣana prabhu pahiṁ āyo.
कृपादृष्टि प्रभु ताहि बिलोका । करहु क्रिया परिहरि सब सोका ॥
kṛpādṛṣṭi prabhu tāhi bilokā, karahu kriyā parihari saba sokā.
कीन्हि क्रिया प्रभु आयसु मानी । बिधिवत देस काल जियँ जानी ॥
kīnhi kriyā prabhu āyasu mānī, bidhivata desa kāla jiyaṁ jānī.

Trans:

When they heard Mandodarī's speech, gods, saints, and sages were all enraptured. Brahmmā, Shiva, Nārad, Sanat-kumār, and all the great seers who have preached the way of salvation, gazed upon Raghupatī with eyes full of tears and were overwhelmed with devotion. Seeing all the women making lamentation, Vibhīshan went to the spot, his heart heavy with grief, and was sorely pained to see his brother's condition. Then the Lord gave an order to Lakshman, who went and did all that he could to console him. At last Vibhīshan betook himself to the Lord, who looked upon him with an eye of compassion and said, "Make an end of sorrow and perform the funeral rites." In obedience to his command he performed his obsequies, wisely bearing in mind the circumstances of time and place.

दोहा-dohā:

मंदोदरी आदि सब देइ तिलांजलि ताहि ।
maṁdodarī ādi saba dei tilāṁjali tāhi,
भवन गईं रघुपति गुन गन बरनत मन माहि ॥ १०५॥
bhavana gaīṁ raghupati guna gana baranata mana māhi. 105.

Trans:

Mandodarī and the others presented the dead with the handfuls of sesame seed and the queens then returned to the palace, recounting all of Raghupatī's excellencies.

चौपाई-caupāī:

आइ बिभीषन पुनि सिरु नायो । कृपासिंधु तब अनुज बोलायो ॥
āi bibhīṣana puni siru nāyo, kṛpāsiṁdhu taba anuja bolāyo.
तुम्ह कपीस अंगद नल नीला । जामवंत मारुति नयसीला ॥
tumha kapīsa aṁgada nala nīlā, jāmavaṁta māruti nayasīlā.
सब मिलि जाहु बिभीषन साथा । सारेहु तिलक कहेउ रघुनाथा ॥
saba mili jāhu bibhīṣana sāthā, sārehu tilaka kaheu raghunāthā.
पिता बचन मैं नगर न आवउँ । आपु सरिस कपि अनुज पठावउँ ॥
pitā bacana maiṁ nagara na āvauṁ, āpu sarisa kapi anuja paṭhāvauṁ.
तुरत चले कपि सुनि प्रभु बचना । कीन्ही जाइ तिलक की रचना ॥
turata cale kapi suni prabhu bacanā, kīnhī jāi tilaka kī racanā.
सादर सिंहासन बैठारी । तिलक सारि अस्तुति अनुसारी ॥
sādara siṁhāsana baiṭhārī, tilaka sāri astuti anusārī.
जोरि पानि सबहीं सिर नाए । सहित बिभीषन प्रभु पहिं आए ॥
jori pāni sabahīṁ sira nāe, sahita bibhīṣana prabhu pahiṁ āe.
तब रघुबीर बोलि कपि लीन्हे । कहि प्रिय बचन सुखी सब कीन्हे ॥
taba raghubīra boli kapi līnhe, kahi priya bacana sukhī saba kīnhe.

Trans:

Again Vibhīshan came and bowed his head. Then the All-merciful called his younger brother and said, "Do you and the monkey prince and Angad and Nala and Nīl, with Jāmvant and the sagacious son-of-wind, all go together in company with Vibhīshan and make the arrangements for his coronation," said Raghunāth. "In deference to my father's commands, I may not enter the city, but I send the monkey and my younger brother to take my place." They all started at once, on receiving the Lord's order, and went and made ready for the installation. With due reverence they seated Vibhīshan on the throne, and after marking his forehead with the royal sign, they sang a hymn of praise, and with clasped hands all bowed the head before him. Then with Vibhīshan they returned to the Lord, and Raghubīr addressed the monkeys with such gracious words as made them all glad.

छंद-chaṁda:

किए सुखी कहि बानी सुधा सम बल तुम्हारें रिपु हयो ।
kie sukhī kahi bānī sudhā sama bala tumhāreṁ ripu hayo,
पायो बिभीषन राज तिहुँ पुर जसु तुम्हारो नित नयो ॥
pāyo bibhīṣana rāja tihuṁ pura jasu tumhāro nita nayo.
मोहि सहित सुभ कीरति तुम्हारी परम प्रीति जो गाइहैं ।
mohi sahita subha kīrati tumhārī parama prīti jo gāihaiṁ,
संसार सिंधु अपार पार प्रयास बिनु नर पाइहैं ॥
saṁsāra siṁdhu apāra pāra prayāsa binu nara pāihaiṁ.

Trans:

He made them glad with words that were sweet as nectar, "It is by your might that the enemy has been defeated, and that Vibhīshan has acquired the kingdom; your glory will live forever throughout the universe. Whoever with sincere devotion shall sing your glorious deeds in connection with me shall cross without an effort the boundless ocean of existence."

दोहा-dohā:

प्रभु के बचन श्रवन सुनि नहिं अघाहिं कपि पुंज ।
prabhu ke bacana śravana suni nahiṁ aghāhiṁ kapi puṁja,
बार बार सिर नावहिं गहहिं सकल पद कंज ॥ १०६॥
bāra bāra sira nāvahiṁ gahahiṁ sakala pada kaṁja. 106.

Trans:

The monkey host would never have been tired of listening to their Lord's words; again and again they all bowed the head and clasped his lotus feet.

चौपाई-caupāī:

पुनि प्रभु बोलि लियउ हनुमाना । लंका जाहु कहेउ भगवाना ॥
puni prabhu boli liyau hanumānā, laṁkā jāhu kaheu bhagavānā.
समाचार जानकिहि सुनावहु । तासु कुसल लै तुम्ह चलि आवहु ॥
samācāra jānakihi sunāvahu, tāsu kusala lai tumha cali āvahu.
तब हनुमंत नगर महुँ आए । सुनि निसिचरी निसाचर धाए ॥
taba hanumaṁta nagara mahuṁ āe, suni nisicarī nisācara dhāe.
बहु प्रकार तिन्ह पूजा कीन्ही । जनकसुता देखाइ पुनि दीन्ही ॥
bahu prakāra tinha pūjā kīnhī, janakasutā dekhāi puni dīnhī.
दूरिहि ते प्रनाम कपि कीन्हा । रघुपति दूत जानकीं चीन्हा ॥
dūrihi te pranāma kapi kīnhā, raghupati dūta jānakīṁ cīnhā.
कहहु तात प्रभु कृपानिकेता । कुसल अनुज कपि सेन समेता ॥
kahahu tāta prabhu kṛpāniketā, kusala anuja kapi sena sametā.
सब बिधि कुसल कोसलाधीसा । मातु समर जीत्यो दससीसा ॥
saba bidhi kusala kosalādhīsā, mātu samara jītyo dasasīsā.
अबिचल राजु बिभीषन पायो । सुनि कपि बचन हरष उर छायो ॥
abicala rāju bibhīṣana pāyo, suni kapi bacana haraṣa ura chāyo.

Trans:

The Lord next addressed Hanumān. "Go to Lankā," said the god, "and tell Jānakī the news and bring me back word of her welfare." Hanumān then entered the city. The demons and demoness no sooner heard than they ran to meet him, and showed him every possible honor and pointed out Sītā to him. From afar off the monkey prostrated himself. She recognized Rāma's messenger. "Tell me, O friend, of my gracious Lord and of his brother; is he well, as also all the monkey hosts?" "All is well, O mother, with the king of Kaushal; he has conquered Rāvan in battle; Vibhīshan has been placed in secure possession of the throne." On hearing the monkey's reply, a great joy was diffused over her soul.

छंद-chaṁda:

अति हरष मन तन पुलक लोचन सजल कह पुनि पुनि रमा ।
ati haraṣa mana tana pulaka locana sajala kaha puni puni ramā,
का देउँ तोहि त्रैलोक महुँ कपि किमपि नहिं बानी समा ॥
kā deuṁ tohi trailoka mahuṁ kapi kimapi nahiṁ bānī samā.
सुनु मातु मैं पायो अखिल जग राजु आजु न संसयं ।
sunu mātu maiṁ pāyo akhila jaga rāju āju na saṁsayaṁ,
रन जीति रिपुदल बंधु जुत पस्यामि राममनामयं ॥
rana jīti ripudala baṁdhu juta pasyāmi rāmamanāmayaṁ.

Trans:

Sītā's soul was overjoyed, her body thrilled, and her eyes streamed with tears, as again and again she cried, "What can I give you, O monkey? There is nothing in the three spheres of creation to be compared to your tidings." "Listen mother: today I have doubtless attained the sovereignty of the entire creation when I find Shrī Rāma safe and sound with his brother after conquering the enemy's ranks on the battlefield."

दोहा-dohā:

सुनु सुत सदगुन सकल तव हृदय बसहुँ हनुमंत ।
sunu suta sadaguna sakala tava hṛdaya basahum̐ hanumaṁta,
सानुकूल कोसलपति रहहुँ समेत अनंत ॥१०७॥
sānukūla kosalapati rahahum̐ sameta anaṁta. 107.

Trans:
"Hearken my son Hanumān: may every virtue find a home in your heart; may you live and prosper forever in the service of Kaushal's king.

चौपाई-caupāī:

अब सोइ जतन करहु तुम्ह ताता । देखौं नयन स्याम मृदु गाता ॥
aba soi jatana karahu tumha tātā, dekhaum̐ nayana syāma mṛdu gātā.
तब हनुमान राम पहिं जाई । जनकसुता कै कुसल सुनाई ॥
taba hanumāna rāma pahim̐ jāī, janakasutā kai kusala sunāī.
सुनि संदेसु भानुकुलभूषन । बोलि लिए जुबराज बिभीषन ॥
suni saṁdesu bhānukulabhūṣana, boli lie jubarāja bibhīṣana.
मारुतसुत के संग सिधावहु । सादर जनकसुतहि लै आवहु ॥
mārutasuta ke saṁga sidhāvahu, sādara janakasutahi lai āvahu.
तुरतहिं सकल गए जहँ सीता । सेवहिं सब निसिचरीं बिनीता ॥
turatahim̐ sakala gae jaham̐ sītā, sevahim̐ saba nisicarīṁ binītā.
बेगि बिभीषन तिन्हहि सिखायो । तिन्ह बहु बिधि मज्जन करवायो ॥
begi bibhīṣana tinhahi sikhāyo, tinha bahu bidhi majjana karavāyo.
बहु प्रकार भूषन पहिराए । सिबिका रुचिर साजि पुनि ल्याए ॥
bahu prakāra bhūṣana pahirāe, sibikā rucira sāji puni lyāe.
ता पर हरषि चढ़ी बैदेही । सुमिरि राम सुखधाम सनेही ॥
tā para haraṣi caṛhī baidehī, sumiri rāma sukhadhāma sanehī.
बेतपानि रच्छक चहुँ पासा । चले सकल मन परम हुलासा ॥
betapāni racchaka cahum̐ pāsā, cale sakala mana parama hulāsā.
देखन भालु कीस सब आए । रच्छक कोपि निवारन धाए ॥
dekhana bhālu kīsa saba āe, racchaka kopi nivārana dhāe.
कह रघुबीर कहा मम मानहु । सीतहि सखा पयादें आनहु ॥
kaha raghubīra kahā mama mānahu, sītahi sakhā payādeṁ ānahu.
देखहुँ कपि जननी की नाईं । बिहसि कहा रघुनाथ गोसाईं ॥
dekhahum̐ kapi jananī kī nāīṁ, bihasi kahā raghunātha gosāīṁ.
सुनि प्रभु बचन भालु कपि हरषे । नभ ते सुरन्ह सुमन बहु बरसे ॥
suni prabhu bacana bhālu kapi haraṣe, nabha te suranha sumana bahu baraṣe.
सीता प्रथम अनल महुँ राखी । प्रगट कीन्हि चह अंतर साखी ॥
sītā prathama anala mahum̐ rākhī, pragaṭa kīnhi caha aṁtara sākhī.

Trans:
Now son, devise some plan by which I may see with my own eyes his dark comely form." Hanumān then returned to Rāma and told him of Sītā's welfare. On hearing her tidings, the Ornament of the solar race called Prince Angad and Vibhīshan. "Both of you accompany the son-of-wind and respectfully escort Janak's daughter here." Forthwith all went to the place where Sītā was; and found a whole host of demoness waiting on her in all humility. Vibhīshan gave prompt instructions to them, who attended her to the bath with all formality. They also decked her with ornaments of every description and then brought a beautiful palanquin duly equipped. Videh's Daughter gladly got on it with her thoughts fixed on the all-blissful Rāma. On all four sides were guards, with staves in their hands, who marched with the greatest gladness of soul. The bears and monkeys all came to look, but the guards in a fury rushed to keep them back. Said Raghubīr, "Attend to what I say: bring Sītā on foot, friends; let the monkeys see her as they would their own mother." Thus said the great Raghunāth and smiled. The bears and monkeys were delighted to hear his commands, and from heaven the gods rained down profusions of flowers. Sītā had been previously lodged in fire; now he sought to bring her back to light.

दोहा-dohā:

तेहि कारन करुनानिधि कहे कछुक दुर्बाद ।
tehi kārana karunānidhi kahe kachuka durbāda,
सुनत जातुधानीं सब लागीं करै बिषाद ॥१०८॥
sunata jātudhānīṁ saba lāgīṁ karai biṣāda. 108.

Trans:
For this reason the All-merciful spoke with seeming harshness. All the demon attendants, when they heard it, began to make lamentation.

चौपाई-caupāī:

प्रभु के बचन सीस धरि सीता । बोली मन क्रम बचन पुनीता ॥
prabhu ke bacana sīsa dhari sītā, bolī mana krama bacana punītā.
लछिमन होहु धरम के नेगी । पावक प्रगट करहु तुम्ह बेगी ॥
lachimana hohu dharama ke negī, pāvaka pragaṭa karahu tumha begī.
सुनि लछिमन सीता कै बानी । बिरह बिबेक धरम निति सानी ॥
suni lachimana sītā kai bānī, biraha bibeka dharama niti sānī.
लोचन सजल जोरि कर दोऊ । प्रभु सन कछु कहि सकत न ओऊ ॥
locana sajala jori kara doū, prabhu sana kachu kahi sakata na oū.
देखि राम रुख लछिमन धाए । पावक प्रगटि काठ बहु लाए ॥
dekhi rāma rukha lachimana dhāe, pāvaka pragaṭi kāṭha bahu lāe.
पावक प्रबल देखि बैदेही । हृदयँ हरष नहिं भय कछु तेही ॥
pāvaka prabala dekhi baidehī, hṛdayam̐ haraṣa nahiṁ bhaya kachu tehī.
जौं मन बच क्रम मम उर माहीं । तजि रघुबीर आन गति नाहीं ॥
jaum̐ mana baca krama mama ura māhīṁ, taji raghubīra āna gati nāhīṁ.
तौ कृसानु सब कै गति जाना । मो कहुँ होउ श्रीखंड समाना ॥
tau kṛsānu saba kai gati jānā, mo kahum̐ hou śrīkhaṁḍa samānā.

Trans:
But Sītā bowed to her Lord's command—pure as she was in thought, word and deed—and said "Lakshman, be you the celebrant of this rite; show me the fire and be quick." When Lakshman heard Sītā's words—so full of detachment, discretion, and piety—his eyes filled with tears and he clasped his hands in prayer; but could not speak a word to his Lord. But seeing Rāma's leaning, he rushed and kindled fire to a large quantity of wood. Sītā beheld the fierceness of the flame, but was glad of heart without a particle of fear. "If, in thought, word and deed, I have never set my heart on anyone other than the Hero of Raghu's line, may this fire, which knows the working of all minds, become cool like a sandal-paste to me."

छंद-chaṁda:

श्रीखंड सम पावक प्रबेस कियो सुमिरि प्रभु मैथिली ।
śrīkhaṁḍa sama pāvaka prabesa kiyo sumiri prabhu maithilī,
जय कोसलेस महेस बंदित चरन रति अति निर्मली ॥
jaya kosalesa mahesa baṁdita carana rati ati nirmalī.
प्रतिबिंब अरु लौकिक कलंक प्रचंड पावक महुँ जरे ।
pratibiṁba aru laukika kalaṁka pracaṁḍa pāvaka mahum̐ jare,
प्रभु चरित काहुँ न लखे नभ सुर सिद्ध मुनि देखहिं खरे ॥१॥
prabhu carita kāhum̐ na lakhe nabha sura siddha muni dekhahim̐ khare. 1.
धरि रूप पावक पानि गहि श्री सत्य श्रुति जग बिदित जो ।
dhari rūpa pāvaka pāni gahi śrī satya śruti jaga bidita jo,
जिमि छीरसागर इंदिरा रामहि समर्पी आनि सो ॥
jimi chīrasāgara iṁdirā rāmahi samarpī āni so.
सो राम बाम बिभाग राजति रुचिर अति सोभा भली ।
so rāma bāma bibhāga rājati rucira ati sobhā bhalī,
नव नील नीरज निकट मानहुँ कनक पंकज की कली ॥२॥
nava nīla nīraja nikaṭa mānahum̐ kanaka paṁkaja kī kalī. 2.

Trans:

The flame was cool as sandalwood as Sītā entered it, meditating on her Lord. "Glory to the king of Kaushal, for whose feet, ever worshipped by Shiva, I cherish the purest devotion." Her shadow and the stain of social disgrace were alone consumed in the blazing fire. Such an action on the part of the Lord had never been seen before: gods, saints, and sages all stood at gaze. The Fire assumed a bodily form and took her by the hand and led and presented her to Rāma, the very Lakshmī celebrated alike in the Vedas and the world, who erst arose as Indirā from the sea of milk. Resplendent with exquisite beauty she shines forth as the left side of Rāma's body, like the blossom of a golden lily beside a fresh blue lotus.

दोहा-dohā:

बरषहिं सुमन हरषि सुर बाजहिं गगन निसान ।
baraṣahiṁ sumana haraṣi sura bājahiṁ gagana nisāna,
गावहिं किंनर सुरबधू नाचहिं चढ़ीं बिमान ॥ १०९क ॥
gāvahiṁ kiṁnara surabadhū nācahiṁ caṛhīṁ bimāna. 109(ka).

जनकसुता समेत प्रभु सोभा अमित अपार ।
janakasutā sameta prabhu sobhā amita apāra,
देखि भालु कपि हरषे जय रघुपति सुख सार ॥ १०९ख ॥
dekhi bhālu kapi haraṣe jaya raghupati sukha sāra. 109(kha).

Trans:

The gods in their delight rain down flowers and make music is the air, while the Kinnars sing and the nymphs of heaven dance, all mounted on their chariots. The beauty of Janak's daughter reunited to her Lord is beyond all measure and bound; the bears and monkeys, in their rapture at the sight, shout "glory to Rāma the beneficent."

चौपाई-caupāī:

तब रघुपति अनुसासन पाई । मातलि चलेउ चरन सिरु नाई ॥
taba raghupati anusāsana pāī, mātali caleu carana siru nāī.
आए देव सदा स्वारथी । बचन कहहिं जनु परमारथी ॥
āe deva sadā svārathī, bacana kahahiṁ janu paramārathī.
दीन बंधु दयाल रघुराया । देव कीन्हि देवन्ह पर दाया ॥
dīna baṁdhu dayāla raghurāyā, deva kīnhi devanha para dāyā.
बिस्व द्रोह रत यह खल कामी । निज अघ गयउ कुमारगगामी ॥
bisva droha rata yaha khala kāmī, nija agha gayau kumāragagāmī.
तुम्ह समरूप ब्रह्म अबिनासी । सदा एकरस सहज उदासी ॥
tumha samarūpa brahma abināsī, sadā ekarasa sahaja udāsī.
अकल अगुन अज अनघ अनामय । अजित अमोघसक्ति करुनामय ॥
akala aguna aja anagha anāmaya, ajita amoghasakti karunāmaya.
मीन कमठ सूकर नरहरी । बामन परसुराम बपु धरी ॥
mīna kamaṭha sūkara naraharī, bāmana parasurāma bapu dharī.
जब जब नाथ सुरन्ह दुखु पायो । नाना तनु धरि तुम्हइँ नसायो ॥
jaba jaba nātha suranha dukhu pāyo, nānā tanu dhari tumhaiṁ nasāyo.
यह खल मलिन सदा सुरद्रोही । काम लोभ मद रत अति कोही ॥
yaha khala malina sadā suradrohī, kāma lobha mada rata ati kohī.
अधम सिरोमनि तव पद पावा । यह हमरें मन बिसमय आवा ॥
adhama siromani tava pada pāvā, yaha hamareṁ mana bisamaya āvā.
हम देवता परम अधिकारी । स्वारथ रत प्रभु भगति बिसारी ॥
hama devatā parama adhikārī, svāratha rata prabhu bhagati bisārī.
भव प्रबाहँ संतत हम परे । अब प्रभु पाहि सरन अनुसरे ॥
bhava prabāhaṁ saṁtata hama pare, aba prabhu pāhi sarana anusare.

Trans:

Having obtained Rāma's permission, and bowing his head at his feet, Matali left with Indra's chariot. The gods too, selfish as ever, came and made this pious prayer seeming to seek the highest truth, "Friend of the destitute, gracious Raghurāī, a God yourself, you have shown mercy to the gods. This sensual wretch, who delighted to harass the whole world, has perished by his own wickedness in his sinful course. You are the Supreme-Spirit, One and Everlasting, ever Unchangeable and Unaffected by circumstances, Without parts or qualities, Uncreated, Sinless, All-perfect, Invincible, Unerring, full of Power and Compassion; Incarnate as the Fish, the Tortoise, the Boar, the Lion-man, and the Dwarf; as Parshurām also and now as Rāma. Whenever, O Lord, the gods have been in trouble, you have taken birth in various forms to put an end to it; but this impure wretch, the persistent plague of heaven, given up to sensuality, greed, pride and passion, this monster of monsters, has been promoted to your sphere and thereat we marvel greatly. We gods are high masters, but in our selfishness we have forgotten the worship of our Lord, and thus we are ever involved in the flood of worldly passions; but now, O Lord, have mercy upon us, for we come to you for refuge."

दोहा-dohā:

करि बिनती सुर सिद्ध सब रहे जहँ तहँ कर जोरि ।
kari binatī sura siddha saba rahe jahaṁ tahaṁ kara jori,
अति सप्रेम तन पुलकि बिधि अस्तुति करत बहोरि ॥ ११० ॥
ati saprema tana pulaki bidhi astuti karata bahori. 110.

Trans:

With clasped hands the gods and saints stood all round about him, thus making supplication; and—his whole body quivering with excess of devotion—Brahmmā at last broke out into this hymn of praise:

छंद-chaṁda:

जय राम सदा सुखधाम हरे । रघुनायक सायक चाप धरे ॥
jaya rāma sadā sukhadhāma hare, raghunāyaka sāyaka cāpa dhare.
भव बारन दारन सिंह प्रभो । गुन सागर नागर नाथ बिभो ॥
bhava bārana dārana siṁha prabho, guna sāgara nāgara nātha bibho.
तन काम अनेक अनूप छबी । गुन गावत सिद्ध मुनींद्र कबी ॥
tana kāma aneka anūpa chabī, guna gāvata siddha munīṁdra kabī.
जसु पावन रावन नाग महा । खगनाथ जथा करि कोप गहा ॥
jasu pāvana rāvana nāga mahā, khaganātha jathā kari kopa gahā.
जन रंजन भंजन सोक भयं । गतक्रोध सदा प्रभु बोधमयं ॥
jana raṁjana bhaṁjana soka bhayaṁ, gatakrodha sadā prabhu bodhamayaṁ.
अवतार उदार अपार गुनं । महि भार बिभंजन ग्यानघनं ॥
avatāra udāra apāra gunaṁ, mahi bhāra bibhaṁjana gyānaghanaṁ.
अज ब्यापकमेकमनादि सदा । करुनाकर राम नमामि मुदा ॥
aja byāpakamekamanādi sadā, karunākara rāma namāmi mudā.
रघुबंस बिभूषन दूषन हा । कृत भूप बिभीषन दीन रहा ॥
raghubaṁsa bibhūṣana dūṣana hā, kṛta bhūpa bibhīṣana dīna rahā.
गुन ग्यान निधान अमान अजं । नित राम नमामि बिभुं बिरजं ॥
guna gyāna nidhāna amāna ajaṁ, nita rāma namāmi bibhuṁ birajaṁ.
भुजदंड प्रचंड प्रताप बलं । खल बृंद निकंद महा कुसलं ॥
bhujadaṁḍa pracaṁḍa pratāpa balaṁ, khala bṛṁda nikaṁda mahā kusalaṁ.
बिनु कारन दीन दयाल हितं । छबि धाम नमामि रमा सहितं ॥
binu kārana dīna dayāla hitaṁ, chabi dhāma namāmi ramā sahitaṁ.
भव तारन कारन काज परं । मन संभव दारुन दोष हरं ॥
bhava tārana kārana kāja paraṁ, mana saṁbhava dāruna doṣa haraṁ.
सर चाप मनोहर त्रोन धरं । जलजारुन लोचन भूपबरं ॥
sara cāpa manohara trona dharaṁ, jalajāruna locana bhūpabaraṁ.
सुख मंदिर सुंदर श्रीरमनं । मद मार मुधा ममता समनं ॥
sukha maṁdira suṁdara śrīramanaṁ, mada māra mudhā mamatā samanaṁ.
अनवद्य अखंड न गोचर गो । सबरूप सदा सब होइ न गो ॥
anavadya akhaṁḍa na gocara go, sabarūpa sadā saba hoi na go.

इति बेद बदंति न दंतकथा । रबि आतप भिन्नमभिन्न जथा ॥
iti beda badaṁti na daṁtakathā, rabi ātapa bhinnamabhinna jathā.
कृतकृत्य बिभो सब बानर ए । निरखंति तवानन सादर ए ॥
kṛtakṛtya bibho saba bānara e, nirakhaṁti tavānana sādara e.
धिग जीवन देव सरीर हरे । तव भक्ति बिना भव भूलि परे ॥
dhiga jīvana deva sarīra hare, tava bhakti binā bhava bhūli pare.
अब दीनदयाल दया करिऐ । मति मोरि बिभेदकरी हरिऐ ॥
aba dīnadayāla dayā kariai, mati mori bibhedakarī hariai.
जेहि ते बिपरीत क्रिया करिऐ । दुख सो सुख मानि सुखी चरिऐ ॥
jehi te biparīta kriyā kariai, dukha so sukha māni sukhī cariai.
खल खंडन मंडन रम्य छमा । पद पंकज सेवित संभु उमा ॥
khala khaṁḍana maṁḍana ramya chamā, pada paṁkaja sevita saṁbhu umā.
नृप नायक दे बरदानमिदं । चरनांबुज प्रेम सदा सुभदं ॥
nṛpa nāyaka de baradānamidaṁ, caranāṁbuja prema sadā subhadaṁ.

Trans:

"Glory to the immortal Rāma, the blissful Harī, the prince of Raghu's line, with his bow and arrows; the lion-like Lord to rend in pieces the elephant of worldly existence; the ocean of perfection, the all-wise, the all-pervading; in whose body is concentrated the incomparable beauty of a myriad Loves; whose virtues are sung by bards, saints, and sages. O Hero of spotless renown, who in thy wrath didst seize Rāvan, as Garud might seize some monstrous serpent; delight of mankind; destroyer of grief and fear; ever unmoved by passion; Lord of supreme intelligence; beneficent incarnation of illimitable perfection; reliever of earth's burdens; wisdom personified; everlasting, all-pervading, without a beginning, the only One—I rapturously adore thee, O Rāma, fountain of mercy. Glory of the line of Raghu, slaying Dūshan and making a king of the ever faithful Vibhīshan. Storehouse of virtue and wisdom; incomprehensible and everlasting, I constantly adore thee, O Rāma, the passionless, the supreme. Mighty of arm, strong in renown, deft in exterminating the hordes of the impious; pre-eminent in auspiciousness; friend and protector even of the undeserving suppliant; I worship the perfection of beauty, the spouse of Lakshmī. Deliverer from the burden of mortality, extern to cause and effect, soul-created destroyer of hideous sin; wielder of the arrows and bow and lovely quiver; lotus-eyed paragon of kings; temple of bliss, Lakshmī's beautiful consort; subduer of pride, lust, lying, and selfishness; irreproachable, imperishable; perceptive and the percept; of all forms alike and yet of no determinate form; like the light of the sun—thus the Vedas have declared, it is no mere quibble of speech—which is separate from it and yet not separate. How fortunate, my Lord, are all these monkeys who reverently gaze upon thy face. A curse, Harī, on the life we gods enjoy without devotion to you, we have all gone astray in the world. Now, as thou art compassionate to the suppliant, have upon us your compassion; be a lion to destroy the elephant-like inconstancy of our purpose; may we practice the reverse of our former ways and live happy, esteeming that happiness which was before a pain. Mercy, O destroyer of the wicked, beautiful jewel, whose lotus feet are cherished by Shambhu and Umā. O king of kings, grant us this boon: the blessing of a constant devotion to thy lotus feet."

दोहा-dohā:

बिनय कीन्हि चतुरानन प्रेम पुलक अति गात ।
binaya kīnhi caturānana prema pulaka ati gāta,
सोभासिंधु बिलोकत लोचन नहीं अघात ॥ १११ ॥
sobhāsiṁdhu bilokata locana nahīṁ aghāta. 111.

Trans:

As Brahmmā made this prayer, his whole body quivered with excess of devotion, and his eyes beholding the ocean of beauty refused to be satisfied.

चौपाई-caupāī:

तेहि अवसर दसरथ तहँ आए । तनय बिलोकि नयन जल छाए ॥
tehi avasara dasaratha tahaṁ āe, tanaya biloki nayana jala chāe.
अनुज सहित प्रभु बंदन कीन्हा । आसिरबाद पिताँ तब दीन्हा ॥
anuja sahita prabhu baṁdana kīnhā, āsirabāda pitāṁ taba dīnhā.
तात सकल तव पुन्य प्रभाऊ । जीत्यों अजय निसाचर राऊ ॥
tāta sakala tava punya prabhāū, jītyoṁ ajaya nisācara rāū.
सुनि सुत बचन प्रीति अति बाढ़ी । नयन सलिल रोमावलि ठाढ़ी ॥
suni suta bacana prīti ati bāṛhī, nayana salila romāvali ṭhāṛhī.
रघुपति प्रथम प्रेम अनुमाना । चितइ पितहि दीन्हेउ दृढ़ ग्याना ॥
raghupati prathama prema anumānā, citai pitahi dīnheu dṛṛha gyānā.
ताते उमा मोच्छ नहिं पायो । दसरथ भेद भगति मन लायो ॥
tāte umā moccha nahiṁ pāyo, dasaratha bheda bhagati mana lāyo.
सगुनोपासक मोच्छ न लेहीं । तिन्ह कहुँ राम भगति निज देहीं ॥
sagunopāsaka moccha na lehīṁ, tinha kahuṁ rāma bhagati nija dehīṁ.
बार बार करि प्रभुहि प्रनामा । दसरथ हरषि गए सुरधामा ॥
bāra bāra kari prabhuhi pranāmā, dasaratha harași gae suradhāmā.

Trans:

Then too came Dashrath, and, when he beheld his son, his eyes were flooded with tears. The Lord and his brother made obeisance before him and their father gave them his blessing. "It is all due, sire, to your religions merit that the invincible demon king has been conquered." On hearing his son's words, his affection increased still more; his eyes streamed and every hair on his body stood on end. Raghupatī understood that his father bore for him the same affection as of before. He therefore looked upon him and after taking thought bestowed upon him absolute wisdom. He did not receive the boon of deliverance from existence. O Umā, Dashrath did not attain final beatitude for the simple reason that he had his heart set upon Devotion maintaining distinct identity from God. Worshippers of God in His embodied form spurn final beatitude. To them Shrī Rāma vouchsafes devotion to His own person. Having again and again prostrated himself before the Lord, Dashrath proceeded with joy to his abode in heaven.

दोहा-dohā:

अनुज जानकी सहित प्रभु कुसल कोसलाधीस ।
anuja jānakī sahita prabhu kusala kosalādhīsa,
सोभा देखि हरषि मन अस्तुति कर सुर ईस ॥ ११२ ॥
sobhā dekhi harași mana astuti kara sura īsa. 112.

Trans:

The Lord, the king of Kaushal, rejoiced together with his brother and Jānakī. At the charming sight Indra, lord of the gods, in his delight chanted this hymn of praise:

छंद-chaṁda:

जय राम सोभा धाम । दायक प्रनत बिश्राम ॥
jaya rāma sobhā dhāma, dāyaka pranata biśrāma.
धृत त्रोन बर सर चाप । भुजदंड प्रबल प्रताप ॥ १ ॥
dhṛta trona bara sara cāpa, bhujadaṁḍa prabala pratāpa. 1.
जय दूषनारि खरारि । मर्दन निसाचर धारि ॥
jaya dūșanāri kharāri, mardana nisācara dhāri.
यह दुष्ट मारेउ नाथ । भए देव सकल सनाथ ॥ २ ॥
yaha dușța māreu nātha, bhae deva sakala sanātha. 2.
जय हरन धरनी भार । महिमा उदार अपार ॥
jaya harana dharanī bhāra, mahimā udāra apāra.
जय रावनारि कृपाल । किए जातुधान बिहाल ॥ ३ ॥
jaya rāvanāri kṛpāla, kie jātudhāna bihāla. 3.
लंकेस अति बल गर्ब । किए बस्य सुर गंधर्ब ॥
laṁkesa ati bala garba, kie basya sura gaṁdharba.
मुनि सिद्ध नर खग नाग । हठि पंथ सब कें लाग ॥ ४ ॥
muni siddha nara khaga nāga, haṭhi paṁtha saba keṁ lāga. 4.

परद्रोह रत अति दुष्ट । पायो सो फलु पापिष्ट ॥
paradroha rata ati duṣṭa, pāyo so phalu pāpiṣṭa.
अब सुनहु दीन दयाल । राजीव नयन बिसाल ॥५॥
aba sunahu dīna dayāla, rājīva nayana bisāla. 5.
मोहि रहा अति अभिमान । नहिं कोउ मोहि समान ॥
mohi rahā ati abhimāna, nahiṁ kou mohi samāna.
अब देखि प्रभु पद कंज । गत मान प्रद दुख पुंज ॥६॥
aba dekhi prabhu pada kaṁja, gata māna prada dukha puṁja. 6.
कोउ ब्रह्म निर्गुन ध्याव । अब्यक्त जेहि श्रुति गाव ॥
kou brahma nirguna dhyāva, abyakta jehi śruti gāva.
मोहि भाव कोसल भूप । श्रीराम सगुन सरूप ॥७॥
mohi bhāva kosala bhūpa, śrīrāma saguna sarūpa. 7.
बैदेहि अनुज समेत । मम हृदयँ करहु निकेत ॥
baidehi anuja sameta, mama hṛdayaṁ karahu niketa.
मोहि जानिए निज दास । दे भक्ति रमानिवास ॥८॥
mohi jānie nija dāsa, de bhakti ramānivāsa. 8.

Trans:

"Glory to Rāma, the home of beauty, the merciful, the refuge of the suppliant; equip with quiver and bow and arrows, triumphing in his mighty strength of arm. Glory to enemy of Dūshan, the foe of Khar, the destroyer of demon host; when my Lord slaying this last monster, all the gods are happy again. Glory to the remover of earth's burdens, whose greatness is indeed vast and unbounded. Glory to Rāvan's merciful foe, the discomforter of the demons. Outrageous was the pride of the king of Lankā, who had reduced to subjection gods and Gandharvs; who relentlessly pursued saints and sages, men, birds, and serpents; a malignant and implacable monster; but who now—the wretch—has obtained his reward. Hearken now, protector of the suppliant, with the large lotus eyes; ere, my pride was inordinate: there was no one to equal me. Now after seeing thy lotus feet, the arrogance that caused me so much misery has passed away. Let others adore the unembodied supreme, the primary existence, whom the Vedas hymn; but my desire is the king of Kaushal, the divine Rāma, visible and material. Together with Sītā and Lakshman, make my heart thy abode. O spouse of Lakshmī, recognize me as thy servant, and grant me Devotion.

छंद-chaṁda:

दे भक्ति रमानिवास त्रास हरन सरन सुखदायकं ।
de bhakti ramānivāsa trāsa harana sarana sukhadāyakaṁ,
सुख धाम राम नमामि काम अनेक छबि रघुनायकं ॥
sukha dhāma rāma namāmi kāma aneka chabi raghunāyakaṁ.
सुर बृंद रंजन द्वंद भंजन मनुज तनु अतुलितबलं ।
sura bṛṁda raṁjana dvaṁda bhaṁjana manuja tanu atulitabalaṁ,
ब्रह्मादि संकर सेब्य राम नमामि करुना कोमलं ॥
brahmādi saṁkara sebya rāma namāmi karunā komalaṁ.

Trans:

Grant me faith, O spouse of Lakshmī, soother of terror, consoler of the suppliant. Thee I adore, O blissful Rāma, prince of the house of Raghu, beautiful as a myriad Loves. Delight of the hosts of heaven, queller of strife; in form as a man of incomparable strength; object of the adoration of Brahmmā, Shankar and all the gods, I worship thee, O Rāma, the gracious, the benign.

दोहा-dohā:

अब करि कृपा बिलोकि मोहि आयसु देहु कृपाल ।
aba kari kṛpā biloki mohi āyasu dehu kṛpāla,
काह करौं सुनि प्रिय बचन बोले दीनदयाल ॥११३॥
kāha karauṁ suni priya bacana bole dīnadayāla. 113.

Trans:

Now in thy mercy, O most merciful, look upon me and direct me what to do." On hearing this tender appeal the protector of the poor made answer:

चौपाई-caupāī:

सुनु सुरपति कपि भालु हमारे । परे भूमि निसिचरन्हि जे मारे ॥
sunu surapati kapi bhālu hamāre, pare bhūmi nisicaranhi je māre.
मम हित लागि तजे इन्ह प्राना । सकल जिआउ सुरेस सुजाना ॥
mama hita lāgi taje inha prānā, sakala jiāu suresa sujānā.
सुनु खगेस प्रभु कै यह बानी । अति अगाध जानहिं मुनि ग्यानी ॥
sunu khagesa prabhu kai yaha bānī, ati agādha jānahiṁ muni gyānī.
प्रभु सक त्रिभुअन मारि जिआई । केवल सक्रहि दीन्हि बड़ाई ॥
prabhu saka tribhuana māri jiāī, kevala sakrahi dīnhi baṛāī.
सुधा बरषि कपि भालु जिआए । हरषि उठे सब प्रभु पहिं आए ॥
sudhā baraṣi kapi bhālu jiāe, haraṣi uṭhe saba prabhu pahiṁ āe.
सुधाबृष्टि भै दुहु दल ऊपर । जिए भालु कपि नहिं रजनीचर ॥
sudhābṛṣṭi bhai duhu dala ūpara, jie bhālu kapi nahiṁ rajanīcara.
रामाकार भए तिन्ह के मन । मुक्त भए छूटे भव बंधन ॥
rāmākāra bhae tinha ke mana, mukta bhae chūṭe bhava baṁdhana.
सुर अंसिक सब कपि अरु रीछा । जिए सकल रघुपति कीं ईछा ॥
sura aṁsika saba kapi aru rīchā, jie sakala raghupati kīṁ īchā.
राम सरिस को दीन हितकारी । कीन्हे मुकुत निसाचर झारी ॥
rāma sarisa ko dīna hitakārī, kīnhe mukuta nisācara jhārī.
खल मल धाम काम रत रावन । गति पाई जो मुनिबर पाव न ॥
khala mala dhāma kāma rata rāvana, gati pāī jo munibara pāva na.

Trans:

"Hearken O king of the gods: my bears and monkeys, who lie on the ground slain by the demons, have lost their life on my account; restore them all to life, wise king of heaven." Hearken, Garud, this request of the Lord's is a mystery that only the greatest sages can comprehend. The Lord could himself destroy and recreate the three spheres of creation; only he wished to do Indra honor. With a shower of ambrosia he restored the bears and monkeys to life. They arose with joy and all betook them to the Lord. The shower of ambrosia fell on both armies; but the bears and monkeys came to life, not the demons. The image of Rāma was imprest upon the demons' soul; thus they were loosed from the fetters of existence and became absorbed in the Divinity. The bears and monkeys were partial incarnations of the gods, and they came to life by the will of Raghupatī. Who is there so kind to the destitute as Rāma, who granted final deliverance even to the host of demons, while that filthy and sensual monster Rāvan obtained translation to the same sphere as the holiest of saints.

दोहा-dohā:

सुमन बरषि सब सुर चले चढ़ि चढ़ि रुचिर बिमान ।
sumana baraṣi saba sura cale caṛhi caṛhi rucira bimāna,
देखि सुअवसरु प्रभु पहिं आयउ संभु सुजान ॥११४क॥
dekhi suavasaru prabhu pahiṁ āyau saṁbhu sujāna. 114(ka).

परम प्रीति कर जोरि जुग नलिन नयन भरि बारि ।
parama prīti kara jori juga nalina nayana bhari bāri,
पुलकित तन गदगद गिराँ बिनय करत त्रिपुरारि ॥११४ख॥
pulakita tana gadagada girāṁ binaya karata tripurāri. 114(kha).

Trans:

After showering down flowers, the gods mounted their splendid chariots and withdrew. Then seeing his opportunity the sagacious Shambhu drew near to Rāma. Most lovingly, with clasped hands, his lotus eyes full of tears and his body quivering all over, Tripurārī uttered this prayer with a choking voice:

छंद-chaṁda:

मामभिरक्षय रघुकुल नायक । धृत बर चाप रुचिर कर सायक ॥
māmabhirakṣaya raghukula nāyaka, dhṛta bara cāpa rucira kara sāyaka.
मोह महा घन पटल प्रभंजन । संसय बिपिन अनल सुर रंजन ॥

moha mahā ghana paṭala prabhaṁjana, saṁsaya bipina anala sura raṁjana.
अगुन सगुन गुन मंदिर सुंदर । भ्रम तम प्रबल प्रताप दिवाकर ॥
aguna saguna guna maṁdira suṁdara, bhrama tama prabala pratāpa divākara.
काम क्रोध मद गज पंचानन । बसहु निरंतर जन मन कानन ॥
kāma krodha mada gaja paṁcānana, basahu niraṁtara jana mana kānana.
बिषय मनोरथ पुंज कंज बन । प्रबल तुषार उदार पार मन ॥
biṣaya manoratha puṁja kaṁja bana, prabala tuṣāra udāra pāra mana.
भव बारिधि मंदर परमं दर । बारय तारय संसृति दुस्तर ॥
bhava bāridhi maṁdara paramaṁ dara, bāraya tāraya saṁsṛti dustara.
स्याम गात राजीव बिलोचन । दीन बंधु प्रनतारति मोचन ॥
syāma gāta rājīva bilocana, dīna baṁdhu pranatārati mocana.
अनुज जानकी सहित निरंतर । बसहु राम नृप मम उर अंतर ॥
anuja jānakī sahita niraṁtara, basahu rāma nṛpa mama ura aṁtara.
मुनि रंजन महि मंडल मंडन । तुलसिदास प्रभु त्रास बिखंडन ॥
muni raṁjana mahi maṁḍala maṁḍana, tulasidāsa prabhu trāsa bikhaṁḍana.

Trans:

"Save me, O prince of the house of Raghu, equipt with thy strong bow and graceful arrows in thy hand; dispeller of the murky clouds of delusion; fire to consume the forest of doubt; delight of the gods; unembodied yet embodied; glorious shrine of perfection; sun of vehement splendor to disperse the darkness of error; a very lion to attack the elephantine monsters: lust, anger, and pride—take up thy abode forever, as in some forest, in the heart of this servant. A severe frost to the lotus growth of sensual desires; gracious beyond all conception; a mount Meru to churn up the ocean of life; dweller of the highest sphere—avert from me the stormy waves of the world—or transport me across them. O king Rāma, dark-hued and lotus-eyed, protector of the poor, soother of the sorrows of the distressed, dwell forever in my heart with Lakshman and Jānakī, delight of the saints, glory of the terrestrial sphere, uprooter of every terror, Tulsīdās' own Lord.

दोहा-dohā:

नाथ जबहिं कोसलपुरीं होइहि तिलक तुम्हार ।
nātha jabahiṁ kosalapurīṁ hoihi tilaka tumhāra,
कृपासिंधु मैं आउब देखन चरित उदार ॥ ११५॥
kṛpāsiṁdhu maiṁ āuba dekhana carita udāra. 115.

Trans:

When your coronation, O my Lord, takes place at Kaushal, I will come to see the glorious ceremony, O greatly compassionate."

चौपाई-caupāī:

करि बिनती जब संभु सिधाए । तब प्रभु निकट बिभीषनु आए ॥
kari binatī jaba saṁbhu sidhāe, taba prabhu nikaṭa bibhīṣanu āe.
नाइ चरन सिरु कह मृदु बानी । बिनय सुनहु प्रभु सारँगपानी ॥
nāi carana siru kaha mṛdu bānī, binaya sunahu prabhu sāraṁgapānī.
सकुल सदल प्रभु रावन मारयो । पावन जस त्रिभुवन बिस्तारयो ॥
sakula sadala prabhu rāvana mārayo, pāvana jasa tribhuvana bistārayo.
दीन मलीन हीन मति जाती । मो पर कृपा कीन्हि बहु भाँती ॥
dīna malīna hīna mati jātī, mo para kṛpā kīnhi bahu bhāṁtī.
अब जन गृह पुनीत प्रभु कीजे । मज्जनु करिअ समर श्रम छीजे ॥
aba jana gṛha punīta prabhu kīje, majjanu karia samara śrama chīje.
देखि कोस मंदिर संपदा । देहु कृपाल कपिन्ह कहुँ मुदा ॥
dekhi kosa maṁdira saṁpadā, dehu kṛpāla kapinha kahuṁ mudā.
सब बिधि नाथ मोहि अपनाइअ । पुनि मोहि सहित अवधपुर जाइअ ॥
saba bidhi nātha mohi apanāia, puni mohi sahita avadhapura jāia.
सुनत बचन मृदु दीनदयाला । सजल भए द्वौ नयन बिसाला ॥
sunata bacana mṛdu dīnadayālā, sajala bhae dvau nayana bisālā.

Trans:

When Shambhu had finished his prayer and had left, then Vibhīshan approached the Lord. Bowing his head at his feet he spoke in pleading tones, "Hearken to my prayer, O Lord, with bow in hand. You have slain Rāvan with all his kindred and all his army and made your unsullied glory known throughout the three spheres. On me, your vile servant, without either sense or breeding, you have in every way shown compassion; now, sire, honor your servant's house and bathe and refresh yourself after the toil of the battle. Inspect my treasure, my palace, and my wealth, and by this condescension make all the monkeys happy. Consider, my Lord, everything that I have as your own, and moreover take me with you to Avadh." When the All-merciful heard this affecting speech, both his great eyes filled with tears.

दोहा-dohā:

तोर कोस गृह मोर सब सत्य बचन सुनु भ्रात ।
tora kosa gṛha mora saba satya bacana sunu bhrāta,
भरत दसा सुमिरत मोहि निमिष कल्प सम जात ॥ ११६क॥
bharata dasā sumirata mohi nimiṣa kalpa sama jāta. 116(ka).

तापस बेष गात कृस जपत निरंतर मोहि ।
tāpasa beṣa gāta kṛsa japata niraṁtara mohi,
देखौं बेगि सो जतनु करु सखा निहोरउँ तोहि ॥ ११६ख॥
dekhauṁ begi so jatanu karu sakhā nihoraum̐ tohi. 116(kha).

बीतें अवधि जाउँ जौं जिअत न पावउँ बीर ।
bīteṁ avadhi jāum̐ jauṁ jiata na pāvaum̐ bīra,
सुमिरत अनुज प्रीति प्रभु पुनि पुनि पुलक सरीर ॥ ११६ग॥
sumirata anuja prīti prabhu puni puni pulaka sarīra. 116(ga).

करेहु कल्प भरि राजु तुम्ह मोहि सुमिरेहु मन माहिं ।
karehu kalpa bhari rāju tumha mohi sumirehu mana māhiṁ,
पुनि मम धाम पाइहहु जहाँ संत सब जाहिं ॥ ११६घ॥
puni mama dhāma pāihahu jahām̐ saṁta saba jāhiṁ. 116(gha).

Trans:

"Hearken brother, all you say is true; your house and treasure are as my own; but thinking of Bharat's condition every moment seems to me as an age. In penitential attire, with emaciated body, he is ever repeating my name in prayer. I entreat you friend, to make an effort so that I may soon be able to see him again. If, on the other hand, I reach there on the expiry of the term of my exile, I do not expect to find my brother alive." And even as the Lord recalled his brother's affection he felt a thrill all over his body again and again. "As for yourself, you shall enjoy sovereignty till the end of creation, inwardly thinking of me all the time; and then you shall ascend to my abode, the final destination of all holy men."

चौपाई-caupāī:

सुनत बिभीषन बचन राम के । हरषि गहे पद कृपाधाम के ॥
sunata bibhīṣana bacana rāma ke, harași gahe pada kṛpādhāma ke.
बानर भालु सकल हरषाने । गहि प्रभु पद गुन बिमल बखाने ॥
bānara bhālu sakala haraṣāne, gahi prabhu pada guna bimala bakhāne.
बहुरि बिभीषन भवन सिधायो । मनि गन बसन बिमान भरायो ॥
bahuri bibhīṣana bhavana sidhāyo, mani gana basana bimāna bharāyo.
लै पुष्पक प्रभु आगें राखा । हँसि करि कृपासिंधु तब भाषा ॥
lai puṣpaka prabhu āgeṁ rākhā, haṁsi kari kṛpāsiṁdhu taba bhāṣā.
चढ़ि बिमान सुनु सखा बिभीषन । गगन जाइ बरषहु पट भूषन ॥
caṛhi bimāna sunu sakhā bibhīṣana, gagana jāi baraṣahu paṭa bhūṣana.
नभ पर जाइ बिभीषन तबही । बरषि दिए मनि अंबर सबही ॥
nabha para jāi bibhīṣana tabahī, baraṣi die mani aṁbara sabahī.

जोइ जोइ मन भावइ सोइ लेहीं । मनि मुख मेलि डारि कपि देहीं ॥
joi joi mana bhāvai soi lehīṁ, mani mukha meli ḍāri kapi dehīṁ.
हँसे रामु श्री अनुज समेता । परम कौतुकी कृपा निकेता ॥
haṁse rāmu śrī anuja sametā, parama kautukī kṛpā niketā.

Trans:

When Vibhīshan heard Rāma's words, he was overjoyed and clasped the feet of the All-merciful. All the bears and monkeys with equal joy clasped the Lord's feet and recited his glorious merits. Then Vibhīshan proceeded to the palace and loaded the chariot with jewels and attire. When he had brought the aerial car Pushpaka and set it before the Lord, the All-merciful smiled and said, "Hearken friend Vibhīshan: step into the car, and when you have risen high in the air, throw down the jewels and dresses." Accordingly Vibhīshan mounted aloft into the heaven and scrambled the raiment and jewels among them all. The monkeys picked up anything they fancied, cramming the precious thing into their mouth; while Rāma and his consort and his brother laughed; so full of playfulness is the All-merciful.

दोहा-dohā:

मुनि जेहि ध्यान न पावहिं नेति नेति कह बेद ।
muni jehi dhyāna na pāvahiṁ neti neti kaha beda,
कृपासिंधु सोइ कपिन्ह सन करत अनेक बिनोद ॥ ११७क॥
kṛpāsiṁdhu soi kapinha sana karata aneka binoda. 117(ka).

उमा जोग जप दान तप नाना मख ब्रत नेम ।
umā joga japa dāna tapa nānā makha brata nema,
राम कृपा नहिं करहिं तसि जसि निष्केवल प्रेम ॥ ११७ख॥
rāma kṛpā nahiṁ karahiṁ tasi jasi niṣkevala prema. 117(kha).

Trans:

He, to whom the saints cannot attain by contemplation, whom the Veda itself fails to fathom, even he in his infinite compassion made merry with the monkeys. O Umā, abstraction, prayer, charity, penance, the different forms of fasting, sacrifice, and vows—all move Rāma's compassion less than pure unadulterated love.

चौपाई-caupāī:

भालु कपिन्ह पट भूषन पाए । पहिरि पहिरि रघुपति पहिं आए ॥
bhālu kapinha paṭa bhūṣana pāe, pahiri pahiri raghupati pahiṁ āe.
नाना जिनस देखि सब कीसा । पुनि पुनि हँसत कोसलाधीसा ॥
nānā jinasa dekhi saba kīsā, puni puni haṁsata kosalādhīsā.
चितइ सबन्हि पर कीन्ही दाया । बोले मृदुल बचन रघुराया ॥
citai sabanhi para kīnhī dāyā, bole mṛdula bacana raghurāyā.
तुम्हरें बल मैं रावनु मारयो । तिलक बिभीषन कहँ पुनि सारयो ॥
tumhareṁ bala maiṁ rāvanu mārayo, tilaka bibhīṣana kahaṁ puni sārayo.
निज निज गृह अब तुम्ह सब जाहू । सुमिरेहु मोहि डरपहु जनि काहू ॥
nija nija gṛha aba tumha saba jāhū, sumirehu mohi ḍarapahu jani kāhū.
सुनत बचन प्रेमाकुल बानर । जोरि पानि बोले सब सादर ॥
sunata bacana premākula bānara, jori pāni bole saba sādara.
प्रभु जोइ कहहु तुम्हहि सब सोहा । हमरें होत बचन सुनि मोहा ॥
prabhu joi kahahu tumhahi saba sohā, hamareṁ hota bacana suni mohā.
दीन जानि कपि किए सनाथा । तुम्ह त्रैलोक ईस रघुनाथा ॥
dīna jāni kapi kie sanāthā, tumha trailoka īsa raghunāthā.
सुनि प्रभु बचन लाज हम मरहीं । मसक कहूँ खगपति हित करहीं ॥
suni prabhu bacana lāja hama marahīṁ, masaka kahūṁ khagapati hita karahīṁ.
देखि राम रुख बानर रीछा । प्रेम मगन नहिं गृह कै ईछा ॥
dekhi rāma rukha bānara rīchā, prema magana nahiṁ gṛha kai īchā.

Trans:

After securing the dresses and ornaments, the bears and monkeys clothed themselves with them and appeared before Rāma. The king of Kaushal laughed again and again to see the monkeys in their motley attire. As he looked upon them all, he was moved with pity, and said in gracious phrases, "It is by your assistance that I have killed Rāvan and thus secured the throne for Vibhīshan. Now return all of you to your several homes; remember me and fear no one." On hearing these words the monkeys were overcome with affection, and all with clasped hands thus reverently addressed him, "What you say, my Lord, is all to your honor; but we are confused on hearing such words. Knowing the low estate of us monkeys, you gave us such a leader: You yourself, O Raghunāth, the sovereign of the universe. When we hear our Lord's words we die of shame: is it possible for a gnat to assist the mighty Garud?" The monkeys were so charmed as they gazed on Rāma's face that in the depth of their devotion they had no desire for their own homes.

दोहा-dohā:

प्रभु प्रेरित कपि भालु सब राम रूप उर राखि ।
prabhu prerita kapi bhālu saba rāma rūpa ura rākhi,
हरष बिषाद सहित चले बिनय बिबिध बिधि भाषि ॥ ११८क॥
haraṣa biṣāda sahita cale binaya bibidha bidhi bhāṣi. 118(ka).

कपिपति नील रीछपति अंगद नल हनुमान ।
kapipati nīla rīchapati aṁgada nala hanumāna,
सहित बिभीषन अपर जे जूथप कपि बलवान ॥ ११८ख ॥
sahita bibhīṣana apara je jūthapa kapi balavāna. 118(kha).

कहि न सकहिं कछु प्रेम बस भरि भरि लोचन बारि ।
kahi na sakahiṁ kachu prema basa bhari bhari locana bāri,
सन्मुख चितवहिं राम तन नयन निमेष निवारि ॥ ११८ग॥
sanmukha citavahiṁ rāma tana nayana nimeṣa nivāri. 118(ga).

Trans:

When the Lord had dismissed them, the bears and monkeys all went their way, cherishing Rāma's image in their heart, exulting with joy and making frequent prayer. The monkey-king, Nīl, the king of the bears, Angad, Nala, Hanumān, Vibhīshan also, and all the other valiant monkey chiefs were so overcome by their feelings that they could not speak a word, while their eyes, streaming with tears, were fixed upon Rāma's person so intently that they had no time to wink.

चौपाई-caupāī:

अतिसय प्रीति देखि रघुराई । लीन्हे सकल बिमान चढ़ाई ॥
atisaya prīti dekhi raghurāī, līnhe sakala bimāna caṛhāī.
मन महुँ बिप्र चरन सिरु नायो । उत्तर दिसिहि बिमान चलायो ॥
mana mahuṁ bipra carana siru nāyo, uttara disihi bimāna calāyo.
चलत बिमान कोलाहल होई । जय रघुबीर कहइ सबु कोई ॥
calata bimāna kolāhala hoī, jaya raghubīra kahai sabu koī.
सिंहासन अति उच्च मनोहर । श्री समेत प्रभु बैठे ता पर ॥
siṁhāsana ati ucca manohara, śrī sameta prabhu baiṭhe tā para.
राजत रामु सहित भामिनी । मेरु सृंग जनु घन दामिनी ॥
rājata rāmu sahita bhāminī, meru sṛṁga janu ghana dāminī.
रुचिर बिमान चलेउ अति आतुर । कीन्ही सुमन बृष्टि हरषे सुर ॥
rucira bimāna caleu ati ātura, kīnhī sumana bṛṣṭi haraṣe sura.
परम सुखद चलि त्रिबिध बयारी । सागर सर सरि निर्मल बारी ॥
parama sukhada cali tribidha bayārī, sāgara sara sari nirmala bārī.
सगुन होहिं सुंदर चहुँ पासा । मन प्रसन्न निर्मल नभ आसा ॥
saguna hohiṁ suṁdara cahuṁ pāsā, mana prasanna nirmala nabha āsā.
कह रघुबीर देखु रन सीता । लछिमन इहाँ हत्यो इँद्रजीता ॥
kaha raghubīra dekhu rana sītā, lachimana ihāṁ hatyo iṁdrajītā.
हनूमान अंगद के मारे । रन महि परे निसाचर भारे ॥
hanūmāna aṁgada ke māre, rana mahi pare nisācara bhāre.

कुंभकरन रावन द्वौ भाई । इहाँ हते सुर मुनि दुखदाई ॥
kuṁbhakarana rāvana dvau bhāī, ihāṁ hate sura muni dukhadāī.

Trans:

When Rāma perceived the strength of their affection, he took them all up into his chariot, and after mentally bowing his head at the feet of Brahmins he directed the car towards the north. A tumultuous noise accompanied the car on its way, all shouting "Glory to Raghubīr!" The throne on which the Lord and his consort were seated was very lofty and magnificent; there Rāma and his bride shone resplendent, like a dark cloud on the peak of Sumeru with attendant lightning. The beauteous car sped swiftly on its way, while the gods in their joy rained down showers of flowers. A delightful breeze breathed soft, cool, and fragrant; the water of the ocean, lakes and streams became unsullied and transparent; omens of good fortune occurred on every side; the heart was glad and all the expanse of ether clear. Said Raghubīr, "See O Sītā, the field of battle: here Lakshman slew Meghnād; here the huge demons that strew the plain were slaughtered by Angad and Hanumān; here fell the two brothers Kumbh-karan and Rāvan, that plague of gods and saints.

दोहा-dohā:

इहाँ सेतु बाँध्यों अरु थापेउँ सिव सुख धाम ।
ihāṁ setu bāṁdhyoṁ aru thāpeuṁ siva sukha dhāma,
सीता सहित कृपानिधि संभुहि कीन्ह प्रनाम ॥ ११९क॥
sītā sahita kṛpānidhi saṁbhuhi kīnha pranāma. 119(ka).

जहँ जहँ कृपासिंधु बन कीन्ह बास बिश्राम ।
jahaṁ jahaṁ kṛpāsiṁdhu bana kīnha bāsa biśrāma,
सकल देखाए जानकिहि कहे सबन्हि के नाम ॥ ११९ख॥
sakala dekhāe jānakihi kahe sabanhi ke nāma. 119(kha).

Trans:

Here the bridge was built and the symbol of the blessed Mahādev adored." the All-merciful and Sītā here both made obeisance to Shambhu. Every place in the forest wherever the gracious god had taken up his abode or rested, he pointed out to Jānakī and told her the names of them all.

चौपाई-caupāī:

तुरत बिमान तहाँ चलि आवा । दंडक बन जहँ परम सुहावा ॥
turata bimāna tahāṁ cali āvā, daṁḍaka bana jahaṁ parama suhāvā.
कुंभजादि मुनिनायक नाना । गए रामु सब कें अस्थाना ॥
kuṁbhajādi munināyaka nānā, gae rāmu saba keṁ asthānā.
सकल रिषिन्ह सन पाइ असीसा । चित्रकूट आए जगदीसा ॥
sakala riṣinha sana pāi asīsā, citrakūṭa āe jagadīsā.
तहँ करि मुनिन्ह केर संतोषा । चला बिमानु तहाँ ते चोखा ॥
tahaṁ kari muninha kera saṁtoṣā, calā bimānu tahāṁ te cokhā.
बहुरि राम जानकिहि देखाई । जमुना कलि मल हरनि सुहाई ॥
bahuri rāma jānakihi dekhāī, jamunā kali mala harani suhāī.
पुनि देखी सुरसरी पुनीता । राम कहा प्रनाम करु सीता ॥
puni dekhī surasarī punītā, rāma kahā pranāma karu sītā.
तीरथपति पुनि देखु प्रयागा । निरखत जन्म कोटि अघ भागा ॥
tīrathapati puni dekhu prayāgā, nirakhata janma koṭi agha bhāgā.
देखु परम पावनि पुनि बेनी । हरनि सोक हरि लोक निसेनी ॥
dekhu parama pāvani puni benī, harani soka hari loka nisenī.
पुनि देखु अवधपुरी अति पावनि । त्रिबिध ताप भव रोग नसावनि ॥
puni dekhu avadhapurī ati pāvani, tribidha tāpa bhava roga nasāvani.

Trans:

Forthwith the chariot arrived at the charming Dandaka forest, and Rāma visited the hermitage both of Agastya and all the other great saints. After receiving the blessing of all the holy men, the Lord of the world came to Chitrakūt. After gratifying the hermits there, the chariot again sped swiftly on. Rāma next pointed out to Sītā the noble Yamunā, that carries away all the impurities of this sinful age. After this he espied the holy Gangā and said, "Sītā, do it homage. See also the king of all holy places, Prayāg, the sight of which puts away all the sins committed in a thousand births. See again the most holy Trivenī, the antidote of sorrow, the ladder of heaven. Now see the sacred city of Avadh, which heals all the three kinds of pain and every disease in life."

दोहा-dohā:

सीता सहित अवध कहुँ कीन्ह कृपाल प्रनाम ।
sītā sahita avadha kahuṁ kīnha kṛpāla pranāma,
सजल नयन तन पुलकित पुनि पुनि हरषित राम ॥ १२०क॥
sajala nayana tana pulakita puni puni haraṣita rāma. 120(ka).

पुनि प्रभु आइ त्रिबेनीं हरषित मज्जनु कीन्ह ।
puni prabhu āi tribenīṁ haraṣita majjanu kīnha,
कपिन्ह सहित बिप्रन्ह कहुँ दान बिबिध बिधि दीन्ह ॥ १२०ख॥
kapinha sahita bipranha kahuṁ dāna bibidha bidhi dīnha. 120(kha).

Trans:

The gracious God and Sītā both did reverence to Avadh. With streaming eyes and quivering limbs Rāma's joy was unbounded. Then came the Lord and with much delight bathed at Trivenī and bestowed gifts of all kinds on the Brahmins and the monkeys joined in that, as well.

चौपाई-caupāī:

प्रभु हनुमंतहि कहा बुझाई । धरि बटु रूप अवधपुर जाई ॥
prabhu hanumaṁtahi kahā bujhāī, dhari baṭu rūpa avadhapura jāī.
भरतहि कुसल हमारि सुनाएहु । समाचार लै तुम्ह चलि आएहु ॥
bharatahi kusala hamāri sunāehu, samācāra lai tumha cali āehu.
तुरत पवनसुत गवनत भयऊ । तब प्रभु भरद्वाज पहिं गयऊ ॥
turata pavanasuta gavanata bhayaū, taba prabhu bharadvāja pahiṁ gayaū.
नाना बिधि मुनि पूजा कीन्ही । अस्तुति करि पुनि आसिष दीन्ही ॥
nānā bidhi muni pūjā kīnhī, astuti kari puni āsiṣa dīnhī.
मुनि पद बंदि जुगल कर जोरी । चढ़ि बिमान प्रभु चले बहोरी ॥
muni pada baṁdi jugala kara jorī, caṛhi bimāna prabhu cale bahorī.
इहाँ निषाद सुना प्रभु आए । नाव नाव कहँ लोग बोलाए ॥
ihāṁ niṣāda sunā prabhu āe, nāva nāva kahaṁ loga bolāe.
सुरसरि नाघि जान तब आयो । उतरेउ तट प्रभु आयसु पायो ॥
surasari nāghi jāna taba āyo, utareu taṭa prabhu āyasu pāyo.
तब सीताँ पूजी सुरसरी । बहु प्रकार पुनि चरनन्हि परी ॥
taba sītāṁ pūjī surasarī, bahu prakāra puni carananhi parī.
दीन्हि असीस हरषि मन गंगा । सुंदरि तव अहिवात अभंगा ॥
dīnhi asīsa haraṣi mana gaṁgā, suṁdari tava ahivāta abhaṁgā.
सुनत गुहा धायउ प्रेमाकुल । आयउ निकट परम सुख संकुल ॥
sunata guhā dhāyau premākula, āyau nikaṭa parama sukha saṁkula.
प्रभुहि सहित बिलोकि बैदेही । परेउ अवनि तन सुधि नहिं तेही ॥
prabhuhi sahita biloki baidehī, pareu avani tana sudhi nahiṁ tehī.
प्रीति परम बिलोकि रघुराई । हरषि उठाइ लियो उर लाई ॥
prīti parama biloki raghurāī, haraṣi uṭhāi liyo ura lāī.

Trans:

The Lord spoke and enjoined Hanumān, "Take the form of a young student and go into the city. Tell Bharat of my welfare, and come back here yourself with the news." The son-of-wind was off at once. Then the Lord visited Bharadvāja. The saint received him with all possible honor, and after hymning his praises gave him his blessing. The Lord prostrated himself at his feet, with his hands clasped in prayer, and then mounted his chariot and went on again. When the Nishād heard that the Lord had come, he cried "a boat, a boat," and summoned his people. The chariot crossed the sacred stream and then stopped on the bank, obedient to the Lord's command.

Then Sītā worshipped the divine Gangā, and again and again threw herself at its feet. In gladness of soul the Gangā gave her this blessing: "Fair lady, may your happiness be without a break." On hearing the news, Guha ran in a transport of love and drew near, bewildered with excess of joy. At the sight of Sītā and the Lord, he fell flat upon the ground quite out of his senses. When Rāma perceived the intensity of his love, he was glad and raised him up and took him to his bosom.

छंद-chaṁda:

लियो हृदयँ लाइ कृपा निधान सुजान रायँ रमापती ।
liyo hṛdayaṁ lāi kṛpā nidhāna sujāna rāyaṁ ramāpatī,
बैठारि परम समीप बूझी कुसल सो कर बीनती ॥
baiṭhāri parama samīpa būjhī kusala so kara bīnatī.
अब कुसल पद पंकज बिलोकि बिरंचि संकर सेब्य जे ।
aba kusala pada paṁkaja biloki biraṁci saṁkara sebya je,
सुख धाम पूरनकाम राम नमामि राम नमामि ते ॥ १ ॥
sukha dhāma pūranakāma rāma namāmi rāma namāmi te. 1.

सब भाँति अधम निषाद सो हरि भरत ज्यों उर लाइयो ।
saba bhāṁti adhama niṣāda so hari bharata jyoṁ ura lāiyo,
मतिमंद तुलसीदास सो प्रभु मोह बस बिसराइयो ॥
matimaṁda tulasīdāsa so prabhu moha basa bisarāiyo.
यह रावनारि चरित्र पावन राम पद रतिप्रद सदा ।
yaha rāvanāri caritra pāvana rāma pada ratiprada sadā,
कामादिहर बिग्यानकर सुर सिद्ध मुनि गावहिं मुदा ॥ २ ॥
kāmādihara bigyānakara sura siddha muni gāvahiṁ mudā. 2.

Trans:

The All-merciful and All-wise Rāma, the spouse of Lakshmī, took and clasped him to the heart and seated him close by his side and asked of his welfare. He was all humility, "Now is all well with me, for I have seen thy lotus feet, the adoration of Brahmmā and Shankar; O Rāma, abode of bliss, fulfiller of desire, thee, thee alone do I worship." Though he was only a poor low Nishād, Harī clasped him to his bosom, as though he were Bharat himself. Dull of soul, says Tulsīdās, is he who is so infatuated as to forget such a Lord. Gods, saints and sages sing with delight these achievements of Rāvan's Destroyer, for they have a sanctifying effect, ever inspire devotion to Rāma's feet, destroy lust and other evil propensities, and they inculcate true wisdom.

दोहा-dohā:

समर बिजय रघुबीर के चरित जे सुनहिं सुजान ।
samara bijaya raghubīra ke carita je sunahiṁ sujāna,
बिजय बिबेक बिभूति नित तिन्हहि देहिं भगवान ॥ १२१क ॥
bijaya bibeka bibhūti nita tinhahi dehiṁ bhagavāna. 121(ka).

यह कलिकाल मलायतन मन करि देखु बिचार ।
yaha kalikāla malāyatana mana kari dekhu bicāra,
श्रीरघुनाथ नाम तजि नाहिन आन अधार ॥ १२१ख ॥
śrīraghunātha nāma taji nāhina āna adhāra. 121(kha).

Trans:

The Lord-God rewards for ever with victory, wisdom and renown, such people of good understanding—who listen to the achievements of Rāma and his victory in the battle. O my mind, this Kali-Yug is the very home of impurity; think well on it and understand: if you abandon the blessed name of Rāma, there is no other savior.

मासपारायण सत्ताईसवाँ विश्राम
māsapārāyaṇa sattāīsavāṁ viśrāma
(Pause 27 for a Thirty-Day Recitation)

इति श्रीमद्रामचरितमानसे सकलकलिकलुषविध्वंसने षष्ठः सोपानः समाप्तः

iti śrīmadrāmacaritamānase sakalakalikaluṣavidhvaṁsane ṣaṣṭhaḥ sopānaḥ samāptaḥ

(Now ends the Sixth-Ascent into the Manasa Lake of Shrī Rāma's Charita which eradicates all the impurities of the Kali-Yug)

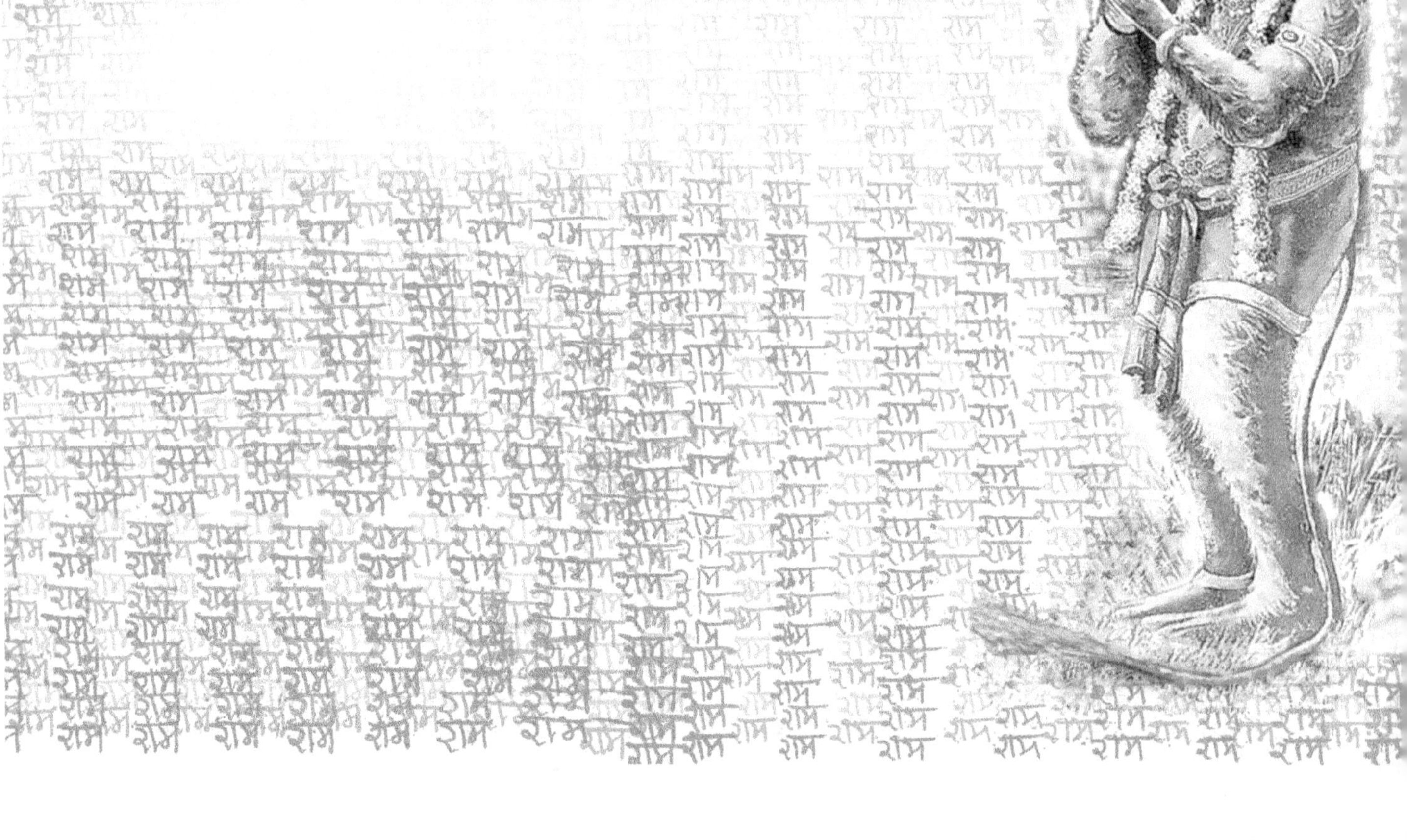

सीताराम सीताराम

ॐ

श्रीजानकीवल्लभो विजयते

śrījānakīvallabho vijayate

श्रीरामचरितमानस

śrīrāmacaritamānasa

सप्तम सोपान - उत्तरकाण्ड

saptama sopāna - uttarakāṇḍa

श्लोक-śloka:

केकीकण्ठाभनीलं सुरवरविलसद्विप्रपादाब्जचिह्नं

kekīkaṇṭhābhanīlaṁ suravaravilasadviprapādābjacihnaṁ

शोभाढ्यं पीतवस्त्रं सरसिजनयनं सर्वदा सुप्रसन्नम् ।

śobhāḍhyaṁ pītavastraṁ sarasijanayanaṁ sarvadā suprasannam,

पाणौ नाराचचापं कपिनिकरयुतं बन्धुना सेव्यमानं

pāṇau nārācacāpaṁ kapinikarayutaṁ bandhunā sevyamānaṁ

नौमीड्यं जानकीशं रघुवरमनिशं पुष्पकारूढरामम् ॥ १ ॥

naumīḍyaṁ jānakīśaṁ raghuvaramaniśaṁ puṣpakārūḍharāmam. 1.

Trans:

Unceasingly I adore Shrī Rāma: the glorious Lord of Sītā, the noblest descendent of Raghu, bright of hue as the neck of peacock; marked with the print of the Brahmin's lotus foot on his chest—proving him to be the highest; the ever gracious, all-beautiful, lotus-eyed; yellow-apparelled; with bow and arrows in his hand, attended by a host of monkeys and served by his brothers; seated on the aerial car Pushpak.

कोसलेन्द्रपदकञ्जमञ्जुलौ कोमलावजमहेशवन्दितौ ।

kosalendrapadakañjamañjulau komalāvajamaheśavanditau,

जानकीकरसरोजलालितौ चिन्तकस्य मनभृङ्गसङ्गिनौ ॥ २ ॥

jānakīkarasarojalālitau cintakasya manabhṛṅgasaḍginau. 2.

Trans:

Beautiful are the lotus feet of the Lord of Kaushal, worshipped by Brahmmā and Shiva, caressed by the tender hands of Jānakī, ever clustered about by the bee-like souls of the devout.

कुन्दइन्दुदरगौरसुन्दरं अम्बिकापतिमभीष्टसिद्धिदम् ।

kundaindudaragaurasundaraṁ ambikāpatimabhīṣṭasiddhidam,

कारुणीककलकञ्जलोचनं नौमि शङ्करमनङ्गमोचनम् ॥ ३ ॥

kāruṇīkakalakañjalocanaṁ naumi śaṅkaramanaṅgamocanam. 3.

Trans:

I worship Shankar, beautiful with the brightness of the jasmine and the moon and the conch-shell; Ambikā's Lord; the compassionate Lord of beautiful lotus eyes; bestower of every success; the annihilator of Lust.

दोहा-dohā:

रहा एक दिन अवधि कर अति आरत पुर लोग ।

rahā eka dina avadhi kara ati ārata pura loga,

जहँ तहँ सोचहिं नारि नर कृस तन राम बियोग ॥

jahaṁ tahaṁ socahiṁ nāri nara kṛsa tana rāma biyoga.

सगुन होहिं सुंदर सकल मन प्रसन्न सब केर ।

saguna hohiṁ suṁdara sakala mana prasanna saba kera,

प्रभु आगवन जनाव जनु नगर रम्य चहुँ फेर ॥

prabhu āgavana janāva janu nagara ramya cahuṁ phera.

कौसल्यादि मातु सब मन अनंद अस होइ ।

kausalyādi mātu saba mana anaṁda asa hoi,

आयउ प्रभु श्री अनुज जुत कहन चहत अब कोइ ॥

āyau prabhu śrī anuja juta kahana cahata aba koi.

भरत नयन भुज दच्छिन फरकत बारहिं बार ।

bharata nayana bhuja dacchina pharakata bārahiṁ bāra,

जानि सगुन मन हरष अति लागे करन बिचार ॥

jāni saguna mana haraṣa ati lāge karana bicāra.

Trans:

There remained only one day to the appointed term; and the people of the city, men and women alike, were sorely distressed in mind, and wasted in the body—in sorrow from Rāma's absence. Despondency reigned all about—when suddenly then auspicious omens of every kind occurred; and at once every heart was gladdened; and the city itself brightened up all around—as if to announce the coming of the Lord. Kausalyā and the other royal dames became all as happy as if any minute expecting to be told "the Lord is here, and with him Sītā and Lakshman." Bharat's right eye and arm throbbed again and again. Recognizing this as a good sign for men, he was glad at heart; and yet he began to ponder deeply once more.

चौपाई-caupāī:

रहेउ एक दिन अवधि अधारा । समुझत मन दुख भयउ अपारा ॥

raheu eka dina avadhi adhārā, samujhata mana dukha bhayau apārā.

कारन कवन नाथ नहिं आयउ । जानि कुटिल किधौं मोहि बिसरायउ ॥

kārana kavana nātha nahiṁ āyau, jāni kuṭila kidhauṁ mohi bisarāyau.

अहह धन्य लछिमन बड़भागी । राम पदारबिंदु अनुरागी ॥

ahaha dhanya lachimana baṛabhāgī, rāma padārabiṁdu anurāgī.

कपटी कुटिल मोहि प्रभु चीन्हा । ताते नाथ संग नहिं लीन्हा ॥

kapaṭī kuṭila mohi prabhu cīnhā, tāte nātha saṁga nahiṁ līnhā.

जौं करनी समुझै प्रभु मोरी । नहिं निस्तार कलप सत कोरी ॥

jauṁ karanī samujhai prabhu morī, nahiṁ nistāra kalapa sata korī.

जन अवगुन प्रभु मान न काऊ । दीन बंधु अति मृदुल सुभाऊ ॥

jana avaguna prabhu māna na kāū, dīna bamdhu ati mṛdula subhāū.

मोरे जियँ भरोस दृढ़ सोई । मिलिहहिं राम सगुन सुभ होई ॥

more jiyaṁ bharosa dṛṛha soī, milihahiṁ rāma saguna subha hoī.

बीतें अवधि रहहिं जौं प्राना । अधम कवन जग मोहि समाना ॥

bīteṁ avadhi rahahiṁ jauṁ prānā, adhama kavana jaga mohi samānā.

Trans:

"The one day that now remains to the fixed time is my only chance; as I ponder thereon, my soul becomes perturbed with anxiety. What is the reason that my Lord has not yet returned? My Lord-God saw my evil nature when he passed me over. Ah! how blessed and truly fortunate is Lakshman in his devotion to Rāma's lotus feet. The Lord knew me to be false and perverse, and therefore he did not take me with him. If the Lord were to consider my actions, there would be no redemption for me even in a hundred million ages. But the Lord never regards the offences of his servants—being most tender-hearted and the very brother to the destitutes. I am firmly persuaded in heart that Rāma will come; the omens are so favorable. But if my life holds out after the term once expires, then I shall be a more despicable wretch than any in the world."

दोहा-dohā:

राम बिरह सागर महँ भरत मगन मन होत ।

rāma biraha sāgara mahaṁ bharata magana mana hota,

बिप्र रूप धरि पवन सुत आइ गयउ जनु पोत ॥१क॥

bipra rūpa dhari pavana suta āi gayau janu pota. 1(ka).

बैठे देखि कुसासन जटा मुकुट कृस गात ।

baiṭhe dekhi kusāsana jaṭā mukuṭa kṛsa gāta,

राम राम रघुपति जपत स्रवत नयन जलजात ॥१ख॥

rāma rāma raghupati japata sravata nayana jalajāta. 1(kha).

Trans:

While Bharat's soul was thus immersed in the sea of Rāma's bereavement, the son-of-wind, disguised in the form of a Brahmin, came like a boat to the rescue. He saw him seated on a mat of sacred grass, with matted hair for a crown, his body all wasted away, his lips muttering the names "Rāma, Rāma, Raghupatī"; his eyes streaming with tears.

चौपाई-caupāī:

देखत हनूमान अति हरषेउ । पुलक गात लोचन जल बरषेउ ॥

dekhata hanūmāna ati haraṣeu, pulaka gāta locana jala baraṣeu.

मन महँ बहुत भाँति सुख मानी । बोलेउ श्रवन सुधा सम बानी ॥

mana mahaṁ bahuta bhāṁti sukha mānī, boleu śravana sudhā sama bānī.

जासु बिरहँ सोचहु दिन राती । रटहु निरंतर गुन गन पाँती ॥

jāsu birahaṁ socahu dina rātī, raṭahu niraṁtara guna gana pāṁtī.

रघुकुल तिलक सुजन सुखदाता । आयउ कुसल देव मुनि त्राता ॥

raghukula tilaka sujana sukhadātā, āyau kusala deva muni trātā.

रिपु रन जीति सुजस सुर गावत । सीता सहित अनुज प्रभु आवत ॥

ripu rana jīti sujasa sura gāvata, sītā sahita anuja prabhu āvata.

सुनत बचन बिसरे सब दूखा । तृषावंत जिमि पाइ पियूषा ॥

sunata bacana bisare saba dūkhā, tṛṣāvaṁta jimi pāi piyūṣā.

को तुम्ह तात कहाँ ते आए । मोहि परम प्रिय बचन सुनाए ॥

ko tumha tāta kahāṁ te āe, mohi parama priya bacana sunāe.

मारुत सुत मैं कपि हनुमाना । नामु मोर सुनु कृपानिधाना ॥

māruta suta maiṁ kapi hanumānā, nāmu mora sunu kṛpānidhānā.

दीनबंधु रघुपति कर किंकर । सुनत भरत भेंटेउ उठि सादर ॥

dīnabaṁdhu raghupati kara kiṁkara, sunata bharata bheṁṭeu uṭhi sādara.

मिलत प्रेम नहिं हृदयँ समाता । नयन स्रवत जल पुलकित गाता ॥

milata prema nahiṁ hṛdayaṁ samātā, nayana sravata jala pulakita gātā.

कपि तव दरस सकल दुख बीते । मिले आजु मोहि राम पिरीते ॥

kapi tava darasa sakala dukha bīte, mile āju mohi rāma pirīte.

बार बार बूझी कुसलाता । तो कहुँ देउँ काह सुनु भ्राता ॥

bāra bāra būjhī kusalātā, to kahuṁ deuṁ kāha sunu bhrātā.

एहि संदेस सरिस जग माहीं । करि बिचार देखेउँ कछु नाहीं ॥

ehi saṁdesa sarisa jaga māhīṁ, kari bicāra dekheuṁ kachu nāhīṁ.

नाहिन तात उरिन मैं तोही । अब प्रभु चरित सुनावहु मोही ॥

nāhina tāta urina maiṁ tohī, aba prabhu carita sunāvahu mohī.

तब हनुमंत नाइ पद माथा । कहे सकल रघुपति गुन गाथा ॥

taba hanumaṁta nāi pada māthā, kahe sakala raghupati guna gāthā.

कहु कपि कबहुँ कृपाल गोसाईं । सुमिरहिं मोहि दास की नाईं ॥

kahu kapi kabahuṁ kṛpāla gosāīṁ, sumirahiṁ mohi dāsa kī nāīṁ.

Trans:

At his sight Hanumān was in ecstasy; and every hair on his body bristled; and his eyes rained down torrents. He felt deeply gratified at heart to see such devotion; then addressing him in words that were as ambrosia to the ears he said, "He, for whose loss you sorrow night and day, the list of whose virtues you are incessantly reciting—the glory of the line of Raghu, the benefactor of the pious, the deliverer of gods and saints—has arrived safely. After conquering the foe in the battle, with the gods to hymn his praises, the Lord is now on his way with Sītā and his brother." On hearing these words Bharat forgot all his pain, like a man dying of thirst has found a stream of nectar, "Who are you, sir, and whence have you come, who have told me such glad tidings?" "I am the son-of-wind, a monkey, Hanumān by name, O fountain of mercy, a servant of the beneficent Raghupatī." On hearing this, Bharat rose and respectfully advanced to meet him. The affection with which he embraced him was too great for heart to contain; his eyes streamed with tears and his body quivered all over. "O monkey, at the sight of you all my sorrows are gone; today I have embraced a friend of Rāma's." Again and again he asked of his welfare, "Hearken brother: what is there that I can give you? After taking thought, I find nothing in the whole world to match this news; I am thus unable to repay my debt to you. Do please recount to me of the ways of my Lord; tell me all." Then Hanumān bowed his head at his feet and told him all Raghupatī's great doings. "Tell me, monkey, did the gracious God ever remember me as one of his servants?

छंद-chaṁda:

निज दास ज्यों रघुबंसभूषन कबहुँ मम सुमिरन करयो ।

nija dāsa jyoṁ raghubaṁsabhūṣana kabahuṁ mama sumirana karayo,

सुनि भरत बचन बिनीत अति कपि पुलकि तन चरनन्हि परयो ॥

suni bharata bacana binīta ati kapi pulaki tana carananhi parayo.

रघुबीर निज मुख जासु गुन गन कहत अग जग नाथ जो ।

raghubīra nija mukha jāsu guna gana kahata aga jaga nātha jo,

काहे न होइ बिनीत परम पुनीत सदगुन सिंधु सो ॥

kāhe na hoi binīta parama punīta sadaguna siṁdhu so.

Trans:

Did the glory of the race of Raghu ever make mention of me, his servant?" On hearing Bharat's modest speech, the monkey was in a rapture and fell at his feet. How can he be other than humble and holy and an ocean of virtue, whose praises Rāma, the Lord of all animate and inanimate creation, himself recites with his lips?

दोहा-dohā:

राम प्रान प्रिय नाथ तुम्ह सत्य बचन मम तात ।
rāma prāna priya nātha tumha satya bacana mama tāta,
पुनि पुनि मिलत भरत सुनि हरष न हृदयँ समात ॥२क॥
puni puni milata bharata suni haraṣa na hṛdayam̐ samāta. 2(ka).

Trans:

"My Lord, you are as dear to Rāma as his own life; that, sir, is the truth." Again and again he embraced Bharat, and his joy was more than his heart would contain.

सोरठा-soraṭhā:

भरत चरन सिरु नाइ तुरित गयउ कपि राम पहिं ।
bharata carana siru nāi turita gayau kapi rāma pahiṁ,
कही कुसल सब जाइ हरषि चलेउ प्रभु जान चढ़ि ॥२ख॥
kahī kusala saba jāi haraṣi caleu prabhu jāna caṛhi. 2(kha).

Trans:

After bowing his head at Bharat's feet, the monkey returned in haste to Rāma and told him that all was well. Then the Lord mounted his chariot and joyfully set forth.

चौपाई-caupāī:

हरषि भरत कोसलपुर आए । समाचार सब गुरहि सुनाए ॥
haraṣi bharata kosalapura āe, samācāra saba gurahi sunāe.
पुनि मंदिर महँ बात जनाई । आवत नगर कुसल रघुराई ॥
puni maṁdira maham̐ bāta janāī, āvata nagara kusala raghurāī.
सुनत सकल जननीं उठि धाईं । कहि प्रभु कुसल भरत समुझाईं ॥
sunata sakala jananīṁ uṭhi dhāīṁ, kahi prabhu kusala bharata samujhāīṁ.
समाचार पुरबासिन्ह पाए । नर अरु नारि हरषि सब धाए ॥
samācāra purabāsinha pāe, nara aru nāri haraṣi saba dhāe.
दधि दुर्बा रोचन फल फूला । नव तुलसी दल मंगल मूला ॥
dadhi durbā rocana phala phūlā, nava tulasī dala maṁgala mūlā.
भरि भरि हेम थार भामिनी । गावत चलिं सिंधुरगामिनी ॥
bhari bhari hema thāra bhāminī, gāvata caliṁ siṁdhuragāminī.
जे जैसेहिं तैसेहिं उठि धावहिं । बाल बृद्ध कहँ संग न लावहिं ॥
je jaisehiṁ taisehiṁ uṭhi dhāvahiṁ, bāla bṛddha kaham̐ saṁga na lāvahiṁ.
एक एकन्ह कहँ बूझहिं भाई । तुम्ह देखे दयाल रघुराई ॥
eka ekanha kaham̐ būjhahiṁ bhāī, tumha dekhe dayāla raghurāī.
अवधपुरी प्रभु आवत जानी । भई सकल सोभा कै खानी ॥
avadhapurī prabhu āvata jānī, bhaī sakala sobhā kai khānī.
बहइ सुहावन त्रिबिध समीरा । भइ सरजू अति निर्मल नीरा ॥
bahai suhāvana tribidha samīrā, bhai sarajū ati nirmala nīrā.

Trans:

Bharat too returned in joy to Ajodhyā and told his Gurū all the news, then spread the word in the palace that Rāma was approaching the city and was safe and sound. At these tidings all the dowager queens started up and ran in haste; but Bharat himself went to them to ease their minds and assure them of the Lord's welfare. When the citizens heard the news, men and women all ran out in their joy; the ladies formed in procession, with stately gait, singing and bearing golden salvers laden with curds, dub grass, the sacred yellow pigment, fruits and flowers and fresh sprigs of the Tulsī plant—each and every thing of good omen. Each ran out just as she happened to be, without stopping to bring either children or old folks. Everyone was asking his neighbor, "Friend, have you seen the gracious Rāma?" Forthwith it knew the Lord was coming, the whole city of Avadh became a quarry of delights. The water of the Sarjū flowed clear as clear could be; and the air was deliciously soft, cool and fragrant.

दोहा-dohā:

हरषित गुर परिजन अनुज भूसुर बृंद समेत ।
haraṣita gura parijana anuja bhūsura bṛṁda sameta,
चले भरत मन प्रेम अति सन्मुख कृपानिकेत ॥३क॥
cale bharata mana prema ati sanmukha kṛpāniketa. 3(ka).

बहुतक चढ़ीं अटारिन्ह निरखहिं गगन बिमान ।
bahutaka caṛhīṁ aṭārinha nirakhahiṁ gagana bimāna,
देखि मधुर सुर हरषित करहिं सुमंगल गान ॥३ख॥
dekhi madhura sura haraṣita karahiṁ sumaṁgala gāna. 3(kha).

राका ससि रघुपति पुर सिंधु देखि हरषान ।
rākā sasi raghupati pura siṁdhu dekhi haraṣāna,
बढ़यो कोलाहल करत जनु नारि तरंग समान ॥३ग॥
baṛhayo kolāhala karata janu nāri taraṁga samāna. 3(ga).

Trans:

Accompanied by his Gurū the citizens, his younger brother and a throng of Brahmins, Bharat went forth to meet the All-merciful, full of affection and joy. Many women mounted the upper stories of their homes to look for the chariot in the sky and, when they espied it, raised their sweet voices in auspicious songs of joy. As the waves of ocean rise and swell at the sight of the full moon, so poured forth the women of the city with a tumultuous sound at the sight of Rāma.

चौपाई-caupāī:

इहाँ भानुकुल कमल दिवाकर । कपिन्ह देखावत नगर मनोहर ॥
ihām̐ bhānukula kamala divākara, kapinha dekhāvata nagara manohara.
सुनु कपीस अंगद लंकेसा । पावन पुरी रुचिर यह देसा ॥
sunu kapīsa aṁgada laṁkesā, pāvana purī rucira yaha desā.
जद्यपि सब बैकुंठ बखाना । बेद पुरान बिदित जगु जाना ॥
jadyapi saba baikuṁṭha bakhānā, beda purāna bidita jagu jānā.
अवधपुरी सम प्रिय नहिं सोऊ । यह प्रसंग जानइ कोउ कोऊ ॥
avadhapurī sama priya nahiṁ soū, yaha prasaṁga jānai kou koū.
जन्मभूमि मम पुरी सुहावनि । उत्तर दिसि बह सरजू पावनि ॥
janmabhūmi mama purī suhāvani, uttara disi baha sarajū pāvani.
जा मज्जन ते बिनहिं प्रयासा । मम समीप नर पावहिं बासा ॥
jā majjana te binahiṁ prayāsā, mama samīpa nara pāvahiṁ bāsā.
अति प्रिय मोहि इहाँ के बासी । मम धामदा पुरी सुख रासी ॥
ati priya mohi ihām̐ ke bāsī, mama dhāmadā purī sukha rāsī.
हरषे सब कपि सुनि प्रभु बानी । धन्य अवध जो राम बखानी ॥
haraṣe saba kapi suni prabhu bānī, dhanya avadha jo rāma bakhānī.

Trans:

On the other hand the Sun of the lotuses of the solar race was pointing out the beauties of the city to the monkeys, "Hearken, Sugrīva, Angad and Vibhīshan; this city is so holy and the country so charming, that although all men speak of Vaikūnth, which is indeed famous in the Vedas and Purānas and celebrated throughout the world, still it is not so dear to me as the city of Avadh; only a rare soul knows of this secret. Here is the delightful city, my birth-place, and to the north the sacred Sarjū, where every man that bathes obtains, without further trouble, an abode near me. The dwellers here are very dear to me; the city makes them my fellow-citizens both here and hereafter and is altogether blessed." The monkeys rejoiced to hear the Lord's words, "What a glory for Avadh, to be thus praised by Rāma!"

दोहा-dohā:

आवत देखि लोग सब कृपासिंधु भगवान ।
āvata dekhi loga saba kṛpāsiṁdhu bhagavāna,
नगर निकट प्रभु प्रेरेउ उतरेउ भूमि बिमान ॥४क॥
nagara nikaṭa prabhu prereu utareu bhūmi bimāna. 4(ka).

उतरि कहेउ प्रभु पुष्पकहि तुम्ह कुबेर पहिं जाहु ।
utari kaheu prabhu puṣpakahi tumha kubera pahiṁ jāhu,
प्रेरित राम चलेउ सो हरषु बिरहु अति ताहु ॥४ख॥
prerita rāma caleu so haraṣu birahu ati tāhu. 4(kha).

Trans:

When the All-merciful Lord God saw all the people coming out to meet him, he willed the aerial chariot close to the city and there alighted on the ground. Having dismounted, he directed the aerial chariot Pushpak to return to Kuber. On receiving Rāma's order it went its way, full of mingled joy and sorrow at the parting.

चौपाई-caupāī:

आए भरत संग सब लोगा । कृस तन श्रीरघुबीर बियोगा ॥
āe bharata saṁga saba logā, kṛsa tana śrīraghubīra biyogā.
बामदेव बसिष्ट मुनिनायक । देखे प्रभु महि धरि धनु सायक ॥
bāmadeva basiṣṭa munināyaka, dekhe prabhu mahi dhari dhanu sāyaka.
धाइ धरे गुर चरन सरोरुह । अनुज सहित अति पुलक तनोरुह ॥
dhāi dhare gura carana saroruha, anuja sahita ati pulaka tanoruha.
भेंटि कुसल बूझी मुनिराया । हमरें कुसल तुम्हारिहिं दाया ॥
bheṁṭi kusala būjhī munirāyā, hamareṁ kusala tumhārihiṁ dāyā.
सकल द्विजन्ह मिलि नायउ माथा । धर्म धुरंधर रघुकुलनाथा ॥
sakala dvijanha mili nāyau māthā, dharma dhuraṁdhara raghukulanāthā.
गहे भरत पुनि प्रभु पद पंकज । नमत जिन्हहि सुर मुनि संकर अज ॥
gahe bharata puni prabhu pada paṁkaja, namata jinhahi sura muni saṁkara aja.
परे भूमि नहिं उठत उठाए । बर करि कृपासिंधु उर लाए ॥
pare bhūmi nahiṁ uṭhata uṭhāe, bara kari kṛpāsiṁdhu ura lāe.
स्यामल गात रोम भए ठाढ़े । नव राजीव नयन जल बाढ़े ॥
syāmala gāta roma bhae ṭhāṛhe, nava rājīva nayana jala bāṛhe.

Trans:

Along with Bharat came the whole population—all emaciated in body by their mourning for Rāma. When the Lord saw Vāmdev and Vasishtha, greatest of sages, he dropped his bow and arrows on the ground and ran to clasp the Gurū's lotus feet—both he and his younger brother, with every hair on their body abristle. The great sage embraced them and asked of their welfare. "By your favor all is well with us." Then the champion of the faith, the King of the Raghu race, made obeisance to all the Brahmins. Next Bharat embraced the Lord's lotus feet, ever worshipped by Shankar, Brahmmā and all the gods and sages. He fell to the ground and refused to rise, until the All-merciful forcibly took and pressed him to his bosom, every hair bristling on his dark-hued body, and his lotus eyes all streaming with tears.

छंद-chaṁda:

राजीव लोचन स्रवत जल तन ललित पुलकावलि बनी ।
rājīva locana sravata jala tana lalita pulakāvali banī,
अति प्रेम हृदयँ लगाइ अनुजहि मिले प्रभु त्रिभुअन धनी ॥
ati prema hṛdayaṁ lagāi anujahi mile prabhu tribhuana dhanī.
प्रभु मिलत अनुजहि सोह मो पहिं जाति नहिं उपमा कही ।
prabhu milata anujahi soha mo pahiṁ jāti nahiṁ upamā kahī,
जनु प्रेम अरु सिंगार तनु धरि मिले बर सुषमा लही ॥१॥
janu prema aru siṁgāra tanu dhari mile bara suṣamā lahī. 1.

Trans:

His lotus eyes streamed with tears and his beauteous body quivered with emotion, as he lovingly clasped Bharat to his heart, even he, the Lord, the sovereign of the three spheres. There is no similitude by which I can express the beauty of the meeting between the Lord and his brother; it was as though Love and Affection in bodily form had met together in a rapturous embrace.

बूझत कृपानिधि कुसल भरतहि बचन बेगि न आवई ।
būjhata kṛpānidhi kusala bharatahi bacana begi na āvaī,
सुनु सिवा सो सुख बचन मन ते भिन्न जान जो पावई ॥
sunu sivā so sukha bacana mana te bhinna jāna jo pāvaī.
अब कुसल कौसलनाथ आरत जानि जन दरसन दियो ।
aba kusala kausalanātha ārata jāni jana darasana diyo,
बूडत बिरह बारीस कृपानिधान मोहि कर गहि लियो ॥२॥
būṛata biraha bārīsa kṛpānidhāna mohi kara gahi liyo. 2.

Trans:

When the All-merciful asked of his welfare, it was with difficulty that Bharat found words to reply. Hearken O Umā: such joy can only be felt, it is beyond speech or intelligence. "Now is all well with me, O Lord of Kaushal. Seeing your servant's distress, you have revealed yourself to him. You have taken me by the hand, All-merciful, when I was sinking in the deep waters of bereavement."

दोहा-dohā:

पुनि प्रभु हरषि सत्रुहन भेंटे हृदयँ लगाइ ।
puni prabhu haraṣi satruhana bheṁṭe hṛdayaṁ lagāi,
लछिमन भरत मिले तब परम प्रेम दोउ भाइ ॥५॥
lachimana bharata mile taba parama prema dou bhāi. 5.

Trans:

Then the Lord smilingly embraced Shatrughan and took him to his bosom, while Bharat embraced Lakshman, his heart over-flowing with love.

चौपाई-caupāī:

भरतानुज लछिमन पुनि भेंटे । दुसह बिरह संभव दुख मेटे ॥
bharatānuja lachimana puni bheṁṭe, dusaha biraha saṁbhava dukha meṭe.
सीता चरन भरत सिरु नावा । अनुज समेत परम सुख पावा ॥
sītā carana bharata siru nāvā, anuja sameta parama sukha pāvā.
प्रभु बिलोकि हरषे पुरबासी । जनित बियोग बिपति सब नासी ॥
prabhu biloki haraṣe purabāsī, janita biyoga bipati saba nāsī.
प्रेमातुर सब लोग निहारी । कौतुक कीन्ह कृपाल खरारी ॥
premātura saba loga nihārī, kautuka kīnha kṛpāla kharārī.
अमित रूप प्रगटे तेहि काला । जथाजोग मिले सबहि कृपाला ॥
amita rūpa pragaṭe tehi kālā, jathājoga mile sabahi kṛpālā.
कृपादृष्टि रघुबीर बिलोकी । किए सकल नर नारि बिसोकी ॥
kṛpādṛṣṭi raghubīra bilokī, kie sakala nara nāri bisokī.
छन महिं सबहि मिले भगवाना । उमा मरम यह काहुँ न जाना ॥
chana mahiṁ sabahi mile bhagavānā, umā marama yaha kāhuṁ na jānā.
एहि बिधि सबहि सुखी करि रामा । आगें चले सील गुन धामा ॥
ehi bidhi sabahi sukhī kari rāmā, āgeṁ cale sīla guna dhāmā.
कौसल्यादि मातु सब धाई । निरखि बच्छ जनु धेनु लवाई ॥
kausalyādi mātu saba dhāī, nirakhi baccha janu dhenu lavāī.

Trans:

After that Shatrughan and Lakshman embraced, remembering no more the intolerable sorrow of separation. Finally Bharat bowed his head at Sītā's feet, both he and his younger brother, with an intensity of delight. The citizens were so glad at the sight of the Lord, that all the sorrow caused by his absence was at once forgotten. Seeing all the people so agitated by affection, the gracious Kharārī practiced an illusion; and appearing at one and the same time in multiplied form, he, in his benignity, brought off greeting everyone with due ceremony individually. The look of compassion, with which Raghubīr regarded them, made every man and woman supremely happy. In a single moment the God embraced them all; this, O Umā, is a mystery that none could comprehend. When Rāma, the perfection of amiability and every virtue, had in this manner made them all happy, he proceeded further. Kausalyā and the other royal dames ran out to meet him, like a cow that has lately calved, at the sight of its little one.

छंद-chaṁda:

जनु धेनु बालक बच्छ तजि गृहँ चरन बन परबस गईं ।
janu dhenu bālaka baccha taji gṛhaṁ carana bana parabasa gaīṁ,
दिन अंत पुर रुख स्रवत थन हुंकार करि धावत भईं ॥
dina aṁta pura rukha sravata thana huṁkāra kari dhāvata bhaīṁ.
अति प्रेम प्रभु सब मातु भेटीं बचन मृदु बहुबिधि कहे ।
ati prema prabhu saba mātu bheṭīṁ bacana mṛdu bahubidhi kahe,
गइ बिषम बिपति बियोग भव तिन्ह हरष सुख अगनित लहे ॥
gai biṣama bipati biyoga bhava tinha haraṣa sukha aganita lahe.

Trans:

Like a cow that has been made to graze in the woods forcibly—leaving its little ones at home—when it draws near to the village at the close of the day, hurries on lowing and with dripping teats—so did all the matrons hastened to embrace the Lord with the utmost affection, lavishing upon him every term of endearment. The cruel pangs of parting had passed away and were replaced by unutterable happiness and delight.

दोहा-dohā:

भेटेउ तनय सुमित्राँ राम चरन रति जानि ।
bheṭeu tanaya sumitrāṁ rāma carana rati jāni,
रामहि मिलत कैकई हृदयँ बहुत सकुचानि ॥ ६क॥
rāmahi milata kaikaī hṛdayaṁ bahuta sakucāni. 6(ka).

लछिमन सब मातन्ह मिलि हरषे आसिष पाइ ।
lachimana saba mātanha mili haraṣe āsiṣa pāi,
कैकइ कहुँ पुनि पुनि मिले मन कर छोभु न जाइ ॥ ६ख॥
kaikai kahaṁ puni puni mile mana kara chobhu na jāi. 6(kha).

Trans:

Sumitrā embraced her son, remembering his devotion to Rāma's feet; Kaekayī too embraced Rāma, but with a heart sadly ill at ease. Lakshman embraced the royal dames one and all and with joy received their blessing; but though he embraced Kaekayī again and again, some anguish of his soul still continued.

चौपाई-caupāī:

सासुन्ह सबनि मिली बैदेही । चरनन्हि लागि हरषु अति तेही ॥
sāsunha sabani milī baidehī, carananhi lāgi haraṣu ati tehī.
देहिं असीस बूझि कुसलाता । होइ अचल तुम्हार अहिवाता ॥
dehiṁ asīsa būjhi kusalātā, hoi acala tumhāra ahivātā.
सब रघुपति मुख कमल बिलोकहिं । मंगल जानि नयन जल रोकहिं ॥
saba raghupati mukha kamala bilokahiṁ, maṁgala jāni nayana jala rokahiṁ.
कनक थार आरति उतारहिं । बार बार प्रभु गात निहारहिं ॥
kanaka thāra ārati utārahiṁ, bāra bāra prabhu gāta nihārahiṁ.
नाना भाँति निछावरि करहीं । परमानंद हरष उर भरहीं ॥
nānā bhāṁti nichāvari karahīṁ, paramānaṁda haraṣa ura bharahīṁ.
कौसल्या पुनि पुनि रघुबीरहि । चितवति कृपासिंधु रनधीरहि ॥
kausalyā puni puni raghubīrahi, citavati kṛpāsiṁdhu ranadhīrahi.
हृदयँ बिचारति बारहिं बारा । कवन भाँति लंकापति मारा ॥
hṛdayaṁ bicārati bārahiṁ bārā, kavana bhāṁti laṁkāpati mārā.
अति सुकुमार जुगल मेरे बारे । निसिचर सुभट महाबल भारे ॥
ati sukumāra jugala mere bāre, nisicara subhaṭa mahābala bhāre.

Trans:

Sītā saluted each of her mothers-in-law and rejoiced greatly to clasp their feet. They asked of her welfare and invoked upon her the blessing, "May your happy wedded life last forever." All gazed on Raghupatī's lotus face and, out of regard for the auspiciousness of the day, checked the tears that welled in their eyes. They waved above his head their golden salvers and sacrificial lamps and again and again contemplated his divine persona. They scattered about him every kind of offering, their heart full of supreme felicity. Time after time Kausalyā fixed her gaze on Rāma—the ocean of compassion and irresistible warrior—and kept pondering within herself, "How can he have killed the king of Lankā? My two boys are so daintily delicate. Is it possible they can have slain the demon's doughtiest champions?"

दोहा-dohā:

लछिमन अरु सीता सहित प्रभुहि बिलोकति मातु ।
lachimana aru sītā sahita prabhuhi bilokati mātu,
परमानंद मगन मन पुनि पुनि पुलकित गातु ॥ ७॥
paramānaṁda magana mana puni puni pulakita gātu. 7.

Trans:

As she looked upon the Lord and upon Lakshman and Sītā, her maternal heart was overwhelmed with felicity and her every limb quivered with emotion.

चौपाई-caupāī:

लंकापति कपीस नल नीला । जामवंत अंगद सुभसीला ॥
laṁkāpati kapīsa nala nīlā, jāmavaṁta aṁgada subhasīlā.
हनुमदादि सब बानर बीरा । धरे मनोहर मनुज सरीरा ॥
hanumadādi saba bānara bīrā, dhare manohara manuja sarīrā.
भरत सनेह सील ब्रत नेमा । सादर सब बरनहिं अति प्रेमा ॥
bharata saneha sīla brata nemā, sādara saba baranahiṁ ati premā.
देखि नगरबासिन्ह कै रीती । सकल सराहहिं प्रभु पद प्रीती ॥
dekhi nagarabāsinha kai rītī, sakala sarāhahiṁ prabhu pada prītī.
पुनि रघुपति सब सखा बोलाए । मुनि पद लागहु सकल सिखाए ॥
puni raghupati saba sakhā bolāe, muni pada lāgahu sakala sikhāe.
गुर बसिष्ट कुलपूज्य हमारे । इन्ह की कृपाँ दनुज रन मारे ॥
gura basiṣṭa kulapūjya hamāre, inha kī kṛpāṁ danuja rana māre.
ए सब सखा सुनहु मुनि मेरे । भए समर सागर कहँ बेरे ॥
e saba sakhā sunahu muni mere, bhae samara sāgara kahaṁ bere.
मम हित लागि जन्म इन्ह हारे । भरतहु ते मोहि अधिक पिआरे ॥
mama hita lāgi janma inha hāre, bharatahu te mohi adhika piāre.
सुनि प्रभु बचन मगन सब भए । निमिष निमिष उपजत सुख नए ॥
suni prabhu bacana magana saba bhae, nimiṣa nimiṣa upajata sukha nae.

Trans:

Vibhīshan, Sugrīva, Nala and Nīl, Jāmvant and the generous Angad, with Hanumān and all the other monkey chiefs assumed beautiful human forms. With most reverent devotion, they applauded Bharat's loving disposition, his penance and his vow. When they saw the citizens' mode of life, they extolled them as well for their attachment to their Lord's feet. Then Rāma summoned all his comrades and bade them clasp the feet of the saint. "Gurū Vasishtha is highly reverenced by my entire race; it is by his favor that we slew the demons in the battle. And hearken holy sir: all these my comrades were the raft that bore me safely out of the waves of the battle. For my sake they staked their lives and they are more dear to me even than Bharat." On hearing the Lord's words, all were greatly overcome. Every moment gave birth to some new rapture.

दोहा-dohā:

कौसल्या के चरनन्हि पुनि तिन्ह नायउ माथ ।
kausalyā ke carananhi puni tinha nāyau mātha,
आसिष दीन्हे हरषि तुम्ह प्रिय मम जिमि रघुनाथ ॥८क॥
āsiṣa dīnhe harasi tumha priya mama jimi raghunātha. 8(ka).

सुमन बृष्टि नभ संकुल भवन चले सुखकंद ।
sumana bṛṣṭi nabha saṁkula bhavana cale sukhakaṁda,
चढ़ी अटारिन्ह देखहिं नगर नारि नर बृंद ॥८ख॥
caṛhī aṭārinha dekhahiṁ nagara nāri nara bṛṁda. 8(kha).

Trans:

Then they bowed their heads at Kausalyā's feet, who rejoiced to give them her blessing, saying "You are as dear to me as Rāma." The heaven was obscured with the showers of flowers as the Root of Joy made his way to the palace, even as throngs of men and women mounted their attics to see their Lord.

चौपाई-caupāī:

कंचन कलस बिचित्र सँवारे । सबहिं धरे सजि निज निज द्वारे ॥
kaṁcana kalasa bicitra saṁvāre, sabahiṁ dhare saji nija nija dvāre.
बंदनवार पताका केतू । सबन्हि बनाए मंगल हेतू ॥
baṁdanavāra patākā ketū, sabanhi banāe maṁgala hetū.
बीथीं सकल सुगंध सिंचाईं । गजमनि रचि बहु चौक पुराईं ॥
bīthīṁ sakala sugaṁdha siṁcāīṁ, gajamani raci bahu cauka purāīṁ.
नाना भाँति सुमंगल साजे । हरषि नगर निसान बहु बाजे ॥
nānā bhāṁti sumaṁgala sāje, harasi nagara nisāna bahu bāje.
जहँ तहँ नारि निछावरि करहीं । देहिं असीस हरष उर भरहीं ॥
jahaṁ tahaṁ nāri nichāvari karahīṁ, dehiṁ asīsa haraṣa ura bharahīṁ.
कंचन थार आरतीं नाना । जुबतीं सजें करहिं सुभ गाना ॥
kaṁcana thāra āratīṁ nānā, jubatīṁ sajeṁ karahiṁ subha gānā.
करहिं आरती आरतिहर कें । रघुकुल कमल बिपिन दिनकर कें ॥
karahiṁ āratī āratihara keṁ, raghukula kamala bipina dinakara keṁ.
पुर सोभा संपति कल्याना । निगम सेष सारदा बखाना ॥
pura sobhā saṁpati kalyānā, nigama seṣa sāradā bakhānā.
तेउ यह चरित देखि ठगि रहहीं । उमा तासु गुन नर किमि कहहीं ॥
teu yaha carita dekhi ṭhagi rahahīṁ, umā tāsu guna nara kimi kahahīṁ.

Trans:

They had made ready all kinds of golden bowls decorated and filled with various articles, which they set at their doors. They busied themselves with wreaths of flowers, flags and banners, all to make a glad show. The roads were all watered with perfumes, and innumerable charming squares were drawn and filled in with the finest pearls. Every kind of festive preparation was taken in hand; the city was en fete and all kinds of music were heard. In different places women scattered their offerings on his path, invoking blessings upon him with their hearts full of joy. Girls wave over his head their golden salvers and sacrificial lamps, singing sweetly the while; yes, salvers for him—who himself is the salve of every ill, the Sun to the lotus growth of Raghu's line. The beauty, the wealth, the magnificence of the city would be a theme for the Vedas, or Sheshnāg, or Shārdā; but the spectacle was too much even for them; how then can any man, O Umā, be able to describe that glory?

दोहा-dohā:

नारि कुमुदिनीं अवध सर रघुपति बिरह दिनेस ।
nāri kumudinīṁ avadha sara raghupati biraha dinesa,
अस्त भएँ बिगसत भईं निरखि राम राकेस ॥९क॥
asta bhaeṁ bigasata bhaīṁ nirakhi rāma rākesa. 9(ka).

होहिं सगुन सुभ बिबिध बिधि बाजहिं गगन निसान ।
hohiṁ saguna subha bibidha bidhi bājahiṁ gagana nisāna,
पुर नर नारि सनाथ करि भवन चले भगवान ॥९ख॥
pura nara nāri sanātha kari bhavana cale bhagavāna. 9(kha).

Trans:

Rāma's absence, like the heat of the sun, had withered the lily-like fair in the Avadh lake; at sunset they blossomed again, at the sight of the moon-god Rāma. Every conceivable auspicious omen occurred and music resounded in the sky, as the Lord God moved towards the palace, a father restored to his people, blessing all with his sight.

चौपाई-caupāī:

प्रभु जानी कैकई लजानी । प्रथम तासु गृह गए भवानी ॥
prabhu jānī kaikaī lajānī, prathama tāsu gṛha gae bhavānī.
ताहि प्रबोधि बहुत सुख दीन्हा । पुनि निज भवन गवन हरि कीन्हा ॥
tāhi prabodhi bahuta sukha dīnhā, puni nija bhavana gavana hari kīnhā.
कृपासिंधु जब मंदिर गए । पुर नर नारि सुखी सब भए ॥
kṛpāsiṁdhu jaba maṁdira gae, pura nara nāri sukhī saba bhae.
गुर बसिष्ट द्विज लिए बुलाई । आजु सुघरी सुदिन समुदाई ॥
gura basiṣṭa dvija lie bulāī, āju sugharī sudina samudāī.
सब द्विज देहु हरषि अनुसासन । रामचंद्र बैठहिं सिंघासन ॥
saba dvija dehu harasi anusāsana, rāmacaṁdra baiṭhahiṁ siṁghāsana.
मुनि बसिष्ट के बचन सुहाए । सुनत सकल बिप्रन्ह अति भाए ॥
muni basiṣṭa ke bacana suhāe, sunata sakala bipranha ati bhāe.
कहहिं बचन मृदु बिप्र अनेका । जग अभिराम राम अभिषेका ॥
kahahiṁ bacana mṛdu bipra anekā, jaga abhirāma rāma abhiṣekā.
अब मुनिबर बिलंब नहिं कीजै । महाराज कहँ तिलक करीजै ॥
aba munibara bilaṁba nahiṁ kījai, mahārāja kahaṁ tilaka karījai.

Trans:

Listen Bhawānī, the Lord knew Kaekayī was ashamed and went to her house first. After comforting her and putting her thoroughly at ease, Harī went on to his own apartments. The All-merciful entered the palace, and every man and woman in the city was happy once more. The Gurū Vasishtha then called the Brahmins, "The day and the hour are now most auspicious; give the glad order, all ye Brahmins, that Rāmachandra today take his seat upon the throne." On hearing Vasishtha's gracious address, the Brahmins were all highly pleased, and the multitudes spoke in endearing terms, "Rāma's inauguration is the desire of the whole world. Now, best of saints, make no delay, but mark the king with the sign of sovereignty."

दोहा-dohā:

तब मुनि कहेउ सुमंत्र सन सुनत चलेउ हरषाइ ।
taba muni kaheu sumaṁtra sana sunata caleu harasāi,
रथ अनेक बहु बाजि गज तुरत सँवारे जाइ ॥१०क॥
ratha aneka bahu bāji gaja turata saṁvāre jāi. 10(ka).

जहँ तहँ धावन पठइ पुनि मंगल द्रब्य मगाइ ।
jahaṁ tahaṁ dhāvana paṭhai puni maṁgala drabya magāi,
हरष समेत बसिष्ट पद पुनि सिरु नायउ आइ ॥ १०ख॥
haraṣa sameta basiṣṭa pada puni siru nāyau āi. 10(kha).

Trans:

The saint thereupon ordered Sumant, who no sooner heard, than went with joy and quickly got ready a multitude of chariots, elephants and horses. Then he dispatched messengers in every direction to acquire stores of all good things, and lastly himself came joyfully and bowed his head at Vasishtha's feet.

नवाह्नपारायण आठवाँ विश्राम
navāhnapārāyaṇa āṭhavāṁ viśrāma
(Pause 8 for a Nine-Day Recitation)

चौपाई-caupāī:

अवधपुरी अति रुचिर बनाई । देवन्ह सुमन बृष्टि झरि लाई ॥
avadhapurī ati rucira banāī, devanha sumana bṛṣṭi jhari lāī.
राम कहा सेवकन्ह बुलाई । प्रथम सखन्ह अन्हवावहु जाई ॥
rāma kahā sevakanha bulāī, prathama sakhanha anhavāvahu jāī.
सुनत बचन जहँ तहँ जन धाए । सुग्रीवादि तुरत अन्हवाए ॥
sunata bacana jahaṁ tahaṁ jana dhāe, sugrīvādi turata anhavāe.
पुनि करुनानिधि भरतु हँकारे । निज कर राम जटा निरुआरे ॥
puni karunānidhi bharatu haṁkāre, nija kara rāma jaṭā niruāre.
अन्हवाए प्रभु तीनिउ भाई । भगत बछल कृपाल रघुराई ॥
anhavāe prabhu tīniu bhāī, bhagata bachala kṛpāla raghurāī.
भरत भाग्य प्रभु कोमलताई । सेष कोटि सत सकहिं न गाई ॥
bharata bhāgya prabhu komalatāī, seṣa koṭi sata sakahiṁ na gāī.
पुनि निज जटा राम बिबराए । गुर अनुसासन मागि नहाए ॥
puni nija jaṭā rāma bibarāe, gura anusāsana māgi nahāe.
करि मज्जन प्रभु भूषन साजे । अंग अनंग देखि सत लाजे ॥
kari majjana prabhu bhūṣana sāje, aṁga anaṁga dekhi sata lāje.

Trans:

The city of Avadh was most elegantly decorated; the gods rained down a continuous shower of flowers. Rāma called and directed his servants, "Go first and assist my comrades at their bath." On receiving this order, his people ran in every direction and quickly bathed Sugrīva and the rest. Next the all-merciful Rāma summoned Bharat and with his own hands untied his knotted coil of hair; the Lord then proceeded to bathe all his three brothers—even he, the gracious Raghurāī, the cherisher of all pious souls. The blessedness of Bharat, and the Lord's tenderness—not a hundred myriads of Sheshnāgs would be able to declare. Finally Rāma unloosed his own matted hair and, after receiving the Gurū's permission, himself bathed. After his bath the Lord put on his ornaments; the beauty of his every limb outshining a myriad Loves.

दोहा-dohā:

सासुन्ह सादर जानकिहि मज्जन तुरत कराइ ।
sāsunha sādara jānakihi majjana turata karāi,
दिब्य बसन बर भूषन अँग अँग सजे बनाइ ॥ ११क॥
dibya basana bara bhūṣana aṁga aṁga saje banāi. 11(ka).

राम बाम दिसि सोभति रमा रूप गुन खानि ।
rāma bāma disi sobhati ramā rūpa guna khāni,
देखि मातु सब हरषीं जन्म सुफल निज जानि ॥ ११ख॥
dekhi mātu saba haraṣīṁ janma suphala nija jāni. 11(kha).

सुनु खगेस तेहि अवसर ब्रह्मा सिव मुनि बृंद ।
sunu khagesa tehi avasara brahmā siva muni bṛṁda,
चढ़ि बिमान आए सब सुर देखन सुखकंद ॥ ११ग॥
caṛhi bimāna āe saba sura dekhana sukhakaṁda. 11(ga).

Trans:

Forthwith Jānakī was attended in the bath with all reverence by her mothers-in-law, who attired her in heavenly apparel with rich jewels for every part of her body. She shone forth on Rāma's left side as the goddess Lakshmī herself, full of beauty and goodness. The royal dames were all overjoyed at the sight and thought their life had been well worth living. Hearken O Garud: upon this occasion Brahmmā, Shiva, and multitudes of sages came to see the Fountain of joy and so did all the gods, mounted on their aerial chariots.

चौपाई-caupāī:

प्रभु बिलोकि मुनि मन अनुरागा । तुरत दिब्य सिंघासन मागा ॥
prabhu biloki muni mana anurāgā, turata dibya siṁghāsana māgā.
रबि सम तेज सो बरनि न जाई । बैठे राम द्विजन्ह सिरु नाई ॥
rabi sama teja so barani na jāī, baiṭhe rāma dvijanha siru nāī.
जनकसुता समेत रघुराई । पेखि प्रहरषे मुनि समुदाई ॥
janakasutā sameta raghurāī, pekhi praharaṣe muni samudāī.
बेद मंत्र तब द्विजन्ह उचारे । नभ सुर मुनि जय जयति पुकारे ॥
beda maṁtra taba dvijanha ucāre, nabha sura muni jaya jayati pukāre.
प्रथम तिलक बसिष्ट मुनि कीन्हा । पुनि सब बिप्रन्ह आयसु दीन्हा ॥
prathama tilaka basiṣṭa muni kīnhā, puni saba bipranha āyasu dīnhā.
सुत बिलोकि हरषीं महतारी । बार बार आरती उतारी ॥
suta biloki haraṣīṁ mahatārī, bāra bāra āratī utārī.
बिप्रन्ह दान बिबिधि बिधि दीन्हे । जाचक सकल अजाचक कीन्हे ॥
bipranha dāna bibidhi bidhi dīnhe, jācaka sakala ajācaka kīnhe.
सिंघासन पर त्रिभुअन साईं । देखि सुरन्ह दुंदुभीं बजाईं ॥
siṁghāsana para tribhuana sāīṁ, dekhi suranha duṁdubhīṁ bajāīṁ.

Trans:

The soul of sage Vasishtha was enraptured as he gazed upon the Lord. He sent at once for a gorgeous throne. Then Rāma took his seat, after bowing his head to the Brahmins, his glory effulgent as the Sun, defying description. As they looked upon Rāma and Sītā, the whole saintly throng was overjoyed. Then the Brahmins repeated their Vedic incantations; while in the heaven above, the gods and saints shouted "Victory-Victory." The sage Vasishtha first himself made the *Tilak* and then ordered the other Brahmins to do the same. His mother rejoiced as she looked upon her son and again and again waved the sacrificial lamp above his head. All kinds of presents were made to the Brahmins and not a seeker remained with a want unsatisfied. At that sight of the Lord of three spheres seated on his throne, the gods beat their kettle-drums.

छंद-chaṁda:

नभ दुंदुभीं बाजहिं बिपुल गंधर्ब किंनर गावहीं ।
nabha duṁdubhīṁ bājahiṁ bipula gaṁdharba kiṁnara gāvahīṁ,
नाचहिं अपछरा बृंद परमानंद सुर मुनि पावहीं ॥
nācahiṁ apacharā bṛṁda paramānaṁda sura muni pāvahīṁ.
भरतादि अनुज बिभीषनांगद हनुमदादि समेत ते ।
bharatādi anuja bibhīṣanāṁgada hanumadādi sameta te,
गहें छत्र चामर ब्यजन धनु असि चर्म सक्ति बिराजते ॥ १॥
gaheṁ chatra cāmara byajana dhanu asi carma sakti birājate. 1.

श्री सहित दिनकर बंस भूषन काम बहु छबि सोहई ।
śrī sahita dinakara baṁsa bhūṣana kāma bahu chabi sohaī,

नव अंबुधर बर गात अंबर पीत सुर मन मोहई ॥
nava aṁbudhara bara gāta aṁbara pīta sura mana mohaī.
मुकुटांगदादि बिचित्र भूषन अंग अंगन्हि प्रति सजे ।
mukuṭāṁgadādi bicitra bhūṣana aṁga aṁganhi prati saje,
अंभोज नयन बिसाल उर भुज धन्य नर निरखंति जे ॥२॥
aṁbhoja nayana bisāla ura bhuja dhanya nara nirakhaṁti je. 2.

Trans:

Drums sounded in the sky, the hosts of Gandharvs and Kinnars sang and the nymphs of heaven danced before the enraptured assembly of gods and saints. Bharat, Lakshman, Shatrughan, with Vibhīshan, Angad, Hanumān and the rest, were there to be seen, each holding severally the umbrellas and chauries and fans and bows, swords, shields and spears. With Sītā by his side, the Glory of the Solar race outshone the beauty of unnumbered Loves; the soul of the gods was fascinated by his exquisite cloud-dark form clad in yellow apparel, and his diadem and bracelets and other marvelous ornaments which bedecked his limbs, and his lotus eyes and stalwart chest and arms—a blessed vision indeed for those so fortunate as to behold.

दोहा-dohā:

वह सोभा समाज सुख कहत न बनइ खगेस ।
vaha sobhā samāja sukha kahata na banai khagesa,
बरनहिं सारद सेष श्रुति सो रस जान महेस ॥१२क॥
baranahiṁ sārada seṣa śruti so rasa jāna mahesa. 12(ka).

भिन्न भिन्न अस्तुति करि गए सुर निज निज धाम ।
bhinna bhinna astuti kari gae sura nija nija dhāma,
बंदी बेष बेद तब आए जहँ श्रीराम ॥१२ख॥
baṁdī beṣa beda taba āe jahaṁ śrīrāma. 12(kha).

प्रभु सर्बग्य कीन्ह अति आदर कृपानिधान ।
prabhu sarbagya kīnha ati ādara kṛpānidhāna,
लखेउ न काहूँ मरम कछु लगे करन गुन गान ॥१२ग॥
lakheu na kāhūṁ marama kachu lage karana guna gāna. 12(ga).

Trans:

The magnificence of the sight and the delight of the assembly are past all telling, O Garud; Saraswatī, Sheshnāg and the Veda may tell it in part, but only Mahādev has learnt all the sweetness of it. After they had all severally hymned his praises, the gods departed, each to his own sphere. Then came the Vedas, in the guise of bards, into the presence of the divine Rāma. The omniscient and compassionate Lord received them with all honor, nor did anyone penetrate the mystery as they thus recited his panegyric:

छंद-chaṁda:

जय सगुन निर्गुन रूप रूप अनूप भूप सिरोमने ।
jaya saguna nirguna rūpa rūpa anūpa bhūpa siromane,
दसकंधरादि प्रचंड निसिचर प्रबल खल भुज बल हने ॥
dasakaṁdharādi pracaṁḍa nisicara prabala khala bhuja bala hane.
अवतार नर संसार भार बिभंजि दारुन दुख दहे ।
avatāra nara saṁsāra bhāra bibhaṁji dāruna dukha dahe,
जय प्रनतपाल दयाल प्रभु संजुक्त सक्ति नमामहे ॥१॥
jaya pranatapāla dayāla prabhu saṁjukta sakti namāmahe. 1.
तव बिषम माया बस सुरासुर नाग नर अग जग हरे ।
tava biṣama māyā basa surāsura nāga nara aga jaga hare,
भव पंथ भ्रमत अमित दिवस निसि काल कर्म गुननि भरे ॥
bhava paṁtha bhramata amita divasa nisi kāla karma gunani bhare.
जे नाथ करि करुना बिलोके त्रिबिधि दुख ते निर्बहे ।
je nātha kari karunā biloke tribidhi dukha te nirbahe,
भव खेद छेदन दच्छ हम कहुँ रच्छ राम नमामहे ॥२॥
bhava kheda chedana daccha hama kahuṁ raccha rāma namāmahe. 2.
जे ग्यान मान बिमत्त तव भव हरनि भक्ति न आदरी ।
je gyāna māna bimatta tava bhava harani bhakti na ādarī,
ते पाइ सुर दुर्लभ पदादपि परत हम देखत हरी ॥
te pāi sura durlabha padādapi parata hama dekhata harī.
बिस्वास करि सब आस परिहरि दास तव जे होइ रहे ।
bisvāsa kari saba āsa parihari dāsa tava je hoi rahe,
जपि नाम तव बिनु श्रम तरहिं भव नाथ सो समरामहे ॥३॥
japi nāma tava binu śrama tarahiṁ bhava nātha so samarāmahe. 3.
जे चरन सिव अज पूज्य रज सुभ परसि मुनिपतिनी तरी ।
je carana siva aja pūjya raja subha parasi munipatinī tarī,
नख निर्गता मुनि बंदिता त्रैलोक पावनि सुरसरी ॥
nakha nirgatā muni baṁditā trailoka pāvani surasarī.
ध्वज कुलिस अंकुस कंज जुत बन फिरत कंटक किन लहे ।
dhvaja kulisa aṁkusa kaṁja juta bana phirata kaṁṭaka kina lahe,
पद कंज द्वंद मुकुंद राम रमेस नित्य भजामहे ॥४॥
pada kaṁja dvaṁda mukuṁda rāma ramesa nitya bhajāmahe. 4.
अब्यक्तमूलमनादि तरु त्वच चारि निगमागम भने ।
abyaktamūlamanādi taru tvaca cāri nigamāgama bhane,
षट कंध साखा पंच बीस अनेक पर्न सुमन घने ॥
ṣaṭa kaṁdha sākhā paṁca bīsa aneka parna sumana ghane.
फल जुगल बिधि कटु मधुर बेलि अकेलि जेहि आश्रित रहे ।
phala jugala bidhi kaṭu madhura beli akeli jehi āśrita rahe,
पल्लवत फूलत नवल नित संसार बिटप नमामहे ॥५॥
pallavata phūlata navala nita saṁsāra biṭapa namāmahe. 5.
जे ब्रह्म अजमद्वैतमनुभवगम्य मनपर ध्यावहीं ।
je brahma ajamadvaitamanubhavagamya manapara dhyāvahīṁ,
ते कहहुँ जानहुँ नाथ हम तव सगुन जस नित गावहीं ॥
te kahahuṁ jānahuṁ nātha hama tava saguna jasa nita gāvahīṁ.
करुनायतन प्रभु सदगुनाकर देव यह बर मागहीं ।
karunāyatana prabhu sadagunākara deva yaha bara māgahīṁ,
मन बचन कर्म बिकार तजि तव चरन हम अनुरागहीं ॥६॥
mana bacana karma bikāra taji tava carana hama anurāgahīṁ. 6.

Trans:

"Hail, visible manifestation of the invisible, incomparable in thy beauty, jewel of kings, who, by the might of thy arm, hast slain Rāvan and the other terrible demons monsters of iniquity. Hail the Lord-God who, incarnate as a human, hast relieved the burdens of the earth, and put an end to her grievous affliction; hail, protector of the suppliant, Lord of compassion, thee we worship, and with thee thy spouse. O Harī, gods and demons, Nagas, men, and all creation, animate and inanimate, have been overcome by thy marvelous delusive power, wearily wandering night and day in the paths of worldly existence, full of the mysteries of fate and wants. If there be any, O Lord, whom thou regardest with compassion, they at once are freed from all their troubles; so prompt to cut short the weariness of existence; have mercy upon us, O Rāma, we implore thee. They, O Harī, who, intoxicated with the pride of learning, respect not the Devotion to you—which takes away the fear of transmigration—might attain to a high rank which even the gods scarce secure, and yet we see them eventually fall from it. They who confidently abandon every other hope and continue thy disciples, by repeating thy name, cross the ocean of life without any difficulty—this is the

Lord whom we invoke. O Mukund, Rāma, spouse of Lakshmī, we ever adore thy lotus feet, object of the worship of Shiva and Brahmmā; by touching the dust of which the sage's wife obtained salvation; from beneath the nails of which flows the Gangā, reverenced by the saints, sanctifier of the three spheres; feet that bear the marks of the flag, the thunderbolt, the elephant-goad and the lotus—and yet sorely pierced by the thorns during thy wanderings in the forest. We adore the uncreated tree, whose root is the primordial germ; whose bark is fourfold, as the Vedas and Purānas declare; whose boughs are six in number and the branchlets twenty-five; with innumerable leaves and abundant flowers; whose fruits are of two kinds: bitter and sweet; with a single creeper ever clinging to it; full of buds and blossoms and fruit, the everlasting tree of creation. Let them preach in their wisdom, who contemplates thee, as the Supreme Spirit, the Uncreated, the Inseparable from the universe, recognizable only by inference and beyond the understanding; but we, O Lord, will ever hymn the glories of thy incarnation. O merciful Lord God, mine of every perfection, this is the boon we ask: that in thought, word and deed and without any variableness we may maintain a devotion to thy holy feet."

दोहा-dohā:

सब के देखत बेदन्ह बिनती कीन्हि उदार ।
saba ke dekhata bedanha binatī kīnhi udāra,
अंतर्धान भए पुनि गए ब्रह्म आगार ॥ १३क ॥
aṁtardhāna bhae puni gae brahma āgāra. 13(ka).

बैनतेय सुनु संभु तब आए जहँ रघुबीर ।
bainateya sunu saṁbhu taba āe jahaṁ raghubīra,
बिनय करत गदगद गिरा पूरित पुलक सरीर ॥ १३ख ॥
binaya karata gadagada girā pūrita pulaka sarīra. 13(kha).

Trans:

When, in the sight of all, the Vedas had uttered this glorious prayer, they became invisible and returned to their home with Brahmmā. Hearken O Garud; then came Shambhu to Raghubīr and with a choking voice and every hair on his body abristle, he made this supplication:

छंद-chaṁda:

जय राम रमारमनं समनं । भव ताप भयाकुल पाहि जनं ॥
jaya rāma ramāramanaṁ samanaṁ, bhava tāpa bhayākula pāhi janaṁ.
अवधेस सुरेस रमेस बिभो । सरनागत मागत पाहि प्रभो ॥ १ ॥
avadhesa suresa ramesa bibho, saranāgata māgata pāhi prabho. 1.
दससीस बिनासन बीस भुजा । कृत दूरि महा महि भूरि रुजा ॥
dasasīsa bināsana bīsa bhujā, kṛta dūri mahā mahi bhūri rujā.
रजनीचर बृंद पतंग रहे । सर पावक तेज प्रचंड दहे ॥ २ ॥
rajanīcara bṛṁda pataṁga rahe, sara pāvaka teja pracaṁḍa dahe. 2.
महि मंडल मंडन चारुतरं । धृत सायक चाप निषंग बरं ॥
mahi maṁḍala maṁḍana cārutaraṁ, dhṛta sāyaka cāpa niṣaṁga baraṁ.
मद मोह महा ममता रजनी । तम पुंज दिवाकर तेज अनी ॥ ३ ॥
mada moha mahā mamatā rajanī, tama puṁja divākara teja anī. 3.
मनजात किरात निपात किए । मृग लोग कुभोग सरेन हिए ॥
manajāta kirāta nipāta kie, mṛga loga kubhoga sarena hie.
हति नाथ अनाथनि पाहि हरे । बिषया बन पावँर भूलि परे ॥ ४ ॥
hati nātha anāthani pāhi hare, biṣayā bana pāvaṁra bhūli pare. 4.
बहु रोग बियोगन्हि लोग हए । भवदंघ्रि निरादर के फल ए ॥
bahu roga biyoganhi loga hae, bhavadaṁghri nirādara ke phala e.
भव सिंधु अगाध परे नर ते । पद पंकज प्रेम न जे करते ॥ ५ ॥
bhava siṁdhu agādha pare nara te, pada paṁkaja prema na je karate. 5.
अति दीन मलीन दुखी नितहीं । जिन्ह कें पद पंकज प्रीति नहीं ॥
ati dīna malīna dukhī nitahīṁ, jinha keṁ pada paṁkaja prīti nahīṁ.
अवलंब भवंत कथा जिन्ह कें । प्रिय संत अनंत सदा तिन्ह कें ॥ ६ ॥
avalaṁba bhavaṁta kathā jinha keṁ. priya saṁta anaṁta sadā tinha keṁ. 6.
नहिं राग न लोभ न मान मदा । तिन्ह कें सम बैभव वा बिपदा ॥
nahiṁ rāga na lobha na māna madā. tinha keṁ sama baibhava vā bipadā.
एहि ते तव सेवक होत मुदा । मुनि त्यागत जोग भरोस सदा ॥ ७ ॥
ehi te tava sevaka hota mudā, muni tyāgata joga bharosa sadā. 7.
करि प्रेम निरंतर नेम लिएँ । पद पंकज सेवत सुद्ध हिएँ ॥
kari prema niraṁtara nema lieṁ, pada paṁkaja sevata suddha hieṁ.
सम मानि निरादर आदरही । सब संत सुखी बिचरंति मही ॥ ८ ॥
sama māni nirādara ādarahī, saba saṁta sukhī bicaraṁti mahī. 8.
मुनि मानस पंकज भृंग भजे । रघुबीर महा रनधीर अजे ॥
muni mānasa paṁkaja bhṛṁga bhaje, raghubīra mahā ranadhīra aje.
तव नाम जपामि नमामि हरी । भव रोग महागद मान अरी ॥ ९ ॥
tava nāma japāmi namāmi harī, bhava roga mahāgada māna arī. 9.
गुन सील कृपा परमायतनं । प्रनमामि निरंतर श्रीरमनं ॥
guna sīla kṛpā paramāyatanaṁ, pranamāmi niraṁtara śrīramanaṁ.
रघुनंद निकंदय द्वंद्वघनं । महिपाल बिलोकय दीनजनं ॥ १० ॥
raghunaṁda nikaṁdaya dvaṁdvaghanaṁ, mahipāla bilokaya dīnajanaṁ. 10.

Trans:

"Hail to thee, Rāma, the spouse of Lakshmī, the pacifier; have mercy on thy servant, harassed with the terrors and troubles of existence. Glorious Lord, sovereign of Avadh, sovereign of heaven, Lakshmī's sovereign, have mercy upon the suppliant, who has fled to thee for refuge. Destroyer of the ten-headed and twenty-armed, remover of earth's sore burden, consumer of the moth-like demon host in the fierce flame of thy fiery arrows; most beauteous ornament of the terrestrial sphere; noblest of all that wield bow, arrows and quiver; radiant as the Sun to disperse the thick darkness of the night of pride, ignorance and egoism; thou hast vanquished the God of Love, who, like a huntsman, had smitten all men to the heart with the arrows of evil desire, as though they were a herd of deer. Now, O Lord Harī, have mercy on us destitute wretches, who have gone astray in the wilderness of sensuality. The many diseases and bereavements, with which the people are stricken, are the yield of their disregard for thy holy feet. The bottomless ocean of existence overwhelms all who cherish no love for thy lotus feet. Poor indeed and vile and wretched forever are they, who have no affection for thy lotus feet. They who take delight in making mention of thy name, have the saints as their constant friends forever, are eternally exempt from passion, greed and arrogance, and regard prosperity and adversity as both alike. Thus it is that thy servants are so happy; the saint abandons forever all confidence in mortification and making simply a vow of perpetual love, serves thy lotus feet with a pure heart. O Raghubīr, mighty and invincible hero, indwelling as a bee in the lotus-like soul of the saints, thy name, O Harī, I repeat in prayer and adore, destroyer of vanity and pride, which are the diseases of life. Humbly I adore without ceasing the spouse of Lakshmī, the supreme abode of goodness, generosity and compassion. O son of Raghu, extirpate every duality from my life; O king of earth, cast a glance on thy humble servant.

दोहा-dohā:

बार बार बर मागउँ हरषि देहु श्रीरंग ।
bāra bāra bara māgauṁ haraṣi dehu śrīraṁga,
पद सरोज अनपायनी भगति सदा सतसंग ॥ १४क ॥
pada saroja anapāyanī bhagati sadā satasaṁga. 14(ka).

बरनि उमापति राम गुन हरषि गए कैलास ।
barani umāpati rāma guna haraṣi gae kailāsa,
तब प्रभु कपिन्ह दिवाए सब बिधि सुखप्रद बास ॥ १४ख॥
taba prabhu kapinha divāe saba bidhi sukhaprada bāsa. 14(kha).

Trans:

Again and again I beg of thee a boon, be gracious and grant it O Shrirang: an unwavering faith in thy lotus feet and a constant communion with saints." After thus hymning Rāma's praises, Shiva returned with joy to Kailāsh. Then the Lord assigned the monkeys the most delightful residences there.

चौपाई-caupāī:

सुनु खगपति यह कथा पावनी । त्रिबिध ताप भव भय दावनी ॥
sunu khagapati yaha kathā pāvanī, tribidha tāpa bhava bhaya dāvanī.
महाराज कर सुभ अभिषेका । सुनत लहहिं नर बिरति बिबेका ॥
mahārāja kara subha abhiṣekā, sunata lahahiṁ nara birati bibekā.
जे सकाम नर सुनहिं जे गावहिं । सुख संपति नाना बिधि पावहिं ॥
je sakāma nara sunahiṁ je gāvahiṁ, sukha saṁpati nānā bidhi pāvahiṁ.
सुर दुर्लभ सुख करि जग माहीं । अंतकाल रघुपति पुर जाहीं ॥
sura durlabha sukha kari jaga māhīṁ, aṁtakāla raghupati pura jāhīṁ.
सुनहिं बिमुक्त बिरत अरु बिषई । लहहिं भगति गति संपति नई ॥
sunahiṁ bimukta birata aru biṣaī, lahahiṁ bhagati gati saṁpati naī.
खगपति राम कथा मैं बरनी । स्वमति बिलास त्रास दुख हरनी ॥
khagapati rāma kathā maiṁ baranī, svamati bilāsa trāsa dukha haranī.
बिरति बिबेक भगति दृढ़ करनी । मोह नदी कहँ सुंदर तरनी ॥
birati bibeka bhagati dṛṛha karanī, moha nadī kahaṁ suṁdara taranī.
नित नव मंगल कौसलपुरी । हरषित रहहिं लोग सब कुरी ॥
nita nava maṁgala kausalapurī, haraṣita rahahiṁ loga saba kurī.
नित नइ प्रीति राम पद पंकज । सब कें जिन्हहि नमत सिव मुनि अज ॥
nita nai prīti rāma pada paṁkaja, saba keṁ jinhahi namata siva muni aja.
मंगन बहु प्रकार पहिराए । द्विजन्ह दान नाना बिधि पाए ॥
maṁgana bahu prakāra pahirāe, dvijanha dāna nānā bidhi pāe.

Trans:

Hearken O Garud; this sacred legend annihilates all the distresses and sins of the world. Anyone who hears this narrative of the royal installation obtains dispassion and discernment. Those with desires, who lovingly sing it, or hear it sung, obtain every kind of happiness and prosperity; and after enjoying in this world a bliss, to which the gods can scarce attain, they are admitted after death into Rāma's own presence. When the liberated soul, the detached from the world, and the worldly, hear it—they obtain respectively: faith, absorption into the divinity, and an ever-increasing prosperity. O Garud, this history of Rāma, that I have repeated, is the delight of a good understanding, a remedy for anxiety and sorrow, a confirmation of detachment, discretion and faith, a splendid raft on which to cross the river of delusion. In the city of Kaushal there ever were some new delights; the people were all happy from the highest to the lowest. All felt an ever growing affection for Rāma's lotus feet—the adored of Brahmmā, Shiva and the saints. Mendicants had clothes given them in abundance and the Brahmins were presented with offerings of every description.

दोहा-dohā:

ब्रह्मानंद मगन कपि सब कें प्रभु पद प्रीति ।
brahmānaṁda magana kapi saba keṁ prabhu pada prīti,
जात न जाने दिवस तिन्ह गए मास षट बीति ॥ १५॥
jāta na jāne divasa tinha gae māsa ṣaṭa bīti. 15.

Trans:

The monkeys were drowned in a joy like that of heaven; all were devoted to the Lord's feet; days and nights passed unnoticed till now six months had been spent.

चौपाई-caupāī:

बिसरे गृह सपनेहुँ सुधि नाहीं । जिमि परद्रोह संत मन माहीं ॥
bisare gṛha sapanehuṁ sudhi nāhīṁ, jimi paradroha saṁta mana māhīṁ.
तब रघुपति सब सखा बोलाए । आइ सबन्हि सादर सिरु नाए ॥
taba raghupati saba sakhā bolāe, āi sabanhi sādara siru nāe.
परम प्रीति समीप बैठारे । भगत सुखद मृदु बचन उचारे ॥
parama prīti samīpa baiṭhāre, bhagata sukhada mṛdu bacana ucāre.
तुम्ह अति कीन्हि मोरि सेवकाई । मुख पर केहि बिधि करौं बड़ाई ॥
tumha ati kīnhi mori sevakāī, mukha para kehi bidhi karauṁ baṛāī.
ताते मोहि तुम्ह अति प्रिय लागे । मम हित लागि भवन सुख त्यागे ॥
tāte mohi tumha ati priya lāge, mama hita lāgi bhavana sukha tyāge.
अनुज राज संपति बैदेही । देह गेह परिवार सनेही ॥
anuja rāja saṁpati baidehī, deha geha parivāra sanehī.
सब मम प्रिय नहिं तुम्हहि समाना । मृषा न कहउँ मोर यह बाना ॥
saba mama priya nahiṁ tumhahi samānā, mṛṣā na kahauṁ mora yaha bānā.
सब कें प्रिय सेवक यह नीती । मोरें अधिक दास पर प्रीती ॥
saba keṁ priya sevaka yaha nītī, moreṁ adhika dāsa para prītī.

Trans:

They had forgotten their homes so absolutely as never even to dream of them, like as the idea of injuring another never enters the soul of a saint. One day Raghupatī summoned all his comrades before him. They came and made reverent obeisance. He seated them by his side with the greatest kindness and thus addressed them in gracious terms, which might well gladden their pious souls, "You have done me excellent service; but how can I praise you to your face? I hold you all most dear, for having left the comforts of your home solely on my account. My younger brother, my crown, my fortune, my wife, my life, my home and loving kinsmen are none of them so dear in my sight as you are. I tell you no falsehood; these are my real sentiments. It is the ordinary rule for a man to cherish his own adherents, but I have a special affection for my servants.

दोहा-dohā:

अब गृह जाहु सखा सब भजेहु मोहि दृढ़ नेम ।
aba gṛha jāhu sakhā saba bhajehu mohi dṛṛha nema,
सदा सर्बगत सर्बहित जानि करेहु अति प्रेम ॥ १६॥
sadā sarbagata sarbahita jāni karehu ati prema. 16.

Trans:

Now, my comrades, return to your homes; there worship me with steadfast faith and maintain your fervent devotion, knowing me to be the eternal and omnipresent benefactor of the universe."

चौपाई-caupāī:

सुनि प्रभु बचन मगन सब भए । को हम कहाँ बिसरि तन गए ॥
suni prabhu bacana magana saba bhae, ko hama kahāṁ bisari tana gae.
एकटक रहे जोरि कर आगे । सकहिं न कछु कहि अति अनुरागे ॥
ekaṭaka rahe jori kara āge, sakahiṁ na kachu kahi ati anurāge.
परम प्रेम तिन्ह कर प्रभु देखा । कहा बिबिधि बिधि ग्यान बिसेषा ॥
parama prema tinha kara prabhu dekhā, kahā bibidhi bidhi gyāna biseṣā.
प्रभु सन्मुख कछु कहन न पारहिं । पुनि पुनि चरन सरोज निहारहिं ॥
prabhu sanmukha kachu kahana na pārahiṁ, puni puni carana saroja nihārahiṁ.
तब प्रभु भूषन बसन मगाए । नाना रंग अनूप सुहाए ॥
taba prabhu bhūṣana basana magāe, nānā raṁga anūpa suhāe.
सुग्रीवहि प्रथमहिं पहिराए । बसन भरत निज हाथ बनाए ॥
sugrīvahi prathamahiṁ pahirāe, basana bharata nija hātha banāe.
प्रभु प्रेरित लछिमन पहिराए । लंकापति रघुपति मन भाए ॥
prabhu prerita lachimana pahirāe, laṁkāpati raghupati mana bhāe.

अंगद बैठ रहा नहिं डोला । प्रीति देखि प्रभु ताहि न बोला ॥
aṁgada baiṭha rahā nahiṁ ḍolā, prīti dekhi prabhu tāhi na bolā.

Trans:

When they heard the Lord's words, all were so overcome that they forgot who they were, or where they were, or where they had come from. With clasped hands and fixed gaze they stood before him, unable to speak from excess of devotion. The Lord perceived the intensity of their love and said all he could to teach them resignation. In his presence they could not answer a word, but still turned their eyes to his lotus feet. Then the Lord called for jewels and robes of honor, of different colors, incomparably beautiful; and first Bharat with his own hands made ready a dress with which he invested Sugrīva. By the Lord's command Lakshman next invested the king of Lankā, to Rāma's great contentment. But Angad remained seated and did not stir. Seeing his love, the Lord did not ask him;

दोहा-dohā:

जामवंत नीलादि सब पहिराए रघुनाथ ।
jāmavaṁta nīlādi saba pahirāe raghunātha,
हियँ धरि राम रूप सब चले नाइ पद माथ ॥ १७क॥
hiyaṁ dhari rāma rūpa saba cale nāi pada mātha. 17(ka).

तब अंगद उठि नाइ सिरु सजल नयन कर जोरि ।
taba aṁgada uṭhi nāi siru sajala nayana kara jori,
अति बिनीत बोलेउ बचन मनहुँ प्रेम रस बोरि ॥ १७ख॥
ati binīta boleu bacana manahuṁ prema rasa bori. 17(kha).

Trans:

but proceeded with the investiture of Jāmvant and Nīl and the rest, who with Rāma's image impressed upon their heart, after bowing their head at his feet, withdrew. Then Angad arose and made obeisance and with weeping eyes and clasped hands uttered his humble petition, steeped as it was with the very essence of devotion:

चौपाई-caupāī:

सुनु सर्बग्य कृपा सुख सिंधो । दीन दयाकर आरत बंधो ॥
sunu sarbagya kṛpā sukha siṁdho, dīna dayākara ārata baṁdho.
मरती बेर नाथ मोहि बाली । गयउ तुम्हारेहि कोंछें घाली ॥
maratī bera nātha mohi bālī, gayau tumhārehi koṁcheṁ ghālī.
असरन सरन बिरदु संभारी । मोहि जनि तजहु भगत हितकारी ॥
asarana sarana biradu saṁbhārī, mohi jani tajahu bhagata hitakārī.
मोरें तुम्ह प्रभु गुर पितु माता । जाउँ कहाँ तजि पद जलजाता ॥
moreṁ tumha prabhu gura pitu mātā, jāuṁ kahāṁ taji pada jalajātā.
तुम्हहि बिचारि कहहु नरनाहा । प्रभु तजि भवन काज मम काहा ॥
tumhahi bicāri kahahu naranāhā, prabhu taji bhavana kāja mama kāhā.
बालक ग्यान बुद्धि बल हीना । राखहु सरन नाथ जन दीना ॥
bālaka gyāna buddhi bala hīnā, rākhahu sarana nātha jana dīnā.
नीचि टहल गृह कै सब करिहउँ । पद पंकज बिलोकि भव तरिहउँ ॥
nīci ṭahala gṛha kai saba karihauṁ, pada paṁkaja biloki bhava tarihauṁ.
अस कहि चरन परेउ प्रभु पाही । अब जनि नाथ कहहु गृह जाही ॥
asa kahi carana pareu prabhu pāhī, aba jani nātha kahahu gṛha jāhī.

Trans:

"Hearken, all-wise, all-merciful and all-blessed, commiserator of the destitute, succour of the distressed; Bālī, in his last moments, placed me in your charge, my Lord. To be the helper of the helpless is the character you support; O benefactor of the faithful, do not abandon me. You, sire, are my spiritual guide, my father and my mother; where can I go, if I leave your lotus feet? Consider yourself and tell me, O king of men: apart from my Lord, what is my home to me? Extend to me your protection, a mere child as I am without knowledge, wisdom, or strength, and regard me as one of the humblest of your servants. Let me perform the most menial office in your palace, if only I may see your lotus feet and thus traverse the ocean of existence." So saying, he fell at the Lord's feet, "O sire, do not again tell me to go home."

दोहा-dohā:

अंगद बचन बिनीत सुनि रघुपति करुना सींव ।
aṁgada bacana binīta suni raghupati karunā sīṁva,
प्रभु उठाइ उर लायउ सजल नयन राजीव ॥ १८क॥
prabhu uṭhāi ura lāyau sajala nayana rājīva. 18(ka).

निज उर माल बसन मनि बालितनय पहिराइ ।
nija ura māla basana mani bālitanaya pahirāi,
बिदा कीन्हि भगवान तब बहु प्रकार समुझाइ ॥ १८ख॥
bidā kīnhi bhagavāna taba bahu prakāra samujhāi. 18(kha).

Trans:

On hearing Angad's piteous prayer, the all-merciful Lord Rāma raised him from the ground and clasped him to his bosom, his lotus eyes streaming with tears. He clothed the son of Bālī in his own robe and jewels and the chain from his own neck, and then the Lord dismissed him with many words of consolation.

चौपाई-caupāī:

भरत अनुज सौमित्रि समेता । पठवन चले भगत कृत चेता ॥
bharata anuja saumitri sametā, paṭhavana cale bhagata kṛta cetā.
अंगद हृदयँ प्रेम नहिं थोरा । फिरि फिरि चितव राम कीं ओरा ॥
aṁgada hṛdayaṁ prema nahiṁ thorā, phiri phiri citava rāma kīṁ orā.
बार बार कर दंड प्रनामा । मन अस रहन कहहिं मोहि रामा ॥
bāra bāra kara daṁḍa pranāmā, mana asa rahana kahahiṁ mohi rāmā.
राम बिलोकनि बोलनि चलनी । सुमिरि सुमिरि सोचत हँसि मिलनी ॥
rāma bilokani bolani calanī, sumiri sumiri socata haṁsi milanī.
प्रभु रुख देखि बिनय बहु भाषी । चलेउ हृदयँ पद पंकज राखी ॥
prabhu rukha dekhi binaya bahu bhāṣī, caleu hṛdayaṁ pada paṁkaja rākhī.
अति आदर सब कपि पहुँचाए । भाइन्ह सहित भरत पुनि आए ॥
ati ādara saba kapi pahuṁcāe, bhāinha sahita bharata puni āe.
तब सुग्रीव चरन गहि नाना । भाँति बिनय कीन्हे हनुमाना ॥
taba sugrīva carana gahi nānā, bhāṁti binaya kīnhe hanumānā.
दिन दस करि रघुपति पद सेवा । पुनि तव चरन देखिहउँ देवा ॥
dina dasa kari raghupati pada sevā, puni tava carana dekhihauṁ devā.
पुन्य पुंज तुम्ह पवनकुमारा । सेवहु जाइ कृपा आगारा ॥
punya puṁja tumha pavanakumārā, sevahu jāi kṛpā āgārā.
अस कहि कपि सब चले तुरंता । अंगद कहइ सुनहु हनुमंता ॥
asa kahi kapi saba cale turaṁtā, aṁgada kahai sunahu hanumaṁtā.

Trans:

Bharat with his brother Shatrughan and Lakshman proceeded to escort him, being greatly moved by his devotion. But Angad's heart was so overflowing with love that he turned again and again for one more look at Rāma. Time after time he prostrated himself upon the ground, crying, "Thus would I stay, if Rāma would only let me." Treasuring up in his mind Rāma's look and voice and gait, his smile too, and his embrace—with a last glance at his face and many words of fervent prayer, he went forth, cherishing his lotus feet in his heart. After escorting all the monkeys with the utmost respect, Bharat and his brothers returned. Then Hanumān clasped Sugrīva by the feet and earnestly besought him, "Let me spend ten days more in Rāma's service and then I will return to your feet, my master." "O Son-of-wind, great is your piety; go, serve the All-merciful." So saying, the other monkeys went their way, but Angad cried: "Hearken Hanumān:

दोहा-dohā:

कहेहु दंडवत प्रभु सैं तुम्हहि कहउँ कर जोरि ।
kahehu daṁḍavata prabhu saiṁ tumhahi kahauṁ kara jori,
बार बार रघुनायकहि सुरति कराएहु मोरि ॥ १९क॥
bāra bāra raghunāyakahi surati karāehu mori. 19(ka).

अस कहि चलेउ बालिसुत फिरि आयउ हनुमंत ।
asa kahi caleu bālisuta phiri āyau hanumaṁta,
तासु प्रीति प्रभु सन कहि मगन भए भगवंत ॥ १९ख॥
tāsu prīti prabhu sana kahi magana bhae bhagavaṁta. 19(kha).

कुलिसहु चाहि कठोर अति कोमल कुसुमहु चाहि ।
kulisahu cāhi kaṭhora ati komala kusumahu cāhi,
चित्त खगेस राम कर समुझि परइ कहु काहि ॥ १९ग॥
citta khagesa rāma kara samujhi parai kahu kāhi. 19(ga).

Trans:

with clasped hands I beg of you to present my service to the Lord and frequently remind him of me." So saying, the son of Bālī started on his way, while Hanumān returned and told the Lord of his devotion; the great god was overjoyed. Now hard as adamant, now soft as the petal of a flower, such, Garud, is Rāma's heart; now who can comprehend it?

चौपाई-caupāī:

पुनि कृपाल लियो बोलि निषादा । दीन्हे भूषन बसन प्रसादा ॥
puni kṛpāla liyo boli niṣādā, dīnhe bhūṣana basana prasādā.
जाहु भवन मम सुमिरन करेहू । मन क्रम बचन धर्म अनुसरेहू ॥
jāhu bhavana mama sumirana karehū, mana krama bacana dharma anusarehū.
तुम्ह मम सखा भरत सम भ्राता । सदा रहेहु पुर आवत जाता ॥
tumha mama sakhā bharata sama bhrātā, sadā rahehu pura āvata jātā.
बचन सुनत उपजा सुख भारी । परेउ चरन भरि लोचन बारी ॥
bacana sunata upajā sukha bhārī, pareu carana bhari locana bārī.
चरन नलिन उर धरि गृह आवा । प्रभु सुभाउ परिजनन्हि सुनावा ॥
carana nalina ura dhari gṛha āvā, prabhu subhāu parijananhi sunāvā.
रघुपति चरित देखि पुरबासी । पुनि पुनि कहहिं धन्य सुखरासी ॥
raghupati carita dekhi purabāsī, puni puni kahahiṁ dhanya sukharāsī.
राम राज बैठें त्रैलोका । हरषित भए गए सब सोका ॥
rāma rāja baiṭheṁ trailokā, haraṣita bhae gae saba sokā.
बयरु न कर काहू सन कोई । राम प्रताप बिषमता खोई ॥
bayaru na kara kāhū sana koī, rāma pratāpa biṣamatā khoī.

Trans:

Next the All-merciful summoned the Nishād and graciously presented him with jewels and raiment. "Return to your home, but ever remember me and in heart, word and deed observe all the ordinance of religion. You, my companion, are as much my brother as Bharat; you must continue to visit the capital every now and then." On hearing these words he was greatly delighted and fell at his feet, his eyes full of tears. With the image of his lotus feet impressed upon his heart, he returned home and declared the Lord's generosity to all his kinsfolk. Witnessing the deeds of Shrī Rāma the citizens repeatedly said, "Blessed is the All-blissful Lord!" Under Rāma's sway the three spheres were full of joy, all sorrow was at end; no one bore enmity against another. All disharmony was obliterated under Rāma's auspices.

दोहा-dohā:

बरनाश्रम निज निज धरम निरत बेद पथ लोग ।
baranāśrama nija nija dharama nirata beda patha loga,
चलहिं सदा पावहिं सुखहि नहिं भय सोक न रोग ॥ २०॥
calahiṁ sadā pāvahiṁ sukhahi nahiṁ bhaya soka na roga. 20.

Trans:

Devoted to religion the people walked in the path of the Vedas, each according to his own caste and stage of life, and enjoyed perfect happiness, unvexed by fear, sorrow, or disease.

चौपाई-caupāī:

दैहिक दैविक भौतिक तापा । राम राज नहिं काहुहि ब्यापा ॥
daihika daivika bhautika tāpā, rāma rāja nahiṁ kāhuhi byāpā.
सब नर करहिं परस्पर प्रीती । चलहिं स्वधर्म निरत श्रुति नीती ॥
saba nara karahiṁ paraspara prītī, calahiṁ svadharma nirata śruti nītī.
चारिउ चरन धर्म जग माहीं । पूरि रहा सपनेहुँ अघ नाहीं ॥
cāriu carana dharma jaga māhīṁ, pūri rahā sapanehuṁ agha nāhīṁ.
राम भगति रत नर अरु नारी । सकल परम गति के अधिकारी ॥
rāma bhagati rata nara aru nārī, sakala parama gati ke adhikārī.
अल्पमृत्यु नहिं कवनिउ पीरा । सब सुंदर सब बिरुज सरीरा ॥
alpamṛtyu nahiṁ kavaniu pīrā, saba suṁdara saba biruja sarīrā.
नहिं दरिद्र कोउ दुखी न दीना । नहिं कोउ अबुध न लच्छन हीना ॥
nahiṁ daridra kou dukhī na dīnā, nahiṁ kou abudha na lacchana hīnā.
सब निर्दंभ धर्मरत पुनी । नर अरु नारि चतुर सब गुनी ॥
saba nirdaṁbha dharmarata punī, nara aru nāri catura saba gunī.
सब गुनग्य पंडित सब ग्यानी । सब कृतग्य नहिं कपट सयानी ॥
saba gunagya paṁḍita saba gyānī, saba kṛtagya nahiṁ kapaṭa sayānī.

Trans:

In the whole of Rāma's dominions there was no one who suffered from trouble of any kind, whether of the body or from the visitation of heaven or the attacks of enemies. Everyone was in charity with his neighbor and contented with the state of life to which he had been born, conformably to the teaching of Scripture and sound morality. The four pillars of religion were established throughout the world; no one even dreamt of sin. Men and women alike were devoted to Rāma's worship and enjoyed all the blessedness of highest heaven. There was no premature death and no sickness even, but everyone was comely and sound of body. No one was in poverty, in sorrow, or distress; no one ignorant or unlucky. All were unaffectedly good and pious, clever and intelligent. All appreciated the merits of his neighbor and was himself learned and wise; everyone was grateful for kindnesses and guilelessly prudent.

दोहा-dohā:

राम राज नभगेस सुनु सचराचर जग माहिं ।
rāma rāja nabhagesa sunu sacarācara jaga māhiṁ.
काल कर्म सुभाव गुन कृत दुख काहुहि नाहिं ॥ २१॥
kāla karma subhāva guna kṛta dukha kāhuhi nāhiṁ. 21.

Trans:

Hearken O Garud; during Rāma's reign there was not a creature in the world, animate or inanimate, that suffered from any of the ills that ordinarily result from time or past conduct or personal temperament and character.

चौपाई-caupāī:

भूमि सप्त सागर मेखला । एक भूप रघुपति कोसला ॥
bhūmi sapta sāgara mekhalā, eka bhūpa raghupati kosalā.
भुअन अनेक रोम प्रति जासू । यह प्रभुता कछु बहुत न तासू ॥
bhuana aneka roma prati jāsū, yaha prabhutā kachu bahuta na tāsū.
सो महिमा समुझत प्रभु केरी । यह बरनत हीनता घनेरी ॥

so mahimā samujhata prabhu kerī, yaha baranata hīnatā ghanerī.

सोउ महिमा खगेस जिन्ह जानी । फिरी एहिं चरित तिन्हहुँ रति मानी ॥
sou mahimā khagesa jinha jānī, phirī ehiṁ carita tinhahuṁ rati mānī.

सोउ जाने कर फल यह लीला । कहहिं महा मुनिबर दमसीला ॥
sou jāne kara phala yaha līlā, kahahiṁ mahā munibara damasīlā.

राम राज कर सुख संपदा । बरनि न सकइ फनीस सारदा ॥
rāma rāja kara sukha saṁpadā, barani na sakai phanīsa sāradā.

सब उदार सब पर उपकारी । बिप्र चरन सेवक नर नारी ॥
saba udāra saba para upakārī, bipra carana sevaka nara nārī.

एकनारि ब्रत रत सब झारी । ते मन बच क्रम पति हितकारी ॥
ekanāri brata rata saba jhārī, te mana baca krama pati hitakārī.

Trans:

The world encircled by its seven seas had only one king, Rāma, the Lord of Kaushal. This was no great matter for him, every hair on whose body is one of the countless spheres of creation. To a man who rightly understands the greatness of the Lord, even this description will seem highly disparaging. But those who understand his divine majesty, Garud, are the very persons who take a delight in these actions of his. They are the special rewards of such knowledge; so declare the greatest of sages and ascetics. Not even Sheshnāg or Shārdā could describe the happiness and prosperity of Rāma's reign. Everyone was generous and kindly disposed to his neighbor and submissive to the Brahmins. Every husband was pledged to a vow of monogamy, and each wife too was devoted to her husband in thought, word, and deed.

दोहा-dohā:

दंड जतिन्ह कर भेद जहँ नर्तक नृत्य समाज ।
daṁḍa jatinha kara bheda jahaṁ nartaka nṛtya samāja,
जीतहु मनहि सुनिअ अस रामचंद्र कें राज ॥२२॥
jītahu manahi sunia asa rāmacaṁdra keṁ rāja. 22.

Trans:

'Danda' (rod) was never seen, save in the hands of the recluse and 'Bheda' (tact) too had ceased to exist except among the dancers in a dancing party. Even so the word 'Jeet' (conquer) was heard only with reference to the mind throughout the realm of Shrī Rāmachandra.

चौपाई-caupāī:

फूलहिं फरहिं सदा तरु कानन । रहहिं एक सँग गज पंचानन ॥
phūlahiṁ pharahiṁ sadā taru kānana, rahahiṁ eka saṁga gaja paṁcānana.

खग मृग सहज बयरु बिसराई । सबन्हि परस्पर प्रीति बढ़ाई ॥
khaga mṛga sahaja bayaru bisarāī, sabanhi paraspara prīti baṛhāī.

कूजहिं खग मृग नाना बृंदा । अभय चरहिं बन करहिं अनंदा ॥
kūjahiṁ khaga mṛga nānā bṛṁdā, abhaya carahiṁ bana karahiṁ anaṁdā.

सीतल सुरभि पवन बह मंदा । गुंजत अलि लै चलि मकरंदा ॥
sītala surabhi pavana baha maṁdā, guṁjata ali lai cali makaraṁdā.

लता बिटप मागें मधु चवहीं । मनभावतो धेनु पय स्रवहीं ॥
latā biṭapa māgeṁ madhu cavahīṁ, manabhāvato dhenu paya sravahīṁ.

ससि संपन्न सदा रह धरनी । त्रेताँ भइ कृतजुग कै करनी ॥
sasi saṁpanna sadā raha dharanī, tretāṁ bhai kṛtajuga kai karanī.

प्रगटीं गिरिन्ह बिबिधि मनि खानी । जगदातमा भूप जग जानी ॥
pragaṭīṁ girinha bibidhi mani khānī, jagadātamā bhūpa jaga jānī.

सरिता सकल बहहिं बर बारी । सीतल अमल स्वाद सुखकारी ॥
saritā sakala bahahiṁ bara bārī, sītala amala svāda sukhakārī.

सागर निज मरजादाँ रहहीं । डारहिं रत्न तटन्हि नर लहहीं ॥
sāgara nija marajādāṁ rahahīṁ, ḍārahiṁ ratna taṭanhi nara lahahīṁ.

सरसिज संकुल सकल तड़ागा । अति प्रसन्न दस दिसा बिभागा ॥
sarasija saṁkula sakala taṛāgā, ati prasanna dasa disā bibhāgā.

Trans:

The trees of the forest were ever full of flowers and fruit; the elephant and the lion dwelt peaceably together. Birds and deer forgot their instinctive animosities and lived in the greatest harmony with one another. The cooing of the birds and the many herds of deer fearlessly roaming the woods made a charming scene. The air was cool, fragrant and exquisitely soft; bees laden with honey made a pleasant humming. Creepers and trees dropped honey to those who asked for it; cows yielded milk to one's heart's content. The earth was ever clothed with crops; even in the Tretā-Yug the conditions of the Satya-Yug prevailed. Conscious of the fact that the Ruler of the earth was no other than the Universal Spirit, the mountains brought to light their mines containing jewels of every description. Every river carried in it excellent water—cool, transparent and pleasant to the taste. The oceans kept within their bounds and scattered jewels on their shores for men to gather. Ponds were all thick with lotuses and every quarter was clear and bright.

दोहा-dohā:

बिधु महि पूर मयूखन्हि रबि तप जेतनेहि काज ।
bidhu mahi pūra mayūkhanhi rabi tapa jetanehi kāja,
मागें बारिद देहिं जल रामचंद्र कें राज ॥२३॥
māgeṁ bārida dehiṁ jala rāmacaṁdra keṁ rāja. 23.

Trans:

The earth was suffused with the radiance of the moon, the heat of the sun was no greater than circumstances required, and the clouds dropt rain whenever asked—in the days when Rāma was the King.

चौपाई-caupāī:

कोटिन्ह बाजिमेध प्रभु कीन्हे । दान अनेक द्विजन्ह कहँ दीन्हे ॥
koṭinha bājimedha prabhu kīnhe, dāna aneka dvijanha kahaṁ dīnhe.

श्रुति पथ पालक धर्म धुरंधर । गुनातीत अरु भोग पुरंदर ॥
śruti patha pālaka dharma dhuraṁdhara, gunātīta aru bhoga puraṁdara.

पति अनुकूल सदा रह सीता । सोभा खानि सुसील बिनीता ॥
pati anukūla sadā raha sītā, sobhā khāni susīla binītā.

जानति कृपासिंधु प्रभुताई । सेवति चरन कमल मन लाई ॥
jānati kṛpāsiṁdhu prabhutāī, sevati carana kamala mana lāī.

जद्यपि गृहँ सेवक सेवकिनी । बिपुल सदा सेवा बिधि गुनी ॥
jadyapi gṛhaṁ sevaka sevakinī, bipula sadā sevā bidhi gunī.

निज कर गृह परिचरजा करई । रामचंद्र आयसु अनुसरई ॥
nija kara gṛha paricarajā karaī, rāmacaṁdra āyasu anusaraī.

जेहि बिधि कृपासिंधु सुख मानइ । सोइ कर श्री सेवा बिधि जानइ ॥
jehi bidhi kṛpāsiṁdhu sukha mānai, soi kara śrī sevā bidhi jānai.

कौसल्यादि सासु गृह माहीं । सेवइ सबन्हि मान मद नाहीं ॥
kausalyādi sāsu gṛha māhīṁ, sevai sabanhi māna mada nāhīṁ.

उमा रमा ब्रह्मादि बंदिता । जगदंबा संततमनिंदिता ॥
umā ramā brahmādi baṁditā, jagadaṁbā saṁtatamaniṁditā.

Trans:

The Lord performed millions of Baji-Medha-Yagyas and conferred innumerable gifts upon the Brahmins. The Defender of the Vedic usage and the champion of righteousness, he transcended the three modes of Nature and was another Indra in opulence. Sītā was ever obedient to her Lord, incomparable in her beauty, her virtue and her meekness, sensible of the majesty of the All-merciful and devotedly attached to his lotus feet. Though there were many man-servants and maid-servants in the palace, all well-skilled in their work, she discharged every domestic duty with her own hands, waiting on Rāma's orders. Any service that might give pleasure to the All-merciful, she herself studied to perform. Without the slightest pride or conceit, she attended on Kausalyā and the other queen dowagers in the palace. Sītā was no other than Goddess Ramā, the Mother of the universe, who is adored even by Brahmmā and other gods and is ever flawless.

दोहा-dohā:

जासु कृपा कटाच्छु सुर चाहत चितव न सोइ ।
jāsu kṛpā kaṭācchu sura cāhata citava na soi,
राम पदारबिंद रति करति सुभावहि खोइ ॥२४॥
rāma padārabiṁda rati karati subhāvahi khoi. 24.

Trans:

The same Lakshmī whose benign look is craved by the gods but who never casts a glance at them, constantly loves Shrī Rāma's lotus feet, forgetting her natural majesty.

चौपाई-caupāī:

सेवहिं सानकूल सब भाई । रामचरन रति अति अधिकाई ॥
sevahiṁ sānakūla saba bhāī, rāmacarana rati ati adhikāī.
प्रभु मुख कमल बिलोकत रहहीं । कबहुँ कृपाल हमहि कछु कहहीं ॥
prabhu mukha kamala bilokata rahahīṁ, kabahuṁ kṛpāla hamahi kachu kahahīṁ.
राम करहिं भ्रातन्ह पर प्रीती । नाना भाँति सिखावहिं नीती ॥
rāma karahiṁ bhrātanha para prītī, nānā bhāṁti sikhāvahiṁ nītī.
हरषित रहहिं नगर के लोगा । करहिं सकल सुर दुर्लभ भोगा ॥
haraṣita rahahiṁ nagara ke logā, karahiṁ sakala sura durlabha bhogā.
अहनिसि बिधिहि मनावत रहहीं । श्रीरघुबीर चरन रति चहहीं ॥
ahanisi bidhihi manāvata rahahīṁ, śrīraghubīra carana rati cahahīṁ.
दुइ सुत सुन्दर सीताँ जाए । लव कुस बेद पुरानन्ह गाए ॥
dui suta sundara sītāṁ jāe, lava kusa beda purānanha gāe.
दोउ बिजई बिनई गुन मंदिर । हरि प्रतिबिंब मनहुँ अति सुंदर ॥
dou bijaī binaī guna maṁdira, hari pratibiṁba manahuṁ ati suṁdara.
दुइ दुइ सुत सब भ्रातन्ह केरे । भए रूप गुन सील घनेरे ॥
dui dui suta saba bhrātanha kere, bhae rūpa guna sīla ghanere.

Trans:

All the younger brothers served the Lord with great fidelity, for their love for Shrī Rāma knew no bounds. Their eyes ever kept gazing on his lotus face in the hope that the benign Lord might give some order to them at any moment. Rāma on his part was most affectionate to his brothers and instructed them on all points of morality. The citizens lived happy, each enjoying a felicity to which the gods might scarce attain. Day and night they made their prayer to God for a fervent devotion to Rāma's holy feet. Two comely sons were born to Sītā: Lava and Kush—so the Vedas and Purānas have declared—both glorious in battle, modest and accomplished and so beautiful that they seemed the very image of Harī. The other brothers also had each two sons, pre-eminent in beauty, virtue, and all good qualities.

दोहा-dohā:

ग्यान गिरा गोतीत अज माया मन गुन पार ।
gyāna girā gotīta aja māyā mana guna pāra,
सोइ सच्चिदानंद घन कर नर चरित उदार ॥२५॥
soi saccidānaṁda ghana kara nara carita udāra. 25.

Trans:

The Supreme Spirit which transcends all intelligence, speech and perception; which is from everlasting; which is unaffected by material phenomena, or the workings of the mind or the properties of things—even he it was who thus exhibited the ideal behavior of a human being.

चौपाई-caupāī:

प्रातकाल सरऊ करि मज्जन । बैठहिं सभाँ संग द्विज सज्जन ॥
prātakāla saraū kari majjana, baiṭhahiṁ sabhāṁ saṁga dvija sajjana.
बेद पुरान बसिष्ट बखानहिं । सुनहिं राम जद्यपि सब जानहिं ॥
beda purāna basiṣṭa bakhānahiṁ, sunahiṁ rāma jadyapi saba jānahiṁ.
अनुजन्ह संजुत भोजन करहीं । देखि सकल जननीं सुख भरहीं ॥
anujanha saṁjuta bhojana karahīṁ, dekhi sakala jananīṁ sukha bharahīṁ.
भरत सत्रुहन दोनउ भाई । सहित पवनसुत उपबन जाई ॥
bharata satruhana donau bhāī, sahita pavanasuta upabana jāī.
बूझहिं बैठि राम गुन गाहा । कह हनुमान सुमति अवगाहा ॥
būjhahiṁ baiṭhi rāma guna gāhā, kaha hanumāna sumati avagāhā.
सुनत बिमल गुन अति सुख पावहिं । बहुरि बहुरि करि बिनय कहावहिं ॥
sunata bimala guna ati sukha pāvahiṁ, bahuri bahuri kari binaya kahāvahiṁ.
सब कें गृह गृह होहिं पुराना । रामचरित पावन बिधि नाना ॥
saba keṁ gṛha gṛha hohiṁ purānā, rāmacarita pāvana bidhi nānā.
नर अरु नारि राम गुन गानहिं । करहिं दिवस निसि जात न जानहिं ॥
nara aru nāri rāma guna gānahiṁ, karahiṁ divasa nisi jāta na jānahiṁ.

Trans:

In the early morning, after bathing in the Sarjū, he sat in his court, in the midst of Brahmins and sages, while Vasishtha recited the Vedas and Purānas. Rāma listening attentively, though he knew them all of himself. He took his meals with his brothers, with the royal matrons looking on with the utmost satisfaction. Then Bharat and Shatrughan, the two brothers, would take Hanumān to some grove, where they would sit down and ask him all about Rāma's enactments, and he would reply out of the depth of his wisdom. It was such a delight to them to hear the glorious narrative that they would beg him to repeat it again and again. In every single house, the sacred legend was told of Rāma's marvelously holy deeds. Men and women alike joined in hymning his praises and day and night passed unheeded.

दोहा-dohā:

अवधपुरी बासिन्ह कर सुख संपदा समाज ।
avadhapurī bāsinha kara sukha saṁpadā samāja,
सहस सेष नहिं कहि सकहिं जहँ नृप राम बिराज ॥२६॥
sahasa seṣa nahiṁ kahi sakahiṁ jahaṁ nṛpa rāma birāja. 26.

Trans:

Not a thousand Sheshnāgs could tell all the happiness and prosperity of the city of Avadh, when Rāma reigned as King.

चौपाई-caupāī:

नारदादि सनकादि मुनीसा । दरसन लागि कोसलाधीसा ॥
nāradādi sanakādi munīsā, darasana lāgi kosalādhīsā.
दिन प्रति सकल अजोध्या आवहिं । देखि नगरु बिरागु बिसरावहिं ॥
dina prati sakala ajodhyā āvahiṁ, dekhi nagaru birāgu bisarāvahiṁ.
जातरूप मनि रचित अटारीं । नाना रंग रुचिर गच ढारीं ॥
jātarūpa mani racita aṭārīṁ, nānā raṁga rucira gaca ḍhārīṁ.
पुर चहुँ पास कोट अति सुंदर । रचे कँगूरा रंग रंग बर ॥
pura cahuṁ pāsa koṭa ati suṁdara, race kaṁgūrā raṁga raṁga bara.
नव ग्रह निकर अनीक बनाई । जनु घेरी अमरावति आई ॥
nava graha nikara anīka banāī, janu gherī amarāvati āī.
महि बहु रंग रचित गच काँचा । जो बिलोकि मुनिबर मन नाचा ॥
mahi bahu raṁga racita gaca kāṁcā, jo biloki munibara mana nācā.
धवल धाम ऊपर नभ चुंबत । कलस मनहुँ रबि ससि दुति निंदत ॥
dhavala dhāma ūpara nabha cuṁbata, kalasa manahuṁ rabi sasi duti niṁdata.
बहु मनि रचित झरोखा भ्राजहिं । गृह गृह प्रति मनि दीप बिराजहिं ॥
bahu mani racita jharokhā bhrājahiṁ, gṛha gṛha prati mani dīpa birājahiṁ.

Trans:

Nārad and Sanat-kumār and all the great sages came every day to Ajodhyā to have a sight of the king of Kaushal. The appearance of the city made them forget all their asceticism: the balconies encrusted with gold and jewels, the splendid pavements laid in diverse colors, the magnificent forts on every side of the city with their brightly painted battlements—as though the nine planets had been mustered in array to beleaguer Indra's capital, Amaravati; the floors beautifully inlaid with colored glass, that the soul of even saint would be distracted at the sight; the glistening palaces, reaching to the sky, with pinnacles that put to shame the brightness of sun and moon; the lattices gleaming with jewels and the jeweled lamps that shone in every room.

छंद-chamda:

मनि दीप राजहिं भवन भ्राजहिं देहरीं बिद्रुम रची ।
mani dīpa rājahiṁ bhavana bhrājahiṁ deharīṁ bidruma racī,
मनि खंभ भीति बिरंचि बिरची कनक मनि मरकत खची ॥
mani khaṁbha bhīti biraṁci biracī kanaka mani marakata khacī.
सुंदर मनोहर मंदिरायत अजिर रुचिर फटिक रचे ।
suṁdara manohara maṁdirāyata ajira rucira phaṭika race,
प्रति द्वार द्वार कपाट पुरट बनाइ बहु बज्रन्हि खचे ॥
prati dvāra dvāra kapāṭa puraṭa banāi bahu bajranhi khace.

Trans:

Beneath the light of jeweled lamps, the houses were resplendent with their thresholds of coral and pillars of precious stones and golden walls, such as the Creator himself might have fashioned, all inlaid with emeralds and gems. The stately palace-courts were lovely with in-worked crystal, and every gate was fitted with folding doors of gold, embossed with diamonds.

दोहा-dohā:

चारु चित्रसाला गृह गृह प्रति लिखे बनाइ ।
cāru citrasālā gṛha gṛha prati likhe banāi,
राम चरित जे निरख मुनि ते मन लेहिं चोराइ ॥२७॥
rāma carita je nirakha muni te mana lehiṁ corāi. 27.

Trans:

In every house was a beautiful and well-furnished picture gallery, where Rāma's achievements were so set forth that the soul of a saint would be ravished at the sight.

चौपाई-caupāī:

सुमन बाटिका सबहिं लगाईं । बिबिध भाँति करि जतन बनाईं ॥
sumana bāṭikā sabahiṁ lagāīṁ, bibidha bhāṁti kari jatana banāīṁ.
लता ललित बहु जाति सुहाईं । फूलहिं सदा बंसत कि नाईं ॥
latā lalita bahu jāti suhāīṁ, phūlahiṁ sadā baṁsata ki nāīṁ.
गुंजत मधुकर मुखर मनोहर । मारुत त्रिबिधि सदा बह सुंदर ॥
guṁjata madhukara mukhara manohara, māruta tribidhi sadā baha suṁdara.
नाना खग बालकन्हि जिआए । बोलत मधुर उड़ात सुहाए ॥
nānā khaga bālakanhi jiāe, bolata madhura uṛāta suhāe.
मोर हंस सारस पारावत । भवननि पर सोभा अति पावत ॥
mora haṁsa sārasa pārāvata, bhavanani para sobhā ati pāvata.
जहँ तहँ देखहिं निज परिछाहीं । बहु बिधि कूजहिं नृत्य कराहीं ॥
jahaṁ tahaṁ dekhahiṁ nija parichāhīṁ, bahu bidhi kūjahiṁ nṛtya karāhīṁ.
सुक सारिका पढ़ावहिं बालक । कहहु राम रघुपति जनपालक ॥
suka sārikā paṛhāvahiṁ bālaka, kahahu rāma raghupati janapālaka.
राज दुआर सकल बिधि चारू । बीथीं चौहट रूचिर बजारू ॥
rāja duāra sakala bidhi cārū, bīthīṁ cauhaṭa rūcira bajārū.

Trans:

Everyone had a flower garden, trimmed with the greatest care, adorned with every kind of choice creeper, and blossoming with perpetual spring. There was ever a pleasant sound of the buzzing of bees, and the air was delightfully cool, soft and fragrant. Birds of all kinds, the children's pets, sweet of note and graceful in flight, peacocks, swans, herons and pigeons, made a charming show on the tops of the houses, cooing and dancing in high glee at the sight of their own shadow. The children taught parrots and *mainas* to repeat the words, 'Rāma, Raghupatī, Savior'. The palace gates were most magnificent and the roads, squares and bazaars all elegantly laid out.

छंद-chamda:

बाजार रुचिर न बनइ बरनत बस्तु बिनु गथ पाइए ।
bājāra rucira na banai baranata bastu binu gatha pāie,
जहँ भूप रमानिवास तहँ की संपदा किमि गाइए ॥
jahaṁ bhūpa ramānivāsa tahaṁ kī saṁpadā kimi gāie.
बैठे बजाज सराफ बनिक अनेक मनहुँ कुबेर ते ।
baiṭhe bajāja sarāpha banika aneka manahuṁ kubera te,
सब सुखी सब सच्चरित सुंदर नारि नर सिसु जरठ जे ॥
saba sukhī saba saccarita suṁdara nāri nara sisu jaraṭha je.

Trans:

The elegance of the bazaars was beyond words, and things could be had even without consideration. How is it possible to sing the riches of the city where the spouse of Lakshmī reigned as king? The cloth-merchants, money-changers and grain-dealers sat at their shops like so many Kubers. Everyone was happy, everyone well-conducted and comely, men and women, young and old, all alike.

दोहा-dohā:

उत्तर दिसि सरजू बह निर्मल जल गंभीर ।
uttara disi sarajū baha nirmala jala gaṁbhīra,
बाँधे घाट मनोहर स्वल्प पंक नहिं तीर ॥२८॥
bāṁdhe ghāṭa manohara svalpa paṁka nahiṁ tīra. 28.

Trans:

To the north flowed the deep and pellucid stream of the Sarjū, with a line of handsome Ghāts and no muddy bank anywhere.

चौपाई-caupāī:

दूरि फराक रुचिर सो घाटा । जहँ जल पिअहिं बाजि गज ठाटा ॥
dūri pharāka rucira so ghāṭā, jahaṁ jala piahiṁ bāji gaja ṭhāṭā.
पनिघट परम मनोहर नाना । तहाँ न पुरुष करहिं अस्नाना ॥
panighaṭa parama manohara nānā, tahāṁ na puruṣa karahiṁ asnānā.
राजघाट सब बिधि सुंदर बर । मज्जहिं तहाँ बरन चारिउ नर ॥
rājaghāṭa saba bidhi suṁdara bara, majjahiṁ tahāṁ barana cāriu nara.
तीर तीर देवन्ह के मंदिर । चहुँ दिसि तिन्ह के उपबन सुंदर ॥
tīra tīra devanha ke maṁdira, cahuṁ disi tinha ke upabana suṁdara.
कहुँ कहुँ सरिता तीर उदासी । बसहिं ग्यान रत मुनि संन्यासी ॥
kahuṁ kahuṁ saritā tīra udāsī, basahiṁ gyāna rata muni saṁnyāsī.
तीर तीर तुलसिका सुहाई । बृंद बृंद बहु मुनिन्ह लगाई ॥
tīra tīra tulasikā suhāī, bṛṁda bṛṁda bahu muninha lagāī.
पुर सोभा कछु बरनि न जाई । बाहेर नगर परम रुचिराई ॥
pura sobhā kachu barani na jāī, bāhera nagara parama rucirāī.
देखत पुरी अखिल अघ भागा । बन उपबन बापिका तड़ागा ॥
dekhata purī akhila agha bhāgā, bana upabana bāpikā taṛāgā.

Trans:

At some distance was a fine spacious Ghāt where all the horses and elephants went to drink. There were also elaborate Ghāts for the citizens' drinking water, where no one was allowed to bathe. The most beautiful of all was the king's Ghāt, which was frequented by men of all four castes. All along the banks were temples to the gods surrounded by pleasant groves. Here and there on the river bank, hermits, sages and anchorites dwelt and meditated; and many bushes of the fragrant Tulsī were there, planted by different holy men. The beauty of the city surpassed all description; its outskirts also were most picturesque. Every sin was effaced by a sight of it, with its woods and groves, its lakes and ponds.

छंद-chamda:

बापीं तड़ाग अनूप कूप मनोहरायत सोहहीं ।

bāpīṁ taṛāga anūpa kūpa manoharāyata sohahīṁ,
सोपान सुंदर नीर निर्मल देखि सुर मुनि मोहहीं ॥
sopāna suṁdara nīra nirmala dekhi sura muni mohahīṁ.
बहु रंग कंज अनेक खग कूजहिं मधुप गुंजारहीं ।
bahu raṁga kaṁja aneka khaga kūjahiṁ madhupa guṁjārahīṁ,
आराम रम्य पिकादि खग रव जनु पथिक हंकारहीं ॥
ārāma ramya pikādi khaga rava janu pathika haṁkārahīṁ.

Trans:

Its matchless lakes and ponds and large and beautiful wells were so charming, with their elegant flights of steps and limpid water, that gods and saints were fascinated by the sight. The many-colored lotuses, the cooing of the numerous birds, and the buzzing of the bees made the spot a delightful one, where the parrots by their clamor, seemed to be inviting travelers to halt.

दोहा-dohā:

रमानाथ जहँ राजा सो पुर बरनि कि जाइ ।
ramānātha jahaṁ rājā so pura barani ki jāi,
अनिमादिक सुख संपदा रहीं अवध सब छाइ ॥२९॥
animādika sukha saṁpadā rahīṁ avadha saba chāi. 29.

Trans:

How is it possible to describe the city, of which Lakshmī's Lord was King? *Anima* and the other superhuman powers diffused through the whole of Avadh, and even so joys and riches of every kind.

चौपाई-caupāī:

जहँ तहँ नर रघुपति गुन गावहिं । बैठि परसपर इहइ सिखावहिं ॥
jahaṁ tahaṁ nara raghupati guna gāvahiṁ, baiṭhi parasapara ihai sikhāvahiṁ.
भजहु प्रनत प्रतिपालक रामहि । सोभा सील रूप गुन धामहि ॥
bhajahu pranata pratipālaka rāmahi, sobhā sīla rūpa guna dhāmahi.
जलज बिलोचन स्यामल गातहि । पलक नयन इव सेवक त्रातहि ॥
jalaja bilocana syāmala gātahi, palaka nayana iva sevaka trātahi.
धृत सर रुचिर चाप तूनीरहि । संत कंज बन रबि रनधीरहि ॥
dhṛta sara rucira cāpa tūnīrahi, saṁta kaṁja bana rabi ranadhīrahi.
काल कराल ब्याल खगराजहि । नमत राम अकाम ममता जहि ॥
kāla karāla byāla khagarājahi, namata rāma akāma mamatā jahi.
लोभ मोह मृगजूथ किरातहि । मनसिज करि हरि जन सुखदातहि ॥
lobha moha mṛgajūtha kirātahi, manasija kari hari jana sukhadātahi.
संसय सोक निबिड़ तम भानुहि । दनुज गहन घन दहन कृसानुहि ॥
saṁsaya soka nibiṛa tama bhānuhi, danuja gahana ghana dahana kṛsānuhi.
जनकसुता समेत रघुबीरहि । कस न भजहु भंजन भव भीरहि ॥
janakasutā sameta raghubīrahi, kasa na bhajahu bhaṁjana bhava bhīrahi.
बहु बासना मसक हिम रासिहि । सदा एकरस अज अबिनासिहि ॥
bahu bāsanā masaka hima rāsihi, sadā ekarasa aja abināsihi.
मुनि रंजन भंजन महि भारहि । तुलसिदास के प्रभुहि उदारहि ॥
muni raṁjana bhaṁjana mahi bhārahi, tulasidāsa ke prabhuhi udārahi.

Trans:

Everywhere men were singing Rāma's praises and even as they sat, this is how they exhorted one another, "Worship Shrī Rāma, the defender of the suppliant, the home of beauty and goodness, of comeliness and virtue, the lotus-eyed and dark-complexioned, who protects his servants as the eyelid does the eye; equipt with lovely bow and arrows and quiver, the champion of the battle; a very sun to rejoice the lotus-like company of the saints; a Garud to consume the terrible serpent Death; whose loving kindness is over all who unselfishly worship Rāma; a huntsman to scatter the deer-like herd of ignorance and greed; a lion to quell the wild elephant Concupiscence; the giver of happiness to his people; a sun to scatter the thick darkness of doubt and sorrow; a fire to consume the dense forest of demons. Who should not worship Raghubīr and Sītā, seeing that he is the breaker of earth's burdens, the frost that kills the insect swarm of manifold desires; the ever uniform, the uncreated and imperishable; the delight of the saints, Tulsīdās' own gracious Lord"

दोहा-dohā:

एहि बिधि नगर नारि नर करहिं राम गुन गान ।
ehi bidhi nagara nāri nara karahiṁ rāma guna gāna,
सानुकूल सब पर रहहिं संतत कृपानिधान ॥३०॥
sānukūla saba para rahahiṁ saṁtata kṛpānidhāna. 30.

Trans:

In such wise the people of the city sang Rāma's praises, while on his part the All-merciful was ever to them, most gracious.

चौपाई-caupāī:

जब ते राम प्रताप खगेसा । उदित भयउ अति प्रबल दिनेसा ॥
jaba te rāma pratāpa khagesā, udita bhayau ati prabala dinesā.
पूरि प्रकास रहेउ तिहुँ लोका । बहुतेन्ह सुख बहुतन मन सोका ॥
pūri prakāsa raheu tihuṁ lokā, bahutenha sukha bahutana mana sokā.
जिन्हहि सोक ते कहउँ बखानी । प्रथम अबिद्या निसा नसानी ॥
jinhahi soka te kahauṁ bakhānī, prathama abidyā nisā nasānī.
अघ उलूक जहँ तहाँ लुकाने । काम क्रोध कैरव सकुचाने ॥
agha ulūka jahaṁ tahāṁ lukāne, kāma krodha kairava sakucāne.
बिबिध कर्म गुन काल सुभाऊ । ए चकोर सुख लहहिं न काऊ ॥
bibidha karma guna kāla subhāū, e cakora sukha lahahiṁ na kāū.
मत्सर मान मोह मद चोरा । इन्ह कर हुनर न कवनिहुँ ओरा ॥
matsara māna moha mada corā, inha kara hunara na kavanihuṁ orā.
धरम तड़ाग ग्यान बिग्याना । ए पंकज बिकसे बिधि नाना ॥
dharama taṛāga gyāna bigyānā, e paṁkaja bikase bidhi nānā.
सुख संतोष बिराग बिबेका । बिगत सोक ए कोक अनेका ॥
sukha saṁtoṣa birāga bibekā, bigata soka e koka anekā.

Trans:

O Garud, from the time of the uprising of the glorious sun of Rāma's power, the three spheres were all suffused with light; many were happy, but many were also sad. First to enumerate the sorrowful: to begin with, the night of ignorance was at an end; owl-like Sin slunk away out of sight; Lust and Anger, like gamblers, were ashamed to show themselves; Formalism, Phenomenal Existence, Time and Nature, were as ill at ease as the *chakor*, Envy, Pride, Infatuation, and Conceit, were like thieves, with nowhere a chance to display their skill. But the ponds of Piety blossomed with the lotuses of Knowledge and Understanding; while Happiness, Contentment, Self-control and Discretion, were like so many *chakwā*s and chakwis when their sorrow is over.

दोहा-dohā:

यह प्रताप रबि जाकें उर जब करइ प्रकास ।
yaha pratāpa rabi jākeṁ ura jaba karai prakāsa,
पछिले बाढ़हिं प्रथम जे कहे ते पावहिं नास ॥३१॥
pachile bāṛhahiṁ prathama je kahe te pāvahiṁ nāsa. 31.

Trans:

When this glorious sun illumines any man's heart, the last named qualities grow and increase; and the first mentioned die away.

चौपाई-caupāī:

भ्रातन्ह सहित रामु एक बारा । संग परम प्रिय पवनकुमारा ॥
bhrātanha sahita rāmu eka bārā, saṁga parama priya pavanakumārā.
सुंदर उपबन देखन गए । सब तरु कुसुमित पल्लव नए ॥
suṁdara upabana dekhana gae, saba taru kusumita pallava nae.

जानि समय सनकादिक आए । तेज पुंज गुन सील सुहाए ॥
jāni samaya sanakādika āe, teja puṁja guna sīla suhāe.
ब्रह्मानंद सदा लयलीना । देखत बालक बहुकालीना ॥
brahmānaṁda sadā layalīnā, dekhata bālaka bahukālīnā.
रूप धरें जनु चारिउ बेदा । समदरसी मुनि बिगत बिभेदा ॥
rūpa dhareṁ janu cāriu bedā, samadarasī muni bigata bibhedā.
आसा बसन ब्यसन यह तिन्हहीं । रघुपति चरित होइ तहँ सुनहीं ॥
āsā basana byasana yaha tinhahīṁ, raghupati carita hoi tahaṁ sunahīṁ.
तहाँ रहे सनकादि भवानी । जहँ घटसंभव मुनिबर ग्यानी ॥
tahāṁ rahe sanakādi bhavānī, jahaṁ ghaṭasaṁbhava munibara gyānī.
राम कथा मुनिबर बहु बरनी । ग्यान जोनि पावक जिमि अरनी ॥
rāma kathā munibara bahu baranī, gyāna joni pāvaka jimi aranī.

Trans:

One day Rāma with his brothers and his special favorite Hanumān went to visit a beautiful grove, where every tree was bright with flowers and fresh leaves. Finding it a good opportunity Sanat-kumār and the others arrived there. Embodiments of spiritual glow, adorned with amiability and other noble qualities, ever absorbed in the rapture of transcendental felicity, they were all youthful to look at, despite their immemorial years. The sages looked upon all with the same eye and were above all diversity; it seemed as if the four Vedas had each assumed a bodily form. They had no covering on their body except the quarters; and their only hobby was to hear the recital of Shrī Rāma's enactments wherever it was carried on. Sanak and his brothers, O Bhawānī, had stayed in the hermitage of the enlightened sage Agastya and the noble sage had narrated to them many a story relating to Shrī Rāma, which are productive of wisdom in the same way as the friction of two pieces of wood produces fire.

दोहा-dohā:

देखि राम मुनि आवत हरषि दंडवत कीन्ह ।
dekhi rāma muni āvata haraṣi daṁḍavata kīnha,
स्वागत पूँछि पीत पट प्रभु बैठन कहँ दीन्ह ॥३२॥
svāgata pūṁchi pīta paṭa prabhu baiṭhana kahaṁ dīnha. 32.

Trans:

When Rāma saw the sages approaching, he rejoiced and prostrated himself before them; then after giving them welcome, the Lord of the yellow robe bade them be seated.

चौपाई-caupāī:

कीन्ह दंडवत तीनिउँ भाई । सहित पवनसुत सुख अधिकाई ॥
kīnha daṁḍavata tīniuṁ bhāī, sahita pavanasuta sukha adhikāī.
मुनि रघुपति छबि अतुल बिलोकी । भए मगन मन सके न रोकी ॥
muni raghupati chabi atula bilokī, bhae magana mana sake na rokī.
स्यामल गात सरोरुह लोचन । सुंदरता मंदिर भव मोचन ॥
syāmala gāta saroruha locana, suṁdaratā maṁdira bhava mocana.
एकटक रहे निमेष न लावहिं । प्रभु कर जोरें सीस नवावहिं ॥
ekaṭaka rahe nimeṣa na lāvahiṁ, prabhu kara joreṁ sīsa navāvahiṁ.
तिन्ह कै दसा देखि रघुबीरा । स्त्रवत नयन जल पुलक सरीरा ॥
tinha kai dasā dekhi raghubīrā, sravata nayana jala pulaka sarīrā.
कर गहि प्रभु मुनिबर बैठारे । परम मनोहर बचन उचारे ॥
kara gahi prabhu munibara baiṭhāre, parama manohara bacana ucāre.
आजु धन्य मैं सुनहु मुनीसा । तुम्हरें दरस जाहिं अघ खीसा ॥
āju dhanya maiṁ sunahu munīsā, tumhareṁ darasa jāhiṁ agha khīsā.
बड़े भाग पाइब सतसंगा । बिनहिं प्रयास होहिं भव भंगा ॥
baṛe bhāga pāiba satasaṁgā, binahiṁ prayāsa hohiṁ bhava bhaṁgā.

Trans:

His three brothers made their obeisance as well and were greatly delighted, as also Hanumān. The saints, as they gazed on Rāma's incomparable beauty, were beside themselves with rapture. With clasped hands they bowed the head before him and could not close their eyes for a moment, so intensely were they fixed on the shrine of beauty, the conqueror of the world, with his lotus eyes and dark-hued frame. When Raghubīr perceived their condition, his eyes streamed with tears and his body quivered with emotion. He took them by the hand and made them sit down and addressed them in these most gracious words, "Hearken reverend sirs: today I am indeed blessed; at the sight of you sin is annihilated. The fellowship of the saints is the greatest of blessings; through such communion the chain of births and deaths is broken without the least exertion.

दोहा-dohā:

संत संग अपबर्ग कर कामी भव कर पंथ ।
saṁta saṁga apabarga kara kāmī bhava kara paṁtha,
कहहिं संत कबि कोबिद श्रुति पुरान सदग्रंथ ॥३३॥
kahahiṁ saṁta kabi kobida śruti purāna sadagraṁtha. 33.

Trans:

To consort with the saints leads to final beatitude, but with the sensual leads one to endless transmigrations: so say the saints themselves, the greatest of the poets, the Vedas, the Purānas and all other Scriptures."

चौपाई-caupāī:

सुनि प्रभु बचन हरषि मुनि चारी । पुलकित तन अस्तुति अनुसारी ॥
suni prabhu bacana haraṣi muni cārī, pulakita tana astuti anusārī.
जय भगवंत अनंत अनामय । अनघ अनेक एक करुनामय ॥
jaya bhagavaṁta anaṁta anāmaya, anagha aneka eka karunāmaya.
जय निर्गुन जय जय गुन सागर । सुख मंदिर सुंदर अति नागर ॥
jaya nirguna jaya jaya guna sāgara, sukha maṁdira suṁdara ati nāgara.
जय इंदिरा रमन जय भूधर । अनुपम अज अनादि सोभाकर ॥
jaya iṁdirā ramana jaya bhūdhara, anupama aja anādi sobhākara.
ग्यान निधान अमान मानप्रद । पावन सुजस पुरान बेद बद ॥
gyāna nidhāna amāna mānaprada, pāvana sujasa purāna beda bada.
तग्य कृतग्य अग्यता भंजन । नाम अनेक अनाम निरंजन ॥
tagya kṛtagya agyatā bhaṁjana, nāma aneka anāma niraṁjana.
सर्ब सर्बगत सर्ब उरालय । बससि सदा हम कहुँ परिपालय ॥
sarba sarbagata sarba urālaya, basasi sadā hama kahuṁ paripālaya.
द्वंद बिपति भव फंद बिभंजय । हृदि बसि राम काम मद गंजय ॥
dvaṁda bipati bhava phaṁda bibhaṁjaya, hṛdi basi rāma kāma mada gaṁjaya.

Trans:

The four sages were rejoiced to hear the Lord's words, and with quivering body they raised this hymn of praise, "Glory to the Lord God, the everlasting, the unchangeable, the sinless, the multiform, the One, the All-merciful. Glory to the unembodied; glory, glory to the universal embodiment, the palace of bliss, the beautiful in his comeliness. Glory to the spouse of Lakshmī, glory to the supporter of the earth, peerless in his splendor, the uncreated, of whom there is no beginning; the fountain of wisdom, the immeasurable, the bestower of honor, whose holy fame is the theme of the Vedas and Purānas; the all-wise, the all-generous, the destroyer of ignorance; the many-named, the nameless, the emotionless; the universe itself, the universal spirit, the indweller of every heart. Abide with us and protect us for ever, O Rāma; dwell in our hearts, tearing asunder the bonds of the world and its miserable contentions and destroying our sensuality and conceit.

दोहा-dohā:

परमानंद कृपायतन मन परिपूरन काम ।
paramānaṁda kṛpāyatana mana paripūrana kāma,
प्रेम भगति अनपायनी देहु हमहि श्रीराम ॥ ३४ ॥
prema bhagati anapāyanī dehu hamahi śrīrāma. 34.

Trans:

O holy Rāma, all-blessed and all-merciful, fulfiller of every desire of the soul, bestow on us the boon of constant love and devotion.

चौपाई-caupāī:

देहु भगति रघुपति अति पावनि । त्रिबिधि ताप भव दाप नसावनि ॥
dehu bhagati raghupati ati pāvani, tribidhi tāpa bhava dāpa nasāvani.
प्रनत काम सुरधेनु कलपतरु । होइ प्रसन्न दीजै प्रभु यह बरु ॥
pranata kāma suradhenu kalapataru, hoi prasanna dījai prabhu yaha baru.
भव बारिधि कुंभज रघुनायक । सेवत सुलभ सकल सुख दायक ॥
bhava bāridhi kuṁbhaja raghunāyaka, sevata sulabha sakala sukha dāyaka.
मन संभव दारुन दुख दारय । दीनबंधु समता बिस्तारय ॥
mana saṁbhava dāruna dukha dāraya, dīnabaṁdhu samatā bistāraya.
आस त्रास इरिषादि निवारक । बिनय बिबेक बिरति बिस्तारक ॥
āsa trāsa iriṣādi nivāraka, binaya bibeka birati bistāraka.
भूप मौलि मन मंडन धरनी । देहि भगति संसृति सरि तरनी ॥
bhūpa mauli mana maṁḍana dharanī, dehi bhagati saṁsṛti sari taranī.
मुनि मन मानस हंस निरंतर । चरन कमल बंदित अज संकर ॥
muni mana mānasa haṁsa niraṁtara, carana kamala baṁdita aja saṁkara.
रघुकुल केतु सेतु श्रुति रच्छक । काल करम सुभाउ गुन भच्छक ॥
raghukula ketu setu śruti racchaka, kāla karama subhāu guna bhacchaka.
तारन तरन हरन सब दूषन । तुलसिदास प्रभु त्रिभुवन भूषन ॥
tārana tarana harana saba dūṣana, tulasidāsa prabhu tribhuvana bhūṣana.

Trans:

Grant us, O Raghupatī, that purifying faith which annihilates every distress and worldly conceit. Be propitious and grant us this boon, O Lord, a very cow of heaven, or tree of Paradise, to satisfy the desires of the suppliant. O Raghunāyak, the Agastya of the ocean of mundane existence, the bestower of blessings which only your servants find it easy to acquire; destroyer of the destroying tortures of love; friend of the friendless; diffuser of equanimity; banisher of vain-hope, fear, of envy and all evil passions; bestower of humility, discretion and detachment; jewel of earthly kings; glory of the world; grant us devotion to thee, the only raft on which to cross the floods of existence; divine swan in the Mānas lake of saintly souls; whose lotus feet are adored by Brahmmā and Shiva; standard of the line of Raghu; bridge for the recovery of the Scriptures; annihilator of time, destiny, nature and phenomenal existence; ark of salvation; healer of every sorrow; glory of the three spheres; Tulsīdās' own Lord."

दोहा-dohā:

बार बार अस्तुति करि प्रेम सहित सिरु नाइ ।
bāra bāra astuti kari prema sahita siru nāi,
ब्रह्म भवन सनकादि गे अति अभीष्ट बर पाइ ॥ ३५ ॥
brahma bhavana sanakādi ge ati abhīṣṭa bara pāi. 35.

Trans:

Having again and again hymned his praises and lovingly bowed the head, Sanat-kumār and his companions returned to Brahmmā's sphere, after obtaining the boon they had so vehemently coveted.

चौपाई-caupāī:

सनकादिक बिधि लोक सिधाए । भ्रातन्ह राम चरन सिरु नाए ॥
sanakādika bidhi loka sidhāe, bhrātanha rāma carana siru nāe.
पूछत प्रभुहि सकल सकुचाहीं । चितवहिं सब मारुतसुत पाहीं ॥
pūchata prabhuhi sakala sakucāhīṁ, citavahiṁ saba mārutasuta pāhīṁ.
सुनी चहहिं प्रभु मुख कै बानी । जो सुनि होइ सकल भ्रम हानी ॥
sunī cahahiṁ prabhu mukha kai bānī, jo suni hoi sakala bhrama hānī.
अंतरजामी प्रभु सभ जाना । बूझत कहहु काह हनुमाना ॥
aṁtarajāmī prabhu sabha jānā, būjhata kahahu kāha hanumānā.
जोरि पानि कह तब हनुमंता । सुनहु दीनदयाल भगवंता ॥
jori pāni kaha taba hanumaṁtā, sunahu dīnadayāla bhagavaṁtā.
नाथ भरत कछु पूँछन चहहीं । प्रस्न करत मन सकुचत अहहीं ॥
nātha bharata kachu pūṁchana cahahīṁ, prasna karata mana sakucata ahahīṁ.
तुम्ह जानहु कपि मोर सुभाऊ । भरतहि मोहि कछु अंतर काऊ ॥
tumha jānahu kapi mora subhāū, bharatahi mohi kachu aṁtara kāū.
सुनि प्रभु बचन भरत गहे चरना । सुनहु नाथ प्रनतारति हरना ॥
suni prabhu bacana bharata gahe caranā, sunahu nātha pranatārati haranā.

Trans:

When Sanat-kumār and his companions had gone their way to Brahmmā's sphere, the three brothers bowed their head at Rāma's feet, but being too diffident themselves to put a question to the Lord, they looked towards Hanumān, wishing to hear from the Lord's own mouth, an explanation which would terminate their doubts. The reader of the heart understood this perfectly and said, "What is it you wish to know, Hanumān?" Then replied Hanumān with clasped hands, "Hearken, all-merciful Lord God: Bharat, Sire, wishes to ask something, but is too diffident to speak out." "Monkey, you know my feelings; there are no secrets between me and Bharat." On hearing the Lord's words Bharat clasped his feet, "Hearken, my Lord, reliever of all the anxieties of the suppliant;

दोहा-dohā:

नाथ न मोहि संदेह कछु सपनेहुँ सोक न मोह ।
nātha na mohi saṁdeha kachu sapanehuṁ soka na moha,
केवल कृपा तुम्हारिहि कृपानंद संदोह ॥ ३६ ॥
kevala kṛpā tumhārihi kṛpānaṁda saṁdoha. 36.

Trans:

I have no doubts whatever, Sire—not a shadow of disquietude or distrust; and this all by dint of your mercy, O All-merciful, All-blessed.

चौपाई-caupāī:

करउँ कृपानिधि एक ढिठाई । मैं सेवक तुम्ह जन सुखदाई ॥
karauṁ kṛpānidhi eka ḍhiṭhāī, maiṁ sevaka tumha jana sukhadāī.
संतन्ह कै महिमा रघुराई । बहु बिधि बेद पुरानन्ह गाई ॥
saṁtanha kai mahimā raghurāī, bahu bidhi beda purānanha gāī.
श्रीमुख तुम्ह पुनि कीन्हि बड़ाई । तिन्ह पर प्रभुहि प्रीति अधिकाई ॥
śrīmukha tumha puni kīnhi baṛāī, tinha para prabhuhi prīti adhikāī.
सुना चहउँ प्रभु तिन्ह कर लच्छन । कृपासिंधु गुन ग्यान बिचच्छन ॥
sunā cahauṁ prabhu tinha kara lacchana, kṛpāsiṁdhu guna gyāna bicacchana.
संत असंत भेद बिलगाई । प्रनतपाल मोहि कहहु बुझाई ॥
saṁta asaṁta bheda bilagāī, pranatapāla mohi kahahu bujhāī.
संतन्ह के लच्छन सुनु भ्राता । अगनित श्रुति पुरान बिख्याता ॥
saṁtanha ke lacchana sunu bhrātā, aganita śruti purāna bikhyātā.
संत असंतन्हि कै असि करनी । जिमि कुठार चंदन आचरनी ॥
saṁta asaṁtanhi kai asi karanī, jimi kuṭhāra caṁdana ācaranī.
काटइ परसु मलय सुनु भाई । निज गुन देइ सुगंध बसाई ॥
kāṭai parasu malaya sunu bhāī, nija guna dei sugaṁdha basāī.

Trans:

But if I may presume on your loving-kindness—for I am your servant and you the benefactor of your faithful people—the Vedas and Purānas, O Raghurāī, have sung in various ways the greatness of the saints; you too have exalted them by your own holy lips, declaring that the Lord has a special affection for them. I would fain hear, Sire, their distinctive marks, O gracious discerner of character and understanding. Instruct me, protector of the suppliant, in the notes that distinguish the good from the wicked." "Hearken brother; the characteristics of the good, as told in the Vedas and Purānas are innumerable. The conduct of the good to the wicked is like that of the sandal tree to the axe, for—see brother—the fragrant wood imparts its perfume to the very iron that cuts it down.

दोहा-dohā:

तातें सुर सीसन्ह चढ़त जग बल्लभ श्रीखंड ।
tāte sura sīsanha caṛhata jaga ballabha śrīkhaṁḍa,
अनल दाहि पीटत घनहिं परसु बदन यह दंड ॥ ३७॥
anala dāhi pīṭata ghanahiṁ parasu badana yaha daṁḍa. 37.

Trans:

For this reason sandalwood, in the form of paste, finds its way to the head of gods and is loved by the world; while the axe, for its punishment, has its edge heated in the fire and is well hammered.

चौपाई-caupāī:

बिषय अलंपट सील गुनाकर । पर दुख दुख सुख सुख देखे पर ॥
biṣaya alaṁpaṭa sīla gunākara, para dukha dukha sukha sukha dekhe para.
सम अभूतरिपु बिमद बिरागी । लोभामरष हरष भय त्यागी ॥
sama abhūtaripu bimada birāgī, lobhāmaraṣa haraṣa bhaya tyāgī.
कोमलचित दीनन्ह पर दाया । मन बच क्रम मम भगति अमाया ॥
komalacita dīnanha para dāyā, mana baca krama mama bhagati amāyā.
सबहि मानप्रद आपु अमानी । भरत प्रान सम मम ते प्रानी ॥
sabahi mānaprada āpu amānī, bharata prāna sama mama te prānī.
बिगत काम मम नाम परायन । सांति बिरति बिनती मुदितायन ॥
bigata kāma mama nāma parāyana, sāṁti birati binatī muditāyana.
सीतलता सरलता मयत्री । द्विज पद प्रीति धर्म जनयत्री ॥
sītalatā saralatā mayatrī, dvija pada prīti dharma janayatrī.
ए सब लच्छन बसहिं जासु उर । जानेहु तात संत संतत फुर ॥
e saba lacchana basahiṁ jāsu ura, jānehu tāta saṁta saṁtata phura.
सम दम नियम नीति नहिं डोलहिं । परुष बचन कबहूँ नहिं बोलहिं ॥
sama dama niyama nīti nahiṁ ḍolahiṁ, paruṣa bacana kabahūṁ nahiṁ bolahiṁ.

Trans:

Without any attachment to sensual objects; store-houses of virtue and generosity; sorrowing in the sorrow of others and finding joy in their joy—is characteristic of a saint. Equable, devoid of animosity; sober, passionless; conquerors of greed and impatience, joy and fear—such are the saints. Tender of heart, compassionate to the poor; with a guileless devotion to me in thought, word and deed; giving honor to all but claiming none for themselves—such saintly souls, O Bharat, are dear to me as my own life. Unselfish, devoted to my name, happy abodes of tranquility, continence and humility; models of contentment, simplicity, benevolence, piety; and devoted to Brahmins—a heart in which such qualities abide can only be the heart of a saint, brothers. The saintly are never disturbed in their quietude, their self-control, their religious observances, or their moral principles; they never utter a harsh word;

दोहा-dohā:

निंदा अस्तुति उभय सम ममता मम पद कंज ।
niṁdā astuti ubhaya sama mamatā mama pada kaṁja,
ते सज्जन मम प्रानप्रिय गुन मंदिर सुख पुंज ॥ ३८॥
te sajjana mama prānapriya guna maṁdira sukha puṁja. 38.

Trans:

they regard praise and blame as both alike—due to their exclusive devotion to my lotus feet. Such are the treasures of virtue, the compendiums of bliss, who are the virtuous, and whom I love as my own soul.

चौपाई-caupāī:

सुनहु असंतन्ह केर सुभाऊ । भूलेहुँ संगति करिअ न काऊ ॥
sunahu asaṁtanha kera subhāū, bhūlehuṁ saṁgati karia na kāū.
तिन्ह कर संग सदा दुखदाई । जिमि कपिलहि घालइ हरहाई ॥
tinha kara saṁga sadā dukhadāī, jimi kapilahi ghālai harahāī.
खलन्ह हृदयँ अति ताप बिसेषी । जरहिं सदा पर संपति देखी ॥
khalanha hṛdayaṁ ati tāpa biseṣī, jarahiṁ sadā para saṁpati dekhī.
जहँ कहुँ निंदा सुनहिं पराई । हरषहिं मनहुँ परी निधि पाई ॥
jahaṁ kahuṁ niṁdā sunahiṁ parāī, haraṣahiṁ manahuṁ parī nidhi pāī.
काम क्रोध मद लोभ परायन । निर्दय कपटी कुटिल मलायन ॥
kāma krodha mada lobha parāyana, nirdaya kapaṭī kuṭila malāyana.
बयरु अकारन सब काहू सों । जो कर हित अनहित ताहू सों ॥
bayaru akārana saba kāhū soṁ, jo kara hita anahita tāhū soṁ.
झूठइ लेना झूठइ देना । झूठइ भोजन झूठ चबेना ॥
jhūṭhai lenā jhūṭhai denā, jhūṭhai bhojana jhūṭha cabenā.
बोलहिं मधुर बचन जिमि मोरा । खाइ महा अति हृदय कठोरा ॥
bolahiṁ madhura bacana jimi morā, khāi mahā ati hṛdaya kaṭhorā.

Trans:

Hear now the characteristics of the impious, association with whom should be scrupulously avoided—for their company ever brings woe, even as a wicked cow ruins by her company a cow of noble breed. The heart of the wicked is a consuming fire, which is ever rekindled at the sight of another's prosperity; and whenever they hear a neighbor abused, they are as glad as if they had picked up a treasure on the road. Devoted to sensuality; choleric, arrogant and greedy; censorious, treacherous, perverse and impure; cherishing causeless animosities against everyone; disliking anything that others like; false in taking, false in giving, false in all matters big or small; speaking plausible words, but ruthless of heart—like the peacock that devours the biggest snake;

दोहा-dohā:

पर द्रोही पर दार रत पर धन पर अपबाद ।
para drohī para dāra rata para dhana para apabāda,
ते नर पाँवर पापमय देह धरें मनुजाद ॥ ३९॥
te nara pāṁvara pāpamaya deha dhareṁ manujāda. 39.

Trans:

injurious to their neighbor, covetous of his wife and wealth and gloating over his misfortunes—men, thus vile and abominable, are ruthless incarnate fiends.

चौपाई-caupāī:

लोभइ ओढ़न लोभइ डासन । सिस्नोदर पर जमपुर त्रास न ॥
lobhai oṛhana lobhai ḍāsana, sisnodara para jamapura trāsa na.
काहू की जौं सुनहिं बड़ाई । स्वास लेहिं जनु जूड़ी आई ॥
kāhū kī jauṁ sunahiṁ baṛāī, svāsa lehiṁ janu jūṛī āī.
जब काहू कै देखहिं बिपती । सुखी भए मानहुँ जग नृपती ॥
jaba kāhū kai dekhahiṁ bipatī, sukhī bhae mānahuṁ jaga nṛpatī.
स्वारथ रत परिवार बिरोधी । लंपट काम लोभ अति क्रोधी ॥
svāratha rata parivāra birodhī, laṁpaṭa kāma lobha ati krodhī.
मातु पिता गुर बिप्र न मानहिं । आपु गए अरु घालहिं आनहिं ॥
mātu pitā gura bipra na mānahiṁ, āpu gae aru ghālahiṁ ānahiṁ.
करहिं मोह बस द्रोह परावा । संत संग हरि कथा न भावा ॥
karahiṁ moha basa droha parāvā, saṁta saṁga hari kathā na bhāvā.
अवगुन सिंधु मंदमति कामी । बेद बिदूषक परधन स्वामी ॥
avaguna siṁdhu maṁdamati kāmī, beda bidūṣaka paradhana svāmī.

बिप्र द्रोह पर द्रोह बिसेषा । दंभ कपट जियँ धरें सुबेषा ॥
bipra droha para droha biseṣā, dambha kapaṭa jiyam̐ dharem̐ subeṣā.

Trans:
Coveting dress, coveting bed, addicted to lust and gluttony, with no fear of the realm of Yama before their eyes, catching their breath as though they had got the ague when they hear of anyone's advancement, but as glad as though they had been made kings of the world, when they see their neighbor in distress; devoted to their own selfish interests, quarrelsome to their kinsfolk, dissolute, avaricious and choleric; disobedient to father and mother, to Guru and Brahmin; dragging down others into the same ruin with themselves, infatuated workers of others' ill; taking no pleasure in the company of the good or in discourse about Hari; oceans of immorality, dull of understanding, lascivious, revilers of the Vedas, masterful with other men's goods, special torment of the Brahmins and the gods, with deceit and treachery in their heart though outwardly fair seeming;

दोहा-dohā:

ऐसे अधम मनुज खल कृतजुग त्रेताँ नाहिं ।
aise adhama manuja khala kṛtajuga tretām̐ nāhim̐,
द्वापर कछुक बृंद बहु होइहहिं कलिजुग माहिं ॥४०॥
dvāpara kachuka bṛm̐da bahu hoihahim̐ kalijuga māhim̐. 40.

Trans:
no such vile wretches of men existed in the first and second Age, and only a few in the third, but in the fourth there are swarms of them.

चौपाई-caupāī:

पर हित सरिस धर्म नहिं भाई । पर पीड़ा सम नहिं अधमाई ॥
para hita sarisa dharma nahim̐ bhāī, para pīṛā sama nahim̐ adhamāī.
निर्णय सकल पुरान बेद कर । कहेउँ तात जानहि कोबिद नर ॥
nirṇaya sakala purāna beda kara, kaheum̐ tāta jānahi kobida nara.
नर सरीर धरि जे पर पीरा । करहिं ते सहहिं महा भव भीरा ॥
nara sarīra dhari je para pīrā, karahim̐ te sahahim̐ mahā bhava bhīrā.
करहिं मोह बस नर अघ नाना । स्वारथ रत परलोक नसाना ॥
karahim̐ moha basa nara agha nānā, svāratha rata paraloka nasānā.
कालरूप तिन्ह कहँ मैं भ्राता । सुभ अरु असुभ कर्म फल दाता ॥
kālarūpa tinha kaham̐ maim̐ bhrātā, subha aru asubha karma phala dātā.
अस बिचारि जे परम सयाने । भजहिं मोहि संसृत दुख जाने ॥
asa bicāri je parama sayāne, bhajahim̐ mohi saṁsṛta dukha jāne.
त्यागहिं कर्म सुभासुभ दायक । भजहिं मोहि सुर नर मुनि नायक ॥
tyāgahim̐ karma subhāsubha dāyaka, bhajahim̐ mohi sura nara muni nāyaka.
संत असंतन्ह के गुन भाषे । ते न परहिं भव जिन्ह लखि राखे ॥
saṁta asaṁtanha ke guna bhāṣe, te na parahim̐ bhava jinha lakhi rākhe.

O my brother, there is no religion like benevolence and no meanness like malevolence. What I now declare to you is the sum of the Vedas and Purānas and the verdict of the philosophers. Men, who in the body, cause suffering to others undergo an enormous series of transmigrations. Men are so infatuated that in their devotion to their own selfish interests they commit many sins and ruin their prospects for the next world. I reveal myself to them, brother, as their destiny and assign them the reward of their deeds, whether good or ill. The truly wise consider the matter thus and worship me, regarding the world only as a burden; they discard action with its results, good or bad, and devoutly adore me, the king of gods and men and saints. Thus have I declared the characteristics of the good and the bad; they who remember them, will not be submerged in the deluge of existence.

दोहा-dohā:

सुनहु तात माया कृत गुन अरु दोष अनेक ।
sunahu tāta māyā kṛta guna aru doṣa aneka,
गुन यह उभय न देखिअहिं देखिअ सो अबिबेक ॥४१॥
guna yaha ubhaya na dekhiahim̐ dekhia so abibeka. 41.

Trans:
Hearken, brother: the multitudinous forms of merit and demerit are all the products of Māyā; the greatest merit is to notice neither; to notice them is an imperfection of knowledge."

चौपाई-caupāī:

श्रीमुख बचन सुनत सब भाई । हरषे प्रेम न हृदयँ समाई ॥
śrīmukha bacana sunata saba bhāī, haraṣe prema na hṛdayam̐ samāī.
करहिं बिनय अति बारहिं बारा । हनूमान हियँ हरष अपारा ॥
karahim̐ binaya ati bārahim̐ bārā, hanūmāna hiyam̐ haraṣa apārā.
पुनि रघुपति निज मंदिर गए । एहि बिधि चरित करत नित नए ॥
puni raghupati nija maṁdira gae, ehi bidhi carita karata nita nae.
बार बार नारद मुनि आवहिं । चरित पुनीत राम के गावहिं ॥
bāra bāra nārada muni āvahim̐, carita punīta rāma ke gāvahim̐.
नित नव चरित देखि मुनि जाहीं । ब्रह्मलोक सब कथा कहाहीं ॥
nita nava carita dekhi muni jāhīm̐, brahmaloka saba kathā kahāhīm̐.
सुनि बिरंचि अतिसय सुख मानहिं । पुनि पुनि तात करहु गुन गानहिं ॥
suni biraṁci atisaya sukha mānahim̐, puni puni tāta karahu guna gānahim̐.
सनकादिक नारदहि सराहहिं । जद्यपि ब्रह्म निरत मुनि आहहिं ॥
sanakādika nāradahi sarāhahim̐, jadyapi brahma nirata muni āhahim̐.
सुनि गुन गान समाधि बिसारी । सादर सुनहिं परम अधिकारी ॥
suni guna gāna samādhi bisārī, sādara sunahim̐ parama adhikārī.

On hearing this utterance of the divine mouth, the brothers rejoiced and their hearts overflowed with love. Again and again they paid him profound homage, while a boundless delight filled the soul of Hanumān also. The Lord of the Raghus then retired to his own palace. In this way he enacted some new sport every day. The sage Nārad came time after time and hymned Rāma's holy acts, every day finding something new to record. He then went to Brahmmā's realm and there recited the whole story. Brahmmā, on hearing it, was so highly pleased that he urged him to repeat it again and again. Sanat-kumār and others marveled at Nārad, and the saints, though absorbed in the contemplation of the Supreme Spirit, forgot their abstraction on hearing his hymn of praise. The highest powers listened reverently.

दोहा-dohā:

जीवनमुक्त ब्रह्मपर चरित सुनहिं तजि ध्यान ।
jīvanamukta brahmapara carita sunahim̐ taji dhyāna,
जे हरि कथाँ न करहिं रति तिन्ह के हिय पाषान ॥४२॥
je hari kathām̐ na karahim̐ rati tinha ke hiya pāṣāna. 42.

Trans:
Even those who are liberated though embodied and are absorbed in Brahmm hear the narrative of Shrī Rāma even by interrupting their meditation. Truly theirs must be a heart of stone who take no delight in the stories of Rāma.

चौपाई-caupāī:

एक बार रघुनाथ बोलाए । गुर द्विज पुरबासी सब आए ॥
eka bāra raghunātha bolāe, gura dvija purabāsī saba āe.
बैठे गुर मुनि अरु द्विज सज्जन । बोले बचन भगत भव भंजन ॥
baiṭhe gura muni aru dvija sajjana, bole bacana bhagata bhava bhaṁjana.
सुनहु सकल पुरजन मम बानी । कहउँ न कछु ममता उर आनी ॥
sunahu sakala purajana mama bānī, kahaum̐ na kachu mamatā ura ānī.

नहिं अनीति नहिं कछु प्रभुताई । सुनहु करहु जो तुम्हहि सोहाई ॥
nahiṁ anīti nahiṁ kachu prabhutāī, sunahu karahu jo tumhahi sohāī.
सोइ सेवक प्रियतम मम सोई । मम अनुसासन मानै जोई ॥
soi sevaka priyatama mama soī, mama anusāsana mānai joī.
जौं अनीति कछु भाषौं भाई । तौ मोहि बरजहु भय बिसराई ॥
jauṁ anīti kachu bhāṣauṁ bhāī, tau mohi barajahu bhaya bisarāī.
बड़ें भाग मानुष तनु पावा । सुर दुर्लभ सब ग्रंथन्हि गावा ॥
baṛeṁ bhāga mānuṣa tanu pāvā, sura durlabha saba gramthanhi gāvā.
साधन धाम मोच्छ कर द्वारा । पाइ न जेहिं परलोक सँवारा ॥
sādhana dhāma moccha kara dvārā, pāi na jehiṁ paraloka saṁvārā.

Trans:

One day, by Rāma's invitation all the Gurūs and Brahmins and people of the city came together; and when the priests and nobles had taken their seat in the assembly, the Comforter of the pious made them this speech: "Hearken to my words, all ye people of the city; I speak without any selfish motive at heart, neither wronging another nor aggrandizing myself; listen and act as may seem good to you. He is my servant and he my best-beloved, who accepts my commands. If I say anything that is wrong, brother, do not be afraid to correct me. All the Scriptures declare that it is a great fortune and a great difficulty surmounted—to be born of a human body, which is a store-house of opportunities, a gate of deliverance. Those who have received it and still attain not to heaven,

दोहा-dohā:

सो परत्र दुख पावइ सिर धुनि धुनि पछिताइ ।
so paratra dukha pāvai sira dhuni dhuni pachitāi,
कालहि कर्महि ईस्वरहि मिथ्या दोष लगाइ ॥४३॥
kālahi karmahi īsvarahi mithyā doṣa lagāi. 43.

Trans:

they reap torment in the next world and beat their head in despair, wrongly attributing the blame to time, fate and God.

चौपाई-caupāī:

एहि तन कर फल बिषय न भाई । स्वर्गउ स्वल्प अंत दुखदाई ॥
ehi tana kara phala biṣaya na bhāī, svargau svalpa aṁta dukhadāī.
नर तनु पाइ बिषयँ मन देहीं । पलटि सुधा ते सठ बिष लेहीं ॥
nara tanu pāi biṣayaṁ mana dehīṁ, palaṭi sudhā te saṭha biṣa lehīṁ.
ताहि कबहुँ भल कहइ न कोई । गुंजा ग्रहइ परस मनि खोई ॥
tāhi kabahuṁ bhala kahai na koī, guṁjā grahai parasa mani khoī.
आकर चारि लच्छ चौरासी । जोनि भ्रमत यह जिव अबिनासी ॥
ākara cāri laccha caurāsī, joni bhramata yaha jiva abināsī.
फिरत सदा माया कर प्रेरा । काल कर्म सुभाव गुन घेरा ॥
phirata sadā māyā kara prerā, kāla karma subhāva guna gherā.
कबहुँक करि करुना नर देही । देत ईस बिनु हेतु सनेही ॥
kabahuṁka kari karunā nara dehī, deta īsa binu hetu sanehī.
नर तनु भव बारिधि कहुँ बेरो । सन्मुख मरुत अनुग्रह मेरो ॥
nara tanu bhava bāridhi kahuṁ bero, sanmukha maruta anugraha mero.
करनधार सदगुर दृढ़ नावा । दुर्लभ साज सुलभ करि पावा ॥
karanadhāra sadagura dṛṛha nāvā, durlabha sāja sulabha kari pāvā.

Trans:

But materialism, brother, is not the proper object of the human body: it is happiness for a very brief period, but ends in misery. The possessor of a human body, who gives himself up to materialism, is like a fool who chooses poison in preference to ambrosia. He is one of whom none can speak well; he throws away the philosopher's stone to pick up a peppercorn. Such a creature drifts forever among the four modes of birth and the eighty-four lakhs of living species, perpetually changing at the will of Māyā, and girded by Time, Fate, Nature and Phenomena. At some time or another, God, of his mercy and without any reason for the favor, gives Jiva a human body, a raft on which he may cross the ocean of existence, with my grace as a fair wind to speed him on his course. With pious teachers at the helm, he easily procures all the equipment of a stout ship, which would otherwise be beyond him.

दोहा-dohā:

जो न तरै भव सागर नर समाज अस पाइ ।
jo na tarai bhava sāgara nara samāja asa pāi,
सो कृत निंदक मंदमति आत्माहन गति जाइ ॥४४॥
so kṛta niṁdaka maṁdamati ātmāhana gati jāi. 44.

Trans:

If thus equipt, he fails to cross the sea, he is an ungrateful wretch, bent on his own destruction.

चौपाई-caupāī:

जौं परलोक इहाँ सुख चहहू । सुनि मम बचन हृदयँ दृढ़ गहहू ॥
jauṁ paraloka ihāṁ sukha cahahū, suni mama bacana hṛdayaṁ dṛṛha gahahū.
सुलभ सुखद मारग यह भाई । भगति मोरि पुरान श्रुति गाई ॥
sulabha sukhada māraga yaha bhāī, bhagati mori purāna śruti gāī.
ग्यान अगम प्रत्यूह अनेका । साधन कठिन न मन कहुँ टेका ॥
gyāna agama pratyūha anekā, sādhana kaṭhina na mana kahuṁ ṭekā.
करत कष्ट बहु पावइ कोऊ । भक्ति हीन मोहि प्रिय नहिं सोऊ ॥
karata kaṣṭa bahu pāvai koū, bhakti hīna mohi priya nahiṁ soū.
भक्ति सुतंत्र सकल सुख खानी । बिनु सतसंग न पावहिं प्रानी ॥
bhakti sutaṁtra sakala sukha khānī, binu satasaṁga na pāvahiṁ prānī.
पुन्य पुंज बिनु मिलहिं न संता । सतसंगति संसृति कर अंता ॥
punya puṁja binu milahiṁ na saṁtā, satasaṁgati saṁsṛti kara aṁtā.
पुन्य एक जग महुँ नहिं दूजा । मन क्रम बचन बिप्र पद पूजा ॥
punya eka jaga mahuṁ nahiṁ dūjā, mana krama bacana bipra pada pūjā.
सानुकूल तेहि पर मुनि देवा । जो तजि कपटु करइ द्विज सेवा ॥
sānukūla tehi para muni devā, jo taji kapaṭu karai dvija sevā.

Trans:

Whoso desires happiness in this world and the next will hearken to my words and imprint them deeply in his heart. It is an easy and a pleasant road, brother—that of my service, as the Vedas and Purānas declare. Knowledge is difficult and beset with impediments, its appliances are cumbrous and it has no grasp on the soul. Though a man endures endless tortures, without devotion he is no friend of mine. Devotion is all-powerful and a mine of every blessing; but men cannot attain to it except by the fellowship of the saints. The saints are not won except by meritorious deeds; their fellowship is the end of mundane existence. Now there is no other meritorious deed in the whole world but this one: to worship Knowers of Brahmm in thought, word and deed; seers and gods are all in his favor who eschews guile and devotes himself to them.

दोहा-dohā:

औरउ एक गुपुत मत सबहि कहउँ कर जोरि ।
aurau eka guputa mata sabahi kahauṁ kara jori,
संकर भजन बिना नर भगति न पावइ मोरि ॥४५॥
saṁkara bhajana binā nara bhagati na pāvai mori. 45.

Trans:

With joined palms I lay before you another secret doctrine: without adoring Shankar man cannot attain devotion to me.

चौपाई-caupāī:

कहहु भगति पथ कवन प्रयासा । जोग न मख जप तप उपवासा ॥
kahahu bhagati patha kavana prayāsā, joga na makha japa tapa upavāsā.
सरल सुभाव न मन कुटिलाई । जथा लाभ संतोष सदाई ॥

sarala subhāva na mana kuṭilāī, jathā lābha saṁtoṣa sadāī.

मोर दास कहाइ नर आसा । करइ तौ कहहु कहा बिस्वासा ॥
mora dāsa kahāi nara āsā, karai tau kahahu kahā bisvāsā.

बहुत कहउँ का कथा बढ़ाई । एहि आचरन बस्य मैं भाई ॥
bahuta kahauṁ kā kathā baṛhāī, ehi ācarana basya maiṁ bhāī.

बैर न बिग्रह आस न त्रासा । सुखमय ताहि सदा सब आसा ॥
baira na bigraha āsa na trāsā, sukhamaya tāhi sadā saba āsā.

अनारंभ अनिकेत अमानी । अनघ अरोष दच्छ बिग्यानी ॥
anārambha aniketa amānī, anagha aroṣa daccha bigyānī.

प्रीति सदा सज्जन संसर्गा । तृन सम बिषय स्वर्ग अपबर्गा ॥
prīti sadā sajjana saṁsargā, tṛna sama biṣaya svarga apabargā.

भगति पच्छ हठ नहिं सठताई । दुष्ट तर्क सब दूरि बहाई ॥
bhagati paccha haṭha nahiṁ saṭhatāī, duṣṭa tarka saba dūri bahāī.

Trans:

Tell me, what pains are involved in the path of Devotion: it requires neither abstract meditation, nor sacrifice, prayer, penance, fasting: only simplicity of character, a mind void of forwardness and absolute content, whatever may befall. If one, who is called a worshipper of mine, trusts in man, tell me where is his trust in me? But why protract my discourse to such a length? These are the practices, brother, by which I am won: avoidance of enmity and rancor, of hope and fear, a constant atmosphere of perfect repose; without home, without pride, without sin, without wrath; placid, provident and wise; ever devoted to the fellowship of the saints; accounting as nothing every object of sense, and even pleasures of heaven and final deliverance upon death; persistent in faith, innocent of wickedness, a stranger to impious skepticism;

दोहा-dohā:

मम गुन ग्राम नाम रत गत ममता मद मोह ।
mama guna grāma nāma rata gata mamatā mada moha,

ता कर सुख सोइ जानइ परानंद संदोह ॥४६॥
tā kara sukha soi jānai parānaṁda saṁdoha. 46.

Trans:

devoted to my name, which is the sum of all my perfections; devoid of selfishness, conceit and vain imagination—such a man's happiness, be assured, is the very sum of transcendental felicity."

चौपाई-caupāī:

सुनत सुधासम बचन राम के । गहे सबनि पद कृपाधाम के ॥
sunata sudhāsama bacana rāma ke, gahe sabani pada kṛpādhāma ke.

जननि जनक गुर बंधु हमारे । कृपा निधान प्रान ते प्यारे ॥
janani janaka gura baṁdhu hamāre, kṛpā nidhāna prāna te pyāre.

तनु धनु धाम राम हितकारी । सब बिधि तुम्ह प्रनतारति हारी ॥
tanu dhanu dhāma rāma hitakārī, saba bidhi tumha pranatārati hārī.

असि सिख तुम्ह बिनु देइ न कोऊ । मातु पिता स्वारथ रत ओऊ ॥
asi sikha tumha binu dei na koū, mātu pitā svāratha rata oū.

हेतु रहित जग जुग उपकारी । तुम्ह तुम्हार सेवक असुरारी ॥
hetu rahita jaga juga upakārī, tumha tumhāra sevaka asurārī.

स्वारथ मीत सकल जग माहीं । सपनेहुँ प्रभु परमारथ नाहीं ॥
svāratha mīta sakala jaga māhīṁ, sapanehuṁ prabhu paramāratha nāhīṁ.

सब के बचन प्रेम रस साने । सुनि रघुनाथ हृदयँ हरषाने ॥
saba ke bacana prema rasa sāne, suni raghunātha hṛdayaṁ haraṣāne.

निज निज गृह गए आयसु पाई । बरनत प्रभु बतकही सुहाई ॥
nija nija gṛha gae āyasu pāī, baranata prabhu batakahī suhāī.

Trans:

On hearing the gracious Rāma's ambrosial speech, they all embraced his feet, "Fountain of mercy, you are our father, our mother, our spiritual guide and our brethren and are dearer than our life. You, O Rāma, have blessed us in body, substance and house and have removed all the sorrows of your suppliants. No one but you could teach us this lesson; for even father and mother are self-interested. The only two disinterested friends in the world are you yourself and your servants, O conqueror of the demons. Every friend in the world has his own object in view; no one, Sire, ever dreams of the highest object." When Raghunāth heard them all speak in such terms of devotion, he was rejoiced at heart; and they, on receiving his permission, returned to their several homes, making the Lord the glorious theme of all their talks.

दोहा-dohā:

उमा अवधबासी नर नारि कृतारथ रूप ।
umā avadhabāsī nara nāri kṛtāratha rūpa,

ब्रह्म सच्चिदानंद घन रघुनायक जहँ भूप ॥४७॥
brahma saccidānaṁda ghana raghunāyaka jahaṁ bhūpa. 47.

Trans:

O Umā, every man and woman among the inhabitants of Avadh was the picture of satisfaction; the supreme felicity of heaven suffused the whole city when Rāma was King.

चौपाई-caupāī:

एक बार बसिष्ट मुनि आए । जहाँ राम सुखधाम सुहाए ॥
eka bāra basiṣṭa muni āe, jahāṁ rāma sukhadhāma suhāe.

अति आदर रघुनायक कीन्हा । पद पखारि पादोदक लीन्हा ॥
ati ādara raghunāyaka kīnhā, pada pakhāri pādodaka līnhā.

राम सुनहु मुनि कह कर जोरी । कृपासिंधु बिनती कछु मोरी ॥
rāma sunahu muni kaha kara jorī, kṛpāsiṁdhu binatī kachu morī.

देखि देखि आचरन तुम्हारा । होत मोह मम हृदयँ अपारा ॥
dekhi dekhi ācarana tumhārā, hota moha mama hṛdayaṁ apārā.

महिमा अमिति बेद नहिं जाना । मैं केहि भाँति कहउँ भगवाना ॥
mahimā amiti beda nahiṁ jānā, maiṁ kehi bhāṁti kahauṁ bhagavānā.

उपरोहित्य कर्म अति मंदा । बेद पुरान सुमृति कर निंदा ॥
uparohitya karma ati maṁdā, beda purāna sumṛti kara niṁdā.

जब न लेउँ मैं तब बिधि मोही । कहा लाभ आगें सुत तोही ॥
jaba na leuṁ maiṁ taba bidhi mohī, kahā lābha āgeṁ suta tohī.

परमातमा ब्रह्म नर रूपा । होइहि रघुकुल भूषन भूपा ॥
paramātamā brahma nara rūpā, hoihi raghukula bhūṣana bhūpā.

Trans:

One day saint Vasishtha came to visit the blessed and glorious Rāma. The prince of the house of Raghu received him with the most profound respect and laved his feet and sipped of the element. "Hearken O Rāma," cried the sage, clasping his hands, "Ocean of mercy, I make this humble submission; even as I watch your doings, boundless bewilderment possesses my soul. Even the Vedas fail to tell your immeasurable greatness—which is beyond the comprehension; how then can I tell it? The business of a family-priest is very contemptible—the Vedas and Purānas and all the Scriptures make small account of it. At first I refused it, but the Creator said to me, "You will be a gainer hereafter, my son; Braham, the Supreme Spirit, will be born in human form as a King, the glory of the race of Raghus."

दोहा-dohā:

तब मैं हृदयँ बिचारा जोग जग्य ब्रत दान ।
taba maiṁ hṛdayaṁ bicārā joga jagya brata dāna,

जा कहुँ करिअ सो पैहउँ धर्म न एहि सम आन ॥४८॥
jā kahuṁ karia so paihauṁ dharma na ehi sama āna. 48.

Trans:

Then I thought to myself: I shall thus attain to him who is the object of all contemplation, penance, charity and sacrifice; what better course can I pursue?

चौपाई-caupāī:

जप तप नियम जोग निज धर्मा । श्रुति संभव नाना सुभ कर्मा ॥
japa tapa niyama joga nija dharmā, śruti saṁbhava nānā subha karmā.
ग्यान दया दम तीरथ मज्जन । जहँ लगि धर्म कहत श्रुति सज्जन ॥
gyāna dayā dama tīratha majjana, jahaṁ lagi dharma kahata śruti sajjana.
आगम निगम पुरान अनेका । पढ़े सुने कर फल प्रभु एका ॥
āgama nigama purāna anekā, paṛhe sune kara phala prabhu ekā.
तव पद पंकज प्रीति निरंतर । सब साधन कर यह फल सुंदर ॥
tava pada paṁkaja prīti niraṁtara, saba sādhana kara yaha phala suṁdara.
छूटइ मल कि मलहि के धोएँ । घृत कि पाव कोइ बारि बिलोएँ ॥
chūṭai mala ki malahi ke dhoeṁ, ghṛta ki pāva koi bāri biloeṁ.
प्रेम भगति जल बिनु रघुराई । अभिअंतर मल कबहुँ न जाई ॥
prema bhagati jala binu raghurāī, abhiaṁtara mala kabahuṁ na jāī.
सोइ सर्बग्य तग्य सोइ पंडित । सोइ गुन गृह बिग्यान अखंडित ॥
soi sarbagya tagya soi paṁḍita, soi guna gṛha bigyāna akhaṁḍita.
दच्छ सकल लच्छन जुत सोई । जाकें पद सरोज रति होई ॥
daccha sakala lacchana juta soī, jākeṁ pada saroja rati hoī.

Trans:

Prayer, penance, pious observances, and doing one's duty in life are different good actions prescribed by the Scriptures. Knowledge, mercy, self-control, bathing at holy places and all the religious practices inculcated by revelation, as also the study of the Vedas and sacred traditions and numerous Purānas, are all the different means to one glorious end: a constant devotion to your lotus feet O Rāma. Dirt cannot be removed by cleansing with dirt; ghee cannot be obtained by churning water; the impurity accumulated within can never be washed away by however many acts—even good ones—and the only final remedy is Devotion. Except by cleansing with the water of loving Devotion, O Lord of the Raghus, the worldly dirt will not wash off. He alone is all-wise—he the philosopher, the scholar, the abode of virtues and possessed of uninterrupted immediate perception, the truly judicious and the possessor of every auspicious attribute—he who is devoted to your lotus feet.

दोहा-dohā:

नाथ एक बर मागउँ राम कृपा करि देहु ।
nātha eka bara māgauṁ rāma kṛpā kari dehu,
जन्म जन्म प्रभु पद कमल कबहुँ घटै जनि नेहु ॥४९॥
janma janma prabhu pada kamala kabahuṁ ghaṭai jani nehu. 49.

Trans:

My Lord, I would ask one boon, grant it, O Rāma, in your clemency: in all my future births may my love for my Lord's lotus feet never diminish."

चौपाई-caupāī:

अस कहि मुनि बसिष्ट गृह आए । कृपासिंधु के मन अति भाए ॥
asa kahi muni basiṣṭa gṛha āe, kṛpāsiṁdhu ke mana ati bhāe.
हनूमान भरतादिक भ्राता । संग लिए सेवक सुखदाता ॥
hanūmāna bharatādika bhrātā, saṁga lie sevaka sukhadātā.
पुनि कृपाल पुर बाहेर गए । गज रथ तुरग मगावत भए ॥
puni kṛpāla pura bāhera gae, gaja ratha turaga magāvata bhae.
देखि कृपा करि सकल सराहे । दिए उचित जिन्ह जिन्ह तेइ चाहे ॥
dekhi kṛpā kari sakala sarāhe, die ucita jinha jinha tei cāhe.
हरन सकल श्रम प्रभु श्रम पाई । गए जहाँ सीतल अवँराई ॥
harana sakala śrama prabhu śrama pāī, gae jahāṁ sītala avaṁrāī.
भरत दीन्ह निज बसन डसाई । बैठे प्रभु सेवहिं सब भाई ॥
bharata dīnha nija basana ḍasāī, baiṭhe prabhu sevahiṁ saba bhāī.
मारुतसुत तब मारूत करई । पुलक बपुष लोचन जल भरई ॥
mārutasuta taba mārūta karaī, pulaka bapuṣa locana jala bharaī.
हनूमान सम नहिं बड़भागी । नहिं कोउ राम चरन अनुरागी ॥
hanūmāna sama nahiṁ baṛabhāgī, nahiṁ kou rāma carana anurāgī.
गिरिजा जासु प्रीति सेवकाई । बार बार प्रभु निज मुख गाई ॥
girijā jāsu prīti sevakāī, bāra bāra prabhu nija mukha gāī.

Trans:

So saying saint Vasishtha returned home. The All-merciful was highly pleased with him in his heart of hearts. Then, being ever gracious to his servants, Shrī Rāma took with him Hanumān and Bharat and his other brothers and in his benignity went outside the city, where he ordered up elephants, chariots and horses. After inspecting them he was pleased and praised them; then he distributed them all—giving each whatever one wished. The Lord, the remover of all weariness, himself acted aweary, and repaired to a cool mango grove, where Bharat spread his own raiment on the ground, and there the Lord took his seat, with all his brothers in attendance. The Son-of-wind now began to fan him; his body quivered with emotion and his eyes filled with tears. There is no one so blessed as Hanumān, nor any so devoted to Rāma's feet, whose love and devotion, O Umā, have again and again been told by the Lord with his own lips.

दोहा-dohā:

तेहिं अवसर मुनि नारद आए करतल बीन ।
tehiṁ avasara muni nārada āe karatala bīna,
गावन लगे राम कल कीरति सदा नबीन ॥५०॥
gāvana lage rāma kala kīrati sadā nabīna. 50.

Trans:

At that time came the Saint Nārad, with his lute in his hand, and began to hymn Rāma's glorious renown, that pregnant theme.

चौपाई-caupāī:

मामवलोकय पंकज लोचन । कृपा बिलोकनि सोच बिमोचन ॥
māmavalokaya paṁkaja locana, kṛpā bilokani soca bimocana.
नील तामरस स्याम काम अरि । हृदय कंज मकरंद मधुप हरि ॥
nīla tāmarasa syāma kāma ari, hṛdaya kaṁja makaraṁda madhupa hari.
जातुधान बरूथ बल भंजन । मुनि सज्जन रंजन अघ गंजन ॥
jātudhāna barūtha bala bhaṁjana, muni sajjana raṁjana agha gaṁjana.
भूसुर ससि नव बृंद बलाहक । असरन सरन दीन जन गाहक ॥
bhūsura sasi nava bṛṁda balāhaka, asarana sarana dīna jana gāhaka.
भुज बल बिपुल भार महि खंडित । खर दूषन बिराध बध पंडित ॥
bhuja bala bipula bhāra mahi khaṁḍita, khara dūṣana birādha badha paṁḍita.
रावनारि सुखरूप भूपबर । जय दसरथ कुल कुमुद सुधाकर ॥
rāvanāri sukharūpa bhūpabara, jaya dasaratha kula kumuda sudhākara.
सुजस पुरान बिदित निगमागम । गावत सुर मुनि संत समागम ॥
sujasa purāna bidita nigamāgama, gāvata sura muni saṁta samāgama.
कारुनीक ब्यलीक मद खंडन । सब बिधि कुसल कोसला मंडन ॥
kārunīka byalīka mada khaṁḍana, saba bidhi kusala kosalā maṁḍana.
कलि मल मथन नाम ममताहन । तुलसिदास प्रभु पाहि प्रनत जन ॥
kali mala mathana nāma mamatāhana, tulasidāsa prabhu pāhi pranata jana.

Trans:

"Look upon me O lotus-eyed, of a merciful attribute, liberator from delusion; dark of hue as the blue lotus; conqueror of lust; bee of the perfumed lotus of soul; Harī, breaker of the might of the demon host; delight of the saints and the pious; exterminator of sin; beneficent to Brahmins as a rain-cloud to the new crops; help of the helpless; befriender of the humble; by the might of whose arm earth's grievous burden has been broken; dexterous destroyer of Khar and Dūshan and Viradh; Rāvan's antagonist; incarnation of beauty; noblest of kings. Glory to the moon of the lotus house of Dashrath, whose glory is renowned in the Purānas, the Vedas and all the Scriptures, and sung by gods and patriarchs and all the saintly throng. O merciful Lord, destroyer of falsehood and pride, infinitely glorious glory of Kaushal, whose name corrects all the impurities of this sinful age and puts an end to the delusions of self, have mercy upon your humble adorer, O Lord of Tulsīdās."

दोहा-dohā:

प्रेम सहित मुनि नारद बरनि राम गुन ग्राम ।
prema sahita muni nārada barani rāma guna grāma,
सोभासिंधु हृदयँ धरि गए जहाँ बिधि धाम ॥५१॥
sobhāsiṁdhu hṛdayaṁ dhari gae jahāṁ bidhi dhāma. 51.

Trans:

Having completed his loving recital of Rāma's praises, the venerable Nārad enshrined the Ocean of beauty into his heart and withdrew to the realm of Brahmmā.

चौपाई-caupāī:

गिरिजा सुनहु बिसद यह कथा । मैं सब कही मोरि मति जथा ॥
girijā sunahu bisada yaha kathā, maiṁ saba kahī mori mati jathā.
राम चरित सत कोटि अपारा । श्रुति सारदा न बरनै पारा ॥
rāma carita sata koṭi apārā, śruti sāradā na baranai pārā.
राम अनंत अनंत गुनानी । जन्म कर्म अनंत नामानी ॥
rāma anaṁta anaṁta gunānī, janma karma anaṁta nāmānī.
जल सीकर महि रज गनि जाहीं । रघुपति चरित न बरनि सिराहीं ॥
jala sīkara mahi raja gani jāhīṁ, raghupati carita na barani sirāhīṁ.
बिमल कथा हरि पद दायनी । भगति होइ सुनि अनपायनी ॥
bimala kathā hari pada dāyanī, bhagati hoi suni anapāyanī.
उमा कहिउँ सब कथा सुहाई । जो भुसुंडि खगपतिहि सुनाई ॥
umā kahiuṁ saba kathā suhāī, jo bhusuṁḍi khagapatihi sunāī.
कछुक राम गुन कहेउँ बखानी । अब का कहौं सो कहहु भवानी ॥
kachuka rāma guna kaheuṁ bakhānī, aba kā kahauṁ so kahahu bhavānī.
सुनि सुभ कथा उमा हरषानी । बोली अति बिनीत मृदु बानी ॥
suni subha kathā umā haraṣānī, bolī ati binīta mṛdu bānī.
धन्य धन्य मैं धन्य पुरारी । सुनेउँ राम गुन भव भय हारी ॥
dhanya dhanya maiṁ dhanya purārī, suneuṁ rāma guna bhava bhaya hārī.

Trans:

Hearken O Umā to this glorious legend, the whole of which I have now told to the best of my accomplishment. But Rāma's acts are hundreds of millions in number and beyond all reckoning—and not even the Veda or Shārdā could recount them all. Rāma is infinite and his virtues are infinite, infinite are his incarnations, his actions and his names. You may count the drops in a shower of rain or the dust on the earth, but Rāma's doings defy enumeration. This holy saga enables one to reach the abode of Shrī Harī; whoever hears it is blessed with unceasing devotion. The whole of the delectable history which Bhusundi repeated to the king-of-birds, has now, O Umā, been told you. I have mentioned only a fraction of Rāma's virtues. Now tell me, Bhawānī, what I am to tell you next." Umā was glad to have heard the blessed story and replied in exceedingly polite and soft accents, "I am thrice blessed, O Slayer of the demon Tripura, to have heard Shrī Rāma's praises, that take away the fear of births and deaths.

दोहा-dohā:

तुम्हरी कृपाँ कृपायतन अब कृतकृत्य न मोह ।
tumharī kṛpāṁ kṛpāyatana aba kṛtakṛtya na moha,
जानेउँ राम प्रताप प्रभु चिदानंद संदोह ॥५२क॥
jāneuṁ rāma pratāpa prabhu cidānaṁda saṁdoha. 52(ka).

नाथ तवानन ससि स्रवत कथा सुधा रघुबीर ।
nātha tavānana sasi sravata kathā sudhā raghubīra,
श्रवन पुटन्हि मन पान करि नहिं अघात मतिधीर ॥५२ख॥
śravana puṭanhi mana pāna kari nahiṁ aghāta matidhīra. 52(kha).

Trans:

By your clemency, O most merciful, I have attained my desire and am no longer in doubt. I know the glory of Rāma—that he is the Lord, the sum of all knowledge and joy. O Lord of resolute mind, my soul knows no satiety as I quaff with the cups of my ears the nectar-like story of Shrī Rāma, which flows from your moon-like mouth.

चौपाई-caupāī:

राम चरित जे सुनत अघाहीं । रस बिसेष जाना तिन्ह नाहीं ॥
rāma carita je sunata aghāhīṁ, rasa biseṣa jānā tinha nāhīṁ.
जीवनमुक्त महामुनि जेऊ । हरि गुन सुनहिं निरंतर तेऊ ॥
jīvanamukta mahāmuni jeū, hari guna sunahiṁ niraṁtara teū.
भव सागर चह पार जो पावा । राम कथा ता कहँ दृढ नावा ॥
bhava sāgara caha pāra jo pāvā, rāma kathā tā kahaṁ dṛṛha nāvā.
बिषइन्ह कहँ पुनि हरि गुन ग्रामा । श्रवन सुखद अरु मन अभिरामा ॥
biṣainha kahaṁ puni hari guna grāmā, śravana sukhada aru mana abhirāmā.
श्रवनवंत अस को जग माहीं । जाहि न रघुपति चरित सोहाहीं ॥
śravanavaṁta asa ko jaga māhīṁ, jāhi na raghupati carita sohāhīṁ.
ते जड़ जीव निजात्मक घाती । जिन्हहि न रघुपति कथा सोहाती ॥
te jaṛa jīva nijātmaka ghātī, jinhahi na raghupati kathā sohātī.
हरिचरित्र मानस तुम्ह गावा । सुनि मैं नाथ अमिति सुख पावा ॥
haricaritra mānasa tumha gāvā, suni maiṁ nātha amiti sukha pāvā.
तुम्ह जो कही यह कथा सुहाई । कागभसुंडि गरुड़ प्रति गाई ॥
tumha jo kahī yaha kathā suhāī, kāgabhasuṁḍi garuṛa prati gāī.

Trans:

They, who become satiated with hearing Rāma's history, know not the relish of its singular savor. The great sages, who have been liberated from mundane existence, listen for ever and ever to the virtues of Shri Rāma. Whoever desires to traverse the ocean of life finds in Rāma's glory a sure secure ship. Even the worldly accept the praises of Harī as pleasant to the ear and grateful to the soul—for is there anyone in the world with ears to hear, who takes no pleasure in Rāma's history? They must be dull of soul indeed and the self-destroyers, to whom Rāma's enactments give no delight. While you have been reciting the 'the Mānas Lake of Harī's renown', I have listened, my Lord, with boundless delight. But this delectable story that you have repeated was declared by Kāgabhusumdi to Garud.

दोहा-dohā:

बिरति ग्यान बिग्यान दृढ राम चरन अति नेह ।
birati gyāna bigyāna dṛṛha rāma carana ati neha,
बायस तन रघुपति भगति मोहि परम संदेह ॥५३॥
bāyasa tana raghupati bhagati mohi parama saṁdeha. 53.

Trans:

Now I marvel greatly, how anyone in the form of a crow could be a votary of Rāma's? And possess such self-control and knowledge and wisdom and such staunch devotion to Rāma's holy feet?"

चौपाई-caupāī:

नर सहस्र महँ सुनहु पुरारी । कोउ एक होइ धर्म ब्रतधारी ॥
nara sahasra mahaṁ sunahu purārī, kou eka hoi dharma bratadhārī.
धर्मसील कोटिक महँ कोई । बिषय बिमुख बिराग रत होई ॥
dharmasīla koṭika mahaṁ koī, biṣaya bimukha birāga rata hoī.
कोटि बिरक्त मध्य श्रुति कहई । सम्यक ग्यान सकृत कोउ लहई ॥

koṭi birakta madhya śruti kahaī, samyaka gyāna sakṛta kou lahaī.

ग्यानवंत कोटिक महँ कोऊ। जीवनमुक्त सकृत जग सोऊ॥
gyānavaṁta koṭika mahaṁ koū, jīvanamukta sakṛta jaga soū.

तिन्ह सहस्र महुँ सब सुख खानी। दुर्लभ ब्रह्म लीन बिग्यानी॥
tinha sahasra mahuṁ saba sukha khānī, durlabha brahma līna bigyānī.

धर्मसील बिरक्त अरु ग्यानी। जीवनमुक्त ब्रह्मपर प्रानी॥
dharmasīla birakta aru gyānī, jīvanamukta brahmapara prānī.

सब ते सो दुर्लभ सुरराया। राम भगति रत गत मद माया॥
saba te so durlabha surarāyā, rāma bhagati rata gata mada māyā.

सो हरिभगति काग किमि पाई। बिस्वनाथ मोहि कहहु बुझाई॥
so haribhagati kāga kimi pāī, bisvanātha mohi kahahu bujhāī.

Trans:

Hearken Purārī: among a thousand men, there may be one who is steadfast in the practices of his religion; among ten-million such, there may be one who loathes sensuality and delights in asceticism; and among ten-million such ascetics—so the Scriptures declare—there may be one who attains to perfect knowledge. Again among a million of such truly wise, one perhaps will attain final beatitude while living; and among a thousand of these it will be difficult to find that perfect bliss of philosophic absorption into the Supreme Spirit. But beyond the religious, the ascetic, the wise, the exempt from transmigration and the absorbed in the divinity, beyond all these rare greats, O King of the gods, there is one yet more difficult to find: a devoted believer in Rāma, who has gone beyond all vanity and illusion of the senses." Said Gaurī, "So tell me, O Lord of the universe, how is it that a crow could attain to that exalted highest dominion of Rāma-Bhakti.

दोहा-dohā:

राम परायन ग्यान रत गुनागार मति धीर।
rāma parāyana gyāna rata gunāgāra mati dhīra,

नाथ कहहु केहि कारन पायउ काक सरीर॥५४॥
nātha kahahu kehi kārana pāyau kāka sarīra. 54.

Trans:

Tell me sire, if he were devoted to Rāma, enamored of wisdom, full of all good qualities and resolute of purpose, what was the reason that he had the body of a crow?

चौपाई-caupāī:

यह प्रभु चरित पवित्र सुहावा। कहहु कृपाल काग कहँ पावा॥
yaha prabhu carita pavitra suhāvā, kahahu kṛpāla kāga kahaṁ pāvā.

तुम्ह केहि भाँति सुना मदनारी। कहहु मोहि अति कौतुक भारी॥
tumha kehi bhāṁti sunā madanārī, kahahu mohi ati kautuka bhārī.

गरुड़ महाग्यानी गुन रासी। हरि सेवक अति निकट निवासी॥
garuṛa mahāgyānī guna rāsī, hari sevaka ati nikaṭa nivāsī.

तेहिं केहि हेतु काग सन जाई। सुनी कथा मुनि निकर बिहाई॥
tehiṁ kehi hetu kāga sana jāī, sunī kathā muni nikara bihāī.

कहहु कवन बिधि भा संबादा। दोउ हरिभगत काग उरगादा॥
kahahu kavana bidhi bhā saṁbādā, dou haribhagata kāga uragādā.

गौरि गिरा सुनि सरल सुहाई। बोले सिव सादर सुख पाई॥
gauri girā suni sarala suhāī, bole siva sādara sukha pāī.

धन्य सती पावन मति तोरी। रघुपति चरन प्रीति नहिं थोरी॥
dhanya satī pāvana mati torī, raghupati carana prīti nahiṁ thorī.

सुनहु परम पुनीत इतिहासा। जो सुनि सकल लोक भ्रम नासा॥
sunahu parama punīta itihāsā, jo suni sakala loka bhrama nāsā.

उपजइ राम चरन बिस्वासा। भव निधि तर नर बिनहिं प्रयासा॥
upajai rāma carana bisvāsā, bhava nidhi tara nara binahiṁ prayāsā.

Trans:

Be pleased to inform me where the crow learnt this holy and delectable history of the Lord's glorious doings; and how did you get to hear it from him? Please tell me, O conqueror of Love, the strange mystery. Garud, again, is very wise and accomplished and one of Harī's most intimate disciples, what was his reason for leaving a company of the saints and going to a crow to hear this story? Describe to me the nature of the dialogue between these two servants of Harī—the crow and the serpent-eater." On hearing Gaurī's artless and charming speech, Shiva was glad and made reverent reply, "A blessing, Sati, on your sanctifying stratagem! Great indeed is your devotion to Rāma's feet. Hearken then, to the all-holy story, the hearing of which puts an end to every sorrow and delusion; for from it, there springs up an implicit faith in Rāma's feet, and then, without any difficulty, men cross the abyss of existence.

दोहा-dohā:

ऐसिअ प्रस्न बिहंगपति कीन्हि काग सन जाइ।
aisia prasna bihaṁgapati kīnhi kāga sana jāi,

सो सब सादर कहिहउँ सुनहु उमा मन लाइ॥५५॥
so saba sādara kahihauṁ sunahu umā mana lāi. 55.

Trans:

This was the very question which the king-of-birds went and put to the crow, as I will reverently explain to you in full. Hearken now Umā with all attention:

चौपाई-caupāī:

मैं जिमि कथा सुनी भव मोचनि। सो प्रसंग सुनु सुमुखि सुलोचनि॥
maiṁ jimi kathā sunī bhava mocani, so prasaṁga sunu sumukhi sulocani.

प्रथम दच्छ गृह तव अवतारा। सती नाम तब रहा तुम्हारा॥
prathama daccha gṛha tava avatārā, satī nāma taba rahā tumhārā.

दच्छ जग्य तव भा अपमाना। तुम्ह अति क्रोध तजे तब प्राना॥
daccha jagya tava bhā apamānā, tumha ati krodha taje taba prānā.

मम अनुचरन्ह कीन्ह मख भंगा। जानहु तुम्ह सो सकल प्रसंगा॥
mama anucaranha kīnha makha bhaṁgā, jānahu tumha so sakala prasaṁgā.

तब अति सोच भयउ मन मोरें। दुखी भयउँ बियोग प्रिय तोरें॥
taba ati soca bhayau mana moreṁ, dukhī bhayauṁ biyoga priya toreṁ.

सुंदर बन गिरि सरित तड़ागा। कौतुक देखत फिरउँ बेरागा॥
suṁdara bana giri sarita taṛāgā, kautuka dekhata phirauṁ berāgā.

गिरि सुमेर उत्तर दिसि दूरी। नील सैल एक सुन्दर भूरी॥
giri sumera uttara disi dūrī, nīla saila eka sundara bhūrī.

तासु कनकमय सिखर सुहाए। चारि चारु मोरे मन भाए॥
tāsu kanakamaya sikhara suhāe, cāri cāru more mana bhāe.

तिन्ह पर एक एक बिटप बिसाला। बट पीपर पाकरी रसाला॥
tinha para eka eka biṭapa bisālā, baṭa pīpara pākarī rasālā.

सैलोपरि सर सुंदर सोहा। मनि सोपान देखि मन मोहा॥
sailopari sara suṁdara sohā, mani sopāna dekhi mana mohā.

Trans:

Listen to the account, O beautiful bright-eyed dame, how I came to hear this story which delivers one from the cycles of births and deaths. You first took birth in the house of Daksha and the name you then bore was Sati. At Daksha's sacrifice you were slighted and in the violence of your indignation yielded up your life. My servants then broke up the sacrifice; but all this is a story that you know already. Afterwards I was sorely troubled at heart, sorrowing for the loss of you, my beloved, and I wandered among the beautiful woods and hills and rivers and lakes, looking at the world, but a sworn ascetic. Far away to the north among the heights of Sumeru is a huge and magnificent purple peak with four glittering pinnacles of gold—so lovely that my soul was enraptured. On each stood one enormous tree, a banyan, a *peepul*, a *pakar* and a mango, and on the top of the mountain was a glorious lake with jeweled steps, which it was a delight to behold—

दोहा-dohā:

सीतल अमल मधुर जल जलज बिपुल बहुरंग ।
sītala amala madhura jala jalaja bipula bahuraṁga,
कूजत कल रव हंस गन गुंजत मंजुल भृंग ॥५६॥
kūjata kala rava haṁsa gana guṁjata maṁjula bhṛṁga. 56.

Trans:

—with its water cool, pure and sweet, its lotuses abundant and of many colors, while flocks of swans murmured their melodious notes and the bees made a delicious buzzing.

चौपाई-caupāī:

तेहिं गिरि रुचिर बसइ खग सोई । तासु नास कल्पांत न होई ॥
tehiṁ giri rucira basai khaga soī, tāsu nāsa kalpāṁta na hoī.
माया कृत गुन दोष अनेका । मोह मनोज आदि अबिबेका ॥
māyā kṛta guna doṣa anekā, moha manoja ādi abibekā.
रहे ब्यापि समस्त जग माहीं । तेहि गिरि निकट कबहुँ नहिं जाहीं ॥
rahe byāpi samasta jaga māhīṁ, tehi giri nikaṭa kabahuṁ nahiṁ jāhīṁ.
तहँ बसि हरिहि भजइ जिमि कागा । सो सुनु उमा सहित अनुरागा ॥
tahaṁ basi harihi bhajai jimi kāgā, so sunu umā sahita anurāgā.
पीपर तरु तर ध्यान सो धरई । जाप जग्य पाकरि तर करई ॥
pīpara taru tara dhyāna so dharaī, jāpa jagya pākari tara karaī.
आँब छाहँ कर मानस पूजा । तजि हरि भजनु काजु नहिं दूजा ॥
āṁba chāhaṁ kara mānasa pūjā, taji hari bhajanu kāju nahiṁ dūjā.
बर तर कह हरि कथा प्रसंगा । आवहिं सुनहिं अनेक बिहंगा ॥
bara tara kaha hari kathā prasaṁgā, āvahiṁ sunahiṁ aneka bihaṁgā.
राम चरित बिचित्र बिधि नाना । प्रेम सहित कर सादर गाना ॥
rāma carita bicitra bidhi nānā, prema sahita kara sādara gānā.
सुनहिं सकल मति बिमल मराला । बसहिं निरंतर जे तेहिं ताला ॥
sunahiṁ sakala mati bimala marālā, basahiṁ niraṁtara je tehiṁ tālā.
जब मैं जाइ सो कौतुक देखा । उर उपजा आनंद बिसेषा ॥
jaba maiṁ jāi so kautuka dekhā, ura upajā ānaṁda biseṣā.

Trans:

On this fair height dwelt a crow, outliving even the end of the world. All the virtues and vices that are produced of Māyā, together with Delusion, Lust and the other errors of judgment which permeate the whole world, never came near this mountain. Hearken Umā with tender affection, while I tell how the crow passed his life here in the worship of Harī. Under the *peepul* tree he practiced meditation; under the *pakar* prayer and sacrifice; in the shade of the *mango* he mentally performed the holy rituals—having no other occupation whatever save the worship of Harī; and under the *banyan* he recited the story of Rāma's adventures, which countless birds flocked to hear. With loving reverence he sung the altering rhythms of Rāma's deeds, in the hearing of all the pure-souled swans that ever dwell in that lake. When I arrived there and saw the sight, an intense joy sprang up in my heart.

दोहा-dohā:

तब कछु काल मराल तनु धरि तहँ कीन्ह निवास ।
taba kachu kāla marāla tanu dhari tahaṁ kīnha nivāsa,
सादर सुनि रघुपति गुन पुनि आयउँ कैलास ॥५७॥
sādara suni raghupati guna puni āyauṁ kailāsa. 57.

Trans:

Assuming for a time the form of a swan, I took up my abode there and after reverently listening to Rāma's praises again, returned to Kailāsh.

चौपाई-caupāī:

गिरिजा कहेउँ सो सब इतिहासा । मैं जेहि समय गयउँ खग पासा ॥
girijā kaheuṁ so saba itihāsā, maiṁ jehi samaya gayauṁ khaga pāsā.
अब सो कथा सुनहु जेही हेतू । गयउ काग पहिं खग कुल केतू ॥
aba so kathā sunahu jehī hetū, gayau kāga pahiṁ khaga kula ketū.
जब रघुनाथ कीन्हि रन क्रीड़ा । समुझत चरित होति मोहि ब्रीड़ा ॥
jaba raghunātha kīnhi rana krīṛā, samujhata carita hoti mohi brīṛā.
इंद्रजीत कर आपु बँधायो । तब नारद मुनि गरुड़ पठायो ॥
iṁdrajīta kara āpu baṁdhāyo, taba nārada muni garuṛa paṭhāyo.
बंधन काटि गयो उरगादा । उपजा हृदयँ प्रचंड बिषादा ॥
baṁdhana kāṭi gayo uragādā, upajā hṛdayaṁ pracaṁḍa biṣādā.
प्रभु बंधन समुझत बहु भाँती । करत बिचार उरग आराती ॥
prabhu baṁdhana samujhata bahu bhāṁtī, karata bicāra uraga ārātī.
ब्यापक ब्रह्म बिरज बागीसा । माया मोह पार परमीसा ॥
byāpaka brahma biraja bāgīsā, māyā moha pāra paramīsā.
सो अवतार सुनेउँ जग माहीं । देखेउँ सो प्रभाव कछु नाहीं ॥
so avatāra suneuṁ jaga māhīṁ, dekheuṁ so prabhāva kachu nāhīṁ.

Trans:

I have thus told you, Girijā, the full account of the circumstances under which I visited the crow. Hearken now to the explanation of the reason for Garud's going to see him. When Raghunāth exhibited the sport of combat, though I understood his action, I was mortified that he should allow himself to be thus bound by Meghnād. Nārad, the sage, then dispatched Garud, the serpent-eater who cut his bonds and came back; but a grievous dejection possessed his soul, as he thought over the Lord's bonds and pondered the matter to himself, "The omnipresent and passionless Supreme Spirit, the Lord of speech, who is absolute master over the vanities of illusion has, I hear, taken birth in the world; but I see no signs of his majesty.

दोहा-dohā:

भव बंधन ते छूटहिं नर जपि जा कर नाम ।
bhava baṁdhana te chūṭahiṁ nara japi jā kara nāma,
खर्ब निसाचर बाँधेउ नागपास सोइ राम ॥५८॥
kharba nisācara bāṁdheu nāgapāsa soi rāma. 58.

Trans:

Can this be Rāma, by the repetition of whose name, men escape from the bonds of existence—if a wretched demon can bind him in snakey coils?"

चौपाई-caupāī:

नाना भाँति मनहि समुझावा । प्रगट न ग्यान हृदयँ भ्रम छावा ॥
nānā bhāṁti manahi samujhāvā, pragaṭa na gyāna hṛdayaṁ bhrama chāvā.
खेद खिन्न मन तर्क बढ़ाई । भयउ मोहबस तुम्हरिहिं नाई ॥
kheda khinna mana tarka baṛhāī, bhayau mohabasa tumharihiṁ nāī.
ब्याकुल गयउ देवरिषि पाहीं । कहेसि जो संसय निज मन माहीं ॥
byākula gayau devariṣi pāhīṁ, kahesi jo saṁsaya nija mana māhīṁ.
सुनि नारदहि लागि अति दाया । सुनु खग प्रबल राम कै माया ॥
suni nāradahi lāgi ati dāyā, sunu khaga prabala rāma kai māyā.
जो ग्यानिन्ह कर चित अपहरई । बरिआईं बिमोह मन करई ॥
jo gyāninha kara cita apaharaī, bariāīṁ bimoha mana karaī.
जेहिं बहु बार नचावा मोही । सोइ ब्यापी बिहंगपति तोही ॥
jehiṁ bahu bāra nacāvā mohī, soi byāpī bihaṁgapati tohī.
महामोह उपजा उर तोरें । मिटिहि न बेगि कहें खग मोरें ॥
mahāmoha upajā ura toreṁ, miṭihi na begi kaheṁ khaga moreṁ.
चतुरानन पहिं जाहु खगेसा । सोइ करेहु जेहि होइ निदेसा ॥
caturānana pahiṁ jāhu khagesā, soi karehu jehi hoi nidesā.

Trans:

Though he did all he could to reassure himself, his understanding was not enlightened; and delusion over-shadowed his soul. Distracted by doubt and full of mental disquiet, he became as subject to delusion as you yourself were. In his perplexity he went to the Rishī of the gods and told him the difficulty that he had in his mind. On hearing his tale, Nārad was moved with great compassion, "Hearken, O bird; Rāma's delusive power is very strong. When he robs the wise of their sense, he makes their infatuation superlative. The same specter that has often disturbed me has now, O king-of-birds, affected you. The mighty error that has taken root in your soul will not be readily removed by any words of mine. You must go to Brahmmā, and do whatever he enjoins you."

दोहा-dohā:

अस कहि चले देवरिषि करत राम गुन गान ।
asa kahi cale devariṣi karata rāma guna gāna,
हरि माया बल बरनत पुनि पुनि परम सुजान ॥५९॥
hari māyā bala baranata puni puni parama sujāna. 59.

Trans:

So saying the teacher of the gods went his way chanting Rāma's praises, again and again in his infinite wisdom, insisting on the might of Rāma's Māyā.

चौपाई-caupāī:

तब खगपति बिरंचि पहिं गयऊ । निज संदेह सुनावत भयऊ ॥
taba khagapati biraṁci pahiṁ gayaū, nija saṁdeha sunāvata bhayaū.
सुनि बिरंचि रामहि सिरु नावा । समुझि प्रताप प्रेम अति छावा ॥
suni biraṁci rāmahi siru nāvā, samujhi pratāpa prema ati chāvā.
मन महुँ करइ बिचार बिधाता । माया बस कबि कोबिद ग्याता ॥
mana mahum̐ karai bicāra bidhātā, māyā basa kabi kobida gyātā.
हरि माया कर अमिति प्रभावा । बिपुल बार जेहिं मोहि नचावा ॥
hari māyā kara amiti prabhāvā, bipula bāra jehiṁ mohi nacāvā.
अग जगमय जग मम उपराजा । नहिं आचरज मोह खगराजा ॥
aga jagamaya jaga mama uparājā, nahiṁ ācaraja moha khagarājā.
तब बोले बिधि गिरा सुहाई । जान महेस राम प्रभुताई ॥
taba bole bidhi girā suhāī, jāna mahesa rāma prabhutāī.
बैनतेय संकर पहिं जाहू । तात अनत पूछहु जनि काहू ॥
bainateya saṁkara pahiṁ jāhū, tāta anata pūchahu jani kāhū.
तहँ होइहि तव संसय हानी । चलेउ बिहंग सुनत बिधि बानी ॥
taham̐ hoihi tava saṁsaya hānī, caleu bihaṁga sunata bidhi bānī.

Trans:

The king-of-birds then went to the Creator and told him his difficulty. On hearing his story, Brahmmā bowed the head to Rāma; and as he thought on his majesty, his heart was filled with love, and he thus mused within himself, "Poets and the wisest of philosophers are subject to delusion. The might of Harī's deceptive power is unbounded; many a time has it made me its puppet, though all things animate and inanimate are of my creation; no wonder then that it has beguiled the king-of-birds." Then said Brahmmā in gracious accents, "Shiva understands Rāma's power. Go to him, O son of Vinata, and ask no questions of any other. There you will find the solution of your doubts." On hearing Brahmmā's advice, the bird went his way.

दोहा-dohā:

परमातुर बिहंगपति आयउ तब मो पास ।
paramātura bihaṁgapati āyau taba mo pāsa,
जात रहेउँ कुबेर गृह रहिहु उमा कैलास ॥६०॥
jāta raheum̐ kubera gṛha rahihu umā kailāsa. 60.

Trans:

Then came the king-of-birds in the utmost distress to me. At that time, Umā, I was on my way to the palace of Kuber, and had left you at Kailāsh.

चौपाई-caupāī:

तेहिं मम पद सादर सिरु नावा । पुनि आपन संदेह सुनावा ॥
tehiṁ mama pada sādara siru nāvā, puni āpana saṁdeha sunāvā.
सुनि ता करि बिनती मृदु बानी । प्रेम सहित मैं कहेउँ भवानी ॥
suni tā kari binatī mṛdu bānī, prema sahita maiṁ kaheum̐ bhavānī.
मिलेहु गरुड़ मारग महँ मोही । कवन भाँति समुझावौं तोही ॥
milehu garuṛa māraga maham̐ mohī, kavana bhām̐ti samujhāvauṁ tohī.
तबहिं होइ सब संसय भंगा । जब बहु काल करिअ सतसंगा ॥
tabahiṁ hoi saba saṁsaya bhaṁgā, jaba bahu kāla karia satasaṁgā.
सुनिअ तहाँ हरि कथा सुहाई । नाना भाँति मुनिन्ह जो गाई ॥
sunia tahām̐ hari kathā suhāī, nānā bhām̐ti muninha jo gāī.
जेहि महुँ आदि मध्य अवसाना । प्रभु प्रतिपाद्य राम भगवाना ॥
jehi mahum̐ ādi madhya avasānā, prabhu pratipādya rāma bhagavānā.
नित हरि कथा होत जहँ भाई । पठवउँ तहाँ सुनहु तुम्ह जाई ॥
nita hari kathā hota jaham̐ bhāī, paṭhavaum̐ tahām̐ sunahu tumha jāī.
जाइहि सुनत सकल संदेहा । राम चरन होइहि अति नेहा ॥
jāihi sunata sakala saṁdehā, rāma carana hoihi ati nehā.

Trans:

He reverently bowed his head at my feet and then told me his difficulty. On hearing his humble petition, I lovingly responded, Bhawānī, "You have met me, Garud, on the road; how can I instruct you? Your doubts will not be settled till you have been for a long time in the company of the saints. There you must listen to the delightful story of Rāma, as sung in diverse manners by the seers, in which the beginning, middle and end is the adorable Lord, the great God Rāma. I will send you, brother, to a place where the story of Rāma is told without respite; go there and listen. As you hear it, all your doubts will vanish; you will have a vehement affection for Rāma's feet.

दोहा-dohā:

बिनु सतसंग न हरि कथा तेहि बिनु मोह न भाग ।
binu satasaṁga na hari kathā tehi binu moha na bhāga,
मोह गएँ बिनु राम पद होइ न दृढ़ अनुराग ॥६१॥
moha gaem̐ binu rāma pada hoi na dṛṛha anurāga. 61.

Trans:

Except in the company of saints there is no talk about Rāma; without that there is no overcoming delusion; till delusion is dispersed, there is no firm affection for Rāma's feet.

चौपाई-caupāī:

मिलहिं न रघुपति बिनु अनुरागा । किएँ जोग तप ग्यान बिरागा ॥
milahiṁ na raghupati binu anurāgā, kiem̐ joga tapa gyāna birāgā.
उत्तर दिसि सुंदर गिरि नीला । तहँ रह काकभुसुंडि सुसीला ॥
uttara disi suṁdara giri nīlā, taham̐ raha kākabhusuṁḍi susīlā.
राम भगति पथ परम प्रबीना । ग्यानी गुन गृह बहु कालीना ॥
rāma bhagati patha parama prabīnā, gyānī guna gṛha bahu kālīnā.
राम कथा सो कहइ निरंतर । सादर सुनहिं बिबिध बिहंगबर ॥
rāma kathā so kahai niraṁtara, sādara sunahiṁ bibidha bihaṁgabara.
जाइ सुनहु तहँ हरि गुन भूरी । होइहि मोह जनित दुख दूरी ॥
jāi sunahu taham̐ hari guna bhūrī, hoihi moha janita dukha dūrī.
मैं जब तेहि सब कहा बुझाई । चलेउ हरषि मम पद सिरु नाई ॥
maiṁ jaba tehi saba kahā bujhāī, caleu harași mama pada siru nāī.
ताते उमा न मैं समुझावा । रघुपति कृपाँ मरमु मैं पावा ॥
tāte umā na maiṁ samujhāvā, raghupati kṛpām̐ maramu maiṁ pāvā.
होइहि कीन्ह कबहुँ अभिमाना । सो खोवै चह कृपानिधाना ॥
hoihi kīnha kabahum̐ abhimānā, so khovai caha kṛpānidhānā.
कछु तेहि ते पुनि मैं नहिं राखा । समुझइ खग खगही कै भाषा ॥
kachu tehi te puni maiṁ nahiṁ rākhā, samujhai khaga khagahī kai bhāṣā.

प्रभु माया बलवंत भवानी । जाहि न मोह कवन अस ग्यानी ॥
prabhu māyā balavaṁta bhavānī, jāhi na moha kavana asa gyānī.

Trans:

Without affection there is no finding Rāma, even though you may take recourse to meditation, prayer, sacrifice, and asceticism. In the region of the north is a beautiful purple mountain, where lives the amiable Kāgabhusumdi, supremely skilled in the method of Rāma's worship, wise and full of all good qualities and very aged. He unceasingly recites Rāma's history and all the noblest of the birds reverently listen to it. Go there and hear all Rāma's excellencies, and your distress born of delusion will then be removed." After I had given him full instructions, he bowed his head to my feet and set out with joy. I did not myself instruct him, Umā, for I understood the mystery of Rāma's grace. Perhaps he had shown pride on some occasion and the All-merciful wished that he should cure himself of this blemish. There was also another reason why I did not detain him; being a bird, he understood bird's language. The Lord's delusive power, Bhawānī, is great; who is so wise as not to be fascinated by it?

दोहा-dohā:

ग्यानी भगत सिरोमनि त्रिभुवनपति कर जान ।
gyānī bhagata siromani tribhuvanapati kara jāna,
ताहि मोह माया नर पावँर करहिं गुमान ॥ ६२क॥
tāhi moha māyā nara pāvaṁra karahiṁ gumāna. 62(ka).

Trans:

Even the vehicle of the Lord of the three spheres, the very crown of philosophers and saints, was overcome by Māyā's deceptive influence: what then to say of pitiful men who have their doubts.

मासपारायण अट्ठाईसवाँ विश्राम
māsapārāyaṇa aṭṭhāīsavāṁ viśrāma
(Pause 28 for a Thirty-Day Recitation)

सिव बिरंचि कहुँ मोहइ को है बपुरा आन ।
siva biraṁci kahuṁ mohai ko hai bapurā āna,
अस जियँ जानि भजहिं मुनि माया पति भगवान ॥ ६२ख॥
asa jiyaṁ jāni bhajahiṁ muni māyā pati bhagavāna. 62(kha).

Trans:

Māyā fascinates Shiva and Brahmmā; why speak of other poor creatures? The saints know this at heart, when they worship the great Lord-God, the Māyā's master, Shri Rāma.

चौपाई-caupāī:

गयउ गरुड़ जहँ बसइ भुसुंडा । मति अकुंठ हरि भगति अखंडा ॥
gayau garuṛa jahaṁ basai bhusuṁḍā, mati akuṁṭha hari bhagati akhaṁḍā.
देखि सैल प्रसन्न मन भयऊ । माया मोह सोच सब गयऊ ॥
dekhi saila prasanna mana bhayaū, māyā moha soca saba gayaū.
करि तड़ाग मज्जन जलपाना । बट तर गयउ हृदयँ हरषाना ॥
kari taṛāga majjana jalapānā, baṭa tara gayau hṛdayaṁ haraṣānā.
बृद्ध बृद्ध बिहंग तहँ आए । सुनै राम के चरित सुहाए ॥
bṛddha bṛddha bihaṁga tahaṁ āe, sunai rāma ke carita suhāe.
कथा अरंभ करै सोइ चाहा । तेही समय गयउ खगनाहा ॥
kathā araṁbha karai soi cāhā, tehī samaya gayau khaganāhā.
आवत देखि सकल खगराजा । हरषेउ बायस सहित समाजा ॥
āvata dekhi sakala khagarājā, haraṣeu bāyasa sahita samājā.
अति आदर खगपति कर कीन्हा । स्वागत पूछि सुआसन दीन्हा ॥
ati ādara khagapati kara kīnhā, svāgata pūchi suāsana dīnhā.
करि पूजा समेत अनुरागा । मधुर बचन तब बोलेउ कागा ॥
kari pūjā sameta anurāgā, madhura bacana taba boleu kāgā.

Trans:

Garud went to Bhusundi's abode, that sturdy-hearted and indefatigable votary of Harī's. At the sight of the mountain his heart rejoiced; the trouble caused him by Māyā's wiles all passed away. After bathing in the lake and drinking of the water, he betook himself under the banyan tree, delighted at heart. There were assembled flocks upon flocks of birds to hear of Rāma's glorious doings; and Bhusundi was just on the point of beginning to recite, when the king-of-birds arrived. All were glad to see him approach, the crow no less than the rest of the assembly. They received him with the utmost politeness and asked of his welfare and conducted him to a seat. Then the crow, after doing him loving homage, addressed him in these winning words:

दोहा-dohā:

नाथ कृतारथ भयउँ मैं तव दरसन खगराज ।
nātha kṛtāratha bhayauṁ maiṁ tava darasana khagarāja,
आयसु देहु सो करौं अब प्रभु आयहु केहि काज ॥ ६३क॥
āyasu dehu so karauṁ aba prabhu āyahu kehi kāja. 63(ka).

सदा कृतारथ रूप तुम्ह कह मृदु बचन खगेस ।
sadā kṛtāratha rūpa tumha kaha mṛdu bacana khagesa,
जेहि कै अस्तुति सादर निज मुख कीन्हि महेस ॥ ६३ख॥
jehi kai astuti sādara nija mukha kīnhi mahesa. 63(kha).

Trans:

"Now am I content, O king-of-birds, in that I have seen you; whatever you may order me, I am ready to do; pray, what is the object of your visit, my Lord?" "You have ever been the image of content," replied Garud in gracious phrase, "seeing that Shiva with his own mouth is ever reverently singing your praises.

चौपाई-caupāī:

सुनहु तात जेहि कारन आयउँ । सो सब भयउ दरस तव पायउँ ॥
sunahu tāta jehi kārana āyauṁ, so saba bhayau darasa tava pāyauṁ.
देखि परम पावन तव आश्रम । गयउ मोह संसय नाना भ्रम ॥
dekhi parama pāvana tava āśrama, gayau moha saṁsaya nānā bhrama.
अब श्रीराम कथा अति पावनि । सदा सुखद दुख पुंज नसावनि ॥
aba śrīrāma kathā ati pāvani, sadā sukhada dukha puṁja nasāvani.
सादर तात सुनावहु मोही । बार बार बिनवउँ प्रभु तोही ॥
sādara tāta sunāvahu mohī, bāra bāra binavauṁ prabhu tohī.
सुनत गरुड़ कै गिरा बिनीता । सरल सुप्रेम सुखद सुपुनीता ॥
sunata garuṛa kai girā binītā, sarala suprema sukhada supunītā.
भयउ तासु मन परम उछाहा । लाग कहै रघुपति गुन गाहा ॥
bhayau tāsu mana parama uchāhā, lāga kahai raghupati guna gāhā.
प्रथमहिं अति अनुराग भवानी । रामचरित सर कहेसि बखानी ॥
prathamahiṁ ati anurāga bhavānī, rāmacarita sara kahesi bakhānī.
पुनि नारद कर मोह अपारा । कहेसि बहुरि रावन अवतारा ॥
puni nārada kara moha apārā, kahesi bahuri rāvana avatārā.
प्रभु अवतार कथा पुनि गाई । तब सिसु चरित कहेसि मन लाई ॥
prabhu avatāra kathā puni gāī, taba sisu carita kahesi mana lāī.

Trans:

Hearken, father; the object for which I came was attained as soon as I saw you. Directly I beheld your most holy hermitage, my delusion was at an end with all my distracting doubts. Now, father, repeat to me with all solemnity the most sanctifying story of Rāma, which is ever delightful and a remedy for every ill: this, my Lord, is what I urgently beg of you." On hearing Garud's prayer, so humble, sincere and affectionate, so graceful and pious, a supreme joy was diffused over his soul and he began the recital of Raghupatī's glory. First, Bhawānī, he expounded with fervent devotion the motive of Rāma's acts. Then he told of Nārad's extraordinary delusion and of Rāvan's incarnation. After this he sang the story of the Lord's birth and then carefully recounted his doings as a child.

दोहा-dohā:

बालचरित कहि बिबिधि बिधि मन महँ परम उछाह ।
bālacarita kahi bibidhi bidhi mana mahaṁ parama uchāha,
रिषि आगवन कहेसि पुनि श्रीरघुबीर बिबाह ॥६४॥
riṣi āgavana kahesi puni śrīraghubīra bibāha. 64.

Trans:
After telling all the details of his boyish performances with the utmost rapture of soul, he next told of the Rishī's coming and of Raghubīr's marriage.

चौपाई-caupāī:

बहुरि राम अभिषेक प्रसंगा । पुनि नृप बचन राज रस भंगा ॥
bahuri rāma abhiṣeka prasaṁgā, puni nṛpa bacana rāja rasa bhaṁgā.
पुरबासिन्ह कर बिरह बिषादा । कहेसि राम लछिमन संबादा ॥
purabāsinha kara biraha biṣādā, kahesi rāma lachimana saṁbādā.
बिपिन गवन केवट अनुरागा । सुरसरि उतरि निवास प्रयागा ॥
bipina gavana kevaṭa anurāgā, surasari utari nivāsa prayāgā.
बालमीक प्रभु मिलन बखाना । चित्रकूट जिमि बसे भगवाना ॥
bālamīka prabhu milana bakhānā, citrakūṭa jimi base bhagavānā.
सचिवागवन नगर नृप मरना । भरतागवन प्रेम बहु बरना ॥
sacivāgavana nagara nṛpa maranā, bharatāgavana prema bahu baranā.
करि नृप क्रिया संग पुरबासी । भरत गए जहँ प्रभु सुख रासी ॥
kari nṛpa kriyā saṁga purabāsī, bharata gae jahaṁ prabhu sukha rāsī.
पुनि रघुपति बहुबिधि समुझाए । लै पादुका अवधपुर आए ॥
puni raghupati bahubidhi samujhāe, lai pādukā avadhapura āe.
भरत रहनि सुरपति सुत करनी । प्रभु अरु अत्रि भेंट पुनि बरनी ॥
bharata rahani surapati suta karanī, prabhu aru atri bheṁṭa puni baranī.

Trans:
Then came the narrative of Rāma's coronation, of the king's vow and the abdication of royal state, the sorrow of the citizens at parting, the colloquy between Rāma and Lakshman, the journey to the forest, the devotion of the boatman, the passage of the Gangā and the stay at Prayāg. He described also the Lord's meeting with Vālmikī and how the god dwelt at Chitra-kūt, the coming of the minister, the death of the king in the city, the arrival of Bharat and the greatness of his affection, how after performing the king's obsequies both Bharat himself and the citizens had gone to join the Lord—Treasury of Bliss; and how after he had said all he could to console them, Bharat took his sandal back with him to Avadh. Next he related Bharat's mode of life, the action of the son of Indra and the Lord's meeting with Atri.

दोहा-dohā:

कहि बिराध बध जेहि बिधि देह तजी सरभंग ।
kahi birādha badha jehi bidhi deha tajī sarabhaṁga.
बरनि सुतीछन प्रीति पुनि प्रभु अगस्ति सतसंग ॥६५॥
barani sutīchana prīti puni prabhu agasti satasaṁga. 65.

Trans:
Then he told of Viradh's death, of how Sarabhanga dropped his body, of Sutīkshan's devotion and the Lord's holy communion with Agastya.

चौपाई-caupāī:

कहि दंडक बन पावनताई । गीध मइत्री पुनि तेहिं गाई ॥
kahi daṁḍaka bana pāvanatāī, gīdha maitrī puni tehiṁ gāī.
पुनि प्रभु पंचबटीं कृत बासा । भंजी सकल मुनिन्ह की त्रासा ॥
puni prabhu paṁcabaṭīṁ kṛta bāsā, bhaṁjī sakala muninha kī trāsā.
पुनि लछिमन उपदेस अनूपा । सूपनखा जिमि कीन्हि कुरूपा ॥
puni lachimana upadesa anūpā, sūpanakhā jimi kīnhi kurūpā.
खर दूषन बध बहुरि बखाना । जिमि सब मरमु दसानन जाना ॥
khara dūṣana badha bahuri bakhānā, jimi saba maramu dasānana jānā.
दसकंधर मारीच बतकही । जेहि बिधि भई सो सब तेहिं कही ॥
dasakaṁdhara mārīca batakahī, jehi bidhi bhaī so saba tehiṁ kahī.
पुनि माया सीता कर हरना । श्रीरघुबीर बिरह कछु बरना ॥
puni māyā sītā kara haranā, śrīraghubīra biraha kachu baranā.
पुनि प्रभु गीध क्रिया जिमि कीन्ही । बधि कबंध सबरिहि गति दीन्ही ॥
puni prabhu gīdha kriyā jimi kīnhī, badhi kabaṁdha sabarihi gati dīnhī.
बहुरि बिरह बरनत रघुबीरा । जेहि बिधि गए सरोबर तीरा ॥
bahuri biraha baranata raghubīrā, jehi bidhi gae sarobara tīrā.

Trans:
He told him also of the purification of the Dandak forest, of the friendliness of the vulture, of the Lord's stay in the woods of Panchwati and how he put an end to the fears of all the saints. Then came the incomparable exhortation to Lakshman and the story of Surpa-nakhā's mutilation. After this he narrated to him the death of Khar and Dūshan, and how Rāvan got all the information, and then the particulars of his talk with Mārich. Then he described the kidnap of the fictitious Sītā and he narrated the theme of Rāma's bereavement. After this he told how the Lord performed the vulture's funeral rites and slew Kabandh and gave salvation to Sabari. He told also of Raghubīr's mourning and how he went to the shore of the lake.

दोहा-dohā:

प्रभु नारद संबाद कहि मारुति मिलन प्रसंग ।
prabhu nārada saṁbāda kahi māruti milana prasaṁga,
पुनि सुग्रीव मिताई बालि प्रान कर भंग ॥६६क॥
puni sugrīva mitāī bāli prāna kara bhaṁga. 66((ka).

कपिहि तिलक करि प्रभु कृत सैल प्रबरषन बास ।
kapihi tilaka kari prabhu kṛta saila prabaraṣana bāsa,
बरनन बर्षा सरद अरु राम रोष कपि त्रास ॥६६ख॥
baranana barṣā sarada aru rāma roṣa kapi trāsa. 66(kha).

Trans:
Of his dialogue with Nārad, his meeting with Hanumān, his alliance with Sugrīva and his taking Bālī's life; of his making Sugrīva the monkey-king, and then taking up his abode on Mount-Prabarshan during the rains. He described also the rains and the autumn and Rāma's indignation and the monkey's alarm:

चौपाई-caupāī:

जेहि बिधि कपिपति कीस पठाए । सीता खोज सकल दिसि धाए ॥
jehi bidhi kapipati kīsa paṭhāe, sītā khoja sakala disi dhāe.
बिबर प्रबेस कीन्ह जेहि भाँती । कपिन्ह बहोरि मिला संपाती ॥
bibara prabesa kīnha jehi bhāṁtī, kapinha bahori milā saṁpātī.
सुनि सब कथा समीरकुमारा । नाघत भयउ पयोधि अपारा ॥
suni saba kathā samīrakumārā, nāghata bhayau payodhi apārā.
लंकाँ कपि प्रबेस जिमि कीन्हा । पुनि सीतहि धीरजु जिमि दीन्हा ॥
laṁkāṁ kapi prabesa jimi kīnhā, puni sītahi dhīraju jimi dīnhā.
बन उजारि रावनहि प्रबोधी । पुर दहि नाघेउ बहुरि पयोधी ॥
bana ujāri rāvanahi prabodhī, pura dahi nāgheu bahuri payodhī.
आए कपि सब जहँ रघुराई । बैदेही कि कुसल सुनाई ॥
āe kapi saba jahaṁ raghurāī, baidehī ki kusala sunāī.
सेन समेति जथा रघुबीरा । उतरे जाइ बारिनिधि तीरा ॥
sena sameti jathā raghubīrā, utare jāi bārinidhi tīrā.
मिला बिभीषन जेहि बिधि आई । सागर निग्रह कथा सुनाई ॥
milā bibhīṣana jehi bidhi āī, sāgara nigraha kathā sunāī.

Trans:

How the monkey king sent out monkeys, who ran in every direction to search for Sītā; how they entered the cave and found Sampāti; how Hanumān, when he had heard all the circumstances, jumped over the mighty ocean; how he made his way into Lankā and bade Sītā be of good cheer; how he laid waste the garden, and admonished Rāvan and set fire to the city and leaped over the sea again. How the monkeys all rejoined Rāma and told him of Sītā's welfare; how Raghubīr with his army went and encamped on the seashore; how Vibhīshan came to meet him and how the sea was put in check;

दोहा-dohā:

सेतु बाँधि कपि सेन जिमि उतरी सागर पार ।
setu bām̐dhi kapi sena jimi utarī sāgara pāra,
गयउ बसीठी बीरबर जेहि बिधि बालिकुमार ॥ ६७क॥
gayau basīṭhī bīrabara jehi bidhi bālikumāra. 67(ka).

निसिचर कीस लराई बरनिसि बिबिधि प्रकार ।
nisicara kīsa larāī baranisi bibidhi prakāra,
कुंभकरन घननाद कर बल पौरुष संघार ॥ ६७ख॥
kuṁbhakarana ghananāda kara bala pauruṣa saṁghāra. 67(kha).

Trans:

how the bridge was built and the monkey host crossed over to the opposite side, and how the valiant son of Bālī went as an envoy. He described the various battles between the demons and the monkeys, the might and valor of Kumbh-karan and Meghnād and their destruction;

चौपाई-caupāī:

निसिचर निकर मरन बिधि नाना । रघुपति रावन समर बखाना ॥
nisicara nikara marana bidhi nānā, raghupati rāvana samara bakhānā.
रावन बध मंदोदरि सोका । राज बिभीषन देव असोका ॥
rāvana badha maṁdodari sokā, rāja bibhīṣana deva asokā.
सीता रघुपति मिलन बहोरी । सुरन्ह कीन्हि अस्तुति कर जोरी ॥
sītā raghupati milana bahorī, suranha kīnhi astuti kara jorī.
पुनि पुष्पक चढ़ि कपिन्ह समेता । अवध चले प्रभु कृपा निकेता ॥
puni puṣpaka caṛhi kapinha sametā, avadha cale prabhu kṛpā niketā.
जेहि बिधि राम नगर निज आए । बायस बिसद चरित सब गाए ॥
jehi bidhi rāma nagara nija āe, bāyasa bisada carita saba gāe.
कहेसि बहोरि राम अभिषेका । पुर बरनत नृपनीति अनेका ॥
kahesi bahori rāma abhiṣekā, pura baranata nṛpanīti anekā.
कथा समस्त भुसुंड बखानी । जो मैं तुम्ह सन कही भवानी ॥
kathā samasta bhusuṁḍa bakhānī, jo maiṁ tumha sana kahī bhavānī.
सुनि सब राम कथा खगनाहा । कहत बचन मन परम उछाहा ॥
suni saba rāma kathā khaganāhā, kahata bacana mana parama uchāhā.

Trans:

the different deaths of all the demons, the fight between Rāma and Rāvan, the death of Rāvan, the mourning of Mandodarī; the enthronement of Vibhīshan and the satisfaction of the gods; the meeting also of Rāma and Sītā and how the gods with clasped hands hymned their praises; how the all-merciful Lord with the monkeys mounted the car Pushpak and set out for Avadh; and how Rāma arrived at his own city; all these glorious doings were sung by the crow. Then he told of Rāma's coronation and described the city and all its kingly polity. The entire history did Bhusumdi tell, as I have told it to you, Bhawānī. When the king-of-birds had heard it all, his soul was in raptures and he cried,

सोरठा-soraṭhā:

गयउ मोर संदेह सुनेउँ सकल रघुपति चरित ।
gayau mora saṁdeha suneum̐ sakala raghupati carita,
भयउ राम पद नेह तव प्रसाद बायस तिलक ॥ ६८क॥
bhayau rāma pada neha tava prasāda bāyasa tilaka. 68(ka).

मोहि भयउ अति मोह प्रभु बंधन रन महुँ निरखि ।
mohi bhayau ati moha prabhu baṁdhana rana mahum̐ nirakhi,
चिदानंद संदोह राम बिकल कारन कवन ॥ ६८ख॥
cidānaṁda saṁdoha rāma bikala kārana kavana, 68(kha).

Trans:

"My doubts are gone, now that I have heard Rāma's full history. By your favor, O best of crows, I feel a devotion to Rāma's feet. A mighty bewilderment possessed me when I saw the Lord bound in battle: Rāma is Knowledge and Bliss personified; how then can he be mortified?

चौपाई-caupāī:

देखि चरित अति नर अनुसारी । भयउ हृदयँ मम संसय भारी ॥
dekhi carita ati nara anusārī, bhayau hṛdayaṁ mama saṁsaya bhārī.
सोइ भ्रम अब हित करि मैं माना । कीन्ह अनुग्रह कृपानिधाना ॥
soi bhrama aba hita kari maiṁ mānā, kīnha anugraha kṛpānidhānā.
जो अति आतप ब्याकुल होई । तरु छाया सुख जानइ सोई ॥
jo ati ātapa byākula hoī, taru chāyā sukha jānai soī.
जौं नहिं होत मोह अति मोही । मिलतेउँ तात कवन बिधि तोही ॥
jauṁ nahiṁ hota moha ati mohī, milateum̐ tāta kavana bidhi tohī.
सुनतेउँ किमि हरि कथा सुहाई । अति बिचित्र बहु बिधि तुम्ह गाई ॥
sunateum̐ kimi hari kathā suhāī, ati bicitra bahu bidhi tumha gāī.
निगमागम पुरान मत एहा । कहहिं सिद्ध मुनि नहिं संदेहा ॥
nigamāgama purāna mata ehā, kahahiṁ siddha muni nahiṁ saṁdehā.
संत बिसुद्ध मिलहिं परि तेही । चितवहिं राम कृपा करि जेही ॥
saṁta bisuddha milahiṁ pari tehī, citavahiṁ rāma kṛpā kari jehī.
राम कृपाँ तव दरसन भयऊ । तव प्रसाद सब संसय गयऊ ॥
rāma kṛpām̐ tava darasana bhayaū, tava prasāda saba saṁsaya gayaū.

Trans:

Seeing all his ways so entirely consistent with humanity, a very grievous doubt arose in my soul. But now I understand that my error was a favor which the All-merciful has been pleased to bestow upon me. To appreciate the blessing of a shady tree, one must first have suffered from the sun's heat. If this delusion had not befallen me, how should I have met you, father, and how should I have heard the delightful story of Rāma, which you have told me so fully in all its details? This is the doctrine of the Purānas and all the Scriptures, the unhesitating assertion of all the seers and sages—that the company of good and holy men can only be attained by one on whom Rāma has looked with an eye of favor. By Rāma's favor I have had sight of you, and by your grace all my doubts are now gone."

दोहा-dohā:

सुनि बिहंगपति बानी सहित बिनय अनुराग ।
suni bihaṁgapati bānī sahita binaya anurāga,
पुलक गात लोचन सजल मन हरषेउ अति काग ॥ ६९क॥
pulaka gāta locana sajala mana haraṣeu ati kāga. 69(ka).

श्रोता सुमति सुसील सुचि कथा रसिक हरि दास।
śrotā sumati susīla suci kathā rasika hari dāsa,
पाइ उमा अति गोप्यमपि सज्जन करहिं प्रकास ॥६९ख॥
pāi umā ati gopyamapi sajjana karahiṁ prakāsa. 69(kha).

Trans:

On hearing Garud's modest and affectionate speech, the crow greatly rejoiced at heart; every hair on his body bristled and his eyes streamed with tears. O Umā, when a good man finds an intelligent and well-disposed listener, who is pious and fond of religious readings and a worshipper of Harī, he reveals to him hidden mysteries.

चौपाई-caupāī:

बोलेउ काकभसुंड बहोरी। नभग नाथ पर प्रीति न थोरी॥
boleu kākabhasuṁḍa bahorī, nabhaga nātha para prīti na thorī.
सब बिधि नाथ पूज्य तुम्ह मेरे। कृपापात्र रघुनायक केरे॥
saba bidhi nātha pūjya tumha mere, kṛpāpātra raghunāyaka kere.
तुम्हहि न संसय मोह न माया। मो पर नाथ कीन्हि तुम्ह दाया॥
tumhahi na saṁsaya moha na māyā, mo para nātha kīnhi tumha dāyā.
पठइ मोह मिस खगपति तोही। रघुपति दीन्हि बड़ाई मोही॥
paṭhai moha misa khagapati tohī, raghupati dīnhi baṛāī mohī.
तुम्ह निज मोह कही खग साईं। सो नहिं कछु आचरज गोसाईं॥
tumha nija moha kahī khaga sāīṁ, so nahiṁ kachu ācaraja gosāīṁ.
नारद भव बिरंचि सनकादी। जे मुनिनायक आतमबादी॥
nārada bhava biraṁci sanakādī, je munināyaka ātamabādī.
मोह न अंध कीन्ह केहि केही। को जग काम नचाव न जेही॥
moha na aṁdha kīnha kehi kehī, ko jaga kāma nacāva na jehī.
तृस्नाँ केहि न कीन्ह बौराहा। केहि कर हृदय क्रोध नहिं दाहा॥
tṛsnāṁ kehi na kīnha baurāhā, kehi kara hṛdaya krodha nahiṁ dāhā.

Trans:

Then answered Kāgabhusumdi, who had great affection for the king-of-birds, "My Lord, you are in every way entitled to my respect—as a vessel of Harī's grace. You had no doubts, infatuation, or delusion; it was only a pretext, sire, for doing a kindness to me. By sending you, O Garud, as a victim of delusion, Raghupatī has conferred an honor upon me. Yet there is nothing wonderful, sir, in that delusion of yours of which you tell me; for Nārad, Shiva, Brahmmā, Sanat-kumār and his brethren, with all the great saints who discourse of the soul—is there one of them who has not been blinded by delusions of Māyā? Again, is there anyone in this world whom lust has not made a puppet of? Who has not been maddened by the thirst for enjoyment and whose heart has not been inflamed by anger?

दोहा-dohā:

ग्यानी तापस सूर कबि कोबिद गुन आगार।
gyānī tāpasa sūra kabi kobida guna āgāra,
केहि कै लोभ बिडंबना कीन्हि न एहिं संसार ॥७०क॥
kehi kai lobha biḍaṁbanā kīnhi na ehiṁ saṁsāra. 70(ka).

श्री मद बक्र न कीन्ह केहि प्रभुता बधिर न काहि।
śrī mada bakra na kīnha kehi prabhutā badhira na kāhi,
मृगलोचनि के नैन सर को अस लाग न जाहि ॥७०ख॥
mṛgalocani ke naina sara ko asa lāga na jāhi. 70(kha).

Trans:

Is there any philosopher, ascetic, or hero in the world, or any learned and accomplished bard, whom Greed has not beguiled; whom the Pride of wealth has not rendered wanton, whom Power has not made deaf, or whom the glance of Beauty has not smitten as an arrow?

चौपाई-caupāī:

गुन कृत सन्यपात नहिं केही। कोउ न मान मद तजेउ निबेही॥
guna kṛta sanyapāta nahiṁ kehī, kou na māna mada tajeu nibehī.
जोबन ज्वर केहि नहिं बलकावा। ममता केहि कर जस न नसावा॥
jobana jvara kehi nahiṁ balakāvā, mamatā kehi kara jasa na nasāvā.
मच्छर काहि कलंक न लावा। काहि न सोक समीर डोलावा॥
macchara kāhi kalaṁka na lāvā, kāhi na soka samīra ḍolāvā.
चिंता साँपिनि को नहिं खाया। को जग जाहि न ब्यापी माया॥
ciṁtā sāṁpini ko nahiṁ khāyā, ko jaga jāhi na byāpī māyā.
कीट मनोरथ दारु सरीरा। जेहि न लाग घुन को अस धीरा॥
kīṭa manoratha dāru sarīrā, jehi na lāga ghuna ko asa dhīrā.
सुत बित लोक ईषना तीनी। केहि कै मति इन्ह कृत न मलीनी॥
suta bita loka īṣanā tīnī, kehi kai mati inha kṛta na malīnī.
यह सब माया कर परिवारा। प्रबल अमिति को बरनै पारा॥
yaha saba māyā kara parivārā, prabala amiti ko baranai pārā.
सिव चतुरानन जाहि डेराहीं। अपर जीव केहि लेखे माहीं॥
siva caturānana jāhi ḍerāhīṁ, apara jīva kehi lekhe māhīṁ.

Trans:

Is there any whom success has not paralyzed? There is not one who has effectually discarded vanity and pride, whom the fever of youth has not overcome, whose glory has not been ruined by self-conceit, whom envy has not besmirched, whom the blast of sorrow has not shaken, whom the serpent of care has not bitten, or whom delusion has not affected. Is there any so well-seasoned of frame that he has not been attacked by desire—as a plank by the weevil? The desire of family, of wealth and of renown is a threefold temptation: whose soul has it not sullied? These all are Māyā's suite; who can describe in full her illimitable might? When even Shiva and Brahmmā stand in awe of her, why speak of other creatures?

दोहा-dohā:

ब्यापि रहेउ संसार महुँ माया कटक प्रचंड।
byāpi raheu saṁsāra mahuṁ māyā kaṭaka pracaṁḍa.
सेनापति कामादि भट दंभ कपट पाषंड ॥७१क॥
senāpati kāmādi bhaṭa daṁbha kapaṭa pāṣaṁḍa. 71(ka).

सो दासी रघुबीर कै समुझें मिथ्या सोपि।
so dāsī raghubīra kai samujheṁ mithyā sopi,
छूट न राम कृपा बिनु नाथ कहउँ पद रोपि ॥७१ख॥
chūṭa na rāma kṛpā binu nātha kahauṁ pada ropi. 71(kha).

Trans:

Māyā's formidable army is spread over the whole world: Lust and the other Passions are her generals; Fraud, Deceit and Heresy her champions. Being the servant of Raghubīr, though known to be a delusion, she can only be dispersed by his favor: this, my Lord, I assert with the utmost confidence.

चौपाई-caupāī:

जो माया सब जगहि नचावा। जासु चरित लखि काहुँ न पावा॥
jo māyā saba jagahi nacāvā, jāsu carita lakhi kāhuṁ na pāvā.
सोइ प्रभु भ्रू बिलास खगराजा। नाच नटी इव सहित समाजा॥
soi prabhu bhrū bilāsa khagarājā, nāca naṭī iva sahita samājā.
सोइ सच्चिदानंद घन रामा। अज बिग्यान रुप बल धामा॥
soi saccidānaṁda ghana rāmā, aja bigyāna rūpa bala dhāmā.
ब्यापक ब्याप्य अखंड अनंता। अखिल अमोघसक्ति भगवंता॥
byāpaka byāpya akhaṁḍa anaṁtā, akhila amoghasakti bhagavaṁtā.
अगुन अदभ्र गिरा गोतीता। सबदरसी अनवद्य अजीता॥
aguna adabhra girā gotītā, sabadarasī anavadya ajītā.

निर्मम निराकार निरमोहा । नित्य निरंजन सुख संदोहा ॥
nirmama nirākāra niramohā, nitya niraṁjana sukha saṁdohā.
प्रकृति पार प्रभु सब उर बासी । ब्रह्म निरीह बिरज अबिनासी ॥
prakṛti pāra prabhu saba ura bāsī, brahma nirīha biraja abināsī.
इहाँ मोह कर कारन नाहीं । रबि सन्मुख तम कबहुँ कि जाहीं ॥
ihāṁ moha kara kārana nāhīṁ, rabi sanmukha tama kabahuṁ ki jāhīṁ.

Trans:

This Māyā, which sets the whole world a-dancing, and whose actions no one can understand, is herself set dancing with all her troupe, like an actress on the stage, O king-of-birds, by the mere play of the Lord's eyebrows. For Rāma is the totality of existence, knowledge, and bliss, the uncreated, the all-wise, the home of beauty and strength; the permeator and the permeated; the indivisible, the eternal; the insoluble, the unerring, the divine energy; the Divinity of whom no qualities can be predicated; beyond the range of speech or perception; all-seeing, irreproachable, unconquered; without personal interests, without form, without illusion; deathless, passionless, blessed for ever; transcending nature; the Lord that in-dwelleth in every heart; the Supreme Spirit, effortless, passionless, imperishable. In the Lord-God delusion finds no sphere. Does darkness ever attack the sun?

दोहा-dohā:

भगत हेतु भगवान प्रभु राम धरेउ तनु भूप ।
bhagata hetu bhagavāna prabhu rāma dhareu tanu bhūpa,
किए चरित पावन परम प्राकृत नर अनुरूप ॥७२क॥
kie carita pāvana parama prākṛta nara anurūpa. 72(ka).

जथा अनेक बेष धरि नृत्य करइ नट कोइ ।
jathā aneka beṣa dhari nṛtya karai naṭa koi,
सोइ सोइ भाव देखावइ आपुन होइ न सोइ ॥७२ख॥
soi soi bhāva dekhāvai āpuna hoi na soi. 72(kha).

Trans:

For the sake of his faithful people, the very God, our Lord Rāma, has become incarnate as a King and for our supreme sanctification has lived as it were the life of an ordinary human—as an actor in the course of his performance assumes a variety of dresses and exhibits different characters but himself remains the same.

चौपाई-caupāī:

असि रघुपति लीला उरगारी । दनुज बिमोहनि जन सुखकारी ॥
asi raghupati līlā uragārī, danuja bimohani jana sukhakārī.
जे मति मलिन बिषयबस कामी । प्रभु पर मोह धरहिं इमि स्वामी ॥
je mati malina biṣayabasa kāmī, prabhu para moha dharahiṁ imi svāmī.
नयन दोष जा कहँ जब होई । पीत बरन ससि कहुँ कह सोई ॥
nayana doṣa jā kahaṁ jaba hoī, pīta barana sasi kahuṁ kaha soī.
जब जेहि दिसि भ्रम होइ खगेसा । सो कह पच्छिम उयउ दिनेसा ॥
jaba jehi disi bhrama hoi khagesā, so kaha pacchima uyau dinesā.
नौकारूढ़ चलत जग देखा । अचल मोह बस आपुहि लेखा ॥
naukārūṛha calata jaga dekhā, acala moha basa āpuhi lekhā.
बालक भ्रमहिं न भ्रमहिं गृहादी । कहहिं परस्पर मिथ्याबादी ॥
bālaka bhramahiṁ na bhramahiṁ gṛhādī, kahahiṁ paraspara mithyābādī.
हरि बिषइक अस मोह बिहंगा । सपनेहुँ नहिं अग्यान प्रसंगा ॥
hari biṣaika asa moha bihaṁgā, sapanehuṁ nahiṁ agyāna prasaṁgā.
मायाबस मतिमंद अभागी । हृदयँ जमनिका बहुबिधि लागी ॥
māyābasa matimaṁda abhāgī, hṛdayaṁ jamanikā bahubidhi lāgī.
ते सठ हठ बस संसय करहीं । निज अग्यान राम पर धरहीं ॥
te saṭha haṭha basa saṁsaya karahīṁ, nija agyāna rāma para dharahīṁ.

Trans:

Such, O Garud, is Rāma's divertissement: a bewilderment to the demons, but a delight to the faithful. Sensual libertines in their dullness of soul impute the Delusion to the Lord like as when, sir, a man whose eyesight is in fault says that the moon is of a yellow color; or when mistaken as to the points of the compass affirms that the sun has risen in the west; or as one on board a ship, who deludes himself with the idea that he is standing still and that the land is moving. When children in play turn round and round, the house, or whatever else it may be, does not turn round; it is only their idle fashion of talking. In this way only, O Garud, can error be ascribed to Harī; never even in a dream is he ever subject to delusion. The wretched dullards, who succumb to Māyā, have a thick veil over their soul, and these are the obstinate fools who raise doubts and lay their own ignorance on Rāma.

दोहा-dohā:

काम क्रोध मद लोभ रत गृहासक्त दुखरूप ।
kāma krodha mada lobha rata gṛhāsakta dukharūpa,
ते किमि जानहिं रघुपतिहि मूढ़ परे तम कूप ॥७३क॥
te kimi jānahiṁ raghupatihi mūṛha pare tama kūpa. 73(ka).

निर्गुन रूप सुलभ अति सगुन जान नहिं कोइ ।
nirguna rūpa sulabha ati saguna jāna nahiṁ koi,
सुगम अगम नाना चरित सुनि मुनि मन भ्रम होइ ॥७३ख॥
sugama agama nānā carita suni muni mana bhrama hoi. 73(kha).

Trans:

How can these clowns understand Raghupatī, addicted as they are to lust, choler, pride, greed, absorbed in domestic affairs, pictures of misery, dwelling at the bottom of a well of darkness. The unembodied phase of the Godhead is easy to understand, but who can comprehend its incarnation? The soul of a saint is bewildered on hearing of all his actions, both natural and supernatural.

चौपाई-caupāī:

सुनु खगेस रघुपति प्रभुताई । कहउँ जथामति कथा सुहाई ॥
sunu khagesa raghupati prabhutāī, kahauṁ jathāmati kathā suhāī.
जेहि बिधि मोह भयउ प्रभु मोही । सोउ सब कथा सुनावउँ तोही ॥
jehi bidhi moha bhayau prabhu mohī, sou saba kathā sunāvauṁ tohī.
राम कृपा भाजन तुम्ह ताता । हरि गुन प्रीति मोहि सुखदाता ॥
rāma kṛpā bhājana tumha tātā, hari guna prīti mohi sukhadātā.
ताते नहिं कछु तुम्हहिं दुरावउँ । परम रहस्य मनोहर गावउँ ॥
tāte nahiṁ kachu tumhahiṁ durāvauṁ, parama rahasya manohara gāvauṁ.
सुनहु राम कर सहज सुभाऊ । जन अभिमान न राखहिं काऊ ॥
sunahu rāma kara sahaja subhāū, jana abhimāna na rākhahiṁ kāū.
संसृत मूल सूलप्रद नाना । सकल सोक दायक अभिमाना ॥
saṁsṛta mūla sūlaprada nānā, sakala soka dāyaka abhimānā.
ताते करहिं कृपानिधि दूरी । सेवक पर ममता अति भूरी ॥
tāte karahiṁ kṛpānidhi dūrī, sevaka para mamatā ati bhūrī.
जिमि सिसु तन ब्रन होइ गोसाईं । मातु चिराव कठिन की नाईं ॥
jimi sisu tana brana hoi gosāīṁ, mātu cirāva kaṭhina kī nāīṁ.

Trans:

Hearken, Garud; I will tell you to the best of my ability a charming story, in illustration of Rāma's power; declaring to you in full, all the particulars of a delusion which befell myself. You, sire, are a vessel of Rāma's grace and cherish a special affection for Harī's actions and are moreover my greatest benefactor; I will therefore conceal nothing from you in this exposition of a great and excellent mystery. Hearken: Rāma's natural disposition is such that he never tolerates pride in his servants. Pride has its root in worldliness and is the cause of many pains and every kind of vexation. Therefore the

All-merciful does away with it, in the greatness of his affection for his servants—in the same way, sire, as when a child has a boil on his body, his mother, with seeming cruelty, cuts it open.

दोहा-dohā:

जदपि प्रथम दुख पावइ रोवइ बाल अधीर ।
jadapi prathama dukha pāvai rovai bāla adhīra,
ब्याधि नास हित जननी गनति न सो सिसु पीर ॥७४क॥
byādhi nāsa hita jananī ganati na so sisu pīra. 74(ka).

तिमि रघुपति निज दास कर हरहिं मान हित लागि ।
timi raghupati nija dāsa kara harahiṁ māna hita lāgi,
तुलसिदास ऐसे प्रभुहि कस न भजहु भ्रम त्यागि ॥७४ख॥
tulasidāsa aise prabhuhi kasa na bhajahu bhrama tyāgi. 74(kha).

Trans:

At first the poor child cries with the pain, but the mother pays no attention to it, her object being to cure the disease. In like manner Raghupatī cures his servants of pride, doing it all for their good. Ah, Tulsīdās, who would not forswear error and worship such a Lord as him?

चौपाई-caupāī:

राम कृपा आपनि जड़ताई । कहउँ खगेस सुनहु मन लाई ॥
rāma kṛpā āpani jaṛatāī, kahauṁ khagesa sunahu mana lāī.
जब जब राम मनुज तनु धरहीं । भक्त हेतु लीला बहु करहीं ॥
jaba jaba rāma manuja tanu dharahīṁ, bhakta hetu līlā bahu karahīṁ.
तब तब अवधपुरी मैं ज़ाऊँ । बालचरित बिलोकि हरषाऊँ ॥
taba taba avadhapurī maiṁ zāūṁ, bālacarita biloki haraṣāūṁ.
जन्म महोत्सव देखउँ जाई । बरष पाँच तहँ रहउँ लोभाई ॥
janma mahotsava dekhauṁ jāī, baraṣa pāṁca tahaṁ rahauṁ lobhāī.
इष्टदेव मम बालक रामा । सोभा बपुष कोटि सत कामा ॥
iṣṭadeva mama bālaka rāmā, sobhā bapuṣa koṭi sata kāmā.
निज प्रभु बदन निहारि निहारी । लोचन सुफल करउँ उरगारी ॥
nija prabhu badana nihāri nihārī, locana suphala karauṁ uragārī.
लघु बायस बपु धरि हरि संगा । देखउँ बालचरित बहु रंगा ॥
laghu bāyasa bapu dhari hari saṁgā, dekhauṁ bālacarita bahu raṁgā.

Trans:

I will now tell you the story, O Garud, of Rāma's grace and my own foolishness; listen attentively. Whenever Rāma assumes human form and goes through his series of mimic actions in the behoof of his votaries, I always betake myself to Avadh and delight to watch his boyish doings. I go and attend the rejoicings at his birth and am glad to stay for five years. The child Rāma is my patron divinity, beautiful in form as a myriad Loves. Ever gazing on the face of my own Lord, O Garud, I give my eyes a treat indeed, and being in the trivial shape of a crow, I keep close to Harī and observe all his child-like sports.

दोहा-dohā:

लरिकाईं जहँ जहँ फिरहिं तहँ तहँ संग उड़ाउँ ।
larikāīṁ jahaṁ jahaṁ phirahiṁ tahaṁ tahaṁ saṁga uṛāuṁ,
जूठनि परइ अजिर महँ सो उठाइ करि खाउँ ॥७५क॥
jūṭhani parai ajira mahaṁ so uṭhāi kari khāuṁ. 75(ka).

एक बार अतिसय सब चरित किए रघुबीर ।
eka bāra atisaya saba carita kie raghubīra,
सुमिरत प्रभु लीला सोइ पुलकित भयउ सरीर ॥७५ख॥
sumirata prabhu līlā soi pulakita bhayau sarīra. 75(kha).

Trans:

Whenever he rambles in play, I flutter about close at hand, and for my food, I pick up the crumbs in the courtyard that fall from his plate. One day Raghubīr played a very quaint frolic." At the remembrance of his Lord's playfulness, every hair on his body stood raised in rapture.

चौपाई-caupāī:

कहइ भसुंड सुनहु खगनायक । रामचरित सेवक सुखदायक ॥
kahai bhasuṁḍa sunahu khaganāyaka, rāmacarita sevaka sukhadāyaka.
नृप मंदिर सुंदर सब भाँती । खचित कनक मनि नाना जाती ॥
nṛpa maṁdira suṁdara saba bhāṁtī, khacita kanaka mani nānā jātī.
बरनि न जाइ रुचिर अँगनाई । जहँ खेलहिं नित चारिउ भाई ॥
barani na jāi rucira aṁganāī, jahaṁ khelahiṁ nita cāriu bhāī.
बालबिनोद करत रघुराई । बिचरत अजिर जननि सुखदाई ॥
bālabinoda karata raghurāī, bicarata ajira janani sukhadāī.
मरकत मृदुल कलेवर स्यामा । अंग अंग प्रति छबि बहु कामा ॥
marakata mṛdula kalevara syāmā, aṁga aṁga prati chabi bahu kāmā.
नव राजीव अरुन मृदु चरना । पदज रुचिर नख ससि दुति हरना ॥
nava rājīva aruna mṛdu caranā, padaja rucira nakha sasi duti haranā.
ललित अंक कुलिसादिक चारी । नूपुर चारू मधुर रवकारी ॥
lalita aṁka kulisādika cārī, nūpura cārū madhura ravakārī.
चारु पुरट मनि रचित बनाई । कटि किंकिनि कल मुखर सुहाई ॥
cāru puraṭa mani racita banāī, kaṭi kiṁkini kala mukhara suhāī.

Trans:

Bhusumdi continued, "Hearken, O king-of-birds, to my story of Rāma's actions, which are ever the delight of his servants. The king's palace was exquisitely beautiful, of gold, constellated with precious stones of every kind. The pleasantness of the courtyard, where the four brothers were always playing, surpasses description. Here Rāma roamed about, to the delight of his mother, diverting himself with childish amusements; his tender frame, dark of hue as a sapphire, with the beauty of unnumbered Loves in every limb; his soft rosy feet like lotus buds, with lustrous nails that outshone the brightness of the moon, decorated with the four-fold stamp of the thunderbolt, the lotus, the elephant-goad and the flag and circled with pretty bangles that made sweet music. Melodious too, the pretty belt about his waist, fashioned of gold and embossed with jewels.

दोहा-dohā:

रेखा त्रय सुन्दर उदर नाभी रुचिर गँभीर ।
rekhā traya sundara udara nābhī rucira gaṁbhīra,
उर आयत भ्राजत बिबिधि बाल बिभूषन चीर ॥७६॥
ura āyata bhrājata bibidhi bāla bibhūṣana cīra. 76.

Trans:

With a belly creased in the three lines of beauty, a navel shapely and deep, and a broad chest gleaming with all the ornaments that befit a child's attire,

चौपाई-caupāī:

अरुन पानि नख करज मनोहर । बाहु बिसाल बिभूषन सुंदर ॥
aruna pāni nakha karaja manohara, bāhu bisāla bibhūṣana suṁdara.
कंध बाल केहरि दर ग्रीवा । चारु चिबुक आनन छबि सींवा ॥
kaṁdha bāla kehari dara grīvā, cāru cibuka ānana chabi sīṁvā.
कलबल बचन अधर अरुनारे । दुइ दुइ दसन बिसद बर बारे ॥
kalabala bacana adhara arunāre, dui dui dasana bisada bara bāre.
ललित कपोल मनोहर नासा । सकल सुखद ससि कर सम हासा ॥
lalita kapola manohara nāsā, sakala sukhada sasi kara sama hāsā.
नील कंज लोचन भव मोचन । भ्राजत भाल तिलक गोरोचन ॥
nīla kaṁja locana bhava mocana, bhrājata bhāla tilaka gorocana.
बिकट भृकुटि सम श्रवन सुहाए । कुंचित कच मेचक छबि छाए ॥

bikaṭa bhṛkuṭi sama śravana suhāe, kuṁcita kaca mecaka chabi chāe.
पीत झीनि झगुली तन सोही । किलकनि चितवनि भावति मोही ॥
pīta jhīni jhagulī tana sohī, kilakani citavani bhāvati mohī.
रूप रासि नृप अजिर बिहारी । नाचहिं निज प्रतिबिंब निहारी ॥
rūpa rāsi nṛpa ajira bihārī, nācahiṁ nija pratibiṁba nihārī.
मोहि सन करहिं बिबिधि बिधि क्रीड़ा । बरनत मोहि होति अति ब्रीड़ा ॥
mohi sana karahiṁ bibidhi bidhi krīṛā, baranata mohi hoti ati brīṛā.
किलकत मोहि धरन जब धावहिं । चलउँ भागि तब पूप देखावहिं ॥
kilakata mohi dharana jaba dhāvahiṁ, calauṁ bhāgi taba pūpa dekhāvahiṁ.

Trans:

with roseate hands and lovely nails, with long and richly braceleted arms, and the shoulders of a young lion, with dimpled neck and rounded chin and face, the perfection of beauty; with lisping speech and ruddy lips, and a pair of dear little pearly teeth above and below, with chubby cheeks and a darling nose, and a smile as winsome as that of the moon, with lotus eyes that loose earth's ties, and forehead gleaming with the mark of yellow pigment, with arched eyebrows and pretty ears, with curly hair black and beautiful, with a thin yellow jacket to set off his body—he fascinated me with his merry glance, as he sported in all his loveliness in the king's courts, dancing at the sight of his own shadow, and having all sorts of antics with me, which I flush to tell. When he laughingly ran to catch me, I flew away; then he showed me a piece of cake.

दोहा-dohā:

आवत निकट हँसहिं प्रभु भाजत रुदन कराहिं ।
āvata nikaṭa haṁsahiṁ prabhu bhājata rudana karāhiṁ,
जाउँ समीप गहन पद फिरि फिरि चितइ पराहिं ॥७७क॥
jāuṁ samīpa gahana pada phiri phiri citai parāhiṁ. 77(ka).

प्राकृत सिसु इव लीला देखि भयउ मोहि मोह ।
prākṛta sisu iva līlā dekhi bhayau mohi moha,
कवन चरित्र करत प्रभु चिदानंद संदोह ॥७७ख॥
kavana caritra karata prabhu cidānaṁda saṁdoha. 77(kha).

Trans:

I came near and the Lord laughed. I flew away again and he fell a-crying. I approached to lay hold of his feet, and he ran off again and again, turning round to look at me. Seeing him play like an ordinary child, I was overcome by bewilderment. Can these be the actions of the Lord, who is the totality of intelligence and bliss?

चौपाई-caupāī:

एतना मन आनत खगराया । रघुपति प्रेरित ब्यापी माया ॥
etanā mana ānata khagarāyā, raghupati prerita byāpī māyā.
सो माया न दुखद मोहि काहीं । आन जीव इव संसृत नाहीं ॥
so māyā na dukhada mohi kāhīṁ, āna jīva iva saṁsṛta nāhīṁ.
नाथ इहाँ कछु कारन आना । सुनहु सो सावधान हरिजाना ॥
nātha ihāṁ kachu kārana ānā, sunahu so sāvadhāna harijānā.
ग्यान अखंड एक सीताबर । माया बस्य जीव सचराचर ॥
gyāna akhaṁḍa eka sītābara, māyā basya jīva sacarācara.
जौं सब कें रह ग्यान एकरस । ईस्वर जीवहि भेद कहहु कस ॥
jauṁ saba keṁ raha gyāna ekarasa, īsvara jīvahi bheda kahahu kasa.
माया बस्य जीव अभिमानी । ईस बस्य माया गुनखानी ॥
māyā basya jīva abhimānī, īsa basya māyā gunakhānī.
परबस जीव स्वबस भगवंता । जीव अनेक एक श्रीकंता ॥
parabasa jīva svabasa bhagavaṁtā, jīva aneka eka śrīkaṁtā.
मुधा भेद जद्यपि कृत माया । बिनु हरि जाइ न कोटि उपाया ॥
mudhā bheda jadyapi kṛta māyā, binu hari jāi na koṭi upāyā.

Trans:

This was what came into my mind, O Garud, for Rāma had sent forth his delusive power to entangle me. But this delusion was in no way harmful to me. I was not so affected by it as other creatures. A special cause, my Lord, was here at work, which I wish you, Garud, to observe attentively. Rāma alone is absolute intelligence; every creature, animate or inanimate, is subject to Māyā. If all had the same perfect intelligence, tell me what would be the difference between God and his creatures. The creature in his pride is subjected to Māyā. Māyā, with all its phenomena, is subject to God. The creature is dependent on others, the Deity is self-dependent; the creature is manifold, Rāma is one. Though the distinctions made by Māyā are false, without Rāma's help they cannot be dispersed, whatever you may do.

दोहा-dohā:

रामचंद्र के भजन बिनु जो चह पद निर्बान ।
rāmacaṁdra ke bhajana binu jo caha pada nirbāna,
ग्यानवंत अपि सो नर पसु बिनु पूँछ बिषान ॥७८क॥
gyānavaṁta api so nara pasu binu pūṁcha biṣāna. 78(ka).

राकापति षोड़स उअहिं तारागन समुदाइ ।
rākāpati ṣoṛasa uahiṁ tārāgana samudāi,
सकल गिरिन्ह दव लाइअ बिनु रबि राति न जाइ ॥७८ख॥
sakala girinha dava lāia binu rabi rāti na jāi. 78(kha).

Trans:

The wisest of men, who hopes for salvation without prayer to Rāma, is like a beast without tail and horns. Though sixteen full moons were to rise at once and all the starry host and the forests on every mountain were set on fire, night would not yield except to the sun.

चौपाई-caupāī:

ऐसेहिं हरि बिनु भजन खगेसा । मिटइ न जीवन्ह केर कलेसा ॥
aisehiṁ hari binu bhajana khagesā, miṭai na jīvanha kera kalesā.
हरि सेवकहि न ब्याप अबिद्या । प्रभु प्रेरित ब्यापइ तेहि बिद्या ॥
hari sevakahi na byāpa abidyā, prabhu prerita byāpai tehi bidyā.
ताते नास न होइ दास कर । भेद भगति बाढ़इ बिहंगबर ॥
tāte nāsa na hoi dāsa kara, bheda bhagati bāṛhai bihaṁgabara.
भ्रम तें चकित राम मोहि देखा । बिहँसे सो सुनु चरित बिसेषा ॥
bhrama teṁ cakita rāma mohi dekhā, bihaṁse so sunu carita biseṣā.
तेहि कौतुक कर मरमु न काहूँ । जाना अनुज न मातु पिताहूँ ॥
tehi kautuka kara maramu na kāhūṁ, jānā anuja na mātu pitāhūṁ.
जानु पानि धाए मोहि धरना । स्यामल गात अरुन कर चरना ॥
jānu pāni dhāe mohi dharanā, syāmala gāta aruna kara caranā.
तब मैं भागि चलेउँ उरगामी । राम गहन कहँ भुजा पसारी ॥
taba maiṁ bhāgi caleuṁ uragāmī, rāma gahana kahaṁ bhujā pasārī.
जिमि जिमि दूरि उड़ाउँ अकासा । तहँ भुज हरि देखउँ निज पासा ॥
jimi jimi dūri uṛāuṁ akāsā, tahaṁ bhuja hari dekhauṁ nija pāsā.

Trans:

In like manner, Garud, without prayer to Harī, the troubles incident to existence cannot be dispersed. Ignorance has no power over a servant of Harī's; it is knowledge, emanating from the Lord, that pervades his whole being. Therefore, O best of birds, there is no destruction for a believer: his faith, as of a servant in his master, is ever ascendant. Rāma smiled to see me bewildered in error; and hear what a strange course he adopted! The secret of this diversion, neither his brother nor his father or mother ever knew. As he crawled on his hands and knees in a hurry to catch me—with his body so dark of hue and his rosy hands and feet—I took to flight, Garud, and he stretched out his arms to lay hold of me. High as I flew into the air, I still saw his arm as close to me as ever.

दोहा-dohā:

ब्रह्मलोक लगि गयउँ मैं चितयउँ पाछ उड़ात ।
brahmaloka lagi gayauṁ maiṁ citayauṁ pācha uṛāta,
जुग अंगुल कर बीच सब राम भुजहि मोहि तात ॥७९क॥
juga aṁgula kara bīca saba rāma bhujahi mohi tāta. 79(ka).

सप्ताबरन भेद करि जहाँ लगें गति मोरि ।
saptābarana bheda kari jahāṁ lageṁ gati mori,
गयउँ तहाँ प्रभु भुज निरखि ब्याकुल भयउँ बहोरि ॥७९ख॥
gayauṁ tahāṁ prabhu bhuja nirakhi byākula bhayauṁ bahori. 79(kha).

Trans:

I mounted even to Brahmmā's sphere, but when I looked back in my flight, two fingers' breadth, O sir, was all the distance between Rāma's arm and me. I cleft the seven folds of the universe and mounted to the utmost height that I could reach, but still I saw the Lord's arm. Then was I dumbfounded.

चौपाई-caupāī:

मूदेउँ नयन त्रसित जब भयउँ । पुनि चितवत कोसलपुर गयऊँ ॥
mūdeuṁ nayana trasita jaba bhayauṁ, puni citavata kosalapura gayaūṁ.
मोहि बिलोकि राम मुसुकाहीं । बिहँसत तुरत गयउँ मुख माहीं ॥
mohi biloki rāma musukāhīṁ, bihaṁsata turata gayauṁ mukha māhīṁ.
उदर माझ सुनु अंडज राया । देखेउँ बहु ब्रह्मांड निकाया ॥
udara mājha sunu aṁḍaja rāyā, dekheuṁ bahu brahmāṁḍa nikāyā.
अति बिचित्र तहँ लोक अनेका । रचना अधिक एक ते एका ॥
ati bicitra tahaṁ loka anekā, racanā adhika eka te ekā.
कोटिन्ह चतुरानन गौरीसा । अगनित उडगन रबि रजनीसा ॥
koṭinha caturānana gaurīsā, aganita uḍagana rabi rajanīsā.
अगनित लोकपाल जम काला । अगनित भूधर भूमि बिसाला ॥
aganita lokapāla jama kālā, aganita bhūdhara bhūmi bisālā.
सागर सरि सर बिपिन अपारा । नाना भाँति सृष्टि बिस्तारा ॥
sāgara sari sara bipina apārā, nānā bhāṁti sṛṣṭi bistārā.
सुर मुनि सिद्ध नाग नर किंनर । चारि प्रकार जीव सचराचर ॥
sura muni siddha nāga nara kiṁnara, cāri prakāra jīva sacarācara.

Trans:

In my terror I closed my eyes, and when I opened them again, I found myself at Ajodhyā. Rāma looked at me with a smile, and as he laughed I was instantly drawn down his throat. Hearken, O king-of-birds, in his belly I saw multitudinous universes, with many strange worlds, each more wonderful than the other, with myriads of Brahmmās and Shivas, with stars and suns and moons innumerable; innumerable Lokpāls and images of Death and Time; numberless mountains and vast plains of earth; seas, lakes, rivers and forests without end, and all the complex machinery of creation; with gods, sages, saints, serpents and kinnars and the four classes of living things, both moving and motionless;

दोहा-dohā:

जो नहिं देखा नहिं सुना जो मनहूँ न समाइ ।
jo nahiṁ dekhā nahiṁ sunā jo manahūṁ na samāi,
सो सब अद्भुत देखेउँ बरनि कवनि बिधि जाइ ॥८०क॥
so saba adbhuta dekheuṁ barani kavani bidhi jāi. 80(ka).

एक एक ब्रह्मांड महुँ रहउँ बरष सत एक ।
eka eka brahmāṁḍa mahuṁ rahauṁ baraṣa sata eka,
एहि बिधि देखत फिरउँ मैं अंड कटाह अनेक ॥८०ख॥
ehi bidhi dekhata phirauṁ maiṁ aṁḍa kaṭāha aneka. 80(kha).

Trans:

such as eye has not seen, nor ear heard, nor has entered into man's mind to conceive, were all the marvels that I saw; how is it possible to describe them? In each universe I stayed a hundred years and in this manner, made the round of all the multitudinous galaxies.

चौपाई-caupāī:

लोक लोक प्रति भिन्न बिधाता । भिन्न बिष्नु सिव मनु दिसित्राता ॥
loka loka prati bhinna bidhātā, bhinna biṣnu siva manu disitrātā.
नर गंधर्ब भूत बेताला । किंनर निसिचर पसु खग ब्याला ॥
nara gaṁdharba bhūta betālā, kiṁnara nisicara pasu khaga byālā.
देव दनुज गन नाना जाती । सकल जीव तहँ आनहि भाँती ॥
deva danuja gana nānā jātī, sakala jīva tahaṁ ānahi bhāṁtī.
महि सरि सागर सर गिरि नाना । सब प्रपंच तहँ आनइ आना ॥
mahi sari sāgara sara giri nānā, saba prapaṁca tahaṁ ānai ānā.
अंडकोस प्रति प्रति निज रुपा । देखेउँ जिनस अनेक अनूपा ॥
aṁḍakosa prati prati nija rupā, dekheuṁ jinasa aneka anūpā.
अवधपुरी प्रति भुवन निनारी । सरजू भिन्न भिन्न नर नारी ॥
avadhapurī prati bhuvana ninārī, sarajū bhinna bhinna nara nārī.
दसरथ कौसल्या सुनु ताता । बिबिध रूप भरतादिक भ्राता ॥
dasaratha kausalyā sunu tātā, bibidha rūpa bharatādika bhrātā.
प्रति ब्रह्मांड राम अवतारा । देखउँ बालबिनोद अपारा ॥
prati brahmāṁḍa rāma avatārā, dekhauṁ bālabinoda apārā.

Trans:

Each world had its own separate Creator, its own Vishnu, Shiva, and Manu, and its own Regents of the spheres; with men, gandharvs, imps and evil spirits, kinnars and demons, cattle, birds and serpents, all the tribes of gods and giants, and every living creature having a shape peculiar to that universe. The earth with its multitudinous rivers, oceans, lakes and mountains, nay, the entire creation in each universe had each a distinctive character. In all these universes I found even myself possessed of manifold incomparable forms. In each world was a separate city of Avadh with its own Sarjū, its own men and women, with Dashrath and Kausalyā and the other queens, and Bharat and his brothers, each in their proper form. Each sphere had its incarnate Rāma with all his child-like sports for me to see.

दोहा-dohā:

भिन्न भिन्न मैं दीख सबु अति बिचित्र हरिजान ।
bhinna bhinna maiṁ dīkha sabu ati bicitra harijāna,
अगनित भुवन फिरेउँ प्रभु राम न देखेउँ आन ॥८१क॥
aganita bhuvana phireuṁ prabhu rāma na dekheuṁ āna. 81(ka).

सोइ सिसुपन सोइ सोभा सोइ कृपाल रघुबीर ।
soi sisupana soi sobhā soi kṛpāla raghubīra,
भुवन भुवन देखत फिरउँ प्रेरित मोह समीर ॥८१ख॥
bhuvana bhuvana dekhata phirauṁ prerita moha samīra. 81(kha).

Trans:

O Garud, I saw every part of the pageant separately repeated, but in my round of the innumerable worlds, I saw no other Lord Rāma. The same child-like ways, the same beauty, the same gracious Raghubīr were what I saw in each successive world that I visited, driven on by the blast of delusion.

चौपाई-caupāī:

भ्रमत मोहि ब्रह्मांड अनेका । बीते मनहुँ कल्प सत एका ॥
bhramata mohi brahmāṁḍa anekā, bīte manahuṁ kalpa sata ekā.
फिरत फिरत निज आश्रम आयउँ । तहँ पुनि रहि कछु काल गवाँयउँ ॥
phirata phirata nija āśrama āyauṁ, tahaṁ puni rahi kachu kāla gavāṁyauṁ.
निज प्रभु जन्म अवध सुनि पायउँ । निर्भर प्रेम हरषि उठि धायउँ ॥

nija prabhu janma avadha suni pāyaum̐, nirbhara prema haraṣi uṭhi dhāyaum̐.
देखउँ जन्म महोत्सव जाई । जेहि बिधि प्रथम कहा मैं गाई ॥
dekhaum̐ janma mahotsava jāī, jehi bidhi prathama kahā maiṁ gāī.
राम उदर देखेउँ जग नाना । देखत बनइ न जाइ बखाना ॥
rāma udara dekheum̐ jaga nānā, dekhata banai na jāi bakhānā.
तहँ पुनि देखेउँ राम सुजाना । माया पति कृपाल भगवाना ॥
taham̐ puni dekheum̐ rāma sujānā, māyā pati kṛpāla bhagavānā.
करउँ बिचार बहोरि बहोरी । मोह कलिल ब्यापित मति मोरी ॥
karaum̐ bicāra bahori bahorī, moha kalila byāpita mati morī.
उभय घरी महँ मैं सब देखा । भयउँ भ्रमित मन मोह बिसेषा ॥
ubhaya gharī maham̐ maiṁ saba dekhā, bhayaum̐ bhramita mana moha biseṣā.

Trans:

Imagine a hundred cycles to have been spent in my wanderings through the different spheres. At last, after all my travels, I came to my own hermitage and there I stayed some little time. When I heard of my Lord's birth at Avadh, I started up in an overwhelming ecstasy of devotion and went and witnessed the rejoicings at his nativity, as I have already described to you. In Rāma's belly I saw many worlds, but what I saw is past all telling. Then again I saw the all-wise Rāma, the Lord of Māyā, the merciful God, and much I questioned within myself, for my understanding was obscured by the mists of delusion. In less than an hour I saw everything; I was a-weary and my soul was bewildered entirely.

दोहा-dohā:

देखि कृपाल बिकल मोहि बिहँसे तब रघुबीर ।
dekhi kṛpāla bikala mohi biham̐se taba raghubīra,
बिहँसतहीं मुख बाहेर आयउँ सुनु मतिधीर ॥८२क॥
biham̐satahīṁ mukha bāhera āyaum̐ sunu matidhīra. 82(ka).

सोइ लरिकाई मो सन करन लगे पुनि राम ।
soi larikāī mo sana karana lage puni rāma,
कोटि भाँति समुझावउँ मनु न लहइ बिश्राम ॥८२ख॥
koṭi bhām̐ti samujhāvaum̐ manu na lahai biśrāma. 82(kha).

Trans:

Seeing my distress, the all-merciful Raghubar laughed; and as he laughed I issued out from his mouth; hearken, O firm of faith. Rāma again began his childish pranks with me. I reasoned with myself in every way I could; but my mind had no peace.

चौपाई-caupāī:

देखि चरित यह सो प्रभुताई । समुझत देह दसा बिसराई ॥
dekhi carita yaha so prabhutāī, samujhata deha dasā bisarāī.
धरनि परेउँ मुख आव न बाता । त्राहि त्राहि आरत जन त्राता ॥
dharani pareum̐ mukha āva na bātā, trāhi trāhi ārata jana trātā.
प्रेमाकुल प्रभु मोहि बिलोकी । निज माया प्रभुता तब रोकी ॥
premākula prabhu mohi bilokī, nija māyā prabhutā taba rokī.
कर सरोज प्रभु मम सिर धरेऊ । दीनदयाल सकल दुख हरेऊ ॥
kara saroja prabhu mama sira dhareū, dīnadayāla sakala dukha hareū.
कीन्ह राम मोहि बिगत बिमोहा । सेवक सुखद कृपा संदोहा ॥
kīnha rāma mohi bigata bimohā, sevaka sukhada kṛpā saṁdohā.
प्रभुता प्रथम बिचारि बिचारी । मन महँ होइ हरष अति भारी ॥
prabhutā prathama bicāri bicārī, mana maham̐ hoi haraṣa ati bhārī.
भगत बछलता प्रभु कै देखी । उपजी मम उर प्रीति बिसेषी ॥
bhagata bachalatā prabhu kai dekhī, upajī mama ura prīti biseṣī.
सजल नयन पुलकित कर जोरी । कीन्हिउँ बहु बिधि बिनय बहोरी ॥
sajala nayana pulakita kara jorī, kīnhium̐ bahu bidhi binaya bahorī.

Trans:

Seeing this miracle and weighing its transcendency I lost my senses. I fell to the ground and no word came to my mouth, except for, "Save me, save me, O savior of all distrest believers." When the Lord saw my agony of devotion, he at once checked the influence of his delusive power. The Lord placed his lotus hands upon my head and—ever merciful to the poor—healed me of all my pain. Rāma, the gracious benefactor of his servants, thus dispelled my infatuation. As I reflected on his mighty power, there first arose in my heart a great transport of delight; and seeing his loving-kindness to his worshippers, my bosom heaved with an unutterable love. With streaming eyes and quivering frame and hands clasped in prayer, I again and again made humble petitions.

दोहा-dohā:

सुनि सप्रेम मम बानी देखि दीन निज दास ।
suni saprema mama bānī dekhi dīna nija dāsa,
बचन सुखद गंभीर मृदु बोले रमानिवास ॥८३क॥
bacana sukhada gaṁbhīra mṛdu bole ramānivāsa. 83(ka).

काकभसुंडि मागु बर अति प्रसन्न मोहि जानि ।
kākabhasuṁḍi māgu bara ati prasanna mohi jāni,
अनिमादिक सिधि अपर रिधि मोच्छ सकल सुख खानि ॥८३ख॥
animādika sidhi apara ridhi moccha sakala sukha khāni. 83(kha).

Trans:

Hearing my loving words and seeing me to be his own devoted servant, he made me this gracious, profound and tender speech: "Kāgabhusumdi, know that I am highly pleased with you; ask of me any boon—be it the supernatural powers of the saints, or fabulous wealth, or deliverance from further transmigration, the sum of all bliss;

चौपाई-caupāī:

ग्यान बिबेक बिरति बिग्याना । मुनि दुर्लभ गुन जे जग नाना ॥
gyāna bibeka birati bigyānā, muni durlabha guna je jaga nānā.
आजु देउँ सब संसय नाहीं । मागु जो तोहि भाव मन माहीं ॥
āju deum̐ saba saṁsaya nāhīṁ, māgu jo tohi bhāva mana māhīṁ.
सुनि प्रभु बचन अधिक अनुरागेउँ । मन अनुमान करन तब लागेउँ ॥
suni prabhu bacana adhika anurāgeum̐, mana anumāna karana taba lāgeum̐.
प्रभु कह देन सकल सुख सही । भगति आपनी देन न कही ॥
prabhu kaha dena sakala sukha sahī, bhagati āpanī dena na kahī.
भगति हीन गुन सब सुख ऐसे । लवन बिना बहु बिंजन जैसे ॥
bhagati hīna guna saba sukha aise, lavana binā bahu biṁjana jaise.
भजन हीन सुख कवने काजा । अस बिचारि बोलेउँ खगराजा ॥
bhajana hīna sukha kavane kājā, asa bicāri boleum̐ khagarājā.
जौं प्रभु होइ प्रसन्न बर देहू । मो पर करहु कृपा अरु नेहू ॥
jauṁ prabhu hoi prasanna bara dehū, mo para karahu kṛpā aru nehū.
मन भावत बर मागउँ स्वामी । तुम्ह उदार उर अंतरजामी ॥
mana bhāvata bara māgaum̐ svāmī, tumha udāra ura aṁtarajāmī.

Trans:

or knowledge and wisdom, self-restraint and philosophy, qualities which, as the entire world know, scarce the gods attain to. Today I will grant you anything; doubt not but ask whatever your soul desires." On hearing the Lord's words I was greatly moved and began to reason thus within myself, "The Lord, it is true, has promised to give me every blessing, but has not said he would give me Devotion. Without Devotion what are any virtues or blessings? Like any quantity of condiments without salt. Of what avail is any good without prayer?" Having thus considered, O Garud, I made reply, "If it be your good pleasure, my Lord, to grant me a boon and if you wish to do me a favor and kindness, I will ask the boon, Sire, which my soul desires; you are generous and know the secrets of the heart:

दोहा-dohā:

अबिरल भगति बिसुद्ध तव श्रुति पुरान जो गाव ।
abirala bhagati bisuddha tava śruti purāna jo gāva,
जेहि खोजत जोगीस मुनि प्रभु प्रसाद कोउ पाव ॥८४क॥
jehi khojata jogīsa muni prabhu prasāda kou pāva. 84(ka).

भगत कल्पतरु प्रनत हित कृपा सिंधु सुख धाम ।
bhagata kalpataru pranata hita kṛpā siṁdhu sukha dhāma,
सोइ निज भगति मोहि प्रभु देहु दया करि राम ॥८४ख॥
soi nija bhagati mohi prabhu dehu dayā kari rāma. 84(kha).

Trans:

Grant me steadfast and sincere Devotion, such as the Vedas and Purānas describe, such as the greatest ascetics and saints search after, but few only find and that by the Lord's grace. O my Lord Rāma, tree of Paradise to the pious, friend of the suppliant, all-merciful, all-blessed, out of your clemency please grant me—The Boon of Devotion."

चौपाई-caupāī:

एवमस्तु कहि रघुकुलनायक । बोले बचन परम सुखदायक ॥
evamastu kahi raghukulanāyaka, bole bacana parama sukhadāyaka.
सुनु बायस तैं सहज सयाना । काहे न मागसि अस बरदाना ॥
sunu bāyasa taiṁ sahaja sayānā, kāhe na māgasi asa baradānā.
सब सुख खानि भगति तैं मागी । नहिं जग कोउ तोहि सम बड़भागी ॥
saba sukha khāni bhagati taiṁ māgī, nahiṁ jaga kou tohi sama baṛabhāgī.
जो मुनि कोटि जतन नहिं लहहीं । जे जप जोग अनल तन दहहीं ॥
jo muni koṭi jatana nahiṁ lahahīṁ, je japa joga anala tana dahahīṁ.
रीझेउँ देखि तोरि चतुराई । मागेहु भगति मोहि अति भाई ॥
rījheuṁ dekhi tori caturāī, māgehu bhagati mohi ati bhāī.
सुनु बिहंग प्रसाद अब मोरें । सब सुभ गुन बसिहहिं उर तोरें ॥
sunu bihaṁga prasāda aba moreṁ, saba subha guna basihahiṁ ura toreṁ.
भगति ग्यान बिग्यान बिरागा । जोग चरित्र रहस्य बिभागा ॥
bhagati gyāna bigyāna birāgā, joga caritra rahasya bibhāgā.
जानब तैं सबही कर भेदा । मम प्रसाद नहिं साधन खेदा ॥
jānaba taiṁ sabahī kara bhedā, mama prasāda nahiṁ sādhana khedā.

Trans:

"So be it," said the prince of the house of Raghu and then continued in these most gracious words, "Hearken, O crow, you are very sagacious, and therefore no wonder that you ask this boon. You crave Devotion, the source of every blessing; there is none in the world so highly favored as you, for the saints cannot grasp it after all their labors, though they consume their whole body in the fire of prayer and meditation. I am pleased to see your sagacity; your prayer for faith is most agreeable to me. Hearken, now, O bird, to the favors I bestow upon you: every good quality shall dwell in your bosom—faith, knowledge, divine wisdom, self-governance, the practice of mystic abstraction and all the secrets of esoteric love. You shall understand the mysteries of every science and with my favor shall need no other help.

दोहा-dohā:

माया संभव भ्रम सब अब न ब्यापिहहिं तोहि ।
māyā saṁbhava bhrama saba aba na byāpihahiṁ tohi,
जानेसु ब्रह्म अनादि अज अगुन गुनाकर मोहि ॥८५क॥
jānesu brahma anādi aja aguna gunākara mohi. 85(ka).

मोहि भगत प्रिय संतत अस बिचारि सुनु काग ।
mohi bhagata priya saṁtata asa bicāri sunu kāga,
कायँ बचन मन मम पद करेसु अचल अनुराग ॥८५ख॥
kāyaṁ bacana mana mama pada karesu acala anurāga. 85(kha).

Trans:

None of the errors that arise from Māyā shall henceforth affect you; you know me to be the Supreme Spirit, without birth or beginning, the immaterial root of all matter. Remember, O crow, that every believer is dear to me; hearken to my words and in thought, word and deed, maintain an unalterable devotion to my feet.

चौपाई-caupāī:

अब सुनु परम बिमल मम बानी । सत्य सुगम निगमादि बखानी ॥
aba sunu parama bimala mama bānī, satya sugama nigamādi bakhānī.
निज सिद्धांत सुनावउँ तोही । सुनु मन धरु सब तजि भजु मोही ॥
nija siddhāṁta sunāvauṁ tohī, sunu mana dharu saba taji bhaju mohī.
मम माया संभव संसारा । जीव चराचर बिबिधि प्रकारा ॥
mama māyā saṁbhava saṁsārā, jīva carācara bibidhi prakārā.
सब मम प्रिय सब मम उपजाए । सब ते अधिक मनुज मोहि भाए ॥
saba mama priya saba mama upajāe, saba te adhika manuja mohi bhāe.
तिन्ह महँ द्विज द्विज महँ श्रुतिधारी । तिन्ह महुँ निगम धरम अनुसारी ॥
tinha mahaṁ dvija dvija mahaṁ śrutidhārī, tinha mahuṁ nigama dharama anusārī.
तिन्ह महँ प्रिय बिरक्त पुनि ग्यानी । ग्यानिहु ते अति प्रिय बिग्यानी ॥
tinha mahaṁ priya birakta puni gyānī, gyānihu te ati priya bigyānī.
तिन्ह ते पुनि मोहि प्रिय निज दासा । जेहि गति मोरि न दूसरि आसा ॥
tinha te puni mohi priya nija dāsā, jehi gati mori na dūsari āsā.
पुनि पुनि सत्य कहउँ तोहि पाहीं । मोहि सेवक सम प्रिय कोउ नाहीं ॥
puni puni satya kahauṁ tohi pāhīṁ, mohi sevaka sama priya kou nāhīṁ.
भगति हीन बिरंचि किन होई । सब जीवहु सम प्रिय मोहि सोई ॥
bhagati hīna biraṁci kina hoī, saba jīvahu sama priya mohi soī.
भगतिवंत अति नीचउ प्रानी । मोहि प्रानप्रिय असि मम बानी ॥
bhagativaṁta ati nīcau prānī, mohi prānapriya asi mama bānī.

Trans:

Attend now to this most holy exposition of mine, which is both simple and true and is contained in the Vedas and other Scriptures. I will reveal to you my own peculiar doctrine; apply your mind to listen and worship me only, abjuring all others. The world is the product of my delusive power, with all its varieties of life, both moving and motionless. I love them all, for all are my creatures; but man is the creature that delights me most. Of men, Brahmins; of Brahmins, those who study the Vedas; of these, such as follow the precepts of the sacred texts; of these again celibates are my favorites and yet more the wise; of the wise I love best the spiritually wise, and of these the best beloved of all are my own servants, who come to me and have no other hope. Again and again I tell you of a truth there are none so dear to me as my own devotee. If Brahmmā himself had no faith in me, he would be no dearer to me than any other creature; while the meanest creature that breathes, if possessed of devotion, is as dear to me as my own soul: this is my doctrine.

दोहा-dohā:

सुचि सुसील सेवक सुमति प्रिय कहु काहि न लाग ।
suci susīla sevaka sumati priya kahu kāhi na lāga,
श्रुति पुरान कह नीति असि सावधान सुनु काग ॥८६॥
śruti purāna kaha nīti asi sāvadhāna sunu kāga. 86.

Trans:

Who would not love a pure, well-disposed and intelligent servant? Hearken, O crow, with attention to the principle laid down both in the Vedas and Purānas:

चौपाई-caupāī:

एक पिता के बिपुल कुमारा । होहिं पृथक गुन सील अचारा ॥
eka pitā ke bipula kumārā, hohiṁ pṛthaka guna sīla acārā.
कोउ पंडित कोउ तापस ग्याता । कोउ धनवंत सूर कोउ दाता ॥
kou paṁḍita kou tāpasa gyātā, kou dhanavaṁta sūra kou dātā.
कोउ सर्बग्य धर्मरत कोई । सब पर पितहि प्रीति सम होई ॥
kou sarbagya dharmarata koī, saba para pitahi prīti sama hoī.
कोउ पितु भगत बचन मन कर्मा । सपनेहुँ जान न दूसर धर्मा ॥
kou pitu bhagata bacana mana karmā, sapanehuṁ jāna na dūsara dharmā.
सो सुत प्रिय पितु प्रान समाना । जद्यपि सो सब भाँति अयाना ॥
so suta priya pitu prāna samānā, jadyapi so saba bhāṁti ayānā.
एहि बिधि जीव चराचर जेते । त्रिजग देव नर असुर समेते ॥
ehi bidhi jīva carācara jete, trijaga deva nara asura samete.
अखिल बिस्व यह मोर उपाया । सब पर मोहि बराबरि दाया ॥
akhila bisva yaha mora upāyā, saba para mohi barābari dāyā.
तिन्ह महँ जो परिहरि मद माया । भजै मोहि मन बच अरू काया ॥
tinha mahaṁ jo parihari mada māyā, bhajai mohi mana baca arū kāyā.

Trans:

A father has a number of children, each different in character, temper and occupation. Say one is learned, another given to austerities, a third spiritually enlightened, another wealthy, the fifth one possessed of valor, another charitable, one all-wise and yet another intent on piety; the father feels the same affection for them all. There is one more son who is in thought, word and deed entirely devoted to his father, never even dreaming of any other duty; and this is the son whom the father loves as his own soul, though he be a perfect ignoramus. In like manner all animate and inanimate beings, including brute beasts, gods, men and demons, in short the entire universe that I have created, is viewed by me with equal compassion; but, amongst them all, if there be one, who forswears vanity and delusion and worships me alone in thought, word and deed,

दोहा-dohā:

पुरूष नपुंसक नारि वा जीव चराचर कोइ ।
purūṣa napuṁsaka nāri vā jīva carācara koi,
सर्ब भाव भज कपट तजि मोहि परम प्रिय सोइ ॥८७क॥
sarba bhāva bhaja kapaṭa taji mohi parama priya soi. 87(ka).

Trans:

whether he be man, eunuch, or woman, whether animate or inanimate, if with all his soul he sincerely worships me—he is my best beloved.

सोरठा-soraṭhā:

सत्य कहउँ खग तोहि सुचि सेवक मम प्रानप्रिय ।
satya kahauṁ khaga tohi suci sevaka mama prānapriya,
अस बिचारि भजु मोहि परिहरि आस भरोस सब ॥८७ख॥
asa bicāri bhaju mohi parihari āsa bharosa saba. 87(kha).

Trans:

O crow, I tell you of a truth that an honest servant is as dear to me as my own life. Remember this and worship me only, abjuring every other hope and assurance.

चौपाई-caupāī:

कबहूँ काल न ब्यापिहि तोही । सुमिरेसु भजेसु निरंतर मोही ॥
kabahūṁ kāla na byāpihi tohī, sumiresu bhajesu niraṁtara mohī.
प्रभु बचनामृत सुनि न अघाऊँ । तनु पुलकित मन अति हरषाऊँ ॥
prabhu bacanāmṛta suni na aghāūṁ, tanu pulakita mana ati haraṣāūṁ.
सो सुख जानइ मन अरु काना । नहिं रसना पहिं जाइ बखाना ॥
so sukha jānai mana aru kānā, nahiṁ rasanā pahiṁ jāi bakhānā.
प्रभु सोभा सुख जानहिं नयना । कहि किमि सकहिं तिन्हहि नहिं बयना ॥
prabhu sobhā sukha jānahiṁ nayanā, kahi kimi sakahiṁ tinhahi nahiṁ bayanā.
बहु बिधि मोहि प्रबोधि सुख देई । लगे करन सिसु कौतुक तेई ॥
bahu bidhi mohi prabodhi sukha deī, lage karana sisu kautuka teī.
सजल नयन कछु मुख करि रूखा । चितइ मातु लागी अति भूखा ॥
sajala nayana kachu mukha kari rūkhā, citai mātu lāgī ati bhūkhā.
देखि मातु आतुर उठि धाई । कहि मृदु बचन लिए उर लाई ॥
dekhi mātu ātura uṭhi dhāī, kahi mṛdu bacana lie ura lāī.
गोद राखि कराव पय पाना । रघुपति चरित ललित कर गाना ॥
goda rākhi karāva paya pānā, raghupati carita lalita kara gānā.

Trans:

Time shall have no power over you, as long as you remember me and be devoted unceasingly." I should never have tired of listening to my Lord's ambrosial discourse; my body quivered all over and my soul rejoiced exceedingly. My mind and my ears experienced a delight, which it is beyond the power of tongue to tell. My eyes had the bliss of beholding my Lord's beauty; but how can they declare it? They have no voice. After he had gladdened me by his manifold teachings, he again began to sport like a child. With streaming eyes and mouth a little awry, he looked at his mother as if he were very hungry. Seeing this she started up in haste and ran and spoke to him with caressing words and clasped him to her bosom; then placing him in her lap she began to suckle him, singing the while of Rāma's charming deeds.

सोरठा-soraṭhā:

जेहि सुख लागि पुरारि असुभ बेष कृत सिव सुखद ।
jehi sukha lāgi purāri asubha beṣa kṛta siva sukhada,
अवधपुरी नर नारि तेहि सुख महुँ संतत मगन ॥८८क॥
avadhapurī nara nāri tehi sukha mahuṁ saṁtata magana. 88(ka).

सोइ सुख लवलेस जिन्ह बारक सपनेहुँ लहेउ ।
soi sukha lavalesa jinha bāraka sapanehuṁ laheu,
ते नहिं गनहिं खगेस ब्रह्मसुखहि सज्जन सुमति ॥८८ख॥
te nahiṁ ganahiṁ khagesa brahmasukhahi sajjana sumati. 88(kha).

Trans:

The citizens of Avadh were ever flooded with the same joy, to attain which the blessed Shiva had to assume his unsightly renunciant garb. Those wise and virtuous, who have once realized even in a dream the least atom of that joy, think nothing, O Garud, of the joys of heaven.

चौपाई-caupāī:

मैं पुनि अवध रहेउँ कछु काला । देखेउँ बालबिनोद रसाला ॥
maiṁ puni avadha raheuṁ kachu kālā, dekheuṁ bālabinoda rasālā.
राम प्रसाद भगति बर पायउँ । प्रभु पद बंदि निजाश्रम आयउँ ॥
rāma prasāda bhagati bara pāyauṁ, prabhu pada baṁdi nijāśrama āyauṁ.
तब ते मोहि न ब्यापी माया । जब ते रघुनायक अपनाया ॥
taba te mohi na byāpī māyā, jaba te raghunāyaka apanāyā.
यह सब गुप्त चरित मैं गावा । हरि मायाँ जिमि मोहि नचावा ॥
yaha saba gupta carita maiṁ gāvā, hari māyāṁ jimi mohi nacāvā.
निज अनुभव अब कहउँ खगेसा । बिनु हरि भजन न जाहिं कलेसा ॥
nija anubhava aba kahauṁ khagesā, binu hari bhajana na jāhiṁ kalesā.
राम कृपा बिनु सुनु खगराई । जानि न जाइ राम प्रभुताई ॥
rāma kṛpā binu sunu khagarāī, jāni na jāi rāma prabhutāī.
जानें बिनु न होइ परतीती । बिनु परतीति होइ नहिं प्रीती ॥
jāneṁ binu na hoi paratītī, binu paratīti hoi nahiṁ prītī.
प्रीति बिना नहिं भगति दिढ़ाई । जिमि खगपति जल कै चिकनाई ॥
prīti binā nahiṁ bhagati diṛhāī, jimi khagapati jala kai cikanāī.

Trans:

After this I stayed some little time at Avadh, a spectator of his delightful boyish plays. Then, by Rāma's blessing, having obtained the boon of devotion, I bowed at my Lord's feet and returned to my hermitage. Since then no delusion has ever affected me, after Rāma accepted me. I have now told you the whole of this strange story of how I was bewitched by Harī's delusive power. From my own experience I warn you, O Garud, that without prayer to Harī your troubles will not yield. Hearken, O king-of-birds: without Rāma's grace, there is no understanding of the Lord's grace; without understanding there is no faith; without faith there is no love; without love there is no consistency in devotion; it slips away, O Garud, like oil on water.

सोरठा-soraṭhā:

बिनु गुर होइ कि ग्यान ग्यान कि होइ बिराग बिनु ।
binu gura hoi ki gyāna gyāna ki hoi birāga binu,
गावहिं बेद पुरान सुख कि लहिअ हरि भगति बिनु ॥८९क॥
gāvahiṁ beda purāna sukha ki lahia hari bhagati binu. 89(ka).

कोउ बिश्राम कि पाव तात सहज संतोष बिनु ।
kou biśrāma ki pāva tāta sahaja saṁtoṣa binu,
चलै कि जल बिनु नाव कोटि जतन पचि पचि मरिअ ॥८९ख॥
calai ki jala binu nāva koṭi jatana paci paci maria. 89(kha).

Trans:

How can there be knowledge without a teacher? How can there be wisdom without dispassion? Or, as the Vedas and Purānas declare, how can man attain to happiness without devotion to Harī? Without innate contentment, sire, none can find peace. A boat will not float without water, though you strain every nerve, enough to kill yourself.

चौपाई-caupāī:

बिनु संतोष न काम नसाहीं । काम अछत सुख सपनेहुँ नाहीं ॥
binu saṁtoṣa na kāma nasāhīṁ, kāma achata sukha sapanehum̐ nāhīṁ.
राम भजन बिनु मिटहिं कि कामा । थल बिहीन तरु कबहुँ कि जामा ॥
rāma bhajana binu miṭahiṁ ki kāmā, thala bihīna taru kabahum̐ ki jāmā.
बिनु बिग्यान कि समता आवइ । कोउ अवकास कि नभ बिनु पावइ ॥
binu bigyāna ki samatā āvai, kou avakāsa ki nabha binu pāvai.
श्रद्धा बिना धर्म नहिं होई । बिनु महि गंध कि पावइ कोई ॥
śraddhā binā dharma nahiṁ hoī, binu mahi gaṁdha ki pāvai koī.
बिनु तप तेज कि कर बिस्तारा । जल बिनु रस कि होइ संसारा ॥
binu tapa teja ki kara bistārā, jala binu rasa ki hoi saṁsārā.
सील कि मिल बिनु बुध सेवकाई । जिमि बिनु तेज न रूप गोसाँई ॥
sīla ki mila binu budha sevakāī, jimi binu teja na rūpa gosām̐ī.
निज सुख बिनु मन होइ कि थीरा । परस कि होइ बिहीन समीरा ॥
nija sukha binu mana hoi ki thīrā, parasa ki hoi bihīna samīrā.
कवनिउ सिद्धि कि बिनु बिस्वासा । बिनु हरि भजन न भव भय नासा ॥
kavaniu siddhi ki binu bisvāsā, binu hari bhajana na bhava bhaya nāsā.

Trans:

Without contentment there is no cessation of desire; so long as desire continues, it is vain to dream of ease and peace. Can desire be subdued without prayer to Rāma? Can a tree ever take root without substratum? Can equanimity be attained without enlightenment? Can you have space without the ether? Without devotion there is no religion, just as there can be no smell without the earth element? Can fame spread without penance, any more than there can be taste in the world without the liquid element? Can virtue be acquired without attendance to the wise, any more than vision can exist, sir, without the element of fire? Can the mind be at rest when ill at ease, any more than the sense of touch is possible without the element of wind? Without faith there is no exercise of supernatural powers, and without prayer to Harī, there is no conquest over the terrors of existence.

दोहा-dohā:

बिनु बिस्वास भगति नहिं तेहि बिनु द्रवहिं न रामु ।
binu bisvāsa bhagati nahiṁ tehi binu dravahiṁ na rāmu,
राम कृपा बिनु सपनेहुँ जीव न लह बिश्रामु ॥९०क॥
rāma kṛpā binu sapanehum̐ jīva na laha biśrāmu. 90(ka).

Trans:

Without faith there is no devotion; without devotion Rāma is not moved; and without the grace of Rāma, no creature can get peace even in dream.

सोरठा-soraṭhā:

अस बिचारि मतिधीर तजि कुतर्क संसय सकल ।
asa bicāri matidhīra taji kutarka saṁsaya sakala,
भजहु राम रघुबीर करुनाकर सुंदर सुखद ॥९०ख॥
bhajahu rāma raghubīra karunākara suṁdara sukhada. 90(kha).

Trans:

Considering that, you of resolute mind—and abjuring skepticism and every doubt—worship Rāma, the heroic son of Raghu, the fountain of mercy, the beautiful, the beneficent.

चौपाई-caupāī:

निज मति सरिस नाथ मैं गाई । प्रभु प्रताप महिमा खगराई ॥
nija mati sarisa nātha maiṁ gāī, prabhu pratāpa mahimā khagarāī.
कहेउँ न कछु करि जुगुति बिसेषी । यह सब मैं निज नयनन्हि देखी ॥
kaheum̐ na kachu kari juguti biseṣī, yaha saba maiṁ nija nayananhi dekhī.
महिमा नाम रूप गुन गाथा । सकल अमित अनंत रघुनाथा ॥
mahimā nāma rūpa guna gāthā, sakala amita anaṁta raghunāthā.
निज निज मति मुनि हरि गुन गावहिं । निगम सेष सिव पार न पावहिं ॥
nija nija mati muni hari guna gāvahiṁ, nigama seṣa siva pāra na pāvahiṁ.
तुम्हहि आदि खग मसक प्रजंता । नभ उड़ाहिं नहिं पावहिं अंता ॥
tumhahi ādi khaga masaka prajaṁtā, nabha uṛāhiṁ nahiṁ pāvahiṁ aṁtā.
तिमि रघुपति महिमा अवगाहा । तात कबहुँ कोउ पाव कि थाहा ॥
timi raghupati mahimā avagāhā, tāta kabahum̐ kou pāva ki thāhā.
रामु काम सत कोटि सुभग तन । दुर्गा कोटि अमित अरि मर्दन ॥
rāmu kāma sata koṭi subhaga tana, durgā koṭi amita ari mardana.
सक्र कोटि सत सरिस बिलासा । नभ सत कोटि अमित अवकासा ॥
sakra koṭi sata sarisa bilāsā, nabha sata koṭi amita avakāsā.

Trans:

Thus have I declared to you, king Garud, according to my ability, the greatness of the Lord's power; nor have I anywhere taken recourse to any studied invention—for I have seen it all with my own eyes. Rāma's greatness, his names, his glory, beauty and perfection, are all boundless and infinite. The saints sing his praises, according to their several ability, but not even the Vedas, Sheshnāg or Shiva could declare them fully. There is no winged creature, from yourself down to a gnat, who can reach to the end of the heaven in his flight. In like manner sire, the greatness of Raghupatī is unfathomable; none can sound the bottom of it. Rāma is beautiful of body—as a myriad Loves; irresistible in the destruction of his foes—as a myriad Durgās; jocund as a myriad Indras; immeasurable in expanse as a myriad firmaments;

दोहा-dohā:

मरुत कोटि सत बिपुल बल रबि सत कोटि प्रकास ।
maruta koṭi sata bipula bala rabi sata koṭi prakāsa,
ससि सत कोटि सुसीतल समन सकल भव त्रास ॥९१क॥
sasi sata koṭi susītala samana sakala bhava trāsa. 91(ka).

काल कोटि सत सरिस अति दुस्तर दुर्ग दुरंत ।
kāla koṭi sata sarisa ati dustara durga duraṁta,
धूमकेतु सत कोटि सम दुराधरष भगवंत ॥९१ख॥
dhūmaketu sata koṭi sama durādharaṣa bhagavaṁta. 91(kha).

Trans:

as masterful in might as a myriad winds; as bright as a myriad suns; as cooling as a myriad moons, soothing all the terrors of existence; as impracticable, inaccessible and interminable as a myriad Deaths, as irrepressible as a myriad fires—such is our very own Lord-God Rāma.

चौपाई-caupāī:

प्रभु अगाध सत कोटि पताला । समन कोटि सत सरिस कराला ॥
prabhu agādha sata koṭi patālā, samana koṭi sata sarisa karālā.
तीरथ अमित कोटि सम पावन । नाम अखिल अघ पूग नसावन ॥
tīratha amita koṭi sama pāvana, nāma akhila agha pūga nasāvana.
हिमगिरि कोटि अचल रघुबीरा । सिंधु कोटि सत सम गंभीरा ॥
himagiri koṭi acala raghubīrā, siṁdhu koṭi sata sama gaṁbhīrā.
कामधेनु सत कोटि समाना । सकल काम दायक भगवाना ॥
kāmadhenu sata koṭi samānā, sakala kāma dāyaka bhagavānā.
सारद कोटि अमित चतुराई । बिधि सत कोटि सृष्टि निपुनाई ॥
sārada koṭi amita caturāī, bidhi sata koṭi sṛṣṭi nipunāī.
बिष्नु कोटि सम पालन कर्ता । रुद्र कोटि सत सम संहर्ता ॥
biṣnu koṭi sama pālana kartā, rudra koṭi sata sama saṁhartā.
धनद कोटि सत सम धनवाना । माया कोटि प्रपंच निधाना ॥
dhanada koṭi sata sama dhanavānā, māyā koṭi prapaṁca nidhānā.
भार धरन सत कोटि अहीसा । निरवधि निरुपम प्रभु जगदीसा ॥
bhāra dharana sata koṭi ahīsā, niravadhi nirupama prabhu jagadīsā.

Trans:

Our Lord is as unfathomable as myriad *Patālās* (Hells); as dreadful as a myriad *Yama*s (Death); as immeasurably holy as myriad places of pilgrimage, whose name obliterates every accumulation of sin. Raghubar is as immoveable as a myriad Himalayas; as profound as a myriad sea; as liberal in the fulfillment of every desire as myriad cows of plenty; and He is our very Lord-God. As illimitable in eloquence as a myriad Shārdās; as skillful in creation as myriad Brahmas; as potent to save as a myriad Vishnus; as potent to destroy as a myriad Shivas; as abounding in wealth as a myriad Kubers; as fertile in phenomena as myriad Mayas; a supporter of the world like a myriad Sheshnāgs—He is the illimitable, incomparable Lord-God, the sovereign of the universe.

छंद-chaṁda:

निरुपम न उपमा आन राम समान रामु निगम कहै ।
nirupama na upamā āna rāma samāna rāmu nigama kahai,
जिमि कोटि सत खद्योत सम रबि कहत अति लघुता लहै ॥
jimi koṭi sata khadyota sama rabi kahata ati laghutā lahai.

एहि भाँति निज निज मति बिलास मुनीस हरिहि बखानहीं ।
ehi bhāṁti nija nija mati bilāsa munīsa harihi bakhānahīṁ,
प्रभु भाव गाहक अति कृपाल सप्रेम सुनि सुख मानहीं ॥
prabhu bhāva gāhaka ati kṛpāla saprema suni sukha mānahīṁ.

Trans:

Incomparable indeed; for, as the Vedas declare, Rāma alone is Rāma's peer, none else can compare with him. If one should compare the Sun to a thousand millions of fire-flies, it would be utterly inadequate. In like manner, the great sages have exercised their ingenuity in describing Harī, and the Lord, appreciating their intention has, of his great clemency, listened kindly and approved.

दोहा-dohā:

रामु अमित गुन सागर थाह कि पावइ कोइ ।
rāmu amita guna sāgara thāha ki pāvai koi,
संतन्ह सन जस किछु सुनेउँ तुम्हहि सुनायउँ सोइ ॥९२क॥
saṁtanha sana jasa kichu suneuṁ tumhahi sunāyauṁ soi. 92(ka).

Trans:

Rāma is an unfathomable ocean of perfection, who can sound it to the bottom? I have told you a little that I have known and heard from the saints.

सोरठा-sorathā:

भाव बस्य भगवान सुख निधान करुना भवन ।
bhāva basya bhagavāna sukha nidhāna karunā bhavana,
तजि ममता मद मान भजिअ सदा सीता रवन ॥९२ख॥
taji mamatā mada māna bhajia sadā sītā ravana. 92(kha).

Trans:

Abjure all selfishness, vanity and pride, and ever worship Sītā's spouse, the great Lord-God, who is moved by sincere devotion, the all-blessed, the all-merciful Rāma."

चौपाई-caupāī:

सुनि भुसुंडि के बचन सुहाए । हरषित खगपति पंख फुलाए ॥
suni bhusuṁḍi ke bacana suhāe, haraṣita khagapati paṁkha phulāe.
नयन नीर मन अति हरषाना । श्रीरघुपति प्रताप उर आना ॥
nayana nīra mana ati haraṣānā, śrīraghupati pratāpa ura ānā.
पाछिल मोह समुझि पछिताना । ब्रह्म अनादि मनुज करि माना ॥
pāchila moha samujhi pachitānā, brahma anādi manuja kari mānā.
पुनि पुनि काग चरन सिरु नावा । जानि राम सम प्रेम बढ़ावा ॥
puni puni kāga carana siru nāvā, jāni rāma sama prema baṛhāvā.
गुर बिनु भव निधि तरइ न कोई । जौं बिरंचि संकर सम होई ॥
gura binu bhava nidhi tarai na koī, jauṁ biraṁci saṁkara sama hoī.
संसय सर्प ग्रसेउ मोहि ताता । दुखद लहरि कुतर्क बहु ब्राता ॥
saṁsaya sarpa graseu mohi tātā, dukhada lahari kutarka bahu brātā.
तव सरूप गारुड़ि रघुनायक । मोहि जिआयउ जन सुखदायक ॥
tava sarūpa gāruṛi raghunāyaka, mohi jiāyau jana sukhadāyaka.
तव प्रसाद मम मोह नसाना । राम रहस्य अनूपम जाना ॥
tava prasāda mama moha nasānā, rāma rahasya anūpama jānā.

Trans:

On hearing Bhusumdi's delectable discourse, the king-of-birds rejoiced and preened his wings. His eyes streamed and his soul was overcome with delight as he meditated on the might of the divine Rāma. He was ashamed to think of his former delusion—when he had taken the everlasting and Supreme Spirit for a mere man. Again and again he bowed his head at the crow's feet, whom, in the greatness of his affection, he regarded as like Rāma. "Without a spiritual guide none can traverse the ocean of existence, though he be the equal of Brahmmā or Shiva. Doubt like a serpent had crushed me in the painful coils of wordy skepticism; but Rāma appeared in your form as an antidote and restored me to life, beneficent as he is to all his votaries. By your favor I have overcome my delusion and have learnt the incomparable mystery of Rāma."

दोहा-dohā:

ताहि प्रसंसि बिबिधि बिधि सीस नाइ कर जोरि ।
tāhi prasaṁsi bibidhi bidhi sīsa nāi kara jori,
बचन बिनीत सप्रेम मृदु बोलेउ गरुड़ बहोरि ॥९३क॥
bacana binīta saprema mṛdu boleu garuṛa bahori. 93(ka).

प्रभु अपने अबिबेक ते बूझउँ स्वामी तोहि ।
prabhu apane abibeka te būjhaum̐ svāmī tohi,
कृपासिंधु सादर कहहु जानि दास निज मोहि ॥९३ख॥
kṛpāsiṁdhu sādara kahahu jāni dāsa nija mohi. 93(kha).

Trans:

After eulogizing him in every possible way and bowing the head before him with clasped hands, Garud said in these humble, affectionate, and winning terms, "In my ignorance, O my Lord and master, I would ask you a question. In your infinite compassion be pleased to instruct me, regarding me as your own peculiar servant.

चौपाई-caupāī:

तुम्ह सर्बग्य तन्य तम पारा । सुमति सुसील सरल आचारा ॥
tumha sarbagya tanya tama pārā, sumati susīla sarala ācārā.
ग्यान बिरति बिग्यान निवासा । रघुनायक के तुम्ह प्रिय दासा ॥
gyāna birati bigyāna nivāsā, raghunāyaka ke tumha priya dāsā.
कारन कवन देह यह पाई । तात सकल मोहि कहहु बुझाई ॥
kārana kavana deha yaha pāī, tāta sakala mohi kahahu bujhāī.
राम चरित सर सुंदर स्वामी । पायहु कहाँ कहहु नभगामी ॥
rāma carita sara suṁdara svāmī, pāyahu kahām̐ kahahu nabhagāmī.
नाथ सुना मैं अस सिव पाहीं । महा प्रलयहुँ नास तव नाहीं ॥
nātha sunā maiṁ asa siva pāhīṁ, mahā pralayahum̐ nāsa tava nāhīṁ.
मुधा बचन नहिं ईस्वर कहई । सोउ मोरें मन संसय अहई ॥
mudhā bacana nahiṁ īsvara kahaī, sou moreṁ mana saṁsaya ahaī.
अग जग जीव नाग नर देवा । नाथ सकल जगु काल कलेवा ॥
aga jaga jīva nāga nara devā, nātha sakala jagu kāla kalevā.
अंड कटाह अमित लय कारी । कालु सदा दुरतिक्रम भारी ॥
aṁḍa kaṭāha amita laya kārī, kālu sadā duratikrama bhārī.

Trans:

You are all wise; perfect in philosophy, intelligent, amiable and upright in your dealings; a store-house of knowledge, sobriety and spiritual intuition; and one of Rāma's favorite servants: what then is the reason, sire, for you having received such a crow form? Explain this to me in full. Tell me also, venerable bird, where you first learnt this excellent history of Rāma's renown. Further, my Lord, I have heard from Shiva that you do not perish at the time of the destruction of all things. The god would never utter an idle word, and therefore my mind is in doubt. For the whole universe, my Lord, with all creatures moving and motionless, serpents, men and gods, is but a mouthful for Death. Death has swallowed up worlds without end and is ever irresistible and strong.

सोरठा-soraṭhā:

तुम्हहि न ब्यापत काल अति कराल कारन कवन ।
tumhahi na byāpata kāla ati karāla kārana kavana,
मोहि सो कहहु कृपाल ग्यान प्रभाव कि जोग बल ॥९४क॥
mohi so kahahu kṛpāla gyāna prabhāva ki joga bala. 94(ka).

Trans:

What is the reason that so terrible a monster as Death has no effect upon you? Be pleased to inform me whether it be the power of your intellect or the virtue of your mystical devotion.

दोहा-dohā:

प्रभु तव आश्रम आएँ मोर मोह भ्रम भाग ।
prabhu tava āśrama āeṁ mora moha bhrama bhāga,
कारन कवन सो नाथ सब कहहु सहित अनुराग ॥९४ख॥
kārana kavana so nātha saba kahahu sahita anurāga. 94(kha).

Trans:

Further, my Lord, be so kind as to explain to me how it was that my delusion vanished directly I approached your hermitage."

चौपाई-caupāī:

गरुड़ गिरा सुनि हरषेउ कागा । बोलेउ उमा परम अनुरागा ॥
garuṛa girā suni haraṣeu kāgā, boleu umā parama anurāgā.
धन्य धन्य तव मति उरगारी । प्रस्न तुम्हारि मोहि अति प्यारी ॥
dhanya dhanya tava mati uragārī, prasna tumhāri mohi ati pyārī.
सुनि तव प्रस्न सप्रेम सुहाई । बहुत जनम कै सुधि मोहि आई ॥
suni tava prasna saprema suhāī, bahuta janama kai sudhi mohi āī.
सब निज कथा कहउँ मैं गाई । तात सुनहु सादर मन लाई ॥
saba nija kathā kahaum̐ maiṁ gāī, tāta sunahu sādara mana lāī.
जप तप मख सम दम ब्रत दाना । बिरति बिबेक जोग बिग्याना ॥
japa tapa makha sama dama brata dānā, birati bibeka joga bigyānā.
सब कर फल रघुपति पद प्रेमा । तेहि बिनु कोउ न पावइ छेमा ॥
saba kara phala raghupati pada premā, tehi binu kou na pāvai chemā.
एहिं तन राम भगति मैं पाई । ताते मोहि ममता अधिकाई ॥
ehiṁ tana rāma bhagati maiṁ pāī, tāte mohi mamatā adhikāī.
जेहि तें कछु निज स्वारथ होई । तेहि पर ममता कर सब कोई ॥
jehi teṁ kachu nija svāratha hoī, tehi para mamatā kara saba koī.

Trans:

When he heard Garud's questions, the crow was pleased and answered him, O Umā, with the greatest possible kindness, "A blessing on your wit, O Garud; your questions are most agreeable. As I listen to your affectionate and becoming enquiries, the recollection of many previous births comes back to me. I will tell you the whole of my history; listen, sire, with full and reverent attention. Prayer, penance, sacrifice, sobriety of mind, self-control, acts of devotion, charity, chastity, knowledge, mystical meditation and spiritual wisdom, all have their fruit in the love for Rāma's feet, without which none can attain to happiness. It was in this body that I learnt devotion to Rāma, and therefore I have a special liking for it. Everyone likes that by means of which he has gained his object.

सोरठा-soraṭhā:

पन्नगारि असि नीति श्रुति संमत सज्जन कहहिं ।
pannagāri asi nīti śruti saṁmata sajjana kahahiṁ,
अति नीचहु सन प्रीति करिअ जानि निज परम हित ॥९५क॥
ati nīcahu sana prīti karia jāni nija parama hita. 95(ka).

पाट कीट तें होइ तेहि तें पाटंबर रुचिर ।
pāṭa kīṭa teṁ hoi tehi teṁ pāṭaṁbara rucira,
कृमि पालइ सबु कोइ परम अपावन प्रान सम ॥९५ख॥
kṛmi pālai sabu koi parama apāvana prāna sama. 95(kha).

Trans:

O Garud, this is a maxim approved by the Vedas declared by the pious that love should be shown to the meanest creature, if you know it to be your friend. Silk is the product of a worm and from it is made beautiful apparel; therefore, vile as the worm is, everyone tends it with the most sedulous care.

चौपाई-caupāī:

स्वारथ साँच जीव कहुँ एहा । मन क्रम बचन राम पद नेहा ॥
svāratha sām̐ca jīva kahum̐ ehā, mana krama bacana rāma pada nehā.
सोइ पावन सोइ सुभग सरीरा । जो तनु पाइ भजिअ रघुबीरा ॥
soi pāvana soi subhaga sarīrā, jo tanu pāi bhajia raghubīrā.
राम बिमुख लहि बिधि सम देही । कबि कोबिद न प्रसंसहिं तेही ॥
rāma bimukha lahi bidhi sama dehī, kabi kobida na prasaṁsahiṁ tehī.
राम भगति एहिं तन उर जामी । ताते मोहि परम प्रिय स्वामी ॥
rāma bhagati ehiṁ tana ura jāmī, tāte mohi parama priya svāmī.

तजउँ न तन निज इच्छा मरना । तन बिनु बेद भजन नहिं बरना ॥
tajauṁ na tana nija icchā maranā, tana binu beda bhajana nahiṁ baranā.

प्रथम मोहँ मोहि बहुत बिगोवा । राम बिमुख सुख कबहुँ न सोवा ॥
prathama mohaṁ mohi bahuta bigovā, rāma bimukha sukha kabahuṁ na sovā.

नाना जनम कर्म पुनि नाना । किए जोग जप तप मख दाना ॥
nānā janama karma puni nānā, kie joga japa tapa makha dānā.

कवन जोनि जनमेउँ जहँ नाही । मैं खगेस भ्रमि भ्रमि जग माहीं ॥
kavana joni janameuṁ jahaṁ nāhīṁ, maiṁ khagesa bhrami bhrami jaga māhīṁ.

देखेउँ करि सब करम गोसाईं । सुखी न भयउँ अबहिं की नाईं ॥
dekheuṁ kari saba karama gosāīṁ, sukhī na bhayauṁ abahiṁ kī nāīṁ.

सुधि मोहि नाथ जन्म बहु केरी । सिव प्रसाद मति मोहँ न घेरी ॥
sudhi mohi nātha janma bahu kerī, siva prasāda mati mohaṁ na gherī.
Trans:

The highest object of every living creature is the love of Rāma. That body alone is sacred and that alone blessed, in which one is able to worship the Hero of Raghu's line. The wise and the learned never extol him who is hostile to Shrī Rāma—even though he may acquire a body as exalted as that of the Creator himself. It was in my present bodily form that my devotion to Rāma first took root, and on that account, sire, I have a great affection for it. Though I can die when I like, I do not give up my body, for without a body, as the Vedas declare, I could not perform worship. At first delusion led me much astray; so long as I remained against Rāma I never had a restful sleep. In different births I practiced different courses of action, essaying mystical contemplation, prayer, fasting, sacrifice and almsgiving. During my peregrinations of the universe, is there any womb in which I have not at some time taken birth? In all my experience, sire, I was never as happy as I am at present. I recollect many previous existences, in which, by the blessing of Shiva, no delusion oppressed my understanding.

dohā-dohā:

प्रथम जन्म के चरित अब कहउँ सुनहु बिहगेस ।
prathama janma ke carita aba kahauṁ sunahu bihagesa,

सुनि प्रभु पद रति उपजइ जातें मिटहिं कलेस ॥९६क॥
suni prabhu pada rati upajai jāteṁ miṭahiṁ kalesa. 96(ka).

पूरुब कल्प एक प्रभु जुग कलिजुग मल मूल ।
pūruba kalpa eka prabhu juga kalijuga mala mūla,

नर अरु नारि अधर्मरत सकल निगम प्रतिकूल ॥९६ख॥
nara aru nāri adharmarata sakala nigama pratikūla. 96(kha).
Trans:

Hearken, king-of-birds: I will now tell you the story of a former birth. To hear it will increase your devotion to the Lord, which is the remedy for every ill. In a former Kalpa, there was a Kali-Yug of the utmost impurity; man and woman were devoted to impiety and all rebelled against the Vedas.

caupāī-caupāī:

तेहिं कलिजुग कोसलपुर जाई । जन्मत भयउँ सूद्र तनु पाई ॥
tehiṁ kalijuga kosalapura jāī, janmata bhayauṁ sūdra tanu pāī.

सिव सेवक मन क्रम अरु बानी । आन देव निंदक अभिमानी ॥
siva sevaka mana krama aru bānī, āna deva niṁdaka abhimānī.

धन मद मत्त परम बाचाला । उग्रबुद्धि उर दंभ बिसाला ॥
dhana mada matta parama bācālā, ugrabuddhi ura daṁbha bisālā.

जदपि रहेउँ रघुपति रजधानी । तदपि न कछु महिमा तब जानी ॥
jadapi raheuṁ raghupati rajadhānī, tadapi na kachu mahimā taba jānī.

अब जाना मैं अवध प्रभावा । निगमागम पुरान अस गावा ॥
aba jānā maiṁ avadha prabhāvā, nigamāgama purāna asa gāvā.

कवनेहुँ जन्म अवध बस जोई । राम परायन सो परि होई ॥
kavanehuṁ janma avadha basa joī, rāma parāyana so pari hoī.

अवध प्रभाव जान तब प्रानी । जब उर बसहिं रामु धनुपानी ॥
avadha prabhāva jāna taba prānī, jaba ura basahiṁ rāmu dhanupānī.

सो कलिकाल कठिन उरगारी । पाप परायन सब नर नारी ॥
so kalikāla kaṭhina uragārī, pāpa parāyana saba nara nārī.
Trans:

In that Kali-Yug, I went to the city of Kaushal and was there born as a working class man, a devoted worshipper of Shiva, but a scornful reviler of all the other gods, intoxicated with the pride of wealth, outrageously boastful, savage of purpose and with a heart full of arrogance. Although I lived in Rāma's capital, I had at the time no knowledge of his greatness. Now I understand the virtue of Avadh, as it has been sung by the Vedas, Purānas and all the Scriptures, that everyone who in any birth has lived at Avadh will eventually become a disciple of Rāma's. A man then knows the virtue of Avadh, when Rāma with bow in hand takes up his abode in his heart. It was an age, Garud, of terrible wickedness; every heart, man or woman, was inclined towards sin.

dohā-dohā:

कलिमल ग्रसे धर्म सब लुप्त भए सदग्रंथ ।
kalimala grase dharma saba lupta bhae sadagraṁtha,

दंभिन्ह निज मति कल्पि करि प्रगट किए बहु पंथ ॥९७क॥
daṁbhinha nija mati kalpi kari pragaṭa kie bahu paṁtha. 97(ka).

भए लोग सब मोहबस लोभ ग्रसे सुभ कर्म ।
bhae loga saba mohabasa lobha grase subha karma,

सुनु हरिजान ग्यान निधि कहउँ कछुक कलिधर्म ॥९७ख॥
sunu harijāna gyāna nidhi kahauṁ kachuka kalidharma. 97(kha).
Trans:

The sinfulness of the age had stifled religion; the sacred book were all neglected and false teachers had published endless heresies, which they had invented out of their own imagination. The people were all overmastered by delusion and greed had stifled all acts of piety. Hearken, most wise Garud, while I describe some of the religious practices of those evil times.

caupāī-caupāī:

बरन धर्म नहिं आश्रम चारी । श्रुति बिरोध रत सब नर नारी ॥
barana dharma nahiṁ āśrama cārī, śruti birodha rata saba nara nārī.

द्विज श्रुति बेचक भूप प्रजासन । कोउ नहिं मान निगम अनुसासन ॥
dvija śruti becaka bhūpa prajāsana, kou nahiṁ māna nigama anusāsana.

मारग सोइ जा कहुँ जोइ भावा । पंडित सोइ जो गाल बजावा ॥
māraga soi jā kahuṁ joi bhāvā, paṁḍita soi jo gāla bajāvā.

मिथ्यारंभ दंभ रत जोई । ता कहुँ संत कहइ सब कोई ॥
mithyāraṁbha daṁbha rata joī, tā kahuṁ saṁta kahai saba koī.

सोइ सयान जो परधन हारी । जो कर दंभ सो बड़ आचारी ॥
soi sayāna jo paradhana hārī, jo kara daṁbha so baṛa ācārī.

जो कह झूँठ मसखरी जाना । कलिजुग सोइ गुनवंत बखाना ॥
jo kaha jhūṁṭha masakharī jānā, kalijuga soi gunavaṁta bakhānā.

निराचार जो श्रुति पथ त्यागी । कलिजुग सोइ ग्यानी सो बिरागी ॥
nirācāra jo śruti patha tyāgī, kalijuga soi gyānī so birāgī.

जाकें नख अरु जटा बिसाला । सोइ तापस प्रसिद्ध कलिकाला ॥
jākeṁ nakha aru jaṭā bisālā, soi tāpasa prasiddha kalikālā.
Trans:

No regard was paid to one's caste or the four stages of life; everyone was bent upon attacking the Scriptures. Brahmins sold the Vedas; kings devoured their subjects; no one regarded the injunctions of Vedas. The right road was any that the most took to fancy; the greatest pundit was the one who talked the loudest. Any who indulged in false pretenses and hypocrisy was universally styled a saint. A wise man was he who plundered his neighbor; every boaster was thought of as a fine fellow, every liar considered a wit and spoken of as celebrity in those evil days. A reprobate, who denied the doctrines of revelation, was counted as enlightened philosopher; and anyone with unkempt hair and nails was celebrated in that debased age as a model of mortification.

दोहा-dohā:

असुभ बेष भूषन धरें भच्छाभच्छ जे खाहिं।
asubha beṣa bhūṣana dhareṁ bhacchābhaccha je khāhiṁ,
तेइ जोगी तेइ सिद्ध नर पूज्य ते कलिजुग माहिं ॥९८क॥
tei jogī tei siddha nara pūjya te kalijuga māhiṁ. 98(ka).

Trans:

To assume the loathsome rags and properties of a mendicant and feed indiscriminately on any kind of food was to be an ascetic, a saint, a subject of veneration in that age of iniquity.

सोरठा-soraṭhā:

जे अपकारी चार तिन्ह कर गौरव मान्य तेइ।
je apakārī cāra tinha kara gaurava mānya tei,
मन क्रम बचन लबार तेइ बकता कलिकाल महुँ ॥९८ख॥
mana krama bacana labāra tei bakatā kalikāla mahuṁ. 98(kha).

Trans:

All kinds of evil-doers were held in honor and respect and the idlest babblers were accepted as preachers in those miserable days.

चौपाई-caupāī:

नारि बिबस नर सकल गोसाईं। नाचहिं नट मर्कट की नाईं॥
nāri bibasa nara sakala gosāīṁ, nācahiṁ naṭa markaṭa kī nāīṁ.
सूद्र द्विजन्ह उपदेसहिं ग्याना। मेलि जनेऊ लेहिं कुदाना॥
sūdra dvijanha upadesahiṁ gyānā, meli janeū lehiṁ kudānā.
सब नर काम लोभ रत क्रोधी। देव बिप्र श्रुति संत बिरोधी॥
saba nara kāma lobha rata krodhī, deva bipra śruti saṁta birodhī.
गुन मंदिर सुंदर पति त्यागी। भजहिं नारि पर पुरुष अभागी॥
guna maṁdira suṁdara pati tyāgī, bhajahiṁ nāri para puruṣa abhāgī.
सौभागिनीं बिभूषन हीना। बिधवन्ह के सिंगार नबीना॥
saubhāginīṁ bibhūṣana hīnā, bidhavanha ke siṁgāra nabīnā.
गुर सिष बधिर अंध का लेखा। एक न सुनइ एक नहिं देखा॥
gura siṣa badhira aṁdha kā lekhā, eka na sunai eka nahiṁ dekhā.
हरइ सिष्य धन सोक न हरई। सो गुर घोर नरक महुँ परई॥
harai siṣya dhana soka na haraī, so gura ghora naraka mahuṁ paraī.
मातु पिता बालकन्हि बोलावहिं। उदर भरै सोइ धर्म सिखावहिं॥
mātu pitā bālakanhi bolāvahiṁ, udara bharai soi dharma sikhāvahiṁ.

Trans:

The man was everywhere subject to the woman and played the buffoon like a dancing monkey. Sudras instructed the twice-born in theology and assuming the Brahminical cord took their infamous gains. Everyone was addicted to sensuality, avarice and violence; and they flouted the gods, the Brahmins, the Scriptures, and the saints. Deserting their own husbands, however handsome and accomplished, women instead adored other strangers—such ill-fated women. Married women appeared without ornaments, widows were bedecked with jewels. Teacher and pupil were of no more account than the deaf and blind: the one would not listen, the other had never read. A spiritual guide who takes his disciple's money but does not take away his misery falls into awful abysmal hells. Father and mother call up their children and teach them such religion alone which fills their belly.

दोहा-dohā:

ब्रह्म ग्यान बिनु नारि नर कहहिं न दूसरि बात।
brahma gyāna binu nāri nara kahahiṁ na dūsari bāta,
कौड़ी लागि लोभ बस करहिं बिप्र गुर घात ॥९९क॥
kauṛī lāgi lobha basa karahiṁ bipra gura ghāta. 99(ka).

बादहिं सूद्र द्विजन्ह सन हम तुम्ह ते कछु घाटि।
bādahiṁ sūdra dvijanha sana hama tumha te kachu ghāṭi,
जानइ ब्रह्म सो बिप्रबर आँखि देखावहिं डाटि ॥९९ख॥
jānai brahma so biprabara āṁkhi dekhāvahiṁ ḍāṭi. 99(kha).

Trans:

People who are devoid of spiritual knowledge talk nothing but of Brahmm—supreme enlightenment, even though in their greed they would kill a Brahmin or their own Gurū for the sake of a single pence. Sudras dispute with the twice-born, "Are you any better than we are? Anyone who understands theology is as good as the best of Brahmins"—thus they scoff insolently.

चौपाई-caupāī:

पर त्रिय लंपट कपट सयाने। मोह द्रोह ममता लपटाने॥
para triya laṁpaṭa kapaṭa sayāne, moha droha mamatā lapaṭāne.
तेइ अभेदबादी ग्यानी नर। देखा मैं चरित्र कलिजुग कर॥
tei abhedabādī gyānī nara, dekhā maiṁ caritra kalijuga kara.
आपु गए अरु तिन्हहू घालहिं। जे कहुँ सत मारग प्रतिपालहिं॥
āpu gae aru tinhahū ghālahiṁ, je kahuṁ sata māraga pratipālahiṁ.
कल्प कल्प भरि एक एक नरका। परहिं जे दूषहिं श्रुति करि तरका॥
kalpa kalpa bhari eka eka narakā, parahiṁ je dūṣahiṁ śruti kari tarakā.
जे बरनाधम तेलि कुम्हारा। स्वपच किरात कोल कलवारा॥
je baranādhama teli kumhārā, svapaca kirāta kola kalavārā.
नारि मुई गृह संपति नासी। मूड़ मुड़ाइ होहिं सन्यासी॥
nāri muī gṛha saṁpati nāsī, mūṛa muṛāi hohiṁ sanyāsī.
ते बिप्रन्ह सन आपु पुजावहिं। उभय लोक निज हाथ नसावहिं॥
te bipranha sana āpu pujāvahiṁ, ubhaya loka nija hātha nasāvahiṁ.
बिप्र निरच्छर लोलुप कामी। निराचार सठ बृषली स्वामी॥
bipra niracchara lolupa kāmī, nirācāra saṭha bṛṣalī svāmī.
सूद्र करहिं जप तप ब्रत नाना। बैठि बरासन कहहिं पुराना॥
sūdra karahiṁ japa tapa brata nānā, baiṭhi barāsana kahahiṁ purānā.
सब नर कल्पित करहिं अचारा। जाइ न बरनि अनीति अपारा॥
saba nara kalpita karahiṁ acārā, jāi na barani anīti apārā.

Trans:

Lecherous after their neighbor's wife, clever only in trickery, imbued with ignorance, violence and selfishness—such are the men who are reckoned as theologians and philosophers. Such is the practices I have seen in every Kali-Yug. Doomed themselves, they drag down others too who tread the path of virtue. They who trouble the world by finding faults in the Vedas, spend a whole Kalpa in each abyss of hell. People of low caste, such as oilmen, potters, dog-feeders, kirāts, kols, and distillers of spirituous liquors, indulge in the sham of shaving their heads and become false religious mendicants, upon the death of their wife or loss of their household goods; and they make Brahmins bow down to their feet. Such men by their own deeds ruin themselves both for this world and also for the next. As for Brahmins they have become unlettered, greedy, sensual, dissolute, stupid and marry low-caste women of lewd character. Sudras practice prayer, fasting and all the other duties of religion, and taking the highest seat expound the Purānas. Everyone practices the duties of some other state of life than his own, and the endless perversions of morality are beyond all description.

दोहा-dohā:

भए बरन संकर कलि भिन्नसेतु सब लोग ।
bhae barana saṁkara kali bhinnasetu saba loga,
करहिं पाप पावहिं दुख भय रुज सोक बियोग ॥१००क॥
karahiṁ pāpa pāvahiṁ dukha bhaya ruja soka biyoga. 100(ka).

श्रुति संमत हरि भक्ति पथ संजुत बिरति बिबेक ।
śruti saṁmata hari bhakti patha saṁjuta birati bibeka,
तेहिं न चलहिं नर मोह बस कल्पहिं पंथ अनेक ॥१००ख॥
tehiṁ na calahiṁ nara moha basa kalpahiṁ paṁtha aneka. 100(kha).

Trans:

In the Kali-Yug different castes are confounded together and everyone is a law to himself. Men practice sin and reap its reward in trouble, terror, sickness, sorrow and bereavement. Overcome by delusion, they walk not in the path of Harī's service—such as is approved by the Scriptures and conjoined with sobriety and discernment—but invent diverse ways of their own.

छंद-chaṁda:

बहु दाम सँवारहिं धाम जती । बिषया हरि लीन्हि न रहि बिरती ॥
bahu dāma saṁvārahiṁ dhāma jatī, biṣayā hari līnhi na rahi biratī.
तपसी धनवंत दरिद्र गृही । कलि कौतुक तात न जात कही ॥
tapasī dhanavaṁta daridra gṛhī, kali kautuka tāta na jāta kahī.
कुलवंति निकारहिं नारि सती । गृह आनहिं चेरि निबेरि गती ॥
kulavaṁti nikārahiṁ nāri satī, gṛha ānahiṁ ceri niberi gatī.
सुत मानहिं मातु पिता तब लौं । अबलानन दीख नहीं जब लौं ॥
suta mānahiṁ mātu pitā taba lauṁ, abalānana dīkha nahīṁ jaba lauṁ.
ससुरारि पिआरि लगी जब तें । रिपुरूप कुटुंब भए तब तें ॥
sasurāri piāri lagī jaba teṁ, ripurūpa kuṭuṁba bhae taba teṁ.
नृप पाप परायन धर्म नहीं । करि दंड बिडंब प्रजा नितहीं ॥
nṛpa pāpa parāyana dharma nahīṁ, kari daṁḍa biḍaṁba prajā nitahīṁ.
धनवंत कुलीन मलीन अपी । द्विज चिन्ह जनेउ उघार तपी ॥
dhanavaṁta kulīna malīna apī, dvija cinha janeu ughāra tapī.
नहिं मान पुरान न बेदहि जो । हरि सेवक संत सही कलि सो ॥
nahiṁ māna purāna na bedahi jo, hari sevaka saṁta sahī kali so,
कबि बृंद उदार दुनी न सुनी । गुन दूषक ब्रात न कोपि गुनी ॥
kabi bṛṁda udāra dunī na sunī, guna dūṣaka brāta na kopi gunī.
कलि बारहिं बार दुकाल परै । बिनु अन्न दुखी सब लोग मरै ॥
kali bārahiṁ bāra dukāla parai, binu anna dukhī saba loga marai.

Trans:

Devotees build themselves costly houses and are carried away by sensuality, forgetful of self-mortification. Ascetics amass wealth, mendicants become householders; the absurdities of the Kali-Yug, sir, are beyond all description. They turn out a well-born and virtuous wife and bring home a strumpet in violation of family custom. A son obeys his father and mother so long only as he sees not a woman's face; as soon as he takes a fancy to his wife's kinsfolk, he looks upon his own family as his enemies. Kings, devoted to criminal trends and with no regard for religion, oppress their subjects with unrighteous judgments. The meanest churl, if he is rich, is accounted noble; a Brahmin is known only by his cord, and any naked wretch is considered an ascetic. Anyone in the Kali-Yug who rejects both Vedas and Purānas is held a worshipper of Harī and a veritable saint. Poets are many, but munificents to encourage and reward are none; plenty are there that find fault with others' virtues, and of the virtuous, there is want. In the Kali-Yug famines are of frequent occurrence and the people perish miserably for want.

दोहा-dohā:

सुनु खगेस कलि कपट हठ दंभ द्वेष पाषंड ।
sunu khagesa kali kapaṭa haṭha daṁbha dveṣa pāṣaṁḍa,
मान मोह मारादि मद ब्यापि रहे ब्रह्मंड ॥१०१क॥
māna moha mārādi mada byāpi rahe brahmaṁḍa. 101(ka).

तामस धर्म करहिं नर जप तप ब्रत मख दान ।
tāmasa dharma karahiṁ nara japa tapa brata makha dāna,
देव न बरषहिं धरनीं बए न जामहिं धान ॥१०१ख॥
deva na baraṣahiṁ dharanīṁ bae na jāmahiṁ dhāna. 101(kha).

Trans:

Hearken Garud; in the Kali-Yug the whole world is instinct with hypocrisy, violence, pride, enmity, heresy, arrogance, ignorance, sensuality and every other evil passion. Men worship the powers of darkness with prayers, fasting, sacrifice, vows and almsgiving; the gods rain not on earth, and the grain is sown but does not germinate.

छंद-chaṁda:

अबला कच भूषन भूरि छुधा । धनहीन दुखी ममता बहुधा ॥
abalā kaca bhūṣana bhūri chudhā, dhanahīna dukhī mamatā bahudhā.
सुख चाहहिं मूढ़ न धर्म रता । मति थोरि कठोरि न कोमलता ॥
sukha cāhahiṁ mūṛha na dharma ratā, mati thori kaṭhori na komalatā.
नर पीड़ित रोग न भोग कहीं । अभिमान बिरोध अकारनहीं ॥
nara pīṛita roga na bhoga kahīṁ, abhimāna birodha akāranahīṁ.
लघु जीवन संबतु पंच दसा । कलपांत न नास गुमानु असा ॥
laghu jīvana saṁbatu paṁca dasā, kalapāṁta na nāsa gumānu asā.
कलिकाल बिहाल किए मनुजा । नहिं मानत क्वौ अनुजा तनुजा ॥
kalikāla bihāla kie manujā, nahiṁ mānata kvau anujā tanujā.
नहिं तोष बिचार न सीतलता । सब जाति कुजाति भए मगता ॥
nahiṁ toṣa bicāra na sītalatā, saba jāti kujāti bhae magatā.
इरिषा परुषाच्छर लोलुपता । भरि पूरि रही समता बिगता ॥
iriṣā paruṣācchara lolupatā, bhari pūri rahī samatā bigatā.
सब लोग बियोग बिसोक हुए । बरनाश्रम धर्म अचार गए ॥
saba loga biyoga bisoka hue, baranāśrama dharma acāra gae.
दम दान दया नहिं जानपनी । जड़ता परबंचनताति घनी ॥
dama dāna dayā nahiṁ jānapanī, jaṛatā parabaṁcanatāti ghanī.
तनु पोषक नारि नरा सगरे । परनिंदक जे जग मो बगरे ॥
tanu poṣaka nāri narā sagare, paraniṁdaka je jaga mo bagare.

Trans:

A woman's only ornament is her tress and she is sorely hungered; the poor are in distress, but are intensely selfish. Fools desire happiness, but have no regard for religion; their narrow mind is hardened and knows no compassion. Men burdened with disease find no rest anywhere; self-conceit and causeless wrangling everywhere. Life is short; man's age is only few years, yet in their pride they reckon on outliving creation. The age of Kali has driven men mad; no one respects the sanctity even of one's sister or daughter. There is no contentment, nor consideration, nor repose; every caste is degraded to the condition of an importunate beggar; there is no contentment, no discernment, no composure. Everyone is aching with sorrow and bereavement; and all thought of the duties connected with caste and stage of life is abandoned. Men are so niggardly that they ignore all self-denial, charity and kind-heartedness; torpor and dishonesty are multiplied exceedingly. Men and women alike all pamper their body and slanderers are spread out everywhere.

दोहा-dohā:

सुनु ब्यालारि काल कलि मल अवगुन आगार ।
sunu byālāri kāla kali mala avaguna āgāra,
गुनउँ बहुत कलिजुग कर बिनु प्रयास निस्तार ॥ १०२क॥
gunaum̐ bahuta kalijuga kara binu prayāsa nistāra. 102(ka).

कृतजुग त्रेताँ द्वापर पूजा मख अरु जोग ।
kṛtajuga tretām̐ dvāpara pūjā makha aru joga,
जो गति होइ सो कलि हरि नाम ते पावहिं लोग ॥ १०२ख॥
jo gati hoi so kali hari nāma te pāvahiṁ loga. 102(kha).

Trans:

Hearken Garud; the Kali-Yug is a mine of impurity and iniquity; but it has one enormous advantage: final emancipation is possible here with little exertion. In the Sat-Yug, Tretā-Yug and Dvapar-Yug solemn worship, sacrifice, and mystical meditation were the appointed means; in the Kali-Yug people attain salvation only by chanting Rāma's name.

चौपाई-caupāī:

कृतजुग सब जोगी बिग्यानी । करि हरि ध्यान तरहिं भव प्रानी ॥
kṛtajuga saba jogī bigyānī, kari hari dhyāna tarahiṁ bhava prānī.
त्रेताँ बिबिध जग्य नर करहीं । प्रभुहि समर्पि कर्म भव तरहीं ॥
tretām̐ bibidha jagya nara karahīṁ, prabhuhi samarpi karma bhava tarahīṁ.
द्वापर करि रघुपति पद पूजा । नर भव तरहिं उपाय न दूजा ॥
dvāpara kari raghupati pada pūjā, nara bhava tarahiṁ upāya na dūjā.
कलिजुग केवल हरि गुन गाहा । गावत नर पावहिं भव थाहा ॥
kalijuga kevala hari guna gāhā, gāvata nara pāvahiṁ bhava thāhā.
कलिजुग जोग न जग्य न ग्याना । एक अधार राम गुन गाना ॥
kalijuga joga na jagya na gyānā, eka adhāra rāma guna gānā.
सब भरोस तजि जो भज रामहि । प्रेम समेत गाव गुन ग्रामहि ॥
saba bharosa taji jo bhaja rāmahi, prema sameta gāva guna grāmahi.
सोइ भव तर कछु संसय नाहीं । नाम प्रताप प्रगट कलि माहीं ॥
soi bhava tara kachu saṁsaya nāhīṁ, nāma pratāpa pragaṭa kali māhīṁ.
कलि कर एक पुनीत प्रतापा । मानस पुन्य होहिं नहिं पापा ॥
kali kara eka punīta pratāpā, mānasa punya hohiṁ nahiṁ pāpā.

Trans:

In the Sat-Yug all were spiritual and wise and crossed the ocean of existence by meditating on Harī. In the Tretā-Yug men performed many sacrifices and dedicating their actions to the Lord and thus attained to salvation. In the Dvapar-Yug men had no other expedient save the worship of Rāma's feet to save their souls. In the Kali-Yug people can cross this turbulent ocean of existence simply by chanting Rāma's praises. In the Kali-Yug neither spiritual abstraction, sacrifice nor knowledge is of any avail; man's only hope is in hymning Rāma name. Anyone who abjures every reliance on every other and simply prays devoutly to Rāma, and sings his praises, will assuredly cross the ocean of mundane existence. The power of his name is thus manifest in the Kali-Yug. The Kali-Yug has another sacred virtue: mental virtues accrue, but mental sins don't count.

दोहा-dohā:

कलिजुग सम जुग आन नहिं जौं नर कर बिस्वास ।
kalijuga sama juga āna nahiṁ jauṁ nara kara bisvāsa,
गाइ राम गुन गन बिमल भव तर बिनहिं प्रयास ॥ १०३क॥
gāi rāma guna gana bimala bhava tara binahiṁ prayāsa. 103(ka).

प्रगट चारि पद धर्म के कलि महुँ एक प्रधान ।
pragaṭa cāri pada dharma ke kali mahum̐ eka pradhāna,
जेन केन बिधि दीन्हें दान करइ कल्यान ॥ १०३ख॥
jena kena bidhi dīnheṁ dāna karai kalyāna. 103(kha).

Trans:

There is no age to compare with the Kali-Yug: in it, if a man has only faith and devotes himself to singing Rāma's holy praises, he crosses over the deep ocean of existence without further trouble. Piety has four well-known pillars, of which one is predominant in the Kali: charity practiced in any way conduces to one's spiritual good.

चौपाई-caupāī:

नित जुग धर्म होहिं सब केरे । हृदयँ राम माया के प्रेरे ॥
nita juga dharma hohiṁ saba kere, hṛdayam̐ rāma māyā ke prere.
सुद्ध सत्व समता बिग्याना । कृत प्रभाव प्रसन्न मन जाना ॥
suddha satva samatā bigyānā, kṛta prabhāva prasanna mana jānā.
सत्व बहुत रज कछु रति कर्मा । सब बिधि सुख त्रेता कर धर्मा ॥
satva bahuta raja kachu rati karmā, saba bidhi sukha tretā kara dharmā.
बहु रज स्वल्प सत्व कछु तामस । द्वापर धर्म हरष भय मानस ॥
bahu raja svalpa satva kachu tāmasa, dvāpara dharma haraṣa bhaya mānasa.
तामस बहुत रजोगुन थोरा । कलि प्रभाव बिरोध चहुँ ओरा ॥
tāmasa bahuta rajoguna thorā, kali prabhāva birodha cahum̐ orā.
बुध जुग धर्म जानि मन माहीं । तजि अधर्म रति धर्म कराहीं ॥
budha juga dharma jāni mana māhīṁ, taji adharma rati dharma karāhīṁ.
काल धर्म नहिं ब्यापहिं ताही । रघुपति चरन प्रीति अति जाही ॥
kāla dharma nahiṁ byāpahiṁ tāhī, raghupati carana prīti ati jāhī.
नट कृत बिकट कपट खगराया । नट सेवकहि न ब्यापइ माया ॥
naṭa kṛta bikaṭa kapaṭa khagarāyā, naṭa sevakahi na byāpai māyā.

Trans:

Every Age has its special characteristic, infused into the soul by Rāma's delusive power. Purity, truth, equanimity and wisdom, combined with joy of soul, are recognized as the outcome of the Golden-Age. A great devotion to truth—though with some admixture of passion—and general happiness are the note of the Silver-Age. Much passion, little truth and some ignorance, with mingled joy and terror of soul, are the note of the Bronze-Age. Great ignorance, less passion and universal antagonism are the outcome of the Iron-Age. The wise understand the proper virtue of each age and forswearing iniquity devote themselves to religion. The influence of the Kali-Yug has no effect on him who cherishes a love for Rāma's feet. A juggler, Garud, may practice the most wonderful deceptions, but they do not impose upon his own servants.

दोहा-dohā:

हरि माया कृत दोष गुन बिनु हरि भजन न जाहिं ।
hari māyā kṛta doṣa guna binu hari bhajana na jāhiṁ,
भजिअ राम तजि काम सब अस बिचारि मन माहिं ॥ १०४क॥
bhajia rāma taji kāma saba asa bicāri mana māhiṁ. 104(ka).

तेहिं कलिकाल बरष बहु बसेउँ अवध बिहगेस ।
tehiṁ kalikāla baraṣa bahu baseum̐ avadha bihagesa,
परेउ दुकाल बिपति बस तब मैं गयउँ बिदेस ॥ १०४ख॥
pareu dukāla bipati basa taba maiṁ gayaum̐ bidesa. 104(kha).

Trans:

The good and evil, which are the creation of Harī's delusive power, can only be dispersed by prayer to Harī: know this and worship Harī, forswearing all sensuality. In that particular Kali-Yug I lived, O Garud, for many years at Avadh, till a famine occurred which compelled me to go to another place.

चौपाई-caupāī:

गयउँ उजेनी सुनु उरगारी । दीन मलीन दरिद्र दुखारी ॥
gayauṁ ujenī sunu uragārī, dīna malīna daridra dukhārī.
गएँ काल कछु संपति पाई । तहँ पुनि करउँ संभु सेवकाई ॥
gaeṁ kāla kachu saṁpati pāī, tahaṁ puni karauṁ saṁbhu sevakāī.
बिप्र एक बैदिक सिव पूजा । करइ सदा तेहि काजु न दूजा ॥
bipra eka baidika siva pūjā, karai sadā tehi kāju na dūjā.
परम साधु परमारथ बिंदक । संभु उपासक नहिं हरि निंदक ॥
parama sādhu paramāratha biṁdaka, saṁbhu upāsaka nahiṁ hari niṁdaka.
तेहि सेवउँ मैं कपट समेता । द्विज दयाल अति नीति निकेता ॥
tehi sevauṁ maiṁ kapaṭa sametā, dvija dayāla ati nīti niketā.
बाहिज नम्र देखि मोहि साईं । बिप्र पढ़ाव पुत्र की नाईं ॥
bāhija namra dekhi mohi sāīṁ, bipra paṛhāva putra kī nāīṁ.
संभु मंत्र मोहि द्विजबर दीन्हा । सुभ उपदेस बिबिध बिधि कीन्हा ॥
saṁbhu maṁtra mohi dvijabara dīnhā, subha upadesa bibidha bidhi kīnhā.
जपउँ मंत्र सिव मंदिर जाई । हृदयँ दंभ अहमिति अधिकाई ॥
japauṁ maṁtra siva maṁdira jāī, hṛdayaṁ daṁbha ahamiti adhikāī.

Trans:

I went to Ujjain—mark me, Garud—a miserable outcast, poor and wretched. After some time I acquired wealth and as before practiced devotion to Shambhu. There was there a Vedic Brahmin who constantly worshipped Shiva and had no other occupation; a very saintly man, learned in divine truth, who served Shambhu but was no reviler of Harī. I hypocritically attended upon this benignant philosopher, and he, sir, seeing me outwardly so submissive, instructed me as his own son, teaching me the Shiva incantations and giving me every kind of good advice. I went to a temple of Shiva and repeated the spells with a heart full of pride and self-conceit.

दोहा-dohā:

मैं खल मल संकुल मति नीच जाति बस मोह ।
maiṁ khala mala saṁkula mati nīca jāti basa moha,
हरि जन द्विज देखें जरउँ करउँ बिष्नु कर द्रोह ॥ १०५क ॥
hari jana dvija dekheṁ jarauṁ karauṁ biṣnu kara droha. 105(ka).

Trans:

Wretch that I was, with a soul full of impurity, low-born and enthralled by delusion, I hated Vishnu, and flew into a passion if I saw any Brahmin, or a worshipper of Harī.

सोरठा-soraṭhā:

गुर नित मोहि प्रबोध दुखित देखि आचरन मम ।
gura nita mohi prabodha dukhita dekhi ācarana mama,
मोहि उपजइ अति क्रोध दंभिहि नीति कि भावई ॥ १०५ख॥
mohi upajai ati krodha daṁbhihi nīti ki bhāvaī. 105(kha).

Trans:

My teacher was distressed to see my manner of life and was always admonishing me; but I became exceedingly angry. Is pride ever pleased by sober counsel?

चौपाई-caupāī:

एक बार गुर लीन्ह बोलाई । मोहि नीति बहु भाँति सिखाई ॥
eka bāra gura līnha bolāī, mohi nīti bahu bhāṁti sikhāī.
सिव सेवा कर फल सुत सोई । अबिरल भगति राम पद होई ॥
siva sevā kara phala suta soī, abirala bhagati rāma pada hoī.
रामहि भजहिं तात सिव धाता । नर पावँर कै केतिक बाता ॥
rāmahi bhajahiṁ tāta siva dhātā, nara pāvaṁra kai ketika bātā.
जासु चरन अज सिव अनुरागी । तातु द्रोहँ सुख चहसि अभागी ॥
jāsu carana aja siva anurāgī, tātu drohaṁ sukha cahasi abhāgī.
हर कहुँ हरि सेवक गुर कहेऊ । सुनि खगनाथ हृदय मम दहेऊ ॥
hara kahuṁ hari sevaka gura kaheū, suni khaganātha hṛdaya mama daheū.
अधम जाति मैं बिद्या पाएँ । भयउँ जथा अहि दूध पिआएँ ॥
adhama jāti maiṁ bidyā pāeṁ, bhayauṁ jathā ahi dūdha piāeṁ.
मानी कुटिल कुभाग्य कुजाती । गुर कर द्रोह करउँ दिनु राती ॥
mānī kuṭila kubhāgya kujātī, gura kara droha karauṁ dinu rātī.
अति दयाल गुर स्वल्प न क्रोधा । पुनि पुनि मोहि सिखाव सुबोधा ॥
ati dayāla gura svalpa na krodhā, puni puni mohi sikhāva subodhā.
जेहि ते नीच बड़ाई पावा । सो प्रथमहिं हति ताहि नसावा ॥
jehi te nīca baṛāī pāvā, so prathamahiṁ hati tāhi nasāvā.
धूम अनल संभव सुनु भाई । तेहि बुझाव घन पदवी पाई ॥
dhūma anala saṁbhava sunu bhāī, tehi bujhāva ghana padavī pāī.
रज मग परी निरादर रहई । सब कर पद प्रहार नित सहई ॥
raja maga parī nirādara rahaī, saba kara pada prahāra nita sahaī.
मरुत उड़ाव प्रथम तेहि भरई । पुनि नृप नयन किरीटन्हि परई ॥
maruta uṛāva prathama tehi bharaī, puni nṛpa nayana kirīṭanhi paraī.
सुनु खगपति अस समुझि प्रसंगा । बुध नहिं करहिं अधम कर संगा ॥
sunu khagapati asa samujhi prasaṁgā, budha nahiṁ karahiṁ adhama kara saṁgā.
कबि कोबिद गावहिं असि नीती । खल सन कलह न भल नहिं प्रीती ॥
kabi kobida gāvahiṁ asi nītī, khala sana kalaha na bhala nahiṁ prītī.
उदासीन नित रहिअ गोसाईं । खल परिहरिअ स्वान की नाईं ॥
udāsīna nita rahia gosāīṁ, khala pariharia svāna kī nāīṁ.
मैं खल हृदयँ कपट कुटिलाई । गुर हित कहइ न मोहि सोहाई ॥
maiṁ khala hṛdayaṁ kapaṭa kuṭilāī, gura hita kahai na mohi sohāī.

Trans:

One day the Gurū called me and instructed me at length in the principles of morality, "The reward, my son, for serving Shiva is a steadfast faith in Rāma. Even Shiva and Brahmmā worship Rāma; of what account then is a measly man? Do you hope to secure happiness, you luckless wight, by persecuting him whose feet even Shiva and Brahmmā adore?" When I heard the Gurū speak of Shiva as a worshipper of Harī, my heart, Garud, was all on fire. I was already such a low-born churl, and after receiving education I became like a snake that has been fed on milk. Arrogant, perverse, ill-starred and ill-bred, I vexed my Gurū day and night. But he was too tender-hearted to be angry and still continued his wise admonitions. The very person from whom a churl obtains promotion is the first he destroys. Hearken friend; smoke is produced by fire, and yet when promoted to cloudship it puts the same fire out. Dust, while it lies on the road, is held in contempt and submits to be trodden under foot of everyone. If the wind carries it aloft, it first darkens that and then gets into the king's eyes or sullies his crown. Hearken, Garud, and thus understand my parable: sensible people should have no dealings with the mean. The wisest of the poets have declared this maxim, it is good neither to quarrel with a churl nor to be friends with him; never have anything to do with them at all, sir. Leave the wicked alone, like a dog. Churl as I was, with a heart full of falsehood and perversity, I paid no heed to the Gurū's friendly admonition.

दोहा-dohā:

एक बार हर मंदिर जपत रहेउँ सिव नाम ।
eka bāra hara maṁdira japata raheuṁ siva nāma,
गुर आयउ अभिमान तें उठि नहिं कीन्ह प्रनाम ॥ १०६क॥
gura āyau abhimāna teṁ uṭhi nahiṁ kīnha pranāma. 106(ka).

सो दयाल नहिं कहेउ कछु उर न रोष लवलेस।
so dayāla nahiṁ kaheu kachu ura na roṣa lavalesa,
अति अघ गुर अपमानता सहि नहिं सके महेस ॥१०६ख॥
ati agha gura apamānatā sahi nahiṁ sake mahesa. 106(kha).

Trans:

One day I was in a temple of Shiva saying my rosary when the Gurū came in, and in my conceit I did not rise to salute him. He was too gentle to say anything, neither did he feel the tiniest iota of resentment, but the grievous sin of slighting a spiritual teacher was more than Shiva could tolerate.

चौपाई-caupāī:

मंदिर माझ भई नभ बानी। रे हतभाग्य अग्य अभिमानी॥
maṁdira mājha bhaī nabha bānī, re hatabhāgya agya abhimānī.
जद्यपि तव गुर कें नहिं क्रोधा। अति कृपाल चित सम्यक बोधा॥
jadyapi tava gura keṁ nahiṁ krodhā, ati kṛpāla cita samyaka bodhā.
तदपि साप सठ दैहउँ तोही। नीति बिरोध सोहाइ न मोही॥
tadapi sāpa saṭha daihauṁ tohī, nīti birodha sohāi na mohī.
जौं नहिं दंड करौं खल तोरा। भ्रष्ट होइ श्रुतिमारग मोरा॥
jauṁ nahiṁ daṁḍa karauṁ khala torā, bhraṣṭa hoi śrutimāraga morā.
जे सठ गुर सन इरिषा करहीं। रौरव नरक कोटि जुग परहीं॥
je saṭha gura sana iriṣā karahīṁ, raurava naraka koṭi juga parahīṁ.
त्रिजग जोनि पुनि धरहिं सरीरा। अयुत जन्म भरि पावहिं पीरा॥
trijaga joni puni dharahiṁ sarīrā, ayuta janma bhari pāvahiṁ pīrā.
बैठ रहेसि अजगर इव पापी। सर्प होहि खल मल मति ब्यापी॥
baiṭha rahesi ajagara iva pāpī, sarpa hohi khala mala mati byāpī.
महा बिटप कोटर महुँ जाई। रहु अधमाधम अधगति पाई॥
mahā biṭapa koṭara mahuṁ jāī, rahu adhamādhama adhagati pāī.

Trans:

A heavenly voice proceeded from the shrine, "You miserable, conceited churl, though your Gurū shows no resentment, being so tender-hearted and of such sublime intelligence, yet I must pronounce a curse upon you, you wretch; I cannot endure such a breach of morality. If I were not to punish you for your wickedness, my scriptural ordinance would be violated. Villains who bear malice against their Gurū are cast for a million ages into the most awful abyss of hell; they then take birth in the brutal most creation and suffer affliction in myriad successive existences. As for you, you guilty wretch, whose soul reeks with impurity, since you kept your seat, as it were some unwieldy boa-constrictor, you shall become a snake; enter into the hollow of some huge forest tree and there remain, vilest of the vile, in the form of vilest creatures."

दोहा-dohā:

हाहाकार कीन्ह गुर दारुन सुनि सिव साप।
hāhākāra kīnha gura dāruna suni siva sāpa,
कंपित मोहि बिलोकि अति उर उपजा परिताप ॥१०७क॥
kaṁpita mohi biloki ati ura upajā paritāpa. 107(ka).

करि दंडवत सप्रेम द्विज सिव सन्मुख कर जोरि।
kari daṁḍavata saprema dvija siva sanmukha kara jori,
बिनय करत गदगद स्वर समुझि घोर गति मोरि ॥१०७ख॥
binaya karata gadagada svara samujhi ghora gati mori. 107(kha).

Trans:

"Alas! Alas!" cried the Gurū, as he heard Shiva's terrible curse; and seeing me all trembling in fear, a profound compassion moved his soul. Devoutly prostrating himself in Shiva's presence, with his hands clasped and his voice choked with emotion as he reflected on my awful fate, he uttered this prayer:

छंद-chaṁda:

नमामीशमीशान निर्वाणरूपं। विभुं व्यापकं ब्रह्म वेदस्वरूपं॥
namāmīśamīśāna nirvāṇarūpaṁ, vibhuṁ vyāpakaṁ brahma vedasvarūpaṁ.
निजं निर्गुणं निर्विकल्पं निरीहं। चिदाकाशमाकाशवासं भजेऽहं॥
nijaṁ nirguṇaṁ nirvikalpaṁ nirīhaṁ, cidākāśamākāśavāsaṁ bhaje'haṁ.
निराकारमोंकारमूलं तुरीयं। गिरा ग्यान गोतीतमीशं गिरीशं॥
nirākāramoṁkāramūlaṁ turīyaṁ, girā gyāna gotītamīśaṁ girīśaṁ.
करालं महाकाल कालं कृपालं। गुणागार संसारपारं नतोऽहं॥
karālaṁ mahākāla kālaṁ kṛpālaṁ, guṇāgāra saṁsārapāraṁ nato'haṁ.
तुषाराद्रि संकाश गौरं गभीरं। मनोभूत कोटि प्रभा श्री शरीरं॥
tuṣārādri saṁkāśa gauraṁ gabhīraṁ, manobhūta koṭi prabhā śrī śarīraṁ.
स्फुरन्मौलि कल्लोलिनी चारु गंगा। लसद्भालबालेन्दु कंठे भुजंगा॥
sphuranmauli kallolinī cāru gaṁgā, lasadbhālabālendu kaṁṭhe bhujaṁgā.
चलत्कुंडलं भ्रू सुनेत्रं विशालं। प्रसन्नाननं नीलकंठं दयालं॥
calatkuṁḍalaṁ bhrū sunetraṁ viśālaṁ, prasannānanaṁ nīlakaṁṭhaṁ dayālaṁ.
मृगाधीशचर्माम्बरं मुण्डमालं। प्रियं शंकरं सर्वनाथं भजामि॥
mṛgādhīśacarmāmbaraṁ muṇḍamālaṁ, priyaṁ śaṁkaraṁ sarvanāthaṁ bhajāmi.
प्रचंडं प्रकृष्टं प्रगल्भं परेशं। अखंडं अजं भानुकोटिप्रकाशं॥
pracaṁḍaṁ prakṛṣṭaṁ pragalbhaṁ pareśaṁ, akhaṁḍaṁ ajaṁ bhānukoṭiprakāśaṁ.
त्रयःशूल निर्मूलनं शूलपाणिं। भजेऽहं भवानीपतिं भावगम्यं॥
trayaḥśūla nirmūlanaṁ śūlapāṇiṁ, bhaje'haṁ bhavānīpatiṁ bhāvagamyaṁ.
कलातीत कल्याण कल्पान्तकारी। सदा सज्जनान्ददाता पुरारी॥
kalātīta kalyāṇa kalpāntakārī, sadā sajjanāndadātā purārī.
चिदानंदसंदोह मोहापहारी। प्रसीद प्रसीद प्रभो मन्मथारी॥
cidānaṁdasaṁdoha mohāpahārī, prasīda prasīda prabho manmathārī.
न यावद् उमानाथ पादारविन्दं। भजंतीह लोके परे वा नराणां॥
na yāvad umānātha pādāravindaṁ, bhajaṁtīha loke pare vā narāṇāṁ.
न तावत्सुखं शान्ति सन्तापनाशं। प्रसीद प्रभो सर्वभूताधिवासं॥
na tāvatsukhaṁ śānti santāpanāśaṁ, prasīda prabho sarvabhūtādhivāsaṁ.
न जानामि योगं जपं नैव पूजां। नतोऽहं सदा सर्वदा शंभु तुभ्यं॥
na jānāmi yogaṁ japaṁ naiva pūjāṁ, nato'haṁ sadā sarvadā śaṁbhu tubhyaṁ.
जरा जन्म दुःखौघ तातप्यमानं। प्रभो पाहि आपन्नमामीश शंभो॥
jarā janma duḥkhaugha tātapyamānaṁ, prabho pāhi āpannamāmīśa śaṁbho.

Trans:

"I adore the Lord of lords, the embodiment of salvation, the omnipresent and all-pervading Supreme Spirit, the image of the Veda. I worship the absolute, the unqualified, the unconditioned, the unwishful; who dwelleth in the heavens and who has the heaven for his soul. I bow before the formless germ of the mystic incantation OM, the transcendental, the Lord that is beyond all speech, understanding, or faculty of the senses; who is the Himalayan king, terrible, and the death of tyrant Death; and yet the most merciful; the grace-abounding refuge of the world. Rugged and stern as the Snowy Mountains, yet radiant with the beauty of a myriad Loves; with the bright waters of the Gangā springing from thy head, with the crescent moon gleaming on thy brow and snakes on thy neck, with tremulous earrings and large eyes and shaggy brows, with benignant face and deep-stained throat, O all-merciful, robed in a tiger's skin, with a necklace of skulls, I worship thee, the universal Lord, even Shankar, whom I love. I adore thee, the fierce, the exalted, the intrepid, the Supreme Lord; the indivisible, the unbegotten, whose glory is that of a myriad suns; tearing up by the root every kind of trouble with the trident in thy hand; Bhawānī's Lord, accessible only by meditation. Unchangeable and ever-blessed Purārī, consummator of earth's cycles, constant bestower of blessings on the pious, sum of all knowledge and felicity, dispeller of delusion, Conqueror of Love, have mercy, O my Lord, have mercy. So long as they worship not the lotus feet of Umā's Lord, neither in this world nor in the next is there any happiness for men, nor peace, nor cessation of misery. O my Lord, clothed about with all the elements, have mercy. I know nothing of meditation, or prayer, or ritual, but at all times and in all places I bow before thee, O Shambhu. Have mercy, O my Lord, on a wretch so sorely afflicted by old age and life's flood of troubles; for thee only I worship, O my Lord Shambhu."

श्लोक-śloka:

रुद्राष्टकमिदं प्रोक्तं विप्रेण हरतोषये ।
rudrāṣṭakamidaṁ proktaṁ vipreṇa haratoṣaye,
ये पठन्ति नरा भक्त्या तेषां शम्भुः प्रसीदति ॥
ye paṭhanti narā bhaktyā teṣāṁ śambhuḥ prasīdati.

Trans:

Anyone who devoutly repeats this hymn to Shiva, as uttered by the Brahmin in his propitiation, upon him will Shiva shower his favor.

दोहा-dohā:

सुनि बिनती सर्बग्य सिव देखि बिप्र अनुरागु ।
suni binatī sarbagya siva dekhi bipra anurāgu,
पुनि मंदिर नभबानी भइ द्विजबर बर मागु ॥ १०८क॥
puni maṁdira nabhabānī bhai dvijabara bara māgu. 108(ka).

जौं प्रसन्न प्रभु मो पर नाथ दीन पर नेहु ।
jauṁ prasanna prabhu mo para nātha dīna para nehu,
निज पद भगति देइ प्रभु पुनि दूसर बर देहु ॥ १०८ख॥
nija pada bhagati dei prabhu puni dūsara bara dehu. 108(kha).

तव माया बस जीव जड़ संतत फिरइ भुलान ।
tava māyā basa jīva jaṛa saṁtata phirai bhulāna,
तेहि पर क्रोध न करिअ प्रभु कृपासिंधु भगवान ॥ १०८ग॥
tehi para krodha na karia prabhu kṛpāsiṁdhu bhagavāna. 108(ga).

संकर दीनदयाल अब एहि पर होहु कृपाल ।
saṁkara dīnadayāla aba ehi para hohu kṛpāla,
साप अनुग्रह होइ जेहिं नाथ थोरेहीं काल ॥ १०८घ॥
sāpa anugraha hoi jehiṁ nātha thorehīṁ kāla. 108(gha).

Trans:

When the omniscient Shiva heard the Brahmin's prayer and saw his devotion, a heavenly voice again sounded in the temple, "Best of Brahmins, ask of a boon." "If my Lord is well pleased with me and will show favor to his servant, grant me first devotion to thy feet and then yet another boon. Overcome by thy delusive power, the ignorant Jiva ever wander astray; be not then wrath with him, O merciful Lord God. Gracious Shankar, be merciful to him. After a little time may thy curse become a kindness;

चौपाई-caupāī:

एहि कर होइ परम कल्याना । सोइ करहु अब कृपानिधाना ॥
ehi kara hoi parama kalyānā, soi karahu aba kṛpānidhānā.
बिप्रगिरा सुनि परहित सानी । एवमस्तु इति भइ नभबानी ॥
bipragirā suni parahita sānī, evamastu iti bhai nabhabānī.
जदपि कीन्ह एहिं दारुन पापा । मैं पुनि दीन्हि कोप करि सापा ॥
jadapi kīnha ehiṁ dāruna pāpā, maiṁ puni dīnhi kopa kari sāpā.
तदपि तुम्हारि साधुता देखी । करिहउँ एहि पर कृपा बिसेषी ॥
tadapi tumhāri sādhutā dekhī, karihauṁ ehi para kṛpā biseṣī.
छमासील जे पर उपकारी । ते द्विज मोहि प्रिय जथा खरारी ॥
chamāsīla je para upakārī, te dvija mohi priya jathā kharārī.
मोर श्राप द्विज ब्यर्थ न जाइहि । जन्म सहस अवस्य यह पाइहि ॥
mora śrāpa dvija byartha na jāihi, janma sahasa avasya yaha pāihi.
जनमत मरत दुसह दुख होई । एहि स्वल्पउ नहिं ब्यापिहि सोई ॥
janamata marata dusaha dukha hoī, ehi svalpau nahiṁ byāpihi soī.
कवनेउँ जन्म मिटिहि नहिं ग्याना । सुनहि सूद्र मम बचन प्रवाना ॥
kavaneuṁ janma miṭihi nahiṁ gyānā, sunahi sūdra mama bacana pravānā.
रघुपति पुरीं जन्म तव भयऊ । पुनि तैं मम सेवाँ मन दयऊ ॥
raghupati purīṁ janma tava bhayaū, puni taiṁ mama sevāṁ mana dayaū.
पुरी प्रभाव अनुग्रह मोरें । राम भगति उपजिहि उर तोरें ॥
purī prabhāva anugraha moreṁ, rāma bhagati upajihi ura toreṁ.
सुनु मम बचन सत्य अब भाई । हरितोषन ब्रत द्विज सेवकाई ॥
sunu mama bacana satya aba bhāī, haritoṣana brata dvija sevakāī.
अब जनि करहि बिप्र अपमाना । जानेहु संत अनंत समाना ॥
aba jani karahi bipra apamānā, jānehu saṁta anaṁta samānā.
इंद्र कुलिस मम सूल बिसाला । कालदंड हरि चक्र कराला ॥
iṁdra kulisa mama sūla bisālā, kāladaṁḍa hari cakra karālā.
जो इन्ह कर मारा नहिं मरई । बिप्र द्रोह पावक सो जरई ॥
jo inha kara mārā nahiṁ maraī, bipra droha pāvaka so jaraī.
अस बिबेक राखेहु मन माहीं । तुम्ह कहँ जग दुर्लभ कछु नाहीं ॥
asa bibeka rākhehu mana māhīṁ, tumha kahaṁ jaga durlabha kachu nāhīṁ.
औरउ एक आसिषा मोरी । अप्रतिहत गति होइहि तोरी ॥
aurau eka āsiṣā morī, apratihata gati hoihi torī.

Trans:

and may the highest blessings attend him; bring it thus to pass, O fountain of mercy." On hearing the Brahmin's speech, so pregnant with charity, the heavenly voice replied "So be it. Although he has committed a grievous sin and I in my wrath have cursed him, yet seeing your goodness I will visit him with a special favor. Brahmins, who are of a forgiving disposition and charitable to their neighbors, are as dear to me as Kharārī himself. Yet my curse, father, cannot be in vain; he shall of a certainty have a thousand lives. But the insupportable misery of birth and death shall not have the slightest effect upon him. In no birth shall his knowledge fail. Hearken Sudra to my judgment. You have been born in Rāma's capital and further you have done me service. By the blessing of the city and by my favor, a devotion to Rāma shall spring up in your bosom. Now hearken, friend, to my solemn declaration: the way to please Harī is by fasting and ministering to the Brahmins. Never again insult a Brahmin; regard the saints in the light of the Everlasting. Indra's thunder-bolt, my mighty trident, the rod of Death and Vishnu's terrible discus, by all these a man may be smitten, yet not die; but a Brahmin's wrath is a fire which shall burn him to ashes. Cherish this counsel at heart and there shall be nothing in the world too difficult for you to obtain. One other blessing I have still to bestow; your goings shall never be impeded."

दोहा-dohā:

सुनि सिव बचन हरषि गुर एवमस्तु इति भाषि ।
suni siva bacana haraṣi gura evamastu iti bhāṣi,
मोहि प्रबोधि गयउ गृह संभु चरन उर राखि ॥ १०९क॥
mohi prabodhi gayau gṛha saṁbhu carana ura rākhi. 109(ka).
प्रेरित काल बिंधि गिरि जाइ भयउँ मैं ब्याल ।
prerita kāla biṁdhi giri jāi bhayauṁ maiṁ byāla,
पुनि प्रयास बिनु सो तनु तजेउँ गएँ कछु काल ॥ १०९ख॥
puni prayāsa binu so tanu tajeuṁ gaeṁ kachu kāla. 109(kha).

जोइ तनु धरउँ तजउँ पुनि अनायास हरिजान ।
joi tanu dharaum̐ tajaum̐ puni anāyāsa harijāna,
जिमि नूतन पट पहिरइ नर परिहरइ पुरान ॥ १०९ग॥
jimi nūtana paṭa pahirai nara pariharai purāna. 109(ga).
सिवँ राखी श्रुति नीति अरु मैं नहिं पावा क्लेस ।
sivaṁ rākhī śruti nīti aru maiṁ nahiṁ pāvā klesa,
एहि बिधि धरेउँ बिबिधि तनु ग्यान न गयउ खगेस ॥ १०९घ॥
ehi bidhi dhareum̐ bibidhi tanu gyāna na gayau khagesa. 109(gha).

Trans:

On hearing Shiva's promise, the Gurū rejoiced and cried Amen. Then, after admonishing me, he returned home, with the image of Shambhu's feet impressed upon his heart. Driven by my fate, I went to the Vindhya mountains and then became a snake, and again after some time quietly dropped that form. Whatever body I assume, Garud, I readily dropped it again, like a man who puts off his old clothes and takes on new. Shiva observed the ordinances of the Veda; while I suffered no pain; thus I assumed many different forms, but my understanding, Garud, never left me.

चौपाई-caupāī:

त्रिजग देव नर जोइ तनु धरउँ । तहँ तहँ राम भजन अनुसरऊँ ॥
trijaga deva nara joi tanu dharaum̐, taham̐ taham̐ rāma bhajana anusaraūm̐.
एक सूल मोहि बिसर न काऊ । गुर कर कोमल सील सुभाऊ ॥
eka sūla mohi bisara na kāū, gura kara komala sīla subhāū.
चरम देह द्विज कै मैं पाई । सुर दुर्लभ पुरान श्रुति गाई ॥
carama deha dvija kai maiṁ pāī, sura durlabha purāna śruti gāī.
खेलउँ तहूँ बालकन्ह मीला । करउँ सकल रघुनायक लीला ॥
khelaum̐ tahūm̐ bālakanha mīlā, karaum̐ sakala raghunāyaka līlā.
प्रौढ़ भएँ मोहि पिता पढ़ावा । समझउँ सुनउँ गुनउँ नहिं भावा ॥
prauṛha bhaem̐ mohi pitā paṛhāvā, samajhaum̐ sunaum̐ gunaum̐ nahiṁ bhāvā.
मन ते सकल बासना भागी । केवल राम चरन लय लागी ॥
mana te sakala bāsanā bhāgī, kevala rāma carana laya lāgī.
कहु खगेस अस कवन अभागी । खरी सेव सुरधेनुहि त्यागी ॥
kahu khagesa asa kavana abhāgī, kharī seva suradhenuhi tyāgī.
प्रेम मगन मोहि कछु न सोहाई । हारेउ पिता पढ़ाइ पढ़ाई ॥
prema magana mohi kachu na sohāī, hāreu pitā paṛhāi paṛhāī.
भए कालबस जब पितु माता । मैं बन गयउँ भजन जनत्राता ॥
bhae kālabasa jaba pitu mātā, maiṁ bana gayaum̐ bhajana janatrātā.
जहँ जहँ बिपिन मुनीस्वर पावउँ । आश्रम जाइ जाइ सिरु नावउँ ॥
jaham̐ jaham̐ bipina munīsvara pāvaum̐, āśrama jāi jāi siru nāvaum̐.
बूझउँ तिन्हहि राम गुन गाहा । कहहिं सुनउँ हरषित खगनाहा ॥
būjhaum̐ tinhahi rāma guna gāhā, kahahiṁ sunaum̐ harașita khaganāhā.
सुनत फिरउँ हरि गुन अनुबादा । अब्याहत गति संभु प्रसादा ॥
sunata phiraum̐ hari guna anubādā, abyāhata gati saṁbhu prasādā.
छूटी त्रिबिधि ईषना गाढ़ी । एक लालसा उर अति बाढ़ी ॥
chūṭī tribidhi īṣanā gāṛhī, eka lālasā ura ati bāṛhī.
राम चरन बारिज जब देखौं । तब निज जन्म सफल करि लेखौं ॥
rāma carana bārija jaba dekhauṁ, taba nija janma saphala kari lekhauṁ.
जेहि पूँछउँ सोइ मुनि अस कहई । ईस्वर सर्ब भूतमय अहई ॥
jehi pūm̐chaum̐ soi muni asa kahaī, īsvara sarba bhūtamaya ahaī.
निर्गुन मत नहिं मोहि सोहाई । सगुन ब्रह्म रति उर अधिकाई ॥
nirguna mata nahiṁ mohi sohāī, saguna brahma rati ura adhikāī.

Trans:

Whatever body I assumed, whether of beast, god, or man, I invariably retained the practice of prayer to Rāma. The one regret that never left me was in the remembrance of the Gurū's mildness of temper and disposition. At last I took birth in the holy form of a Brahmin, a rank to which—as the Vedas and Purānas declare—it is difficult even for gods to attain. So joining in play with other children, I enacted all of Rāma's boyish sports. When I grew bigger, my father gave me lessons; but I neither understood, nor attended, nor gave my mind to anything; every other inclination clean deserted me and I was wholly absorbed in my devotion to Rāma's feet. Tell me, O king-of-birds, is there anyone so foolish, as to abandon the cow of plenty to tend to a she-donkey? I was so overwhelmed with love that naught else pleased me, and my father was quite tired of trying to teach me. After my parents had succumbed to fate, I went into the forest, to adore the Savior of beings. Wherever I discovered any great saints living in the woods, I frequently visited their hermitage and bowed before them, asking them all about Rāma's excellencies and listening, O Garud, with delight to what they told me. I went about everywhere hearing the tales of Harī's goodness, for by the blessing of Shambhu there was no check to my movements. The three kinds of evil concern had left me and I had only this one great longing at heart: "Ah, when I shall behold Rāma's lotus feet? Only then I shall account my life to have been worth living." Every sage, to whom I asked, told me thusly, "The Lord is present in all his creatures." But this doctrine of the Impersonal-God did not satisfy me; I felt an overpowering devotion towards the Incarnation of the Supreme-with-Form.

दोहा-dohā:

गुर के बचन सुरति करि राम चरन मनु लाग ।
gura ke bacana surati kari rāma carana manu lāga,
रघुपति जस गावत फिरउँ छन छन नव अनुराग ॥ ११०क॥
raghupati jasa gāvata phiraum̐ chana chana nava anurāga. 110(ka).
मेरु सिखर बट छायाँ मुनि लोमस आसीन ।
meru sikhara baṭa chāyām̐ muni lomasa āsīna,
देखि चरन सिरु नायउँ बचन कहेउँ अति दीन ॥ ११०ख॥
dekhi carana siru nāyaum̐ bacana kaheum̐ ati dīna. 110(kha).

सुनि मम बचन बिनीत मृदु मुनि कृपाल खगराज ।
suni mama bacana binīta mṛdu muni kṛpāla khagarāja,
मोहि सादर पूँछत भए द्विज आयहु केहि काज ॥ ११०ग॥
mohi sādara pūm̐chata bhae dvija āyahu kehi kāja. 110(ga).
तब मैं कहा कृपानिधि तुम्ह सर्बग्य सुजान ।
taba maiṁ kahā kṛpānidhi tumha sarbagya sujāna,
सगुन ब्रह्म अवराधन मोहि कहहु भगवान ॥ ११०घ॥
saguna brahma avarādhana mohi kahahu bhagavāna. 110(gha).

Trans:

Remembering the Gurū's words and with my mind fixed on Rāma's lotus-feet, I wandered about hymning his praises and my love every moment grew yet more and ever more. On one of the peaks of mount Meru under the shade of a Banyan sat the Saint Lomas. On seeing him I bowed my head at his feet and addressed him in most humble strains. No sooner, O Garud, had the beneficent sage heard my meek and submissive speech than he graciously enquired, "Say, O Brahmin, with what purpose you have come." Thereupon I replied, "Fountain of mercy, you are omniscient and all-wise; teach me, sire, how to worship the Incarnate-God."

चौपाई-caupāī:

तब मुनीस रघुपति गुन गाथा । कहे कछुक सादर खगनाथा ॥
taba munīsa raghupati guna gāthā, kahe kachuka sādara khaganāthā.
ब्रह्मग्यान रत मुनि बिग्यानी । मोहि परम अधिकारी जानी ॥
brahmagyāna rata muni bigyānī, mohi parama adhikārī jānī.

लागे करन ब्रह्म उपदेसा । अज अद्वैत अगुन हृदयेसा ॥
lāge karana brahma upadesā, aja advaita aguna hṛdayesā.
अकल अनीह अनाम अरुपा । अनुभव गम्य अखंड अनूपा ॥
akala anīha anāma arupā, anubhava gamya akhaṁḍa anūpā.
मन गोतीत अमल अबिनासी । निर्बिकार निरवधि सुख रासी ॥
mana gotīta amala abināsī, nirbikāra niravadhi sukha rāsī.
सो तैं ताहि तोहि नहिं भेदा । बारि बीचि इव गावहिं बेदा ॥
so taiṁ tāhi tohi nahiṁ bhedā, bāri bīci iva gāvahiṁ bedā.
बिबिधि भाँति मोहि मुनि समुझावा । निर्गुन मत मम हृदयँ न आवा ॥
bibidhi bhām̐ti mohi muni samujhāvā, nirguna mata mama hṛdayam̐ na āvā.
पुनि मैं कहेउँ नाइ पद सीसा । सगुन उपासन कहहु मुनीसा ॥
puni maiṁ kaheum̐ nāi pada sīsā, saguna upāsana kahahu munīsā.
राम भगति जल मम मन मीना । किमि बिलगाइ मुनीस प्रबीना ॥
rāma bhagati jala mama mana mīnā, kimi bilagāi munīsa prabīnā.
सोइ उपदेस कहहु करि दाया । निज नयनन्हि देखौं रघुराया ॥
soi upadesa kahahu kari dāyā, nija nayananhi dekhauṁ raghurāyā.
भरि लोचन बिलोकि अवधेसा । तब सुनिहउँ निर्गुन उपदेसा ॥
bhari locana biloki avadhesā, taba sunihaum̐ nirguna upadesā.
मुनि पुनि कहि हरिकथा अनूपा । खंडि सगुन मत अगुन निरूपा ॥
muni puni kahi harikathā anūpā, khaṁḍi saguna mata aguna nirūpā.
तब मैं निर्गुन मत कर दूरी । सगुन निरूपउँ करि हठ भूरी ॥
taba maiṁ nirguna mata kara dūrī, saguna nirūpaum̐ kari haṭha bhūrī.
उत्तर प्रतिउत्तर मैं कीन्हा । मुनि तन भए क्रोध के चीन्हा ॥
uttara pratiuttara maiṁ kīnhā, muni tana bhae krodha ke cīnhā.
सुनु प्रभु बहुत अवग्या किएँ । उपज क्रोध ग्यानिन्ह के हिएँ ॥
sunu prabhu bahuta avagyā kiem̐, upaja krodha gyāninha ke hiem̐.
अति संघरषन जौं कर कोई । अनल प्रगट चंदन ते होई ॥
ati saṁgharaṣana jauṁ kara koī, anala pragaṭa caṁdana te hoī.

Trans:

Thereupon, O Garud, the great saint spoke briefly though reverently of Rāma's virtues; and then, being himself a philosopher devoted to the mystery of the transcendental, and thinking that I had fully mastered the subject, he began a sermon on the Formless Brahmm—the unbegotten, the indivisible, the immaterial, the sovereign of the heart; unchangeable, unwishful, nameless, formless; approachable only by analogy, indestructible, incomparable; beyond the reach of thought or sense, spotless, immortal, emotionless, illimitable, blessed forever; identical with yourself, you and he being as absolutely one as a wave and its water; so the Vedas declare. The saint gave me the fullest possible instructions, but the worship of the Impersonal had no hold upon my soul. Again I cried, bowing my head to his feet, "Tell me, O holy father, how to worship the Incarnate. Devotion to Rāma, O wisest of sages, is like the element of water and my soul is, as it were, a fish; how can it exist without it? In your mercy, please instruct me so that I may see Rāma with my own eyes. When I have seen my fill of the Lord of Avadh, then I shall listen to your sermon on the Un-embodied." Again the saint discoursed of the incomparable Harī, and demolishing the dogma of Incarnation, expounded God as altogether void of qualities. But I rejected the theory of the abstract and with much obstinacy, insisted on the concrete manifestation. For every answer of his, I had a rejoinder ready. The saint at last showed signs of anger. Mark me, sir; I was so disrespectful that resentment was aroused even in the heart of a philosopher. An excessive amount of friction will strike fire even out of sandalwood.

दोहा-dohā:

बारंबार सकोप मुनि करइ निरुपन ग्यान ।
bāraṁbāra sakopa muni karai nirupana gyāna,
मैं अपनें मन बैठ तब करउँ बिबिधि अनुमान ॥ १११क॥
maiṁ apaneṁ mana baiṭha taba karaum̐ bibidhi anumāna. 111(ka).

क्रोध कि द्वैतबुद्धि बिनु द्वैत कि बिनु अग्यान ।
krodha ki dvaitabuddhi binu dvaita ki binu agyāna,
मायाबस परिछिन्न जड़ जीव कि ईस समान ॥ १११ख॥
māyābasa parichinna jaṛa jīva ki īsa samāna. 111(kha).

Trans:

Again and again the saint angrily expounded his theory, while I sat still and argued the matter from every point of view in my own mind, "Can there be anger without duality, or duality without ignorance? Can a soul, dull, circumscribed and subject to delusion, ever be at par with God?

चौपाई-caupāī:

कबहुँ कि दुख सब कर हित ताकें । तेहि कि दरिद्र परस मनि जाकें ॥
kabahum̐ ki dukha saba kara hita tākeṁ, tehi ki daridra parasa mani jākeṁ.
परद्रोही की होहिं निसंका । कामी पुनि कि रहहिं अकलंका ॥
paradrohī kī hohiṁ nisaṁkā, kāmī puni ki rahahiṁ akalaṁkā.
बंस कि रह द्विज अनहित कीन्हें । कर्म कि होहिं स्वरूपहि चीन्हें ॥
baṁsa ki raha dvija anahita kīnheṁ, karma ki hohiṁ svarūpahi cīnheṁ.
काहू सुमति कि खल सँग जामी । सुभ गति पाव कि परत्रिय गामी ॥
kāhū sumati ki khala saṁga jāmī, subha gati pāva ki paratriya gāmī.
भव कि परहिं परमात्मा बिंदक । सुखी कि होहिं कबहुँ हरि निंदक ॥
bhava ki parahiṁ paramātmā biṁdaka, sukhī ki hohiṁ kabahum̐ hari niṁdaka.
राजु कि रहइ नीति बिनु जानें । अघ कि रहहिं हरिचरित बखानें ॥
rāju ki rahai nīti binu jāneṁ, agha ki rahahiṁ haricarita bakhāneṁ.
पावन जस कि पुन्य बिनु होई । बिनु अघ अजस कि पावइ कोई ॥
pāvana jasa ki punya binu hoī, binu agha ajasa ki pāvai koī.
लाभु कि किछु हरि भगति समाना । जेहि गावहिं श्रुति संत पुराना ॥
lābhu ki kichu hari bhagati samānā, jehi gāvahiṁ śruti saṁta purānā.
हानि कि जग एहि सम किछु भाई । भजिअ न रामहि नर तनु पाई ॥
hāni ki jaga ehi sama kichu bhāī, bhajia na rāmahi nara tanu pāī.
अघ कि पिसुनता सम कछु आना । धर्म कि दया सरिस हरिजाना ॥
agha ki pisunatā sama kachu ānā, dharma ki dayā sarisa harijānā.
एहि बिधि अमिति जुगुति मन गुनऊँ । मुनि उपदेस न सादर सुनऊँ ॥
ehi bidhi amiti juguti mana gunaūm̐, muni upadesa na sādara sunaūm̐.
पुनि पुनि सगुन पच्छ मैं रोपा । तब मुनि बोलेउ बचन सकोपा ॥
puni puni saguna paccha maiṁ ropā, taba muni boleu bacana sakopā.
मूढ़ परम सिख देउँ न मानसि । उत्तर प्रतिउत्तर बहु आनसि ॥
mūṛha parama sikha deum̐ na mānasi, uttara pratiuttara bahu ānasi.
सत्य बचन बिस्वास न करही । बायस इव सबही ते डरही ॥
satya bacana bisvāsa na karahī, bāyasa iva sabahī te ḍarahī.
सठ स्वपच्छ तव हृदयँ बिसाला । सपदि होहि पच्छी चंडाला ॥
saṭha svapaccha tava hṛdayam̐ bisālā, sapadi hohi pacchī caṁḍālā.
लीन्ह श्राप मैं सीस चढ़ाई । नहिं कछु भय न दीनता आई ॥
līnha śrāpa maiṁ sīsa caṛhāī, nahiṁ kachu bhaya na dīnatā āī.

Trans:

Can pain under any circumstances be the same as pleasure? Can the possessor of the philosopher's stone suffer poverty? Can an oppressor be free from anxiety or a sensualist remains without reproach? Can a man's family prosper if he persecutes the Brahmins? Can religious observances be practiced by a man careful only for bodily comforts? Can sound doctrines be acquired by communion with the wicked? Can an adulterer attain to the felicity of the Blessed? Can a searcher after the Supreme Spirit escape from transmigration? Can a reviler of Harī be ever happy? Can a kingdom stand without knowledge of diplomacy? Can sin co-exist with a recital of Harī's virtues? Can spotless renown be acquired without religious merit? Can anyone be disgraced except by sin? Is there any gain like devotion to Harī, as hymned by the Vedas, the saints and the Purānas? Is there any loss, sir, in the whole world, like that of being born as a man and yet not worshipping Harī? Is there any other sin so bad as detraction, or any virtue, O Garud, so great as charity?" Thus I reasoned to myself with much ingenuity and could not listen with patience to the saint's instruction. Again and again, I maintained the doctrine of the Incarnation, till at last the saint uttered these angry words: "O fool, I have given you the most advanced teaching, but still you are not convinced and persist in your replies and rejoinders. You have no confidence in my veracious discourse, but like a crow suspect everything. Wretch, as your soul is so exceedingly self-opinionated, you shall at once be changed into a crow." I took the curse on my head, and felt neither frightened nor humiliated.

दोहा-dohā:

तुरत भयउँ मैं काग तब पुनि मुनि पद सिरु नाइ ।
turata bhayauṁ maiṁ kāga taba puni muni pada siru nāi,
सुमिरि राम रघुबंस मनि हरषित चलेउँ उड़ाइ ॥११२क॥
sumiri rāma raghubaṁsa mani harașita caleuṁ uṛāi. 112(ka).

उमा जे राम चरन रत बिगत काम मद क्रोध ।
umā je rāma carana rata bigata kāma mada krodha,
निज प्रभुमय देखहिं जगत केहि सन करहिं बिरोध ॥११२ख॥
nija prabhumaya dekhahiṁ jagata kehi sana karahiṁ birodha. 112(kha).

Trans:

Immediately I was turned into a crow. Then again I bowed my head at the saint's feet and mindful of Rāma, the jewel of the line of Raghu, I joyfully flew away. O Umā, they who devote themselves to Rāma's feet and abjure lust, pride and choler, they see their Lord present in everything: with what then can they quarrel?

चौपाई-caupāī:

सुनु खगेस नहिं कछु रिषि दूषन । उर प्रेरक रघुबंस बिभूषन ॥
sunu khagesa nahiṁ kachu riși dūșana, ura preraka raghubaṁsa bibhūșana.
कृपासिंधु मुनि मति करि भोरी । लीन्ही प्रेम परिच्छा मोरी ॥
kṛpāsiṁdhu muni mati kari bhorī, līnhī prema paricchā morī.
मन बच क्रम मोहि निज जन जाना । मुनि मति पुनि फेरी भगवाना ॥
mana baca krama mohi nija jana jānā, muni mati puni pherī bhagavānā.
रिषि मम महत सीलता देखी । राम चरन बिस्वास बिसेषी ॥
riși mama mahata sīlatā dekhī, rāma carana bisvāsa biseșī.
अति बिसमय पुनि पुनि पछिताई । सादर मुनि मोहि लीन्ह बोलाई ॥
ati bisamaya puni puni pachitāī, sādara muni mohi līnha bolāī.
मम परितोष बिबिधि बिधि कीन्हा । हरषित राममंत्र तब दीन्हा ॥
mama paritoșa bibidhi bidhi kīnhā, harașita rāmamaṁtra taba dīnhā.
बालकरूप राम कर ध्याना । कहेउ मोहि मुनि कृपानिधाना ॥
bālakarūpa rāma kara dhyānā, kaheu mohi muni kṛpānidhānā.
सुंदर सुखद मोहि अति भावा । सो प्रथमहिं मैं तुम्हहि सुनावा ॥
suṁdara sukhada mohi ati bhāvā, so prathamahiṁ maiṁ tumhahi sunāvā.
मुनि मोहि कछुक काल तहँ राखा । रामचरितमानस तब भाषा ॥
muni mohi kachuka kāla tahaṁ rākhā, rāmacaritamānasa taba bhāșā.
सादर मोहि यह कथा सुनाई । पुनि बोले मुनि गिरा सुहाई ॥
sādara mohi yaha kathā sunāī, puni bole muni girā suhāī.
रामचरित सर गुप्त सुहावा । संभु प्रसाद तात मैं पावा ॥
rāmacarita sara gupta suhāvā, saṁbhu prasāda tāta maiṁ pāvā.
तोहि निज भगत राम कर जानी । ताते मैं सब कहेउँ बखानी ॥
tohi nija bhagata rāma kara jānī, tāte maiṁ saba kaheuṁ bakhānī.
राम भगति जिन्ह कें उर नाहीं । कबहुँ न तात कहिअ तिन्ह पाहीं ॥
rāma bhagati jinha keṁ ura nāhīṁ, kabahuṁ na tāta kahia tinha pāhīṁ.
मुनि मोहि बिबिधि भाँति समुझावा । मैं सप्रेम मुनि पद सिरु नावा ॥
muni mohi bibidhi bhāṁti samujhāvā, maiṁ saprema muni pada siru nāvā.
निज कर कमल परसि मम सीसा । हरषित आसिष दीन्ह मुनीसा ॥
nija kara kamala parasi mama sīsā, harașita āsișa dīnha munīsā.
राम भगति अबिरल उर तोरें । बसिहि सदा प्रसाद अब मोरें ॥
rāma bhagati abirala ura toreṁ, basihi sadā prasāda aba moreṁ.

Trans:

Hearken, O king-of-birds; the saint was no way in fault; it was Rāma who had bestirred his soul. The All-merciful had confounded his intellect and thus made a trial of my love. When the Lord God had proved the thoroughness of my devotion, he restored the saint his senses. On beholding my great amiability and preeminent confidence in Rāma, the holy man was much astonished; repenting again and again, he courteously called me near. After consoling me in every possible way, he gladly taught me the spell by which Rāma is invoked, and in his infinite compassion told me how to meditate on his blessed child form. The beauty and sweetness of this form of devotion pleased me so well; and I have already told you all about it at the beginning. The saint kept me there for some little time and recited the whole of poem called Ramchartimanas—the Lake brimful of Rāma and his enactments and glories. When he had reverently completed the narrative, he finally addressed me in these gracious words, "By the blessing of Shambhu, my son, I discovered this secret and delectable fountain of song; I know you to be one of Rāma's most devoted servants and therefore I have told it all to you. Never repeat it, my son, in the presence of any whose heart is void of Rāma's love." The saint reiterated his instructions again and again, and I lovingly bowed my heat at his feet. He touched my head with his lotus hands and gladly gave me his blessing, "Henceforth by my favor an unalterable devotion to Rāma shall dwell forever in your heart.

दोहा-dohā:

सदा राम प्रिय होहु तुम्ह सुभ गुन भवन अमान ।
sadā rāma priya hohu tumha subha guna bhavana amāna,
कामरूप इच्छामरन ग्यान बिराग निधान ॥११३क॥
kāmarūpa icchāmarana gyāna birāga nidhāna. 113(ka).

जेहिं आश्रम तुम्ह बसब पुनि सुमिरत श्रीभगवंत ।
jehiṁ āśrama tumha basaba puni sumirata śrībhagavaṁta,
ब्यापिहि तहँ न अबिद्या जोजन एक प्रजंत ॥११३ख॥
byāpihi tahaṁ na abidyā jojana eka prajaṁta. 113(kha).

Trans:

Be forever Shri Rāma's best-loved; an illimitable store-house of all good qualities; changing your form at will and choosing your own time for death; a treasury of knowledge and asceticism. And may every hermitage—where you hereafter abide and make your prayer to the blessed Lord-God—be unapproachable by the spirit of Ignorance within the space of one league all around.

चौपाई-caupāī:

काल कर्म गुन दोष सुभाऊ । कछु दुख तुम्हहि न ब्यापिहि काऊ ॥
kāla karma guna doșa subhāū, kachu dukha tumhahi na byāpihi kāū.

राम रहस्य ललित बिधि नाना । गुप्त प्रगट इतिहास पुराना ॥
rāma rahasya lalita bidhi nānā, gupta pragaṭa itihāsa purānā.
बिनु श्रम तुम्ह जानब सब सोऊ । नित नव नेह राम पद होऊ ॥
binu śrama tumha jānaba saba soū, nita nava neha rāma pada hoū.
जो इच्छा करिहहु मन माहीं । हरि प्रसाद कछु दुर्लभ नाहीं ॥
jo icchā karihahu mana māhīṁ, hari prasāda kachu durlabha nāhīṁ.
सुनि मुनि आसिष सुनु मतिधीरा । ब्रह्मगिरा भइ गगन गँभीरा ॥
suni muni āsiṣa sunu matidhīrā, brahmagirā bhai gagana gaṁbhīrā.
एवमस्तु तव बच मुनि ग्यानी । यह मम भगत कर्म मन बानी ॥
evamastu tava baca muni gyānī, yaha mama bhagata karma mana bānī.
सुनि नभगिरा हरष मोहि भयऊ । प्रेम मगन सब संसय गयऊ ॥
suni nabhagirā haraṣa mohi bhayaū, prema magana saba saṁsaya gayaū.
करि बिनती मुनि आयसु पाई । पद सरोज पुनि पुनि सिरु नाई ॥
kari binatī muni āyasu pāī, pada saroja puni puni siru nāī.
हरष सहित एहिं आश्रम आयउँ । प्रभु प्रसाद दुर्लभ बर पायउँ ॥
haraṣa sahita ehiṁ āśrama āyauṁ, prabhu prasāda durlabha bara pāyauṁ.
इहाँ बसत मोहि सुनु खग ईसा । बीते कलप सात अरु बीसा ॥
ihāṁ basata mohi sunu khaga īsā, bīte kalapa sāta aru bīsā.
करउँ सदा रघुपति गुन गाना । सादर सुनहिं बिहंग सुजाना ॥
karauṁ sadā raghupati guna gānā, sādara sunahiṁ bihaṁga sujānā.
जब जब अवधपुरीं रघुबीरा । धरहिं भगत हित मनुज सरीरा ॥
jaba jaba avadhapurīṁ raghubīrā, dharahiṁ bhagata hita manuja sarīrā.
तब तब जाइ राम पुर रहऊँ । सिसुलीला बिलोकि सुख लहऊँ ॥
taba taba jāi rāma pura rahaūṁ, sisulīlā biloki sukha lahaūṁ.
पुनि उर राखि राम सिसुरूपा । निज आश्रम आवउँ खगभूपा ॥
puni ura rākhi rāma sisurūpā, nija āśrama āvauṁ khagabhūpā.
कथा सकल मैं तुम्हहि सुनाई । काग देह जेहिं कारन पाई ॥
kathā sakala maiṁ tumhahi sunāī, kāga deha jehiṁ kārana pāī.
कहिउँ तात सब प्रस्न तुम्हारी । राम भगति महिमा अति भारी ॥
kahiuṁ tāta saba prasna tumhārī, rāma bhagati mahimā ati bhārī.

Trans:

May neither time nor fate, merit, demerit nor circumstance ever cause you any vexation. May the unspeakably delightful mysteries of Rāma, the esoteric as well as the exoteric doctrines of the Chronicler and Purānas, be all comprehended by you without any difficulty, and may your affection for Rāma's feet increase day by day. May every desire that you form in your mind, by the blessing of Harī, be ever easy of attainment." On hearing the saint's benedictions—mark me, O firm of faith—this solemn voice rang from Brahmmā's abode, "May your words come to pass, O wisest of sages: he is my votary in thought, word and deed." When I heard the heavenly voice I rejoiced and was so drowned in love that all my doubts vanished. After making humble petition I received the saint's commands, and bowing again and again at his lotus feet, I took my leave and arrived with joy at this hermitage, having obtained by my Lord's favor an inestimable boon. During my stay here, mark me, O king-of-birds, seven and twenty cycles have elapsed. I incessantly repeat Rāma's praises, and the birds in their wisdom reverently listen. Whenever Raghubīr, in behoof of his votaries, takes upon him the form of a man at the city of Avadh, I go and stay at his capital and delight myself with the spectacle of his childish sports. Again, cherishing in my heart the image of the child Rāma I return, O Garud, to my own hermitage. I have now told you the whole history of the reason for which I was changed into a crow and have replied, sir, to all your questions. The efficacy of faith in Rāma is truly marvelous.

दोहा-dohā:

ताते यह तन मोहि प्रिय भयउ राम पद नेह ।
tāte yaha tana mohi priya bhayau rāma pada neha,
निज प्रभु दरसन पायउँ गए सकल संदेह ॥ ११४क॥
nija prabhu darasana pāyauṁ gae sakala saṁdeha. 114(ka).

Trans:

Therefore I love this form, in which my devotion to Rāma's feet has been exhibited, in which I have been favored with the sight of my Lord and all my doubts have been removed.

मासपारायण उन्तीसवाँ विश्राम
māsapārāyaṇa untīsavāṁ viśrāma
(Pause 29 for a Thirty-Day Recitation)

भगति पच्छ हठ करि रहेउँ दीन्हि महारिषि साप ।
bhagati paccha haṭha kari raheuṁ dīnhi mahāriṣi sāpa,
मुनि दुर्लभ बर पायउँ देखहु भजन प्रताप ॥ ११४ख॥
muni durlabha bara pāyauṁ dekhahu bhajana pratāpa. 114(kha).

Trans:

For my obstinacy in upholding the doctrine of devotion I was cursed by the seer, but eventually I obtained a boon which even the saints find difficult: see the efficacy of prayer.

चौपाई-caupāī:

जे असि भगति जानि परिहरहीं । केवल ग्यान हेतु श्रम करहीं ॥
je asi bhagati jāni pariharahīṁ, kevala gyāna hetu śrama karahīṁ.
ते जड़ कामधेनु गृहँ त्यागी । खोजत आकु फिरहिं पय लागी ॥
te jaṛa kāmadhenu gṛhaṁ tyāgī, khojata āku phirahiṁ paya lāgī.
सुनु खगेस हरि भगति बिहाई । जे सुख चाहहिं आन उपाई ॥
sunu khagesa hari bhagati bihāī, je sukha cāhahiṁ āna upāī.
ते सठ महासिंधु बिनु तरनी । पैरि पार चाहहिं जड़ करनी ॥
te saṭha mahāsiṁdhu binu taranī, pairi pāra cāhahiṁ jaṛa karanī.
सुनि भसुंडि के बचन भवानी । बोलेउ गरुड़ हरषि मृदु बानी ॥
suni bhasuṁḍi ke bacana bhavānī, boleu garuṛa haraṣi mṛdu bānī.
तव प्रसाद प्रभु मम उर माहीं । संसय सोक मोह भ्रम नाहीं ॥
tava prasāda prabhu mama ura māhīṁ, saṁsaya soka moha bhrama nāhīṁ.
सुनेउँ पुनीत राम गुन ग्रामा । तुम्हरी कृपाँ लहेउँ बिश्रामा ॥
suneuṁ punīta rāma guna grāmā, tumharī kṛpāṁ laheuṁ biśrāmā.
एक बात प्रभु पूँछउँ तोही । कहहु बुझाइ कृपानिधि मोही ॥
eka bāta prabhu pūṁchauṁ tohī, kahahu bujhāi kṛpānidhi mohī.
कहहिं संत मुनि बेद पुराना । नहिं कछु दुर्लभ ग्यान समाना ॥
kahahiṁ saṁta muni beda purānā, nahiṁ kachu durlabha gyāna samānā.
सोइ मुनि तुम्ह सन कहेउ गोसाईं । नहिं आदरेहु भगति की नाईं ॥
soi muni tumha sana kaheu gosāīṁ, nahiṁ ādarehu bhagati kī nāīṁ.
ग्यानहि भगतिहि अंतर केता । सकल कहहु प्रभु कृपा निकेता ॥
gyānahi bhagatihi aṁtara ketā, sakala kahahu prabhu kṛpā niketā.
सुनि उरगारि बचन सुख माना । सादर बोलेउ काग सुजाना ॥
suni uragāri bacana sukha mānā, sādara boleu kāga sujānā.
भगतिहि ग्यानहि नहिं कछु भेदा । उभय हरहिं भव संभव खेदा ॥
bhagatihi gyānahi nahiṁ kachu bhedā, ubhaya harahiṁ bhava saṁbhava khedā.
नाथ मुनीस कहहिं कछु अंतर । सावधान सोउ सुनु बिहंगबर ॥
nātha munīsa kahahiṁ kachu aṁtara, sāvadhāna sou sunu bihaṁgabara.
ग्यान बिराग जोग बिग्याना । ए सब पुरुष सुनहु हरिजाना ॥
gyāna birāga joga bigyānā, e saba puruṣa sunahu harijānā.

पुरुष प्रताप प्रबल सब भाँती । अबला अबल सहज जड़ जाती ॥
puruṣa pratāpa prabala saba bhāṁtī, abalā abala sahaja jaṛa jātī.

Trans:

They who knowingly reject such devotion and labor merely for wisdom are fools. Who would leave at home the cow of plenty and go out to look for the *Ak* plants to acquire milk? Hearken Garud; all who abandon the worship of Harī and seek to prosper by any other means are wretched blunderers who try to swim across the ocean without a boat." On hearing Bhusumdi's speech, O Bhawānī, Garud was glad and said in gentle tones, "By your favor, my Lord, every doubt, anxiety, error and delusion has been removed from my heart. Through your clemency I have heard the holy tale of Rāma's achievements and have gained peace. There is still one matter, sir, about which I would ask; in your infinite compassion be pleased to enlighten me. The saints and sages, the Vedas and Purānas, all say there is nothing so difficult of attainment as Wisdom. But the saint told you, father, that there is nothing so estimable as Devotion. Explain to me, most gracious Lord, all the difference between Devotion and Wisdom." The sagacious crow was pleased to hear Garud's question and courteously replied, "In essence, there is no difference between Devotion and Wisdom—for both put an end to the troubles incident to existence. Great sages nonetheless point out some difference between the two, my lord; now listen to the same with rapt attention, O chief of the birds. Wisdom, dispassion, Yoga and Realization—mark me—are all masculine in conception, O Garud! Now the masculine character is altogether strong, while the feminine is weak and submissive by nature.

दोहा-dohā:

पुरुष त्यागि सक नारिहि जो बिरक्त मति धीर ।
puruṣa tyāgi saka nārihi jo birakta mati dhīra,
न तु कामी बिषयाबस बिमुख जो पद रघुबीर ॥ ११५क ॥
na tu kāmī biṣayābasa bimukha jo pada raghubīra. 115(ka).

Trans:

That man alone can forswear woman who be self-restrained and resolute; and it is impossible for the sensual voluptuary who has no regard for Harī's feet.

सोरठा-soraṭhā:

सोउ मुनि ग्याननिधान मृगनयनी बिधु मुख निरखि ।
sou muni gyānanidhāna mṛganayanī bidhu mukha nirakhi,
बिबस होइ हरिजान नारि बिष्नु माया प्रगट ॥ ११५ख ॥
bibasa hoi harijāna nāri biṣnu māyā pragaṭa. 115(kha).

Trans:

Even a saint and a philosopher, O Garud, is distracted at the sight of a woman, with her fawn-like eyes and moon-bright face. It is God Vishnu's own Māyā that manifests itself in the form of a woman!

चौपाई-caupāī:

इहाँ न पच्छपात कछु राखउँ । बेद पुरान संत मत भाषउँ ॥
ihāṁ na pacchapāta kachu rākhauṁ, beda purāna saṁta mata bhāṣauṁ.
मोह न नारि नारि कें रूपा । पन्नगारि यह रीति अनूपा ॥
moha na nāri nāri keṁ rūpā, pannagāri yaha rīti anūpā.
माया भगति सुनहु तुम्ह दोऊ । नारि बर्ग जानइ सब कोऊ ॥
māyā bhagati sunahu tumha doū, nāri barga jānai saba koū.
पुनि रघुबीरहि भगति पिआरी । माया खलु नर्तकी बिचारी ॥
puni raghubīrahi bhagati piārī, māyā khalu nartakī bicārī.
भगतिहि सानुकूल रघुराया । ताते तेहि डरपति अति माया ॥
bhagatihi sānukūla raghurāyā, tāte tehi ḍarapati ati māyā.
राम भगति निरुपम निरुपाधी । बसइ जासु उर सदा अबाधी ॥
rāma bhagati nirupama nirupādhī, basai jāsu ura sadā abādhī.
तेहि बिलोकि माया सकुचाई । करि न सकइ कछु निज प्रभुताई ॥
tehi biloki māyā sakucāī, kari na sakai kachu nija prabhutāī.
अस बिचारि जे मुनि बिग्यानी । जाचहिं भगति सकल सुख खानी ॥
asa bicāri je muni bigyānī, jācahiṁ bhagati sakala sukha khānī.

Trans:

Here I maintain no private theory of my own. I only declare the doctrine of the Vedas, Purānas and the saints. A woman is never enamoured of another woman's beauty: this, O enemy of the serpents, is a strange phenomenon. Observe: Māyā and Devotion are both of the feminine gender, as everyone knows. Again, Devotion is the beloved of Rāma, while he regards Māyā as a mere dancing girl. Rāma being thus amiable to Devotion, Māyā is greatly afraid of her. Devotion for Rāma is incomparable and illimitable, and he in whose heart she abides is ever blessed. Māyā, at the sight of her, is confounded and can do nothing of her own power. Knowing this, the most enlightened sages attest Devotion to be the source of every blessing.

दोहा-dohā:

यह रहस्य रघुनाथ कर बेगि न जानइ कोइ ।
yaha rahasya raghunātha kara begi na jānai koi,
जो जानइ रघुपति कृपाँ सपनेहुँ मोह न होइ ॥ ११६क ॥
jo jānai raghupati kṛpāṁ sapanehuṁ moha na hoi. 116(ka).

औरउ ग्यान भगति कर भेद सुनहु सुप्रबीन ।
aurau gyāna bhagati kara bheda sunahu suprabīna,
जो सुनि होइ राम पद प्रीति सदा अबिछीन ॥ ११६ख ॥
jo suni hoi rāma pada prīti sadā abichīna. 116(kha).

Trans:

This mystery of Raghunāth's, no one can grasp all at once; but whoever does comprehend it by his favor, is never subject to any delusion even in sleep. Further now, hearken with your best intelligence to the distinction between Wisdom and Devotion, by the hearing of which, is induced the imperishable devotion to Rāma's feet.

चौपाई-caupāī:

सुनहु तात यह अकथ कहानी । समुझत बनइ न जाइ बखानी ॥
sunahu tāta yaha akatha kahānī, samujhata banai na jāi bakhānī.
ईस्वर अंस जीव अबिनासी । चेतन अमल सहज सुखरासी ॥
īsvara aṁsa jīva abināsī, cetana amala sahaja sukharāsī.
सो मायाबस भयउ गोसाईं । बँध्यो कीर मरकट की नाईं ॥
so māyābasa bhayau gosāīṁ, baṁdhyo kīra marakaṭa kī nāīṁ.
जड़ चेतनहि ग्रंथि परि गई । जदपि मृषा छूटत कठिनई ॥
jaṛa cetanahi graṁthi pari gaī, jadapi mṛṣā chūṭata kaṭhinaī.
तब ते जीव भयउ संसारी । छूट न ग्रंथि न होइ सुखारी ॥
taba te jīva bhayau saṁsārī, chūṭa na graṁthi na hoi sukhārī.
श्रुति पुरान बहु कहेउ उपाई । छूट न अधिक अधिक अरुझाई ॥
śruti purāna bahu kaheu upāī, chūṭa na adhika adhika arujhāī.
जीव हृदयँ तम मोह बिसेषी । ग्रंथि छूट किमि परइ न देखी ॥
jīva hṛdayaṁ tama moha biseṣī, graṁthi chūṭa kimi parai na dekhī.
अस संजोग ईस जब करई । तबहुँ कदाचित सो निरुअरई ॥
asa saṁjoga īsa jaba karaī, tabahuṁ kadācita so niruaraī.
सात्त्विक श्रद्धा धेनु सुहाई । जौं हरि कृपाँ हृदयँ बस आई ॥
sāttvika śraddhā dhenu suhāī, jauṁ hari kṛpāṁ hṛdayaṁ basa āī.
जप तप ब्रत जम नियम अपारा । जे श्रुति कह सुभ धर्म अचारा ॥
japa tapa brata jama niyama apārā, je śruti kaha subha dharma acārā.
तेइ तृन हरित चरै जब गाई । भाव बच्छ सिसु पाइ पेन्हाई ॥
tei tṛna harita carai jaba gāī, bhāva baccha sisu pāi penhāī.

नोइ निबृत्ति पात्र बिस्वासा । निर्मल मन अहीर निज दासा ॥
noi nibṛtti pātra bisvāsā, nirmala mana ahīra nija dāsā.
परम धर्ममय पय दुहि भाई । अवटै अनल अकाम बनाई ॥
parama dharmamaya paya duhi bhāī, avaṭai anala akāma banāī.
तोष मरुत तब छमाँ जुड़ावै । धृति सम जावनु देइ जमावै ॥
toṣa maruta taba chamām̐ juṛāvai, dhṛti sama jāvanu dei jamāvai.
मुदिताँ मथै बिचार मथानी । दम अधार रजु सत्य सुबानी ॥
muditām̐ mathai bicāra mathānī, dama adhāra raju satya subānī.
तब मथि काढ़ि लेइ नवनीता । बिमल बिराग सुभग सुपुनीता ॥
taba mathi kāṛhi lei navanītā, bimala birāga subhaga supunītā.

Trans:

Attend, my dear, to this unutterable utterance, which in truth is incapable of expression—and only mentally conceived: The soul is a particle of the divinity, immortal, intelligent, pure and naturally blissful. But sir, being overcome by Māyā, it is caught, as it were a parrot or monkey. The enfeebled intellect is bound with a knot, which though imaginary is difficult to untie. Thus the soul becomes worldly; there is no loosing the knot and it knows no happiness. The Vedas and Purānas have declared many remedies; but there is no getting free—perhaps the entanglement is rather increased. The inside of the heart is full of the darkness of delusion and it cannot see how the knot can be untied. When God brings about such a complication, escape is knotty tough. If, by Harī's favor, a spirit of sincere piety—alike a beautiful cow—comes and dwells in the heart, then the prayers, penance and fasts and all the religious observances and acts of devotion, which the Vedas have inculcated as meritorious practices, are as it were a green pasture for the cow to graze in. The calf, which fills her teats with milk, is love; the heel-rope with which she is bound is the spirit of quietism; the milk-bowl the faith; and the herdsman who tends her is the spotless soul. After drawing off the milk of sound religion, it is set to boil on the fire of continence. Forbearance then cools it with the breath of patience; and perseverance is the rennet that coagulates it into curds. Again, contentment is the maid who churns it in the bowl of discretion, with self-restraint for the stick, and truth and good words as the cord. By such churning, is produced the butter of pure, excellent and holy asceticism.

दोहा-dohā:

जोग अगिनि करि प्रगट तब कर्म सुभासुभ लाइ ।
joga agini kari pragaṭa taba karma subhāsubha lāi,
बुद्धि सिरावै ग्यान घृत ममता मल जरि जाइ ॥ ११७क॥
buddhi sirāvai gyāna ghṛta mamatā mala jari jāi. 117(ka).

तब बिग्यानरूपिनि बुद्धि बिसद घृत पाइ ।
taba bigyānarūpini buddhi bisada ghṛta pāi,
चित्त दिआ भरि धरै दृढ़ समता दिअटि बनाइ ॥ ११७ख॥
citta diā bhari dharai dṛṛha samatā diaṭi banāi. 117(kha).

तीनि अवस्था तीनि गुन तेहि कपास तें काढ़ि ।
tīni avasthā tīni guna tehi kapāsa teṁ kāṛhi,
तूल तुरीय सँवारि पुनि बाती करै सुगाढ़ि ॥ ११७ग॥
tūla turīya sam̐vāri puni bātī karai sugāṛhi. 117(ga).

Trans:

After kindling the flame of meditation and applying actions both good and bad, Intelligence allows the ghee of wisdom to cool, but bums all the scum of selfishness in the fire. Then Intelligence, master of highest wisdom, takes this absolutely pure ghee, and filling with it the lamp of the soul sets it on the stand of equanimity. Then extracting from the cotton the soul's three conditions and the three properties, it works up the clean fiber of the fourth state and fashions it into an excellent candle.

सोरठा-sorațhā:

एहि बिधि लेसै दीप तेज रासि बिग्यानमय ।
ehi bidhi lesai dīpa teja rāsi bigyānamaya,
जातहिं जासु समीप जरहिं मदादिक सलभ सब ॥ ११७घ॥
jātahiṁ jāsu samīpa jarahiṁ madādika salabha saba. 117(gha).

Trans:

In this manner is kindled a splendid torch of knowledge, and the gnat-like swarms of vanity and other vices on approaching it are consumed by it.

चौपाई-caupāī:

सोहमस्मि इति बृत्ति अखंडा । दीप सिखा सोइ परम प्रचंडा ॥
sohamasmi iti bṛtti akhaṁḍā, dīpa sikhā soi parama pracaṁḍā.
आतम अनुभव सुख सुप्रकासा । तब भव मूल भेद भ्रम नासा ॥
ātama anubhava sukha suprakāsā, taba bhava mūla bheda bhrama nāsā.
प्रबल अबिद्या कर परिवारा । मोह आदि तम मिटइ अपारा ॥
prabala abidyā kara parivārā, moha ādi tama miṭai apārā.
तब सोइ बुद्धि पाइ उँजिआरा । उर गृहँ बैठि ग्रंथि निरुआरा ॥
taba soi buddhi pāi um̐jiārā, ura gṛham̐ baiṭhi graṁthi niruārā.
छोरन ग्रंथि पाव जौं सोई । तब यह जीव कृतारथ होई ॥
chorana graṁthi pāva jauṁ soī, taba yaha jīva kṛtāratha hoī.
छोरत ग्रंथि जानि खगराया । बिघ्न अनेक करइ तब माया ॥
chorata graṁthi jāni khagarāyā, bighna aneka karai taba māyā.
रिद्धि सिद्धि प्रेरइ बहु भाई । बुद्धिहि लोभ दिखावहिं आई ॥
riddhi siddhi prerai bahu bhāī, buddhihi lobha dikhāvahiṁ āī.
कल बल छल करि जाहिं समीपा । अंचल बात बुझावहिं दीपा ॥
kala bala chala kari jāhiṁ samīpā, aṁcala bāta bujhāvahiṁ dīpā.
होइ बुद्धि जौं परम सयानी । तिन्ह तन चितव न अनहित जानी ॥
hoi buddhi jauṁ parama sayānī, tinha tana citava na anahita jānī.
जौं तेहि बिघ्न बुद्धि नहिं बाधी । तौ बहोरि सुर करहिं उपाधी ॥
jauṁ tehi bighna buddhi nahiṁ bādhī, tau bahori sura karahiṁ upādhī.
इंद्री द्वार झरोखा नाना । तहँ तहँ सुर बैठे करि थाना ॥
iṁdrī dvāra jharokhā nānā, taham̐ taham̐ sura baiṭhe kari thānā.
आवत देखहिं बिषय बयारी । ते हठि देहिं कपाट उघारी ॥
āvata dekhahiṁ biṣaya bayārī, te haṭhi dehiṁ kapāṭa ughārī.
जब सो प्रभंजन उर गृहँ जाई । तबहिं दीप बिग्यान बुझाई ॥
jaba so prabhaṁjana ura gṛham̐ jāī, tabahiṁ dīpa bigyāna bujhāī.
ग्रंथि न छूटि मिटा सो प्रकासा । बुद्धि बिकल भइ बिषय बतासा ॥
graṁthi na chūṭi miṭā so prakāsā, buddhi bikala bhai biṣaya batāsā.
इंद्रिन्ह सुरन्ह न ग्यान सोहाई । बिषय भोग पर प्रीति सदाई ॥
iṁdrinha suranha na gyāna sohāī, biṣaya bhoga para prīti sadāī.
बिषय समीर बुद्धि कृत भोरी । तेहि बिधि दीप को बार बहोरी ॥
biṣaya samīra buddhi kṛta bhorī, tehi bidhi dīpa ko bāra bahorī.

Trans:

The unalterable persuasion of the identification of the soul with God is its pre-eminently brilliant flame; and the happiness that results from this knowledge of self is the light it diffuses, by which it destroys the erroneous distinctions which are born of the world. Delusion and all the other forms of darkness that attend upon tyrant Ignorance are then utterly dispersed. Thus Intelligence, having procured a light, sits in the chamber of the heart and tries to loosen the knot. And should he succeed in untying it, the soul obtains its object. But when Māyā, O Garud, sees him loosening the knot, she creates many difficulties and sends forth, sir, innumerable *Riddhi*s and *Siddhi*s as obstacles and for exciting his concupiscence. In some way or other, by force or by fraud, they get near and try to put out the lamp by a side puff. If Intelligence is altogether wise, he perceives their hostile intent and will not look at them. Should he escape free from this danger, it is the gods then who proceed to attack him. The faculties of sense are the so many portals, at each of which a god sits on guard. When they see any sensual air stirring, they at once throw the doors wide open. If the blast penetrates the chamber of the soul, it forthwith extinguishes the lamp of Wisdom. When its light is put out, there is no untying the knot, for Intelligence is undone by this blast of sensuality. Neither the senses nor the gods approve of Wisdom; they are always inclined to sensual enjoyment. When Intelligence has been thus fooled by the breath of sensuality, who can then light the lamp again as before?

दोहा-dohā:

तब फिरि जीव बिबिधि बिधि पावइ संसृति क्लेस ।
taba phiri jīva bibidhi bidhi pāvai saṁsṛti klesa,
हरि माया अति दुस्तर तरि न जाइ बिहगेस ॥ ११८क॥
hari māyā ati dustara tari na jāi bihagesa. 118(ka).

कहत कठिन समुझत कठिन साधत कठिन बिबेक ।
kahata kaṭhina samujhata kaṭhina sādhata kaṭhina bibeka,
होइ घुनाच्छर न्याय जौं पुनि प्रत्यूह अनेक ॥ ११८ख॥
hoi ghunācchara nyāya jauṁ puni pratyūha aneka. 118(kha).

Trans:

Then the soul is again subjected to all the manifold miseries of transmigration. O Garud, Harī's delusive power is a trackless ocean that none can traverse. Wisdom is difficult to describe, difficult to understand, difficult to master, and if by any lucky chance a right judgment be formed, still many impediments block the way.

चौपाई-caupāī:

ग्यान पंथ कृपान कै धारा । परत खगेस होइ नहिं बारा ॥
gyāna paṁtha kṛpāna kai dhārā, parata khagesa hoi nahiṁ bārā.
जो निर्बिघ्न पंथ निर्बहई । सो कैवल्य परम पद लहई ॥
jo nirbighna paṁtha nirbahaī, so kaivalya parama pada lahaī.
अति दुर्लभ कैवल्य परम पद । संत पुरान निगम आगम बद ॥
ati durlabha kaivalya parama pada, saṁta purāna nigama āgama bada.
राम भजत सोइ मुकुति गोसाईं । अनइच्छित आवइ बरिआईं ॥
rāma bhajata soi mukuti gosāīṁ, anaicchita āvai bariāīṁ.
जिमि थल बिनु जल रहि न सकाई । कोटि भाँति कोउ करै उपाई ॥
jimi thala binu jala rahi na sakāī, koṭi bhāṁti kou karai upāī.
तथा मोच्छ सुख सुनु खगराई । रहि न सकइ हरि भगति बिहाई ॥
tathā moccha sukha sunu khagarāī, rahi na sakai hari bhagati bihāī.
अस बिचारि हरि भगत सयाने । मुक्ति निरादर भगति लुभाने ॥
asa bicāri hari bhagata sayāne, mukti nirādara bhagati lubhāne.
भगति करत बिनु जतन प्रयासा । संसृति मूल अबिद्या नासा ॥
bhagati karata binu jatana prayāsā, saṁsṛti mūla abidyā nāsā.
भोजन करिअ तृपिति हित लागी । जिमि सो असन पचवै जठरागी ॥
bhojana karia tṛpiti hita lāgī, jimi so asana pacavai jaṭharāgī.
असि हरि भगति सुगम सुखदाई । को अस मूढ़ न जाहि सोहाई ॥
asi hari bhagati sugama sukhadāī, ko asa mūṛha na jāhi sohāī.

Trans:

The path of Wisdom is like the edge of a scimitar; for those who fall on it, Garud, there is no escape. If any traverse the path in spite of its difficulty, they attain to the supreme sphere of beatitude. But this exalted felicity is immensely hard of attainment—as is declared by the saints, the Purānas, the Vedas and all the Scriptures. Now contrast this with Devotion: By the worship of Rāma, sir, that same beatitude comes freely of its own accord. As water cannot stay without some support, however much you may try to make it, in like manner, mark me, Garud, the joy of final salvation cannot be secured without the worship of Harī. The wisest of Harī's worshippers know this, and thinking lightly of the soul's deliverance from the body, crave much rather for Devotion than Wisdom. By Devotion, without any trouble or difficulty, the ignorance that arises from mundane existence is utterly destroyed with no effort on our part—just like we eat for our gratification and make only that effort, but the digestion happens automatically, on its own without conscious effort. What fool is there who does not welcome such easy path of Devotion to Rāma, which is at the same time such delightful?

दोहा-dohā:

सेवक सेब्य भाव बिनु भव न तरिअ उरगारि ।
sevaka sebya bhāva binu bhava na taria uragāri,
भजहु राम पद पंकज अस सिद्धांत बिचारि ॥ ११९क॥
bhajahu rāma pada paṁkaja asa siddhāṁta bicāri. 119(ka).

जो चेतन कहँ जड़ करइ जड़हि करइ चैतन्य ।
jo cetana kahaṁ zaṛa karai zaṛahi karai caitanya,
अस समर्थ रघुनायकहि भजहिं जीव ते धन्य ॥ ११९ख॥
asa samartha raghunāyakahi bhajahiṁ jīva te dhanya. 119(kha).

Trans:

Impossible it is to cross this ocean of transmigration, except by cultivating the same feeling towards Shri Rāma as a servant cherishes towards his master. Worship then the lotus feet of Shri Rāma, knowing this to be the culmination of every doctrine. Raghunāth can make the living dead and the dead alive; blessed are the souls that worship Rāma.

चौपाई-caupāī:

कहेउँ ग्यान सिद्धांत बुझाई । सुनहु भगति मनि कै प्रभुताई ॥
kaheuṁ gyāna siddhāṁta bujhāī, sunahu bhagati mani kai prabhutāī.
राम भगति चिंतामनि सुंदर । बसइ गरुड़ जाके उर अंतर ॥
rāma bhagati ciṁtāmani suṁdara, basai garuṛa jāke ura aṁtara.
परम प्रकास रूप दिन राती । नहिं कछु चहिअ दिआ घृत बाती ॥
parama prakāsa rūpa dina rātī, nahiṁ kachu cahia diā ghṛta bātī.
मोह दरिद्र निकट नहिं आवा । लोभ बात नहिं ताहि बुझावा ॥
moha daridra nikaṭa nahiṁ āvā, lobha bāta nahiṁ tāhi bujhāvā.
प्रबल अबिद्या तम मिटि जाई । हारहिं सकल सलभ समुदाई ॥
prabala abidyā tama miṭi jāī, hārahiṁ sakala salabha samudāī.
खल कामादि निकट नहिं जाहीं । बसइ भगति जाके उर माहीं ॥
khala kāmādi nikaṭa nahiṁ jāhīṁ, basai bhagati jāke ura māhīṁ.
गरल सुधासम अरि हित होई । तेहि मनि बिनु सुख पाव न कोई ॥
garala sudhāsama ari hita hoī, tehi mani binu sukha pāva na koī.
ब्यापहिं मानस रोग न भारी । जिन्ह के बस सब जीव दुखारी ॥
byāpahiṁ mānasa roga na bhārī, jinha ke basa saba jīva dukhārī.
राम भगति मनि उर बस जाकें । दुख लवलेस न सपनेहुँ ताकें ॥
rāma bhagati mani ura basa jākeṁ, dukha lavalesa na sapanehuṁ tākeṁ.
चतुर सिरोमनि तेइ जग माहीं । जे मनि लागि सुजतन कराहीं ॥
catura siromani tei jaga māhīṁ, je mani lāgi sujatana karāhīṁ.
सो मनि जदपि प्रगट जग अहई । राम कृपा बिनु नहिं कोउ लहई ॥
so mani jadapi pragaṭa jaga ahaī, rāma kṛpā binu nahiṁ kou lahaī.
सुगम उपाय पाइबे केरे । नर हतभाग्य देहिं भटभेरे ॥
sugama upāya pāibe kere, nara hatabhāgya dehiṁ bhaṭabhere.
पावन पर्बत बेद पुराना । राम कथा रुचिराकर नाना ॥
pāvana parbata beda purānā, rāma kathā rucirākara nānā.

मर्मी सज्जन सुमति कुदारी । ग्यान बिराग नयन उरगारी ॥
marmī sajjana sumati kudārī, gyāna birāga nayana uragārī.
भाव सहित खोजइ जो प्रानी । पाव भगति मनि सब सुख खानी ॥
bhāva sahita khojai jo prānī, pāva bhagati mani saba sukha khānī.
मोरें मन प्रभु अस बिस्वासा । राम ते अधिक राम कर दासा ॥
moreṁ mana prabhu asa bisvāsā, rāma te adhika rāma kara dāsā.
राम सिंधु घन सज्जन धीरा । चंदन तरु हरि संत समीरा ॥
rāma siṁdhu ghana sajjana dhīrā, caṁdana taru hari saṁta samīrā.
सब कर फल हरि भगति सुहाई । सो बिनु संत न काहूँ पाई ॥
saba kara phala hari bhagati suhāī, so binu saṁta na kāhūm̐ pāī.
अस बिचारि जोइ कर सतसंगा । राम भगति तेहि सुलभ बिहंगा ॥
asa bicāri joi kara satasaṁgā, rāma bhagati tehi sulabha bihaṁgā.

Trans:

I have thus stated and expounded the Science of Wisdom, or Gyan; hear now the virtue of that jewel called Devotion. Devotion to Rāma is a glorious philosopher's stone; in whosoever heart it dwells, Garud, there night and day is an infinite splendor—a lamp that never requires to be fed with oil. Delusion and poverty come not near; no blast of covetousness ever extinguishes it. The gloom of overpowering Ignorance is dispersed; the swarms of gnats are all destroyed. Neither vile lust nor any other vice approaches the soul in which Devotion abides. It changes poison to ambrosia, enemies to friends, and without this jewel no one can attain to happiness. Those grievous mental diseases, by the influence of which all living creatures are rendered miserable, have no effect upon him in whose heart is the jewel called Devotion; not even in a dream can he feel the slightest iota of pain. They are the true paragons of wisdom—who labor persistently to secure this jewel. Although this jewel is manifest all around, yet without Rāma's grace none can find it. There are easy devices for finding it, but luckless wights attempt harder methods. The Vedas and Purānas are the holy mountains, the legends of Rāma it's many glorious mines; the pious are the discoverers; and good counsel is their pick-axe; while wisdom and asceticism, O Garud, are their eyes. Any creature who looks for it with faith succeeds in finding the Jewel of Devotion—in itself a mine of every blessing. I have in my mind this conviction sir: that a servant of Rāma's is greater than Rāma himself. Rāma is the sea, the good and pious are the rain-clouds. Harī is the sandal tree and the saints are the winds that diffuse its perfume. Faith in Harī is a delight and the crown of all desire, but it cannot be had without the saints. Anyone, Garud, who understands this and communes with the saints will find Devotion to Rāma easy to attain.

दोहा-dohā:

ब्रह्म पयोनिधि मंदर ग्यान संत सुर आहिं ।
brahma payonidhi maṁdara gyāna saṁta sura āhiṁ,
कथा सुधा मथि काढ़हिं भगति मधुरता जाहिं ॥ १२०क॥
kathā sudhā mathi kāṛhahiṁ bhagati madhuratā jāhiṁ. 120(ka).

बिरति चर्म असि ग्यान मद लोभ मोह रिपु मारि ।
birati carma asi gyāna mada lobha moha ripu māri,
जय पाइअ सो हरि भगति देखु खगेस बिचारि ॥ १२०ख॥
jaya pāia so hari bhagati dekhu khagesa bicāri. 120(kha).

Trans:

The Supreme Spirit is the ocean, wisdom is mount Mandara and the saints are the gods, who churn out the nectar in the form of sacred legends, which has Devotion as its sweetness. Wielding the shield of Self-control, and with wisdom as the sword with which to slay the enemy: Pride, Greed and Delusion—the Devotion to Harī always persists supremely triumphant; ponder and realize this, O king-of-birds."

चौपाई-caupāī:

पुनि सप्रेम बोलेउ खगराऊ । जौं कृपाल मोहि ऊपर भाऊ ॥
puni saprema boleu khagarāū, jauṁ kṛpāla mohi ūpara bhāū.
नाथ मोहि निज सेवक जानी । सप्त प्रस्न मम कहहु बखानी ॥
nātha mohi nija sevaka jānī, sapta prasna mama kahahu bakhānī.
प्रथमहिं कहहु नाथ मतिधीरा । सब ते दुर्लभ कवन सरीरा ॥
prathamahiṁ kahahu nātha matidhīrā, saba te durlabha kavana sarīrā.
बड़ दुख कवन कवन सुख भारी । सोउ संछेपहिं कहहु बिचारी ॥
baṛa dukha kavana kavana sukha bhārī, sou saṁchepahiṁ kahahu bicārī.
संत असंत मरम तुम्ह जानहु । तिन्ह कर सहज सुभाव बखानहु ॥
saṁta asaṁta marama tumha jānahu, tinha kara sahaja subhāva bakhānahu.
कवन पुन्य श्रुति बिदित बिसाला । कहहु कवन अघ परम कराला ॥
kavana punya śruti bidita bisālā, kahahu kavana agha parama karālā.
मानस रोग कहहु समुझाई । तुम्ह सर्बग्य कृपा अधिकाई ॥
mānasa roga kahahu samujhāī, tumha sarbagya kṛpā adhikāī.
तात सुनहु सादर अति प्रीती । मैं संछेप कहउँ यह नीती ॥
tāta sunahu sādara ati prītī, maiṁ saṁchepa kahauṁ yaha nītī.
नर तन सम नहिं कवनिउ देही । जीव चराचर जाचत तेही ॥
nara tana sama nahiṁ kavaniu dehī, jīva carācara jācata tehī.
नरक स्वर्ग अपबर्ग निसेनी । ग्यान बिराग भगति सुभ देनी ॥
naraka svarga apabarga nisenī, gyāna birāga bhagati subha denī.
सो तनु धरि हरि भजहिं न जे नर । होहिं बिषय रत मंद मंद तर ॥
so tanu dhari hari bhajahiṁ na je nara, hohiṁ biṣaya rata maṁda maṁda tara.
काँच किरिच बदलें ते लेही । कर ते डारि परस मनि देहीं ॥
kām̐ca kirica badaleṁ te lehī, kara te ḍāri parasa mani dehīṁ.
नहिं दरिद्र सम दुख जग माहीं । संत मिलन सम सुख जग नाहीं ॥
nahiṁ daridra sama dukha jaga māhīṁ, saṁta milana sama sukha jaga nāhīṁ.
पर उपकार बचन मन काया । संत सहज सुभाउ खगराया ॥
para upakāra bacana mana kāyā, saṁta sahaja subhāu khagarāyā.
संत सहहिं दुख परहित लागी । परदुख हेतु असंत अभागी ॥
saṁta sahahiṁ dukha parahita lāgī, paradukha hetu asaṁta abhāgī.
भूर्ज तरू सम संत कृपाला । परहित निति सह बिपति बिसाला ॥
bhūrja tarū sama saṁta kṛpālā, parahita niti saha bipati bisālā.
सन इव खल पर बंधन करई । खाल कढ़ाइ बिपति सहि मरई ॥
sana iva khala para baṁdhana karaī, khāla kaṛhāi bipati sahi maraī.
खल बिनु स्वारथ पर अपकारी । अहि मूषक इव सुनु उरगारी ॥
khala binu svāratha para apakārī, ahi mūṣaka iva sunu uragārī.
पर संपदा बिनासि नसाहीं । जिमि ससि हति हिम उपल बिलाहीं ॥
para saṁpadā bināsi nasāhīṁ, jimi sasi hati hima upala bilāhīṁ.
दुष्ट उदय जग आरति हेतू । जथा प्रसिद्ध अधम ग्रह केतू ॥
duṣṭa udaya jaga ārati hetū, jathā prasiddha adhama graha ketū.
संत उदय संतत सुखकारी । बिस्व सुखद जिमि इंदु तमारी ॥
saṁta udaya saṁtata sukhakārī, bisva sukhada jimi iṁdu tamārī.
परम धर्म श्रुति बिदित अहिंसा । पर निंदा सम अघ न गरीसा ॥
parama dharma śruti bidita ahiṁsā, para niṁdā sama agha na garīsā.
हर गुर निंदक दादुर होई । जन्म सहस्र पाव तन सोई ॥
hara gura niṁdaka dādura hoī, janma sahasra pāva tana soī.
द्विज निंदक बहु नरक भोग करि । जग जनमइ बायस सरीर धरि ॥

dvija niṁdaka bahu naraka bhoga kari, jaga janamai bāyasa sarīra dharī.

सुर श्रुति निंदक जे अभिमानी । रौरव नरक परहिं ते प्रानी ॥
sura śruti niṁdaka je abhimānī, raurava naraka parahiṁ te prānī.

होहिं उलूक संत निंदा रत । मोह निसा प्रिय ग्यान भानु गत ॥
hohiṁ ulūka saṁta niṁdā rata, moha nisā priya gyāna bhānu gata.

सब कै निंदा जे जड़ करहीं । ते चमगादुर होइ अवतरहीं ॥
saba kai niṁdā je jaṛa karahīṁ, te camagādura hoi avatarahīṁ.

सुनहु तात अब मानस रोगा । जिन्ह ते दुख पावहिं सब लोगा ॥
sunahu tāta aba mānasa rogā, jinha te dukha pāvahiṁ saba logā.

मोह सकल ब्याधिन्ह कर मूला । तिन्ह ते पुनि उपजहिं बहु सूला ॥
moha sakala byādhinha kara mūlā, tinha te puni upajahiṁ bahu sūlā.

काम बात कफ लोभ अपारा । क्रोध पित्त नित छाती जारा ॥
kāma bāta kapha lobha apārā, krodha pitta nita chātī jārā.

प्रीति करहिं जौं तीनिउ भाई । उपजइ सन्यपात दुखदाई ॥
prīti karahiṁ jauṁ tīniu bhāī, upajai sanyapāta dukhadāī.

बिषय मनोरथ दुर्गम नाना । ते सब सूल नाम को जाना ॥
biṣaya manoratha durgama nānā, te saba sūla nāma ko jānā.

ममता दादु कंडु इरषाई । हरष बिषाद गरह बहुताई ॥
mamatā dādu kaṁḍu iraṣāī, haraṣa biṣāda garaha bahutāī.

पर सुख देखि जरनि सोइ छई । कुष्ट दुष्टता मन कुटिलई ॥
para sukha dekhi jarani soi chaī, kuṣṭa duṣṭatā mana kuṭilaī.

अहंकार अति दुखद डमरुआ । दंभ कपट मद मान नेहरुआ ॥
ahaṁkāra ati dukhada ḍamaruā, daṁbha kapaṭa mada māna neharuā.

तृस्ना उदरबृद्धि अति भारी । त्रिबिधि ईषना तरुन तिजारी ॥
tṛsnā udarabṛddhi ati bhārī, tribidhi īṣanā taruna tijārī.

जुग बिधि ज्वर मत्सर अबिबेका । कहँ लगि कहौं कुरोग अनेका ॥
juga bidhi jvara matsara abibekā, kahaṁ lagi kahauṁ kuroga anekā.

Trans:

Garud asked further in loving tones, "Since, my Lord, you are pleased to be gracious to me, acknowledge me as your disciple and resolve me these seven questions: Tell me first, O staunchest of the faithful, what form is the most difficult for a Jiva to obtain? Next consider and tell in brief what is the greatest pain and what the highest pleasure? Also, expounding on their innate disposition, what are the essential characteristics of the good? And of the wicked? And further, what is the highest religious merit as made known in the Scriptures? And say what is the most awful sin? And what are the diseases of the soul? Omniscient as you are and richly endowed with compassion, do please settle my doubts." "Listen, my son, with the greatest reverence and devotion, while I briefly exposit my views on them. The human form is the most excellent of all, and the desire of every living creature, whether moving or motionless. It is the ladder that connects hell and heaven and final emancipation and is the bestower of the blessings of wisdom, continence and faith. Men who have attained to this form and yet do not worship Harī show themselves, in their infatuation for the world, greater fools than any fool living, clutching at bits of glass while they throw away the philosopher's stone which they had in their hands. Next, there is no pain in the world so great as poverty and no pleasure like that which results from communion with the saints. It is an essential characteristic of the good, O Garud, to be charitable to others, in thought, word and deed. The good take pains to help their neighbors, but wicked wretches take pains to trouble them. The good in their compassionateness resemble the birch tree and constantly submit to the greatest distress in order to benefit others. The wicked, like the hemp, have their skin flayed off and perish in agony, merely to supply cords to bind people. Observe O enemy of serpents, the wicked do mischief, even when they have no object of their own to gain—like a serpent or a rat. They would kill themselves to ruin another's prosperity, like the hail which dissolves after destroying the crops. The rising of the wicked is as much a cause of calamity to the world as that of the infamous planet Ketu is known to be. The rise of the good is ever productive of happiness, as when the moon rejoices the world by scattering the darkness. Next, the highest religious merit, as declared in the Scriptures, is to do no harm to any creature. There is no sin as heinous as the abuse of another. He, who abuses Harī or his Gurū, becomes a frog and is born a thousand times in that form. He, who abuses a Brahmin, after suffering in many Hells, will be born into the world in the form of a crow. They, who have the presumption to abuse the gods or the Scriptures, will fall into the hell called Raurava. They, who delight to abuse the saints, will be changed into owls, as loving the night of error and hating the sun of knowledge. The fools who abuse everyone will be born again as bats. Hearken now, my son, to the diseases of the soul from which all people suffer pain. Delusion is the root of all ailments and from these again spring many pains. The flatulence of lust, the phlegm of insatiable greed, and the bile of passion constantly inflame the breast, and when these three combine, sir, there results a miserable paralysis of the whole system. Who can tell the names of all the diseases represented by the various obstinate sensual cravings?—such as the leprosy of selfishness, the itch of envy, the rheumatic throbs of joy and sorrow, the consumption that burns at the sight of another's prosperity, the horrible open sore of a malignant spirit, the excruciating gout of egoism, the sciatica of heresy, hypocrisy, vanity and pride, the terrible leprosy of greed, the violent tertian ague of the three kinds of covetousness, the two fevers of jealousy and indiscrimination. But why continue the interminable list of diseases?

दोहा-dohā:

एक ब्याधि बस नर मरहिं ए असाधि बहु ब्याधि ।
eka byādhi basa nara marahiṁ e asādhi bahu byādhi,
पीड़हिं संतत जीव कहुँ सो किमि लहै समाधि ॥१२१क॥
pīṛahiṁ saṁtata jīva kahuṁ so kimi lahai samādhi. 121(ka).

नेम धर्म आचार तप ग्यान जग्य जप दान ।
nema dharma ācāra tapa gyāna jagya japa dāna,
भेषज पुनि कोटिन्ह नहिं रोग जाहिं हरिजान ॥१२१ख॥
bheṣaja puni koṭinha nahiṁ roga jāhiṁ harijāna. 121(kha).

Trans:

A man dies even of one disease; but these incurable diseases which constantly harass the soul are many in number, how then can it find rest? Pious and religious observances, penance, meditation, sacrifice, prayer and alms-giving, are so many different remedies; but the disease, O Garud, does not abate.

चौपाई-caupāī:

एहि बिधि सकल जीव जग रोगी । सोक हरष भय प्रीति बियोगी ॥
ehi bidhi sakala jīva jaga rogī, soka haraṣa bhaya prīti biyogī.

मानस रोग कछुक मैं गाए । हहिं सब कें लखि बिरलेन्ह पाए ॥
mānasa roga kachuka maiṁ gāe, hahiṁ saba keṁ lakhi biralenha pāe.

जाने ते छीजहिं कछु पापी । नास न पावहिं जन परितापी ॥
jāne te chījahiṁ kachu pāpī, nāsa na pāvahiṁ jana paritāpī.

बिषय कुपथ्य पाइ अंकुरे । मुनिहु हृदयँ का नर बापुरे ॥
biṣaya kupathya pāi aṁkure, munihu hṛdayaṁ kā nara bāpure.

राम कृपाँ नासहिं सब रोगा । जौं एहि भाँति बनै संयोगा ॥
rāma kṛpāṁ nāsahiṁ saba rogā, jauṁ ehi bhāṁti banai saṁyogā.

सदगुर बैद बचन बिस्वासा । संजम यह न बिषय कै आसा ॥
sadagura baida bacana bisvāsā, saṁjama yaha na biṣaya kai āsā.

रघुपति भगति सजीवन मूरी । अनूपान श्रद्धा मति पूरी ॥
raghupati bhagati sajīvana mūrī, anūpāna śraddhā mati pūrī.

एहि बिधि भलेहिं सो रोग नसाहीं । नाहिं त जतन कोटि नहिं जाहीं ॥
ehi bidhi bhalehiṁ so roga nasāhīṁ, nāhiṁ ta jatana koṭi nahiṁ jāhīṁ.
जानिअ तब मन बिरुज गोसाँई । जब उर बल बिराग अधिकाई ॥
jānia taba mana biruja gosāṁī, jaba ura bala birāga adhikāī.
सुमति छुधा बाढ़इ नित नई । बिषय आस दुर्बलता गई ॥
sumati chudhā bāṛhai nita naī, biṣaya āsa durbalatā gaī.
बिमल ग्यान जल जब सो नहाई । तब रह राम भगति उर छाई ॥
bimala gyāna jala jaba so nahāī, taba raha rāma bhagati ura chāī.
सिव अज सुक सनकादिक नारद । जे मुनि ब्रह्म बिचार बिसारद ॥
siva aja suka sanakādika nārada, je muni brahma bicāra bisārada.
सब कर मत खगनायक एहा । करिअ राम पद पंकज नेहा ॥
saba kara mata khaganāyaka ehā, karia rāma pada paṁkaja nehā.
श्रुति पुरान सब ग्रंथ कहाहीं । रघुपति भगति बिना सुख नाहीं ॥
śruti purāna saba graṁtha kahāhīṁ, raghupati bhagati binā sukha nāhīṁ.
कमठ पीठ जामहिं बरु बारा । बंध्या सुत बरु काहुहि मारा ॥
kamaṭha pīṭha jāmahiṁ baru bārā, baṁdhyā suta baru kāhuhi mārā.
फूलहिं नभ बरु बहुबिधि फूला । जीव न लह सुख हरि प्रतिकूला ॥
phūlahiṁ nabha baru bahubidhi phūlā, jīva na laha sukha hari pratikūlā.
तृषा जाइ बरु मृगजल पाना । बरु जामहिं सस सीस बिषाना ॥
tṛṣā jāi baru mṛgajala pānā, baru jāmahiṁ sasa sīsa biṣānā.
अंधकारु बरु रबिहि नसावै । राम बिमुख न जीव सुख पावै ॥
aṁdhakāru baru rabihi nasāvai, rāma bimukha na jīva sukha pāvai.
हिम ते अनल प्रगट बरु होई । बिमुख राम सुख पाव न कोई ॥
hima te anala pragaṭa baru hoī, bimukha rāma sukha pāva na koī.

Trans:

Every creature in the world is diseased of duality, distracted alternately by sorrow and joy, by fear and love. I have mentioned only some of the diseases of the soul; they touch everyone, but few only detect them. On detection the wretches diminish somewhat, but these tormentors of the faithful are not completely destroyed. When fed on the unwholesome diet of materialism, they spring up even in the soul of a saint, how much more then in that of ordinary mortals? By the grace of Rāma every disease is extirpated, if the treatment is conducted in the following manner: With a holy teacher for physician, faith for a prescription, indifference to worldly pleasures as the regimen, devotion to Harī for life-giving drugs and a soul full of faith as the vehicle in which it is administered. By this treatment the disease is easily subdued: otherwise all your efforts go for nothing. You may know, sir, that the mind is free from disease as soon as it gains strength in self-control, with a daily increasing appetite for good resolutions and a weakness in cravings for material pleasures. After bathing in the pure stream of divine knowledge, the whole soul is suffused with faith in Rāma. This, O king-of-birds, is the doctrine of Shiva, Brahmmā, Shuk-dev, Sanat-kumār, Nārad and all the sages, who have been eminent in theological speculation: "Practice devotion to Rāma's lotus feet."—The Vedas and Purānas and all the Scriptures declare this; without faith in Rāma there is no happiness. It would be easier for water to stay on the back of a tortoise, or for the son of a childless woman to be slain, or for flowers of every description to bloom in the air, than for any creature to be happy in opposition to Harī. Sooner shall thirst be satisfied by drinking of a mirage, or horns sprout on the head of a hare, or darkness extinguish the sun, than any creature find happiness if he has turned his face away from Rāma. Sooner shall fire appear out of ice than anyone oppose Rāma and yet find happiness.

दोहा-dohā:

बारि मथें घृत होइ बरु सिकता ते बरु तेल ।
bāri matheṁ ghṛta hoi baru sikatā te baru tela,
बिनु हरि भजन न भव तरिअ यह सिद्धांत अपेल ॥ १२२क॥
binu hari bhajana na bhava taria yaha siddhāṁta apela. 122(ka).

मसकहि करइ बिरंचि प्रभु अजहि मसक ते हीन ।
masakahi karai biraṁci prabhu ajahi masaka te hīna,
अस बिचारि तजि संसय रामहि भजहिं प्रबीन ॥ १२२ख॥
asa bicāri taji saṁsaya rāmahi bhajahiṁ prabīna. 122(kha).

Trans:

Sooner shall butter be produced by churning water, or oil squeezed out of sand, than the ocean of existence be traversed without prayer to Harī: this is an indisputable conclusion. The Lord can change a gnat into Brahmmā or make Brahmmā himself even less than a gnat. A wise man will consider this and discard all doubt and worship Rāma.

श्लोक-śloka:

विनिश्चितं वदामि ते न अन्यथा वचांसि मे ।
viniścitaṁ vadāmi te na anyathā vacāṁsi me,
हरिं नरा भजन्ति येऽतिदुस्तरं तरन्ति ते ॥ १२२ग॥
hariṁ narā bhajanti ye'tidustaraṁ taranti te. 122(ga).

Trans:

I declare to you my considered view, and my words can never be untrue: those, who worship Rāma, are able to cross this most formidable ocean of existence.

चौपाई-caupāī:

कहेउँ नाथ हरि चरित अनूपा । ब्यास समास स्वमति अनुरुपा ॥
kaheuṁ nātha hari carita anūpā, byāsa samāsa svamati anurupā.
श्रुति सिद्धांत इहइ उरगारी । राम भजिअ सब काज बिसारी ॥
śruti siddhāṁta ihai uragārī, rāma bhajia saba kāja bisārī.
प्रभु रघुपति तजि सेइअ काही । मोहि से सठ पर ममता जाही ॥
prabhu raghupati taji seia kāhī, mohi se saṭha para mamatā jāhī.
तुम्ह बिग्यानरूप नहिं मोहा । नाथ कीन्हि मो पर अति छोहा ॥
tumha bigyānarūpa nahiṁ mohā, nātha kīnhi mo para ati chohā.
पूँछिहु राम कथा अति पावनि । सुक सनकादि संभु मन भावनि ॥
pūṁchihu rāma kathā ati pāvani, suka sanakādi saṁbhu mana bhāvani.
सत संगति दुर्लभ संसारा । निमिष दंड भरि एकउ बारा ॥
sata saṁgati durlabha saṁsārā, nimiṣa daṁḍa bhari ekau bārā.
देखु गरुड़ निज हृदयँ बिचारी । मैं रघुबीर भजन अधिकारी ॥
dekhu garuṛa nija hṛdayaṁ bicārī, maiṁ raghubīra bhajana adhikārī.
सकुनाधम सब भाँति अपावन । प्रभु मोहि कीन्ह बिदित जग पावन ॥
sakunādhama saba bhāṁti apāvana, prabhu mohi kīnha bidita jaga pāvana.

Trans:

I have told you, my Lord, Harī's unparalleled achievements, in full or in brief, as my ability served me, and this, Garud, is the crowning dogma of the Scriptures: to abandon sensuality and worship Rāma. Whom else can you serve if you forsake the Lord Raghupatī—who was compassionate even to such a wretch as myself. You are wisdom itself and superior to delusion, but you showed me, my Lord, a great kindness in that you asked me for Rāma's history, which is so holy that it delights the soul, even of Shuk-dev and Sanat-kumār and Shambhu. The company of the good is hard to get in the world, even for once, even for a single moment. See, Garud, and consider for yourself: I am now a master in the worship of Raghubīr—and though I was the vilest of birds and in every way abominable; the Lord has made me famous as a purifier of the world.

दोहा-dohā:

आजु धन्य मैं धन्य अति जद्यपि सब बिधि हीन ।
āju dhanya maiṁ dhanya ati jadyapi saba bidhi hīna,
निज जन जानि राम मोहि संत समागम दीन ॥ १२३क॥
nija jana jāni rāma mohi saṁta samāgama dīna. 123(ka).

नाथ जथामति भाषेउँ राखेउँ नहिं कछु गोइ ।
nātha jathāmati bhāṣeuṁ rākheuṁ nahiṁ kachu goi,
चरित सिंधु रघुनायक थाह कि पावइ कोइ ॥ १२३ख ॥
carita siṁdhu raghunāyaka thāha ki pāvai koi. 123(kha).

Trans:

Blessed, blessed indeed am I today, notwithstanding my meanness: for Rāma has acknowledged me as one of his own servants and has admitted me to the communion of the saints. I have spoken, my Lord, according to my ability and have concealed nothing; but Rāma's doings are a very ocean, who can find the bottom of them?"

चौपाई-caupāī:

सुमिरि राम के गुन गन नाना । पुनि पुनि हरष भुसुंडि सुजाना ॥
sumiri rāma ke guna gana nānā, puni puni haraṣa bhusuṁḍi sujānā.
महिमा निगम नेति करि गाई । अतुलित बल प्रताप प्रभुताई ॥
mahimā nigama neti kari gāī, atulita bala pratāpa prabhutāī.
सिव अज पूज्य चरन रघुराई । मो पर कृपा परम मृदुलाई ॥
siva aja pūjya carana raghurāī, mo para kṛpā parama mṛdulāī.
अस सुभाउ कहुँ सुनउँ न देखउँ । केहि खगेस रघुपति सम लेखउँ ॥
asa subhāu kahuṁ sunauṁ na dekhauṁ, kehi khagesa raghupati sama lekhauṁ.
साधक सिद्ध बिमुक्त उदासी । कबि कोबिद कृतग्य संन्यासी ॥
sādhaka siddha bimukta udāsī, kabi kobida kṛtagya saṁnyāsī.
जोगी सूर सुतापस ग्यानी । धर्म निरत पंडित बिग्यानी ॥
jogī sūra sutāpasa gyānī, dharma nirata paṁḍita bigyānī.
तरहिं न बिनु सेएँ मम स्वामी । राम नमामि नमामि नमामी ॥
tarahiṁ na binu seeṁ mama svāmī, rāma namāmi namāmi namāmī.
सरन गएँ मो से अघ रासी । होहिं सुद्ध नमामि अबिनासी ॥
sarana gaeṁ mo se agha rāsī, hohiṁ suddha namāmi abināsī.

Trans:

As he pondered on Rāma's manifold perfections, the all-wise Bhusumdi was yet more and more enraptured. "He, whose greatness the Scriptures have declared to be unutterable, whose might and majesty and dominion are unbounded, whose feet are adored by Shiva and Brahmmā, even he, Raghurāī, has in his infinite compassion, shown favor to me. Never have I seen or heard of such benignity; to whom, O Garud, can I compare Rāma? Strivers and perfect souls, deified anchorites, miracle-working saints, liberated and the unworldly-minded, inspired bards and rigid ascetics, spiritualists, self-mortified divines, those knowing the secrets of Karma and those who have renounced all action, Yogis, and valiant heroes, great ascetics and wise men, pious souls and men of erudition and even men who have realized the Self, whosoever it be—none of them can cross the deep ocean of existence but by serving the Lord-God. Again and again, and yet again, I bow myself before Rāma. I worship the Immortal Lord, with whom all who take refuge are sanctified, though even guiltier than was I.

दोहा-dohā:

जासु नाम भव भेषज हरन घोर त्रय सूल ।
jāsu nāma bhava bheṣaja harana ghora traya sūla,
सो कृपाल मोहि तो पर सदा रहउ अनुकूल ॥ १२४क॥
so kṛpāla mohi to para sadā rahau anukūla. 124(ka).

सुनि भुसुंडि के बचन सुभ देखि राम पद नेह ।
suni bhusuṁḍi ke bacana subha dekhi rāma pada neha,
बोलेउ प्रेम सहित गिरा गरुड़ बिगत संदेह ॥ १२४ख॥
boleu prema sahita girā garuṛa bigata saṁdeha. 124(kha).

Trans:

He, whose name is an elixir of life, the healer of every kind of trouble, may he, in his mercy, remain ever gracious both to me and to thee." Hearing Bhusumdi's words and perceiving his admirable devotion to Rāma's feet, Garud replied in loving tones and with every doubt at an end,

चौपाई-caupāī:

मैं कृतकृत्य भयउँ तव बानी । सुनि रघुबीर भगति रस सानी ॥
maiṁ kṛtakṛtya bhayauṁ tava bānī, suni raghubīra bhagati rasa sānī.
राम चरन नूतन रति भई । माया जनित बिपति सब गई ॥
rāma carana nūtana rati bhaī, māyā janita bipati saba gaī.
मोह जलधि बोहित तुम्ह भए । मो कहँ नाथ बिबिध सुख दए ॥
moha jaladhi bohita tumha bhae, mo kahaṁ nātha bibidha sukha dae.
मो पहिं होइ न प्रति उपकारा । बंदउँ तव पद बारहिं बारा ॥
mo pahiṁ hoi na prati upakārā, baṁdauṁ tava pada bārahiṁ bārā.
पूरन काम राम अनुरागी । तुम्ह सम तात न कोउ बड़भागी ॥
pūrana kāma rāma anurāgī, tumha sama tāta na kou baṛabhāgī.
संत बिटप सरिता गिरि धरनी । पर हित हेतु सबन्ह कै करनी ॥
saṁta biṭapa saritā giri dharanī, para hita hetu sabanha kai karanī.
संत हृदय नवनीत समाना । कहा कबिन्ह परि कहै न जाना ॥
saṁta hṛdaya navanīta samānā, kahā kabinha pari kahai na jānā.
निज परिताप द्रवइ नवनीता । पर दुख द्रवहिं संत सुपुनीता ॥
nija paritāpa dravai navanītā, para dukha dravahiṁ saṁta supunītā.
जीवन जन्म सुफल मम भयऊ । तव प्रसाद संसय सब गयऊ ॥
jīvana janma suphala mama bhayaū, tava prasāda saṁsaya saba gayaū.
जानेहु सदा मोहि निज किंकर । पुनि पुनि उमा कहइ बिहंगबर ॥
jānehu sadā mohi nija kiṁkara, puni puni umā kahai bihaṁgabara.

Trans:

"By your discourse I have attained my end, now that I have learnt the delectable doctrine of faith in Rāma. My love to his feet increases ever more and more and the trouble created by Māyā is clean gone. You have been my raft in the sea of delusion and have bestowed on me, my Lord, the most exquisite delight. I can in no way requite you; but again and again I prostrate myself at your feet. Full to overflowing with love for Rāma you are so blessed, sire, that none can equal you. Saints, trees, rivers, mountains and the earth, all operate for the good of others. The hearts of the saints is like butter—so the poets say, but they say not well; for butter melts when itself is tried by the fire, but the saints are so good that they melt at others' trials. Now has my life become worth living, for by your favor my doubts have disappeared. Regard me ever as your servant." Again and again, O Umā thus spoke the noblest of birds.

दोहा-dohā:

तासु चरन सिरु नाइ करि प्रेम सहित मतिधीर ।
tāsu carana siru nāi kari prema sahita matidhīra,
गयउ गरुड़ बैकुंठ तब हृदयँ राखि रघुबीर ॥ १२५क॥
gayau garuṛa baikuṁṭha taba hṛdayaṁ rākhi raghubīra. 125(ka).

गिरिजा संत समागम सम न लाभ कछु आन ।
girijā saṁta samāgama sama na lābha kachu āna,
बिनु हरि कृपा न होइ सो गावहिं बेद पुरान ॥१२५ख॥
binu hari kṛpā na hoi so gāvahiṁ beda purāna. 125(kha).

Trans:

After affectionately bowing his head at his feet, Garud proceeded to Vaikūnth, with Rāma's image impressed upon his heart. O Girijā, there is no blessing like that of communion with the saints; it is attainable only by Harī's grace so the Vedas and Purānas declare.

चौपाई-caupāī:

कहेउँ परम पुनीत इतिहासा । सुनत श्रवन छूटहिं भव पासा ॥
kaheuṁ parama punīta itihāsā, sunata śravana chūṭahiṁ bhava pāsā.
प्रनत कल्पतरु करुना पुंजा । उपजइ प्रीति राम पद कंजा ॥
pranata kalpataru karunā puṁjā, upajai prīti rāma pada kaṁjā.
मन क्रम बचन जनित अघ जाई । सुनहिं जे कथा श्रवन मन लाई ॥
mana krama bacana janita agha jāī, sunahiṁ je kathā śravana mana lāī.
तीर्थाटन साधन समुदाई । जोग बिराग ग्यान निपुनाई ॥
tīrthāṭana sādhana samudāī, joga birāga gyāna nipunāī.
नाना कर्म धर्म ब्रत दाना । संजम दम जप तप मख नाना ॥
nānā karma dharma brata dānā, saṁjama dama japa tapa makha nānā.
भूत दया द्विज गुर सेवकाई । बिद्या बिनय बिबेक बड़ाई ॥
bhūta dayā dvija gura sevakāī, bidyā binaya bibeka baṛāī.
जहँ लगि साधन बेद बखानी । सब कर फल हरि भगति भवानी ॥
jahaṁ lagi sādhana beda bakhānī, saba kara phala hari bhagati bhavānī.
सो रघुनाथ भगति श्रुति गाई । राम कृपाँ काहूँ एक पाई ॥
so raghunātha bhagati śruti gāī, rāma kṛpāṁ kāhūṁ eka pāī.

Trans:

I have now finished the all-holy story, by the hearing of which the bonds of existence are loosened, the very tree of Paradise abounding in mercies for all who approach it, and which causes and stimulates devotion to Lord Rāma's lotus feet. Sins engendered of thought, word and deed are all absolved in those who listen attentively to this legend. Pilgrimages to shrines, recourse to all the means of grace, meditation, self-control, perfection in wisdom, works of religious merit, devotional practices, fasting and alms-giving, continence, temperance, prayer, penance and manifold sacrifices, tender-heartedness to all living creatures, ministering to Brahmins and Gurūs, learning, morality and exalted intelligence, in short all the forms of discipline, which the Vedas have recommended, have but one aim, O Bhawānī: devotion to Rāma. Such devotion—as the Scriptures describe it—is attained by a rare few by the grace of Rāma.

दोहा-dohā:

मुनि दुर्लभ हरि भगति नर पावहिं बिनहिं प्रयास ।
muni durlabha hari bhagati nara pāvahiṁ binahiṁ prayāsa,
जे यह कथा निरंतर सुनहिं मानि बिस्वास ॥१२६॥
je yaha kathā niraṁtara sunahiṁ māni bisvāsa. 126.

Trans:

But even though the sages found it scarce attainable, anybody can easily acquire it now, by the repeated hearing of this story, if he does so with faith.

चौपाई-caupāī:

सोइ सर्बग्य गुनी सोइ ग्याता । सोइ महि मंडित पंडित दाता ॥
soi sarbagya gunī soi gyātā, soi mahi maṁḍita paṁḍita dātā.
धर्म परायन सोइ कुल त्राता । राम चरन जा कर मन राता ॥
dharma parāyana soi kula trātā, rāma carana jā kara mana rātā.
नीति निपुन सोइ परम सयाना । श्रुति सिद्धांत नीक तेहिं जाना ॥
nīti nipuna soi parama sayānā, śruti siddhāṁta nīka tehiṁ jānā.
सोइ कबि कोबिद सोइ रनधीरा । जो छल छाड़ि भजइ रघुबीरा ॥
soi kabi kobida soi ranadhīrā, jo chala chāṛi bhajai raghubīrā.
धन्य देस सो जहँ सुरसरी । धन्य नारि पतिब्रत अनुसरी ॥
dhanya desa so jahaṁ surasarī, dhanya nāri patibrata anusarī.
धन्य सो भूपु नीति जो करई । धन्य सो द्विज निज धर्म न टरई ॥
dhanya so bhūpu nīti jo karaī, dhanya so dvija nija dharma na ṭaraī.
सो धन धन्य प्रथम गति जाकी । धन्य पुन्य रत मति सोइ पाकी ॥
so dhana dhanya prathama gati jākī, dhanya punya rata mati soi pākī.
धन्य घरी सोइ जब सतसंगा । धन्य जन्म द्विज भगति अभंगा ॥
dhanya gharī soi jaba satasaṁgā, dhanya janma dvija bhagati abhaṁgā.

Trans:

He is all-wise, he is an accomplished scholar, he is renowned throughout the world for learning and beneficence, he is truly pious and his kinsfolk's savior—whose soul is enamored of Rāma's feet. He is perfect in morality and supremely intelligent, he has a thorough understanding of scriptural doctrine, and he is an inspired bard and a man of fixed purpose—who, without hypocrisy, worships Raghubīr. Blessed is the land where the Gangā flows; blessed is the wife who is faithful to her husband; blessed is the king who governs justly; blessed is the Brahmin who swerves not from his duty; blessed is the wealth which is used to the best advantage; blessed is the creed which most conduces to works of piety; blessed is the hour which brings communion with the saints; blessed is the life which is staunch in devotion to the twice-born.

दोहा-dohā:

सो कुल धन्य उमा सुनु जगत पूज्य सुपुनीत ।
so kula dhanya umā sunu jagata pūjya supunīta,
श्रीरघुबीर परायन जेहिं नर उपज बिनीत ॥१२७॥
śrīraghubīra parāyana jehiṁ nara upaja binīta. 127.

Trans:

Blessed is the family, yea—mark me, O Umā—worthy of veneration throughout the world and truly holy, in which is born a humble worshipper of the divine Raghubīr.

चौपाई-caupāī:

मति अनुरूप कथा मैं भाषी । जद्यपि प्रथम गुप्त करि राखी ॥
mati anurūpa kathā maiṁ bhāṣī, jadyapi prathama gupta kari rākhī.
तव मन प्रीति देखि अधिकाई । तब मैं रघुपति कथा सुनाई ॥
tava mana prīti dekhi adhikāī, taba maiṁ raghupati kathā sunāī.
यह न कहिअ सठही हठसीलहि । जो मन लाइ न सुन हरि लीलहि ॥
yaha na kahia saṭhahī haṭhasīlahi, jo mana lāi na suna hari līlahi.
कहिअ न लोभिहि क्रोधिहि कामिहि । जो न भजइ सचराचर स्वामिहि ॥
kahia na lobhihi krodhihi kāmihi, jo na bhajai sacarācara svāmihi.
द्विज द्रोहिहि न सुनाइअ कबहूँ । सुरपति सरिस होइ नृप जबहूँ ॥
dvija drohihi na sunāia kabahūṁ, surapati sarisa hoi nṛpa jabahūṁ.
राम कथा के तेइ अधिकारी । जिन्ह कें सतसंगति अति प्यारी ॥
rāma kathā ke tei adhikārī, jinha keṁ satasaṁgati ati pyārī.
गुर पद प्रीति नीति रत जेई । द्विज सेवक अधिकारी तेई ॥
gura pada prīti nīti rata jeī, dvija sevaka adhikārī teī.
ता कहँ यह बिसेष सुखदाई । जाहि प्रानप्रिय श्रीरघुराई ॥
tā kahaṁ yaha biseṣa sukhadāī, jāhi prānapriya śrīraghurāī.

Trans:

Though at first I kept it secret, I have now to the best of my ability told you the whole story. I saw the extreme devotion of your soul, and it is for this reason that I have declared to you Rāma's history. It is not to be repeated to any perverse wretch, who will not give his mind to understand the tale of Harī's sportive manifestations, nor to any covetous, choleric or sensual person, who worships not the Lord of all animate and inanimate creation. Neither must it ever be told to a persecutor of the Brahmins; even should he be as great a king as Indra. They are fit for instruction in Rāma's history, who dearly love the communion of the saints, who have a great affection for the feet of their Gurū and the precepts of morality, and are submissive to the Brahmins: these are fit recipients, aye. They will derive a special delight from it, who love Rāma as they love their own life.

दोहा-dohā:

राम चरन रति जो चह अथवा पद निर्बान ।
rāma carana rati jo caha athavā pada nirbāna,
भाव सहित सो यह कथा करउ श्रवन पुट पान ॥१२८॥
bhāva sahita so yaha kathā karau śravana puṭa pāna. 128.

Trans:

Whoever wishes to love Rāma's feet or to attain to final deliverance should devoutly fill the pitchers of his ears with the water of this legend.

चौपाई-caupāī:

राम कथा गिरिजा मैं बरनी । कलि मल समनि मनोमल हरनी ॥
rāma kathā girijā maiṁ baranī, kali mala samani manomala haranī.
संसृति रोग सजीवन मूरी । राम कथा गावहिं श्रुति सूरी ॥
saṁsṛti roga sajīvana mūrī, rāma kathā gāvahiṁ śruti sūrī.
एहि महँ रुचिर सप्त सोपाना । रघुपति भगति केर पंथाना ॥
ehi mahaṁ rucira sapta sopānā, raghupati bhagati kera paṁthānā.
अति हरि कृपा जाहि पर होई । पाउँ देइ एहिं मारग सोई ॥
ati hari kṛpā jāhi para hoī, pāuṁ dei ehiṁ māraga soī.
मन कामना सिद्धि नर पावा । जे यह कथा कपट तजि गावा ॥
mana kāmanā siddhi nara pāvā, je yaha kathā kapaṭa taji gāvā.
कहहिं सुनहिं अनुमोदन करहीं । ते गोपद इव भवनिधि तरहीं ॥
kahahiṁ sunahiṁ anumodana karahīṁ, te gopada iva bhavanidhi tarahīṁ.
सुनि सब कथा हृदय अति भाई । गिरिजा बोली गिरा सुहाई ॥
suni saba kathā hṛdaya ati bhāī, girijā bolī girā suhāī.
नाथ कृपाँ मम गत संदेहा । राम चरन उपजेउ नव नेहा ॥
nātha kṛpāṁ mama gata saṁdehā, rāma carana upajeu nava nehā.

Trans:

The story of Rāma, as I have now told it you, O Umā, has power to subdue the impurity of this evil age and to remove all the impurities of the soul. It is a healing remedy for every disease of life, as is declared by those learned in the Veda. It has seven beautiful stairs, which are so many paths as it were leading to the goal of Devotion to the Lord of the Raghus. He alone who enjoys the utmost grace of Shrī Harī can set his foot on that path. They, who guilelessly recite this history, obtain success in everything their soul desires. They who hear, or repeat and gladly assent to it, traverse the depths of existence as they would a mere puddle." Umā was greatly pleased to have heard the whole history and cried in joyous tones, "By my Lord's favor my doubts have been dispelled, and my love for Rāma's feet has sprung up anew.

दोहा-dohā:

मैं कृतकृत्य भइउँ अब तव प्रसाद बिस्वेस ।
maiṁ kṛtakṛtya bhaiuṁ aba tava prasāda bisvesa,
उपजी राम भगति दृढ़ बीते सकल कलेस ॥१२९॥
upajī rāma bhagati dṛṛha bīte sakala kalesa. 129.

Trans:

Through your grace, O Lord of the universe, I have now attained my desire: a firm faith in Rāma has resulted, and all my troubles are at an end."

चौपाई-caupāī:

यह सुभ संभु उमा संबादा । सुख संपादन समन बिषादा ॥
yaha subha saṁbhu umā saṁbādā, sukha saṁpādana samana biṣādā.
भव भंजन गंजन संदेहा । जन रंजन सज्जन प्रिय एहा ॥
bhava bhaṁjana gaṁjana saṁdehā, jana raṁjana sajjana priya ehā.
राम उपासक जे जग माहीं । एहि सम प्रिय तिन्ह कें कछु नाहीं ॥
rāma upāsaka je jaga māhīṁ, ehi sama priya tinha keṁ kachu nāhīṁ.
रघुपति कृपाँ जथामति गावा । मैं यह पावन चरित सुहावा ॥
raghupati kṛpāṁ jathāmati gāvā, maiṁ yaha pāvana carita suhāvā.
एहिं कलिकाल न साधन दूजा । जोग जग्य जप तप ब्रत पूजा ॥
ehiṁ kalikāla na sādhana dūjā, joga jagya japa tapa brata pūjā.
रामहि सुमिरिअ गाइअ रामहि । संतत सुनिअ राम गुन ग्रामहि ॥
rāmahi sumiria gāia rāmahi, saṁtata sunia rāma guna grāmahi.
जासु पतित पावन बड़ बाना । गावहिं कबि श्रुति संत पुराना ॥
jāsu patita pāvana baṛa bānā, gāvahiṁ kabi śruti saṁta purānā.
ताहि भजहि मन तजि कुटिलाई । राम भजें गति केहिं नहिं पाई ॥
tāhi bhajahi mana taji kuṭilāī, rāma bhajeṁ gati kehiṁ nahiṁ pāī.

Trans:

This glorious dialogue between Shambhu and Umā is fruitful in blessings and destructive of sorrow; it puts an end to transmigration, disperses doubt, delights the devotees and is dear to the saints. To the worshippers of Shrī Rāma, nothing is so dear as this narrative of Shrī Rāma. By Raghupatī's favor I have sung to the best of my ability his holy and gracious deeds. In this, the last age of the world, there is no other means of salvation, neither abstraction, sacrifice, prayer, penance, neither vows nor religious ceremonial; just think only of Rāma, sing only of Rāma, and give ear only to Rāma's infinite perfections. Let the soul give over its perversity and worship him, whose special characteristic it is to sanctify the fallen—as is declared by saints and seers, by Veda and Purānas. Is there anyone who has worshipped Rāma and not found salvation?

छंद-chaṁda:

पाई न केहिं गति पतित पावन राम भजि सुनु सठ मना ।
pāī na kehiṁ gati patita pāvana rāma bhaji sunu saṭha manā,
गनिका अजामिल ब्याध गीध गजादि खल तारे घना ॥
ganikā ajāmila byādha gīdha gajādi khala tāre ghanā.
आभीर जमन किरात खस स्वपचादि अति अघरूप जे ।
ābhīra jamana kirāta khasa svapacādi ati agharūpa je,
कहि नाम बारक तेपि पावन होहिं राम नमामि ते ॥१॥
kahi nāma bāraka tepi pāvana hohiṁ rāma namāmi te. 1.
रघुबंस भूषन चरित यह नर कहहिं सुनहिं जे गावहीं ।
raghubaṁsa bhūṣana carita yaha nara kahahiṁ sunahiṁ je gāvahīṁ,
कलि मल मनोमल धोइ बिनु श्रम राम धाम सिधावहीं ॥
kali mala manomala dhoi binu śrama rāma dhāma sidhāvahīṁ.
सत पंच चौपाईं मनोहर जानि जो नर उर धरै ।
sata paṁca caupāīṁ manohara jāni jo nara ura dharai,
दारुन अबिद्या पंच जनित बिकार श्रीरघुबर हरै ॥२॥
dāruna abidyā paṁca janita bikāra śrīraghubara harai. 2.
सुंदर सुजान कृपा निधान अनाथ पर कर प्रीति जो ।
suṁdara sujāna kṛpā nidhāna anātha para kara prīti jo,
सो एक राम अकाम हित निर्बानप्रद सम आन को ॥
so eka rāma akāma hita nirbānaprada sama āna ko.
जाकी कृपा लवलेस ते मतिमंद तुलसीदासहूँ ।
jākī kṛpā lavalesa te matimaṁda tulasīdāsahūṁ,
पायो परम बिश्रामु राम समान प्रभु नाहीं कहूँ ॥३॥

pāyo parama biśrāmu rāma samāna prabhu nāhīṁ kahūm̐. 3.

Trans:

Listen foolish mind: is there any creature who has worshipped Rāma, the purifier of the fallen, and not found salvation? The wretches whom he has redeemed are countless, such as the harlot Pinglā and Ajāmil, the huntsman Vālmikī, the vulture Jatāyu, and the elephant. Even Abhir, Yavan, Kirāt, Khasiā, Chandāl, and other embodiments of pollution are purified if they, but once, repeat his name. O Rāma, I adore thee. Anyone who reads, or hears, or recites this history of the glorious son of Raghu, washes out the stains of the world and the stains of his own soul and without any trouble, goes straight to Rāma's sphere in heaven. Nay, the Chief of the Raghus cures the perversities, caused by the fivefold ignorance, of those men who treasure up in their heart even a few Chaupāis of this narrative that appeal to them as most charming. If there is anyone who is all-beautiful, all-wise, full of compassion and full of loving kindness for the destitute—that is Rāma and Rāma alone. Who else can compare with him in benevolence, as a selfless friend and bestower of final deliverance? There is no other Lord like Shri Rāma, by whose favor, however slight, even I, the dull-witted Tulsīdās, have found perfect peace.

दोहा-dohā:

मो सम दीन न दीन हित तुम्ह समान रघुबीर ।

mo sama dīna na dīna hita tumha samāna raghubīra,

अस बिचारि रघुबंस मनि हरहु बिषम भव भीर ॥१३०क॥

asa bicāri raghubaṁsa mani harahu biṣama bhava bhīra. 130(ka).

कामिहि नारि पिआरि जिमि लोभिहि प्रिय जिमि दाम ।

kāmihi nāri piāri jimi lobhihi priya jimi dāma,

तिमि रघुनाथ निरंतर प्रिय लागहु मोहि राम ॥१३०ख॥

timi raghunātha niraṁtara priya lāgahu mohi rāma. 130(kha).

Trans:

There is no one as pathetic as I am and no one as gracious to the piteous as you, O Raghubīr: remember this, O glory of the race of Raghu, and rid me of the grievous burden of existence. As an amorous person is infatuated over their lover, and just as a greedy miser hankers after money, so for ever and ever, may you be always dear to me, O Rāma.

श्लोक-śloka:

यत्पूर्वं प्रभुणा कृतं सुकविना श्रीशम्भुना दुर्गमं

yatpūrvaṁ prabhuṇā kṛtaṁ sukavinā śrīśambhunā durgamaṁ

श्रीमद्रामपदाब्जभक्तिमनिशं प्राप्त्यै तु रामायणम् ।

śrīmadrāmapadābjabhaktimaniśaṁ prāptyai tu rāmāyaṇam,

मत्वा तद्रघुनाथमनिरतं स्वान्तस्तमःशान्तये

matvā tadraghunāthamaniratam svāntastamaḥśāntaye

भाषाबद्धमिदं चकार तुलसीदासस्तथा मानसम् ॥१॥

bhāṣābaddhamidaṁ cakāra tulasīdāsastathā mānasam. 1.

Trans:

The same esoteric Mānas-Rāmāyana, the Holy Lake of enactments of Shrī Rāma, that was brought to fore, in days of yore, by the blessed Shambhu, the foremost amongst poets—with the object of developing unceasing devotion to the beautiful lotus-feet of our beloved Lord: the all-merciful Rāma—has been likewise rendered into the common lingo by Tulsīdās for dispersing the gloom of his own soul, which it does—rife as it is with the name Rāma that alone gives this work a substance.

पुण्यं पापहरं सदा शिवकरं विज्ञानभक्तिप्रदं

puṇyaṁ pāpaharaṁ sadā śivakaraṁ vijñānabhaktipradaṁ

मायामोहमलापहं सुविमलं प्रेमाम्बुपूरं शुभम् ।

māyāmohamalāpahaṁ suvimalaṁ premāmbupūraṁ śubham,

श्रीमद्रामचरित्रमानसमिदं भक्त्यावगाहन्ति ये

śrīmadrāmacaritramānasamidaṁ bhaktyāvagāhanti ye

ते संसारपतङ्गघोरकिरणैर्दह्यन्ति नो मानवाः ॥२॥

te saṁsārapataṅgaghorakiraṇairdahyanti no mānavāḥ. 2.

Trans:

This glorious, purifying, blessed most limpid holy Mānas Lake of Shrī Rāma's enactments ever begets happiness. Verily, it bestows both Wisdom and Devotion; and it washes away delusion, infatuation and impurity; and brimful with a stream of love it inundates one with bliss supreme. Never scorched by the burning rays of the sun of worldly illusions are those who take a plunge in this most Holy-Lake of the Glories of Shrī Rāma.

मासपारायण तीसवाँ विश्राम

नवाह्नपारायण नवाँ विश्राम

māsapārāyaṇa tīsavāṁ viśrāma

navāhnapārāyaṇa navāṁ viśrāma

(Pause 30 for a Thirty-Day Recitation)

(Pause 9 for a Nine-Day Recitation)

इति श्रीमद्रामचरितमानसे सकलकलिकलुषविध्वंसने सप्तमः सोपानः समाप्तः

iti śrīmadrāmacaritamānase sakalakalikaluṣavidhvaṁsane saptamaḥ sopānaḥ samāptaḥ

(Now ends the Seventh-Ascent into the Manasa lake of Shrī Rāma's Charita which eradicates all the impurities of the Kali-Yug)

— सीताराम सीताराम सीताराम सीताराम सीताराम सीताराम सीताराम सीताराम सीताराम सीताराम सीताराम सीताराम सीताराम सीताराम सीताराम —

श्री राम-स्तुति — śrī rāma-stuti

श्री रामचन्द्र कृपालु भजु मन हरण भवभय दारुणं ।
śrī rāmacandra kṛpālu bhaju mana haraṇa bhavabhaya dāruṇaṁ,
नवकंज-लोचन कंज-मुख कर-कंज पद कंजारुणं ॥ 1
navakaṁja-locana kaṁja-mukha kara-kaṁja pada kaṁjāruṇaṁ.
कंदर्प अगणित अमित छवि नवनील नीरद सुंदरं ।
kaṁdarpa agaṇita amita chavi navanīla nīrada suṁdaraṁ,
पट पीत मानहु तड़ित रुचि शुचि नौमि जनक सुतावरं ॥ 2
paṭa pīta mānahu taṛita ruci śuci naumi janaka sutāvaraṁ.
भजु दीनबंधु दिनेश दानव-दैत्य-वंश निकंदनं ।
bhaju dīnabaṁdhu dineśa dānava-daitya-vaṁśa nikaṁdanaṁ,
रघुनंद आनँदकंद कोशलचंद दशरथ नंदनं ॥ 3
raghunaṁda ānaṁ̐dakaṁda kośalacaṁda daśaratha naṁdanaṁ.
सिर मुकुट कुंडल तिलक चारु उदारु अंग विभूषणं ।
sira mukuṭa kuṁḍala tilaka cāru udāru aṁga vibhūṣaṇaṁ,
आजानुभुज शर-चाप-धर संग्राम-जित-खरदूषणं ॥ 4
ājānubhuja śara-cāpa-dhara saṁgrāma-jita-kharadūṣaṇaṁ.
इति वदति तुलसीदास शंकर-शेष-मुनि-मन-रंजनं ।
iti vadati tulasīdāsa śaṁkara-śeṣa-muni-mana-raṁjanaṁ,
मम हृदय कंज निवास करु कामादि खल-दल-गंजनं ॥ 5
mama hṛdaya kaṁja nivāsa karu kāmādi khala-dala-gaṁjanaṁ.

श्री रामचन्द्र कृपालु भजु मन हरण भवभय दारुणं ...
śrī rāmacandra kṛpālu bhaju mana haraṇa bhavabhaya dāruṇaṁ ...

श्री हनुमान-स्तुति — śrī hanumāna-stuti

मंगल-मूरति मारुत-नंदन । सकल-अमंगल-मूल-निकंदन ॥ 1
maṁgala-mūrati māruta-naṁdana, sakala-amaṁgala-mūla-nikaṁdana.
पवन-तनय संतन-हितकारी। हृदय विराजत अवध बिहारी ॥ 2
pavana-tanaya saṁtana-hitakārī, hṛdaya virājata avadha bihārī.
मातु-पिता गुरु गनपति सारद। सिवा-समेत संभु सुक-नारद ॥ 3
mātu-pitā guru ganapati sārada, sivā-sameta saṁbhu suka-nārada.
चरन बंदि बिनवौं सब काहू। देहु रामपद-नेह-निबाहू ॥ 4
carana baṁdi binavauṁ saba kāhū, dehu rāmapada-neha-nibāhū.
बंदौं राम-लखन-बैदेही। जे तुलसी के परम सनेही ॥ 5
baṁdauṁ rāma-lakhana-baidehī, je tulasī ke parama sanehī.

मंगल-मूरति मारुत-नंदन ...
maṁgala-mūrati māruta-naṁdana ...

(तुलसीदास कृत विनय-पत्रिका से)
(From the Vinay-Patrika of Goswāmi Tulsīdās)

श्री हनुमान चालीसा — śrī hanumāna cālīsā

दोहा - dohā

श्रीगुरु चरन सरोज रज निज मन मुकुर सुधारि । बरनऊँ रघुबर बिमल जस जो दायक फल चारि ॥
śrīguru carana saroja raja nija mana mukura sudhāri, baranaūṁ raghubara bimala jasa jo dāyaka phala cāri.
बुद्धि हीन तनु जानिकै सुमिरौं पवन कुमार । बल बुद्धि बिद्या देहु मोहि हरहु कलेश विकार ॥
buddhi hīna tanu jānikai sumiraum pavana kumāra, bala buddhi bidyā dehu mohi harahu kaleśa vikāra.

चौपाई - caupāī

जय हनुमान ज्ञान गुण सागर । जय कपीश तिहुँ लोक उजागर ॥ 1
jaya hanumāna jñāna guṇa sāgara, jaya kapīśa tihuṁ loka ujāgara.
राम दूत अतुलित बल धामा । अंजनिपुत्र पवनसुत नामा ॥ 2
rāma dūta atulita bala dhāmā, aṁjaniputra pavanasuta nāmā.
महाबीर बिक्रम बजरंगी । कुमति निवार सुमति के संगी ॥ 3
mahābīra bikrama bajaraṁgī, kumati nivāra sumati ke saṁgī.
कंचन बरन बिराज सुबेषा । कानन कुंडल कुंचित केशा ॥ 4
kaṁcana barana birāja subeṣā, kānana kuṁḍala kuṁcita keśā.
हाथ बज्र और ध्वजा बिराजै । काँधे मूँज जनेऊ साजै ॥ 5
hātha bajra aura dhvajā birājai, kāṁdhe mūṁja janeū sājai.
शङ्कर स्वयं केशरीनंदन । तेज प्रताप महा जग बंदन ॥ 6
śaṅkara svayaṁ keśarīnaṁdana, teja pratāpa mahā jaga baṁdana.
विद्यावान गुणी अति चातुर । राम काज करिबे को आतुर ॥ 7
vidyāvāna guṇī ati cātura, rāma kāja karibe ko ātura.
प्रभु चरित्र सुनिबे को रसिया । राम लखन सीता मन बसिया ॥ 8
prabhu caritra sunibe ko rasiyā, rāma lakhana sītā mana basiyā.
सूक्ष्म रूप धरि सियहिं दिखावा । बिकट रूप धरि लंक जरावा ॥ 9
sūkṣma rūpa dhari siyahiṁ dikhāvā, bikaṭa rūpa dhari laṁka jarāvā.
भीम रूप धरि असुर सँहारे । रामचन्द्र के काज सँवारे ॥ 10
bhīma rūpa dhari asura saṁhāre, rāmacandra ke kāja saṁvāre.
लाय संजीवनि लखन जियाये । श्री रघुबीर हरषि उर लाये ॥ 11
lāya saṁjīvani lakhana jiyāye, śrī raghubīra haraṣi ura lāye.
रघुपति कीन्ही बहुत बड़ाई । तुम मम प्रिय भरतहिं सम भाई ॥ 12
raghupati kīnhī bahuta baṛāī, tuma mama priya bharatahiṁ sama bhāī.
सहस बदन तुम्हरो जस गावैं । अस कहि श्रीपति कंठ लगावैं ॥ 13
sahasa badana tumharo jasa gāvaiṁ, asa kahi śrīpati kaṁṭha lagāvaiṁ.
सनकादिक ब्रह्मादि मुनीशा । नारद शारद सहित अहीशा ॥ 14
sanakādika brahmādi munīśā, nārada śārada sahita ahīśā.
जम कुबेर दिगपाल जहाँ ते । कबि कोबिद कहि सकै कहाँ ते ॥ 15
jama kubera digapāla jahāṁ te, kabi kobida kahi sakai kahāṁ te.
तुम उपकार सुग्रीवहिं कीन्हा । राम मिलाय राज पद दीन्हा ॥ 16
tuma upakāra sugrīvahiṁ kīnhā, rāma milāya rāja pada dīnhā.
तुम्हरो मंत्र बिभीषन माना । लंकेश्वर भए सब जग जाना ॥ 17
tumharo maṁtra bibhīṣana mānā, laṁkeśvara bhae saba jaga jānā.
जुग सहस्त्र जोजन पर भानू । लील्यो ताहि मधुर फल जानू ॥ 18
* juga sahastra jojana para bhānū, līlyo tāhi madhura phala jānū.
प्रभु मुद्रिका मेलि मुख माहीं । जलधि लाँघि गये अचरज नाहीं ॥ 19
prabhu mudrikā meli mukha māhīṁ, jaladhi lāṁghi gaye acaraja nāhīṁ.
दुर्गम काज जगत के जेते । सुगम अनुग्रह तुम्हरे तेते ॥ 20
durgama kāja jagata ke jete, sugama anugraha tumhare tete.

राम दुआरे तुम रखवारे । होत न आज्ञा बिनु पैसारे ॥ 21
rāma duāre tuma rakhavāre, hota na ājñā binu paisāre.
सब सुख लहैं तुम्हारी शरना । तुम रक्षक काहू को डर ना ॥ 22
saba sukha lahaiṁ tumhārī śaranā, tuma rakṣaka kāhū ko ḍara nā.
आपन तेज सम्हारो आपै । तीनौं लोक हाँक ते काँपै ॥ 23
āpana teja samhāro āpai, tīnauṁ loka hāṁka te kāṁpai.
भूत पिशाच निकट नहिं आवै । महाबीर जब नाम सुनावै ॥ 24
bhūta piśāca nikaṭa nahiṁ āvai, mahābīra jaba nāma sunāvai.
नासै रोग हरै सब पीरा । जपत निरंतर हनुमत बीरा ॥ 25
nāsai roga harai saba pīrā, japata niraṁtara hanumata bīrā.
संकट ते हनुमान छुड़ावै । मन क्रम बचन ध्यान जो लावै ॥ 26
saṁkaṭa te hanumāna chuṛāvai, mana krama bacana dhyāna jo lāvai.
सब पर राम तपस्वी राजा । तिन के काज सकल तुम साजा ॥ 27
saba para rāma tapasvī rājā, tina ke kāja sakala tuma sājā.
और मनोरथ जो कोउ लावै । तासु अमित जीवन फल पावै ॥ 28
aura manoratha jo kou lāvai, tāsu amita jīvana phala pāvai.
चारों जुग परताप तुम्हारा । है परसिद्ध जगत उजियारा ॥ 29
cāroṁ juga paratāpa tumhārā, hai parasiddha jagata ujiyārā.
साधु संत के तुम रखवारे । असुर निकंदन राम दुलारे ॥ 30
sādhu saṁta ke tuma rakhavāre, asura nikaṁdana rāma dulāre.
अष्ट सिद्धि नव निधि के दाता । अस बर दीन्ह जानकी माता ॥ 31
aṣṭa siddhi nava nidhi ke dātā, asa bara dīnha jānakī mātā.
राम रसायन तुम्हरे पासा । सदा रहउ रघुपति के दासा ॥ 32
rāma rasāyana tumhare pāsā, sadā rahau raghupati ke dāsā.
तुम्हरे भजन राम को पावै । जनम जनम के दुख बिसरावै ॥ 33
tumhare bhajana rāma ko pāvai, janama janama ke dukha bisarāvai.
अंत काल रघुबर पुर जाई । जहाँ जन्म हरिभक्त कहाई ॥ 34
aṁta kāla raghubara pura jāī, jahāṁ janma haribhakta kahāī.
और देवता चित्त न धरई । हनुमत सेइ सर्ब सुख करई ॥ 35
aura devatā citta na dharaī, hanumata sei sarba sukha karaī.
संकट कटै मिटै सब पीरा । जो सुमिरै हनुमत बलबीरा ॥ 36
saṁkaṭa kaṭai miṭai saba pīrā, jo sumirai hanumata balabīrā.
जय जय जय हनुमान गोसाईं । कृपा करहु गुरु देव की नाईं ॥ 37
jaya jaya jaya hanumāna gosāīṁ, kṛpā karahu guru deva kī nāīṁ.
यह शत बार पाठ कर जोई । छूटै बंदि महा सुख सोई ॥ 38
yaha śata bāra pāṭha kara joī, chūṭai baṁdi mahā sukha soī.
जो यह पढ़ै हनुमान चालीसा । होय सिद्धि साखी गौरीसा ॥ 39
jo yaha paṛhai hanumāna cālīsā, hoya siddhi sākhī gaurīsā.
तुलसीदास सदा हरि चेरा । कीजै नाथ हृदय महँ डेरा ॥ 40
tulasīdāsa sadā hari cerā, kījai nātha hṛdaya mahaṁ ḍerā.

दोहा - dohā

पवन तनय संकट हरन मंगल मूरति रूप । राम लखन सीता सहित हृदय बसहु सुर भूप ॥
pavana tanaya saṁkaṭa harana maṁgala mūrati rūpa, rāma lakhana sītā sahita hṛdaya basahu sura bhūpa.

* Here Juga (which equal 12,000 Divine-Years per Vedic-Time-Scale) is used as a number; sahastra is 1000; jojana is 8 miles. The distance to Bhanu (Sun) 12,000x1000x8 = 96 million miles is given out in this 18th Chaupai. This estimate by Tulsīdās from sixteenth century India is within 3.3% of modern day calculations.

श्री हनुमान आरती — śrī hanumāna ārati

आरती कीजै हनुमान लला की । दुष्ट-दलन रघुनाथ कला की ॥ 1
āratī kījai hanumāna lalā kī, duṣṭa-dalana raghunātha kalā kī.
जाके बल से गिरिवर काँपै । रोग दोष जाके निकट न झाँपै ॥ 2
jāke bala se girivara kāṁpai, roga doṣa jāke nikaṭa na jhāṁpai.
अंजनि-पुत्र महा बल दाई । संतन के प्रभु सदा सहाई ॥ 3
aṁjani-putra mahā bala dāī, saṁtana ke prabhu sadā sahāī.
दे बीरा रघुनाथ पठाये । लंका जारि सीय सुधि लाये ॥ 4
de bīrā raghunātha paṭhāye, laṁkā jāri sīya sudhi lāye.
लंका-सो कोट समुद्र-सी खाई । जात पवनसुत बार न लाई ॥ 5
laṁkā-so koṭa samudra-sī khāī, jāta pavanasuta bāra na lāī.
लंका जारि असुर संहारे । सियारामजी के काज सँवारे ॥ 6
laṁkā jāri asura saṁhāre, siyārāmajī ke kāja saṁvāre.
लछिमन मूर्छित पड़े सकारे । आनि सजीवन प्रान उबारे ॥ 7
lachimana mūrchita paṛe sakāre, āni sajīvana prāna ubāre.
पैठी पताल तोरि जम-कारे । अहिरावन की भुजा उखारे ॥ 8
paiṭhī patāla tori jama-kāre, ahirāvana kī bhujā ukhāre.
बायें भुजा असुरदल मारे । दहिने भुजा संतजन तारे ॥ 9
bāyeṁ bhujā asuradala māre, dahine bhujā saṁtajana tāre.
सुर नर मुनि आरती उतारे । जै जै जै हनुमान उचारे ॥ 10
sura nara muni āratī utāre, jai jai jai hanumāna ucāre.
कंचन थार कपूर लौ छाई । आरति करत अंजना माई ॥ 11
kaṁcana thāra kapūra lau chāī, ārati karata aṁjanā māī.
जो हनुमानजी की आरति गावै । बसि बैकुंठ परमपद पावै ॥ 12
jo hanumānajī kī ārati gāvai, basi baikuṁṭha paramapada pāvai.

आरती कीजै हनुमान लला की । दुष्ट-दलन रघुनाथ कला की ...
āratī kījai hanumāna lalā kī, duṣṭa-dalana raghunātha kalā kī ...

°°
°°

सियावर रामचन्द्र की जय
siyāvara rāmacandra kī jaya
पवनसुत हनुमान की जय
pavanasuta hanumāna kī jaya
गोस्वामी तुलसीदास की जय
gosvāmī tulasīdāsa kī jaya

Guide to Pronunciation

(T)	(D)	(IPA)	
a	अ	ə	Vowel. The sound of short vowel 'a' is inherent in almost all consonants. Sounds like 'u' in **us**.
ā	आ	a:	Vowel. Long 'a'. Sounds like f**a**r.
ai	ऐ	ɛ:	Vowel. Long 'ai'. Sounds like **a**nti, N**a**ncy.
au	औ	ɔ:	Vowel. Long 'o' Sounds like s**aw**, s**ou**ght, g**o**t.
b	ब	b	Consonant. Sounds like **b**us.
bh	भ	bʱ	Consonant. Aspirated version of above. Sounds like a**bh**or.
c	च	tʃ	Consonant. Sounds like **ch**irp.
ch	छ	tʃʰ	Consonant. Aspirated version of above. Sounds approx. like hit**chh**iker, or the sound of sneeze 'a**ch**oo'.
d	द	d̪	Consonant. Sounds like **th**us.
ḍ	ड	ɖ	Consonant. Sounds like guar**d**.
ḏ	ड़	ɽ	Consonant. Retroflex flap. Sounds approx. like guar**dh**ouse.
dh	ध	d̪ʱ	Consonant. Aspirated version of above. Sounds approx. like wi**th**out.
ḍh	ढ	ɖʱ	Consonant. Sounds approx. like bi**rd**.
ḏh	ढ़	ɽʱ	Consonant. Aspirated retroflex flap. Sounds approx. like bi**rdh**ouse.
e	ए	e:	Vowel. Short 'ai'. Sounds like pr**ay**.
g	ग	g	Consonant. Sounds like **g**um.
gh	घ	gʱ	Consonant. Aspirated version of above. Sounds like a**gh**ast.
h	ह	ɦ	Consonant. Sounds like **h**urt.
ḥ	◌ः	-	Vowel modifier. Sounds like **h**um.
i	इ	i	Vowel. Short 'e'. Sounds like **i**t.
ī	ई	i:	Vowel. Long 'e'. Sounds like **ea**t.
j	ज	dʒ	Consonant. Sounds like **j**ust.
jh	झ	dʒʱ	Consonant. Aspirated version of above. Sounds approx. like he**dgeh**og.
k	क	k	Consonant. Sounds like **c**ut.
kh	ख	kʰ	Consonant. Aspirated version of above. Sounds like si**kh**.
l	ल	l	Consonant. Sounds like **l**earn.
ḷ	ऌ	l̩	Vowel. Vocalic l. Sounds like sick**le**.

(T)	(D)	(IPA)	
m	म	m	Consonant. Sounds like **m**uch.
ṃ	◌ं	-	Vowel modifier. Pure nasal after a vowel as in Luftha**n**sa.
n	न	n	Consonant. Sounds like **n**un.
ṅ	ङ	ŋ	Consonant. Sounds approx. like ha**n**g.
ñ	ञ	ɲ	Consonant. The palatal nasal has sound similar to o**ni**on.
ṇ	ण	ɳ	Consonant. Sounds like be**n**t.
o	ओ	o:	Vowel. Short 'o'. Sounds like **o**ld.
p	प	p	Consonant. Sounds like **p**urse.
ph	फ	pʰ	Consonant. Sounds like **f**un.
r	र	r	Consonant. Sounds like **r**un.
ṛ	ऋ	r̩	Vowel. Vocalic r. Sounds like int**ere**sting.
ṝ	ॠ	r̩:	Vowel. Long Vocalic r.
s	स	s	Consonant. Sounds like **s**um.
ś	श	ʃ	Consonant. Sounds like **sh**ut.
ṣ	ष	ʂ	Consonant. Sounds approx. like wor**sh**ip.
t	त	t̪	Consonant. Difficult to approximate but think of it like **t**hought without the sound 'h'.
th	थ	t̪ʰ	Consonant. Sounds like **th**ought.
ṭ	ट	ʈ	Consonant. Sounds like **t**usk.
ṭh	ठ	ʈʰ	Consonant. Aspirated version of above. Sounds approx. like gues**th**ouse.
u	उ	ʊ	Vowel. Short 'u'. Sounds like b**oo**k.
ū	ऊ	ʊ:	Vowel. Long 'u'. Sounds like b**oo**t.
v	व	ʋ	Consonant. Sounds like **w**ord.
y	य	j	Consonant. Sounds like **y**up.
m̐	◌ँ	-	Vowel modifier. Sounds like French bo**n** viva**n**t.

(D) Devnagri character — Column 2

(T) Equivalent Transliteration — Column 1

(IPA) Associated (International Phonetic Alphabet) symbol — Column 3

(Table sorted on Column 1)

The table on the opposite page should prove useful in learning to pronounce Devnāgrī words. Important points are highlighted below:

VOWELS

Trans-literation	Devnāgrī Vowel in Standalone-Form	Description	Devnāgrī vowel in Mātrā-Form (examples shown with consonant स)
a	अ	Vowel, short 'a', sounds like the **u** in s**u**m	स
ā	आ	Vowel, long 'a', sounds like the **a** in saga	सा
i	इ	Vowel, short 'i', sounds like the **i** in s**i**t	सि
ī	ई	Vowel, long 'i', sounds like the **ee** in s**ee**k	सी
u	उ	Vowel, short 'u', sounds like the **u** in s**u**per	सु
ū	ऊ	Vowel, long 'u', sounds like the **oo** in s**oo**t	सू
e	ए	Vowel, short 'ai', sounds like the **ay** in s**ay**	से
ai	ऐ	Vowel, long 'ai', sounds like the **a** in s**a**g	सै
o	ओ	Vowel, short 'o', sounds like the **o** in s**o**ul	सो
au	औ	Vowel, long 'o', sounds like the **aw** in s**aw**	सौ

▪ Vowels are written in Standalone form, or in Mātrā form with a consonant. Listed above are the 5 main vowels, in their short & long tones. More vowels exist.

▪ Short vowels (**a, i, u, e, o**) are pronounced a certain way and their long equivalents (**ā, ī, ū, ai, au**) receive additional stress on those short sounds.

▪ ऋ (**ṛ**) is another vowel. In Mātrā form it is written as the curve below some constant; e.g. कृ - k**ṛ** ('c**r**unch').

▪ **ṃ ṁ m̐** are modifiers which have the effect of nasalizing the preceding sound.

▪ **ḥ** is a vowel modifier: a rough breathing that causes the preceding vowel to echo.

CONSONANTS

For the most part Consonants sound just as in English; but do please be cognizant of the following:

▪ Devnāgrī Consonants are mostly pronounced with the inherent sound of short **a** at the end*, unless another vowel modifies that sound. e.g. consider म-ma ('**mu**st') versus the vowel modified म-m like:

मा-mā ('**mar**k'), मि-mi ('**mi**ss'), मी-mī ('**mee**k'), मु-mu ('**mu**dra'), मू-mū ('**moo**n'), मे-me ('**may**'), मै-mai ('**ma**n'), मो-mo ('**mo**re'), मौ-mau ('**mau**l'), मं-maṁ ('**mum**').

*Exception: A Devnāgrī consonant in its pristine form (e.g. म् [in rare use and] which has a diacritic mark) or a half form (e.g. सम्मान) will not have the sound of short vowel 'a' at end.

▪ **c** is always pronounced like the **ch** in **ch**uck. [so then expect words like clear would be written as **k**lear]

▪ **ch** may also be approximated to **c** but with added aspiration like in the sneezing sound.

▪ **d** is soft like in **th**us. **ḍ** is hard like in **d**irt.

▪ **g** is hard like in **g**ranite.

▪ **ṅ** sounds approx. like the **ng** in hu**ng**. **ñ** is the ny sounds like the **ni** in o**ni**on.

▪ **s** without the diacritic is like the normal **s**, as in **s**um.

▪ **ś** and **ṣ** have very subtle difference that may be ignored, and can be approximated to the **sh** in **sh**ut.

▪ **ṭ** is hard like in **t**ough. **t** is soft. Difficult to approximate but try saying **t**hird without the h.

▪ Unlike English, Devnāgrī distinguishes between un-aspirated consonant and aspirated consonants (with a succeeding **h)**. So we have **bh, ch, dh, ḍh, gh, jh, kh, ph, th, ṭh** etc. as shown in the table.

ABOUT RĀMCHARITMĀNAS AND TULSĪDĀSA

Cheerfully and lovingly recited by all the devotees of Bhagwān Rāma, Rāmcharitmānas, the Epic-of-Rāma, is a veritable fount of Devotion and Wisdom known to dispel away evil and ignorance. Established through all the regions of earth, this timeless saga of the ancient most Being Rāma has been narrated by many a great Rishīs of past; and once again to trumpet it in the Kali-Yug, the holy story of Rāma, Lord of Hanumān, has been penned by the wonderful saint Tulsīdās—from a quill fashioned with the very feathers of a Param-Haṁsa, the divine bird of highest discrimination and wisdom—and written dipped in the sweetness of Nectar of Devotion.

Tulsīdās, born in India in the sixteenth century, was an illustrious saint, philosopher, poet, and a supreme devotee of Bhagwān Rāma, the incarnate Supreme Being. He composed many poems in praise of Shrī Rāma, with Rāmcharitmānas being his most celebrated epic. Though he was an eminent Sanskrit scholar he chose to write in Awadhī, the language of the populace, so that all could sing the glories of Lord God Rāma.

The potency and beauty of Tulsīdās' poetry is unparalleled in the history of literature. Rāmcharitmānas, intended as the religious instruction for all—literate or illiterate, even those who have absolutely no knowledge of the Vedas—is the quintessence of Sanātana-Dharma; and the verses of Rāmcharitmānas may be compared to Mantras: containing the gist of the highest truths culled from the Vedas and Purānas.

By churning the wealth that is contained in many religious works and in many discourses based on Dharma, the nectar of Rāmcharitmānas—comprising of the highest knowledge and most sublime devotion—has been raised by Rishī Tulsīdās. As ghee is created from milk for the benefit of a beloved, even so has Rāmcharitmānas been churned out by Tulsīdās for the sake of Rāma Devotees—simply out of compassion and love that only a parent can have for their child. Our repeated obeisance to the parent of every Devotee: Bhakta Shiromanī Param Rāma Bhakta Sant Rishī Tulsīdās Jī.

The Vedas and Purānas are oceans of wisdom; and when the intellect of a seer like Tulsīdās shines upon them, then, seared from its fieriness, some of that sapience evaporates; and further, when those cumulous clouds of profundity condense under the cooling influence of compassion of that saint's lovesome heart, then they pour in as snow upon the sublime heights of Himalayas called the Rāmcharitmānas; and then from those lofty heights, multiple streams of the wonderful confluence of Wisdom and Devotion are seen forevermore in a relentless flow: as the Gangā of Rāma-Kathā, for the thirsting humanity.

Within Rāmcharitmānas, Tulsīdās has caught the essence of the mystic susurrations of Vedic chants; and their ancient rhythm has become woven into a simple rustic poetry in his artful words and deft hands. Verily the bright searing heat from the sun of Vedic wisdom is seen congealed into the cooling beams of full-moon light in Tulsīdās' verses sublime—which bring restful solace to one and all who have read them just but once. And these verses of Rāmcharitmānas—when sung or heard, whether understood or not—when their charming beauty has inundated you with bliss, and when their sound floats away driven by the dictates of the laws of nature—then they do not mingle far but remain suspended in space, clinging around you, and they wrap you in an aura of hushed serenity which carries you on a cloud of calm, through the intensity of entire day.

(*Above culled from books in the:* **Upanishad Vidya Series.** *Authored by:* **Vidya Wati**)

ABOUT SUNDARAKĀNDA AND TULSĪDĀSA

Such souls are truly blessed: who drink of the nectar which is the name 'Rāma'—which nectar has been churned out of the all-pervading ocean of Brahmn—which nectar may be availed of as much as desired but never becomes depleted—which nectar remains ever present on the moon-like beautiful face of Lord Shankar increasing his beauty—which nectar is the sole remedy for all worldly afflictions—which nectar is the provider of all bliss—which nectar is the very life of mother Jānakī Sītā.

Blessed is our Lord God Sītā-Rāma and blessed the devotees of Sītā-Rāma: who remain ever absorbed in the joy of devotion to their Lord; who have thrown their heart as fish into the nectarine lake of love for the beautiful name Sītā-Rāma—two redeeming words, easy to remember, most delightful to hear, utter, sing; which satisfy every wish, and are the highest gain in this world and the next.

Blessed are such noble souls, who have heard the word, and who now understand, and who find themselves almost there; or who, in the spirit of devotion, have taken their first plunge; but the blessed-most are those who have already attained eternal happiness in the sea of serenity called Sītā-Rāma. But what about the rest of us? How will I secure my own release from this endless cycle of transmigration? Having Bhakti and submission to our Lord is the surest means of gaining deliverance from the cruel cycle of births and deaths—easy to say, but how do we attain to that? How far is it from here to there? And how do we get there? Who will be gracious to me? Who will inspire me with devotion to the lotus feet of Sītā-Rāma? In these difficult times, how is one to inculcate Devotion to the Lord's feet, and furthermore sustain it?

The answer is Tulsīdās' Rāmacaritamānas.

Yes, Rāmacaritamānas, the divine song—which emerged from the beautiful Mānas Lake of Lord Shiva's soul—which is the celestial river replete with Rāma's bright renown that has been in a relentless flow for eons—in whose holy torrents are swept away all the impurities of the Kali-Yug, whether they be in the form of tiny blades of grass or mighty trees tall—in the proximity of which you find your soul in an overflowing swell of ecstatic devotion—and submerged in whose streams you find your heart welling with joy and rapture.

Verily Rāmacaritamānas imparts Bhakti—as millions over the ages have discovered and aver. Its recitation helps us inculcate the habit of constantly remembering Bhagwān Rāma: to focus our minds upon Him, and His Holy Name. This is the supreme easy path of Sanatana Dharma known as Bhakti-Yog—finding God through Devotion. Bhakti for Sītā-Rāma, Hanumān, is the infallible remedy for all worldly ills and misfortunes which you see spreading like wildfire in this Kali-Yug.

Not just imparting the highest bliss of emancipation, Rāmacaritamānas delivers at every level—be it worldly or spiritual. After a hard day's toil, one finds a fount of rejuvenation within the verses of Tulsīdās; and just as a fish feels fresh when submerged in water, so too our souls feel invigorated by taking a dip in the Ocean of Bliss called Rāma—which Ocean exists within Rāmacaritamānas: the holy water of divine enactments and stories of Lord Rāma—which deeds were recorded by Lord Shiva Himself; and which have percolated down to us through several different narrators—with Goswāmī Tulsīdās being the latest in the long chain. Tulsīdās recorded the Rāmacaritamānas in his rustic poetry and his books are like pitchers full of ambrosia for gaining everlasting peace within our soul.

With the blessings of Lord Shiva, the verses of Rāmacaritamānas have acquired the power of Mantras. Each verse within Rāmacaritamānas is like a Siddha-Mantra—this the multitudes have testified over the centuries. Not only does Rāmacaritamānas bring the Supreme Being nearer to our hearts than ever before—making spiritual liberation and deliverance easily available—but the worldly benefits she brings to us are endless too. As myriads of devotees have verified through experiences of direct grace, Rāmacaritamānas, the Epic of Rāma, is like a Kāmadhenu—the celestial cow—which yields whatever the devotee seeks from her, be it some worldly remedy or spiritual enlightenment.

Amongst the people, Sundarakāṇḍa, the fifth ascent into Rāmacaritamānas has become the most popular Canto of the great Epic. Often it is often sung independently and is considered a book in itself. It is called Sundara because it is Beautiful, and it is Beautiful for its various reasons; especially since the sorrowful events of Ayodhyā-Kānd, this episode rekindles hope.

The Fifth Canto of Rāmacaritamānas bridges many ends and in it one finds many wishes being granted—which span the spectrum of human desires. In the same vein, numerous Rāma devotees over the centuries have averred, after direct realization, that the Pāṭha (recitation) of Rāmacaritamānas (or her proxy, the Sundarakāṇḍa) has the power to grant you any wish which you harbor in your heart; and during their recitation, they use the Samputṣ of certain verses taken from within the Rāmacaritamānas to get their desired wish.

Samput or Samputịkaran is a Mantra which adds potency to the verses being hymned; in essence, it is a Mantra within a Mantra. Considered very powerful, Samput Mantras are mostly Chaupaīs or Dohās from within the Rāmacaritamānas itself; or they are the various chants of 'Rāma'—the King of Holy Mantras.

There are many Mantras in Rāmacaritamānas which are used to ward off troubles and afflictions as well as to gain the favor of our Lord God. For instance many parents will do the Pāṭha of Sundarakāṇḍa on the birthday of their children or loved ones using the following Mantra:

अजर अमर गुननिधि सुत होहू । करहुँ बहुत रघुनायक छोहू ॥
ajara amara gunanidhi suta hohū, karahuṁ bahuta raghunāyaka chohū.

which means: **May you, dear, become ageless, deathless and a treasury of virtues and the very beloved of Shrī Rāma.** This is the boon which mother Sītā bestows upon Hanumān in verse 5.17.3 of Rāmacaritamānas (the 3rd Chaupaī leading up to Dohā 17 of the Fifth Canto, Sundarakāṇḍa). Similarly, to gain the favor of Lord God and for the welfare and general well-being of their family, people will add the following Samput Mantra during their weekly Sundarakāṇḍa Pātha:

मंगल भवन अमंगल हारी । द्रवउ सो दसरथ अजिर बिहारी ॥
maṁgala bhavana amaṁgala hārī, dravau so dasaratha ajira bihārī.

meaning: **He, who is the bane of all woes and an Abode of Bliss, who sports in the courtyards of King Dasrath, may that compassionate child Rāma, be ever kind to me.** This verse is spoken by Lord Shiva to Uma at Rāmacaritamānas 1.112.4.

Above culled from our book:
Sundarakanda -- The Fifth-Ascent of Tulsi Ramayana with English Translation & Transliteration by Subhash Chandra
(ISBNs: 978-1-945739-05-7 (Paperback),
978-1-945739-15-6 (Hardcover),
978-1-945739-90-3 (Journal),
978-1-945739-91-0 (Journal Hardcover)

Some other Books you may like

Below is reproduced from **Sundarakanda: The Fifth-Ascent of Tulsi Ramayana, by Subhash Chandra.** ISBNs: **978-1-945739-05-7 / 978-1-945739-15-6 / 978-1-945739-90-3 / 978-1-945739-91-0**

(Excerpts shown below are in reduced font-size)

शलोक-śloka:

शान्तं शाश्वतमप्रमेयमनघं निर्वाणशान्तिप्रदं
śāntaṁ śāśvatamaprameyamanaghaṁ nirvāṇaśāntipradaṁ
ब्रह्माशम्भुफणीन्द्रसेव्यमनिशं वेदान्तवेद्यं विभुम् ।
brahmāśambhuphaṇīndrasevyamaniśaṁ vedāntavedyaṁ vibhum,
रामाख्यं जगदीश्वरं सुरगुरुं मायामनुष्यं हरिं
rāmākhyaṁ jagadīśvaraṁ suraguruṁ māyāmanuṣyaṁ hariṁ
वन्देऽहं करुणाकरं रघुवरं भूपालचूडामणिम् ॥१॥
vande'haṁ karuṇākaraṁ raghuvaraṁ bhūpālacūṛāmaṇim. 1.

Trans:

I adore the Lord of the universe—immeasurable, all pervading and eternal, the very theme of Vedanta, beyond ordinary means of cognition, the all-merciful God of gods constantly worshipped by Brahmmā, Shambhu and Shesha; the dispeller of all sins, bestower of the supreme beatitude of emancipation, a veritable mine of compassion, the Lord God Hari appearing through his Māyā in the form of man, the King of kings, the chief of Raghus—Shrī Rāma.

नान्या स्पृहा रघुपते हृदयेऽस्मदीये सत्यं वदामि च भवानखिलान्तरात्मा ।
nānyā spṛhā raghupate hṛdaye'smadīye satyaṁ vadāmi ca bhavānakhilāntarātmā,
भक्तिं प्रयच्छ रघुपुङ्गव निर्भरां मे कामादिदोषरहितं कुरु मानसं च ॥२॥
bhaktiṁ prayaccha raghupuṅgava nirbharāṁ me kāmādidoṣarahitaṁ kuru mānasaṁ ca. 2.

Trans:

There is no other craving in my heart, O Lord, and I speak the truth and you know my inmost thoughts—for you are the indwelling Spirit in the hearts of all—do please grant me, O crest-jewel of Raghus, the intense-most devotion to Thy Holy Feet; and make my heart clean of lust and every other sin.

अतुलितबलधामं हेमशैलाभदेहं दनुजवनकृशानुं ज्ञानिनामग्रगण्यम् ।
atulitabaladhāmaṁ hemaśailābhadehaṁ danujavanakṛśānuṁ jñānināmagragaṇyam,
सकलगुणनिधानं वानराणामधीशं रघुपतिप्रियभक्तं वातजातं नमामि ॥३॥
sakalaguṇanidhānaṁ vānarāṇāmadhīśaṁ raghupatipriyabhaktaṁ vātajātaṁ namāmi. 3.

Trans:

Repeatedly I bow to the son-of-wind-god: repository of immeasurable might, with his body shining like a mountain of gold, the very blazing fire that devours the forest in the shape of demons; the abode of virtues, the noblest messenger of Raghupati, foremost amongst the wise, the chief of the monkeys: Shrī Hanumān, the most beloved devotee of Shrī Rāma.

चौपाई-caupāī:

जामवंत के बचन सुहाए । सुनि हनुमंत हृदय अति भाए ॥
jāmavaṁta ke bacana suhāe, suni hanumaṁta hṛdaya ati bhāe.
तब लगि मोहि परिखेहु तुम्ह भाई । सहि दुख कंद मूल फल खाई ॥
taba lagi mohi parikhehu tumha bhāī, sahi dukha kaṁda mūla phala khāī.
जब लगि आवौं सीतहि देखी । होइहि काजु मोहि हरष बिसेषी ॥
jaba lagi āvauṁ sītahi dekhī, hoihi kāju mohi haraṣa biseṣī.
यह कहि नाइ सबन्हि कहुँ माथा । चलेउ हरषि हियँ धरि रघुनाथा ॥
yaha kahi nāi sabanhi kahuṁ māthā, caleu haraṣi hiyaṁ dhari raghunāthā.
सिंधु तीर एक भूधर सुंदर । कौतुक कूदि चढ़ेउ ता ऊपर ॥
siṁdhu tīra eka bhūdhara suṁdara, kautuka kūdi caṛheu tā ūpara.
बार बार रघुबीर सँभारी । तरकेउ पवनतनय बल भारी ॥
bāra bāra raghubīra saṁbhārī, tarakeu pavanatanaya bala bhārī.
जेहिं गिरि चरन देइ हनुमंता । चलेउ सो गा पाताल तुरंता ॥
jehiṁ giri carana dei hanumaṁtā, caleu so gā pātāla turaṁtā.
जिमि अमोघ रघुपति कर बाना । एही भाँति चलेउ हनुमाना ॥
jimi amogha raghupati kara bānā, ehī bhāṁti caleu hanumānā.
जलनिधि रघुपति दूत बिचारी । तैं मैनाक होहि श्रमहारी ॥
jalanidhi raghupati dūta bicārī, taiṁ maināka hohi śramahārī.

Trans:

Hearing the heartening speech of Jāmavaṁt, Hanumān greatly rejoiced in his heart and said, "Endure these hardships my brothers, and with roots, herbs, fruits as your food, await here my return—till I am back with the news of Mā Sītā. My objective will surely be accomplished—I experience this great exhilaration in my heart." Saying so he bowed his head to them all; and then, with the image of Shrī Rāma enshrined in his heart, and full of exuberance, Hanumān sallied forth. There was a majestic rock by the seashore and Hanumān sprang upon its top in mere sport. Then again and again invoking the name of Raghubīr, the son-of-wind leaped with all his might. And the hill upon which he had planted his foot instantly sank—recoiling into the nethermost world. And just like an exceeding unerring arrow fired by Raghupati, Hanumān sped away. On the way—and knowing Hanumān to be the emissary of Shrī Rāma—the deity presiding over the Ocean told Maināk, "Relieve him of his fatigue."

दोहा-dohā:

हनूमान तेहि परसा कर पुनि कीन्ह प्रनाम ।
hanūmāna tehi parasā kara puni kīnha pranāma,
राम काजु कीन्हें बिनु मोहि कहाँ बिश्राम ॥१॥
rāma kāju kīnheṁ binu mohi kahāṁ biśrāma. 1.

Trans:

[Mount Maināk raised himself up from the sea and stood before, in welcome,] but Hanumān merely touched it with his hand, and saluting to it said, "There can be no rest for me until I have accomplished the work of Shri Rāma."

सीताराम सीताराम सीताराम सीताराम सीताराम सीताराम सीताराम सीताराम सीताराम सीताराम सीताराम सीताराम सीताराम सीताराम सीताराम सीताराम सीताराम सीताराम सीताराम सीताराम
सीताराम सीताराम सीताराम सीताराम सीताराम सीताराम सीताराम सीताराम सीताराम सीताराम सीताराम सीताराम सीताराम सीताराम सीताराम सीताराम सीताराम सीताराम सीताराम सीताराम

Below is reproduced from **Bhagavada Gītā, the Holy Book of Sanatana Dharma, by Sushma.** ISBNs: **978-1-945739-39-2** (Journal format) / **978-1-945739-36-1** (Paperback)/ **978-1-945739-37-8** (Hardback)

(Excerpts shown below are in reduced font-size)

न त्वेवाहं जातु नासं न त्वं नेमे जनाधिपाः ।
na tvevāhaṁ jātu nāsaṁ na tvaṁ neme janādhipāḥ
न चैव न भविष्यामः सर्वे वयमतः परम् ॥२-१२॥
na caiva na bhaviṣyāmaḥ sarve vayamataḥ param (2-12)

There never was a time indeed when I—or you or any of these kings—did not exist; nor it is that hereafter any of us shall cease to be.

देहिनोऽस्मिन्यथा देहे कौमारं यौवनं जरा ।
dehino'sminyathā dehe kaumāraṁ yauvanaṁ jarā
तथा देहान्तरप्राप्तिर्धीरस्तत्र न मुह्यति ॥२-१३॥
tathā dehāntaraprāptirdhīrastatra na muhyati (2-13)

Even as the embodied soul attains in this body the states of childhood, youth and old age—even so it obtains another body upon death; the wise do not get deluded witnessing such changes.

मात्रास्पर्शास्तु कौन्तेय शीतोष्णसुखदुःखदाः ।
mātrāsparśāstu kaunteya śītoṣṇasukhaduḥkhadāḥ
आगमापायिनोऽनित्यास्तांस्तितिक्षस्व भारत ॥२-१४॥
āgamāpāyino'nityāstāṁstitikṣasva bhārata (2-14)

From the contact of the sense-organs with sense-objects, there arise heat and cold, and even so pleasures and pains; but these are all transitory and fleeting and are subject to coming and going—so therefore just endure them, O Bhārata.

नासतो विद्यते भावो नाभावो विद्यते सतः ।
nāsato vidyate bhāvo nābhāvo vidyate sataḥ
उभयोरपि दृष्टोऽन्तस्त्वनयोस्तत्त्वदर्शिभिः ॥२-१६॥
ubhayorapi dṛṣṭo'ntastvanayostattvadarśibhiḥ (2-16)

The unreal has no existence, and the real never ceases to be—the conclusion of both is clearly perceived to its stark reality by the knowers of Truth.

अविनाशि तु तद्विद्धि येन सर्वमिदं ततम् ।
avināśi tu tadviddhi yena sarvamidaṁ tatam
विनाशमव्ययस्यास्य न कश्चित्कर्तुमर्हति ॥२-१७॥
vināśamavyayasyāsya na kaścitkartumarhati (2-17)

That One—by which this entire universe is pervaded—know That to be imperishable; verily no one can bring about the destruction of that Immutable Principle.

य एनं वेत्ति हन्तारं यश्चैनं मन्यते हतम् ।
ya enaṁ vetti hantāraṁ yaścainaṁ manyate hatam
उभौ तौ न विजानीतो नायं हन्ति न हन्यते ॥२-१९॥
ubhau tau na vijānīto nāyaṁ hanti na hanyate (2-19)

He who thinks of It to be a slayer, and who thinks of It as slain, both of them are ignorant—for verily the Self neither kills, nor gets killed.

नैनं छिन्दन्ति शस्त्राणि नैनं दहति पावकः ।
nainaṁ chindanti śastrāṇi nainaṁ dahati pāvakaḥ
न चैनं क्लेदयन्त्यापो न शोषयति मारुतः ॥२-२३॥
na cainaṁ kledayantyāpo na śoṣayati mārutaḥ (2-23)

Weapons do not cut the Self; and fires burn It not; and water cannot drench It; nor can It the winds dry.

न जायते म्रियते वा कदाचिन् नायं भूत्वा भविता वा न भूयः ।
na jāyate mriyate vā kadācin nāyaṁ bhūtvā bhavitā vā na bhūyaḥ
अजो नित्यः शाश्वतोऽयं पुराणो न हन्यते हन्यमाने शरीरे ॥२-२०॥
ajo nityaḥ śāśvato'yaṁ purāṇo na hanyate hanyamāne śarīre (2-20)

The Self is never born, nor does it ever die; nor does it come into existence by the body coming into being. Verily the Soul is unborn, immutable, constant, eternal and ancient-most. Even though the body is slain, the indwelling Self always persists unslain.

वासांसि जीर्णानि यथा विहाय नवानि गृह्णाति नरोऽपराणि ।
vāsāṁsi jīrṇāni yathā vihāya navāni gṛhṇāti naro'parāṇi
तथा शरीराणि विहाय जीर्णान्यन्यानि संयाति नवानि देही ॥२-२२॥
tathā śarīrāṇi vihāya jīrṇānyanyāni saṁyāti navāni dehī (2-22)

Discarding worn-out garments, just as a person puts on new garbs, in like fashion does the embodied Self—casting off outworn bodies—enters into other newer ones.

—❧—

अव्यक्तादीनि भूतानि व्यक्तमध्यानि भारत ।
avyaktādīni bhūtāni vyaktamadhyāni bhārata

अव्यक्तनिधनान्येव तत्र का परिदेवना ॥२-२८॥
avyaktanidhanānyeva tatra kā paridevanā (2-28)

Beings have the Unmanifest as their beginning; and upon death they return to that Unmanifest again. Between birth and death—only during the interim—do the beings become manifest; so wherefore lament for them, O Bhārata?

—❧—

देही नित्यमवध्योऽयं देहे सर्वस्य भारत ।
dehī nityamavadhyo'yaṁ dehe sarvasya bhārata
तस्मात्सर्वाणि भूतानि न त्वं शोचितुमर्हसि ॥२-३०॥
tasmātsarvāṇi bhūtāni na tvaṁ śocitumarhasi (2-30)

The indwelling Self, within the bodies of all, is eternally indestructible, O Bhārata; therefore, you ought not to grieve for any being.

—❧—

यावानर्थ उदपाने सर्वतः सम्प्लुतोदके ।
yāvānartha udapāne sarvataḥ samplutodake
तावान्सर्वेषु वेदेषु ब्राह्मणस्य विजानतः ॥२-४६॥
tāvānsarveṣu vedeṣu brāhmaṇasya vijānataḥ (2-46)

All the purposes which a small reservoir serves, is served entirely by a vast lake full of water. Likewise the purpose which all the Vedas serve, is already attained by one who is in complete knowledge of Brahama.

—❧—

योगस्थः कुरु कर्माणि सङ्गं त्यक्त्वा धनञ्जय ।
yogasthaḥ kuru karmāṇi saṅgaṁ tyaktvā dhanañjaya
सिद्ध्यसिद्ध्योः समो भूत्वा समत्वं योग उच्यते ॥२-४८॥
siddhyasiddhyoḥ samo bhūtvā samatvaṁ yoga ucyate (2-48)

Established in Yoga, perform Karma renouncing all attachments, O Dhananjaya, remaining unconcerned as to the outcome—be it failure or success; this equanimity of mind is what is called Karma-Yoga.

—❧—

कर्मजं बुद्धियुक्ता हि फलं त्यक्त्वा मनीषिणः ।
karmajaṁ buddhiyuktā hi phalaṁ tyaktvā manīṣiṇaḥ
जन्मबन्धविनिर्मुक्ताः पदं गच्छन्त्यनामयम् ॥२-५१॥
janmabandhavinirmuktāḥ padaṁ gacchantyanāmayam (2-51)

Endowed with wisdom, renouncing the fruits born of action, attaining self-realization, freed from the shackles of births and deaths—verily a Yogī enters that abode which is void of sorrows.

—❧—

यदा संहरते चायं कूर्मोऽङ्गानीव सर्वशः ।
yadā saṁharate cāyaṁ kūrmo'ṅgānīva sarvaśaḥ
इन्द्रियाणीन्द्रियार्थेभ्यस्तस्य प्रज्ञा प्रतिष्ठिता ॥२-५८॥
indriyāṇīndriyārthebhyastasya prajñā pratiṣṭhitā (2-58)

When one can altogether withdraw the senses from the sense-objects—even as a tortoise its limbs—then his wisdom is said to be steady.

—❧—

विषया विनिवर्तन्ते निराहारस्य देहिनः ।
viṣayā vinivartante nirāhārasya dehinaḥ
रसवर्जं रसोऽप्यस्य परं दृष्ट्वा निवर्तते ॥२-५९॥
rasavarjaṁ raso'pyasya paraṁ dṛṣṭvā nivartate (2-59)

Sense enjoyments can be restricted through physical restraint by an abstemious being, but a relish for them may still persist; even this relish ceases when the highest bliss of the Supreme is realized.

—❧—

कर्मेन्द्रियाणि संयम्य य आस्ते मनसा स्मरन् ।
karmendriyāṇi saṁyamya ya āste manasā smaran
इन्द्रियार्थान्विमूढात्मा मिथ्याचारः स उच्यते ॥३-६॥
indriyārthānvimūḍhātmā mithyācāraḥ sa ucyate (3-6)

The fool who outwardly restraining the organs of action sits dwelling upon the senses-objects through the mind—that man of deluded intellect is called a hypocrite.

—❧—

यस्त्विन्द्रियाणि मनसा नियम्यारभतेऽर्जुन ।
yastvindriyāṇi manasā niyamyārabhate'rjuna
कर्मेन्द्रियैः कर्मयोगमसक्तः स विशिष्यते ॥३-७॥
karmendriyaiḥ karmayogamasaktaḥ sa viśiṣyate (3-7)

But he who controls the sense-organs through the mind—performing Karma-Yoga through the organs of actions while remaining unattached—that wise one excels, O Arjuna.

सीताराम सीताराम सीताराम सीताराम सीताराम सीताराम सीताराम सीताराम सीताराम सीताराम सीताराम सीताराम सीताराम सीताराम सीताराम सीताराम सीताराम सीताराम सीताराम सीताराम
सीताराम सीताराम सीताराम सीताराम सीताराम सीताराम सीताराम सीताराम सीताराम सीताराम सीताराम सीताराम सीताराम सीताराम सीताराम सीताराम सीताराम सीताराम सीताराम सीताराम

Below is reproduced from Vivekachūḍāmani of Shankaracharya, **the Fiery Crest-Jewel of Wisdom** by Vidya Wati. ISBNs: **978-1-945739-41-5** (Journal format) / **978-1-945739-44-6** (Paperback) / **978-1-945739-79-8** (Pocket-sized) / **978-1-945739-45-3** (Hardback)

(Excerpts shown below are in reduced font-size)

—❧—

लब्ध्वा कथञ्चिन्नरजन्म दुर्लभं तत्रापि पुंस्त्वं श्रुतिपारदर्शनम् ।
labdhvā kathañcinnarajanma durlabhaṁ
tatrāpi puṁstvaṁ śrutipāradarśanam ,
यस्त्वात्ममुक्तौ न यतेत मूढधीः स ह्यात्महा स्वं विनिहन्त्यसद्ग्रहात् ॥४॥
yastvātmamuktau na yateta mūḍhadhīḥ
sa hyātmahā svaṁ vinihantyasadgrahāt (4)

He who, having by some means obtained this privileged human birth born a man—and furthermore having knowledge and learning and grasp of the sacred scriptures—does not exert himself for self-liberation, that fool is certainly committing suicide thereby—for he imperils himself by holding as life-support those very things which themselves are tenuous and unreal.

—❧—

ब्रह्म सत्यं जगन्मिथ्येत्येवंरूपो विनिश्चयः ।
brahma satyaṁ jaganmithyetyevaṁrūpo viniścayaḥ ,
सोऽयं नित्यानित्यवस्तुविवेकः समुदाहृतः ॥२०॥
so'yaṁ nityānityavastuvivekaḥ samudāhṛtaḥ (20)

"*Brahama* alone is Real (self-existent), and the universe non-Real (not self-existent)"—the insight, discernment, and firm conviction by which one comprehends this Vedic dictum: that is designated to be *Viveka* (or Discrimination between the Real and the non-Real).

—❧—

अहङ्कारादिदेहान्तान् बन्धानज्ञानकल्पितान् ।
ahaṅkārādidehāntān bandhānajñānakalpitān ,
स्वस्वरूपावबोधेन मोक्तुमिच्छा मुमुक्षुता ॥२७॥
svasvarūpāvabodhena moktumicchā mumukṣutā (27)

An intense yearning for Freedom—to be released of all bondages, from that of egoism to that of body, to be relieved of all thralldoms superimposed by dint of Ignorance—by realizing one's Real Nature: that is designated to be *Mumukshutā* (or Longing for Liberation).

—❧—

मोक्षकारणसामग्र्यां भक्तिरेव गरीयसी ।
mokṣakāraṇasāmagryāṁ bhaktireva garīyasī ,
स्वस्वरूपानुसन्धानं भक्तिरित्यभिधीयते ॥३१॥
svasvarūpānusandhānaṁ bhaktirityabhidhīyate (31)

Among the means most conducive to Liberation, *Bhaktī* holds a supreme spot. A constant contemplation and seeking of one's true Self, one's Real Nature—that is designated to be *Bhaktī* (Devotion).

—❧—

ऋणमोचनकर्तारः पितुः सन्ति सुतादयः ।
ṛṇamocanakartāraḥ pituḥ santi sutādayaḥ ,
बन्धमोचनकर्ता तु स्वस्मादन्यो न कश्चन ॥५१॥
bandhamocanakartā tu svasmādanyo na kaścana (51)

A father may have his sons and others to redeem him from his financial debts, but there is no one other than one's own Self to deliver one from the within bondages that are upon the Self (and which are self-imposed).

—❧—

तस्मात्सर्वप्रयत्नेन भवबन्धविमुक्तये ।
tasmātsarvaprayatnena bhavabandhavimuktaye ,
स्वैरेव यत्नः कर्तव्यो रोगादाविव पण्डितैः ॥६६॥
svaireva yatnaḥ kartavyo rogādāviva paṇḍitaiḥ (66)

Therefore—just as in the case of bodily diseases and internal maladies—the wise should strive personally and with every means in his power, to free himself from the bondages of this dreadful transmigratory disease of repeated births and deaths.

—❀—

मा भैष्ट विद्वंस्तव नास्त्यपायः संसारसिन्धोस्तरणेऽस्त्युपायः ।
mā bhaiṣṭa vidvaṁstava nāstyapāyaḥ saṁsārasindhostaraṇe'styupāyaḥ
येनैव याता यतयोऽस्य पारं तमेव मार्गं तव निर्दिशामि ॥४३॥
yenaiva yātā yatayo'sya pāraṁ tameva mārgaṁ tava nirdiśāmi (43)

Fear not, O learned one, there is no death for thee; verily there is a sovereign means of crossing this sea of relative existence. That very supreme path, treading which our ancient sages of yore have managed to go beyond—that very way I shall now inculcate to thee.

सीताराम सीताराम सीताराम सीताराम सीताराम सीताराम सीताराम सीताराम सीताराम सीताराम सीताराम सीताराम सीताराम सीताराम सीताराम सीताराम सीताराम सीताराम सीताराम सीताराम
सीताराम सीताराम सीताराम सीताराम सीताराम सीताराम सीताराम सीताराम सीताराम सीताराम सीताराम सीताराम सीताराम सीताराम सीताराम सीताराम सीताराम सीताराम सीताराम सीताराम

Below is reproduced from Ashtavakra Gita, **A Fiery Octave in Ascension** by Vidya Wati. ISBNs: **978-1-945739-42-2** (Journal format) / **978-1-945739-46-0** (Paperback) / **978-1-945739-48-4** (Pocket-sized) / **978-1-945739-47-7** (Hardback)

(Excerpts shown below are in reduced font-size)

—❀—

अहं कर्तेत्यहंमानमहाकृष्णाहिदंशितः ।
ahaṁ kartetyahaṁmānamahākṛṣṇāhidaṁśitaḥ ,
नाहं कर्तेति विश्वासामृतं पीत्वा सुखी भव ॥१-८॥
nāhaṁ karteti viśvāsāmṛtaṁ pītvā sukhī bhava (1-8)

May thou
—who have been bitten by the deadly serpent of egoism,
who persist delirious in its venom,
hallucinating, "I am the Doer"—
drink of the antidote of faith
—partake of the curative reality—
which avers: "I am not the Doer";
and replete with that nectar,
may thou abide ever glad.

—❀—

एको विशुद्धबोधोऽहमिति निश्चयवह्निना ।
eko viśuddhabodho'hamiti niścayavahninā ,
प्रज्वाल्याज्ञानगहनं वीतशोकः सुखी भव ॥१-९॥
prajvālyājñānagahanaṁ vītaśokaḥ sukhī bhava (1-9)

Burn down this wilderness of Ignorance in the
Fiery Knowledge-of-the-Self,
the essence of which Truth is the firm conviction that proclaims,
"I am the One Reality,
the all-pervading pristine Consciousness";
and thus freed of pain grief sorrows,
may thou abide in supreme happiness.

—❀—

कूटस्थं बोधमद्वैतमात्मानं परिभावय ।
kūṭasthaṁ bodhamadvaitamātmānaṁ paribhāvaya ,
आभासोऽहं भ्रमं मुक्त्वा भावं बाह्यमथान्तरम् ॥१-१३॥
ābhāso'haṁ bhramaṁ muktvā bhāvaṁ bāhyamathāntaram (1-13)

Giving up the mistaken identification with the body—the external crust;
and rid also of identifying yourself
as being the ego and mind
—the superimposed delusions which are but reflections of the Ātmā—
meditate on yourself as being none of these but purely the Ātmā:
Immutable Consciousness,
the One without a second.

—❀—

यथा न तोयतो भिन्नास्तरङ्गाः फेनबुद्बुदाः ।
yathā na toyato bhinnāstaraṅgāḥ phenabudbudāḥ ,
आत्मनो न तथा भिन्नं विश्वमात्मविनिर्गतम् ॥२-४॥
ātmano na tathā bhinnaṁ viśvamātmavinirgatam (2-4)

Just as
the waves foam and bubbles
are identical to the water of which they are made, even so
this seemingly real universe
has emanated from the Param-Ātmā,
and is none other than the Ātmā
—my Self.

—❀—

प्रकाशो मे निजं रूपं नातिरिक्तोऽस्म्यहं ततः ।
prakāśo me nijaṁ rūpaṁ nātirikto'smyahaṁ tataḥ ,
यदा प्रकाशते विश्वं तदाहं भास एव हि ॥२-८॥
yadā prakāśate viśvaṁ tadāhaṁ bhāsa eva hi (2-8)

My innate essence is a Fiery Light—
and other than the effulgence of Consciousness
I am nothing else.
When the universe shines forth,
it does so borrowing the glow of my brilliance. Through and through everything
which is manifest anywhere,
there is nothing except for the Fiery Ātmā
shining all splendorous.

—❀—

मत्तो विनिर्गतं विश्वं मय्येव लयमेष्यति ।
matto vinirgataṁ viśvaṁ mayyeva layameṣyati ,
मृदि कुम्भो जले वीचिः कनके कटकं यथा ॥२-१०॥
mṛdi kumbho jale vīciḥ kanake kaṭakaṁ yathā (2-10)

All this here, emerges out of me;
it exists in me;
and within me again it becomes dissolved
—like an earthen jar returning to its
component clay,
...or a wave
blending back into the water again,
...or a gold bracelet
melting into the pureness of its element
—having become bereft of form
bereft of name.

—❀—

द्वैतमूलमहो दुःखं नान्यत्तस्याऽस्ति भेषजम् ।
dvaitamūlamaho duḥkhaṁ nānyattasyā'sti bheṣajam ,
दृश्यमेतन् मृषा सर्वमेकोऽहं चिद्रसोमलः ॥२-१६॥
dṛśyametan mṛṣā sarvameko'haṁ cidrasomalaḥ (2-16)

The notion of duality
is at the root of all grief and misery.
There is no other cure for sorrow
except the realization of the Truth, that
"There are no two here—it is all just One."
All this perceived multifariousness
is just an apparition,
and behind it all is just the One pristine Reality void of defilements,
comprised in bliss and consciousness.

—❀—

नाहं देहो न मे देहो जीवो नाहमहं हि चित् ।
nāhaṁ deho na me deho jīvo nāhamahaṁ hi cit ,
अयमेव हि मे बन्ध आसीद्या जीविते स्पृहा ॥२-२२॥
ayameva hi me bandha āsīdyā jīvite spṛhā (2-22)

I am not this body
—and nor had I ever a body—
I am not the Jīva,
I am nothing but a Pure Consciousness.
This indeed was my bondage:
that I once had this 'me' and 'mine';
and that I thirsted for life
in greed, desires, covetousness;
and that I fancied little bites of joys
—while in fact
the entire ocean of bliss was just I myself.

—❀—

यत् पदं प्रेप्सवो दीनाः शक्राद्याः सर्वदेवताः ।
yat padaṁ prepsavo dīnāḥ śakrādyāḥ sarvadevatāḥ ,
अहो तत्र स्थितो योगी न हर्षमुपगच्छति ॥४-२॥
aho tatra sthito yogī na harṣamupagacchati (4-2)

Even suffering the state of mirthful revelries
—those ravishing spheres of pleasures which even gods like Indra yearn for
disconsolately—
the yogi finds no excitement existing in them
—being that he always abides
in That-Ocean-of-Bliss
where such morsels of delights
are but tiny fleeting waves
...flapping away

—❀—

न ते सङ्गोऽस्ति केनापि किं शुद्धस्त्यक्तुमिच्छसि ।
na te saṅgo'sti kenāpi kiṁ śuddhastyaktumicchasi ,
सङ्घातविलयं कुर्वन्नेवमेव लयं व्रज ॥५-१॥
saṅghātavilayaṁ kurvannevameva layaṁ vraja (5-1)

There is nothing at all here attached to which you lie bound in fetters.
Pure and taintless you already are—
so what is that you must needs give up?

Renounce simply the idea of a body—
set aside this composite organism to rest.
Give up identifying yourself with this assemblage of skin, bone, organs.
Abide Dissolved,
knowing that you are not anything material
but the Ātmā pure.

—❀—

यस्य बोधोदये तावत्स्वप्नवद् भवति भ्रमः ।
yasya bodhodaye tāvatsvapnavad bhavati bhramaḥ ,
तस्मै सुखैकरूपाय नमः शान्ताय तेजसे ॥१८-१॥

tasmai sukhaikarūpāya namaḥ śāntāya tejase (18-1)

Salutation to that Fiery Light—
self-effulgent, self-existent, independent,
which is pristine consciousness
which is tranquility,
which is bliss,
which is abiding existence—
in whose dawn,
this dark delusive universe
—which has you enslaved—
vanishes away
like the dream of a dark night.

—❀—

व्यामोहमात्रविरतौ स्वरूपादानमात्रतः ।
vyāmohamātraviratau svarūpādānamātrataḥ ,
वीतशोका विराजन्ते निरावरणदृष्टयः ॥१८-६॥
vītaśokā virājante nirāvaraṇadṛṣṭayaḥ (18-6)

With their delusions dispelled,
those who abide cognized of the Self
—the fiery glow of pure consciousness shining within—
their distress is now at end;
and they live free of sorrows
—in a completeness of Bliss.

—❀—

क्व विक्षेपः क्व चैकाग्र्यं क्व निर्बोधः क्व मूढता ।
kva vikṣepaḥ kva caikāgryaṁ kva nirbodhaḥ kva mūḍhatā ,
क्व हर्षः क्व विषादो वा सर्वदा निष्क्रियस्य मे ॥२०-९॥
kva harṣaḥ kva viṣādo vā sarvadā niṣkriyasya me (20-9)

Whither went concentration?
...and what happened to all those distractions?
...whither the deluded soul?
...and whither the burdensome bag of delusions?
...where went charms and delights of the world?
...and where went sorrows?
For me, it has all coalesced into a oneness.
Bereft of any karmas,
I am just the Ātmā now.

सीताराम सीताराम सीताराम सीताराम सीताराम सीताराम सीताराम सीताराम सीताराम सीताराम सीताराम सीताराम सीताराम सीताराम सीताराम सीताराम सीताराम सीताराम सीताराम सीताराम
सीताराम सीताराम सीताराम सीताराम सीताराम सीताराम सीताराम सीताराम सीताराम सीताराम सीताराम सीताराम सीताराम सीताराम सीताराम सीताराम सीताराम सीताराम सीताराम सीताराम

---

www.ingramcontent.com/pod-product-compliance
Lightning Source LLC
Chambersburg PA
CBHW081332080526
44588CB00017B/2592